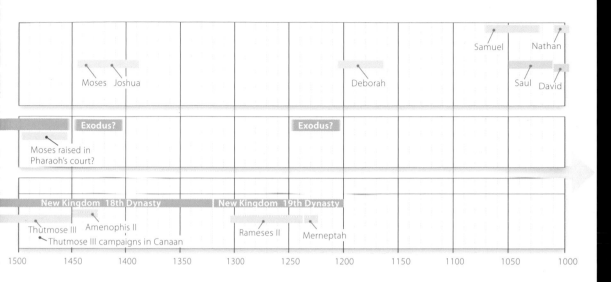

Samuel   Nathan

Moses Joshua   Deborah   Saul   David

Exodus?   Exodus?

Moses raised in
Pharaoh's court?

New Kingdom 18th Dynasty | New Kingdom 19th Dynasty

Thutmose III   Amenophis II   Rameses II   Merneptah
    Thutmose III campaigns in Canaan

| 1500 | 1450 | 1400 | 1350 | 1300 | 1250 | 1200 | 1150 | 1100 | 1050 | 1000 |

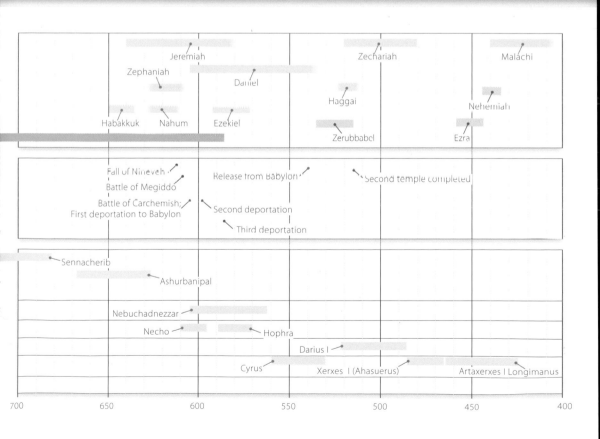

Jeremiah   Zechariah   Malachi

Zephaniah   Daniel

Haggai

Nehemiah

Habakkuk   Nahum   Ezekiel

Zerubbabel   Ezra

Fall of Nineveh   Release from Babylon   Second temple completed
Battle of Megiddo
Battle of Carchemish;
First deportation to Babylon   Second deportation

Third deportation

Sennacherib

Ashurbanipal

Nebuchadnezzar

Necho   Hophra

Darius I

Cyrus   Xerxes I (Ahasuerus)   Artaxerxes I Longimanus

| 700 | 650 | 600 | 550 | 500 | 450 | 400 |

THE BAKER
ILLUSTRATED
BIBLE
COMMENTARY

THE BAKER
ILLUSTRATED
BIBLE
COMMENTARY

Edited by

Gary M. Burge and Andrew E. Hill

BakerBooks

a division of Baker Publishing Group
Grand Rapids, Michigan

Published by Baker Books
a division of Baker Publishing Group
P.O. Box 6287, Grand Rapids, MI 49516-6287
www.bakerbooks.com

Printed in China

Library of Congress Cataloging-in-Publication Data

Burge, Gary M., 1952–
    The Baker illustrated Bible commentary / Gary M. Burge and Andrew E. Hill.
      p. cm.
    Includes bibliographical references.
    ISBN 978-0-8010-1308-9 (cloth)
    1. Bible—Commentaries. I. Hill, Andrew E. II. Title. III. Title: Illustrated Bible commentary.
    BS491.3.B87 2012
    220.7—dc23   2011024828

12   13   14   15   16   17   18   7 6 5 4 3 2 1

Interior design by Brian Brunsting

Contents

Preface

Evangelicals believe that the Bible is the Word of God. This means that when the Bible is read with care and joined to the work of the Spirit (2 Cor. 3:16–18), it can become an unparalleled source of strength, wisdom, and instruction in the ways of God (Ps. 19:7–8; 2 Tim. 3:16). Each generation needs to reexamine God's Word and ask how it can be effectively applied to the specific needs that exist. To assist in this task, commentaries are written. They are designed not to replace Scripture but to aid the understanding of it. That is the purpose of this commentary. It was written to help the average reader understand what the biblical text says.

All of the writers for this commentary are evangelical Christians who are technical scholars in their field. They all have a knowledge of the original language of the text and have studied it extensively; many have already written elsewhere on the same material that they address in this volume.

The commentators have also written so that persons without technical training can understand the Bible. Many excellent books have been written by scholars for scholars, but that was not the design of this work. Certainly, if scholars read this commentary, they will see the academic scaffolding behind it. But this commentary was written primarily to assist the pastor, student, church school teacher, or interested layperson in grasping the meaning of Scripture and applying it to his or her life.

This commentary tackles problematic questions but also calls attention to the spiritual and personal aspects of the biblical message.

The authors have certainly attempted to clarify existing difficulties, but that, in itself, was not deemed a sufficient goal. That the Word be allowed to speak to our needs was also considered an important purpose.

Although this commentary is not a textbook on systematic theology, important points of biblical theology are brought out. The great doctrines of the faith, relating to matters such as creation, redemption, sanctification, and resurrection, are discussed in the appropriate places.

The writers were encouraged to include material from their latest research when this would be helpful, so fresh material and ideas can be found here for the reader's interest and benefit.

The writers were chosen for their knowledge of the biblical text, not for their denominational point of view. Hence, writers representing a variety of theological perspectives are included in this volume. It could well be that at certain points differences might exist, but no attempt was made to impose an artificial unity on what is here. Charitable disagreement is common to our life as Christians and you may find such disagreements within these pages. The one thing that binds all the writers together is a common fidelity to the Bible as the Word of God. The sincere desire of the writers of this commentary is that its use will make the Scriptures more intelligible and that by knowing God's Word believers will come to a more penetrating, meaningful, and life-changing understanding of God and his purposes.

The present volume is a complete revision of the *Evangelical Commentary on the Bible* (Grand Rapids: Baker, 1989), edited by Dr.

Walter Elwell and published almost twenty-five years ago. Every commentary section that was retained has been revised and updated. But in addition we have made way for new scholars whose expertise in the Scriptures and vibrant faith in Christ are well known. This edition is generously supplemented with maps, charts, photos, and illustrations intended to further enrich and inform personal study by complementing the analysis of the biblical text with visual perspectives.

Our prayer is that these efforts will strengthen the church and its mission in the world. We believe that an enduring faith is established by a devout and sincere knowledge of the Scriptures through which we understand our God and may follow him rightly.

Andrew E. Hill, PhD
Old Testament Editor

Gary M. Burge, PhD
New Testament Editor

Contributors

Paul N. Anderson. PhD, Glasgow University. Professor of Biblical and Quaker Studies, George Fox University, Newberg, Oregon.

Hermann J. Austel. PhD, University of California, Los Angeles. Distinguished Professor of Old Testament and Bible Exposition, Northwest Baptist Seminary, Tacoma, Washington.

Mark J. Boda. PhD, University of Cambridge. Professor of Old Testament, McMaster Divinity College, Hamilton, Ontario, Canada.

Keith Bodner. PhD, University of Aberdeen. Professor of Religious Studies and Stuart E. Murray Chair of Christian Studies, Crandall University, Moncton, New Brunswick, Canada.

Mervin Breneman. PhD, Brandeis University. Escuela de Estudios Pastorales, San José, Costa Rica.

Jeannine K. Brown. PhD, Luther Seminary. Professor of New Testament, Bethel Seminary, St. Paul, Minnesota.

Gary M. Burge. PhD, University of Aberdeen. Professor of New Testament, Wheaton College, Wheaton, Illinois.

Lynn H. Cohick. PhD, University of Pennsylvania. Associate Professor of New Testament, Wheaton College, Wheaton, Illinois.

Hélène Dallaire. PhD, Hebrew Union College. Associate Professor of Old Testament, Denver Seminary, Littleton, Colorado.

Peter H. Davids. PhD, University of Manchester. Professor of Biblical Theology, St. Stephen's University, St. Stephen, New Brunswick, Canada.

Barry C. Davis. PhD, Trinity International University. Senior Pastor, Evangelical Free Church of China–International Church, Hong Kong.

James A. Davis. PhD, Nottingham University. Adjunct Associate Professor of New Testament, Fuller Theological Seminary Texas, Houston, Texas.

James R. Edwards. PhD, Fuller Theological Seminary. Bruner-Welch Professor of Theology, Whitworth University, Spokane, Washington.

Richard J. Erickson. PhD, Fuller Theological Seminary. Associate Professor of New Testament, Fuller Theological Seminary Northwest, Seattle, Washington.

Janet Meyer Everts. PhD, Duke University. Associate Professor of Religion, Hope College, Holland, Michigan.

Roy E. Gane. PhD, University of California, Berkeley. Professor of Hebrew Bible and Ancient Near Eastern Languages, Andrews University, Berrien Springs, Michigan.

Gene L. Green. PhD, University of Aberdeen. Professor of New Testament, Wheaton College, Wheaton, Illinois.

Victor P. Hamilton. PhD, Brandeis University. Professor Emeritus of Old Testament Studies and Scholar-in-Residence, Asbury University, Wilmore, Kentucky.

Andrew E. Hill. PhD, University of Michigan. Professor of Old Testament Studies, Wheaton College, Wheaton, Illinois.

Robert D. Holmstedt. PhD, University of Wisconsin–Madison. Associate Professor of Near and Middle Eastern Civilizations, University of Toronto, Toronto, Ontario, Canada.

Walter C. Kaiser Jr. PhD, Brandeis University. President Emeritus and Colman M. Mockler Distinguished Professor of Old Testament, Gordon-Conwell Theological Seminary, South Hamilton, Massachusetts.

Reggie M. Kidd. PhD, Duke University. Professor of New Testament, Reformed Theological Seminary, Orlando, Florida.

Sheri L. Klouda. PhD, Southwestern Baptist Theological Seminary. Assistant Professor of Biblical Studies, Taylor University, Upland, Indiana.

Max J. Lee. PhD, Fuller Theological Seminary. Associate Professor of New Testament, North Park Theological Seminary, Chicago, Illinois.

Gary A. Long. PhD, University of Chicago. Professor of Old Testament, Bethel University, St. Paul, Minnesota.

Tremper Longman III. PhD, Yale University. Robert H. Gundry Professor of Biblical Studies, Westmont College, Santa Barbara, California.

Elmer A. Martens. PhD, Claremont Graduate School. Professor Emeritus of Old Testament and President Emeritus, Mennonite Brethren Biblical Seminary, Fresno, California.

Scott E. McClelland. PhD, University of Edinburgh. Director of San Francisco Urban Program, Westmont College, Santa Barbara, California.

Douglas J. Moo. PhD, University of St. Andrews. Blanchard Professor of New Testament, Wheaton College, Wheaton, Illinois.

Stephen Motyer. PhD, London School of Theology. Lecturer in New Testament and Hermeneutics, London School of Theology, London, England.

V. Henry T. Nguyen. PhD, University of Aberdeen. Assistant Professor, Loyola Marymount University, Los Angeles, California

David W. Pao. PhD, Harvard University. Associate Professor of New Testament,

Trinity Evangelical Divinity School, Deerfield, Illinois.

R. D. Patterson. PhD, University of California, Los Angeles. Distinguished Professor Emeritus, Liberty Baptist Theological Seminary, Lynchburg, Virginia.

D. L. Petter. PhD, University of Toronto. Associate Professor of Old Testament, Gordon-Conwell Theological Seminary, South Hamilton, Massachusetts.

Elaine Phillips. PhD, The Dropsie College for Hebrew and Cognate Learning. Professor of Biblical Studies, Gordon College, Wenham, Massachusetts.

Robert S. Rayburn. PhD, University of Aberdeen. Pastor, Faith Presbyterian Church, Tacoma, Washington.

Eckhard J. Schnabel. PhD, University of Aberdeen. Professor of New Testament, Trinity Evangelical Divinity School, Deerfield, Illinois.

Thomas R. Schreiner. PhD, Fuller Theological Seminary. James Buchanan

Harrison Professor of New Testament Interpretation, Southern Baptist Theological Seminary, Louisville, Kentucky.

Richard L. Schultz. PhD, Yale University. Carl Armerding and Hudson T. Armerding Professor of Biblical Studies, Wheaton College, Wheaton, Illinois.

Gary V. Smith. PhD, The Dropsie College for Hebrew and Cognate Learning. Professor of Christian Studies, Union University, Jackson, Tennessee.

Willem A. VanGemeren. PhD, University of Wisconsin. Professor of Old Testament and Semitic Languages, Trinity Evangelical Divinity School, Deerfield, Illinois.

Herbert M. Wolf. PhD, Brandeis University. Former Associate Professor of Theological Studies, Wheaton College, Wheaton, Illinois.

Gregory T. K. Wong. PhD, University of Edinburgh. Associate Professor of Old Testament, Evangel Seminary, Hong Kong.

Abbreviations

ANET	*Ancient Near Eastern Texts Relating to the Old Testament.* Edited by J. B. Pritchard. 3rd ed. Princeton, 1969	KJV	King James Version
		NASB	New American Standard Bible
BDAG	Bauer, W., F. W. Danker, W. F. Arndt, and F. W. Gingrich. *Greek-English Lexicon of the New Testament and Other Early Christian Literature.* 3rd ed. Chicago, 1999	NEB	New English Bible
		NET	New English Translation
		NIV	New International Version (2011 edition)
		NIV 1984	New International Version (1984 edition)
ca.	circa (about, approximately)		
cf.	compare	NJB	New Jerusalem Bible
chap(s).	chapter(s)	NJPS	*The Tanakh: The Holy Scriptures: The New JPS Translation according to the Traditional Hebrew Text*
COS	*The Context of Scripture.* Edited by W. W. Hallo. 3 vols. Leiden, 1997–		
e.g.	for example	NKJV	New King James Version
ESV	English Standard Version	NLT	New Living Translation
HALOT	Koehler, L., W. Baumgartner, and J. J. Stamm. *The Hebrew and Aramaic Lexicon of the Old Testament.* Translated and edited under the supervision of M. E. J. Richardson. 5 vols. Leiden, 1994–2000	NRSV	New Revised Standard Version
		RSV	Revised Standard Version
		TDOT	*Theological Dictionary of the Old Testament.* Edited by G. J. Botterweck and H. Ringgren. Translated by J. T. Willis, G. W. Bromiley, and D. E. Green. 8 vols. Grand Rapids, 1974–
HCSB	Holman Christian Standard Bible		
i.e.	that is	TNIV	Today's New International Version

Old Testament Introduction

The Old Testament consists of thirty-nine books, written and collected over a period exceeding a thousand years. Sacred to both Jews and Christians, this collection was the Bible used by Jesus, Paul, and the early church. It was the Old Testament from which the first Christians drew their doctrine, upon which they grounded their lives, in which they found prophetic references to Jesus and themselves, and from which they derived comfort, strength, encouragement, and vision for the future.

The books are of unequal length (Obadiah being barely a page long, Psalms having 150 chapters), written mostly in Hebrew. (Small portions of Ezra, Jeremiah, and Daniel are written in Aramaic, a language similar to Hebrew.) These books exhibit great diversity of literary style, including narrative, poetry, sermons, dialogue, prayers, hymns, songs, letters, and prophecies. They also show great linguistic diversity.

While there were many other books written in antiquity, some of which are mentioned in the Old Testament (the book of Jashar in Josh. 10:13, for example), these were not preserved and used as sacred literature by the Israelites. But under the guidance of God, those books that he had inspired were gathered together, until, at last, the collection of writings was complete. There the Word of God to his people was to be found.

The books, as found in the Protestant Bible (the Roman Catholic Bible adds another small collection called the Apocrypha), are arranged in the order of law–history–poetry–prophecy.

The legal and historical material (Genesis–Esther) begins with the creation of the world, continues through Israel's waxing and waning

The Desert of Zin, one location where the Israelites journeyed during the exodus (e.g., Num. 20:1). This key period in Israel's history is a recurring theme throughout the Old Testament.

fortunes, and ends with Israel's return to its homeland after seventy years of exile in Babylon. Some overlap occurs in the accounts, and the material does not run in strict chronological order, but it is history in the fullest sense of the word. Here are events of life, often broadly conceived on a national scale, where nations rise and fall, but also seen on a personal level, where the faith and courage or pride and deceit of individuals is the focus of attention.

The poetic books (Job–Song of Solomon) were grouped together mainly because they are almost entirely in poetic form. These books deal with very personal issues, from devotion to God, to the trials of faith, to human love and the inevitability of death.

The prophetic books contain the complex message of Israel's prophets. These messages are urgent, direct, contemporary, morally informed, and filled with warning, promise, or judgment. There is also a universality about them that reaches out to the nations surrounding Israel; indeed, they speak to any nation at any time.

In spite of the great diversity of the Old Testament books, a profound unity remains as well. What gives the Old Testament its focus is the doctrine of a personal God who created the world and, in spite of the world's defection from him because of sin, has not given up on it. God's fatherly concern was expressed in his selection of a nation to represent him to humankind, and through which he would offer salvation to anyone willing to accept it. The many theological themes to be found in the Old Testament are all part of this presentation of God as the Creator, Sustainer, and Redeemer of the world.

The writers of the New Testament look back upon the Old Testament as foreshadowing, indeed prophesying, their own day. God was preparing the world for a full and final revelation of himself in his Son, Jesus Christ, in the types and shadows that he used in earlier times. "In the past God spoke to our ancestors through the prophets at many times and in various ways, but in these last days he has spoken to us by his Son" is how the writer of Hebrews puts it (Heb. 1:1–2). Jesus is seen as the fulfillment of all that went before and as the summation of all God's dealings with humankind. His life, death, and resurrection marked the end of the old and the beginning of the new. Because the Old Testament pointed directly to Jesus, the early Christians used it as their own Bible and structured their lives according to its spiritual teachings. These two testaments, the Old and the New, comprise one Bible and tell the story of God's redemptive work to reclaim, restore, and reinhabit his creation marred by human sin. Marvelously and mysteriously, God chose to do this work of re-creation as an "insider," through the incarnation of Jesus the Messiah—who is "making all things new" (Rev. 21:5 NASB).

The Pentateuch

The "Pentateuch," literally the "five books," is the Greek name for what the ancient Hebrews called the "Torah" (or "Law"). The Hebrew word, however, more properly means "instruction," because the Pentateuch contains the legal, doctrinal, and ritual basis upon which Hebrew covenantal life was established. The five-book division of the Pentateuch is somewhat artificial, since the work is better understood as a unified, literary whole. The Pentateuch is a five-volume book, a five-part miniseries that tells a story. It narrates the story of creation, the fall of humanity, and God's response to the human predicament in the form of both judgment and deliverance. The unifying theme of God's story is his promise to restore humanity by means of covenant relationship. He makes a series of covenants or treaties, first with Noah, then with Abraham and his descendants, and ultimately with the people of Israel at Mount Sinai after their exodus from Egypt under Moses's leadership. The Pentateuch artfully blends historical reporting and theological interpretation, using a diversity of literary genres, including prose narrative, lofty poetry, and legal treatise.

Genesis ("origin") deals with creation, primeval human history, and the patriarchal period of Israelite life, ending with the twelve tribes living in Egypt. Exodus tells how, by God's power, these tribes were delivered from enslavement and welded into a covenant nation during a four-decade wilderness experience. Leviticus contains the detailed prescriptions for sacrificial worship, along with regulations for community living. Numbers deals with events at the beginning and end of the wilderness period to provide a representative description of the entire desert sojourn. Deuteronomy is a covenant-renewal document that furnishes a detailed description of what the Sinai covenant meant for the Israelites.

Together, the five books show God as the sole Creator and Sustainer of the universe. The Torah teaches that humanity was created to worship God and have fellowship with him. In particular it describes how the Hebrews were chosen from all the nations to witness to God's existence and power in the world. Their way of life was to reflect his high moral and spiritual qualities, and they were commanded specifically to

Handwritten Torah scroll from the 1740s on display at the Ramhal Synagogue, Acre, Israel

behave as a priestly kingdom and a holy nation. In a superstitious pagan world they were to be examples of obedience and faithfulness to the one true God's revealed will for humankind. If they behaved in this way they would be blessed richly, but if not they would experience divine judgment.

The Pentateuch forms the historical, religious, and theological basis for the entire course of Hebrew history. Its legal and moral implications undergirded the instruction of the Hebrew wisdom tradition and laid the foundation for all prophetic teachings, which included the promise of a redeeming Messiah. In his ministry Jesus fulfilled all that the Law and the Prophets had spoken concerning him, and the new covenant that he instituted in his death, burial, and resurrection became the basis of all Christian faith.

Genesis

VICTOR P. HAMILTON

Introduction

Authorship

Moses's name does not appear in the book of Genesis as it does in the other four books of the Pentateuch, nor is another author identified. For that reason, strictly speaking, Genesis is an anonymous book. There is no real problem with acknowledging this, for the majority of the books in the Old Testament are anonymous. Who wrote Kings? Who wrote Judges? We do not know. The presence of so many anonymous books in the Old Testament invites the reader to focus exclusively on what is said rather than on who said it. Content trumps source.

Jewish and Christian tradition alike have attributed Genesis to Moses. This position is based more on inference, or the lack of a more appealing alternative, than on clear textual data in Genesis. When the New Testament uses phrases such as "Moses and all the Prophets" (Luke 24:27) or "Moses and the Prophets" (Luke 16:29), we know that Jesus is speaking of the first two sections of the three-sectioned Hebrew Bible (Law, Prophets, Writings). As "Prophets" stands for Joshua, Judges, Samuel, Kings, Isaiah, Jeremiah, Ezekiel, and the twelve Minor Prophets, "Moses" stands for the Torah, Genesis through Deuteronomy. Jesus thus marks Genesis as Mosaic.

Most critical biblical scholars outside evangelical circles find the above conclusion both unconvincing and unacceptable. In its place they offer the Documentary Hypothesis, or the JEDP theory, which rejects both the Mosaic authorship of Genesis (and the rest of the Pentateuch) and its literary unity. It is alleged that multiple authors are indicated by (1) the presence of doublets (two creation accounts, two flood stories, two banishments of Hagar and Ishmael) that contain contradictory and mutually exclusive information, (2) several distinctly different writing styles and theological perceptions, and (3) the use of multiple names for deity (Elohim, Yahweh, Yahweh-Elohim), often in a single story.

Specifically, four documents are posited. The first is J (for in it the name for deity is Yahweh/Jehovah), which was written in the time of David and Solomon in Jerusalem. The second is E (Elohim is the name for deity here), written about a century later somewhere in northern Israel. After these two documents were spliced, D (for Deuteronomy, or parts of Deuteronomy) was produced in the late eighth or seventh century BC. Finally, around the time of the exile or shortly thereafter (550–450 BC), the P (for priestly) materials were added. Subsequently someone edited all of the documents to give us our Pentateuch. There are currently multiple reconfigurations of the JEDP sequence; for example, one would place J last, and another reverses D and P (i.e., from Deuteronomy: Priestly to Priestly: Deuteronomy).

There are two possible (evangelical) explanations for the origin of Genesis. First, Genesis

1–50 could have originally existed as tablets. Moses then arranged these tablets in chronological order and added the material about Joseph. This makes Moses the compiler (not author) of Genesis. Second, Genesis may have been composed around the time of the exodus from Egypt. Emphasizing as it does the promise of God to Israel's forefathers and the origins of the patriarchs, Genesis would be an appropriate composition to read to the tribes before they departed for Sinai. The most likely author of such a composition would be the person designated to lead them to Sinai—Moses.

Structure and Content

One structure found within Genesis is an introduction (1:1–2:3) followed by ten sections (2:4–50:26), each of which is introduced by the formula "these are the generations of" (2:4; 5:1; 6:9; 10:1; 11:10; 11:27; 25:12; 25:19; 36:1+9; 37:2). Five times the formula is followed by narrative (2:4; 6:9; 11:27; 25:19; 37:2). In these verses the NIV understandably translates "generations" as "account of." Five times the formula is followed by a genealogy: either a vertical genealogy (a genealogy that focuses on one line of descendants; 5:1; 11:10) or a horizontal genealogy (a genealogy that highlights subgroups; 10:1; 25:12; 36:1). Through both narrative and genealogy Genesis traces a specific line of descendants from Adam to Jacob as a reflection of God's will for one people. All ten uses of this phrase, except for the first one (2:4), end with the name of a person (Adam, Noah, etc.). The first of these ten ends, by contrast, with "the heavens and the earth." Together human beings join with the heavens and the earth to form God's creational family.

It is debatable whether the phrase "these are the generations of" introduces what follows (a superscription) or whether it concludes what has just preceded (a subscription or colophon). In favor of the first interpretation is the fact that the phrase is always followed by the genitive of the progenitor (e.g., "This is the account of Shem," 11:10), never of the progeny. In favor of the second interpretation is the fact that often

(e.g., 5:1; 37:2) the preponderance of information given about the person named in the phrase comes before the phrase, not after it.

Additionally we may note that Genesis covers multiple generations in chapters 1–11 but only four generations in chapters 12–50. Patriarchal history is the more crucial segment and hence receives a more extensive treatment. Similarly, note that while only two chapters are given to a rehearsal of creation (chaps. 1–2), thirteen and a half are devoted to Abraham (12:1–25:11). Why six times as much space for Abraham as for Adam and Eve? Or why consign the narration of the fall to one chapter (3), while there are twelve chapters for Joseph (37; 39–48; 50), a marginal character not in the Abraham–Isaac–Jacob–Judah chain?

This does not mean that the creation story is less important than the Abraham story, or that the fall narrative is less significant than the Joseph narrative. Longer does not mean more crucial any more than shorter means less important. But it does say something about focus and emphasis. Presumably the creation story, confined to Genesis 1–2, could have been stretched over a dozen chapters or so, but it was not. Genesis does not address itself exhaustively to questions such as, What is humankind? or, What is humankind's origin? Rather, it addresses questions like, What does it mean for a person to follow God in faith? (hence the Abraham story) or, How does God use the life of the one who will honor him? (hence the Joseph story).

Genesis, as the title suggests, is a book about beginnings, specifically the beginning of humankind (chaps. 1–11) and the beginning of a single family (chaps. 12–50). Genesis 1–11 begins with a world untouched by sin. That pristine situation will not reoccur until Revelation 21. The untarnished world of Genesis 1–2 is shattered by Adam and Eve's dissatisfaction with their creaturely status, and their coveting of a godlike stature. Sin puts a wedge within relationships established by God. There is alienation between humankind and God, between humankind and

the animals, between man and woman, between man and land, between man and himself.

In chapters 4–11 sin snowballs. Genesis 3 may be read as the cause and 4–11 as the effects of sin. Cain, Lamech, the sons of God, the contemporaries of Noah, and the tower builders all follow in Adam and Eve's footsteps. Fratricide, polygamy, lust, violence, and self-aggrandizement are the fruits of disobeying God.

Paul says that where sin increased, grace increased all the more (Rom. 5:20). Clearly we have abounding sin in Genesis 3–11. Do we also have abounding grace? May Paul's dictum be applied to Genesis 3–11 and beyond? True, God banishes Adam and Eve from the garden, and he makes Cain a refugee, but note that *before* God banishes Adam and Eve he clothes them; *before* he exiles Cain he places a protecting mark on him; *before* God sends the flood he announces to Noah a covenant that will come on the heels of that flood. The God of 3–11 is a God of judgment *and* a God of grace.

Even the whole patriarchal section (chaps. 12–50) may be read as God's plan of redemption through one family (and eventually one person

out of the family) for the sin-infested world of Genesis 3–11. Thus Genesis 3–11 may be read as the problem, and Genesis 12–50 as the solution.

To that end, running throughout the patriarchal narratives is the theme of promise: (1) the promise of a son, (2) the promise of descendants, (3) the promise of land, (4) the promise of God's own presence, and (5) the promise of spiritual influence among the nations. At every major point the patriarchs are buoyed by the "I will" of God. God's covenant with the patriarchs is primarily unilateral rather than reciprocal. He is the one who commits himself through self-imposed oath to the fulfillment of this covenant and these promises. Only secondarily is human behavior introduced as a contingency factor. "You will" is subordinated to "I will" in Genesis 12–50.

Genesis makes it clear that the greatest threats to the promises of God are seldom external ones. Generally, the most potentially damaging threat to the divine promises is the bearers of those promises. Note, for example, how frequent are deception scenes in 12–50: Abraham and Pharaoh; Abraham and Abimelek; Isaac and Abimelek; Jacob and Esau; Jacob and Isaac; Jacob and Laban; Laban and Jacob; Joseph's brothers and their father; Judah and Tamar; Joseph and his brothers. All of these produce strife and alienation, and many an anxious moment. Yet an Abraham or a Jacob is never exiled from Canaan along the lines of the punishment meted out to Adam and Eve or to Cain. Nor are they reprimanded by God for their highly questionable behavior and tactics. Silence does not exonerate them. Silence does indicate, however, the primary focus of Genesis 12–50—God's election of and commitment to one family as the means for world redemption. God will no more lay aside the family of Abraham as his chosen vessel than he will scuttle the church and establish a surrogate institution.

Commentary

1. Primitive History (1:1–11:32)

A. The creation of the world (1:1–2:3). The Bible does not begin by attempting to prove the existence of God. It simply assumes this fact. But it does begin by describing God's creation of the heavens and the earth (1:1–2). This phrase may be an illustration of what is known as merism, the expression of totality through the use of opposites. Thus verse 1 is simply saying that God created everything. This he did in the beginning, which is the Hebrew way of saying, "a long time ago," without stipulating how long ago it was. John begins his Gospel with the same prepositional phrase (John 1:1), but surely means something different by it. The whole verse may be interpreted as a statement of the fact of an action that is described in detail in 1:2–2:3. The NIV renders the Hebrew word for "heavens" as "sky" elsewhere in Genesis 1 (1:8–9, 14–15, 17), and "earth" as "land" (1:10–12, 24), leading to the possible translation of Genesis 1:1 as "In the beginning God created the sky and the land."

The earth is described as formless and empty. This pair of words occurs again only in Jeremiah 4:23 and Isaiah 34:11, both in the context of divine judgment. One may not conclude, however, that Genesis 1:2 refers to something that is the result of God's fury. The two words designate a state of material devoid of order, a peopleless wilderness, prior to God's meticulous work on it.

Some have connected the Hebrew word for "deep" with the Akkadian goddess of chaos, Tiamat. Not only is this linguistically suspicious, but Genesis 1 itself rules it out, for here the deep is the impersonal watery mass

This Assyrian tablet describes the celebration of the god Marduk's defeat of Tiamat, goddess of chaos.

that covered the world before God brought about the created order. Over this deep hovers the Spirit of God. The verb here is employed elsewhere of birds (Deut. 32:11). The translation "Spirit of God" is preferable to "wind of God." The traditional interpretation makes better sense of the "us" in verse 26. It is the Spirit who holds things together.

There are a number of elements common to the creation day units: (1) introduction—"and God said"; (2) the creative word—"let there be"; (3) fulfillment of the word—"and it was so"; (4) a name-giving/blessing—"God called"; (5) the divine commendation—"and God saw that it was good"; (6) the concluding formula—"and there was evening, and there was morning—the _____ day."

Actually light is the only item created by fiat alone (1:3–5). Everything else in Genesis 1 is created by fiat plus some divinely instigated type of activity. Note that the darkness is not called "good," and that there are sources of light in the universe (day one) besides sunlight (day four). It is appropriate that the one who is light (1 John 1:5) should as his first creative act call forth the light to penetrate and push back the darkness.

One Hebrew word designates heaven both as the place where God dwells and the place where birds fly (1:6–8). The second sense is used here. The Hebrew word may be translated "expanse, firmament, vault" and is that element that divides heavenly waters from terrestrial waters.

In a second work of separation, land is separated from seas, just as in verse 6 waters

were separated from waters (1:9–13). Vegetation is created immediately—"Let the land produce vegetation." The productive power of the earth is a God-given gift.

For a specific reason the moon is called (only here) the lesser light, and the sun is called (also only here) the greater light (1:14–19). Among Israel's neighbors sun and moon were designations for deities. Not so in God's world! In fact, they are not light proper, but carriers of the light. They are lamps, and their duties are spelled out to show their status as servants. They are not arbiters of humanity's destiny.

Day five parallels day two. On the second day the habitat was created (sky separating waters), and on the parallel day the creatures that live in that habitat (birds and fish) are created (1:20–23). The land can "produce" vegetation (1:11) and animals (1:24), but the sea does not "produce" fish and the sky does not "produce" birds. Only the earth/land (a feminine word in Hebrew) is life-producing.

Here, however, for the first time we see the Hebrew verb for "create" applied to a specific creature. The choice of this verb is to emphasize a uniquely divine act. It never has a human subject. By contrast, Genesis 1 also uses "make/made" with God (1:7, 16, 25–26, 31), a verb that frequently has a human subject. One verb ("create") underscores the uniqueness of God as Creator. The other verb ("make") draws attention to the parallel between divine and human productivity.

Day three brings about the environment (land and vegetation); day six brings about those beings (animals/humankind) that inhabit that environment (1:24–31). Unlike the other days the sixth day is alone designated by the article: "*the* sixth day." And when it is completed God evaluates only this day's work as *very good*. These two facts indicate the climactic nature of the sixth day.

Humanity's creation is preceded by the phrase "let us make mankind" (1:26). While

9

we should hesitate to read this as a clear-cut statement about the Trinity, a matter about which the Old Testament is essentially silent, neither should we interpret it mythologically ("God said to the other gods") or angelically ("God said to the angels"). It does suggest that there is a distinction of personalities in the divine being. God, so to speak, can step outside of himself and speak to himself. May it be that God is addressing his Spirit (1:2)? Quite possibly the divine plurality of 1:26a anticipates the human plurality of man and woman of 1:26b.

God creates humankind in *his image, his likeness*. Humans are animals, but they are more than animals. Humans are godlike, but they are less than God. "Image" emphasizes humanity's close similarity to God, while "likeness" stresses that this similarity is not exact. God and humanity are not indistinguishable. Verse 27 clearly states that the distinction of the sexes (male and female) is also of divine origin. One's sexuality is far from a biological accident.

A sacred tree, possibly symbolizing life (Nimrud, Assyria, 865 BC), similar to the Tree of Life in Genesis 2:9

As the divine image bearer, humanity is to subdue and rule over the remainder of God's created order. This is not a license to rape and destroy everything in the environment. Even here he who would be lord of all must be servant of all. This is indicated, among other ways, by the fact that God created his image bearers as vegetarians (1:29–30).

Everything God created thus far is called "good" or "very good." The seventh day alone is called "holy" (2:1–3). It is significant that the word "holy" is applied in Scripture first to the concept of time, not to space. Pagan mentality would place a premium on space and holy places; time and history are viewed as cyclical.

The absence of the phrase "and there was evening, and there was morning—the _____ day," after the seventh day indicates that God is not resting because he is exhausted but is desisting from his work of creation. It is not so much a date as it is an atmosphere. The seventh day, like man and woman (1:28), is blessed. If "blessed" in 1:28 is meant to confer the power to beget new life, might "blessed" in 2:3 mean the same?

B. Adam and Eve (2:4–25). Genesis 1 says little about how God created humankind. It simply notes that God created male and female,

adding a few remarks about their relationship to the rest of creation. Genesis 1 emphasizes humankind as *created with* authority; Genesis 2 emphasizes humankind as *under* authority.

This section (2:4–7) is introduced as "the account of the heavens and the earth"; this is the first of ten units in Genesis introduced with "account of" (or, "story of, descendants of"). In a sense man is viewed as the offspring of the heavens and the earth. But it is an earth without vegetation and water (2:5), except for subterranean streams (2:6).

God is pictured as a potter. He forms man from the dust. Perhaps we should translate dust as "mud" or "clay," for potters do not work with dust. The idea of God creating man from the earth is mentioned elsewhere in the Old Testament (Job 4:19; 10:8; Ps. 90:3; 103:14; 104:29; 146:4). Not only is God potter, he is animator as well. God breathes the breath of life into man.

The Garden of Eden (2:8–14) is located in the east, but an explicit location is not given. The word "Eden" may be connected with Sumerian-Akkadian *edinu* ("wilderness, flatland"). Three times (2:8, 10; 4:16) the word refers to the geographical location of the garden. That the garden is planted after man's creation indicates that the Lord God did not live there.

The trees in this garden produce edible fruit. But two trees are given special significance: the Tree of Life and the Tree of the Knowledge of Good and Evil. There are only a few references to the Tree of Life in the Old Testament (Prov. 3:18; 11:30; 13:12; 15:4) and a few in the New Testament (Rev. 2:7; 22:2, 14, 19). Humans are not dependent on this tree for life, for they already have life (man was "a living being" [2:7] before the Tree of Life [2:9]). What they are dependent on is a proper relationship with God. Accordingly there seems to be no need for this living, primal human pair to eat of the Tree of Life immediately, although later that might change.

Work is not a result of the fall; manual labor is prefall. Adam is put into the garden to work it and to take care of it (2:15–17). God has been doing the work thus far, and now he shares that responsibility with his image bearer. Even before Genesis 3, then, a biblical work ethic is sounded.

With this assignment comes an additional word from God. In Genesis 2 God creates two institutions. The first is law, the purpose of which is to teach people to live under authority. The second is marriage, the purpose of which is to teach people to live for someone other than themselves.

God reminds Adam of his ample provision for humankind: "You are free to eat from any tree." The Lord is not stingy. Then he follows that with a single prohibition: "You must not eat from the tree of the knowledge of good and evil" (2:17). There is much debate about the meaning of the phrase "knowledge of good and evil." One popular suggestion is that this knowledge is sexual knowledge, for when the couple eat from this tree they immediately realize they are naked (3:7). But why would God want to withhold sexual knowledge from those he just created male and female? A second popular interpretation of the phrase is that "good and evil" means everything (a merism), and what was forbidden was the acquisition of omniscience. But then 3:22 would teach that Adam and Eve, when they disobeyed, actually became omniscient. The serpent would be proved correct that disobedience to God brings only gains and advantages.

A third possibility, and the one accepted here, is that the knowledge of good and evil means the ability and power to determine what is good and what is evil. Of course, this is God's prerogative alone. He has never delegated moral autonomy to any of his creatures. This suggestion is lent credibility by the fact that the phrase "good and evil" is most often used in the Old Testament where some kind of a decision or discernment is demanded (Deut. 1:39; 1 Kings 3:9).

Interestingly it is God who determines that it is not good for man to be alone (2:18–25). There is no indication that Adam himself was dissatisfied with his circumstances. After making his evaluation, God proposes a solution (2:18). God will provide a helper for Adam. God already is Adam's helper (but a superior helper). The animals are also Adam's helpers (but inferior helpers). This helper, then, must be one that will be equal to him. Furthermore she is to be suitable for him. The Hebrew word for "suitable" suggests something that completes a polarity, as the North Pole is "suitable" to the South Pole. One without the other is incomplete.

To that end God parades the animals before Adam (2:19–20). The force of this stresses that Adam himself chooses who his partner will be. Rather than force a decision on Adam, God allows the man to make a free decision. Man is not free to choose what is right and wrong, but he is free to choose his life partner.

After the scene with the animals is over, God administers anesthesia to Adam; and while the man is in a deep sleep, God makes woman from one of his ribs (a Hebrew word, incidentally, that is translated "side" everywhere else it appears in the Old Testament). Actually the text says that the Lord "built" woman.

When Adam says that the woman is "bone of my bones and flesh of my flesh" (2:23) he is giving the ancient equivalent of our "in weakness and in strength." One of the meanings of the verb behind the Hebrew noun "bone" is "to be strong." Flesh, on the other hand, represents weakness in a person.

The man is to leave his father and mother (neither of which Adam has!) and cleave to his wife. Elsewhere in the Old Testament these are covenant terms. When Israel forsakes God's covenant she "leaves" him. And when Israel is obedient to God's covenant she "cleaves" to him. Already Genesis 2:24 is saying that marriage is a covenant simply through the use of covenant terminology.

The climax of creation is this: the man and his wife are both naked. How appropriate! Physical nudity? Yes. But there are other kinds of nakedness. The verse is claiming a total transparency between this primal couple.

C. The fall (3:1–24). There are only four chapters in the Bible where Satan is not implicitly present in the world, the first two and the last two. The Bible begins and ends with him out of existence. But between Genesis 3 and Revelation 20 he is a factor to be reckoned with. The Hebrew word for "serpent" may be connected either with an adjective/noun meaning "bronze" (suggesting something that is shiny), or with a verb meaning "to practice divination." Two things are said about the serpent (3:1–7). First, a word about his character—he is crafty, subtle. These terms translate a neutral word that in the Old Testament may describe either a commendable ("a prudent man" in Prov. 12:16, 23) or a reprehensible (the "crafty" in Job 5:12 and 15:5) trait. Second, there is a word about the serpent's origin—he was made by God. This point is stressed to make it plain that the serpent is not a divine being, not a coequal with God.

The serpent's first tack is to suggest to Eve that God is sinister, that in fact God is abusing her. This is the force of his question in verse 1. "Would God let you see and touch these trees (i.e., raise the desire), but not let you eat *any* of them? A God who would do something like that certainly does not love you." Eve responds with a little hyperbole of her own ("you must not touch it," 3:2) in her defense of God.

The serpent's second tack is to deny the truthfulness of God's word (3:4) and to suggest that disobedience, far from bringing any disadvantages, will in fact bring an advantage—"you will be like God" (3:5). That God has already made the couple in his likeness (1:26) is moot. The serpent is suggesting another kind of likeness, a self-aggrandizing kind of likeness.

No further conversation ensues between the two. Verse 6 tells us that the temptation appealed, in the following order, to (1) Eve's physical appetites, (2) what she could see, and (3) her imagination. Note the thrust in this temptation. The serpent does not ask homage from Eve. Rather he indirectly suggests that she shift her commitment from doing God's will to doing her own will.

God does not track down this wayward couple. He simply walks in the garden in the cool of the day (3:8–13). Hearing his sound, they hide from him. This is as foolish as Jonah, who thought he could actually run from the presence of the Lord. Neither trees nor distance can put one out of the reach of the "Hound of Heaven." You can run, but you cannot hide.

The Lord begins with a question just as the serpent has—"Where are you?" (3:9). This question does not mean that God is ignorant of Adam's whereabouts. Rather it is God's way of drawing Adam out of hiding, to give Adam and Eve the opportunity to face God themselves. God does not just direct monologues toward us. He asks questions, and he listens carefully to the answers given. Maybe God at times appears to limit his knowledge in order to really listen. Individuals who know everything are seldom good listeners. They would rather talk than listen.

Adam does two wrong things. First, he hides rather than face the truth (3:10). His fear drives him from God rather than to God. Second, he blames his spouse and God. Adam refuses to admit that even complicity is a way of being involved in wrongdoing. Eve is not any better than her husband. She too looks for a scapegoat (the serpent, 3:13). What Adam and Eve have in common

Impression from a cylinder seal showing Bashmu, a serpentine creature with two front legs, being attacked by a deity

is their refusal to accept personal responsibility for their actions.

The consequences of sin are detailed in 3:14–19. Only the serpent is cursed. God does not curse those he created in his image. Phrases like "crawl on your belly" and "eat dust" may be understood as metaphorical expressions denoting the serpent's submission. (Compare the statement made of Israel's messianic king in Ps. 72:9, "His enemies lick the dust.") He is now himself a servant. True, snakes do "crawl on their belly" as a means of locomotion (possibly one reason why later biblical law prohibits the consumption of marine life that crawls on the ocean's bottom; Lev. 11:10; Deut. 14:10), but they do not eat dust. Wherever God curses, it is in response to somebody's behavior. Wherever God blesses, it is normally an act flowing out of his gracious will. For every time the Bible speaks of God cursing, it speaks multiple times of God blessing.

God also tells the serpent that he is to be on the losing side of a battle between the seed of the woman and himself. In this eventual showdown, his head will be crushed by the seed of the woman. Is the "seed" collective or singular? The Hebrew allows for either, but the Septuagint has "he." (The Latin Vulgate even has "she"!) Not without good reason many have referred to Genesis 3:15 as the protoevangelium, "the first good news." An as-yet-unidentified seed of the woman will engage the serpent in combat and emerge victorious. It is likely that Eve does not comprehend this word. But the snake is not left in the dark—he is to be cursed, a crawler, and crushed. The closest that the language from Genesis 3:15 comes to surfacing in the New Testament is in Paul's word about Christ's reigning "until he has put all his enemies under his feet" (1 Cor. 15:25), or even better, "The God of peace will soon crush Satan under your feet" (Rom. 16:20).

God speaks to Eve about her role as mother and as wife (3:16). Here are the two points where, in biblical thought, a woman experiences her highest fulfillment. And at these two points there will be pain and servitude. It may well be that we should read these words in verses 16–19 not as prescriptions but as descriptions by God himself of what it means to be separated from him. Note that in chapter 1 God created male and female to rule jointly. Now in chapter 3 male rules female (same Hebrew verb). The word for desire in verse 16 is used again in 4:7 (sin's desire to have Cain). Is Eve's desire for Adam normal desire or is it a desire for domination as in 4:7? Given the fact that later this woman's first son murdered her second son, maybe the pain is not the physical pain of birthing but the pain she will experience in seeing the violence in her family.

God speaks to Adam about his role as a worker. Here is where the male experiences his highest fulfillment. And for him too there will be pain. If we read these words as divine mandates, then we should not see these speeches of God as his way of "getting even" or "teaching a lesson" to Adam and Eve. They may in fact be love gifts from God, his way of wooing the couple back to himself. Why should a person who once walked in perfect fellowship with God and is now separated from the garden want to get back to God if he sees no need for that, and his life is essentially problem free? For Adam that involves trying to till a cursed ground. It is not labor but the difficulty of that labor. Sin always puts a wedge between things or people. In Genesis 3 it puts a wedge between God and humans, between man and woman, between man and himself, and now between man and the soil.

It is interesting that on the heels of this divine word (3:20–24) Adam names his wife "Eve," which is connected with the word for "life, living." It is a name of dignity and reflects the eventual joy of motherhood she will experience. Here is hope in the midst of judgment.

Adam gives a name (as he did to the animals in 2:20), but the Lord clothes Adam and Eve with garments of skin. The important thing here is garments rather than skins. God provides a covering for this naked couple, but it is a divine covering, not a human covering (3:7). Throughout the Old Testament one of the meanings of "to atone" is "to cover." It is no wonder that God's righteousness is compared to clothing, as is unrighteousness ("filthy garments"). Think

The cherubim in Genesis 3:24 may have been like the winged composite creature shown here guarding the temple at Ain Dara, Syria.

of the father in Luke 15:22, who clothed his bedraggled, wayward son with the "best robe" upon the son's return to the father's house. It is important to note that God covers the couple *before* he expels them. Here is grace before law.

The Lord banishes Adam and Eve from Eden (not because of what they have done, but because of what they might do if allowed to remain in the garden) and restricts reentry to Eden via cherubim and a flaming sword. Adam has indeed become "like one of us" (3:22) but not in the sense the serpent said he would. Anytime a person believes he can decide for himself what is right and wrong, he becomes god. He has usurped the divine prerogative.

D. Cain and Abel (4:1–26). Cain and Abel, Adam's sons, are born after the fall (4:1–16). Eve connects Cain's birth with the verb "to bring forth." In Hebrew this verb (*qanah*) sounds like "Cain" (*qayin*). Eve has been allowed to share in the creative work of God. Unlike Cain's, Eve does not explain Abel's name. "Abel" is the word "vanity" appearing in Ecclesiastes 1:2—"Abel of Abels, all is Abel"—unless "Abel" is to be connected with a cuneiform word meaning "son." Traditionally understood, his name reflects the transitory nature of his existence.

Abel is a shepherd, and Cain is a farmer. Both brothers bring offerings voluntarily to the Lord suitable to their vocations. There is no indication in the text that one offering is inferior to the other.

The Lord looks favorably on the presentation of Abel's fatty portions. We should not spend a lot of time trying to answer why God accepted Abel's offering and rejected Cain's. Genesis 4 does not supply an answer but rather shifts its concerns to another matter: how does one respond when God says no? Those who try to discern a reason for the acceptance/nonacceptance of the offering usually focus on the quality of the gifts or the motives of the givers. Perhaps a better clue is to be found in the fact that Cain offered a gift to God that came from the soil, or ground, which God cursed in 2:17–19.

Cain is very angry and his face is downcast. Cain is the first angry and depressed man in the Bible. (For others in the Bible whose anger is directed at God and his actions see 1 Sam. 15:11; 2 Sam. 6:8; Jon. 4:1; Luke 15:28.) He should be able, however, to overcome these feelings before they overcome him ("if you do what is right," 4:7). Cain still retains the power of decision. Sin is now crouching, demonlike, at Cain's door. A serpent in a garden and now sin at the door. What is Cain to do? The last portion of verse 8 may be read as a command ("you *must* master it"), an invitation ("you *may* master it"), or a promise ("you *will* master it").

Cain kills Abel in the field (Cain's?). Tragically civilization's first recorded crime of murder arises over a conflict involving the practice of one's religion by two individuals who worship the same God. First, man fell out of relationship with God. Now he falls out of relationship with his brother. How can Cain love God, whom he cannot see, when he cannot love Abel, whom he can see? God's question to Cain is followed by the famous question: "Am I my brother's keeper?" (4:9). The answer to that question, incidentally, is no. "To keep" means to be responsible for, to control, to exercise authority over. That is why God is repeatedly called Israel's "keeper." We are not called to be our brother's keeper but our brother's lover. Abel's blood cries out because the earth will not receive and cover over innocent blood.

As a consequence, Cain is to be driven from the land and become a wanderer. The ultimate penalty for a Hebrew is not death, but exile, a loss of roots.

Unlike his father and mother, Cain complains about the harshness of his sentence (4:13). He will be forced to become a nomad; God will hide his face; Cain will become the object of blood revenge (4:14). This last phrase assumes a populated earth, indicating the existence of others besides Adam, Eve, and Cain. To that end God places a mark on Cain before he expels him. This will protect Cain from recrimination (and for other protecting marks see

Exod. 12:13; Ezek. 9:4–6; Rev. 7:3). Here again is mercy before judgment. What clothing is to Adam and Eve, the mark is to Cain. Note that in neither Genesis 3 nor 4 do the disobedient repent of their sin. Cain dwells in Nod, which sounds like the verb "to wander."

In light of the reference to Adam and Eve's "other sons and daughters" (5:4), does Cain marry an unnamed sister? Or are there women represented among "whoever finds me" (4:13)?

Now Cain the wanderer has become Cain the city builder (4:17–24). Does this indicate that the divine penalty has been mitigated? Or is this further proof of Cain's self-determination? The city Cain builds might even be an early version of the later "cities of refuge" to which a manslayer might flee, and hence be the protecting mark for Cain.

Although out of fellowship with God, Cain is still able to multiply and fill the earth. Several of his descendants are worthy of note. Lamech (4:19) is both polygamous and given to titanic revenge (4:23). Lamech fathers four children: Jabal ("to lead flocks"), Jubal ("Trumpet"), Tubal-Cain ("Cain" = "forger"), and Naamah (close to Hebrew "pleasant," as in "Naomi"). The skills of shepherding, music, and metallurgy are attributed to the fallen line of the Cainites. Many of history's most significant cultural advances have come from people who stand outside the orbit of the God of Scripture.

Genesis 4:25–26 should not be understood as a sequel to verses 17–24. Cain's genealogy does not extend six generations before Adam fathers a child again. Adam and Eve's third child is called Seth, here connected with a verb meaning "he has granted." Eve has lost Abel to death and Cain to exile. Seth is a replacement for Abel, not for Cain.

In a chapter given over so much to names, how appropriate it is to read that at this time men begin to call on the name of the Lord (Yahweh). Long before God revealed himself fully as Yahweh to one people called Israel (Exod. 3:6), or even to the patriarchs, there is at least a small group of people who grasp the identity of the true God. Not until 12:8 will another individual (Abraham) "call on the name of the LORD."

E. From Adam to Noah (5:1–32). A genealogy stretching over ten generations traces the lineage from Adam to Noah. Only in the last section does this vertical genealogy become a horizontal one (5:32).

In the description of each generation, the same literary structure is followed: (1) the age of the father at the birth of the firstborn, (2) the name of the firstborn, (3) how many years the father lived after the birth of this son, (4) a reference to the fathering of other children, and (5) the father's total life span.

The names of Adam's progeny are Seth, Enosh, Kenan, Mahalalel, Jared, Enoch, Methuselah, Lamech, and Noah. The genealogical data about Noah are only partially given in verse 32, and are not completed until 9:28–29.

Two things need to be said about these individuals. First, there is close or exact similarity between some of the names in the Sethite list (5:1–32) and some of the names in the Cainite list (4:17–24). There is, for example, a Cainite Lamech (4:18–24) and a Sethite Lamech (5:25–28), a Cainite Enoch (4:17) and a Sethite Enoch (5:21). Also, names like Irad (4:18) and Jared (5:15), Methushael (4:18) and Methuselah (5:21) are very close to each other. These similarities do not force us, however, to assume that the respective genealogies are imaginary, or that both chapters 4 and 5 are dependent on a stock genealogy. Two separate lines, with two names common to each, are traced.

The second item of interest in chapter 5 is the unusually long life spans. Methuselah's is longest (969 years). Some would dismiss these figures as totally impossible. While they are indeed high, the numbers are quite ordinary when laid alongside another document from the ancient world known as the Sumerian King List (ca. 2000 BC; see photo). It begins with an introductory note about the origin of kingship. Then it gives a list of eight preflood kings who reigned a total of 241,200 years. One of these

Tablet containing the Sumerian King List

kings, Enmenluanna, reigned 43,200 years. The shortest reign is 18,600 years. Furthermore it is difficult to distinguish whether some of the earlier entries in the king list are gods, mortal, or both. The farther one goes back, the less the distinction between deity and humanity is maintained. Not so in Genesis 5. Push humanity as far back as possible and one encounters only "earthling" (a literal translation of "Adam"). The chasm between the finite and the infinite is never blurred in the Bible. The long life spans may also be a reflection of God's blessing on the Sethites. Longevity in Old Testament thought is a sign of divine blessing on the godly (see Deut. 4:25; 5:33; 30:20).

One of the names in this passage is well known—Enoch. It is not without significance that he is the seventh (the perfect position) in this genealogy. Unlike everyone else in the chapter, whose death is recorded, Enoch is "taken away." (For other divine "takings" see 2 Kings 2:1 [Elijah]; Ps. 49:15; 73:24.) Perhaps long life is not the greatest blessing one can experience. To be elevated into God's presence is better. It is ironic that the one man in Genesis who does not experience death (Enoch) fathers history's oldest individual (Methuselah). That Enoch walked with God is a virtue and a privilege he shares with Noah (6:9) and is one we are all urged to emulate (Mic. 6:8).

F. The flood (6:1–8:22). **6:1–22.** Few episodes in Scripture defy dogmatic interpretation as does Genesis 6:1–4. The sons of God marry the daughters of men; and Nephilim are said to be on the earth. Until this point Genesis has dealt only with the sins of individuals—Cain, Lamech, Eve, Adam. Now the emphasis is on the sin of a group, the sons of God. Who are these sons of God? The term "sons of God" elsewhere in the Old Testament designates angels (see Job 1:6; 38:7; Ps. 29:1; 89:7). The New Testament, however, teaches that angels do not marry (Matt. 22:29–30; Mark 12:24–25; Luke 20:34–35). Furthermore, if the angels are the villains, then why is God's anger directed against *humans*? Recall, however, that in the following flood story all of God's creation suffers for the sin of humanity.

The sons of God, if not angels, may be the Sethites (the godly line), while the daughters of men are the Cainites (the ungodly line). The trespass would be the unequal yoking together of believer and unbeliever. This interpretation is not without its problems, but it is quite entrenched in Christian tradition.

Whatever the correct interpretation, the union is illicit, for God is provoked. It is interesting that the reference to God's displeasure (6:3) comes before the reference to the Nephilim (6:4). This shows that God's annoyance is with the nuptial arrangement itself. More than likely, the 120 years does not refer to a shortened life span (for only Joseph lives less than 120 years in Genesis) but to a period of grace before the flood commences. As such it may be compared with Jonah 3:4, "forty more days and Nineveh will be overturned." The text does not say that the Nephilim ("those who were made to fall") are the offspring of this alliance. Rather they are contemporaries of the other two parties (sons/daughters/Nephilim). According to Numbers 13:33, they form part of the pre-Israelite population of Palestine.

There is a clear-cut reason for the flood (6:5–22). The sons of God see how beautiful the daughters of men are. The Lord sees how terrible the earth has become (wickedness). The problem is not only what humankind *does*; even their *thoughts* are evil. Sin is both extensive and intensive. Verse 6 says God repents (KJV); the NIV reads that he "regretted" (NIV 1984 "was grieved," 6:6). In the majority of cases when the Hebrew verb for "repent" is used, surprisingly the subject is God. It is important to observe that God is not on this occasion angry or vengeful, but grieved, hurt. That is, 6:6 emphasizes God's "tender" emotions rather than his "raw" emotions.

Noah stands out among his peers. He is righteous and blameless and walks with God. Thus verse 9 supplies the answer to why Noah finds favor in the Lord's eyes (6:8). Divine favor is not something Noah wins; it is something he finds. The essence of favor or grace is that it cannot be defined by the recipient's worthiness. It always comes from another source. To say that Noah (or any of us) found grace is to say grace found Noah (or us).

God spoke to himself his first intention to destroy the earth (6:7). Now he shares that information with Noah (6:13), just as he later tells Abraham that he intends to destroy Sodom (18:17–21).

Noah is told to build an ark about 450 feet long, 75 feet wide, and 45 feet high. It is really a ship, but Genesis calls it an "ark." The only other place this Hebrew word is used is in Exodus 2, to refer to "the ark" into which baby Moses is placed. In both instances an individual destined to be used by God is saved from drowning by being placed in an ark. Again, note the announcement of a covenant (6:18) before the flood starts. Here again is grace before judgment.

7:1–24. God now repeats his earlier word to Noah (6:18–20) to enter the ark (7:1–10). What the narrator earlier observed about Noah's character (6:9), God confirms (7:1). This time Noah is told to take aboard, in addition to his family, seven of every kind of clean animal and two of every kind of unclean animal. In 6:19–20 and 7:15–16 we read that Noah is to take *two* of all living creatures. Is this a discrepancy, and thus evidence for the blending in Genesis 6–9 of two flood stories? One pair or seven pairs? Not necessarily. Genesis 6:19–20 and 7:15–16 provide general information. Noah is to bring aboard pairs of animals. In 7:2, specific information is given about how many pairs—seven. It is not surprising that God desires salvation of the clean animals. But why spare the unclean animals? Does God's compassion extend to them too?

Noah is given a week's warning before the flood begins. The Hebrew word for "rain" in verse 4 is different than the word for "rain" in verse 12. That used in verse 12 designates a heavy downpour. Thus the rain of verse 4 is no shower—it is to last forty days and forty nights. Noah does what God says (7:7–9) and God fulfills his word (7:10).

As the flood starts (7:11–16), again we find the deliberate use of repetition and summarization. This is a characteristic of epic composition. Note: the flood (7:6), entry into the ark (7:7–9), the flood (7:10–12), entry into the ark (7:13–16). Actually there are two references to the flood's beginning: verse 10 and verse 11. The additional data given in verse 11 are about the two sources of the rain: the springs of the great deep and the floodgates of heaven. But verse 12 refers only to the second of these.

Although Noah's wife, sons, and daughters-in-law are also saved, there is no reference to their character. Their salvation is due to their husband/father/father-in-law. Interestingly it is "God" who commands the group to enter the ark (7:16a), but "the LORD" who shuts them in (16b). Perhaps this shift to God's more personal name suggests that God is the protector of the ark.

As the waters rise (7:17–24), verses 13–16 focus on the action inside the ark, while verses 17–24 focus outside the ark. To be outside the ark is akin to being outside the garden. Salvation inside the ark is total; destruction outside the ark is total.

The reference to 150 days (7:24) includes the forty days of rainfall, plus the length of time before the floodwaters begin to diminish (40 + 110 = 150; not 40 + 150 = 190). This is confirmed by 8:4, which states that the ark rested on a mountain peak five months later (second month to seventh month). This period of time represents five months of thirty days.

8:1–22. Suddenly the story shifts; God remembers Noah (8:1–2). Not Noah's righteousness or blamelessness or his walk with God. Just Noah. There are seventy-three instances in the Old Testament where God is said to "remember." This remembrance moves God to send a wind over the earth. One Hebrew word (*ruah*) translates "wind" and "Spirit." In 1:2 it is the Spirit who hovers over the waters. Twice the divine *ruah* encounters the waters, first restraining them, now evaporating them. The sun plays no role in the drying up of the waters. In pagan myths this is exactly what happens. The ark finally comes to rest on the mountains of Ararat (in modern Armenia and eastern Turkey).

Noah must now determine whether the waters have receded sufficiently for dry land to reappear (8:6–14). To find out, Noah sends out first a raven, then a dove (twice). God does not tell Noah when the ground has dried out even though he did tell him about when the flood would start and exactly how to build the ark. Here Noah moves from being the passive recipient of revelation to being the active investigator of what and when the next move is.

The raven does not return because, as a carrion eater, it is able to feed on the animal corpses on the mountaintops. The dove, by contrast, is a valley bird that feeds off food in the lower areas, the last to dry out. This is why it returns to the ark.

In verses 13 and 14 we have two Hebrew words for "dry," just as we had two words for "rain" in chapter 7. The first (8:13) means to be free of moisture. The second (8:14) refers to the complete absence of waters. Thus the choice of verb and the progression from verse 13 to verse 14 is logical.

Twice God speaks in 8:15–22, once to Noah (8:15–17), and once to himself (8:21–22). Between these two speeches is the departure of Noah from the ark (8:18–19) and his act of worship (8:20). Even though the dove does not return, Noah does not leave the ark until God tells him. God, and only God, can give the green light.

The divine soliloquy is composed of a negative statement (8:21) and a positive one (8:22). In spite of man's congenital proclivity to sin, the God of mercy will not exterminate him (8:21). There will be predictability in the natural world (8:22). And all this will be a gracious gift from God. No rites associated with fertility cults will bring about this condition. Only grace will.

G. Noah after the flood (9:1–29). Genesis 9:1–17 spells out in more explicit detail what God revealed to Noah in 8:20–22 about the postflood stage. That God talks to Noah as he does in verse 1 ("Be fruitful and increase in

Mount Ararat, the area where Noah's ark came to rest (Gen. 8:4)

number and fill the earth") indicates that Noah is a second Adam. These are the same imperatives addressed to Adam in chapter 1. But the world of Genesis 9 is not exactly the same as the world of Genesis 1. For one thing, man is now allowed to kill animals for food and add meat to his diet (9:2–3). Just as Genesis 2 stated a permission followed by a prohibition, Genesis 9 provides the same sequence: permission (9:2–3)–prohibition (9:4). Interestingly even animals are now held accountable for crimes (9:5–6).

God now proceeds to establish his covenant with Noah (9:8–11) and with the animals. The covenant is unilateral. That is, it is one that lays all obligations on God and no obligations on man. It is a covenant in which the Almighty binds himself to a certain course of action—never again to destroy the earth by a deluge.

To cement that covenant God establishes a sign both with Noah and with unborn generations. He will put his rainbow in the clouds. The Hebrew language does not distinguish between a rainbow and a bow (weapon). One word covers both. In what is a radical reinterpretation of divine power, the bow ceases to function as a sign of God's militancy and begins to function as a sign of God's grace. A rainbow is a bow without an arrow.

We are perhaps surprised to read that the bow is in the sky for God's benefit—"Whenever . . . the rainbow appears . . . I will remember." Perhaps there is a play here on the verbs "see" and "remember." The flood story began with God "seeing" (6:5, 12) the unrestrained evil in the world. It ends with God "seeing" the rainbow. The flood story reaches a turning point when God "remembers" Noah (8:1). It reaches a climactic point when he "remembers" his covenant.

The story of Noah in 9:18–27 focuses on Noah's nakedness and not on his drunkenness. Why Noah is nude we do not know. Is he in a drunken stupor, or is he preparing to have intercourse with his wife? One of his sons—Ham—sees his father's nakedness. To be sure, this phrase (see Leviticus 18) may mean to have sexual relations

with a relative (incest). More than likely, here it simply means that Ham sees Noah's genitalia. Shem and Japheth, on the other hand, cover their father's nakedness, much as God did with Adam and Eve's in 3:21. (Note again the emphasis here on "seeing" and "not seeing.")

As a result of Ham's involvement, Noah curses not Ham but his grandson Canaan. This may illustrate the "eye for an eye" principle of justice. The youngest son of Noah sins, and as a result, a curse is placed on Ham's youngest son. Other interpretations are possible. This is the only instance of a humanly imposed curse in the five books of Moses; furthermore, they are the first recorded words in Scripture from Noah's mouth. Throughout the flood he was active, but he never spoke, not even once.

Noah also blesses the Lord of Shem, and Canaan is to be slave to both Shem (9:26) and Japheth (9:27). God has talked about the future (9:8–17). Now Noah talks about the future (9:25–27).

H. The table of nations (10:1–32). The account of Noah's descendants begins with a list of Noah's sons in this order (10:1): Shem, Ham, Japheth; but in the verses that follow that order is reversed: Japheth, Ham, Shem. The Japhethites (10:1–5) are peoples (seven are identified) most remote from Palestine, and most of the nations/places mentioned here are in the Mediterranean islands and Asia Minor. We recognize names like Magog and Meshek from the book of Ezekiel. Javan represents early Greeks (Ionians) in the Aegean area. Madai represents the Medes. The Kittites are to be associated with Cyprus, and the Rodanites are from the island of Rhodes, by the southwest coast of Turkey.

Ham has four sons, the most surprising of them being Canaan. The fourth generation is traced only through Cush. Most of the peoples in this section (10:6–20) are Gentiles with whom Israel has had unpleasant relationships. For example, Cush represents Ethiopia; Mizraim (KJV), Egypt; and Put, modern Somaliland.

Most interesting here is Nimrod (10:8–12). So well known is he that he has established a reputation as a mighty hunter, and verse 9 provides the only time the Lord appears in this genealogy. Nimrod is not only the Bible's first hunter (to be coupled with Esau [Gen. 25:27; 27:30]); he is the Bible's first king (10:10). This refers probably to his martial prowess. The four cities he founds— Babylon, Uruk, Akkad, and Kalneh (?)—are all to the east of Canaan, not to the south-southwest,

BABEL AND THE PLAIN OF SHINAR

as is Egypt. Does this indicate that Egyptian power extended at one point as far east as the Euphrates?

Shem fathers four sons. This section (10:21–32) is last in this list because it is the most crucial of the three. In this section we discover the name Eber, the connection of which with "Hebrew" should be obvious. "The earth was divided" in Peleg's time (10:25). This may mean that the Semitic groups were divided into two branches. Or, because Peleg is related to an Akkadian word meaning "canal," it may mean that Peleg was involved in the construction of irrigation canals. Or it may contain a hint of the tower of Babel story in which people were divided from each other.

Geographically Genesis 10 ranges as far east as Persia (Elam), as far south as Ethiopia (Cush), as far north as the Aegean Sea (Caphtorites), and as far west as Egypt and Libya. Theologically the list affirms God's blessing on Noah's progeny. Israel, or Eber-ites, have no monopoly on attributing their existence to God. It is not incidental that Jesus sends out seventy (or seventy-two) disciples (Luke 10:1). Jesus

is reflecting the Genesis 10 list of the seventy nations in the then-known world, sending his disciples into every part of that world.

I. The tower of Babel (11:1–9). The whole world with which verse 1 begins has just been described at length in chapter 10. Further, we read, this world has one language and a common speech. This is puzzling, for already in Genesis 10 we have read, three times, about the descendants of Noah, who were divided on the basis of their respective languages (11:5, 20, 31). There are four possible ways of handling this. One is to maintain that the two chapters contradict each other. A second way is to suggest that chapter 10 refers to local languages and dialects, while chapter 11 refers to an international language, a lingua franca. A third approach is to suggest that chapter 10, although actually falling after 11:1–9, is placed ahead of chapter 11, lest chapter 10 be read as a manifestation of God's judgment on the Noahites. Finally, this could be an instance of a general description of an event (chap. 10) followed by one that provides more details about the event (11:1–9). We have already seen this

Partially reconstructed ziggurat at Ur

the former section some people wanted to make a name (Hebrew *shem*) for themselves, and 11:10–32 is the family tree of Shem. The list is much like that in 10:21, 24–25. Four of the names are repeated—Arphaxad, Shelah, Eber, and Peleg. Additionally some of the names are to be identified with place names in northwest Mesopotamia (e.g., Serug/Sarugi; Nahor/Nakhur). This lends historical credibility to the genealogy.

pattern with Genesis 1 as a general overview and Genesis 2 as a sequel that adds greater detail.

Shinar is the land of Babylonia. The tower the people want to build is probably a ziggurat, a seven-staged tower (see photo). In addition they want to build a city, and thus join Cain (4:17) in such an enterprise. In itself this is not sinful. Nor is it sinful to wish to build a tower that reaches to the heavens. The sin comes in the purpose: "so that we may make a name for ourselves" (11:4). "Name" means reputation. They want to erect an edifice that will memorialize them.

It is difficult to miss the irony or humor in verse 5. The people want to build a skyscraper, but the Lord still comes down to see the city and the tower. Once again there is an emphasis on somebody seeing something. This is the first of several times in the Bible that God "comes down" (e.g., Gen. 18:21; Exod. 3:8). He did not need, by contrast, to come down to speak with Adam or with Noah.

Note that God does not halt the project while it is under construction. Nor does he destroy it once it is completed. What God does is judge the language, not the tower or the city. The people's tongues, and not their hands, feel the wrath of God. This gives rise to the name Babel, which means in Hebrew "to confound, confuse." The Babylonians themselves call their city *bab-ili* or *bab-ilani*, "gate of the god(s)," which is reflected in the Greek *Babylōn*.

J. The Shemites (11:10–32). Here is another ten-generation genealogy stretching from Shem to Terah/Abraham. A possible connection between 11:1–9 and 11:10–32 is that in

Abraham, however, comes from Ur of the Chaldeans (11:28), which is in southern Mesopotamia. There is a great deal of evidence to support a movement of Terahites from Ur north to Harran, which provides support for linking Abraham with lower Mesopotamia and the patriarchs with northern Mesopotamia. There is no indication that Abraham ever regretted leaving Ur or Harran. This is different from his offspring, who frequently regretted leaving Egypt and wanted to return there (Exod. 16:3; 17:3; Num. 14:3).

2. Abraham (12:1–25:18)

A. The call of Abram (12:1–9). God's first word to Abram is an imperative: *leave!* The three things he is to leave behind are arranged in ascending order: country, people, father's household. The imperative is followed by a series of promises relating to progeny, reputation, and blessing. There is quite a contrast between 11:4 ("we may make a name for ourselves") and 12:2 ("I will make your name great"). The climax of the divine "I wills" is that all peoples on earth (Genesis 10) will be blessed through Abram. Abram is to be not only a recipient of the blessing but also a channel through which this blessing may flow to others.

This all happens when Abram is seventy-five years old. God gets involved for the first time in the life of this septuagenarian.

Abram's response is prompt: "So Abram went" (12:4). First the Lord speaks to Abram (12:1). Then God appears to him (12:7). Now that Abram has moved into Canaan (Shechem, Bethel), God makes a further promise to him: "To your offspring I will give this land." Abram does not yet have even one child, and here is God talking about offspring. First God speaks (12:1–3), then Abram journeys (12:4–6). Next God appears, then Abram worships (12:7). The paragraph begins with the promise to make for Abram a great "name" and concludes with Abram calling on the Lord's "name."

B. Abram in Egypt (12:10–20). A famine sends Abram to Egypt. He is certain that, once there, the Egyptians will abduct Sarai and murder him. Why he thinks that or how he knows this is not clear. Since God is certain about Abram's future (12:1–9), why cannot Abram himself be as certain?

Abram asks Sarai to identify herself to Pharaoh as Abram's sister (which is partially the truth). The logic of Abram's move is clear enough. As brother to the woman involved he can be ignored; as husband to the woman he would have to be eliminated. Think of David, who orchestrated Uriah's death to get Bathsheba.

There are two flaws in Abram's ruse. First, it is laced with deception (not the first time we have met this in Genesis; it is as old as chap. 3). Second, it is a plan in which Sarai has to make herself vulnerable. Indeed, Genesis 12:10–20 describes actual adultery rather than potential adultery, for Sarai is taken into Pharaoh's palace. Conspicuous throughout this event is Sarai's silence. Does she approve? Does she oppose? Does she submit silently? Will she sacrifice her life for Abram's?

As a result Pharaoh falls under God's wrath, albeit he has sinned in ignorance. This is an immediate fulfillment of 12:3, "Whoever curses you I will curse." Perhaps Abram did this for a good purpose, so he thought. If he is slain what will happen to God's promises? They will be aborted. Abram must do anything to prevent

this. One of the great foibles of this man of God is in believing that now and then the Almighty is in need of a helping hand. If this is his thinking, then it suggests that Abram believes he is indispensable to God's plan and promises but Sarai is not. God can always give him, he may think, another Sarai, a more fertile Sarai.

C. Abram and Lot separate (13:1–18). The Negev is the desert region south of Palestine. It is through this region that Abram, his wife, and Lot (he also goes to Egypt) travel on their way back to Canaan. Abram is a wealthy man (13:2), but his wealth is not necessarily an evidence of divine blessing for obedience. Back in his own backyard, Abram's first priority is to renew his life of worship (13:4).

There is a problem, however. Not a problem with outsiders, but inside the family. Abram and Lot each have so much that the land cannot support them both. This leads to quarreling among their respective employees (13:7). This incident demonstrates that the blessings of God can create either possibilities or problems. How we handle these blessings determines whether they remain blessings or become sources of friction.

Abram moves quickly to settle the strife. He foments strife in 12:10–20. Here he settles it. As the elder person, Abram would have been fully within his rights to decide who gets what portion of land. As the younger, Lot would have to accept passively what was left over or assigned to him.

It is not always propitious to exercise one's prerogatives. Abram believes that. Voluntarily he gives priority of choice to his nephew. Note the change between the Abram of 12:10–20 and the Abram of 13:1–12. In the first instance he is obsessed with himself, his safety, his future. He must become deceitful. In the second instance Abram assigns himself position number two. He empties himself of patriarchal authority.

All of this action takes place north of Jerusalem in the area of Benjamin. From here the lush Jordan Valley can be seen (13:10). Lot chooses the plain of the Jordan, which is comparable to Eden and Egypt. A person is known by his choices. Lot's choice puts him in contact with Sodomites, people whose lives are contrary to God's way (13:13).

Only after the difference is settled does God get involved. He has been watching two of his children hammering out their differences, allowing each to live with the consequences of his choice. God speaks to Abram now that Lot has departed. For a second time God gives Abram a series of promises. The first is land (13:15) and the second is innumerable offspring (13:16). Abram is to lift up his eyes (13:14) and lift up his feet (13:17). Twice in this chapter Abram builds an altar. He settles in Mamre, which is approximately twenty miles south of Jerusalem. Hebron is two miles south of Mamre.

D. Abram rescues Lot (14:1–24). Four powerful kings from the east head an assault against five minor Palestinian kings (14:1–13). It is impossible to identify the four kings with certainty. Amraphel means "the mouth of god has spoken," and he is the king of Shinar (i.e., Babylonia). Arioch matches the name Arriyuk and is a good Hurrian name. Kedorlaomer means "servant of Lagamar" (an Elamite god). Tidal is the Hebrew equivalent of the Hittite regnal name Tudhalia, borne by several Hittite kings.

These four kings engage the five petty kings in battle near the Valley of Siddim, where the Dead Sea now is. Verse 4 suggests that the battle is instigated by an attempt of the minor kings to establish independence. To quell the revolt, these kings march, according to place names in verses 5–7, from Syria to the Gulf of Aqaba, then north again to Kadesh.

In the midst of these hostilities Lot is captured (14:12). He is now suffering one of the consequences of his choice. Abram is informed of this, and it is here that we find the interesting phrase "Abram the Hebrew" (14:13). In the one chapter where Abram engages in military activity he is spoken of as a "Hebrew." Some have suggested a possible relationship between "Hebrew" and "Habiru,"

the latter being those who in times of war hired themselves out as mercenaries. In light of Lot's selfish behavior in chapter 13, one might excuse Abram for being indifferent when news of Lot's abduction reaches him. But no, his heart is bigger than that. Furthermore, it is not only his nephew that Abram rescues but the prisoners of war taken from cities like Sodom and Gomorrah. So before Abram prays for these cities (chap. 18), he puts his life on the line for them.

Abram does not have to rescue Lot singlehandedly (14:14–16). He has 318 trained men. This indicates that Abram is anything but a nomadic shepherd who passes time counting sheep and stars. He is a powerful individual with a substantial number of troops on call.

How does one man with an army of 318 men go against four major kings and their armies? Certainly not head-to-head. It is a nocturnal battle (14:15). Perhaps this story about the retrieval of Lot and the success of Abram anticipates the degree of success God pictures for his people Israel, even though they too will be a minority.

On his way home Abram meets the king of Sodom in the Valley of Shaveh (14:17–24). Melchizedek is identified as king of Salem. This is most certainly an abbreviation for Jerusalem. Melchizedek means "my king is righteous/justice." Further, he is described as priest of God Most High (14:18). It was common in pagan cultures for the king to be head of both state and church. Not so in Israel, except for one who properly bears the function of prophet, priest, and king.

He blesses Abram (14:19) and God (14:20a), and Abram responds with a tithe from the war booty (14:20b). It is to Melchizedek's credit that he knows the real reason why Abram was victorious. It is God, and not Abram's military sagacity, who has won the battle. It is no wonder that Hebrews 7 relates Melchizedek and Christ typologically. The story concludes with Abram conversing with the king of Sodom (14:22–24). He insists that the king take the war spoils. One king already enriched him (12:10–20). He does not want that to happen again.

E. God's covenant with Abram (15:1–21). "After this" (15:1) must refer to the harrowing experiences Abram encountered in chapter 14. He has reason to be afraid of the possible repercussions of his rescue mission. God's word to him, then, is most appropriate (15:1–6): "Do not be afraid, Abram." God is Abram's shield, not his 318 servants. And God himself is Abram's reward.

Abram has a major concern. He is still childless, and apparently resigned to that fact. For he is prepared to designate his servant Eliezer as the heir to his estate (15:2). This procedure reflects a law from Nuzi in ancient Mesopotamia that says a childless father might adopt a servant and name him as heir.

God's first word to Abram is about himself. His second word (15:4–6) is about Abram. First, there is the promise of a natural heir (15:4), and then there is the promise of legions of descendants (15:5). This is the third time Abram receives promises (12:1–7; 13:14–17), and it is sufficient evidence for Abram. He believes the Lord. He is willing now to stake his life on the reliability of the promises of his Lord. The Hebrew verb "to believe" is the source of "amen." Whenever one believes, he is saying "amen." God's response to Abram's amen is to credit it to him as righteousness. This is, of course, the great text on which Paul builds the truth about justification by faith (Rom. 4:1–3; Gal. 3:7–9). Yet, even though Abram has just "believed the Lord," that does not end his questions directed at God (15:8). And God does not seem annoyed by his questions.

God's covenant with Abram is confirmed by a ritual (15:7–21). Abram is to bring a heifer, a goat, a ram, a dove, and a young pigeon. The heifer and the ram he is to cut in two and arrange in parallel rows. The most frequent way in Hebrew to say "make a covenant" is "cut a covenant." The only other reference in the Old Testament to this kind of covenant ritual is Jeremiah 34:18. Abram cuts the animals and

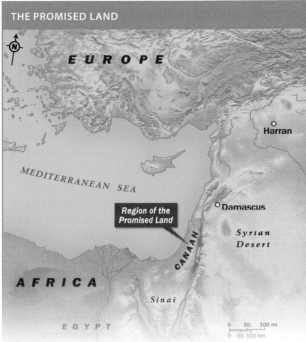

THE PROMISED LAND

EUROPE

Harran

MEDITERRANEAN SEA

Region of the Promised Land

Damascus

Syrian Desert

CANAAN

AFRICA

Sinai

EGYPT

0   50   100 mi
0   50 100 km

God cuts the covenant, all of which leads to the cutting of circumcision in chapter 17. The penalty for failing to be circumcised, in turn, is to be "cut off" (17:14).

In a deep sleep Abram observes a smoking firepot and a blazing torch pass between the portions of animal flesh. These fiery elements can only be symbols of God himself, for in the Bible fire represents the presence of God. The ritual here is dramatic. It is as if God is placing himself under a potential curse: "Abram, if I do not prove faithful to my word, let the same thing happen to me as to this heifer and ram." Abram thus believes the Lord.

Abram will not himself possess this land (15:13–16). Only when the sin of the Amorites (i.e., Canaanites) has reached its final stage of decay will the land pass to Israel. Although this is generations away, God already knows exactly the boundaries of the promised land (15:18–21).

F. Hagar and Ishmael (16:1–15). How does one handle the problem of childlessness, especially in a society that places a premium on having children? To the contemporary reader

Abram and Sarai's method appears quite strange and highly suspect. Sarai offers her maidservant Hagar to Abram. He cohabits with her, and he fathers a child—Ishmael. This child then becomes Sarai's child. Such a procedure, however illicit it may sound to us, is well documented in ancient literary sources such as the Code of Hammurabi and in the texts from Nuzi.

Still one wonders to what degree Abram's belief in the Lord (15:6) informs his action in 16:1–4. If there is a vivid contrast between the Abram of the first half of chapter 12 and the second half of chapter 12, then we observe an equally vivid contrast between the Abram of chapter 15 and that of chapter 16.

Hagar does not help the situation. She despises (the Hebrew word rendered "curse" in 12:3) her mistress, for she can bear a child while Sarai cannot. Sarai is understandably incensed (16:5). Abram is of little help. He refuses active involvement with his lame "do with her whatever you think best" (16:6). As a result Hagar is banished from the premises.

God finds her at a spring on the road to Shur (a word meaning "wall"), which runs from Egypt to Beersheba. He engages her in conversation by asking her questions (16:8), to which he knows the answers.

It is the angel of the Lord who meets Hagar in the wilderness; this is the first time he appears in the Bible. But in verse 13 the text says that it is God who speaks with her. The angel of the Lord and the Lord—distinct, yet the same. All sorts of explanations, usually along the lines of form-critical concerns (what was the original form of the story?), have been offered to explain this "incongruity." Might we see here, as we saw in the "us" of 1:26 and 11:7, a hint of God's trinitarian nature?

The child born of this union between Hebrew patriarch and Egyptian servant girl is Ishmael. The name means "El [God] has heard," but the explanation given for the name is that the Lord has heard. This shows there is no real difference between El(ohim) and Yahweh as names of deity.

Ishmael is to be "a wild donkey of a man" (16:12). He will live the life of a Bedouin, a nomad, and at the same time he will be warlike. For all this emphasis on Ishmael's involvement with hostility, his descendants, the Ishmaelites, never are in conflict with Israel, nor are they the objects of God's judgment. David had an Ishmaelite brother-in-law (1 Chron. 2:17), and an Ishmaelite was one of the key overseers in his administration (1 Chron. 27:30).

Now it is Hagar's turn to name somebody. And she names God—she is the only one to do this in all the Bible. She calls him "You are the God who sees me" (and, again, note the emphasis on seeing, as in previous chapters), or in Hebrew, *El Roi*. She names the well where this all takes place Beer Lahai Roi, "well of the Living One who sees me." Hagar ran away from Sarai and ran into God. These names stress not the gift she has received (a child) but the Giver of that gift. A distraught, frightened, pregnant, non-Israelite slave girl encounters God in a desert and is never the same again.

G. The covenant of circumcision (17:1–27). Nothing of real significance happens in Abram's life between the ages of eighty-six (16:16) and ninety-nine (17:1), indicating that Abram at times lived for over a decade with no recorded revelation from God. God now appears to him as *El-Shaddai* (see NIV note for 17:1), meaning either "God Almighty" or "God of the Mountain." God's self-identification is followed by a moral imperative: "walk before me faithfully and be blameless" (17:1). We observed in chapter 15 that all of the obligations of the covenant fell on God. Chapter 17 lends a bit of balance to that. Abram does not have license to live as he pleases. His behavior is to reflect the character of the one who called him.

In the course of conversation God tells Abram that his name will be changed from "Abram" ("father is exalted") to "Abraham." The only difference between the two is the syllable *ha* in the new name. The explanation "father of many nations" is arrived at on the basis of "Abraham" being assonant with Hebrew *ab–hamon,* "father of a multitude." Every one of the major characters in Genesis 11–50 undergoes a name change, except Isaac. A new name indicates a new destiny.

The name change is followed by another series of promises about progeny (17:6–7) and land (17:8), and here the point is made that Abraham is to keep the covenant. He is not to play fast and loose with the word of the Lord.

There are four great imperatives addressed to Abraham: walk, be blameless, keep, and circumcise. Verses 9–14 focus on the last of these. This is not something presented to Abraham as an option. It is mandatory. It is to be administered to every male after his eighth day of birth. It extends even to servants (17:12) and thus is not an elitist ritual. Circumcision functions as a sign of the covenant. Earlier the rainbow was a sign of God's covenant with Noah. The sign here must be for the benefit of the recipient. By an ineradicable mark cut into his flesh, the believer is constantly reminded that he is God's special child. The sign speaks of God's mercies and his expectations. Obviously the sign of the covenant, circumcision, applies only to Abraham's male descendants, that is, half of his family. The sign relates to male sexual activity and procreation, which is a key to the fulfillment of God's covenant; accordingly male sexual activity needs to be disciplined and dedicated to God.

Sarai is to become Sarah, not a significant name change; thus her new name is not explained as is Abraham's, but she is the only woman in the Bible to have her name changed. Something more important than her name is to change. The condition of her womb is to change (17:16). She is to give birth not only to children but to kings (17:15–17).

Abraham laughs (17:17). Here we have the first of three instances linking laughter with the name Isaac (see also 18:12; 21:6). It is unclear whether it is the laughter of joy or of unbelief. Verse 18 (Abraham's concern for Ishmael) and verse 17 (Abraham's realism) favor the latter interpretation. Both he and his wife are beyond child-producing and child-bearing years. Often God seems to insist on the impossible to increase dependence on him.

True, God will bless Ishmael (17:20), but his covenant is with Isaac (17:21). Ishmael is not lost, damned, or condemned, but he is clearly placed outside the covenant family, although a recipient of divine promises.

Abraham's implementation of the divine directive (17:11–14) is not carried out until verses 23–27. Sandwiched between is the promised birth of Isaac. One wonders if Abraham ever questioned circumcising Ishmael since he was not to be a link in the covenant chain.

II. The Lord of birth and death (18:1–33). This chapter highlights the forthcoming birth of Isaac and the forthcoming death of Sodom. In this contrast between the beginning of life and the end of life, Abraham has opportunity first to be host, then to be intercessor. As host he entertains three men by his home at Mamre (18:1–15). One of these is obviously the Lord (18:1). The other two must be angelic companions, both of whom essentially drop out of the story after verse 9. The number three should not be pressed for any trinitarian significance.

Circumcision was practiced in other cultures throughout the ancient Near East, such as Egypt. This relief depicting a circumcision was found in the Temple of Khonspekhrod at Luxor.

Abraham serves the three visitors a meal and watches while they eat (18:8). The supernatural character of these visitors is evidenced by the fact that they know Abraham is married, and they also know his wife's name. This probably shocks Abraham. He does not recognize his visitors, but his visitors know all about him. There stands with Abraham one whom he does not know.

Sarah overhears the announcement about her forthcoming pregnancy. It is an incredible promise. Under her breath Sarah laughs—another play on the name Isaac—for she and Abraham are too old, a feature later shared by Zechariah and Elizabeth (Luke 1:7). Sarah, however, needs to see beyond her lord (Abraham) and see her Lord. Not only is she unbelieving, but she denies that she is (18:15). Let us, however, cut Sarah some slack. God speaks of their forthcoming child only to Abraham, never to her, and apparently Abraham never shares that information with her. Otherwise why would she be so startled when she overhears the conversation?

Even God has intimates to whom he bares his soul, and Abraham is one of these. God knows Abraham and therefore is not hesitant to inform Abraham about his intentions for Sodom (18:16–33).

What God hears is the outcry against Sodom and Gomorrah. This word is used in the Old Testament normally to describe the cry of the oppressed who are brutalized by their taskmasters. Ezekiel 16:49–50 makes it clear that Sodom's sin was social as well as sexual immorality.

God himself conducts a personal inspection of the city (18:21)—or at least he intends to. Abraham now stands before the Lord. (Some commentators feel that the original text may have been "The Lord stood before Abraham.")

Abraham is convinced that the judge of all the earth will do right. He has no doubts about the integrity and consistency of God. Therefore he speaks plainly with God. This is no place for clichés and shibboleths. He asks if God would refrain from judging Sodom if there were fifty righteous people in the city. Eventually he jumps not by fives but by tens, and finally he asks if God would spare Sodom for the sake of ten righteous people. Abraham believes that the presence of a few who are godly has a saving influence on the many who are ungodly. It is interesting to reflect what this story has to say about petitionary prayer, prayer as dialogue, and an omniscient, sovereign God who is moved to action or inaction by the intercessions of the faithful. Unlike Noah, who never intercedes for his sinful generation, Abraham will speak boldly to God on behalf of sinful Sodom.

I. The destruction of Sodom and Gomorrah (19:1–38). Like his uncle Abraham, Lot has opportunity to play host to two angels (19:1–11). Even before they can retire for the night, Lot's house is surrounded by the townspeople, who demand that Lot hand over his guests so that the townspeople, as the NIV puts it bluntly, might "have sex with them" (19:5). This clearly points to the fact that part of the sin of the Sodomites is sexual depravity.

Lot offers to turn over his two daughters as surrogates for the two angels. Perhaps he considers this the lesser of two evils. As host he must allow no harm to come upon his guests while they are under his roof. That was an ancient Near Eastern law of hospitality. This does not mean that Lot was justified in his action. Here the daughters are used, but in verses 30–38 the tables are turned and they are the ones in charge.

Lot and his family are warned about God's judgment on Sodom and are given a chance to escape (19:12–19). Nothing has been said about Lot's righteousness, as was the case with Noah. But in many ways the Noah story and the Lot story are parallel. A chosen family is spared the judgment of God.

Lot's sons-in-law ignore his warning, thinking he is joking. Lot's family does not take him seriously. Even Lot himself hesitates (19:16) when given the ultimatum. Lot is exempted from death because the Lord is merciful.

Lot turns down the suggestion that he flee to the mountains and asks instead for refuge in the village of Zoar. Zoar means "small," and is connected with Lot's reference in verse 20 to the place as a very small one. Lot will be saved.

Only verses 24 and 25 describe the actual catastrophe. The disaster is a combination of volcanic activity and earthquake. Lot's wife still longs for Sodom; she looks back, and that is the end of her. Verse 29 provides a second reason why God spares Lot: he remembers Abraham. This is the second time Lot owes his life to his uncle. He has been delivered from capture and now from death. Lot's connections with Abraham save him from Sodom's doom. Lot's wife's connections with Lot do not save her.

Lot ends up in the mountains, even after earlier stating that he would not go there. Lot gets drunk after the disaster, as did Noah. And while drunk, he is taken advantage of by a family member, as was Noah. His two daughters get him drunk and then sleep with him (19:30–38). As a result two sons are born: Moab ("by the father") and Ben-Ammi ("son of my parent"), from whom come the Moabites and Ammonites. The story says more about Lot than anything. He is shortsighted, insensitive, and unattractive. His relationship with God does not measure up to that of his uncle.

J. Abraham and Abimelek (20:1–18). For a second time Abraham finds himself an alien in a foreign land, with Sarah by his side (see chap. 12). And for a second time he resorts to deceit. He again asks Sarah to identify herself as his sister. This time he is in Gerar, a city of the Philistines, and the king is Abimelek. On this occasion Abraham does not draw attention to Sarah's striking beauty as he did in 12:11, but this is almost twenty-five years later.

Unlike chapter 12, which presents a case of actual adultery, this chapter deals with potential adultery. Sarah is taken, but before Abimelek can cohabit with her, God speaks to him in a dream. Three times in the Bible God appears to non-Israelites in order to warn them against carrying out their intentions: here, Genesis 31:24 (Laban), and Numbers 22:12 (Balaam). This part of the story is also unlike chapter 12. There Pharaoh discovered Sarah's true identity only when plagues were unleashed on his kingdom. Here knowledge is communicated not through an act of God but through a word of God.

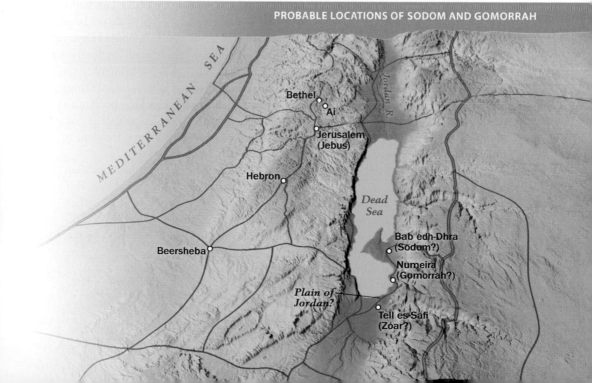

PROBABLE LOCATIONS OF SODOM AND GOMORRAH

Interestingly God identifies Abimelek's near adultery as "sinning against me" (20:6). It is not a sin against people as much as it is a sin against God. For he is the one who created the marriage relationship, and his guideline was one man for one woman, one woman for one man. Think of David, who said, "Against you, you only, have I sinned" (Ps. 51:4), after committing adultery and having the husband eliminated.

Not only is Abraham a liar; he is a prophet (20:7). One of the functions of a prophet is to represent someone before God. The prophet is an intercessor par excellence. Abraham is to pray for Abimelek, although he will never pray for barren Sarah as Isaac will for barren Rebekah (Gen. 25:21).

Unlike in chapter 12, Abraham offers a lame excuse, which he believes justifies his ruse: "there is surely no fear of God in this place" (20:11). There is no Hebrew word for "religion." The expression "fear of God" is as close as it comes. Here specifically, "fear of God" means consideration for the rights and safety of outsiders.

Abimelek is more gracious than Pharaoh. The latter expelled Abraham as a persona non grata. Abimelek, on the other hand, opens his territory to Abraham (20:15); additionally he earmarks an appreciable sum of money for Sarah to cover any ignominy she has had to endure (20:16). Although not worshipers of the Lord, Abimelek and Pharaoh in chapter 12 have enough moral sense to know you do not take somebody else's wife.

The irony in all this is that Abraham can pray for the salvation of the depraved Sodomites, and God responds. Abraham can pray for barren Philistine women, and God responds. Yet Sarah is still barren.

K. Friction inside and outside the family (21:1–34). One of the characteristics of Abraham's faith is his ability to wait and to be patient—at least most of the time. Twenty-five years earlier God promised Abraham a son (chap. 12). Now that promise becomes reality (21:1–7) after some false hopes and false moves. Appropriately, and following an earlier directive,

Abraham names the child Isaac, meaning "he laughs." Who laughs? God? Isaac? Abraham? Then Abraham circumcises Isaac (21:4).

For a third time somebody laughs, and here it is Sarah (21:6–7). This is a joyful laughter, and her joy will be contagious.

How quickly festivities can turn into friction (21:8–21). Sarah sees Ishmael mocking Isaac after Isaac has been weaned (about three years). Actually the Hebrew word for "mocking" is "to laugh." Ishmael was "Isaac-ing" Isaac. Paul's choice of "persecuted" in Galatians 4:29 indicates that Isaac and Ishmael were not engaged in harmless play.

Sarah is enraged. Laughter turns to shouting: "Get rid of that slave woman and her son" (21:10). She is too angry to call either of them by name. Abraham is more impressive here than he was in the earlier situation involving Hagar and Sarah. He protests (21:11) and makes sure that Hagar and Ishmael leave with provisions (21:14), but how long will a bottle of water and a couple of sandwiches last for a mother and her son in the desert?

This story has often been read as standing in bold contrast to that in chapter 16. For instance, it is maintained that the Ishmael of chapter 16 is a lad of sixteen years or so, while the Ishmael of chapter 21 is but an infant whom Hagar carries on her shoulders and "throws" under the tree to watch him die. A closer reading of chapter 21, however, shows that Ishmael is anything but an infant (as Ishmael's mocking of Sarah and Isaac suggests, 21:9). Chapter 21 is not a second account of the same incident in chapter 16, but a sequel to it.

Sarah does not feel much compassion for this banished mother and son. But God does. Note again, as in an earlier chapter, the intermingling in verse 17 of God and angel of God. God opens

This ancient well stands next to the archaeological site of Beersheba, which was named for the oath Abraham made there (Gen. 21:31).

his heart, and he opens Hagar's eyes to a well of water.

The problem in 21:22–34 is not over two boys but over a well belonging to Abraham that has been seized by Abimelek. To begin with, Abimelek requests honest, open dealings with Abraham, to which Abraham commits himself. Abraham lived in the Negev area. It is a hot, dry place, averaging less than seven or eight inches of rain per year. Understandably, in such an arid region, access to wells would be vitally important.

To attest that the well is indeed his, Abraham makes a treaty with Abimelek and presents animals to him, including seven live lambs. They are a witness to Abraham's honesty. As a result the place is called Beersheba, which can be translated either as "well of seven" or "well of oath." In Hebrew "to swear an oath" is "to seven." It is to Abraham's credit that he is able to prevent what could have been a major altercation. Apparently he is better at keeping peace internationally than he is at home.

L. Abraham's test (22:1–24). Sometime later God tests Abraham. It is not clear how much later, but Isaac is old enough to carry wood for a fire and carry on an intelligent conversation with his father. For the first time the verb (but not the idea) "test" occurs in the Bible. As early as chapter 12 God tested Abraham when he told him to leave Ur with his family, and Abraham went out not knowing "where he was going" (Heb. 11:8). As a matter of fact, Abraham's life begins and ends, as far as divine speech goes, with two imperatives: "Leave." "Take." And just as he is told to leave three things in chapter 12, here in chapter 22 he is told to take (1) his son, (2) his only son, (3) Isaac whom he loves. Each expression becomes more intense.

Abraham and Isaac leave Beersheba and travel three days to Mount Moriah. There is only one other reference to this site in the Old Testament, 2 Chronicles 3:1, and this passage tells us that Moriah is Jerusalem. Not one word is said about that emotion-filled three-day journey. What were Abraham's thoughts? Did he pray: "If it be possible, let this cup pass from me" (Matt. 26:39 KJV)? He certainly was quite vocal with God back in chapter 18. Why not here? Has he learned from what happened in chapter 18? Or is it a case of Abraham praying for the deliverance of sinners but refusing to pray for the deliverance of his own family?

Abraham does not expect this to be the last he will see his son. ("We will come back to you," 22:5.) Yet this story is as much an illustration of Isaac's faith as it is of Abraham's. He willingly submits to his father (22:9), when in point of fact he could have tied up his father, had he so decided.

Only when the knife is raised (22:10) is Abraham stopped by the Lord's angel. This test has proved that Abraham "fears God." That was the expression used by Abraham back in 20:11. To fear God in chapter 22 means to believe his word fully and absolutely and to be loyal to his directives.

In a nearby bush a ram is caught by its horns. Actually the Hebrew says "another ram." Ancient and modern versions have missed the point when they render "a ram" or

"a ram behind him." Isaac was the first ram. Here is the second one.

Abraham calls the name of this place "The LORD will provide." The name he chooses does not draw attention to himself but to his Lord. He does not name the place "Abraham believed." He focuses on God's mercy and faithfulness, not on his own obedience.

This place-naming is followed by one of the few instances where God's promises flow out of Abraham's performance: "because you have done this . . . I will . . ." (22:16–17). These verses actually bring the story to its climax. The story would be without a proper conclusion had it stopped at verse 14. It is not difficult to see why the New Testament interprets the binding of Isaac as a forerunner of the binding of one greater than Isaac. Notice, however, that at the most fundamental point the parallel between Isaac and Jesus breaks down. Jesus died. Isaac did not. To that degree the ram (and not the "lamb" father and son were looking for) is as much a Christ figure as Isaac.

Verses 20–24 report the birth of children to Nahor, Abraham's brother. In the midst of this story is the name Rebekah, thus preparing us for the next generation of patriarchs. Most of the names in this genealogy are the ancestors of cities and tribes around Israel. They are precisely the peoples who are to be blessed through Abraham's offspring (22:18).

M. The death of Sarah (23:1–20). Sarah dies at the age of one hundred and twenty-seven, thirty-seven years after the birth of Isaac. She is conspicuously absent from the events of chapter 22. The last city she lives in is Kiriath-arba, "city of the four," which is another name for Hebron. Abraham is not a man without emotion. He mourns and weeps for her.

For at least a third time in Genesis Abraham is an alien and a stranger. His hosts this time are the Hittites. Every time a key figure in Genesis 12–50 interacts with non-Israelites (Egyptians, Philistines, Hittites), those "outsiders" come across as decent, courteous, law-abiding, moral people. This is the opposite of the people Israel

encounters in Exodus and beyond. "Hittites" may be a name for non-Semitic peoples living in Canaan, or it may be a synonym for "Canaanites." Most likely it refers to the Hittites of Asia Minor, part of whom made their way into southern Canaan, where they established an enclave. In favor of this interpretation are the many authentic Hittite elements in the story.

For example, Abraham wants to buy only the cave of Machpelah on the property of Ephron the Hittite (23:9). Instead Ephron insists that Abraham purchase the entire field, cave and all (23:11). According to the Hittite law code one who bought a field from another had to assume feudal obligations for the field. By requesting only a part, Abraham is trying to avoid these obligations.

Abraham pays four hundred shekels of silver for the field. This seems a high price, given the fact that many generations later Jeremiah will pay seventeen shekels of silver for a field at Anathoth (Jer. 32:9). On more than one occasion, God has promised Abraham that he will "give" him this land. Here, however, Abraham buys land, and only a parcel of it at that. The transaction is carried out the usual way, at the gate of the city. Nowhere in this event is God involved. He never addresses Abraham after chapter 22.

N. Isaac and Rebekah (24:1–67). Abraham loses one family member (a wife), then gains another (a daughter-in-law). He is now old (somewhere between 137 and 175). Isaac is near forty (25:20) and still single. To remedy this situation Abraham sends a servant (Eliezer of chap. 15) to Aram Naharaim ("Syria of the two rivers") to obtain a bride for Isaac.

Abraham makes two specific requests. The girl must not be a Canaanite. Isaac must not be unequally yoked. But are Mesopotamian girls any less "pagan" than Canaanite girls? Second, Isaac and his bride must return to Canaan. Isaac is not to make Aram Naharaim a home away from home, for God has said to Abraham "to your descendants I will give this land" (24:7 RSV). All this is sealed by an oath (24:9).

The servant proposes a test to determine who Isaac's bride will be by suggesting to God that the girl who offers to water his camels be the one for Isaac (24:14). This is the servant's way of placing the success of his mission in the Lord's hands. He will not try to manipulate or orchestrate the events.

Rebekah is now introduced. She is a hard worker (24:15), beautiful (24:16a), chaste (24:16b), courteous (24:18), and thoughtful (24:19). The gifts the servant gives Rebekah are not bridal gifts. These will come later (24:53). They are, instead, an expression of appreciation for her kindness.

The girl is more than ready to give the servant a night's lodging in her family home. All of this produces an outburst of praise to God by the servant.

That Rebekah tells her mother's household (24:28) about the stranger must mean that her father, Bethuel, is dead. (The word "Bethuel" in 24:50 has no strong textual support and probably should not be read there.)

It is noteworthy that Laban should greet the servant as "blessed by the LORD" (24:31). Where would he have picked up either the name or the theology? If the God of Israel could reveal himself to Abimelek in a dream, could he not also have made himself known in some way to Laban?

Once settled in, the servant relates to Laban the purpose of his mission (24:34–41). It is most interesting that the servant relates the part about not staying in Aram Naharaim, even if he has to return empty-handed, and that while he is in Laban's family room in Aram Naharaim. Then he relates to Laban his first encounter with Rebekah (24:42–49).

Laban responds quickly and positively. In verse 57 Rebekah is consulted for her thoughts on the matter. She is not asked, however, if she wants to marry Isaac. Laban has already settled that. She is asked whether or not she desires to accompany the servant to his master's land. Assyrian law protected a woman's right to stay in her own homeland.

In verses 62–67 Isaac and Rebekah meet for the first time. He is out in the field meditating (24:63)—the Hebrew word is uncertain. As Isaac draws nearer, she veils herself (24:65). They are married, and only now does Isaac's grief at the death of his mother subside. Isaac is one of two husbands in Genesis said to love his wife. The other is his son Jacob (29:18, 30).

O. Abraham and Ishmael (25:1–18). Abraham remarries after Sarah's death, and his second wife's name is Keturah. Even though he himself felt he was past the age of fathering children before Isaac, he now produces six more children (25:2). The places represented by these names are all Arabian. The best-known of them (from the books of Numbers and Judges) is Midian. These six children of Abraham do not supplant Isaac as the son of promise (25:5).

Abraham lives until he is 175 years old (25:7–11). This means, according to 12:4, that he lived exactly one hundred years in the land of promise. Of interest is the fact that Ishmael and Isaac are both involved in the burial of their father. Ishmael, though exiled, returns for his father's funeral. Two other brothers (Esau and Jacob), long separated from each other, also meet for their father's funeral (35:29). That the text says Abraham is "gathered to his people" (25:8) indicates that death was never conceived of as extinction.

Ishmael fathers twelve children (25:12–18), more than his father did. Ishmaelites are located in the northwestern part of the Arabian peninsula. The text does not say, as it did of Abraham, that Ishmael lived a life "full of years." It is surely not accidental that two genealogies of nonchosen peoples, Ishmael's in 25:12–18 and Esau's in 36:1–40, bracket the Jacob narrative. God's call to the chosen family is to be a means of blessing to all the other families.

3. Jacob (25:19–36:43)

A. Esau and Jacob (25:19–34). Like Sarah, Rebekah is unable to bear children. Isaac's prayers reverse this situation, however (25:21).

Rebekah conceives and gives birth to twins, Esau and Jacob. Unlike Sarah, Rebekah is addressed directly by God (25:23).

It is Rebekah who is given the startling prophecy that of the two children she is carrying, the older (Esau) will serve the younger (Jacob). This is a departure from the normal procedure, where priority went to the firstborn. That the prophecy is made before the birth of the children stresses that Jacob's elevation is due to God's grace and decree and is not based on any merit in Jacob. For reasons that are not evident Rebekah never shares this oracle with her husband. (Would he have even believed her? Plus, it becomes apparent later that Isaac was overly fond of Esau.) If she had, she would not have had to urge Jacob to pretend to be Esau to get his father's blessing in chapter 27.

As they grow older Esau becomes an excellent hunter, while Jacob remains a quiet man. Esau's strength is his weakness. Famished from a hunt, he is willing to abandon his birthright in return for some red stew (on which see Heb. 12:16). His stomach overrules his conscience. Jacob wants more than a gentleman's agreement. He insists on an oath from Esau, just in case Esau has second thoughts. Although Esau will later swear at Jacob, he is content here to swear to Jacob. No commentary is made about Jacob's exploitation of his brother, or of his modus operandi in getting the birthright. God has not said "the younger shall exploit the older."

B. Isaac and Abimelek (26:1–35). This is the one chapter in Genesis devoted exclusively to Isaac. And it does not show him at his best. He imitates his father in the wife-as-sister deception. The one difference is how Abimelek is informed about the woman's identity. Abimelek sees Isaac caressing Rebekah. This can only be sexual fondling, and Abimelek is able to draw the right conclusion. Abimelek shares some of the moral values of the patriarchs. He too believes adultery is wrong and that it brings guilt on people.

Isaac fares well (26:12–14), but there is a problem. The Philistines have filled in the wells

Isaac's father has dug; Isaac proceeds to open them up again. He then digs his own wells, only to have the Gerarites claim ownership of them. The quarreling here is reminiscent of that between Abraham's servants and Lot's. Isaac gives the wells names that reflect this dispute: Esek ("contention"), Sitnah ("enmity"); but then he does better with Rehoboth ("wide places") and Shibah ("seven").

All of this concludes with a covenant between Isaac and Abimelek, solemnized by a covenant meal. The Philistines recognize a spiritual dimension in Isaac's life (26:28–29). Perhaps this is because of the mature way in which he handles the dispute. He does not lower himself to the level of the disputants. But Isaac, now at peace with neighbors, still has domestic problems. Esau marries outside the faith.

C. Jacob's deceit (27:1–40). Isaac, now advanced in age and gradually losing his eyesight, requests Esau to go out into the fields and hunt some wild game (27:1–4). It is paradoxical that Esau lost his birthright after he returned from a hunt, and he is about to lose the blessing after he leaves for a hunt.

Rebekah suggests that Jacob pretend to be Esau and thus obtain the blessing through deceit (27:5–17). This includes presenting Isaac with some choice delicacies that she will prepare, plus covering Jacob with Esau's clothes and the exposed parts of his body with goatskins. At no point does Jacob question the propriety of this course of action. He does know that if his disguise fails, it will bring a curse on him (27:12). Rebekah, however, accepts full responsibility if anything goes wrong. Rebekah is very similar to Sarah. Sarah advances Isaac's position by banishing Ishmael. Rebekah advances Jacob's position by cutting Esau out of the picture. We cannot be sure if both mothers were acting from self-interest or whether they believed they were through their actions furthering the divine agenda. Interestingly both mothers never see nor talk to their sons after these respective episodes.

This is no innocuous prank. It is deadly serious. Either way it will bring Jacob problems.

If the plan is thwarted his brother will curse him. Deception is bad enough. To deceive one's own father is even worse. To deceive a father who is senile and physically handicapped is reprehensible. Of course Isaac was not above using deceit himself if circumstances warranted (chap. 26). Here Isaac has become Abimelek, and Jacob has become Isaac (27:18–29). Like father, like son! What makes Jacob's deception utterly dastardly is his reference to God's help in the allegedly quick capturing of the game (27:20), when in fact his mother prepared it.

The truth comes out—plainly and painfully (27:30–40). It is Jacob, not Esau, whom Isaac has blessed. But a word once spoken cannot be recalled. This is the reason, by the way, for the many injunctions in the Old Testament against speaking too much, making rash vows, injudicious talk, and so forth. There is an irrevocable quality attached to words. One cannot "unsay" them.

For a second time there is a play on Jacob's name, this time by Esau (27:36). He is correctly called Jacob, says Esau, for twice now Jacob has supplanted him. The Hebrew words for "Jacob," "heel," and "supplant" are alike. Isaac blesses Esau (27:39–40), but it is hardly a positive word from the father.

D. Jacob flees to Harran (27:41–29:14). Rebekah now has a second problem on her hands. The first was to get the blessing away from Esau. The second is to get Jacob away from Esau. She accomplishes this by urging Jacob to go to Mesopotamia until Esau calms down (27:41–46). She also reminds her husband about Esau's two Hittite wives (27:46). In effect she says to Isaac: "You do not want another Hittite daughter-in-law, do you?"

For a second time, and with full awareness of whom he is blessing, Isaac gives Jacob a warning, some advice about marriage, and a blessing (28:1–9). Isaac nowhere rebukes his son for his earlier antics, any more

than God rebuked Abraham or Isaac for similar ruses. Silence, however, should not be taken as approval. The purpose of the Genesis stories in chapters 11–50 is to illustrate the election of one family through whom nations will be blessed, the promises made to that family, and God's commitment to those promises. Esau, still holding on, tries to buy a little favor with his parents by marrying a non-Canaanite girl (28:6–9). Jacob imitated him. Now he will imitate Jacob.

Somewhere between Beersheba and Harran, at a site referred to nebulously as "a certain place" (28:11), Jacob makes preparations to go to sleep. Here we have the third instance of God communicating via a dream (28:10–22; cf. Gen. 15:12; 20:3). Presumably all three of these revelations took place at night.

In his dream Jacob sees a stairway or ramp stretching from heaven to earth, with angels ascending and descending on it. The KJV has "ladder," and not "stairway" (NIV). The latter suggestion has gained wide acceptance for two reasons. First, it allows comparison with the Babylonian ziggurat, or tiered tower, and its stairways; and, second, two-way traffic on a ladder is inconceivable. However, this latter point is a moot one, and for that matter, why do angels even need anything on which to ascend and descend? The traditional "ladder" may be retained.

This is the first time God speaks to Jacob. And he does not rebuke Jacob for any previous

Jacob set up a pillar at Bethel (Gen. 28:18), similar to this sacred standing stone at the temple in Shechem.

indiscretions. On the contrary, he gives Jacob promises that include descendants, land, spiritual influence, and God's own presence (28:13–15)—promises made to a heel-grabbing Jacob who has bilked Esau and pulled the wool over Isaac's eyes, and who is fleeing, not entering, the land of promise.

Jacob's response to this is strange: he is afraid. Whenever God showed himself to Abraham, Abraham never trembled. Maybe the best parallel here is Adam, who was afraid in the garden when the Lord's presence became apparent. In Jacob's case, is this fear born of awe of God's presence, of his own spiritual insensitivity, or of a guilty conscience?

Jacob calls this place "Bethel," which means "God's house/abode." No longer is it just a place, a site, but it is now El's dwelling place. Only later in the narrative are we informed that previously the shrine was called Luz (28:19). To memorialize this encounter with God, Jacob takes the stone he laid his head on and erects it as a pillar (a phenomenon that later becomes illicit in certain contexts, but is permissible in patriarchal times).

Jacob's vow is of interest in that it picks up on the promise of verse 15 but excludes verse 14. It is God's presence and a safe return to the land from which he has fled that concerns Jacob. The climax of the vow is that Jacob will commit himself to tithing (28:22). This moves the Bethel encounter out of the realm of emotion exclusively and into the realm of self-denial and stewardship.

"Eastern peoples" (29:1) is used as a general designation for anybody living east of Canaan. Jacob meets a number of shepherds milling around the well, which is covered by a large stone. Happily these shepherds know who Laban is and the state of his health. And even better, Laban's daughter Rachel comes to the well while Jacob is there. All of this is not fortuitous, but an indication of God's guidance (29:1–14).

Jacob urges the shepherds to water their flocks and return them to pasture. When they protest that this would be a breach of formalities, Jacob himself rolls away the stone. All this may be deliberately designed by Jacob to buy some time alone with Rachel. Jacob's kissing of Rachel should be seen as the custom of the day and not as an act of indiscretion or a good way to end a courtship before it begins.

E. Jacob, Leah, and Rachel (29:15–30:24). Laban has two daughters, Leah ("cow") and Rachel ("ewe lamb") (29:15–30). Rachel is the younger and the one Jacob finds more attractive. Jacob's suggestion that he work seven years in return for her hand in marriage is a magnanimous offer. He goes to this extreme in hopes of guaranteeing his marriage with Rachel. Laban agrees to the proposal (29:19).

On the night of the wedding feast, Laban manages to substitute Leah for Rachel. It is unlikely that a heavily veiled Leah could dupe Jacob. Probably Laban was able to succeed only because Jacob was drunk. We are not told about Leah. Was she drunk too? Did she have any say in the matter? Did she believe she was entitled to marry Jacob? Or does she passively submit to her father's orders? There can be no doubt that this scenario contrasts with the event of chapter 27. The perpetrator of deceit is now the victim of deceit. Jacob surely wondered why Laban did not offer the explanation found in verse 26 earlier. But no trickster can let the cat out of the bag prematurely.

Leah gives birth to four sons—Reuben, Simeon, Levi, and Judah (29:31–35). Jacob never names the children. Leah does, and the significance of each name is explained by a Hebrew phrase that contains a word or words that sound like the proper name.

Most intriguing here are the births of Levi and Judah. From these sons come two of the most crucial institutions of the Old Testament—priesthood and kingship. Both institutions have their origin in an unwanted marriage laced with deception and bitterness. Paul is correct; God does work in all things for good (Rom. 8:28).

The competition between Leah and Rachel means more children for Jacob (30:1–24).

Reflecting an allowable custom of her day, Rachel gives her maidservant Bilhah to Jacob as a surrogate wife, much as Sarah gave Hagar to Abraham. Bilhah gives birth to Dan and to Naphtali. As with the names in 29:31–35, the meaning of each name is explained by a Hebrew phrase reflecting the circumstances of the child's birth. In verse 7 "a great struggle" may be translated "wrestlings of God." In chapter 30 it is Rachel who wrestles with God. In chapter 32, Jacob wrestles with God. Throughout these brief birth scenes Leah and Rachel speak often, and when they do they frequently speak about God (e.g., 29:32; 30:6). By contrast Jacob speaks only once in the birth accounts of his eleven children, and that one time he does speak (30:2) is to berate Rachel.

Zilpah, Leah's maid, also bears two children, Gad and Asher (30:9–12). This is more than Rachel can take. She believes, mistakenly, that if she can just get some mandrakes, now in Reuben's possession, she will be able to conceive. Mandrakes are herbs that give off a distinct odor and produce a fruit like a small orange. They were thought to aid in conception, an idea helped along no doubt by the fact that the Hebrew words for mandrake and love are from the same root word. Verses 22–24, however, make it clear that it is not mandrakes that bring fertility to Rachel. She gives birth to Joseph not because of magic but because God remembers her and opens her womb.

F. Jacob and Laban (30:25–31:55). Earlier Rachel said to Jacob, "give me children" (30:1). Now Jacob says to Laban, "give me my wives and children." It is time for him to head back to Canaan. To that end, he asks that Laban give him the speckled and spotted sheep and goats as his wages (30:25–43).

Laban believes that Jacob is giving himself the short end of the deal (very few irregular animals will be bred from this), and so he quickly agrees to Jacob's proposal.

Jacob, however, knows more about crossbreeding and the laws of heredity than Laban knows—and more than Laban gives him credit for knowing. Through exposure to a visual stimulus (branches of certain trees, which Jacob marks with white stripes) the monochromes give birth to multicolored young. In the process, not only does Jacob get more flocks than Laban bargained for, but he gets healthier flocks as well. Now it is Laban's turn to be outwitted.

Jacob's rods may be compared with Rachel's mandrakes. It is God, not the mandrakes, who bestows fertility on Rachel. Similarly, it is a dream revelation from God (31:10–12), not the rods per se, that makes it possible for Jacob to obtain a decent wage from his uncle. In both instances, success is due to the providence of God rather than to magic.

All factors indicate that it is high time for Jacob to bid adieu to Laban (31:1–21). The attitude of Laban and his sons (31:1–2) and a direct revelation from God (31:3) confirm this. Jacob is careful, however, to share this with his wives, not with his father-in-law. They concur immediately with Jacob, for Laban now considers them, in their judgment, only as foreigners. Jacob is careful to make his move while Laban is out shearing his sheep. Rachel takes only what she can carry—the clothes on her back and her father's household gods. It is unlikely she takes these gods as decorations for her new living quarters, or even for divine protection on their trip to Canaan. Some have suggested that she takes the gods in an attempt to establish Jacob as the legitimate heir of Laban's possessions. But there are problems with this explanation as well.

That Laban catches up with Jacob in seven days means either that Laban moved incredibly fast, or else his home was not as far from Canaan as Mesopotamia (31:22–42). He is enraged, and an enraged man is an irrational man. God comes to him in a dream at night (as with Abimelek in chap. 20), warning Laban to do no physical harm to Jacob. If Jacob is to get any hard knocks it will be from God, not Laban.

Laban seems to be most upset by the fact that he believes Jacob has stolen his gods. This is ironic. Can gods be stolen? Can deity be kidnapped? In nonbiblical thought, yes. If you make your gods or buy your gods, then they become vulnerable.

Rachel is as deceptive as her father and her husband. She is the one who has stolen the gods, without telling Jacob. Jacob did not tell Laban he was leaving, and Rachel did not tell Jacob she had taken Laban's gods. She pretends that she is having her menstrual period, and is thus unable to move as Laban conducts his search. Not only are the gods stolen, but now they suffer a further indignity—they are stained by Rachel's blood. Jacob has his chance to rebuke Laban. Note his interesting reference to the Lord as the "Fear of Isaac" (31:42), a name for God that appears in the Old Testament only here and in verse 53.

Rather than part in bitterness, Jacob and Laban choose to part amiably, and this is to their credit. Accordingly they make a covenant. To memorialize this moment they raise a pillar of stones, which Laban names "Jegar Sahadutha" (Aramaic), and which Jacob names "Galeed" (Hebrew; both terms mean "the heap of witness"). The site is also called "Mizpah," meaning "watchpost." Both pledge not to intrude on the peace of the other or to become belligerent toward the other. Laban seals this covenant, interestingly, with a reference not to his own gods but to the God of Abraham. Is this religious courtesy and ecumenism, or is Laban moving toward belief in the one true God?

G. Jacob and Esau (32:1–33:20). 32:1–32. It has been at least twenty years since Jacob last saw Esau. Time heals all wounds, so the saying goes. Sometimes time intensifies wounds. Jacob is far from believing that with Esau all is forgotten and forgiven. To that end he makes preparations to meet Esau, with fear and trepidation (32:1–21). The skeletons in Jacob's closet are now coming out. Jacob moves from crisis to crisis, from hot water to hot water. Laban confronted him in chapter 31, and now he is about to meet Esau.

Jacob is as diplomatic as possible. He identifies himself, through his messengers, as "your servant" (32:4, not "your brother"), and he refers to Esau as "my lord" (32:5).

Terrified to learn that Esau has four hundred men with him, Jacob divides his entourage into two, breathes a quick prayer, and prepares a lavish gift for Esau. Jacob reveals his purpose for these presents: "I will pacify him" (32:20). Appeasement, then, is a must for Jacob. The Hebrew for "pacify" reads literally "cover his face." Note Jacob's position: his gifts go on ahead of him.

Jacob, in chapter 28, was interested only in getting away from Esau. But God met him unexpectedly. Here Jacob is thinking only of how to prepare for Esau. Again, unexpectedly, God meets him (32:21–32).

The action begins at night when a man (?) wrestles with Jacob. Incidentally, the verb for "wrestle" and the place where this match occurs, Jabbok, are from the same root, one of the many wordplays in this story. This wrestling continues until daybreak. Given the fact that this "man" is indeed the all-powerful God, could he not have bowled Jacob over in a split second with a little fling of his finger? No! For here is a God assuming human form, taking on flesh so to speak, and putting aside his awesome power. Jacob displays a few admirable characteristics. One of these is a confession of unworthiness: "What is your name?" (32:27). "Jacob," he answers. "Jacob" is not only *who* he is, but *what* he is. Here is an explicit case where a name is descriptive of one's nature. Who am I? Trickster. Supplanter. Heel-grabber.

A second commendable virtue is Jacob's consuming hunger for God. "I will not let you go unless you bless me" (32:26). One result of this meeting with God is that Jacob's name is changed to Israel, which in the explanation given is connected with a Hebrew verb meaning "to contend with, strive." As with Abraham in chapter 17, a new name indicates a new destiny. The first evidence of real spiritual transformation in Jacob's life is that he receives a new name.

God first gives a name, and then Jacob gives a name. He calls the site "Peniel" (Penuel is a variant), meaning "the face of God." Jacob is doubly surprised. He has a new name, and he has seen God and lived to tell about it. But his hip is not healed. Jacob leaves, no, limps away from Peniel. That limp will be a constant reminder to him of this experience with God. Finally, Jacob's run-in with God carries influence well beyond his own lifetime (32:32, though this particular dietary prohibition is not spoken of in later legislation).

33:1–20. Jacob is about to see Esau again. He lines up his family in order of least loved to most loved (33:2). There is one difference. Before Jacob met God at Peniel he would stay "behind" (32:16, 18, 20). Now he goes "on ahead" of his entourage (33:3a). Not only did Jacob receive a new name at Peniel, but he received new courage as well.

The narrator refers to Esau as Jacob's "brother" (33:3b) as does Esau of Jacob (33:9). Jacob, however, still addresses Esau as "my lord" (33:8, 14–15), and refers to himself as "your servant" (33:5).

Jacob insists that Esau accept the gifts he has brought, and Esau takes them only reluctantly. He who earlier took twice from Esau now demands that Esau take something from him. One cannot help but be impressed with the "outsider" Esau on this occasion. He is not angry or vengeful. In running to Jacob and then embracing him and kissing him, he acts much like the father upon the return of the prodigal son (Luke 15).

When Esau suggests that Jacob follow him back home to Seir, Jacob offers an excuse why he cannot and promises to come to Seir later, a promise that Jacob likely has no intention of keeping. Apparently there is still a bit of Jacob in him. Jacob goes to Shechem, and there purchases a piece of land for a quarter of the amount his grandfather paid for his land.

Even before going to Shechem he goes to Sukkoth ("huts, booths"). The altar he builds he calls El Elohe Israel ("God, the God of Israel [Jacob]"). Does not that bring to completion the word of the Lord to Jacob in 28:13, "I am

the LORD, the God of your father Abraham and the God of Isaac"? Now he is the God of the third generation too. Jacob is reconciled with God in chapter 32. He is reconciled with his brother in chapter 33. Anyone who does not love his brother cannot love God (1 John 4:20).

H. The rape of Dinah (34:1–31). Life has not treated Jacob well. As a young man he was forced to flee from home. In the wilderness he met God and was afraid. Then he was tricked and embarrassed by Laban. He fled Laban. At Peniel he wrestled with God and limped away. Before and after that he agonized over meeting Esau. And now his one beloved daughter, Dinah, is violated. The tragic event is comparable to one in David's life. He too has many sons, but only one daughter, Tamar, who is also sexually violated (2 Samuel 13).

The criminal is Shechem, son of Hamor. He is called a Hivite in verse 2. An ancient version of the Bible renders this as "Horite" (i.e., Hurrian), showing perhaps that the original settlers of Shechem were Hurrians.

Jacob's sons (but not Jacob himself) are understandably incensed. Hamor attempts to appease them with the offer of peaceful coexistence. One more time we encounter an instance of deception in Genesis. Jacob imitates his father, who imitated his father. And now Jacob's sons imitate their father. Simeon and Levi are the ringleaders. They let on that it is proper for Dinah to marry a Hamorite only if all the males are circumcised.

Three days later, when the pain from the operation would be greatest, Dinah's brothers strike with a vengeance. Holy war is declared against the Hamorites. Jacob protests the excesses of their retaliation, but his sons defend their action as noble. A vigilante mentality always insists that the answer to violence is more violence. Jacob himself has been set free from such a mindset. The last verse of chapter 34 and the last verse of Jonah (Jon. 4:11) provide the only two instances in the Old Testament of a scene that concludes with an unanswered question.

I. Jacob returns to Bethel (35:1–29). Jacob continues to evidence spiritual maturity. He is, for instance, sensitive to anything that is at cross-purposes with the presence of God in his life. That is why he orders the removal of foreign gods (probably those Rachel brought from Laban's house) and the change of clothes (symbolizing spiritual renewal). Even the rings in their ears are removed. Wherever Jacob goes the power of God is manifest (35:5).

Jacob now renames Bethel "El Bethel" ("God of the House of God"). More important than Bethel as a site of cherished memory is the remembrance of the God who met him there. Last, God repeats Jacob's new name, Israel. This is not another tradition parallel to 32:28. Why then repeat it? May the repetition indicate that it is only when Jacob is reconciled to Esau that Jacob indeed becomes Israel? This reminder is then followed by a reiteration of the divine promises (35:11–13).

Still, there are a few more unpleasant, grief-producing series of incidents for Jacob. Rebekah's nurse dies. His beloved Rachel dies in giving birth to Benjamin ("son of the right [hand]"). Reuben, his firstborn, commits incest. Finally, his father Isaac dies. None of the other patriarchal figures ever had to endure the tragedies that Jacob did. From chapter 28 on, hardly a chapter passes without some unsettling or disturbing incident taking place.

J. Esau's descendants (36:1–43). Chapter 36 is not among the more exciting chapters of Genesis. It is given entirely to a listing of Esau's descendants. The structure is much like that of chapter 25, where the record of Abraham's death (25:7–11) is followed by Ishmael's genealogy (25:12–18). Here the account of Isaac's death is followed by Esau's genealogy.

The names include Esau's immediate family (36:1–19), the sons of Seir (36:20–30), and a list of Edomite kings (36:31–39) who "reigned in Edom before any Israelite king reigned" (36:31). This would suggest that they are all pre-Saul. A footnote in the earlier edition of the NIV (1984) suggests an alternate reading: "before an

Israelite king reigned over them." That would mean they are all pre-David. Repeatedly these individuals are referred to as "chiefs" (36:15, 18–19, 29–30, 40). This term is used in the Old Testament for Edomite leaders.

It is interesting that the second-longest chapter in Genesis is devoted to a genealogy of a marginal person—Esau—and that the story of Jacob should conclude by talking extensively (there are over two hundred names!) about the future of Esau. For that fact, the rest of Genesis (chaps. 37–50) is mostly a narrative about Joseph, also a marginal nonpatriarchal individual, and not the son of promise through whom the covenant is perpetuated. Esau is not Jacob, but he is not a nobody either. God has been gracious to him, as is implied by Esau's testimony to the "plenty" he now enjoys (33:9).

4. Joseph (37:1–50:26)

A. Joseph and his brothers (37:1–36). Joseph gives his brothers three reasons to dislike him. First, he "snitches" on them (37:2). Second, their father openly loves Joseph more than any other of his children (37:3–4). Third, he has two dreams that his brothers interpret as arrogant and egotistical (37:5–11). The younger brother will have authority over the older brother, just as Jacob did over Esau. Even Jacob is jolted by Joseph's second dream. Will he too bow the knee to his son? Jacob's "will your mother and I . . ." (37:10) must be understood as a posthumous reference to Rachel, for she has already died.

The Bible makes no comment, other than the brothers' response, about the motivation for Joseph's telling these dreams. Could he not anticipate that sharing them would inevitably produce antagonism? Probably Joseph, at the young age of seventeen, did not think it through that far. What he is doing is sharing the sense of destiny that God is opening up before him with anybody who will listen. God has a plan for Joseph's life, and that plan involves leadership and authority. For sharing this sense of excitement about God's will for his future, he is sold by his own flesh as a slave. That was not

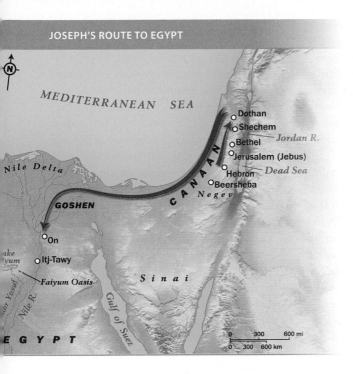

JOSEPH'S ROUTE TO EGYPT

again belief in an afterlife. Joseph, meanwhile, is sold to an Egyptian officer, Potiphar. It is most likely that Joseph is not yet able to make the connection between his dreams of destiny and this devastating experience. Little does he know that this is but the first event God will use to implement his plan for Joseph's life, although God never speaks, nor is he spoken to or about, throughout the entire chapter.

B. Judah and Tamar (38:1–30).

Momentarily Joseph drops out of the narrative to be replaced by his brother Judah. Judah marries a Canaanite girl by whom he has three children: Er, Onan, and Shelah. Er marries Tamar, but he is put to death by God for an unspecified sin. As a result Tamar is left a childless widow.

It is then the responsibility of the next eldest son, Onan, to father a child by his sister-in-law to bear the name of the deceased. This custom is known as levirate marriage (Latin *levir*, "brother-in-law"), and is spelled out in detail in Deuteronomy 25:5–10. The institution is reflected in the New Testament story about the woman who was married to seven husbands (Matt. 22:23–28). In the resurrection, Jesus is asked, to whom will she belong?

Onan refuses to exercise his responsibility most likely in order to guarantee he will get his hands on his older brother's inheritance, and as a result dies. He who would in one sense keep his brother alive dies himself.

The third son, Shelah, is too young. Tamar is to return for a while to her father's home. When Shelah grows a bit older, Judah will send for her.

Like many promises, this is never carried out. Judah forgets his word to Tamar, intentionally or inadvertently. She takes matters into her own hands. Disguising herself as a prostitute (the normal Hebrew word for harlot is used in verse 15, but the Hebrew word for "shrine

part of the dream! Where does this nightmare fit into God's glorious future for Joseph?

Joseph travels from Hebron to Shechem to Dothan in search of his brothers. This is no small trip by any means. Joseph would have traveled approximately one hundred miles. The brothers realize that this is their moment for getting even with their brother and his grandiose dreams (37:12–36). They will kill him by throwing him into a cistern, where he will surely die of starvation and exposure.

Reuben, desirous of avoiding bloodguilt, suggests an alternative, as does Judah (37:21–22, 26–27). In the end Joseph is sold as chattel to Midianites (i.e., Ishmaelites).

Meanwhile the brothers put Joseph's coat into goat's blood to convince their father that Joseph has been attacked and killed by a wild animal. Once again we encounter deception. Jacob, the master deceiver, is deceived by his own sons.

He buys their ruse—hook, line, and sinker. Jacob's affirmation that he will "go down to the grave to my son" (37:35 NIV 1984) shows prostitute" occurs in 38:21–22), she seduces her father-in-law. He impregnates her and she bears twins by him, Perez ("breaking out") and Zerah ("scarlet"). Judah is quick to condemn Tamar for her blatant immorality (38:24) but draws back and blushes when his own sin is exposed. As with Jacob and Leah a key child is born of Judah and Tamar, Perez, who will continue the messianic line (Matt. 1:3).

One more time we have a story built around deception. It is Judah this time who is deceived. There are a number of parallels between this story and the ones in chapters 37 and 39. Joseph's morality in the face of temptation may be contrasted with Judah's immorality. In chapter 37 Jacob is deceived; in chapter 38 Judah is deceived. In both instances the truthfulness of the situation is confirmed by the presentation of evidence. Jacob "knows" Joseph is dead because of the bloodied coat. Judah knows he is the father of Tamar's children when she produces his seal, cord, and staff.

C. Joseph and Potiphar's wife (39:1–23). Joseph finds himself in the employ of Potiphar, a high-ranking official of Pharaoh. What goes through the mind of the bewildered teenager, who has been uprooted violently from his home, sold as a servant, made to live with strangers, and purchased off the trading block and is now dwelling in a foreign country?

Joseph has two things going for him. First, the Lord is with him. Joseph may not know this—at least not yet, for although the Lord is with Joseph, the Lord does not keep Joseph out of trouble and danger. This is the only chapter in the Joseph story (excluding chaps. 38 and 49, where Joseph is either absent or minimally present), where "Lord" appears, and it appears seven times, all by the narrator. In addition to the divine presence, Joseph is a diligent worker, one who impresses his master with his conscientious industriousness. Joseph is to Potiphar what Jacob was to Laban. Both of these non-Israelites experienced blessings because a child of Abraham was in their midst. Joseph oversees everything except Potiphar's food (39:6).

Potiphar's wife finds herself romantically drawn to this young, handsome, unattached Hebrew. At a propitious moment she propositions him. Joseph adamantly refuses to become her lover for two reasons. First, it would be a disservice to his master, who has trusted him (39:8–9a). Second, it would be a sin against God (39:9b). Joseph's words help us understand the difference between guilt over sin and godly sorrow over sin. Guilt means we are sorry for our sins because we know they are ruining our lives and may keep us out of heaven. Godly sorrow means we are sorry for our sins because we know they grieve the heart of God. It is Joseph's commitment to high moral principle that keeps him free from an illicit affair. How different he is from David!

In a last-ditch attempt to get rid of Joseph for rejecting her, the wife grasps a section of his cloak, and then spreads the vicious lie that Joseph tried to rape her. That cloak is her incriminating evidence. She passes the same lie on to her husband. She cannot call Joseph by his name but refers to him as "that Hebrew slave" (39:17).

We do not know why Potiphar put Joseph into prison rather than killing him. Did Potiphar have reason to be suspicious of his wife's story? Had she done something like this before? Maybe Potiphar trusts Joseph more than he trusts his wife. If that is the case, Potiphar is appropriately cautious. You can release an innocent man from incarceration, but you cannot resurrect him.

Many have observed the parallel between this story and the thirteenth-century-BC Egyptian story The Tale of Two Brothers. In the latter, one brother is married, and one is not. In the married brother's absence, the wife tries to seduce her brother-in-law, who refuses her. She then complains to her husband, when he returns, about the "initiative" taken by the younger brother. Eventually the truth emerges, and the wife is slain for bearing false witness.

Even in prison Joseph is productive and is quickly given authority (39:21–23). The Lord is with him. Joseph shares a sense of destiny, and it gets him a pit and a ride to Egypt. He is committed to being morally pure, and it lands him in jail. What is to be made of these paradoxes?

D. Joseph's interpretation of dreams (40:1–41:57). Joseph finds himself in custody with two of Pharaoh's officers, the cupbearer and the chief baker (40:1–23). Potiphar's house would have to be in the capital city of the empire. That is the only way Joseph would end up in the same prison as Pharaoh's officials.

Both officials have dreams relating to their position. The cupbearer dreams of three blossoming branches on a grapevine. He squeezes the grapes into Pharaoh's cup and puts the cup in his hand (40:9–11). The baker dreams of three baskets of bread on his head, and of birds, which eat the bread out of the basket (40:16–17).

Joseph is not a skilled dream interpreter by nature. He makes that plain when he says, "Do not interpretations belong to God?" (40:8). He knows who is to get the credit. It is not without significance that in an ancient world filled with guilds of dream interpreters (oneiromantics), with whom every king surrounded himself, the Old Testament seldom mentions this. To be sure, dreams are common, but there are only two places in the Old Testament where *A* interprets *B*'s dreams. Those two incidents involve Joseph and Daniel, one at the beginning and one at

the end of the Old Testament. And both times they interpret the dreams of a non-Israelite.

The cupbearer's dream anticipates a happy future. Joseph tells him that within three days Pharaoh will take up his case. The verdict will be a good one. The cupbearer will be restored to his position.

The baker's dream does not bode well for his future. Birds in the flood story were a good omen, but here they are a threat. Within three days Pharaoh will literally lift up the baker's head—he will die.

Joseph has one little favor to ask. He requests that when the cupbearer is restored to his position, he use his influence to get Joseph released from jail, for Joseph is there because of a false charge. The cupbearer, however, forgets him.

Here are the thorns in Joseph's flesh: his brothers, Potiphar's wife, and now the cupbearer. The first abused him. The second lied about him. The third forgets him. Joseph has more than sexual temptations to confront. There is the temptation to be resentful, to be angry, to be depressed, and even to be cynical. How will he rise above these?

For two years Joseph has been imprisoned for a crime he did not commit.

In the ancient world dreams were thought to be messages from the gods. This portion of the Gilgamesh Epic describes Gilgamesh's dream and its explanation by Enkidu.

For two years the cupbearer forgets about him completely. That is all about to change, for Pharaoh has two dreams, the interpretation of which eludes the wise men of Egypt and its magicians (41:1–57).

In the first dream seven fat cows are eaten by seven lean cows. In the second dream seven healthy heads of grain are swallowed by seven thin heads of grain. One would think that the dreams should have been essentially self-explanatory. They both have to do with the number seven, and with something good and healthy being overcome by something unhealthy. At least the magicians might have guessed at it. Does God not only make the difficult discernible but also the easy indiscernible?

It is ignorance that opens the door for Joseph. Suddenly the cupbearer recalls Joseph. Little notes such as the fact that Joseph shaves (41:14) serve to authenticate the Egyptian milieu of the story. The Egyptians, unlike the Hebrews, were always clean shaven. Only the pharaoh wore a beard, and even that was an artificial one.

Joseph is able both to interpret Pharaoh's dreams (41:25–31) and to explain why Pharaoh had dual dreams (41:32). In addition to making known the future to Pharaoh (seven years of plenty followed by seven years of famine), Joseph suggests a future course of action in order to prepare for the lean years.

Such foresight commends Joseph to Pharaoh, who immediately gives Joseph a position of leadership and invests him with the symbols of authority that go with that office. Also, Joseph obtains a wife (Asenath, daughter of Potiphera) and a new Egyptian name—Zaphenath-Paneah.

Joseph fathers two children, Manasseh and Ephraim (41:50–52). The first name is connected with the verb "to forget" (i.e., "he made me forget"), and the second is connected with the verb "to be fruitful" (i.e., "he made me fruitful"). These two names point to a God who can both heal one of painful memories and make one useful and productive even in the most debilitating circumstances. The text mentions no problem with Joseph marrying an Egyptian, as there was with Esau marrying a Hittite.

For the first time something happens to Joseph in which he is not a victim. Only now do the silent workings of God begin to dawn on him. Joseph is beginning to discover that God is truly with him.

E. Joseph's brothers in Egypt (42:1–38). There must be at least seven years between the end of chapter 41 and the beginning of chapter 42, for there is now the reality of famine, which Joseph has predicted.

It is interesting to observe Joseph's strategy in dealing with his brothers. First, he pretends to be a stranger. Second, he speaks harshly to them. Third, he accuses them of being spies. Fourth, he repeats that accusation. Fifth, he tests their integrity by insisting that one brother stay behind while the others return to Canaan and bring back their youngest brother. Finally, he slips the money they give him for the grain back into their sacks, creating the impression that they are thieves.

To say the least, Joseph has made it as difficult for the brothers as possible. Some would say that this is vindictiveness on the part of Joseph. Here is his chance to reciprocate, and he relishes the moment. A more likely suggestion is that Joseph is testing (see 42:15) his brothers. Are they any different than when he last saw them? Will the brothers really recognize the terrible nightmare through which they put Joseph if they have to endure some suffering of their own? The frequent references to Joseph's weeping (42:24; 43:30; 45:1–2, 14–15; 46:29; 50:1, 17) show that such harshness is but a facade.

It is not difficult to see why the brothers would not recognize Joseph. It has been at least twenty years since they last saw him. Also, he is clean shaven and uses an interpreter. Even his selection of Simeon (42:24) as the one to stay behind may be an attempt not to give his hand away too soon. Had he chosen Reuben, as one would expect, then maybe the brothers would have started putting two and two together. For it was Reuben who spoke up in Joseph's defense (42:22; 37:21–22).

All of this produces more turmoil for Jacob. His own unhappy experiences are not yet ended. They are still dogging him, and will continue to do so to the grave.

F. The second journey to Egypt (43:1–34). Because of the continuing famine, Joseph's brothers must return to Egypt to procure additional grain. This time it is Judah who comes to the fore. It is he who reminds Jacob of the terms Joseph set for any future purchase of food. Before he will release any supplies, they must bring Benjamin with them.

Judah says nothing about the charge that they were spies. Nor does anybody seem to have much to say about Simeon. He is miles away, incarcerated somewhere in Egypt. Judah, however, is willing to go surety for Benjamin (43:8–9), and this convinces Jacob to send Benjamin. Either Judah is using a bit of delightful hyperbole (43:10), or else there was a protracted, heated debate on what was best for the family to do.

Jacob reluctantly agrees. The brothers will return to Egypt, with Benjamin, and take some gifts to appease Joseph, much as Jacob brought a gift to Esau to appease him. Jacob also doubles the amount of silver that Joseph put back into their sacks (43:12). Jacob may be without food, but he is not without money.

For the first time in many years Joseph sees his younger brother Benjamin, and his emotions get the better of him. After getting control of himself, he serves a sumptuous dinner, with extra portions for Benjamin. Why all this lavish attention on Benjamin?

G. Judah's plea (44:1–34). Joseph's final plan to "incriminate" his brothers is to send them back to Canaan again. But before they leave he slips his silver cup into Benjamin's grain sack. This is Pharaoh's cup, and the one with which he practices divination. Water divination was a common practice in Egypt, a method of determining the future. One might read the pattern of drops that fell from a cup, or one might

throw something into the water in the cup, which would form patterns that were omens.

The brothers maintain their innocence. Why do such a stupid thing, they ask? This incident reminds us of Rachel's theft of her father's gods. Laban hunted Jacob down and accused him of being a thief. Jacob protested, claiming innocence, and even pronounced a curse on any person who did take them.

Imagine the brothers' horror when the silver cup is found in Benjamin's sack. Until this point, the brothers do not have a clue that all this has been staged by Joseph. They believe that all this is happening because of divine retribution (44:16).

One of the most moving speeches in all of Scripture is Judah's plea for Benjamin (44:18–34). This is quite a different Judah than the one we read about in chapter 38. He is the intercessor par excellence, and even offers himself as a substitute for Benjamin—"take me, but let him return." And Judah's concern is as much for his father as it is for his young brother.

Joseph's strategy, however wrenching, is producing positive changes in his formerly calloused brothers.

H. Joseph makes himself known (45:1–28). It is now two years into the famine. That means it has been twenty-two years since Joseph has seen his father. Unable to hide his identity any longer, Joseph weeps aloud and identifies himself to his brothers: "I am Joseph!" So astonished are they that they cannot respond (45:3). Doubtless they now expect the worst. However, Joseph is above vindictiveness and retaliation. An eye for an eye and a tooth for a tooth is not his procedure. Instead he shares with his brothers a beautiful interpretation of what has happened to him. He affirms that it was to save lives that God sent him ahead. And quite possibly "to save lives" may refer to Hebrew lives and Egyptian lives. Not only are Jacob's relatives spared because of Joseph, but so are the Egyptians. It was not the brothers who sold him, but God who "sent" him. It is unlikely that Joseph saw it in exactly that light twenty-two years earlier.

Now the truth of Romans 8:28, long before it was written, shapes Joseph's attitudes.

He becomes a bit more specific in verse 7 when he says, "God sent me ahead of you to preserve for you a remnant." It now becomes clear that Joseph is the divine means for the salvation of his family. Even though he is not the son through whom the covenant promise is passed, he is the son that God uses to keep the flame alive.

Joseph promises them land if they move to Egypt. They will live in Goshen, a fertile area in the northeast delta region. Unlike many immigrants who are consigned to desolate places, Jacob and his sons will move into lush land where harvests will be bountiful. Goshen is the perfect place for Jacob to settle his family. Here they can live without close contact with the native Egyptian people.

As the brothers head back to Canaan they do so with Egyptian carts, new clothes, food, and provisions, with something extra for Benjamin (45:21–23). Joseph's injunction that they not quarrel on the way (45:24) shows that he has not forgotten what his brothers are capable of doing.

Jacob is stunned to learn that Joseph is still alive. And well he should be. Actually he needs little convincing— only the Egyptian carts. In spite of advancing age, he is now most eager to see his son. It is not clear why the father called Jacob in verses 25–27 is now called Israel in verse 28. Jacob, a name overladen with pejorative overtones, would be inappropriate at a moment of ecstasy and euphoria. Israel, the new name, the name of new direction, is the better one to use at this happy time.

I. Jacob in Egypt (46:1–50:14). 46:1–34. Jacob prepares to head down to Egypt to see Joseph (46:1–34). On the way he stops at Beersheba and offers sacrifices to the Lord. Isaac, his father, has built an altar there (26:25). It is significant that the Lord speaks to Jacob after Jacob has worshiped.

The last time God confronted Jacob was at night (32:22–32). The first time God spoke to Jacob was through a dream (28:10–12). The last time God speaks to Jacob is through a vision at night. God's first word to Jacob was nothing but promises for his future (28:13–15). His last word to Jacob is similarly promissory (46:3–4). This is exactly the same with Abraham. God's first word (12:1–3) and his last word (22:15–18) are promises. The lives of these two patriarchs are bracketed by the "I will" of God. This structure underscores the cruciality of promise as the major theme of Genesis.

The number of those who go to Egypt, excluding Jacob's daughters-in-law, is sixty-six (46:26). This number is obtained by the deletion of Er and Onan (46:12), who are already dead; by the deletion of Joseph, Ephraim, and Manasseh,

Joseph tells his brothers, "You shall live in the region of Goshen, and be near me" (Gen. 45:10). Seen here is the modern-day region of Tell ed-Dab'a, where Goshen was located.

who are already in Egypt; plus the inclusion of Jacob's daughter, Dinah (70 – 5 + 1 = 66).

Judah, always the go-between, is sent ahead to prepare for the meeting of father and son (46:28). Few events in Scripture can match the emotion-filled intensity of this reunion. Tears are many. Words are few. Jacob's only reason for not wanting to die has been erased. He knows Joseph is alive, and he has seen him again.

Joseph urges his family to identify themselves as shepherds to Pharaoh. The reason for this is clear enough. Goshen, with its scrub-covered plains, was an excellent area for cattle. This fact would encourage Pharaoh to allow the Jacobites to settle in Goshen.

47:1–31. Joseph carefully orchestrates the meeting between Jacob and his sons and Pharaoh. Everything goes smoothly. Pharaoh knows this territory well and requests that the royal cattle be put under the supervision of one of Joseph's brothers (47:6). Goshen is identified in verse 11 as the district of Rameses. This must be an editorial note, for the area did not acquire this name until the thirteenth century BC.

Jacob's autobiography is far from positive. He tells Pharaoh: "My years have been few and difficult" (47:9). True, Jacob (147 years) does not live as long as his father (180 years) or his grandfather (175 years), but more than life span is in mind here. Looking back over his past, Jacob sees a few bright moments, but they have been eclipsed by a constant series of setbacks, family problems, tragedies, and nightmares.

Joseph must continue to oversee the country. He collects the money the people use to purchase the grain. When the money is all gone, he accepts livestock as payment. When the livestock is all sold, he accepts land as payment. Only the priests are exempt from this administrative policy.

Life is not prosperous for the Egyptians, but at least they are alive, and for this they are grateful to Joseph. Their words, "you have saved our lives" (47:25), confirm that the "save lives" of 45:5 includes Egyptians. Already God is

fulfilling his promise to Abraham that nations will be blessed through him. The Egyptians are blessed by Joseph's presence. They do not die. They survive a catastrophe, thanks to Joseph.

Just before he dies, Jacob summons Joseph to him. The phrase "put your hand under my thigh" (47:29) lends solemnity to the occasion of the oath. (The same procedure is mentioned in 24:2.) Joseph binds himself by oath not to inter Jacob in Egypt. Jacob's "swear to me" directed to Joseph (47:31) may be compared with his "swear to me" directed long ago to Esau (25:33). But there is a world of difference between the conniving Jacob of chapter 25 and the dying Jacob of chapter 47. Jacob wants no burial plot in Egypt. This is not, he knows, God's destiny for his people. He wants to leave when they leave.

48:1–22. Before Jacob blesses his own sons, he blesses the two sons of Joseph. Advanced age plus debilitating illness indicate that Jacob is near death. In a bedside conversation he reminds Joseph of God's earlier workings in his own life (48:3–4; cf. 35:11–12).

Jacob refers to Ephraim, then Manasseh (48:5), reversing the order of verse 1. This anticipates the reversal of order that will be spelled out later in the chapter. Jacob will adopt these two sons, which explains why Manasseh and Ephraim are reckoned as sons of Jacob.

Jacob's eyes may be failing, but his spiritual insight is not. Joseph lines up Manasseh, the firstborn, opposite Jacob's right hand, and Ephraim, the younger son, opposite Jacob's left hand. In this way the right hand of blessing will be placed on the head of Manasseh. Joseph believes he has arranged everything correctly.

There are limits, however, to Joseph's knowledge. He may interpret dreams and predict famines, but he does not know the future of his own two sons. Jacob surprises Joseph by crossing his hands and placing his right hand on Ephraim, the younger. This is ironic. Jacob, the younger, usurped Esau; and now this same Jacob blesses the younger (grand)son. The way of God repeats itself two generations later. Joseph is still ignorant. He thinks his father's eyesight or else his mind is the problem. But Jacob knows exactly what he is doing. Ephraim will become a more prominent tribe than Manasseh. But both are to become a source of blessing for all Israel (48:20). This quiets Joseph, and now he sees the rightness of his father's action.

Jacob is about to leave Joseph, but God will not (48:21). The word for "ridge" in verse 22 is the word for Shechem, which, we recall, after Joshua's day became part of the territory of Ephraim. But where did Jacob engage in militarism? To think, if Jacob had stayed in Canaan and chosen not to visit Egypt, he never would have seen Joseph or Joseph's sons or had this happy opportunity to be a prophet of God.

49:1–33. Most of Genesis 49 is poetry. The content is mostly concerned with Jacob's blessing of his twelve sons. We use the word "blessing" in a general sense, for there is little actual blessing in the chapter. Only Joseph is literally blessed (49:25–26). We retain the title "Jacob's blessing" primarily because of verse 28: "This is what their father said to them when he blessed them." Some of the sections read more like a curse than a blessing.

Verse 1 would suggest that the words that follow are Jacob's addressed to individuals—his twelve sons. Verse 28, however, extends the perspective: "All these are the twelve tribes of Israel."

One of the reasons this chapter is problematic is that it is so difficult to translate from the original. Indeed, it is probably the most difficult chapter in Genesis. Just a glance at the many footnotes in the NIV, which suggest alternate readings, will bear this out.

Reuben, the firstborn, is disqualified from the rights of primogeniture because of his earlier incestuous behavior (35:22). Eventually the Reubenites settled in the Transjordan as one of the minor tribes. Simeon and Levi lose out because of their violence against the Shechemites (chap. 34). Indeed, Simeon was absorbed into Judah, and Levi was dispersed among the other tribes. These are the only three sons whose fate in Genesis 49 is explicitly connected with earlier material in the Genesis narrative. They provide a further illustration of more pain in Jacob's life. Even on his deathbed, he is reminded of outrageous acts committed by members of his family.

Judah is not disqualified because of his immorality (chap. 38). Clearly Judah is cut out for a place of preeminence and royal leadership. Verses 11–12 confirm the messianic thrust of this section. Judah will usher in an age of abundance and prosperity.

Zebulun will live by the seashore. There is a maritime dimension to the Israelite way of life that is not always appreciated. Issachar will occupy fertile farmland but will be too capitulatory. Dan will emerge as a power in the period of the judges—like a serpent, small but victorious. Gad will also settle in the Transjordan and will be attacked by nomadic groups. Asher inhabits fertile land in western Galilee. Naphtali is also a northern tribe, but the thrust of verse 21 is by no means clear.

Joseph is to be a prosperous tribe and is to be victorious over his enemies. But all this prosperity and victory is due to the presence of God. Six times in verses 25–26 some form

Painting from a tomb at Beni-Hassen, Tunisia, showing Semitic people arriving in Egypt. Once Jacob and his sons migrated to Egypt, their descendants remained there until the exodus.

of "bless" appears. Benjamin is to have warlike qualities and is compared to a wolf. (Note the frequent use of animal imagery in this chapter: oxen—49:6; lion's cub, lion, lioness—49:9; donkey—49:11, 14; snake, horse—49:17; doe, fawns—49:21; wolf—49:27.)

Jacob now dies. The chapter returns to "sons" (and not tribes)—a parallel to its beginning (49:1).

50:1–14. Both Jacob (50:2) and Joseph (50:26) are embalmed (i.e., mummified), a standard Egyptian practice. The seventy days of mourning for Jacob were also traditional in Egypt. Joseph has a little easier time leaving Egypt with Pharaoh's permission than did Moses. Joseph is a man of his word. He does return to Egypt after he and his brothers have buried their father (50:14). This is quite a different trip to Egypt for Joseph than the one recorded in chapter 37, when he went to Egypt *because of* his brothers. Now he goes to Egypt *with* his brothers. Joseph is held in such high esteem that a large Egyptian entourage participates in Jacob's burial (50:7). Even the Canaanites are impressed.

J. Joseph's reassurance (50:15–21). Now, however, the brothers feel that Joseph will retaliate since their father is out of the way. Nowhere is it recorded that Jacob gave to his other sons the directives that verse 16 claims he did. Either the brothers are fabricating this, or they are recalling a legitimate word that did not make it into the biblical record. To that degree the brothers' quotation of their father's words is unverifiable (as is Absalom's referencing his own earlier words in 2 Sam. 15:8).

Their apprehension is all for naught. They fail to see that Joseph is different, that he is compassionate and forgiving, that he is unlike his brothers. "Am I in the place of God?" (50:19) he asks. Then Joseph follows with the classic line: "You intended to harm me, but God intended it for good" (50:20). The best evidence of spiritual maturity in Joseph's life is his ability to relate all the experiences of his life, good and bad, to the sovereign will of God. The Hebrew behind "intended" is the same as "plans" in the famous passage from Jeremiah 29:11, "I know the plans I have for you . . . plans to prosper you . . . plans to give you hope and a future."

K. Joseph's death (50:22–26). Joseph dies at the age of a hundred and ten years (50:22), which in Egyptian literature is the ideal length of human life. Moreover Joseph lives long enough to see his great-grandchildren (50:23), a privilege shared by no other patriarchal figure. There is no question that one day Joseph's family will leave Egypt. "Take my bones with you when you leave," he says (50:25, author's translation). Joseph, of course, is not aware of the titanic struggle that awaits God's people as they seek release from bondage. But having seen the reality and power of God in his own life, he has every reason to believe that God is quite capable of finishing what he started.

Select Bibliography

Brueggemann, Walter. *Genesis.* Interpretation. Atlanta: John Knox, 1982.

Fretheim, Terence E. "Genesis." In *The New Interpreter's Bible.* Edited by Leander E. Keck. Vol. 1. Nashville: Abingdon, 1994.

Hamilton, Victor P. *The Book of Genesis.* 2 vols. New International Commentary on the Old Testament. Grand Rapids: Eerdmans, 1990, 1995.

Kidner, Derek. *Genesis.* Tyndale Old Testament Commentaries. Downers Grove, IL: InterVarsity, 1967.

Sarna, Nahum. *Genesis.* JPS Torah Commentary. Philadelphia: Jewish Publication Society, 1989.

Waltke, Bruce K., and Cathi J. Fredricks. *Genesis: A Commentary.* Grand Rapids: Zondervan, 2001.

Walton, John H. *Genesis.* NIV Application Commentary. Grand Rapids: Zondervan, 2001.

Wenham, Gordon J. *Genesis.* 2 vols. Word Biblical Commentary. Waco: Word, 1987, 1994.

Exodus

Elaine Phillips

The book of Exodus reports the most dramatic events in the Hebrew Bible. After the Israelites spent 430 years in Egypt (Exod. 12:40) God delivered his people from oppression, brought them into the bonds of covenant relationship at Mount Sinai, and established his sanctuary in their midst. The exodus was a foreshadowing of the deliverance from the bondage of sin accomplished by the atoning death of Jesus Christ as the Passover lamb (1 Cor. 5:7; 1 Pet. 1:18–19).

Title

The Hebrew title of the book, *Shemot* ("names"), is based on the first key word of the text. It refers to the names of the children of Israel who went down to Egypt, and it establishes continuity, in spite of the centuries of intervening silence, with the events that closed Genesis. The English title, Exodus, comes from the Greek Septuagint title and addresses the theme of the first part of the book.

Date and Historicity

The historicity of the exodus has prompted extensive scholarly debate, accessible in standard texts on the history of Israel. The following commentary is written from the perspective that the exodus was a historical event during which the Israelites were freed from their bondage to Pharaoh in Egypt. That there is no mention of the event in the Egyptian sources is not

surprising; temple inscriptions were designed as positive propaganda, reminding the deity that the pharaoh had ruled well. The devastation of the country and the stunning defeat of the Egyptian army demonstrated the opposite. In addition, written words were viewed as magically powerful; an event might repeatedly recur if committed to writing. The reverse was also true; if something was not written down, it was as if it had never happened. Finally, the mud flats of the delta regions are far from ideal for preserving buildings, let alone documents. From the perspective of Israelite historiography, it is unlikely that later writers would concoct such a humiliating narrative if it were not true.

There are two positions regarding the date of the exodus, each having significant supporting data as well as unanswered questions. The early date, primarily based on 1 Kings 6:1, is 1446 BC, placing the exodus during the eighteenth dynasty. According to Exodus 2:23 the ruling pharaoh died shortly before the exodus. In fact, the eighteenth dynasty's Thutmose III died circa 1450 BC. If the exodus occurred in 1446 BC, Amenhotep II (1450–1426) was pharaoh at the time. Thutmose III's immediate predecessor was Hatshepsut, a formidable woman who was both the wife and half sister of Thutmose II. She coreigned with Thutmose III for a period of time and exercised considerable power in Egypt. Hatshepsut's character could fit the biblical picture of the daughter of Pharaoh who rescued Moses. Akhnaton (Amenhotep IV), a late eighteenth-dynasty pharaoh, briefly championed a form of monotheistic worship of the sun. If the effects of God's miraculous work on behalf of Israel had an impact in Egypt as it had on the nations around (Exod. 18:1; Josh. 2:10; 1 Sam. 4:8), perhaps the brief turn away from polytheism was one of them.

The late date locates the event in the middle of the thirteenth century BC. New Kingdom palaces and temples had storage facilities associated with them, perhaps the focus of the Israelites' labor at Pithom and Rameses (Exod. 1:11). The name Rameses does not occur in dynastic lists until the nineteenth dynasty, and Rameses II (1290–1224) was recognized as the preeminent builder among the pharaohs. It is logical that the city of Exodus 1:11 was named in his honor. If so, Israel was still in Egypt at the start of Rameses II's reign. Nevertheless, Pharaoh Merneptah (1224–1214) recorded a conflict with a group named Israel already in the land of Canaan. Locating the exodus in the nineteenth dynasty encounters difficulties regarding the length of Rameses II's rule, the need for a change in pharaohs, and the necessary time to accommodate the wilderness wanderings and get Israel into the land by the time Merneptah became pharaoh.

Authorship

It is not improbable that Moses, reared in the highly literate court of Pharaoh, was capable of recording the history of his people, the events that they experienced, and the stipulations of God's covenant. There are direct indications of his writing in Exodus 17:14 and 24:4, 7. Nevertheless, the Documentary Hypothesis regarding the composition of the Pentateuch poses four distinct sources, JEDP, originating considerably later than Moses. The two earliest narrative strands, distinguished primarily on the basis of the divine names, Yahweh (J) and Elohim (E), are dated to the ninth and eighth centuries respectively. At the time of Josiah's reform (621 BC) is

when Deuteronomy (D) was composed. That corpus was supplemented by a collection of priestly materials (P), dated to the postexilic period. While such a complete rejection of Mosaic authorship is not necessary, later editing of the Pentateuch is entirely possible.

Theological Themes

More important, however, than the quest for underlying sources are the timeless theological themes of revelation, redemption, and relationship that are intertwined in the narrative. God revealed himself to Moses at Horeb (Sinai), reasserting the covenant relationship already established with Abraham, Isaac, and Jacob, and declaring his intention to rescue the people from bondage. He revealed himself to the Israelites in the mighty acts that led to their deliverance at the Sea of Reeds, and he revealed the words of the Sinai covenant. God gave instructions for the tabernacle and priesthood, essential provisions for the wayward people to maintain their relationship with God.

Head of a nineteenth-dynasty pharaoh, possibly Rameses II

Redemption means paying a price to buy back either persons or property. God's powerful deliverance of his people, called redemption (Exod. 6:6; 15:13), is linked with the firstborn. Israel was God's firstborn; because Egypt would not allow God's firstborn to go free, the Egyptians would pay with their own firstborn sons (Exod. 4:21–23). Even so, this was not without cost to Israel. Their firstborn males were to be consecrated to the Lord, animals sacrificed and firstborn sons redeemed, commemorating the payment of the blood of Egyptian firstborns on behalf of God's own firstborn (Exod. 13:11–16). This provides the cultural and theological backdrop for Jesus's declaration that he would give his life as a ransom for many (Mark 10:45) and Paul's affirmation of the redemptive blood of Christ (Eph. 1:7), the firstborn over all creation (Col. 1:15). Undergirding these Exodus themes is the truth of God's sovereignty. He is able perfectly to accomplish his good purposes, carrying out his will and working through the course of human history.

Commentary

1. From Bondage to Freedom (1:1–15:21)

The events in Exodus must be read against the backdrop of Joseph's words to his brothers:

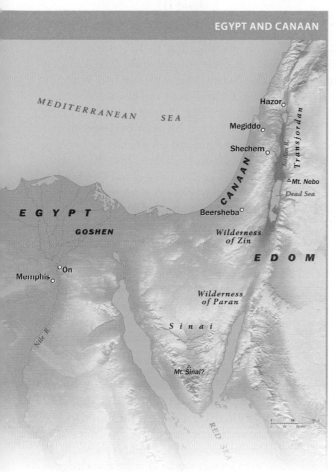

EGYPT AND CANAAN

MEDITERRANEAN SEA

Hazor

Megiddo

Shechem

Jordan R.

Transjordan

C A N A A N

△Mt. Nebo

Dead Sea

E G Y P T

GOSHEN

Beersheba

Wilderness of Zin

E D O M

Memphis

°On

Wilderness of Paran

S i n a i

Nile R.

Mt. Sinai?

RED SEA

After the death of Joseph the Israelites were extraordinarily prolific; five verbs are reminiscent of Genesis 1, "They were fruitful, and swarmed, and multiplied, and were very, very strong and the land was filled with them" (1:7; author's translation). Even the passive form of the last clause suggests that their presence was overwhelming and potentially threatening.

B. Oppression of Israel (1:8–22). Fearing that the growing number of Israelites would join the enemies of Egypt in the event of war and leave the country, the king determines to deal "shrewdly" with them. Ironically each phase of his plan is a failure. The Israelite slaves were a necessary part of the Egyptian economy (Exod. 14:5); their efforts were invested in public projects and were represented in the store cities and hard field labor. These descriptions are consistent with Egyptian evidence in which foreign slaves are depicted in the arduous process of making bricks.

When the first phase of harsh labor fails to control the number of Israelites, Pharaoh commands the Hebrew midwives to kill newborn boys when they observe them literally "on the stones" (1:16), possibly referring to two stones positioned for the actual birth process. This expression, however, may have a further level of meaning. It is used one other time in the Hebrew Bible (Jer. 18:3) in conjunction with pottery. In Egyptian religious art the potter's wheel was associated with the god of creation, Khnum, who would shape each person at conception on his stone wheel. Perhaps the Hebrew expression is an adaptation of that idiom and refers to the child still forming in the womb. If so Pharaoh expects the midwives to do a prenatal examination, a practice within the technical expertise of ancient Egypt, and kill the unborn children they determine to be male.

"But God sent me ahead of you to preserve for you a remnant on earth and to save your lives by a great deliverance" (Gen. 45:7). Initially Israel had flourished in Egypt, but ruthless oppression by a new dynasty was the crucible in which their suffering prepared them for deliverance. God visited them in that suffering, using a fearful Moses to confront the systemic evil of polytheistic Egypt, represented by Pharaoh.

A. Connection with the past (1:1–7). The explicit naming of the sons of Jacob echoes the words of Genesis 46:8, "These are the names of the sons of Israel who went to Egypt," and abbreviates what follows there. Likewise, the reference to seventy descendants echoes Genesis 46:27.

Shiphrah and Puah are likely representative of a larger group of midwives, members of what was a prestigious profession in ancient Egypt. Fear of God motivates them to disobey the king of Egypt, preserve the lives of the infants, and present the matter to Pharaoh in a less-than-truthful fashion. This is the first recorded instance in the Bible of civil disobedience in the face of an immoral law. In return God blesses these women with families, an example of the measure-for-measure justice evident throughout the Scriptures. The two midwives are named while Pharaoh is not. Not only is this ironic; it also fits with patterns in Egyptian texts. No names are appended to the title Pharaoh until the tenth century BC.

The third phase of Pharaoh's scheme is outright infanticide. Pharaoh's determination to exterminate Hebrew boys in water will be repeated in just measure as the Egyptians meet their end in water.

C. Birth, preservation, and preparation of Moses (2:1–25). The parents of Moses, Amram and Jochebed (Exod. 6:20), are both of the tribe of Levi.

The extreme measures taken to deal with newborn Israelite males were relatively recent at the time of Moses's birth because Aaron is three years his elder (Exod. 7:7). Miriam is old enough to watch the basket into which their mother puts Moses after she can no longer hide him. When she puts her son into the Nile it is in keeping with the edict, with the added protection of an ark. Originally an Egyptian word, the Hebrew word *tebah* is used only here and of Noah's ark (Gen. 6:14–16). Each craft saves the life of a critical servant of God from the destructive force of water.

It is possible that Jochabed lodged the basket in a side channel of the Nile, knowing that was where Pharaoh's daughter would be bathing. Even though the boy is recognized as a Hebrew child, Pharaoh's daughter defies the decree, accepts Miriam's bold offer to find a nurse for him, and adopts him as her son. There is evidence from the eighteenth dynasty of bringing foreign princes to be trained in Pharaoh's court. Nevertheless, in the context of the official policy toward the Israelites, these actions are extraordinary. The name that Pharaoh's daughter gives to Moses has both Hebrew and Egyptian connotations. *Mosheh* is a Hebrew participle suggesting his being drawn out of the water and also his drawing the people out of Egypt. In Egyptian it means "son" and is related to several names of the eighteenth dynasty. Thutmose, for example, would mean "son of the god Thoth."

As his mother nurses him, Moses develops a strong and profound sense of his identity as a Hebrew. In the court of Pharaoh, "Moses was educated in all the wisdom of the Egyptians and was powerful in speech and action" (Acts 7:22). This means acquiring the ability to write, likely access to literary works, and the knowledge of "court etiquette" that would serve him well in the future confrontations with Pharaoh. After Moses kills an Egyptian and it becomes known, he flees to the wilderness of Midian (2:11–15). There he gets married and shepherds his father-in-law's sheep for forty years. Contrary to all appearances this aspect of Moses's training and experience is indispensable, as he learns the terrain and the precious water sources of the Sinai Peninsula and gains skills necessary for leading recalcitrant groups. Although the wilderness is barren and forbidding, it is where God chooses

A papyrus basket from ancient Egypt, similar to the basket used by Moses's mother (Exod. 2:3)

to reveal himself both to Moses and later to God's covenant people. The name of Moses's son, Gershom, is telling; it speaks of his sense of alienation, both in his current circumstances and from his Hebrew and Egyptian identities (2:22).

With the death of Pharaoh (2:23) there is potential for instability; the outcry of the enslaved Israelites may reflect this sociopolitical development. Instead of the government responding, however, it is God who hears, who remembers his covenant, who sees, and who knows. And God will work through this unlikely fugitive. Because it was established practice for a new pharaoh to release captives and allow fugitives to return, Moses is able to reenter the court.

D. Moses's call and commissioning (3:1–4:17). The call of Moses is a radical break from everything that has gone before. Moses is shepherding Jethro's flocks near Horeb, the mountain of God, when the burning bush attracts his attention. The Hebrew word for bush (*seneh*) appears in the Bible only five times and sounds similar to Sinai. Fire is formless, powerful, luminous—a perfect means of representing God. Although the messenger appears in the flaming bush, it is the Lord who speaks with Moses; the messenger has nothing to say. God identifies himself as the God of the covenant with Abraham, Isaac, and Jacob and declares he has "come down" (3:8) to deliver his people because he sees, hears, and knows their suffering. Although God's promise of the land flowing with milk and honey was never part of the descriptions of the land in Genesis, here it comes as an invitation to the enslaved people. Most likely the milk refers to goats' milk and the honey was from dates.

Moses raises a series of objections because he understands the dangerous and apparently impossible nature of his calling. Each of God's responses presses him toward an altered perspective. The dialogue unfolds with terse questions from Moses and expansive responses from God.

When Moses initially asks, "Who am I?" (3:11), God's response redirects Moses's attention from the intimidating prospect of Pharaoh to the ultimate goal of worshiping God. The promise of a sign confirming that God has sent him is a challenge; it will not be manifested until the completion of the entire enterprise. Nevertheless, when the people finally *worship* God on the mountain, they are indeed no longer *serving* Pharaoh—the Hebrew word for "worship" and "serve" is the same.

Ostensibly on behalf of the Israelites, Moses next asks in effect, Who are *you*? Who will be authorizing this demonstration of massive civil disobedience? At the same time, since his own new vocation is dependent on God's presence, it is also important for him to know who God is. In response God reveals the essence of his covenant name and his intention to fulfill the covenant promise regarding the land. The meaning of the Hebrew phrase *ehyeh asher ehyeh* (3:14) is "I AM WHO I AM" (NIV) or "I will be what I will be" (cf. NIV note) and follows directly on Exodus 3:12, "I will be with you." Repetition of the verb form confirms that the Lord is the eternally self-existent and sustaining source of all that is, entirely sufficient for all past, present, and future trials and triumphs. He is God of the fathers, God of the people in bondage, and God of the *continuing* covenant. The root of this verb is the basis for the divine name Yahweh, which is characteristically translated "LORD."

The Lord promises that the elders of Israel will listen to Moses and together they will request permission from Pharaoh to go for three days to offer sacrifices in the wilderness to the Lord, the God of the Hebrews. It would not have been unusual for a group of slaves to make a pilgrimage to a shrine. Nevertheless the king of Egypt will send them forth only after God's wonders have been performed in their midst. God further promises that the Egyptians will be favorably disposed to give valuable articles to the departing Israelites.

In spite of hearing God's plan for the entire enterprise, Moses is still fearful of the Israelites' incredulous response. Thus God demonstrates two signs as witnesses. As the first sign, Moses's rod becomes a serpent when he casts it to the ground, and it returns to its natural state when he puts out his hand to take it up again. The Hebrew word for serpent is *nahash*, the appropriate term in the Sinai region; when Moses replays the sign in Pharaoh's court at the Nile (Exod. 7:9–10), the rod becomes a crocodile (Hebrew *tannin*). The second sign is the appearance and subsequent removal of leprosy on his hand. Leprosy ominously signifies punishment for disobedience. Finally, if the people do not believe the first two signs, Moses is to pour Nile water onto dry ground and see it become blood, a preview of the first plague.

Unconvinced, Moses returns to his own perceived inadequacy, claiming that he is "slow of speech and tongue" (4:10). While this appears to contradict Stephen's witness in Acts that Moses was "powerful in speech and action" (Acts 7:22), Moses has been out of the Egyptian court for forty years. Stephen's perspective represents Moses's activities throughout the entire process of leaving Egypt. After Moses first addresses Pharaoh and apparently fails, he raises the issue again, stating twice that he is literally "uncircumcised of lips" (Exod. 6:12, 30). God reminds Moses that he is the creator of all human abilities and impediments but promises his presence with Moses as he speaks (literally "with [his] mouth"; 4:12).

Even though Moses stubbornly begs God to send someone else, God continues with his intention to use Moses, indicating that Aaron will be his mouthpiece. Providentially, in the context where Pharaoh considers himself a deity, for Moses to operate through a spokesperson-prophet for whom he would be "like a god" (4:16; 7:1) will raise his level of credibility in the court.

E. Return to Egypt (4:18–31). As Moses is en route to Egypt, the Lord declares that his signs and wonders will parallel the hardening of Pharaoh's heart. God's hardening and Pharaoh's responsibility in hardening his own heart are inextricably interwoven. In both Israelite and Egyptian contexts the heart was viewed as the center of volitional, intellectual, emotional, and spiritual capacities. Three Hebrew words are used for hardening: *hazaq*, "to strengthen" (4:21; 7:13, 22; 8:19; 9:12, 35; 10:20, 27; 11:10; 14:4, 8, 17); *qashah*, "to be difficult, harsh, or hard" (7:3; 13:15); and *kabed*, "to be heavy" (7:14; 8:15, 32; 9:34; 10:1). *Hazaq* has implications of power in order to perform a function. *Kabed* would have been particularly significant in the Egyptian context. After death the heart was weighed in a scale opposite a feather. If the heart outweighed the feather the deceased would suffer judgment. Pharaoh's weighty heart would have indicated that he did not after all perfectly embody the gods Horus and Re and their authority.

The form of *hazaq* in God's initial statement that he will harden Pharaoh's heart (4:21) suggests God's direct involvement and the recurrence of Pharaoh's rejection. As the signs commence, the condition of Pharaoh's heart is described (Exod. 7:13–14): it is strong (*hazaq*) and heavy (*kabed*), and the first plague only strengthens (*hazaq*) Pharaoh's heart, as the Lord has said (Exod. 7:22). In chapter 8 Pharaoh causes his heart to be heavy (*kabed*), it is strong (*hazaq*), and he does not listen (Exod. 8:11). Listening implies obedience; Pharaoh refuses to bend. Chapter 9 includes all three aspects: his heart is heavy, the Lord strengthens it, and Pharaoh causes it to be heavy. When he acknowledges his sin, asking for forgiveness, it is short-lived; and he sins further in turning back to his old pattern. In the last plagues before the death of the firstborn, the Lord hardens and strengthens Pharaoh's heart; the same is true as Pharaoh changes his mind after Israel departs (Exod. 14:4, 8). Under God's sovereign design Pharaoh's choices determine the continuing pattern of his life. This tragic and complex process is the context for Paul's comments in Romans 9:16–18, as he wrestles with the implications of God's sovereignty.

Pharaoh has exalted himself above humans in his assumption of deity and in his treatment of Israel as subhuman; thus God deprives him of his free will and binds him in rebellion, making him subhuman. Pharaoh's refusal to free Israel, God's firstborn, results in the slaughter of the Egyptian firstborn, another instance of measure-for-measure justice.

There is a thematic link between this mention of firstborn and the next puzzling incident (4:24–26). The Lord encounters Moses on the way back to Egypt, threatening to kill "him" (either Moses or the firstborn son) because Moses has not circumcised his son. Even though Zipporah, his Midianite wife, knows the proper action, her epithet suggests revulsion on her part. Nevertheless she immediately circumcises her son. While her repeated charge that Moses is a "bridegroom of blood" is cryptic, there are several possible symbolic connections to consider. The sign of the covenant with Abraham is circumcision, and those who are not circumcised will be cut off, just as the foreskin is cut off (cf. Gen. 17:14). When Moses fled from Egypt forty years prior, he may have intentionally rejected the practices that defined him as an Israelite. Since he is the chosen deliverer of God's people, his failure to live up to the covenant stipulations threatens both his immediate family and the larger covenant family descended from Abraham. To make that right involves the shedding of blood. Further, the matter of protecting the Israelite firstborn in Egypt will also involve shedding the blood of a Passover lamb. The rabbis of late antiquity repeatedly affirmed the connection between the blood of circumcision and that of the Passover sacrifice.

F. God of Israel versus the gods of Egypt: The initial request (5:1–6:1).

God's command to "let my people go" recognizes the Hebrews' demeaned status as state slaves, entirely subjugated to Pharaoh. Later, in response to his arrogant declaration that he does not recognize the Lord and will not send Israel out to worship the Lord, Pharaoh is told, "You shall know that I

am the Lord" (Exod. 7:17 NASB). Increasing the workload of the people is an insidious move to turn the Israelites against Moses. In brick-making the requisite straw is a binding agent; when it decays, the released acid makes the material more plastic and prevents shrinking and cracking. The Israelites' situation deteriorates, but there is a purpose: Instead of sanctioning a temporary journey into the desert, Pharaoh will drive the Israelites out, and the mighty hand of God will accomplish the task. Notably, however, the purposes of God are accomplished through difficult and bitter experiences.

G. Covenant Lord and his ministers (6:2–30).

Exodus 6:3 implies that the patriarchs did not know the name Yahweh even though it appears in Genesis. The verse immediately following, however, says, "I *also* established my covenant with them," suggesting that the preceding statement could be a positive one, translated as a question: "I appeared . . . as El Shaddai *and* (by) my name, did I not make myself known to them?" The verb "to make known" appears in other passages with connotations of experiencing revelation.

While God did reveal himself by the name Yahweh to the patriarchs, the full implications of that name were not yet evident. Moses has complained that God has done nothing; this is God's response to Moses. Now Israel will know from experience that God is the covenant Lord, about to redeem them and give the Sinai covenant. The name El Shaddai appears in Genesis 35:11 just after God reiterates Jacob's name change to Israel and restates the covenant promises as given to Abraham and

Mud bricks made with straw

Isaac. Continuity is established with Genesis, and at the same time God's declaration here changes the identity and future of Israel as his community. Genesis contains a wider variety of divine names, but from this point in Exodus onward, the names El and El Shaddai are used infrequently except in poetic texts. The expression "outstretched arm" (6:6) was used by eighteenth-dynasty pharaohs to express their conquering arm. The promise that the Lord will redeem Israel with an "outstretched arm" indicates that the Lord will demonstrate his superiority over Pharaoh.

The partial genealogy (6:14–25), focusing on Levi, establishes the position of Moses and Aaron. Jochebed's name means "the Lord is glory." She is the first person in the biblical text to carry a name including part of the divine name. The wife of Aaron, Elisheba, is from the tribe of Judah, thus uniting the priestly and royal lines. Genealogies, such as this one, were significant indicators of continuity, life, and vitality.

H. Moses and Aaron confront Pharaoh (7:1–13). Because Moses will be as God to Pharaoh, and Aaron will be Moses's spokesperson, this encounter will unfold with Moses being Pharaoh's "equal." Egypt considered Pharaoh divine, eternal, and in control of the elements of nature, all of which will be overturned by the "signs and wonders." The declaration "Thus saith" (NIV "This is what the LORD says" [e.g., Exod. 7:17]), also used in Egyptian texts, indicates to Pharaoh that he is being challenged by the deity of the Hebrews. God will harden Pharaoh's heart so that, even in the face of tremendous miracles, he will reject the word of God. God will deliver his people from Egypt with "mighty acts of judgment" (7:4), and Egypt will indeed know who the Lord is.

The initial confrontation in this cosmic battle pits Aaron's rod against Egyptian religious symbols. The shepherd's crook was symbolic of Pharaoh's sovereignty, and the cobra was goddess of Lower Egypt. The cobra worn on Pharaoh's headdress was designed to terrify enemies and affirm Pharaoh's power. When Aaron flings down his rod and it becomes a serpent, swallowing the rods of the Egyptians, it is more than supernatural one-upmanship; it is a stunning demonstration that God is attacking and disordering the very fabric of Pharaoh's realm.

Pharaoh's court included magicians and sorcerers, most likely members of the priestly caste and teachers of wisdom. There is evidence of Egyptian magical practices that involved turning rods into snakes (Westcar Papyrus). The initial signs performed by Moses and Aaron are imitated by those who dabble in the arts of magic and deception and who appeal to the darker supernatural powers that keep the people in blindness. The root of the Hebrew word translated "by their secret arts" (7:11) implies "to enwrap or envelope," suggesting secrecy. Because the magicians are able to effect the same supernatural demonstrations, this first sign appears ambiguous, contributing to the hardness of Pharaoh's heart.

I. Nine plagues (7:14–10:29). The plagues are purposeful manifestations of God's sovereign power. In response to Pharaoh's challenge (Exod. 5:2) the plagues demonstrate to him and to Egypt the identity and power of God (7:5, 17; 9:14–16; 14:4). The "strong hand" that Pharaoh presumes to wield is Yahweh's attribute (see 6:1 KJV). The mighty acts of God gain freedom for Israel, confirming that they are God's people (8:22–23) and he is their God (10:1–2). These events make an indelible mark on the corporate memory of Israel (Ps. 78:1–8, 44–51; 105:28–36). Pharaoh was raised up that God's name might be proclaimed in all the earth (Exod. 9:16). Jethro hears and joins with the Israelites in worshiping God (Exod. 18:8–12). Rahab tells the spies that the inhabitants of Canaan have heard of God's activities (Josh. 2:8–11). Centuries later the Philistines express their fear of the God who struck the Egyptians with the plagues (1 Sam. 4:8). The plagues directly challenge the Egyptian worldview, bringing judgment on all the gods of Egypt (Exod. 7:4; 10:2; 12:12; Num. 33:4). The last two plagues are especially sharp attacks because the sun was the primary deity, and Pharaoh was its earthly representative, responsible for maintaining cosmic order. God mobilized creation on behalf of his children, using timing and intensifying aberrations in the natural order, many of which the Egyptians had deified. Finally, these plagues foreshadow the cosmic eschatological plagues, including hail, fire, blood (Rev. 8:6–8), and locusts (Rev. 9:1–11). The two unnamed witnesses of Revelation 11:6 will have power to shut up the sky, turn the waters into blood, and strike the earth with every kind of plague. In this foreshadowing the sovereign God is reducing the natural order to chaos, and yet it is chaos under his control.

The regular inundation of the Nile began midsummer and continued until September or October. A large flood upriver in the Blue Nile increased the small organisms that gave a reddish color to the water, absorbed oxygen, and caused death. If that late-summer event is the first plague, then the whole series takes well over half a year. This would enable the Egyptians to replenish the livestock after multiple attacks on domestic animals.

As each of the plagues tears at the foundations of Egyptian economy, Pharaoh appears to capitulate, requesting that Moses pray for relief and declaring that they can go and worship (8:8, 28; 9:28; 10:17, 24). As the devastation increases, Pharaoh even acknowledges his sin, seeking forgiveness (9:27; 10:16–17), and Moses consistently serves as mediator. The plagues stop as Moses calls on the Lord in response to Pharaoh's plea for relief, interceding on behalf of this supremely evil ruler. Nevertheless, Pharaoh's heart grows increasingly obdurate.

7:14–8:15. When Aaron strikes the water of the Nile with the staff, all of it turns bloodred, bringing

death. The idiomatic use of "blood" to indicate color is evident in Joel 2:31 and 2 Kings 3:22. This strikes at the heart of Egypt's economy and religion. Agricultural productivity depended on rich alluvial deposits on the floodplains. Ironically the Nile was considered to be the lifeblood of Osiris, god of the underworld, who brought new life after each inundation. There is blood in every place where water collects, even on the "vessels of wood and stone" (7:19), perhaps idolatrous objects. The river, canals, and ponds were affected by the flowing surface waters of the Nile as it flooded. Further inland, where the water percolated through soils, they could dig for potable water. Water was a precious resource in Egypt, and Pharaoh fails to control its provision. Worse yet, when his magicians reproduce the same miracle, they contribute to further devastation of his people just to make a point against the God of Moses and Aaron, a case of destructive ideology (7:24).

Seven days later, with Aaron as agent, frogs entirely overwhelm the land (8:1–15). Heqt, a frog-headed Egyptian goddess, was an emblem of fertility, presumably assisting women in childbirth. The uncontrollable proliferation of frogs even in the bed of Pharaoh himself is the height of humiliation. As with the bloodred waters, however, the Egyptian magicians repeat the phenomenon. Nevertheless, at this point Pharaoh begins to

The Nile River, whose flooding was necessary for the agricultural productivity of ancient Egypt

negotiate through Moses, and God responds to Moses's prayer. The frogs are removed the next day, although the stench remains.

8:16–32. The next two plagues are a natural result of putrid water and dying frogs. Vermin, possibly gnats or lice, followed by dense swarms of flies, descend on the land. The vermin are a plague on both humans and domestic animals, while the land is ruined because of the flies. The Hebrew word for "ruin" also appears in Genesis 6 regarding the devastation caused by both the wholesale sin of humankind and the floodwaters of judgment. The magicians capitulate at the third plague when they fail to produce gnats, acknowledging "the finger of God" (8:19), by which they mean God's power evident in the rod. Up until this point, Egypt has suffered double onslaught as Pharaoh tried to keep up with Moses. With the plague of flies, God announces and makes a distinction between the Egyptians and the Israelites who live in Goshen. Pharaoh poses the alternative of worship in the land, a futile attempt to keep it under his control.

9:1–12. The plague on the livestock (9:1–7) is the first to destroy property, particularly transport animals as well as those that provide food, dealing a shattering blow to the entire economy. In addition to the economic implications, there may also have been religious repercussions since both Apis and Hathor were bovine deities. The Lord continues the distinction between the Egyptians and the Israelites.

The plague of boils (9:8–12) brings physical suffering directly to humans. Pharaoh's own magicians are humbled and unable to stand in the presence of Moses. The reports of the fifth and sixth plagues are terse, and Pharaoh's role is reduced to the indications that his heart is hard, he will not listen, and he will not let the people go.

9:13–10:29. With the third set of three plagues the onslaught intensifies. The extensive descriptions are interwoven with articulation of God's purposes and Pharaoh's acknowledgment of his moral culpability. Following Moses's warning, some of Pharaoh's officials are convinced and preserve their property by following the instructions. The hail (9:13–35) would have occurred in February, when the barley and flax were ripe (9:31). It may be that Pharaoh's insincere admission of sin was designed to negotiate relief for the crops that ripened later. Moses next warns that the crops not devastated by the hail will be destroyed by an invasion of locusts (10:1–20). Pharaoh's entire system is eroding; in spite of his divine stature his officials challenge his authority, appealing to the potential utter ruin of Egypt. He recalls Moses and Aaron, but when he learns that they will all be leaving to worship, Pharaoh declares his intent to keep women and children as hostages.

The ninth plague (10:21–29) attacks the sun god, Amun-Re. It is a darkness "that can be felt" (10:21), possibly the *sharav*, a dry heat wave in which winds from the Arabian desert raise fine dust in the air, often obscuring the sun. Furthermore, in the ancient world, darkness was terrifying and dangerous, palpably "felt" in that sense. Amun was the god most closely linked with Pharaoh as a divine figure. In fear, Pharaoh orders Moses to leave with all the people and worship the Lord. He will not, however, allow them to take their livestock; thus the impasse continues, with Pharaoh threatening death if Moses should appear before him again.

J. Warning of the tenth plague (11:1–10). Probably still in Pharaoh's presence, Moses tersely announces the conditions, significantly ahead of the actual plague. At midnight as every firstborn died, the outcry of Egypt, parallel to Israel's anguished cry, would have been horrifying. God would again distinguish between Israelites and Egyptians, and Pharaoh's servants would beg the Israelites to leave. This chapter brings closure to the narrative of signs and wonders, promising that Pharaoh will drive the Israelites out and their Egyptian neighbors will send them away wealthy, notably because of Moses's stature. This culminating plague also points ahead to the Passover.

K. Instructions for Passover (12:1–28). While the Hebrew word translated "Passover" (*pesah*) appears frequently with reference to the sacrificial animal for the festival, the related verb (*pasah*) is not so common. In Isaiah 31:5 it appears in poetic parallelism and clearly indicates protection. Thus, when the Lord sees the blood on the door frames, he will "protect" the doorway, not permitting the destroyer to enter and strike down the people. This compellingly foreshadows the protective blood of Christ, the Passover lamb, as he bore the destructive wrath of God against sin (1 Cor. 5:7).

This section includes instructions both for the Passover in Egypt and for its commemoration on an annual basis. The liturgical component keeps alive for each successive generation the memory of God's deliverance, particularly engaging the children. The Lord gives both sets of instructions to Moses, and Moses passes them along to the elders of Israel. Central to the Passover in Egypt is the lamb; in the celebration for generations to come, the emphasis switches to the unleavened bread.

The Israelites are instructed to take a one-year-old male lamb or kid without defect on the tenth day of the month and keep it until the fourteenth day. The four days of guarding the animal would ensure its unblemished state. One animal suffices for each extended household. The entire community will slaughter the animals at the same time. Hyssop, a plant with small leaves, bundled together, used for sprinkling the blood, has aromatic properties that counter the stench of blood. The Israelites are to consume indoors the roasted sacrifice with bitter herbs and bread made without yeast. They are not to break any bones of the sacrificial animal (Exod. 12:46; cf. John 19:36). In time the bitter herbs came to represent the bitterness of slavery and unleavened bread the purifying from the leaven of sin. Yeast affects the entire loaf of bread; so also the pollution of sin ranges much farther than its original starting point. Fermentation also leads ultimately to decay and death, a compelling representation of the results of sin. Jesus identifies the "yeast of the Pharisees" as hypocrisy (Luke 12:1), and Paul

uses the figure to address the need to deal in a radical way with sin in the Corinthian congregation (1 Cor. 5:6–8). In the generations to come, those who eat leaven during the festival are to be cut off from Israel, the most severe of punishments (12:19).

L. Tenth plague and departure of Israel (12:29–42). The Lord passes through the land, striking down all the firstborn in Egypt, both human and animal. The firstborn of Pharaoh would have been considered divine; traditionally the god Amun visited the mother of the pharaoh-to-be. Utterly humiliated, Pharaoh summons Moses and Aaron in the night, orders them out, and seeks their blessing. Pharaoh first calls the people Israelites at this point (12:31), giving recognition to them as a national entity.

The Israelites ask for silver, gold, and clothing from Egyptians, and in doing so they receive token "payment" for the years of slave labor. That Israel goes out with provisions fits with the torah regulations that freed slaves be provisioned (Deut. 15:13–15). Further, these materials constitute the voluntary offerings for the construction of the tabernacle (Exod. 25:1–7; 35:4–29). In the Old Testament pattern plunder is taken when Israelites are victorious, as they are here. The Lord gives Israel favor in the eyes of Egypt, suggesting that the Egyptians view this as "paying off" Yahweh in order to escape any further devastation. The Hebrew verb translated "plunder" may also mean "save," perhaps signaling some positive outcome for Egypt as they essentially gave this offering to the Lord.

The biblical text uniformly presents the number of the Israelites during the period of the exodus and wanderings as approximately six hundred *elep* fighting men (cf. Num. 1:46; 11:21; 26:51). Traditionally the Hebrew word *elep* is translated as "thousand." With the addition of women and children, those who exited Egypt would have been in excess of two million persons. The entire population of Egypt was probably about five million in the fourteenth century BC. If the Israelites were so numerous it is not clear why they were so terrified by the

Egyptian forces or the forthcoming battle with the nomadic Amalekites in 7:8–16. Further, Israel is described as having too few people to occupy the entire promised land right away (Exod. 23:29–30; cf. Deut. 7:7). The word *elep*, however, can also mean "troop, leader, group, or clan," according to context. The average number of males per family was eight or nine and likewise the number of men in a troop was nine or ten. Perhaps the total number of people leaving Egypt was approximately twenty thousand, still indicative of their multiplying (Exod. 1:7) and an attestation to God's clearly miraculous provision. A mixed multitude joins the Israelites along with large numbers of flocks and herds (12:38). These may have been a conglomeration of fellow Semitic-speaking peoples in Egypt under bondage to Pharaoh.

M. Instructions for commemoration (12:43–13:16). Israel is to observe the annual celebration, keeping vigil for generations to come because the Lord has kept watch that night. The reenactment of each aspect of the Passover will remind Israel of their previous distress, God's mighty deliverance, and the terrible price of freedom. To ensure corporate memory and continuity of the tradition, the redemption of the firstborn and eating unleavened bread are designed to prompt children's questions. The phrase "like a sign on your hand and a reminder on your forehead" (13:9, 16) is also part of the command to teach children the torah (Deut. 6:4–9) and is the basis for wearing phylacteries.

Eating unleavened bread for seven days (13:7) continues to identify and unite the community of Israel, even apart from the temple. The combined Festival of Passover and Unleavened Bread crosses the boundaries between home and family, where it began, and the corporate community at the central place of worship. Deuteronomy 16:2 indicates that God's people are to sacrifice at the location he will choose as a dwelling for his name. When major reforms occur during the reigns of Hezekiah (2 Chron. 30) and Josiah (2 Chron. 35), central to each

is the corporate celebration of Passover at the cleansed temple. God's redemption means deliverance from sin followed by transformed lives.

An additional element of the annual celebration is the consecration of firstborn males (13:11–16), a reminder that the firstborn is the Lord's and that he required of the Egyptians their firstborn. In the case of livestock this means sacrifice. Firstborn sons are redeemed; a price is paid as a substitute. Only members of the covenant people can participate in the Passover celebration. For males, this means circumcision (12:48).

N. Deliverance at the sea (13:17–14:31). The Hebrew phrase *yam sup* means "sea of reeds." This may refer to the region north of the Gulf of Suez, which, in antiquity, was characterized by large, shallow lakes and extensive swamps. The water level was higher four thousand years ago, and the north end of the Gulf of Suez may have merged with the Bitter Lakes region, all of it being called *yam sup*. It would not have been navigable without the miracle that dries it up and allows the Israelites to walk across on dry ground. Furthermore, this body of water is deep enough that the Egyptians are engulfed when the waters return. The strong east wind (14:21) causes walls of water to pile up on both sides of its path as well as to the west. When Moses again stretches out his hand over the sea, it drowns the Egyptians who have turned around and are fleeing west.

As the Israelites exit Egypt their path is not the well-fortified international trade and military route heading toward Philistine country, because they are not ready for major battle. In addition God's design is to make them appear confused in the desert so that Pharaoh will pursue them, resulting in Egypt's catastrophic defeat and final victory for the Lord. God's presence in the pillar of cloud and fire guides Israel as they travel both day and night. This is an urgent journey.

The Philistines were among the sea peoples whose migration to the ancient Near East occurred during the early twelfth century BC,

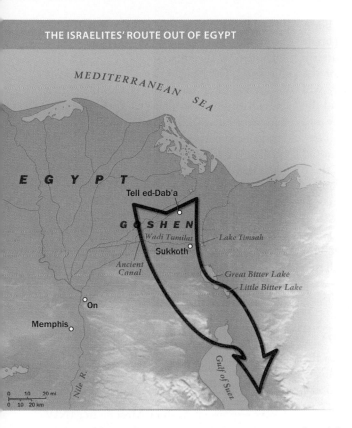

THE ISRAELITES' ROUTE OUT OF EGYPT

MEDITERRANEAN SEA

EGYPT

Tell ed-Dab'a

GOSHEN

Wadi Tumilat · Lake Timsah

Sukkoth

Ancient Canal

Great Bitter Lake

Little Bitter Lake

On

Memphis

Nile R.

Gulf of Suez

0 10 20 mi
0 10 20 km

his elite fighting corps. In fear the Israelites cry out to the Lord and reproach their visible leader, Moses. Five times in 14:12–13 they mention Egypt, a familiar and thus seemingly desirable place in these terrifying circumstances. Each step of the deliverance is accompanied by uncertainty, fear, and the resultant need to trust God. Moses encourages the Israelites with the promise of God's deliverance, but he also appeals to the Lord, who instructs him to raise the rod in order to dry up the sea (14:16). Echoing the creation narrative, the dry ground emerges and the chaos of water is subdued. Because it takes all night for the waters to dry up, the angel of God and the pillar of cloud come between the army of Egypt and the Israelites.

As the Egyptians pursue the Israelites into the sea, they see God's intervention and express their conviction that the Lord is fighting for Israel. In contrast it is not until the Israelites see Egyptians lying dead that they fear the Lord and put their trust in him and in Moses. The text does not mention that Pharaoh himself perishes, and there is no evidence of a change of pharaoh at the critical points in either the early- or late-date schemes.

O. Song of victory (15:1–21). Poetry, a powerful vehicle for remembrance, was commonly used in Egyptian texts to emphasize a prose narrative. This is the first poetic rendition of God's mighty deliverance, but the events are rehearsed again in Psalms 78 and 106. Both Moses and Miriam teach the song to the Israelites. The first part addresses the events that have already occurred, hailing God as the majestic warrior whose mighty acts completely nullify the claims of Pharaoh to be divine. This song celebrates victory over a powerful and evil enemy in graphic images. The right hand of Yahweh has shattered the enemy; his burning anger

evidenced by reliefs from the reign of Rameses III. This was well after the exodus no matter which date is supposed for that event. Later editing of the text may have introduced this familiar designation of the coastal plain area, always controlled by more powerful, cosmopolitan political forces who were characteristically enemies of Israel. It is noteworthy that, when the Israelites battle Philistines centuries later, those Philistines allude to the memorable events in Egypt (1 Sam. 4:8). It is also possible that while the major migration of the sea peoples occurred in the twelfth century, there had been smaller groups of them already resident in the land.

Moses takes the bones of Joseph (13:19) to fulfill the oath taken by the sons of Israel (Gen. 50:25), drawing together the promises in Genesis with their fulfillment in Exodus. (See Heb. 11:22.)

Intending Israel's annihilation, Pharaoh calls out all the chariots of Egypt along with consumes them as fire would chaff. The bombastic words of Pharaoh are followed by simply the breath of the Lord destroying them utterly.

Verse 13 transitions to promises for the future. The major enemies whom they will encounter, Philistines, Edom, Moab, and the Canaanites, will be terrified into silence and allow the people to pass by. Because the international coastal route traversed what would be later known as the plain of Philistia, these people are listed first, although recorded conflict with the Philistines would not occur until significantly later. The others appear in the order in which the Israelites encounter them. The poem does not end with victory in the land but with worship in God's sanctuary, where he will rule as sovereign. This is a prophetic look forward from the perspective of Moses and Miriam; neither of them will set foot in the land.

2. Tests in the Wilderness (15:22–18:27)

Neither the route of the Israelites to the mountain of God nor Mount Sinai itself can be identified with certainty, but the traditional location of the mountain in the southern part of the Sinai Peninsula is fitting. The region is rugged, far from the traveled northern routes across Sinai, and isolated from those routes by a barren and desolate wilderness. The Israelites' journey is fraught with difficulties, and their faith is tested. Likewise they test God. The Israelites' wilderness journey is mirrored

in the lives of believers who have experienced profound joy in redemption only to be overwhelmed by the frustrations of life in a sinful world. The Israelites' penchant for quickly forgetting God's provision is a reminder that human nature has not changed. Each generation can see itself with chagrin in the increasingly strident and perpetually unhappy Israelites. The challenge is to be committed to obedience and trust that the Lord, fully in keeping with his character (Exod. 3:14), will be faithful to provide what is necessary. Further, leaders of God's people are inevitably the target of unjustified criticisms, obliged to sacrifice personal feelings for community well-being and "pray for them which despitefully use you" (Matt. 5:44 KJV). Paul declares that these events occurred as examples so that God's people through the centuries would learn not to set their hearts on evil things (1 Cor. 10:1–13).

A. Bitter waters (15:22–27). In the desert, three days without water is a crisis. The bitter water the Israelites find fits well with the salinity of the swampy area north of the Gulf of Suez. God's response is to show Moses a tree (NIV "piece of wood") to cast into the waters in order to restore them. The Hebrew word translated "showed" literally means "taught" and is related to the word "torah" (instruction). As Jewish rabbis of late antiquity discussed what kind of a tree might sweeten bitter

Jebel Musa, the traditional site of Mount Sinai

waters, one of their suggestions was that the tree symbolized torah itself; this verb strengthened that interpretation. Knowledge of torah was viewed as a sufficient antidote to deal with the bitter experiences of life.

At this point, God states his intention to test the Israelites. Although the specific contents of the decree and the law are not articulated, the people are to obey God's voice as they hear it and to heed the forthcoming commandments. The reward will be freedom from the diseases that God brought on the Egyptians. This may be a reference to far-reaching effects of the plagues, evidence of which they have seen. After the crisis, God brings them to a place with multiple springs. Twelve may symbolize the tribes, and seventy may represent the elders appointed later (Numbers 11).

B. Threat of starvation (16:1–36). A month later in the Desert of Sin the Israelites' circumstances are so bleak that they voice their desire to return to Egypt, representing their previous estate in rosy colors complete with pots of meat and all the food they want. Their grumbling against Moses and Aaron prompts a response from the Lord; the Israelites will see manifested in the wilderness the glory and power of God in his benevolent provision. They will have meat in the evening and bread in the morning to meet their daily needs. In this context, while both are promised, manna is the focus of the narrative. A year later (Num. 10:11), the quail are prominent. These are not disparate accounts of the same incident. Rather, the year at Mount Sinai, characterized by ongoing rebellion on the part of the people, makes them disdain the tedium of daily manna (Num. 11:6). While in this first instance God responds in mercy, their subsequent complaint results in severe judgment (Num. 11:31–34).

The quail are a natural seasonal event in Sinai, while the manna is a daily and miraculous provision. Even the name expresses the Israelites' wonder at this substance: "They said to each other, 'What is it [*man hu*]?' For they did not know what it was [*mah-hu*]" (16:15).

The name *man* (what) sticks. It appears as thin flakes like frost, is white like coriander seed, tastes like wafers made with honey, and looks like resin (Num. 11:7–8). While it could be identified with a sticky, granular insect excretion of the Sinai Peninsula, the miraculous nature of God's extensive, egalitarian, and continuous provision is evident. Moses commands Aaron to place a jar containing an omer of manna before the Lord as a memorial of God's faithful provision during the entire wilderness experience. It will be parallel to the bread of the Presence instituted in the tabernacle structure. After celebrating the Passover in the land, the Israelites cease to receive manna (Josh. 5:10–12).

Prior to giving the torah at Sinai, the Lord institutes the Sabbath observance in conjunction with providing manna. It is miraculously preserved from the sixth day until the seventh in contrast to its spoilage every other day, and the Israelites are not to collect it fresh on the seventh. Although they are not to be greedy and hoard from one day to the next, the perversity of human nature is sadly evident in that, no matter what the people are commanded to do, some of them do not obey. The Sabbath is called a *shabbaton shabbat qodesh* (literally "a day of rest, a holy rest"; 16:23). *Shabbat* means a complete stop, bringing wholeness to the time preceding it. *Shabbaton* is superlative, indicating the *greatest* degree of rest. For this previously enslaved population, the Sabbath comes as a joyous gift. It is a time to leave the tedium and anxiety of work. It is also the culmination of the creation time cycle, and God sanctified it (Gen. 2:2–3), a fact included in the Ten Commandments, as Israel is commanded to remember the Sabbath by sanctifying it just as the Creator did (Exod. 20:8–11). When God's people observe the Sabbath, they are re-presenting God's acts of creating, completing, and resting. Further, the Sabbath will be the sign of the Sinai covenant, and desecrating the Sabbath is punishable by death (Exod. 31:12–17). Because the Sabbath was and is an intrinsic part of nurturing the relationship between God and his people, its importance transcends the stipulations of the Sinai covenant.

C. Thirst in the desert (17:1–7). Traveling at the command of the Lord, the Israelites journey to Rephidim, find no water, and quarrel with Moses to the point where he fears for his life. God promises Moses, "I will stand there before you by the rock at Horeb. Strike the rock, and water will come out" (17:6). In Paul's recital of the lessons to be learned from the wilderness events, he states that the people drank "from the spiritual rock that followed them, and the Rock was Christ" (1 Cor. 10:4 NRSV). Unpacking the symbolic connections, there is an intimation that God himself is struck.

Massah is related to the Hebrew verb *nasah*, meaning "to test," and Meribah comes from *rib*, "to strive or quarrel." A similar incident with the recurrence of the name Meribah occurs when the people arrive at Kadesh Barnea (Num. 20:1–13). Nevertheless God's instructions to Moses at Kadesh Barnea are different. He is to speak to the rock instead of striking it, as in this instance. Because Moses there responds in anger, striking the rock twice and lashing out at the people, he is punished; God refuses to allow him to enter the land.

These incidents are paradigmatic for the psalmist (Ps. 95:7–11) and for the author of Hebrews 3–4, both of whom are concerned about unbelief and hardness of heart in the face of God's evident provision. The exhortation to enter the "Sabbath-rest" (Heb. 4:9–10) means leaving the life of disobedience and unbelief.

D. Attack from enemies (17:8–16). The Israelites present a threat to the nomadic Amalekites' water sources in the wilderness. Thus the Amalekites viciously attack weary Israel, cutting off stragglers, with no fear of the Lord (Deut. 25:17–18). The rod of God raised up by Moses is a visible symbol indicating that the battle is the Lord's. When Moses tires and his hands sink, the Amalekites prevail until Aaron and Hur, representing the tribes of Levi and Judah, sustain him. Almost uniformly, the church fathers saw in Moses's symbolic action the uplifted cross of Christ, effecting victory over spiritual enemies (e.g., *Epistle of Barnabas* 12; Justin Martyr, *Dialogue with Trypho* 90–91; Tertullian, *Answer to the Jews* 10). This is the first mention of Joshua, whose name means "the Lord saves." In the aftermath of the battle the Lord declares his perpetual enmity toward the Amalekites, who sporadically reappear on the stage of Israel's history. They attack Israel in the period of the Judges (Judg. 6:3). Saul disobeys God by not putting to death Agag, the king of the Amalekites (1 Samuel 15). First Chronicles 4:41–43 records the destruction of the remnant of Amalekites in the days of Hezekiah. Mordecai, from the tribe of Benjamin (Esther 2:5), sees the downfall of Haman, the Agagite (Esther 3:1), who plotted the destruction of the Jews.

In the first reference to writing in the Bible, Moses is commanded to record the sacred ban on Amalek on a

Moses calls the Lord "my Banner" (or "Standard"; Exod. 17:15), such as these standards carried before the Egyptian king Narmer (ca. 3150 BC).

scroll (17:14). Writing is presented here in conjunction with and as the basis for oral recitation; both are sources for the tradition. Moses builds an altar, calling it "The LORD is my Banner [or "Standard"]" (17:15). The Hebrew word for "banner," *nes*, refers to an upraised symbol and rallying point in battle (cf. Isa. 11:10). The next verse (17:16) could possibly read, "Because a hand was upon the standard (*nes*) of the LORD, the battle is the LORD's," instead of "Because a hand was upon the throne (*kes*) of the LORD . . ." (author's translation). The first Hebrew letters of each of these words (*n* and *k*) look similar and could be easily exchanged by a scribal error. In the former rendering the verse would then refer to Moses's upraised hands with the rod (the visible rallying point) of God.

E. Reuniting with family (18:1–12). At some point after the incident en route to Egypt from Midian (Exod. 4:24–26), Moses sent Zipporah back to her father, possibly because the rigors of confronting Pharaoh would be overwhelming. She also would have been a foreigner in the Israelite context. Moses knows what it feels like to be an outsider, as the name of his first son, Gershom, testifies (18:3). Although it is not clear when his second son was born, the boy's name, Eliezer, affirms that God is Moses's helper (18:4), delivering him from death at the hand of Pharaoh. The children's names symbolize the wilderness experiences for repeated generations of God's people.

Horeb (Sinai) seems to have been on the edge of Midianite territory, and it was where God initially appeared to Moses (Exod. 3:1). When Jethro hears all that the Lord has done for Israel, he testifies to the greatness of the Lord God above all other gods and brings sacrifices to express his allegiance. The burnt offering atones for sin (Lev. 1:4). In communion with Aaron (the priest of Israel) and the elders, this priest of Midian eats in the presence of God.

F. Settling disputes (18:13–27). Jethro immediately contributes to the community's well-being. Seeing the congestion created by large numbers of people coming to Moses with legal disputes, he advises Moses to delegate responsibility. As Moses represents the people before God and teaches them, qualified persons can serve under him, caring for set numbers of people. Those selected are to fear God, to be people of truth, and to hate dishonest gain. Jethro's return home is temporary, as he reappears to help Israel again after their Sinai sojourn (Num. 10:29–32).

3. Covenant at Sinai (19:1–24:18)

God's revelation comes to the people in the wilderness, characteristically a place for purification and for meeting God. The covenant encompasses the whole of Israel's life. Their community comes into existence at the gracious will of God, and they are expected to exercise appropriate societal and individual responsibilities as his people. Even though there are affinities between the covenant and the Hittite treaty pattern, this relationship between God and the entire people is unique. Furthermore the setting in a narrative context is unique.

Exodus 20 begins the instructive words (torah, or law) of God for the recipients of the covenant. Torah reveals God's holiness, indicating that there are specific standards of right and wrong; violations of those moral standards warrant punishment. Torah repeatedly calls the people of God to be holy as he is holy; it articulates purity and cleanliness standards for life lived in the presence of God. And torah reveals the depths of human sinfulness as those standards are repeatedly broken. Paul makes this point forcefully in Romans 3:9–20. No one is righteous, but through torah individuals become conscious of sin. Because torah demonstrates what sin is and how completely humans are captured by it, it serves to lead to Christ (Gal. 3:24; see also Rom. 7:7–13). Torah also sets the basic standards by which social structures function. Finally, Hebrews 10:1 suggests that the righteousness and goodness evident in torah is a shadow of the perfection and justice that will prevail when this world's injustices have finally been overcome. This is a source of hope in a disheartening and fallen world.

These instructions address every aspect of life as a unified whole. Many scholars have rejected the three categories of moral-ethical, civil-social, and ritual-ceremonial torah as arbitrary and have intrepreted the text by use of principalism. This method (1) identifies what the law meant to its original audience, (2) evaluates the differences between the initial audience and successive generations of believers, and (3) develops universally applicable principles from the text that correlate with New Testament teaching. To be sure, the instructions are interwoven in the text in a way that defies firm boundaries around each of the three categories. Nevertheless, such a conceptual framework makes sense of the complex web of laws and underscores certain emphases as they appear. Thus to speak of moral-ethical torah means affirming there are fundamental principles of right and wrong that transcend cultural and temporal boundaries. Civil-social torah addresses social structures and provides for proper administration of justice in a given cultural context. Specific formulations would change, but the general principles remain the same because all social systems are composed of sinful humans. Many actions that violate moral torah end up in the court system. Ritual-ceremonial torah prepares the covenant community to approach God in worship and insists that all of life is conducted in the presence of God. While worship environments change, the fundamental need of sinful human beings to have a way into the presence of a holy God remains the same.

A. Preparations to receive the covenant (19:1–25). As covenant mediator, Moses goes up and down the mountain multiple times (19:3, 7–9, 10, 14, 20–21, 24–25), communicating to Israel God's promises and the procedures for purification, and communicating to God Israel's expressed intention to be obedient. After Moses's third trip up the mountain he objects to God's repetition of the command to go down and warn the people (19:20–22), but in fact the people are still not fully prepared for God's

direct revelation and need additional warning. Even so, they are able to endure only the Ten Commandments; after that they request that Moses serve as mediator (Exod. 20:19). Referring to the activities of Moses in this setting, Paul notes that "the law was given through angels and entrusted to a mediator" (Gal. 3:19; see also Acts 7:53; on the angels' role in the giving of the law, see Deut. 33:2; Heb. 2:2).

The promises of God follow his reiteration of his strong care for them, since he has borne them on eagle's wings to their present safe haven (19:4). The image of the eagle conveys both power and protection (Deut. 28:49; 32:11). The promises set Israel apart from all nations but are conditional on their obedience. Israel will be God's treasured possession, a kingdom of priests, and a holy nation (19:5–6). In these promises we see the Israelites' transformation from slaves of Pharaoh to honored members of God's kingdom. "Kingdom of priests" unites political and sacred vocations; they are to function among the nations as mediators of God's blessings. Peter invokes these promised roles of Israel, emphasizing that Christians' privileged status as God's treasured possession inspires praise (1 Pet. 2:9). In the eschatological fulfillment of these covenant promises the four living creatures and the elders extol God for making those whom the Lamb has purchased with his blood to be a kingdom and priests to serve God (Rev. 5:10).

Meeting with God comes only after disciplined preparation. The people have to purify themselves, washing their clothes and setting boundaries around the mountain (19:10–11). The warning against mingling religious observance and sexual practice (19:15) is likely due to sacred prostitution characteristic of the surrounding nations. Whoever touches the mountain will be either shot with arrows or stoned, so that symbolically the people avoid direct contact with one guilty of presumptuous sin (19:13).

The descent of God on the third day is preceded by thunder, lightning, a thick cloud, and a loud trumpet blast (19:17). He arrives amid billowing smoke, raging fire, and violent trembling of the mountain. The event is beyond the capacity of any words to capture its essence, and the accompanying phenomena inspire the greatest dread and humility. God does indeed come down, an expression of his condescension, but the people are called to meet him in humble fear. These are important truths in light of contemporary trivializations of "mountain-top experiences" as places for self-indulgence. When God manifests himself, it is the prelude to his demand for transformed lives. Coming to grips with the terrible implications of his holiness is essential.

The author of Hebrews contrasts the terror inspired by this drama with the joy of approaching Mount Zion and the heavenly Jerusalem, the city of the living God, through Jesus, the mediator of the new covenant (Heb. 12:18–24). Nevertheless that writer knows that the holy nature of God has not changed one iota, so he urges his audience to worship God with fear and awe because God is a consuming fire (Heb. 12:28–29).

B. Ten Commandments and the people's response (20:1–26). When Jesus is asked which commandment is the most important, he affirms two fundamental principles that characterize the Law and the Prophets: "Love the Lord your God with all your heart and with all your soul and with all your mind and with all your strength," and "Love your neighbor as yourself" (Mark 12:28–34; Matt. 22:34–40; Luke 10:25–27). The Decalogue (literally the "Ten Words," or the Ten Commandments) itself opens with "the Lord your God" (20:2) and closes with "your neighbor" (20:17). The first four of the Ten Commandments address the relationship of humans to God, affirming his unassailable right as Creator to the worship and undivided adoration of his people. The last six compactly articulate the absolute justice and goodness that must attend all human interactions. There are both positive and negative commandments, guarding against death and pointing the way

to life. The commandments are designed to direct love to the proper object by ruling out those things that quench or distort love. All of the commandments are addressed to members of the community of Israel, with singular forms of the verbs. Each individual is to hear and obey, and the community is to be of one heart and mind. In rabbinic tradition the people only hear the Lord utter the first two; after that Moses serves as mediator. The textual basis for this is the change in pronoun: God is referred to in the first person in the first two commandments but in the third person after that.

20:1–17. Because God identifies himself as the Israelites' redeemer, the *first commandment* prohibits other gods; all of the people's lives are to be shaped by singular loyalty to God. They have been living for centuries in Egypt, surrounded by elements of nature that are deified. They will be moving into Canaan, where the same practices are evident. Contemporary secular culture offers a plethora of choices ("other gods") where no allegiance is required, and in fact any wholehearted allegiance is viewed as suspect. God's people are called to be radically bound by love for God.

The *second commandment*, against making images, bowing down to them, or serving them, could refer both to images of Yahweh and to those of rival deities. Because the latter possibility was already addressed with the first commandment, this one primarily forbids any attempt to make a visible representation of God himself that would domesticate and trivialize his awesome majesty. Nevertheless the prohibition also applies to any of the elements of nature that so easily become objects of worship, especially those closely associated with the presence of God. The restriction is comprehensive, from the heavenly bodies to creatures in the sea. The people are easily tempted to attribute power to these various objects; an idol is the means of capturing that power and using it. It reduces God to something that could be managed for the self-satisfaction of the one who fashions the idol.

Idolatry was a sore temptation to which the Israelites succumbed throughout their history; their heinous idolatry repeatedly brought judgment on them, culminating in exile from the land. The stinging condemnation of idolatry as opposed to worship of God the Creator in Isaiah 41–44 is echoed in Romans 1. Colossians 3:5 indicates that greed is idolatry. God, who has bound his people to himself with covenant love, is jealous and will punish those who abuse his covenant love and refuse to be devoted exclusively to him (Exod. 20:5a). The Hebrew adjective translated "jealous" is used only of God; it is the divine response to apostasy. Successive generations suffer the consequences of their forefathers' choices to live in rebellion against God. Often children are the tragic victims of these choices. This warning is countered by the promise of unfailing covenant love (Hebrew *hesed*) to thousands (of generations) of those who love God and keep his commandments (20:5b). In this single verse both the justice and the mercy of God are evident.

A literal translation of the *third commandment* reads, "You shall not lift up the name of the Lord your God to emptiness because God will not hold guiltless the one who lifts up his name to emptiness" (20:7). Uttering God's name in the service of any objective outside God's purposes is a serious affront to his glory and majesty. The ambiguity of the expression "lift up . . . to emptiness" allows a wide application, from swearing falsely in lawsuits to frivolous use of God's mighty name. In the Israelite context one who deliberately blasphemed the name of God with a curse was put to death (Lev. 24:10–16). By the first century, Jews were careful to substitute other terms so as to avoid breaking this commandment. Matthew consistently uses the term "kingdom of heaven" rather than "kingdom of God." "Lifting up the name" may suggest taking an oath in a legal context. In its wider application infractions of this commandment occur with sad frequency within the believing community, which too often lightly and frivolously jokes about God.

The Israelites had already been taught the Sabbath procedures when they received the manna (Exodus 16). In Exodus 20:8, the *fourth commandment* says to "remember" the Sabbath; in Deuteronomy 5:12 the word is "keep." Both focus on the objective of setting the Sabbath apart, "keeping it holy." Remembering establishes continuity with their past tradition; keeping implies protecting and guarding it for the future. God himself rested after creation (20:11), building into the very fabric of his created order the necessity of rest. As God set the day apart and blessed it, Israel is to remember and do the same. There is nothing in all the ancient Near East that corresponds to this gift from God to his people. The Sabbath is determined not by the movement of celestial bodies but by a simple seven-day cycle.

In Deuteronomy 5:15 keeping the Sabbath commemorates God's rescue of Israel from Egypt. Because the exodus event foreshadows the redemption that Christians experience in the risen Christ, it is not surprising that Jesus infuses the Sabbath with even greater meaning when he says, "The sabbath was made for humankind, and not humankind for the sabbath; so the Son of Man is lord even of the sabbath" (Mark 2:27–28 NRSV). Jesus did not lessen the importance of the Sabbath but redirected the attention of the people to the necessary heart attitude of reverent worship of their Creator and Redeemer. The first-century Jewish legal experts systematized thirty-nine principal categories of forbidden work (Mishnah *Shabbat* 7:2) because the Sabbath was the sign of the Sinai covenant and infractions meant the death penalty. They were concerned to determine just what actions beyond those noted in Scripture (Exod. 16:29; 34:21; 35:3; Num. 15:32–36; Neh. 10:32; 13:15–18; Jer. 17:21, 24, 27) were forbidden. Sabbath observance in its original intent, however, was viewed as a positive and restorative command, providing release from anxious toil and ambition.

The *fifth commandment* (20:12) is in a pivotal position between the first group, which addresses humankind's relationship with God, and the second, which attends to interactions on the human level. Parents bring new life into the world, and they are to be accorded corresponding honor. This is a comment on the value of life and the order established by God, whom parents represent to their children. While this is a call to children to esteem their parents, it is likewise a call to parents to be worthy of the honor. Observing that this is the first commandment with a promise, Paul indicates that it should be from parents that children learn how to love and serve God (Eph. 6:2–4). Clearly human parents often fail in this enterprise, some more drastically than others. Part of the honor accorded them is, in those cases, forgiveness and exerting every effort to live at peace (cf. Heb. 12:14). Maligning parents who have been a severe detriment to one's life only leads to bitterness. The punishment for cursing parents is death (Exod. 21:17); rebellion and disobedience receive a like punishment (Deut. 21:18–21). The Hebrew word translated "honor" literally means "to be heavy" or "give weight to" and may be directed to those children who are already adults and responsible for providing for their parents. This aspect of the commandment seems to underlie Jesus's rebuke of the Pharisees in Mark 7:9–13. Finally, the promise regarding the land may refer to the fact that poor family relationships will mean forfeiting the family property.

From this point the commandments are tersely articulated, allowing for considerable re-presentation in specific sociohistorical contexts. The *sixth commandment* (20:13) prohibits murder and always refers to illegal killing. The Hebrew term for "murder" refers to intentional and deliberate taking of human life; most examples of where the term is used address improper homicide that clearly is damaging to the community. In Hebrew, two entirely different words are translated "to kill" and "to put to death." The primary concerns here are not the death penalty or warfare. Murder is the most drastic antihuman action, violating the image of God. Satan was a murderer, knowing that introducing sin meant introducing death. Subsequent stipulations in the torah deal with such issues as manslaughter, going to war, and capital punishment. The punishment for murder is the death penalty (Exod. 21:12).

With the *seventh commandment* (20:14), God forbids adultery. Violation of the marriage covenant leads

A tablet containing Sumerian laws of Ur-Nammu. Among the many law codes archaeologists have discovered from the ancient Near East, this collection of laws is the oldest, dating to just before 2000 BC.

only to disaster, graphically illustrated on the human level in Proverbs 5:1–23; 6:20–29; 7:1–27. The gift of sexuality is both rapturous and potentially destructive to individuals and whole communities, as it evokes desires that can overwhelm reason. Thus sexuality must be disciplined in a context of fidelity so that family stability and honor are maintained. Marriage symbolizes the intimate covenant love between God and his people; broken marriages represent the spiritual adultery of the people of Israel (Hos. 1:1–2:23; Mal. 2:13–16). All manner of unacceptable sexual practices are rampant in the land that the Israelites are going to possess, and God warns them soberly against these perversions, stating unequivocally that such perversions defile the land (Leviticus 18). As with all of the commandments up to this point, adultery is punishable by death (Lev. 20:10). So also are other sexual aberrations (Lev. 20:11–16). Jesus makes very strong comments about adultery and divorce, calling his audiences back to the principle of two becoming "one flesh" (Mark 10:2–12; Matt. 19:3–12; cf. Gen. 2:24).

The *eighth commandment* prohibits stealing (20:15). Underlying this commandment is the intrinsic value and freedom of persons and property. While God is the ultimate possessor of all creation, he has given stewardship and ownership of specific aspects of the creation to human beings, and that ownership is not to be violated. Subsequent chapters of Exodus address details regarding judicial procedures for the variety of possible infractions. The penalty for property theft is restitution (Exod. 22:1–4), but if a person is stolen (kidnapped), the penalty is death (Exod. 21:16).

The *ninth commandment* forbids false testimony and has specific application to witnesses in court (20:16). The penalty for false witnesses is severe (Deut. 19:16–21). The rest of Scripture presents lying in general as a heinous offense. The book of Proverbs repeatedly warns of the damage that false speech does, declaring that a lying tongue and a false witness who pours out lies are detestable to the Lord (Prov. 6:16–19).

Jesus strikes at the root of the problem, calling the devil the father of lies and a murderer from the beginning (John 8:44). The end of liars, along with such offenders as murderers, the sexually immoral, and idolaters, will be the lake of fire (Rev. 21:8). Distortions of the truth lead to ruined reputations, lack of trust, irreconcilable pain, and loss of life. Sadly, multiple biblical as well as contemporary illustrations demonstrate these consequences, both on the level of individuals and in terms of systemic and ideological shaping of truth.

Finally, the *tenth commandment*, against coveting (20:17), completes the circle created by this comprehensive statement of ethics. Coveting means an insatiable craving to serve oneself at any cost, a clear violation of the first two commandments. It is the heart attitude that surfaces in acts of murder, adultery, theft, and false witness. When Jesus challenges the self-righteous rich young ruler to give up all his possessions and follow Jesus, the ruler acknowledges that his heart is too attached to his wealth (Matt. 19:16–22).

20:18–26. Having seen and heard the manifestation of God's presence, the people are afraid and ask Moses to mediate. Moses attests to the protective value of fear, as it will keep them from sin (20:20). While the people remain at a distance, Moses approaches the thick darkness. Evidence of God's overpoweringly dreadful presence and continuing mystery, the thick cloud shrouds his manifestation, so often portrayed as blazing fire. From this point forward, all of God's revelation will be mediated through Moses, the continuing prophetic office, and finally the incarnate Word.

God's initial words to Moses repeat the warning against idolatry and give preliminary directives about constructing earthen and stone altars (20:22–26). This passage may affirm the use of sacrificial altars besides the central one at the tabernacle, and later the temple. That such did exist is clear both from the biblical text (1 Kings 18:30) and from archaeological finds, notably the horned altar at Beersheba.

The warning against revealing nakedness in verse 26 may allude to the connection in the surrounding Canaanite culture between worship and sexuality.

C. Covenant stipulations (21:1–23:19). These specific stipulations interweave civil torah, social rules, moral injunctions, and prescriptions for worship, and none is privileged above the others. The initial civil-social instructions are presented as case law, specific for their ancient Near Eastern culture; about halfway through, the tone changes to imperatives addressing issues of justice, mercy, and proper worship. The bulk of the material establishes procedures to administer justice in this newly forming social entity and is designed for their life together in the land. In order to deal with some of the seemingly less-than-ideal stipulations included in the book of the covenant, some scholars have proposed applying trajectory theology. This interpretive model sees the laws articulated in the Sinai covenant as ethically more advanced than those in the surrounding cultures, but as only approximating the ideal to which they point. Further progress toward that ideal may then be found in New Testament practical theology and in some Western social structures, although not everything in the latter represents an improvement on the biblical material.

21:1–23:9. Primary social issues addressed in this section include the treatment of Hebrew slaves, personal injuries, theft and property damage, sexual abuses, and mistreatment of the disenfranchised. Such factors as intentionality, gender, and whether one is a slave or free affect how civil torah is implemented in that sociocultural setting. Israelites are not to pervert justice for ill motives, and balance in the administration of justice is essential. The measure-for-measure principle—"eye for eye, tooth for tooth, hand for hand" (21:23–25; see also Lev. 24:17–22; Deut. 19:16–21)—does not imply that literal hands and eyes are to be removed but that the punishment must fit the crime; it is meant to curb the all-too-human tendency for revenge and to ensure equal treatment across sociological

boundaries. The text affirms the possibility of compensatory payments in place of strict measure-for-measure action (21:26–27). The Hebrew verb for "to make restitution" is *shalem*, which means to set right and restore well-being (*shalom*). These guidelines were established for court procedures. Jesus addresses the personal need to eschew any desire for retaliation by giving even more than is required (Matt. 5:38–42).

21:1–36. The master-servant relationship was part of the widespread ancient socioeconomic structure, and the Israelites, emerging from their own harsh bondage, are to be particularly sensitive to mistreatment of slaves. The Hebrew word *ebed* means both "slave" and "servant." Because there is provision for selling oneself into bondage in order to deal with unmanageable debt (22:3), hope for freedom is essential. A male servant does not have to buy his freedom but can leave at the end of six years if he chooses to do so (21:2). If, however, he loves his master, or his master has given to him a wife whom he loves, he can continue to serve his master (21:5–6). Because it was common practice in the ancient Near East for a master to "breed" slaves by giving the slave a wife, the slave might not have an emotional attachment to his wife and might leave by himself. Becoming a permanent slave was a major step, and thus an oath was taken in the presence of the judicial authorities, who represented God. If freedom means freedom in poverty, the slave may choose to remain secure in the master's household.

Women were in a different position (21:7–11). In that social context it was not possible for a woman to live independently apart from the protection of father, husband, or master. When a father sold his daughter to be a servant in a stable household, that ensured her security and could involve marriage either to the new master or to his son. This explains why she is not allowed automatically to go free after six years (cf. Deut. 15:12). The ambiguity of the passage is heightened by the provision for redeeming her if she is not pleasing (21:8) and even the possibility of her going free if her master does not provide her with the basics of food, clothing, and marital rights (21:10–11). This is a freedom for which she does not have to pay. However these particular factors fit together, she is not to be cast off, either by being sold to foreigners (21:8) or by becoming marginalized and abused in the extended family context (21:10).

In regard to personal injury and abuse (21:12–35) the matter of intentionality is prominent. If an individual dies as the result of a premeditated attack, the killer is to be put to death. If, on the other hand, "God lets it happen" (21:13), then there is a system to protect the slayer from those who would take revenge. This is briefly mentioned in Exodus and developed significantly in conjunction with the cities of refuge (Num. 35:6–34; Deut. 19:1–13). Dishonoring parents by physical or verbal abuse, a violation of the fifth commandment, is punishable by death. So also with stealing persons, or kidnapping (21:15–17).

The same life value is put on women and men in the category of personal injury, but slaves are treated differently than are nonslaves. Whereas injury to a free person means the assailant has to compensate for lost time (21:19), if a person injures his own slave, no punishment is required because the slave is his property (21:21). Injury to a free woman requires measure-for-measure punishment (21:22–25). In the case of a slave, compensation is effected by granting the slave freedom (21:26–27). If a bull gores a slave, compensation is made to the owner of the slave, but the punishment is not as rigorous (21:32). Masters can discipline slaves but not to the point of death (20:20–21). Otherwise the slave can be avenged. These instructions oscillate between humane justice and the concern for economics, as slaves represented a financial investment and were viewed as property. Even so, there are no other ancient Near Eastern legal codes that protect slaves from maltreatment by masters.

The case in Exodus 21:22–25 is complicated by the woman's pregnancy. If, as a result of the blow, "her children" come out (21:22 ESV) but there is no serious injury, the punishment is a fine. Serious injury necessitates just retribution. While there is some potential ambiguity in the text, it seems likely that the injury addressed in this case is that which occurs to the woman. The fine applies to the prematurely born or miscarried children (see 21:22 NIV and note).

The owner is responsible in the case of an ox that is known to be lethal (21:29–32). This same situation is also treated in the ancient Near Eastern codes of Eshnunna and Hammurabi. The animal is to be destroyed because of the sanctity of life. If the owner was aware that the animal was dangerous and did nothing to address the situation, he too is subject to stoning, although a ransom payment can be an alternative.

22:1–23:9. Because the society was agricultural, the cases regarding theft and property damage have primarily to do with animals and land produce (22:1–15). While theft in general means a twofold restitution, the relative value and necessity of certain animals means that the payback when they are stolen is significantly more: five head of cattle for an ox and four sheep for one sheep. Oxen were working animals, and their loss would have had significant productivity implications. Likewise, flocks were valuable for milk, fleece, flesh, and hides. There is even concern for justice for the housebreaking thief (22:2–3). If he is fatally struck at night the homeowner is not liable, but the latter is held responsible during a daytime theft if his defensive assault is lethal.

Cases of negligence and loss (22:5–15), where identifying the responsible party is difficult, are brought before God or the judges (Hebrew *elohim* can mean either). An oath taken before the Lord that the temporary keeper did not commit a crime in regard to the property is to be sufficient. The verb *shalem* recurs throughout the section, implying that making restitution means restoring the social fabric.

A man who seduces a virgin and sleeps with her (22:16–17) is to take responsibility by paying the bride-price and marrying her. Even if her father refuses to allow her to marry, the seducer still has to pay the bride-price. The same stipulation is part of a much larger discussion of sexual improprieties in Deuteronomy 22:13–30. Likewise the brief mention of the death penalty for having sexual relations with an animal (22:19) is among numerous abuses detailed in Leviticus 18. The prohibitions in Exodus 22:18–20 address practices that are abominations. The serious nature of these infractions is evident in that the punishment involves the practice of *herem*, giving over to destruction those who have deliberately rejected the Lord (22:20).

Four groups are repeatedly the objects of God's deep compassion—widows, orphans, aliens, and the poor (22:21–24). Just as God has heard the cry of the Israelites when they were in Egypt, so he promises to hear and respond with justice to the cry of disenfranchised persons. If Israelites treat widows or orphans unjustly, the number of widows and orphans in Israel will increase because God will kill the malefactors! Those who are financially disadvantaged are not to be abused, either in matters of justice or in financial dealings. The need for a loan demonstrates devastating poverty; paying interest would relegate the person to perpetual economic distress (22:25). While there is evidence of loans with interest in the commercial and urban ancient Near East, the Israelites' well-being depended on the land's productivity, a more tenuous situation. Israelites could add interest to loans for foreigners because they were likely traveling with commercial and trade interests and, being more mobile, posed a greater financial risk. Both the individual and society were equally responsible to meet the needs of those who were in poverty; singular as well as plural verbs are woven into the commands.

The command not to blaspheme (22:28) may refer to God or to judges (Hebrew *elohim*); in this context it may have primary reference to the latter. Blasphemy trivializes authority, whether divine or human. The Israelites are also reminded to give to the Lord their firstborn and to demonstrate their separation by not eating improperly killed meat (22:29–31).

The principles that close the section on social and civil torah (23:1–9) acknowledge the fundamental evil of lying, hatred, and greed and call for truthfulness as the basis of justice. No special consideration is to be given to social status, whether rich or poor. The specific mandate to help the animal of one's enemy would be a way of demonstrating evidence of forgiveness within the community.

23:10–19. The summary of Sabbath guidelines (23:10–12) highlights social and humanitarian concerns. The complex of seventh-year procedures, expanded in Deuteronomy 15, provides for the poor as does the Jubilee (Leviticus 25). Even the command to observe one day in seven brings refreshment to the members of extended households that most need it: slaves, aliens, and working animals.

Each of the three major pilgrim festivals (23:14–17) is described at greater length and with alternative names in parallel passages (Lev. 23:1–44; Num. 28:16–29:40; Deut. 16:1–17). Once the temple is built, a male appearing before the Lord means pilgrimage to Jerusalem. Passover (not mentioned here) and the seven-day Feast of Unleavened Bread are combined, with greater emphasis being given to the latter. The Feast of Harvest (Weeks and Pentecost) celebrates the first fruits of the crops and traditionally commemorates the gift of torah three months after leaving Egypt. The Feast of Ingathering, at the end of the year, is also called the Feast of Tabernacles. All are celebrations of God's provision for Israel. In response, celebrants are to bring something back to God; they are not to appear before him empty-handed.

Four ritual guidelines follow (23:18–19). They are not to offer sacrificial blood, the cleansing agent, with anything that contains yeast because the latter symbolizes that which is evil. The fat portion, always given over to the Lord (Lev. 3:9–17), is not to be left until morning. That would represent disdain for what belongs to the Lord. The best of the first fruits belongs to God. Finally, a young goat is not to be cooked in its mother's milk. Although this last prohibition appears three times in the Torah (Exod. 34:26; Deut. 14:21), no reason is articulated. It may have been a Canaanite religious practice or a magical rite from which Israelites were to be separate.

D. Preparing the way to the land (23:20–33). The accompanying angel, identified with the Lord himself, will bring the Israelites into the land inhabited by idolatrous people groups. The Israelites are to demolish all the idols and sacred stones lest they engage in practices that would threaten their fragile allegiance to the Lord God (23:24). The brief statement of blessings for covenant obedience (23:25–26) is a microcosm of those articulated in Leviticus 26:1–13 and Deuteronomy 28:1–14. The Hebrew word *tsirah* ("hornet") is used only two other times, both in conjunction with the conquest (Deut. 7:20; Josh. 24:12). It might mean "plague" or could figuratively refer to the succession of pharaohs whose campaigns in Canaan had devastated the economy and military fortifications. There is a phonetic similarity between *mitsrayim* (Egypt) and *tsirah*. That the people are not sufficiently numerous to move into the land all at once suggests that their numbers were not in the millions.

The borders indicated in verse 31 present a western "front" at the Mediterranean Sea and across Sinai to the southwest, and an eastern boundary out to the desert in the Transjordan and extending northeast to the Euphrates River. This interpretation is contingent on understanding the "Sea of Reeds" as the same body of water that the Israelites crossed as they exited Egypt, which is not necessarily consistently the case in the biblical text. (See, for example, Num. 21:4.) These boundaries are never realized, even under the united monarchy of David and Solomon.

E. Covenant ratification (24:1–18). Only Moses is allowed to approach the Lord (24:1–2). Those invited to ascend the mountain are granted a vision of the God of Israel while the people worship at a distance. The representative leaders include Aaron, Nadab and Abihu, and the seventy elders. Nadab and Abihu are the eldest two sons of Aaron (Exod. 6:23), who later bring unauthorized fire into the presence of the Lord and are consumed by fire (Lev. 10:1–2). One of the possible explanations of that rash deed stems from this ceremony. Their privileged position here goes to their heads, and they presume to be able again to enter into the Lord's presence when the tabernacle proceedings are inaugurated. The seventy elders are recognized leaders (cf. Num. 11:16).

Moses repeats to the people what the Lord has said, they promise to be obedient, and Moses writes down the contents of the covenant in preparation for the ratification ceremony (24:3). Moses also builds an altar and sets up the symbolic twelve stones, and young Israelite men sacrifice burnt offerings and fellowship offerings (24:4–5). While the purposes and procedures for these sacrifices are later detailed in Leviticus 1–4, the offerings are already known to the Israelites, as their idolatrous worship of the golden calf demonstrates (Exod. 32:6). Possibly, as Moses wrote these accounts later, he described what happened in terms that were familiar to those who knew the sacrificial procedures. The Israelite young men, representative of the people, slaughter the animals, while Moses mediates by sprinkling the blood (24:6).

The purpose of the whole burnt offering is to atone for sin in general (Lev. 1:4), while the fellowship offering is an expression of gratitude and, by virtue of its name (an offering of "peace" or "wholeness," related to Hebrew *shalom*), a symbol of restored relationship. The participants partake of the fellowship offering in God's presence. The blood of these sacrifices represents life given to make atonement (cf. Lev. 17:11), and half is put on the altar prior to reading the book of the covenant (24:6–7). When Moses sprinkles the other half on the people, he essentially ordains them as the "kingdom of priests" with the words "This is the blood of the covenant" (24:8). The words of Jesus at the

Last Supper are an echo: "This is my blood of the covenant, which is poured out for many for the forgiveness of sins" (Matt. 26:28). Hebrews 9:19–22 re-presents this ceremony, expanding the list of objects that are sprinkled with the blood, and focusing on the blood as the means of cleansing and as necessary for forgiveness.

The Israelites' vision of God corresponds in abbreviated fashion to significant aspects of Ezekiel's vision into heaven. The clear pavement of sapphire under God's "feet" sets apart the presence of God's throne just as does the "vault, sparkling like crystal" above the heads of the living creatures and below the throne (Ezek. 1:22–26). Some of these same features reappear in the final throne vision of Revelation 4. In every case the glory of God overwhelms its audience. Not only do these invited participants see God; they eat and drink in his presence, symbolizing the relationship established by this covenant.

Following the communal meal (24:9–11) the Lord summons Moses to ascend the mountain and receive the tablets of stone on which the Lord has written the torah (24:12). Joshua, not part of the covenant ratification group, accompanies Moses. Aaron and Hur, of the tribes of Levi and Judah, are appointed as caretakers in their absence (24:13–14). Moses is called into the cloud, leaving the human sphere and venturing where no one has ever gone. The glory of God appears to the people as a fire that is consuming (24:15–17). It is no wonder they question if Moses will ever return. Moses remains on the mountain for forty days and nights to receive the instructions for the construction of the tabernacle and the preparation of the priesthood (24:18; cf. 25:40; 26:30; 27:8). When the glory of the Lord covers the mountain, it is a prelude to his presence manifested in the forthcoming tabernacle, God's dwelling in the midst of his people. The tabernacle is only a copy and shadow of God's heavenly dwelling (Heb. 8:5; 9:24).

4. Instructions for Sanctuary and Priesthood (25:1–31:18)

The significance of the tabernacle and its ministers is evident in the amount and placement of text devoted to these topics. After the covenant is articulated and confirmed (Exodus 20–24), God gives instructions about his sanctuary (Exodus 25–31; 35–40) before he outlines the sacrificial procedures in Leviticus 1–10. The two distinct units on the sanctuary are separated by the devastating golden calf incident, in which Israel breaks the fundamental bond of the covenant. Yet, God determines to dwell in their presence; completion of the structure and ordination of the priests demonstrate God's mercy.

The tabernacle is called a "sanctuary," a place set apart. The courtyard around the sanctuary defines that space. At the same time, the term for "tabernacle" means "dwelling place." God has chosen to dwell in their midst; the tabernacle prefigures the incarnation of the Word of God: "The Word became flesh and tented among us" (John 1:14, author's translation). John continues, "We beheld his glory," drawing his readers' attention back to the manifestations of divine glory in conjunction with the tabernacle, which is also called the "tent of meeting," indicative of God's intention to meet his people wherever they are on their journey. The Sinai event is continued in the tabernacle, combining God's presence and his mobility.

The tabernacle is a powerful visual lesson about approaching the holy covenant God. It is exquisitely constructed, remarkably extravagant, and representative of the beauty and perfection of the Master of the Universe as he comes to dwell in his people's midst. The pathway is via blood sacrifice and subsequent symbolic cleansing. The very process of taking the life of the animal, the mess, the bloodshed, and the pain, are all grim reminders that sin is a horrifying and dreadful thing in the presence of God. None of this speaks of "coziness" with God.

A. Contributions (25:1–9). The precious materials for the tabernacle (25:2–7; 35:20–29) are likely from the wealth that the Israelites took with them when they left Egypt. Out of grateful hearts, the people voluntarily give metals, fabric and yarns in colors of royalty, land and sea animal skins, wood, oil, spices, and precious stones. Moses is allowed to see the divine blueprint (25:9), a concept not foreign in the ancient Near East.

B. Ark of the covenant (25:10–22). The ark, an acacia-wood box overlaid with gold (25:10–11), will be the sole object in the Most Holy Place. It contains the tablets of the testimony from Mount Sinai, the permanent statement of the covenant relationship. In the ancient Near East it was standard practice to deposit tablets recording treaty relationships. The ark symbolizes the footstool of God's throne, evoking the image of God as sovereign. At certain points in Israel's history, this chest will also hold the pot of manna and Aaron's rod (Exod. 16:34; Num. 17:10; Heb. 9:4; see 1 Kings 8:9; 2 Chron. 5:10). The ark has a cover above which extend the wings of two cherubim facing each other (25:17–22). The Hebrew verb meaning "to cover" is used primarily in conjunction with the atonement provided by the blood sacrifice. When Moses enters the Tent of Meeting he hears the voice of God speaking to him from between the two cherubim above the atonement cover (Exod. 33:11; Num. 7:89). The cherubim figures represent celestial beings standing guard between the throne of God and the earthly spheres (Gen. 3:24; Ezek. 1:1–28; 10:1–22).

C. Table and lampstand (25:23–40). The table for the bread of the Presence (25:23–30) is placed on the north side in the Holy Place of the tabernacle (26:35). Twelve loaves of bread are regularly set out before the Lord on behalf of the Israelites (Lev. 24:5–9), a reminder of God's faithful provision, most notably of manna in the wilderness. Accompanying the table are plates, ladles, pitchers, and bowls for pouring out offerings. On the south side (Exod. 26:35) is an

elaborate lampstand with six branches extending out from a central shaft, three on each side (25:32). Altogether there are seven lamps on the stand (37:23). Each of the branches has multiple cups to hold oil for burning. The lamps inside the tabernacle are to be tended and kept burning continually (Exod. 27:21; Lev. 24:2–4), the pure radiant light of God's presence constantly driving away the dark powers of evil. A symbolic connection between the lamps and the Spirit is suggested in Zechariah 4:1–14 and Revelation 1.

D. Tabernacle (26:1–37). The tabernacle is portable (cf. Num. 4:24–33) with upright frames and crossbars of manageable size and silver bases for the frames (26:15–26, 29). The use of acacia wood (26:15, 26, 32) reflects the Sinai environment, as this tree grows most frequently in that relatively barren terrain. Four layers of curtains, likewise in segments for easy assembly and dismantling, cover the structure. The innermost layer is fine linen with figures of cherubim worked into the material (26:1). Longer curtains, protective coverings, are

Model of the ark of the covenant from the tabernacle model at Timna Valley Park, Israel

made of goat hair, ram skins, and the hides of animals whose habitat was apparently the Red Sea (26:7–14; NIV 1984 "hides of sea cows"). The Hebrew word for these hides is used only in conjunction with the tabernacle, and it is not entirely clear just what type of creature the hides came from.

A separate and finely made linen curtain covers the entrance (26:36). It is protected from the outside elements by an extra length of the goat hair curtain. Inside the tabernacle another curtain, also adorned with cherubim, partitions off the Most Holy Place, in which the ark is kept (26:31–35). Only the high priest entered the Most Holy Place, and that occurred only on the Day of Atonement. At the moment Jesus dies this curtain is rent asunder from top to bottom (Matt. 27:51). Hebrews 10:20 affirms that Jesus, in his role as our great High Priest, makes a "new and living way opened for us through the curtain."

E. Altar and courtyard (27:1–21). The altar for sacrifices is placed in the courtyard. The raised "horn" on each of the four corners likely served the practical purpose of containing the burning wood and sacrifices heaped on the altar. The horns of the altar came to be identified as a place of refuge from someone seeking to take a person's life (1 Kings 1:49–53; 2:28). The altar, of acacia wood with a bronze overlay, is hollow and thus transportable (27.1–2, 8). The curtained courtyard of the tabernacle delineates the sacred space. It is one hundred by fifty cubits, with the entrance on the east side (27:12–13).

F. Priestly attire (28:1–43). The mediating role of the high priest as he represents Israel before God is symbolized in the priestly attire. The ephod (28:6–14), a finely crafted garment of linen with strands of gold interwoven among blue, purple, and scarlet yarn, is worn over the priest's robe. It has shoulder pieces on which are engraved the names of the children of Israel. Aaron bears these names before the Lord as a memorial.

The breast piece (28:15–29) is a square piece of material attached to the ephod, folded double and worn over the heart. It has twelve stones, one for each of the tribes. The Urim and the Thummim, for making decisions (cf. Num. 27:21), are put into the breast piece. The command to take judicial issues to the priests, who will give decisions in the Lord's presence, likely refers to their use of the Urim and Thummim (Deut. 17:9–10). It is not clear how the Urim and Thummim functioned or even what the words mean. The traditional suggestion is that Urim means "lights" (from Hebrew *or*) and Thummim, "perfections" (from Hebrew *tom*); a confirming light would indicate a positive answer. Not every incident where they may have been used, however, so easily fits into the pattern of casting lots with simple positive or negative answers (cf. Judg. 1:2; 20:18; 2 Sam. 5:22–25).

The high priest is to wear a blue robe (28:31–35) with pomegranates and bells alternating around the hem. Pomegranates were among the seven fruits of the land (Deut. 8:8), symbolic of God's good blessings. Some suggest the bells were for the benefit of those outside, who would be concerned for the high priest's safety in the presence of the Lord. If they could hear him, they would know he had not perished in God's terrifying presence, a matter of particular concern after the incident with Nadab and Abihu (Leviticus 10). The text indicates that the bells have to do with God's attention to the high priest in his representative dress. The entire worship ritual is a mutual communicative process that utilizes the full sensory experience. To speak of sounds and smells appealing to God is not primitive anthropomorphism (giving God human attributes) but recognizes something profoundly rich about the senses in the expressed relationship between the Creator and his worshiping creatures.

Aaron is also to wear a linen turban bearing a gold plate that says, "holy to the LORD" (28:36–38). In this way he will carry aspects of the guilt of Israel. All of the priests are to wear white linen underclothes and carefully constructed tunics, sashes, and headbands, symbolic of purity (28:39–43).

G. Consecration of priests (29:1–46). Once dressed, the priests are consecrated for service, a process described in greater detail in Leviticus 8. Because the priest is the covenant mediator, the bull to cover his own sin is sacrificed first (29:10–14). While the blood of this animal is sprinkled before the curtain (Lev. 4:6), placed on the altar of incense, and poured out at the base of the outside altar, its fat portions are burned on the sacrificial altar as an offering to the Lord, and its flesh and hide are to be burned outside the camp in a ceremonially clean place.

The first of two rams is a whole burnt offering (29:15–18), the blood of which is sprinkled on all sides of the altar. The blood of the second ram (29:19–21), the ordination offering, is sprinkled on all sides of the altar, and also put on the right ear lobes, thumbs, and big toes of Aaron and his sons. Traditionally this represents their need for care in how they listen, what they do, and how they conduct themselves. This procedure also applies to a person who has been cleansed from an infectious skin disease (Lev. 14:28). These actions symbolize the comprehensive efficacy of the sacrificial blood to make the person presentable before God.

The fat of the offerings (29:22–26) is always the Lord's. The fat portions of the ordination offering, together with unleavened bread, a cake made with oil, and a wafer, are lifted up, symbolically being given to God, and then burned as "a pleasing aroma to the Lord." This expression or some variation of it is used more than forty times in the Old Testament, almost always in conjunction with God's acceptance of both thanksgiving and propitiatory sacrifices. It is a profound acknowledgment of God's participation in accepting offerings from his people. Idols are unable to smell (Ps. 115:6); by way of contrast God can, and that is one way of articulating his pleasure. Amos 5:21–22, declaring God's rejection of sacrifices from an unacceptable people, literally reads, "I will not smell your assemblies. . . . I will not look upon your best peace offerings."

The parts of the ordination offering that are eaten (29:31–34) belong solely to the priests. Aaron and his sons are to lay their hands on its head, representing their identification with this living creature whose life will be a substitute for theirs. The consecration of the priests is an intricate, seven-day process and one that must be completed perfectly. Leviticus 8–9 indicates that Moses, Aaron, and the priests fulfill all the requirements; in response, the glory of the Lord appears to all the people, and fire consumes the Lord's offerings on the altar.

The burnt offering of two lambs (29:31–34) is to be made twice daily, once in the morning and once at evening, affirming the continuing relationship between God and his people at that place where he has determined to dwell and where he will meet with them (29:44–46). The tabernacle is "set up on the first day of the first month in the second year" (40:17). Thus it is ready for the celebration of Passover.

H. Incense altar, half-shekel contribution, wash basin, oil, and incense (30:1–38). The altar for incense is to be positioned in front of the curtain separating the Holy Place from the Most Holy Place (30:6), although there is some ambiguity regarding which side it was on. Possibly it was a second article in the Most Holy Place (cf. Heb. 9:3–4). When the incense was ignited, the cloud provided protective covering (Lev. 16:13) as the high priest went into the Most Holy Place once a year. In addition, incense is burned regularly every morning and evening (30:7–8). Neither profane incense nor any other substance is to be burned on the incense altar (30:9). This elucidates the horrifying narrative of Nadab and Abihu, who offer "unauthorized fire" before the Lord (Lev. 10:1) and forfeit their lives as a result. The cloud of incense will come to be symbolic of the prayers of the saints (Ps. 141:2; Rev. 5:8). The imagery and theology of Exodus infuse the book of Revelation, as it looks forward to perfect worship in the very presence of God.

The half-shekel payment, collected in conjunction with the census, maintained the cultic system. It is called atonement money and serves as a reminder that the members of the community have been ransomed (30:12). While the original statement sounds like a one-time payment, it was collected at later points in history when the temple was being repaired (2 Kings 12:4; 2 Chron. 24:9; 34:9) and seems to have been the precedent for an annual assessment (cf. Matt. 18:24–27).

The basin and its stand are to be made of bronze (30:17), which comes from the mirrors of the women serving at the entrance to the Tent of Meeting (38:8). If Aaron and his sons do not wash their hands and feet in the basin before entering the tent, they will die (30:20–21). The altar is in front of the entrance to the tabernacle, and the basin is between the tent and the altar (40:6–7). Thus, there is a "path" into the presence of God. First, sacrificial blood is shed at the altar. Then, cleansing is necessary, and finally the cloud of incense precedes the priest into the presence of God and protects the priest.

All the cultic articles in the tent as well as the priests are to be consecrated with the fragrant anointing oil (30:22–33). A portion of the salted, pure, and sacred incense is to be placed in front of the Testimony in the tabernacle (30:34–38). The pleasing aroma is a contrast to the stench of death. Used in conjunction with royalty and worship, spices were exceedingly precious in the ancient Near East. The Israelites may have acquired these materials from traders along their journey. Because salt both preserves and enhances flavor, it was an appropriate additive to incense and offerings that represented the relationship with the everlasting covenant God (cf. Lev. 2:13).

I. Spirit-filled artisans (31:1–11). The Holy Spirit fills Bezalel, the artist who oversees the work, with practical wisdom (31:1–5). God also appoints his assistant, Oholiab, and gives them the ability to teach all the artisans (31:6; cf. 35:30–36:2). The artists are God's agents, as they fashion all the furnishings according to the pattern Moses has seen on the mountain (31:7–11).

J. Sign of the covenant (31:12–18). The Lord's Sabbath is the sign of this covenant. As the tabernacle is a reflection of God's dwelling in heaven, the Sabbath sanctifies time, reflecting the fact that God himself was refreshed after his creative activity (31:17). God is holy; the people are holy because he makes them so, and they are to keep the Sabbath holy as a lasting covenant. Observing the Sabbath and embracing the holiness of God are of one piece. Thus, those who desecrate the Sabbath are to die, a twice-stated warning (31:14–15). While the activities that constitute "work" are not fully specified, Exodus 35:3 prohibits lighting a fire on the Sabbath.

5. Apostasy at Sinai (32:1–34:35)

Moses's role as covenant mediator is particularly poignant in these chapters. Repeatedly he appeals to the Lord on behalf of the wayward people, seeking God's forgiveness and promise of his continuing presence with them. Neither comes automatically, but Moses persists, even offering himself as a substitute. Finally, in asking to see God's glory, Moses is given assurance of God's forgiveness (Exod. 34:6–7).

A. The golden calf (32:1–29). While Moses is on the mountain receiving the instructions regarding the tabernacle and the special position and function of Aaron as the high priest, Aaron succumbs to the popular demand that he take over for Moses, who has been gone for a disturbingly long time (31:1).

The calf may represent Israel's return to the gods of Egypt, flagrant idolatry. On the other hand, when Aaron fashions the calf, declares it is the god who has brought them out of Egypt, and proclaims the next day a festival to the Lord, he apparently does not view himself as engaged in wholesale apostasy (32:1–5). Ezekiel's vision of cherubim involves calves' feet and a face like an ox (Ezek. 1:5–10). When the temple is constructed according to plans that the Spirit has given David (1 Chron. 28:11–13), the great basin stands on twelve bulls (2 Chron. 4:3–4). In Moses's absence, perhaps the people choose to celebrate the Lord as a warrior, symbolically representing him as a strong bull, the pedestal on which Yahweh stands. If so, the Lord is not replaced by an idol but misrepresented, a far more insidious danger. Aaron has broken the second commandment, led the people astray with language that sounded orthodox, and allowed them to get wildly out of control. That they "rose up to play" (32:6 NASB) possibly implies sexual activity (cf. Gen. 26:8, which uses the same Hebrew term for Isaac's "caressing" Rebekah). This incident is a sobering reminder that the very heart of religion can be fraught with danger. It is also a humbling reminder that leaders of God's people need intercession and forgiveness.

God's words to Moses contain an ominous distancing. He calls the Israelites "*your* people, whom *you* brought up out of Egypt" (32:7) and declares his intention to destroy them and make Moses into a great nation; this is a significant temptation to Moses, who has already endured immense distress on account of the people. Nevertheless, he intercedes for them even before descending from the mountain, asking God to turn from his anger and his destructive intentions and remember the covenant with Abraham, Isaac, and Israel (32:11–13). In response to Moses's plea, God chooses not to bring disaster on the people. The Hebrew word *naham* means to change one's course of action. It can apply both to humans and to God. With regard to humans, the term is generally translated "repent." When God "changes course," it means that his intention, articulated at a given point in response to specific circumstances, has been altered to best address current developments (cf. Gen. 6:6–7 [NIV "regretted"]; 1 Sam. 15:11; Jon. 4:2). In ways that are beyond human comprehension, this is part of the complexity of God's sovereignty.

When Moses descends the mountain, he carries two tablets, written both front and back (32:15). These are likely two complete copies of the covenant, one for Yahweh as suzerain and one for the vassal, Israel. Both copies would be put into the ark as a witness on behalf of the people. When Moses sees that the people have rebelled so blatantly against the covenant, in an action laden with symbolism he hurls and breaks the tablets. Then he burns the calf, grinds it, and makes the people drink the powder mixed with the water (32:19–20). The same types of destructive actions are found in a text from Ugarit about the death of Mot (the Canaanite god of death and the netherworld), conveying a picture of complete destruction. These are literary patterns; whether or not metal burns is not the issue. There are possible parallels with the later legislation regarding the wife suspected of adultery (Num. 5:5–31). Curses are written on a scroll and washed off into water, and the woman must drink this bitter water. If she is guilty it will enter her and cause suffering. In this case, the idolatrous Israelites have committed spiritual adultery by breaking their marriage covenant with the Lord. Here, unlike Numbers 5, the Israelites' guilt is not in question.

Aaron does not manifest great strength of character. His response to Moses's inquiry sets the responsibility almost entirely on the Israelites and their fundamentally evil nature (32:21–24). Worse yet, he reduces his active role in fashioning the calf to a passive one: "I cast it into the fire, and this calf came out" (32:24 NKJV). It seems that the destruction of the calf prompts a riot among the people, and the Lord calls on those who are faithful to him to kill the idolaters (32:25–29).

Statuette of a god standing on a bull, using it as a pedestal

The choice made by the tribe of Levi, Aaron's own tribe, is not an easy one (32:26). Killing three thousand people who are continuing in flagrant disobedience is a horrifying task and a severe punishment for not standing up for righteousness in the first place. The weight of responsibility Aaron must have felt would undoubtedly have been crushing. Yet, in the sovereign workings of God, he will be the ideal human high priest, fully aware of his own weakness, knowing God's mercy and forgiveness, and able to deal gently with those who stray (Heb. 5:2).

B. Moses intercedes for the people (32:30–33:17). Recognizing that the heinous sin still needs to be addressed, Moses continues his role as mediator, declaring his willingness to sacrifice himself (32:30–32). In response, God declares that the Israelites will go forward to the covenant land, but they have forfeited the fullness of God's presence. Instead, God's angel will accompany them (32:33–34; cf. 23:20–23). Paradoxically, God's threat to withdraw his presence is for Israel's protection. He knows their ongoing rebellion against him will bring just punishment of sin (33:1–3). The forgiving mercy of God is always balanced with his sovereign justice; neither can be minimized.

The placement of Exodus 33:7–11 is significant. The Tent of Meeting is set up "outside the camp some distance away," symbolic of God's removal from their immediate presence. This tent existed prior to the construction of the "official" tabernacle, the one whose pattern was shown to Moses on the mountain, the one at which Aaron would officiate, and the one that would represent God's dwelling *with* his people. Now they are at a critical juncture. Will God continue with his expressed intention to dwell in their midst, or will it be only Moses who will meet face-to-face with God? In a remarkable response to Moses's persistence, God reverses his decision to remove his presence (33:12–17). He promises again to go with them, thus restoring their distinct position from all the nations on the earth. Because Moses finds favor with God, the Lord declares that he will grant all of Moses's requests for God's presence, his favor, and rest (33:14). The expression "know you by name" is used of no one else in the Bible, but it appears twice here (33:12, 17).

C. Revelation of God's glory (33:18–34:9). At this point, Moses, who already has entered into the cloud, requests to see the glory of God, the visible manifestation of the complete power, perfection, and radiance of God's person. This manifest presence of God with his people has already been demonstrated in the wilderness, where the cloud was the vehicle for God's glory. In Exodus 24:17, his presence appears as the brilliance of fire to all Israel. Subsequently, the glory of God will be manifested in the tabernacle, and later the temple (Exod. 40:34–35; Lev. 9:23; 1 Kings 8:10–11).

Moses is allowed to experience what he is capable of seeing without being taken from this world by the overwhelming presence of God. Proclaiming his prerogative to exercise abundant mercy, God promises to hide Moses in the cleft of a rock and cover him "with [his] hand" while he causes his goodness to pass in front of Moses and proclaims his name in Moses's presence (33:19–22). God's "back" (33:23) suggests traces of the divine presence. In a stunning display of grace, God descends in the cloud of glory, stands with Moses, and proclaims his covenant name, Yahweh, and his covenant character of compassion, mercy, patience, unfailing covenant love, forgiveness, and justice (34:5–7). Forgiveness has been the focus of Moses's persistent entreaty; this declaration of God emboldens Moses to ask once more that Israel be forgiven and accepted as God's inheritance (34:8–9). God's justice means he will most certainly punish those who are guilty. Only there could rest the true goodness and integrity of his name and character. Repetition of "the LORD" (34:6) may echo the repetition in Exodus 3:14. These elements of the Lord's name echo throughout the history of Israel as they persist in demonstrating their human failings and as God lavishes on them mercy and forgiveness.

D. Restating the covenant (34:10–35). The Lord restates his promise to work wonders for his covenant people as he drives out the inhabitants of the land (34:10–11). The warnings against becoming entangled in the false worship of the Canaanites are even more emphatic. To avoid the problem, the Israelites are not to intermarry or make treaties with any who live in the land (34:15–16). The latter warning is ignored in the case of the Gibeonite coalition that comes to Joshua and the Israelites requesting a treaty (Joshua 9). The Israelites are to break down standing stones and Asherah poles, ridding themselves of any temptation to provoke God to jealousy (34:13). While the identity of Asherah within the ancient Near East pantheon is complex, she was related to fertility rituals and was the consort of one of the chief gods.

In Exodus 34:17–26, the Lord restates significant elements of the torah, commencing with the warning against making idols and emphasizing the festivals that will take place in the context of the sanctuary, a reassurance that God's presence will continue to be with them and a clear rejection of the false feast that Aaron has instituted. (On the restriction regarding cooking a kid in its mother's milk in Exodus 34:26, see commentary on 23:10–19.) Then the Lord tells Moses to write the words of the covenant, the initial Ten Commandments, which has previously been shattered. It is clear that when Moses writes the words, it is as if God has written them (compare 34:1 with 34:28).

Moses's intimate interactions with God result in his own visible transformation. His face is radiant with a brilliance so fearsome that he has to veil his face before the rest of the Israelites (34:29–35). The expression translated "his face was radiant" in the NIV is not used this way elsewhere in the Old Testament. It is related to the word for "horn" and prompted earlier translations and representations to

depict Moses with horns. Doubtless, however, these were rays of light. The glory of the Lord thus moves from the mountain to Moses and finally to the tabernacle. This veil has both positive and negative implications for the people. On the one hand, that his face reflects the presence of God reassures them. On the other, it is only Moses who can mediate; the veil serves as a reminder of their apostasy. There was a phenomenon in the ancient Near East of veiling one's face when speaking with the gods, but here the veil covers Moses's face when he is not in God's presence. Instead, he reflects God's glory to the people. Paul draws on this figure in 2 Corinthians 3:7–18, declaring that the radiance faded away while the veil was over Moses's face and contrasting that fading glory associated with Moses and the engraved tablets with the unfading glory of the ministry of the Spirit. Those

Michelangelo's famous statue of Moses (St. Peter in Chains Church, Rome) depicts Moses with horns, based on some translations of Exodus 34:29–35.

who are in Christ, like Moses, reflect the Lord's glory but do not need to wear the veil, as we are "transformed into his image with ever-increasing glory, which comes from the Lord, who is the Spirit" (2 Cor. 3:18).

The condition of this people who has fallen so far is no different from that experienced by believers, representatives of frail humanity, throughout the ages. Moses, as their leader and mediator, is painfully aware of the seriousness of their condition before the Lord. He persists in his expressed desire for assurance because he knows the reality of the wrath of the Lord against sin. He does not take lightly or easily God's grace. He fasts again for forty days and forty nights (Deut. 9:9, 18), recognizing his need to be prepared to be the covenant mediator who will declare the word of God. This fasting is a prototype of that of Jesus Christ, who in preparation for his role as the perfect mediator of the new covenant will fast in the Judean wilderness for forty days and nights. Just as the Ten Commandments are written again, graciously given to instruct and restore the Israelites to a right relationship with their covenant Lord, the Word incarnate came to instruct and fully restore fallen humankind.

6. Assurance of God's Presence (35:1–40:38)

A. Sabbath (35:1–3). While the Sabbath regulations closed the initial instructions regarding the tabernacle, they appear at the beginning of the description of its completion. The connection between sanctified place and time is an intimate one. This is more abbreviated but has the new prohibition regarding lighting a fire.

B. Establishing the tabernacle (35:4–40:38). The voluntary donations are received in terms of both materials and skills. Not only does the Spirit fill Bezalel and Oholiab to produce the artistry demanded by this structure; all who are skilled come and contribute those skills (35:4–36:6). The expression "all who were willing" is repeated throughout, emphasizing that their offerings come from hearts aware of God's great mercy and ready to obey the

Lord. So overwhelming is the response that there is more than enough, indicative of their transformation from self-centered living to extravagant and lavish worship of God. Moses even has to order them to stop making and bringing gifts (36:6).

The order in which the instructions are executed is somewhat different from the order in God's description to Moses on the mountain. The tent itself is the first to be completed, followed by the most significant articles in the tabernacle: the ark, table, lampstand, and the altar of incense along with the anointing oil and the sacred incense (36:8–37:29). Moving out to the courtyard, next are fashioned the altar for offerings and the wash basin (38:1–8). A new detail at this point is the mention of the bronze mirrors of the women who serve at the entrance to the Tent of Meeting (38:8). There is some ambiguity regarding the function of these women. The verb simply implies they are qualified to serve in the workforce, but a potentially ominous side of this activity is evident in 1 Samuel 2:22, where Eli's sons are sleeping with the women who serve at the entrance of the tabernacle. After the actual construction, Moses records the amounts of precious metals, the total of which is in the vicinity of six tons (38:21–28).

Once they finish the place, the priestly garments are prepared. Obedience is a constant drumbeat throughout this section (39:1–31). The people prepare the attire "just as the LORD commanded Moses," and then the entire work is brought to Moses (39:32–41). He sees the evidence of their obedience and blesses them (39:42–43). Then the Lord gives Moses final instructions for placement and anointing of the furnishings and consecration of the priests (40:1–15). Moses does as the Lord commands and finishes the work (40:16–33). Exodus closes on a note of joyous hope with the glory of the Lord present with his people and guiding them on their journey (40:34–38). God's people are assured of the reality of that presence in the ongoing wilderness experiences of despair and death. Even though that will be forthcoming, God's presence never leaves them, even accompanying them into the exile in Babylon and bringing them back—a second exodus.

Select Bibliography

Brueggemann, Walter. "Exodus." In *The New Interpreter's Bible*. Edited by Leander E. Keck. Vol. 1. Nashville: Abingdon, 1994.

Childs, Brevard. *Exodus*. Old Testament Library. Philadelphia: Westminster, 1974.

Enns, Peter. *Exodus*. NIV Application Commentary. Grand Rapids: Zondervan, 2000.

Hoffmeier, James K. "The Arm of God versus the Arm of Pharaoh in the Exodus Narratives." *Biblica* 67 (1986): 378–87.

———. *Israel in Egypt: The Evidence for the Authenticity of the Exodus Tradition*. Oxford: Oxford University Press, 1996.

Humphreys, Colin J. "How Many People Were in the Exodus from Egypt?" *Science and Christian Belief* 12 (2000): 17–34.

Kemp, Barry J. *Ancient Egypt: Anatomy of a Civilization*. London: Routledge, 1989.

Morschauser, Scott. "Potters' Wheels and Pregnancies: A Note on Exodus 1:16." *Journal of Biblical Literature* 122 (2003): 731–33.

Motyer, J. Alec. *The Message of Exodus*. The Bible Speaks Today. Downers Grove, IL: InterVarsity, 2005.

Sarna, Nahum M. *Exodus*. JPS Torah Commentary. Philadelphia: Jewish Publication Society, 1991.

Stuart, Douglas K. *Exodus*. New American Commentary. Nashville: Broadman & Holman, 2006.

Wheeler, Gerald. "Ancient Egypt's Silence about the Exodus." *Andrews University Seminary Studies* 40 (2002): 257–64.

Youngblood, Ronald. *Exodus*. Chicago: Moody, 1983.

Leviticus

Roy E. Gane

Introduction

Leviticus is part three of a five-part series (the Pentateuch) that moves from origins of planet Earth and of the Israelite people (Genesis) to their arrival at the border of the promised land (Deuteronomy). Leviticus begins with "Then" (or "And"), continuing the story of the Israelites' epic journey from Egypt through the wilderness to Canaan, which commenced in the book of Exodus. They spend one year of this journey at Sinai, as recorded in Exodus 19 through Numbers 10, which includes the whole book of Leviticus. There God prepares his people for the future by giving them his law, confirming his covenant with them, establishing the sanctuary and its services, and organizing them into a disciplined army. The basic narrative framework of Leviticus is sandwiched into a month between Exodus (40:2, 17) and Numbers (1:1, 18), when the Israelites have already been encamped in the Sinai wilderness for almost a year (see Exod. 19:1).

When the Lord moves into his sanctuary residence (Exod. 40:34), it becomes the place of divine-human meeting. Here he conveys most of the instructions recorded in Leviticus from the beginning of the book (Lev. 1:1; cf. Exod. 29:42–43 and Num. 7:89, replacing an earlier oracular "Tent of Meeting" in Exod. 33:7–11). However, some messages included in Leviticus were communicated to Moses on Mount Sinai (Lev. 7:38; 25:1; 26:46; 27:34), the earlier place

of divine revelation (Exod. 24:15–18; 34:4–5). So it appears that thematic reasons affected selection of the book's materials.

Title

The Hebrew name of Leviticus is taken from its first word: *Wayyiqra*, "Then he [the Lord] called." This name is fitting because the book records more direct divine speech than any other biblical book. The title "Leviticus" is the Latin form of the Septuagint Greek name *Leuitikon*, which characterizes the book as concerning Levites. The book barely mentions the Levite tribe (25:32–33), but much of Leviticus relates to ritual matters supervised by priests belonging to this tribe.

Genre

Leviticus consists mainly of instructions from the Lord, arranged in a series of divine speeches to Moses for the Israelites as a whole (e.g., Lev. 1:2; 4:2; 7:23, 29), for the priests (6:25; 21:1, 17—to Aaron for all priests), or just for the high priest (16:2). These instructions generally take the form of legal prescriptions to be applied on any number of future occasions. However, the book contains two narratives describing events that generated some additional legislation (Lev. 8:1–10:20; 24:10–23).

The legal genre that dominates Leviticus is also prominent in some other biblical books, especially Exodus and Deuteronomy, the laws of which have many parallels with those in

Leviticus (e.g., laws regulating servitude in Exodus 21, Leviticus 25, and Deuteronomy 15). This genre can be subdivided into ritual law, governing practices relevant to the sanctuary (e.g., Leviticus 1–7), and nonritual law. Nonritual law includes moral or ethical law, which is generally stated in apodictic formulation as direct statement of principle ("You shall [not] . . ."; e.g., 18:20; 19:3–4, 11–12), and civil law. Civil law, usually in casuistic (case law) formulation (e.g., "If . . . then . . ."), applies timeless moral principles within the ancient Israelite context and often stipulates penalties to be administered under the judicial system of the Israelite theocratic government (e.g., 24:15–21).

Some interpreters have suggested another subdivision or category of the legal genre: health law. Undoubtedly rules regarding diet (11:1–46; 17:10–14), diagnosis of disease and quarantine (13:1–59), and sanitation (15:5–12; cf. Deut. 23:13–15) would have an effect on health. But nowhere in the Pentateuch is a health motivation attached to a particular law. Rather, God promises health to those who obey all of his commands (Exod. 15:26). This implies that health is affected by every aspect of a person's life.

Modern Application

Basic moral and health principles are timeless, but the Israelite sanctuary (or temple) and judicial system ceased operation long ago. So modern people, who live under a different form of government, cannot keep the ritual laws or administer civil penalties as specified in the Bible even if they want to. However, they can greatly benefit by applying underlying timeless principles to the extent that they can do this within their respective contexts.

Leviticus teaches God's faulty people how to worship and live with their Redeemer in close proximity as he dwells among them. The book reveals the divine character in relation to human nature and the Lord's plan to forgive and cleanse sinners through sacrifice. Much of Leviticus concerns rituals, but the scope of the book is broader than the ceremonial system. From the center at the Lord's sanctuary headquarters, holiness is to extend outward to all of the covenant people in every aspect of their lives. Thus Leviticus is the charter for fulfilling the Lord's promise that his chosen people are to be his "kingdom of priests" and "holy nation" (Exod. 19:6).

Christians who inherit this promise in spiritual terms (1 Pet. 2:5, 9) and desire intimacy with God (Ps. 23:6; Rev. 21:3) through the priesthood of Christ (Heb. 4:14–16; 10:19–25) can learn a great deal from timeless principles of divine-human interaction encapsulated in Leviticus. Most important, they can gain a deeper understanding of the sacrifice of Christ, which was typified by the ancient Israelite sacrifices (cf. John 1:29). Sacrifice is necessary for God to extend mercy without compromising justice, the other side of his character of love. While only Christ's sacrifice is ultimately effective in reconciling sinners to God (Heb. 10:1–18), the Israelites were to experience the hope of that unique event and receive grace through faith by enacting powerfully dramatic rituals. Since Christ's once-for-all sacrifice is so rich, different kinds of Israelite sacrifices were necessary to teach various aspects of it.

The tabernacle model at Timna Valley Park, Israel

Date and Authorship

Leviticus belongs to the larger Pentateuch (Torah) collection. The authorship of the Pentateuch is anonymous, but traditionally it has been attributed to Moses. Jesus and his disciples accepted Mosaic authorship (Matt. 8:4; 19:8; Mark 7:10; 12:26; Luke 24:44; Acts 3:22; Rom. 10:5), which accords with the fact that Exodus, Leviticus, Numbers, and Deuteronomy identify Moses as the primary mediator of divine revelation, who recorded such communications in writing (Exod. 24:4; 34:27–28; Deut. 31:9). Basic Mosaic authorship does not rule out some later editing (e.g., the death of Moses in Deuteronomy 34) in the production of inspired canonical books that have been transmitted to us (2 Tim. 3:15–16).

Modern historical-critical theory denies Mosaic authorship, detaching the origin of pentateuchal books from their narrative setting. Rather than seeing Leviticus as authoritative divine instruction, critics view it as the literary production of later priests concerned with promoting their own ideals and interests. Because there is no hint of monarchy in Leviticus, many critics have assumed that the book must have been assembled to address the Jewish community after the fall of the Judahite monarchy in 586 BC. For them the wilderness sanctuary is fictitious, a retrojection into the distant past to provide the backdrop for a credible human claim to divine authority.

Some historical-critical interpreters find evidence that the language and contents of Leviticus fit the historical context of preexilic Israel. If so, the book reflects a ritual system that actually operated in the first (Solomon's) temple. However, placing authorship of the book during the First Temple period does not account for the absence of monarchy in Leviticus and still detaches the book from the wilderness setting of divine revelation to Moses.

Comparison and contrast between Leviticus and other ancient Near Eastern texts (especially ritual, legal, and treaty texts) and cultural artifacts from the second millennium BC indicate that there is no compelling reason why the book could not have originated before the monarchy during the second millennium BC, in harmony with its explicit narrative context, although editing and updating of language could have taken place later.

Like other peoples of the second millennium BC, early Israelites possessed a complex ritual and legal system. They shared many aspects of culture with those around them, but significant features of the biblical instructions were countercultural, in accordance with the Lord's distinctive theology. For example, death was holy for Egyptians, but for Israelites things associated with death were ritually impure and restricted from contact with the sacred sphere (e.g., Lev. 21:1–6, 10–12). Also, the "bread of the Presence" ritual encapsulated a message that was opposite to that of non-Israelite food presentation offerings: rather than signifying that the Lord's people fed him, the bread offering acknowledged that he provided food for them (see commentary on 24:5–9 below).

The ritual portions of Leviticus contain selected details regarding activities, with little explanation of meanings attached to the activities. This suggests that the text was written when its ritual system was actually performed. The text has the stated purpose of guiding priests and other participants, who could observe what was going on. So they did not need all the details and explanations that would characterize a text describing rituals that were imaginary or no longer performed.

Structure

Interpreters of Leviticus have viewed its logical structure in various ways according to factors such as literary style (including a combination of genres), vocabulary, rhetorical features, topics, divine speeches, repetitions (e.g., between chaps. 18 and 20), and sacred space. Perhaps it is most helpful to recognize that the book progressively introduces concepts in a way that is logical for the purpose of teaching.

The book begins with basic instructions for three voluntary forms of sacrificial worship (burnt, grain, and well-being offerings), at least two of which were already known to the Israelites (burnt and well-being; Exod. 10:25; 18:12; 24:5) but adapted to the new ritual system of the sanctuary (Leviticus 1–3). Then it adds two new mandatory kinds of sacrifice (purification and reparation offerings) to remedy some moral faults (4:1–6:7). Following are additional instructions regulating the five kinds of sacrifices (6:8–7:38), knowledge of which is essential for understanding combinations of ritual types employed at the initial consecration (chap. 8) and inauguration (chaps. 9–10) of the sanctuary's ritual system.

Next, Leviticus presents rules governing physical ritual impurities associated with the birth–death cycle of mortality, which must be separated (in some cases by sacrifices) from the sphere of holiness and life (chaps. 11–15). Special rituals on the yearly Day of Atonement, culminating the first major part of Leviticus, remove both moral faults and physical impurities from the sanctuary and the Israelite community (Leviticus 16). Following are reiterations of some instructions regarding sacrifice and purity, with additional warnings and explanations (chap. 17). Many scholars have regarded Leviticus 17 as commencing a so-called Holiness Code of laws that concludes with chapter 26, but the ritual concerns of chapter 17 have much in common with the earlier chapters.

The subsequent portion of Leviticus (chaps. 18–26), united by the refrain, "I am the LORD" (e.g., 18:2, 4–6), exhorts the Israelites to live holy lives in accordance with the will and character of their holy God, who is the authority behind the laws presented here (cf. 11:44–45). Holy lifestyle rules out sexual aberrations and idolatry (chap. 18) and governs a comprehensive variety of divine-human and human-human interactions (chap. 19). Chapter 20 contains additional instructions, penalties, and exhortations regarding some cases in chapters 18 and 19.

The following sections regulate priestly lifestyle and holy offerings (21:1–22:16), call for periodic observance of sacred times of worship (chap. 23), and make provision for regular rituals inside the sanctuary (24:1–9). Holy life rejects assault and blasphemy (24:10–23) but observes sacred times of rest for the land and release from debt-servitude (chap. 25). Life in harmony with all the Lord's instructions is the condition for maintaining a positive, beneficial covenant relationship with him (chap. 26).

Notice the progression of holy things in Leviticus 18–25 from all Israelites (chaps. 18–20) to priests (21:1–22:16), animal offerings (22:17–33), time (chap. 23), light (from oil) and bread in the outer sanctum of the sanctuary (24:1–9), God's name, as well as human and animal life (24:10–23), and the promised land (chap. 25).

Chapters 25–26 are a unit delivered to Moses on Mount Sinai (25:1; 26:46), which deals with treatment of the land and blessings and curses associated with it. The comprehensive covenant blessings and curses of chapter 26 bring the book to a logical conclusion, but rules for dedications of persons, animals, and real estate must follow in chapter 27 (often regarded as an appendix) because they partly depend on the Jubilee release of land (27:17–18, 21, 23–24), which is explained in chapter 25.

Outline

1. Sacrificial Worship (1:1–7:38)
   A. Voluntary Sacrifices (1:1–3:17)
   B. Mandatory Sacrifices as Moral Remedies (4:1–6:7)
   C. Additional Instructions regarding Sacrifices (6:8–7:38)
2. Establishment of Ritual System (8:1–10:20)
   A. Consecration of Sanctuary and Priests (8:1–36)
   B. Inaugural Priestly Officiation and Divine Acceptance (9:1–24)
   C. Divine Nonacceptance of Inaugural Ritual Mistake (10:1–20)
3. Impurities and Ritual Remedies (11:1–17:16)
   A. Separating Physical Impurities from Persons (11:1–15:33)

Commentary

1. Sacrificial Worship (1:1–7:38)

A. Voluntary sacrifices (1:1–3:17). **1:1–17.** According to Genesis, sacrificial worship and priesthood originated long before the Israelites departed Egypt (Gen. 4:3–5; 8:20; 12:7–8; 13:4, 18; 14:18; 22:13; 31:54; 46:1). In Leviticus some earlier categories of sacrifice (burnt offerings and "sacrifices") continue. Also continuing are a number of aspects of sacrifice, such as the need for invoking divine acceptance by a pleasing aroma, restriction of victims to animals and birds that were fit to eat, offering of fat portions, an element of substitution, and remedying sin. However, Leviticus incorporates some key differences affecting sacrificial worship. The Israelites are to transport a portable bronze altar with them and rely on priests, who are entitled to sacrificial portions, to officiate for them at a tabernacle that serves as the earthly residence of the deity.

Leviticus 1:2 introduces the first overall topic of the book in the style of case law: "When anyone among you brings an offering to the Lord . . ." The first subcase, prescribing the burnt offering of herd animals (1:3–9), sets up a pattern of activities that must be performed if the offerer chooses to offer that kind of sacrifice. At strategic points the text indicates meanings or interpretations attached to the activities.

The offerer performs the first action of the burnt offering ritual proper by laying one hand on the head of the animal (1:4a). This gesture has no inherent meaning; however, the Lord attaches to it the meaning of ensuring that the animal is accepted on behalf of this particular person, who is transferring ownership of the victim to the Lord.

The sacrifice accepted by God will "expiate" (Hebrew *kipper*) for this offerer (1:4b; NIV "make atonement"). *Kipper* is usually translated "atone," which in English means to reconcile (to be "at one"). However, *kipper* signifies removing an impediment to the divine-human relationship by making amends through offering a sacrifice of "food" as a token payment of an obligation or "debt." If the debt is for sin (rather than physical impurity; see below), reconciliation is completed by subsequent divine forgiveness. Thus, a priest who officiates a purification offering thereby makes atonement (*kipper*) on behalf of the offerer, meaning that the obligation regarding the sin is removed

This portion of the Standard of Ur (ca. 2500 BC) may show men bringing their animals as offerings.

from the offerer, in order that the individual may be forgiven by God (see commentary on 4:1–5:13). This use of the Hebrew verb for the idea of "expiate" or "remove" is related to the meaning of the Akkadian cognate *kuppuru*, "wipe" (including "wipe off"). Payment of debt for sin ransoms life (Lev. 17:11; for *kipper* as "ransom," cf. Exod. 30:12, 15–16) because sin leads to death (cf. Rom. 6:23).

Next, the offerer is to slay (slit the throat of) the bull (1:5a), and the priest dashes its blood around the sides of the altar, which is located at the entrance of the Tent of Meeting (1:5b). Explanation of this action, for which no precedent is recorded in Genesis, comes later, in Leviticus 17:11: The life of the flesh is (symbolically) in the blood, which the Lord gave to the people in order to ransom (Hebrew *kipper*) their lives by having it applied to his altar (cf. Exod. 12:7, 12–13, where Passover blood at dwelling entrances preserves lives).

Subsequent burnt offering activities are listed without explanation until the end of the unit provides the overall meaning or function of the ritual: The priest makes the burnt offering go up in smoke (this verb is from the same Hebrew root as "incense") as an "aroma pleasing to the LORD" (1:9). So the altar is the means of access to the heavenly dwelling place of God (cf. Ps. 11:4; 1 Kings 8:30).

Most translations of Leviticus 1:9 describe the burnt offering as "an offering (made) by fire." However, the Hebrew word could include sacred offering portions that are not burned (Lev. 24:9; Deut. 18:1), and the term is never used for purification offerings (so-called sin offerings), even though they are burned. Some scholars have related the term to a cognate Ugaritic word meaning "gift," a concept that fits the contexts in which the Hebrew word appears. Sacrifices to the Lord were generally prepared as food gifts (Lev. 3:11, 16; 21:6, 8; Num. 28:2).

Use of food to signify or build a positive relationship with the deity was related to hospitality in which a person signified friendship by offering food to a guest, who could be a divine messenger (Genesis 18; Judges 6, 13). However, because the Lord does not need to consume food (Ps. 50:13), he receives it in the form of smoke as a kind of incense. This interaction with the supernatural being makes the activity system a kind of acted out prayer (cf. Rev. 8:3–4).

Leviticus 1:10–13 continues instructions for burnt offerings by outlining the procedure if the victim will be a flock animal. Verses 14–17 prescribe the process if it is a domesticated bird, which a poor person could afford (cf. 5:7–13). The offerer simply hands the bird to the priest, so there is no need for a separate hand-laying gesture to clear up any potential ambiguity regarding the offerer's identity.

In Leviticus 1, units of instruction are arranged in descending order of the cost of a burnt offering victim. Sacrifices of domesticated (never game) animals always represent financial cost (cf. 2 Sam. 24:24), but Israelites could bring what they could afford. Offerings of the poor have no less value in God's sight than more expensive gifts (cf. Mark 12:41–44).

Although animal sacrifices involved cost to those who offered them, they were only small tokens by which Israelites accepted God's infinitely greater gift of ransom for their lives, which no human being could provide (Lev. 17:11; Ps. 49:7–9). God had provided the Israelites with all their property (Deut. 8:18), and he graciously initiated sacrifice as the means of making amends with him (see above). So sacrifices expressed faith in God's free grace (cf. Eph. 2:8–9).

Grace has come to ultimate fulfillment in Christ, who has given his lifeblood to ransom life (Matt. 20:28; 26:28). Just as the burnt offering was consumed on the altar, Christ's sacrifice consumed his human life (Heb. 7:27; 1 John 3:16). Just as the smoke of the burnt (literally "ascending") offering ascended heavenward like incense to be accepted by God, Christ ascended to his Father immediately after his resurrection (John 20:17). Then he returned to be with his disciples for forty days, at the end of which they saw him taken up to heaven (Acts 1).

2:1–16. Leviticus 2 provides instructions for offerings of grain. The Hebrew expression for "grain offering" here is a technical (more narrow) usage (2:3–5); in Genesis 4 the same term refers to the vegetable and animal "offering" or "tribute" of Cain and of Abel (cf. Judg. 3:15, 17–18). Numbers 15 specifies that burnt offerings and "sacrifices" (i.e., sacrifices from which the offerers eat) always require accompanying grain and drink (wine) offerings. Along with the animal portions, these accompaniments complete the Lord's "meal" (cf. Genesis 18). A grain offering is a sacrifice—that is, an offering to the Lord for his utilization—even though it involves no death or blood (cf. Rom. 12:1, "living sacrifice").

Grain offerings consist of choice flour, with oil and frankincense (2:1), but are to be unleavened (2:4–5, 11). They can be presented in various forms (2:4–7), and there is a special subcategory for first fruits of the harvest (2:14–16). The Lord's token portion is a handful containing some of the grain and oil but all of the frankincense (2:2, 16). A priest burns the Lord's portion on the altar, and the remainder belongs to the priests (2:2–3, 9–10) as their commission for serving as God's agents. So the priests eat from the Lord's food, just as special servants and friends of a monarch or governor eat at his table (1 Sam. 20:29; 2 Sam. 9:7, 13; 1 Kings 2:7; 18:19; Neh. 5:17; cf. 2 Kings 25:29–30; Dan. 1:5).

Verses 11–13 give the following rules regarding grain offerings that applied to all sacrifices. First, leaven and honey are excluded from the altar (2:11–12), presumably because leaven causes fermentation and honey is susceptible to fermentation. Fermentation was associated with decomposition and therefore death, which was antagonistic to the sphere of holiness and life. Paradoxically, the altar was "most holy" (Exod. 29:37), even though dead animals were placed on it. Such sacrificial death was uniquely necessary to ransom human life.

Second, sacrifices are salted in order to place them in the context of the permanent covenant with God (2:13; cf. Ezek. 43:24 of salting animals). As a preservative, salt appropriately signifies the permanence of a covenant (Num. 18:19; 2 Chron. 13:5).

3:1–17. Leviticus 3 outlines the "sacrifice of well-being." Unlike the burnt offering, the victim here can be female, only its suet (fat) goes up in smoke on the altar, the priest's commission consists of edible portions (Lev. 7:31–34), and the offerer eats the remainder (7:15–16). There are no well-being offerings of birds because they are too small to be divided between the Lord, priests, and offerers.

Notice the progression of instructions for voluntary rituals from the burnt offering (none of which is to be eaten by a human; chap. 1) to the grain offering (from which only a priest can eat as his "agent's commission"; chap. 2; cf. Lev. 7:9–10) to the well-being offering (which is eaten by the offerer[s] as well as a priest; chap. 3; cf. 7:15–16, 31–36). The order is away from exclusive utilization by the Lord toward sharing

Grain offerings or incense would most likely be burned on an offering stand such as this one from Megiddo.

with human beings. A shared meal expresses mutual goodwill and trust (cf. Gen. 31:54).

Leviticus 3:16–17 adds the general rule that all suet belongs to the Lord, and therefore the Israelites are never to eat it. Neither are they to eat blood—that is, meat from which the blood was not drained out at slaughter (cf. Gen. 9:4). But the text avoids saying that blood belongs to the Lord; it never went up in smoke to him as part of his "food."

Well-being offerings were given to celebrate joyfully a healthy relationship with God (cf. Lev. 7:12; 1 Sam. 11:15) and did not serve to atone for specific sins. Nevertheless, they were still sacrifices carrying a basic element of ransom (Lev. 17:11), which makes divine-human interaction possible in a fallen world. Even praise to God is made possible by sacrifice, without which we could have no access to God. Just as ancient Israelites ate meals shared with the Lord, Christians enjoy peace with God through Christ (Rom. 5:1), who invites them to spiritually partake of him through his words (John 6:48–58, 63).

B. Mandatory sacrifices as moral remedies (4:1–6:7). Two new kinds of mandatory sacrifices protect the holy sphere centered at God's earthly residence. These are the purification (so-called sin) and reparation ("guilt") offerings. The purification offering removes defilements caused by sins (4:1–5:13) and by physical conditions (chaps. 12–15) that can affect the state of the sanctuary (15:31; 16:16). The reparation offering remedies various kinds of sacrilege (5:14–6:7).

The Hebrew word for "purification offering" is generally rendered "sin offering" because it is the same as the word for "sin," which it remedies (e.g., 4:3, 14). This sacrifice does expiate or atone for moral faults involving violation of divine laws, so that the offerer can receive forgiveness (e.g., 4:20, 26, 31, 35). However, elsewhere the same kind of sacrifice expiates in the sense of purifying the offerer from severe physical ritual impurities, which are not sins in the sense of moral faults and required no

forgiveness (Lev. 12:7–8; 14:19–20). The common denominator among physical impurities is association with mortality, the state resulting from sin (Rom. 6:23).

The translation "sin offering" confuses the distinction between sins and physical impurities, incorrectly implying, for example, that a woman somehow sins by giving birth (Lev. 12:6, 8). Such category confusion can tend to reduce a person's sense of accountability for making right choices: if automatic or involuntary physical impurities (e.g., Lev. 15:19; Deut. 23:11) were sins, people automatically sin all the time and cannot do anything about it. The rendering "purification offering," referring to purification from either sins or physical impurities, avoids the confusion and correlates with the fact that the verb from the same root can also mean "purify" (Lev. 8:15).

No Israelite sacrifices remedied defiant sins (Num. 15:30–31). The purification offering expiated inadvertent violations of divine commands (Leviticus 4; Num. 15:22–29), the deliberate sin of failing to answer a public adjuration to testify (Lev. 5:1), or forgetting to perform a duty to undergo ritual purification or to fulfill an oath (5:2–4). Sinners were responsible for bringing sacrifices only when they knew that they had sinned (cf. James 4:17).

The reparation offering (see below) is for inadvertently misappropriating something sacred (5:14–16); the possibility of sacrilege, even when the cause of a sense of guilt is not known (5:17–19); and deliberately misusing God's name in a false oath to defraud another person (6:1–7). The burnt offering already functioned as an expiatory sacrifice, so we can assume that it continued to remedy all the other expiable (nondefiant) cases that were not taken over by the purification and reparation offerings.

In the New Testament, there is only one sacrifice for all kinds of sin: Christ's sacrifice (John 1:29; Heb. 9:28). Even sins for which there was no forgiveness through the Israelite ritual system (Acts 13:38–39)—namely, defiant sins—are remedied through this one sacrifice.

This explains how King Manasseh could be forgiven (2 Chronicles 33): through the coming sacrifice of the Messiah.

A reparation offering remedies a sin of taking property, which carries a specific value. The sinner is required to make reparation before bringing a sacrifice by restoring what was taken from the wronged party (God or another Israelite), plus paying a penalty of one-fifth or 20 percent (5:16; 6:5), unless the offender does not know the nature of the sin (5:17–18). The purification offering lacks prior reparation, and only its suet is burned on the altar (unlike the burnt offering). However, it compensates by emphasizing blood, which represents ransom for life (Lev. 17:11). In other sacrifices blood is dashed on the sides of the altar in the court, but purification-offering blood is applied higher and more prominently on the horns of the outer altar or of the golden incense altar in the outer sanctum (4:7, 18, 25, 30, 34).

4:1–5:13. In Leviticus 4, there are two main kinds of purification offerings. If the offerer is a chieftain or ordinary person, the priest is to daub the blood on the horns of the outer altar (4:25, 30, 34), burn the suet on the altar, and eat the remaining meat (6:26, 29). Purification-offering suet is not considered a food "gift" (contrast Lev. 3:3, 5, 9, 11 of the well-being offering), apparently because it is a mandatory token fulfillment of an obligation or debt.

Sins of communitywide significance committed by the high priest (4:3–12) or the whole community (4:13–21) require the high priest to sprinkle blood seven times in the outer sanctum (in front of the inner veil), daub blood on the horns of the incense altar, and dispose of the remaining blood at the base of the outer altar (4:5–7). Blood is especially prominent in three ways: vertically on the altar horns, horizontally by coming closer to God's place of enthronement in the Most Holy Place (cf. Exod. 25:22;

Num. 7:89; 2 Sam. 6:2), and by the fact that there are two applications of blood (not including disposal). The officiating high priest is also the offerer, or part of the offerer (when the community sinned), so he is not allowed to eat the meat, which is disposed of by incineration (4:11–12, 21).

Both kinds of purification offering have the same effect: to expiate for the sinner "from" (with NJB; not "for" or "concerning") his or her sin—that is, to remove the guilt from the sinner, so that the person can be forgiven (Lev. 4:26). The priest accomplishes expiation, but only God can forgive. Until he forgives, full reconciliation is not complete. When Jesus forgave like this, he claimed divinity (Mark 2:5–7).

Leviticus 5:1–13 continues the instructions for the purification offering of ordinary people that began in 4:27. Here sins remedied are not inadvertent but hidden, in that they involve deliberate neglect or forgetfulness (5:1–4). The sinner can perceive the need to bring a sacrifice only by realizing or experiencing guilt (5:2–5; cf. 4:22, 27; with NJPS), not by another person pointing out the fault (cf. 4:23, 28), because nobody else necessarily knew about it. One who becomes aware of a need for expiation is required to confess before bringing the sacrifice to the sanctuary (5:5). So the confession is not to a priest.

A reconstructed horned altar at Beersheba

A sinner who cannot afford a flock animal is allowed to bring a less expensive sacrifice of two birds: one for a purification offering, supplemented by another for a burnt offering (5:7–10). The pair is functionally equivalent to the purification offering of a single flock animal. The purification offering is performed first because it is a token debt payment, which has to be taken care of first before the burnt offering gift can be accepted.

An even poorer sinner is allowed to bring a purification offering consisting only of flour, without the oil or incense (5:11–13) that would have been included in a (nonexpiatory) grain offering (Lev. 2:1). The ritual provides expiation, prerequisite to divine forgiveness, just like blood sacrifices (cf. Heb. 9:22—*almost* everything is purified with blood). A substitute of grain (cf. Matt. 26:26) was a concession so that not even the poorest sinner would be left behind.

5:14–6:7. Leviticus 5:14 introduces the reparation offering. This unit naturally follows the preceding one because the Hebrew term for "reparation offering" is a technical usage of the word that can mean "remedy" or "penalty for guilt" (cf. 5:6–7). The procedure itself is reserved for the additional instructions in 7:1–7.

The reparation offering teaches several concepts:

1. Only after sinners make wrongs right to the best of their ability will God accept their sacrifices (cf. Matt. 5:23–24).
2. It is not enough for sinners to put things right as best they can; they still need expiation provided by sacrifice (see Isa. 53:10—the messianic suffering servant is the ultimate "reparation offering").
3. Divine forgiveness is available to those who are unable to identify their sins.

C. Additional instructions regarding sacrifices (6:8–7:38). The earlier basic instructions were for all Israelites (Lev. 1:2; 4:2), but here the priests receive additional guidance regarding their role (6:9, 14, 20, 25). The unit on well-being offerings, which were also eaten by the people, is logically reserved until the end (7:11–36).

Instructions regarding the burnt offering (6:8–13) are concerned with ensuring that the sacred altar fire, lit by God himself (cf. 9:24), will never go out. The burnt offering is the basic, regular altar sacrifice that is to burn throughout each day and night (6:9; cf. Exod. 29:38–42; Num. 28:1–8).

Leviticus 6:14–18 expands on the grain-offering procedure, specifying where (sanctuary court) the members of the priestly family (males) are to eat their most holy portions. Verses 19–23 prescribe a special, regular grain offering of each high priest as his personal tribute to God. He occupies a high position, but the Lord is his superior.

Verses 24–30 regulate allocation and eating of purification-offering meat. As with the grain offering, the meat is most holy, must be eaten in the sacred court, and conveys holiness (implying ownership by the sanctuary) to things by touch, and the priest may not eat it if he also benefits from the same sacrifice as offerer (as when the blood is brought inside the tabernacle; Lev. 4:3–21).

Purification offerings are most holy, but their blood and meat are paradoxically treated as though they are contaminated: what they contact is to be washed or destroyed (6:27–28; cf. 11:32–33, 35; Num. 31:20–23). This contamination can come only from the offerer, from whom it is removed, and it conveys to the altar residual pollution from sin or physical ritual impurity when blood from the same sacrifice is applied to the altar's horns. This explains why special purification offerings are needed to remove such defilements from the sanctuary on the Day of Atonement (Lev. 16:16).

In ancient Israel purification-offering blood served as a carrier agent to remove pollution, as in a living body. There was nothing wrong with the blood, which cleanses faulty people (cf. Heb. 9:14; 1 John 1:7). Not only can expiation be regarded as removal of debt that stands between God and human beings (cf. Matt. 6:12); it also cleanses from defilements that separate them from him (cf. 1 John 1:9). Amazingly, God makes himself vulnerable by allowing their pollutions to affect his holiness so that he can restore them (2 Cor. 5:21).

Leviticus 7:1–7 outlines the procedure of the reparation offering, which is similar to the purification offering, except that the blood is dashed on the sides of the outer altar. Its suet serves as a food "gift," even though the sacrifice is mandatory, because it follows payment of reparation to the wronged party. Verses 6–10 specify priestly ownership of reparation-offering meat and summarize priestly agents' commissions of the other sacrifices (vv. 8–10).

Verses 11–36 provide additional instructions for varieties of the "sacrifice" of well-being, which the people are to eat. Anyone who (intentionally) violates the sanctity of a well-being offering by eating its meat while impure incurs divine punishment (7:19–21), in keeping with the principle that interaction with the holy God requires purity (cf. Matt. 5:8).

A summary at the end of Leviticus 7 (vv. 37–38) lists sacrifices in the order of their presentation in 6:8–7:36 but looks ahead to chapter 8 by inserting the "ordination offering" before the well-being offering. The ordination offering is similar to the well-being offering in that it includes special grain accompaniments (Lev. 8:26–28, 31; cf. 7:12–14) and the breast belongs to the officiant (8:29; cf. 7:30–31).

2. Establishment of Ritual System (8:1–10:20)

Chapters 8–10 describe a one-time event: founding the Israelite ritual system by consecrating and inaugurating its sanctuary and priesthood. Once this is done, regular and cyclical rituals will serve the Lord and maintain his presence at his earthly dwelling place (e.g., Exod. 29:38–46; 30:7–8; Num. 28:1–29:40), and expiatory rituals will restore divine-human relationships when problems resulting from human faultiness arise (e.g., Lev. 4:1–6:7).

A. Consecration of sanctuary and priests (8:1–36).
Leviticus 8 reports fulfillment of the divine instructions for the consecration service (Exod. 29:1–44; 30:26–30). Special anointing oil (cf. Exod. 30:22–33) conveys permanent holiness to objects and authorizes persons because God has given the oil that function as an extension of his presence (cf. Exod. 29:43). Moses, the prophet (cf. Deut. 18:15; 34:10), officiates sacrifices as temporary priest (Lev. 8:14–32) in order to set up the permanent priesthood.

Purification and burnt offerings (8:14–21) prepare for the unique ordination offering (8:22–32). Although the purification offering is on behalf of the priests, it also purifies and further consecrates the outer altar (8:15; cf. Exod. 29:36–37). Since the priests and altar are in the process of consecration, the purification offering does not leave a residue of defilement on the altar (contrast Lev. 6:27; see commentary on 6:8–7:38).

The Hebrew term for the "ordination offering" refers to "filling" the hand (cf. Exod. 28:41; 29:9)—that is, authorizing for a function. Moses daubs some blood on the right ears, thumbs, and big toes of the priests (8:23–24). This implies their commitment to ministry, as a life-and-death contract in blood, to hear and obey, do, and go according to the Lord's will. Moses also takes some anointing oil and some blood that has been applied to the altar and sprinkles them on the priests and their vestments to consecrate them (8:30). Thus they are bonded to the Lord by blood (cf. Exod. 24:6, 8). Their strict confinement to the sacred precincts during seven days of repeating the ordination sacrifices reinforces the fact that they now belong to the holy sphere as the Lord's servants (8:33–35).

It is striking that both the outer altar and the priests are consecrated by anointing and with sacrificial blood (8:11–12, 15, 23–24, 30). From the Hebrew term for "anointed," referring especially to the high priest (Lev. 4:3, 5, 16; 6:22), comes the English word "messiah." The prophesied Messiah (Dan. 9:25–26) is

Christ (from the Greek for "anointed one"), who has been consecrated as the heavenly high priest (Heb. 5:5–10). He qualified for that role through his own sacrificial blood (see Heb. 13:10–12).

B. Inaugural priestly officiation and divine acceptance (9:1–24). The final phase of establishing the ritual system is to initiate the priests by having them officiate their first sacrifices at the altar. Expiatory pairs of purification and burnt offerings are repeated, first for the priests (9:8–14) and again for the rest of the community (9:15–16). Although the priests are consecrated, they are still faulty human beings. So before they can mediate for their people, they need expiation for themselves (unlike Christ—Heb. 7:26–27). Then Aaron performs grain and well-being offerings (9:17–21) and blesses the people (9:22; cf. Num. 6:22–27). Sacrificial worship to the Lord and blessing people in his name go together.

Moses and Aaron enter the sacred tent, which is permitted only for authorized priests. The fact that Aaron emerges alive to bless the people again (with Moses) means that the Lord has accepted him as priest. This is confirmed by the appearance of the Lord's glory at that moment (9:23). Then divine fire consumes the sacrifices that have started burning on the altar (9:24; cf. 1 Kings 18:38), overwhelming the people with

Aaron's sons died for burning incense inappropriately (Lev. 10:1–2). On this stele, a priest burns incense to honor the god Ra-Horakhty-Atum (Egypt, ca. 900 BC).

evidence of divine favor and acceptance for their benefit.

C. Divine nonacceptance of inaugural ritual mistake (10:1–20). Tragedy strikes before the priests have even finished their postrequisite duties, such as eating their portions. Two sons of Aaron offer incense to the Lord with unauthorized fire, rather than the divinely lit altar fire (cf. Lev. 16:12). Thus, they put human power in place of divine power, failing to glorify the Lord as holy (see 10:3). Ministering with kindling ignited by humans is unacceptable to God, and the same kind of divine fire that has favorably consumed the altar sacrifices now consumes Nadab and Abihu (10:1–2).

The Lord's presence is an awesome force, like a nuclear reactor. His protocols had to be carried out to the letter if he were to dwell among faulty, mortal people without destroying them. Priestly failure in this regard could affect the safety and well-being of the people, both physically and in terms of their attitude toward God's nature and character.

The surviving priests are sanctified, so they are forbidden to mourn (10:6–7, as in 21:10–12, at the strict standard for the high priest). Thus the God of Israel rejects death as evil and therefore alien to his holy nature, which his priests are to represent. This separation between holiness and death is in stark contrast to the religious culture of Egypt, where death was considered holy because it was the passage of the soul (which was immortal) to another phase of life.

In the middle of Leviticus 10 is a divine speech that prohibits the priests from entering the sacred tent while under the influence of alcohol and summarizes the priestly roles of distinguishing between categories (holy and profane, impure and pure) and teaching the people all the Lord's rules (10:8–11). Placement of the speech here could imply that Nadab and Abihu erred due to impaired judgment because they were intoxicated.

Moses reminds the surviving priests in detail regarding their portions of the inaugural sacrifices (10:12–15) to ensure that no more mistakes will derail the ritual system at the vulnerable moment of its inception. When he finds that they have already incinerated the remainder of the people's purification offering (10:16), which they should have kept to eat (6:26, 29; unlike their own purification offering, which they correctly incinerated because it was on their behalf—9:11), he is understandably furious (10:16–18).

Moses's rebuke clarifies the role of priestly consumption of purification-offering meat: This is a privilege, but it is also a requirement; by consuming the meat, priests bear the culpabilities (NIV "take away the guilt") of the offerers as part of the mediatorial process of expiating for the offerers (10:17). Thus, priests participate in the role of God, who bears culpability (Exod. 34:7; NIV "forgiving wickedness" translates the same Hebrew expression used in Lev. 10:17) when he extends mercy to sinners. The fact that Christ bore the culpabilities for our sins as our priest and died for those sins as our sacrificial victim, combining the two roles in himself, proves that he died as our substitute. Moses accepts Aaron's explanation that at this time of divine judgment on his family, he (with his surviving sons) did not feel worthy to partake of the purification offering meat (10:19–20).

3. Impurities and Ritual Remedies (11:1–17:16)

A. Separating physical impurities from persons (11:1–15:33). **11:1–47.** Leviticus 11 picks up the themes of eating meat (Lev. 10:12–20) and making category distinctions (Lev. 10:10; cf. Deut. 14:1–29) and addresses general dietary rules to all Israelites. The priests are especially consecrated as the Lord's house servants, but all Israelites are holy in a wider sense. So they are to emulate the holiness of their God (11:44–45), from whom impurity is to be kept separate (cf. Lev. 7:20–21), by separating themselves from specified physical impurities (chaps. 11–15). In chapter 11 this means abstaining from eating meat of creatures regarded by God as "unclean" in the sense of unfit to eat.

Some impurities are temporary and it is permitted to incur them, provided that proper purification is carried out, but an impure kind of creature is permanently prohibited as food. This impurity is not physical dirt, nor does the Bible indicate that an impure creature is not good for other things; indeed, all creatures were created "good" (Gen. 1:20–25).

Noah already knew the difference between clean and unclean animals (Gen. 7:2, 8–9; 8:20), but Leviticus 11 enumerates the distinctions in detail within the broad categories of creatures inhabiting and moving in the different zones of planet Earth: land, air, and water (11:46; cf. Gen. 1:1–31). There are simple criteria for recognizing clean land animals (split hooves and cud chewing), water creatures (fins and scales), and some edible kinds of insects (jointed legs to leap). For birds there are no criteria; the text only lists the forbidden species. Among land-swarming creatures there is no distinction in terms of fitness for eating; all are unclean.

Scholars have proposed possible reasons why a given creature should be permitted or prohibited for eating, such as dietary impact on human health, the need to teach respect for animal life, and reflection of the creation ideal of life, which excludes animals linked to death. However, the Bible never states such a rationale. God's people are to obey his instructions simply because they trust him.

Some kinds of animal carcasses convey temporary impurity to persons who merely touch them (11:24–40). Of these, carcasses of some rodents and reptiles additionally defile any object that they contact. But there is a striking exception: They do not contaminate a water spring or cistern (11:36). This principle that a source of purity would not be defiled explains how Jesus is not defiled when he touches lepers or is touched by a woman with a hemorrhage and power goes forth from him to heal them (Luke 5:12–14; 8:43–48).

Regarding the categories of edible and inedible animals (not including any additional temporary impurities), Leviticus 11 only presents categorical permissions or prohibitions, without any ritual remedies. The fact that such basic dietary distinctions long preexisted Israel (Gen. 7:2, 8) suggests that they are permanent and universal for God's people, who are to emulate divine holiness (cf. 1 Pet. 1:14–16; 2:9). Daniel risks his life to maintain his holiness by not defiling himself with a forbidden diet, even though he is far from the temple and the land of Israel, and God blesses him for his choice (Daniel 1).

12:1–15:33. Leviticus 12–15 moves to physical ritual impurities that originate in human beings. These include healthy or unhealthy flows of blood from reproductive organs (Leviticus 12, 15), emissions of semen or unhealthy genital flows of other kinds (chap. 15; cf. Deut. 23:10–11), and skin disease (Leviticus 13–14). Numbers 19 includes the impurity of corpse contamination.

These impurities are not mere physical dirtiness but conceptual categories excluded from contact with the sacred. Their common denominator is association with the birth-death cycle of the state of mortality that results from sin (cf. Rom. 5:12; 6:23). These rules and remedies do not apply to Christians, whose high priest ministers in heaven (Heb. 4:14–16; 8:1–2) rather than in an earthly temple. However, we can learn from them about human nature in relation to God. He is the Lord of life and does not want himself to be misrepresented as comfortable with death, which was never part of his ideal plan. He saves people from

(not in) their mortality to give them eternal life (John 3:16).

12:1–8. Most ritual impurities originating in humans pertain to the birth-death cycle, so this section of Leviticus logically begins with the impurity of a woman who gives birth. This impurity arises from the genital flow of blood that normally follows birth. Birth of a girl keeps the mother impure twice as long as if she bears a son. The text does not explain the reason for this. At birth a girl may produce some vaginal discharge, which can include blood, so perhaps the mother also bears the child's impurity in this case. Alternatively, perhaps the mother's initial period of heaviest uncleanness is shortened to seven days (and therefore her subsequent purification from lighter impurity is proportionally shortened) if she has a boy so that she will not transmit impurity to him by contact (cf. 15:19) at or following the time of his circumcision on the eighth day (12:3; cf. Gen. 17:12). But circumcision is to be performed at home rather than at the sanctuary, so it is unclear why such mitigation of impurity would be necessary.

The mother's impurity is a serious one, lasting a week or more. Therefore, she is to complete the purification process by offering a pair of sacrifices: a burnt offering and purification offering. As elsewhere, the purification offering is performed first and the combination functions as a larger purification offering (cf. Lev. 5:7–10; Num. 15:24, 27). A mother who cannot afford a sheep may bring a bird for the burnt offering (cf. Lev. 1:14–17). This is what Mary offers after the birth of Jesus (Luke 2:24). Notice that women are allowed, and in some cases even commanded, to participate in sacrificial worship (cf. generic language in Lev. 2:1; 4:27; 5:15).

A female's need for purification does not devalue her as a human being. She is the source of precious new life, but through no fault of her own it is mortal life. So she needs only cleansing from her impurity (12:7–8), not forgiveness.

13:1–14:57. While Leviticus 12 concerns a healthy condition, chapters 13–14 give instructions for diagnosis of and ritual purification from an unhealthy state: skin or surface disease. In humans this complex of conditions, some of which resemble psoriasis, is not the same as modern leprosy (Hansen's disease). The translation "leprosy" (e.g., KJV, NASB) stems from confusion concerning the translation in the Greek Septuagint. Analogous surface maladies could take the form of mold in garments (13:47–59) and fungus in walls of houses (14:34–53).

For Leviticus the concern is not spread of the disease itself but that the disease makes persons, garments, or dwellings ritually impure; they therefore have to be kept separate from the holy realm until symptoms abate, when they can be purified. Here ritual purification does not heal (unlike the miracle of Naaman; 2 Kings 5:14); it only follows healing.

Authoritative diagnosis of suspected skin disease and evaluation of its healing is left to experts: the priests. Symptoms, manifested by appearance, mainly involve discoloration of skin spots or hairs, or abnormal skin texture. Diagnosis of mold in garments of fabric or leather, worn over the skin, is analogous to that of skin disease (13:47–59).

The ritual impurity of surface disease was contagious, severe, and associated with death (Num. 12:12). So persons diagnosed with this condition are required to adopt the appearance of mourners, warn others of their presence (13:45), and dwell outside the Israelite camp in order not to defile it, because the holy God is in residence there (13:46; cf. Num. 5:2–3).

Leviticus 14 outlines ritual purification of persons if they are healed (14:1–32) and of houses if fungus abates (14:33–53). The section on houses includes some diagnostic criteria, but the unit is here because the emphasis is on purification. Houses, like garments, are closely connected with their owners, so the Lord's concern for the purity of his people extends to them.

Skin disease generates such potent impurity that purification requires several stages. Repeated pronouncements that the person is pure (14:8–9, 20) mean "pure enough for this stage." Compare the way Jesus heals a blind man in stages so he can experience restoration as a process (Mark 8:22–25).

If a priest certifies that an individual is healed from skin disease (cf. Matt. 8:4), a bird is slaughtered over "living" water (i.e., from a flowing source). The priest then dips a live bird, together with cedar wood, red yarn, and hyssop, in the life liquid, consisting of the living water and the lifeblood of the slain bird (14:1–6). The priest sprinkles some of the life liquid on the person and sets the live bird free, representing departure of the impurity transferred to it (14:7; cf. 16:10, 21–22 and somewhat parallel ancient Mesopotamian and Anatolian rituals). Nothing is offered to God, so this is not a sacrifice, but it begins to transfer the person from impurity and death to purity and life.

After additional purification, the person is pure enough to enter the camp, but not one's tent (14:8). By the eighth day, the individual is pure enough to offer sacrifices at the sanctuary (14:9–20). Apparently the reparation offering is for the possibility of sacrilege (cf. Lev. 5:17–19) because in some instances the "stroke" of skin disease could be perceived as coming from God (cf. 14:34; as divine punishment, see Num. 12:10; 2 Kings 5:27; 2 Chron. 26:19–21).

There is striking similarity between use of oil and the blood of the special reparation offering on the extremities of the formerly skin-diseased person (14:25–29) and use of oil and blood in the consecration of the priests (Lev. 8:12, 23–24, 30). The formerly skin-diseased person did not become holy as would a priest, but purification restored status among the holy people (broadly understood), who were eligible for limited contact with the holy sphere. This powerful enactment of return to purity and life would reassure those who had suffered not only physically but also from fear regarding their relationship with God.

Fungus in houses could be a problem in Canaan (14:33–53). As with garments, priestly diagnosis could have different results, depending on the behavior of the infestation. In Leviticus, though, it is priestly pronouncement, not mere presence of fungus, that makes a house and its contents impure. This reinforces the fact that impurity is a conceptual category.

Purification of a "healed" house involves a ritual that parallels the first-day purification of a person healed from skin disease (14:49–53; cf. vv. 4–7). The idea that a dwelling can be purified by expiation to benefit its owner (14:53) paves the way for understanding purification of the Lord's sanctuary on the Day of Atonement (chap. 16).

15:1–33. Leviticus 15 covers a variety of healthy and diseased genital discharges. It treats genital discharges of males and then females in chiastic order moving from abnormal male (15:2–15) to normal male (15:16–18) to normal female (15:18–24) to abnormal female (15:25–30). The transition from male to female is with sexual intercourse (15:18), which involves both genders. Genital flows could be involuntary (diseased discharges, nocturnal emission, menstruation) or voluntary (intercourse). Abnormal urethral discharge of males could be caused by a kind of gonorrhea (not modern venereal gonorrhea). In females, a chronic vaginal discharge of blood could result from a disorder of the uterus.

Minor impurities lasting one day until evening require the remedy of bathing (15:16–18). More serious impurities lasting a week (menstruation) or more (abnormal flows) indirectly convey impurity by touch.

Purification of a person healed from an abnormal or diseased discharge requires two stages: (1) waiting seven days plus ablutions and (2) purification and burnt offerings on the eighth day. Water and sacrifice, involving blood, are the agents of purification, with blood sacrifice providing the stronger remedy (cf. John 19:34; 1 John 5:6).

Near the end of chapter 15 is a concluding warning to separate the Israelites from their impurities so that they will not die when they defile the Lord's sanctuary in their midst (15:31). This points ahead to chapter 16, which addresses the problem of the sanctuary's defilement.

B. Separating defilement from sanctuary and community (16:1–34). Once a year on the tenth day of the seventh month, called the "Day of Atonement" (Lev. 23:27–28; 25:9), it is necessary for the high priest to purge the sanctuary of the evils that have reached it and accumulated there throughout the year. These evils consist of severe physical ritual impurities, expiable "sins," and rebellious "transgressions" (16:16). The impurities and expiable sins affect the entire sanctuary when purification offerings that remove these evils from their offerers contact parts of the sanctuary. (See Lev. 6:27 and commentary on 6:8–7:38.)

Notice the "part for all" principle here, which also explains how blood on one part of an altar can affect the whole altar (cf. Lev. 8:15; Exod. 30:10), how daubing blood and oil on extremities can affect whole persons (Lev. 8:23–24; 14:17–18), and how a whole animal from which part (blood) was taken into the sanctuary to purge it will absorb evils (16:27–28).

During the Second Temple period, bathing for ritual purity (as prescribed in Leviticus 15) often occurred in a mikvah, a ritual bath. The mikvah shown here was excavated near the southern wall of the Temple Mount in Jerusalem.

Indication of the way rebellious faults can defile the sanctuary comes later, in Leviticus 20:3 and Numbers 19:13, 20: These egregious sins (worshiping Molek and wantonly neglecting to be purified from corpse contamination) automatically contaminate the sanctuary from a distance when they are committed. These sins must be removed from the sanctuary, but the remedy does not benefit the sinners themselves. Rather, they are condemned to the terminal divine penalty of "cutting off," which denies them an afterlife.

Some scholars hold that every instance of sin or severe physical impurity automatically defiled the sanctuary so that the purpose of purification offerings throughout the year was to purge the sanctuary from these evils on behalf of the sinners. However, this kind of automatic defilement and sacrificial expiation to benefit the sinners were mutually exclusive: One who automatically defiled the sanctuary was terminally condemned, which meant that such a person had no opportunity to receive forgiveness through sacrifice (cf. Num. 15:30–31).

The high priest purges the sanctuary by applying the blood of a bull (on behalf of himself and his [priestly] household) and of the Lord's goat (for the people) to each division of the sanctuary from the inside out, as we would expect for a housecleaning job (16:14–19). This process reverses the flow of defilements into the sanctuary that have occurred when purification offerings removed evils from their offerers at the sanctuary. The purgation procedure in the outer sanctum follows the pattern set in the inner sanctum (16:16; cf. 16:14–15), which means that the blood is applied once on the horns of the incense altar (cf. Exod. 30:10) and seven times in front of it (reversing the order in Lev. 4:6–7, 17–18).

The Day of Atonement purification offerings are supplemented by two burnt offerings for the same offerers: priests and people (16:24). After purging the sanctuary with blood, the high priest transfers the culpabilities and sins of Israel to a live goat belonging to "Azazel" by confessing while placing both hands on its head. Then he banishes the goat as a ritual "garbage truck" into the wilderness to Azazel, thereby permanently removing the moral faults of the Israelites from their camp (16:10, 21–22).

Azazel, the meaning of whose name remains mysterious (certainly not "[e]scapegoat"), is a party capable of owning a goat (16:8, 10), but he is not the Lord. The Lord treats him in a hostile manner by sending Israel's toxic moral waste to be "dumped" in his territory, implying that he is the source of the moral faults, to which they are returned. This nonsacrificial elimination ritual ("purification ritual," not "purification offering") teaches that after the Lord's sacrifice bears all of the people's responsibility for their sins as their substitute, a demonic archenemy of the Lord bears responsibility for his own part in their sins as the originator of sin (cf. Genesis 3), tempter (1 Chron. 21:1; Matt. 4:1, 3; 1 Cor. 7:5; Rev. 12:9), and maliciously accusing witness (Deut. 19:16–19; Zech. 3:1; Rev. 12:10). The live goat does not represent Christ (Heb. 13:11–12 refers to purification offerings in Lev. 4:5–7, 11–12, 16–18, 21, not Azazel's goat).

Throughout the year, Israelites received sacrificial expiation that either was prerequisite to forgiveness (Lev. 4:20, 26, 31, 35) or purified them from physical ritual impurities (12:7–8; 14:19–20; 15:15, 30). But on the Day of Atonement, as a result of the sanctuary's purification, people who have already been forgiven receive another kind of expiation that now *purifies* them from all their expiable sins (16:30). This is a second stage of expiation for the same sins, beyond forgiveness, which provides moral (rather than physical ritual) purification. No text dealing with the Day of Atonement (Lev. 16; 23:26–32; Num. 29:7–11) mentions forgiveness from sin at all.

Expiation beyond forgiveness is necessary because the process of forgiving truly guilty people affects God's sanctuary or place of enthronement, founded on his righteous and just principles of administration (cf. Ps. 97:2) and representing his name or reputation (cf. Deut.

12:5, 11, 21; Ezek. 20:9). He would be just if he vindicated the innocent and condemned the guilty (Deut. 25:1; 1 Kings 8:32). But he also mercifully forgives the guilty, thereby upsetting the balance between justice and mercy and taking on himself a burden of judicial responsibility (cf. 2 Sam. 14:9). The fact that God bears this kind of responsibility when he forgives (Exod. 34:7; the phrase translated "forgiving wickedness" is literally "bearing culpability"; see commentary on 10:1–20) explains why his priests bear it as his representatives (Lev. 10:17) and why his sanctuary bears accumulated "defilement" (representing a problem) from forgiven sins.

On the Day of Atonement, God vindicates his reputation for justice concerning his treatment of two kinds of sins: (1) expiable sins of faulty but loyal people, which he has already forgiven, and (2) inexpiable sins, for which the disloyal are already condemned. The cleansing of his sanctuary through sacrifice represents this vindication. While the high priest is doing this for the people, those who have been loyal thus far are to reaffirm their loyalty to God by practicing self-denial (e.g., through fasting) and abstaining from work (16:29, 31) in order to receive the benefit of moral cleansing (16:30). Vindication of their Judge simultaneously vindicates the forgiveness that he has granted them. Those who fail to show loyalty in these ways are "cut off" or destroyed (Lev. 23:29–30). So the Day of Atonement is Israel's "Judgment Day."

The New Testament teaches that, because of the sacrifice of Christ, which pays our debt for sin, God is right when he justifies a person who has faith in Jesus (Matt. 6:12; Rom. 3:21–26). But God's justice still requires that he judge believers (Rom. 14:10–12; Heb. 10:30; 1 Pet. 4:17) to show that their faith continues (Col. 1:23) and is alive because it works through love (Gal. 5:6; James 2:18–26). This judgment considers works (cf. Eccles. 12:14; Dan. 7:10) not because a person is made righteous by one's own performance but because works provide evidence of faith, by which believers receive God's gift of grace (Eph. 2:8–9). This evidence of faith does not inform God, who already knows everything and can read thoughts (1 Cor. 4:5); rather, it demonstrates to his created beings, who cannot read thoughts of faith, that he is fair when he extends mercy. Thus the judgment in the New Testament has the same function as the ancient Day of Atonement judgment: to vindicate the character of God, which perfectly balances mercy and justice in love (cf. Ps. 85:10).

C. Additional instructions regarding sacrifices and impurity (17:1–16). Leviticus 17 serves as a transition. While it shares contents with earlier chapters, its style of exhortation, with emphasis on motivations and penalties, is characteristic of later chapters. The instructions in this chapter counter disloyalty to God by prohibiting Israelites from offering idolatrous sacrifices in the open country to male goats or goat demons, with which the Israelites have committed (spiritual) promiscuity (17:5, 7; cf. 20:5; Exod. 34:15; Deut. 31:16). This material aptly follows instructions for the Day of Atonement since such illicit sacrifices appear related to (and perhaps a reaction to?) dispatch of a male goat to Azazel in the wilderness (Lev. 16:10, 21–22).

Leviticus 17 reinforces earlier instructions regarding the authorized place of sacrificial slaughter (17:1–9; cf. e.g., 1:3; 3:2), draining blood at slaughter (17:10–14; cf. 3:17; 7:26–27), and the need to purify oneself after eating a clean animal that dies without slaughter by a human (17:15–16; cf. 11:39–40). The main new element is the prohibition against slaughtering any sacrificeable kind of herd or flock animal without offering it as a sacrifice at the sanctuary. Any violator incurs bloodguilt for illicitly shedding blood, in this case of an animal that should have been offered to the Lord, and is condemned to the divine penalty of "cutting off" (17:3–4).

There is a close connection between the topics in this chapter. The blood now has to be drained out at the sanctuary to ensure that the Israelites do not eat meat with its blood.

Blood contains life, so the Lord assigns it the function of ransoming human lives when it is applied to his altar (17:11). Thus, he provides a powerful rationale for not eating meat with its blood: respect for animal life and reverence for his blood ransom, without which people would perish (cf. Matt. 20:28; 26:28; Heb. 10:26–29).

The blood of a wild game animal is not assigned to the altar, but the moral principle of respect for life (cf. Exod. 20:13) still applies (Lev. 17:13). The prohibition of eating meat from which the blood is not drained at the time of slaughter goes back to God's initial permission to eat meat in the days of Noah (Gen. 9:4), long before Israel existed. So it is not surprising that in the New Testament, abstaining from blood and what has been strangled is treated as timeless moral law (with prohibitions against pollution from idols and immorality) that remains in effect for Gentile Christians (Acts 15:20, 29). Draining blood does not apply to animals that died in other ways, whether naturally or by predators, but an Israelite who eats such meat incurs ritual impurity (17:15–16).

4. Holy Lifestyle (18:1–27:34)

A. Holiness of people (18:1–20:27). Aspects of sexuality were introduced in chapters 12 and 15, where the focus was on separating remediable physical ritual impurity from the holy sphere centered at the sanctuary. Here the concern is with avoiding moral impurity (18:24, 30), for which there is no ritual remedy.

18:1–30. Leviticus 18 begins by explaining the purpose of the instructions that follow. God's laws are good for his people, so by cause and effect, those who keep his laws can live (18:5). This means that his principles enable the people to live long in the land that he has given them (cf. Exod. 20:12) rather than be expelled from it and die as the Canaanites do (18:24–30). This is not a legalistic approach to gaining eternal life through one's own works. Gaining eternal life faces the problem that everyone has already sinned and the law is powerless to help those who have broken it (cf. Rom. 3:19–26; Gal. 3:10–14).

The remainder of chapter 18 forbids several kinds of sexual practices. Prohibition of idolatrous and cruel worship of the god Molek (18:21) seems out of place here until we see the parallel with the law regarding adultery: just as you shall not (literally) give your penis for seed (or sperm) to your neighbor's wife (18:20), you shall not give of your seed (or offspring) to be presented to Molek (18:21). This recognizes the parallel between physical and spiritual adultery (disloyalty to God; cf. Lev. 17:5, 7 and the commentary on 17:1–16) and the close relationship between the sexual and religious practices of the Canaanites, which will later become a lethal snare to the Israelites (e.g., Numbers 25).

Leviticus 18:6 states the general prohibition of incestuous sexual relations, which is euphemistically expressed in terms of approaching a blood relative to uncover nakedness. A blood relative obviously includes one's full sister or daughter, who do not need to be mentioned, but verses 7–16 specify other relations by blood or more indirectly through marriage to which the prohibition of incest applies or extends.

Verses 17–18 forbid sexual liaisons (including marriage) with two women who are related to each other: a woman and her daughter or granddaughter (18:17), and a woman as a rival in addition to her sister in a bigamous situation while the first wife is still alive (18:18). This reminds the reader of some biblical narratives recounting painful rivalries between wives, whether literal sisters (Genesis 29–30) or not (1 Samuel 1), in polygamous households. Pointing beyond literal sisters are passages in which the Hebrew expression "a woman to her sister" refers to feminine counterparts (e.g., curtains in Exod. 26:3, 5, 6; wings in Ezek. 1:9, 23; 3:13). So although the prohibition of Leviticus 18:18 in its context refers to literal sisters, it alludes to "sisters" in the extended sense of any two women, and thereby tends to discourage all polygamy.

Reiteration of one of the Ten Commandments in verse 20 (against adultery; cf. Exod. 20:14) accords with the fact that the divine commands in Leviticus 18 regarding sexual lifestyle are categorical statements of moral principles. Neither the scope nor observance of these principles depends on the ancient Israelite cultural or ritual context. Therefore, these are timeless laws against immorality (cf. Acts 15:20, 29).

Within the moral law context of chapter 18 is the prohibition against having sexual intercourse with a woman during her menstrual period (18:19; cf. Ezek. 18:6, also within a moral context), implying that it too has ongoing application. According to Leviticus 20:18, the problem with such intercourse is that it exposes the woman's source of blood through sexual activity, apparently showing disrespect for life.

Modern "political correctness" seeks to slide homosexual practice out from under divine condemnation, but the nontechnical language of 18:22 is unambiguous: for a man to sexually lie with another man as with a woman is abominable to God. Censured here is not simply homosexual tendency, but acting on it. Also violating the creation order of sexual expression between one human male and female (Genesis 2) is bestiality (18:23), which was well known in ancient times and is unfortunately still with us. Oh that Leviticus were not so relevant!

19:1–37. Leviticus 19 contains a remarkably diverse group of laws, mixing moral or ethical injunctions with religious or ritual instructions. Such a combination of categories is not found elsewhere in the ancient Near East, where religious and ethical laws are separated in different collections. This combination of ethics and religion in the Bible emphasizes that for God's people, every aspect of life is holy and under his control. Thus, the heading in 19:2 calls for the Israelites to be holy as the Lord their God is holy, and the following laws teach them how to emulate his holy character (cf. Lev. 11:44–45) in the ways they interact with him and each other. The principle underlying all of God's laws occurs at the end of the first half of the chapter: love for one's fellow or neighbor (19:18). Near the end of the second half of the chapter, such love is extended to the resident alien (19:34).

The following table lists the topics of the divine commands in Leviticus 19, along with references to laws on similar topics presented earlier in the Pentateuch. Indirect relationships are indicated by references in parentheses. Significant repetitions, which help to reveal the structure of chapter 19 (in two halves), are in bold within the list of topics.

Verse(s)	Topic of law	Related passages
3	**Revere** mother and father	Exod. 20:12
3	**Keep the Lord's sabbaths**	Exod. 20:8–11
4	No **turning** to idols or making cast images	Exod. 20:3–6
5–8	No **profaning** well-being offering by eating it on third day	Lev. 7:16–18
9–10	Leave some of harvest for gleaning by poor and **alien**	
11	No stealing	Exod. 20:15
11	No deceiving, lying	(Exod. 20:16)
12	No swearing falsely by God's name	Exod. 20:7
13	No economic exploitation	(Exod. 20:15)
14	No wronging handicapped persons; **fear God**	
15	Judge fairly	
16	No slandering	Exod. 20:16
16	No seeking to profit by another's death	(Exod. 20:13, 15)
17	Reprove rather than hate	
18	**Love** your fellow rather than get revenge or bear a grudge	
19	No mixtures in animal breeding, sowing, or garments	
20–22	Reparation offering to remedy sex with betrothed slave girl	Exod. 20:14; Lev. 6:1–7
23–25	No eating fruit of new tree until fifth year after fourth-year offering	
26	No eating meat over or with blood	Gen. 9:4; Lev. 3:17; 7:26–27; 17:10–12
26	No divination	(Exod. 20:3)

Verse(s)	Topic of law	Related passages
27	No cutting side-growth of hair and beard	(Exod. 20:3)
28	No gashing oneself for the dead	(Exod. 20:3)
28	No tattooing	(Exod. 20:3)
29	No **profaning** daughter by making her a prostitute	(Exod. 20:14)
30	**Keep the Lord's sabbaths**	Exod. 20:8–11
30	**Revere** the Lord's sanctuary	
31	No **turning** to occult	(Exod. 20:3)
32	Respect the elderly; **fear God**	
33–34	**Love** rather than oppress the **alien**	
35–36	Use honest measures for scales	(Exod. 20:15)

There is a logical flow of topics, although it is not immediately apparent. The first half of the chapter begins with the need to respect the human and divine parties involved in creating people (19:3): parents (mother first here) and God, who rested (sabbathed) at creation (cf. Gen. 2:2–3). Respect for God rules out unfaithfulness to him through idolatry (Lev. 19:4) or profaning a well-being offering (19:5–8). Another restriction on food that shows respect for God is to leave some of the harvest for disadvantaged people to glean (19:9–10). Such concern for others, especially the underprivileged, calls for honesty (19:11–14), fairness (19:15–16), and love rather than hate (19:17–18).

The second half of the chapter commences: "You shall keep my statutes" (19:19). Again, topics begin with a connection to creation in terms of reproduction of animals and crops (from which come materials for garments), human beings, and new fruit trees (19:19–25). Respect for the holy Creator also rules out eating meat over or with (life)blood (19:26a), divination that seeks knowledge of the future apart from God (19:26b), pagan mourning practices (19:27–28; cf. 21:5, 10), and profaning one's daughter by making her a prostitute (19:29). Continuing the theme of creation, verse 30 repeats, "You

shall keep my sabbaths," which first appeared at the beginning of the chapter after, "You shall each revere [literally "fear"] his mother and his father" (19:3), but here in verse 30 is followed instead by, "And you shall revere ["fear"] my sanctuary" (cf. Lev. 26:2; author's translations). The sanctuary is the place of holiness and life where God's presence resides, so it is associated with creation (cf. Exod. 31:12–17, immediately following instructions for constructing the sanctuary).

Just as 19:4 forbids turning to idols, verse 31 prohibits turning to occult sources of knowledge, which includes the spirits of the dead. It is forbidden to pay attention to the dead (including ancestors) in that way, but elderly living persons should be treated respectfully (19:32, as in 19:14 regarding the handicapped). Concern for other people continues with loving the resident alien (19:33–34; cf. 19:9–10) and practicing honesty in business (19:35–36; cf. 19:11).

Much of the legislation in chapter 19 reiterates or is related to principles of the Ten Commandments (Exod. 20:3–17). The first nine commandments are clearly represented, and the principle of the tenth (against coveting; Exod. 20:17) is implied behind laws against stealing, exploiting, and seeking to profit by another's death. Notice that whereas Exodus 20:16 is against harming someone by giving testimony (in court), the biblical law against lying in general is in Leviticus 19:11.

A number of laws in chapter 19 have to do with basic ethics of kindness and decency (especially to

God commanded the Israelites not to "turn to idols or make metal gods" (Lev. 19:4), such as this bronze figurine representing the Canaanite god Baal.

vulnerable people) arising from unselfish love, which is the basic principle of all divine law and revelation (Matt. 22:37–40). The fact that love can be commanded (19:18) shows that it is a principle, not only an emotion. Unlike human lawgivers, God can hold people accountable for such inner attitudes because his knowledge penetrates to thoughts (1 Kings 8:39; Ps. 44:20–21; 94:11).

Rationales for some laws are not immediately apparent. Prohibitions of mixtures between kinds in animal breeding, sowing, or garments (19:19; cf. Deut. 22:9, 11) seem to emphasize a distinction between the earthly sphere, in which each species generates life according to its kind, and the supramundane or holy sphere represented at the sanctuary, where mixtures can be appropriate (Exod. 25:18–20; 26:1, 31; cf. cherubim in Ezek. 1:5–12; 10:8–22 and mixed supernatural creatures in ancient Near Eastern art). The connection between mixtures and holiness is reinforced by Deuteronomy 22:9, where sowing another crop in a vineyard results in the entire harvest becoming holy, which would mean that it is forfeited to the sanctuary. The earthly sanctuary and the temple that replace it are now gone, so it appears that the need for maintaining such distinctions, at least with regard to mixed materials in garments, is no longer a divine requirement.

In ancient Israel, illicit sex with an engaged woman was treated as a form of adultery and was normally punishable by death to both parties if the woman consented and to the man alone if he raped her (Deut. 22:23–27). However, in Leviticus 19:20–22 the woman is a slave, lacking the right of consent that could make her culpable. Since the nature of the offense depends on the woman's role, which in this case is ambiguous, the man also escapes capital punishment. However, he must offer a reparation offering because he has broken God's moral law by committing sacrilege in the sense of violating the sanctity of the woman's marriage, even before it is consummated.

Following the prescribed treatment for new fruit trees (19:23–25) shows grateful acknowledgment of the Lord's sovereignty over the land that he has provided. The horticultural practice of removing the buds of an immature tree rather than letting it prematurely produce edible fruit would also increase the yield (19:23).

A cluster of three laws prohibit doing certain things to one's body: cutting side-growth of hair and beard, gashing oneself for the dead, and tattooing (19:27–28). Mention of "the dead" here reveals that these were pagan mourning practices involved in ancestor worship (cf. Deut. 14:1–2; Jer. 48:37; 1 Kings 18:28).

20:1–27. Leviticus 20 is a highly effective reinforcement of chapter 18, so that these two chapters frame chapter 19 in a unified section concerning Israelite lifestyle. However, chapter 20 also reiterates parts of chapter 19, so it serves as a fitting conclusion to the section as a whole. By contrast with the apodictic formulations (straightforward statements of principle: "You shall . . ." or "You shall not . . .") of chapter 18, chapter 20 uses casuistic formulations to emphasize a variety of severe punishments: if a person does (offense), as a result that person will suffer (penalty).

Leviticus 18:21 briefly forbids Molek worship, but 20:1–5 places this case up front, adding stoning by the community plus the divine penalty of "cutting off." Sympathizers are also to be "cut off." The Molek worshiper loses the present life by stoning, and by "cutting off" he or she loses the life to come (cf. Matt. 10:28). "Cutting off" is punishment for defiling the Lord's holy sanctuary and profaning his holy name by giving of one's offspring to Molek. This defilement occurs when the egregious cultic sin is committed (20:3; cf. Num. 19:13, 20). But the sinner has no opportunity for sacrificial expiation. There is no evidence here or anywhere else that expiable sins, which may be remedied through purification offerings, automatically defile the sanctuary like this when they are committed.

Going astray after Molek is expressed metaphorically in terms of promiscuity (20:5), which helps to explain why Molek worship appears in chapters 18 and 20, with sexual offenses. Another kind of "promiscuity" punishable by "cutting off" is to turn to occult sources of knowledge (20:6; cf. 19:31). The Israelites are to sanctify themselves (rather than defile themselves by idolatry and the occult) by keeping God's laws because the (holy) Lord is their God (20:7–8; cf. 11:44–45; 19:2). They are able to do this because the Lord has made them holy (20:8; see also Exod. 31:13; Lev. 21:8; cf. Phil. 2:12–13).

In Leviticus 19, a call to holiness is followed by a command to revere parents (Lev. 19:2–3). Similarly, in chapter 20 the call to holiness (20:7–8) is followed by the death penalty for cursing parents (20:9). Continuing the concern for family relationships, verses 10–21 reiterate a number of sexual laws presented in chapter 18, this time with penalties attached to each.

An exhortation (20:22–26) recapitulates the endings of chapters 18 and 19. The Lord has separated the Israelites from other peoples to be holy to himself, so they must separate between clean and unclean animals. The idea of separation links two themes: creation, in which the Lord separated elements (Gen. 1:4, 6, 7, 14, 18), and separation or dedication of persons to holy service of God. As holy people, the Israelites are responsible for making some category distinctions (see Lev. 10:10, of priests). By implication, members of the "kingdom of priests" and "holy nation" (Exod. 19:6) serve as ambassadors of God's creation order and its corresponding purity (cf. 1 Pet. 2:9).

B. Holiness of priests and offerings (21:1–22:33). Priests are held to special standards in order to keep their holiness separate from impurities of various kinds (21:1–9). They are to properly represent God and not profane his name or reputation (21:6; 22:2).

Priests are forbidden to engage in pagan mourning practices (21:5; cf. 19:27–28) and prohibited from even participating in burying the dead and thereby incurring corpse contamination, except for with close blood relatives (21:1–4). Their holiness (21:8) prevents them from marrying women who have been promiscuous, "pierced" or "profaned" (i.e., probably raped), or divorced (21:7). Thus the lives of priests are to model ideal life in order to portray the Lord's holiness as ideal.

Family members of the Lord's ministers are also responsible for protecting their reputations, which affects people's perceptions of God. A priest's promiscuous daughter profanes herself and thereby profanes her father, who is God's representative (21:9).

The highest lifestyle standards apply to the specially anointed high priest, who is closest to God (21:10–15). He is prohibited from even approaching a corpse (literally "dead soul" [21:11], as in Num. 6:6), with no exceptions, and can marry only a virgin from his people. Leviticus 21:16–23 continues the idea that the inner sphere of the Lord is as close to ideal life as possible by limiting the privilege of officiating sacrifices to priests without physical defects, just as sacrificial victims must be unblemished (Lev. 1:3, 10; 22:17–25; cf. Heb. 4:15—Christ as high priest is morally unblemished). However, a defective descendant of Aaron can eat sacred food (Lev. 21:22). Nevertheless, physical ritual impurity disqualifies any of Aaron's descendants from eating sacred food (22:1–7).

Priests are not allowed to incur impurity by eating meat from animals that died naturally or were killed by predators (22:8; contrast 17:15–16, of other Israelites). However, their dependents are authorized to share some kinds of holy meat (but not the most holy; 22:10–13).

Leviticus 22:17–25 lists permanent defects that disqualify animals from being given to God. The Hebrew word for "defect" is the same as that used for physical blemishes of priests (21:17–23). Again, the holy realm is ideal, and it would be an insult to the Lord to offer him a poor gift (Mal. 1:6–14). Additional criteria for acceptable sacrifices, apparently based on respect for life, exclude an animal that is too young and slaughter of an animal and its young on the same day (22:26–28).

Chapter 22 ends with an exhortation (22:31–33). God has sanctified the Israelites by bringing them into a special relationship with himself. Correspondingly, they are to sanctify him by treating him as the source of holiness and by obeying him.

C. Holiness of time (23:1–44). The liturgical calendar in Leviticus 23 lists Israel's special appointments with the Lord throughout the year, which are to be proclaimed as sacred occasions. Following the initial introduction (23:1–2) is a reminder to keep the seventh-day Sabbath (23:3), which is the foundation of all sacred time. Then a second introduction (23:4) precedes enumeration of annual festivals, thereby setting them apart from the weekly Sabbath. Weekly Sabbath rest is established for all inhabitants of planet Earth by the Lord's example of celebrating his creation (Gen. 2:2–3; cf. Mark 2:27), but the festivals are commemorations of God's redemption, leading, and blessing in the history and agricultural life of the Israelite nation.

Leviticus 23 refers to annual festivals prescribed earlier (Exod. 12:1–50; 23:14–17; 34:18, 22–23; Lev. 16:1–34) and adds new instructions. It lists festivals in chronological order throughout the year, beginning with the first month in the spring. There are four festival occasions in the spring and four in the autumn, in the seventh month. The following table lists the festivals, verses in chapter 23 that refer to them, the festival's dates, and the durations in days.

Festival	Verse(s)	Dates	Days
Spring			
Passover	5	month 1, day 14	1
Unleavened Bread	6–8	month 1, days 15–21	7
Elevated Sheaf	9–14	day after Sabbath	1
Weeks	15–21	Elevated Sheaf plus 50 days, day after Sabbath	1

Festival	Verse(s)	Dates	Days
Autumn			
Trumpets	23–25	month 7, day 1	1
Day of Atonement	26–32	month 7, day 10	1
Booths	33–36, 39–43	month 7, days 15–21	7
Concluding Holiday	36, 39	month 7, day 22	1

Notice the overall chiastic symmetry in the days of duration, with the one-plus-seven-day contiguous festivals of Passover and Unleavened Bread at the beginning, balanced by the seven-plus-one-day contiguous festivals of Booths and the Concluding Holiday at the end.

Timing of the festivals of the Elevated Sheaf and Weeks is based on the agricultural cycle rather than fixed dates. The Israelites are to bring a sheaf of the first grain harvested and give it to a priest as a first fruits offering. At the sanctuary on the day after the next weekly Sabbath, the priest is to lift it (not wave it) in a gesture of dedication to the Lord (23:10–11), implicitly acknowledging the Lord's ongoing creative power and thanking him. Counting from this day (including the first day), the Festival of Weeks (or Pentecost, in Acts 2:1; 20:16; 1 Cor. 16:8) comes on the day after the seventh Sabbath, that is, on the fiftieth day (23:15–16).

In the Second Temple period, it was assumed that the timing of the Elevated Sheaf was tied to the beginning of the Festival of Unleavened Bread. This raised a question regarding which there was fierce debate: Does "the day after the Sabbath" (23:11, 15) refer to the first weekly Sabbath after Passover or to the ceremonial Sabbath (partial rest day) at the beginning of Unleavened Bread (23:7)? The Sabbath between Jesus's crucifixion as the ultimate Passover sacrifice (1 Cor. 5:7) and his resurrection as the first fruits (1 Cor. 15:20) is described as, literally, a "great day" (John 19:31), meaning that the ceremonial and weekly Sabbaths happened to be the same day that year. So he was the fulfillment either way.

In addition to the weekly Sabbath, there are seven ceremonial days of rest that can occur on various days of the week (23:7–8, 21, 24, 27, 35–36). Six of them require only rest from laborious or occupational work. But the Day of Atonement is like the weekly Sabbath in that all work is excluded (23:27) so that God's people can completely focus on him.

Each festival has a distinct character. Passover and Unleavened Bread commemorate the traumatic and glorious historical circumstances of Israel's birth as a nation, when the Lord delivered his people from Egyptian bondage (cf. Exodus 12–13). Several festivals joyfully celebrate God's agricultural provision for his people through the stages of harvest from the beginning of the barley (Elevated Sheaf) and wheat (Weeks) harvests to completion of the harvest season (Booths and Concluding Holiday).

Bread and other produce are among the items shown in this offering scene from an Egyptian tomb painting (ca. 1991–1784 BC)

Leviticus 23:37–38 concludes the liturgical calendar, but verses 39–43 add further instructions regarding the Festival of Booths to give it a dimension of historical commemoration. Temporary shelters or booths reenact the period when the Lord provided for his people during their wilderness journey (23:40–43). So when they enjoy the bounty of the land, they are to remember that it is a gift from God.

A Festival of Trumpets, celebrated in the autumn on the seventh new moon, involves a reminder announced by a (trumpet or horn) signal (23:24). In Numbers 23:21 the same Hebrew word for the signal refers to acclamation of the Lord as king in the war camp of his people (cf. Psalm 47). This concept of divine kingship fits the context of the Festival of Trumpets: a reminder of the Lord's sovereignty prepares his people for the great Day of Atonement ten days later, when he judges between his loyal and disloyal subjects (23:26–32).

D. Holiness of light and bread (24:1–9). In addition to cyclical festivals observed by all Israelites, regular rituals are to be performed by the priests, as the Lord's house servants, in the outer sanctum of his sanctuary. These rituals include arranging the lamps to provide light every day and placing bread on the golden table every Sabbath (24:1–9). This passage returns to the Sabbath, where chapter 23 began.

Verses 1–4 reiterate Exodus 27:20–21, where the Lord commands the Israelites to provide olive oil for the lamps to burn from evening until morning (cf. Exod. 25:37; 30:7–8). The fact that his light is on throughout each night implies that he stays awake to guard Israel (Ps. 121:4). The sanctuary is his palace, but he is no ordinary monarch.

Exodus 25:30 mentions that special "bread of the Presence" is to be regularly placed before the Lord's presence on the golden table. Leviticus 24:5–9 provides the details, including twelve loaves (one for each Israelite tribe), two arrangements or piles, frankincense on each pile, and changing the bread every Sabbath to signify an eternal covenant between the Israelites (twelve tribes) and the Lord.

Other ancient Near Eastern peoples fed their gods twice per day, but Israel's deity needed no human food, even once a week, for his own utilization (Ps. 50:12–13). Bread was offered to him, but he retained only the incense as a token portion and gave all the bread to his priests. The covenant bread was renewed on the Sabbath, which itself was an eternal covenant and sign between the Lord and his people to commemorate his creation (Exod. 31:12–17). So the Israelites did not feed God, but placed bread or basic food before him to acknowledge their dependence upon him as their ongoing Creator and Provider in residence (cf. Ps. 145:15–16; Dan. 5:23).

Light and bread are powerful symbols of the Lord's care for the Israelites. In the New Testament, Christ claims to fulfill these roles for all people by calling himself "the light of the world" (John 8:12; 9:5), "the bread of life" (John 6:35, 48), and "the living bread that came down from heaven" (John 6:51). He provides not merely for the present mortal existence, but for eternal life through the breaking of his body, represented by "new covenant" bread (John 6:51; Luke 22:19).

E. Holiness of God's name, and human and animal life (24:10–23). This passage, like the narrative in Leviticus 10, recounts failure by a member of the community that led to his death. This time it is an ordinary person who brawled and blasphemed. So his case becomes the occasion for additional divine legislation regarding blasphemy and assault.

The blasphemer is the son of an Israelite woman and an Egyptian man. So it appears that he belongs to the "mixed multitude" that left Egypt with the Israelites (Exod. 12:38 NASB). The identity of his mother is more important than that of his father. She is Shelomith, daughter of Dibri, of the tribe of Dan. Ironically, the name Shelomith is from the same Hebrew root as the noun for "well-being" or "peace" and the verb for "make restitution" (see Lev. 24:18, 21); Dibri is from the same root as the verb "speak" and the noun "word"; and Dan is derived from the verb "judge" (Gen. 30:6). An Israelite hearing this story would understand that the mother's identity summarizes the situation: Her son is *judged* for disturbing the *peace* and for *speaking* against God.

The half-Israelite man "went out among the Israelites" (24:10), implying that he initiated the altercation when he entered the encampment of the full Israelites. In anger he blasphemously pronounced "the Name"—that is, the sacred personal name of Israel's deity (Hebrew *yhwh*, usually translated "the LORD")—and cursed (24:11). The fact that the ensuing legislation deals with anyone who curses God (24:15) suggests that the blasphemer's curse was against the Lord himself, in violation of Exodus 22:28. Since a curse was regarded as a kind of weapon, he has assaulted God.

The blasphemer has broken the third of the Ten Commandments by taking God's name in vain (Exod. 20:7) and has assaulted God and man. Therefore, the Lord directs that the Israelites stone him outside the camp, after those who hear his utterance lay their hands on his head as a symbolic action (24:14), apparently to return evil back to its source (cf. Lev. 16:21) so that the originator will bear punishment for his own sin (cf. 24:15).

Verses 15–22, between the death sentence (24:14) and its fulfillment (24:23), specify penalties for anyone who commits similar crimes. Assault on a person resulting in a permanent physical defect (the Hebrew word is the same as for defects disqualifying priests and sacrificial animals in chaps. 21–22) is punishable by pure retaliatory justice (cf. Exod. 21:23–25; Deut. 19:19–21). The penalty is so severe because inflicting permanent disfigurement is a kind of sacrilege that diminishes the sacred life of a person made in the image of God (cf. Gen. 9:6), who belongs to a "kingdom of priests" and a "holy nation" (Exod. 19:6).

In its time the principle of retaliation (pioneered by some laws of Hammurabi, an Old Babylonian king of the early second millennium BC) advanced justice by ruling out disproportionate revenge (cf. Gen. 4:23–24) and by mandating equal-opportunity punishment among various social and economic classes. Christians know about retaliation from the words of Jesus (Matt. 5:38–39). Jesus did not repeal the penalties of the law in their judicial contexts; rather, he spoke against personal application of retaliation and advocated a higher ideal: waging peace in the face of adversity.

F. Holiness of promised land (25:1–55). This chapter continues the theme of Sabbath, which is prominent in chapters 23 and 24, by prescribing rest for the promised land. Analogous to the weekly Sabbath, sabbatical rest for the land is to occur every seventh year (25:1–7; introduced in Exod. 23:10–11). Such a year is a sacred time when the land will revert to its natural state and everyone will live off whatever the land produces by itself. This implies a regular exercise of faith: The Israelites need to depend on their Creator to provide enough food.

Leviticus 25:8–55 introduces a super-Sabbath for the land and its inhabitants: the Jubilee year. After seven sabbatical years, totaling forty-nine years, the Jubilee year comes every fiftieth year (cf. timing of the Festival of Weeks in Lev. 23:15–16). So the Jubilee follows the seventh sabbatical year and coincides with the first year of the following sabbatical year cycle. Thus, there are two fallow years in a row. Consequently, the Israelites have to rely on the divine blessing of a bumper crop in the year before the fallow begins (25:20–22; cf. Exod. 16:5, 22, 29).

The Israelite calendar year began in the spring (Exod. 12:2), and the religious climax in the autumn began on the first day of the seventh month (Lev. 23:24—with a horn signal), which has become the Jewish New Year (Rosh Hashanah). However, the book of Leviticus dictates that commencement of the Jubilee year is signaled by horn blasts on the Day of Atonement, the tenth day of the seventh month (25:9). The name Jubilee (25:10) comes from a Hebrew word for "ram" (*yobel*), an animal that provided horns to blow for signals (Josh. 6:4–6, 8, 13; cf. Exod. 19:13).

The Jubilee provided release of two kinds: return of ancestral agricultural land to its original owners and release of persons from servitude. Israelites could lose their inherited property and freedom due to poverty, which could result from a factor such as crop failure. Once a farmer sold his land for living expenses or to pay off debt,

if he had no relative to redeem the property for him, he would no longer have the means to support himself in his agrarian society and could be constrained to voluntarily sell himself and his family members into servitude so that they could survive (25:25–41). Servitude could seize him involuntarily if he defaulted on a loan, for which he and his dependents were collateral (cf. 2 Kings 4:1).

Deuteronomy 15:1–2 calls for remission of debts at the end of every seven years, which would reduce the incidence of debt slavery. Exodus 21:2 and Deuteronomy 15:12 mandate release of Israelite slaves after six years. But how would such persons independently support themselves after they regained their freedom? Leviticus 25 provides the solution: A servant can be retained up to a maximum of forty-nine years, but with a higher standard of living like that of a hired worker (25:39–43). The servant is released in the Jubilee year, when he regains his land, on which he can support himself and his family. Such servitude would be far from ideal, but it would sustain life until a farmer had the opportunity to begin again.

Some Mesopotamian kings occasionally corrected social inequities by proclaiming remissions of commercial debts and release of private slaves. Israel's divine monarch instituted a superior system (whether the Israelites later followed it or not) that was regular and did not depend upon the whim of a human ruler.

While modern Westerners cannot observe the Jubilee legislation as such because we lack the systems of ancestral land ownership and debt servitude that it regulates, we can learn much from Leviticus 25 about our responsibility to treat the poor and our workers with kindness. The Lord forbids taking advantage of people in economic distress (see 25:36–37, prohibiting charge of interest). If members of our society remember that they owe everything they have to God and are his tenants (cf. 25:23, 38), their generosity will contribute to alleviating poverty.

G. Covenant blessings and curses (26:1–46).
Leviticus 26:1–2 recalls the first laws in chapter
19 (vv. 3–4, regarding parents, Sabbath, and
idolatry), but in reverse order and with revering the Lord's sanctuary in place of revering
one's mother and father (as in Lev. 19:30). This
chiasm frames the intervening chapters, containing a wide variety of laws governing many
aspects of life. So when 26:3 refers to keeping
God's laws as the condition for enjoying the
covenant blessings, the whole collection of
divine statutes is in view. Repetition of two
of the Ten Commandments at the outset in
verses 1–2—against idolatry and for keeping
the Lord's Sabbath—is significant. Obeying
these commands is crucial for showing loyalty
to God.

Most of chapter 26 consists of conditional
blessings for faithfulness to the Lord's covenant stipulations (26:3–13) and curses for
failure to obey (26:14–39). Such contrasting of
blessings and curses (cf. Deuteronomy 27–30,
plus Hittite and Assyrian political treaties) was
an important feature of ancient Near Eastern
treaty formulations. It served the persuasive
function of encouraging compliance and discouraging noncompliance with the covenant
or treaty stipulations established by the superior party.

Israel's superior party was the omnipotent
deity, so his blessings and curses covered a
breathtaking array of effects, including conditions in nature that would affect well-being on
the promised land. The Lord clearly desired
to lavish blessings on his people to show the
benefits of a positive relationship with him
(26:3–13). But he could not bless them if they
were disloyal to him, or he would send a false
message about himself.

Much longer than the list of blessings is
the series of curses (26:14–39), which threaten
escalating severity if the Israelites refuse to learn
from their mistakes. This litany of horrors is
among the most powerful warnings in the Bible.
But while the Lord chastises his chosen people
in a mighty attempt to teach them and prevent

ultimate disaster, he will not utterly destroy
their nation.

Prominent among the sins listed in the
curses are idolatry and failure to give the land
its sabbatical rest. God will make the punishment of his people fit their crimes. If they do not
respect the holiness of the Lord of the Sabbath,
he will punish them sevenfold, and the land will
rest while they languish in exile.

The end of Leviticus 26 has a stunning turnaround: If the remnant of Israelites in exile
humbly confess and repent, God will restore
his covenant with them. No expiatory animal
sacrifices are prescribed for this situation because none could be adequate. The Lord will
simply respond to a belated choice to return
to him. Thus the book of Leviticus recognizes
the power of divine grace, the imperative of
true repentance, and the limitation of its ritual
system in remedying the problem of sin.

The tragic trajectory described in chapter
26 is not supposed to happen, but it does in
the subsequent history of Israel, culminating
in exile (2 Chron. 36:21—"until the land had
enjoyed its sabbaths," NASB). Daniel, in exile
in Babylon, desperately seeks the turnaround
through his impassioned prayer of confession
and repentance (Dan. 9:3–19). In response, a
heavenly messenger promises national restoration, and, at the end of a super-Jubilee cycle of
seventy sabbatical year periods, the Messiah
will come (Dan. 9:20–27).

H. Holiness of dedicated items (27:1–34).
Leviticus 27 focuses on the sacred sphere of
the sanctuary, thereby reminding the reader
of the early chapters of Leviticus. This chapter
provides instructions for donations (including
through vows) to God. Donated items become
the property of the sanctuary, administered by
the priests. Such items can include persons
valued according to their capacity for physical
labor, presumably to assist sanctuary personnel
in some way (27:2–8; cf. 1 Sam. 1:11, 22, 28;
2:11), animals (27:9–13), houses (27:14–15),
and fields (27:16–25). Firstborn animals cannot
be donated because they already belong to God

(27:26–27). A special kind of dedication makes a human, animal, or landholding most holy and irrevocably devoted to permanent sanctuary ownership or destruction (27:28–29). Tithes, like firstborn animals, automatically belong to God (27:30–33). Some kinds of items can be redeemed from the holy domain after they are donated.

The blessings and curses of chapter 26 have conditionally probed into the future possibility of exile, but chapter 27 concludes Leviticus on a positive note. It brings the original Israelite audience back to the present, when the functioning sanctuary is at the center of their life with God.

Select Bibliography

Gane, Roy E. *Leviticus, Numbers*. NIV Application Commentary. Grand Rapids: Zondervan, 2004.

Milgrom, Jacob. *Leviticus: A Book of Ritual and Ethics*. Continental Commentary. Minneapolis: Fortress, 2004.

Rooker, Mark F. *Leviticus*. New American Commentary. Nashville: Broadman & Holman, 2000.

Ross, Allen P. *Holiness to the Lord: A Guide to the Exposition of the Book of Leviticus*. Grand Rapids: Baker Academic, 2002.

Tidball, Derek. *The Message of Leviticus: Free to Be Holy*. The Bible Speaks Today. Downers Grove, IL: InterVarsity, 2005.

Wenham, Gordon. *The Book of Leviticus*. New International Commentary on the Old Testament. Grand Rapids: Eerdmans, 1979.

Figurines like these from Mesopotamia (ca. 2900–2330 BC) found at Tell Asmar, Iraq, were placed in temples in connection with a vow.

Numbers

Roy E. Gane

Introduction

Numbers constitutes episode four of a larger five-part composition, the Torah, or Pentateuch. This foundational block of Scripture recounts the dramatic and often convoluted story of divine-human interaction in the early development of humanity and of the Israelite nation. The first verse of Numbers already indicates that it is not a self-standing work: "Then the LORD spoke to Moses in the wilderness of Sinai, in the tent of meeting, on the first of the second month, in the second year after they had come out of the land of Egypt, saying" (Num. 1:1 NASB). Like Leviticus, Numbers begins with the conjunction *waw* ("and" or "then") and a verb form that continues a narrative sequence of events by reporting new communication from the Lord at the sanctuary. Information provided by earlier books is necessary for identifying the "Tent of Meeting" and the people referred to in the phrase "after they had come out."

The reminder of Israelite departure from Egypt and present location in the wilderness of Sinai introduces Numbers as continuing the travel story that commenced in Exodus. The people have entered the wilderness of Sinai in the third month after they left Egypt (Exod. 19:1). For eleven months, the Lord has established them as a theocratic nation by formalizing his covenant with them, giving them laws, directing construction of his sanctuary residence among them, and providing instructions for ritual worship and purity (Exodus 19–Leviticus 27). Numbers commences with a new phase of divinely guided organization: arrangement of the Israelites in a war camp to prepare them for moving on and conquering the land of Canaan, which God has promised them. This phase begins on the first day of the second month in the second year after they departed from Egypt (Num. 1:1), and they set out from the wilderness of Sinai only twenty days later (Num. 10:11–12).

The first ten chapters of Numbers present an ideal of order and harmony. There is every reason to believe that with the Lord leading and empowering his people, the journey to and conquest of Canaan should be rapid. But because of persistent Israelite rebellion, there is disappointment and delay. The outlook improves in the latter part of the book, with several notable victories over other nations (chaps. 21, 31), but these only bring the Israelites to the eastern side of the Jordan River, still outside Canaan (36:13).

Title

The Hebrew title of the book—*Bemidbar*, "In the Wilderness" (taken from 1:1)—is apt in describing its setting. The English title, "Numbers," is from Latin *Numeri*, derived from the earlier Septuagint Greek *Arithmoi*, which primarily refers to two sets of census lists. These summaries of the adult generation that left Egypt (chaps. 1–4) and the younger generation finally permitted to enter Canaan (chap. 26) are major pillars in the literary structure of the book (see below).

Theological Themes

God's treatment of the Israelites is much more severe in Numbers than in Exodus. In Exodus, he rescues them and provides water and food when they complain (chaps. 14–17), and they are punished only after they commit themselves to a covenant with him (chap. 24) and break it by turning to idolatry (chap. 32). Divine punishments in Numbers are among the most dramatic in the Bible and escalate in severity, with high body counts.

God's behavior in Numbers raises the question of theodicy (justification of divine character). However, he had repeatedly delivered the Israelites (Exodus 12; 14; 17) and miraculously sustained them with manna (cf. Exodus 16) every day for a year before they left the wilderness of Sinai, so he could justifiably hold them increasingly accountable for trusting that he would provide. He lavished grace upon them, but they steadfastly refused to develop a trusting heart relationship with him or learn from their mistakes when he disciplined them.

The story of extreme conflict in the wilderness serves as a warning to later people of God (1 Cor. 10:1–11), but it also gives hope. The fact that the Lord can bring the Israelite nation through drastic situations to victory implies that he can save anyone else, provided they choose to follow the example of Moses, Caleb, and Joshua rather than Korah, Dathan, and Abiram. It is possible to safely journey with God and be his holy people.

Date and Authorship

Tradition and the New Testament regard Moses as the primary human author of the Pentateuch, including Numbers (e.g., Matt. 8:4; 19:8; Mark 7:10). Modern historical-critical scholars attribute most of Numbers, like Leviticus, to a much later "priestly source." However, they acknowledge incorporation of some earlier materials, such as "the Book of the Wars of the Lord" (Num. 21:14–15) and a proverbial saying about the Amorite city of Heshbon (21:27–30).

Some extrabiblical inscriptions are relevant to the dating of Numbers. Two silver amulets, discovered in 1979 at a tomb above the Hinnom Valley outside ancient Jerusalem, are inscribed with the priestly blessing found in Numbers 6:24–26 (see photo). They date to the end of the seventh century BC or the beginning of the sixth. So, if the blessing is a quotation from Numbers rather than vice versa, composition of at least this portion of Numbers must predate the amulets. Eighth-century-BC inscriptions on plaster walls at Deir 'Allā, just east of the Jordan River, tell about a prophet of the gods called Balaam son of Beor. This evidence supports the idea that there was a preexilic historical figure by that name, as in Numbers 22–24.

One could wish that archaeological data from places listed in the itinerary of Numbers 33 would help us to date the Israelite presence there. But archaeological evidence of nomadic lifestyle, even of large groups, has a very short life span. Therefore, the ancient Israelite tent encampment has left no lasting footprint, and a

Ketef Hinnom silver amulets, inscribed with the priestly blessing found in Numbers 6:24–26 number of stations along the itinerary have not even been identified. However, the borders of the promised land in Numbers 34 imply a chronological framework because they coincide with those of the Egyptian province of Canaan during the fifteenth to thirteenth centuries BC. So the ideal shape of the territory of Israel, displacing the Asiatic portion of the Egyptian Empire, appears to have been formed during that period.

Like Leviticus, Numbers supports the exclusive authority and livelihood of a centralized Aaronic priesthood (Num. 3:10, 38; 16:35; 17:1–11; 18:1–32). This could be taken to support the theory that Numbers was written by self-serving priests, who stood to gain by persuading the Israelites of their obligations toward the elite religious dynasty. However, such a theory does not adequately reckon with other factors. These books do not hesitate to point out and emphasize failures of priests (Lev. 10:1–2; 16:1; Num. 3:4; 26:61), including Aaron himself (Num. 20:12, 23–24). Furthermore, they lay onerous responsibilities and restrictions on priests (Lev. 16:2, 13; 21:1–15; Num. 18:1).

Debates over the authorship of Numbers will continue for the foreseeable future. However, at present there seems to be no compelling evidence that the book's basic material could not have originated from the early time it describes, that is, before Israelite entrance into Canaan and development of the monarchy. (See further in the introduction to the commentary on Leviticus.) We do not know the process by which Numbers was formed and edited into its final canonical shape. But 33:2 explicitly states that at least some of the book is based on records written by Moses, whose inspired leadership and prophetic communication from God preserved and shaped his nation.

Structure

The main divisions of Numbers are 1:1–10:10, 10:11–25:18, and 26:1–36:13. These sections begin with the census of the first generation (chaps. 1–3), departure from the Sinai wilderness to continue the journey toward Canaan (10:11–36), and the census of the second generation (chap. 26). Recapitulation of the census after journeying (census 1—journey—census 2) indicates an overall A B A′ structure.

The literary texture of Numbers is complicated and enriched by interplay between narrative and legal (including ritual law) genres. Shifts in narrative-legal texture further support the A B A′ structure of the book: 1:1–10:10 and 26:1–36:13 emphasize instructions, but 10:11–25:18 focuses on negative narrative events. There is a dynamic relationship between narrative and law: narrative shows how Israel responds to God's instructions and how he reacts to their responses, including by giving more instructions. Some of these additional instructions are supplements to laws previously given (e.g., 5:5–10 [cf. Lev. 6:1–7]; and Num. 9:1–14 [cf. Exod. 12:1–13]). Reminders of the earlier laws, which are necessary for supplementing them, provide didactic reinforcement of divine principles.

Section one (1:1–10:10) is dominated by divine instructions given within a narrative framework. Some instructions or commands only apply to the temporary situation of the war camp (Num. 1:1–2:34; 5:1–4) and initial establishment of the ritual system (7:11). Others are formulated as ongoing laws that continue to apply after the conquest (5:5–6:27). Some instructions mix temporary or initial and ongoing aspects (Num. 3:1–4:49; 8:1–26; 9:1–10:10). In addition to providing settings for divine communication (with the narrative situation generating the need for law in Num. 9:1–14), narrative also reports fulfillments of divine commands (e.g., Num. 1:54; 2:34; 5:4).

Section two (10:11–25:18) consists mainly of narratives recounting significant events during the forty-year journey from Mount Sinai to the steppes of Moab, just east of the Jordan River. All of the human failures and divine punishments in Numbers are described within this range of chapters. Some divine commands (e.g., Num. 11:16–20; 12:4, 14; 13:1–2; 14:25) and fulfillments appear in these narratives. Chapters

15 and 18–19 contain ongoing laws. The Balaam story in chapters 22–24 is distinct in that its setting is away from (although directed toward) the Israelite encampment and that it presents only a positive picture of God's covenant people.

Section three (26:1–36:13) is similar to section one (1:1–10:10) in that it begins with a census and mainly consists of divine instructions in a narrative framework. These instructions include commands for the temporary or initial situation (Num. 26:1–65; 31:1–2; 25:1–30:16; 33:50–56), ongoing laws (chaps. 27–30, 36, with the situation calling for law in 27, 36), or both (chaps. 34–35). Most of chapter 33 (vv. 1–49) is a narrative synopsis of the Israelite itinerary.

Embedded in the narrative framework of Numbers are not only laws but also units belonging to several other genres, such as census report (1:20–46), blessing (6:24–26), prayer (11:11–15; 12:13), diplomatic correspondence (20:14–20), poetry (21:17–18, 27–30), prophecy (24:3–9, 15–24), and itinerary (33:1–49). This literary variety enhances interest for the hearer or reader and highlights the multifaceted nature of the wilderness experience.

Outline

1. Preparations for Resuming Journey (1:1–10:10)
   A. Military Organization (1:1–2:34)
   B. Organization of Sanctuary Personnel (3:1–4:49)
   C. Laws and Blessing for Purity and Holiness (5:1–6:27)
   D. Sanctuary Supplies and Service (7:1–8:26)
   E. Passover and Final Organization (9:1–10:10)
2. Wilderness Journey with God (10:11–25:18)
   A. Departure from Sinai Wilderness (10:11–36)
   B. Escalating Rebellion (11:1–14:45)
   C. Laws concerning Loyalty versus Disloyalty (15:1–41)
   D. Rebellion of Korah and Aftermath (16:1–18:32)
   E. Law of Purification from Corpse Impurity (19:1–22)
   F. From Failure to Victory (20:1–21:35)
   G. Balaam's Failed Attempts to Curse Israel (22:1–24:25)
   H. Apostasy with the Baal of Peor (25:1–18)
3. Preparation for Occupation of the Promised Land (26:1–36:13)
   A. Organization of the Younger Generation (26:1–27:23)
   B. Calendar of Communal Sacrifices (28:1–29:40)
   C. Law of Vows (30:1–16)
   D. Punishment of Midianites (31:1–54)
   E. Allotment of Land in the Transjordan (32:1–42)
   F. Itinerary (33:1–49)
   G. Instructions for Conquest and Settlement of Canaan (33:50–36:13)

Commentary

1. Preparations for Resuming Journey (1:1–10:10)

A. Military organization (1:1–2:34). Preparation for completing the trip to Canaan and conquering that land requires organization of the Israelites as a sacred fighting force. This process includes a military census (Numbers 1), arrangement of tribes in a holy war camp and assignment of their marching order (chap. 2), as well as a census of sanctuary personnel (members of the Levite tribe) and allocation of their duties (chaps. 3–4).

The military census numbers able-bodied adult males along tribal lines, implying that military divisions correspond to tribes and their subunits. Organizing the army in this way would have had two major advantages. First, tribal hierarchy supplied a naturally effective military chain of command. Second, Israelites fighting alongside members of their extended families would have a strong vested interest in supporting each other.

Twenty years old and upward (with no upper limit) is considered fighting age (1:3, 18, 45). Compare Leviticus 27, the previous chapter of the Pentateuch, which places a premium on the valuation of males twenty to sixty years of age, based on their capacity for work benefiting the sanctuary (1:3).

Following a tally of men in each tribe, except for Levi, the grand total is 603,550 (1:46). If we add younger and infirm males, the tribe of Levi (22,000 aged a month old and upward; Num. 3:39), the "mixed multitude" that left Egypt with the Israelites (Exod. 12:38), and a corresponding number of females, the total population under the leadership of Moses could easily be between two and three million.

This is a lot of people to survive and move in a wilderness setting, where logistics would be daunting for a small fraction of this number. In addition, the Israelites took a large number of livestock with them (Exod. 12:38). Consequently, most scholars do not accept the census figures as historical and have tried to reduce the population of Israel in various ways. For example, the Hebrew word for "thousand" can also refer to a tribal subunit, or clan (e.g., Judg. 6:15; 1 Sam. 10:19), so some have regarded the 603,000 figure as 603 contingents consisting of far less than 1,000 members each.

A number of factors have thwarted attempts to cut the census figures down to a humanly manageable size:

1. Several biblical books agree that the number of Israel's able-bodied men during the early periods of the exodus, conquest, and judges was high (Exod. 12:37; 38:26; Num. 26:51; Judg. 20:2, 15, 17).

2. Internal consistency in Numbers 1–3 requires reading the 603,550 total (1:45) as an ordinary number. This figure is the sum of the tribal tallies, which include not only thousands but also hundreds and tens. The Israelite firstborn males from a month old and upward total 22,273 (Num. 3:43), which includes single digits. The difference between the firstborn and the 22,000 Levites (1:39), who replace them as God's special servants, is 273 (1:46), for whom five shekels apiece, totaling 1,365 shekels, are given to the priests (1:50). These are calculations of ordinary math (cf. Exod. 30:12–16; 38:25–26).

3. In Numbers 31:32–40, large numbers of captured animals are formatted the same way as the numbers in the census reports of chapters 1 and 26. One could hardly speak of tribal or military contingents of animals.

Large numbers of Israelites at the time of the exodus and wilderness journey are in harmony with two themes in the Pentateuch. First, there was explosive Israelite population growth in Egypt that alarmed Pharaoh but fulfilled God's covenant promise to Abraham that he would have innumerable

Temple relief of Rameses II's war camp (Abu Simbel, Egypt)

descendants (Gen. 13:16; 15:5; 16:10; Exod. 1:1–22). Second, deliverance from Egypt (including at the Red Sea) and survival in the wilderness were totally impossible without mighty, divine miracles (cf. Exod. 19:4; 20:2).

Numbers 2 arranges twelve tribes (not including Levites) in four major divisions, consisting of three tribes each. The Israelite war camp has the shape of a hollow square, with the residence of the divine king protected in the middle. Strikingly similar is the war camp around the palatial tent of Pharaoh Rameses II (ruled 1279 to 1212 BC) pictured in his temple at Abu Simbel in southern Egypt (see photo).

Including the Levites, there are thirteen tribes descended from the twelve sons of Israel (formerly Jacob). There are thirteen because Jacob granted Joseph a double inheritance by adopting his two sons, Ephraim and Manasseh, who each became a tribe (see Genesis 48). The Levite tribe is to camp inside the hollow square, around the sanctuary, in order to guard its sanctity and thereby protect the Israelites from an outbreak of divine retribution (Num. 1:53; 3:23, 29, 35). Moses, with Aaron and his priestly family, camps in front of the sanctuary's entrance in order to guard its most vulnerable point. Any nonpriest who presumes to usurp priestly function is to be put to death (Num. 3:38).

B. Organization of sanctuary personnel (3:1–4:49). The Levite tribe (including priests) is not included in the military census because it is responsible for taking care of the Lord's sanctuary (Num. 1:47–53; 2:33). Nonpriestly Levites are to serve as assistants to the priests. In addition to the regular care and guarding of the sanctuary and its contents, the Levites are responsible for packing up, transporting, and reassembling the tabernacle when the Israelites journey from one place to another.

The Levites belonging to the three subdivisions of their tribe are counted in two censuses. The first reports 22,000 Levite males at least a month old (3:39). A census of the firstborn males, a month old and upward, from other tribes yields a total of 22,273 (3:40–43). These reports are placed together because the Levites have been chosen to serve God's sanctuary, and as such they redeem and replace the firstborn males of the other tribes (3:44). The second census of the Levites numbers mature males at the prime of life from thirty to fifty years of age, preliminary to organizing them as the sanctuary workforce (chap. 4).

The Lord claimed the firstborn males when he saved them from destruction of the firstborn in Egypt, but they are to be redeemed rather than sacrificed as firstborn animals are (Exod. 12:29; 13:2, 12–15; 22:29; 34:20; Num. 8:17). Instead of using the firstborn of the various tribes as his priests and their assistants, God transfers this privilege to the Levites because of the loyalty they showed by executing apostate Israelites at the time of the golden calf incident (Exod. 32:25–29; Deut. 10:8). By substituting for the firstborn, the Levites redeem them by substitution (cf. Num. 35:25, 28, 32), but the 273 firstborn over the number of Levites has to be redeemed with five shekels apiece (3:45–51).

C. Laws and blessing for purity and holiness (5:1–6:27). The Israelite camp is sanctified by the presence of the Lord's sanctuary in its midst. Therefore, the community within the camp is to be ritually and ethically pure.

5:1–31. Males or females with severe physical ritual impurities are required to stay outside the camp so that they will not defile its sphere of holiness that surrounds the sanctuary (5:1–4). This is no ordinary public health quarantine. Leviticus 13:46 already commanded that individuals afflicted by skin disease are to dwell apart. But exclusion of persons contaminated by genital discharges and corpses (5:2) goes beyond the rules in Leviticus 15 and Numbers 19 because life in the sacred war camp demands a standard that is higher than usual.

Numbers 5:5–10 continues the theme of solving problems that males or females cause with regard to the sacred realm. However, this passage turns to a topic of deliberate ethical sin: men or women wronging other persons through unfaithfulness or sacrilege (Hebrew *maal*) against the Lord (by taking false oaths; cf. Lev. 6:2–3). This topic was already treated in Leviticus 6:1–7, dealing with cases remedied by reparation offerings (so-called guilt offerings). But Numbers 5 adds the requirement of confession (5:7; cf. Lev. 5:5 for other sins that are not simply inadvertent), and provision to pay reparation to a priest if the wronged person dies and has no kinsman to whom it can be given (Num. 5:8–10).

Thus far, supplementary instructions in 5:1–4 and verses 5–10 serve as potent reminders (in reverse, chiastic order) of the entire systems regulating physical ritual impurities from human sources (Leviticus 12–15) and expiation for moral faults (Lev. 4:1–6:7). The next law (Num. 5:11–31) picks up the factors of men and women, impurity, the moral fault of unfaithfulness (*maal*), and giving something to a priest. This time the case involves the possibility that a woman becomes ritually impure by having sexual intercourse (cf. Lev. 15:18) with the wrong man, thereby committing unfaithfulness against her husband. A husband suspecting that adultery has occurred, even though witnesses are lacking, is to bring her to the sanctuary.

In biblical law, this is the only kind of case in which the Lord himself renders the verdict at his sanctuary through a ritual procedure. The Lord's verdict is revealed by the presence or absence of punishment. If a woman is guilty, her punishment will fit the crime by afflicting her sexual organs and making her sterile (5:16–28).

God does not entrust such a case to a regular Israelite court, which would have been all-male in that society. Men naturally would have tended to sympathize with a suspicious husband, which meant that an innocent woman could have difficulty obtaining a fair hearing and could be unjustly condemned to death (cf. Lev. 20:10; Deut. 22:22). Only women needed this level of protection, which explains why there is no corresponding law for a suspected adulterer.

The ritual procedure is a kind of litmus test in which the woman takes into her body a holy substance, holy water, the sacredness of which is enhanced by adding some dust from the earthen floor of the holy tabernacle. It is a basic principle of the sanctuary and its ritual system that holiness is compatible with purity but antagonistic to impurity (cf. Lev. 7:20–21). So if a morally pure woman drinks the holy water, there will be no problem. But if she is guilty of adultery, combining holiness with her moral impurity will cause a destructive physical reaction with a permanent effect worse than wearing a scarlet letter *A* for *Adultery*.

An innocent woman vindicated in this way by the all-seeing Lord himself would be completely freed from any social stigma of suspicion. Her husband could enjoy full confidence that she was faithful, and their marriage could be healed. A less potent ceremony would not have the same effect. (Compare parallels in Luke 7:37–50, but Jesus forgave a woman rather than vindicating her.)

6:1–27. The next law in Numbers, regarding temporary Nazirites (6:1–21), continues the theme of holiness versus impurity, involving factors such as treatment of hair, binding speech, and drinking (or not). Any Israelite man or woman could voluntarily take a special Nazirite vow of separation in order to be holy to the Lord for a period of time that he or she would specify. A holy lifestyle during the period of dedication would include abstaining from drinking intoxicating beverages or consuming any grape products, letting one's hair grow without cutting it, and avoiding the severe physical ritual impurity of corpse contamination (6:3–8).

Through the Nazirite vow, the Lord makes it possible for nonpriestly Israelites to enjoy a high level of sanctity connected to himself. In terms of holy lifestyle, priests were prohibited from imbibing wine or other fermented drinks only when they entered the sanctuary (Lev. 10:8–11). But such beverages are prohibited at all times to Nazirites (6:3), whose standard in this regard is higher. Ordinary priests were permitted to become impure by participating in burial of their closest relatives (Lev. 21:1–4). But the holiness of Nazirites is like that of the high priest in barring them from going near any corpse at all (6:6–7; Lev. 21:11).

The expression for "corpse" in Leviticus 21:11 and Numbers 6:6 is "dead *nepesh*." The KJV of Genesis 2:7 translates the Hebrew word *nepesh* as "soul": "And the LORD God formed man of the dust of the ground, and breathed into his nostrils the breath of life; and man became a living *soul*." A person who loses the breath of life and dies is no longer a living soul or being (*nepesh*) but a dead *nepesh*, that is, a corpse. So a person is a *nepesh*, whether alive or dead, rather than having a "soul" that continues conscious existence after death (cf. Ps. 115:17; Eccles. 9:5).

Nazirites, then, avoid corpse contamination, but people could suddenly die near them. Although this prohibited defilement would be incurred inadvertently, it would abruptly abort the period of Naziriteship. Therefore, the (now former) Nazirite is to undergo purification for corpse contamination (cf. Num. 19:11–19) and shave his or her defiled hair on the seventh day (6:9).

On the eighth day, the person is to bring a pair of sacrifices to the sanctuary (purification offering [so-called sin offering] and burnt offering) to receive expiation for the inadvertent sin of violating the prohibition (6:10–11). In addition, a reparation offering (so-called guilt offering) expiated for inadvertent sacrilege: depriving the Lord of the remaining days of the vow and the dedicated hair that was to grow during that period (6:12; cf. Lev. 5:14–16). Having rededicated his or her head (of hair) and the same duration of separation as before, the Nazirite begins the vowed period of time all over again (6:11–12). God takes seriously a person's commitment to spend special time with him!

An Israelite who successfully completes the Nazirite period is to culminate his or her sacred dedication through a special group of rituals (6:13–21). First is a pair of sacrifices, listed as a burnt offering and purification offering (6:14; cf. Lev. 12:6, 8). However, the purification offering is actually performed first (6:16; cf. Lev. 9:7–16, 22). This purification offering has puzzled scholars. Elsewhere in the Israelite sacrificial system, this kind of sacrifice expiates for nondefiant (including inadvertent) sins (Lev. 4:1–5:13) and physical ritual impurities (Lev. 12:6–8; 14:19, 22, 31; 15:15, 30). But in this case there is no mention of the Nazirite sinning or becoming impure.

The key to the function of this purification offering is found in the close parallel between the offerings of the Nazirite and those of the priests at the time of their consecration (Exodus 29; Leviticus 8). Each set of sacrifices includes a purification offering, burnt offering, a sacrifice partly eaten by the offerer(s) (i.e., ordination offering of the priests; well-being offering of the Nazirite), and unleavened grain items in a basket. In the context of the priestly initiation, the purification offering apparently serves to raise Aaron and his sons to a higher level of ritual purity in preparation for completing their consecration. Similarly, the Nazirite is already basically pure, but the purification offering enhances purity to a high level before the climax of Naziriteship: shaving the dedicated

An Egyptian tomb painting depicting the wine-making process. Wine and related products were forbidden to a Nazirite (Num. 6:1–4).

hair and offering it to the Lord on the fire under the well-being offering (6:18). Thus the hair, which is a token part of the Nazirite, is permanently sacrificed to God. The Israelite ritual system never comes closer to human sacrifice than this.

The priests are consecrated at the beginning of their ministry as lifelong servants of God. Nazirites, on the other hand, are brought to a kind of consecration at the end of temporary periods of dedication to special holiness. After a concluding dedication of priestly portions, Naziriteship is over (6:19–20). The high level of religious intensity is costly for a Nazirite (6:21; cf. Acts 21:23–24) and cannot be sustained. But for a brief, shining, and memorable moment, an ordinary Israelite can experience exceptional closeness to God.

The Bible also attests a lifelong Nazirite: Samson, whom the Lord dedicates before his miraculous birth to perform a special task of deliverance (Judges 13). Samuel and John the Baptist are similar to Samson in some ways (1 Sam. 1:11; Luke 1:15), although they are not called Nazirites. Jesus was not a Nazirite (Hebrew *nazir*; cf. Matt. 11:19), although linguistic confusion with his identity as a Nazarene (someone from Nazareth, derived from the Semitic root *nsr* rather than *nzr*) has inspired centuries of artists to give him the long hair of a Nazirite. Nevertheless, his life of dedication to a special mission of deliverance ended, like Samson's, with the sacrifice of his life (Judges 16; Matthew 27). But this end is also a new beginning because it serves as his sacrifice of consecration to eternal priesthood following his resurrection (Hebrews 7).

After the Aaronic priests are consecrated (Leviticus 8), they officiate inaugural sacrifices (chap. 9). Then Aaron raises his hands toward the people and blesses them (Lev. 9:22; cf. v. 23). In Numbers 6, after the concluding ceremony of elite Naziriteship, which somewhat parallels priestly consecration (see above), verses 22–27 instruct the priests how to orally bless all the people in order to place the Lord's name on them so that he will bless them. Invoking him as the deity of all Israel affirms that the entire nation, not only priests or Nazirites, is to be God's own possession, "a kingdom of priests and a holy nation" (Exod. 19:5–6).

To give assurance that the blessing will be effective, the Lord himself gives the words to the priests (6:24–26). Because this is a request for divine blessing, it is a kind of prayer (paralleling the requests of the Lord's Prayer, Matt. 6:11–13). The blessing is formulated as poetry, with three pairs of expressions. The first member of each pair wishes for God to be favorably disposed toward his people (bless, make his face shine, lift up his face). The second member wishes for his aid (guard, be gracious, give well-being). All benefits flow from a positive relationship with the Lord, which he freely offers.

D. Sanctuary supplies and service (7:1–8:26). Following this reminder of Aaron's blessing at the time when the ritual system was inaugurated (see Lev. 9:22), Numbers 7 fills in some details regarding establishment of the sanctuary: gifts for the sanctuary presented by chieftains on behalf of their twelve tribes (not including Levi). The gifts belong to two main categories. First is a practical offering of carts and oxen that the Levites will use to transport the sanctuary (7:1–9; cf. chap. 4). Second is a set of offerings for the dedication of the altar when it is consecrated (7:10–88; cf. Lev. 8:11, 15).

Chronologically, the report of these gifts belongs with Leviticus 8–9. However, Leviticus focuses on ritual procedures. So the report is placed in Numbers because the presents are from the tribal chieftains (cf. chaps. 1–2) for the sanctuary infrastructure, including the work of the Levites (cf. chap. 4).

The offerings of the chieftains are practical gifts, honor the Lord's altar, and acknowledge his sovereignty over their tribes. Numbers 7:89 emphasizes the dynamic nature of this sovereignty by reporting that when Moses enters the sanctuary (cf. Lev. 9:23), the Lord speaks to him from between the cherubim over the ark of the covenant (cf. Exod. 25:22).

Numbers 7 refers to establishment of the outer altar (7:10–88) and the Most Holy Place (7:89). Numbers 8 then adds a reminder of the outer sanctum, or Holy Place, reiterating the instruction for the priest to mount the seven sanctuary lamps so that they will shed light in front of the golden lampstand to illuminate the area (8:1–4; cf. Exod. 25:37).

Continuing the theme of founding the sanctuary system, Numbers 8:5–26 describes the ceremony of ritually purifying and setting apart the Levite workforce (cf. chap. 4). Some interpreters have mistakenly supposed that cleansing the Levites removed sin. Thus the NRSV, NASB, and NLT say that they "purified themselves from sin" (8:21, summarizing the activities specified in 8:7). It is true that the Hebrew word here is a form of the verb that often means "to sin" (e.g., Lev. 4:2–3, 14, 22). However, the same verb can also refer to purification from physical ritual impurity alone (Lev. 14:49, 52; Num. 19:12–13, 19–20; 31:19–20, 23). The cleansing procedures for the Levites in Numbers 8:7 only have to do with removing ritual impurity (especially corpse contamination; cf. Num. 19:9, 13, 20–21; 31:23), not sin in the sense of moral fault. They need this purification before they can safely come close to holy things in order to do their work at the sanctuary.

To complete their purification, the Levites offer a purification offering and a burnt offering (8:12). This pair of sacrifices functions as the equivalent of a larger purification offering (here for the entire Levite workforce), with the burnt offering supplementing the quantity of

This mosaic from a fifth-century-AD synagogue (Beth Shean, Israel) depicts the Most Holy Place, lampstands, incense shovels, and ram's horns.

expiation provided by the purification offering (cf. Lev. 5:6–9; Num. 15:22–29). The goal in this instance is for Aaron to make expiation for the Levites in order to purify *them* (8:21). This rules out the theory that the purpose of all purification offerings was to purify the sanctuary alone, never the offerer(s) (see further Leviticus 4; 16).

Numbers 4 stipulated that the Levite workforce must consist of men from thirty to fifty years of age (e.g., Num. 4:3, 23, 30). However, 8:23–26 puts the beginning age at twenty-five. The ages in chapter 4 may apply only to the period when it is necessary to perform the sensitive and potentially hazardous duty of moving the sanctuary from place to place (cf. 1 Chron. 23:24–27; 2 Chron. 31:17; Ezra 3.0).

E. Passover and final organization (9:1–10:10). God reminds Moses in the first month of the second year after they have left Egypt to observe the Passover festival at its proper time on the night of the fourteenth day of the month (9:1–3). This reminder chronologically precedes the Lord's command on the first day of the second month to carry out a military census (chap. 1). But the book's placement of the second Passover just before a second exodus, this time from the Sinai wilderness (chap. 10), gives the festival an impact of resumptive repetition: In the continuation of God's deliverance from Egypt, his people are picking up where they left off and continuing to the promised land.

Some are not able to participate in Passover because they are ritually impure through corpse contamination (9:5–6; cf. Lev. 7:20–21;

Num. 5:1–4). So God graciously provides the solution of an alternate Passover date a month later for any Israelites or resident aliens unable to participate at the normal time due to their impurity or absence on a long journey (9:6–14).

Speaking of absence on a long journey, verses 15–23 recount God's guiding Israel to Canaan through the movements of his glory cloud (cf. Exod. 13:21–22; 14:19–20, 24; 40:34–38). It is crucial for his people to stay with him and follow his leading.

A system of signals, consisting of two trumpets blown by priests, is established for making announcements to the large community—announcements such as precise times when tribal divisions are to set out after the cloud lifts from the tabernacle (10:1–10). Putting priests in charge of the signals emphasizes that the Israelites are under divine control. Trumpet calls are to vary according to the number of trumpets, kinds of blasts, and the number of blasts. These variables will communicate different messages. For instance, one kind of blast indicates assembly and celebration at the camp, and another signals moving out to travel or to make war.

2. Wilderness Journey with God (10:11–25:18)

A. Departure from Sinai wilderness (10:11–36). At last, on the twentieth day of the second month of the second year after the Israelites left Egypt, the divine cloud lifts from "the tabernacle of the Testimony" (10:11 NIV 1984). This is only twenty days after the Lord has commanded Moses to carry out the military census (1:1), and a week after the alternative Passover, on the fourteenth day of the second month (9:11).

When the Israelites set out from the wilderness of Sinai in accordance with the procedures that the Lord has specified (10:12–28; cf. 2:1–34; 4:1–49), the Levites move the sanctuary and its sacred objects (10:17, 21), and the ark of the Lord's covenant leads the way (10:33). References to the Lord's covenant and testimony in Numbers 10 remind the audience that the Israelites' bond to the Lord requires them

to serve him with respect, trust, loyalty, and obedience, all of which will be in short supply on various occasions recounted in the following chapters.

According to Numbers 2:17, the sanctuary and Levites are to travel in the middle of the four major tribal divisions. In chapter 10 the Kohathite Levites, carrying the sacred objects, do set out between the second and third divisions (10:21). However, the Gershonite and Merarite Levites with the tabernacle have departed earlier (10:17). This makes it possible for the Gershonites and Merarites to reach their destination and set up the tabernacle before the Kohathites arrive (10:21). Then the sacred objects can go directly into their places rather than remaining on the shoulders of the Kohathites while the tabernacle is reassembled.

Moses seeks the assistance of Hobab, his Midianite brother-in-law, to locate good camping places and be the "eyes" of Israel (10:29–32; cf. Exod. 2:18, 21). This would at first glance seem to be in tension with the notice that the ark of the covenant goes before the Israelites to seek a resting place for them (10:33). But the Lord's role in guiding Israel does not rule out human participation and cooperation in working out details that are within the framework of his plan.

B. Escalating rebellion (11:1–14:45). **11:1–12:16.** Journeying through wilderness is a lot more strenuous than camping at Mount Sinai. The Israelites have not gone far when they start to complain, and God is incensed. His fire blazes among them, causing damage in the outer part of their camp (11:1). It is not clear whether anybody is hurt, but the people are traumatized. They cry to Moses, who intercedes with the Lord through prayer, and the fire dies down. Moses dubs the location Taberah, "place of burning," as a reminder that divine fire has blazed there (11:2–3).

This brief episode contains the DNA of much of the Israelites' wilderness experience. Elements that recur and develop with variations include rebellious complaining, divine wrath in response, intercession by Moses, subsiding of divine wrath after infliction of some damage, and remembrance of the experience as a lesson for the future.

Another element is implicit in the notice that the Lord targets the outskirts of the camp, where the "mixed multitude" would have had their tents. Because they did not belong to the Israelite tribes, they would have camped outside the four main tribal divisions that surrounded the sanctuary (cf. Lev. 24:10). These non-Israelites or partial Israelites cast in their lot with the Israelites when they departed from Egypt (Exod. 12:38). The fact that the Lord strikes the area of the mixed multitude at Taberah suggests that they instigated or led the chorus of complaining.

The next episode explicitly begins with the mixed multitude, described as inferior "rabble," or a bunch of vagabonds. Their intense craving for meat infects the Israelites and incites them to weep again (11:4). The people prefer Egyptian food to manna, and life under Pharaoh to their present situation under the leadership of God and his servant Moses (11:5–9; cf. v. 20). Still slaves at heart (cf. Acts 7:39), they rebel against the cost of freedom.

God is angry again, but this time Moses is upset too. Rather than interceding, he bitterly objects that God has laid the burden of all the people and their unreasonable request on him (11:10–15). The Lord treats Moses with patience and understanding (cf. 1 Kings 19:4–8), providing two solutions for his dilemma.

First, God has him appoint seventy elders, who are already recognized as leaders, to help him govern the Israelites. Then if the people become unhappy, these tribal representatives will absorb the impact and have a vested interest in calming them down. Notice how God works with existing social structures that are already familiar and credible to the Israelites.

The Lord legitimates the participation of the seventy elders with Moses as mediators between himself and the people by taking some of the divine Spirit that is on Moses and putting it on

them. They demonstrate their gift of the Spirit by prophesying just once (Num. 11:16–17, 24–25). The text does not record their words; the point is the fact of their prophesying rather than the content.

Most of the elders prophesy while they are assembled around the sanctuary. However, two have not answered the call to go from their place of encampment to the sanctuary. Nevertheless, the Spirit finds them and they prophesy too. Their breach of protocol alarms Joshua, Moses's assistant. Rather than seeking to "quench the Spirit" (cf. 1 Thess. 5:19–20), as Joshua suggests, Moses only wishes that all of the people would similarly receive the Spirit (Num. 11:26–30). He understands that the Spirit has confirmed the call of the two men, in spite of their apparent reticence, and it is not his place to get in God's way (cf. Acts 10:44–48; 11:15–18).

The Lord's second solution for Moses is to miraculously provide all the Israelites with an abundance of meat, without depleting their livestock. He does this by sending a wind to divert millions of quail from the sea to the area of the Israelite camp (11:31; cf. Exod. 16:13). Quail have relatively heavy bodies, so they tire easily on long flights, especially if winds are not in their favor. Therefore, it is not surprising that quail flying a few feet ("about two cubits," which is about three feet) above the ground (with NKJV, NIV 1984; not left on the ground to a depth of two cubits, as NIV, NRSV, NASB, NJPS, and NJB read) would be easy prey for the Israelites to knock out of the air.

The ravenous Israelites work around the clock to gather a huge number of the hapless birds, at least ten homers (originally donkey loads, or about ten and a half bushels) of quail each (11:32). Flocks consisting of millions of migrating quail have been recorded as recently as the 1900s. But the remarkable number in Numbers 11, combined with the timing in response to the Israelites' cry for meat, would be due to divine intervention (cf. 11:23).

Abundantly giving the people what they want is not weakness on God's part but a way to discipline them. He provides enough meat for them to eat it every day for a whole month, but this is to make them come to loathe it, in order to teach them a lesson for rejecting him and questioning why they ever left Egypt (11:18–20).

The Lord has told Moses to command the Israelites to consecrate themselves in preparation for eating the meat that he will provide (11:18). This implies that receiving God's miraculous gift will be a sacred event, like a sacrifice from which the offerer could eat (cf. 1 Sam. 16:5). But the people turn it into an orgy of greed and a feeding frenzy. Disgusted by their lack of restraint or respect for him, he does not waste time by giving them a month to experience their punishment but immediately strikes many dead with a plague. The place is named after the new cemetery there: Kibroth Hattaavah, "The Graves of Craving" (11:33–34). The name provides the Israelites (and us) with a potent reminder of the Lord's attitude toward greed and gluttony.

At Hazeroth (11:35), Moses has to endure a more personal kind of attack on his leadership from Miriam and Aaron, his own sister and brother: "Miriam and Aaron spoke against Moses because of the Cushite woman he had married: 'He married a Cushite woman!' They said, 'Has the LORD spoken only through Moses? Has He not spoken through us as well?'" (Num. 12:1–2 NJPS).

Miriam is named before Aaron, suggesting that she is the instigator. Criticism of Moses's marriage is a way to lower him closer to the level of his sister and brother, who have also received the prophetic gift and therefore believe that they should have a greater role in leading Israel than Moses is giving them. This sibling rivalry is about power.

It is surprising that Miriam and Aaron describe Moses's wife as "Cushite," which means "Ethiopian." Some interpreters have speculated that he took a black African wife, whether in place of or in addition to Zipporah. But aside from this verse, there is no clear record of Moses

marrying anyone but Zipporah, a Midianite (Exod. 2:16, 21). Nor is there any indication that she has died. The Midianite relatives of Moses were mentioned recently in Numbers 10, when the Israelites departed from Mount Sinai (Num. 10:29).

Labeling Moses's wife as Cushite appears to reflect a racial slur by Miriam and Aaron rather than state an objective fact. If so, they are belittling Zipporah for the darker color of her Midianite skin by likening her to an Ethiopian (or Nubian). They are choosing to regard Moses's marriage to this non-Israelite (although descended from Abraham; Gen. 25:1–2), whom they view as inferior, as diminishing his leadership.

Moses does not attempt to defend himself against Miriam and Aaron, due to his extreme humility (Num. 12:3—not likely written by Moses to honor himself). He is not confident in himself but is completely confident in and zealous for the Lord, under whom his ego is subsumed. Undoubtedly this was a key to his unique access to God and his unparalleled career as a leader whom the Lord was able to use in order to accomplish his purposes.

God does not deny the prophetic gifts or leadership roles of Aaron and Miriam (cf. Mic. 6:4). Rather, he rebukes them for speaking against Moses, who is more than a prophet, communicating with him face-to-face (12:4–8). Then Miriam is struck with a disease that gives her skin an appearance like snow, whether flaky or white or both (12:10; cf. the commentary on Leviticus 13:1–14:57). Apparently Miriam receives the blow because she is the prime culprit in diminishing Moses's sacred role, a sin of sacrilege (cf. the same divine punishment for sacrilege in 2 Kings 5:27; 2 Chron. 26:19–21). The punishment of skin disease, especially if it makes Miriam an ugly white color, also exquisitely fits the crime of casting contempt on Moses's wife for the dark pigment of her skin.

If a skin disease were inflicted on Aaron, its impurity would disqualify him from priestly service and profane his high-priestly garments

(Lev. 13:1–59; cf. 22:1–9). Nevertheless, he is punished by anguish at seeing the repulsive living death of his sister. He is the appointed ritual mediator for all Israel, but he confesses their sin to Moses and begs for Moses's intercession (12:11–13; cf. Job 42:7–9).

The Lord implicitly agrees to heal Miriam but requires that she remain outside the camp for seven days to bear her shame (12:14–15) and presumably because she is ritually impure (cf. Lev. 13:46; Num. 5:1–4). A person healed of skin disease is permitted to enter the camp (but not his or her tent) after the purification ritual of the first day (Lev. 14:8). So it appears that God delays healing Miriam for a week. In this episode is a major warning for all Israel: If not even Miriam and Aaron can get away with undermining divinely appointed leadership, do not imagine that anyone else can!

13:1–14:45. The next crisis is much more serious and negatively affects the Israelites for decades to come. It comes at a major moment of decision as the national war camp approaches the southern border of Canaan and camps at Kadesh (13:26; Kadesh Barnea in Num. 32:8 and Deut. 1:19). Will the Israelites go ahead and take the land that the Lord has promised to them?

According to Numbers, Moses follows the Lord's command to send a group of scouts or spies, consisting of a leader from each tribe (except Levi), to explore Canaan (13:1–16). Deuteronomy presents the idea of sending scouts to obtain military intelligence as coming from the people and accepted by Moses (1:22–23). The two books do not contradict each other but emphasize different aspects of the same account: The people propose sending scouts and Moses agrees (Deuteronomy); he of course takes the matter to God, who approves and commands Moses to go ahead with the plan (Numbers).

Moses undoubtedly assumes that the report of the scouts, who are credible representatives from the various tribes, will be glowing and will motivate the people to leave the wilderness and enter the promised land. Archaeologists have discovered that during this period (Late Bronze Age), much of the hill country was sparsely settled and lacked extensive fortifications. So the scouts should have found this area vulnerable to conquest.

After a major expedition, the scouts return to the Israelite encampment with impressive samples of fruit and affirm that the land is indeed "flowing with milk and honey" (cf. Exod. 3:8, 17; 13:5). But they quickly move on to describe military obstacles. Rather than pointing out a route of least resistance to gain an initial foothold in the hill country, they summarize the nations living throughout Canaan, including on the Mediterranean coast and along the Jordan Valley. This gives the Israelites the impression that the promised land is impenetrable (13:21–29).

The fact that it is necessary for Caleb, the scout from Judah (cf. 13:6), to quiet the people before offering his minority report shows that their dismayed reaction is already causing an uproar. He emphatically makes the motion that Israel should and can take the land, "for we are well able to overcome it" (13:30 NKJV, NRSV). He has seen the same obstacles as the other scouts, but includes God in "we," believing that the Lord can overcome Israel's enemies and fulfill his promise.

The Israelite spies describe the cities in Canaan as fortified (Num. 13:28), perhaps similar to this Iron Age fort at Arad in Judah.

The other scouts jump in to counter Caleb. Determined to discourage their people, the negative scouts stoop to contradicting themselves and distorting the truth. They now give a bad report of the land they have earlier praised, claiming that it "devours its inhabitants" (13:32 NASB). Whatever they mean by this, it does not make sense that nations living in such a land would flourish (including growing to great stature) and therefore pose a major threat to invaders from outside (13:31–33).

Faithless as they are, the Israelites do not see through the contradictions but accept the faithless majority report. The next day, they are considering replacing Moses and Aaron with a leader who will take them back to Egypt. Joshua and Caleb make a final, passionate appeal, but the people respond by saying they should be stoned (14:1–10). Thus the people condemn themselves and seal their fate.

The Lord wants to exterminate the Israelites and make Moses a great nation instead. Moses intercedes, as he has earlier, after the golden calf episode (14:11–19; cf. Exod. 32:9–13). He appeals to God's need to maintain his reputation in the world by fulfilling his promise to bring his people into their land. Moses also appeals to the Lord's gracious character by citing his self-proclaimed slowness to anger, loving-kindness, and forgiveness (14:18; cf. Exod. 34:6–7).

God agrees to forgive the Israelites as Moses has requested, which means that he withdraws his threat to destroy the entire nation. But it does not mean that rebellious individuals within the nation will go unpunished, in this case adding up to the entire generation of adults that he has brought out of Egypt, except for faithful Caleb and Joshua. He will not kill the people outright and thereby harm his international reputation but will keep them in the wilderness, the home that they have chosen, until they all die natural deaths and their children grow up to replace them. He refuses to reward rebellion by giving a home in the promised land to disloyal people connected with him. To do that would be to send the world a wrong message

about his glorious and holy character (see 14:21) and damage his purpose of blessing all nations through the descendants of Abraham (Gen. 12:3; 22:18).

To make sure the connection between the Israelites' punishment and the scout fiasco will be remembered, the extra time in the wilderness will be forty years, a year for each day that the scouts explored Canaan (14:20–35). The ten faithless scouts, who are especially culpable, immediately die from a plague as "first fruits" of death in the wilderness (14:36–38).

In response to the divine sentence, the Israelites admit their sin and claim readiness to obey God by entering Canaan, which now seems like a better option. But they have already definitively proven their pathological lack of faith, without which God cannot give them the land. Their opportunity has passed. Nevertheless, they presumptuously disregard Moses's warning and vainly attempt to storm Canaan by themselves, without the Lord (14:39–45).

If the Israelites had entered Canaan when it was time to go, they would have enjoyed the advantage that their enemies were terrified because of what the Lord had recently done to the Egyptians (Exodus 7–14), not to mention the Amalekites who attacked them on the way to Mount Sinai (Exod. 17:8–13). Now the Israelites' defeat by other Amalekites, along with Canaanites (14:45), removes the fear that these and other nations had of them. By snatching defeat out of the jaws of victory, the adult Israelites make it harder for their children to take Canaan later on.

C. Laws concerning loyalty versus disloyalty (15:1–41). After the tumultuous narrative events of the previous chapter, the collection of laws in Numbers 15 seems like an anticlimax. The first part of the chapter concerns offerings to the Lord, including expiatory sacrifices (15:1–29). Then the topic shifts to inexpiable sin (15:30–36), and finally a visible reminder of loyalty to God attached to Israelite garments (15:37–41). Looking at the chapter as a whole reveals its relevance between the reports of major rebellions in chapters 14 and 16. The theme is encouragement to loyalty and warning against disloyalty.

The first law specifies accompanying grain and wine offerings for all burnt offerings and sacrifices of herd or flock animals (15:1–16). The Hebrew term rendered "sacrifice" refers to a kind of sacrifice from which an offerer is permitted to eat (especially a well-being offering; Lev. 3:1–17; 7:11–36). The fact that some kinds of animal sacrifices require accompaniments to make them complete meals for the deity (cf. Gen. 18:6–8) is already known to the Israelites (e.g., Exod. 29:40–41; Lev. 23:13, 18; Num. 6:17). However, Numbers 15 systematically specifies amounts of grain and drink offerings corresponding to sacrificial victims of different sizes.

This law regarding sacrifices reminds the Israelites of their basic obligation to serve the Lord. But the fact that Israel continues to enjoy the privilege of worshiping him is due to divine grace. The introduction to the law—"When you come into the land . . ."(15:2 NRSV)—is striking in light of the previous chapter. Whether the legislation was actually given just after the events of chapter 14 or placed here for thematic reasons, it reinforces the promise that the (next generation of) Israelites will indeed live in Canaan. The next law regarding the obligation to offer a loaf of the first batch of dough from the grain harvest (15:17–21) is introduced with the same message (15:18).

The following legislation concerns purification offerings as remedies for inadvertent sins of the entire community (15:22–26) or of an individual (15:27–29). Notice how Numbers 15 roughly follows the order in Leviticus, which prescribes burnt, grain, and well-being offerings in chapters 1–3 and purification offerings in chapter 4.

Numbers 15:27–29 simply reiterates the requirement of a female goat as the purification offering of an individual, adding only the stipulation that the animal be a year old (cf. Lev. 4:27–35). However, 15:22–26 significantly

modifies the sacrifice for the community. In Leviticus 4:13–21, the sin of the community requires only the purification offering of a bull, the same as for the sin of the high priest (Lev. 4:3–12). But in Numbers 15, the community's sin calls for a pair of sacrifices: a burnt-offering bull, with its grain and drink accompaniments, in addition to a male goat as a purification offering. The purification offering would actually be performed first (cf. Lev. 5:7–10; Num. 8:8, 12). This pair serves the function of a purification offering, but the burnt offering greatly augments the quantity of the sacrifice and its expiation in order to benefit the whole community (cf. Num. 8:12, 21—for all Levites).

There are sacrificial remedies for inadvertent sins (15:22–29) but not for a sin committed "with a high hand." In such a case, the perpetrator is condemned to the terminal divine punishment of "cutting off"—that is, denial of an afterlife (15:30–31). This contrast has confused scholars, who have interpreted "high-handed" sin as any deliberate wrongdoing. They are confronted with the contradiction that the Israelite ritual system does provide expiation for some deliberate sins (Lev. 5:1; 6:1–7; cf. Num. 5:5–10).

The problem vanishes when "high-handed" is properly understood as "defiant" (cf. Exod. 14:8; Num. 33:3). Numbers 15 does not deny that nondefiant deliberate sins can be expiated. But it contrasts inadvertent sins, which are always nondefiant and therefore expiable, with defiant sins in order to implicitly warn against the latter, for which there is no remedy. This warning is highly relevant to the surrounding narrative context of the book of Numbers, which features rebellious, defiant sins, both of individuals and of the entire community (chaps. 14, 16).

A brief story of a man caught gathering wood on the Sabbath (15:32–36), which occurs sometime during the Israelite wilderness experience, is placed here for a thematic reason. The story provides an implicit example of defiant sin, even though his action is not labeled "high-handed." The Israelites have been repeatedly prohibited from work on the seventh-day Sabbath (e.g., Exod. 16:29–30; 20:8–11), and the penalty for violation is death and "cutting off" (Exod. 31:12–17; 35:2–3—prohibition against kindling a fire). So the man has no excuse and is clearly rebelling against the Lord's authority. By insisting on working when God has provided rest, he is a microcosm of his faithless generation, which prefers slavery to the Lord's deliverance. There is no doubt that he will die; the only question is the manner of his execution. The Lord provides the answer: stoning by the community outside the camp (in order not to defile it).

The last section in Numbers 15 instructs each of the Israelites to put tassels or fringes, with bluish (or violet) cords attached to them, on the corners of their garments (15:37–41; cf. Luke 8:44—fringe of Jesus's garment). The purpose is to provide them with a tangible reminder to obey the Lord's commandments and be holy rather than literally "scouting" after their hearts and eyes (cf. Num. 13:2, where the same Hebrew verb refers to the scouts exploring Canaan), which are causing the people to commit promiscuity in the figurative sense of disloyalty to God (cf. 14:33). In other words, they should make their decisions according to the word of the Lord, rather than on the basis of their feelings and senses.

In this Egyptian relief of Seti's invasion of Canaan, tassels (such as those described in Num. 15:38–39) can be seen on the garment of a fallen warrior.

Bluish color was associated with royalty because this kind of dye (extracted from certain snails found at the Mediterranean coast) was expensive. It was also used for priestly garments (Exodus 28). So the cords will remind the Israelites that all of them constitute "a kingdom of priests and a holy nation" (Exod. 19:6; cf. 1 Pet. 2:9—priesthood of all Christian believers).

D. Rebellion of Korah and aftermath (16:1–18:32). Numbers 16 is one of the most harrowing and dramatic chapters in the entire Bible. It reports the ill-fated rebellion of Korah and company (16:1–40) and the subsequent uprising of the Israelite community to protest their "martyrdom" (16:41–50).

In the wake of the scouting episode (chaps. 13–14), a large and powerful contingent of leading Israelites blames Moses and Aaron for keeping the Israelites in the wilderness until the adult generation will die. The attack against the Lord's appointed leaders is two-pronged. Korah, a Kohathite Levite closely related to Moses and Aaron (cf. Exod. 6:18; Num. 3:19, 27), leads a group of Levites in challenging the exclusive right of Aaron and sons to the exercise of religious leadership through the priesthood. Dathan, Abiram, and On, from the tribe of Reuben, more specifically target the role of Moses.

The basic argument of the rebels is that Moses and Aaron have wrongly appropriated excessive power over the Israelites, who are all holy (16:3). Indeed, the law regarding tassels at the end of the previous chapter affirms the holiness of each member of God's chosen community. But there, holiness is tied to obedience to God's commands (15:40); it is not unconditional. Moses and Aaron have not seized power; the Lord has appointed them as his servants. So Korah and company are challenging God's leadership.

Moses offers a counterchallenge: if Korah and company want to go ahead and try to be priests, they can show up at the sanctuary the next morning and burn incense along with Aaron. They will find out whether God accepts them or Aaron as holy priests (16:5–11, 16–17). This challenge of a duel with censers is deadly serious. Did the Levites not believe God when he had warned that any nonpriest who usurped priestly prerogatives would be put to death (Num. 3:10, 38)?

The next day, Korah and his colleagues presume to show up at the sanctuary and burn incense. With them comes the whole community, which Korah has persuaded to turn against Moses and Aaron. God is about to instantly destroy the community, but due to the intercession of Moses and Aaron, he only warns that everyone must get away from the dwellings of the chief rebels (16:18–24).

Moses goes to the Reubenite encampment of Dathan and Abiram to pass on the warning to the people there. In response to their sizzling challenge (16:12–14), he proposes another deadly counterchallenge: if God makes the ground swallow them and all that belongs to them, the Israelites will know that they have despised the Lord when they claimed that he had not sent Moses. This immediately happens. Having reached for higher status, they are lowered into the nether region (16:25–34).

Then divine fire consumes the two hundred and fifty unauthorized men who are offering incense (16:35; perhaps including Korah—cf. 16:40), just as it slew two sons of Aaron when they burned incense with unauthorized fire (Lev. 10:1–2). The divine fire has sanctified the censers of the rebels, so they now belong to the sanctuary. The high priest's son puts them to good use by having them hammered out as a plating on the outer altar in order to warn nonpriests not to follow the example of the rebels and share their fate (16:36–40).

The people were already sympathetic to the complaints of Korah and company. So the next day, they accuse Moses and Aaron of killing the Lord's people. Remarkably, they refuse to accept miraculous retribution on Korah and company as coming from God himself. The implication

is that Moses and Aaron are employing some kind of black magic. Thus the people attribute the work of God to an evil force (cf. the unpardonable sin in Matt. 12:24–32).

Again the Lord warns Moses and Aaron to get away so that he can instantly consume the Israelites (16:45; cf. 16:21). But this time he has no fuse left and does not wait for their intercession. Aaron's rapid mediation with incense to make atonement (meaning "propitiation" here) saves most of them, but 14,700 die of a quickly spreading plague before his incense can reach them (16:41–50). The action of Aaron, who literally stands "between the living and the dead" (16:48), demonstrates the value and urgency of intercession, which Christians can do through prayers (e.g., Matt. 5:44; James 5:14–18), which ascend to God like incense (Rev. 5:8; cf. 8:3–4).

To put a final end to challenges against the priesthood of Aaron and his descendants, God tells Moses to set up a positive test with staffs from the tribal leaders and Aaron, which cannot be viewed as black magic (Num. 17:1–7). By the next day, Aaron's staff (cf. Exod. 7:9–10, 12, 19; 8:5, 16–17) has miraculously blossomed and already produced ripe almonds (Exod. 25:33–34, 37:19–20), proving that the holy God, the Creator of life, has chosen him to be priest.

Moses deposits Aaron's rod back in the sanctuary in front of the covenant "Testimony" (NIV 1984; cf. NIV "covenant law"—i.e., the stone tablets of the Ten Commandments; see also Exod. 25:16, 21), as a perpetual sign of the Lord's choice (17:8–11). According to Hebrews 9:4, Aaron's staff was kept inside the ark of the covenant, along with the tablets and a jar containing a sample of manna (cf. Exod. 16:33–34).

The Lord has convinced the Israelites that it is better to die a natural death in the wilderness than to further incur his retributive justice. But now they are terrified that they might all perish like the rebels (cf. 16:34) if any of them approaches the sanctuary (17:12–13). God's answer is to make the priests and other Levites subject to divine wrath if somebody should violate the boundaries and rules protecting the sanctuary's holiness. If a nonpriest, including a Levite, attempts to usurp any priestly function, only that person will be put to death. If the unauthorized individual succeeds in transgressing a priestly prerogative, the priests will also die (18:1–7; cf. vv. 22–23; 1:51; 3:10, 38). This is serious incentive to guard the sanctuary and its priestly service!

God compensates the priests and Levites for their important, hazardous responsibilities and continual vigilance, which would make it hard for those on duty to make a living any other way. Unlike the other tribes, Levi will not inherit a territory in Canaan in order to pursue an agricultural livelihood. Rather, God allots all the tithes (tenth portions; cf. Gen. 14:20; 28:22; Lev. 27:30–32; Neh. 10:38; Mal. 3:8–10) of the Israelites' agricultural produce to the Levites. To the priests he assigns a permanent ("covenant of salt"; 18:19) entitlement from sacred gifts, including portions of sacrifices, plus a tithe of the tithes received by the Levites (18:8–32). Similarly, Christian ministers have the right to material support for spiritual service (Luke 10:7; 1 Cor. 9:13–14).

E. Law of purification from corpse impurity (19:1–22). Leviticus and Numbers have repeatedly mentioned the severe physical ritual impurity of corpse contamination (Lev. 21:1–4, 11; Num. 5:2; 6:6–12; 9:6–12), the possibility of purification from it on the seventh day after defilement (Num. 6:9), and the means of cleansing through sprinkling water of purification (Num. 8:7; cf. v. 21). Numbers 19 explains the nature of the water and specifics of the sprinkling. A comprehensive remedy for corpse contamination comes as a relief after all the deaths that have occurred from chapter 11 onward.

Numbers 19:1–10 outlines the procedure for producing the most powerful active ingredient in the "water of purification," which is the cleansing agent. This ingredient consists of ashes of a reddish cow that is sacrificed as "a purification offering" (19:9 NRSV; against NKJV, NASB, NIV, which mistakenly render purifying or purification "from sin"). Rather

than applying the blood to an altar, the officiating priest sprinkles some of it seven times in the direction of the sanctuary, thereby linking the ritual to God (19:4).

This sacrifice for a physical ritual impurity (not a "sin" in the sense of moral fault) is unusual in several respects: (1) it is performed outside the Israelite camp to avoid polluting the sanctuary, (2) it is completely burned up to produce a long-lasting supply of ashes for the entire nation, and (3) the officiating priest adds several elements to the burning in order to enhance the cleansing properties and volume of the ashes. These elements are cedar wood, hyssop, and red yarn (cf. Lev. 14:4, 6, 49, 51–52; Ps. 51:7). The reddish color of the cow, along with the (at least partly) reddish cedar wood and red yarn, suggests that the ashes are the functional equivalent of dehydrated blood, which is red.

The most unusual feature of the reddish-cow ritual is its effect on those who participate in burning the cow and storing its ashes: they incur minor ritual impurity that requires laundering clothes, bathing in water, and waiting until evening (19:7–10). Similarly, a pure person who later contacts water of purification containing some of the ashes in order to sprinkle them on a corpse-contaminated person or thing also becomes impure (19:21). Paradoxically, the ashes make pure persons impure but cleanse contaminated persons. This has puzzled scholars for many centuries.

Two concepts unlock the mystery. First, water containing the cow's ashes removes corpse contamination by absorbing impurity from the person or thing on which it is sprinkled. This explains why a pure person who touches the water receives impurity from it. Second, the burning cow is viewed as a unit both in time and space. So when tiny parts of it in the form of ashes later absorb impurity, the whole cow becomes impure at the time of its burning. Therefore, those who participate in the burning become secondarily contaminated.

The reddish-cow purification offering uniquely shows how a sacrifice can expiate *future* evils. The offering of the cow yields a store of ashes that will serve the community for an extended period of time, therefore covering ritual impurity that has not yet occurred at the time the cow is burned. Sprinkling water that contains these ashes then conveys on the unclean person the purification brought about by the previous offering. By a similar dynamic, Christians today can benefit from Christ's sacrifice, which bore their mortality and sins many centuries before they were even born.

Numbers 19:11–22 explains (1) how one can know what a corpse has contaminated (including everything and everyone in the same enclosed space), (2) how to formulate the "water of purification" (some reddish-cow ashes plus fresh water), (3) when it must be sprinkled (third and seventh days), and (4) the penalty for automatically defiling the sanctuary by deliberately neglecting to be purified (divine penalty of "cutting off," with no opportunity for forgiveness through expiatory sacrifice). Notice that the fresh (from a flowing source) water mixed with the ashes is literally "living" water (10:17; cf. Gen. 26:19; Lev. 14:5–6; John 4:10–11; 7:38), an appropriate remedy for impurity resulting from death.

F. From failure to victory (20:1–21:35). Following the remedy for corpse impurity (chap. 19), we learn in chapter 20 that Miriam, Aaron, and Moses will share the fate of the adult generation by dying without entering Canaan. Miriam dies when the Israelites arrive (again?) at (the same or another) Kadesh (20:1). The text does not say why she is denied entrance to Canaan, but the last time we have heard from her is in Numbers 12, where she is punished with skin disease for undermining Moses.

Also at Kadesh, the reaction of Moses and Aaron to an uprising of the older generation ("brothers" of Korah and company who left Egypt) against them due to lack of water results in their exclusion from Canaan (20:2–13). God tells Moses to take his rod, but he and Aaron are to call water from a rock by speaking to it (20:8), rather than striking it, as Moses has done

at Rephidim (cf. Exod. 17:1–7). This would have been a greater miracle because speaking could not physically dislodge a plug to an aquifer.

Moses loses patience with the people, calling them "rebels." He fails to glorify God by rhetorically asking, "Must we [Moses and Aaron] bring you water out of this rock?" He fails to follow the divine instruction, instead raising his hand (20:10–11; cf. 15:30–31—defiant sin with a "high hand" [RSV]) and striking the rock twice. Aaron's role is passive: he fails to speak to the rock with Moses.

Water flows from the rock anyway, but because the brothers have not treated God as holy (at Kadesh, which means "holy") by showing trust in him before the community, they cannot lead the Israelites into the promised land (cf. Num. 27:14). As leaders, they have a high level of accountability to properly represent God to their people (cf. Lev. 10:3).

Numbers 20:14–21 records diplomatic correspondence from (the same or another) Kadesh, near the end of the wilderness period, between Moses and the king of the Edomites. These people are descended from Esau and therefore related to the Israelites (cf. Genesis 36). For some reason, the Israelites want to enter Canaan from the east, rather than from the south, as they expected to do decades earlier (Numbers 13–14). To enter from the east, they need to pass through Edom. But Moses's appeal to kinship ties between the two nations is to no avail. Consequently, the Israelites are forced to make a long detour around Edom. During this journey, Aaron dies on Mount Hor (20:22–29). Before Aaron dies, Moses transfers his holy high-priestly garments to Eleazar, Aaron's son, presumably to keep them from becoming impure.

While the Israelites are traveling eastward under the southern part of Canaan, the Canaanite king of Arad attacks them (21:1), just as the Amalekites assaulted them at Rephidim soon after Moses brought water from a rock there (Exodus 17). The Israelites have withdrawn from the Edomites' show of force (20:20) because they are relatives (cf. Deut. 2:4–5). But there is no reason to refrain from retaliating against unprovoked Canaanite aggression. So the Israelites vow to devote (Hebrew root *ḥrm*, of irrevocable dedication to God; cf. Lev. 27:28–29) the towns of this king to the Lord for total destruction, and their holy war is successful with God's help. God does not allow other nations to pick on his chosen people with impunity (cf. the fate of Amalek in Exod. 17:13–16; 1 Sam. 15:1–35).

The Israelites dub the location "Hormah" (from the root *ḥrm*), referring to sacral destruction (21:2–3). Ironically, it was Hormah to which the Amalekites and Canaanites beat back the presumptuous Israelites when they attempted to storm Canaan without God (Num. 14:45). Thus the Israelites gain victory at a place of former defeat.

Victory is soon followed by another failure. The people become impatient during the tedious and taxing extra trip around Edom, complain of lack of food and water, and ungratefully express loathing for the manna. Divine punishment comes in the form of deadly poisonous "fiery serpents" (KJV, RSV), apparently referring to fiery pain from their bites (21:4–6).

Moses intercedes, but rather than simply removing the threat as he has at Taberah (11:2), the Lord makes healing from snakebite conditional on trust in him as expressed by looking at a bronze snake mounted on a pole (21:7–9). This is not magic, as many have supposed (including later Israelites who worshiped the object; 2 Kings 18:4), but a test of faith. All are free to accept or reject the means God has provided and will live or die with the consequences. Why

A bronze serpent found at an ancient shrine in Timna, Israel, similar to the bronze snake made by Moses (Num. 21:9)

a statue of a snake? In this way the people confront the source of their trouble, which they have brought upon themselves.

Jesus likens himself on the cross to the bronze serpent that Moses raised up (John 3:14–18; cf. 12:32). By becoming sin for us, Jesus enables us to become righteous (2 Cor. 5:21; cf. Gen. 3:1–24).

Moving northward, the Israelites cross the Wadi (river valley) Zered (21:12). Deuteronomy 2:14 notes that by this point the last Israelites belonging to the generation of fighting-age men who rebelled thirty-eight years before at Kadesh (Numbers 14) have died. Now the nation can go ahead and enter Canaan.

At Beer (pronounced Be-er), which means "Well," the Israelites celebrate the divine gift of water that they have received by cooperating with God through digging a well (21:16–18— this is a refreshing change from their complaining about lack of water). Again the Israelites gain victory in an area of past failure (cf. 21:3).

Numbers 21:21–35 recounts Israelite conquests of the Transjordanian territories of Sihon, king of the Amorites, and Og, king of Bashan. The Israelites only want to pass through to a point east of Jericho in order to penetrate Canaan from there, but these kings will not let them do so in peace. These military engagements provide the Israelites with valuable experience, plus encouragement that they can take the promised land by cooperating with God.

G. Balaam's failed attempts to curse Israel (22:1–24:25). Undaunted by opposition, the Israelites continue northward through Moabite territory to a location across the Jordan River from Jericho, within striking distance of Canaan. Balak, king of Moab, is understandably alarmed, particularly because Israel has defeated Sihon (22:1–3), who previously defeated Moab (Num. 21:26). He does not know that God has instructed Israel not to disturb the Moabites or Ammonites, who are their relatives descended from Lot (Deut. 2:9, 19). So Balak, allied with Midianites, attempts to hire Balaam to weaken Israel by cursing her so that his army can prevail against this intruder. A curse invoking supernatural intervention was a kind of weapon in the ancient Near East, potentially of mass destruction, which explains why curses were taken so seriously in biblical law (Exod. 21:17; Lev. 20:9; 24:15; Num. 5:18–27).

Balaam enjoyed an international reputation as an effective prophet and diviner. He was from Aram in northern Mesopotamia (northeastern Syria, three to four hundred miles from Moab; Num. 22:5; cf. 23:7; Deut. 23:4) and communicated with the Lord of the Israelites (22:8–12). Perhaps he knew the Lord through their Aramean relatives (cf. Gen. 25:20; 28:5; 31:24; Deut. 26:5).

Balaam initially obeys God, who forbids him to curse the Israelites because they are blessed (22:12–13; cf. Gen. 12:2–3; 22:16–18). God gives him permission to go with Balak's second delegation if the men come to call him. In the morning Balaam goes with them, but God is angry with him for doing so (Num. 22:20–21). This could be because God is testing him by permitting him to have what he wants, but he makes a bad choice (cf. chap. 11 and the provision of meat for Israelites at Kibroth Hattaavah). More likely, however, the messengers set out to return home without calling him and he took off after them anyway, violating the Lord's condition. This would explain why he is accompanied only by his two servants, why he is so upset when his female donkey slows his hot pursuit, and why God is so angry (22:22–33).

This episode involving the donkey is full of irony. The donkey sees what the seer or visionary does not: the angel of the Lord blocking the way as an "adversary" (KJV, RSV; Hebrew *satan*; 22:22–23). When the donkey miraculously speaks, Balaam dialogues with her as if this were a usual occurrence, and she has the better of the argument. Balaam accuses her of treating

him badly and says he would kill her if he had a sword, but she saves his life from the sword of the angel. When the Lord opens Balaam's eyes and he sees the angel, he prostrates himself on the ground, a similar reaction to that of his donkey the third time she saw the angel. Once the distinguished prophet is blinded by profit and sets out to destroy Israel, he is diminished to a level below that of a donkey.

When he meets Balak, Balaam makes it clear to the king that he is bound by what God will put in his mouth (22:38; cf. vv. 20, 35). This is Balaam's escape clause: If he should fail to curse Israel, it is not his fault.

Balak takes Balaam to Bamoth Baal, "The High Places of Baal," where he can see the edge of the Israelite community in order to aim his curses by line of sight (22:41). This is the first of three attempts to have Balaam curse Israel (22:41–23:12; 23:13–26; and 23:27–24:13). On each occasion, Balak takes Balaam to a vista point where he can see the Israelite encampment, Balaam directs Balak to build seven altars there and offer sacrifices to invoke the Lord, and God gives Balaam a blessing on Israel to pronounce in the hearing of Balak. Balak becomes progressively more angry, but Balaam keeps repeating his escape clause.

Balaam's inspired blessings do not say a negative word about the Israelites. To outsiders they are the chosen people whom God cherishes, blesses, and protects from curses. Their problems are strictly "in-house."

Balaam's first blessing is short (23:7–10). Its thrust is that he cannot curse the Israelites, a separate nation of numerous people, because God has not cursed them. His second speech (23:18–24) points out that God will not change his mind to bless Israel, and Balaam cannot undo his blessing. Furthermore, God is with them as their king in the midst of a royal war camp to protect them, including from occult attacks. He has brought them out of Egypt and is their strength in battle. This is a warning not to oppose them.

After two failed attempts, Balaam sees his opportunity to claim Balak's reward slipping away. So the third time he does not go off by himself to seek the Lord, as he has before, but simply gazes toward Israel and intends to pronounce a curse without God's interference (24:1–2; cf. 23:3–5, 15–16). But the Spirit of God comes upon him anyway (cf. Num. 11:26).

Balaam's third blessing (24:3–9) begins by describing him as one who receives divine revelation through the senses of sight and hearing. The words "who falls down, but with eyes uncovered" (24:4 NRSV) likely refer to his experience when he met the "angel of the Lord" (22:31). But they could also ominously allude to his downfall in spite of possessing extraordinary insight from God. His moral fall is already under way, and he is pursuing a perverse course with his eyes open, knowing what he is doing.

Balaam goes on to extol the magnificence of Israel's encampment and to prophesy the greatness of her future king, who will be exalted above Agag, the later king of Amalek (1 Sam. 15:8–9, 20, 32–33). The latter portion of this speech uses vivid imagery to expand on a theme of the second blessing: God is the strength of the Israelites, and they will destroy their enemies. The final words echo God's blessing to Abraham: "Blessed is everyone who blesses you, and cursed is everyone who curses you" (24:9 NRSV; cf. Gen. 12:3).

Three times Balaam has attempted to strike the Israelites. From Balak's perspective, Balaam has struck out and is fired (24:10–11). Before leaving, Balaam gives Balak a bonus cluster of four oracles (24:15–24), bringing the total of his inspired speeches to seven. These four are prophecies of breathtaking scope, predicting fates of various peoples in the future and thereby introducing the biblical genre of oracles against nations (e.g., Amos 1:3–2:3; Isa. 13:1–23:18; Jer. 46:1–51:64; Ezek. 25:1–32:32).

According to the first oracle, an Israelite monarch ("star," "scepter") will conquer Moab and its neighbor, Edom (24:15–19). King David will fulfill this (2 Samuel 8). In the second oracle, Amalek will perish (24:20). Samuel and King Saul will accomplish this (1 Samuel 15). The remaining oracles (24:21–24) are against the Kenites and Ashur (Assyrians or another group?) and mention ships from Cyprus (NASB, RSV "Kittim"; Isa. 23:1, 12; Jer. 2:10; Ezek. 27:6) afflicting Ashur and Eber. These verses present serious interpretive difficulties, but Balaam's point seems to be further emphasis on the contrast between blessed Israel and other nations, which are not similarly blessed.

H. Apostasy with the Baal of Peor (25:1–18). Balaam and Balak have parted ways (Num. 24:25), apparently for good. But Balaam returns to advise Balak (and undoubtedly claim a reward) to defeat the Israelites through another strategy (Num. 31:8, 16), which is recounted in chapter 25. Balaam understands that the Israelites' blessing is conditional on their faithfulness to the Lord. If they can be enticed to worship another deity, the Lord will cease to protect them. To lure the Israelites into such worship, the Moabites deploy time-tested ways to a man's heart: food and sex.

The diabolical plan works like a charm. Moabite women seduce Israelite men and invite them to sacrificial feasts, at which they participate in idolatrous worship of a local god, the Baal of Peor. Thus they commit both physical and spiritual promiscuity. Consequently, God is angry with Israel (25:1–3). He has warned the Israelites of this kind of danger (Exod. 34:15; cf. Rev. 2:14). The stakes are incredibly high. Apostasy of the former generation with the golden calf almost aborted his covenant with Israel (Exodus 32). Now the next generation is derailed just before entering Canaan.

The tribal leaders are especially culpable for leading the way into disloyalty. To root out the evil (cf. Deuteronomy 13) so that the Lord's retributive wrath against the whole nation will subside, the Lord commands that they be executed and their bodies exposed out in the open rather than buried (25:4; cf. 1 Sam. 31:10; 2 Sam. 21:3–14). Similar exposure by suspending an executed person's body from a tree or stake meant that the individual was cursed by God (Deut. 21:22–23; cf. Gal. 3:13). Such shameful treatment would also serve as a deterrent.

Moses issues the execution order and weeps at the sanctuary with the other members of the community (25:5–6). They have several reasons to weep: apostasy, executions, and a divine plague (cf. 25:8). Just then Zimri, the son of a Simeonite chieftain, appears and brazenly brings Kozbi, daughter of a Midianite chieftain, to a tent chamber at the encampment of his relatives (25:6; cf. vv. 8, 14–15). No doubt their intention is sexual.

Phinehas, son of the new high priest, puts a quick end to the openly high-handed offense by dispatching the couple with his spear. God accepts this act of retribution as expiation for Israel, and the plague abruptly ceases (25:7–8; cf. v. 13). This is not substitutionary atonement that benefits the wrongdoers, but expiation in the basic sense of purging them from the community (cf. Lev. 16:10; 2 Sam. 21:3–6).

The Lord rewards the loyal zeal of Phinehas—which saves the Israelites from the Lord's zeal in holding them accountable for an exclusive covenant connection with him—by giving him a covenant promise of a priestly dynasty (25:10–13). Compare the Lord's reward for the Levite executioners at the time of the golden calf apostasy (Exod. 32:25–29; Deut. 10:8).

Before Phinehas's vigorous action stops the virulent plague, 24,000 die (25:9). This is the highest body count from any divine punishment on the Israelites during the wilderness period, even much higher than the 14,700 slain in the aftermath of the revolt by Korah and company (Num. 16:49; but cf. 2 Sam. 24:15—70,000 in the time of David). God holds members of the new generation accountable to learn from the experiences of their parents.

According to Deuteronomy 2:9, the Lord has told the Israelites not to fight the Moabites. But the Midianites, who are allied with Moab (Num. 22:4, 7), are under no such protection. Their complicity (as revealed by the role of Kozbi; 25:18) in triggering the destruction of a large number of Israelites by divine agency is tantamount to a declaration of war. So God

The plains of Moab, where Israel camped before entering the promised land and chose to worship Baal of Peor (Num. 25:1–5)

declares war on them (25:16–18; cf. chap. 31). Of course, the fact that a high-ranking Israelite official kills the daughter of a Midianite chieftain would have made the Midianites even more hostile to Israel.

3. Preparation for Occupation of the Promised Land (26:1–36:13)

A. Organization of the younger generation (26:1–27:23). The remaining chapters of Numbers focus on preparations for the Israelites to enter Canaan, including a census of the new adult generation, instructions for apportionment of territory, and more laws. A fresh census (Numbers 26) is necessary for organization because the generation counted in the earlier census (chaps. 1–3) is now gone. The second census also verifies that only Caleb and Joshua remain of those numbered in the first census (26:64–65).

The census is undertaken after the plague (26:1), which has reduced the Israelites by 24,000. Nevertheless, the total of the military census (not counting Levites) is 601,730 (26:51), only slightly down from the total of 603,550 in the earlier census (Num. 1:46). Some tribes have fared better than others, no doubt largely due to the degrees of their loyalty or disloyalty to God. The size of territories allotted to tribes in Canaan is to be proportional to their populations (26:52–56). This indirectly ties land awards to behavior during the wilderness period.

Numbers 26 includes genealogical review, in order to outline tribal structure, as well as some brief historical notes. One of these notes provides startling new information: when Korah, Dathan, and Abiram and their families perished (26:9–10; cf. 16:27–35), Korah's sons (named in Exod. 6:24) did not die (26:11). No explanation is given, but presumably they separated themselves from the rebellion in some way. So in spite of everything, Korah's line continued and his descendants composed a number of psalms (Psalms 42; 44–49; 84–85; 87–88).

Regarding allocation of tribal land, the daughters of Zelophehad recognize a problem for their family. Their deceased father is survived only by daughters, who are not eligible to inherit part of Canaan. Consequently, he will be posthumously punished by having no part of the promised land to which his name will be attached in order to perpetuate his memory (27:1–4; cf. Ruth 4:1–22). The solution they propose calls for them to inherit their father's possession along with their uncles (27:4). Moses brings their case to the Lord, who rules in their favor and expands this legal precedent to cover related cases in the future (27:5–11; cf. 9:6–14).

Moses knows that he, like Zelophehad, will not enter Canaan because of the debacle at the waters of Meribah, meaning "strife" (Num. 20:12–13). Now God reminds him of this and tells him to ascend a mountain belonging to the Abarim range on the western side of the Moabite plateau, which includes Mount Nebo. From there he will see the promised land and then die, as Aaron has (27:12–14; cf. 20:23–29; Deut. 32:49).

Since Moses's end is near, he petitions God to appoint his successor so there will be a smooth transition of leadership and Israel will not be vulnerable. The Lord designates Joshua, "a man in whom is the Spirit" (27:15–18 NASB, ESV; see NIV note). Joshua has the right experience as Moses's assistant (cf. Exod. 24:13; 33:11; Num. 11:28), Israel's military leader (Exod. 17:8–13), and a faithful scout (Numbers 13–14). But the Spirit is his most essential qualification.

Moses follows God's directions by transferring some of his authority to Joshua so that the Israelites will follow his leadership. The ceremony is simple and clear: Moses lays his hands on Joshua, as a gesture of transfer, and commissions him before the high priest and the community (27:18–23; cf. Acts 6:3–6). Moses shares power with Joshua until he dies not long after this (Deuteronomy 34). Then Joshua is dependent on the high-priestly oracle of the Urim and Thummim for divine guidance (27:21; cf. Exod. 28:30) because he cannot communicate with the Lord face-to-face, as Moses did (Num. 12:8; Deut. 34:10).

B. Calendar of communal sacrifices (28:1–29:40). Following the Baal of Peor episode (chap. 25), chapters 28–29 supplement the liturgical calendar of Leviticus 23 and thereby remind the Israelites of their worship obligations to the Lord (cf. chap. 15). Numbers 28–29 specifies public sacrifices (with grain and drink accompaniments) to be offered for all Israel on particular days of the year. The order is the same as in Leviticus 23, moving from smaller to larger time cycles and progressing through the annual festivals from spring to autumn. Leviticus 23 begins its list of sacred occasions with the weekly seventh-day Sabbath (Lev. 23:3), but Numbers 28 first reiterates Exodus 29:38–42, regarding the foundational sacrifice of the ritual system: the morning and evening regular burnt offering, performed every day of the year (Num. 28:1–8).

All other sacrifices are in addition to the daily burnt offering of two male yearling lambs, which serve as "food" for God (28:2). Other ancient Near Eastern peoples fed their gods twice per day, but the Lord only "enjoyed" his daily food as a token of human faith in the form of smoke; he did not need nourishment from it (cf. Ps. 50:12–13).

The weekly Sabbath is to be honored with two additional lambs (28:9). Changing the bread of the Presence on the Sabbath (Lev. 24:8) also highlights this day. The fact that the Israelite ritual system honors the Sabbath does not make the timeless moral requirement for rest on this weekly birthday of the world (Exod. 20:8–11; cf. Gen. 2:2–3) a ritual law. Nor does enforcement of this rest by the theocratic community (Num. 15:32–36) make it basically a civil law, or its refreshing benefit for humans and animals make it only a health law (Exod. 23:12).

Leviticus 23 omits new moon festivals, but they are included in Numbers 28; additional monthly sacrifices consist of an impressive group of burnt offerings (two bulls, one ram, seven lambs with accompaniments) plus one purification offering (28:10–15). This sets up the basic pattern for additional sacrifices offered during the yearly festivals. Notice the prominence of the sabbatical number seven and its multiples in this list.

Numbers 28–29 concentrates on clusters of calendrical sacrifices that honor God on special days by supplementing the morning and evening burnt offering. It does not give details concerning, or necessarily even mention, unique rituals that were performed on only one day of the year, such as the day of the raised (so-called wave) sheaf (only Lev. 23:9–14) and the Day of Atonement (Leviticus 16; only cursory reference in Num. 29:11).

Sacrifices were an integral part of the biblical Israelite festivals (cf. Exod. 23:15; Deut. 16:16). Because the sacrificial system is no longer functioning, it is impossible for anyone to fulfill an obligation to God by performing rituals on these sacred occasions (cf. Col. 2:16–17—typological "shadows" on festivals, new moons, and sabbaths [not including basic Sabbath rest], chiastically referring to the sections of Numbers 28–29 in reverse). However, adaptations of aspects of the festivals that can be voluntarily carried out in a postsacrificial environment can serve a useful teaching purpose to emphasize remembrance of salvation history.

C. Law of vows (30:1–16). Aside from the communal sacrifices, Israelites can offer individual sacrifices for various reasons, including to fulfill vows (cf. Lev. 7:16; Num. 6:13–21; 15:3). Vows are binding promises to the Lord that cannot be broken (30:2). This is no problem if the person making the vow is independent, including a widow or divorced woman (30:9). However, there could be a problem if an unmarried daughter or a wife makes a vow.

Ownership of family property, including livestock that could be sacrificed, was under the jurisdiction of men in Israelite society. If a daughter or wife binds herself by a vow to make a sacrifice, and if her father or husband forbids her to spend an animal for this purpose, she will be culpable before God. Another problem could arise if a married woman contracts a vow to practice physical self-denial (30:13), which could include sexual abstinence that deprives her husband.

To absolve women from guilt if they are unable to fulfill their vows, and to prevent domestic tensions, God provides a way out in Numbers 30: a father or husband can annul his daughter's or wife's vow when he first hears of it, but not after that, or "he [husband but also implicitly father] shall bear her culpability" (30:15, author's translation). If he does annul it, she will be automatically forgiven (30:5, 8, 12). This is the only instance of such automatic forgiveness in the Israelite religious system.

This legislation shows the high priority that God places on harmony in the home. He is willing to forgo his right to what women vow in order to preserve peace. Notice that God worked with the patriarchal culture as it was rather than engaging in social engineering (cf. Num. 27:1–11, regarding female inheritance).

Numbers 30 does not deal with the problem that a man's vow of physical self-denial could involve sexual abstinence that would deprive his wife. Perhaps males were unlikely to make such vows. But the apostle Paul taught that Christian marriage partners should abstain from sexual relations only temporarily and by mutual agreement (1 Cor. 7:3–5).

D. Punishment of Midianites (31:1–54). The Baal of Peor episode has left Moses with some unfinished business to be accomplished before his death: carrying out retributive justice on the Midianites for their role (31:1–2; cf. 25:17–18). This will be the last military operation before the Israelites enter Canaan, where Joshua alone will be in charge.

Moses's strong hand against these people, even though he is related to another group of Midianites by marriage (Exodus 2), will serve notice that nations who try to destroy the chosen people, even by deception, will surely be held accountable. If this seems harsh, we should remember that there was no United Nations organization in the predatory ancient Near East. People who showed weakness soon ceased independent existence.

The operation commanded by God is a holy war that deploys a symmetrical army of twelve thousand, composed of one thousand soldiers from each of the twelve tribes (31:3–5; cf. Rev. 7:4–8—twelve thousand from each "tribe"; 14:1, 3). The army is accompanied by a priest equipped with sacred utensils and signal trumpets (31:6) to sound blasts that will call the Israelites to remembrance before the Lord so that he will give victory over the enemy that has oppressed them (Num. 10:8–9). Lest there be any doubt as to the connection with the Baal of Peor debacle, the priest is Phinehas. The campaign is an extension of the retribution that he has carried out on Kozbi, the Midianitess (Num. 25:6–8, 14, 18).

The successful holy war results in massive destruction (31:7–18). But it is not mandated as devotion (Hebrew *herem*) to the Lord for total annihilation of everyone and everything (including animals), such as the Israelites carried out on the kingdom of Arad, which had directly attacked them (Num. 21:1–3; cf. later Josh. 6:1–27; 1 Sam. 15:1–35). So the Israelites spare young female virgins, who can be assimilated into the community through marriage (cf. Deut. 21:10–13) or become servants, and they keep livestock and goods.

Initially the army also spares male children and all the (nonvirgin) women, but Moses commands that they be slain. The women are culpable for causing the Israelite apostasy by implementing Balaam's counsel (31:9, 14–18), and the boys presumably could become a threat in the future. Speaking of Balaam, the army has killed him along with the five tribal kings of the Midianite alliance (31:8).

The operation results in a lot of death. So purification from corpse contamination has to be carried out on any Israelites who are involved, as well as captive girls. They cannot enter the camp for a week until this is accomplished (31:19, 24; cf. 5:1–4). Instructions for cleansing objects with fire or water (31:20–23) supplement the earlier directions for sprinkling the water of purification (Num. 19:14–18).

Captured humans and animals are divided equally between the army and the rest of the Israelites (cf. 1 Sam. 30:23–25), with levies from each half going to the priests as a contribution to the Lord (one five-hundredth) and to the Levites (one-fiftieth), respectively (Num. 31:25–47; cf. Gen. 14:20—tithe to priest after battle; Num. 18:25–28—Levites receive nine times as much tithe as priests). Apparently the girls could be used as servants to assist with menial work related to the sanctuary (cf. Josh. 9:27).

The army officers take a head count and find that they have not lost a single man in the war, which is obviously due to divine protection. To ransom the lives of their soldiers for taking this census (see Exod. 30:11–16), without the need for their troops to pay anything, they set aside to the Lord a rich offering of their own share of the plunder: 16,750 shekels of gold (31:48–53; cf. Judg. 8:26). This is deposited in the sanctuary as a reminder of the ransom (31:54). The required ransom for a census was one-half shekel of silver per person (Exod. 30:13), which would have amounted to six thousand silver shekels for the twelve-thousand-man army. But the officers present several times that value, probably implying that their donation additionally expresses voluntary thanks to the Lord.

E. Allotment of land in the Transjordan (32:1–42). The promised land consisted only of Canaan, west of the Jordan River. Apparently the Israelites are planning to abandon the territories east of the Jordan that they have taken from Sihon and Og (Numbers 21). But the Reubenite and Gadite cattlemen see that these lands are an ideal pastureland and ask for them instead of possessions in Canaan (32:1–5). This creates a misunderstanding with Moses, who delivers a blistering oration expressing his assumption that they are rebellious, faithless cowards like the previous generation, seeking to avoid the fight for Canaan and discouraging other Israelites (32:6–15).

The men of Gad and Reuben win Moses's approval by solemnly pledging to serve in the front lines of the combined Israelite army until Canaan is conquered, after which they will return to their families and livestock in the Transjordan (32:16–32). Moses is concerned because they will receive their reward before fulfilling their obligation, thereby compromising their motivation. So he holds them strictly accountable to God (especially in 32:23), who alone can enforce compliance of two entire tribes. Moses officially assigns the Transjordanian territories to the people of Gad and Reuben, and also half of the tribe of Manasseh, who take possession and install infrastructure to safeguard their families and livestock during their extended absence (32:33–42).

F. Itinerary (33:1–49). This itinerary reviews the past by listing noteworthy stages in the long Israelite journey from Egypt (cf. Exodus 12) to the plains of Moab. Some sites in this list are associated with events briefly mentioned here and detailed elsewhere in Exodus and Numbers, but other places appear only here. Many of the locations have been lost and remain unidentified.

Numbers 33 lists only one stop at Kadesh (33:36–37). The Israelites arrived there early in the wilderness period (Num. 13:26) but came to the next place in the fortieth year (33:37–38). They spent a long time at Kadesh (Deut. 1:46) and then traveled through unnamed sites for thirty-eight years (Deut. 2:1–3, 14). It appears that they subsequently came to the same or another Kadesh and moved from there toward the Transjordan (Num. 20:14–22:1; 33:37–49). If so, the history of the bulk of the wilderness period was erased by numbing monotony: a lost trail of tears and unmarked graves.

This itinerary serves several purposes. First, it demonstrates how God led his people and miraculously sustained them in largely uninhabitable wilderness. Second, the length and convolutions of the trip show the consequences of Israelite unfaithfulness. Third, the itinerary summarizes and concludes the wilderness period. The rest of Numbers looks ahead to conditions in the promised land.

G. Instructions for conquest and settlement of Canaan (33:50–36:13). The Lord has promised to drive out the corrupt inhabitants of Canaan before the Israelites (Exod. 23:28; 33:2; 34:11, 24; Lev. 20:23). It is now crucial that the Israelites cooperate with God in completing the expulsion of the Canaanites and destroying all artifacts of their religious culture. Any remnants will cause trouble and result in God treating the Israelites like Canaanites (33:50–56), implying that the Israelites will apostatize as they have with the Baal of Peor (chap. 25). This theme of totally expelling the Canaanites is further developed in Deuteronomy (Deut. 7:1–5, 17–26; 20:16–18) and dominates the history of later failure in the book of Judges.

At the time of the second census, God introduced a fair plan for apportioning conquered Canaan by lot: tribal groups would receive territory in proportion to their population (Num. 26:52–56). Now he reiterates that (33:53–54) and specifies further details necessary for dividing the land among nine and a half tribes (not including those that settled in the Transjordan; 34:13–15; cf. chap. 32): its boundaries, coinciding with those of the Egyptian province of Canaan (34:1–12),

and the tribal chieftains responsible for administering allocation under the supervision of Eleazar the high priest and Joshua (34:16–29; cf. Josh. 14:1–19:51).

The Levite tribe, which makes its basic living from tithes and offerings for service to God, will not receive territories like the other tribes (cf. Num. 18:20, 23–24). However, the other tribes are to give the Levites dwelling places consisting of forty-eight towns surrounded by pastures (35:1–8). An unstated benefit would be unification of the Israelites under God by distributing his special servants among them.

Six of the Levite towns, three on each side of the Jordan, are designated as cities of refuge. Accidental manslayers can flee to these from avengers of blood, kinsmen of those who died, in order to survive and receive fair trials by the community. If the examination of circumstances surrounding a death shows that the defendant did not intentionally cause the death, the defendant will be safe within the city of refuge (but nowhere else) until the death of the current high priest and then will be free to return home. However, a person who commits first-degree murder, as attested by more than one witness, is to be executed, with no ransom permitted for that person's life (35:6, 9–34).

As in chapter 30, God provides a way to carry out his principles within the context of an existing culture. He does not ban the institution of blood vengeance, but ensures justice. He is realistic concerning human feelings and does not attempt to set up a conflict of interest by obliging avengers to protect those who kill their relatives. By requiring manslayers to remain in cities of refuge, God emphasizes the gravity of taking human life. Even accidental killing causes moral pollution of the land, except cities of refuge, until the high priest's death (35:32–34). If Israelite moral pollution of the

The region of Kadesh Barnea, where the Israelites camped on several occasions during their wilderness wanderings (e.g., Num. 33:36–37). It was in this area that Moses struck the rock.

land (also by illicit sexual practices and idolatry) accumulates, the people will be exiled from it (Leviticus 18, 20).

Why would the high priest's death free a manslayer? An animal sacrifice for inadvertent sin (Leviticus 4) could not expiate for inadvertently taking the life of a human being, for which only the life of the killer can suffice (35:33). But instead of execution of the manslayer, God accepts the natural death of the high priest, who can bear culpabilities of his people (cf. Exod. 28:38; Lev. 10:17). According to the New Testament, Christ accomplished substitutionary expiation by bearing all human sin as Priest and unnaturally dying for that sin as sacrificial victim (1 Tim. 2:5–6; Heb. 7:25–27; 9:11–12, 14–15, 26, 28; 10:5–14).

Relevant to the topic of apportioning land (Numbers 34–35, within which legislation regarding Levite cities of refuge is subsumed), Numbers 36 is a postscript to chapter 27, regarding inheritance by the daughters of Zelophehad. Leaders of their clan perceive a potential problem: if these women join another tribe by marriage, they will transfer their landholding to that tribe. The Jubilee return of ancestral land to original inheritors (cf. Leviticus 25) cannot fix the problem because they are the heiresses (36:1–4).

Again the Lord's word through Moses solves the matter within the culture (cf. Numbers 30): these and other daughters who inherit should simply marry within their father's tribe to preserve his property. Zelophehad's daughters comply (36:5–12). This passage demonstrates cooperation with God, social justice and harmony, and formation of new families belonging to the generation that will finally inherit the promised land. It provides an upbeat, forward-looking conclusion to the records of divine instructions included in the book of Numbers (36:13).

Select Bibliography

Ashley, Timothy R. *The Book of Numbers*. New International Commentary on the Old Testament. Grand Rapids: Eerdmans, 1993.

Brown, Raymond. *The Message of Numbers*. The Bible Speaks Today. Downers Grove, IL: InterVarsity, 2002.

Cole, R. Dennis. *Numbers*. New American Commentary. Nashville: Broadman & Holman, 2000.

Gane, Roy E. *Leviticus, Numbers*. NIV Application Commentary. Grand Rapids: Zondervan, 2004.

Milgrom, Jacob. *Numbers*. JPS Torah Commentary. Philadelphia: Jewish Publication Society, 1990.

Olson, Dennis T. *Numbers*. Interpretation. Louisville: Westminster John Knox, 1996.

Wenham, Gordon. *Numbers*. Tyndale Old Testament Commentaries. Downers Grove, IL: InterVarsity, 1981.

Deuteronomy

WALTER C. KAISER JR.

Introduction

For all too many, this book sounds to them like "Duty-onomy." But how could that be, when Deuteronomy has been praised as the heartbeat and the most influential book of the Old Testament? If we add the testimony of Jesus, Paul, and the early church, Deuteronomy may well be the most significant book in the whole canon of Scripture. In fact, there are some 103 allusions or references to Deuteronomy in the Gospel of John alone. While it represents the climax of the five books of Moses, it is also a prophetic book; Moses was among the first and the greatest of Israel's prophets.

Title

The English title for this book comes from the Greek translation of Deuteronomy 17:18, which speaks of the king having "a copy of the law." The Greek Septuagint inaccurately rendered this verse as *deuteronomion*, meaning "second law." However, this book is not a second law but a renewal of the covenant Moses made at Mount Sinai, which site is also called Mount Horeb.

Rather than giving a title for each book, the Hebrew Bible follows the ancient custom of naming a book by its opening line. In Hebrew, Deuteronomy starts with, "these are the words"; therefore it was simply called *Debarim*, "The Words."

Structure

There are at least three different ways this book can be examined: (1) as the three great speeches of Moses, (2) as a text exhibiting the form of the vassal treaties of the great kings of the second millennium BC, or (3) as an expanded exposition on the Decalogue, the Ten Commandments.

Using the repeated rhetorical markers of "These are the words" (1:1), "This is the law" (4:44), and "These are the terms" (29:1), it is possible to detect the three key speeches/sermons of Moses, each with a distinct focus: learning from history (1:1–4:43), explaining the law of God (4:44–28:68), and renewing the covenant (29:1–30:20).

The archaeological discovery of some fifty to sixty extrabiblical treaties of sovereign kings with their vassal kings from around 1400 BC has provided us with echoes of a similar structure for

Vassal treaty between the Hittite king Mursili II and Talmi-sharruma of Aleppo (c. 1300 BC)

Deuteronomy. Especially significant have been the Hittite treaties from the second millennium BC, whose patterns are paralleled section for section in the same order as those in Deuteronomy.

Hittite Treaty	Deuteronomy
A Preamble—The King Who Makes the Treaty	1:1–5
An Historical Prologue—Events Leading Up to the Treaty	1:6–4:49
The Stipulations—Allegiance Required to the Covenant	5:1–26:19
The Blessings and Curses	27:1–28:68
The Witnesses	30:19; 31:19, 26
Arrangements for Succession and Preservation	29:1–31:30

The third structure proposed for Deuteronomy finds the Decalogue governing the central section of this book (see Kaufmann and Braulik). One way of viewing this development is to notice how the commandments are explained in order:

Commandment	Deuteronomy
1	6:1–11:32
2	12:1–13:18
3	14:1–29
4	15:1–16:17
5	16:18–18:22
6	19:1–22:8
7	22:9–23:14
8	23:15–24:7
9	24:8–25:4
10	25:5–26:19

Thus Deuteronomy is the most complete exposition of the Ten Commandments as they are set forth in Exodus 20 and Deuteronomy 5 (apart from their explanation, in part, in the book of the covenant [Exodus 21–23]).

Date and Authorship

Both Jewish and Christian writers have generally affirmed Moses's authorship of the entire Pentateuch over the centuries. For example, Sirach 24:23 assumes this, as do Philo, Josephus, and several New Testament sources (e.g., Matt. 19:8; Mark 12:26; John 7:19, 23; Acts 15:5; 1 Cor. 9:9; Heb. 9:19; 10:28).

Despite this almost universal testimony, there is an alternative view that associates Deuteronomy with the reform conducted by King Josiah in 621 BC. This view appeared as early as the fourth century AD in Athanasius, John Chrysostom, and Jerome. But no systematic treatment of this opinion appeared until AD 1805, when the German scholar Wilhelm de Wette proposed that Deuteronomy was written just before Josiah's time as a law book for the religious reforms he would lead. Later, at the turn of the nineteenth century, Julius Wellhausen put this theory into its classic form, supposing that this book in part, or the whole, was the so-called D document, which became the main plank in the literary and source criticism of the JEDP theory for the origin of the Pentateuch.

More recently, however, some scholars have reinstated Moses as the author of the first five books, called the Torah, because of the work of Kenneth Kitchen and Meredith G. Kline. Instead of the book exhibiting the end product of a series of redactions reaching its final form (Deuteronomy as a whole) in the seventh century BC, the book follows the same structural unity and integrity as the second-millennium (i.e., around 1400 BC) ancient Near Eastern vassal treaties. If the book had been written in the first millennium, as the King Josiah thesis would argue, Deuteronomy would generally lack the historical prologue (1:6–4:49). While one seventh-century-BC treaty with a historical prologue has been found recently, the above argument is still strong when viewed in light of the preponderance of the evidence. Add to this the fact that the prophets exhibit a good number of passages that are reminiscent of Deuteronomy (such as the law on the boundary mark in Deut. 19:14 and Hos. 5:10; the use of a double standard in Deut. 25:13–14 and Amos 8:5; the triennial tithe in Deut. 14:28

and Amos 4:4; and the authority of the priest in Deut. 17:12; 24:6 and Hos. 4:4–5), and it makes a good case for a date around 1400 BC, or thereabouts.

Theological Themes

Some twenty-five times Deuteronomy stresses that the land of Canaan was a gift from Yahweh to Israel. The land is not that nation's own possession by any natural right or effort; it belongs to the Lord. It is theirs only because the Lord has sworn on an oath to give it to the patriarchs: Abraham, Isaac, and Jacob. This concept of the "land" is the fourth most frequent noun in the Old Testament, appearing 2,504 times.

The main purpose for writing this book can be found in the love God continued to pour out on Israel. Over and over again God proclaims: "The LORD did not set his affection on you and choose you because you were more numerous than other peoples, for you were the fewest of all peoples. But it was because the LORD loved you and kept the oath he swore to your ancestors that he brought you out with a mighty hand and redeemed you from the land of slavery, from the power of Pharaoh king of Egypt" (Deut. 7:7–8; cf. 4:37; 14:1–2; 26:18–19).

Some sixteen times in this book, Israel is also called on to "remember" what God has done for them, especially in their redemption from Egypt. But such recollections serve them well for the present and project into the future in the final acts of God in history. The act of remembering is not a purely cognitive one; it also presumes and includes action based on that memory.

Outline

1. Moses's First Sermon: "Look What God Has Done" (1:1–4:43)
   A. Introduction (1:1–5)
   B. His Command to Go into the Land (1:6–8)
   C. Learning from the Sins of the Past (1:9–46)
   D. Warning Not to Fight Brethren (2:1–23)
   E. Witnessing First Fruits of the Coming Campaign (2:24–3:11)
   F. Warning against a Premature Conclusion (3:12–22)
   G. Denying Entrance to a Failed Leader (3:23–29)
   H. Seeking God with All Our Hearts (4:1–43)
2. Moses's Second Sermon: "Applying the Decalogue" (4:44–28:68)
   A. Focusing on the Core of God's Guidance (4:44–5:33)
   B. Loving God with All Our Might (6:1–25)
   C. Defending the Faith (7:1–26)
   D. Remembering Not to Forget All God Has Done (8:1–20)
   E. Resisting Pride and Self-Righteousness (9:1–10:11)
   F. Knowing What the Lord Requires of Us (10:12–22)
   G. Keeping the Faith Vital (11:1–32)
   H. Honoring God in Our Worship (12:1–31)
   I. Extolling the Excellencies of God's Word (12:32–13:18)
   J. Living as People of the Name (14:1–16:17)
   K. Appointing Leaders to Lead (16:18–18:22)
   L. Upholding the Sanctity of Life (19:1–21:23)
   M. Showing Respect for All Forms of Life (22:1–12)
   N. Respecting Marriage and Sexual Relationships (22:13–30)
   O. Portraying a Caring Community of God (23:1–25:19)
   P. Taking Time to Celebrate God's Goodness (26:1–19)
   Q. Renewing the Covenant with Our God (27:1–26)
   R. Distinguishing between the Blessings and Curses (28:1–68)
3. Moses's Third Sermon: "Realizing We Too Were There at Sinai" (29:1–30:20)
   A. Hearing the Things Revealed to Them and Their Children (29:1–29)
   B. Anticipating the Future for Israel (30:1–20)
4. Epilogue (31:1–34:12)

A. Parting Words for the New Leader
(31:1–8)
B. Renewing the Covenant in the Seventh Year (31:9–13)
C. Installing the New Leader (31:14–18)
D. Singing Moses's Swan Song
(31:19–32:47)
E. Preparing to Die (32:48–52)
F. Moses's Final Blessing (33:1–29)
G. Moses's Death (34:1–12)

Commentary

1. Moses's First Sermon: "Look What God Has Done" (1:1–4:43)

A. Introduction (1:1–5). In what will be the style of the prophets of Israel, the book begins with, "These are the words Moses spoke" (1:1; cf. Jer. 1:1; Hos. 1:1). Moses is to "proclaim . . . all that the LORD had commanded," and to "expound [make clear] this law," thus Deuteronomy is "preached law," the torah of God explained with divine authority and clarity, showing its sufficiency for those times and ours (1:3, 5).

Most of the place names cannot be identified, but the location certainly is north of the Dead Sea on the east side of the Jordan River.

Moses's first sermon takes place in "the fortieth year, on the first day of the eleventh month" (1:3). Miriam has died already in the first month (Num. 20:1), and Aaron too died on the first day of the fifth month (Num. 33:38) of that same year, soon to be followed by Moses. Israel will cross over the Jordan without Moses on the tenth day of the first month of the forty-first year (Josh. 4:19). Almost incidentally we are told that it is a mere "eleven days" from Horeb/Sinai to Kadesh Barnea (1:2), but Israel has managed to turn eleven days into almost forty years!

The defeats of Sihon and Og are both a prelude to what God will do across the Jordan and visible evidence that the Lord will continue to fulfill his promises to his people. These two kings were among the Amorites, a people group known as far back as 1900 BC in the Egyptian Execration texts. They were defeated by the Israelites, as also described in Numbers 21:21–35, prior to Israel's crossing the Jordan.

B. His command to go into the land (1:6–8). Moses's story begins at Mount Horeb, which name Deuteronomy prefers for Mount Sinai (except in 33:2). Most scholars locate Horeb in the southern part of the Sinai Peninsula and not

ISRAEL CONQUERS THE TERRITORY OF SIHON AND OG

at Jebel Halal, about twenty-two miles west of Kadesh Barnea. The Lord their God gave the order at Horeb to move out; they had "stayed long enough at [that] mountain" (1:6). Israel was instructed to enter the Amorite territory from the south and go directly into the hill country, then to attack the Jordan Valley ("the Arabah"), next the western low country of the Shephelah, and then the territory in the Negev around Beersheba, and then to head toward Lebanon and as far as the Euphrates River to the northeast (1:7). Right from the beginning of this book, the theme of the land takes a dominant role, as God has promised it to Abraham's descendants in Genesis 15. God was reminding them, and Moses is reminding them now, that all this land has been promised to the patriarchs (1:8), as indeed it has (Gen. 12:7; 15:18–21; 17:8; 26:3; 28:13–14; 35:12).

C. Learning from the sins of the past (1:9–46). Moses goes on: prior to God's supplying the law on Sinai, Moses's father-in-law, Jethro, advised Moses to decentralize the legal process so that he would have assistance from appointed leaders and judges. Otherwise, the burden of this people would be too heavy for him to carry alone (1:9, 12; cf. Exod. 18:13–26). This advice he followed with God's approval.

Now, having left Horeb, as Israel was poised to enter the Amorite territory from the south they proposed that spies first be sent out to reconnoiter the land, which proposal Moses and the Lord approved (Num. 13:1–3). The promise of God was clear: twice over Moses declared on the authority of God that he had given them the hill country and the land (1:20–21). Therefore it was incumbent upon Israel to go up and to possess what had been promised to them rather than to be afraid or discouraged.

The spies returned with the report that the land indeed was good and brought along some fruit ("cluster of grapes," Num. 13:23) from the Valley of Eshkol (1:25). Nevertheless, the people decided to "rebel" (a technical term for breach of covenant terms) against the command of God because of the report by ten of the twelve spies that advised the land was unassailable. Only Joshua and Caleb thought the land could be conquered despite the presence of the Anakim giants (cf. Num. 13:26–33). Caleb and Joshua, unlike the other ten, feared God, not the obstacles (Num. 14:7–9, 24). Fear of the giants and the obstacles robbed the people of the victory that was as sure as God's promise was. The lesson was: rebellion against our God does not pay. They had turned their backs on God and his way.

But, Moses continues, another lesson followed just as quickly (1:27–40): willful unbelief against our God does not pay either. Rather than esteeming the name (Mal. 3:16) and the power of God greater than any force they had uncovered in their espionage, they "grumbled in [their] tents" and announced, "The LORD hates us" (1:27). What a warped view of God's nature and the obstacles or difficulties they faced! In their view, God's love—seen in all his miraculous works on their behalf—was exceeded by the strength and height of the enemy and the walls of the Canaanite cities (1:28).

Worst of all, the Israelites had a warped theology of disbelieving God and a warped sense of safety and security for their children (1:29–33; 37–40). The battle was not theirs but God's. However, no amount of reassurance would replace their adamant belief that the ten spies were correct. In fact, the "little ones," who they worried would be taken captive, would be the only ones who would enter the land (1:39) along with Caleb and Joshua as the sole representatives of that older generation. It was the people's constant griping that also cost Moses his opportunity to finish the job and to lead them into the promised land (1:37; Num. 20:1–13; Ps. 106:32–33). Trouble came to him because of them.

A third and final lesson from this episode, Moses tells the people, is this: arrogant presumption against God does not pay either (1:41–46), for the people of that generation took matters into their own hands when they learned that their disobedience would cost them thirty-nine more years of wandering and denial of their entrance into the promised land (1:41–45).

The principle is that God's people cannot accomplish spiritual things through the energy of the flesh. Without the presence of God, defeat on the battlefield is inevitable—and that is what happened. The beaten people came back and wept before the Lord (1:45).

D. Warning not to fight brethren (2:1–23). In this chapter Moses recounts, for a change, a number of times Israel obeyed. They began by turning away from the promised land and traveling "around the hill country of Seir" (2:1). Then they turned north (2:2). Israel was not to provoke the descendants of Esau to war, for God had already given this hill country to Edom (2:5); instead, Israel was to purchase food and water from them for silver (2:6). God had already so blessed Israel that they "lacked nothing" (2:7 KJV, RSV).

Likewise, Israel was not to harass Moab (2:9), for just as God had dispossessed the Horites (also called Hurrians) of their land and had given it to Edom (2:12), so he had driven the Emites out of the other land he had now given to Moab (2:10). The name Anak was also known in the early Egyptian Execration texts. The Anakim were remembered by the name Rephaim as well, listed earlier as original inhabitants of the promised land, who were defeated by the invader Kedorlaomer (Gen. 14:5).

Israel crossed the brook Zered, the southern boundary of Moab, after thirty-eight years had gone by since they left Kadesh Barnea (2:14)—enough time for an entire generation of

fighting men to have perished. All that time, it should be noticed, the hand of the Lord had been against them (2:15).

Now that that generation had expired, they were forbidden once again to harass the Ammonites, for God had also given these descendants of Lot their territory, replacing the Zamzummites (called Zuzites in Gen. 14:5). Despite the fact that the Zamzummites too were as strong and powerful as the Anakites, the Lord destroyed them to make room for the Ammonites. He is Lord of history—yes, of all nations!

A similar dispossession had occurred in the coastal region of the Gaza Strip, where the Avvites once lived. But the Caphtorites came from Caphtor, which is probably the island of Crete, and destroyed the Avvites (2:23). The Caphtorites were also known as the Philistines, who played such a large role in the land that their name was given by the Romans to the land of Palestine in the second century AD, after the Bar Kokhba rebellion.

E. Witnessing first fruits of the coming campaign (2:24–3:11). The battle for the Transjordan would now begin. Sihon the Amorite, king of Heshbon, was among those who had been under God's watchful eye as he waited for the sin of the Amorites to fill up the cup of iniquity (Gen. 15:16). Their sin had now flowed over the top of that cup; therefore, God would put the Amorites in the power of Israel.

Even though God's judgment was sure, God had Moses send messengers seeking peaceful passage through Sihon's territory. Sihon ruled over the area east of the Jordan and the Dead Sea from the Arnon River in the south to the

Silver coils. To purchase something for silver, as the Israelites were instructed to do in Seir (Deut. 2:6), one would cut off the correct weight from the coil.

Jabbok River in the north. Heshbon may have been his capital, located some fifteen miles east of the northern end of the Dead Sea. Moses's messengers promised to "stay on the main road" (2:27) and to consume only what they purchased, as they had done in Edom and Moab. Sihon, however, firmly refused since, as Moses says, the Lord had "made his spirit stubborn and his heart obstinate in order to give him into your hands" (2:30).

The same battle recorded in Numbers 21:23–26 is lengthened here as the battle of Jahaz (2:32). This site is known in Jeremiah 48:34, Isaiah 15:4, and in lines 18–20 of the archaeological find called the Mesha Stone. The battle was a disaster for Sihon, his army, and their whole country. Sihon is the first to suffer the judgment of "total destruction," referred to in Hebrew as *herem*, as the entire land was put under the ban and "devoted" or "dedicated" to destruction (2:34; the term occurs five other times in Deuteronomy: 3:6 [twice]; 7:2; 13:16; 20:17). This concept of *herem*, except for its single occurrence outside the Bible on the Mesha Stone, is found only in the Bible. As the act of dedicating the cities and peoples of Canaan to God for destruction demonstrated, Canaan belonged exclusively to the Lord. Therefore, what was not killed or burned, such as silver, gold, or iron, was to be placed in the sanctuary of the Lord. This is not the ordinary ethic of the Bible with respect to the treatment of people groups, but an extraordinary one. It was the prerogative of the original Israelite inhabitants of Canaan, thereafter only to be realized in the future in the final destruction of all evil.

In like manner, the Lord gave Og, king of Bashan, into Israel's hands (3:1–11). His territory, far to the north and east of the Sea of Galilee, was known for its plush pastures and remarkable cattle (Amos 4:1; Mic. 7:14). This Rephaite giant, Og, famous for his thirteen-foot-long and six-foot-wide king-sized bed (some commentators incorrectly say it was a basalt sarcophagus), fell before the troops of God as easily as had Sihon (also reported in

Num. 21:32–35). No obstacle proved invincible to Israel.

F. Warning against a premature conclusion (3:12–22). Moses then tells of the distribution of the land in the newly won Transjordanian territory to two and a half tribes (3:12–17; fully described in Num. 32:1–42). Deuteronomy makes no reference to the conflict that arose over this decision. Reuben was given the territory from the Arnon north to the hill country of Gilead, with half of that area (the land previously held by Sihon) given to Gad. Og's territory, which was the other part of Gilead and all of Bashan, was given to the half tribe of Manasseh; the other half of the tribe would need to wait until Joshua made the distribution on the west side of the Jordan, which is recorded in Joshua 17:7–11. One of Manasseh's descendants, Jair, "took" the whole of the Argob up to the borders of two small states of Maakah (around the Jordan just south of Mount Hermon) and Geshur (located east of the Sea of Galilee). The Geshurites and the Maakathites appear never to have been dispossessed of their lands, but seem to have survived as small, partially independent states for centuries (Josh. 13:13; 2 Sam. 3:3; 13:37; 15:8). Jair renamed his territory Havvoth Jair; the word *Havvoth* could come from a Hebrew word meaning "settlements" or the plural for the word meaning "life" (just as German *Leben*, "life," is seen in Eisleben, Germany, for example).

Even though many take the expression "to this day" to mean a later hand added this note, the same expression is used in Moses's reference to the victory over Egypt in the Hebrew text of Deuteronomy 11:4 (not rendered in the NIV) and in Joshua 9:27 about what happened to the Gibeonites. This expression, then, may well mean something like "and so it remained" or it was "irrevocable" (Harman, 51).

While some of the tribes worried that this early distribution would excuse these two and a half tribes from the battle for Canaan on the west side of Jordan, that was a premature conclusion; in 3:18 Moses tells that he directed all able-bodied men in these two and a half tribes to cross over "ahead of the other Israelites" and to stay until the job was done.

Finally, Moses points out that what God has done to Sihon and Og is to serve as a lesson to Joshua that the Lord will do the same to all the kingdoms in the west (3:21). Joshua is not to be afraid: "the LORD your God himself will fight for you" (3:22).

G. Denying entrance to a failed leader (3:23–29). Moses tells how he pleaded with God, whom he addressed as "Sovereign LORD" (in Hebrew the compound name is *yhwh* [Yahweh] in combination with *adonay*, each typically translated as "Lord"; 3:24), a form distinctively used in the Abrahamic and Davidic covenants. Moses appealed, "Let me go over and see the good land beyond the Jordan" (3:25). After all, he argued, God's anger had come on him because the people had made him angry. The incident was when he struck the rock instead of merely *speaking* to the rock (Num. 20:1–13). God seems to have agreed that Moses was indeed provoked by the people in doing this rash act (Ps. 106:32–33), but God determined that Moses had failed publicly in the act of leadership, therefore he would not be allowed to

continue leading God's people. Despite Moses's repeated request for God's overruling his judgment against his role as leader (Deut. 1:27; 3:26; 4:21; cf. 31:2; 32:48–52; 34:4), God would not relent. Moses surely was forgiven, but the consequences of his act as a leader still remained.

H. Seeking God with all our hearts (4:1–43). Chapter 4 is one of the great sermons of the Bible. This sermon finds its focus and heart in verse 29, "But if . . . you seek the LORD your God, you will find him if you seek him with all your heart and with all your soul." Years later the prophet Jeremiah will appeal to this text in his letter to the Hebrew exiles in Babylonia (Jer. 29:13).

Based on the preceding historical review, Moses here transitions to exhorting Israel as he calls them to follow God's instruction. The reason or purpose for observing God's guidance in his laws is "so that you may live" (4:1). Few phrases are repeated more frequently in this book (e.g., 5:33; 6:2; 11:21; 25:15; 30:6), climaxing in 30:15–20 as a call to life as God means it to be lived. This life is found only by belief and trust in the word of God, which is inviolable, with no lessening (subtracting from) or increasing (adding to) that word (4:2). Israel's wisdom and understanding of these laws will be a witness to the nations (4:5–8).

Moreover, the only way anyone is going to be able to find God is by not forgetting these teachings or letting them slip from his or her life (4:9). Even though none of the Israelites see any form of God (4:12, 15), they still hear God speak directly from heaven (4:10). Since God has no form, Israel must not make any image or assumed likeness to him, for this would defame God's majesty (4:16–19). The Living God will brook no rivals, for zeal for

A carving on a fourth-century-AD sarcophagus lid showing Moses striking the rock

his own character would consume all pretenders (4:24).

Heaven and earth are called as witnesses (4:26; cf. 30:19; 32:1; Isa. 1:2; Jer. 2:12; Mic. 6:1–2) against all who worship foreign gods and who have become corrupt (4:25). The threat of scattering the Israelites among the nations and of a pending exile is predicted even before they enter the land (4:27–28; cf. Lev. 26:33; Deut. 28:64–68). But when the distress of those "later days" finally hits, if they will "return" (4:30) both spiritually and physically back to God and come back to the land, God will once again be found by them, for he is a "merciful God" and "he will not abandon or destroy [them] or forget the covenant with [their] ancestors" (4:31). God's character is indeed the foundation of all his promised plans for Israel and all who will later believe.

There is one more reason why all must seek the Lord with all their being: there is no one else like the Lord himself. Three questions (4:32–34) ask whether anyone has ever encountered anything like what Israel has experienced: Has anyone ever heard God speaking out of the fire and lived? Or seen such miraculous signs and wonders? Or seen what God did for Israel in Egypt? It is all impressive evidence of God's "love" and "Presence" (4:37).

The Lord God has no rivals; therefore, all believers must live in accordance with God's law. How else will the other nations come to experience the uniqueness of Yahweh unless they also see the ethical distinctiveness of God's obedient people (4:39–43)? That is why three cities of refuge are set up for those who kill unintentionally to have a place of safety (4:41–43)—Israel's ethic is distinctive.

2. Moses's Second Sermon: "Applying the Decalogue" (4:44–28:68)

A. Focusing on the core of God's guidance (4:44–5:33). **4:44–49.** As in Deuteronomy 1:1 and 29:1, so 4:44 introduces the next sermon with the similar rhetorical expression: "This is the law." It begins with a summary of the story already rehearsed in chapters 1–3, a use

of repetition that is not uncommon in other ancient Near Eastern narrative texts.

5:1–33. Before reiterating the law, originally given at Sinai, here in the plains of Moab, Moses emphasizes the importance of the "ear" as the organ for listening and responding—"Hear, Israel" (5:1). But Moses also gives three important principles prior to giving the Ten Commandments.

First, Moses declares the *continuity* of the covenant: "not with our ancestors . . . but with us" (5:3). This has the force of "not simply with them alone," but also refers to all who later will hear and obey. Therefore, even though the original proclamation of the Decalogue, the ten words, was given to the fathers of this generation, it is nonetheless given to the present generation as much as if they too had been present. Since God is a living God, each succeeding generation is simultaneously addressed and called to the same degree of obedience.

Second, while Moses speaks metaphorically of the Lord addressing the father's generation "face to face" (5:4–5), it is no less a *direct* speaking to later generations as well. This is no impersonal encounter or an abstract duty, but a personal relationship with the Lawgiver himself.

Third, the environment of the law is God's *redemptive grace* (5:6), for he has brought them up out of Egypt. These laws are not given so that persons can gain salvation by works but because God has already redeemed them; they now want to do what he has said. These ten words are the Magna Carta, a covenant of grace, anchored in God's first step toward us: redemption.

Commandment 1 (5:7). We are to have no other gods before the Lord. Therefore, we must have a God (versus atheism); we must have Yahweh as our God (versus idolatry); we must have the Lord alone (versus polytheism); and we must love, fear, and serve this Lord with all our heart and soul (versus ritualism).

Commandment 2 (5:8–10). We are not to make for ourselves an idol in the form of anything anywhere. Hebrew has fourteen words for idols or images, so prevalent was this pagan practice of false worship. Forms of idolatry, however, can be material and external as well as spiritual and internal.

The penalty or sanction for this commandment comes with the magisterial reminder that God is a jealous, zealous God who demands exclusive worship (5:9). His anger is roused by all that opposes the good, right, fair, and just, rather than by envy or a spirit of getting even; it is an emotion roused by evil and sin to take up the cause of righteousness. Often children repeat the sins of the parents going on into the third or fourth generation, but in no way must either the fathers or the children stand responsible for the sins of the other (Deut. 24:16).

Commandment 3 (5:11). The prohibition against using God's name in vain includes more than just the misuse of the name by which God is known. It also refers to his nature (Ps. 20:1), his teaching or doctrine (Ps. 22:22; John 17:6, 26), or his ethical directions (Mic. 4:5). It forbids not only using his name to curse but also all trite or purposeless and frivolous uses of this name.

Commandment 4 (5:12–15). The call to observe the Sabbath is not intended to be a word of bondage but one of liberation and cessation of work, leading to genuine rest. The nature of this command is mixed: it is moral, mandating that God has a right to a portion of our time in worship, service, and rest. But it is also ceremonial in that it spells out the seventh day, the Jewish Sabbath, as that rest day. However, the same law that points to the seventh day also forecasts that the eighth day, on certain feast days, is to be holy to the Lord and a day in which no normal work is to be done (Lev. 23:16, 21, 24, 35, 36, 39). This points to the coming work of Christ and anticipates Sunday worship in honor of the resurrection of Jesus.

Commandment 5 (5:16). The sanctity of the family calls for esteeming and prizing highly parents and all those in authority over us as we defer to them with respect and honor. When this command also enjoins our obedience to parents and those over us, it is qualified as "in the Lord" (Eph. 6:1). Parents, governors,

magistrates, teachers, and pastors are to be shown respect, but nowhere are their wills or wishes to be substituted for the will of God. The promise of long life with this commandment is unique, though all the commandments have the promise of life standing over them (Deut. 4:1; 8:1; 16:20; 30:15–16).

Commandment 6 (5:17). The sanctity of life is affirmed with the use of one of seven Hebrew words that refer exclusively to taking life by malice and forethought or premeditation. This prohibition does not include accidental homicide, self-defense, just war, or the like, for which other Hebrew words are used. So sacred is life that no "substitute/ransom" can be accepted for premeditated murder (Num. 35:31), whereas other capital crimes presumably could be atoned for with substitutes.

Commandment 7 (5:18). The sanctity of marriage carries out the case made for monogamous relationships in Genesis 2:23–24. Adultery is not just the violation of a pledge made to another person, but it also violates the covenant made with God (Prov. 2:17; Mal. 2:14). It is a sin against God as well as against one's partner (Gen. 29:9).

Commandment 8 (5:19). The sanctity of property calls for a recognition that God owns everything (Ps. 24:1; 115:16). Therefore, stealing is an act of putting possessions ahead of God when goods and wealth are voluntarily to be shared with all.

Commandment 9 (5:20). The sanctity of truth is based on the fact that flouting the truth is an act of despising God, whose very being and nature is truth. Lying is always wrong, for God commands truth-telling (Ps. 27:12; 35:11; Prov. 6:19; 14:15).

Commandment 10 (5:21). The sanctity of motive includes all thoughts, desires, and inner instincts that lead to the above nine actions. This command seeks a state of contentment for God's men and women, for "godliness with contentment is great gain" (1 Tim. 6:6).

God announced these commandments, Moses says, in a "loud voice" (5:22) as the mountain was ablaze (5:23). Instead of continuing to hear God's voice directly, the people urged Moses to go up to God on their behalf and tell them what God had said (5:26). However, all that God would say, they promised, "We will listen [to it] and [we will] obey" (5:27). This pleased God: "Everything they said was good" (5:28). The Lord just wished that this would always be true of them.

B. Loving God with all our might (6:1–25). Here begins the detailed explanation of the commandments, as some of their implications are spelled out more fully. This instruction will be given so that all may "fear the LORD" (6:2). Few expressions in the Old Testament embrace more what it is to listen, love, and serve God than to "fear God."

These verses do not suggest any type of entitlement, as if the promise is that if we always fear and obey God we will always receive anything we want. We do not trade in spiritual capital for material prosperity in some kind of name-it-and-claim-it economy. Instead, it is our privilege to honor so great a Lord.

The famous Shema passage of verse 4 (in Hebrew, *shema*, "hear," is the first word in the verse) is one that is on the lips of orthodox Jews morning and night, and one they wish to be on their lips when they die. To this verse, Jewish practice dictates that they also add Deuteronomy 15:13–21 and Numbers 15:37–41. Twice over, the covenantal name Yahweh appears in this verse. But the emphasis is on the Hebrew *ehad*, meaning "one" (if it is an adjective) or "alone" (if it is an adverb). Either way, the point is that our God is

unique, with no rivals. To worship other gods is to chase after nothingness.

Since God is the one and only God, verse 5 commands us to "love" him (one of fourteen times in Deuteronomy). We are to love him with "all [our] heart," which in this case refers to our mind and intellect (Jer. 5:21; Hos. 7:11), and with "all [our] soul," which refers to our total being, life, and vitality.

Parents in Israel are to make sure that conversation about such things is a daily part of their children's lives. There is to be no excuse for neglecting their children's spiritual welfare. As families eat together, they are to talk around the table about the Lord. Later on many Jewish families will take verses 8–9 literally, making small boxes with these verses inside strapped to their foreheads, called phylacteries (see photo), and attaching similar boxes to their doorposts, called mezuzas. However, these words are meant to be taken metaphorically, for they echo similar words in Exodus 13:9, 16 regarding the consecration of the firstborn. Moreover, Moses directs that these words are to be "on your hearts" (6:6) and that much more is meant by "these commandments" than merely the words of verses 4–9—it encompasses all the commandments.

But with the blessing of God to come as they enter the land of Canaan and receive his gracious gifts, they must "be careful that [they] do not forget the LORD" (6:12). Forgetting what God has done would seriously impoverish Israel's spirituality, for pride takes over as they begin to think that it all happened by their own strength.

Fearing God is one of the best ways to express our love and devotion to him (6:13). Moses contrasts *slavery* in Egypt (6:21) to *service* to God (6:13). Israel's deliverance from bondage is to set her free to confess and serve a wonderful Lord. Idolatry, which is a form of covetousness, must be avoided,

A modern-day phylactery

for God is a jealous God (see commentary on 5:9). Rejected are all forms of worthless service, which include hedonism (the god of enjoyment), social approval (the god of how I am regarded), overweaning ambition (the god of what I must achieve), and materialism (the god of all that I can get).

Since the Israelites have received all these demonstrations of the Lord's favor and power, they must not force the Lord for still more miracles (6:16). They did that at Massah (Exod. 17:7; Deut. 9:22), but their faith must be as simple as the child's question (reminiscent of Exod. 13:14) of verse 20, "What is the meaning of the stipulations, decrees and laws?" The answer is always to tell the story all over again of God's mighty acts in the exodus. Because of God's grace, obedience is as natural as for any grateful person who has been snatched from death's door. God is to be confessed and honored before all mortals, without casualness, overfamiliarity, or triteness. Recalling God's fulfilled promises is a mandatory feature of being part of the family of God, for if we forget, we will experience the consequences and certainly come to grief.

C. Defending the faith (7:1–26). Destroying the Canaanites will really be the work of the Lord, for he will "drive [them] out" (7:1). The same Hebrew verb is also used for "loosening" or "taking off" a sandal (Exod. 3:5; Josh. 5:15); thus the Lord will free Israel from these seven nations just as one loosens a sandal from the foot. Elsewhere Canaan is listed as having eleven nations (Gen. 10:15–18), or ten (Gen. 15:19–21), six (Exod. 3:8; 33:2), or three (Exod. 23:28).

Israel is to "destroy them totally" (Hebrew *haram*, a verb meaning "to devote to the ban" or "to dedicate to destruction"). All the spoil belongs to the Lord and is banned from any human use. This principle is best illustrated in the Achan story (Josh. 7:1–26). This type of dedication is an involuntary dedication (the opposite of Rom. 12:1–2, which is a voluntary offering of ourselves up to God).

Since the territory will not all be available immediately (7:22), Israel is to beware of intermarriage (7:3), the foreign cult apparatuses of sacred stones (7:5), the fertility pole of Asherah (7:5), and foreign altars. This whole chapter is very similar to Exodus 23:20–33.

Israel is called to be a "holy people," a "treasured possession" (7:6; the Hebrew term for "treasured possession" means a moveable asset, like jewels; cf. Exod. 19:5; Deut. 14:2; 26:18; Mal. 3:17).

Though Israel is the smallest of all peoples, the only explanation for God's choice of them is that he "loved" them (7:7–8)—an unmerited love. In verse 8 a new term appears, "redeemed you," which in Hebrew means "set you free" or, as used in the sacrifices, refers to "a ransom that delivers by the use of a substitute." Two other important terms show up in verse 9: "know," a technical expression of the covenant, like "choose" (cf. Amos 3:2), and "covenant of love," which has the word "covenant" standing alongside of Hebrew *hesed*, "faithful love" (appearing 248 times in the Old Testament), one of the most beautiful terms, and equated very closely to "grace."

Over against those enjoying God's faithful love are those who "hate him" (7:10), as shown by their disobedience and rejection of God's word. It is either "love God" or "hate him"; there are no middle alternatives.

For those who love the Lord, there are innumerable blessings (7:12–15), but Israel must destroy those the Lord gives over to them (7:16–26). God will send "hornets" (7:20) among their enemies, which some interpret metaphorically as leprosy, but which others more convincingly link to the invasion of the Egyptians over the years prior to Israel's conquest of the land, since Egyptian pharaohs had a type of hornet in their insignia. Another divine promise is a panic sent by God on these enemies (7:23). No one will be able to stand against Israel, for they will be standing against God himself!

D. Remembering not to forget all God has done (8:1–20). This chapter is bracketed in verses 2 and 18 by "remember," thus reminding the people of the danger of letting slip from memory all God has done for them. In Hebrew, "to remember" is not purely cognitive but also implies an action resulting from our calling it to mind. As the Lord "remembered" Hannah, she became pregnant (1 Sam. 1:19). As the great Puritan preacher Stephen Charnock advised, "Oh if we did remember [God's] former goodness, we should not be so ready to doubt of his future care" (Charnock, 1:114).

Verse 3 contrasts self-dependence with dependence on God and his word. That is why God fed the Israelites with manna in the wilderness, "to teach [them] that man does not live on bread alone, but on every word that comes from the mouth of the LORD" (used by Jesus in his temptation by the devil in Matt. 4:4). The use or nonuse of God's word will gauge the attitude and direction of the people. Even the hard experiences (8:5) are meant to be educational, just as a father's discipline of his own son.

The vivid portrayal of the land with all its richness (8:7–9) is repeated in very similar terms in the Egyptian story of Sinuhe from 1800 BC. But this extravagance is accompanied with a warning that they must "be careful . . . not [to] forget" the Lord or all that he has commanded them. Forgetting the Lord and disobeying his commandments seem to be tied together in practice (8:10–14), for both lead to disaster. The gifts must not replace the Giver, for often widespread prosperity leads to gross ingratitude.

The desert experience (8:15–16) was most unpleasant when Israel encountered venomous snakes (Num. 21:4–9) and lack of water (Num. 20:1–13). But even there God provided food (Exod. 17:1–7) and water (Num. 20:13). Nevertheless, God "confirms his covenant" (8:18), which is a reaffirmation of his long-standing promise. But if forgetfulness prevails, then that generation too will be destroyed (8:19–20; cf. Mal. 4:6).

E. Resisting pride and self-righteousness (9:1–10:11). The victory Israel is about to achieve will be the Lord's doing, not Israel's.

It will be an expression of God's grace and not of this nation's prowess. Once again Israel is summoned to listen (9:1), as in Deuteronomy 6:4–9. They will face the giants (Anakim), of whom they were previously terrified (Deut. 1:28), but the emphatic thrice-repeated "he" in the Hebrew of verse 3 reminds them of the initial words of the Ten Commandments, "I am the LORD your God":

> "He [is the one] who goes over before you
> as a consuming fire" (ESV; cf. 4:24);
>
> "He will destroy them";
>
> "He will subdue them before you."

But God's intervention on their behalf is not to be credited to their "righteousness" or their "integrity" (9:5–6), for they are a stiff-necked people (9:6). Moses easily illustrates the evidence for Israel's disobedience and stubbornness (9:7–29): at Sinai with the golden calf (9:8–21; cf. Exod. 32:1–34:35), at Massah (9:22; cf. Exod. 17:1–7), at Taberah (Num. 11:1–3), at Kibroth Hattaavah (Num. 11:31–34), and at Kadesh Barnea (9:23; Num. 13:1–14:45). So far was Israel from God that he told Moses they were "your people" (9:12)—God was ready to "blot out their name" (9:14) and make a new nation out of Moses. But the God who had prepared Moses to also intercede on their behalf was the same God who was merciful and gracious to all who would turn and repent. Moses, however, "lay prostrate before the LORD" for "forty days and forty nights because the LORD had said he would destroy [them]" (9:25). Moses also prayed for Aaron (9:20)—even the high priest needed forgiveness.

Moses tells the people that he made three requests of God (9:26–27): (1) that God would not destroy his inheritance; (2) that God would remember his ancient promise to the patriarchs: Abraham, Isaac, and Jacob; and (3) that God would overlook Israel's stubbornness and sin.

So God told Moses that new tablets were to be chiseled out of stone (10:1), and Moses was to come back up the mountain once again as God personally rewrote the same words that were on the first set of tablets that Moses had smashed in disgust at the people's sin. Unlike other commands, which God gave through the mediation of Moses, these came directly from the Lord, hence their importance and significance. These stone tablets were to be put into a "chest" or "ark" (10:2–3).

This probably was not the same permanent receptacle made by Bezalel (Exod. 37:1) but was a temporary box.

Verses 6–9 seem intrusive, but the end of verse 5 leads naturally into the Levites, who are charged with the moving and keeping of the ark (10:8–9). The Levites' work, Moses says, is threefold: (1) they are responsible for carrying the ark of God; (2) they are to stand and minister before the Lord; and (3) they are to pronounce blessings in the name of the Lord, meaning they are to bring the people into a relationship with the Lord by proclaiming his salvation and by instructing the people in the law (33:10; Mal. 2:4–5). As a consequence (10:9), the Lord is the Levites' inheritance even though they did not receive one among their fellow Israelites.

The outcome of Moses's prayers and fasting is noted in verses 10–11. The Lord again shows mercy to the people and restates his promise.

A tablet containing the legal sayings of Lipit-Ishtar (Mesopotamia, ca. 1930 BC). This collection is concerned with issues of justice, similar to those in Deuteronomy 10:17–18.

F. Knowing what the Lord requires of us (10:12–22). Moses's style changes in 10:12, as marked by the words, "And now." The interrogative "What does the LORD your God ask of you" is echoed in Micah 6:8. Moses gives five answers to this rhetorical question: (1) "to fear the LORD," (2) "to walk in obedience to him," (3) "to love him," (4) "to serve the LORD your God with all your heart and with all your soul," and (5) "to observe the LORD's commands and decrees . . . for your own good" (10:12–13). But this is no call to formalism, for the people must spiritually "circumcise [their] hearts" (10:16), a concept repeated in Deuteronomy 30:6; Jeremiah 4:4; 9:26; Ezekiel 44:7, 9; in Paul's call for obedience from the heart (Rom. 2:28–29); and in Stephen's speech (Acts 7:51).

This leads into a description of the incomparability of God, emphasized by three adjectives: "great . . . , mighty and awesome" (10:17). Furthermore, this awesome God "shows no partiality," "accepts no bribes," "defends the cause of the fatherless and the widow," and "loves the foreigner," "giving [the foreigner] food and clothing" (10:17–18). No wonder, then, that "he is [our] praise" (10:21 KJV, RSV).

G. Keeping the faith vital (11:1–32). Chapter 11 brings to a close the section that began with the Ten Commandments in chapter 5 and its exposition of the central principle of the ten words before he gives the exposition of these commandments in chapters 12–26. The fundamental commandment is to "Love the LORD your God" (11:1), with "commandment" appearing in the singular form (cf. Deut. 6:5). They are to keep his "charge" or "requirements," this word used uniquely here in Deuteronomy.

Even though those in the new generation are not the eyewitnesses of God's mighty acts in the past or of his "discipline" (the Hebrew term has not just the idea of punishment, but his "chastening instruction"), nevertheless many others did witness the exodus (11:4) and the revolt of Dathan, Abiram, and the sons of Eliab (11:6; cf. Num. 16:1–50). No mention is made of Korah's role in this revolt; he died in it, but his children did not (Num. 26:9–11; cf. Ps. 106:17–18, which mentions only Dathan and Abiram).

For the second time in this chapter the Israelites are called to "observe therefore all the commands" (in Hebrew, "commandment" is singular here, indicating the wholeness of the law) God is giving to them (11:8), setting the stage for future life in the land (11:8–17). For example, whereas Egypt was a land with scarce rainfall, necessitating hard work in the irrigation of the land by foot pedals to lift the water, Canaan is a land that "drinks rain from heaven" (11:11). Thus, there is theology in

meteorology, as faithfulness to God is correlated with the amount of water in the rain gauges (11:13–15; cf. Lev. 26:3–4).

Israel must be careful not to be enticed into thinking that Baal—the Canaanite god of rain, fertility, and agricultural fecundity—is responsible for the fertility of Canaan. While we are not taught that prosperity always proves obedience to God, neither can we prove that suffering necessarily implies personal guilt. Nevertheless, God does remain in control of even the climate, fertility, and all that affects human life (11:16–17).

Verses 18–32 conclude this section of chapters 5–11 and draw the major themes of this section together. Moses's teaching is to be impressed on their hearts and souls, which calls for a total commitment, as noted in the great Shema ("*Hear*, O Israel") of chapter 6. The promise of military success is given once again (11:22–25), repeating Deuteronomy 7:12–24.

This leaves Israel with a present and future choice: "a blessing and a curse." There are no bases for any apathy or mediating alternatives (11:26–28). Moses arranges that when they enter Canaan, a symbolic ceremony is to take place on either side of Shechem, on Mount Gerizim and Mount Ebal. A fuller description of this ceremony appears in Deuteronomy 27:1–26, while its actual occurrence takes place in Joshua 8:30–35. The blessings are to be recited (apparently antiphonally) on Mount Gerizim (the mountain to the south) and the curses from the other half of the congregation on Mount Ebal (to the north). This ceremony is to be conducted at the heart of the foreign religious territory as the true word of God will come into conflict with Canaanite pagan falsehood.

H. Honoring God in our worship (12:1–31). In the middle of Moses's second speech (which began at 5:1), a fresh heading in 12:1 begins the central section of the book (12:12–26), which elaborates on commandments 2–10. This, then, is the "preached law," where

Figurine of El, head of the Canaanite gods, which the Israelites were warned not to worship (Deut. 11:16)

Moses applies the law he gave forty years earlier. However, this division must not be made too sharply, for all the laws in 12:12–26 are given in response to the principles laid down in 12:1–5.

Chapter 12 calls for honoring God exclusively in our worship, which fills out what is meant by the second commandment and its prohibition "no other gods." The warning in 12:4 (cf. 12:30–31), "You must not worship the LORD your God *in* [*your own*] *way*" (emphasis mine), repeats the concern of Leviticus 18:3, "You must not do as they do." Canaanite religion included both male and female prostitution, which the Lord "hates" (12:31) and finds "detestable" (Deut. 18:9). Canaanite worship is completely unacceptable (12:1–4).

Israel is to gather together at the *place* of worship God will describe. No specific case is made for "Jerusalem" at this point, as many scholars incorrectly infer. At this place of worship seven distinct offerings are to be brought (12:6): (1) burnt offerings, (2) sacrifices, (3) tithes, (4) heave offerings (literally, what is lifted up in your hand), (5) vowed offerings, (6) freewill offerings, and (7) firstlings. All syncretistic types of worship or joint services with the pagans are off-limits to the people of God.

Even before they enter Canaan some are already worshiping as they see fit (12:8). The choice of a central place to worship is in God's hands, not theirs (12:11).

Whereas verses 1–12 use the second person plural, verses 13–28 use the second person singular, personalizing the instructions in anticipation of an eventual centralized worship center. In the new land where they are going, some of the people will now be scattered as far as away two or three days' journey from the sanctuary. Therefore, when they prepare meat for eating, it will not be necessary to bring the animals to the central sanctuary. However, care must be taken not to eat the blood, for it represents life (12:16, 23; Lev. 17:11). Verses 30–31 warn of certain religious traps: idle inquiry about other gods and the drive not to stand out among others as strange. The danger

is that, if they are too curious or want to fit in, God's people will imitate what they see other people doing and therefore will do things that displease God.

I. Extolling the excellencies of God's word (12:32–13:18). The word God gives to Moses is not to be added to or have anything taken away from it (12:32; cf. Rev. 22:18–19). God will confirm his true prophets with accompanying "miraculous signs or wonders" (13:1 NIV 1984). The message of these prophets must also be in accord with what God has previously revealed (13:2–5). In the last days false prophets will come who can produce miraculous signs, but their teaching will not be in harmony with what God has previously taught (Matt. 24:23–24; Gal. 1:7–8; 2 Thess. 2:8–9; 1 John 4:1).

God's word is more to be preferred than human relationships (13:6–11), for our commitment to the Lord comes before loyalty to our families. Even the tenderest of human ties must not keep us from avoiding all perversions of the word of God (cf. Jesus on loving father or mother *more than* him; Matt. 10:37). False teaching about Scripture is to theology what cancer is to the body; it must be "cut out."

Israel must never automatically assume that rumors about people violating God's word are true; they must (1) "inquire," (2) "probe," and (3) "investigate it thoroughly" (13:14). If the rumor of error is confirmed, those "troublemakers" (Hebrew "sons of Belial" = "worthless, good-for-nothing dudes") must be "put under the ban" (Hebrew *haram*; cf. 4:24). Likewise, believers are called to act just as decisively in 2 John 7–11. But if there is obedience to God's commands, then he will show mercy and compassion (13:17).

J. Living as people of the name (14:1–16:17). **14:1–29.** Chapter 14 is an exposition on the third commandment. It involves matters not only of speech but of living as well. If Israel is God's "firstborn," his "son" (Exod. 4:22–23), then they are called to bear the image and character of the living God in their persons and in their lifestyles (Exod. 19:6; see Harman, 155–63).

For example, in the face of death, they are not to lacerate or mutilate their bodies, as if that would keep them in contact with the dead, or to cut off locks of their hair (14:1–2; v. 2 is a verbal repetition of 7:6). Ugaritic tablets from Ras Shamra, Syria, suggest such practices were part of the cult of the dead and fertility rituals.

The creatures listed in verses 4–21 are categorized as they are in Leviticus 11:1–23—in the order of their primary habitat, just as they appear in the creation account: land (14:4–8), water (14:9–10), and air (14:11–20). The basis for dividing these creatures up into clean and unclean is not immediately apparent, but it may involve hygienic reasons, avoidance of heathen religions, and the fact that those who ate unclean flesh were producers of death. Surely the use of the word "detestable" (14:3) or "abominable" is linked with offensive Canaanite practices not tolerated by God (Deut. 7:25–26; 12:31; 13:14).

Eating the bodies of creatures already dead is also prohibited (14:21), but the reason is not hygienic, for they can be given to a foreigner to eat; the distinction is in the fact that Israel is to be holy to the Lord, which calls for a separation in their actions.

Cooking a kid in its mother's milk is likewise forbidden (14:21; cf. Exod. 23:19; 34:26) because it seems that it replicated the pagan practices seen in a broken Ras Shamra text, which says, "cook the kid in milk, the lamb in butter." This law, however, has nothing to do with keeping meat and milk products and dishes separate.

Finally, the third commandment also involves the matter of tithing (14:14–29), as mentioned earlier (Deut. 12:6, 11, 17). The tithe expresses the joy the tither feels in acknowledging that God has provided all he or she has. It includes one-tenth of all the Israelites' produce (cf. Gen. 28:22) and the "firstborn" of their herds (14:23). The tithe is also another way to deny that any Canaanite fertility rites or practices have brought this increase. It is another way of refusing to take God's name and work in vain.

A triennial tithe is to be collected for the care of the Levites, foreigners, fatherless, and widows who live in their towns (14:28–29). Failure to offer any of the tithes both dishonors God and robs him of what is due him (Mal. 3:6–12).

15:1–16:17. Deuteronomy 15:1 transitions to an exposition of the fourth commandment, with its concern for the Sabbath and the use of time. In this connection, two topics are raised: cancellation of debts (15:1–11) and the release of slaves (15:12–18).

Every seventh year there is to be a release (Hebrew *shemittah*, from the root meaning "to let fall"); as in Exodus 23:11, the land is to be left fallow, but here the debts also are to be remitted. This year of release is part of the symbolism of the Jubilee year, wherein personal freedom is restored and alienated property is recovered. The only exception is the foreigner's debt: it remains (15:3).

Despite the ideal that "there need be no poor people among you" (15:4), the existence of the poor (15:7, 11) shows there is an incomplete obedience to God's rule or remission of debts. Jesus's words at his anointing in Bethany (Matt. 26:11; Mark 14:7) are probably taken from Deuteronomy 15:11.

The seventh year is also a year of emancipation of indentured Hebrew slaves (15:12–18). Israelites could indenture themselves for a maximum of six years (their land could not be used as collateral on debts since God owned the land). Since the whole nation has once been slaves in Egypt, but were redeemed by the Lord, they too must act accordingly (15:15). Some versions, such as the KJV and NIV, translate in verse 18 "double" or "twice," but here (and in Jer. 16:18) the Hebrew word means "an equivalent," since the slave has saved the master six years of wages.

The topic of the firstborn, which was raised in 14:23, is now reasserted, as it concerns bringing them to the central sanctuary as offerings (15:19–23). As is the practice in Deuteronomy, the principle is first stated in the opening verse (15:19)—all of life belongs to God as the Giver and Source of life. However, the animal must be without defect.

The first of the feasts is Passover (16:1–8), which is to take place in the month of Aviv (our late March–early April). The name Passover probably comes from the verb "to pass over," as when God had the death angel "leap/pass over" the houses of the Israelites in Egypt just before the tenth plague of the death of the firstborn in Egypt (Exod. 12:29–31). It is also the time of the barley harvest and the seven additional days of eating unleavened bread (16:3), since they needed to leave Egypt in "haste" (the Hebrew term, meaning to move in a hurry along with fear and trepidation, is used only in Exod. 12:11, here, and in Isa. 52:12).

This sacrifice is to begin at the "place" (16:2, 6, 7) that God will choose for his name to dwell, thus replacing the sites of Exodus 12:3. It is to be eaten with unleavened bread (symbolizing haste) and "the bread of affliction" (16:3; to remind them of their hard labor in Egypt).

On the day following the seven weeks after Passover comes the Feast of Weeks (16:9–12)—hence "the Fiftieth [Day]" (based on the Greek Septuagint of Lev. 23:16) or "Pentecost" (cf. Acts 2; it is also known as the Feast of the Harvest [Exod. 23:16] or the Feast of Firstfruits [Num. 28:26])—which arrives sometime in our May or early June, during the wheat harvest. All are to give voluntarily and proportionately as God has blessed them. A common meal with the whole family is to be eaten in the "place" where God will set his name and shared with the Levites, foreigners, orphans, and widows to recall the years of their slavery in Egypt and God's kindness to them.

The Feast of Tabernacles (16:13–15; also called the Feast of Ingathering [Exod. 23:16], the feast to the Lord [Lev. 23:39], or the feast [Ezek. 45:25; John 7–8]) celebrates the end of the agricultural activities (our September to October) in a communal thanksgiving celebration. Once again, the emphasis is on the "place" (16:15) the Lord will choose for his name to dwell. At each of these three feasts every man

in Israel is to come to the central sanctuary, but they are to bring their gifts, for none is to appear "empty-handed" (16:16; cf. Exod. 23:15). This is the only feast the prophets make reference to as they describe the final ingathering into God's kingdom (Zech. 14:16–19).

K. Appointing leaders to lead (16:18–18:22). The teaching now moves to discussing what the fifth commandment means, for more is intended than simply honor and respect to one's parents—it involves respect for all whom God has placed in authority over his people.

First, "judges and officials" (16:18–20) are to rule "fairly," without "pervert[ing] justice," "show[ing] partiality," or "accept[ing] a bribe." Failure to exercise absolute fairness will result in their failure to live and possess the land (16:20) that God is giving to them.

Israel's source of authority must not be replaced by an idol such as an Asherah pole or a sacred stone (16:21–22), nor should any defective sacrifice be accepted in legal matters; the same rule that is in force for worship is in force here too (17:1).

Three rules of evidence are given in 17:2–7. Justice demands that (1) a thorough investigation be conducted (17:4), (2) the evidence must be supported by two or three witnesses (17:6), and (3) the accusers must face the accused (17:7). The purpose of these safeguards is to "purge the evil from among [them]" (17:7).

As was true in the wilderness, where the difficult cases came to Moses (Exod. 18:13–27), so now as Israel settles into the land there is to be a supreme tribunal, which meets at the central sanctuary, for cases that are too difficult for local judges (but it does not serve as an appellate court; 17:8–13). The law will teach them how to act (17:11). Anyone who shows "contempt" (17:12–13) for the judgment rendered is to be put to death so evil will be purged from the nation.

When the time comes when Israel will desire a king (17:14–20), this desire must not be to replace the theocracy with an autocratic or tyrannical rule. A king for the nation has

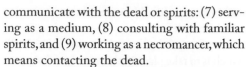

been envisaged as far back as the time of the patriarchs (Gen. 17:6, 16; 35:11; 49:10). In the days of Samuel, the people will desire a king, but the objectionable point to their demand is that they want a king "such as all the other nations have" (1 Sam. 8:5; cf. 8:19–20). But contrary to that copycat standard, God imposes four conditions on the king: (1) he must be the one the Lord chooses (17:15); (2) he must not multiply horses, which is where other nations put their trust for military prowess (17:16); (3) he must not acquire many wives in a harem or great riches (17:17); and (4) he must make a copy of his own scroll of the law to have with him and to read all the days of his life (17:19–20). This observance of the law will keep the king on the straight path and prevent him from getting arrogant.

Verses 1–8, on respect and honor for priests and Levites, cover the ground more fully traced in Numbers 18 (see already Deut. 12:12, 19; 14:27–29). The priests come from the Levites, but not all Levites are priests. The Levites are not to receive a tribal allotment, for the Lord is their inheritance (18:2). They are to receive the first fruits of the land (18:4) and to minister in the Lord's name (18:5). If a Levite desires to move to the "place" of the central sanctuary, he is not to be discriminated against (18:6–8).

The prophets in Israel make up the final category (18:9–22). Three classes of false Canaanite fortune-telling are warned against in nine verbs in verses 9–11. The first three pagan practices pretend to foretell the future: (1) making one's son or daughter pass through fire, (2) divination, and (3) sorcery. Another class of three false practices claims to influence or change the future: (4) interpreting omens, (5) engaging in witchcraft, and (6) casting spells. The third class of false prophecy pretends to

communicate with the dead or spirits: (7) serving as a medium, (8) consulting with familiar spirits, and (9) working as a necromancer, which means contacting the dead.

There are three reasons why God's people are not to try to get supernatural information or divine revelation by going any of these nine routes: (1) it is an abomination to the Lord (18:12); (2) God's people should be blameless before him (18:13); and (3) God will send his prophet to relay the true knowledge of God (18:15–22).

There are five tests for a true prophet of God: (1) the prophet must be Hebrew (18:15, 18), (2) the prophet must speak in the name of the Lord (18:18, 22), (3) what the prophet says must come to pass (18:22), (4) the prophet may perform confirming signs and wonders (13:1), and (5) what the prophet says must conform to previous revelation from God (13:2).

L. Upholding the sanctity of life (19:1–21:23). The application of the sixth commandment has broader implications than simply prohibiting murder. First, a provision is made for a humanitarian zone (19:1–13), called "cities of refuge" in Numbers 35:6–32. Thus, the right of asylum is provided for at three evenly distributed cities in Canaan, just as three cities of refuge have been provided in the Transjordan. In Joshua 20:1–9 we learn these added cities are Kedesh, Shechem, and Kirjath Arba (Hebron). These places of refuge are not for murderers but for those who unintentionally cause someone's death. The illustration of an ax flying off the handle and killing a victim while the two are chopping wood (19:5) shows that although such a case still involves a killing, the offender can be protected in one of these cities, for it was "without

Clay models of livers, which were used for divination, a practice forbidden to the Israelites (Deut. 18:10, 14)

malice aforethought" (19:6; cf. Num. 35:22–28). Provision is also made for an additional three cities to come later, making a total of nine, if Israel ever enlarges its territory (19:8–9), but there is no evidence Israel ever raised the number to nine.

In cases where there is a predetermined plot to murder someone, the elders of the offender's city can extradite the murderer from the city of refuge (19:11–13) so that justice will be served. The death of the murderer will bring cleansing to the land (19:13).

Neither is removing a neighbor's boundary stone to be permitted, for it is God who distributed the land and set the boundaries (19:14; cf. Prov. 22:28; 23:10; Hos. 5:10).

A person cannot be convicted on the testimony of one witness (19:15) or by a false and malicious witness (19:16). The disputants are required to "stand in the presence of the Lord" (19:17), and if the priests and judges find one to be a liar, then the false witness has to suffer the penalty he hoped the one he defamed would get (19:19). The *lex talionis* is invoked—"eye for eye, tooth for tooth" (19:21)—which does not mean individual personal vengeance is available to the one falsely accused but instead is a stereotypical formula for the judges that says in effect: "Make the punishment fit the crime."

Also included under the topic of killing are the wars of the Lord (20:1 20). Israel differs widely from her neighbors in that she is never allowed to expand her territories by conquest of surrounding nations, for going into battle is solely the Lord's decision. Israel has no need to prove her greatness by her military strength, power, or possessions, for her greatness is to be found in who her Lord is. Her wars are not "holy wars" but "Yahweh wars" (20:1–4). She has nothing to prove by conquering others.

Rather than chapter 20 being a militaristic chapter, it comes off as being antimilitaristic, as it calls for a reduction in the size of the army and the release of some who are probably the youngest and most fit soldiers. Four groups are exempted and qualify for immediate release

from this nonstanding army: (1) those who have just built a new house (20:5), (2) those who have planted a new vineyard and not yet seen its fruit (a five-year period; 20:6), (3) those who are engaged to be married, but have not done so as yet (20:7; plus a one-year reprieve after being married [24:5]), and (4) those who are psychologically spooked about going into battle, lest discouragement spread among the troops (20:8).

Cities outside of Canaan are to be offered terms of peace (20:10, 15) first of all, but those in Canaan are to be destroyed because of their accumulated wickedness and the threat of religious syncretism in Israel (Deut. 7:1–6, 25–26). Idolatry must not creep into the land via the back door.

These wars are to be ecologically sensitive as well: fruit trees are not to be cut down or destroyed (20:19–20). Moreover, a captive woman is to be treated mercifully, for if she is later married to an Israelite, she must never be sold or treated as a slave. Without a Geneva Convention, the rules for the conduct of war in this chapter are most humane.

Special provisions are made for a murder committed by an unknown assailant (21:1–9) with no witnesses. The whole community must take responsibility as the elders and the judges measure to find out what town is closest to the murder. That town is to take a young heifer and make atonement for this killing; only then can the guilt on the nation be expiated.

Four subject areas are considered that either resulted from warfare or from the required death penalty: (1) marrying a prisoner of war (21:10–14); (2) establishing the rights of the firstborn, especially in loss of life that brought some families into a polygamous situation (21:15–17); (3) reinforcing the penalty for a rebellious son (21:18–21); and (4) limiting the time a person accursed by God can be impaled on a tree (21:22–23).

Since war brides are people and not chattel or slaves, husbands of those brides are limited in their authority after the potential wives meet four conditions (21:12–13) and are married. Even in this case life is precious to God and is to be treated as such by all.

Neither can favoritism be shown in a polygamous family to the son of the wife the husband loves. The rights of the firstborn son who is son of the unloved wife are not to be reallocated to the son of the loved wife (21:16–17). The firstborn son is to receive a "double share" (21:17; cf. 2 Kings 2:9).

For a son who is blatantly rebellious, the parents are not to take the law into their own hands but to take him to the elders in the gate of the city, and on the elders' judgment, the son is to be stoned (21:20–21). Likewise, a man hung on a tree must not be left there overnight (21:22–23), for as a criminal he is under God's curse; thus his body left there would desecrate the land.

M. Showing respect for all forms of life (22:1–12). Nine laws conclude this section on the value of life. To begin, a straying ox or sheep is not to be ignored but is to be restored to its owner (22:1–4). Assistance must be given, for this "fellow Israelite" (Exod. 23:4–5 reads "enemy" in this place) is a person in need (cf. Luke 10:30–37, where Jesus identifies a person in need as our "neighbor"). The same obligation applies to helping the fallen beast of an enemy get to its feet (22:4).

The interchange of clothing between men and women (22:5), which seems harmless enough on the face of it, is read as an attempt to blur basic sexual differences. Lucian of Samosata and Eusebius describe the practice of masquerading in garments of the opposite sex in the worship of the goddess Astarte. The New Testament declaration (Gal. 3:28) that there is neither male nor female refers to one's status in God's sight and not to matters of dress.

Divine care and concern extend beyond domestic animals (22:6–7), for one is not to take the mother bird along with the young bird(s); the respect for the provision of life coming in the future, and for motherhood, are both evident in these verses.

In a world of flat roofs there was always the danger someone might fall, and guilt for that person's life might follow (22:8). Therefore, a parapet or fence must be built to prevent this eventuality, just as the Code of Hammurabi (ca. 1700 BC; see photo) stipulates in laws 229–40; modern backyard fences around a swimming pool to prevent accidental drowning exemplify the same principle.

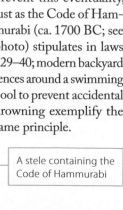

A stele containing the Code of Hammurabi

Three laws deal with mixing dissimilar things (22:9–11). The mixing of two kinds of seed violates the purity of the seed for next year's crop. Hybrids may be fine where seed companies exist to supply next year's seed; but it is tragic for those who want to preserve part of their own crop for next year's seed. Likewise plowing with an ox and donkey yoked together is unnatural, for the strength of the two is not equal. The mixing of material in one's clothing may again be the difference in the strength of the two different fibers, but since the word for "mixture" or "woven together" in verse 11 is thought to be Egyptian, it may have pagan connotations that are now lost to us.

The law of the tassels (22:12) on the four corners of one's garment gives Israel a distinctive dress. The symbolic meaning of the tassels is explained in Numbers 15:37–41.

N. Respecting marriage and sexual relationships (22:13–30). Even though the only reference to adultery in this whole section, which extends to 23:14, is in 22:22, the focus is nevertheless on expanding the implications of the seventh commandment. The sin of adultery was called the "great sin" in Genesis 20:9 (KJV) and in the ancient Near East. The rest of chapter 22 in Deuteronomy is concerned with six cases of those betrothed or married and the question of chastity.

The first case concerns the virginity of a betrothed woman when her new husband makes a false accusation against her and thus comes to dislike (in Hebrew, "hate") her (22:13–17). He is accusing her either of not being a virgin at the time of their marriage or of already being pregnant when he married her. Since the elders are involved, the offenses are against society as a whole and not just personal and against individuals. A false accusation (22:18–19) requires a fine of one hundred shekels of silver to be paid to the woman's father (cf. the fifty shekels David pays for the purchase of Araunah's threshing floor [2 Sam. 24:24]). However, if the accusations prove correct, she has done an "outrageous thing" (22:21; in Hebrew, a "foolish"

or "immoral act," from the root for "fool" or "folly"); therefore she must be stoned to death.

When a man commits adultery with a married woman (22:22), it is destructive to the social order and the family. Both the man and the woman must die, as in the Code of Hammurabi 129, though Proverbs 6:26–35 suggests the death penalty could have a substitute.

Two other cases of seduction are now considered (22:23–27). In one case, the seduction takes place in the city and consent is assumed, for the woman could have called out for help in town. In the other case, the seduction occurs in the country; a rape is presumed since no one could have heard her call for help. If the woman is not betrothed (22:28–29), the man is to pay the equivalent of a bride-price (but in Exod. 22:16–18 the woman's father can refuse to give her in marriage).

The final situation (22:30) is a man married to his father's wife (his mother or stepmother), where presumably his father has died. The literal Hebrew expression for "dishonoring the father's bed" is the euphemism "to uncover his father's skirt." Incestuous marriages were found among the Hittites and some African societies where the son married the wives of his dead father—but not in Israel.

O. Portraying a caring community of God (23:1–25:19). **23:1–14.** Deuteronomy uses for the first time the full expression "the congregation/assembly of the Lord." Those who are excluded from this congregation are self-inflicted eunuchs (23:1), bastards (23:2), and Ammonites or Moabites up to the tenth generation (23:3–6); however, Edomites and Egyptians can enter that congregation after the third generation (23:7–8).

Since castration was imposed on some of the personnel of the Canaanite sites of worship (23:17–18), Israel is forbidden to do the same. However, eunuchs who are faithful to God are included in the family of God (Isa. 56:3–5; cf. Acts 8:27, 38). Illegitimate children are also excluded. Whether these are children of mixed-racial marriages with non-Israelites or those who come from incestuous relations, it is not possible to say. The Ammonites and Moabites refused Israel passage through their land, and they also hired Balaam to curse Israel (Numbers 22–24), whereas Edom is Israel's brother (Esau) and Israel had for a time been shown kindness in the land of Egypt.

Verses 9–14 express concern for cleanliness in the camp of Israel. First, "everything impure" is addressed (23:9), followed by rules for a "nocturnal [seminal] emission" (23:10–11). All defecation is to be done outside the camp (23:12–13), by using a special tool to dig the hole and to cover it. If Israel wants God's presence to deliver them in battle, the camp has to be kept clean and holy (23:14) since God is present in the camp.

23:15–24:7. With 23:15 we enter into a discussion of the implications of the eighth commandment, relating to theft. Five laws (23:15–25) are given in the second-person singular, perhaps highlighting the importance of individual responsibility within the covenant community. Even the rules on divorce (24:1–4) and kidnapping (24:7) represent a metaphorical and real theft of life.

Other ancient Near Eastern countries required the extradition of runaway slaves, but Israel did not, for it would imply a covenant relationship with that foreign country and the slave was not to be oppressed but helped (23:15–16). Male and female prostitution are forbidden. The Hebrew terminology for such prostitution comes from the root meaning "holy" or "set apart." In this one word, "holy," the sacred and the secular come into mortal conflict.

Neither is "interest" to be charged to a poor Israelite (23:19–20), whereas it can be charged to a foreigner, since the foreigner does not stand in the same relationship to the people of God. Moreover, one is not obligated to make vows, but once they have been made voluntarily, they must be kept (23:21–23). As evidence of Near Eastern hospitality to passersby, travelers can slake their hunger as they journey along by helping themselves to the fruit or grain that grows along the roadway, but they are not to gather additional amounts to put into a basket (23:24–25); the same principle applied to Jesus's disciples as they journeyed along the wayside (Matt. 12:1–8).

Contrary to traditional thought, Deuteronomy 24:1–4 does not make divorce mandatory; rather, it deals only with remarriage to the same partner after a divorce has occurred. The circumstances are described in verses 1–3 with the consequences coming in verse 4; some translations incorrectly make the consequence come in the second part of verse 1. The ground for the divorce (24:1), "something indecent," is not adultery (for which capital punishment is appropriate) or trivial (as in rabbinical writings), but something shameful probably connected with sexual relations. The provision of a "certificate of divorce" is to protect the woman, who otherwise never knew where she stood depending on the whims of her husband. Even if the second marriage fails, there is to be no return to the first marriage, for the woman will have become "detestable" in God's sight (24:4). Care has to be exercised in maintaining the purity of marriage lest sin and defilement be brought on the land.

Further examples of theft can be seen in (1) not exempting from army service for one year a man recently married (24:5), (2) removing a household's pair of millstones for security when they are needed each day to grind the daily food (24:6), and (3) stealing a person by force and treating him or her as a slave (24:7). This last example is a capital offense.

24:8–25:4. The implications of the ninth commandment begin in 24:8; they concern the refusal to give false testimony against one's neighbor by thinking and acting fairly toward the possessions and persons of others.

The first illustration comes from Miriam's case of leprosy (a disease that may include anything from a skin disease all the way to Hansen's disease; 24:8–9) as a result of her libel against Moses (Num. 12:10–15). That was no way for Miriam to act or think! Similarly, though loans to fellow Israelites are forbidden, use of some kind of security is permitted (24:10–13). However, the rights of the debtor are to be respected by not entering a person's house to select what could be put up as security and by not taking a person's cloak beyond sunset since it is needed to keep warm at night. A third illustration (24:14–15) concerns paying workers each day before sunset for their work, since they have no resources otherwise to get food and the necessities of life for that day. In the case of individual sins, children are not to bear the brunt for their father's sins nor vice versa. King Amaziah will show how this works when he executes those who have killed his father but spares their children, citing this verse (24:16; cf. 2 Kings 14:5–6).

Special neighborly care is to be shown in giving justice to the foreigner, the orphan, and the widow (24:17–18). They are also to be remembered by leaving some of the gleanings in the harvest fields, the olive harvests, and the grape pickings for their subsistence (24:19–22), as Ruth 2 illustrates. The Israelites are to recall that all of them once were slaves in Egypt as well (24:22).

Neighborly love dictates that when corporal punishment for a crime is required, it should not exceed the limits of human dignity (25:1–3). Forty lashes is the limit, later restricted to thirty-nine to make sure the limit will not be exceeded. That same care for others is seen in farmers removing the muzzle from the ox that is drawing a threshing wedge of sharp stones round and round over the grain so that the ox can feed as it works. Not only are love and kindness to be shown to God's creatures (cf. Deut. 22:6–7; Prov. 12:10), but in an a fortiori argument—that is, deducing the greater from the lesser—it has application to the farmers who thereby themselves are made more gentle and kind as they show the same kindness and generosity to their animals. That is why the apostle Paul, in 1 Corinthians 9:9 and 1 Timothy 5:18, can make the same application to showing kindness to those who teach the word of God. His point is the same: pay your pastors or you will become rough and without kindness and gentleness in your personality, like the miserly farmers who muzzle their oxen.

25:5–19. The tenth and last commandment, about not coveting, is applied in 25:5–16. Thus, all acts beginning even with the thoughts of

Deuteronomy 25:4 says not to muzzle oxen while they tread grain, as they are seen doing in this Egyptian wall painting.

coveting and all mental processes leading up to it are forbidden here.

The opposite of coveting is set forth first in the case of levirate (from Latin *levir*, meaning "a husband's brother") marriage (25:5–10). In this case, the brothers live together and one of them dies. The widow is not to marry outside the family, because the brother-in-law, apparently even if already married, is to marry her and see that an heir is raised up for his deceased brother (25:5). If the brother-in-law objects and refuses to fulfill his obligation, his renunciation must be accompanied by a symbolic act. The widow of the man's brother must remove his sandal and spit in his face, saying, "This is what is done to the man who will not build up his brother's family line" (25:9; cf. Gen. 38:1–10; Ruth 4:7–8). That man's house will forever be known as "The Family of the Unsandaled" (25:10).

In another case, a woman is not allowed to stop an attacker of her husband by seizing the attacker's private parts (25:11–12), for besides questions of modesty, there is the threat of preventing the man from having any future descendants.

Another case deals with the use and the possession of dishonest weights (25:13–16). Some disregarded this teaching, as Amos 8:5 shows, but this is but another evidence of coveting what is not theirs.

The concluding instructions regarding the treatment of the Amalekites (25:17–19) may be an appendix to the legislation concerning the treatment of foreigners given previously in Deuteronomy 23:3–6 or a transitional paragraph bridging the discussion of the future addressed in chapter 26. Given the shameless way the Amalekites acted in attacking the rear line of march—the sick, the young, and the stragglers (Num. 14:39–45; Deut. 1:42–44)—Israel is to blot the Amalekites out after Israel has been given rest after conquering Canaan.

P. Taking time to celebrate God's goodness (26:1–19). Chapter 26 concludes the long exposition of the Ten Commandments that began in chapter 6. The emphasis is still on

the land God has given the Israelites. Verses 1–11 describe a ceremony involving a sample of the fruit of the land that is to be placed in a basket and brought to the "place" God's name will dwell. The man bringing the basket will declare before the priest that he has come to the land God has pledged to give Israel. The priest will then take the basket, place it in front of the altar, and confess what almost amounts to a creed (see von Rad, 1–76). Their "father" is Jacob, the "wandering Aramean," who while not actually being an "Aramean" yet married Aramean wives (Leah and Rachel) and lived in Aram Naharaim for twenty-one years. Eventually he went down to Egypt, with only seventy persons, yet they became a great and powerful nation. But when the Egyptians enslaved them, they cried out to God and the Lord delivered them from Egypt miraculously and brought them to this place, a land flowing with milk and honey (26:5–10). While there is no reference to Sinai, it is incorrect to assume as von Rad does that this was not an ancient part of the story. Verse 11 emphasizes that it is Yahweh, not Baal, the fertility god of the Canaanites, who gives these gifts and therefore is to be worshiped and given praise for "all the good things."

A second ceremony will come in the third year of their occupying the land at the central sanctuary: the giving of the tithes (26:12–15) for the needy. Once again there is a formal declaration along with a prayer for Yahweh's blessing. The individuals offering the tithe then declare that they are not ritually unclean nor have they entered into any pagan rituals such as "mourning" (cf. Hos. 9:4) or offered anything to the dead.

Now that the heart of the covenant law has been heard, in its broad principles and its exemplary specifics (5:1–25:15), a fresh commitment to the covenant on the plains of Moab is appropriate (26:16–19), as took place following the reading of the book of the covenant at Sinai (Exod. 24:7). No formal ceremony is mentioned, but the words echo language used elsewhere of just such an event. Israel promises they will fully obey all God has said, for they are his "treasured possession" (26:18; cf. Exod. 19:5–6; Deut. 7:6; 14:2). Israel will be given "praise, fame and honor high above all the nations" (26:19) if they will so live in obedience.

Q. Renewing the covenant with our God (27:1–26). Israel is to conduct a reaffirmation of the covenant after she enters the land (27:1–8). The people are to set up large stones coated with plaster, as was done in Egypt, on which the law is written (cf. Josh. 24:26–27). Moses is now referred to in the third person, which has not happened since 5:1. An altar is to be erected on Mount Ebal, where the curses are to be recited and which is chosen as the place of sacrifice for both burnt offerings and peace/fellowship offerings. Ebal may have been chosen to show that even in the place of cursing God can remove sin and restore mortals once again to fellowship.

The conclusion to the ceremony (27:9–10) brings the announcement that "you have now become the people of the LORD your God." The people are then exhorted, "Be silent"—a common climax to such solemn events (cf. Neh. 8:11; Hab. 2:20; Zeph. 1:7; Zech. 2:13).

The nation is then divided evenly into six tribes each on Mount Gerizim and Mount Ebal, facing each other (27:11–26). Those on Mount Gerizim are to recite the blessings of the covenant; those on Mount Ebal are to recite twelve curses from the law (corresponding to the number of tribes). The Levites in each group pronounce the blessings and curses antiphonally, to which the people respond by saying, "Amen" (27:15–26). The core of these blessings and curses comes from the commandments, and the purpose of the ceremony is to bind both people and land to God's law.

R. Distinguishing between the blessings and curses (28:1–68). After describing the renewal of the covenant for the time when Israel enters Canaan, the text returns to the plains of Moab, where Moses one more time reminds Israel of the blessings and curses. In 28:3–6, six successive phrases begin in Hebrew with "blessed." In verses 16–19, there are six corresponding curses (though the third and fourth are interchanged). Again, in their total the blessings and curses match the number of the tribes, but the curses give the reversal of the very things promised in the blessings.

The exposition of blessings is given in a chiastic pattern in verses 7–14, ranging from foreign relations (28:7, 12b–13) to domestic affairs (28:8, 11–12a) to the central matter, the covenant of the Lord (28:9–10; see Harman, 237). The main reason for the curses is that the people will forsake their God (28:20–26); thus they will suffer the same defeat their enemies would have suffered had Israel obeyed. The curses are also in a chiastic pattern: incurable disease (28:27, 35), madness (28:28, 34), continual oppression (28:29, 33), and frustration (28:30–32; see Harman, 242).

To a disobedient and idolatrous nation, God will bring a nation from afar to lay siege and take them into exile (28:49–57). The high fortified cities will not be a deterrent to the enemy. So severe will be the siege that cannibalism and fights over the afterbirth will ensue among the besieged Israelites.

Unimaginable terrors await Israel if she rebels (28:58–63). The result will be a reversal of the patriarchal promises. Moreover, the Lord will scatter the Israelites among the nations of the world (28:64–68), where they will find no resting place. Life itself will be a drudgery as they once again sell themselves as slaves, as happened in Egypt.

3. Moses's Third Sermon: "Realizing We Too Were There at Sinai" (29:1–30:20)

A. Hearing the things revealed to them and their children (29:1–29). Moses opens his final sermon with words very similar to 1:1. Once again, Moses draws on recounting God's works in the past (29:1–8) as the basis for the exhortation that follows (29:9–15). Though Moses begins by speaking of God in the third person (29:2, 4), in verse 5 the Lord speaks in the first person, thereby showing how the words of

Moses and those of God blend into each other almost imperceptibly. As the people stand in God's presence to renew their allegiance to him, all are included: wives, children, servants, and anyone with any type of authority. Thus all Israel enters into a binding covenant with the Lord.

This is followed by stern warnings against apostasy, hypocrisy, or rebellion (29:16–29). Care is to be taken that their hearts do not turn from the Lord. Seeds of sedition and rebellion would be as devastating in their outcome as an insidious root that gives poisonous fruit (29:18). For those who nominally confess their commitment to the Lord, disaster awaits them, for physical circumcision depends for its reality on spiritual circumcision (Jer. 9:25–26; Rom. 2:29).

Even curious speculation into God's will is no substitute for obeying what is known of God's will (29:29). Israel is not held accountable for the "secret things belong[ing] to the Lord"; they and their children have enough to do, based on what has been revealed to them through Moses.

B. Anticipating the future for Israel (30:1–20). The future for Israel is carried even beyond the exile, for with a future change of heart on the part of Israel, God will restore this banished people to their land once again (30:1–10). God will once more "restore your fortunes" (30:3)—that is, bring the people back from captivity (cf. Ps. 126:1; Jer. 29:14; Ezek. 29:25). The Lord will circumcise their hearts, "so that [Israel] may love him with all [their] heart and with all [their] soul, and live" (30:6). Now the curses will revert to Israel's enemies (30:7).

For the third time in Deuteronomy (11:26–28; 28:1–3; 30:11–20) God sets before them a choice of either life or death (30:15). God's word has not been concealed or hidden from them; no, it is right there in their mouths and in their hearts (30:14). This is the same word of faith that Paul preaches in Romans 10:6–8. God's righteousness is not accessed by any works of the law; in both testaments it is gained by believing and confessing the same Lord who has given his man of promise, the Messiah.

God has set "life and prosperity" as well as "death and destruction" before them (30:15). "Prosperity" is the Hebrew term *tob*, "good"; it is also a covenantal term (Deut. 12:28; Ps. 23:6). Therefore, love and obedience to God will bring life and the covenantal blessings.

The last part of the covenant renewal is an appeal to heaven and earth to witness all the blessings and curses that have been fairly set before the people (30:19–20). Often in the prophets, God calls on his creation to verify what he has done and said as third-party witnesses. The words to Israel that linger as the ceremony comes to an end are "choose life" (30:19). Only in choosing life will this or any other generation enjoy what God has promised to Abraham, Isaac, and Jacob (30:20).

4. Epilogue (31:1–34:12)

A. Parting words for the new leader (31:1–8). At the age of 120 years, Moses knows he is no longer able to lead this nation, nor will he cross over the Jordan River with them: "The LORD your God himself will cross over ahead of you" (31:3). God will do to those Canaanites what he has done to Sihon and Og, the Amorite kings in the Transjordan (31:4–5). People and leader alike are to "be strong and courageous" (31:6), for God is not about to forsake his people.

Moses summons Joshua, the man who has served for years under Moses's mentoring (Exod. 17:9) and to whom has been given a good measure of authority (Num. 27:18–23; Deut. 1:38). Joshua is given a commission to exhibit God's strength and courage as he now will lead Israel into the land of promise (31:7–8).

B. Renewing the covenant in the seventh year (31:9–13). Moses writes down the law and gives it to the priests, who carry the ark of the covenant, for deposit there. This law is to be read publicly every seventh year, in the year of "canceling debts" (Hebrew *shenat shemittah*, "year of release," a sabbatical year; 31:9–13; cf. 15:1). At the Feast of Tabernacles, during the harvest time, in that sabbatical year, the people will be reminded to consecrate themselves afresh to the Lord.

C. Installing the new leader (31:14–18). Moses and Joshua are to appear at the entrance to the tabernacle so all the people can witness that it is God who is commissioning Joshua and not Moses alone (31:14–18). The glory of the Lord, which has been their guide throughout the wilderness journey (31:15; Exod. 13:21; 33:9–11; Num. 9:15–23), appears at Joshua's installation. One more time God uses the occasion to warn Israel of the dreaded curses that will come upon them if they stray from what his law teaches.

D. Singing Moses's swan song (31:19–32:47). So that later generations can have a witness, Moses and Aaron are given a song, which they are to teach to the Israelites and have them sing (31:19). This song will serve as a testimony against them when they turn away from God (31:21).

When Moses has finished writing in a book the words of the law (31:24), he orders the Levites to put it into the ark of the covenant. It too will serve as a witness against the lawlessness of God's people, for they have been instructed and guided in the way they ought to go. Now that all is ready, the priests are to assemble Israel to hear Moses's song (31:28–29). Then Moses recites the words of the song from the beginning to the end as the people listen (31:30). This will be one of three songs Moses composes: Exodus 15:1–18, Psalm 90:1–17, and this one, Deuteronomy 31:30–32:44.

Usually the greatness of God is seen through his actions, but in this song a strong emphasis is placed on a series of metaphors and similes. For example, five times God is described as the "Rock" (32:4, 15, 18, 30–31), which was an ancient name for God (Gen. 49:24; Ps. 18:2). "Rock" has the idea of stability and dependability, along with being a place of refuge (Ps. 19:14; 31:3–4; 71:3). Jesus likewise uses a rock as an illustration of his own word in the story of the house that is built on a rock (Matt. 7:24–27). Another metaphor is "Father" (32:6, 7), which

speaks of God's close relationship to his children in this world. Again God is "Creator" (32:6) and is "like an eagle" (32:11). God the "eagle" will "hover over" his believers as he did over creation itself (Gen. 1:2) to catch those who have not yet learned to fly. This is because the Lord regards his children as "the apple of his eye" (32:10), another metaphor expressing the centrality and significance of mortals to God.

Israel is called "Jeshurun" (32:15; 33:5, 26; and one other time in the Bible, Isa. 44:2), which comes from Hebrew *yashar*, "upright, straight" (some scholars think it implies a diminutive ending of -*un*, meaning "little upright one," but this diminutive meaning is unattested). The irony, however, is that Israel is the very one who rejects her Creator, her Rock, her Eagle. She kicks and grows fat and bloated with food and then abandons her God. Israel even sacrifices to "demons" (NIV 1984; NIV "false gods"; this Hebrew word is used only in 32:17 and Ps. 106:37), or idols, which are not gods at all.

Israel is not to omit singing the fourth stanza of this hymn (32:15–43), for God's word should cause shivers to run up and down the spines of his people who turn away from him. God will abandon Israel during that generation and hide his face from them as he kindles his anger against them and scatters them (32:19–26). However, for all those in any of the nations who renounce their apostasy, they along with Israel will eventually rejoice as God takes vengeance on his enemies and makes atonement for his land and for his people (32:43). So, "See now that I myself am he!" says the Lord (32:39). If God be for them and for the nations that believe, who can be against Israel or all who believe?

Moses and Joshua (here called by his older name, "Hoshea," meaning "salvation"; cf. Num. 13:8, 16) finish teaching this song to Israel (32:44–47). The words of this song will be "life" to them if they obey God's teaching.

E. Preparing to die (32:48–52). On the same day that Moses and Joshua finish teaching this song to the people, Moses is told to ascend

Mount Nebo in Moab (32:48), where he is to die. He has received advance warnings of this in Numbers 27:12–14, because he and Aaron were guilty of hitting the rock when God wanted them only to speak to the rock (Num. 20:2–13; cf. Deut. 32:51) and to show the power of his word. From a distance Moses sees Canaan, the land God has promised for some six hundred years.

F. Moses's final blessing (33:1–29). Before Moses dies, he gives his blessing to the tribes of Israel, just as Isaac (Gen. 27:27) and Jacob (Gen. 49:1–28) have done. Here for the first time he is called "the man of God," thus linking him with the prophets of whom this same title is used later on (1 Sam. 9:6, 10). These deathbed blessings played a key role in the Near East and were valid in a court of law even though they were given orally and often were in a poetic form, which makes their interpretation and translation quite difficult (cf. the various Bible versions for somewhat different translations of this chapter).

Moses begins by likening the coming of God on Mount Sinai to a glorious sunrise (33:2), attended by myriads from his heavenly armies. Just as the Song of Moses (32:1–43) pictures a bleak future, this chapter promises prosperity and glory.

Moses's blessing begins with the eldest son, Reuben (33:6), whose tribe is not to become extinct, despite the rebellion of Dathan and Abiram (Num. 16:1–30). The tribe of Judah (33:7), which seems to have assimilated the tribe of Simeon (Josh. 19:1–9), is to have great success against all its enemies. The tribe of Levi (33:8–11) is given unique ministry tasks because of its faithfulness in responding to God's word, especially when others did not. The tribe of Benjamin (33:12) is specially loved by the Lord, as Jacob loved Benjamin. The tribes of Joseph's two sons, Ephraim and Manasseh (33:13–17), are promised the best gifts from the land and great military success. The tribes of Leah's sons Zebulun and Issachar (33:18–19) are given commercial success in the future, whether on the

seas or on the sands (of the beaches or deserts?). The tribes of Bilhah's sons, Dan and Naphtali (33:22–23), are promised northern territories: Dan at the foot of Mount Hermon in the city of Dan, and Naphtali, the northern territory extending down to the Sea of Chinnereth (Sea of Galilee) on the west side of the Jordan River. Finally, the tribe of Asher (33:24–25) is given oil in which to bathe their feet and solid protection against their enemies, for "[his] strength will equal [his] days" (33:25).

Moses concludes his blessings by praising Israel's God, to whom no one can compare (33:26). Because Israel has such an awesome God, "Who is like you [Israel], a people saved by the Lord?" (33:29). Eventually even Israel's enemies will "cower before [them]" (33:29) because of Israel's God.

G. Moses's death (34:1–12). Moses climbs to the top of Mount Nebo, apparently alone, from which vantage point God allows him a panoramic view of the promised land, from the north in Gilead all the way south into Judah and the Arabah.

There Moses dies at the age of 120, and the Lord buries him in Moab in an unmarked grave, unidentified to this day (34:6). Israel mourns for him thirty days (34:8).

Because Moses has laid his hands on him, Joshua is "filled with the spirit of wisdom" (34:9). However, no prophet like Moses has ever risen since his day (34:10), one to whom God spoke directly. Nor have any other mortals seen or performed the miracles Moses did in plain view of all Israel (34:12).

Select Bibliography

Barker, Paul A. *The Triumph of Grace in Deuteronomy: Faithless Israel, Faithful Yahweh in Deuteronomy.* Carlisle, UK: Paternoster, 2004.

Block, Daniel I. *Deuteronomy.* NIV Application Commentary. Grand Rapids: Zondervan, 2008.

Braulik, G. "The Sequence of the Laws in Deuteronomy 12–26 and in the Decalogue." In *A Song of Power and the Power of Song: Essays on the Book of Deuteronomy*. Edited by Duane L. Christensen. Winona Lake, IN: Eisenbrauns, 1993.

Charnock, Stephen. *The Complete Works of Stephen Charnock*. 5 vols. Edinburgh: James Nichol, 1864.

Craigie, Peter C. *The Book of Deuteronomy*. New International Commentary on the Old Testament. Grand Rapids: Eerdmans, 1976.

Harman, Allan. *Deuteronomy: The Commands of a Covenant God*. Ross-shire, UK: Christian Focus, 2001.

Kaufmann, Stephen A. "The Structure of the Deuteronomic Law." *Maarav* 1 (1978–79): 105–58.

Kline, Meredith G. *The Treaty of the Great King*. Grand Rapids: Eerdmans, 1963.

McConville, J. Gordon. *Grace in the End: A Study in Deuteronomic Theology*. Grand Rapids: Zondervan, 1993.

Merrill, Eugene H. *The Book of Deuteronomy*. New American Commentary. Nashville: Broadman & Holman, 1994.

Millar, J. Gary. *Now Choose Life: Theology and Ethics in Deuteronomy*. Downers Grove, IL: InterVarsity, 1998.

Thompson, J. A. *Deuteronomy*. Tyndale Old Testament Commentaries. Grand Rapids: Eerdmans, 1974.

Von Rad, Gerhard. *The Problem of the Hexateuch and Other Essays*. Translated by E. W. Trueman Dicken. New York: McGraw-Hill, 1966.

Wright, Christopher. *Deuteronomy*. New International Biblical Commentary. Peabody, MA: Hendrickson, 1996.

A view from the top of Mount Nebo, looking across the Dead Sea to the land of Israel. From this mountain, Moses had his final view of the promised land (Deut. 34:1–4).

The Historical Writings

The Historical Writings include the books of Joshua through Esther. These compositions describe the life and growth of the Israelite nation once they entered and occupied the land of covenant promise. Beginning with the book of Joshua, these books trace the people's history through the turbulent period of the judges and explain how the monarchy came to be formed. The events leading to the establishment of two separate kingdoms, Israel and Judah, are described, including the devastation of the two at the hands of foreign nations and the events that followed this catastrophe.

Like the other people groups of the biblical world, the Hebrews developed a tradition of history writing to record and preserve the story of their national experience. Since the Israelites were by nature a religious community, the historical books have distinctive theological overtones. Thus, the main focus of the historical literature is God and his covenant relationship with Israel, not simply important figures or key events. Indeed, the narratives of Israel's history demonstrate this understanding of covenant theology by showing how God blessed his people when they obeyed his will, and the punishments that followed when they lapsed into Canaanite idolatry. Despite periodic revivals of covenantal faith, the Israelites proved unable to resist the attractions of false gods and were exiled as a result, despite many warnings from God's prophets.

The return of Judah from captivity in Babylonia, recorded in Ezra and Nehemiah, marked a new beginning for Hebrew national life. The idea of a Davidic kingdom gave way to a religious community governed by a priesthood. The reorganization of postexilic Israel around the law of Moses was designed to restore covenant holiness in God's people. It was thought that such a move would both prevent Hebrew exile and preserve Hebrew ethnic identity. Eventually this reordering of Hebrew society around Mosaic law laid the seedbed for the legalism, exclusivism, and sectarianism characteristic of Judaism in the Gospel accounts of the New Testament.

Mount Carmel, the site of Elijah's showdown with the prophets of Baal (1 Kings 18:16–40). Worship of Baal and other false gods was a problem throughout Israel's history.

Joshua

Gregory T. K. Wong

Introduction

The book of Joshua traces the historical fulfillment of the Lord's promise to the patriarchs and Moses to give Israel a national homeland in Canaan. This fulfillment of the land promise is of great significance in relation to the Abrahamic covenant, in which the Lord promised to bless Abraham by making his descendants into a great nation. In order for this to happen, three things were needed: descendants from Abraham becoming a nation, a constitution to govern this nation, and a land for this nation to dwell in. In Genesis 12 to Exodus 18, one learns about the calling of Abraham, how the Lord miraculously provided a son for him in old age, how through this son, descendants arose, how these descendants eventually went down to Egypt and multiplied, and how the Lord brought them out from Egypt to become a nation. In Exodus 19 through Leviticus, plus portions of Numbers and Deuteronomy, one learns about the giving of the law that serves as a constitution for the nation, binding its people to the Lord and allowing him to rule as king in their midst. The final element is the land, and it is primarily in the book of Joshua that one sees the Lord's promise of land to Abraham's descendants begin to be fulfilled. Therefore, to the extent that the book focuses on how Israel takes possession of Canaan with the Lord's help,

it highlights the Lord's covenant faithfulness to his people.

Authorship

Although the book is named after Joshua, the central character of the narrative material, nowhere within the book or within Scripture is the identity of the book's author revealed. There is no compelling reason to rule out Joshua himself as the author of the bulk of the material within the book. After all, 8:32 and 24:26 show that Joshua was capable of making and indeed did make records of historical events. If he wrote the book in his old age, years after the events narrated in the first half of the book had transpired (cf. 23:1), then the intervening years could conceivably explain the recurring phrase "to this day" that frequently punctuates the narration, especially in the first half of the book (4:9; 5:9; 6:25; 7:26; 8:28–29; 9:27; 10:27; 13:13; 15:63; 16:10). In fact, if 6:25 is taken literally, then Rahab must have still been alive when that episode was recorded. This suggests that the events narrated may well have been written down within a generation of their having taken place. But even if Joshua did write the bulk of the book, he could not have recorded his own death and burial and written about what happened after his death, in 24:29–33. So either editorial work was done on the book after Joshua had written the bulk of it, or an unknown author wrote the book not long after Joshua's death.

Structure

The book of Joshua is roughly divided into three major sections plus an epilogue. The first section (1:1–12:24) concerns Israel's effort to take possession of the land. This can be further divided into two subsections: 1:1–5:15 records what Israel does to prepare for war, while 6:1–12:24 records the actual military campaigns and their results. The second section (13:1–21:45) concerns the allotting of the land to the various tribes, plus the setting up of cities of refuge and Levitical cities. The final section (22:1–24:28) recounts a potential crisis and Joshua's two parting speeches, with a focus on covenant faithfulness as a necessary condition that will make it possible for the people to continue living in the land. The epilogue (24:29–33) records the death and burial of Joshua.

Theological Themes

Although the book of Joshua was written to trace the historical fulfillment of the Lord's promise to the patriarchs and Moses to give Israel a national homeland in Canaan, throughout the narration there is also a strong emphasis on the fact that Israel's success is a direct result of obedience. This can be seen in that the author seems to have taken great care to show that almost every significant step Israel takes is exactly as Joshua commanded, and that Joshua, in turn, follows exactly the Lord's instructions (4:3–9, 15–17; 5:2–3; 6:3–20; 7:13–25; 8:1–8, 18, 27; 10:24, 40; 11:6, 9). On other occasions, it is also emphasized that Joshua and the Israelites have followed exactly the commands Moses left behind, which he, in turn, received from the Lord (4:12; 8:30–35; 11:12, 15, 20, 23; 14:2, 5; 17:4; 20:1–3, 7–9; 21:1–3; 22:1–2). Thus, throughout the book, Israel's many successes are presented as resulting directly from obedience at every level, from leader to people.

Conversely, disobedience is also clearly presented as an obstacle to success. First, the past generation's forty years of wilderness wandering is presented as resulting from disobedience (5:6). Then within the conquest narrative, the one significant defeat Israel suffers is also attributed to the disobedience of one man in their midst, Achan (7:1, 10–12), who violated clear instructions regarding the devoted things. Not until Achan and all that belongs to him has suffered the consequences and been eradicated from among the people is Israel able to enjoy success again. Thus, by both positive and negative examples, the author has made it abundantly clear that the condition through which Israel enjoys success is obedience.

But while obedience may be the condition through which Israel enjoys success, the author also leaves no doubt that Israel's success comes directly from the Lord. For not only is the crossing of the Jordan (3:1–17) a spectacular miracle calculated to remind one of the crossing of the Red Sea (cf. Exod. 14:1–31), but also the appearance of the commander of the army of the Lord before their first battle (5:13–15), the ritualistic rather than military approach through which the wall of Jericho is brought down (6:6–20), and the miracle of the sun and moon standing still in the battle against the southern coalition (10:12–14) all point to the Lord's miraculous intervention rather than Israel's own military prowess as the ultimate source of victory. Even in the more conventional battles, such as Israel's second attempt to take Ai and the campaign against the northern kings, military strategies such as the use of ambush and the hamstringing of horses and burning of chariots are presented as coming directly from the Lord (8:2; 11:6). This emphasis on the Lord as Israel's ultimate source of victory thus reinforces again the great importance of obedience as a condition for success.

Outline

1. Taking the Land (1:1–12:24)
   A. Preparation for War (1:1–5:15)
   B. Campaigns of War (6:1–12:24)
2. Distributing the Land (13:1–21:45)
   A. Land Yet to Be Possessed (13:1–7)
   B. Distribution of Land to the Tribes and to Joshua (13:8–19:51)

Commentary

1. Taking the Land (1:1–12:24)

A. Preparation for war (1:1–5:15). The beginning of the book marks the beginning of a new era. Moses, the servant of the Lord who led the Israelites out of Egypt and brought them to the threshold of the land promised to their forefathers, is now dead (1:1). The task of leading the people into Canaan to take possession of the land has now fallen on Joshua, the one chosen by the Lord to succeed Moses (cf. Num. 27:12–23; Deut. 31:1–8, 14,

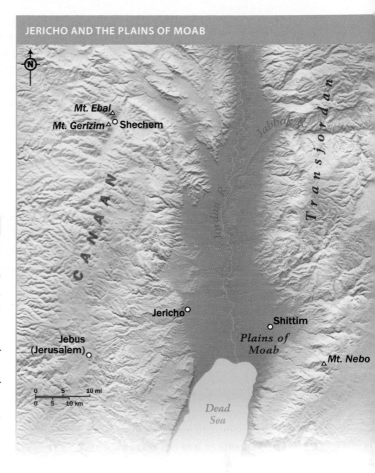

JERICHO AND THE PLAINS OF MOAB

23). But as much as the book focuses on Israel's success in taking possession of the land under Joshua's leadership, the actual account of battles with the Canaanites does not begin until Joshua 6. Joshua 1–5 thus concerns the preparation Joshua and Israel have to make before they are battle-ready. Such preparation begins with the Lord's commission to Joshua and his promise to him and to Israel (1:1–9).

1:1–18. Perhaps to impress on Joshua the new leadership role he now must play, the Lord begins by reminding him of the death of Moses (1:1). The rest of the Lord's speech can be divided roughly into two parts: the first is intended for both Joshua and the Israelites (1:2–4, using "you" plural throughout), while the second is for Joshua alone (1:5–9, switching to "you" singular).

The message to both Joshua and the Israelites consists of a command and a promise: a command to set out from their camp on the plains of Moab and cross the Jordan into Canaan (1:2) and a promise that God will give them all the land within the prescribed boundary on which they have set foot, just as he promised to Moses (1:3–4). That boundary is further specified to be between the desert in the south and Lebanon in the north, and between the Euphrates River in the east and the Mediterranean Sea in the west. Note, however, that the mention of "the Hittite country" in 1:4 is not a reference to the ancient Hittite Empire centered in modern Turkey in the second millennium BC. Rather, it is a reference to Syria, "the land of the Hatti," mentioned also in Akkadian inscriptions in the first millennium BC.

As for the message to Joshua, it consists of two promises (1:5) and three commands (1:6–9). The first promise guarantees success in that no one will be able to stand against him during his lifetime. The second, providing the basis for that success, is that the Lord's presence will be with Joshua just as it was with Moses. In light of these two promises, the first command, repeated three times in 1:6–7, 9, is for Joshua to be strong and courageous, essential qualities that will enable him to lead the people against hostile forces to inherit the land. The other two commands, however, are slightly different. Although the earlier promise that no one will be able to stand against Joshua sounds unconditional, the following two commands provide further qualifications. In 1:7 the success previously promised is now tied to the command to obey unswervingly the entire law given by Moses. And to the extent that obedience must come from knowledge, 1:8 further commands Joshua to constantly meditate on that law, so that he may obey it and enjoy success.

Having received the Lord's commands and promises, Joshua then goes to the leaders of the people to convey to them the Lord's will (1:10–11). Just as the Lord has commanded in 1:2, Joshua now tells the people to get ready to cross the Jordan in three days to take possession of the land the Lord will give them.

Having spoken to the leaders, Joshua then addresses especially the two and a half Transjordan tribes (1:12–18). Having asked for and received land east of the Jordan, these two and a half tribes promised Moses that they would send their armed men across the Jordan in solidarity with the other tribes to help them take possession of their land (Numbers 32). Now that the Israelites are finally ready to cross the Jordan, Joshua wants to make sure that the promise they previously made will be honored.

The two and a half tribes answer Joshua in the affirmative, and pledge not only to obey him just as they have obeyed Moses but also to put to death any who refuse to obey him. In this, they show their full acceptance of Joshua's leadership as successor of Moses. In fact, when the two and a half tribes invoke a blessing for the Lord to be with Joshua as he was with Moses and encourage Joshua to be strong and courageous (1:17–18), their unknowing use of the very words the Lord has earlier spoken to Joshua must have shown Joshua that the Lord and the people were now unified in vision and purpose.

2:1–24. Before crossing the Jordan, Joshua decides to send out a reconnaissance mission especially to spy out Jericho, the first city of which they will be engaging the local population in battle. Given Joshua's earlier decision to cross the Jordan in three days, he probably intends this reconnaissance mission to be brief, as the spies can conceivably go, stay overnight, and return again the next day. But as it turns out, the mission takes slightly longer than Joshua anticipated (cf. Josh. 2:22–23).

There is some debate as to whether Rahab was a common prostitute or a cultic prostitute who would have played a more highly regarded role in Canaanite religion. But regardless of which, her house would have been a place where the presence of male strangers would arouse the least suspicion, thus likely explaining why the spies choose to stay at her place. Nonetheless, the spies' cover is apparently blown, as the king of Jericho finds out about their presence and sends word to Rahab commanding her to turn them over.

Instead of obeying, Rahab brings the spies to the rooftop and hides them under some stalks of flax. Then, cleverly admitting that the spies have indeed been there, she makes up a story about them having left before the closing of the city gate at dusk and sends the pursuers after them. She then goes to the spies to explain her actions and to make a request. She tells them that her people have heard about the Israelites' miraculous crossing of the Red Sea and their subsequent destruction of the two Transjordanian kings Sihon and Og, which has brought great fear to her people (2:9–11). Bracketing this disclosure, however, is Rahab's declaration of her faith in the Lord and in what he will accomplish for his people. She begins her speech in 2:9 by first expressing her certainty that the Lord has given the land of Canaan to the Israelites. And in 2:11, she concludes by openly declaring that the Lord, the God of Israel, is God in heaven above and earth below. In doing so, Rahab has highlighted her personal faith response to the information both she and her people have received, thus setting up an implicit contrast between her willing submission to the Lord's sovereignty and her people's refusal to submit.

Having made her declaration, she then asks the spies to swear in the Lord's name and provide a sure sign that they will show kindness (Hebrew *hesed*) to her and her family by sparing them from death, reminding them that she has first shown kindness to them on her own initiative. So the spies swear to show kindness and faithfulness to her when the Lord delivers the city to them, as long as she keeps quiet about their visit.

Here some have questioned the propriety of the spies' promise to Rahab in light of the Lord's clear command in Deuteronomy 7:1–3 and Deuteronomy 20:16–17 to destroy without mercy all the local population in the land Israel was to take possession of. To these interpreters, the spies' promise to Rahab would amount to an act of disobedience. However, a strong case can be made that the spies do not do anything inappropriate.

First, there is no rebuke from Joshua when the spies return to camp and report what happened (2:23). In fact, Joshua makes sure the spies' promise to Rahab is honored when the Israelites finally take Jericho (cf. 6:17, 22–25).

Second, in spite of the spies' promise, the Lord still brings about a miraculous victory over Jericho (cf. 6:1–21). This suggests that the promise to Rahab is deemed acceptable to the Lord (cf. Achan's sin and Israel's subsequent defeat at Ai in 7:1–15).

Third, the Lord's earlier commands for Israel to totally destroy the local population both came with the explicit justification that otherwise the local population would lead Israel astray with their idolatry (Deut. 7:4; 20:18). But in the case of Rahab, she has already placed her faith in the Lord and backed it up by hiding the spies from her own people. Her turning to the Lord thus effectively eliminates the threat of her turning Israel away from the Lord and, hence, the reason not to show mercy. The fact that Rahab and her family later become part of the covenant community (cf. 6:25; Matt. 1:5) only proves the genuineness of her faith.

Fourth, the spies' promise of kindness (*hesed*) is in fact in line with the unspoken rules of the giving and receiving of *hesed* between individuals in the Old Testament. Although *hesed* is often translated as "kindness," when applied to dealings between human beings, the predominant idea behind *hesed* seems to be the appropriate demonstration of benevolence demanded by specific underlying relationships. Thus, a request or demonstration of *hesed* is often based on previous *hesed* received (cf. Gen. 21:23; 1 Sam. 15:6). In fact, the receipt of *hesed* without reciprocating is often considered an act of betrayal (cf. Judg. 8:23; 2 Chron. 24:22). In Rahab's case, therefore, not only has she already taken the initiative to show *hesed* by hiding the spies, her request of *hesed* is also based on the *hesed* she has already shown. The spies will thus be acting dishonorably if they refuse to return the *hesed*.

Finally, the positive portrayals of Rahab in two New Testament books that seem to address audiences with Jewish background also imply a high regard for Rahab within Jewish and early Christian traditions (cf. Heb. 11:31; James 2:25), thus vindicating the decision to spare her and her family.

Having received the promise she sought, Rahab then lets the spies outside the city wall by a rope through her window, but not before giving them further instructions to help them escape their pursuers (2:15–16). In return, the spies give her instructions regarding how she and her family can be kept safe when the

Israelites invade the city (2:17–20). Following Rahab's instructions, the spies hide for three days until their pursuers have left before returning to the Israelites. They then report all that has happened, confidently declaring that the Lord has indeed given the land into their hands (2:22–24).

3:1–4:24. Once the spies have returned, Joshua and the Israelites set out from Shittim toward the Jordan to cross it. A series of instructions is given in 3:2–6 especially concerning the place of the ark as the procession moves toward the Jordan. The ark, carried by the priests and signaling the Lord's presence and guidance, is to lead the way, with the people following after it. But the people are cautioned not to follow too closely but to maintain a distance of a thousand yards, presumably in deference to the Lord's holiness (3:3–4). The fact that some distance needs to be kept between the people and the ark does not mean, however, that the people are then exempt from maintaining a high standard of purity before his presence. Hence, Joshua also instructs the people to consecrate themselves the day before the crossing, so that there will be nothing to hinder the Lord from doing wonders among them (3:5).

As the Israelites approach the Jordan with the ark ahead of them, the Lord gives Joshua further assurances and instructions (3:7–8). Promising to begin exalting Joshua before the Israelites so that they will know that the Lord is with him as he was with Moses, the Lord gives additional instruction regarding the imminent crossing of the Jordan. In light of the more detailed instructions Joshua gives the Israelites in 3:9–13, compared with the brief instructions Joshua receives in 3:8, it is likely that the author chose not to report fully the Lord's instructions in 3:8. Certain detail is thus left until Joshua speaks to the people, so as to avoid excessive repetition.

Even though Joshua's fuller instructions to the people most likely come directly from the Lord, a slight change in emphasis can be detected. In his speech to Joshua, the Lord states that events to follow will serve to exalt Joshua before the people so that they will know the Lord's presence with him (3:7). But in Joshua's speech to the people, he declares instead that events to follow will serve to demonstrate that the living God is among his people and will fulfill his promise to dispossess the local population for them (3:10). This seems to show that Joshua is determined to exalt only the Lord before the people, even though he is aware of the Lord's intention to exalt him.

The enigmatic instruction in 3:12 to choose twelve men, one from each tribe, is likely in anticipation of further instructions to be given in 4:2.

Joshua 2:15 describes Rahab's house as "part of the city wall." This pillared house with a back wall adjoining the city wall was found among the archaeological remains at Beersheba.

Concerning the actual crossing of the Jordan, the instructions Joshua conveys from the Lord are that the priests are to go ahead until their feet are standing in the Jordan. The waters flowing downstream will then be miraculously cut off, such that they will stand in a heap (3:8, 11, 13).

When the people do exactly as told, the water from upstream indeed stops flowing and stands in a heap some distance away. As the priests carrying the ark stand still in the middle of the Jordan, the entire nation crosses over on dry ground (3:14–17). In fact, to emphasize the miraculous nature of this crossing, the narrator even notes that all this happened during the river's flood stage, when the water level would have been higher than normal (3:15). To the extent that this crossing of the Jordan shares similar features with one of Moses's more spectacular miracles, the crossing of the Red Sea (cf. Exod. 14:21–22), it indeed sends a clear message to Israel that the Lord is with Joshua just as he was with Moses (cf. 3:7).

When the whole of Israel has crossed over, the Lord gives further instructions concerning the twelve men chosen earlier (4:2–3; cf. 3:12). They are each to take a stone from the middle of the river, where the priests carrying the ark stand, and carry it to the camp where they will be spending the night. In 4:2–3, as in 3:7–8 earlier, the author has chosen to provide initially only a brief excerpt of the Lord's instructions to Joshua, leaving the rest of the details to be disclosed in Joshua's instructions to the twelve (4:4–7). Joshua's instructions explain that the twelve stones are to form a memorial for the Israelites so that, should their descendants ask about the meaning of the stones, the story will be retold about how the Lord miraculously brought his people across the Jordan.

The exact implementation of Joshua's instructions is reported in 4:8. Although 4:9 could be understood as the setting up of a second memorial of twelve stones in the middle of the river, it is more likely a "fast-forward" report of the twelve stones taken from the river

to set up as a memorial at the Israelite camp. This anticipates the more detailed account to be given in 4:20–24.

A new section begins in 4:10, which culminates in the priests coming up to the other side of the Jordan with the ark. But to lead up to this point, the author first "rewinds" his narrative slightly to when the people were still crossing the Jordan in order to provide details that were not disclosed earlier (cf. 3:17). These include the people's hurried crossing (4:10), the crossing of the armed Transjordanian tribes (4:12; cf. 1:12–18), and the number of battle-ready who crossed over as around forty thousand (4:13). That the ark and the priests carrying it cross over only after the rest have done so is also mentioned in 4:11, in anticipation of the more detailed account of how this happens (4:15–18). But the fact that the Lord has brought honor to Joshua that day just as he had promised (cf. 3:7) is emphasized in 4:14, such that the people revere (literally "fear") Joshua all the days of his life just as they have previously revered Moses.

After the people have crossed over, the Lord tells Joshua to command the priests carrying the ark to come up from the Jordan (4:15–17). As Joshua does, and the priests come up, the water of the Jordan immediately returns to its previous flood position (4:18), again highlighting the miraculous nature of Israel's crossing.

The commemoration of this historic event is dealt with in 4:19–24. The date of the crossing is clearly recorded in 4:19. As the Israelites are camping out at Gilgal, on the eastern border of Jericho, Joshua sets up the twelve stones taken from the Jordan as a memorial there (4:20).

The instructions to the people that accompany the setting up of the stones in 4:21–24 are basically consistent with Joshua's earlier instructions in 4:6–7. In both instances, Joshua highlights the function of the stones to provide opportunities for future generations to be told about the miraculous crossing of the Jordan. But in 4:21–24, Joshua brings up two additional points. First, he explicitly compares the miraculous crossing of the Jordan to the miraculous crossing of the Red Sea (4:23). Second, he discloses two further results of this miraculous crossing of the Jordan (4:24): in relation to the Lord's people, it was meant to spur continuous reverence for the Lord, and hence, obedience; but in relation to the surrounding nations, it was intended to be a concrete demonstration of the Lord's power. Indeed, immediately following this disclosure, it is reported that kings in both the hill country (Amorite) and the coastal plains (Canaanite) west of the Jordan react with great fear when they hear about Israel's miraculous crossing (5:1).

5:1–15. Despite the fact that the Israelites are now camping right by Jericho, further spiritual preparation is necessary before they will be ready to battle the indigenous population and take possession of the land. Such preparation is reported in 5:2–15.

The first thing Israel is required to do is to circumcise all their men (5:2–9). The command of the Lord and Joshua's obedience are reported in 5:2–3. Note that the word "again" in 5:2 does not necessarily mean that Joshua has already circumcised some of the men but simply that circumcision was performed before Israel left Egypt and must now be performed once again (cf. 5:4–7). The name of the place where the Israelites are circumcised, Gibeath Haaraloth (5:3), literally means "hill of foreskins." The name must have been given after the event to commemorate what happened there.

The circumstances that necessitate the command to circumcise are as follows (5:4–7). When the Israelites first left

Egypt, all the men were circumcised. But no circumcision had taken place during the forty years when Israel was wandering in the wilderness. Now that the generation who was of fighting age when they left Egypt has died under the Lord's discipline for unbelief, the generation born during the wilderness years has remained uncircumcised.

But why is it important for the Israelites to be circumcised at this point? To begin, circumcision is a concrete sign of the Abrahamic covenant (Gen. 17:9–14). More significantly, it is precisely on the basis of this covenant (cf. Gen. 15:7–21) that Israel is now seeking to take possession of the land before them. It is therefore understandable that, before delivering the land into their hands, the Lord would first demand a demonstration of covenant faithfulness. Such a demonstration also requires a corresponding demonstration of faith, since there is an implicit danger to Israel's obedience. After all, the Israelites, having just set foot on hostile land and now camping near the enemy, would have been extremely vulnerable to the enemy's attacks after the procedure (cf. Gen. 34:13–29).

But the people obey by faith, and when they do, the Lord declares that their past disgrace of having been slaves in Egypt will be rolled away (5:9). This is presumably because their demonstration of faith and covenant faithfulness now guarantees that they will no longer be slaves, as they are poised to take possession

The Lord commanded Joshua to circumcise using a flint knife (Josh. 5:2), such as this one from predynastic Egypt (4000–3100 BC).

of their own land. The fact that they camp at Gilgal while they are healing from circumcision further drives home the Lord's declaration, for the name Gilgal puns with the Hebrew verb meaning "roll away" (*galal*).

The next event in their spiritual preparation is the celebration of the Passover on the fourteenth day of the month (5:10), in accordance with the law (Exod. 12:6; Lev. 23:5; Num. 9:2–3; 28:16). Note that this celebration is possible only because Joshua has circumcised all Israelite males four days previous, for the law stipulates that only those who are circumcised are eligible to celebrate the Passover (Exod. 12:43–49).

While the text provides no further detail about this celebration, it is disclosed that on the day after the celebration, the Israelites have their first taste of the produce from the land (5:11). This is followed by an end to the provision of manna (5:12), thus signaling the beginning of a new era in which, instead of the Lord having to provide for Israel's daily needs, the people will henceforth be sustained through the produce of the land they will soon possess.

If the above were all intended to raise Israel's confidence ahead of their impending battles to take possession of the land, then the final confidence booster comes when the Israelites begin moving toward Jericho for their first military encounter with the indigenous population (5:13–15). As Joshua looks up, he sees a man standing before him with a drawn sword in his hand. Wanting to ascertain whether he is friend or foe, Joshua asks if he is for or against them. But the answer he gets is neither. The man identifies himself as the commander of the army of the Lord, implying that his role is not so much to help, but to assume command in the Lord's battle. Joshua is thus being reminded that the battle is ultimately not Israel's battle with the Lord to provide help, but the Lord's battle with Israel needing to submit to his command.

Realizing who the man is, Joshua then prostrates himself and asks what message the Lord has for him. But the commander simply tells Joshua to remove his sandals because where he is standing is holy. This instruction almost replicates exactly the Lord's instruction to Moses in Exodus 3:5. But in both instances, the holiness of the place probably has less to do with the particular geographic location than with the manifestation of the Lord's presence. Taking off one's sandals is presumably an expression of humility, since in Deuteronomy 25:7–10, 2 Chronicles 28:15, and Isaiah 20:2–4, being without sandals is deemed a sign of humiliation. Thus, the commander's message to Joshua reinforces the need for Joshua to humbly submit himself before the Lord.

B. Campaigns of war (6:1–12:24). After the focus on preparation for battle in chapters 1–5, chapters 6–11 now describe the actual battles, with chapter 12 being a summary of results. The battles themselves can roughly be divided into three main campaigns, focusing respectively on the central (6:1–8:35), southern (9:1–10:28), and northern regions (11:1–23).

6:1–8:35. The first campaign described is in the central region.

6:1–27. The campaign in the central region begins with the battle against Jericho. Anticipating the arrival of the Israelites and fearing their power (cf. Josh. 2:10–11), the inhabitants of Jericho choose to shut themselves up in their walled city rather than go out in battle. But the Lord has special instructions for Joshua regarding how to breach Jericho's wall.

Consistent with the narrative style of the author (cf. Josh. 3:7–13; 4:2–7), the battle account is presented through layers of near repetitions, with each layer expanding further on the information previously provided. The main thrust of the Lord's instructions to Joshua is first reported in 6:2–5; it concerns the key participants and the order of the procession, as well as different actions to be taken for the first six days versus the seventh day. Joshua's subsequent instructions to the people are reported in three stages (6:6–7, 10, 15–19), each followed by the people's obedient response (6:8–9, 11–14, 20–21). Note here that Joshua's instructions to the people contain details previously unmentioned in the Lord's instructions, as does the report of the people's actions contain details previously unmentioned in Joshua's instructions. In Joshua's instructions to the people (6:6–7), for example, not only does he repeat the Lord's instructions concerning the seven priests carrying seven ram's horns in front of the ark and armed men marching around the city, he also includes a previously unmentioned detail about an armed guard going ahead of the ark. The report of the actual execution (6:8–9) in turn contains descriptions not only of priests and the armed guard marching ahead of the ark but also of the priests blowing their horns as they march, followed by the rear guard. The author's use of this expanding layer of repetition likely serves two purposes. First, by repeating the core instructions from the Lord both in Joshua's instructions to the people and in the report of the people's actions, the author is thus able to highlight the exact obedience of both Joshua and the people. Second, by leaving out less critical details in the initial report of the Lord's instructions and only introducing them subsequently, the author is also able to retain interest by injecting variety into the repetitions.

After the activities on the first six days have been reported, 6:15–26 then focuses on the climactic events of the seventh day. As per instructions from the Lord (6:4), the people march around the city seven times on the seventh day. Just before the trumpet blast at the end of their seventh circle around the city, Joshua gives further instructions regarding what to do with the city after it is taken (6:17–19). Specifically—except for Rahab and her family, who will be spared for helping the spies—the city and everything in it will be devoted to the Lord. Nothing will be available for the Israelites to take for themselves as spoil. In fact, the people are clearly warned that taking any of the devoted items for themselves will bring not only destruction to the taker but also trouble for the entire camp.

As to what is meant by devoting something to the Lord, the Hebrew verb *haram* is commonly translated in the NIV as "totally/completely destroy" (Num. 21:2–3; Deut. 2:34; 7:2; 13:16; 20:17; Josh. 2:10; 10:1, 40; 11:11–12; Judg. 1:17; 1 Sam. 15:8–9, 20; 1 Chron. 4:41; Isa. 34:2, 5; Jer. 50:21, 26). The related noun *herem*, "devoted thing," is thus often understood as signifying something set apart for destruction (cf. Lev. 27:29; Deut. 7:26; Josh. 7:12; 1 Kings 20:42; Isa. 43:28). However, Leviticus 27:21, 28; Numbers 18:14; and Micah 4:13 suggest that the concept may also have a more positive nuance where devoting something to the Lord refers to an irrevocable dedication of something valuable to the Lord for his use.

Thus, whether a devoted item would be destroyed or retained actually depended on what that item was. While items of value were sometimes retained for the Lord's use, items deemed offensive to the Lord, such as idol worshipers and their idols, were generally destined for destruction. That is why, as much as Jericho and everything in it are declared "devoted to the LORD" (6:17), the silver and gold and articles of bronze and iron are not to

An aerial view of the archaeological site of Jericho

be destroyed, but go into the Lord's treasury (6:19). That the latter are also considered part of the "devoted things" is evident in 7:1, 21, where the "devoted things" Achan has taken include not only the Babylonian robe destined for destruction but also the silver and wedge of gold that were destined for the Lord's treasury. Thus, in the context of Joshua 6–7, "devoted things" refers to all items declared off limits to Israel because they have been irrevocably dedicated to the Lord, regardless of whether they are to be destroyed or put into the treasury. Note, however, that the instruction about the devoted things in 6:17–19 is probably mentioned in anticipation of the following episode, where the violation of that instruction leads to an unexpected defeat at Ai.

Outside Jericho, when the Israelites shout together at Joshua's signal, its walls miraculously collapse, so that the Israelites are able to charge into the city to take it (6:20). Since the entire city has been devoted to the Lord, all living things, including livestock, are destroyed. The only exceptions are Rahab and her family, who are brought out by the two spies in accordance with the oath sworn to her (6:21–23). And with the exception of the silver and gold and the articles destined for the Lord's treasury, the rest of the city is burned (6:24).

The successful campaign then concludes with a few final notes. First, it is reported that Rahab and her family are allowed to live among the covenant community (6:25). The comment that she lives among the Israelites "to this day," if taken literally, suggests that the account must have been penned within Rahab's life span. But some have understood the "she" in the last clause of 6:25 as representative, thus not necessarily suggesting that it is Rahab herself but her family and descendants who are still living among the Israelites "to this day." And while some see this comment as a subtle rebuke against the Israelites for allowing non-Israelites to become part of the covenant community, the comment is more likely an endorsement of that decision

by testifying to the genuineness of Rahab's faith (see commentary on Josh. 2:1–24).

Second, 6:26 reports a curse Joshua pronounces on Jericho that whoever attempts to rebuild the city will suffer the loss of sons even as construction takes place. Here the rebuilding Joshua has in mind may be more the refortification of the city with walls and gates rather than the construction of houses for dwelling. For although there is evidence that the city was inhabited between its initial destruction and its eventual rebuilding during the time of Ahab (cf. Josh. 18:21; Judg. 3:13; 2 Sam. 10:5), it is only in association with its refortification in Ahab's days that Joshua's curse is literally fulfilled (cf. 1 Kings 16:34).

Finally, in 6:27 it is noted that, as the Lord's presence with Joshua has been amply demonstrated through this victory, Joshua's fame spreads throughout the land.

7:1–26. With such an auspicious start, one would naturally expect a string of victories to immediately follow. But as the Israelites move westward toward Ai, they experience a surprising defeat. To prepare the readers for this unexpected development, the author preemptively discloses in 7:1 the reason for defeat, namely, that Achan has secretly taken some of the devoted things for himself. Notice that although it is evident throughout the narrative that this violation is entirely Achan's own, both the author in 7:1 and the Lord in 7:11 speak of Israel as a whole having acted unfaithfully regarding the devoted things. This is in line with the principle of corporate responsibility often held during biblical times, where the action of one can implicate the whole. This, in fact, was precisely Joshua's warning in 6:18, that any violation of the Lord's commands would endanger not only the individual involved but also the entire community.

The reason for the impending defeat having been disclosed, the author traces the series of events from its beginning. Fresh from the conquest of Jericho, Joshua repeats his former strategy by sending spies to spy out their next

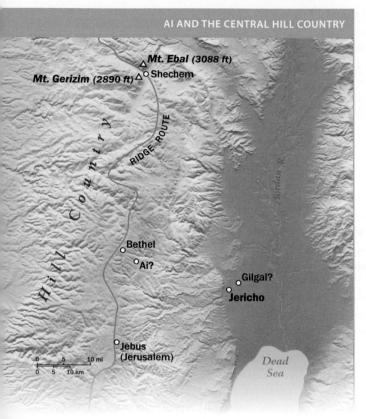

AI AND THE CENTRAL HILL COUNTRY

Mt. Ebal (3088 ft)

Mt. Gerizim (2890 ft) Shechem

Hill Country

RIDGE ROUTE

Jordan R.

Bethel

Ai?

Gilgal?

Jericho

Jebus
(Jerusalem)

Dead
Sea

0   5   10 mi
0   5   10 km

would have been better for them not to have crossed the Jordan, as their defeat by the small army of Ai will surely embolden their enemies to band together to annihilate them. But like Moses, Joshua also seeks to motivate the Lord to act on their behalf by pointing to the disrepute he will suffer if he allows them to be destroyed by the Canaanites (7:9; cf. Num. 14:13–16).

The Lord's response (7:10–15) seems to hint at a slight impatience with Joshua's melodrama, as he tells him to get up and stop lying prostrate before him. He then tells Joshua that the real problem has to do with sin. Disclosing the nature of the sin, the Lord further threatens to withdraw his presence unless the devoted things among them are destroyed. This is followed by a series of instructions designed to rectify the problem. Joshua is to tell the people to consecrate themselves and inform them of the real reason behind their defeat. The need to consecrate is most likely in preparation for the Lord's presence as he undertakes to personally identify the culprit. The people are told to present themselves tribe by tribe before the Lord the following morning. The tribe chosen will then come forward clan by clan, then family by family, and then the male representatives of households one by one, until the culprit is identified. The culprit, together with all that belongs to him, will then be destroyed by fire for violating the Lord's covenant.

The following day, everything goes as instructed, and Achan is singled out (7:16–18). On Joshua's urging, Achan admits that he has taken among the devoted things a Babylonian robe, the equivalent of about 5 pounds of silver, and approximately 1.25 pounds of gold, and has hidden them in the ground inside his tent (7:19–21). When the items are retrieved and

target, Ai. Brimming with confidence, the spies return to report that a mere two to three thousand men will be sufficient to defeat Ai's much smaller army. But in the ensuing battle, the Israelites are defeated, resulting in the loss of thirty-six lives. With that, the fragile confidence of the Israelites is broken, as their hearts melt like water. Although some scholars cite the Israelites' overconfidence as part of the reason for their defeat, the text unambiguously cites Achan's sin as the only factor (7:1, 11).

Joshua and the elders of Israel appear before the ark of the Lord in mourning attire and lay prostrate on the ground until evening. Then Joshua, not yet realizing what has caused the defeat, starts complaining to the Lord. Using language reminiscent of Israel's earlier complaints under Moses (cf. Num. 14:3; 20:4–5; 21:5), he asks why the Lord has brought them across the Jordan to be destroyed. He even asserts that it brought before the congregation, the Israelites take Achan, the stolen goods, and all that belongs to him to a valley. There they stone him to death along with his family and livestock, in accordance with the principle of corporate responsibility. The corpses are then burned along with Achan's other belongings, and a pile of rocks marks the place of execution. The valley is named Achor, perhaps partly because it sounds like Achan and partly because the word, meaning "trouble," reflects Joshua's final pronouncement before the execution that the Lord will bring trouble to Achan because he has brought trouble to Israel (7:25–26).

8:1–29. With the Lord's anger turned away, the stage is set for a second attempt to take Ai. The Lord encourages Joshua by telling him to go up again to attack Ai, and even promises victory in advance. The Lord instructs Joshua to do to Ai and its king exactly as he did to Jericho and its king; however, he allows livestock to be kept this time as spoil for the Israelites. As for military strategy, the Lord commands an ambush (8:1–2).

Here again, the author chooses not to disclose all the detailed instructions concerning the ambush in the Lord's speech to Joshua. It is only at the end of Joshua's instructions to the thirty thousand warriors chosen for the mission, when Joshua charges them to do what the Lord has commanded (8:8), that it becomes clear that the entire plan must have originated directly from the Lord.

The basic plan is this: Joshua will take some men and launch a frontal attack on Ai. But about five thousand (8:12) are to quietly set up an ambush behind the city. When the men of Ai come out to fight, Joshua and his men will pretend to flee, thus luring the enemy away from the city in pursuit. The ambushing force will then take the now largely defenseless city, setting it on fire (8:3–7).

Everything goes according to plan (8:10–19). As Joshua and his men pretend to flee, all the men of Ai pursue, leaving the city open and defenseless. At the right moment, the Lord tells Joshua to hold out his javelin toward Ai, a detail previously unmentioned, but obviously understood by all as a sign for the ambushing force to attack. The ambushing force thus takes the defenseless city and sets it on fire. Apparently, Joshua continues holding out his javelin throughout the entire battle, until all the enemy has been destroyed (8:26).

The climactic turning point of the battle is skillfully described in 8:20–22 with a quick juxtaposition of two different perspectives. From the perspective of the men of Ai, one can almost feel their sense of doom when, realizing something is wrong, they look behind them only to see their city going up in smoke. But by the time they turn to face their enemy again, those fleeing before them just moments ago have already turned around and started attacking. They are thus caught between enemies coming from both directions and have nowhere to escape (8:20). From the perspective of Joshua and his men, however, the pivotal moment they have been waiting for is seeing the smoke rising from the burning city. Realizing immediately that the ambush has succeeded, Joshua then turns his fleeing men around and starts attacking, even as the ambushing force emerges from the city to join the battle from the opposite direction (8:21–22).

So the army of Ai is totally annihilated, and their king is captured and executed, as are the rest of Ai's citizens. But the livestock the Israelites take for themselves, just as the Lord instructed.

Joshua has the city burned and reduced to rubble, and the body of the king of Ai is hung on a tree after his execution (8:29). The point of the latter practice is not entirely clear, although the same thing is also done to the five kings Joshua later kills (Josh. 10:26). The fact that in both cases Joshua has the corpses taken down at sunset seems to point to an application of Deuteronomy 21:22–23. If so, then the hanging of the corpses probably serves to convey God's curse, while the removal of the corpses before evening is to prevent desecration of the land.

After the corpse of the king of Ai is taken down, Joshua has rocks piled over it at the entrance of the city gate as a memorial for Israel's victory.

8:30–35. Joshua and the Israelites then travel north to the vicinity of Mount Ebal to hold a covenant renewal ceremony. Such a move is probably prompted by several considerations. To begin, Moses left clear instructions that such a ceremony should take place after Israel crossed the Jordan into the land the Lord would give them (Deut. 11:29–30; 27:1–26). Although Moses did not specify at what point after their entrance into the land such a ceremony should take place, with the Israelites freshly coming off two significant victories and being sufficiently close to Mounts Ebal and Gerizim geographically, this is probably a suitable occasion to express their gratitude to the Lord while fulfilling Moses's charge. Besides, in light of Achan's recent covenant violation, this will also be a good time for Israel to renew her corporate commitment to the Lord.

The ceremony basically follows what Moses prescribed. Joshua builds an altar using uncut stones, on which the people present burnt offerings and fellowship offerings (8:30–31; cf. Deut. 27:5–7). On some large stones coated with plaster (cf. Deut. 27:2, 4), Joshua copies the entire law of Moses (8:32; cf. Deut. 27:3, 8). The Israelites are then divided into two groups according to tribal affiliation: one in front of Mount Ebal and the other in front of Mount Gerizim, both facing the ark between them, carried by priests and Levites (8:33; cf. Deut. 27:12–13).

Joshua reads all the words of the law to the assembly, including the blessings and curses (8:34). Although here, the author never mentions whether the Levites declared loudly the covenant curses, as Moses commanded in Deuteronomy 27:14–26, the emphatic statement in 8:35 that Joshua does not leave out any of Moses's commands suggests that all the instructions in Deuteronomy 27 must have been read out and followed.

Notice also the repeated mention of "foreigners" (i.e., non-Israelites) among the participants of the ceremony (8:33, 35). These foreigners probably include descendants of non-Israelites who left Egypt with the Israelites (cf. Exod. 12:38), Rahab and her family (Josh. 6:25), and possibly others like her who have chosen to put their faith in Israel's God and become part of the covenant community. Their presence among the Israelites thus shows the Lord's willingness to extend his grace to all who will put their faith in him, regardless of ethnicity. This, incidentally, is also demonstrated in the next episode, concerning the Gibeonites.

9:1–10:43. The second major military campaign described is in the southern region.

9:1–27. To provide a context for the Gibeonites' use of deception to win a reprieve for themselves, it is first reported that news of Israel's victories has so concerned the kings west of the Jordan that they have decided to join forces to attack the Israelites (9:1–2). But before the

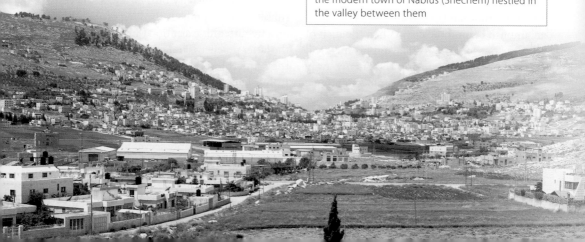

Mount Ebal (right) and Mount Gerizim (left), with the modern town of Nablus (Shechem) nestled in the valley between them

actual account of that battle (10:1–43), the author introduces a different approach taken by a coalition of four Gibeonite cities (cf. 9:17) as a foil to the kings' military action.

At this point, the Israelites have returned to their base camp in Gilgal (9:6). Having heard about the destruction of Jericho and Ai, the Gibeonites decide that, instead of fighting the Israelites, they will seek an alternative solution to preserve their lives. From the tactics they take and by their own admission (9:24), it is clear that the Gibeonites are aware of the Lord's command to totally destroy inhabitants of cities within the land but to spare inhabitants in distant cities if they are willing to be subjected to the Israelites (Deut. 20:10–18). That is why they decide to pretend they are from a distant land, willing to subject themselves so that their lives might be spared. They load their donkeys with worn-out sacks and old wineskins, put on worn clothes, and bring with them dry and moldy food (9:4–5). They are even careful enough to mention only Israel's earlier victories under Moses instead of the more recent victories over Jericho and Ai, so as not to arouse suspicion that they actually live closer than they have claimed (9:10). The Israelites, without inquiring directly of the Lord, fall for the ruse and make a treaty with the Gibeonites, and the leaders of the assembly ratify it by oath.

Three days after the treaty, however, the Israelites hear that the Gibeonites are actually nearby neighbors. But because they have already made a treaty with them by oath in the Lord's name, they cannot attack them when they arrive at their cities. Understandably, the people grumble against their leaders, who, by hastily making a treaty, have placed the nation in a no-win situation. For while Deuteronomy 7:1–5 and 20:16–18 clearly stipulate that nations dwelling in the land given to Israel must be totally destroyed, Numbers 30:2 dictates that sworn oaths must be kept. Israel is therefore caught between two competing obligations—the keeping of one can only mean the breaking of the other.

In the end, the leaders choose to honor the treaty they made with the Gibeonites to avoid incurring the wrath of the Lord for breaking an oath they swore in his name (9:19–20). Is this the right decision? There are reasons to believe so.

First, although the Gibeonites did use deception to secure a treaty with the Israelites, their action seems to be motivated by a proper fear of the Lord and his people. For in contrast to the other Canaanite kings who reacted to the Israelite threat by waging war against her and her allies (cf. 9:1–2; 10:1–5; 11:1–5), the Gibeonites, who are actually known to be good fighters (10:2), come willingly to be subjected to Israel (9:24–25). Thus, while they may not have made as direct and unambiguous a proclamation as Rahab did, their submissive attitude nonetheless points to an implicit faith.

Second, in deciding to spare them, Joshua and the leaders also seem to take the necessary steps to ensure that the Gibeonites will pose minimal threat to the religious integrity of the nation. After all, it is clear from Deuteronomy 7:1–4 and 20:16–19 that the command to destroy the Canaanites without mercy is primarily motivated by a need to remove any apostatizing influence from within Israel. But by making the Gibeonites woodcutters and water carriers specifically for the altar at the Lord's chosen shrine (9:23, 27), Joshua in effect makes it very difficult for them to continue their former religious practice since their main sphere of activity will now be confined to Israel's religious center.

Finally, while the author's comment that the Israelites do not inquire of the Lord in making a treaty with the Gibeonites (9:14) certainly presents the treaty as something that should not have happened, the Israelites' final decision to honor the treaty does not result in the kind of wrath from the Lord seen in the Achan episode. On the contrary, when the Gibeonites are later attacked and the Israelites go to their defense in honor of the treaty, the Lord still takes an active role in that battle to give the Israelites a miraculous victory (10:6–15). In fact, the author's subtle disapproval of the treaty notwithstanding, he recognizes that the Lord is fighting for Israel (10:14).

In addition, during the time of David the Lord actually brings a famine on Israel because Saul, in his zeal, tries to annihilate the Gibeonites in violation of the treaty ratified under Joshua. It is only after retribution is made as seven of Saul's descendants are handed over to the Gibeonites to be executed that the Lord heals the land (2 Sam. 21:1–14). This signals the Lord's full acceptance of Joshua's treaty with the Gibeonites despite the way the treaty came about. Thus, the sparing of the Gibeonites in Joshua 10, while not ideal, does not seem to be regarded by the Lord as a covenant violation.

10:1–43. If the destruction of Jericho and Ai was already enough to raise consternation among the Transjordanian kings (cf. 9:1–2), then news about the Gibeonites' voluntary subjection to Israel must have brought even greater alarm. After all, Gibeon was larger and certainly more important than Ai, and their warriors had a reputation of being good fighters (10:3). No wonder, then, that five of the southern kings, led by Adoni-Zedek, king of Jerusalem, immediately spring into action by launching a joint military campaign (10:1–27). Instead of directly attacking the Israelites, however, they target Gibeon on account of their treaty with the Israelites, perhaps wanting to test the strength of that treaty and hoping that a punishing defeat of Gibeon will

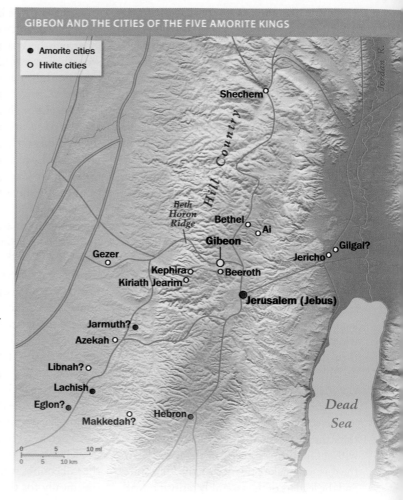

GIBEON AND THE CITIES OF THE FIVE AMORITE KINGS

dissuade other wavering Canaanite cities from following Gibeon's example.

So, the Gibeonites send word to Joshua, and using language of a vassal to their overlord ("do not abandon your servants"; 10:6), request help in the face of the impending attack. As Joshua mobilizes his troops in response to the Gibeonites' plea, the Lord further encourages Joshua by promising victory (10:7).

To launch a surprise attack, Joshua and his men march throughout the night from Gilgal. As battle commences, the Lord participates directly in three ways. First, he throws the enemy into confusion before the Israelites (10:10). Then, as the enemies flee south toward Azekah and Makkedah, the Lord hurls large hailstones down on them, such that more are killed by the hailstones than through direct combat with the Israelites (10:11). Finally, in response to Joshua's prayer, the Lord miraculously lengthens the day by a full day, temporarily halting the earth and the moon in their orbits so that the sun and the moon stand still until the Israelites finish defeating their enemies (10:12–13). In fact, that spectacular miracle is also recorded in the Book of Jashar (10:13), about which little else is known other than that it also contained David's lament for Jonathan (cf. 2 Sam. 1:18). This unprecedented and hitherto unmatched intervention of the Lord in response to Joshua's bold prayer thus prompts the author to declare in no uncertain terms that the Lord is fighting for Israel (10:14).

Regarding the miraculous standing still of the sun and the moon, there is a plethora of attempts to explain what exactly happened, and no unanimity as yet exists. Instead of seeing a miraculous astronomical event, some argue that the description of the sun and the moon standing still is merely poetic language that is not meant to be taken literally. But while 10:12–13a is indeed presented in poetic form, the report in 10:13b that the sun stands in the middle of the sky and does not hasten to go down for a full day is written in prose and cannot be dismissed simply as poetic language. Others appeal to the ancient Near Eastern custom of observing the movement of celestial bodies for omens and argue that 10:12–13 refers to the naturally occurring monthly alignment of the sun and moon happening on the wrong day. To the Canaanites, this would signal a bad omen and would thus deflate their morale. The problem with this interpretation is that the language of 10:13b, taken at face value, seems to affirm that the sun remains in the sky without going down for a full day, not that

its alignment with the moon is off by one day. Thus, the traditional, literal understanding is still to be preferred over all other options.

The premature report of the Israelites' return to Gilgal in 10:15 is most likely in anticipation of their eventual return in 10:43. For it is clear from 10:16–42 that after their initial victory, the Israelites do some follow-up pursuit and engage in further fighting, returning to Gilgal only after the entire southern campaign comes to a successful end.

The five enemy kings are among those who manage to flee south to Makkedah, and once there, they hide themselves in a cave (10:16). When Joshua is told where the kings are hiding, he gives orders for large stones to be rolled over the mouth of the cave and for guards to be stationed to prevent them from escaping. The Israelites then pursue the rest of the enemy troops. After annihilating most of them, they return to their interim camp in Makkedah, where Joshua has the captured kings brought before them. Telling his commanders to put their feet on the kings' necks to force them into a submissive pose, and using this to visually symbolize the kind of victory the Lord will continue to give, Joshua then executes the kings and has their corpses hung on trees until evening, just as he did with the king of Ai (cf. Josh. 8:29). After the corpses are taken down, Joshua has them thrown into the cave where they were hiding and turns the cave into a memorial for

The Assyrian king Tiglath-pileser III here places his foot on the neck of a captured enemy, as the Israelites do in Joshua 10:24.

Israel's victory by having large stones piled over its mouth.

Now that they have come all the way down to Makkedah, Joshua and the Israelites take the opportunity to strike a number of Canaanite city-states located in the vicinity, beginning with Makkedah itself and moving on to Libnah, Lachish, Eglon, Hebron, and Debir (10:28–43). Of these city-states, Lachish, Eglon, and Hebron belong to the coalition that originally launched the attack against Gibeon to start this war. Although Makkedah, Libnah, and Debir are not specially included as part of the main coalition (cf. 10:3), they must have also played supportive roles. As the Israelites move from city to city in this southern campaign, and as the Lord gives these cities into their hands, they apply the principle of *herem* (see commentary on 6:1–27) and totally destroy each city, leaving no survivor behind. Note, however, that when the king of Gezer and his troops come to Lachish's aid, only those who come are destroyed. As Gezer is located some distance north of this cluster of southern cities, Joshua apparently does not take a detour to attack Gezer. That is why, according to 16:10 and Judges 1:29, Gezer remains among the cities to be dispossessed.

With the Lord fighting for them, Joshua and the Israelites thus succeed in taking control of the entire region south of Gibeon by decimating its major cities (10:40–42). They then return to their base camp in Gilgal.

11:1–23. Chapter 11 turns to the third major campaign, in the northern region. Just as Israel's victories over Jericho and Ai spur the southern kings into action, their victories over the southern kings now prompt the northern kings to join forces against them (11:1–15). This northern coalition, led by Jabin, king of Hazor, is much broader and significantly larger than the coalition of southern kings, perhaps reflecting the degree of alarm the Israelites have now stirred up among the Canaanites. The exact number of kings and cities involved is unclear, but they seem to come from the region north of the Valley of Jezreel and south of Mount Hermon, around the Sea of Chinnereth (Sea of Galilee). Note that the region of Mizpah in 11:3 refers neither to the city associated with Jephthah in Gilead (cf. Judg. 10:17; 11:11) nor to the city in Benjamin that is part of Samuel's circuit (1 Sam. 7:16) but to the Valley of Mizpah, just south of Mount Hermon, mentioned also in 11:8. That these kings are much more powerful than their southern counterparts can be seen in that they possess a large number of horses and chariots, the latter representing the most advanced military technology of the time. Their number is also compared to the sand on the seashore, subtly highlighting the comparative disadvantage of the Israelite contingent.

As this vast enemy coalition gathers at the Waters of Merom, ready to fight the Israelites, the Lord not only

An excavated Canaanite palace undergoing reconstruction at the archaeological site of Hazor. Notice the large stone slabs on the left in the foreground—the cracking is evidence of burning, possibly during Joshua's conquest (Josh. 11:10–11).

encourages Joshua with a promise of victory but also provides the military strategy that will enable the Israelites to neutralize the enemy's technological advantage. As chariots must be drawn by horses, the Lord tells Joshua to hamstring the horses and then to burn the chariots when the horses falter (11:6).

Armed with the divine plan, Joshua surprises his enemies by boldly taking the offensive against them at their base camp (11:7). As Joshua follows the Lord's instructions, the Lord hands the enemy over to the Israelites. They strike the enemy down and pursue them until they are completely destroyed. Then the Israelites return to Hazor, whose king led this northern coalition. Applying the principle of *herem* (see commentary on 6:1–27), Joshua has the king executed and the people totally destroyed. The city is also burned (11:10–11).

From there, the Israelites attack and take the remaining royal cities that are part of the coalition, again applying the principle of *herem*, in accordance with Moses's command (Deut. 7:1–2; 20:16–17). The goods and livestock the Israelites plunder for themselves. Only they do not burn these cities, as they did Hazor. In all this, they follow exactly what the Lord has prescribed through Moses.

At this point, the author jumps ahead and summarizes Israel's accomplishments under the leadership of Joshua (11:16–23). By annihilating various kings and their people, the Israelites have effectively taken control of the whole land from south (Mount Halak, southwest of the Dead Sea) to north (Baal Gad, below Mount Hermon, north of the Sea of Chinnereth), including the wilderness in the southwest (the Negev), the Jordan Valley (the Arabah), the hill countries of Judah and Ephraim, and the western foothills between the hill countries and the coastal plains. This does not mean that the Israelites have taken every single city within the area mentioned (cf. Judg. 1:19–36). But to the extent that they have already taken the most important cities in each of the regions, the entire land is as good as in their hands.

Thus, the assertion that Joshua has conquered the whole land (11:16, 23) should not be taken too literally, but simply as a forward-looking statement in anticipation of an imminent reality. Notice, however, that in 11:16–17 the coastal plains are not included as part of conquered territory. Instead, much of this area, especially the southern plains occupied by the Philistines, is included in 13:2–5 as land yet to be taken.

Furthermore, although earlier accounts of victories over the southern and northern coalitions in 10:1–11:15 seem to give the impression that the land has been conquered quickly, the author is careful to note in 11:18 that the campaign against the indigenous population was a continuous effort that took time. But through it all, except for those living in the Gibeonite cities, none have sought peace with the Israelites. This is due to the Lord's hardening their hearts so that they would seek war with Israel and be annihilated. To put this in perspective, however, one must remember that in Genesis 15:16, when the Lord foretells the return of Abraham's descendants to the promised land after their Egyptian enslavement, he implies that the delay in allowing Abraham's descendants to take possession of the land is because the sin of the Amorites has not yet reached its full measure. Thus, the hardening of the hearts of the indigenous population (11:20) should be viewed as the Lord's judgment on a people whose sin has reached a stage that demands judgment.

Note also the singling out of the destruction of the Anakites for special mention (11:21–22). This is probably because it was the Anakites who initially so intimidated the Israelites that they were unwilling to enter into the land (cf. Num. 13:31–33). Incidentally, in that episode Joshua was one of only two spies who had confidence in Israel's ability to defeat them with the Lord's help (Num. 14:6–9). The mention of the destruction of these very people and their cities, with the exception of a small pocket of survivors in the coastal plains, thus vindicates Joshua's faith in the Lord and provides a fitting conclusion to a summary highlighting Israel's success under Joshua's leadership.

12:1–24. To supplement the above summary, a list of defeated kings is also provided, including both those defeated under Moses's leadership east of the Jordan (12:1–6) and those defeated under Joshua's leadership in the west (12:7–24). The two major kings defeated east of the Jordan were Sihon, king of Heshbon, and Og, king of Bashan. The area over which they ruled extended from the Arnon Gorge in the south at around the midpoint of the Dead Sea (also known as the Sea of Arabah or the Salt Sea) to Mount Hermon in the north, encompassing the entire eastern side of the Jordan Valley. This territory Moses gave to Reuben, Gad, and the half tribe of Manasseh (cf. Num. 32:1–42; Josh. 13:8–13).

In the list of thirty-one kings defeated by Joshua west of the Jordan, sixteen from the south-central region are first enumerated (12:9–16), followed by fifteen from the north-central region (12:17–24). The overall area they represent essentially corresponds to that described in 11:16–17.

Two further observations are noteworthy. First, some of the kings in the list (e.g., the kings of Geder, Hormah, Arad, Adullam, Tappuah, and Hepher) were not mentioned in the earlier accounts of the campaigns against the southern and northern coalitions (10:1–11:15). The exact circumstances of their defeat are unknown; they may represent follow-up victories that took time to accomplish. Second, the defeat of these kings does not mean that in every case the Israelites have successfully taken their cities. For example, 10:16–27 records the killing of the king of Jerusalem, but there is no explicit mention of the city being taken in 10:28–42. Indeed, Judges 1:21; 19:11–12; and 2 Samuel 5:6–9 suggest that the Israelites never took full control of the city until the reign of David. Similarly, 10:33 spoke of the king of Gezer being killed while he and his troops came to the aid of Lachish, but according to Judges 1:29, the Israelites are still unable to take full possession of the city. Other cities the

Israelites were apparently unable to dispossess immediately despite their kings appearing on the list include Taanach, Meggido, and Dor (cf. Judg. 1:27); Aphek (if this is the Aphek in Asher; cf. Judg. 1:31); Bethel (cf. Judg. 1:22); and Hormah (cf. Judg. 1:17)—the eventual conquests of the last two take place only after the death of Joshua (cf. Judg. 1:1).

2. Distributing the Land (13:1–21:45)

A. Land yet to be possessed (13:1–7). Joshua 13:1–21:45 constitutes a new section within the book, as the main focus is no longer taking possession of the land but distributing the land to the various tribes. Timewise, this section also marks a break from the previous section, as this land distribution apparently takes place some years later, when Joshua is already well advanced in age (13:1). In fact, it may well be the combination of Joshua's age and the reality of there being large areas of land yet to be possessed that prompts the Lord's command for Joshua to distribute the land to the tribes (13:1–7). This seems to signal the beginning of a new strategy: instead of a central figure leading the nation in its military campaigns, each of the tribes must now assume primary responsibility for taking possession of the area allotted to it.

The land yet to be possessed is listed in 13:2–5. From the places cited, it is clear that this is not meant to be a comprehensive list of every city that remains to be taken but a list of particular regions where Israel has yet to establish a solid foothold. These include the coastal plains in the southwest, where the Philistines dominate; the coastal region in the northwest that stretches from Aphek, west of the Sea of Chinnereth/Galilee, northward through Sidonian territory to northern Lebanon; and the rest of Lebanon, to the east. Notice that none of the three regions mentioned here is included in the catalog of land taken in 11:16–17 and 12:7–8. Particularly regarding the inhabitants of the northern region in Sidonian territory and Lebanon, the Lord further promises to dispossess them before the Israelites and wants to make sure that the area is included in the distribution of land to the remaining nine and a half tribes (13:6–7).

B. Distribution of land to the tribes and to Joshua (13:8–19:51). 13:8–33. Before recounting the actual land distribution to the nine and a half tribes, the author first summarizes the arrangements already made for those who will not be participating in the distribution. This is further broken down into a general (13:8–14) and a more specific (13:15–33) summary.

In the general summary, Moses's prior giving of land east of the Jordan to the two and a half tribes is first mentioned, along with the extent of that land. But the comment that the Israelites did not dispossess the Geshurites and Maakathites (13:13) shows that, even for these tribes, their task is far from completed.

The arrangement regarding the tribe of Levi is also brought up in 13:14 because, like the two and a half tribes, it also will not be receiving an inheritance in the upcoming land distribution. For it was ordained that instead of land the Levites would receive sacrificial offerings made to the Lord as their inheritance (cf. Num. 18:20–24; Deut. 18:1–2).

Having summarized in general terms the inheritance already received, the author describes in detail the specific extent of land inheritance of the two and a half tribes. Reuben receives the southernmost portion of land east of the Jordan, from the Arnon Gorge around the midpoint of the Dead Sea to the plateaus just above its northern tip (1:15–23). Gad receives roughly half of Gilead, from its border with Reuben northward to the southern tip of the Sea of Chinnereth (13:24–28). And the half tribe of Manasseh receives the rest of Gilead north of Gad including all of Bashan (13:29–31). As for the Levites, their not receiving any land inheritance is mentioned again (cf. 13:14), with additional emphasis that the Lord himself, and not just the sacrificial offerings, is their inheritance (13:33; cf. 13:14).

14:1–5. With the nonparticipants accounted for, the author then moves on to record the outcome of the land distribution. Introductory remarks (14:1–5) specify the people involved (Eleazar the priest, Joshua, and the tribal leaders) and the method of distribution (by drawing lots, as the Lord commanded Moses in Num. 26:52–56). The nonparticipating tribes are again mentioned, together with a brief explanation of their nonparticipation. But the arrangement for the Levites not to receive any land inheritance is now juxtaposed with two new pieces of information: the descendants of Joseph will now be considered two tribes, and even though the Levites will not receive a land inheritance, they will be given cities to live in throughout the land where they can graze their livestock (cf. Josh. 21:1–45).

14:6–19:51. The process of distribution actually involves two rounds, with the first round taking place in Gilgal (14:6–17:18) and the second round taking place later in Shiloh (18:1–19:51). The first round apparently involves only two and a half tribes: Judah, Ephraim, and the remaining half tribe of Manasseh.

14:6–17:18. As the men of Judah come forward to receive their land (14:6–15:63), Caleb speaks up to make a special request (14:6–12). In 14:6, Caleb is introduced as a Kenizzite. According to Genesis 15:19, the Kenizzites were a Canaanite people during the time of Abraham. When and how Caleb and his family became a part of the covenant community remains unclear. But by the time of the exodus, Caleb's family has apparently been well integrated into the tribe of Judah, such that not long afterward, when Moses sends spies to spy out the land, Caleb is selected as the representative of Judah (Num. 13:1–16). In this, Caleb belongs to a group including Rahab of Jericho, Ruth the Moabitess, and Uriah the Hittite, all of whom have become an integral part of the covenant community by their faith.

What Caleb requests is that the Lord's promised land reward to him through Moses be honored. To make his case, Caleb first summarizes events that took place some forty-five years ago, when he was sent out as one of the spies (14:6–9; cf. Num. 13:1–14:38). He especially highlights the contrast between his response and the response of the other spies, and he recounts the Lord's subsequent promise to give him the portion of land that he personally walked through as he spied out the land (Num. 14:24; Deut. 1:34–36). Then, testifying to the Lord's faithfulness in keeping him alive through the wilderness years and beyond, Caleb declares that he is just as strong and ready to take on the enemy as before (14:10–11). He then requests to be given the hill country, as the Lord has promised, and expresses confidence that, with the Lord's help, he can drive out the Anakites, known both for their physical build (cf. Num. 13:33; Deut. 9:2) and for their large and well-fortified cities (14:12).

So Joshua gives Hebron, located at the heart of the hill country, to Caleb as an inheritance (14:13–15). The author's parenthetical note that the city was originally named after one of the mightiest Anakites further highlights Caleb's faith, as the challenge before him has now become obvious.

Once Caleb has been given his special inheritance, the portion of land allotted to Judah is then recorded in detail (15:1–63). The extent of Judah's allotment is first described by its boundaries (15:1–12). While its eastern (15:5a) and western (15:12) boundaries are fairly straightforward, being the Dead/Salt Sea to the east and the Mediterranean/Great Sea to the west, its southern (15:2–4) and northern boundaries (15:5b–11) require a more detailed description. Judah's southern boundary is essentially the same as the southern boundary of Canaan described in Numbers 34:3–5. This

The modern city of Hebron

means Judah's allotment will include the southernmost portion of the land. Moreover, with the southern boundary extending along the Wadi of Egypt (15:4) and the northern boundary along the northern slope of Ekron (15:11), Judah's allotment effectively includes the entire territory of the Philistines yet to be possessed (cf. Josh. 13:2–3).

The inheritance of Caleb within Judah's allotment is reiterated in 15:13–14, with a further note that Caleb eventually is able to defeat three Anakites to take possession of Hebron. Having taken Hebron, Caleb also marches against Debir. Although Hebron and Debir were among the cities destroyed by Joshua earlier (cf. Josh. 10:36–39; 11:21), some Anakites who escaped to Philistine territory (cf. Josh. 11:22) must have subsequently returned to reestablish the cities. Upon Caleb's promise to give his daughter Aksah in marriage to whoever can take Debir, Caleb's nephew Othniel captures the city and takes Aksah as his wife (15:15–17). Aksah's subsequent request and Caleb's giving of the upper and lower springs to her in addition to land in the Negev (15:18–19) further clarifies the extent of land inheritance belonging to Caleb and his clan. (See also commentary on Judg. 1:1–2:5.)

While in 15:1–12, the extent of Judah's allotment is presented in terms of geographic boundaries, in 15:20–62, the same allotment is now presented in terms of towns and villages grouped into four main geographic regions. These include twenty-nine towns and their villages in the Negev in the south (15:21–32), thirty-nine in the western foothills plus three Philistine cities that were, strictly speaking, located on the coastal plains (15:33–47),

thirty-eight towns in the hill country (15:48–60), and six in the desert area along the west coast of the Dead Sea (15:61–62). Note that concerning the towns in the Negev, even though 15:32 counts twenty-nine towns, the list in 15:21–32 actually contains thirty-six names, thus presenting a difference of seven. This discrepancy is hard to account for.

Some suggest that it may be because some of the towns originally allotted to Judah in the Negev are later given to Simeon (19:1–6). But the number of towns thus reassigned is nine (Moladah, Hazar Shual, Beersheba, Ezem, Eltolad, Hormah, Ziglag, Ain, and Rimmon), not seven. Besides, two of the foothill towns (Ether and Ashan) listed as belonging to Judah in 15:42–44 are similarly reassigned to Simeon. Yet no numerical discrepancy exists between the number and names of towns in the foothills.

The section on Judah then closes with a note concerning Judah's failure to dispossess the Jebusites living in Jerusalem (15:63). This is somewhat curious, as Jebus (Jerusalem) technically falls outside Judah's allotment, on the Benjamin side of the border (cf. 15:8; 18:17, 28). The town is thus Benjamin's responsibility to dispossess (cf. Judg. 1:21). It is possible that the note is included to reflect the failure of Judah to permanently remove the Jebusites from Jerusalem despite an initially successful assault against the city under Judah's leadership (cf. Judg. 1:8).

Next to receive their allotment are the one and a half Joseph tribes (16:1–17:18). Notice that, although the allotment will be further divided between Ephraim and the remaining half tribe of Manasseh, the two portions

The Amarna letters, one of which is pictured here, are important for understanding the political situation in fourteenth century-BC Canaan. In this letter the king of Gezer writes for help to defend his city against an enemy (probably not referring to the Israelites).

appear to be regarded as a single allotment (cf. 17:14). The description of the allotment begins in 16:1–3 with a delineation of its southern boundary. This is followed by descriptions of the actual territories of Ephraim (16:5–10) and Manasseh (17:1–13).

The boundaries of Ephraim are very roughly delineated, with its southern boundary first described briefly (16:5–6a; cf. 16:1–3), followed by its eastern boundary going from north to south (16:6b–7), and its northern boundary going from east to west, ending at the Mediterranean Sea (16:8). Joshua 16:9 further discloses that some of Ephraim's towns and villages are actually located inside the territory of Manasseh, although the names of these towns are not provided. In fact, unlike the description of Judah, no specific name of any of Ephraim's towns is mentioned, except for Gezer (16:10). Apparently, despite the death of Gezer's king and army (cf. Josh. 10:33), the Ephraimites did not dispossess the Canaanites there but merely subjected them to forced labor. Canaanites were thus allowed to live among the tribe's population.

Regarding Manasseh's allotment (17:1–13), a difficulty here concerns the identity of those receiving land east and west of the Jordan. The NIV translation of 17:1–2 gives the impression it is the Gileadites among Makir's descendants who receive land in Gilead and Bashan east of the Jordan. If so, this means those eligible for land west of the Jordan should be the remaining non-Gileadite clans of Manasseh. The problem, however, is that the six clans mentioned in 17:2 (Abiezer, Helek, Asriel, Shechem, Hepher, and Shemida) are all descendants of Gilead. In fact, according to Numbers 26:30–32, these six may constitute the entire Gileadite clan. If so, then who is receiving land east of the Jordan?

To solve this problem, two things should be noted. First, 17:1 can actually be translated as follows: "This was the allotment for the tribe of Manasseh, the firstborn of Joseph, and specifically, for Makir, the firstborn of Manasseh, the father of [the region] Gilead. Because he [Makir] was a warrior, he took Gilead and Bashan." In this translation, reflected in most other major English versions, it is not the descendants of Gilead who receive Gilead and Bashan but, more generally, the descendants of Makir. This is consistent with Joshua 13:29–31, Numbers 32:40, and Deuteronomy 3:13–15, where the half tribe of Manasseh receiving land east of the Jordan is always spoken of with reference to Makir and not as descendants of Gilead. In fact, in the Hebrew text, both mentions of Gilead in 17:1 have a definite article attached to the name, thus signaling that the Gilead referred to in both cases is the geographic area Gilead and not Makir's son Gilead.

Second, it is clear from 1 Chronicles 2:21 that Makir also has an unnamed daughter, whose grandson Jair captures a number of settlements east of the Jordan (Num. 32:40–41; Deut. 3:13–14) and, together with his sons, controls twenty to thirty towns in Gilead and Bashan (13:30; Judg. 10:3–5; 1 Chron. 2:22). Furthermore, 1 Chronicles 7:16–17 suggests that Makir also had other sons besides Gilead, even though these are not mentioned elsewhere. This means when 13:31 speaks of "half of the sons of Makir" receiving land east of the Jordan, it may well be referring to descendants from Makir's daughter and other sons, thus leaving the six clans descending directly from Gilead eligible to receive land west of the Jordan. While this would mean none of the Gileadite clans actually receive land in Gilead, one should remember that the clans were named after a person whose name bore no direct relationship with the geographic area that happened to share the same name.

Like Caleb in 14:6, five daughters of Zelophehad from one of the Gileadite clans also come forward to make a request (17:3–6). When Moses was still alive, these daughters had already asked for an inheritance so that even though their father had no son, his name would still be preserved through land passed on to the daughters (Num. 27:1–4). Moses made an inquiry of the Lord on that occasion, and the Lord not only ruled in the women's favor but also issued a decree allowing a man's nearest relative, including a daughter, to inherit his property should he die with no son (Num. 27:5–11). So, as the five daughters remind Joshua and the leaders of the Lord's prior ruling through Moses, Joshua also gives them a land inheritance.

The extent of Manasseh's allotment west of the Jordan is then described in terms of geographic boundaries (17:7–11), with special emphasis on its southern boundary, shared with Ephraim (17:7–10a). Its northern and eastern boundaries border the tribal territories of Asher and Issachar and are mentioned only very briefly (17:10b). But just as some Ephraimite towns are located inside Manassite territory (16:9; 17:9), some towns belonging to Manasseh are also located within the territories of Asher and Issachar (17:11). These include Beth Shan, Ibleam, Dor, Endor, Taanach, and Megiddo, most of which are located around the edge of the Valley of Jezreel. Yet faced with the determination of the Canaanites living there, the Manassites are unable to occupy these towns. Like the Ephraimites, they can do no more than subject the Canaanites to forced labor when they are stronger militarily.

Perhaps to provide further insight into the failures of the Joseph tribes, a dispute between them and Joshua is then recorded (17:14–18). It begins with the Joseph tribes complaining to Joshua about the inadequacy of their single allotment (cf. 16:1) in view of their great number. In response, Joshua challenges them to take on the Perizzites and Raphaites, who control parts of the hill country within their allotment, so that they can clear the forest for more space. But they reply that even then there would still be insufficient space for them, as they are unable to take Beth Shan and the towns around the Valley of Jezreel because the plain-dwelling Canaanites there possess technologically superior military hardware—iron chariots. (Note that according to historians of material culture, the iron chariots referred to here were likely not entirely made of iron but rather of wood with some iron reinforcement.) Joshua disputes the tribes' assertion. Not only challenging them once more to clear the forest in the hill country, Joshua goes further by telling them that even though the Canaanites are strong and have technologically superior military hardware, the Joseph tribes should still be able to dispossess them.

Although the author ends the exchange without providing any resolution, what bears asking is whether Joshua's perspective or that of the Joseph tribes represents a more accurate reflection of reality. To answer the question, it must first be noted that Joshua never disputes the Joseph tribes' presentation of facts. The Joseph tribes were indeed numerous, and the Canaanites living on the plains indeed had iron chariots. What he disputes, however, is the tribes' assertion that they are no match against the enemy's technologically superior military hardware. And Joshua seems to have history on his side. After all, the Israelites faced technologically superior military hardware before in the form of chariots (cf. Josh. 11:4). Yet they were able to overcome them with the Lord's help (Josh. 11:7–9). In fact, not long afterward, during the days of the judges, Barak's ability to defeat Sisera's army of nine hundred iron chariots (cf. Judg. 4:3, 13) will also retroactively vindicate Joshua's optimism.

18:1–19:51. For reasons undisclosed, the first round of land distribution apparently comes to a halt after Judah and the Joseph tribes receive their inheritance. By the time the process resumes (18:1), the main administrative center has shifted from Gilgal, where the Israelite camp has been based throughout the military campaigns (cf. Josh. 4:19–20; 9:6; 10:7), to Shiloh, where the tent of meeting is now set up.

Joshua begins this second round of land distribution by impatiently asking how long the Israelites are going to wait before taking possession of the land (18:3). This suggests that some time must have passed since the last round of land distribution. It also suggests that Joshua must have been hoping for more progress in actual land possession before drawing lots for tribes whose inheritance would include some of the land yet to be possessed.

Joshua's instructions for the remaining seven tribes are for each tribe to send three men so that together they will form a team to map out the land. The tribes that have already received their inheritance will essentially be allowed to keep what has already been allotted to them, with the Levites not receiving any land inheritance. Those involved in mapping out the land will then divide the land into seven portions, with each of the seven tribes receiving a portion through drawing lots (18:4–8).

The first lot comes out for Benjamin, and the description of its inheritance, the most detailed among the seven tribes, includes both a delineation of its boundaries (18:11–20) and a list of its major cities (18:21–28). Where its tribal boundaries are concerned, its northern boundary (18:12–13) is essentially the same as the southern boundary of the Joseph tribes delineated in Joshua 16:1–3, except that instead of continuing westward toward the Mediterranean, Benjamin's boundary takes a sudden southward turn after Beth Horon to connect with the tribe's southern boundary just north of Kiriath Jearim. The line that extends between Beth Horon and Kiriath Jearim thus becomes the tribe's western boundary (18:14). From north of Kiriath Jearim at the tribe's southwest corner, Benjamin's southern boundary (18:15–19) extends eastward until it reaches the Jordan, essentially tracing Judah's northern boundary as delineated from the opposite direction in Joshua 15:5b–9. Note that Geliloth in 18:17 may well be another name for Gilgal (cf.

DISTRIBUTION OF THE PROMISED LAND

within the territories of Judah because Judah has received more land than it needs (19:1, 9). That is why many of the towns listed as belonging to Simeon are also found in an earlier list of Judahite cities in the Negev and the foothills (cf. Josh. 15:26–32, 42). The territories of Simeon are thus located toward the southwest corner of Judah.

Incidentally, there is evidence to suggest that Simeon did not hold on to its inheritance but eventually migrated northward. First Chronicles 4:27–31 seems to suggest that by the reign of David, towns once allotted to Simeon have already been taken over by the Judahites, who outnumber the Simeonites. Further information from 2 Chronicles 15:9 suggests that by the reign of Asa early in the divided monarchy, Simeon has already resettled within Ephraim-Manasseh territory in the northern kingdom, with 2 Chronicles 34:6 suggesting that this is still the case during the reign of Josiah. In addition, according to 1 Chronicles 4:38–41, during the reign of Hezekiah some Simeonites will also migrate (presumably from the regions of Ephraim-Manasseh, where they have resettled) to Gedor east of the Jordan to take advantage of the rich pastureland there. And according to 1 Chronicles 4:42, about five hundred of these will eventually move further south from Gedor into the hill country of Seir. Not only can these developments be seen as a fulfillment of Jacob's prophecy against Simeon in Genesis 49:7, but they also explain why, at the imminent division of the kingdom after Solomon, Jeroboam is promised ten tribes in the north as Rehoboam is allowed to take Benjamin in addition to Judah in the south (cf. 1 Kings 11:28–39). For by then, Simeon will have already effectively become a northern tribe through migration.

The third lot belongs to Zebulun (19:10–16); the description of its inheritance includes a delineation of boundaries as well as a towns list, albeit a very brief one. The delineation of the tribe's boundaries begins roughly at the midpoint of its southern boundary, at Sarid,

Josh. 15:7). On the east, the tribe is bounded by the Jordan River (18:20).

Regarding cities belonging to the tribe, these are divided into two lists: the first lists twelve cities in the east (18:21–24), and the second lists fourteen cities in the west (18:25–28). Included among the western cities are the three Gibeonite cities Gibeon, Beeroth, and Kephirah (cf. Josh. 9:17). The other Gibeonite city, Kiriath Jearim, located at the border between Judah and Benjamin, apparently falls within the territory of Judah (cf. Josh. 15:60; Judg. 18:12).

The second lot comes out for Simeon; the description of its inheritance includes only a list of towns and no delineation of tribal boundaries (19:1–9). What is noteworthy is that the inheritance of Simeon actually lies and extends westward past Dabbesheth to the ravine at Jokneam, and eastward to Daberath at Mount Tabor. At Daberath, it loops northward and eastward past Rimmon and Hannathon, on its northern boundary, before turning south again at the Valley of Iphtah El, presumably to complete the circle as it ends back at the ravine of Jokneam. As such, the tribe's inheritance seems to be landlocked, bordering Manasseh in the south, Asher in the west and northwest, Naphtali in the east and northeast, and possibly Issachar in the southeast. Of the twelve towns that belong to Zebulun, only five are cited by name. (Note that Bethlehem in 19:15 is not the Bethlehem in Judah but a border town close to Asher, in the west.)

Next is the allotment for Issachar (19:17–23). The tribe's inheritance is described primarily by a list of towns (19:17–21), including several (e.g., Jezreel, Shunum, Haphariam, and Kishion) located at the northeastern part of the fertile Valley of Jezreel. Although there is a brief attempt to delineate a northern boundary from Mount Tabor past Beth Shemesh to the Jordan (19:22), with the Jordan understood as the tribe's eastern boundary, the delineation is incomplete, as no southern and western boundaries are described. However, from 17:11 one can surmise that its western and southern boundaries probably loop just south of Megiddo, Taanach, Ibleam, and Beth Shan.

The allotment for Asher is next (19:24–31), with the names of some of its towns incorporated into the delineation of its boundaries. Its southern boundary begins north of Mount Carmel in the west, and extends eastward until it meets Zebulun at the Valley of Iphtah El. Then it turns northward and goes all the way past Kabul, Neiel, Abdon, and Kanah, into Sidonian territory, before turning westward and southward again, eventually ending at the Mediterranean coast after passing Tyre.

Then comes the allotment for Naphtali (19:32–39), which is described both with respect to its boundaries (19:33–34) and its fortified cities (19:35–38). As with Zebulun, the delineation of its boundaries begins roughly at the midpoint of its southern boundary, at Heleph. Eastward, it passes Adami Nekeb and Jabneel until it reaches the Jordan. Westward, the tribe's southern boundary goes past Aznoth Tabor, then along its border with Zebulun until it reaches Hukak. The tribe's western boundary then extends northward from Hukak along its border with Asher, while its eastern boundary is the Jordan. A northern boundary is not specified for the tribe, perhaps because a few natural barriers, such as Mount Hermon and the Litani Gorge, render such description unnecessary.

The final lot is for Dan (19:40–48), and its allotment is described only by a list of towns. These towns are mostly clustered around the area to the northwest of Judah, just south of Ephraim, with at least two towns (Zorah and Eshtaol) falling within Judah's border and two more (Shaalabin and Aijalon) possibly falling inside Ephraim's boundary. The rest, including Ekron, which have earlier been allotted to Judah (cf. Josh. 15:45), seem to be located in the northern part of the territory controlled by the Philistines. From this list of towns, it is clear that Dan was originally to be a southern tribe like Judah and Simeon. But as is immediately noted in 19:47, Dan is unable to take possession of its allotted territory, so the tribe eventually moves north. Having conquered Leshem (alternatively known as Laish in Judg. 18:7, 27), they rename the town Dan after their ancestor and settle there, thus becoming one of the northernmost tribes. (For a more detailed account of this event, see Judges 18.)

The land having been thus allotted to all the tribes, the tribes then honor Joshua by giving him the town he has requested (19:49–51). Perhaps as a testimony to his humility, Joshua does not request an important or well-established town but the small and obscure Timnath Serah, which is located in the hill country within the territory of his own tribe, Ephraim. This is a town Joshua will have to build up himself; not only does he settle there, but he is also buried there eventually (Josh. 24:30). The town is otherwise not mentioned in the Old Testament.

C. Cities of refuge and Levitical towns (20:1–21:45). With the entire land allotted to all the tribes, the Lord then gives further instructions to Joshua regarding cities of refuge (20:1–9). Cities of refuge are first mentioned in Exodus 21:12–13, with further instructions regarding them reported in Numbers 35:6–33 and Deuteronomy 19:1–13. These are essentially centers of asylum where individuals who have unintentionally killed another can go and seek protection from avengers. For ancient Israel allowed blood vengeance: a close relative of a murder victim could seek the life of the victim's killer without such an act of vengeance being considered murder (cf. Num. 35:16–21, 27). But the law also distinguishes between premeditated murder and unintentional manslaughter; only those guilty of the former deserve death (Num. 35:16–25; Deut. 19:4–6, 11–13). Thus, cities of refuge are established primarily to ensure that those guilty of unintentional manslaughter will not be undeservedly killed, so that the land will not be polluted by unnecessary bloodshed (Deut. 19:10).

Thus, according to the law, an individual who has unintentionally killed another can flee to a city of refuge. The individual will need to explain the case before the elders at the city gate, and if the elders' preliminary judgment is that the person is innocent of premeditated murder, they will admit the petitioner into the city to be protected from avengers until a formal trial before the assembly (20:4–6; cf. Num. 35:12, 24). If declared innocent of murder at that trial, the individual will then be returned to the city of refuge to remain and to continue receiving protection until the death of the high priest who was serving when the individual was admitted (Num. 35:25). Only then will the person be allowed to return home with guaranteed immunity from blood vengeance. Otherwise, a premature departure from a city of refuge will mean the forfeiting of any protection from avengers (cf. Num. 35:26–28).

What the establishment of cities of refuge seems to highlight, then, is the Lord's concern for fairness and the protection of human life, so that even in the pursuit of justice, unwarranted bloodshed can be prevented. But the obligation for those guilty of manslaughter to remain in cities of refuge until the death of the high priest also shows that manslaughter is not without consequences. Thus in reality, cities of refuge served not only as places of asylum but also as a form of lesser punishment for those who have taken a human life, even if unintentionally.

So, the Israelites set aside six towns as cities of refuge, as the Lord instructed. In accordance with Numbers 35:6, 9–15, all six are Levitical towns (cf. 21:11–13, 21, 27, 32, 36, 38), with three located west of the Jordan (Kedesh, Shechem, and Hebron) and three in the east (Bezer, Ramoth Gilead, and Golan). The cities are equally spread out on each side of the Jordan, with two in the north (Kedesh and Golan), two in the central region (Shechem and Ramoth Gilead), and two in the south (Hebron and Bezer), to ensure sufficiently easy access throughout the land.

Then the Levites, who did not receive an allotment as per prior arrangements, come to the leaders and remind them of the Lord's command to provide towns for them to live in with pastureland for their livestock. So, in accordance with Numbers 35:1–8, each tribe assigns a number of towns with surrounding pastureland to the Levites (21:1–42). Note that these towns are not to be construed as "inheritance" for the Levites because the Lord has already ordained that they are not to receive any inheritance in the form of land that can be passed on permanently to their descendants (Num. 18:23–24; Deut. 18:1–2). The Levitical towns are therefore merely towns for them to live in where their pasturing rights are guaranteed. In fact, 21:11–12 suggests that these towns are not even exclusively reserved for the Levites, but must be shared with inhabitants of the tribes to which these towns belong. Thus, while Hebron is among the towns given to the Levites, the surrounding fields and villages remain the possession of Caleb and his descendants, who presumably live there as well.

The total number of towns thus assigned to the Levites is forty-eight (21:41; Num. 35:6); these include the six cities of refuge (21:13, 21, 27, 32, 36, 38; cf. Num. 35:6). The forty-eight towns are basically divided into four allotments. The three major clans that descended from Levi's three sons, Gershon, Kohath, and Merari (cf. Gen. 46:11; Exod. 6:16–19; Num. 3:17–20; 26:57; 1 Chron. 6:1, 16–19), each receive an allotment. Because the descendants of Aaron the priest, who belong to the Kohathite clan, are entitled to a special allotment apart from the allotment for the nonpriestly Kohathites, this clan ends up receiving two allotments.

A summary of the results of the four allotments is presented in 21:4–8, with the details of specific towns in each allotment listed in 21:9–40.

The first lot belongs to the priestly clans of the Kohathites: they receive a total of thirteen towns and their surrounding pastureland in the south from Judah, Simeon, and

Benjamin (21:4, 9–19). The next lot belongs to the nonpriestly Kohathites: they receive ten towns and their surrounding pastureland in the coastal plains and central hill country from Dan, Ephraim, and the western half of Manasseh (21:5, 20–26). The third lot belongs to the Gershonites: they receive thirteen towns and their surrounding pastureland in the north from Issachar, Asher, Naphtali, and the eastern half of Manasseh (21:6, 27–33). The final lot belongs to the Merarites: they receive twelve towns and their surrounding pastureland from Zebulun, Reuben, and Gad. Of the four lots, this is the only one where the towns received are located in two disconnected regions. The four towns received from Zebulun are located north of the Valley of Jezreel, west of the Jordan, but the remaining eight towns received from Reuben and Gad are mainly located in the central-southern region east of the Jordan (21:7, 34–40).

It may be of interest to note variations between the current list of Levitical towns and a similar list found in 1 Chronicles 6:54–80. Some of the differences are minor, and mainly concern vocalization or name endings (e.g., Holon in 21:15 vs. Hilen in 1 Chron. 6:58; Almon in 21:18 vs. Alemeth in 1 Chron. 6:60; Be Eshtarah in 21:27 vs. Ashtaroth in 1 Chron. 6:71; Mishal in 21:31 vs. Mashal in 1 Chron. 6:74). Others can be accounted for by a scribe's copying errors, such as the omission of Eltekeh and Gibbethon (cf. 21:23) from 1 Chronicles 6:69, and Gath Rimmon in 21:25 being mistakenly copied from the same name in 21:24 instead of Ibleam (cf. 17:11), which appears as Bileam in 1 Chronicles 6:70 due probably also to scribal error. Yet other differences are significant (e.g., Kibzaim in 21:22 vs. Jokmeam in 1 Chron. 6:68; Dimnah and Nahalal in 21:35 vs. Rimmono and Tabor in 1 Chron. 6:77), and these may be due to the existence of competing textual traditions.

Once all matters pertaining to land distribution have been addressed, the author then closes the section with a summary highlighting the Lord's faithfulness in giving the land to the Israelites as he has promised their forefathers (21:43–45). While the summary may sound idealistic and overly optimistic, the fact remains that as far as the events narrated in the book are concerned, the Lord did give Israel's enemies into their hands such that none could stand before them. And while the reality is that Israel's work is far from done, as evidenced by the land still to be possessed (cf. Josh. 13:1–7; 18:1–3), the Lord nonetheless has given Israel the land he swore to their forefathers, which they have now begun taking possession of and settling in. And should Israel continue to remain faithful and obedient to the Lord as they have thus far demonstrated, there is no reason why they should not continue to make progress until they have taken full possession of the land.

3. Staying in the Land (22:1–24:28)

The final three chapters of the book, consisting of an account of a potential conflict (22:1–34) and two speeches (23:1–24:33), each with its unique setting, do not immediately appear to constitute a natural literary unit. But these episodes do share a common concern. While the near conflict is triggered by a potential covenant violation that threatens to jeopardize the welfare of the entire community, Joshua's two speeches also warn of the destructive potential of any covenant violation. Thus, the common concern is that in order to remain in the land that the Lord has given to her, Israel must vigilantly guard against any violation of the covenant. Failure to do so will lead to a reversal of fortune, so that instead of taking full possession of the land and settling in it, Israel will be destroyed from the land.

A. Dealing with potential covenant violation (22:1–34). With the land now essentially under Israelite control and its distribution to the tribes completed, Joshua dismisses the Transjordanian tribes at Shiloh with his blessing (22:1–8). This provides a fitting closure to the narrative within the book, which begins with Joshua urging the Transjordanian tribes to cross over to fight with their brothers until they have taken possession of the land (1:12–15). But before the two and a half tribes return to their own inheritance, Joshua charges them to remain faithful to the Lord by loving and serving him and obeying his commandments (22:5). They are then sent away not only with Joshua's blessing but also with a significant amount of plunder (22:6–8).

But as they reach Geliloth, which may be another name for Gilgal (cf. 15:7; 18:17), they decide to build an imposing altar right at the border of Canaan before crossing over to return home. The rationale behind this move is not immediately disclosed. Instead, the reader is told of the reaction of the Israelites in Canaan when they hear about it. Convinced that this setting up of a second altar is a willful violation of the Lord's command not to offer sacrifices except at the Tent of Meeting (cf. Lev. 17:8–9), the Israelites in the west gather at Shiloh ready to go to war with the Transjordanian tribes.

Fortunately, before war breaks out, the Israelites in the west first send a delegation to see if it will be possible to turn their brothers from their errant ways. So Phinehas son of Eleazar the priest, who has already distinguished himself by his zeal for the Lord (cf. Num. 25:6–13), accompanied by ten leaders representing the nine and a half tribes in the west, crosses over the Jordan to confront their brothers. Citing the incident at Peor as an example, where the Lord sent a plague upon the nation because of her apostasy (cf. Num. 25:1–9), the delegation rebukes the

Transjordanian tribes for breaking faith and turning away from the Lord (22:16–17). Then, using Achan's sin regarding the devoted things as a further example to remind them that acts of rebellion can carry grave consequences for the entire community, the delegation offers to share the land in the west if the Transjordanian tribes are unhappy that their land is defiled (22:18–20).

It is not entirely clear what the delegation means when they speak of the land being defiled. If they thought the Transjordanian tribes had offered sacrifices on the newly built altar before crossing over, they could have associated that with ritual cleansing and concluded that the Transjordanian tribes must have considered their land defiled. Others have suggested that, with the altar and the Tent of Meeting located in the west, the land in the east may have been considered defiled since it did not have any visible representation of the Lord's presence.

To the delegation's accusation, the Transjordanian tribes make a detailed response (22:21–29). Invoking the Lord as a witness and inviting both the Lord and the western tribes to take action against them if they have harbored any rebellious intention (22:21–23), the Transjordanian tribes explain that the altar they built was never meant for actual sacrifices (after all, the altar is located on the Canaanite side). Instead, it is a replica of the official altar, meant to serve as a witness to their determination to worship the Lord at his sanctuary in the west. But they feared that a future generation of westerners might one day cut them off from being part of the covenant community on account of the natural barrier imposed by the Jordan. They were also worried that this might cause their descendants to stop fearing the Lord. Thus, the Transjordanian tribes decided to build the replica as a witness to future generations on both sides of the Jordan that those in the east are also committed to worshiping the Lord and offering sacrifices at his chosen sanctuary in the west.

Pleased with what they hear, the delegation declares that the faithfulness of the Transjordanian tribes has assured them of the Lord's continued presence, as the nation has now been delivered from the Lord's potential judgment (22:30–31). When the delegation returns to the west and reports their findings, the Israelites praise God and no longer talk of war. The Transjordanian tribes then name the replica altar "A Witness Between Us—that the LORD is God" (22:34).

B. Covenant exhortations and renewal (23:1–24:28). Joshua's speech in 23:1–16 is often referred to as his farewell speech, as it takes place a long time after the Lord has given Israel rest from the attacks of her enemies, when Joshua has already become very old (23:1). In fact, Joshua himself suggests that it will not be long before he will pass away (23:14). So, gathering the leaders together as representatives of all Israel, Joshua charges them to remain faithful to the Lord and warns them of the dire consequences of disobedience.

Joshua first reminds the people of how the Lord has fought for them against their enemies, and how he will continue to dispossess their enemies for them until they have taken full possession of the land. The fact that the inheritance the tribes received also includes land still occupied by the nations is itself a clear indication of the Lord's intention to have Israel eventually take full possession of the land (23:3–5).

In light of this potential reality, Joshua, using words reminiscent of what he once heard from the Lord (cf. 1:7), exhorts the people to be strong and to be careful to obey the law of Moses without turning from it to the right or to the left (23:6). In particular, Joshua emphasizes how important it is for them not to associate with the nations that remain among them, and especially not to worship and serve other nations' gods. Instead, Israel must remain faithful to the Lord (23:7–8).

Joshua then gives the people a positive and a negative reason for his command. On the positive side, he reminds them that the Lord's past help in driving out nations far greater and more powerful than they makes it incumbent upon them to "love" the Lord by remaining faithful (23:9–11). On the negative side, he also warns that if they start forming alliances and intermarrying with the remaining nations, then the Lord will no longer dispossess the nations before them but will allow these nations to ensnare and torment the Israelites until they perish from the land (23:12–13; cf. Deut. 7:1–6).

To further drive home his point, Joshua then emphasizes the certainty of what he has just told them (23:14–16). For just as the leaders know from their own experiences that the Lord has been faithful to fulfill all his good promises when they act faithfully, he will likewise make good all his threats if they violate his covenant and start worshiping and serving other gods. His anger will then burn against them until he has destroyed them from the land.

Some time later, Joshua gathers the tribes of Israel and their leaders at Shechem and speaks to them again (24:1–28). Because of the similarity in subject matter between the two speeches, some consider them merely different reports of the same speech. However, the two speeches likely represent two different occasions. While those present for the first speech are mainly leaders representing all Israel (23:2), 24:1 seems to suggest that all the tribes are also present for the second speech. Moreover, while the first speech seems to be delivered in a less formal setting, with Joshua sharing parting instructions with the nation's leaders, the second is delivered in the context of a covenant renewal ceremony in which formal responses are demanded and an official memorial is set up.

Two observations further support the view that the occasion depicted in Joshua 24 is a formal covenant renewal ceremony. First, that the people are described as presenting themselves "before God" (24:1) suggests the presence of the ark. Second, the choice of Shechem, located in the valley between Mount Ebal and Mount Gerizim, as the setting is probably due in part to the fact that the last covenant renewal ceremony (Josh. 8:30–35) also took place there. Assuming that the stones on which the law was written last time (8:32) were still standing, they would serve as a powerful reminder to the people of their previous commitment even as Joshua challenged them again to choose to serve the Lord.

Speaking on behalf of the Lord, Joshua begins by first recounting his benevolent involvement in the nation's history. In secular ancient Near Eastern treaties, this recounting of the historical basis of a covenant is a common feature, serving as the preamble. Here, the recounting begins with the call of Abraham (Gen. 12:1–9), highlighting how the Lord has brought him to Canaan and given him descendants, including Isaac, Jacob, and Esau. Mentioning Jacob's migration to Egypt (Gen. 46:1–47:31), the Lord then speaks of sending Moses and Aaron to bring the Israelites out of Egypt. In the process, the Egyptians were destroyed at the Red Sea (Exodus 3–15). (For the reference in 24:7 to placing darkness between the Israelites and the Egyptians, see Exod. 14:19–20.)

Then after allowing the Israelites to wander for some time in the wilderness, the Lord gave them victories over two Amorite kings east of the Jordan (Num. 21:21–35). And when Balak the Moabite king sent Balaam to curse the

The ancient site of Shechem (foreground) and modern Nablus at the foot of Mount Gerizim

Israelites, the Lord also protected them by repeatedly turning Balaam's intended curses into blessings (Numbers 22–24).

Having led them across the Jordan, the Lord also gave victory to Israel when indigenous populations west of the Jordan fought against them (6:1–11:23). Some commentators understand the hornets in 24:2 as a reference to the repeated incursions of the Egyptians into the region before the arrival of the Israelites. Through these victories, the Lord gave Israel a land with well-established infrastructure ready to be occupied and used.

The history of the Lord's past benevolence having been recounted, Joshua then challenges the people to make a clear choice regarding their allegiance. If they choose to fear and serve the Lord, then they need to get rid of their former gods and serve him faithfully. Otherwise, they could also choose to serve the gods of their forefathers or the gods of the Amorites around them. But as for Joshua and his household, they have made their choice to serve the Lord (24:14–15).

Now that the people have been reminded of the Lord's past benevolence and they themselves recall the Lord's deliverance, protection, and giving of land and victory over their enemies, the people declare that they too will choose to serve the Lord (24:16–18). But Joshua, in an attempt to impress on them the serious consequences implicit in their choice, replies that they are unable to serve him (24:19). He explains that because the Lord is a holy and jealous God, if they choose to serve him and then start turning to other gods, he will hold them accountable and bring disaster on them until they are destroyed.

But the people reaffirm their determination to serve the Lord. So, challenging them to serve as witnesses against themselves regarding their commitment, Joshua tells them to get rid of the foreign gods among them and yield their hearts to the Lord. As the people agree to do so, Joshua makes a covenant for them and records it in the book of the law of God, which is kept beside the ark of the covenant (cf. Deut. 31:24–26). He sets up a large stone beneath the oak on this sacred site as a memorial and witness to the agreement between the people and the Lord. Then he dismisses the people to return to their inheritance.

4. Epilogue: Death and Burial Notices (24:29–33)

The book closes with a report of three burials, beginning with Joshua's (24:29–30). Perhaps as a testimony to the positive influence Joshua has had on the nation, it is also noted that Israel served the Lord throughout the lifetimes of Joshua and of the elders who outlived him who had experienced the Lord's mighty deeds (24:31). The author of the book of Judges, however, then gives this note a more ominous spin: the generation after Joshua and the elders no longer knows the Lord or his deeds and thus does evil by serving other gods (see Judg. 2:10–13).

Two final notes involve the burial of Joseph's bones in Shechem and the death and burial of Eleazar the high priest. The burial of Joseph's bones represents the fulfillment not only of his dying wish (cf. Gen. 50:24–25) but also of the Lord's promise to the patriarchs to bring their descendants back to Canaan to inherit the land promised to them.

Select Bibliography

Butler, Trent C. *Joshua*. Word Biblical Commentary. Waco: Word, 1983.

Hess, Richard S. *Joshua*. Tyndale Old Testament Commentaries. Downers Grove, IL: InterVarsity, 1996.

Howard, David M., Jr. *Joshua*. New American Commentary. Nashville: Broadman & Holman, 1998.

Hubbard, Robert L. *Joshua*. NIV Application Commentary. Grand Rapids: Zondervan, 2009.

Woudstra, Marten H. *The Book of Joshua*. New International Commentary on the Old Testament. Grand Rapids: Eerdmans, 1981.

Judges

GREGORY T. K. WONG

Introduction

Title

Containing some of the most shocking stories in the Old Testament, involving murders (4:18–21; 5:24–27; 15:6–7), fratricide (9:3–5), human sacrifice (11:32–39), gang rape (19:22–26), dismemberment (19:29), and even toilet humor (3:20–25), the book of Judges records events that took place in Israel's Dark Ages, between the initial conquest of the land and the eventual establishment of the monarchy. The book is so named because the period is predominantly ruled by a series of leaders raised up by the Lord, known as "judges" (*shopetim* in Hebrew).

Typically in the Old Testament, the act of judging (from the Hebrew root *shpt*) is associated with judicial responsibilities such as justice arbitration and the upholding of an individual's rights (cf. Exod. 18:13–26; Deut. 1:16; 19:17–18; 25:1–2; Mic. 4:3; Zech. 8:16). Within the book of Judges, however, except for Deborah (4:4), none of the judges are portrayed as having any judicial responsibilities. Instead, they are primarily military leaders who wage wars to deliver Israel from foreign oppressors. While such a use of "judge" may seem atypical within the Old Testament, evidence from other ancient Semitic cultures does testify to the use of *shpt* to designate a local governor. In particular, Akkadian texts from Mari (around 1800

BC) mention a high official known as "judge" (*shapitum*) whose responsibilities included not only the government of town and country and the administration of justice but also military leadership such as troop deployment and local defense. In this respect, the *shapitum* seems to show certain parallels to the judges featured in the biblical book.

Date and Authorship

The author of the book remains largely unknown. Although Jewish tradition attributes the book to the prophet Samuel, there is no solid evidence to support the claim. The most that can be said is that the author was an Israelite devoted to the Lord.

Similarly, there is scant evidence from within the text to allow a pinpointing of the date of composition. While the mention of "king" in 17:6; 18:1; 19:1; 21:25 is often seen as referring to the human kings that will eventually rule Israel, thus placing the composition of the book in the monarchical period, the likelihood that the "king" may actually be a reference to the Lord (see commentary on 17:6) nullifies its use in dating. The mention of "captivity of the land" in 18:30 is also of little help, as it is unclear whether it refers to the sixth-century-BC Babylonian captivity or the earlier eighth-century-BC exile of the northern kingdom by Assyria. In fact, the phrase itself is highly unusual because elsewhere it is often a specific place that is spoken of as being exiled, such as Israel, Judah, or Jerusalem (cf. 2 Kings 17:23; 25:21; Jer. 1:3). That is why some scholars suggest that "the land" (Hebrew *haarets*) may be an error for what originally read, "the ark" (Hebrew *haaron*), the phrase thus referring to the capture of the ark by the Philistines in 1 Samuel 4:11. These uncertainties surrounding 18:30 thus limit its usefulness in matters of dating.

That said, however, the vividness of detail found in 3:12–16:31 does suggest that the narratives of the judges may have come into existence not much later than the events themselves. In fact, scholars generally agree that most of these stories had probably been circulating in oral form within Israelite society for an extended period of time before they were collected and written down by the author of the book. While the conscious framing of the narratives of individual judges into recurring cycles (see commentary on 2:6–3:6) suggests that the original source material was subjected to some editing, the embedding of other literary genres such as poetry (5:2–31) and fable (9:8–15) within the narratives also suggests that the author was careful to preserve as much as possible the sources in their original form.

Structure

The book can roughly be divided into three main sections. It begins in 1:1–3:6 with a double introduction that highlights Israel's failures in the military and spiritual realm. This is followed in 3:7–16:31 by a series of narratives concerning the exploits of the various judges. Finally, 17:1–21:25 provides a fitting conclusion, as two narratives concerning largely nameless characters illustrate the extent to which chaos and anarchy have taken hold in Israelite society.

While there is no reason to doubt the historicity of the events narrated, it should be noted that the overall selection and arrangement of material within the book seems to be guided more by literary and theological concerns than by a desire to present a comprehensive and chronological account of the period. This is evident from the neat schematization that characterizes most of the book. For example, both the conquest report in 1:1–36 and the narratives of the judges are arranged roughly along the same south-to-north trajectory that begins with Judah and ends with Dan, the former according to the geographic location of the tribes and the latter according to the judges' tribal affiliation. In both cases, this trajectory also coincides with a progressively deteriorating trend (see commentary for details). This neat schematization suggests that the author may have arranged his material primarily to reflect his particular theological interpretation of the period's history rather than to provide a strictly chronological account of what happened.

Furthermore, most of the twelve judges mentioned in 3:7–16:31 (among the leaders discussed in this section, Barak and Abimelek are not referred to as judges) are from different tribes. The enemies, with the exception of the Philistines common to both Shamgar and Samson, likewise come from different ethnic groups. This suggests that these narratives were likely selected for their representative function to show that, collectively, judges from all tribes were chosen to deal with enemies from every ethnic background.

Outline

1. Introducing the Era of the Judges (1:1–3:6)
   A. Military Failures (1:1–2:5)
   B. Spiritual Failures (2:6–3:6)
2. Exploits of Israel's Judges and Leaders (3:7–16:31)
   A. Othniel (3:7–11)
   B. Ehud (3:12–30)
   C. Shamgar (3:31)
   D. Deborah and Barak (4:1–5:31)
   E. Gideon (6:1–8:35)
   F. Abimelek (9:1–57)
   G. Tola and Jair (10:1–5)
   H. Jephthah (10:6–12:7)
   I. Ibzan, Elon, and Abdon (12:8–15)
   J. Samson (13:1–16:31)

3. Chaos in Israelite Society (17:1–21:25)
   A. In the Areas of Religious and Military Practices (17:1–18:31)
   B. In the Areas of Social Norms and Political Decisions (19:1–21:25)

Commentary

1. Introducing the Era of the Judges (1:1–3:6)

A. Military failures (1:1–2:5). The book of Joshua ends with the death and burial of Joshua (Josh. 24:29–30). The book of Judges begins with an extended report of Israel's military progress after Joshua's death (1:1–36). Having received prior instructions to destroy the Canaanites and take possession of their land (Num. 33:51–53; Deut. 1:8; 7:1–4, 16), Israel begins by asking the Lord which tribe should lead the way in battle. After Judah is chosen and promised victory, the tribe takes leadership by inviting Simeon, whose allotted land falls within Judah's boundary (cf. Josh. 19:1–9), to join them in battle.

Judah meets with a string of initial successes, including at Bezek, where they capture its leader and become the instrument of divine vengeance by doing to him what he had previously done to other defeated kings. Then Judah engages the enemy in three different regions: the hill country, the southern land (Negev), and the lowlands (Shephelah), with the results summarized in the report that follows.

In the hill country, under the leadership of Caleb and his family, Judah is able to take Hebron and Debir (cf. Josh. 14:6–15; Judg. 1:20). While Caleb's promise to give his daughter

Chariots, mentioned in Judges 1:19, are also featured in many Assyrian battle scenes, such as in this relief (Nineveh, 645–635 BC).

Aksah as a reward to whoever is able to capture Debir may seem objectionable to modern sensibilities, in so doing, Caleb is also ensuring that Aksah will be married to a valiant warrior who is able to fulfill the Lord's command to dispossess the enemy. Besides, Caleb's readiness to grant Aksah a blessing (translated "a special favor" in the NIV [1:15]) in the form of springs of water reinforces his overall benevolent intention toward his daughter.

Regarding the Negev, after briefly noting that the Kenites have relocated there with some Judahites, the author reports that Judah helps Simeon destroy Zephath. The city, previously allotted to Simeon (cf. Josh. 19:4, using the city's new name), is then renamed Hormah.

As for the lowlands, 1:18 reports that Judah is able to take the Philistine cities of Gaza, Ashkelon, and Ekron.

But Judah's war effort is not without setback. According to 1:19, despite the tribe's success in the hill country, it is unable to dispossess the Canaanites in the plains because the enemy there has iron chariots. For some the mention of iron chariots exonerates Judah since its failure is only due to the enemy's superior technology. A careful consideration of other mentions of "iron chariots" suggests otherwise. After all, when the Joseph tribes suggested in Joshua 17:14–18 that the enemy's iron chariots were too strong for them, Joshua dismissed this by affirming the tribes' ability to conquer enemy territory in spite of the iron chariots. In fact, Barak's ability to defeat Sisera in Judges 4, even though the latter has nine hundred iron chariots (4:3), proves

Joshua's point. Thus, rather than exonerating Judah, the mention of iron chariots in 1:19 actually highlights the tribe's failure.

After the lengthy report on Judah, the author then quickly moves through the rest of the Transjordanian tribes, following a roughly south-to-north trajectory. The next tribe to the immediate north is Benjamin, who fails to dispossess the Jebusites living in Jerusalem. Despite the assertion in 1:8 that Judah took Jerusalem, Jerusalem is actually part of the territory allotted to Benjamin (Josh. 18:28). Thus, Benjamin has ultimate responsibility to dispossess it. The capture of the city reported in 1:8 may merely represent an initial victory where Judah, in obedience to the Lord's command to lead the way (cf. 1:1–2), launches a successful initial assault. What 1:21 highlights, then, is Benjamin's failure to follow up on that initial victory to permanently take possession of what has been allotted to them.

As the northward progression continues, the focus moves to the two Joseph tribes, whose allotments are immediately north of Benjamin. Here, the joint effort of the two tribes is first reported (1:22–26) before the individual efforts of Manasseh (1:27–28) and Ephraim (1:29) are reported.

At first glance, the joint effort spells success for the two tribes, as they not only enjoy the Lord's presence (1:22) but also are able to conquer Bethel/Luz (1:23–26). But on closer examination, the success at Bethel/Luz is perhaps not all that it appears. First, that the Joseph tribes need to cut a deal with a local inhabitant to be shown a way into Luz seems to suggest an inability to take the city without such help. Second, since the man spared promptly goes away and builds a new Luz, the spirit of Luz is not vanquished but lives on merely at a different location.

The Bethel/Luz episode is then followed by a series of short reports concerning individual tribes, including Manasseh and Ephraim as well as the northern tribes of Zebulun, Asher, Naphtali, and Dan. All these tribes fail to dispossess the cities allotted to them in Joshua

16–19. Here, it should be noted that Dan was originally allotted land on the southern coastal plains next to Judah (Josh. 19:40–46). Unable to take possession of that land, the tribe eventually moved to the far north (cf. Josh. 19:47; Judg. 18:1–31), so that it ends up last on the list.

Taken as a whole, this tribal conquest report seems designed to highlight a pattern of progressive deterioration. Four stages of deterioration can be discerned: (1) Judah and Simeon are able to dispossess some of the Canaanites, such that there is no mention of the Canaanites having to live among them. (2) Benjamin to Zebulun are unable to dispossess the Canaanites, but seem to be in a dominant position, as they allow the Canaanites to live among them. (3) Asher and Naphtali are also unable to dispossess the Canaanites but seem to be in a subordinate position, as they have to live among the Canaanites. (4) Dan is stymied by Amorites and is unable even to set foot on their allotted land.

B. Spiritual failures (2:6–3:6). Given the Lord's specific commands for Israel to take possession of the land and destroy its inhabitants (Num. 33:51–56; Deut. 1:8; 7:1–4, 16), it is not surprising that an angel of the Lord is sent to confront the people for their disobedience in making covenants with the local population rather than dispossessing them (2:1–5). Announcing the withdrawal of his earlier promise to dispossess the local population for them (cf. Deut. 7:1–2, 17–24; 9:1–5; 11:22–25; 31:3), the Lord warns that those spared by the Israelites will end up being a source of future trouble for them. On hearing this, the people weep, which explains the subsequent naming of the place as Bokim, meaning "weepers."

After reporting Israel's military failures, the narrative then shifts to the people's spiritual failures (2:6–3:6). Since the spiritual failures occur simultaneously with the military failures, the author traces how they came about by taking the reader back to the death of Joshua. The wording of 2:6–9 is very similar to Joshua 24:28–31 and highlights the fact that, while under the leadership of Joshua and the elders who had personally experienced the Lord, the people continued to serve him. But after the death of Joshua and that generation of elders, another generation grew up without any knowledge of the Lord or what he had done for Israel. This ushers in an era of spiritual decline, where the nation's history seems to be locked in a series of downward spirals.

A recurring vicious cycle is introduced in 2:11–19, and this becomes the pattern according to which most of the subsequent narratives about the judges are organized. The cycle essentially consists of five stages: (1) the people do evil in the eyes of the Lord by worshiping idols (2:11–13); (2) the Lord, in his anger, gives Israel into the hands of foreign oppressors (2:14–15a); (3) the people cry out to the Lord in their distress (2:15b, 18b); (4) the Lord raises up judges to deliver the nation from its oppressors (2:16, 18a); (5) the land has rest (not specifically mentioned in 2:11–19, but recurring in many of the subsequent narratives of the judges).

But after each judge dies (and sometimes even while the judge is still living; cf. 8:27), the people inevitably return to idolatry, thus initiating the cycle all over again (2:17, 19).

Two further comments need to be made about this cyclical pattern. First, the people's crying out in stage three is not to be understood as acts of repentance but simply as cries for help. That is why in 10:14, the Lord, in anger, tells the people to "cry out" to the gods they have chosen instead. That being the case, the Lord's intervention in stage four is to be understood as a gracious and compassionate act to the undeserving rather than a response to genuine repentance.

Second, note also that the cycles are not simply static recurrences, but according to 2:19 each represents a further deterioration from the one before. This is also discernible in the narratives of the judges, such that a particular theme found in one narrative will reappear in a subsequent narrative but show trends of worsening. Moreover, even the cycle itself breaks

down as it progresses. Thus, beginning with the Jephthah cycle, the land is no longer said to be at rest after each deliverance, and in the Samson cycle, there is no longer any report of the people crying out to the Lord when they are oppressed. (Instances of this deteriorating trend in the narratives of the various judges will be pointed out in the relevant sections of the commentary that follows.)

As in 2:1–5, where Israel's military failures result in rebuke and the withdrawal of the Lord's promise to dispossess the nations, so too the report of Israel's spiritual failures is also followed by a similar rebuke and withdrawal of earlier promises. The content of 2:20–21 is not substantially different from 2:1–3, except for the further disclosure that the presence of the nations also serves to test the extent of Israel's obedience (2:22; 3:4) and to teach warfare to a generation without battle experience (3:1–2). Unfortunately, regarding the test, Israel clearly fails, as 3:5–6 reports that the people not only live among the local population but have also intermarried with them in violation of the Lord's explicit commands (cf. Deut. 7:1–4). And as Deuteronomy 7:4 foresaw, intermarriage has indeed led to apostasy, as the Israelites also "served their gods."

2. Exploits of Israel's Judges and Leaders (3:7–16:31)

The book now moves into a section where the exploits of Israel's various judges constitute the main focus. But despite the highly individual character of these narratives, the section as a whole is intricately tied to the material in the preceding section. This can be seen in that elements of the cyclical pattern found in 2:11–19 regularly appear at the beginning and end of each major judge narrative to form a frame. The narratives about the major judges in this section are thus to be understood as concrete illustrations of the cyclical pattern introduced in 2:11–19.

A. Othniel (3:7–11). Unlike the other narratives to follow, the narrative of the Judahite judge Othniel is very brief and consists primarily of stereotypical phrases already found in 2:11–19. Othniel is the only major judge presented without any discernible character flaw. It is likely that the author has intentionally set him as an ideal paradigmatic model against which subsequent judges are to be compared.

Following the expected pattern, the cycle begins with Israel doing evil in the eyes of the Lord by worshiping idols. This results in the Lord giving the nation into the hands of Cushan-Rishathaim, a king who likely comes from northern Mesopotamia (Aram Naharaim is literally "Aram of two rivers," referring probably to the Euphrates and the Habur). Israel is subjected to him for eight years. But as the people cry out to the Lord, the Lord raises up Othniel by sending his Spirit on him. He defeats Cushan-Rishathaim in battle and brings rest to the land for forty years, until his death.

B. Ehud (3:12–30). After the death of Othniel, Israel once again does evil in the eyes of the Lord (3:12). The Lord then empowers Eglon, king of Moab, who, with the Ammonites and Amalekites, oppresses Israel for eighteen years (3:13–14). Israel then cries out to the Lord, who responds by raising up Ehud as deliverer.

Ehud is first introduced in 3:15–16 as a "left-handed man," which in Hebrew is literally "a man restricted in his right hand." Considering that Ehud is from the tribe of Benjamin, which literally means "son of my right hand,"

This figurine from Tyre, which may represent the Canaanite god Baal as a warrior (1400–1200 BC), is an example of the type of idol that the Israelites rebelliously persisted in worshiping (Judg. 2:19).

that a judge from the tribe of right-handers is restricted in his right hand immediately presents Ehud as an unlikely candidate for a deliverer.

To carry out his assassination (3:17–26), Ehud appears before Eglon as a tribute bearer for Israel. Because of his left-handedness, Ehud is able to smuggle his sword into the palace by strapping it to his right thigh, where no one would normally expect a weapon to be carried. After presenting the tribute, Ehud pretends to leave with his entourage, only to turn back near Gilgal with claims of a secret message for Eglon. The meaning of the word translated "stone images" in 3:19, 26 is uncertain, but it likely refers to the engraved boundary stones that mark national borders. If so, the fact that Ehud turns back alone at the border after having sent his own entourage on might have convinced Eglon that he indeed had a secret message to convey that he did not want his colleagues to know about.

Ehud's actual words are not without ambiguity. The Hebrew word for "message" in 3:19–20 can equally mean "word" or "thing." Thus, while Eglon thinks Ehud has a divine message for him, Ehud may be thinking about the thing (weapon) he has prepared for Eglon on behalf of the Lord.

When Eglon unsuspectingly dismisses his attendants and rises to receive what he thinks is a divine oracle, Ehud quickly deploys his hidden sword and plunges it into Eglon's belly.

There is some debate regarding what comes out in 3:22 after the blade goes in, as represented by the translations in the NIV. The reading in the 1984 edition suggests that it is the sword that comes out from Eglon's back, but the 2011 translation ("his bowels discharged") represents the understanding that the obscure Hebrew word is a reference to fecal matter coming out of Eglon as he dies. If the latter is correct, then the accompanying smell would explain why the servants later think their king is relieving himself (3:24). By the time these servants lose patience and open the locked door only to find their king dead, Ehud has already escaped back to Israel.

Rallying his people with the declaration, "The LORD has given Moab, your enemy, into your hands" (3:28), Ehud and his army then block off the fords of the Jordan, thus cutting off possible Moabite reinforcement from across the river. Having struck down ten thousand Moabites, Israel then subjects Moab to them for the next eighty years (3:27–30).

C. Shamgar (3:31). The account of the next judge, Shamgar (3:31), is very brief, and reminds one of Samson (13:1–16:31) because of the unusual weapon and the Philistine enemy both share in common. The name Shamgar son of Anath, however, is a non-Israelite name, possibly of Hurrian or Syrian origin. Although not much else is known about him, his inclusion as one of the judges shows that the Lord uses even non-Israelites to deliver his people.

D. Deborah and Barak (4:1–5:31). **4:1–24.** Before long, Israel again does evil in the eyes of the Lord, resulting in the Lord's selling them into the hands of the Canaanite king Jabin and his commander Sisera. Possessing superior technology in the form of iron chariots, they oppress Israel for twenty years (4:1–3).

Israel's cry to the Lord is followed immediately by the appearance of Deborah (4:4–5). This and the description of her as "leading" (literally "judging"; see RSV) Israel give the impression that Deborah must be the next judge in focus. But Deborah's role within the narrative, primarily having to do with speaking (4:5–6, 9, 14), is more consistent with her being a prophetess (4:4) than a judge. In addition, although she is said to be "judging" Israel, this "judging" is immediately qualified in 4:5 as judicial in nature. As this is the only time within the book where the "judging" of one of Israel's leaders is so qualified, it may be intended to distinguish Deborah's judging from the kind of military deliverance associated with the book's other judges. In fact, 4:14 seems to suggest that after giving the rallying cry, Deborah does not join in the battle. Nor is she mentioned again in the rest of the chapter describing Israel's victory. Thus, Deborah is not actively involved in the military aspect of Israel's deliverance.

Rather, it is Barak whom the Lord calls to fight against Sisera and into whose hands (the singular "your" in 4:7, 14 clearly refers to Barak) the Lord promises to give Sisera. This suggests

Mount Tabor, where the Israelite troops assembled before the battle with Sisera (Judg. 4:7)

that it is really Barak and not Deborah who is meant to occupy the role of the deliverer judge. That subsequent references to the judges in 1 Samuel 12:11 and Hebrews 11:32 mention only Barak by name but not Deborah also seems to confirm that both Jewish and early Christian traditions view Barak rather than Deborah as the deliverer judge.

When Deborah sends for Barak and commissions him on behalf of the Lord to fight Sisera (4:6–9), Barak makes his acceptance conditional on Deborah's willingness to go with him. Given the Lord's clear promise of victory (4:7), Barak's response seems to betray a lack of faith. This is especially so since, in the Ehud narrative, the similar prospect of the Lord giving the enemy into Israel's hands (3:28) is sufficient to prompt immediate participation from the people. No wonder, then, that Barak's response is met with the Lord's disapproval, such that the honor of capturing and killing Sisera will now go to a woman.

After recounting the gathering of troops on both sides and Deborah's rallying cry (4:10–14), the author briefly reports the battle itself in 4:15–16. Although no detail is given regarding how the victory comes about, 5:19–22 suggests that the Lord has sent a heavy rainstorm, thus flooding the Kishon River and rendering Sisera's iron chariots inoperable as the wheels get stuck in the mud. That may be why even Sisera himself has to flee on foot (4:15, 17).

Sisera's escape takes him to the tent of Jael, wife of Heber the Kenite (4:17–21). Earlier, in 1:16, it was reported that the Kenites had associated themselves with the people of Judah in the south. But according to 4:11, Heber has moved away from the rest of his people toward the north. He has apparently made a peace treaty with Jabin, whose army Sisera commands (4:17). This friendly relationship thus paves the way for Jael's offer of hospitality to be accepted without suspicion. Jael's provision of a blanket, and of milk when Sisera merely asks for water, probably further enhances Sisera's trust. The irony is that when Sisera instructs

Jael to answer in the negative when asked if anyone (literally "a man") is there (4:20), little does he realize that what he means to be a lie actually turns out to be true because the only man in that tent will soon be brutally killed by his hostess. Thus, Deborah's prophecy (4:9) is fulfilled, as Barak arrives only to find Sisera already dead by the hand of a woman (4:22). With Sisera dead and his army destroyed, the Israelites build on that momentum until Jabin is finally destroyed as well (4:23–24).

5:1–31. The victory likely prompts a national celebration, which may be the setting for the following song (5:1–31). A careful consideration of the content of the song suggests, however, that this may not be merely a hymn celebrating victory but a politically charged attempt to promote participation in wars against foreign oppressors.

The song itself can roughly be divided into two parts, each introduced by a refrain calling on the people to praise the Lord (5:2, 9). In both refrains, the leaders (princes) of Israel are mentioned, along with the people who willingly volunteered themselves for battle. That both calls to praise are prompted by this willing participation of leader and people alike suggests that the focus of the song is not just on the victory but also on the theme of participation.

In the first part, the call for praise (5:2) is followed by a call to foreign kings to listen (5:3). Then 5:4–5 describes the appearance of the Lord in a thunderstorm, apparently marching ahead of his people into battle against the enemy. Storm imagery is commonly associated with the appearance of a deity in both Canaanite literature and the Old Testament (cf. 2 Sam. 22:10–15; Ps. 68:7–8; 77:16–18; 97:2–5; Isa. 29:6; Nah. 1:3–5). In this case, such imagery appropriately anticipates the heavy rain and the subsequent flooding of the Kishon that contributes to the defeat of Sisera's army (cf. 5:20–22).

The significance of the Lord's coming from Seir/Edom in 5:4 is uncertain, but in Deuteronomy 33:2 and Isaiah 63:1, the Lord is also depicted as coming from Seir and Edom, with Seir being further connected with Sinai in Deuteronomy 33:2. The mention of these southern locations likely reflects an early tradition in which the Lord's dwelling is believed to lie in the south.

The plight of the people is next described in 5:6–8, as village life is portrayed as having ceased and the main roads as having been abandoned. According to 5:8, the root cause of this decimation is that the people have forsaken the Lord and chosen new gods. As the Lord gave his people into the hands of foreign oppressors in judgment, war came to the city gates, where an army would have gathered before marching out. That there is neither shield nor spear among Israel's army speaks both of the desperation of the situation and of the valor of those who would still volunteer themselves for battle. No wonder, then, that 5:8 is followed immediately by the refrain in 5:9, as the second part of the song begins with another call to praise prompted by the willing participation of leaders and people.

This second call to praise is followed in 5:10–11 by an exhortation to travelers passing by—both the ruling class, who would ride on donkeys (cf. 10:4; 12:14), and commoners, who would walk on foot—to consider the message of the singers at the watering places. The fact that the message to be considered concerns the righteous acts not only of the Lord but also of his warriors in Israel again suggests that the overall focus of the song is on both the Lord's intervention on behalf of his people and the role the people play in battle. The actual account of such acts then follows in the rest of the song.

The recitation begins with the Lord's people going down to the city gates to join the battle (5:11, 13). This is followed by a roll call that includes the participating tribes (5:14–15) as well as the nonparticipating tribes who chose to stay behind (5:15–17). Although the impression given in 4:6, 10 is that only Zebulun and Naphtali fought in the battle, apparently other tribes also participated. That the nonparticipating tribes are also listed suggests again that the main concern of the song is not just to celebrate a victory but also to present a polemic against nonparticipation.

Among the list of participating and nonparticipating tribes are two designations that are nontribal: Makir in 5:14, and Gilead in 5:17. Since the geographic area known as Gilead, covering the mountainous area east of the Jordan, was occupied by Gad and the half tribe of Manasseh, the reference in 5:17 is likely to these one and a half tribes. As for Makir, the clan so named also represents the descendants of a son of Manasseh (cf. Gen. 50:23; Num. 26:9). Since Gilead in 5:17 already includes the Manassites who settled east of the Jordan, the reference to Makir in 5:14 probably refers to those who have settled west of the Jordan. The use of Makir and Gilead thus likely serves to distinguish the two halves of Manasseh, who took different stances with regard to war participation.

Thus, according to this roll call, five and a half tribes—Ephraim, Benjamin, the western half of Manasseh, Zebulun, Issachar, and Naphtali (actually not mentioned until 5:18)—participated, while four and a half tribes—Reuben, Gad and the eastern half of Manasseh, Dan, and Asher—did not. When this is compared to the support Ehud received from all Israel (3:27), one can discern the beginning of a deteriorating trend. Subsequent judges will receive even less support from the people as they battle foreign enemies.

In the account of the battle itself (5:18–22), not only is the contingent from Zebulun and Naphtali depicted as having fought valiantly to prevent foreign kings from carrying off plunder (5:18–19), but forces of nature apparently also joined in to wreak havoc for the enemy's horses (5:20–22). Here, as is common in Canaanite mythology, the stars likely represent the source of the rain that caused the Kishon River to flood and thus impeded the movement of the horses drawing the enemy's chariots. This involvement of the natural forces thus speaks of the Lord's intervention on behalf of his people, thereby making it inexcusable for any Israelite not to participate as well.

The song returns to the theme of participation versus nonparticipation as the city of Meroz is singled out and its people twice cursed because they did not participate in the Lord's battle (5:23). In contrast, Jael is twice called most blessed (5:24), apparently for her involvement in killing Sisera, the details of which follow in 5:25–27.

Functionally, 5:25–27 seems to be a hinge paragraph, as it connects both with the immediately preceding verse to explain Jael's blessedness and also with the following section to offer a contrast with Sisera's mother. For, 5:25–27 and 5:28–30 both focus on a woman in relation to Sisera. If Jael's offer of milk in 5:25 is meant to portray her as a mother figure, then here is a mother figure who kills, in contrast to the description of Sisera's real mother, who waits in vain for her son to return. But ironically, it is the mother figure who kills that is praised, while the real mother who waits is taunted. For the "oo" in 5:31 has effectively cast the real mother among the enemies of the Lord, while by her action, Jael has proven herself to be among those who love the Lord.

The entire narrative about Barak and Deborah then concludes with the note that the land rested for forty years (5:31).

E. Gideon (6:1–8:35). 6:1–40. The cycle is to begin anew when Israel again does evil in the eyes of the Lord. This time, the Lord hands his people over to a coalition led by the Midianites, who for seven years have impoverished them through regular pillaging of crops and livestock. As expected, Israel cries out to the Lord (6:1–6).

Whereas in previous cycles Israel's cry was met almost immediately with the raising up of

The Canaanite pantheon included goddesses, such as Astarte (seen here on a Late Bronze Age plaque), consort to Baal, and Asherah (Judg. 6:25).

a deliverer judge (3:9; 3:15; 4:3, 6–7), this time, the Lord sends a prophet to rebuke the people for their ingratitude and disobedience, evident in their worship of foreign gods (6:7–10). One can sense the Lord's increasing frustration with his people's repeated waywardness, something that will become even more apparent at the beginning of the Jephthah narrative in 10:10–16.

Nonetheless, an angel of the Lord, who turns out to be the Lord himself (cf. 6:14), appears to Gideon (6:11–24). The Lord affirms to Gideon his presence and addresses him as a mighty warrior. But Gideon merely questions why, if the Lord is indeed present, Israel has not experienced the kind of miraculous deliverance known during the exodus. In response, the Lord commissions Gideon to save Israel out of Midian's hand. But Gideon simply stresses his clan's weakness and his own insignificance.

To counter Gideon's protestation, the Lord reiterates his presence, but Gideon still demands a sign. Not until the angel disappears, after causing fire to flare from a rock to consume the offering Gideon brought, does Gideon realize he has been in the presence of the divine. Upon assurance from the Lord that he will not die even though he has seen the angel face-to-face, Gideon builds an altar to the Lord and names it "The LORD Is Peace" (6:24), perhaps to commemorate the Lord's declaration of peace in 6:23.

That same night comes Gideon's first mission (6:25–32), as the Lord commands him to tear down the idolatrous Baal altar and Asherah pole his father sponsored for the community. In their place, Gideon is to build a proper altar to the Lord and offer a bull as burnt offering. Although Gideon does as he is told, because he is afraid of his family and the men of the community he carries out his mission under the cover of night. This betrays a lack of faith, as his previous and subsequent need for signs also seems to confirm.

The following morning, when the townsfolk discover what has been done and that the perpetrator is Gideon, they demand his death. Gideon himself seems strangely absent in this episode, and it is left to his father, Joash, to save Gideon as Joash challenges Baal to contend for his own altar. Reflecting this challenge, Gideon is also called Jerub-Baal, meaning "Let Baal contend with him" (i.e., Gideon).

As enemies from the east cross the Jordan and camp at the Valley of Jezreel, the Spirit of the Lord comes upon Gideon, prompting him to summon the necessary troops in preparation for battle (6:33–35). Positive responses come from three northern tribes—Asher, Zebulun, and Naphtali—as well as Gideon's tribe, Manasseh.

But at this point, instead of moving forward boldly, Gideon again manifests a lack of faith. Even though he is aware that the Lord has promised to save Israel by his hand (6:36–37; cf. 6:16), Gideon needs further assurances (6:36–40). After asking for a sign and receiving confirmation from the Lord as his piece of fleece becomes wet while the surrounding ground remained dry, Gideon asks for the reverse to happen, probably to make sure that the previous sign was not caused naturally by the sun evaporating the dew on the ground faster than the dew that had saturated the fleece. The Lord graciously accommodates the second request.

7:1–25. Having been assured, Gideon sets up camp almost directly south of the Midianites (7:1). But before battle commences, the Lord has further instructions regarding the number of Gideon's troops (7:2–8). Concerned that in the aftermath of the impending victory, Israel will boast of its own strength rather than the Lord's deliverance, the Lord wants the number of troops reduced so that it will be clear to all

that the credit for the victory is entirely his. So the Lord tells Gideon to let all who fear to return home, and the number of troops goes from thirty-two thousand to ten thousand. But this is still too many in the Lord's estimate. So a second round of elimination takes place by a stream in which 9,700 who knelt to drink are sent back, leaving only three hundred, who lapped water like a dog.

Here, although many have offered explanations for why those who lapped are chosen over those who kneeled—much of the speculation has to do with the alertness of the soldiers as reflected by their drinking pose—the text itself is silent on the matter. Since the main issue here is the number of troops and not the quality of the soldiers, perhaps the only reason why the lappers are chosen over the kneelers is that there are fewer of them (note in 7:4 that the group to be chosen is not specified beforehand). For if the victory is to be entirely the Lord's doing, then what kind of soldiers are involved is really immaterial.

The night before battle, the Lord, probably because he is aware of Gideon's propensity to fear especially in light of the drastic troop reduction, takes the initiative to offer Gideon a final reassurance (7:9–15). Having affirmed once again that he will give the Midianites into Gideon's hands, the Lord then tells Gideon to go down to the enemy camp to receive further encouragement. Notice, however, that this instruction to go down is an option to be exercised only if Gideon is "afraid to attack" (7:10). That Gideon chooses to exercise this option thus indicates his insufficient faith in spite of the Lord's repeated promises (cf. 6:16; 7:7, 9). It is only after he has gone down to the enemy camp and heard even the enemy affirming the same promise the Lord has already made to him (7:14) that Gideon finally worships God and is ready to fight.

When Gideon returns to the Israelite camp, he gives his troops specific instructions for battle (7:15–18). The strategy is unconventional, as Gideon's three hundred men are equipped primarily with trumpets and empty jars with torches inside them. But this is the Lord's battle, since he has purposely pitched an army of three hundred against a coalition innumerable and like swarms of locusts (cf. 7:12).

Curiously, however, Gideon includes his own name in the battle cry, as he instructs his troops to shout "For the LORD and for Gideon" at the designated moment (7:18). Considering that after Midian is defeated the Israelites invite Gideon and his descendants to "rule over" them because they see him as the one who has saved them out of the hands of Midian (8:22), one has to wonder if the inclusion of Gideon's name on the same level as the Lord's in the battle cry contributes to Israel's eventual misattribution of credit to Gideon alone. This is even more ironic in light of the fact that the Lord's explicit aim in reducing the troops earlier was to ensure that the credit due him would not be usurped by another (7:2).

The unconventional battle strategy proves to be entirely successful (7:19–25), and the Midianites flee, probably taking the noise and light to be indicative of a much larger Israelite contingent. In the process, the Lord confuses the Midianites and their allies, and they end up attacking each other.

As the Israelites pursue, Gideon sends word to the Ephraimites, asking them to block the fords of the Jordan so that the enemy will not be able to escape back to their eastern homeland. The Ephraimites are thus able to capture and kill two Midianite generals, although two Midianite kings and some of their troops manage to escape.

8:1–35. After killing the two generals, the Ephraimites launch a strong complaint against Gideon for failing to involve them earlier (8:1–3). But Gideon credits the Ephraimites with the more significant accomplishment, and a potential internal conflict is averted.

As Gideon and his three hundred men continue to pursue the escaped Midianite kings east of the Jordan, he seeks help from two Israelite towns, Sukkoth and Peniel (8:4–9).

Each, however, refuses to help, and in response, Gideon threatens punishment on his return. Indeed, after successfully capturing the two Midianite kings (8:5–12), Gideon makes good on his threat and returns to the two uncooperative towns (8:13–17). He threshes the elders of Sukkoth with thorns and briers and also tears down the tower of Peniel, as he earlier promised (cf. 8:7, 9). But he also kills the men of Peniel (8:17), something that seems excessive, especially when compared to Deborah and Barak's mere verbal rebuke of those who had similarly refused to help (cf. 5:15–17, 23). But the trend will only worsen, as Jephthah later slaughters forty-two thousand Ephraimites over the similar issue of noncooperation (12:1–6).

Gideon then turns his attention to the two captured kings (8:18–20). Having asked about the men they killed at Tabor and received confirmation that they were his brothers, Gideon exacts revenge by executing the two kings, but not before telling them that, had they spared his brothers, he would have spared them. Here, Gideon clearly means what he says, as his statement is accompanied by a most serious oath formula invoking the personal name of the Lord. But if so, his statement is problematic in at least two ways.

First, even from the beginning of conquest, the standard practice seems to have been the killing of defeated enemy kings, be it in battle or in its aftermath (cf. Deut. 2:32–33; 3:3; Josh. 8:29; 10:22–26, 28, 30, 33, 37, 39, 40; 11:10, 12). Within Judges, Adoni-Bezek's death in 1:7 could very well represent this kind of execution. In fact, even in the period of the monarchy, both Saul's sparing of the Amalekite king Agag in 1 Samuel 15 and Ahab's sparing of the Aramean king Ben-Hadad in 1 Kings 20:29–43 result in judgment from the Lord. This means Gideon actually has no legitimate basis to consider sparing the two Midianite kings.

Second, Gideon's statement also reveals that his pursuit of the two kings may have been motivated more by personal vendetta than a desire to deal the nation's enemy a decisive defeat.

This makes one wonder if Gideon's punishment of the two uncooperative towns is not also motivated similarly by personal revenge. In hindsight, his openness to sparing the two Midianite kings makes his killing of the men of Peniel even harder to justify.

After executing the two kings, Gideon takes the ornaments off their camels' necks. This curious detail is significant in that such ornaments, along with the pendants and purple garments mentioned in 8:26, were status symbols often associated with royalty. Perhaps not coincidentally, Gideon's interest in such items is followed immediately by the report of the people's offer of kingship to him (8:22–27).

Admittedly, kingship is never explicitly mentioned in the people's offer. But the verb "to rule over" (Hebrew *mashal*) is often associated with kingly rule (cf. Josh. 12:2, 5; 1 Kings 4:21; 2 Chron. 7:18). In fact, in Judges 9:2, Abimelek persuades the Shechemites to let him "rule over" them, and as a result, they make him king (Judg. 9:6, 16). Furthermore, Israel's offer to Gideon is for a dynastic rule that passes from father to son, and this suggests royalty since the office of judge was not passed down this way (cf. Judg. 12:9–11).

To such an offer, Gideon dutifully declines, declaring piously that only the Lord should rule over them. His declaration notwithstanding, there are numerous indications that Gideon actually does harbor kingly ambitions. After all, he seems to covet royal paraphernalia and takes them for himself (8:21, 26). Some also understand his asking for gold earrings (8:24) as a request for tribute, which was the privilege of kings. This accumulation of wealth, together with having many wives and concubines (8:30–31), is also a decidedly kingly trapping, against which the Lord already warned in the rules he laid for Israelite kingship (cf. Deut. 17:17). Finally, the fact that Gideon personally names one of his sons Abimelek (8:31), meaning "My father is king," also hints at his kingly ambition. This is why some scholars actually see Gideon's answer not so much as a decline of

Israel's offer but as an acceptance couched in pious clichés. But regardless of whether Gideon actually accepts the offer, his seventy sons apparently do end up ruling (*mashal*, as in 8:22–23) in Gideon's place after his death (cf. Judg. 9:2).

Regarding the manufacturing of the golden ephod (8:27), it should be noted that an ephod was originally an item of clothing worn by those in priestly offices. There is also a tradition in which the ephod had a special function in relation to oracular inquiries (1 Sam. 23:6, 9; 30:7). Although the text is silent on Gideon's motive for manufacturing the golden ephod, it seems reasonable to speculate that it may be to establish his hometown as an alternative worship center where people can inquire of the Lord. However, this ill-advised move ends up ensnaring both Gideon's family and all Israel, as the golden ephod turns into an object of idolatry.

The narrative about Gideon ends with a summary of his major accomplishment, the years of peace under his judgeship, and notes about his family and his place of burial (8:28–32). This is followed by further comments on the people's spiritual state (8:33–35), with special attention to their apostasy and their failure to show covenant faithfulness to Gideon's family. This last point then introduces the following narrative, which details Israel's lack of covenant faithfulness.

F. Abimelek (9:1–57). The narrative begins with an account of Abimelek's rise to power (9:1–6). As indicated in 8:31, Abimelek is a son of Gideon by his Shechemite concubine. Going to his relatives in Shechem, Abimelek asks the city's leaders to support him over Gideon's seventy sons as sole ruler. Seeing that Abimelek has both legitimacy as Gideon's son and blood relationship with them that Gideon's other sons lack, the Shechemites throw their support behind Abimelek by providing him with the necessary funds to stage a coup. Abimelek then hires some reckless fellows and goes back to Ophrah, where he murders his seventy half brothers on a stone.

The leaders of Shechem and Beth Millo then gather to crown Abimelek king. Here, although some see the extent of Abimelek's rule as largely restricted to Shechem and its surroundings, 9:22 suggests that it includes all Israel. After all, Abimelek usurped the power of his seventy half brothers, whose rule had probably included all the territory formerly ruled by their father. Besides, "the Israelites" in 9:55 seems to refer to Abimelek's followers. Thus, although it is initially the leaders of Shechem and Beth Millo who crown Abimelek king, the rest of Israel may have eventually accepted his leadership as well.

Jotham, Gideon's youngest son, somehow escapes the massacre. When he hears that Abimelek has been made king, he goes up Mount Gerizim just outside Shechem and proclaims a message of rebuke against Abimelek and the Shechemites (9:7–21).

Jotham begins with a fable about trees searching for a king (9:8–15). There is some debate as to whether the fable is against the idea of monarchy in general or only speaks to the particular situation concerning Abimelek and the Shechemites. Those who support the former interpretation point out that, since the fable suggests that honorable and productive people have no desire to become king, but only the unworthy aspire to it, kingship must therefore be an inherently bad idea. While such a reading is possible, it is more likely that by casting Abimelek as the thornbush and the Shechemites as trees looking for a king, Jotham is making the point that those who are foolish enough to choose an unworthy candidate as king should be wary of the destructive potential of their choice.

In the fable, the thornbush boastfully demands that the other trees take refuge in its shade to show their sincerity (*emet* in Hebrew, translated by the NIV simply as "really" [9:15]).

The archaeological remains of Shechem (foreground), at the base of Mount Gerizim (background)

Otherwise, it threatens to let fire come out to consume even the cedars of Lebanon. Playing on the word *emet* and using it in a slightly different sense to mean "integrity" in 9:16, 19 (translated "honorably" in the NIV), Jotham then sarcastically wishes both parties mutual happiness if the Shechemites have indeed acted with *emet* in making Abimelek king. But accusing them of not having done so since they sponsored the murder of Gideon's seventy sons even though Gideon has delivered them from Midian's oppression, he curses them with mutual destruction by fire, and then quickly makes his escape.

The rest of the narrative then focuses on how Jotham's curse is fulfilled, as the Lord brings just retribution to both Abimelek and the Shechemites (9:22–57).

After Abimelek has governed Israel for three years, the Lord sends an evil spirit between Abimelek and the leaders of Shechem (although the NIV has "the citizens of Shechem," the Hebrew refers specifically to the "leaders") in order to repay both for their roles in the murder of Gideon's sons.

The conflict begins with the leaders of Shechem placing men in the hills to rob passersby, presumably to enrich themselves at the expense of Abimelek, who apparently does not live in the city. Matters soon escalate further with the appearance of Gaal, whose words in 9:28–29 imply that he is a descendant of Hamor, the father of Shechem, after whom the city may have been named (cf. Genesis 34). By appealing to closer ties with the city than those of the existing ruler, the tactic Gaal uses to turn the Shechemites against Abimelek is ironically what Abimelek used earlier to turn the Shechemites against Gideon's seventy sons. In this, one can already sense the outworking of just retribution, as the treachery Abimelek used against his half brothers is now being used against him.

However, Abimelek has a loyal deputy in the city's governor, Zebul, who reports back to him all that is going on. Upon Zebul's advice,

Abimelek brings along his men, fights, and defeats Gaal. Then he turns against the city that has betrayed him and destroys it, killing its people. This prompts the Shechemites in a nearby tower to go and hide in a stronghold at a pagan temple. But Abimelek sets fire to the stronghold, killing all those inside. Jotham's curse is thus partly fulfilled, as these Shechemites are literally destroyed by fire. Inasmuch as those who helped Abimelek kill his half brothers are now themselves killed by Abimelek, the Shechemites finally receive their just retribution.

As for Abimelek, not until he takes his campaign of revenge to Thebez does he finally meet his just retribution. Although Thebez is not previously mentioned, Abimelek's attack on the town suggests that it must have been aligned with Shechem in some way. As the townsfolk there have also locked themselves in a tower, Abimelek decides to use the same strategy he did before by setting the tower on fire. But as he approaches the entrance, a woman drops an upper millstone from above and hits Abimelek on the head, seriously wounding him. To avoid the shame of being killed by a woman, Abimelek asks his armor bearer to kill him. Thus even in the manner of his death, there is poetic justice. For he who killed on a *certain* stone (Hebrew *ehad*, meaning "one" or "a certain" in 9:5) is now killed by a *certain* woman (9:53, again *ehad*) dropping a stone on his head. Thus, God finally brings just retribution to all the perpetrators (9:56–57).

G. Tola and Jair (10:1–5). After the death of Abimelek, 10:1–5 briefly introduces two more judges: Tola and Jair. These two, plus the three listed in 12:8–15, are commonly referred to as minor judges because of the brevity of their accounts. Because these accounts contain no reports of military exploits against foreign enemies but only odd domestic details, some see the so-called minor judges as a different kind of judge from the so-called major judges. Thus, while the major judges are military leaders who fight foreign oppressors, the minor judges are thought to be administrators during times of peace. But such a distinction may not be necessary or accurate.

First, there are hints that some of the minor judges may also have played military roles. Tola, for example, is said in 10:1 to have arisen to "deliver" Israel (RSV), with the Hebrew root *ysh'* ("save" or "deliver") being used nineteen times out of twenty in the book to speak of deliverance from foreign enemies (cf. Judg. 2:16, 18; 3:9 (twice), 15, 31; 6:14–15, 36–37; 7:2, 7; 8:22; 10:12–14; 12:2–3; 13:5). Jair too may have played a military role, as other traditions about him in Numbers 32:41 and Deuteronomy 3:14 depict him also as a military hero.

Second, the distinctive framework used for the minor judges that provides the exact duration of office (as opposed to forty or eighty years of rest for the land for most of the major judges) and specifies the place of burial is also used for Jephthah (12:7). This suggests that in the earliest tradition, Jephthah may have been grouped together with the minor judges. If so, the fact that Jephthah was also a deliverer judge means that one cannot rule out the possibility that the other minor judges also had military exploits against foreign oppressors. It would thus be difficult to maintain a functional difference between the major and minor judges.

Third, at the end of the Gideon narrative, the information about his wives and children, as well as his place of burial (8:30–32), is also not dissimilar to the information given for some of the minor judges, such as Jair (10:4), Ibzan (12:9), and Abdon (12:14). This again shows that the difference between the major and minor judges may not be that significant, and the brevity of the accounts of the minor judges may only be due either to some of the traditions about them having been lost or to the fact that their exploits did not fit the rhetorical purpose of the book's author.

H. Jephthah (10:6–12:7). **10:6–11:40.** The new cycle that begins with sin, oppression, and crying out to the Lord is again reported in 10:6–16, but with greater detail than before. The

"evil" the Israelites commit is clearly specified as apostasy, and the people's deteriorating spiritual state is highlighted both by the long list of foreign gods they have come to serve and by the explicit statement that they have forsaken the Lord and no longer serve him. The mention of the Philistines together with the Ammonites in 10:7 as people into whose hands the Lord has sold Israel perhaps anticipates also the Samson cycle. In the narrative featuring Jephthah, however, the focus is on the Ammonites. In addition, although the Ammonite oppression seems to be most keenly felt by the tribes east of the Jordan, 10:9 makes it clear that the western and southern tribes, such as Judah, Benjamin, and Ephraim, are also affected, so that the crisis is justifiably presented as national.

This time, not only is Israel's crying out to the Lord reported, but their confession that accompanies their crying out is also quoted (10:10). But instead of immediately providing a deliverer as he did in the Othniel, Ehud, and Barak cycles, the Lord, for the second time, responds with a rebuke. It even comes directly from him rather than through a prophet, as in the Gideon cycle. To make matters worse, the Lord initially refuses to save his people, telling them instead to go and cry out to the various gods they now serve. This leads to a second round of confession from the people, accompanied by concrete action as they get rid of the foreign gods among them and return to the Lord.

While it may be easy to assume that the Lord's eventual willingness to save his people indicates that he accepts their repentance, the text suggests otherwise. The Hebrew root *qtsr*—translated as "could bear no longer" in 10:16—often conveys the idea of being weary (2 Kings 19:26 = Isa. 37:27; Zech. 11:8) or impatient (Exod. 6:9; Num. 21:4; Job 21:4; Prov. 14:17, 29; Mic. 2:7). Particularly in 16:16, the word is used in relation to Samson being wearied to death by Delilah's constant nagging and prodding. Thus, what 10:16 seems to suggest is that the Lord's eventual action for his people comes not so much out of his acceptance of their repentance but out of compassion regarding their misery or even a sense of weariness from their constant pleading.

But instead of waiting for the Lord to raise up a deliverer for them, Israel's leaders decide to find a deliverer for themselves when the Ammonites are called to arms (10:17–11:11). They initially offer to make anyone willing to lead the attack against the Ammonites the head of all Gilead (10:18), but when no one apparently responds, they approach Jephthah to enlist him for the job (11:4).

In a brief flashback that serves to introduce the new hero (11:1–3), it is disclosed that, as an illegitimate son of Gilead, Jephthah has earlier been driven out by his half brothers over inheritance issues. This apparently happened with the blessing of the elders of the community (cf. 11:7). He then settled in Tob, where he gathered around him a group of ruffians and likely made a living from raiding. He must have made quite a name for himself, thus explaining why the elders of Gilead turn to him when no one else takes up their open offer.

In approaching him, the elders initially seem uncomfortable with the idea of making Jephthah head of their people. Thus, they only offer to make him commander, a military office clearly inferior to that of "head" of the people. Whether or not Jephthah knows about the earlier open offer is uncertain, but clearly considering the elders' offer insufficient, Jephthah does not respond favorably. The elders thus revise their offer, this time agreeing to make him head of Gilead. With that, Jephthah finally agrees to go with them. As the Gileadites make Jephthah both head and commander over them, Jephthah solemnizes the agreement before the Lord at Mizpah.

Notice that unlike Gideon, who initially had doubts about his own ability to deliver Israel, Jephthah shows no such reservations. At a time when Israel is oppressed by the Ammonites, what these negotiations show is that, unlike the judges before him, Jephthah, in his final consent to play the role of deliverer, is mainly motivated by self-interest rather than a concern for the people's suffering. This theme of a judge increasingly acting out of self-interest, which first surfaced with Gideon (see commentary on Judg. 8:18–20), continues through Jephthah and will eventually culminate with the final judge in the book, Samson.

The region around the Jabbok River, the northern boundary of the territory Israel is accused of stealing from the Ammonites (Judg. 11:13)

Jephthah's back-and-forth dialogue with the Ammonite king through messengers is reported in 11:12–28. While this may appear to be some form of negotiation, Jephthah's words are not conciliatory and may actually be more a challenge to war. In response to Jephthah's inquiry into the reason behind the hostility, the Ammonite king accuses the Israelites of having taken his land when they first came out of Egypt (11:12–13). Specifically, the land in question concerns the area occupied by Reuben and Gad between the rivers Arnon and Jabbok east of the Jordan.

Jephthah's lengthy reply essentially consists of four points. First, he maintains that when Israel came out of Egypt, she did not take any of the land belonging to the descendants of Lot or Abraham, such as the Moabites, Ammonites, and Edomites (11:15–18). Second, he argues that the land in question was actually taken from the Amorites, as the Lord gave the Amorite king Sihon and his army into Israel's hands when they attacked Israel (11:19–22). Third, Jephthah asserts that since Israel's God has given that land to his people, and since that land has been in their possession for three hundred years without Ammon ever having challenged that right, Israel will continue to keep that land just as Ammon will keep what their god has given them (11:23–26). Notice that in so saying, Jephthah is not affirming the reality or authority of the Ammonite god. After all, he is involved in a dispute with war implications and is not conducting a theological debate. Therefore, he may simply be using language his opponent will understand to make a point. Fourth, having made that point, he warns that as the Ammonites' hostility was uncalled for, they should beware that the Lord, who is the ultimate judge, will decide the dispute (11:27).

When the Ammonite king chooses not to respond any further (11:28), Jephthah takes active steps to prepare for war (11:29–31). As the Spirit of the Lord comes upon him, he crosses Gilead and Manasseh, presumably to mobilize his troops. But 11:30–31 also records a vow he makes to the Lord, promising to sacrifice as burnt offering whatever comes out of his house to meet him when he returns safely from war.

Now because what ends up being sacrificed is his daughter, it is worth asking if Jephthah intended the sacrifice to include humans. While some suggest that he never meant to include humans, the fact is that had he only intended an animal to be sacrificed, he would not react as he does when he sees his daughter coming out to meet him. He would instead greet her gladly and look around for the first animal. Therefore, even though Jephthah certainly does not expect the victim to be his daughter, he must have been open to the possibility that a human being could be sacrificed. If so, this indicates two things.

First, Jephthah has apparently allowed pagan religious practices to exert a stronger influence on him than the clear stipulations of the Mosaic law (cf. Deut. 12:31; 18:10). Second, to make such a high-staked vow on the eve of battle, even after the Spirit of the Lord has come upon him, betrays a desperation that points to a lack of faith. And to the extent that he is willing to put at stake a human life, whereas Gideon only asks for signs involving pieces of fleece, one can argue that Jephthah's lack of faith represents a deterioration from Gideon.

The battle itself and the subsequent victory against the Ammonites are described with surprising brevity in 11:32–33, and the focus promptly shifts to Jephthah's homecoming (11:34–40).

The tragedy is highlighted in 11:34, when Jephthah's unnamed daughter, described as an only child, comes out dancing in celebration of her father's return, oblivious to the vow that will soon doom her. No wonder, then, that Jephthah reacts with great distress when he realizes what he has done. But the daughter, perhaps showing a greater awareness of the demands of the law than her father, urges him to fulfill his vow, using language that echoes Numbers 30:2, as she tells him to "do to me according to what has gone out of your mouth" (NRSV). All she asks for is two months, so that she can mourn with friends the fact that she will never have the chance to experience married life. He grants her request, which subsequently gives rise to a custom in which every year, Israelite women commemorate Jephthah's daughter for four days.

12:1–7. Whether the events recorded in 12:1–7 happen before or after the sacrifice of Jephthah's daughter is uncertain. But in the aftermath of the Ammonite war, the Ephraimites cross over the Jordan to complain to Jephthah, just as they did earlier to Gideon (8:1), about not having been asked to participate in the war. This time, they even threaten to burn down Jephthah's house in retaliation. But while Gideon answered diplomatically to avert an internal conflict, Jephthah, who has earlier shown a willingness to patiently dialogue with the enemy (11:12–28), simply counteraccuses the Ephraimites of refusing to help when asked, and calls out the Gileadites to fight them. Using the same strategy Ehud (3:28) and Gideon (7:24) used when fighting enemies who had crossed over from the other side of the Jordan, Jephthah has his troops cut off the point of crossing at the Jordan to prevent the Ephraimites from returning to their home base. Then, using a dialectal peculiarity to determine tribal identity, Jephthah has forty-two thousand Ephraimites killed.

From this, one can see that the tendency toward internal conflict that first emerged with Gideon (8:1–17) has now escalated both in scope and intensity with Jephthah, until it eventually culminates in the slaughter of almost the entire tribe of Benjamin in the civil war recorded in 20:12–48.

Note also the absence of any mention of years of peace as the Jephthah narrative comes to a close in 12:7. Thus, the cyclical structure that characterizes the narratives of the major judges is also breaking down as the overall narrative continues.

I. Ibzan, Elon, and Abdon (12:8–15). For the three so-called minor judges listed in 12:8–15, Ibzan, Elon, and Abdon, see the earlier commentary on Judges 10:1–5. The only thing to note here is that the Bethlehem with which Ibzan is associated is likely not the famous Bethlehem in Judah but a city of the same name located within the territory of Zebulun (cf. Josh. 19:15). For within the book, the other Bethlehem is almost always referred to specifically as Bethlehem of Judah (cf. Judg. 17:7–9; 19:1–2, 18).

J. Samson (13:1–16:31). **13:1–25.** After another note of the Israelites doing evil in the eyes of the Lord and the Lord giving them into the hands of the Philistines, the narrative of the final judge begins somewhat unusually, with his birth narrative (13:1–25). The announcement of miraculous birth to a barren woman is a familiar biblical theme (cf. Gen. 18:9–15), and the careful instructions given by the angel to Manoah's wife further heighten the expectation that the child to be born will be special. Specifically, it is disclosed that the child is to be a Nazirite from the womb, and his mission will be to begin the deliverance of Israel from the Philistines.

Regarding the Nazirite status, a comparison of the instructions given by the angel with the Nazirite rule in Numbers 6:1–21 shows both similarities and differences. The similarities include the prohibitions against fermented drinks and the cutting of hair. The differences involve the involuntary nature, and hence, the permanency of the Nazirite status, as well as the stipulation against unclean food. For according to Numbers 6, the Nazirite vow is normally a voluntary vow that is binding only for a specific period. In Samson's case, however, he is set apart involuntarily, while still in his mother's womb, a fact evident through the requirement of the mother to also not drink fermented drink or eat unclean food for the duration of the pregnancy, presumably to safeguard the Nazirite status of the son in her womb. As for the duration of this Nazirite status, unlike those who would take the vow voluntarily, for Samson, it seems to be permanent. At least this seems to be how Samson's mother understands it, for she states in 13:7 that Samson will be a Nazirite of God from the womb until his death.

In addition, while one of the stipulations the angel specifies involves prohibition against unclean food, such a prohibition is not found in Numbers 6. Instead, Numbers 6 emphasizes avoiding contact with the dead. But as different as these two stipulations seem to be, both essentially concern ceremonial cleanliness (cf. Num. 6:7). Since Samson's mission as a deliverer who will most likely kill in combat effectively renders it impractical for him to stay away from dead bodies, the stipulation against unclean food may represent an attempt to highlight the continued necessity for ceremonial cleanliness notwithstanding the nature of his mission.

After her encounter with the angel, the woman goes and tells her husband about her experience. Manoah, perhaps wanting to confirm the matter for himself, prays for the man of God to appear to him. The angel does, and after he confirms to Manoah what was said earlier to his wife, Manoah offers to prepare a meal for him, not realizing he is an angel. In a scene reminiscent of Gideon's encounter with the angel of the Lord (6:20–23), it is only after flame blazes from the altar and the angel goes up with the flame that Manoah realizes he has seen an angel. Like Gideon, he also fears for his life, until his wife convinces him they will be safe.

The wife eventually gives birth to Samson, and it is immediately reported that the Lord blesses him as he grows up, and the Spirit of the Lord begins to stir in him. All these only heighten expectations of greatness. But such expectations are immediately put to the test, as chapter 14 recounts the events surrounding his near marriage to an unnamed Philistine woman.

14:1–20. Having noticed the Philistine woman in Timnah, Samson goes to his parents demanding that they get her for him as a wife. The parents, alarmed that he wants to marry a non-Israelite who belongs to the occupying power, try in vain to suggest that he find someone from among their own people. But Samson is insistent, and using an expression that

will eventually appear again in the epilogue's refrain (cf. 17:6; 21:25), he justifies his request by declaring that the woman is literally "right in his eyes" (14:3).

Given the blatant disapproval of marriages with foreigners already expressed in Judges 3:5–6, it seems obvious that Samson's desires in this matter should be viewed negatively. But the supplementary information provided by the narrator, that Samson's parents are ignorant of the Lord's plan to seek an occasion against the Philistines, suddenly seems to cast that evaluation in doubt. Is Samson right to seek a marriage alliance with the Philistines?

To answer the question, one should consider the following. First, that the Lord has planned to use Samson's proposed marriage as an occasion to strike the Philistines does not necessarily imply his approval of Samson's action. After all, in Genesis 45:5–8 and 50:19–20, Joseph speaks of God's having a plan to preserve many, which overlapped his brothers' plan to harm him, but that clearly does not mean God approved of the brothers' wicked deeds. Second, the point of the narrator's comment may be precisely to highlight the Lord's determination to deliver his people in spite of Samson. For as the narrative progresses, it becomes clear that, rather than being committed to striking the Philistines, Samson seems all too eager to form marriage and sexual alliances with their women. Therefore if it were not for the Lord's intervention, Samson would probably never have fulfilled his mission to begin delivering Israel from the Philistines. Finally, the fact that the narrator needs to supply this extra information is proof itself that the readers are expected to agree with the parents' perspective. The comment is therefore designed not so much to exonerate Samson but to further clarify why Samson is allowed to continue this undesirable course of action.

At Samson's insistence, the parents give in. As Samson goes down to Timnah again, presumably to seek the woman's hand in marriage, a young lion attacks him just as he is approaching the vineyards (an ominous note since a Nazirite

231

is supposed to avoid any product of the vine). But the Spirit of the Lord comes upon him and he tears the lion in two with his bare hands. When he reaches Timnah, he speaks to the woman, who, for the second time (see 14:3), is described as someone he considers "right in his eyes" (14:7).

Having returned home, he makes another trip down to Timnah to marry the woman. At the place where he previously killed the lion, he finds inside its carcass a swarm of bees and some honey, which he scoops up and eats. He even brings some back with him for his parents, who, ignorant of the source of the honey, eat it as well. In so doing, Samson both violates his Nazirite status by eating unclean food and also brings ritual defilement to his parents, as food contaminated by a carcass is considered unclean even to ordinary Israelites (see Lev. 11:39–40).

But not only does Samson violate the food stipulation of his status, he also appears to violate the stipulation against fermented drink. In 14:10, he is said to have "held a feast, as was customary for young men." In days before there was a variety of beverage choices, wine and fermented drink were commonly served at such feasts. In fact, the Hebrew words for "wine" and "fermented drink" found in the stipulations for Nazirites (Num. 6:3–4) and for Samson (Judg. 13:4, 7, 14) are explicitly associated with the word for "feast" elsewhere in the Old Testament (1 Sam. 25:36; Esther 5:6; 7:2, 7, 8; Isa. 5:12; Jer. 51:39; Dan. 1:16). If Samson conducted himself as was customary for bridegrooms of his day, then he would certainly have consumed such drinks.

Caught up in the festivity of the occasion, Samson challenges his thirty Philistine groomsmen to a timed riddle with the wager set at thirty sets of clothing. Since the riddle involves Samson's earlier experience of eating honey out of the lion's carcass, the groomsmen obviously cannot guess the answer. So they threaten Samson's wife-to-be with death, and she, in turn, keeps nagging Samson until he gives in and tells her the answer. She then reveals the answer

to the groomsmen, who naturally win the bet. Samson, realizing that he has been betrayed by his wife-to-be (thus the comment about "plowing with my heifer") and not having the means to pay the wager, then goes down to Ashkelon, kills thirty Philistines, and takes their clothes to pay up. Then without consummating his marriage, he angrily returns to his father's house. With the groom gone, the bride is given to one of the groomsmen instead.

15:1–20. The narrative unit in chapter 15 recounts the series of events that takes place in the aftermath of the failed marriage. Having had time to calm down, Samson returns to the house of his would-be wife with a gift, apparently wanting to continue the relationship from where he has left off. Although the mention of the wife's room does not necessarily imply physical intimacy, the response of the father-in-law, first refusing to let him in, then explaining that the woman has already been given to another, and finally offering the supposedly more beautiful younger daughter as replacement, suggests an understanding that Samson wants to consummate the marriage. Having been rebuffed, Samson angrily promises revenge on the Philistines, and then sets on fire their entire harvest. This is particularly devastating as it is the time of the harvest (cf. 15:1), which means that the Philistines' months of hard work is now in vain. When the Philistines discover that Samson was behind the deed, they take it out on the would-be wife and her father by burning them to death. This prompts an angry Samson to seek further revenge by slaughtering many Philistines.

This causes the Philistines to demand more revenge, as they go up to Judah and set up camp. Sensing trouble, representatives from Judah inquire about the reason for the Philistines' military presence. Having discovered that it is related to Samson, three thousand men from Judah go to Samson's hiding place to confront him. From their words, it is clear that by then, these Israelites from Judah have become content to be ruled by the Philistines, such that they prefer keeping the status quo peacefully rather than upsetting their overlords for any reason. Can this be why no report is made of the people crying out to the Lord when the Philistine oppression is introduced in 13:1? Thus, another stage of the cyclical structure that characterizes the narratives of the major judges has quietly broken down.

But not only are these men from Judah content to live under Philistine rule, they are even ready to side with their oppressors, as they inform Samson that they will tie him up and hand him over to the Philistines. In this, the theme of Israelites refusing to stand with their judges, which first emerged with Deborah and Barak (Judges 5) and continued with Gideon (Judg. 8:4–17) and Jephthah (Judg. 12:1–7), has reached its nadir.

Having made them promise not to kill him, Samson allows himself to be tied up. But as he is about to be handed over to the Philistines, the Spirit of the Lord comes upon him, such that the ropes that tie him melt away. Finding the jawbone of a donkey, Samson uses it to kill a thousand Philistines. This results in the place being named Ramath Lehi, meaning "Jawbone Hill."

But no sooner has he experienced this great deliverance than Samson prays a prayer that betrays a lack of faith. Interestingly, the circumstances of this prayer seem calculated to remind one of the prayers by Gideon (Judg. 6:33–40) and Jephthah (Judg. 11:29–31). For all three prayers are preceded by the coming of the Spirit of the Lord upon the judges, prompting them to take concrete action against the enemy. All three prayers also represent the first utterance the respective judges made to the Lord after the coming of the Spirit. While one would naturally expect these to be prayers of faith, they are, unfortunately, just the opposite.

For Samson, his prayer is essentially for his thirst to be quenched. But the way he phrases his request is manipulative. While acknowledging the great deliverance the Lord has just given him, Samson, however, uses it as a means

of coercion, suggesting that the very deliverance will have been in vain if he is allowed to die of thirst and fall back into the hands of the Philistines. In this respect, his prayer compares unfavorably to Gideon's prayer for signs and Jephthah's desperate vow. For while the prayers of Gideon and Jephthah are made before their respective confrontation with the enemy, Samson's manipulative prayer comes after he has just won a great victory. Thus, one can argue that Samson shows even less faith than his two predecessors.

Nonetheless, the Lord answers his prayer by opening up a hollow from which water comes, and the spring comes to be known as En Hakkore, meaning "Spring of the Caller."

16:1–31. The brief unit in 16:1–3 recounts Samson's involvement with a prostitute in Gaza, which provides another demonstration of his extraordinary strength. But more important, sandwiched between the narrative involving the Philistine woman he almost marries and the one about Delilah, whom he supposedly loves (16:4), this brief story is likely included to clarify Samson's root problem. Lest one think that Samson is simply unlucky in love, the presence of this episode suggests that the "love" he seemingly seeks may be no more than the satisfaction of his sexual appetite.

Samson's downfall through his involvement with Delilah is next recounted in 16:4–22. Although the text has not specified Delilah's race, that she lives in Philistine territory and has connections with the Philistine rulers makes it almost certain that she is ethnically Philistine. That she lives in the Valley of Sorek also bodes ill for Samson, for the name means "choice vines," thus suggesting something that should be out of bounds for a Nazirite like Samson.

The Philistine rulers, understanding the futility of their attempt at vengeance unless they can overcome Samson's extraordinary strength, promise Delilah money for uncovering the secret of his strength. The first three times Delilah tries to coax the secret out of Samson, he lies to her, but unable to withstand her constant nagging, he finally gives in. In his final disclosure, Samson is able to explain accurately the significance of his uncut hair, thus suggesting that he must have been aware all along of the circumstances of his birth and the calling with which he has been entrusted. Sadly, he never takes that calling seriously. The secret of his strength having been disclosed, his hair is cut while he is asleep. With the only visible symbol of his Nazirite status now gone, the Lord and his supernatural strength leave Samson. After he is captured, Samson's eyes, which seem to have been a major source of his repeated transgressions (cf. 14:1, 2, 8; 16:1), are gouged out, and he is taken to Gaza and imprisoned. But foreshadowing what is to come, 16:22 reports that his hair is beginning to grow back.

Celebrating Samson's capture, the Philistines gather to give credit to their god Dagon for this turn of events (16:23–30). To add insult to injury, they have Samson brought out to entertain them. Perhaps feigning tiredness, Samson requests to lean on the pillars supporting the temple, and there, prays for strength for one

last time. As he pushes hard on the supporting pillars, the temple collapses, killing all who are in it, including himself. Note, however, that consistent with the portrayal of Samson in these narratives, even his final prayer is motivated by personal vendetta, in order to avenge the loss of his eyes. Thus, one can say that everything Samson does against the Philistines is motivated by self-interest rather than a concern for God's people. Nonetheless, it is reported that he killed more Philistines in death than when he was alive. His body is apparently recovered from the ruins and brought back for burial near his hometown (16:31).

Before leaving the Samson narrative, it must be pointed out that Samson's life has often been seen as a microcosmic reflection of Israel itself, as the two share much in common. Both are set apart by God before birth (Israel is chosen through Abraham even before it becomes a nation), but in spite of this special calling, Samson cannot resist the lure of foreign women, much as Israel cannot resist the lure

These column bases in a Philistine temple from the Iron Age (Tel Aviv, Israel) may be similar to the pillars knocked down by Samson (Judg. 16:29–30).

of foreign gods. In fact, these attractions seem almost obsessive, such that, even though these foreign women/gods bring nothing but trouble (cf. Judg. 2:11–15; 3:7–8, 12–14; 4:1–2; 6:1–5; 10:6–9; 13:1 for Israel), each keeps returning for more. In times of trouble when Samson (Judg. 15:18; 16:28) and Israel (Judg. 3:9, 15; 4:3; 6:6; 10:10) cry out to the Lord in distress, the Lord delivers. But eventually, when Samson, like Israel, has been enticed once too often, the Lord, the source of Samson's strength, leaves him (16:19), just as the Lord, the source of Israel's strength, will eventually also leave her and will no longer deliver his people (cf. 2 Kings 17:1–23; 24:20–25:21; 2 Chron. 36:14–21; Ezek. 8:1–11:25). Of course, that withdrawal of the Lord from delivering Israel will come much later in the nation's history. But if these narratives were written before the nation's fall, perhaps Samson's end is meant to serve as a warning for Israel before she travels down a similar path. Unfortunately that is a warning Israel did not heed.

3. Chaos in Israelite Society (17:1–21:25)

While the last five chapters have often been referred to as the epilogue of the book, scholars have struggled to understand its connection with what precedes. For unlike the previous section, these narratives feature neither any judge nor any foreign enemy. Instead they seem to concern largely nameless individuals within Israelite society, with the focus being on internal chaos generated entirely from within. Structurally, the cyclical framework that organizes much of the preceding material also no longer organizes the epilogue. Instead, it is the refrain "In those days Israel had no king" (17:6; 18:1; 19:1; 21:25) that seems to bind together two extended narratives, each featuring a Levite.

These stark contrasts notwithstanding, one can nonetheless discern a certain continuity between the epilogue and earlier parts of the book. The deteriorating trend regarding internal conflict featured in the narratives of the judges, for example, continues to worsen, culminating in the near annihilation of the tribe of Benjamin

in a civil war in 20:1–48. And the apostasy repeatedly mentioned in the previous sections is also given a closer look in the epilogue, as the case of how one family's syncretistic worship eventually results in the idolatry of an entire tribe is featured in 17:1–18:31.

A. In the areas of religious and military practices (17:1–18:31). The first of two extended narratives begins in 17:1–5, with the return of some stolen silver by one of only two named characters within the epilogue. The specification of his name is probably for ironic purposes, as Micah, meaning "Who is like the Lord," is someone who turns out to be an idol worshiper. In any event, after he returns the silver to his mother, likely out of fear for the curse she has placed, the mother invokes a blessing from the Lord, presumably to cancel out her earlier curse. She then decides to dedicate the silver to the Lord, but bizarrely, to have an idol made. Note that, although the text speaks of "a carved image and a cast idol" (cf. ESV, NIV 1984) this may be a figure of speech called hendiadys, in which the two actually represent the same thing: a carved image overlaid with molten metal (so NIV). For the pronoun in the last clause of 17:4 is actually singular in Hebrew; thus, "It was put in Micah's house."

As it turns out, Micah has his own household shrine, which already houses an ephod and some idols. In addition, he has established his own sons as priests, which is a clear violation of the law, as Micah is an Ephraimite (see 17:1) and Exodus 28:41–43 and Numbers 25:10–13 stipulate that only a specific group of Levites can serve as priests. It is at this juncture that the full refrain "In those days Israel had no king; everyone did as they saw fit" appears for the first time in 17:6. The phrase "everyone did as they saw fit" is likely an allusion to Deuteronomy 12:8, where "everyone doing as they see fit" is specifically prohibited in the context of not worshiping the Lord just anywhere but at the place chosen by him. But while this first appearance of the refrain may be intended to draw attention to Micah's illegitimate worship, the other appearances of this refrain within the epilogue, be it in full (21:25) or reduced (18:1; 19:1) form, are probably intended to serve as a commentary on the general anarchy of the period.

The identity of the "king" in the refrain is debatable. While most scholars see it as a forward-looking reference to the human kings who will eventually rule over Israel in the monarchic period, a case can be made that the "king" actually refers to the Lord himself. After all, the Lord's kingship over Israel is a tradition that was established relatively early in Israel's history (cf. Exod. 15:18; Num. 23:21; Deut. 33:5). Gideon's answer to Israel's kingship offer in 8:23 also implies an understanding that the Lord is king over the nation. Besides, if "king" is meant to refer to a human king, then the statement "In those days Israel had no king" is strictly speaking not true. Because even within Judges, Abimelek is presented as having been made king (9:6, 16, 18) and having ruled over "Israel" for three years (9:22). But if "In those days Israel had no king" simply means the Lord was not honored as king over Israel during this period, then what this provides is a much-needed spiritual diagnosis for the anarchy spoken of in the second half of the refrain.

As the story continues, the focus briefly shifts to a young Levite who has been living in Bethlehem of Judah but who is now traveling in search of another place to stay, presumably where he will find new employment (17:7–13). Already this information raises all kinds of questions. First, Bethlehem is not one of the Levitical cities listed in Joshua 21:9–16, so why was he living there previously? As for his search for a new place of residence and employment, since Deuteronomy 18:6–8 guarantees a means of livelihood and employment at the main sanctuary for any Levite leaving a Levitical city, why does he need to travel around looking for employment? If these already hint at the Levite's disregard for Levitical stipulations, then the most egregious violation would be his eventual acceptance of Micah's offer to

serve as his priest (17:10–12). For not only is the household shrine illegitimate, but, as one discovers later, this Levite is also not a direct descendant of Aaron or Phinehas but of Moses (18:30) and is thus just as ineligible to serve as priest as Micah's sons (cf. Exod. 28:41–43; 29:44; Num. 25:10–13). Micah's confidence in the Lord's blessings because he now has a Levitical priest (17:13) is thus greatly misplaced.

The setting changes briefly in 18:1 as new characters are introduced who will play significant roles in the continued unfolding of the story. But first, the shortened version of the refrain appears again in 18:1a, perhaps to highlight the fact that the events to be narrated will again illustrate the anarchy that results from the Lord not being honored as king.

The inability of the Danites to take possession of their allotted land has already been disclosed in Joshua 19:47 and Judges 1:34. What the tribe has done to compensate for that inability is now described in detail in 18:1b–31. The tribe decides to send out five spies to look for alternative land. The spies come to Micah's house and decide to spend the night there. When there, they recognize the voice (perhaps the southern accent) of the Levite and inquire about his presence. After the Levite tells them everything, they ask him to inquire of God regarding their mission and receive a favorable answer. They then continue their journey, eventually reaching Laish.

Here, the author seems to have gone out of his way to present Laish as a peaceful community. Its residents are described in 18:7 as living in "safety" and "at peace" (NIV 1984 "unsuspecting"), both words related to the same Hebrew verb *batah*, which means "to trust." Furthermore, the Hebrew word translated as "secure" in the NIV is from the root *shqt*, used in 3:11, 30; 5:31; and 8:27 to describe the land as enjoying peace after the judges have routed the oppressors. As such, the word indicates the absence of conflict (cf. Josh. 11:23; 14:15; 1 Chron. 22:9; 2 Chron. 14:1, 4–5; 20:30). The isolation of this peaceful community is also highlighted by the fact that they live at a distance from their neighbor, the Sidonians, and they apparently have no dealings with anyone else.

Having found this ideal community, the spies return to their tribe, and emphasizing the goodness of the land and the unsuspecting nature of the community (18:9–10), they urge their kinsmen to go and attack them. Here, although the author has not directly evaluated this recommendation, the fact that attacking peaceful (*shaqat*) and unsuspecting (*batah*) people is considered an evil plan in later prophetic writing (cf. Ezek. 38:10–12) should cast some light on how this recommendation is to be viewed.

So six hundred Danites set out toward Laish. When they pass by Micah's house, the spies mention the idols at his shrine, and the Danites decide to go and take them. The Levite at Micah's shrine initially tries to stop them, but upon the Danites' offer to make him priest for their entire tribe, he takes the idols and joins the group. When Micah discovers the robbery, he goes after the Danites with some men and catches up with them. But the Danites threaten

them with violent deaths, and Micah, realizing that his party is outnumbered, turns back.

The Danites arrive at Laish, and emphasizing for the third time the peaceful (*shaqat*) and unsuspecting (*batah*) nature of the city's residents, the author tells of the slaughter of this people and the burning of their city. The Danites then rebuild the city and rename it after their eponymous tribal ancestor, Dan. They also set up the idol they have stolen from Micah and worship it there. Shockingly, it is disclosed only at this point that the young Levite who became priest to the tribe is actually none other than Jonathan, grandson of Moses! The fact that he and his sons continue to serve as priests for Dan thus demonstrates powerfully the extent and rapidity of moral, social, and religious decline in Israel, if even descendants of Israel's lawgiver are behaving lawlessly.

B. In the areas of social norms and political decisions (19:1–21:25). **19:1–29.** How appropriate, then, that as the first extended narrative ends

A Middle Bronze Age mud-brick gate at Dan (ancient Laish, ca. 1800 BC; see Judg. 18:29)

and the second begins, the refrain "In those days Israel had no king" appears again in 19:1, bridging the two stories and subtly reminding the readers that those were days when "everyone did as they saw fit" (17:6; 21:25).

The second extended narrative begins with the attempt of another Levite to woo back a concubine who has left him to return to her father's house (19:2–10). Here, although the text clearly states that she has been unfaithful (from the Hebrew verb meaning "to prostitute"), some scholars suggest that the word may have come from an orthographically similar Hebrew verb that means "to be angry." This is because, according to Leviticus 20:10, the penalty for adultery would have been death, and it would thus be inconceivable for the concubine's family to take her back and let her stay for four months, let alone for the Levite to come wooing, given the circumstances. But as others have pointed out, since Israelite law did not allow for divorce by a woman, the very act of the concubine walking out on her husband may have been sufficient for her to be regarded as having acted unfaithfully without her actually having committed adultery with another man.

In any event, the Levite, probably realizing that he is at fault in causing her departure, comes after her to woo her back. He is warmly welcomed by the father-in-law and persuaded to stay and enjoy the hospitality for three days. Intending to leave on the fourth day, he is persuaded to stay for yet another night, until he finally insists on leaving on the fifth day. So despite the day being already half gone when they set off, the Levite leaves with his concubine and servant.

The journey home (19:11–29) turns out to be disastrous. When they approach Jebus (the former name for Jerusalem), the day is almost gone. The servant suggests staying overnight in the city, but the Levite refuses, pointing out that Jebus is a non-Israelite city and implying that it might be unsafe due to its lawlessness. The decision is to travel at least to Gibeah in Benjamin before spending the night.

However, when they arrive at Gibeah's city square, contrary to expected social norms, no one offers hospitality to them, until an old Ephraimite temporarily residing in the city takes them in.

Things soon take a decided turn for the worse. In an even graver violation of social norms that echoes the Sodomite incident in Genesis 19, while guest and host are enjoying a meal, men of the city surrounded the house demanding that the Levite be handed over for sexual abuse. Like Lot in Genesis 19, the old man of Judges 19 goes out to the mob, begging them not to commit the evil deed (19:23; cf. Gen. 19:6). And like Lot, he also offers them two women as substitutes, only here, he takes the liberty of including the Levite's concubine as well since he has only one daughter (19:24; cf. Gen. 19:8). But just as in Sodom, the mob refuses (19:25; cf. Gen. 19:9).

Note the irony that permeates this turn of events. Had the Levite even remotely thought he would encounter in Jebus the kind of danger he does in Gibeah, his rejection of the servant's suggestion to stay in Jebus would not have been so mild. Yet the lawlessness encountered turns out to be far worse in Israelite Gibeah than it would have been in non-Israelite Jebus. In fact, it is so bad it mirrors what happened in Sodom (Gen. 18:20; 19:1–29), a city that represents the epitome of depravity and deserving judgment in the Old Testament (cf. Deut. 29:23; Isa. 3:9; Jer. 23:14; Lam. 4:6; Ezek. 16:48). The social and moral degradation that has befallen Israel is thus made amply clear.

With the situation at an impasse, as the mob rejects the old man's offer, the Levite takes things into his own hands and shoves his concubine out the door, whereupon she is raped and abused all night until morning. When the Levite gets up the next morning to go on his way, he finds her lying at the doorway. In a show of unbelievable callousness, he simply tells her to get up so that they can be on their way. Receiving no response from her and probably discovering then that she is dead, he loads her up on his donkey, takes her corpse home, and cuts her into twelve pieces, sending them to the twelve tribes of Israel presumably to demand retribution.

19:30–20:48. The receipt of cut-up human body parts apparently achieves its intended result. The tribes react with disgust and anger, and except for Benjamin, gather together at Mizpah to discuss the appropriate response (19:30–20:13). The Levite is asked to explain what happened, and he gives a story that is at best only a half-truth, as he exaggerates the danger ("The men of Gibeah came after me . . . , intending to kill me" [20:5]) and leaves out entirely his own role in the death of his concubine. His story causes an outrage, so that those gathered decide to attack Gibeah to punish its residents. They first send men to Benjamin, demanding that they hand over the offenders. But in an act of misplaced tribal solidarity, Benjamin decides to stand with the offenders, thus causing a civil war (20:14–48).

The Benjamite army gathers at Gibeah in anticipation of war. In response, the Israelites also muster their troops and go up to Bethel to inquire of the Lord regarding which tribe should lead the charge (20:18). The question they ask and the answer they receive mirror a similar exchange found at the beginning of the book (1:1–2), except here, the Lord's answer does not come with a promise of victory. So the Israelites go to battle and promptly suffer a loss of twenty-two thousand men. They return to inquire of the Lord whether they should go again, and again receive instructions from the Lord to go (20:23). But as they go, they are again defeated, losing eighteen thousand men. So they return to inquire of the Lord yet a third time, this time even suggesting the possibility of quitting, only to finally receive a promise of victory (20:26–28). As these initial defeats are the only times in the Old Testament that Israel follows the Lord's instructions and yet loses in battle, one should rightly ask what happened.

The problem likely has to do with Israel's opponent at war. Benjamin is part of the covenant community, yet the rest of Israel seems intent to treat it as if it were a foreign enemy. For according to 21:1, 7, 18, one of the oaths Israel took prior to the war obliged them not to give their daughters in marriage to any Benjamite. Considering that intermarriage was explicitly prohibited only with the non-Israelite population in the land (Deut. 7:3), this oath to ban intermarriage with Benjamin almost implies the excommunication of Benjamin from the covenant community. This is corroborated by the Israelites' conduct of war, such that upon defeating the Benjamites, they proceed to burn their cities and kill all their citizens (20:48). In so doing, they subject Benjamin to the same destruction to which they subjected the foreign nations they conquered (cf. Josh. 6:21, 24; 8:24–26; 10:28–40; 11:10–15). Since the law only called for such destruction within Israel in cases of communal apostasy (Deut. 13:12–18), as heinous as Gibeah's crime was and as wrong as it was for Benjamin to stand with the perpetrators, their offenses do not warrant the treatment they receive. Add to that a second oath that binds every Israelite community to participation in the war against Benjamin on pain of death (21:5), and a picture emerges of Israel determined to deal with the Benjamites in the harshest possible way, as if they were no longer a brother.

Yet Israel never seeks the Lord's guidance in deciding on such a course of action. In fact, their first inquiry of the Lord is made only immediately prior to battle, and even then, it only concerns the identity of the tribe to lead the charge. While this question was appropriate at the beginning of the book (1:1) because the Lord had already commanded the destruction of the Canaanites in the land (Deut. 7:1–4; 20:16–18), he has not issued a similar command regarding a tribe of Israel, even a sinful one. So it is entirely possible that the Lord's selection of Judah without promising victory and his subsequent sending of the Israelites out twice to be defeated are expressions of his displeasure over their presumption and maliciousness toward a brother within the covenant community.

And this is not entirely lost on Israel either, judging by their response. For after the first defeat, when Israel makes a second inquiry of the Lord, instead of referring to their opponents simply as "the Benjamites" (cf. 20:18), they now add "our fellow Israelites" (20:23). The question also changes to one they should have asked initially, "Shall we go up again to fight?" But despite such changes, the Lord, perhaps wanting to drive home his displeasure, sends them out again to suffer another defeat. So for the third time, Israel comes before the Lord, this time involving "the whole army" (20:26), and not just weeping before the Lord (cf. 20:23) but also fasting and presenting burnt offerings and fellowship offerings (20:26), presumably to show their repentance. And instead of simply asking whether they should go up again to fight, this time they even suggest an alternative by adding "or not [literally "or shall I stop"]?" (20:28).

But the Lord finally promises victory, perhaps not so much because Israel's show of repentance is genuine, but because Benjamin too needs to be disciplined for siding with offenders. The Israelites' subsequent conduct of war shows that whatever remorse they have shown is soon forgotten after they receive the Lord's promise of victory, for they go out and do exactly what they have planned to do all along, almost annihilating the entire tribe of Benjamin.

The battle strategy Israel adopted was likely inspired by memory of their victory against Ai in Joshua 8. The two bear remarkable resemblances in that both involve a fake defeat to lure the enemy out, an ambushing unit to take the largely defenseless city, and the setting of the city on fire so that the smoke will serve as a signal to those in the front line to turn around and attack. And at first glance, both battles meet with great success.

21:1–25. However, a sign that the victory against Benjamin is not all it appears is that what follows is not celebration but nationwide mourning as the Israelites realize belatedly that

a tribe among them is on the verge of disappearing (21:1–3). But instead of acknowledging their responsibility in the matter, Israel actually tries to put the blame on the Lord (20:3).

The solutions Israel comes up with to repopulate Benjamin (21:4–24) are highly ironic. Faced with the challenge of finding women for the six hundred Benjamites left without violating the oath they swore earlier not to give them their daughters in marriage, the Israelites inquire if any among them has failed to participate in the war with Benjamin. Discovering that the town of Jabesh Gilead has not participated, the assembly then sends warriors to the town to carry out their earlier oath to put to death any community not participating in the war. Only, the warriors are instructed to spare all the virgins so that they can be given to the Benjamites as wives.

But that still leaves them two hundred virgins short. Knowing that young women go out dancing at an annual festival to the Lord at Shiloh, the elders tell the remaining Benjamites to hide at the vineyard and to each abduct a young woman when they come out dancing. This way, since the parents did not willingly give their daughters to them in marriage, their collective oath will not be violated. The Benjamites then go and do accordingly.

The irony is that the war against Benjamin initially took place to avenge the raping to death of one woman: the Levite's concubine. But by killing off an entire Israelite town to obtain virgins and by allowing the forcible abduction of young women at Shiloh, the Israelites have essentially sanctioned what amounts to the rape of six hundred young women. The remedy is thus far worse than the crime it sought to rectify.

It is no wonder, then, that as the book comes to a close, the refrain "In those days Israel had no king; everyone did as they saw fit" appears yet once more to sum up the era of the judges (21:25). Because this was an era when the Lord was not honored as king, everyone ended up doing as they saw fit.

Select Bibliography

Block, Daniel I. *Judges, Ruth*. New American Commentary. Nashville: Broadman & Holman, 1999.

Harris, J. Gordon, Cheryl A. Brown, and Michael S. Moore. *Joshua, Judges, Ruth*. New International Biblical Commentary. Peabody, MA: Hendrickson, 2000.

Webb, Barry G. *The Book of Judges: An Integrated Reading*. Journal for the Study of the Old Testament Supplement 46. Sheffield: Sheffield Academic Press, 1987.

Wilcock, Michael. *The Message of Judges*. The Bible Speaks Today. Downers Grove, IL: InterVarsity, 1992.

Younger, K. Lawson, Jr. *Judges, Ruth*. NIV Application Commentary. Grand Rapids: Zondervan, 2002.

Ruth

D. L. PETTER

Date and Authorship

This heart-wrenching yet refreshing story unfolds "in the days when the judges ruled" (1:1). This places the account chronologically somewhere between circa 1380 and 1050 BC. The book was likely composed by an unnamed author relying on oral sources at a later period in Israelite history, one that seems to coincide with David and the early monarchy (Ruth 4:7, 17). Historically, the period of the judges represents a setting when religious syncretism provoked military aggression resulting in societal unrest, a cycle that perpetuated itself until the Lord graciously intervened by raising up a judge (Judges 2). As a literary bridge, the notification in 1:1 points the reader back to the last verse in Judges, where it concludes, "In those days Israel had no king; everyone did as they saw fit" (Judg. 21:25). It also points forward to the closing genealogy in Ruth, mentioning David (4:18–22), which anticipates 1–2 Samuel, when kingship is formally grafted into the covenantal community. In this way Ruth functions as a literary hinge with respect to its placement in the English Bible (an arrangement based upon the Greek Septuagint).

Theological Themes

Ruth recounts the private and domestic affairs of a family of four from Bethlehem, with literary artistry full of suspense and emotion. Even the most casual reader recognizes themes of divine providence, mercy, and provision for the less privileged. An equally notable and repetitive theme concerns the idea of redemption, particularly evident in Boaz's crucial role as kinsman-redeemer.

Collectively, these themes, which are communicated through speech rather than narration, unveil the main point driving the narrative. Ruth finds both a physical and spiritual home in Israel. But how can a Moabite secure a home in Israel and even be included in David's lineage? These are pertinent questions given Deuteronomic law, which forbids Israelite associations with Moabites, a chided enemy. Moreover, how can Israel's renowned king come from mixed ancestry? The book of Ruth not only lauds the Lord's merciful hand of guidance on Naomi and Ruth but also addresses these intriguing questions in light of the bigger picture of Israelite history.

1. Setting: Famine and Family Tragedy (1:1–5)
2. Widows and Their Worries: Back to Bethlehem (1:6–22)
   A. Back to Bethlehem (1:6–7)
   B. The Nature of Naomi's Worries/Naomi's Resolve and Confession (1:8–15)
   C. Ruth's Resolve and Confession (1:16–17)
   D. In Bethlehem (1:18–22)

Commentary

1. Setting: Famine and Family Tragedy (1:1–5)

The grim opening of this story grips the reader on three counts. First, it is neither a prosperous nor a fruitful time in the nation's life (1:1). Second, and not unrelated, the people of Israel face famine (1:1). The fact that a famine prevails in Bethlehem, in Judah's "house of bread," together with the religious crisis dominating the landscape indicates an unpleasant visitation by the Lord on the land. The Lord promised famine as one among many of his acts of judgment for covenantal waywardness (Lev. 26:18–20; Deut. 28:24; Jer. 24:10; 27:8–13; 29:17; 34:17; 38:2; Ezek. 6:11; 7:15; 12:16). The writer now zooms in on one specific family and their attempt to deal with these circumstances. Elimelek, his wife Naomi, and their two sons Mahlon and Kilion relocate from Bethlehem to the neighboring fields of Moab in search of food. Their relocation to Moab suggests that in spite of previous tumultuous relationships between Moab and Israel (Numbers 22; 25),

relative peace prevails at the time the family uproots (Judg. 3:11; 5:31). Although the stated motivation of finding food provides a logical rationale for moving, one wonders if it does not point to the fragile nature of Elimelek's faith, much like the faith of Israel's patriarchs who went to Egypt in time of famine (Gen. 12:10; 26:1; 41:54–57). However one interprets their journey, the family attempts to face their crisis practically by securing necessary food.

Third, after arriving on foreign soil, the family meets a series of tragedies. More precisely, we read Elimelek's obituary. Elimelek dies and is survived by his wife and two sons. While this is tragic for Naomi, the widow would have taken a measure of comfort, and even hope, in the fact that she had two sons—heirs and people who could look after her in her old age (Deut. 25:5–10; Lev. 25:25). But this is not meant to be.

After Elimelek dies, both sons marry Moabite women. The fact that Mahlon and Kilion forge relationships with Moabite women, however, is suspicious. For men from Bethlehem to marry Moabite women is problematic under the Mosaic economy. Even though the Moabites are related to Israel by virtue of Lot's incestuous relationship with his older daughter (Gen. 19:36–37), the biblical record mandates their separation as early as the time of Moses. Two critical events provide a rationale. First, the king of Moab hired a Mesopotamian prophet to curse Israel on four occasions when the nation was on the verge of taking possession of the promised land (Num. 22:4–6; 23:1–24:25). The Lord, however, turned the curses into blessings because of his relentless commitment to Abraham: "Whoever curses you I will curse" (Gen. 12:3; Num. 24:10–24). Second, by invitation of some Moabite women, the Israelites polluted themselves by worshiping a foreign deity, Baal of Peor (Num. 25:1–3; 31:15–16). On account of these two events, Moabites have been excluded from Israelite religious practices (Deut. 23:3–4).

Israelites were prohibited from making political and marriage alliances with foreigners due to the possibility of religious enticement toward deities other than Yahweh (Deut. 7:1–3; Exod. 34:11–16). Although the Moabites are not specifically mentioned in Deuteronomy and Exodus, and regardless of their family ties to Israel, they are treated like nonfamily members or "foreigners" elsewhere. Solomon receives condemnation in Kings, as do the Jews of Ezra and Nehemiah's day, because these married, among other foreigners, Moabite women (1 Kings 11:1–8; Ezra 9:1–6; Neh. 13:23–27). Conjoining Israelite relatives to a list with foreigners illustrates the severity of the separation. Essentially, the Israelites were to treat the Moabites like nonfamily members and have nothing to do with them because of conflicting religious practices. Although the narrator refrains from passing specific judgment on Elimelek's sons, their marriages to Ruth and Orpah should be interpreted as anything but neutral.

After about ten years, the situation moves from bad to worse for Naomi. Another tragedy strikes: both of Naomi's sons die. Without sons or grandchildren, she is now utterly hopeless for the well-being of her own future, not to mention the painful effects for Ruth and Orpah. The deaths of Mahlon and Kilion signal death for the continuation of the family name and inheritance, essentially a loss of a home and identity.

Thus a heavy and mournful atmosphere obtains at the outset, due to famine and three deaths. Furthermore, the likely cause of famine (national disobedience), the move to Moab (perhaps a display of fear not faith), and the marriages to Moabite women (relationships not sanctioned by Israelite law) create suspicion for a reader aware of Mosaic legislation. This marriage of emotions (sorrows with suspicion) invites an interpretation that, *perhaps*, the ongoing struggles that face Elimelek's family are somewhat self-imposed. Regardless, from famine in Judah to family tragedy in a foreign land, Naomi and her two daughters-in-law face great loss. It seems a dark and dismal future awaits them.

2. Widows and Their Worries: Back to Bethlehem (1:6–22)

A. Back to Bethlehem (1:6–7). Against this grim setting Naomi confronts some important news in the fields of Moab. She learns that famine no longer threatens Judah. Since Hebrew and Moabite are closely related languages, perhaps this accounts for her ability to understand the conversation.

That a famine no longer prevails in Bethlehem indicates a pleasant visitation by the Lord on his land and people. Indeed, he promised bread as one among many of his acts of mercy for covenantal faithfulness (Deut. 28:3–5, 8, 11–12; Lev. 26:3–5). Thus, the news of food in Bethlehem is linked to the Lord's favor, a connection that the writer implicitly emphasizes. With this bit of "good news" Naomi realizes that the way forward for all concerned is the way back to her home in Bethlehem. The three women set out for their trip to Judah. For Naomi it represents a return trip, but for Ruth and Orpah it entails a journey into the unknown.

B. The nature of Naomi's worries/Naomi's resolve and confession (1:8–15). On journeying back to Bethlehem, Naomi has second thoughts regarding the benefits of bringing Ruth and Orpah home with her. She openly shares her worries and concerns with them. Her sentiments are not communicated through narration but by three speeches (1:8–9, 11–13, 15). In each we witness a display of her sentiment to care for Ruth and Orpah, which translates into a relentless resolve to persuade them to keep their homes in Moab. The heart of her concern is that the women have homes, places of refuge, security, provision, and above all identity (1:9; 3:1; 4:11, 12, 18). Naomi wants Yahweh to give them patrimonial roots typical to the current tribal social structure. Accordingly, she does not allow her personal sentiments to prevail over the practical matters facing these women. Naomi deliberately and selflessly distances herself from the emotional ties that, undoubtedly, bind them.

In the first speech Naomi questions if it may not be better for each of them to return to "your mother's home," to "the home of another husband," places where each would be guaranteed to find the needed security and assistance (1:8–9). She stirs up doubt about their choice to relocate. To travel with Naomi will entail a journey into the unknown, a life lived on foreign soil with its accompanying hardships. By appealing to their Moabite blood ties, Naomi tries to free them of ongoing obligations to her, a nonblood relative and a foreigner. Naomi understands that the death of her sons technically severed continued familial obligations between her, Orpah, and Ruth. Her speech concludes with a benediction asking the Lord to grant them reciprocating kindness (1:8). This speech represents Naomi's first attempt to persuade her daughters-in-law.

After the benediction Naomi kisses them, and off they are supposed to go. Naomi's resolve, however, is met with resistance at a deep level, something witnessed by the women's tears and words (1:9). They argue, "We will go back with you to your people" (1:10). The statement reveals that their ties to Naomi are deeper than to their own mothers. Clearly their desire for Naomi's well-being mirrors their mother-in-law's concern for Orpah and Ruth. They pledge their commitment not to abandon her. Far from naively following her, however, they acknowledge the great cost involved. The use of the possessive "your people" in 1:10 identifies the level of risk for them in finding a new home in Judah. It reflects the distance between Naomi's people, the Israelites, and the Moabite women. It expresses the cross-cultural experience that awaits them. Nonetheless, Orpah and Ruth put Naomi first. They disregard the risks and doubts raised by Naomi, and in so doing they rival their mother-in-law's resolve.

Naomi retorts with an honest and humble confession (1:11–13), a second speech attempting to persuade them to keep their hope of a home in Moab rather than Bethlehem. Naomi initially appeals to insurmountable practical difficulties, items the women cannot dispute.

The region around modern Bethlehem

Because Naomi has nothing to offer them by way of future marriage options, she warns, once a widow always a widow as long as they remain with her. As widows they can hope for nothing more than poverty and destitution, an empty and bleak future. While she can bear the precarious nature of her own situation, Naomi does not want to subject Ruth and Orpah to such circumstances.

Naomi also appeals to a religious drawback. As is typical of the ancient Near Eastern mindset, Naomi attributes divine disfavor as the source of her inexplicable suffering (1:13). For this reason, Naomi cautions her daughters-in-law that the Lord's hand of disfavor may continue to affect them adversely and is a valid reason to reconsider. Thus Naomi hones in on the negatives both practically and religiously in the hope that the women will relent.

With this second speech both women reach a final decision. Orpah departs, determined to make Moab her home once again (1:14). The author narrates and reports the outcome of the conversation, allowing the reader to pass silent judgment on both Orpah's decision and Naomi's resolve to keep these women in Moab. There is little doubt that Naomi's resolve should be characterized as selfless and genuinely concerned for the women's physical well-being. The narrative firmly establishes this. But one wonders if Naomi is not too caught up in the practical (finding Ruth a home) to the neglect of the spiritual benefits these women might have accrued by going to Bethlehem (i.e., finding refuge in the Lord,

A warrior god from Moab, possibly Chemosh (cf. Ruth 1:15)

the God of Israel). Again, the author allows room for this possible interpretation.

Reluctant Ruth, by contrast, clings to Naomi (1:14). Ruth's gesture indicates a staunch loyalty to the relationship, a loyalty much like one gives in marriage (Gen. 2:24; 1 Kings 11:2) or in service to the kingdom (2 Sam. 20:2). This prompts Naomi's third and final attempt to persuade Ruth to find her home in Moab, not Judah (1:15). Her method includes pressuring Ruth to be like her sister-in-law, as well as arguing that living in Moab is preferred due to the established deity and territorial associations familiar to Ruth (1:15). By this statement Naomi declares that Ruth belongs to Moab, her people are the Moabites, and her god is Chemosh (Num. 21:27–30). Naomi dissuades her from making what would amount to a radical change in the status quo. Yet even after this compelling attempt, Ruth's resolve remains intact.

C. Ruth's resolve and confession (1:16–17). For the first time Ruth speaks. She interprets Naomi's previous injunctions to journey back to Moab (along with Orpah) as abandonment of her mother-in-law, something Ruth resolutely refuses (1:16). Her words, which are followed by an oath (1:16–17), indicate her relentless resolve to stay with Naomi and help the reader to grasp the profound sentiment behind Ruth's physical gesture of clinging to Naomi (1:14).

In general, Ruth is expressing covenantal loyalties to Naomi in much the same way Jonathan pledges to David, along the lines of other covenants between equals in the Bible.

Ruth elects to extend her familial relationship of obligation already established with Naomi through marriage to Mahlon (4:10) regardless of his death. These renewed loyalties translate into a radical change for Ruth, specifically, a change in ethnic identity. In short, Ruth pledges to become an Israelite. Her commitment to Naomi is such that it entails becoming an Israelite even though the text does not state this explicitly until later (4:11–12, 13–17). Old alliances (social, religious, and political) must be discarded so as not to threaten the obligations involved with the renewed relationship. Ruth's specific statement about wanting to be buried in Naomi's homeland seems to capture her willingness to embrace a new land and ethnicity (1:17). Indeed, archaeology has shown a connection between mortuary data and the ethnic identity of the deceased. Furthermore, a change in ethnic identity meant a change in religion, since the two were bound together.

It is not surprising, therefore, that in the oath sealing her commitment to Naomi, Ruth invokes the name of the Lord rather than Chemosh to sanction the renewed relationship (1:17). The oath also indicates just how far Ruth is willing to go to serve Naomi. Ruth asks that the Lord hold her liable unto death if she does not keep her commitment to Naomi, thereby placing herself under Deuteronomic obligations. Outside of the book of Ruth, this oath formula appears only in 1 Samuel 20:13.

Generally speaking, native Israelites swear by Elohim (God), not Yahweh (the Lord) in oaths that employ the deity to punish the oath taker if he or she does not follow through with the promised actions. The preference for the more generic Elohim over Yahweh (a specific term that resonates with covenant; Exodus 3; 6) suggests a deliberate distance between the deity and the one taking the self-maledictory oath. A native Israelite would, however, use the name of the Lord in a common oath formula, such as "as the Lord lives." In the latter, omission of the self-maledictory piece allows the oath taker freedom to use the more personal divine

name. Accordingly, the name functions like a verbal signature, a guarantee of the genuine desire to do what is being pledged.

Ruth implores the Lord to punish her if she does not do all that is in her power to care for Naomi (1:17). This entails nothing less than a change in ethnicity and religion. That Ruth calls on the Lord and not Elohim perhaps underscores the influence of Naomi's faith on her while in Moab. The oath demonstrates her full assimilation to Elimelek's family and culture. But it also shows Ruth is "swearing by the true God (rather than some other being who might be designated as 'god') . . . reflecting the strength of her emotion and commitment" (Revell, 203).

The fact that Ruth willfully becomes an Israelite and embraces the Lord by moving to Judah is somewhat typical of one in the ancient world adopting the god of the land to which they have moved. Her actions are atypical, however, when viewed against the average Israelite who, at that time, tended toward adopting foreign gods alongside the Lord. This syncretism (fusing two or more originally different beliefs into one) so dominant at the time the story unfolds is something Ruth chooses not to embrace. Ruth does what few Israelites are able to do, embrace and fully commit to Yahwistic religion yet discard all opposing religious alliances. In a very real sense, Ruth clings to the Lord by clinging to Naomi. Because her actions stand in stark contrast to those of the typical Israelite in this regard, at numerous and even awkward times in the story the author reminds the reader of Ruth's Moabite ethnicity (1:22; 2:2, 21; 4:5, 10). Ruth the Moabitess is a model Israelite in that she embraces Yahweh fully and exclusively. But she is also a model Israelite in showing kindness according to Mosaic law. Furthermore, Ruth's naturalization process is crucial for the story line and the upcoming betrothal narrative (3:7–15). It legitimizes her marriage to an Israelite man, unlike her first marriage, to Mahlon.

Thus the covenantal loyalties described in these verses, her burial desires, and the oath using the Lord's name seem to reflect that necessary break with her past (not syncretism), a break that has religious, social, and political ramifications. Indeed, the journey to her future home is such that it will require the kind of break and assimilation Ruth is pledging to Naomi.

D. In Bethlehem (1:18–22). After such a statement of loyalty and fidelity, Naomi's pleas stop, and they set out for Judah as originally intended (1:18). When Naomi arrives in Bethlehem without Elimelek, Kilion, and Mahlon, she shocks the city on account of the great loss so apparent in her life (1:19). When confronted by the women in town, Naomi reveals the theological grid that informs her situation (1:20–21). She interprets her pitiful condition (once full but now empty) as caused by both "the Almighty" and "the LORD," in personal opposition. This explains why she requests they no longer call her Naomi but Mara, a name change that in Hebrew reflects the bitterness she has experienced.

The notification that their arrival in Bethlehem (1:18–22) coincides with the beginning of the barley harvest in March to April confirms the correctness of what Naomi heard in the fields of Moab (1:6). But the women's successful trip is not the sole concern of the chapter. With the conversation between Naomi and Ruth exhibiting mutual resolve and powerful confessions, the author is establishing the exemplary characters of these women. Furthermore, the grim atmosphere is beginning to turn to a more hopeful tone for Naomi, reflecting a hope that becomes more fully developed in what follows.

3. A Worthy Woman Meets a Worthy Man (2:1–23)

A. Ruth finds work (favor) in Boaz's field (2:1–3). The author introduces the reader to a new character (2:1). Before offering a name introduction, the writer gives information about this person that will be vital to the development of the plot. First, the character happens to be a distant male relative of Naomi's husband. Second, this relative is designated as a "man of standing" (2:1). The very existence of someone related to Elimelek and Naomi gives the reader cause to hope that Naomi's misfortunes may change due to legal responsibilities a living family member had to a deceased relative's family (Lev. 25:25; Deut. 25:5–10). Only after these introductory items do we learn that the person's name is Boaz. Indeed, Boaz will be the means that allows the widows to find food, favor, and ultimately a restored home. The scene is now set for the "coincidental" meeting between Ruth and Boaz.

At Ruth's initiative and in accordance with standard Mosaic practice that encouraged the poor

Harvesting scene from the Tomb of Menna (Luxor, Egypt, ca. fourteenth century BC). Notice the two women gleaning in the field and the waterskin hanging on the tree.

and needy to find sustenance by gleaning in another's field, she sets out (2:2). Upon Ruth's arrival at the field we are told promptly that it belongs to Boaz, a person from Elimelek's family (2:3). Here the mention of Boaz's name appears first, and then his kinship tie to Elimelek follows, a reverse of 2:1. By supplying the field owner's name first and the kinship tie second, the author creates a tangible hope that Ruth might actually meet Boaz, a necessary rendezvous, one that could potentially help the distressed women. Thus both hope and suspense build as the story unfolds. In Bethlehem there exists a family member who could rescue Naomi (hope). But without the ability to find him, the women have no chance in reestablishing a home (suspense). The chance encounter turns out to be a sovereign setup of circumstances. Boaz notices Ruth and, as a result, she finds escalating favor with him.

B. Boaz reaches out to Ruth, and Ruth responds with gratitude (2:4–16). Boaz speaks for the first time in the narrative (2:4). He exchanges a blessing with his workers, which shows his cordial nature and the good relationship he shares with them. Next Boaz notices a new worker. Once made aware of the worker's identity, Boaz kindly reaches out to her and, in so doing, reveals the strength of his own character in three ways (2:5–7).

First, he goes beyond the Mosaic mandate (the requirement to leave food for the poor in the fields; Deut. 24:19) by providing for her need to drink, encouraging her to stay in his field, and offering her protection (2:8–9). Boaz also showers Ruth with exceptional favors by allowing her to have a meal with him and the reapers and by granting her special access to wheat pieces deliberately left by the reapers (2:14–16).

Second, Boaz recognizes and honors Ruth's conduct and reputation. He acknowledges her displays of loyalty to Naomi and family, loyalties that were costly and translated into personal denial and sacrifice (2:11).

Third, he pronounces a blessing on her and asks that she be rewarded richly by "the LORD, the God of Israel, under whose wings you have come to take refuge" (2:12). The latter statement represents Boaz's own commentary on Ruth's gestures that have won her a great reputation. He understands that Ruth's change of ethnic identity is religious in nature. Ruth has put her trust in the Lord rather than in her familiar Moabite deities. The Hebrew term translated here as "refuge" appears mainly, although not exclusively, in the Psalms and reflects one's personal

and private association with the Lord rather than the national or territorial association (e.g., Ps. 7:1; 11:1; 16:1). Furthermore, the compound designation Boaz uses here, "the LORD, the God of Israel," deliberately distinguishes the Lord from foreign gods, namely, Chemosh, Moab's chief deity. Thus Boaz seems to be acknowledging that Ruth is a follower of Yahweh. He affirms that her Abrahamic-like abandonment to uproot geographically, no matter how difficult, has brought her to a good place spiritually. He confirms Ruth's religious assimilation rather than her religious syncretism. Boaz's words function as a testimonial of Ruth's character. Indeed, Ruth is doing what she previously pledged to Naomi, to become an Israelite (1:16–17). Furthermore, Boaz's statement reveals that he views Ruth functionally as an Israelite. In these three ways, Boaz's speech reveals his strong reputation and character. Through his acts of kindness, Boaz becomes the answer to his own prayer, as the LORD blesses Ruth when Boaz showers her with practical favors and recognition.

Ruth then responds with gratitude. Even as she formally responds to Boaz (2:10), his initial query about the identity of the woman in his field reveals her hardworking nature (2:7). Her physical gesture of bowing down to the ground reflects a deep humility and submission to an elder. Her words that follow illumine more of the integrity of her heart. Regardless of Ruth's naturalization process, she still considers herself "a foreigner," a point further illustrated in the remark, "I do not have the standing of one of your servants" (2:10, 13). These statements reflect Ruth's perception about her origin and not her current status as an Israelite. She assumes her foreign origin naturally disqualifies her from benefiting from Boaz's generosity. Her overall response is characterized with grace and gratitude (2:10, 13). Thus, through the unexpected meeting and conversation, the author has established the noble characters of Ruth and Boaz. It equally exposes the unseen hand of Yahweh providentially at work. Indeed, a worthy woman meets a worthy man (2:1; 3:11).

C. Ruth returns home with a favorable report (2:17–23). The practical outworking of Boaz's initial favor translates into the abundance of food Ruth brings back to Naomi after her first day on the job, approximately twenty to twenty-five pounds, or twenty-five liters—enough for roughly five days (2:17). Boaz meets the immediate practical needs of two desperate women. He continues to do so for about three months, the duration of two harvests (2:23). However, later that evening Naomi informs Ruth (the reader already knows this; 2:1) of Boaz's ability to meet an even greater need (2:20).

On account of Ruth's fruitful workday and the owner's obvious generosity, Naomi pronounces a blessing on this man without knowing his identity (2:19). However, once Naomi learns that Boaz is the man Ruth worked for, she bubbles over with enthusiasm and pronounces a second blessing on him. But the latter arises because of the concrete knowledge Naomi now possesses. Not only is Boaz a man of stellar character and wealth, a relative, and known to Ruth, but he happens to be a close relative described by Naomi as "one of our kinsman-redeemers" (2:20 NIV 1984; NIV "guardian-redeemers").

Mosaic legislation defines a redeemer as a male, near blood relative who has the responsibility for rescuing, protecting, and helping weaker relatives. His responsibilities might include such things as buying back land belonging to relatives that was sold or forfeited, defending legal interests of that relative, executing a relative's killer, or siring and raising children with the wife of the deceased relative in order to perpetuate the family name (Lev. 25:25–28; Deut. 25:5–10).

The mention of Boaz as kinsman-redeemer injects even more hope into the narrative, a hope only previously alluded to with Boaz's introduction, the unexpected meeting between Ruth and Boaz, and the favors Boaz bestows on Ruth (2:1, 3, 14–16). Thus Boaz's crucial role in the story line now unfolds with more specificity. Furthermore, Boaz's affirmation of Ruth's covenantal loyalties to the Lord sets the stage for the upcoming betrothal narrative.

Threshing floor outside Bethlehem

4. Ruth's Proposal (3:1–18)

A. Naomi navigates a plan (3:1–5). Ruth works in Boaz's field for about three months and continues to live with Naomi (2:23). But living together was never Naomi's long-term plan for Ruth. Now that Boaz and Ruth have providentially met, and given that Boaz bears a legal family responsibility, Naomi attempts to secure a new home and identity for Ruth. She hopes to restore the coveted family name and reputation along with any inheritance. Naomi seizes the opportunity to inform Boaz of his responsibility by sending Ruth to communicate to him at the threshing floor.

B. Ruth reaches out to Boaz at the threshing floor (3:6–9). In submission to Naomi, Ruth follows a set of instructions puzzling to a reader removed from Israelite laws and customs. First, Ruth "uncovered his feet and lay down" (3:7). Although she might be uncovering his literal feet, it is possible that she is exposing his private parts, given the euphemistic use of "feet" for genitals and sexual relations elsewhere in the Bible (Isa. 7:20; Deut. 28:57). Second, once he awakes and learns of her identity, Ruth asks specific instructions of him. Her words to Boaz, "Spread the corner of your garment over me, since you are a kinsman-redeemer" (3:9 NIV 1984), indicate a desire for marriage (Ezek. 16:8; Deut. 22:30). As an Israelite, Ruth proposes marriage to Boaz. Her conduct represents an interpretation and contextualization of Israelite law governing a widow's social standing. However, in light of forbidden Israelite and Moabite relations, she is still taking a great risk, regardless of her solid reputation. For this reason, Naomi and Boaz take precautionary measures as they instruct Ruth.

C. Boaz responds with gratitude and a requirement (3:10–15). Boaz's response further shows that he is a man of integrity and noble character. He allays her fears and without hesitation happily obliges. His unequivocal acceptance of her proposal relies on the fact that she is a woman of noble character (3:11). Indeed, as a new Israelite, Ruth is a worthy woman. He deems it honorable that Ruth has pursued and preferred him (3:10). It is unfathomable given the writer's intentionality in bolstering Boaz's godly and reputable character that he would agree to marry "Ruth, the Moabite" if she had not changed her ethnic identity.

Although Boaz agrees to the proposal and responds with gratitude, a potential threat looms (3:10–13). There exists another man whose legal rights to meet Ruth's needs surpass his own due to closer familial ties. The law requires that Boaz appeal to this person before agreeing to Ruth's request (3:10–13). Now there are two possible places where Ruth might find a home! Boaz cautions Ruth but assures her of his strong desire to provide for her.

D. Ruth returns home (3:16–18). Again Boaz does not send Ruth back to Naomi "empty-handed" (3:17). He gives her an ample supply of barley and causes her to return with another favorable report (3:14–15). As before, the favor extended to Ruth concerns more than abundance of food; now it entails Boaz's verbal commitment to marry Ruth and give her a new home and identity in Israel. Tension still remains, however, as to the full outcome. What will become of Ruth and Boaz? As long as this "other man" exists it remains to be seen whether her new home will be with Boaz.

5. Boaz's Acceptance (4:1–12)

A. The legal decision made (4:1–6). The escalating tension and suspense finally reach a climactic outcome. By taking the reader directly to the city gate, the place where legal decisions are heard and decided, the author highlights Boaz's urgency in attending to the matter as anticipated by Naomi (3:18). Reaching a decision entails assembling Boaz and the redeemer to sit and discuss the matter in the company of ten elders, the number required for legal and marriage benedictions (4:1–2). Once Boaz fully airs the matter with the nameless kinsman-redeemer, the latter determines he cannot fulfill his obligations for personal reasons (4:3–6). The curious omission of the redeemer's personal name represents the author's way of giving a high profile to the *act* of redemption, the necessary event to secure restoration for both women. In fact, the terms "redeem" and "kinsman-redeemer" appear multiple times in chapter 4. The repetition reflects the importance of the event. "The redeemer" is relinquishing his rights to Boaz (4:6). Boaz accepts his obligations, which entail marrying Ruth, purchasing the land, and giving money to Naomi in the form of property (4:9–10; Deut. 25:5–10).

B. The decision confirmed (4:7–12). The decision is now confirmed by a sandal exchange and two speeches: one by Boaz (4:9–10) and the other by the gathered witnesses (4:11–12). The sandal exchange functioned like a receipt for business conducted. Accordingly, it indicates a formal transference of property reflecting possession (Josh. 1:3). Boaz's public and verbal affirmation functions as a ratifying oath sealing the business deal (4:9–10). His statement reveals the intent of the Mosaic legislation: perpetuating the name of the dead. But it also shows how the legislation is contextualized given Naomi's age. Rather than marry widowed Naomi as prescribed in the law, Boaz agrees to marry "Ruth the Moabite, Mahlon's widow." This designation, different from the previous one, is uniquely suited to the legal proceedings. Out of necessity, it emphasizes Ruth's legal social status as a widow. Together with the sandal exchange it represents a formal declaration of what Boaz gains.

Finally, the public and verbal affirmation of the elders and witnesses concludes the business transaction (4:11–12). The witnesses affirm the rightness of the decision by declaring a blessing on Boaz's new household: for Boaz's wife they ask for fruitfulness akin to Rachel's and Leah's. They wish Ruth to be like a matriarch in Israel, a key indicator of Ruth's changed status. They deem her a formal and legitimate member of the house of Israel. For Boaz personally they ask that he be famous in Bethlehem. Indeed, as father of Obed and husband of Ruth, Boaz (already prominent and famous for his acts of kindness) will receive greater renown as an

ancestor of David. And for his entire household they ask the blessing of children, such as was found in Perez's house. By recalling Perez, they are reminded of how his birth parallels the birth of Obed in that it represents the continuation of a threatened lineage through the providence of the Lord and the active role of another wise widow named Tamar (Gen. 38:24–30).

Thus, business in town is terminated. Boaz now has the legal right to marry Ruth. The witness of the Israelite elders and the blessings they pronounce underscore how Ruth, now an Israelite, has the right to receive the blessings of Abraham concerning fruitfulness and prosperity. It shows how an enemy of Israel becomes blessed by pledging allegiance and faithfulness to the Lord.

6. The Marriage: Family Fortunes and Fruitfulness (4:13–17)

Boaz at last marries Ruth. Although she experienced infertility when previously married to Mahlon, the Lord enables her to conceive with Boaz as he enabled Sarah, Rebekah, and Rachel (Gen. 21:1–2; 25:21–25; 30:22–24). The significance of this cannot be overstated. The fact that barren Ruth conceives is a hallmark of the promises to Abraham. More specifically, like the birth of Isaac in the patriarchal narratives, it suggests that David comes from "promise." In contrast to the opening of the book, where the town's women noticed Naomi's emptiness, they now acknowledge her fullness and the Lord's goodness toward her in the birth of a grandson. In Boaz she has an honorable relative, one who has met her practical needs. Through Ruth, Naomi has experienced deep love and commitment, such as might have been supplied by the ideal of seven sons. And by gaining a grandson Naomi is assured of full restoration to the family name. They ask, as they did for Boaz, that the child be renowned in Israel.

Following this the neighborhood women, not the parents, name the child. They name him Obed, or "the one who serves." Indeed, their benediction on Obed is realized by the statement, which reveals Obed's ties to Israel's famous King David, "[Obed] was the father of Jesse, the father of David" (4:17). Not only will Obed serve Naomi, but Obed, as grandfather of King David, will in turn serve Israel. Accordingly, Obed will receive a renowned reputation. As mother of Obed and wife of Boaz, Ruth (already famous for her acts of kindness) will receive greater renown as an ancestor of David. Thus for the first time in the book the author discards Ruth's Moabite designation. It is no longer necessary because her marriage to Boaz formalizes her assimilation into Israel. Although once empty, Naomi has now received fullness from the Lord's sovereign and merciful hand in her old age.

Thus the "naturalization" process that Ruth undergoes enables her to marry Boaz. Ruth finds a new home in Israel, the answer to Naomi's passionate concern. Ruth also finds a spiritual home by trusting in Israel's God. Her functional change in ethnic identity, whereby she transfers membership to Israel, also explains how a Moabite can be included in David's line, the enthusiastic witness of the Israelite elders verifying Ruth's Israelite membership, and the outpouring of blessings and fruitfulness in Ruth's life. The evidence suggests that David's ancestry is neither mixed nor suspicious. In fact, the noble woman and man lauded in the story are no less than the ancestors of the founder of the Judean dynasty. Therefore, the book not only introduces David in a way the books of Samuel and Chronicles do not, but it also appears to be an attempt to legitimize David's rule so as to free it from any scandal that could have surfaced during or after his reign.

7. Conclusion: Future Fruitfulness (4:18–22)

The concluding genealogy provides proof that their marriage has future implications for the house of Israel. Although deliberately limited in scope, it lauds the fruitfulness of the house of Perez. In describing him as an ancestor of David, the genealogy shows the nature of the restoration afforded to Tamar and to the descendants of Jacob (Gen. 38:29; 46:12). It equally shows

the nature of the restoration given to Ruth and Naomi through Boaz. But the genealogy also points forward to the physical and spiritual restoration Israel will experience from King David (2 Samuel 7). The genealogy of David's family at the end of Ruth declares that Yahweh's previous promise to Abraham, "and kings shall come forth from you" (Gen. 17:6 RSV), stands for the future regardless of Israel's present temperament toward the Lord (1:1). Indeed, without this providentially driven betrothal narrative there would have been no King David in Israel.

Although Naomi wanted to establish a home and identity for Ruth, the Lord ultimately builds a home for her in a way Naomi could never have fathomed. On account of Jesus, the great Son of David and the ultimate kinsman-redeemer (Matt. 1:1; Luke 1:68), those who take refuge in him find a new identity as children of God (John 1:12) and a new home as citizens of the eternal kingdom of God (Matt. 19:28–30; Rom. 14:17).

Select Bibliography

Alter, Robert. *The Art of Biblical Narrative.* New York: Basic Books, 1981.

Berlin, Adele. "Ruth." In *Harper's Bible Commentary.* Edited by James Luther Mays. San Francisco: Harper & Row, 1988.

Campbell, Edward. *Ruth: A New Translation and Commentary.* Anchor Bible. New York: Doubleday, 1975.

Hubbard, Robert L., Jr. *The Book of Ruth.* New International Commentary on the Old Testament. Grand Rapids: Eerdmans, 1988.

Nielsen, Kirsten. *Ruth.* Old Testament Library. Louisville: Westminster John Knox, 1997.

Revell, E. J. *The Designation of the Individual: Expressive Usage in Biblical Narrative.* Kampen, Netherlands: Kok Pharos, 1996.

Smith, Mark S. "'Your People Shall Be My People': Family and Covenant in Ruth 1:16–17." *Catholic Biblical Quarterly* 69 (2007): 242–58.

Younger, K. Lawson, Jr. *Judges, Ruth.* NIV Application Commentary. Grand Rapids: Zondervan, 2002.

1–2 Samuel

HERBERT M. WOLF
REVISED BY ROBERT D. HOLMSTEDT*

Introduction

The books of 1 and 2 Samuel are named after the prophet Samuel, who served as the last judge of Israel and who anointed both Saul and David to be kings of Israel. The books thus provide a transition between Judges, with its underlying argument for the unifying nature of a monarch, and 1 and 2 Kings, which tell the story of the Israelite monarchy. Originally 1 and 2 Samuel were one book, a unity attested by the earliest existing copy, the larger Samuel scroll among the Dead Sea Scrolls (4QSamᵃ), which partially preserves the text from what we know as 1 Samuel 1:11 to 2 Samuel 24:20. Jewish tradition continued to treat the books as one until the fifteenth century; this is most easily seen in the Masoretic marginal notes, which mark 1 Samuel 28:24 as "half of the book by verses." At the same time, the division between 1 and 2 Samuel is natural enough, since 1 Samuel ends with the death of Israel's first king, Saul, leaving 2 Samuel to focus on the reign of David. The division into two books occurred already in antiquity, likely due to space concerns; it was first divided by the translators of the Greek Old Testament (Septuagint), who referred to the two

as the books of First and Second Kingdoms. The Latin Bible (Vulgate) called these books First and Second Kings and the books that followed, Third and Fourth Kings.

It is worth noting that the story of David does not end in 2 Samuel 24, but continues through 1 Kings 1, and his death is not mentioned until 1 Kings 2:10–11. Thus, not only is the division between 1 and 2 Samuel artificial, but the entirety of Joshua–Judges–Samuel–Kings reads, in their final forms at least, as a single, four-volume work that tells the story of the Israelite history in Canaan, from entrance to exile. Moreover, all four contain themes and explicit textual links to the book that apparently gave the historian of the final work his focus: Deuteronomy. It is thus important that as sensitive readers we bear in mind that with 1–2 Samuel we are stepping into the middle of an ongoing story. So, while Samuel, Saul, and David take center stage in this work, the central characters of the larger story are the Lord and Israel.

The Argument of 1–2 Samuel

In asking what 1–2 Samuel is about, we must remember that history-writing, whether ancient or modern, is never simply about "recording

---

* Herb Wolf was one of my teachers at Wheaton College; I studied Old Testament, Hebrew, and Ugaritic with him. It is to his memory that I dedicate this revision. While I have added to and revised the original text, I have been very selective and have tried to retain as much of the original as possible. What changes I have made were done in the spirit of the original commentary.

the facts." Instead, a historian chooses which facts to include, orders them, and sometimes even dresses them up. This is done in order to make an argument about some person, event, or period in history—that is, to explain why something happened or to explain a person or event's larger significance (see Frykenberg). The challenge with the biblical history writings is that it is often difficult to reconstruct enough of the historians' settings to be able to identify accurately the specific underlying arguments in their books. Even so, it is helpful to ask oneself as one reads a book like 1–2 Samuel, Why is this event included? or, Why is it told this way?

As a whole, 1–2 Samuel describes two critical transitions in the story of Israel's beginnings: from charismatic judges to prophets and from tribalism to monarchy. Each shift revolves around three or four figures. Eli, Samuel, Gad, and Nathan represent the shift from judge to prophet; Samuel, Saul, and David move Israel from a loose tribal association to centralized governance in the form of a dynastic monarchy. Within this overarching context of transition, one issue stands at the center and drives the historian's argument: kingship.

Many scholars nowadays assert that the historian's use of sources, some that were antimonarchy and others that were promonarchy, have left a confusing mix of narrative voices in the final book. Indeed, there is no doubt that both views can be discerned in the book, but if we assume a skillful historian behind the end product, we need not take the tension simply as a remnant of a complex compositional background; rather, the tension was more likely a deliberate rhetorical strategy allowing the historian to maintain two stances at once: as a political pragmatist the historian recognizes both the fact of the monarchy's existence and that a monarchy provides a long-term solution to deal with outside threats (so also Judges); as a theological idealist the historian balks both at the challenge the monarchy makes to God's kingship and the authority of the prophets and at the power of the monarchic authority to corrupt the king and so lead Israel astray (so also 1–2 Kings).

Even the early chapters, before a king is mentioned, contribute to the argument about monarchy: on the one hand, oppression by the Philistines implicitly picks up the argument at the end of Judges—Israel suffers chaos because there is no king (cf. Judg. 17:6; 18:1; 19:1; 21:25); on the other hand, the victory of the Lord over the Philistine god Dagon in 1 Samuel 5 suggests that if the Israelites had just been loyal their divine king would have provided peace for them. This issue of kingship hovers just below the surface of the entire narrative in the form of three questions: (1) Will Israel continue to recognize the Lord as its true king even though they now have a human monarch? (2) Who has greater authority, prophet or king? and (3) Who will be the next monarch?

Human versus divine monarch. Fundamental to the historian's view was the belief that God as the divine king deserved the loyalty and worship of his people and that he also demonstrated his power to the nations. The request for a human king was thus seen as a rejection of the Lord, both his ability to protect his people and, to some degree, his authority. Typologically and theologically the request for a king mirrors the Israelites' request at Sinai that Moses receive the Ten Commandments on their behalf—in both cases, the people elect to place a barrier between themselves and the Lord. It is thus not surprising that the historian views the institution of monarchy with disappointment and suspicion.

In fact, nowhere does the juxtaposition of anti- and promonarchy voices come out more clearly than in 1 Samuel 8–12—the chapters that describe the monarchy's origin. The first and last episodes in this sequence present Samuel and the people in a discussion about the merits of a monarchy, and both render the judgment that it is, at its core, a rejection of the Lord as Israel's king. As bookends to the entire sequence, 1 Samuel 8:1–22 and 12:1–25 ensure a negative evaluation of the establishment of the monarchy. The middle episode (10:17–27), in which Samuel summons the people to Mizpah for the official selection of Saul, is also a negative evaluation of the monarchy. Not only does Samuel remind the people of their disloyalty to the Lord by asking for a king, but their future king is found hiding among the luggage! It is an ignominious start for the monarchy.

In contrast, the second episode (9:1–10:16) asserts that the monarchy will be used by God for Israel's deliverance. Moreover, the fourth episode (11:1–15) illustrates this benefit, with Saul's first victory as the newly chosen king. Thus the historian has used both positive and negative stories about the institution of the Israelite monarchy. The positive stories reflect the recognition that being united under a central leader has great benefit. Throughout the ancient Near East, kings were responsible for maintaining justice and hearing legal cases, and 1–2 Kings on occasion depicts a ruler deciding such cases. The negative stories reflect the historian's distrust of monarchy as an institution of power and wealth that can deter obedience to the command of the Lord (a view echoed in Deut. 17:14–17). These stories also reflect the historian's view that Israel's choice of a king was first and foremost a rejection of the Lord as their king and military leader (1 Sam. 8:7; 10:19), and, secondarily, a rejection of Samuel (8:8). Why is the rejection of Samuel important to the historian? Because it reflects a fundamental tension in the hierarchy of authority between king and prophet.

Prophet versus king. A second kingship-related thread in the stories of Samuel and Saul and David, Gad, and Nathan is the prophetic

challenge to monarchic decisions. The common view throughout the ancient Near East was that the king served as the deity's vice-regent, thus assuming a close alliance between the king and the deity. This alliance is described in this book (2 Sam. 7:14) and elsewhere (Ps. 2:7; 89:27–28) using adoption and the father-son relationship as metaphors. The relationship between prophet and king that is unfolded in Samuel, however, undercuts that view: for the historian, the prophet stood between the Israelite king and the Lord, so that a prophet like Samuel could even replace a sitting king by anointing a new one. This superiority of the prophet is strikingly portrayed in a story about David escaping one of Saul's attempts to kill him (1 Sam. 19:18–24). This bizarre episode draws on the fact that one of the characteristic behaviors marking prophets was that they fell into ecstatic states. In this story not only do all of Saul's messengers begin to prophesy, but even Saul himself falls into a prophetic frenzy when they approach Samuel's encampment. The prophetic aura functions almost like a force field to keep Saul and his servants at bay, thus demonstrating the true power of prophet versus king.

As much as 1–2 Samuel is a history of the rise of the Israelite monarchy, it is a history of the dominance of prophets over kings. It expresses prophetic misgivings about kings and their tendencies—above all, their tendency to ignore the word of God through the prophet in preference for the desires

The top register of the Hammurabi Stele (eighteenth century BC) shows Hammurabi commissioned by the god Shamash to administer justice.

of the people. And at each step it shows the prophet Samuel and, to a lesser extent, his prophetic successors, Nathan and Gad, in charge of the flow of events, anointing kings, limiting their powers, and dismissing them from office when they refuse to yield to the divine word announced by the prophet.

The historian's shaping of the key episodes, from the choice of Saul to both Nathan's and Gad's rebukes of David, reflects his deep preference for the priority of prophets over the institution of the king. It is a theologically driven preference for the less institutionalized office of the judge and the highly charismatic office of the prophet that seems to lie behind the negative evaluation of kings that permeates this narrative of the rise of the monarchy. The role of the prophet was considered superior to that of kings, based on the pattern of Moses as the prophet par excellence in Deuteronomy 18.

Who shall rule? Finally, a question that becomes agonizing is that of succession. David is anointed in 1 Samuel 16 but is not installed as king of Judah in Hebron until 2 Samuel 2 and, finally, as king of all Israel in Jerusalem until 2 Samuel 5. It thus takes twenty-one chapters to answer if and how David will actually succeed Saul.

After David becomes king, God promises that David's family will remain the royal family forever and his descendants will follow him on the throne. This promise later figures into the development of an expectation for an "anointed one" (Messiah) from the line of David to deliver the Jewish people from the oppression of foreign rule. Yet the promise does not ensure a smooth transition of power, and David himself witnesses struggles over who will succeed him. He endures an outright rebellion by one son, Absalom (2 Samuel 13–20), and, if we look ahead to 1 Kings 1–2, wrangling between two more sons, Adonijah and Solomon, which ends fatally for Adonijah. Typologically, there are parallels between Moses and David in that Moses also faced rebellion, had his authority challenged (even by his brother and sister), and

faced the issue of succession. Similarly, David's story, including its continuation into Kings, mirrors some elements of the patriarchal narratives in Genesis. For Genesis, an ongoing issue is who will carry on the promise made to Abraham and whether the successor is or will become worthy; this topos finds expression in Samuel-Kings and the historian's evaluation of each king against the model of David, who, like Abraham, is an imperfect first recipient of his respective promise.

Title and Authorship

The book is named 1–2 Samuel not primarily on the basis of authorship but on the centrality of the figure of Samuel in the first half of the work: his birth is narrated in the first chapter and his death is reported in 1 Samuel 25:1. Even so, it appears that early interpreters took the association to indicate authorship—at least for the first half of the work, up to Samuel's death—since the Babylonian Talmud asserts that "Samuel wrote 'his' book, Judges, and Ruth" (*Baba Batra* 14b). There are tantalizing hints that Samuel (or perhaps his followers) left a set of traditions. In 1 Chronicles 29:29 there is an interesting reference to "the words of Samuel the seer, the words of Nathan the prophet, and the words of Gad the seer" (author's translation). Like Samuel, Nathan and Gad were prophets who were closely associated with David. Gad accompanied David during his years as a fugitive from Saul (1 Sam. 22:5), and Nathan was the one who ministered to David throughout his reign (2 Sam. 7:2; 12:1). Thus it is possible that the traditions mentioned by the writer of 1–2 Chronicles overlap with or perhaps lie behind 1–2 Samuel, much like the Book of Jashar that is mentioned as a source in 2 Samuel 1:18. Perhaps the historian who finalized 1–2 Samuel made use of several earlier sources, although it must be stressed both that most such theories are all but impossible to prove and that it matters little for the interpretation of the final form, the received biblical book.

Structure and Composition

Structurally, the book can be divided into four sections based on thematic emphases: 1 Samuel 1–15 (Samuel and Saul), 1 Samuel 16–2 Samuel 8 (the rise of David), 2 Samuel 9–20 (David's reign), and 2 Samuel 21–24 (epilogue). The first section describes the transition from the period of the judges to the monarchy and includes a number of stories about the ark of the covenant. In the second section, we are told about David's rise to the throne and how his dynasty is established.

The third section is sometimes called the "Succession Narrative" or "court history" of David. Linked with 1 Kings 1–2, these chapters trace the rivalry among David's sons as they vie for the right to succeed him as king. That these perceived thematic sections align with the historian's intended flow is affirmed by four summaries that act as transitional markers: 1 Samuel 7:15–17, for Samuel as a judge; 1 Samuel 14:47–52, for Saul's reign; 2 Samuel 8:15–18, for David's reign; and 2 Samuel 20:23–26, listing David's officials.

Though it may be useful to read the book in the four parts mentioned above, the unity of the work as a whole should not be overlooked. One example of the intentionality of the final structure is the use of poems to mark the beginning (Hannah's song in 1 Samuel 2), the middle (David's elegy for Saul and Jonathan in 2 Sam. 1:19–27), and the end (David's

The Apology of Hattusilis. Tablet from Boğazköy (ancient Hattusas), thirteenth century BC, Hittite Empire.

song in 2 Samuel 22 and David's last words in 2 Samuel 23).

Research into the composition of the three thematic sections suggests that one or all may have existed as separate works in some form before being combined and edited into the larger narrative. For instance, considerable attention has been focused on the literary and rhetorical similarities between 1 Samuel 16–2 Samuel 8 and an ancient Hittite text called the Apology of Hattusilis (see photo). Like David, Hattusilis I (1275–1250 BC) took over the throne under unusual circumstances and was accused of being a usurper. But even if the interpretation of this middle section as a dynastic defense, an "apology," is accurate and helpful for interpretation, it is not clear if the writer of 1–2 Samuel used the apology as a source; that is, it is difficult to discern whether it ever functioned independently of the other chapters or if it was created in its current form during the composition of the book as a whole.

The events described in these books cover a period of approximately one hundred and thirty years, from the birth of Samuel around 1100 BC to the end of David's reign in circa 970 BC. David reigned seven years over Judah and thirty-three years over all Israel (2 Sam. 5:4–5) from circa 1010 to 970 BC, but the length of Saul's reign is unclear. Apparently the text of 1 Samuel 13:1 became damaged or was miscopied by scribes, because both Saul's age when he became king and the length of his reign are uncertain. Similarly, the length of Samuel's tenure as a prophet and judge can be only approximated, although from 1 Samuel 8:1, 5 we learn that Samuel is an old man when the people ask him to select a king for them.

In all likelihood, the material in 1 Samuel is arranged in chronological order, but this is not always the case in 2 Samuel. For example, the establishment of the Davidic covenant (2 Samuel 7) may have occurred after the military victories described in 2 Samuel 8, because 7:1 says that "the LORD had given him rest from all his enemies." Likewise, the victories over the Ammonites and Arameans discussed in 2 Samuel 10 may be either an elaboration of the battles described in 2 Samuel 8:3–12 or a completely different set of earlier engagements. Perhaps the lack of chronological order may be partly explained by the theory that 2 Samuel 7 and 8 conclude the "apology of David."

The final four chapters of 2 Samuel are regarded as an epilogue, partly because of their uncertain chronology. The account of the Gibeonites' revenge against the family of Saul is given in chapter 21, but it probably preceded the revolt of Absalom (chaps. 15–18). In 16:7–8 a descendant of Saul named Shimei curses David for shedding the blood of the family of Saul, and this may very well be a reference to the executions David permits in chapter 21. At the end of chapter 21 the author describes four battles against the Philistines, which are not likely in chronological order. The chronological issues notwithstanding, the epilogue serves as a transition between Samuel and Kings: the final episode describes David's purchase of the location that will eventually become home to Solomon's temple.

Date

As with the issue of literary sources or traditions, so too the date of the book remains greatly disputed. Some scholars continue to treat the materials in 1–2 Samuel as a sort of running history contemporaneous with the events described; that is, the narratives were

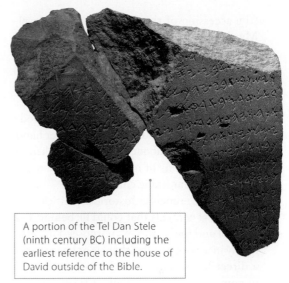

A portion of the Tel Dan Stele (ninth century BC) including the earliest reference to the house of David outside of the Bible.

composed during or soon after Samuel, Saul, and David lived. In this view, even if a later editor combined earlier materials, the earlier sources were left largely intact. Although the lives of the figures themselves (since we assume that they did indeed exist) provide the logical terminus a quo, references like "Israel and Judah" (1 Sam. 11:8; 17:52; 18:16) and "the kings of Judah" (27:6) suggest that a more likely earliest date lies after the division of Solomon's kingdom into north and south had taken place, perhaps in the late tenth century BC. The opposition faced by Solomon and his son and successor, Rehoboam, would have furnished a likely occasion for a vigorous defense of David's dynasty such as we have in 1–2 Samuel and 1 Kings.

But the historicity of the figures in the book and the date of the book's writing are not necessarily connected. While recent archaeological finds (such as the Tel Dan Stele, which likely mentions the "house [i.e., dynasty] of David"; see photo) suggest that more of "biblical" Israel existed in the tenth century than a few recent scholars are willing to admit, it is also legitimately possible to push the date quite a bit further away from the tenth century. If 1–2 Samuel is of a piece with 1–2 Kings and since the last edition of Kings belonged to the exile (the accession of the Babylonian king Awel-Marduk in 561 BC is mentioned in 2 Kings 25:27), it is only logical that the received form of 1–2 Samuel took shape some four hundred years removed from David. A work that, on the one hand, celebrates King David and provides a future hope for the monarchy by means of God's promise to David and that, on the other hand, carries a warning about the havoc wreaked by the inevitable sins of monarchs fits the needs and reality of an exilic context.

There are numerous historical, political, and theological contexts that could lie behind 1–2 Samuel and the historian's purposes. Unfortunately in a work like this there is not necessarily a direct link between the historian—who is unnamed—and the content, as there is in, for example, some of the prophetic books, such as Micah or Haggai. Thus, the explicit connections that we find in some books between the text and the historical context are missing or extremely subtle. While it can be beneficial to investigate how the book might have fit into various contexts, all but the hints in the text itself (see above on the book's argument) have been lost to us. Thus, strong assertions about setting and purpose should be received with some suspicion. The only hard fact is the text as we have it, and the most significant context is that the book was ultimately intended for inclusion in Scripture.

Outline

1. A Period of Transition (1 Sam. 1:1–15:35)
   A. Eli and Samuel (1:1–7:17)
   B. The Early Years of Saul's Reign (8:1–15:35)
2. David's Rise to the Throne (1 Sam. 16:1–2 Sam. 8:18)
   A. David's Fame (16:1–17:58)
   B. David's Struggles with Saul (18:1–27:12)
   C. Saul's Final Battle (28:1–31:13)
   D. David Unifies Judah and Israel (2 Sam. 1:1–5:25)
   E. David Established as King (6:1–8:18)

3. David's Successes and Failures (9:1–20:26)
   A. David's Success (9:1–10:19)
   B. The Turning Point (11:1–12:31)
   C. Rebellion (13:1–20:26)
4. Epilogues (21:1–24:25)
   A. The Gibeonites' Revenge (21:1–14)
   B. Victories over the Philistines (21:15–22)
   C. David's Song (22:1–51)
   D. David's Last Words (23:1–7)
   E. David's Mighty Men (23:8–39)
   F. David's Census (24:1–25)

Commentary

1. A Period of Transition (1 Sam. 1:1–15:35)

After the turbulent days of the judges, the people of Israel looked forward to better times. The economic and spiritual condition of the nation was deplorable, even though the Lord dwelled among his people and had appointed the priests to be their leaders.

A. Eli and Samuel (1:1–7:17). 1:1–2:11. Samuel's importance can be seen in the lengthy account of his birth. There are no birth narratives for Saul and David, even though they are kings. The story of Samuel's birth is a testimony to the faith of his mother, Hannah (1:1–8). Like Sarah and Rachel, Hannah has great difficulty becoming pregnant, and barrenness was considered to be a mark of the Lord's disfavor. To make matters worse, her husband, Elkanah, has another wife who has several children and who taunts Hannah the way Hagar scorned Sarah (Gen. 16:4). Although no reason is given for Hannah's barrenness, it is likely not the result of some sin, for verses 3–8 tell how she often accompanies her husband to the house of God. The yearly festival referred to in verse 3 might be the Feast of Tabernacles, celebrated at the end of the summer to commemorate God's provision for Israel in the Sinai desert after the exodus (Lev. 23:43) and to give thanks for the summer harvest.

Though deeply discouraged, Hannah takes her problem to the Lord and to the high priest Eli at the tabernacle, which at that time was located at Shiloh, about twenty miles north of Jerusalem (1:9–18). In great earnestness, Hannah makes a solemn promise that if the Lord will give her a son, she will dedicate him to the Lord's work. By promising that "no razor will ever be used on his head," Hannah effectively places her son under the restrictions of a Nazirite vow, which also involved total abstinence from the fruit of the vine (Num. 6:1–3). Long hair was a symbol of an individual's commitment to the work of the Lord. Through her vow, Hannah voluntarily places Samuel in the same position in which God put Samson, whose mother had also been sterile for years (Judg. 13:3–5). Both Samson and Samuel were to be Nazirites for life, though the vow was normally for a limited period.

Eli watches as Hannah prays, concludes that she is drunk, and admonishes her accordingly. But Hannah is not drunk, simply absorbed in her anguished prayer. To Eli's credit, once he realizes his mistake, he blesses her. But Eli's mistaken assessment is an important signal for the audience: it is used by the historian to indicate Eli's lack of discernment (which is also seen in his inability to deal with his sons) and to comment on the spiritual conditions of Israel in general.

Upon Hannah's return home to Ramah (about five miles north of Jerusalem), "the LORD remembered her," as he had remembered the barren Rachel centuries earlier (1:19–20; Gen. 30:22). In due time Hannah gives birth to a son and names him Samuel. There is a wordplay in the Hebrew text that is missed in English but which the historian used to foreshadow the prophet-versus-king theme mentioned in the introduction. When Samuel is born, Hannah names him so because she requested him from the Lord (1:20). Even though the explanation suggests as much, the name Samuel does not sound like the Hebrew word for "requested" or "asked," which is a theme word in the section (see also 1:27–28). Instead, the name Saul

During Hannah's day, the tabernacle may have stood in this area of the ancient site of Shiloh.

means "requested," and Samuel perhaps means "his name is El" (although the name's precise meaning remains obscure). However, the name Samuel also sounds similar to the phrase "God had heard," so there might be a subtle wordplay intended. The name itself might connect the son to God's merciful answer to Hannah's request. The explanation for the name that the historian gives in the text subtly contrasts Samuel with Saul and thus foreshadows God's (and the historian's) opinion that a good prophet is always better than a monarch.

After the birth of Samuel, Elkanah returns to Shiloh to offer the annual sacrifice in fulfillment of a vow he has made. Hannah does not accompany her husband, but nurses Samuel until he is weaned, probably at three years of age. True to her promise, she then brings him to the tabernacle and turns him over to Eli (1:21–28). On this occasion she also sacrifices a bull in fulfillment of her vow (Num. 15:8–10) and reminds Eli that she has prayed for a child in his hearing. Here the emphasis is not on the Nazirite vow (1:11) but on the surrender of the child for a "whole life" of service.

While still at the sanctuary, Hannah again prays to God, this time lifting her heart in praise of his goodness (2:1–11). She rejoices not so much in her son, Samuel, but in the Lord who has given him to her: he is the "Rock," the all-powerful God who provides security for his people. Hannah testifies that God humbles the proud and the rich and exalts the weak and the poor (2:3–9). Mary will later mention these reversals in her song of praise (Luke 1:51–53), and for both Hannah and Mary it is the birth of a son that brings such great blessing. The final couplet of Hannah's song (2:10) is used to foreshadow Samuel's role in establishing a monarchy for the Israelites.

2:12–36. One of the saddest episodes of this part of the story is the disintegration of the family of Eli. The weakness and gloom of Eli contrast sharply with the faith and joy of Hannah. If the sons of the priests are "scoundrels," the condition of the nation is desperate indeed. Ironically,

Eli's sons sin in the way they handle the sacrifices—the very animals brought to make atonement for sin! According to the law of Moses the priests were allowed to eat part of the meat of the sacrificial animals (except for the burnt offerings), but certain restrictions applied (Lev. 7:31–37). The fat was always considered the Lord's portion and had to be burned on the altar (Lev. 3:16). Yet Hophni and Phinehas take the meat before the fat is burned and apparently ignore the custom of boiling the meat (2:15). In spite of the complaints of the people, the priests refuse to change and treat "the LORD's offering with contempt" (2:17). Such an attitude brought death to two of Aaron's sons several centuries earlier (Lev. 10:1–3).

In sharp contrast to the sin of Eli's sons are the Lord's blessings on Samuel and his family (2:18–21). Once a year Samuel's parents visit him, and his mother brings a robe that she has made. Apparently he wore this under the linen ephod, an apronlike garment worn by all the priests (1 Sam. 22:18). On one of the early visits, Eli blesses Elkanah and Hannah with the promise of additional children (2:20). Over the years three sons and two daughters are born to Hannah (2:21).

Faced by the mounting reports about the wicked deeds of his sons, Eli directly confronts them (2:22–25). Among other things, they are guilty of sexual immorality with women who serve at the entrance to the tabernacle. Such women are mentioned only in Exodus 38:8, but the exact nature of their function is not given. It is possible, though unlikely, that they were temple prostitutes like those present in Canaanite shrines to promote the overall fertility of the land (Num. 25:1–3), even though this practice was forbidden in Deuteronomy 23:18. Oblivious to their father's belated warnings, Eli's sons continue in their sinful ways. And for the second time in the chapter, Samuel's behavior is directly compared with that of Eli's sons (2:26): in contrast to Hophni and Phinehas, as he grows up Samuel pleases both God and men.

That God will not let Eli's sons' behavior go unpunished—nor Eli's failure to rein them in—is confirmed by a visit from an unnamed prophet (2:27–36). Called "a man of God" (9:6, 10), this prophet makes it clear that part of the blame is Eli's—he honors his sons more than God by failing to oppose their sinful ways.

In light of the unfaithfulness of Eli's sons, the prophet announces that disaster will strike Eli's family, and his descendants will not live out their days peacefully. This prediction is fulfilled when Eli's sons—Hophni and Phinehas—both die on the same day (1 Sam. 4:11), a grim parallel to the sudden death of Aaron's sons Nadab and Abihu (Lev. 10:1–3). Instead of having choice parts of meat from the sacrifices, Eli's descendants will have to beg for "a loaf of bread" (2:36). Honor and prestige will be replaced by disgrace and poverty.

3:1–21. Samuel's calling is told in 3:1–10. For the third time in the book, we read that Samuel ministers "before the LORD" (3:1). He serves as a kind of apprentice priest, and at this point is probably about twelve years old. The Lord begins to speak to Samuel one night while he is sleeping in his usual place near the tabernacle. Apparently it is close to dawn, because verse 3 mentions that the golden lampstand in the Holy Place is still burning. Every evening olive oil was brought in to keep the lamps burning until morning, when the flame either grew dim or went out (Exod. 27:20–21; 2 Chron. 13:11). The ark of the covenant was in the Most Holy Place, and it was from the ark that God used to speak with Moses (Num. 7:89). In this setting, then, it is altogether fitting for God to call a new Moses to lead his people. At first, Samuel thinks that Eli is calling him, but after Samuel has made three trips to Eli's bed, the aged priest realizes that God is calling the boy.

Unfortunately for young Samuel, and especially for Eli, the divine message is one of judgment against Eli (3:11–21). Action that makes the ears tingle (3:11) is nothing short of catastrophe, and destruction lies ahead for Eli's family. Eli has failed to restrain his sons,

who treat the Lord with much contempt, even though he did try to warn them (2:22–25). They will never be forgiven for their stubborn rebellion, regardless of the number of sacrifices they handle.

Having observed Eli's sons in action, Samuel may not have been surprised at the severity of the Lord's message, but he must have wondered what he should tell Eli. This problem is solved when Eli uses a curse formula (3:17) to insist that Samuel tell him everything. When Samuel complies, Eli accepts God's sentence and reacts the way Hezekiah does when he learns that his descendants will be exiled to Babylon (Isa. 39:8). In an era when "everyone did as they saw fit" (Judg. 21:25), God takes appropriate measures to judge the wicked. Since Samuel's account of God's revelation is the same as the announcement the man of God gave to Eli (2:27–36), Eli has no doubt that God has spoken to Samuel. As time goes by, Samuel's message is fulfilled, and "all Israel" recognizes that he is a genuine prophet (3:20). Chapter 3 begins with the observation that visions are given only rarely, but it ends with a reference to God's repeated revelations to Samuel. Here is a young man through whom the Lord will speak to his desperate people.

4:1–22. In fulfillment of the prophecies of chapter 3, Eli's family suffers a devastating blow in the wake of a battle with the Philistines some years later (4:1–11). The conflict takes place near Aphek, a city about twenty miles west of Shiloh and somewhat north of the main Philistine territory along the Mediterranean Sea. According to Judges 13–16, the Philistines controlled the tribe of Judah and were putting pressure on tribal regions to the north. Unlike Samson, Israel's army cannot gain the victory and in fact loses about four thousand (or four "companies" of) men. (Note that the same Hebrew word for "thousand" may also mean "company [of men]" as well as a "tribal clan." Interpreters both modern and ancient likely have often misunderstood which meaning was intended in a given passage, because geographically and agriculturally the land of Canaan was simply unable to support the large numbers that are mentioned—or misinterpreted—in the Old Testament.)

Distraught, the rest of the soldiers wonder why the Lord has abandoned Israel, for they—like the surrounding nations—believe that the people with the strongest gods win battles (1 Kings 20:23). The soldiers recall how the ark of the covenant accompanied Israel's armies when they crossed the Jordan River and defeated the city of Jericho (Josh. 3:11, 17; 6:6, 12). The ark was God's footstool and symbolized his presence more than any other part of the tabernacle (4:4). Thus, the men reason that the ark will guarantee victory over the Philistines. The Philistines likewise believe that the presence of the ark is a bad omen, for they have heard about the plagues with which the Lord afflicted Egypt (4:8).

In reality the Philistines have little to worry about, for the ark is not a magical talisman; its mere physical presence cannot compel the Lord to give Israel a victory—especially when Eli's two wicked sons, Hophni and Phinehas, accompany the ark to the battlefield. Their presence dooms Israel, and in the ensuing battle another thirty thousand (or thirty "companies" of) men die, including Eli's two sons. The ark is captured. It is an unmitigated disaster.

Eli's family suffers disaster as well (4:12–22). A messenger with "his clothes torn and dust on his head" brings news of Israel's defeat to Shiloh (4:12). When Eli hears the commotion, he asks what has happened. According to verse 13, Eli had serious misgivings about taking the ark to battle. Old and feeble at age ninety-eight, Eli falls off his chair and breaks his neck when he hears the extent of the catastrophe, especially the news about the capture of the ark. This is worse than the report that his own two sons have been killed. Following the style of the book of Judges, the author notes that Eli "had led Israel forty years" (4:18), and his leadership had proved ineffective.

Death continues to stalk Eli's family: his daughter-in-law dies in childbirth after learning what has happened to her husband and father-in-law. Before succumbing, she names her baby boy Ichabod, meaning "where is glory," because of the capture of the ark. It is as though the cloud of glory that normally fills the Most Holy Place around the ark has left Israel. Since the Lord was "enthroned between the cherubim" above the ark (4:4), the loss of the ark symbolizes graphically his abandonment of Israel. He has refused to be manipulated by his own people.

5:1–7:1. After their triumph over Israel, the Philistines intend to celebrate their good fortune, but the Lord has other plans. After its capture, the ark is taken to the coastal city of Ashdod, about thirty-five miles west of Jerusalem and one of the five main centers of the Philistines (5:1–12). There they place it in a temple beside the image of Dagon, a god of grain worshiped in many parts of the Fertile Crescent and the Philistines' leading deity. According to popular theology, Israel's defeat would have meant that Dagon was more powerful than the Lord, but the ensuing events illustrate for the audience the power of Israel's deity, the Lord. Twice the image topples to the ground before the ark, and the second time Dagon's head and hands break off.

Meanwhile, the Lord afflicts the people of Ashdod with tumors of some sort, and the disease follows the ark to Gath, a city several miles to the east. Death comes to many, and the people panic, as do the residents of Ekron, about eleven miles northeast of Ashdod. The spread of the plague confirms the original reaction of the Philistines when the ark was brought into the Israelites' camp (4:7–8). They have heard how Israel's God struck the Egyptians with terrible plagues, and now they are experiencing a similar plague firsthand. Instead of having a prized trophy of victory, the Philistines possess an instrument of judgment that demonstrates the power of the Lord and the corresponding weakness of Dagon.

After seven difficult months, the Philistines are ready to send the ark back to Israel (6:1–9).

But they want to make sure they do not offend the Lord any further, so they consult with their religious leaders. The leaders urge them to send a gift with the ark to compensate for the way they have dishonored Israel's deity. This guilt offering consists of "five gold tumors and five gold rats" (6:4), representing the five main cities of the Philistines and reflecting the symptoms and likely medium of the plague (that is, the

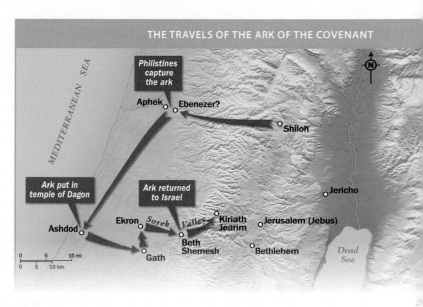

THE TRAVELS OF THE ARK OF THE COVENANT

Philistines capture the ark

Aphek   Ebenezer?

Shiloh

MEDITERRANEAN SEA

Ark put in temple of Dagon

Ark returned to Israel

Jericho

Ashdod   Ekron   Sorek Valley   Kiriath Jearim   Jerusalem (Jebus)

Beth Shemesh   Bethlehem   Dead Sea

Gath

0   5   10 mi
0   5   10 km

rats may have carried the disease as a bubonic plague). Through this offering and the return of the ark, the Philistines hope to bring an end to the plague.

To carry the ark, the priests suggest that a new cart be used, one that is "ceremonially clean." The cart is to be drawn by "two cows that have calved and have never been yoked." According to Numbers 19:2, in some cases a cow was not to be used in a sacrifice if it had been under a yoke. In relation to the new cart, it was likely a common ritual belief that the most appropriate instrument for dealing with a sacred object was something new—that is, something not used for nonreligious purposes. The two cows not only were usable for sacrificial purposes but may have been used by the Philistines as divination tools. If two cows would not only walk away from home and their unweaned calves but do so pulling a cart, even though they had never been yoked, then it would be clear (and it was!) that the Hebrew God was behind the entire event.

When the Philistines hitch the cows to the cart and send them on their way, the cows head straight up the Sorek Valley to Beth Shemesh, a city of Judah close to the Philistine border. The implication of the cows' actions would have been

obvious to the Philistines: the Israelite God had indeed been against them. Providentially Beth Shemesh was also a city belonging to the priests (cf. Josh. 21:16), who were responsible for the ark of the covenant. The people are harvesting wheat, which usually took place in May or June. When they see the ark they are overjoyed and proceed to sacrifice the cows as a burnt offering. They place the ark on a large rock, which becomes a monument to this event (6:18).

Tragedy strikes, however, when God puts seventy men to death for looking into the ark (6:19). According to the law of Moses, the sacred articles of the tabernacle were to be treated with great reverence. Not even the Levites could look at the holy things without risking death (cf. Num. 4:20). Since the ark was the most sacred object and since it was closely associated with the presence of God, access to it was very restricted. Not even the high priest could look into the ark without endangering his life, a reminder that being in the presence of God required ritual purity.

Distraught at the death of the men, the rest of the townspeople follow the example of the Philistines and look for another city where they can send the ark. Kiriath Jearim, located about fifteen miles northeast of Beth Shemesh, accepts the ark, and a man named Abinadab is given custody of it (7:1). The ark was probably not put back in the tabernacle because of the destruction of Shiloh by the Philistines. Although the tabernacle itself is moved in time, it will not have a more permanent home for many years.

7:2–17. Approximately twenty years elapse before the Israelites gain any lasting relief from Philistine oppression. Finally, Samuel senses that a genuine repentance is under way, so he challenges the people to rid themselves of their "foreign gods," identified as their "Baals and Ashtoreths" (7:2–6). Throughout the period of the judges, many Israelites worshiped these deities. Baal was the Canaanite god of rain and agriculture and, ironically, was sometimes described as the son of Dagon. The Ashtoreths were female deities such as Astarte (the Babylonian Ishtar), goddess of fertility, love, and war. As in Judges 10:16, the Israelites stop worshiping these gods and return to being loyal to the Lord. Samuel gathers "all Israel" at Mizpah, about seven and a half miles north of Jerusalem, and promises to pray for them. As they fast and confess their sin, they pour out water before the Lord, perhaps symbolic of their earnestness and wholehearted commitment to God.

Believing that the Israelites have gathered at Mizpah for military reasons, the Philistines attack them (7:7–12). In light of their repentant attitude, the people of Israel beg Samuel to pray for them, which he does, as well as sacrificing a burnt offering. True to his covenant promise, the Lord intervenes on behalf of his beleaguered people and thunders against the Philistines. Apparently the Lord sends a storm similar to the ones that routed the Amorites (Josh. 10:11–12) and bogged down the chariots of Sisera (Judg. 5:20–21). Thunder, hail, and heavy rain cause panic among the Philistines and send them fleeing to the west and south. Recognizing that it is the Lord's victory, Samuel sets up a stone as a monument and calls it Ebenezer, which means "stone of help."

After this victory, the Israelites gain the upper hand over the Philistines and at least temporarily put an end to Philistine oppression. During this time of peace, Samuel travels to many towns in the tribe of Benjamin, serving as a judge and spiritual leader (7:13–17). Since Samuel ministers as a priest and prophet, he builds an altar to the Lord in his hometown of Ramah.

Here we can identify a literary strategy that the historian has continued from the books of Joshua and Judges: events that may have focused on one or two tribes or concerned a small regional conflict are placed in the context of the entire people and country. In 1–2 Samuel this literary device is used to broaden the scope of Samuel's reputation and authority. For instance, Samuel's yearly circuit as a judge is limited to Bethel and Mizpah, in the central hill country down to Gilgal, near Jericho in the Jordan Valley (7:16). Yet, he is said to have gathered "all Israel" at Mizpah (7:5), and the historian asserts that "all Israel from Dan to Beersheba" knows of Samuel's prophetic abilities (3:20). What this information illustrates is the historian's interest in making clear that events and people associated within a limited area often have broader implications for the entire nation.

B. The early years of Saul's reign (8:1–15:35).
8:1–22. Even though Samuel has led the people well as a judge, he will be the last to hold this charismatic office. Under pressure from the people, Samuel anoints Saul as the first king and thereby ushers in a new era of Israel's history. Saul's initial years as king are promising, and it appears that the unified nation will be a powerful one.

Unlike most judges, Samuel appoints his sons to succeed him, but, like Eli before him, Samuel proves to be an unsuccessful parent: his sons are dishonest and create serious problems for both Samuel and the nation. Using the misconduct of Samuel's sons as a pretext, the elders ask Samuel to appoint a king over Israel (8:1–9). They want what they perceive to be the stability and strength of a monarchy, as in the nations around them. By this request the people effectively reject the leadership of Samuel, and more important, the kingship of the Lord. From the standpoint of faith, the people choose to remove themselves one step from trust in God, with a human monarch standing between them and their divine king. Thus the Israelites repeat the mistakes of their past, for their ancestors made a similar choice at Mount Sinai, instructing Moses to listen to God and speak for them while they stood at a distance (Exod. 20:18–21).

To help the people see the implications of their request, Samuel tells them what it will be like to have a king (8:10–22). Using the policies of other ancient Near Eastern kings as a pattern and reflecting a similar caution in Deuteronomy 17:14–20, Samuel warns the Israelites how their sons and daughters will be drafted into the king's service and how government officials will take control of fields and vineyards. In addition to the tithe required by the law of Moses, the king will demand an additional 10 percent of crops, flocks, and livestock. Samuel asserts that eventually the people will feel like the king's slaves and will cry out to God for relief, just as they have cried for help during times of foreign oppression.

Ignoring the urgency of Samuel's arguments, the people remain firm in their desire for a king. Their minds are made up even though Samuel has pointed out the painful consequences of establishing a monarchy. When Samuel takes their decision to the Lord, God tells him to "give them a king" (8:22).

9:1–10:27. The Lord's choice is a man named Saul, who belongs to a prominent family from the tribe of Benjamin (9:1–13). He is tall—a head taller than anyone else—but he is looking for lost donkeys and not a crown when he encounters Samuel. After searching the tribal areas of Ephraim and Benjamin, Saul is ready to give up the search, but his servant suggests that they consult a highly respected man of God. Fortunately the servant has a small amount of silver to give to the prophet, for payment of

some sort was customary (see 1 Kings 14:3). When the two men ask about the prophet, they are told that he is on his way to bless a sacrifice at the local high place. High places were shrines located on hills and contained, among other things, an altar. Later writers will associate high places with the worship of gods other than the Lord. Although both King Hezekiah (2 Kings 18:4) and King Josiah (2 Kings 23:8) are later praised for removing the high places in Judah and centralizing worship at the Jerusalem temple, it is clear that high places continue to be used even after the temple is built, particularly during times that are described as filled with sin and apostasy.

Unknown to Saul, the Lord has told Samuel that he is to anoint a man from Benjamin as king of Israel the very day of their meeting (9:14–10:1). The Hebrew verb *mashah*, "to anoint," from which the noun "messiah" ("anointed one") is derived, is used of a king for the second time in the book in verse 16 (see 1 Sam. 2:10). In Exodus it was priests who were anointed for service (Exod. 29:7; 40:12–15), but from this point on "the anointed one" is usually the king. Anointing indicated that a person had been set apart for a particular task and that the Lord would enable the person to perform the appointed task. The anointing oil was a symbol of the Holy Spirit, who empowers both Saul and David after they are anointed (see 1 Sam. 10:6; 16:13).

Note also the reason that the Lord gives Samuel for anointing a king, the day before Saul shows up: "For I have seen the suffering of my people, because their outcry has come to me" (9:16 NRSV). Similar language is used in connection with God's call to Moses in Exodus 2:23. The intertextual allusion suggests that the historian viewed the establishment of the monarchy on par with the choice of Israel's greatest leader.

When Saul meets Samuel, the prophet surprises him by announcing that the lost donkeys have been found and that "all the desire of Israel" is directed to Saul as the new king

(9:20). Saul protests that the tribe of Benjamin is not very prominent (although it was neatly situated between the powerful tribes of Judah and Ephraim). During the period of the judges Benjamin was nearly wiped out in a civil war that seemed to end its influence permanently (Judg. 20:46–48). Like Gideon before him (Judg. 6:15), Saul protests that his clan is too small and insignificant to be considered for such an honor. But Samuel insists that Saul join the invited guests at the high place for a meal after the sacrifice, and Samuel reserves for Saul a choice part of the animal, the thigh. Normally the right thigh of fellowship offerings belonged to the priests (see Lev. 7:33–34), so the people realize that Saul is in line for special honor.

Saul stays with Samuel that night, during which he likely receives instruction about his coming responsibilities and the challenges he will face. The next morning Saul and his servant prepare to leave, but Samuel sends the servant ahead while he gives Saul "a message from God" privately (9:27). Then, taking a flask of olive oil, Samuel pours it on Saul's head and anoints him king. So begins Samuel's key role as a king maker, and Israel's monarchy is launched. A new era has begun.

Before Saul leaves, Samuel gives him some signs as further proof that God has indeed chosen him to be king (10:2–8). Samuel predicts the location at which Saul will meet various individuals and what they will do, demonstrating again that he is a legitimate prophet of the Lord (see Deut. 18:21–22). The third sign is the most significant, for it deals with Saul's empowering by the Spirit of God. A group of prophets will approach Saul playing musical instruments. While the band of prophets is prophesying, Saul will join with them and the Spirit of the Lord will come upon him in power, just as it came upon Othniel (Judg. 3:10), Gideon (Judg. 6:34), and Jephthah (Judg. 11:29). Each of these judges was designated as God's chosen leader in this fashion, and the same is true for both Saul and David.

When God gives an individual an assignment, he also supplies divine power to perform that assignment. In Saul's case Samuel indicates that he will be "changed into a different person" (10:6), which likely refers to the ecstatic state or prophetic frenzy that will overcome Saul in the encounter with the Spirit of the Lord. The event might reflect the historian's pro-prophet stance by asserting that some prophetic ability is necessary for a monarch to be acceptable. Whatever the precise significance, Saul recognizes that God is with him to bless and strengthen him.

Even though Saul will have the authority of a king, verse 8 is a reminder that he also needs to obey the word of God. At

Anointing of kings occurred in Egypt as well as in Israel (1 Sam. 10:1). In this coronation scene from Kom Ombo, the pharaoh is anointed by the gods as life is poured from the jars.

a forthcoming gathering at Gilgal—the sacred town near the Jordan River—Saul is instructed to wait a full week for Samuel to advise him.

The rapid fulfillment of signs leaves little doubt that God has spoken through Samuel (10:9–16). Saul's participation in prophesying startles his friends, and they ask, "Is Saul also among the prophets?" (10:11). By this time the curiosity of Saul's uncle has been aroused, but when he questions Saul about his visit with Samuel, Saul says nothing about the anointing. As rumors about Saul begin to multiply, Samuel summons the people to reveal God's choice of king (10:17–27). Before proceeding with the selection, however, he scolds the people for rejecting the Lord and reminds them that God has rescued them from Egypt and saved them out of all their calamities. Even with a king, Israel has to remember that it is God who is the source of their strength and salvation.

The selection of the king was probably accomplished through casting lots in conjunction with the Urim and Thummim handled by the priest (see Exod. 28:30; 1 Sam. 14:41–42). By this means the tribe of Benjamin and the clan of Matri are chosen, and finally Saul himself is singled out. Knowing that he will be selected, Saul has hidden himself among the baggage (10:22); this response foreshadows the type of character flaws and lack of faith that will come out later in his interactions with David. When Saul is finally presented to the people, they shout with enthusiasm, "Long live the king!" (10:24).

At this point, Samuel reminds the people of "the rights and duties of kingship" (10:25), likely the same regulations, built on Deuteronomy 17:14–20, with which he tried to deter them from choosing a monarchy in 1 Samuel 8:10–22. Given Samuel's prophetic perspective on monarchy, the depositing of this document about kingship "before the LORD" suggests that above all the people and the monarch must remember who is the true king of Israel.

When Saul returns to his hometown of Gibeah he enjoys the support of many valiant men.

The tribe of Benjamin was renowned for its excellent warriors, and now one of their number is king of the whole land. Some of the people are dubious about Saul's abilities, however, and openly withhold their support.

11:1–15. Before long Saul has a chance to prove himself, when the Ammonites besiege the city of Jabesh Gilead, a town just east of the Jordan River, about forty miles northeast of the area of Benjamin (11:1–5). The Ammonites also lived in the Transjordan and had captured a large section of Israel's territory before Jephthah drove them out (Judg. 11:29–33).

Note that the great Samuel scroll from the Dead Sea Scrolls found at Qumran (4QSamª) provides a transition between the end of chapter 10 and the beginning of chapter 11, a transition that most scholars take to be the original text that was lost by scribal errors. Before this scroll was discovered, the received text of this episode had long been puzzling. What are the reasons for the Ammonites' sudden aggression against Jabesh Gilead? Why would Nahash, the Ammonite king, demand mutilation as the terms for surrender? Such mutilation was only appropriate for rebels or escaped prisoners of war, not for the subjects of newly conquered cities outside one's domain. The text of 4QSamª provides the necessary material to make sense of the rather abrupt beginning of 1 Samuel 11. Some Bible versions have added this material to the text of 1 Samuel (e.g., NRSV, *The Message*); the NIV includes it in a footnote at 11:1:

> Now Nahash king of the Ammonites oppressed the Gadites and Reubenites severely. He gouged out all their right eyes and struck terror and dread in Israel. Not a man remained among the Israelites beyond the Jordan whose right eye was not gouged out by Nahash king of the Ammonites, except that seven thousand men fled from the Ammonites and entered Jabesh Gilead.

From this lost piece we learn that Nahash has previously reconquered area in the Transjordan that belonged to Ammon before the Israelite tribes or Reuben and Gad laid claim to it. In order to preclude recrimination, he mutilates the men so that they will not be able to effectively lead future campaigns against him. During the fighting, seven thousand (or seven "companies" of) Reubenite and Gadite warriors flee north to the Gileadite city Jabesh Gilead. Nahash's attack on that city is punishment for sheltering the warriors he has defeated, whom he now considers his subjects. His insistence on mutilation reflects the fact that those harboring his enemies deserve the same punishment.

Since the people of Jabesh Gilead have close family ties with the tribe of Benjamin (cf. Judg. 21:12–14) and since Saul has been appointed king over all the tribes, they appeal to Saul for help. Saul hears the news when he comes in from plowing the fields, an indication that his kingly responsibilities are not yet very extensive.

For the second time, "the Spirit of God came powerfully upon him" (cf. 1 Sam. 10:6, 10) as Saul, like the judges before him, goes into action against the enemy (11:6–15). Asserting his authority as king, Saul cuts up two oxen and sends the pieces throughout the land to indicate that death is in store for those who do not respond to the crisis. More than three hundred thousand (or three hundred "companies" of) soldiers gather. Following the strategy used by Abraham and Gideon, Saul surprises the enemy in the middle of the night and thoroughly defeats them. Jabesh Gilead is saved and Saul is a hero.

On the heels of victory the people want to execute those who opposed the selection of Saul as king, but Saul refuses to go along with the idea. This is a day to rejoice, because God has given them a great victory. Samuel suggests that everyone assemble at Gilgal, the town near the Jordan where Joshua and his army celebrated the conquest of Canaan (Josh. 10:43). There they present fellowship offerings to thank the Lord for his goodness to the nation and to confirm Saul as king.

12:1–25. Like Moses and Joshua, Samuel does not relinquish his leadership without challenging the nation to be faithful to the Lord. The theme of covenant renewal that characterizes the whole book of Deuteronomy and Joshua 24 is emphasized once again in Samuel's farewell.

Since the wickedness of Samuel's sons was a factor behind the initial request for a king (cf. 8:3–5), Samuel begins his speech with an examination of his own conduct as leader (12:1–5). He challenges the people to point out any instance where he has wronged anyone or used his position for financial gain. By pointing to his own clean record Samuel hopes to provide an example for Saul and future kings.

As Samuel seeks to establish the monarchy on a sound footing, he reminds the Israelites of the way God has provided for them in the past (12:6–15). When they cried for relief in Egypt, the Lord sent Moses and Aaron to deliver them from slavery. When their own sinfulness brought oppression in Canaan, God raised up heroes such as Gideon, Barak, and Jephthah to rescue them from the enemy. God would have saved them from the recent Ammonite attack even if no king had been appointed. Although the Lord used Saul to deliver Jabesh Gilead, the monarchy brings with it a new danger. Will the people put their trust in a human leader at the expense of their faith in the Lord? Samuel warns that both the people and the king must serve and obey the Lord. The covenant structure remains the same, for the Lord demands the unwavering allegiance of all the people.

To impress on the Israelites the evil inherent in their request for a king—and their rejection of God as king—the Lord sends thunder and rain in the dry season (12:16–18). The wheat harvest normally occurred in June, and it rarely rained in Israel during the summer. The people stand in awe as their forefathers did at Mount Sinai, when God revealed his power in thunder and lightning (Exod. 19:16; 20:18). God spoke through Moses, and now he is speaking through Samuel, and the message must be taken seriously.

In 1 Samuel 7:8 the people asked Samuel to pray when the Philistines attacked. Now that God has revealed himself they ask Samuel to pray for them again (12:19–25). Like the generation at Mount Sinai, they are afraid they might die. Samuel assures them that the Lord will not reject them, but he urges them to "serve the LORD with all your heart" (12:20). God has done "great things" for them (12:24), and he will continue to work wonders on their behalf (cf. Ps. 126:2). And Samuel promises to keep praying for them and teaching them how to live. Although he is retiring as the military and judicial leader, he will continue to function as a prophet for the nation and as an advisor for the king.

13:1–22. After the victory over the Ammonites east of the Jordan, Saul turns his attention to the Philistines, Israel's perennial enemy along the Mediterranean coast. Undoubtedly the Philistines were worried about Israel's upstart king and likely wanted to attack him before he became too established and powerful.

Since the initial conquest under Joshua, the cities that were most solidly under Israel's control were located in the hill country, an area about two thousand feet above sea level that ran from north to south through much of central Palestine. Saul's capital of Gibeah was located there, but this did not stop the Philistines. As chapter 13 begins, the Philistines have pushed to within five miles of the capital (13:1–7). Jonathan, Saul's oldest son, attacks the Philistine outpost at Geba, and thus angers the Philistines. They amass an army supported by three thousand (or three "companies" of) chariots, and the Israelites withdraw to Gilgal, by the Jordan. Some of Saul's soldiers hide "in caves and thickets, among the rocks, and in pits and cisterns" (13:6).

Saul starts with three thousand (or "companies" of) troops, but while he delays at Gilgal, some of the men grow fearful and begin to "scatter," leaving Saul with a final tally of six hundred. He is waiting for Samuel to come and offer sacrifices as he has promised to do (cf. 1 Sam. 10:8). After seven days Saul violates Samuel's command: he offers the sacrifices himself with the hope of gaining God's blessing on the upcoming battle. When Samuel finally arrives,

The remains of Saul's palace at Gibeah

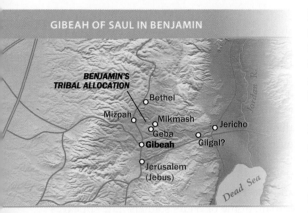

GIBEAH OF SAUL IN BENJAMIN

have their farming tools sharpened, but in time of war no plowshares were beaten into swords. Only Saul and Jonathan had a sword or spear; the rest of the troops used slingshots, bows and arrows, or even ox-goads. No wonder many of Saul's men deserted!

13:23–14:52. When all seems lost, Jonathan leads a daring attack on the Philistine position north of the Mikmash pass (14:1–14). At the time Saul is still near Gibeah, trying to take care of national business as he sits under a pomegranate tree. No one else knows that Jonathan and his armor bearer are embarking on a dangerous mission. Jonathan believes that God will intervene on behalf of his people and save them from "those uncircumcised men" (14:6). As Jonathan and his armor bearer make their way across the Mikmash pass, the Philistines spot them and challenge them to come up and fight. This response is a sign to Jonathan "that the LORD has given them into [the hand of Israel]" (14:10). The Philistines mock Saul's troops for hiding in holes and refer to the Israelites as "Hebrews," a term sometimes used by foreigners in a disparaging way (cf. Gen. 39:17). This usage might be related to the word's apparent etymology, from a term meaning "movers," or it might refer to the Israelites' origins in the hill country, as in "hillbillies." Clearly the Philistines expect to make short work of the two men, but convinced that God is with them, Jonathan and his armor bearer fight and kill about twenty men. Their faith has been vindicated.

As confusion grows among the Philistine forces, the Lord sends the whole army into a panic by shaking the ground (14:15–23). The earth tremor frightens the Philistines, and they fight among themselves in all the confusion and flee the battleground. It is the same sort of panic that was behind the victory at Mizpah (1 Sam. 7:7–12) and the defeat of the Midianites under Gideon (Judg. 7:22).

Saul's lookouts at Gibeah report the commotion to their commander, and Saul immediately consults Ahijah the priest, apparently about using the ark to address the Lord. Before

he condemns Saul's action and announces that his son will not succeed him on the throne (13:8–15). Instead, God will now choose "a man after his own heart" to rule Israel (13:14; 16:7). This phrase "a man after his own heart" does not, contrary to popular interpretation, refer to the Lord's particular favor of David or some special quality of David's; rather, it refers to the Lord's divine right and freedom to choose a new king. Thus it might be better translated "a man according to his [the Lord's] choosing." This new choice is motivated by Saul's guilt in ignoring the Lord's command through his prophet. In subsequent years, all of Israel's kings will be responsible to obey the law of Moses and the instructions of the prophets (cf. Jer. 25:4). If a king is guilty of wrongdoing, often a prophet will appear on the scene to announce God's judgment.

In spite of mounting difficulties, Saul and Jonathan return to Gibeah, only a few miles from the Philistines at Mikmash. The Philistines send out raiding parties to plunder and to demoralize the people, and Saul is unable to stop them (13:16–22). One reason for Israel's predicament is a lack of weapons. According to verse 19 the Philistines have established a monopoly on the production of iron and have refused to share the secret. They may have learned how to smelt iron from the Hittites of Asia Minor, who used iron to great advantage prior to 1200 BC. The Israelites had to pay the Philistines to receiving an answer from the Lord, however, Saul takes his men to the battle and finds the Philistines in total confusion. As word about the battle spreads, the soldiers who earlier abandoned Saul rejoin his forces to take part in the chase, just as the ranks of Gideon swelled once the Midianites were on the run (Judg. 7:23). Since Saul has done almost nothing to bring about the defeat of the Philistines, the credit for the victory is not his. It is the Lord who has rescued Israel. The victory leaves Israel with some security in their own heartland and keeps the Philistines at a safe distance for years to come.

As in the case of Jephthah's victory over the Ammonites, in Judges 11:32–35, the celebration of the Philistines' defeat ends abruptly because of an ill-advised oath (14:24–30). In an apparent attempt to win the Lord's favor, Saul has put a curse on anyone who eats any food before the coming evening. The curse demonstrates Saul's poor judgment, because the weary troops need to be refreshed so they can continue the pursuit of the Philistines. To make matters worse, Jonathan did not hear the curse and eats some honey along the way. He immediately receives some much-needed strength but is upset when someone tells him about his father's oath.

As a direct result of Saul's curse the rest of the troops transgress a purity restriction known also from the law of Moses (14:31–35). They are famished after chasing the Philistines into the western foothills, so when they are finally allowed to eat, they butcher animals without properly draining the blood. By eating blood they break the Lord's command (see Lev. 17:11; Deut. 12:16), because blood was normally to be poured out in sacrifices and was considered sacred. Saul builds his first altar at this time, perhaps to atone for the actions of his men and to express thanks to God for the great victory over the Philistines.

After the soldiers eat and regain some strength, Saul proposes they continue to pursue the Philistines during the night to follow up the victory. The men agree, but when Ahijah inquires of the Lord—presumably through the Urim and Thummim—there is no answer. Saul reasons that someone must have broken his oath and prays that the Lord might identify the guilty party. Using the same Urim and Thummim to cast lots, Saul and the priest discover that Jonathan is the culprit (14:36–46). Even though Jonathan has only "tasted a little honey" (14:43), Saul asserts that he must die. The troops protest Saul's decision, for they know that Jonathan is the one whom God has used to bring about an amazing victory. Why should he be put to death for being courageous? Whatever their arguments were, which are not specified, the people convince Saul to let Jonathan live, a happy outcome. Even so, the entire event signals that Saul's judgment and leadership ability is already in decline and suffering from the reversal of God's blessing (13:10–14). Moreover, the complications caused by Saul's curse prevent the Israelites from taking full advantage of the disarray of the Philistines. Many of the Philistines make it safely back to their coastal cities and resume their attacks, eventually bringing about the death of Saul and the collapse of Israel (31:1–13).

The first main section of 1–2 Samuel ends with a summary of Saul's rule as king (14:47–52). Even though Saul continues to rule for a bit longer (until the end of 1 Samuel), chapter 15 marks the transition to David's rise to the throne.

Along with his victories over the Ammonites and Philistines, Saul enjoyed some success against Moab and Edom to the east and south and against the king of Zobah, a region in the Beqa'a Valley north of Israel. None of these other battles are recorded in Scripture, but chapter 15 does describe the victory over the Amalekites.

Saul's sons are listed in verse 49, although Ish-Bosheth, who succeeds him as king briefly, is not named (see 2 Sam. 2:8). Saul's two daughters, Merab and Michal, are also mentioned. Michal will play an important role as David's first wife. The key military figure is Saul's cousin, Abner, who commands the army throughout his reign.

15:1–35. As in the last chapter, Saul wins an important victory but makes a serious mistake (15:1–9). This time the enemy is the Amalekites, a Bedouin people that attacked the Israelites after they came out of Egypt (Exod. 17:8–16). In accord with the Lord's harsh words about Amalek given to Moses, Samuel tells Saul to attack the Amalekites and "totally destroy" all their people and animals (15:3). This technical term for complete destruction was also applied to the Canaanites when Joshua invaded the land. Because of the wickedness of the people, God decreed that everybody and everything should be wiped out (Josh. 6:17–18). No plunder of any kind could be taken.

Saul musters a sizable army and heads south to carry out his mission. Before attacking, he warns the Kenites, a seminomadic community, to move out of the area. Unlike the Amalekites, the Kenites have been friendly to Israel, and Moses in fact married a Kenite woman. Once the Kenites leave, Saul battles the Amalekites, chasing them to the eastern border of Egypt and wiping out all of the people. But he unwisely spares the king, Agag, and "the best of the sheep and cattle" (15:9).

Saul's incomplete obedience creates an immediate crisis for the incipient monarchy because the Lord is grieved that he has made Saul king (15:10–21). Samuel knows that

The Mesha Stele (eleventh century BC), shown here, records King Mesha's total destruction of a city as commanded by his Moabite god, Chemosh; Saul is given a similar order in 1 Samuel 15:3.

Saul's future is bleak. Saul's sin and the sin of his soldiers brings deep sorrow to God, and judgment is sure to follow. As he returns from the victory, Saul sets up a monument in his own honor, revealing an attitude of pride. Then he goes to Gilgal, where he was confirmed as king years earlier (11:14–15) but where he will now lose the kingship.

When Samuel meets him, Saul greets him warmly, but Samuel quickly dispenses with the niceties and instead responds by asking why the sheep and cattle have been spared. Saul tries to shift the blame to the soldiers, claiming that the animals were saved so that they might be sacrificed to the Lord. Even if the army had a spiritual purpose in mind, Samuel asserts that it was wrong to spare the animals. Saul protests vigorously, arguing that he did in fact carry out the assigned mission.

Samuel's response to Saul gives the classic position about the relationship between sacrifice and obedience (15:22–31). Stated bluntly, "To obey is better than sacrifice" (15:22). Without question, the offering of sacrifices was an integral part of worship in ancient Israel and was valued highly, but it was an empty ritual without the proper motivation and piety. A rebellious and arrogant attitude nullified the effect of any sacrifice. Many of the prophets will wrestle with this issue and assert that a large number of sacrifices will never atone for injustice, oppression, or pride. Genuine repentance and obedience are necessary accompaniments to the presentation of sacrifices. Since Saul has deliberately disobeyed the Lord's command, the Lord rejects him as king.

Alarmed by the severity of Samuel's pronouncement, Saul finally admits his sin and begs forgiveness, but Samuel condemns him again and turns to leave. As he does so, Saul, who has taken hold of his robe, accidentally tears it. The action proves symbolic of the fact that the Lord has "torn the kingdom of Israel" from Saul and given it to David (15:28). Lest there be any doubt about the certainty of God's word, Samuel reminds Saul that God "does not lie or change his mind" (15:29). Ironically, verse 29 is an allusion to Balaam's words to the king of Moab warning him that God had fully determined to bless Israel (Num. 23:11–12). For Saul, God's word has become a curse.

Although at first (15:26) Samuel refuses to accompany Saul to the place of worship, he finally agrees to go with him. If he had not gone, the break between the prophet and the king would publicly weaken Saul's authority and thus that of the monarchy in general. The "honor" of verse 30 is probably the honor of Samuel's presence at Gilgal, where the sacrifices were offered.

Another reason why Samuel goes to Gilgal is to deal with Agag, king of the Amalekites, whom Saul has spared (15:32–35). Normally victory was not complete until the opposing king was killed, especially if it was a war of "total destruction" (cf. 15:3). Like Joshua, who executed the five Amorite kings (Josh. 10:26), and Gideon, who killed the two kings of Midian (Judg. 8:21), Samuel strikes down Agag. It may seem like a strange role for the aged prophet and priest, but Samuel here is functioning as the "judge" in his military duties. That Samuel has to play the judge, even after the establishment of a monarchy, is yet another sign that Saul is failing.

2. David's Rise to the Throne (1 Sam. 16:1–2 Sam. 8:18)

As noted in the introduction, these chapters serve as a defense of the dynasty of David, providing a full account of David's rise to the throne and explaining why someone from the tribe of Judah replaces Saul of Benjamin. One of the key points in this "apology" is that Saul has disqualified himself as king by his actions, paving the way for the accession of David.

A. David's fame (16:1–17:58). **16:1–23.** The Old Testament contains many stories about the young and the obscure and how they become successful, but perhaps none is loved more than the story of David. Born the youngest of eight sons in the town of Bethlehem, David becomes a hero overnight and achieves a level of fame and fortune unmatched in Israelite tradition. As musician, poet, prophet, warrior, diplomat, and statesman, in his versatility and ability David sets the standard for all the monarchs that follow him, from his son and successor Solomon to the kings of the north and south after the monarchy splits. Before David is allowed to develop some of these gifts, however, he first has to survive Saul's anger and jealousy.

After the series of disasters that marks Saul's first years (military victories marred by Saul's lack of faith and judgment), the Lord sends Samuel to Bethlehem, a town six miles south of Jerusalem, to anoint a new king (16:1–13). This was the setting for the story of Ruth and Boaz, and it is one of their great-grandsons that Samuel anoints (Ruth 4:17). Samuel is afraid Saul might kill him, but the Lord shows Samuel how to disguise the purpose of the visit by offering a sacrifice in Bethlehem. When he arrives there, the elders' reaction—they meet Samuel with some trepidation—perhaps reflects that they either share his concern about a potential negative reaction from Saul or are worried that Samuel has come to reprove them. Whatever their worries, Samuel calms their fears. He has come only to offer a sacrifice. He then invites Jesse and his sons to come to the sacrifice with him.

When they arrive Samuel is impressed by the oldest son, Eliab, a tall and handsome man. But the Lord reminds Samuel that he considers the inner qualities of an individual rather than the outward appearance. None of Jesse's seven sons present at the sacrifice is the chosen one, so Samuel insists that the youngest son be brought from tending the sheep. When David arrives, he too is handsome and fit, but as the youngest he is the unlikeliest choice; even so, the Lord chooses him to shepherd the people of Israel (cf. 2 Sam. 5:2). On the spot and with his family looking on, Samuel anoints David with oil as the new king-designate. "From that day on the Spirit of the LORD came powerfully upon David," as it has come upon Saul at the earlier anointing (16:13; cf. 10:6–10). Throughout the rest of his life, David will enjoy the empowering of the Spirit on his work and ministry.

While David is receiving the Spirit of the Lord, it departs from Saul. In fact, the language and juxtaposition of these statements in verses 13–14 suggest that the historian saw these events as simultaneous and related. Not only, though, does Saul lose the divine spirit; the Lord sends an evil spirit to torment him. (We must remember that the Hebrews' perspective on good and evil was that God created and controlled them both; see Isa. 45:7.) Saul's jealousy and depression are made worse because of the influence of this evil spirit, and at times it will drive Saul to violence (cf. 1 Sam. 18:10–11). According to verse 23, the evil spirit affects Saul sporadically.

In an attempt to help Saul find relief from the evil spirit, Saul's attendants suggest that he secure a musician to play soothing music. Ironically, the man they recommend is none other than David (16:14–23). In addition to his ability as a shepherd, David knows how to play the harp, and he has a fine personality. He also enjoys divine favor (16:18). By bringing David to his court, Saul gives his successor valuable training, during which David might have made important personal and political connections. Saul likes David very much and asks Jesse if David might remain in his service. While the court service introduces David to the inner workings of the monarchy, what catapults David into the public eye is his heroic victory over Goliath, an event that also betokens his later successes and eventual domination of the Philistines.

17:1–58. The setting of young David's famous first military victory is the Valley of Elah, about fifteen miles west of Bethlehem. The Philistines have amassed their troops there in an apparent attempt to reassert control over the emerging Israelite monarchy. Instead of trying to engage the Israelites in full battle, the Philistines send out a champion fighter named Goliath to challenge the Israelites to send out a soldier of theirs for one-on-one combat. The outcome of the battle will thus hinge on the struggle between the two men. This custom was known also among the Greeks, and Homer's *Iliad* contains the famous example of Achilles' victory over Hector. Apparently the Hittites of Asia Minor also practiced individual combat to a limited extent. According to 2 Samuel 2:15, a later war between Israel and Judah will be settled by a twelve-man "team" representing each side. In view of Goliath's great size and strength, it is easy to see why the Philistines are

The Valley of Elah, the site of David's defeat of Goliath (1 Samuel 17)

counting on him. According to the received Hebrew text, he is six cubits and a span tall (i.e., about nine feet, nine inches) and his armor weighs about one hundred and twenty-five pounds. (Other textual traditions, such as the Greek Septuagint, the Dead Sea Scroll text 4QSamᵃ, and Josephus give Goliath's height as four cubits and a span, which would put him at six feet, nine inches tall. This is still significantly taller than the height of the average Iron Age male, which was just over five feet. The textual sources all agree on the weight of his armor, which is more than even most modern soldiers carry in the field.) When Goliath hurls his challenge toward the Israelites, Saul and his men cower in fear. Their defeatist attitude is reminiscent of the fear of the ten spies who saw the "giant" residents of Hebron prior to the conquest (Num. 13:31–33).

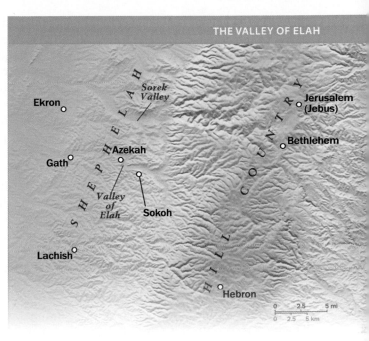

THE VALLEY OF ELAH

As tension mounts at the battle scene, we are told that David's three oldest brothers are among Saul's troops, listening to Goliath's defiant challenge for forty days. David is back in Bethlehem taking care of the sheep, for Saul's condition has apparently improved. Anxious about his older sons, Jesse decides to send David to visit the troops and take some food to his brothers and their commander. It is not hard to imagine that young David would have welcomed the chance to see the excitement of impending conflict and to find out why no battle had taken place yet. When he arrives at the scene, he soon discovers the problem and witnesses Goliath stepping forward to shout his defiance against Israel. David also sees the Israelites again shrink back in fear.

Although no one has yet volunteered to fight Goliath, Saul offers substantial rewards to the man who can defeat him. Wealth and honor will be his, along with exemption from

taxes for his father's family. The victor will also receive Saul's daughter in marriage, with no further bride-price expected. Normally a sizable amount of silver or valuables had to be paid by the groom to the family of the bride, though military exploits were sometimes substituted. Saul's offer is attractive, but who can stand a chance against the Philistine champion?

David is the first one to express any interest, taking youthful umbrage at Goliath's defiance of "the armies of the living God" (17:26). As David tries to encourage the troops, he is severely reprimanded by his oldest brother, Eliab. Eliab may have been jealous of David's anointing or he may have felt guilty for not volunteering to fight Goliath himself, but in any event his assessment of his brother is misguided. David is not trying to avoid family chores, nor is his heart conceited and wicked. With a combination of faith and naïveté that belongs predominantly to young men, David simply questions the Israelites' fear and before long informs King Saul that he will fight the "uncircumcised Philistine." In view of David's age and inexperience, however, Saul at first rejects his offer. But David reminds Saul that as a shepherd he has killed a lion and a bear, both of which are far more agile than Goliath. David is confident that since God has saved him from wild animals, he will also save him from Goliath.

Convinced of David's faith and courage, Saul gives him his blessing and offers David his own armor. But the armor does not fit David, nor will the bulky equipment be helpful since it would inhibit his movement. Instead, he takes his shepherd's staff, his sling, and five smooth stones from the stream and goes to face Goliath.

After waiting for forty days, Goliath is disappointed and disgusted when he sees the youthful, unarmed David coming toward him. How much glory is there in killing a defenseless youth? David listens to Goliath's curses and then acknowledges that his main weapon is "the name of the LORD Almighty" (17:45). Like Saul's son, Jonathan, David believes that the battle is the Lord's and that victory does not depend on who has the best weapons or the most soldiers. As with all the great acts of Israel's warrior God, such as the parting of the Red Sea (Exod. 13:17–15:21) or the fall of Jericho's walls (Josh. 5:13–6:27), so the death of Goliath will demonstrate the power of Israel's God.

As Goliath moves in to silence his brash opponent, David slings one of the stones with unerring accuracy. It strikes the Philistine on the forehead, perhaps killing him instantly or at least incapacitating him (17:49). David then removes Goliath's sword from the scabbard and cuts off his head. Stunned by this turn of events, the Philistines flee back toward the coast, to their cities of Gath and Ekron, with the Israelites in hot pursuit. As David predicted (17:46), many of the Philistines are killed along the way. David puts Goliath's weapons in his own tent and later dedicates the sword to the Lord, taking it to the tabernacle (21:9) as a way of acknowledging that God gave him the victory. According to verse 54, David takes Goliath's head to Jerusalem. This may refer to a later time after David has conquered Jerusalem (2 Sam. 5:1–9), or David may have displayed Goliath's head in the Jebusite city

as a warning that Jerusalem would suffer a similar fate in the future.

Saul's questions about David's identity seem peculiar in light of David's earlier service as a court musician (16:18–23), not to mention the discussion between the two before David fought Goliath. Since David did not stay at the court permanently, however, it is possible that Saul has forgotten his name or at least the name of his father. Alternately, many scholars take this literary bump, as well as many others like it in this episode, as an indication that at least two popular traditions about young David were edited together by the historian. (See the comments on composition in the introduction.)

B. David's struggles with Saul (18:1–27:12). **18:1–19:24.** In spite of, or perhaps because of, the beneficial results that David's triumph brings to Israel as a whole, Saul soon becomes jealous of David and begins to treat him as a rival to the throne. Perhaps Saul suspects that David is the "neighbor" who will replace him as king (15:28).

After a brief period of promotions and honor, David becomes persona non grata in Saul's court, and the king tries several methods to get rid of him. Saul's attitude is diametrically opposed to that of his son Jonathan, who does all he can to help David. Jonathan admires David greatly and comes to be his close friend (18:1–7). Both men are courageous warriors who depend on the Lord for victory, and both are national heroes. Out of his love for David, Jonathan makes a covenant with David and gives him clothes and weapons as a pledge of his friendship. Jonathan's sword, in particular, must have been highly treasured by David. In spite of Saul's increasing ill will toward David, he continues to give David additional military assignments and a high rank in the army due to David's ability and successes.

When Saul and David return home after another defeat of the Philistines, the women of the land come out to greet them with singing and dancing, much like when Miriam and the women of Israel celebrated the victory over the Egyptians at the Red Sea (Exod. 15:20). Since David has killed Goliath, his name is included along with Saul's as the women sing their praises: "Saul has slain his thousands, and David his tens of thousands" (18:7). The refrain must have been sung throughout the country because even the Philistines know about it (1 Sam. 21:11).

When Saul hears the refrain, he is infuriated and his jealousy and suspicion of David increase (18:8–16). Coupled with the influences of another "evil spirit from God" (18:10), this jealousy drives Saul to hurl his spear at David while the young warrior is temporarily back at his musician's post. Saul misses twice, and then, frustrated, sends David back to the battlefield. He recognizes that the Lord is with David but somehow hopes that the Philistines will kill him in battle. When David wins additional battles, the people love him all the more and Saul's apprehensions increase.

When David killed Goliath, he won the right to marry Saul's daughter, Merab (18:17–30). Saul, however, adds further military responsibility as a condition of marriage (18:17). As the oldest daughter, Merab would have given her husband an important claim in the matter of succession to the throne. David politely refuses her hand, a decision for which we are not given any reason. In any event, when Saul's other daughter, Michal, is offered to David, he agrees to the marriage in spite of the required bride-price. Saul hopes that one of the Philistines will kill David, but instead, David and his men double the bride-price by killing two hundred Philistines. Saul is forced to make good on his offer, and Michal becomes David's wife. Twice the text states that Michal is in love with David (18:20, 28), so the marriage begins on a positive note in spite of the disgruntled father-in-law. Both Saul's position and his state of mind are becoming more and more precarious while David's standing steadily improves.

Unable to bring about David's death at the hand of the Philistines, Saul appeals to his close associates to kill David. But Jonathan warns David and tells him to go into hiding. Jonathan then tries to persuade his father that David is a friend, not an enemy (19:1–7). After all, he argues, David risked his life to save Saul and Israel from the Philistine threat. Jonathan's appeal convinces Saul, and he promises not to harm David. In fact, David is restored to Saul's service in the court.

The reconciliation does not last long, however; and it may be David's continued success as a general that triggers a new outburst of jealousy and violence (19:8–17). For the third time, an evil spirit afflicts Saul, and as in 18:10, David's music does not soothe the king. Again Saul throws his spear at David, and again he misses. It is the last time David will dare to be in the presence of the increasingly unstable king.

David returns to his own home, but Michal convinces him to flee that night. Like Rahab with the two spies, Michal lowers David through a window so he can escape undetected. She then buys time for David by putting an idol in his bed and telling Saul's messengers that David is sick. When Saul learns that Michal helped David escape, he is upset with her. She explains that David threatened her life unless she assisted him. Michal's actions underscore her allegiance to her husband over her father.

Saul is thwarted in his attempt to capture David (19:18–24). David, deciding to take refuge with Samuel in Ramah, only a short distance from Saul's capital at Gibeah, pours out his troubles to Samuel, who takes him to the nearby residence of the prophets. When Saul's men come to capture David, the Spirit of God comes upon them and compels them to prophesy. After two more groups of messengers have the same experience, Saul himself comes in search of Samuel and David. On the way to Naioth the Spirit of the Lord also falls upon Saul, causing him to prophesy and strip off his clothes, a sign of an ecstatic state. Literarily this is an important juncture, since the prophetic frenzy that overtakes Saul here at his last meeting with Samuel mirrors what happened after Samuel first anointed him (10:11–12). Thus,

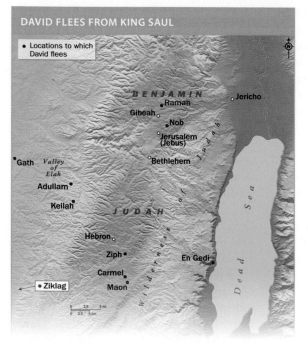

DAVID FLEES FROM KING SAUL

- Locations to which David flees

BENJAMIN
Ramah
Gibeah
Nob
Jerusalem (Jebus)
Jericho

Gath Valley of Elah
Bethlehem

Adullam
Keilah

JUDAH

Hebron
Ziph
Carmel
Maon
En Gedi

Ziklag

Dead Sea

his table. David uses the situation as a test of Saul's intentions. He asks Jonathan to give Saul a false excuse for his absence and to note Saul's response: if Saul accepts the excuse, David is safe, but if Saul is angered, his desire to kill David remains.

Sensing that Saul's jealousy might make future contact with David impossible, Jonathan takes David outside for a long talk (20:11–23). He promises to carry out David's wishes at the festival and to let David know if he should stay or flee. But beyond that, Jonathan wants to reaffirm his covenant with David. According to verse 13, Jonathan fully expects David to be the next king, and he wants David to promise that he will be kind to Jonathan's family even after he takes the throne. Often a king from a new dynasty would put to death the descendants of the previous king. David reaffirms his oath to show "unfailing kindness" to Jonathan and his family (20:14–15). When he becomes king, David will remember his oath to Jonathan and make special provision for his crippled son Mephibosheth (2 Sam. 9:7).

All hope that Saul might be reconciled to David is dashed by what takes place at the New Moon festival (20:34–42). Saul assumes on the first day that David has a legitimate reason to be absent, but on the second day he explodes. When Jonathan tells Saul about the sacrifices in Bethlehem, Saul realizes that he will not have another chance to kill David, so he takes out his anger on Jonathan. Saul cannot understand how Jonathan could side with David when David is the one standing between him and the throne. In utter frustration, Saul hurls his spear across the table at Jonathan. He has clearly never been able to accept Samuel's announcement that his kingdom will not endure, and in his obsession to kill David, Saul manages to alienate his own son as well.

The next day Jonathan goes to the field where David is hiding to give him the prearranged signal (20:35–42). Jonathan shoots an arrow

Saul's anointment began with Samuel and was marked with the sign of prophecy, and it ends with Samuel and is again marked by prophecy as well as the symbolic removal of his garments, representing his removal as the anointed king.

Although Jonathan is Saul's oldest son and is expected to succeed him on the throne, he has become close friends with Saul's chief rival. Jonathan sees that David is God's chosen and does not allow his own ambition to oppose God's will.

20:1–42. Within a short period of time David's status has changed from national hero to fugitive. Disappointed and confused, David seeks out Jonathan for an explanation of Saul's erratic behavior (20:1–10). Jonathan assures David that Saul would not harm him. But he does agree to sound out his father regarding his current feelings about David. The next day is the New Moon festival, a holiday on the first of the month, marked by rest and special offerings (20:5). Verse 27 indicates that it is a two-day festival. Since David is Saul's son-in-law and has held a high position in the army, Saul evidently expects David to be present at beyond the boy who is with him as a sign that David must flee. Because Jonathan knows he might be watched, they have not planned to meet and talk, but after the boy returns to town, David ignores the danger. The two have a tearful parting, and Jonathan reminds David of their sworn friendship and of the Lord's involvement in their families forever. Judging from his praise of the fallen Jonathan in 2 Samuel 1:26, David greatly values their friendship.

21:1–22:23. The next several years David spends as a fugitive, moving from place to place trying to avoid Saul. Most of the time he stays within the borders of his own tribe of Judah, although on two occasions he lives under Philistine jurisdiction.

David stops first at Nob, where the tabernacle is located, a town just northeast of Jerusalem (21:1–9). When he arrives alone, the high priest Ahimelek is startled and wonders what is wrong. David deceitfully replies that Saul has sent him on a secret mission, and then he asks for some food. The only food available is the bread of the Presence, the loaves kept in the Holy Place as a symbol of God's provision. Normally this bread was eaten only by the priests (Lev. 24:9), but Ahimelek agrees to give it to David provided that he and his men are ceremonially clean. This involves, in particular, abstinence from sexual relations (Exod. 19:15). Jesus refers to David's action as an example of doing what is right in an emergency even though it was, strictly speaking, "unlawful" (Mark 2:25–26).

After receiving the bread, David also takes with him the sword of Goliath that he dedicated to the Lord after his great victory. According to 22:10 and 15 Ahimelek inquires of the Lord to give David some much-needed guidance.

All of this time Ahimelek is unaware of David's flight from Saul, since David has lied about the purpose of his visit. This deception may have helped David obtain what he needed, but it costs the priests dearly when Saul finds out what they have done for David (22:17–18).

Finding a safe hiding place in a small country is not easy, so David seeks out an area where Saul will be unlikely to follow him (21:10–15). It is nevertheless surprising that David goes immediately to Philistine territory and to Gath, the hometown of Goliath! He must have hoped that no one would recognize him, but he is immediately identified as "the king of the land" and a warrior like Saul (21:11). (It is unlikely that the Philistines would have been privy to David's anointed status, and so in the phrase "the king of the land" we almost certainly see the historian's hand, reminding the audience through even the mouth of Israel's enemies that David was the true king.)

David's response is to pretend to be insane, with the hope that they will not detain him. Upon seeing his behavior, Achish, the king of Gath, refuses to let him stay in the city. Although David will later return to Gath (1 Sam. 27:1–2), for the time being it is too dangerous.

After his narrow escape David travels about twelve miles further inland, to the cave of Adullam, in the western foothills (22:1–5). This is close to the place where he killed Goliath, in the Valley of Elah. Word of his whereabouts reaches his family and other individuals who are in trouble with Saul's regime. About four hundred malcontents join him and are molded by David into an effective and loyal fighting force. Managing this motley crew would have been both extremely difficult and an excellent preparation for ruling the entire land. Since Saul will have likely taken measures against the rest of David's family, David asks the king of Moab to allow his parents to live there for a while.

At this time we are introduced to the prophet Gad, who advises David and who is associated with a record of David's reign (1 Chron. 29:29). It is Gad who gives David a choice of three options after David sins by taking a census of the land (2 Sam. 24:11–14).

Aware that David now has a growing group of supporters, Saul is worried about a conspiracy against his life (22:6–10). He knows that Jonathan is a close friend of David's, and he is afraid that other high officials might have been tempted to defect to David's side. If any are so inclined, Saul warns them that David is from the tribe of Judah and most of them are from Benjamin: will David give them high positions and valuable property if he becomes king?

To prove his loyalty to Saul, Doeg the Edomite, Saul's head shepherd, reports what he has seen when David received help from Ahimelek the priest. The implication is that Ahimelek might be the next leader to join David.

Armed with this new information, Saul immediately sends for Ahimelek and the rest of the priests (22:11–15). He accuses Ahimelek of conspiring against him by giving valuable assistance to a traitor. Ahimelek protests that he had not realized that David was regarded as an outlaw and a fugitive. Moreover, Ahimelek complains, he perceived no reason to suspect David: David is the king's own son-in-law and a respected military leader who has accomplished much for the whole nation. Besides, David told Ahimelek that he was on a secret mission for Saul (see 1 Sam. 21:2).

Ahimelek's reasoning is sound, but Saul has moved beyond reason (22:16–23). When Saul orders the guards to kill the priests, they are unwilling; but Doeg the Edomite is willing and executes the priests. Doeg's actions do not help relations between Edom and Israel, and David later treats the Edomites harshly (cf. 2 Sam. 8:12–14).

Not only does Saul order the death of eighty-five priests, but the whole town of Nob is put to the sword, including women and children. It is the sort of total destruction normally reserved for Israel's worst enemies. Only one person escapes and reaches David with the news: a son of Ahimelek named Abiathar. When David hears about the massacre, he admits that his deception has contributed heavily to the priests' deaths. Abiathar remains with David and uses the ephod with the Urim and Thummim to inquire of the Lord for David. Meanwhile Saul is left without any guidance from prophet or priest.

The general movement of David's flight is toward the south and east and the more rugged areas of Judah. But with the help of local residents, Saul is able to track him closely.

23:1–24:22. Throughout his time as a fugitive David protects the cities of Judah from their enemies. When the Philistines steal grain from the threshing floors of Keilah, a city in the western foothills about ten miles northwest of Hebron, David and his men attack them and drive them off (23:1–6). Even though David is no longer in Saul's employ, he continues to enjoy mastery over the Philistines. The victory nets David considerable plunder, especially livestock (23:5).

While David and his men stay in Keilah, Saul hears about it and prepares to besiege the city (23:7–13). David learns of Saul's plans and inquires of the Lord through Abiathar. In spite of all that David has done for the people of Keilah, the Lord indicates that they will hand him over to Saul. The failure to extradite a fugitive was a significant provocation and thus a common cause for war in the ancient Near East, so the city elders did not want to risk the horrors of a siege. Since David is equally unwilling to fight Saul, he and his men—six hundred by now—leave the safety of the walled city.

David heads for the Desert of Ziph, south of Hebron, and the Lord protects him in the hills there. One day encouragement comes through an unexpected visit from Jonathan, Saul's son (23:14–18). In this final meeting between the two dear friends, Jonathan assures David that he will become king and that Jonathan will serve under him. Before parting, the two reaffirm the covenant they have made.

In contrast to Jonathan the people of Ziph are eager to help Saul capture David, so they relay David's precise location to the king (23:19–29). Saul thanks them, saying, "The LORD bless you for your concern for me" (23:21). But as in verse 7, when Saul thought that God had handed David over to him, the king is badly mistaken. God has abandoned him and is frustrating his every move. In this instance Saul and his men have David cornered in the Desert of Maon when news comes that the Philistines are attacking the land. The timing is providential from David's perspective and allows David and his men to escape to the caves of En Gedi.

David's new hideout is an area with many caves along the high cliffs. The whole region between the Dead Sea and the hill country of Judea consisted of steep valleys and gorges cut by the streams and wadis that flowed into the Dead Sea. En Gedi means "spring of the goats" because of the excellent water source located there.

When Saul returns to pursue David he happens to relieve himself in the same cave where David and his men are hiding (24:1–7). Apparently Saul is alone, leading David's men to proclaim this as the Lord's timing, with the implication that David should kill Saul. David does not kill Saul but instead sneaks up behind Saul and cuts off a corner of his robe.

After Saul leaves the cave, David calls out to him and tells him what he has done (24:8–15). Holding up the piece of the robe as evidence of his mercy, David asserts that he is not trying to wrest the throne from Saul and that he is not guilty of treason. Instead, he has committed the matter to the Lord, who will decide the case as a righteous Judge. Just as war was considered a contest between the gods of the rival nations, so this personal battle will be settled by the Lord in favor of the righteous party. According to verse 14 David is no more dangerous than a dead dog or a flea, and yet Saul is consuming time and energy in an effort to eliminate him.

Confronted by clear evidence that David has spared his life, Saul expresses remorse for seeking to kill David and admits that he has treated David badly (24:16–22). Echoing the words of his son Jonathan (23:17), Saul recognizes that David will indeed be the next king of Israel, but he makes David promise that as the new ruler he will not wipe out Saul's descendants. In the light of this apparent reconciliation, it appears that David's years as a fugitive are over; but David has learned that Saul's word cannot be trusted (cf. 1 Sam. 19:6). Subsequent events indicate that before long Saul resumes his pursuit of David.

25:1–44. To make matters worse for David, the prophet Samuel dies (25:1). The revered

The area of En Gedi, where David hides from Saul in 1 Samuel 23:29. Notice the caves in the cliffs and the greenery in the gorge, which indicates the water below.

leader who has presided over the beginning of the monarchy and has anointed both Saul and David is gone. He was a great figure in Israel's history, playing important spiritual and political roles in the tradition of Moses. Thus, David is left without one of his strongest supporters.

After his meeting with Saul, David continues to live in the region south of Hebron. The "Carmel" mentioned in verse 2 was near Ziph and Maon, not the Mount Carmel of Elijah near the Mediterranean Sea in the northern part of the country. While living in Carmel, David and his men work for a wealthy man named Nabal, protecting his flocks and herds (25:2–13). When sheepshearing time arrives, David expects to be given meat and bread in exchange for his labors. Normally this was a time of feasting for all the family and workers. When Nabal receives David's request from the ten men he has sent, he refuses to give him anything, calling David a nobody, a deserter.

News of Nabal's insulting remarks spurs David to action. If Nabal will not pay willingly, David will take his pay by force and kill Nabal's family in the process. Bent on revenge, David sets out with four hundred men.

Nabal has an intelligent and beautiful wife named Abigail who is wiser than her stingy husband (25:14–22). When she hears what Nabal has said to David, she follows the advice of one of the servants and takes matters into her own hands. Quickly she prepares a sizable gift of meat, bread, raisins, and figs and sends them to David. She herself mounts a donkey and heads in the same direction. As she approaches, David has just invoked a curse on himself that will take effect if he does not put to death all the males in Nabal's household (25:22).

When Abigail begins her plea for mercy, she immediately disassociates herself from her husband (25:23–35). She admits that he is a scoundrel and that he deserves to die. To reinforce her point Abigail makes a play on her husband's name, which sounds like the Hebrew word meaning "fool." (The name itself likely derived from a word meaning "noble,"

or perhaps his real name was suppressed and "Nabal" was used because of the character of the man.) In spite of his wealth, no one has anything good to say about him, least of all his wife.

Nine times Abigail refers to David as "my lord" or "my master," an indication of her deference to David. Abigail's implicit assessment of David contrasts sharply with her explicit assessment of her husband. Thus Nabal serves as a foil for David, whose wisdom is touted throughout the passage. David's wisdom and mercy on Nabal in this episode epitomize, in the historian's view, the differences between Saul, the first king, and David, the eventual second king. In the end Abigail admits her husband's guilt but appeals to David's mercy and good sense: taking revenge on members of his own tribe of Judah will tarnish David's image as a wise and fair leader.

David thanks Abigail for her kind words and acknowledges that the Lord has used her to keep him from avenging himself. Instead of acting like the king he is destined to be, he has almost behaved like a brigand chief.

When Abigail returns home she finds Nabal very drunk. At sheepshearing time drunkenness and partying were common, and Nabal has enjoyed it to the hilt. The next morning Abigail tells him about her meeting with David, after which Nabal suffers a stroke or perhaps a heart attack. About ten days later he dies. David interprets Nabal's death as the Lord's judgment for mistreating him and probably many other people as well (25:36–44). The realization that the Lord has upheld his cause against Nabal gives David the confidence that God will decide the dispute with Saul in his favor also.

The death of Nabal also releases Abigail from marriage and gives David the freedom to take her as his wife. From David's standpoint, marriage to the widow of a prominent citizen of Judah will help him politically, and a new wife is compensation for the loss of Michal, whom Saul has given to another man to weaken David's claim to the throne. David never accepts

Saul's imposed divorce, however, and later takes Michal back as his wife (2 Sam. 3:13–16).

26:1–27:12. David again refuses to kill Saul (26:1–12). As in 24:2, Saul takes three thousand (or three "companies" of) men to track David down in the Desert of Ziph, where he narrowly escaped from Saul earlier (23:24–28). David's scouts tell him where Saul and his army are camping for the night, and David himself comes close enough to see where Saul and Abner are lying down. With characteristic boldness, David decides to pay a visit to the camp, accompanied by Abishai, his nephew who will later become one of his top generals (2 Sam. 18:2). It seems like a foolish idea, but the Lord has put Saul's army "into a deep sleep" (26:12). David and Abishai creep right up to Saul, and Abishai sees a golden opportunity to get rid of Saul. But as in the cave at En Gedi (24:6), David refuses the easy way out. Besides, the death of Nabal proved how rapidly God can strike down the enemy—without any help on David's part. So David and his nephew take Saul's water jug and spear and leave the camp.

When they reach a hill a safe distance away, David calls out loudly to Saul's cousin Abner, the army commander (26:13–25). He scolds Abner for failing to guard the king and points out the security breach that has occurred. Awakened by the commotion, Saul reacts to David's voice exactly as he has in 24:16: "Is that your voice, David my son?" David responds with another assertion of innocence and wonders aloud why Saul continues to chase him. He feels like a partridge relentlessly pursued by a hunter. If God has incited Saul against him, David is willing to make things right with the Lord and bring him an offering. If other men have urged Saul to pursue David, he calls on God to judge them.

As in 24:16–22, Saul seems convinced by David's arguments and especially by the spear in David's hand. The king admits he has acted like a fool and promises to leave David alone. In verse 25 Saul predicts that David "will do great things and surely triumph," implying

that eventually David will be king. Saul almost sounds like Balaam, who wanted to curse Israel but instead wound up predicting that Israel would crush their enemies (Num. 24:17).

Sad to say, this second set of conciliatory words is no better, and Saul soon forgets what he has promised. Frustrated and discouraged, David decides to find refuge in Philistine territory, where Saul will not likely venture (27:1–12). It is a calculated risk, because the Philistines might kill him and because the Israelites might consider him a traitor and might never welcome him back. These risks notwithstanding, David goes to the Philistines and uses the time to his benefit. David learns valuable information about their military tactics and about ironworking, and he also makes friends with some of the Philistines. Indeed, after he becomes king, several contingents from Philistia serve as faithful mercenary troops under him (2 Sam. 15:18).

As he did earlier (1 Sam. 21:10–15), David goes to Achish of Gath and asks for asylum. The historian provides no reason why this time the Philistines are not suspicious of David, but one may speculate that his reputation as an outcast and an enemy of Saul has become well established. Moreover, David's six-hundred-man army could have served Achish as a valuable mercenary force. Whatever the reasons, David is allowed to live in Ziklag, a town in the transition zone between Philistia and southern Judah; the town is listed as Israelite in Joshua but has come under the control of the Philistines. While there David and his men have more freedom than they would have had in Gath.

During his time in Ziklag, David actually benefits the Israelites much more than the Philistines. Although he tells Achish that he is conducting raids against areas of Judah, instead he is attacking Israel's enemies. Joshua was not able to conquer the land of the Geshurites in the south (Josh. 13:2), but now David soundly defeats them (27:8). Like Saul, David also successfully fights the Amalekites. Whenever he attacks a town, he leaves no survivors to complain to the Philistines, but he does take flocks, herds, and other valuables. David's deception works, and Achish naively thinks that David has completely turned against the Israelites.

C. Saul's final battle (28:1–31:13). 28:1–29:11. Throughout his reign Saul has battled the Philistines in an attempt to keep them from expanding beyond their coastal strongholds. With David's help he has won many crucial victories, but now David is living among the Philistines, and Saul is left without the Lord's favor.

David knows that eventually he will be called on to fight against Saul (28:1–6). As a mercenary of Achish, he will have to join with the rest of the Philistine forces. Although it is unthinkable for David to fight against his own people, he has the Philistines convinced that he is ready and eager to fight Saul. His actual statements, however, are ambiguous and leave the reader wondering if he ever intended to fight against Israel. Whether David would have fought against his own people is left an open question in the narrative, since the Philistine military leaders reject his involvement before battle commences (29:3–9).

The Philistines assemble their troops at Shunem, in the Valley of Jezreel near the Sea of Galilee, and the Israelites gather at Mount Gilboa, toward the eastern end of the valley. Saul is terrified and turns to inquire of the Lord, but the Lord has long since broken off contact with Saul. Revelation from God normally came through dreams, prophets, or priests, but Saul has massacred the priests himself (22:18), and Samuel is dead. Apparently, Saul is not in touch with any other prophet.

Saul goes to Endor, a few miles north of Mount Gilboa, to inquire of a medium (28:7–14). Since Saul himself has apparently expelled the mediums and spiritists from the land earlier in his reign, he disguises himself and takes only two men with him. The disguise seems to work until the medium sees the spirit of Samuel coming up out of the ground, at which time she recognizes Saul. Consulting the dead is referred to in Deuteronomy 18:11 and Isaiah 8:19, and although it is strongly condemned by the biblical writers as characteristic of the spiritual corruption of other nations, its effectiveness is not denied. It was likely a fairly common practice in many periods of Israel's history. Thus, we cannot fault Saul for seeking recourse in this way. An unusual aspect of this account is the description of Samuel as "spirit" (28:13 NIV 1984; NIV "a ghostly figure"), a word that means "God," "gods," or at least "divine beings." This is one of the few hints in the Old Testament of some sort of dynamic existence after death and is thus all the more intriguing.

While Saul prostrates himself on the ground Samuel begins to speak, complaining about being disturbed in this fashion (28:15–19). The grave was to be a place of rest, where the righteous "enter into peace" (Isa. 57:2). Saul explains that the situation is desperate and that he has called for Samuel with the hope that perhaps in his mercy God will once again deliver Israel against great odds. He wants a glimmer of hope, a word of encouragement from Samuel, who himself has witnessed God's miraculous intervention against the Philistines (1 Sam. 7:10–11).

Unhappily Samuel's response is anything but encouraging and contains the same grim words

Mount Gilboa

he spoke at his last meeting with Saul after the battle with the Amalekites (1 Sam. 15:22–29). Because Saul has failed to carry out God's fierce wrath against the Amalekites, he has lost the right to rule, and the next day he and his sons will die (28:18–19). Just as Eli and his sons died the same day the Philistines defeated the Israelites (1 Sam. 4:11, 18), so Saul and his family will fall before the same enemy. In both cases, Samuel announces God's word of judgment prior to the catastrophe.

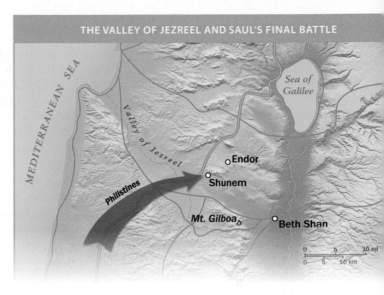

THE VALLEY OF JEZREEL AND SAUL'S FINAL BATTLE

MEDITERRANEAN SEA

Valley of Jezreel

Philistines

Endor

Shunem

Mt. Gilboa

Beth Shan

Sea of Galilee

Recognizing that all hope is gone, Saul falls to the ground in despair (28:20–25). He is also completely exhausted, because he has eaten nothing all day in preparation for his encounter with Samuel. At the urging of the woman and his men, Saul finally agrees to eat something, and the woman butchers a fattened calf. In spite of his pitiful condition Saul is still the king, and she gives him the best she has.

As the battle draws near, David and his men are lined up on the Philistine side (29:1–11). They are "at the rear with Achish," an indication of the esteem in which Achish holds David (not necessarily that David wants to stay out of the battle if possible). However, in light of the success that David has previously had in fighting against the Philistines, the other Philistine commanders are nervous about his presence. They are concerned that he might rejoin the Israelite side during the battle and be reconciled to Saul. In point of fact, in an earlier battle a number of renegade Israelites had switched back to their own side when the Philistines began to suffer losses (1 Sam. 14:21).

Achish protests that he has no reason to doubt David's loyalty to his new allies, but he is clearly outvoted by the other commanders. When he breaks the news to David, David acts surprised and hurt. Clearly, however, the orders save him from the horns of a dilemma. Up to this point he has consistently refused to touch the Lord's anointed and he has secretly helped the Israelites even while in exile. At this point, to fight against the people over whom he expected to be king would no doubt have been unpalatable and likely affected negatively the Israelites' acceptance of David as the next king.

30:1–31. While David and his men are north with the Philistine armies, the Amalekites decide to get revenge for David's earlier attacks against them (30:1–6). David's city of Ziklag is burned and all of the women and children are taken captive. David and his men are heartbroken. The men even blame David and threaten to stone him, just as an earlier generation grumbled menacingly against Moses (Exod. 17:4). Yet in the midst of this opposition and his own personal sorrow at the loss of his two wives, "David found strength in the LORD his God" (30:6).

Since Abiathar the priest is there and can inquire of the Lord by means of the ephod, David determines that he can overtake the raiders (30:7–20). Encouraged, he and his men head to the southwest in pursuit. Only four hundred men are strong enough to keep up the pursuit, for they have already covered many miles in the three-day journey back home. Fortunately they receive valuable information from an Egyptian member of the raiding party who has been abandoned after taking ill. Revived by food and drink, he reveals that the Amalekites have taken advantage of all the parties involved in the war in the north by attacking several areas belonging to Judah and the Philistines (30:14). The amount of the plunder may have slowed them down, because David finds them celebrating enthusiastically. Apparently the Amalekites think they are a safe distance away from any pursuers, but David soundly defeats them and recovers all of the captives and plunder. Mourning turns to joy as the men are reunited with their families. It is a great triumph, reminiscent of Abraham's recovery of the people and goods of Sodom after his daring pursuit of the four northern kings (Gen. 14:15–16).

After their return, a dispute arises over the distribution of the plunder (30:21–31). Should the two hundred men who could not keep up with the others receive an equal share of the goods? As a wise and fair leader David insists that all the shares be the same, for the victory was the work of the Lord and none of the men can claim credit for it. The same God who handed over Goliath to David has handed over the Amalekites. Because the plunder is so abundant David also sends presents to the elders in a number of the towns of Judah. Those towns are mostly to the south of Hebron, where David and his men tried to hide from Saul (23:24–25) and where

A depiction of heads hung on a city wall and bodies hung up on poles—similar to the fate of King Saul's body at Beth Shan (1 Sam. 31:10)—on a bronze strip from the palace of Shalmaneser III (858–824 BC).

David received valuable assistance. A number of these places had probably been plundered by the Amalekites and were no doubt grateful for the gift of goods and livestock.

31:1–13. Saul fights the Philistines in the Valley of Jezreel, and for the first time their chariots may have given the Philistines a decided advantage. But even more important is the fact that God has abandoned Saul, weakening the armies of Israel (31:1–6). As the battle rages three of Saul's sons are killed, including Jonathan, the crown prince and David's close friend. One son—called Ish-Bosheth or Esh-Baal—survives, and he will serve as king briefly. Saul's leading general, Abner, also somehow lives through the battle. Saul himself is critically wounded by the archers and asks his armor bearer to finish him off. When the armor bearer refuses to kill him, Saul falls on his sword, thus taking his own life. It is a tragic ending to a reign that began in such a promising fashion.

With their leaders gone and the army in full flight, the Israelites abandon their cities and flee, allowing the Philistines to take full control of the whole region (31:7–13). The next day the Philistines cut off Saul's head, as David did to Goliath (cf. 17:51). Word of the Philistines' triumph is announced in their temples, giving glory to their gods. Just as David placed Goliath's sword in the tabernacle as a trophy of victory (21:9), so Saul's armor is placed in the temple of their goddesses. Saul's body is hung on the wall of the public square of Beth Shan.

When the men of Jabesh Gilead hear how Saul's body is being displayed ingloriously, they cross the Jordan, take down his body and those of his sons, and return home. They remember how Saul rescued their city from the threat of the Ammonites when he first became king. Because the bodies have been mutilated, they are cremated rather than buried, though the bones are to some extent preserved and buried. Years later, David has the remains of Saul and Jonathan transferred to the family tomb of Saul's father, Kish, in one of the towns of Benjamin (2 Sam. 21:11–14). To mourn the death of Saul, the people of Jabesh Gilead fast for seven days.

D. David unifies Judah and Israel (2 Sam. 1:1–5:25). **1:1–27.** When Saul dies it appears that Israel's experiment with the monarchy has been a failure. Philistine control has increased rather than decreased, and Israel is on the verge of splitting into north and south because of the dispute between Saul and David. Within seven years, however, David is able to unify the people of Judah and Israel, defeat the Philistines, and establish a strong national presence in the Near East. Israel's golden age is about to begin.

It must have been with a heavy heart that David awaited news of the battle in the north. Although an Israelite defeat would hasten David's rise to the throne, it would also bring hardship and sorrow to the young nation.

Three days after David's return to Ziklag, he learns the outcome of the battle (1:1–16). An Amalekite who has escaped from the scene describes how he himself put Saul out of his misery. His account differs from that of 1 Samuel 31. Most likely the Amalekite claims credit for killing Saul with the hope of getting a reward from David. He undoubtedly reached Saul before the Philistines did, saw his dead body, and took the crown as plunder. Having confirmed the death of Saul and Jonathan, David and his men tear their clothes as a sign of their grief. David displays no joy whatsoever over Saul's death and in fact orders that the Amalekite be executed because he testified that he had killed the Lord's anointed. It is obviously not lost on the historian how ironic it is that an Amalekite

is executed for Saul's death since Saul's downfall began with the failure to destroy the Amalekites (1 Sam. 15:18–19; 28:18). In light of David's recent conflicts with the Amalekites (1 Samuel 30), the young man's hope for a reward was slim to begin with.

David's harsh treatment of Saul's alleged murderer is an important part of David's "apology." To avoid the charge of being a usurper, David expresses displeasure with anyone who hastens the demise of Saul and his family. When Saul's son Ish-Bosheth is assassinated, David likewise orders the execution of the two assassins (4:10–12). No one in the tribe of Benjamin can say that David is supporting those who have killed his political rivals.

David composes an elegy in honor of Israel's fallen leaders (1:17–27). Known as the "lament of the bow," it may have been sung by Israel's warriors while they practiced their technique with the bow and arrow in the hope of avoiding defeat in battle. According to verse 18, this lament was also included in the Book of Jashar, a collection of battle accounts that appears to have been used as a source for biblical texts (cf. Josh. 10:12–13).

The lament begins and ends with the line, "How the mighty have fallen!" as David eulogizes Saul and Jonathan and emphasizes their accomplishments. Nowhere in the poem does David mention Saul's weaknesses, failures, or jealousy; instead he links father and son as an effective team, victorious in battle and benefactors of the nation's citizens. The second line of the lament (1:20) has the form of a command aimed at David's audience, but it functions as a wish, that the Philistines will not gloat over Israel's defeat (although they do in fact spread the news throughout the land, 1 Sam. 31:9). Turning his attention to the scene of the battle (1:21), David pronounces a curse on the mountains of Gilboa, as if the terrain itself were responsible for Israel's defeat. Out of reverence for the royal men who have been slain there, David wishes that the soil would lie barren in sympathetic mourning over the terrible catastrophe. Although David honors the memory of Saul in several verses, his greatest praise is reserved for Jonathan. Jonathan made a covenant with David, linking their families forever (1 Sam. 20:14–16), but his loyalty to Saul kept him by his father's side in this final and fatal conflict.

2:1–32. During Saul's reign, the people of Judah were also torn between loyalty to the king and loyalty to the local hero David, whom Saul had declared an outlaw. Since David had cultivated the friendship of the elders of Judah even while allegedly an ally of the Philistines (1 Sam. 30:26), his leadership status is clearly established. Nonetheless, after Saul's death David takes nothing for granted and seeks the Lord's guidance before moving to Hebron, the most important city of Judah, centrally located in the hill country nineteen miles south of Jerusalem. There, where Abraham had lived for many years and where the patriarchs were buried, David is publicly crowned as king over Judah (2:1–7). He has waited about fifteen years since his private anointing by Samuel in Bethlehem (1 Sam. 16:13), but the time to rule has finally arrived.

Realizing that Saul's supporters in the north will not readily accept him as king, David seeks to establish good relations with them immediately. He demonstrates his respect for Saul by thanking the men of Jabesh Gilead for burying him. By their brave actions they have shown kindness to Saul, and David promises to treat them kindly and fairly. Although this message is an indirect request for them to recognize David as king, the northern tribes refuse to acknowledge him for another seven years.

The general of Saul's army, his cousin Abner, has managed to survive the Battle of Gilboa and emerged as the most powerful figure of the northern tribes. Instead of unifying the nation under David, Abner decides to place Saul's remaining son, Ish-Bosheth, on the throne of Israel (2:8–11). His reasons for doing so are not entirely clear, but later on even Ish-Bosheth suspects that Abner wanted the throne for himself (3:6–8). The name Ish-Bosheth means "man of

shame," but this was a later development, a sort of derogatory nickname. Originally his name was apparently Ish-Baal, or Esh-Baal, meaning "man of Baal" (1 Chron. 8:33). Baal was the name of a prominent Canaanite god, but in Hebrew the word also meant "lord" or "master"; it was even sometimes used to refer to God. It is not clear whether Saul's son's name reflects a strain of syncretistic Baal worship by Saul's house or refers to God—that is, "man of the Lord." Similarly, Jonathan's son Mephibosheth was originally named Merib-Baal (1 Chron. 8:34). Whatever the original intent of these names, later tradition often changes the "Baal" to "Bosheth" ("shame") to emphasize that worshiping Baal was "a shameful thing." Thus, it is possible that the tradition includes an implicit condemnation of Saul for Baal worship, whether that is justified or not.

Abner makes Ish-Bosheth king in Mahanaim, a city in the Transjordan that functioned as a "capital in exile." He is called king of "all Israel" (2:9), but it is not likely that he exercised much control over the tribal areas west of the Jordan, where the Philistines apparently controlled many of the cities. An additional problem is the "two-year" reign of Ish-Bosheth (2:10), which is hard to reconcile with David's seven-and-a-half-year reign over Judah (2:10–11). Does this mean that it took five years before all the northern tribes recognized Ish-Bosheth as king, or do the two years refer to the time it took for him and Abner to reestablish control over the area west of the Jordan?

With two kings vying for control of the land, conflict between the forces of David and Ish-Bosheth is inevitable (2:12–17). The first battle takes place at Gibeon, about six miles north of Jerusalem, close to Saul's former capital at Gibeah. Abner brings in troops from the Transjordan, while David's army is led by his nephew Joab, a loyal and effective commander to whom David has become greatly indebted. At times he is ruthless and quick to assassinate his foes, but David seems unable to punish him. In his opening battle, twelve men fight for each side in a kind of representative warfare similar to the one-on-one combat between David and Goliath. The result is indecisive, so a full-scale battle ensues. The civil war is underway, and David's men win handily.

As the men of Israel flee the scene, Joab's brother Asahel, who is a very swift runner, chases Abner (2:18–23). Asahel knows that if he can kill Abner, Ish-Bosheth's "kingdom" might collapse completely, giving David control of the whole nation. Abner is much older and unable to outrun Asahel, but he does not want to anger Joab by killing his brother. He fears that Joab might seek revenge, even if the death takes place in battle. When no other alternative remains, Abner strikes Asahel with the butt of his spear, perhaps to stop but not kill him. The blow is a powerful one, however, and Asahel dies immediately.

After the death of their brother, Joab and Abishai keep up the chase until sunset, when Israel's resistance stiffens (2:24–32). Abner calls for a truce, because the terrible results of civil war are already becoming clear to him. In light of the number of fatalities, Joab agrees to the truce, and the battle is finally over. Both armies march all night to return to their respective capitals by morning. Only nineteen of David's men have perished, compared with three hundred and sixty casualties for Abner and Benjamin.

3:1–4:12. In the years that follow, David continues to enjoy success in the conflict with Ish-Bosheth. One sign of David's increasing strength is the number of sons born to him in Hebron (3:1–5). Since none of the six have the same mother, we learn that David has taken four more wives. One of these—Maakah, daughter of the king of Geshur—was probably married to David for political reasons, to make an alliance with the Aramean city-state northeast of the Sea of Galilee. It is Maakah's son Absalom who will kill David's firstborn, Amnon, and then lead a rebellion against his own father.

The modern village of el-Jib surrounds the site of ancient Gibeon (foreground), where David's men fought Ish-Bosheth's (2 Sam. 2:12–17).

Apparently Ish-Bosheth resents the fact that Abner is the power behind the throne, and in his jealousy he accuses Abner of wanting to seize the throne himself (3:6–11). The specific issue is whether Abner has slept with Saul's concubine, because a king's concubines normally became the property of his successor. Abner reacts to the charge by ending his allegiance to Saul's family and vowing to "transfer the kingdom" to David (3:10). In his reply Abner admits that he knows the Lord has promised the throne to David. Abner's reaction is more than Ish-Bosheth has bargained for, but his fear of Abner keeps him from raising any objections.

Abner immediately opens negotiations with David to discuss the conditions under which David might become the ruler of the entire nation (3:12–21). David is willing to work out an agreement, but only if Saul's daughter Michal is returned to him. During David's years as a fugitive, Saul forced Michal to divorce David, but David has continued to regard her as his wife. His marriage to Saul's daughter would have measurably strengthened his claim to succeed Saul as king, particularly in the eyes of the northern ten tribes.

In the decision-making process, the role of the elders is an important one. As the heads of families and tribes, the elders have a voice in the selection and retention of a king (1 Sam. 15:30; 2 Sam. 5:3; 1 Kings 12:3), though their influence will decrease over the years as the dynastic model of monarchy becomes more entrenched. Knowing that many of Israel's leaders have favored David all along, Abner encourages them to support him openly. Abner pays special attention to Saul's tribe of Benjamin, who is the hardest to convince. Satisfied that the leaders of Israel will be willing to make a treaty with David, Abner personally goes to Hebron, where David prepares a feast in his honor. From all indications, David's coronation over all Israel is not far off.

There is one member of David's inner circle who is not happy about the move toward unity (3:22–27). David's nephew, Joab, his top military commander, tries to convince David that Abner has come as a spy and that he cannot be trusted. In all likelihood, Joab feared that if the merger took place, he might lose his job to Abner. Joab has also never forgiven Abner for killing his brother Asahel during the Battle of Gibeon years before (2:23). Since Abner has not traveled very far from Hebron, Joab uses an excuse to bring him back secretly and then stabs him to death. Although Joab justifies his action on the basis of blood revenge, David's reaction to Abner's death exposes Joab's treachery. Abner killed Asahel only after repeated warnings and as a last resort to save his own life. Moreover, it took place in the middle of a battle and was not comparable to Joab's premeditated murder of Abner.

When David learns what Joab has done, he does everything possible to express his displeasure and to indicate that he was not personally involved (3:28–29). David goes so far as to place a curse on Joab and his descendants, asking God to punish them with disease, starvation, or violent death (3:29). David himself leads the mourners and weeps at Abner's tomb, and he also composes a short lament in Abner's honor (3:33–34). To emphasize his sorrowful attitude David fasts the rest of the day.

By regarding Abner's death as a great tragedy, David convinces the nation that he was not implicated in the murder, and the fragile alliance with the northern tribes remains intact. At the same time, David probably should have taken some direct disciplinary action against Joab, who seems not to have lost any power.

David's failure to discipline his officers and his sons constitutes one of his greatest weaknesses, and it will nearly cost him the kingdom some years later. Just before he dies David will tell Solomon to bring Joab to justice for his crimes, and shortly thereafter he is executed (1 Kings 2:5–6, 29–35).

With Abner gone, Ish-Bosheth's weakness as a leader is evident even to the tribe of Benjamin (4:1–12). Not long after Abner's death, two of Ish-Bosheth's military officers gain entrance into the king's house and stab him to death. Then they cut off his head and take it to David at Hebron, hoping to be rewarded for their action. When they arrive, the two brothers connect their assassination with the Lord's vengeance "against Saul and his offspring" (4:8). To their surprise, David does not rejoice at the news of Ish-Bosheth's death but instead orders that the murderers themselves be put to death. Once again David claims no responsibility for the elimination of any rival—whether Saul or Abner or Ish-Bosheth. In each case he is angry and dismayed. The bodies of the assassins are hung near the pool in Hebron as a warning to all and as a sign that David believes in justice.

After the death of Ish-Bosheth, there is no other member of Saul's family who could be considered a serious contender for the throne. Jonathan does have a son named Mephibosheth, but he was crippled as a child (4:4). Years later David will make sure that he is well cared for in fulfillment of his covenant with Jonathan (2 Samuel 9).

5:1–25. In recognition of their need of a strong leader, the tribes of Israel journey to the southern capital to anoint David (5:1–5). Many soldiers, representing all of the tribes, come together to make an agreement with David and to acclaim him as king. They acknowledge that the Lord has chosen him and that he has demonstrated his leadership ability over the years. Even during Saul's reign, some soldiers from the northern tribes have defected to David (1 Chron. 12:1–22), but now the entire nation rallies around him. David is almost thirty-eight years old, and he will remain king until he is seventy. In the next thirty-three years David strengthens the nation and extends her borders in every direction. Before David dies, Israel has become a stable and secure force in the region between Egypt to the south and

ISRAEL DURING THE TIME OF KING DAVID

the Phoenician city-states and Mesopotamia to the north.

David makes many excellent choices during his lifetime, but none is better than his decision to make Jerusalem the capital of the united nation (5:6–8). Although Jerusalem briefly belonged to the Israelites (Judg. 1:8), they were unable to retain control of the city, leaving the Jebusites to rule it. Some biblical texts associate the name Jebus with the city (Josh. 15:8; 18:28; Judg. 19:10; 1 Chron. 11:4–5), which is really a reference to the ethnicity of the residents.

Some scholars connect the Jebusites with the Hurrians, a people who exercised considerable influence in Mesopotamia and Asia Minor from 1800 to 1200 BC. The precise meaning of the name Jerusalem is unclear, but it might mean "foundation of peace" or "foundation of [the god] Shalem." The city was also known by the shorter form Salem (Gen. 14:18) and by the name Zion, mentioned for the first time here in 5:7 (the etymology of "Zion" is also unknown).

In David's time, Jerusalem was a hill covering about eleven acres, located on the border between Judah and Benjamin, making it an ideal neutral site for one who wanted to unite the north and the south. Deep valleys on every side except the north surrounded Jerusalem, so it could be easily defended, which explains the Jebusites' confidence that David will not be able to capture the city (5:6). Jerusalem also possessed an excellent water source, the Gihon spring in the Kidron Valley, east of the city. But it may have been the "water shaft" running from the Gihon spring into the city that David's men used to gain entrance into Jerusalem or at least to block the city's water supply (5:8).

David takes immediate steps to fortify his new capital (5:9–16). His building efforts are aided by an alliance with Hiram, king of Tyre, one of the primary Phoenician city-states. Sending the famed cedars of Lebanon and skilled craftsmen, Hiram helps David build a palace. The Phoenicians were also excellent sailors who controlled the seas, and over the years the Israelites will trade them crops for merchandise. Both sides will profit from the alliance, which will become even stronger during the reign of Solomon. David acknowledges that his success is due to the Lord, who is making Israel a great nation, as he has promised.

As long as David is only the king of Judah, the Philistines do not seem upset by his rule. In fact, they may have considered him a vassal king, one step removed from the role he played under Achish as a mercenary commander. But once David becomes king of all Israel, the Philistines realize that he is a threat to their control

of the northern parts of Israel (5:17–25). So before David has a chance to get established, the Philistines launch an attack, perhaps even before David has captured Jerusalem. It seems unlikely that they would allow him to enjoy the safety of a fortress if they could engage him in battle before this occurred.

Although David has not fought against the Philistines for several years, he has not lost his battle sense and once again emerges victorious. Both battles are fought west of Jerusalem and determine who will control the central hill country. After the first battle, the Philistines abandon their idols, just as the Israelites have lost the ark of the covenant in the days of Eli. (First Chronicles 14:12 adds that David burns the idols; this addition reflects the Chronicler's interest in having David act in accord with Moses's command [see Deut. 7:5].) The second battle begins after David hears "the sound of marching in the tops of the poplar trees" (5:24). This is the signal that the Lord and his angels are leading the way into battle. Just as the Lord went ahead of Barak as he moved against the army of Sisera (Judg. 4:14), so he enables David to rout the Philistines and chase them back to the coastal plain.

E. David established as king (6:1–8:18).
6:1–23. After a long wait marked by years of valuable training, David has now become the king of Israel. Because he is God's new choice as king, the Lord gives him and his descendants the right to rule forever, and he gives David victory over all his enemies.

The ark of the covenant represents God's presence more than does any other article in the tabernacle (1 Sam. 4:4), so David has it brought to Jerusalem. The ark has been in Kiriath Jearim, about nine miles west of Jerusalem, since the days of Eli and Samuel, but the time has come to move the ark to the new national capital. To emphasize the importance of the ark, David and his men lead a triumphant celebration, complete with singing and dancing. It is the type of celebration that usually accompanies a military victory and is David's way of proclaiming that

God deserves the recognition and glory for Israel's triumphs.

In his zeal to honor the Lord, David places the ark on a new cart, the way the Philistines have done (6:1–11; see 1 Sam. 6:7). While a new cart is pure and this is an appropriate means of transporting a sacred object, it is also contrary to what is specified in Numbers 7:9; thus the historian likely sees in the next event a form of divine punishment. When the oxen pulling the cart stumble, a man named Uzzah—at whose home the ark has been kept—reaches out to steady the ark. As he does so, he is struck dead. There are many proposed explanations for this enigmatic event, but none is entirely satisfying, and the text provides no hint. There is no indication that Uzzah somehow sins or is ritually impure. The historian of 1–2 Chronicles ascribes Uzzah's death to the non-Levitical mode of transport (1 Chron. 15:13). Whatever the reason, David is angry at the Lord's action and

so disturbed that he leaves the ark in the house of Obed-Edom.

Three months later David is encouraged by the blessing that God has brought to the household of Obed-Edom (6:12–19). Realizing that the Lord is no longer angry, David prepares once more to bring the ark to Jerusalem. (The Chronicler adds that "those who were carrying the ark" were Levites, thus making the second attempt fall in line with Mosaic law [1 Chron. 15:15].) After the ark bearers have taken six steps and are still alive, David offers sacrifices in thanksgiving. As the procession continues amid music and shouting, David deliberately dresses like one of the Levites, putting on a robe of fine linen and a linen ephod, a garment usually reserved for the priest. When his wife Michal sees him dressed in this fashion, leaping and dancing before the Lord, she is shocked.

David does not try to bring the tabernacle to Jerusalem but sets up a special tent for the ark. Instead, Moses's "Tent of Meeting" remains at Gibeon, about six miles northwest of Jerusalem (cf. 2 Chron. 1:3). David wants to build a permanent temple to honor the ark, as we

This stepped-stone structure, called the Millo, located in the ancient city of David in Jerusalem, may have supported a royal building such as David's palace.

learn in 2 Samuel 7. With the ark safely in Jerusalem, David sacrifices burnt offerings and fellowship offerings and gives gifts of food to all the people. This was also a custom at the coronation of a king, and, since the ark was the footstool of God's throne, David may have been emphasizing God's role as the great king over Israel.

Michal's reaction to David's behavior during the celebration is harshly critical. She apparently feels that the king should not have displayed such enthusiasm, behaving like "any vulgar fellow" (6:20). Perhaps she is afraid that David will be like her father Saul, whose ecstatic prophesying episodes bore some similarities to David's behavior (cf. 1 Sam. 19:24). In any event, David rebukes her by reminding her of the context for his behavior, that it was in recognition that God is Israel's true king and David but a servant. Moreover, the historian juxtaposes this exchange with the report that Michal never has any children, implying that the Lord is similarly critical of her response.

7:1–29. After the Phoenicians have built a palace for David out of the cedars of Lebanon, David wants to build a magnificent temple for the Lord (7:1–7). At first the prophet Nathan encourages him, but then the Lord reveals to Nathan that David will not be allowed to construct the temple. The reason is not explicit in 2 Samuel and differs from the Chronicler's explanation, that David is a man of war who has shed much blood and that his son Solomon will be "a man of peace and rest," who will be allowed to build the temple (1 Chron. 22:8–9). The implicit reason in Samuel seems to concern the direction of authority: who is whose benefactor?

Note David's reasoning: he sees the disparity between his dwelling and that for the ark of the Lord and proposes to rectify this. God's response is interesting. After God notes his previous practice, that he has never dwelt in a house before, he addresses David's concern that God not be angry over the disparity by pointing out that none of the previous leaders have been punished for not building God a temple. But underneath this all, it seems that the Lord's rejection of David's proposal is in fact aimed at the suggestion that David might be the Lord's patron. The use of first-person pronouns ("I") in the Hebrew of the verses that follow stresses the Lord's role as David's patron. Over against David's proposal to serve as benefactor for the Lord, the Lord asserts his role as benefactor to David (a role that is emphasized again in 7:11–12). Whereas it was commonplace in the ancient Near East for kings to build temples for their deity, this story restricts the king from making the deity indebted to him. And yet, the historian has to balance the direction of patronage with the fact that a temple is eventually built for God. Thus, it is assigned to David's successor (7:13).

While God does not allow David to build his temple, he does reveal through Nathan that he will continue to bless David and the entire nation (7:8–17). God promises to make David's name great, just as he promised to do for Abraham (Gen. 12:2). Powerful leaders will no longer oppress Israel the way the Egyptians or other neighboring peoples did during the period of the judges. Although Joshua helped plant the nation in the land promised to Abraham, David will plant them more firmly (7:10).

To encourage David even further, the Lord announces that instead of David building him a "house," God will build David a "house," meaning a dynasty. Unlike the judges or Saul before him, David's family will continue to rule for generations. The son who immediately succeeds him (Solomon) will build the Lord's temple, and his kingdom will be powerful and secure. In addition to all this, God promises to maintain a special father-son relationship with each king, assuring him of divine counsel. As the Lord's "son," however, the king is required to obey his commands faithfully. If the Davidic king sins, God will punish him, but he will not take the throne away from David's family (1 Kings 11:34). Eventually a king will arise who will reign "with justice and righteousness" (Isa. 9:7), and the Spirit of the Lord will rest on him in a powerful way (Isa. 11:2). Many of the later prophecies about the Messiah draw on this great promise to David.

In response to what he has heard from Nathan, David enters the tent he has set up for the ark and worships the Lord (7:18–29). As he prays he addresses the Lord seven times as the "Sovereign Lord," a title that stresses God's control over the nations and his covenant relationship with Israel. It is a title frequently used in prayer. David marvels that God has made such promises to him and his family. Unlike Saul, who became proud in his role as king, David seems to have maintained some degree of humility.

At the same time David acknowledges God's greatness and uniqueness and his choice of Israel to be his special people. David realizes that God's promises to him are intimately connected with God's favor for Israel in the past, as in the exodus from Egypt (7:23). With a grateful heart David prays that God will keep his promises.

8:1–18. The battles described in chapter 8 may have taken place over a period of years. Almost all of the nations adjacent to Israel's borders fought against David, perhaps in an attempt to keep him from expanding or simply from becoming too influential over the important trade routes winding through Israel. But by defeating them, David becomes the head of an influential kingdom (8:1–6). One of his first foes is Moab, with whom he has earlier been allied (1 Sam. 22:3–4). Another foe north of Israel and northwest of Damascus is the powerful Aramean kingdom of Zobah. By his victory over King Hadadezer of Zobah, David establishes a presence to the north of Israel. The Aramean kingdom between Israel and Zobah was centered in Damascus, located about sixty-five miles northeast of the Sea of Galilee and an important trade center. Damascus was closely allied with Zobah, and when these Arameans come to the aid of Hadadezer, David also subdues them and places garrisons in Damascus. Israel remains in control of this Aramean stronghold until well into Solomon's reign.

As a result of his military success, David receives significant wealth in the form of plunder and tribute payments from surrounding nations (8:7–14). Bronze, silver, and gold begin to pile up in Jerusalem. Even friendly neighbors such as Tou, king of Hamath, send gifts of precious metal to David. In recognition of the Lord's blessing on his rule, David dedicates many of these articles to the Lord, and later on they are used in the construction of the temple. David's victory over the Edomites gives him control of the rich copper mines south of the Dead Sea, adding further to his wealth.

Unlike the reign of many of the later kings, David's rule is characterized by justice and righteousness (8:15). The historian juxtaposes this statement with the preceding description of David's success to create a causal connection: David is successful due to his loyalty to God (8:15–18). David is assisted by several able administrators, including a "recorder" and a "secretary." The former may have been the head administrator of royal affairs and the latter something like our secretary of state. Neither position is mentioned in the summary of Saul's role in 1 Samuel 14:49–52, and this difference may indicate the growth of Israel as an administrative entity. Zadok the priest is mentioned for the first time here (8:17). A descendant of Eleazar son of Aaron, Zadok replaces Abiathar as the leading priest under Solomon, and his descendants hold the high priesthood throughout the rest of the monarchy. Strangely, David's sons are also called "priests," though the NIV 1984 translates the word as "royal advisers" (8:18). Sometimes priests did fulfill the role of advisors (cf. 1 Kings 4:5), but some scholars feel that David and his sons may have been priests of an order especially assigned to, and in this case including, members of the royal house. David did wear a linen ephod when he brought the ark to Jerusalem (6:14), and he is closely involved with the worship of the Lord throughout his reign. In later ancient translations, the reference to David's sons as priests is often toned down to, for example, "great men" or "princes," likely to avoid the suggestion that legitimate non-Levitical priests existed after Moses's day.

3. David's Successes and Failures (9:1–20:26)

Although for the most part David is a pious and effective ruler, his sin with Bathsheba is a terrible stain on his record. In the years that follow his adultery, David faces a rebellion led by his own son Absalom and another led by a Benjamite named Sheba. Jerusalem and all Israel are shaken by these events, and David struggles to maintain his throne. Because of the turmoil in his own family, the question of who will succeed him as king becomes an important one.

A. David's success (9:1–10:19). Early in his career David is known as a wise and fair leader (1 Sam. 30:24–25), and when he becomes king he continues to handle problems with great skill. His kindness to Jonathan's son Mephibosheth demonstrates his genuine compassion for others. As a military leader, David has known only victory in battle ever since his triumph over Goliath, and the Ammonites and Arameans learn about his military prowess the hard way.

In light of the covenant God has made with David promising to show kindness to his family forever, it is fitting that David remembers the covenant he made with Jonathan. When most kings came to power they sought to eliminate any survivors of the preceding king, but not David (9:1–5). Bound by covenant to his best friend, Jonathan, David is loyal to his oath and eager to take care of any of Jonathan's descendants. Ziba, who was Saul's chief steward, tells David about Mephibosheth, Jonathan's crippled son, who is living in the Transjordan with a wealthy man named Makir.

We do not know if Mephibosheth knew anything about his father's covenant with David, but he certainly does not anticipate that David will treat him so royally (9:6–13). Not only does David give him the income from Saul's land, but Mephibosheth is allowed to eat at David's table "like one of the king's sons" (9:11). Ziba and his family are given the responsibility of working the land for Mephibosheth, and from 16:3–4 we learn that Ziba really wanted control of Saul's land himself. For the time being, however, Ziba seems willing to serve Mephibosheth, and, unlike others who later rebel against David, Mephibosheth remains loyal to the king the rest of his life.

In light of the frequent fighting between Israel and the Ammonites, we might well wonder how and why the Ammonite king Nahash previously assisted David (10:1–5). Perhaps Nahash harbored David in some way while he was fleeing from Saul. Regardless, the old animosity is not far below the surface, and David's attempt to congratulate the new king is interpreted as a spy mission. David's men are badly mistreated. In the ancient Near East, beards were shaved only during times of personal or national catastrophe as a sign of deep mourning. By cutting off the men's garments at the buttocks, the Ammonites treat the messengers as prisoners of war. Humiliated, David's men cross the Jordan River and stay at Jericho until their beards grow back.

The Ammonites realize that David will regard their insulting behavior as an act of war, so they summon a substantial number of their Aramean allies for the upcoming battle (10:6–19). The small kingdoms of Beth Rehob, Maakah, and Tob lay to the east and north of the Sea of Galilee, with Zobah a little further to the north. (Note that David conquered Zobah and its ruler, Hadadezer, in chapter 8, after which there is no hint that he loses control of the region; this thus suggests that the events in this part of 2 Samuel are not in strict chronological order.) Faced by a powerful coalition, David sends Joab to engage the enemy in battle. As the leading general, Joab himself leads the best troops against the Arameans, and he sends Abishai to fight the Ammonites at their capital city of Rabbah, about thirty miles east of Jericho. Encouraging one another in the Lord, Joab and Abishai attack, with excellent results. The

Ammonites take refuge behind the walls of their capital city while the Arameans head north. Hadadezer, king of Zobah, hires reinforcements from across the Euphrates, while David himself takes the men back across the Jordan to meet this new threat. In spite of the additional troops the Arameans fall before David, and a number of kings are forced to subject themselves to him. Initially, David intends to punish the Ammonites, but when the dust settles he finds himself in control of much of the land between Israel and the Euphrates.

B. The turning point (11:1–12:31). **11:1–27.** At a time when David and his people seem to be thriving, the king commits adultery and murder. Although David repents and the Lord forgives his sin, this whole episode marks a major turning point in David's rule. From this point on David faces serious challenges from his own family and fellow Israelites and in the process nearly loses the throne.

Like Samson before him, David is guilty of sexual immorality, with all its consequences. While committing adultery is bad enough, David compounds the problem by committing murder as well. The second crime is intended to cover up the first—but he soon finds out that nothing is hidden from the Lord.

The historian starts the narration of this scene by noting that kings customarily return to the battlefield after the rainy season ends in April and May (11:1). This provides a gauge by which to judge David's choices. David and Joab want to complete the conquest of the Ammonites, so the army is sent to put Rabbah under siege. But David stays home, a decision contrary to custom and one that places him in the way of temptation. Thus he becomes involved with Bathsheba, the wife of one of his soldiers, Uriah the Hittite (11:1–5).

To make it appear that her husband has made her pregnant, David calls Uriah back from the battlefront under the guise of gaining information about the progress of the campaign (11:6–13). David sends Uriah home to relax with his wife, but Uriah refuses to go home

and enjoy himself when the rest of the army is exposed to hardship in the open field. His dedication contrasts sharply with David's self-indulgence. Sexual intercourse made a man ceremonially unclean and unfit for battle for a few days, and it appears that Uriah wanted to get back into action quickly. David keeps Uriah in Jerusalem one more day, hoping that he will sleep with his wife. To break down Uriah's defenses, David sees to it that Uriah is made drunk, but even so, he does not go home.

Frustrated by the self-discipline of Uriah, David now takes more desperate measures to cover up his sin (11:14–27). In a painful bit of irony, David uses Uriah as a messenger to send a letter to Joab asking that Uriah be placed in a very dangerous position in the front line. With Uriah dead, David will then marry his widow and legitimize the birth of Bathsheba's child. Joab complies by sending Uriah too close to the wall of Rabbah, where he is killed by Ammonite arrows. Joab clearly knows that this tactic is unwise and in the aftermath anticipates the king's displeasure at losing soldiers in this way (11:20–21), but we can surmise it is his loyalty to David that leads him to follow David's instructions. By way of contrast, David's loyalty to Uriah is nonexistent. Though Uriah is one of David's top thirty-seven soldiers (23:39) and more than willing to risk his life for David and for Israel, David mercilessly steals his wife and arranges for his death. Since only Joab suspects foul play, it looks like the perfect crime. Bathsheba mourns for her husband (perhaps seven days; cf. Gen. 50:10), then slips into the royal harem. It all looks very innocent, but the Lord notices. In his eyes David has broken the last five Mosaic commandments in this one brief episode. The consequences will be devastating.

12:1–31. The same prophet who told David about the eternal dynasty God has promised him (7:11–16) now appears to deliver a very difficult message (12:1–12). Although many months have passed since David's sin, he has apparently not reckoned with the significance of his deeds. Nathan's visit changes everything, as David listens to a parable and pronounces a death sentence on himself. The ewe lamb in Nathan's parable is Bathsheba, and the poor man is Uriah. David as the reigning king is guilty of misusing the power God has given him. The king is regarded as the shepherd of Israel, and David now realizes what he has done to his flock.

After pointing out David's guilt, Nathan announces that David will be punished the same way he has sinned. Violent death will strike his own family, and in subsequent years, three of his four oldest sons will die by the sword. Confronted by the prophetic word of God, David finally realizes the true nature of his actions (12:13–19). After David admits his sin (his contrition is only implied), Nathan informs him that God has forgiven him and will spare his life (cf. Psalm 51).

Notice the confrontation between the prophet and the king. Especially telling is that David's misdeed is characterized as despising the word of the Lord (12:9) and is thus cast as an offense against the prophetic office. Moreover, the analogy Nathan uses in his story of the rich man who steals the poor man's sheep is just the sort of behavior Samuel warned is characteristic of kings: kings are takers, and they will appropriate what you cherish (see 1 Sam. 8:10–18). Thus this passage betrays the same critique of kings and advances the image of prophets as dominant over kings.

In the years that follow, David continues to reap the consequences of his sins with Bathsheba and Uriah, starting with the death of Bathsheba's baby. For seven days David prays and fasts for the sick child with the hope that in his grace, God might also spare this little one. But the child dies, and David tastes the first bitter fruit of his sins. In spite of his pain, David accepts the death of the child as the Lord's will and does not continue to lament (12:20–25). Encouraged by the knowledge that his own sin is forgiven, David goes into the house of the Lord and worships.

Some time later Bathsheba has another son, whom they name Solomon, which is formed from *shalom*, the Hebrew word for "peace" or "well-being." He is also called Jedidiah, "beloved of the Lord." Both names perhaps reflect what David hopes for and expects of this son; both names also aptly preview the historian's assessment of Solomon's reign.

After a long delay, the historian returns to the subject of the siege of Rabbah (12:26–31), where David probably should have been in the first place. More than a year has gone by since Joab began the siege. At Joab's insistence, David participates in the final assault on the Ammonite capital and receives the honor for the victory. Of unusual interest is the seventy-five-pound gold crown taken from the king, part of the substantial plunder found in the city. Additional loot is taken from the other Ammonite cities, and the captives are put to work on

In the ancient world, conquered enemies often became slave labor (see 2 Sam. 12:31). This panel from the palace of Sennacherib (Nineveh, 700–692 BC) shows prisoners of war pulling ropes to haul a stone bull as part of a construction project.

various building projects. Slave labor of this sort played an important role in the construction activities of many ancient Near Eastern rulers.

C. Rebellion (13:1–20:26). 13:1–39. Although the Lord did not explicitly forbid polygamy, the story recounted in 13:1–14 illustrates why multiple marriages are unwise. Hatred and jealousy among half brothers was a constant problem and sometimes led to murder (cf. Judg. 9:5), especially when one's own sister is violated (cf. Genesis 34). It is unlikely that the heart of the matter in this story is an unlawful relationship: while Leviticus 18:9 and 20:17 forbid sexual relations with one's sister (half sister or not), taking a "wifster" (wife-sister) was commonplace if not encouraged, particularly in royal families. (This ensured, for instance, that any claims to the throne were kept within the family.) This episode probably reflects a power play by Amnon, perhaps to keep another pretender to the throne in line; in other words, Tamar is simply a tragic tool for getting at Absalom.

Taking the advice of his cousin Jonadab, Amnon pretends to be sick and asks that Tamar might visit him. When she is alone with him in the bedroom, his long-awaited chance comes. Tamar attempts to deter Amnon by suggesting his position as heir apparent to the throne could be placed in jeopardy by his action. Finally, in what is likely a last-ditch ruse to buy time, she suggests that David will allow the two of them to get married. In spite of these protests, Amnon refuses to listen and rapes her (which hints at his true motivation, the humiliation of Absalom).

Unlike the young prince Shechem, whose love for Dinah increases after he sleeps with her (Genesis 34), Amnon's love is not genuine and is surpassed by his hate for his rival. Thus, Amnon quickly has Tamar removed from his house: his purposes have been accomplished (13:15–22). Shamed and rejected, Tamar leaves in mourning, throwing ashes on her head and tearing her beautiful ornamental robe that signifies her status as a virgin daughter of the king.

Amnon's hatred for Tamar and Absalom is more than equaled by Absalom's hatred for Amnon once Absalom finds out about the violation, with all its implications for himself.

Like Dinah's brothers in Genesis, Absalom responds against the guilty party with vengeance. David is also deeply upset over what has happened, but, strangely, he does nothing to punish Amnon. At the very least he should have announced that Amnon's deed disqualified him as a contender for the throne. Just as Jacob's oldest son Reuben lost the birthright by sleeping with his father's concubine (Gen. 35:22; 49:4), so Amnon should have forfeited any right he had to the throne. Perhaps David is reluctant to take any action against Amnon because he himself has been guilty of adultery. David's failure to discipline Joab, Amnon, and Absalom and to control the strife within his family in general constitutes a major character flaw and reflects the tragic course on which he has set his family by his mistreatment of Bathsheba and Uriah.

In spite of his intense hatred for Amnon, Absalom waits two years before taking revenge on his half brother (13:23–33). He chooses a normally festive occasion, the time of sheep shearing, to invite his brothers to visit his land in Ephraim, in the center of Israel. To make it look legitimate, he invites David to join them, but when David turns down the invitation, Amnon is invited as the king's representative. Apparently none of the other brothers suspect anything either, until a somewhat drunk Amnon is struck down by Absalom's men, after which they all flee in fear for their own lives. At first there is a rumor that all the king's sons have been killed. David's nephew Jonadab—who is partly responsible for the whole situation in the first place—correctly insists that only Amnon has been killed. By killing Amnon, Absalom gains revenge for the rape of Tamar and eliminates a rival for the throne. With Amnon dead, Absalom is apparently the oldest surviving son.

While the rest of David's sons flee southward toward Jerusalem, Absalom heads north, toward the safety of his maternal grandfather's kingdom of Geshur (3:3), northeast of the Sea of Galilee (13:34–39). David used the same strategy himself when he sought refuge in his great-grandmother Ruth's native land of Moab (1 Sam. 22:3). In one stroke David loses Amnon by death and Absalom by flight. Absalom's absence allows David time to postpone a decision about how to punish him. As time passes, the king recovers from the loss of Amnon and his heart grows softer toward Absalom.

14:1–33. Since David responded so well to Nathan's indirect approach in 12:1–7, Joab decides to use the same method with reference to his cousin Absalom (14:1–11). The story told by the wise woman bears some resemblance to the struggle between Amnon and Absalom, but it is disguised to the extent that David can make an objective decision before applying it to his own case. He rules in the woman's favor and in doing so creates tension between his ruling and his banishment of Absalom. Once David has solemnly promised to spare the guilty son from death, the wise woman of Tekoa cautiously applies the decision he has made to his own situation with Absalom (14:12–20). Her reference to the reconciliation of a "banished person" to God may be an allusion to David's own restoration after he committed murder; it is also a powerful metaphor for God's love of and desire for all sinners. As a final argument, the woman refers to David's ability to make just decisions, such as a divine messenger would make. Although this may be partly flattery, David does possess excellent judgment—except when it comes to those close to him. By this point in the conversation David realizes that Joab has sent the woman to him and he believes that Joab is right about Absalom.

Grateful that the king has taken his "indirect" advice, Joab goes to Geshur to bring Absalom home (14:21–27). When he arrives in Jerusalem, Absalom is not allowed to see David, an indication that while he has been allowed back from exile, he is not fully restored into the king's house. Because of his good looks,

Absalom soon becomes very popular. There is special mention of his thick hair, which serves to enhance his vigorous appearance. In the ancient world, kings and warriors were often depicted with long hair as a sign of strength and courage. The birth of sons was also an evidence of manliness, and Absalom had three of them. He also had a daughter named after her aunt, Tamar.

After two years in Jerusalem Absalom demands to see the king to find out what his status really is (14:28–33). He wants David either to punish him or forgive him and to do so openly. Since Joab was instrumental in Absalom's return to Jerusalem, Absalom calls on his cousin for help once more. This time Joab is reluctant to even talk about the problem, until Absalom has Joab's barley field set on fire. This brings Joab on the run, and a visit with the king soon follows. In their face-to-face confrontation David kisses Absalom as a sign that he is forgiven and restored to the royal family. There is no indication that Absalom has repented of Amnon's murder, so it seems that some disciplinary action is in order—perhaps a clear statement that Absalom will never be king. Although Absalom may have known that he would not be David's choice as king, public censure might have made it more difficult for Absalom to gain support for his rebellion.

15:1–37. For four years Absalom develops a strategy to increase his popularity and chances for the throne (15:1–12). Pretending to be a champion of justice, Absalom wins the hearts of the people by agreeing with their complaints against the king. Handsome and charming, he personally meets large numbers of people near the city gates of Jerusalem, thereby ingratiating himself to the general populace.

All this time David apparently suspects nothing, so when Absalom asks permission to go to Hebron, David raises no objection. It sounds innocent enough, much like Samuel's announcement that he would offer a sacrifice in Bethlehem—just before he anointed a king in place of Saul (1 Sam. 16:2–3). Hebron was the site of the cave of Machpelah, where Abraham and Sarah were buried, so it was a popular national center. But it was also the city where David was anointed king by both Judah and all Israel—and where Absalom was born.

By now Absalom is probably close to thirty years old and David about sixty. Very few individuals know about Absalom's plans, not even the guests he has invited from Jerusalem. From the outset, however, Absalom enjoys the support of key individuals, especially David's top advisor, Ahithophel. With their help, the revolt has a good chance of succeeding.

Up to this point in his career David has never suffered a defeat in battle, but he is forced to flee his beloved Jerusalem in the face of Absalom's revolt (15:13–23). David does not want to subject the city to the horrors of war, so he takes his men and heads east toward the Jordan River, unsure how much support he would have if he stayed.

Accompanying David in his flight are the men who have been with him since the time he was a fugitive from Saul, as well as several contingents of mercenary troops from Philistine territory. According to 8:18 the Kerethites and Pelethites are commanded by David's general Benaiah, and the six hundred Gittites are probably from the city of Gath, where David and his men earlier served as mercenaries. Ironically, the foreign troops are most loyal to David, although David releases Ittai the Gittite from any additional obligation. Ittai refuses the generous offer, though, and pledges his loyalty to David. In the showdown against Absalom, Ittai will play a key role (2 Sam. 18:2).

Since David has been a protector of the priests and since he has brought the ark to Jerusalem, it is fitting that the priests and the ark accompany him in leaving the capital. Both Zadok and Abiathar are with him, and their presence seems to ensure God's blessing on David. Yet once they are safely out David sends the ark back to Jerusalem. It is particularly interesting that while David makes a declaration of trust in how the Lord will allow events to unfold, he also sets up a veritable spy network

using the priests Zadok and Abiathar, whom he is sending back (15:24–29).

Leaving his trusted companions behind, David continues his sorrowful trek up the Mount of Olives. At the summit he meets Hushai, another of his close advisors, who has heard the news about Absalom (15:30–37). David asks Hushai if he is willing to return to Jerusalem and become an advisor to Absalom. In this way he might contradict the advice of Ahithophel and talk Absalom into a bad decision.

16:1–17:29. To make matters more confusing, David encounters two members of the tribe of Benjamin along the way (16:1–13). The first is Ziba, Mephibosheth's servant, and the second is an angry relative of Saul named Shimei.

David knows Ziba from their earlier meeting, when David asked him to work for Jonathan's son Mephibosheth (9:9–10). Now that David is headed toward the Transjordan, Ziba brings him some much-needed supplies. The amounts of bread and raisins are identical to those Abigail gave to David at an earlier time of crisis (1 Sam. 25:18) and help Ziba accomplish his objective. Apparently Ziba does not enjoy his subservient position and so tells David that Mephibosheth is hoping to regain control of his grandfather Saul's kingdom. Since David is uncertain about the extent of the revolt, he believes the lie about Mephibosheth and gives Ziba control of Saul's estate. It is a clever move by Ziba, who profits from the political crisis.

On the eastern side of the Mount of Olives and still only about two miles from Jerusalem, David is confronted by Shimei, a man from the same clan as Saul's family (16:5). Still frustrated by the transfer of power from Saul to David, Shimei takes out his anger on David by cursing him and pelting him with stones. Calling David a troublemaker and a wicked man, Shimei asserts that God is punishing David for shedding the blood of the household of Saul. This may be a reference to the execution of seven of Saul's descendants because of the Gibeonite problem (2 Sam. 21:1–9) or a more general allusion to casualties in the civil war between David and the remnants of Saul's family. By throwing stones at David, Shimei implies that David should have been stoned to death for his crimes.

On the other hand, David's men feel that Shimei deserves to die for cursing the king. According to the law, slander of this sort was akin to blaspheming God (Exod. 22:28). But David does not allow anyone to strike Shimei down, perhaps because he knows his own sin was behind his troubles and he deserves harsh words. By committing the matter to God, David hopes that the Lord will turn the curse into a blessing. Although David will later spare Shimei's life again (2 Sam. 19:23), eventually Shimei is executed by Solomon (1 Kings 2:46).

When Absalom arrives in Jerusalem he is congratulated by Hushai the Arkite, the man David hopes will be able to nullify the counsel of Ahithophel. In spite of Absalom's suspicions, Hushai is able to convince him that he will serve the new king because he is David's son.

As expected, Ahithophel gives Absalom some shrewd advice (16:15–23), recommending that he sleep with his father's concubines. Usually a king's concubines belonged to his successor, so by this action Absalom strongly asserts his kingship. At the same time he states his complete contempt for his father. By sleeping with the concubines in a tent pitched on the roof, he also ensures that all Israel knows what he is doing.

Given the skill and the reputation of Ahithophel, it comes as a shock to see his advice rejected in 17:1–14. Ahithophel recommends that Absalom pursue David immediately, before he has a chance to escape very far or to organize his forces. If he had killed David quickly, then David's supporters would likely have paid allegiance to Absalom and the nation would not have been divided by a long and bloody civil war. It is a good plan, but Hushai tries to buy time for David by pointing out the fallacies in Ahithophel's suggestion. He refers to David's reputation as a fighter and warns that he will not be captured so easily. Appealing to Absalom's

ego, Hushai urges him to gather a huge army and make sure that he can defeat David's men.

As the historian asserts, it is in accord with God's planning that Absalom chooses to follow the bad advice of Hushai and in doing so brings ruin on himself. God will not allow Absalom to usurp the throne at David's expense, and thus God answers David's prayer. Moreover, because of Ahithophel's subsequent suicide, Absalom loses the services of his top advisor permanently.

Delighted with Absalom's decision, Hushai decides that he will nonetheless take no chances and will warn David to cross the Jordan River as soon as possible (17:15–22). If he delays and if Absalom changes his mind and begins the pursuit immediately, David will be in grave danger. Following their prearranged plan, Hushai sends word to David through the sons of Zadok and Abiathar. Unfortunately they are spotted and have to hide in a well on the eastern slope of the Mount of Olives. In a ruse similar to that used by Rahab (Josh. 2:5), the woman hiding the men sends the pursuers on ahead. This enables the two messengers to avoid capture and to cover the fifteen miles to the Jordan River. Near the fords of the Jordan the men urge David to cross the river at once lest Absalom attack him before daybreak.

Convinced that Absalom will lose the war with David and that he and the other leading rebels will be put to death for treason, Ahithophel decides to commit suicide (17:23–29). It is a tragic end for one whose counsel has been sought so avidly. His death is a sign to Absalom and his followers that their cause is doomed.

Meanwhile, David heads for the city of Mahanaim, north of the Jabbok River, the same city that Ish-Bosheth used as his capital (2:8). By this point Absalom has brought a sizable army across the Jordan, led by Amasa, a cousin or half cousin of both Joab and Absalom. Cut off from the luxury and resources of Jerusalem, David and his men receive valuable supplies from Makir and Barzillai, wealthy Israelites in the Transjordan. David will never forget their kindness (1 Kings 2:7). More surprising is the aid he receives from the son of the king of the Ammonites, whose brother David defeated in battle (see 2 Samuel 10).

18:1–19:8. As the battle draws near, David's men are commanded as usual by his nephews Joab and Abishai (10:9–10), but this time a mercenary contingent is led by Ittai from Gath (18:1–8). David volunteers to go with them but is dissuaded in view of the fact that the enemy wants above all to see him dead. As the troops march out to battle, David urges them to be gentle with Absalom. Since David and his men are outnumbered they choose the rugged terrain of "the forest of Ephraim" as the battle site (18:6). Aided by this unusual setting, David's men outmaneuver the army of Israel and kill twenty thousand (or twenty "companies" of) men. Experienced and intensely loyal to David, his men win a decisive victory and save the throne for him.

During the course of the battle Absalom somehow becomes separated from his men, and his head—or possibly his thick hair—is caught in a low-hanging oak tree (18:9–18).

Unable to extricate himself, Absalom is soon at the mercy of Joab, who plunges three javelins into his heart. In spite of David's specific order not to harm Absalom, Joab likely realizes that without Absalom the revolt will collapse. Although Joab had been instrumental in bringing Absalom back from exile (2 Sam. 14:1–20), upon his revolt Joab clearly felt no pity for the handsome prince. Absalom's body is thrown into a large pit, and a pile of rocks is heaped over him. The irony of this ignoble burial is not lost on the historian; he points out that Absalom previously erected "a monument to himself" near Jerusalem (18:18).

Whenever an important battle was in progress, the people who sent out the troops anxiously awaited news of the outcome. Naturally everyone hoped for good news, and the messenger was called "the one who takes the good news." Sometimes, however, the news was anything but good, such as the time Eli was told about Israel's crushing defeat (1 Sam. 4:12–17). As Joab prepares to dispatch a messenger, he realizes that from David's perspective the news about Absalom's death is bad (18:19–29). For

This burial monument from the first century AD, located in the Kidron Valley, has been traditionally identified as the tomb of Absalom.

this reason, Joab hesitates to send Ahimaaz son of Zadok, who has served as a messenger before (cf. 2 Sam. 17:17, 21). If David sees him coming, he will anticipate good news, and Joab does not want the king to get his hopes up. So Joab sends a foreigner, a Cushite, to take the news, although a little later he allows Ahimaaz to run behind him. By taking a different route, Ahimaaz outruns the Cushite and reaches David first. He tells the king about the victory but is unaware of Absalom's fate. Judging from his questions, David seems to be more interested in Absalom's condition than the outcome of the battle.

When the Cushite arrives, he gives David the information he wants in an indirect but clear way. David is crushed and begins to mourn his son's death (18:30–19:4). The pain is so great that David wishes he had died instead of Absalom. Over the years the tension between father and son has been great, but clearly David has no desire for such a violent outcome. Though the troops return in triumph, their shouting and celebrating are quickly stilled in response to David's mourning. Instead of congratulating his men, David continues to grieve uncontrollably over the death of Absalom. Although David's response is understandable in his capacity as a father, it ignores his responsibilities as the king and military leader. For this reason Joab confronts David and rouses him from his despondency (19:5–8). In a short and sarcastic speech, Joab accuses David of ignoring the fact that his soldiers have just risked their lives to win a crucial victory and that they deserve the king's profound thanks. By behaving as if he has lost the battle, David stands the chance of losing the support of the very men who have been so loyal to him. David responds to Joab's plea, and his presence in the city gate consoles the men.

19:9–43. After the rebellion collapses, the people in the northern tribes blame themselves for what has happened. They reflect on all the good things David has done for the country and decide they want him to return as king (19:9–15). When David hears about this sentiment, he sends word to the elders of his own tribe of Judah to see how they feel. Although the rebellion was launched in Judah, David is willing to forgive them for their actions. In fact David even announces that he will make Absalom's general Amasa the new commander of his army. It is possible that David has found out about Joab's role in the death of Absalom and decided to punish his military chief. Encouraged by David's forgiving spirit, the men of Judah enthusiastically urge him to return.

When David reaches the eastern banks of the Jordan River opposite Jericho, he is met by the man who cursed him as he fled from Jerusalem (19:16–23). This time Shimei is accompanied by a thousand (or a "company" of) other Benjamites, who may fear that Shimei's disrespect will bring David's wrath on the whole tribe. Bowing low, Shimei apologizes for his earlier behavior and begs David's forgiveness. David's men are not impressed by Shimei's "repentance" and urge the king to execute him. But in light of the end of the civil war and David's restoration to power, he determines that this is a time for conciliatory action, not revenge. David never fully forgives Shimei, however, and on his deathbed asks Solomon to find a way to put him to death (1 Kings 2:8–9).

Another piece of unfinished business has to do with Mephibosheth, Jonathan's son, who was accused of participating in the revolt (19:24–30). He wanted to join David in exile but was left behind by his steward Ziba. Since the time David left Jerusalem, Mephibosheth has remained in an unkempt condition as a sign of deep mourning. Aware that as a descendant of Saul, he does not deserve David's favor, Mephibosheth nonetheless politely asks David to rethink his decision to give Saul's estate to Ziba. Uncertain as to who is telling the truth, David decides to divide the inheritance between Ziba and Mephibosheth.

On a more pleasant note, David says goodbye to Barzillai, who sustained him during the difficult days in the Transjordan (19:31–39).

Although David wants him to live in Jerusalem, Barzillai declines the invitation because of his advanced age. At eighty he is too old to appreciate the finer things of life in the capital. He does agree to send Kimham (probably his son) to Jerusalem, and David is glad to oblige. The king never forgets the help Barzillai gave him, and he asks Solomon to treat his sons well even after David's death (1 Kings 2:7).

The split between David and Absalom is symptomatic of the more basic division between north and south, the ten tribes of Israel and the tribe of Judah (19:40–43). As the various tribes scramble to be present when David crosses the Jordan and reenters the promised land, some of the northern tribes have not yet arrived. Apparently the men of Israel feel that the absence of these tribes could be interpreted as lack of support for David. There remains the lingering suspicion that David is partial to his own tribe, whereas the ten tribes constitute the bulk of the nation. So, at a time when David seems to have won back the hearts of the people, friction is already developing between the North and the South.

20:1–26. In spite of their recent affirmation of loyalty to David, the ten northern tribes are quick to defect under the leadership of Sheba (20:1–7). Using a rallying cry that will be repeated when the kingdom is divided after Solomon (1 Kings 12:16), Sheba reasserts the power the tribe of Benjamin lost after the death of Saul. David enters Jerusalem without fanfare and tries to deal with the new crisis. But first he dismisses his ten concubines from the palace and places them under guard in separate quarters since they are linked with the first rebellion, when Absalom slept with them.

True to his promise, David appoints Amasa commander over the army and orders him to take action against Sheba. When Amasa moves too slowly, David asks the veteran general Abishai to take charge, again ignoring his strong-headed nephew Joab. Yet when the troops are sent out, one contingent is "Joab's men" (20:7), and before long Joab will lead them himself.

The other troops include the Kerethites and Pelethites, who were loyal to David during Absalom's rebellion.

About six miles north of Jerusalem Amasa catches up with the army, presumably bringing additional troops (20:8–13). As Joab steps forward to greet him, he stabs Amasa in the stomach with a dagger, once again eliminating someone who threatens his position as commander in chief. Joab knows how deeply obligated David is to him. As in the case of Shimei, David in his dying days finally asks Solomon to punish Joab for his treachery (1 Kings 2:5–6). After the death of Amasa, Joab takes charge of the army, placing his brother Abishai in the familiar role of second in command.

Meanwhile, Sheba shows respect for David's army by retreating to Abel Beth Maakah, a city north of the Sea of Galilee (20:14–22). After gathering additional troops, he takes refuge inside the walls of the city. When Joab reaches Abel Beth Maakah, he surrounds the city and tries to batter down the wall. Usually this was accomplished by repeatedly hitting the wall with a large metal-tipped wooden beam. When the people inside the city see the damage being done, they are understandably upset. The city is known for the wisdom of its residents, so one of the wise women asks to speak to Joab. Joab explains what he wants, and the woman sees to it that the head of Sheba is thrown over the wall. The refusal to extradite a political foe was a legitimate reason for war in the ancient world, and earlier David himself was forced to leave a walled city to avoid being handed over to Saul (1 Sam. 23:7–13).

Without a leader the revolt collapses, and the northern tribes acknowledge David as their king. They continue to serve David and his son Solomon for more than forty years, until they revolt successfully under Jeroboam I about 930 BC.

Each of the major divisions of 1 and 2 Samuel ends with a list of the officials of Saul or David (1 Sam. 14:49–52; 2 Sam. 8:15–18) and each list is slightly longer than the previous list, indicating the gradual development in the size of the royal cabinet. The major change in the list in 20:23–26 is the addition of Adoniram, who "was in charge of forced labor" (20:24). As the kingdom expands, David employs Canaanites and prisoners of war in various building projects, and during Solomon's reign even some Israelites will be used on occasion for this purpose. Adoniram continues in this position throughout Solomon's reign, so he must have been appointed in the final years of David's rule. Another administrative change is the appointment of Ira the Jairite as "David's priest," whose role may have been closer to that of a royal advisor.

4. Epilogues (21:1–24:25)

Like the book of Judges, the two books of Samuel end with nonchronological epilogues arranged in a chiastic A-B-C-C′-B′-A′ pattern. There are two incidents describing God's wrath against Israel (chaps. 21, 24) and several short accounts of the victories of David and his men (21:15–22; 23:8–39). Between these two clusters of heroic achievements are two poems written by David praising the Lord for his deliverance (22:1–23:7). Although their overall purpose remains opaque, the function of the two middle sections, David's song and last words, is transparent, as is that of the final chapter, which prepares for Solomon's building of the temple in 1 Kings 5–6.

A. The Gibeonites' revenge (21:1–14). Because of the possible reference to this chapter in 2 Samuel 16:7–8, it is likely that the Gibeonite problem was resolved prior to the revolt of Absalom. There is no clue in 1 Samuel as to when Saul became involved with the Gibeonites.

When Joshua was conquering the promised land, he was tricked into making a treaty with the Gibeonites, guaranteeing that they would not be put to death (Josh. 9:15, 20). Since the city of Gibeon was located in the tribal territory of Benjamin, not far from Saul's capital, at some point during his reign Saul violated this treaty by attacking and killing some of the Gibeonites. As punishment, the Lord afflicts

Israel with three years of famine during David's reign (21:1–6).

When David discovers the reason for this famine, he confers with the Gibeonites who have survived. Since the death of the guilty can turn away God's wrath, David agrees with the Gibeonites' request that seven of Saul's male descendants should be killed at Gibeah, Saul's capital. The number seven was probably chosen because it represented completeness.

As David assumes the responsibility of handing over Saul's descendants, he spares Jonathan's son Mephibosheth in light of the covenant they made. But David turns over to the Gibeonites the two sons of Saul's concubine Rizpah and the five sons born to Saul's daughter Merab (21:7–14). Ironically, Merab should have been David's wife as a reward for killing Goliath. The seven are put to death in April during the barley harvest, and the family of Saul is effectively wiped out.

Normally the dead were buried quickly, but not in the case of those whose bodies were exposed "before the Lord" (21:6) to atone for sin involving the whole nation (cf. Num. 25:4). So Rizpah heroically guards the exposed bodies of her sons until the rains pour down as an indication that the drought that has caused the famine is over. David then orders that the bones of the deceased be buried in the tomb of Saul's father, and he shows his respect for the whole family by transferring the remains of Saul and Jonathan from Jabesh Gilead to Benjamin.

B. Victories over the Philistines (21:15–22). Revenge is also the motive in a series of battles between the Philistines and Israelites. Ever since David's victory over Goliath, the Philistines have tried to take revenge, but without success. Four specific Philistine warriors are mentioned, and each of them—like Goliath—is tall and powerful. All four are "descendants of Rapha," probably a reference to the gigantic Rephaites (Deut. 2:11; Josh. 12:4).

According to verse 19 a man named Elhanan "killed Goliath the Gittite" (NIV 1984; see NIV note). Unless this is a different Goliath from the warrior in 1 Samuel 17, we seem to have a competing account of his death. In the parallel passage in 1 Chronicles 20:5, this difficulty is smoothed out by specifying that Elhanan "killed Lahmi the brother of Goliath." Some commentators argue that Elhanan may be another name for David, since monarchs often had personal names and throne names. Others have suggested that Elhanan, not David, was the man who killed Goliath and that the hero story was later transferred to David, perhaps in the course of its telling through the generations. If we choose not to smooth the issue out by identifying Elhanan as David or suggesting two Goliaths, then we should understand the David and Goliath story as one akin to George Washington and the cherry tree—it may not be historically factual but it is true in a larger sense, since it accurately reflects the man's character. After all, the whole account of David's rise to the throne

Philistines were one of the Sea Peoples, whose capture by Rameses III is depicted here in a relief from Medinet Habu (Luxor, Egypt, twelfth century BC).

is predicated on his ability to defeat the Philistines, and the story of the slaying of Goliath is used as the catalyst for his amazingly quick move into the national spotlight.

C. David's song (22:1–51). Just as 1–2 Samuel begins with Hannah's song of thanksgiving for the birth of Samuel (1 Samuel 2), it ends with David's song of praise for God's deliverance from his enemies. The song appears in almost identical form in Psalm 18. In both passages the same historical heading referring to Saul and other enemies introduces the hymn.

When David was fleeing from Saul he was forced to take refuge in a number of caves (22:2–4). These hideouts are sometimes called "strongholds"; the same word is applied to the Lord in verse 2 ("fortress"). David thus acknowledges that God is the true source of his security and the one whom he can call on for help.

In words that anticipate the experience of Jonah, David describes his difficulty as if he had been drowning (22:5–7). The cords of death were wrapped around him like seaweed. Because of his extreme danger, death seemed close indeed. In his predicament, David called out to the Lord for help, and in his heavenly temple God heard his cry.

The next verses (22:8–16) describe a theophany—the coming of God to defeat his foes. The imagery is similar to the description of God's appearance on Mount Sinai, when he descended in a thick cloud amid thunder and lightning. The earth shook as God spoke with Moses before the awestruck Israelites (Exod. 19:16–19). So powerful was God's voice that it sounded like thunder. In Judges the Lord sent a thunderstorm to bog down the chariots of Sisera and give Israel a surprising victory (Judg. 5:4–5, 20–21). There may also be an allusion in 2 Samuel 22:16 to the demise of the Egyptians at the Red Sea, where the waters were rebuked by a strong wind (Exod. 14:21). The cherubim mentioned in verse 11 are said to be transporters of the throne of God in Ezekiel 10, and this throne symbolizes the authority of the mighty king.

Just as God delivered his people in time past, so he reached down and rescued David from his powerful enemy (22:17–20). Instead of being hemmed in and confined, David was brought "into a spacious place" (22:20) and given freedom from danger and oppression.

Grateful for God's intervention, David reflects on God's goodness to those who serve him and live righteously (22:21–30). His assertion of innocence does not mean that he is claiming to be sinless but that he is seeking to live in accord with God's word (22:23). Since David is the king, he has an obligation to set an example for the rest of the nation and lead a godly life. His realization that God brings down the proud and exalts the humble (22:28) repeats an underlying theme of 1 and 2 Samuel. In his own struggle with Saul, David becomes well aware of what pride can do to a king out of touch with God.

David also knows that God responds in kind to the attitudes and actions of human beings. Those who are hostile toward God will eventually find that God will be hostile toward them (Lev. 26:27–28). Those who seek first God's kingdom and his righteousness will discover that he will bless them in remarkable ways (Matt. 6:33). Because of David's faithfulness as king, God has given him military victories, fame, and fortune.

Returning to the themes introduced in verses 2–4, David spells out in greater detail what God has done for him (22:31–46). With a sense of exuberance David tells how the Lord gave him strength, speed, and stability, enabling him to overwhelm the enemy. David describes the plight of his foes (22:38–43), who were crushed and trampled under his feet. When they cried for help the Lord did not answer; no one came to their rescue.

God delivered David from his enemies within the borders of Israel and in foreign lands. Though it had seemed that he was on the verge of dying, David was made "the head of nations" (22:44). As his enemies fell before him one by one, the kingdom of Israel grew into an empire stretching from Egypt to the Euphrates River. The covenant blessing promised by Moses has become a reality.

David knows that he does not deserve the credit for his success, so in the final verses of this song (22:47–51) he exalts "God, the Rock, my Savior!" (22:47). Through the prophet Nathan, God made a covenant with David, promising that his dynasty would last forever (2 Sam. 7:12–16); and David acknowledges that the Lord's "unfailing kindness" (22:51) was a guarantee that the covenant would remain valid. Such a faithful God is one whom David wishes to praise "among the nations" (22:50).

D. David's last words (23:1–7). The second song contained in the appendixes is much shorter than the first and gives us the last poetic piece attributed to David. Many psalms associated with David are in the book of Psalms, but this brief poem is not paralleled in the Psalter. As in chapter 22, David acknowledges God's blessing on his life and in particular refers to the way the Spirit of the Lord spoke through him (23:2). Ever since he was anointed as king, the Spirit has rested on him and inspired him to write and sing the psalms loved by believers down through the centuries.

Empowered by the Lord, David has been able for the most part to rule in righteousness, bringing peace and prosperity to the whole nation. His rule became the standard against which all other rulers of Israel and Judah are judged and the pattern for at least some messianic expectations. As his own life comes to an end, David rejoices that God has made with him "an everlasting covenant" (23:5), assuring his descendants of continuing rule. According to verses 6–7 and Psalm 110, this will ultimately mean the destruction of wicked men when Christ places his enemies under his feet.

E. David's mighty men (23:8–39). Like any commanding general, David knew the value of faithful, dedicated followers. Without the help of skilled warriors, he could not have established a powerful kingdom. Thirty-seven of his men deserved special credit for their courage and commitment.

A group called "the Three" fought so valiantly that they are singled out above the rest

(23:8–12). Josheb-Basshebeth killed eight hundred men at one time. In another memorable battle against the Philistines, Eleazar son of Dodai single-handedly struck down the Philistines after the rest of the Israelites had retreated. The third hero, Shammah son of Agee, performed a similar exploit against the Philistines. Refusing to flee with the rest of the troops, Shammah stood his ground and successfully fought the enemy by himself.

Another story about three heroes—probably not the same three just mentioned—tells how they broke through Philistine lines to get water from the well near the gate of David's hometown of Bethlehem (23:13–17). The incident may have occurred while David was a fugitive from Saul or just after he had been anointed king over all Israel. When the three men brought the water to David, he refused to drink it and poured it out as an offering before the Lord. By doing this he acknowledged God's goodness in giving him followers who would risk their lives for him.

Two other men performed exploits that were comparable to those of "the Three" (23:18–23). David's nephew Abishai once saved David's life by killing a Philistine giant who had threatened David (2 Sam. 21:16–17). Here we are told that he was also responsible for killing three hundred men in battle. Benaiah son of Jehoiada was in charge of the Kerethites and Pelethites, two valuable mercenary bands that constituted the royal bodyguard, and later Benaiah will replace Joab as commander of Solomon's army (1 Kings 2:35). On the way to becoming a leader, Benaiah gained fame for killing two of Moab's finest soldiers and "a huge Egyptian" who was first disarmed and then killed with his own spear. In the best tradition of Samson, Benaiah also killed a lion in "a pit on a snowy day" (23:20).

While not quite attaining the stature of the aforementioned heroes, another thirty warriors constituted an elite group of mighty men (23:23–39). They came from many parts of Israel, including Saul's capital city of Gibeah. Most of the individuals are otherwise

unknown in Scripture, except for Joab's brother Asahel, who died in the civil war against Abner (2 Sam. 2:23), Uriah the Hittite, the husband of Bathsheba, and Bathsheba's father, Eliam. The figure of thirty-seven given in 2 Samuel 23:39 apparently includes "the Three," Abishai and Benaiah, and possibly Joab, the indefatigable commander of the whole army.

F. David's census (24:1–25). For the second time in the appendixes David has to face the wrath of God (cf. 2 Sam. 21:1–14), but this time he bears more of the blame. It is a hard lesson for David and his people, though the chapter ends on a note of worship that paves the way for the building of the temple.

A comparison of verse 1 with 1 Chronicles 21:1 reveals a startling difference about the identity of the one who incites David to take a census (24:1–9). According to 2 Samuel it is the Lord, whereas 1 Chronicles names Satan as the instigator. The change in the texts highlights a theological difference between the historian of 1–2 Samuel and the historian of 1–2 Chronicles. The majority of Old Testament writers held a worldview in which the Lord, as the Creator of all, was also responsible for both peace and disaster (or "evil"; Isa. 45:7). Of course, in the case of the census, it is not simply that God incites David to do something wrong (which is little different from sending the evil spirit to torment Saul in 1 Sam. 16:14); rather, what is really troubling is that God would then turn and punish David for doing the very thing he has incited him to do. It is no wonder that the historian of 1–2 Chronicles would have reworked this passage. Yet there is more to the replacement of the Lord with "Satan": the view of the Chronicler represents a later theological development in thinking, one that imposes a strict separation between good and evil. Such a clean separation does not exist in most of the Old Testament.

It is worth pausing to consider the Old Testament view of "Satan." Contrary to popular thinking, for the ancient Israelites this figure was not the personification of evil, the archnemesis of God—this view developed in later Judaism and Christianity. Rather, "satan" in the Old Testament describes a character (human or divine) who functions as an adversary or opponent, or even a prosecutor in legal contexts (cf. 1 Sam. 29:4 [David]; 2 Sam. 19:22 [Abishai]; 1 Kings 5:4; Ps. 109:4). Even in the book of Job, the "satan" is not evil but is associated with the group of divine beings called the "sons of God" whose duty it is to serve the Lord (Job 1:6; 2:1; see NIV notes). The "satan" in Job is a sort of divine prosecutor whose task is to ferret out hypocrisy.

Sometimes the taking of a census was perfectly acceptable (Numbers 1; 26), so David's sin must here involve the motivation behind the census. In all probability David is guilty of pride as he glories in the size of his armies and the numerous victories he has won. Backed by faithful, highly skilled troops and courageous leaders, David may be overlooking his need to trust in the Lord, the one who gave Goliath into his hands. Even Joab recognizes that it is wrong to take this census, but David insists that he go ahead with it.

For almost ten months Joab and the other commanders travel throughout Israel, starting in the Transjordan and then counting all the able-bodied men west of the river. The total comes to eight hundred thousand (or eight hundred "companies of men") from Israel and five hundred thousand (or five hundred "companies of men") from Judah. After Joab and his men return David recognizes how wrong he has been and confesses his sin before the Lord (24:10–14). Earlier he repented of his adulterous relationship with Bathsheba when the prophet Nathan confronted him (2 Sam. 12:13). This time the prophet Gad is sent to David, offering the king a choice of three calamities. Faced with the prospect of three years of famine, three months of military defeat, or three days of plague, David chooses the final option, believing that the Lord will somehow be merciful in spite of the plague.

True to his word the Lord strikes Israel with a plague more severe than that connected with the Baal of Peor episode in Numbers 25 (24:15–17). Seventy thousand (or "clan groups") die as the angel of the Lord moves through the land, bringing relentless judgment. When the angel comes to Jerusalem the Lord has mercy on his chosen city as David cries out on behalf of the people.

As the angel with a drawn sword stands near him, David is ordered to build an altar to the Lord (24:18–25). The place where he sees the angel is the threshing floor of Araunah the Jebusite, located

Threshing sledge and fork on a threshing floor. David buys the threshing floor of Araunah to build an altar to the Lord (2 Sam. 24:18–25).

north of Jerusalem on a hill overlooking the city. Chronicles refers to this hill as Mount Moriah, and it will become the very site on which Solomon later builds the temple (2 Chron. 3:1). When David asks Araunah for permission to buy the threshing floor, the Jebusite agrees and even offers to give it to David along with oxen and wood for the offering. But David insists on paying for it, refusing to sacrifice burnt offerings that cost him nothing. He pays fifty shekels of silver for the threshing floor and the oxen, and according to 1 Chronicles 21:25 he pays six hundred shekels of gold for the whole site.

When the altar is built, David presents burnt offerings and fellowship offerings as a symbol of his renewed commitment to the Lord. These two offerings were also presented in the midst of an earlier national calamity during the time of the judges (Judg. 20:26), and Solomon will sacrifice numerous burnt offerings and fellowship offerings at the dedication of the temple. Coupled with David's confession and repentance, the sacrifices make atonement for sin, and God answers his prayer in behalf of the land. The plague ends as the Lord has mercy on his covenant people.

Select Bibliography

Anderson, A. A. *2 Samuel.* Word Biblical Commentary. Dallas: Word, 1989.

Arnold, Bill T. *1 & 2 Samuel.* NIV Application Commentary. Grand Rapids: Zondervan, 2003.

Frykenberg, R. E. *History and Belief: The Foundations of Historical Understanding.* Grand Rapids: Eerdmans, 1996.

Gordon, Robert P. *1 & 2 Samuel.* Library of Biblical Interpretation. Grand Rapids: Zondervan, 1986.

Hamilton, Victor P. *Handbook on the Historical Books.* Grand Rapids: Baker Academic, 2001.

Klein, Ralph W. *1 Samuel.* Word Biblical Commentary. Waco: Word, 1983.

McCarter, P. Kyle, Jr. *1 Samuel.* Anchor Bible. New York: Doubleday, 1980.

———. *2 Samuel.* Anchor Bible. New York: Doubleday, 1984.

Nelson, Richard D. *The Historical Books.* Interpreting Biblical Texts. Nashville: Abingdon, 1998.

Tsumura, David Toshio. *The First Book of Samuel.* New International Commentary on the Old Testament. Grand Rapids: Eerdmans, 2007.

1–2 Kings

Keith Bodner

Introduction

The final line of the book of Judges—"In those days there was no king in Israel, each one did what was upright in his own eyes" (author's translation)—might imply that a monarchy will usher in a new era of peace and stability for God's people. Such an era is *not* reported in 1–2 Kings. Instead, some four hundred years of Israelite history are narrated, and at times the political landscape is even more chaotic than in the book of Judges, as if that were possible. Some of the most colorful, disturbing, inspiring, and theologically subtle material in all of Scripture is presented to the reader of 1–2 Kings, a long work that rewards careful study and reflection.

Literary Features

Like 1–2 Samuel, 1–2 Kings was originally a single volume that eventually was divided into two parts, which together recount and evaluate the story of Israel's royal experiment. The customary title "Kings" might be slightly misleading since royal figures are only part of the cast of characters. To be sure, kings and their antics, rivalries, major feuds, minor squabbles, petty agendas, inspiring reforms, brave leadership decisions, and flawed pretensions form the backdrop and the necessary plotlines; but other characters also shape the story. Most prominent among these characters are the prophets, with a remarkable range of personalities and gifts. Nathan is instrumental in securing Solomon's throne, while Ahijah of Shiloh pronounces its demise. Elijah confronts Ahab and hundreds of Baal prophets and later throws his mantle on Elisha of Abel-Meholah in the north. Micaiah speaks of Ahab's last days, while Huldah speaks of the doom about to befall the southern kingdom of Judah. Along with an anonymous fraternity of prophets that often seems to be hovering in the background, this diverse group of spokespeople confronts the various kings and their times and brings a sense of accountability and historical memory to the table that might otherwise be lacking.

Whether it entails speaking a word in crisis (e.g., Isaiah in 2 Kings 19) or dispensing advice on policy (e.g., Elisha in 2 Kings 6:22), new contours of the prophetic office are detailed as the narrative progresses. Not only are we given insight as to how prophets operated during this stretch of history; there also are hints dropped along the way as to how things might work in the future. Moreover, there is a host of minor characters that populates the narrative, ranging from courtiers like Benaiah and Obadiah (who serve Solomon and Ahab, respectively), to the servant Gehazi (last seen testifying about Elisha's word in 2 Kings 8) and the high priest Jehoiada (instrumental in bringing the tyrannical reign of Athaliah to an end). Towering above all these characters—whether royal, prophetic, or part of the supporting cast—is the ultimate king, the God of Israel. The real king in this story has rebellious subjects and global concerns, yet comes across as remarkably long-suffering and pastoral. Although there is a wealth of divine patience, as the story moves to a conclusion discipline is exacted and God's people are humbled. Relentlessly faithful and more sovereign than readers might expect, in the pages of 1–2 Kings the Lord creatively refuses to be boxed in by anyone and resists easy labels or stereotyping.

Literary and Historical Context

Rather than read in isolation, the 1–2 Kings narrative is best studied as one chapter within a larger story. The collection of books beginning with Joshua and ending with 1–2 Kings—known in the Hebrew canon as the Former Prophets—represents a continuous narrative, the long story of Israel's experience in the land of promise between entry and exile. These books are often referred to as the Deuteronomistic History, since the book of Deuteronomy provides the theological backbone of the narrative. As an address from Moses to the people of Israel on the borders of Moab looking into the land of promise, Deuteronomy articulates the parameters of covenant faithfulness, and it is this standard by which the various kings and leaders of the future are measured. For example, Deuteronomy 11:26–28 says, "See, I am setting before you today a blessing and a curse—the blessing if you obey the commands of the LORD your God that I am giving you today; the curse if you disobey the commands of the LORD your God and turn from the way that I command you today by following other gods, which you have not known." There is, in other words, a consistent exhortation in Deuteronomy to "choose life" (cf. Deut. 30:19) and a summons to partake of the available blessings and the many advantages of not forsaking covenant relationship. A necessary corollary, as Deuteronomy also intones, is the possibility of cursing should the Israelites eschew such responsibilities.

Furthermore, Deuteronomy also anticipates the advent of kingship in Israel. Deuteronomy 17:18–20 lays out a number of criteria by which the king shall reign and concludes:

When he takes the throne of his kingdom, he is to write for himself on a scroll a copy of this law, taken from that of the priests, who are Levites. It is to be with him, and he is to read it all the days of his life so that he may learn to revere the LORD his God and follow carefully all the words of this law and these decrees and not consider himself better than his brothers and turn from the law to the right or to the left. Then he and his descendants will reign a long time over his kingdom in Israel.

It cannot be baldly asserted, therefore, that in principle Deuteronomy and the Deuteronomic History are against the notion of the monarchy. Instead, the institution *can* work if strictures are in place. Of course, kingship is intimated elsewhere in the Torah. In Genesis 17 both Abraham and Sarah are told that "kings" will issue from them, and the last words of Jacob include a reference to "the scepter" not departing from Judah (Gen. 49:10). Kingship also features in the Former Prophets. The book of Joshua foregrounds the prominence of the tribe of Judah, while Judges provides an introduction to the story of kingship on many levels (not least the account of Abimelek in chapter 9, and the final line of the book as quoted above). When the elders of Israel request a king in 1 Samuel 8, God himself condescends to the request and so begins the protracted royal struggle between Saul and David, culminating in the latter's eventual coronation and subsequent enthronement in Jerusalem.

In terms of the overall composition, 1–2 Kings forms the last installment of the long story of Israel's experience in the land. Indeed, the beginning of 1 Kings—with the aged David near the end of his tenure—seems to be something of a resumption from the narrative thread of 2 Samuel 20, the story of civil war that, save for the actions of Joab and the wise woman of Tekoa, could have been a disaster for the Davidic kingdom. Despite the rebellion's suppression, seeds are planted that

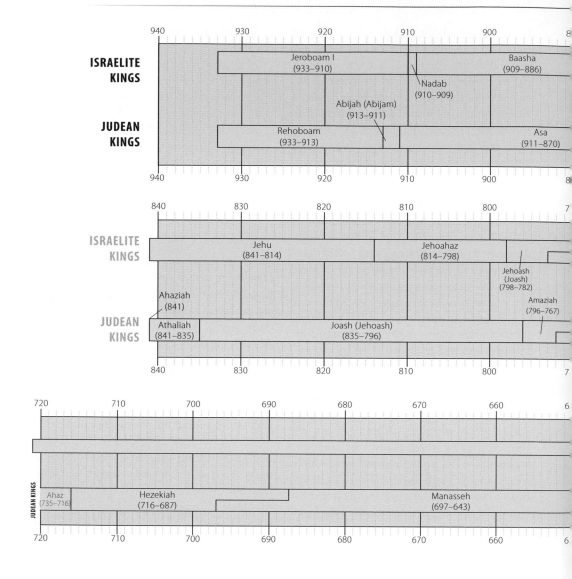

germinate when the northern tribes break away in 1 Kings 12. But prior to that, the Davidic torch is passed to Solomon, whose accession (in roughly 960 BC) and reign dominate the opening half of 1 Kings. The era of Solomon is certainly impressive on the outside, with the achievement of the temple and the glittering erection of his palace complex. Yet Solomon's reign is darker than commonly thought, incorrigibly marred by a series of concessions (such as becoming a son-in-law to Pharaoh) and great apostasy. Solomon does not bequeath the

best legacy to his son Rehoboam: within a week or so of Rehoboam's accession, the kingdom is permanently divided into north and south (933 BC).

Although Rehoboam manages to reign in the south and retain Jerusalem as the capital of Judah, Jeroboam presides over a northern kingdom that increasingly drifts into idolatrous instability. One could argue that at times the south fares no better, yet there is comparatively more stability because of the divine promise to David in 2 Samuel 7, where God guarantees

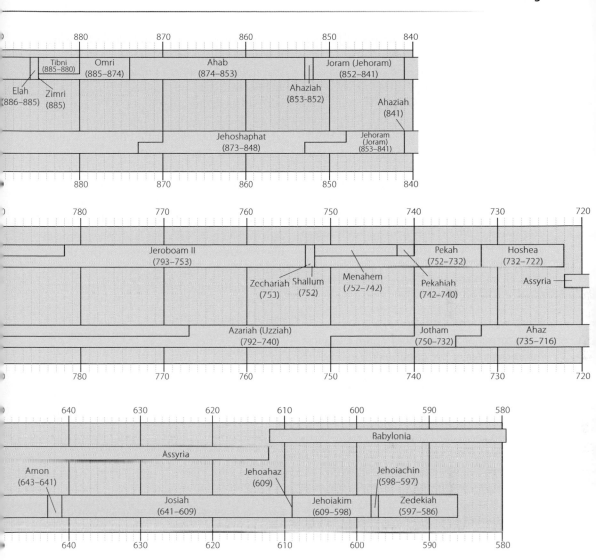

that a Davidic descendant will always be on the throne; much of the narrative in 1–2 Kings confirms that this promise is the difference between the north and the south. An acute rise in prophetic activity is particularly visible after the division of the kingdom, and correspondingly there also is a rise in international hostilities. Israel was plagued with plenty of foreign conflicts before—preeminently with the Philistines—but during the period of the divided monarchy the scale increases, with a number of Aramean and Assyrian offensives.

Such antagonism, coupled with an increasingly syncretistic worship and a string of ineffective northern leaders, reaches a climax with a devastating Assyrian invasion that results in the fall of the northern kingdom and the pillaging of Samaria (722 BC). The miraculous survival of the south (with Jerusalem still intact) is slowly countered by a mounting Babylonian presence in the region, and the days of the southern kingdom as a viable political entity are numbered. Nebuchadnezzar's sack of Jerusalem in 586 BC results in the demolition of the temple, and his deportation of a large number of Judeans inaugurates the period of exile.

When surveying the end of the book, we can discern an "envelope structure" between the start and finish of Kings. Just as 1 Kings begins with an aged king, so 2 Kings ends with an imprisoned king at the mercy of the Babylonians; therefore Kings begins and ends with the same issue: uncertainty about succession. The repetition of this issue is not arbitrary; it is, rather, part of the theology of hope central to the book, and to the Former Prophets as a whole. In other words, the future of Israel does not lie with a formal monarchy but rather with the promises and character of God, who out of this royal mess will bring forth a messiah.

Methods of Interpretation

In terms of method and approach, most commentaries of late combine three kinds of reading strategies for 1–2 Kings: historical, theological, and literary. Although there has been some recent controversy over matters of Israelite history, such epistemological matters lie beyond the scope of our inquiry here. With the crisis of modernity, it is not a bad thing that reading habits (since the Enlightenment) have changed and criteria for certainty now have different rules. Contemporary interpreters are far more aware that 1–2 Kings presents more than merely some banal quest for "objectivity," as though that represents the highest standard of truth. On the contrary, 1–2 Kings is filled with the author's *assessment* from start to finish (sometimes overt, at other times submerged just below the surface of the text). In this work we are dealing with theological narrative, which presents an intersection between human actions and divine sovereignty. In terms of theology, then, when reading this text the interpreter should attend to matters of theological significance, such as the role of prayer and the efficacy of the prophetic word. The best methodology incorporates the results of historical analysis with theological reflection.

That being said, there is little doubt 1–2 Kings is a sophisticated work of historiography, one that utilizes a number of different sources and archival materials and combines regnal formulas with other dating procedures. As mentioned above, 1–2 Kings is but one chapter in the larger the Deuteronomistic History. In addition, Martin Noth and other scholars in his wake have affirmed that the author(s) of 1–2 Kings experienced the Babylonian exile and from this vantage point were inspired to produce a story of Israel and a history of the nation's downfall. While Noth was fairly pessimistic in his conclusions, later redactors of this theory (such as Gerhard von Rad) were more positive, suggesting that the purpose of the author(s) was decidedly constructive: just as the nation was exiled because of disobedience, God has by no means given up on his people, and the examples of the past become a guide for the future. By any measure, a text with a high level of historical sophistication is presented here.

Even as matters of history continue to be debated, what is increasingly agreed on is the narrative artistry and literary sophistication of 1–2 Kings, with enhanced appreciation of the narrative dynamics at work in the story. It is this literary dimension (with issues of plot, characterization, point of view, irony, ambiguity, and spatial setting) that we will touch on during the course of our commentary. It would not be an overstatement to label 1–2 Kings as dramatically worthy of its regal subject matter, and all the vicissitudes of Israel's four-hundred-year experiment with kingship are worth studying, pondering, and preaching. There is much for God's people even today to hear in these pages. What is important is *not* that kings such as David, Solomon, and Hezekiah are flawless and worthy of emulation (because this is simply not the case—there are many shades of gray in these complex figures); instead what is continually stressed is the character of God, who keeps his promises and refuses to give up on a nation—even one on a passage to exile.

Commentary

1. 1 Kings 1:1–22:53

A. Accession of a younger son (1:1–53). First Kings begins with a point of contrast: back in 1 Samuel the young David is introduced as a man of action and seemingly boundless energy; now, his aged condition creates a situation in which Israel's king is more acted on than acting. The opening scene (1:1–4) reveals that the servants of David have implemented a search for a young maiden whose body heat will increase the king's waning temperature. It is unlikely that the servants are proposing a medicinal remedy; on the contrary, this rather appears to be a cover story either to prove the aged king's virility to a doubting constituency or to produce an heir to the throne. Despite a plethora of offspring, at this point in the story David has not explicitly named his successor. The servants' political motivation is evident when Abishag is found, from the village of Shunem, in Issachar—a nice union of north and south. The servants' plan, however, is foiled as the king (literally) "knows her not," and thus the reader concludes that the successor to David's throne can only be one of his (surviving) sons.

If there is a power vacuum, Adonijah is determined to step into it (1:5–10). As the oldest son of David—after the untimely deaths of his older brothers—Adonijah enlists the support of key allies (Joab the military commander, plus Abiathar the priest) and holds a feast for leading dignitaries. Like Absalom before him, Adonijah flaunts his royal pretensions with an entourage of chariots and runners, and also like Absalom he receives very little paternal discipline from David. Factions are apparent in the Davidic court: some officials are invited to join Adonijah, while others (including Nathan the prophet and the younger brother Solomon) are not. The comparison with Absalom—despite good looks and popularity—is an ominous sign for Adonijah's stately ambitions.

One gets the feeling that this is a dangerous place of political maneuvering, an impression enhanced in the next scene (1:11–14), featuring Nathan's conference with Bathsheba, the mother of Solomon. After outlining Adonijah's recent activities—boldly stating that Adonijah has "become king"—Nathan instructs Bathsheba to pose a question to King David regarding Solomon's accession: "My lord the king, did *you* not swear [an oath] to me your servant: 'Surely Solomon your son shall be king after me . . . '?" (1:13). No such oath is recorded in 2 Samuel, and a reader may have expected that such a momentous oath would have been mentioned *if* it was sworn. A slight irony will emerge here: Bathsheba is instructed to ask David about an (alleged) oath-swearing, and her own name means "daughter of swear an oath"! But still, the question remains as to why Nathan would counsel Bathsheba in this manner. We recall that Nathan has had dealings with David and Bathsheba before. In 2 Samuel 12:25, Nathan is sent by God to bring a new name for baby Solomon; in the book of Genesis a change of name involves a change of destiny, so Nathan may well infer—reasonably enough—that Solomon is destined to be his father's successor. Time is of the essence, given that

Adonijah is simultaneously hosting a feast with his powerful cadre of associates.

Bathsheba (1:15–21) is duly granted an audience in the king's private chamber, with Abishag in the room, a presence that foregrounds the rivalry of succession. Yet instead of asking the king a question (as Nathan directs), she utters an emphatic statement ("*you* yourself swore [an oath]," 1:17) and explains about the feasting of Adonijah. While she is concluding her story, as if on cue, Nathan arrives (1:22–27) and asks a set of questions of his own about the succession. Whether or not David ever did swear an oath about Solomon now becomes immaterial: he claims that he did and gives orders that Solomon is to be crowned in his stead (1:28–31). The anointing ceremony (1:32–40) is supervised by the trio of Nathan, Benaiah, and Zadok, with Zadok deploying the horn of oil in the midst

of considerable pomp—loud enough to make the earth quake.

The tremors can be felt as far away as Adonijah's banquet, an event taking place simultaneously with Solomon's anointing ceremony. Jonathan son of Abiathar (of the line of Eli and thus acquainted with rejection!) brings the crushing news (1:41–48) to Adonijah, exhaustively detailing the accession of Solomon. This breathless report disperses the guests and sends Adonijah to the horns of the altar, setting the stage for a confrontation between the two brothers (1:49–53). Throughout the entire transaction leading up to his enthronement, Solomon has not lifted a finger, so to speak, and certainly has not been allocated any direct speech. In the final scene of the chapter, this is poised to change. With limited options, Adonijah asks for an oath of amnesty, rather ironic in light of the earlier "oath" issues with Nathan and Bathsheba. However, Solomon does not give any kind of oath to his older brother; instead, he offers conditional terms, to the effect that if Adonijah shows himself to be a worthy man all will be well (but if not, he will die). One assumes that the freshly crowned Solomon will be the judge of whether or not Adonijah acts in a worthy manner. Solomon's first words are important for his characterization: the speech to Adonijah shows a glimpse of his wisdom, but one wonders to what ends this wisdom will be used.

B. Security clearance (2:1–46). David himself mentions Solomon's "wisdom" during his long speech to his heir, the last words of David in the narrative (2:1–12). The speech has two parts, beginning with an injunction to walk in the ways of torah, reminiscent of great speeches of the Former Prophets such as Joshua 1. David also

Four-horned incense altar from Megiddo (1000–586 BC). Clinging to the horns of the altar, as Adonijah did (1 Kings 1:50), indicated a wish for amnesty for those who feared retribution.

reiterates the divine promise he was given in 2 Samuel 7, but one notices that the language is slightly modified: the promise is unconditional when delivered to David, but here the king stresses that the promise is *conditional* upon his descendants' faithfulness. On the one hand, David simply could be extending some hard-earned advice, since his own life could have been much easier had he always walked in torah. On the other hand, maybe it foreshadows that Solomon himself might have struggles with faithful obedience. Either way, the second part of the speech gets worse, as David provides a list of leaders Solomon should "deal with": Joab, Barzillai, and Shimei. While Barzillai is to eat at the royal table, the other two are to be dispatched to Sheol, on rather dubious pretexts it must be said. The combination of keeping the commandments of the Lord and homicide creates a sense of uneasiness as David breathes his last, and Solomon takes sole possession of Israel's throne. In verse 12 the narrator highlights that the kingdom is "firmly established," perhaps undercutting any need for violence toward opponents.

The kingdom may be firmly established, but Adonijah appears to savor some further ambitions (2:13–18). Having been sentenced to virtual house arrest at the end of chapter 1, Adonijah takes a risk in deciding to confer with Bathsheba—but not nearly as great a risk as in requesting Abishag. The reader has already seen that any play on a member of the royal harem is tantamount to a claim on the throne itself, as the actions of Abner (2 Sam. 3:7) and Absalom (2 Sam. 16:22) grimly illustrate. Whether Adonijah is motivated by love or power, this must be perceived as a bizarre strategy that underestimates his younger brother: why would Solomon consent to such a marriage that strengthens his older brother's claim? While Bathsheba agrees to take Adonijah's suit to her son, we have just seen her execute an audacious undertaking on her son's behalf, and surely she is not going to give up that easily. In her conference with Solomon (2:19–25) that takes place while *both* are

seated on royal thrones, she undersells the "small" request of Adonijah (which is anything but). Solomon's reaction is aggressive: he interprets the proposition as treasonous and unleashes a rare double oath toward Adonijah. The double oath is ironic. Adonijah previously wanted an oath from Solomon and was denied; now he gets a twofold portion. Benaiah—who did not attend Adonijah's party in chapter 1—is summoned to carry out the death sentence, and he will have no shortage of contracts as the rest of the chapter unfolds.

Attention soon shifts to other foes. David did not mention Abiathar, but Solomon takes initiative (2:26–27) and banishes the priest to his hometown—though the king says he is worthy of death! While Abiathar's "crime" is unstated, one guesses it is that he sided with Adonijah, despite a history of loyalty to David. At the same time, Solomon's order intersects with a prophetic word spoken against the house of Eli (1 Sam. 2:27–36), reminding the reader that such utterances invariably find fulfillment in the narrative. Ironically, Solomon himself will be the subject of such a prophetic word later in the story.

Meanwhile, Joab hears about Abiathar's treatment and flees to the horns of the altar (2:28–35). One recalls that David gave Solomon orders about Joab, but why is Joab worthy of death? After all, he has been a staunch ally of David, participating in the cover-up of Uriah, and his liquidation of dangerous challengers such as Abner and Amasa undoubtedly benefited David. A plausible reason is that Joab must die as a penalty for supporting a rival, sending a strong message to any other pretenders that *this* is how such miscreants are treated in the Solomonic administration. Knowing the game, Joab becomes the second character to cling to the horns of the altar in as many chapters. Joab does win a moment of reprieve when Benaiah hesitates to strike him down in the inner sanctum, but Benaiah's conscience is assuaged by a lengthy speech from the king explaining that such a homicide is justifiable, considering

Joab's past conduct. With effective use of some royal hyperbole that cannot be taken at face value, the king's speech is sufficient to militate against Benaiah's ethical sensibilities: Joab is struck down, it would seem beside the altar, and for all his loyalty to David is buried "in the wilderness." Fittingly enough, after Joab is buried there are two promotions for new labor, as Zadok is elevated over Abiathar and Benaiah is put in charge of the army, a position previously held by Joab.

David had also given instructions about Shimei, a member of the tribe of Benjamin and a supporter of the Saulide regime, one who made the politically incorrect decision to curse David and call him a "man of blood." At the fords of the Jordan David swore an oath to Shimei (2 Sam. 19:23), but David also said that Solomon was a wise man and would know what to do (1 Kings 2:9). Solomon now addresses Shimei (2:36–46) and commands him to build a house and remain in Jerusalem, with a severe restriction on travel. In light of Adonijah's demise, it might have been wise for Shimei to "hear" (a Hebrew wordplay on the name Shimei) Solomon's injunction, but chasing some fugitives to Gath, Shimei temporarily leaves the city. It does not appear that Shimei was up to any malfeasance, but like Adonijah, he underestimates Solomon, who is informed of the trip to Gath and launches into another long speech denouncing an opponent and exalting the security of his own throne.

When Benaiah is dispatched once more, the reader knows the expected result. What is slightly unexpected is the final line of the chapter (2:47), echoing verse 12, "The king commanded Benaiah son of Jehoiada, and he marched out, reached out against him, and he died, and the kingdom was established in Solomon's grip" (author's translation). The repetition of the verb "establish" serves to reinforce a key truth: Solomon's ruthless purge was unnecessary, as God had already established his kingdom. While figures like David and Solomon are often glorified in the popular imagination,

in fact this narrative functions to draw attention to some of the murky ways in which Solomon uses his gifts. This account of Solomon is not best read as a set of tidy moral lessons; on the contrary, it is an honest and rigorous critique of Israel's failed leadership.

C. Wise options (3:1–28). If there have been any lingering doubts with respect to Solomon's decision making, then such doubts are not eradicated in the opening lines of the next chapter (3:1–2), as Solomon becomes a son-in-law to Pharaoh. In one respect it is obvious why an ancient Near Eastern king would desire such an alliance, as military and economic advantages would certainly accrue in an arrangement of this type. Yet a main purpose of the exodus is so Israel can be liberated from Egypt, not form partnerships where future ensnarement becomes a possibility. Moreover, the law of Moses—in which Solomon is enjoined to walk—counsels against such marriages (e.g., Deut. 7:3). The announcement of a marriage alliance with Pharaoh is thus not mere historical decoration; it is a programmatic statement about how Solomon's kingship will *operate*. When the elders of Israel asked for a king "like other nations" back in 1 Samuel 8, they hardly conceived that they would be getting a player on the world stage. The notice about the people continuing to sacrifice on the high places—worship installations perched on hilltops originally having Canaanite roots—underlines the idea of Israel moving toward a kingship model that is indebted to the surrounding nations and stands in uneasy tension with torah.

To be sure, the next section of the chapter (3:3–9) begins with a notice that Solomon loves the Lord, although the announcement is slightly qualified since the king himself also frequents the high places. The way Solomon demonstrates his love is by walking in the "statutes of David his father," but it will be Solomon's other loves that prove problematic in due course. For now the king cannot be faulted for *quantity* of sacrifices, and at the great high place of Gibeon—a spatial setting first introduced in Joshua 9—he offers a vast amount. The dream at Gibeon, where God appears and invites Solomon to ask for anything he wants, has often been viewed positively by past interpreters. Indeed, Solomon's response is effusive and correct: he asks for, literally, a "listening heart," which could also be translated "obedient heart." God's response (3:10–15) is equally long, and on the surface, it looks like a commendation for Solomon's choosing wisdom over riches, long life, or the death of his enemies (although there cannot be too many enemies left in Israel after the purge in chap. 2). But the fact that God gives him riches and honor *anyway* can be read in two ways: it might be a sign of approval for the king, or it might be a test. How will Solomon handle the gifts that God bestows? Will he stay faithful until the end of his long life?

Solomon's wisdom is immediately put to the test, as two harlots bring a challenging suit before the king (3:16–28). In the absence of any witnesses or DNA testing, it is a matter for the king to decide between the two claimants. The ingenious solution of calling for the sword not only resolves the maternal mystery but also marks the first time in Solomon's career that the sword will have been used for a positive purpose (as opposed to slaying political rivals). The public opinion poll at the end of the chapter is revealing: the people "fear" the king (NIV "held the king in awe"), aware that he has been given wisdom from God; and they no doubt hope that such responsibility will not be abused.

D. Constructive criticism (4:1–10:29). We assume this text is written for an audience that has experienced the crisis of Jerusalem's collapse, as an unflinching narrative designed to rebuild the faith of Israel in exile and beyond. Up to this point in 1 Kings, Solomon has established his kingdom and been given tremendous gifts, though small seeds of doubt have also been planted.

4:1–34. The next major section of the narrative recounts the highlights of the reign. Amid great construction projects, a critical element will emerge as well. At first glance chapter 4 might appear to be just some mundane lists, but in fact there are some important components of the plot contained here. For instance, the opening list (4:1–6) provides a directory of the king's administrative captains, and several names stick out. Abiathar the priest is still officially on the books (despite banishment), and there is a reminder that Benaiah has been promoted over the army (loyalty seems to be a common thread in the rest of Solomon's council). Almost hidden at the end of the list is Adoniram, in charge of the forced labor (cf. 2 Sam. 20:24, a policy started under David). The term "forced labor" ominously appeared in Exodus 1:11 and will become a central grievance that precipitates the division of the kingdom in chapter 12. In terms of genre, scholars draw attention to similar lists of offices from Egyptian and Assyrian kings, a further indication that Solomon's court is modeled on the surrounding nations.

The next itemization is of the twelve "district governors" whose designated tasks include providing daily bread for the burgeoning royal house (4:7–19) and collecting revenues. The stress on surnames and Solomon's own family suggests a degree of patronage, and conspicuous by its absence is any mention of Judah. Recent commentators point out that the king overhauls the taxation system by restructuring the traditional tribal arrangement into new taxation districts. If there are going to be exciting building projects, someone has to pay for them. The political advantage of changing the boundaries is clear: old party lines and borders are shifted, and the king enjoys increased centralization and a streamlined method of ensuring monthly income. Regardless of one's assessment of the ethical ramifications of Solomon's highly organized system of taxation, the success of the scheme is beyond dispute (4:20–28). From the Euphrates to Egypt, there is sumptuous prosperity, a blossoming court, and an absence of foreign incursions, and the district governors are able to collect a vast amount of food. Still, there is a note slipped in about a vast number of horses, something warned against in Deuteronomy 17:16. The people are living "in

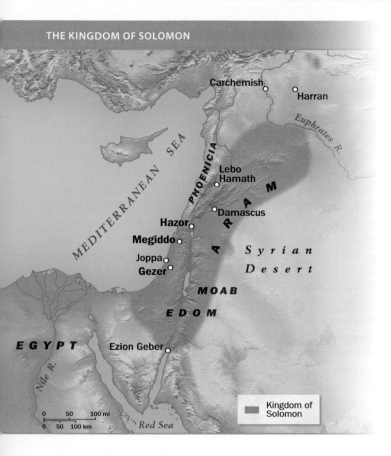

THE KINGDOM OF SOLOMON

short distance, it would seem, between broadness of mind and arrogance.

5:1–18. The next phase of the narrative outlines the construction projects (palace and temple), but amid all the architectural glory there will also be a subtle criticism of the royal administration. Without much background information, we learn that Hiram king of Tyre sends envoys to Solomon (5:1), having heard of his accession. The city of Tyre was a thriving commercial and colonial center; Joshua 19:29 refers to it as "fortified," and Herodotus mentions a venerable ancient temple. This is not Hiram's first appearance in the Former Prophets. Back in 2 Samuel 5, an unprompted Hiram sent timber and craftsmen to build a palace for David. Here he sends a delegation to Solomon, and the narrator informs us that he "loved" David (NIV "on friendly terms with")—the same verb used to describe Solomon's "love" for the Lord. Hiram does not verbalize any message, so the reader is left to infer what Hiram is really after. Solomon, however, does respond in his typically lengthy manner (5:2–6), and he starts by bringing up the temple. This is Solomon's first explicit mention of the temple, and it is spoken to a foreign king. Solomon asserts that David was unable to build a temple because of besetting wars, and we have to refer back to 2 Samuel 7 to figure out if this is a valid claim. Regardless, Solomon is interested in the cedars of Lebanon and skilled workers. The cedars of Lebanon will shortly become a prophetic metaphor of towering pride (e.g., Isa. 2:13; Zech. 11:1).

security" (NIV "in safety"), but at what price, and for how long?

The cosmopolitan dimension of Solomon's court is emphasized in the final section (4:29–34). The report underscores the king's God-endowed wisdom, which exceeds the greatest sages of the day, and his far-reaching fame. Solomon's intellectual authority extends even to matters of flora and fauna, with no shortage of audience. Even foreign kings journey to hear this original Renaissance man, a composer of songs and proverbs. A key question remains: how will these remarkable capabilities and the extraordinary gift of such wisdom be used? According to the NIV translation of 4:29, Solomon has "breadth of understanding," a phrase that could literally be rendered "broadness of mind." In Proverbs 21:4, ironically, the same phrase is translated "proud heart." There is a

Hiram's initial response (5:7–12) is an outburst of praise, surprising in the mouth of a foreign monarch. Hiram then delineates what he will do (float the logs by sea) and finally mentions his own expectations in the transaction: food for his household. A number of commentators argue that Hiram gets the better of the deal, but Solomon is willing to make it because of the unique quality of timber. He wants, in other words, both the materials and the highly skilled artisans that Hiram could supply, and in return provides a huge quantity of produce for Hiram's court. We have seen a marriage arrangement with Egypt; now there is a northern alliance. Pharaoh will prove a rather ruthless father-in-law, and while Hiram will never invade Israel, his presence will find its way into the very center of Israelite worship. In terms of Solomon's preparations for building (5:13–18), the king gathers a workforce of "conscripted laborers"—slightly toned down in the NIV, but again the same word as Exodus 1:10, "forced labor." But at least there are rotating crews, who have superintendents in charge. The king appears to be acting unilaterally, since there is no mention of prophets or priests. Israel certainly has a king like the other nations—hopefully Israel's worship will be different.

6:1–37. Formal commencement of temple construction is prefaced with an important temporal notice (6:1). The project begins 480 years after the exodus, locating it at roughly the halfway point between the exodus *from* Egypt and exile *to* Babylon. How have the people of Israel fared in the promised land? Have they received a passing grade? The temple project thus becomes a type of midterm exam of Israel's faithfulness. Further, construction begins in the month of "Ziv, the second month." Here we have a conflation of two different calendars: the old Canaanite agricultural calendar ("Ziv") and also Babylonian ("the second month"). The halfway point between (past) captivity in Egypt and (future) captivity in Babylon is brought to the fore just as the building begins.

Starting with the external structure, the size of the edifice is delineated (6:2–10). A careful sketch of the dimensions is given, including windows (for natural lighting or ventilation) and side chambers. There is also a note about tools *not* to be used in the temple precinct, creating a sacred ambiance even during construction. Yet even in this floor-to-ceiling description some scholars are uneasy, as they believe that aspects of the blueprints have been borrowed from architectural models of the surrounding nations, including Canaanite and Phoenician designs. Since Hiram's workers are involved, this would not be overly surprising.

The pivot point of this section comes in the form of an unmediated divine word, an interruption of sorts directly from God to Solomon (6:11–13). In my view, the chapter is built around this theological utterance, where God furnishes the king with a careful warning by means of an "if . . . then" equation. If the king does not walk with God, it is possible that God will abandon his people, and therefore even the nicest temple does not grant immunity from obedience.

There is no recorded response from the normally loquacious Solomon to this divine word. Instead, the "tour" of the building site continues (6:14–36) with an almost bewildering degree of ornate specificity. While it is easy to get lost amid the details, at least "the ark" has considerable prominence and functions as a reminder of God's provision, promise, and presence. One hopes that God's word of caution is not lost in the midst of the tour, but it is possible that occasionally God's people are more caught up with building programs than relationship and covenant. The concluding lines of the chapter (6:37–38), though, imply that there is much to admire in this project. The garden plants (flowers and palm trees) and cherubim remind us of the creation narrative, and the reference to "seven" years to "finish" the sanctuary is the same language used in the opening chapters of Genesis. If the fidelity of the king and the worshiping community is as pure as the gold used in the temple, then there is reason for optimism at this key point in Israel's history.

7:1–51. The next section begins with another temporal notice (7:1), informing the reader that Solomon took thirteen years to build his own house. On the one hand, it might be a simple matter of practicality: the palace is vast, and therefore requires more time. On the other hand, there could be a subtle comment on the king's priorities, and where his attention will eventually be diverted. The NIV recognizes the latter by capturing the contrastive element of the Hebrew text ("however").

What cannot be denied is the impressiveness of the palace (7:2–12). Named "The House of the Forest of Lebanon" (RSV; cf. KJV), the central palace is a massive structure that must have been quite a feat of engineering. The "palace" is not limited to a single building; included in this larger development are centers of public administration, with courtyards, the "Hall of Justice," and a separate residence for Pharaoh's daughter (a reminder of the marriage alliance with Egypt). Historians inform us that Egyptian monarchs were not quick to give their daughters in marriage, so perhaps Pharaoh's daughter is worthy of special treatment in Solomon's harem.

Erecting the palace compound must have been a very expensive undertaking, since its size virtually dwarfs the temple. Is the temple the most noticeable structure in Jerusalem or more of an appendage in the royal facility?

After the palatial digression, the interior design of the temple becomes the focus (7:13–40). A signal moment is the arrival of Huram, expressly summoned by Solomon. Huram lays claim to an international pedigree: his mother is a "widow" from the northern tribe of Naphtali, while his father was a skilled artisan from Tyre—thus Huram can boast of having both Israelite and Phoenician roots. Huram may have had a hybrid genealogy, but there is no doubting his considerable talents, attested by the substantial catalog of his works: the central columns (emblematically named Jakin ["established"] and Boaz ["strength"]), the Sea (a water tank, perhaps symbolizing how chaos is subdued in the sanctuary), along with movable stands and equipment (ideally a celebration of the Lord's kingship). During this guided tour of the temple furnishings it seems as if the reader is given the king's perspective of these magnificent works. We trust that all is done with genuine piety and not with a desire to keep up with the other nations. Huram's consultancy draws to a close with an inventory (7:41–51) of his aesthetically pleasing designs, along with a dedication of the objects collected during David's (many) battles,

> The Ain Dara temple in Syria (tenth–ninth century BC) is similar to Solomon's temple in its architectural design.

suggesting that the treasuries are well stocked and the temple is a place of material prosperity.

8:1–66. Even though two long chapters describe the building and contents of the temple, nothing substantial has yet happened. That is poised to change in the next major unit of the narrative, a stretch of text that describes the first activities and ceremonies in the newly built house. The king summons the elders (8:1–11) during the month of "Ethanim" (seventh month). Coinciding with the Feast of Tabernacles, this is an ideal time to bring the ark into the temple due to the number of people in the city and the sense of occasion that the feast carries. Among the assembled dignitaries are representatives of the "tribes" of Israel—rather than the reorganized tax districts enumerated in chapter 4—as well as priests and Levites (a group that has not been prominent so far in Solomon's reign). The temple is essentially publicized as the successor to the portable sanctuary and betokens that "place" described in Deuteronomy (e.g., 12:5). In the midst of the ceremony is a prompt from the narrator that the ark is empty *except* for the tablets of the law, reinforcing the obligation of obedience. As the sanctuary is filled with divine glory (echoing Exodus 40), there is a powerful reminder of God's commitment to his people.

Despite a bevy of priests on hand, it is the king who presides as the master of ceremonies (8:12–21). Just before moving into his formal address, Solomon supplies a "quotation" (see Deut. 4:11) in response to the enveloping presence of God, followed by his own comment that God will reside in the temple "forever." In light of the end of 2 Kings, God certainly will not dwell there forever, but it is an apt quotation for the occasion. Along with the requisite praise, Solomon's address also features a considerable amount of emphasis on the electoral status of the Davidic line. Although the success of the ceremony cannot be refuted, the opportunity is also taken (in this very public setting) to promote Solomon's kingship. It would probably be unfair to say that the king's opening words are

overtly political, but at the same time—given all the elders who are assembled, from a host of interest groups—the publicity cannot hurt.

Solomon's exhaustive prayer (8:22–53) merits extensive analysis, but several facets can at least be noted: the mention of the conditional dynamic for the Davidic line is laudable; an almost "exilic" spirituality emerges, there is an inclusive embrace of the foreigner, and there is sizable reference to the necessity of individual and corporate forgiveness for crimes and misdemeanors. A number of commentators point out that when the prayer as a whole is surveyed, it is evident that Solomon's public discourse features an impressive theological synthesis that must appease the various interest groups assembled. Even if there is a fair bit of promotion of the Davidic line, there is also an unambiguous recognition of God's transcendence, and one guesses that the prayer must have had an overwhelmingly positive reception. The concluding stage of the ceremony (8:54–66) comprises a corporate blessing by the king (with a call for fully committed [Hebrew *shalom*] hearts), abundant sacrifices, and a joyful dismissal. If the nation can remain this united, then Solomon's leadership will bequeath an enduring legacy.

9:1–28. After a chapter fraught with spectacle and discourse of great acclaim, a more forceful speech (9:1–9) occurs, as God again appears to Solomon, just as at Gibeon in chapter 3, where Solomon asked for a "listening heart" (see commentary on 3:1–28). God's word here begins with a stunning acknowledgment that he has heard the king's prayer, he has sanctified the temple, and his eyes will always be on it. But immediately the word continues with an intense admonition about the king's personal conduct, with a rather ominous mention of serving and paying homage to "other gods." The consequences of royal disobedience involve more than the king alone: there are implications for all Israel, and a dire warning of eviction from the land that houses the temple. Should exile occur, Israel will become a "proverb" (NIV "byword"), an ironic situation considering the superscription to the book of Proverbs. The glorious "house" that Solomon has just finished building will be desolate; and without theological vigilance, it could become a temple of gloom.

God's speech makes it clear that the king's office is a position of trust. Again, there is no response from Solomon, but it is not accidental that the next part of the chapter unfolds a series of transactions from the king's reign. Indeed, this section looks like an abrupt switch to a collection of somewhat random miscellany, but this is far from the case; there is a common thread woven throughout. The first report is of further dealings with Hiram (9:10–23), without whose assistance there would have been a rather different temple. One immediately recalls that the portable tabernacle in the wilderness was built with freewill offerings of God's people; by contrast, the permanent temple in Jerusalem was procured through international trade and forced labor. Hiram's "payoff" in the end is a number of villages in northern Israel; from the exilic point of view, land for gold is not a good investment. Real estate deals are beyond the king's purview. In addition to partnership with Hiram, Solomon has also made a marriage alliance with Pharaoh, who proves to be a meddlesome father-in-law. The plethora of royal building ventures is carried out by means of forced labor, with a range of projects. The final section of the chapter (9:24–28) notes the relocation of Pharaoh's daughter, Solomon's religious observances, and naval activities with Hiram. The foray into shipbuilding is a lucrative one, netting Solomon an enormous quantity of gold to deposit in his burgeoning coffer. Overall, however, one senses that this entire section of the text is designed to imply that the king—who has asked for a "listening heart"—might be acoustically challenged. It has taken twenty years for Solomon to build both temple and palace, but now, at the halfway point of his career, time is running out to avert a plague on *both* of the king's houses.

10:1–29. The state visit of the iconic Queen of Sheba (10:1–13) is justly famous, although not much is known about her, and the location of Sheba—possibly in Arabia—is uncertain (mentioned in the gospels as "the ends of the earth," e.g., Matt. 12:42). An exotic visitor of immense wealth and stature, the queen is almost an alter ego of Solomon himself. She comes to test Solomon with "riddles" (NIV "hard questions"), a term most recently seen in the Samson story; Israel's urbane monarch passes the test with flying colors. Her theological affirmations on one level are astonishing, but on another level we wonder how much is standard courtly rhetoric, in the same manner as Hiram's fulsome praise in chapter 5. Since Hiram is parenthetically mentioned in verse 11, the comparison is plausible. Solomon passes the test of the Queen of Sheba, but hers is not the only test that the king will face.

The amount of gold that the queen gives Solomon actually pales in comparison to Solomon's yearly income, outlined in the next section of the chapter (10:14–25). With 666 talents per annum, the question quickly becomes: what on earth can he do with it all? Solomon does not lack creative ideas, as the gold is used for crafting shields, a massive throne, and household utensils, and as a commodity for international business. Despite all the sparkle, this section of the chapter cannot be properly understood apart from Deuteronomy 17:16–17, the so-called regulations of the king:

> The king, moreover, must not acquire great numbers of horses for himself or make the people return to Egypt to get more of them, for the LORD has told you, "You are not to go back that way again." He must not take many wives, or his heart will be led astray. He must not accumulate large amounts of silver and gold.

God has given assurance in chapter 3 that Solomon will be rich, and it is impossible to deny that reality here in the latter stages of chapter 10. Most likely a host of people would have been impressed by such riches and could well have pointed to such prosperity as sure signs of God's blessing and favor. In just a few short years the nation of Israel has achieved a completely new position as a competitor on the worldwide stage. As I suggested earlier, however, Solomon's enormous wealth has the elements of a test: how will the king handle these resources? Will these riches be used faithfully, or—as in the parable of the soils in Mark 4—will they prove to be a snare? Deuteronomy 17 advises against multiplying gold because of the sinister potential that causes so many to wander astray. That same text further proscribes the accumulation of horses, yet horses get a lot of attention in the closing stages of this chapter (10:26–29). Notably, the price for importing a horse from Egypt is given *in silver*, meaning the king could afford lavish numbers because of his gigantic income. In the book of Job the horse is symbolic of war and power. Here in 1 Kings 10 the horse has a similar symbolic dimension entailing military arrogance. Finally, Deuteronomy 17 also warns against the king's multiplying of wives, a subject reserved for the final chapter on Solomon's reign.

E. Divided heart, divided nation (11:1–12:33). It cannot be an accident that right after a lengthy description of Solomon's stockpile of gold and horses, we are moved directly into the stage of the narrative commonly referred to as the king's fall. In fact, "fall" might not be the most accurate term: in light of the warning signs throughout, we may have anticipated that the Solomonic enterprise would come crashing down before too long. Judgment is delayed—surely because of God's forbearance—but the entire nation is implicated in Solomon's apostasy.

11:1–43. The first installment (11:1–13) begins abruptly: "But Solomon loved many foreign women, and Pharaoh's daughter" (author's translation), once again in opposition to Deuteronomy 17. The number of wives is staggering and must be meant to reflect the vast network of political alliances formed by Solomon. The wives and concubines are only one element, however, as the section continues with a long chronicle of idolatry, mentioning a plethora of deities and installations for their worship that Solomon sponsors, including the spatial setting of the Mount of Olives. Solomon is negatively compared with his father David, who, for all his faults (and he had his share of wives), could not be impeached for idolatry, seemingly the thrust of verse 4. Once more God speaks to Solomon, but this time the warnings are over and a decision is announced: the king's divided heart will lead to a divided nation. Reminiscent of the earlier conflict between Saul and David, an underling will arise to inherit the kingdom, yet one tribe will remain under the aegis of the Davidic house, on account of the promise articulated in 2 Samuel 7.

By means of a flashback (11:14–22) the audience is also informed that Solomon's kingdom had some serious opposition. When the reader is told that the Lord raised up Hadad of Edom, we note that the specific Hebrew term *satan* ("adversary") is used, a stunning contrast with Solomon's earlier declaration to Hiram (5:18) that no *satan* can be found on any side. This is a graphic illustration that Solomon's words can be hollow. In fact, Solomon's adversaries may be more subtle, since Hadad—like Solomon himself—marries into the Egyptian royal family, and therefore Solomon and Hadad may well share the same father-in-law. Ironically, Hadad is willing to return to his homeland only *after* the death of the fearsome Joab, whom Benaiah executes under orders of the king. As it turns out, Hadad of Edom is not the only adversary, since Rezon of Damascus is also listed as a foe (11:23–25). Several commentators observe that neither Rezon nor Hadad is portrayed as actually doing anything but rather as creating general mischief. When read in tandem, the account of the careers of Rezon and Hadad anticipates that of the next adversary, Jeroboam. Furthermore, both Rezon and Hadad symbolize and foreshadow God's use of the Assyrian and Babylonian leaders against the people of Israel.

Solomon's opponents are not only external but internal as well. Jeroboam (11:26–40) is of northern provenance, and his industriousness captures the king's attention, in such a way that he is rewarded with a key promotion over the northern labor force. But Solomon is not the only one to notice Jeroboam: for no specified reason, Jeroboam receives an oracle, delivered by Ahijah of Shiloh. Ahijah has no introduction and has not appeared previously in the narrative, but his hometown of Shiloh is certainly acquainted with rejected houses and divine judgment (see 1 Sam. 4:12–22; cf. Ps. 78:60; Jer. 7:12, 14). The crux of Ahijah's oracle is transmitted by means of a wordplay, as he tears Jeroboam's robe (Hebrew *salmah*) to underscore the tearing of the kingdom from Solomon (Hebrew *shelomoh*). One purpose of a wordplay in Hebrew is to signal a reversal of fortune. Like the kingdom of Saul (who is on the wrong end of a garment-tearing episode in 1 Samuel 15), Solomon's kingdom—with all the building projects that impress a consumer culture—is about to be dismantled. We should bear in mind that Ahijah's word makes clear that Jeroboam's kingship is conditional from the outset, predicated on his "listening" (exactly what Solomon has not done). If he is obedient, he will have a lasting kingdom.

No response from Jeroboam is recorded, but Solomon reacts by trying to kill Jeroboam. It is a mystery how Solomon finds out, since verse 29 describes Jeroboam and Ahijah as "alone out in the country," but the remark does foreground the conflict between the king's power and the prophet's word that will be with us until the end of 2 Kings. To save his life, Jeroboam—like others before him—flees to Egypt. The king of Egypt, as we have seen, has a habit of harboring Solomon's opponents.

A short obituary for King Solomon closes the chapter (11:41–43), with mention of his deeds and wisdom, but no word about his negligible commitment to orthodoxy and his vacuous worship of the Lord. He is succeeded by his son Rehoboam, but the reader knows that the son has inherited a kingdom on the threshold of partition.

12:1–33. The story of the schism begins in Shechem (12:1–19), most recently the site where the rogue Abimelek was declared king back in Judges 9. For Rehoboam's coronation ceremony, Jeroboam returns from Egypt and is present (as de facto leader?) along with a delegation, which lodges its principal complaint: the long hours and harsh working conditions under Solomon are making it difficult to happily dwell under fig and vine. The advice of the elders to Rehoboam indicates that the northerners' claim is not unreasonable, and the elders' advocacy of servant leadership—surely not something Solomon ever embodied—reveals *their* wisdom. That Rehoboam rejects their counsel and secures a second opinion from his cronies (described as "young men," in contrast to the elders) does not speak well of his political acumen. The cronies are also crude, as it is more likely that the NIV's "little finger" in verse 10 should be more coarsely understood as a reference to male genitalia. Rehoboam heeds most of their counsel, but verse 15 represents a powerful intersection of the divine will and human folly: it is the Lord's will that the kingdom should divide, and simultaneously Rehoboam's inept leadership is the vehicle for the fulfillment of the prophetic word spoken by Ahijah. Rehoboam's obstinacy is met with a song, featuring recycled lyrics first sung by the leader of the rebel alliance in 2 Samuel 20, Sheba son of Bikri. Evidently the song has remained popular in the northern imagination during the reign of Solomon and now resurfaces with a vengeance, as it becomes the rallying cry whereby the kingdom is drastically reduced, just as Ahijah's prophetic word declared. Sending Adoniram—first mentioned in 2 Samuel 20 as well, and the one under whose direction the people toiled in forced labor—to calm the cries of the madding crowd may not have been the brightest ploy, and Rehoboam barely escapes without being stoned himself.

In response to the crowning of Jeroboam, the gathering of a substantial host (12:20–24)

THE DIVIDED KINGDOMS OF ISRAEL AND JUDAH

MEDITERRANEAN SEA

Dan

Sea of Galilee

Mt. Carmel

ISRAEL

Samaria

Shechem

Bethel

Jerusalem

Lachish

Dead Sea

JUDAH

mind reveals that he is paranoid about southern loyalties. He takes counsel (like Rehoboam) and quickly builds alternative cultic objects and sites of worship. Golden calves may not be particularly original (see Exodus 32), but their installation at the extremities of the northern kingdom is designed to divert the populace from participating in temple worship at Jerusalem. For similar reasons, Jeroboam also changes the calendar of religious observance, erects high places, and opens up the priesthood to non-Levites.

F. Northern exposure (13:1–16:34). **13:1–34.** The main story line of 1 Kings 13 features an interlude on the prophetic word, an anomalous chapter that in various ways contributes to the overall plot of the narrative. The first scene (13:1–10) takes place at Bethel, probably in the shadow of the newly constructed golden calf. It features a confrontation between Jeroboam and an unnamed man of God from Judah. The unexpected interruption as the new king is paying homage at this alternative place of worship grabs the reader's attention. More dramatic than withered hand and sign fulfilled is the mention of the proper name "Josiah," a highly specific prediction and uncommon kind of prophetic utterance that speaks deep into the future. That it is spoken by a man from Judah would have the effect of further unsettling Jeroboam, who we know is paranoid about the people's loyalty returning to the line of David. This utterance declares that the line of David will not only survive but also eventually produce a spiritual deliverer who will triumph over the very site of idolatrous installation where Jeroboam's hand has been withered. Jeroboam's motives for hospitality and the offer of a gift are not elaborated, but

is either a reflection on Rehoboam's improved leadership abilities or, more likely, a declaration of loyalty by the south to the line of David. Only a prophetic word spoken by Shemaiah (mentioned only here) averts a civil war. This word is directed to Rehoboam and "the remnant" of the people (KJV), and the smartest thing Rehoboam does is to listen. As a virtual opposite, the policy initiatives of Jeroboam (12:25–33) are rather different. Jeroboam then fortifies Shechem and the northern town of Penuel (as though he is expecting trouble), and a glimpse into Jeroboam's the man of God's refusal on the grounds of divine commandment should be noted, since (not) eating and drinking is a common element in the next section of the chapter.

The enigmatic dialogue between the man of God from Judah and the old prophet from Bethel (13:11–32) yields at least two main points. First, one purpose of the conversation is to raise the issues of false prophecy and the motives of the northern prophet for lying. The motives are complicated by the seemingly legitimate word of the Lord announcing condemnation in verses 21–22, underscoring that God can even use dubious prophets to accomplish his purposes. Second, the animals in the story play an interesting role, as the lion (by not eating) and the donkey (by not bolting) exhibit more self-restraint than the man of God, resulting in a critique of the prophetic office, which will be scrutinized in the days ahead. The final lament of the old prophet—and his desire to be buried beside his southern counterpart—indicates that even the strange old prophet from Bethel understands the efficacy of the prophetic word spoken by the man of God from Judah, and the desire to have his bones next to the bones of the man of God reminds the reader of what will eventually happen to human bones on the altar of Bethel. By repeating the recalcitrance of Jeroboam in the denouement of this perplexing narrative (13:33–34), the writer alerts us to the ultimate fate of Jeroboam's house, but even the scare of a withered hand is not enough to dissuade him from a heretical course of action.

14:1–31. From the account of two anonymous prophets we are taken back to a story about a more familiar figure, Ahijah of Shiloh, once more interacting with Jeroboam, although this time by proxy (14:1–16). Jeroboam's scheme to disguise his wife fits into the motif of "royal disguise" that has been seen before (Saul in 1 Samuel 28) and will occur later (Ahab in 1 Kings 22), as kings clothe themselves in other raiment in an attempt to thwart a prophetic word. Despite blindness, Ahijah is able to see through the disguise because of a divine word;

hence his surprise greeting of Jeroboam's wife even before she enters the house. Jeroboam's wife is welcomed with a long oracle of doom that resists an easy summary, but the capstone is that another king will be raised up in place of Jeroboam (who has not, as Ahijah first directed, been obedient), and the nation will be scattered "beyond the Euphrates River" (14:15). No sooner does the ineffectively disguised wife return home (14:17–20) than her son dies, and despite a proper funeral, it is a grim confirmation that it is hard to deceive a blind (true) prophet of the Lord. Jeroboam is succeeded by Nadab, who inherits a kingdom under judgment. Given the recent events surrounding the prophetic word, the reader knows it is just a matter of time before Jeroboam's house goes the way of the house of Eli.

A narrative pattern of periodic switching back and forth between north and south leads to a return to Rehoboam (14:21–31); how does this southern king fare while his northern counterpart is on the wrong end of a prophetic utterance? The notice about Jerusalem as the chosen city prefaces a catalog of Judah's transgressions. The southern kingdom does not appear much more virtuous than the north. Hence it must be the promise to the line of David that allows them to survive, even to the point of incursions by the king of Egypt. Rehoboam's obituary includes another reference to his mother (one of his father's many foreign wives), and the succession of Abijah evokes the recent memory of Jeroboam's son of the same name, who dies because of the sin of his father.

15:1–32. The opening lines of chapter 15 indicate that time will now largely be measured by kings and their reigns. Abijah's (also called Abijam) accession occurs in Jeroboam's eighteenth year (15:1–8), and he quickly builds up a sinful résumé. Rather than being disqualified, however, his line is preserved because of God's commitment to the line of David, with whom Abijah is unfavorably compared. Verse 5 is startling; in rhetorical terms, it has to be in the same category as David's last words to Solomon, with the stress on the necessity of obedience. Constant conflict with his northern counterpart is the hallmark of Abijah's three-year reign (one wonders what happened to the prophetic word of Shemaiah), until he is succeeded by his son Asa. More narrative space is allocated to the reign of Asa (15:9–24), probably because he has a longer and more fruitful reign.

There are some initial fears that Asa and Abijah share the same mother (Maakah), an incestuous tension that the NIV dispels by translating the Hebrew term normally rendered "mother" as "grandmother" in verses 10 and 13 (a plausible solution). Regardless, Maakah is dismissed from her position of "great lady" (NIV "queen mother") when Asa implements a systematic reversal of his father's policy by eliminating idolatrous paraphernalia. One blemish in an otherwise comprehensive purge is leaving the "high places" intact, sites that we will hear about again in due course.

The Asa narrative features introductions to two other characters. Baasha will formally enter the stage in the next section of 1 Kings 15 but here gets a brief cameo because of an aggressive campaign to control the key southern access point of Ramah. It is this aggression that leads to the introduction of Ben-Hadad, an official title for the Syrian kings, several of whom will appear in the story. Asa uses national resources of palace and temple to broker a "covenant" with Ben-Hadad; buying off the Syrian king enables Asa to shift the balance of power, and with his own conscripted labor he reallocates the building material of Ramah to his own defensive fortifications. There is no specific commendation or censure of Asa's actions here, but such alliances will loom large throughout the narrative of the divided kingdom. Asa's obituary in the closing lines of this section mentions, for the second time in 1 Kings, a document called "The book of the annals of the kings of Judah" (15:23), presumably some sort of record the author draws from. Finally, there is the curious note about Asa's "diseased" feet, and commentators theorize everything

from leprosy to venereal disease. After a long reign that spans seven northern kings, this is a painful way for Asa to exit the stage.

In the north, the house of Jeroboam is under a prophetic sentence, so when Nadab inherits the throne of Jeroboam his father, one has guarded expectations (15:25–32). A mere two years passes before the prophetic sentence announced by Ahijah of Shiloh is ruthlessly executed by Baasha, ironically the son of (another) Ahijah. Baasha is probably a mere agent in fulfilling the prophetic word, so the reader should be prepared for a similar dynamic unfolding later in the story. As it stands, Baasha is the general of the army when he usurps the throne during a siege, a common theme throughout the history of the northern kingdom. Lacking the same dynastic guarantee as Judah, northern kings will often be deposed by their senior underlings.

15:33–16:34. At some point during the twenty-four-year reign of the usurping Baasha (15:33–16:7), the prophet Jehu arrives with a strong denunciation. The fact that Baasha does a good imitation of Jeroboam is the initial reason for the prophetic word, as the hitherto unmentioned Jehu announces that the house of Baasha will experience an identical fate. Jehu's confrontation certainly anticipates prophetic activity in the next major section of 1 Kings (chapters 17–22), and his phrase "from the dust" (16:2) evokes memories of Hannah's song in 1 Samuel 2:8. Further, the dismal mention of dogs eating the royal corpse(s) will become a familiar refrain before long. After Baasha is buried in (yet another northern capital city) Tirzah, he is succeeded by Elah his son (16:8–14), whose two-year reign marks the end of the short-lived Baasha dynasty. Just as Baasha conspired against Nadab, so Zimri (one of Elah's officials) conspires against Baasha's son. But that is where the comparisons end: Nadab was occupied with a foreign conflict, but Elah meets his doom far closer to home, while getting drunk with a colleague. When Zimri assassinates Elah and reigns in his stead, it is a sober moment, as Jehu's word about the house of Baasha finds its fulfillment.

The account of Zimri (16:15–20) is bizarre for a number of reasons. First, the length of time that he reigns is a meager seven days, and in that one week he somehow finds time to walk in all the sins of Jeroboam—an impressive execution of idolatry. Second, his dismissal begins with rumor, and when Omri (the commander of the military) is crowned, it appears for a moment that there are two kings in the north. Third, Zimri's incendiary end is recorded from his own point of view ("when Zimri saw that the city was taken"), yielding a suicidal finish to the shortest reign in Israelite history. For more information on the conspiracy he wrought, we are referred to the northern annals, and primary attention turns to Omri. Although his reign is recorded in only a handful of verses, Omri (16:21–28) is the most influential northern king since Jeroboam. He achieves full control once the threat of the rival Tibni expires, after what seems to be a four-year struggle, with the death of Tibni himself. Most recent commentators note that Omri garners a couple of extrabiblical notices (in the Moabite stone and Assyrian records), but spiritually his legacy in Israel was decidedly negative. Otherwise, Omri's reign is significant for two reasons. First, he purchases and builds the capital of Samaria, a strategic location; according to archaeologists, this impressive fortification lasts for the rest of the northern

kingdom. Second, Omri sires a modest dynasty (a number of descendants will sit on the throne after him), a reasonable achievement considering the volatility of the north.

The first of Omri's descendants is Ahab (16:29–34), whose initial claim to fame is that he exceeds in evil all who precede him—quite an accomplishment, given Jeroboam's range of heterodoxies. The narrative cannot resist a piece of sarcasm: as though it were trivial to commit such atrocities, Ahab plunges even further by marrying Jezebel, the Sidonian princess. Under the leadership of this royal couple, the worship of Baal and Asherah (the Canaanite storm god and his female consort) flourishes. The manner of Ahab's introduction sets the stage for the prophetic contest that follows, especially since the final lines of the chapter refer back to Joshua 6:26, where a curse is directed at one who attempts to rebuild Jericho. Thus during the preliminary account of Ahab's reign, we are made aware of the ultimate power of the "word of the LORD," as Hiel of Bethel belatedly discovers.

G. Prophetic contests (17:1–22:53). 17:1–24. After the report about Hiel of Bethel and the fulfillment of the word of the Lord spoken through Joshua many centuries before, Elijah the prophet bursts onto the scene (17:1) without much introduction (like Ahijah, Shemaiah, and

Asherah statuette

Jehu before him), though he seems to originate from a settlement beyond the Jordan River. Elijah's initial confrontation with Ahab consists of a single sentence about rain, an important narrative signal of a key theme in this stretch of text. As numerous scholars maintain, there is a theological confrontation in this text as well: where does ultimate power reside, in the word of a king or a foreign deity, or in God's word? Thus the conflict between Ahab and Elijah is brought to the forefront in this struggle: who controls the rain, the Lord or Baal? This is the essence of the theological contest between king (whose name means "my father's brother") and prophet (whose name means "my God is the Lord"). That God immediately directs Elijah (17:2–6) to the Kerith Ravine ("Cutoff Creek") has threefold significance: rain will be cut off until God speaks to Elijah, Elijah will be cut off from Ahab until prompted otherwise, and meanwhile Jezebel will be cutting off the Lord's prophets in a purge of her own (see 1 Kings 18:4). During this famine, however, Elijah is supplied with food by ravens "morning and evening," reminiscent of Israel's wilderness experience, when there was no option but for God's people to be fed by him. Ravens are unclean birds (Deut. 14:14) and are therefore a surprising instrument for sustaining the prophet, paving the way for other astonishing moments in this narrative. Compared with the last few chapters, there is a slightly different literary technique deployed here in 1 Kings 17, which comes after the lengthy parade of northern kings and their futilities.

When the water supply of Cutoff Creek is cut off, it creates an opportunity for a shift in spatial setting, and Elijah's sojourn to the Sidonian widow dovetails with a number of broader themes in the story (17:7–16). The widow, vulnerable in the present, acquainted with grief and loss in the past, is gathering sticks for a last supper amid arid sterility. But she submits to the (counterintuitive) prophetic word and experiences life, as a substitute for death. Elijah's journey deep into Sidonian

territory demonstrates God's sustaining power in a situation akin to "exile," and the word of the Lord spoken in a distant land transfuses hope in perilous times. In fact, we see in this episode the power of God even beyond the borders of Israel, indeed, in the very backyard of Jezebel! Not only does Jezebel's god(dess) lack efficacy, but there is some humor here: God hides his prophet deep in the queen's territory (cf. Luke 4:25–26).

Such themes, however, are threatened when the widow's son takes ill (17:17–24). Yet the son's restoration is accomplished through prophetic mediation and thus encourages a rejection of the royal paradigm espoused by Ahab and Jezebel: what rulers (of any nation) are ultimately helpless to give, the prophetic word achieves. In this scene the reader hears the testimony of a non-Israelite about the God of Israel and his chosen prophet. It is the God of Israel who sends Elijah, just as it is the God of Israel who sends rain, who delivers from death, and whose word transcends any other authority. Elijah's declaration to the widow ("your son lives" [RSV]) echoes his earlier word to Ahab ("as the Lord lives") and underscores the theme of *the God of life* that continues throughout this narrative stretch.

18:1–46. By way of review, the first Hebrew word of 1 Kings 17 is "and he said," centralizing the spoken word that is a key element of this section. Elijah has earlier said to Ahab that there will be no rain "these years," a vague temporal indicator that suspends *royal chronology* and replaces it with *prophetic time*. Noticeably, the next installment of the story begins in the "third year" of prophetic time (18:1), as God announces that he will send rain. The next segment of the chapter (18:2–15) is best viewed through the lens of Obadiah, a figure whose actions and words glance back to the previous chapter and set the stage for the conflict on Mount Carmel. Obadiah is a high-standing member of Ahab's court, but the meaning of his name ("servant of the Lord") reflects a tension: on the one hand he is literally "over the house" of Ahab (NIV "his palace administrator," 18:3), but behind the scenes he is aiding the prophets, surely against the wishes of his employers. Obadiah "hides" the prophets and "sustains" them with supplies (18:4), just as God earlier told Elijah to "hide" (17:3), and Elijah was "sustained" by the ravens. Enlisting the help of Obadiah, King Ahab searches for water to keep the animals alive so they do not have to be "cut off." Obadiah must have been shocked to find the missing prophet during this quest for unwithered grass, and his long speech provides Elijah with a summary of the events that have taken place while he has been in hiding: Obadiah fears Ahab, but he also fears the Lord. By reciting his résumé to the prophet, Obadiah provides an instance of what literary critics refer to as "contrastive dialogue," whereby his voluminous outpouring is answered by a terse command: announce to

Ahab, "Behold, Elijah!" (NIV "Elijah is here," 18:8). Rain will fall only at Elijah's word, but to the long-suffering Obadiah he is a man of few words.

The confrontation between Elijah and the prophets of Baal on Mount Carmel (18:16–40) is a dramatic and well-known episode, and three aspects of Elijah's words should be highlighted. First, the prophet's accusation (literally, he asks the people, "how long will you hobble on two sticks?") encapsulates the vacillating tendencies of the general population. Ahab and the prophets of Baal are not Elijah's only opponents in this contest: also on trial is the spiritual paralysis that stems from a lack of real conviction. Obadiah at least shows that it is possible to have some faithfulness even in a brutal regime. By agreeing to the test of fire, the people tacitly agree that they have not been entirely loyal to God. Second, the mocking voice of Elijah (including pejorative remarks about Baal, such as "maybe he is sleeping") is met with complete silence from the rival deity.

> The Muhraqa Monastery, built to commemorate Elijah's victory over the prophets of Baal (1 Kings 18), is located up the hill from the traditional site of the contest.

This contest is about the power of speech, yet Baal has no voice here. When Elijah rebuilds the altar, the reader may think about the latter part of the book of Isaiah (e.g., chap. 44), where a satirical invective launched at various deities and competing worldviews is followed by a rebuilding of the faith of Israel. Third, the turning point of the episode is the intercessory prayer of the prophet, and for a community in exile, this surely speaks of the possibility of restoration. The final scene (18:41–46) features a slight ridicule in the warning to Ahab: the king needs to hurry up, because the long-awaited rain will cause his chariot to get stuck in the mud!

19:1–21. When Ahab's chariot returns home, he reports the news (19:1–2) to his wife Jezebel, whose murderous threats reveal her destructive tendencies. After taking on Ahab, hundreds of false prophets, and the general population, why is Elijah so scared of Jezebel's threat? Perhaps Jezebel is more scary than anything else Elijah has faced, or her intimidating message is the last straw. Either way, Elijah crosses the southern border (19:3–7) with an apparent case of prophetic depression, exclaiming to God, "Enough!" After the pyrotechnics of Mount Carmel, there is a movement from the prophet's external conflict to an internal struggle, where *he* has become like the widow of Sidon and needs to be revived like the widow's son in chapter 17. Some intriguing parallels begin here (and continue throughout the rest of the chapter) with the desert narratives and the career of Moses in Exodus and Numbers, with a constellation of shared images and words: forty days, the mountain of Horeb, visions, provisions of food by God, and a successor—suggesting that even great leaders need periodic renewal.

Once more Elijah is sustained by a meal, then sent on a journey (19:8–18) deep into the wilderness of Israel's history. As a spatial setting, the mountain of Horeb was a site of revelation, evoking memories of God's consuming presence. We are unsure how to understand Elijah's complaint ("I am the only one left") in light of Obadiah's claim of hiding one hundred prophets in caves, but God now proposes to pass by the prophet in the cave at Horeb. Like Moses, Elijah experiences dramatic signs and a thunderous display. In Elijah's case, however, they are followed by a "sound of sheer silence" (NIV "gentle whisper") and a repetition of the question "What are you doing here?" The prophet's feeling of isolation is countered by a task list for him—not only providing introductions to some characters who will follow in the story but comforting Elijah as well. The anointing of Elisha as successor, we will see, is vital for the dismantling of Ahab and Jezebel's kingdom, and thus Elijah's apprentice will be the prophetic catalyst for the fall of Ahab's house. When passing the mantle to Elisha (19:19–21), the senior prophet appears almost gruff with his new protégé. It has been suggested that Elisha hails from a wealthy family (twelve pairs of oxen), and apart from the obvious symbolism of the number twelve and connections with the twelve stones of the previous chapter, this scene implies that Elisha leaves a relatively secure lifestyle for all the risks of the prophetic vocation. That the chapter ends with yet another meal is appropriate (given all the food in 1 Kings 19), but the sacrifice of the oxen confirms that for Elisha there is no going back.

20:1–43. Given the reinstatement of Elijah, it is noteworthy that neither he nor Elisha features in 1 Kings 20. Instead, we get a different kind of prophetic intervention in this chapter, prompted by the aggression of Ben-Hadad and his allies (20:1–12). The considerable demands of Ben-Hadad give the impression that he has some leverage; the backstory would be that Israel is experiencing foreign hostilities under Ahab, and therefore abandoning orthodoxy does not always bring socioeconomic benefits. Some witty repartee between the two kings indicates that Ahab has a sense of humor, but it really looks like he is about to get horse-whipped. Despite Elijah's protest that he is the "only one left," an anonymous prophet confronts Ahab (20:13–22) with an announcement of improbable victory. Although the NIV renders the instruments for victory as, "the junior officers of the provincial commanders," another way of understanding the Hebrew text is captured by the NASB ("the young men of the rulers of the provinces"), thus enhancing the improbability of any victory, since we may not even be dealing with military personnel but rather regional administrators! Certainly Ben-Hadad is not overly stressed, as we infer from his drunken babble as he imbibes in his tent at high noon with his thirty-two royal allies. As predicted by the prophet, the purpose of Ahab's subsequent victory is to acquaint the king with this reality, "I am the LORD," and the same prophet alerts Ahab that Ben-Hadad will soon attack again.

As it turns out, the sequel has its own set of surprises (20:23–34), beginning with a snippet of a theological and strategic debate inside the Aramean camp, as the officials claim that Israel has "gods of the hills" and those drunken kings need to be replaced with some serious soldiers. Even though there is a narrative description of Israel's army resembling "two small flocks of goats" (20:27) compared to the massive Aramean host, an announcement to Ahab from a man of God (probably different from the earlier prophet) again forecasts victory. Ben-Hadad has two lucky escapes despite losing the battle. First, he is not crushed by the wall (which falls like the one in Jericho many years ago), and second, he receives a pardon from Ahab. Normally, showing mercy to an opponent on the ropes is commendable, but here the unexpected release of the royal prisoner of war (after securing a favorable trade agreement) leads to a serious prophetic condemnation in the final scene of the chapter (20:35–43). As in 1 Kings 13, this episode features one prophet deceiving another and an attacking lion. The disguised prophet, unlike Jeroboam's wife, is successful, eliciting a self-condemning sentence from Ahab, whose response ("resentful and sullen" [RSV]) prepares the reader for the next episode.

21:1–29. Ahab has wreaked havoc in Israel through apostasy and by marrying Jezebel; now he turns to appropriating his neighbor's property (21:1–4). Naboth's refusal to sell or barter his inheritance is consistent with torah (e.g., Lev. 25:23; Num. 27:8–11), yet the king's reaction, as in the previous chapter, is to return home "resentful and sullen." Ahab does not apply further pressure on Naboth—does he realize that Naboth is simply following the law?—but when he is met by Jezebel (21:5–7) we immediately realize that she is not beholden to Israelite law in the same way. Her reaction to the situation again shows her malevolence, but it is unclear whether Ahab expected this kind of response and that his Sidonian wife would concoct a scheme. Regardless, Jezebel's plan of writing deadly letters (21:8–16) evokes poignant memories of David's dispatching of Uriah back in 2 Samuel 11. This time, however, it is the queen who writes in the king's name, with her request to employ a pair of "sons of Belial" (NIV "scoundrels," 21:10) to liquidate Naboth. The false charge carries a death sentence, and Naboth is duly stoned—a murder, all because he refuses to sell out. Samuel the prophet warned that vineyards would be taken (see 1 Sam. 8:14) if Israel would choose the path of kingship, and such a warning is now a dreadful reality for Naboth.

The elders of the city might be fooled by Jezebel and Ahab, but not God's prophet Elijah, who unexpectedly arrives (21:17–24) to deliver a judgment. The spatial setting for this confrontation is "Naboth's vineyard," the very place the crime is set in motion. Ahab is seemingly held liable for Jezebel's atrocity, but the latter is not exempt; like her husband, Jezebel will suffer the ignominy of dogs consuming her remains. The scene is interrupted with a penetrating aside (21:25–26) about Ahab's vile conduct, reinforcing a key moment from the start of the chapter: Naboth refuses to sell his property, but Ahab has sold himself to do evil, incited by his wife Jezebel. The concluding interaction between Elijah and Ahab (21:27–29) has a pair of incongruous moments. First, Ahab's response appears humble, with clothing and deportment customary for those in mourning. Second, one might be skeptical about Ahab's humility, but God remarks on the king's contrition to Elijah—the object of Ahab's wrath on more than one occasion—and actually expresses commendation. Is there a mitigation of divine wrath? The days of Ahab's house are numbered, but God's capacity to extend grace should not be underestimated.

22:1–53. After the interlude at Naboth's vineyard, the narrative focus returns to the long-standing conflict with Aram (22:1–6), where the southern king Jehoshaphat—who will be formally introduced later in the chapter—appears as an ally of Ahab. Despite sparing Ben-Hadad's life earlier, Ahab is now interested in launching a hostile offensive against the northern outpost of Ramoth Gilead. Jehoshaphat seems to be the weaker partner in this alliance with Ahab against the Arameans, but his abrupt request to first seek God's counsel indicates that his voice is taken somewhat seriously. The reader knows that Ahab and Jezebel sponsor (false) prophets, and it is the compromised response of these employees that prompts Jehoshaphat (22:7–9) to request a genuine prophet of the Lord. Ahab's depiction of Micaiah makes it clear that they have encountered one another in the past, and Micaiah is summoned (22:10–15) before an assembly that is aggressively pro-Ahab and obviously prepared to say or do anything to placate the king (e.g., the goring antics of Zedekiah in 22:11).

Evidently Ahab has been trumped by Micaiah's sarcasm on previous occasions, and it is ironic that the king implores the prophet (22:16–28) to "tell me nothing but the truth *in the name of the Lord*" (22:16) in the midst of a plethora of false prophets on the royal payroll. By contrast, Micaiah's bold oracle informs Ahab that a "deceiving spirit" has emanated from the divine council and spread falsehood (22:22–23), a rather dramatic theological idea to say the least. Micaiah's presence must be

destabilizing for the rest of the prophets, such that it garners a slap in the face, literally, from the iron-horned Zedekiah (22:24). Deuteronomy 18:21–22 outlines the test for a prophet, and Micaiah tacitly appeals to this tradition in his spar with Zedekiah, proclaiming that *his* word will be authenticated. Ahab—under a death sentence from Micaiah—does his best to thwart the prophetic word through disguise (like Jeroboam's wife in chapter 14) but learns the hard way (22:29–40) that it is impossible to outmaneuver a true prophetic utterance. A seemingly random archer drawing his bow "in innocence" (NIV "at random") sends a bleeding Ahab back to town, where the dogs partake of the fulfillment of Elijah's earlier word and Micaiah's recent oracle. Despite lacking a disguise, Jehoshaphat survives the battle, and several highlights of his reign are recounted (22:41–50), including his building of a fleet of trading ships and his failure to remove the high places. Meanwhile, Ahab's death results in the accession of his son Ahaziah (22:51–53), who inherits his parents' predilection for heterodoxy.

2. 2 Kings 1:1–25:30

A. Chariots and fire (1:1–2:25). Although the first chapter of 2 Kings begins with a notice about Moab's rebellion (1:1–2), this thread will not be picked up until chapter 3. More pressing for the moment is Ahaziah's awkward nosedive that reveals something about his character: he is not willing to consult the God of Israel but rather opts for an alternative deity (literally "Baal the fly," here located in the Philistine city of Ekron) to learn his prospects for recovery. The impotence of this god is further enhanced when Ahaziah's messengers (1:3–12) are intercepted by a prophet with a memo of doom for the king, and since Ahaziah is able to recognize Elijah from their description, the two must have had prior dealings. Not only is the bedridden Ahaziah under a death sentence; he is singularly unsuccessful in bringing Elijah into custody: instead of apprehending the prophet, two successive groups are arrested by fire at the top of a mountain, much like the sacrifice was consumed by fire on Mount Carmel back in 1 Kings 18. The third captain has the sense to beg for mercy (1:13–18), and one gets the impression that if the angel of the Lord had not intervened, Elijah would have continued to call down fire. Ahaziah, like his father, tries in vain to nullify the prophetic word but discovers to his grave chagrin that such a task is beyond any earthly monarch. It is curious that Ahaziah has no son to succeed him, since the next chapter addresses the (formal) succession of Elijah by Elisha.

An extraordinary chapter narrates the stunning conclusion of Elijah's career and the beginning of Elisha's as a public figure. One aspect that emerges early in the narrative (2:1–8) is the tenacity of Elisha, in dealing with both his master and the persistent questions from the "company of the prophets" (literally "sons of the prophets"). Elijah's upcoming experience is evidently common knowledge in prophetic circles, and yet Elisha's tenacity early in the chapter foreshadows his difficult request in verse 10. Furthermore, the parting of the waters of the Jordan is reminiscent of the wilderness years, carrying the implication that Elisha ("God is salvation") will be the new Joshua ("the LORD is salvation") for these times. As Elijah and Elisha cross the river (2:9–18), the unexpected invitation for Elisha to "ask" for something evokes memories of Solomon in 1 Kings 3. A number of commentators understand the phrase translated literally "two mouthfuls of your spirit" (2:9) as a reference to inheritance (see Deut. 21:17), and perhaps Elisha wants a double portion to avoid prophetic burnout or a repeat of Elijah's depression. He certainly witnesses Elijah's departure, and tearing his clothes in two pieces is similar to sacrificing his oxen in 1 Kings 19 and anticipates his taking up of Elijah's mantle in verse 13. Notably, like Elijah he too poses a question to God ("Where now . . . ?"), and his public profile begins with an answered prayer. All the while, the band of prophets have been watching, and their banal questions must function as comic relief after the

unparalleled departure of Elijah; but also, this group observes firsthand the events of Elisha's succession and stands in contrast to the "official" prophets of the Ahab court.

A couple of memorable events (2:19–25) mark the beginning of Elisha's public activity, as he retraces the journey (Jordan River, Jericho, and Bethel, then on to Mount Carmel and Samaria) of Elijah at the beginning of the chapter. The healing of water with salt is somewhat offset by the bitter curses and bear-mauling of the forty-two youths from Bethel, yet both illustrate that a prophet's response to "evil" can bring both healing and destruction. The entrance of the female bears as agents of judgment reminds us of the devouring lions earlier in the narrative.

B. Days of Elisha (3:1–8:29). 3:1–27. Because Ahaziah did not have a son, his brother Jehoram (Joram) succeeds him, with mixed results (3:1–3): he betters his parents by eliminating some vestiges of Baal worship but persists in the ways of Jeroboam—the negative standard by whom the rest of the northern monarchs are measured. The rebellion of the king of Moab was mentioned at the outset of chapter 1 but is now explained (3:4–12) as a failure to deliver the requisite sheep quota, prompting military action from Jehoram (aided by the kings of Judah and Edom). There are some immediate similarities with Ahab's campaign in 1 Kings 22, including the summoning of Judah's king Jehoshaphat, who once more volunteers his forces and—in response to Jehoram's complaint about no water in the desert of Edom—requests the aid of a prophet. There is a state visit from this triumvirate of kings (3:13–19) to the prophet Elisha, who sounds every bit as gruff as his master upon catching sight of Jehoram, and just as sarcastic as Micaiah. Only the presence of Jehoshaphat (who describes Elisha as, literally, a "water pourer" [3:11]—exactly what he will become later in the chapter) assuages the prophet, whose request for a "harpist" is odd. Music has been connected with prophecy before (see 1 Samuel 10), and the request for a stringed instrument might be in the same vein—and none of the assembled kings seems to have a problem with it. Elisha ends up having an encouraging word: dig some ditches, for not only will there be water in the desert but Moab will be overthrown.

As Elisha forecasts (3:20–25), the land is miraculously filled with water, and the defeat of Moab begins at "the time for offering the sacrifice," a description similar to the reference to Elijah's actions at Mount Carmel back in 1 Kings 18:36. The water brings life for the three kings (Israel, Judah, and Edom), but brings death for Edom, as an optical illusion fools them into thinking the kings have slaughtered each other. The victory is tarnished, however, by an utterly baffling turn of events (3:26–27). While it comes as no shock that the king of Moab engages in child sacrifice after his last stand proves ineffective, the penultimate phrase, "and the fury against Israel was great," defies easy interpretation. Two kinds of sacrifices are contrasted here: the sacrifice for God's people outlined by torah (3:20), and the kind of abominable sacrifice practiced by certain foreign rulers. The king of Moab becomes like the injured Ahaziah in chapter 1, a king who lacks a successor—a not-so-subtle critique of the house of Ahab and its policy of imitating the surrounding nations.

4:1–44. Early in Elijah's career a Sidonian widow is sustained during a famine through a supply of oil; Elisha is involved with something similar (4:1–7), except this time the widow of a deceased Israelite prophet is the beneficiary. Here, one guesses the oil is limited so as to facilitate trust in the prophetic word without fostering complacency, even as it delivers her from the immediate threat of her creditors—and thus the woman is *not* childless. Elisha's care for the widow sets the tone for the rest of the chapter, as another female character features in the next episode (4:8–37). The two women are in different straits: the widow was in debt and stood to lose her offspring, while the next woman is married and affluent, yet has no children to lose. This finely crafted episode has three movements, beginning with the announcement and subsequent birth of a son. The reader is given a first glimpse of Elisha's aide-de-camp, Gehazi (a supporting actor in the next chapter as well), and through dialogue with Gehazi, it becomes apparent that the woman has needs that material wealth cannot satisfy. Through the prophet's intervention, this elderly couple now have an heir—unlike Ahaziah and the king of Moab.

Plaque with a harpist (Mesopotamia, 2000 BC). Elisha requests a harpist in 2 Kings 3:15.

The second movement revolves around sickness and death. In the woman's case, barrenness was replaced by fertility, but fertility has now (after the passage of some time) been routed by illness that leads to death. Earlier the woman pleaded, "Did I not say, 'Do not deceive me'?" (4:28 KJV), and now surely she feels the victim of false hope. But the third movement of the episode involves intercession and revival, and the woman's journey to Mount Carmel (recalling the God who answers by fire) is "Elisha-like" when she says she will not leave the prophet, just as Elisha once said to his master. Her perseverance is likewise rewarded with a double portion of rescue from death. Right after the account (3:27) about an appalling child sacrifice, we have a narrative about the prophet as a catalyst in the birth and "resurrection" of a promised son, against all odds. In some ways this mirrors the story of God's people: death and exile are not the end of the story.

Two feeding anecdotes (4:38–44) round out the chapter, and while the accounts may seem randomly patched together, there are some organic connections to the chapter as a whole. In the first story there are two problems: not only is there a famine, but the one meal for the prophetic guild is laced with poison ("death in the pot"). Flour once more is used to bring life (see 1 Kings 17:12), and death is averted just as with the son (4:32–35). In the second story—presumably at the end of the famine—first fruits are brought to the community of prophets, and despite the incredulity of Elisha's assistant, there is more than enough for everyone to partake of the crop.

5:1–27. There is a change of focus in the next episode (5:1–3) that begins with some role reversal: Naaman is the commander of the Aramean forces and a palpable foe of Israel, yet he has leprosy and is told of a (potential) cure by his wife's servant girl who was kidnapped from Israel. As Naaman eventually visits Elisha (5:4–10), the overarching concerns of the story become evident. First, there is concern even for the non-Israelite—in this case Naaman,

the military commander who was probably in charge of the raids (5:2). The word of Elisha begins to transcend traditional boundaries, paving the way for a rather more expansive view of salvation, and anticipating later prophetic oracles (e.g., Isaiah 49). Second, Elisha seems to have at least a functional relationship with the king of Israel, and despite the fact that both kings have a deficient view of the situation, the prophet's intervention creates peace (*shalom*) instead of more war. Naaman's initial frustration (5:11–18) eventually gives way to submission to the prophetic word, resulting in healing for the Aramean soldier. At first he is disappointed, wanting something akin to the fire of Carmel rather than a still small voice! But the healing journey elicits a spectacular confession from an inveterate enemy, and the reader cannot help but notice a discrepancy: while the nation of Israel is descending into a spiral of idolatry, here is a foreigner who pledges to honor God alone. Such commitment is only enhanced when the newly converted Naaman asks for a wheelbarrow of earth, since he has to—on official duty—enter the equivalent of a Baal temple but is determined that his allegiance will not waver.

Though Elisha refuses any recompense, his servant Gehazi has a rather different view of the matter (5:19–27), and Gehazi's avaricious behavior begins with an oath ("as the LORD lives," ironic in light of the healing of the boy in the previous chapter). After Gehazi secures a useful amount of material goods, the awkwardness of his interview with Elisha is captured in Gehazi's words: (literally) "Your servant didn't walk here and here" (5:25; NIV "Your servant didn't go anywhere"). The chapter begins and ends with leprosy, but with startling reversal, as Gehazi and his descendants will forever embody the decision to pursue Naaman and hoodwink him for some silver and new clothes. A contrast emerges between Gehazi (a servant lad) and the captured Israelite at the beginning of the story (a servant girl). The girl in exile has deeper acquaintance with the prophetic word than the insider Gehazi, who spends day and night with the man of God. These two young people see Naaman differently, and it is the young girl in captivity who displays vastly more theological insight than her counterpart.

6:1–7:2. Elisha has enjoyed a fair bit of interaction with the band of prophets (literally "sons of the prophets") to this point; further activity is the subject of the first episode of this chapter (6:1–7), recovering the borrowed (literally "asked for") ax head. In this account, a miracle occurs when the man complies with the prophet's directive, even if seemingly arbitrary ("When he showed him the place . . ."), just as with Naaman the Aramean. Even the sons of the prophets need such periodic reminders, as do foreign lepers and servants like Gehazi. Keeping such matters in mind, the narrative shifts to the court of the king of Aram (6:8–14), who suspects a mole in his camp because all of his secret locations are somehow known to Israel. Elisha's growing fame is evident, since an officer of Aram understands that the prophet is responsible. As Gehazi can testify (see 5:26), the prophet often has inside information, and in this instance it is presented in an almost slapstick manner. A large posse having been sent to arrest the prophet, Elisha and his (unnamed) servant awake (6:15–23) to find the house surrounded. The reader observes that blindness and insight are key components of this scene, as the servant glimpses the matter from Elisha's perspective (a vast multitude of the heavenly host surrounds them) while the Aramean troops are struck with blindness and led to Samaria by the very man they were sent to capture. If the captured Arameans are expecting the worst, such expectations are thwarted as the prophet orders hospitality for the prisoners and so transforms a situation of hostility into a season of peace.

The peace is temporary, however, as Ben-Hadad continues his offensive and besieges Samaria (6:24–7:2). A city under siege invariably faces scarcity and massive inflation, and here mothers are driven to contemplate cannibalism (see Deut. 28:53–57 for a warning). When the king of Israel is apprised of the situation, he directs his outrage at Elisha; no motive is stated, but one guesses that he wanted to destroy the captured Aramean soldiers earlier (6:21), while the prophet let them live. The king orders the death of Elisha, but as the king of Aram knows full well, Elisha is an elusive foe. Not only does Elisha avoid assassination, but he also speaks a radical word about reversal. However, as in the repartee between Micaiah and Zedekiah in 1 Kings 22:24–28, Elisha encounters some opposition. The supporting officer's expression of incredulity is met with a retort from the prophet, namely, that the fulfillment of the prophetic word shortly will come back on him like a stampede.

7:3–20. If Elisha's utterance is implausible, the instruments used for delivering such a word are even more unlikely (7:3–12), as four lepers have their march to surrender turned into a discovery of an empty Aramean camp. This group of outcasts must be as hungry as the mothers in 6:29, and so we can appreciate their joy at this find. Their pricks of conscience introduce an important word: *good news* (7:9). In the biblical economy, good news generally refers to big events such as rescue from captivity, the end of exile, and the reversal of oppression (see Isa. 40:9; 52:7–10). Reporting the news to the palace (7:13–20) launches an investigation team, confirming the empty camp and flooding the market with affordable food just as Elisha has forecast. In this case, the fulfillment of the prophetic word is yet another miracle in this stretch of text, where a divine interruption occurs in order to draw attention to particular facets of God's character, and the prophetic word here turns apparent hopelessness into a moment of salvation. As for the skeptical officer (7:2), he is sadly trampled during the resulting pandemonium at the gate (7:17), a hard way to learn the benefits of submission to the prophet's authority.

8:1–29. The next episode is introduced with a flashback to seven years earlier (8:1–6), when Elisha advises the Shunammite woman to sojourn outside of Israel during a famine. Because she has to reclaim her land from the king, one wonders if the king somehow appropriated the land in her absence. There is a miracle of timing: at the very moment the king is asking Gehazi about Elisha's mighty deeds, the woman shows up with her (revived) son! Gehazi's cameo is almost as astonishing, since he was last seen at the end of chapter 5 "white as snow"—it is not clear why he is in the king's presence, but his animated testimony aids the restoration of her property. The prophet's reputation continues to be a major theme (8:7–15), as Ben-Hadad consults him about his illness. The ensuing interaction between Elisha and Hazael of Damascus is significant for two reasons. First, it brings us back to the very outset of Elisha's career in 1 Kings 19:15–17, when God informs Elijah that Hazael's reign will be destructive. Now, closer to the end of Elisha's career, that cryptic word is poised for fulfillment. Second, Elisha's tears during the interview with Hazael become hauntingly appropriate when Hazael smothers Ben-Hadad's face with a wet rag. The same prophet who knows about Aramean troop movements (2 Kings 6:8–10) knows that Hazael—like Shakespeare's Macbeth—is about to become a murdering usurper.

After a lengthy hiatus, attention returns to the south with regnal summaries of two kings of Judah. The eight-year reign of Jehoram (8:16–24) represents a downturn, and marrying into the northern royal family does not look good on his résumé. However, a repetition of the Davidic guarantee ensures that the southern kingdom will continue; otherwise, the most noteworthy event in Jehoram's tenure is the revolt of Edom. Jehoram is succeeded by his son Ahaziah (8:25–29), who does "evil in the eyes of the LORD" during his reign of a single year. Joining the northern king Joram in an offensive against Hazael in the final scene, Joram is injured. Ahaziah's visit to the convalescing Joram sets the stage for a new chapter to unfold.

C. Jehu's ascendancy (9:1–10:36). Without any prior notice, Elisha commissions an unnamed member of the prophetic guild to anoint Jehu king of Israel (9:1–13). The prophet is instructed to take a "flask" of oil. The only other king to be anointed with a flask is Saul; the allusion to his ill-starred reign may signal that Jehu's term in office might be complicated. A brief comparison between Elisha's instruction and the other prophet's words to Jehu highlights a discrepancy: the prophet's report to Jehu (9:6–10) is considerably longer. It is unclear whether such "additions," including the command to massacre Ahab's house for revenge, are authorized by Elisha. Does this prophet speak for Elisha or on his own initiative? Moreover, why is the assembled group so quick to proclaim Jehu as king? Were they plotting an overthrow? A storm is brewing on the horizon because Joram is still king over Israel and presently has a visitor, Ahaziah of Judah.

Jehu's charioteering (9:14–29) is hall-of-fame caliber ("he drives like a maniac," in the words of one eyewitness), and such driving cannot augur well for the rival house of Ahab. Recruiting allies over the course of his wild ride, Jehu finally confronts Joram, at Naboth's vineyard of all places. This spatial setting reinforces the idea that judgment day has arrived for Ahab's dynasty, just as Elijah spoke in 1 Kings 21:20–24. Jehu's archery is above censure (as he hits the royal target "between the shoulders," 9:24), but it is Jehu's remarks after killing Joram that merit attention. Turning to Bidkar, he outlines justification for his actions in light of Elijah's oracle—one that Jehu claims to have heard. This is not reported in 1 Kings 21, but due to the relative accuracy of the words, Jehu should probably be given the benefit of the doubt. Despite Joram's warning (he shouts "Treachery!" in 9:23), Ahaziah is also killed by Jehu, making it a painfully effective day for regicide. Joram and Ahaziah are dead, but Jezebel still remains, and one senses that her demise is imminent (9:30–37). Characteristically, she exits the stage with a flourish, after one last stand in Jezreel. With freshly arranged hair, she includes in her greeting to Jehu the term "Zimri" (see 1 Kings 16:15–20). By alluding to

Zimri and his one-week reign of terror, Jezebel invites Jehu to partner with her if he wants a longer kingship. Jehu categorically rejects her offer, and some eunuchs duly throw her out the window, and she is trampled by oncoming horses and chariotry. It almost seems an afterthought when Jehu finally gives orders to bury her, and only scant remains can be found, giving Jehu one more opportunity to point out the fulfillment of Elijah's word.

To this point Jehu has not had much time for anything but rapid destruction. In the next episode (10:1–17) he appears more calculating. There is a grisly irony with Jehu's letters: through a letter Jezebel secured the death of Naboth in Jezreel, and now by a similar means Jehu destroys Ahab's offspring by sending correspondence to the same address. Jehu's intimidating epistle—not dissimilar to Jezebel's—does not leave much room for negotiation, and so for the second time in recent memory the leadership of Jezreel is purged, and the heads of Ahab's seventy sons are delivered to Jehu in baskets. (It is unclear whether or not the number seventy is symbolic and if the word "sons" indicates direct descendants.) Jehu seizes the opportunity to once more cite the prophet Elijah and continue his purge of the Ahab administration. Ahaziah's relatives are not exempt; they seem oblivious to recent events of destruction but are quickly apprised of Jehu's policy of elimination. Jehu recruits one further character—Jehonadab son of Rekab—whose descendants feature prominently in Jeremiah 35. By all accounts the Rekabites are a conservative group of traditionalists, worth commandeering for their political capital.

If Jehu seemed deceptive in his letters, such inclinations are exponentially increased in the next scene (10:18–27). To be sure, there is no lack of drama in the episode: Jehu's devious claim to worship Baal with great fervor, his threat that anyone who misses the event will be killed, everyone jammed into the temple literally "mouth to mouth" (10:21; NIV "until it was full from one end to the other"), and the end result of Baal's temple becoming a public lavatory. It certainly looks like a revolution, but its effectiveness will have to be measured over the long haul. For all his undisputed zeal, Jehu does not achieve the best of grades when his reign is finally evaluated (10:28–36). While ridding the land of Baal worship earns divine approval (for this he is given a four-king dynasty, smaller than Omri!), the reader also learns that Jehu was involved in worship of the golden calves and did not offset the incursions of Hazael into Israelite territory. Several commentators note that Jehu's eradication of idolatry did not go far enough: the reform does not seem to have penetrated his own life to the same degree.

D. Twilight for Samaria (11:1–17:41). 11:1–21. Ahaziah, we recall, was related by marriage to the house of Ahab and was

This panel from the Black Obelisk of Shalmaneser III (858–824 BC) shows Jehu kneeling before the Assyrian king and records the tribute paid by Israel.

assassinated by Jehu. Attention now turns to the southern kingdom (11:1–3), where Ahaziah's mother Athaliah assumes power by destroying "the whole royal family." Jehu has just purged the house of Ahab; now Athaliah (the daughter of Ahab and probably Jezebel) purges her own house. But the violent actions of one woman are counteracted by the resourceful actions of another (the otherwise unmentioned Jehosheba), and the fact that a young son (Joash) is hidden away in the temple precincts suggest a pocket of faithfulness within the inner circle of Judean leadership.

The anti-Athaliah conspiracy (11:4–16) reaches its zenith after seven years, and its careful choreography is rewarded with success. Her arrest takes place in the temple and is led by Jehoiada the priest, who arms the Carites with the ancient weapons of King David. We note the symbolism here, as the aged weapons of David are used to dislodge a pretender and secure the throne for a legitimate descendant of David. Jehoiada is labeled as the high priest in the next chapter. As for the prominent role played by the "Carites," this is a group who make no other appearance in the story. One theory links them with the Kerethites of 2 Samuel 8:18, a foreign militia group hired for royal security. Regardless, the Carites facilitate the end of Athaliah, and the view of many citizens seems to be that Athaliah is not a legitimate monarch (hence their "rejoicing" in 11:14). She is given no regnal formula, and her own words ("Treachery! Treachery!"; NIV "Treason! Treason!") ironically rebound on her. Like Jezebel, Athaliah finds her demise in a place where horses trample (see 1 Kings 9:33). The formal circumstances of coronation (11:17–21) for the seven-year-old Joash include a covenant ceremony (led by the priest) and eradication of Baal worship (the first and only mention of a Baal priest named Mattan—a foil for Jehoiada in this episode). The narrator's comment that "the city was calm" has a useful parallel in Isaiah 14:7, and this episode hints at the possibilities for the temple and its personnel to create peace in the land.

12:1–21. During Joash's reign (12:1–3) there is a reversal of Athaliah's policies, as Joash "did what was right in the eyes of the LORD," under the vigilant tutelage of Jehoiada. Part of his achievement might be credited to his mother from Beersheba, a city in the far south of Judah, as far as possible from northern corruption. The high places remain, however, and in this context the mention of incense burning and deviant sacrifices might serve as a bit of an ominous foreshadowing. A major undertaking during Joash's reign is the restoration of the temple (12:4–16). Although no motive is stated, one suspects that this rebuilding project is part of the long road away from apostasy. It is curious, therefore, that the priests are apparently negligent in their appointed tasks of renovation, and for that matter, that it takes Joash twenty-three years to make inquiries. During the reign of Athaliah it is likely that the Baal priest Mattan got a better deal, so perhaps the priests are simply recouping past losses. Jehoiada's solution of a voluntary offering chest—to be counted by representatives of both king and temple—is an effective one, and the proper accounting procedure results in everyone getting a fair share. It takes well over twenty years to combat a couple generations' worth of corruption.

Elisha recently wept over the damage that Hazael of Damascus would inflict (1 Kings 8:12), and after Joash's renovations of the temple, Hazael launches an offensive (12:17–21). While Joash buys him off and temporarily averts a crisis, he does so by emptying the temple, which had successively been restocked since the days of Asa (who also buys off the Aramean army in 1 Kings 15:18). The restoration of the temple under Joash was undoubtedly positive, but this action colors his reign with ambivalence. As for the end of Joash, it is a sad irony that he leaves the narrative because of "treachery" (12:20; NIV "conspired"), the same term used by Athaliah when she is ambushed in the temple (11:14). The motives of Joash's assassins are not clear (2 Chronicles 24 gives another perspective), but the fact that the conspirators put Joash's own son on the throne (unlike in northern rebellions) suggests a degree of disillusionment with his reign.

13:1–25. The reader knows that Jehu's dynasty will last four generations, and the accession of Jehoahaz after his death (13:1–9) represents the next installment. Like the majority of his predecessors, Jehoahaz walks in the sins of Jeroboam. There is, though, one remarkable moment in Jehoahaz's term of office that merits consideration: during a severe Aramean invasion, the king entreats the Lord, who responds favorably, much like during the turbulent times of the judges. A "savior" (RSV) or "deliverer" (NIV) of unspecified identity (Elisha?) is raised up (13:5), and if verse 7 describes the state of the armed forces when the king cried out, the divine intervention occurs when Israel's defenses have been decimated. Even though the northern kingdom has been guilty of widespread apostasy, God still responds to earnest prayer, and one would think this reality gives hope to anyone in exile. The next generation, under Jehoash (13:10–13), does not fare much better, and there is no record of a royal prayer such as that in verse 4 (although Jehoash is triumphant over Judah in battle).

Jehoash's sixteen-year reign does have one momentous event, and it is reported by means of a flashback (13:14–21) dealing with the prophet's illness and a royal visitation. Jehoash's words mirror what Elisha says when Elijah is taken up in 1 Kings 2, and his grief for the ailing prophet appears sincere. Even a recalcitrant king knows the power of a good prophet, and for a moment Jehoash seems to glimpse that Israel's only chance lies with the power of God, not military force. Several commentators note that Elisha's instructions to the king with the arrows might have a rough parallel with the actions of other prophets such as Ahijah in 1 Kings 12, where the prophetic signs function as a kind of test as well. Jehoash passes the test with shooting the arrows but fails when it comes to striking them on the ground. Whether his enthusiasm or spirituality is censured here is

unclear, but unlike Elisha, Jehoash certainly does not get a double portion as the prophet leaves the stage. Elisha may not exit the narrative as dramatically as his master, Elijah, but his grave site is known, and even his bones can raise the dead. Near the beginning of the chapter God answers a prayer, and now near the end (13:22–25) the narrator comments on the Lord's benevolence toward his people. As Elisha has forecast, Jehoash launches three winning assaults against Aram; things could have gone better, but the northern kingdom also could have fared much worse. There has been remarkable divine forbearance until this point, but one is unsure how long it will hold out.

14:1–29. Amaziah of Judah replaces his slain father (14:1–7) and is described as having something of a divided heart: some faithfulness mingled with compromise. Notably, he takes revenge for his father's death, presumably on Jozabad son of Shimeath and Jehozabad son of Shomer for their role in 12:21. For some reason the king acts within limits prescribed by Deuteronomy 24:16, but he himself will be struck down later (14:19), possibly in retaliation. His most impressive achievement is his victory over the Edomites described in 14:7, where renaming the city—some identify Sela as "Petra"—is probably self-aggrandizing behavior that reinforces his victory, anticipating his royal pride in the next scene. In all likelihood fortified by this triumph over Edom, Amaziah proceeds to throw down the gauntlet to his northern counterpart Jehoash (14:8–14), perhaps eager to shake off the northern yoke now that he is in the ascendancy. Jehoash shows himself adept at prophetic satire and uses the metaphors of a scrub bush (Judah) versus a towering cedar (Israel) to tell the aggressive king to rest on his laurels and quit while he is ahead. Jehoash correctly predicts that this confrontation will not end well for the south. Amaziah's hearing impairment proves very expensive, and the face-off at Beth Shemesh results in a major loss for Judah and a crippling of Jerusalem. Sadly, this is not the last time the city will be invaded and looted, with prisoners taken. The same royal pride will resurface in the Babylonian conquest in the days ahead.

The regnal notice for the northern king Jehoash may seem out of place or a duplication of the earlier note, but it does serve to effectively introduce the demise of Amaziah (14:15–22). Overall, Jehoash scores higher in terms of military and political effectiveness, especially when Amaziah dies as an embarrassed victim of an internal plot. The narrative does not spell out the identity of the conspirators, though it is possible that relatives of those liquidated in 14:6 are responsible, or perhaps a group that was upset with the recent debacle with the north. Amaziah is replaced, as in previous cases, by his son. The southern kingdom, because of God's guarantee, always has a descendant of David on the throne. The north, by contrast, is subject to constant upheaval and dynastic instability, and hence the immediate consequence of Jeroboam II's reign (14:23–29) is that Jehu's dynasty is nearing its end. For the moment, however, Jeroboam II is not unsuccessful: despite an evil disposition, he does oversee an expansion of Israel's landholdings to an extent not seen since the days of the Solomonic empire. This reclamation project is undertaken at the prompting of the prophet Jonah, whom the reader later meets in the book that bears his name. For the second time in as many chapters the narrator reflects on the quality of divine mercy (vv. 26–27), and so it is that Israel's dominance during this period is due less to Jeroboam II's acumen and more to God's grace—to the point that he saves them through the king's hand. It is as though the Lord is continually reaching out, as in the days of the judges.

15:1–38. The ignoble demise of Amaziah results in the succession of his son Azariah (also called Uzziah) to the throne of Judah (15:1–7), one of the better kings who enjoys a long reign, but one who also fails to do anything about the high places (whether because it was politically incorrect to do so, or because he lacked the requisite spiritual discernment). It is conspicuous that Azariah/Uzziah is struck with leprosy, with no precise explanation given except that "the Lord" is responsible. The affliction is severe enough to warrant confinement and limit his duties, and after his partition there is a coregency with his son Jotham.

A rapid parade of northern kings follows—few of whom are distinguished in any way, or particularly competent—beginning with Zechariah (15:8–12). The entire stretch of text is fraught with violent overthrows and coups, and Zechariah's short tenure provides an overture. We suspected Jehu's dynasty was nearing the end, and the king's public assassination by Shallum brings to fulfillment the prophetic word spoken to Jehu. Shallum's identity is obscure, and the report of his one-month reign gives little detail (15:13–16) other than his death at the

Relief of Tiglath-Pileser III (Nimrud, Assyria, ca. 728 BC), referred to as Pul in 2 Kings 15:19

hands of Menahem from Tirzah. Some scholars reconstruct a political background, suggesting that some leaders were interested in fostering ties with Aram while others were more enticed by an Assyrian alliance. Such a theory gains plausibility with the report of Menahem's reign (15:17–22), as he gathers substantial revenues to pay off Pul (another name for the Assyrian king Tiglath-Pileser III) during what must have been a sizable invasion; the reader needs no reminder that making deals with foreign kings is always a perilous enterprise. It is almost surprising when Menahem's son Pekahiah succeeds him on his death (15:23–26), but the familiar pattern of usurpation continues with Pekah's treacherous takeover (15:27–31). The twenty-year reign of the penultimate king of Israel is dominated by an increasing Assyrian presence in the region. Reports that Assyrian incursions are gaining in frequency and scope does not bode well for Israel or Judah.

Indeed, Judah is not exempt from the growing Assyrian pressure. Jotham's political career in Judah began with coregency in 15:5, but his formal reign commences when he accedes to the throne after the death of his father (15:32–38). Jotham manages to rebuild the "Upper Gate" of the temple, but this project is eclipsed by mounting anxiety over external matters, such as the northern alliance (Israel and Aram) against Judah. Yet there is a powerful assertion in verse 37 that even the growing maelstrom of international hostility is under the aegis of divine sovereignty.

16:1–20. Hostility toward Judah is not abated, and in fact it increases in the next segment of the story, the reign of Ahaz (16:1–20). The Ahaz administration has a bad start: previous kings were censured for not removing the high places, but Ahaz goes a step further by actually worshiping at these installations. Even worse, he adheres to the terrifying practice of child sacrifice, and such conduct presages a litany of compromises and surrenders in this chapter. Ahaz follows the ways of the nations that the Lord drove out, and his egregious conduct

paves the way for such nations to return. Ahaz's deal with Assyria is prompted by the so-called Syro-Ephraimite pact of aggression (see also Isaiah 7): the kings of Aram and Israel want Judah to join in against Assyria, and to signal their ambitions the port of Elath is seized. Ahaz resists the invitation by pilfering the treasury and pleading for Assyrian assistance. Ahaz opts for submission, and the king of Assyria is all too willing to fulfill his end of the bargain by decimating Damascus. In the aftermath of destruction Ahaz is invited to the humbled city of Damascus, and the reader now realizes that submission to Assyria comes at an even steeper price. In an attempt to ingratiate himself with his new master, Ahaz sends blueprints for the redesigned altar of the temple in Jerusalem after a foreign prototype, and thus the place of worship becomes corrupted as a place of political servitude. It is hard to determine the degree of complicity on the part of Uriah the priest, but he certainly does not appear to be a "Jehoiada" for these times. After sixteen years Ahaz dies and is succeeded by Hezekiah, a son who inherits a legacy of Assyrian accommodation.

17:1–41. A heightening sense of inevitability of the northern kingdom's doom is poised for climax. In Deuteronomy 8:19 Moses warned, "If you ever forget the LORD your God and follow other gods and worship and bow down to them, I testify against you today that you will surely be destroyed." Such a warning has not been sufficiently heeded and finds its grim realization during the truncated reign of the woeful Hoshea (17:1–6), who probably regrets attacking and usurping Pekah in 16:30. Curiously, Hoshea is described in better terms than previous kings of Israel, but his attempt to rebel against Assyria and seek assistance from Egypt is rewarded with incarceration and a three-year siege of Samaria by the new king, Shalmaneser. Once the city is captured, the population is deported to various outposts of the Assyrian Empire.

In the lengthy catalog of indictments against the northern kingdom (17:7–23), it is as though the author comes out from behind the curtain to address the audience directly. The catalog is self-explanatory and requires little commentary, and scholars agree that it constitutes a theological explanation for the fall of the north. It is not just the leaders who are guilty—although they are implicated beyond doubt—but there has been widespread collaboration of all the people in covenant unfaithfulness and chasing after what the NIV translates as "worthless idols" (or "vanities," the same word that begins Ecclesiastes). Interlaced in the midst of the catalog is also an assessment of Judah, and the southern kingdom is just as guilty. Judah survives for the time being, however, because of the promise to David. But in this context is laced a profound sense of caution, as though Judah is given one more chance to avoid the disaster that has just engulfed the north.

The city of Samaria is hit hard by the Assyrians, but the deportation of the population is only half the story (17:24–41). By resettling different groups of Mesopotamian deportees in the "towns of Samaria," the king of Assyria also introduces a cornucopia of new deities and attendant ideologies into the land. Lion attacks (see 1 Kings 13) only serve to bring back a local priest to conduct basic theological education; whether a priest of Samaria is to be understood as a pillar of orthodoxy is not under discussion, but what results is a hybrid syncretism. Samaria, as the epicenter of northern corruption, was a snare to Judah before the collapse, and there are hints that it will continue to be so in the future, albeit in a different guise with a different population. This religious threat may prove more trouble in the end than Assyria's military, but for the moment, Judah has its hands full with that situation.

E. Hezekiah's Assyrian crisis (18:1–20:21). **18:1–37.** Although the destruction of Samaria has taken place, the Assyrian ambition is far from quenched. The accession of Hezekiah occurs in less than enviable circumstances, but the early report of his reign ushers in a spring of hope after a long winter of despair (18:1–8). Part of his comprehensive housecleaning includes

pulverizing the bronze snake, a venerated object from the days of Moses. One recalls that Moses made the snake for healing, but now this great symbol has to be destroyed, as it has become irredeemably corrupted. Such actions earn Hezekiah the highest commendation from the narrator—even to the point that his rebellion against Assyria and defeat of the Philistines is praiseworthy. While Hezekiah is undertaking his reforms, we are reminded that the northern kingdom is dismantled by the Assyrians (18:9–16). Working their way south into Judah, they find that the "fortified cities" are no match for them; with Jerusalem firmly in the Assyrian sights, Hezekiah has little option except to grovel and pay a hefty fine.

The amount Hezekiah pays, scholars tell us, is ridiculously high, and to generate enough gold the temple has to be stripped right down to the baseboards. Although the fine is paid, it seems to avail little, as the highest-ranking officials of Assyria still show up in Jerusalem (18:17–25). The confrontation with the field commander happens at the "aqueduct," a poignant spatial setting that strongly suggests a possible siege. With a long speech, he lampoons Hezekiah's strategic initiatives with Egypt and the recent religious reforms. The Assyrian ambassador claims, boldly, to speak for the Lord! After Hezekiah's representatives request Aramaic (18:26–37), the orator calls the bluff: not only does he respond in Hebrew, but he ups the rhetoric a notch, talking about the gloomy realities of a siege. As the reader knows, history is on his side (e.g., 2 Kings 6:24–29, and the cannibal mothers). The "war of the words" reaches a crescendo with a verbal assault on the person of the king, followed by lavish promises about peace and security, promises that must be more appealing than drinking urine. The speaker sounds like a passionate prophet talking about a land of milk and honey—and he intones that Assyria is like a juggernaut crushing every land and god! In light of this onslaught, the self-control of the people indicates the kind of respect they have for their leader.

19:1–37. To this point in the confrontation Hezekiah has been represented by proxy, through leading representatives within his circle of advisors. Now his personal response is detailed (19:1–4), and his impulse is to send a message to the prophet Isaiah—who makes his first appearance in the text at this point. Earlier we are told that Hezekiah "trusted" the Lord (18:5); the practical ramification is that he is willing to call on the prophet here rather than make an arrest (cf. 6:30–31). Dressed for a funeral and citing proverbial metaphors about difficult childbirth (meaning no hope for the future), the king pleads for prayer on behalf of "the remnant" against an infinitely superior and mocking oppressor. Isaiah's response sets up a confrontation between two counselors, and he now appears as a counterpart to the king of Assyria's representative (19:5–13). Isaiah's message is unequivocal: the onslaught will not finally succeed. It is unlikely that the Assyrians are aware of this message, but they continue their southern offensive and send a further message to Hezekiah—rather more terse this time—about his certain defeat. On receiving this deadly epistle, Hezekiah visits the temple (19:14–19) and, presumably in the presence of the ark, utters an intense supplication. The relative postures of the two kings seem to be a point of issue: one is powerful and all about military hardware, whereas the other is powerless and all about prayer.

The Assyrian field commander scaled considerable rhetorical heights in his long speeches of the previous chapter. Isaiah also sends a message (19:20–34), seemingly unsolicited, and the field commander's bravado pales before the oracle of Isaiah. In Isaiah's poetic economy, the powerful king is mocked by a young lady, as he eventually returns with a hook in his nose. The words for the king of Assyria are highly personal, informing him that his sweeping victories are not because of his logistics but because of God's foresight to use the Assyrians as part of his divine plan. Hezekiah is also given a sign (encouraging him to give patient leadership to the remnant *who will survive*), and the immediate crisis will be resolved as God will defend Jerusalem "for my sake and for the sake of David my servant" (19:34). While no response of Hezekiah is preserved, the resolution of the conflict surely provides some vindication for prophet and king (19:35–37). The same "angel of the LORD" who visits Elijah with bread in 1 Kings 19:7 now visits the vast Assyrian army with death. As for Sennacherib, he too spends time in a temple, like Hezekiah. But according to this text Nisrok does not undertake on behalf of his supplicant, as Sennacherib is cut down with the sword, courtesy of his own offspring.

20:1–21. Although the Assyrian threat has spectacularly subsided, Hezekiah's struggles are the subject of a pair of episodes in 2 Kings 20 that pertain to the king's person and his progeny. In the first (20:1–11), by means of a flashback the reader discovers that in the midst of the Assyrian attack, Hezekiah was gravely ill. A precise diagnosis of Hezekiah's sickness is not the point; rather, this sophisticated literary technique allows Hezekiah's illness to become a moment of parabolic reflection on the Assyrian invasion and its aftermath. Hezekiah is threatened with certain death, just like the city, yet he prays and is miraculously delivered. For the sake of God's promise, Jerusalem too is delivered, but just as Hezekiah is given fifteen more years, Jerusalem's time is ultimately limited. The purpose for the "shadow sign" is to demonstrate that God can turn back the time of judgment, should he be willing. It is entirely intentional, therefore, that the next episode about emissaries from the king of Babylon (20:12–19) follows the account of Hezekiah's recovery. Ostensibly arriving to offer congratulations to the king, the Babylonian diplomats get an extensive tour of the royal precincts. The temporal note "at that time" implies that the visitors arrived while the Assyrian crisis was still going on and thus provides a clue as to the real motives: the Babylonians are seeking an ally in the west against Assyria. Their exact motives (and the motives of Hezekiah, for that matter) quickly become peripheral as the episode continues. Isaiah, having given a series of powerful words of hope, does not appear thrilled at the presence of the envoys, and his words are scathing. This is not, Isaiah declares, the last time the Babylonians will lay eyes on the treasures of Jerusalem, for the time is coming when the treasures will be forcibly exported there. Hezekiah's reaction is staggeringly shortsighted: his own descendants will be emasculated, but he is happy that he will retire in peace. Some interpreters try to defend the king, but it is hard to deny that Hezekiah's response puts a real damper on an otherwise remarkable reign. The chapter ends with a regnal summary (20:20–21), including the ingenious engineering feat still called "Hezekiah's tunnel" to this day.

F. *Babylon rising (21:1–24:17)*. **21:1–26.** The visit of the Babylonian dignitaries is a prelude to the role Babylon plays through the end of 2 Kings. Hezekiah is succeeded by his son Manasseh, and a reader could be forgiven for expecting good things from this era. The fifty-five-year reign of Manasseh, though, is described in the worst possible terms (21:1–18), and under his leadership more evil is done than even in the dispossessed nations. It is hard to believe that such an all-inclusive program of idolatry can be implemented in light of the recent deliverance from the Assyrians, but it earns Manasseh a unique prophetic censure: a group of prophets, speaking with unanimity, condemns the king and forecasts disaster for the nation. Manasseh is likened to Ahab, and the fate of Jerusalem is likened to that of Samaria, hardly a flattering set of comparisons. It is also said that Manasseh filled Jerusalem with innocent blood literally from "mouth to mouth" (NIV "end to end"), a phrase that last occurred in 2 Kings 10:21, when Jehu purged the land of Baal worship. The shedding of innocent blood, as several commentators note, points to massive injustices alongside religious apostasy. When Manasseh dies, there is no sign of improvement under his son Amon (21:19–26), who engages in the same evil practices as his father. Amon falls victim to a conspiracy led by his officials,

who are summarily executed by the "people of the land." One recalls that the "people of the land" were active in the overthrow of Athaliah in 2 Kings 11, so it is most likely the same kind of popular uprising here. Furthermore, the installation of the eight-year-old Josiah is reminiscent of young Joash's replacing Athaliah.

22:1–23:30. Josiah's arrival has been long anticipated. Back in 1 Kings 13, the man of God from Judah arrived in Bethel, and with the highly unusual disclosure of a proper name hundreds of years ahead of time, prophesied that this son of David's house would obliterate the altar of this northern shrine. Given such advance billing, there is a sense of great expectation when Josiah's reign begins after he is installed by the people of the land (22:1–2). His father and grandfather were the worst royal tandem ever, and so it is against the odds that Josiah earns the unique commendation of not turning "to the right or to the left" (see Deut. 5:32) as he does what is upright in God's sight.

Like Joash before him, Josiah sponsors renovations of the temple (22:3–10). Just after the halfway point of Josiah's reign, during the routine duties of paying workers and supervising the project, a discovery is reportedly made by the high priest Hilkiah: the book of the law ("the Torah"). It is not hard to imagine how the book was eschewed during the reigns of Manasseh and Amon, and whether a cadre of priests kept it hidden or it was literally lost, the book is back on the radar after a long absence. The book is not only found, but it is also read in the king's presence. Considerable scholarly energy has been expended on identifying the contents of this book, but most agree that Deuteronomy must form a significant portion of this scroll that is read aloud before the king. Josiah's response (22:11–13) confirms as much: his actions (garment tearing) and his words (calling for a prophet) parallel the response of Hezekiah to the fearful oratory of the Assyrian field commander. Josiah understands these words to have a similar kind of present-tense reality, and a similar threat.

By calling for a prophetic interpretation, Josiah shows his immediate concern is to take a drastically new course of action. His officials are dispatched (22:14–20) to "inquire" of the Lord, the same request that Jehoshaphat made back in 1 Kings 22. The officials go to Huldah, who has not been mentioned in the story before; she resides in Jerusalem and is part of a prominent family circle. She addresses two different audiences: first the nation, then the king himself. As for Judah, the prognosis

JOSIAH DIES IN BATTLE AT MEGIDDO

is dire: "disaster" (literally "evil") is forecast. Huldah's words are in line with the unified prophetic declaration of 21:10–15. As for the king, Huldah's words affirm his personal piety and laudable reaction to the words read from the scroll. His reward is somewhat counterintuitive: he will journey to the grave in peace (Hebrew *shalom*) and not lay eyes on the evil that will befall Judah. Since Josiah dies rather violently at the end of the next chapter, some have pointed to inexact prophecy here. But on the contrary, the manner of Josiah's death is "peaceful" when compared with Jerusalem's invasion, which is now dead ahead on the horizon.

Although the prophetess Huldah has unequivocally announced certain doom, the king calls together Judah's leadership for a public reading of the "Book of the Covenant" and a covenant renewal ceremony (23:1–14). Commentators often point to texts such as Joshua 24 as an analogue, or, more recently, to the ceremony led by Jehoiada (2 Kings 11:12). After the assembly, a host of idolatrous installations are removed, not just the typical Baal and Asherah equipment, but also all the paraphernalia associated with practices like child sacrifice,

astral deities, and chariots dedicated to solar worship. From the highly detailed description of the removal one sees the vastness of the installations, here pictured with more specificity than at any other point (even chapter 17, with its catalog of northern abuses). Not only are these installations recent (as in the eras of Manasseh and Amon), but such activity goes as far back as the syncretism of Solomon as well.

There was an early hint in 23:4 that Bethel would not be exempt from the reforms, and singled out for special attention is the altar of Bethel (23:15–20) constructed by Jeroboam. Not only does the destruction of the altar fulfill the prophetic utterance spoken long ago; it also indicates Josiah's willingness to travel outside of Judah, and even to Samaria. After Josiah's return to Jerusalem, it is symbolically appropriate that the Passover is celebrated (23:21–25), as Deuteronomy 16:5–6 outlines that this most important feast—commemorating the saving events of the exodus from Egypt—needs to be held in the place that God "chooses." It has been many days since the land has seen this celebration, maybe since the time of Joshua 5 (although see 2 Chronicles 30). But on the heels of another commendation of Josiah is a further reminder of imminent destruction (23:26–30), and even these extensive and far-reaching reforms are not enough to offset Josiah's end or Judah's invasion. The shadow of judgment does not move backward, as in the days of Hezekiah, and the story is marching inexorably toward exile. Josiah's untimely death at Megiddo takes place, literally and figuratively, between two superpowers as he tries somehow to thwart the Egyptians who are coming to aid Assyria. His death resembles his reform movement in Judah; although brave and passionate, he is unable to stem the rising tide of Babylon.

23:31–24:17. A fair bit of narrative space is dedicated to Josiah's kingship, but now there is a sense of narrative acceleration as we move more quickly to the end, beginning with the short and profoundly ineffective reign of Josiah's son Jehoahaz (23:31–35). Under the control of Pharaoh Necho, Jehoahaz is transferred as a prisoner from Riblah in Syria to Egypt and has to pay a fine (although it is a pittance compared with Hezekiah's fine, showing how economically crippled the nation is). Jehoahaz dies in Egypt, in a house of bondage, with an Egyptian king once more acting aggressively against God's people. The brief reign of Jehoahaz will be typical, since there will be no political autonomy for Judah from now until the end. Instead, Judah's affairs are seemingly determined by foreign superpowers. The reader is reminded, however, that these nations are not operating of their own volition, but are subject to "the LORD's command." This includes the first Babylonian invasion of the land during the reign of Jehoiakim (23:36–24:7), who is, like his predecessor, subservient to a more powerful king. Historians inform us that Jehoiakim made several alliances, bouncing back and forth before Babylon forcibly won the day. When Jehoiachin assumes the throne (24:8–17), Babylonian hostility has reached the point of a siege on Jerusalem. No doubt aware of the kind of exigencies created by a siege, the king and company surrender and are taken into exile. During the visit of the Babylonian envoys way back in 2 Kings 20, Isaiah warned that all the valuables would be taken from the treasury, and that word begins to be fulfilled during the days of Jehoiachin. With the king in Babylon, his uncle Mattaniah takes his place (I assume that Mattaniah changes his own name to Zedekiah, perhaps hoping for a change of destiny in the process).

G. Judah's captivity (24:18–25:30). Zedekiah may have changed his name, but he is powerless to change the times. It is under his leadership (24:18–25:12) that the kingdom of Judah reaches its end.

For some reason, Zedekiah rebels (or "acts audaciously") against the king of Babylon, in all likelihood by siding once more with Egypt (25:1–12). Whatever Zedekiah was hoping to achieve through such a rebellion did not happen, and Nebuchadnezzar's retribution is fierce: Jerusalem becomes a city under siege, and the siege is a long one. Finally, the wall is breached (historians point to a date of 586 BC for this

A Babylonian inscription (550–400 BC) recording Nebuchadnezzar's attack on Jerusalem (see 2 Kings 25)

event), resulting in the worst day in the history of God's people. Rather than surrender like Jehoiachin ten years earlier, Zedekiah and his sycophants flee, but they are duly overtaken, and the last thing Zedekiah ever sees is the execution of his sons. Blinded, he is marched to Babylon; in retrospect, he should have changed his name to Ichabod, "where is the glory?" Meanwhile, the city of Jerusalem is looted, and a high percentage of the population is likewise sent into exile. A careful description is provided for the dismantling of the temple (25:13–21), but there is no mention of any idolatrous paraphernalia, only implements and vessels known from the blueprints of the Torah.

Judah is sent into captivity, but Nebuchadnezzar does install a provisional government for those who remain (25:22–26), with Gedaliah (grandson of Josiah's official in chapter 22) as the superintendent in the town of Mizpah. His directive to settle down and serve the Babylonians does not sit well with a faction led by Ishmael, whose "royal" bloodline receives no elaboration (though some interpreters point to Elishama, David's son in 2 Sam. 5:16). This faction is probably pro-Egypt, because Egypt is where they head after the assassination of Gedaliah, motivated by fear of Babylonian reprisal. One can immediately sense that this moment—with a remnant of the people in Egypt—functions as an important preface to the final scene of the chapter (25:27–30), indeed, of 1–2 Kings as a whole. God's people are now in exile and needing an exodus, just like in the days of old. With the last king of Judah chained in Babylon, such hope looks slim. But Jehoiachin's parole in the concluding lines of the book becomes a reminder that God's promise to the house of David will endure. The promise will not end with a restoration of the monarchy but with a movement toward the messiah.

Select Bibliography

Brueggemann, Walter. *1 & 2 Kings*. Smith & Helwys Bible Commentary. Macon, GA: Smyth & Helwys, 2000.

Fretheim, Terence E. *First and Second Kings*. Interpretation. Louisville: Westminster John Knox, 1999.

Hens-Piazza, Gina. *1–2 Kings*. Abingdon Old Testament Commentaries. Nashville: Abingdon, 2006.

Long, B. O. *2 Kings*. Forms of the Old Testament Literature. Grand Rapids: Eerdmans, 1991.

Provan, Iain W. *1 and 2 Kings*. New International Biblical Commentary. Peabody, MA: Hendrickson, 1995.

Römer, Thomas C. *The So-Called Deuteronomistic History: A Sociological, Historical, and Literary Introduction*. New York: T. & T. Clark, 2005.

Seitz, Christopher R. *Prophecy and Hermeneutics: Toward a New Introduction to the Prophets*. Studies in Theological Interpretation. Grand Rapids: Baker Academic, 2007.

Seow, C. L. "1 & 2 Kings." In *The New Interpreter's Bible*. Edited by Leander E. Keck. Vol. 3. Nashville: Abingdon, 1999.

Sweeney, Marvin A. *I & II Kings*. Old Testament Library. Louisville: Westminster John Knox, 2007.

Walsh, J. T. *1 Kings*. Berit Olam. Collegeville, MN: Liturgical Press, 1996.

Wray Beal, Lissa M. *The Deuteronomist's Prophet: Narrative Control of Approval and Disapproval in the Story of Jehu (2 Kings 9 and 10)*. Library of Hebrew Bible/Old Testament Studies 478. New York: T. & T. Clark, 2007.

1–2 Chronicles

Mark J. Boda

Authorship and Date

By beginning with Adam and ending with Cyrus, 1–2 Chronicles provides an overview of history from the creation of the world until the foundation of the community to which it is addressed, in the Persian period. Mention of the figure Cyrus (2 Chron. 36:22–23, 539 BC), the coin "daric" (1 Chron. 29:7, ca. 515 BC), and Persian-period Davidic descendants (1 Chron. 3:17–24, ca. 450 BC) places the author of this book no sooner than the mid-fifth century BC. Allusions to Chronicles in books from the Second Temple period (1 Maccabees, Sirach, Dead Sea Scrolls) and its inclusion in the Old Greek translation suggest it was composed prior to the mid-third century BC. The community in and for which it was written was controlled largely by a group who had returned to Jerusalem after exile in Mesopotamia, rebuilt the temple, restored its services, yet remained under the hegemony of a foreign power, most likely the Persians (see Ezra-Nehemiah, Haggai, Zechariah, Malachi). The author is anonymous, but the emphasis placed on and familiarity with the practices of the nonpriestly Levites suggests someone within this guild.

Sources

The Chronicler responsible for this book constantly refers to sources from which further information could be culled and possibly from which he has drawn elements in his account. These sources range from records of various prophets (e.g., 1 Chron. 29:29; 2 Chron. 9:29) to the book of the kings of Judah and Israel (e.g., 2 Chron. 16:11; 25:26), none of which are extant. A close comparison of the accounts and lists in Chronicles and other Old Testament books reveals heavy reliance on the books of Samuel and Kings for narrative material (approximately 50 percent) and reliance on the Torah, Joshua, Psalms, Ruth, Ezra, and Nehemiah for many of the lists. A comparison between Chronicles and these sources offers insight into the historiographic intention of the Chronicler. It shows that the Chronicler is a master at gathering and combining sources as he constructs his history of Israel for his Persian-period audience.

Structure

Due to its length this work is typically divided into two parts (1 and 2 Chronicles), but it constitutes a single literary work. This composition is divided into four basic sections, beginning with an elongated review of the genealogies of Israel within the world (1 Chronicles 1–9), which not only depicts an ideal Israel united by Judah (David), Levi (temple), and Benjamin but also implicitly traces the story of Israel among the nations from Adam (1 Chron. 1:1) to Saul (1 Chron. 9:35–44). The narrative proper begins in chapter 10, with the death of Saul, designed to both contrast and prepare for the account of David in 1 Chronicles 10–29. The focus of this account is on David's preparations for the temple, first by transporting the ark to Jerusalem and legislating worship at this site, second by identifying the site of the temple, and third by providing the materials and personnel necessary for Solomon's construction of the temple. This is the focal point in the third major section of the book in 2 Chronicles 1–9, the account of Solomon. The idyllic rendition of Solomon's reign provides a firm foundation and exemplary pattern for the second temple in the Chronicler's day but also suggests an enduring hope for a future ideal royal figure. The post-Solomonic narratives in 2 Chronicles 10–36 trace the rise and fall of Judah's various monarchs, each providing an example to warn or encourage the Chronicler's audience. The book closes with a reminder of the divine hope expressed through the Persian-sponsored reconstruction of the temple and the divine challenge for others to return and join this worshiping community.

Theological Themes

The Chronicler expresses key theological principles through his rendition of the history of Israel. At the core of his theology is the proper worship of Yahweh at the temple in Jerusalem. While not ignoring the Torah legislation for worship revealed through Moses, in particular priestly sacrificial activity, the Chronicler consistently embraces Davidic innovations for the worship at the temple with focus on the verbal worship performed by the nonpriestly Levites. Faithfulness to covenant values expressed in the Torah, especially those related to exclusive worship of Yahweh at Jerusalem through legitimate means, is essential to the Chronicler's depiction of the history of Israel. Programmatic is Solomon's prayer at the dedication of the temple, which identifies the temple as the place of renewal for disobedient Israel (2 Chronicles 6). Key also is Yahweh's subsequent response in 2 Chronicles 7:12–16, which identifies the path to renewal as seeking, humbling, praying, and repenting, activities that will result in the blessing of God. This blessing is depicted throughout Chronicles in terms of construction projects, military success, abundant progeny, popular support, and long rule. Those who act unfaithfully and abandon Yahweh lack these blessings and are cursed. The Chronicler gives much attention to the prophetic office, citing many figures of classical prophecy (Isaiah, Jeremiah) as well as depicting priestly, Levitical, and even imperial figures as functioning prophetically. One can also discern within the

Artist's rendering of Solomon's temple

Chronicler's history a vision for Israel beyond that of the Chronicler's present community. Although the Chronicler does not see a place for the northern kingdom as a political structure independent from Davidic rule, he consistently embraces northerners who submit to Davidic rule and worship at the temple in Jerusalem. The depiction of an ideal David and Solomon and exemplary figures like Hezekiah and Josiah, the inclusion of an elongated Davidic genealogy in 1 Chronicles 3, and regular references to the enduring nature of the dynastic promise to David reveal the Chronicler's hopeful agenda for the reemergence of Davidic rule for the restoration community. The close link between temple and kingship throughout Chronicles reveals that the reconstruction of the temple foreshadows the renewal of the Davidic dynasty.

For Christians 1–2 Chronicles reveals the spiritual posture of a community into which their messiah Jesus would come. The importance of the faithful gathered around the second temple to the recognition of Jesus after his birth (see Luke 1–2) and the preparation for Jesus's ministry by the priestly prophet John's call to repentance are part of the enduring legacy of the Chronicler, who looked for an ideal Davidic ruler. This book has enduring relevance for a church in need of penitential renewal, reminding the followers of the Messiah Jesus that God continues to act in history, as his eyes "range throughout the earth to strengthen those whose hearts are fully committed to him" (2 Chron. 16:9).

Outline

F. The Accounts of Ahaziah, Athaliah, and Joash (22:1–24:27)
G. The Account of Amaziah (25:1–28)
H. The Account of Uzziah (26:1–23)
I. The Account of Jotham (27:1 9)
J. The Account of Ahaz (28:1–27)
K. The Account of Hezekiah (29:1–32:33)
L. The Account of Manasseh (33:1–20)
M. The Account of Amon (33:21–25)
N. The Account of Josiah (34:1–35:27)
O. The Final Royal Accounts, Exile, and Restoration (36:1–23)

Commentary

1. The Genealogies of Israel (1 Chron. 1:1–9:44)

The book of 1–2 Chronicles begins with nine long chapters of genealogies. Through these genealogies the Chronicler lays the foundation for the story of Israel, which will shift to narrative form in 1 Chronicles 10, with the final scene of Saul's life. The genealogy in 1 Chronicles 1 identifies Israel's roots among the nations of the world, showing that the story of Israel is intertwined with that of other nations. Chapters 2 8 provide details on the various tribal lineages within Israel, arranged in chiastic fashion with the two key tribes that survived the exile, Judah (2:3–4:23) and Benjamin (8:1–40), bracketing the entire list and the priestly tribe, Levi, at its center (chap. 6). Between these tribes are placed the northern tribes (chaps. 5, 7).

Such genealogies are used for a variety of purposes in ancient literature. They define sociological functions (identifying military,

One genealogy from ancient literature is the Assyrian King List (seventh century BC), which records all the Assyrian kings down to Tiglath-Pileser I (1115–1076 BC).

priestly, and royal personnel), highlight relationships between various groups of people (here relationships with the broader world and between various tribes), initiate the narrative plot by using people's names to summarize earlier phases of the story, and foreshadow key theological themes and literary structures used later in the work. Chapters 1–9 are thus not composed of irrelevant lists but rather lay the foundation for this book and the community that read it. This constitutes a genealogical tradition that will be continued in the books of Matthew and Luke, finding its culmination in the person of Jesus the Messiah, son of David, son of Abraham, son of Adam, son of God (Matt. 1; Luke 3).

A. God's chosen people among the nations (1:1–2:2). The first genealogy begins with Adam (1:1) and ends with the family of Israel (2:1–2), laying the foundation for the core of this genealogical section in chapters 2–8, which will focus on the various tribes of Israel. The genealogy in 1:1–4 is linear; it traces a single line of descendants from Adam to Seth to Noah, ignoring the line of Cain. Beginning with verse 5, the genealogy shifts to a segmented genealogy, one that traces multiple lines emerging from the final character mentioned. Thus Noah has three sons (1:4), and so the genealogies of these sons are provided in reverse order: Japheth (1:5–7), Ham (1:8–16), and Shem (1:17–26). From these three, descendants related to the final genealogical group

(Shem) become the focus of the next group of genealogies. Thus, Abram/Abraham's line emerges from the line of Shem (1:24–28), and the lines of his two key sons, Isaac and Ishmael, are traced in reverse order with Ishmael first (1:29–31), followed by the sons of Abraham through Keturah (1:32–33), and finally and most importantly, Isaac (1:34). The chosen line of Isaac is then traced in reverse order of election, first Esau and related peoples (1:35–54), followed by Israel (2:1–2).

This opening genealogy is an important reminder that Israel has arisen out of the nations and that its destiny is to bring blessing to these nations. The Chronicler's audience was well aware of the recent exilic experience among the nations. Although the return to the land was a signal of a new day for the nation (2 Chronicles 36), the postexilic community would continue to live under the hegemony of the nations. The restoration that Jesus inaugurated was not identified as a return to political independence but rather as a kingdom that would be spread by the gospel throughout all nations. In this way then, Israel's identity here is a foreshadowing of Christian identity, that community of the Messiah who would take the blessing of Abraham to the Gentiles.

B. Judah (2:3–4:23). While the genealogies in chapter 1 traced the chosen line last, the genealogies of Israel in chapters 2–8 place the enduring chosen lines at the beginning (Judah), center (Levi), and end (Benjamin). Although fourth-born of Israel (2:1–2), Judah is given primacy among the tribes, placed in first position, with the longest list. This genealogy of Judah is bracketed by an introduction to all the sons of Judah in 2:3–9 and a short description of the nonelect clans in 4:17–23. Genesis 38 explains the origins of these various clans. Judah's Canaanite wife Bathshua produced Er, Onan, and Shelah, with only the last surviving and having offspring. Judah's unknowing tryst with his Canaanite daughter-in-law Tamar produces the twins Perez and Zerah. The short description in 4:17–23 quickly traces the descendants

through the two insignificant Judahite lines of Zerah and Shelah, while the dominating central core of this genealogy in 2:10–4:16 lists the descendants of Perez through Hezron. The focus of this central genealogy is clearly the royal line of David from the family of Ram (2:10–17; 3:1–24), with David in the preferred seventh position from beginning and end of the list of Jesse's children in 2:10–17. David's royal descendants, provided in detail in 3:1–24, continue well after the fall of the kingdom to the time of the Chronicler, evidence of the Chronicler's enduring royal hope.

The first and longest genealogy among the tribes is that of Judah, not surprising in light of the fact that descendants of this tribe formed the majority of the postexilic audience, for which Chronicles was written, and that royal descendants of this tribe (Davidic dynasty) functioned as the central characters of the book. This focus on Judah reminds the reader that Israel's hope was tied especially to the small Judahite community that survived the exile, rebuilt the temple, and reestablished communal and spiritual rhythms. It is into this community that Jesus of Nazareth, son of David, would arise and fulfill the messianic hopes of old.

C. Simeon (4:24–43). It is not surprising to find a short genealogy of Simeon following the review of Judah. Simeon's territory is closely associated with Judah's inheritance throughout the book of Joshua (cf. Josh. 15:26–32; 19:1–9), and Judges 1 reveals how Judah and Simeon cooperated in their conquest of the land. Ultimately Simeon would be swallowed up by Judah, a reality foreshadowed by Jacob's curse in Genesis 49:7 on Simeon for his violent treatment of the Shechemites in Genesis 34:25–30. The Chronicler uses Simeon as a foil against which one can see Judah's blessing more vividly (1 Chron. 4:27).

D. Northern Transjordan tribes (5:1–26). Enclosed within the genealogical structure of the Chronicler's present-day community (Judah, chaps. 2–4; Levi, chap. 6; Benjamin, chap. 8) are two genealogical sections devoted to the northern tribes (chaps. 5, 7). The first recounts the lines of the northern tribes Reuben and Gad and half the tribe of Manasseh, who settled in the Transjordan (that region east of the River Jordan; Josh. 1:10–18). While these genealogies are bracketed by reminders of the failures of these tribes (5:1–2; 5:25–26), the inclusion of their genealogies as well as accounts of faithful victory (see 5:18–22) reveals the Chronicler's positive stance toward these tribes. For the Chronicler there is hope for a unified Israel, assembled around the Davidic monarch and his Levitical servants.

E. Levi (6:1–81). At the center of the genealogies in Chronicles is the tribe of Levi, those responsible for the temple and its worship, which will become the dominant theme of the narrative of 1–2 Chronicles. The Chronicler traces first the Aaronide priestly lines (6:1–15) then the nonpriestly Levitical clans (6:16–30). The respective duties of these two groupings are presented in reverse order, beginning with the nonpriestly Levites (6:31–48) and then the priests (6:49–53). Here the Chronicler lays out his vision for cooperation among all descendants of Levites in the worship at the temple, foreshadowing the innovations of David in 1 Chronicles 11–29. While the focus of the priests is on making atonement for Israel by offering sacrifice and incense (6:49), the focus of the nonpriestly Levites is to minister in music (6:31–32) and perform other duties (6:48). The territory for both priests and Levites is outlined in 6:54–81, revealing how the material needs of these clans were to be met, even as they provided spiritual service for the tribes throughout the land. The worship of Yahweh is the core calling of the people of Israel, and so the tribe of Levi is placed at the center of this genealogical review. It is Jesus who will assume and transcend the role of Levi in the new covenant (see Heb. 5, 7–10).

F. Northern Cisjordan tribes (7:1–40). The list of genealogies in 1 Chronicles 7 complements the list of northern tribes in 1 Chronicles 5, this time listing the genealogies of the

Cisjordan (those tribes on the western side of the River Jordan), northern tribes, which included Issachar, Benjamin, Naphtali, Manasseh, Ephraim, and Asher. In light of the focus of chapter 8 on the tribe of Benjamin, it is odd that Benjamin is included here among the northern tribes. This suggests Benjamin's identity as the tribe caught between the dominant northern (Ephraim) and southern (Judah) tribes. The absence of the tribes of Dan and Zebulun may be a painful reminder of the consequences of the disobedience of the northern tribes. However, the list of the other northern tribes reveals the Chronicler's affirmation of these northern groups and hope for a unified Israel rallied around the temple (Levi, chap. 6) and led by a Davidic monarch (Judah, chaps. 2–4). Allusion to an Israel united around Jesus is seen in his calling of the Twelve and the fulfillment of the restoration vision of Joel 2:28–32 in Acts 2.

G. Benjamin (8:1–40). An elongated genealogy of Benjamin concludes the Israelite genealogies in chapters 2–8, forming with Judah (chaps. 2–4) a bracket around the entire complex at whose center is the tribe of Levi (chap. 6). Benjamin's place here is related to the fact that it is descendants of Judah and Benjamin who will form the core of the restoration community after the exile (see Ezra 1:5) and that the narrative of Israel in 1 Chronicles 10–2 Chronicles 36 will begin with a focus on the fate of Israel's first king, the Benjamite Saul (1 Chron. 10:1–14; cf. 8:29–40).

H. God's chosen remnant from the nations (9:1–44). After providing a detailed genealogical vision of Israel in chapters 2–8, the Chronicler returns to the broader context of Israel's place among the nations, complementing the introductory genealogy in chapter 1. In 1 Chronicles 9 Israel again emerges from the nations, this time as a restoration community after the exilic nightmare. It is this restoration community to which the Chronicler's audience would trace itself. The Chronicler's present Israel (chap. 9) has the same potential as the Israel of chapters 2–8, which emerged from the nations in chapter 1.

Chapter 9 concludes with a repetition of 8:29–40, functioning here as a transition between the genealogies in chapters 1–9 and the narrative account in 1 Chronicles 10–2 Chronicles 36, which begins with the account of Saul's death in 1 Chronicles 10.

2. The Account of David (10:1–29:30)

With chapter 10, 1 Chronicles shifts from its genealogical introduction to the story of the Davidic monarchy. This story begins with the tragic death of Saul, revealing Saul's role as a foil against which one may see the brilliance of David. The account of David comprises two main sections divided by the story in chapter 21, which reveals how the temple site was chosen. Driving the first main section (chaps. 10–20) is David's passion for the centralization of worship in Jerusalem, while driving the second main section (chaps. 22–29) is David's provision of personnel, support, and materials for the temple

to be constructed by his son Solomon. Both sections give some attention to military matters, revealing David's role in creating a secure kingdom where worship would be possible.

This section foreshadows the future role of David's scion Jesus of Nazareth, the one who taught that the Father was seeking worshipers who would worship neither at Jerusalem nor Gerizim, but rather would worship in spirit and truth (John 4:24). Christ's death and resurrection opened this way to the Father, the ultimate centralization of worship for the whole world.

A. The defeat and death of Saul (10:1–14). The genealogies ended in the previous chapter with the Benjamite Saul, revealing that one of the roles of genealogies was to provide a quick summary of the story of the world and Israel from Adam (1:1) to Saul (9:39). The chapter begins with the dramatic story of the defeat of Saul's army on Mount Gilboa by the Philistines and his suicidal death (10:1–7). So powerless is this first king of Israel in his dying moments that when the king is wounded and facing imminent death, his armor bearer refuses to save him the dishonor of death by the Philistine

The ancient site of Beth Shan, where Saul's body was taken by the Philistines and placed on public display to highlight the victory over Israel (1 Chron. 10:10; cf. 1 Sam. 31:10)

archers. Reference to his whole house dying together (10:6) is a poignant reminder of the demise of Saul's dynasty, setting the stage for the rise of David in the following chapter. First Chronicles 10:8–12 relates the aftermath of the battle, focusing on the shameful dishonoring of the body of Saul by the Philistines. The placement of Saul's head and armor in Philistine shrines emphasizes the religious character of this victory and Saul's association even in death with Canaanite spirituality. In the end Saul's kin at Jabesh Gilead (see Judg. 21:1–25; 1 Sam. 11:1–11) retrieve the bodies of Saul's family from the Philistines, observing proper mourning rites (cf. 2 Sam. 1:11–12, 17–27; 3:35; Ps. 35:13–14). This chapter closes with a theological reflection, in 10:13–14, that links his death to divine judgment due to Saul's serious offenses against God, which included not following Yahweh's instructions (cf. 1 Samuel 13; 15), consulting a medium (1 Sam. 28:1–25; cf. Deut. 18:9–14), and not inquiring of Yahweh through appropriate means. The priority of the Chronicler is thus the attentive seeking of Yahweh's will through appropriate means followed by careful obedience to that revealed will. Saul's negative example sets the stage for both positive and negative examples of later kings and their people. Important is the final sentence of the chapter, which signals the transition from Saul to David, identifying Yahweh as the instigator of this transition and creating expectation of a new and positive era for Israel.

B. Establishing David's rule (11:1–47). In contrast to the writer of 1–2 Samuel, who depicts the civil war between those loyal to the dynasty of Saul and those loyal to David, in 11:1–3 the Chronicler immediately moves to the anointing of David by all the tribes of Israel, which followed that civil war. The absence of the depiction of David's struggle for the throne is the first sign that the Chronicler is presenting a glorified image of David (and Solomon), one that functions to justify the present second temple activities and to inspire future royal hope. The people's speech

here highlights David's early qualifications for kingship (11:2), referring to him as a shepherd, a common ancient Near Eastern royal image of one who cares for a vulnerable people (cf. Ps. 78:70–72), and as a ruler or leader, using the same Hebrew term often used by Yahweh to refer to his royal vice-regents (cf. 1 Sam. 9:16; 10:1; 13:14). Anointing and public confirmation here are the essential signs of the community's recognition of Yahweh's election of the royal figure. Oil was most likely used for the anointing, representative of Yahweh's blessing on and presence in the leader.

David's first action in Chronicles is to conquer and fortify Jerusalem (11:4–9), the first of a series of steps in 1 Chronicles 11–29 that highlight David's fixation with temple worship in Jerusalem. Description of early building programs in the fortification of Jerusalem will become a typical sign in Chronicles of Yahweh's blessing on a faithful king. Here this is made explicit with the reference to the presence of Yahweh Almighty at the end of 11:9.

Chapter 11 closes with a list of the names and exploits of David's military heroes, who are depicted as indicative of the full support of "all Israel" (11:10). This focus on "all Israel" is important to the Chronicler's vision for the nation, united around their Davidic ruler in worship of Yahweh at Jerusalem. The list of military men begins with the exploits of "the Three" (11:11–19). Each of these military figures is credited with a major military victory against incredible odds, the final one cast in language suggestive of sacrifice (blood, he poured it out before the Lord; cf. Num. 28:7). Verses 20–25 relate the exploits of two additional leaders: Abishai, the brother of Joab, David's general, who rises to commander of possibly a second squad of "the Three" in 11:11–19; and Benaiah son of Jehoaida, who although not attaining to the level of "the Three" gains renown among "the Thirty" by killing two men, a lion, and a giant Egyptian. The list of mighty men in 11:26–47 most likely represents members of the Thirty, that faithful inner circle of warriors loyal to

David who provided protection for the newly anointed king.

C. Supporting David's rule (12:1–40). What follows in 1 Chronicles 12 is a depiction of David as a leader who attracts Israel's loyalty long before the end of Saul's life. In this the Chronicler has shifted to an earlier period of history than that depicted in 1 Chronicles 11.

The first section, 12:1–22, depicts those who supported David prior to his establishment of Hebron as his first capital. It is not accidental that the first group listed is linked to Saul's own tribe of Benjamin and his hometown, Gibeah. Others who support David are not only from the expected southern tribe of Judah but also from the northern tribes of Gad and Manasseh. Locations listed here, Ziklag (1 Sam. 27:1–6) and his stronghold in the desert (see Adullam in 1 Sam. 22:1–5, En Gedi in 1 Sam. 23:29, unnamed ones in 1 Sam. 24:22; 2 Sam. 5:17), are typical of David's experience while on the run from Saul and prior to his settlement in Hebron as his capital. This list and account are an important reminder of early support of David by all Israel. Amasai's Spirit-inspired speech in 12:18 not only voices the loyalty of these defectors to David but also reminds the reader of divine blessing and presence within David.

Verses 23–38a provide further examples of support for David, now after the death of Saul. Again emphasis is placed on "all Israel" as evidence of support, with accompanying numerical values provided for all thirteen tribes of Israel (12:24–37) who affirm David's kingship. The list moves geographically from south to north in the Cisjordan (Judah, Simeon, Levi; Benjamin, Ephraim, Manasseh, Issachar, Zebulun, Naphtali, Dan, Asher) and then the Transjordan (Reuben, Gad, Manasseh). The numbers used here most likely refer to military units, both large (thousand) and small (hundred).

Chapter 12 closes with a picture of the entire nation gathered around David at Hebron, unified and celebrating his ascension to the throne (12:38b–40). The accent on joy will become typical throughout the Chronicler's account.

The Chronicler's depiction of Israelite support for David stands in stark contrast to the struggle depicted through 1–2 Samuel. Through this the Chronicler continues to offer an idealized portrait of David, one that legitimizes the second temple of his present day and creates expectations for the return of royal rule.

D. Transferring the ark: First attempt (13:1–14). First Chronicles 13 reveals that David's military strength and popular support makes possible his main agenda of the worship of God at the temple in Jerusalem. This chapter represents the first of two attempts to move the ark from Kiriath Jearim (cf. 2 Samuel 6) to Jerusalem, the second successful attempt occurring in 1 Chronicles 15. The narrative begins with David's consulting the people (13:1–4), continuing the motif of the entire nation ("all Israel") unified around their monarch. David's appeal to the assembly emphasizes the role of the people as a whole ("if it seems good to you"), but also of Yahweh ("if it is the will of the LORD our God") in decision making. It is ironic that while in his speech David distances himself from his predecessor Saul, whose lack of inquiry led to his downfall (cf. 10:13–14), David does not properly inquire of Yahweh as to how to move the ark, which would place inquiry at the heart of the nation. Although he discerns the will of the people (13:4), he does not discern the will of Yahweh (cf. 1 Chron. 15:13).

Verses 5–8 then describe how David and all Israel proceeded to Kiriath Jearim to transport the ark to Jerusalem. According to Exodus 25:10–22 the ark was housed in the Most Holy Place in the tabernacle, represented either Yahweh's royal throne or his footstool, and contained symbols of his miraculous provision (manna, Aaron's rod) and covenant relationship with Israel. Its presence in Kiriath Jearim followed its loss to the Philistines (1 Samuel 4–6). David has arranged for its transport on a cart guided by the sons of Abinadab, Uzzah and Ahio, and accompanied by the worship of the people with musical instruments, a theme typical of the books of Chronicles.

In 13:9–12, however, tragedy strikes as Uzzah reaches out his hand to steady the ark when the oxen stumble. In this the commoner Uzzah violates a holy object, that is, one dedicated for Yahweh alone, which was to be approached only by sacred personnel. It is not accidental that the location of this event is at a threshing floor (13:9), a foreshadowing of a later threshing floor that will mark the site of the temple in which the ark will finally rest (1 Chron. 21:18). David's anger and fear (vv. 11–12) reminds the reader of the mysterious character of Yahweh's will and the need for God's servants to make inquiry of and submit to that will. David's searching question in verse 12 will be answered by the provision of the Levites in chapter 15.

The chapter ends in 13:13–14 with the ark resting in the home of Obed-Edom, where it brings divine blessing. This only increases the tension created by this incident, ensuring that the ark will eventually find its way into Jerusalem so as to bring blessing on the nation as a whole.

E. The world stage (14:1–17). Before resolving the tension introduced in chapter 13, the Chronicler reminds the reader of the divine blessing on David, expressed here as elsewhere in Chronicles through depictions of building activity, abundant progeny, and military victory. While chapters 11–12 focused on the support David enjoyed within the nation, chapter 14 begins and ends with notes on the respect he receives from surrounding nations (14:1, 17). In 14:1 David receives messengers and artisans from Hiram's royal court at Tyre, signaling his newfound status among the kings of the ancient Near East. In light of this the Chronicler provides a summative note in 14:2, describing David's realization that his new position was caused by Yahweh's election and for the sake of his people. In this he truly functions as a mediatorial figure between Yahweh and his people, one who will be a conduit of divine blessing to the nation. In 14:3–7 the Chronicler lists the progeny born to David in his new capital at

Jerusalem, here contrasting Saul, whose progeny was lost in 1 Chronicles 10:6.

First Chronicles 14:8–16 then comprises two accounts of David's military victories over the Philistines, that force which had defeated Saul in 1 Chronicles 10. These two accounts accentuate the contrast between David and Saul, as David inquires of Yahweh for guidance (14:10, 14; cf. 10:13–14) and sees Yahweh go before him as divine warrior. David's actions here also reveal the missing element in his unsuccessful attempt at moving the ark in chapter 13, which will soon be rectified in chapter 15. These episodes provide a normative pattern for royal leadership in the Chronicler's Israel, one that seeks and obeys Yahweh's will. First Chronicles 14:17 brings closure to the chapter, returning to the point at which chapter 14 began by reminding the reader of David's international recognition caused by Yahweh. Throughout this chapter David's success is explicitly linked to Yahweh's election and action, an important reminder that apart from Yahweh, David has no significance or potential.

F. Transferring the ark: Second attempt (15:1–29). After the reminder of Yahweh's blessing on David, exemplified in his newfound status among the nations, the Chronicler finally provides the resolution to the plot introduced in chapter 13. The majority of the chapter (15:1–24) describes David's preparation to transport the ark from the home of Obed-Edom (see chap. 13) to Jerusalem. This time David prepares a place for the ark to be laid in Jerusalem (15:1) and assembles "all Israel" in Jerusalem (15:3). The account of the preparations is dominated by the identification of the Levites as the appropriate personnel for transporting the ark (15:2, 4–24), ignorance of which is explicitly identified as the cause of the failure in chapter 13. The Levitical role extends beyond merely carrying the ark to surrounding it with oral worship. This will be typical of the Chronicler's account of Israel's worship, showing how David sets in motion a new phase of worship in Israel, one that will employ musical voice and instrument alongside the sacrifices established by Moses (see 1 Chronicles 16).

At the end of the chapter (15:25–29) the Chronicler focuses on the laity of Israel, emphasizing the unity of Israel around this worship event but also David's priestly role, akin to both that of the Levites (robe of fine linen) and that of the priests (linen ephod). The account closes, however, with the dark figure of the Saulide Michal accentuating the brightness of David as a normative character, dancing and celebrating before Yahweh. By bringing the ark into Jerusalem, David identifies this city as the capital of his nation and Yahweh as the king he serves. It also reveals that worship lies at the heart of David's agenda for Israel and his capital city, an agenda that will quickly consume the Chronicler's account (see 1 Chronicles 22–29).

G. The ark in Jerusalem and the tabernacle in Gibeon (16:1–43). First Chronicles 16 continues the account in chapter 15, which traces the movement of the ark from the house of Obed-Edom (see 1 Chronicles 13) to the city of Jerusalem. By the end of chapter 15 the ark was entering the city accompanied by the music of the Levites, the joy of the people, and the dancing of David, the priestly Levitical king.

In 16:1–3 the Chronicler traces how the ark is set inside the tent prepared by David in 15:1. This is followed by a celebration in which David worships Yahweh through two voluntary offerings described in the Torah: the burnt (Leviticus 1) and peace (Leviticus 3) offerings. He then blesses the people in word and deed. By these two acts David again functions in his mediatorial role, positioned between God and people to bless and bring blessing. First Chronicles 16:4–37 recounts David's regularization of the aural worship so integral to the movement of the ark in chapter 15. With the Levitical function to transport the ark on the cusp of being rendered obsolete by a permanent shrine (temple), David reveals new roles for the Levites in relation to the ark, among which musical ministry is primary. For this next phase of history, the sacred shrine will have two locations, with the tabernacle remaining at Gibeon and the ark in a tent in Jerusalem. Of the Levitical clans appointed in 15:17 to transport the ark, Asaph

This Iron Age (tenth-century-BC) temple to Yahweh at Arad shows that other competing worship sites may have existed besides Jerusalem and Gibeon.

is responsible for musical worship at the tent in Jerusalem (16:5, 37).

First Chronicles 16:4 outlines the three basic types of songs that David commissions the Asaphites to compose for praise at the ark: petition, thanksgiving, and praise. It is these three types of psalms that dominate the Psalter, and not surprisingly the psalm provided in 16:7–36 is an amalgamation of three psalms from the Psalter, each representative of a different type of psalm: 1 Chronicles 16:8–22 being a portion from Psalm 105, a psalm of thanksgiving; 1 Chronicles 16:23–33 being a portion of Psalm 96, a psalm of praise; and 1 Chronicles 16:34–36 being a portion of Psalm 106, a psalm of petition. While the Asaphites are responsible for verbal worship at the ark, of the Levitical clans appointed in 15:17 to transport the ark, according to 16:39–42 Heman and Jeduthun (Ethan) are responsible for the tabernacle in Gibeon (16:39, 41). There Zadok, descendant of the priest Aaron, will sacrifice the daily offerings (Exod. 29:38–43; Num. 28:1–8) alongside these musical Levitical clans. The content of their musical worship is cited in verse 41: "to give thanks to the LORD, 'for his love endures forever.'" Ultimately this duality of worship centers would cease, but not until the temple was built by Solomon.

Chapter 16 ends with a focus on the community as a whole in 16:43, as both David and the people return to their own homes, David specifically to bless his family. This echoes the earlier blessing of Obed-Edom's household in 13:14. The blessing that earlier eluded David is now a reality because of the presence of the ark within David's capital.

H. Dynasty and temple (17:1–27). With the ark now safely in Jerusalem, David turns to the obvious contrast between his own house (palace) and Yahweh's tent (17:1). Interestingly, the court prophet Nathan rashly affirms David's intention (17:2), but immediately that night Yahweh appears to Nathan in a dream, overturning the prophet's words.

What follows in 17:3–15 constitutes Yahweh's revelation to Nathan, beginning in 17:4 and 7 with the introductory formula typical of prophetic speech. These introductory formulas divide the speech into two parts, with verses 4–6 questioning the necessity of a permanent house for Yahweh and verses 7–14 affirming the leadership of David. Interestingly, verses 4b and 10b form a complete sentence, the first verse claiming that David is "not the one to build me a house to dwell in," and the second claiming that "the LORD will build a house for you." In this lies the irony, formed by a play on the word "house," which here in verse 4b means a temple and then in verse 10b a dynasty. Rather than David, the house (palace) builder, building a house (temple) for Yahweh, Yahweh will build a house (dynasty) for David, which will then build a house (temple) for Yahweh. In this David and Solomon's destinies are made inseparable, as will be seen in the Chronicler's presentation of David's preparations for the temple in 1 Chronicles 22–29. Also significant in this prophetic speech is the covenantal promise in 17:13: "I will be his father, and he will be my son." In this one can discern the reciprocity essential to all the covenants between God and humanity throughout the Old Testament, elsewhere expressed as "I will be your God and you will be my people" (cf. Gen. 17:7–8; Exod. 6:7; Jer. 31:33). In the New Testament this same promise will be applied not only to Jesus (Heb. 1:5) but also to the entire messianic community (2 Cor. 6:18). In 17:16–27 David responds to Yahweh's covenantal invitation.

In 17:16–21 David humbly expresses his unworthiness at such an invitation from God. His reference to "servant" places himself at the service of Yahweh but also in company with other figures such as Moses, Joshua, and the prophets. In 17:20–22 David expresses the unique character of Yahweh among the gods and by extension the unique character of Israel among the nations. This uniqueness is highlighted by a rehearsal of the salvation story of Israel divided into the phases of exodus, conquest, and election. The prayer closes with David's clear acceptance of the invitation to covenant in 17:23–27, which emphasizes the enduring nature of the covenant and the promises to his dynasty, both based on the eternal character of praise due Yahweh. Through both Nathan's prophecy and David's response, the Chronicler accentuates the endurance of the Davidic covenant, suggesting his future hope for the renewal of the Davidic line.

I. Victory over the nations and administration in Israel (18:1–17). First Chronicles 18–20 follows up on the statements made in the dynastic oracle in chapter 17, showcasing Yahweh's fulfilling his promise to subdue all David's enemies and make his name great on the earth (see 1 Chron. 17:8, 10) and revealing why David's involvement in blood and war (1 Chron. 22:8–10) will make his son Solomon the candidate for building the temple (1 Chron. 17:11–12). David's many victories will provide the peace essential for the building projects Solomon will undertake and also the wealth necessary for such projects. The first section of chapter 18, 18:1–6, focuses on David's military victories over the Philistines (Gath), Moab, Zobah, and Damascus, groups representative of southwestern (Philistines), southeastern (Moab), and northern (Zobah/Damascus) powers outside traditional Israelite lands. Control of Philistia and Moab gave David the ability to tax the two great international trunk highways (Way of the Sea, King's Highway), providing resources to sustain a royal court. Zobah and Damascus were centers of (at times) powerful Aramean kingdoms to the north of Israel. Damascus was key since both the international highways intersected at this geographical location. References to these nations becoming "subject" to David and offering him "tribute" (18:2, 6, 13) is suggestive of vassal relationships in the ancient world in which a royal overlord would allow a conquered people a measure of political autonomy as long as they sent tribute regularly to the overlord.

First Chronicles 18:7–11 provides a list of various spoils dedicated to Yahweh, from both the northern regions (Hadadezer of Zobah and Tou of Hamath) and the south (Edom, Moab, Ammon in the Transjordan, Philistia in the southwest, and Amalek, in the southern Transjordan). While the battles that result in the tribute from the northern region and from Philistia and Moab are recorded in 18:1–6, the battle with the Ammonites is recorded in 1 Chronicles 19 and with the Edomites in 18:12–13. Key to these various accounts are the Chronicler's theological statements in 18:6 and 13, which remind the reader that Yahweh is the source of David's universal victory. David is successful not only in conquering the regions lying outside of traditional Israelite lands but also in developing the internal administration of the kingdom (18:14–17). It is clear not only that it is important to have proper organization for this new kingdom (vv. 15–17) but also that a premium is placed on the quality of this rule, described in verse 14 as "just and right for all his people" (cf. Psalm 72).

J. Victory over Ammon and Aram (19:1–19). Chapter 19 continues the series of accounts in 1 Chronicles 18–20 that traces David's victories over his enemies, which are a fulfillment of Yahweh's promise to him in 1 Chronicles 17:8–10, as well as justification for why David as man of blood and war is not allowed to build the temple (1 Chron. 22:8–10). First Chronicles 19:1–5 highlights the incident that causes tension with the Ammonites. It appears that Ammon has been on friendly terms with David, possibly because David and the father Nahash shared a common enemy in Saul (see 1 Sam. 11:1–11; 12:12). The death of Nahash and accession of his son Hanun introduces ambiguity into the relationship between the two kingdoms, not surprising in times of leadership transition in the ancient world. Hanun's suspicion of David's intent leads to his shameful treatment of Israelite messengers, whose hair is shaved and nakedness revealed (cf. Isa. 47:2–3). Such treatment of messengers is a rebuff of the one who sent the messengers and in this case a cause for war.

In the first battle, in 19:6–15, David sends his general Joab. It appears that Hanun does not possess appropriate resources to challenge David, since he needs to hire mercenaries from Aramean states to the north (Aram Naharaim, Aram Maakah, Zobah). These mercenaries are placed out front, where their powerful chariots can take advantage of the open fields, while the Ammonites remain near the city. Joab's strategy is to divide his army into two groups, the first of which he will lead against the Arameans, and the second of which his brother Abishai will lead against the Ammonites near the city. However, the battle is short-lived, as both Arameans and Ammonites retreat and the Israelites return to their land. The fighting is not yet over, as the Arameans decide to turn against David in 19:16–19. In this case David takes command of the Israelite army against an Aramean coalition led by Hadadezer of Zobah (see above on 18:1–6) and his general Shophak. The battle, which takes place at the River Jordan, is a decisive victory again for Israel.

K. Victory over Ammon and Philistia (20:1–8). First Chronicles 20 contains the final two accounts of David's military victories over the nations surrounding Israel, which compose 1 Chronicles 18–20. First Chronicles 20:1–3 brings closure to David's battle against the Ammonites, which began in 19:1–15. Joab, David's general, led the Israelite army on that occasion and, while putting Ammon to flight, decided not to besiege their city. The account turns first in 19:16–19 to describe David's victory over the Arameans, some of whom had retreated with the Ammonites, and only now in 20:1–3 describes David's defeat of the Ammonite capital city of Rabbah. It is interesting that here the Chronicler's source introduces the tragic story of David and Bathsheba (see 2 Samuel 11–12), but the Chronicler makes no mention of Bathsheba—not surprising in light of

> Remains of a second-century-AD Roman temple to Hercules mark the site of ancient Rabbah, the capital of the Ammonites during the time of David.

the glorious presentation of David throughout Chronicles. The final section of 1 Chronicles 18–20, 20:4–8, focuses on the exploits of David's men over a series of Philistine giants. This is an appropriate ending to this section on David's exploits, since it began with David's conquest of Gath (1 Chron. 18:1). This account closes the complex of stories devoted to David's military victories, which are appropriate following the dynastic oracle in chapter 17. However, these stories also prepare the way for 1 Chronicles 21, where David's foolish census for military purposes will prompt divine discipline.

L. The census (21:1–30). The Chronicler largely ignores the failings of the two founding figures of the Davidic dynasty, David and Solomon. While not a single failure is attached to Solomon, two of David's failures are included in Chronicles. Interestingly, both of these failures are related to David's naïveté in ritual matters, both are related to events key to Jerusalem's new role as worship center in Israel, both result in the death of innocent figures, and in both David functions as a priestly leader offering sacrifices. Thus, through these failures David accomplishes a positive mission: the centralization of worship at Jerusalem.

Chapter 21 begins in 21:1–6 with the revelation that Satan has enticed David to count his people, contrasting the assertion in 2 Samuel 24:1 that it was Yahweh who incited/enticed David to do so. The Hebrew term *satan*, which means "adversary," is used of both human (e.g., 1 Sam. 29:4) and heavenly (e.g., Job 1:6–9) beings, in both military (e.g., 1 Kings 5:18) and legal (Ps. 109:6) contexts. While it is clear that this is a military context, it is uncertain whether this is a human or heavenly figure. Evidence for a human figure is seen in the use of the phrase "rose up against" (2 Chron. 20:23) and the presence of other instances of human military opponents in chapters 18–20; but evidence for a heavenly figure occurs in Zechariah 3:1, which includes the same Hebrew phrase translated in 1 Chronicles 21:1 as "rose up against" (NIV "standing at"), as well as in Job 1–2, which uses

"incited." David's error here lies not in the act of counting itself, since such counting occurs elsewhere in 1–2 Chronicles (cf. 1 Chron. 9:1; 11:11; 12:24), but in his failure to perform the rituals demanded by the Torah (Exod. 30:11–16), that is, payment of a half shekel for each person over twenty years old. Joab's attempt to avoid guilt by not counting all the tribes reveals his lack of knowledge of the Torah legislation.

David's foolish act prompts divine discipline in 21:7–14. No description is given of what prompted David's admission of sin and request for absolution. Yahweh's response with the choice of three deadly options (famine, military defeat, plague) is not inconsistent with David's request for absolution. Each of these represents mitigated punishment, a judgment less than the sin deserves, which is typical in Old Testament approaches to sin (see Num. 14:17–23; Exod. 32:30–35). It is in 21:15–27 that this event takes on even greater significance. As the death angel is about to strike Jerusalem, David cries out for God's mercy, admitting his culpability again and asking God to strike him and his family rather than the people. In response Yahweh demands that David build an altar and sacrifice offerings to avert judgment. The site for this altar belongs to a man named Araunah, a Jebusite, one of the pre-Davidic inhabitants of Jerusalem. The final section of chapter 21, 21:28–22:1, makes clear that through David's failure Yahweh identifies the site of his temple, which will be a place of penitential prayer and sacrifice.

M. Initial provision and commission to build the temple (22:1–19). This chapter begins, in 22:1, with the reminder that David's failure in chapter 21 in relation to counting the army resulted in the identification of the site of the temple and altar in Jerusalem. With this site identified, the remainder of the account of David is dominated by David's preparations for the building of the temple. Chapters 22 and 28–29 form a bracket around an inner core in chapters 23–27, which comprises lists of personnel essential for the temple and its proper function.

First Chronicles 22:2–5 describes David's provision of materials for the temple construction. The regular use of terms for large amounts throughout these verses accentuates the grandeur of the project. Reference is made to Solomon's youth and inexperience, a reminder that David and Solomon together will build this sanctuary, with David providing the building materials, personnel, and services and Solomon guiding the construction and dedication after his father's death.

The importance of Solomon's role is made clear in 22:6–16, as David commissions him, rehearsing the encounter with God in 1 Chronicles 17, explaining why Solomon, the man of peace, will build the temple rather than David, the man of war, and then blessing his son in words reminiscent of Joshua's commissioning in Deuteronomy 31:2–8 and Joshua 1:1–9. As Joshua fulfilled Moses's ultimate goal of taking the people into the land, so Solomon will fulfill David's ultimate goal of building the temple. Solomon, however, is not going to do this alone, but is to be supported by the people according to 22:17–19. In these closing verses of chapter 22, David commissions "all the leaders of Israel," reminding the reader once again of the importance of the community as a whole to the support of the temple, a key value for the Chronicler as he addresses his own postexilic community gathered around the second temple. Here seeking Yahweh with one's entire being (heart and soul) is equated with building the sanctuary. The stimulus for such support is the presence of God ("Is not the LORD your God with you?"), and the ultimate goal is the praise of the name of God.

N. Personnel for temple and kingdom (23:1–27:34). First Chronicles 23–27 is dominated by lists of personnel within the kingdom appointed by David for the support of the temple and its services after his death. While such lists are rarely appreciated by modern readers, they are as key to the Chronicler's rhetorical strategy as his introductory genealogies in chapters 1–9. They accentuate David's thorough preparation for the temple construction and worship by provision of personnel for both temple and state.

23:1–25:31. First Chronicles 23:1 sets these lists into the context of the final phase of David's life. While chapters 22 and 28–29 focus on David's provision of the necessary material resources, chapters 23–27 focus on the equally important provision of human resources for the proper operation of the temple. In this way the Chronicler depicts David and Solomon as a temple construction team. First Chronicles 23:2, with its use of the language of assembly ("gathered together"), introduces the many lists in chapters 23–27, the end of which will be signaled by the reference to David's summons of the various groups in 28:1. First Chronicles 23:3–5 orients the reader to the many lists of Levites that will appear throughout chapters 23–27 (23:6–24; 24:20–31; 25:1–31; 26:1–19, 20–28, 29–32), identifying the age of those counted (thirty or older), the total number (thirty-eight thousand), and the various responsibilities (construction supervisors, officials, judges, gatekeepers, musicians).

The initial list that follows in 23:6–24 provides a basic orientation to the three foundational clans of Levites, each reviewed in order, with Gershon in 23:7–11, Kohath in verses 23:12–20, and Merari in 23:21–23; the list ends with a summary in 23:24. The roots of the priestly line of Aaron within the tribe of Levi are identified in 23:13, although a fuller account is not provided until chapter 24. First Chronicles 23:13 identifies four roles for the Aaronide priests: consecration of most holy things (Exod. 28:38; Lev. 22:2–3), offering of sacrifices (Lev. 6:8–7:38), ministry before Yahweh (Exod. 28:35), and blessing of the people (Num. 6:22–27). This allusion to Aaron and the priestly tasks in the midst of the Levitical lists prompts the orientation provided by 23:25–32, which explains the roles of nonpriestly Levites under the new circumstances of temple worship. They are to assist the priests in the temple by giving attention to courtyards and side rooms, purification rites, baking products, and measuring devices, as well as by offering verbal praise alongside the various sacrifices at the temple. There is thus a place for all members of the tribe of Levi at the temple, something that would have been helpful for shaping worship in the Chronicler's own day.

The list in 24:1–19 then focuses on the Aaronic priestly line in Israel. After referring in passing to the tragedy that befell Aaron's sons Nadab and Abihu (Lev. 10:1–2; Num. 3:4), the list focuses on the two remaining clans established by Aaron's other two sons, Eleazar and Ithamar. Two priestly figures assist David, the one Zadok from the clan of Eleazar and the other Ahimelek son of Abiathar from the clan of Ithamar (cf. 1 Chron. 15:11; 18:16). The ultimate dominance of the former (Eleazar) over the latter is recorded in 1–2 Kings, Ezekiel, Ezra, Haggai, and Zechariah and is evident in the larger numbers associated with Zadok's clan here in chapter 24. There is, however, a role for the clan of Ithamar in the temple, and this is determined by sacred lot, which divides the responsibilities into twenty-four divisions—if on annual rotation, this would mean each clan covered half a month, or if biannual rotation, then a month each. Verse 19 emphasizes the need for these priestly clans to follow the regulations established by Yahweh through Aaron. Following this priestly list, the Chronicler returns to a list of a select group of nonpriestly Levitical clans from the lines of Kohath and Merari in 24:20–31. While this list expands the information

David appointed men to play cymbals, harps, and lyres at the house of God. Here are two harpists in a ninth-century-BC Assyrian relief from Ashurbanipal's palace at Nimrud.

found in the earlier list of 23:12–23, key here is the link to the priestly appointment seen in the casting of lots before David, Zadok, Ahimelek, and priestly and Levitical leaders (cf. 24:5–6).

First Chronicles 25:1–31 recounts the commissioning of Levitical musicians from the clans of Asaph, Heman, and Jeduthun, appointments foreshadowed by the account in chapters 15–16, which placed the Asaphites in the Jerusalem tent (16:37) and the Hemanites and Jeduthites in the Gibeonite tabernacle (16:41–42). According to 1 Chronicles 6:33–47, these three families were each from a different Levitical clan outlined in 23:6–24, with Heman from Kohath, Asaph from Gershon/-m, and Ethan/Jeduthun from Merari. Here in 25:1 Levitical music is explicitly identified as "prophesying," and in 25:2–5 the various clan heads are associated with prophetic activity. This link between Levitical music and prophecy is seen elsewhere in the Chronicles (2 Chron. 20:21–22; 29:25, 30; 35:15). Here we see an expansion of the prophetic role into the worship of Israel. While prophetic communication in the Old Testament is typically delivered in nonmusical verbal form or action, here prophecy is delivered through musical media, as the Levites give thanks and praise to Yahweh (25:3), accompanied by musical instruments (25:1). There are, however, precedents for connection between prophetic utterance and music in 1 Samuel 10:5 and 2 Kings 3:15 (cf. 1 Sam. 16:23). As with the priestly appointments earlier, in chapter 24, so here the musicians are appointed by sacred lot and divided into twenty-four clans, suggesting a parallel Levitical ministry of music alongside the priestly ministry of sacrifice at the temple.

26:1–27:34. First Chronicles 26:1–19 traces David's commissioning and organizing of the Levitical gatekeepers, whose lineage is traced to the clans of Kohath and Merari. The list in verses 1–11 is divided into three groups, followed (as in earlier lists) with a description of the selection process and vocational function in verses 12–19. The selection process here echoes that of earlier Levitical and priestly appointments in chapters 24–25 (sacred lot), and the gatekeepers' responsibility was to protect the gateways into the temple precincts. According to 1 Chronicles 9:23, 27, this responsibility entailed guarding the entrance, patrolling at night, and opening the gates in the morning. Not surprisingly, the total number of gatekeepers adds up to twenty-four, but this time the number does not refer to rotation of duty as in earlier lists. Rotation according to 1 Chronicles 9:24–25 was every seven days.

Following the list of gatekeepers the Chronicler provides the list of Levitical treasurers in 26:20–28. The two Levitical groups responsible for the treasuries hailed from the line of Gershon (26:21–22) and Kohath (26:23–28). Two types of treasuries are defined here (26:20), the first relating to the house of God, and the other to dedicated gifts. The latter contains plunder dedicated to the temple from military victories (vv. 26–28). Not only Levitical treasurers but also Levitical administrators were commissioned by David according to 26:29–32. These administrators, drawn from the Levitical clan of Kohath, were not directly related to worship activities on the temple mount, functioning instead as "officers and judges" throughout the land (see Deut. 16:18–20) with responsibility for both "secular" and "sacred" matters (see 26:30, 32; cf. 2 Chron. 19:5–11). The list of these Levitical administrators functions as a segue to lists of other Davidic personnel not directly associated with the sacred duties at the temple in chapter 27.

First Chronicles 27:1–15 enumerates David's military, including the various levels in the army's chain of command. Verse 1 makes it clear that David's army was not an ad hoc force but rather a standing army on defined rotation, able to defend Israel constantly. First Chronicles 27:16–22 lists the leaders of the tribes of Israel, leaving out the two tribes of Gad and Asher, separating Aaron from the rest of Levi, and dividing the Joseph tribes into three groups (Ephraim, half Manasseh, half Manasseh), to bring the total number to thirteen. By placing this list of tribal leaders at the end of his list of material in chapters 23–27, the Chronicler is foreshadowing their appearance in chapters 28–29 to pledge their support for Solomon and his temple project (cf. 28:1; 29:6). In a short note in 27:23–24 following the lists of army and tribal leaders, the Chronicler reveals that David's sin in 1 Chronicles 21 was not related to breaking the prohibition of counting those over twenty years of age (cf. Num. 1:3, 45), a prohibition based here on Yahweh's promise of innumerable descendants to Abraham (cf. Gen. 22:17), since Joab did not complete the count. (See above on 1 Chronicles 21:1–6 for the nature of David's sin.) The list in 27:25–31 presents twelve overseers of David's royal property throughout the land, ranging from those supervising treasuries (v. 25) to those supervising agricultural activity (vv. 26–31). Such resources were essential for the sustenance of an ancient royal court and army. The final list in chapters 23–27 (27:32–34) identifies the seven key advisors at the core of David's court who would offer him wisdom to rule the kingdom.

O. Commissioning Solomon (28:1–21). After the long series of lists in chapters 23–27, which traces David's provision of the support personnel for the temple, the Chronicler provides a second scene of commissioning, echoing the earlier one in chapter 22. While in 22:5 David speaks of his future preparations for the temple, in 29:19 he reflects over his past preparations. First Chronicles 28:1 introduces this second commissioning, noting how David has assembled the secular leadership just reviewed in chapter 27. What follows in 28:2–8 is David's address to this gathered assembly of leaders, which echoes the themes and vocabulary of the earlier speech in 22:7–16. The majority of the speech (28:2–7a) focuses on the privileges enjoyed by Solomon, with greater emphasis placed in this speech on Yahweh's choice of Solomon (28:5–6; cf. 28:10; 29:1). Verse 7b introduces the incredible responsibility laid on Solomon to carry out and follow God's commands. Before turning to Solomon in verses 9–10, however, in verse 8 David first charges the leaders of Israel to fulfill the same demands imposed on Solomon, fulfillment of which will ensure the enduring possession of the land. David then turns to Solomon in 28:9–10, calling him to acknowledge and serve God with all his being and identifying the two possibilities before Solomon (seek or forsake) and their attendant results (finding God and being rejected by God). These two possibilities echo the "two ways" placed before Israel as they were poised to enter the promised land (Deut. 30:15). Yahweh's omniscience discourages any hypocrisy and ensures a just divine response. Fundamental to the service Solomon will render Yahweh is the building of the temple (28:10).

David's commission to Solomon is followed in 28:11–19 by David's provision to Solomon of detailed written plans for the temple structure, work assignments, and worship articles. Verses 12 and 19 point to the divine source of these plans: the Spirit and the hand of Yahweh. After handing over these plans to Solomon, David delivers his final charge to his son in 28:20–21, using language of encouragement reminiscent of Moses's commissioning of Joshua in Deuteronomy 31:7, 23; Joshua 1:6–7, 9, 18 and echoing the earlier commission of 1 Chronicles 22:6–16. David's call to courage is not based primarily on the extensive resources that David has provided for the project (28:21) but first and foremost

on the theological premises that God will be with Solomon and will not fail or forsake him as he pursues this massive task (28:20).

P. Charging the assembly (29:1–30). Having addressed Solomon in front of the assembled leaders in chapter 28, David now turns to the entire assembly in 29:1–5. Most of this speech expresses the reasons why the leadership needs to fully engage (29:5) in the temple project. These include the inexperience of his successor Solomon (29:1a), the magnitude of the task ahead (29:1b), and the generous example of David in the past (29:2) and present (29:3–5).

The response of the leadership in 29:6–9 is described as willing, wholehearted, and substantial, prompting the joy of both the people and the king. This joy prompts the response of David to God in 29:10–19, one that begins with general praise of Yahweh as Creator of all things (29:10–13), shifts to the unworthiness of David and his nation, who are merely returning to God what he first gave them (29:14–17), and concludes with requests for his people and Solomon that God may stir their inner affections to obedience to the law and completion of the temple project (29:18–19). This prayer then prompts from the assembly in 29:20–22a a response of praise to Yahweh and homage to the king followed by a sacrificial celebration in God's presence. It is at this celebration that Solomon is then crowned king (29:22b–25) a second time. Solomon's first coronation in 1 Chronicles 23:1 was a private affair enacted by David. This second event is performed by the people. Examples of a two-stage royal appointment with one private and the other public can be seen in the lives of Saul (1 Sam. 10:1; 11:12–14) and David (1 Sam. 16:13; 2 Sam. 2:1–7; 5:1–5). Reference is made here also to the anointing of Zadok as priest, something important to the Zadokite priests, who will serve as high priests in the second temple of the Chronicler's day (see Zech. 3:1–10; 6:9–15). The embrace of Solomon by the people (29:23) and military (29:24) is explicitly linked to a divine act in 29:25.

The account of David's reign concludes in 29:26–30 with a summary note, emphasizing that he ruled over a unified Israel ("all Israel") and experienced exemplary blessing (long life, wealth, honor). The final verses recount various resources used by the Chronicler for his account, all linked to prophetic figures who served during the life of David. Such resources bolster the authenticity of this account to the Chronicler's ancient audience.

3. The Account of Solomon (2 Chron. 1:1–9:31)

A substantial portion of the account of David (1 Chronicles 22–29) is devoted to a description of David's preparations for the succession of his son. These preparations are focused almost exclusively on Solomon's function as temple builder and patron. The Solomon who emerges after the death of David at the end of 1 Chronicles 29 is a Solomon without tarnish. While two failures of David are incorporated into his account, both events key to the creation of Jerusalem as the central place of worship in Israel (1 Chronicles 13; 21), not one failure is attributed to Solomon in 2 Chronicles 1–9. Like the transition from Saul to David in 1 Chronicles 10–11, the transition from David to Solomon is smooth and lacking conflict. This idyllic portrait of the past lays the foundation and provides direction for realities within the Chronicler's present community, especially in relation to the second temple and its services. Furthermore, it engenders future hope for a community struggling under enduring imperial rule, which knows well the prophetic messianic hope.

A. Ascending the throne (1:1–17). The account of Solomon begins with a summary note in 1:1 stating that Solomon takes firm control of the kingdom. While Solomon has been largely passive throughout 1 Chronicles 22–29, he now leaps into action. His success in this shift is attributed by the Chronicler to the presence of Yahweh. In 1:2–12 Solomon convenes an assembly of all Israel and its leaders (military, officials, tribal and family heads), leading them to the tabernacle at Gibeon. While David brought the ark into Jerusalem, housing it in a tent where verbal worship was conducted (1 Chron. 16:1, 37–38), the rest of the tabernacle has remained in Gibeon, where both sacrificial and verbal worship are conducted (16:39–42). Although the ark is in Jerusalem, it is to Gibeon that Solomon goes with the people to inquire of Yahweh and sacrifice burnt offerings. Seeking Yahweh in proper ways is key to the presentation of proper kingship throughout 1 Chronicles, negatively portrayed in the life of Saul (1 Chron. 10:13–14), positively displayed in the life of David (1 Chron. 13:3), and expectantly encouraged in the life of Solomon (1 Chron. 22:19; 28:8–9). There in Gibeon, Yahweh appears to Solomon, inviting him to ask for anything as he begins his reign. Solomon chooses wisdom (1:8–10), which Yahweh promptly gives him, noting that such a choice will yield also wealth and fame (1:11–12). This interchange between Yahweh and the new king is followed by a summary statement in 1:13 that, together with 1:1, isolates verses 2–12 as foundational to the account of Solomon in chapters 1–9. In 1:14–17 the Chronicler immediately recounts the military and economic prosperity of Solomon. Similar material will recur at 2 Chronicles 9:25–28, forming a bracket around the entire Solomon account and reminding the reader of the fulfillment of Yahweh's promises given at Gibeon.

B. Preparing for the temple project (2:1–18). While 1 Kings shows the impact of Solomon's new divine gift of wisdom on the administration of the kingdom, especially in areas of justice, 2 Chronicles immediately shows its impact on what, for the Chronicler, is Solomon's main purpose, the building of the temple. Second Chronicles 2:1 functions as a summary note, signaling the beginning of Solomon's building projects, which include a royal dwelling for both Yahweh (temple) and himself (palace). In 2:2 Solomon organizes the workforce for the temple project, numbering the workers and separating them into three groups: carriers, stonecutters, and foremen. Solomon next sends a letter to Hiram in 2:3–10. Hiram is first introduced in Chronicles at 1 Chronicles 14:1–2, where this king of the Phoenician city of Tyre acknowledges the new reign of David. Tyre was located to the northwest of Israel along the Mediterranean coast. Its control of the forests of the Lebanon mountains to its east made it an important source for construction projects in the ancient Near East. As is typical of ancient political relationships, emphasis is placed on the past relationship between the two political states, and here Solomon uses this past relationship as the basis for his request for materials for his temple project. Solomon carefully identifies the purpose of this temple, emphasizing the incomparability of Yahweh among all gods, particularly important as he interacts with this foreign leader. Solomon asks for not only materials but also craftsmen who will train his workers in finer construction techniques.

Hiram's reply in 2:11–16 not only affirms that Solomon's reign is being recognized and legitimated in similar ways to the reign of his father (cf. 1 Chron. 14:1–2) but also grants Solomon his requests for material and human resources. Particular emphasis is placed on the figure Huram-Abi, the description of whom is designed to link him to the craftsman Oholiab, who worked on the earlier tabernacle project in the wilderness (Exod. 35:31–36:1). More details of the enumeration mentioned in 2:2 are provided in 2:17–18, the two forming a bracket around the key interchange between Solomon and Hiram in 2:3–16.

C. Building the temple structure (3:1–17). Having made arrangements for materials and personnel for the temple project in chapter 2, Solomon now begins construction in chapters 3–4. Second Chronicles 3:1–2 is another of the many summary notes used throughout Chronicles. Here the note identifies the location of the temple with two earlier key sacrificial traditions, which involved the angel of the Lord: the provision of sacrifice to Abraham in order to save the life of young Isaac on Mount Moriah in Genesis 22 (see esp. 22:13–14) and the provision of sacrifice to David on the threshing floor of Araunah to save Jerusalem in 1 Chronicles 21.

Second Chronicles 3:3–17 traces the creation of the physical structures of the temple site. Laying the foundation (3:3) was an important stage in the construction of sacred shrines in the ancient Near East (see Ezra 3:1–13; Isa. 28:16; Hag. 2:15–19; Zech. 4:6–10), not only to ensure that the building endured, but also because the building needed to rest on undefiled ground. The use of pure gold in the entrance room (3:4) is a key signal to worshipers that they

An aerial view of the Jerusalem Temple Mount, located on Mount Moriah, the site of Solomon's temple

are approaching the presence of deity. The main room (3:5–7) is equivalent to the Holy Place in the earlier tabernacle structure (Exod. 26:33). The iconography of trees and angelic beings suggests a heavenly paradise. While the Holy Place of the tabernacle contained one lampstand and one table (for the bread of the Presence), according to chapter 4 this room contains ten gold lampstands, ten tables, and ten small basins. The Most Holy Place (3:8–14) is constructed in a perfect square, the use of fine gold appropriate for the place of God's manifest presence. While the cherubim in the tabernacle were simply part of the ark (Exod. 25:10–21), the cherubim in the temple are standing side by side and facing the entrance to the main hall, guarding the throne room of Yahweh. A cherubim motif is woven into the curtain (3:14) that, along with doors (see 4:22), separates and protects this special room from the main hall (cf. Exod. 26:31–33). Two pillars stand in front of the temple, their names Jachin ("he will establish") and Boaz ("in him is strength"), signifying the enduring quality of the temple and the kingdom of those who will worship there.

A shrine model from the tenth century BC. The two pillars bearing the roof are reminiscent of the central columns, Jakin and Boaz, in Solomon's temple (2 Chron. 3:17).

D. Creating the temple furnishings (4:1–22). Having reviewed the construction of the building structure in chapter 3, the Chronicler now focuses attention on the creation of the various furnishings and utensils to be placed within the temple to facilitate worship. Second Chronicles 4:1–8 provides an account of the fashioning process. The bronze altar, which has sixteen times the surface area of the former altar in the tabernacle (Exod. 27:1–8), replaces David's temporary altar at this site (1 Chron. 21:26). It is positioned in the inner court of the temple area.

"The Sea," replacing the large basin in the tabernacle (Exod. 30:17–21), is made of bronze and placed on a foundation of twelve oxen. It is used for ritual cleansing, key for approaching the holy presence of Yahweh. Ten smaller basins, placed within the main room of the temple, are for washing utensils used in the sacrificial process. Matching these ten basins are ten gold lampstands and ten tables, the former providing light inside the temple and the latter platforms for the bread of the Presence (cf. 4:19). Before providing lists of the items just described, the Chronicler describes the creation of the outer courtyard structures, which will hold the bronze altar and the Sea, in 4:9–10. Two courtyards are created, one inner courtyard for the priests and another, larger, outer courtyard supposedly for nonpriests (see 1 Kings 7:12).

The account concludes with lists of the furnishings and utensils created for the temple in 4:11–22. The lists are divided into two parts, tracing first the accomplishments of the Tyrian artisan Huram-Abi (see 2 Chron. 2:11–16 above) in 4:11–18 and then those of Solomon in 4:19–22. Huram-Abi's items are all made of bronze and placed in areas outside the sanctuary proper, while Solomon's are all made of gold and placed in the sanctuary itself. This distinction between these two figures identifies Solomon as the lead craftsman and Huram-Abi as his assistant (cf. 4:11).

E. Transferring the ark in Jerusalem (5:1–14). The summary note at the beginning of chapter 5 signals a new phase in the account of the temple-building process. Whereas chapter 2 traced the preparation phase, and chapters 3–4 the construction phase, chapters 5–7 trace the dedication phase. In 5:1 the Chronicler notes that the construction is finished, naming David's gifts for the temple (1 Chron. 18:10–11; 26:26–27; 29:1–5) at this point to remind the reader of the role of both David and Solomon in making this possible. With everything in place, it is time now to transfer the ark from the tent David has provided in Jerusalem to the Most Holy Place, on the temple mount above the city (5:2–10). Solomon times this to coincide with the festival of the seventh month, most likely a reference to the Feast of Tabernacles, which was one of the mandatory feasts of Israel and was held from the fifteenth to the twenty-first of the month (Lev. 23:34, 39; Num. 29:12–34). With the leadership of the nation gathered in Jerusalem, the Chronicler depicts the Levites carrying the ark from Zion to the temple (5:4–5), Solomon in the midst of his people sacrificing animals (5:6), and the priests then carrying the ark into the Most Holy Place (5:7–10).

With the transfer complete (5:11–14), the Levites break into song, which prompts Yahweh to fill the temple with his presence and glory, making the work of the priests impossible. While this is strikingly reminiscent of the conclusion to the tabernacle account in Exodus 40:34–35, where Moses was unable to enter the tent of meeting, here David's Levitical innovation of verbal worship (see 1 Chronicles 16) overshadows the traditional role of the priests, reminding readers that this is a new era of Israel's relationship with Yahweh. God's presence here reflects his pleasure not only in the praise of his people but also in the temple itself, which was made for him.

F. Dedicating the temple—Solomon's speech and prayer (6:1–42). In response to the descent of God's presence, in 6:1–2 Solomon states the significance of the present shift from the "dark cloud" to his "magnificent temple." It is clear from the later statements in this chapter (6:18, 21, 25, 27, 30, 33, 35, 39) that, while Yahweh rules from heaven, the temple is now the place of his special manifest presence on earth, from which he exercises his rule on earth. Before addressing the people, Solomon blesses them (6:3), following the pattern established by his father in 1 Chronicles 16:2. The speech to the people that follows (6:4–11) sets the tone for the dedication of the temple. While mindful of the redemptive story of Israel (exodus), Solomon emphasizes God's election of Jerusalem and David (6:4–6). Use of the term "leader" (6:5; cf. 1 Chron. 11:2) suggests David's role as Yahweh's vice-regent on earth. With this foundation in mind, Solomon then shifts to his own election by Yahweh to build the temple (6:7–9), concluding with a rehearsal of his own experience of the fulfillment of Yahweh's promises in the events recounted throughout 2 Chronicles 1–5 (6:10–11).

Having rehearsed the narrative-theological foundation for this dedication, Solomon then expresses a long prayer to Yahweh in 6:12–42. The location of this prayer is identified as a bronze platform constructed in the outer courtyard of the temple area before the assembly. The first section of the prayer (6:14–17) again rehearses theology foundational to the temple, that is, the incomparability of Yahweh and his election of the Davidic dynasty. It is clear that the temple itself is proof of Yahweh's faithfulness to David, but Solomon sees this day as confirmation that David's dynasty will be perpetual. For the Chronicler's audience, then, the temple engendered hope in God's enduring promises to the royal house. The second part of the prayer (6:18–40) accentuates the role of the temple as a place of prayer, providing the many scenarios that will prompt the prayer of the people either at or toward the temple in Jerusalem. The accent on prayer in Solomon's address to Yahweh here continues the emphasis on the innovation of verbal worship throughout the account of David (see 1 Chronicles 16). While the temple remains a place of sacrifice, administered by the priests, with David and Solomon there is a greater emphasis on verbal praise fostered by the nonpriestly Levites and prayer uttered by the people. Several of the scenarios in verses 18–40 focus on the necessity of penitential prayer as a disciplined people seek God's favor. This sets the agenda for the prayers of later generations (e.g., Ezra 9; Nehemiah 1; 9; Daniel 9). Solomon's prayer concludes in 6:41–42 with Solomon's request for God's enduring presence in the temple and perpetual acceptance of the Davidic dynasty. The Chronicler's generation longed for both of these as much as did Solomon of old.

G. Dedicating the temple—Yahweh's response to Solomon (7:1–22). In response to Solomon's request for God's manifest presence at the end of his prayer in 6:41–42, in 7:1–2 Yahweh fills the temple as he did in 2 Chronicles 5:13–14, again making impossible the ministry of the priests. The manifest presence of Yahweh triggers the reverential praise of the people in 7:3, who proclaim the same words that prompted the first filling of the temple in 5:13–14. Not only the Levites but also the people are caught up in the praise of Yahweh. The dedication festivities conclude with the sacrificial celebration of the Feast of Tabernacles in 7:4–10. In view here is the dedication of both the temple (7:5) and the altar (7:9). Again David's name is mentioned by the Chronicler (7:6, 10), reminding the reader of his role together with Solomon in the creation of the temple. Hamath lay in the most northern region of Syria, with Lebo Hamath (entrance to Hamath) referring to its southern boundary. The Wadi of Egypt refers to the boundary river that lay between the Negev Desert, which began in southern Judah, and the Sinai region. For these two locations as indicative of the land of Israel see Numbers 13:21; 34:5–8; Joshua 13:5; 15:4, 47. The nation is united around both temple and monarch. Second Chronicles 7:11 represents a final summary for the temple building and dedication account, noting the completion of both temple and palace (cf. 2 Chron. 5:1).

The construction of Solomon's palace receives little attention in Chronicles, although it is mentioned in passing in 2 Chronicles 2:1, 12. The mention here of the palace sets up the concluding divine speech in 7:12–22, which focuses on Yahweh's acceptance of and vision for the temple (7:12–16) and dynasty (7:17–22). In his section on the temple (7:12–16), Yahweh articulates an agenda for renewal that sets the tone for the remainder of the presentation of the books of Chronicles. Yahweh warns that he will bring natural disaster (drought, locusts, plague) on the people if they are disobedient (7:13), but reveals that these are intended as discipline to turn the people back to himself (7:14). Such renewal will involve humility, prayer, seeking God's face, and turning from wicked ways and will result in forgiveness of the people and healing of the land (that is, reversal of the natural disaster). This vocabulary will be repeated constantly throughout the remainder of 2 Chronicles, identifying both positive and negative exemplars of this agenda. On the negative side it will be those who abandon and are unfaithful toward Yahweh who will receive Yahweh's discipline. In his section on the Davidic dynasty (7:17–22), Yahweh reminds Solomon of the need for faithfulness by the royal house and introduces the dark potential for those who do not embrace the agenda of renewal introduced in 7:13–14. Particular attention is given to the fate of the temple.

H. Other pursuits (8:1–9:31). Having completed his description of Solomon's temple building (chaps. 2–7), the Chronicler now offers some insight into Solomon's other activities, which reveal the ways Yahweh blesses Solomon for his faithfulness to the temple project. This new phase of the account begins with a summary note in 8:1, which identifies the period in view as after the completion of the temple. The first set of activities (8:2–11) is secular and includes construction projects and the organizing of human resources. Urban areas in view range from the north (8:2–4) to the south (8:5–6). Solomon is credited with completing the conquest of the land, left unfinished in Joshua and Judges (8:7–8), and conscripting some of these people groups to be his laborers; Israelites instead served as his military and officials (8:9–10). Although married to

Pharaoh's daughter, Solomon is careful not to defile Jerusalem by her presence (8:11). While most of chapters 8–9 is focused on Solomon's nontemple activities, 8:12–16 is a reminder of the enduring significance of the sacred. This section traces Solomon's sacred activities as patron of sacrifice (8:12–13) and verbal worship (8:14–15), fulfilling the ordinances laid out by Moses and David.

The remainder of the account in 8:17–9:28 returns to the earlier focus in 8:2–11 on Solomon's secular activities, tracing his economic achievements, international fame, military resources, and border expansions. Solomon partners and interacts with foreign figures, from Hiram of Tyre in the north (see 2 Chronicles 2) to the Queen of Sheba and the kings of Arabia in the south. With Solomon partnering with the maritime Phoenician Hiram at Elath on the Gulf of Aqaba, it is not surprising then to see interest from Sheba and Arabia (Ps. 72:15; Isa. 60:6; Jer. 6:20; Ezek. 27:22; 38:13). Solomon's stature among the nations is described in incomparable terms (9:9, 11, 19–20, 22, 27). The account of Solomon concludes in 9:29–31 with a summary note typical throughout 1 and 2 Chronicles. Reference to prophetic sources here and in David's summary note in 1 Chronicles 29:29–30 bolsters the authority of this account. Absent from the end of the account of Solomon, however, is any reference to Solomon's failure, which leads to the division of the nation. This flawless Solomon is being presented not merely as a past figure but as one who legitimates the present temple in the Chronicler's day and foreshadows a future renewal of the dynasty.

4. The Post-Solomonic Accounts (10:1–36:23)

With 2 Chronicles 10 the Chronicler's positive ideal of the Davidic-Solomonic kingdom becomes the exemplar against which all future generations will be evaluated. In general the tone is negative, although there are several key positive examples that approximate the earlier ideal, especially Hezekiah (chaps. 29–32) and Josiah (chaps. 34–35). The northern kingdom is largely ignored as a political entity in the post-Solomonic account, although those northern Israelites who join the South are

The remains of the six-chambered Solomonic gate at Hazor (tenth century BC), one of Solomon's building projects focused on fortifying strategic cities

affirmed. While the accounts of Athaliah and especially Ahaz constitute the nadir of the post-Solomonic account, it is especially Hezekiah and secondarily Josiah who represent its high points. Ironically, though, after Josiah the nation enters a different phase in its political life, controlled now by foreign nations and so in a state of exile until the edict of Cyrus at the tail end of the book (35:20–36:23). The historiographic principles used to describe, evaluate, and explain the events in the post-Solomonic account were set out in the speech of Yahweh in 2 Chronicles 7:13–15. On the one hand, those who seek Yahweh, who humble themselves, pray, and repent, are those who experience Yahweh's blessed success and prosperity exemplified in construction projects, military resources and success, abundant progeny, popular support, and long life. On the other hand, those who abandon and are unfaithful to Yahweh lack these blessings.

A. The reign of Rehoboam (10:1–12:16). It is in times of royal succession that there is the greatest danger of upheaval in the ancient Near East, in particular after a long and prosperous reign, and the transition from Solomon to his son Rehoboam is no exception. The first section of Rehoboam's account, 10:1–11:4, traces the schism in the kingdom that follows Solomon's death. Having traveled to Shechem for his coronation (cf. Judges 9), the Davidic heir Rehoboam is confronted by demands for reduction in royal taxation and labor burdens from the people, led by Solomon's former nemesis, Jeroboam son of Nebat (cf. 1 Kings 11:26–40). The composition of this rebellious flank is depicted as "all Israel," although it becomes clear by verse 17 that the tribe of Judah has remained faithful to Rehoboam. Ignoring the wise advice of Solomon's advisors, Rehoboam follows the foolish advice of his young friends and gambles away the kingdom. Fearing for his life, Rehoboam flees south to Jerusalem to gather reinforcements but is dissuaded from retaliation by the prophetic figure Shemaiah. In 2 Chronicles 13:6–7 Abijah will blame this

schism on Jeroboam and his followers for taking advantage of the young Rehoboam. But Shemaiah's speech in 2 Chronicles 11:4 reminds the reader that this schism was rooted in the will of Yahweh, even if 11:19 suggests that their enduring revolt is an unacceptable circumstance.

Rehoboam's obedience to the prophet in 11:4 foreshadows the second phase of his reign, one characterized by faithfulness, which follows in 11:5–23. Here Rehoboam becomes an exemplar of the Chronicler's historical principle, showing that with obedience and religious reform (11:13–17) comes divine blessing in the form of military fortification (11:5–12) and abundant progeny (11:18–23). It is interesting that the religious reform is linked to the return of priests and Levites from the north who rejected Jeroboam's illegitimate religious innovations (see further 1 Kings 12:25–33). This emphasis on the key role played by priestly and especially Levitical figures is typical of the Chronicler. Their return suggests that already in this second phase of Rehoboam's reign, it is expected that the northern tribes will submit again to the Davidic rule. The list of sites in 11:6–10 suggests a kingdom limited to the Judean hill country and the foothills in the west, with only one site (Gath) on the coastal plain and nothing in the far south (Negev).

There is, however, a third phase to Rehoboam's rule, depicted in 12:1–13a. Rehoboam's success leads to his downfall as he "abandon[s]" and is "unfaithful" toward Yahweh, vocabulary typical of the Chronicler's depiction of negative characters (see above on 2 Chron. 7:12–22). As expected, such disobedience leads to divine discipline in the form of an attack by Shishak king of Egypt (931–910 BC), whose campaign in western Asia is attested in Egyptian records (*ANET* 242–43, 263–64). This divine discipline prompts a penitential response from Rehoboam and his leaders, one in which they humble themselves and declare God's justice. Such repentance is a positive model for the Chronicler (see 2 Chron. 7:12–22) and leads to a mitigated punishment for Rehoboam, as

Yahweh promises not to destroy him and his kingdom entirely. The statement in 12:8 that foreign hegemony has a didactic role, to teach them "the difference between serving me and serving the kings of other lands," suggests that the circumstances of the Chronicler's audience under Persian rule were not seen as the nation's final state. Rehoboam thus embodies three key models for the Chronicler: the positive model of obedience, which results in blessing, the negative model of disobedience, which results in discipline, and the positive model of repentance, which results in renewed blessing. These models will reappear constantly in the accounts to follow in 2 Chronicles 13–36. The account of Rehoboam ends with the summary note in 12:13b–16, typical of the reigns throughout 2 Chronicles 10–36. Although exemplifying certain positive values, in the end he is deemed an evil king, especially because he did not set his heart on seeking Yahweh (see commentary on 2 Chron. 7:12–22).

B. The reign of Abijah (13:1–22). As is typical throughout 2 Chronicles 10–36, the royal accounts begin with a summary note, signaling the accession of a new royal figure (13:1–2a). With the death of his father, Rehoboam, Abijah the crown prince becomes king. By dating the beginning of his reign to the reign of a northern king (something common in Kings but not in Chronicles), the Chronicler prepares the reader for the fundamental tension in his reign, his battle against the founder of the northern kingdom, Jeroboam, in 13:2b–19 (see 2 Chronicles 10).

In what may appear to be a suicidal act, the much weaker Abijah invades Jeroboam's kingdom. However, Abijah's speech in 13:4–12 reveals that this invasion is an act of faith, based on the theological foundation of the Davidic covenant. Jeroboam's rebellion against Rehoboam is clearly treated as illegitimate, even if 2 Chronicles 11:4 does reveal that this act lay within the permissive will of Yahweh. Called a "covenant of salt," possibly a reference to the quality of salt for preservation and purification

and/or the use of the salt at covenant agreement meals (see Num. 18:19; cf. Gen. 26:30; 31:54; Lev. 2:13), the Davidic covenant is not an option for the nation. Abijah's attack on Jeroboam focuses particularly on his creation of a countercult at Bethel and Dan, complete with golden calves and non-Aaronide priests to rival the worship at the legitimate shrine in Jerusalem sponsored by the Davidic house and administered properly by the Aaronic priesthood according to Yahweh's requirements. Jeroboam's quantitative advantage is soon bolstered by qualitative advantage through the use of clandestine military strategy.

Faced with such overwhelming odds, Abijah has no option but to trust in Yahweh (13:14, 18), who acts on behalf of his people (13:15–16). This battle is a turning point for both Jeroboam and Abijah (13:20–21), the former never regaining power and experiencing the fatal judgment of God and the latter increasing in power and experiencing the divine blessing of progeny. In 13:22–14:1 the short account of Abijah comes to a close with a summary note. Reference to a prophetic source for this reign reminds the reader of the authority of this account. While no explicit theological evaluation is offered for Abijah, his speech and the outcome of his reign confirm his status as a normative character in Chronicles. Abijah is a reminder that the division of the kingdom and rebellion against the Davidic house was not to be an enduring circumstance within Israel. Through this the Chronicler expresses a future hope for the Davidic house for his Persian period audience.

C. The reign of Asa (14:1–16:14). As is the trend throughout the post-Solomonic account in 2 Chronicles, the reign of Asa begins with a summary note, describing his accession after the death of his father Abijah in 14:1–2. Asa's reign is divided into three basic phases, with an early phase of preliminary religious fidelity rewarded by military success (chap. 14), a middle phase of heightened religious renewal in response to the prophetic word (chap. 15), and a later phase of infidelity through foreign alliance and plundering of the Jerusalem temple that leads to prophetic attack and decline (chap. 16). Second Chronicles 14:3–8 depicts Asa's early religious reforms (see 2 Chron. 17:3), described more generally as seeking (see 2 Chron. 7:12–22) and obeying God (14:4, 7) and specifically as removing illicit worship sites and objects (14:3, 5), which rival the centralized worship at the temple in Jerusalem. This normative activity prompts the blessing of God, exemplified in the fortification of the land (14:6–7), a large military force (14:8), and peace and rest (14:5, 7; cf. 14:1). This idyllic picture of peace and rest, however, is shattered in 14:9–15 as the Ethiopian king Zerah advances up the Way of the Sea—that key tributary that ran along the Philistine coast and connected Africa with Europe and Asia—getting as far as the Mareshah Valley, one of five key valleys that ran from the coastal plain to the Judean hill country. As his father Abijah's speech in 2 Chronicles 13 highlighted the faith of a godly leader, so Asa's prayer here reveals his faith in God's resources. As in Abijah's battle against the more powerful Jeroboam, Yahweh fights on behalf of Judah (cf. 2 Chron. 13:16), defeating the Ethiopian army, which retreats south past Gerar.

This Ethiopian attack on Judah does suggest that something may be amiss in Asa's kingdom, and it is precisely this that comes to the fore in 15:1–19. Returning from his battle against the Ethiopians, Asa is confronted by the prophet Azariah, who reminds the king that the divine presence the nation has just experienced depends on the nation's presence (covenant faithfulness) with Yahweh. In language typical of 1–2 Chronicles (see commentary on 2 Chron. 7:12–22), the king is presented with a choice between seeking and

forsaking God. This prompts Asa to perform more extensive religious reforms, now removing idols from outlying areas and repairing the central shrine in Jerusalem, even though still certain high places (outlying shrines) are left standing. The festal celebration in 2 Chronicles 15:10–15 depicts in communal terms an appropriate response to the prophetic call to seek God, here identified as seeking "with all their heart and soul" expressed through an oath. As in the early phase of Asa's reign (14:5, 7), the result is the divine blessing of "rest" (15:15).

The final phase of Asa's reign in 16:1–10, however, is tragic. When Jeroboam's son Baasha regains territory his father lost to Asa's father Abijah (see 2 Chronicles 13), Asa responds by entering into a military alliance with the Syrian king Ben-Hadad, whose territory lay to the north of Baasha (thus Asa surrounded Baasha and forced him to fight on two fronts). The use of resources from the temple to entice Ben-Hadad into an agreement is despicable. Once again a prophet arises to confront Asa, and Hanani contrasts Yahweh's faith during Asa's early reign as he faced the great Ethiopian army (chap. 15) with Asa's unbelief when facing the much smaller Israelite army (chap. 16). The words of promise, that Yahweh is searching the earth to

The stylized trees in this bronze model of a cultic site (Susa, twelfth century BC) are reminiscent of Asherah poles, one of the objects of false worship that faithful kings destroyed during religious reforms.

strengthen those who are fully committed to him, are used to judge this king who has refused to trust Yahweh in his moment of need (16:9). The contrast between the early and late Asa is accentuated further by his conflicting treatment of the prophet who delivers the divine word. In 15:8 he took courage and responded positively, but in 16:10 he imprisons Hanani. Asa's alliance with Ben-Hadad introduces a negative precedent that will escalate in frequency and negative results in the coming accounts of Judean kings. Judah is called to faith in Yahweh alone, who will fight on their behalf. In the face of much greater imperial forces in the Persian period, the Chronicler's audience is called to trust Yahweh alone to establish his kingdom.

Second Chronicles 16:11–14 brings closure to the account of Asa with a typical summary note. The tragedy of Asa's life is accentuated in his closing years, as the man whose name probably means "God is (my) physician" (*HALOT* 4:73) is plagued by diseased feet and yet refuses to seek help from Yahweh rather than physicians. This contrasts the young Asa who sought Yahweh's help against the mighty Ethiopian army.

D. The reign of Jehoshaphat (17:1–20:37).
17:1–18:34. The account of Jehoshaphat begins with an abridged summary note in 17:1a, with more information provided in the concluding summary note in 20:31–34. Much as the reign of his father Asa (cf. 2 Chron. 17:3; 20:32; 21:12), Jehoshaphat's reign begins on a high note (17:1b–19), with an initial phase of faithfulness (17:3–4) that is rewarded with the divine blessings of military, political, and economic success (17:5, 10–19). Jehoshaphat goes beyond merely removing false worship practices and sites from his nation (17:3–6) by positively facilitating instruction among the people (17:7–9). He commissions five officials, nine Levites, and two priests for itinerant teaching of the law throughout his kingdom. The account stresses the written character of their source for teaching, noting how they took with them "the Book of the Law of the LORD" to the

various towns of Judah. Although the books of Chronicles stress the centralization of worship at the temple in Jerusalem and with it greater opportunities for the involvement of Levites in verbal worship alongside the sacrificial activity of the priests, here a decentralization of teaching reveals his desire to keep the people from returning to their former ways. The reference to the fear of Yahweh falling on the surrounding kingdoms reveals the power of such teaching. For the Chronicler's audience this is a reminder of the importance of teaching the written word to ensure central and pure worship among his own generation.

Although initiating reforms that will ensure faithfulness among his people (teaching), Jehoshaphat makes a foolish mistake by entering into an alliance with Ahab king of Israel to the north in 18:1–34. This is ironic in light of the fact that Jehoshaphat spent his initial days fortifying his kingdom against this northern power (17:1–2). Little does he know the tragic outcome of this alliance, since it will be sealed by the marriage of his son Jehoram to Ahab's daughter Athaliah (2 Chron. 18:1), whose bloody purge will nearly extinguish the Davidic line (22:10–12). A pact with Ahab's kingdom would have been tempting, especially since Ahab's marriage to the Phoenician princess Jezebel reveals that he had already developed an alliance with the Phoenician city-states. That Ahab is the more powerful partner is suggested by the fact that Jehoshaphat travels to Ahab's capital, Samaria. Once there, he is pressured by his new ally to assist him in recovering Ramoth Gilead, one of Ahab's fortress cities on the Transjordanian plateau south of the Golan region and overlooking the River Yarmuk. But Jehoshaphat displays his earlier spiritual sensibilities by exhorting Ahab to inquire of Yahweh.

Unsatisfied with the positive response of Ahab's four hundred non-Yahwistic prophets (most likely prophets of Asherah or Baal; see 1 Kings 18:19), Jehoshaphat demands a prophet of Yahweh. Ahab reluctantly produces Micaiah son of Imlah, who has consistently spoken negatively of Ahab. Ahab knows something is amiss when Micaiah encourages him to enter battle, promising victory. In response to Ahab's demand for the truth, Micaiah explains his experience in the divine council of Yahweh, a scene strikingly reminiscent of the prophetic commissioning scene in Isaiah 6. Prophets are the only human participants who are allowed into the divine council (Jer. 23:16–22), joining heavenly counterparts who also carry out tasks for Yahweh. In this context Micaiah listens in on a discussion in the divine council, as Yahweh asks for a volunteer to entice Ahab to enter battle. One heavenly participant agrees to prompt Ahab's prophets to encourage Ahab into battle. Micaiah is thus truly speaking the word of the Lord when he encourages Ahab to enter the battle. After Ahab throws Micaiah into prison, Ahab and Jehoshaphat proceed to the battle for Ramoth Gilead. Ahab's supremacy over Jehoshaphat is confirmed by his instruction that Jehoshaphat wear his royal robes while Ahab disguises himself. While this sets up Jehoshaphat as the only royal target, Ahab's folly is in thinking he can thwart Yahweh's will. As expected, the opposing army does target Jehoshaphat, but the Davidic king's cry to God saves him (18:31). In contrast, Ahab, relying on his crafty strategy, is mortally wounded by a "random" arrow, confirming Micaiah's earlier word of judgment (18:27).

19:1–20:37. As Jehoshaphat returns home from the battle at Ramoth Gilead he is confronted by the prophet Jehu son of Hanani (19:1–3). This is reminiscent of Azariah's confrontation of Jehoshaphat's father, Asa, upon his return from the battle against the Ethiopians in 15:2, a battle in which the earlier royal also cried out for help in the midst of overwhelming odds (2 Chron. 14:9–15). While the *timing* of the prophetic confrontation is similar to that in chapter 15, the *content* of Jehu's prophetic message to Jehoshaphat is similar to the message delivered by Jehu's father, Hanani, to Jehoshaphat's father, Asa, in 16:7–10: both upbraid the Davidic king for entering into

an inappropriate alliance. In contrast to his father, Asa, who throws Hanani into prison, Jehoshaphat responds appropriately. First, the king who sent his officials, Levites, and priests to teach the people about the Torah (chap. 17) goes himself through the breadth of the land, from furthest south (Beersheba) to furthest north (hill country of Ephraim), encouraging them to return to God (19:5). Second, the king whose name means "Yahweh judges" establishes an impartial judicial infrastructure (cf. Deut. 16:18–17:13) in the fortified cities and Jerusalem to encourage faithfulness to the Torah through accountability (19:6–11).

These reforms in chapter 19, however, do not spare Jehoshaphat from the serious military challenge that arises in 20:1–30, even though his victory is an example of God's reward for those who obey and trust in him. Jehoshaphat's enemy in this chapter is composed of people groups in the southern Transjordan: (from north to south) Ammon, Moab, and Edom (although see NIV note). Jehoshaphat is informed of this army's advance when it reaches En Gedi, an oasis halfway up the western side of the Dead Sea. With this force within forty miles of Jerusalem, Jehoshaphat and his people (men, women, children, babies; see 20:13) gather together to seek Yahweh's help through communal fasting (20:4) and prayer (20:5–12). Jehoshaphat founds his prayer on Yahweh's omnipotent rule, then he recalls the vision of the temple as a place where Yahweh will hear prayer (a thought articulated by Solomon at the dedication of the temple in 2 Chronicles 6). Jehoshaphat then focuses on the inappropriateness of this attack by Ammon, Moab, and Edom, especially in light of Israel's mercy toward them before the conquest of the land. The divine response to this prayer comes from a Levite who functions as a prophetic voice with the Spirit of the Lord descending on him. The trend of a prophetic role for Levites seen earlier in Chronicles (see 1 Chronicles 25) is developed further here. For a prophet to respond to such a prayer is appropriate, as God comforts his people and proclaims salvation, even offering a military strategy that will ensure victory.

In the following scene, the king plays an important role in encouraging the people before they go into battle. The victory is prompted here not by military action but rather by men (most likely Levites) singing praise. Yahweh miraculously intervenes, setting ambushes that provoke the combined forces of Ammon, Moab, and Edom to turn on one another. Jehoshaphat and his men only have to collect the plunder from the defeated armies (20:25), respond in praise to Yahweh (20:26), and return to Jerusalem with joy (20:27–28). The concluding summary note for Jehoshaphat is divided into two sections, 20:31–34 and 21:1, split by a short account in 20:35–37, which depicts Jehoshaphat's inappropriate economic alliance with Ahab's son Ahaziah of Israel, which ended in disaster with the destruction of their fleet of ships. This event shatters the idyllic later portrait of Jehoshaphat, reminding the reader again that foreign alliances are inappropriate. In so many ways Jehoshaphat is a powerful renewal figure in Judah, serving personally as a catalyst of repentance and trust among the people and creating institutions for instruction and justice. However, his proclivity for alliances with the northern kingdom brings him much tragedy, ultimately threatening the Davidic dynasty and the independence of the southern kingdom.

E. The account of Jehoram (21:1–20). The death of Jehoshaphat initiates a period of crisis that will endure for the next three reigns, beginning with Jehoram and Ahaziah and ending in the tragedy caused by the queen Athaliah. It is interesting that the names of the two kings here are also names of northern kings (Ahab's son was Ahaziah and his grandson was Jehoram), clear indications of the influence of the northern kingdom introduced by Jehoshaphat's alliance with Ahab and the marriage of Ahab's daughter Athaliah to Jehoshaphat's son Jehoram. The account of this son Jehoram begins in 21:1–7 with an expanded introductory summary note highlighting the evil behavior of Jehoram from

the very beginning of his reign. By assassinating all contenders for the throne, Jehoram introduces the key motif of dynastic endangerment, which will reappear throughout chapters 21–22 (21:17; 22:8–9; 22:10–12). The Chronicler's note in verse 7 is a careful reminder that the consistent survival of the dynasty through these tragedies can be traced to the covenantal promise of Yahweh to David of an enduring lamp, signifying permanence (cf. Job 18:5; Prov. 13:9; 24:20). In the end it will take this endangerment to purify the Davidic line from the religious influence of the northern Omride dynasty.

According to 21:8–11, Jehoram's abandonment of Yahweh (21:10; see 2 Chron. 7:12–22), detailed in 21:11 as building high places and fostering inappropriate worship, is the cause of two revolts against Jehoram: by Edom, in the southern Transjordan, and by Libnah, a city in the southwestern territory of Judah. Jehoram even receives a prophetic word of judgment from the prophet Elijah in the form of a letter in 21:12–15. The appearance of the northern prophet Elijah is appropriate for a southern king so influenced by the north. The comparison to Ahab in verse 13 is a poignant reminder of the source of Jehoram's infidelity, while the contrast to his grandfather Asa and his father, Jehoashaphat, is a reminder that Jehoram has squandered most of their accomplishments in terms of both territory gained and religious reforms enacted. Elijah prophesies an ominous end to Jehoram's life (see 21:18–19). Verses 16–17 provide further description of the divine judgment on Jehoram, depicting the attack of a combined group of Philistines and Arabs, people groups living on the southwestern and southern borders of his kingdom. Their attack threatens the survival of the royal family, only the crown prince Ahaziah surviving, which is tragically similar to Jehoram's purge of his own family at the outset of his reign in 21:1–7. As if this loss of life were not enough, finally the Chronicler depicts a crisis in Jehoram's health (21:18–19), an event that constitutes the fulfillment of Elijah's prophecy in 21:12–15.

Jehoram's account ends in typical fashion, with a concluding summary note in 21:20, repeating the information already supplied in 21:5. Jehoram is one of the darkest figures in the Chronicler's account of the southern kingdom, exemplifying what awaits the king who abandons the Lord.

F. The accounts of Ahaziah, Athaliah, and Joash (22:1–24:27). **22:1–12.** With the death of Jehoram, the Chronicler introduces the reign of his son Ahaziah (also known as Jehoahaz and Azariah; see NIV note on 21:17; 22:6), the only survivor of the bloody attack of the Philistine-Arab coalition in 2 Chronicles 21:17. This typical summary note (22:1–5a) makes clear the influence of Ahaziah's mother, Athaliah, that daughter of Ahab (son of Omri) whose marriage to Ahaziah represented an unhealthy alliance between the dominant and illegitimate northern kingdom of Israel and the legitimate southern kingdom of Judah. The Chronicler links Athaliah's influence, as well as that of other counselors from Ahab's northern kingdom, to the evil that Ahaziah did in the eyes of the Lord. As in the case of his grandfather Jehoshaphat, who forged the relationship with the northern kingdom, Ahaziah's alliance with his northern cousins involves supporting them against King Hazael's Aramean forces (22:5b–9a; cf. 2 Kings 8:7–15). Ironically, the site of the battle is Ramoth Gilead, the same site at which Ahab and Jehoshaphat fought together in 2 Chronicles 18:28–34. This time, however, the outcome of the battle will mean death for both northern and southern kings. The northern king Joram (son of Ahab) is wounded in the battle, and when his nephew the southern king Ahaziah comes to pay his respect, both kings are assassinated by Jehu: Joram at Jezreel and Ahaziah in Samaria.

In 22:7 the Chronicler links the downfall of Ahaziah to the will of God, who is responsible for the destruction of the house of Ahab. These two events are intricately linked, since the eradication of the house of Ahab means a significant purge of the royal house in Judah

as well. In his abridged concluding summary note in 22:9b, the Chronicler ironically notes the positive qualities of Jehoshaphat ("who sought the LORD with all his heart"), even though it was Jehoshaphat who introduced the fateful alliance and intermarriage into the Davidic line. The final statement that no one is powerful enough to retain the kingdom can be explained by Jehu's destruction of the "princes of Judah" and "the sons of Ahaziah's relatives." While the divinely affirmed Jehu thoroughly destroys the royal family of Ahab and stikes down all the adult males of the royal family of Ahaziah, it is the evil Athaliah who will nearly complete the job in 22:10–12, which is ironic since this aids the purification of the Davidic royal house of northern influences. The story here traces the efforts of two women, the first being Athaliah daughter of Ahab, who seeks to snuff out the lamp of David's dynasty (cf. 21:7) and the second, Jehosheba, who as daughter of Jehoram and sister of Ahaziah (see 2 Kings 11:2) rescues the Davidic dynasty from extinction. Jehosheba is also the wife of the high priest Jehoiada and so is able for six years to provide sanctuary for the sole surviving Davidic heir, the young Joash son of Ahaziah.

23:1–21. After six years the high priest Jehoiada, husband of Jehosheba, finally makes his move to dethrone Athaliah and enthrone the legitimate and sole Davidic heir, Joash. It is Jehoiada who controls the plot from beginning to end, his success signaled by the closing note in 23:21 that the city is quiet because Athaliah has been slain. Jehoiada gathers help from sacred and secular groups to overthrow Athaliah at the time of the changing of the guard at the temple. It will be the weapons David gave to the temple treasury that will grant military resources to Jehoiada to preserve the Davidic dynasty. In this passage one can discern the rituals related to the inauguration of a king, which include gathering both sacred and secular leaders of the nation at a key location, anointing the royal individual with oil, sounding the trumpet, and chanting, "Long live the king." Jehoiada carefully protects the sanctity of the sacred precincts, instructing his troops to avoid the temple precincts and even ensuring that Athaliah's blood is not shed in the temple. With Athaliah dead, Jehoiada leads the people in a covenant renewal, which binds people and king together. Although a priest, Jehoiada affirms the role of the Levites in the temple services (23:18–19), further evidence for the Chronicler of the necessary role played by the Levites in his own day. Not only does Jehoiada ensure there is new leadership over the temple; he also guarantees in verse 20 that Joash is supported by the secular leadership of the land, as he, together with the military, royal, and family leaders, seats the young king on the royal throne in the palace. In this narrative, which depicts the renewal of a Davidic house on the brink of destruction, the Chronicler shows the key role played by the priestly house. In his own day priests would again have an opportunity to preserve the nation until the renewal of the royal house (see Zech. 3:1–10; 6:9–15).

24:1–27. Although Joash has already played a role in the narrative, it is in chapter 24 that the account of Joash begins properly, with his accession summary note in 24:1–3. Joash's reign is divided into two phases: the first (24:4–16), during Jehoiada's lifetime, is the righteous phase, and the second (24:17–22), after Jehoiada's death, unrighteous. Second Chronicles 24:3 focuses particular attention on Jehoiada's choice of wives for Joash, an important topic in light of the previous crisis created by Jehoshaphat's unwise intermarriage with the northern royal house. Joash's reforms during the lifetime of Jehoiada (24:4–14) are focused on the restoration of the temple, a necessity after the inattention and plundering (2 Chron. 24:7) of Athaliah's reign. Joash devises a system for the collection of resources from throughout the land, but when no progress is made he is forced to confront his mentor Jehoiada. Alluding to a tax authorized by Moses (Exod. 30:11–16), Joash then changes his tack, creating instead a centralized system in which the resources are to be brought to Jerusalem. The initial phase of inaction, the confrontation between Joash and Jehoiada, and the involvement of both priestly and royal officials for counting and disbursing the collection (24:11–14) suggest some measure of tension between temple and palace, which is ultimately resolved. Both people and leaders respond with an abundance of resources.

Second Chronicles 24:15–16 constitutes a concluding summary note, in this case not for a royal figure, as usual, but rather for Jehoiada the high priest. This is key for the depiction of Joash, whose reign is divided into two phases, based on the presence and absence of Jehoiada. It also grants Jehoiada honor commensurate with that of the kings of Judah, so that he overshadows even his disciple Joash (see 24:25–27). Jehoiada provides a model for high priests who serve in the Chronicler's generation, revealing the role that a high priest can play in the preservation and restoration of the Davidic line.

With Jehoiada's death, however, there is a significant shift in the account of Joash, who reverses his early reforms in 24:17–22. In a scene reminiscent of Rehoboam earlier (2 Chronicles 10), Joash listens to the advice of unwise counselors, abandoning the temple and shifting allegiance to the goddess Asherah, consort of El, the chief god of the Canaanite pantheon. Before divine discipline falls on the nation, Yahweh graciously sends prophets to prompt repentance, culminating with Jehoiada's son Zechariah. That an individual from sacred ranks plays a prophetic role is typical of the presentation in Chronicles (see 1 Chron. 25:1–31; 2 Chron. 20:1–37; 29:1–36; 34:30; 35:15), but there is great tragedy here in Joash's murder of the son of the one who saved his life and also in the fact that the murderous act takes place in the holy space that Jehoiada so carefully protected when ridding the nation of Athaliah (2 Chron. 23:7, 14–16, 19). Second Chronicles 24:23–25a showcases the key principle in Chronicles that those who abandon Yahweh receive his retribution, in this case in the form of military defeat and assassination. Joash is defeated by much weaker Aram, from Damascus, a kingdom to the north of traditional Israelite lands. As is typical in the ancient Near East, this defeat is followed by the assassination of the king in his bed.

The account of Joash concludes in typical fashion, with a summary note in 24:25b–27. The brevity of this note, especially in comparison to that on Joash's mentor Jehoiada in 24:15–16, and the comment that Joash is denied a proper royal burial are indications of the Chronicler's low esteem for Joash. The emphasis on prophecy and temple restoration is an important reminder of the key agenda of the Chronicler for his own generation, who are called to care for the temple and to give careful heed to God's word.

G. The account of Amaziah (25:1–28). The assassination of Joash opens the way for the accession of his son Amaziah, whose reign is introduced by the summary note in 25:1–4. In contrast to his father, Joash, Amaziah's doing "what was right in the eyes of the Lord" (25:2), yet not "wholeheartedly," is suggestive of the two different phases of his reign, the first positive (25:5–12) and the second negative (25:13–24). Both phases are structured by the same pattern: (1) Amaziah arouses divine anger, (2) a prophetic figure confronts the king, (3) the king responds with a question, (4) the prophetic figure responds, (5) the king obeys or disobeys, and (6) a battle results in success or failure. In the first phase of 25:5–12 Amaziah prepares for battle against Edom but is confronted by "a man of God" (a term for a prophet or miracle

worker; see 1 Sam. 2:27; 9:6–10; 1 Kings 12:22) who attacks the king for including mercenaries from the northern kingdom among his forces. Judah's reliance on northern military resources (2 Chronicles 18) was what caused the near extinction of the Davidic line in 2 Chronicles 22. Although reluctant to lose his initial investment in these troops (25:9), Amaziah obeys and experiences victory against the Edomites, called here the sons of Seir, the mountain region traditionally associated with Edom. The Valley of Salt is in the lower Dead Sea region.

This victory over the Edomites, however, will lead to Amaziah's downfall in the second phase of his reign in 25:13–24. Although Yahweh has given him the victory (see vv. 8–9), Amaziah bows down to the gods of his conquered foe. This arouses divine anger, and so again Yahweh sends a prophet to confront the king. This time, however, Amaziah ignores the divine warning and ensures divine judgment. Ironically, this judgment will come through the hand of the northern kingdom, whose mercenaries are rejected by Yahweh in 25:5–12 and will be prompted by Amaziah's vengeful challenge of the northern king Joash. The fateful battle takes place at Beth Shemesh, which guarded Jerusalem from its vantage point in the Sorek Valley along the western boundary of traditional

The ancient site of Beth Shemesh with the Sorek Valley in the background

Judahite territory. Judah's loss will lead to the capture of both king and capital, plundering of temple and palace, and destruction of city defenses. The concluding summary note in 25:25–28 not only brings closure to the account of Amaziah but also depicts his demise as judgment from God. The Chronicler traces the conspiracy against Amaziah to his apostasy from God. He flees from Jerusalem to another of the fortified cities to the southwest of Jerusalem, Lachish. There he is caught by the conspirators and killed. Amaziah showcases key theological principles developed throughout Chronicles. God brings judgment on the disobedient, but does offer warning through the prophetic word.

H. The account of Uzziah (26:1–23). With the assassination of his father in a palace coup, Uzziah comes to the throne at age sixteen (26:1–5). The Chronicler evaluates Uzziah (called Azariah in the book of Kings; cf. 2 Kings 14:21) positively, noting that he did right in the eyes of Yahweh, but qualifying this by reference to the mentoring influence of an otherwise unknown figure named Zechariah. In keeping with the Chronicler's theological principles, such righteous behavior is rewarded with prosperity, exemplified in Uzziah's signature achievement of rebuilding Elath, an Israelite southern seaport on the Gulf of Aqaba. Doing right is described here as seeking after God and is linked to the fear of God, that human response of awe and submission before almighty Yahweh Creator (cf. Deut. 5:5, 22–27, 29; 6:1–6; Prov. 1:7).

The initial phase of Uzziah's reign in 26:6–15 is typified by offensive military success on all his borders, including the west (Philistines, 26:6–7), south and east (Arabs, 26:7), east (Transjordan, 26:8), and south (Negev, 26:8), success that gives him control of the two main international highways through which the trade of the ancient world flowed. There are also defensive fortifications within the land (26:9–10, 15) and the amassing of a large and efficient army (26:11–14). But this initial success, to be linked to the influence of the godly Zechariah (see similarly Jehoiada's influence on Joash in 2 Chronicles 24), comes to an end in 26:16–21, when Uzziah's pride corrupts him. Violating the clear laws governing the holy space in the temple and ignoring the priests' concerns, Uzziah invades the holy place to burn his own incense. God's judgment falls on the king as an unclean skin disease breaks out on his forehead (see Leviticus 13–14). This condition is the beginning of the end for Uzziah, who will live out the remainder of his reign isolated from the rest of the community, with his son Jotham as coregent. Loss of health is a sign of God's displeasure with figures in Chronicles (e.g., 2 Chron. 21:18–20).

Second Chronicles 26:22–23 brings closure to the account of Uzziah, with a summary note that identifies prophetic works as the source of the information. Although he exemplified many good characteristics as he followed the lead of Zechariah, in the end his name would be associated with the judgment of Yahweh.

I. The account of Jotham (27:1–9). The account of Jotham is considerably brief, most likely reflecting the short period he reigns after his father Uzziah's death. In the introductory summary note in 27:1–2, the Chronicler parallels Jotham with his father in terms of positive accomplishments while distancing him from his father's breach of the sacred precincts of the temple (see 2 Chron. 26:16–21). Jotham is evaluated as doing right in Yahweh's sight, even though the people act corruptly. The list of Jotham's accomplishments in 27:3–6 reveals the blessings that accompany those who do right (see esp. 27:6). Special focus is placed on military defense through building activities in and outside Jerusalem and military offense in his campaign against the Ammonites. Control of Ammon meant the economic benefit for three years from taxes on goods moving along the King's Highway between Asia, Arabia, Africa, and Europe. The closing summary note in 27:7–9 reminds the reader of the contrast between Jotham and his father Uzziah, the former's account explicitly mentioning his burial in the city of David.

J. The account of Ahaz (28:1–27). With the accession of Jotham's son Ahaz there is a radical shift in the evaluation of the Chronicler, who judges Ahaz as *not* doing what is right in Yahweh's sight, in the introductory summary note in 28:1–2a. Ahaz represents a pregnant moment in the post-schism history of Israel, since during his reign the illicit northern kingdom comes to an end. Unfortunately, far from the ideal conditions established by his ancestor David (28:1), Ahaz's kingdom continues the illicit ways of the northern kingdom. From the Chronicler's perspective Ahaz takes the nation to its darkest level prior to the exile. The specific description of Ahaz's evil activities is provided at the outset of 28:2b–7, as the Chronicler lists the violations of Yahweh's demand that worship take place through appropriate means at the appropriate place. His offenses include the worship of Baal, one of the key gods in the Canaanite pantheon; child sacrifice, a practice prohibited in Deuteronomy 18:10–11 (cf. 2 Chron. 33:6); and burning incense at sites other than the temple. The Valley of Ben Hinnom bordered the south and west sides of Jerusalem and was not a designated location for worship activities. As is typical throughout 2 Chronicles, such illicit behavior is met with divine discipline, here in the form of military defeat, at the hands of first the Arameans and then Israel, both key threats from the north (see Isaiah 7).

Second Chronicles 28:8–15 represents one of the few times the Chronicler focuses on characters from the northern kingdom, but in this case a prophet (Oded) confronts the victorious northern army (with its capital at Samaria), calling them to care for their southern military captives in a merciful way (strikingly similar to the actions of the Good Samaritan in Jesus's parable in Luke 10). Against the brightness of this northern response, the darkness of Ahaz's behavior in the south in 28:16–25 will be seen even more clearly. Faced with further divine discipline through military attacks from the east

(Edom) and west (Philistia), Ahaz will not only use treasures from the temple to try to enlist the great Mesopotamian imperial power Assyria for help to deal with his smaller enemies but also will sacrifice to the gods of the conquering Arameans. Trusting in such imperial and heavenly powers, however, only exacerbates Judah's situation. It also leads to the closure of the temple and construction of altars throughout the kingdom. Identified as the worst leader of Judah, Ahaz is disqualified from burial in the royal tombs (28:26–27).

K. The account of Hezekiah (29:1–32:33). While Ahaz represented the lowest point in the history of Judah after Solomon and before the exile, Hezekiah represents the highest point. In the introductory summary note of 29:1–2 the Chronicler offers his theological evaluation of this great king, describing him unreservedly as doing right in the sight of Yahweh and comparing him to the ideal monarch, David.

The account proper begins with Hezekiah's foundational achievement, the cleansing and rededication of the temple in 29:3–36. While his father Ahaz closed the temple and abandoned its services (2 Chron. 28:24), Hezekiah's first move is to reopen the temple. His motivational speech in verses 4–11 identifies the important role played by the priests and Levites in such renewal of the temple and its worship, a message relevant to his own generation. Hezekiah places priority on making a covenant with Yahweh, that is, a relationship with expressed obligations by both partners (see especially the two foundational covenants with Abraham, Genesis 15; 17 and with Israel at Sinai, Exodus 20; 24). Levites and priests respond to Hezekiah's call, purifying themselves and then the temple. The fact that it takes sixteen days to clean out the temple indicates the dysfunction of Ahaz's reign. What follows in verses 20–36 is a detailed description of the rededication of the temple, all guided by Hezekiah (see 28:24). Music plays a role alongside sacrifice at this dedication, in line with the priorities of David and Solomon when first the ark and then the temple were dedicated.

With the temple purified and rededicated, the Chronicler then depicts in 30:1–31:1 Hezekiah's renewal of the festal rhythms of Israel. In view are the Feasts of Passover and Unleavened Bread. The condition of the temple inherited by Hezekiah from his father precludes celebration of these festivals at their legislated times (the fourteenth to the twenty-first days of the first month; Exod. 12:1–13:22; 23:14–17; 34:18–23; Lev. 23:1–44; Deut. 16:1–17), and so they are celebrated one month later (see the provision in Num. 9:1–14). Hezekiah initiates this celebration by sending a proclamation via couriers throughout the land from Beersheba in the far south to Dan in the far north. The extent of the land is indicative of the era after the fall of the northern kingdom, Hezekiah's kingdom representing the first renewal of the united kingdom since the idyllic era of David and Solomon (1 Chronicles 10–2 Chronicles 9), to which Hezekiah's reign is compared in 30:26. Hezekiah's letter in 30:6–9 is a powerful call to repentance, identifying a return to faithful temple worship as a penitential act. So also Hezekiah's prayer in 30:18–20 echoes the vocabulary of God's earlier promise to Solomon in 2 Chronicles 7:14, reminding the people of God's willingness to forgive and heal those who seek God.

Water from the Gihon Spring gushes into Hezekiah's tunnel (eighth century BC), carved as a protected means to bring water within the walls of Jerusalem (cf. 2 Chron. 32:4).

After purifying and dedicating the temple (chap. 29) and celebrating the first festivals (chap. 30), in 31:2–21 the Chronicler details Hezekiah's reformation of worship practices. Hezekiah reflects the priorities of David's innovations in worship, providing both the sacrificial and verbal dimensions of worship at the temple, with the former facilitated by the priests and the latter by the Levites. In view is a festal calendar that demands daily, weekly, monthly, and yearly events (31:3). Prompted by the personal example of their king, the people give beyond Hezekiah's expectations. These many gifts demand careful attention to a system for the distribution of the contributions among the priests and Levites of the land (31:11–20). According to 31:21 Hezekiah embodies the values of the Chronicler, as one who seeks God with all his heart and so enjoys success.

The presentation of Hezekiah in 2 Chronicles is dominated by his religious reforms related to the temple and its services. But the final phase of the account is largely devoted to a summarized version (cf. 2 Kings 18–20) of Yahweh's rescue of Hezekiah's kingdom from the clutches of the Assyrian Sennacherib (32:1–24), whose own versions of these events have been discovered (see *COS* 2.119B:302–3). That Judah would face the Assyrians was inevitable, especially after the incorporation of the Aramean and Israelite kingdoms, directly north of Judah, into the Assyrian Empire. The text depicts Hezekiah's extensive preparations for this Assyrian challenge, including protecting water sources, refortifying wall structures, accumulating weaponry, and organizing the military. The voice of Hezekiah comes to the fore once again in 32:7–8, as he encourages his officers with the theological reality that Yahweh is greater than the Assyrian arm of flesh. This short speech is dwarfed by the long speeches of Sennacherib to Hezekiah and his people (32:10–19), designed to undermine their confidence. In the end the Chronicler simply records the fact that both Hezekiah and Isaiah cry out in prayer to heaven and God answers with his mighty angel, who defeats the Assyrian army.

According to 32:25–31 Hezekiah is not perfect; he struggles with pride. Although the account here does not provide details on this pride, the parallel account in 2 Kings 20 as well as 2 Chronicles 32:31 reveals that his pride leads him to show his royal accomplishments to envoys from a potential ally, the Babylonian king Marduk-Baladan, whose rebellion against the Assyrians is attested in ancient Near Eastern records (see *COS* 2.118J; 2.119A; cf. Verse Account of Nabonidus). The way Hezekiah deals with this flaw when facing divine discipline is, ironically, exemplary, as the southern king and his community humble themselves and repent. This opens the way for divine blessing in the form of economic success and construction projects. The account closes in 32:32–33 with the typical concluding summary note, which reports his burial among the kings of Judah amid the glorification of his people. Hezekiah was an exemplary figure for the Davidic house, one who reopened the temple in Jerusalem and reinstituted its service of worship.

L. The account of Manasseh (33:1–20). The Chronicler's primary source, the book of Kings, depicts Manasseh as the worst character, that king who seals the fate of Judah (2 Kings 21:12–15; 23:26–27; 24:3–4; cf. 24:20). While not ignoring Manasseh's disobedience, the Chronicler presents this king as a role model, one whose repentance after an exilic punishment to Babylon showcases the Chronicler's agenda for renewal for his own generation. His account begins with the typical accession summary note in 33:1–2, where the Chronicler's theological evaluation of him is extremely negative, with its link to the Canaanite nations that preceded Israel's arrival. To be like these nations is to risk experiencing their fate (see 33:9).

The specifics of Manasseh's evil are provided in 33:3–9, which first outlines his sponsorship of decentralized cult practices at the high places (sacred sites on higher ground, nearer the heavens), with their worship of the Canaanite deities Baal and Asherah. Second, it describes Manasseh's despicable innovations in the Jerusalem temple cult of the worship of celestial bodies, complete with dedicated altars in the two courts (see 2 Chron. 4:9) and even a carved image. Like his grandfather Ahaz (2 Chron. 28:2), Manasseh reverts to various divinatory practices, including child sacrifice in the Valley of Ben Hinnom, the valley that formed the southern and western boundaries of Jerusalem. Reference at two points to God's eternal choice of Jerusalem (33:4, 7) is a poignant reminder that ultimately it is not God who has failed Israel, but Israel who has failed God and so experiences exile (33:8). What follows in 33:10–17 is a classic depiction of repentance. After rejecting God's gracious warning through his prophetic word (33:10), Manasseh is severely punished by Yahweh through the Assyrians, who take him off to Babylon, a region under their control (33:11). There, however, Manasseh has a change of heart, described by the Chronicler in his dominant theological idiom (33:12; see 2 Chron. 7:12–22). After restoring him to his kingdom, Yahweh blesses him with success in building projects and military fortifications (33:13–14). Manasseh's repentance is depicted as more than just words. He removes his illicit innovations from the temple and city (33:15) and restores proper worship of Yahweh (33:16), even though the people fall short of exclusive central worship in Jerusalem (33:17). The closing summary in 33:18–20 balances the two sides of Manasseh's reign, both his prayer and his sins.

M. The account of Amon (33:21–25). In a short account the Chronicler describes the evil of Manasseh's son Amon, using the typical structure of introductory accession summary (33:21–22a), events of his reign (33:22b–23), and concluding summary note (33:24–25). Comparison between Amon and his father accentuates the penitential model of Manasseh so important to the Chronicler (see 2 Chron. 7:12–22; 33:10–17). As expected, Amon's evil leads to his untimely assassination at the hands of palace officials.

N. The account of Josiah (34:1–35:27). The Chronicler's high opinion of Josiah is evident from the opening accession summary note in 34:1–2, where he is compared to his ancestor David, an honor bestowed in 2 Chronicles 10–36 only on Hezekiah (2 Chron. 29:2). Rising to power in the final third of the seventh century BC, a period that saw the shift of imperial power from Assyria to Babylon, would give Josiah the political space to enact his key religious reforms (34:3–33) in three phases: his eighth (34:3a), twelfth (34:3b–7), and eighteenth (34:8–33) years. The last reform is initially focused on the reconstruction of the temple, supported through the contributions of a united Israel (34:8–13). This physical restoration, however, is soon eclipsed by the discovery of a law book (most likely the book of Deuteronomy), which prompts the deep contrition of Josiah, who seeks a prophetic word from God. This word is delivered by the prophetess Huldah, who, after delivering a word of judgment on Israel for its illicit worship of other gods, commends the penitential example of Josiah. Josiah leads the nation in a covenant renewal, in which they pledge their desire to follow God, but he also rids the nation, including also the tribal territories of the former northern kingdom, of its detestable idols.

This restoration of the temple and renewal of the people lays the foundation for the reinstatement of the festal calendar at the temple in 35:1–19. In focus are the closely related Festivals of Passover and Unleavened Bread. Josiah's actions and speech in verses 1–6 highlight his careful attention to follow the Torah legislation established by Moses and the further legislation established by David and Solomon. Sacrificial animals are provided by Josiah (35:7), his officials (35:8), and Levites (35:9), and the sacrifices are offered in the prescribed way by the priests and Levites (35:10–14), accompanied by music (35:15). Comparisons to the time of Samuel raise the profile of Josiah considerably. What is surprising, however, is the quick downfall of Josiah in 35:20–24. On his way to support his Assyrian ally against the rival coalition of Babylon and Media, Pharaoh Necho II (609–594 BC) demands passage through Josiah's land. Josiah foolishly challenges this more powerful, Egyptian monarch in the Valley of Jezreel, a large open plain immediately north of Megiddo. Interestingly, the Chronicler identifies Necho as one who delivers the word of God and Josiah's death as the result of his disobedience. With the death of Josiah, Judah will no longer enjoy independent status, and the exilic nightmare has begun. Beginning with the demise of Josiah, foreign monarchs (Necho of Egypt, Nebuchadnezzar of Babylon, Cyrus of Persia) will control Judah's destiny.

The account of Josiah concludes with a summary note in 35:25–27 that focuses on Israel's grief over Josiah's death and Josiah's acts of devotion to Yahweh. Jeremiah's "laments" for Josiah should not be confused with the biblical book of Lamentations, which focuses instead on the city of Jerusalem in a later era.

O. The final royal accounts, exile, and restoration (36:1–23). From the Chronicler's perspective the death of Josiah seals the fate of Judah and for all intents and purposes the exile has begun. Foreign rulers now take political control over the nation, and more important the narrative, as Necho, Nebuchadnezzar, and Cyrus, along with prophetic figures, act and speak for Yahweh. Throughout the accounts in this chapter the Chronicler regularly depicts the kings going into exile with temple treasures and makes no mention of their deaths. The lack of death notice, typical of all these kings in chapter 36, suggests hope for the Davidic line to reemerge after the exile. The link of royal figure and temple treasures suggests an intertwining of their fates, so that the reemergence of the temple in 36:22–23 brings hope for the reemergence of the royal line.

Josiah's death brings his son Jehoahaz to the throne (36:1–3), but his reign will last a mere three months. After heading north to assist the losing cause of the Assyrians (see 2 Chron. 35:20–24), Necho inherits the Levant, setting up his headquarters in Aramean territory just north of the traditional lands of Israel. From there (Riblah) Necho summons Jehoahaz to depose him and send him to exile in Egypt (cf. 2 Kings 23:33).

Necho replaces Jehoahaz with his brother Eliakim, changing his name to Jehoiakim and demanding heavy tribute (36:4–8). Jehoiakim will see his Egyptian master lose control of the Levant to the rising ancient Near Eastern power Babylon, led first by Nabopolassar and then by his son Nebuchadnezzar (see 2 Kings 24:1–7). Although at first submitting to this new eastern power, Jehoiakim soon rebels and faces the punishment of Nebuchadnezzar, implicitly linked by the Chronicler to the evil Jehoiakim does in the eyes of Yahweh. The term used for evil here is the same used to characterize Ahaz (2 Chron. 28:3) and Manasseh (33:2; 34:33), showing that Jehoiakim deserves this divine discipline.

With his father in exile Jehoiachin ascends to the throne (36:9–10), but his reign lasts only three months and ten days. He also is evaluated negatively by the Chronicler, who describes his divine discipline as exile to Babylon (for the fate of Jehoiachin see 2 Kings 25:27–30 and the record of his royal provisions in exile in *ANET* 308). Nebuchadnezzar appoints Zedekiah (36:11–20), Jehoiachin's uncle, as puppet king of Judah (see *COS* 1.137:468). After eleven years of submission Zedekiah rebels against his overlord, an action paralleled by the apostasy of both Zedekiah and his people from Yahweh by following the detestable practices (same word used of Ahaz, Manasseh, and Jehoiakim in 2 Chron. 28:3; 33:2; 34:33; 36:8). The prophetic voice again breaks in as God's last act of compassion to avoid discipline, but to no avail. The city falls to Nebuchadnezzar, who kills the people; despoils the royal and temple treasures; destroys the temple, wall, and palaces; and exiles the survivors.

In 36:21 the Chronicler notes how the exile provides an opportunity for the land to enjoy the Sabbath rest required in the Torah (Leviticus 25). The figure seventy often appears in reference to the exile (Jer. 25:12; 29:10; Dan. 9:2; Zech. 1:12; 7:5). Symbolic of a generation (Isa. 23:15–18; Ps. 90:10), it is linked in the ancient world to the length of destruction for a rebellious city. Although the period between the date of the final destruction of Jerusalem in 587–586 BC and that of Cyrus's decree in 539 BC is shy of fifty years, as noted in the commentary on 35:20–24, the death of Josiah in 609 BC seems to mark the beginning of the exile in Chronicles, resulting in a period of seventy years.

The conclusion to 1–2 Chronicles, in 36:22–23, expresses both the Chronicler's hope and his challenge in his own generation. In 539 BC, after amassing a large empire surrounding the Babylonian Empire, Cyrus will conquer Babylon and inherit the traditional lands of Judah and Israel and their exiles in Mesopotamia. God's sovereign fulfillment of Jeremiah's prophecy is seen in Cyrus's proclamation that promises the rebuilding of the temple and invites the exilic community to return to the land. Similar policies of Cyrus toward his conquered nations can be seen in the famous Cyrus Cylinder, which describes his restoration of sanctuaries and their gods in southern Mesopotamia. Once again the Chronicler depicts a foreign emperor acting on behalf of Yahweh, here in fulfillment of earlier prophetic expectation (Jer. 25:12; 29:10; cf. Isa. 44:28; 45:1, 13; Jer. 51:11, 28).

Select Bibliography

Boda, Mark J. *1–2 Chronicles*. Cornerstone Biblical Commentary. Wheaton: Tyndale, 2010.

Braun, Roddy L. *1 Chronicles*. Word Biblical Commentary. Waco: Word, 1986.

Dillard, Raymond B. *2 Chronicles*. Word Biblical Commentary. Waco: Word, 1987.

Hill, Andrew E. *1 & 2 Chronicles*. NIV Application Commentary. Grand Rapids: Zondervan, 2003.

Japhet, Sara. *I & II Chronicles*. Old Testament Library. Louisville: Westminster John Knox, 1993.

Johnstone, William. *1 and 2 Chronicles*. Journal for the Study of the Old Testament Supplements 253–54. Sheffield: Sheffield Academic Press, 1997.

Jones, Gwilym H. *1 & 2 Chronicles*. Old Testament Guides. Sheffield: JSOT Press, 1993.

Klein, Ralph W. *1 Chronicles: A Commentary*. Hermeneia. Minneapolis: Fortress, 2006.

Knoppers, Gary N. *I Chronicles: A New Translation with Introduction and Commentary*. 2 vols. Anchor Bible. New York: Doubleday, 2004.

McConville, J. G. *I & II Chronicles*. Daily Study Bible. Philadelphia: Westminster, 1984.

Selman, Martin J. *1 Chronicles*. Tyndale Old Testament Commentaries. Downers Grove, IL: InterVarsity, 1994.

———. *2 Chronicles*. Tyndale Old Testament Commentaries. Downers Grove, IL: InterVarsity, 1994.

Thompson, J. A. *1, 2 Chronicles*. New American Commentary. Nashville: Broadman & Holman, 1994.

Tuell, Steven S. *First and Second Chronicles*. Interpretation. Louisville: Westminster John Knox, 2001.

Williamson, H. G. M. *1 and 2 Chronicles*. New Century Bible Commentary. Grand Rapids: Eerdmans, 1982.

Ezra-Nehemiah

MERVIN BRENEMAN

Introduction

The combined book of Ezra-Nehemiah gives us a glimpse of the drama and struggles of the Israelites as they return to Judah from captivity in Babylon to reestablish their community centered on the worship of the one true God. But it is more than a simple chronicle of events; Ezra-Nehemiah uses narration to teach and guide the community in its faith and everyday life.

Many studies of the history of Israel give little attention to the postexilic community. However, in God's redemptive plan, every period is important for the continuity and fulfillment of that plan. This small community of returned exiles was used by God to preserve and give to the world the inspired Scriptures of the Old Testament. These people kept alive the faith, worldview, and messianic hope that God had been progressively revealing for centuries. They prepared the way for the coming of the Messiah. Thus the work of Ezra, Nehemiah, and the people in restoring the temple worship (Ezra 1–6); in renewing emphasis on the Torah (Ezra 7–10); in the restoration of the wall and development of the community (Nehemiah 1–7); and in the cultural revitalization, the spiritual renewal, and the community consolidation (Nehemiah 8–13) all has strategic importance in God's eternal redemptive plan.

Historical Context

In regard to the historical setting, the narrative of both Ezra and Nehemiah concerns the small postexilic community of Jews in Judah. These Jewish people had a vital interest in their own history. They knew that they were descendants of Abraham and Jacob, with specific promises from God regarding his purpose for the Jewish people. At the same time, they were prone to discouragement because of their precarious position in the vast Persian Empire. They were also surrounded by hostile communities.

After the glorious reigns of David and Solomon, the Jewish kingdom was divided (931 BC) into the northern and southern kingdoms. Both 1–2 Kings and 1–2 Chronicles describe the struggle to maintain faith in Yahweh. God raised up prophets to warn the people of their sinful, rebellious ways and to prophesy that destruction and captivity would occur unless the people repented.

In 722–721 BC the Assyrian Empire conquered the northern kingdom, exiling much of the population to other parts of the empire. The southern kingdom, with the Davidic dynasty, continued until 587–586 BC, when it was conquered by the Babylonian Empire. Most of the surviving population was taken captive to Babylon.

Although the Babylonian conquerors were less brutal than the Assyrians, the Jews were still captives in a foreign land. They had not believed Jeremiah's warnings about God's judgment (e.g., Jer. 1:14–16; 4:15–18; 6:6–8), preferring to believe the false prophets who said God would never let Jerusalem fall.

The Jews faced a serious test of their faith during the captivity. Now they realized that Jeremiah was right since his prophecies were fulfilled (Jer. 29:10–14). This realization helped many to believe Jeremiah's positive message that God still had a purpose for them and that they would return to Palestine. Largely through the messages of Jeremiah and Ezekiel, the faith of Israel survived the captivity.

However, after the people had waited nearly fifty years, the return seemed remote. Then, in 539 BC, the Persian king Cyrus I suddenly moved to capture Babylon. His army took the city practically without a struggle. Thus Cyrus controlled the whole Babylonian Empire, including Palestine.

The Assyrians had been brutal, transporting captives to different parts of the empire and massacring whole populations. The Babylonians were somewhat less cruel but followed the same practice of taking whole populations captive and deporting them. Cyrus, however, encouraged conquered peoples to continue their own religions and cultures. When he took over Babylon he allowed the Jews and other captive peoples to return to their homelands.

The Persian Empire dominated the political scene of the ancient Near East from its capture of Babylon in 539 BC until its defeat by Alexander the Great in 330 BC (see Table 1 for a chronological picture of the period). The Persian Empire reached its most developed organization and its greatest extent in the reign of Darius I (522–486 BC). It extended from Egypt, Thrace, and Macedonia in the west to the Indus Valley in the east. Under Darius the empire was divided into twenty satrapies, which were further divided into provinces. The Persian "satraps" were virtually kings over their huge satrapies. Their provinces were supervised by governors, normally from local descent. Thus, in Ezra and Nehemiah, Zerubbabel and Nehemiah are called governors.

Judah was a small province; its area was between 950 and 1,150 square miles (compare to the state of Rhode Island, 1,214 square miles). The northern boundary passed through Mizpah and Gibeon and on to the Jordan River. The southern boundary was between Beth Zur and Hebron. During the time of the exile the Edomites took over much of southern Judah, since the Edomites were driven from their homeland by the Nabatean Arabs.

Archaeology indicates that Judah was sparsely populated and quite poor during this time. Although when Judah and Jerusalem fell in 587 BC most of the survivors were carried as captives to Babylon, a few Jews remained in the land. A group of

Assyrian relief from Sennacherib's palace at Nineveh (700–692 BC) showing captives from one of Sennacherib's military campaigns

Table 1: Chronological Overview of the Persian Empire, 539–330 BC	
Persian Ruler	**Key Historical and Biblical Events**
Cyrus the Great, 550–530 BC	Captures Babylon in 539; Issues edict for Jews' return to Judah in 538
Cambyses II, 530–522	Conquers Egypt
Darius I, 522–486	Invades Greek mainland in 490, defeated at Marathon; Permits rebuilding of temple in Jerusalem, completed between 520 and 516
Xerxes I, 486–465	Attempts to conquer Greece, defeated at Salamis in 480; Book of Esther begins in 483; Esther becomes queen in 479
Artaxerxes I, 464–424	Ezra to Jerusalem in 458; Nehemiah, in 445
Darius II, 423–404	
Artaxerxes II, 404–359	
Artaxerxes III, 359–338	
Artaxerxes IV, 338–336	
Darius III, 336–300	Alexander burns Persepolis in 330

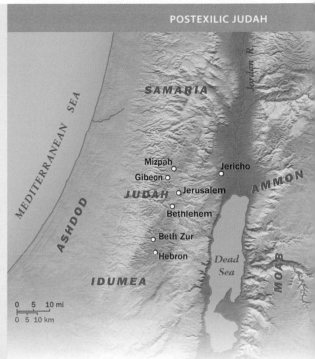

POSTEXILIC JUDAH

them fled to Egypt (2 Kings 25; Jeremiah 41). Some Jews who had fled to neighboring areas returned to Judah, but the area remained poor. Nehemiah 11:25–35 mentions Jews from a number of towns in the Negev and Shephelah that were outside the boundaries of Judah mentioned above. There were also quite a few Jews in Galilee and other parts of Palestine in the time of the Maccabees (ca. 176 BC). This helps explain why some "people of the land" are mentioned in Ezra-Nehemiah (Ezra 9:11; Neh. 9:24; cf. 9:10).

The Jewish community during the time of Ezra and Nehemiah was small and fragile. There were enemies on every side. Samaria was on the north, where Sanballat was governor. On the east was Ammon-Gilead, where Tobiah was governor. Geshem was governor of Arabia-Idumea on the south, and on the west was the Philistine province of Ashdod.

The Persian king Artaxerxes I commissioned both Ezra and Nehemiah to go "up to" Jerusalem to help the struggling community. The exact dates of Ezra's and Nehemiah's arrivals in Jerusalem have been disputed in biblical scholarship. The traditionally accepted date for Ezra's arrival is 458 BC. This is based on Ezra 7:7–8, assuming the arrival occurred during the seventh year of Artaxerxes I (464–424 BC). Nehemiah was commissioned by Artaxerxes to restore the broken-down walls of Jerusalem and arrived there thirteen years later in 445 BC (Neh. 2:1). Some scholars disagree, questioning why Ezra would have waited thirteen years for the public reading of the law (Nehemiah 8), or why, after Ezra's reforms, Nehemiah would still find mixed marriages. So it is suggested that perhaps Ezra arrived in the seventh year of Artaxerxes II, who reigned from 404 to 359, which places Ezra's arrival in 398. This calls into question the two passages that put Ezra and Nehemiah together (Neh. 8:9; 12:36). It has also been suggested that the "seventh" year in Ezra 7:7–8 might be a textual error for the thirty-seventh year, 428. (Although there is virtually no manuscript support for this view, some scholars prefer it because this would require less time between Ezra's arrival and the public reading of the law.)

Despite the problems encountered in reconciling the relationship of Ezra and Nehemiah as co-reformers, taking the biblical text as it stands has proven to be the best solution. Hence this commentary supports the traditional dates of 458 for Ezra's arrival and 445 for Nehemiah's arrival.

Ezra was commissioned by the Persian king to teach the people "the laws of your God" (Ezra 7:25). Ezra had a deep and long-lasting influence on the postexilic Jewish community. The Persian king recognized the distinctive religious faith of the Jews; yet they were part of the Persian Empire. This even affected their language. The Jews now spoke Aramaic, which had become the international language of the empire. Ezra changed the script of the Scriptures from the old rounded letters to the Aramaic square letters so the people could read it. He provided help for those who could not understand the Scriptures read in Hebrew at the public reading of the law in Nehemiah 8. Thus it is understandable that the correspondence with the Persian government in Ezra 4:7–6:18 and 7:12–16 is written in Aramaic. The remainder of Ezra-Nehemiah is written in Hebrew. Although the people spoke Aramaic, they considered Hebrew their native language.

In Ezra 1:3, 5; 7:28 the Jews are invited to "go up" to Jerusalem. The transition from Babylon to Jerusalem is evident throughout the narrative. The name Jerusalem occurs eighty-six times in Ezra-Nehemiah. It was of utmost importance to the Jews that they reestablish the "house of God" in Jerusalem.

Composition

In regard to the composition and construction of Ezra-Nehemiah, the books of Ezra and Nehemiah both receive their names from their principle characters. In the Hebrew Bible and in the Talmud the two books are considered one book in two parts. Since the time of Origen (AD 185–253) and throughout most of church history, Ezra and Nehemiah have been considered separate books. In modern times opinions have fluctuated; some scholars have considered them written as two separate books. Recent studies, however, tend to sustain the view that Ezra-Nehemiah was composed as one work.

Several blocks of material are evident in Ezra-Nehemiah: (1) the narrative of the first return (Ezra 1–6); (2) the Ezra memoirs, apparently written by Ezra (Ezra 7–10); and (3) the Nehemiah memoirs (Nehemiah 1–7 and much of 11–13). How then was this book composed? Although some details of the process remain unknown, apparently the author-editor used these three blocks of material, along with some other documents such as inventories, lists of returnees, and letters. With his own summary notations, he joined them into one work, the book of Ezra-Nehemiah.

Authorship

Who was the author of Ezra-Nehemiah? The most likely candidate seems to be Ezra himself. It has been suggested that Ezra-Nehemiah was written by the same author who compiled 1–2 Chronicles, since the two works have some points of view in common. However, the different context, focus, and structure of each would indicate different authors for Ezra-Nehemiah and 1–2 Chronicles.

When was Ezra-Nehemiah written? The memoirs of Ezra and those of Nehemiah certainly were written first, perhaps at different periods. Since there are no people or events mentioned in Nehemiah that require a date later than 400 BC, we can assume it was finished sometime before then. If Ezra was the final author, Ezra-Nehemiah must have been completed around 420 BC.

Literary Features and Structure

Most of Ezra-Nehemiah consists of narrative. Typical of biblical narrative, it combines three types of writing: historical, literary, and theological. Some contemporary writers have been skeptical of its historical value. These critics compare biblical history with ancient Greek historical writings, which were partially fictitious. Likewise, since biblical narrative teaches certain theological truths, these critics doubt its historical accuracy.

However, the fact that Ezra-Nehemiah uses literary techniques and teaches theological truths in no way implies that the events it describes did not actually occur. It is now generally understood that no historical writing can be completely objective. Every writer expresses some point of view. We should rather be thankful that God, in order to give us his revelation, used and inspired writers who could convey his point of view and could use narrative techniques to help us understand what they intended to communicate. As we read and study Ezra-Nehemiah we should recognize the various narrative techniques the author uses, along with the theological principles he wishes to convey.

History is important in the biblical perspective. Israel's experiences with God (for example, the patriarchal narratives or the exodus event) as recorded in the Pentateuch left a permanent imprint on the Jews, resulting in two basic convictions: (1) that God acts in history and (2) that God communicates and interprets the meaning of these acts through Scripture. Much of the negative criticism of biblical history is based on a worldview, currently in vogue, that denies these basic convictions.

At least half of the Bible is historical narrative, normally presented in the form of stories. Ezra-Nehemiah is largely composed of stories. Story writers call attention to their viewpoints and purposes through structure and by literary techniques such as characterization, omission, repetition, key words, contrast, comparison, irony, climax, and resolution. Divine inspiration does not obliterate these techniques but guides the authors in their use.

Biblical narratives or stories normally include a recognizable plot, usually with (1) an introduction or exposition, which explains the background, the characters, and other necessary information; (2) a rising tension, often depicted through contrasts and conflicts; (3) a climax or breaking point in the tension; and (4) a solution or unraveling of the plot tension. The viewpoint or evaluation of the author can often be seen in how the solution to the tension in the plot is explained.

Does the structure of Ezra-Nehemiah fit this pattern? Recent studies have attempted to show that it does, helping the reader clearly see the author's purpose.

The structure of Ezra-Nehemiah helps us discern its main emphases. The entire work can be divided into four main blocks: three principle "missions" and a fourth section, a "concluding resolution" to the entire plot.

1. The first mission is the return of the Jews to Judah to reestablish themselves in the promised land and to build the house of worship under the leadership of Sheshbazzar and Zerubbabel (Ezra 1–6).
2. The second mission is that of Ezra, teacher and scribe, to "appoint magistrates and judges to administer justice" and to teach "the law of your God and the law of the king" (Ezra 7–10; see 7:25–26).
3. The third mission is that of Nehemiah to lead the people in restoring the wall around Jerusalem (Nehemiah 1–7).
4. The fourth section, although it may be considered a continuation of Nehemiah's mission, brings the whole narrative to a conclusion by highlighting the consolidation of the covenant community (Neh. 7:5–13:31).

These different sections are surprisingly similar in their construction, and through them we can see three basic themes: (1) the continuation of the people of God, with emphasis on the community rather than on powerful leaders;

(2) the construction of the house of God, with its strong emphasis on worship; and (3) the importance of the authority of written texts, primarily the law of God, but also the law of the king and written resolutions of the community.

The book of Nehemiah also displays community development and renewal processes similar to those described in modern sociological studies. In Nehemiah 1–2 we can see an "innovation process." A society begins to change when someone (or some group) is concerned about community problems, investigates their causes, finds solutions, and persuades the community to take action.

Theological Themes

An amazingly complete biblical theology is implicit throughout Ezra-Nehemiah, which includes all the basic Old Testament teachings about God: his creation (Neh. 9:5–6), his infinite knowledge and power (Neh. 1:6, 10; 4:14; 6:16; 9:10–11), his sovereignty over all the nations (Ezra 1:1; 5:5, 11; 7:27; 8:22; Neh. 2:8; 4:14, 20), his covenant with Israel (Ezra 9:6–15; Neh. 1:5–11; 9:5–37), his judgment (Ezra 9:7, 13–15; Neh. 13:18), and his mercy (Ezra 3:11; Neh. 9:9, 17, 19). Of special interest is how this theology is worked out in the restoration of the Jewish people both physically and spiritually, which is the basic theme of Ezra-Nehemiah.

As we notice several theological emphases in Ezra-Nehemiah, we should not miss their relevance for God's people today.

The author highlights God's sovereignty and providence in the continuity of his plan and his people. The text constantly emphasizes that God moved the Persian kings to allow the return, to allow the construction of the temple, and to favor the work of Ezra and of Nehemiah. In the events of their day, the Jews saw parallels to the manifestations of God's sovereignty and providence in the exodus, the wilderness journey, the conquest of Canaan, and all their history. They commemorated these events in their annual feasts. All this deepened their conviction that they embodied the continuity of God's people.

The author insists that God's holiness requires his people's separation from evil. Perhaps some of Ezra's and Nehemiah's actions seem too stringent to us; but we must remember how important it was to God for this community to maintain its identity as God's people—if they failed, they might face another exile.

Ezra-Nehemiah underlines the centrality of God's Word in the life of the community. God's law is a recipe for a healthy society. Under Ezra's and Nehemiah's leadership the people recognize the law's authority, repent of their disobedience, decide to obey, and confirm their decision in writing and by definite action.

Throughout Ezra-Nehemiah we see an emphasis on worshiping and glorifying God. The convictions in the people's hearts lead to genuine worship. What we believe determines our priorities and our decisions. The first returning exiles build the altar to worship God before they build the temple. The emphasis on worship and God's Word leads to renewal movements, with a focus on repentance, definite decisions for change, renewed worship, and specific followup. But that is not the end of the matter, for the people document their decisions and make special efforts to continue the changes.

The author artfully combines theology and history: a living faith based on a vital theology produces dynamic application. Here we will mention three significant themes in Ezra-Nehemiah that greatly affect their future history: prayer, renewal, and consolidation.

Prayer is emphasized throughout Ezra-Nehemiah. Ezra calls for a time of fasting and prayer before making the trip to Jerusalem. In Ezra 9, Ezra's prayer marks a turning point in the community. Nehemiah spends four months in prayer before approaching the king with his request. The statement "because the gracious hand of my God was upon me, the king granted my requests" (Neh. 2:8) recognizes that response as an answer to prayer. Nehemiah constantly turns to God in prayer. Indeed, the whole Bible emphasizes prayer, yet most believers admit they do not pray enough. Jacques Ellul, a famous political philosopher, has stated that a Christian can have more political influence on their country in earnest prayer than by being a politician.

Renewal, while closely related to prayer, is also a distinct key factor in the history of Ezra-Nehemiah. Some historians have used the figure of the "hinges" of history, key events or turning points in the history of a nation. Many historians recognize the Wesleyan revivals in Britain and the Great Awakenings in the United States as such hinges or turning points. The renewals in the postexilic community were also hinges in the history of Israel. We see this in Ezra 9 and again in Nehemiah 8–10. These renewals made a difference in people's attitudes and brought unity and purpose, which resulted in the people working together to build the temple and restore the wall.

Consolidation of the community through unity and mutual dedication is important in the last section of Ezra-Nehemiah (Nehemiah 8–13). In Nehemiah 8–10 the people renew their covenant with God and rededicate themselves to obedience to the Torah. This spiritual revival is also a revitalization of their Jewish culture (Neh. 9:38–10:39).

Consolidation of the restoration community also requires taking care of details. If Jerusalem is to be a vital religious center, more people will have to live there. So, many of the Jews voluntarily give up their preference to live in the suburbs outside Jerusalem in order to populate the city itself and thus consolidate the decisions they have just made.

Consolidation of the community is strengthened by celebration, a great and joyous dedication of the completion of the wall (Nehemiah 12). One wonders why this is not celebrated sooner. But it certainly fits the emphasis here on consolidation. Such celebrations, directed at honoring God for what he has done, enhance the unity and dedication of the people.

Consolidation of the restoration community is also achieved by discipline and caring for administrative details. The litany of reforms in Nehemiah 13 may seem to be an anticlimax to the story of Ezra-Nehemiah; however, even a renewed community includes human frailties. God uses consecrated leaders to address these details and lead the community forward to fulfill God's purposes.

Outline

Commentary

1. The First Mission: The Return of the Jews to Judah (Ezra 1:1–6:22)

A. Cyrus's proclamation (1:1–4). Ezra 1:1–4 provides a general introduction to

Ezra-Nehemiah. The first verse sets the pace, beginning with a specific time in history: "In the first year of Cyrus king of Persia" (539 BC). The author purports to give us historical facts. While the book is historical narrative, it does not pretend to give a complete history of the period. Rather, the author selects the material that can best present his message.

Immediately the author indicates the basic premise of his message: "in order to fulfill the word of the LORD." God is in charge of history; he has proclaimed his will through his prophets. He "moved the heart" of Cyrus to set forth the proclamation found in verses 2–4.

The proclamation itself also suggests certain theological themes: "The LORD, the God of heaven" (1:2), the emphasis on his people, and the stated purpose to "build the temple of the LORD, the God of Israel" (1:3). These elements give the impression that a Jew could have written the proclamation, although Cyrus may have consulted with the Jews prior to his pronouncement.

This introduction to the first mission is packed with theological premises. It takes for granted the providence of God, the emphasis on written law and prophecy, and the importance of written proclamations (cf. Exod. 36:6; 2 Chron. 30:5). Therefore, while this may be

seen as an introduction to the first part of Ezra, it may also be understood as the introduction to the whole book.

The reference to Jeremiah in 1:1 no doubt is to Jeremiah 25:11 (cf. Jer. 29:10; 2 Chron. 36:21). It is not clear how we should calculate the seventy years mentioned in the Jeremiah passages (but not mentioned here). It could be from circa 606 BC, when the land was desolated, until the time of Cyrus, or it could apply to the time between the destruction of Jerusalem in 587–586 BC and the completion of the second temple in 516.

When the author says, "The LORD moved the heart of Cyrus" (1:1), he likely is alluding to the same expression used in Jeremiah 51:11 and Isaiah 41:2. He must have also known the more specific prophecies of Isaiah 44:28 and 45:1, 13. The author certainly emphasizes God's sovereignty and fulfillment of prophecy. He attributes the great events about to be described to both the supernatural source—"the LORD moved" (literally "Yahweh stirred up")—and the human instrument, "the heart of Cyrus."

At the end of the first mission or stage of the work (Ezra 6:14), the author again repeats this emphasis on the divine and human instruments: "They finished building the temple according to the command of the God of Israel and the decrees of Cyrus, Darius and Artaxerxes, kings of Persia." The same emphasis is reiterated in

Cyrus Cylinder (Babylon, after 539 BC)

each of the three missions or stages of the work in Ezra-Nehemiah. In matters both divine and human, the focus is on the written documents: the decrees of the kings and the law of God. The author thus underlines the authority of the written Word of God.

The proclamation in 1:2–4 is the famous Edict of Cyrus. (Another record of it is found in Ezra 6:3–5.) It seems to give the impression that Cyrus believed in Yahweh, the God of Israel. However, inscriptions from that time indicate that Cyrus made similar proclamations to other ethnic captives, honoring their gods and returning the people and their idols to their homelands. The Cyrus Cylinder, a long inscription found in Babylon (see photo), states that the god Marduk chose Cyrus to free Babylon and restore the former worship to that god. This is a typical attitude in polytheistic culture, where many gods are worshiped. Cyrus wanted to secure the favor of them all.

The decree does not command the Jews to return to Jerusalem, but certainly it encourages them to do so. In verse 4 it is not altogether clear if "survivors" refers only to fellow Jews or also to other neighbors. Its primary focus may be on the fellow Jews, but in the light of verse 6, it is likely that others also participated in this generosity.

The Persian kings respected the religious convictions of their subject peoples. They supported their temples and religious activities as a means to keep peace throughout the empire. Likewise the Jews could expect help from the empire's treasuries to provide silver, gold, and livestock for the sacrifices and offerings in their temple. What joy the returning Jews must have experienced as they realized that God was keeping his promises to bring them back to their land and to restore their house of worship!

B. Preparations for the return (1:5–11). The three divisions of Ezra-Nehemiah dealing with the three main missions of the people (Ezra 1:1–6:22; 7:1–10:44; Neh. 1:1–7:73) seem to have a parallel structure: preparation for the

work, the beginning of the work, opposition to the work, resolution of the conflict or opposition, and the conclusion. Some of the elements are more prominent than others, but they all follow the same general order in each division.

This section on the preparation for the first mission begins with a summary statement (1:5–6). Again we notice the emphasis on God's providence ("Everyone whose heart God had moved") and on the purpose of the mission ("to build the house of the LORD"). The rebuilding of the worshiping community in Jerusalem is a noble mission. But not all the people are willing to return to Jerusalem. Many Jews have adapted to their context in Babylon and opt to stay there. They realize that to return is a hard and dangerous mission.

This was written to present teachings that are still valid today. In God's work he takes the initiative; he moves in peoples' hearts. But the people also have to "decide" to act, to obey God's leading. In any mission or project, the people need a goal. For the returning Jews, their immediate objective is to build the house of God in Jerusalem.

The phrase "all their neighbors assisted them" (1:6) reminds us of the exodus experience, when the Egyptians gave generous gifts to the Israelites before they left Egypt (Exod. 12:35–36). Here it appears that those who give also included non-Jewish neighbors. No doubt the author had in mind the exodus parallel since throughout Ezra-Nehemiah there are exodus motifs. In Isaiah as well, the return from Babylonian exile is pictured as a second exodus. This must have encouraged the people as they prepared their long trip to Jerusalem, and later as they compared this event with the great work of God in the exodus from Egypt.

We see the king's generosity in 1:7–8. Cyrus made it his policy to help support the practices of the local religions in the areas under the rule of the Persian Empire. In ancient times, when one country or king conquered another, the god of the conquering people was considered the victor over the conquered people's gods. The ruling king took the subject's idols and religious utensils as plunder and symbols of his own god's supremacy and put them in his temple. This is what Nebuchadnezzar did with treasures and articles from the Jerusalem temple when he conquered Judah. Now Cyrus allows the Jews to take many of the vessels that Nebuchadnezzar carried off to Babylon and return them to the temple of God, which they have been commissioned to build. This is a significant act by Cyrus; it shows his sincere interest in the well-being of his subject peoples.

We see the author's concern for detail in the list of articles that are returned to the temple in Jerusalem. They represent considerable value and were considered important, as seen in their mention again in Ezra 5:13–15. The inventory list does not pretend to list all the vessels, since it includes only 2,490 of the 5,400 articles mentioned in verse 11. The inventory list further attests God's power to preserve and sustain—both people and temple artifacts are restored to the land of covenant promise.

Sheshbazzar is mentioned only in Ezra 1:8, 11 and 5:14, 16. Ezra 5:14 says Cyrus has appointed him as governor, and 5:16 says he lays the foundation of the temple. But we see no more of him; rather, in Haggai 1:1, Zerubbabel is called the governor of Judah, and he is also mentioned in Zechariah 4:6; Ezra 2:2; and Nehemiah 7:7.

In this first chapter several themes emphasized throughout Ezra-Nehemiah stand out: (1) the people of God—the restoration community is the continuation of God's people from Abraham until the present (Ezra-Nehemiah tends to put the emphasis on the "people" rather than on outstanding leaders, shown by the fact that the author mentions the heads of families. It is true that Ezra and Nehemiah stand out as important leaders; however, the intent of the author is to emphasize even more the people as a whole.); (2) the "house of God," with its focus on worship and a holy community; and (3) written documents and their function to guide the faith and life of the community.

The chapter ends with a statement that must have excited the first readers: "when the exiles came up from Babylon to Jerusalem" (1:11). In the news of the great cities of that day, this would not have received much attention. But as we look at God's plan throughout the Bible, this event has great importance. For through this small, apparently weak community, God will continue to fulfill his plan to give to the entire world his revelation in Scripture and his salvation in Christ Jesus.

C. The list of returnees (2:1–70). The modern reader may wonder why this long list of names is included in the narrative. Why would the original readers be interested in this list? Since Israel, God's covenant people, descended from Jacob, their family records were always important to them. Here their genealogy is especially important to show they are the continuation of the preexilic Jewish community. Each person wanted to confirm his or her identity as part of the covenant community, which also served to emphasize their separation from the Samaritans and other surrounding peoples. In many cases this identity and continuity was also important for land rights. Many of them realized that they were part of God's continuing plan; notice their rejoicing: "Our mouths were filled with laughter, our tongues with songs of joy" (Ps. 126:2).

But today we do not put much emphasis on genealogies, so what value does this chapter have for us? First, it helps us to understand the context of Ezra. The list also confirms Jeremiah's word that the exile would be limited to approximately seventy years and the people would return. Again it emphasizes the continuity of this people with the preexilic covenant community. Today we also need this emphasis on the common people, on our families, on our identity in Christ, on the fact that each member of the community is important in God's work.

In Ezra 2:1, the reference to "province" probably means the province of Judah, which was far away from the administrative center of the Persian Empire. The people's records also indicated where their family inheritance was located; thus they endeavored to return to the same place, "each to his own town."

The list begins, in 2:2, with the names of eleven leaders. Virtually the same list in Nehemiah 7 includes twelve names (perhaps a conscious effort to create analogy with the twelve tribes of Israel).

It is interesting that Zerubbabel is mentioned instead of Sheshbazzar. Sheshbazzar disappears very quickly, and Zerubbabel, grandson of King Jehoiachin, continues as leader of the group. According to the curse on Jehoiachin (Jer. 22:28–30), no one of his line could ever sit on the throne of David. Zerubbabel led the first group of returnees but was not king. In fact no descendant of Solomon reigned in Judah during the period of the Second Commonwealth (538 BC–AD 70). The Nehemiah mentioned in 2:2 is apparently not the Nehemiah who will rebuild portions of the Jerusalem wall. However, we do not know when this list was compiled. It is quite possible that the final author copied the same list that was used in Nehemiah 7.

Although the leaders are mentioned, the real emphasis is on all the "people of Israel." During the divided monarchy, the northern kingdom is usually referred to as Israel and the southern kingdom as Judah. The use of Israel here, however, emphasizes that this restoration community is heir to the biblical covenants rather than referring to the northern kingdom.

The names of many people are listed in 2:3–61, first the lay families, then the different groups of families with religious duties. Within the lay families, some are listed according to family names (2:3–20), while others are listed according to the place of their family inheritance (2:23–35).

Although some of these names occur elsewhere, as do eleven in Ezra 8, they are not necessarily the same persons. "Pahath-Moab" means "governor of Moab"; this ancestor might have governed part of the Moab area sometime during the monarchy. Instead of "Gibbar" (2:20), Nehemiah's list has "Gibeon," so the list of place names may start with verse 20.

The names of towns mentioned in 2:21–35 apparently indicate places where the families lived before the exile. Only Bethlehem and Netophah are south of Jerusalem; the others lie north of Jerusalem. Lod, Hadid, and Ono (1:33) are near Joppa on the coast.

The lists of temple ministers are given in 2:36–58. Although Ezra-Nehemiah emphasizes the worship, spiritual life, and holiness of the people, it is significant that the "lay" people are listed before the priests and their helpers. Before the exile there were twenty-four family groups of priests; here only four are mentioned, but the totals indicate more than four thousand persons. Thus the priests compose about 10 percent of those returning from exile.

In comparison, the number of Levites that return is very small. (Levites were descendants of the tribe of Levi but not from the priestly family of Aaron.) Later, when Ezra endeavors to bring more Levites back from Babylon, only thirty-eight will respond. Could the lack of interest be due to the fact that Levites did not inherit land, since the Lord was their inheritance

The list of temple officers inscribed on this Ugaritic tablet (Ras Shamra, thirteenth century BC) provides an example of ancient record keeping.

(Josh. 13:33; 14:3–4; 18:7; 21:1–41)? It is interesting to note that in Numbers 18:21, 26, the tithe laws indicate that there were many more Levites than priests at that time.

The temple servants are named in 2:43–54. Who were they? The list includes many foreign names. In Ezra 8:20, some of those who return to Jerusalem are temple servants—"a body that David and the officials had established to assist the Levites." We know that David's bodyguard was composed of foreign men. In Numbers 31:47 Moses gives some of the Midianite captives to the Levites. So this group may have been at least partly composed of individuals from non-Israelite descent. Based on Joshua 9:27, Jewish rabbinic tradition says the temple servants are Gibeonites.

The "descendants of Solomon's servants" (2:55–58) must have been a similar group. Solomon's servants may have been temple workers recruited from the local non-Israelite population. The total (2:58) includes both groups of servants. From the 49 clans mentioned, there are only 392 persons.

Although Jewish families normally kept family registers (see Neh. 7:5; 1 Chron. 7:5), apparently some of the returnees have lost their records (2:59–63). Also, it is possible that some are proselytes, converts to Judaism. The Babylonian towns from which they have come are mentioned. Some of those lacking genealogical records are priests (2:62–63). Moses commanded that only descendants of Aaron could "burn incense before the LORD" (Num. 16:40). In the course of time some are able to find their credentials. The descendants of Hakkoz (2:61) apparently are accepted as priests some eighty years later, if "Meremoth son of Uriah, the priest" in 8:33 is the same "Meremoth son of Uriah, the son of Hakkoz" in Nehemiah 3:4, 21.

A Persian word is used for "governor" (2:63; also in Neh. 7:65, 70; 8:9; 10:1); here it probably refers to Sheshbazzar. The "Urim and Thummim" were small pebbles or precious stones that the high priest used as lots to determine

God's specific will in certain cases (Num. 27:21; 1 Sam. 14:37–42).

What can we learn from the totals mentioned in 2:64–69? The total listed, 43,360, is the same in Nehemiah 7 and 1 Esdras 5:41, so it appears to be correct. The itemized details listed add up to less; some persons and items were omitted in the catalogs. The large number of menservants and maidservants (a ratio of approximately one to six, 2:64–65) indicates that some returnees were wealthy. There are also quite a few horses, which were used by the wealthy. However, there are many more donkeys, which were used by the poor.

Just as is true today, the spiritual temperature of a community can be seen in their freewill offerings (2:68–69). The phrase "some of the heads of the families gave freewill offerings" would indicate that some others have a different attitude. As will be seen later, some of the returnees are more interested in their own fortunes than in God's work in the community. However, the offering is relatively large, which indicates that there is a certain measure of wealth in the community. Some eighteen years later, when Haggai is preaching, there is apparently more poverty (Hag. 1:7–11).

The chapter ends on a positive note (2:70): the people and some of the temple personnel settle in their towns. Some of the priests and temple servants live in Jerusalem itself. Chapter 2 prepares us for the great work of building the temple in order that the covenant community can renew their worship of God as prescribed in the law of Moses.

D. The work begun (3:1–6). The returnees have their priorities correct; they first build the altar in order to offer sacrifices and worship to God. The author plunges quickly into the project at hand, and specifies the time (autumn of 537 BC). The seventh month, Tishri (our September–October), traditionally was important for its religious ceremonies. On the first of the month the New Year and Feast of Trumpets were celebrated (Lev. 23:23–25). Although not mentioned here, the Day of Atonement was the tenth day (Leviticus 16). From the fifteenth day until the twenty-first was the celebration of the Feast of Tabernacles, mentioned in verse 4.

There are several emphases here: (1) the unity and continuity of the community ("The people assembled as one man," 3:1); (2) beginning by putting God first (worship); and (3) following the written law of Moses (3:2, 4). The people do not wait until the temple is rebuilt to build the altar and offer sacrifices to God. In 3:3, "despite" (NIV) could also be rendered "because of"; the people know they have enemies—they know they need God's protection.

Although there is a noticeable emphasis on all the people, Joshua and Zerubbabel are mentioned as leaders. Some see a conflict with Ezra 5:16, where Tattenai's letter to king Darius says Sheshbazzar laid the foundations of the temple. It may be that Sheshbazzar was named governor by Cyrus, but Zerubbabel was his assistant and soon was put in charge. Ezra-Nehemiah does not mention it, but Haggai 1 notes that Joshua is the high priest at this time, apparently the most important leader of the community.

Although Ezra is not yet in Jerusalem, the author repeats the emphasis on doing everything as written in the law of Moses (3:4–6). First they build the altar according to the instructions given by Moses (cf. Exod. 27:1–8; 31:2–5; 38:1–7). They are careful to celebrate the Feast of Tabernacles just as was written (Lev. 23:33–43). They not only are careful to celebrate Tabernacles; they also immediately begin to offer the regular burnt offerings as stipulated by Moses (Exod. 29:38–43), as well as the New Moon sacrifices and all the other regular sacrifices and "freewill offerings."

The people are united in their desire to worship God, trust him, and obey him. They are eager to build the temple, but they put worshiping God first. Many times Christians allow even "God-ordained" projects to come before their genuine interest in God's glory. We must remember that genuine worship is always first in God's priorities. These Jews knew that only in God's power could they survive in their

precarious situation. Since then, God's people have often rediscovered that worshiping and praying together is the best way to deal with difficult situations.

E. Rebuilding the temple (3:7–13). The temple project is well planned. The people have funds, both from the freewill offerings (2:68–69) and from the Persian treasury. The "authorization" by Cyrus (3:7) includes permission and expenses for securing and transporting the lumber from the mountains of Lebanon.

Again the continuity of this community with the preexilic community is emphasized, here by conscious parallels with the construction of Solomon's temple. Just as Solomon did, the Jews send to Lebanon for lumber (cf. Ezra 3:7 with 2 Chron. 2:16); both constructions begin in the second month (3:8; 2 Chron. 3:2); both are overseen by Levites (3:9; 1 Chron. 23:4); and both temples are celebrated with songs, instruments, and thanksgiving (3:10–11; 2 Chron. 5:11–13). In this celebration the restoration community also follows what was "prescribed by David" (3:10).

Even though they have only built the altar and laid the foundation for the temple, the people rejoice and praise God. They give God the glory and look forward to what he will do in the future. Certainly this shows their faith in God, that he will continue to protect them and guide them. However, there are some who are not so happy (cf. Hag. 2:3). Apparently older people remember the splendor of Solomon's temple in comparison with the simplicity of this temple. Haggai goes on to prophesy, "The latter glory of this house will be greater than the former" (Hag. 2:9 NASB), which was ultimately fulfilled when Jesus came to this second temple (cf. Luke 2:27, 32).

Ezra 3 has a wealth of teachings for God's people today. We see the importance of the continuity of God's people through whom God continues to fulfill his redemptive plan. We see the dedication of this small, seemingly insignificant community both in their enthusiasm to get on with God's work and in their decision to make worship and obedience to God's written word the foundation of their work and life.

Throughout Ezra-Nehemiah there is an emphasis on the authority of written documents, especially on God's written word. This community accepted the authority of the Pentateuch, the five books of the Law. Some scholars suggest that they must have had only portions of the Pentateuch available to them. However, it is significant that in Ezra-Nehemiah stipulations from all parts of the Pentateuch are found.

F. Opposition to the work (4:1–24). 4:1–5. Following the preparation and beginning of the work in the first mission, the work faces opposition. In 4:1–3, the opposition begins as soon as the neighboring peoples hear that the Jews are "building a temple for the LORD."

Even before they build the altar, the Jews fear "the people around them" (literally "the peoples of the lands"; 3:3). In earlier times, the phrase "people of the land" (singular) referred to the landowning families of the ruling class. Later it referred to the "poor people of the land" (Hag. 2:4). In Ezra (in plural form) it refers to the surrounding peoples (e.g., those from Samaria, Ammon, Ashdod, Edom, and Moab). They are persons mostly of foreign descent. Some are mixed Jews, whose ancestors intermarried with people brought in by the Assyrians (cf. 2 Kings 17:24–25). Some are Jews in Judah or nearby lands whose faith has become diluted with local religious beliefs.

But the author calls the peoples enemies. At first glance it appears that they want to help. They even claim that they worship the same God. But the rest of Ezra-Nehemiah shows their deep hatred of the Jews. The returned exiles reject their help. Are they too separatist? Should they have accepted help from these neighbors? This is a dilemma similar to that which Christians often face, and this issue is often a divisive factor in churches or denominations. Certainly there are many considerations involved in such complex decisions. From whom should Christian ministries and projects accept help? Will accepting this help compromise the unique gospel message of God's grace? Will it limit our freedom to follow Christ? What resources does the church have in making such decisions?

In this case the Jewish leaders recognize that these neighbors are enemies. Perhaps the neighbors become more antagonistic because of this rejection, but the Jewish leaders recognize the stakes involved. The most intense opposition comes from Samaria, just north of Judah. These neighbors might have been offering sacrifices to Yahweh, but they were also worshiping other gods (2 Kings 17:33). They are a mixed people. Some Jews remained in the northern kingdom when the majority went into captivity to Assyria in 721 BC. They were mixed with other captive peoples whom the Assyrian king Esarhaddon (681–669 BC, cf. Ezra 4:2) had moved there. These are the ancestors of the Samaritans often mentioned in the New Testament. The Assyrian king Ashurbanipal (669–633 BC) also brought other captive peoples to Samaria (Ezra 4:10).

The Samaritans' basic beliefs were quite different from those of the returned exiles. As polytheists they worshiped many gods, among whom was Jehovah. They did not give sole allegiance to the one true God; they did not submit to the authority of his Word. The Jewish leaders recognize that the Samaritans' motives are subversive. The returned exiles, the "people of God," are concerned to maintain their purity and the truth of God's revelation. We can praise God that they did, for through this community all the world has received the Bible and God's glorious message of salvation.

Ezra 4:4–5 is a résumé of the opposition during the reigns of the Persian kings Cyrus (550–530 BC), Cambyses II (530–522 BC), and Darius I (522–486 BC). As we continue to see, there are enemies on every side of this small community. Part of the enmity must have been the enemies' envy of the Jews; also they feared that a rebuilt Jerusalem would take away from their own authority in the region. The word translated "hired" (4:5) also means "bribed." The "counselors" they hire or bribe probably are Persian officials that have power to obstruct the work. The opposition continues through all the remainder of Cyrus's reign, through the reign of Cambyses II, to the second year of Darius (520 BC). It is designed to discourage the Jews and prevent them from rebuilding the temple or the city of Jerusalem. The last phrase in verse 5 looks ahead to verse 24, after the parenthetic paragraphs of 4:6–23.

4:6–24. Ezra 4:6–23 is a parenthetic statement that tells how opposition to the Jews continued in the time of kings Xerxes I (486–465 BC) and Artaxerxes I (464–424 BC). Thus, this parenthesis must include a period of nearly eighty years, from the events of Ezra 5 (520 BC) until the early part of Artaxerxes' reign, before Nehemiah is sent to Jerusalem (445 BC). Why does the author skip ahead chronologically? He apparently thought it important to emphasize the continuing opposition, possibly to justify the decision to reject the neighbors' help and to emphasize the significance of the achievements recorded in chapters 5 and 6.

The opposition described here is opposition to the building of the wall. But apart from verse 6, details of the activity during the reign of Xerxes are not given. Some building activity on the walls may have begun at that time, which could explain the reference to the wall "broken down" and the gates "burned" in Nehemiah 1:3.

The next part of Ezra, which describes Ezra's mission to Jerusalem (Ezra 7–10), takes place in the reign of Artaxerxes I. So Ezra would have been familiar with these events.

The letter to Artaxerxes (4:7–16) was written and signed by important officials in Samaria and elsewhere in this western satrapy, "Trans-Euphrates" (literally "Beyond the River," 4:10). Judah was one small area of this large satrapy. Since the officials of different areas in this satrapy allied themselves against the Jews, we cannot blame Artaxerxes for taking the letter seriously. In addition, the king was very concerned about Persian control in this part of the empire at this time, for an Egyptian revolt, supported by the Greeks, began in 460 BC.

Ezra 4:7 notes that the letter is written in Aramaic. The author of Ezra-Nehemiah apparently had copies of the letters and other documents in Aramaic, which is probably why Ezra 4:7–6:18 is written in that language.

The phrase "written in Aramaic script and in the Aramaic language" is literally "written Aramaic, translated Aramaic." The NIV note gives an alternate rendering, "written in Aramaic and translated." The first rendering would suggest that it was written in the Aramaic language (which became the diplomatic language in the Persian Empire) and in the Aramaic script (which refers to the "square" script in distinction from the "cursive" script, which was still in use for Hebrew). The alternate rendering probably

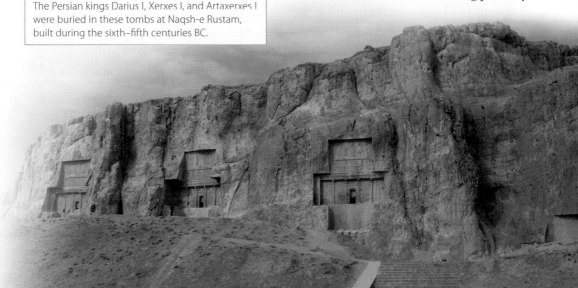

The Persian kings Darius I, Xerxes I, and Artaxerxes I were buried in these tombs at Naqsh-e Rustam, built during the sixth–fifth centuries BC.

means the letter was translated into Persian for the king. Both renderings fit the context.

The Jews learned to speak Aramaic during the Babylonian exile; thus Aramaic was the language of the returned exiles and continued to be the language of the Jews until the time of Christ. The two languages, Hebrew and Aramaic, are quite similar, so most Jews likely continued to use the Scriptures in Hebrew. But sometime in the period between the two Testaments it became necessary when the Hebrew Scriptures were read to also give an interpretation (or paraphrase) in Aramaic. This gave rise to the Targums, translations or paraphrases, in Aramaic, of the Hebrew Scriptures.

Ezra 4:12–16 quotes the letter to Artaxerxes. In Nehemiah 2 this same king authorizes Nehemiah to repair the walls of Jerusalem, so this must have been earlier in his reign. The letter is quite derogatory of the Jews and exaggerates their faults, for this small community did not pose any great threat to the empire. But given the precarious situation of this part of the Persian Empire, the king was sensitive to the possibility of any more rebellions. The three different words for royal revenue in 4:13 ("taxes, tribute or duty") emphasize the importance of taxes in the Persian Empire. When Alexander the Great conquered Persia, he found huge storehouses of many tons of gold and silver.

The expression "in the archives of your predecessors" (4:15) refers to the records kept by former kings, including the Babylonian kings, since the Persian kings considered themselves the Babylonians' successors. All these kings kept records of their governments and of transactions with their vassals.

Ezra 4:17–22 gives King Artaxerxes' reply to the letter. Again, in 4:18, translation is mentioned. Apparently the king needed the Aramaic translated into his Persian language. The letter confirms that many times in the past Jerusalem has rebelled against the ruling kings. This must refer to the Babylonian kings and perhaps the Assyrian kings. The "powerful kings" (4:20) no doubt refers to David, Solomon, and some others who ruled areas beyond Judah.

The effects of the opposition are seen in 4:23–24. The neighboring officials do not lose any time in forcing the Jews to comply, to stop their building activities. If this refers to a time some years before Nehemiah's coming to Jerusalem, it may again help to explain the broken walls and burned gates of Nehemiah 1:3. The clause "so that the city will not be rebuilt until I so order" (4:21) is significant, for it gives the king a possibility to change the policy in the future. Thus, in Nehemiah 2, he is free to specifically commission Nehemiah to rebuild the city. Certainly this shows God's providence and the confidence that the king has in Nehemiah.

The theme of opposition and conflict is seen throughout the Bible, from Genesis 3 to Revelation 20. The New Testament makes it clear that anyone who follows Christ will confront opposition, from Satan and his emissaries and from human beings whom the devil uses. Throughout history there have been constant attempts to destroy God's people, the Jews and later also the Christians.

Ezra-Nehemiah reminds us that as God's people we are engaged in a struggle, a conflict with the forces of evil. Paul says, "In fact, everyone who wants to live a godly life in Christ Jesus will be persecuted . . ." (2 Tim. 3:12). Likewise, any work of God will confront opposition. But Ezra-Nehemiah also reminds us that God knows how to give the victory; he is faithful and will fulfill his purpose in our lives and in the work he gives us to do.

Ezra 4:24 appears to refer to verse 23, but in reality it refers back to Ezra 4:5, since verse 23 clearly refers to the time of Artaxerxes and is still part of the parenthesis. So 4:24 brings the account back to where it left off in 4:5, in the reign of Darius. It prepares the reader for chapter 5. The second year of King Darius was 520 BC, the same year that Haggai was preaching in Jerusalem (Hag. 1:1).

G. Resolution: The temple building continued and finished (5:1–6:22). 5:1–17. Ezra 5:1 takes up the account from 4:24. Sixteen years have passed since 4:1, when the neighboring "enemies" were able to halt the work. The people have good excuses for not trying to build the temple; after all, their neighbors stopped them when they tried to build. But according to Haggai (1:9–10), who was preaching in Jerusalem at that time (520 BC), they have become more interested in building their own houses and are guilty of putting their own comfort

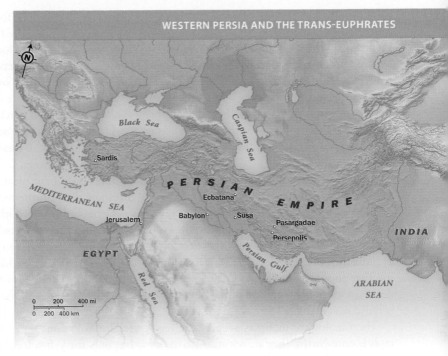

WESTERN PERSIA AND THE TRANS-EUPHRATES

before their responsibility to God. God expects the people to put forth more initiative for his work.

Ezra 5 and 6 provide an amazing account of how God works everything together to fulfill his purposes. This marks an important year in Jerusalem: it is the first time since the days of Jeremiah that a prophet of God has preached in Jerusalem. God sends two prophets, Haggai and Zechariah, to inspire the Jews to get back to work on the temple. The first chapter of Haggai, which refers to these same events, is a wonderful example of how God uses the preaching of his messenger to stir up his people from their lethargy, in this case to renew their work on the temple construction. But what about the neighboring enemies and the Persian authorities? When the people take the initiative to renew the work, God also works in the Persian authorities. They question the activity but give the Jews a fair chance to state their case before the Persian king. Certainly God's providence is evident in every detail, for the authorities find that Cyrus has decreed that the

Jews should rebuild their temple. Now, Darius reconfirms the decree, including the stipulation that the government is to provide funds and supplies for the work and that anyone who changes this edict should be put to death. The whole episode should help Christians today to rely on God to open doors that seem closed and to work in the hearts of both leaders and all the people, to fulfill his purposes.

Haggai delivers his messages between August and December of 520 BC, and the temple construction is renewed in September. Zechariah gives his messages beginning in October of 520 (Zech. 1:1). Zerubbabel and Joshua are mentioned as leaders here, and many times in Haggai and Zechariah. However, Zerubbabel is not mentioned again in Ezra-Nehemiah, not even in the celebration at the completion of the temple. Some have suggested that he may have died before that event.

Who was Tattenai (5:3)? He is called "governor of Trans-Euphrates." Apparently the area of Babylon and "Beyond the River" (referring to the Euphrates River) were two parts of one very large satrapy, and Tattenai was ruler of the part called "Beyond the River." So he and the others mentioned were Persian officials in charge of keeping order in this part of the empire. Their request is legitimate. The author here calls attention to God's providence: "But the eye of their God was watching over the elders of the Jews" (5:5). This explains why the officials allow the Jews to continue until they have an official reply from the king.

This positive attitude on the part of the Persian officials is further seen in the details they include in their letter to the king. The Jews' answer is very honest and transparent, even acknowledging that Jerusalem was destroyed as punishment from God (5:12). It is surprising that the Persian officials include all these details, and their suggestion to the king (5:17) is quite reasonable.

The theological maturity seen in the Jews' reply is noteworthy. They are not afraid to testify of their faith in God. They understand that God works in history, that their captivity was not due to God's failure but to his discipline on them. The prophets have told them this would happen; now they believe them.

Cyrus is called "king of Babylon" (5:13); was he not the king of Persia? Yes, but Cyrus issued his decree as king of Babylon. Inscriptions have been found in which Cyrus is also called king of Babylon.

Sheshbazzar is named again in 5:14. He was the fourth son of king Jehoiachin; Zerubbabel was the son of Jehoiachin's oldest son, Shealtiel (see Matt. 1:12). Here Sheshbazzar is credited with laying the foundation of the temple. In Ezra 3:10 it appears that Zerubbabel is in charge of the work. We cannot be sure of all the details, since the work was started in 536 BC and the present episode takes place in 520 BC. Perhaps Zerubbabel was working under Sheshbazzar's authority, or there may have been a need to redo some of the work begun earlier.

6:1–12. King Darius does as Tattenai's letter suggests: he orders a search to see if Cyrus really has issued such a decree (Ezra 6). We would expect the decree to be found in the archives at Babylon or in Susa, the Persian capital. However, the document is found in Ecbatana, the summer capital of the Persian kings. It is written on a scroll rather than on a tablet. Since they were now writing their official documents in Aramaic, they used parchment.

Darius's reply first quotes a copy of the decree archived in the treasury. The variation in some details between Cyrus's decree in Ezra 1 and this document means this copy was likely a résumé used for the records of the treasury.

Cyrus and Darius both were concerned that their subject peoples could correctly celebrate their religious rites. Cyrus put emphasis on the people's traditions, so his decree emphasized building the temple on the original site. But the "ninety feet high" (sixty cubits) might be a mistake in the original decree or in this letter, for Solomon's temple was ninety feet long but only forty-five feet high. In 1 Kings 6:36, "three courses of dressed stone and one course of trimmed cedar beams" are mentioned (see 6:4), but in regard to the inner courtyard.

Where did the Persians acquire all these specific details? It is possible that Cyrus received them from a Jewish scribe. This concern for detail and accuracy is also seen in the correspondence between this report (6:5) and the information the Jews have given to Tattenai (5:15).

The answer from King Darius (6:6–12) is very direct and very detailed. The phrase "stay away from there" (6:6) translates a legal term that indicates the accusations against the Jews have been rejected. Comparable documents from the Persian treasury to other subject peoples include similar details. However, the specific mention of the wheat, salt, wine, and oil to be used in the Jewish sacrifices (6:9) may suggest that a Jewish scribe helped with the details.

These details for the sacrifices are all specified in Leviticus 1–7. The people offered to God ingredients that make up part of everyday life. But how would these sacrifices represent praise and worship from the hearts of the people if the Persian king has paid for them? Notice the different reason for sacrifices in the hearts of non-Jews: to appease and supply food for the gods. But in the biblical perspective, God does not need these ingredients; the sacrifices expressed faith in God's redemption and the people's thankfulness, love, and dependence on God. There is no indication later that the Jews depend on the Persians to supply these sacrifices. We can be thankful that under the new covenant our Savior has fulfilled all these offerings (Heb. 10:10–14); thus in gratitude to him we submit wholeheartedly to his lordship in our lives (Rom. 12:1–2).

The language of 6:11–12 reflects both Persian laws and Jewish theology. It was common to include very strong punishment for those who broke Persian laws (cf. Dan. 2:5; 3:29); the statement, "May God, who has caused his Name to dwell there," may be another indication that a Jew helped prepare the decree.

6:13–22. The remainder of chapter 6 describes the completion and dedication of the temple.

6:13–18. Tattenai and the other officials immediately obey the king's decree. This indicates the degree of order in the Persian Empire at the time. It is amazing how quickly the small community of Jews finishes the temple once they trust God and decide to do it with all their heart. It is less than four and a half years; they began in September of Darius's second year (520 BC) and finish in March of his sixth year (516 BC).

Again, notice the emphasis on God's providence in 6:14–15. God uses the preaching of the prophets Haggai and Zechariah, the command of God, the decrees of the Persian king, and the

Cattle were used for offerings (e.g., Ezra 6:17) as well as food throughout the ancient Near East. This painting from the tomb-chapel of the Egyptian official Nebamun (ca. 1350 BC) depicts him inspecting a cattle herd.

people to complete the work. Again we see an example of Romans 8:28, "In all things God works for the good of those who love him." Certainly this group of returned exiles rejoiced in what God had done.

We might wonder why King Artaxerxes is included here if he comes on the scene only many years later. Again, the author looks ahead and includes the building project under Artaxerxes. The Aramaic text here does not include the word "temple"; literally it says, "And they finished building according to the command" (6:14).

The dedication of the temple is described in 6:16–18. There is a conscious comparison with Solomon's dedication of the first temple in 1 Kings 8. The temple is called the house of God, and there is a large number of fellowship offerings. The one hundred bulls, two hundred rams, and four hundred male lambs here are much less than what is offered in 1 Kings, but this is a small group of people in comparison. These are fellowship offerings, in which only small portions were burned in sacrifice; the meat is eaten by the people in a joyous feast together before the Lord.

There is a conscious emphasis on the continuity of the people of God, not only in the parallels to the dedication of the first temple, but also in other details. The sin offering consists of twelve male goats, "one for each of the tribes of Israel," even though most of the returned exiles are from the tribes of Judah and Benjamin. This continuity is also seen in the installation of the priests and Levites in their divisions and groups "according to what is written in the Book of Moses" (6:18). It is interesting that the author of 1 Chronicles emphasizes David's work of organizing the priests and Levites (1 Chronicles 23–25), another indication that 1–2 Chronicles and Ezra-Nehemiah do not come from the same author. The emphasis on the Book of Moses and its accepted authority also indicates that the people must have had the Pentateuch long before this.

6:19–22. Soon after the dedication of the temple the people celebrate the Passover. Beginning in 6:19 the text is again written in Hebrew; the portion in Aramaic ends in verse 18. It is calculated, according to our calendar, that the temple was completed on March 12, 515 BC, and the Passover would have begun on April 21. So, only a few weeks after the dedication of the temple the Jews had another important celebration.

Celebrations were important in the life of the Jews. These gatherings gave them opportunity to worship together, to remember God's great works throughout their history, to be taught from the law, and to have joyous times of fellowship. The Passover celebrated their deliverance from the bondage of Egypt. The events of the exodus from Egypt left a lasting effect on Israel. We can see it in three major areas of emphasis during Passover: (1) God's acts in history; (2) redemption and the language of redemption throughout the Bible; and (3) justice and concern for the poor, the widows, and orphans, the unprotected persons in society.

Although the Jews celebrated the Passover every year, it is usually mentioned in relation to some important event in Israel's life (Num. 9:5;

Josh. 5:10; 2 Kings 23:21; 2 Chron. 30:1–27; 35:1–27). The revival movements under Hezekiah (2 Chronicles 30) and under Josiah (2 Chronicles 35) are both closely linked to the Passover celebration.

It was very important for the priests and Levites to be ceremonially clean to lead in the celebration of the Passover. As prescribed in Exodus 29 and Numbers 8, this involved a rather complicated process of washing, sacrifice, and anointing. In fact, in Hezekiah's time the people had to delay the Passover a month because they lacked sufficient ceremonially pure priests (2 Chronicles 30).

The statement, "together with all who had separated themselves from the unclean practices of their Gentile neighbors in order to seek the LORD" (6:21), needs explanation. The returned exiles are not the only Jews in Judah at this time. Although the Babylonians carried most of the people away captive, some were left in Judah. Other Jews may have lived in the neighboring regions. No doubt many had accepted the customs of their neighbors. The zeal and dedication of the returned exiles draw them back to Judah and to the faith of their fathers.

The Jewish leaders at times seem very strict, but they are willing to accept these Jews who were not exiled to Babylon if these Jews definitely decide to follow the law of Moses. That means two basic decisions: (1) they must separate themselves from the unclean practices of their Gentile neighbors, and (2) they must seek the Lord, which implies a sincere attitude of worship and obedience to God.

These decisions are similar to those every Christian must make. Following Christ has ethical implications; it implies renouncing what is displeasing to God. It also means seeking God, walking with the Lord in obedience, and following where he leads.

This first section of Ezra-Nehemiah concludes on a note of victory and thanksgiving for what God has done (6:22). The people worship God with joy during this whole week of the Feast of Unleavened Bread. This was a separate feast from Passover, but the two were always celebrated together.

Worship is constantly associated with joy, because in worship the worshiper is conscious of God's presence, his mercy, his love, and his work in the world. Here what the Jews have just experienced is a special motive for joy. The Lord has filled them with joy "by changing the attitude of the king of Assyria, so that he assisted them in the work of the house of God" (6:22). They are aware that all this has come about because God changed the king's attitude. God works out all the details.

But why is Darius called the king of Assyria? Certainly the author of Ezra-Nehemiah gives very accurate details throughout the work. He must have a special purpose in calling Darius the king of Assyria. A glimpse at the history of that time indicates that, at least in the minds of many, there was continuity in the empires of Assyria, Babylon, and Persia, the times of Gentile domination. Herodotus once calls Babylon the capital of Assyria (*Histories* 1.178). Nehemiah, in his prayer, speaks of the hardships the Jews have had "from the days of the kings of Assyria until today" (Neh. 9:32). The author here likely had something similar in mind. Clearly there was a tremendous change of attitude between the Assyrian kings on the one hand and Cyrus and Darius on the other. So the Jews have reason to rejoice and praise God.

The events of this "mission" in Ezra 1–6 are important in God's plan of redemption. Although Solomon's temple was larger and more beautiful, it existed for a little less than four hundred years. This temple, of which Haggai says, "The glory of this present house will be greater than the glory of the former house" (Hag. 2:9), will be the scene of the presence of the coming Messiah, and will exist for some 585 years, until AD 70. (Although sometimes language about Herod's embellishment of the temple gives the impression that it was a third temple, it was nevertheless still the second temple. In Jewish history the period of the second temple continues from 515 BC to AD 70.)

2. The Second Mission: The Return under Ezra (7:1–10:44)

A. Introduction and preparation (7:1–28). Chapter 7 begins the second stage of the rebuilding of the community in Ezra-Nehemiah. Fifty-seven years have passed since the accounts of chapters 5 and 6. The author does not pretend to give a complete history of the period; rather, he chooses the events that were significant for the continuation of the Jewish community. Here he introduces Ezra.

7:1–10. Ezra has all the necessary credentials for the mission assigned to him. The Jews have always emphasized their genealogy, but it was especially important for the priests and Levites, such as Ezra. The genealogy in 7:1–5 is similar to that of 1 Chronicles 6:3–14; however, it omits some names between Meraioth and Ezra. Seraiah was high priest in the time of King Zedekiah and was killed by the Babylonians (2 Kings 25:18–21). That was some one hundred thirty years before this time. "Son of Seraiah" can also mean "descendant of Seraiah." Zadok was made high priest instead of Abiathar, the descendant of Eli (1 Kings 2:35).

The author continues to give Ezra's credentials. He is a scribe and a teacher (7:6; the NIV translates the typical word for scribe as "teacher" here). God's hand is on Ezra, and he has the king's favor. Also, other Jews accompany him to Jerusalem, and there is special mention of the "Levites, singers, gatekeepers and temple servants." Notice that these distinctions in the temple personnel have continued from before the exile.

This introduction of Ezra concludes with his arrival in Jerusalem (7:8–9). The date mentioned is, by our calendar, August 4, 458 BC, although we see later their departure from Babylon is delayed twelve days (8:31). There may be an intended parallel with the dates of the exodus (Exod. 12:2; Num. 33:3), since the return of the exiles is seen as a second exodus (cf. Isa. 11:11–16). The trip would have been some eight or nine hundred miles. It took just over three and a half months, an average of about ten miles a day. The author recognizes

Ezra, Example of an Effective Teacher

The author of Ezra-Nehemiah emphasizes the role of the whole people of God instead of glorifying the leaders. Yet we can learn much from the examples of the humble leaders God uses to encourage and guide his people.

Ezra is a good example of an effective teacher. He is "well versed in the Law of Moses"—the Hebrew term for "well versed" means "skilled" and carries the connotation of "quick." In Proverbs 22:29 the term means "diligent." A good teacher is diligent in studying God's Word. "Ezra had devoted [literally "directed the heart toward"] himself to the study and observance of the Law of the LORD, and teaching its decrees" (7:10).

The requirements of a good teacher are not confined to study and research but also include a spiritual emphasis, a walk with the Lord. Ezra devotes himself to obeying the word of the Lord, thus earning the respect and confidence of the king, "for the hand of the Lord his God was on him" (7:6, 14–21). Not only does Ezra have knowledge, but, as the king notes, he also has "the wisdom of God" (7:25); thus the king also gives Ezra administrative responsibilities.

A good teacher does not look for personal glory but gives glory to God. In Ezra 7:27, Ezra praises God for what has been accomplished. At the same time, recognizing that God's hand is on him gives him courage to enlist others to share the work with him (7:27–28).

In Ezra 8 we notice more characteristics of Ezra: his ability to organize the helpers (8:15), his initiative to secure more help (8:17), his honesty and sensitive conscience (8:22), and his dependence on God (8:21, 23), which also motivates others to worship the Lord (8:35).

Teachers frequently present reams of material but do not require accountability of their students. Both in teaching and in administration, Ezra gives an example of delegating responsibilities and requiring accountability (8:24–26, 34).

The depth of a teacher's character and spiritual life has an impact on his or her students. In chapter 9 we see Ezra's earnestness in prayer; he identifies with the people's need for repentance and forgiveness (9:10). He understands God's ways, holiness, justice, and mercy (9:13). He is an example of piety, repentance, and a humble attitude (10:1). His teaching and example lead to action on the part of the people (10:3, 4, 8).

Though Ezra is not mentioned again until Nehemiah 8, he must have continued teaching, for in Nehemiah 8 the people assemble and ask Ezra "to bring out the Book of the Law of Moses." In this chapter we see that God uses Ezra, the scribe, the teacher, to bring about a revival among the people, based on God's written word. He reads the book of the law to them for hours (Neh. 8:3), leads the people in praise (Neh. 8:6), and has his helpers assist in understanding the word. His follow-up consists of continued teaching and leading the people to obey God's teachings (Neh. 8:13–18). Those who teach God's Word today can certainly learn from Ezra's example.

God's providential protection on the dangerous trip, for the people travel without military escort—while carrying a considerable amount of silver and gold, on roads often infested with robbers. This small group of emigrants certainly has reason to praise the Lord.

The author calls attention to Ezra's lifelong devotion to studying, obeying, and teaching "the Law of the LORD" (7:10). (See box, "Ezra, Example of an Effective Teacher.") The law of the Lord must have included the whole Pentateuch, the five books of Moses. The Old Testament understands the law not as a heavy burden but as a recipe for a healthy society. The Decalogue, or Ten Commandments, gives in brief form an outline of biblical ethics. Each commandment represents a whole area of ethical behavior. For example, "You shall not commit murder" shows the sanctity of human life and our responsibility not only to avoid homicide but to help preserve life. These implications of the commandments are spelled out in the rest of the Old Testament and in Jesus's Sermon on the Mount (Matthew 5–7).

Up until the time of the exile the priests were the guardians and teachers of the law. After the exile the scribes become more important. Ezra is both a priest and a scribe; according to Jewish tradition he had a lot to do with the transition. This scribal tradition was important for the preservation of the Scriptures. Unfortunately the scribal establishment later became too legalistic (see Matthew 23).

How can we maintain a correct balance between the "pharisaism" that Jesus criticized and the syncretism of our day, which dilutes the authority of Scripture, blurs the biblical worldview, and erodes the essence of the gospel? One answer is to follow Ezra's example of seeking the Lord, putting emphasis on obeying God's Word, and being a doer and not only a hearer of the Word. And just as in Ezra's case, those who teach God's Word need "the hand of the Lord on them" (7:28).

7:11–28. Ezra has received official recognition from the Persian king. The letter of Artaxerxes (7:12–26) is in Aramaic. Some wonder whether it could be from the Persian king, since it has many Jewish details. Again, the king would have had a Jewish advisor, maybe Ezra himself. The letter also includes many details with a distinctive Persian flavor, such as "king of kings" and "seven counselors."

The letter presents five stipulations: (1) it authorizes Ezra to go to Jerusalem and to appoint magistrates and judges to administer justice (7:14, 25); (2) it provides funds to purchase sacrifices and temple vessels (7:15–19); (3) it requires the treasurers of Trans-Euphrates to give supplies to Ezra; (4) it prohibits charging taxes to temple personnel; and (5) it authorizes Ezra to teach and require obedience to "the law of your God and the law of the king" (7:25–26).

The Jews are free to go with Ezra or stay in Mesopotamia; many choose to stay, mainly in the Babylon area. The "seven advisors" (7:13) is reminiscent of the statement by Herodotus (*Histories* 1.14) that the king had an advisory council composed of the heads of the seven leading families in Persia.

The king entrusts to Ezra a surprising amount of silver and gold. This could have made the trip more dangerous because of robbers on the way. It certainly indicates that the king trusts Ezra. The articles to "deliver to the God of Israel" are those mentioned in 8:25, donated by the king and his officials.

Why does the king command the provinces to give so much support to the Jews (7:21–22)? The Persian kings wanted the favor of all the gods. In addition, it was important to

Persians referred to their king as the "king of kings," as illustrated by the cuneiform inscription on this silver bowl of Artaxerxes I (fifth century BC), which reads in part: "Artaxerxes, the great king, king of kings, king of countries, son of Xerxes the king, son of Darius. . . ."

Artaxerxes that there be peace in this area of his empire, for in 460 BC there was a revolt in Egypt, and in this same year, 458, he sent a Persian army to Egypt.

Ezra does not boast of what he has accomplished; rather, his heart immediately turns to praising God for his work in the heart of the king (7:27–28). Again, there is an emphasis on God's providence. "To bring honor to the house of the LORD" (literally "to beautify") could explain why Artaxerxes was included in 6:14. The fact that Ezra understands that God's hand is on him gives him courage to invite others to join him in the mission to Jerusalem. Similarly, when a Christian knows they are in God's will and God is working in their life and ministry, it provides courage to get others involved in the ministry.

B. The return to Jerusalem (8:1–36). Ezra 8 recounts the trip to Jerusalem but first mentions the family heads of those who accompany Ezra (8:1–14). This is not the same list as in Ezra 2, though the two lists have many names in common. Instead of starting with the lay families, then listing the priests, Levites, and temple personnel, as in chapter 2, here the list begins with the priestly families, followed by a descendant of David, and then concludes with twelve lay families. Throughout the chapter we see an emphasis on the number twelve, certainly to represent all Israel. In the Ezra material Israel is mentioned twenty-four times, but Judah only four. In this list only the men are listed; in Ezra 2, the women are included in the numbers. Here the men counted in the twelve families number fifteen hundred. Therefore, with women and children there may have been as many as five thousand in the caravan to Jerusalem.

All the family names in 8:3–14 are also in Ezra 2. That would indicate that those who return to Jerusalem now have relatives in Jerusalem from the first emigration. The phrase "the last ones" (8:13) may indicate that no others from that family have remained behind; the other families still have relatives in Babylon.

The preparation for the journey is described in detail in 8:15–30. If there were some five thousand people, we can see the wisdom of taking a few days to organize them. Ezra discovers there are no Levites who have offered to return to Jerusalem. Since his mission is centered on worship in the temple, the need for sufficient temple personnel is urgent. Ezra knows where to search for Levites: he sends helpers to "Kasiphia"—the Hebrew says "Kasiphia, the place" (8:17). That expression, "the place," in the Old Testament sometimes designates a place of worship (Deut. 12:5; Jer. 7:3, 6–7). It has been suggested there may have been a school for training temple personnel in Kasiphia.

The numbers surprise us: only eighteen Levites, but two hundred and twenty temple servants, who were helpers for the Levites. Ezra sees this provision also as evidence of God's hand on the mission.

Paramount in any preparation for ministry is the spiritual preparation, through prayer and fasting. Ezra and the people realize they are undertaking a very dangerous mission. The almost four-month journey is in itself a risky adventure. Life in the little community in Judah is still precarious. But they know God's hand is on them; they know they have to depend completely on him. So, they begin with fasting and prayer (8:21–23).

This journey normally was dangerous, for there were bandits on the way. With the great amount of silver and gold they will be carrying, it will be doubly dangerous. In addition, after telling the king that God takes care of his people, Ezra cannot conscientiously ask for a military escort. We see here a tremendous example of faith, of absolute dependence on the Lord. Ezra's example and teaching bring forth a similar response of faith in the people.

Ezra also understands the need for administrative preparation. As a good leader, he delegates responsibility to capable helpers. The value of the money and temple vessels they carry is staggering. As the notes in the NIV indicate, it included twenty-five tons of silver, three and three-quarters tons of gold, and many silver and gold vessels for the temple.

Ezra points out that all these riches as well as these men in charge of them are "consecrated to the Lord." "Consecrated" is literally "holy" and demonstrates the basic meaning of "holy": "set apart for God." The men in charge are the priests and the heads of families. Consecration and holy lives are requirements for the material as well as the spiritual aspects of God's work.

Responsible stewardship requires careful records as well as consecrated administrators. The money and articles have been carefully weighed and registered. The men in charge of the valuables are responsible to take care of the treasures on the trip, then weigh them out again before the priests, Levites, and family heads in the temple in Jerusalem (8:28–29). That this was done is recorded in 8:33–34.

The description of the trip to Jerusalem (8:31–36) is very brief. The trip officially was to begin on the first day of the first month (7:9), but they are delayed until the twelfth day due to the need to recruit Levites and temple servants (8:15–20). The nearly four-month trip must have been quite an adventure. But the only detail given is that God keeps them safe from "enemies and bandits," for which they give God the glory. Of the many good examples we find in Ezra's ministry, this is one we should remember every time we arrive safely from a trip. According to Ezra 7:9 they arrive on the first day of the fifth month (August 4).

The treasures are presented to Meremoth in the temple. It does not say he is a priest but that he is the son of Uriah the priest. Nehemiah 3:4 lists Uriah as the son of Hakkoz, but in Ezra 2:61 the sons of Hakkoz could not be installed as priests because their genealogical records were lacking. If this is the same family, possibly by this time they have been accepted in the priesthood.

The author again emphasizes the careful record that has been kept of the money and articles (8:34). Since the Persian government kept careful records, we can assume that Ezra sent a record back to the king.

The last paragraph (8:35–36) notes that these returned exiles give priority to worshiping the Lord. Again the author mentions "twelve bulls for all Israel"; this community represents the whole people of Israel. The documents with the "king's orders" are delivered to the Persian authorities. These include the authority for Ezra to administer Jewish law to his fellow Jews.

C. Opposition from within: The crisis of intermarriage (9:1–15). In this second movement of the book (Ezra 7–10), the crisis or conflict is the problem of mixed marriages with pagan neighbors. It is an outright disobedience of God's commands and threatens the future of the covenant community. This episode takes place four months after the events of chapter 8 (see Ezra 10:9). Ezra has been teaching God's written word. He does not try to do everything himself; his policy is to prepare leaders through teaching the law of God. Throughout this chapter there are many allusions to and echoes of passages in the Law and the Prophets. Ezra's teaching is bearing fruit; the leaders become conscious of the critical situation in regard to mixed marriages.

Ezra's dismay and humility are seen in 9:1–5. There is a conscious allusion to passages in the Pentateuch that name these various inhabitants of Canaan (9:1; cf. Deut. 20:17). Although most of these people groups—all except the Ammonites, Moabites, and Egyptians—no longer existed in Ezra's time, the inclusion of the entire list emphasizes Moses's strong prohibition against intermarrying with the neighboring pagan peoples. "Holy race" (9:2) also alludes to the Pentateuch and points out the contrast between what God's people should be and what they are in reality. They are unfaithful to their covenant with God. Intermarriage with these peoples involves compromising the covenant relationship with God, the acceptance of "detestable practices," and opening the community to the influence of a pagan worldview.

All through the Bible God calls his people to be separate from the world (1 John 2:15–17).

Sometimes they have gone to extremes in a legalistic fashion, which the prophets and Jesus condemn. But this chapter combines various passages from Moses and the Prophets to show that the basic commands are applicable to new situations. We need the Holy Spirit's guidance and the sound teaching of God's Word to correctly apply the Bible's ethical principles. The New Testament commands believers not to marry unbelievers (2 Cor. 6:14). Any commitment that competes with our commitment to Christ makes us guilty of "unfaithfulness." This can be applied to other areas of life, such as marrying Christian beliefs with current un-Christian philosophies. It often results in reducing the "Christian" message to a simple code of rules for good behavior and negates the power of Jesus's gospel.

When Ezra realizes what is happening, he is horrified; he becomes very emotionally involved. His actions in 9:3 depict very deep consternation. The "tunic" refers to the undergarment and the "cloak" to a long outer garment. Tearing one's garments was a sign of extreme grief.

"Everyone who trembled at the words of the God of Israel" (9:4) denotes readiness to obey God's words. In the postexilic period "tremble" was used to describe those who strictly observed the law. If we "tremble" at God's Word, we will also "tremble" at sin.

Ezra's action shows the depth of his spiritual life; his first reaction is to fall on his knees and pray. Both Ezra and Nehemiah constantly turn to God in prayer and worship. They believe that God hears prayer and answers; they know that God's work depends on the prayer of his people. Some of the Jewish leaders led the people into this practice of intermarriage; now, Ezra and his disciples lead the people in prayer, repentance, confession, and renewed obedience to God.

Ezra's prayer of confession (9:6–15) gives further insight into his spiritual life. He begins his prayer with confession of sin (9:6–7). He starts out on a personal note and with a humble attitude toward God. Then he immediately changes to "we" and "our." In other words, he

does not take a proud, selfish attitude—"Look what they have done!" Rather, he identifies with the people. True, we are each individually responsible for our obedience to God. But each one is also a part of the community, the people of God. What affects one or a few members of the community in reality affects all. The Bible teaches that we are each other's keepers. Some are guilty, but others have condoned or permitted the behavior of the guilty. So Ezra includes himself in this confession.

Due to the preaching of the prophets, especially Jeremiah and Ezekiel, the Jews now understand that their demise and captivity was a direct consequence of their nation's disobedience and apostasy. This destruction and humiliation "at the hand of foreign kings" (9:7) must refer to their suffering under three empires: Assyria, Babylon, and Persia.

Ezra recognizes God's goodness even in the midst of subjection to foreign rule (9:8–9). He recognizes that it is due to God's mercy that the Jews can return to their land, build the temple, and count on God's protection.

The "remnant" (9:8) refers to those who have returned from the Babylonian exile. The word "remnant" is used with several meanings in the Prophets. It refers to those who will return from exile (Jer. 42:2; Zech. 8:6, 11–12); to a "remnant" that will return to God (Isa. 10:21), at the time when Gentiles will participate in a return (Isa. 11:10–16); and to Israel in the messianic age (Jer. 23:3; 31:7; Zech. 14:2). Paul mentions a "remnant" of Jews "chosen by grace" (Romans 11).

"But now, O our God, what can we say after this?" again highlights Ezra's recognition of disobedience (9:10–12). He repeats God's commands that they have disobeyed, from several Old Testament books (Lev. 18:25–28; Deut. 4:5; 9:4; 1 Kings 14:24; and Ezek. 37:25), so Ezra and the people must have been familiar with these Scriptures.

The final paragraph of the prayer (9:13–15) represents Ezra's plea for mercy, although not in the form of a direct petition to God. Rather, he recognizes before God how evil the people have been, how unreasonable their rejection of God's commands. Ezra confesses that God has shown more mercy than the people deserve; what they really deserve is punishment for their present disobedience. Because of this, he throws himself and his people on God's mercy.

D. Resolution: The covenant to change (10:1–44). Ezra is not ashamed to let his great emotional distress be seen and heard by the public. This is an example of how God can use the sincere emotional expression of a righteous person to bring conviction on the whole congregation. Ezra's leadership is noteworthy; he does not force the people to submit to him. He trusts God to work among the people. Then, their representative, Shekaniah, comes to Ezra and urges him to lead the way in changing the situation.

The law required the people to put away their foreign wives. This seems like a very harsh remedy, but we must remember the urgency of maintaining the Jewish community. We also should understand that these foreign women would most surely be taken back into their own parents' extended family. Also, in the light of Malachi (Mal. 2:14–16), who preached shortly before this time, it appears that some of these men had divorced their Jewish wives to marry the women from the surrounding pagan peoples.

The priestly leaders and the representatives of the Jewish families take "the oath" (10:5), which is really a renewal of their covenant with God. Again Ezra leaves the plans in the hands of others, while he withdraws alone to continue in fasting and prayer. He is a good leader, and he realizes that there can be no genuine change without God's work in the hearts of the people.

The community leaders take very wise and definite action: they call an assembly to involve all the people (10:7–17). The province of Judah was small, so all could travel to Jerusalem within three days. The penalty for not appearing seems harsh, but it is within the authority the Persian king has given to Ezra. "To forfeit" one's property here means to have it put under the ban; thus the property of those who fail to attend the assembly will be given to the temple treasury (Lev. 7:21).

This takes place some four and a half months after Ezra's arrival in Jerusalem. It is the rainy season and probably quite cold, so although the people repent and agree they should correct the situation, they wisely decide to take time to treat each case in order. Only a few oppose the proposed solution.

Ezra again takes the lead in naming the commission to judge the cases. The judging process takes three months. Each one who is guilty must appear before the commission. They go with the elders and judges of their hometown, which indicates a concern that justice be done in each case.

Those guilty of intermarriage are named and called (10:18–44). The list names 111 men guilty of taking foreign wives (or 110 if the term translated as "Maknadebai" in 10:40 is not a proper name and is read instead as "from the descendants of Zakkai"). Seventeen are priests, ten are Levites—correcting community problems must start with the leaders. The other eighty-four are from the rest of the community. Some think this is a small number from a community of possibly thirty thousand people and suggest there must have been more who were guilty. But there is no evidence there were more. Ezra and the leaders are diligent in maintaining the identity of the covenant community in a pagan world.

What can we learn from this episode? In a different context the application of biblical principles may not be exactly the same. But like postexilic Israel, we must be aware of the danger of moral and spiritual apathy. Similarly, we face moral and spiritual crises in our time that require strong leadership and definitive community action on the part of God's people.

3. The Third Mission: Nehemiah Restores the Wall (Neh. 1:1–7:73a)

The first seven chapters of Nehemiah and all or most of chapters 11–13 are considered part of the Nehemiah memoirs; they are written in first person. The name Nehemiah means "the Lord comforts," a fitting name for one whom the Lord uses to encourage the discouraged exiles. Nehemiah is a very capable leader; he has a deep trust in God and is a careful organizer and a man of action.

A. Preparation (1:1–2:10). **1:1–11.** The events in Nehemiah 1 take place in Susa, the winter residence of the Persian kings, 150 miles north of the Persian Gulf. The events of Esther and the vision of Daniel 8 also take place in Susa. Darius I built a palace there (during the years 518–512 BC). The time (Neh. 1:1) is November–December (the month Kislev), 445 BC (the twentieth year of Artaxerxes I). The previous years have been difficult for Artaxerxes I in the western part of his empire. A revolt in Egypt (460–455 BC) and a brief rebellion by the satrap of Trans-Euphrates (448 BC) have certainly made the king sensitive to happenings in Palestine.

The report Nehemiah receives from his brother, and others who come from Jerusalem, is not very encouraging. The reference to the broken-down wall and burned gates (1:3) may indicate damage still unrepaired from the earlier sack of Jerusalem by Nebuchadnezzar, or, more likely, may indicate the results of the opposition from the Jews' enemies mentioned in Ezra 4:12. The news has a very deep impact on Nehemiah (1:4). He weeps and spends many days mourning, fasting, and praying. The following prayer must represent the content of his prayer during the next four months, for verses 1:12 and 2:1 indicate that four months pass between 1:1 and Nehemiah's petition to the king in 2:1.

The content of Nehemiah's prayer is noteworthy. It includes (1) a cry for God to hear (1:6), (2) an appeal to God's covenant with Israel (1:5, 9), (3) confession of sin, (4) identification with the people ("we Israelites," 1:6), (5) a recognition of the cause of their captivity (1:8), (6) an appeal to God's promise (1:9), (7) a reminder to God that these returnees are his redeemed people (1:10), (8) a plea for God to answer (1:11), and (9) a petition for favor with the king (1:12). Many of these same themes appear in the prayers of Ezra 9, Nehemiah 9, and Daniel 9.

Nehemiah's sensitivity to the people and his dedication to constant prayer indicate his

Assyrian relief showing a cupbearer (left) with King Ashurnasirpal (Nimrud, 865–860 BC). Nehemiah served as a cupbearer (Neh. 1:11).

godly character. He has a deep understanding of God and his word as revealed in the five books of the Pentateuch. Apparently, during this extended time of prayer, Nehemiah realizes that God is calling him to take action and to lead the project for revitalizing the struggling community in Judah. He is wise enough not to enter suddenly with a petition to the king. Rather, through extended times of prayer and careful planning, he awaits God's timing to approach the king.

The fact that Nehemiah mentions here his position as "cupbearer to the king" (1:11) may indicate that he now understands God has put him in this strategic position for a purpose. The cupbearer had a high position in the Persian court. The king apparently cares for Nehemiah and recognizes his many abilities, for he is about to give him political power to help his people and even overturn official decrees against them. The Jews in Judah are not yet aware of it, but God is about to change their sorry situation.

2:1–10. Nehemiah finally presents his request to the king (2:1–8). The month Nisan (March–April) marks four months since Nehemiah received news of the difficult situation in Jerusalem. The account does not tell us if it is a special feast or perhaps a family or staff dinner; it does mention that the queen is sitting beside the king. Why has the king not noticed his cupbearer's sadness before? The last sentence in Nehemiah's prayer (1:11) suggests that prior to this he has hidden his sadness but now he senses that it is time to approach the king with his concerns. Although Nehemiah has prayed and planned, he is afraid (2:2), for he knows the danger of anything that might raise the king's suspicion.

Nehemiah's reply has been well planned. The king apparently understands that Nehemiah wants to make a request. The king's question is so direct (2:4), and Nehemiah is so aware of the great importance of his answer, that he first, in his heart, prays to God before he answers. This prayer, like most of his nine prayers recorded in the book, is short. But such prayers are possible and effective because of his evident life of prayer and dependence on God.

Nehemiah's answers to the king's questions (2:4, 6) indicate that he has a growing realization that God is calling him to go to Jerusalem and has carefully planned even the details of this project. The king is immediately interested in the project and generously approves Nehemiah's requests. Perhaps it is because of his confidence in Nehemiah and the strategic importance of Palestine, near the western limit of his empire. But Nehemiah himself gives the basic reason: "because the gracious hand of my God was upon me" (2:8). Throughout the book, Nehemiah emphasizes God's providence, his working out details to fulfill his purpose.

The account gives very few details of Nehemiah's trip to Jerusalem. He apparently has to visit the officials of Trans-Euphrates to make arrangements for the trip and the supplies he will need. The local rulers, Sanballat and Tobiah (2:10), are quite disturbed when they realize the intent of the trip.

These neighboring governors will very strongly oppose any projects to restore Jerusalem. Not only will they present opposition from without; their connections within the Jewish community will later cause opposition from within. A grandson of the high priest Eliashib is a son-in-law of Sanballat (Neh. 13:28). The family name of Tobiah, a Hebrew name, was prominent in Ammon during the Persian period. Tobiah may have been a descendant of Jews who fled to Ammon after the destruction of Jerusalem (Jer. 41:15). Both Tobiah and his son Jehohanan have connections with influential families in Judah through marriage (Neh. 6:17–19).

B. The work begun (2:11–3:32). 2:11–20. After arriving in Jerusalem and resting three days, the first thing Nehemiah does is survey the situation. No doubt, even in these three days, he is gathering information and getting acquainted with the leaders of the people. But he wisely does not yet tell them of his project. He needs time to survey the existing remains

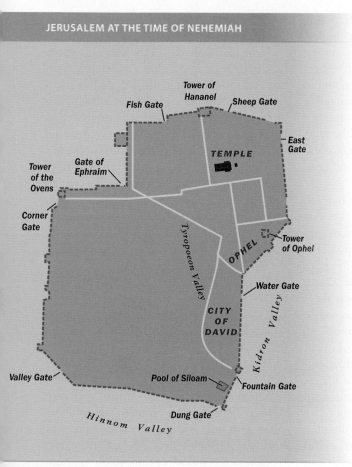

JERUSALEM AT THE TIME OF NEHEMIAH

for the overflow from the Pool of Siloam. From there, because of the debris from the destroyed wall, he goes by foot on up the valley. He does not say how far; if he went the entire distance it would be somewhat less than a mile.

Now Nehemiah is ready to present his project to the people (2:17–18). He is aware that the project cannot go forward without the wholehearted cooperation of the leaders and the people. As a good leader, he knows how to motivate them. He identifies himself with the people (2:17, "the trouble we are in"); he emphasizes their critical situation; he is committed to take action and participate with the people; and he shares his own testimony of "the gracious hand of my God upon me" for this project. Nehemiah shows us how a godly leader can influence the people to trust God and work together.

The author again mentions the neighboring enemies of Judah: Sanballat, Tobiah, and Geshem (2:19–20). They apparently fear that a revitalized Jerusalem and Judah will reduce their influence and power in the region. Their mocking and ridicule are designed to discourage the Jews from cooperating with Nehemiah. Nehemiah's brief but meaningful answer puts the emphasis on God's sovereignty and power; he reminds the neighbors that they do not share the same convictions, legal claims, or historical legacy as the returned Jews.

The roster of builders reveals a lot about the disposition of the people to work together and about Nehemiah's abilities to organize the work (3:1–32). Although it is in the third person and includes details even to the finishing touches on the gates (6:1 and 7:1), it is likely part of the Nehemiah memoirs. It constitutes one of the most detailed biblical descriptions of Jerusalem.

of the walls and their condition. He knows God has called him to this work but is careful to await the correct time to present the project to the leaders and all the people.

Nehemiah describes his secret (by night) inspection of the condition of the walls (2:13–16). The places he describes are in the southern part of the city, the part traditionally known as the City of David. He does not mention places around the northern parts of Jerusalem. The Valley Gate overlooks the Tyropoeon Valley on the west side of the city. The Dung Gate is near the southern end, where the Tyropoeon and Hinnom valleys meet. Nehemiah follows the wall turning north on the east side, to the Fountain Gate, overlooking the Kidron Valley. The "King's Pool" may be a retaining pool

3:1–32. The reconstruction of the northern and western walls is described in 3:1–15, starting at the Sheep Gate, near the northeastern corner of Jerusalem. Eliashib, grandson of Joshua (Neh. 12:10), who was the leader when the temple was rebuilt (Ezra 5:2), along with his fellow priests, rebuilds the Sheep Gate and the wall as far as the Tower of Hananel. There are two towers in the north wall; this is the only side of Jerusalem not defended by steep hills.

The fact that this part of the wall and the Tower of Hananel are the only parts dedicated here, apart from the entire dedication celebration (Nehemiah 12), may have theological significance. This tower is mentioned in only two Old Testament passages outside of Nehemiah (Jer. 31:38; Zech. 14:10), both in the context of the eschatological restoration of Jerusalem. Thus its prominence in Nehemiah and its dedication here by the priests may be seen as pointing to a theological vision that extends the sacredness of the temple, the house of God, to the entire "holy city" (cf. Neh. 11:1, 18) of Jerusalem.

The workers are sometimes identified by families and sometimes by their hometowns. The comment concerning the nobles of Tekoa (3:5) indicates that some Jews are not cooperating. Since Tekoa is near the area controlled by Geshem the Arab, this might be a factor. The Jeshanah Gate is also called the Old Gate.

Men and women from all walks of life share in the work; the account mentions goldsmiths and perfume makers (3:8), as well as sons of political rulers (3:9, 12). The small villages all over the area of Judah are represented. The work of restoration involves many different skills, as noted in 3:15.

The account continues with the construction of the eastern wall (3:16–32). The landmarks in this section are mostly houses and buildings instead of gates, since the wall on the east side did not follow the former wall but was built higher on the ridge. Nehemiah's leadership skills are evident in his recognizing special effort by workers such as Baruch (3:20) and in his assigning workers to build the wall near their own houses (3:21–24, 26). "The hill of Ophel" (3:26) is part of the ridge between the City of David and the temple area (2 Chron. 27:3; 33:14). The East Gate (3:29) may be where the Golden Gate was located later. Meshullam (3:30) is related through marriage to Tobiah's family and later is reprimanded by Nehemiah for giving Tobiah the use of one of the rooms in the temple construction.

Chapter 3 is more than a series of construction details; it has significance in the moral and religious life of the Jewish community. The wall is symbolic of separation from pagan influence (cf. Neh. 13:19–22). It gives the people a renewed sense of identity; it reverses their situation of shame, humiliation, and defeat. Also, it is symbolic of God's presence and expands the sanctity of the temple, God's house, to include the whole of Jerusalem.

The chapter also contains teaching for Christians today. The people's willingness and enthusiasm to work together is a challenge for any church. Even those who live far from Jerusalem join in the work. It is an example of the Old Testament ideal of a community of brotherly love. The result is also a powerful testimony to their neighbors. Why does the work progress? Both the faith and decision of the whole community and the wise, godly leadership of Nehemiah are crucial. (See box, "Nehemiah, Example of a Godly Leader.")

C. Opposition to rebuilding the wall (4:1–6:14). Any effective work for God can expect opposition, from either humans or evil powers, or both. The ability of a leader can be judged by how he or she confronts crises and reacts to opposition. We can learn from Nehemiah's example as he faces different kinds of opposition. This lengthy section depicts the progress in reconstructing the wall in spite of and in response to opposition, both from without and within the community.

4:1–23. The first attack is in the form of ridicule (4:1–6). Sanballat is angry when he learns that the Jews are rebuilding the wall. The world's response to God's work is often anger, for it makes people uncomfortable by challenging their values and worldviews. In this case Sanballat also sees it as a threat to his influence in the area. So he attempts to make their efforts appear useless. Certainly the burned stones would be almost useless and the rubble would hinder the work. Tobiah joins the opposition by exaggerating the weakness of the wall. Together they attempt to stop the work. Psychological warfare often resorts to lies (as archaeologists have found that Nehemiah's wall was nine feet thick).

Nehemiah's first response is to turn to God in prayer, a good example for us. He reminds

Aramaic inscriptions of the name Tobiah appear in two halls of the "castle of the slave" (Amman, Jordan, second century BC), indicating that it may have been built by a descendant of the Tobiah who opposed rebuilding Jerusalem's walls (Neh. 4:7).

God that his people are being despised. Then he asks God to judge and punish those who oppose his work. Apparently Nehemiah also motivates the people to work all the harder (4:6).

When Sanballat and Tobiah realize their ridicule is not working, they mobilize the other surrounding peoples to join them in a more aggressive plot. This includes Ashdod on the west, the Arabs on the south, and Ammon on the east. Again, Nehemiah, along with the people (4:9), responds immediately and clearly with prayer and precaution, trust and good management.

The next phase of the opposition adds the element of difficulties from within to the plot development (4:10–14). The continued intense labor, the massive amount of rubble from the former destruction, and now the threat of armed attack are causing the people to become discouraged. In addition, the Jews who live near the neighboring enemies are exaggerating the danger, creating more anxiety in the hearts of the workers.

Again, Nehemiah takes definite action. He posts guards with weapons at the weaker points in the wall. He wisely organizes the guards according to families for mutual encouragement. Then he calls the leaders and workers together and encourages them to trust God, who is powerful to deliver, and to defend their families (4:14). The enemies again realize their plans have failed; Nehemiah praises God for frustrating their plot (4:15).

Nehemiah understands the need for further precautions, so he divides the workforce, equipping half the men with armor and weapons and posting them at strategic points (4:16–23). Some keep their weapons in their hands even while they carry building materials. Nehemiah also prepares

Nehemiah, Example of a Godly Leader

Although Ezra-Nehemiah emphasizes the role of all the people, certainly Nehemiah serves as a marvelous example of godly leadership. God used him to lead and consolidate the people in a critical time of their history.

Nehemiah is an example in his relationship with God. His call to special service was not spectacular, but as he prayed for his people, far away in Jerusalem, he was sensitive to God's voice calling him (Nehemiah 1). He was a man completely committed to God, willing to humbly sacrifice himself for the Lord and for his people. He was a man of faith who constantly called on God and recognized God's powerful hand in all he did. He had a profound understanding of God's Word (1:8) and was a man of prayer. These qualities are just as essential for those called to administrative tasks as for pastors and teachers.

Nehemiah combined prayer and careful planning in his ministry. He prayed four months before presenting his project to the king (2:1–2) and sought God's wisdom for decisions throughout his ministry. He also carefully planned his strategy and actions (2:6–9, 11–15) and took time to evaluate the current situation before each decision. When working with a community, a leader must also be able to motivate people. Nehemiah had a special ability to motivate the people and then to delegate responsibilities in a wise manner.

A godly leader must be a people-person. Nehemiah sympathized with the feelings of the people (1:4; 2:17), listened to their problems (3:10, 23; 4:10; 5:1–4), and was sensitive to their needs. He joined with them in the work (4:23; 5:16). He was generous in sharing his own goods (5:10, 14–18). Nehemiah's love and tactfulness in dealing with people is seen in how he wisely presents his project to the people (2:17–18), encourages them (4:14), assigns work crews near their own homes (3:10, 23), and resolves conflicts (5:6–9).

How a leader confronts opposition is often an indicator of leadership ability. Nehemiah's wisdom, trust in God, courage, action, firmness, and honesty in the face of many types of opposition are excellent examples for every leader.

Can an administrative leader have an impact on the spiritual life of a community? Nehemiah's emphasis on the Word of God, worship, humility, repentance, faith, and recommitment played a key role in the renewal of the community. His insistence on putting decisions in writing, obedience to God's Word, and vigilance in holy living were vital for continued renewal.

Nehemiah probably never appeared in the news reports of the great Persian Empire. But in God's plan for the survival of this community, through which came the Bible and eventually our Savior, his leadership has eternal importance. So too a Christian leader today may never share in the limelight but may still have lasting significance in the kingdom of God.

for mobilizing the defense at specific points if necessary (4:20). He asks the people from outside Jerusalem to stay in the city during the night while the crisis continues. Unfortunately opposition to God's work today also requires precautions, delays, and increased resources (cf. Eph. 6:10–18), along with the same faith that we see in Nehemiah, who reminds the people that "our God will fight for us" (4:20).

5:1–19. Nehemiah not only must face opposition from without; now he has to face opposition from within the Jewish community (5:1–19). Christian leaders today find the same to be true, and it tests a leader's character even more than opposition from without. In this case the nobles and officials, the powerful and the well-off in the community, are treating unjustly the underprivileged, the needy, and the poor.

This exploitation or oppression by one's fellow human beings is one of the most detrimental evils in any society. It is one of the major themes of the prophets, who denounced Israelite society for condoning the injustice in their midst. According to the prophets, exploitation was one of the major causes for the exile (Isa. 1:15–17; 58:6; Jer. 7:5–7; 21:12–14; Amos 2:6–8; 5:11–12; Mic. 2:2). It was an indication that the people were becoming insensitive to

God's laws and principles revealed to them through Moses.

This problem must have been developing before Nehemiah arrives on the scene, since over ninety years have passed since the first return from exile in 538 BC. But now the intense work on the wall and the external opposition increase the strain on the economy. The need for workers to stay in Jerusalem adds to the hardship of the local workforce and finally brings forth their "outcry" (5:1). The same Hebrew word was used for the "[out]cry" of the Israelites under the Egyptian oppression in Exodus 3:9.

The law of Moses is part of God's covenant with Israel as a people. The individual is important but is expected to act in benefit of the whole community. Therefore the individual's relations to fellow Jews should never be purely business transactions; they should also be spiritual service pleasing to God. Thus, the Mosaic law provides regulations to maintain a respectable level of equality in the community and also provides ways to alleviate poverty when it exists: (1) Those in dire need can sell the crop value of their land until the next Jubilee year; then the land reverts to the original owner (Lev. 25:8–17). (2) Those with means are to help the poor. No interest is to be charged on loaned money, nor is food to be sold to the poor for profit (Lev. 25:35–38). (3) People in extreme poverty can sell themselves to one with means, to serve for six years. When Israelite servants are set free, their masters must give them liberal supplies of animals and food (Deut. 15:12–15). (4) All debts are to be canceled every seven years (Deut. 15:1–2).

The description of the problem (Neh. 5:1–5) and the reaction of Nehemiah (5:6–11) indicate that the community has been disobeying these laws. So Nehemiah becomes angry; but before acting, he wisely ponders the situation, its causes, and its possible solutions (5:7). His course of action to resolve this conflict between social classes serves as a good guide for resolving conflicts today. First, he separates the people from the problem. He sees the conflict as a community problem rather than a class conflict (5:8). Second, he shows that the wealthy leaders' actions are hurting the whole community (5:9). He focuses on community interests rather than positions. Third, he proposes a solution that will benefit the whole community (5:10–12). A good leader considers a variety of possibilities before deciding what to do (cf. 5:7). Fourth, Nehemiah bases his solution on principles set forth in God's law (5:10–13). Fortunately, the nobles and officials voice their agreement and promise to do as Nehemiah asks (5:12).

In this whole crisis Nehemiah shows courage, diplomacy, firmness, wisdom, and carefulness. He recognizes that oral promises are often forgotten, so he requires the nobles and officials, in the presence of the priests, to take an oath that they will do as they promised. Official oaths of this kind were put in writing and kept on record. The whole episode ends with praise to God for this happy resolution.

Nehemiah's leadership style, alluded to in 5:10, is now further explained (5:14–19). The twelve years (5:14) include time after the events of these chapters but certainly indicate the unselfishness and generosity of his leadership at this time. His concern for the poor and needy and his decision to relinquish his income to alleviate the taxes on his fellow citizens serve as an example to all the leaders. Likewise, his trust in God, his moral integrity, and his wise leadership certainly have a lasting impact on the community.

6:1–14. Now that the internal crisis has been alleviated, the account turns again to the opposition from without, this time by trickery. Apparently Sanballat and his allies, having failed in their former tactics, decide the only way to stop the revitalizing of the Jewish community is to eliminate their leader. They are desperate, for now only the gates must be finished to complete the wall. Their first attempted "trick" is to entice Nehemiah to a diplomatic meeting. Nehemiah recognizes their attempt to trick him, so he firmly answers that he is occupied in more important matters (5:3).

The next tactic of the enemies is to publish an open letter to spread rumors of rebellion against Persia that will damage the work and perhaps cause the Persian king to stop it, as in Ezra 4 (Neh. 6:5–9). Such tactics are often used today to discredit Christian leaders. How should one respond? Nehemiah simply states clearly that their letter is full of lies and prays to God for strength to continue the work.

The final deception is very subtle. Shemaiah is a prophet, and apparently a priest (cf. Delaiah, 1 Chron. 24:18). He tries to cause Nehemiah to fear and shut himself in the temple. How is Nehemiah to know if this is a prophetic message from God or a false message? He discerns that it is not from God because (1) a leader should not fear, and (2) Nehemiah, a layman, is prohibited from entering the temple (6:11–13). He realizes that Sanballat and Tobiah are using their contacts within the community to either intimidate or kill him. There are also apparently other prophets who do not support the wall-building project.

D. Resolution: The wall completed; community consolidation begun (6:15–7:73a). Finally, the wall is completed (6:15–19)—what a note of victory! This is an important milestone, which greatly encourages the people. It testifies to what can be accomplished when the community works together under good leadership. The celebration for the wall's completion is described in Nehemiah 12. Elul is the sixth month; the year starts with Nisan (Neh. 2:1), the first month in the religious calendar. But if the work is completed in fifty-two days, it is not clear exactly when the project was started. The twenty-fifth of Elul would be mid-September or the beginning of October.

The effect of this "victory" on the enemies is evident. They lose their self-confidence, and they fear (6:16). As long as they can convince themselves that this work is not legal and not of God, they can remain comfortable in their unbelief. However, when they realize that God has his hand in the project, they have reason to fear.

"In those days" means "throughout that period" (6:17), not only the present moment. It no doubt is included here to emphasize God's power in what has been accomplished and also that the opposition may continue and will require continued diligence on the part of the community. This will not be easy, for Tobiah has influence on some of the important people in the community as well as on the priests. Tobiah's name and that of his son Jehohanan ("The Lord has shown mercy") may indicate that Tobiah considered himself a worshiper of the same God as this Israelite community.

Now that the wall-building project is completed, Nehemiah turns to the need to organize and consolidate the community (7:1–5). First on his agenda is the security of the city. The gatekeepers are normally assigned to the security of the temple. Why does Nehemiah assign them to the gate of the city and assign to work with them the Levites and singers? Certainly one reason is the lack of personnel and the great danger from the surrounding enemies. Another reason is that the whole purpose of the Jerusalem community is to worship God. As we have seen, Nehemiah considers the city an extension of the temple and therefore part of the house of God—thus, the city's sanctity. The Hanani that Nehemiah puts in charge of the city is the same brother that first visited him in Susa and informed him of the sorry situation of Jerusalem (1:1–3).

The next step in the consolidation is to remedy the lack of population in Jerusalem (7:4–72). The people prefer to live in the villages out in the countryside. How can Nehemiah persuade some to live in Jerusalem? He seeks and receives God's guidance, then plans to call a meeting of the leaders and all the people in order to take a census. He begins with a list of those who came from Babylon ninety-three years ago (in 538 BC). The list occupies the next sixty-seven verses (7:6–72).

The list apparently interrupts the flow of the Nehemiah memoirs at 7:5. That narrative continues again in 11:1—although Nehemiah

7:73 sounds like part of the memoirs and seems to fit between 7:4 and 11:1. Why did the author insert this list here? Why is a repetition needed? Studies in literary narrative technique indicate that such repetitions help to show the intentions of the author. Here the two appearances of the list (Ezra 2 and Nehemiah 7) form an "inclusio," a kind of frame to bind together these three "missions" (Ezra 1–6; 7–10; Nehemiah 1–7). It also underlines the importance of the people, the whole community. The census itself must have gone on to include newer arrivals and family changes. So the list also helps tie together the past and the present of the community.

This list is almost exactly the same as the list in Ezra 2. There are differences in the spelling of some names and a few differences in verses 70–72. These verses appear to be summarized in Ezra 2:68–69; therefore some think the list of Ezra 2 is a copy of Nehemiah 7.

4. The Consolidation of the Covenant Community (7:73b–13:31)

This final section of Ezra-Nehemiah focuses on the reordering, revitalization, and consolidation of the covenant community. The other three sections lead up to this final time of renewal, victorious celebration, and dedication of what God has done in and through his people. The events may not be in exact chronological order but are arranged according to the author's purpose. Some think the events of chapter 13 may well have occurred at an earlier time. Also, some think that chapters 8–10 were part of the Ezra memoirs and fit between the fifth month (Ezra 7:9) and ninth month (Ezra 10:9) of his account. They suggest that the phrase "Nehemiah the governor" (Neh. 8:9) is a later editorial addition to make it compatible with Nehemiah's time. However, there may have been various times of reading the law; furthermore, it is unlikely that this large convocation and revival occurred immediately after Ezra's arrival in Jerusalem. Even though Ezra and Nehemiah do not mention each other in their separate memoirs, there is no reason to conclude that the two of them were not active in Jerusalem at the same time.

A. Spiritual renewal according to the Torah (7:73b–12:26). Now that the reconstruction of the wall is finished, no time is wasted in making sure the community keeps its priorities in order. The people recognize the influence that times of spiritual renewal have had in their own past history under Asa (2 Chronicles 14–15), Hezekiah (2 Chronicles 29–31), and Josiah (2 Chronicles 34–35). The seventh month was an ideal time to seek another renewal, for the first day was the Feast of Trumpets, which later was also celebrated as the New Year. The Day of Atonement was celebrated on the tenth day, and the Feast of Tabernacles began on the fifteenth of this month. In the sabbatical year, the proclamation of the cancellation of debts was made during this feast (Deut. 31:11–13).

This spiritual renewal provides an excellent example of how such renewals revitalize a community. The same characteristics and ingredients of all genuine revivals are present here: (1) emphasis on God's Word (8:1–5), (2) praise to God and celebration (8:6, 10), (3) the Holy Spirit's humbling work in the hearts of the people (8:9), (4) confession of sin and repentance (9:2, 6–18), (5) reestablishing a meaningful prayer life (9:4–37) and (6) a new commitment to obey God (9:38–10:39).

7:73b–8:18. Ezra has not been mentioned since the events of Ezra 10 (458 BC or soon after). He must have been successfully teaching the law of Moses, because now, in 445, the people call on him to lead in making the word of the Lord the moral basis of their community. The initiative for this revival comes from the people, both men and women, young people and children ("all who were able to understand," 8:2). We have seen the emphasis on "the people" throughout Ezra-Nehemiah; it is significant that the word "people" is used twelve times in this section (8:1–12).

Paul says in 2 Timothy 3:16 that all Scripture is inspired by God and profitable "for teaching, rebuking, correcting and training in righteousness." Certainly Nehemiah 8 challenges Christians today to seek renewal through God's

Word. First, it emphasizes that all the people need to know and use God's teachings, as Moses made clear (Deuteronomy 6). In later Judaism, the scribes and Pharisees gave the impression that the common people could not discern God's will directly from Scripture. The early church returned to the Mosaic principle. Over time, the official church "experts" fell into the same error as the scribes and Pharisees. The Protestant Reformation again put emphasis on every believer's use of the Bible. Again today there is a tendency to neglect this emphasis.

God's work in the people's hearts is evident in every verse. All the people are attentive to hear the reading of the scroll for some six hours (8:3). Their reverence and eagerness to hear what God

In this eleventh-century-AD Targum, the biblical text (here Exod. 12:25–31) is translated verse by verse, first presenting the Hebrew and then translating it into Aramaic. A similar technique may have been used in Nehemiah 8:8.

says to them shows the Holy Spirit's work in this renewal (8:7). They are eager to worship the Lord (8:6). Those who are prepared to teach instruct the people (8:7), so they can all understand (8:8). Since their everyday language now is Aramaic, some undoubtedly have difficulty understanding the Hebrew; this is thought to have been the beginning of the Targums (Aramaic paraphrases of the Hebrew Old Testament), if the help the teachers are giving is to explain the text in Aramaic.

Again, we see the Holy Spirit's work in the people's hearts as they weep when they recognize they have not been obeying God (8:9). True revival causes repentance but then results in joy (8:10). As Nehemiah says, "This day is sacred"; times of revival are always sacred times for God's people. Although what happens here should happen in every worship service, throughout history God has also greatly used these special times of revival.

Chapter 8 emphasizes the need to continue the renewal. All the families are eager to "give attention to the words of the Law" (8:13). This leads to a renewed celebration of the Feast of Tabernacles (8:14–17) and continued reading of the law of God (8:18).

9:1–38. This revival continues with the people's heartfelt confession of sin, praise, and petition to God (9:1–37). Their attitude reveals the depth of this renewal; instead of being eager to finish the Feast of Tabernacles and get back to normal life, they gather together for another reading of the law. Not only are they sorry for their past failures; they are serious about making a definite change. They spend at least half the day in hearing the law of God, confession, and praise (9:3). Then they dedicate time to prayer.

Apparently the Levites lead in the long prayer that follows (9:5–37). In form and content it is similar to the historical psalms (Psalms 78; 105–6; 135–36). The prayer is packed with theology. First the Lord (Yahweh) is recognized as the only God. He created everything and is worshiped by all the "multitudes of heaven" (9:6). The prayer emphasizes God's grace in choosing Abraham, in making Israel his covenant people. God continues to shower on them his love and mercy through all their history: in miraculously redeeming them from bondage in Egypt, in leading them through the desert and providing their needs, and in giving them his revelation through Moses.

The prayer has a penitential emphasis; the people recognize that their nation has constantly failed (9:16–17, 26–30), that God has been just in punishing them, and that he has been merciful when they have again turned to him (9:17–25, 27–28, 30).

The last part of the prayer asks God to notice their present suffering. They again recognize that it is their just punishment for their failures (9:33–35). They emphasize their condition as subjects of foreigners. True, the Persians were not as cruel as the Assyrians and Babylonians, but their heavy taxation kept the people in poverty. Interestingly, the prayer does not end with a plea for God to show mercy. The people know God will be merciful if they really turn to him and obey his commands. Therefore they make a "binding agreement" (9:38), which is really a covenant. Not only do they make the agreement verbally, but they make and sign, with an oath, an official legal document stating they will obey carefully all God's commands (10:29). They describe specific actions they will take to maintain their religious duties (10:30–39), summarizing with the promise, "We will not neglect the house of our God."

10:1–39. The list of signers in 10:1–27 is similar to the lists of Ezra 2 and Nehemiah 7. There apparently were some others not in this list. The mention of those who "separated themselves from the neighboring peoples" (10:28) may indicate that some Jews who returned from the surrounding areas are included. The

covenant includes not only the heads of families but also their wives and children "who are able to understand" (10:28).

The duties specified in 10:30–39 are based on the Pentateuch, but those laws are applied to this new situation. This illustrates early Jewish biblical exegesis. For example, the rule concerning intermarriage (Exod. 34:11–16; Deut. 7:1–4; 20:10–18) is slightly different here. The Sabbath laws must also be clarified. Originally the Jews would not have bought and sold among themselves on the Sabbath, but now non-Jewish neighbors are trying to sell them grain, even on the Sabbath. Hence, the laws pertaining to the Sabbath forbid buying and selling grain (10:31).

What can Christians today learn from this chapter? Certainly we are not under the law. But the laws of Moses teach the ethical principles that show God's will for his people in all times. The Sabbath teaches us the importance of setting apart one day out of seven for worship and service to God. The sabbatical year indicates social principles for a healthy society: equality, justice, responsibility to the needy, and responsibility to the environment. The chapter teaches us to submit to the authority of God's Word, to recognize the holiness of the Christian community, and to take seriously our commitment to Christ (cf. Rom. 12:1–2). It teaches us to be faithful in supporting those in full-time Christian service.

11:1–12:26. Nehemiah's concern about the lack of population in Jerusalem (Neh. 7:4–5, 35) is taken up again in chapter 11. The author follows a very logical sequence in this final section (Nehemiah 8–13). First are the revival and the people's covenant to be faithful to God. The next step in the consolidation of the community, as well as the community's worship, is the repopulation of Jerusalem. After this we will see another emphasis on the genealogical list, then the dedication of the wall (Nehemiah 12).

11:1–36. Most of the people prefer to live in the villages outside of Jerusalem, including many priests, Levites, and temple servants. It is beneficial for those who serve in religious matters to live among the common people. But the parenthetical sentence in 11:3–4 suggests that it is an anomaly for them to live far away while other people live in Jerusalem. The whole community decides to choose by lots those who should live in Jerusalem. Some offer voluntarily to move to the city (11:2).

The list of those who move to Jerusalem (11:4–24) can be compared to a parallel list in 1 Chronicles 9. There are quite a few differences, so apparently neither is copied from the other. Both lists begin with the laypeople: the Chronicles list includes some families from tribes of the former northern kingdom; Nehemiah's list, only Judah and Benjamin.

The families of priests are listed in 11:10–14. Some of their different tasks are mentioned. Good administration is needed to achieve harmony in the work with such a large number of priests. The Levites (11:15–18) also have many different duties. Only two are mentioned: the outside work of the house of God and the direction of praise and prayer. Mattaniah is the great-grandson of Asaph, who is mentioned in the titles to various psalms. The director of praise and prayer certainly has a great influence on the faith and life of any believing community. The surprisingly small number of Levites in comparison with the large number of priests reflects the situation described in Ezra 8:15–20.

The list of gatekeepers here is very brief (11:19); in 1 Chronicles 9:23–26 more details are given, and some of the gatekeepers are Levites. The remaining verses in this list give miscellaneous details. Some of the priests and Levites continue to live in the villages (11:20). The temple servants do not have to move; they already live in Jerusalem (11:21). Mattaniah must be of considerable age since his grandson Uzzi is the chief officer of the Levites (11:22).

The list of villages where the people lived (11:25–36) helps us to outline the area of Judah. It includes the area of Benjamin. However, it is possible that a few of the villages mentioned had a partially Jewish population and were outside the actual borders of Judah, such as Ono,

near the northwest corner of Judah, and some villages in the south, where Geshem and the Arabs may also have lived.

12:1–26. Why, before describing the final celebration and dedication of the wall (Neh. 12:27–43), does the author present another list of priests and Levites (12:1–26)? He again emphasizes the covenant community's historical continuity with preexilic Israel. He provides a way of dating specific events in their history, reverting to the method used before the monarchy, when successive periods were remembered by the lifetimes of the high priests (Num. 35:28). With the loss of Hebrew kingship, it is important to designate alternative historical markers. Also, by naming the priests and Levites, the author indicates the importance of each individual in God's work (cf. Ephesians 4), even though throughout Ezra-Nehemiah he is careful to emphasize the whole people rather than one or two great leaders.

Twenty-two names are given in 12:1–7. Nearly all are seen again in 12:12–21 to show the continuity of the priestly houses. Fifteen of those who signed the special "binding" covenant in Nehemiah 10:2–8 had these family names, although there are some spelling differences. Since originally there were twenty-four priestly divisions (1 Chron. 24:7–19), and the same was true in later Judaism, two names may have dropped out of this list (12:1–7), or perhaps no representatives of those families were among the returnees.

The list in 12:8–9 provides additional information to Ezra 2:40–42, which includes only the names of Jeshua, Kadmiel, and Hodaviah. As the NIV note at Ezra 3:9 indicates, Judah (Yehudah) may be the same as Hodaviah.

The genealogy of the high priestly family is given in 12:10–11. Joshua was high priest at the time of the first return (538 BC) and at the time of Haggai and Zechariah (520 BC). Eliashib was high priest in Nehemiah's time; therefore Joiakim was high priest between those two.

The priestly families in the time of the high priest Joshua were named in 12:1–7. Now the author gives the priestly families in the time of Joiakim's high priesthood (12:12–21). Compared to the list of priests who signed the covenant (10:2–8, in Nehemiah's time), this list contains six additional names. It may simply indicate that in 10:2–8 some priests did not sign the covenant.

Additional information concerning the Levites is given in 12:22–26. Some see a contradiction between verse 22, where Johanan is high priest after Joiada, and verse 23, where he is "son of Eliashib." It has been suggested that he was a brother of Joiada; but more probably we should read "descendant of Eliashib" in 12:23. According to the Elephantine Papyri, a Johanan was high priest in 410 BC, in the reign of Darius II. Since names are often repeated in family lines, it may not be the same Johanan. These verses (12:22–23) indicate that careful records were kept by the Jewish leaders.

The phrase "one section responding to the other" (12:24) refers to antiphonal singing, which David instituted. According to Nehemiah 11:17, Mattaniah, Bakbukiah, and Obadiah (12:25) were singers; thus they should be included in 12:24. The final note (12:26) again gives the impression that Ezra and Nehemiah worked together in Jerusalem, at least some of the time.

B. Celebration and dedication (12:27–43). The first-person account, which broke off at 7:5, resumes at 12:27. Nehemiah describes the dedication of the wall following the spiritual renewal and the people's covenant to obey God. He understands the divine emphasis on celebrations. God calls his people to thankful worship and rejoicing (Deut. 12:7, 12, 18; 14:26; 16:11–15; 26:11; 27:7). Times of celebration and thankful worship unite the community, draw the people closer to God, and motivate them to rededicate their lives to the Lord.

The completion of the wall is the climax of a series of wonderful manifestations of God's guidance and power: the decree of Cyrus (Ezra 1:1–4) has brought about freedom from captivity, the temple has been constructed, and the Jewish community has been revitalized and renewed. The restoration of the wall of Jerusalem has been completed, extending the sanctity of the temple to include the whole city. It is time to remember what God has done and unite in joyous praise to him.

Elaborate preparations are undertaken to make the celebration meaningful (12:27–30). Special effort is put forth to bring the Levitical singers and musicians from far and near to prepare for the great musical celebration. "Songs of thanksgiving" (12:27) signifies "thanksgiving choirs" and is translated "choirs" in verses 31, 38, and 40. Since this is a celebration centered on God, the priests and Levites first purify themselves through the prescribed ceremonies; then they

The top layers of stone (extending from the foreground to the tower) are thought to be remnants of Nehemiah's wall, built in the middle of the fifth century BC.

sanctify, through sacrifices, the people, the gates, and the wall.

The dedication is quite impressive, and the sounds of singing, musical instruments, and rejoicing can be heard far and wide (12:43). There are two choirs that march on top of the wall and sing antiphonally. They begin the procession at the Valley Gate (cf. Neh. 2:13). Ezra leads the first choir proceeding south (to the right, counterclockwise) to the Dung Gate and the Fountain Gate, up the steps to the City of David, and on to the Water Gate on the east. The second choir proceeds in the opposite direction (clockwise), as Nehemiah and the other officials follow them. They go past the Tower of the Ovens, the Gate of Ephraim, the Jeshanah Gate, the Fish Gate, the Tower of Hananel, and the Tower of the Hundred, and on to the Sheep Gate, stopping at the Gate of the Guard. After this spectacular celebration they go into the temple and continue the rejoicing and worship with singing and "great sacrifices" (12:43). The sacrifices symbolize their dedication to God. Truly the whole city of Jerusalem has become sanctified.

C. Conservation of the renewed community (12:44–13:31). How does a revitalized community continue the renewal experience? Certainly the history of Israel and the church illustrates the human tendency to drift away from communion with God. Preserving and continuing renewal requires a constant vigil on the part of the community and its leaders. This may be the reason Ezra-Nehemiah ends with examples of actions to avoid such apostasy (13:4–31).

The phrases "on that day" (12:44 [NIV "at that time"]; 13:1) and "in those days" (13:15, 23) refer in general to a period of time, not necessarily to specific days. The author uses them as a narrative technique to unify the material from 12:44 to 13:31. Apparently he wishes to show the contrast between their promising beginning (12:44–13:3) after the renewal and dedication experiences and their later backsliding after Nehemiah's absence (13:4–31).

12:44–13:3. After the dedication, the people begin well. The comments in 12:44–13:3 likely refer in general to the period after the covenant of Nehemiah 10 and the dedication of the wall (Nehemiah 12) and are added here before resuming the Nehemiah memoirs (13:4–30). These comments confirm that the community really is being faithful to the covenant they signed in chapter 10. They are bringing the tithes and offerings according to the law (12:44). They are not neglecting the house of God (cf. Neh. 10:39). The statement "for [because] Judah was pleased with the ministering priests and Levites" highlights an important truth: when worship and pastoral leaders serve according to Scripture and in order to please God, the "spiritual" level of the community remains high, and the people give generously for God's work (12:47). Nehemiah and the leaders wisely organize the administration to correctly follow the law of God, as they promised in Nehemiah 10:29. Likewise, the next paragraph (13:1–3) indicates they are taking seriously their promise of separation in 10:30. This sounds like a harsh decision; however, foreigners could become part of Israel through conversion (Ruth 1:16–17).

13:4–31. The situation then changes. The practices condemned in this section all involve disobedience to God's commands. The first is a failure to maintain the sanctity of the temple and to fulfill other religious responsibilities (13:4–14). The second is disobedience to God in regard to keeping the Sabbath holy (13:15–22), and the third is disobedience in regard to marriage with non-Jews (13:23–29).

The phrase "before this" (13:4) refers to a period prior to Nehemiah's return to Jerusalem after he has been absent for a time. But it does not tell us how long before. Some suggest that the events of this chapter occurred earlier than the dedication ceremony; however, it is best to consider it later, during the time Nehemiah has returned to his service for King Artaxerxes (13:6). Why does Nehemiah call him "king of Babylon"? The Persian kings occasionally used this title (cf. Ezra 5:13), for they considered their empire the continuation of the Babylonian

Empire. It is also possible the king was living in Babylon at this time.

The high priest is not in charge of the storerooms, so this "Eliashib the priest" (13:4) surely is not the Eliashib who was high priest. Earlier it was mentioned that Tobiah the Ammonite had a negative influence on some of the important people in Jerusalem. He is married to a Jew (Neh. 6:10). Eliashib certainly has betrayed his responsibility in allowing Tobiah to use a storeroom of the temple court for his own purposes. Since this was the place designated for storing the people's offerings, it no doubt is one cause for the disruption in the Levites' ministry (13:10–11).

Nehemiah resolves the problem by expelling the Ammonite, purifying the desecrated areas, and putting responsible, trustworthy men in charge of the storerooms (13:12–13). When order is restored, the people again are faithful in giving their support for the priests and Levites.

Nehemiah also notices the backslidden condition of the people in their failure to keep the Sabbath (13:15–22). When the people drift away from the Lord, they become lax in obeying God's will. The Old Testament puts a lot of emphasis on keeping the Sabbath. The concept of a Sabbath was unknown in the ancient world outside of Israel. God instituted it as a means of keeping his people centered on his priorities; it emphasizes the sanctity of time and symbolizes that all our time belongs to God.

Although in the New Testament, believers are not under the law in a legalistic manner, the inclusion of the Sabbath in the Ten Commandments would indicate God's will that one day a week be set aside and dedicated to worship and rest. Because of Jesus's strong teaching against the legalistic observance of the Old Testament Sabbath, and his repeated postresurrection appearances on the first day of the week, the early Christians began to worship God together on the Lord's Day (Sunday) to commemorate Jesus's resurrection. It gradually took the place of gathering on the seventh day. Throughout the centuries of church history there has been much discussion concerning our responsibility in regard to the Lord's Day. Christians throughout the world follow Jesus's example of putting emphasis on "how to sanctify" the Lord's Day, by making it a day of rest, worshiping together, and serving God.

Nehemiah warns the Jews that by desecrating the Sabbath they will again bring down God's wrath on their nation. The initiative for the commercial activity has come from non-Jewish neighbors. Apparently many of the Jews are taking advantage of their offers. Even the Levites who have been assigned to guard the city gates are somehow neglecting their duty. Nehemiah takes specific action to completely stop all buying and selling on the Sabbath. He also finds it necessary to reassign the Levites to guard the gates.

The repetition of the phrase "in those days I saw . . ." (13:15, 23) underlines a characteristic of Nehemiah's good leadership; he is aware of what is happening among the people throughout the whole region. He sees another area where the people are disobeying God's standards: intermarriage with pagan neighbors. Even the family of the high priest has become involved (13:28). Like Ezra, who confronted the same problem earlier (Ezra 10), Nehemiah realizes the danger this poses to God's purpose for the Jewish community. Again he takes definite action, including purifying the priests and Levites "of everything foreign" (13:30).

Although Nehemiah is best known for reconstructing the walls of Jerusalem, he concludes his memoirs, and the author concludes Ezra-Nehemiah, with this emphasis on maintaining the renewed Jewish community's worship and commitment to God. Today we can be thankful that God used both Ezra and Nehemiah to reestablish and maintain this community through which he fulfilled his purpose in giving his revelation, the Bible, and the Savior to the entire world.

Select Bibliography

Blenkinsopp, Joseph. *Ezra-Nehemiah*. London: SCM, 1989.

Breneman, Mervin. *Ezra, Nehemiah, Esther*. New American Commentary. Nashville: Broadman & Holman, 1993.

Clines, David J. A. *Ezra, Nehemiah, Esther*. New Century Bible Commentary. Grand Rapids: Eerdmans, 1984.

Fensham, F. Charles. *The Books of Ezra and Nehemiah*. New International Commentary on the Old Testament. Grand Rapids: Eerdmans, 1982.

Holmgren, Fredrick Carlson. *Ezra and Nehemiah: Israel Alive Again*. International Theological Commentary. Grand Rapids: Eerdmans, 1987.

Kidner, Derek. *Ezra and Nehemiah*. Tyndale Old Testament Commentaries. Downers Grove, IL: InterVarsity, 1979.

Klein, Ralph W. "Ezra and Nehemiah." In *The New Interpreter's Bible*. Edited by Leander E. Keck. Vol. 3. Nashville: Abingdon, 1999.

Throntveit, Mark A. *Ezra-Nehemiah*. Interpretation. Atlanta: John Knox, 1992.

Williamson, H. G. M. *Ezra, Nehemiah*. Word Biblical Commentary. Waco: Word, 1985.

Esther

Hélène Dallaire

Introduction

The book of Esther, one of two biblical books highlighting a female character, provides the story of a young Jewish girl named Hadassah (Esther), who lives among the Jewish diaspora in Persia. Esther plays a major role in the deliverance of the Jews who were destined to be destroyed and annihilated at the hand of the evil Haman. Also central to the narrative is her cousin Mordecai, whose discovery of Haman's plot to annihilate the Jews is pivotal. Mordecai's rise from common man to nobility is one of several examples of role reversal, where the underdog unexpectedly becomes the hero of the story.

Ahasuerus, the Persian king, is also important to the story line; he consistently allows nobles in the royal palace to influence his decisions, causing him to vacillate and waver on matters related to ruling the kingdom. Early in the story his wife, Queen Vashti, is deposed from her royal throne after refusing to attend her inebriated husband's banquet where her exquisite beauty was to be displayed before the guests. Her overthrow gives place for Esther to enter the scene and to become God's instrument of deliverance.

Esther's story testifies to God's sovereignty and his faithfulness to deliver his people wherever they may be—in the promised land or in exile. Though God is never mentioned by name in this book, the reader encounters God at every turn. No event in the narrative is coincidental; every segment is divinely orchestrated, and in the end, God is glorified.

Historical Context

The story of Esther takes place during the reign of Ahasuerus of Persia, between the years 486 and 465 BC, after King Cyrus had allowed the Jews to return to their homeland and to rebuild the temple in Jerusalem (538 BC). Scholars' views on the dating of the book range from mid-fifth to mid-third centuries BC. Those who advocate for an early date point to (1) the presence of Persian loan words and the scarcity of Greek words, (2) the author's familiarity with the geography of Susa, and (3) the close similarities between the Hebrew of Esther and the language of Chronicles. Advocates for a late date suggest that the opening statement, "This is what happened during the time of Xerxes, the Xerxes who ruled over 127 provinces," places the author at a temporal vantage point removed from the events. Also noted is the lack of interest in the land of Israel and the absence of religious practices, features that distance the story from the events of Ezra and Nehemiah.

Canonicity

The inclusion of the book of Esther in the canon was originally disputed in both Jewish and Christian circles. According to rabbinic literature, the absence of God's name, the secularity of the book, and the addition of Purim to the feasts of the Torah contributed to this controversy (e.g., Babylonian Talmud *Megillah* 7a). In the writings of early church fathers, the book was rejected by some because of its nationalistic and genocidal tone (e.g., Melito of Sardis, Athanasius, Gregory of Nazianzus, Theodore of Mopsuestia), while it was accepted by others who adopted Josephus's list of alphabetic canonical texts (e.g., Origen).

Historicity

Among scholars, some advocate for a historical interpretation of the book, while others support the notion that the narrative was written as an imaginative story of a comedic style composed solely for entertainment purposes. Scholarly arguments for a nonhistorical interpretation include (1) the absence from Persian records of a queen named Esther, (2) the fact that Persian queens were of noble birth and not from ethnic minorities, (3) the unprecedented idea that Persian kings would have consulted with legal advisors to make decisions, and (4) the unlikelihood that Persia, a country that favored ethnic minorities and allowed the Jews to return to their homeland, would have issued an edict to annihilate Jews.

King Xerxes I (Ahasuerus) with attendants, depicted in a relief from the remains of his palace at Persepolis

Although these arguments have some merit, each one can be refuted in turn: (1) not every queen is mentioned in ancient Persian records, (2) biblical characters who became prominent leaders were often born outside of noble families, (3) Israelite and foreign rulers frequently consulted with their advisors before deciding important matters (e.g., Pharaoh, Gen. 41:8; Rehoboam, 1 Kings 12:6–9), and finally (4) history shows that nations that once favored Jewish presence in their midst sooner or later allowed the rise of anti-Semitism.

According to historical records, no Persian king has ever had a Jewish queen named Esther. However, in Herodotus's writings, Amestris (Esther? See Herodotus, *Histories* 7.114, 9.112) is introduced as the wife of King Xerxes I, the biblical Ahasuerus. Most scholars associate Mordecai with the court official Marduka mentioned in a text from Borsippa, who served the Persian king as inspector in the citadel of Susa. Biblical records tell us that not all Jews who lived in exile chose to return home to the province of Yehud (Judah). Some opted to remain in Persia, where they had established deep familial roots. Mordecai and Esther lived among them and were by this time well integrated into Persian culture.

Literary Features

The book of Esther is meticulously woven together with intricate literary features that include "doublets" (e.g., two eunuchs, twice casting of lots), "keywords" (e.g., feasts, edicts), "humor" (e.g., legislation of husbandly authority), "incongruence" (e.g., minority killing majority), and "exaggeration" (e.g., extravagant banquets). The story highlights frequent cases of "reversal," or a sudden turn of events (peripety). Noteworthy examples of this last item are the following: (1) Vashti's dethronement (2:1) followed by Esther's coronation (2:17); (2) Haman's empowerment (3:10) ending with his fatal disempowerment (7:10); (3) Mordecai's humble beginnings (2:5) finding him as grand vizier in the royal court (10:2–3); (4) the book opening with two Persian banquets (1:3, 9) and ending with two Jewish banquets (8:17; 9:18); (5) the king first endorsing an anti-Jewish edict (3:13) and eventually sanctioning a pro-Jewish decree (8:11); and (6) the planned annihilation of the Jews (3:6–7) turning into the annihilation of the enemies of the Jews (8:11–9:1).

Genre

Scholars have proposed various genres for the narrative, from Jewish novella to historical wisdom tale, comedic narrative, court legend, historicized myth, short story, folklore, and burlesque (literary farce). There is sufficient internal data for the book to be considered historical (e.g., name of Persian king, Jewish communities in exile, origin of Purim festival), and when this is combined with the rhetorical and literary features (e.g., humor, exaggeration, peripety), the narrative represents a historical-comedic masterpiece.

Commentary

1. The First Two Feasts—Vashti Is Deposed (1:1–22)

The book of Esther begins with a description of its historical background. The events of the book occur when the city of Susa is serving as the capital of Persia and the empire includes 127 provinces (possible hyperbole) that extend from India to Ethiopia (Cush). During the third year of his reign, Ahasuerus organizes a lavish banquet that will last 180 days and at which event he will display before the male nobility of his kingdom his affluence and his distinguished fame as the ruler of the vast Persian Empire. Ahasuerus's banquet, the longest feast mentioned in the Bible, is marked by indulgence in wine and strong drink, gastronomic extravagance, and excessive reveling (1:4–8), as was common in royal feasts of this period (Herodotus, *Histories* 1.133–35). The event corresponds well with the war council of 483 BC, when the king assembled his officials to plan a campaign to conquer Greece. While the king is entertaining his guests in the palace, his wife Queen Vashti also holds a feast for women in another section of the royal citadel (1:9).

On the seventh day of the celebration, while King Ahasuerus is in high spirits and drunk with wine, he commands seven eunuchs to bring Queen Vashti to his palace in order to display her magnificent beauty. To the king's

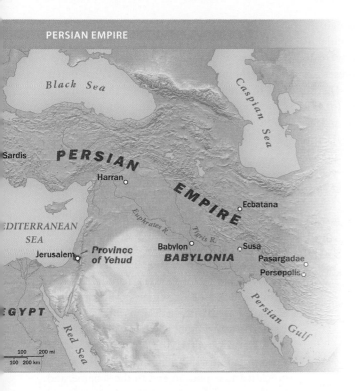

PERSIAN EMPIRE

Black Sea

Caspian Sea

Sardis

PERSIAN

Harran

EMPIRE

Ecbatana

MEDITERRANEAN SEA

Euphrates R.

Tigris R.

Jerusalem

Province of Yehud

Babylon

BABYLONIA

Susa

Pasargadae

Persepolis

EGYPT

Red Sea

Persian Gulf

100   200 mi
100 200 km

suffer great personal losses shortly after becoming inebriated.

Though Vashti holds a position of authority, her status is noticeably subordinate to that of the king's aristocrats. Not only is she subjected to her husband's narcissistic caprices, but she is also at the mercy of his court officials, whose masculinity seems to have been threatened by her refusal to parade herself before them. Drawing on their alleged legal expertise, the king's officials pronounce the harshest possible judgment on the queen. She is publicly dethroned. The anxiety of the king's advisors has been fueled by the unlikely hypothesis that women would rebel en masse against the patriarchal system of the day and destroy the peace of the kingdom (1:16–18). How ironic that the decision to depose one queen opens wide the door through which another queen will deliver the entire Jewish population of Persia.

astonishment, Queen Vashti categorically refuses to obey the orders and leaves her husband publicly humiliated and irate in the presence of his awaiting guests (1:12). It is likely that the queen has previously experienced such ordeals when the king's drunkenness has seriously affected his ability to make moral decisions. Her unflinching response to the king's request seems to indicate so. The biblical text provides a number of accounts where reckless decisions are made by drunk leaders. For example, King Belshazzar (Dan. 5:2), Nabal (1 Sam. 25:36), and Amnon (2 Sam. 13:28)

2. The Third Feast—Esther Becomes Queen (2:1–20)

In chapter 2, physical beauty and sexual attraction become once again major themes of the story. In chapter 1, the author informed us that Vashti was stunning. After her removal from royalty, the king's attendants seek

> The Persian Empire (550–330 BC) boasted four capital cities: Susa, Pasargadae, Ecbatana, and Persepolis. The magnificent archaeological remains of Persepolis, pictured here, attest to the wealth of the empire.

attractive young virgins from all the provinces of the empire and bring them to the citadel of Susa. Following twelve months of beauty treatments, these young women are to be presented to the king as would-be queens (2:2–4). The young virgins who have been chosen for the royal pageant are confined inside the palace and triply secure in the citadel of Susa, in the royal harem, under the watchful eye of a eunuch named Hegai. Once in the harem, the young women seemingly have very little contact with the outside world (2:11).

Mordecai the Jew (2:5; 5:13), of the tribe of Benjamin, appears on the scene as Esther's older cousin who has adopted her after the death of her parents and who has raised her in his own household. Mordecai is a second- or third-generation exiled Jew who is well entrenched in the culture of Persia and who has risen through the ranks in the courts of the king. His prominent position is in many ways a fulfillment of the words of the prophet Jeremiah, who pronounced to the exiles decades earlier to

> build houses and settle down; plant gardens and eat what they produce. Marry and have sons and daughters; find wives for your sons and give your daughters in marriage, so that they too may have sons and daughters. Increase in number there; do not decrease. Also, seek the peace and prosperity of the city to which I have carried you into exile. Pray to the LORD for it, because if it prospers, you too will prosper. (Jer. 29:5–7)

After hearing of the search for beautiful young women, Mordecai decides to release Esther into the care of Hegai but seeks daily confirmation of her welfare from the officials in the harem (2:8–11). Not only is Mordecai concerned with Esther's physical and emotional well-being, but given the potential dangers of living as a Jew in a foreign land, he is worried that her Jewish identity might be revealed and might draw unnecessary attention (2:19–20).

Following the elaborate process of a royal beauty pageant, radiant Esther enters the royal residence, wins the favor of the king, and becomes the new queen of Persia. What better way to commemorate the event than to have a coronation banquet, proclaim a national holiday, and distribute gifts throughout the kingdom (2:15–18)?

3. Mordecai Rescues the King (2:21–23)

All seems to go well in the kingdom. The king's anger against Vashti has subsided, a new queen has been appointed, and the celebrations that accompany the coronation have blessed everyone. Yet trouble is brewing on the horizon, as Bigthana and Teresh, two eunuchs of the king, openly devise a plot to assassinate him (2:21). While sitting at the king's gate, Mordecai discovers the plan, and without delay he informs Queen Esther. In turn, Esther makes the plot known to the king and credits Mordecai with providing this crucial life-saving information. The king's quick reaction puts an end to the scheme, and Bigthana and Teresh are investigated, found guilty, and condemned to death (2:23). Disaster is averted, and Mordecai's name is appropriately inscribed in the annals of the king.

4. Haman's Plot to Annihilate the Jews (3:1–15)

After being exalted to the highest seat of honor, pompous and egotistical Haman begins to receive reverence and admiration by all, except by Mordecai, who refuses to bow down and kneel before him at the king's gate (3:2). His courageous behavior mirrors that of Shadrach, Meshach, and Abednego, who categorically refuse to bow before the statue of Nebuchadnezzar, a daring move that earns them a visit to the fiery furnace (Dan. 3:1–21). In both accounts, God intervenes, delivers his servants from certain death, and exalts them to positions of leadership in the kingdom.

Informed by royal officials that Mordecai is a Jew, Haman devises a plan to exterminate both Mordecai and his people by a royal decree sealed with the signet ring of the king.

The decree commands the leaders of all the provinces of Persia "to destroy, kill and annihilate all the Jews—young and old, women and little children—on a single day, the thirteenth day of the twelfth month, the month of Adar, and to plunder their goods" (3:13). The edict is obtained by Haman through deceptive means that dehumanize the Jews and present them as an unassimilated people who habitually disobey the king's laws (3:8). Convinced by Haman's arguments, the king condemns the entire Jewish population of the kingdom to death.

After the decree is sent out to all the provinces, the king and Haman sit down in the palace to celebrate the event. Meanwhile outside the palace, the mood grows somber, and the inhabitants of Susa become confused and mystified by the sudden news of the impending "final solution" (3:15). The Hebrew word translated "confused" (*nabo kah*) appears in only two other passages in the Hebrew Bible. In Exodus 14:3, after the Israelites experience the original Passover in Egypt and leave their homes with the plunder of the Egyptians, they find themselves "confused" (*nebukim*) as they wander between their former homes and the Red Sea. In Joel 1:18, the cattle are said to be "wandering aimlessly" (*naboku*), without pasture, as the day of the Lord approaches. In these three cases, feelings of disorientation, bewilderment, and vulnerability describe the condition of the communities, and such is the atmosphere in Susa.

This stone tablet from Persepolis was inscribed during the reign of Xerxes I (Ahasuerus) and includes a list of the countries that he ruled.

5. Mordecai's Petition to Esther (4:1–17)

Contributing to the state of confusion is distraught Mordecai, whose wailing is heard throughout the city, and whose transformed outward appearance—the wearing of sackcloth and ashes—is noticeably out of character for a man of his social status (4:1). In the Bible, sackcloth and ashes typically accompany laments and mourning for the dead, and in certain cases, fasting for the deliverance of a people (e.g., Gen. 37:34; Lam. 2:10–12). Mordecai's demeanor and unusual garb appropriately reflect the mood of the Susan community.

When Esther hears about Mordecai's distress, she is deeply troubled and seeks to find out the reason for her cousin's unusual behavior. Mordecai sends a detailed report to Esther describing Haman's edict and his offer to pay a sum of money into the royal treasury in order to have all the Jews killed. Together with this report, Mordecai gives a copy of the royal decree to Esther and pleads with her to request an audience before the king in order to intercede on behalf of her people (4:8).

Upon learning that Esther has not been summoned to appear before the king for over thirty days, Mordecai urges Esther to take the greatest risk of her life and request a special royal audience. According to the law of Persia, a refusal by the king would result in certain death for the queen. Although Esther lives a privileged life in the royal palace, she finds herself desperately constrained, unable to communicate directly with her cousin Mordecai

outside and unable to freely approach the king inside. The glory of queenship begins to fade as Esther faces the realities of her confined existence. But, prompted by Mordecai's urgency, she accepts the challenge, knowing full well that her decision could cost her her life (4:11). Esther quickly heeds Mordecai's famous words, "And who knows but that you have come to royal position for such a time as this?" (4:14). She urgently calls a fast and declares, "If I perish, I perish" (4:16).

6. The Fourth Feast—Esther's First Banquet (5:1–8)

After three days of fasting, Esther clothes herself with royal garments and makes her way to the palace where her fate and that of her people will be determined. When the king sees Esther entering his chamber, he extends his royal scepter and invites her to make her petition known to him (5:2). The king offers her "up to half the kingdom" (5:3), an idiom that is not to be taken literally but rather signifies that the petitioner has gained great favor in the eyes of the king (see Mark 6:23).

In response to the king's question, Esther invites the king and Haman to a private banquet on that day in her royal quarters. Without delay, the king accepts, and he and Haman make their way to Esther's residence. Reclining on the couch with a drink in his hand, the king inquires once again concerning Esther's petition. Seemingly without hesitation, Esther craftily withholds the answer to the question and invites her two guests to join her again the next day for another banquet at which she will disclose her request (5:7). The purpose for Esther's calculated delay is never revealed.

7. Haman's Hatred of Mordecai (5:9–14)

Full of joy and inebriated, Haman leaves Queen Esther's banquet and returns home to boast of his great wealth and honored position in the courts of the king. On the way home, Haman encounters his nemesis Mordecai, who refuses once again to bow before him (5:9). Seething with rage, pretentious Haman vows revenge.

After bragging to his family and friends about the special privileges he has received from the royals, Haman expresses severe discontentment at Mordecai's refusal to honor him (5:13). Haman's concerned wife, Zeresh, quickly recommends an unconscionable solution, one that will both humiliate Mordecai and vindicate her husband: "Have a pole set up, reaching to a height of fifty cubits, and ask the king in the morning to have Mordecai impaled on it. Then go with the king to the banquet and enjoy yourself" (5:14). Delighted with his wife's suggestion and convinced that the king will concur, Haman has the pole set up (more likely than a gallows for hanging [see NIV 1984], since impalement was a common form of execution by the Persians) in preparation for his revenge.

8. The King Rewards Mordecai (6:1–14)

Afflicted by insomnia, King Ahasuerus requests that the royal records be read to him. Providentially, the report of Mordecai's heroism regarding his disclosure of the assassination plot is read by the attendant. Rather than falling asleep, the king becomes intrigued by the details of the account and asks if the hero has been honored for his bravery (6:3). The king's attendant replies that nothing has been done to honor him. Eager to recompense the one who saved his life, the king asks who is in the court in order to discuss the best possible way to honor this brave man. The timing could not be better! Haman has just entered the courtyard to approach the king with his despicable request for permission to impale Mordecai (6:4).

Summoned to the king's presence, Haman rushes to his side anticipating that his request will be quickly granted. The king asks Haman: "What should be done for the man the king delights to honor?" (6:6). Who other than himself would narcissistic Haman consider worthy of the king's honor? Haman offers what he considers to be the most ingenious proposition of his life, one that will exalt him above everyone in the kingdom, or so he thinks! He proposes that the honoree should be dressed in royal garb and be paraded through the city streets on a royal horse with attendants proclaiming: "This is what is done for the man the king delights to honor" (6:9). Without hesitation, the king agrees and commands Haman to personally grant this royal treatment to Mordecai the Jew.

How devastating for egomaniac Haman to realize that the lavish reward he has devised is to be granted to his nemesis Mordecai and not to him. Once again, Haman's hopes are shattered, and his mood quickly changes from exhilaration to devastation, a clear example of the recurring reversal motif. How could this be happening

to him? How can he now petition the king to have Mordecai killed? With these questions haunting him, Haman obeys the king's orders and parades Mordecai through the city streets in the exact manner he has suggested to the king earlier that day. What a disgrace for Haman!

Humiliated by the events, Haman rushes home to his wife and advisors and tells them everything that happened to him that day (6:12). After listening to the distressing report, his counselors utter one of the most critical statements of the narrative, a declaration that provides a needed ray of hope for the Jews of the empire: "Since Mordecai, before whom your downfall [Hebrew *napal*] has started, is of Jewish origin, you cannot stand against him—you will surely come to ruin [*napal*]" (6:13). The repetition of the key Hebrew word *napal* ("to fall") is significant, as it foreshadows Haman's impending fall from nobility (cf. 7:8). No sooner has Haman's disgrace been predicted than he is whisked away to Esther's second banquet (6:14).

9. The Fifth Feast—Esther's Second Banquet and Haman Impaled (7:1–10)

The moment has now come for Esther to make her petition known to the king. Only with great care can she proceed with her accusation of Haman, since he is the grand vizier of the kingdom and she is only a vulnerable queen. Will the king believe her story? Will she obtain the favor needed to prevent the execution of the royal decree? As these thoughts race through her mind, Esther reveals to the king the impending plan to slaughter and annihilate her people (7:3–4). Startled by the details of this looming atrocity, the king immediately asks Esther for the name of the instigator (7:5). Without hesitation, Esther turns and points to Haman, who is seized with horror at the potential consequences of his conspiracy (7:6). Enraged, King Ahasuerus bolts out of the banquet hall and exits to the garden in order to regain his composure and decide the fate of Haman.

Upon his return, King Ahasuerus finds foolish Haman fallen (Hebrew *napal*) on the couch where Esther is reclining, begging her for mercy. Furious at this outrageous behavior, the king cries out: "Will he even molest the queen while she is with me in the house?" (7:8). One of the royal attendants who has witnessed the unfolding events informs the king that Haman has recently set up a pole in order to impale Mordecai, the recent honoree. Without wavering, the king declares: "Impale him on it!" (7:9). Haman is now condemned to death, the very fate he has devised for Mordecai and the Jews of Persia (7:5–10). At once, the king's fury is appeased and hope is renewed for the Jewish population of the kingdom.

10. The King's Edict to Spare the Jews (8:1–17)

The day of Haman's execution ironically becomes the day of Esther and Mordecai's exaltation, a clear reversal of events. Following Haman's death, King Ahasuerus gives Haman's estate to Queen Esther and rewards Mordecai by giving him the royal signet ring that was used to seal the first decree against the Jews (8:1–2). Although Haman is now dead and gone, Mordecai and Esther face the grim reality that their ordeal is far from over. Unless the unchangeable law established by Haman is canceled, overturned, or neutralized, the Jews will continue living in peril for their lives. Mordecai and Esther have to act swiftly in order to prevent the massacre and annihilation of their own people.

Once again, Queen Esther approaches the king, this time with a tearful and deeply emotional plea (8:3). She receives immediate favor and is given permission for her and Mordecai to issue a new royal decree that will allow the Jews from Persia to defend themselves against their enemies (8:8). The new decree, originally written in the Persian language, is dictated by Mordecai and transcribed into the scripts and languages of all peoples and provinces in Persia (8:9). Although Esther is the one who pled before the king, the focus quickly shifts to Mordecai, who assumes the leadership in issuing the new decree. By this time, Mordecai has

replaced Haman in the royal courts, another striking case of reversal.

The composition and diffusion of this new legal document echo with great precision Haman's earlier verdict. In both cases, (1) royal secretaries are summoned (3:12 // 8:9), (2) the decree is written in the languages of the empire (3:14 // 8:9), (3) the decree is written in the name of the king and sealed with his signet ring (3:12 // 8:10), (4) couriers are dispatched (3:13 // 8:10), (5) the edict gives permission to kill and annihilate enemies (3:13 // 8:11), (6) the events are to take place on the thirteenth of Adar (3:13 // 8:12), and (7) the decree is issued by messengers throughout the city of Susa (3:15 // 8:14).

In both cases, the people of the city of Susa react with deep emotions. Following Haman's decree, the people of Susa are confounded and the Jews fear for their lives (3:15). Following Mordecai's decree, the city of Susa holds "a joyous celebration," and the Jews of every province cheer with dancing and feasting (8:15–17).

11. The Jews Triumph over Their Enemies (9:1–17)

Eleven months have passed since Haman's original decree to annihilate the Jews. The day anticipated by all has now come, and contrary to earlier expectations, the Jews emerge as victors rather than victims. Haman's planned catastrophe has turned into deliverance, and his intended terror has turned into feasting. Once again, a reversal of fortune has occurred: "*The tables were turned* and the Jews got the upper hand over those who hated them" (9:1).

The events of the day are costly for the enemies of the Jews, as more than seventy-five thousand lose their lives. What was originally intended to be a defensive approach is described in the chapter in offensive terms, virtually depicting the Jews as calculated aggressors who violently annihilate all who hate them (9:5–10). Scholars have struggled with the grim details of this chapter, questioning the merciless slaughter of Persian women and children, the excessive number of people who are killed, and Esther's request to continue the killing for a second day when apparently the Jews have already killed "all their enemies with the sword" (9:5). Some have suggested that Esther's request to continue the slaughter and to have Haman's sons impaled reveals her vindictive and bloodthirsty nature. Others have justified her behavior by pointing to her need to ensure complete safety for her people and to remove all possible future enemies from the kingdom. Public humiliation by impaling is not unique to the book of Esther. This practice was common in the ancient Near East (as depicted in the relief of the Assyrian siege of Lachish) and occurs in other biblical accounts (e.g., 1 Sam. 31:8–10, Saul and his sons).

For the Jewish communities of Persia, there is a renewed sense of security: "The people of all the other nationalities were afraid of them, and all the nobles of the provinces, the satraps, the governors and the king's administrators helped the Jews, because fear of Mordecai had seized them" (9:2–3). The Jews can now live peacefully throughout the kingdom of Persia, at least as long as Mordecai and Esther remain influential in the courts of the king.

12. Purim (9:18–32)

With the endorsement of the king, Mordecai sends a letter to all the Jews of the kingdom and institutes the feast of Purim (or "lots"). Since then, on the fourteenth and fifteenth of Adar, Jewish communities around the world celebrate the triumph of the deliverance of the Jews of Persia (9:28). During this feast, the book of Esther is read in synagogues, and active participation by the congregation is strongly encouraged. Cheers are shouted at the mention of Esther and Mordecai, while hisses and jeers are yelled at the mention of Haman. Families commemorate the event by "giving presents of food to one another and gifts to the poor" (9:22).

13. Mordecai Is Exalted (10:1–3)

Surprisingly, the book ends with an exposition of Mordecai's fame rather than a description of Esther's accomplishments. Queen Esther's role seems to have faded, while Mordecai is exalted and granted the ultimate reward. His deeds are recorded in the royal annals, and his "acts of power and might, together with a full account of his greatness" (10:2), are recompensed by the king with a promotion to the highest position in the royal courts, second in command to the king himself (10:3).

Humiliation by impaling, as shown in an Assyrian relief (Nineveh, 700–692 BC) of the siege of Lachish (cf. Esther 9:14)

Conclusion

The story of Esther begins and ends with a feast, and throughout the whole book, banquets, celebrations, parties, and festivities fill the story line. Food and drink abound, as lavish affairs show off wealth and power, celebrate important events, and commemorate victories.

The content of the book is entertaining and comical, and its characters are colorful and amusing. But even more significant, the book of Esther underlines numerous biblical truths. Among them, Haman's story confirms that "pride goes before destruction, a haughty spirit before a fall" (Prov. 16:18). Esther and Mordecai highlight the importance of fasting and contrition in order to receive direction from God (Esther 4:3; 9:31; 1 Pet. 3:12). Most of all, the book of Esther confirms that God is faithful to keep his promises and to deliver his people from oppression and destruction wherever they may be in the world (Ps. 124:1–8; Rom. 8:31).

The book of Esther reveals God's eternal love and providential care for his people. Dispersed in exile, the Jews were at the mercy of ruling powers and anti-Semites. But as depicted in the book of Esther, God's chosen people are never alone. At home or away, they dwell in his presence, receive his protection, and delight in his abundant provision.

Although God's name is conspicuously absent from the book, every "coincidental" turn of events carries his inimitable imprint. God's omnipresence is felt throughout the narrative as he orchestrates events, responds to the faithful, thwarts the plans of enemies, delivers his people from annihilation, and restores their covenantal hope for a future.

Select Bibliography

Allen, Leslie C., and Timothy S. Laniak. *Ezra, Nehemiah, Esther.* New International Biblical Commentary. Peabody, MA: Hendrickson, 2003.

Baldwin, Joyce G. *Esther.* Tyndale Old Testament Commentaries. Downers Grove, IL: InterVarsity, 1984.

Bechtel, Carol M. *Esther.* Interpretation. Louisville: Westminster John Knox, 2002.

Berlin, Adele. *Esther.* JPS Bible Commentary. Philadelphia: Jewish Publication Society, 2001.

Day, Linda. *Esther.* Abingdon Old Testament Commentaries. Nashville: Abingdon, 2005.

Fox, Michael V. *Character and Ideology in the Book of Esther.* 2nd ed. Grand Rapids: Eerdmans, 2001.

Jobes, Karen H. *Esther.* NIV Application Commentary. Grand Rapids: Zondervan, 1999.

Kahana, Hanna. *Esther: Juxtaposition of the Septuagint Translation with the Hebrew Text.* Leuven: Peeters, 2005.

Klein, Lillian R. *From Deborah to Esther: Sexual Politics in the Hebrew Bible.* Minneapolis: Fortress, 2003.

Levenson, Jon Douglas. *Esther.* Old Testament Library. Louisville: Westminster John Knox, 1997.

Millgram, Hillel I. *Four Biblical Heroines and the Case for Female Authorship: An Analysis of the Women of Ruth, Esther, and Genesis 38.* Jefferson, NC: McFarland & Company, 2008.

The Poetic Books

The ancient Hebrews were a people skilled in composing forceful, elegant poetry. Nearly one-third of the Hebrew Bible is actually written in this manner. For example, the prophets used poetic oracles to teach covenant theology, and the powerful *qinah* or "dirge meter" was used both to pronounce doom upon disobedient Israel and to lament the devastation when the pronounced judgment was fulfilled. One section of the Old Testament is referred to specifically as the Poetic Books. Among these books, Psalms, Proverbs, and Song of Solomon are entirely poetic in form. The other two books in this division of the canon, Job and Ecclesiastes, contain poetic portions.

Unlike English poetry, which often focuses on rhyme, Hebrew poetry is characterized by rhythm: both rhythm of sound (including patterns of stressed and unstressed syllables, assonance and alliteration, and wordplay) and rhythm of thought (typically described as various types of parallelism). Poetic parallelism takes many forms, including the use of synonymous words, matched word pairs, opposite words, and progressive or sequential words and phrases. Hebrew poetry is the language of the heart; it is rich in metaphor and vibrant with word pictures.

Poetry has advantages over prose in that, through the use of throbbing rhythms, it can convey a message with elegance, emotion, and emphasis in such a manner as to make it memorable. Poetry is therefore an extremely important instrument for teaching. One way that the ancient Hebrews used the Psalms was to instruct the nation in its faith and history. Another function of the Psalms was devotional, as they examined the relationship between God and humankind in the varied circumstances of life—especially the circumstances that led to questions of theodicy, God's role in addressing the problem of evil in the world. These devotional compositions stressed the supreme might of Israel's God, his hatred of sin, the responsibilities of the covenant relationship, and the fate of the nation if it disobeyed or rejected his will. The Psalms also reveal a deity who cares greatly for

This ancient statuette depicts a person playing a lyre, an instrument mentioned frequently in Psalms.

451

his people and longs to shower his covenant love upon them.

As a collection of sung prayers, Psalms became the hymnbook of ancient Israel. Long after prophetic oracles had been fulfilled and the nation of Israel dispersed, the Psalms continued to minister to God's ancient people and remain still a centerpiece of Jewish worship. The Christian church incorporated this treasured legacy into its own worship in varying ways and continues to rejoice in the rich spirituality of the Psalms.

The Poetic Books also include a number of writings known as wisdom literature, especially Proverbs, Job, and Ecclesiastes. Hebrew wisdom literature was similar in many ways to its ancient Near Eastern counterpart, as all societies seek to cope with the uncertainties of human existence and ensure their survival by handing down the accumulated knowledge of experience and observation. The concept of "the fear of the Lord" was foundational to the Hebrew wisdom tradition. For Israel, wisdom and the knowledge of God were inseparable since God is the source and dispenser of insight and understanding. Much of Hebrew wisdom is instruction and practical commentary on the law of Moses, designed to help the people of God navigate life safely and successfully.

Job

GARY A. LONG

Introduction

On the surface, the book of Job is a simple story: Job, a pious man, is struck down in the prime of life. He and his friends strive to understand the reasons for his calamities. God appears and Job is restored.

Dig deeper, though, and one quickly understands why this book commands the attention it does among scholars, clerics, and interested readers. Crosscurrents, complexities, ambiguities, and contradictions play out. It soothes and it frustrates. Sitting squarely within the biblical corpus of wisdom literature, the book is, in part, a counterpoint to the theology of piety and sin developed in Proverbs, represented in the words of Job's friends. We encounter biblical point/counterpoint in substantive fashion.

We enter now into the world of Job, the literary work and the character. Here in the introduction, the path ahead is first to recognize that literature like Job had company. We will then consider the book's interpretive hurdles, and, in light of some of those hurdles, consider how one may make sense of the final form we encounter in the Bible.

Mesopotamian Parallels

We should not be surprised to encounter Job-like literature outside of Job. Suffering is universal, and contemplating unexpected suffering in the face of believing that one has faithfully lived out the will of a deity is clearly Mesopotamian. Though Job shares similarities with some Mesopotamian literature, comparisons to the *entirety* of Job do not stand.

An important characteristic blossoms when one looks at the dialogues in Job and the Mesopotamian parallels. Sophistication and high literary art are seemingly found within an author's ability to revisit and to recraft a point into many elaborations, much like musical variations on a theme. Yes, there is development, to be sure, but repetition lies at the core.

Sumerian. "Man and His God," or "Sumerian Job" (*COS* 1.179:573–75), is the earliest Mesopotamian example to explore social and physical suffering among the pious. The demons Namtar and Asag play a role in the suffering of a virile young man. Only after the man affirms that "never has a sinless child been born to its mother" (line 104), and at the city gate publicly declares his sins (line 115), does he receive restitution. Accepting this sufferer's prayer, the god fully restores him "to joy" and protects him with guardian spirits. Sumerian Job, in the end, then, embraces a traditional or orthodox understanding of retributive theology (that the good prosper and the wicked are punished). This tale lacks dialogue, so robustly used within biblical Job, telling its story through monologue and the narrator's voice. Unlike biblical Job, this tale offers no challenge to traditional retributive theology.

Akkadian. "Dialogue between a Man and His God" (*COS* 1.151:485) is the earliest known Akkadian exploration of human suffering, coming from the Old Babylonian period, circa 1800–1600 BC. Its fragmentary nature shrouds our understanding, but it clearly explores a man suffering illness who is eventually restored by divine favor.

From the Kassite period, circa 1600–1200 BC, comes the "Poem of the Righteous Sufferer," known also from the words of the opening line as *Ludlul bel nemeqi* ("I Will Praise the Lord of Wisdom") (*COS* 1.153:486–92; see photo). Throughout the poem, we hear in monologue the voice of the sufferer, Shubshi-meshre-Shakkan, a prosperous gentleman. The opening line is truly apropos. Praise opens and closes his tale, and nothing undermines genuine adoration. Shubshi-meshre-Shakkan loses status, respect, and his wealth. His body, racked with pain, wastes away from debilitating disease and acute affliction. His calamity is punishment from the god Marduk, who later restores him fully. A story line of praise-calamity-restoration-praise does not include the rhetoric of protesting innocence found in Job.

"A Sufferer's Salvation" (*COS* 1.152:486) is a fragmentary Akkadian text (Ras Shamra 25.460) that comes from the city-state of Ugarit, near the shores of the Mediterranean in Syria, in the Late

The Babylonian "Poem of the Righteous Sufferer" (also called *Ludlul bel nemeqi*) from the library of Ashurbanipal (seventh century BC)

Bronze Age (ca. 1550–1200 BC). In a similar vein to the "Poem of the Righteous Sufferer" (or, *Ludlul bel nemeqi*), a protagonist—a single voice—is afflicted, then brought back from the brink of death by Marduk, a cause for grateful praise: "I praise, I praise, what the lord Marduk has done. . . . He thrust me away, then gathered me in, He threw me down, then lifted me high" (lines 29, 38–39).

The Babylonian Theodicy (*COS* 1.154:492–95), a text from circa 1100–1000 BC with a later Seleucid-era (after 300 BC) commentary found in Sippar, near Babylon, is usually regarded as the closest parallel to Job's poetic core (3:1–42:6). In form, the Babylonian Theodicy is a dialogue between one sufferer and one friend. The sufferer shuns established understanding, rejecting the idea that god rewards the good and punishes the transgressor. The sufferer's own life verifies his claim. From youth, "with prayer and supplication" he pursued the will of god, yet he suffers. The friend resolutely affirms the long-standing tradition the sufferer shuns. In content, Job (particularly chapters 3–27) and the Babylonian Theodicy share similar rhetoric, yet on the whole they are really quite dissimilar. Most agree that the Theodicy and Job share little beyond a common intellectual pursuit scholars call Wisdom tradition, known among their respective societies.

Date

To speak of a date for a book within the Hebrew Bible is not without complexity. First, by date, does one mean the *origin* of a story? Or does one mean the date of a book's *final composition*—that is, the form that draws from, compiles, or edits earlier oral or written stages and is preserved, essentially, in extant manuscripts like the Dead Sea Scrolls or Masoretic Text?

Stories can be fluid. At any one cross section in time, they may have different versions, diverse storytellings. Further, as they travel down through time, they may change, embracing different details. One sees such difference clearly within the pages of the Christian canon. (1) Second Timothy 3:8 names the Egyptian magicians who combat Moses: "Just as Jannes and Jambres opposed Moses . . ." Nowhere, though, does the Hebrew Bible mention these names. The magicians are anonymous (Exod. 7:11, 22). The *Damascus Document*, however, mentions "Jannes and his brother" rising up against Moses (5:17–19), and *Targum Pseudo-Jonathan* cites both names (Exod. 1:15). (2) Jude matter-of-factly talks about a dispute between Michael and the devil over Moses's body (Jude 9). You will read no such detail in the Hebrew Bible, but the dispute is attested in later literature, including Clement of Alexandria (*Fragments on the Epistle of Jude*), Origen (*On First Principles* 3.2.1), and *Pseudo-Oecumenius* at Jude 9. Stories can have multifaceted lives, and for Job we must keep these questions and issues particularly in mind.

Rabbinic and early Christian voices speak to a wide range of suggested dates. The discussion of rabbinic voices in *Baba Batra* 15a–b of the Babylonian Talmud is illustrative. One opinion holds that Job lived in the time of Jacob and married Dinah, his daughter. Rabbi Joshua ben Levi ben Lahma believed that Job was contemporary with Moses. Another says, "The span of Job's life was from the time that Israel entered Egypt until they left it." Raba said that Job lived in the time of the spies. Rabbi Nathan opined that Job "was in the time of the kingdom of Sheba," basing his claim on "the Sabeans attacked" (Job 1:15). The Sages placed him in the time of the Chaldeans (Job 1:17). Rabbis Johanan and Eleazar both stated that Job was among those who returned from the Babylonian exile, living in Tiberias. Rabbi

Joshua ben Korhah situated Job in the time of Ahasuerus (Persian). One rabbi even suggested, "Job never was and never existed, but is only a typical figure." Early Christian scholarship, in essence, echoes the rabbinic voices.

Scholarship from the last century to the present generally favors a range from the sixth through fourth centuries BC. Let us consider the data.

Early Date. Job's world, fashioned within the text, points to a hoary antiquity, a time similar to, if not before, the world of the patriarchs encountered in the pages of the Bible. Job's wealth is measured in large part by his possessions—animals and servants (1:3; 42:12; cf. Gen. 12:16; 32:5–6). Rather than the later shekel, the monetary unit is the *qesitah* (42:11; Gen. 33:19). Job offers sacrifice without intervention of a priestly class. His life span exceeds those of the patriarchs. Never do we read explicitly of events and notions important to an Israelite: Abraham, exodus, conquest, or exile. Never do we encounter the thought of monarchy, the temple, or the prophets. Admittedly, several of these characteristics could be linked not to chronology but to geography. The story does begin, after all, "In the land of Uz there lived a man whose name was Job."

The name Job seems to occur in cognate languages in the second millennium BC and thus is an "old" name (see commentary on 1:1–5). Close variants are found in the Egyptian Execration texts (early second millennium), at Mari (eighteenth century), at Alalakh (both eighteenth and fifteenth centuries), and at Ugarit (fourteenth century).

The prophet Ezekiel lists three names that apparently had become synonymous with "righteousness": Noah, Daniel, and Job. The prophet envisions a country's devastation by beasts then sword then plague (Ezek. 14:15–19). In this context, God, through Ezekiel, utters, "Even if these three men—Noah, Daniel and Job—were in [the country], they could save only themselves by their righteousness" (Ezek. 14:14), and "even if Noah, Daniel and Job were in it, they could save neither son nor daughter. They would save only themselves by their righteousness" (Ezek. 14:20). The context suggests that these men shared a righteousness that saved even their children. Though this is not an unimportant issue, our focus here will remain on these names as insight into dating.

At first blush, with the biblical canon in mind, all three can qualify as "righteous." Noah and Job are *explicitly* declared so (Gen. 6:9; Job 1:1). Daniel, the character in the biblical book by the same name, is *not* explicitly declared righteous, but one could argue that his disposition and behavior qualify him for such a label. Of the three, Noah is clearly a figure of righteousness placed in *antiquity*, Job perhaps so, given the world in the text; Daniel certainly is not, given his life in exilic Babylon.

But life, culture, and literature never occur in a vacuum. For many decades now, scholars have increasingly understood Daniel to be someone else. The city of Ugarit introduced the world to another Daniel, found in the Legend of Aqhat (*COS* 1.103:343–56), a story written roughly between 1550 and 1200 BC. Spelled with precisely the same consonants as Ezekiel's Daniel (the spelling in the book of Daniel has an additional consonant), Daniel is a pious and respected man known for his just verdicts at the city gate. That this is the Daniel whom Ezekiel has in mind is further suggested by Ezekiel 28:3. Here Ezekiel speaks against Tyre, for which Ugarit was a cultural ancestor: "Are you wiser than Daniel?" Most scholarship now understands that Ezekiel drew on three *ancient* characters of renown, Job being among them.

These features suggest an early *origin* and perhaps a long-standing story or at least portions of one. Other elements, however, point to a later time.

Late Date. Identifying concepts and morpho-syntactic linguistic determiners in the narrative bookends (1:1–2:13; 42:7–17), Avi Hurvitz has argued that the form of the story as we have received it likely could be no earlier than the exile (sixth century BC) (Hurvitz, 30). These same linguistic characteristics are not present in the poetic core (3:1–42:6). The core presents its own linguistic conundrums that make definitive statements elusive. Further, one must be cautious because any one language is not uniform at any one moment in time. Any assertion that this or that feature is here and not there must be expressed tentatively. With that in mind, the overall evidence seems to suggest that the poetic core (or portions of it) is earlier than the narrative prose as we have it.

Most commentators point to the presence of the Adversary (Hebrew *hassatan*, which in Job is not a personal name but a noun, *satan*, with the definite article, *ha*) as a nod to the postexilic period. We will take up this topic in more detail below in the commentary, under 1:6–12.

The "Chaldeans" (1:17) may indicate a later date. As a people, they first appear textually in the ninth century BC, living in the southern Euphrates-Tigris basin and toward Elam. In time, the Bible will use the label as a synonym for the Neo-Babylonian Empire and region associated with Nabopolassar and Nebuchadnezzar. In Job, Chaldeans are marauders. Are they one and the same? We cannot know for sure. When they "appear" in the ninth century, they are well established. We can therefore assume a vibrant prehistory. That said, the ubiquitous use of "Chaldean" throughout the Bible for a first-millennium-BC people and region and as an anachronism when it refers to Ur of the Chaldeans (Gen. 11:31) may well be echoed in Job.

"Sabeans" (1:15) and "Sheba" (6:19) might express first-millennium-BC realia. Though different in the NIV, the words are identically spelled in Hebrew (*sheba*). In Job 1:15 *sheba* attacks, carrying off Job's herds. Job 6:19 parallels the "caravans of Tema" with the "merchants of *sheba*." Controlling trade, particularly in the eighth to fifth centuries BC, Tema sat on a major artery known as the "incense road," which united the region of *sheba* in southwest Arabia with Syria and the Mediterranean. The *sheba* in Job might be this southwest Arabian region.

Equally plausible is that the story has in mind the vicinity of Wadi-Esh-Shaba in northwest Arabia, two hundred miles south of Tema. Marvin Pope believes that this northern *sheba* is mentioned by Assyrians Tiglath-Pileser III and Sargon II (mid to late eighth century BC); the "Saba," allied with Arabs, appear to be border raiders in the Assyrian annals (Pope, 13).

Job, then, in its canonical form, complete with narrative bookends and poetic core, nods to second- through mid-first-millennial phenomena that are packaged, in part, in language of the exilic or postexilic world. Do we have an early story with updated features or a late story with a created, archaized, patriarchal-like world, scrubbed of subsequent history? Ezekiel 14 suggests that Job the character had a long-standing tradition, but that is not the same as saying the story as we encounter it in the Bible and that tradition are precisely one and the same.

Composition

The journey to Job's becoming a biblical book is important, extremely complex, and shrouded in uncertainty. We would do well to ponder two underlying methodological principles when considering composition and sources. The first is to separate *fact* from *hypothesis*. The second—Occam's razor—is that hypotheses should not be multiplied beyond necessity. Job, in its extant, canonical form is *one* book, all together. That is *fact*. Burden of proof resides among the ranks of hypotheses that argue for compositional stages, and the voice of "hypothesis" should be humble and wary. However, naïveté about process is equally unwelcome.

Over the course of the past century, a consensus grew among scholarship that Job developed in stages. (1) An "original" Job was an oral story about a pious man. Elements of the current bookends are the only remnants of this early story. A now-missing middle exists no more but likely had three friends speaking critically of God, with Job refusing to utter anything unkind. (2) Keeping the bookends, a more ambitious story line explored the notion of Job challenging God's treatment of him while three friends affirmed traditional wisdom. A wisdom poem (28), Job's final soliloquy (29–31), and a speech by God (38:1–42:6) were inserted after the dialogues and before the epilogue. (3) Perhaps perceived as a more decisive refutation of Job, the Elihu character was next introduced (32–37).

"Job-by-stages" does have merit as a way of understanding some of Job's vexations, which we will discuss more fully below, under "Structure." The present bookends and poetic

Assyrian soldiers pursue Arabs fleeing on their camels in this relief from the North Palace at Nineveh (645–635 BC).

core appear dissonant. The friends recite well-affirmed traditional proverbial wisdom, yet they are scolded. Job becomes increasingly impatient and short with God, yet Job is fully exonerated. The Adversary appears in the prologue but is then hooked off the stage, never again seen or mentioned. Elihu, a fourth friend, is entirely overlooked in the epilogue. An understandable response has been to proffer a story developed by insertions and deletions by many hands over time. A century's prominence on compositional elements, however, was increasingly affirmed for what it was: an emphasis that shortchanged the *fact* that, whatever its compositional history, Job has a final, canonical form that must be taken seriously.

Structure

The relationship between Job's narrative bookends—the prologue (1–2) and epilogue (42:7–17)—and its poetic core (the rest of the book) is arguably complex, some might say strained. Notwithstanding works that argue for Job's overall unity, Bruce Zuckerman's following words summarize well the bulk of understanding among scholarship:

> The book of Job therefore appears to be at odds with itself; and however one may attempt to resolve its contradictory nature, the result never seems to be quite successful. Like oil and water, the Prose Frame Story and the Poem naturally tend to disengage from one another despite all efforts to homogenize them. (Zuckerman, 14)

David Clines offers one of the more sobering reflections on the whole of Job.

> The book of Job has an unequalled power to compel in its readers a suspension of disbelief. We cheer its hero on even though we know that he labours under a huge misapprehension, believing he is being declared a heinous sinner by God even while we know that God is counting him his boast. That suspension of disbelief on the level

of the plot has its analogy on the level of its ethics, in that a book that is fundamentally concerned with cosmic morality has embedded in it at key moments deeply troubling ethical difficulties.
>
> What is truly amazing about the book is that for the most part its readers do not even notice that there are any ethical problems. Whole volumes devoted to the book of Job rhapsodize about its theological depth and its grand vision of the governance of the universe without a glance at the act of gross divine injustice against Job that is the springboard of the whole drama—the unprovoked and unjustifiable assault of heaven upon Job's person and property. And that is just one of the several ethical problems the book raises. (Clines 2004, 248–50)

For all its grandeur, Job offers some difficult, nagging questions. (1) Why, really, does Job go through the suffering he does? (2) Why does Job have to be kept in the dark about the reasons for his suffering? (3) Why does God respond in the overpowering fashion he does? (4) Why does the book, at the end, apparently reaffirm the principle of retribution, against which Job has fought but for which the friends have argued (Clines 2004, 233–50)?

In similar vein, as we visit the bookends versus the poetic core, we encounter, so it seems, somewhat disparate stories. If we emphasize the bookends, the story of Job is a testing of the motivation behind the protagonist's blameless behavior. The prologue centers on the Adversary and a contest: can a human love God for God's sake alone? Is it devotion, without qualification, to God regardless, or is it devotion as a means to be and remain prosperous? Two rounds of calamity later, Job has not sinned "by charging God with wrongdoing" (1:22) or "in what he said" (2:10). In the epilogue, the Adversary is gone, the three consoling friends are chided, and Job is reinstated. The curtain can close.

If, however, we accentuate the poetic core, the story flirts with skepticism and explores whether the upright and the wicked get expected consequences. Job maintains that he is pious; the friends, including Elihu, argue that Job's calamities demonstrate that he is not. Job, the almost-silent, serene, and patient transforms into Job, the boisterous and impatient. Job feels victimized throughout by God and unable to have a hearing. Job's words in chapter 24, in fact, argue that prosperity among those who act unjustly or violently verifies that God is derelict in addressing injustice. God, of course, finally does appear but seemingly will have none of it, effectively shutting Job down. "Who is this that darkens my counsel with words without knowledge?" (38:2). "Would you discredit my justice? Would you condemn me to justify yourself?" (40:8). God, throughout his speeches, emphasizes chaos and the myopia of human understanding, justifying neither Job nor the friends.

But let's explore more closely the whole and specifically the shift from poetic core to final bookend. God indicts only three friends, Eliphaz, Bildad, and Zophar: "I am angry . . . because you have not spoken of me what is right, as my servant Job has" (42:7). This creates tension. First, God has earlier rebuked Job. Second, although the friends are declared wrong, they are correct about the doctrine of retribution. Job *is* innocent, and he *is* rewarded! It is as they have argued. The righteous prosper.

The desire for a neat, unified message is understandable. A univocal text, theologically, seemingly affirms the notion of God-as-Author who speaks *consistently* throughout the whole of Scripture. Philosophically, such a text supports a supposition that truth is best communicated by logical, noncontradictory propositions. But univocality is not universally justified. It is not found in biblical parallel historical accounts, not in the message of Proverbs versus Ecclesiastes, and not in Job.

What do we make of Job as a whole? How do we go forward understanding the final casting of this book?

Brevard Childs offers an important framework. (1) Though Job has component parts,

they interact with each other, begging for a holistic treatment, and (2) any interpretation of the holistic treatment must keep the tensions (Childs, 543–44).

In recent years, Mikhail Bakhtin has influenced biblical studies, particularly his notion of "polyphony," rooted in his perception that human experience has both centrifugal and centripetal forces. One force thrusts us out, encountering ever more variety, ever different voices, ever more complexity. Another force gathers one in, highlighting sameness and unity. Life is polyphonous. For Bakhtin, Dostoevsky's literary art achieved a polyphonic ideal. Wayne Booth offers the following insight about Dostoevsky, through Bakhtin's eyes:

> [Dostoevsky] genuinely surrenders to his characters and allows them to speak in ways other than his own. Heroes are no longer diminished to the dominating consciousness of the author; secondary characters are no longer encompassed by and diminished to their usefulness to heroes—or to the author. Characters are, in short, respected as full subjects, shown as "consciousnesses" that can never be fully defined or exhausted, rather than as objects fully known, once and for all, in their roles—and then discarded as expendable. . . . In the finest fiction, the author's technique will not be marshaled to harmonize everything into a single unified picture and to aid the reader to see that picture. (Bakhtin, xxii–xxiii)

Time may likely show that Bakhtin has been oversummoned among biblical scholars, but Job—the literary work—and polyphony are not incompatible colleagues. Carol Newsom aptly observes, "No one voice can speak the whole truth. Rather, the truth about piety, human suffering, the nature of God, and the moral order of the cosmos can be adequately addressed only by a plurality of unmerged consciousnesses engaging one another in open-ended dialogue" (Newsom 2003, 24). In polyphony, authors, readers, and characters do not "give up holding passionately to claims of truth. But such positions are held in humility, as one engages in the discipline of seeing how one's position appears from the perspective of another" (Newsom 2003, 262). Indeed, among the other members of wisdom literature, the divergence between the respective voices of Proverbs and Ecclesiastes on life demonstrates further the interaction of multiple voices. In Job we should likely not go searching for tidy univocality. Rather, we should experience Job for its mirror reflection on calamity's untidiness. We should note the *processes* of processing tough circumstances.

Therein do we find a core value of this book. It is not primarily addressing *whether* the innocent suffer or *why* they do, though it speaks to these. And we do not encounter definitive, all-encompassing insight into God's relationship with suffering. Rather, the book, again, mirrors what a God-fearing innocent—at least this paradigmatic innocent—*does* when tragedy strikes. The book's greatest value is the insight and evaluative contemplation that arises from looking in on Job's uneven actions and the polyphonous words and ideas he hears and he himself speaks. The focus is on Job and his journey.

Synopsis

(Job 1–2)	Blameless, upright, and full of wealth,
	    Job has family, flock, and health.
	A deity's boast, a challenger's dare:
	    "Job's virtue will crumble, just lay him bare!"
	Challenge accepted, calamity rife,
	    nothing left but ailing life.
	Three friends arrive, in mournful silence,
	    days and nights, no words, in alliance.

(3)	"Curse my birth!" Silence is broken.

(4–27)	Counsel by friends, in turn, is spoken,
	"Upright don't perish,
	    their lives, not nightmarish."
	Diffident, defiant, on they natter,
	    indignant becomes their chatter.

(28)	Exhausted with friends and his stigma, ponder does Job on wisdom's enigma,
(29–30)	gladness past and present-day sadness,
(31)	a court to boast his lack of badness.

(32–37)	Voice *for* God, brash Elihu offers
	    insight he's sure the friends have not
	    proffered.

(38–42:6)	Voice *of* God roars and expresses
	    He understands all world's processes.
	Behemoth, Leviathan, creatures of chaos;
	    Humans crave order, they think they're the
	    bosses.
	But order and chaos are life's forces.
	    Job sits silent, God's voice he endorses.

(42:7–17)	Three friends are indicted,
	    Job with new life, united,
	    restored, completely a-righted.

Outline

Book Outline

Poetic Core

PROLOGUE 1–2	Job's Opening Soliloquy, 3	1st Cycle, 4–14	2nd Cycle, 15–21	3rd Cycle, 22–27	Wisdom 28	Job's Closing Soliloquy, 29–31	Elihu 32–37	God & Job 38–42:6	EPILOGUE 42:7–17
		Eliphaz, 4–5 Job, 6–7 Bildad, 8 Job, 9–10 Zophar, 11 Job, 12–14	Eliphaz, 15 Job, 16–17 Bildad, 18 Job, 19 Zophar, 20 Job, 21	Eliphaz, 22 Job, 23–24 Bildad, 25–26(?) Job, 27:1–12 Zophar(?), 27:13–23(?)					

Narrative "Bookends"

Commentary Outline

Commentary

This commentary does not explore the book chapter by chapter. Every reader can experience the book in that fashion. Rather, we have focused on sections and characters, attempting to present to the reader a vista that sees the whole of them in a less fractured setting than the setting in the story. This context will then complement a chapter-by-chapter reading.

1. Prologue and Epilogue (1:1–2:13; 42:7–17)

A significant poetic story plays out between these two bookends, but few doubt a close connection between Job's prologue and epilogue, and for good reason. Both are composed in prose, stitched throughout with similar thread. (1) When speaking with the Adversary, God speaks of Job as "my servant Job" (1:8; 2:3). When speaking to the three friends, God uses precisely the same phrase four times (42:7–9). (2) "A *foolish* woman" is Job's indictment of his wife's response (2:10); folly is in view in Job 42:8. (3) The banquetlike gathering in the epilogue (42:10–11) has the thread of similar feasting in the prologue (1:4–5). (4) Sympathy and comfort recur (2:11; 42:11). (5) The number of livestock is precisely doubled in the epilogue (1:3; 42:12).

(6) A baseline of the number of children is in mind in both (1:2; 42:13). From another angle, in the introduction, under "Composition" and "Structure," we have already rehearsed some of the arguable dissonance between the bookends and the poetic core, uniting even further the former. With fear of oversimplification, we can say that much of the dissonance arises from Job's carte blanche reinstatement, which accords more with the moral world of the narrative than with the poetic core. The ending clashes with the complexity developed in the poetic core.

But we embrace the advice of Childs, mentioned above: though Job has component parts, they interact with each other, begging for a holistic treatment, and any interpretation of the holistic treatment must keep the tensions (Childs, 543–44). Whatever the path to the form of Job we now have, the epilogue serves as denouement. For the narrative story of the bookends, the epilogue offers a rather simple, smooth, expected reversal of fortune. For the *whole* of Job, it creates, as we have said now several times, unexpected dissonance with many details. Incongruity notwithstanding, one commonly and understandably encounters efforts to soften or explain it away in a vein similar to "in the end, we are invited to interpret [Job's blessing] as arising of God's freedom enacted toward Job" (Janzen, 267).

If one embraces the dissonance—keep in mind the polyphony that permeates the story—the *whole* book explores the various aspects of the complex matrix of suffering and divine-human relationships. "The dissonance both recognizes and refuses the reader's desire for closure to the story and a definitive resolution of the issues it has raised" (Newsom 1996, 634). A reader is thrown toward more contemplation about the book's issues. The story is merely a morsel for a reader's thought process, not a full meal.

A. Prologue (1:1–2:13). **1:1–5.** The scene: Earth. Here we are introduced to Job and his exemplary piety, which even embraces actions on behalf of family.

Job's name (Hebrew *iyyob*) appears to be not uncommon. W. F. Albright suggested, from cognate evidence from the second millennium BC, that *iyyob* should be seen as a Hebrew form traceable to an earlier Semitic form *ayyabu*, a sentence name meaning, "Where (is) father?" (Albright, 226). Robert Gordis suggested that the name is linked to a single root, *'yb* "to hate," suggesting a meaning of "hated" or "persecuted one" (Gordis 1978, 10). J. Gerald Janzen embraced both, arguing that "word-plays through secondary etymology are a common device in biblical narrative" (Janzen, 34). Historical evidence supports Albright's analysis more strongly, but it is not impossible that, secondarily, the very name *iyyob*/Job teases out the main character's predicament.

Evidence places Uz, Job's homeland, in two different spots. (1) A locale near Edom is supported by several texts. Jeremiah mentions the kings of Uz immediately after mentioning Egypt and just before mentioning Philistine cities, Edom, Moab, Ammon, then Phoenicia (Jer. 25:19–22). Lamentations places Edom and Uz in parallel (Lam. 4:21), and, in the often eponymous nature of the Genesis narrative, one of the sons of Dishan, an Edomite chieftain, is Uz (Gen. 36:28). (2) Other texts support a location northeast of Israel. Genesis 10:23

and 1 Chronicles 1:17 claim Uz as a son of Aram, thus associating Uz with the Arameans. In Genesis 22:21, Uz is the firstborn of Abraham's brother Nahor and is thus affiliated with Upper Mesopotamia ("Nahor" appears as a geographical entity in the Mari letters of the early second millennium BC). One likely cannot reconcile the evidence. But a nod to the book's genre and place within wisdom literature may tip the scales toward Transjordanian Edom. Job is the greatest among "all the people of the *East*" (Hebrew *qedem*; 1:3). In praise of Solomon's wisdom, we are told that it surpassed a people known for their great wisdom, "the [people] of the *East* (Hebrew *qedem*; 1 Kings 4:30). Lamentations' parallelism of Edom and Uz suggests that Uz is a poetic referent associated with Edom. Perhaps it is fitting, then, that biblical Job lives in and around Edom, a region of Qedem, a home of legendary wisdom.

Job as "blameless," "upright," a God-fearer, and one who "shunned evil" (1:1) connects the book strongly with Proverbs. Proverbs 2:7; 2:28; and 28:10 speak of the blameless and the upright, using the very same words. Proverbs 3:7 admonishes the reader, again with the same vocabulary, to "fear the LORD and shun evil" (see also Prov. 14:16; 16:6). Job is an exemplary model of the proverbial ideal. Job's status is a foundation to the problem explored by the book: the suffering of one who has fulfilled wisdom's expectations of proper behavior. Job's "regular

The Transjordanian region of Edom, one possible location for Uz, Job's homeland

custom" (1:5) of ritual purifica- tion and sac- rificing burnt offerings serves as an explicit example of Job's piety.

In verse 5 we are introduced to an interesting au- thorial feature related to the Hebrew root *brk*, which the storyteller uses seven times in Job. The author forces the reader to negotiate between the root's primary meaning, "bless" (1:10, 21; 42:12), and an oppo- site meaning, "curse" (1:5, 11; 2:5, 9). A meaning for this root is also found outside of Job (1 Kings 21:10, 13). Thought a euphemism, the antitheti- cal meanings in Job draw attention—one has to stop and decide on the meaning.

The numbers related to Job's possessions hint at the storyteller's craft. *Seven* sons and *three* daughters are "paralleled" by *seven* thousand sheep and *three* thousand camels. Sons number- ing seven appears to be a cultural concept of blessing or a full complement of male progeny (1 Sam. 2:5; Ruth 4:15).

1:6–12. The scene: the heavens. Amid an assembly of divine beings, the Adversary and God consider Job's behavior. Contemplating the Adversary's challenge about Job's motivations, God agrees to allow Job to be tested.

A council composed of divine beings is on the stage here. NIV's "angels" too easily mis- directs the modern reader. The idea of a divine council of deities is systemic throughout the ancient Near East. As but one example, the ancient West Semitic deity El presided over such a council (*COS* 1.86:241–74). A divine council underlies other texts in the Hebrew Bible (1 Kings 22:19–23; Isa. 6:1–8; Ps. 29:1; 82:1, 6; 89:5–7; Dan. 7:9–14), though the NIV's translation of the passages arguably shrouds, at times, the Hebrew's rhetoric and affinities with the cultural parallels.

This procession of four gods on a Neo-Hittite orthostat is similar to images featuring the gods gathering for a divine council.

One of the members of the heavenly council, "Satan" (so NIV) arrives with other members to present himself to the celestial ranks and to report on his affairs. "Satan," however, is not here a name but a role (as evidenced by the use in Hebrew of the noun *satan*, "accuser, adversary," with the definite article [*hassatan*]). The Adversary here is a skeptic or realist who has a good read on human nature in general. The concept of "satan" is certainly not uni- form and shows development. A *satan* has the *function* of a "messenger" sent by Yahweh to impede Balaam (Num. 22:22, literally "a mes- senger of Yahweh placed himself in the way as a *satan* to [Balaam]"). The *satan* increasingly becomes an adversarial being in postexilic biblical writing (after 539 BC). In Zechariah 3:1–2, *hassatan* is rebuked by a messenger of Yahweh. In 1 Chronicles 21:1 *satan* is appar- ently for the first time a personal name and a being responsible, in the Chronicler's mind, for standing against Israel and inciting David. To read into Job the much-later and present theological notions of Satan as the devil is to misunderstand this Joban character. One com- mentator has tried to capture the idea by British parliamentary parlance: His Majesty's Loyal Opposition (Janzen, 262). In Job, the Adver- sary appears to be in the habit of patrolling the earth looking for indictable behavior. In this scene, he stands within the heavenly council to report his findings.

Preemptively, through a rhetorical question, God himself boasts of Job in precisely the same terms as the narrator, "blameless and upright." The Adversary, with insight into normative human nature, responds with rhetorical questions of his own, focusing on Job's motivation: "Does Job fear God for nothing? Have you not put a hedge around him?" Removing the protection would expose Job as no paragon of piety. God accepts the challenge. His role may be exonerated by pointing out that *the Adversary* is the true agent of Job's destruction. Though true, the view is likely overly optimistic and guilty of hand-washing. God and the Adversary, at the end of the day, have joined hands and together will see Job ruined (see further comments below under 2:1–7a).

1:13–22. The scene: Earth. Four reports describe the systemic ruin of Job's property and children.

A joyous day ends with unspeakable calamity. After describing a cheerful day of feasting, the narrative introduces four messengers bringing news of four catastrophic events. The rhetoric is formulaic and repetitive. Human predators and what most likely are natural events alternate as the destructive agents.

Sabeans attack, carrying off oxen and donkeys. "Fire of God," most likely lightning, consumes the sheep. Chaldeans sweep away the camels, and a "mighty wind" collapses Job's oldest son's house. In each episode, individuals called *nearim* (literally "young ones") are killed. In the first three, *nearim* are "servants." In the fourth, translated as "them" (1:19), they are Job's sons and daughters.

Job lies ruined. He tears his outer robe and shaves his head, typical expressions of grief and mourning (Gen. 37:29; Isa. 15:2; Jer. 7:29; *COS* 1.86:268 = actions of 'Ilu when he hears of Ba'lu's death in the Ugaritic Ba'lu myth). He falls to the ground and "worships," the common word for obeisance before divinity (Gen. 24:26)

and royalty (1 Sam. 24:9). His words express a cultural proverbial expression of human fate (Eccles. 5:15): "Naked I came . . . naked I will depart." The proverbial idiom is followed by a religious one, which orients the events around the activity of God: "The LORD gave and . . . has taken away." In expressing "may the name of the LORD be praised," Job has contradicted the Adversary. Yet, in somewhat teasingly ironic rhetoric, Job has also fulfilled the Adversary's prediction. The Hebrew root *brk* (translated as "be praised"; see comments on 1:1–5) is once again at play here. In Job 1:11, the Adversary claimed that Job would *brk* God—"curse" God. Here Job does *brk* God, but in light of the narrator's assessment of Job's actions in verse 22, Job clearly has "blessed" him.

2:1–7a. The scene: the heavens. We are whisked up again to the assembly of divine beings in council, where, in almost precise repetition of the previous heavenly scene, God and the Adversary contemplate Job.

One can imagine God reveling somewhat in his dialogue with the Adversary. Begrudgingly, the latter must agree with God that Job, devastated by the turmoil of the previous scene, has nevertheless maintained his "integrity" (from the same Hebrew root as "blameless"; cf. 1:1), his spotless character (2:3). It is possible to see confident gloating through the last few words of verse 3: "You incited me against him to ruin him *without any reason*." In the Hebrew, the term is a recurrence of the Adversary's own term at the opening of his rhetorical question in Job 1:9 ("Does Job fear God *for nothing*?"). But unlike its initial use in the Adversary's mouth, the term can also denote "in vain" (Mal. 1:10 RSV; cf. Ps. 109:3, "without cause"). God could well be celebrating that it was in vain that the Adversary set in motion the events that transpired. He lost.

More plausibly, though, and more troublingly for the reader, one likely encounters God's implicit admission that the Adversary was successful first in that he incited God to ruin Job and second in that it was "without any reason"; that is, it was gratuitous or undeserved. If correct, we view an increasingly darker underbelly to this book. Not only has God agreed to allow Job to suffer once "without any reason," but he is about to agree to yet another round.

The Adversary is quick with his next challenge, this one against Job's own person. "Skin for skin," because of its enigmatic terseness, is a phrase that has received much attention. As with most interpretation, the immediate textual environment is vital: "A man will give all he has for his own life" (2:4). The words and the context suggest that the Adversary, in effect, is saying that a person will give anyone else's skin to save their own (Gordis 1978, 20). Struck with physical ailments, Job will curse (Hebrew root *brk*; see comments on 1:1–5) God, or so the Adversary boasts.

2:7b–10. The scene: Earth. The Adversary afflicts Job's body. Job responds to his wife's presence and words, and he is affirmed as one who "in all this, did not sin."

Job's affliction has received much attention; commentators have understandably taken on the role of physician and attempted to provide a diagnosis. Whatever the disease, it is one that affected his skin and, more important, one that likely evoked the stigma of divine displeasure. Job's disease is one with which God promises to curse the Israelites if they fail to obey the covenant (Deut. 28:35).

Illness and the activity of the gods were closely linked in the ancient world. This Neo-Assyrian amulet depicts Lamashtu (the large figure standing on the donkey), who was believed to cause many illnesses. The amulet would be placed above the bed of a sick person to call on the gods for healing.

The narrative of a fragmentary Aramaic text from the Dead Sea Scrolls, known as the *Prayer of Nabonidus* (4Q242/4QPrNab ar), describes how the Babylonian king was afflicted by this same disease. Only after a Jewish exile forgives his sins and instructs him to pray to "God Most High" is the king healed.

Job's wife enters, focusing on her husband's "integrity," the same word affirmed by God above in Job 2:3. The wife's words are rich—and ambiguous. Job's wife may believe that holding on to integrity is now a futile act. It no longer pays out the dividend of "the good life." But, given the self-conscious exploration of the book and the arguments of the soon-to-arrive friends, his wife may be setting a theme similar to that of the friends: "Why are you holding on to your *own, self-centered* integrity that has you falsely clinging to the notion that you are pious? Calamity undermines your claims of piety! Curse [Hebrew root *brk*] God, and then you will die!" Her motivation is also unclear. Her words could be callous indifference (as they are widely understood to be)—just die! Or she could be offering loving compassion—death would have to be a better condition for him than the present misery.

The Septuagint expands the wife's presence, giving her more to say. Her words there remind the reader of cultural realities. She *herself* has grievously suffered. Her children, of course, are

465

gone. But *her* income, *her* status, *her* reputation—because of her cultural dependency on her husband—are gone as well.

The Hebrew expression underlying the narrator's affirmation of Job's character is literally that Job does not sin "in/with his lips." This led the rabbinic commentator Rashi to suggest that Job does sin, not *with his lips* but *in his heart* or *thoughts*. Though this is intriguing, it is better to keep in mind that the omniscient storyteller has carefully woven Job's blamelessness and uprightness throughout the story so far. The expression at hand should not serve as a new hedge to Job's blameless character. That said, Janzen does compare the differences between Job's first response (1:20–22) and his second here, arguing that Job's initial stalwart confidence in God, God's ways, and himself has eroded (Janzen, 51–55). If so, we may see an *editorial* nod in producing the final, canonical version of Job. Already in the narrative prologue, we may see a patient Job transforming into the increasingly impatient Job of the poetic core.

2:11–13. The scene: Earth. Three friends arrive and in silence sit with Job, mourning.

Most believe that Job's three friends are geographical neighbors. Underlying NIV's "sympathize" is a Hebrew word that refers to a motion of nodding the head as an expression of commiseration. Sympathy so deep as to be devoid of words, expressible only through this movement, is understandable here. One may note the use of three and seven again (see 1:1–5). *Three* friends sit silent for *seven* days and nights.

B. Epilogue (42:7–17). The scene: Earth. God scolds Job's three friends, demanding that they offer sacrifices and that Job pray on their behalf. That action complete, Job is restored, blessed again with possessions, family, and a long life to enjoy them.

An entire poetic story has played out since the last scene in the prologue (2:11–13). We now encounter the only scene of the epilogue. God's words, particularly his affirmation about Job, to the three friends carve out a chasm between this scene and the poetic dialogue. If one feels compelled to harmonize, it is hard to imagine how to do so successfully. God asserts, "You have not spoken of me what is right, as my servant Job has" (42:7–8). The Hebrew word *nekonah* underlies NIV's "what is right," a term that denotes "correct." How does one mesh God's praise that Job has spoken "what is right" with his earlier rebuke that Job has spoken "words without knowledge" (38:2), which Job acknowledges later in his response to God (42:3)? One scholar, in fact, is compelled to say that in "Job's speeches can be found examples of some of the most anti-Yahwist sentiments of which we have any record in literature (9:15ff.) . . . [filled with] . . . audacity, defiance, and self-righteousness" (Polzin, 184). God's praise fits well with the bookends-only story line (1:1–2:13; 42:7–17), where Job's actions and words are a model of an acquiescent, soft-spoken affirmation of God's ways. But we do encounter a hurdle in that same story line when we consider the friends. They speak no words in it. The final "cut" of Job, though, envisions friends uttering God-censurable words. Most agree that Job, no matter what the proposed stages, had that component. Beyond that, disagreement quickly arises. What appears clearest is that both Job and the friends have indeed spoken, that God comments on those characters here in the epilogue, and that scholars have left us with two general paths to follow. One path strives to harmonize; the other does not.

Efforts to harmonize vary. (1) God, in his final praise, is hereby declaring that Job, despite vitriolic and seemingly contrary-to-God moments, is free from blame. Job's words are *nekonah* because they are "truth," "correct and consistent with the facts"; that is, they "correspond with reality . . . devoid of dissembling and flattery" (Habel, 583). (2) Even in his accusations, Job "has truly identified the fact that his terrible trials have transpired within God's world, a world for which God may properly and finally be held responsible" (Janzen, 264). (3) God is focusing on the correct elements within Job's words, particularly Job's "denying that sin is always punished with affliction and his holding fast to his innocence" (Pope, 350). (4) Job has spoken *to* God *directly*, not just *of/about* God, as the friends have done (Phillips, 41). (5) Job has been genuinely groping for truth, never turning his back on God. The friends' reductionistic theology, which underpins their counsel to confess sin in order to return to prosperity, would have led Job *away* from God and truth (Carson, 378–79). (6) Finally, in our representative samplings, no disharmony is even acknowledged (Dhorme, 648).

The other path celebrates the dissonance as purposeful and meaningful. God requires that the friends take seven bulls and rams to Job, who is to offer the animals as burnt sacrifices on his friends' behalf and then to pray. The number of animals is large and is somewhat reminiscent of the sacrifice of seven bulls and seven rams on seven altars in the Balaam story (Num. 23:1, 4, 14, 29–30). The effect of all this is seen in God's words to the friends: "I will accept [Job's] prayer and not deal with you according to your folly" (42:8). The NIV's translation leads the reader to see that the friends have somehow, somewhere in the story, committed folly. But we may be missing one of the most striking, and troubling, instances in the Hebrew Bible of attributing human feelings to God. We must consider two things: the structure of the utterance and the behavior in mind. (1) The words underlying Job 42:8 are a common idiom in the Hebrew Bible: "do *x* with *y*," where *y* is a person or entity and *x* is the behavior or concept, such as "loving-kindness," or "a morally reprehensible act" (Hebrew *nebalah*). Earlier, for example, Job has uttered, literally, "life and loving-kindness you have done with me" (10:12). God, in Job 42:8, literally says, "[I will] not do with you all a morally reprehensible act." (2) The behavior or concept here in Job 42:8, *nebalah*, many times throughout the Hebrew Bible refers to morally repugnant conduct (Gen. 34:7; Deut. 22:21; Josh. 7:15; Judg. 19:23; 20:6, 10; 2 Sam. 13:12; Jer. 29:23). Are the *friends* being accused of morally shocking behavior? If so, what is

it? No quorum unites commentators on what it would be. Another direction is to consider that God, in a didactic, wisdom story, is musing hypothetically about his own behavior. *God* does not want to commit *nebalah* against the friends, and Job's actions will appease God. In fact, one recent reading of Job argues that the story has earlier shown God guilty of *nebalah* when he granted the Adversary's requests to devastate an innocent man. In the epilogue, God is here putting a restraint in place for himself from further *nebalah*. Job has remained the constant one: an innocent intercessor in the beginning, an innocent intercessor at the end (Guillaume and Schunck, 457), though, as we will see, one who has not understood the bigger picture. One can understand some translators' and commentators' inclinations to see the friends as having acted with *nebalah*, but one must embrace an unprecedented understanding of the idiom—not impossible, but probably not the most prudent given the data.

When Job prays on behalf of the friends, God restores Job with twice as much as before. Brothers, sisters, and former friends all make their way to comfort and console him, each one giving him "a piece of silver" and a gold ring.

Job's flocks are doubled (1:3; 42:12), reparation elsewhere in the Hebrew Bible for one who has lost property through theft or a negligent trustee (Exod. 22:4, 7, 9). A new family of "seven sons and three daughters" is born to Job, the same as in the beginning (1:2). The Hebrew word for "seven," however, is considered by many to be a dual form: seven-twice, that is, fourteen. The Targum of Job, in fact, uses that very number. One may note that in 1 Chronicles 25:5, Heman, King David's seer, is given fourteen sons and three daughters "through the promises of God to exalt him." If this is all correct, Job's sons are doubled but his daughters are not. A conventional answer to this disparity is that, with culture in mind, males were a blessing while females were usually not an index of status and wealth. In fact, daughters could be a source of worry and concern (Sirach 26:10–12;

467

42:9–11). That said, the story of Job focuses on the daughters and their extraordinary beauty and makes the point that Job "granted them an inheritance along with their brothers." A final gesture of Job's bounty is his length of life. Over the course of 140 more years, Job is able to see his descendants down to the fourth generation. Living to see one's children's children (two generations) is already a blessed life (Ps. 128:6). Job, again, has doubled that.

So the epilogue of this story in its present form within the Masoretic Text produces dissonance. The affirmation that Job has spoken "what is right" calls out to the reader to consider again what Job has in fact said: God is derelict in addressing injustice (Job 24). God's Job-silencing speeches argue that order and chaos are the full experience of life. Human arrogance that expects order is what God dismantles. Chaotic forces have played havoc on Job. Yet God, in a sense, has unleashed them by allowing the Adversary to act. With a subtle nod of restoring Job to double his former life, God may actually be "owning up." Job receives reparation a thief or negligent trustee must pay out. Is this simply coincidence? And the friends have repeatedly urged Job to understand the world in ways that the epilogue verifies. For Eliphaz, as an example, God "injures, but his hands also heal" (5:19), just as the epilogue shows. As mentioned above, a reader is thrown toward more contemplation about the book and its message—a teasing morsel, not a completed meal.

2. Job's Opening Soliloquy (3:1–26)

The silence among the array of characters at the end of the prologue is shattered. The outburst is striking. Here, psychologically, Job moves from silence to give voice, in the company of others, to his calamity. Out of his anguish, Job curses his existence, focusing primarily on the day of his birth. Imagery of light and darkness, day and night weaves the soliloquy together. His outcry is beyond a response to his friends. It flows from the calamities that have befallen him. His sorrow, pain, and confusion fumble about together as raw emotion. None of the

prologue's detached, sterile setting has seeped in. Because of language similar to the Psalter's own laments, the psychological and interpretive effects of Job's words convey a suffering typical of all humanity, though extreme. Yet in Job the reader is somewhat of a voyeur. The psalmists' laments, often through generality, draw a reader in, and both share the despair. Though most recognize and understand Job's emotion, the precise details of his calamity serve as a small hedge, keeping distance. Like Job's friends, we look on and overhear his words, and they are not quite ours.

Job's soliloquy here and the one later in chapters 29–31 frame the three cycles of dialogues between Job and the friends.

3:1–10. The narrator tells us that Job opens his mouth to curse (the Hebrew root here is not *brk*, used in the prologue; see comments on 1:1–5), literally, "his day." In Job's soliloquy, we discover quickly that "his day" is about his origins: the day of his birth, the night of his conception. The NIV's wording of 3:3, which has in mind only a *birth*, diminishes Job's brilliant interplay. His words fade skillfully between the day of his birth and the night of his conception (3:3a: day; 3:3b: night; 3:4–5: day; 3:6–10: night). Day and night both merge and separate. The day of birth is, of course, different from the night of conception, yet both this day and night compose a day, the particular "day" that is the sum total of his creation. God's first words in the cosmos's creative process were "let there be light" (Gen. 1:3). About his own "creative" process, his birth, Job wails "That day—let there be darkness!" (3:4; NIV "may it turn to darkness"), a potent exclamation and a fitting curse for a *day*.

Given cultural parallels, one could expect in Job 3:8 something to do with "sea" in a poetic line that also has "Leviathan." In fact, "sea" does occur in the NRSV of Job 3:8 (cf. NIV note). From Ugaritic texts, Leviathan is one of several monsters associated with deified sea, that is, Yammu. They are forces of chaos. The Hebrew text is teasing in this respect. The

Hebrew Masoretic Text has literally "cursers of day" (*orere yom*), but many prefer a conjectural emended reading, "cursers of sea" (*orere yam*), thus giving a translation like "Let the Sea-cursers damn it [the night], those skilled to stir Leviathan" (Pope, 26). All this has the advantage of well-known mythological connections found in ancient Levantine cultures—those on the eastern Mediterranean seaboard—and in the Hebrew Bible (Ps. 74:13–14; Isa. 27:1), since it too is a product of Levantine people. But perhaps the word purposely plays with the early audience. The choice of *yom* ("day") for an expected *yam* ("sea") blends the expected mythological imagery with the storyteller's poetic examination of "day." The audience "gets it."

3:11–19. This section begins with "why." Job's attention shifts away from cursing "his day" to focus on questioning why he could not have died at birth. If such were the case, he would now be "asleep and at rest" (3:13). We have here a portal into the then-cultural concept of afterlife. Sheol—the word is not explicitly mentioned—the resting place of all who have died, is a preferable place to be. His wish balances extremes. Sheol's dreadfulness is diminished; Job's misery is heightened. Sheol here is little more than a peaceful realm where human status and rank are equalized—Job desires it! But Sheol elsewhere is a dark (Job 10:21–22; 17:13), snatching-away (Job 24:19), entangling, destructive enemy (Ps. 18:4–5)—Job prefers this? His present life is truly miserable.

Job's train of thought is first to question rhetorically why life-sustaining persons had to be present at his birth (3:11–13). If they had not been there, he would be in peaceful rest in the company of now-dead kings and rulers. In death, the infant and the great, the wicked and the weary, the captive and the slave, share rest.

Why Job focuses on kings and rulers is somewhat of a mystery. Their "footprint" on earth may rival Job's own precalamity presence. To use the most substantive among human dwellers as examples of life's transience and futility

is fitting. Their buildings now lie in ruin, their wealth left behind.

The last few verses (3:17–19) hone in on what Job desires most at this moment: peaceful rest from a baneful existence. The wicked, the weary, captive, slave, small, and great, now dead, all enjoy what Job wishes. The wicked have no more turmoil, the weary enjoy ease, and the captive lies deaf to the insults and demands of the slave master. They are all free.

3:20–26. "Why" opens this new section, which focuses on the plight of a sufferer, here and now on earth, before the grave. The nostalgia in the previous verses of what might have been gives way to what is.

Light reappears, still unwanted. Earlier, Job desired darkness (3:3–10). Now, in third-person point of view, a shift away from first person, Job explores how light torments the tormented. Why then does God provide it, Job rhetorically poses. The imagery of treasure hunters taps into the frenetic adrenaline rush of discovered treasure and is powerful in Job's mouth for describing a sufferer's hunt for death. But efforts are frustrated. Death does not come, and light floods in.

Shifting back to the first-person point of view, Job soberingly describes his own pain (3:24–26). Sighs are his food; groans are his water. His fears are realized. Rest—a theme throughout his soliloquy—is all he desires, yet his final words are painful: "but only turmoil," literally "but agitating trouble has come."

3. Three Cycles of Dialogue (4:1–14:22; 15:1–21:34; 22:1–27:23)

Job has no idea how true his last few words are. He has spoken them of his past. He will soon discover that they anticipate his future. The frustrating dialogues with the friends lie ahead—agitating trouble has indeed come.

Eliphaz, Bildad, and Zophar will by and large collectively affirm a traditional doctrine of divine retribution: God rewards good and punishes evil. Job will declare his innocence. The friends will increasingly grow frustrated with Job. Job will progressively become agitated with them and with God. The tension that arises from listening in on the characters cannot be resolved by omnisciently declaring the friends wrong and Job correct. Rather, we experience firsthand through their respective words the complexity of understanding suffering and the diversity of response to it. Polyphony is at play, mirroring real life.

Is this section truly a *dialogue*? Are the participants really responding to each other? A fairly widespread scholarly consensus says no. At the very most, the consensus concedes enough of an interaction for the sides to become irritated with what is being said.

The conversation does not sustain a point-by-point debate, and one does walk away from the dialogues feeling that the participants have largely talked past one another. This is understandable, given the very

Job's friends sprinkled dust on their heads to demonstrate their grief over his condition (Job 2:12). This practice was known in Egypt as well, as depicted in this painting of a woman putting dust on her head in mourning (tomb of Nebamun, ca. 1350 BC).

response to Eliphaz, for example, one feels the pathos welling up within Job over the discord between his life's reality and Eliphaz's counsel (Job 6–7). The same can be said for Job's reaction to Bildad and Zophar. Such features do interweave the dialogues, with the strongest stitching being disagreements or counterpoints. And once again the interweaving features of dialogue are found primarily in the opening verses of each speech. In the dialogues one does not find a parry matching every thrust, but fencing sabers are drawn and do touch.

In the main, however, the dialogues speak to a level beyond the characters sitting together. They constitute a disputation that explores, more globally, traditional ideology on misfortune. Job-as-sufferer and friends-as-advisors serve as vehicles to a conversation of grander scale. Wisdom literature is exploring itself.

different starting points. Job cannot begin where the friends do because he does not fit their paradigm.

The consensus is chiefly true, but it appears to be overstated. The first several verses of each speech arguably acknowledge past comments of other characters. In Job's first

Does each of the three friends have a distinct personality? Consensus asserts that Eliphaz is more distinct than the other two. Assessments of him as the oldest and most urbane are typical. Many see Bildad and Zophar together as less courteous and less tactful than Eliphaz, and some make Zophar much less restrained than Bildad.

Does each represent a particular point of view? Here things get a bit more muddled. Even those who argue for distinct perspectives argue them primarily from the first cycle. Whatever may be true from the first round of speeches becomes increasingly cluttered in the second and third rounds. With this important caveat in mind, and drawing primarily from the first round of speeches, one can nevertheless draw some generalities.

Eliphaz, firmly grounded in the principle of retribution, as are all three friends, grants a higher level of piety to Job than the other two (4:6) and, drawing on that, offers more consolation and encouragement. Bildad is certain that the wicked set their own misfortune because the world operates on God-ordained principles. Job's children are an example of that rule at work. Zophar, more certain of Job's sin than the other two, focuses on Job's miserable circumstances as the foundation to denounce him for sin that, because of his calamity, he surely has committed. His intent seems more to frighten Job into repenting of those sins (Job 21). As the dialogues continue, the friends' voices seem to merge almost into a collective character set against Job. The words of the friends narrow down to their communal undergirding that retribution befalls the sinful. Nearing the end of the dialogues, even Eliphaz, a champion for some level of Job's piety, is frustrated: "Is not your wickedness great? Are not your sins endless? . . . Submit to God and be at peace with him; in this way prosperity will come to you" (22:5, 21). Traditional proverbial wisdom, personified through Eliphaz, Bildad, and Zophar, is affirmed: the pious are rewarded, the impious are not; indeed, they are afflicted. But Job cannot embrace this wisdom, and neither can the omniscient reader. Eliphaz, Bildad, and Zophar, through their parroting of traditional human wisdom, register wisdom's failure to penetrate *fully* into and make sense *completely* of human suffering.

We will say more below (under "Job's Words") about Job's character throughout the dialogues. Suffice it to say here that he is on a journey, one that revisits a couple of prominent themes while at the same time moving forward in thought and understanding.

The dialogues through the first two cycles establish a symmetry: friend followed by Job. In the third cycle, however, the symmetry is disrupted, particularly after the final Eliphaz-Job interchange (22:1–24:17). From there, the text as we have received it shows the following characteristics.

1. The content of Job's reply to Eliphaz in 24:18–25 abruptly begins to sound like any of the three friends.
2. Bildad's third speech is very short (25:1–6) and lacks a customary direct response to Job, typical of his first two (8:2–7; 18:2–4).
3. Job's reply in 26:2–4 is grammatically a second-person address, "you," and specifically second-person *singular*. Hebrew makes a clear distinction in its grammar between second-person singular and plural. Until now, though, Job generally responds to *a* friend by using second-person *plural* forms. The Hebrew reader understands that Job has all along been saying "y'all," as it were, in response to a single friend's words. There are a few exceptions (12:7–8), but the plural is statistically the preference. Job, then, if we follow the received text, somewhat uncharacteristically addresses the friend here as singular. However, when a friend refers to Job in the second person, each generally uses singular forms, as expected (an exception is Bildad in 18:2–4).
4. In the middle of Job's reply to Bildad (Job 26), the narrator interjects, "And Job continued his discourse" (27:1), and does so again at Job 29:1, a point again

where Job seemingly has been speaking all along. Up to now, the narrator has interjected only to change speakers and has used different wording, "Then *x* replied."

5. Zophar has no third speech.

Most scholarship rearranges, in some fashion, the contents of Job 24:18–27:23. Clines has charted an array of proposals for the puzzle (2006, 629). How does one go forward through the maze?

Measured against two previous cycles, the third exhibits a different pattern and rhetoric, at times at odds with expectations. These are good grounds to question exactly what it is we have received. Do we have a corrupted text, a play with misplaced lines? If we do, we have no clear evidence from the earliest renditions. The Targum of Job, the Septuagint, and manuscripts display no reorientation.

If one affirms the text as is, without changes, one is also affirming the empirical over the hypothetical. A host of reconstruction, after all, may create a text that never existed except in the minds of scholars. Without changes, interpreters argue the following. Bildad's short speech and Zophar's absence accurately reflect the exhausted, frustrated state of the arguers. The rhetoric in Job's mouth of ideas that have been spoken by the friends is either straightforward citation or sarcastic parroting.

Preferring empirical evidence over hypothetical should not easily be pushed aside. But the cumulative weight of the characteristics we rehearsed above about the "post-Eliphaz" material in the third cycle warrants, in our opinion, some reassignment. We go forward with utmost caution and without entrenched conviction, but we think the following represents a helpful direction.

- Though sometimes Job 24:18–25 is reassigned to a friend, Job is still speaking here, in line with the Masoretic Text. We understand the grammatical mood of the language not to be declarative, as the NIV translates, but optative (that is, a hypothetical projection or wish of a situation or condition; see NJPS). Job *wishes* that God undid the wicked; he is not *declaring* it so.

- Bildad's second speech constitutes all of Job 25–26. Further, we are inverting Job 26:2–4 and Job 25:2–6, thus putting his speech into the following order: 25:1; 26:2–4; 25:2–6; 26:5–14 (Clines 2006, 618–41). In this reassignment, Bildad addresses Job, in the initial portion of a speech, in second-person singular rhetoric, which the friends have done in the previous cycles. This avoids the dilemma of why, if one keeps Job 26:2–4 in Job's mouth, he would shift to singular person address when he has previously statistically preferred the plural. The narrator at Job 27:1 informs the reader that Job is now about to speak. Here, and at Job 29:1, the narrator uses different wording: "Job continued his discourse." Something unique is going on, but what? At Job 29:1, though Job has been speaking since 27:2 according to the Masoretic Text, scholarship, with few exceptions, sees Job 28 as an interlude, an independent poem about wisdom interjected between the dialogues and Job's closing soliloquy (Job 29–31). For Job 29:1, one might argue that the different phrasing is a nod—perhaps from the literary narrator but more likely from an editor—that we are turning from something "non-Joban" (the wisdom poem) to Job. The same phrase in Job 27:1 could be a similar nod: something "non-Joban" (Bildad's speech) to Job. Why we should encounter new phrasing is unclear, but I suggest that the dilemma of editors bumping up against what always was or what had become an opaque, problematic story has had a hand.

- Job's response to Bildad is Job 27:1–12, which follows the Masoretic Text's assignment.

- Zophar actually does appear in the third cycle, though not introduced. Job 27:13–23 is assigned to the third friend.

A. Eliphaz's words (4:1–5:27; 15:1–35; 22:1–30). Eliphaz is likely the eldest. Deference to age underpins the story of Job. Elihu's opening words, after he has heard the three cycles of speeches, make it clear that the three friends are older than he (32:6–9). Of the three friends, Eliphaz appears most conciliatory toward Job. Job is not wicked. Far from it, Job is righteous; but, as with all humanity, Job cannot be perfect. The calamity Job is experiencing is divine discipline for something untoward. All humanity must deal with something of this sort. Job needs only to address the imperfection and move on. Though Eliphaz becomes harsher through the cycle of speeches, he remains the most encouraging and grants the most to Job. Even when frustrated to the point of declaring Job's sins as "endless" (22:5), Eliphaz's redemptive intent beckons Job to "submit to God and be at peace with him" (22:21).

4:1–5:27: First cycle. Eliphaz seems intent on encouraging Job here, drawing from self-proclaimed experience and a quiver full of rhetorical devices: parable, proverb, vision report, beatitude, doxology, and exhortation. Everyone, he offers, is guilty of some error. Suffering is divine discipline (5:17–19) that addresses human impurity. It is those who repent and acknowledge God who are blessed and free from calamity. Job is still alive, and this is testimony that Job is still redeemable. God is ready to heal (5:18). But Eliphaz cannot accommodate a righteous person, one with no known or unknown sin, experiencing calamity. For all of Eliphaz's experience and understanding, then, Job's *true* situation remains impossible in Eliphaz's worldview. That worldview leads Eliphaz to offer words of encouragement that are, in fact, bitterly cruel to Job:

"Where were the upright ever destroyed?" (4:7);

"[A fool's] children are far from safety, crushed in the court without a defender" (5:4);

"You will know that your children will be many" (5:25).

Words meant to support Job and sustain the dogma behind them actually indict the cruelty of Eliphaz's—traditional wisdom's—narrow dogma. Eliphaz's words, seemingly an effort to reflect on suffering, are more appropriately read as an attempt to silence the words of a sufferer thought by a nonsufferer to be unacceptable and harsh.

4:1–6. Eliphaz first acknowledges Job's fragile condition before expressing his own need to speak. Verifying what we know already about Job from the prologue, Eliphaz wants Job to consider his past good works, his own words of encouragement to others. Job needs now to hear his own advice. Job, in Eliphaz's mind, has lost sight of who he is, who he was. In rich imagery, Eliphaz hones in on Job as one who has shored up, who has supported, but now falters and grows weary. Drawing from the past will buoy Job. It is in 4:6 that we encounter the bedrock of Eliphaz's theology: pious reverence confidently invites God's favor. The phrase translated "your piety" is particularly meaningful. Eliphaz says literally, "your *reverence*" (Hebrew *yirah*). One of the core tenets of biblical wisdom is reverence (*yirah*) for Yahweh. The phrase and the concept permeate the wisdom books. Proverbs, the "guidebook," as it were, for the theological perspective of the friends, develops precisely how, in the practice of life, the reverence (*yirah*) of the Lord is the beginning of wisdom and knowledge. No Hebrew-speaking audience can miss encountering the word *yirah* here and understanding the very pointed, powerful theological underpinning.

4:7–11. If 4:6 expresses the bedrock of Eliphaz's theology, 4:7–11 is the first stratum of development. Job, Eliphaz is certain, only needs to reflect on "truth": "Who, being innocent, has ever perished? Where were the upright ever destroyed?" (4:7). Eliphaz draws deeply from his world experience. A lifetime of observation can only verify for Eliphaz the veracity of his theology. Eliphaz articulates his insight lushly, with figurative imagery drawn from agriculture (4:8–9) and the animal kingdom (4:10–11). Fields planted with evil produce evil, and they are scorched by hot desert winds—"the breath of God." Lions are commonly a metaphor for the wicked (Prov. 28:15; Ps. 17:12; 35:17). The wicked are lions with broken teeth, without food, and with cubs vulnerably scattered. In short, the impious do not thrive, they perish. The irony here, and it will continue to build throughout Eliphaz's speeches, is that the depth of Eliphaz's world experience, from which he draws so deeply to console Job, is still too shallow to allow for a Job.

4:12–21. We continue to encounter Eliphaz's wealth of experience. Eliphaz relies further on knowledge derived from an auditory night vision, similar to that of a prophet. He describes the details of its onset (4:12–16), then recites the words he received from some unidentifiable "form" that spoke with "hushed voice" (4:17–21). In this additional stratum of Eliphaz's theology, a central point of the vision's message is that no human is *fully* or *perfectly* just. Eliphaz, as a voice of traditional wisdom, helps us see that though the dyad of the just and the wicked is firm, things are not so pristinely straightforward. The pious, then, as wisdom envisions them, can expect some of the misfortune fully reserved for the wicked. The implication for Job, therefore, is to (re)embrace this truth, to repent of what all humans share. In so doing, Job will end his temporary downturn of fortune, an effect rooted in his own human imperfection. The voice of the amorphous presence builds its case on a familiar rhetorical device: minor to major, or "how much more?" First, the voice's rhetorical question is almost banal—a mortal more righteous, more pure than God?! On the heels of the resounding rhetorical no comes the minor example of servants and angels (4:18) followed by the major

example of humans (4:19–21). If God places no trust in his inner circle, how much more humanity. At face value, the apparition's voice, which Eliphaz has embraced, paints a rather hopeless picture for humanity (4:20–21). Is Eliphaz here affirming that achieving wisdom is impossible, despite all the contrary rhetoric of the wisdom tradition? No. Rather, one should use the weight of wisdom tradition as a counterbalance. It is easy for any reader, any interpreter to overparse, overliteralize what could be seen as a candidate for rhetorical flourish and hyperbole to make a point. Here the driving point is a disparity in purity between God and mortal. The point is made!

5:1–7. Eliphaz, through his initial rhetorical question, states that Job has no one among the heavenly realms to answer him (5:1). Job's circumstances are part of the human condition. Reciting a proverb (5:2), Eliphaz admonishes Job not to continue to play a role best played by the fool (5:3–5). He continues to draw on his experience in such matters (5:3). Job must understand that suffering is not natural (5:6); indeed, suffering is brought on by humans themselves (5:7). This last verse is the heart of Eliphaz's consolation here. Job should not feel victimized by outside forces. Something within Job's human condition is responsible.

5:8–16. Job must acknowledge the human-originated cause behind his plight and appeal to God. Eliphaz, if he were in Job's shoes, would certainly make a case to the deity (5:8). Eliphaz offers a doxology (5:9–16) of rather stereotypic language, affirming God as an adjuster of moral and social order, so that, in the end, "injustice shuts its mouth."

5:17–27. A beatitude (5:17a)—"blessed is . . ."—begins Eliphaz's final words to Job in this speech. He has amassed imagery to affirm God as sustainer in the middle of calamity (5:19–23) and in its aftermath (5:24–26). His final exhortation affirms the veracity of his well-examined words, again a nod to experience. Job must now simply apply them to himself.

15:1–35: Second cycle. Eliphaz, in response to Job's argumentative stance, reprimands Job through a flurry of rhetorical questions and bold statements. Age is thematically important in Eliphaz's words here (15:10, 17–18), for it—with its twin of wisdom—outweighs Job's understanding of reality. We recognize, with more clarity, that Eliphaz believes that Job's rhetoric is undermining the very core of established, and for Eliphaz, *correct* religion (15:4). The long run of words about the wicked (15:20–35) is not Eliphaz's description of Job, but it likely serves as cautionary. Eliphaz, throughout his three speeches, sees Job not as an impious, sin-permeated person. Job, at his core, is righteous but suffers at the moment from disciplinary calamity. Job has *done* something wicked but *is* not wicked. For Eliphaz, Job's failings are that he seems unwilling to recognize that all humanity is contaminated (15:14) and, further, that he is not responding to his suffering in a manner befitting someone who should know better. Job's own words and his rage against God (15:13) convict Job (15:6).

15:1–16. Opening each point with rhetorical questions, Eliphaz challenges Job's right, in light of the latter's words, to speak as a wise man (15:2–6). Eliphaz claims that he and the friends have the reliable authority of age-tested wisdom on their side (15:7–10), shaming Job for his rage filled words (15:11–13) and pointing out once again the intrinsic crookedness within humanity. We hear the echo of *yirah* (NIV's "piety" in 15:4), spoken earlier by Eliphaz (see comments on 4:2–6), and, like an echo, what we hear again is not quite what we heard first. In Eliphaz's first speech, Job's piety, his *yirah* or reverence for God, was to be his confidence for a hopeful future. Job, now through his blustering "rage," undermines *yirah*. Eliphaz's claim that age-old wisdom is on his side begins with his rhetorical question to Job, "Are you the first man ever born?" (15:7). Eliphaz likely does not have in mind Adam of the Genesis account. Eliphaz's "first man" is "born" "before the hills" with access to God's council. Eliphaz is likely

alluding to a cultural mythological tale, remnants of which possibly undergird Ezekiel's depiction of the king of Tyre (Ezekiel 28), and are found in Psalms, Philo, the Apocrypha, the Midrash, the gnostics, and the patristic writings (Gordis 1936, 86). Eliphaz's point is clear: Job is arrogant. Age and communal consensus are the pillars of wisdom and understanding. How dare one lone mortal take these on, and do so by rejecting soft-spoken divine consolation with raging outbursts (15:11–13). Eliphaz again draws from his first speech (4:17–19) to reiterate that no human is perfect (15:14–16). Job has been declaring himself innocent (9:21; 13:23). Eliphaz has been listening. "What is man, that he could be pure," is Eliphaz's rebuttal in 15:14, attempting to break through Job's entrenchment.

15:17–35. Eliphaz again highlights experience, introducing his focus on the plight of the wicked by declaring that his insight is not *his*; it is the collective voice of sages throughout time (15:17–20). In the balance of his speech he describes the miserable life of the wicked, who "shakes his fist at God and vaunts himself against the Almighty" (15:25). Though Eliphaz likely has not placed Job among the wicked as he envisions them, lines that imply fist-shaking and taking on God are surely meant as strong admonition. The wicked suffer torment, distress, and ruin, and receive it in full before their time (15:32). Prosperity that the wicked may enjoy is short-lived. Eliphaz's last few words (15:35) respond in part to something Job has said. In Job's last speech of the first cycle, he has claimed that God is behind life's destructive forces (12:14–25). Eliphaz will hear none of that: the *wicked*, not God, "conceive trouble and give birth to evil" (15:35).

22:1–30: Third cycle. Finishing up his last speech in the second cycle, Job has flatly denied the principle of retribution. Eliphaz, urbane statesman, is pushed to the edge. Job is entrenched; he is immovable. He must be convinced of his guilt. God derives no benefit from wise and righteous mortals; he gains nothing from blamelessness. Job's *yirah* (NIV's "piety" in 22:4; see comments on 4:2–6) certainly would not bring rebuke. Thus, for Eliphaz, Job must see that his calamity is payment for sin, which he now boldly details (22:6–11). Eliphaz accuses Job of inappropriately challenging God (22:13–14), a path that leads to sure ruin (22:15–20). Eliphaz leaves Job with a final appeal: "Submit to God" (22:21). Though his words are harsh, the humane side of Eliphaz dimly shines through. How could it not be a good thing for Job to submit everything in his life to God? He wishes the best for Job. Only Job and we, the elevated reader, know that such an act now would be arguably dishonest for Job. In Job's words ahead, he will insist on a hearing to present his case to God.

22:1–11. Eliphaz again opens a speech with a flood of rhetorical questions. The first two couplets focus on human righteousness's having little meaningful effect on God (22:2–3). The second two couplets address Job, making the point that he is with sin (22:4–5). A no is the response to the first three couplets, but a resounding yes is Eliphaz's expectation for the last, "Is not your wickedness great? Are not your sins endless?" (22:5). Earlier Job has begged God to tell him where he has gone wrong (10:2; 13:23). In God's absence, Eliphaz steps in, providing the particulars. With gusto and terminology typical of a prophet, Eliphaz lays out sins before Job. And they are damning: (1) exploitation (22:6) and (2) inhumane treatment of the destitute (22:7–8) and those especially under God's watch, the widow and orphan (22:9). Has Eliphaz *seen* Job behave this way? No, Job could not have *really* committed these sins and be declared blameless by God himself. In a later speech, Job explicitly denies a self-constructed similar list (Job 31). Is Eliphaz maliciously libeling Job? Perhaps, but more likely, no. For Eliphaz, God unbiasedly punishes the wicked. Job is being punished. Job must be wicked. Considering the gravity of Job's "punishment," Eliphaz offers a list of sins Job *might* have committed.

22:12–20. Job has earlier turned a truism about God's great knowledge on its head to argue that no rational principle separates those who receive blessing and those who receive despair (21:22–26). Eliphaz wants to reclaim Job's God-disparaging comments (22:13–14), laying out that such a course leads assuredly to ruin (22:15–18). In the end, the righteous win the day (22:19–20), because of *God*.

22:21–30. Thus, Eliphaz continues, "Submit to God . . . accept instruction from his mouth." Only if Job returns to the Almighty can he be assured of restoration. Prosperity will return, and one's course of action will be accomplished because of harmony with God (22:27–28). Eliphaz's last words are ironic. The efficacy of the righteous allows them to deliver those who are not innocent. In Job 42:8, Job will intercede for Eliphaz and his friends.

B. Bildad's words (8:1–22; 18:1–21; 25:1–26:14). Bildad grants less piety to Job than does Eliphaz and appears a bit more patient than Zophar. Bildad argues, at first, with comparison. Job is alive, his children are not. He urges Job to sift through his life to make sure that he is free of the guilt that has taken his children's lives (8:4–6). Bildad develops a plant metaphor to teach Job the truth that the impious wither (8:11–19), though, for a season, they sometimes flourish (8:16–19). Bildad is certain that the wicked receive the judgment they deserve (18) and that God is in charge of a predictable world order (25–26).

8:1–22: First cycle. Unlike Eliphaz, Bildad's first response to Job acknowledges nothing laudable. Suffering is punishment. Job is suffering, ergo, he is being punished. With a mixture of reprimand and instruction, Bildad wishes Job to understand that long-standing wisdom (8:8–10) affirms the principle of retribution. The death of Job's children illustrates the point (Job 3–4), as do plants that wither without water (8:11–15) or are torn out by the roots (8:16–19).

8:1–7. Job's words in response to Eliphaz counter a long-standing "rule": suffering is punishment. To Bildad, Job is a "blustering wind." Bildad likely is not being sarcastic but is acknowledging the destructive force of Job's howling words. There is order, a God-ordained order, by which life operates. Bildad's rhetorical questions in Job 8:3 flow out from that understanding, which Bildad will develop later in Job 26:5–14. God does not pervert justice; he does not pervert doing what is right. The combination of the Hebrew words in parallelism and the concepts they have in mind is at the very core of God's nature, extolled throughout the Psalms (72:2; 89:15; 97:2) and among the prophets (Hos. 2:19; Amos 5:24). To illustrate the point that God does what is right, Bildad throws Job's children at him. When they "sinned against [God], he gave them over to the *penalty* of their sin" (8:4). Like Eliphaz (5:8, 17–26), Bildad calls on Job to supplicate the Almighty (8:5) and offers the hope of a bright future (8:7). Once pure and upright, Job will experience God's protection (8:6).

8:8–10. Eliphaz was the first to appeal to experience, primarily his own (4:8, 12–21; 5:27). Having heard Eliphaz draw on personal experience and having seen Job remain unimpressed, Bildad implores Job to heed experience based on long-standing ancestral tradition. He may well have in mind even the primordial (Deut. 4:32). Job must pay attention to the ages.

8:11–19. This section is not without its interpretive hurdles. What is clear is that Bildad first draws on the image of a withering, water-starved papyrus plant to illustrate the

Papyrus plants commonly grew in marshes along the Nile (cf. Job 8:11), as illustrated in this Egyptian painting of a hunt (tomb of Nebamun, ca. 1350 BC).

outcome for the impious (8:11–13). But does the next plant imagery (8:16–19) offer a *second* illustration of the plight of the wicked (Clines 1989, 209–10) or a *contrast* with the first, describing the enduring nature of the blameless despite a harsh environment (Gordis 1978, 521; Newsom 1996, 402–3)? In favor of the latter is a textual environment where Bildad is contrasting fates (8:4, 20–22). Contrasting the blameless and the wicked with tree imagery is used in Psalm 1 and Jeremiah 17:5–8. Verse 19, an extremely abstruse verse, must be saying, for this interpretation, that the plant survives: "such is the plant's joy, that from the dust later it will sprout." The ambiguity of the Hebrew text allows for this. The NIV understands the imagery as a second illustration of the wicked. Though the wicked appear at times to thrive in good conditions (8:16) or when otherwise they should not (8:17), they will be uprooted (8:18) and the area overgrown with other, desirable plants (8:19). If this second interpretation is correct, Bildad seems to have aspects of Job's life in mind. Wealth and prestige were but for a season. Children are now uprooted, and Job himself will likely be uprooted if he does not return to God.

8:20–22. Here Bildad clearly articulates what his rhetorical questions had in mind in Job 8:3: God does not reject the blameless or strengthen the evildoer. Echoing his earlier plea to call on God to correct the wrong (8:5–7), Bildad, in traditional psalmlike rhetoric and categories, addresses Job directly and again affirms the possibility of a bright, restored future with enemies gone.

18:1–21: Second cycle. Bildad continues to dislike what he's been hearing. He finds Job insulting. Bildad, with rich imagery, hammers his point that the wicked receive the judgment they deserve.

18:1–4. Bildad, having opened his first speech with "How long?" (8:2), begins his second speech with a similar but more emotive form: "*How much more* must we listen to insulting speechifying?" Bildad feels belittled by Job's persistent responses and is sure that Job considers his friends stupid. Bildad addresses Job not with Hebrew second-person singular forms but with plural, a one-time anomaly here—all the friends elsewhere use the singular when they talk directly to Job. Clines lists no fewer than eleven possibilities for this phenomenon (Clines 1989, 409–10). As in his first speech (8:3), Bildad, through rhetorical questions, expresses his outrage over Job's position, one that insanely would dismantle universal order (8:4). Job clearly considers himself overly important and is overstepping.

18:5–19. Bildad turns his attention fully to the wicked and their ultimate demise, a core value of his universal moral structure. His imagery, in part, taps into light and its absence (18:5–6), entrapment (18:7–10), and scorched earth (18:15–19). Is Bildad describing Job? No and yes. To the extent that Job's calamity is rooted in impiety, yes, but Bildad's words focus beyond the mere man to the grander vista of all humanity. The light of the wicked will darken (18:5–6), a common proverbial concept (Prov. 13:9; 20:20; 24:20). The stride of the wicked is hobbled, and their legs lead them into an array of traps (18:7–10). The shortened, lumbering gait makes the wicked particularly susceptible to the myriad of entrapments Bildad mentions—no less than six ways for the lower body to be ensnared.

Bildad then explores death's assault on and appetite for the wicked (18:11–14). The word "terrors" hedges in this section (18:11, 14). Understanding the Hebrew of verses 12–13 is difficult and allows a different rendering than the NIV's translation. Pope translates: "The Ravenous One confronts him, Calamity ready at his side. He eats his skin with two hands, First-born Death with both his hands" (Pope, 132; similarly Habel, 280). Bildad likely has in mind common Levantine mythological motifs. In the Ba'lu myth among the Ugaritians living on the northern Levantine coast in the second millennium BC, the god Mot (literally "Death"; the related Hebrew word is used in 18:13) is a ravenous eater, consuming by "double handfuls" (*COS* 1.86:264–65). Speaking to the goddess 'Anatu, Mot later boasts, "I went searching. . . . There were no humans for me to swallow, no hordes of the earth to swallow . . . [and then] I met up with Mighty Ba'lu, I took him as (I would) a lamb in my mouth, he was destroyed as a kid (would be) in my crushing jaws" (*COS* 1.86:270). For Bildad, death devours not Ba'lu but, in similar fashion, the wicked.

Scorched earth and obliteration are Bildad's next themes (18:15–19). Fire and sulfur burn down the safe haven of the wicked. Sulfur, of course, renders land infertile (cf. Deut. 29:23), the case here with roots and branches withering.

The wicked are obliterated from the earth, banished to darkness, with complete extinction.

18:20–21. Bildad steps back and views the scene through the eyes of the global observer. The geographical merismus of "west" and "east" expresses the totality of human existence, much as "heaven and earth" express totality of everything known. The words of Bildad's summary (18:21) are either his own or his own as expressed through the global observers. The wicked are judged, devastatingly so.

25:1; 26:2–4; 25:2–6; 26:5–14 (?): Third cycle. *25:1.* We have rehearsed above under "Three Cycles of Dialogue" the reasons for the reassignment of these texts to Bildad. Bildad has just heard Job cry out for a hearing before God himself. There Job would be vindicated, but, Job complains, God is inaccessible and ineffective, if not negligent. The wicked thrive. Job closes with a wish that God would undo the wicked (24:18–25). To those words of Job comes Bildad's last reply: God is in absolute charge of a predictable world order. Job wishes to stand before God himself? Impossible! No human is pious enough. Awe and dominion belong to God; no maggot human can stand up to that. Bildad would have Job deny human worth and affirm that unflinching absolute power lies at the core of divine essence (Clines 2006, 640).

26:2–4. Eliphaz, early on, was the first to praise Job for his past help and counsel (4:3–6). Bildad, having heard Job undermine traditional understanding and now indict God for cosmic negligence, shakes his head in disbelief. "How is it possible that this man ever helped the powerless and offered sound advice? How is it that he utters what he does?"

This Neo-Assyrian cylinder seal may illustrate the creation epic, in which the gods fight the chaos monster Tiamat.

25:2–6. Bildad now crafts his theme: the dominion, awe, and order of God. The second line of his thesis statement (25:2b) is literally "maker of peace in his heights." The NIV has understood this terse, somewhat cryptic line correctly, though the ideas behind it are too easily overlooked. The idea of deities involved in conflict, especially with forces like chaos, is an ancient Near Eastern and biblical backbone. Chaos, as a concept, is in mind here, since Bildad alludes to creation "nothingness" (26:7; NIV "empty space"; the same Hebrew word is used in Gen. 1:2 [NIV "formless"]) and Rahab (26:12–13). Rahab is a chaos monster set among ancient cultural mythologies where creation forces defeat chaos. Leviathan is another such monster, as are Yammu and Tehom. The latter is alluded to in Genesis 1:2 as the "deep" (Hebrew *tehom*, "primeval sea") and is cognate with Babylonian Tiamat, the personified primeval ocean that Marduk defeats in the Babylonian creation epic, *Enuma Elish.* At Ugarit, Yammu (the god of the sea), along with other chaos monsters, is defeated by Ba'lu or 'Anatu (*COS* 1.86:248–49). God himself has defeated such forces (Gen. 1:2 and the Genesis creation account as the triumph of order; Isa. 51:9–10; Ps. 89:9–10). This is Bildad's primary point in the balance of his speech. After painting the canvas with cosmic battle and victory, Bildad turns his attention to Job. Does Job really plan to confront God, this being who defeated chaos and who established world order? Will Job really declare his innocence? The very claim itself, coming from a mortal, is an affront to order and proper understanding. Unthinkable.

26:5–14. Bildad continues to expound on God's awe and his dominion, particularly over forces of chaos. Bildad first looks down to the netherworld (26:5–6). Sheol (NIV's "Death" in 26:6) itself cannot escape. There the "dead" tremble. The Hebrew term for "dead" (26:5) here refers to the shadowy dead who reside in Sheol, situated, in the mind of the Hebrew culture, at the bottom of the sea (26:6; Ps. 88:6–7; Jon. 2:2–6). Isaiah uses the term to refer to heroic dead kings (Isa. 14:9). Though Bildad likely has the general inhabitants of Sheol in mind, we could also expect the additional overlay of past heroic figures. Even they quiver. Having looked down below, Bildad looks toward the famous mythic mountain Zaphon, which underlies the NIV's "northern skies" (Hebrew *tsapon*). Zaphon is indeed geographically north of Israel, but Bildad's imagery here is more complex. Mount Zaphon, which lies about thirty-seven miles north of ancient Ugarit, was the long-standing home of Baal and the divine assembly. It was the seat of power. The Hebrew Bible, in Psalms particularly, takes imagery from neighboring cultures and supplants the former deities, for example, with Yahweh as supreme God. Human experience commonly takes cultural icons—established, meaningful ways to understand something—and adapts them. Bildad appears to be saying that God has stretched out Zaphon over chaos (NIV "empty space," 26:7; cf. Gen. 1:2, "formless"). As Zaphon represents a seat of authority and rule, so God has stretched out dominion over chaotic forces. Additionally, "earth" (26:7), his creation, triumphs over chaos. The pair, Zaphon and earth, seems to be a merism similar to "heaven and earth."

God has control over rain clouds, life-giving waters that subdue the chaotic powers of destruction (26:8). In Job 26:9, it is unclear whether God covers the "full moon" or his "throne." The Masoretic Text reads "throne" (Hebrew *kisseh*), but many suggest, including the NIV, reading "full moon" (Hebrew *keseh*). Given the underlying concept of Zaphon, Bildad is here saying that God shuts off from

view his *throne*, spreading his clouds over it (so NJPS). God's base of operation, as it were, is hidden from humanity. The cosmological understanding behind Job 26:10–11 is opaque. The clearest concept is the "pillars of heaven" (26:11), which are likely the great mountains that hold up the sky, known in Akkadian as "the foundations of heaven." Bildad now turns to the epic battle that most ancients considered at the heart of order and chaos (26:11–13). God has subdued (not NIV's "churned up") the sea (Hebrew *yam*), Rahab, and an elusive serpent. We have already noted the well-known mythologies underpinning these words. One should not avoid seeing the connection between *yam* here and Yammu at Ugarit (see commentary on 3:1–10). Rahab and serpentine creatures are additional chaotic forces. Isaiah has similar concepts in mind when he says that Yahweh will punish Leviathan, the serpent of the sea (Hebrew *yam;* Isa. 27:1). Bildad concludes (26:14) that the great cosmic plain he has just described is but the "outer fringe," the "faint whisper" of what God can do.

C. Zophar's words (11:1–20; 20:1–29; 27:13–23?). All three friends share a core assumption about Job: he is guilty of sin. But beyond that, they do differ. In the first cycle, Eliphaz grants Job's suffering as but a hiccup in a near perfect life. Bildad would have Job focus on the moral lesson of Job's children: they are dead; Job is not. Job is therefore more pious than they but still has within him impurity, which he must address (Job 18). Zophar is straight to the point: sin—so much sin, in fact, that God has even forgotten some of it (11:6). Job must repent of his sin; he then will be restored (Job 11). The wicked have no profit in their endeavors and suffer an inescapable end (Job 20), which Zophar explores further in his third speech (27:13–23).

11:1–20: First cycle. Zophar has a scathing rebuke for Job (11:2–3). He, unlike Eliphaz, after all, has heard more things said by the time he takes his turn. He indicts Job's self-assessment as a "flawless" person. Job is myopic,

Zophar contends, for if God were to respond, Job would hear of the vast depths of wisdom that he obviously has not yet seen. Job would recognize that he is so flawed that God himself has forgotten some of Job's sin (11:4–6). God is limitless, encompassing all, giving him a vantage point nothing else shares. From that point, God recognizes deceit in humanity, and, to an extent, he sees it in Job (11:7–12). Zophar finishes his speech by reassuring Job that if he expunges the sin within him, he will be restored, made secure again, resting in safety (11:13–19), unlike the wicked (11:20).

11:1–6. "When words are many, sin is not absent, but he who holds his tongue is wise" (Prov. 10:19). Such a traditional proverbial outlook seems to underpin Zophar's first words to Job (11:2). This generic "truth" he then applies specifically to Job. Job's prattle, insisting on his innocence, may silence lesser men but not Zophar (11:3–4). If God could speak, he would show Job how shortsighted he is (11:5). Zophar insists that God's actions toward Job have been tempered by restraint (11:6). Zophar may not here expect that God will indeed appear, but Job increasingly desires an appearance. Remarkably and ironically, when God later does break into the conversation, much of what he says echoes Zophar's expectations—a display of power and a taunt of Job's limited understanding.

11:7–12. Zophar develops his theme of secrets and mysteries. On the whole this section has buried within it the kernel of God's later speeches. Both probe the limitless boundaries of God and his knowledge: higher than the heavens, deeper than Sheol, longer than the earth, wider than the sea (11:7–9). Job, then, must recognize that if placed before the Almighty, he would find that God perceives all and easily ferrets out the deceitful (11:10–11). A case may fall short on human evidence, but God's evidence will be copious. Zophar then quips out what surely is a clever witticism complete with Hebrew alliteration (11:12), though precisely what it says and what Zophar means by saying it is not entirely clear. The saying contemplates,

literally, a "hollow" person's ability to become learned. After this, things get muddy. One option is that such a person will become wise only when a wild ass is born a human being (NJPS). The NIV represents another direction: that a witless person will no more become learned than a wild donkey will be born to a human. At first glance, Zophar seems to mean that he believes Job incapable of true wisdom. Yet Zophar's following words encourage Job to pursue the right path (11:13–20). In context, then, Zophar appears to be challenging Job not to be a hollow man.

11:13–20. Zophar's instruction to Job now follows. If Job can learn from Zophar's words, he is well on the road away from hollowness. Job must direct himself toward God and expunge all iniquity (11:13–14). With that done, brighter days lie ahead—a response to Job's imagery at the end of his previous speech in Job 10:22. Restoration and rest are around the corner (11:15–19). But, for the wicked, only their last dying breath awaits them (11:20).

20:1–29: Second cycle. The second cycle of the friends' speeches has depicted the fate of the wicked. For Eliphaz, that image is what Job is not; Job is not wicked at the core (Job 15). For Bildad, that fate *may* lie ahead for Job. Bildad's disturbing depiction of the disastrous end to the wicked seems to trace out a trajectory meant to correct Job's path (Job 18). For Zophar, that picture is what Job cannot avoid without serious change. In his second speech, Zophar recites conventional words on the fate of the wicked. Hearing no words of remorse yet from Job, Zophar is sure this fate *is* what lies ahead. He paints a bleak picture, arguably the bleakest among the friends. Zophar first explains his need to respond (20:2–3). He then joins in on the chorus of aged experience (20:4; compare 8:8–10; 15:7–10) to contribute his insights. The wicked are but a flash who suffer utter destruction (20:5–11). With imagery drawn from gastronomy, Zophar concocts the dish of evil's self-destroying poison (20:12–23). He then draws from imagery of sword and disaster to highlight the unavoidable end that awaits the wicked (20:24–28). His summation is clear: all this happens to the wicked by the hand of God (20:29).

27:13–23 (?): Third cycle. We have rehearsed above under "Three Cycles of Dialogue" the reassignment of these texts to Zophar. Chapters 24–27 are, as we mentioned above, muddled and at face value somewhat out of step with the previous cycles. As it is, Zophar has no third speech, and Job utters words that sound like Bildad's and Zophar's. I place this section, warily, within Zophar's mouth. If indeed he is speaking, we do not hear the customary introductory direct, second-person confrontation. Rather, we hear almost an echo of his previous discourse with imagery very similar to that found in Job 20:24–28. The devastating end of the wicked comes by sword, plague, destruction of home, and terror. Job's own calamity involved a few of these. Such allusions, and Job's pain, cannot be underestimated.

D. Job's words (6–7; 9–10; 12–14; 16–17; 19; 21; 23–24; 27:1–12). Within the first cycle (Job 4–14), Job at first highlights his anguish, his desire to be crushed (6:9), and his displeasure with his friends' counsel (6:14–23). Job cannot envision a return to happiness (7:7). Headed to the netherworld of Sheol, he is confused as to why God should pay so much attention to humans in general and Job in particular. Job, however, begins to flirt with the idea of a court case with God himself (9:3–4, 19) but quickly muses on the absurdity of a human dealing with the divine (9:32). God is powerful and overwhelming. Insistent on his rightness, Job expresses the shame he lives under, preferring never to have left the womb, an echo from his soliloquy (Job 3). Reacting to charges of guilt by all three friends, Job insists that nonhuman witnesses would attest to his guiltlessness (12:7–9). The real culprit is God, who is powerful and who abuses the world with that strength (12:14–25). Job revisits the notion of working out a case against God (13:13–28) but ends the first cycle focused on the desperation

of the human condition, that humans die and reside in Sheol without help (Job 14).

In his first speech of the second cycle, Job graphically details his mistreatment by God (Job 16–17) and yet again looks to a courtroom, becoming increasingly passionate about it. Job speaks of having a witness in heaven, ready to testify on high (16:19). Indeed, this vindicator, this kinsman-redeemer (19:25), will take his place should Job fall to the grave (16:18, 22; 19:26). Job, however, would much rather confront God in person (19:26b–27), a thought he sets aside in his last speech, where he returns to contemplate how the wicked prosper (Job 21).

Job, at the start of the third cycle (Job 22–27), returns to the court case, no longer focusing on a vindicator. Job now insists on seeing God to set out his own case, but he soon despairs. God, he declares, is unfindable (23:8–9). His assertion is no glowing affirmation of God's sovereignty. Job's pain is profound. Whatever God wishes, he will do (23:13). Humans be cursed, or at least humans who suffer injustice be cursed, for God, right under his nose, allows success for the wicked (Job 24). This state of affairs verifies that God is derelict in addressing injustice. Until his death, Job will nevertheless maintain his integrity and blamelessness (27:1–12).

6–7; 9–10; 12–14: First cycle. *6:1–7:21.* Job will not be silent, and he certainly does not embrace the advice that Eliphaz, with good intention, has offered and suggested he take (5:27). Job first focuses on his plight (6:2–13). He is weighed down with unbearable misery, shot through with God's poisonous arrows. Job is on his last gasp. He wants to die. Indeed, more in line with the way Job feels about God, he wants God to crush him, to complete the job he started.

Job turns to address his friends, spiritedly throwing accusations at them (6:14–30). He has expected comfort and sympathy; he has received none. Though only Eliphaz has spoken, Job condemns them all for turning their backs on expected loyalty (NIV's "devotion," Hebrew *hesed*). By doing so, they forsake "the fear [pious reverence] of the Almighty"—a very telling statement out of Job's mouth. This bond should be the foundation of acceptance and support, but frightened by Job's plight, they accuse him of wrong. Job wants none of it: "Be so kind as to look at me. Would I lie to your face?" (6:28). Job is innocent. The friends should affirm this.

Job now turns his attention toward God, ruminating on what it is to be a human and his own place as one (7:1–21). Forced labor and hired labor (7:1–2) are the lots of humanity, and his own life

On this inscribed shell, a Mesopotamian god faces a seven-headed monster, one of the chaos monsters related to the sea in ancient Near Eastern mythology.

drags on through such unsatisfied emptiness (7:3–5). Time, on one hand, may halt, yet he also considers how it swiftly flashes by. This too is his life, a breath quickly over (7:6–10). The stranglehold of futility and mortality forces Job to cry out to God in complaint, asking a fundamentally important theological question (7:11–21): why does God concern himself with humanity? Job revisits the common ancient Near Eastern notion of cosmic battle among divinities (7:12; cf. 3:8). He asks whether he is the "sea" (Hebrew *yam*) or "the monster of the deep" (Hebrew *tannin*). At Ugarit, divinized chaos creatures Yammu and Tannin, precise cognate parallels, are defeated. Job's point is clear. Job is thoroughly unimportant, he is no chaos monster. Why should God be taking him on as though he were? Why is a human worth God's time? Why does God look so intently on such an impotent figure within the cosmos? Why, if a human should sin, can God not easily forgive?

9:1–10:22. In reply to Bildad, Job's rhetorical question about a mortal being right before God (9:2) holds the spark of the fire that will increasingly consume Job's mind (9:2–13). Here he ignites the idea of standing before God in court (9:3), but he quickly lets the flame die down, overwhelmed by the disparity between human and divine (9:4–13). In hymnlike doxology, with motifs paralleled elsewhere in the Bible or the ancient Near East, Job explores the destructive (9:5–7) and creative (9:8–10) omnipotence of God.

A lawsuit with God is impossible. For Job, God is both judge and enemy (9:14–24). There is no higher court, yet this one who hears cases also overwhelms and crushes. God is an oppressive presence, destroying both blameless and wicked, mocking the despair of the innocent. This judge of judges is guilty of subverting justice among humanity, blinding justice in a land filled with wickedness.

Job turns to himself, contemplating how swiftly the days of a life pass and how joyless his are (9:25–35). He then returns to the nagging thought of court. Job truly is a moth to a flame. Job is disadvantaged, condemned guilty by God, frightened silent by his terror. If only there were someone else who could arbitrate justly, Job could speak and defend his innocence. But such is not the case.

Miserable circumstances give a voice to Job (10:1–7). He boldly announces what he will say to God. Through three fields of questioning, Job tries to peel back the motives behind God's treatment of him. Is God pleased by defrauding his creation (10:3)? Does God have another perspective of right and wrong, different from humans (10:4)? Does God live under a constraint of mortality, a brevity of his own life, that he is so quick to target Job (10:5–7)?

Job is himself a creation of God (10:8–17). Why would God seek so hard now to destroy him? God's intent all along, despite showering favor in the past (10:12), was to create a being to be scoured for sin (10:13–14). Job highlights his affliction and God's aggression.

Overwhelmed with despair over a God he believes responsible for willful barrages and attacks, Job echoes earlier thoughts (10:18–22). He wishes he had never been born, but having been born, he wishes God would turn away, to grant Job a moment of joy before he slips away into the gloom and shadow of death.

12:1–14:22. Job's final speech in the first cycle, divided into three chapters in the Hebrew Bible, can also be split into two major sections: Job addresses his friends (12:2–13:19), and Job addresses God (13:20–14:22).

Job is sharply sarcastic toward his friends as he opens his mouth (12:2–13:19). Oh, yes, they understand everything! But Job is no dolt. He knows no less than others. He seems to recognize that, from others' point of view, his situation has turned him into a laughingstock. Contempt quickly replaces respect among those who witness the fall of a respected person (12:5). Job further digs at his friends' notion that they know more than he (12:7–10). In parody Job parrots their style and counsel, even using second-person *singular* deixis ("you" singular), which the *friends* use when *they* speak to Job. Job parodies their argument: even simpleminded animals know that God is judging you, Job. Job continues his platitudes by reciting what appears to be a well-known proverb (12:11). Elihu too will quote this saying (34:3), which also appears in similar form in Sirach 36:24. As the palate (NIV "tongue") discriminates between what is tasty and what is not, so the ear judges and assesses the arguments it hears. The point of the proverb, uttered within its contexts, is to invite

the hearer to agree with the speaker. The friends, of course, are being attacked by Job's parody of them: agreeable voices speaking from age and the ages (12:11–12). Having caricatured his friends' counsel, Job turns to hymnic rhetoric, with a negative spin (12:13–25). Through the language of doxology—praise to God and his ways—Job cuts away at the traditional wisdom that lies at the heart of his friends' counsel. Job's own voice and nonsatirical comment is heard in Job 13:1–2, which is best linked with what has been said in chapter 12. Job's eyes and ears have encountered all this knowledge and wisdom, and forming an inclusio, Job repeats what he said earlier: what you know, I know; I am not inferior to you (13:2; 12:3). Yet, for Job, this brand of wisdom does not account for his situation. His is different, and no small part in the issue is that the friends misrepresent God and his ways (13:3–19). The friends smear Job with lies (13:4), but based on Job's following comments, the lies are not so much about Job as about God (13:7–12). Job believes he is speaking honestly about God, and emboldened by his belief that the friends speak deceit, he demands that they remain silent. He, meanwhile, is ready to appear in court.

Job now addresses God directly (13:20–14:22). A day in court is possible for Job if God would withdraw his overpowering, oppressive presence. In a less intimidating, more neutral courtroom, there Job presents his case. "What wrong have I committed? Why do you treat me the way you do?" Job's legalese fades as we encounter his words in 14:1–22. Job's query about God's treatment of him has blossomed into contemplation on the desperation of the human condition, that one eventually dies and resides without help in Sheol. Sheol here is not the comfort that it was to Job earlier (3:13–19; 7:8–9), a place where he will rest and be far from God. Sheol is now the problem because Job wishes at present to confront God. Sheol will deny Job that satisfaction. We face imagery of Job's impotence in relation to God. Humanity is a fragile flower (14:2). Though human hope be cast as a mountain, God embodies all the forces that erode it to nothing (14:18–22). Does the very image of human hope as a substantial geological feature shed light on Job's psychological disposition, his own growing tenacity to get at God, his own hope? Perhaps so, for Job will thunderously continue to insist on meeting up with God. Yet he clearly holds this hope in tension with his perception of a God who, through death and the underworld, is separated and alienated from humanity.

16–17; 19; 21: Second cycle. *16:1–17:16.* Eliphaz has just argued that Job is arrogant in his rejection of conventional wisdom, that it is the *wicked* who suffer torment, distress, and ruin and receive it in full (15:32). Job's opening remarks (16:1–6) ridicule his friends: "Will your long-winded speeches never end?" (16:3). He too, if he were in their shoes, could say the same things they say, but now that he recognizes the devastation of his life and his exception to the rule, he would be more encouraging than they. His friends are no friends.

Job's alienation from the traditional response about calamity is potently seen in his address now directly to God (16:7–17). Job takes up, understandably, a lament similar to his opening soliloquy (Job 3). In rhetoric similar to that of Lamentations 3:1–20, Job describes himself as a persecuted and oppressed man. The persecutor, the enemy, is God himself. This powerful lament is painted onto the canvas with images of aggression drawn from beasts, swords, arrows, and warfare.

But, at a point where lament is elsewhere known to re-embrace God, rediscover hope, and extol God's goodness (Lam. 3:21–39), Job cries out, as though in court, for his blood to be avenged and for an advocate to vindicate him (16:18–21). Job is in no frame of mind to make nice.

His urgency is rooted in his assessment that he has little life yet to live, and once dead he will never again have an opportunity to face God (16:22–17:16). In these verses Job expresses the one thing about which he is certain—his

death. His words convey hopelessness mixed with criticism for his friends and the view they express.

19:1–29. Though Job seems to jab right back at Bildad by opening with Bildad's own first words from his previous speech, "How long" (19:2; cf. 18:2; NIV does not reflect the precise repetition in the Hebrew), Job, as is now the pattern, has all the friends in mind (19:1–6). The friends continue to grieve, humiliate, and abuse Job. The friends' abuse, however, is matched by God himself (19:7–12). Job, again using figurative images of assault (cf. 16:7–17), utters a lament of God's mistreatment of him.

As Job continues his lamentation, the shift from figurative language now arguably to nonfigurative lays out another level of pathos (19:13–20). He is literally without family, friends, and household. He is in reality repulsive to look at. Once an elder commanding respect through the East, he is scorned now even by children. Job's point is that he is truly pitiful (19:21–22). God himself has struck him down. Why then should the friends persist in their insatiable quest of maligning Job?

We encounter here one of the most well-known and cited of Joban passages (19:23–29), its popularity contributing one more layer to the many layers of encumbrances that surround it. The text itself is difficult. A "Christianization" of the text has led to notions of Christ as Redeemer. The NIV's capitalized spelling of "Redeemer" reflects that line of thinking and plays no small role in perpetuating it. Christian interpretation, further, has found here "proof" for bodily resurrection. But there is another way to view these verses. Job has become increasingly frustrated that he has no access to defend his case before God, a theme heard in his last speech (16:18–17:16). There as well, Job has teased out the notion of a witness in heaven, an advocate (16:18–21). To that thought, to that wish for a supporter on high, Job now adds a belief that, should he die without facing God, his "kinsman-redeemer" (Hebrew *goel*; NIV "redeemer") will take his case and confront

God. The *goel*—an Israelite sociological phenomenon—is a near relative whose role is to assist a family or family member in dire straits. Whether the distress was lost property (Lev. 25:25–28), murder of a family member (Deut. 19:6–12), or lack of progeny (Deut. 25:5–10), the *goel* was to correct the situation. This "family advocate," this "righter of wrongs," is what Job has in mind. The identity of this *goel* is not clear, but a more important aspect is the *goel*'s function. In Job 19:25–26a, Job states his confidence that his *goel* is alive and ready to take up Job's cause in the (likely) event of Job's death. Job's preference, though, is expressed in 19:26b–27. Job, while still alive (NIV's "in my flesh"), would rather stand before God to defend himself. The NJPS captures these lines well:

> But I know that my Vindicator
> lives;
> In the end He will testify on
> earth—
> This, after my skin will have been
> peeled off.
> But I would behold God while still
> in my flesh,
> I myself, not another, would behold Him;
> Would see with my own eyes:
> My heart pines within me.

Job has been developing this thought about an advocate. These verses are the strongest expression we hear from him. Job hereafter will never again mention such a figure. Here on out, when Job returns to the courtroom with God (Job 23; 31), he speaks only of wanting to be in front of God. Though he is confident that his case will be heard in court one way or another, Job yearns for a face-to-face confrontation!

21:1–34. In the second cycle of speeches, the friends have focused on how the wicked are treated according to their tradition-inspired insight. Job, up to now, has focused on his own dire circumstances and his wish to confront God directly. Here he turns to the topic his friends have been addressing. But his voice is a counterpoint: the wicked prosper!

Job addresses his friends with an appeal to listen (21:2–6). The thoughts he is about to articulate are bold and shocking. They undermine the moral order as it is understood by conventional wisdom, the position of Job's friends. Job himself trembles at the implications.

The wicked live on in prosperity (21:7–16). They live to old age, seeing generations of children. They are secure, never feeling God's judgment. They enjoy life thoroughly and consciously reject God and God's ways. God does nothing.

What tradition affirms as a rule Job offers as exception (21:17–21). For tradition, even if in one generation a wicked person does not receive full retribution, the next generation will. But Job will have none of that. His prayer is that the wicked should receive punishment here and now. Even if the doctrine of retribution were true, it would be irrelevant, for death is the great equalizer (21:22–26). In death everyone experiences the same fate. Everywhere it is common that evil prospers in life and enjoys reputation in death (21:27–34). This is universally true, claims Job. One simply needs to ask the traveler.

23–24; 27:1–12: Third cycle. *23:1–24:25.* Job's previous speech (Job 21), where he challenged conventional wisdom, was a pause from the crescendo of his desire to stand before God. In these chapters, Job returns to the elusive courtroom.

Job has earlier expressed his confidence in a vindicator (16:18–21) or kinsman-redeemer (19:23–29) to prosecute his case after his death. But Job wants none of that now (23:2–7). Perceiving no activity on God's end, Job realizes that *he* must be the one to track down God. But whether Job goes east, west, north, or south, he cannot find him (23:8–12). Though God is hidden from Job, Job confidently asserts that God is nevertheless well aware of him. God knows full well that Job is guiltless despite God's treating him as though he were not. To Job's mind, however, God does whatever he pleases

(23:13–17). Job's words are not a glowing affirmation of God's wonderful omnipotence. Job feels hopeless, terrified of this being and the treatment Job has received from him.

Job has focused on himself as an inhabitant of a moral world where God has gone missing. He turns now to consider the many others who suffer and cry out for justice (24:1–17). In his previous speech (Job 21), Job's point was that prosperity among the wicked is proof of a God-abandoned, topsy-turvy moral world order. Here his proof is the way the wicked are able to prey successfully on the poor and powerless. The examples Job amasses are not about religious apathy or syncretistic worship. God's abdication is proved through a myriad of heinous acts of social injustice and social oppression.

Verses 18–25 are sometimes reassigned to one of Job's friends. Those who understand the verbal mood as declarative (a declaration that God undoes the wicked) consider these verses to be out of step with Job's disposition and more akin to the attitude of the friends. But the grammatical mood of the language is not declarative, as the NIV translates; rather, it is optative (a hypothetical projection or wish; see NJPS). Job continues to speak here. He is not *declaring* that God undoes the wicked but *wishing* that God would. Having painted a canvas with bloodred strokes of injustice and criminality, Job attempts in these verses to paint a serene landscape as he wishes it would be. But that landscape is not a reality. His final words that boast the truth of his viewpoint are a defiant challenge to his friends.

27:1–12. Job continues in the vein of his words in 23:8–12. Through a series of oaths, Job defends the integrity and veracity of his position. He is right and righteous and is therefore unwilling to agree with his friends' position. Job launches an imprecatory attack on any enemy who would continue to assail him and ends his speech intent on instructing his friends on God's

ways, criticizing them for their "meaningless talk," or nonsense.

4. Wisdom: Where Is It? (28:1–28)

The reader encounters here magnificent literary art, but there is no consensus on how it interacts with the book as a whole. At face value, of course, this chapter is a continuation of Job's speech, but therein lies the dilemma. The contrast of this chapter when compared to what Job has been saying and what he will shortly say (Job 29–31) is striking. Does it belong better in the mouth of one of the friends? The common reply is no, for it seems to lack their characteristic rhetoric and the focus on retributive justice so interwoven within their responses.

By all accounts it appears to be a self-contained reflection on wisdom and where one may find it. The impasse between Job and

The suffering Job, with his wife and a friend standing nearby (sarcophagus of Junius Bassus, AD 359)

his friends has increasingly heightened. One wonders whether the storyteller is here sending down a sounding to find our bearings. None of the characters has yet found wisdom. We have seen firsthand the limitations of human understanding. The storyteller therefore embarks, in Greek choruslike fashion, on a contemplative musing about wisdom.

The poem opens by considering earth's precious metals and stones and the valiant attempts of humans to mine them (28:1–11). The human quest to extract earth's valuable nuggets serves as a foil for the rest of the poem, which explores human failure, in contrast to God's success, to mine wisdom. Verses 12–27 form two parallel structures: 28:12–19 and 28:20–27. Each unit opens with essentially the same rhetorical question (28:12, 20), followed by a declaration that neither humanity (28:13, 21) nor deified cosmic realms ("deep," "sea," "destruction/Abaddon," and "death"; 28:14, 22) can locate and dig out wisdom. The first unit then explores how wisdom cannot be bartered for the earth's wealth (28:15–19). The second unit, in contrast, affirms God's access to wisdom, encountered first in the act of creation (28:23–27).

The reflection ends (28:28) with the most traditional of clichés (Prov. 1:7; 3:7; 9:10). What is the point at this moment in the story? Norman Habel offers insight (Habel, 392–93). The cliché surely cannot be the final word to Job's dilemma, for "reverence" (Hebrew *yirah*; see commentary on 4:2–6) toward God has not given Job, in this instance, insight to understand his crisis. The friends have maintained, particularly Eliphaz in Job 4:6, that pious reverence (*yirah*) confidently invites God's favor. Not only has Job vigorously argued against the traditional understanding, but he himself has teasingly admitted his rejection of traditional reverence of God (6:14). Job is not buying the cliché.

The cliché, further, echoes the opening line of Job (1:1). There Job "feared God and shunned evil." In Job 28:28, the fear of the Lord is wisdom and to shun evil is understanding. But clearly neither reverence of God nor shunning evil protected Job or gave him insight into his predicament. In fact, Job's following words (Job 29–31) rehearse the life of a man who shunned evil but has received it in immeasurable quantity. Thus the storyteller seems to offer up the cliché as a foil. The traditional cliché is not acceptable to Job. Piety and avoidance of evil have not resulted in wisdom and understanding. Job has wanted and will continue to want justice and direct access to God.

5. Job's Closing Soliloquy (29:1–31:40)

After Eliphaz, Bildad, and Zophar's contributions to the story, Job longingly recalls the good days of old (29) as contrast to his present social and physical maladies (30), strongly insisting on his innocence (31).

29:1–25. Job recalls grand days of his past. He recounts his flawless conduct and God's constant favor. We journey with Job, this honored and revered figure, as he moves from his family circle (29:2–6), outward to his seat among the nobles at the city gate (29:7–11), to his fatherly care for the marginalized within his society (29:12–17). He anticipated a long, full life (29:18–20), devoted to enhancing life for others (29:21–25).

30:1–31. Having listened in on Job's self-assessment of days gone by, the reader is now in a position to understand more clearly Job's social, psychological, and physical suffering. Job turns to his present, awful circumstances, structured rhetorically through the repetition of "now" (30:1, 9, 16) and "surely" (30:24). Job speaks with layered pejoratives against those at the bottom of the social order who now have nothing but derisive contempt for him: *young lads* born to the *dogs* of society, banished like *thieves, huddled in underbrush*, eating *broom root* (30:1–8). Their contempt for Job has led to mistreatment (30:9–15), and Job laments the painful atrophy of body and life (30:16–19). Job cries out to God, declaring him cruel and savage (30:20–23) and expressing his disbelief that such evil could befall him (30:24–31).

31:1–40. Job now turns to defend his position with a testimony of integrity similar to those found in Egyptian mortuary texts, where the deceased, speaking to Osiris and other gods, lists offenses that the deceased has *not* committed. Job's integrity is seen through the transgressions he is not guilty of committing. He expresses a series of oaths grouped by topic. The form throughout is a variation on "If *a* has done *b*, may *c* happen to *a*" (for example, 31:7–8). The first group of oaths focuses on sexual ethics (31:1–12), the second on social justice (31:13–23), the third on avoiding misplaced loyalty (31:24–28), and the fourth on offenses that would erode social fabric, such as gloating over an enemy's misfortune or failure to extend hospitality to a stranger (31:29–34). Job metaphorically signs this writ of oath (31:35), wanting nothing less than a hearing with God himself (31:35–37). Job has done nothing wrong. And, as if adding a postscript of yet one more thing just remembered, Job utters his last oath centered on ecological stewardship (31:38–40). Job's speeches end here.

This chapter helps to validate further what Job knows about himself and what the reader knows through the narrator: Job is a pious man of honor. The values that Job upholds are also values that God holds dear. The reader can see this common ground between Job and God, one that could serve for reconciliation and resolution. But God does not choose that path, leaving the reader with a story line that "challenges many of Job's assumptions about God and the relationship between God and the world" (Newsom 1996, 551).

6. Elihu's Words (32:1–37:24)

Elihu? Has he been here the whole time? He is not one of the three friends introduced in the prologue, and he is not mentioned in the epilogue. Yet from his own words he has been nearby and listening in, remaining silent in the presence of men older than he. But now he can no longer restrain himself.

We have seen above under "Composition" that many think the Elihu character is a late insertion. Not mentioned earlier or later by the narrator, and not acknowledged by human characters or God, Elihu admittedly has the earmarkings of a surgical insertion. Be that as it may, he is alive and well in the version before us, and we must reckon with him and his words at this juncture.

Elihu, as a character, is young, brash, self-important, and dogmatic. Many find him quite unlikable. Elihu, as a speaker in the story, though, stands as a Janus-like figure, facing back to comment on what has been said, and facing forward, anticipating some of God's rhetoric. Elihu pushes back against the four. Suffering is not *always* caused by sin, argues Elihu against the theology of Eliphaz, Bildad, and Zophar. Rather, through two means—dreams and illness—God can speak to humanity to guide them along a better path. Turning slightly to Job, Elihu does not accept the former's claim that God is unjust. And turning in the opposite direction to face what is about to come, Elihu speaks of God's mystery, unknowable motives, and ways in creation and nature. In comparison, Job is powerless and ignorant. Elihu's final description of theophany heralds God's entrance into the story at Job 38.

7. God's Speeches (38:1–41:34) with Job's Responses (40:3–5; 42:1–6)

The polyphony in the words and ideas that have cut across the respective characters' monologic points of view grinds nearly to a halt with God's thunderous voice. Job finally gets to stand before God. The wish is granted. But, teasingly, this will be no dialogic interchange. This is monologue. God has a different set of values, other premises than those held by Job. God's barrage of questions, though in the form of an invitation to dialogue, are here rhetorical and meant to silence, the outgrowth of confronting one whose words are "without knowledge" (38:2).

Commentator upon commentator explores the conundrum of whether God's speeches engage Job's arguments, and if so, how. Has God *really* answered? If he has answered, has he answered in full or suitably? Job is certainly, in a sense, left speechless. Is that because he has heard a satisfying response or because he has been crushed into silence?

38:1–38: God. God appears out of the storm to confront Job. God will be doing the talking now, the accumulative effect of which is overwhelming. The rhetorical "Who?" "Where?" "Have you?" "If you know, tell me," pound at Job. Does Job truly understand the cosmos: earth's structure (38:4–7); the forces of the sea (38:8–11); dawn (38:12–15); the depths of the sea and the gates of death (38:16–18); light and darkness (38:19–21); storm (38:22–30); the movement of constellations (38:31–33); the control of weather (38:34–38)?

38:39–39:30: God. Abruptly God turns his attention to wild animals: lion (38:39–41); mountain goat and deer (39:1–4); wild donkey (39:5–12); ostrich (39:13–18); war horse (39:19–25); hawk and eagle (39:26–30). Understanding the ways of such creatures is beyond the human.

40:1–2: God. God has held the cosmos and wildness of nature under the light of scrutiny to explore the mystery beyond human understanding. God now demands an answer from Job.

40:3–5: Job. One might expect the disputation to begin here in earnest. Job has wanted this moment to stand and to plead his case before God. Four words are all Job needs to signal his complete and utter withdrawal (40:4). The white flag of surrender is buoyed by the action of clapping his mouth shut with his hand.

Hippopotami on an Egyptian relief (tomb of Ka-Gemni, Saqqara, 6th Dynasty). The Behemoth in Job 40 may be a hippopotamus.

40:6–14: God. God's second speech begins with a challenge. Job is again told to brace himself in the face of what will be a second wave. God, through the rest of his speech, will again direct Job to consider animals. But here they are two great creatures, one of land and one of sea: Behemoth and Leviathan.

40:15–24: God. In form, Behemoth (Hebrew *behemot*) is nothing more than a plural of the Hebrew word for "animal" (*behemah*). Yet, from Job's context, this is *a* beast and one that is particularly powerful and awesome. The storyteller may well have crafted this word specifically for this story. From the description, Behemoth may be a hippopotamus, connected in Egypt with the deities Seth and Horus. Behemoth may also be a water buffalo or related to the bull figures so prominent in Mesopotamia. Or Behemoth may be a literary fiction, drawing from well-known imagery but representing a sort of everybeast of a type that complements Leviathan. Behemoth, a creation of God, as is Job (40:15), is a primordial beast of calm repose, approachable only by its Maker. God's query whether one can catch it provides the segue to the next creature.

41:1–34: God. Can Job catch Leviathan? Likely not a crocodile, Leviathan is a creature of epic mythic presence (see commentary on 3:1–10). Leviathan is a wild, chaotic force, and, whereas Behemoth evoked images of repose, Leviathan is fierce, fearless, menacing, and violent. God ends his second speech by describing this beast as one who looks down on all who are arrogant and proud (41:33–34). This is shocking to the common conception that Leviathan, as chaos, is to be thwarted and defeated. Here the creature is celebrated for its well-deserved pride.

42:1–6: Job. Job can do nothing but confess his unworthiness and lack of understanding. But Job's last words (42:6) are anything but clear. Job may be saying any of the following, and choosing one over the other depends on how one understands God's speeches and Job's reaction:

1. I despise myself and repent (sitting) on dust and ashes—an act of humbleness (so NIV);
2. I take back/retract myself (my words) and repent on dust and ashes;
3. I now reject and forswear dust and ashes—Job now rejects his symbols of mourning;
4. I retract my words and have changed my mind about dust and ashes—Job has changed his mind now about the human condition;
5. I retract my words and am comforted about dust and ashes—Job is at peace with the human condition;
6. I recant and relent being but dust and ashes—being human and not God he thus now understands that he must recant (so NJPS) (Newsom 1996, 629).

What does one make of these speeches? Just how is God answering Job? Newsom's insight is worth our time (Newsom 2003, 239–41, 252–56). God and Job are vastly different. Their respective understandings of reality are worlds apart. Therein lies a problem. Job's voice, especially in his closing soliloquy (Job 29–31), and God's speeches stand in contrast to each other, perhaps in contest with one another. The space and territory each occupies affects their respective outlooks. (1) Even though God has not appeared to Job, Job nevertheless views God as looking in on him and humanity (31:4, 6, 14–15). God is "with" Job, though

not physically. But God abolishes the notion that Job is truly with God ("Where were you?" 38:4). God purges Job from attendance at and knowledge associated with the foundations of the cosmos. Job is *not* close to God. (2) God's and Job's spaces are vastly different. Job's sphere has centered on his family, his friends, his land, and his place in society. God's space, in his speeches, has reached to the remotest portions of the cosmos: earth's foundations, primordial sea, gates of death, and storehouses of weather.

The accumulative weight of God's focusing on the wild and the chaotic is also key. The friends and Job, ironically, have both affirmed moral *order*, though in different ways. The friends are rooted deeply in the traditional paradigms of order related to punishment and reward. Job's view of moral order underpins his cry to confront God with charges of derelict behavior. Job has expectations, rooted in his understanding of God's *orderly* nature. God, rather, highlights the feral and chaotic. God crescendos to Leviathan, the epitome of chaos. Throughout, God appears not to be condemning or engaged in thwarting these forces. Disconcertingly, he seems to be celebrating them.

We are left at the very end with God, Leviathan, and Job. Perhaps we should see the latter two as antithesis, each representing but one aspect of the totality of existence. Neither order nor chaos alone is the full image. Most telling is the celebration of Leviathan's pride (41:33–34), the very last words of God. Leviathan is not here humbled. Job is! Job's pride has been addressed and dismantled. That pride, as Newsom has argued, characteristic of all humanity, is the *expectation* of and *demand* for order (Newsom 2003, 252). Job, in his last full speech where he rehearsed his days of orderliness compared to his present chaos (Job 29–31), voices the human drive for order, control, and safety, particularly for those close to us—the motive behind Job's sacrifices on behalf of his family. His, and ours, is a passion to thwart or deny the tragic. The expectation, now seen as the *arrogance*, that everything should be orderly and go well underlies the crushing devastation one feels at the catastrophic, the appalling, the dreadful, and the awful. The image of Leviathan—the uncontrollable—exposes the human self-deception about order. Order *and* chaos are antithetic complements of existence. They are opposites, yet they are complete-ments. Job falls silent. He understands this now.

Herein is irony. Zophar, early on, argued that if God could speak, he would show Job how shortsighted he is, how atrophied his understanding of universal truth is (11:5). Of course, Zophar expects God to bring Job around to the friends' understanding of truth. But Zophar's view is every bit as gaunt as Job's. All the friends have missed the mark, measured by God's words. God's condemnation of them is understandable. They have understood only the orderly side of life.

8. A Final Word

When Job finishes his last word, the storyteller moves to the epilogue (see commentary on prologue), and, as mentioned before, we encounter dissonance. Both Job and friends have spoken from half-full perspectives, and Job has earlier claimed that God is derelict about injustice (Job 24). Yet the friends are rebuked, and Job is exonerated. Why this is so is not crystal clear. The bookends alone give us a story arguably more simple. The bookends with the poetic core throw complexity our way.

It is understandable to feel frustrated. We leave the book uncertain why a heavenly dare had to be so cruel to Job and why the book, in its epilogue, reaffirms the principle of retribution, for which the friends have argued, against which Job has fought, and which God has declared an atrophied understanding of life. The book and its insights elude neat tidiness. We want clear answers, ready answers in life, and we especially want them from the Bible. But the elusive answer is biblical, seen elsewhere in the parable, particularly as used by Jesus, and the riddle (e.g., Prov. 1:6).

With the whole book in mind, the return to order in the face of God's contemplation and celebration of the wild and chaotic severs monologic understanding of the book. There is chaos, and there is order. Both forces play out. But taking a clue that only the "Maker" can approach the chaotic force that is Behemoth (40:19), the book acknowledges that God somehow stands beyond the grip of such forces.

Think about Job and ourselves as readers. Consider where we were in our respective understandings at the beginning of the story. We have journeyed far. And though the book has decided on a "happy ending," that is not the sum total. The journey through competing polyphonic ideas and ideals that remain in tension has Job and us leave as different people.

Select Bibliography

Albright, W. F. "Northwest-Semitic Names in a List of Egyptian Slaves from the Eighteenth Century B.C." *Journal of the American Oriental Society* 74 (1954): 222–33.

Bakhtin, Mikhail. *Problems of Dostoevsky's Poetics.* Theory and History of Literature 8. Translated and edited by Caryl Emerson. Minneapolis: University of Minnesota Press, 1984.

Carson, D. A. "Mystery and Faith in Job 38:1–42:16." In *Sitting with Job: Selected Studies on the Book of Job.* Edited by Roy B. Zuck. Grand Rapids: Baker Books, 1992.

Childs, Brevard S. *Introduction to the Old Testament as Scripture.* Philadelphia: Fortress, 1979.

Clines, David J. A. *Job 21–37.* Word Biblical Commentary. Nashville: Thomas Nelson, 2006.

———. "Job's Fifth Friend: An Ethical Critique of the Book of Job." *Biblical Interpretation* 12 (2004): 233–50.

———. *Job 1–20.* Word Biblical Commentary. Dallas: Word, 1989.

Dhorme, E. *A Commentary on the Book of Job.* Translated by Harold Knight. London: Thomas Nelson and Sons, 1967.

Gordis, Robert. *The Book of Job: Commentary, New Translation, and Special Studies.* Moreshet 2. New York: Jewish Theological Seminary of America, 1978.

———. "The Significance of the Paradise Myth." *American Journal of Semitic Languages and Literatures* 52 (1936): 86–94.

Guillaume, Philippe, and Michael Schunck. "Job's Intercession: Antidote to Divine Folly." *Biblica* 88 (2007): 457–72.

Habel, Norman C. *The Book of Job.* Old Testament Library. Philadelphia: Westminster, 1985.

Hurvitz, Avi. "The Date of the Prose-Tale of Job Linguistically Reconsidered." *Harvard Theological Review* 67 (1974): 17–34.

Janzen, J. G. *Job.* Interpretation. Atlanta: John Knox, 1985.

Newsom, Carol A. *The Book of Job: A Contest of Moral Imaginations.* New York: Oxford University Press, 2003.

———. "The Book of Job: Introduction, Commentary, and Reflections." In *The New Interpreter's Bible.* Edited by Leander E. Keck. Vol. 4. Nashville: Abingdon, 1996.

Phillips, Elaine A. "Speaking Truthfully: Job's Friends and Job." *Bulletin for Biblical Research* 18 (2008): 31–43.

Polzin, Robert. "Framework of the Book of Job." *Interpretation* 28 (1974): 182–200.

Pope, Marvin H. *Job: Introduction, Translation, and Notes.* Anchor Bible. Garden City, NY: Doubleday, 1973.

Zuckerman, Bruce. *Job the Silent: A Study in Historical Counterpoint.* New York: Oxford University Press, 1991.

Psalms

Barry C. Davis

Introduction

The Psalms are designed to comfort and to disturb—to minister to our anguish and yet to break us from the complacency of our lives. They do not want us to walk away feeling merely "blessed." They want us, at times, to feel bludgeoned, battered, and torn apart. They attack our sensibilities—shaking us to the very roots of our beings—yet they resonate within us with the realization that, perhaps for the first time in our lives, we truly have been understood.

The psalmists expect us to enter with them into the glorious worship of our God—we like that. The psalmists also expect us to join with them in calling for and rejoicing over the destruction of the enemies of our God—for some reason, we feel less than comfortable about that. Some psalms we relate to: we have walked the lonely or tragic path that the psalmist has walked; other psalms make little sense to us: we may even question the psalmists' reasons for writing them. We wonder how a godly person could write a psalm that expresses personal depression or rage at God, hopelessness, bitterness, or caustic invective. We also marvel and are incredulous that a person experiencing deep personal struggles or the deceptive attacks of an enemy could record words that draw us into the highest heaven—words that make our spirits soar or perhaps cause us to feel a glimmer of hope in the midst of our overwhelming sorrow.

Yet, whether we find a given psalm particularly appealing, feel revulsed by it, or simply read it "because it is there," each of the 150 psalms is designed to guide us, discipline us, alter our thoughts and attitudes, or mold us into being more and more like the God of the Bible, the God whom we serve.

The Psalms sit fixed on the pages of the text, unmoved and unchanged like granite. Their words remain always the same; their meaning never changes. Yet, each time we read them, we are different, and God uses them to intrude in our lives and burn his eternal truth into us so that in each meeting with the familiar and the not-so-familiar psalms, we feel we have encountered them again for the first time.

Even a cursory look at the Psalms reveals that their authors intended them to be sung aloud (often following set tunes accompanied by various instruments), read aloud

Statue of a harpist from the tomb of Nykauinpu, Giza

(sometimes antiphonally or responsively), or meditated on. The Psalms are written at times for private use—to express deep feelings of anguish, contrition, or gratitude; at times for informal gatherings of believers—to teach and encourage one another and to praise God; and at times for formal worship services, specific celebrations, or national events. New Testament believers continued many of these practices (cf. Luke 20:41–44; Eph. 5:19; Col. 3:16).

Composition, Authorship, and Structure

Under God's guidance, the 150 psalms tell a unified story—a story of hope in the midst of the chaos of life. They begin with a picture of life as it should be: the righteous always triumphing, the wicked always losing. In other words, Psalm 1 portrays life in an ideal world, not the world that many, if any, of us experience.

Psalm 1, however, establishes one of the key themes of the Psalter: the battle between the righteous and the wicked.

Psalm 2 presents the second major focus of the book of Psalms: the messianic hope—the Messiah who intervenes in the epic battle between good and evil, defeating his enemies and bringing victory to his people.

That messianic victory drives the Psalter (and life for the believer) to its ultimate conclusion—to Psalm 150—to the free, unencumbered joy of praising God. Like Psalm 1, Psalm 150 is not a reality of present-day life. Even the delight experienced and expressed in corporate worship is often tainted by our exhaustion from a

Ivory book cover showing David dictating the Psalms (tenth–eleventh century AD)

week of work or by our worries about family problems, careers, personal failures, future plans, or what's for lunch. The unspoiled, exuberant expression of praise to God—and seeing those around us also freely proclaiming the wonder of our God—is in its purest sense an experience reserved for us in heaven.

The psalmists are realists. They recognize that life is less than perfect, that it is, in fact, downright difficult. They know that life is not as it should be or as it will be, so they recorded the psalms in between Psalms 1 and 150 to present a picture of life as it is—that is, a picture of the realities of life where there is pain and suffering, where good does not always triumph, and where evil (at times, or even much of the time) seems to overwhelm. On occasion, God graciously gives us an inside glimpse to the world of Psalms 1 and 150, but for the most part we live in the world of the in-between psalms.

The 150 psalms of the Psalter were written over a period of approximately one thousand years—from the time of Moses (Ps. 90), if not earlier, to the time of Ezra (Ps. 119?), Haggai and Zechariah (Psalms 146? and 147?), or later (if the Septuagint, the second-century-BC Greek translation of the Hebrew Scriptures, is correct). The superscriptions of the Hebrew text identify seven different authors as having written one hundred of the psalms (crediting David with seventy-three of them), the remaining fifty being anonymous (the Septuagint alleging five individuals as writing fourteen of them). Note, however, that there is debate regarding what a superscription actually means when it declares a given psalm to be "of David," "of Asaph," or "of" anyone else. Most argue that the Hebrew preposition translated "of" is intended to mean "written by," whereas some favor other grammatically possible meanings, such as "written about," "written for" (i.e., commissioned by), or "written to."

Through the centuries, God guided the writing, collating, and editing of the Psalter, linking certain psalms into unified groups (e.g., Ps. 22–24; 56–60; 93–100; 107–18; 120–34; 146–50). The compilers and editors brought the individual psalms together into five books and then, at the linking of the five books into one, possibly added similar words of praise to the concluding psalm of each of the first four books (even though that psalm might not be a praise psalm itself). In drawing those books together to convey God's intended story, the compilers emphasized either God's covenant relationship with Israel by the use of his name Yahweh (NIV = LORD) or his power and authority over all peoples, by using his general title Elohim (NIV = God), as noted below.

Book	Chapters	Concluding Praise	Yahweh	Elohim
1	1–41	41:13	277	48
2	42–72	72:18–19	31	188
3	73–89	89:52	43	59
4	90–106	106:48	101	19
5	107–50	146–50	226	28

Each of the five books contributes to the overall story of the Psalms, with each book advancing a different perspective on that story.

By presenting how the author reacts to the crises he or others are facing, the first chapter of each book sets the emotional tone for its respective book. The flow of these "first chapters" reveals a deepening of despair from book 1 to book 3. In book 3, that despair begins to shift to a sense of hopefulness—hopefulness that grows into bold confidence by the end of book 5.

Although the first chapters present what may appear to be a straight-line path from confidence to discouragement to exuberant delight, the individual psalms within each book do not rigidly follow this pattern. At times, they project more or less optimism or pessimism than do their respective first chapters, but those psalms nevertheless do tend to reflect, in some ways, the tone of that first chapter.

Psalms 1 and 2 are introductory chapters to the entire Psalter. As noted above, they lay out the major themes of good versus evil and the messianic hope, respectively.

In Psalm 3, the first psalm of book 1, David exhibits fearless confidence in God's control over all things. Despite the fact that he has been dethroned by his son Absalom and is fleeing for his life, David expresses no doubts whatsoever that God will give him victory in the midst of what arguably could be considered one of the greater tragedies of David's life. Book 1 is very positive. Note, for example, the difference between the tone of Psalm 23 (book 1) and that of Psalm 88 (book 3). Both speak about being close to death, but whereas Psalm 23 is quite upbeat, Psalm 88 is anything but.

Psalm 42 (book 2) reveals that discouragement has set in. The author conveys the sense that life used to be happy but is now sad. He remembers God; he knows that God is good; yet he finds himself in despair and has to steel his courage to place his hope in God.

Hopelessness is the operative word for the first half of Psalm 73, the opening chapter of book 3. The psalmist, a leader among God's people, is so depressed that he is ready to forsake the way of righteousness and to join with the arrogant oppressors. They prosper; he knows only failure. Then one day, when he is at his lowest, he discovers God's perspective on life: the wicked may have victory in this life, but the righteous will have victory for all eternity. The psalmist's bitterness turns to hope. He knows that, with God's help, he will ultimately succeed.

Book 4 continues the move toward joyful confidence in God. Moses, the author of Psalm

90, gains further understanding that God, not the wicked, holds sway over all that transpires in life. Moses also realizes that the true source of their crisis is not their enemies but God, who is judging them (Moses and his people) for their sins. Moses then calls on God to help them walk humbly and joyfully before him. Interestingly, by the end of book 4 (and prominently in book 5), the command "Hallelujah" (i.e., Praise the LORD), not seen previously in the Psalter, bursts forth in glorious splendor.

Psalm 107 begins book 5 by declaring that God guides his people and deals with them wonderfully when they turn back to him. God defeats the wicked and gives victory to the upright, even though he does not remove his people from the problems of life. The remainder of book 5 advances hope and confidence in God. It concludes with five psalms of joyous praise—the final psalm being essentially pure praise for who God is and what he does.

Having seen that the Psalter tells a story, how then should we study it to determine God's intended meaning and how that meaning might impact our lives?

Methods for Reading the Psalms

Although there are many ways to study the Psalms, those who seriously read through the psalms generally use four prominent methods. A brief discussion of those methods follows.

First, the devotional method is the reading of the various psalms of the Psalter in no particular order, but reading individual psalms or portions of psalms for the purpose of receiving a blessing from God. Its strengths include the following: it requires a minimal amount of time to complete, focuses on the emotional aspects of the psalms, and seeks to affect the reader's own spirit. As for its weaknesses, the devotional approach to the Psalms may rip verses out of their proper context or lead to an inadequate understanding of the theology of the passage and, as a result, leave the reader ill equipped to face the realities of life or to defend the faith when questioned.

Second, the historical-context method is the reading of the Psalter in no particular order, but reading a given psalm in light of its original historical context. Strengths: it seeks to return to the point of original inspiration of a given psalm; provides a sense of historical validation; and attempts to understand the psalm in the context of the original author, setting, and readers. Weaknesses: it cannot always re-create the original context fully enough to ensure that a psalm is being understood in its original setting (e.g., "a psalm of David" may have been written when David was a shepherd, when he was anointed as king but not yet ruling and was being chased by King Saul, when he was ruling as king, when he was forced off the throne by Absalom, or when he returned to the throne), may require the use of extrabiblical sources to be able to understand the Scripture, and may assume that the "event" a psalm describes is inspired just as is the composition of the text about the event.

Third, the functional-genre method is the reading of a psalm in light of its function within the worship practices of the ancient people of Israel—that function being understood generally as fulfilling one of (though not limited to) the following roles: hymns, community laments, thanksgiving songs of the individual, laments of the individual, or poems of mixed type—enthronement, victory, processionals, songs of Zion. Strengths: it helps readers understand the meaning of a given psalm in light of other psalms that were written according to a similar pattern, it fits well with the view that the psalms were designed to meet the needs of the religious community, and it accounts for the use of the Psalter by the community of believers and by individual believers. Weaknesses: it offers no conclusive proof that the psalms were ever used in ancient times according to the categories cited in the definition above, it tends to overlook subtle differences among the various psalms of a given functional category, and it may generate confusion, since there is a lack of consensus among scholars regarding the definition and details of the various categories of worship practices.

A more popular approach to the functional-genre method is the classification of psalms according to their content or style; for example, psalms reflecting the human soul in its cry for God: extreme distress (6; 69; 77), joy (1; 16; 24; 40; 103; 107), or thirst for God (42–43; 63); psalms focusing on God himself: adoration (34; 45; 48; 95–100), contrasting him to idols (14; 53; 115; 135), God as refuge (18; 46; 61–62; 90–91), or God as eternal king (47; 93; 97; 99); psalms relating to the Messiah (based on New Testament references) (2; 8; 16; 22; 24; 31; 34–35; 40–41; 45; 61; 68–69; 72; 89; 96–98; 103; 109–10; 118); psalms invoking a curse (i.e., imprecatory psalms) (35; 58–59; 69; 83; 109; 137); and acrostic (alphabet) psalms (9–10; 25; 34; 37; 111–12; 119; 145).

Fourth, the literary-context method is the reading of a psalm in light of its context within the written Word of God, that is, reading it in the context of the psalms that surround it just as one would read Genesis 13 in the context of Genesis 12 and 14. Strengths: it views the 150 psalms of the Psalter as a literary unit and requires each psalm to be interpreted in light of that literary context, recognizes the canonical nature of the psalms, and accounts for the arrangement of the psalms and for the editing of the Psalter. Weaknesses: it removes the meaning of a psalm from its original historical context, downplays the role of the original author of a given psalm, and requires that the doctrine of inspiration encompass not only the work of the original author but also the work of the ancient editors and compilers of the Psalter—up to and including the point in time when the Psalter reached its final canonical state.

This commentary on Psalms adheres to the literary-context method of interpretation and on occasion discusses the interconnections between various psalms. Because space is limited, only a few connections are cited. You are encouraged to look for additional linkages.

Some of the linkages between psalms may be identified by observing the following:

similar themes; repeated terms, phrases, or even complete verses; a question asked in one psalm being answered in the next; the ideas at the end of one psalm flowing into the beginning of the next; or words rarely used in the Psalms or in Scripture appearing in both psalms. There are also other legitimate connections that can be made among sequential psalms. Applying these guidelines reveals the following interconnections (among others) in Psalms 107–18:

1. Each of the twelve psalms exhibits either key word or thematic (or both) connections with every other psalm in the group.
2. An inclusio (i.e., a repeated verse) surrounds the group (cf. 107:1; 118:29).
3. There is a tendency for the psalms that are sequentially closer to one another to have stronger key-word ties than for those that are farther apart.
4. Three themes are interwoven through these psalms: God deserves praise (10 of 12 psalms), God delivers his people (10 of 12), and God dominates the created order (6 of 12).
5. Psalms 111–13 all begin with the command "Praise the LORD"; Psalms 115–17 all end with that same command.
6. Psalm 111 ends with a discussion of fearing the Lord; Psalm 112 continues that discussion.
7. Psalms 107–9 display a plea for deliverance; Psalms 111–13 offer praise for having been delivered; Psalm 110 connects the two groups by presenting God the Messiah as the deliverer (who deserves the praise of Psalms 111–13).

To be able to understand the meaning of individual psalms requires not only that we study them in their literary context but also that we interpret them in light of the principles of Hebrew poetry. Neglecting to understand Hebrew poetic form may result in incorrect interpretations of a given psalm.

Chart 1   Examples of Parallelism in Hebrew Poetry

A. Synonymous Parallelism

1. Complete   A B C D / A′ B′ C′ D′

	A	B	C	D
Ps. 94:16	Who	will rise up	for me	against the wicked?
	A	**B′**	**C**	**D′**
	Who	will take a stand	for me	against evildoers?

	A	B	C	
Ps. 46:7	The LORD Almighty	is	with us;	
	A′	**B**	**C′**	
	the God of Jacob	is	our fortress.	

2. Incomplete   A B C / A′ B′ –

	A	B	C
Ps. 96:13b	He will judge	the world	in righteousness
		B′	**C′**
		and the peoples	in his faithfulness.

	A	B	C
Ps. 24:1	The earth	is the LORD's,	and everything in it,
	A′		**C′**
	the world,		and all who live in it.

3. Incomplete with Compensation   A B C –/ A′ B′ – D

	A	B	C	
Ps. 96:1	Sing	to the LORD	a new song;	
	A	**B**		**D**
	sing	to the LORD,		all the earth.

	A	B	C	
Ps. 98:5	make music	to the LORD	with the harp,	
			C	**D**
			with the harp	and the sound of singing.

B. Antithetical Parallelism

1. Complete   A B C / A′ B′ C′

	A	B	C
Ps. 18:26	to the pure	you show yourself	pure,
	A′	**B**	**C′**
	but to the devious	you show yourself	shrewd.

	A	B	C
Ps. 30:5a	For his anger	lasts	only a moment,
	A′	**B**	**C′**
	but his favor	lasts	a lifetime.

2. Incomplete   A B C / A′ B′ –

	A	B	C
Ps. 119:67	Before	I was afflicted	I went astray,
	A′		**C′**
	but now		I obey your word.

	A	B	C
Ps. 30:7	LORD,	when you favored me,	you made my royal mountain stand firm;
		B′	**C′**
		but when you hid your face,	I was dismayed.

3. Incomplete with Compensation   A B C –/ A′ B′ – D

	A	B	C	D	
Ps. 1:6	For the LORD	watches over	the way	of the righteous,	
			C′	**D′**	**E**
			but the way	of the wicked	leads to destruction.

	A	B	C	
Ps. 147:6	The LORD	sustains	the humble	
		B′	**C′**	**D**
		but casts	the wicked	to the ground.

Continued

C. Synthetic Parallelism

1. Continuous "Narration" A B C » — » D E F

	A	B		
	that I may walk	before the LORD		
Ps. 116:9			C	D
			in the land	of the living.

2. Disjointed "Narration" A B C « — » D E F

	A	B			
	They have freely scattered their gifts	to the poor,			
Ps. 112:9		C	D	E	
		their righteousness	endures	forever;	
			F	G	H
			their horn	will be lifted high	in honor.

Hebrew poetry is not based on either a rhyme scheme or meter; instead, it operates on the basis of a parallelism of ideas. That is to say, the second line of a couplet plays off the first, at times bolstering or restating in different words the thought of the first line (synonymous parallelism), at times showing a contrasting idea (antithetical parallelism), and at times completing the thought or moving in a different direction (synthetic parallelism).

For example, in Chart 1, the author of 94:16 (synonymous parallelism: complete) records God's seemingly asking for two different groups of people to accomplish two different actions against two other groups of people. Knowing the concept of synonymous parallelism, however, we realize that God is seeking one individual (or one group of people) to act (rise up/take a stand) on his behalf in opposition to all (the wicked/evildoers) who do not care about him.

In 96:13b (synonymous parallelism: incomplete), the words "he will judge" apply to both lines. The psalmist, moreover, is not indicating that God will judge one group of people, called "the world," by means of righteousness and another group, called "the peoples" (people groups?) by his faithfulness. "The world" and "the peoples" are one and the same, and God will judge that one group by both his righteousness and his faithfulness.

The antithetical parallelism (incomplete with compensation) of 1:6 reveals that those whom God watches over will remain, whereas those whom he does not watch over will be destroyed.

In the two examples of synthetic parallelism, the second line of the continuous "narration" example (116:9) simply completes the thought of the first line, whereas the second and third lines of the disjointed "narration" (112:9) do not have a direct connection to the first line. (Note: the word "narration" is in quotation marks to remind us that we are still reading poetry, not a narrative text, and that the various rules of poetry apply.)

Key Terms

Following are brief discussions of selected terms appearing in the Psalter or in typical analyses of Hebrew poetry.

Acrostic or alphabet psalms. Psalms in which typically the first word of each verse begins with a different letter of the Hebrew alphabet, running in sequence from the beginning to the end of the alphabet (25; 34; 37; 111–12; 119; 145). Not all acrostic psalms are complete (9–10; 145). Psalm 119 is unique in that it begins the first word of eight verses in a row with the same letter of the alphabet, moves on to the next letter of the alphabet in the following eight verses, and continues doing so throughout the remainder of the psalm, completing the alphabet in that way. A given author may have written an acrostic psalm to provide a memorization aid or to suggest that he had "covered" the topic of the psalm "from a to z."

Chiasm/chiastic structure. Within a verse, a chiastic structure indicates that the first part of the first line parallels the last part of the second line, while at the same time the last part of the first line matches up with the first part of the second line. The chiastic structure strengthens the interconnections between the ideas. Psalm 2:10 provides the following example:

A   you kings
   B   be wise
   B′   be warned
A′   you rulers on the earth

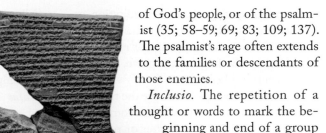

Acrostics are found in Akkadian literature as well. This royal prayer of Ashurbanipal (Neo-Assyrian period) is written as an acrostic that forms the message "I am Ashurbanipal" when read down the left edge.

When observed in a sequence of verses within a psalm (e.g., 67:1–7; 126:2–3), a chiastic pattern appears as follows (note: the pattern may contain fewer or more elements—with the central item[s] in the structure being presumed to be emphasized):

A   (first idea)
   B   (second idea)
     C   (key idea)
   B′   (second idea restated, typically in different words than before)
A′   (first idea restated, typically in different words than before)

Imprecatory psalms. These psalms call for the brutal destruction of the enemies of God,

of God's people, or of the psalmist (35; 58–59; 69; 83; 109; 137). The psalmist's rage often extends to the families or descendants of those enemies.

Inclusio. The repetition of a thought or words to mark the beginning and end of a group of verses or psalms (e.g., the word "blessed" appears in 1:1 and 2:12 to set Psalms 1 and 2 apart as a unit of thought; see also the repetition of an entire verse in 107:1 and 118:29 that links all of the psalms from 107 through 118 together).

Messianic psalms. Any psalm that makes reference in any of its verses to the coming Messiah. The surest way to label a psalm as messianic is to discover other passages of Scripture that make reference to a verse or idea in the psalm and do so in a context of a discussion regarding the Messiah.

Praise and lament. The primary (though not exclusive) communicative components of the individual psalms are the expressions of praise and lament. These expressions may have been originally the spontaneous outbursts of emotion of the psalmists or the reasoned thoughts of worshipers in quiet moments of meditation or prayer. The fact that the psalms are now written documents, on the one hand, lessens to some extent their spontaneity or freshness; on the other hand, it intensifies the reflective moment, moving each psalm from mere words on a page to that which calls for—demands—our attention and response.

Selah. The precise meaning of the term "Selah" (appearing seventy-four times in the Psalter) is unknown. Some of the more frequently offered interpretations are that it means a musical interlude, a pause for meditation, or a crescendo of music.

Sheol. This term has a range of meanings, including a pit in the ground, a grave, the place of the dead, and hell.

The righteous. The psalmists use the title "the righteous" to indicate all who are committed to God, irrespective of whether or not they are living godly lives. In other words, all who have a personal interest in God are identified as "the righteous."

The wicked. The psalmists use the title "the wicked" to indicate all who have no interest in God, irrespective of whether or not they are living sinful lives. In other words, all who do not have a personal relationship with God are identified as being "the wicked."

Outline

1. Book 1 (1:1–41:13)
2. Book 2 (42:1–72:20)
3. Book 3 (73:1–89:52)
4. Book 4 (90:1–106:48)
5. Book 5 (107:1–150:6)

Commentary

1. Book 1 (1:1–41:13)

Psalm 1. This psalm forces readers to make a choice: serve God and succeed or follow the world and lose. Yet the author of this psalm and those of the remaining psalms know that life is not so simple. The righteous do not always get ahead; the ungodly do not always fail. This psalm describes how life ideally should play out on earth and how it ultimately will turn out in eternity. It establishes a key theme traced throughout the Psalms: the righteous (those committed to God) contrasted to the wicked (those with little interest in God).

To experience true happiness, believers reject the ways of those who do not serve God and embrace God's truth, considering the implications of truth for all aspects of life (1:1–2). Doing so brings stability, refreshment, and fruitfulness to life (1:3).

Following the world makes one as stable as dust in a windstorm, whether on earth or in eternal judgment (1:4–5). God gives absolute success to those with whom he has an intimate relationship (1:6).

Psalm 2. Whereas in 1:2 the righteous meditate on God's truth, in 2:1–2, the wicked plot (literally "meditate") God's destruction and that of the Messiah (the Anointed One). Psalm 2 inaugurates the second major theme of the Psalms: the Messiah as final resolver of the problems believers encounter.

The nations rage at God, seeking their own way, but God laughs at their folly, countering with his own fury that shakes them to their core (2:3–5).

The psalmist reveals the relationship between God and his appointed king (Father and Son—2:6–7). This king will reign over the earth with absolute power (2:8–9). All people are urged to yield themselves joyfully to the Lord and to his Son (2:10–12). Verse 12 echoes Psalm 1—rejecting God's Son brings ultimate destruction (1:6); embracing him brings blessing (1:1–2).

Psalm 3. Building on the introductory psalms, Psalm 3 sets the tone for book 1—the righteous under attack, emboldened by the divine protector to face difficulties with confidence. The superscription places David in a crisis that rips his kingdom and family apart (cf. 2 Samuel 15–19—Absalom deposing David; God reestablishing David's kingship).

This psalm exhibits a four-part structure: (1) enemies in overwhelming numbers declare that God will not give the psalmist victory (3:1–2); (2) God responds to the psalmist's cries for help, giving protection and success (the "lifting of one's head" indicates the achievement of victory, not the overcoming of discouragement—cf. Ps. 27:6; 110:7) (3:3–4); (3) God from his "holy hill" (cf. 2:6) gives the psalmist peace in the midst of crisis (3:5–6); and (4) the psalmist (despite enemy dissuasion—3:1–2) confidently seeks God's help for his people (3:7–8).

Psalm 4. Facing different challenges in Psalm 4 than in Psalm 3, the psalmist resolves them using similar methods and experiences similar results. In Psalm 3, David encounters physical assault (3:1); here, he is grieved by their ungodly lives (4:2, 6). In both psalms, he calls to God for help, certain that God will respond positively (3:4; 4:1, 3, 7) and provide security despite the chaos (3:5; 4:8). His adversaries, however, do not recognize God as the true source of help (3:2; 4:6).

David issues seven commands to the ungodly (4:3–5): "know" that God favors the righteous (not those who dishonor him); "tremble" (NIV "in your anger") because of encountering God (cf. Ps. 18:7; 77:16, 18; 99:1); "do not sin"; "search" your hearts at night (cf. the righteous's peaceful sleep, 4:8); "be silent" (in God's presence); "offer" true sacrifices (unlike those you offer to idols, 4:2); and "trust" in God. By contrast (4:7–8), those who please God receive superabundant joy, peace (i.e., wholeness, things as they should be), and security.

Psalm 5. David presents the stark contrast between the righteous and the wicked (cf. Psalm 1). The righteous seek God, and God blesses them. The wicked, however, have no access to God because God abhors their acts.

David (one of the righteous) opens with a personal plea to God for help yet does not detail the specifics of his problem (5:1–3). Next David unveils God's feelings toward the wicked, either through his own reactions or through their acts (5:4–6). David then declares his desire to worship God and seeks his guidance in the face of

his enemies (5:7–8). By contrast, David pleads to God to not even hear the words of the wicked but to condemn the wicked because they cannot be trusted (5:9–10). God, however, should welcome the righteous because they place their hope and love in him; he is, moreover, the one who envelops them with his kindness (5:11–12).

Psalm 6. Suffering physically and emotionally (6:2–3)—totally exhausted (6:6–7)—David seeks relief from God's discipline (6:1–4) and from the pressure of his enemies (6:7–8, 10).

In verses 1–5, David pleads for God to show mercy rather than the heat of his rage (6:1–2). No longer able to stand the torment (6:2–3), David cries to God for deliverance. He appeals via three lines of argumentation: (1) his own interminable suffering (6:2–3), (2) God's undying love (6:4), and (3) his own desire to praise God while still alive (6:5).

In verses 6–10, David denounces his enemies as the cause of his misery (6:6–7). His tears that his enemies rejoice over are the same tears that move God to shame and terrify those same enemies (6:8–10).

The psalmists understand the reality of the afterlife. They know they will praise God even in death (e.g., Ps. 44:8; 52:9; 145:1). In 6:5, David highlights the silence of the tomb—that no one buried there can be heard on earth to praise God.

Psalm 7. God is a righteous judge who battles daily those deserving judgment, whether they are his people or his people's enemies (7:6, 8, 11–13). Yet the psalmist does not run from that judge; instead, he seeks refuge in,

Psalm 7:12 describes God as sharpening his sword and stringing his bow. The use of such military imagery to describe deity was common in the ancient world. In this Neo-Assyrian relief, the god Ashur is shown with a drawn bow, accompanying Ashurnasirpal II into battle.

deliverance by, and justice from him (7:1, 6, 8). The psalmist—fully confident of his innocence of charges against him—even risks allowing God to judge him, either by his enemies or by himself, knowing that such judgment might result in his death (7:4–5, 8).

Although the psalmist seeks protection from his all-too-powerful enemies (7:1–2), he knows that God will ultimately judge them (7:11–13) or their own actions will crash down on them (7:14–16). The psalmist, who seeks God as a powerful protector who overthrows his enemies (7:6, 8), praises God most for his righteousness (7:17).

Psalm 8. David interweaves two contrasting themes: significance and seeming insignificance.

Significance—God's greatness (8:1); seeming insignificance—helpless infants (8:2—cf. Matt. 21:16); significance—God's use of infants to defeat his enemies (8:2).

Significance—God's expansive creation (8:3); seeming insignificance—comparatively tiny human beings (8:4); significance—God takes an interest in humans (8:4).

Seeming insignificance (?)—God makes humans lower than angels (8:5); significance—God makes humans to rule over his creation (8:6–8).

Significance—God's greatness (8:9).

David assumes that God is the Creator of heaven and earth, which are not themselves self-existing or self-sustaining. God empowers humans to conquer against overwhelming odds (8:2) and to manage what is beyond their ability to comprehend (8:6–8). David surrounds the psalm with an inclusio of praise regarding God's majesty (8:1, 9).

Psalm 9. Psalm 9:1–2 echoes 7:17 via a high degree of repetition of Hebrew words. David declares that he will sing praise to God's name, telling of his wonders (quite probably the wonders in Psalm 8).

Other connections exist between chapters 7 and 9. Two different verbs translated "judge" and the noun translated "righteousness" in 7:8 also appear in 9:8 (cf. 9:4 and Prov. 31:9). In addition,

9:15–16 links back to 7:14–16, describing the truism that those who sin stumble over their own sins to their own detriment.

The remainder of chapter 9 reveals God's protection of those who trust and serve him in righteousness (9:9–10, 12–13) and his destruction of those who oppose him (vv. 3, 5–6). God's people are to praise him and declare his great works to the world (9:11).

A partially hidden acrostic, beginning in Psalm 9 and concluding in Psalm 10, suggests a linkage between the two psalms.

Psalm 10. Whereas Psalm 9 announces that God at times protects and delivers his people from the afflictions that bring them close to death, Psalm 10 indicates that God may not necessarily enact that deliverance quickly; he may allow the enemies of his people to inflict terrifying suffering on them over long periods of time.

The psalmist begins with a question: Where are you, God, when I need you most? The enemy is boastful and self-absorbed, rejoicing in greed and rejecting God (10:2–4). This foul-mouthed enemy sneers at God's people, destroying the helpless—seemingly never experiencing tragedy, only success (10:5–10), and somehow escaping God's judgment (10:11–13).

Despite describing two divergent pathways of life, the psalmist(s) of Psalms 9 and 10 draw(s) the same conclusion: God rules over the wicked and the righteous alike. He deeply cares about suffering of his people and ultimately mercifully overcomes their problems (9:9–10, 12, 16–18; 10:14, 16–18).

Psalm 11. If David flees for his life, seeking protection from earthly things rather than from God, he will be deserting the foundational truths of his life (11:1–3). David knows that God, who is firmly fixed on his heavenly throne, understands the thoughts of the righteous and the wicked and executes a very different judgment on the two groups (11:4–7).

The two judgments anticipated in verses 6 and 7 may depict eternal judgment (suffering the fire of hell or enjoying the face of God in heaven—cf. 11:4), or they may be metaphoric representations of God's censure of unbelievers and gracious reward of believers on earth.

Psalm 12. A psalm about words—the deceitful, destructive words of the godless (12:2–4); the true, unfailing word of the Lord (12:5–6). The beginning and the ending of the psalm present God's enemies as dominant in a world where the righteous are few in number (12:1–2, 8). Although the psalmist knows that he is not the sole believer in God on earth (cf. "us" in 12:7), he feels overwhelmed by a world filled with self-centered, self-aggrandizing oppressors. He seeks God's help, knowing that God will do what he promises (12:1, 3, 5–7). Yet, even though God one day will rise and conquer on behalf of his people (12:5), he has not yet done so, and the world remains the playground of those who rejoice in evil (12:8).

Psalm 13. Manifested in a fourfold cry to the Lord—"how long" (13:1–2), David's emotional stress exposes four agonized concerns: (1) that he may have become "invisible" to God, that is, that God will no longer act on his behalf; (2) that God is angry with him, intentionally turning away from him; (3) that his frustrations and personal suffering may never end; and (4) that he will not find relief from enemy oppression. David pleads for answers—his life and happiness depend on what God does or does not do (13:3). If God does not help him, the enemy wins and rejoices over him (13:4). If God helps him, he triumphs and rejoices in God's deliverance (13:5–6).

Psalm 14. The world is filled with those who take little interest in God, living in ways displeasing to him (e.g., corruptness, vileness, destroying God's people, taking advantage of the helpless) (14:1–4, 6). God, however, lives with his people, protecting them (14:5–6).

Note: Psalm 53 essentially replicates Psalm 14, except for 14:5–6 (Ps. 53:5). Psalm 14:5–6 fits particularly well the flow from Psalms 13–15. In 14:5–6, David focuses primarily on God's relation to those who are special to him (i.e., the righteous and the poor/afflicted). Those

verses, together with the remainder of the psalm, address David's concerns (Psalm 13) and set the stage for his discussion (Psalm 15) regarding those whom God allows to be close to him.

Psalm 14 ends much like Psalm 13: God's people will rejoice individually (13:5–6) or corporately (14:7) when he delivers them from their problems.

Psalm 15. With whom does God like to keep company (15:1)? David answers: those who live with integrity (15:2); who avoid harming others, by words or actions (15:3); who act as God acts toward the wicked (despising them) and toward the upright (honoring them) (15:4); and who are willing to suffer righteously, not taking advantage of a helpless person, even to their own detriment (15:4–5). Based on the questions asked and the answers given, some argue that Psalms 15 and 24 form part of the ancient liturgy sung upon entrance to worship at the temple.

Psalm 15 advances the concept of the ideal person (cf. Psalm 1), showing how the godly person pleases God and successfully handles life's challenges (described in later psalms).

Psalm 16. True goodness is found only in God and in those who are his followers (16:1–4). David finds delight in the holy ones who serve God (16:3) but not in those who turn to other gods—not even being willing to raise a glass in their honor at their death (16:4). He knows that God gives him a good life and guides him through it (16:5–7).

David concludes the psalm with several enigmatic statements: always seeing God (16:8a), God being at his right hand (16:8b), resting secure that the grave will not be the end (16:9–10), and having eternal delight at God's right hand (16:11). The New Testament indicates that David is writing not about himself but about the coming Messiah, Jesus (Acts 2:25–31; 13:35–37). Thus one thousand years in advance, David announces the resurrection of Jesus the Messiah.

Psalm 17. In five of the twelve direct commands/entreaties in this psalm (cf. 17:1, 6), David asks God to hear his prayers. In the remaining seven (cf. 17:7–8, 13–14), he desires God's protection and support. In the three indirect commands, David seeks God's favorable assessment regarding his attitudes and actions (cf. 17:2) and desires that God would overwhelm him with his presence (17:15—literally "when [I am] awakened, may you [fully] satisfy [me] with your likeness").

David portrays his enemies as violent, hardhearted, arrogant people who, like wild animals, steal what they can and circle ever closer to him, determined to devour him mercilessly (17:4, 9–12). While pleading for help, David expresses gratitude for God's unyielding compassion toward those whom he loves (17:14–15).

Psalm 18. David fully believes that God controls his enemies (18:3, 17, 40, 43, 48), death (18:4–5), nature (e.g., mountains, hail, lightning, rain clouds, water, sea—18:6–15), angels (18:10), and darkness (18:11, 28). David also has complete confidence that he has a relationship with that all-powerful God. Not only is the Lord David's God (18:2, 6, 21, 28–29), but he is also David's rock, fortress, shield, support, and Savior (18:1–2, 18, 46).

God gives David a remarkable victory over his enemies—empowering him to fight, honoring him after the battle, and causing the defeated nations to tremble before him (18:31–45). God does all this because he delights in David, and David remains faithfully obedient to him by living humbly and blamelessly, with God as his refuge (18:20–30).

David praises his God and determines to praise him throughout the nations. God's kindness to David extends through all generations (18:46–50).

Psalm 19. God's heavenly creation sings forth his message nonstop (19:1–2). Throughout the earth, the sun daily blazes God's truth for all to see (19:3–6).

God's written word is also a faithful proclaimer of God's message. Utilizing synonymous parallelism (19:7–9), David cites six names by which God's word is known: the law, statutes, precepts, commands, fear, and ordinances. Five of these six names are commonly recognized; the sixth, "the fear of the LORD," is not. David clearly wants his readers to recognize God's word as an awesome terror to be reckoned with. In 19:7–10, he also highlights numerous benefits of knowing and applying God's word.

David concludes by expressing his desire that God's word and ways would reign in his heart and that God would be pleased with all that he thinks and does (19:11–14).

Psalm 20. In 20:1–5, reflecting David's prayer in Psalm 19, the people of Israel express to the king their desire that God would help him, would accept his sacrifices, would give him the longings of his heart, and would deliver him.

The king responds, declaring that God delivers his anointed (i.e., King David himself) by his great strength (20:6).

Concurring with David's acknowledgment of God as the sole source of his victory, the people announce their intention to put their total confidence in God. To do anything less— such as to trust in military might—would be to court disaster (20:7–8). The people then seek God's deliverance for themselves (20:9).

Psalm 21. In an inclusio of praise to God for his strength, David and his people delight in their God (21:1, 13). Between those two declarations, David reveals God's exercise of strength toward his servant (21:2–7) and against his enemies (21:8–12).

God responds to the desires of the king's heart, overwhelming him with riches, long life, military success, and eternal blessings (21:2–6). God, moreover, makes the king immovable, because the king trusts in him (21:7).

In 21:8–12, David depicts God as controlling, consuming, and conquering his foes—foes who are unable to withstand the onslaught of God's strength.

As does Psalm 1, Psalm 21 reveals that God has very divergent destinies for the righteous and the wicked, both in this world and in eternity.

Psalm 22. New Testament authors clearly portray Psalm 22 as messianic; they do so either by citing it directly, as in 22:1 (Matt. 27:46; Mark 15:34); 22:18 (John 19:24); 22:22 (Heb. 2:12), or by referring to it, as in 22:7 (Mark 15:29); 22:8 (Matt. 27:43); 22:15 (John 19:28); and 22:16 (John 20:25).

Psalm 22 begins with deep anguish, a sense of being deserted by God, who does not answer the sufferer's prayers (22:1–2). The psalm concludes both with praise to God for responding favorably to the pleas of the helpless and with a declaration that God's message is a message for the ages (22:22–31). The inner portion of the psalm acknowledges God's worthiness to be praised for delivering those who trust him (22:3–5). Yet, feeling as though he has been deserted both by God and by humans (22:6–18), the speaker cries out to God for deliverance from those ravenous beings who hold his life in the balance (22:19–21).

Psalm 23. God brings comfort to the terrified psalmist, who, like the speaker in chapter 22, is on the edge of death (23:4). The speaker in chapter 22 anguishes over the horrific acts inflicted on him and over God's apparent desertion in the time of his greatest need. In stark contrast, in chapter 23,

In Psalm 23:6, David says that he "will dwell in the house of the LORD forever." In the ancient Near East, one way an individual's continual presence in the house of the deity would be represented was by placing a votive figure, like the one pictured here, in the temple (Sumer, Early Dynastic Period, 2900–2330 BC).

the psalmist joyfully and fully drinks in God's comfort (23:2–3).

Whereas in Psalm 22, the speaker maintains confidence in the Lord despite not being delivered from death by him, in Psalm 23 the author expresses full confidence in the Lord because God provides for his needs in times of weakness (23:1–3), guides and protects him in near-death experiences (23:4), and honors him abundantly in the midst of immediate danger (23:5).

David concludes by announcing that God aggressively pursues (not simply follows) him in this life and ensures that he will dwell with him in the next (23:6).

Psalm 24. In Psalm 23 David suggests that God's pursuit (23:6) is the basis by which he has eternal fellowship with God, but he fails to indicate what role he plays in securing that fellowship. Here in 24:4–6 David provides an answer: he is committed to the true God and to no other, and God has vindicated him, that is, declared him righteous. (That he has "clean hands" and a "pure heart" does not imply a sinless life; otherwise God would have no need to vindicate him.)

David also declares that God, the Creator and owner of the world (24:1–2), allows those who seek his face, faithfully serving him, to join him in his holy place (24:3–6). (Some believe Psalm 24 to be a component of the "entrance-to-worship" liturgy [cf. Psalm 15]). Furthermore, the time has come (God's people need to be prepared) for this all-powerful king of glory to return to his rightful place to reign among his people (24:7–10).

Psalm 25. Has David (cf. 24:4–6) lived a completely godly life? Psalm 25:7, 11, 18 clearly says no. David confesses his sin and seeks God's help. Yet, despite being a sinner, he is strongly committed to the Lord (25:1–2, 5, 15, 20–21). Near the beginning and the ending of this psalm, David declares that his hope is in God (25:5, 21) and prays that God would never allow him to be shamed by his enemies (25:2, 20; though, as David says, no one who trusts in God is ever truly put to shame—25:3). Throughout this acrostic psalm, David shifts back and forth from a desire for God's guidance along the right path (25:4–5, 8–9, 12–14) to a plea for God's mercy because he and his people have followed the wrong path (25:6–7, 10–11, 15–22).

Psalm 26. Once more (cf. 24:4), David boldly proclaims what appears to be a belief that he is without sin . . . or does he? With confidence, David declares himself to be blameless (26:1, 11), willing to be tested by God (26:2), faithful to God's word (26:3), an avoider of sin and sinners (26:4–5), and a man of worship in the midst of a godless society (26:5–12). But does he believe that he is perfect, without sin?

Though sounding much like the Pharisee in Jesus's parable (cf. Luke 18:9–14) who conceitedly announces his "spiritual greatness," David speaks truth about his actual godliness and, like the tax collector in that parable, recognizes his need for God's mercy (26:11). David trusts God fully; he does not waiver in his belief in the true God of Israel (26:1).

Psalm 27. Confidence in the Lord permeates David's thought (27:1, 3, 5, 10). He places his trust in the Lord and urges himself to increase that commitment (27:4, 8, 14).

The description of David's dedication here parallels that found in chapters 23–26. Psalm 27, however, emphasizes potential or real enemies and problems far more than those other psalms (27:3–6, 10–12). Yet, despite facing such dangers, David declares that he is not afraid, because God is his light, salvation, stronghold, protector, helper, and displayer of good (27:1, 5, 9, 13). As a consequence, David pleads with God never to turn him away but to allow him to remain in his presence always (27:4, 7, 9, 11–12).

Psalm 28. David's problems in Psalm 28 are more intense than in recent psalms. Yet his thoughts here parallel those in Psalm 27: a desire for God to hear his cry for mercy (27:7; 28:2), a plea to God not to treat him as he treats the wicked (27:12; 28:3), and an appeal to God not to desert him (27:9; 28:1).

David fears God's silence. He needs God's positive response for help; otherwise he would be like those who have died (28:1–2). Likewise, he fears experiencing God's negative response of judgment—like that deserved by God's enemies. They need God's judgment; he needs God's mercy (28:2–5). David, however, realizes that God does deal with him in mercy, as his protector, deliverer, and shepherd (28:6–9). David's fears are unfounded, for he experiences the joy of the Lord (28:1–2, 6–7).

Psalm 29. A powerful psalm of repetition—David over and over again proclaims the greatness of God—a greatness that extends over the forces of nature and overwhelms his heavenly host and his awed people.

David combines repetition with metaphoric language to drive his message about the power of God forward. Furthermore, he concludes each repetitive section with a different focus: angels (mighty ones) are to worship God, literally, "in [the] beauty of holiness" (29:2); God's majesty makes this world's glory seem as if it were nothing (29:5–6); and humans are to worship God, proclaiming, "Glory!" (29:9). Glory to God, who rules over the forces of the earth, who reigns forever, and who empowers his people and gives them peace (29:10–11). The ending is unexpected: God's terrifying power brings peace.

Psalm 30. God delivers David from a near-death encounter with his enemies (30:1–3); as a result, David praises God (30:4–5). God then establishes David, making his life secure

(30:6–7a). But God seemingly deserts David; so, in anguish, David cries out to him for mercy, for life, and for the ability to praise his faithfulness (30:7b–10). God once more turns David's mourning into rejoicing (30:11–12).

Psalm 30 is the finale of a four-act play that reveals how David's hopes and concerns in chapters 27–29 play out in the drama of his life. David firmly believes that if God were to establish him in his tabernacle, then he would be lifted up above his enemies (27:5–6); so he pleads to God for mercy—to preserve him from his enemies (27:7, 12; 28:2–3; 30:8–10). God answers David's prayer; he also keeps David from death (30:1–3). David then praises God for delivering him and for sparing his life (28:1–2, 6; 30:2–3, 9). Throughout these difficult times, David's confidence in the Lord never waivers (27:3; 30:6). He fears, though, that God might hide himself from him (27:9)—something that God apparently does (30:7); in the end, however, God transforms David's sorrow into joy (30:11–12). David, like other believers overwhelmed by God's majesty (29:1–11), declares that he will praise his God (30:12).

Psalm 31. In all three major stanzas of this psalm (31:1–8, 9–13, 14–22), David expresses strong confidence in God, even in the face of godless enemies who seek to ruin his life. David's focus in the first and third stanzas is on God—how God is a refuge, a protector, and a deliverer from the snares set by David's enemies. David cries out to the righteous and true God to act with unceasing love to deliver him from his enemies' lies and deceit, so that their contempt may never put him to shame. God, David declares, is good, sheltering him from his enemies.

In the middle stanza, David draws attention to the negative impact that his enemies have had on his life. Their contemptuous acts have worn him down, leaving him a broken man with no friends but God to help.

Despite David's exhaustion and feelings of "terror on every side," he knows he has experienced God's marvelous grace. He concludes this psalm (31:23–24) by encouraging those who follow the Lord: Love and serve God faithfully—he will sustain you; he will judge your enemies.

Psalm 32. This psalm is the first of three sequential psalms that offer God's blessings (cf. 32:1–2; 33:12; 34:8—cf. Ps. 1:1; 2:12).

In 32:1–2, David introduces two blessings that point to God's forgiveness, and he extends the second to encompass those who conceal no sin. Experientially, David knows these blessings to be true. After he attempted to hide his sin but discovered that God relentlessly ripped joy from his life (32:3–4), David's confession and God's forgiveness ensure God's blessing.

David, acknowledging God as a refuge and encourager, urges others to pray before their troubles arise (32:6–7).

Before concluding, David interjects words of encouragement and challenge from God. He plays off God's words by challenging his readers to willingly trust God, whose love envelops them, and to praise him (32:10–11).

Psalm 33. Psalm 33 begins with a series of commands (occurring in this combination in no other chapter of Scripture) to praise God with joyful music (33:1–3), because he is a God of perfection who loves what is best for humans

Psalm 33:2 states, "Praise the LORD with the harp; make music to him on the ten-stringed lyre." A lyre player is depicted here on the Standard of Ur (2600–2400 BC).

(33:4–5). He is also the Creator, whose commands brought creation into existence (33:6–9). Intimately involved in his creation, he oversees it to accomplish his plans (33:10–15). God alone—not governments, military might, or individual power—is able to deliver safely from trouble those who trust him (33:16–19). God's people rely on him for protection; he, whose unceasing love they crave, is their reason for rejoicing (33:20–22; cf. 33:1–3).

Psalm 34. Continuing the upbeat mood of Psalm 33, Psalm 34 presents almost no suggestion of deep anguish. David's attitude is curious in light of the superscription, which highlights a troubled time in his life (cf. 1 Sam. 21:10–15; Abimelek = Achish).

David speaks of trials in generic terms, not dwelling on the heartache, but on God's good work toward those facing difficulties (34:4–6, 18–19).

David portrays God as paying special attention to the righteous, hearing their cry for help, delivering them (immediately?), and condemning their enemies (cutting off from the earth all memory of them) (34:4, 15, 17, 19, 21). God redeems all who take refuge in him (34:22).

In this psalm, confidence outweighs trepidation. Of the five occurrences of words translated "fear(s)," only one conveys the negative sense of terror (34:4); the others (34:7, 9 [2×], 11) speak of the affirmative "fear the Lord."

Psalm 35. David describes the dark side of life, where his enemies pursue him, set traps for him, and rejoice when he falls. His enemies dominate the "headlines"—God being far less prominent in Psalm 35 than he is in Psalm 34. Every command in Psalm 35, however, is directed toward God, with David imploring God to defend him, defeat his enemies, or rescue him (contrast Psalm 34). Yet, despite their differences, Psalms 34 and 35 conclude that God delivers the upright.

Throughout Psalm 35, David seeks God's help (35:1–3, 17, 22–25), desiring his enemies to falter because of the misery they have caused

him (35:4–8, 11–16, 19–21, 26). He also declares his intent to praise God when God overcomes those enemies (35:9–10, 18, 28).

Verse 27 is a rarity in the Psalms—David indicates that some people apparently support him. He urges them to praise God for watching over him.

Psalm 36. Psalm 36 is a proverbial psalm; essentially every verse describes either the wicked and how they act (36:1–4, 11–12) or God and the godly and how they act (36:5–10). Only rarely does David reveal his presence (36:1, 9, 11).

Being self-absorbed and intentionally destructive of others, the wicked care nothing about God (36:1–2, 4). They enjoy that which is sinful and harmful rather than that which is good (36:3–4).

God, however, displays a rich love toward all people regardless of their status (36:5–7, 10). He deals with them justly, protecting and delivering them (36:6–7). Thus the godly recognize him as the source of life and light, in whom is bountiful pleasure (36:8–9).

David wants to avoid the attacks of the wicked and their destiny—when they fall, they are unable to rise again (36:11–12).

Psalm 37. Psalm 37 is a psalm of promise for those who seek the Lord—a psalm of disaster for those who fail to do so. Time is short for the wicked (37:1–2, 9–10). Their day of success is only for the present, and their success is due, in part, to their taking advantage of the helpless and powerless (37:12–14, 35–36).

In sharp contrast, David highlights God's abundant provision for all who turn to him (37:6, 19). God meets their present needs and deepest desires, offering the righteous a wonderful future (37:4, 18, 37). He is their helper, upholder, protector, and deliverer who never deserts them (37:23–25, 39–40). They are therefore exhorted to enjoy him, follow him, and rely on him always (37:3–5).

Thus God's people should never be troubled by or envious of the success of the ungodly (37:7–8). God's followers should give and give abundantly, even though they may have very little of this world's goods (37:16, 26).

Psalm 38. Despite the advice David gives in Psalm 37, he does not always follow God's way. Psalm 38 shows David grieving over his personal sin and over the intense judgment that God is enacting against him (38:1–8, 18). At times, he recognizes his judgment in the way that others treat him (38:9–12).

Having no solution to his problems other than to rely on God's deliverance from his sin and his enemies (38:13–20), David pleads to God for a quick resolution of his problems (38:21–22).

Although confession of sins, regret for having committed sins, and fear of subsequent judgment do occur elsewhere in book 1 (cf. Ps. 6:1–3; 32:1–5), they are rare, making Psalm 38 unique up to this point in the Psalter (cf. Ps. 44; 51; 78; 95; 106).

Psalm 39. David declares that life is frustratingly short (39:4–6; cf. Job 7:7; Ps. 144:4). Sin makes life miserable and senseless (39:6, 12; cf. Ps. 89:47; Eccles. 1:2); God's judgment increases the agony of that short and miserable life (39:9–11; cf. Ps. 38:18; Jer. 30:14–15; Heb. 12:11). Any attempt to hide personal frustrations (to maintain a "good testimony" for the sake of others) only intensifies the heartache (39:1–3; cf. Job 9:24–29). David then cries out to the one who can make some sense out of the vapor of life, but God does not unravel the enigmas of his life (39:7–8, 12–13; cf. Deut. 29:29).

Psalm 39 blends well with Psalm 38: life seems all too short and the misery of life all too real. Running from the world or from God may seem like the best way to deal with problems but in reality is not. Rediscovering the joy of life requires a relationship with God—having him both close (in his compassion) and far away (in his discipline).

Psalm 40. At the end of Psalm 39 (v. 12), David anxiously pleads to God to respond to his needs. In 40:1, he makes an intense effort to wait for God's answer to his "cry (for help)" (a term rarely occurring in Scripture, but appearing in both 39:12 and 40:1). God transforms David's situation from one of misery to one of praise that others can observe and respond to (40:2–3). Interestingly, in Psalm 39, David indicates that he has been silent before both God and unbelievers (39:1–2, 9) because of his feeling that life is both short and meaningless (39:4–5, 10–11). But in 40:9–10, David openly proclaims God's love and truth. What makes a discouraged David a joyful David is the truth about the coming sacrificial death of the Messiah (40:5–8; cf. Heb. 10:1–10). Life and death now make sense to David. He still has problems beyond number (40:12), but he knows that the one who has plans beyond number for his people (40:5) gives abundant joy to all who trust him (40:16). Previously David agonizingly waited for God to resolve his concerns (40:1); now he hopes that God will not take as long to handle his many other problems (40:17).

Psalm 41. In 40:17, David states that he is "poor and needy." Now, at the beginning of Psalm 41, he declares that God takes a special interest in those who help the weak, blessing them when they encounter enemies, disease, or other difficulties (41:1–3).

The mood of this psalm changes quickly. David seeks forgiveness for having wronged God (41:4); he also seeks God's help to get revenge on his enemies who have been scheming against him (41:5–10). Some have been quietly spreading rumors about him, others openly slandering his good name, and still others praying for his death. Even a very good friend has betrayed him (41:9 has messianic implications; cf. John 13:18).

David concludes much like he begins, with a focus on his helplessness. In 41:1–3, he pronounces a blessing on those who help the weak. In 41:11–13, he "blesses" God, who helps him in his weakness.

2. Book 2 (42:1–72:20)

Psalm 42. Psalm 42 sets the tone for book 2—though enemies overcome the psalmist, God does not vanquish them quickly. The author uses repetition to convey this sense of discouragement. Twice the naysayers mock: "Where is your God?" (42:3, 10). Three times the psalmist bemoans that he is "downcast" (42:5–6, 11; cf. 43:5; 44:25 ["brought down"]—these are the only occurrences of this verb in Scripture); twice that he is "disturbed" (42:5, 11). Even when he records statements suggesting hope, he immediately dismisses them as not being a reality in his life. When his heartache continues "day and night" despite God's presence with him, he wonders whether God has forgotten about him completely (42:3, 8–9).

Despite being physically apart from his normal places of worship (42:1–2, 4), the psalmist does not abandon his God, who appears less and less responsive. Just the opposite, he consistently declares his fervent desire to be with and to live for his God (42:1–2, 4, 5–6, 11).

Psalm 43. Psalm 43:2 parallels 42:9, and 43:5 essentially duplicates 42:5, 11; however, Psalm 43 is not simply a smaller version of Psalm 42. Psalm 43 explodes with greater emotional intensity than does Psalm 42—there are more commands and entreaties (significantly more considering the relative sizes of the two psalms). In the parallel verses (43:2 and 42:9, respectively), "stronghold" (i.e., "fortress") evokes more forceful imagery than does "rock," and "rejected" is more actively intentional than "forgotten." Even the word "go," in "Why must I go about mourning" (43:2), suggests a pacing back and forth, an agitation, rather than mere motion (42:9).

In Psalm 43, the psalmist implores God to defend him in the world court—to free him from the grasp of the godless (43:1). Convinced that God has abandoned him to his oppressors (43:2), he begs God to return him to Jerusalem, where he can worship God (43:3–4). Yet, seeing little hope, all he can do is to fortify his courage and maintain his confidence in God (43:5).

Psalm 44. The psalmist here presents four key ideas: (1) God has the power to deliver his people from their enemies, having done so in the past (44:1–8). (2) God has rejected the present generation of Israel, delivering them into their enemy's hands (44:9–16). (3) God has rejected them despite their faithfulness to him (44:17–22). (4) Although God has rejected them, they plead to him for deliverance, because he alone is their Redeemer (44:23–26).

God alone has the power to deliver his people to freedom or to bondage. Apart from his will, neither human efforts nor weapons are able to effect any form of deliverance (44:3, 5–7, 9–14). Furthermore, God does what he wants to do, whether or not doing so makes any sense to his people (44:9–14, 17–22).

The psalmist concludes by appealing to God for help solely on the basis of God's unfailing love (44:26; cf. 44:3).

Psalm 45. The psalmist depicts the king as a man (literally "fairer than the sons of man") eternally blessed by God (45:2)—a mighty warrior of excellent character, more powerful than the nations (45:3–5). This king is none other than God (45:6–7; cf. Heb. 1:8–9 and ancient Hebrew tradition). His very garments exude fragrance; he is admired and honored from far and wide (45:8–9). The king, the author declares, is to be married to a non-Israelite woman of royal birth who is to honor (literally "bow down to"—a verb typically describing worship) him (45:10–11). Others will honor this royal union (45:12–17).

Although the psalmist may have used imagery from a royal wedding, his words indicate this wedding to be that of the Messiah. Who then is the royal bride so beautifully dressed? Combining Revelation 19:7–8 with Hebrews 1:8–9 produces one conclusion only: the church.

Psalm 46. God's people are with their God; he is with them (46:1, 5, 7, 11). He overcomes their troubles, whether those troubles arise from nations or nature (46:2–3, 6, 8–9). The Most High is a refuge and fortress—the Lord of heavenly armies and the God of his people (46:1, 4, 7, 11). In his presence, all are to keep silent and honor him (46:10). He is the God to end all wars (46:8–9).

Psalm 46 flows naturally from the picture of the royal wedding in Psalm 45, in which the psalmist calls out to God, as king, to prepare for war and to ride victoriously (45:3–4). He overcomes his enemies and rules forever (45:5–6). Psalm 46 carries forward that theme: God overthrows the nations, desolating them, destroying their weaponry, and receiving their honor (46:6–10). Thus God is the strong protector of his people in whatever crisis they may face (46:1, 7, 11).

Psalm 47. Once more, the psalms speak of God as a conquering king (cf. Psalms 44–46). Here the author declares: God is to be praised and feared as the vanquisher of nations and as king of kings (47:2–3, 7–9).

The psalmist favors words of praise that are relatively rare in the Psalter. The particular words used to say, "clap . . . hands," appear only here in the Psalms, as does the combination of words that forms the concept of "shout . . . with cries of joy" (47:1). A different word for "shouts of joy" (47:5) surfaces in the Psalter only four other times. The remaining word of praise in this psalm, rendered "sing praises" (47:6 [3×], 7), does enjoy a moderate frequency of usage in the Psalter. That the psalmist chooses less frequently occurring words of praise makes Psalm 47 somewhat unusual in its style.

Psalm 48. A psalm that highlights the grandeur, power, and victories of Jerusalem gives even greater praise to the God who dwells there. The psalmist begins and ends with God (48:1, 14) and specifically references God in seven other verses (48:2–3, 7–11). He presents God as the possessor and ruler of Jerusalem and as its righteous warrior, defender, and judge. As a consequence, in the midst of Jerusalem's beauty is Jerusalem's true strength (48:3).

Within Jerusalem, God's people are secure and joyful, for he guides them always (48:8, 11, 14). They take great comfort in living there, being free to meditate on God's unending love and to declare his praise (48:8–11).

Psalm 48 speaks of Jerusalem (Zion) more than any other psalm in Scripture.

Psalm 49. Psalm 48 closes with a reminder of death (God guides us "to the end," literally to death). Psalm 49, a wisdom psalm, delves deeper into that topic, answering the question: how can one be secure in the afterlife?

The psalmist warns against fearing or envying the rich (49:5–6, 16); their wealth is insufficient to buy eternal redemption for others or for themselves (49:7–13) and does not even follow them in their deaths (49:17–20). Death is the great equalizer—all humans die (49:10, 12); but after death God redeems the righteous to rule with him (49:14–15).

Psalm 50. In Scripture, only here (50:1) and in Joshua 22:22 does the appellation "the Mighty One, God, the Lord" appear—an appropriate introduction to a psalm about the power, majesty, and judgment of God.

Asaph discusses how to please such a terrifying God, who reigns among his people (50:2–3; cf. 48:4–8). He observes that God's judgment categorizes people into two groups (cf. Psalm 49): true worshipers and those who are not (despite their religiosity). True worship is not based on a (God-created) sacrificial system— God does not need sacrifices (50:9–13), and he despises hypocritical worship (50:16–21). True worship flows from a heart of thanksgiving (50:14, 23). Only true followers of God will experience from God both deliverance from trouble (50:15) and ultimate salvation (50:23).

King David established (what many have called) "music guilds," with Asaph being a leader of one of those guilds. The guilds (from generation to generation) led temple worship (praying, praising, and preaching, as well as composing, directing, and playing the music) (1 Chron. 15:16–19; 16:4–7; 25:1–6; Ezra 3:10; Neh. 11:22; 12:46).

Psalm 51. David's sin (i.e., adultery with Bathsheba; cf. 2 Sam. 11:1–12:14) and the thought of its horrific offense to God devastate him. He labels his adultery as transgression, iniquity, evil, and sin (note: Psalm 51 has a higher concentration of these terms than any other psalm in the Psalter).

In every section of the psalm, David pleads for God to do a transforming work in him (51:1–2,

9–10, 12, 14). He desires a newness of spirit within him that will allow him to delight freely in God (51:7–10, 12). He also pleads that God would not remove him from his position as king (as he has done with Saul; 1 Sam. 15:28; 16:14), by taking the Holy Spirit from him (51:11—note: he is not afraid of losing his salvation; cf. 51:12).

The conclusion of Psalm 51 echoes key ideas from Psalm 50: Jerusalem as a place that God blesses (50:2; 51:18), and God's desires regarding true sacrifice—that is, a humbled, repentant heart that pours out thanks to God (50:5, 8–14, 23; 51:16–17, 19).

Psalm 52. David expresses outrage at one who could act so treacherously as to slaughter the priests and people at Nob (see the superscription; 1 Sam. 21:7–19) and enjoy doing so (52:1–4). Such an individual epitomizes the self-centered person who takes pride in plotting and carrying out evil.

Together, Psalms 51 and 52 show the difference between those who are broken by their sin and those who embrace their sin, and the diametrically opposite end states of each (52:5–9).

Psalm 53. Appropriately placed between two psalms in which David scathingly denounces heinous plots and acts against God's people, Psalm 53 deplores the character and dealings of those who reject God, and it applauds God's righteous judgment of such people.

Psalm 53 essentially replicates Psalm 14. Like other psalms in book 2, Psalm 53 favors the use of Elohim (God) over that of Yahweh (LORD); wherever the name Yahweh appears in Psalm 14, Psalm 53 either does not include it or records Elohim instead (53:2, 4, 6). Furthermore, 53:5 combines portions of 14:5–6 and offers encouragement to God's people (rather than denunciations to the wicked)—encouragement much needed by those under attack from the likes of Doeg (Psalm 52) and the Ziphites (Psalm 54).

Psalm 54. Recording the actions of those who have no interest in God, David cries to God for help (54:1–2), presenting his reasons for needing help (54:3), his confidence in God

(54:4–5), and his commitment to praise God for helping him (54:6–7).

David does not focus primarily on those chasing him but on God, who can deliver him. He relies on God's character, power, and integrity to keep his word (54:1, 5). He presents a crucial difference between himself and his enemies: he turns to God; they do not (54:2–3; cf. 53:1, 4). God is David's deliverer, vindicator, protector, and sustainer (54:1, 4, 7). Being rescued from near destruction, David determines to offer a sacrifice of thanksgiving to God (54:6; cf. 50:23; 51:16–17, 19; 52:9).

Psalm 55. Unable to handle his enemies and the emotional strain they cause him, David seeks God's help (55:1–8, 16–19). His enemies are relentless in their destructive work, terrorizing not only him but also the people of the city (55:9–11). Unexpectedly, despite facing a multitude of enemies, David zeroes in on one unnamed individual—a friend who has become a traitor to him (55:12–14, 20–21; cf. 41:9, cited by Jesus [John 13:18] regarding his betrayer). This betrayal disturbs David more than the havoc caused by all his other enemies.

Once again (cf. 52:7; 53:1–4; 54:3), David identifies the wicked as those who do not care about God (55:19). Such people face God's wrath; God's people, however, find him to be a place of security (55:22–23).

Psalm 56. The psalmist's enemies continue to mount their vicious, debilitating attacks. In Psalms 52 and 53, they attack God's people. In Psalms 54, 55, and here in 56, they target David. David describes these personal attacks as relentless: all day long they trample him down (56:1–2), twist his words (56:5a), and plot to ruin him (56:5b–6).

In the midst of those dangers, David trusts God and is emboldened to face his enemies without fear (56:3–4). He seeks both God's intervention against his enemies (56:7, 9) and God's involvement in his own life and sufferings (56:8–9). David once again proclaims his trust in God, who has kept him from faltering (56:10–11, 13).

Psalm 57. Two psalms in a row, David pleads to God for mercy (or grace) (56:1; 57:1 [2×]). Nowhere in the Psalter does any psalmist ever seek mercy (or grace) from his enemies.

In this psalm, although David speaks about his problems (57:1, 3–4, 6), his greater interest is in his relationship to God (57:1–2, 7–9) and in God Most High, who is intimately involved in the psalmist's concerns (57:2–3) and yet is far beyond the heavens (57:5, 10–11).

Psalm 57 forms a major component of Psalm 108, with 57:7–11 being essentially the same as 108:1–5.

Psalm 58. David's frustration escalates. The wicked do not merely fail to judge rightly; they aggressively seek ways to act unjustly—with a vengeance (58:1–2). These people are not novices to sin; they are skilled practitioners of it, honing their sinful ways from before birth (58:3). Interestingly, David earlier (51:5) notes his own sinfulness from birth. The difference between David and the wicked of this passage is that whereas he confesses his sin and desires to live uprightly before God, they become increasingly like out-of-control cobras, striking to kill whenever and whomever they can (58:4–5).

David's frustration explodes in an imprecatory prayer. Outraged at the unrestrained wickedness surrounding him, he calls for God's unrestrained judgment to fall hard on them (58:6–9). Smash their teeth, rip out their teeth; destroy them before they can live full or meaningful lives.

The righteous, David declares, will rejoice in this slaughter of the wicked and will recognize their God as a powerful and just God (58:10–11). David uses the final verse of the psalm to loop back to the first to reveal the stark contrast between the unjust judges who practice injustice and the just Judge, who destroys injustice.

Psalm 59. About to be unjustly attacked, David pleads to God to rescue him (59:1–5). David's enemies, like packs of wild dogs, show no fear of David or of God (59:6–7); but God mocks their idiocy (59:8–10).

Perhaps for the only time in the Psalter, David seeks God's mercy for his enemies, but only so that they might be object lessons for his people (59:11). Then, after the lesson is learned, David hopes that God will destroy these prideful sinners (59:12–13).

David's enemies howl through the night (59:14–15), whereas David, whom God preserves through the night, praises God for his unfailing love (59:16–17). Thus David, who at the beginning of the psalm seeks deliverance, now at the end of the psalm pours out gratitude to God for having delivered him.

Psalm 60. References to the Valley of Salt (see the superscription) appear only four other times in Scripture (2 Sam. 8:13; 2 Kings 14:7; 1 Chron. 18:12; 2 Chron. 25:11), each time, as here, linked to a battle in which David's army slaughters ten thousand or more people. Although the battle is a success, David writes as though he were under attack, perplexed that God might have deserted Israel. Yet, even if that were true (60:1–3, 10), David announces that he has not abandoned God (60:11–12).

In the first (60:1–5) and last (60:10–12) sections, David reveals his fears that God is fighting against Israel. In the first section, he prays that God would rescue his people from the dangers of the battle; in the last section, he seeks God's help against his enemies. The middle section (60:6–9) divulges the extent of the battle.

With only minor variations, 60:5–12 appears intact as Psalm 108:6–13.

Psalm 61. David longs always to be under God's protective care (61:1–4) and to live long so that he may daily serve God (61:5–8). Being far from home and feeling a tremendous need for God's protection, David expresses his desperation through several rare phrases—three that appear only here in Scripture: "heart grows faint," "rock . . . higher than I," and "shelter [secret place] of your wings" (61:2–4).

David believes that God will allow him to dwell near him because God has accepted

David's vows and given David an eternal inheritance with the faithful (61:5–8).

Psalm 62. The near repetition of 62:1–2 in 62:5–6 conveys David's ability to remain confident despite experiencing danger (62:3–4) and provides the foundation for his charge to God's people to rely on him as their powerful protector (62:7–8). David concludes (62:9–12) by reinforcing his already-stated views: the world system, being transitory, cannot be relied on; it is God alone, being powerful and loving, who can and must be relied on.

Psalm 63. The third of three consecutive psalms in which David expresses no anguish and few problems, Psalm 63 emphasizes David's yearning for and complete reliance on his glorious God.

Throughout much of David's life, his spiritual nature trumps his physical nature. In Psalm 62, he prefers God to the powers of this world and to his own desires (62:9–10). Here (63:1–6), he declares that God is more precious to him than the physical needs of life—or even than life itself. God is his protector and sustainer (63:7–8); his enemies will no longer live to spread deception, but he and all who worship God will sing God's praise (63:9–11).

Psalm 64. The wicked do not fear God but believe they are invincible. They expend much effort enacting evil plans; but God acts quickly against them. Their evil structures collapse; they themselves are destroyed. The evil they intended to do (64:2–6), God does to them (64:7–8a).

There is no cliff-hanger at the end of this psalm. God acts decisively (64:7–8a); all people will be overwhelmed by his amazing work (64:8b–9)—they then are to draw near to him and praise him (64:10).

Psalm 65. Psalm 64:10 exhorts people to praise God; Psalm 65 describes that praise which begins in Jerusalem (65:1), is echoed by all peoples (65:2, 5, 8), and is proclaimed throughout the earth by creation itself (65:9–13).

God resolves humanity's deepest needs: forgiving people, drawing them to him, blessing them (65:3–4). Those overwhelmed by their own sin God overwhelms by demonstrating his righteous power in creation (65:3, 5–7), using creation to provide abundantly for the world (65:9–13).

Psalm 66. All people (friend and foe alike) must praise God (66:1–4), whether he accomplishes awe-inspiring works in creation (66:5–7), disciplines people (66:8–15), or answers prayers (66:16–20).

God's greatness, moreover, overshadows any fears that the psalmist might have about his enemies (66:3, 7).

Although the psalmist does not assume that God will answer his prayers (whether he is serving God or sinning against him, 66:17–19), he determines to keep the vow to God he made when he was in trouble (66:13–14). God may do as he likes (66:8–15), but humans are to serve and praise him (66:2, 4, 8, 16, 20).

Psalm 67. The psalmist utilizes a chiastic structure to emphasize the fact that all people should praise God, who rules with uprightness. He begins (A—67:1–2) and ends (A′—67:6–7) by focusing on God's blessing his people and the nations (i.e., those needing to be saved and to fear God). He builds the second stages of the structure with two identical declarations (B—67:3; B′—67:5): "May the peoples praise you, O God; may all the peoples praise you." Then, in the central point of the psalm (C—67:4), the psalmist focuses on the reason why the world should praise God—he is the righteous judge who directs all nations.

Psalm 68. God, who goes forth conquering (68:1–4), provides for the helpless (68:5–14), delivers his people (68:15–23), and returns to receive justly deserved praise (68:24–35).

When God enters into battle, the wicked crumble (68:2); the righteous rejoice and praise God (68:3–4).

In victory, God's compassion reaches to those whom society often forgets: the orphans, the widows, the lonely, the poor, and the women who remain at home during the battle (68:5–14). By contrast, God covers the ground with his enemies like fallen snow (68:14).

The defeated nations, represented by the peaks of Bashan, envy Jerusalem because God dwells there (68:15–16).

After ascending to heaven taking the defeated with him (for judgment?), God returns to receive tribute from the defeated nations (68:18; cf. Eph. 4:8), to execute judgment on his enemies, and to help the righteous (68:19–23).

The psalm concludes with God's triumphal entry into his temple, with all of his people in grand array (68:24–27), the nations worshiping the glorious king (68:28–35).

Psalm 69. Writing a psalm with messianic implications (69:9, 21, cf. Matt. 27:34, 48; John 2:12–17; 19:28–29), David unleashes his emotions. David faces overwhelming and unjustified attacks, yet God, who knows David's problems, does not respond (69:1–5, 19). David suffers because of his stand for God and fears that others may falter in their faith because of him (69:6–12). He desires that they instead take courage (69:30–32).

David continues sinking; God remains hidden (69:13–21). David's enemies openly ridicule him (yet no believers come to his rescue) (69:19–21). No longer able to control his emotions, David spews out vitriolic imprecation

The entry of the deity into the sanctuary, such as is described in Psalm 68:24, is vividly illustrated at the temple at Ain Dara (Syria, tenth–ninth century BC) by giant footprints carved into the stone walkway.

against his enemies, calling down God's unhindered destruction on them (69:22–28). Having vented his rage, David again seeks God's help, declaring his confidence that God will accomplish great things for his people (69:29–36).

David reminds his readers about two important matters: God desires heartfelt gratitude more than animal sacrifice (69:30–31; cf. 40:6; 50:8–13; 51:16–19), and God cares deeply about the needy and the helpless (69:32–33; cf. 68:5–6, 10; 70:5; 72:4, 12–13).

Psalm 70. David extensively uses repetition of both words and ideas in Psalm 70 to emphasize his key points. (1) being "poor" and "needy," David desperately needs help; (2) his enemies rejoice in having the upper hand over him; and (3) God alone can resolve David's problems, after which he (and others) will be able to rejoice in God.

Verses 1 and 5 form an inclusio around the psalm to highlight David's plea that God respond immediately.

David's use of the word "seek" in verses 2 and 4 (NIV 1984) sets up a contrast between those who seek David (i.e., to kill him) and those who seek God (i.e., to serve him)—the former are to experience distress, the latter joy.

Psalm 71. The author presents his ideas in Psalm 71 in a stair-step fashion: (A) God is good to the psalmist even though he has not yet rescued him from the troubles his enemies are causing him (71:1–13); (B) the psalmist has full confidence in God and will praise him (71:14–16); (A′) God is good to the psalmist even though he has not yet rescued him from the troubles he is causing him (71:17–21); (B′) the psalmist has full confidence in God and will praise him, for he has begun his deliverance (71:22–24).

Several ideas occurring in Psalm 71 carry on the thoughts of previous psalms: God is hidden from the psalmist (71:12; cf. 69:17); God is urged to hurry his work of deliverance (71:12; cf. 70:1, 5); the enemies scorn the psalmist—the psalmist desires them to be scorned, and they are (71:1, 13, 24; cf. 69:7, 10, 19–20; 70:2–3); and the enemies openly rejoice over the tribulations of the psalmist (71:10–11; cf. 70:3).

Psalm 72. The parallel structure of 72:1–2 reveals that Solomon (the king who is also the royal son [of David]) desires God to give him both justice and righteousness so that he might judge God's people (the "afflicted ones") with righteousness and justice. When Solomon rules in that manner, the nation (represented synecdochically by "mountains" and "hills") will prosper, and he will deliver the helpless (72:3–4). This king is a blessing both to his people and to the nations, who in turn will acknowledge his greatness and serve him (72:5–17).

Solomon recognizes that God deserves the credit for his success. God is the giver of justice and righteousness (72:1–2); he is the performer of all the great works highlighted in this chapter; and he is the truly glorious one (72:18–19).

3. Book 3 (73:1–89:52)

Psalm 73. In a moment of earthly realism and spiritual insanity, Asaph believes that the wicked always succeed; the righteous never get ahead—Psalm 1 turned upside down.

The wicked have wealth, health, and no worries (73:2–7). Claiming divine and human authority, they debase others (73:8–9) and live the good life (73:10). Having no fear of God, they believe that he has no idea what they are doing (73:11).

Regretting living a godly life because it brings him only misery, Asaph encapsulates the lives of the wicked in two words: prosperity and peace (73:12–14). His theology and his reality are in conflict (73:15–16).

Asaph, a worship leader at the temple, gains a new perspective on reality: there is a different destiny for the wicked than for the righteous (73:17–20, 23–24, 27). Regretting his bitterness and foolishness (73:21–22) and remembering God's faithfulness (73:26), Asaph declares that he will proclaim God's truth (73:28).

Psalm 74. Beginning with national discouragement and ending essentially where it begins, Psalm 74 leaves Israel's problems unresolved.

Enemies, like rampaging barbarians, have desecrated and destroyed the temple, hacking to pieces its delicate engravings (cf. 1 Kings 6:29–36) and burning it to the ground, yet God does nothing, except retain his anger at his people (74:1–3). Using five arguments, Asaph appeals to God to act: (1) your dwelling place has been desecrated (74:2–3); (2) your enemies have acted with power and arrogance (74:4–8); (3) you are a God of infinite power, who controls creation (74:12–17); (4) you have a covenant with your people, and your people are oppressed and needy (74:19–21); and (5) your enemies mock you (74:10, 18, 22–23). Despite Asaph's appeal, God remains unmoved.

Psalm 75. Asaph alternates between his own words (75:1, 6–9) and God's words (75:2–5, 10). Speaking on behalf of God's people, Asaph offers thanksgiving to God for his marvelous works (75:1). He then proclaims God's warning against a self-absorbed world (75:2–5). God declares to the world that he is a righteous judge who holds the world together (while people are shaken by earthquakes) (75:2–3; "pillars" metaphorically represents the "foundations" of the earth). God directs his judgment toward those who think they are greater than he (75:4–5; note: "horns" represents power). Asaph concurs that God is a judge who honors some (75:6–7) and pours out his wrath on others (75:8). Asaph concludes by praising God (75:9; cf. 75:1). God, not Asaph, is the speaker of the final verses, since God alone possesses the power to fulfill those words (cf. 75:6–8).

Psalm 76. God stands glorious—a victorious conqueror (76:1–2, 4); his enemies lie strewn across the battlefield—their war machine a shambles (76:3, 5–6). He silences their bravado. Their kings encounter God's power and wrath, and they fear him (76:5, 7–8, 12).

God brings judgment to some, deliverance to others (76:8–9). The defeated, no longer boastful, are to present gifts of homage to the eternal King (76:11; cf. Ps. 68:29; Isa. 18:7).

At the beginning of this psalm, God's people know him; at the end, the world knows and fears him (76:1–2, 12). (Salem [76:2] is an early name for Jerusalem.)

Psalm 77. Discouraged with life's problems, Asaph turns to God in extended prayer but finds no resolution to his troubles (77:1–2). Thinking about God seems to exacerbate his problems, causing him to lose sleep (77:3–4). Pondering the past brings no comfort, only questions: has God given up on his people (77:7)? Has God's eternal character faltered (77:8)? Does God no longer care about Israel (77:9)?

Still discouraged, Asaph determines to think specifically about God's mighty works toward Israel and his power over nature (77:10–20). Asaph gains a correct perspective on God and praises him (even though his problems remain).

Asaph records his transformation through various grammatical tactics. He uses first-person singular verbs to introduce his grief (77:1–6) and the reversal of his attitudes (77:10–12). He highlights God's power through language taken from nature (e.g., water, lightning, whirlwind), setting 77:16–19 off by an inclusio consisting of the names of famous Israelites who experienced God's power (77:15, 20).

Psalm 78. Psalm 78 begins in hope (with Israel's forefathers transmitting God's word from generation to generation; 78:1–7) and ends in hope (with God establishing his dwelling place among his people and choosing his servant David to shepherd his people; 78:65–72). In between, Asaph records God's miraculous works on Israel's behalf (78:12–16, 23–29, 42–55, 65–66), Israel's trivializing of those miracles and rejection of God's word (78:8–11, 17–20, 22, 32, 36–37, 40–42, 56–58), God's merciful but powerful judgment against his people (78:21, 30–31, 33, 38–39, 59–64), and Israel's repentance, short-lived as it was (78:34–35).

In typical Hebrew style, Asaph does not always write in strict chronological order; he writes to convey truth in whatever order best makes his point. Asaph also includes information not previously known; for example, plagues of grasshoppers, frost, and lightning (78:46–48, cf. Exodus 7–12) and a band of angels that leads the way for the Lord's destruction of the firstborn of Egypt (78:49).

Psalm 79. Asaph portrays a gruesome picture of Jerusalem's destruction (by Babylon?): the temple and the city ruined; bodies strewn about unburied, food for wild animals (79:1–4). Asaph issues the plaintive cry "How long, O Lord?"—a cry not concerned about how long Israel's enemies will dominate them but how long God will be angry with his own people (79:5). Immediately thereafter, and to the end of the psalm, Asaph alternates between his desire for God to act with vengeance against Israel's enemies (79:6–7, 10, 12) and his plea for God to show mercy toward his people—and that God's people, in turn, would honor him (79:8–9, 11, 13).

Psalm 80. Psalms 77–80 use shepherding metaphors to depict God as Israel's shepherd or as the one who establishes Israel's shepherd. God shepherds his people from slavery in Egypt to freedom in the promised land (77:20; 78:52–55). He then chooses David, a literal shepherd, to shepherd his people (78:70–72). As shepherd, God guides his people during their exile in Babylon and (if the psalmist's prayers are answered) out of Babylon (79:13). In 80:1,

Asaph appeals to God in his role as shepherd for that deliverance.

Asaph weaves this psalm around three obvious (80:3, 7, 19), and one obscure (80:14), refrains. In the parallel refrains, Asaph builds the name of God, from "God" (80:3) to "God Almighty" (80:7) to "Lord God Almighty" (80:19), as though his pleading were growing increasingly intense. The obscure refrain (using a different form of the same first verb than do the other refrains) calls out, not "restore us," but "restore yourself to us" (NIV "return to us"). Asaph revises "make your face shine upon us" to "look down from heaven and see," and replaces a desire for deliverance with a desire to be cared for.

Immediately preceding each refrain, Asaph fleshes out Israel's need for restoration. In 80:1–2, Israel needs deliverance, but God is not acting on Israel's behalf. In 80:4–6, God is actually judging Israel. In the final two sections (80:8–13, 15–18), God has brought about his wrath on Israel. Asaph then asks God to specially care for (empower) the (Davidic) king (a possible reference to the messianic king who sits at the right hand of the Father) (80:17).

Psalm 81. In 80:4–6, God's people complain that he does not answer their prayers, but allows their enemies to triumph over them, forcing them to eat bitterness. In Psalm 81, God responds: despite my delivering you from slavery (81:5–6, 10) and guiding you through the wilderness (81:7), you serve other gods—you do not obey me. Turn to me, and I will resolve your problems (81:14–16).

In Psalms 77, 78, 80, and 81, the references to Joseph (or to Ephraim and Manasseh) indicate that God still cares about the northern kingdom, which had previously gone into captivity. God's plan is to restore all his people, both south and north.

Psalm 82. The question "how long," in the form found in 82:2, appears five other times in the Psalter, always directed toward God (cf. Ps. 6:3; 74:10; 80:4; 90:13; 94:3). Our passage is the exception. In 80:4, God's people challenge him with the words "how long"—"how long" will you fail to respond to us? In 81:13–16, God answers them in generic terms: "Listen to me . . . follow my ways." Now, in 82:1–2, God gives them specifics. He redirects their question back to them: "How long" will you, O Israel, contradict all that I have taught you, by supporting the wicked and forsaking the helpless? Defend the defenseless; rescue those dominated by the world (82:3–4).

In verses 1 and 6, God refers to his people as "gods" (cf. John 10:22–39). He uses that term metaphorically to describe those who are in a

> Psalm 80:1 refers to God as "Shepherd of Israel, you who lead Joseph like a flock."

position to receive God's word and to live it out before others (particularly, before the helpless).

No true believing Israelite would ever claim to be a "god" to be worshiped and obeyed (as is the sole right of the Lord; Deut. 6:4). Most certainly, in Psalm 82 God does mean that his people are "gods" as he is God, unless, God forbid, he is declaring that he himself can and does sin like the "gods" do (cf. 82:2). The true God, the Blessed One of Israel, cannot sin (1 Sam. 15:29; 2 Cor. 5:21; 1 Pet. 2:22; 1 John 3:5).

Psalm 83. An imprecatory psalm—God, destroy your enemies and ours! Asaph, however, does not describe in detail how he wants God to slaughter Israel's enemies; the imprecation, therefore, is relatively mild.

Asaph seeks God's help (83:1) because their mutual enemies have one terrifying purpose: annihilate Israel (83:2–5). Their enemy is formidable, consisting of Israel's neighbors to the east, south, and west—with Assyria covering the northern flank (83:6–8).

Asaph cites two decisive victories that God achieved over Midian—the first during Deborah's judgeship (83:9–10), the second during Gideon's (83:11–12). In both battles, Israel was at a great disadvantage. Asaph wants God, like wind, fire, and storm, to shame Israel's enemies (83:13–16a, 17), so that the world, seeing that destruction, will recognize God's greatness (83:16b–18; cf. 82:8).

Psalm 84. Away from Jerusalem, perhaps in battle, the psalmist longs to be at God's temple. He is "jealous" of the birds that live there, because they are close to God in his special dwelling place (84:1–4).

The psalmist also "envies" those who take pilgrimages to the temple. They gain strength and joy as they approach it; God even transforms for them the Valley of Baka ("the valley of weeping") into a place of blessing (84:5–8). (Note: whether the Valley of Baka is a literal or symbolic place is uncertain.)

A way for the psalmist to return to the temple soon is for God to grant Israel's king (shield, anointed one) victory over his enemies;

so the psalmist prays to that end (84:9). (Note: the "shield" metaphor and the four-times-mentioned name "Lord Almighty" [literally "Lord of armies"] suggest a battle.)

Even better than victory ("dwell[ing] in the tents of the wicked") is being at the temple. Yet God can still wonderfully bless those who are not so privileged, if they serve God faithfully (84:10–12).

Psalm 85. After judging his people for their sins, God forgives them fully and brings them back from their captivity (85:1–3). Yet God remains grieved by what they have done and has not removed all of the negative consequences of their sins (85:4–6).

Israel has the hope of God's salvation of peace—perhaps even for the current generation, if they trust him fully (85:7–9). Even though all is not well in Israel, God still blesses his people in many different ways (85:10–13).

("Folly" [85:8] is translated in the NIV as "confidence" in Job 4:6, the difference being whether one walks away from God's paths or on them.)

Psalm 86. An inclusio of hearing and answering prayer (86:1, 7) surrounds David's requests to the pardoning and compassionate God for protection and deliverance.

David then (86:8–10) declares that the world should praise God for his great works. Similarly, David announces that, because God has worked wonderfully on his behalf, he wants to know God better and praise him forever (86:11–13).

David begins the final section by describing the sinfulness of his enemies and the greatness of his God (86:14–15). He concludes the section, in reverse order, by speaking well of God (seeking God's help) and then desiring the downfall of his enemies, because God has been good to him (86:16–17).

Psalm 87. Zion, that is, Jerusalem—God's holy mountain, God's chosen dwelling place, the perfection of beauty from where its Maker shines, a city loved by the Lord, the place from where God judges (bringing joy to its people)

521

(Ps. 2:6; 9:11; 50:2; 78:68; 97:8; 132:13)—that city of God forms the focus of Psalm 87.

Five heathen nations will one day know the true God (87:4; cf. 68:31–32; Zeph. 3:9–10):

Egypt (Rahab; cf. Isa. 30:7) and Babylon—powerful enemies that took God's people into exile;

Philistia—perennial harasser and subjugator of God's people;

Tyre—commercial powerhouse that exploited Israel;

Cush—composed of Ethiopia, Sudan, and Somalia, an empire that, at one time, together with Egypt, was the object of Israel's misplaced hope (cf. Isa. 20:5).

These five nations will one day find their hope and joy in Zion and be proud to have God's people in their midst (87:4).

Psalm 88. Compared to Psalm 23, another psalm about near-death experiences, Psalm 88 shows considerably greater despair. Psalm 23 reflects the upbeat nature of book 1, Psalm 88 the agony of book 3.

Facing death, the psalmist multiplies prayers, but they go unanswered (88:2, 9, 13). Misery sets in; hopelessness runs rampant; his theology of an afterlife is bludgeoned (88:10–12; cf. 44:8; 45:2; 49:15). When he is down, God forces him even deeper in the flood of his terror, into the darkness of sorrow and death (88:14–18).

Psalm 88 ends with hopeless depression. No one comforts the psalmist except darkness, his closest friend. God has thrust his loved ones into the eternal pit and has pushed the psalmist to the edge of that pit, making him an abomination even to the dead (88:3–8, 18).

Psalm 89. This psalm presents a stark contrast from the previous psalm of despair—or does it? From the outset, this psalm explodes with praise to God (89:1–37). Yet, were it not for the "added" verse of praise to end book 3 (89:52), this psalm would end much like Psalm 88 does, with the psalmist bearing the brunt of God's wrath (89:38–49)—plus the extra burden

of his enemies' scorn (89:50–51). Verses 1–37 and verses 38–51 are seemingly diametrically opposed, yet both sets of verses proclaim truth.

The psalmist's words are shocking. He almost portrays God as a liar who promises wonderful things but reneges on his promises. Were this psalm not the final psalm of book 3, the reader might assume that the author intended for the final verse of blessing (editorially added, see the introduction) to be read sarcastically: Blessed be the Lord forever . . . who casts aside his anointed one, exalts his enemies, and allows them to revile him (89:38–45, 50–51).

4. Book 4 (90:1–106:48)

Psalm 90. Moses contributes to the ongoing conversation about death (cf. 88:3–6, 11, 15; 89:47–48) the concepts of returning to dust (90:3), being transitory like grass (90:5–6), and having a short life span with great sorrow (90:9–10).

With this discussion about death, Moses interweaves praise to God (90:1–2), acknowledgment of Israel's sin as the reason for God's anger (90:7–11), and hope that God will allow them to live meaningful lives (90:12–17).

Psalm 91. Psalm 91 is a psalm of encouragement: God is a great protector, who surrounds the believer (and the chapter—91:1–4, 14–16); those who seek him fully have nothing to fear (91:5–13).

God does not promise the psalmist that he will not see danger, sickness, or terror; rather, he will protect him from the tragedies of life (91:3–10).

The psalmist uses anthropomorphisms—shadow, feathers, wings—to depict God's protective care (91:1, 4).

Verses 11–12 have messianic implications, with Satan referencing these verses in his temptation of Christ (Matt. 4:6–7; Luke 4:10–11).

In Psalm 91:4, God is said to provide refuge "with his feathers" and "under his wings." The image of wings as shield and shelter is visualized by this statuette of the Egyptian goddess Isis with outstretched wings.

God's protection and presence accompany those who love the Lord as their God; God meets their needs (91:14–16).

Psalm 92. Psalm 92 begins and ends with praise to God (92:1–5, 15). In between, the wicked flourish but are quickly defeated (92:6–9). The righteous also flourish but (unlike the wicked) remain productive throughout their lives (92:10–14).

In 91:5–6, the righteous fear nothing at night/in the darkness or by day/at noon; here (92:2), they praise God in the morning and at night. Thus dedicated believers, who have nothing to fear at any time, should offer praise at all times.

Verses 8–10 uniquely span the contrast between the wicked and the righteous. These verses present an inclusio of exaltation—first directed toward God (92:8) and last toward God's servant (92:10). Verse 9 declares the destruction of those who are at odds with God—a destruction that the righteous see (92:11; cf. 91:8).

Psalm 93. This psalm flows almost as the waves of the sea, beginning small, building to its crest, then starting over again. This wave building begins in verse 1a: "The LORD reigns"—"he is robed in majesty"—"the LORD is robed in majesty and is armed with strength." Each line is important in its own right; each subsequent line adds impact to what has gone before.

The next wave, rising in verse 1b, expresses its full force in verse 2, conveying the theme of an immovable foundation. The author describes first the established world, next God's eternally established throne, then finally God himself, who is "beyond establishment" (he is eternal).

Verses 3 and 4 have their own internal waves, verse 3 emphasizing the powerful roar of the waves lifting up their voice (to proclaim God's power to the world?) and verse 4 continuing the mightiness of the water imagery, concluding that God is even more powerful than his awesome and fearsome creation.

Verse 5 seems to defy the wave pattern—there is no crescendo within it, no completion of any previously identified wave. But closer inspection reveals that 93:5 is perhaps the convergence of all the previous waves: the king's words are unshakable; his house is eternally majestic.

Psalm 94. The psalmist cries out to the avenger God to judge the wicked because of their attacks on God's people, particularly on the helpless (e.g., widows, foreigners, and orphans) (94:1–6).

The wicked arrogantly assume that God has no idea what they are doing (94:7). Yet their beliefs about God are illogical; for the one who created the ability to hear, see, and think most certainly knows all about their sinful actions (94:8–11).

This all-knowing, compassionate God justly disciplines his people so that they might follow his truth (94:12–16). Likewise, he deals with his enemies in justice, issuing a judgment that results in their destruction (94:20–21, 23). God, however, protects his people (94:17–19, 22).

Psalm 95. The psalmist again introduces his ideas using a stair-step structure: (A) call to praise God (95:1–2); (B) reasons for praising God (95:3–5); (A´) call to praise God (95:6); (B´) reasons for praising God (95:7a). He then alters his structure to challenge his readers to live godly lives (95:7b–11).

In 95:1–2, the psalmist encourages Israel to praise God (in words and music) as their faithful deliverer, because (95:3–5) he is greater than both the idols of human creation and creation itself.

Completing the stair-step structure, the psalmist (95:6) urges people to praise God as our Creator. In verse 7a, he declares that God is praiseworthy because he is our God (i.e., we have a relationship with him) and our shepherd.

In 95:7b–8, the shift is abrupt: a temporal adverb ("Today"), a conditional clause ("if"), and a prohibition ("do not harden your hearts"). In typical Hebrew fashion, the psalmist pronounces his contemporaries guilty of sinning together with their forefathers (cf. Heb. 3:15). That earlier generation failed to receive God's blessing; this generation must make sure that it does not do the same (95:9–11).

Psalm 96. The author uses fourteen imperatives from ten different verbs to encourage people to praise God. In the Psalter, Psalm 96 is tied for fifth (with Psalm 80) in frequency of imperatives used, behind Psalms 150, 117, 100, and 134 (all except Psalm 80 being praise psalms).

The author records those imperatives in 96:1–3 and 7–10a, ending each cluster with a command to proclaim God's greatness before the nations, because he is greater than the nations' gods (96:4–5), and he rules as the nations' judge (96:10b–13).

In 1 Chronicles 16:8–36, David offers a psalm of thanks that appears, with a few variations, in Psalm 96:1–13a (1 Chron. 16:23–33); Psalm 105:1–15 (1 Chron. 16:8–22); and Psalm 106:47–48 (1 Chron. 16:35–36).

Psalm 97. Psalm 97 is the third of six psalms in sequence that focus on God's greatness. Psalms 97 and 99 are the only psalms in that group that do not call for singing or shouting for joy to the Lord. Both begin by declaring that "the LORD reigns," that he is beyond human comprehension (shrouded in darkness, 97:2; above the angels, 99:1), and that his throne is unlike any human throne. Both then provide their own reasons why God is to be praised.

Psalm 97 depicts the raw power of God by which he destroys his enemies (97:3), shakes the earth's foundations (97:4–5), and amazes the heavens (97:8). The forces of evil are no match for him and are in fact subject to him (97:7). Thus, God's people delight in him because he is greater than any other power this world knows or serves (97:8–9).

The psalmist then commands God's people to reject the world's ways and to joyfully embrace God, who protects them against that world (97:10–12).

Psalm 98. Whereas Psalms 95–97 speak about God being greater than idols, Psalms 98–100 make no mention of idols whatsoever. Nevertheless, these two groupings contain many common themes.

Psalm 98 focuses on praising God. Verses 1–3 and 7–9 offer reasons why he deserves praise. Verses 1–3 encourage praise because, in his strength, God delivers his people, thereby demonstrating that he is a righteous God who loves his people and never forsakes them. Verses 7–9 urge praise because he is coming to judge the world with correct and evenhanded decisions.

Verses 4–6 command that joyful praise be made to God in song and music but specify no reason for such praise (perhaps because none is ever necessary for God's creation to worship him).

Psalm 99. Concluding each of his calls to worship by proclaiming that God is holy (99:3, 5, 9), the psalmist uses those calls as refrains for the psalm's three sections (99:1–3, 4–5, 6–9).

Verses 1–2 present God as ruler over all peoples (Jews and Gentiles). The refrain (99:3) calls everyone to acknowledge God's holiness.

Verse 4 depicts God as an upright judge who dispenses evenhanded justice in Israel (cf. 96:10; 98:9). The refrain (i.e., 99:5) seeks obedience to God—the holy ruling arbiter over their lives.

The final section (99:6–9) pictures God responding to Israel's needs, lifting the burden of their sins, yet disciplining them for those sins. The final holiness refrain (99:9—more detailed than the other two) issues another call for God's people to worship him.

Psalm 100. An invitation for all to praise God joyfully, Psalm 100 creates an atmosphere of thanksgiving (without concern about enemies, without seeking anything from God) in which essentially every word declares God's marvelous goodness or urges God's people to exhibit grateful hearts to their Maker and shepherd.

Psalm 100 reflects the thoughts of numerous other psalms: shouting joyfully to God (98:4); worshiping (serving) him (2:11); acknowledging him as our Maker (95:6); recognizing him as our shepherd (79:13); rejoicing in his courts (96:8); blessing his name (145:1); and understanding that he is good (34:8), his love endures forever (106:1), and his faithfulness never ends (119:90).

Psalm 101. Following the introductory verse of praise in Psalm 101, David shifts immediately to the two-front war being waged between righteousness and wickedness, in the human soul and in the world. He presents that war in a stair-step fashion, declaring that he (A) will live in righteousness—maintaining integrity of heart (101:2); (B) will not put up with the unrighteous—shunning evil in the world (101:3–5); (A´) will live with the righteous—bringing them into his business (101:6); and (B´) will not put up with the unrighteous—expunging them from his house and kingdom (101:7–8). David is determined to live a holy life and to make Israel a place where holiness flourishes.

Psalm 102. God's unresponsiveness plus the psalmist's anguish and lonely suffering form the foundation of this psalm (102:1–7, 9–10). The psalmist senses that his battles with life are hopeless (102:8, 11)—life is short, and God seems to be shortening it even more (102:23). Yet God is his only hope, so he pleads with him for mercy (102:12–17, 24) on the basis of his eternality and creation's temporality (102:24–28). He hopes that future generations will be able to praise God because God showed him mercy (102:18–22).

Psalm 103. In nearly every verse, David expresses adoration toward God for his character or acts. In Psalm 103:1–5, he remembers God's goodness to him: forgiving him, healing him, preserving his life, meeting his needs. David notes that God also demonstrates his care for others (103:6–8).

God is not a machine, automatically condemning us as he well could (103:9). Likewise, he is not always fair to us—sometimes he shows mercy when we deserve punishment (103:10).

Furthermore, God acts compassionately toward those who serve him, eradicating their sins, which have brought about the terrible shortness of life (103:11–18). This

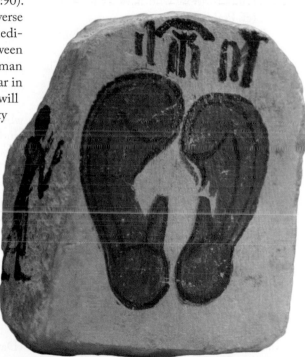

The psalms often ask God to "turn your ear" to hear the psalmist's prayer (Ps. 17:6; 31:2; 71:2; 88:2; 102:2). In ancient Egypt, votive tablets like the one pictured here included depictions of the deity's ears to help the supplicants visualize the gods listening to their pleas.

God, who rules over creation, deserves praise from his creation (103:19–22).

Psalm 104. Another psalm of praise, Psalm 104 announces God's greatness primarily in relation to the creation. The heavens and the earth, the sun and the moon, seas and rivers, mountains and valleys, animals, birds, fish, vegetation—all reveal God's handiwork.

God is worthy of praise! So, for the first time in the Hebrew Scriptures (104:35), the command "Hallelujah" ("Praise the LORD") appears. In the Psalter, this command occurs only in books 4 and 5. A similar command—"Bless the LORD" (NIV "Praise the LORD")—acts as an inclusio around Psalm 104 (104:1, 35) and appears in the Psalter also only in books 4 and 5.

In 104:35, "sinners" parallels "wicked" and thus refers to those who have no interest in God (cf. Psalm 1).

Psalm 105. Psalm 105 begins a trilogy of "historical" psalms that together sketch Israel's history from Abraham to the postexilic era—contrasting God's faithfulness to Israel's unfaithfulness. It presents Israel's history up to their entrance into the land (105:6–11; 43–45). Although God causes Israel to suffer greatly (105:16, 25), he delivers them and provides for them abundantly (105:26–45).

A psalm of reversals: God gives his people the land, but they cannot live in it (105:8–13); he protects them from human oppression, but uses nature to oppress them (105:14–16); God allows a favored son to become a slave to make him a ruler among his enslavers (105:17–22); God causes his people to multiply, resulting in their enslavement, so that he might deliver them (105:24–44). God's purpose is that Israel would obey his word (105:45) and Gentiles would hear his truth (105:22).

Psalm 106. This psalm presents the depraved side of Israel's life in Egypt, but more particularly, in the wilderness and in the land.

In twenty different verses, the author depicts thirty-four examples of sin—even that Israel offered their children as sacrifices to idols! He also unfolds God's reactions to Israel's disobedience: delivering them from their enemies, scattering them, causing plagues and death, abhorring them, nearly destroying them, remembering his covenant with them, relenting of his intended judgment.

Surrounding the intense action in the psalm are the psalmist's exhortations to praise God, declare his greatness, and live godly lives (106:1–3, 47–48). He, a sinner, also seeks God's grace for himself (106:4–6).

In the concluding verses, the author prays that God would deliver his people from exile so that they might thank and praise him (something the author himself does in the final verse).

5. Book 5 (107:1–150:6)

Psalm 107. Psalms 106 and 107 begin essentially the same way, then quickly go their separate ways. Psalm 106 closes book 4 with God's rebellious people suffering in exile. By contrast, Psalm 107 opens book 5 declaring that God has answered Israel's desperate cry (106:47), having delivered them from their distress.

Verses 1–32 depict four different acts by which God delivers his people—each act including a cry for help and a refrain urging those whom God delivered to thank him for his loving-kindness and great works. Verses 33–42 reveal God's control over creation and how he helps the downtrodden. Verse 43 both concludes the second section and echoes, in reverse order, the challenge of each refrain of section one (107:8, 15, 21, 31).

Psalm 108. Three themes link Psalms 107 and 108: God's sovereignty over the created world, God's people exalting him, and God's deliverance of his people.

The fact that the author of Psalm 108 (David) is committed to the Lord (108:1–5) allows him to boldly trust God for deliverance, even though God has rejected his people (108:6, 11–13). The author, however, has not yet been rescued, so he calls out to God (108:6; seeking human help would be futile, 108:11–13), and he hears God's full assurance that he will enact his deliverance soon (108:7–10).

Psalm 108 is basically a compilation of Psalms 57:7–11 (108:1–5) and 60:5–12 (108:6–13).

Psalm 109. The frustration of Psalm 108 continues in Psalm 109—David still has not been released from his attackers, who abuse him verbally, deceptively accuse him, and despise his kindness. Knowing that no human help would make any difference against his enemies (plural) who surround him (cf. 108:12), David begins his counterattack by enlisting God's help (109:1–5).

Seeking God's wrath to crush his enemy (singular), David unleashes one of the strongest imprecations in Scripture (109:6–20). He wants his enemy to be pronounced guilty (in God's court?) and to die—with his family becoming destitute beggars, who receive no love in this life and are eternally condemned in the next.

Following his scathing imprecation, David (who is destitute and afflicted) hopes God will show him kindness by shaming his enemies (plural) and frustrating their attacks (109:21–29).

Being confident of deliverance, David affirms that God gives victory to his people who are in need (109:30–31).

Psalm 110. Psalm 110 has messianic implications (for Ps. 110.1 see Luke 20:43; Acts 2:35; Heb. 1:13; and for Ps. 110:4 see Gen. 14:18–20; Heb. 5:1–7:28).

Psalm 110 sits at a key juncture in the Psalter. In Psalm 107, the author pictures God as a powerful deliverer. In Psalms 108 and 109, the psalmist, in need of deliverance, calls out to God for help. Yet, at the end of each of those psalms, he still faces his adversaries' attacks. Psalm 110 relieves the tension as to whether God will respond favorably or whether he has irretrievably rejected his people. In Psalm 110, God the Messiah conquers the nations of the world (110:5–6). Psalms 111–13 reveal that, having experienced victory, God's people are then able to rejoice freely.

Set in heaven, 110:1 introduces the psalm's main characters: the LORD (Yahweh), the Lord (Adonai), and the enemies. The LORD announces both that he will conquer the Lord's enemies (110:1) using the Lord's scepter (royal authority, power) (110:2) and that the Lord is an eternal priest of a special priestly order (110:4). The Lord then moves forth in his strength to destroy his enemies (110:5–6). In verse 7, after the battle is over, the Lord refreshes himself and lifts his head, signifying that he has secured a complete victory.

Psalm 111. An acrostic psalm and a praise psalm, Psalm 111 is the first of three sequential psalms beginning: "Praise the LORD." This psalm praises God for freeing Israel from bondage to the nations—thus fulfilling his promise (110:5–7).

In 111:1, the author determines to publicly praise God. Then, in verses 2–9, he does so, speaking of God's memorable works, which are worthy of thoughtful study—works by which the righteous and compassionate God redeems and cares for his people.

In light of God's character and works, the author (111:10) declares that true spirituality arises from having right attitudes toward God and right actions for God. He then concludes with praise for God.

Psalm 112. Psalm 112 (a praise psalm and an acrostic psalm) illustrates what the wise person of 111:10 looks like and becomes.

Those who fear God share their possessions with the needy, treat all people fairly, and serve God faithfully (112:5–7, 9). God blesses them and their descendants abundantly (112:2–3). Interestingly, those who fear God and delight in his word (112:1) display godlike attributes of grace and compassion (111:4; 112:4). Like God, they provide for the needy (111:5; 112:5, 9); their righteousness, like God's, continues forever (111:3; 112:3, 9).

In verse 10, the psalmist abruptly shifts to the reaction of those who have no interest in God. They are so bothered by the righteous person's acts that it tears up their insides; their hopes are obliterated.

Psalm 113. Verse 1 of Psalm 113 begins: "Praise the LORD." Verse 9 concludes: "Praise the LORD," thereby forming an inclusio of praise around this psalm—and, together with 111:1, an inclusio enveloping Psalms 111–13.

The psalmist announces that God cares for those who are the poor, the needy, the downtrodden (113:7–9). He urges that praise be made to God across time and in all locations (113:2–4). Our God, the psalmist declares, is unlike any other god: he is beyond creation but humbles himself to enter creation and to fulfill the deepest needs of those whom the world despises as forgotten and shamed by God (113:5–9).

Psalm 114. Despite sitting between two groups of praise psalms, Psalm 114 does not contain the word "praise." Nevertheless, Psalm 114 is most definitely a praise psalm, presenting praiseworthy examples of God's incredible power.

Using synonymous parallelism, the author indicates that the same group of people departs from a foreign nation and becomes the people among whom God establishes his royal residence (114:1–2). Creation is terrified, not by that departing nation, but by the God of that nation (114:3–6)—the Red Sea parts (Exod. 14:21–22); the Jordan River ceases flowing (Josh. 3:15–16); and mountains and hills shake

(Judg. 5:4). The whole earth (Ps. 114:7–8) is to tremble before such an omnipotent God, who also causes water to flow out of solid rock (Num. 20:11; Deut. 8:15).

Psalm 115. The Creator God alone deserves praise; he does whatever he pleases (115:1, 3, 16, 18). By contrast, the nations' idols (though visible; cf. the question of 115:2) are unable to accomplish anything (115:4–7). Their riches and physical attributes are given to them, but they are not alive to use them. Tragically, their makers and followers become like them (115:8; contrast dedicated believers in the Lord who become like him—Psalm 112).

God's people are to trust in him (not in their own sufficiency or in idols) (115:1, 8–11). The true God helps and blesses all who follow him (115:9–15). He loans out the earth to humans, where they are to worship him who is worthy of praise (115:16–18). Those who die no longer praise God among the living, for they are in Sheol (115:17). Yet true believers will praise the Lord in this life and forevermore: "Praise the LORD" ("Hallelujah" concludes 115:18).

Psalm 116. Tied closely to 115:17–18, Psalm 116 speaks of the psalmist's relief at surviving an encounter with death and of his subsequent praise to God. Furthermore, just like Psalm 115 (and Psalm 117), Psalm 116 concludes with the words, "Praise the LORD."

In 116:1–11, the author intertwines his gratitude to the Lord for delivering him from his near-death experience (116:1–2, 5–7, 9) with a delineation of his reactions during that experience (116:3–4, 8, 10–11). In the remaining verses, he announces his commitment to carry out his vows, to offer a sacrifice of thanksgiving, and to praise (116:12–19). Before God's eyes, his death is precious (116:15; cf. 72:13–14), so he determines to praise God publicly (116:14, 18–19).

Offering prayers to deity was common in the ancient world. Here a Hittite relief from the eighth century BC shows King Warpalas praying in front of the storm god Tarhunza.

Psalm 117. The shortest chapter of the Bible, Psalm 117, opens and closes with, "Praise the LORD" (as does Psalm 113).

Whereas the psalmist of Psalm 116 declares that he will complete his vows in the presence of God's people (116:14, 18–19) and the writer of Psalm 118 challenges the people of Israel to praise God (118:1–4) in Jerusalem (118:27–28), the author of Psalm 117 urges the Gentiles of the world to praise God (117:1). In verse 2, he cites God's love and faithfulness as the reasons why God is to be praised. "Praise the LORD."

Psalm 118. Verses 1 and 29 of Psalm 118 form an inclusio, highlighting the importance of showing gratitude to God because of his nature and love. Verse 29 and 107:1 form an inclusio around Psalms 107–18, grouping these psalms together as praise psalms.

The author uses repetition within sequential verses to emphasize God's compassion (118:1–4); God's presence, which gives confidence (118:6–7); God's protective care, which surpasses that of human powers (118:8–9); and God's empowerment, which gives victory against overwhelming forces (118:10–12). Verses 13–18 show God's resolution to the psalmist's near-death experience, which was caused by his enemies (beginning in 118:5).

Including messianic allusions (118:22–23; cf. Matt. 21:42), the psalmist reemphasizes his commitment to God and urges his readers also to thank God (118:19–29).

Psalm 119. An acrostic psalm—the first letter of each verse of every eight verses being a different letter of the Hebrew alphabet (in alphabetical order)—Psalm 119 proclaims the greatness of God's word. The psalmist uses 12 different terms (e.g., law, word, statutes, decrees) over 180 times to unfold the significance of God's truth. He intends those words to be understood synonymously, that is, without distinctions among them.

Except for 119:1–3, 115, the author directs the entire psalm to God, expressing his devotion to God's word. With a nuanced pattern, he begins most stanzas with positive affirmation regarding God's truth. He generally projects discouragement (due either to his own shortcomings or to enemy challenges) and seeks God's help (before or after the statements of consternation). Most often, he expresses delight in or determination to obey God's word. On occasion, all eight verses reveal positive confidence; on no occasion do all eight verses portray hopelessness or dismay.

Psalm 120. Psalm 120 (beginning fifteen sequential psalms known as the Songs of Ascents, songs presumably sung by pilgrims journeying upward to Jerusalem) depicts its author separated from his desired place (120:5–6) and needing God to resolve his dilemma (120:1).

If the psalmist is speaking literally (120:5–6), then he is living among barbaric unbelievers near the southeastern end of the Black Sea (Meshek) and in the wilderness (with the nomads of Kedar). If, however, he is speaking metaphorically then the Israelites surrounding him are the deceptive warmongers. In either case, life's frustrations are wearying him. He is among untrustworthy and antagonistic people (120:1–2, 5–7). He seeks God's help while uttering a harsh imprecation against those who plague him (120:3–4). Although still facing his problems, he is confident that God is resolving them (120:1, 7).

Psalm 121. A psalm of protection—with each occurrence of the verb translated "to keep" or "to watch over" (121:3, 4, 5, 7 [2×], 8), the psalmist depicts God as protecting his people. God shields them from death (121:3; cf. 66:9), from nature's attacks (121:5–6), and from evil things (121:7).

God is the source of help (121:1–2), who never ceases offering that help (121:3–4)—the one who protects against danger from inanimate sources (121:5–6) and against evil (harm) from animate sources (121:7–8).

The hills (121:1) are likely either those filled with danger through which pilgrims passed (thus wondering where their Protector was) or those surrounding Jerusalem, which pilgrims scanned in anticipation of seeing Mount Zion (thus locating God's dwelling place).

Psalm 122. Thankful that people encouraged him to go to Jerusalem (122:1), David again stands within Jerusalem's walls (122:2), impressed by its design with everything crowded together (as it should be) (122:3), and by the crowds, in obedience to God's command, streaming in to praise God (122:4).

More than merely a destination point, Jerusalem is a place to receive God's justice and blessing (122:5–6). Those who consider Jerusalem should pray that God would bring his peace and goodness to it (122:6–9).

Psalm 123. In this, the second of only two psalms in the Psalter in which the psalmist lifts his eyes (cf. 121:1), the author focuses his attention on the God of heaven (123:1), never taking his eyes off him (123:2). Fully committed to doing God's will, the psalmist pleads for God's favor until both he and God's people receive it (123:2–3). They need God's help because those at ease (the proud)—the self-lifted-up ones (the arrogant)—deride them (123:3–4). The psalmist knows that the only way he and God's people will endure their enemies' attacks is to direct their eyes to the truly exalted one.

Psalm 124. In Psalm 124 David conveys Israel's feelings of hopelessness and powerlessness and Israel's need to rely on God. In verses 1–5, he reveals that Israel has no measure of control whatsoever—the enemy's "tidal wave" drags God's people under, leaving them powerless against the constant battering. Until God acts, Israel can do nothing to secure freedom (124:6).

Yet, in verse 7, David declares, "We escaped!" He does not assume, however, that Israel engineered its own escape; he knows that God is the one who breaks Israel's bondage (124:8).

In an inclusio around the enemy's attacks (124:2b–5), David presents God as Israel's sustainer (124:1–2a) and protector (124:6). He emphasizes Israel's debilitating terror via metaphoric language and repetition in the attack-and-deliverance sequence (124:3–7).

Psalm 125. Throughout the Psalter, the psalmists record only three elements that cannot be shaken (unless God shakes them): the earth, Mount Zion (Jerusalem), and those who trust in the Lord/live godly lives. The author of Psalm 125 (v. 1) references the latter two elements. (Note: being "unshakable" does not mean not being affected by external forces, but rather, not being moved off God's unshakable foundation.)

God's presence ensures this immovable security (125:2); he does not allow his people's enemies to rule over them forever (to protect them from following their captor's evil ways) (125:3; cf. Deut. 7:1–4).

The psalmist seeks God's blessing for true believers (whose foundation is sure) (125:4) but his judgment for those who walk with the wicked (whose foundation is not the true God) (125:5).

Psalm 126. The author structures Psalm 126 to highlight two points: God's great work (126:1–3; cf. 125:3–4) and the anticipated joy of future blessings (126:4–6).

In verse 1, God has returned his people from exile; they are ecstatic. In verses 2–3, the chiastic structure emphasizes God's marvelous work: (A) the people rejoice (126:2a); (B) God has done great things (126:2b); (B′) God has done great things (126:3a); (A′) the people rejoice (126:3b).

In 126:4, the author asks God to continue his wonderful work. In verses 5–6, in stair-step fashion, he presents the hoped-for transformation: (A) the people sow in sorrow (126:5a); (B) they reap with joy (126:5b); (A′) the people sow seeds in sorrow (126:6a); (B′) they reap sheaves with joy (126:6b). (People sow in tears because today's food [the seed] must be sown for next year's harvest.)

Psalm 127. Success comes when God blesses an endeavor and the responsible parties do what they must do (127:1, 3).

Solomon's practical experience confirmed this principle. By God's blessing, Solomon's hard work accomplished great things (cf. Eccles. 2:4–10; 5:18–20; 6:2; 12:13–14). Work wisely, then go to sleep trusting God for the results (Ps. 127:2).

Solomon observes that one blessing God may choose to give to a family is children; that blessing, moreover, may allow families to accomplish much and to gain status within society (127:3–5). Humans do their part, God does his, and the family is blessed in multiple ways.

Psalm 128. Psalms 127 and 128 present similar themes: God blesses believers in their work (127:1; 128:1–2) and in their families (127:3–5; 128:3). Psalm 128 emphasizes the importance of trusting God more prominently than does Psalm 127, using "fearing God" as an inclusio around the blessings (128:1, 4). Furthermore, Psalm 128 extends an individual's blessings throughout that person's lifetime and includes a national blessing (128:5–6); Psalm 127 does neither.

Psalm 128 concludes: "Peace be upon Israel"—a blessing that also concludes Psalm 125 (v. 5). Both psalms emphasize the importance of trusting God.

Psalm 129. The blessing in Psalm 128:6—"Peace be upon Israel"—now makes sense. It is not generic but eminently practical: Israel's enemies, for all too long, have been venting their rage on Israel (129:1–3). Israel needs peace.

Oppressors ran roughshod over Israel but could not defeat God's people (129:2–3), because God overcame those who opposed him, setting his people free (129:4).

Verses 5–8 convey a mild imprecation: those who despise God's special place on earth (Zion) are to be humiliated (129:5), to become worthless, and to face a premature death (129:6–7). No one is to seek God's blessing for such people (129:8).

Psalm 130. In stair-step fashion, the psalmist seeks the Lord (130:1–2, 5–6) and proclaims that God graciously frees people from their sins (130:3–4, 7–8).

Pleading directly for God's mercy (130:1–3), the author cries to God from the "depths"—a specific term always indicating (metaphorically or literally) a dangerous, even deadly situation or place. He continues revealing the intensity of his feelings through repetition, comparing his waiting to that of a night guard on sentry duty who longs for the comfort of daylight (130:5–6).

Verses 3–4, 7–8 focus on God's merciful forgiveness and redemption of sinners, thereby suggesting that "depths" (130:1) refers to the psalmist's grief over the devastating impact of personal and national sin.

Psalm 131. Contentment (131:1–2) comes from resting in God—not in self-seeking (considering oneself above others, perhaps even better than God; cf. Ps. 10:4), not in conceit (i.e., looking down on others as being of no account; cf. Prov. 30:12–13), not in achieving high status (Jer. 45:5), and not in doing miraculous things (as God alone does; cf. Ps. 72:18).

David humbles himself before God, taking satisfaction in being in God's compassionate and protective arms (much like a child does who delights in holding on to his or her mother; 131:2).

Psalm 131:2–3 link back to 130:5–7. Hope (131:3) implies confident waiting—the opposite of what 131:1 describes.

Psalm 132. In a psalm with messianic implications, the author reveals David's commitment to build a house for God (132:2–5) and God's commitment to David and his descendants (132:11–12) and to Jerusalem, his dwelling place (132:14–18).

Two petitions for God to act graciously toward David (132:1, 10) introduce the main sections, whereas a reference to spiritual clothing closes each section (132:9, 16–18).

Repetition of thought abounds, whether in the same verse through parallelism (132:2, 4–5); in consecutive verses through chiastic structure (132:11b—A; 132:12a—B; 132:12b—B´; 132:12c—A´); or in nonadjacent verses through essentially the same words (132:9, 16), through the use of synonyms (132:5, 7–8, 13–14—dwelling place and resting place), through the echoing of ideas (132:2, 11—David and God swear oaths to each other; 132:8, 14—your/my resting place), or through words rarely occurring in the Psalter (132:9, 16—"priest" appears only three other times in the Psalter).

Psalm 133. Oneness among God's people brings genuine delight (133:1).

David describes his feelings about unity via two illustrations. First (133:2), he points to Aaron's consecration as high priest—an event signifying a free-flowing channel of oneness between God and his people. Second (133:3), David speaks metaphorically of the pristine and heavy dew of Mount Hermon dripping down on the mountains of Zion—bringing life to the land.

The downward flow of the oil (133:2) and dew (133:3a) reflects the "downward flow" of God's blessing on his people (133:3b).

Psalm 134. The third of four sequential psalms that reference those who serve God as priests, Psalm 134 encourages communication between those "night-shift" priests (134:1–2) and God himself (134:3).

The exact phrases of Psalm 134 are rare in Scripture. "Praise [bless] the LORD" (134:1–2) appears only seven times total; "all . . . servants of the LORD" (134:1–2) only once elsewhere. "Who minister [stand] . . . in the house of the LORD" (134:1) occurs only two other times; "lift up your hands" is unique to verse 2. Even "may the LORD bless you" (134:3) is rare—five times total; likewise the title "the Maker of heaven and earth" (134:3) appears only five times.

Psalm 135. The words rendered "praise" and "bless" (NIV "praise") dominate the beginning (135:1–4) and concluding sections (135:19–21) of Psalm 135.

Comparing verses 5–7 and verses 15–18 reveals contrasts between God and idols: God's ability to control creation—idols' inability to control themselves. In verses 8–14, God powerfully overthrows idol-worshiping nations for the benefit of his people.

Psalms 135 and 136 share three themes: God's rule over creation (135:6–7; 136:6–9), God's deliverance of Israel from Egypt (135:8–9; 136:10–15), and God's protection of Israel in the wilderness (135:10–12; 136:16–22).

Psalm 136. The repeated clause, "His love endures forever," drives the pace of Psalm 136, building momentum with each subsequent verse. This repetition suggests that everything God does is a result of his never-ending love.

An inclusio of thanksgiving (136:1–3, 26) emphasizes the one who is to receive the gratitude of all people—that is, God, who displays goodness (136:1), who is greater than any other spiritual force (136:2), who is more powerful than all other rulers (136:3), and who is beyond all creation (136:26).

The psalmist highlights God's acts in creation (136:4–9), in the exodus (136:10–15), in the wilderness wanderings (136:16–22), and in the ongoing provision for his people and his creation (136:23–25).

Psalm 137. Despite being in exile, the author does not plead to God for deliverance in Psalm 137. Instead, he focuses on the anguish of being separated from Jerusalem.

Two emotions pervade this psalm. In 137:1–6, the psalmist experiences sadness thinking about home. Nevertheless, he determines never to forget Jerusalem. Should he ever stop remembering, he desires never to make music or sing again.

In 137:7–9, venting rage in an imprecation directed at the Edomites for encouraging the Babylonians, the psalmist takes pleasure in knowing that Edom will one day face judgment (cf. Obad. 1–21).

Psalm 138. Facing trouble in the midst of pagan nations, David remains confident in God. In fact, he develops this psalm as a thanksgiving psalm ("praise" in 138:1–2, 4 being the same word as "thanks" in 136:1–3, 26), hoping that the idol-worshiping kings will one day give thanks to the true God (138:4–5).

The God of the universe being intimately involved in his life, David prays that he will continue to bless and remember him (138:6–8).

Psalm 139. Binding the psalm together by describing God's intimate knowledge of his life and desires (139:1–3, 23–24), David writes about an all-knowing, everywhere-present, intimately involved God and expresses righteous rage against those who oppose him.

God knows everything about David's actions and thoughts—things even David does not know (139:1–6). Yet God still cares for David—a reality that David cannot fathom.

Proclaiming God's omnipresence (139:7–12), David declares that time and space do not confine him. God can guide and protect David wherever he is.

David marvels at God's creativity in forming humans (139:13–18). He is amazed that God constantly thinks about them and mercifully preserves them.

Because enemies of such a God deserve destruction, David (139:19–24) declares his hatred for them. Recognizing his fallibility, however, he seeks God's guidance in his life.

Psalm 140. As ungodly people slander and attack God (139:19–21), so they slander and attack David (140:1–5). David calls for their destruction (139:19; 140:9–11).

Using "Selah," David divides Psalm 140 into four parts (see NIV note). In the first two sections, he presents parallel cries to God for protection against those who falsely assail his character (140:1–3) or set traps to ruin him (140:4–5). In section three (140:6–8), he appeals to God for help—making the basis of his appeal their personal relationship. David concludes (140:9–13) with an imprecation against his attackers, basing his appeal to God on his needs and godly character.

Psalm 141. Desiring not to become like those whom he despises, David seeks God's protection from himself. He wants God to keep him from practicing

wickedness (141:1–5a), to keep the wicked away from him (141:5b–7), and to keep him from the wicked (141:8–10).

David uses contrasting imagery to conclude the first and second sections of this psalm: the oil of joy (141:5) and the horror of death (141:7). He completes the psalm by expressing his hope that the wicked would fall into their own death traps (141:9–10; cf. 140:5, 9).

Psalm 142. David uses three couplets to communicate the thrust of psalm 142. In verses 1–2, he cries out to God his complaint against his attackers. In verses 4–5, he recognizes that he has no refuge in this world, except God ("refuge," in 142:4, meaning a place to which to flee; in 142:5, a safe, protected shelter). In the final couplet (142:6–7), David seeks deliverance because his enemies overwhelm him (142:6) and because others then would recognize God's graciousness (142:7).

In the unpaired verse (142:3), David introduces the components of his complaint: he is no match for his powerful enemies, but his God knows (and can solve) his problem.

David prays, "Let the wicked fall into their own nets, while I pass by in safety" (Ps. 141:10). The use of nets to entrap prey (here, a herd of deer) is illustrated in this Assyrian relief (Ashurbanipal's palace, Nineveh, 645–635 BC).

Psalm 143. Many elements of Psalm 143 parallel those of Psalm 142. David cries out to God for mercy (142:1; 143:1) because his enemies are beyond his capability to handle (142:6; 143:3). He wants God to rescue him (142:6; 143:9) from his enemies' grasp (142:7—prison; 143:3—darkness). His spirit is worn down (142:3; 143:4); he needs God's protective care (142:5; 143:9).

In Psalm 143, David, unable to worship God freely, seeks freedom from his enemies. He is near to death—exhausted, simply trying to survive (143:1, 3–4, 7, 9, 11–12). Yet, even under such circumstances, he meditates, prays, and trusts God (143:5–6, 8).

Not deserving God's mercy, David hopes that God will extend grace to him (143:2, 7–8, 10). Through all this, he remains spiritually close to God (143:10, 12).

Psalm 144. In five sequential psalms, David seeks God's help in terrible crises. Psalms 140–43 highlight his desperation because of his enemies' overwhelming power and, at times, picture his physical or spiritual life succumbing to pressure. By contrast, Psalm 144 depicts God as a conquering warrior, who sweeps down from heaven on behalf of helpless people and, with great power, defeats their enemies (144:3–6). That same God at times overwhelms his people with blessings at home, in business, and in the world (144:12–15).

Not currently experiencing that blessed life, David offers a repeated prayer (144:7–8, 11) that God deliver him. After the first plea, he declares that he will praise God for the victory; after the second plea, that God will greatly bless his people (144:9–10, 12–15).

Psalm 145. David conveys a sense of "totality" in three different arenas: time, people, and God's works and ways.

Time: David declares that he and all people will praise God every day and forever (145:1–2, 21—an inclusio of praise to God). God's reign, moreover, lasts forever (145:13).

People: God provides for all people, especially for those who suffer and call on his name (145:9, 14–16, 18). He cares for all his people, overcomes all the wicked, and receives praise from all people forever (145:20–21).

God's works and ways: he is righteous and gracious in all that he does, showing mercy to all his works (i.e., people) (145:9–10, 17).

The praise of Psalm 145 prepares the way for the praise psalms that conclude the Psalter.

Psalm 146. Psalms 146–50 all begin and end with, "Praise the LORD."

The psalmist warns against trusting earthly powers, whose plans end at death (146:3–6), and encourages trusting God, who fulfills his promises forever (146:6) and ceaselessly cares for those facing physical, emotional, and personal struggles (146:7–9). He favors the godly and obstructs the wicked (146:8–9). The psalmist will praise the eternal God all of his life (146:1–2, 10); God's people are to do likewise (146:10).

Psalm 147. The author emphasizes three truths: God is beyond humanity; God is involved in humanity; and God is to be praised by humanity. Surrounding the psalm with calls for praise (147:1, 20) and strategically positioning similar calls (147:7, 12), the psalmist creates three sections that highlight God's immanence and transcendence (147:2–6, 8–11, 13–20).

Immanence—God helps the hurting (147:2–3), benefits the godly but opposes the ungodly (147:6, 10–11, 19–20), and meets the needs of humans and animals (147:9, 13–14).

Transcendence—God directs the universe (147:4), comprehends what humans cannot even imagine (147:5), and controls nature (147:8, 15–18).

Psalm 148. Whereas the previous two psalms conclude by emphasizing that Israel's God reigns eternally (146:10) or that God gives his word uniquely to Israel (147:19–20), Psalm 148 ends by revealing that God empowers Israel and has a special relationship to Israel (148:14).

Enclosing this praise psalm with the command, "Praise the LORD" (148:1a, 14d), the author begins each section (148:1b–6, 7–14c) with a similar command and indicates from where that praise is to arise: from heaven and from earth (148:1b, 7a, respectively). Then, after identifying specific beings or objects that are to offer praise (148:1c–4, 7b–12), he concludes each section with, "Let them praise the name of the LORD," and gives reasons why such praise should be given (148:5–6, 13–14c).

Psalm 149. This psalm emphasizes the necessity of praising and humbly serving God. The author binds together the psalm's two sections (149:1–4, 5–9) by revealing privileges given to the saints: praising God publicly, praising him privately, and doing his will (149:1, 5, 9).

God's people are to praise him because he takes joyful interest in them and blesses those who humble themselves before him (149:1–4). God's people, moreover, are to honor him by carrying out his judgment on those who oppose God (149:6–9). This judgment does not originate from the saints' own hatred of their enemies but from the recorded decision of God (149:9) and is a judgment that they are to inflict because of their love for God (149:6).

Psalm 150. All people everywhere (on earth and in the heavens) (150:1, 6) are to praise God for who he is and what he does (150:2)—to praise him with music and dance (150:3–5).

Verse 6 clarifies a concern that may arise throughout the Psalter: does God care only about Israel and not about the nations? Verse 6 declares that God's interest extends to all people everywhere.

After recording eleven direct commands to praise God (150:1–5), the author uses an indirect command: "Let everything that has breath praise the LORD" (150:6). This shift slows down the pace of the psalm, giving readers time to ponder its truth—everyone in the world is to praise God. The author then concludes with one final direct command: "Praise the LORD."

Select Bibliography

Allen, Leslie C. *Psalms 101–150.* Word Biblical Commentary. Dallas: Word, 1983.

Bullock, C. H. *Encountering the Book of Psalms.* Grand Rapids: Baker Academic, 2001.

Craigie, Peter C. *Psalms 1–50.* Word Biblical Commentary. Dallas: Word, 1983.

Kidner, Derek. *Psalms.* 2 vols. Tyndale Old Testament Commentaries. Downers Grove, IL: InterVarsity, 1973, 1975.

Longman, Tremper, III. *How to Read the Psalms.* Downers Grove, IL: InterVarsity, 1988.

Tate, Marvin E. *Psalms 51–100.* Word Biblical Commentary. Dallas: Word, 1990.

VanGemeren, Willem A. *Psalms.* Expositor's Bible Commentary. Edited by Tremper Longman III and David E. Garland. Grand Rapids: Zondervan, 2000.

Wilson, Gerald H. *Psalms.* NIV Application Commentary. Vol. 1. Grand Rapids: Zondervan, 2002.

Proverbs

Richard L. Schultz

Introduction

There are few Old Testament books as attractive to the modern reader as the book of Proverbs. Four reasons for this appeal can be suggested: the brevity of its basic unit, its universal and timeless nature, the practical focus and range of its everyday subjects, and its rhetorical appeal to modern intellectuals. Nevertheless, each of these features presents its own unique challenges. First, the individual proverbs often appear to be arranged somewhat arbitrarily, so that readers seem compelled to interpret each one without the benefit of literary context. Second, the book of Proverbs shares so many formal, verbal, and conceptual elements with ancient Near Eastern proverbial collections that its claim to be part of the uniquely inspired Word of God has been questioned. In addition, Proverbs appears to reflect few of the central themes of Old Testament theology. Third, the pragmatic emphasis of the book, especially within the proverbial collections, obscures its theological foundations, some of which may be implicit and

presupposed. Fourth, the terseness of expression and frequent juxtaposition of clauses, especially in the original Hebrew, impede the attempt to translate or interpret those proverbs with the usual degree of certainty.

Title and Authorship

The book of Proverbs contains several proverbial collections, each of which has its own brief title (10:1; 24:23; 25:1; 30:1; 31:1) or introductory section (22:17–21). The initial title in 1:1 ("The proverbs of Solomon son of David, king of Israel") identifies the book's dominant (but not only) literary form and author. This title is expanded in 1:2–7, which state the objectives and foundational premises of this wisdom text in a manner that parallels 22:17–21 and several Egyptian instructional texts. The

This tablet from Nippur (eighteenth century BC) containing Sumerian proverbs is one of many such proverbial collections from the ancient Near East.

titles of the proverbial collections in Proverbs 10:1 and 25:1 similarly associate their contents with Solomon, which fits the portrayal of his reign in 1 Kings and 2 Chronicles. According to 1 Kings 3:12, God granted Solomon a "wise and discerning heart" that manifested itself in his judicial decisions, international relations, the temple construction project, encyclopedic knowledge, and literary compositions. These are described most fully in 1 Kings 4:29–34, which makes several important claims: (1) Solomon's wisdom was God-given and surpassed that of all of his contemporaries. (2) During the united monarchy under Solomon, some Israelites had sufficient knowledge of and access to wisdom writings of the East (probably Mesopotamia, not Arabia) and Egypt to warrant such a comparison between Solomon and his contemporaries and to establish Solomon's international reputation. (3) Solomon's literary output included more than three thousand proverbs (which could have included many of the 950 verses in the book of Proverbs), as well as more than one thousand songs.

In light of these qualifications, Solomon's traditional association with Old Testament wisdom writings (including Ecclesiastes and Song of Songs) is understandable. This has even led some scholars to claim that he is the author of the entire book of Proverbs, viewing Agur (in Prov. 30.1, "gatherer") and Lemuel (in 31:1, "belonging to God"), as symbolic designations for Solomon. Nevertheless, many contemporary scholars deny that the present canonical book contains any proverbs or instructions that originated with Solomon. James Crenshaw states bluntly: "Wisdom and Solomon have nothing to do with each other" (Crenshaw, 40). Ultimately, the validity of biblical claims regarding Solomonic wisdom depends on one's view of the reliability of biblical historiography. If Solomon was, in reality and not simply in legend, an incomparably wise ruler and sage, it is certainly plausible that many of the proverbial sayings that he personally formulated would be preserved in the canonical anthology ascribed to him.

To posit Solomonic authorship for some of the contents of the proverbial collections by no means demands his editorial responsibility for the entire book. Taking Proverbs 1:1 seriously does not exclude the extensive contribution of other unknown sages, authors, and editors. According to the talmudic tractate *Baba Batra* (15a), "Hezekiah and his men wrote Isaiah, Proverbs, the Song of Songs, and Qoheleth." The textual basis for this is Proverbs 25:1, which may suggest a larger compositional or editorial role played by a scribal group in the time of Hezekiah, two centuries after Solomon—this group perhaps even added the introductory prologue in 1:8–9:18. As already noted, there are several additional authors mentioned in the titles to the individual subcollections of proverbs and sayings. Proverbs 30 constitutes "the sayings of Agur son of Jakeh—an oracle"; Proverbs 31 contains, similarly, "the sayings of King Lemuel—an oracle his mother taught him." (Neither Agur nor Lemuel is mentioned elsewhere in biblical or extrabiblical sources.) Proverbs 22:17 ("Pay attention and listen to the sayings of the wise") and 24:23 ("These also are sayings of the wise") are usually taken as titles that introduce additional proverbial collections from anonymous sages. The Greek translators of these verses, however, viewed neither of them as constituting an introductory title, and the insertion of the subheadings "Sayings of the Wise" and "Further Sayings of the Wise" into the NIV text simply reflects a Bible editor's interpretation. Given the nature of proverbial wisdom, which often has an oral origin, it is likely that Solomon and other contributors to the book of Proverbs both coined and collected proverbial sayings.

Date

Seeking to determine the date of an anthology like the book of Proverbs is a tenuous undertaking. First of all, one must distinguish between the date of origin of individual proverbs, the date of their compilation into collections, and the date of the editing of the book of Proverbs, which certainly could have gone through several editions before the final canonical edition was completed. Second, the universal and timeless nature of the individual proverbial sayings and instructions makes them difficult to date. Third, the striking formal differences between Proverbs 1–9 and 10–31 require separate treatments of the two major sections of the book. Most scholars view chapters 10–31 as being earlier than 1–9, citing several of its striking features in support of this claim. From a form-critical perspective, Hermann Gunkel and his early followers claimed that the shorter forms (e.g., two-clause proverbial sayings in chaps. 10–31) are earlier than the longer instructional discourses (e.g., 1:8–19). From a conceptual standpoint, the figure of personified wisdom as developed in Proverbs 1–9 is seen to be dependent on later Persian or Greek models. In terms of content, Proverbs 1–9 is considered late due to its highly reflective theological content that closely links wisdom and its acquisition to personal piety and divine endowment. As a result, Proverbs 1–9 is commonly understood as a prologue that was composed much later to serve as a theological introduction to chapters 10–31.

There is no evidence, however, that any of the proverbial collections ever circulated in Israel independently from chapters 1–9. Apart from chapters 1–9, a proper framework for understanding the purpose and theological basis for chapters 10–29 is lacking. Furthermore, the arguments in support of a postexilic origin for Proverbs 1–9 have been countered by Egyptologists, such as Kenneth Kitchen, who note that proverbial collections preceded by lengthy prologues, the personification of abstract qualities such as wisdom, and similar theological and personal ethical reflection are found in various Egyptian and Mesopotamian wisdom collections dated to the third and second millennia BC, that is, prior to the time of Solomon (Kitchen, 134–36). Divergent claims regarding the dating of texts within chapters 10–31 usually focus on the contents of those texts rather than on their language. Two features

figure prominently in such discussions. Some scholars, such as William McKane, distinguish, for example, between secular-individualistic, community-focused, and moralistic-Yahwistic proverbs, which then are ascribed to different phases of Israel's intellectual and religious development (McKane, 10–22). Other scholars posit diverse socioeconomic backgrounds (or "life settings," e.g., tribal, agrarian, scribal, royal) as giving rise to individual proverbs and collections. It is rather questionable to suggest, however, that only farmers can formulate proverbs about crop growth (e.g., 14:4). In any case, these issues have little bearing on how one should understand these individual proverbs within their present canonical-compositional collections. Nevertheless, given the book's association with Solomon and its frequent focus on the duties of a king or courtier, it is likely that the book as a whole was composed in a royal-scribal setting. This does not preclude individual proverbs from originating in a tribal or rural setting, nor is there reason to believe that the canonical book was not intended to have a much broader readership.

Literary Features

A wide range of literary forms are used in the book of Proverbs, not all of which are native to or typical of wisdom discourse. These include the instruction (chaps. 1–9), individual sentence (primarily chaps. 10–30), numerical saying (6:16–19; 30:15–31, possibly also a riddle), beatitude (3:13; 8:32, 34; 28:14), acrostic (i.e., alphabetic sequence, 31:10–31), and allegory (5:15–23). Especially in chapters 1–9, stylistic devices, such as the call to attention (4:1; 5:1), rhetorical question (6:27–28), and personal observation and reflection (4:3–8; 7:6–23), are commonly employed. By far, the dominant form is the individual sentence or proverb. Most proverbs take the form of the wisdom saying, which consists of a declaration formulated with indicative verbs, including participles. In chapters 1–9 and 22–24, however, the admonition (a command or a prohibition), expressed with imperative verb forms, is also common. Admonitions typically contain a motivational clause that seeks to persuade the addressee to heed the instruction by noting promised benefits for obedience or adverse consequences for ignoring it ("Do not love sleep or you will grow poor; stay awake and you will have food to spare," 20:13). Often this takes the form of an appeal to discernment on the basis of experience or common sense ("Do not lust in your heart after her beauty or let her captivate you with her eyes. . . . Can a man scoop fire into his lap without his clothes being burned?" 6:25, 27). Alternatively, it can involve an explicit reference to the way of life or death or to Yahweh ("Do not exploit the poor because they are poor and do not crush the needy in court, for the LORD will take up their case and will plunder those who plunder them," 22:22–23).

Ted Hildebrandt has helpfully described a proverb as a "short, salty, concrete, fixed, paradigmatic, poetically-crafted saying" (Hildebrandt, 234). The meaning of the Hebrew word for "proverb" is disputed, based on the meaning of the related verbal root or Semitic cognate word. The most commonly suggested meanings for "proverb" are (1) a comparison or noted similarity (from the verb "to resemble") or (2) a powerful word (from "to rule"). As noted above, an individual proverb in the book of Proverbs usually consists of two parallel lines. The second line continues and completes the theme and thought of the first line by means of emphatic restatement or supplementary comment, striking comparison, contrast, illustration, or reference to the consequences of specific actions. This can be illustrated

by 18:22–23 ("He who finds a wife finds what is good / and receives favor from the LORD" [supplementation]; "A poor man pleads for mercy, / but a rich man answers harshly" [contrast]). Individual proverbial assertions can be categorized according to the kind of comment they make regarding a given topic, such as classification (14:15; 27:7; 29:5), comparison (25:13; 26:14), evaluation (17:16; 22:1), and act-consequence (15:13; 19:20).

Structure and Theological Themes

Proverbs is best understood as a carefully edited anthology. This has a number of implications for how the book should be interpreted. First of all, chapters 1–9 function as a theological introduction to biblical wisdom and an interpretative introduction to the proverbial collections that follow. After the divine origin and God-centered orientation of wise behavior has been established in the prologue, even the "secular" proverbs in chapters 10–31 are to be read through this theological lens. Second, chapters 10–29 in turn often echo and offer numerous practical everyday illustrations of the theological principles set forth in chapters 1–9, including those exemplified by Lady Wisdom and Lady Folly. Third, even though many individual proverbs may have had an independent oral existence prior to their incorporation within the collections of the canonical book, they are now to be interpreted within the context of their present

Many of the ancient proverb collections still in existence today are practice writing tablets from scribal schools. This Egyptian relief showing two scribes is from the Tomb of Mere-Ruka, Sakara (ca. 2300 BC).

literary collections, in which various ordering principles can frequently be identified. Numerous individual proverbs are repeated fully or in part elsewhere within the book and thus have a different emphasis or application in each of their respective contexts (compare, for example, 13:14 with 14:27). Fourth, chapters 30–31 form a literary bracket with chapters 1–9 (i.e., a theological prologue and epilogue; note the verbal links between 9:10 and 30:3 as well as 31:30) around the proverbial collections. Within this bracket, 30:1–9 (a sage's confession and prayer) and 31:1–9 (a queen mother's charge) offer complementary summaries of wise behavior, and 31:10–31 describes Lady Wisdom (from chaps. 1–9) incarnated as a real-life, if somewhat idealized, wife.

As Proverbs 1:7 already makes clear ("The fear of the LORD is the beginning of knowledge"), biblical wisdom involves more than intellectual prowess. Rather, wisdom is better defined as *the ability—divinely bestowed and acquired through a lifelong process—that enables one in various situations to make and carry out decisions pleasing to God and ultimately socially and personally beneficial*. With "wisdom" (Hebrew *hokmah*) serving as the broader term, related words, such as "understanding," "knowledge," "prudence," "insight," and "discernment," express various intellectual and practical aspects of wise behavior. This is in contrast to the terms related to folly, which convey varying degrees of personal blame and hope for corrective change, from naïveté (Hebrew *peti*, 1:4) to hard-core mockery of God-fearing wisdom (Hebrew *lets*, 9:7) and practical atheism (Hebrew *nabal*, 17:21; cf. Ps. 14:1; 53:1). Wisdom theology is rooted in creation, which reflects God's sovereign ordering of all things (3:19–20) and enables one to derive insights even from the observation of this in nature (6:6). But it is also rooted in the "law" of God (Hebrew *torah*, Deut. 4:44 and Prov. 6:23), claiming the same authority as the Mosaic instruction and promising the same benefits (and consequences) as are associated with obedience (and disobedience)

to the covenantal stipulations (e.g., long life in the land; compare Deut. 4:40 and Prov. 2:21). Wisdom theology's foundational principle is the fear of the Lord (Prov. 1:7; 8:13; 9:10; 31:30), which involves not simply sincere reverence for God but also reliance on him and the avoidance of evil, and is essentially the Old Testament equivalent of saving faith in the New Testament. Thus the acquisition of wisdom is a lifelong process to be furthered through instruction and observation as well as through discipline and correction. This covenantal foundation and the broad ethical demands flowing from reverence for Yahweh distinguish Proverbs from the more utilitarian, courtly emphasis of Egyptian instructional literature, despite the many themes, stylistic features, and objectives that these texts share.

Outline

1. Foreword (1:1–7)
2. Prologue: Introducing the Way of Wisdom (1:8–9:18)
   A. The Initial Appeals of the Parents and Lady Wisdom (1:8–33)
   B. The Commendation of Wisdom (2:1–4:27)
   C. Warnings against Folly, Especially Sexual Infidelity (5:1–7:27)
   D. Wisdom's Final Appeals (8:1–9:18)
3. Proverbial Collections: Advanced Instruction in Wisdom (10:1–29:27)
   A. The Original Solomonic Collection (10:1–22:16)
   B. Sayings of the Wise: Admonitions for Societal Relationships (22:17–24:22)
   C. More Sayings of the Wise: The Necessity of Honesty and Diligence (24:23–34)
   D. The Later Solomonic Collection (25:1–29:27)
4. Epilogue (30:1–31:31)
   A. Agur's Message: Relying on God's Word, Learning from His Work (30:1–33)
   B. The Message of Lemuel's Mother: A Call for Royal Justice (31:1–9)
   C. Lady Wisdom Exemplified (31:10–31)

1. Foreword (1:1–7)

Proverbs 1–9 serves as the theological introduction to the canonical book, giving a foundational introduction to biblical wisdom—its nature, sources, acquisition, and value. Chapters 10–29 build on this foundation, offering a plethora of illustrations of what wisdom and its opposite, folly, look like in everyday life. In effect, Proverbs 1–9 offers the "Wisdom 101" course, while Proverbs 10–29 presents "Wisdom 201." Proverbs 1 is introductory both to the book as a whole and to the prologue in particular, introducing all of the prominent elements of chapters 1–9. Within this theological introduction, 1:1–7 forms the foreword, giving the book's title, purpose, and central theme.

The title (1:1) presents King Solomon as the primary author, raising the possibility of an initial edition of the book that contained only Solomonic proverbs, perhaps ending at 22:16. Interestingly, outside of this preface and the titles to the Solomonic collections (Prov. 10:1; 25:1), the word "proverb" occurs only in 26:7, 9. The purpose statements in 1:2–6 are grammatically linked to verse 1. these Solomonic proverbs are presented in order to achieve specific pedagogical and behavioral goals. Verse 5, which interrupts the sequence, describes how wise individuals will respond to this challenge. Verses 2a and 3–4 refer to the contents of the instruction. The book of Proverbs is designed to help its readers experience wise discipline, the theory and practice of proper living. Appropriately, the first wisdom term employed here is the general term "wisdom" (Hebrew *hokmah*; there are almost one hundred occurrences in Proverbs of this or a related form of the word). "Discipline" (NIV "instruction") designates the process of learning to live consistently according to wisdom principles through training, modeling, and correction. Verses 2b and 6 suggest that one must also learn the skill of interpreting and properly applying various wisdom forms, something that the fool is unable to do (Prov.

26:7, 9). Several of the Egyptian instructions, including the Instruction of Amenemope, contain similar purpose statements. Verse 3b indicates that biblical wisdom is not simply the art of successfully navigating around the twists, turns, and submerged boulders of life; it also involves the pursuit of justice, equity, and fairness in interpersonal, especially legal and commercial, relationships.

Verses 4–5 introduce those potentially benefiting from this instruction. The primary addressees are the "simple," who presumably are also "young." The "simple" (Hebrew *peti*) are inexperienced, even naive, the stereotypical "freshmen," but also open-minded and not yet set in their ways. Even the beginner in wisdom's school can receive the necessary instruction to meet life's challenges. The NIV takes verse 5 as an admonition; it also could be translated as a statement. In either case, a distinguishing characteristic of the truly wise is that they continually augment their wisdom resources. The wise individual devotes special attention to the various subgenres through which the insights of the wise are expressed, including enigmatic sayings that need to be solved ("riddles," 1:6; cf. Judg. 14:12 and 1 Kings 10:1) Verse 7a concludes the foreword by introducing the foundational theological principle or motto of the book of Proverbs. The phrase "the fear of the LORD" also occurs in Proverbs 9:10, thus bracketing the book's introductory section (also 1:29; 2:5; 8:13, and nine times in chaps. 10–31). To fear the Lord is not to cower in terror before an unknowable deity; rather, it entails a life lived in constant awareness of one's dependence on and obligation toward the sovereign Creator. This expression distinguishes biblical wisdom from all other types of human learning. Ancient Near Eastern wisdom literature outside of Israel never presents wisdom as rooted in one's relationship to a deity. The "beginning" refers to the essential foundation without which no growth in understanding can take place. Verse 7b concludes the preface by distinguishing fools, who alone despise the benefits of wise discipline (cf. 1:2), from those addressed in these introductory remarks.

2. Prologue: Introducing the Way of Wisdom (1:8–9:18)

A. The initial appeals of the parents and Lady Wisdom (1:8–33). Proverbs 1:8–19 contains the first parental lesson out of ten (or more) in the prologue, exhibiting the basic structural features that the additional lessons will follow. On the basis of posited Egyptian literary models, scholars have often divided up this section into a number of originally independent "lectures." Nevertheless, a convincing case can be made that the prologue as a whole presents a carefully composed and unified argument. Michael Fox lists the following three features as typical in these lessons: (1) the *exordium*, or introduction, consisting of an address to the

audience, an exhortation to hear and remember the teachings, and motivational statements that extol the teachings' excellence and value to their possessor; (2) the *lesson*, or teaching proper; and (3) the *conclusion*, or summary statement, which generalizes the lesson's principle (Fox, 45).

This first lesson contains three addresses to the son (1:8, 10, 15), each followed by imperatives (commands or prohibitions), thus dividing the instruction into three sections. Verses 8–9 contain the introductory call to attention and the benefits of doing so; verses 10–14 offer an anticipatory warning against yielding to the temptation to join a violent gang; and verses 15–19 present the admonition proper, followed by reasons for heeding it. The command to "listen" occurs at least twelve times in Proverbs, eight of these in chapters 1–9, and emphasizes the importance of being receptive to the guidance of a parent or sage. In conformity to the ancient Near Eastern instructional genre, Proverbs is directed at young sons, preparing them to lead an effective public life of service, perhaps in the royal court (since Solomon is the designated author). The Egyptian texts, however, never refer to a mother's instruction, as in verse 8, which suggests that the home is the setting for such training. The lessons learned there will adorn the youth like a garland or wreath (1:9; 4:9) or decorative chains (Song 4:9).

Those unambiguously labeled as "sinful" seek comrades in their devious, violent, unprovoked, and unjustified actions, for which they possess an enormous appetite (1:10–12), offering the enticing promise of sharing the battle "plunder" (1:13; cf. Deut. 20:14 and Josh. 11:14, which use the same word). Verse 15 introduces the major image and theme of the two ways in Proverbs, which can refer either to

The Instructions of Shurrupak to His Son Ziusudra, a collection of Sumerian proverbs found on this tablet from 2400 BC, begin similarly to Proverbs 1:8: "Shurrupak gave instructions to his son." Other versions add, "My son, let me give you instructions: you should pay attention!"

specific decisions or actions or to one's general life choices or lifestyle. Paul quotes this description of frivolous bloodshed in Romans 3:15. Proverbs 1:17 introduces a proverbial saying that suggests that a bird is cleverer than these evil schemers, who in setting an ambush for others are actually lying in wait (1:11, 18) for their own lives!

In 1:20–35, wisdom is presented not simply as an abstract capacity or skill but as a person who directly addresses those most lacking in wisdom. Although the nature and origin of Lady Wisdom (Hebrew *hokmah* is a feminine noun) have been much discussed, this figure is best understood as both a poetic personification of a divine attribute and a foil, or conceptual antithesis, to the promiscuous or foolish woman. The designation for Lady Wisdom is literally "wisdoms," possibly an intensive plural, implying that she embodies the fullness of wisdom qualities (similar to the plural form *elohim* for God and the plural *behemot*—literally "beasts"—for Behemoth [Job 40:15]). The presence of a female figure justifies the use of the language of romantic love, as the author portrays the acquisition of wisdom as something profoundly personal, enjoyable, beneficial, and lifelong.

In this section, Lady Wisdom is presented as a prophetlike figure who seeks to rescue fools from the error (and consequences) of their ways, in effect assuming a mediatorial role between God and humanity. According to the fourfold description of Lady Wisdom's location (1:20–21), she calls out to those engaged in the business of everyday life, where commerce, communication, and legal affairs are conducted. She rebukes both the naive and the hardened mockers for clinging to their folly and repeatedly spurning her corrective counsel (1:22–27). As a result of their resistance, when "calamity" strikes, the roles will be reversed (1:26). These youths will then call out for help (1:28; cf. 1:24), only to be ignored and mocked by her and abandoned to bear their self-inflicted—and potentially fatal—troubles alone (1:28–33).

B. The commendation of wisdom (2:1–4:27).

2:1–22. With Proverbs 2, the parental speaker begins a positive recommendation of wisdom, which encompasses three lengthy exhortations (chaps. 2–4). Proverbs 2 lays the foundation, describing the source and primary benefits of wisdom, while chapters 3–4 offer more detailed descriptions of the values of wise behavior. One striking emphasis in Proverbs 2 is the acquisition of wisdom as the result of both intensive human effort and divine endowment, while the remaining instructions focus on the first of these two, human effort. Furthermore, the instruction in chapter 2 differs from the others in Proverbs 1–9 in that it contains no imperative verbal forms in the Hebrew text. If one pays close attention to the sequence of conjunctions (i.e., if, then, for, thus), a clear structure emerges. Three (or four) conditions for obtaining wisdom are set forth in 2:1–4, followed by 2:5–8 and 2:9–19, which portray, respectively, the general and specific protection that wisdom offers all who attain it. Verses 20–22 conclude the instruction by describing the ultimate benefits of following the way of wisdom.

Proverbs 2:1–4 assumes that the son sincerely desires to obtain wisdom. A clear progression is discernible in the sequence of verbs employed in setting forth the conditions, moving from passive to active engagement. The first step is receptivity: "accept" (the same Hebrew verb occurs also in 1:3; 4:10; 8:10; 10:8; 21:11; and 24:32). The child must welcome the parental instruction and store it up as valuable and authoritative "commands" (cf. Ps. 119:11). Verse 2 describes holistic engagement involving the ear and heart, while verse 3 notes the urgency of the undertaking, as one cries aloud for wisdom. Verse 4 forms the climax of the quest for wisdom; the same persistence required of one seeking precious metals is demanded of the one who wishes to become wise (cf. Job 28).

The initial rewards for persevering in one's quest for wisdom are set forth (2:5–8). The first result is somewhat surprising. Rather than becoming exceedingly wise or successful, one first must develop true piety, understanding what it means to fear the Lord. The quest for true wisdom inevitably leads first to God, since, according to verse 6, he is its ultimate source, and it is his exclusive prerogative to grant wisdom to every earnest seeker.

Wisdom's primary benefit according to this instruction is protection during one's journey through life. Remarkably, the quester has been transformed in the process, becoming "upright," "blameless," "just," and one of God's "faithful ones." What God "holds . . . in store" for those who "store up" (using the same Hebrew verb) the parents' words (2:1) is "success" (the Hebrew word denotes "top grade" wisdom, which brings success, 2:7). God also serves as a protective shield for the blameless, perhaps an allusion to his earlier promise to Abraham (Gen. 15:1), of whom he made a similar demand (Gen. 17:1).

The second benefit is described in 2:9–11 ("Then . . ."). In seeking wisdom, one develops not only an intimate relationship with God but also an intimate understanding of moral rectitude (2:9; cf. 1:3). Since wisdom now pervades the command center of one's life and acquiring knowledge has become an enjoyable task, personal discretion assumes the role previously carried out by God (2:8) of protecting the youth from the dangers brought about by wrong choices and missteps (2:11). Divine wisdom will help the youth get on the right path and stay on it. Verses 12–19 then describe the two primary threats to the moral integrity of the youth: perverse men (2:12–15) and seductive women (2:16–19). These two groups are described in a similar fashion, using participial verbal forms to emphasize their habitual modes of speaking and the good that they leave behind (2:13, 17).

In verse 16, the dangerous woman is introduced for the first time in Proverbs; a fuller portrait of this woman is given in Proverbs 5–7. This person's designation as a "strange" (Hebrew *zarah*; 2:16; 5:3, 20; 7:5; cf. 22:14; see also commentary on 5:1–23) woman or a "foreigner" (2:16; 5:20; 6:24; 7:5; cf. 20:16; 23:27; 27:13) in some translations has spawned

extensive discussion regarding the import of these designations. The NIV's translation of these words as "adulterous" and "wayward" woman, respectively, clearly involves an interpretive paraphrase. There is no indication in the text of Proverbs, however, that either designation reflects Israelite fear of foreigners or even the fear that a foreign wife's pagan religious practices will undermine Israelite devotion to Yahweh. The descriptions of this individual in Proverbs 1–9 suggest, rather, that she is a married, adulterous Israelite woman, who is "estranged" from her husband and from society in general by virtue of her promiscuity. More significantly, she represents all forms of socially destructive sexual behavior. Unlike the wicked men of 2:12–15, who do not present a direct threat to the son unless he joins them on their "crooked" paths that presumably will not reach the desired destination, a single encounter with the seductress can be fatal, and 2:19 expresses this threat comprehensively.

Verses 20–22 introduce the ultimate benefits of staying on the right path: good companions (2:20), long life in the land (2:21), and avoiding the fate of the wicked (2:22). These verses use language reminiscent of the covenantal promises and threats regarding the land. (For example, Deut. 28:63 uses the same rare verb translated "torn" in Prov. 2:22.) In effect, covenantal promises to the nation are being extended to the individual who embraces wisdom. Such an individual will remain in the land under God's favor rather than be cut off (the same Hebrew verb is used in the Mosaic law to describe divine judgment; see Lev. 7:20, 21, 25, 27; 17:4, 9–10, 14; 18:29).

3:1–35. Chapter 3 continues the positive recommendation of wisdom. Based on thematic development, the chapter can be subdivided into four subsections: 3:1–4, 5–12, 13–26, 27–35. Verses 1–4 set forth additional advantages of preserving wisdom instruction. The words "teaching" and "commands" (Hebrew *torah* and *mitsvah*, 3:1, also in 6:20, 23; 7:2) are commonly paired with reference to Mosaic law (cf. Exod.

24:12; Josh. 22:5). Parental instructions are authoritative, not simply good advice. To "forget" involves not simply letting something slip one's mind; it entails failing to act accordingly. Observing this exhortation, the son is assured, will result in a long and satisfying life (3:2; cf. Exod. 20:12; Eph. 6:1–3). This promise is problematic, since many people know someone who lived a wise, God-fearing life only to die young. Bruce Waltke (2004, 107–9) explains that proverbs teach the ABCs of morality, emphasizing their ultimate validation in the future despite temporary exceptions. This would be confirmed if the first phrase, literally "length of days" (cf. Deut. 30:20; Ps. 21:4; 23:6; 91:16; 93:5; Lam. 5:20), refers to an extension of life beyond clinical death, but this is unclear. "Love and faithfulness" (Hebrew *hesed* and *emet*; cf. Prov. 14:22; 16:6; 20:28) should be publicly displayed ("bind . . . around") and permanent traits ("write . . . on," 3:3). Such fidelity to one's divine-human and human-human commitments will lead to divine and human favor (3:4; cf. Luke 2:52). These two relationships are in turn further unfolded in 3:5–12 and 27–35, respectively.

Proverbs 3:5–10 continues the pattern of verses 1–4, the odd-numbered verses containing commands and the even verses promised results. Verses 5–6 encourage complete reliance on God and his revealed will—rather than on oneself—in all decisions and actions. As a result, God will help one to head straight for the goal and avoid unnecessary detours. Verses 7–8 continue the theme of life direction, with verse 7a paralleling verse 5b. The phrase "in your own eyes" directs one's attention back to verse 4, "in

the sight [literally "eyes"] of God and man"; here it is a question of whose approval one values. Ironically, although Proverbs repeatedly emphasizes the quest for wisdom, the greatest folly is to assume that one has arrived (3:7a), for that fosters self-reliance. Verse 7b underlines the inseparable relationship between wisdom, piety, and obedience. Reverence for God compels a person to avoid all that is displeasing to God (Prov. 8:13; 16:6; 23:17; cf. 13:19), and living a life that thus avoids destructive behavior will enhance one's physical well-being (4:22).

Verses 9–10 imply that trusting God completely includes trusting him with one's material needs by returning a portion of one's wealth. Verse 9 contains a rare mention of sacrifices in Proverbs; the offering of first fruits is described

Proverbs 3:16 says of Wisdom, "Long life is in her right hand; in her left hand are riches and honor." The same concept is visually portrayed in an Egyptian stele (tomb of Horemheb, Saqqara, 18th dynasty): life (the ankh) is held in the gods' right hands and power and authority (the scepter) in their left.

in Exodus 23:19 and Deuteronomy 18:4. The assurance in verse 10 speaks of abundance but not necessarily of miraculous multiplication (cf. Israel's corporate covenantal promises: Lev. 26:3–5; Joel 2:23–24). Verses 11–12 serve as a counterpart to verses 5–6, encouraging the youth, as in verse 1, to be receptive to instruction. Here the Lord is compared with a loving parent who, of necessity, dispenses both discipline and corrective rebuke (the pair appears nine times in Proverbs, always in this order; cf. Deut. 8:5; Heb. 12:5–6).

A threefold recommendation of wisdom is given in 3:13–26. (1) The person who finds personified wisdom will experience a happy, pleasant, and lengthy life (3:13–18; "blessed" begins and concludes the unit). By use of several richly evocative metaphors, wisdom is described as incomparably more profitable than precious metals or gems, as offering tranquil paths, and as a life-giving and life-enhancing tree (Prov. 11:30; 13:12; 15:4; cf. Gen. 2:9; 3:22, 24; Rev. 2:7), which is truly worth hugging! (2) The very same treasures that a person can "find" or "gain" according to 3:13 were foundational when God created the cosmos (3:19–20; Proverbs 8 expands on this claim). Divine knowledge is reflected in God's superintendence of nature in both catastrophic (Gen. 7:11) and everyday (Job 36:28) circumstances. If wisdom and understanding were essential even for God in carrying out his creational and providential tasks, how much more should we as humans consider their acquisition indispensable for carrying out our responsibilities in God's world! (3) The final unit modifies the instructional form by abbreviating the charge (3:21) and expanding the explanation (3:22–26). You should hang on to your specialized skills in advising and decision making, for they literally can save lives (as detailed in 3:23–26; cf. 1:33) and enhance your reputation (3:22; cf. 1:9).

Proverbs 3:27–35 describes the impact of acquired wisdom on interpersonal relationships, thus corresponding to 3:5–12. These verses suggest that one can avoid "the ruin that overtakes

the wicked" (3:25; both 26 and 32–34 point to divine causality) by not treating others wickedly. Verses 27–30 are parallel in formulation, each beginning with a negative imperative ("do not") followed by a qualifying phrase. The first two verses address good deeds that should not be neglected, while the next two deal with evil deeds to be avoided. (Don't harm the one who has not harmed you!) The fifth negative imperative, in 3:31, warns against envying a violent person, presumably because no punishment for such actions is apparent, leading one to copy those ways. Verses 32–34 give the rationale for this prohibition by noting God's response. Above all, such people are detestable to the Lord (3:32). This is the first of twenty-one occurrences of the word *toebah* in Proverbs (here, what the Lord "detests"; translated as "abomination" in the KJV), which designates morally or cultically abhorrent practices (e.g., aberrant sexual relationships, idol worship, occult activities, child sacrifice, eating unclean food, sacrificing defective animals, business fraud). The godly, however, are offered friendship with God, literally his "secret counsel" (NKJV; cf. Ps. 25:14; 55:14; Amos 3:7). Various proverbs suggest that one's behavior can influence the well-being of one's entire household (3:33)—they often share one's attitudes and actions and will share also in one's fate. Five different designations for the "bad" person appear in 3:31–35, as well as four designations for the "good." Verse 35 characterizes the preceding actions and attitudes under the general rubrics of wisdom and folly as moral categories and presents their well-deserved consequences: honor or shame.

4:1–27. Proverbs 4, which concludes the positive commendation of wisdom, consists of three instructions, each of which begins with a direct address (4:1, 10, 20). In 4:1–9, which utilizes several terms from the preceding section, the father passes on counsel from his own father that is marked by another metaphorical presentation of wisdom as a woman. Verse 1 uses "my sons" rather than "my son" for the first time in the book (cf. Prov. 5:7; 7:24;

8:32), which, along with the reference to the mother in Proverbs 1:8 and 6:20, suggests that a parent rather than a professional teacher (as some claim) is speaking here. The call to heed is grounded not in consequences but rather in an awareness of one's family heritage. The grandfather's words are quoted in 4:4b–9. Obedience brings life (4:4b = 7:2a)—this is a promise not of eternal life but of an existence enhanced both qualitatively and quantitatively, as developed in the preceding instruction (3:2, 18, 22). "Get" (Hebrew *qanah*, 4:5, 7) is a favored term, used fourteen times in Proverbs. There is an intimate relationship between retaining (godly) parental instruction and acquiring wisdom and understanding, and the latter should be one's top priority. The metaphorical Lady Wisdom is hinted at in 4:5 (since one can "get" or "acquire" a wife; cf. Ruth 4:5), but she emerges clearly in verses 6–9 (similar to 3:13–18): you should not "forsake" (also 4:2) wisdom but rather lovingly embrace her. In return, wisdom will guard (2:11) and grace you like a crown.

A second instruction follows in 4:10–19, which, like 1:10–19, warns against following the "way" or "path" (i.e., mode of behavior; 4:11, 14, 19) of the wicked rather than wisdom's way. The twofold path is a common motif within the wisdom tradition and is found throughout the Old Testament and New Testament (e.g., Prov. 13:16, 28; Ps. 1:6; 119:29–30; Jer 6:16; 21:8; Matt. 7:13–14; 2 Pet. 2:15). In a culture in which this-worldly prosperity was often viewed as a sign of divine blessing and an early death as a divine curse, no greater motivation could be given to a youthful audience than the promise of a long, good life marked by steady progress rather than stumbling (4:10–12; cf. 3:6). Verses 16–17 explain why one should completely avoid the "path" of evildoers (4:14–15): such individuals are obsessed with carrying out wicked and violent actions. It literally makes their day, being as essential to their existence as bread and wine. Verses 18–19 offer an additional reason. The way of the righteous person just keeps getting brighter as one proceeds along it, while the way of the wicked is always utterly dark. (Note the poetic justice in the contrasting uses of "stumble" in 4:12, 16, 19.)

A final section, 4:20–27, is dominated by positive imperatives, again promising life to those who keep to the right path (4:22, 23; cf. 10, 13). The contrast in verse 21 between losing sight of and retaining these words within the heart involves not simply memorizing them but rather consistently keeping them in mind when deciding what actions to take in a given situation. Sustained health is a frequently emphasized component of the promise of life (4:22) resulting from wise living. One should watchfully protect the heart from all harmful influences, such as twisted talk and crooked conversation (4:24; also 6:12). This must become a top priority, because life-determining decisions flow forth from the heart as control center. Verses 24–27 describe how to safeguard one's heart. (Proverbs 4:20–27 begins and ends with the same command, "turn" [literally "turn aside from"].) Wisdom and folly engage the entire person: ear (4:20), eyes and eyelids (4:21, 25), body/flesh (4:22), heart (4:21, 23), mouth and lips (4:24), and feet (4:26–27). The concluding verses take up the path metaphor, warning the youth, as in chapter 2, to get on the right track and then to avoid getting sidetracked (cf. Deut. 17:20; 28:14; Josh. 1:7; 23:6; 2 Kings 22:2; 2 Chron. 34:2).

C. Warnings against folly, especially sexual infidelity (5:1–7:27). Proverbs 5–7 forms the second major section of the prologue. Whereas the lessons in chapters 2–4 primarily involve the commendation of wisdom and its benefits, those in 5–7 offer warnings against folly (i.e., against harmful relationships) and its consequences, especially involvement with "the loose woman." Instruction regarding sexual issues (5:3–6, 8–20; 6:24–35; 7:16–19) is supplemented by ethical instruction on other topics (6:1–19) and framed by introductory and concluding material (5:1–2, 7, 21–23; 6:20–23; 7:1–4).

5:1–23. Proverbs 5 differs from chapters 6–7 in its positive commendation of marital fidelity and its delights. A general warning against the "strange" (KJV) or "adulterous" (NIV) woman (5:3–6; see commentary on 2:1–22), which expands on 2:16–19, follows the usual call to attentiveness (5:1–2). Acquiring discretion (5:2) is critical because the loose woman is so dangerously seductive to those who lack it. Sweet (Song 4:11) and smooth flattering talk (5:3; cf. 2:16; 6:24; 7:5, 21) may constitute an irresistible combination, but in 5:4 the woman is unmasked. In reality she is like gall and a double-edged sword. The NIV's "gall" is literally "wormwood" (5:4; cf. Jer. 23:15; Lam. 3:19), a nonpoisonous (despite NLT's "poison") plant known for its bitter taste and use in eradicating intestinal worms. The phrase "in the end" introduces an important concept in Proverbs (5:4; cf. 5:11; 14:12, 13; 16:25; 19:20; 20:21; 23:18, 32; 24:14, 20; 25:8; 29:21). The wise person sees beyond the attractive (or painful) present to the ultimate consequence (or benefit), as summarized in Ecclesiastes 7:8. This attractive woman is headed downward toward death (5:5) due to her careless-ness (5:6). The same Hebrew verb translated here as "she gives no thought" (5:6), denoting scrutinizing attention, occurs in 4:26 and 5:21. In Proverbs, ignorance of what one is doing (i.e., staggering down a crooked path like a drunkard [cf. Isa. 29:9] or a blind person [Lam. 4:14]) and of its consequences is characteristic

of the foolish individual (see also Prov. 4:19; 7:23; 9:13, 18).

A specific warning against this woman follows in 5:7–14, with the introductory phrase "now then" calling for an appropriate response to what verses 1–6 have just presented (cf. 7:24; 8:32). The farther away from danger one stays, the less likely one is to be drawn in by her wiles (5:8) and suffer for it (5:9–11). Three consequences are noted. (1) You will "lose your honor" (or "splendor," 5:9a)—perhaps referring, in light of verse 9b, either to possessions amassed through payment for years of hard work or, more likely, to service rendered to a cruel taskmaster (or an angry husband; cf. 6:34–35)—as a penalty for being caught in the act (5:9–10). (2) With poetic justice, the young man who yields to the "strange woman" (5:3, Hebrew *zarah*) will end up giving his strength to satiate "strangers" (5:10, Hebrew *zarim*)—the son has more to lose than his virtue! (3) He also will experience physical anguish and debilitation (5:11); venereal disease could be the cause. The remorseful fool rages angrily (5:12–14). He has learned too late the high cost of rejecting discipline and correction (cf. Prov. 1:7, 30) offered by parents or teachers (financial and physical ruin and social ostracism), barely avoiding an even worse fate (e.g., death).

In 5:15–20, the speaker shifts abruptly to a call for sexual fidelity and praise of marital bliss.

Clay plaque from Ur of an affectionate couple (2000–1750 BC)

Sexual pleasure within the context of marriage is addressed in verses 15, 17a, 18–19; sex outside of marriage is discouraged in verses 16, 17b, 20. The parental charge begins with a vivid but tasteful water metaphor (reminiscent of Song 4:12, 15), developed positively in verse 15 and negatively in verse 16 (cf. 7:18; 9:17; Song 5:1). The repeated use of "your" in 5:15–18 emphasizes the exclusivity, not the possessiveness, of the relationship between husband and wife. Verse 15 describes an intentional, private, refreshing "drink," verse 16 a promiscuous, public, and polluted "overflow" or "spill" (NLT). Thus the initial warning not to yield to the woman's allure, lest one be forced to share one's prized possessions (i.e., wealth) with strangers, is followed by a warning against voluntarily sharing one's most valuable "possession" (i.e., his wife) with strangers (5:17, 20) due to a permissive lifestyle. Verses 18–20 describe the exhilaration of marital sexuality. One's lifelong partner (cf. Prov. 2:17; Mal. 2:14), or "loving doe" (5:19; cf. Song 2:7; 3:5), is a source of both delight and intense pleasure. There is a striking progression in the verbal sequence in verses 18–19: "praise her . . . enjoy her . . . and continually be intoxicated by her [also 7:18] until you stagger!" (author's translation). That the son should trade such pure ecstasy for the thrill of an illicit liaison is inconceivable (5:20).

The father's warning against sexual indiscretion is sealed by a theological rationale (5:21–23). God carefully notes and assesses everything that a person does (5:21), and a lack of self-discipline as well as sinful folly (5:23; cf. 5:12–13) can capture, hold fast, and even destroy a person. Abandoning one's wife for the lure of the seductress may cause one's head to spin, but it can be a fatal misstep (the same Hebrew verb, "stagger," occurs in 5:19–20 [NIV "intoxicated"] and 23 [NIV "led astray"]).

6:1–35. The next lesson, in 6:1–19, treats several topics related to financial affairs (6:1–5), work (6:6–11), and negative character traits (6:12–19), followed by another lesson on sexual morality (6:20–35). A common tone unites the chapter, as the father warns his child, either explicitly or implicitly, against loans (6:1–5), laziness (6:6–11), evildoers (6:12–15), a catalog of detestable actions (6:16–19), and the prostitute (6:20–35).

6:1–19. In the first section (6:1–5), the parent/speaker begins exceptionally by immediately sketching a dangerous scenario the youth should escape. The subject of guaranteeing loans is addressed elsewhere in Proverbs (11:15; 17:18; 20:16; 22:26; 27:13) and is illustrated by Judah's actions in Genesis 43:8–9; 44:30–34. Whether one formally seals the deal with a neighbor or a stranger, one has in effect been trapped by one's words. Since such a transaction is not regulated by Mosaic legislation, there is only one thing to say: "Free yourself" (6:3, 5) immediately, no matter what it takes. Compassion for a financially strapped friend is not the issue here; intentionally jeopardizing one's economic well-being is an action to be avoided at any cost.

The next section (6:6–11), regarding laziness, is linked to the preceding unit in three ways. Both involve actions that negatively affect one's financial well-being, warn against sleeping at the wrong time (6:4, 9), and employ the imperative "go" (6:3, 6). This is the first of many appearances of the lazy man (NIV "sluggard") in the book (Prov. 10:26; 13:4; 15:19; 19:24; 20:4; 21:25; 22:13; 24:30; 26:13–16). In a book that emphasizes deliberate, decisive, and diligent behavior, laziness is a serious character flaw. Ancient Near Eastern (and contemporary) wisdom commonly turns to nature to illustrate positive and negative behavioral patterns, and the ant has much to teach the slacker (6:6–8; also 30:25), including initiative, diligence, and timely preparations for future needs. The speaker seeks to rouse the slothful person from any form of excessive repose (i.e., sleep, slumber, or rest; 6:9–10), thereby avoiding a truly rude awakening: being suddenly overpowered by poverty (6:11; cf. 24:33–34).

While lazy individuals are their own worst enemies, others are far more dangerous. Five characteristic actions of those labeled "trouble-makers" and "villains" are noted in verses 12–15, which lack any conceptual connection with the two preceding sections. The word translated "troublemaker" is a Hebrew compound word, familiar from the KJV "sons of Belial," meaning "without profit"—that is, useless. The term occurs twenty-seven times in the Old Testament (cf. 16:27; 19:28); it is used to describe the men of Gibeah who gang-rape the Levite's concubine (Judg. 19:22; 20:13) and the sons of Eli (1 Sam. 2:12). "Villains" are destructive abusers of power; both are perverse societal menaces. Their twisted words, devious (though obscure) gestures, and perverted minds constantly foment dissension (6:14). Just as for the lazy, sudden disaster awaits them (6:15). Their actions hardly seem to warrant such harsh divine punishment compared with the bloodthirsty band of thieves similarly threatened in Proverbs 1:26–27. Wisdom ethics, however, gives greater value to the integrity and well-being of the family and the community than to an individual's personal preferences.

In justifying this threat, a list of seven detestable vices follows in 6:16–19 (cf. Prov. 26:25). The "numerical" form of verse 16 (i.e., "There are six . . . , seven"; cf. Job 5:19) is found in various types of Old Testament literature, most notably in Proverbs 30:18–31, as well as in Ugaritic and Akkadian texts. This form places climactic emphasis on the final element, which is here quite similar to 6:14b. Far from advocating a mechanical link between deed and consequence, Proverbs affirms that Yahweh ultimately upholds justice in his world. The word "detestable" (KJV "abomination"; Hebrew *toebah*; see commentary on 3:1–35) occurs frequently in Proverbs, compared to, for example, Deuteronomy. Each of the first five actions in this vice list involves a body part, in a sequence moving downward from head to foot, indicating the totality of one's involvement in mischief (6:17–18). The final two vices (6:19) diverge stylistically, perhaps involving actions that depend on the preceding five. Since the order here is climactic, attacking the integrity of the family or clan unit

(through instigating disputes, 6:19b) is viewed as more heinous than perverting the legal system (through false witness, 6:19a; cf. 12:17; 14:5, 25; 19:5, 9; 21:28; 25:18).

6:20–35. This next lesson resumes the typical instructional form, with an extended call to heed the parental counsel (6:20–23) preceding the specific warnings (6:24–35). It also takes up the topic of Proverbs 5, developing the grave consequences of sexual immorality more fully. Presumably one ties the commands of both parents "around your neck" (6:21) in order to keep them plainly in view when deciding which direction to head. Verse 22 cites three daily situations in which such instruction proves useful, offering guidance, protection, and a conversation partner—metaphorically speaking, both a proper path to follow and a light to illumine it (6:23a; cf. Ps. 119:105).

In particular, this counsel is intended to keep the youth from the immoral woman (6:24; NIV "your neighbor's wife"), who can ruin his life. This smooth-tongued temptress, already familiar from chapters 2 and 5, is called literally "a woman of evil." This expression occurs only here in the Old Testament; the Septuagint may have read a similarly written word, translating "married woman." The admonition in verse 25 consists of a twofold warning. The negative command, "Do not lust in your heart after her beauty" (6:25a), recalls the tenth commandment (Exod. 20:17; Deut. 5:21), which employs the same Hebrew verb, while the NLT's "Don't let her coy glances seduce you" (6:25b) vividly captures the process. The remainder of the instruction (6:26–35) details the dangers that one will thereby avoid. While every prostitute has her price, the adulteress will, metaphorically speaking, stalk you like prey (6:26; cf. Job 10:16; Mic. 7:2). This is the first reference to prostitution in Proverbs (cf. 7:10; 23:27; 29:3); however, the emphasis here is clearly on adultery (cf. 6:29, 32, 34).

Two additional vivid comparisons are made. (1) Whoever commits adultery is playing with fire and bound to get burned (6:27–29). "No one . . . will go unpunished," in verse 29, recalls the covenantal formulation in Exodus 20:7; 34:7; Numbers 14:18; Deuteronomy 5:11; and Nahum 1:3 (see also Prov. 11:21; 17:5; 19:5, 9; 28:20). (2) Whoever "steals" what belongs to another, whatever the motivation (e.g., being sex starved; 6:30), will be punished when caught (6:29–35; the Mosaic law mandates only twofold restitution, compared to the sevenfold requirement here; cf. Exod. 22:3–4, 7). Here the consequences for violating the eighth and seventh commandments are contrasted (Exod. 20:14–15). Anyone committing adultery lacks judgment (6:32, literally "lacks heart"; NIV "has no sense"), since it is a self-destructive act (similarly 7:22–23), as verses 33–35 detail. Lasting shame will be the least of his problems! The rage of a cheated husband knows no bounds; no restitution payment or bribe will assuage his jealous desire for revenge (Prov. 27:4; Song 8:6). And it all began with a few flattering words and some eye makeup (6:24–25).

7:1–27. The extensive warning against the "wayward" or "adulterous" woman concludes with a final lesson in chapter 7, which focuses on the temptation. Its structure is quite similar to that of the preceding lesson, consisting of a call to heed (7:1–4), a nearly identical purpose statement functioning as a warning (to "keep you from . . . ," 7:5; cf. 6:24) and an extended illustration (7:6–23), and an explicit warning (7:24–27; cf. 6:25). Once again, the goal of the instruction is to preserve and enhance life (7:2; cf. 4:4). Accordingly, these wisdom-imparting commands are to be treasured (cf. Prov. 2:1), carefully preserved both externally and internally (cf. Prov. 3:3; 6:21), as diligently protected as the pupils of one's eyes (= "the apple of your eye," 7:2), and welcomed as "family" (7:4). A wordplay binds the

introduction together: *keep* my words (7:1), and they will *keep* you safe (7:5).

The temptation is portrayed as a scenario observed by the speaker through the window of his home (7:6). The victim is portrayed as easy prey—and not completely innocent: young, naive (cf. Prov. 1:4), lacking judgment (cf. 6:32), and heading for her house just as night falls (7:7–9). The adulteress is shockingly goal-oriented, heading straight toward him, clothed like a prostitute to cunningly camouflage her actual marital status, a familiar sight around town, defiant, brazen, and aggressive (7:10–13). As Waltke sums it up, "she 'rapes' dull men by clever deceit" (Waltke 2004, 374), literally ambushing them (7:12; cf. 1:11, 18). Her seductive speech seals the deal (7:21; hence the repeated warnings: 2:16; 5:3; 7:5). Her reference to recently fulfilled vows suggests both fidelity in worship and fresh meat to dine on (7:14). The youth alone is the object of her attention and affection, or rather, of her lust (7:15, 18; contrast 5:19); her bed has been specially prepared and perfumed for him (7:16). Multicolored imported linens and exotic fragrances indicate her wealth and provide an enticing love nest. Best of all, they can enjoy a secret, all-night tryst without any fear of getting caught (7:19–20).

Her mission is successful: "All at once he followed her" (7:22a). Instead of describing the anticipated sensual ecstasy, the description concludes with three animal similes (7:22b–23). Having yielded to his animal instincts, the

Proverbs 7:23 likens succumbing to temptation to "a bird darting into a snare," as depicted in this painting of men using a net to catch quail (tomb of Nebamun, Egypt, ca. 1350 BC).

youth is reduced to a doomed beast. He is as oblivious as an ox headed for slaughter, a stag stepping into a noose (following the Septuagint; NASB follows the Masoretic Text: "as *one in* fetters to the discipline of a fool"), or a bird darting into a snare. Certain death awaits all four (cf. 6:26, 32). Perhaps *now* the sons will pay closer attention (7:24) when warned against straying onto her path (7:25). Suddenly the simple scenario observed through a window is replaced by a broad mural portraying a multitude of similarly stupid victims who once crowded the highway that headed straight down to hell—or at least a dead end in the local cemetery (depending on one's interpretation of *Sheol*, 7:26–27).

D. Wisdom's final appeals (8:1–9:18). In Proverbs 8–9, personified Wisdom makes her final appeal, speaking again in the first person to her young audience.

8:1–36. Chapter 8 offers a lengthy discourse commending wisdom, which can be divided into four sections. In verses 1–11, wisdom's surpassing value is asserted, while verses 12–21 portray wisdom's "associates" and attributes. Wisdom's worth is then further affirmed in a description of its ancient origin—at the time of creation (8:22–31), before wisdom assumes the role of the parent/sage in directly urging the "sons" to heed her counsel (8:32–36).

8:1–11. Lady Wisdom's appearance here is reminiscent of Proverbs 1:20–33, with 8:1–3 paralleling 1:20–21 and 8:5 similar to 1:22, although her message in chapter 8 is more positive. She stations herself in places of prominence, commerce, and heavy traffic, where as many will hear her voice as possible (8:1–3). She does not confine herself to the temple or palace—or to the covenant people of Israel—for her appeal is to all humanity, in particular to those most in need of understanding (8:4–5). In verses 6–9 she stresses the moral excellence rather than the eloquence of her speech: it is trustworthy, right (cf. Prov. 1:3; 2:9), reliable, righteous, honest (cf. Prov. 24:26), and faultless, devoid of any deception or perversion. Thus

her instruction is more valuable than the most precious metals (8:10; 3:14); indeed, wisdom is incomparably desirable (8:11 = 3:15, briefly abandoning the personification for a third-person reference to wisdom).

8:12–21. The mention of wisdom in verses 1 and 11 leads to verse 12, in which wisdom refers to herself for the first time: "I, wisdom . . ." In the Hebrew text, the repeated use of the independent pronoun "I" in 8:12, 14b, 17 punctuates the section (8:12–21), as wisdom gives an extensive self-introduction. Whereas 1:2–6 simply introduces various terms associated with wisdom, in 8:12 these are presented as wisdom's housemates. Verse 13a seems to interrupt the flow. The expression "fear of the LORD," however, occurs strategically in Proverbs 1–9 (1:7, 29; 2:5; 8:13; 9:10). Here it grounds wisdom's attitude toward arrogance, evil, and corruption. Together with the description of her speech in the preceding section, it clearly demonstrates that wisdom is primarily a moral, not an intellectual, enterprise. Verse 14 emphasizes precisely those attributes essential for all government officials (8:15–16): counsel and ingenuity, discernment and power (the Hebrew term for "power" occurs only here in Proverbs; it most commonly refers to the power possessed by God). "I have insight" in 8:14b is literally "I *am* insight"; that is, insight is "part of her very essence" (Waltke 2004, 402) but is also available to all who welcome her.

In verse 17, "I" introduces a subunit bracketed by "those who love me" (8:17–21). Wisdom's "love" here involves bestowing her rich gifts on all who desire her, not just on rulers. Those "who seek me find me" (8:17b) evokes passages such as Deuteronomy 4:29; Jeremiah 29:13; and Matthew 7:7 (also Matt. 6:33, which describes how "all these things will be given to you as well"). Verse 19 grounds the claim in verse 10, and wisdom's "fruit" is not simply material wealth (8:18). "Righteous(ness)"/"just" occurs five times in chapter 8 (vv. 8, 15, 16 [see NIV note], 18 [NIV "prosperity"], 20). Since wisdom walks about on just paths (cf. Prov.

12:28; Ps. 23:3), practicing what she preaches, she gives goods only to her lovers (8:20–21).

8:22–31. A new section commences by associating wisdom not with earthly rulers (as in 8:15–16) but with Yahweh, the Creator of the universe (8:22). This section then proceeds to describe wisdom's ancient origin and earliest activities. Although God is the subject of all verbs in verses 22–29, wisdom's close association with him is emphasized repeatedly. A number of interpretive difficulties are found in this section. God's first action is to create/bring forth or to acquire/possess wisdom. In the Old Testament, the Hebrew verb *qanah* can be used to express both of these activities. Elsewhere in Proverbs (cf. 1:5; 4:5, 7; see commentary on 4:1–27) and in the majority of its Old Testament occurrences, "acquire" is the most likely nuance of *qanah*. In 8:22 it could simply affirm that God *already possessed* (having previously acquired) wisdom when he began his work of creation, and some Greek translations interpret it similarly. In Genesis 4:1, probably Genesis 14:19, 22, and Psalm 139:13, the verb describes instead the act of bringing something into being. The Greek Septuagint and Aramaic Targum translate the verb as "create" in Proverbs 8:22. More importantly, other verbs in this section also speak of wisdom's origin or birth (e.g., "formed" in 8:23, "given birth" in 8:24–25), without implying the involvement of any divine sexual partner. The interpretation of the verb *qanah* has played a significant role in christological discussions, since many early Christian interpreters, including Tertullian, Origen, and Athanasius, identified "wisdom" in Proverbs 8 with Jesus, on the basis of texts like Colossians 1:15 and 2:3. Ironically, some contemporary interpreters find instead in Proverbs 8 support for an ancient Israelite goddess! It is best simply to understand wisdom here as a personified divine trait.

Verses 22–29 have many images and terms in common with other poetic creation texts, such as are found in Job, Psalms, and Isaiah, except this language is subordinated to the section's emphasis on the "priority" of wisdom, both temporally ("before" and "when" occur repeatedly in these verses) and in importance. These descriptions express God's wise planning and sovereign control (using seven different Hebrew verbs) rather than either a primitive, prescientific cosmology or revelatory knowledge of the universe's makeup. In 8:30–31, the focus shifts to wisdom's role ("Then I was . . . I was"). The rendering "the craftsman" or artisan in NIV 1984 (8:30a) is one of several suggested translations for Hebrew *amon*, supported by its use in Jeremiah 52:15 and a similar word in Song of Solomon 7:1. It could refer either to wisdom or, more likely, to Yahweh, who constructs the cosmos in this section. The NIV reads "constantly" (literally "faithful"), which is supported by "always" (literally "at every time") in 8:30b. A preferable option is "little child" (literally "one looked after"; see NIV note), as in Lamentations 4:5 and Esther 2:20 ("bring up"), which Fox takes verbally as "growing up" (Fox, 287). This is supported by the references earlier to wisdom's birth and by the actions described in 8:30b–31 (cf. Isa. 66:12, which translates "delight" as "dandled"; the other verb here can be translated "laugh/play"). Wisdom was continually beside God, delighting (see Psalm 119, regarding God's law) and reveling in what he was creating day by day. More specifically, she was celebrating the creation of planet Earth and of humanity. If wisdom has been delighting in us since the creation, should we not delight in wisdom as well?

8:32–36. "Now then, my children," in 8:32, signals the transition to application. Exceptionally, wisdom replaces the parent here. By heeding wisdom's instructions ("listen" occurs three times) *day by day*, one can become wise (8:33–34). Two contrasting claims conclude this discourse (8:35–36). To find wisdom is to find life and to obtain divine favor (cf. Prov. 12:2; 18:22), whereas to miss wisdom is to be self-destructive, since wisdom-haters are death-lovers (cf. 8:17, 21).

9:1–18. The prologue comes to a climax in chapter 9 with invitations to two rival banquets,

553

raising the question of which voice the sons will heed and whose meal they will share—wisdom's or folly's? The two descriptions are similar in structure and formulation (9:1–6, 13–18) and are separated by a theological interlude (9:7–12). Therefore, it is helpful to compare the two rather than consider them separately. The "Woman of Wisdoms" (9:1, an intensive plural, also 1:20) is competing with Lady Foolishness (9:13, only here in the Old Testament). The former, Wisdom, is characterized as diligent and prosperous by her extensive preparations of house (its seven columns imply perfection) and banquet and her employment of servants (9:1–3a). The latter, Folly, makes no preparations and is labeled explicitly as loud, gullible, and ignorant (9:13). Both own a house (9:1, 14) and station themselves "at the highest point of the city" (9:3b, 14b). Both call out (9:3a, 15a), issuing an identical general invitation (9:4 = 9:16), although the latter's audience is specifically described as following a straight course until she detours them (9:15). Both offer a free meal. Wisdom shares her food and self-mixed wine (9:5), while Folly provides only stolen water and pilfered food (9:17), their source adding flavor to the menu. Both scenes conclude by noting the consequences of accepting the respective invitation (9:6, 18). Wisdom calls

for the simple to abandon their naive ways (or naive companions) and henceforth proceed with discernment. Folly on the contrary conceals the fate of her dinner guests: her gravy will be followed by the grave (similar to Prov. 7:26–27)! By concluding the introductory section of Proverbs on this tragic note, the author/sage not only extends a final warning but also implies that not all his youthful readers will heed it.

This outcome is already anticipated by the intervening section, verses 7–12. This section, which contrasts two potential audiences for wisdom's correction, ironically begins and ends by referring to the mocker. Some will reject the painful message and hate and abuse the messenger (9:7–8a); others will continually receive and benefit from the message (cf. Prov. 1:5) and understandably love the messenger (9:8b–9). The pairing of the mocker, one of the worst types of fools, with the wicked in verse 7 and the wise with the righteous in verse 9, underlines the near interchangeability of these two categories in Old Testament wisdom teaching.

> Wisdom lives in a house of seven pillars (Prov. 9:1), similar to the two sets of seven pillars that mark the colonnade of the court of Amenhotep II (18th dynasty) at the Temple of Luxor, Egypt.

The foundational place of reverence for Yahweh is affirmed once more (9:10; cf. 1:7), while personal knowledge of the utterly Holy One (an intensive plural; cf. Isa. 6:3) will not be mentioned again until Proverbs 30:3. The section begins by addressing the sage as one who instructs others (9:8–9). It concludes, however, by highlighting one of wisdom's prime benefits—an extended life span (9:11)—and by emphasizing that both wisdom and folly, despite their social consequences, make the greatest impact on the individual (9:12). Thus the way is prepared for wise individuals to profit from the various proverbial collections that begin in chapter 10.

3. Proverbial Collections: Advanced Instruction in Wisdom (10:1–29:27)

If one views Proverbs 1–9 as a basic introduction to proverbial wisdom, then chapters 10–29 serve as the advanced course. Or, to express it differently, the prologue presents and commends wisdom, while the collections that follow illustrate the scope and variety of situations in which wisdom is advantageous (without absolutely guaranteeing success) if employed properly and in a timely manner. Proverbs 1–9 also gives the reader a theological lens through which to read the individual proverbs. Although many of them seem to be secular and even mundane, viewing individual proverbs through the lens of (1) the fear of the Lord as foundational, (2) wisdom as both divine gift and human acquisition, and (3) the wise as righteous and fool as wicked will transform one's evaluation and application of them. Furthermore, regardless of the original social setting that gave rise to such sayings, in terms of interpretation their life setting is now less important than their book setting. The assertions and admonitions of individual verses are now qualified, expanded, explained, generalized, or illustrated by the verses that surround them.

All interpreters of Proverbs acknowledge that chapters 10–31 constitute an anthology containing various proverbial collections diverse in style, content, and origin. What is disputed is the extent (or even the existence) of compositional design within and between the various collections. Stated simply, is the order (and literary context) of the individual proverbs significant and therefore to be taken into consideration when interpreting each verse? Or should one view each proverb as an independent literary unit and interpret it as such? The second approach has dominated commentaries in the past and is adopted in the recent commentary by Tremper Longman III (see Longman 2006). For more than two decades, however, the first approach has been explored in numerous learned monographs and briefer studies and employed by most contemporary commentators, most fully by Bruce Waltke (see Waltke 2004–5). Those skeptical toward this newer approach dismiss alleged compositional patterns as *imposed* rather than *identified* by the interpreter, asserting that "whoever seeks, will find," or, at the very least, "if there's any doubt, don't [claim any editorial intentionality]."

Several lines of evidence converge in support of this newer viewpoint, without demonstrating that every proverb and every collection exhibit editorial design. (1) Since the ancient sages devoted themselves to analyzing and ordering their world, it is likely that they also gave order to their literary compositions. (2) Some of the ancient Near Eastern instructional texts, especially from Egypt, contain thematic groupings of proverbs. (3) Ted Hildebrandt has demonstrated that there are dozens of paired proverbs within the book, which should be taken together (as "proverbial pairs") (Hildebrandt 1988). (4) The repetition of words, phrases, clauses, half-verses, and entire verses within individual or adjoining chapters is too frequent to be coincidental. (5) Such repeated clauses or verses sometimes appear to mark the beginning and end of sections or subsections. (6) Consecutive proverbs frequently offer comments on the same general or specific topic. Since reading is essentially a sequential process, it is natural to read each succeeding proverb in light of those that immediately precede it. (7) The center of the book is marked by the highest concentration of references to Yahweh and the king, the same verbs being used with reference to both subjects. On the basis of these seven features, we will seek to point out, where possible, striking indications and implications of compositional design in the following chapters.

A. The original Solomonic collection (10:1–22:16). **10:1–15:33.** Proverbs 10–15 is characterized by the predominance of contrasting (i.e., antithetical) parallelism within the individual proverbs and an emphasis on the righteous/wicked (e.g., 10:3, 6–7, 11, 16, 20, 24–25, 28–30, 32) rather than on the wise/fool (10:1, 8, 13–14, 23).

10:1–32. Chapter 10 offers a clear illustration of how the newer approach highlights possible connections between verses. A new title in verse 1a indicates that a new section/collection begins here. If one analyzes these verses in terms of positive and negative behavior or outcomes, a pattern emerges (see Table 1).

In the first subunit (10:1–5), verse 1b offers a general description of the effects that wise and foolish children have on their parents, while verse 5 concludes the subunit by noting the specific behaviors that elicit this response. Verse 2 compares the relative worth of "ill-gotten treasures" and righteousness, while verse 3 offers an explanation. The Lord provides for the righteous while preventing the wicked from satisfying their cravings. Verse 4 implicitly qualifies such provision; it may come through diligent labor rather than by just relaxing and waiting for it. Those who indulge in the latter behavior bring poverty upon themselves (10:4a) as well as disgrace upon their parents (10:5).

The second subunit (10:6–11) emphasizes the impact of both edifying and harmful speech, culminating in verse 11: a righteous person's words can be life-giving. The second line of each verse describes the fate of the wicked/fool. Notably, both verses 8b and 10b, and 6b and 11b, are identical, which is unlikely a coincidence; such repetition is emphatic. Verse 7a explains

Table 1: Examples of Contrasting Parallelism in Proverbs 10

First subunit		
10:1	+	–
10:2	–	+
10:3	+	–
10:4	–	+
10:5	+	–

Second subunit		
10:6	+	–
10:7	+	–
10:8	+	–
10:9	+	–
10:10	–	–
10:11	+	–

the "blessings" of the righteous, while verse 7b offers a contrast.

The third subunit (10:12–21) begins by contrasting hatred (also in 10:18) with love, the latter half of the verse being quoted in James 5:20 and 1 Peter 4:8. One who hates foments discord, while one who loves overlooks offenses. The wise "store up" (cf. Prov. 2:1; 7:1) knowledge (10:14a) rather than relying on amassing wealth like the rich do (10:15a) and are assured that their "wages" as righteous individuals are "life" itself (10:16a). That is because a lack of judgment can result in a physical beating (10:13b) and even death (10:21b). They also realize that not only poverty (10:15b) but also one's careless words (10:14b) can be ruinous. The effects of speech are again prominent in this subunit (10:13–14, 18–21); the restraint of the wise in this area adds value to their words (10:19). The righteous/wise not only experience life but also can lead others to life (10:16a, 17a, also 21a; cf. 10:11a).

The fourth subunit (10:22–26), which Waltke labels "Pain and Pleasure" (Waltke 2004, 473), begins by referring to the Lord's blessing as bestowing wealth without pain (10:22; the same Hebrew root is translated "grief" in 10:10;

cf. 10:14–16). Employing a lazy person, however, can be a painful experience (10:26). This subunit is framed by synthetic proverbs rather than antithetical, as in verses 23–25. The foolish/wicked and the wise/righteous find pleasure in different things (10:23) and with contrasting results (10:24–25).

The final subunit (10:27–32) consists exclusively of positive-negative verses. Following the introductory thematic reference to the "fear of the LORD" in verse 27a, reinforced by the "way of the LORD" in verse 29a, the first half of each verse mentions the "righteous" (or "blameless," in 10:29a). Verses 28–30 affirm their stability, while verses 31–32 focus on their speech. The fear of the Lord not only extends the life of the righteous but also governs their tongues, ruling out any perversity. Although not every succeeding chapter can be analyzed here in such detail, similar patterns, links, and associations are often evident.

11:1–31. As Proverbs 11 begins, verses 1–2 introduce the specific theme of (commercial) integrity and the general theme of wisdom respectively before describing some benefits of honesty and righteousness in 11:3–6. The repetition of "by" in verses 3b and 6b indicates how the wicked bring about their own doom (11:7). Three paired verses are linked next. The righteous are "delivered" (11:8–9; NIV "rescued"), which produces joy in the "city" because of their civic contributions (11:10–11), in contrast with the destructive speech of the wicked (11:9a, 11b), who do not preserve neighborhood confidences (11:12–13). The community focus introduced in verse 10 continues in verse 14, which affirms the guidance provided by wise advisors. It concludes in verse 15, which echoes the sentiment of Proverbs 6:1–5.

The next section introduces a positive pair: a gracious woman and a kind man (11:16–17), who themselves benefit from their attitude. She gains honor, while the ruthless *only* get rich, harming themselves in the process of earning deceptive wages; this ultimately will end not in comfort but in death, since their perversity makes God their foe (11:16b, 17b, 18a, 19b, 20a—which parallels 11:1). To sum up, the wicked will not escape punishment, unlike the righteous (11:21). Verse 22 offers a qualification to verse 16a, since "gracious" (NIV "kindhearted") can have a broad range of nuances. She may be charming, but if she loses her good judgment, she will quickly turn ugly.

The following unit is framed by verses 23 and 27, which both refer to the unspecified "good" (Hebrew *tob*) that the righteous desire, allowing a broad application. Since they seek "only" good for themselves and others, they will get what they are looking for; ironically, so will the wicked (11:27b)! Verses 24–26 describe the paradoxical nature of two contrasting attitudes toward one's possessions—one type of "good." The generous keep on giving to others while continuing to prosper (contingent, of course, on God's blessing, 11:26b), while stingy hoarders may experience "only" impoverishment.

Those who trust in wealth rather than in God (11:28, perhaps therefore hoarding it; contrast 3:5) put themselves at risk. Fools can easily ruin not only themselves but also their whole households. The fool will thus be reduced to debt slavery and leave nothing for the family to inherit except wind (11:29, the source of the 1960 movie title; cf. Eccles. 1:14). The righteous, however, will flourish and nourish like a healthy tree (11:28b, 30a). The soul-winner's favorite verse, 11:30b (e.g., NIV 1984 "he who wins souls is wise"), could stem from a faulty translation. The expression "to take souls" normally means to kill, as the Greek Septuagint apparently translates (cf. Prov. 1:19). Given the associations in this verse with the righteous, the wise, and a tree of life (cf. Gen. 2:9), however, a negative meaning is unlikely. One should then read verse 30b in light of verse 30a, as recommending either that wise people pick for themselves the fruit of this tree, thereby enjoying "lives" (an intensive plural; cf. NIV "the one who is wise saves lives"), or that they take others to this tree, without its fruit being limited to *eternal* life. Verse 31 offers an emphatic summary of the opposite "rewards" of the righteous and the wicked, anticipating requital during their earthly sojourn.

12:1–28. Proverbs 12 begins with three general proverbs (12:1–3). Verse 1 indicates the necessary attitude toward instruction and correction (i.e., love; cf. Prov. 4:6), which, according to verse 2, is displayed by a good person who gains God's approval (cf. 11:1, 20, 27) and thus is established as righteous, unlike those who futilely pursue success through evil (12:3).

Verse 4 introduces a domestic context with the virtuous wife (cf. Prov. 31:10), who contributes to her house standing firm (12:7, similar to 12:3). These verses reveal a progression from character (12:4) to plans (12:5) to words (12:6) to consequences (12:7), with the negative clauses developing from disgraceful behavior to deceitful advice to destructive words to downfall and doom.

Proverbs 12:8–12 focuses on work. One's reputation should be derived from one's prudence (12:8), not from one's pretense (12:9). On the farm, righteousness expresses itself even in one's treatment of animals (12:10) and wisdom in diligently tilling the field to produce plentiful crops (12:11). Metaphorically speaking, employing a wordplay connected to agriculture, the righteous person's "root" yields fruit (12:12). An additional word repetition is suggestive:

those who lack sound judgment (12:11b) will likely lack bread (12:9b). The wicked, however, are not content to "chase fantasies" (12:11b), preferring a "snare" to capture prey (12:12a; cf. KJV "net"; the NIV's "stronghold" substitutes the object for the instrument—the meaning here is disputed).

Speech is the focus of the lengthy unit 12:13–23. Ironically connected to the preceding verse (12:12a), evil persons can themselves be "snared" (NIV "trapped") by their own defiant utterances (12:13a), although one's lips can bear good "fruit" as well (12:14a). The wise heed spoken advice, while fools think they need none (12:15). The shrewd also ignore an insult, while fools immediately respond by displaying their vexation (12:16; cf. 9:7). In a legal setting, honest rather than deceitful testimony is sought (12:17); both inside and outside the court, words can hurt or heal (12:18). Truth will ultimately prevail, much to the joy of those promoting peace, but lies will be exposed, as will the deceitful hearts that spawned them (12:19–20). Trouble will therefore overwhelm the wicked,

According to Proverbs 12:11, "Those who work their land"—like the figure in this wooden model, who is plowing with two oxen (Egypt, second millennium BC)—"will have abundant food."

while the righteous will be spared (12:21; cf. 22:8), because the Lord detests lying lips while approving of those who are trustworthy (12:22; cf. 12:2). Thus speech is a key area in which the wise and the foolish greatly differ. The wise do not tell all they know; the foolish loudly proclaim their folly (12:23, also 12:15–16).

Work's reward is mentioned in passing in verse 14b; in verses 24–27, the contrast between the diligent and the lazy frames a brief unit. The diligent will rise to exercise authority over others or at least enjoy hearty meals, while the lazy will descend to conscripted labor or at least go hungry (12:24, 27). Verse 25 recalls another important power from the preceding section—the healing power of the tongue (cf. 12:18b). If one modifies the vowels of its first word, 12:26 affirms that "the righteous has an advantage over his neighbor" (Heim, 157), as illustrated in verse 27, since the righteous are, in Proverbs' conceptual world, both wise and diligent. Verse 28 concludes the chapter, contrasting the "way of the wicked" (12:26) with the "way of righteousness" (12:28), which leads not simply to a long and full life but even to an unending life (literally "no death"; NIV "immortality"; see also Waltke 2004, 518).

13:1–25. Following an introductory proverb affirming the receptivity of the wise (13:1), Proverbs 13:2–6 briefly takes up themes of the previous chapter, linked by the repetition of "appetite, soul" (Hebrew *nepesh*, which occurs four times in 13:2–4). One's words can fill one's life with either luscious or foul fruit, and thus restraint in speech is essential (13:2–3), just as diligent labor enables one to fulfill one's desires (13:4). The righteous eschew false words (NLT "lies"), thereby protecting their lives (13:5a, 6a). The wicked, in contrast, enjoy broadcasting odious scandal (cf. same verb in Gen. 34:30; Exod. 5:21) and suffer the consequences (13:5b, 6b).

Wealth and poverty are examined in 13:7–11. Wealth can be feigned (13:7) or life-saving (13:8a) and can rapidly disappear if acquired dishonestly rather than through sustained effort (13:11). Those living in poverty, in contrast,

cannot respond to a painful rebuke (13:8b; cf. 13:1b), much less a death threat. Verse 9 affirms that the righteous shine more brightly than the wicked, whom God will extinguish (cf. Prov. 20:20; 24:20), and in this context more brightly than the wealthy, who may soon fade. Verse 10b echoes the sentiment of 13:1a: wisely accepting advice is the opposite of arrogant quarreling (13:10a).

A lengthy unit on fulfillment versus frustration follows in 13:12–19, as indicated by the expression "a longing fulfilled," which brackets the section in verses 12b and 19a. This allows one to interpret verses 13–18 as indicating how wise and foolish actions lead to contrasting outcomes: a sick heart or a life-giving tree (13:12). Wise actions include obeying God's commands, heeding wise instruction and correction (13:13–14, 18), acting prudently (13:15–16), and serving reliably (13:17). Such behavior will result, respectively, in reward, a fountain of life, favor, healing, and honor—a truly "sweet" outcome (13:19a)!

A parent's legacy is the focus of 13:20–25. According to verses 22 and 24, the legacy can be both material and moral in nature. The righteous are rewarded with "good things" (13:21b), such as fertile fields producing abundant food (13:23a, 25a). A "good person" can pass these things on to heirs (13:22a), though wealth can be lost both through one's own misdeeds (13:22b) and through injustice (13:23b). In a society in which child abuse is far too prevalent, the call to apply the rod conscientiously as an expression of parental love (13:24) strikes one as antiquated. Here one should note (1) that the rod is mentioned seven times in Proverbs, and its "pedagogical effectiveness" in instilling wisdom is praised (29:15); (2) that God is our model for loving correction (3:11–12); and (3) that the parent's primary educational tool is not the rod but wise instruction, as exemplified in 13:20, which can be translated imperatively (following alternative Hebrew readings): "Walk with the wise and become wise" (so the NIV).

14:1–35. Commentators disagree regarding how to subdivide Proverbs 14. Striking here is the opening clause (14:1a, "The wise woman builds her house"), which echoes 9:1. It is followed by the first of three occurrences of "the fear of the LORD" in the chapter (14:2, 26–27). One's conduct reflects one's attitude toward God (14:2). Wise behavior is constructive; folly is destructive (14:1, 3; the NIV 1984 emends KJV's "rod of pride" to "rod to his back"). Verse 4 offers a homey illustration of how one wisely builds a house: without oxen there is less cleanup work to do in the barn, but less harvested grain as well.

The focus of 14:5–7 is speech, both in a legal setting (14:5; cf. 12:17) and in general. Mocking fools cannot obtain wisdom; therefore, their words will be devoid of true knowledge (14:6–7).

Proverbs 14:8–15 addresses self-perception and self-deception, framed by the phrase "the prudent give thought to their ways/steps" (14:8, 15). The prudent perceive where they are heading, while fools do not have a clue! Mockers do not even take sin (and the resultant need to make amends) seriously, while the upright do and receive (divine) approval (14:9). One can be equally clueless about another person's private pains and pleasures and their commingling (14:10, 13, both with "heart"). Verse 11 is linked to its context by the word "upright" (cf. 14:9, 12) and its use of the house motif (cf. 14:1). It also reflects the seamless alternation (and virtual equation) of wisdom/folly and righteousness/wickedness in Proverbs. Verse 12 continues the main theme: one may be deceived about the deadly destination of a "way" that appears to be straight (or "upright"; cf. Prov. 12:15; 16:2). A backslider is punished for choosing wrong "ways," while the "good" are rewarded (14:14). Hence, only the gullible will believe whatever they are told (literally "every word"); the prudent are more reflective (14:15).

This concluding verse also introduces the next development in thought (14:16–18). In carefully considering their "steps," the wise display their reverence for God by making a wide detour around evil (14:16a; cf. 3:7; 4:27). Fools, however, exhibit reckless, uncontrolled behavior, which is conduct the uncorrected, naive person naturally inherits (14:15a, 16b–18a). The prudent, in contrast, easily acquire knowledge to augment their skill set for dealing with life's challenges (14:18b; cf. 14:6b, 15b).

Proverbs 14:19–24 initially describes two unexpected attitudes (see "evil . . . good" in 14:19, 22). The wicked bow down before the righteous, though probably against their will (14:19), and the poor are hated even by their peers, while many love the rich, though probably for questionable reasons (14:20). Such an attitude toward the needy merits condemnation as sin, since they of all people deserve kind treatment (14:21). Those who, in fact, "plan what is good" will both practice and experience steadfast love (NIV "love and faithfulness"; Hebrew *hesed* and *emet*; cf. Prov. 3:3; 16:6). But merely planning good (i.e., "mere talk") accomplishes little—no pain, no gain (14:23). Accumulated wealth is a "crowning" achievement for the wise (cf. 14:18, 35), while all that fools multiply is folly (14:24).

Life-and-death matters are addressed in 14:25–27. Verse 25 affirms the life-saving power of a truthful witness in a capital case (cf. 14:5 in the context of speech), while a proverbial pair describes three metaphorical benefits of reverence for God (14:26–27). It provides a secure fortress to protect one's children and a life-giving fountain (cf. Prov. 13:14), while keeping one from deadly snares, since those who fear God will avoid both evil and divine punishment and will experience God's favor and blessing. Verses 30 and 32 also concern life and death. Verses 28–35 are framed by national concerns: the value of a large population (14:28), the even greater value of a righteous population (14:34), and the king's understandably strong response to a servant's shameful actions (14:35). The intervening proverbs could then be taken as describing some of those shameful actions (as well as their opposites). Short-temperedness, envy, and oppression of the poor, as expressing contempt for one's Maker and refuge (14:29–32), are juxtaposed with patience, tranquility, and kindness to the needy (cf. 14:21), and wisdom so striking that even fools—and the king—take note (14:33; cf. 14:35a).

15:1–33. The covenantal name Yahweh occurs nine times in Proverbs 15 (and also in chap. 3), giving this instruction a more explicitly theological tone. Verses 1–4 focus on speech, with verse 1 taking up the motif of (the king's) anger from 14:35. It notes that a gentle answer can roll back the waves of anger (the Hebrew word for "answer" occurs four times: 15:1, 23; 16:1, 4), while a painful word further stirs it up. Waltke comments regarding verse 2a: "Instead of brutalizing people with their knowledge of the cause-effect relationship in God's ordained moral order, the wise state it kindly, sensitively, and gently with an aim to save their audience, not to condemn and destroy it" (Waltke 2004, 614). Verse 3 reminds us that this cause-effect nexus is not mechanistic but rather is upheld by an ever-observant God. Verse 4 corresponds to verse 1, contrasting the soothing and spirit-crushing power of the tongue, using the favored analogy of the life giving tree (cf. Prov. 3:18; 11:30; 13:12). Mention of individuals who reject correction (i.e., fools and mockers) brackets the next section (15:5–12), giving it a focus on the benefits of instruction. Great treasures as well as great knowledge are available to those who will heed it (15:6–7). More important, one living a righteous life experiences God's favor and love (15:8–9) rather than animosity leading to divine discipline or death, as God punishes wayward actions and attitudes (15:10–11).

The reference to the human heart in 15:7b and 11b is taken up in verses 13–15, which juxtapose the value of a joyful/cheerful heart with that of a discerning one and contrast two metaphorical menus (15:14b, 15b). Verse 14b also parallels verse 2b, illustrating the saying: "Garbage in, garbage out." Two "better-than" proverbs (15:16–17) take up the meal imagery

as well as the heart attitudes of the preceding verses (discernment [v. 14] ← fear of the Lord [v. 16]; joy [v.15] ← love [v. 17]), debunking society's elevation of wealth and plenty. One's heart attitude is more important than one's circumstances. Verse 18 concludes the unit by suggesting one source of turmoil and animosity—a hot-headed individual. Such a person is also repeatedly mentioned as a social menace in Egyptian instructional texts.

By contrasting the sluggard's thorn-impeded path with the superhighway of upright people (literally "straight ones"), verse 19 identifies laziness as a moral issue. Verbal links connect the following verses. Only a discerning individual walks "straight" (15:21b). A father finds joy in a wise son (15:20; cf. 10:1); one lacking sense, in folly (15:21); and an audience, in an apt answer (15:23; cf. 15:1). Verses 22–23 highlight two important features of wise counsel: more is better, and timing is everything (Eccles. 10:11).

Proverbs 15:24–29 contrasts five actions, individuals, and consequences, three of which explicitly mention God: the way of the prudent leading upward to life (15:24), the attitude of the proud bringing down their house (15:25), the plans of the wicked provoking God's displeasure (15:26), the deeds of one who pursues illicit gain troubling their family (15:27; cf. Josh. 6:18; 7:25), and the careful words of the righteous being heard by God (15:28–29). The righteous reflect before replying (15:28a; cf. 15:23); the wicked blurt out evil (15:28b; cf. 15:2b). Therefore, the Lord distances himself from the wicked while hearing the prayer of the righteous (15:29; cf. 15:8).

This major section, Proverbs 10–15, concludes with 15:30–33. (According to Waltke 2005, 5–6, these verses serve rather to introduce the next major section.) Verses 31–32 use a form of the word "hear" (NIV "heed"). Although hearing good news can cheer and refresh the "heart" (15:30), heeding correction can preserve life, give one a home among the wise, and impart sound judgment (literally "heart"; cf. "lacking of heart," 15:21; 15:31–32). Such receptivity to wisdom's instruction is rooted in the fear of the Lord, which teaches one that humility always precedes honor (15:33).

16:1–22:16. The second section of the major proverbial collection, presumably also "Solomonic," gives counsel for rulers and for everyday life. Whereas contrasting (antithetical) proverbs dominate Proverbs 10–15, in chapters 16–22 the second line of a proverb more frequently reinforces or completes the assertion in the first. Although the thematic contrast between the wise and the foolish continues, the contrast between the righteous and the wicked is far less prominent than in chapters 10–15. For example, "righteous" (Hebrew *tsaddiq*) occurs thirty-nine times in chapters 10–15 but only ten times in chapters 16–22. Similarly, "wicked" (Hebrew *rasha*) occurs forty-two times in chapters 10–15 but seventeen times in 16–22.

16:1–33. Chapter 16 constitutes the center of the book, the rabbinic editors marking verse 17 as the middle verse. Therefore, it is significant that the second greatest concentration of "Yahweh" (or "LORD") and the greatest concentration of "king" (cf. chap. 25) in the book occur here. The relationship between divine and delegated rule is explored in

16:1–15; verses 10–11 mark the transition. Several terms refer to both God and king (e.g., "detests" [respectively, 16:5, 12]; "atone/appease" [16:6, 14]; "take pleasure in" [16:7, 13]; "establish" [16:9, 12]), supporting this comparison.

God's sovereign involvement in human affairs is expounded in verses 1–9—a theological gold mine. (Corresponding affirmations begin and conclude the chapter in 16:1, 33.) We can order our thoughts, but God facilitates effective speech (16:1). He evaluates our motives, even if they are hidden to us (16:2). Thus we can commit our activities to him to give them lasting value (16:3). Every human action receives an appropriate divine response (literally "answer"), including the evil day awaiting the wicked (16:4). He detests and will punish their arrogant behavior (16:5). Though "steadfast love" (NIV "love") in dealing with others can make amends for their failures, God-fearers will avoid such evil in the first place (16:6). God, however, can enable those pleasing him to live in harmony even with their foes (16:7). Therefore, the righteous needy are really better off than the wicked wealthy (16:8). Verse 9 summarizes: we can responsibly make plans (echoing 16:1a), but God "establishes" our steps (so the NIV in 16:3b, 9b).

The righteous king (16:10–15) will model similar attitudes and surround himself with like-minded aides, experiencing similar divinely bestowed success. He will exalt just verdicts, standards, actions, and words (16:10–13), which will temper how he wields

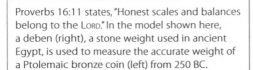

Proverbs 16:11 states, "Honest scales and balances belong to the LORD." In the model shown here, a deben (right), a stone weight used in ancient Egypt, is used to measure the accurate weight of a Ptolemaic bronze coin (left) from 250 BC.

his delegated authority over life and death (16:14–15).

As one crosses the midpoint of the book of Proverbs, wise and foolish speech are again described (16:16–30). Verses 16–19 are introductory and sound familiar notes: wisdom's supreme value (16:16) and a straight road that avoids both evil and disaster (16:17). The familiar proverb "Pride goes before a fall" contrasts the parallel clauses of verse 18. In context, and paired with verse 19, it illustrates what the "upright" of verse 17 will avoid. Wisdom gives life stability.

Proverbs 16:20–24 concerns wise speech. Heeding instructions and trusting in the Lord (16:20) are both characteristic of the humble (16:19). A sage's reputation for insight, a spoonful of rhetorical sugar, and skilled speech issuing from a wise heart all serve to "promote instruction" (16:21, 23). This encourages others to drink from discretion's life-giving fountain rather than being chastened like fools (16:22). The holistic benefits of "pleasant" or "gracious words" are emphasized in 16:24 (cf. 12:18; 13:17; 15:4).

The destructive speech of fools offers a striking contrast (16:25–30). Proverbs 16:25 is identical to 14:12, perhaps repeated here to underline this contrast, while 16:26 is linked to 16:24 by the word "soul/appetite" (Hebrew *nepesh*; see also commentary on 13:1–25). As a general proverbial statement, it describes the inner forces that produce external actions—both good and evil. Words can burn like fire (16:27), igniting discord, separating intimate friends (16:28), and luring the unsuspecting onto harmful bypaths (16:29). Evil lips can even be used to gesture to one's accomplices in carrying out one's perverse plots (16:30).

The chapter closes in 16:31–33 by summarizing central wisdom themes. Righteous conduct leads to a long life (16:31), and conquering oneself (literally "one who governs his spirit") is more significant than conquering a city (16:32). Above all, life is not a crapshoot; God ultimately controls everyone's destiny (16:33).

17:1–28. There are fewer internal verbal and conceptual links within chapter 17 than in the preceding chapters, making it difficult to discern subunits. There is a domestic emphasis, with "house" in verses 1 and 13; "son/child" in verses 2, 6, and 25; and "brother" in verses 2 (NIV "one of the family") and 17; while friendship is mentioned in verses 9 and 17–18. The initial verses portray unexpected values or incongruous situations (17:1–8). A dry morsel eaten in tranquility is deemed better than fresh meat eaten amid strife (17:1; cf. 15:16–17). The disturbed home motif continues in verse 2, with a wise servant supplanting a son as heir. God assesses the purity of one's heart attitudes (17:3), unlike the wicked, who apparently prefer listening to malicious words (17:4)—such as mockery of the poor and their calamity, as well as of their Maker—thereby provoking punishment (17:5). Some people view their grandchildren or parents, rather than a rich wardrobe, as their crowning glory (17:6; cf. 16:31). Excessive speech is inappropriate for a senseless person and, even more so, deceitful speech for a ruler (17:7). Bribes, however, often work like a lucky charm, bringing success rather than reprisal (17:8).

The verses that follow highlight beneficial and destructive relationships (17:9–20). One's response to an offense can either deepen or destroy a friendship (17:9; cf. 16:28). A well-intentioned rebuke (from such a friend) can make a deep impact (17:10), while a rebel may receive a harsher message (17:11). A fool on the loose is more dangerous than an angry she-bear (17:12), such as a fool who repays good with evil, bringing unending disaster on his home (17:13). Similarly, provoking strife releases flood waters, causing great damage (17:14), while perverting justice provokes divine displeasure (17:15). Even given sufficient cash, a fool will not acquire wisdom (17:16). A true friend constantly offers loving support, especially when there is trouble (17:17). There is, however, a limit to the assistance that one can wisely give: don't secure a friend's debts (17:18; cf. 11:15).

Whereas some love their friends (17:17), others show affection for sin and strife, erecting pretentious, perverse, and thus precarious barriers between themselves and others, and so inviting disaster (17:19–20).

Proverbs 17:21–28 portrays a foolish child causing grief in the family (17:21–22, 25) and a wicked person (by juxtaposition, presumably the same individual) perverting justice (17:23, 26). Such a person lacks a proper perspective (17:24), as well as proper restraint in speech and in controlling emotions (17:27–28).

18:1–24. The thematic emphasis of Proverbs 18:1–8 is the fool's speech. Accordingly, 17:27–28 could be viewed as introductory or transitional. The theme is launched by introducing three types of speakers: the antisocial person, the fool, and the wicked. The antisocial person (literally "one who separates himself"; cf. 17:9) pursues self-gratification, leading him to irrationally provoke quarrels (18:1; cf. 17:14; 20:3). The fool "takes fatuous pleasure in his morally bankrupt heart's exposing itself" (Waltke 2005, 70), rather than in gaining understanding (18:2). Contempt for others accompanies the wicked person, and the feelings are mutual (18:3). One can drown in words, but wise speech is a continual source of refreshment (18:4). One must not show partiality to the wicked, thereby skewing justice (18:5), but sooner or later their words will bring them down (18:6–7). Verses 8–9 close the unit by introducing two more destructive individuals: the gossip, whose juicy rumors are eagerly devoured, and the slacker, who is also a societal saboteur (cf. Prov. 26:22).

The next unit begins with an ironic proverbial pair (18:10–11). Whereas the righteous seek refuge in the towering character of their God, the rich vainly consider their wealth as making them invulnerable to trouble's assault. Such haughty thoughts (literally "high heart," a wordplay) precede doom, while the humility of the righteous is rewarded (18:12; 12b = 15:33b). Haughtiness also leads one to respond before considering what a conversation partner has to say; this can also lead to humiliation (18:13),

and perhaps even to a crushed spirit, which is worse than disease (18:14). In contrast, the ears of the wise eagerly listen and learn (18:15).

Disputes, especially within a legal context, are dealt with in 18:16–21. Accordingly, "gift" probably refers to a bribe or private present that secures an unfair advantage for a person rather than to generosity or giftedness (18:16; cf. 21:14). Verse 17 affirms the persuasive power of a well-crafted argument—at least, prior to cross-examination. Verse 18 commends the alternative of casting lots to settle a dispute, since God, rather than elders, then determines the outcome (16:33; Jon. 1:7). This is preferable to leaving the offended person less approachable than a fortified city (18:19; cf. 18:11). The proverbial pair in verses 20–21 describes speech's dual effects and fits the disputational context well. The words that we speak can satisfy like fruit, but we may have to harvest and eat our words (18:20). No wonder people love (and should fear) the tongue's ability to dispense both life and death (18:21).

Proverbs 18:22–24 fits well with the initial emphasis on companionship, especially the poor person's lack thereof in 19:1–7. Verse 22 begins with the most intimate of human relationships, affirming that finding a (wise) wife is valuable (cf. 8:35; 19:8) and an indication of divine favor. The poor, however, often find themselves alone, their pleas for compassion rebuffed by the rich (18:23). Yet even with companions you can come to ruin if you lack a true friend (literally "one who loves"), who will stick with you in a crisis (18:24; cf. 15:9 [a divine friend?]).

19:1–20:4. The initial verses of chapter 19 continue the theme of companionship, with an emphasis on the poor (19:1–9). Despite the social ostracism experienced by the poor, it is better for them to maintain their integrity in word and deed than to resort to perverse speech like a fool (19:1). Lacking knowledge, the fool rushes ahead and slips (or NKJV "sins," 19:2). When his own folly thus subverts his course, he angrily blames God (19:3). New companions flock to the wealthy while abandoning the poor (19:4). Whereas a fool with "twisted" or "perverse" lips may self-destruct (19:1b, 3), a false witness will be directly punished by God (19:5). People flock to the ruler (not "generous man" [NASB, ESV], 19:6) as to the rich, seeking the best friend that money can buy. In contrast, the poor are even hated by their siblings and abandoned by companions. No words can bring them back (19:7). Verse 8 is connected to 18:22 and 19:2 by the Hebrew word for "good": to find a wife is to "find what is good," to lack knowledge is "not good," and by preserving understanding one literally "finds good" (and therefore "prospers"). The unit concludes by repeating verse 5, changing only the last word. Those acquiring sound judgment love their lives (19:8a), while profuse liars will perish (19:9b).

Verses 10–15 focus on the court and the home. Verse 10 is transitional: it is not fitting for fools to enjoy luxury, not because it is undeserved, but because they cannot use it well (cf. Prov. 26:1). Similarly, slaves are unsuited for leadership roles (also 30:22), especially if lacking wisdom (cf. 14:35; 17:2). In context, the high value of forbearance and forgiveness is applied to the king, who will either refresh like dew or rage like a lion—but it could apply to a courtier as well (19:11–12). Verses 13–15 juxtapose a dysfunctional and a healthy household. In the dysfunctional home, a foolish son ruins the father's estate, probably through chronic laziness (19:15), while his quarrelsome wife irritates like a leaky roof. In the healthy household, the estate is preserved and enhanced through the skill of the God-given wife.

These contrasting homes prompt a mini lesson on parental instruction (19:16–29) similar to Proverbs 1–7, with imperatives (commands or exhortations) in 19:18, 20, and 27 and references to Yahweh ("the LORD") in verses 17, 21, and 23. Heeding instruction, rather than living carelessly, preserves life (19:16). An alternate reading verse 16b is "be put to death" (i.e., by God), suggesting that "his ways" (NIV 1984) refers instead to God. This is supported by verse 17: showing kindness toward the poor (thus

resolving 18:23) is one of God's foundational "ways." Thus parents who neglect discipline designed to instill wisdom in their children are actually seeking their premature death (19:18) and may end up repeatedly bailing them out of trouble (19:19)! Whereas verse 18 directly addresses the parent, verse 20 directly addresses the child: wisdom, not subordination, is the ultimate goal. Verse 21 juxtaposes valuable human counsel and sovereign divine counsel (19:20a, 21b); divine counsel always prevails. The human longing for "loyal love" (Hebrew *hesed*; NIV "unfailing love") in verse 22a recalls 18:24, while verse 22b echoes 19:1. The NIV's alternate translation for verse 22a ("Greed is a person's shame") is influenced by 22b but less likely. Reverence for God leads to a life marked by fulfillment and protection from harm (19:23). A contrasting portrait of inconceivable laziness (19:24) recalls the vice that first prompted this lesson (19:15). The mocker is immune to discipline's benefit and knowledge (19:25), resulting in the kind of son who disgracefully mistreats his parents (19:26; cf. 19:13a). Thus the lesson concludes by ironically reversing 19:20 in 19:27.

Proverbs 19:28–20:4 describes several foolish menaces to society who deserve a beating. This reference to "beatings" serves to bracket chapter 20 (19:29; 20:30), while the word "mock" links 19:28–20:1. Such "fools" include the worthless (Hebrew *beliyyaal*) witness and the wicked, who gulps down (Hebrew *yeballa*, a wordplay) evil (19:28); the drunken brawler (19:1); raging, roaring royalty (20:2; cf. 19:12a); the instigator of quarrels (20:3); and the destitute sluggard (20:4).

20:5–30. Verses 5–13 consider challenges to accurate assessment. The metaphor "deep waters" in verse 5 is unclear but probably negative (cf. Prov. 18:4 and Ps. 69:2, 14). The sometimes dubious intentions of a person are hidden in the depths of the heart, but a discerning person can bring them to the surface for a closer look. Similarly, not everyone proclaiming "loyal love" is to be taken seriously, for faithful friends are rare (20:6). Those leading a life of integrity, leaving a trail of blessing, are clearly identifiable as righteous (20:7). The trained eye of the king is capable of distinguishing between the righteous grain and wicked chaff (20:8), but anyone claiming complete purity and innocence is self-deceived (20:9). One can deceive others by using falsified weights and measures, but these provoke divine displeasure (20:10). Waltke rejects the traditional understanding of verse 11, translating it, "Even a youth in his evil deeds dissembles. So is his conduct pure, or is it upright?" (Waltke 2005, 120, 137–38), since the Hebrew word for "actions" usually refers to *evil* deeds. This interpretation fits well in the thematic sequence. Taken with verse 9, however, which also refers to "pure" behavior, the proverb more likely affirms that, even as a youth, one can distinguish oneself as pure and upright by one's *conduct* rather than by one's *claims*, just like the elderly righteous (20:7). Verse 12 refers again to God's role in assessment (20:10 and 12 end with "them both"): he endows humans with the sensory organs that make this possible (20:12). Verse 13 concludes the unit, linking to verse 12 by the phrase "open your eyes" (NIV "stay awake"), also countering verse 4. Perhaps it should be taken metaphorically: open your eyes and perceive accurately where laziness will take you!

The next verses (20:14–17) move into the realm of commerce, where hyperbole and haggling prevail (20:14), knowledge-rich lips are rare gems (20:15), debts should be carefully secured (20:16), and fraudulent practices can turn a "sweet" deal sour (20:17). Before undertaking something big, seek wise counsel, being careful to avoid those who might betray your trust (20:18–19).

The final section (20:20–30), in which several verses take up ideas occurring earlier in the chapter, focuses on the outcome of or retribution for one's actions, specifically by God (20:22–24, 27) and the king (20:26, 28). Those who curse their parents will be extinguished (20:20). An inheritance obtained prematurely may not lead to happiness in the end (20:21).

The weighing of the heart in a scene from the Book of the Dead, dated to the Ptolemaic Period (fourth–first century BC)

Taking revenge usurps a divine prerogative (20:22; cf. Rom. 12:19). God detests deceptive standards (and will punish, 20:23; cf. 20:10), but in fact he sovereignly directs our steps and destinies, surpassing human comprehension (20:24). Those making hasty vows set a trap for themselves (20:25). The wise king separates out the wicked as chaff and gives them a good "threshing" (20:26; cf. 20:8). The Lord's searchlight shines through (or illumines) the king, exposing the "inmost being" of individuals to him (20:27; cf. 20:5). It is the king's "steadfast love" (NIV "love") as ruler, however, that stabilizes his rule, not the delegated authority he wields (20:28). Youth and old age may have their respective advantages (20:29), but all can benefit from the type of divine "beating" that removes evil from one's "inmost being" (20:30, same expression as in 20:27).

21:1–31. Some interpreters take the initial verses of chapter 21 with the preceding section, since the king is mentioned in 20:26, 28 and 21:1. Chapter 21, however, is framed by proverbs asserting Yahweh's sovereignty over human outcomes (21:1, 30–31, similar to 16:1, 33). Three "Yahweh" (or "LORD") proverbs set the tone for a new section, which encompasses the entire chapter. God can direct the decisions (literally "heart") of even the most powerful human beings, like a watercourse, to specifically benefit those who please him and abundantly irrigate their lives (21:1). "Weighing the heart" is a common ancient Egyptian image of divine judgment; God's assessment of human ways is complete and accurate (21:2; cf. 16:25). His priority concerns what is actually just and right(eous), not simply proper ritual or what people think is (up)right (21:2a, 3; cf. 21:8b). His assessment includes the unrestrained intents of the wicked (21:4, literally "broad heart"). The NIV 1984's "lamp" contrasts with Yahweh's "lamp" in 20:27, but what this lamp illumines remains unclear. Following the NIV instead, the wicked are like an uncultivated field, which produces only sinful weeds. The following verses expand on the yield of the

wicked. Unlike the plans of diligent individuals, who profitably carry out their plans, haste (and lack of planning) makes waste (21:5; cf. 14:23). Treasures gained through deception are as temporary as a vapor (Ecclesiastes' favorite word), for those who own such treasures are seeking death (21:6, NIV alternate translation) through their crooked path marked by violence and injustice (21:7–8a).

The next subsection (21:9–19) is framed by two similar proverbs (21:9 = 25:24; 21:19; reinforced by references to the wicked in 21:10, 18). Both express a preference for peace with privation (house roof, wilderness) over a contentious companion and introduce a thematic emphasis on the wicked's impact on communal life—and their punishment (even a wife is considered "wicked" if inciting contention). Controlled by their evil desires, they show neighbors no compassion and ignore the cries of the poor (21:10, 13a). When such incorrigible mockers are punished (literally "fined") by local officials, even the naive can learn a lesson (21:11; cf. 19:25). More significantly, the Righteous One (correctly capitalized in the NIV) observes the wicked and brings disaster on their homes. Now their cries are those that go unheeded (21:12–13). The wicked may offer a covert bribe to placate the righteous wrath directed toward them, but they will cower in terror if justice is carried out, much to the joy of the righteous (21:14–15). Whoever wanders away from the prudent path will join only *one* community—the community of the departed (21:16). The contextual message of verse 17 is suggested by the concept of "joy" that it shares with verse 15: take pleasure in justice achieved rather than loving pleasure itself, as represented by wine and cosmetics. Verse 18 is not to be taken theologically. Rather, as Kidner summarizes it (Kidner, 144), the treacherous wicked are the "'expendable' members of society," who will face disaster rather than the upright righteous.

Whereas the preceding subsection focuses on the wicked, 21:20–29 highlights the advantages of wisdom. Not only do the wise have

567

plenty of fine fare stored up, but as those who pursue righteousness and loyal love, they find life, prosperity (literally "righteousness," a metonymy of reward for relationship; cf. 22:4), and honor as well (21:20–21). Wisdom makes them powerful and spares them from speech-provoked trouble (21:22–23), unlike the deadly folly of four characters: insolent mockers, craving sluggards, hypocritical worshipers, and ruthless perjurers (21:24–28). The wicked brazenly feign strength, while the upright discern the import of their decisions and conduct (21:29). Verses 30–31 conclude the section by reminding the reader that, despite its many benefits, human wisdom cannot prevail against God's sovereign plans. And although one can strategically prepare for battle, victory is God's gift.

22:1–16. An initial thematic emphasis in Proverbs 22 is God's sovereignty over wealth and poverty. Verse 1 asserts a countercultural value: a good reputation (literally "a name"; cf. Eccles. 7:1) and good favor (cf. Prov. 3:4), presumably through one's wise conduct, are more worthy of pursuit than substantial wealth. The claim of verse 2 is not that God is the creator of a socioeconomic hierarchy; rather, both rich and poor are under his sovereign care and control. Accordingly, wealth may be one reward for humble reverence toward God (22:4; cf. 21:21). Verses 3 and 5 describe the contrasting walks of the shrewd/righteous and the untrained/perverse. The former warily avoid "evil" (NASB; NIV: "danger"); the latter follow a thorn-filled path and "pay the penalty" (22:3b; literally "are fined," continuing the financial theme). Verse 6 (though lacking in the Greek Septuagint) is a favorite proverb on biblical parenting, but its translation and import are disputed, since the exact meaning of the Hebrew for "his way" is unclear. Taken in context, *his* way could refer back to the fear of Yahweh in verse 4a (i.e., *God's* way) in contrast to the way of the perverse in verse 5a. In Proverbs youth is associated with gullibility and the need for wise instruction (cf. Prov. 1:4; 7:7) by parents and others. Once launched in the right direction, the child will

likely stay on course throughout life. Verse 15, which is linked to 22:5–6 by the verb "stays/drive far from" and the training theme, supports this interpretation. Folly is an innate part of a child's makeup and must be removed by discipline while the child is still young.

The second subsection, addressing the mistreatment of the poor and indicating that some poverty is self-inflicted, is bracketed by 22:7 and 16. Those who thus wickedly abuse their power will be divinely punished (22:8), while those who generously care for the poor will be divinely rewarded (22:9). Other fools (22:15) afflicting society include the mocker (22:10), the treacherous (22:12b), the lazy (22:13), and the adulteress (22:14, here portrayed as a potential agent of divine punishment). Both the king and the Lord, however, are looking for those whose words are marked by purity, grace, and knowledge to befriend and support (22:11–12a).

The first major collection of proverbs concludes in 22:16.

B. Sayings of the wise: Admonitions for societal relationships (22:17–24:22). Since the discovery and translation of the Egyptian Instruction of Amenemope in the 1920s, scholars have noted its striking parallels with this section of Proverbs and debated the nature of that relationship. In a 1996 essay, Paul Overland lists seventeen verbal or thematic parallels between the texts, claiming that the author of Proverbs 22–24 excerpted and summarized the Instruction of Amenemope. Most Old Testament scholars are so convinced of this alleged literary dependence that they emend the Hebrew text in at least five places to conform to the Egyptian text and speculatively subdivide Proverbs 22:17–24:22 into thirty "sayings" to correspond to the thirty chapters of the Instruction of Amenemope (e.g., NIV). More caution is warranted, however, since these parallels (1) derive from only eight of the thirty chapters, (2) are confined to 22:17–23:11, (3) occur in Proverbs in a puzzling order (i.e., 2, 3, 16, 1, 4, 5, 12, 13, 17, 14, 15, 9, 10, 11, 6, 7, 8), and (4) are quite similar to other Old Testament and ancient Near Eastern texts. Moreover, even if the Israelite sage has borrowed from Egyptian wisdom here because it accurately expresses how God "set up the world," the sage has transformed that wisdom by theologically refocusing it to promote reverence for Yahweh.

Rhetorically, 22:17–24:22 is similar to Proverbs 1–9 in the prevalence of imperative verb forms, including the call to heed these "sayings of the wise" (compare 22:17 with 4:20 and 5:1), followed by explanatory (i.e., motivation) clauses. Unlike Proverbs 10:1–22:16, this unit consists not of individual proverbs but of a series of admonitions on various topics, most of them being two or more verses in length.

22:17–23:11. The primary purpose of this instruction (22:17–21) is not pragmatic (i.e., to train capable court advisors; see 22:18, 21) but faith-related ("that your trust may be in the LORD," 22:19a). The number "thirty sayings" in 22:20a reflects an emendation of the text based on the "Amenemope hypothesis." The alternate reading "formerly" in the NIV 1984 accurately translates the Hebrew word that corresponds to the temporal expression "today" in 22:19b.

The social topics that follow have been encountered previously in chapters 1–9 and 10–22. The first section highlights harmful attitudes and actions regarding wealth and possessions (22:22–23:11). You should not exploit or devastate the poor or legally disadvantaged, because Yahweh will come to their defense and do to you as you did to them (22:22–23, an inclusio with 23:10–11). It is equally hazardous to have anger-controlled companions and become like them (22:24–25). You should also avoid cosigning on loans because you may end up losing more than your shirt (22:26–27)! Verse 28 warns against violating the property rights of others (cf. 23:10). Verse 29 affirms the value of developing professional skills (cf. 22:21 and Ps. 45:1). Lacking any imperative (i.e., command or exhortation; cf. 22:22, 24, 26, 28), 22:29 may serve to introduce the next topic.

Proverbs 23:1–3 and 6–8 are linked by the repeated phrase "do not crave his delicacies"

(22:3a, 6b; cf. Sirach 31:12–32:2), suggesting that the focus in verses 1–3 is not on improper *conduct* when your abilities bring you into the presence of a powerful person. (One can also translate "what" in verse 1b as "who" [see NIV note]; the word is perhaps intentionally ambiguous.) Drastic measures may be needed to curb an uncontrolled appetite or inordinate desire (22:2–3). Such food may be "deceptive," intended as a test of your self-discipline rather than simply as a calorie-rich diet. Verses 4–5 support this interpretation, warning against exhausting efforts to acquire fleeting riches. Verses 6–8 involve a begrudging host (literally "one evil of eye"), complementing the equally deceptive host of verses 1–3. The much cited translation of verse 7a, "as he thinks in his heart, so is he" (NKJV; cf. NIV alternate) is possible but uncertain; the Greek Septuagint translates "like a hair in his throat." Forget the flattery intended to win his favor, for both his food and his feigned hospitality may prove nauseous!

Verse 9 is linked to verse 8 by the motif of wasted words. A discerning person exercises restraint in attitudes, actions, and speech (23:1b, 4b, 9a). Proverbs 23:10–11 concludes the section by warning against the illegal acquisition of property (cf. 22:28), especially at the expense of the weak and needy (i.e., orphans). In wording identical to the initial warning in 22:22–23, it is expressed that God will take up their legal cause as their "family protector" (Waltke 2005, 245, Hebrew *goel*).

23:12–24:22. The second half of the instruction focuses on the wise, responsive child, paralleling Proverbs 1–9 more fully than does the first half of the instruction. (The Hebrew root *hkm*, "wisdom," occurs eight times in these verses.) It begins with a renewed call to accept experience-rich instruction (23:12, literally "discipline"; cf. 22:17), followed by a warning against neglecting the "discipline" (23:13–14) of the young, and presumably foolish, person. Verse 13b is ironically ambiguous: rather than killing the youth, the rod of correction may actually save the youth's life (cf. 22:15). Verse

14b, literally "deliver his soul from Sheol," may even speak of avoiding the *ultimate* fate of the wicked. The son is directly addressed and encouraged to live wisely in 23:15–16, 19, 26; 24:13–14, 21 (cf. also 23:22–25), punctuating the section, with an admonition to fear Yahweh in 23:17 and 24:21 framing it. The resultant joy of the parents is mentioned as a motivation in 23:15–16, 24–25. The foundational warning is against envying sinners (23:17; 24:1; 24:19). Their apparent "success" will be short-lived, while sustained zeal for God and a life marked by wisdom gives one a lasting, even an eternal, hope (23:18; 24:14). Specific admonitions then condemn (1) gluttony and especially drunkenness as leading to rags, not riches (23:20–21), as well as a plethora of physical, emotional, and mental afflictions (23:29–35), and (2) promiscuity with a prostitute or adulteress, who first captivates (just like wine, 23:31) and then takes one captive (23:27–28; cf. 22:14).

Proverbs 24:1–22 contrasts evil plotting (24:1–2, 8–9, 15–16) with wise planning (24:3–7). Repeated warnings against envying the wicked (24:1, 19–20) frame the subunit. Unlike evil men who plan destruction (24:1–2), wisdom is constructive and enriching (24:3–4; cf. 9:1 and 14:1), supremely powerful and effective (24:5–6), and too lofty and unattainable for fools (24:7).

Accordingly, those who devise ways to harm others gain a reputation as a master schemer or conspirer (24:8; cf. 12:2; 14:17). Ironically, this capacity for forging shrewd plans is viewed positively in Proverbs 1–9 (the same Hebrew noun the NIV translates as "schemer" in 24:8, it translates as "discretion" in 1:4; 2:11; 3:21; 5:2; 8:12). Such actions are described further as foolish, sinful, and socially repulsive (24:9). In light of the preceding verses, verses 10–12 apparently then challenge the wise to use their "strength" (24:5, 10) to rescue the potential victims of such deadly plots—or of any life-threatening crisis (24:11). Feigning ignorance will not suffice when they are confronted by the omniscient discerner of human motives

(24:12; cf. 16:2; 21:2), protector of lives, and rewarder of deeds.

The previous contrast from 24:1–9 resumes in verses 13–14, describing wisdom as "honey" for the soul, which gives one a secure and lasting "future hope." The call to eat this good "honey" is followed by three warnings regarding one's attitude toward the wicked. First, we should not act like them in plotting against the righteous, knowing that God will help them get back on their feet again while causing the wicked to stumble (24:15–16). Second, we should not gleefully celebrate our enemies' downfall, lest God be displeased with our heartless disdain toward fellow human beings and cut short their punishment (or perhaps redirect his attention to us; 24:17–18; cf. 17:5; Job 31:29). Third, we should neither be vexed by (cf. Ps. 37:1, 7–8) nor envy them, since, unlike the wise, evildoers have "no future hope." Instead, they will be extinguished like a lamp (24:19–20). Therefore, the best course for the son to take is to fear both God and his agent, the king, rather than making common cause with dissenters, since both of them are capable of suddenly turning his ordered life into a rubble heap (24:21–22).

C. More sayings of the wise: The necessity of honesty and diligence (24:23–34). A new collection of proverbs (24:23–34) is introduced in verse 23a simply as "also of the wise," the word "sayings" being added by the translator. It addresses two familiar themes: honesty, especially in legal settings, and diligence in one's work. The basic claim is stated in verse 23b: judicial partiality is not good. Acquitting the guilty rightfully provokes widespread, even national, outrage and condemnation, as the people call on God to curse those who pervert justice but to bless richly those who legally correct wrongdoers (24:24–25). Verse 26 broadens the theme: a straightforward response, whatever the setting, is as much an expression of devoted love as a kiss on the lips. Verse 27 introduces the second theme, diligence, by calling for proper preparations, provisions, and priorities. Then verses 28–29 complete the first theme, warning against being a perjurer or a hostile witness (cf. Prov. 3:29–30) motivated by a desire for revenge. The collection concludes with a colorful description of the sluggard's irrational behavior, along with its consequences (24:30–34; cf. 6:10–11). The rundown condition of the vineyard is a precursor to the resultant poverty, offering the observant sage a valuable lesson.

D. The later Solomonic collection (25:1–29:27). A second "Solomonic" proverbial collection begins in 25:1, extending through 29:27. These were "compiled" or edited two centuries after the reign of Solomon, during the reign of Hezekiah.

25:1–27:27. The first subsection of this collection is on relating wisely to rulers, neighbors, family, and social menaces. In these chapters God is rarely mentioned (only 25:2, 22) and numerous comparisons are used (in the NIV, "like" occurs more frequently in chaps. 25–27 than in all of chaps. 10–24).

25:1–28. Chapter 25 focuses on how to relate properly to various groups within society, frequently employing proverbial pairs (i.e., two consecutive related verses) to do so. Verses 2–5 lay the foundation for verses 6–15, which address court officials, although one could apply them more broadly. Verses 2–3, which have the ideal ruler in view, affirm a hierarchy in authority of God–king–subjects. The purposes of both God as Creator and monarch as shrewd and insightful statesman may remain inscrutable, but the latter should be honored for his skills. Accordingly, the wise king strengthens the realm by removing the wicked from positions of influence (25:4–5). The wise courtier therefore avoids self-promotion and public disgrace by approaching the great with humility (25:6–7; cf. Luke 14:8–10). Verses 8–10 warn against committing similarly rash

Proverbs 25:12 compares the rebuke of a wise judge to "an earring of gold or an ornament of fine gold," such as this beautiful gold earring from the area of Iran (eighth–sixth century BC).

actions in the legal sphere, also resulting in public shame. These specific examples of foolish speech are followed by proverbs about valued speech. A fitting word, even in the form of a timely rebuke, is beautiful (literally "golden," 25:11–12). Thus a reliable envoy is as refreshing as snow, while one who makes inflated, unfulfilled promises is as disappointing as rainless clouds (25:13–14). Finally, a gentle but persistent tongue can break down even the strongest ruler's resistance (25:15).

Two proverbs regarding honey frame a section offering instruction on how to be a good neighbor, which employs vivid comparisons (25:16, 27): too much of a good thing can be bad! (1) Don't become burdensome through overly frequent visits, thereby possibly turning friend into foe (25:16–17). (2) Don't betray trust in a time of crisis, assaulting others through false testimony (25:18–19; cf. 26:18–19). (3) Don't be insensitive in a time of sorrow (25:20). The NIV translates "on a wound" for the NIV 1984's "on soda." The point of either comparison would be that the so-called friend's behavior would only make matters worse. (4) Be generous in a time of need, thereby possibly turning an enemy into a friend and receiving divine payback (25:21–22, quoted in Rom. 12:20). The meaning of "heap burning coals on his head" (cf. Prov. 6:28), unfortunately, remains obscure, since causing a foe great pain sounds contrary to the biblical injunction against taking revenge. Perhaps referring metaphorically to some ancient ritual, the burning probably refers here to psychological pain produced by benevolent actions, resulting in remorse and, hopefully, reconciliation.

The instructions in 25:16–22 are followed by sayings (25:23–28) about various types of unwelcome individuals: the deceptive (25:23, literally "tongue of hiddenness"; Ps. 101:5), the quarrelsome (25:24 = 21:9), the compromising (25:25–26, literally "a righteous one [whose foot] slips before the wicked"; cf. 10:30), and those obsessed with honor (25:27); each of them, to some degree, lacks self-restraint (25:28). The repetition of "search out" and "honorable" in verse 27 from 25:2–3 (an inclusio; the Hebrew for "honorable" the NIV translates as "glory" in 25:2) and "honey" from verse 16 suggests that the NIV 1984's "seek one's own honor" is misleading. Rather, the proverb warns against a preoccupation with the sources or nature of honor (cf. 22:4; Longman 2006, 459: "Nor is it honorable to investigate honor").

26:1–28. Proverbs 26 describes, and by implication warns against, a series of dysfunctional and often dangerous members of society, beginning with the fool (26:1–12). How should one respond to fools (26:1–5)? It is just as inappropriate to honor them as it is to curse the innocent. But in the latter situation, God will defuse the curse (26:1–2). The corrective rod is a more fitting means of dealing with fools (26:3), though a well-considered corrective word may also be effective, as long as one neither speaks as foolishly as they do nor affirms them in their folly (26:4–5). It is foolhardy to honor fools by employing them as messengers (26:6–10; e.g., the failure of Ahimaaz in 2 Sam. 18:19–33), for such an arrangement may harm the employer (26:6), the fool, who is incapable of using proverbial sayings properly (26:7–9), and others as well (26:10). This is because fools disgustingly repeat their folly rather than learn from their mistakes and are self-deluded regarding their capabilities (26:11–12).

Next in line is the sluggard, who is similarly self-deluded (26:13–16; compare 26:16a and 12a). This portrait employs proverbs similar to those found elsewhere in the book (compare 26:13 with 22:13; 26:14 with 6:9–10; 24:33; and 26:15 with 19:24). Whereas those who meddle in someone else's dispute hurt only themselves (26:17, i.e., being bit by a stray dog), the one

who considers deceiving others to be a game is like a crazed archer (26:18–19). Similarly, the gossip or slanderer (26:20–22; 26:22 = 18:8) enjoys adding the charcoal of rumors to fiery quarrels—or igniting them in the first place. The series climaxes in an extensive description of the hateful person (26:24, 26, 28; NIV 1984 "malicious man"; NIV "enemies"), whose warm and witty words disguise a corrupt and conniving heart (26:23–25). Ultimately, however, such people's hidden and harmful malice will be publicly exposed and recoil upon them (26:26–28; cf. Ps. 7:15–16).

27:1–27. Proverbs 27 offers more general advice on a wide range of topics. A primary emphasis in 27:1–22 is on one's relationship with friends (27:6) or companions/neighbors (27:9, 10, 14, 17). As in chapters 1–9, a parent addresses a child here (27:11), framing the section by warning against arrogant self-confidence and self-praise (27:1–2, 21) and, by implication, against becoming a fool (27:3, 22). The destructive, jealous rage of a fool (27:3–4) is juxtaposed with the beneficial, though painful, corrective word of a genuine true friend and is contrasted with the reticence of a so-called friend and a foe's feigned affection (27:5–6). Two general proverbs follow. Verse 7 may simply illustrate how circumstances dictate tastes (although both are distorted); however, in context, the *sweet*-tasting, bitter food may refer to the "wounds from a friend" (27:6). The Hebrew verb *nadad* (27:8) designates one forced to flee (NIV) from home like a bird (rather than one unfaithfully straying, as in NIV 1984) and thereby being deprived of the *sweet* counsel of a close companion (NIV "pleasantness," 27:9). Whereas verse 8 pities the one forced to flee, perhaps due to a crisis, verse 10 admonishes this one not to forsake a proven friend in such a situation, who will more readily supply concrete assistance than a distant relative.

The parent's charge to "my child" or "my son" to be wise (27:11) could involve avoiding obvious "danger" (or "evil," 27:12 = 22:3), including guaranteeing a stranger's debt (27:13).

Being a good companion or neighbor requires a degree of self-restraint (27:14), unlike the conduct of the quarrelsome wife, who lacks this and cannot be turned off, so to speak (27:15–16; cf. 19:13). Rather than irritating one another, friends should "sharpen" each other (27:17). (Similarly, reliable servants benefit others and deserve honor [27:18].) Just as water can reflect one's face, in the case of intimate friends "one human heart reflects another" (27:19 NRSV)—including those who are insatiable and incorrigible (27:20–22).

Chapter 27 concludes with advice concerning the material benefits of carefully attending to one's flocks and herds (27:23–27). It is linked to verse 1 by verse 24 in affirming the tenuousness of wealth and power, while offering concrete advice for securing the former.

28:1–29:27. Chapters 28–29, on righteousness and a nation's welfare, together conclude this anonymous proverbial collection. They are similar to chapters 10–15 *stylistically* in their dominant use of contrasting parallel clauses and *thematically* in their repeated contrast between the righteous and the wicked (Hebrew *rasha* occurs five times each in chaps. 28 and 29 but is absent from chap. 27; cf. commentary on 16:1–22:16). Some interpreters consider these chapters to be "rules for rulers," although fewer than one-fourth of the verses refer to either rulers or their subjects. More striking is the emphasis on traditional Hebrew piety here. Proverbs 28:12, 28 and 29:2, 16 are parallel, dividing these chapters into four subsections: 28:1–11; 28:12–28; 29:1–16; 29:17–27. According to these verses, the stability and mood of a nation directly depend on whether the righteous or the wicked are in charge and "thriving."

28:1–11. The initial subsection begins by contrasting the psychological states of the wicked and the righteous (28:1). Discernment (28:2, 5, 7, 11) and heeding God's commands (28:4, 7, 9) are crucial both in government (28:2–6) and in the home (28:7–11). Hebrew *torah* is better understood here as referring to divine "law" (NIV 1984) than to human

"instruction" (NIV, 28:4; cf. "seek the LORD" in 28:5, only here in Proverbs). A nation where these are lacking will be marred by instability and chaos (28:2), oppression of the poor (28:3), and badly skewed values (28:4–6). A discerning child also avoids those who are self-indulgent (28:7) and exploitation of the poor (28:8), enjoying instead answered prayer (28:9), good things (28:10), and keen insight into the true character of others (28:11).

28:12–28. The second subsection is framed by descriptions of the contrasting responses of citizens to the righteous and wicked leaders (28:12, 28; cf. 11:10). A close relationship with God and moral uprightness are crucial, especially for rulers (28:15–16). This involves acknowledging and abandoning one's sins and shuddering at the thought of disobeying God (28:13–14), for example, through the perversity and violence of unjust gain or bloodshed (28:15–18). The keys to prospering are honest, hard work (28:19a, 20a; cf. 12:11), coupled with a trust in God rather than in one's own efforts, which expresses itself in generosity toward the poor (28:25b–27). This approach stands in stark contrast to get-rich-quick schemes involving bribery, stinginess, flattery, rationalized robbery, and greed (28:21–25a), which are doomed to fail or even to provoke divine judgment (28:19b, 20b, 22b, 27b).

29:1–16. The third subsection is doubly framed by proverbs concerning the importance of heeding and consistently giving correction (29:1, 15) and the contrasting responses to or consequences of the righteous or wicked rule (29:2, 16). This juxtaposition suggests that an undisciplined child may grow up to become not only a disgraceful son but also a disgraceful ruler. This is reinforced by verses 3–4, which describe, respectively, a son who squanders an inheritance on prostitutes and a ruler who destroys a country by taking bribes. A major responsibility for a king is to protect the rights of the poor (29:7, 14), for both the poor and the powerful owe their very existence to God (29:13; cf. 22:2). The remaining verses in this section introduce various foolish types, who undermine a nation's stability and disturb its tranquility (29:8a, 9b, 11a). These include flatterers, who end up snaring themselves with their words (29:5–6), provocative mockers (29:8), disrupters of the legal system (29:9), bloodthirsty foes of all who are godly (29:10), and unrestrained and deceptive courtiers (29:11–12).

29:17–27. The fourth subsection begins with a call to discipline one's children (29:17, the only imperative [command] in the chapter), bolstered by the assurance that the child will in turn become a source of parental relief and delight (cf. 29:3). As previously in the chapter, the stage shifts in the following proverb (29:18) from the family to the nation. The familiar but misleading KJV wording, "Where *there is* no vision, the people perish," has led to the common misuse of this proverb to justify long-range planning, which the NIV has corrected. The mention of divine "revelation" (the same Hebrew term refers to a prophet oracle, as in 1 Sam. 3:1; Isa. 1:1) and the people "casting off restraint" recalls the golden calf incident in Exodus 32:25, where the same verb is translated

by the NIV as "running wild" and "out of control." Observing God's "law" (NIV 1984; NIV: "instruction"; Hebrew *torah*; see commentary on 28:1–11), however, will bring a nation his blessing. Alternatively, the proverb may claim for the wisdom instruction genre the same inspired and authoritative status normally associated with Old Testament prophetic and legal texts. The emphasis on constraining improper behavior continues in the following verses. Like a child, a servant needs discipline (29:17, 19), but mere words may not suffice, especially if people have previously indulged that servant (29:19, 21). Those who cannot control their tongue, temper, or ego are prone, respectively, to folly, sin, and humiliation (29:20, 22, 23). And partnering with the wrong individuals, such as thieves, is self-destructive, pressuring one to refuse one's duty to offer legal testimony out of fear of others rather than trust in God for one's safety (29:24–25; cf. 28:25). Although people may think that a personal meeting with a ruler will guarantee the meeting of their needs, justice comes from God alone (29:26). In light of the divine standards emphasized in this section, the

Proverbs 29:19 says that servants require more than verbal discipline. Some masters understood the need for corporal punishment as license to beat their slaves, such as in this Egyptian painting (Tomb of Menna, 1400–1390 BC).

mutual antipathy between the righteous and the wicked is easy to understand (29:27; cf. 29:10).

4. Epilogue (30:1–31:31)

Although the final two chapters of Proverbs contain the wisdom of two more sages, from a thematic-theological standpoint they form an epilogue that corresponds to and serves to complete the prologue (Proverbs 1–9; parallels will be noted below). The words of Agur son of Jakeh and of King Lemuel are both called an "oracle," a term otherwise applied to prophetic utterances (30:1; 31:1; cf. the opening verses of Nahum, Habakkuk, and Malachi), perhaps thereby claiming divine origin and authority (so the NIV's "an inspired utterance"). Less likely, the Hebrew word *massa* could designate a region in the Arabian Peninsula named after one of Ishmael's descendants (i.e., Massa; cf. Gen. 25:13–14; 1 Chron. 1:29–30; see NIV 1984 note), making the authors non-Israelite.

A. Agur's message: Relying on God's word, learning from his work (30:1–33). In the Greek Septuagint, Proverbs 30:1–14 is placed before 24:23, while 30:15–33 is located after 24:34, leading some to suggest that Agur's words end with verse 14. The initial section expresses Agur's earnest personal piety and echoes various Old Testament texts (30:1–9). Just as verse 1b moves from a claim of physical weakness ("I am weary, God") to confidence ("but I can prevail"), verses 2–3 move from intellectual weakness to confidence, since the Hebrew syntax of verse 3 expresses a contrast: "I have not formally studied wisdom, but I have personal knowledge of the Holy One" (author's translation; cf. Prov. 9:10). The content of the rhetorical questions in 30:4, which describe the unique heavenly access and creative power of the "Holy One," remind one of Deuteronomy 30:12 (cf. Job 11:7–8) and Job 26:8, respectively; they are similar in form to those in Isaiah 40:12–14 and Job 38–39. The final question ("What is his name, and what is the name of his son?"), without directly referring to Jesus Christ, anticipates his coming as the one whom the first question describes (cf. John

3:13). The following confession shifts the focus from God's work to God's word (30:5–6). These verses quote both Psalm 18:30 (= 2 Sam. 22:31; cf. Ps. 119:140) and Deuteronomy 4:2; 12:32 (cf. Rev. 22:18–19), by implication claiming the same "flawless" status for Agur's wisdom as that invoked by the use of the word "oracle" in verse 1a. The section concludes with a simple but earnest prayer (and the only one expressed in the book), invoking divine aid in avoiding empty and deceitful speech and in procuring only sufficient material resources (cf. Matt. 6:11) to avoid the opposite temptations of impious self-sufficiency and hunger-induced theft.

In the remainder of the chapter (30:10–33), the numerical saying becomes the dominant form. In these often riddlelike proverbs, which draw striking examples from nature, the final item is emphasized. These verses also can be attributed to Agur, since no other author is named. The first subunit (30:10–17) consists of proverbs loosely connected with each other by repeated words or themes. Three consecutive verses refer to damaging the reputation of another: one who desecrates God's name by stealing, one who slanders a servant before his master, and one who denigrates father and mother (30:9–11; being cursed/cursing link 30:10–11). Verses 11–14 describe four disreputable types: despisers of parents, the self-righteous, the arrogant, and the greedy. Avarice, the vice of the fourth of these, is described as cutting open the poor in order to devour them. This is illustrated in the animal world by the leech, whose twin suckers (literally "daughters") keep crying for more. It culminates in a numerical saying that lists four insatiables: the realm of the dead, the barren womb, parched soil, and fire. The subunit is rounded off by verse 17, which again describes the disrespectful, disobedient child (cf. 30:11) with a sinful eye (cf. 30:12–13) that will be pecked out by, presumably divinely dispatched, scavenging birds.

A series of four numerical proverbs follows (30:18–31). There are four wonder-evoking movements (literally "ways," 30:18–19): a soaring eagle, a slithering snake, a ship cutting through the waves, and a young couple enjoying sexual union. Upon completion, none of these actions leaves behind any obvious traces. The sage hastens to concede, however, that such natural "laws of motion" can be perverted. The adulteress, who "eats and [then] wipes her mouth," removing every trace of her sexual snack (30:20; contrast Song 5:1), recalls the various destructive meals described in 30:14–17 (cf. 30:22b and 25b). Four developments shake the planet by disturbing the established or ideal social order (30:21–23): a male servant elevated to king, a "hardened fool" (NIV "godless fool"; Hebrew *nabal*; see "Structure and Theological Themes" in the introduction) apparently rewarded with plenty, a married woman who is disliked (cf. Deut. 21:15–17; 22:13, 16; 24:3), and a female servant who supplants her mistress. Four small, weak but wise animals achieve remarkable success (30:24–28): ants are amply supplied with food, rock badgers are protected by inaccessible cliffs, locusts advance irresistibly, and lizards are at home in the royal palace. A final numerical saying describes those known for their stately strut (30:29–31): the fearless lion, the rooster, the male goat, and the king accompanied by troops. That such a regal stride may be pretentious for the rooster and goat is suggested by the concluding verses, which draw warnings from the preceding numerical sayings (30:32–33): one should not act like a "[hardened] fool," exalting oneself, hatching schemes, and provoking quarrels by stoking anger.

B. The message of Lemuel's mother: A call for royal justice (31:1–9). The closing "oracle" (NIV "inspired utterance") is ascribed to King Lemuel (whose name means "belonging to God"), who simply passes on what his mother has taught him (31:1). Like chapter 30, Proverbs 31:1–9 clearly belongs to this oracle, while the remaining verses of the chapter could constitute an independent section, although lacking a new title/author ascription. Whereas in Proverbs 1–9 King Solomon admonishes his "son(s)" to acquire and practice wisdom, in Proverbs 31 the queen mother lovingly but strongly admonishes her son regarding the demands and duties of his royal office, addressing three topics. First, she warns against sexual dissipation, which could wipe out his career (31:3; cf. 5:9–10). Second, she warns against drunkenness, which could cloud his mind, distracting or hindering him from administering the law of the land, especially on behalf of the oppressed (31:4–5). She recommends a better use for his supply of alcoholic beverages: rather than drinking it himself and *forgetting* his duties, he should give it to the dying and suffering, briefly helping them to *forget* their miserable circumstances (31:5–7). Finally, and more importantly, she calls on him to be a vocal advocate for the rights of the voiceless and vanquished, judging rightly on their behalf (31:8–9). Rather than focusing on royal prerogatives, pomp, and power, Lemuel's mother emphasizes his responsibilities toward the weakest of his subjects. (Compare the Solomonic description of the king's ultimately unsatisfying pursuit of personal pleasure in Eccles. 2:1–11.)

C. Lady Wisdom exemplified (31:10–31). Proverbs 31:10–31 is stylistically distinct from the preceding set of admonitions. (The only imperative [command] is in the final verse.) In a twenty-two-verse alphabetic poem, in which each succeeding verse begins with the next Hebrew letter, a woman is presented who embodies all of wisdom's skills and virtues, from *a* to *z*. In context this section serves to counterbalance the initial admonition against sexual promiscuity in verse 3. At the same time, it takes up the sustained contrast within Proverbs 1–9 between Lady Wisdom and Lady Folly, presenting a woman who is both capable and virtuous, one who consistently practices what the book preaches in both the domestic and public spheres. By implication, Lemuel (or any young man) is urged to marry a woman who resembles this idealized but not unrealistic portrait. Like King Lemuel, she properly uses her strength (31:3, 10, 29) and opens her mouth (31:8–9, 26), caring for the poor and needy (31:9, 20) as well as for her family.

This description is clearly structured. Verses 10–12 affirm her great value in general terms, while verses 13–27 describe her activities in detail, warranting a concluding call in verses 28–31 to praise her. Several of the terms and images used here occurred previously in chapters 1–9. Such a woman is a rare gem (31:10; cf. 3:15; 8:11), a partner in whom her husband can place his complete confidence (31:11a). Like a victorious warrior, she will bring him rich spoil, consistently benefiting rather than harming him throughout life (31:11b–12). Through her industry and ingenuity, she augments the family's income and nourishes her household (31:13–18; cf. 31:24), much like a merchant ship or a lioness rising before dawn to stalk prey (31:15; NIV "food"; cf. Job 4:11). She produces both textiles and grapes for sale and invests in real estate. Her commercial trade is so profitable that their household lamps have oil to spare (31:18b—she is not sleep deprived, cf. 31:15a). Her balanced concerns are expressed through repetition in verses 19–20. She stretches out her hands to spin thread and to care for the poor and needy. She is unafraid of severe weather or the future—she fears God alone (31:21a, 25b, 30b)—for her family's clothing and bedding are luxurious, not merely adequate (31:21b–22). The mention at this point in the text of her husband's role and respect in the city administration (31:23) suggests that these are contingent on her manifold contributions to the household. Her most distinctive "clothing," however, is not fine linen and purple but rather "strength and dignity" (31:22b, 25a). Furthermore, her speech, like that of the sage, is marked by wisdom and faithful instruction (31:26). In sum, she vigilantly oversees the affairs of her home, exhibiting no traits of the lazy (31:27).

Not surprisingly, although not to be taken for granted, her children and husband praise her, publicly extolling her unsurpassed character

A young woman grasps a spindle with her fingers, as in Proverbs 31:19, in this relief fragment from Susa (eighth–seventh century BC).

and accomplishments, and the town's leading citizens should as well (31:28–29, 31). As the book concludes, the foundational and lasting benefits of reverence for God (31:30; cf. 1:7; 2:5; 8:13; 9:10) are contrasted with the fleeting attractions of personal charm and physical beauty. The wise son will do whatever it takes in order to make this woman his lifelong partner, and the wise reader will pay whatever it costs in order to engage in a lifelong journey along "the way of wisdom" (4:11) so vividly set forth and illustrated throughout the book of Proverbs.

Select Bibliography

Crenshaw, James L. *Old Testament Wisdom: An Introduction.* 2nd ed. Louisville: Westminster John Knox, 1998.

Fox, Michael V. *Proverbs 1–9.* Anchor Bible. New York: Doubleday, 2000.

Heim, Knut Martin. *Like Grapes of Gold Set in Silver: An Interpretation of Proverbial Clusters in Proverbs 10:1–22:16.* Beihefte zur Zeitschrift für die alttestamentliche Wissenschaft 273; Berlin: Walter de Gruyter, 2001.

Hildebrandt, Ted A. "Proverb." In *Cracking Old Testament Codes: A Guide to Interpreting the Literary Genres of the Old Testament*. Edited by D. B. Sandy and R. L. Giese Jr. Nashville: Broadman & Holman, 1995.

———. "Proverbial Pairs: Compositional Units in Proverbs 10–29." *Journal of Biblical Literature* 107 (1988): 207–24.

Kidner, Derek. *Proverbs*. Tyndale Old Testament Commentaries. Downers Grove, IL: InterVarsity, 1964.

Kitchen, K. A. *On the Reliability of the Old Testament*. Grand Rapids: Eerdmans, 2003.

Longman, Tremper, III. *How to Read Proverbs*. Downers Grove, IL: InterVarsity, 2002.

———. *Proverbs*. Baker Commentary on the Old Testament Wisdom and Psalms. Grand Rapids: Baker Academic, 2006.

McKane, William. *Proverbs: A New Approach*. Old Testament Library. Philadelphia: Westminster, 1970.

Overland, Paul. "Structure in *The Wisdom of Amenemope*." In *"Go to the Land I Will Show You": Studies in Honor of Dwight W. Young*. Edited by J. E. Coleson and V. H. Matthews. Winona Lake, IN: Eisenbrauns, 1996.

Schultz, Richard L. "Unity or Diversity in Wisdom Theology?—A Canonical and Covenantal Perspective." *Tyndale Bulletin* 48 (1997): 271–306.

Waltke, Bruce K. *The Book of Proverbs: Chapters 1–15*. New International Commentary on the Old Testament. Grand Rapids: Eerdmans, 2004.

———. *The Book of Proverbs: Chapters 16–31*. New International Commentary on the Old Testament. Grand Rapids: Eerdmans, 2005.

Ecclesiastes

RICHARD L. SCHULTZ

Introduction

There are few Old Testament books as intriguing and as difficult to interpret as Ecclesiastes. The book speaks directly to a contemporary society seeking desperately for meaning in life while involved in the often-reckless pursuit of material and personal success.

Yet it also contains numerous assertions that appear not only to contradict other biblical texts but also to be at odds with other passages within Ecclesiastes itself. Although such statements prompted some early rabbinic discussion concerning the nature of the book's inspiration, there is no evidence that its canonicity was ever in doubt.

What quickly becomes clear when one surveys the diverse understandings offered by ancient and contemporary interpreters of the book is that one's decision regarding some basic issues largely shapes the interpretation of the book as a whole. For example, how should we translate the oft-repeated Hebrew word *hebel* (KJV "vanity"; NIV "meaningless")? Or what is the point of the refrainlike call to "eat and drink and find satisfaction in [one's] work" (2:24; 3:12–13, 22; 5:18–19; 8:15; 9:7–9)? Interestingly, even though most contemporary scholars question the traditional ascription of the book to Solomon, this opinion appears to have little impact on their overall assessment of the message of Ecclesiastes.

Title, Authorship, and Date

The familiar English title of the book, Ecclesiastes, is a Greek word meaning "assembly member, assembler," which simply translates its Hebrew title "Qoheleth," the author's preferred self-designation. The word "Qoheleth," in turn, is a transliterated participle that the NIV consistently renders as "the Teacher" (KJV, NASB "the Preacher").

Despite the fact that the book never mentions King Solomon by name, he has traditionally been viewed as the author. There are three primary reasons for this ascription: (1) the author is described in 1:1 as "son of David, king in Jerusalem," although the word "son" could designate any royal descendant. When this is combined with 1:12, which describes him further as "king over Israel in Jerusalem," only Solomon could be intended if "Israel" refers to the united monarchy. (2) The speaker's first-person claims about his personal achievements and acquisitions correspond closely to the narrative descriptions of Solomon's reign in 1 Kings. (Compare, for example, Eccles. 1:16 and 2:4–10 with 1 Kings 3:12; 4:29–34; 5:13–18; 7:1–8; 9:17–19; 10:14–29; also Eccles. 7:20 with 1 Kings 8:46 and Eccles. 7:28 with 1 Kings 11:1–3.) (3) The claims of 1 Kings 4:29–34 that Solomon not only possessed unsurpassed wisdom but also authored numerous proverbs make him a plausible author who not only could test life's offerings to the full but also commend his discoveries to his people in a literary form. The cumulative effect of this textual support is sufficiently weighty that even most scholars who reject Solomonic authorship nevertheless assume that a later author has, as it were, slipped into the famed king's sandals in order to view the rich opportunities and cruel realities of life through his eyes. For them Solomon is simply the pseudonymous author of or the fictive voice in the book.

Those questioning the traditional authorship note specific elements of the book's language, content, and concepts that they view either as incompatible with Solomonic authorship or, more generally, with a date of composition early in the Israelite monarchy (i.e., tenth century BC). Despite the traditional association of Solomon with both Proverbs and Ecclesiastes, there are striking differences between the Hebrew of Proverbs and that of Ecclesiastes, the latter containing numerous grammatical forms and specific words that occur elsewhere only in exilic or postexilic Old Testament books or in Aramaic or postbiblical (Mishnaic) Hebrew. Words such as *pitgam* (8:11, "sentence") and *pardes* (2:5, "garden") are taken as indicating Persian influence and thus a date after the exile.

In the objections to Solomonic authorship based on the book's *content*, at least four points

Solomon's unsurpassed wisdom is depicted in this carved ivory codex binding (tenth–eleventh century AD) portraying his judgment between two women who lay claim to the same child (I Kings 3:16–28).

are raised. (1) The fact that Solomon is never mentioned by name in the book, the speaker instead being referred to (1:1–2; 7:27; 12:8–10) or referring to himself (1:12) as "Qoheleth," is taken as indicating that the author is an anonymous sage. (2) A king like Solomon would not repeatedly criticize the abuses of royal power (e.g., 5:8–9; 8:9–11). (3) It is unlikely that the book's skepticism toward the benefits of wisdom and righteousness could stem from the same author as the optimistic or positivistic claims of Proverbs. (4) The book appears to allude to or depend on specific events and socioeconomic conditions from the Persian period.

An additional point is raised based on the book's *concepts*: Some of the emphases and specific expressions of Ecclesiastes are similar to those found in Greek philosophy, especially Stoicism and Epicureanism.

A minority of scholars still support a Solomonic origin for the book, which would put its composition in the mid-tenth century BC. According to an Aramaic translation of the book, Solomon authored the book during a time of religious apostasy, which occurred late in his life. The book itself, however, does not support such a claim (cf. 12:9–10) or suggest a specific period of his life. Those rejecting the traditional author, including many conservative scholars, tend to date the book no earlier than the late postexilic period, with an increasing number supporting a third-century-BC date.

Although a detailed defense of Solomonic authorship in response to the preceding objections cannot be offered here, the following points may be noted. The *language* argument certainly is weightier than the *content* argument. After a thorough examination of the linguistic evidence, however, Daniel Fredericks concludes that a preexilic date for Ecclesiastes is defensible and that the book should not be dated later than the exilic period (Fredericks, 13). Given the relative paucity of surviving Hebrew and Aramaic texts from this period, any effort to use specific linguistic features to set an absolute date for any biblical composition is fraught with difficulties, and the editorial updating of a wisdom book such as Ecclesiastes is a reasonable explanation for the existence of "late" features. With regard to the content argument, the author may call himself "the Teacher" to emphasize the specific hat he is donning in this book in addressing a broad range of topics and a broad audience, drawing on common wisdom themes and sources. And one can identify at least as many parallel concepts in ancient Mesopotamian or Egyptian texts as in Greek compositions. In the following interpretive comments, a Solomonic *perspective* will be assumed throughout, based on our conclusions regarding the *possibility* but not the *necessity* of a Solomonic origin for the book's teachings. Accordingly, we will avoid tying this perspective too tightly to any concrete historical setting, either monarchic or postexilic.

Literary Features

Although the question of authorship is not insignificant, issues related to the compositional unity, rhetoric, genre, structure, and overall purpose of Ecclesiastes have a much greater impact on its interpretation. Seemingly contradictory statements have led interpreters to identify multiple voices within the book. Compare, for example, 5:10 ("whoever loves wealth is never satisfied with his income") with 10:19

("money is the answer for everything") or 1:18 ("with much wisdom comes much sorrow; the more knowledge, the more grief") with 7:11 ("Wisdom, like an inheritance, is a good thing and benefits those who see the sun"). One explanation is that a skeptical speaker verging on heresy has been (later) countered editorially by the addition of an orthodox perspective. Some understand the concluding verses, 12:13–14, as a pious postscript that serves to reject all that precedes it within the book. It is preferable, however, to view this repeated juxtaposition of divergent, even opposing, proverbs as the intentional rhetorical strategy of the author, who seeks as sage to examine human pursuits from all sides in order to assess realistically both their benefits and limitations and advocate a balanced perspective.

Striking similarities and differences between Ecclesiastes and a wide range of biblical and ancient Near Eastern texts have complicated efforts to identify its genre, since it is arguably unique. The book begins with a lengthy first-person section (1:12–2:26, although first-person statements continue through chap. 10), but the lessons drawn from these experiences are quite unlike those of other royal autobiographical texts, such as the Cuthaean Legend of Naram-Sin. Ecclesiastes lacks the sustained wrestling with divine injustice that marks Job and a number of Mesopotamian texts, such as the Babylonian Theodicy, as well as the pervasive cynicism of texts such as the Dialogue of Pessimism. The book itself suggests that its teachings result from an intentional and wide-ranging examination of all that is done under the sun, not simply for self-discovery but also for the benefit of others (compare 1:13 and 2:3 with 12:9–10).

Structure and Theological Themes

Many interpreters despair of finding any structural framework or logical development within the central section of the book, chapters 3–11. They dismiss any attempt as a creative imposition on a loose collection of miscellaneous topics and sayings. This commentary, however, will seek to demonstrate that the sage who authored this book sought not only to find order in his world but also to order his discoveries. In light of his initial thesis stated in 1:2 that everything is utterly "temporary" (Hebrew *hebel*, used thirty-eight times in the book), he seeks to determine what nevertheless has lasting value (1:3, NIV "gain"; Hebrew *yitron*) in such a world. To this end, he proceeds to analyze and assess the foundational activities and dimensions of life under the "sun": human achievements and wisdom (1:12–2:26), time and eternity (3:1–22), social relationships (4:1–16, followed by an admonitory interlude in 5:1–9), and wealth (5:10–6:9). As a result of his investigation, he comes to understand that seemingly bad days can bring about good (6:10–7:14), that righteousness and wisdom offer only limited protection in this world (7:15–29), that one must submit to the government despite injustice (8:1–17), that in the light of death one must make full use of one's opportunities (9:1–10), and that one should embrace wisdom and avoid folly (9:11–10:20). Despite having emphasized the elusive nature and ephemeral value of many

The Harper's Song—part of which appears in the hieroglyphs above the blind harper in this relief (Tomb of Intef, Saqqara, 1333–1307 BC)—contains thematic similarities to the book of Ecclesiastes.

of our most prized possessions and achievements, the author concludes by affirming the value of vigorous and joyful engagement in life, tempered by reverence for God (11:1–12:7), until death overtakes us.

The book of Ecclesiastes draws on Genesis 1–3 repeatedly; it refers to God as the "Creator" (12:1), who created humans from the dust of the ground and imparted the "spirit" to them (3:20–21; 12:7), and who makes "everything beautiful in its time" (3:11). In a fallen world, though, human (Hebrew *adam*) efforts are marked by wearisome "labor" or "toil" and produce no lasting results. In Ecclesiastes, God's most frequent activity is "giving" (used thirteen times of God). He gives both toil (1:13; 2:26; 3:10) and enjoyment in life (2:24, 26; 3:13; 5:18), wisdom and knowledge (2:26; cf. 12:11), wealth and honor (5:19; 6:2), and the numbered days of one's life (5:18; 8:15; 9:9). God remains sovereign (6:10; 9:1), and his work incomprehensible (3:11; 7:14; 8:17; 11:5). Ultimately every person will encounter him as judge (3:15; 5:6; 7:16–17; 11:9; 12:14), though the present delay in divine justice can be quite troubling (3:16–17; 8:12–13) and uncertainty regarding the future can lead to debilitating doubt and even despair (3:22; 6:12; 7:14; 8:7; 9:1, 12; 10:14).

Though God's work is inscrutable, he has "set eternity" within the human heart (3:11), and the appropriate human response is to "revere" him (3:14; cf. 5:7). This exhortation is balanced by Ecclesiastes' dominant encouragement to find joy in the everyday experiences of life (2:24–25; 3:12–13; 5:19–20; 8:15; 9:7–8; 11:8–10), which recurs almost like a refrain and progresses in the course of the book from an assertion to a command. Without these twin pursuits, life is reduced to futility (i.e., "chasing after the wind," 1:14, 17; 2:11, 17, 26; 4:4, 6; 5:16; 6:9), without rest (2:23; 4:6; 5:12; 8:16), satisfaction (4:8; 5:10; 6:3, 7, 9), or mean-ing (2:17–23; 4:8). Despite these difficulties, Ecclesiastes repeatedly emphasizes that life is not without "gain." Wisdom, wealth, and wife, though temporary, should be embraced and enjoyed as divine gifts. The book encourages us therefore to "accept our lot" (especially 5:18–19; 9:9), even though the present is difficult and the future is veiled (2:12, 18; 6:12; 7:14; 9:3; 10:14; 12:7).

Outline

Commentary

1. Introductory Remarks (1:1–11)

A. Title (1:1). The book begins with a title that attributes these "sayings" to "Qoheleth." Deuteronomy 1:1; Nehemiah 1:1; Proverbs 30:1; 31:1; Jeremiah 1:1; and Amos 1:1 intro-duce their books similarly as containing the words of a specific individual, without neces-sarily claiming thereby that this person wrote or edited the present canonical book. Although often left untranslated as the proper name Qo-heleth, this word is more likely a professional title, literally "the Assembler" of the people. The same Hebrew verb is used in 1 Kings 8:1–2 when Solomon *assembles* (Hebrew *qahal*) the Israelite leaders prior to the temple dedication celebration, in which the whole assembly of Israel participates. Instruction is then the as-sumed purpose for which the author *assembles* the people. Alternatively, the word could de-scribe him as the "assembler" or author/editor of wise sayings (cf. 12:9–10). It is clear from the royal activities and achievements noted in chapters 1–2 that the book sets forth "Solo-mon's"—rather than a later monarch's—wis-dom, whether as the actual originator of its teachings or merely as a literary foil or voice for a later author. In biblical scholarship, it has become conventional to refer to the author as Qoheleth, thus distinguishing him from the historical king. In calling himself Qoheleth (1:12), he may be emphasizing his role as sage rather than as ruler. The third-person references to Qoheleth could point to the work of an editor.

B. Theme verse: Everything is ephemeral (1:2). The main body of the book is bracketed by Solomon's foundational assessment of life "under the sun" (1:2 and 12:8). As noted above, how one understands the Hebrew word *hebel* (NIV "meaningless"), which occurs five times in this verse, largely determines how one char-acterizes the basic message of the book. There have been numerous suggestions, although no single English word adequately renders its contextual meaning throughout the book—for example, absurdity, contradiction, irony, opacity, vanity (KJV and NASB), naught. Psalm 144:4 offers a helpful indicator of its possible meaning: "Man is like a breath [*hebel*]; his days are like a fleeting shadow." *Hebel* is also the Hebrew spelling of Abel, the first human to die (Gen. 4:8), and all humans have experienced similarly the transient or otherwise insubstantial nature of their life and achievements. Since all human endeavors under the sun are stamped with a *t* for temporary, such pursuits often seem to be futile or even senseless, but this gives no warrant for translating the word consistently as "meaningless" in the book, as the NIV does. The repetition of the word in verse 2 is emphatic, similar to "Song of Songs" and "holy of holies"; that is, *everything* is utterly temporary.

C. Goal of the investigation (1:3–11). How should one then live in such a world? The phrase "under the sun" is used exclusively in Ecclesiastes (twenty-nine times, with the variant expressions "see the sun" [6:5; 7:11; 11:7] and "under the heavens" [1:13; 2:3; 3:1]). It designates the earthly realm of existence and activity as humans experience and view it apart from divine revelation regarding the final judgment and the eternal dimension. Qoheleth largely restricts himself to the former perspective throughout the book, while not denying thereby that the latter exists. Verse 3 suggests that verse 2 is not making a blanket nihilistic claim regarding the created world but rather prompting a thorough search for what ultimately remains as "gain" or profit from one's work. This investigation dominates the first half of the book. The underlying Hebrew word *yitron* is a commercial term that occurs only in Ecclesiastes. Verses 4–11 offer a poetic overview and suggest the provisional answer that little or nothing is gained. In the realm of nature, despite the relative permanence of the earth (1:4), one observes constant movement. This is emphasized by the dominance of participial forms and the sixfold use of the verb "go" in verses 4–7. There is no progress, however, for the sun (1:5; cf. Ps. 19:4–6), wind (1:6), and rivers (1:7) repeatedly run the same courses.

In the realm of the human senses (speaking, seeing, hearing, 1:8), there is effort without satisfaction. Weary words (rather than NIV's "things are wearisome") cannot fulfill. In the realm of human activities, nothing fundamentally new is done or discovered, despite claims to the contrary (1:9–10). Even the memory of the proudest achievements of the past or present generation (cf. 1:4a) will soon fade (1:11).

2. Everything under the Sun Is Examined (1:12–6:9)

A. Human achievements and wisdom (1:12–2:26). In the first major section of the book, Qoheleth examines various aspects of life "under the sun" (1:12–6:9), intermittently evaluating what he has experienced or observed. In an extended autobiographical section (1:12–2:26), Qoheleth relates his personal experiences. He first examines by means of wisdom (1:13; cf. 7:23) the gain that comes through a life marked by achievements and pleasures and then examines wisdom itself. He relates his findings in these two realms first in summary form (1:12–15; 1:16–18) and then more fully (2:1–11; 2:12–16) before drawing both negative and positive conclusions (2:17–26).

1:12–18. The opening summary exhibits a parallel structure, as Qoheleth sets forth his qualification (1:12, 16), his purpose (1:13a, 17a), the result (1:13b–14, 17b), and an explanatory saying (1:15, 18). His first qualification—that he ruled over (all) Israel in Jerusalem (1:12)—applied only to David and Solomon. Verse 13 emphasizes his single-minded effort (literally "I gave my heart," also 1:17; 7:21; 8:9, 16) to examine human activities in depth and in breadth, despite their unpleasant nature ("heavy burden"; a better translation is NJPS's "unhappy business"). Surprisingly, for reasons to be explained in chapter 2, all of these activities appear to be as futile (Hebrew *hebel*) as "chasing after the wind" (1:14; also 1:17; 2:11, 17, 26; 4:4, 6, 16; 6:9, cf. 5:16; 8:8). Expressed proverbially (1:15; cf. 7:13), capturing the wind is as impossible as

This Egyptian painting (tomb of Nebamun, ca. 1350 BC) illustrates the role of dancers and musicians to delight the heart, such as Qoheleth sought with his male and female singers (Eccles. 2:8).

restoring something that has been damaged or counting something that is not there.

Solomon was reputedly the wisest individual and exhibited unrivaled theoretical and practical skills (cf. 1 Kings 10:7). Thus he was uniquely qualified to assess wisdom's worth (1:16). Interpreters have taken the phrase "more than anyone who has ruled over Jerusalem before me" (cf. 2:9) as pointing to a later Davidic king as speaker, since Solomon would not make such a claim with David as his only predecessor. This conclusion is unwarranted, since even the postexilic author of 1 Chronicles 29:25 makes a strikingly similar assertion regarding Solomon. Although Qoheleth seeks to understand wisdom better by studying its opposites, "madness and folly" (1:17), wisdom itself is experienced as a mixed blessing. As the concluding proverb asserts (1:18), increased wisdom and knowledge are accompanied by increased vexation and pain. No amount of wisdom and knowledge will enable one to explain or resolve all of life's challenges.

2:1–16. Qoheleth's actual test is related in this strongly autobiographical section that has striking parallels with the Solomonic narrative in 1 Kings. Verse 10 might give the impression that these verses express his later sober reflections on an earlier period of sensual excesses, but the emphasis is rather on the intentional and restrained nature of his investigation (2:3b: "my mind still guiding me with wisdom"; verse 9b: "In all this my wisdom stayed with me"). He begins by testing himself with "pleasure." The NIV translates the same Hebrew word as "pleasure" in 2:2, 10 and 7:4, but as "happiness" in 2:26; "gladness" in 5:20; 9:7; and "enjoyment" in 8:15. He ultimately will see the "enjoyment" of life as something good. Here he simply notes that pleasure soon fades and thus accomplishes little (2:1b, 2b), while indulging in laughter (or NJPS "revelry") is madness (2:2a). As one form of pleasure, he tries stimulating his senses with wine (2:3a). The parallel expression, literally "to grasp folly," is puzzling, since nowhere else in the book does Qoheleth admit engaging in foolish behavior. Perhaps this merely reflects his following judgment that such activities are not "worthwhile" pursuits for individuals "during the few days of their lives."

Next, Qoheleth details his private architectural and horticultural projects (2:4–6), personal acquisitions of slaves, herds and flocks, and treasures (2:7–8a), and sources of musical and sexual delight (2:8b). The NIV notes that the translation "harem" for Hebrew *shiddah* is uncertain. A similar Hebrew word, *shad*, means "breast" and occurs together with the word translated here as "delights" in Song of Solomon 7:6–7, supporting this understanding (compare Judg. 5:30, literally "a womb or two"). He summarizes his unrivaled status and accomplishments (2:9) and opportunities for self-gratification (2:10a) and concludes positively (2:10b) that his heart (i.e., the core of his being) "took delight in all [his] work" and in the fruits of his labors. Such efforts ultimately can be viewed as only temporary and futile, like pursuing the wind, since they bring no lasting gain or benefit (2:11, answering the question posed in 1:3). Precisely why this negative conclusion is warranted will be explained in 2:17–23.

Next, in 2:12–16, Qoheleth investigates wisdom and its converse, madness and folly (2:12a; cf. 1:17). Verse 12b is viewed by some commentators as unintelligible or displaced but may serve to anticipate 2:18–21, which also deals with the king's successor. Verse 12b, translated literally, asks, "For what kind of person is it who will come after the king, in the matter of what has already been done?" (so Eaton, 68). Verses 12–15 contain a sequence of verbal actions that set forth Qoheleth's epistemological process. These will be repeated, with some variations, throughout the book: (1) verse 12—"I turned . . . to consider" (selection of object of examination), (2) verse 13—"I saw" (observation), (3) verse 14—"I came to realize" (reflection), (4) verse 15—"I thought/said in my heart" (conclusion). His observations affirm the traditional assessment of wisdom's relative benefit (2:13; Hebrew *yitron*, as in 1:3). He also states this proverbially (2:14a): the wise are able to see where they are going, unlike the fool, who constantly stumbles about in the dark. Yet, in his quest for *lasting* gain,

Qoheleth must recognize that both the wise and the foolish share the common destiny of death, the ultimate equalizer (2:14b–15). The NIV's "fate" implies a predetermination not suggested by the more neutral Hebrew word *miqreh* ("occurrence" or "what befalls a person"). This word is used seven times in the book, always referring to death. The inevitability of death makes Qoheleth question the value of his pursuit of wisdom, for he concludes that, in the end, this too is temporary (2:15). Not only will his wisdom perish with him, but he and his wisdom also will soon be forgotten (2:16; cf. 1:11).

2:17–26. This leads to Qoheleth's concluding evaluation of this area of investigation. On the negative side (2:17–23), he claims to have hated life. All work, especially his own life's work, was "grievous" or burdensome to him (cf. Eccles. 1:13b), a futile pursuit of lasting gain (2:17–18a). His strong emotions here appear to contradict his previous assessment of the delight he derived from his labor (2:10b, but note 2:11) until he explains his response. First, upon death, a potentially foolish heir will take control of all that Qoheleth has accrued through his efforts, wisdom, and skill. This heir has not contributed to its acquisition and, unfortunately, may have no inclination to steward it well (2:18b–21). Second, one's work life is marked by pain and vexation (NIV "grief"), and even by sleepless nights (2:22–23).

On the positive side (2:24–26), Qoheleth affirms that life, along with its daily activities such as eating, drinking, and working, can be enjoyed—but only as a divine gift and not apart from God. (NIV's "without him" here follows Septuagint, Syriac, and some Hebrew manuscripts; the Masoretic Text reads "apart from me.") God grants "wisdom, knowledge, and happiness" to the one "who pleases him" (NIV; literally "good before him"). In contrast, the "sinner" (Hebrew *hote*; contra NJPS, "him who displeases") may gather possessions only to pass them on without ever enjoying them, if God withholds that ability. Ecclesiastes 7:26

and 8:12–13 (cf. also 9:2, 18) indicate that this benefit has a moral basis rather than resting on God's "unpredictable and totally arbitrary pleasure" (so Loader, 32). Qoheleth thus concludes his first inquiry by issuing for the first time his repeated call to "eat, drink, and enjoy one's work" (not simply its by-products).

B. Time and eternity (3:1–22). Next Qoheleth turns to the examination of how time, viewed against the backdrop of eternity, affects human efforts to engage in profitable activities.

3:1–8. He begins with a highly structured "Catalogue of Times" (Fox, 193), which affirms and illustrates that "there is a time for everything" (3:1–8), certainly the book's best-known text. The poem begins with an initial summary claim regarding time and every human purpose (Hebrew *hepets*; 3:1). It is disputed whether this verse is to be taken descriptively (i.e., there is a predetermined time to acknowledge or be passively submitted to) or prescriptively (i.e., there is a proper time for action to seek or for making an appropriate response). This is followed by seven (symbolizing completeness) couplets of paired actions (i.e., 7 × 2 × 2 = 28). The fourteen pairs of terms employ merism, a figure of speech that designates a sphere by means of polar opposites (e.g., Gen. 1:1 "the heavens and the earth" = the cosmos; Ps. 1:2 "day and night" = continually). Although some interpreters claim that the author has made no attempt to order the activities progressively or in terms of their importance, J. A. Loader has identified an alternating pattern of values that is quite attractive. By labeling the actions within each pair as either generally "favorable" (F) or "unfavorable" (U), Loader (34–35) discovers the following pattern:

v. 2: FUFU; v. 3: UFUF; v. 4: UFUF; v. 5: FUFU; v. 6: FUFU; v. 7: UFUF; v. 8: FUUF. Also noteworthy is the fact that the Catalogue begins in v. 2a with birth and death and concludes with war and peace in v. 8b, both pairs describing fundamental human experiences.

Following Loader's lead, a coherent development can be traced in this poem, but its point remains unchanged even if one finds this interpretation strained and thus unconvincing. Verse 2 describes the beginning and end of animal and plant life, as determined by God, although "uproot" most likely does not refer to harvesting (cf. Zeph. 2:4). The NIV's "to be born" is literally "to give birth." Verse 3 describes the destruction and repair or construction of a body and a building, as determined by humans. Verse 4 describes opposite moods, which might accompany the preceding actions, in both their emotional ("weep . . . laugh") and ceremonial ("mourn . . . dance") expressions.

Verse 5 describes the treatment of stones and people in terms of joining and separating. It is unclear what *gathering* stones refers to, but it must have a negative connotation (as in judicial stoning) if Loader's analysis is correct. Verse 6 describes the treatment of possessions similarly, emphasizing their unintentional or intentional loss. The verb translated "scatter" in verse 5 is translated as "throw away" in verse 6. Similar to verse 4, the first terms in verse 7 describe proper responses to tragedy in both gesture and speech (cf. 2 Sam. 13:31, Job 2:12–13). The poem concludes with the primal emotions of love and hate and their societal effects in war and peace. Through this catalog of a wide variety of opposite actions and emotions, the poem presents a selective but comprehensive portrait of human life "under the sun."

3:9–22. The meaning and implications of this introductory poem must be determined by the verses that follow it, regardless of whether it was written specifically for this context or incorporated from elsewhere. Verse 9 poses the book's foundational question again (1:3): In light of the just-highlighted ordering of the times, what gain can be achieved through one's labor? An answer is given in verses 10–15, qualified further in verses 16–21, and reinforced in verse 22. In observing the divinely assigned tasks that occupy humans, Qoheleth concludes that God "has made everything beautiful *in its* *time.*" The NIV's "burden" in verse 10 for Hebrew *inyan* is too negative. Verse 11 may echo the creation narrative (Gen. 1:31), also taking up the key word of the preceding section, "time" (occurs twenty-nine times in 3:1–8, but only ten times in the rest of Ecclesiastes). All such activities have their appropriate or fitting occasion within God's sovereign ordering of the times. To the extent that one can discern these times, one should either delay action or act decisively (8:5: "the wise heart will know the proper time"; cf. also Eccles. 5:2, 4; 8:3; 10:10–11). Yet these times find their true significance—as merely temporal pursuits—against the backdrop of the sense of perpetuity (NIV "eternity"; Hebrew *olam*) that God has placed in every human heart. The traditional translation of this important Hebrew word is defensible here, even though it is sometimes used in terms of relative rather than absolute duration (i.e., "permanently," as in Exod. 21:6). Though realizing that more can be observed "under the sun," humans are unable to fully comprehend God's work (3:11b).

How should one respond to the fact that God grants beautiful times as well as a glimpse of eternity? With respect to time, Qoheleth reiterates his conclusion from 2:24–26. He affirms that there is no better course for humans than to enjoy life as a divine gift and to do what is good (3:12–13; cf. 7:20). With respect to eternity, he acknowledges that only divine actions transcend the transience of the "under-the-sun" world and the need for revision (cf. Deut. 4:2; 12:32). The best course for humans, then, is to revere God, since, unlike humans, who cannot produce anything fundamentally new (cf. Eccles. 1:9–10), God can even "call the past to account" (3:14–15). This rendering is supported by 3:16–17, which continues the theme of divine judgment. An alternative translation of the difficult wording of verse 15b is "God seeks out the persecuted," which does not fit the context as well, or "God can seek (successfully) that which already has been pursued" (in vain by others), which contrasts with verse 15a.

The opening phrase of 3:16–22, "and I saw something else," links this section with 3:10 rather than with chapter 4. Here Qoheleth describes something that does not appear to be very "beautiful in its time." In the place where justice should be administered, wickedness is being perpetrated instead (3:16). He offers two responses to this dilemma, each introduced by "I thought." First, he is confident that God has set a *time* for executing judgment. (The Hebrew phrase for "a time for every activity" in 3:17 is identical to 3:1.) Furthermore, God temporarily allows such wickedness to prevail in order to "test" (or "clarify for"; cf. Eccles. 9:1) humans, so that they will discover that, left to themselves, they are mere beasts (3:18), a point emphasized by a striking use of assonance (Hebrew *shehem-behemah hemmah lahem*).

This thought leads the author to return to his earlier assertion regarding the equalizing effect of death (2:14–16) and draw out further similarities. From an under-the-sun perspective, humans and animals share a common destiny, and their deaths are indistinguishable. Both are marked by transience, utterly dependent on their life-sustaining "breath" (Hebrew *ruah*, 3:19, but translated as "spirit" in 3:21). Genesis also describes both animals and humans as "living beings" (Gen. 1:24 [NIV "living creatures"; 2:7; cf. ESV). Both are on their return trip to the dust (3:20), paraphrasing Genesis 3:19. The author nevertheless stops short of equating the two, distinguishing their final direction in verse 21. The NIV 1984's alternate translation offers a literal (and the only defensible) rendering of the *unemended* Masoretic Text: "Who knows the spirit of man, which rises upward, or the spirit of the animal, which goes down into the earth?" (see also Eccles. 12:7). This point is obscured by most modern translations, which view the rhetorical question in verse 21 as a denial of any distinction between man and beast. The section concludes with a brief reiteration of verses 12–15: enjoy your time-bound lot in life, since your (eternal?) future remains veiled (3:22).

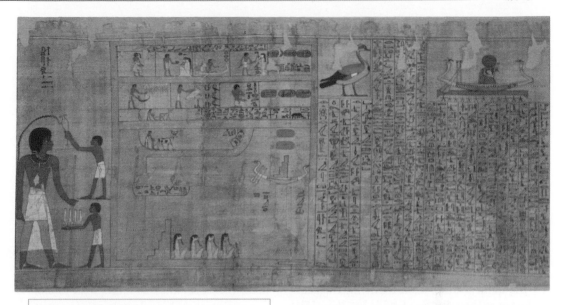

Just as Qoheleth speculated on the fate of humans and animals after death (Eccles. 3:19–21), other ancient Near Eastern cultures formulated various conceptions of the afterlife. For example, this illustration from the Egyptian Book of the Dead (papyrus, ca. 1450 BC) pictures the "Field of Reeds" where the dead would find plentiful water supplies to support their agricultural activities.

C. Social relationships (4:1–16). Next, Qoheleth examines life in society. Chapter 4 can be analyzed as a coherent unit. If one subdivides it into four subsections (i.e., 4:1–3, 4–6, 7–12, 13–16), each of them displays the following features: (1) a thematic emphasis on the value of companionship, (2) no mention of God, (3) no positive resolution to the observed problem, (4) the verb "I saw" (4:1, 4, 7, 15), (5) the inclusion of a "better than" saying (4:3, 6, 9, 13), and (6) a reference to "two" (4:3, 6, 8–12; cf. 4:13). He portrays humans in these successive scenarios as oppressed without comfort, envious, isolated, and inconstant.

4:1–3. The first subunit focuses on injustice, which was introduced in the preceding section (3:16–17). Thematic continuity is suggested by the introductory phrase "Again I looked and saw . . ." Three forms of the same Hebrew root "oppression . . . oppressed . . . oppressors") give focus to this theme. To suggest that a king like

Solomon could not be speaking here because he could (and should) have taken action to end such human abuse misses the point of this chapter, since he is involved here in making global observations. That which especially shocked him is introduced by Hebrew *vehinneh*, left untranslated in the NIV (but NASB "And behold . . ."). It was not simply the tears and the power imbalance but rather the fact that no one came alongside the oppressed to comfort them that was so painful (cf. Job 16:2; Ps. 69:20). The use of exact repetition in 4:1 is emphatic and a favored stylistic technique of the author (cf. 3:16). This observation is followed in verses 2–3 by one of the most negative-sounding (i.e., unbiblical, though see Job 3:1–26; Jer. 20:14–18) claims in the book—that the dead are better off than the living and those never born better off still! This statement is qualified, however, by a surprising reason: they have not "seen the evil that is done under the sun." Although the Hebrew verb for "see" in Ecclesiastes can denote personal experience as well as observation from a distance, it should not be limited to the former here. Qoheleth will continue to wrestle with the problem of theodicy (i.e., divine injustice); here he focuses on those condemned to suffer *alone*.

4:4–6. The second subunit gives Qoheleth's analysis of the workplace: all diligent and skillful labor is motivated solely by competitive envy. This may strike us as a rather cynical (and inaccurate) assessment, but it is typical of wisdom pedagogy to generalize and universalize in order to make a point. (There is no indication that Qoheleth's efforts, as recounted in chap. 2, had a similar motivation.) Without explaining why, he notes that seeking to keep up with the Joneses is futile. Lest one think he is thereby questioning the value of diligent efforts, he counters with a proverb and a better-than saying (4:5–6). These verses are linked by three references to "hands." Only fools avoid work—to their own ruin (literally "and eats his own flesh"; cf. Prov. 6:10–11 = Prov. 24:33–34). Working solely to supply one's material needs, if accompanied by "tranquility," is preferable to striving constantly for more (literally "two fistfuls," cf. Prov. 17:1).

4:7–12. The third subunit also focuses initially on the workplace, with thematic continuity signaled by the opening words "Again I saw," similar to verse 1. For the first time in the book, the author uses *hebel* (i.e., something senseless) in his observation rather than in his concluding statement. "There was" typically introduces a specific example or case study in Ecclesiastes (e.g., 2:21; 7:15; 8:14; contrasted with "there was no . . . ," e.g., 4:1; 7:20). Unlike the individual in the preceding scenario, who works constantly with an eye on others, this individual has no one to look to (similar to the first scenario, 4:1). Lacking a partner or any relative with whom to share the accrued wealth, this person labors without end and without contentment. This theme will be developed more fully in 5:10–6:9. Then this "workaholic" is stopped short by the obvious question: why am I working so hard while depriving myself of any enjoyment? This makes no sense and turns work into a "miserable business." Companionship is preferable to isolation, for partners can share together in the fruits of their labors. The author then expands on the benefits of companionship in 4:10–12. These verses are not to be viewed as an independent section, since they lack the key elements of the other subunits (i.e., "I saw," a

"better" saying). Despite the popularity of these verses as a wedding text, they refer rather to one's needs during a journey: assistance after falling (4:10), warmth when sleeping (4:11), and backup when attacked (4:12). The concluding proverb about "a cord of three strands" can be traced back to ancient Sumer.

4:13–16. The fourth subunit begins uniquely with a better-than saying, which introduces the evaluative comparison between two successive monarchs (4:13–14). King 1 is old but unexpectedly foolish, no longer receptive to corrective advice. King 2 is still a youth and of ignoble birth but nevertheless wise and therefore "better." The Hebrew word for "poor" in verse 13 and 9:15–16 refers to one's lowly social status (i.e., a commoner) rather than to one's financial situation. King 2 was born into poverty in King 1's kingdom and rose to power after being imprisoned. The NIV's "hypothetical" translation in verse 14 ("may have come . . . may have been") is unnecessary; a concrete chronological sequence of monarchs is being described here. Commentators both ancient and modern have sought to identify these individuals with Old Testament figures such as the Pharaoh and Joseph or various Hellenistic rulers, but none sufficiently fit these details. Qoheleth gives special attention to the fickleness of their subjects in verses 15–16. The masses (literally "all the people he was before," i.e., whom he led, as in Num. 27:17) thronged to the side of youthful King 2 when he replaced King 1. Unfortunately, those of the next generation of subjects "were not pleased" (or "may not be pleased") with King 2, for the crowd's adulation quickly dies out, regardless of how one governs.

D. Warnings against wrong attitudes toward God and government (5:1–9). Ecclesiastes 5:1–9 offers an interlude before Qoheleth concludes his investigation of life under the sun. This section is distinct from the one that immediately precedes it, as indicated by the repeated references to God, the dominance of imperative verb forms, and the complete absence of first-person verb forms. Here for the first time in the book, the author directly addresses the reader. This section, addressing one's attitude toward God (5:1–7) and government (5:8–9), in its context may serve to warn against rash responses to the preceding observations of the incongruities and injustices of life under the sun.

In 5:1–7, the author cautions the reader to exercise restraint in various cultic activities, particularly while making vows that involve subsequent voluntary offerings. The occasion is not specified, although vows in the Old Testament often involve leveraging divine protection and favor. (See, for example, Gen. 28:20–22; Judg. 11:30–31; 1 Sam. 1:11; and 2 Sam. 15:7–8; wisdom literature seldom addresses such matters.) This section is framed by positive charges (5:1, 7), while four negative admonitions dominate verses 2–6. Whenever you head for the temple, Qoheleth tells the worshiper, you should draw near (a technical cultic term) in order to *listen* to God rather than to *tell* him something. Otherwise, you will "offer the sacrifice of fools," probably referring here to excessive words uttered before God (5:2–3, 7). Such foolish words have their source in a foolish heart (5:2; cf. Matt. 12:34). Folly in the Old Testament is a moral category with a cognitive dimension; such individuals are ignorant and thus do wrong. These instructions reflect Qoheleth's conclusion in chapter 3 regarding discerning the proper time: it can be just as harmful to act too hastily (5:2) as to act too slowly (5:4). Verse 2 emphasizes the *difference* rather than the *distance* between God and humans. Our words directed toward God should be kept to a minimum not because they are futile but because they should be sincere and weighty. Just as multiplied concerns spawn dreams, so verbosity results in foolish speech (5:3), both of these by-products being equally insubstantial (Hebrew *hebel*, 5:7a). Verses 4–6 are verbally dependent on the Mosaic legislation in Deuteronomy 23:21–23 regulating vows. A shocking sequence of consequences can follow a voluntary but legally binding rash pledge: divine displeasure (5:4), sin, divine wrath, and divine judgment (all in 5:6). Telling the temple

messenger who comes to collect the promised sacrifice (cf. Mal. 1:13–14) that such a vow was "a mistake" (Hebrew *shegagah*; cf. 10:5; Num. 15:25) is an attempt to downplay it as an "inadvertent" sin. Such an excuse is excluded by this explicit warning, and a deep reverence for God (5:7b) will avert such a cultic disaster (cf. Lev. 19:5–8).

Ecclesiastes 5:8–9 is probably the most difficult passage in the book to interpret. It is loosely linked with verses 1–7 by the reference to a "higher" authority and by the negative admonition in verse 8. Verse 8 takes up the theme of injustice and oppression again (cf. Eccles. 3:16; 4:1). Upon observing the blatant deprivation of human rights, one should not be stunned or appalled by this "activity" (NIV "such things"; Hebrew *hepets*, as in Eccles. 3:1). The NIV's "be surprised" is too weak a translation for the Hebrew verb here. The reason for this admonition is literally that "a high one is keeping watch over a high one, and high ones over them." If one views the author's basic attitude toward government as positive, this statement could be taken as pointing to the benefits of hierarchical levels of jurisdiction, especially if one takes the plural as a superlative (i.e., the highest one, God). "Do not be upset—other officials are keeping an eye on the situation!" Or, more cynically, it could be understood as retorting, "What do you expect, when every bureaucrat is protecting another?" The Hebrew word used here for "district" is taken by some as a certain indicator of the book's late date of composition, since in Nehemiah and Esther the same term frequently designates the Persian satraps. But the term also occurs in 1 Kings 20:14, 15, 17, and 19, referring to provincial commanders in the time of Elijah.

The wording of verse 9 is even more ambiguous. The fact that it begins with the key Hebrew word *yitron* ("profit") suggests that it is making a positive rather than a negative assertion. Literally, it claims: "But a profit of a land in all is this: a king served by a field (or: a king for a tilled field)." The latter option fits better with the book's overall treatment of the theme (esp. in chap. 8). Despite potential abuses of power, human government is a God-ordained and beneficial institution.

E. Wealth (5:10–6:9). Qoheleth concludes his examination of foundational human activities with an extensive and highly structured analysis of wealth. This section can be subdivided into three distinct scenarios involving wealth on the basis of the threefold use of "I saw" (5:13; 5:18; 6:1) as well as the striking verbal and conceptual parallels between 5:10–12 and 6:7–9. Two negative portraits (5:13–17; 6:1–6) frame a positive one (5:18–20). These three observations are in turn framed by an introduction and a conclusion (5:10–12; 6:7–9), which state the basic inadequacy of riches for providing lasting "gain." In sum, they do not last and also cause problems. This section offers a clear example of the misleading nature of the biblical chapter divisions and also illustrates the author's pattern of touching on

These gold plaques are part of the four hundred gold, silver, bronze, and stone jewelry items found in a ceramic jug under the floor of a house at Beth Shemesh (thirteenth century BC). This cache of valuables has long outlived its owner, demonstrating Qoheleth's point that just as everyone comes into the world empty-handed, "so they depart" (Eccles. 5:15).

a topic briefly at one point in the book (e.g., 4:4–9) and then treating it more fully later.

5:10–12. The introduction begins with a proverb: whoever loves money (and lots of it) will never find lasting satisfaction therein (5:10), because an increase in one's goods attracts more consumers. As a result, the owner watches wealth vanish, with minimal personal benefit (5:10–11). Furthermore, wealth can deprive its owner of sleep (cf. Eccles. 2:23; 8:16), whether due to an overly rich meal (NASB "full stomach") or the fear of a sudden financial reversal. Such problems do not plague the simple laborer (5:12).

5:13–17. The first scenario continues this negative portrayal, offering minimal details and thus facilitating a broader application. Hoarded wealth can harm its owner, perhaps through distorting values and lifestyle, leading either to decadence or to miserly self-deprivation (5:13). Verse 17 along with 4:8 may support the latter interpretation, in describing life as lived "in the dark" (contrasted with light in Eccles. 2:13; 11:7–8), plagued by psychological, physical, and emotional pain (cf. Eccles. 2:23).

Wealth also can be easily lost. The Hebrew expression for "some misfortune" (also in 1:13; 4:8) may refer here to a "bad investment" (NASB; cf. NJPS: "unlucky venture") or some other sudden reversal of fortune (5:14a). Having lost all, this person is left as bereft of possessions (literally "naked"; Job makes a nearly identical claim in Job 1:21) as at birth and "empty-handed," despite strenuous labor, with nothing to pass on to an heir (5:14b–15). This leads the author to a related thought, a second "grievous evil" (5:16; cf. 5:13), namely, that *all* individuals end up departing as "naked" as when they arrived in this world. They can achieve no lasting "gain," since they are, in effect, toiling "for the wind" (5:16).

5:18–20. The second scenario stands in stark contrast to the empty existence just sketched. Verses 18–20 describe wealth enjoyed through divine enablement; God is mentioned four times in these verses. The NASB captures the tone of the introductory phrase better than the NIV: "Here is what I have seen to be good and fitting" (the Hebrew word for "fitting" is also used in 3:11 [NIV "beautiful"]). For the fourth time in the book, eating, drinking, and "finding satisfaction" in one's work (literally "seeing good") during this brief life is commended. In this context, the sage clarifies that God's gift extends beyond wealth and possessions to the ability to partake of food, to accept one's lot, to enjoy one's work, and even to avoid hyperfocusing on the brevity and difficulties of life. The closing claim that "God keeps him occupied with gladness of heart" should be understood as a strong affirmation of the value of life, despite everything, rather than as a cynical concession that such gladness merely provides a brief distraction.

6:1–6. The final scenario, which presents another weighty "evil" (cf. Eccles. 8:6) that Qoheleth has observed, is closely linked to the preceding unit. Here too God grants an individual the ability to achieve wealth, possessions, and the resultant deference (as Solomon himself enjoyed, according to 2 Chron. 1:1–2), in principle supplying everything one could possibly desire. But, in this case, God prevents this individual from benefiting (literally "eating") from these goods. Instead, God allows an outsider rather than another family member to consume them (6:2), as previously envisioned in Ecclesiastes 2:26—the height of futility! In verses 3–6, the situation is intensified. The individual whose appetite (or "soul") is not satisfied by that which is good (6:3; cf. 6:6) is so miserable that even the hyperbolic experience of prime Israelite blessings (i.e., fathering one hundred children, 6:3, and living for two thousand years, 6:6), cannot compensate for this lack. Stating it extremely, not being born in the first place would be preferable, like a stillborn child that in its fleeting (Hebrew *hebel*) and obscure existence misses much but also is spared much (cf. Eccles. 4:2–3). The mention in verse 3 of being deprived of a proper burial is somewhat puzzling. One possibility is to relate this to the stillborn: "then even without a burial, I say the stillborn is better off . . ." (so Murphy, 45; similarly NJPS; cf. Job 3:16). Alternately, the

once wealthy and respected person of verse 2 is presented as being deprived of even the final honor of burial (compare Jer. 22:19) and thus failing to enter into rest, in contrast with the stillborn (6:5). Ultimately all are headed for the same destiny of death (6:6; cf. 3:20).

6:7–9. The conclusion parallels the introduction (5:10–12). All human efforts simply serve to fill the mouth, but they cannot satisfy the appetite (6:7; cf. 5:10). Verse 8 fits somewhat awkwardly between verses 7 and 9, though it parallels 5:11b in its formulation. In context, if wealth ultimately cannot satisfy, then the wise are no better off *in this respect* than the fool, nor is the poor person who has learned the proper conduct for societal survival. Better is "what the eye sees" as a present possession (i.e., a bird in the hand) than "the roving of the appetite" (i.e., two in the bush, 6:9a). Being content with what one has is a gain, while pursuing satisfaction through further acquisition is futile. The final occurrence in the book of the phrase "a chasing after the wind" concludes its first major subdivision.

3. Positive Attitudes in the Light of Injustice and Uncertainty (6:10–10:20)

After examining the major areas of life in his quest for lasting—or even limited—gain, Qoheleth proceeds in the second major section of the book (6:10–10:20) to inculcate positive attitudes regarding "how should we then live," a foundational query of Francis Schaeffer. This presents a special challenge in a world marked by "transience" (Fredericks's translation of *hebel*) and uncertainty and marred by injustice. In particular, the author is intent on clarifying the contributions and limitations of wisdom in this endeavor. This shift in purpose is marked by the increased use of imperative verb forms, which, apart from 5:1–9, are completely absent from the first major section. In addition, the repeated use of the phrases "cannot know" and "cannot find out" replaces "chasing after the wind." In the process, Qoheleth addresses the problems posed by God's "twisting" of the times, such as bad things happening to good people, bad government, the inescapability of death, and the limited benefits of godly or wise behavior.

A. Recognize that bad days can bring about good (6:10–7:14). Qoheleth seeks to demonstrate in this first subsection that seemingly "bad" days can bring about good.

6:10–12. Properly speaking, these verses are transitional, serving to summarize one section and introduce (or frame, with the parallel verses 7:13–14) the next. Ecclesiastes 6:10 marks the middle verse of the book, as indicated by the masoretic editors. Here the author sets forth some basic assertions: (1) The world is unchangeable (6:10a; cf. 1:9; 3:15). (2) The limitations of human beings are well known, namely that one cannot successfully contend with God, who is mightier, as Job also learned (6:10b–11). Since multiplying words before him only serves to increase their vacuity, nothing can be gained thereby (similarly Eccles. 5:3, 7). (3) Disputing God's actions is not only futile but also senseless, since one possesses insufficient knowledge of what is truly good for a person during their short life span, which passes as quickly as a shadow (6:12a, cf. Job 14:2). That is because no one can offer reliable information regarding the shape of future events (6:12b), regardless of whether the word "after" here refers to one's immediate (7:14) or *postmortem* (3:22) future.

7:1–12. The general nature of the rhetorical question in 6:12 ("Who knows what is good for a man in life?") becomes apparent in this central section of the unit. Here the author employs a series of traditional proverbs in order to affirm, somewhat ironically, nine things that are good or better (all with Hebrew *tob*), many of which initially appear to be undesirable. The major emphasis here is that *wisdom* can be acquired or augmented in the hard times of life. The Hebrew root for wisdom occurs seven times in these verses. The initial proverb (7:1a), which uses a wordplay to tout the superiority of a good name (Hebrew *shem*) over a good perfume (Hebrew *shemen*), could have a number of applications. For example, following 5:10–6:9, it could affirm the superiority of character to wealth, as in Proverbs 22:1. Linked to 7:1b–4, however, the verse most likely refers to one's reputation at death and the aromatic oil used in preparing a corpse for burial. A good name makes a more lasting impression than a good smell. Similarly, the sorrowful reflection on death at a funeral is better for the "heart" (four times in 7:2–4) than the levity of a birthday celebration. This is because the former makes a deeper impact, as people are confronted thereby with their own

The sarcophagus portrayed here has a perfume cone on the top of its head, representing the "fine perfume" (Eccles. 7:1) or aromatic oils associated with preparing bodies for burial or the afterlife (Book of the Dead, ca. 1391–1353 BC).

mortality. Additional difficult lessons can be learned, for example, through preferring a sage's painful rebuke to the frivolous and perhaps flattering song of fools (7:5). Verse 6 explains the inferiority of the latter: a fool's levity is as noisy and useless as thorns (Hebrew *hassirim*) used for fuel under a cooking pot (Hebrew *hassir*, another wordplay), for both soon fade away (Hebrew *hebel*).

Such hard-won insights, unfortunately, are constantly at risk (7:7–10). Oppression (as in Eccles. 4:1; 5:8, contra NIV's "extortion") can drive even a wise person mad, while a bribing gift can destroy the core of one's being (literally "heart"). Perseverance and patience are to be valued over pride (literally "better long of spirit than high of spirit"), hasty and persistent reactions to provocation, and plaintive comparisons (7:8–10). Verses 11–12, which conclude the central section by comparing wisdom and wealth, support the possibility that verse 1a may continue the main theme of 5:10–6:9. Both wisdom and inherited property are beneficial, providing protective "shelter" for their owner, but sagacity is superior in its ability to preserve life, as affirmed in numerous proverbs.

7:13–14. These concluding verses parallel the introductory verses (6:10–12) and are dominated by three positive imperatives, beginning with "Consider [literally "see"] the work of God!" (KJV). Alluding to the reminder that humans are not *able* to contend with the superior strength of God in 6:10b, the author asks in 7:13: "Who is *able* to straighten what he has made crooked?" Here the author takes up the proverb of Ecclesiastes 1:15 and ascribes this "twisting action" to God. Humans cannot change what God has ordained. So Qoheleth charges us, in pleasant times, to enjoy them and, in unpleasant times, to reflect on the fact (literally "see") that both good and bad days come from God and serve *his* sovereign purposes, although we as humans cannot find out anything about the future (7:14).

B. Recognize that righteousness and wisdom offer only limited protection (7:15–29). This unit can be clearly distinguished in style from the preceding unit. First-person verbs detailing Qoheleth's investigative procedure, as well as his discoveries, structure 7:15–29 but are absent from 6:10–7:14. Note the following examples: "I have seen" (7:15), "all this I tested by wisdom and I said" (7:23; cf. 1:13), "so I turned my mind to understand" (7:25), "I find" (7:26), "this is what I have discovered" (7:27), "I found" (7:28), "this only have I found" (7:29). Furthermore, in this section the focus is on the righteous person (Hebrew *tsaddiq*) for the first time (7:15, 16, 20). The question at issue is how wisdom literature's prominent "retribution doctrine" that righteousness (as well as wisdom) is richly rewarded while wickedness (as well as folly) is punished (e.g., Prov. 10:3, 7, 16, 24–25, 30) can be squared with one's everyday observations.

7:15–19. Qoheleth begins by citing two contrary examples: a righteous man who perishes (prematurely) in his righteousness and a wicked man who lives long in his wickedness. The Hebrew preposition translated here as "in" could be understood either as "in spite of" or "due to"; either way the jarring observation stands (7:15). This apparent injustice prompts some rather pagan-sounding advice: do not be overrighteous, overwise, overwicked, or a fool (7:16–17). According to some interpreters, this constitutes a recommendation of moderation in all things, "the golden mean," as if a little godlessness is perfectly acceptable as long as one does not attract God's attention! Although numerous suggestions have been made, a contextually plausible solution may be to see here a presentation of varying *degrees* of righteousness: relative (7:15), pretentious (7:16), and absolute (7:20).

Several linguistic clues support this interpretation: (1) Nowhere else in the Hebrew Bible does a form of "to be" (Hebrew *hayah*) occur with "righteous" as a command or exhortation (cf. Ezek. 18:5). Usually, "being" righteous is expressed in Hebrew simply through a verbal form of the root *tsdq* (e.g., Job 9:2, 15, 20). (2) The verb form of the word translated "be overwise" can, in some constructions, mean "to pretend to be," most notably in Numbers 16:3 (to lord it over; i.e., act like a chief), 1 Samuel 21:14–15 (to pretend to be crazy), and 2 Samuel 13:5–6 (to feign illness). Conversely, the similar formulation of the parallel admonitions in verse 17 weakens this grammatical evidence: Do not act wickedly overmuch (cf. "*over*righteous"); do not "be [Hebrew *hayah*; cf. Prov. 3:7] a fool!" The explanation for this is perhaps to be found in the parallel questions that conclude verses 16–17. On the one hand, the person who seeks to exhibit exaggerated righteousness and wisdom in order to avoid a fate similar to that of the righteous person of verse 15 will be in for a big shock. The NIV's "destroy yourself" is too strong here (cf. Isa. 59:16; 63:5, which use the same verbal form). On the other hand, the one who concludes that divine justice is blind and thus plunges headlong into ungodly and foolish behavior may end up dying prematurely (literally "before [his] time," contrast Eccles. 3:2). Therefore, the author concludes (7:18) that the God-fearer will take hold of both warnings (7:16a, 17a), thereby escaping both fates (7:16b, 17b, rather than NIV's "avoid all extremes"). Proverbially speaking (7:19), acting wisely in such a situation offers a person more protection than a city council, as will be illustrated more fully in 9:13–18.

7:20–24. The following verses continue to develop the theme by conceding that no one is completely righteous (7:20–22) or wise (7:23–24). Accordingly, how righteous does one have to be before claiming to be treated unjustly by God? There is no one who never sins (7:20), especially in speech (7:21–22). A similar acknowledgment is made in Solomon's prayer in 1 Kings 8:46 // 2 Chronicles 6:36 and in Proverbs 20:9. "Cursing" here (Hebrew *qillel*) may have the weaker sense of merely denigrating or insulting someone. It is possible to understand verses 23–29 as constituting a new subsection that focuses on wisdom. "All this" in verse 23 probably refers backward to the preceding observations and deliberations in 7:15–22 rather

than forward. In seeking the depth of wisdom necessary to comprehend such matters, he falls far short of his goal. This is because "what is" or "what has been" (NIV "whatever exists") under the sun is "far off and most profound" and thus beyond human discovery (7:24).

7:25–29. This leads to a more modest search. These verses use the Hebrew word for "seek" three times (7:25, 28, 29; NIV "search"), for "discover/find" seven times (26, 27 [2×], 28 [3×], 29), and for "scheme [of things]" three times (7:25, 27, 29). The third word is a mathematical term, literally "calculation" (NASB "explanation"). In his quest for a wise explanation and his effort to "understand the stupidity of wickedness and the madness of folly" (7:25), Qoheleth makes three discoveries:

1. Wicked and foolish women are dangerous, even life-threatening, but one can escape their snare (7:26). This verse echoes the descriptions of the adulteress and Lady Folly in Proverbs 2:16–19; 5:3–6; 7:5–23; and 9:13–18, but it certainly does not refer to all women (cf. Eccles. 9:9).

2. In this world, things just do not "add up" (7:27–28a). Exemplary human beings (Hebrew *adam*, not *ish*, "male"), for example, in their righteousness and wisdom, are extremely rare, only one in a thousand. Qoheleth's reported failure to find the woman he was seeking (7:28b) sounds rather misogynistic, but it is not necessarily normative or expressing a blanket condemnation of the female gender. Possible explanations include that this conclusion reflects Solomon's personal experience (after seven hundred wives and three hundred concubines, 1 Kings 11:3!), the preceding reference to the foolish woman in verse 26, or Eve's role in the fall, according to Genesis 3 (in light of the possible reference to it in 7:29). An intriguing alternative noted by Michael Fox is that "Qoheleth could *understand* one man in a thousand but not a single woman" (Fox, 271).

3. God did not make humans this way. The author concludes with his most significant discovery or "explanation" ("This only have I

found," 7:29), drawing again on Genesis 1–3. Although originally created morally "upright" (cf. Prov. 20:11; 21:8), individuals soon sought out "many schemes." Alternatively, the repetition here of two key words from the opening verse of this subsection ("search" and "scheme," 7:25) may merely express his intellectual resignation: "they have engaged in too much reasoning" (so NJPS). If one understands 7:15–29 as basically constituting a coherent discourse unit, then the former interpretation is more likely.

C. Recognize that one must submit to the government despite injustice (8:1–17). In chapter 8, Qoheleth takes up the topic of the role of government and judicial authority, especially in relationship to "evil" (the Hebrew root for "evil" occurs seven times in Ecclesiastes 8). This section is remarkably similar in some of its perspectives to Romans 13, though not necessarily Paul's source. Both texts note the theological basis as well as the personal benefits of submission to authority, although Ecclesiastes 8 focuses more on the latter than Romans 13. Here the author addresses more fully how the wise person should relate to authority that is sometimes used to perpetrate rather than punish injustice (cf. Eccles. 3:16–17; 4:1–3, 13–16; 5:8–9). This unit is framed by brief reflections on wisdom (8:1, 16–17) that link it to what precedes and follows.

8:1. Following the failed quest for wisdom related in 7:23 and the previous use of the who question in the book (cf. Eccles. 2:25; 3:21–22; 6:12; 7:13, 24), one expects a negative response to the questions in verse 1a: No one is truly wise or understands such things. Verse 1b, however, suggests a more modest but positive claim: the wise are remarkable, being able to interpret sayings such as the following proverb about wisdom's transformative effect on a person (cf. Job 29:24; Prov. 21:29).

8:2–15. The section can be divided into two parts. Verses 2–8 urge and offer a rationale for allegiance to the monarch, while verses 9–15 set forth Qoheleth's personal observations and reflections on justice. The positive injunction to carry out the king's command (8:2a) is followed

by two related negative admonitions in verse 3a. First, do not withdraw hastily from his presence. This refers to leaving his service, as in Ecclesiastes 10:4, rather than simply violating court protocol. Second, do not stand up for (i.e., participate or persist in) a bad cause (literally "a bad matter"; NJPS "a dangerous situation," also in 8:5a), such as an insurrection. These instructions are reinforced in 8:5a, while the remaining verses offer a threefold rationale: (1) due to the loyalty oath taken by the subject before God (8:1b), (2) due to the monarch's superior position and power (8:3b–4), and (3) in order to stay out of harm's way (8:5). The phrase "time and procedure" in verses 5b–6a should be taken as a hendiadys (two words representing a single concept; here, "a judgment-time"), since verse 6a echoes 3:1 and 3:17. The development of thought in verses 6–8 is somewhat unclear, but the repetition of the Hebrew root for "have power" in verses 4, 8 (twice), and 9 suggests a thematic connection. Misery weighs heavily on the wise (8:6b) in part because they know neither what will happen to change things nor when it will occur (8:7). Rather than taking matters into their own hands, however, the wise will wait for the appointed time of judgment to arrive (8:5). Then the powerful ones (8:4) will finally meet their match. The king cannot exert authority over the wind (or over his spirit, Hebrew *ruah*, possibly a deliberate wordplay) or over his death. Moreover, just as no one is exempted from duty in wartime, so wickedness will not free its perpetrators from the consequences of their actions (8:8).

The related theme of injustice is developed in verses 9–15 through personal observations. Verse 9 is transitional, summarizing verses 2–8 ("All this I saw," cf. Eccles. 7:23) as "a time when a man lords it over others to *their* hurt." This follows the NIV's footnote and is contextually preferable to the NIV's "his own," despite verse 8b and 5:13. "Then too" (in such a situation), he observes a disturbing inequity, the exact details of which are difficult to translate (8:10). This is complicated by the presence of a well-attested ancient textual variant. The NIV follows the variant: godless and sacrilegious individuals *"receive praise"* and a proper burial. The other reading, which probably is preferable, offers a contrast: the wicked are buried, "while such as acted righteously [the same Hebrew verb as used in 2 Kings 7:9] *are forgotten* in the city" (so NJPS), perhaps implying that they are deprived of a similar burial. Not only do the wicked seem to escape punishment (8:10), but the delayed execution of sentences for crimes also prompts others to perpetrate evil (8:11). Despite observing that prolific sinners often still live a long life (8:12a), Qoheleth reaffirms his core theological conviction that those who fear God will *ultimately* be better off than the godless (8:12b–13). Now, however, just the opposite occurs, as Job also repeatedly complains, with righteous individuals apparently receiving what the wicked deserve and vice versa (8:14, expanding on 7:15). Verse 14 begins and ends by labeling this state of affairs as *hebel*, "meaningless," for it temporarily makes godly living seem senseless. Somewhat surprisingly, Qoheleth concludes this consideration of long-delayed justice with his familiar commendation of the enjoyment of life (8:15). Since we can neither avoid suffering injustice nor expedite divine judgment, we might as well seek those sources of happiness that can sweeten ("accompany") our labor under the sun.

8:16–17. These verses are transitional, describing the ongoing quest for wisdom, which is also mentioned in verse 1. The formulation of verse 16 closely parallels verse 9, while verse 17 echoes 7:23–29 in its repeated references to seeking and not finding. The author concludes that, although one can investigate God's work thoroughly, one cannot fully comprehend what occurs on earth, despite strenuous efforts and exaggerated claims. What remains opaque, in particular, is the relationship between our own stressful work and God's sovereign work.

D. Recognize that, in the light of death, one must redeem the time (9:1–10). Chapters 9–10 of Ecclesiastes address the subjects of how one

should live in light of the certainty of death and in light of the theoretical and practical limits of wisdom. The exact demarcation of these respective sections is less clear. Ecclesiastes 8:16–17 could serve as the introduction to 9:1–10, and 9:11–12 could be taken as addressing either the first or the second topic. Verse 11 refers to the wise, while verse 12 may refer to death, and the use of first-person verbs in chapter 9 (vv. 1, 11, 13, 16) is inconclusive.

As in Ecclesiastes 7:23 and 8:9, commentators are not unified regarding whether "all this" (twice in 9:1) points backward or forward. The NIV translation here paraphrases a difficult Hebrew text; the remainder of verse 1 could express the *goal* rather than the *result* of his examination. In light of his preceding observations regarding injustice under the sun, Qoheleth affirms that the requiting of the deeds of both the righteous and the wicked is in God's sovereign control. Love and hate could be a merism (as in Eccles. 3:8), expressing the full range of emotions that may motivate one's actions, probably human rather than divine (as in 9:6). These emotions are associated exclusively with humans in the book (Eccles. 2:17–18; 3:8; 5:10; 9:9). How a specific person will be treated by others and treat others remains unknown, for both those classified as "good" and those labeled "bad" share common experiences under the sun, as well as the common destiny of death (9:2, as in 2:14–15; 3:19).

What is crucial, then, is how one responds to the universal fact of death (9:3–6). How sad it is when the human heart is dominated by evil and folly throughout life, and afterward one simply joins the dead (9:3). But where there is life, there is hope, whether you are a wretch (i.e., dog) or a royal (i.e., lion). The NIV's "is among" and alternative "be chosen" reflect two ancient variant readings. The author's claim elsewhere that death is preferable to life (cf. Eccles. 4:2; 6:3) must be tempered in light of his comments here and in the following verses, though the exact content of this "hope" (or "confidence," as in 2 Kings 18:19) is unspecified. Verses 5–6 contrast the living and the dead, describing the latter as having no further participation or portion in life under the sun and being forgotten (cf. Eccles. 1:11; 2:16). Here it should be kept in mind that this is not the only statement in the Old Testament—or in Ecclesiastes—about what follows death.

While the dead know (or experience) nothing, the living know that they will die (9:5), which, according to Ecclesiastes 7:1–4, can have a profound effect on how the *wise* live. Thus Qoheleth concludes his deliberations on death with his final climactic commendation of joy, only here expressed as an imperatival charge (9:7–9): eat and drink with a merry heart! Celebrate life continuously with "party clothes" and rich oils (Ps. 23:5; 104:15; Esther 8:15; also Epic of Gilgamesh, Tablet 10)! Share this joy with your marriage partner! This is not a license for unbounded self-indulgence (cf. also Eccles. 11:9), for it is balanced by a call to strenuous, skillful, and

Ecclesiastes 9:5–6 says, "The dead know nothing; . . . even their name is forgotten." This is vividly depicted in a relief from the temple of Hatshepsut at Karnak. The chiseled marks to the left of the god Horus show where the figure of Hatshepsut was erased by her successor Thutmosis III so her memory would be forgotten.

smart work (9:10). What is the basis for such advice? (1) Such a course of action bears God's stamp of approval, since it is his gift (9:7b; cf. 3:13; 5:19), our lot in life, and the reward for our labor (9:9b). (2) Our opportunities for both

work and pleasure under the sun are limited. Our days are *hebel*, and we all are headed for the realm of the dead (i.e., Sheol, 9:9a, 10b).

E. One should embrace wisdom and avoid folly (9:11–10:20). If one understands "his hour" and "evil times" (literally "his time," "bad time") in 9:12 as referring to death (as in 7:17), then one can view 9:11–12 as the conclusion of the discourse on death. It is preferable, however, to view these verses as the introduction to the following section on the benefits of wisdom in contrast with folly. This chapter strongly resembles the book of Proverbs in both form and content and is more loosely organized than the rest of Ecclesiastes.

9:11–10:1. Qoheleth begins by noting some of wisdom's limitations, introducing them with "I saw" (9:11, 13). First, success in various human activities, such as victory, wealth, or social favor, is not guaranteed either by physical skill, such as speed and strength, or by mental prowess (using three wisdom terms). This is because "time and chance," a hendiadys designating unexpected events, can happen to anyone (9:11). Since even death (i.e., "his time") can approach without warning, catastrophe can strike as suddenly as a fishnet or a bird trap captures its unsuspecting prey (9:12).

Second, wisdom can be unappreciated. Verses 13–15 present a brief scenario that features another "wise commoner" (as in Eccles. 4:13–16). That individual single-handedly delivered his small city when it was besieged by a powerful and well-equipped king. Sadly, no one later remembered his contribution, presumably by rewarding or promoting him (cf. Eccles. 2:16). This interpretation is preferable to seeing here merely a *potential* delivery, through "remembering" during the crisis that such a capable person lived there. Verses 16–17 draw some conclusions from this situation. Although wisdom is superior to military might, some wise people are despised and their words not heeded (9:16), even though their calm counsel is more worthy of attention than the shouts of a ruler of fools (9:17). Ecclesiastes 9:18–10:1 notes a third limitation, that despite wisdom's superiority (9:18a parallels 9:16a), a single sinner can destroy much that is beneficial. The NIV's "sinner" correctly renders the Hebrew participle *hote* (cf. 2:26; 7:26; 8:12; and 9:2) and is preferable to NRSV's "bungler" and NJPS's "error." This limitation is vividly reinforced by the proverb in 10:1. Just as a few dead flies can cause the finest perfume to stink and ooze, so a little folly, which wisdom theology equates with sin and godlessness, can overpower an impressive display of wisdom.

10:2–20. The exposition of wisdom's limitations in 9:11–10:1 as contingent, unappreciated, and fragile could lead to the conclusion that it is not such a valuable commodity after all. This section continues, however, by focusing instead on fools and folly, sometimes in contrast to the wise and wisdom. It is somewhat arbitrary to separate verses 2–20 from the preceding, especially since their unity largely consists of their common theme.

First-person verbs occur in 10:5 and 10:7, just as in 9:11 and 9:13, and both 10:1 and 10:2 offer direct comparisons. The subsection begins with a general characterization of the

fool. Fools suffer from a congenital heart defect, a flaw at the very center of their being, which skews all of their actions and attitudes (10:2). (Contrary to contemporary practice, right and left are seldom contrasted in the Old Testament [but see Gen. 48:13–14, 17–20].) The resultant ineptitude is set forth in verse 3 (cf. 10:15): in performing everyday tasks, fools lack "sense" (literally "heart," cf. Prov. 10:21), broadcasting their folly to all (cf. Prov. 12:23).

In 10:4–7 and 16–20, folly in high places is portrayed: verses 4–7 begin with an admonition directed to the wise (10:4), while verses 16–20 end with one (10:20). If a ruler is angry with you, do not act rashly (10:4; cf. 8:2), for your calmness may help him to avoid committing great sins (as Prov. 29:22 also acknowledges). The NIV, in translating the Hebrew root *hata* (cf. 9:18) as "errors" rather than "sins" (only here of almost six hundred Old Testament occurrences), takes this word as referring instead to the *cause* of the ruler's anger (as in Prov. 10:12). The former interpretation is supported by verse 5: Qoheleth has observed the type of "evil" or harmful "error" (here *shegagah*, as in Eccles. 5:6) that powerful leaders can promote. Social structures are turned upside down, with fools and servants being promoted and wealthy leaders and princes demoted (10:6–7). The Egyptian Admonitions of Ipu-wer contain similar descriptions. That "the rich" are contrasted here with fools suggests that these may be those who enjoy the fruits of divine favor, wisdom, and diligence (cf. Eccles. 5:19; Prov. 8:18, 21; 10:4, 22; 14:24).

The contrast between the wise and the foolish is taken up again in 10:8–15. Verses 8–9 describe four workplace injuries, while verses 10–11 explain how two of these, a woodcutting injury and a snake bite (the fourth and the second), can be prevented through the timely use of wisdom, as expressed in the NASB ("Wisdom has the *advantage* of giving success"; Hebrew *yitron* is also used in 10:11: "no *profit*"). The wise person sharpens the ax blade *before* chopping and charms the snake *before* it strikes. By implication, the fool instead relies on "brawn over brains" and gets bit. Verses 12–14 describe the fool's speech. Unlike the gracious words of the wise, which can benefit both the speaker (cf. Prov. 22:11), probably the emphasis here, and the listeners (cf. Prov. 25:11–13), the fool's lips harm the speaker (10:12, literally "swallow him up"). This is not surprising, since their words go from bad to worse (10:13), as their verbal stream flows unabated (10:14a; cf. 5:3, 7) despite a lack of certain knowledge (10:14b, echoing 6:12 and 8:7). No wonder the fools' work is tiring: they wear themselves out in carrying out the simplest of tasks, such as finding the way to town (10:15; cf. 10:3)!

The section concludes with a further description of folly in high places (10:16–20). Verses 16–19 contrast two countries. One is ruled by those ill prepared for such a task (10:16a), either due to youthful inexperience or, more likely, low social status. Thus the NIV's "servant" for Hebrew *naar*, contrasted with one "of noble birth" in verse 17, is preferable to the NIV's alternative "child," as in 1 Kings 3:7 and Isaiah 3:4–5. This country's leaders put pleasure before business (10:16b). Proverbially speaking, they carelessly allow the place to get run down (10:18), while living out the self-indulgent motto expressed in verse 19. The other, more fortunate, country is ruled by a king who is well prepared for that role and by leaders who limit eating to its proper time (as in Eccles. 3:1) and purpose ("for strength," 10:17). The subsection concludes with another warning, perhaps prompted by the preceding portrait of administrative failure (10:20; cf. 10:4; 5:8; 8:3). Since nothing is to be gained thereby, avoid cursing or denigrating (Hebrew *qillel*, as in Eccles. 7:21–22) the all-powerful king even in your thoughts (contra NASB's "bedchamber," which imposes synonymy), since such thoughts may ultimately find expression in words. You may think you are safe from the influential rich in the privacy of your bedroom, but be careful—the room may be bugged (or birded)!

4. Final Charge (11:1–12:7)

The book of Ecclesiastes climaxes in a lengthy section dominated by imperative verbs (11:1, 2, 6, 8–10; 12:1; "Remember" in 12:6 is added by the NIV for the sake of clarity).

Here the author issues his final challenge to the reader, addressing three major topics, which Derek Kidner (96) succinctly summarizes as "Be bold!" (11:1–6), "Be joyful!" (11:7–10), and "Be godly!" (12:1–7). Several repeated words serve to link these three subunits: disaster/trouble(s) (11:2, 10; 12:1 [all the same Hebrew word]), clouds (11:3–4; 12:2), rain (11:3; 12:2), light (11:7; 12:2), darkness (11:8; 12:2), remember (11:8; 12:1).

A. Be bold (11:1–6). The first subunit addresses the question, how should one act when so much remains unknown or unknowable (11:2b, 5, 6b)? Some commentators take verses 1–2 as offering commercial advice: send your merchandise across the sea, expecting a profit (11:1), as Solomon did in 1 Kings 10:22 (cf. Prov. 31:14). And spread the risk, perhaps by using multiple ships, or diversify your investments, so that you will not be bankrupted by some unexpected catastrophe (11:2; cf. 5:14). In light of striking parallels in Egyptian wisdom instructions, however, these verses are more likely an encouragement to "strategic" philanthropy, as encouraged in Proverbs 19:17 and Luke 16:9. For example, the Instruction of 'Onchsheshonqy (an Egyptian wisdom tradition from ca. 200 BC) advises, "Do a good deed and throw it into the flood. / When it subsides you will find it" (Simpson, 519), and the Instruction of Ptahhotep (ca. 2200 BC) recommends, "Gratify your friends with what has come into your possession, / . . . No one knows what will come to pass when he considers tomorrow, / . . . But one can bring happiness (to) friends when there is need" (Simpson, 139). In other words, freely give away some of your goods—with hopeful patience and fearless generosity.

Verses 3–6 encourage decisive, unhesitant action despite uncertainty. Verse 3 describes

Ptahhotep II, an important Egyptian official during the 5th dynasty (ca. 2465–2325 BC) who composed the Instruction of Ptahhotep, is shown with his son in this painting from his tomb at Saqqara.

two processes of nature: rain, which is somewhat predictable, and the direction a tree falls, which is unpredictable and which humans cannot control. Constantly watching the wind that can knock down a tree or the clouds that will bring rain, while waiting for more favorable weather conditions, can keep one from either sowing or reaping (11:4). Despite our ignorance regarding such natural phenomena, we must act. The NIV distinguishes two examples in verse 5: the path of the wind (as in 11:4a; cf. John 3:8) and the formation of a fetus in a pregnant woman. But it is preferable to see here a wordplay with Hebrew *ruah* designating *wind* in verse 4 and *spirit* in verse 5. The use of this word in Ecclesiastes 8:8 is similarly ambiguous, perhaps intentionally. Thus, only one example is noted: how the life-breath (as in Eccles. 3:21; 12:7) enters a fetus. This and more fall under the rubric of the "work of God" (cf. Eccles. 7:13; 8:17). God sovereignly accomplishes all things, often in ways that are humanly unknowable, and the NIV's "the Maker" incorrectly narrows the scope of divine action here. The subunit ends with positive counsel (11:6), which parallels verse 1: Sow your seed continually and untiringly (similar to Eccles. 9:10a)—probably referring here to a wide range of human endeavors (cf. John 4:37; 1 Cor. 9:11; 2 Cor. 9:6; Gal. 6:7)—since you cannot know in advance which efforts will prosper.

B. Be joyful (11:7–10). The second subunit presents Qoheleth's final commendation of joyful living, although the typical reference to eating and drinking is lacking here. The subunit begins by affirming that it is good to be alive (11:7, literally "to see the sun"; cf. 6:5). We should enjoy the light of each day God grants us, not knowing how many we will have and keeping in mind the many dark and meaningless days to follow (11:8). The reference here is to our death, as in 6:4, rather than to difficulties during life, as in Ecclesiastes 5:17. Such unencumbered happiness is clearly more attainable when one is young and vigorous. Therefore, the author encourages the young to "follow the ways of your heart and whatever your eyes see" (11:9). This sounds like aimless self-indulgence, which disturbed rabbinic interpreters, who saw in this counsel a direct contradiction of Numbers 15:39 ("that you may . . . not prostitute yourselves by going after [the lusts of] your own hearts and eyes"; NIV adds "the lusts of"). In light of the regulative role of the heart referred to in Ecclesiastes 2:3 (cf. Prov. 16:9), the contrast made in 6:9 ("Better what the eye sees than the roving of the appetite"), and the concluding reminder in this verse that God will ultimately judge the individual on the basis of these activities, this advice is better understood as "Let your conscience be your guide and be content with what you have!" This fits better with 11:10, which encourages the young person to avoid those things that can detract either psychologically (cf. Eccles. 2:23; 5:17; 7:9) or physically (cf. Eccles. 5:13; 12:12) from the enjoyment of life, because youthful vigor (perhaps literally "dark hair") is fleeting (Hebrew *hebel*).

C. Be reverent (12:1–7). The final subsection is closely linked to the preceding. Whereas the preceding verses challenge the young to enjoy life while they can while keeping in mind the dark days to come, 12:1–7 begins by challenging them to keep God in mind while they are still young, before unpleasant days come (12:1a). As the lengthiest of the three, it offers a context for the preceding calls to decisive action and joyful living. The direct command to "remember" God is rare in the Old Testament (elsewhere only Neh. 4:14; Jer. 51:50; cf. Deut. 8:18), as is the description "your Creator" (elsewhere only Isa. 43:1). "Remember" here is a logical extension of the imperative "know" in 11:9b, while "Creator" is a fitting title for the source of life's everyday gifts, given the book's frequent allusions to the Genesis 1–3 narrative. The remainder of the text offers a threefold motivating contrast with "the days of your youth," each commencing with the word "before" (12:1b–2, 6). Verse 1b contrasts the present enjoyable days with the coming "days of trouble" (cf. "bad times," Eccles. 7:14), when life will not or no longer will be pleasing.

In 12:2 those days of light (11:7) are contrasted with gloomy cloud-shrouded days, when all celestial light sources are darkened. The description here reminds one of the cataclysmic day of the Lord, as announced by the prophets (cf. Isa. 5:30; 13:10; Ezek. 32:8; Joel 2:2, 31; Amos 5:20; Zeph. 1:15). The description of that "day" in verses 3–5, which expands on this image, indicates that the end of the individual's life is in focus here rather than the eschatological end of the world. These verses contain a partially allegorical portrayal of the debilitating effects of old age, offering a striking contrast to the youthful traits of 11:9–10. This is accomplished through the description of an estate where "business as usual" has ceased, perhaps due to the storm of verse 2 or a resident's death, as verse 5 implies. The imagery is enigmatic and its meaning, accordingly, disputed, although the basic point of the scenario is clear. Verse 3 describes the reactions of four individuals or groups, namely, the male and female owners and household servants. The male housekeepers (= arms, cf. 2 Sam. 15:16) shake, while the "strong" men (= legs, probably designating financial or character strength) bend or grow crooked. The miller maids (= molars) have become too few to grind, while the view through the windows for the ladies of leisure is obscured (= eyes, cf. Judg. 5:28; 2 Kings 9:30). The double doors to the street (= ears, possibly lips, cf. Job 41:14) are shut tight, so that outdoor noises grow faint (12:4a). On edge, one is startled by any sudden noise, such as a bird call, or one sleeps so lightly that the least sound awakens. The sound of the female singers (= voice) is made low (12:4b; cf. Isa. 29:4). According to verse 5a, one then becomes fearful of heights and unknown travel dangers, the phobias of old age. This is accompanied by the appearance of white hair (the color of almond blossoms), a limping gait (the grasshopper dragging itself along), and the loss of sexual desire (the ineffective caper, a stimulant or aphrodisiac).

An explanation of the preceding description is offered in 12:5b: humanity is heading for its eternal, or enduring, house, while paid mourners already begin their procession through the streets. Recently, the translation "dark house" has been suggested, based on one possible meaning of the Hebrew root *'lm*, the description of the dead in 6:4, and the aptness of this description for a tomb. Given the use of *olam* (from the same Hebrew root) elsewhere in the book (Eccles. 1:4, 10; 2:16; 3:11, 14; 9:6), however, a meaning for this use is more likely in 12:5. In Ecclesiastes, this word designates that which lasts in contrast with that which is only temporary. Thus understanding "eternal house" here as referring specifically either to the grave or to an eternal residence in heaven (similar to John 14:2–3) is unwarranted. This is reinforced in the third contrast set forth in verses 6–7, which begins with several images of death: a broken decorative cord with its attached bowl (perhaps an oil lamp, as in Zech. 4:2–3) and a shattered water jar and well wheel. Unlike the language of verse 3–5, verse 6 probably is not intended to be taken allegorically (i.e., anatomically). Rather, it simply emphasizes the finality, irreversibility, and destructiveness of death: the light goes out and thirst goes unquenched. The subunit concludes in verse 7 with a more literal contrast. Whereas the dust *returns* to the earth (the phrase echoes Genesis 3:19 and 2:7; cf. Job 10:9), the "spirit," or life-breath, *returns* to God, who originally issued it. This verse thus parallels Ecclesiastes 3:20–21. The reference in verse 7b to God as "giving" the human spirit (Hebrew *ruah*) recalls his description as Creator in verse 1a and offers a final rationale for "remembering" him. One should avoid reading too much into "returning to God" (despite Eccles. 5:2: "God is in heaven"), since Psalm 104:29 and

Relief showing a procession of mourners (tomb of Merymery, Saqqara, ca. 1391–1353), as described in Ecclesiastes 12:5

Job 34:14–15 speak similarly of God gathering the spirits of both animals and humans.

5. Concluding Explanatory Remarks (12:8–14)

A. Theme verse: Everything is ephemeral (12:8). The concluding remarks are preceded by the repetition of the theme verse, which affirms that everything is utterly ephemeral. The preceding verses (12:1–7) offer the book's final and most dramatic illustration of the brevity of life. Verse 8, which is similar in formulation to Ecclesiastes 1:2, thus forms with it a literary bracket around Qoheleth's investigations and findings. This observation has led several commentators to identify a distinct prologue in 1:1–11 or 1:3–11 and an epilogue in 12:8–14 or 12:9–14, which have been added by a later narrator/editor who introduces, incorporates, and then evaluates Qoheleth's autobiographically oriented reflections in 1:12–12:7. Such a suggestion is not inherently problematic, since 1:1 and 12:9–12 in particular are editorial in nature and similar to ancient Near Eastern colophons. As will be noted below, many of the key words in this section occur repeatedly throughout the book, though sometimes with a different nuance. This fact could support either a common author or an editor's intentional imitation. The more significant consideration is how one assesses this proposed editor's attitude toward Qoheleth's wisdom. Since the nineteenth century, there have been interpreters, including those responsible for the Scofield Bible notes, who have understood this so-called appendix to Ecclesiastes as a full-blown rejection of Qoheleth's unorthodox views. These views are therefore corrected or countered by the orthodox ending (12:13–14). In mathematical terms, one places a large "minus" sign before the parenthesis around 1:12–12:8, saying, in effect: "Not that but rather this." According to this interpretation, it probably was only the later addition of 12:13–14 that succeeded in shoehorning this book into the Hebrew canon.

B. Hermeneutical reflections (12:9–14). Even if this concluding section stems from a second author, there is no compelling reason to interpret these verses as offering a critique rather than an explanation of the book's compositional purpose and a hermeneutical guide to its proper understanding. Interestingly, in the Hebrew text, verses 9 and 12 begin identically (NJPS "A further word" or "and furthermore"), while verse 13 begins with, literally, "a final word" (cf. Eccles. 3:11; 7:2), possibly thereby dividing this section into three parts. Verses 9–10 describe Qoheleth's (i.e., the Teacher's) purpose, procedure, and product, which parallel in some respects the narrative description of Solomonic wisdom in 1 Kings 4:29–34. Qoheleth was a wise person who publicly instructed the people. For that purpose, he pondered (literally "listened carefully to" or "weighed"), thoroughly investigated, and edited many proverbs. The NIV's translation of 12:10 emphasizes the intentional aesthetic, stylistic, and moral quality of these words. Another option is to take this verse as referring to Qoheleth's efforts both to find (i.e., collect) apt sayings and to compose truthful sayings himself (cf. Prov. 22:20–21).

The effect of such wisdom sayings is described in 12:11–12. In referring to the "words of the wise," he appears to make a broader, even canonical, claim, since an identical phrase is used in the prologue to Proverbs (1:6, also 22:17; Eccles. 9:17). Such sayings are effective, even if painful (as in Eccles. 7:5; cf. Ps. 141:5), like cattle prods that get you moving in the right direction. Furthermore, those who master such anthologies are secure, like firmly planted nails (see NASB; cf. Isa. 41:7), since these words are given by a "shepherd." This has traditionally been understood as claiming God, Israel's shepherd, as the ultimate source of wisdom. Alternatively, the entire verse could be understood as developing the metaphor of a goad whose sharp embedded tip is deftly wielded by a shepherd (so Fox, 353–56). Although the Old Testament consistently acknowledges the divine origin of wisdom (e.g., 1 Kings 4:29; 5:12; Ps. 51:6; Prov. 2:6; Eccles. 2:26) and frequently describes God as a shepherd, these two concepts are not combined elsewhere. Interestingly, Psalm 78:72 notes that King David employed wisdom in shepherding Israel, while Ecclesiastes 12:9 implies that Qoheleth viewed public instruction as a proper means for guiding the people. Verse 12 is difficult to translate. The NJPS prefers "A further word" (as in 12:9, similarly NKJV), while the NIV translates the Hebrew phrase as "in addition to" (as in Esther 6:6). Here the editor adopts the typical wisdom form of address, "my son," which does not occur elsewhere in Ecclesiastes but is prevalent in Proverbs 1–9 and 23–24. He warns the "son" against devoting equal attention to the countless other books that are not of similar origin, quality, or benefit. The NKJV offers a different suggestion: "Be admonished by these" (i.e., the texts of 12:11), unlike the king described in Ecclesiastes 4:13.

In 12:13–14 is a summary of Qoheleth's basic message, the "bottom line" after all of his words have been heard: "Fear God and keep his commandment, for this pertains to every human" (contra NIV's "this is the whole duty of man"). Verse 14 offers the motivation for heeding this charge. The coming comprehensive judgment of God will encompass every human deed, including those carefully concealed from others. These verses do not constitute an orthodox corrective, since they state nothing that the main body of the book has not affirmed previously: (1) the value of revering God (3:14; 5:7; 7:18; 8:12–13), (2) the need to obey God's commands (e.g., 5:4–6, which cites Deut. 23:21–23 regarding vows; cf. also 8:5, literally "a command-keeper"), and (3) the certainty of divine judgment, either under the sun or after death (3:15, 17; 5:6; 7:17; 8:12–13; 11:9; possibly 8:5–6). Despite the diverse and sometimes disturbing course of Qoheleth's reflections and conclusion, at the core he has not strayed from the central convictions of the Israelite faith.

Select Bibliography

Eaton, Michael A. *Ecclesiastes*. Tyndale Old Testament Commentaries. Downers Grove, IL: InterVarsity, 1983.

Fox, Michael V. *A Time to Tear Down and a Time to Build Up: A Rereading of Ecclesiastes*. Grand Rapids: Eerdmans, 1999.

Fredericks, Daniel C. *Coping with Transience: Ecclesiastes on Brevity in Life*. Sheffield: JSOT Press, 1993.

Keddie, Gordon J. *Looking for the Good Life: The Search for Fulfillment in the Light of Ecclesiastes*. Phillipsburg, NJ: Presbyterian and Reformed, 1991.

Kidner, Derek. *A Time to Mourn, and a Time to Dance: Ecclesiastes and the Way of the World*. Downers Grove, IL: InterVarsity, 1976.

Loader, J. A. *Ecclesiastes: A Practical Commentary*. Translated by J. Vriend. Grand Rapids: Eerdmans, 1986.

Longman, Tremper, III. *The Book of Ecclesiastes*. New International Commentary on the Old Testament. Grand Rapids: Eerdmans, 1998.

Murphy, Roland E. *Ecclesiastes*. Word Biblical Commentary. Dallas: Word, 1992.

Ogden, Graham. *Qoheleth*. 2nd ed. Sheffield: Sheffield Phoenix Press, 2007.

Provan, Iain. *Ecclesiastes, Song of Songs*. NIV Application Commentary. Grand Rapids: Zondervan, 2001.

Simpson, William K., ed. *The Literature of Ancient Egypt*. 3rd ed. New Haven: Yale University Press, 2003.

Whybray, R. N. *Ecclesiastes*. New Century Bible Commentary. Grand Rapids: Eerdmans, 1989.

Song of Solomon

ANDREW E. HILL

Introduction

Title

This book takes its title from the superscription (1:1) and is variously labeled the Song, Songs, Song of Songs, Song of Solomon, and the Best Song. The alternative name, Canticles, is derived from the Latin Vulgate.

Genre and Literary Features

The Song is placed among the books of wisdom and poetry in the Septuagint and most English versions. While not wisdom literature in the strict sense, the Song shares some affinities with wisdom in that the work is associated with wise King Solomon (1 Kings 4:29–34), concerns itself with the mystery of humans created male and female, and offers instruction (at least implicitly) on human behavior as it relates to sexuality and marriage. The Song is grouped first among the five festival scrolls (Megilloth) in the Hebrew canon, and in later Judaism it was designated to be read as part of the Passover celebration.

Like Psalms, Proverbs, and Lamentations, the Song is entirely poetic in literary form (with the exception of the superscription). The distinguishing feature of Hebrew poetry, and all poetry in the ancient Near East, is rhythm of sound and rhythm of thought. Rhythm of sound is the regular pattern of stressed or unstressed syllables in lines of poetry, including the repetition of sounds through alliteration and assonance. Rhythm of thought is the balancing of ideas in a structured or systematic way. The primary vehicle for conveying this thought rhythm is word parallelism, in which similar or opposite ideas are offset in the lines of poetry (e.g., earrings/strings of jewels, 1:10; mountains/hills, 2:8; opened/left, gone, 5:6). Sometimes this poetic parallelism arranges ideas synthetically or climactically, in that each idea in the successive lines of the verse builds on the previous one (e.g., wall/windows/lattice, 2:9).

Poetry is a language of images often given to making comparisons by utilizing simile and metaphor. This is especially true of the Song as lyrical love poetry. Frequently the Western reader finds these comparisons humorous or even uncomplimentary (e.g., "your waist is a mound of wheat," or "your nose is like the tower of Lebanon," 7:2, 4), not to mention difficult to understand. The bold language and vivid imagery of the love poetry sometimes shock and embarrass the modern reader (e.g., 7:8). In part this may be due to the idyllic overtones of the Song. Although the Song is not an idyll in the technical sense, today's technologically sophisticated audience experiences uneasiness when encountering these kinds of unfamiliar pastoral scenes.

The Song does conform, however, to literary conventions of love poetry in the second millennium BC. For example, the Egyptian love songs of the New Kingdom (ca. 1570–1085 BC) contain many of the same themes and employ similar figures of speech (see Longman, 49–52; Garrett and House, 49–57). The garden motif as erotic symbol and lyrics in praise of the rapture and mystery of human sexual love are prominent. Simile and metaphor abound, including descriptive songs that compare the physical features of the lovers to exotic flora and fauna. Songs of desire calling the partners to love, to partake of delicate foods, and to drink spiced wine to refresh "lovesickness," and even the attention to fine apparel and exquisite perfumes and ointments are commonplace in the literature. When the Song is viewed against this literary backdrop, its strangeness is diminished and appreciation for its simple beauty and sensitive treatment of the subject matter is enhanced.

Specific literary forms and formal features identified in the love poetry of the Song include descriptive songs, in which each lover sketches the other in highly figurative language (4:1–7; 6:4–7; 7:1–9); self-description (1:5–7; 8:10); songs of admiration, calling attention to the lover's adornment (1:9–11; 4:9–11); songs of desire, characterized by an invitation to love (1:2–4; 8:1–4); and search narratives, recounting

Egyptians used imagery similar to that found in the Song of Solomon. In this garden scene, King Tutankhamun appears with his queen, who is holding lotus flowers and mandrakes and wearing a perfume cone on her head (Egypt, fourteenth century BC).

the maiden's energy and persistence in seeking her lover (3:1–4; 5:2–7).

Several more technical literary devices recognized in the Song include oath formulas (2:7; 3:5; 5:8; 8:4); the teasing song, as the lovers banter in their desire to unite (2:14–17; 5:2–7); the boasting song, in which the maiden flaunts her uniqueness (6:8–10); the urgent call to love, usually prefaced with an imperative verb (2:5, 17; 4:16; 7:11–13; 8:14); and the game of love, composed of the search narrative (5:2–7), an oath formula (5:8), the "teasing question" posed by the friends (5:9), the maiden's answer song (5:10–16), another teasing question from the friends (6:1), and finally, the "formula of belonging" (6:2–3).

Structure

There are as many outlines for structuring the content of the Song as methods of interpretation. While the book contains repeated phrases and lines (e.g., "how beautiful you are, my darling" [1:15; 4:1, 7]; "my beloved is mine" [2:16; 6:3]; "who is this?" [3:6; 6:10; 8:5]; "my sister, my bride" [4:9, 12; 5:1]; and "daughters of Jerusalem, I charge you" [2:7; 3:5; 5:8; 8:4]), only the charge to the daughters of Jerusalem in 2:7; 3:5; and 8:4 appears to serve as a refrain perhaps marking strophic structure.

The speeches or direct discourse provide clues for dividing the text, yet the speakers remain largely unidentified. Speech content can aid in the identification of the speaker, but this is not conclusive. The terse language and cryptic nature of the poetry often make ascertaining the exact extent of a given speech no easy task. These efforts to assign the speeches to specific participants in the love story are complicated by the question of the exact number of characters in the story. No wonder many biblical commentators consider the Song a rather random assortment of love poems collected into an anthology (see Longman, 42–43 ; Ryken, 272–74). This commentary on the Song views the poetry as a loosely unified composition and "reweaves" the narrative along the lines of a three-character love story in a series of sequential events.

Authorship and Date

Traditional biblical scholarship has ascribed the Song of Solomon to King Solomon and dated the poetry to the late tenth century BC—largely on the strength of the superscription to the book (1:1; see Provan, 235–36). Some ancient Jewish traditions credit the work to King Hezekiah, the Judahite ruler accorded a prominent place in the preservation of the Israelite wisdom literature (Prov. 25:1; cf. 2 Chron. 32:27–29; see Murphy, 6n17).

The problems of authorship and the date of the Song are closely related. The inconclusive nature of the book's title further complicates the matter. The Hebrew phrase *lishlomoh* (1:1) may be understood variously as "of/to/for/about Solomon" (cf. the notations in, e.g., Ps. 3:1; 4:1; 5:1). Thus this title may imply that Solomon wrote the poetry, that the poems were dedicated to him, or that they are songs composed about him.

Scholarly appeal to other criteria related to authorship proves no more useful in establishing the identity of the writer of the Song. Though Solomon's name occurs six times elsewhere in the book (1:5; 3:7, 9, 11; 8:11, 12), and other passages attest to his sagacity and literary skill

(e.g., 1 Kings 4:29–34), these references assert nothing concerning his authorship of this poetry. Instead, they merely confirm Solomon's role as a key figure in the love story.

The exotic vocabulary (e.g., perfume, 1:12; saffron, calamus, aloes, 4:13–14) and the author's knowledge of Palestinian flora and fauna (including fifteen species of animals and twenty-one varieties of plants) might suggest Solomonic authorship (cf. 1 Kings 4:33).

As the previous discussion indicates, however, neither the Solomonic references nor the language of the poetry yields solid evidence for ascertaining the authorship of the "best of songs." Unhappily, the results are similar when these various criteria are examined and applied to the problem of dating the Song.

The presence of Aramaic influence and Persian and Greek loan words has caused biblical commentators to assign dates to the book ranging from Israel's united monarchy (tenth century BC) to the Persian and Greek periods (ca. 500–300 BC).

The juxtaposition of Jerusalem and Tirzah in a poetic couplet (6:4) is often suggested as a clue to fixing the date of the Song, since Tirzah was the capital city of the northern kingdom during the reigns of Baasha, Elah, Zimri, Tibni, and Omri (ca. 900–870 BC). But the city may have been used by Jeroboam I as a secondary royal residence (cf. 1 Kings 14:17) and was likely a prominent and beautiful city long before it became the capital (cf. Josh. 12:24).

Additionally, the indiscriminate mention of geographical localities found in both the northern and southern kingdoms (e.g., Jerusalem, 1:5; En Gedi, 1:14; Sharon, 2:1; Gilead, 4:1) may suggest the united monarchy, when these places were part of the same political realm. The preponderance of northern and eastern cities and regions (e.g., Bethrabbim, Carmel, Damascus, Gilead, Hermon, Heshbon, Lebanon, Mahanaim, Sharon, Shulam, and Tirzah), however, better argues for the time of the divided monarchy and a northern provenance for the writing of the book.

One final factor influencing informed opinion on the authorship and date of the Song deserves mention. The interpretive method adopted by the individual translator/commentator in large measure determines how one outlines the text and understands the poetry with respect to the number of characters in the story and plot development, and ultimately colors the way one arranges and evaluates the various strands of evidence bearing on the question of authorship and date.

For example, those who contend the love story is a two-character drama are likely to focus attention on the exotic vocabulary, the plethora of references to flora and fauna, and the apparent unity of geography within the poems and opt for a date in the Solomonic age, if not Solomonic authorship (see the discussions in Carr, 19–20; Garrett and House, 22–25). By contrast, those who view the poetry depicting a love triangle with King Solomon cast as the "villain" would tender a northern kingdom provenance and an early-divided-kingdom date (e.g., Waterman as cited in Pope, 24). The scholar employing the typological or cultic approach to the Song will likely emphasize the late lexical features of the text and the device of "literary fiction" in the poetry where Solomon simply represents the "great lover" and will conclude that the book should be dated to the Persian period (e.g., Murphy, 4).

Although awareness of these complexities connected with authorship and date is crucial to any study of the Song, caution and restraint are clearly in order since no consensus exists even among conservative biblical scholars. Despite this inability to firmly establish an author and date for the Song of Solomon, the lack of concrete knowledge on these two issues in no wise diminishes the beauty of the poetry or the power of its message.

Given the uncertainties associated with the superscription and the unusual nature of the book's vocabulary and style, the Song is best regarded as an anonymous composition. The weight of the literary, historical, and linguistic evidence as currently assessed points to a northern kingdom provenance and an early (preexilic) date for the writing of the book. Attempts to be more precise than this are tenuous and return relatively little benefit for the overall comprehension of the message and meaning of the love songs.

Methods of Interpretation

No single Old Testament book has proven more perplexing for biblical interpreters than the Song of Solomon. Centuries of careful study, analysis, and commentary by biblical scholars of various traditions and theological persuasions have produced little interpretive consensus.

First, the theme or topic of the Song has confused, shocked, and embarrassed both Jewish and Christian interpreters—so much so that the rabbis and early church fathers debated the value of the Song and its place in the biblical canon for generations. What merit is there in a book that contains no suggestion of worship, no hint of social concern, no affirmation of faith in God, indeed not even any mention of God (save the possible reference to "the very flame of the LORD" [NIV note] in 8:6)? What value in a book vaunting human affection, physical passion, and erotic sexual love?

Second, the nature and structure of the poetry does not lend itself to ready analysis. Aside from the ambiguous references to King Solomon, clear historical parallels and allusions are wanting. Much of the language of the book is unusual if not unique and obscure, making translation and interpretation difficult. By definition lyrical poetry is brief in length, concentrated in meaning, and often lacking smooth transitions, posing a dilemma for commentators seeking to divide the book into smaller logical units. In turn, this makes for uncertainty in identifying the number of different characters in the love story and assigning these smaller units of speech to specific individuals.

The *dramatic* approach has been part of church tradition since the third century AD (e.g., Origen as cited in Carr, 32). Based largely on the analogy of later Greek drama, this approach understands the Song as an ancient

Hebrew play. The poetry is considered a dramatic script intended for royal entertainment. Speeches are assigned to the principal characters of the melodrama (whether two or three, depending on the identification of the shepherd as one and the same with the king), with the daughters of Jerusalem (or harem) represented by a female chorus. Attempts to divide the Song into acts and scenes often require significant emendation of the text, and efforts to cast the book as Greek drama are forced and artificial.

Unlike allegory, the *typological* method tends to recognize the historical elements of the book (whether it commemorates Solomon's marriage to Pharaoh's daughter or recounts the king's wooing of the Shulammite maiden) but subordinates the literal presentation of Old Testament history to a correspondent New Testament pattern or parallel (see the discussion in Carr, 24-25; Bullock, 228). The traditional "type/antitype" fulfillment is God's covenant relationship to Israel for the Jewish interpreter or Christ's relationship to the church as his bride for the Christian interpreter. Thus the expression of love in the Song may illustrate the truth of God's relationship to his creation or his chosen people, or Christ's relationship to the church. This despite the fact that the Song itself gives no hint that it is intended as typology, nor does the New Testament make any significant use of the Song, either by direct quotation or indirect allusion.

The *cultic* or *mythological* approach views the Song as a Hebrew adaptation of Mesopotamian fertility cult liturgy (see the discussion in Garrett and House, 81–83). The annual ritual was a reenactment of the ancient myth recounting the goddess Ishtar's searching for her dead lover in the netherworld and finally restoring him to life through sexual union, thus ensuring creation's continued fertility. It is assumed that the cultic associations of the Song were forgotten or consciously changed to make the book acceptable to the Israelite faith.

The *wedding cycle* approach assumes the Song is an amalgam of nuptial poems (see the discussion in Pope, 141–45). The series of songs honoring the bride and groom were eventually formalized into a cycle of recitations that were incorporated into the wedding celebration. The Song does contain numerous parallels to ancient Jewish wedding customs and to this day is chanted or sung as an integral part of the orthodox Jewish wedding ceremony.

While the historical aspects of the book are not denied, the *didactic* view understands the poem as a vehicle for instruction and simply subordinates

Sacred marriage texts from the ancient Near East, such as this Sumerian tablet from Nippur (1974–1954 BC), recount the love affairs of the gods.

the circumstances surrounding the occasion of the book in favor of the moral and didactic purposes of the literature. The book is seen to present the purity and wonder of sexual love, to promote ideals of simplicity, faithfulness, and chastity, and to instruct on the virtue of human affection and the beauty and holiness of marriage.

The *allegorical* method is the oldest and most popular approach to the Song. Here it is important to distinguish between allegory as a literary type and allegorizing as an interpretive method. Allegory is defined as an obvious symbolic representation in literature, or simply, extended metaphor. Allegory says one thing but conveys another, deeper, hidden meaning. The allegorizing of a text occurs when the interpreter understands a given passage as an allegory even though the author did not intend it as such (as in the case of the Song). The allegorical method may relate historical events in symbolic form or the symbolism may be nonhistorical, but the approach tends to emphasize the role of the poetry as a vehicle for some hidden spiritual truth (see Bullock, 228). As applied to the Song, the allegorizing method has predominantly yielded insights for Jewish interpreters on the spiritual truth of God's covenant relationship to Israel, or for Christian interpreters on Christ's relationship to his church and the individual believer.

The *literal* approach takes the Song at face value and interprets the love poetry for what it appears to be—a sensual, even erotic expression of emotion and passion as two young lovers voice their desire for each other (see Bullock, 231–32; Carr, 34–35; Ryken, 271–72). The literal interpretive stance makes no attempt to apologize for the frankness of language or boldness of imagery in the poem by resorting to typology or allegorizing. Nor does it seek to justify the biblical treatment of the subject of human love and sexuality, since God made man male and female and sanctioned their union as one flesh at creation. Whether composed by him or not, for some the love poetry of the

Song is believed to reflect real events associated with the reign of King Solomon. For others, the collection of poems celebrating human love and sexuality has no particular historical associations. In either case, those opting for a more literal approach to the love poems must assume the lovers in the Song are married (or eventually get married), though this is nowhere made explicit in the book.

One popular approach considers the book a collection of a series of (random?) love poems with no historical connection and no intended plot structure ("a kind of erotic psalter," Longman, 43). Another literal approach views the book's poetry as a unified composition, but with no historical connection and no intended plot (e.g., Gledhill, 37; Hess, 34–35). For example, the headings for the speech units in the NIV assume two primary characters, "She" and "He" (designated in the NIV 1984 as the "Beloved" and the "Lover"), and the paragraph structure implies movement from the love of courtship to the intimacy of marriage.

In keeping with the storytelling nature of the Hebrew people, this commentary assumes a three-character love story and adopts the literal-historical approach in combination with elements of the didactic approach. The book is likely a northern kingdom satire on the reign of Solomon and his exploitation of women (ironically to his own demise), and a memorializing of the exemplary character of the Shulammite maiden, who rejects the wooing of the king because of her faithfulness to her shepherd lover.

Outline

3. The Shulammite Maiden Rejects the King (7:10–8:4)
4. The Shulammite Maiden and Her Shepherd Lover Are Reunited (8:5–14)

Commentary

1. The Shulammite Maiden (1:1–3:5)

A. Superscription (1:1). The title of the book, both English and Hebrew, is taken from the first verse. Literally translated, the verse reads, "the song of songs, which is of Solomon." The expression "song of songs" is an idiom for the superlative in Hebrew—"the best song." The word "song" is a generic term for any happy, festival song (cf. Isa. 24:9; 30:29). The possessive pronoun attributing the work to Solomon, if original, is ambiguous at best.

B. The king and the maiden banter (1:2–2:2). The opening sections of the poem find the maiden in the royal court of King Solomon, with no indication as to how she came to be there (although 6:11–12 implies she was taken from the countryside against her will). Those who espouse a three-character Song recognize 1:9–2:2 as a dialogue between the king and the maiden but understand her speeches as projections directed to the shepherd lover she has left behind and not as direct responses to Solomon's flattery.

1:2–4. In the anxiety and confusion of her separation from her home in the northern hill country and her shepherd lover, the maiden recalls the tenderness of his affection and the pleasure she experienced when kissing him (1:2–4a). The pleasure of the lover's kiss is likened to wine, a connection well attested in ancient literature (4:10; 5:1; 7:9; Prov. 9:2, 5). More than the physical sensations of lovemaking, the maiden recalls and longs for the sense of belonging and security she enjoyed in the presence of the shepherd lover.

A pun occurs in verse 3 in that the words for "perfume" and "name" sound alike in Hebrew. The name of a person and his or her character and personality were inseparable in the ancient mind. Remembering the sweet fragrance of the shepherd's cologne causes the maiden to glory in the strength and richness of the shepherd's character. Like the aroma of expensive ointment, the shepherd's personality attracts all the young maidens. A sense of urgency surfaces in the maiden's plea for the lover to rescue her from her plight, indicated by the use of an imperative verb ("take me away"). The maiden is not asking to be brought into the king's private chambers! Rather, she implores the shepherd to rescue her from the royal harem before Solomon violates her sexually and destroys their relationship.

The shift to the first-person plural (1:4b) marks the end of the maiden's speech and may represent a dramatic interjection in the poem. The "we" is thought to be the women of the royal harem. Apparently they recognize the unique nature of the maiden's love for her absent shepherd, and they extol her sincere affection and faithfulness. Indeed, this admixture of these qualities in the chemistry of a male-female relationship merits more praise than wine.

1:5–8. Perhaps the interjection of the harem women reminds the maiden of her visage in contrast to theirs (1:5–7). Unlike the soft and white-skinned harem women, she is black or dark, yet very beautiful. Like the tents of the Transjordanian nomads woven of black goat hair, the maiden has been tanned dark brown by exposure to the sun while working in her family's vineyards. The curious stares of the other women prompt self-justification. No reason is given for her brothers' anger, though they do reappear later in the poem (8:8–9). It is possible that it is no more than wordplay, as she has been "burned" by the sun and "burned" by the anger of her brothers. The vineyard she has neglected is her own person. The duration and intensity of her outdoor activity have interrupted or even canceled normal hygenic and cosmetic routines. The imperative, "Tell me" (1:7), addressed to the absent shepherd parallels that of verse 4 and underscores the distress of the maiden's situation. If the shepherd can call to her from among all the flocks and shepherds seeking refuge from the noonday heat in the shade of rocks and trees, her search for him will be expedited.

The shift to the feminine form (1:8) marks a different speaker, probably the women of the royal harem. The phrase "most beautiful of women" is repeated three times in refrains by the harem women (1:8; 5:9; 6:1), and it echoes a constant theme in the poem—the flawless beauty of the maiden. Verse 8 has puzzled interpreters in that the women's instructions to follow the sheep tracks and then graze her young goats nearby in hopes of finding the shepherd seem nonsensical because they encourage the very behavior the maiden wishes to avoid.

1:9–15. Solomon now enters the scene, and his first words are an attempt to divert the maiden's attention from the shepherd to himself through flattering speech and the presentation of costly gifts (1:9–11). Complimentary comparisons of women to animals are a common feature of ancient Near Eastern love poetry (cf. Garrett, 522–23). In the Song the maiden is likened to a mare (1:9), dove (1:15), goats and sheep (4:1–2), and gazelle fawns (4:5), while the shepherd is compared to the gazelle or stag (2:9, 17). The maiden's rustic beauty excites interest in the king in the same way a mare might attract attention among Pharaoh's stallions. The radiance of the maiden's countenance is enhanced by her jewelry and ornamentation, an important part of female dress in the Old Testament world. The shift back to the first-person plural in verse 11 may indicate that the harem women are speaking again, although this is not clear. Ornaments crafted especially for the maiden are ordered, the reference to gold and silver perhaps indicating expensive and exquisite jewelry befitting her rapturous beauty.

The juxtaposition of the "king" and "my beloved" in the maiden's soliloquy (1:12–14) indicates they are not one and the same person. While the king entertains at a royal banquet (whether publicly or privately is unclear), the maiden's own perfume incites erotic imaginations of the shepherd lover. The intensity of her romantic response is reinforced by the mention of three separate fragrances. "Spikenard" (NEB) was an exotic and expensive ointment derived from plants native to India; myrrh was an aromatic resin manufactured from the gum of a species of tree in southern Arabia. The sachet, or necklace with a pouch, was a common way to use myrrh as a perfume. The myrrh was mixed with a fat or oil base and placed in a hollow pod or wrapped in a cloth or leather pouch and worn as a necklace or bracelet. As body heat melted the fat, the aroma of the solid stick of myrrh was released.

The king continues to laud the captivating comeliness of the maiden (1:15), twice repeating the word "beautiful." The expression "your eyes are doves" is obscure. Both the maiden and shepherd are described as having "dove

A woman with a perfumed cone on her head (tomb of Menna, Egypt, fifteenth century BC)

eyes" (1:15; 4:1; 5:12), and the dove is elsewhere one of the metaphors used of both lovers (2:14; 5:2; 6:9). The dove is a symbol of peace, purity, and tenderness in the Old Testament. The eyes are thought to reveal inner character, so "dove eyes" may suggest qualities of innocence, purity, loyalty, and fidelity evident in the lovers.

1:16–2:2. The maiden's initial response may have given Solomon false hope, as she repeats his very words. However, she quickly lets it be known that her words are intended for another and that she does not belong in the presence of the king (1:16–2:1). The scene of her lovemaking is pastoral, in grassy fields and under spreading trees—not the palace precincts. In her modesty she compares herself to the more common wildflowers of the countryside, flowers of Sharon not far from her home in Shulam.

The king's final simile, a weak attempt to play on the maiden's words, falls on deaf ears (2:2). He continues to exalt her beauty above the "thorns" of his harem, oblivious to the fact that the banter has another dimension. This other dimension is intimated by the satirical repetition of "my" in the opening exchange of speeches (1:9, 13, 14, 15, 16; 2:2, 3) and demonstrated more clearly in the maiden's next discourse.

C. The maiden seeks her shepherd lover (2:3–3:5). 2:3–7. The literary form of this section is the boasting or admiration song, common in ancient love poetry. The maiden touts her lover and rejoices in the delight his lovemaking arouses in her. The cultivated fruit tree in the midst of a wild wood calls attention to the uniqueness of her lover. To "sit in his shade" (2:3) suggests cool refreshment and the comfort and protection of the lover's physical proximity. The fruits sweet to her taste are the elements of his lovemaking. In contrast to Solomon's banquet, the maiden imagines her own wedding feast with her shepherd's pure and faithful love as her banner or emblem of betrothal (2:4; cf. Ps. 20:5; 60:4). Overcome with exhaustion in the ecstasy of lovemaking, the maiden requests refreshment with foods the ancients believed

possessed powers to restore and enhance romantic energies and capabilities. These aphrodisiacs included raisins, apples, raisin cakes, pomegranates, and spiced wine (2:5; 4:13; 7:8, 12–13). The "raisin cakes" (NJB, NASB) embodied considerable erotic symbolism, as they were associated with the rites of the ancient fertility cults (cf. Jer. 7:18; 44:18–19).

The maiden's charge to the daughters of Jerusalem, or harem women, in her company is a recurring refrain in the poem (2:7; 3:5; 8:4). The refrain marks major breaks in the text of the poem and usually occurs in the context of physical intimacy. "By the gazelles and by the does of the field" is a rustic oath formula underscoring urgency and seriousness in her entreaty. Love is not to be stirred until the partners have taken full satisfaction in the intimate physical delights of each other's company.

2:8–13. The imperative verbs in the opening and closing verses, 2:8 and 13, signal an intensification of emotion in the maiden as she continues to dream about the shepherd lover left behind. The repetition of "Arise, my darling" in verses 10 and 13 is an envelope construction making this a separate stanza in the unit. Dwelling on her lover and the sweetness of his affection moves the maiden to fantasize that he has come to rescue her from the king's harem. The analogy to the wild animals of the hill country continues, perhaps a subtle foil between the freedom the "stag" enjoys and the confinement of the "doe" behind the walls, lattices, and windows of the palace complex. The stag, staring, gazing, bounding from window to window seeking a glimpse of his doe, is the picture of both crestfallen loneliness and energetic impatience. Winter is over and the spring season has come, evidenced by the blooming flowers, nesting birds, and early fruit of the fig orchards (2:11–13). Love is awakened; it is now time for the lovers to be rejoined in their natural setting. The certainty of warmth and spring growth following the winter rains no doubt images the ever-budding affections of the lovers. The two-character interpretation of the poem strains at this point to make sense of the plot. If Solomon is the lover, why must he come from the hills and peer through garden lattices for a glance of the maiden? If the maiden is confined in the palace precincts and Solomon and the lover are one in the same, why must she (even in a dream) steal through the streets of Jerusalem pursuing her lover? The anthology-of-love-poems approach considers this poem an invitation by the man to the woman to join him in a tryst (and addressing the issue of morality by assuming the context of marriage based on a canonical reading of the Songs [e.g., Longman, 116; cf. p. 70]).

2:14–15. The comparison of the maiden to a nesting rock dove echoes 2:12 and maintains the springtime imagery of the previous section. The "dove" is a pet name for the maiden (1:15; 4:1; 5:2, 12; 6:9) and a common symbol of love and fertility in the ancient Near East (cf. Garrett, 523). "Face" (literally "appearance") and "voice" are paired in chiasmus in verse 14 in the maiden's memory of the playfulness of their love. The meaning of verse 15 is obscure. It may be a literal reference to measures taken in the vineyards to prevent spoilage by foxes (since the maiden worked the vineyards prior to her abduction, 1:6), or it may be a symbolic statement of the blossoming love shared by the two and a veiled expression of their desire to prevent the relationship from being "ruined" by the foxes (intruders or rivals?) before it matures.

2:16–17. The vivid memory of the shepherd and the vibrance of the intimate moments she shared with him during the spring season(s) in the vineyards elicits an affirmation of love and loyalty from the maiden. Verse 16 is repeated in 6:3 and emphasizes the exclusiveness of their relationship. "Browsing" or "feeding" among the lilies is a metaphor for the lover's enjoyment of the maiden's physical charms (cf. 6:2). "Until the day breaks" is a poetic idiom for the dawn. The joy and pleasure of the physical intimacies shared through the night are ended at daybreak. As the sun rises and chases away the shadows of night, so the shepherd lover turns and runs

like a stag back into the hills. Like the dove, the gazelle or stag has connections with Mesopotamian fertility rites, being a model of sexual prowess (cf. 2:8–9; see Longman, 119–20).

The expression "my beloved" in verse 16 is the favorite epithet of the maiden for the rustic shepherd lover. The word occurs more than thirty times in the book, and elsewhere in the Old Testament the term can mean "uncle" or "relative" (Num. 36:11; 2 Kings 24:17; Amos 6:10) or even refer to lovemaking (Prov. 7:18; Ezek. 16:8; 23:17; cf. Song 1:2; 4:10). In extrabiblical literature the cognate word for the Hebrew signifies "darling (sexual) partner," and it is employed in ancient love poetry and fertility cult liturgies with erotic connotations (cf. *TDOT* 3:143–44). The term may even be a euphemism for the breasts or genitals (cf. 7:12).

3:1–5. The opening line of this "search narrative" in 3:1 confirms that the entire section (2:3–3:5) is to be understood as the recounting of the maiden's fantasy as she pines for her absent lover. The dream or fantasy concludes dramatically with her frantic search of the city for the shepherd and the passionate reunion of the lovers in the deserted streets of Jerusalem. The plural "nights" implies that the fantasy or dream is a recurring one (NEB "night after night") or that it lasts all night long (NIV). The refrain in verses 1–2 continues the pattern of repeated phrases and lines throughout the entire stanza (e.g., 2:7 and 3:5; 2:10 and 2:13) and accentuates the earnestness and persistence of the maiden's search. Soon after encountering the watchmen or night police making their rounds, the maiden locates her lover and the dream sequence ends ideally. Her second night-search fantasy has no such happy ending (5:2–8). In her joy and relief the maiden clutches her lover and refuses to release him from her embrace— almost a prophetic foreshadowing of how she intends to respond to the shepherd lover should they ever be reunited (cf. 8:1–4). The leading of the lover into her mother's house may signify the formalizing of their love relationship (i.e., parental approval and a public wedding; cf. 8:8,

13). The phrase "to the room of the one who conceived me" (3:4) is probably a reference to the sexual consummation of their relationship. Only then will she freely give him the "nectar of her pomegranates" and the delicacies of her love (8:2). The first stanza of the poem concludes (3:5) with a word-for-word repetition of the charge previously made to the harem women.

2. The King Woos the Shulammite Maiden (3:6–7:9)

A. The king's first proposal (3:6–5:8). The two-character approach to the Song identifies this unit as a segment of what was probably a longer royal nuptial song honoring the marriage of Solomon and the maiden and celebrating the consummation of their love (cf. Psalm 45). However, this understanding of the poem cannot adequately account for the maiden's second night search for her lover, nor her charge to the harem women concerning the absent lover and their response (5:8–9). The refrain in 3:5 and 8:4 is followed by the same question: "Who is this coming up from the desert?" Here the question is posed by the harem women, and it introduces the pericope under discussion.

3:6–11. The verses seem to be a lyrical flashback, reminding the maiden of how she came to be a part of the royal harem. The "who" in verse 6 is probably the maiden, since the accompanying demonstrative pronoun *this* is feminine singular in form. The king has returned to the royal city in all his splendor with yet another beautiful woman from the kingdom for his ever-expanding harem. (This sight was no doubt fairly common in the capital, as Solomon had 140 women in the harem at the time of this episode [6:8], and a total of 1,000 women populated the royal harem by the end of his reign [1 Kings 11:1–8].) The convoy of armed bodyguards suggests a tour or review of the empire, not a military campaign. The Hebrew word translated "palanquin" (NRSV; NIV: "carriage"; NJB: "litter"; NASB: "traveling couch") is unique in the Old Testament, and its derivation is uncertain. The NJB understands two different vehicles in the royal procession—the litter that transports the Shulammite maiden and the exquisitely constructed portable throne (palanquin) on which Solomon is carried. The crown the king wears is not the diadem of kingship but a wedding wreath.

4:1–15. The king's rehearsal of the maiden's beauty and his invitations to love constitute this longest single unit in the poem. The first half of the passage is a descriptive song with highly figurative language and is bounded by the inclusio, "How beautiful you are, my darling" (4:1, 7). The descriptive song mixes pastoral, domestic, and urban images common in ancient love poetry (e.g., myrrh, lilies, pomegranates, etc.). The language of the love poem now becomes increasingly erotic and explicit. The import of the descriptive song is the maiden's flawless beauty from head to toe (literally, from eyes [4:1] to breasts [4:5]); she mirrors the beauty, freshness, and innocence of the natural world and the strength and elegance of the manmade world. The phrases "mountain of myrrh" and "hill of incense" (4:6) are more difficult to understand. This may be a generic allusion to all the physical charms of the maiden or another erotic figure of speech signifying the breasts or vulva. Either way the king's objective is transparent—to fully possess *all* the maiden's physical charms through intimate sexual relations. Portions of the descriptive song (4:1–3) are repeated later in the king's second poetic sketch of the maiden (6:5–7). The phrase "until the day breaks" also occurs in 2:17. There the Shulammite encourages the shepherd to take full satisfaction in her love all night. Here the king foists his desire for the same on the maiden.

The two imperatives in verse 8 mark the transition from descriptive song (4:1–7) to a song of admiration (4:9–11) as Solomon continues to woo the maiden. Geographically the Shulammite has been brought to Jerusalem from her home in the northern hill country. Now the king urges that she break from her past socially and emotionally by accepting his proposal for love and marriage. She has ravished his heart with her physical beauty and sensual charm, as the admiration song calling attention to her adornment confesses. "Sister" and "brother" are titles of endearment spoken commonly between lovers in the poetry of the ancient Near East (4:9–10, 12; cf. Garrett, 526; Carr, 121). "Bride" is better understood as "betrothed one," in that her relationship to Solomon has not yet been consummated sexually. The girl remains a virgin, a garden locked up and a sealed spring. The garden metaphor is also a popular motif in ancient Near Eastern love poetry (cf. Carr, 59–60). The female character is often depicted as an orchard, a garden full of choice fruit and exotic plants. The trees and plants mentioned are predominantly those associated with the accoutrements of romance and lovemaking (e.g., spices, oils, perfumes, and even foods and potions considered aphrodisiacs), all serving to heighten the erotic and the sensual.

A royal couple is depicted in a garden setting in this painting from Amarna (fourteenth century BC).

4:16–5:1. The two-character interpretation understands this section as the climax of the love poem. According to this view, the maiden has succumbed to the king's passionate wooing, willingly offering him the "fruit of her garden," and the king happily "possesses" the garden, consummating their marital relationship. This approach assumes that the imperative "awake" (4:16) in the lovers' dialogue is conjunctive, not disjunctive. Yet in previous speeches the maiden has used the imperative verb disjunctively, indicating her address or response is intended not for the king but for another. The two-character approach also fails to adequately explain how the maiden remains a virgin (who has stored up her "delicacies" for her lover [7:12–13] and stood like "a wall" against the amorous advances of the king [8:10]) until she is reunited with

her lover at the end of the poem. The maiden imagines and yearns for the breezes of fate to waft the fragrance of her love to her true lover, alluring him to deliver her from the confines of the royal harem. Interestingly enough, this very sequence of events constitutes the maiden's second night-search fantasy (5:2–8). She can only invent the absent shepherd lover's ideal response to her invitation.

The harem women may be speaking in 5:1c, applauding the lovers' faithfulness and encouraging their continued enjoyment of the pleasures of lovemaking. The "friends" may also be guests and companions of the lovers (perhaps at a wedding feast?), advising them to take full satisfaction in the physical intimacies of the marriage bond.

5:2–8. That King Solomon is not the lover the maiden has invited to enter her "garden" is made clear by this second lengthy search narrative. Her wishful thinking in 4:16–5:1 becomes a reality, if only in a night vision. The one she has longed for, the one to whom she has pledged her love, stands at her very door! The shepherd identifies himself by making mention of his dew-drenched hair, hardly unusual for one who sleeps outside and tends flocks through the night, but most unusual for a king with the reputation for self-indulgent luxury.

The maiden's hesitation and excuse-making delay her answering the door, turning the lover away. The reason for her behavior is unclear. Her reaction may be attributed to fear of another disappointment, fatigue, or disbelief, or perhaps even a fatalistic resignation to her present plight. Her continued shouts and frantic searching for the departed lover avail nothing, save incurring the wrath of the night watchmen, who partially strip and beat her (for disturbing the peace, mistaking her for a prostitute, or for a second offense in violating the harem curfew?).

The two-character view considers this a temporary lapse in the marriage of the king and the maiden because he is late in returning home (cf. Carr, 131). The maiden pouts in her self-pity, lamenting the postponement of the tryst she has anticipated. When the lover finally arrives, she greets him with apathy and indifference, then later regrets her action and seeks to make amends. This view not only distorts the literary intentions of the search-find motif in love poetry but also tarnishes the idyllic love relationship portrayed everywhere else in the poem. The anthology-of-love-poems approach notes the actions of the two characters as "odd," but emphasizes the creation of mood over any real-life experience (cf. Longman, 161).

The charge to the harem women is a partial repetition of Song of Solomon 2:7 and 3:5, and, like 3:5, signals another major break in the poem. The maiden is either asking the women

to inform her lover she is forlorn, weak, and lovesick because of his absence or rhetorically stating she is not exhausted from lovemaking (cf. 2:5).

The cultic interpretation of the Song highlights this second night-search narrative (in combination with the occurrence of "beloved" in the singular) as a vestige of Canaanite fertility cult influence in the Song (cf. Pope, 149–53). The maiden is thought to be the goddess searching for her lover, the god Dod, who died and rests in the netherworld. Upon finding him she renews him with sexual intercourse, commemorated annually in the ritualistic marriage of the king to a virgin in his harem. This approach ignores the immediate context of the lovers' dialogue, discounts a more literal interpretation of the search narrative, and dismisses the other preexilic citations of the word "beloved."

B. The king's second proposal (5:9–7:9). 5:9–6:12. The subsequent material introduced in 5:9 constitutes one of the more stylized sections of the poem (5:9–6:12). The highly figurative descriptive speeches are placed within the framework of a series of transitional interrogative interjections by the harem (5:9; 6:1, 10, 13). The harem women are bewildered by the maiden's behavior. Their confusion is voiced in the form of a query to the Shulammite. What is so special about her lover that she refuses the king? There is also the practical matter of seeking justification for the charge given to them earlier (5:8).

5:9–16. The answer to the question posed by the harem women (5:9) takes the form of a descriptive song reciting the lover's good looks (5:10–16). Once the harem women witness his handsome features, they will know why he is "better than others." The descriptive song is characterized by romantic exaggeration, and several of these similes and metaphors have their antecedents in the earlier descriptive songs praising the maiden's beauty. The only thing remarkable about the passage is its subject matter, as descriptive songs about male characters in ancient love poetry are exceptional.

The comeliness, strength, and splendor of his physical appearance no doubt reflect the incomparable inner qualities of character and personality the lover possesses. This man is her lover—reason enough to spurn the wooing of the king and sufficient rebuttal to the harem's interrogation.

6:1–3. Convinced that the maiden's lover is indeed better than others and worthy of such loyal devotion, the harem women accept the maiden's charge (6:1). They too will join the quest for the absent lover, if she can only provide some clue as to his whereabouts so they might commence searching.

The maiden's enigmatic response (6:2–3) almost defies explanation. Is she speaking literally of his vineyard or of a secluded garden haunt the lover frequented? If she is, she should go there and seek him out instead of combing the city streets and enlisting the help of the harem women. Is she confined to the palace precincts? Elsewhere the garden motif has represented the physical intimacies of lovemaking. But if the maiden is understood as speaking figuratively about herself, the response still carries little meaning for the location of the absent lover. Perhaps the mutual pledge of loyalty (6:3) offers a

Aside from Song of Solomon 5:10–16, this Sumerian love poem from Nippur (2037–2029 BC) provides one of the few descriptions of male beauty in ancient love poetry. It starts, "Bridegroom, dear to my heart, goodly is your beauty, honeysweet."

solution: the bond of love between the two is so strong that in spite of his physical absence the lover continues to "browse among the lilies" of his garden in the mind and heart of the maiden.

6:4–10. If the descriptive song in 7:1–9 is ascribed to the shepherd lover, then 6:4–9 is Solomon's final speech in the poem and represents his last attempt to betroth and wed the Shulammite maiden. Tirzah (the name means "beauty") was a Canaanite stronghold appropriated by Jeroboam I (ca. 930–909 BC; 1 Kings 14:17; 15:21, 23) as the first royal city of the northern kingdom. Later the city was fortified and refurbished as the primary residence of the Omride dynasty (ca. 885 BC; 1 Kings 16:8, 15, 17, 23). The "queens" and "concubines" are a reference to Solomon's harem, while the "virgins" or "maidens" are probably the countless number of women of marriageable age in the realm. The two-character interpretation of the poem argues (most unconvincingly!) that the love of the king (Solomon) and the maiden (perhaps Abishag) is pure and genuine since there are only 140 women in the royal harem at the time (cf. Carr, 148).

The final question posed by the harem women (6:10) is rhetorical in that it is not so much a question directed toward the maiden as a statement about her unrivaled beauty. The verse may well represent part of the chorus by which the queens and concubines praise the extraordinary beauty of the maiden (6:9). The interrogative "Who is this?" is identical in form to the expression in 3:6 and also appears in 8:5. The threefold repetition of the question constitutes a perfect foil, summarizing the drama of the love poem:

> 3:6 *Who is this?* The maiden arriving in Jerusalem with Solomon, bereft of home and lover.
>
> 6:10 *Who is this?* The maiden unsurpassed in beauty, unmatched in loyal devotion, praised by the harem women.
>
> 8:5 *Who is this?* The maiden freed, reunited with her lover, and returning to her village home.

The celestial similes not only portray the radiance, brightness, and freshness of the maiden's appearance but also celebrate her uniqueness. The sun and moon dominate the heavens without equal. The phrase "majestic as the stars in procession" (NIV) repeats the last line of 6:4 and is better translated "terrible like an army with banners" (so RSV). The image conveys the awesome splendor associated with army troops in dress parade.

6:11–12. This section is crucial to the understanding of the Song, and yet verse 12 is the most difficult line of the poem to translate and interpret sensibly. (See the variations in the major English versions.) Literally rendered, the verse reads "I did not know, my soul, (it/he) set me in the chariot of Amminadab." The confusion results from the ambiguous syntax in the verse, especially the relationship of "my soul" to the verbs in the line. (Here the Septuagint actually changes the first verb ["know"] from first to third person and reads "my soul did not know" to solve the problem.) Is "my soul" the subject or object of "did not know" or the subject of "set me"? If the latter, then "my soul" is a figure for another person (hence the translations "my desire" [NJB, NIV] or "my fancy" [NRSV], in reference to the lover). The maiden uses many terms of endearment for her lover, but "my soul" is not one of them. Perhaps the maiden here recounts her abduction by Solomon and

transport to Jerusalem upon venturing into the orchard of nut trees near her home one spring.

6:13–7:9. As previously noted, imperative verbs often signal significant shifts in speech patterns or breaks in the dramatic action of the poem. This section (6:13–7:9) marks the maiden's last appearance among the harem women and records Solomon's final attempt to woo and wed the Shulammite. The women urge her to return (6:13a), apparently to dance. The fourfold repetition of their plea emphasizes their urgency and the seriousness of the situation (the maiden's departure from the harem?). The verse implies that the maiden has been or intends to go somewhere away from the palace confines. Presumably the shepherd has arrived to claim the maiden as his own, or she has refused to participate in the harem dance (at the wedding feast—perhaps her own?). Whatever the reason, it is the maiden's continued refusal of the king that finally induces him to release her from the harem and any betrothal obligations.

The maiden has no interest in being a court spectacle for the friends of the king. The Shulammite has no intention of submitting to inspection by the male onlookers in attendance (the verb "look" is masculine in form: "Why should you men look?") This exchange (6:13b) contains the only Old Testament occurrence of the appellative "Shulammite" (see the discussion in Longman, 192). Shulam was probably the home of the maiden. The location of the site is unknown, but the village of Shunem near Mount Tabor in the region of Galilee is regarded as the most likely identification. The meaning of the last line eludes interpreters. The phrase literally means "the dance of the two armies" (NIV "Mahanaim," a proper name; NJB "two rows"; NEB "the lines"). Exact meaning notwithstanding, the maiden shuns the idea of being made an exhibition at the court dance (see the discussions in Carr, 155; Garrett, 528).

The answer to the maiden's question (7:1–9) is predictable: "Dance for us because your physical beauty infatuates us." The two-character interpretation makes this another descriptive song about the maiden by the king or bridegroom. This portrait of the maiden's physical charms moves up from the feet instead of down from the head (cf. 5:1–5). The reference to the king as a third party in verse 5 has led many to assign verses 1–5 to the friends of the bridegroom or royal (male) onlookers. Prominent in the descriptive song are the graphic sketches of the distinctively sexual aspects of the maiden's anatomy (thighs, pudenda, belly, and breasts). The repetition of "how beautiful" in verse 6 (cf. 7:1) may indicate that the king or bridegroom now joins in the adoration of the maiden (recalling the ecstasy of the sexual intimacies experienced the previous night according to the two-character interpretation). The language of the passage is the most erotically explicit of the poem.

The three-character understanding of the poem views the passage as Solomon's last attempt to betroth the maiden and add her permanently to the ranks of the royal harem. The descriptive song of the bawdy onlookers (7:1–5) is particularly sexual in focus, lacking the sensitivity and dignity of the more euphemistic sensual symbolism encountered earlier in the poem, as well as the mutuality of the sexual experience. The "grasping" and "climbing" and the breast/genital orientation of the king's speech (7:6–9) invoke images of conquest, self-indulgence, lust, and self-gratification. Again, the gentleness, tenderness, willing surrender, and reciprocation in lovemaking as a shared experience by the lovers seems absent. Thus the passage provides an effective foil for the two kinds of human love, contrasting the purity and genuineness of one-to-one love of the Genesis-creation-account ideal with the one-to-many love found in the royal harem.

3. The Shulammite Maiden Rejects the King (7:10–8:4)

The maiden, for the final time, affirms her love for another, the shepherd lover out in the countryside. It is this concluding assertion of loyalty and faithfulness that gains the maiden's release from the claims of the king and the confines of the royal harem. Perhaps in recognition

of her great virtue and unswerving loyalty, the king permits the maiden to return to her northern village. Her persistent rejection of the king's wooing and her unfading devotion to her absent lover must have won Solomon's favor, as it has won that of the harem women. She has remained a garden locked up and a spring enclosed (4:12), a wall fortified with towers (8:10), and now her desire to freely give the love she has stored up to her shepherd lover is apparently granted (7:12–13). The beauty of sexual love is represented in the fertility symbols of the vineyards, pomegranates, and mandrakes ("every delicacy," 7:13). The maiden's desire to share love's intimacies with the shepherd is so overwhelming she almost wishes he were a brother so any public display of affection would not incur the contempt of the villagers.

In escorting the shepherd to her mother's home the maiden accomplishes two goals: she gains approval from her mother and the brothers of the shepherd, and she fulfills her dream of consummating their vows in the place where she was "schooled" by her mother in the art of romance and lovemaking. "Spiced wine" and mandrake apples were renowned aphrodisiacs in Egypt and Mesopotamia. The phrase "nectar of my pomegranates" (8:2) has distinctly erotic connotations, the woman's breasts being identified with pomegranates in Egyptian love poetry (cf. Carr, 167; Hess, 230). The love repose the maiden imagined in 2:6 will soon be a reality, as the awakening of love fancied in 4:16 now comes to fruition. The refrain closing this major section of the poem carries the full force intended by the writer. The maiden and the shepherd have been rejoined in love.

4. The Shulammite Maiden and Her Shepherd Lover Are Reunited (8:5–14)

Admittedly, the collage of poetic units constituting the conclusion of the Song presents numerous difficulties for the interpreter. The problem in identifying the character speaking, determining the extent of that speech, and then assigning those speech units to the appropriate characters is so acute that many commentators regard these last ten verses as a separate collection of poetic fragments appended to the Song by later scribes or editors. The dissimilarity of the material with the rest of the poem, along with the moralizing tendencies of 8:6–7, is cited as further evidence of the disjunctive nature of this section (cf. Murphy, 195). The anthology-of-love-poems approach identifies four separate poems in the section of 8:5–14 (8:5–7, 8–10, 11–12, 13–14; see Longman, 206–22).

The interrogative "Who is this?" echoes 3:6 and 6:10, and as in the other two instances, the maiden is the object of the question (8:5a). Here it is probably the maiden's brother (or her brothers) who calls attention to the pair approaching arm in arm by questioning his companions in the field or vineyard.

The Hebrew verb forms in 8:5b–7 have masculine suffixes, indicating the maiden is speaking to her lover. The apple-tree motif of 8:5b occurred previously, in the context of the maiden's description of the lover and her delight in his lovemaking (2:3–6). While it is clear that the maiden initiates the love-play and that the passage makes reference to marital love, verse 5b defies explanation. Perhaps the verse is an oblique statement about the cycle of love in humanity—lovemaking, conception, birth, life, and love aroused, leading to lovemaking and conception in the next generation. This then is the maiden's poetic declaration that she is fulfilling her destiny in life by her love relationship with the shepherd.

Seals (8:6) were pieces of stone or metal inscribed with personalized markings and were tantamount to an individual's signature. The seal was an important emblem of ownership and possession in the ancient world. When stamped, the impression of the seal registered the seal-bearer's claim whether in economic or legal documents, or even on private property (cf. Hess, 238; Garrett, 529–30). The maiden requests that the seal of her lover be stamped indelibly on her heart. Then he, and he alone,

will have claim to the maiden's love. Why? The proverbial statements of verses 6–7 help explain the didactic purposes of the poem and serve as the climax to the foil of the maiden's one-to-one love and Solomon's one-to-many love. Genuine human love is as permanent as death, and the righteous jealousy of this affection will never surrender possession of the loved one, just as the grave tenaciously clings to the dead. True love burns bright and intense, "a raging flame" (8:6, NRSV). This phrase literally reads "flame of Yah" and has puzzled translators and interpreters. If this is a reference to Yahweh, the verse implies God himself kindles the flames of human love. Finally, the flames of genuine human love are unquenchable in the face of life's surging flood tides. The worth, the value, of this kind of love is beyond calculation. The wealth of a household, indeed the wealth of an empire (even Solomon's), cannot purchase the loyalty, devotion, true passion, and faithfulness of genuine human love.

The maiden's brothers recall her growth and development from their "little sister" into a mature woman ready for a life of her own (8:8–9). The earlier anger of the brothers (1:6) was likely their jealous protection of their sister's chastity against the designs of overzealous suitors in an attempt to prevent premature love before the proper time for her marriage. The phrase "on

In Song of Solomon 8:6, the maiden asks her lover to "place me like a seal over your heart." Ancient seals such as this one, which is stamped into a storage jar handle, denoted ownership. The design contains the wording "lmlk" ("belonging to the king") above a winged sun disc and the place name "Sokoh" (eighth–seventh century BC).

the day she is spoken for" (8:8) implies this was the purpose of the lovers' return to her home village—the granting of approval for marriage. If she proves worthy of such a union (i.e., if she has preserved her virginity), they will dutifully provide her with the dress, ornamentation, and dowry befitting such a momentous occasion.

In reply to the conditional pledge of her brothers, the maiden avows that she has guarded her chastity and remains a virgin (8:10–12). Despite her abduction and the wooing of Solomon, she has remained a garden locked, a spring sealed, a reservoir of faithful love. Implicit in the maiden's boast of chastity is her maturing and blossoming womanhood and her readiness for wedlock ("my breasts are like towers"). "His eyes" is a reference to the shepherd lover, and "bringing contentment" suggests his recognition of the rightness and the wholesomeness of their relationship.

The term "vineyard" has consistently been a metaphor for the person of the maiden (including her sexual charms). The strongest support for the three-character interpretation of the Song is found here. The maiden's "vineyard," her love and sexual delicacies, belonged to her and were hers to give. Solomon had let out his vineyard (his own person and his own sexual energies) to "tenants" (i.e., the women of the royal harem). Whether two hundred women (cf. the 140 in 6:8) or the one thousand women (1 Kings 11:3), Solomon has made his choice—including the ugly consequences that surfaced later in his reign (cf. 1 Kings 11:1–8). The maiden has preserved her "vineyard" from the exploitation and corruption of harem love and now experiences the joy of freely giving it to her *one* lover.

The shepherd addresses either those who live in the maiden's village or the maiden herself (8:13). If the former, he is seeking public approval and support from the clan for his marriage to the maiden or else calling for shouts of celebration in response to the wedding feast. If the latter, he beckons the maiden for a song confirming her desire for him and commitment to a life of love even rivers cannot wash away (8:7).

The maiden's response (perhaps part of a nuptial song) is immediate and complete (8:14). Her invitation to love, oft repeated, will finally, joyously be realized. The maiden will pour out her love long stored, and the lovers will eat, drink, feast, and linger over love's delicacies. Love will not be aroused until its desire has been fulfilled (2:7; 3:5; 8:4). The gazelle/stag simile calls to mind an early fantasy of the maiden (2:8–13). The erotic symbolism of the poem's concluding verse is simple and appropriate. The maiden tenderly invites the shepherd to playfully, happily commune with her in all the jubilation, ecstasy, and mystery of sexual love.

Select Bibliography

Bullock, C. Hassell. *An Introduction to the Old Testament Poetic Books.* Chicago: Moody, 1979.

Carr, G. L. *The Song of Solomon.* Tyndale Old Testament Commentaries. Downers Grove, IL: InterVarsity, 1984.

Garrett, Duane. "Song of Songs." In *Zondervan Illustrated Bible Backgrounds Commentary.* Edited by John H. Walton. Grand Rapids: Zondervan, 2009.

Garrett, Duane, and Paul R. House. *Song of Songs/Lamentations.* Word Biblical Commentary. Nashville: Thomas Nelson, 2004.

Gledhill, Tom. *The Message of the Song of Songs.* Downers Grove, IL: InterVarsity, 1994.

Hess, Richard S. *Song of Songs.* Baker Commentary on the Old Testament Wisdom and Psalms. Grand Rapids: Baker Academic, 2005.

Jenson, Robert W. *Song of Songs.* Interpretation. Louisville: Westminster John Knox, 2005.

Longman, Tremper, III. *Song of Songs.* New International Commentary on the Old Testament. Grand Rapids: Eerdmans, 2001.

Murphy, Roland E. *The Song of Songs.* Hermeneia. Minneapolis: Fortress, 1990.

Pope, Marvin. *Song of Songs.* Anchor Bible. Garden City, NY: Doubleday, 1977.

Provan, Iain. *Ecclesiastes/Song of Songs.* NIV Application Commentary. Grand Rapids: Zondervan, 2001.

Ryken, Leland. "The Song of Solomon." In *Words of Delight: A Literary Introduction to the Bible.* 2nd ed. Grand Rapids: Baker Academic, 1993.

The Prophetic Books

The Prophetic Books record the messages of persons inspired and called by God to minister to the spiritual condition of the covenant people. They include the books of Isaiah through Malachi and constitute a section of the biblical canon also called simply "the Prophets." The books of the Prophets are subdivided into the Major Prophets (Isaiah, Jeremiah, Ezekiel, and Daniel) and the Minor Prophets (Hosea, Joel, Amos, Obadiah, Jonah, Micah, Nahum, Habakkuk, Zephaniah, Haggai, Zechariah, and Malachi). The term "prophet" comes from a Greek word, and has often been interpreted as either a "forthteller" or a "foreteller." The principal Hebrew term for "prophet," however, means "one called" to proclaim a message of divine origin. The prophets announced good and bad tidings alike, depending upon the circumstances, over a period of several centuries.

The prophets sometimes received their messages directly from God, but on other occasions indirectly in visions and dreams. Although there were prophetesses in Israel, only men seem to have made public proclamations that were recorded. Prophets came from various social levels. Some were of obscure origin, such as Elijah, while others were priests (Ezekiel and possibly Jeremiah). Isaiah was probably a highly placed court official in Judah, while Daniel, though not strictly a prophet in the usual sense, was a

The prophets Daniel, Ezekiel, Jeremiah, and Isaiah stand at the southwest entrance of the Skara Domkyrka, Sweden.

distinguished statesman of Hebrew origin in a foreign court.

The purpose of prophecy was to confront the nation of Israel with the demands of traditional covenantal faith based on the instruction of the Mosaic law, to condemn idolatrous practices in Israel, and to promise punishment if such behavior continued or blessing if the people heeded the call to repentance and returned to faith in God. Predictions of a Messiah and a new kingdom of righteousness are notable elements of prophecy, along with the assurance of a new covenant, the latter being established by the Christ-event.

The prophets' messages were based on a thorough knowledge of the law of Moses, and the individuals received their proclamations as part of their spiritual communion with God. Two themes, especially, course through the books of the Prophets—the appropriate worship of God and the practice of social justice—giving them currency across the ages. Their words were recorded in somewhat different ways, but written accounts probably would have been made at or shortly after the time of oral delivery. The collections of the prophets' oracles into books or anthologies likely occurred in stages, taking final form sometime after the death of the prophet. Their proclamations glorified God as supreme Lord, revealed his will for the nation, and demanded a high level of dedication and spiritual living among the Israelites. Their declaration of God's redemption in history was climaxed by the work of Jesus, who came to fulfill all that the Law and the Prophets had spoken concerning him. The prophetic writings are among the great spiritual treasures of the Christian church.

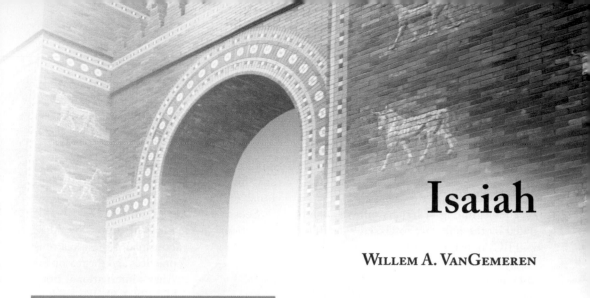

Isaiah

WILLEM A. VANGEMEREN

Introduction

Isaiah the Prophet

Little is known about the prophet Isaiah other than that he loved Jerusalem, freely associated with Judah's kings, was married, and had two children. The name Isaiah means "Yahweh is salvation." His name and the names of his sons—Shear-Jashub ("a remnant will return"; see NIV note for 7:3) and Maher-Shalal-Hash-Baz ("quickly to the plunder, swift to the spoil"; see NIV note for 8:1)—were symbolic to the nation (8:18). These three names capture the essence of the book: (1) Yahweh is the source of salvation; (2) Yahweh will spare a remnant for himself; and (3) Yahweh's judgment is certain to come.

The prophet's relationship to the royal house of David has been a subject of speculation. The prophet moved easily into and out of the palace and had access to the king. He was respected by Ahaz and Hezekiah. Though this relationship does not prove that Isaiah was of royal lineage, it is clear that he held a respected position in the court. The tradition of Isaiah's royal lineage cannot, however, be demonstrated. Isaiah was, nevertheless, very familiar with court protocol and life in Jerusalem. He was respected in the court of Jerusalem even when he criticized the ruling classes.

Isaiah's father, Amoz, is not to be identified with the prophet Amos, who ministered a generation earlier in the northern kingdom.

The spelling of these two names is different both in Hebrew and in English. Isaiah was a highly educated man who lived mainly in Jerusalem. He ministered to God's people roughly from 742 to 700 BC in an era of great political tumult.

What little is known about Isaiah's death is derived from extrabiblical sources. There are several traditions that, when taken together, strongly suggest Isaiah may have suffered martyrdom under Manasseh, who succeeded Hezekiah.

Isaiah was a "son of Jerusalem." The book is full of Isaiah's love and concern for the city. He believed the city was representative of the people as a whole.

Clearly Isaiah was well acquainted with the city of Jerusalem, the temple (1:11–15), the ways of the rich, and the suffering of the poor. Because of his love for Jerusalem, he never delights in the messages of doom to the city and her inhabitants. He pictures the city as a "shelter" in a vineyard (1:8), and he gratefully speaks about God's mercy and desire to call a remnant who will return to Jerusalem after the exile and share in the joy God has prepared for the city and her population:

> But be glad and rejoice forever
> in what I will create,
> for I will create Jerusalem to be a
> delight
> and its people a joy. (65:18)

Even though it is nowhere clearly stated where Isaiah was born and raised, all indications point to a man who knew the city of Jerusalem, walked in it, and loved it as the city God had chosen in which to establish his name and glory.

Historical Context

The beginning of Isaiah's ministry can be dated by the reference to Uzziah's death (ca. 740 BC) in 6:1. Under Uzziah, Judah gained remarkable economic achievements (2 Chron. 26:6–15) and made an attempt to reassert herself as a political power. Following Uzziah's death, Judah would be cast into the midst of a stream of international developments that would leave her a vassal state of the Assyrian Empire. During his ministry, Isaiah witnessed the fall of Aram (Syria) and Israel as well as the desolation of Judah by the Assyrians.

Succeeding Uzziah, Jotham (750–732 BC) ruled a nation that was materially strong but corrupt in her values and apostate in her adherence to Yahweh. Hosea and Amos had condemned the excesses of wealth and injustice in the north, and Isaiah brought the same condemnation against the southern kingdom. Jotham died in peace while the Assyrian fist was being raised toward Aram, Israel, and Judah. Tiglath-Pileser III ("Pul" in 2 Kings 15:19) subjugated cities lying

A painting of the prophet Isaiah by Duccio di Buoninsegna (AD 1308–11)

on the route from Nineveh to Damascus. When Jotham died, the handwriting was on the wall.

A king who plays a more prominent role in the book of Isaiah is Ahaz. He ruled over Judah from 732 to 716 BC. Though Ahaz was not the kind of man to seek a prophet's counsel, God sent him a word of encouragement through Isaiah (chap. 7).

Second Chronicles enumerates a list of objectionable practices instituted by Ahaz and explains the idolatrous practices and the reason for Ahaz's international troubles (28:2–8). The book of Isaiah presents Ahaz as a man imprudent in political affairs. The alliance of Rezin, king of Aram, and Pekah, king of Israel, was intended to create a buffer against the expansionist drive of Assyria. In order to accomplish this, the allied kings needed Ahaz to join their confederacy. When he refused, Rezin and Pekah marched against Ahaz, intending to dethrone him and to set up a king in Ahaz's place who would be sympathetic to their political scheming (2 Kings 16:5; Isa. 7:6). Ahaz was greatly disturbed about the Syro-Ephraimite alliance. Into this context, Isaiah brought God's word. Isaiah challenged Ahaz not to fear their power, and instead to look to God's presence in Jerusalem as the strength of Judah. Ignoring God's word, Ahaz looked for a political solution and asked Tiglath-Pileser of Assyria to help him (2 Kings 16:7). Tiglath-Pileser swiftly reacted to the threat on the western front. In 734 BC he marched through Phoenicia as far as Philistia, conquering as he went. In the following years he invaded Judah, which was reduced to a vassal state. Ahaz went to Damascus to celebrate Assyria's victories, and while there he saw an altar, a replica of which he constructed and set up in the temple court (2 Kings 16:10–16).

Ahaz's son Hezekiah was a godly king who sought counsel from the prophet Isaiah in times of national and personal tragedy. He ruled from 715 BC until his death, in 686 BC. During his rule he instituted many reforms (2 Kings 18:4, 22), including the celebration of the Passover (2 Chronicles 30). He witnessed the fall of Israel, which was overrun by the Assyrians when Hoshea refused to pay tribute to them. Shalmaneser IV began the campaign, and his successor, Sargon II, destroyed Samaria and exiled her population in 722 BC. Assyria's hegemony in the Syro-Palestinian region grew. In 711 BC, Sargon descended on Ashdod in Philistia because it was thought Ashdod had conspired against Assyria (Isa. 20:1). At Sargon's death (705 BC), Sennacherib took over. He faced an immediate coalition of Egypt, Philistia (except for Ekron), Babylon, and Judah (2 Kings 18:7), organized by Hezekiah. The southern king had hoped that the time had come to throw off the hegemony of Assyria, believing that Judah had the power to lead the conspiracy. This rebellion was quick to spark the anger of Sennacherib. On his way to Judah, he put down various rebellions in Mesopotamia, Phoenicia, and Philistia. His forces moved through Judah and may have taken as many as forty-six cities (some of which may be listed in Isa. 10:28–32 and Mic. 1:10–16). As Sennacherib approached Jerusalem, Hezekiah attempted to pacify Sennacherib's anger by sending him an abundance of tribute (2 Kings 18:13–16). Despite Hezekiah's attempt to divert the Assyrian forces, Sennacherib's march toward Jerusalem continued.

Finally, Sennacherib besieged Jerusalem. Hezekiah was locked in Jerusalem, surrounded by Assyrian forces. He had prepared well for the siege, but the Assyrians had the fortitude to wait for the surrender of Jerusalem. However, as Hezekiah and Jerusalem trustfully waited, the Lord intervened miraculously to deliver Jerusalem from the grasp of the Assyrian forces (2 Kings 19:35–36).

Literary Features

As far as literary style, the prophet Isaiah is a master of the Hebrew language. He knows how to express himself well and has a distinctive literary quality in his writing.

First, Isaiah uses rich vocabulary. Many of Isaiah's words are unique, occurring only once or just a few times in the whole Hebrew Bible. Both Isaiah's extensive vocabulary and choice of expression show his ability to use the Hebrew language in a highly poetic style with a variety of parallel forms.

In addition to variety in vocabulary, the book's brilliant and imaginative descriptions of war and of social and rural life, such as the parable of the vineyard in chapter 5, demonstrate Isaiah's familiarity with these areas of Israelite society. Isaiah is an extremely gifted preacher who knows exactly how to use the right illustration as he communicates God's revelation.

Many literary devices were available to him in the Hebrew literary tradition: personification, metaphor, simile, wordplay, alliteration, song, and satire. If one compares Isaiah with a book like 1 Samuel, both of them being nevertheless inspired, the difference in style becomes apparent. Isaiah captures the imagination with his use of various images, his sentences flowing one into the other, the tightly knit imagery demonstrating Isaiah's intimate familiarity with the world in which he lived.

Critical commentaries on Isaiah divide the material into three major divisions: chapters 1–39 are thought to have come from the eighth-century prophet Isaiah; chapters 40–55 from a sixth-century prophet known as Deutero- (or Second) Isaiah; chapters 56–66 from a fifth-century source known as Trito- (or Third) Isaiah. However, three arguments may be advanced in support of the unity of Isaiah.

First, Jesus and the apostles held to the unity of Isaiah. Whenever they quoted from the book of Isaiah, whether from the beginning or the end, they always referred to the prophet Isaiah. The Gospel of John has an interesting passage that combines two quotations from Isaiah, and each comes from a different section. John comments on the unbelief of the people at Jesus's time by referring to Isaiah 53:1 and on the effect of their unbelief by appealing to Isaiah 6:10. In this instance, one quotation comes from Isaiah 1–39 and another from Isaiah 40–66, yet both of them are introduced as the words of Isaiah: "This was to fulfill the word of Isaiah the prophet" (John 12:38) and "as Isaiah says elsewhere" (John 12:39). So whether in the first or second part of Isaiah, the whole of the prophecy is seen as being the work of one author: Isaiah.

Second, many of the dissimilarities between the critical divisions of Isaiah can be explained by a change in subject matter. The first division emphasizes the Lord's coming judgment on all flesh, whereas the latter part of the book of Isaiah emphasizes the comfort and consolation given to the remnant, for whom God still has a future. In fact, the second section begins with these words: "Comfort, comfort my people, says your God" (40:1). The theme of comfort is characteristic of most of the chapters in the second division. Though there may be some indication of judgment, the main message is one of comfort.

Moreover, even though the emphasis in the first part is on judgment, there is also a message of restoration. A brief comparison of two sections on the restoration (35:7–10 and 43:19–21) reveals a number of common elements: water, the road, animals, and the statement that the people of God do not have to be afraid. The shift in emphases also serves as an explanation for the dissimilarities in vocabulary and theme.

Third, despite some dissimilarities between the three divisions, there is wide recognition of similarities linking the three. The "blindness" and "deafness" terminology (6:9–10; 32:3; 35:5; 42:18–20; 43:9), the Jerusalem theme (1:27; 36:2; 40:2; 66:13), the expression "Holy One of Israel" (1:4; 41:14; 60:14), and the "highway" theme (35:8; 40:3) are examples of common links recognized between the three sections.

Theological Themes

The scope of the book takes us beyond Isaiah's days to the new heavens and the new earth. The prophecy spans the preexilic, exilic, and postexilic eras, the coming of the Messiah, the messianic age, the church, and the final consummation. The book unfolds God's plan for the redemption of his people. The meaning of Isaiah's name, "Yahweh is salvation"—also translated as "salvation is of the Lord" or "salvation of Yahweh"—reveals the purpose of the book.

The message of the gospel is found throughout the prophecy, and as a matter of fact the prophet concludes with it.

A portion of the Isaiah Scroll (ca. 100 BC), part of the Dead Sea Scrolls from Qumran

"As the new heavens and the new earth that I make will endure before me," declares the LORD, "so will your name and descendants endure. From one New Moon to another and from one Sabbath to another, all mankind will come and bow down before me," says the LORD. (Isa. 66:22–23)

Salvation is not to be limited to Israel only, for Isaiah as the "evangelical" prophet speaks also to Gentiles.

Outline

Commentary

1. Prophecies against Judah (1:1–12:6)

The first twelve chapters of Isaiah may be compared to a painting with three panels (a triptych). Isaiah's call to be a prophet (chap. 6) is at the center, while the other two parts of the triptych concern judgment and hope. The first section (chaps. 1–5) is in the form of a covenantal lawsuit, and the third section (chaps. 7–12) presents God's word of judgment and hope in the historical situation of the growing

Assyrian Empire. A holistic approach to these chapters presents the reader with Yahweh's holiness (6:3), Isaiah's prophetic calling (6:8), the finality of God's judgment (6:11–13a), and the hope for the remnant (6:13b). Each motif is developed throughout the triptych. The prophet begins with Yahweh's charges against Judah and Jerusalem (1:2–31) and concludes with the new song of the remnant who have discovered that the Holy One of Israel is still in the midst of his people (12:6). The focus, then, of all twelve chapters is on the Holy One of Israel, who cleanses Isaiah (6:7), and who, through the process of judgment, cleanses his people from all their sins and defilement (4:3–4).

A. Judgment and comfort: Part one (1:1–2:5). Isaiah calls on heaven and earth to witness against God's people in language reminiscent of Moses's Song of Witness (Deut. 30:19; 32:1; cf. Mic. 6:1–2). God's people have severed their relationship with Yahweh, their Father (1:1–4). Though Yahweh has treated them as sons, and Judah has received great benefits, the people foolishly abandon their heritage. They have become fools, who do not "know" and "do not understand" (1:3). Their folly has led to open rebellion against their suzerain (covenant) Lord. They have forsaken their loyalty to Yahweh and replaced it with hatred and apostasy. They are not children of God but "a brood of evildoers" (1:4). They have rejected "the Holy One of Israel," the God who not only sovereignly rules over his people but also has promised to dwell in their midst so as to sanctify them.

Yet the Lord has severely judged Judah not to destroy her but in order to get her attention (1:5–9). Her wounds symbolize the extent to which God has patiently dealt with his people. He has used wars, oppression, desolation, and famine in order to bring his people to their senses and to himself. The desolation may very well reflect the situation in 701 BC, when Sennacherib despoiled the land, destroyed the cities, and nearly took the city of Jerusalem. Were it not for the grace of God, Judah would have been destroyed like Sodom and Gomorrah. The leaders were at fault for bringing judgment on Judah. Clearly God did not intend to destroy her from under the face of the sun. The "Daughter Zion" (Jerusalem, remnant) is spared like "a shelter" (1:8). The intent of God's judgment is purification, and to that end Yahweh is patient and merciful.

The leaders are corrupt, like the people of Sodom and Gomorrah (1:10–17; Gen. 18:20). They are reminded of God's law, which requires righteousness as a prerequisite for bringing offerings and sacrifices (Deut. 33:19). The prophet is not antagonistic to offerings and sacrifices, feasts and festivals, and prayer; but he knows

Isaiah 1:8 describes Jerusalem "like a city under siege," similar to the attack against a city portrayed in this Assyrian relief (728 BC).

that God rejects any act of worship at any time, even in the holy court of his temple, when it is little more than an empty ritual. Worship must be pure. The requirements of ritual purity must be kept, and sacrifices are to be offered from a pure heart. The intensity of God's hatred of their worship affects sacrifices, convocations, and individuals. In their rebellion against God, they have maintained "religion," but in their practices they are corrupt. They cannot merit God's grace by their "pious" activities. Their "hands are full of blood" (1:15), because they have disregarded the rights of the needy. It is impossible to pray for relief from the enemy as long as no compassion is shown to the oppressed.

The proper response, then, to the grace of Yahweh is obedient faith (1:18–20). Obedient faith entails the willingness to remove and cleanse oneself from the evil of one's generation, to love one's neighbor, and to receive divine cleansing and forgiveness. True repentance results in faithful obedience, as an expression of gratitude and the willingness to obey God. The remnant that has survived the ordeal may again be restored to enjoy God's blessings. God has graciously opened up a future for them, but for those who rebel, judgment is sure to come.

In a lament, the prophet speaks about the filth of Jerusalem (1:21–26). Rather than resembling pure silver in the practice of justice, righteousness, and faithfulness, the city's silver has become dross (1:21–22). Isaiah reflects on the era of David and Solomon as one in which Israel was characterized by justice, righteousness, and loyalty to the Lord, because these leaders upheld God's law. But Jerusalem has become faithless, like a harlot. She is as worthless as wine diluted with water. People and leaders are all alike: each one is out for him- or herself. Yahweh, the great and merciful king, has seen their insensitivities and will come to the defense of the poor. He will bring them through another judgment in order to remove the "foes." God's "enemies" are all those who do not do his will, and it is significant that he addresses the covenant community. One is reminded of Jesus's

words that whoever is not for him is against him (Matt. 12:30; Luke 11:23).

God will certainly distinguish between the righteous and the wicked (1:27–31). The future belongs to the remnant, which repents by *doing* righteousness, but judgment will make an end of rebels and idolaters. Isaiah then compares the people as a whole to the effects of a drought in which the leaves of an oak fall off and the garden is burned up (1:30). However, the oak still stands and the garden is still there. Hard times may come upon the godly, but they will persevere. The wicked, however, will be utterly consumed as by fire.

In four verses (2:1–4) Isaiah describes the nature of God's kingdom: its glory, its extent, and its effect. The glory of God's kingdom is so great that it will be recognized by the nations. God's kingdom will not be limited to the Jews in Jerusalem or Judea but will extend to the nations, who will desire to be instructed by the people of God. The language is centripetal; the people are coming to one center to be instructed. The knowledge of God will be among the nations; and the nations, having been disciplined in the ways of God, will live in accordance with God's word. The universal knowledge of God is the precondition for the rule of God, which brings peace to the earth. The promises of verse 4 are especially reassuring in an age marred by terrorism and nuclear warfare. However, we must keep in mind that as long as nations make decisions for themselves without respect to God, there is little possibility for peace. The prophet envisions a time when Yahweh himself will rule the nations and will make decisions for them; then and only then will there be a state of shalom, when weaponry can be changed into implements of peace. Before this glorious vision may be realized, there is one precondition: men must respond in full submission to the Lord (2:5). It is possible to be inspired by the vision of the messianic age, but inspiration should lead to obedient faith.

B. Judgment and comfort: Part two (2:6–4:6). Isaiah now focuses on how God's people have rebelled (2:6–22). First, he singles out their rampant materialism, idolatry, and acceptance of pagan practices. He includes all pagan cultures by referring to the superstitions from the east and west (diviners of the Philistines). Judah, though isolated geographically, has opened herself to foreign cultures. This fits well with the period of Uzziah, when Judah made alliances with nations so as to maintain commercial and military relations. Their strength was in negotiation, and not in Yahweh. The people possessed silver and gold, horses and chariots, and idols. Judah was no different from other nations. God's judgment would show that idols would provide no help, that gold and silver could not save his people in the hour of disaster, and that the nations would be impotent in the hour of need. God's judgment comes against any and every monument of human pride. Yahweh alone will be exalted. The "day" of God's judgment (2:12) is a reference to an era in which God reveals his wrath. The emphasis on arrogance in this passage fits well with the imagery of the cedars of Lebanon, the oaks of Bashan, the mountains and hills, the high towers and fortified walls, and the stately ships (literally "ships of Tarshish"), which sailed the seas and brought crafts and products from other nations into the finest homes of Jerusalem. All these objects symbolize human pride and autonomous accomplishments. Humanity will have to face God, who comes to quell the rebellion of his subjects. Yahweh's day is the day of his self-exaltation, which excludes humanity and any reasons for pride.

Isaiah now charges the people with open rebellion (3:1–15). Their leaders are particularly responsible. He charges the leaders with irresponsibility and injustice, which have caused the poor to become poorer. This charge is also to be understood in the light of the previous charge of rebellion (2:8–9). The combination of corrupt leadership and widespread, open rebellion has resulted in social and moral upheaval. The Lord's judgment, however, will result in an even more catastrophic disruption of life in Judah. He will take away their food and water. He will remove the divinely ordained officers and will instead put over the people corrupt leaders who are immature and lacking in experience, like "youths" and "children" (3:4), and who will contribute to further social and moral decay in Judah. In addition, judgment comes in the form of the collapse of the economy and political structures. The ruins and the absence of qualified leaders reflect the situation in Judah after the ravages of Nebuchadnezzar (586 BC). Though God's judgment will result in terrible lawlessness, the righteous remnant must take heart, knowing that they will be rewarded. The Lord brings a suit against the corrupt leaders who have taken advantage of their office.

Yahweh charges the daughters of Jerusalem with pride and seduction (3:16–4:1). The men of Jerusalem are selfish, materialistic, and oppressive, but they have partners in their wives and lovers, who have an insatiable desire to beautify themselves, enrich themselves, and compete with each other. The brief description of the "fine" women is followed by the effects of the day of Yahweh: all their pretty things will be removed, they will go around filled with mourning, and their men will fall in battle. Their glory will turn to shame. The severity of their loneliness will be so great that these women will fight over a man in order to remove the disgrace of their childlessness.

The prophet's theme now changes abruptly, for in 4:2–6 Isaiah speaks about the new messianic era. While human pride is gone, there is a future for the remnant who have humbled themselves in the presence of the Lord. Isaiah develops the theme of the messianic kingdom, begun in 2:1–5, by speaking about the people as "the Branch of the Lord." This "Branch" is not the branch of a tree but a new shoot out of the ground; it refers to the survivors of the day of judgment. "Branch" may also signify the Messiah of David, as in Jeremiah 23:5; 33:15 and Zechariah 3:8; 6:12, but the more general designation of messianic "people" fits the context best. The "fruit of the land" (4:2) describes the blessedness of the land, as the people are restored to God's blessings.

The messianic era is characterized here as an era of restoration. The remnant, the people of God, has survived God's judgment. The day of the Lord has been a day of terror but also one of purification. The filth of corruption, the fires of rebellion, and the folly of God's people have been removed; those who are left are now described as holy; and their names are recorded in the book of life. Having consecrated for himself a new people who will be responsive to him, God assures them of his glorious presence. The glory of the Lord, revealed to Israel in the wilderness, will protect only those who are holy and over whom his judgment has passed.

C. Judgment (5:1–30). Isaiah may have sung his parabolic poem about the vineyard (5:1–7) at a wine festival, surprising his listeners with the application. He sings about a "friend" (NIV "loved one") who gives himself with exacting care to the preparation of a vineyard. The vineyard, however, produces only sour grapes. Isaiah asks what else this "friend" could have done for the vineyard. The rhetorical question must be answered! The prophet then explains that the vineyard represents the people of Israel and Judah and that the Lord is the keeper of the vineyard. He deeply cared for his people and lavished on them his grace and love, expecting justice and righteousness as the appropriate fruits. Instead of justice and righteousness, the people have responded with bloodshed, which has elicited a cry of distress from the downtrodden.

Six woes (5:8–24) explaining the nature of oppression, bloodshed, and the cry for justice (5:7) are directly related to the parable of the vineyard. In these six woes Isaiah has painted for us a portrait of God's people near the end of the eighth century. The portrait is that of social elites who have perverted justice, morality, religious values, and the wisdom that flows out of the fear of the Lord. In his description of the rich, Isaiah gives us a candid glimpse, not only of the Judean society of his day, but

of the besetting sins of human society at any time and place. The first woe (5:8–10) is against economic opportunists who amass more and more material wealth. They flaunt the inalienable relationship of the people to "God's land" (Lev. 25:13–16). They accumulate houses and fields at the expense of the economically disadvantaged. Their houses will be in ruins, and their vineyards and fields will not produce enough to make a living. The picture in these verses is one of loneliness: houses that were once full of parties will be no more. A ten-acre vineyard will produce only one bath (6 gallons) of wine; a homer of seed (6.4 bushels) will yield only a little over half a bushel.

The second woe (5:11–17) pertains to drunkards who spend all their time feasting and drinking. They cannot wait to begin their day with a drink and prepare banquets in order to attract others who enjoy drinking. Isaiah does not say much about the source of the money with which their wine and strong drink are purchased, but it may be deduced from the context that the wine has been obtained with the money and labors of the poor. In their drunken stupor, they are ignorant of the ways of God. They will go into exile as fools who did not know that the day of the Lord was coming on all. Death will inevitably overtake those who know nothing but the joys of life.

The third woe (5:18–19) pertains to those who corrupt justice. They have no sense of the holiness of God and even scoff at the thought of the coming judgment.

The fourth woe (5:20) is pronounced against those who corrupt religious values. They do not know the difference between good and evil, darkness and light, bitter and sweet. They confound their own conscience and the consciences of others. The revelation of God is no longer a light for their path because their standards have confused the clarity of God's revelation.

The fifth woe (5:21) is to those who have exchanged the wisdom of God for the folly of man.

The sixth woe (5:22–23) also applies to drunkards. Here Isaiah describes the drunkard as a man who feels strong in his drinking. He enjoys power. While he feasts, he is getting rich at the expense of others.

While there are hints at the coming judgment of God throughout the woes, the prophet provides greater detail toward the end (5:25–30). Clearly social position does not deter judgment, because the ultimate polarity is between sinful people and a holy God (5:16). When God enters into judgment, he comes as the great king (Lord Almighty) and the Holy One of Israel. Because they have spurned his law and his covenant, the anger of the God of Mount Sinai will burn against his own people. He will mercilessly strike his people with blow upon blow. Fierce and untiring enemies will come at God's command. With rapidity and catastrophic power they will destroy and exile God's people. The

day of the Lord is not a day of restoration and light, but full of darkness, anxiety, and gloom.

D. Isaiah's call (6:1–13). The prophet dates his vision of God's glory (6:1–4) to the year in which King Uzziah died. Scholars have tried to understand the significance of this dating, but it is enough to recognize that this is one way of connecting chapter 6 to the context of the Syro-Ephraimite War (see Isa. 7:1). A vision of the Lord appears to the prophet. He sees Yahweh sitting on the throne, exalted in the temple. The prophet concentrates not on the throne or on the Lord seated on it but on "the train of his robe" as it fills the temple, which is filled with the glorious presence of the Lord. He touches the earth in his power and glory, and yet the earth and the earthly temple cannot contain him. The appearance of the Lord, transcendent in his majesty and yet immanent in his presence, is represented in the language of a theophany. It affects all things on earth: the doorposts and thresholds of the temple, for instance, shake as in an earthquake. When the Lord appeared on Mount Sinai, his revelation was preceded by an earthquake, lightning, and darkness (Exod. 19:16). Isaiah finds himself gazing at a ceremony in which the seraphim announce the glorious presence of the Holy One of Israel. The seraphim are like men in appearance, with faces and feet; however, they are unlike men in that they have six wings, with which they cover themselves in the presence of the Lord. As they hover in his presence, they call out, "Holy, holy, holy."

The holiness of the Lord is a most important doctrine in the teaching of Isaiah. Yahweh's holiness is an expression of his separateness from the corruption of his people. He is the Holy One of Israel, and in this sense he is the "wholly

On this ancient throne, from Pharaoh Tutankhamun, winged serpents form the armrests and would flank the king as he sat (fourteenth century BC).

other" one. Israel and Judah will not be able to experience the loving-kindness of the Lord until they have been cleansed and sanctified; only then can they experience the presence of the Holy One of Israel. The seraphim ascribe holiness to "the Lord Almighty" ("the Lord of Hosts"). He is the great King over "the host" of heaven (Deut. 4:19; 1 Kings 22:19; Isa. 40:26) and over the earth, which as part of his kingdom "is full of his glory" (6:3). The word "glory" is also important to the message of Isaiah. It signifies the majesty and splendor of the presence of Yahweh. Over against all the wealth of the rich and the royal courts of earthly kings is the king of glory, whose judgment will destroy human kingdoms and frustrate human plans. When the king of glory establishes his kingdom and extends it from shore to shore, the fullness of his glory will become evident. The seraphim already see the whole earth full of his glory.

In an appropriate response to the impact of the vision of God's holiness, presence, and glory, Isaiah calls out, "Woe to me!" (6:5). The prophet fears for his life, as he is particularly aware of his uncleanness—he *represents* the sinful nation (6:5–7). In response, one of the seraphs takes with special tongs a burning coal from the altar and touches Isaiah's mouth. The ceremony is reminiscent of the incense altar (Exod. 30:1–10), which was lit by a burning coal taken from the altar (Lev. 16:12–13). Before Isaiah is able to speak to the Lord, he must be forgiven. This forgiveness is personal. Once Isaiah has been purified, he is permitted to speak in the heavenly council and receives his commissioning.

In his heavenly council Yahweh asks the question, "Who will go for us?" (6:8). Isaiah volunteers, and Yahweh immediately commissions him (6:8–13). The commission consists of a declaration that Isaiah's ministry is going to be hard and long. His message will prick the conscience of people, but they will harden themselves against God and his word. Isaiah is shown the desolation of the land and the exile of the population. The emphasis is on judgment,

devastation, and desolation. But there is hope, for the "holy seed" will remain. Isaiah begins chapter 1 with the "brood of evildoers" (literally "seed of . . .") and concludes chapter 6 with a ray of hope ("holy seed").

The messages of the first part of the triptych (chaps. 1–5—Judah's sin, God's judgment, the remnant, and the messianic kingdom; see beginning of commentary on 1:1–12:6) are not set in historical context. This changes with the historical reference to the year of Uzziah's death (6:1), and the third part of the triptych (chaps. 7–12) begins with events associated with Ahaz. When Ahaz came to the throne, the Aramean (Syrian) power was about to be eclipsed. The Arameans were already feeling mounting pressure from the east, as the Assyrians were moving westward. God's word comes to Israel, Aram, Assyria, and Judah. Everything that happens on earth results from God's sovereign rule.

E. Crisis in perspective (7:1–8:22). The Arameans have made an alliance with the Israelites in order to create a united front against Assyria. In order to further their goals, they plan to dethrone Ahaz and place their own man ("the son of Tabeel," 7:6) on the throne in Jerusalem.

The prophet and his son Shear-Jashub (whose name signifies the hope that "a remnant will return") meet Ahaz at the upper pool. Ahaz is shaken by the alliance and needs counsel (7:1–9).

Isaiah calls on Ahaz to face the crisis from God's perspective. These two mighty kingdoms, Israel and Aram, are nothing more than "two smoldering stubs of firewood" (7:4) who will soon come to an end. The challenge (7:9) is a pun created by the assonance of the Hebrew words translated "stand firm" and "stand"; the NIV makes an attempt to reflect this. Aram came to an end in 732 BC, and Assyria exiled Israel in 722 BC.

The emphasis on God's presence in this crisis receives special significance in the naming of a child: Immanuel (7:10–17). Isaiah challenges Ahaz to ask for a sign, so that he might "stand firm in [his] faith" (7:9). The king piously refuses. Knowing that Ahaz has set his heart on a political solution, Isaiah rebukes him (7:13). Ahaz is impatient with the solution of faith and looks toward Assyria for a novel approach. The Lord, however, has a sign for Ahaz, the house of David, and all who would hear it. The sign is the "Immanuel" (7:14).

Much controversy has surrounded the meaning of the sign: what is the meaning of "virgin," and who is the child? The validity of the sign lies in a miracle or event and must be of significance to Ahaz. The birth of Christ was a miracle but would have been of little relevance to Ahaz in his time. If the sign was to strengthen the word of God in Ahaz's time, it may have been that Isaiah spoke of a woman in the royal court or of his own wife (8:1–4, 18). The child could not be Hezekiah, however, since he was already born by this time. Though Isaiah's son is not *the* Immanuel, he is a *sign* of the Immanuel, in that Judah is spared. Through Isaiah, God assures Judah that his promises to David (2 Sam. 7:11–16) will come to pass. The Lord has not abandoned the house of David! He marshals the Assyrians to remedy this crisis situation.

As problematic as the interpretation of this passage is, the quotation in Matthew is authoritative. It focuses on Jesus the Messiah as *the* Immanuel, the Savior sent by the Father. Ahaz may have looked for a fulfillment and witnessed the desolation of Aram, but he did not understand the fullness of the prophetic witness.

Ahaz's policy pushes him into direct contact with Assyria (7:18–25). He appeals to Tiglath-Pileser (the "razor hired"). Others have looked to Egypt. The clash for power in the Mediterranean Basin will result in great devastation. Assyria is God's appointed means and will "shave" Judah; that is, he will exact tribute (7:20). Judah will be impoverished and will only survive on "curds and honey" because its luxuriant vineyards and cultivated fields will become grazing land for cows and sheep.

The birth of Isaiah's second son is significant (8:1–4). To properly emphasize its significance,

he writes on a large scroll the name "quick to the plunder, swift to the spoil." This he does in the presence of two witnesses: Uriah the high priest and Zechariah. Then he has relations with his wife, "the prophetess," and out of that union a child is born. The child's name signifies judgment on Israel and Aram and a contemporary fulfillment of 7:14. Thus, in a short time the Assyrian forces will carry off the "plunder" of Damascus and Samaria.

The people have rejected the Lord and his promises to David (symbolized by the waters of Shiloah; 8:6). They have lost heart over the Israelite-Aramean alliance, not trusting in God. Yet God is sovereign over the nations (8:5–10). He permits the Assyrians to "flood" the Mediterranean Basin with their forces. The Euphrates River (8:7) symbolizes Assyrian strength. It will overpower the nations but will not destroy Judah, because of the Immanuel-presence of the Lord. The "outspread wings" in 8:8 are a figure of God's protection of his people (cf. Ps. 91:4). God has set the bounds of Assyria's power.

The prophet calls on the nations to recognize that they are pawns in the hands of God. The Lord effectively works out all his plans. The nations cannot stand up against the God who has promised to protect his people. He is Immanuel! There also seems to be an eschatological dimension here, as it foreshadows the end of human resistance to God's plans. God's plan will be done on earth, as it is in heaven.

Isaiah is warned not to identify with the secular values of his contemporaries (8:11–15). Those who follow the Lord are not to give in to the prevailing political and economic winds of their age. As secularism and humanism grow stronger and the believing community is increasingly pressured in a world without God, Isaiah reminds us to look at the world from God's perspective: the world is under his judgment, and the Lord himself should be the object of our fear. The name of the Lord is a "stone of stumbling" (8:14–15 KJV) to those who keep their political options open. The people do not listen to his message because they are hardened.

Rather than enjoying God's protection, they plot their own course with self-reliance. He is the Lord of Hosts and the Holy One, who offers sanctuary to those who fear him alone.

As the "stone," he evokes a response of either faith or rejection, causing an offense that will snare the people of Jerusalem.

Isaiah leads the godly remnant to find shelter in the Lord (8:16–22). The Lord has instructed Judah through Isaiah, whose teachings are consonant with the testimony and law of Moses. His teaching of judgment and hope is summarized in the names Maher-Shalal-Hash-Baz, Shear-Jashub, and Isaiah (8:18).

As for the rest of the people, God's judgment will find them out if they continue to reject the prophetic call to repentance. The judgment is described as desolation, devastation, famine, and despair from which there is no escape. It is a time without hope for the future, because God appears to be at a great distance from his people. In their abandonment they will even consult the dead. Isaiah calls on them to seek the light of the Lord's testimony and law as revealed in his own message (8:20). Otherwise, they will come to realize the futility of reliance on kings and nationhood.

F. The Messiah (9:1–7). In 733 BC, Tiglath-Pileser III besieged Damascus, invaded the region of Galilee, including Zebulun and Naphtali, and incorporated it into his kingdom (2 Kings 15:29) in fulfillment of God's word. "Gloom" and "distress" result from oppression and separation from Yahweh's covenantal love. But the Lord will graciously turn humiliation into glory. How? By the coming of the Messiah of David (9:1–7). Although the northern tribes have rejected David's dynasty in favor of Jeroboam (1 Kings 12:1–20), their salvation will come from the very one whom they rejected. The new era will be characterized by great joy. The Messiah will free his people from their enemies and bring the actualization of the Davidic ideal.

The child (9:6) is the Immanuel (7:14). He is God's gift to humanity's predicament. He is fully human ("child," "born," "son"), but he is also divine, with all the perfections of kingship in himself: supernatural wisdom, might, paternal beneficence, and peace. This son will reign forever in justice, righteousness, and peace. The certainty of his kingdom is guaranteed by "the zeal of the LORD" (9:7).

G. The wrath of God (9:8–10:34). The Lord's mercy is demonstrated in his patience with the corrupt northern kingdom. However, they are not responsive. The shadow of God's outstretched hand hangs over Samaria (9:12, 17, 21; 10:4; cf. 5:25; Amos 4:6–12). His judgment is relentless in view of the stubborn persistence of evil in Israel.

The attack of the Arameans and Philistines (ca. 737 BC) weakens Israel, but Israel does not view this military defeat as an expression of the Lord's discipline. Instead, the leaders seize it as a political opportunity. Foolish Israel cannot see that the Lord has raised up the Assyrians to chasten her (9:8–12)!

This era is marked by civil wars and coups d'état (9:13–21; 2 Kings 15:8–30). All classes of people ("head and tail," "branch and reed") will ultimately suffer at the hands of the Lord: young and old, rich and poor, political and religious leaders alike. All Israel is characterized by perversity ("ungodly"), evil, and impiety (NIV 1984 "vileness"; the Hebrew Masoretic Text and NIV have "folly").

Godlessness and chaos are twins. Anarchy destroys the fiber of Israel's life like a fire (9:20–21). It spreads first through the underbrush and finally destroys everything. The Lord permits the anarchy, but he is still in control. The destructive forces of civil war and anarchy are also described metaphorically as a ferocious and uncontrollable appetite.

At the root of Israel's troubles is its resistance to God's just laws (10:1–4). Injustice prevails at the expense of the oppressed. In time, all Israel will be oppressed, but there will be no help forthcoming from the Lord. His anger will see to the righteous execution of his decree against Israel.

The Lord has granted Assyria's rise to power (10:5–19). He permitted Assyria to enrich herself as he sent her on his holy mission to reduce those nations that had provoked his wrath. Assyria's lust for power, however, is unbridled. She is a tyrant who boasts of her victories over cities and nations. The boast displays an attitude of autonomy and evidences no fear of God. Since Samaria has fallen (722 BC) and the Lord did not rescue it, how can Jerusalem expect to be rescued? The Assyrian advance has swept from Carchemish on the Euphrates to Jerusalem, and who can stop it? The Lord. Isaiah interrupts his sarcastic poem about Assyria's pride with a brief prose section (10:12), containing the Lord's response to Assyria's taunt. He will punish Assyria. Assyria is nothing more than God's instrument.

The nature of the judgment is then given in poetic form (10:13–19) and is likened to a fire and a wasting disease. Assyria claimed that her wealth and strength came by clever strategy and irresistible power. Nations were despoiled, being impotent to resist the might of

Assyria, but the God of Israel was witness and will judge Assyria. When he is through with Assyria, her power will be at an end. Assyria's warriors will be rendered powerless by a "wasting disease" (10:16), and Assyria's pomp will be easily reduced, even as a fire destroys a forest. Nonetheless, the Lord's "Light," which assures Judah of a future, will bring Assyria to an end.

The Lord's mercy is for the remnant's sake (10:20–23). Jerusalem was besieged in 701 BC, and the country was desolated. Yet after the siege was lifted, even this remnant did not return to the Lord. Therefore, destruction has been decreed and will ultimately bring down both Judah and Jerusalem. Through the ministry of the prophets, a true remnant is sensitized. They will return and rely on the Lord. The expectation of repentance and restoration is symbolized

The mighty warrior king trampling his enemies (see Isa. 10:6) is seen in many reliefs from the ancient Near East. Here the Assyrian king Ashurnasirpal tramples over an enemy soldier as he leads the chariot charge (865–860 BC).

in Isaiah's son Shear-Jashub ("a remnant will return," 7:3).

The Lord, who dealt graciously with his people in Egypt and rescued them from the Midianites in the days of the judges, will come to the rescue of his people once more (10:24–27). The victory belongs to the Lord. The promise of his wrath passing from Judah to the enemy has eschatological overtones. The prophet looks forward to the period of restoration as the end of the Lord's wrath and the beginning of deliverance from the oppressors. In a real sense, believers in Jesus are the remnant, who have been rescued from the wrath of God (1 Thess. 1:10), but who still await full deliverance from the enemies of God (2 Thess. 1:6–10).

The picture of the Assyrian advance from 10:9–11 is continued in 10:28–34. The Assyrians are closing in on Jerusalem, devastating city after city. The Assyrian march need not be construed as historical. The poetic imagery permits Isaiah to project the advance on Jerusalem from the direction of Samaria, as if it has just been conquered. The period between Samaria's fall (722 BC) and Jerusalem's siege (701 BC) is not his concern. He brings out a sense of panic. What will happen now? Will the Lord be faithful to his promise to remain with Judah? The answer is yes. God will first "lop off the boughs" by stopping Assyria's advance, and later he will cut down the might of Assyria. In less than a hundred years, Assyria will not be reckoned among the nations. God's word is true.

H. The Branch from Jesse (11:1–16). The threat to the Davidic dynasty (Isaiah 7) has passed. Ahaz has survived the attack, and Aram and Israel have been conquered by Assyria. In chapter 9 the prophet speaks about "a son" to whom the everlasting government will be given and whose throne will be established with justice, righteousness, and peace. In chapter 11 Isaiah again takes up the theme of the messianic rule.

Assyria and all world powers will fall like "lofty trees" (10:33), but the Lord will raise up his Messiah as a "shoot" (11:1–9). This shoot does not spring from one of the branches of a tree; its origin is the roots. The Messiah is a shoot from the roots of David's dynasty. The new leadership over God's people must come from David's dynasty, but it is also separate from the old dynastic interests. Kingship may cease in Judah, but God's promise to David will be kept. The messianic shoot does not conform to the old way. He introduces God's rule on earth, symbolized by the presence of the "Spirit of the LORD" (11:2).

The new stage in God's kingdom will combine the old (the Davidic covenant) and the new (the era of the Spirit). The presence of God's Spirit on the Messiah will be evident in his rule of wisdom, justice, righteousness, faithfulness, and peace, complete with the absence of evil and the universal knowledge of God. The messianic era is an idealization of the period of David and Solomon's rule over Israel. The qualities of the Messiah make him fit to protect his people. His relationship with God is beyond criticism, as he fears God and delights to do his will. He will protect the needy and execute judgment on the wicked without mercy. He favors his subjects with a rule of righteousness and faithfulness and will establish a paradisal renewal of the earth in which his peace extends even to nature; all people will know God.

The Messiah of the root of Jesse will be a "banner for the peoples" (11:10–16). He gathers the scattered remnant of Israel and Judah from the nations in a "second" exodus. They will freely come from Egypt (Upper = Pathros and Lower), Cush (Nubia/Ethiopia, the Upper Nile region), Elam (east of Babylonia), Shinar (Babylonia), Hamath (region north of Damascus), and the Mediterranean coastlands. He will join together the twelve tribes and rule over a restored Israel. Nothing can stand in the way of God's purpose. He will even dry up the Red Sea ("Egyptian" sea), make the Euphrates passable, and make a highway from Assyria and Egypt to Israel. The restoration from exile will be more glorious and more extensive than the first exodus. The fulfillment of this prophecy began in the restoration from exile and extends to the fullness of time, when Christ came to gather both Jews and Gentiles into his flock (John 10:16).

I. Songs of praise (12:1–6). Two brief hymns (12:1, 4–6) and an oracle of promise (12:2–3) make a fitting conclusion to the first division of Isaiah (chaps. 1–12). The prophet renews the promise of full and free salvation and calls on the godly to join him in confident trust in God. As the "strength" of his people, Yahweh is able to accomplish all that Isaiah has predicted: universal peace, the presence of God, the restoration of the remnant, the Messiah's rule, and the universal knowledge and fear of God.

The hymns focus on two aspects of deliverance: God's comfort of his people (12:1) and the proclamation of his acts of salvation to the nations (12:4–6). The day of judgment is against all flesh, and God alone will be "exalted." The righteous have been delivered from the finality of judgment and know the Lord as the "exalted," Holy One of Israel. The era of restoration is marked by redemption, proclamation, rejoicing, and the renewal of God's presence among his people.

Isaiah calls on the nations to exalt Yahweh's name because of what he does on behalf of his own. This expression of hope by God's own will result in responses of faith and praise by the nations. The expression of hope takes the form of thanks and songs of praise. Therefore, Isaiah calls on the remnant to drown out their sorrows in songs of joy in and expectation of their deliverance by the Holy One of Israel. If God's own people can live in joyful expectation of the final redemption, the world will take notice.

The people who were restored to the land of Judah after the exile had reason to celebrate and give thanks to God for the redemption they had experienced. The fullness of that redemption, however, was not yet theirs. The day to which the prophet refers in verse 1 extends from the restoration after the exile all the way to the return of the Lord Jesus Christ.

Chapter 12 forms a transition between chapters 1–11 (Yahweh's judgment on Judah) and chapters 13–23 (Yahweh's judgment on the world). The focus of chapter 12 grants us an insight into the plan of God by revealing that, while God is angry with this world (including the Jews), he still holds out his arms to all who will exalt his name, whether they are Jews or Gentiles.

2. Oracles against the Nations (13:1–23:18)

These messages are called "oracles." The word "oracle" (literally "burden") is a technical term and occurs in the heading of Isaiah's speech against each nation (13:1—Babylon; 17:1—Damascus; 19:1—Egypt; 23:1—Tyre; cf. also 21:1, 11, 13; 22:1; 30:6). Similar collections are found in Jeremiah 46–51 and Ezekiel 25–32. This collection of oracles forms the second major division of Isaiah and prepares the reader for the "Apocalypse of Isaiah" (chaps. 24–27).

A. Babylon (13:1–14:23). Isaiah views the Lord's judgment on Babylon as an expression of his rule over the earth (13:1–16). He commands the armed forces of the nations. The "holy ones" are the warriors mustered and consecrated for battle (13:3 NIV 1984). The Lord sovereignly rules over the nations, who serve him without knowledge of their being the instruments of the establishment of his kingdom. The descriptions of the ensuing battle and the day of the Lord take on universal proportions. The nations of the earth are involved. The day of the Lord as a time of great destruction on earth is near. Humanity is totally helpless. Heaven and earth heave when God expresses his anger with sinful man. Few survive, and even those who escape will come to a painful end.

The cosmic description of the day of the Lord is applied to Babylon's fall (13:17–22). As an expression of his sovereignty, God will also turn against mighty Babylon. The fall of Babylon will be great. In colorful language Isaiah portrays the devastation caused by her enemies. The enemies are the Medes (13:17), who together with the Persians conquered Babylon under the leadership of Cyrus the Persian (539

BC). They will have no pity. Her doom is that of a deserted city. The desolation of Babylon is graphically portrayed by its becoming the haunt of wild animals, like Sodom and Gomorrah. This prophecy was not completely fulfilled when Cyrus entered Babylon; the transfer of power was rather quiet. It seems that the prophet extends the perimeter of application to all world kingdoms and empires. Babylon is symbolic of all evil, pride, oppression, or power that exalts itself against the Lord. This power will be broken (cf. Rev. 18:2–24). Thus Yahweh deals with any kingdom that exalts itself against him and his anointed people.

In the midst of a description of the world in flames, Isaiah encourages God's people with a message of comfort (14:1–4a). When Babylon comes to its end, the Lord will restore the exiled people to the land. There is a hint of the cosmic effect of Israel's restoration in that the nations, too, will join in Israel's future either as converts (14:1) or as servants (14:2). The era of restoration marks the freedom of God's people. As an expression of joy, God's people take up a dirge (a traditional funerary song) mocking the end of the oppressors. It is a taunt (14:4)—not to be taken literally, but as a hyperbolic statement of the end of the aggressor. This explains the mythological allusions, as Isaiah portrays the end of Babylon in its own religious language.

The king of Babylon typifies world power. When the aggression of the oppressor comes to an end, the whole earth is at rest (14:4b–8). The nations, likened to trees, rejoice that Babylon no longer cuts down nations and kingdoms like a woodsman.

The mortality of Babylon is poetically set forth in the mythological language of Babylon's own religious conceptions (14:9–10). Babylon considered itself ruler over life and death. Kings, leaders, and people died in the many campaigns and battles waged by the Babylonians. They found rest in the netherworld. But with the end of Babylon, spirits in the netherworld stir themselves up as the king of Babylon knocks and desires to enter. There is a sudden commotion, as the news of Babylon's fall is announced. Babylon the great has fallen. It too is subject to powers greater than itself.

Babylon's fall is great (14:11–15). The king is compared to the "morning star, son of the dawn" (14:12). As the morning star is not the sun, which distinguishes day from night, the king of Babylon is not God. However, in Babylon's drive to rule the world, its pride was unlimited (Dan. 4:30), and it acted as God on earth. In its imperial ambitions it acted no differently than the ancient people who built a city to make a name for themselves (Gen. 11:1–9). Likewise, Babylon's goal was to reach into heaven and to take the place of the Most High. But it too will be cast down. The greater the aspirations, the worse the fall. Isaiah uses this dramatic interlude to build up suspense. Will the spirits of the netherworld welcome the king of Babylon?

The spirits first gaze with amazement at the beggarly and weak king, covered with maggots. They respond with unbelief, mocking the mortality of Babylon. At this, they cast him out of the netherworld (14:16–20a). There will never be any rest for the king of Babylon and his offspring. He does not get the burial of a hero but is like a soldier missing in action. The spirit of Babylon is doomed to roam.

God has reserved a time of judgment for all evildoers (14:20b–21). They may flourish and thrive, but then they are suddenly cut off. In Old Testament language the king and his sons, representative of the spirit of Babylon, will be cut off forever. Their memory will be forgotten. Thus the Lord will do to all evildoers. In the biblical conception of Babylon, as we have seen, Babylon represents the spirit of humanity without God, the spirit of autonomy, the spirit of secularization, and the spirit of antichrist. For God's kingdom to be established, the Lord must deal with any manifestation of evil.

The application is clear. Babylon must fall by the will of the Lord (14:22–23). Its judgment is sealed, and in its final state it is likened to a swamp, good only for animals (14:23).

B. Assyria (14:24–27). Yahweh is angry not only with Babylon but also with Assyria (cf. 10:5–34). Regardless of the question of which nation is guilty of the greater sin, all nations are under God's condemnation. The counsel of the nations will be frustrated, but his counsel will stand. These words are Yahweh's solemn assurance to his people that he will establish his kingdom on earth.

C. Philistia (14:28–32). The oracle against Philistia is dated by the year in which Ahaz died. The historical background is far from certain. It may be that Philistia made an effort to lead Judah, Edom, and Moab in an insurrection against Assyria (ca. 715 BC) that was put down by Sargon II in 711 BC. The Philistines have hoped for the end of Assyria's dominance, but Isaiah warns them that they will be put down several times (711, 701, 586 BC) until they are finally no more. The metaphors of the snake, viper, and a venomous serpent (14:29) have been variously interpreted. They possibly refer to the several Assyrian and Babylonian campaigns, each one growing in severity. The word "root" (14:29) denotes the offspring of the serpent. The Philistines are thus assured that the danger is far from over. Their own offspring (literally "root") will come to an end by famine and subsequently by the sword. The enemy from the north (14:31) is Assyria and Babylonia. Philistia, the archenemy of God's people, will also come to an end. The Lord, however, has established his kingdom on earth, and only the humble who seek him will find refuge in it. Regardless of the political changes and the message of the emissaries of the nations, God's people must seek the Lord and his kingdom.

D. Moab (15:1–16:14). The oracle concerning Moab is largely in the form of a lament and is partially repeated in Jeremiah 48:29–38. The judgment on Moab is marked by severity and utter frustration.

An enemy will come from the north and free the refugees to migrate southward along the King's Highway into Edom (15:1–9). Isaiah movingly and sympathetically pictures the fall

Isaiah 16:1 says to "send lambs as tribute." In this Assyrian relief, sheep and goats are being led away from a captured town (palace at Nimrud, 728 BC).

of Moab's cities: Kir, Dibon, Nebo, Medeba, Heshbon, Elealeh, and Jahaz. With the fall of these cities, ranging from the far north to the south, Moab has come to an end. The refugees clutch in their hands whatever they can carry and move southward, wailing over their misfortunes. Isaiah joins in the lament and evokes sympathy for the Moabites. They were, after all, Israel's relatives through Lot (Gen. 19:36–37), and David was a descendant of Ruth the Moabitess (Ruth 4:17). The brooks have dried up, and the waters of Dimon (Dibon?) are filled with blood (15:6, 9). Thus, they cross the "Ravine of the Poplars" (Wadi Zered) into Edom.

From Edom (Sela; cf. 2 Kings 14:7) the Moabites send emissaries requesting asylum (16:1–5). They come with lambs as "tribute," thus recognizing Judah's supremacy. The prophet explains why it is important to seek sanctuary in Judah. First, oppression will cease from the world. Second, the messianic kingdom will be established, when a king will rule on David's throne with faithfulness, justice, and righteousness.

Moab is insincere in her request for sanctuary with God's people. They desire refuge from the enemy but not in the Lord and his Messiah. The heart of pride, conceit, and empty boasts has not changed. Therefore, judgment has overtaken them. Still, Isaiah laments the fall of Moab (16:6–12). He grieves over the ruined vineyards, fields, and orchards. The songs of joy at harvest time have been changed into songs of mourning. The produce once exported to other nations has ceased. Moab's gods are unable to rescue her.

The date of Moab's doom is given: "within three years" (16:13–14; literally "the years of a hireling"). The beginning of Moab's disasters may have come in the Assyrian campaigns. Moab came to an end.

E. Damascus and Israel (17:1–14). The oracle against Damascus (a major city in Syria) is brief in comparison to the other oracles. It seems that this oracle is intimately connected with the judgment of Israel and the judgment on the nations. The structure of the chapter is far from simple. After the declaration of the oracle against Damascus, the prophet three times employs the introductory formula "in that day" (17:4, 7, 9), and the last section is introduced

with the word "woe" (17:12). But if we look at the chapter from a literary perspective, we observe two major motifs in verses 1–3: destruction and the disappearance of glory. These motifs recur in verses 4–6, but in the reverse order, thus forming a chiastic structure. Verses 7 and 8 contain an invitation to repent, whereas verses 9–11 explain the reason for the destruction of the northern kingdom.

Finally, the last three verses give God's judgment on the nations who have been involved in the judgment of Israel and Damascus. The historical background of the oracle against Damascus can best be understood in the context of the Syro-Ephraimite alliance (ca. 734 BC). Ephraim and Damascus thought they could free themselves from the yoke of Tiglath-Pileser III. As we have seen in our analysis of chapter 7, the prophet has forewarned the nations that their alliance will not undo the Davidic dynasty in Judah, nor will they succeed in destabilizing Assyria. Instead, both nations will shortly come to an end, which happened to Damascus in 732, when it was taken by Tiglath-Pileser III, and to Samaria

A scene featuring Assyrian archers and a battering ram, from one of Tiglath-Pileser III's campaigns (738–737 BC) prior to his defeat of Damascus in 732

in 722, when it was taken by Shalmaneser V and Sargon II.

The oracle against Damascus is addressed to the Aramean nation, against which the prophet has already spoken (chaps. 7–8). He portrays the city of Damascus in ruins and utter desolation (17:1–3). The flourishing city traces its ancestry back to a desert oasis. It developed from a caravansary to a major commercial center. The judgment reverses the progress of Damascus; it will again be a place where flocks are pastured (17:2). Since Ephraim and Aram have consolidated their strength, both nations will come to an end and their glory will be wasted.

Isaiah compares Israel's future to a grain harvest in the Valley of Rephaim (17:4–6). Twice David fought there and defeated the Philistines (2 Sam. 5:17–25). The valley was important for the cultivation of grain needed for Jerusalem. The law of gleaning allowed for the poor to pick any ears of grain left after a harvest (Lev. 19:9–10; 23:22; Deut. 24:20–22). The future of Israel is likened to the scanty remains left to the poor for gleaning. Israel is also likened to the few olives left in an olive tree that has been shaken thoroughly during the harvest (17:6).

Verses 7–8 constitute a beautiful interlude in which Isaiah describes the future conversion of the remnant. The verb for their conversion is not the usual verb ("to repent"/"to return") but rather it is "to look." The people must recognize that Yahweh is "their Maker" and "the Holy One of Israel" (17:7). Therefore, they must refrain from looking to their illegitimate altars as the source of deliverance.

The fall of Israel results in exile so that the countryside will be characterized by depopulation (17:9–11). The reason for the judgment is given in verse 10. The people have forgotten the God of their salvation, their Rock, who could provide a refuge. Instead of committing themselves fully to Yahweh they have given themselves to pagan nature cults. The character of these cults is not clear; they may have been the cults of Adonis. It may very well be that at these sites there were also gardens symbolic of the powers

of the deities. However, these people who do everything to appease the deities by cultivating the ceremonial gardens are assured that they will not be able to reap the benefits of their worship; rather, they will reap sickness and pain.

Isaiah uses alliterative devices to impress on his hearers that God's judgment will affect a great multitude of the nations (17:12–14), which are described in terms of the raging sea and "the roaring of great waters" (17:12). It is as if the nations are going beyond the bounds set by God as they storm and foam, but God comes with a rebuke set in the language of a theophany. Yahweh's coming is associated with a wind and a whirlwind. The power of Yahweh is so great that the nations suddenly appear like chaff or tumbleweeds. Thus it will be with the nations: one moment they are terrifying but the next moment they are no more. Isaiah adds one final phrase to encourage the godly remnant that God will deal justly with those who have oppressed his own.

F. Cush (18:1–7). Whereas 17:12 began with the Hebrew word for "woe" to introduce a general prophecy to the nations, this chapter begins with "woe" in verse 1 and focuses its prophecy on a more specific geographic region. As far as the time reference is concerned, it may be that the prophecy against Cush (Ethiopia) came some twenty years after the prophecy against Damascus (ca. 734 BC). In chapters 29–30 the prophet charges the people of Judah with independence from God and reliance on Ethiopia. In 705 BC Hezekiah sought an alliance with Ethiopia. This was because the Ethiopian king Shabaka controlled Upper Egypt as far as the Nile Delta. Apparently the Ethiopians had taken Egypt (715 BC) and negotiated an alliance with Hezekiah. From Isaiah's description of the Ethiopians, it would seem that the Judeans stood in amazement of them because they were able to subdue the great power of Egypt. However, chapter 18 brings out God's judgment on this powerful people while intimating that God has a place reserved for them in his overall kingdom purposes.

The literary imagery is very artistic, creating a mental picture of this distant nation (18:1–2). The land of Ethiopia was known as a place from whence the locusts came; and therefore, Isaiah describes it as "the land of whirring wings" (18:1). The reference also depicts the Ethiopians as being able to cover and dominate an area very rapidly. The Ethiopians are described as people who send their ambassadors across the water by means of papyrus vessels (18:2). "The water" probably is a reference to the Nile River, but it is unlikely that the papyrus vessels were used on as grand a scale as is suggested in verse 2. If we keep in mind Isaiah's artistic purposes, however, we have before us a picture of a people who hasten to send their emissaries in light vessels to wherever their mission takes them. There is a certain ironic twist because the Lord has his own mission to the Ethiopians (18:3–6). He calls on his "swift messengers" to declare his word to the Ethiopians, who are further described as tall and "smooth-skinned"—an awe-inspiring people who have been able to expand their territory by trampling down their adversaries. Isaiah keeps us in suspense as to the nature of God's message, by turning his attention to the inhabitants of the world. They must wait for the "banner" to be raised and the trumpet to be blown. God also waits, withholding judgment, as he looks at the plotting of the nations. He hovers over them from his dwelling place like the shimmering heat or an isolated cloud. Suddenly, the Lord seizes the moment and cuts down the nations like the branches of a grapevine (18:5). A vinedresser prunes the vines over the summer for cosmetic purposes and to increase the grape harvest. Once pollinated, the flower bears fruit, but the fruit takes three to four months to mature. God is likened to a vinedresser who, instead of waiting for the fruit to mature, comes in the heat of the summer to his vineyard and cuts off the shoots and the spreading branches, leaving these for the animals or for the birds of the air (18:5–6).

The people so carefully described in verse 2 are described in the same way in verse 7. They are still tall and awe-inspiring, but this time they are coming not as messengers of war but as worshipers of Yahweh. They are bringing gifts to Yahweh in Jerusalem. Instead of Judah bringing gifts to Ethiopia to placate her king and to join in her cause of rebellion against the Assyrians, the Ethiopians come to Mount Zion to placate the king of Judah. In this way Isaiah moves from the historical circumstances and context in which the prophecy has been written to an eschatological description. The eschatological hope of the psalms is that the people of Ethiopia might also experience the salvation of the Lord and that they too might be inhabitants of the New Jerusalem.

G. Egypt (19:1–20:6). Yahweh comes on a cloud in judgment on Egypt, especially on her religious system (19:1–4). With the collapse of her religion, Egypt's social order falls apart. Egyptian will turn against Egyptian, city against city, and province against province. The hegemony of Pharaoh's rule will be impotent in the face of these forces, and he must submit. The religious and political establishment thus abdicates to foreign rule and religious expressions.

In the second stanza (19:5–10), Isaiah portrays the end of Egypt's economy. The Nile River and its many canals form the essential system of economic support in Egypt. Because of lack of water, the reeds, flax, and fish languish, and agriculture becomes impossible. Reeds were used for the production of papyrus, baskets, and simple artifacts. Flax was the raw product used in Egypt's extensive production of linen. Egypt exported both her papyrus and linen and was economically dependent on these products. Another basis of her economic support came from the fish industry, but that too is devastated by drought. All people will mourn over the great depression.

The third stanza (19:11–15) points out the folly of Egypt's counselors and princes. The intellectual elite are unable to avert the disaster. All are affected by God's judgment. The one who caused all Egypt to cry out on the night of the tenth plague (Exod. 12:29) will bring Egypt to her knees again.

In 19:16–25, the prophet repeats the phrase "in that day" six times (19:16, 18, 19, 21, 23, 24). He speaks about the day in which great "terror" will overtake the Egyptians. The terror will be similar to the time when Israel came out of Egypt after Yahweh demonstrated his power in the ten plagues.

In Egypt itself five cities will speak the language of Judah (19:18). Because Jews settled in Egypt during the exile, Isaiah may be referring to the great Jewish centers in Migdol, Tahpanhes, Noph (Memphis), Pathros, and Alexandria. It is not clear what is meant by the "City of the Sun" (the NIV note explains that most Hebrew manuscripts read "City of Destruction," 19:18), which commentators identify with Heliopolis. The Greek Septuagint suggests the reading "The City of Righteousness." The issue also remains whether one can be certain about the identification of these five cities. To a large extent, the identification rests on our knowledge of Jewish communities in Egypt. Perhaps we should see "five" as symbolic for "many."

In addition to cultural assimilation, the Egyptians will also assimilate religiously with the people of Judah. There will be an "altar" dedicated to Yahweh in the midst of Egypt and a "monument" (19:19) as a memorial to his redemptive power. The Egyptians will come with voluntary sacrifices in order to keep the vows that they have made to Yahweh, the God of Israel. They were struck with plagues in the past, but now they will experience healing from Yahweh himself.

The last verses speak about a highway extending from Egypt to Assyria, following the Fertile Crescent. The highway is symbolic of universal salvation, as it extends from west to east. The nations will join Israel in the worship of the Lord, and Israel and the nations together will be known as the blessed of the Lord.

The occasion of the prophecy of Egypt's fall (20:1–6) is the conquest of the city of Ashdod by Tartan, the supreme commander of the forces of Sargon II. At this time the Lord commands

"Sargon king of Assyria" (Isa. 20:1) is depicted in his chariot in this Neo-Assyrian relief (721–705 BC).

Isaiah to walk about "stripped and barefoot" for three years (20:2). The period of three years need not be exactly thirty-six months, because in oriental fashion, any portion of a year is considered a year. The behavior of the prophet has a calculated effect. The Lord requires this of his servant because it will be "a sign and portent" against Egypt and Ethiopia to symbolize the way in which they will be carried off as exiles by the Assyrians. This prophetic word was partially fulfilled in 671 BC, when Esarhaddon conquered Lower Egypt, including the city of Memphis, and in 665 BC, when Ashurbanipal conquered Thebes, in Upper Egypt. Apparently Judah and Philistia continued to look to Egypt for help both in the rebellion of 705–701 BC and during the last days of Judah, when Zedekiah was looking for Egypt to help the weak state of Judah against the rising power of Nebuchadnezzar.

H. Babylon, Edom, and Arabia (21:1–17). These oracles are linked by the theme of the prophet's office of watchman (21:6, 8, 11–12). Isaiah is waiting to see what the Lord is doing and proclaims what he sees as an oracle.

In the oracle concerning Babylon (21:1–10), the meaning of "Desert by the Sea" (21.1) is not exactly clear. It may possibly be the territory of Babylon north of the Persian Gulf. Isaiah compares the attack of Elam and Media on Babylon to whirlwinds coming from the desert. The prophet experiences great anguish when he understands the dire vision. He feels like a woman in labor and like a man who staggers. Anguish and fear fill his heart and incapacitate him. He sees the prepared tables, the banquets, and the drinking of the Babylonians, but he cannot reach the officers to warn them. They are unprepared; their shields have not even been oiled for battle (21:5). The prophet dramatizes his empathy to portray the sudden fall of Babylon. The picture fits in well with the feast of Belshazzar in Daniel 5. Though Isaiah expresses a longing for the "twilight" of deliverance from Babylon, his empathy keeps him from rejoicing. It is a day full of horror.

Next, the Lord commands him to serve as a watchman and to report on any movement. A man in a chariot gives him the awaited report: "Babylon has fallen" (21:9; cf. Rev. 18:2). This is God's word of deliverance to his people.

The meaning of "Dumah" (21:11–12) is uncertain. It may be a corruption of the word "Edom." This fits well with the reference to Seir (21:11), where the Edomites settled. Twice an Edomite calls on the watchman (Isaiah) to predict the end of "the night" of distress. Isaiah responds that the morning of "hope" will come but can say no more.

The Dedanites (21:13–15) were an Arabian tribe of caravanners and traders located close to Edom. The caravanners are not coming to Tema for commercial purposes, but to hide away in the "thickets" (desert shrubs) of Arabia as refugees from slaughter. They come south to Tema for food and water. They have encountered a strong enemy (Assyrians?), who has put them to flight with sword and bow.

The people of Kedar (21:16–17) were also known as caravanners and were respected for their prowess with bows and arrows. These warlike archers were able to protect the caravans as they migrated across the Arabian desert, but they are not able to defend themselves. In a prosaic statement, the prophet concludes the oracles by saying that disaster will also come on Kedar.

I. Jerusalem (22:1–25). "The Valley of Vision" (22:1, 5) is an obscure reference to Jerusalem. The context of this oracle (22:1–14) is best set in the events of 701 BC, when Sennacherib's siege of Jerusalem was lifted. Judah lay in ruins and Jerusalem had paid a dear price for freedom. The leaders had not been loyal, and the soldiers were butchered without honor. While the people rejoice in their freedom, Isaiah is disconcerted. He must weep bitterly over what has happened to his people. The prophet speaks of another day, a day determined for the destruction of Jerusalem. The recent events, catastrophic as they were, are a picture of the Valley of Vision that

God is preparing for all those who do not respond appropriately.

Isaiah looks out at "the Valley of Vision," which was occupied shortly before by foreign troops (represented here by Elam and Kir, 22:5–7). The ravages of war are all around. Isaiah reminds the people of their anguish and nervous industry as they set out to repair the walls with stones taken from their houses and to store water for the long siege. But they have not looked to the Lord for help. They respond to crisis situations but do not respond to their sovereign God.

With the lifting of the siege, the people care even less for God. They are filled with a self-congratulatory spirit as they celebrate mock victory. The Lord will not forgive their callousness. His judgment on Jerusalem stands firm.

The arrogance of Jerusalem is symbolized in Shebna's desire for power and recognition (22:15). The precise circumstances of Isaiah's outburst against Shebna (22:15–19) are not stated, but Isaiah characterizes him as too ambitious (22:16). He will be disgraced, and Eliakim will take over his office with suitable honor. Eliakim did succeed Shebna in office (see Isa. 36:3; 37:2), while Shebna maintained a prominent position as secretary (36:3). However, even Eliakim's position was not permanent (22:20–25). In a sense, Shebna and Eliakim represent the attitude of the people of Judah: arrogant and filled with selfish ambition. The fall of these men symbolizes, therefore, the ultimate fall of Jerusalem.

J. Tyre (23:1–18). The prophetic word against Tyre is singularly difficult. There are three main difficulties: the change of addressees (Sidon, 23:2–4, 12; Tyre, 23:1, 6–9, 15–18; Phoenicia, 23:10–12), textual problems, and the historical fulfillment of the prophetic word. The cities of Phoenicia were subjugated by Assyria (701 BC), Nebuchadnezzar, and Alexander the Great (332 BC).

The prophet begins the oracle with an indirect reference to the ships of Tarshish, the large vessels that plied the seas (23:1–5). The rumor of Tyre's destruction is spread all around the Mediterranean area. From Larnaka, the port of Cyprus, to the ports around the Mediterranean, it is known that "the marketplace of the nations" (23:3) has ceased doing business. Egypt too will hear. Its reaction is anguished.

Isaiah calls on the people of Tyre to flee to Tarshish on the Atlantic coast southwest of Spain (23:6–9). Even though the prophet may not have the exact region of Tarshish in mind, he is at least calling on the people to flee the catastrophe that will befall Tyre. The city had enjoyed great prosperity. It was an ancient commercial center where tycoons ruled like princes. From Tyre these "princes" ruled over colonies and commercial empires. Because of its natural harbor, the history of Tyre goes back well into the third millennium BC.

The exultation of Tyre, however, has turned to lamentation. The ancient city has come to an end, and the glory of Tyre has been defiled. The prophet assures the people of God that whatever happens to the great cities of Phoenicia (Tyre and Sidon) is the Lord's doing.

The people of Phoenicia can no longer depend on the trade advantages of Tyre (23:10–14). They will have to build up their own land. The Lord will judge Tyre, and his judgment is inescapable. The Babylonians/Assyrians (23:13—the text is difficult) are the instruments

The inscription on this lintel from a seventh-century-BC tomb indicates that it belonged to a "royal steward," whom many identify as the Shebna mentioned in Isaiah 22:15.

of his judgment. The ruin of Tyre, Sidon, and Phoenicia affects all maritime trade.

Tyre is compared to an old prostitute unable to attract interest (23:15–18). Its abandonment will last "seventy years" (cf. Jer. 25:12; 29:10). The round number is symbolic of judgment and restoration. After a period of time the people will be restored, but they must also recognize that a portion of their income must be set apart for the Lord of Hosts (cf. Isa. 60:4–14). "Set apart" is related to the word "holy," and the prophet purposely uses this phraseology to indicate that the silver and the gold once used for secular purposes would be consecrated for God's kingdom.

The prophecy, while it reflects historical events, has eschatological overtones. It is difficult to find a precise fulfillment for the restoration of Tyre except that in the middle of the third century BC Tyre again became a trading city. However, Tyre did not send a portion of its revenues to support the temple worship in Jerusalem. Tyre, representing all of the port cities and trading capitals of the world, is symbolic of God's judgment on national wealth if that wealth is not used for the kingdom of God.

3. The Apocalypse of Isaiah (24:1–27:13)

These four chapters are known as Isaiah's "apocalypse" because in them the prophet Isaiah introduces God's universal judgment, the renewal of the earth, the removal of death and the effects of sin, the deliverance of his people, and the victorious and universal rule of God. The chapters do not possess the usual characteristics of apocalyptic literature (visions, symbolic numbers, animals), but Isaiah gives a glimpse of the future deliverance of God's people and the establishment of his kingdom on earth after the judgment. The revelation is a witness to the power of God to keep his people, even in the face of all the turmoil they may experience on this earth. Likewise, Isaiah 24–27 stands as a witness of God's power to judge this present world order and to create a new people for himself.

A. God's judgment (24:1–23). In a couple of brief strokes Isaiah presents the extent of devastation effected by God's judgment on the earth (24:1–13). The whole earth lies contorted or twisted, as by an earthquake (NIV "he will ruin its face," 24:1). The devastation is nondiscriminatory and complete, in accordance with the word of the Lord. This destruction is the result of humanity's grievous sin against God and his covenant of preservation (Gen. 9:9–17). His curse rests on all of creation. Humanity has transgressed against God's holy ordinances governing the family, morality, preservation of life, and true worship. Therefore, God's judgment must come upon all. All have sinned; all are covenant breakers, without exception. Yet God is faithful to his promises in the Noahic and Abrahamic covenants by preserving a remnant.

The earth is compared to a city after the ravages of fire, war, and earthquake. It lies in ruins. The people left in it are the survivors of the "gaiety" (NIV 1984) and "joy" of the past (24:11), which are symbolized by wine (24:7, 9). The songs of the revelers have come to an abrupt end, but a new song is being raised.

The joy of the redeemed remnant (24:14–16a) is like that of redeemed Israel, just as they joined Moses in a song celebrating the glory of Yahweh as king over his people (Exod. 15:1–18). From one end of the earth to the other, the redeemed of Israel praise the Righteous One. Jews and Gentiles together constitute the blessed remnant.

Isaiah returns again to the theme of universal judgment (24:16b–23). "I waste away" in verse 16b is variously translated as "woe to me" (NASB) or "I pine away" (RSV). The prophet represents all God's children, yearning for the day of redemption and yet fearing the momentary expression of God's great wrath on earth. It is a day full of "terror and pit and snare" (24:17), from which no one can escape. It is like a violent earthquake and a universal flood similar to Noah's flood. All powers, spirits, demons, and forces of evil will be cast out of heaven and imprisoned in a "dungeon" (24:21–22; cf. 2 Pet.

2:4; Rev. 19:20–21; 20:10). Then the kingdom of God will be established with great triumph. The ultimate purpose of the judgment is that Yahweh alone may reign over this earth. The picture of Yahweh, the Lord of Hosts, reigning from Mount Zion and sharing his glory with all of his elders is a beautiful picture that anticipates the visions of the apostle John, as he describes the glory of the Lamb on his throne, surrounded by the elders (Rev. 4:10; 5:8–14).

B. The redemption of God's people (25:1–26:6). The prophet's song of thanksgiving (25:1–5) celebrates God's victory over the enemies of his people as if it has already taken place. He is a refuge for his needy people in any age. Regardless of the exigencies of the present and the uncertainty of the future, the godly hold fast to their faithful God. The righteous are exhorted to look forward to the downfall of the capitals of the kingdoms of this world, namely, the centers of political and economic power, where ruthless tyrants rule. Isaiah provides a glimpse into God's perspective of history as an assurance to the godly that Yahweh protects his people regardless of the intensity of their adversities. He will bring down evil and provoke their enemies to jealousy.

The Lord invites all obedient nations (24:14–16; 25:3) together with the Jews to a banquet on Mount Zion (25:6–8; cf. 24:23). Yahweh himself has prepared a rich banquet of the finest food and drink in order to celebrate his goodness. Since it is the godly who have been the helpless and needy (25:4), the eschatological banquet is described in the language of comfort and assurance. The Lord will take care of his people by providing for all their needs, a fact symbolized by the choice food and drink. He will also remove "the shroud" ("sheet") of mourning, as he deals with "death" and its causes. The heavenly Father himself will comfort his children by wiping away their tears (25:8; cf. Rev. 7:17; 21:4). He will "remove [their] disgrace" and share his honor with them.

Then God's children will respond with thanksgiving and confidence in God's saving power (25:9–10a). True to character, Isaiah suddenly bursts out in hymns as he reflects on the great salvation and permanent establishment of God's kingdom (24:21–23; 25:6–8; 26:1–6). God's children wait (NIV "trusted") for divine deliverance (25:9).

Moab is symbolic of all of the nations (25:10b–12). This may be inferred from the connection between this section and the section that described the ruthless nations and the palaces of the strangers (25:1–5). Though Moab has not been Israel's greatest enemy, it too will be brought down. It will be trampled like straw being trampled down in manure (25:10). Though its inhabitants will try to save themselves, they will fail. God has purposed to bring down Moab's pride.

The song of the redeemed (26:1–6) is not merely a song of thanksgiving but a celebration of trust in God, whose "city" of salvation will be glorious (cf. Psalm 46). The godly community awaits the moment of their redemption. In this section Isaiah addresses those who trust in Yahweh, encouraging them to wait in hiding for a little while until the Lord completes his judgment on the wicked.

The new song on the lips of the godly is a song of trust in the Lord, who protects his people as if they were in "a strong city" surrounded by "walls and ramparts" (26:1). God saves the inhabitants of his city, and Isaiah here describes those inhabitants as "righteous" (26:2) and faithful (26:2–3). The humble will be raised, while the proud and the oppressors will be brought low. The "old" people had a history of faithlessness and apostasy; the inhabitants of the "strong city" must be a people of integrity and loyalty. God will reward these people with his peace.

C. A prayer for God's people (26:7–21). Isaiah further describes the nature of the people of God. He is aware that it may be a long time before God's purposes are fully realized on earth. In order to encourage the godly community to persevere in righteousness and faithfulness, he offers a prayer of wisdom, confidence, and petition.

He prays that God's people may be wise (26:7–10). Wisdom is the mark of godliness in the Old Testament, as it expresses dependency on Yahweh and his word. At the same time, however, it is not a slavish dependency in which the godly wait for Yahweh to approve every decision they make. They walk in accordance with his judgments ("laws," 26:8) with a constant desire for God and with the hope that the nations will do God's will on earth. Isaiah prays that godly wisdom may triumph over evildoers (26:7–11).

He also expresses confidence in the Lord, who will show his zeal for his people when he establishes peace for them (26:12–15). He will punish the wicked, who have no share in God's redemption, but will "enlarge" his people and extend their borders (26:14–15). He raises up his own people and will rule over them exclusively.

Isaiah prays that the time of distress will soon pass and that, out of the suffering, the Lord may raise up a new people (26:16–19). God alone can initiate the era of restoration, and those who share in it will "wake up and shout for joy" (26:19).

The Lord responds to the prayer with the assurance that he will avenge Israel's enemies because of their sins (26:20–21). Even though the bloodshed has seemingly been covered up, justice will prevail. The Lord will reveal everything that has been hidden. He encourages the godly to wait until his purposes for this present world have been fulfilled.

D. Deliverance of Israel (27:1–13). God will finally give a death blow to "Leviathan" (27:1), symbolic of the rebellious heavenly host (27:1–13; cf. 24:21). The descriptions "gliding" and "coiling" are also used to describe Leviathan in Ugaritic (Canaanite) literature. The Old Testament uses the language of Canaanite mythology in order to express God's control over evil, chaos, and rebellion. The New Testament also employs this symbolic language (Rev. 12:7–10). Leviathan is the master of the sea, whose punishment marks the end of rebellion in heaven and on earth.

Isaiah develops his vineyard poems (5:1–7) into an eschatological picture (27:2–6). Though the vineyard has been destroyed because of its utter worthlessness, God remains faithful to his people. Because the leaders were responsible for the ruined vineyard (3:14), the Lord himself assumes responsibility for its care. He watches, waters, and protects it. He will make war against anyone ("briers and thorns," 27:4) who opposes his people. He prevents those conditions he has previously permitted to ruin the vineyard (5:6). He is not angry but desires reconciliation with even hostile opponents.

His purpose for the vineyard is success on a grand scale. The root must be well established before the blossoms will produce their fruit in "all the world" (27:6). The kingdom of God gradually extends as God's new people are grafted in. These new people are expected to conform to God's justice and righteousness.

Isaiah 27:7–11 is obscure and intrusive. These verses are best regarded as a reflection on suffering. The Lord cleanses his people by exile and judgment (27:8; NIV "by warfare and exile"; literally "measure by measure"). They must abandon idolatry and return to the Lord. Even so, God does not kill off his people as he did his opponents, whose "fortified city stands desolate" (27:10). Outside the walls, their farms are so devastated by drought that tree branches are used to kindle fires.

Nothing can hinder the return of the tribes of Israel from Egypt and Assyria, because the Lord himself has ordained it (27:12–13). This is his harvest (27:12; cf. Rev. 14:15). The "great trumpet" (ram's horn) ushers in the eschatological kingdom, when the restoration takes place. The prophet uses the language of inclusion and welcome as he refers to the borders from the Euphrates to the Wadi of Egypt (Wadi El Arish, fifty miles southwest of Gaza), from where people will come to worship the Lord on Mount Zion. This word found partial fulfillment in the restoration from exile (539 BC). The New Testament extends the symbolism to God's worldwide harvest, when Jesus returns (Matt.

24:31; 1 Cor. 15:52; 1 Thess. 4:16). The trumpet blast marks the end of humanity's rule and the introduction of the full reign of God on earth.

4. Oracles of Woe (28:1–33:24)

The material in these chapters is loosely connected by the repetition of "woe" (28:1; 29:1, 15; 30:1; 31:1; 33:1) and seems to date to the period of Judah's troubles with Assyria, during the reign of Hezekiah.

A. Ephraim (28:1–29). This section comes from a time before the fall of Samaria when the enemy of Israel was already on the horizon. Assyria is likened to "a hailstorm and a destructive wind" and "a driving rain and a flooding downpour" (28:2). Imagery of overflowing water is also found in Isaiah 8, where the prophet describes the coming judgment on Israel and Aram. The northern kingdom is likened to a "fading flower" (28:1) because the beautiful and fertile valleys characteristic of Ephraim would soon be overrun by Assyrian troops. The agricultural advantages of the northern kingdom were significant. It had excellent soil, large valleys, and finely terraced hills on which the people were able to farm and enjoy their olive groves. With all of the advantages of the northern kingdom, the people had become independent and proud. Even as the wind

and rain had given economic prosperity to the northern kingdom, God's judgment, likened to wind and rain, would destroy Ephraim. The freely given covenant blessings did not elicit an appropriate response from Ephraim. The beauty of Ephraim, like a ripe fig, will be enjoyed by foreigners (28:4).

In contrast to the self-exalting pride of Ephraim, the Lord will establish his glorious kingdom of justice and strength (28:5–6). The nobles of Ephraim cannot protect the people because of their drunken stupor, but the Lord will protect and strengthen the remnant that survives in Judah. The enemy will be stopped, and kingship and theocracy will continue there by divine decree.

Judah's status was no better than Ephraim's. Even though Judah existed another 150 years after the fall of Samaria, the situation in the southern kingdom was generally no better than that in the northern kingdom (28:7–13). For this reason Isaiah strongly condemns Judah. In fact, his language is stronger against the southern kingdom than against the northern kingdom. He accuses Judah's leaders of drunkenness, an unteachable spirit, scoffing, and self-confidence.

Though the Lord is gracious in sparing Judah, its religious leaders are incapable of rendering decisions and of proclaiming the visions of God because of their drunken stupor.

Terraced hillsides in Israel

While sitting by their filth (28:8), they mock Isaiah, speaking like a babbler who is explaining his message to babes and infants or like a kindergarten teacher who begins by teaching sounds: "*tsav latsav tsav latsav / qav laqav qav laqav*" (28:10). By mimicking the sounds, the religious leaders express the intensity of their hatred for God's word.

To this mockery, Isaiah responds with God's word of judgment. Whereas the Lord has given the land to Israel as a place in which they might receive his blessings, foreign invaders will come and speak like babblers. The people who have rejected the warnings of approaching judgment as unintelligible and irrelevant will hear the same message from these foreign invaders. Then, however, it will be too late, because they will be taken captive. The prophets of whom Isaiah speaks are the false prophets called to share visions and give judgments but unable to do so because they are prostrate in their own vomit.

The leaders of God's people are unteachable, and for this reason they have little to teach others. They mock the prophet by asking the rhetorical question, "Who is it he is trying to teach?" (28:9). They think he is nothing more than a repetitious schoolteacher.

These four characterizations (drunkenness, unteachable spirit, scoffing, and self-confidence) portray Jerusalem's leaders as completely insensitive to Yahweh's law and to the covenant. They have broken away from Yahweh and are unable to lead his people back to righteousness. Yahweh's words of response are directly related to chief accusations the prophet has made. First, foreign enemies will come into the country and take it. As the foreign forces will be using foreign languages (28:11), the people themselves will feel like uncomprehending children. Whereas God has encouraged the people to find rest and repose for their souls (28:12), they instead will be taken into exile by the enemy. In addition to this, the confidence and scoffing of the people will turn to terror. The people thought they were invincible. They put their confidence in

the security of Jerusalem, their leaders, the temple of Yahweh, and the priests. However, on the day of God's judgment, they will not be able to stand because Jerusalem will be trampled down. The people themselves will go from terror by day to terror by night. That day will bring no peace or comfort. The prophet likens this to a time when the bed is too short and the blanket too small (28:20). Isaiah further exhorts the people to cease their scoffing lest the judgment of God be intensified.

The political leaders also scoffed at the prophet. They did not believe that trust in the Lord ("a tested stone," 28:16) was the answer to Judah's political woes. Instead, they had relied on a covenant with Egypt. The prophet facetiously calls this treaty "a covenant with death" and the guaranteed protection a "lie" and a "falsehood" (28:14–22). They firmly believed that they had power to avert the judgment, which is likened to a flood.

Set over against the false security of political alliances is Yahweh, the "tested stone," a "cornerstone" who provides a solid foundation for all who trust in him (28:16) and order their lives in accordance with his absolute standards of justice and righteousness. He, however, will not provide any refuge to those who have made foreign alliances. Death will overtake them, and Yahweh will execute his judgment. Then their self-made remedies, like a short bed and a narrow blanket, will not work. The Lord will do a work, not to save, as he did at Mount Perazim in David's day (2 Sam. 5:20–25), but to destroy. The decree has gone forth from the Lord Almighty.

The wise farmer does not plow continuously but organizes his operation so as to have a time and place for plowing, sowing, and harvesting (28:23–29). Even in the process of harvesting, the farmer knows exactly which tools will obtain the desired harvest. So it is with God. He sovereignly and wisely administers his rule.

B. Ariel (29:1–24). The background of the prophecy against Ariel may best be found in the years preceding 701 BC. A power struggle had taken place between Sennacherib and the eastern nations, making it possible for the western nations to rebel. During these years, Hezekiah turned to Egypt for help (30:1–2; 31:1). This political option was reasonable; Sennacherib was busy on the eastern front. The alliance between Aram, Phoenicia, Judah, and Egypt made it imperative for Sennacherib to deal quickly and decisively with his eastern problems and then turn his attention to the west. During the intervening years, the psychological mood in Judah was very positive. The people felt less threatened and were hoping for a strong political and economic resurgence. Yet Isaiah had already prophesied that Assyria was to be the instrument of God's judgment—even on Judah (8:7–8; 10:5).

With the possibility of an independent Judah on the horizon, the people viewed the prophet's words with skepticism. After all, it had seemed that the prophet spoke about a doom greater than could be realized. The future of Judah would be determined by the people and their political skills rather than by the word of God.

The prophet preaches the word of the Lord in these optimistic times (29:1–4). He addresses Jerusalem as "Ariel" (Lion of God), though it is uncertain why; there is no scholarly consensus on the meaning of the term. Some have proposed that this may be an ancient Canaanite name for Jerusalem; others have suggested that the gates of Jerusalem may have had lions as a part of their decoration.

Isaiah first brings a woe on Jerusalem, the city where David lived and where the temple stands. In spite of its ties with the temple and David's dynasty, Yahweh plans to bring down Jerusalem. The future of Jerusalem will be filled with distress, lament, and mourning, because Yahweh has turned against the people and surrounded them like an enemy surrounds a city. Isaiah describes Jerusalem in a state of humiliation, likening it to a conquered city whose inhabitants are pushed down into the dust begging for mercy from their conquerors

(29:4). The voices of the dead also cry out from the dust.

Jerusalem will be covered by the multitude of her enemies, which are compared to fine dust or chaff (29:5–8). The future of Jerusalem looks bleak because Yahweh himself comes against his people, who have been enjoying security but are relying on Egypt for their survival.

The devastation, compared to thunder, loud noise, winds, tempest, and fire, is reminiscent of Yahweh's revelation on Mount Sinai (Exod. 19:16–19). This is a prophetic proclamation of the judgment to come on the day of the Lord.

Though Yahweh has given up Ariel to the nations, he protects the remnant of his people. The nations who rise against Judah and Jerusalem will leave empty. The prophet likens the reaction of the nations to that of a hungry or thirsty man who has dreamed of being satisfied but in the morning wakens to find he has not actually eaten or drunk (29:7–8).

This will be the experience of any nation that fights against the people of God. They will have a measure of victory, but it will not last. Yahweh is still with his people. How comforting these words are to the people of God living at any time and in any place! Regardless of how God's people may fail, he has a plan to redeem a people for himself and will continue to work out the goals that he has decreed from eternity.

There are some who believe that the prophet's words are not meant for them but possibly for others in another time. They are blind to the revelation of God (29:9–14) and are like those who stagger in a drunken stupor (29:9) and those who have fallen into a deep sleep that renders them unable to hear and respond to the warning of imminent judgment. There is a real danger in not applying the word of God to one's own time or in lacking interest in how the word of God may be applied.

Assyria's siege of Jerusalem was imminent. In 701 BC they surrounded Jerusalem after devastating the countryside of Judah and leveling her fortified cities. It was only then that the people began to see; it was too late, however;

they had not responded appropriately to the prophetic message.

Isaiah concludes with a warning to the people at large (29:13–14). He again accuses them of hypocrisy (cf. chap. 1). The people come into the courts of the temple to pray and sacrifice, but their real love is not for Yahweh. Their wisdom is the wisdom of this world, and at that time the wisdom of the world dictated that Jerusalem ally herself with Egypt. The wisdom of that time perished, as subsequent events have shown. God, however, calls his people to a wisdom that comes from on high. He will stun them with his wonders of judgment and devastation. The future of the people lies, therefore, not in their own scheming and planning, nor in self-confidence, but in Yahweh himself.

The prophet renews his proclamation of "woe" on the people who plan and scheme as if Yahweh does not know or see (29:15–24). The people are the clay and the Lord is the potter, but the clay is skeptical and critical of the potter's abilities (29:16).

Thus far Isaiah has portrayed a number of the people's reactions: apathy (29:9–10), disbelief in the relevance of the prophetic word for their time (29:11–12), formalism and hypocrisy (29:13–14), and dependence on human scheming and planning apart from God (29:15–16). Yet, however dark the day may be, God still has a message of salvation for his people. Isaiah now calls to spiritually sensitive people—those known as deaf, blind, poor, afflicted, and needy. The deaf and the blind are those who have suffered the judgment of God and now respond to his revelation. The afflicted and the needy are those who have experienced God's judgment and whose hearts search for the living God. The spiritual remnant will hear the word of God, see the salvation of the Lord, and rejoice in Yahweh himself.

The focus of this section is on the work of the Lord in history. The Holy One of Israel, who destroys cruel people and oppressors, gives cause for joy to people who have faith in him. The promise is to the "redeemed" children of Abraham, his spiritual seed (29:22). The promises concern the work of final restoration begun in history. The Lord will transform them into a holy people who will serve him from the heart.

C. Foreign alliances (30:1–33). The background of chapters 30 and 31 lies in the diplomatic mission to the Ethiopian ruler Shabaka, who extended his rule as far as the Nile Delta. Because of the increase in Shabaka's power, the Judean aristocracy considered the possibility of an alliance between Shabaka, Hezekiah, the Philistines, and the Phoenicians against the Assyrian king Sennacherib (705–701 BC).

The leadership of Judah relied on political solutions to political problems (30:1–7). They made every attempt to solve their problems creatively, without consulting the Lord. Instead of finding "protection" and "refuge" (30:2) in the Lord, they looked to Egypt for help against Assyria. Ultimately, however, their plan failed; Egypt used Judah to its own advantage, and Judah was disgraced.

The stubbornness and folly of Judah's leaders are highlighted by the description of the desert and the caravans that traverse the desert from Judah through the Negev and the Sinai to Egypt. Isaiah describes the desert as a place filled with anguish and loneliness, a desolate area to travel. Apparently the Via Maris (or Way of the Sea), which was the usual route between Judah and Egypt, was not open because the delta was controlled by the Egyptian Saite dynasty. Thus, the best road was not available for the Judean caravans, and they had to take the more difficult desert route to Egypt.

The desert is filled with dangers. The purpose of the reference to the animals is to make it clear that the people of Judah sent their emissaries through a torturous terrain filled with difficulties in order to get absolutely nowhere! The leaders of Judah go to great pains to have a caravan laden with precious objects sent to Egypt to obtain the favor of the Egyptians for their own political purposes. But Egypt is not able to help.

The last part of verse 7 is somewhat difficult in its description of the situation in Egypt. It is possible to read this as a question: "Is this the mighty one (Rahab) sitting still?" Apparently, the efforts of the Judeans to buy security would be futile because their fine treasures could not guarantee that Egypt would be in any position to help. As it turned out, the Egyptians were defeated by Sennacherib at Eltekeh. The areas of Phoenicia, Philistia, and Judah were taken, and Jerusalem was surrounded by Sennacherib in 701 BC.

In 30:8–17 Isaiah returns to the theme of rebelliousness. Judah has been rebellious against Yahweh for some time, rejecting both his law and his prophet. In order to remind the future generations, Isaiah is commanded to write on a tablet the testimony (or witness) of God against Israel and Judah. The language of the witness is reminiscent of Moses's Song of Witness (Deuteronomy 32) and of Joshua's stone of witness (Josh. 24:26–27). The history of Israel and Judah is incriminating evidence against the people. They have been called to be Yahweh's people, but in essence they are false sons who have not responded appropriately.

Isaiah's words are a testimony to those who hate the word of God and thereby the Holy One of Israel. God's word becomes for them a word of judgment. If they persist in their self-reliance, they will suffer a sudden fall. They are like a wall that has been standing for a long time but already shows evidence of weakness by a protrusion. The wall may stand for many years but will suddenly cave in; so will Judah (30:13–14).

Israel is also like a piece of pottery. A potter's jar may be beautiful and may function very well. When shattered, however, it is of no use. One cannot even use the sherds to take coals of fire from the hearth or to dip water from a pool (30:14).

Before destruction comes upon Judah, Isaiah calls on the people to return to the Holy One of Israel. Salvation does not lie in heroic acts but rather in repentance and trust in Yahweh. Faith and repentance are requisites for true salvation. Instead of turning to Yahweh, Judah has shown a history of unwillingness to return, responding instead by relying on horses and military power. Since they are intent on rejecting Yahweh's gracious invitation, Yahweh deals with the people accordingly. They rely on horses; in their haste they will have to flee as though they are on horses. Instead of experiencing God's blessing, whereby a thousand enemy troops are routed by one Israelite (30:17a), they will experience the opposite—the entire nation fleeing from a handful of enemy troops (30:17b).

The grace of God is still evident in the remnant that will remain. They will be like a small military outpost—a flagstaff on a mountaintop or a banner on a hill. Few will be left, but there will still be some to whom the Lord will continue to show his grace.

The first effect of God's grace is that the sorrow of the people will be removed (30:18–26). Those who have been weeping and crying because of their great distress are assured that Yahweh will answer their prayers and will heal all their hurts. Yahweh comes to heal the wounds of his people and to assure their well-being—physical as well as spiritual. Another way in which Isaiah describes the grace of Yahweh on his people is by delineating his blessings. The grace of God is free. How different is God's guidance; he leads his people into the way that leads to blessing! Isaiah poetically describes the blessings of rain and sun. This combination makes it possible for crops to grow and produce abundantly, for animals to roam and be satisfied, and for people to have plenty of bread and water. In the land Yahweh blesses, there will no longer be any evidence of idolatry.

Isaiah returns to the theme of Yahweh's justice with respect to his enemies (30:27–33). The enemies of whom he is speaking are the Assyrians in particular (30:31), but Isaiah's words may be applied to all the enemies of God's people.

First, Isaiah describes the greatness of Yahweh's wrath. He comes in burning anger, symbolized by smoke and fire, in order to completely wipe out the enemy. Fire, wind, and flood (30:27–28, 30–31) are the prophet's favorite metaphors for the wrath of the Lord. The nations are put into a sieve and shaken back and forth so that the wicked might be removed. Isaiah also likens Yahweh's judgment to "a bit" that leads the people to their destiny (30:28). None of the wicked will remain. The destiny of the nations is also described as the destruction of the wicked in the Valley of Topheth, south of Jerusalem (30:33). Here Yahweh will set up piles of wood on which the bodies of the enemies of his people will be placed, and with the breath of his mouth he will set these stacks of wood aflame.

The destruction of the wicked is cause for joy among the people of God, who have been suffering under the ruthless power of their enemies. They are portrayed as singing in the night as during the days of a festival. They will be glad, and not afraid, because their faith is in the Rock of Israel (30:29). There will be ritual rejoicing as they make music with their tambourines, lyres, and other instruments. They cannot help Yahweh in his war against the enemies; it is Yahweh's war. Instead, they must wait quietly with assurance that, when Yahweh is finished with his enemies, the victory will also belong to them.

D. Judgment and hope (31:1–32:20). Isaiah charges Judah's leaders with seeking autonomy by depending on Egypt's military superiority (31:1–9). In the ancient world, superiority generally belonged to those kings who had a great number of horses and chariots. In order to fight military power with military power, Judah relied on the force Egypt would be able to provide against the great power of Assyria. It became proverbial in Judah that the opposite of reliance on Yahweh was the reliance on horses and chariots (cf. Ps. 20:7).

Isaiah calls on the people to look to the Holy One of Israel for wisdom and help. If they do not, his wisdom will turn against them, and his hand will destroy both his enemies and all who do not lean on him. The people must remember that all who do not look to Yahweh for their protection have abandoned the Holy One of Israel, who is powerful to put down human inventiveness and all the powers that oppose him.

Yahweh can protect his people! The prophet likens him to a lion, intent on getting his prey even when many shepherds make a loud noise to scare him off, and to fluttering birds, intent on scaring away a would-be intruder to protect their young in the nest. The Lord is strong like a lion as he destroys the enemies and caring like a bird as he protects Judah (31:4–5).

In order to assure themselves of Yahweh's protection, the people must respond with willing submission and repentance. The future belongs to those who repent by returning to the Lord in faith and turning from paganism.

Isaiah describes the effect of Yahweh's anger on the Assyrians. They will fall by God's decree and not by the sword of man, and the young men will become forced laborers. The Lord's wrath, symbolized by "fire" and "furnace" (31:9), is in Jerusalem. He has a purpose for Jerusalem and will not permit it to fall.

The future age will be characterized by righteousness and justice (32:1–8). The king, leaders, and people will be concerned with the pursuit of wisdom from above. The wise man is blessed in that he represents God's blessedness; he is "a shelter," "a refuge," "streams of water in the desert," and shade (32:2). No longer will God's people be characterized by deafness and blindness, but all will hear, see, and act in accordance with the word of God. They will hasten to do his will on the earth in contrast to the past, when they hastened to do their own will. In their pursuit of godly wisdom, they will hate folly and wickedness. The wise person pursues what is noble (i.e., godly wisdom). The wise people of God will no longer take their counsel in accordance with earthly standards and be primarily concerned with earthly matters, but rather they will have new standards and concern about the things that pertain to God himself.

The "women" finding rest are characterized by having confidence in the future (32:9–14).

These women are described as women of ease and complacency (32:9), not wanting to be troubled. They seem to be happy with the way things are, when they should be beating their breasts (32:12), trembling (32:11), dressed in sackcloth (32:11), and troubled (32:11) because of the thorns and briers that rob the land of productivity. The women of Jerusalem are sitting back in ease while sin destroys the fruit of righteousness and bankrupts the city, leaving her abandoned and forsaken.

Isaiah now returns to the description of the era of righteousness (32:15–20). The only way in which folly will change to wisdom and the devastation of the land to blessedness is by a divinely ordered transformation. Restoration is the work of the Spirit, bringing about a return of the blessings of God on his people and on the earth. The creation will be renewed, wisdom enthroned, righteousness established, and peace restored to the people of God. The wise will experience the blessings of God in every area of their lives.

Reliance on Yahweh is one of the major emphases in these chapters. In response, God's people wait for the fullness of redemption. As Christians, we believe the day of redemption is closer since the coming of the Lord Jesus. Yet, along with the saints of the Old Testament, we must have a real sense of hope and longing for the fullness of redemption to which the prophet bears witness.

E. Distress and help (33:1–24). God's judgment ("woe") rests on those who have enjoyed absolute power in this world (33:1–6). Because they have caused great devastation on this earth, they must answer to the Lord. When he comes he will sound a loud battle cry (33:3) to avenge himself on the nations.

This judgment on the ungodly is in response to the prayer of the godly. The godly have been asking for Yahweh's grace to appear to them because they have been suffering while ruthless hordes were controlling the world. Their hope has been that Yahweh's strength might be revealed to them in salvation. Yahweh comes as King (33:5), seated on his throne of judgment to dispense justice and righteousness. The benefits of Yahweh's rule for his people are many: salvation, a firm foundation, and wisdom. The godly experience salvation and practice wisdom and knowledge in the fear ("awe") of the Lord.

Isaiah shows that the benefits of the messianic kingdom will be limited to the godly (33:7–16). The enemies of the kingdom from both within and without will be destroyed. For this reason, the prophet addresses the men of Ariel (33:7). Scholars are in general agreement that the phrase "brave men" (NIV) may be understood as a reference to Ariel (cf. Isa. 29:1).

The proud cry because their plots have been frustrated. They have not been able to avert the very thing that they feared. The highways will become desolate, the judicial processes will be interrupted, and the land will be devastated by enemies.

Yahweh will arise in judgment. The works of the godless will consist of little more than "chaff" and "straw" (33:11). All their selfish efforts within the covenant community will be burned up. Who, then, can come through the consuming fire? Only those who have walked righteously and have spoken uprightly and have hated bribery and oppression (33:15; cf. Ps. 15:1–5; 24:3–5). The godly will receive protection and provision from the Lord.

The godly will see not only Yahweh's coming in great vengeance and fury to judge the wicked but also the glory of Yahweh in its full and radiant beauty (33:17–24). The realm of Yahweh's rule will be extended, but there will be no place for the wicked in his kingdom. Zion, the city of God, will be full of peace like a river where no hostile ships can sail (33:21).

Yahweh the majestic one will be for his people and will provide for them a river of life (33:21; Rev. 22:1). The songs of Zion celebrate the glory, beauty, and rivers (or springs) found in the city of Zion. Yahweh will be present as the king, judge, and lawgiver of his people. He will rule, guide, and teach his people so they will know how to live in his presence. The new age will bring renewal and a deep awareness of forgiveness.

5. Cataclysmic Judgment (34:1–17)

Again Isaiah returns to the theme of God's anger against the world. God's judgment will effect complete destruction, leaving the world uninhabited.

In powerful language Isaiah calls on all nations, who are the object of the Lord's anger, to hear the word of God (34:1–4). The judgment is likened to a great slaughter or sacrifice (34:1–2). On the earth, the slain will be everywhere; corpses will stink and blood will cover the mountains. In the heavens, constellations will disappear.

Isaiah focuses on Edom as representative of the nations (34:5–17). Yahweh's judgment on Edom will be similar to what he will do to the whole world. Edom is under the "ban" of the Lord (34:5). The term "ban" (Hebrew *herem*) expresses Yahweh's decree to destroy a people for his own purposes. The sword will pierce Edom and fill the country with blood, as though a great sacrifice has taken place. The day of God's judgment is the day of vengeance on his enemies and of the vindication ("retribution") of his people.

After the destruction of its people and animals, the land itself will become worthless and desolate forever because of the brimstone and pitch that will cover it (34:10). It will revert to a wilderness with thorns and nettles, a place fit only for wild animals.

All things will be subject to God's judgment. When Yahweh comes in judgment, there will be no way of escaping. Yet there is the promise that those who belong to Yahweh are heirs of the new age.

6. The Day of God's Glory (35:1–10)

The discussion in Isaiah 35 complements that of the day of the Lord's vengeance (34:8; 35:4). Here the prophet portrays the glories that await the people of God (35:1–7). Whereas the "day of vengeance" (34:8) is characterized by the sword and desolation, the day of the Lord's deliverance is characterized by his glory and sustenance. Isaiah brings out the nature of the glorious kingdom, which will affect all creation—people as well as nature itself. Although the country has been laid desolate like the wilderness because of Yahweh's judgment, the desolation will give way to the glory of Lebanon and the majesty of Carmel and Sharon. There will be rejoicing, gladness, blossoming, and shouts of joy. The people will see the glory of their God reflected in the restoration of nature. They will also experience a sense of renewal, as he assures them that their "salvation" includes a salvation from their enemies and restoration. There is no place for fear in God's kingdom.

> Isaiah 35:2 describes the "splendor of Carmel and Sharon." This aerial view shows the fertile Sharon plain, located between Joppa and Mount Carmel.

Restoration comes to those who are in need: the blind, the deaf, the lame, and the mute (35:5–6). The people who rejected God's way and suffered the consequences in judgment and alienation will again be the objects of his unmerited favor. They, like Israel of old, will see God's glory, experience his presence, protection, and guidance, and taste of his provisions in the wilderness.

The word of promise pertains to the postexilic community following the Jews' return to Palestine from Babylon and Persia (35:8–10). Yet the language of these verses transcends the experience of any ordinary road. The highway is characterized by two qualities: holiness and joy. Its use is limited to those who are holy and have been cleansed from defilement. The people who walk in it are described as "the redeemed" (35:9–10), who are in right relationship with God. The highway is the place where God brings full deliverance to his people and where he supplies their physical and spiritual

needs. Hence, those who walk on the highway will be full of joy as they march toward "Zion" (35:10). The redemption of which the prophet speaks will culminate in that day when Jesus comes to restore the present earth to himself.

7. Hezekiah (36:1–39:8)

These chapters are virtually identical to the account recorded in 2 Kings 18:13–20:19. The historical background of Isaiah 36 and 37 lies in the events of 701 BC, when the forces of Sennacherib devastated Judah and her fortified cities. Several years prior to this (705–702 BC), Hezekiah became sick. His illness and prayer are recorded in chapter 38, while his foolish act of revealing the royal treasures to the Babylonian envoys is found in chapter 39.

A. Challenge and deliverance (36:1–37:38). The pious response of Hezekiah to the intimidation of the Assyrian field commander is also recorded in 2 Kings 18:13–19:37. Isaiah omits the account of Hezekiah's submission and payment of tribute (2 Kings 18:14–16). Apparently the canonical emphasis in Isaiah is on the Assyrian pride, the godly response of Hezekiah, and God's miraculous deliverance.

Sennacherib's field commander accuses Hezekiah of overtly rebelling by forming an alliance with Egypt (36:1–22). He attempts to undermine confidence in the Lord by playing down Hezekiah's reforms, threatening the people with intimidation, falsely arguing that the Lord is not able to deliver them, and claiming that the Lord is on his side. Hezekiah's officers report the threats to Hezekiah with their clothes torn as a token of mourning. They themselves have not answered the challenges in accordance with the royal command.

The historical reconstruction of the international events that led to Jerusalem's deliverance is a complex problem (37:1–38). The trust of the king, Isaiah's restraint from saying "I told you so," the prayer of Hezekiah, and the word of the

Assyrian relief of Sennacherib from the throne-room at Khorsabad (721–705 BC)

Lord through Isaiah reveal remarkable wisdom on the part of Hezekiah and Isaiah and the great concern of the Lord for the Davidic kingship and Jerusalem. This is fully consistent with Isaiah's emphases on Zion and God's protection of his people against foreign invaders (chaps. 28–33).

B. Hezekiah's illness (38:1–22). Hezekiah's psalm of lament and thanksgiving has no parallel in 2 Kings. The superscription "a writing" (Hebrew *miktab*, 38:9) may be a corrupt form of the musical term *miktam*, a heading found in Psalms 16; 56–60. The text of the psalm contains several serious difficulties and is similar in content to Jonah's prayer (Jonah 2) and Job's speeches (e.g., Job 7).

In lamenting his early death, Hezekiah compares it to pulling down a tent and to material taken off the loom before being completed (38:12). Like a bird, he made a noise in his anguish, but it seemed as if the Lord, like a lion, was intent on mauling him to pieces.

In the restoration from sickness, he experiences the joy of health and God's never-failing love. In response to God's kindness, he vows to walk humbly before God, to praise him, and to declare to the next generation the "faithfulness" of the Lord.

C. Envoys from Babylon (39:1–8). The account of the Babylonian messengers sent by Marduk-Baladan parallels that of 2 Kings 20:12–19. It functions here as a transition to the oracles of comfort (chaps. 40–48), which presuppose the exilic situation of Judah in Babylon. Because of Hezekiah's pride in his possessions, Isaiah proclaims God's judgment of exile into Babylon on another generation. Hezekiah's generation will escape that judgment, but the exile of Judah is inevitable.

8. The Beginning of Restoration (40:1–48:22)

A. Prologue (40:1–11). Isaiah 40:1–11 gives the context for reading chapters 40–48. The people of God have gone into exile because of their sins, but Isaiah affirms that the exile will end. The exile is therefore an expression of God's judgment. It is first a just judgment; second, it

is a form of restitution for damages. Israel and Judah not only have abandoned Yahweh but also have detracted from Yahweh's glory by giving it to idols. The exile was a time in which God's people could reflect on what they had done; this period of reflection was a way of paying the damages in order to be restored to fellowship with Yahweh. The statement "she has received from the Lord's hand double for all her sins" (40:2) is an allusion to the Old Testament laws of restitution (Exod. 22:4, 7, 9).

At God's appointed time a proclamation of "comfort" comes to his people (40:1–5). Yahweh will come to help his own. In the Hebrew text the verb "comfort" is in the plural, but it is not clear who the comforters are. The prophet and those who follow him are charged with giving comfort to God's people. The message of comfort was also proclaimed by Jesus and is continued by all faithful ministers of the word of God. The content of the message pertains to the coming era of the renewed relationship between Yahweh and his people, an era in which forgiveness is proclaimed and experienced. The fulfillment of this word takes us from the time of the restoration from exile all the way to the return of Jesus and the establishment of the new heavens and earth. It is for this reason that Isaiah 40–66 is so important for the church of Jesus Christ; we too are the beneficiaries of the fulfillment of the promises of God's word.

The announcement of the coming salvation takes place in the desert (40:3), representative of the experience of alienation. Precisely where the people of God are in need of deliverance comes the announcement to them that the Lord is coming. All of nature prepares for his theophany, making a giant road through valleys and across mountains. The promise is given that all "people" (literally "flesh") will see the "glory of the Lord" (40:5).

The prophet again hears a voice commanding him to speak of what he has seen (40:6–8). He explains the vision in terms of blessing and judgment. The judgment of the Lord will come upon all flesh, because they are nothing but grass and like the flowers of the field—here today and gone tomorrow. When the sovereign Lord comes in power to rule, the nations will be like nothing in his presence.

The emphasis on promise is more obvious. The "word of our God endures forever" (40:8)—this is the word of promise pertaining to the coming era of restoration. "Good news" must be proclaimed to Zion so that everyone may hear. The good news is focused in the presence of the Lord: "Here is your God!" (40:9). He comes with power against the adversaries and with a reward for his own. The divine warrior delivers and leads his own people like "lambs." What a Savior! What a gospel!

B. Disputations (40:12–31). The prophet raises five questions in the context of the proclamation of the establishment of Yahweh's kingship. These five questions, rhetorical to a large extent, are a literary device to remove any doubt from the minds of the godly as to the certainty of the establishment of the kingdom and to instill a sense of awe for Yahweh himself.

By means of the questions introduced by the word "who" (40:12–17; cf. Job 3:8–22), Isaiah affirms that Yahweh alone is the Creator God. He needs no counselors. His sovereignty extends to all of creation, and especially over the nations, which are like a "drop" in the bucket or like a piece of "dust" on the scales (40:15).

Yahweh is unique in that no one can compare him with anything the human mind may imagine (40:18–20). He is not to be likened to idols, which are powerless and fully dependent on human craftsmanship.

The God of Israel is seated "above" the earth (40:21–24). He is the great king, the sovereign judge over all the world. Yahweh himself oversees all that the nations do. At *his* time he will bring the nations to judgment. Even as grass is scorched and dried up, so Yahweh will bring the nations to nothing.

Yahweh is the Creator God whose might is revealed in the stars of the sky (40:25–26). The Babylonians deified the stars and constellations, but they too are the work of the Creator God.

The people are disheartened. They wonder whether God is truly able to establish his kingship (40:27–31). Yahweh may be the Creator of heaven and earth, know all of his creation by name, and hold the judges and rulers of this earth accountable for their actions, but does he still have concern for his people? The prophet affirms Yahweh's concern for their situation by focusing their attention on God's nature. He is the everlasting God, Yahweh, the covenant God, the Creator of heaven and earth. He tirelessly works out his plan of salvation for his people. Their restoration is based on his nature. He will renew the strength of his people, but this is contingent on their willingness to submit themselves to him.

C. Deliverance (41:1–44:23). **41:1–29.** The message of consolation (41:8–20) is enclosed by two arguments against the nations (41:1–7, 21–29). These arguments are addressed particularly to Israel to assure her that the nations are subject to God's power.

The nations are called to come before God's tribunal (41:1–7). Through a series of questions and answers, Yahweh announces the imminence of the judgment for the rebellious nations who are foolishly hoping that their idols will protect them. The instrument of God's judgment here ("one from the east") is ambiguous (41:2; cf. 41:21).

He answers his own question with the declaration, "I, the LORD—with the first of them and with the last—I am he" (41:4). The nations respond foolishly to the sovereignty of Israel's God. They renew their commitment to idols. The prophet mocks those involved in the manufacture of idols. They take the raw materials, beat them smooth with a hammer, and then solder them together. The irony in this passage highlights the folly of dependence on objects made by humans for protection against the power of the nations and especially against the power of Yahweh, the God of Israel.

Israel will be restored to her former status because, as Redeemer, Yahweh will be loyal to his "servant" (41:8–20). Therefore, God's people need not fear the nations.

Though Israel has been guilty of many offenses and has consequently gone into exile, she is still God's servant because of Abraham and Jacob. The election and calling of God are freely given, and his love extends to "the ends of the earth" (41:9). The depth of his care and the strength of his might comfort his disheartened people. He gives strength and will remove any obstacle or opposition. He is Yahweh, the Redeemer, the Holy One of Israel. Although his people are as insignificant as a "worm" by themselves (41:14), they will become like a "threshing sledge," pulverizing and crushing any obstacle (41:15–16). Their fear will turn to great joy in the Holy One of Israel.

Yahweh the Redeemer is able to meet all the needs of his people, whether spiritual or physical. Yahweh will extend his comfort to those who are poor in spirit. He will do everything in order to restore his people to himself. The verbs ("I will make . . . I will turn . . . I will put . . . I will set") express some of the many ways in which Yahweh shows concrete concern for his people. He will not forsake them in their need. Instead, he will provide the thirsty with water and will change conditions so that his people will see the evidences of his love.

The argument of 41:21–29 is a continuation of the first section of the chapter (41:1–7). The deities of the nations are unable to do what God does. He can declare from the beginning what is going to happen. He can give signs. He has power over all nations. He can bring adversity as well as prosperity. By contrast, the gods of the nations are powerless. They cannot respond. Therefore, the nations must know that as long as they depend on their gods they are actually without protection. As in 41:2, one who is unnamed will be raised up by Yahweh, the God of Israel, to bring about God's plan. His victories are the outworking of his plans. The Lord, who knows the future, reveals the good news of his accomplishments in history according to his plan for his own people. The idols are mere vanity.

The identity of the servant of the Lord has long been a subject for discussion. In this context several arguments favor identifying the servant first with Israel (see 41:8–9) and then in a greater way with the Messiah, in whom the perfection of servanthood is found. The language about the election, calling, and particular tasks of the servant fits in very well with the Old Testament language about Israel. The Servant Songs (42:1–9; 49:1–13; 50:4–9; 52:13–53:12) clearly reveal God's expectations of Israel and also how the Messiah, the faithful Servant-Son, alone fulfilled all God's expectations, especially in his vicarious suffering.

42:1–17. The servant is described as one in whom Yahweh has delight and whom he has elected (42:1–4). The language of election is an affirmation of the servant's continued existence and takes us back to the Abrahamic covenant, where God himself swore that he would be faithful to his covenant with Abraham's descendants.

The description of the Holy Spirit being "on" the servant is an Old Testament expression signifying a renewal of God's presence, by which God's servant is better equipped to serve him. The servant's task is to bring "justice" to the nations (42:1, 4), which is identical to the purpose of the coming messianic king (Isa. 9:7; 11:4). "Justice" here signifies neither religious nor legal practices, but the rule of Yahweh on earth. The servant is tender, gentle, and faithful characteristics embodied also by Jesus Christ. The nations are waiting for their inclusion in the kingdom. The ministry of the servant will last until the fullness of the kingdom has been established.

Yahweh the Creator God has called the servant to be a light to the nations (42:5–9). He will make the servant's mission a success by extending the covenant to the Gentiles. The messianic nature of Israel is to so affect the earth that all nations will be blessed through her and will join with her in expressing their faith in Yahweh.

Yahweh's jealousy for his glory ensures his continued presence with his people. He will open the eyes of the blind, free the prisoners, and do whatever is necessary to establish his kingdom on earth, in fulfillment of his word to the patriarchs (Gen. 12:1–3) and through the prophets. The restoration of the Jews and the inclusion of the Gentiles express the new age planned and revealed beforehand.

Isaiah leads the godly community, including the Gentiles, to praise Yahweh, the victorious king (42:10–13; cf. 44:23; 49:13; 52:9). The nations are called on to join together with the godly of Judah to sing "a new song" (42:10). The prophet gives two reasons for praising Yahweh. First, Yahweh has created a new era. He has opened up a new perspective by redeeming his people to be "a light to the nations" (42:6 RSV, NASB). Even the people in the wilderness of Kedar and in the Edomite city of Sela are invited to join in praise of the God of Israel (42:11). Second, his people praise him because the Lord rouses himself for battle like a mighty warrior (Exod. 15:3, 16). Zealous for his kingdom, he will not allow enemy nations to trample his rights.

Yahweh has been patient with the nations for a long time (42:14–17). Now he is ready to act on behalf of his people. When he comes, nothing can stop him. He is like a woman in labor who must give birth. He has the power to destroy and to make things desolate, yet he also has the power to redeem his people. His people are the blind who need light and guidance. Yahweh will build his kingdom while judging the nations and demolishing paganism.

42:18–43:28. Israel is a blind and deaf servant (42:18–43:7). Because of her unwillingness to respond to Yahweh, she was oppressed and exiled as an expression of Yahweh's anger. Israel's exile was evidence of God's rejection, but her redemption is an expression of his love.

Israel's formation was not a mistake. God elected ("created," "formed") Israel. He made them to be his people by calling them to be his. He loves his people and will do anything to redeem them. Regardless of how difficult the circumstances or how far he has to bring his people, *he is with them.* He is their God by covenant, the Holy One who has consecrated them, their Redeemer. He will give up nations such as Egypt, Cush (Ethiopia), and Seba (a region south of Ethiopia) in exchange for the remnant of his people, his "sons" and "daughters," who are called by his name (43:6–7). Thus, both the experience of rejection and the affirmation of redemption are the outworking of God's will and are expressions of his fatherly concern for his children.

Over against the magnificent portrayal of the future of God's people is present reality: Israel is still blind and deaf (43:8–13). In spite of this condition, however, God still has a future for them. They will be witnesses to his majesty and authority over the nations. He cannot use the nations for this purpose because they have given themselves over to idolatry. God's people should know only Yahweh, having experienced his deliverance.

The phrases "I am he" (43:10) and "I am God" (43:12) signify that only Yahweh, the God of Israel, is God. He is also the powerful Redeemer who has already shown his ability to his people. Yahweh as the God of his people has revealed himself by words as well as deeds so that all might know that he is the only true God.

In their need Yahweh reminds his people repeatedly that he is their Redeemer, the Holy One of Israel, "the LORD" (Yahweh), their king (43:14–21). In their self-doubt, they must never doubt him. The God who redeemed his people from Egypt will bring down Babylon and deliver his people from exile. The old, old story of the Passover and the miraculous journey through the Red Sea is dwarfed in comparison with the "new thing" (43:19). This "new thing" refers to the new era of forgiveness, restoration, and God's presence. The servant of Yahweh, the people whom he has chosen, will be refreshed. The rivers of water speak not only of the spiritual refreshment but also about the manner in which Yahweh will take care of the physical needs of his people in bringing them out of exile and into the promised land.

The very purpose of the deliverance is that the people may praise Yahweh upon experiencing the blessings of redemption and restoration.

The postexilic Jewish community enjoyed the benefits of restoration from exile, resettlement in the land of Canaan, and the physical and spiritual blessings of God's presence. This progressive restoration was intensified in the coming of the Messiah, who gives the water of life (John 4:14). Yet the *final* restoration of all things will bring with it the climactic fulfillment of these words.

God's people do not deserve his love (43:22–28). They have failed to honor him as God by neglecting to present offerings and sacrifices. But the nature of God does not change. He is compassionate and gracious and ready to forgive his people (Exod. 34:6–7; Ps. 103:3, 11–14). Because of God's unchanging love, the prophet calls on the people to turn from their state of sin and return to Yahweh.

From its beginnings, Israel has been a nation of sinners. Kings, priests, and false prophets rebelled against the Lord. Israel can in no way claim innocence in a case against God. Therefore, Israel has been destroyed and disgraced. God is vindicated in his judgment.

44:1–23. Regardless of Israel's past, she is still the servant of Yahweh (44:1–5). Her future lies in her election. Israel is transformed by God's grace into a new creation, the nature of which is described in a threefold way. First, the Spirit of the Lord is poured on the people (44:3). The presence of the Spirit is an expression of God's intent to use the people as his servants and to equip them for his service. Second, the blessing of God will rest more markedly on the people's offspring (44:3–5). The very process of internal renewal affects generations to come. In contrast to the past generations of faithlessness (43:27), there will now be generations of faithful people, blessed by the Lord. Third, the covenant will be renewed not only with Israel but also with Gentiles who will call on the Lord and join in Israel's heritage (44:5).

The certainty of the future of God's people is guaranteed by Yahweh's kingship (44:6–23). He is Yahweh, king of Israel, Redeemer, and Lord of Hosts. There is no god like him, because he foretells what is to come. Since the God of Israel knows and controls the future, his people need not fear. God's purpose for them will stand; they *will* be his witnesses.

How different are idols from the "Rock" of Israel! The prophet depicts the folly of idolatry in the form of a satire. Idols are, after all, the work of humans and are characterized by several human limitations. First, even the best artisans have human limitations. Second, idols are nothing more than creations fashioned by the best of human instruments. Third, idols are also limited by the materials from which they are made. They are made from wood, a material hardly appropriate for the production of precious objects. How can one distinguish which piece of wood is more appropriate for worship and which is to be used to kindle a fire? Clearly the whole idol industry is the work of humans and is characterized by the physical limitations of human weaknesses, the instruments, and the material itself. The pursuit of idolatry is irrational and leads to irrationality. Idolatrous people will not be able to respond appropriately to Yahweh because their eyes are shut and their hearts are hardened (44:20). They are given to immorality and idolatry and have no way of turning back.

This section closes with a restatement of the uniqueness of Israel's God (44:21–22). The Lord has elected, called, and forgiven his people. He calls them to repent by returning to him, their Redeemer. The greatness of God's forgiveness and love is brought out in a hymn in which nature is called on to rejoice in the outworking of God's plan of redemption. Nature itself awaits the fulfillment of this plan and the revelation of the glory of God's people.

D. Yahweh's sovereignty (44:24–47:15). **44:24–45:25.** Yahweh is the Redeemer and has the power to renew his people (44:24–28). Within Yahweh are two creative forces: the force to create (re-create) and the force to redeem. Yahweh is the Creator of the heavens and the earth. However, he also re-creates everything in accordance with his purpose. This restoration (re-creation) makes the earth habitable for his people—an integral part of their redemption. Every act in the progression of redemption confirms his word. While in exile, Israel needed the reassurance that Jerusalem would be repopulated and rebuilt and that the temple would be restored. The power of Yahweh in creation, renewal, and redemption stands in stark contrast to the impotence of the practitioners of magic and divination. Yahweh overturns the signs of the diviners and negates the wisdom of the sages. In spite of all the Babylonian claims to wisdom and magical powers, he will raise up a foreign king, Cyrus the Persian, to initiate a new stage in the history of redemption. The postexilic era of reconstruction is a resumption of his redemptive activities, which will culminate in the new heavens and earth and in the New Jerusalem.

Isaiah 45:1–8 develops the role of Cyrus in God's redemptive plan. Cyrus has been raised up and empowered by Yahweh to accomplish God's kingdom purposes. He has been anointed for the particular purpose of accomplishing God's work on earth. Therefore, it is even possible to call him "the anointed one," a designation generally limited to the kings of Israel and Judah.

God's purpose in raising up Cyrus is twofold. First, he will be raised up for the sake of Israel in order to be an instrument of redemption (45:4). Second, he will cause the nations to recognize that Yahweh, the God of Israel, is the only true God. He alone has power to change light into darkness, adversity into prosperity, and vice versa (45:7). The very designations "I am the LORD" and "I, the LORD, do all these things" (45:6–7) express the authority of the God of Israel in fulfilling his covenantal obligations and general governance of the earth. This indirect encouragement to Israel is to assure those living in darkness and those experiencing adversity that Yahweh has the power to reverse their situation.

In another hymn (45:8), the prophet rejoices in the salvation of the Lord, which is expressed in a temporal extension of his righteous rule. Cyrus is the instrument, but the Lord is the author of it all.

Isaiah then calls on the nations to present their argument in the very presence of God (45:9–13). Since they do not have confidence in the God of Israel, they have questioned what Yahweh is doing. Yahweh is the potter and humankind is nothing but clay in his hands. Yahweh's particular concern with the earth extends to humanity at large.

The Creator God is the Redeemer God who will establish righteousness on earth, beginning with the restoration from exile and the rebuilding of Judah.

The nations—represented by Egypt, Cush, and Seba (45:14)—will seek the favor of God's people, having witnessed in the events of history that God is present with them (45:14–17). It is likely that verse 15 continues their confession, as the nations have not known the God of Israel and express a desire to know the Savior of Israel. Israel's salvation is of the Lord and is therefore lasting; idolatry brings only disgrace and ruin.

Yahweh, the Creator of heaven and earth, shows his peculiar interest in mankind by revealing that he created the earth to be inhabited (45:18–19). He will never destroy it. Therefore, he chose the seed of Jacob and revealed himself to them. His word is open ("not . . . in secret"), righteous (NIV "the truth"), and "right" (45:19). He has revealed his decrees, and their fulfillment confirms that he is victorious and faithful.

The survivors of God's judgment are invited to judge for themselves (45:20–25). Idols cannot foretell or control the future. Only Yahweh, the God of Israel, is able to execute his righteous plans for redeeming his people. The nations must turn to Yahweh and join freely in God's salvation—or else under compulsion at the great judgment of the nations.

At the final judgment of God, all nations will be "put to shame" (45:24). "Shame" is that state in which one is without help, without escape, without God, and thus completely disgraced. The righteous will rejoice in the victory, glory, and praise that Yahweh will extend to them. They will find that Yahweh is truly righteous in that he brings about all his promises. Not only will they rejoice in Yahweh's victories, but they will also be assured that their descendants will be the beneficiaries of God's goodness.

46:1–47:15. The fall of Babylon is first portrayed by the carrying off of her gods (46:1–13). The exile of Babylon's gods is symbolic of God's intervention on behalf of Israel. The inability of Babylon's gods to save her stands in stark contrast to the power of Yahweh. Therefore, the prophet concludes by calling on Israel to listen and respond to God because his salvation is near.

As their gods are being carried off, the people of Babylon make every effort to save them, but to no avail. Bel is the title given to Marduk, god of the capital city of Babylon. His title is related to the Hebrew word *baal* ("Lord," "Master"). The god of the city of Borsippa was Nebo, Marduk's son, to whom belonged wisdom and learning. The political power represented by Bel and the wisdom represented by Nebo will be unable to deliver the idols of Babylon, much less the people.

In contrast, God has taken pains to carry and care for Israel, like a mother, and purposes to remain faithful. His signature affixed to this promise is "I am God" (46:9).

The Babylonian gods are incapable of hearing or delivering those who depend on them. Not so with Yahweh, who answers his people when they call on him in their distress.

Yahweh has revealed that he alone is God, the Creator, the planner and executor of everything that has taken place on earth. His plan includes Cyrus, who is compared to a "bird of prey" (46:11). Though stubborn Israel does not deserve it, God's salvation is very near. The future of God's people is based on God's full and free salvation. The Lord will be victorious ("righteous").

Isaiah 46:1–2 describes the gods of Babylon being carried off into captivity. Such a scene is portrayed in this Assyrian relief, which shows soldiers carrying away the gods of the enemy they have just defeated (palace at Nimrud, 728 BC)

Babylon is portrayed as a "virgin" who will lose her genteel, cultured life (47:1–4). Her status will be reduced to that of a slave girl who, scantily dressed, works with the millstones and grinds flour. The virgin daughter of Babylon is symbolic of the whole empire. The judgment on Babylon is an expression of the vindication of the Redeemer and Holy One of Israel, who delivers his people from their oppressors.

Babylon is also portrayed as "the eternal queen" (47:5–7). She ruled over the nations like a queen mother, but showed no mercy to the subject nations. She showed no accountability to God as she ruled.

The fame of Babylon is a claim to autonomy, but also to deity (47:8–11). The language "I am" and "there is none besides me" (47:8) is the language usually reserved for Yahweh and his claim that he alone is God.

Although the Babylonians have used all kinds of magic spells to secure their future, sudden disaster will overtake them. Though Babylon has used her wisdom to plot military strategies and avert political and economic disasters, she cannot match the wisdom and power of God. A disaster has been planned, and there is no way Babylon can ward off the purposes and plan of God. Whereas Babylon prided herself on her ability to predict and prevent, the God of Israel suddenly overwhelms her in his judgment.

The prophet sarcastically urges the people to devote themselves a little more to their magic and sorceries: there may still be some answers forthcoming from the established Babylonian systems of divination (47:12–15). However, these systems will prove ineffective against the God of Israel. The prophet moves on to another well-developed area of Babylonian religion: astrology. With strong irony, he calls on Babylon to turn to the astrologers and the many counselors, that they may be able to save Babylon from her fall. The counselors and astrologers are compared to stubble, which is quickly burned and of little use.

The prophet began by portraying Babylon's gods being carried into exile (46:1–2) and concludes with the inability of her wise men, astrologers, and diviners to help the nation out of her great trouble. Her religious, political, and intellectual systems will completely break down.

Human political, religious, and intellectual systems may work for a long time, as did the system in Babylon. They may be revitalized and altered to meet changing conditions; however, any system that works for its own glory and for human autonomy, whether national or individual, cannot deliver people at the time when deliverance is most needed. By means of this solemn statement, the prophet has contrasted the failure of human systems over against a God who is able to deliver and establish his eternal kingdom.

E. Proclamation of restoration (48:1–22). Yahweh has planned everything that has happened and will happen on this planet. However, the events themselves are directed toward the creation of a new era. Though God's people may fail, Yahweh himself remains faithful to introduce and bring in that new era. The new era is not eschatological in the sense that it is far off. Instead, like the judgment, it is always near. The restoration of the Jewish people from exile introduced this era in a grand way. Its future lies hidden in the revelation of God's name, which will be manifested in the glory, righteousness, and salvation of his people.

Though God's people claim to lean on Yahweh, swear by Yahweh, and point to Jerusalem as the holy city, they do not show their covenant relationship in their daily lives (48:1–8). They are faithless, without any righteous deeds, and stubborn. Though they claim to belong to Yahweh's "city," the city of the great king (48:2), their lifestyle is in direct rebellion against him. Though Yahweh has revealed that all rebellious people will be exiled, they receive the good news of a "new" beginning. It is the new era in which Yahweh begins the restoration of Israel, which will eventually include a re-creation of the heavens and the earth. It will be a time especially characterized by fulfillment of the promises of God.

By means of repetition the prophet calls attention to the ground of salvation (48:9–11). He repeats the expression "for my own name's sake" three times (48:9, 11). The reason for the future salvation does not lie in Israel but in God himself. For the sake of his own honor he restrains his anger. The restraint of God is a loving restraint; he does not unleash the fullness of his anger on his people. Yahweh is intent on purifying a people unto himself through adversity.

The name Yahweh signifies that God keeps covenant by fulfilling all of the promises he has made (48:12–16). He is the first and the last (48:12). By "the first," the prophet signifies the God who has been involved in the work of creation and with his people in exile. By "the last," Isaiah signifies the new era, which is to be introduced at the fall of Babylon and the decree of Cyrus, also designated the era of "new things" (48:6). Yahweh himself directs the history of redemption from beginning to end. He has not spoken or dealt secretly but rather has made it clear that he has planned everything that comes to pass, including the mission of the servant (48:16). The identity of the servant is not made clear, and opinions vary (Cyrus, the prophet himself, the messianic servant).

Yahweh is the Redeemer of his people, their covenant God and teacher (48:17–19). The Teacher God instructs his people so that they might succeed. However, Israel has been unresponsive and, as such, has missed the fullness of the covenantal blessings. Instead of seeing their population explode to the point of being like the sand of the seashore, they have seen their number reduced. Instead of experiencing the peace that comes from Yahweh's victories over the enemies, they have been subjugated. Israel has lost God's great blessings because of its stubbornness.

The prophet calls the people to leave Babylon (48:20–22). The coming out of Babylon marks the beginning of the era of restoration. For that reason it is important to begin seeing that all of the blessings of restoration, beginning with the return from exile and extending to the coming of Jesus Christ, are expressions of the new covenant. Though Jesus would come more than five hundred years later, the benefits of Israel in the land are benefits based on and in anticipation of the finished work of Christ. Though in one sense they are still under the old covenant, in a greater sense they are already under the new covenant. The people respond to Yahweh and his word. The Spirit of God is present in a greater way after the exile than before. There is a real joy among the people of God because they have experienced the return from exile as a token of God's redemption and kingship.

For this reason the people are to joyfully proclaim what God has done on their behalf. All the nations must hear that Yahweh has restored his people to be his servants. Yahweh has been faithful to his promises by providing water out of the rock. The God of the exodus will continue to redeem his people. However, the effect of redemption is limited to those who have the spiritual marks of Abraham.

9. Reconciliation and Restoration (49:1–55:13)

A. The servant of the Lord (49:1–13). These verses portray the various characteristics of the servant of God and call on the nations to pay attention to the servant even though he is despised by them.

The servant of God is not to be judged by his present or past status but rather by his election (49:1–6). Yahweh himself has called and named his servant. The prophet intimates that there is a twofold purpose in the servant's calling. On the one hand, he is to proclaim the word, which the prophet likens to a "sharpened sword." On the other hand, he is to be like a "polished arrow" (49:2). The sword speaks of the prophetic ministry in which the servant, filled by the word of the Lord, speaks that word, which is able to penetrate the hearts and souls of people. The arrow, as an instrument of warfare, symbolizes God's judgment on those who do not respond. Yahweh himself will be glorified by his servant. He will continue to use his servant to speak to

Israel as well as to the nations. Yahweh's word will not return to him void, so the servant is guaranteed that his prophetic mission will be successful.

The servant responds by looking at his own condition. He realizes that he has not been successful and asks why he must continue to labor. God's response is that he will shortly reward the servant with success. The tribes of Jacob will be restored as a part of God's mission, that they might be a "light" to the nations.

Who is the "servant"? According to 41:8–9; 44:2; and 49:3, "servant" is a prophetic designation for the restored people of God, Israel. Yet, according to 49:1–6, the servant has a mission to the nation and to the Gentiles. These words are applicable to the restored community of Jews in Judea and the Diaspora, but in a greater sense they apply to the mission of our Lord (see Luke 2:32; Acts 26:23). Since that time the mission of the servant has become the mission of the church, the new people of God.

The success of the servant's mission depends on Yahweh (49:7). He, "the Redeemer" and "the Holy One of Israel" (two times), is faithful to his election. Though the servant may be ridiculed, impoverished, persecuted, and oppressed, the kingdom of God will be established on earth, and all the sons of the great king will receive glory. The nations and kingdoms outside of the kingdom of God will be put down. Isaiah 49:7 contains an allusion to the nature of the mission of Jesus Christ. He suffered, and through his suffering obtained glory. Jesus, after his resurrection and glorification in heaven, is the great judge, who will put down all unsubmissive nations and is the one before whom all the nations must eventually lie prostrate.

The phrase "the time of my favor" signifies the era of Yahweh's gracious acceptance of his people (49:8–13), denoting an era of proclamation of freedom. It marks the renewal of the covenant and the fulfillment of God's promises. The renewal of the covenant finds expression in God's redemption, protection, provision, and guidance. He will remove obstacles and gather his people from all over the Diaspora.

The prophet then bursts into another hymn of praise. Nature observes and participates in the care, comfort, and relief of the afflicted children of God (49:13).

B. Zion's surprise (49:14–21). "Zion" here is a metaphor for the people of God who lament, asking whether the Lord has completely forgotten them. Yahweh, like a mother, can never forget his children.

Zion is also likened to a mother bereft of her children and abandoned in the ruins. The Lord assures her that he will never forget her because she is "engraved . . . on the palms of my hands" (49:16). The scattered will return and be so numerous that the land will be too small. The land and its cities will be restored, and its enemies will be kept away. The fulfillment of these words applies to postexilic Judaism and extends until the renewal of this earth.

C. Israel's restoration (49:22–26). The nations themselves will become instruments of the redemption of God's people. They will cooperate with God's plans so that the people of God may draw comfort and not be disappointed. The Lord will bring down the nations that seek to harm his people and will not submit to him. "The Mighty One of Jacob" will fight the battle for them, that the nations may know that he is Yahweh, the Deliverer and Redeemer of his people.

D. Sin and obedience (50:1–11). Because of the great guilt of the people of God and their lack of responsiveness, Yahweh has justly exiled them (50:1–3). In the past he called them tenderly, but there was no response. He has the power to avert the exile, as seen in the plagues on Egypt, but he acts freely, deciding to let it happen. Yet, even though he sent them away, he has not divorced or sold Israel to the creditors.

Who is this obedient and suffering servant (50:4–9)? Since his suffering is not unto death and he seems to be untouched by the rejection of humanity, the servant is probably the prophet himself. The prophet, in pursuit of his prophetic mission, directs himself to the people of God in the hope of being heard and understood. Instead, he is reviled. If 50:4–9 is a restatement of 49:1–6, it is also possible to identify the servant with faithful Israel as a good disciple of the Lord.

The servant has a mission to encourage the "weary"—the dejected Jews in exile and all who long for God's redemption. The authenticity of the message is guaranteed by the Lord himself, who teaches and opens the ear of the servant. The servant is a responsive disciple who executes and speaks whatever has been taught. Even in the face of unbelief and opposition he does not hesitate, because of his unique relationship with God and because of his conviction that the Lord will contend for him. No one can bring a charge against him. Over against the victorious outworking of God's plans are the unbelievers, who will perish.

The response to the ministry of this servant may be one of faith or further obstinacy (50:10–11). He calls for a wise response rather than a continuation in folly and dark ways. If people continue to insist on walking by their own light, the judgment of God will overtake them, and there will be no escape. These verses also form an appropriate transition from chapters 49–50 to 51:1–52:12.

E. Everlasting salvation (51:1–52:12). The theme of the restoration of the people of God is developed in nine strophes (verse units) (51:1–3, 4–6, 7–8, 9–11, 12–16, 17–23; 52:1–2, 3–6, 7–12). These strophes are connected by the repetition of imperatives ("listen," 51:1, 4, 7, 21; 52:8; "look," 51:1–2; "awake," 51:9, 17; 52:1; and "depart," 52:11), promises of comfort, and references to creation and redemption.

God's words of comfort (51:1–3) are addressed to those who still fear the nations among whom they are dwelling. They believe but have not yet come to the point where their faith is a conquering faith. There are many lingering questions. Will Yahweh restore his people to the land? Will he multiply his people again? Will their enemies prevail once more?

The pursuit of righteousness focuses on God's ordering of all things in accord with his promises. The prophet encourages all who long for the fulfillment of God's word by pointing to God's work in the past. He promised to multiply Abraham and Sarah's descendants and to bless them (Gen. 17:2, 5–6, 16), and so he did (51:1–2). Their solidarity with Abraham, as they come from the same "rock" and "quarry" (51:1), should be comforting because God is the same and his promises do not change. Since the people are looking for God's grace, he will comfort Zion. The Lord will restore the land and the people, so that the work of restoration points back to the Garden of Eden. His people will again experience his presence, as in Eden, and will rejoice in the beginning of God's restoration.

Only the godly constitute the "new people of God," with whom he renews his covenant (51:4–6). They receive the words of assurance that God's rule ("instruction," "my justice," 51:4) will extend beyond Israel to the nations. They will also see the light. The present heaven and earth must be made into a new creation, characterized by God's triumphant and everlasting rule. Israel and the nations join together in eager expectation of the new heaven and earth.

The comfort of God is limited to those who have appropriated for themselves the knowledge of his righteous rule and salvation (51:7–8). They do not wait passively; they are God's agents in establishing the new age. They firmly believe in God's plan for them and for the world. Yet in their weakness they need encouragement. These verses essentially repeat the previously given words of comfort: God will judge the wicked and restore all things to his divinely purposed order.

In a most urgent way, reminiscent of the psalms of lamentation (cf. Ps. 44:23), the prophet calls on the Lord to act on a scale grander than the exodus from Egypt (51:9–11).

Then, God revealed his strong arm by redeeming his people and inflicting plagues and death on the Egyptians (Exod. 7:14–12:23). When God acts in history, the redeemed will experience his deliverance. Their sorrow and sighing will be turned into an everlasting life of great joy.

The Creator God is the Redeemer God. He is the maker of heaven and earth *and* Zion. He comforts his people like no one else (51:12–16). His own need not be afraid of people who by their very nature are mortal. He shall free them so magnificently that the oppressors will be unable to oppose his power. He is the Lord, the great warrior whose name is Yahweh of Hosts ("LORD Almighty," 51:15). The word of the Lord is true, and he will protect his own until he has accomplished the restoration of all things.

The prophet brings the people back to their own situation (51:17–23). When God's judgment came on them, there was no word of comfort. The suffering of judgment is metaphorically described as a "cup" (51:17). The "cup" is an expression of the fullness of the anger of the Lord: "ruin and destruction, famine and sword" (51:19). Now, he graciously rouses them from their drunken stupor. The Lord who judged them will again defend his people. He removes the cup of judgment from them. He encourages them in that their lot will fall on their oppressors.

In response to their prayer ("awake, awake," 51:9), the Lord calls his people to wake up from their stupor (52:1–2). He has sovereignly and graciously exchanged the shame of their exile and alienation for the glory of his presence. Jerusalem, the "mother city," will again be a glorious queen. Her reproach will be removed when the ungodly desist from oppressing. Only a holy people will inhabit the holy city.

Israel's bondage in Egypt and her exile in Babylon were not due to God's inability to deliver them. He freely handed them over, and freely he will deliver them (52:3–6). His purpose

> God's strength is symbolized through the mighty or outstretched "arm of the Lord" (Isa. 51:9; cf. Ps. 77:10–15). In Egyptian reliefs, the pharaoh's strength is often portrayed in a similar way, with his "mighty arm" ready to strike. Here, Rameses III has one arm raised and the other grasping the hair of his enemies (Medinet Habu, twelfth century BC).

was that they might witness that he is Yahweh, who is constant and faithful to his people.

The good news of God's kingship is freely proclaimed in Zion (52:7–12). The anger of God has subsided. He has cleansed his people and returns to dwell again in their midst. Only those who are "pure," untouched by the defilements of this world, may experience his presence as in the days of the exodus. However, the new exodus is unlike the exodus under Moses in two ways. First, they need not hasten (52:12) because God will protect them. He will "bare his holy arm" (52:10) so that all the nations will submit to him in fear. Second, he himself will go before them, instead of merely showing his presence symbolically in the cloud of glory or the ark of the covenant. God's people, the recipients of his fatherly comfort, will be led home triumphantly.

F. The Suffering Servant (52:13–53:12). The servant of the Lord will share the throne with God himself, as he will be "lifted up and highly exalted" (52:13–15). He will succeed in his mission, for which reason he is described as acting "wisely" (52:13). He does what is right and pleases God. The Lord will raise him up to glory. The nations who marvel at his appearance, because the servant was greatly humiliated in his suffering, will witness his glory.

The kings and nations were amazed when they heard about the suffering servant, and so are the godly in Israel (53:1–3). Therefore, the question "Who has believed?" is raised. The question is meant not only to draw attention to the servant but also to introduce the servant as the means of redemption. Yahweh has chosen to reveal his "arm" through the servant. The "arm of the LORD" is a symbol of the Lord's judgment as well as of his deliverance (cf. Ps. 98:1). In this context it is the means of deliverance for those who trust in the suffering servant.

The servant was characterized by humility. Isaiah compares him to a "tender shoot" coming forth out of "dry ground" (53:2). He was an ordinary human being and not a king or potentate. The servant was unimpressive and readily rejected by humans.

The suffering servant was one who knew sorrows and fully identified with humankind. Not only was he born with little chance of success; he was also extremely vulnerable. He lived as a man among humans. The rejection of the servant is graphically described: he was "punished," "stricken," and "afflicted" (53:4–6). He took upon himself the very curse of God. Since God's curse comes on any who break his covenant, the servant either was a great sinner or carried the sins of others. In addition, he is described as one who was "pierced" (wounded), "crushed," and "punished" (53:5). He suffered in order that he might bring restoration ("peace" and "healing") between God and humanity.

His experience of suffering is characterized by people's violence, by his own innocence and patience, and most importantly by God's acceptance. The servant himself did nothing wrong (53:7–9). He did no violence, nor did he speak in a deceptive way. Why then did Yahweh lay such suffering on him? The reason for the suffering must be found in the nature of the judgment of God. The Lord brought him through torture, judgment, death, and finally burial. In these verses Isaiah describes how the servant was oppressed and afflicted, how he did not receive a just sentence. He was put to death and buried like a criminal. Even though his suffering was unjust, the servant accepted his humiliation quietly, patiently, and obediently. He is compared to a lamb led to the slaughter or to a sheep being sheared (53:7). Quietly he received the judgment from God because he bore that judgment for others.

The servant suffered not for himself but rather to bear "our suffering," "our transgressions," and "our iniquities" (53:4–5). The benefits of the vicarious suffering of the servant include reconciliation to God and forgiveness. He carried the sins and guilt of the people; therefore, he was able to bring the people of God back into fellowship with their heavenly Father. All humankind has gone astray, but through the suffering of the servant there is still the possibility for peace and healing.

The servant's death was not in vain (53:10–12). He had done the Lord's will, even when he was crushed. He suffered as a human "offering for sin" and as a rebel against God for the sake of rebels. Because God was pleased not only to crush him but also to accept his life as an offering, the effects of his death are many: life, "offspring" (53:10), success, and honor. Through him many may be justified. The servant suffered on behalf of others. They share in his benefits if they turn to him as the means of forgiveness by reconciliation with the heavenly Father.

Of whom is the prophet speaking? It is tempting to read the New Testament association of the Suffering Servant with the Lord Jesus. But would Isaiah have understood it this way? Isaiah's own testimony does not provide the clues for the identification of the servant. It could be Israel's suffering on behalf of Israel, or the suffering of the prophet himself or any prophet, or that of a Moses-like figure. The apostolic interpretation of the text opens and closes with the identification of the servant. On the one hand, the apostles encourage God's people to suffer with patience and endurance for the sake of the kingdom. They modeled this vicarious lifestyle. On the other hand, they also point to Jesus Christ as the paradigm. Instead of seeing a one-to-one correspondence between the Suffering Servant and Jesus, the apostles showed that the relationship between Jesus and the members of his church is such that the suffering continues. The suffering of Jesus Christ is analogical to that of the church throughout her history.

G. The new covenant (54:1–17). The prophet calls on the covenant people to rejoice because of the change in their condition (54:1–10). The sufferings of the past and present will give way to a new era. The people are compared to a "barren woman" (54:1), a widow (54:4), and a woman separated from her husband (54:6).

The blessedness of the reversal from barrenness and desolation is the reward of the servant. The new age will resemble God's graciousness to Sarah, who was barren (Gen. 11:30) but who by God's promise became the mother of nations

and kings (Gen. 17:16). The mother's "tent" will be full (54:2), and the land will be repopulated.

The description of the new condition serves to encourage the people of God not to be afraid or ashamed. In the past they have been ashamed because of the disgrace they carried. However, the Lord assures them that their shame will be removed. The hope for the future lies in the Lord himself. He will again take his people to himself, because he is their maker and husband. He is their great king ("the Lord of Hosts"; NIV "Lord Almighty), their Redeemer, the Holy One of Israel, who desires to sanctify his people; he is God of the whole world.

This is a description of the covenant God, who graciously renews the covenant with his people. He has abandoned them for a short time only to renew his love with great compassion—*forever*. The length and intensity of the love of God cannot be compared with the shortness of his wrath. The Lord assures his people by oath that he will never be angry with them again. He will never again use exile as an expression of his animosity toward his people. The certainty of the covenant lies in Yahweh himself. The Lord swears that he will never remove his covenantal blessings of peace, mercy, and kindness from his people. The ground for the restoration of the Jewish people lies in the Lord's oath to be gracious to all those who call on him. This covenant blessing has been extended by Jesus Christ to all who call on him.

The prophet contrasts the situation of the desolate Jerusalem with its glorious future (54:11–17). It has been attacked and disgraced and received no pity or compassion, but the glory of the mother city will be great. She will be completely rebuilt as the New Jerusalem.

Within the city itself the people are blessed, with a blessedness limited to the righteous. Their children will know the Lord and will be blessed by him. They will experience the presence and protection of God. They will not fear because Yahweh will destroy every enemy. Nothing can separate them from him. They enter into their heritage from the Lord.

After the exile the Jews experienced some of the benefits of Yahweh's blessing as they were restored to the land and lived in the city of Jerusalem and in Judea. But the people of God are still looking forward to the revelation of their glorious city, the New Jerusalem, which will come from above (Rev. 21:2). While on this earth, we rejoice in the love God has shown for his church, we rejoice in having children who know the Lord, and we rejoice in his presence and protection. However, our hope still lies in the day in which our Lord Jesus Christ will reveal his glory.

H. Assurance (55:1–13). Yahweh's invitation to the people is not an esoteric one (55:1–5). His call is like the cry of a vendor selling his wares in the marketplace. The Lord calls on anyone and everyone to turn to him as the one who is able to provide for their needs. The open proclamation of the Lord assures that whoever desires may come, including Gentiles. He promises to take care of *all* humanity's needs. This redemption is gracious and free.

The gift of God is an everlasting covenant, such as the Lord made with David (2 Sam. 7:8–16). The people of God will join with the Davidic Messiah in leading nations into the covenant fellowship. The nations will submit to the witness-bearing role of God's people.

The prophet joins the invitation of Yahweh with a call to the people to have faith in him and to openly show their faith by repentance from their evil works (55:6–9). There is still the possibility of reconciliation and forgiveness. Yahweh is greater than man; as such, his thoughts cannot be likened to man's thoughts. Man's thoughts are evil for evil, but Yahweh can be gracious even when he has been hurt, dishonored, and disobeyed. *Now* is the day for the people to come to Yahweh in faith. The prophet calls on the people to respond by signing the contract and seeking him in the present moment.

The certainty of free redemption and the free offer of the gospel lie in Yahweh himself (55:10–13). As long as the moment of grace is *here*, Yahweh's invitation will not return to him void. He has planned to call out a people to himself, and in this he will succeed. The prophet likens the power of the word to the rain and the snow, which are useful in germinating the seed and permitting it to develop. The word of the Lord concerns the redemption and restoration of all things.

Redemption begins with the postexilic developments. Yahweh calls on the people to depart from Babylon and assures them that they will be restored to the land; indeed, the land itself will be restored so that, instead of briars and thorns, cypress and myrtle will grow up. Even nature joins with the people of God in the restoration and now awaits further restoration. The redemption of God's people from exile is a sign to all the godly that Yahweh is the Redeemer. He calls on his people to have faith in him for their free redemption. The one who led Israel from Egypt and provided for them in the wilderness with manna, meat, and drink again proves himself faithful by redeeming his people from Babylon. Redemption is the sign of the covenant. From the moment of the restoration from exile, all the godly are assured that the new heavens and the new earth and the New Jerusalem will be established, because God is the Redeemer.

10. The Glory and Responsibility of Zion (56:1–66:24)

A. Response to redemption (56:1–8). Salvation is the act of God in which he gathers his people, both Jew and Gentile, and unites them with himself and with one another (56:1–2). To these he extends the privilege of being subjects under his righteous rule along with all its benefits.

The proper response of the people of God is that of covenant loyalty. The Lord expects his people to act like him. He expects that the people who have been justified and thereby have entered into a relationship with him will act in accordance with his own standards. There is a blessing for all who keep the covenant.

The Sabbath is singled out as the sign of the covenant and is representative of all the commandments (56:3–8). How one relates to the Sabbath is an indication of how one relates to the other commandments. The Sabbath commandment, therefore, is a barometer of one's spiritual condition.

The Gentile ("foreigner") and the eunuch both show their commitment to the covenant Lord by keeping the Sabbath. In the past the eunuch could not be a part of the covenant community; there were also limitations on foreigners (Deut. 23:1–8). However, the renewed covenant is extended to those who were previously unfit.

The Lord responds to the needs of those who join his covenant. The eunuch is assured that he will have a remembrance among the people of God. His name will be remembered forever. Foreigners who have been kept away from the worship of the Lord in Jerusalem are assured that they too will be able to bring sacrifices and worship the Lord.

The temple will be known as the "house of prayer" for all nations (56:7). The prophet looks forward to the new era in which Jews and Gentiles will worship God together. Our Lord Jesus Christ brought together the two folds—the Jews and the Gentiles (Eph. 2:14).

The prophet proclaims the word of God to the people of his time and at the same time issues a warning to future generations. Since the prophet warns God's people against the dangers of apostasy, faithlessness, and formalism, the exhortation of the prophet still speaks to issues that the people of God face today.

B. Unfaithful leaders (56:9–57:2). The leaders are called "watchmen" (56:10; cf. Isa. 52:8; Ezek. 3:17; 33:7). Leaders, whether civil or religious, charged with responsibility for the people of God are likened to "mute" and greedy dogs (56:10–11)—irresponsible in discharging their responsibility for instructing God's people and greedy for material gain.

The struggle between righteousness and wickedness extends even to Zion. The wicked are those who enjoy the benefits of the covenant community without committing themselves fully to God and to his righteous purposes. As long as evil is in the world, its dark power seems to overshadow the glory of Zion.

C. Unfaithful people (57:3–13a). Isaiah goes on to compare the people of God to bad "seed" (NIV "offspring," 57:3). They are nothing but rebels because they love idolatry in all its forms. They have given themselves over to idolatry and immorality.

The beardless faces on these men shown in the throneroom scene of Sargon II likely indicate that they are eunuchs (Khorsabad, 721–705 BC).

Isaiah describes the extent of Judah's apostasy. Wherever they are, the people are corrupt, whether they go to the ravines (57:6) or to the hills (57:7), whether they stay at home (57:8) or go to Sheol (57:9).

The wicked will be left to themselves. The Lord has been patient in not destroying them thus far. Because they have shown no sign of repentance or fear of him, however, they will not stand in the judgment of God. They will fall with the rest of humanity.

D. The future of God's people (57:13b–21). In contrast to the greedy and idolatrous ways of the wicked, the righteous and devout, who walk uprightly and commit their way to the Lord, will have a future. What a contrast between verses 1–2 and 13b! The perishing will have a glorious future, because they have made the Lord their refuge.

The Lord himself initiates the full redemption of his children. All obstacles will be removed for his coming. He is the exalted king, "the high and exalted One," who lives "in a high and holy place" (57:15). He reaches down to save, revive, and even dwell with the devout, "who [are] contrite and lowly in spirit" (57:15). The holy God will allow the humble to dwell with him on his "holy mountain."

If God were to be continually angry, the righteous would also lose heart. Therefore, he revives the spirit of his people by words of comfort. He assures the humble that they will receive all they need for this life and the life to come. In healing his people, the Lord gives them rest and consolation, guidance and protection, and joy. They will be at peace with God. The wicked are compared to a "tossing sea" (57:20). They will never have a lasting peace.

Thus, the prophet assures the godly that the Lord is intent on providing restoration for his people, though it may take a long time. While on earth, the righteous experience some rest and peace. However, these are but tokens of the grace of God. The fullness of rest and peace will come when the Lord has fully restored the heavens and the earth and when the wicked are no more.

E. True religion (58:1–14). The prophet again calls on the people to look on themselves in terms of their commitment. The people did indeed practice fasts and the Sabbath, which were derived from the law. However, just as syncretism and paganism are abominable to God, so is religious formalism. It is not enough for people to *conform* to the law of God if in one or more ways they continue to sin against it. The prophet emphasizes true religion and the rewards of true godliness.

The prophet shows what true religion is not (58:1–9a). True religion includes obedience to the law of God and a delight in the presence of God; but when sought for a reward, it degenerates into formalism or pharisaism. The love of God must show itself in love of one's neighbor. Godliness is shown not by appearing outwardly pious but by being sensitive to the suffering of people.

The Lord regards those who fast in humility. To fast in humility is to have regard for God and for others. This regard for others is expressed by giving people a sense of importance and freedom, by giving people food, and by speaking and acting in a way that brings honor to the people of God. Fasting as an act of humility and contrition can be acceptable to God only if it is an expression of love for God and neighbor.

True godliness shows itself in concern for justice and a love of the Sabbath (58:9b–14). Justice is God's concern and therefore cannot be limited to the Jewish people under the law. God is concerned with oppression, slander, and unrighteous acts. The glorious presence of God will dawn on the righteous. The godly are likened to a well-irrigated garden (58:11). They are God's appointed instruments of restoration. Such is the ministry of healing and reconciliation God has given to his people—then as well as now.

This understanding of God's desire for justice informed what keeping the Sabbath should entail. The Sabbath was a day in which the people were to give themselves to the worship of the Lord. While doing so, they were also to think about ways of enriching themselves. The prophet calls the people to look on the Sabbath as a day that the Lord has given to them on which to rest. To rest from one's labors is, first, not to think about personal gain, and second, to do what is right. To call the day a delight is to think about ways in which other people, too, may delight in the day. The Sabbath day is most appropriate as a day on which to do works of mercy in order to give an experience of light and joy to the oppressed and distressed.

F. Responsibility (59:1–21). The postexilic experience was marked by disillusionment; God's promises pertaining to the new era were not completely fulfilled. The early church also had to adjust to delay (see 2 Pet. 3:3–10). Isaiah explains that the delay is not because God cannot deliver. Instead of charging God with injustice or unfairness, the community of believers must look at its own sins and shortcomings (59:1–8). It is guilty of murder, untruth, and injustice, and is buried in all kinds of evil. Israel looks like the nations instead of God's people. The people are like mothers of evil who hatch vipers and cover sin with a veneer as thin as cobwebs.

The community lament contains a moving confession of sin and an expression of Israel's longing for the day of redemption (59:9–15a). It will be a day of "light" and rejoicing; darkness and mourning will be dispelled. In the confession, the community expresses sorrow for its shortcomings. The people have sinned against their neighbors. They have scorned justice, fidelity, and integrity and crushed the honest man. The dawning of God's kingdom is related to, but not dependent on, God's people ordering their lives in harmony with his purposes.

Because of the absolute moral bankruptcy of the people, no one is able to deliver them. Only the Lord, whose arm is strong to deliver, can deal with his people (59:15b–21). Isaiah describes the Lord as a warrior readying himself to aid the godly. He puts on the breastplate, representative of "righteousness," the helmet, representative of "salvation," and the garments,

signifying his "vengeance" and "zeal" (59:17; cf. Eph. 6:14–17). God is concerned about the remnant, and he expresses his concern by coming to judge the wicked, who will be punished according to their deeds. The Lord may delay his judgment, but he sees everything, including the affliction of his people and the evil done to those who call on his name.

The Redeemer God will reveal his glory to the ends of the earth, singling out Zion for his kingdom. The covenant will be renewed by the pouring of his Spirit on them and their children forever, so that all God's people will be inspired to know, do, and speak according to his word. Paul cites these words in his argument that God will redeem apostate Israel, which has rejected the Messiah (Rom. 11:27).

G. The glory of Zion (60:1–62:12). 60:1–22. The delay in the revelation of God's victorious kingdom concerns God's people, but God still expects them to live in accordance with his rule by practicing justice, righteousness, love, and peace. The word of the Lord (59:21) will be fulfilled.

The revelation of God extends his glory and light—characteristics of the Lord himself—to his people (60:1–9). Glory and light will surround them, enabling the nations to see God through restored Israel. The repetition of the words "light," "brightness," "shining," and "glory" creates a poetic effect.

The light in combination with "thick darkness" sets the background of a theophany. The response of the nations will be twofold. First, they will desire inclusion in the new era that will dawn on Zion (60:3). Second, they will cooperate by contributing to the welfare of Zion (60:4–9). The resources of the nations will be used to "honor . . . the LORD . . . the Holy One of Israel." Riches, herds, flocks, and ships of Tarshish will all be submitted to God.

The tribute and labor of the nations will be used to rebuild Zion as an expression of God's compassion and justice (60:10–14). The enemies and oppressors of Zion will receive their just deserts. The walls and gates symbolizing God's kingdom are not for protection; the gates will always be open (60:11). The Lord will share the spoils of his victory with his people. Furthermore, he will reestablish his glorious presence in their midst. Zion will be called the "City of the Lord" and "Zion of the Holy One of Israel" (60:14; cf. Ps. 48:1–14).

The Redeemer God will restore the fortunes of Zion (60:15–18). They have been forsaken but will become "the everlasting pride" and "the joy of all generations" (60:15). They will know that he is their Redeemer. His governance will be not only just but glorious as well. He will prosper his people greatly with a kingdom of peace and righteousness, in which his victorious rule brings lasting salvation and joy.

The glory of the New Jerusalem is in the experience of God's presence (60:19–22; cf. Rev. 21:23; 22:5). The people will all be "righteous"; that is, they will enjoy the benefits of his kingdom: the new creation. The certainty of fulfillment is guaranteed by his signature: "I am the Lord." He will restore everything, especially the New Jerusalem.

61:1–62:12. Judah and Jerusalem have been assured that Yahweh has a plan for a remnant of the people. They will return from exile. The Lord has promised to restore heaven and earth, to restore the people to himself, and to hasten the day of redemption. The announcement of the year of the Lord's favor means that the Lord is reconciled to humanity and that humanity may obtain forgiveness from God. In chapter 61 the Lord himself, together with the prophet, confirms the eternal covenant, which cannot be broken.

The person of whom the prophet speaks in 61:1–7 is a servant of God. (Technically this is not a Servant Song.) The presence of the Spirit of God (61:1) and the anointing and proclamation suggest the servant's purpose. The servant of the Lord, who has been called to proclaim the good news, can be none other than the prophet himself. He has been called to proclaim the acceptable year of the Lord to those in exile, but in a fuller sense the proclamation of

the servant applies to the ministry of our Lord (Luke 4:18–19).

The messages of comfort begin with a call to loudly proclaim the good news of the Lord's forgiveness and restoration of his people. The prophetic proclamation consists particularly of the preaching of "the year of the Lord's favor" (61:2). In the restoration from exile, the prophets were instrumental in bringing the good news to the captives. Jesus further proclaimed the good news and focused on himself as the one bringing in the era of restoration. He also promised that he would accomplish all when he returns. The year of restoration is not limited to one particular day or year, but extends from the postexilic restoration to the full restoration of heaven and earth.

The proclamation of the acceptable year of the Lord is directly connected to the proclamation of the day of vengeance. The one focuses on God's kindness to his people, whereas the other focuses on God's judgment on the wicked.

"The year of the Lord's favor" is also a prophetic reference to God's administration of grace, which culminates in the restoration of all things. This restoration includes the promises of forgiveness and full fellowship with God and the removal of physical problems, obstacles, and mourning. It is the year of Jubilee, the year of liberation (Lev. 25:10). Jesus applied this word to his healing of the blind, deaf, and lame as a token that God is concerned about our whole being, including our physical welfare.

Finally, the acceptable year of the Lord proclaims comfort to all the people of God. The prophet calls the new people of God "oaks of righteousness" and the "planting of the Lord" (61:3). Instead of being rejected, the people of God will be accepted and prepared for a great and glorious future.

This redemption, however, is not to be limited to the eschatological future. The prophet quickly moves from the restoration of the people to the restoration of the land. God is also concerned with the ruins and assures his people that the cities will be rebuilt and that this will be funded by the wealth of the nations. The new position of the people of God is expressed by the word "priests" (61:6). They will be priests of the living God, while others take care of menial tasks.

Spiritual benefits are mixed with God's concern for physical well-being. The people have been disgraced in exile, but they are assured that they will have a double portion in the land. The Lord knows that his people have suffered double for all of their sins (Isa. 40:2), and he gives back what they have missed during the exile. The purpose of the acceptable year of the Lord is to prepare the Lord's people for the fullness of redemption. While they are on earth they receive the first fruits of redemption. The Jews after the exile experienced restoration of the cities, help from the nations, and productivity of the land. They were comforted by God's grace physically as well as spiritually. Since the coming of our Lord Jesus Christ the people of God are now made up of Gentiles as well as Jews. Our heavenly Father has assured us that he is concerned about our physical well-being. Moreover we are the recipients of the grace, comfort, and forgiveness of God. Yet this message speaks of a greater era in which our heavenly Father will restore heaven and earth through the ministry of Jesus Christ.

Isaiah 61:3 describes God's people adorned with "oil of joy" and a "garment of praise." In this painted wood stele from Egypt, the Lady Taperet (right) is depicted similarly, dressed elegantly with a perfume cone in her hair (tenth or ninth century BC).

The new era is forever, because the covenant is forever (61:8–9). God knows how his people can be unpredictable and faithless; therefore, the outworking of the covenant is not dependent on them. He is faithful. His covenant will accomplish the purpose for which he has made it: that his people may be blessed.

The prophet likens the glory prepared for God's people to the adornments of a bride, bridegroom, and priest (61:10–11). She will serve the Lord in the presence of the nations as a priest, adorned with "a crown of beauty" (61:3), anointed with the "oil of gladness" (61:3), and clothed in "a garment of praise" (61:3). The new era of the priesthood of all believers will introduce a renewal of God's kingdom.

The prophet prays that the era of God's victorious kingship, bringing full "salvation" to his people, may come soon (62:1–5). Then the nations will recognize the glory of Zion, which was trampled down by the enemies of God. The new names given are descriptive of the new era: "Hephzibah" ("my delight is in her") instead of "Deserted," and "Beulah" ("married") instead of "Desolate" (62:3–4). The Lord will rejoice over his people.

Out of concern for his people, the Lord has appointed watchmen (62:6–12). The watchmen are not needed for the protection of the city, for

Yahweh makes his people secure. The watchmen pray day and night for the full restoration of the people of God. The Lord responds to the prayer by an oath of assurance that he will never again do what he has done to his people. Redemption is certain to come, and the prophet calls the people to prepare themselves for the Savior's coming.

The people receive a new name. God sets them apart as a holy people and the redeemed of the Lord: "The Holy People," "The Redeemed of the LORD," "Sought After," "The City No Longer Deserted" (62:12; see also 60:14, 18; 62:4). These names for the new people of God signify the new relationship, the glory, and the purpose of the people of God.

H. The day of vengeance (63:1–6). Since the Lord is righteous and speaks righteously, the day of vengeance is the day of redemption of God's people (63:4). In his verdict as the great judge, he assures the people that he truly is able to save them. Because of his righteousness, his concern for his people, and his great anger, the Lord comes to this world as the great warrior (63:1). The portrayal of the judgment of Edom is a picture of God's judgment on the whole earth.

The day of the vindication of the Lord is an expression of the day of the Lord, an eschatological event in which God brings his cataclysmic judgment upon all the earth.

I. A prayer for God's people (63:7–64:12). Isaiah publicly proclaims the acts of the Lord's love (Hebrew *hesed*) for his people, whom he adopted as his sons and daughters (63:7–14). He redeemed them in the expectation that they would be loyal to him. However, they were unfaithful and opposed his will ("grieved his Holy Spirit," 63:10).

The past era of grace and compassion is over. The godly look back over the history of redemption with a renewed longing to be included. In the past God raised up Moses, and no one could oppose his will. God showed the power of "his glorious arm" (63:12). He brought the people through the Red Sea and safely into the promised land by his divine will. The past reveals that nothing stands in the way of God's will and presence.

The prophet leads God's people in a prayer for redemption (63:15–64:12). He grounds the petition on God's promise to establish his sanctuary as a footstool among his people (63:15, 18), on the father-son relationship (63:16), and on the covenantal relationship with the tribes (63:17–19). Now it seems that they have never been called by his covenant name.

The prayer also focuses on the revelation of God. As the people pray that the Lord might descend to shake the mountains and show himself in his glorious fire, they call on him to come to their aid by taking vengeance on their enemies and by redeeming his faithful people. The people confess that they are not ready for him because they are sinners, unclean, hopeless, and objects of wrath. But they pray that the Lord may forgive and forget their sins. They call on the Lord as their Father and wait for his compassion. They confess his authority and their helplessness and need of forgiveness, restoration, and fellowship. They remind him that the land, the cities, Jerusalem, and the temple are in ruins.

J. God's response (65:1–25). The Lord is ready to respond in a most self-giving way (65:1–7). But the people are still too engrossed in sin. They show themselves to be idolaters and have little concern for spiritual purity, as they keep vigils among the graves and eat pork—against God's explicit commandment. They are like Gentiles. They respond with a self-made holiness. The Lord in turn will respond in judgment. Even as the Lord has promised not to be silent until he has accomplished the redemption of his people, so he will not be silent until the enemies of his kingdom have been put down.

God assures his own that he knows them and will separate the ungodly from the godly (65:8–16). On one hand, God promises his grace to the remnant. On the other, he makes it clear that his judgment will rest on the ungodly until they are no more.

The prophet likens the covenant community to a cluster of grapes. Not all the grapes in a cluster are good; some are spoiled and others are unripe. However, some may still produce wine and obtain a "blessing" on the cluster. For the sake of the whole, God will be patient with the community; his judgment will be selective. Yahweh will reward those who seek him, whereas he will judge the wicked.

The ungodly have forgotten the Lord and have given themselves over to idolatrous practices. They are unresponsive and rebellious toward him. They will mourn their disgrace, whereas the righteous will rejoice in the Lord because of the many benefits he has extended to them. The Lord assures his own that they will be satisfied both with food and drink and with their new name, which represents their restored status. Instead of the troubles associated with the "old era," they will experience the fullness of the restoration God has promised to all his people: the new heavens, the new earth, and the New Jerusalem.

It is tempting to think of the state of restoration (65:17–25) as the eschatological, everlasting state of the new heavens and the new earth. Even though the prophet portrays the blessings of the people of God in a final way, he is addressing those in exile, assuring them that they will have a future. The Lord will again rejoice in his people. Because the Lord has blessed them, their former troubles are forgotten. The "former" era is the experience of judgment and exile. The Lord will create a "new era"—"new heavens" and a "new earth" (65:17). The new era is characterized by the joy of the people of God because Yahweh himself rejoices over his people. The sorrow of past sufferings will cease because of the comfort of the Lord. The new era is described in terms of physical health and longevity, the enjoyment of God's benefits in physical ways, answers to prayer, and peace and the absence of malice and corruption. Even their children will know the Lord and will be blessed by him.

Those who returned from exile experienced these blessings to some extent; however, many of them were only partially realized. Jesus reaffirmed that it is the Father's will to restore the heavens and the earth. He showed his concern for the physical and spiritual needs of people. Jesus has also pointed us to the great future that awaits all who have faith in him. He will bring in the new era in an even greater way. Then Christians will enjoy the fullness of God's benefits, spiritual as well as physical. Isaiah 65:17–25 is thus a continual reminder of the Christian's heritage in Jesus Christ.

K. Judgment and restoration (66:1–24). The last chapter of Isaiah provides a complementary answer to that of chapter 65. The Lord affirms the certainty of his judgment on idolatry and religious hypocrisy among his people and the blessings of the new age on faithful Jews and Gentiles. The extension of the new age to the Gentiles is a further development beyond chapter 65 and is in full harmony with the prophet's teaching on the universal nature of God's kingdom.

It was tempting for Old Testament believers to localize God's kingship. They knew that God ruled over the whole earth and that his throne was in heaven. They had also been taught that the earth, and especially the temple in Jerusalem, was his footstool. To approach the temple was to approach God. For that reason, it was important to approach the Lord with gifts befitting his sovereignty and royal splendor. But rather than being the place of true worship, the temple had become a place where people came to pacify their own consciences; they were trying to atone for their own misdeeds without exhibiting a spirit of true contrition. In their corruption, injustice, and hatred, they were presenting sacrifices offensive to the Lord.

The prophecy of Isaiah concludes with God's concern for true worship (66:1–6). God desires to have fellowship with those who show sensitivity to his word by acts of obedience, love, and justice. The love of God is evident in those who are humble and contrite in spirit. They may suffer in an unjust world, but he promises to vindicate them. On the other hand, he will avenge himself on those within the community of faith who worship in their own ways, not having a heartfelt love for God and for their brothers and sisters in the faith.

The judgment of God clearly comes against all those who have opposed his kingdom (66:7–9). The noise coming from the temple (66:5–6) is the sound of the Lord himself, who has come to defend his children by bringing retribution on the wicked.

The Lord invites all to rejoice with Mother Jerusalem. Those who love her in adversity and prosperity will be rewarded with joy, fullness of life, peace, and comfort (66:10–14). These benefits are further guaranteed to all who love the Lord Jesus Christ.

As God's people are encouraged that the Lord is going to be with his children, he also assures the enemies that his vengeance will come upon them (66:15–17). His coming is depicted in prophetic imagery: fire, chariots, whirlwinds, and swords. The effect of Yahweh's judgment is that the wicked will be slain. The prophet gives the scene of God's judgment on the wicked in order to assure the ungodly who have been members of the covenant community that they too will be under God's judgment. Those who have made their own rules of sanctification and defilement will be consumed together with the wicked.

In quick strokes the prophet describes how many nations will be instrumental in bringing together the people of God (66:18–23). They will be instrumental in restoring the Jews to full participation in the kingdom of God. But in the very process, they too will see the glory of the Lord. The Lord himself will set a sign among the nations by sending messengers who will proclaim the glorious acts of God. The restoration of the Jews to the land, God's continued care for the Jewish people, and God's acts of redemption (including the finished work of our Lord Jesus Christ and the work of missionaries and evangelists) will result in many nations (including the Jews) bringing sacrifices to the Lord and serving as priests and Levites in God's presence. They will gather together from festival to festival and enjoy covenant fellowship from generation to generation.

The prophet introduced the coming judgment and its effects in verses 15 and 16. He returns to this motif in the last verse of the prophecy (66:24), a perpetual reminder that God's judgment on the wicked is everlasting and that those who have been condemned to separation from him in life will suffer eternal separation in death.

Select Bibliography

Childs, Brevard S. *Isaiah*. Old Testament Library. Louisville: Westminster John Knox, 2001.

Grogan, G. "Isaiah." In *The Expositor's Bible Commentary*. Edited by Frank E. Gaebelein. Vol. 6. Grand Rapids: Zondervan, 1986.

Motyer, J. Alec. *The Prophecy of Isaiah*. Downers Grove, IL: InterVarsity, 1993.

Oswalt, John N. *Isaiah*. NIV Application Commentary. Grand Rapids: Zondervan, 2003.

———. *Isaiah 1–39*. New International Commentary on the Old Testament. Grand Rapids: Eerdmans, 1986.

———. *Isaiah 40–66*. New International Commentary on the Old Testament. Grand Rapids: Eerdmans, 1998.

Ridderbos, Jan. *Isaiah*. Bible Student's Commentary. Grand Rapids: Zondervan, 1985.

Webb, Barry G. *The Message of Isaiah: On Eagles' Wings*. The Bible Speaks Today. Downers Grove, IL: InterVarsity, 1996.

Young, Edward J. *The Book of Isaiah*. 3 vols. Grand Rapids: Eerdmans, 1965–72.

Jeremiah

ELMER A. MARTENS

Introduction

The book of Jeremiah is one of unusual intensity. The destiny of God's people is at stake. A prophet, against great odds, alerts his people to a monumental crisis. He argues persuasively, sometimes feverishly, for a specific course of action to avert the impending doom. His counsel, though given in the name of God, is rejected, and the catastrophe about which he has warned happens. Life is miserable. People are killed or deported. The people's king is tortured. Property is destroyed. The temple is burned. Their land is lost. A 250-year national history has come to an end.

Historical Context

What brought on the political crisis in the land of Judah at the turn of the sixth century was a moral and religious depravity traceable to the long reign of Manasseh, Judah's most evil king (686–643 BC). Manasseh reintroduced Baal worship and set up altars to foreign gods in the Jerusalem temple area, not to mention other practices of the most bizarre kind (2 Kings 21:6). For offenses not nearly as gross, Israel, Judah's northern neighbor, had been invaded by the Assyrians in 722 BC. Its capital, Samaria, had been captured. Judah, the prophet Jeremiah warned, would face a greater tragedy.

Yet "crisis" could hardly describe Judah during Josiah's reign (641–609 BC). Manasseh before him had been a vassal of the Assyrians. But with Assyrian power waning, Josiah enlarged Judah's territories. Times were prosperous. It even seemed that Josiah would turn the nation to God. When the scroll, possibly Deuteronomy, was discovered in the temple in 622, he took strong measures to reform Judah's religious life (2 Kings 22–23). But the reforms turned out to be temporary. A number of prophetic oracles in the first six chapters of Jeremiah date from Josiah's reign. They claim that the situation, for all its apparent calm, is serious.

To aggravate matters, Jehoiakim (609–597 BC), Josiah's son, reversed the direction set by Josiah. He, in fact, returned to pagan idols and even practiced child sacrifice. Despite wealth being drained to Egypt, to whom Judah had become a vassal, Jehoiakim built himself a showy palace. He failed to compensate the laborers, nor did he care for society's poor. He callously disregarded the God of Israel, whose message was read to him from a scroll prepared by Jeremiah. He sliced the written columns as they were read and tossed them into the fire (Jeremiah 36).

Such brazen disregard for God propelled the people into a national crisis both religious and political. Josiah, the highly respected king, had been killed in 609 BC at Megiddo in an attempt to halt the Egyptians, who were moving northward to the aid of an ailing Assyria. A fast-moving Babylonian, Nabopolassar, had captured Nineveh, Assyria's capital, in 612 BC.

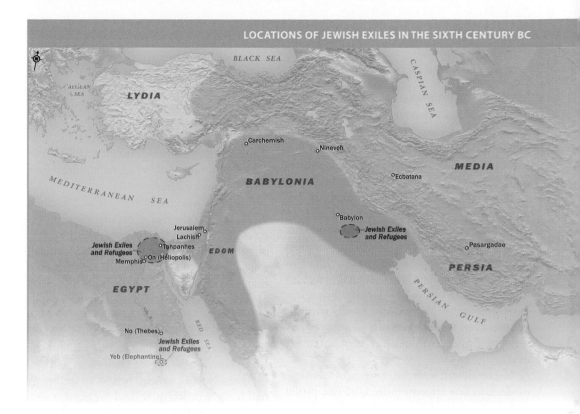

LOCATIONS OF JEWISH EXILES IN THE SIXTH CENTURY BC

With a decisive victory over Egypt at the Battle of Carchemish in 605 BC, Nebuchadnezzar, who succeeded Nabopolassar to the throne, was about to swallow the little countries of Syria-Palestine, including Judah.

He swept down the Mediterranean coast soon after 605 BC, and in response to Jehoiakim's maneuvers, attacked Jerusalem. He took the elite of that city, including Jehoiachin, the recently inaugurated king who followed Jehoiakim, captive to Babylon. In its last two decades Judah had five different kings. With the Babylonian attack in 597 BC, disaster had come to Judah, as God's prophet had warned.

Nebuchadnezzar appointed Zedekiah to be his vassal king in Jerusalem. God's messenger Jeremiah threatened further disaster if king and people would not turn from their evil, their lying, their violence, their injustice, and their flirting with strange gods. Zedekiah was a vacillating king, controlled and confused by rival political parties, the strongest of which urged

alliance with Egypt. At one point Zedekiah made a courageous social and religious move. He followed the Mosaic law and released the slaves—but days later he went back on his word (Jeremiah 34). Widespread corruption reached crisis proportions. God's agents the Babylonians were on hand. When Zedekiah rebelled against his overlord in 589 BC, Nebuchadnezzar laid siege and after eighteen months broke into the city. He destroyed it, including the palace and the four-hundred-year-old temple.

More persons were taken captive to Babylon. Gedaliah was appointed governor. One of his own countrymen, an Israelite, assassinated him. Fearing revenge from the Babylonians, some Jews left to settle in Egypt. Even after all this, little had been learned, so it seemed, because there too people preferred a pagan deity, the Queen of Heaven, to the worship of the God of Israel.

The story line of the book of Jeremiah stretches from 627 BC, the year of Jeremiah's call to be a prophet, to 562 BC, the last chronological marker mentioned in the book's appendix. For Judah those years were the most convulsive in its history.

Jeremiah the Prophet

One of God's spokespersons during these troubled decades was Jeremiah. His contemporaries included Zephaniah, Habakkuk, Nahum, and Ezekiel. Born, it is believed, into a priestly family in 640 BC, Jeremiah was commissioned by God in 627 BC. As a youth, Jeremiah witnessed Josiah's reform and was almost certainly supportive of it, though explicit endorsements are not found in the book. Jeremiah gave most of his oracles during the reigns of Jehoiakim and Zedekiah. When Jerusalem fell, Jeremiah was singled out by the Babylonians for preferential treatment. Yet he chose to stay with his people, even when, against his counsel, they went to Egypt. Nothing is known about his death.

Jeremiah's message, largely one of warning, made him few friends; indeed, he was pitted against kings, prophets, priests, and society at large. Throughout the book, he reprimands Jehoiakim for his extravagance. He prophesies woe for Jehoiachin and urges Zedekiah to submit to the Babylonians rather than to resist them. Jeremiah charges his peers, the prophets, with complicity. He brands them liars. He rails at them for talking about peace when God is about to inflict disaster. He writes to the exiles, naming the prophets of whom they should beware. As for the priests, they, like the prophets, dislike him. So do the ruling officials. Jeremiah languishes in a mud dungeon because of their schemes and comes close to death. A sermon at the temple brings him a near-lynching by the incensed crowd. At times he is forced, along with Baruch his scribe, into hiding.

God asks him to engage in symbolic actions. Jeremiah buys a new garment, then promptly buries it in the sand. He buys a jar and, in an object lesson to the city elders, smashes it before their eyes. He wears an ox yoke as he lays out God's word to dignitaries from neighboring nations; he was a prophet not just to Israel but to the nations.

Jeremiah was an intense man. His emotions for his people ran deep. He agonizes over the messages God asks him to give. He is disgusted by the evil around him and devastated because of the lack of response. Even the joy of being God's servant vanishes on occasion. He is so depressed that he curses the day of his birth. No other prophet allows us such a deep look into his interior life.

Jeremiah was courageous, for he presented God's word at the risk of his life. He was persevering. For more than twenty years, he called on people to repent but without result. Jeremiah was gentle, tender, and sensitive. He felt pain that God would have to mete out punishment. He uncompromisingly delivered God's unpopular but necessary warnings. The word of God was to him like a fire and like a hammer. More than 150 times one reads, "This is what the LORD says," or similar expressions.

In the New Testament period, some identified Jesus with Jeremiah, and for good reason (Matt. 16:14). Both were opposed to the religious establishment. Each preached repentance. Each warned about the fall of Jerusalem. Both had a small band of supporters. Both endured the rejection of the masses. Jesus's passion story has its counterpart in the Passion Narrative of Jeremiah (chaps. 26–44). According to one count, there are forty quotations from and allusions to Jeremiah in the New Testament. Many are found in the book of Revelation; the most striking is Hebrews 8, which quotes the new covenant passage in full (Jer. 31:31–34).

Theological Themes

In simple terms, one could say that Jeremiah's message for his society centers on the interplay between God, people, and land.

Between God and people there was a covenant. It consisted of a commitment for God to be God of his people and a demand for the people to be God's kind of people. Covenant was an intimate arrangement that called for loyalty from the covenant partners. The covenant had been established at God's initiative when he called Abraham and later when he delivered his people from bondage into freedom. In the opening oracles, this covenant is depicted using marriage as the primary metaphor (chaps. 2–3).

But Israel's sporadic disloyalty became chronic, and therein lay the crisis. The relationship between God and Israel was strained to the breaking point. In fact, God declares that the covenant is broken. Through repeated exhortation, encouragement, and warnings, however, God intends to salvage the covenant.

The presupposition for God's message to Judah about the covenant is also the backdrop for God's message to nations: God the Lord is the sovereign Lord. The title "Lord of Hosts" (NIV "LORD Almighty"), though common in the Old Testament, is concentrated in Jeremiah, where it appears eighty-two times. That title, with its military overtones, emphasizes God as supremely in command. As sovereign dispatcher, God was the one who sent Nebuchadnezzar, his "servant," against Jerusalem. Because God is God, idolatry is both intolerable and foolish. As supreme Creator, God is able to make his purposes stand, whether for Israel or for the nations. With him nothing is impossible (32:17).

God delights in righteousness. Of prime value, therefore, is not human wisdom, strength, or riches but a knowledge of God, who "exercises kindness, justice and righteousness on earth," for, he says, "in these I delight" (9:24). His wrath is against all unrighteousness; and Judah was grossly unrighteous. For this reason, perhaps, God's wrath is a secondary theme in the book.

The shape of evil, as Jeremiah exposes it, on the part of nations, is a disregard of the sovereign God, and on the part of Israel, a rejection of the covenant God. Jeremiah addresses a stinging rebuttal to all who substitute images for the sovereign God (10:1–16), or to nations who worship deities other than God, such as Chemosh, Molek, or Marduk. Arrogance and ego obsession also come under the judgment of God.

In Judah an assortment of evils jeopardized the covenant relationship. Preponderant among them was injustice. The poor, the disadvantaged, and the marginal people were neglected and even exploited. Violence and sexual license had become common. Lying and deceit were widespread national ailments that affected even religious persons. Prophets, for example, sanctioned the evil plans of others with their benedictions (23:14–18). Religiously the people were stiffnecked. They refused to listen to God's word, and refused, too, to take correction.

Israel had set God aside; people were secure in the land—or so they thought. They were wrong! Covenant breaking, the severing of ties between people and God, has consequences—among them the dislocation of people from their land. Repeatedly Jeremiah warns that a northern foe will invade Judah. Havoc will come to Jerusalem. Worst of all, for those who escape death, Jeremiah says, there will be the loss of land and an ordered life. People will be taken into exile. God's judgment on the sin of covenant disloyalty in his people did indeed affect their land. Drought came and eventually they lost their land.

God judges all sin—also that of nations. They too, according to Jeremiah, will suffer loss of life and property. Empires will shatter and nations will go into exile. Removing people from their land and returning them to their land are both acts of God. The land of Israel, while a geographical territory, eventually becomes a symbol of the good life, the life with God. Land was something like litmus paper in chemistry: it was an indicator of where one stood spiritually and theologically. Loss of land is not the last word, however. The salvation word is about land too. Israel will also return to its land. More than that, she will recover what was lost, and good times will come again (chaps. 30–31). Central to these good times will be a spiritual return to God. In fact, God will make a new covenant—certainly the high point in Jeremiah's message—in which people will be given a new heart and will know God immediately and intimately (31:31–34).

God will save his people. The announcement of good news is sealed, as was the announcement of bad news, by a symbolic action. Jeremiah buys property to show that after the exile normal routines will be resumed.

Jeremiah's message raises questions appropriate in every age. What is the nature of the relationship between God and his people? What is the shape of evil in church or society? Where and by whom is God's message freely proclaimed? When is the message of repentance appropriate? What is the word from God to modern nations on the brink of global disaster? To what extent and in what way is a believer to be involved in society, especially in its political life? To what degree is the good life "guaranteed"?

Literary Features

The book has several distinctive features. It is the longest, by word count, in the Bible. Several short sections are duplicated in scattered places. The book has an appendix, taken largely from 2 Kings 24–25. The book as a "prophetic" book supplies an amazing amount of historical information. Similarly, there is more of a biography of the prophet, including Jeremiah's emotional pilgrimage, than in any other prophetic book. Among personal interest stories are Jeremiah's symbolic actions.

This Hebrew bulla (possibly a forgery) was made with a stamp inscribed, "(belonging) to Brekhyahu son of Neriyahu the scribe," which is the same name as Jeremiah's scribe, "Baruch [Brekhyahu] son of Neriah [Neriyahu]" (Jer. 36:4).

The first twenty chapters plus the first two in the "Book of Comfort" are mostly poetry. The poetry is vigorous and expressive, filled with metaphor. Metaphors such as that of the marriage between God and Israel are drawn from Hosea. The prose sections are much like Deuteronomy in style—a fact that has spawned numerous theories about the relationship between Deuteronomy and Jeremiah. Often-occurring expressions include "they/you did not listen"; "stiff-necked"; "the LORD Almighty"; and "I will be their God, and they will be my people." Much of the book is punctuated with exclamation marks.

Structure and Authorship

The book appears scrambled because it is not chronologically or even topically arranged. In addition, the Greek text (Septuagint) is one-eighth shorter and places chapters 46–51 in the middle of the book (after 25:13). There have been many theories on how the book came to be composed. One possibility is that the scroll Jehoiakim burned was dictated a second time. Since it contained warnings, it is likely, though not stated, that part or all of chapters 1–20 were part of that scroll (see 36:32). Since Baruch was Jeremiah's scribe, and since the narratives about Jeremiah appear in the third person, it has been suggested that chapters 26–45, excluding the Book of Comfort (30–33), are his work. In summary, Jeremiah himself as "author" would be responsible for chapters 1–20 (25), 30–33, and 46–51. Baruch may have been the author-compiler of chapters 26–29 and 34–45. An editor may have added the appendix (chap. 52).

More helpful than trying to determine authorship is attention to the book as it now lies before us. Several different blocks of material can be distinguished. The warnings and threats to Judah, sermonlike, dominate chapters 1–20. Stories from Jeremiah's experience are found in chapters 21–29 and 34–45 to illustrate the wicked society. The Book of Comfort (30–33) has a tone totally different from the rest of the book. The oracles against the nations (46–51) put the reader on the world stage. The book tells about the experiences of a prophet; it surveys nations. Most of all it acquaints us with God, and that with a passion.

Outline

Commentary

1. Jeremiah's Credentials (1:1–19)

The stage is set for the book of Jeremiah by introducing person, place, event, and historical time (1:1–3). The person is Jeremiah, whose name probably means "the Lord is exalted." He is from a priestly line. It is unclear whether Jeremiah came from the family of Abiathar, a priest exiled by David to Anathoth (1 Kings 2:26–27). The place is Anathoth, the modern Anata, two to three miles northeast of Jerusalem. The event is the coming of the word of God, which means that the subsequent book has a divine quality to it.

The time frame extends from Josiah through Jehoiakim to Zedekiah, Judah's last king. This list omits two three-month reigns: Johoahaz (609) and Jehoiachin (598–597). Jeremiah's life coincides with the final years of Judah and its collapse. The prophet lives through Josiah's reform, Nebuchadnezzar's siege of Jerusalem in 597, the reign of the vacillating Zedekiah, and the capture and burning of Jerusalem in 587, as well as the horror of Gedaliah's assassination.

The introduction, while appropriate for the entire book, is, to be formal, limited to chapters

1–39, since Jeremiah's ministry did not conclude with Zedekiah (1:3; cf. chaps. 40–44). Almost certainly, therefore, the book grew in stages.

The date for the prophet's call (1:4–10) is 627 BC, the thirteenth year of Josiah's rule, when Jeremiah is in his middle or late teens. The dialogue points to an intimacy between the Lord and Jeremiah.

God's "forming" activity recalls Genesis 2:7. "To sanctify" is to set apart, usually for some service. The word order emphasizes the unexpected: "A prophet to the nations I have appointed you" (author's translation). The word for "prophet," said to mean "speaker" or even "gushing at the mouth," is more appropriately defined, according to the Hebrew root, as "one who is called." Prophetic work was exemplified by Moses (Deut. 18:18) and is depicted in Exodus 7:1.

Jeremiah registers an excuse (1:6). The word translated "youth" (NASB) or "child" (KJV) suggests inexperience and inadequacy as well as age. God identifies the given reason (inability to speak) as well as the unspoken but deeper reason (fear). The fear is met with the so-called divine-assistance formula, "I am with you" (1:8, 19; cf. Gen. 28:15; Matt. 28:20).

The installation ceremony has a personal touch. Jeremiah's primary vocation is speaking, though he will engage in sign acts (chaps. 13, 19, 32). The gift of words recalls Moses (Deut. 18:18).

Jeremiah's ministry is to extend beyond Judah/Israel to other nations. He is called to demolish false securities (Jer. 7:1–15) and to root out the cancer of idolatry and social corruption. Deconstruction precedes construction. Much of Jeremiah's message is about threat and punishment; good news, as in the Book of Comfort (30–33), is less characteristic. Excerpts of his six-part job assignment, to uproot and tear down, to destroy and overthrow, to build and to plant, are noted in 18:7–9; 24:6; 31:28; 42:10; and 45:4.

Two objects—a flowering branch and a boiling pot—are used to further clarify the call (1:11–16). There is a wordplay between "almond" (Hebrew *shaqed*) and "watch" (Hebrew *shaqad*). Almond trees are among the first to flower in spring and so become "watching trees." The word over which God is watching is the promise to Jeremiah.

The boiling pot, likely tilting northward, represents an unnamed northern army (later to be identified as Babylon; cf. chap. 39). The reason for disaster, variously nuanced throughout, is basically that the people have forsaken God. This summary accusation and the announcement of disaster foreshadow two themes that will dominate chapters 2–10.

Jeremiah's commission is restated in 1:17–19. "Gird up your loins" (NASB) points to promptness in obeying an order (1 Kings 18:46) and means "Get going!" Jeremiah, like Jesus, will face strenuous opposition from religious officialdom. He will be opposed by kings, by princes, by priests, and by the people. But God will make him as strong as a fortified city. To call Jeremiah a weeping prophet is not incorrect, but the projected portrait is of a man of steel. His unbending personal courage is most impressive.

2. Sermons Warning of Disaster (2:1–10:25)

A. A marriage about to break up (2:1–3:5). The prophet's opening sermon, dated prior to Josiah's reform in 621, is direct, even abrupt. The first scene (2:1–3) shows God with his people, who are like a new bride on a honeymoon. But almost at once there is trouble. The last scene (3:1–5) puts divorce talk squarely at the center. It is a case of a ruined marriage.

God does not want a divorce. Through these verses rings the pathos of a hurt marriage partner. The strong feelings that accompany the marriage breakup are caught in the questions God poses, the quotations from the people, and the picturesque language about wells, donkeys, camels, lions, yokes, vines, brides, and prostitutes.

Here is sweet talk about a honeymoon, nostalgic talk about good times, angry talk about people turning to Baal, and exasperated talk about guilty people who claim innocence.

Evidence of the partner's neglect, her arrogance, self-sufficiency, idolatry, injustice, and physical/spiritual adultery is cited. There is no outright call to repent—yet. Pleas for a people to reconsider are frequent.

The initial honeymoon (2:1–3) has been called the "seed oracle" for chapters 2–3, where the themes are expanded. The "house of Jacob" technically refers to all descendants of Jacob, which includes the ten tribes exiled by the Assyrians in 722 BC as well as the people in the southern territories of Judah and Benjamin, who have, at the time of speaking (627–622), been spared an invasion.

The partners share courtship memories of good days: the exodus and Sinai. To that covenant, the people, like a bride wanting to please, responded, "We will do everything the LORD has said; we will obey" (Exod. 24:7). "Devotion" (Hebrew *hesed*, 2:2) is a strong word indicating covenant love. As the first fruit is choice fruit, so Israel was special to God. As a protective bridegroom, God would not allow the slightest injury to be inflicted on his bride. God and Israel were intimate and close.

Then there was trouble (2:4–8). Neither the leaders nor the people asked the Lord for orientation. Ironically, the priests, whose major duty was to teach the law—a law that called for the worship of the Lord—did not bother about the Lord. The prophets, who were to rebuke transgressions, instead now themselves prophesied by Baal. Each group of leaders mishandled its responsibility.

Baal was the god of the Canaanites, a god of weather and fertility. Among the archaeological discoveries in the 1930s at Ugarit on the Mediterranean are stories that depict him as young, lusty, and aggressive. But God's favors, not Baal's, made crops productive.

God as partner spelled benefits. To walk after Baal was of no profit. "Worthless" is Jeremiah's customary word for idols (8:19; 10:8, 15; 16:19). Disregard for God, departure from God, and courtships with another god spelled deep trouble for the covenant.

In 2:9–13, a court lawsuit gets under way. It is the Lord Yahweh versus Israel. God the prosecutor claims that Israel's behavior is unprecedented. Were one to go west to the island of Cyprus in the Mediterranean or east to the Kedar tribes in Arabia, one could not find an example of a pagan people switching allegiance to another god. Israel's action is irrational. She has exchanged God, with his deliverance at the exodus, his law at Sinai, his care of the people in the wilderness, and his blessing of Canaan for a god of no worth. It is a bad bargain. The move is shocking. The heavens are court witnesses.

Israel is like a man who decides to dig for water despite the artesian well on his property. Beyond the hard work of digging the cistern and lining it with plaster, he faces the problem of leaky cisterns, not to mention stale water. The unsatisfactory "cisterns" (Egypt and Assyria) are described in 2:14–19. Living (fresh) water is at hand (Isa. 55.1, John 4.1–26). Enough has been said to dispose the court in favor of God and against Israel.

In five questions, God both accuses his marriage partner and brings her to reconsider her ways (2:14–19). The first question (2:14a), about status, implies a negative answer: No, Israel's destiny was not to be some servant or slave. Second, God raises a question about Israel's ravaged condition (2:14b). Since the lion was the insignia for Assyria, that country may be in view. Noph, which is ancient Memphis,

Jeremiah 2:8 criticizes "following worthless idols," such as this figurine of the god Baal (Megiddo, Late Bronze Age).

was the capital of the pyramid-building Pharaohs. Tahpanhes was a Nile Delta fortress city. Egypt had "cracked [Israel's] skull." The expression certainly refers to a defeat or humiliation brought on by Egypt, possibly a raid into Israel's choice lands. The third question is about assigning blame (2:17). The fourth and fifth questions concern direction (2:18). Will Israel go for help to Egypt, which has already mistreated her? Or to Assyria, which has invaded the ten northern tribes and occupies the area just north of Jerusalem?

The summary accusation is that Israel has forsaken her covenant partner (2:19) and that there is no reverence or appropriate fear of God. The title "Lord of Hosts" (NIV "LORD Almighty") speaks of power and rulership.

God's pleas fail. Hard evidence must now be marshaled (2:20–28). While some Hebrew manuscripts read, "I broke your yoke," it is preferable, given the line of argument, to follow those ancient manuscripts that read, "For of old you broke your yoke" (2:20). The yoke continues the figure of a partnership, a binding relationship. The Canaanite god Baal was worshiped on hilltops and in the shelter of large, spreading trees—a practice noted in Hosea 4:13 and forbidden in Deuteronomy 12:2.

Figures of speech follow in profusion. The vine, Israel, is of a good variety. The soda and soap (mineral and vegetable alkalis) metaphor stresses the deeply ingrained nature of Israel's evil. The young camel, wobbly on its feet, illustrates how directionless Israel is as she crisscrosses her ways. The donkey at mating time illustrates the passion with which Israel pursues the Baals even in the valley, which, if the Hinnom Valley, would be the place for child sacrifice.

In sarcasm, God warns Israel in all this pursuing of other gods not to stub her toe (to use a modern idiom) or to overexert and so become thirsty. Israel, self-consciously determined to do evil, responds in fiery language. The wood posts and stone pillars mentioned in 2:27 were both worship objects in the Baal cult.

Courtroom language continues (2:29–37). God complains of breach of covenant, as exemplified by the way Israel handles correction, treats the prophets, and announces her independence: "I am free" (cf. 2:31). Her deliberate desertion is incomprehensible, since God and people, like bride and wedding gown, belong together.

Four additional accusations undermine any protests of innocence: (1) Israel has sought other lovers, and in such an abandoned way as to teach the professionally wicked women, the prostitutes, a thing or two; (2) Israel is guilty of social violence by killing off innocent ones; (3) Israel is guilty of lying by claiming she has not sinned; (4) flighty behavior puts her in league once with Egypt, next with Assyria, but not with the Lord.

God's patience is huge but not infinite. A court sentence is missing but is implied in the announcement of Israel's exile from her land (2:37), for to go with hands on one's head is to go as a captive.

Israel acts as though she can at any time sweet-talk her way back to God (3:1–5). Not so. The law forbade a divorced husband from returning to his former, now-married wife (Deut. 24:1–4). Israel is now "married" to Baal.

Israel has not simply been overtaken by temptation. As an Arab is ready to ambush, so Israel has deliberately planned to be promiscuous. Language of harlotry has a double meaning: physical unfaithfulness in marriage and spiritual disloyalty to God (sacred prostitution was part of Baal worship). Israel's immature appeals to a supposedly indulgent father only add to the ugly picture of her evil.

B. A story of two sisters (3:6–4:4). Two sisters, Israel to the north and Judah to the south, are each characteristically tagged: "ever-turning" (backsliding; NIV "faithless") Israel, and "wicked" (runaway; NIV "unfaithful") Judah. In 722 BC Assyria captured Samaria and occupied Israel. In Jeremiah's time Judah was still an independent nation, but the Assyrian garrison was only a few miles away. God argues that Judah is more evil than Israel. For Israel, distressed because of God's punishment, there is an earnest plea to return to God. For Judah, there is a short but very stern warning (4:3–4). The passage is piled with wordplays on the word "turn," which in its various forms occurs sixteen times. The messages date early in Jeremiah's ministry, during Josiah's reign, possibly between 625 and 620 BC.

Ever-turning Israel is accused of harlotry (3:6–10). Harlotry, with its overtones of desertion from the marriage partner and illicit sex, is a graphic way of describing Israel's unfaithfulness to God. God's harsh action in divorcing Israel by sending her into exile should have been a lesson to Judah, who not only saw all that happened but was herself severely threatened by the Assyrians (2 Kings 18–19). Stone pillars, sometimes representing the male sex organ, and trees or wood poles representing the female deities were standard Baal symbols.

Instead of making the expected judgment speech, God issues a plea for ever-turning Israel to turn once more, this time to him (3:11–18). The wordplay can be caught in the translation "Come back, backsliding Israel" (3:11). Verses 12–14 contain three exhortations in as many verses: return, acknowledge, return. The word "turn" is one of two words used for the idea of "repent."

The appeal is persuasive. God advances reasons for Israel to return: (1) he is merciful; (2) repentance is demanded because of the breach of covenant; (3) he is still Israel's husband; (4) good things will follow if they repent. Among these good things are return from exile, godly leaders, shepherds, prosperity, a holiness extending to the entire city of Jerusalem rather than just the ark, a transformed heart, fulfillment of an earlier promise that nations would be blessed through Israel, and a returned and unified people.

The ark was a box in which were kept the stone tables of law that symbolized the presence of God. It had been relocated during Josiah's reform into the most holy area in the temple

(2 Chron. 35:3). To do away with the ark would be radical in the extreme. In the new era all of Jerusalem would contain God's presence. Also striking in these announcements is Israel's return to the land from the exile, a frequent subject in Jeremiah (24:6; 30:1–3; 31:17; 32:37).

God advances further motivations for the people to return to God (3:19–4:2). Verse 19 is not so much a statement as it is a thought, a dream. For a moment we see inside God's mind. He schemes how he can give his people the very best, and he has pleasant thoughts of how in response Israel would in love call out "My Father" (cf. 31:9). Imagery moves between marriage and family.

The dream is shattered, yet it continues. Hypothetically, we must understand, God envisions a change, as though he hears voices calling to him from out of Israel's perversion. A dialogue between God and Israel follows. In imagination, so one must suppose, Israel does an about-face. The people who said they wanted nothing but to go after alien gods (Jer. 2:25) now declare the Lord Yahweh to be their God. A liturgy of a model repentance follows. They admit they were wrong and that from the mountains (the place of noisy Baal worship) no help could come. The shameful gods are Baals. Here is no attempt to look good. Here is no excuse and no belittling of evil. The speech, however, is God putting words in Israel's mouth.

For this reason the divine response begins with "if" (4:1). Ever-turning Israel might turn, yet fail to turn to God. Turning to God demands action as well as words. Negatively it means throwing away the detestable things—all that is ungodly. Positively it means a change in behavior to just and righteous dealings. Then Israel can rightfully make promises by invoking the name of the Lord. Meeting the conditions means good things to nations who will be blessed and who will give the Lord praise; for God's eye is not on his people alone but on other peoples as well.

After the message to Israel (3:11–4:2), Jeremiah turns to his immediate audience, the city of Jerusalem and the territory of Judah (4:3–4). This group will be the focus of the book until chapter 30. Israel appeared ready to change, and so the plea. But Judah is hard, and therefore a threat.

The call is for drastic action. The hard soil of stubbornness is to be broken before good seed is sown—otherwise it will still fall among thorns. In spiritual renewal one cannot shortcut repentance. The exhortation turns from agricultural to physiological symbolism (4:4). Circumcision for Israel was a physical sign of the covenant (Gen. 17:1–14). Since it signified a people spiritually linked with God, circumcision talk came to be associated with the heart. The circumcision of hearts refers to removing whatever spiritually obstructs (Deut. 10:16). The sense is of giving oneself totally to God's service.

God's anger—a very frequent theme in the book—will go forth as a fire so hot that stopping it is impossible.

C. Trouble from the north (4:5–6:30). The story now shifts from marital language to military language. In his capacity as a watchman, Jeremiah sees a God-appointed nation from the north about to invade Palestine.

In earlier prophets a judgment speech classically included an accusation followed by an announcement. In Jeremiah both elements appear, but not in the usual order. In broad strokes, however, one can identify the sequence: announcement (4:5–31); accusation (5:1–13); threat and further accusation (5:14–31); warning (6:1–9); further warning (6:10–20); and second announcement (6:22–30). The announcement is about the invader. God's accusation attacks Judah's lack of moral integrity, spiritual dullness and social injustice, and widespread covetousness and corruption. Laced within announcements, accusations, and warnings are expressions of the prophet's great sorrow and appeals by God to a people to wash their hearts and to walk in the old paths.

Urgency is the note in 4:5–18. Through short, commandlike calls, people are urged to leave their fields and hurry into the walled cities, Zion (Jerusalem) in particular. The destroyer from the north, frequently mentioned in subsequent chapters, is unnamed but later identified as Babylon (27:6). The large Assyrian Empire, which had dominated the Middle East for 150 years, crumbled quickly after the rise of Nabopolassar, the Babylonian, in 626 BC. This oracle is likely early in Jeremiah's ministry, before 621 BC or between 612 BC and 608 BC.

The power of this nation is lionlike (4:7). Before it the leaders, both political and religious, lose their courage.

Verse 10 is the first of the prophet's many personal responses. Jeremiah is markedly affected by the message he preaches. Boldly he faces God with the contradiction—as listeners would see it—between what was promised and what is. The deceit is not to be attributed to God; it is Jerusalem's wickedness that accounts for the impending disaster.

The burst of the invading nation on the scene is graphically pictured as a windstorm of hurricane proportions. The announcement of the army's march is sounded first from Dan, Israel's northern border town, and then from Mount Ephraim, roughly in the middle of Palestine, thirty miles north of Jerusalem. Like a security force, the enemy directly surrounds Judah's cities. Nor need Judah ask why. Her rebellion has brought disaster on her.

The upcoming invasion is not a skirmish, but an onslaught that will demolish everything (4:19–31). Like a photographer using a zoom lens, the prophet first gives an initial picture of the devastation of the whole earth (4:23–26), then a wide-angle shot of all the land (4:27), and finally a close-up of what happens in a town (4:29). The earth becomes chaotic, formless, and empty, as it was before the creation (Gen. 1:2). There are four references to nonlife (earth, heaven, mountain, hill) and four mentions of life (humanity, birds, fruitful land, cities). Behind that army is God's wrath. God is fully committed to this action of judgment and will not be dissuaded.

This description of devastation is bracketed by expressions of pain and hurt. Jeremiah is bent over with pain, as with prophetic perception he hears the war trumpet and sees the war flag. The invaders are like murderers who will strangle Judah to death.

God complains that his people are as those who have not known (i.e., experienced) him;

they are unwise and undiscerning. Proof of their lack of discernment is that Judah, sitting atop a dynamite keg, misreads the situation: with trouble about to break in on her, she is primping herself with cosmetics and jewelry. She is preparing to meet her lovers, who are really her murderers.

So far, statements about Judah's evil have been only sketches. Now the people (not only Jeremiah) are commanded to investigate the moral situation by means of a citywide poll (5:1–13) to show statistically, so to speak, that the place, like Sodom and Gomorrah (Gen. 18:23–33), totally lacks persons of integrity. And worse—people are outrightly defying the Lord. The poll gives warrant for God's severe judgment.

Were there even only one who would seek after truth, God would pardon the city! "Doing justice" (NIV "who deals honestly," 5:1) refers to honorable and upright relationships, not only in the law court, but in every social contact or transaction. Justice is a prime requirement of God's people. Some merely mouth the words of an oath ("As the LORD lives"). Taking the oath, however, is not proof that people mean it.

Jeremiah participates in the research. The poor are not excused because they are poor but are faulted for hard-heartedness. The leaders, who have every advantage, fail the test. Besides, they lead in breaking the relationship (yoke) between people and God. Deliberate defiance and covenant breaking will bring God's judgment—attack by wild animals.

God responds to the statistical research. Like a highly sexed male horse, Judah goes neighing adulterously after another man's wife (5:8). Prosperity apparently led to luxury, which led to sexual liberties. God will judge sexual promiscuity. The people disparagingly suggest that God does not know what is going on, or if he does, he is too nice to punish! Vineyard language of pruning (5:10) is figurative for enemies "pruning" Israel. In mercy God stops short of complete destruction. There is a difference between punishment and annihilation.

Lions stride along the lower section of the facade from the throne room of Nebuchadnezzar's southern palace in Babylon (sixth century BC). Jeremiah 4:7 appropriately compares Babylon to a "lion [who] has come out of his lair."

The people conclude that God will not punish them. God will give to Jeremiah fiery words that will devastate the people's arguments (5:14–19). Babylon, still unnamed, will demolish Judah's fortresses and consume stored provisions as well as current harvests. The sense of verse 16 is that their arrows are deadly. War casualties are many.

A second round of announcements and accusations begins in 5:20, in which greater stress is put on the evils that necessitate severe judgment. Specifically, Judah has spurned the Creator God, and within society, including even religious life, people practice injustice (5:20–31).

God presents himself as the Creator, basically the God of space and time. God curbs the mighty sea and ensures the regularity of the seasons. Yet his people, unimpressed, have violated God's limits and have no awe before him. Irreverently, their eyes and ears are closed to God's wonders. Along with the evils of omission are evils of defiant action. In a rebellious spirit they have deserted their God, much to their own hurt, for the rains have ceased. Sinning people cheat themselves out of what is good.

On the human plane there are likewise sins of action and sins of neglect. Evil persons, like hunters of game, fill their traps (cages) to the limit. By their clever maneuvers, they exploit other people. Their riches have accumulated, due to their deceptive schemes. They are described as overstepping even the usual evils. They have neglected the defense of orphans and other marginal people who do not have access to power. God makes careful treatment of the disadvantaged a measuring stick for social righteousness (cf. Mic. 2:1–5; Isa. 3:13–15).

Corruption has penetrated even the religious arena. Prophets prophesy falsely. The priests are conniving power grabbers who use their position unethically. For these evils God would judge any other nation. And Israel is no exception.

Earlier, people hurried into the city for safety (4:5). But now the invader (compared to a nomadic shepherd whose flocks eat away the pasture) has moved southward to Benjamite territory just north of Jerusalem (6:1–9). Verse 2 is best taken as "I will destroy fragile Zion."

Attacks are made early in the day. The commander barks orders; the attackers are determined. The Lord, now on the side of the enemy, adds his orders to build a ramp up against the city wall (cf. Jer. 21:4). Oppression, violence, and plundering are the reasons for this turn of events. God may, if Judah does not take warning, do even worse by turning completely away and not restraining the enemy at all. The enemy will make a thorough search, like a grape gatherer reaching into the vine branches, for the last fugitive.

With language heightened in intensity, additional reasons are given for the invasion (6:10–20): disinterest in God's message; covetousness; corrupt religious leaders who fail to be radical but instead do easy counseling, assuring peace and well-being; callousness about evil; intentional disobedience; and rejection of God's word. Sacrifices continue with rare incense from Sheba in Arabia and specialties possibly from India. But these are unacceptable because of Judah's moral condition.

Even so, Jeremiah gives warning; God counsels Judah to return to the older, tried lifestyle and calls forth watchmen (prophets). The warning, however, is not heard because of stopped-up (uncircumcised) ears, nor is the counsel heeded, nor is ear given to the prophets. God will therefore unleash his anger. Nations are called to witness that such proceedings are just. Jeremiah's personal outrage seems to ignite God's anger, for in the interchange both become increasingly exasperated.

Throughout the larger block (4:5–6:30) more and more details about the invader from the north have been supplied. Here the army is depicted as advancing fully armed and altogether cruel and merciless (6:21–30). The defenders are hopelessly enfeebled. Escape routes are cut off. Jeremiah anticipates sackcloth rituals of mourning for those slain.

The foe from the north has been said to be the Scythians, but that is hardly likely since their invasion is historically questionable. Since in mythology the mountain of the north was not only the home for the gods but also the source of evil, some have advocated that Jeremiah used this myth to generate fear and foreboding. Most likely, even though the enemy remains unnamed and may initially not have been known to Jeremiah, the "northerner" was the Babylonian army.

Jeremiah is to assay the worth of metals (6:27). Lead was added to silver ore so that when heated, it would remove alloys. Here there is ore, but not enough silver. Jeremiah's conclusion: these are (literally) "rebels of rebels." There is no true Israel. This negative judgment is elsewhere tempered with some words of hope. But now, refine as one will, there is no precious metal, only scum silver at best, which is to be rejected. On this hopeless note ends a passage that has included strong warnings, earnest appeals for change, and dire threats.

D. Examining public worship (7:1–8:3). The basic mode of poetry in 2:1–10:25 is interrupted by a prose sermon. The sermon, a sharp attack on moral deviations and misguided doctrinal views about the temple, stirs up a vehement response, as we learn from a parallel account in Jeremiah 26:1–15. Attack on venerated tradition is risky business (cf. Acts 7). The sermon, on worship, leads to some instructions designed to correct misguided worship (7:16–26) and to halt bizarre worship (7:27–8:3). It is a prelude to further talk about siege (8–10). Similarly, the sermon of chapters 2–3 precedes the announcement of the northern invader (4:5–6:30).

The famous temple sermon (7:1–15) at once identifies the points at issue: a call to behavioral reform and a challenge to belief about the temple. The first point is amplified in verses 5–7, the second in verses 8–12. A biting announcement concludes the sermon, which was preached early in the reign of Jehoiakim.

The temple gate, perhaps the so-called New Gate (Jer. 26:10), from which Jeremiah spoke, belonged to the three-hundred-year-old Solomonic temple. The call to reform is given without preamble but with specifics. Practicing justice—that is, the observance of honorable relations—is a primary requirement. Specifically, "doing justice" (as contrasted to the Western notion of "getting justice") means coming to the aid of those who are helpless and otherwise the victims of mistreatment, often widows, orphans, and strangers.

To shed innocent blood is to take life by violence or for unjust cause. The gift of land was outright; the enjoyment of that gift was conditional. The theme of land loss and land repossession is frequent in Jeremiah (16:13; 24:6; 32:41; 45:4).

A second consideration is a popular chant that had become a cliché: "the temple of the LORD." Its popularity arose from the teaching that God chose Zion, and by implication, the temple (Ps. 132:13–14). A century earlier, with the Assyrian threat, God had shielded and spared the city (2 Kings 19). Any threat to the city's safety was apparently shrugged off with the argument that God would protect his dwelling place under any circumstance. A theology once valid had become stale, even false.

Jeremiah points to violations of the Ten Commandments (7:9, Exod. 20:1–17). It is incongruous that people who steal and go after Baal, this Canaanite nature deity of weather and fertility, should claim immunity on the basis of the temple. Brashly these worshipers contend that standing in the temple, performing their worship, gives them the freedom to break the law. The temple, like a charm, has become a shelter for evildoers. Theirs is (eternal) security, so they think. Yet God sees not only their "holy" worship, but their unholy behavior.

The clincher in Jeremiah's sermon comes from an illustration in their history more than four hundred years earlier (7:12–14). Shiloh, located in Ephraimite territory some twenty miles north of Jerusalem, was the worship center when Israel entered the land (Josh. 18:1). Eli was its last priest. It was destroyed, likely by the Philistines, in 1050, according to Danish archaeologists. Samaria, the capital of Israel, was taken by the Assyrians in 722. God threatens to do to Jerusalem what he did to Shiloh and Samaria. The people's worship is misguided in two ways (7:16–26): they offer to the Queen of Heaven (7:16–20), and they offer to God but without moral obedience (7:21–26).

The Queen of Heaven (7:18) was Ishtar, a Babylonian fertility goddess. Worship of Mesopotamian deities became popular with Manasseh (2 Kings 21:1–18; 23:4–14). Such apostate worship was anything but secret since it involved entire families. Cakes, round and flat like the moon or possibly star-shaped or even shaped like a nude woman, were offered as food to this deity. But any worship of gods other than the Lord Yahweh is a violation of the first commandment. Violations bring dire consequences.

The tone of 7:21 is sarcastic: "Very well, heap up offerings—as many as you want—and gorge yourselves" (author's translation). Some offerings required participants to eat meat; others, such as burnt offerings, were to be offered in their entirety. God did, of course, give commandments in the wilderness about sacrifices (Leviticus 1–7).

External worship practices are empty without a devoted heart. Three factors should encourage obedience: (1) the promise of covenant, a part of God's initial design (7:23a; Exod. 6:7; the formula occurs twenty times in the Bible); (2) total well-being (7:23b); and (3) prophets to encourage it (7:25).

Again the people are charged with failure to receive correction (7:27–8:3). The result is the disappearance of truth and integrity and a turning to a bizarre religion. God's punishment will be as outlandish as their practice is bizarre. Anticipating that awful death, Jeremiah is commanded to cut his hair and to cry on the bare hilltop, as was customary to mark a calamity.

Vandalism in worship exists. Representations of other deities were brought into the temple reserved for the Lord Yahweh. The Valley of Hinnom, also known as Topheth, is immediately south of old Jerusalem. Topheth

The goddess Ishtar, "the Queen of Heaven" (Jer. 7:18), is represented on this clay plaque from ancient Mesopotamia (1792–1750 BC).

("fire pit") was a worship area (high place) in this valley. Child sacrifice was introduced by Ahaz and Manasseh (2 Kings 16:3; 21:6), abolished by Josiah (2 Kings 23:4–7), but renewed by Jehoiakim.

The judgment speech of 7:32–8:3 predicts that the deaths either through plague or military slaughter will be so overwhelming that the valley's new name will be Valley of Killing. The sacrifice area will become the cemetery. None will be left to chase off vultures who feed on corpses. Bones of past kings will be exhumed by the enemy as an insult. The astral deities, so ardently served and worshiped, will look coldly and helplessly on.

E. Treachery, trouble, and tears (8:4–10:25). "Oh, that . . . my eyes [were] a fountain of tears!" (9:1). It is from such expressions in this section that Jeremiah has been called the weeping prophet. The prophet aches for his people. Trouble will be everywhere, and it will be terrible. Crops will fail; fields and properties will be taken over by strangers; and the dreaded foe from the north will be on the way.

Things will never be the same. And the reason is that God's people have forsaken God's law (8:9; 9:13). Specifically, they have not repented of their evil. They speak lies, and they prefer wooden self-made idols to the living God. Desolation will come. The emotional outpourings of sorrow are a new dimension in the development of the theme of judgment.

As the book now stands, this kaleidoscope of accusation, threat, and lament—mostly in poetry—follows the temple sermon, which is in prose. One can discern three rounds of presentation: 8:4–9:2; 9:3–25; 10:1–25. Three sections occur in each round:

the people's sins (8:4–13; 9:3–9; 10:1–16)

the coming trouble (8:14–17; 9:10–16; 10:17–18)

sorrow in the minor key (8:18–9:2; 9:17–22; 10:19–25)

8:4–9:2. Those who stumble ordinarily get up. Those who find themselves on a wrong road turn around. Not so Israel (8:4–13). The word "turn" occurs five times in verses 4–5. Like horses with blinders, Israel stubbornly charges ahead. Israel has less sense than birds or animals, whose instinct at least returns them to their original place or owner.

There are four other problems: (1) *Pseudo-wisdom.* Judah prides herself in the possession of the law, possibly a reference to the newly found law book (Deuteronomy?) in 621 under Josiah (2 Kings 22:1–10). "The lying pen of the scribes" (8:8) does not refer to miscopying or questionable interpretations as much as to leaving a corrupt society unchallenged. (2) *Greed.* All strata of Hebrew society crave the accumulation of wealth. (3) *Lying.* Religious leaders treat Israel's serious wounds (her crisis of wickedness) lightly. They say, "All is well." The duty of prophets was to expose evil, not to minimize it. One can be occupied with God's word yet have an unscriptural message.

Topheth, or the Valley of Hinnom, located outside the southern walls of the old city of Jerusalem (see Jer. 7:31–32).

(4) *Failure to feel shame.* The prophet, in contrast to Israel, knows what time it is.

The list of harmful consequences continues (8:14–17). It is now the people who understand that the human evils of the enemy's advancing cavalry and poisoned water, as well as natural evils such as poisonous snakes, are God's agents. Sarcastically it is noted that people leave the fields only to die in the cities. Resistance is futile. Poisonous adders cannot be charmed; horses, like modern cruise missiles, are unstoppable.

We have here not a dispassionate onlooker but a tender caregiver torn up over the news of the coming disaster (8:18–9:2). Verse 18 is variously translated because of alternate readings in Hebrew and Greek texts. It is best read: "My grief is without healing" (see Thompson, 303 n. 1).

The prophet, perhaps imaginatively, hears the cry of a now-exiled people. Plaintively they ask about God, their king ("Lord" and "King" are in parallel in 8:19). At the same time, the prophet hears God saying in effect: "I can't stand their idolatry." Listening once more, the prophet detects the hopeless cry of those in exile who approach a dreaded winter without provisions. The early harvests of grain (May–June) and the later harvests of fruits (September–October) are over. This agricultural allusion may be a way of saying, "We counted on help (our own or that of others), but nothing came of it."

The prophet identifies with the people ("*my* people"—found three times in 8:21–22; 9:1). Since they are crushed, he is crushed. The prophet is beside himself with grief. Exhausted, he cries and wishes for his head to be a never-ending fountain so that he could cry more (9:1). On the other hand, he would like to get away from it all. The people's sins disgust him. Prophets did not stand at a distance lobbing bombshells; they were closely involved with their listeners.

9:3–25. Lying, mentioned only in 8:10, is now treated in full as a major problem (9:3–9). Deception has replaced integrity as a way of life.

The usual translation of 9:3 pictures the tongue as a bow and lies as arrows. Equally possible and more stinging (and more in line with 9:8) is the translation that makes the lies the bow and the tongue the arrow. Out of a false person come falsehoods. In any case, lies have a lethal quality about them. Verse 4 has a clever turn of phrase: "Jacob" is synonymous with "deceiver"; hence, literally, everyone deceives ("Jacobs") his brother.

For any other nation such flagrant violation of truth and integrity would mean God's punishment. Should Israel be spared? It is as though God throughout wrestles with the issue of what is the just and right thing to do.

The "I" of verse 10 is Jeremiah, who once more responds emotionally by weeping at the prospect of punishment (9:10–16). The desolation is complete. No mooing of cattle and no sound of birds are heard. All signs of life are gone (cf. 4:25). The "I" of verse 11 is God. Scattering among the Gentiles will be a fate for some, death by the sword the fate for others. The title "Lord Almighty" (NIV)—that is, "Lord of Heaven's Armies"—does not leave the outcome of his decision in doubt.

Such destruction calls for an explanation. In a nutshell the reasons are faithlessness to the law (in which they boasted, 8:8), disobedience to the Lord, a godless lifestyle, and long-practiced idolatry of the Canaanite variety. Other reasons are given in 9:3–9.

Voices of wailing in response to the total destruction come from three quarters (9:17–22). First, professional women mourners, usually engaged to prompt crying at funerals and calamities, are hurriedly summoned to lament this awful disaster. Second, wailing is heard from Jerusalem itself, where plundered fugitives explain that they must vacate their dwellings and leave their land because all is ruined. Third, since in the future, mourners will be in great demand, the professionals are urged to train daughters and neighbors in the art of mourning.

The epidemic is described metaphorically: "Death has climbed in through our windows"

(9:21). Alternatively, "death" may be a personification of the demonlike figure Lamastu, known from Akkadian literature.

In 9:23–26, the Lord describes proper boasting. The connection of verses 23–24 with the foregoing is not at once clear. The "wise" have been noted in verse 12 and again in verse 17. "Wisdom" and "riches" could refer to the royal lifestyle under Solomon. Jehoiakim gloried in riches, in contrast to his father, Josiah, for whom knowing God was important; knowing God meant caring for the disadvantaged. The Hebrew word for "know" obviously goes beyond possessing information!

Kindness or covenant love is voluntary help extended to those in need. Justice includes honorable relations in every transaction. Judged by this quality alone, the situation described in the foregoing verses is nauseating. Righteousness is that inner disposition of integrity and uprightness that issues in right action.

The nations listed (9:26) were likely in a military alliance against Babylon. The historical situation is assumed to be 597, when Nebuchadnezzar led an attack against Jerusalem. For Israelites to hear their country named along

Astral symbols representing the gods and their "signs in the heavens" (Jer. 10:1) adorn the top of this stone boundary marker (Mesopotamia, 1125–1100 BC).

with others must have been shocking. Yet this emphasizes that inner obedience is more crucial in God's sight than mere outward compliance.

10:1–25. The blistering tirade against idols (10:1–16) is directed against "Israel," which as an umbrella term includes both Israel and Judah. Here Judah is particularly in view. Judah is warned about the astral deities commonly worshiped in Babylon. Some scholars claim an exilic setting for the poem and many deny its unity and that Jeremiah wrote it. The contrast between homemade idols and the living God has seldom been better drawn. With cutting sarcasm, the Lord describes the process of shaping, stabilizing, and clothing these gods. The contrast between the idol and God is heightened by alternating a mocking poem with a doxology: idols (3–5), God (6–7), idols (8–9), God (10), idols (11), God (12–13), idols (14–15), God (16).

The idols are nonfunctioning, a "work of errors" (NKJV). They are an embarrassment to their makers and will be the object of divine punishment. Fear, quite inappropriate before idols, is necessary before God.

To clinch the contrast with the unnamed figurines, God is given a name: Yahweh, the Lord of Heaven's Armies, Lord Almighty. The name "Portion of Jacob" (10:16) points to God's lively interest in people. He is also known as "King of the nations" and "King" (10:7, 10). From a statement about his incomparability (God is in a class by himself) and his function as Creator, the writer moves to God's crowning activity: his election and shaping of Israel to be his special people.

The crisp word about picking from the ground the fugitive's bundle announces the theme of coming trouble heard throughout these chapters (10:17–18). God serves notice, as to a tenant, that he will sling out (cf. the same word in Judg. 20:16) the inhabitants. There is about this a tone of final warning.

Judah is without shelter and without family (10:19–25). Blame properly falls on her leaders, chiefly kings, who have failed to seek God. The destruction comes at the hand of the northerner—still unnamed but later identified as Babylon.

Instead of taking satisfaction in his announcement coming true, Jeremiah interjects, "This is my sickness, and I must endure it" (10:19). Jeremiah speaks again in verse 23. Given the dull-hearted leaders, he is unsure of his next step. The request to be corrected may be for himself or may be made on behalf of the people. The prayer for God's anger to fall on the Gentiles could be a quotation from the people (cf. Ps. 79:6–7). Like the prayers for vengeance (Psalms 109; 137), while not representing the New Testament ideal of loving enemies, the prayer at least turns the situation over to God instead of taking it in hand personally.

3. Stories about Wrestling with People and with God (11:1–20:18)

The preceding chapters, though grim with dark announcements and heavy accusations, have had a formal cast. Only rarely has the prophet expressed personal anguish. In chapters 11–20, however, Jeremiah as a person is much more at center stage. In these stories Jeremiah wrestles hard to persuade his audience of their serious situation. He engages in sign acts. Here also we observe a man wrestling with God as he deals with frustrations and discouragements. The so-called laments or confessions—seven of them—are unique windows into the prophet's interior life (11:20–23; 12:1–4; 15:10–11, 15–21; 17:14–18; 18:18–23; 20:7–13).

A. Coping with conspiracies (11:1–12:17). Two scenes of conspiracy dominate these two chapters. The first is a conspiracy of a covenant people against its covenant God (11:9–13). In the second conspiracy, in the private arena, plotters conspire to do away with Jeremiah (11:18–19). The double conspiracy leads to two personal encounters with God in which the prophet pours out his complaint (11:20; 12:1–4). In each case God answers, but not necessarily as Jeremiah expected (11:21–23; 12:5–17).

Covenant has been a presupposition in the foregoing chapters, but it is now made explicit (11:1–8). Covenant is more than a contract. "Contract" suggests negotiation and terms, has generally to do with goods or services, and is task oriented. "Covenant," while it is not without terms, is a bonding between two persons that has a mutual relationship as its goal. At stake is intimacy and loyalty. The intimacy factor is pinpointed in the covenant formula: "You will be my people, and I will be your God" (11:4). The loyalty component is explicit in the command, "Obey." The charge that Israel has not obeyed is repeated more than thirty times, in chapters 7, 11, 26, 35, and 42.

"This covenant" (11:2) may be the renewed covenant under Josiah (2 Kings 23). More likely, because the context is "ancestors" and Egypt, it is the Sinai covenant (Exodus 19–24). Since the Josianic covenant was a renewal of the earlier covenant, we may properly see in these verses Jeremiah's aggressive preaching on behalf of the reform launched by Josiah in 621 BC.

Deliverance was the presupposition for covenant. The idiom "land flowing with milk and honey" (11:5) suggests paradise and in Western idiom could be rendered "God's country." Set in between these grace gifts is a call to obedience. To "obey," very frequent in verses 2–8, is to comply with the will of another.

Covenant, it has been suggested, has close parallels with ancient political treaties. These treaties concluded by invoking strong curses on the party that failed to observe the treaty terms (cf. Deut. 27:15–26). God threatens to set these curses in motion. By saying "Amen" (11:5), Jeremiah consents to this understanding of covenant and invites his audience to stand with him on common ground.

Jeremiah 11:9–13 is in the pattern of the traditional judgment speech, which begins with an accusation and ends with an announcement. The accusation becomes the reason for, and shapes the nature of, the announcement.

The accusation is conspiracy. Both Judah and Israel have conspired to return to old ways. In defiance they have gone after other gods. In political language this is an act of treason. Jeremiah puts it boldly and shockingly: they "have broken the covenant" (11:10).

God closes the door to any change of mind by forbidding prophetic intercession (11:14–17). The sense of verse 15 is that Judah/Israel, God's beloved, has no business in his temple (perhaps meaning the land) because she has plotted numerous times against him. Sacrifices, which she still offers, are called "consecrated meat" to suggest her notion that only the outward matters.

Now Israel, a highly desirable and potentially productive olive tree, is hit by a lightning storm and destroyed. Covenant curses have been activated.

To pronounce the covenant broken is to stir opposition (11:18–23). The men of Anathoth, Jeremiah's townsfolk, are almost certainly his immediate family (cf. 12:6). Embarrassed, then incensed, they eventually plot murder. People who resent a disconcerting message resort to silencing or eliminating the messenger (cf. Amos 7:12; Jesus in John 19; Stephen in Acts 7:54–59).

The episode triggers an appeal by Jeremiah to God for him to deal with the plotters. As a righteous God, he tests "the heart and mind" (11:20). The Hebrew word the NIV translates as "heart" is literally "kidneys," which were thought to be the seat of emotion. The heart (NIV "mind") symbolized thought and will. Together, the two terms represent a person's internal motives. Commendably, the prophet refrains from retaliation. His prayer is in accord with the teaching, "'Vengeance is mine, I will repay,' says the Lord" (Rom 12:19 NASB).

God's response to bring disaster on the plotting townsfolk must be seen as a miniature scene showing how God can be expected to deal with covenant partners who conspire. Verses 20–23 make up Jeremiah's first personal lament.

The second of Jeremiah's seven personal laments touches on God, the wicked, the prophet himself, and the land (12:1–4). Jeremiah uses court language and asks for justice, or right dealing. "Righteous" is a term of relationship describing integrity and uprightness. On what grounds can God prosper evil persons? It is an old question. The wicked discount God by claiming that God will not have final jurisdiction over them.

The prophet protests his innocence, a feature of other laments. Moral corruption has ecological effects, death among them (12:4; Hos. 4:1–3).

Jeremiah 12:5–17 is a reply to the questions of verses 1–4. There are two answers. The first is to rebuke Jeremiah, saying essentially, "If such (little) problems upset you, how will you successfully deal with weighty issues?" The Jordan Valley has its jungles—a considerable obstacle course. Here is no offer of sympathy nor divine coddling, but a call to toughen up. Far harder to explain than the success of the wicked is God's overturning of his own people.

Verses 7–13, a second answer, give a partial response to the evil about which Jeremiah has complained. God will judge that wicked people even though it is his inheritance, his special people. Already surrounding nations have beset her, as a flock of birds is known to peck at an odd speckled bird (12:9). Or perhaps the scene is one of a hen with hawks circling overhead. The raids of hordes, including the Moabites and Ammonites, could be in view in verse 10. Kings were commonly called shepherds in the ancient Near East.

Successively God loses his vineyard, his field, and in fact, his entire portion. As in the previous lament (11:20–23), Jeremiah's challenge to God's justice becomes an excuse to reiterate the now-familiar announcement of coming destruction. One clue to the question about justice lies in the future, when God will punish his people.

God's justice, about which Jeremiah has inquired, means that the nations who as God's agents bring desolation will themselves be judged (12:14–17). This of course raises other issues, not addressed here but elaborated elsewhere (Isa. 10:5–7). One does not harm God's possession, his people, without receiving harm in turn. But later on God will restore Moab and Ammon (Jer. 48:47; 49:6). He will bless Egypt (Isa. 19:24). The agenda of justice has become the agenda of compassion. God's missionary purpose must not go unnoticed (Isa. 2:1–4; 19:16–25).

B. Pride ruins everything (13:1–27). The ruined girdle (13:1–11) is the first of several sign acts, dramatized attention-getters, for people who have stopped listening. Sign acts consist of a divine command, the report of compliance, and an explanation. The girdle, or loincloth (Hebrew *ezor*), is more than a belt; it is like a short skirt that reaches down to the knees but hugs the waist.

Jeremiah's symbolic act has a double message, the first of which is the evil of pride. God detests pride (2 Chron. 32:24–26; Prov. 8:13). Arrogance, an exaggerated estimate of oneself, brings the disdain of others and accounts for the evils of verse 10. Second, the sign act pictures the way in which God would take proper pride in Israel, who, like the girdle worn around the waist, would be close, as well as beautiful. That hope was dashed.

Wine at harvest was put into storage jars. Two-foot-tall clay jars held about ten gallons each. Jeremiah states the obvious (or is it a riddle?) in order to secure assent (13:12–14). Those drunk with actual wine or with divine intoxication (Jer. 25:15) are civil and religious rulers as well as ordinary citizens. The smashing of these jars suggests the violent clash between these groups, with resulting factions. The entire social structure will disintegrate.

A discussion of pride precedes a miscellaneous collection of evils, all of which justify harsh punishment (13:15–27). To "give glory" (13:16) is literally to give weight or to make God, not self, prominent. To look for light is to look for the time of salvation. The picture is one of a traveler in the mountains overtaken by nightfall. The captivity, indeed Judah's wholesale exile, is here first mentioned (13:19), even though the northern agent (Babylon) has been announced earlier (4:6). In the invasion, the fortified cities of the Negev in the south will be surrounded and blockaded, becoming inaccessible.

Jerusalem is addressed as a woman in verses 20–22. Those persons and countries whom Judah enlisted as allies will be appointed by the enemy to rule over them. Like civilian women in wartime, so Judah will be violated. She will be disgraced, stripped from head to toe, and exposed.

Jeremiah 13:12–14 uses the image of smashing together wine-filled jars, such as these storage jars from Hazor (ninth–eighth century BC).

C. Dealing with drought (14:1–15:21). If past chapters have emphasized God's punishment of his people through the sword, these two deal primarily with drought. Famine pushes the people to pray, even to acknowledge their sinfulness. God refuses to help; no relief is in sight. The prophet is pained by the people's plight, and, in a different way, by his own. Chapter divisions here obscure two symmetrical halves (14:2–16 and 14:17–15:9). In each there is a description of the famine (14:2–6; 14:17–18), a prayer (14:7–9; 14:19–22), and a divine response (14:10–16; 15:1–9).

The droughts (plural) are vividly depicted in their effect on high-ranking people, farmers, and animals (14:1–9). City gates, more like open areas comparable to modern malls, were places for merchandizing and legal transactions. All has come to a standstill because of the downturn in the economy. To "cover the head" (14:3) was a cultural expression of embarrassment or frustration.

When people's livelihood is in jeopardy, they pray. There is recognition of evil (literally "crookedness, perversity") and acknowledgment of their continual "turning" and their sin (literally "missing the mark"). "For the sake of your name" (14:7) refers to the name Yahweh, which means, "I am present to save." To "bear your name" (14:9) is to belong to God. People chide God for being uninvolved and for failure of nerve. They seek consolation from old assurances and, in bargaining fashion, ask that God forget their sins.

The finality of God's "No!" to the people's prayer is evidenced in his forbidding prophetic intercession (14:10–18). All access to God such as fasting and sacrifice is barred (cf. Isa. 58:3–11). False prophets who kept announcing good times and "true peace" were Jeremiah's constant irritation. His experience of seeing victims of sword (animals put out of misery) in the field and hunger in the city totally contradicts any optimism. The conclusion: the prophets and priests, who are called to show the way, wander aimlessly. "They do not know" (14:18 NASB;

cf. NLT) may mean that they do not know the mind of the Lord.

Suffering, such as hunger, is not necessarily sin-related; however, this famine is a judgment (14:19–22). Hope for an answer lies in the Lord's name, his covenant, and his creation power. "Do not dishonor your glorious throne" (14:21) is an appeal on the basis of the temple (Jer. 17:12).

Again intercession is ruled out (15:1–9). Moses and Samuel, both prophets, interceded at critical times. God fulfills an earlier announcement not to hear pleas for help (Jer. 11:11). Manasseh, who ruled Judah fifty years earlier, was Judah's most wicked king (14:4; 2 Kings 21:1–8). A generation is being punished for another's sin, but also for its own sin.

By sword or other means God will annihilate the men, leaving widows. Once-proud mothers of many sons will gasp in their confused, possibly demented state. The covenant promising many descendants has been reversed.

Two laments from the prophet follow (15:10–21). Both are in response to the droughts and, more particularly, Jeremiah's devastating announcement that God will destroy his people.

Jeremiah claims he is not to be faulted for the nagging and the widespread antagonism against him. He would rather not have been born (15:10). God's assurance is for his safety. Verse 12 is a reference to the strong northern killer nation who, like iron, will not be broken in his advance. While to Jeremiah the enemy will show mercy, the land generally will be plundered. People will be removed from their land. The response to the prophet's woes, instead of softening the announcement, hardens it yet more.

The lament of verses 15–18 is by one who shirks further engagement. The prayer for vengeance falls short of the Christian teaching to love enemies. "When your words came" may refer to the discovery of the scroll in the temple (2 Kings 22:13). High joy (to be called by the name of the Lord of Heaven's armies and so be on the winning side) is followed by loathsome misery, hot indignation, and isolation. (Jeremiah did not marry; 16:2.) Jeremiah has disgust for his enemies and difficulty stabilizing his personal life, and he is disappointed in God, who has become a problem. Dry streambeds give a Palestine traveler the mirage of water.

God's answer deals with all three parts of the lament. First, Jeremiah is to turn, a word that often (though not here) means "to repent." The wordplay is represented in the translation "If you change your heart and come back to me, I will take you back." Second, he must not take his cue from others. Third, God recalls the promise of his presence given at the time of Jeremiah's call (Jer. 1:19). The prophet who levels with God finds that God levels with him.

D. Much bad news, some good (16:1–17:27). These two chapters are a mixture. God privately instructs Jeremiah not to socialize; God speaks publicly about keeping the Sabbath. The people of God will be exiled; but there will be a restoration. A prophet turns to God in his frustration; Gentiles turn en masse to God in conversion. There are mini essays; there are proverblike sayings. However, the theme remains unchanged: sin is pervasive and judgment will be certain and terrible.

God gives Jeremiah three commands about his social life (16:1–13). The reason for each command arises out of the coming disaster. First, Jeremiah is to be celibate. Having children, which was highly desirable, is forbidden him, for all existing families will disappear. Gruesome death will come to children from terrible diseases, the enemy's sword, and famine.

Second, Jeremiah must not attend funerals or extend comfort. The reason: God has withdrawn his covenant blessings of peace, covenant love, compassion, and favor. So must the prophet withdraw his involvement. Cutting oneself to show grief, though forbidden (Lev. 19:28; Deut. 14:1), was apparently practiced (Jer. 16:6).

Third, Jeremiah is to avoid weddings and all parties as a way of announcing the end of all joyful socializing. Judah has deserted God because of the stubbornness of an evil heart

(16:12; cf. 3:17; 7:24; 9:14; 11:8; 13:10; 18:12; 23:17). Forewarned of the reason for the disaster, Judah would be able to survive.

Placing promise oracles next to judgment oracles is not new (16:14–18; see Hos. 1:9–10). The oracle is repeated in Jeremiah 23:7–8, where it better suits the context. The statement of 16:14–15 is not to deny the exodus event but to emphasize that the return from exile will be even more impressive.

Verse 16 notes that fishermen with nets will catch the masses, while hunters will catch the stragglers, so that no one will escape. The language about idols is filled with disgust.

Ironically, while Judah turns from God to idols, Gentiles, world over, turn from idols to God (16:19–21). The vision is refreshing and overpowering (cf. Jer. 12:14–17; Isa. 2:1–4; 45:14–25; Zech. 8:20–23). Gentiles are saying about these gods what God says about them. God speaks in verse 21. He will teach the Gentiles in the sense of giving them an experience of his power.

The judgment speech in 17:1–4 consists of an accusation and an announcement. Sin written indelibly on the heart will one day be replaced by God's law written on the heart (Jer. 31:33). Horns were corner projections on an altar to which the animal was tied and on which the atoning blood was put. Asherah poles were wooden carvings erected to honor the astral goddess Asherah, known in Babylon as Ishtar.

The announcement summarizes the disaster. "My mountain" (17:3) refers to Mount Zion in Jerusalem, where the temple stood. High places were hilltop areas set apart for the worship of Canaanite gods. By default, the people will lose their belongings, their land, and their freedom. The cause is twofold: Judah's sin and God's anger.

In the parable of 17:5–8 the issue is in what or whom one "trusts" (literally "throws oneself forward," 17:5). Jeremiah's announcements, if taken seriously, would trigger military preparations. But on a national scale confidence was not to be placed in human leadership (even a new king) or in military resources. The prospect for nations or individuals leaning on human strength is death and isolation.

In stark contrast, God-trusting persons are "blessed" or empowered, like a tree planted by water, which "does not fear when heat comes" (17:8). Similar comparisons between the godly and ungodly are made in Psalm 1 and Matthew 7:13–14.

Three separate and only loosely related wisdomlike pieces are joined together (17:9–13). The heart, the seat of the will, is searched and explored and diagnosed as deceptive. "Deceitful" is a variant for "Jacob" (deceiver, heel-grabber). The term "incurable" (NIV "beyond cure," 17:9) reflects Jeremiah's despair in the human situation. The antidote is a heart transplant (31:33).

The proverb of verse 11 emphasizes both the wrongfulness of riches acquired by devious means and the way such riches are vulnerable to attack and loss. A partridge or calling bird is said to gather the eggs of other birds and then brood on them to hatch them.

Verse 12 continues the motif of contrasts begun in verse 5. The temple is the place of God's dwelling and hence the place of safety. "Written in the dust" (17:13) points to some disgrace or may mean "consigned to the netherworld" and thus death, quite opposite to "written in the book [of life]" (Dan. 12:1; cf. Exod. 32:32).

Another lament as a personal response interrupts the attention focused on the nation (17:14–18). It depicts Jeremiah, however, as one who trusts the Lord. To be "saved" (17:14) is to be brought from restrictive places to the freedom of open spaces. Jeremiah's personal request for healing and salvation arises from the mocking taunts of others. They jeeringly ask about the unfulfilled announcements of disaster—a question likely asked prior to the first Babylonian invasion of Judah in 605. Jeremiah protests his innocence. Nor has he wished for the catastrophic event.

The harshness of his prayer for disaster to come on his opponents can be appreciated if

his opponents are understood as those opposing God. "Double destruction" (17:18), it has been argued, is proportionate destruction (cf. 16:18).

The people are exhorted to observe the Sabbath (17:19–27; Sabbath laws are given in Exodus 20:8–11; 23:12; 34:21; Num. 15:32–36). "Be careful" is a frequent admonition in Deuteronomy. The instruction is to desist from public trading and from work generally.

Reform and renewal start with specifics. Some have suggested that of the Ten Commandments Jeremiah singled out the fourth because it was the easiest to observe; besides, it was a tangible sign of the covenant (Exod. 31:16–17). As with God's instructions generally, so here, difficulty ensues for those who disregard them; blessing follows those who obey. After two three-month reigns (Jehoahaz; Jehoiachin) the promise of a stable monarchy (17:25–26) would be important. Political stability and religious commitment provide the setting for the good life.

Appropriate sacrifices will be brought from the whole land. Verse 26 names the regions: Benjamin, a territory adjoining Judah to the north; the Shephelah, foothills west of Jerusalem; the hill country, the range from Ephraim south; and the Negev, in the desert south. In the gates, the very place of desecration, fiery destruction will begin should the Sabbath not be observed.

E. A pot marred, a pot smashed (18:1–19:15). These two chapters describe two sign acts. Both involve clay pots. In the first a marred pot is a prelude to a call to repentance—a call that is defiantly rejected. In the second sign act, a pot is smashed as a visual message about the coming catastrophe upon the city of Jerusalem. God's sovereignty is evident throughout.

If one includes chapter 20, one can see two symmetrical halves, the second half of each (2 and 4 below) more elaborate and precise than the first:

1. Pottery making/smashing 18:1–10; 19:1–13
2. God shapes disaster 18:11–17; 19:14–15

3. Attack on the prophet 18:18; 20:1–16
4. A response of lament 18:19–23;
   20:17–18

The sign act or symbolic action is in the traditional form: (1) an instruction, (2) a report of compliance, and (3) an interpretation.

The potter's equipment consisted of two stone disks placed horizontally and joined by a vertical shaft. The lower would be spun using the feet; the other, at waist level, had on it the clay for the potter's hand to shape.

"Uprooted," "torn down," and "destroyed," as well as "built up" and "planted" (18:7, 9), recall words from Jeremiah's call, which occur there, as here, in the context of nations generally (Jer. 1:10; cf. 24:6).

It is not so much that God offers a second chance but that, just as the potter is in charge and decides what to do when things go other than planned, so God is in charge and at any given moment has the option of choice. In some sense at least, prophetic announcements are conditional. God is not arbitrary; repentance makes a difference.

Egyptian statuette showing a potter working at a potter's wheel (ca. 2477 BC)

The principle stated in verses 6–8 is next applied to Judah (18:11–17). Their decision to follow their own stubborn heart is confirmed by their explicit statement.

God assesses their decision as "horrible" (18:13)—unlike the decision of other nations (Jer. 2:10–11). The argument in verse 14 is that it is contrary to nature for snow to leave Lebanon. The seriousness of coming disaster is described by responses of others to it: scorn (18:16) is hissing or whistling in unbelief. God's "face" (18:17) is language for blessing and favor.

The decision to follow personal plans puts into effect plans to do away with the prophet (18:18–23). Priests, wise men, and prophets, along with kings, represent that society's leaders.

Jeremiah's prayer incorporates elements similar to those in his other laments (see Jer. 11:18–23; 12:1–4; 15:10–21; 17:14–18). There is personal petition, complaint, and a call for God to bring vengeance. Evil has been paid him for the good he has done—specifically, he has sought the well-being of those now turned against him. The question of 18:20 could also be a question asked by his persecutors, who think of their actions as good.

We are shown an angry prophet. Against families (women, youths, children) Jeremiah would bring famine and sword. Even more, he prays God to forestall any atonement for their sins. Here is a lapse in prophetic intercession. Even acknowledging that Jeremiah leaves the matter in God's hands, he falls short of Jesus's response to his enemies: "Father, forgive them" (Luke 23:34). One may, however, in Jeremiah's response see mirrored how God in justice might deal with those opposing him.

The terrible message of doom is first made vivid to the elders by means of a smashed pot; later the same message is announced to all the people (19:1–15). Egyptians wrote names of enemies on pottery jars and then smashed them, believing that such action magically triggered disaster.

F. Terror on every side (20:1–18). Here is the first one-on-one announcement of the coming catastrophe (20:1–6). Pashhur might well have been among the religious leaders taken by Jeremiah on a tour to see Topheth (19:1–15). Magor-Missabib (20:3), which means "terror on every side," catches the emotional dimension of the coming disaster. The name is a reversal of Pashhur, which, though Egyptian, in Aramaic might mean "fruitful on every side." Babylon, now named for the first time in the book (20:4), will be Pashhur's destiny, not because he arrested Jeremiah, but because he collaborated in the big lie of announcing continued safety (Jer. 8:10–11). In keeping with the principle of corporate personality or social solidarity, Pashhur's household will share his fate.

The lament in 20:7–13 follows the classical lament pattern: complaint, statement of confidence, petition, and praise. Jeremiah's address to God is daring. "Deceived" (20:7) is elsewhere rendered as "entice" or "seduce" (Exod. 22:16), but may here be used in the sense of "persuade," though with a sinister purpose (Prov. 24:28). God has victimized the prophet. Jeremiah cries out as an innocent sufferer. To shout violence is the equivalent of the modern "Emergency!"

Jeremiah's personal frustration in dealing with an irresictible urge to speak is compounded by external opposition. "Friends" (20:10) is a tongue-in-cheek designation. His "support system" has collapsed. They mock him with the slogan of his own message, "Terror on every side."

The statement of confidence about God as warrior (20:11) harks back to Jeremiah's call (1:8, 19). God's vengeance contrasts with the enemy's vengeance. Praise within a lament is a standard component; one-third of all the psalms are classified as laments, and all but one (Psalm 88) contain praise. In contrast to other laments, this one is not followed by a response from God.

The classical statement of cursing in 20:14–18 likely describes another occasion; otherwise its link with verse 13 presents a schizophrenic prophet. Or, this may be not Jeremiah's curse, but a standard outcry made by people caught in calamity. Cursing the day of one's birth stops short of cursing God (cf. Job 3:2–10). Sodom and Gomorrah, totally destroyed, are the two cities of verse 16 (cf. Gen. 19:24–28). The speaker, in his vexation of spirit, would have preferred to be stillborn or unborn. The death wish, if it is Jeremiah's, arises not only out of personal despair but also out of the shocking public scene.

4. Challenging Kings and Prophets (21:1–29:32)

The preceding chapters have introduced the message of doom (2–10) and the reason for that message (11–20). Beginning with this section we are more securely locked into datable historical, though chronologically disarranged, events. We hear of kings: Josiah, Jehoiakim, Jehoiachin, Zedekiah. We meet prophets: Hananiah, Ahab, Zedekiah, Shemaiah. The leaders bear major responsibility for Judah's evil condition. Prose narrative dominates, which speaks of Jeremiah in the third person.

A. Addressing rulers and governments (21:1–23:8). **21:1–22:9.** The first of two delegations (21:1–10) from Zedekiah to Jeremiah is to be dated to 588 BC. Nebuchadnezzar, the famous ruler of Babylon (605–562), had earlier invaded Judah (597) and had appointed Zedekiah as king. Zedekiah, apparently persuaded by his advisors to invite Egypt's help, had rebelled (cf. Jer. 52:3). Now Nebuchadnezzar was back.

The delegation wonders whether God might intervene, as he did when Hezekiah was threatened by Sennacherib and the Assyrians (2 Kings 19:35–36). Pashhur (21:1) is not to be identified with the priest of 20:1–6; this Pashhur later calls for Jeremiah's death (38:1–6). Zephaniah (21:1) is not to be confused with the priest (Jer. 29:25, 29). He is a member of a later delegation (Jer. 37:3–10) and appears in 2 Kings 25:18. Jeremiah as an intermediary is approached for information.

Jeremiah's answer is bad news. Judah's weapons will be turned back on them, possibly through Babylonian capture, or because of confusion during a rapid retreat. Judah faces a God who fights not for her but against her. "Outstretched hand" (21:5) is holy-war language.

The fate of Zedekiah and his officials—death by the sword of Nebuchadnezzar—is fulfilled in Jeremiah 52:8–11. Jeremiah's counsel for the people to surrender peacefully to the Babylonians (also called Chaldeans) brands him a traitor.

The passage about God-pleasing government (21:11–22:9) is in two symmetrical parts (21:11–14 and 22:1–9):

	21:11–14	22:1–9
Instruction	21:11–12	22:1–3
Announcement	21:13–14	22:4–9

The instruction is first to the royal dynasty generally, almost as if by way of review (21:11–12; Deut. 17:18–20; 1 Kings 3:28). Jeremiah walks downhill from the temple to the palace to address a specific ruler of David's line, possibly Zedekiah (22:1–3). The initial call in either case is for the king to be a guardian of justice, which may be defined as "love in action" or "honorable relations." Clearly "justice" goes beyond legal court decisions and is expressed in social concern for the oppressed and for the marginal people, those readily exploited or cheated.

The announcement in the first half (21:13–14) assumes a history of failure. God is poised to move against Jerusalem (not named, but inferred from the feminine forms; cf. 21:5). Jerusalem has valleys on three of its sides; the rocky plateau is Mount Zion. "Forests" refers to the pillars in the palace or to the palace itself, called "Palace of the Forest of Lebanon" (1 Kings 7:2).

The announced promise in the second half (22:4–9) is of good things for the royal house or dynasty and is followed by a warning.

22:10–30. The verdicts about Judah's kings may at one time have been isolated statements. Or, if Zedekiah is the king to whom 21:11–22:9 is addressed, they may have been spoken for his benefit.

Jehoahaz's failures are detailed first (22:10–12). The dead king (22:10) is Josiah, Judah's king for thirty-one years who died in battle at Megiddo in 609 BC, apparently in an attempt to halt the Egyptians. He who is exiled is Shallum, whose regal name was Jehoahaz, the fourth-oldest son of Josiah (1 Chron. 3:15). He came to the throne at age twenty-three, in 609 BC, and ruled only three months. Pharaoh Necho of Egypt declared his suzerainty over Judah by taking Jehoahaz captive, first to Riblah, north of Damascus, and then to Egypt, where he died (2 Kings 23:31–34; 2 Chron. 36:1–4).

Jeremiah's sharpest and most extended critique is directed at the despot Jehoiakim, who ruled 609–597 (22:13–23; see 2 Kings 23:34–24:6). Midway through his eleven-year reign he became a vassal of the Babylonians. Jeremiah attacks Jehoiakim's ostentation and covetousness in connection with a new palace built, as archaeologists in the 1960s have suggested, at Ramat Rachel.

A woe statement (22:13; cf. 22:18, where "woe" is translated "alas"), while common in Jeremiah (23:1; 48:1), is more frequent in Isaiah

Casemate wall remains from a royal citadel (seventh century BC) at Ramat Rachel, where Jehoiakim may have built his palace (Jer. 22:13–14)

(Isa. 5:8, 11, 18, 20–21). Unrighteousness is lack of inner integrity, and injustice is failure to be honorable in transactions. Justice was to be a ruler's first concern (21:11; 23:5; Mic. 3:1–3). Specifically, Jehoiakim cheated his workers out of pay or resorted to forced labor. Because of the heavy tribute to Egypt, he may have been unable to pay (2 Kings 23:35).

Large rooms, windows, cedar paneling—a luxury (cf. Hag. 1:4)—and red paint signal showiness. Jehoiakim was obsessed with acquiring wealth and with shedding innocent blood. "Oppression" (22:17), in its verb and noun forms, occurs more than fifty times in the Old Testament. In many contexts the term carries nuances of force or violence, and sometimes misuse of power. In more than half the occurrences, the context also specifies poverty.

Jehoiakim's insensitivity to the urgency of the times is in contrast with Josiah's overriding concern to do what was right and just. Concretely this meant acts of compassion and caring for the poor. Knowing (i.e., experiencing) God consists of such caregiving (cf. Jer. 9:23).

People will not hold Jehoiakim, who wants so much to be a "somebody," in regard, nor will they express loss at his death or care for his supposed accomplishments, his "splendor." The oracle with the catchword "Lebanon" (22:20, 23) is directed in the feminine to Jerusalem.

The accusation is that of disobedience. Shepherds are civil rulers; "allies" refers to Egypt, Assyria, Moab, and the like, who will be driven off by the wind (fulfilled in 597) (22:22).

Jehoiachin, known as (Je)Coniah, was Jehoiakim's eighteen-year-old son who succeeded him and reigned for three months in 598–597 (22:24–30; 2 Kings 24:8–12). The signet ring (22:24) was used to stamp official correspondence. The queen mother was Nehushta (22:26; cf. 2 Kings 24:8). Jeremiah's prediction was fulfilled in 597 (2 Kings 24:15). The last comment about Jehoiachin is about improved conditions in exile, where he died (Jer. 52:31–34).

"Pot" (22:28) is a term for a degraded quality of jar. The address to land is likely a call for a

witness (22:29; cf. 6:19). The threefold iteration marks intensity (cf. Isa. 6:3). Jehoiachin had seven sons (1 Chron. 3:17–19), none of whom ruled. Zerubbabel, Jehoiachin's grandson, returned to Jerusalem to become governor, not king. Since Zedekiah, Judah's last king, preceded Jehoiachin in death, Jehoiachin in effect marked the end of a 350-year Davidic dynasty.

23:1–8. The righteous branch is celebrated in 23:1–6. A general woe is spoken to all rulers, known in the ancient world as shepherds (cf. Ezekiel 34). God notes and repays officials who have misused their office. The charge "you have scattered" refers to the scattering into exile that will be the result of sins such as child sacrifice, which kings condoned and even encouraged. "Tend" (23:4) is used both for caregiving and for supervision in the sense of paying attention. Restoration to the land of those scattered will be a chief theme of the Book of Comfort (chaps. 30–33, esp. 30:3; 31:17) and Ezekiel (11:17; 20:42; and 37:21).

"Branch" is familiar language in discussion of royal family trees (Isa. 10:33–11:4) and serves as a messianic title (Isa. 4:2; Zech. 3:8; 6:12). This promise, one of the few messianic promises in Jeremiah, is echoed in 33:15–16. Justice and righteousness will be the trademark of the coming ideal king, as it was to have been of all kings. The name "the LORD Our Righteous Savior" (23:6) memorably embodies God's concern for justice. Since in Hebrew this name (*yhwh tsidqenu*) is similar to Zedekiah's (*tsidqiyahu*; "My justice is Yahweh"), some have thought that this oracle has allusions to Judah's last king. If so, then all of Judah's last kings, beginning with Josiah, would have been named (22:10–23:6). It is better, since the oracle is in the future tense, to see in it the description of the ideal king, who from our vantage point is Jesus, the Messiah.

The oracle about a glorious return from exile (23:7–8) is elaborated in chapters 30–31. The exodus from Egypt was significant in shaping a people. So will the "new" exodus of the exiles, the descendants of Israel, inaugurate a new era. The "return" took place in 538 BC and partially fulfilled the oracle, which promised more spectacular things. It has been noted that a god-sized problem was given a God-sized solution.

B. Addressing prophets and their audiences (23:9–40). The challenge to leaders continues. The address to the kings, the civil leaders (21:1–23:6), is followed by an address to the religious leaders, the prophets and priests (23:9–40). They are faulted for giving leadership in Baal worship, for personal immorality, and for being out of touch with God's message for their time. Their message either is self-originated or comes by dreams or is borrowed from others.

Jeremiah's denunciation of his peers is sad before it is harsh (23:9–10; cf. 9:1–6). Confronting persons with their evil is difficult for a caring person. However, so strong and overpowering are God's words to him that, like a drunken man, he feels himself out of control. Since elsewhere the figure of drunkenness is used for those on whom God's wrath comes (Jer. 13:13–14; 25:15–16), we perhaps should see here a man absorbing punishment intended for his colleagues.

Verse 10 depicts the results for which the prophets are held accountable. "Adulterers" may literally refer to faithless marriage partners (Jer. 5:8). Like Hosea before him (Hosea 1–3), Jeremiah uses adultery to depict the faithlessness of a people to their God. Curses follow covenant breaking. The environment (land) is affected by the people's immorality (cf. Hos. 4:1–3). Drought and famine are described in chapters 14–15.

The word "godless" begins the accusation and ends the announcement against the corrupt clergy (23:11–15). "Godless" translates a Hebrew word meaning "to pollute," "to defile," or "to profane." It means to live in opposition to all that is right. The wickedness in the temple is described elsewhere (2 Kings 16:10–14; 23:7; Ezek. 8:6–18). The prophets' fate is compared to walking in slippery places in the dark.

Two groups of prophets are identified, the second more evil than the first. Samaria was the capital of the ten northern tribes; it fell to the Assyrians a century earlier in 722. The horrible scene in Jerusalem consists of immoralities comparable to those in Sodom and Gomorrah, cities known for their thoroughgoing corruption. The charge of adultery is laid against Ahab and Zedekiah. Lying suggests that these are special "con men."

Jeremiah warns of disaster, but false prophets speak soothing platitudes of presumptuous optimism. They tell people what they want to hear. In this crisis of prophetic ministry, each side accuses the other. Bitter food and poisoned water (23:15) are both results of army invasions. Food will be in short supply; water sources could be poisoned by the enemy.

The false prophets' messages are misleading and wrong; they are self-induced and not God-originated (23:16–22). The prophets give their benediction to God-despisers (23:17). False prophets make things easy.

Prophetic ministry calls for careful listening and looking during the divine briefing session (23:18, 22). Verses 19–20 must be understood as the council's "decision": a whirlwind of wrath from God will crash on the heads of evildoers. Meanwhile, false prophets, altogether out of touch with the purposes of God's heart, predict peaceful times. When the future judgment comes, the people will understand it clearly.

Dreams are essentially (though not completely) discounted as a vehicle of divine communication (23:23–32). Fascination with dreams has become a substitute for interest in God's name. As though sifting chaff, a true prophet ought to distinguish ordinary dreams from God's firelike word, to which Jeremiah gave testimony in 20:9. God's word, like a hammer, has force; dreams are inconsequential fluff. Reaching for a message to proclaim, these prophets resort to stealing a word from fellow prophets, either their contemporaries or those of an earlier time.

God is against pseudoprophets who plagiarize, misrepresent him, and wish to be sensational. Prophets are called to expose evil. Those who fail to do so do not help God's people.

In the next passage the prophet puns on a word that can mean either "oracle," a weighty message, or "burden," something that is physically carried. The abruptness of frequent questions in 23:33–40 gives a sense of confusion, no doubt purposely, so as to characterize the religious scene.

Jeremiah alone is depicted as having the true word from the Lord. The word is that God will abandon his people. Verses 37–38 chide the people, who, it would seem, go from prophet to prophet to get new or better-sounding messages.

C. Divine anger (24:1–25:38). From concerns about kings and prophets, we move in rapid succession to the future: Judah's, Babylon's, and that of other nations. In his anger—a key theme—God consigns Judah to seventy years of desolation, Babylon to devastation, and all the nations to destruction.

24:1–10. Either in a vision or in actuality, Jeremiah sees two baskets of figs. These stand for two major population groups. The date is 597 BC. Judah now has two rulers: one exiled and one reigning. With whom does the future lie? Two baskets of figs, possibly brought to the temple as a first fruit offering (Deut. 16:9–12), evoke the Lord's answer.

In the interpretation, the future surprisingly is with the exiles, though the reason, apart from God's initiative and choice, is not given. God can plan calamity or good. The words "build," "plant," "tear down," and "uproot" (24:6) were important in Jeremiah's call (1:10). The covenant formula—"They will be my people, and I will be their God"—captures God's design for bondedness. Here spiritual restoration follows physical return to the land; elsewhere, spiritual restoration seems to precede the homecoming (cf. Jer. 31:18–22).

The survivors in the homeland feel that God's future with his people will be with them. The obvious conclusion, however, is the wrong conclusion. Some Jews may have been carried to Egypt with Jehoahaz (2 Kings 23:34); others went there later (Jer. 43:7). The siege of 597 had not completely fulfilled the prophecies for disaster, as some may have thought. Jeremiah overturns popular beliefs.

25:1–38. Chronologically, 25:1–14 precedes chapter 24. The date, when allowance is made for variant practices in counting regnal years, can be synchronized with Daniel 1:1 to be 605 BC. Soon after the battle of Carchemish in 605 BC, between the Egyptians and the Babylonians (46:2), Nebuchadnezzar succeeded Nabopolassar as king. In 609 BC Jehoiakim followed the godly Josiah to the throne. Since Josiah's rule began in 640 BC, the thirteenth year (25:3) was 627/6 BC. In much of the book Jeremiah has spoken in the first person; here (as also in 20:1–6; 21:1–10; 26:12–15) he is referred to in the third person.

The summary of the prophet's ministry is in the form of an accusation. It emphasizes the people's failure to listen, a charge made more than thirty times in the book. "Again and again" (25:4) translates an idiom about early rising ("persistently and without interruption"). A spiritual turnaround is here linked, as elsewhere, with continued occupancy in the land. Prophets reinforce the first of the Ten Commandments through their warnings (25:6, Exod. 20:3).

The announcement in 25:9–10 identifies the northerner with Nebuchadnezzar of Babylon for the first time. "My servant," also used to describe the prophets, is used here in the sense of "agent." Surrounding nations, such as Edom and Moab, like Judah were in Babylon's path to Egypt. "Completely destroy" (25:9) is a chilling term from the language of holy warfare, where it means "to destroy as in a sacrifice, leaving no survivor."

Social life (marriages), business (millstones), and home life (light) will cease. Seventy years (25:12), if intended literally, are best calculated from 605 (an early Babylonian attack) to 535 (the first return came in 538). Other uses of the number, including in Assyrian texts, suggest the number seventy to be a symbol for indefinite time (Ps. 90:10). Whether the seventy years is understood literally or symbolically, God will bring certain judgment against Babylon for its pride (cf. Jer. 50:31). The punishment fits the crime.

As in a vision, the prophet sees the cup of God's wrath (25:15–29). It contains God's fury, which is associated with sword and destruction (25:16, 27; Isa. 51:17–23; cf. Lam. 4:21; Rev. 18:6). As wine intoxicates and confuses, so will nations gag on this "wine." God's people in Judah are the first to drink. The scene of destruction and the resulting aspersions cast on Judah are presumably repeated for the other nations mentioned.

The roster of nations—nations from every point on the compass—begins with Egypt in the south and ends with Babylon to the east. These two were the superpowers of that century. "Foreign people" in Egypt and in Arabia (25:20, 24) designate smaller, usually adjacent kingdoms and allies. Uz bordered the desert east of Jordan. The Philistine city-states lay between Judah and the Mediterranean.

Edom was to the south of Judah; Moab and Ammon were to the east. Tyre and Sidon were in the north. Dedan, Tema, and Buz were in the Arabian desert. Zimri is unknown. Sheshak (25:26) is a code name for Babylon formed by substituting *b b l* (letters in the second and twelfth positions in the alphabet) with their counterparts when numbering the alphabet backward. Jeremiah, as foretold (1:10), is a prophet to the nations.

Jerusalem is the city that bears God's name. If God's people are not spared because of their sin, how will others, whose sin is presumably greater, fare?

The poem of 25:30–38, a repetition and reflection of verses 15–29, begins and ends with an angry God. The poem is charged with emotion. With vigor and vehemence God moves against Judah/Israel and all humanity.

Beyond massive deaths of the "flock," the leaders, the high and mighty ones, along with their own deaths, face the dismantling of all they have known.

D. Jeremiah versus the people (26:1–24). Numerous accusations against the kings, prophets, and people in preceding chapters are confirmed in the incidents that follow. A sermon on repentance brings a near lynching (chap. 26). A yoke with its sign message of surrender serves to unmask a false prophet (chaps. 27–28). A letter discloses sinister power plays (chap. 29). It has been argued, quite plausibly, that Baruch compiled these vignettes from Jeremiah's life.

Chapter 26 supplies details surrounding the temple sermon recorded in 7:1–15. Here (26:1–6) the focus is on the audience's response. In 609, Pharaoh Necho of Egypt, who humiliated Judah to vassal status, appointed Jehoiakim king (2 Kings 23:34–35). The public address given early in his reign, likely in 609/8, appeals for general repentance (cf. 25:4–7).

Verse 3 appeals to the principle laid out in Jeremiah 18:7–8: God does not desire the death of the wicked (Ezek. 33:11). Shiloh (26:6), north of Jerusalem in Ephraimite territory, was the central worship place during the time of the judges (1 Samuel 1–4). It was destroyed, likely by the Philistines, in the middle of the eleventh century, more than four hundred years before

Neo-Babylonian drinking cup made of clay (sixth–seventh century BC)

Jeremiah. The threat is against both the prized three-hundred-year-old temple and the cherished city of Jerusalem. For a nation that just lost its revered king, Josiah, and had been subjugated by Egypt, further disaster seemed intolerable.

Priests and prophets, whose livelihood depended on the temple, are enraged (26:7–16). Promoters of "civil religion," they fail to hear the call to repent. They interpret the threat against temple and city (both held to be divinely chosen) as blasphemy, which called for the death penalty (Lev. 24:10–16; 1 Kings 21:13). Court trials were held in the city gate area. Ostensibly Jeremiah is on trial; in reality the people are on trial.

Jeremiah answers the leaders' question; he is divinely deputized. Instead of qualifying the message, he reiterates it together with another appeal. The crowd, initially on the side of the priests and prophets, comes over to the side of the officials.

The elders invoke precedent for sparing Jeremiah (26:17–24). A century earlier, Micah, like Jeremiah, threatened destruction for both temple and city in the name of the Lord (Mic. 3:12). Hezekiah's response is recorded in 2 Kings 18:4 and 2 Chronicles 29–31. The evil his repentance forestalled was perhaps Sennacherib's advance on Jerusalem.

Baruch, the likely compiler of this section, adds verses 20–23 to indicate the risk Jeremiah takes. Elnathan, a high official, possibly Jehoiachin's father-in-law (2 Kings 24:8), will later urge restraint on behalf of Jeremiah (Jer. 36:25). Ahikam of the Shaphan family was the father of Gedaliah, governor of Judah after 586 BC (Jer. 40:5). An additional indignity for the prophet Uriah was burial as a stateless citizen, likely in the Valley of Kidron (2 Kings 23:6).

E. Submit to Babylon's yoke! (27:1–28:17). The northerner Babylon has come. Jeremiah has preached repentance (25:5). Now he "meddles" in foreign policy and urges submission to Babylon rather than resistance or revolt. This unusual counsel, given not as a politician but as a prophet, is pressed on the visiting envoys, on Zedekiah himself, and on the priests and people.

Each group is instructed to submit to Babylon; each is warned not to heed false prophets.

The sign act of carrying a wooden yoke makes the message memorable: surrender to Nebuchadnezzar (27:1–11). It comes early in Zedekiah's reign, likely 593. In 597 Nebuchadnezzar appointed Zedekiah to rule (2 Kings 24:15–20). The plot by a coalition of surrounding small states, who like Judah are in Nebuchadnezzar's grip, is to revolt. The time for revolt seems auspicious since Nebuchadnezzar is attending to some revolts nearer home. Also, Pharaoh Necho of Egypt died in 594, and his successor is engaged in wars.

Envoys are on hand in Jerusalem to persuade Zedekiah or were perhaps invited by him. Jeremiah, as a prophet to the nations (1:10), gives them the Lord's word: *submit!*

The yoke is likely an ox yoke consisting of leather straps and a carrying frame. It is one of Jeremiah's several sign acts (chaps. 13, 19, 32, 43). The accompanying message is compelling.

Ancient kings surrounded themselves with prophets and soothsayers. The latter were forbidden in Israel (Lev. 19:26; Deut. 18:10–11). Jeremiah brands as liars prophets who give their support to the planned insurrection. Jeremiah fights for a hearing both inside and outside of Judah. Everywhere he preaches his unwelcome message of disaster (and now of surrender), it is contested and contradicted.

The same message is given to the king and to the people—as the plurals of verse 12 indicate (27:12–15). False prophets, such as Hananiah, also speak in the Lord's name. To follow these prophets is to follow a lie (Hebrew *sheqer*—a much used word in Jeremiah [37×]). It is the way of kings to meet force with force; to submit is alien strategy.

The twofold refrain continues: submit to Babylon; be warned against false prophets (27:16–22). The temple, in which the priests had vested interests, is prominent. Some temple articles had been carried off by Babylon in 605 (Dan. 1:2) and again in 597 (2 Kings 24:13). Optimistically, false prophets predict these will be speedily recovered. Jeremiah announces *eventual* recovery. True prophets are marked by intercession.

The year 594–593, in which there was plotting of a revolt, must be assigned to both chapters 27 and 28, if one takes "of that same year" (28:1) seriously. Hananiah, whose name means "the Lord is gracious," hailed from Gibeon, a town five miles northwest of Jerusalem (28:1–11). He is repeatedly called "prophet" (28:1, 5, 10, 12, 15, 17). Both Jeremiah and Hananiah speak in the name of the Lord Almighty. Hananiah, however, directly contradicts Jeremiah's announcement in 27:16–22. While both predict the return of temple furnishings (27:22; 28:3), it is the time of their return that is at issue: two years (so Hananiah) or seventy years (so Jeremiah—25:12; 29:10). Hananiah also announces Jehoiachin's return. The people now hear conflicting interpretations of the yoke sign act; the onus for a decision about the true prophet is on the people.

Jeremiah proposes two tests for the accuracy of a prophecy. Former prophets, given similar societal conditions, prophesied disaster. Examples would be Amos (2:4), Hosea (4:6), and Isaiah (3:13–15). The first test then is one of consistency with tradition. A second test has to do with the fulfillment of a prediction. Hananiah meets Jeremiah's symbolic action with one of his own: he breaks the yoke. In so doing he endorses the proposed revolt against Nebuchadnezzar.

Jeremiah, who was clearly speaking for himself in verse 7, now speaks in the name of the Lord Almighty (28:12–17), branding Hananiah a liar. A pun on the word "sent" could be rendered: "I did not send you, but now I am sending you right off the face of the earth" (28:15–16). Prophetic predictions to individuals other than kings are relatively rare. The preaching of rebellion calls for the death penalty (Deut. 13:5; 18:20). Two months later there is one less false prophet.

F. A pastoral letter (29:1–32). Jeremiah's letter to the Judean captives in Babylon advises

them to adjust to the new circumstances and warns about false prophets and manipulators.

A brief explanation of the letter is given first (29:1–3). A full title for God opens the letter before Jeremiah exhorts the people to work and pray (24:4–9). God is the ultimate agent of the exile. Jeremiah counsels the people to resume work because the exile will be long and not short, as the false prophets are announcing. His advice is also intended to forestall notions the exiles might have about revolting or assisting those who do. The exiles, who live in colonies (Ezek. 3:15), seem to have considerable freedom.

To pray to God on behalf of the city (Babylon) is essentially to pray for one's enemies. Prayer can be directed to the Lord in Babylon and not only in Jerusalem, the Lord's land. Jeremiah urges intercession and good citizenship. False prophets are active in Babylon as well as in the homeland. Their announcements and dreams are in response to people's wishful thinking. And so both people and prophets are accountable for the lies.

God has good plans (29:10–14). Seventy years, counting from 605, the battle of Carchemish, would extend to 535 BC. Babylonian supremacy ended when Cyrus the Mede took Babylon in 539 BC. Jeremiah refers to restoration of the land, a promise, even if in the distance, to encourage homesick captives. God desires to bless his people, and his plans are firm (Isa. 46:10). "Prosper" (29:11) translates the Hebrew word *shalom*, a term denoting well-being, wholeness, harmony, and peace. Seeking God will be characteristic of the new "heart" (29:13; cf. 24:7). "Hope and a future" (29:11) is a Hebrew form that could be rendered "a future full of hope." Along with physical restoration to the land, there will be spiritual restoration to God.

Prophets in Babylon, of whom Ahab and Zedekiah are examples, are optimistic about the rapid return to normalcy in Jerusalem. Jeremiah insists that the problems in Jerusalem have not yet peaked (29:15–19). Jerusalem's king, Zedekiah, like the bad figs of the vision in 24:8–10, will come to grief. The reason for the disaster is that people have not listened. The exiles' failure to listen makes the good plans of verses 10–14 all the more remarkable.

The letter to the exiles continues with an exposé of the prophets Ahab and Zedekiah, of whom nothing more is known (29:20–23). They operate under false pretenses and without a mandate. Their fate, execution by burning, is foretold; otherwise, there is no record of it. In Judah the decimation of Jerusalem would prompt curses of others; a counterpart in the exile would be the curse occasioned by the two prophets. The reason for their fate is sin in both their personal life (adultery) and in their vocational life (speaking lies).

In a power maneuver calculated to diminish Jeremiah's influence, Shemaiah in Babylon by unilateral action appoints Zephaniah as priest (29:29–34). The priest was also head of the temple police (cf. Jer. 20:1). Shemaiah, more concerned about "political" points of view than temple service, instructs Zephaniah to arrest persons, madmen like Jeremiah, whose views differ from his own. For an unknown reason, Zephaniah discloses the contents of the letter

The "flow" of the material is a problem. Perhaps verse 29 is a parenthetical explanation. This would mean that Jeremiah reviewed the contents of Zephaniah's letter (29:25–29)—all the more likely if we omit, "This is what the Lord . . . says" in verse 25. Or, the rehearsal of the incident (29:24–29) is an insert, perhaps by Baruch, to help the reader make sense of Jeremiah's announcement about Shemaiah (29:31–34). Still another possibility is that verses 30–32 represent a later letter from Jeremiah, since Shemaiah in his letter refers to instructions, presumably from Jeremiah's pastoral letter.

5. The Book of Comfort (30:1–33:26)

As now arranged, the book so far has had several urgent warnings, some earnest pleas, and many dire announcements of coming disaster. By contrast, chapters 30–33 fulfill that part of Jeremiah's assignment that called for building and planting (1:10). Now come promises of return from exile, of a secure and stable society in the homeland, and of an intimate relationship once again of people with their God. The "book" proper is in poetry (30–31); the prose expansion (32–33) continues the theme of a bright prospect.

A. Coming back to the land (30:1–24). Generally the address is to "Israel"; other names for these people are Jacob, Rachel, and Ephraim. The specific word to Judah is short (31:23–24, 38–40). The theme of the book is the future (30:1–3).

Cries of fear indicate a people in great trouble (30:4–11). The setting could be the Assyrian capture of Samaria in 722, the Babylonian invasion of Jerusalem in 587, or any calamity, past or future. Childbirth is a frequent illustration in Jeremiah of great distress, anxiety, and pain (4:31; 6:24; 13:21; 49:24). Verses 4–7 are the backdrop against which the following promises of comfort must be seen.

The reference to breaking the yoke in 30:8 recalls Jeremiah's sign act. Two nations that held Israel captive were Assyria and Babylon. "David their king" (30:9) can hardly refer to the

God promises to "break the yoke off their necks" and free his people from bondage (Jer. 30:8). Such bonds are depicted on a section of bronze band from the Balawat gates (859–824 BC), showing prisoners yoked at the neck.

tenth-century monarch, but refers rather to one of his descendants, or as the ancient Aramaic Targum paraphrases, the Messiah. "Do not be afraid" is salvation language (30:10). "Save," with its sense of release from confinement, is an apt term to describe being freed from exile. "I am with you" is the divine-assistance formula (30:11).

Using the metaphor of injury and healing, the oracle of 30:12–17a sets the tone for the specific announcements that will follow. The "wound" (30:12; literally "brokenness") is figurative for the calamity, namely, the takeover of the country by a foreign power and the removal of its population into exile. It is beyond healing in the sense that the pain of punishment for sin must be endured.

The God who has afflicted is the God who will heal. God will deal decisively with the agents of punishment. The reasons for God's dealing with them are not given here but elsewhere (see Jeremiah 46–51).

"Because you are called an outcast" (30:17b) introduces a new oracle and a new theme: rebuilding a ruined city and living in it to the full (30:17b–24). The sorry plight is depicted before the promise of reversal is given. The nations' disparaging statements about God's people move God to action. "I will restore the fortunes" is now applied to buildings and to society. Laughter replaces terror and agony. Honor replaces reproach. A leader from within replaces a foreign (or, like Zedekiah, a foreign-appointed) overlord.

Verses 23–24 are to be understood as a guarantee by oath of good times ahead. Good times are possible if the enemies are removed. The verses repeat 23:19–20, where they are the conclusion of the heavenly council. What seems too good to be true will really happen.

B. Coming back to God (31:1–40). This chapter is striking for its news and its exuberance. The recovery of the land (chap. 30) is followed by the recovery of a relationship with God (chap. 31). God is pictured successively as father, shepherd, mother, and covenant maker.

The announcement of the coming restoration is given first to the exiles (31:1–9), then to the nations (31:10–14), then to Israel (31:15–22).

The covenant formula (31:1) is the basis for the great trek (31:7–9). A reference to distress prepares for promise. The refugees from both the Assyrian invasion of Israel in 722 BC and the Babylonian invasion of 586 BC survive. Only here in Jeremiah is God the subject of love.

"Again," used three times and in Hebrew each time in first position, anticipates the reconstruction process, the return of joyful times, uninterrupted economic pursuits, and vigorous religious activity. Jeremiah prays for those left alive and dispersed in various places. If people from Ephraim (a name for the northern kingdom) come to Zion (Jerusalem), it will mean a united Israel in worship.

The "land of the north" (31:8) likely refers to the Habor River region, to which the Assyrians took the northern kingdom captive. The weeping in the new exodus may be tears of reform from sin, tears of joy for deliverance, or both. God, the Father, is the initiator of the trek and its protector.

Nations, even distant islands, hear the message of Israel's regathering, of her return, and of her abundance (31:10–14). Such a message would reverse the slurring byword spoken by them about Israel's destroyed cities.

Laments, in one sense, stir God to action. The hope-filled future of 29:11 is now elaborated as Jeremiah describes the return of the prodigal (31:15–22).

"Ephraim" (31:18) here designates the ten northern tribes. The pun on "turn," translated "restore," "return," "stray," intermingles turning to (or away from) God and (re)turning to the land. Israel's repentance is like that earlier prescribed. "Beating the breast" (literally "thighs") was a gesture of great feeling, especially of remorse.

God's response is motherlike. The word for "compassion" (31:20) is a derivative from the term for "womb." God reprimands and rebukes Israel for her sins. Still, the two, God and Ephraim, have found each other and have been reconciled.

Verses 21–22 round off a promise introduced in verses 3–6. Verse 22 has evoked much discussion. The "new thing" is puzzling. Some interpretations put forward are (1) a role reversal such that women, rather than men, become aggressive; (2) in the poem two women—Rachel and Virgin Israel—"encompass" (NKJV, NASB) the man Ephraim; (3) a messianic promise in which a woman (Mary) "encompasses" the God-man, Jesus (so Jerome in the fourth century); (4) a proverb whose meaning is lost to us but which may describe a topsy-turvy situation; and (5) formerly God encompassed Israel; now Israel will embrace God—certainly a new thing. The last interpretation is preferred; it anticipates the new covenant of verse 31.

Jeremiah 31:23–26 focuses on Judah, the southern kingdom, in contrast to Israel, the northern kingdom. "O righteous dwelling" (31:23 NIV 1984) refers to the temple on Mount Zion, God's dwelling. A restored people will be a worshiping people. Farmers, settled on their land, often clashed with roaming shepherds who disregarded property rights. These will now coexist peacefully. The unexpected reference to sleep in 31:26 may mean: "This is all too good to be true."

The concluding section is in three parts, each beginning with "days are coming" (31:27–30, 31–37, 38–40). God promises to plant or repopulate the territories that have been decimated. God watched over Jeremiah's first assignment announcing destruction; he will watch over the second one announcing recovery. The proverb about grapes and blunt teeth restates (and exaggerates) Exodus 20:5 and Numbers 14:18. Complaints that the children's miseries (the exile) were the result of the fathers' sins (Manasseh) will cease. People are individually accountable.

In the justly famous salvation oracle of 31:31–37, an unprecedented announcement takes shape. A covenant, differing from a contract, is an arrangement of bonding between persons. The old covenant from Sinai (Exod. 19:5–6) was broken and is no longer operative. A fresh arrangement, not a covenant renewal, is put into effect. It is God's prerogative and his initiative (cf. repetitions: "I will . . ." and "declares the LORD").

In Jeremiah's analysis, the heart is deceitful and stubborn (3:17; 7:24; 9:14; 11:8; 17:1, 9). God's law or teaching in the heart is the equivalent of a new heart. The objective of the Sinai covenant, "I will be their God, and they will be my people," remains. Ancient nations associated their gods with territories. The binding of a deity to a people is unique in world religions.

"Knowing God" is more explicitly "experiencing God." The new covenant marks the end of the teaching profession. The new covenant passage, the longest Scripture quoted in the New Testament (Heb. 8:7–12), is said to be fulfilled in Christ. Quite possibly, judging from verse 33, originally only Israel was in view. Later, Judah was included (31:31). The New Testament promise includes the Gentiles.

Just as the first half of the poetic Book of Comfort ends with an oathlike statement (30:23–24), so also here (31:35–37). The creation is an expression of the "Lord of Hosts" (NIV "LORD Almighty," 31:35). The decrees in 31:36 are the laws that govern the natural elements of the universe. Israel's continuous existence as a people is guaranteed by the natural ordering of the universe.

The repeated announcement of a return of the exiles to the homeland and the rebuilding of a city climax in the specifics of 31:38–40. The place-names specify the extent of the rebuilt and enlarged Jerusalem. More important than the boundaries is the fact that the city will be for the Lord, holy and permanent.

C. A property purchase (32:1–44). The prophet's purchase of a field becomes a sign. After the fiery destruction of Jerusalem, people will eventually return to the city. Normal commerce will resume.

The purchase takes the form of a sign act (32:1–15; cf. 13:1–14; 19:1–13; 27:1–7). The instruction is brief; so is the initial interpretation. Most attention is given to the report of compliance. A man who through poverty or debt was about to forfeit his land was to solicit a next of kin to buy it (Lev. 25:25–28; cf. Ruth 4:7).

The business transaction is given in detail—one of the fullest records we have on such matters. Scales were used to weigh bars or rings of silver. Seventeen shekels of silver equaled seven ounces. The two copies of the transaction, either transcribed on clay tablets, as is known from Mesopotamia, or on papyrus, as is known from Egypt, would be identical. The unsealed copy would be accessible. The sealed copy would be opened only if the unsealed copy were tampered with or lost. The accompanying divine message (32:15) confirms the announcements of hope found elsewhere in the book, some of which undoubtedly preceded this sign act.

An Old Babylonian contract for the purchase of a house, which was paid for in silver rings (ca. 1812–1793 BC)

Apparently the purchase happens quickly and certainly without the prophet's forethought. Jeremiah is perplexed about his own action (32:16–25). Given the state of siege and his own prediction that Babylon will capture Jerusalem, his investment seems foolish. His prayer extols God as Creator. Recalling God's power in creation brings fresh perspective in prayer. The name "Lord of Hosts" (NIV "Lord Almighty," 32:18) refers to God's rule of both celestial bodies and military armies. The name, therefore, is a bridge between God's work in creation and in history.

In reply, the Lord first addresses the immediate circumstance of the invasion and then elaborates on the sign act of the purchase (32:26–35). "Is anything too hard for me?" (32:27) puts into question form Jeremiah's opening assertion (32:17). Judah's sins—the list is familiar—are said to have provoked God's anger.

Judgment, however, is not the last word (32:36–44). The regathering of a dispersed people and their return to the homeland are familiar themes, especially in the Book of Comfort. The everlasting covenant is called the "new covenant" in 31:31–34, where themes of a covenant people and a new heart are taken up.

God's beneficent intentions are not in doubt. Bustling commercial activity will characterize Benjamin, which is adjacent to Judah in the north, the hill country farther north, and cities in the Negev, such as Beersheba.

D. Things great and unsearchable (33:1–26). Positive announcements about a glorious future for city and people tumble over one another in this passage. Divine pardon, energetic praise songs, enterprising shepherds, established royal and priestly lines, and a united and permanent people—all are part of the kaleidoscope of future assurance. In content the chapter duplicates and slightly expands chapters 30–31.

The promise of restoration extends to both city and country (33:1–13). When judgment has been completed, wholeness will be God's gift. God's general stance of goodwill contrasts with the wrath that precipitated the destruction.

Both Judah and Israel are in view. God mercifully forgives sin and iniquities. The city of Jerusalem and God's people generally are intended as a prime exhibit of his goodness, which should prompt repentance. Celebrations will mark the future, in stark contrast to earlier mourning. The empty land will be populated. "Will again pass . . . who counts them" (33:13) refers to the shepherd's taking nightly inventory of the flock. Life will be back to its routine.

The city's safety is not separate from a spiritual realignment. "Just" describes observable behavior that is correct before God; "right" describes inner integrity. The promise to David (2 Sam. 7:13) is guaranteed by the fixed appointment of day and night. The covenant with the Levites (Num. 25:12–13; Mal. 2:5) is similarly guaranteed. The Davidic and Abrahamic covenants (2 Sam. 7:8–16; Gen. 15:1–21; 17:1–27) are the background for verse 26.

The popular opinion that "it is all over" would be understandable, even if inaccurate, following the demise of Israel in 721 BC and Judah in 586 BC. The strong guarantees (33:25–26) essentially repeat 31:36–38, except that the continuation of the Davidic monarch is of paramount concern.

6. Case Studies in the Failure of Leadership (34:1–39:18)

Incidents from the reigns of two kings, Jehoiakim and Zedekiah, are told in chapters 34–39. The actors include Jeremiah, princes, and the Rekabite family. The stories, not chronological, are prelude to the fall of Jerusalem (chap. 39). "Fire" and "burning" are key words. The stories are a forceful commentary on ungodly leadership and on spiritual rebellion. Here is the account of the total rejection of the word of God, whether received via a scroll or from a prophet. Both ungodly leadership and spiritual rebellion are reasons for the burning destruction of chapter 39.

A. Going back on one's word (34:1–21). Chapters 34 and 35, when taken together, display a similar pattern:

Prophetic revelation formula	34:8a	35:1
Report of incident	34:8b–11	35:2–11
Prophetic revelation formula	34:12a	35:12–13a
Retelling of incident	34:12b–16	35:13b–16
General announcement	34:17–20	35:17
Particularized announcement	34:21–22	35:18–19

While the issues in the two stories are very different—national policy in the one case and diet in the other—the main idea in both is integrity in covenant keeping. The fickle King Zedekiah contrasts with the tenacious Rekabites. In both, Jeremiah complains, "You have not obeyed" (34:17; 35:16).

Jeremiah's message deals with Zedekiah's personal safety (34:1–7; cf. 21:1–10). "Burn it down" and "burned" are prominent terms in chapters 34–38, anticipating the burning of Jerusalem. Zedekiah's gruesome fate (34:3; cf. 2 Kings 25:7) stops short of a violent death. A funeral fire, perhaps the burning of spices, indicates the citizenry's goodwill. The promise of verse 4 is conditional on Zedekiah's surrender to Babylon.

Persons in poverty or in a crisis of debt made themselves available as slaves. Mosaic law called for the release of slaves every seventh year (Exod. 21:1–11). The seriousness of siege apparently brings compliance with God's law, perhaps to secure God's favor, and the people of Jerusalem free their slaves. Freed slaves would defend the city better; owners need not be responsible for their provisions. When the siege slackens in the summer of 588 BC because the Babylonians leave to fend off the Egyptians, the king and others promptly go back on their word.

The incident inspires a sermon. Covenant making must be taken seriously. The rescinding of covenant is ultimately an offense against God, for it disregards God's stipulations. To profane or desecrate is to make commonplace, to rob something of its special character, to render something holy unholy. What if God in his covenant making waffled, as did Zedekiah?

A paraphrase of the pun on freedom could read: "Since you have not freed up the slaves, I [God] am freeing you up for the sword, pestilence, and famine—and for anyone who wants you." An accompanying ritual in covenant making included a "walk" between the two halves of a slain animal (34:18–19; Gen. 15:9–17). The practice is known from non-Israelite writings. This ritual symbolized that covenant violators would be subject to the fate of the slain calf. The announced disaster is a consequence of Zedekiah's violation. He will not be exempt, even though, for the moment, he has reason for optimism. God will "turn" the Babylonians around; they will be back.

B. Obedience (35:1–19). In nonhistorical sequence, but as a contrast to chapter 34, the story of the Rekabites focuses on uncompromising obedience.

The account (35:1–11) is from the year 601 (see 35:11). The Rekabites are from the clan of the Kenites, a people who associated themselves with Israel (1 Chron. 2:55). The Rekabites were a conservative, if not reactionary, group. No evaluation of the rightness or wrongness of their views is given, but their tenacity for obedience is applauded. Theirs is the prospect of a perpetual ministry.

Jeremiah's commentary on the incident (35:12–19) contrasts the absolute and unquestioning obedience of the Rekabites to their ancestor with Judah's disobedience to the Lord Yahweh. The people's refusal to learn a "lesson" (Hebrew "discipline" or "correction," 35:13) is a repeated accusation (2:30; 5:3; 7:28; 17:23). An example of this refusal occurs in 7:1–15. Themes about disobedience (34:17; 35:17b) and disaster (34:18–22; 35:17a) alternate in this and the preceding chapter.

C. The burning of a scroll (36:1–32). Like Zedekiah (chap. 34), Jehoiakim scorns the

law of God. Incidentally, chapter 36 provides a glimpse into how books of the Old Testament came to be.

God commands Jeremiah to write on a scroll (36:1–7). His restriction (36:5) may have resulted from his controversial temple sermon (7:1–15) or his "lecture" to the elders (19:1–20:6). Jeremiah had censured Jehoiakim for his extravagance and extortion in building a palace (22:13–23). Since the scroll was read three times in one day it may not have been that extensive. The purpose of the reading, despite the accusations and warnings, is to bring the people to a spiritual turnaround.

The scroll is read three times: at the temple to the people, in the secretaries' room to the scribes, and at the royal winter apartment to the king and his officials (36:8–26). The reverence with which the scribes treat the message shows that some spiritual sensitivity remains in Judah (36:11–18). It also indicates the credibility of Jeremiah. The officials, however, show contempt. The hiding of Jeremiah and Baruch is well advised in view of 26:20–23. To tear their clothes (36:24) would be a sign of self-humiliation. The report seems deliberately to contrast Jehoiakim with his father, Josiah (cf. 2 Kings 22:11–20).

Severe judgment comes on Jehoiakim, who rejects a word intended to spare him. As Jehoiakim tried to blot out God's word, so his own house will be blotted out. His punishment—to have no descendants on the throne—contrasts with God's promise to David (2 Sam. 7:12–16). Jehoiakim's son, Jehoiachin, who ruled for three months, ends the family rule.

D. Troubling a prophet (37:1–38:28). Chapter 36 reports on efforts to do away with the word of God by burning it. These two chapters tell of attempts to do away with the prophet. Arrested without cause, Jeremiah is held in a dungeon, put in a prison, and then thrown into a miry hole to die. Even so, he is sought out by King Zedekiah, whose city is now under siege, for some favorable word.

The pattern of organization in chapters 37–38 parallels that of chapter 36.

Introduction	36:1–4	37:1–2
Story in three movements: three readings, three interviews	36:5–26	37:3–38:13
Message to the king	36:27–31	38:14–23
Destiny (scroll, prophet)	36:32	38:24–28

A key word throughout is "burn"; the word's use in conjunction with Jehoiakim (36:25, 27–29, 32) corresponds to its use in conjunction with Nebuchadnezzar (37:8, 10; 38:17, 18, 23). The first is an internal threat; the second is an external threat. The officials, still somewhat conciliatory in chapter 36, are single-minded toward evil in chapters 37–38. Attempts to destroy the written word (chap. 36) and the speaker of that word (chaps. 37–38) suggest that the rejection of God's message is total. So judgment follows (chap. 39). Still God, who announced judgment already in Jehoiakim's reign (chap. 36), waits for more than a decade before bringing it.

A lull in the two-year Babylonian siege of Jerusalem prompts Zedekiah to inquire of Jeremiah (37:1–10). An example of his failure to pay attention to the words of the Lord (37:1) is Zedekiah's reenslavement of freed slaves (chap. 34). Intercession is understood to belong to the prophet's ministry. Prayer could ensure the Babylonians' permanent departure. Jeremiah's message is simple: the Babylonians will be back!

Jeremiah's message to surrender to Babylon (27:12) causes suspicion about his patriotism. The charge in the arrest is that Jeremiah is defecting to the enemy (37:13). Others have already defected (38:19; 52:15).

From a vaulted cell in a dungeon at Jonathan's house, Jeremiah is summoned personally by Zedekiah for a message from the Lord.

Thanks to Zedekiah's generosity and Jeremiah's bold request, Jeremiah, though still confined, is given improved conditions. With his limited wartime ration of bread, Jeremiah suffers the effects of siege along with the others.

Severe famine contributes to the city's final collapse (2 Kings 25:3).

Jeremiah's pacifist position enrages the officials (38:1–13). Their information may have come from Pashhur, a member of an earlier delegation (Jer. 21:1–10), or Jehukal (37:3–9), or through personal contact. Religious leaders earlier demanded a death sentence for Jeremiah (26:1–15). The officials are wrong in holding that Jeremiah is not seeking the good of the people. Zedekiah, like Pilate centuries later (Matt. 27:24–26), hands the prophet over to his accusers. Dissension among leaders bodes ill for any country's future.

By disposing of Jeremiah in a cistern, the officials seek his death without physically laying hands on him. It is a foreigner, Ebed-Melek, from the land of Cush, south of Egypt, who pleads for Jeremiah to be spared. The care with which Jeremiah is taken from the dungeon suggests that he is severely emaciated. Ebed-Melek, whose name means "servant of the king," is rewarded for his trust in the Lord; his life is spared when calamity strikes (39:15–18).

Zedekiah makes a second and last attempt at an interview with Jeremiah (38:14–27). Some see this as another version of the earlier visit (37:17–21), but divergent details (two different dungeons; two different precipitating occasions) argue for two accounts. The place is in the temple, where state officials would have little reason to go.

Jeremiah paints the consequences of a refusal to surrender (38:21–22). Palace women will become the property of a conqueror. The city will be burned down. The king, habitually indecisive, is isolated. Jeremiah is under no obligation to disclose full information.

E. The fall of Jerusalem (39:1–18). From a narrative point of view this chapter is the climax of the book. Repeated threats have now been fulfilled. Chapters 34–38 provide the reasons for the catastrophe; chapters 40–44 tell of the sequel.

The siege begins in January 588, lasts some eighteen months, and ends in July 587.

Zedekiah breaks faith and rebels against the Babylonians. They respond with an invasion (2 Kings 25:1–12 = Jer. 52:4–16). Babylonian officials are named, as are Judah's officials (38:1).

The king's fate accords with Jeremiah's announcements. The city is burned, as Jeremiah so often predicted, and its citizenry is exiled, also as foretold. The poorer class remains.

Jewish defectors or his own intelligence sources inform Nebuchadnezzar about Jeremiah. Gedaliah will shortly be appointed governor (40:7). For his deed of kindness to Jeremiah, Ebed-Melek escapes with his life. The Lord honors those who trust in him.

7. After the Catastrophe (40:1–45:5)

The capture of Jerusalem touches off a sordid set of events. The assassination of Gedaliah leads to strife, insecurity, and fear of Nebuchadnezzar's reprisal. Consequently some trek off to Egypt, against Jeremiah's advice. There the familiar godless lifestyle persists; more judgment speeches follow.

A. Trouble from within (40:1–41:18). A fresh beginning quickly turns sour with Ishmael's struggle for power over Gedaliah.

This relief from an Assyrian palace at Nineveh shows a family being taken into exile after the capture of the city of Lachish (700–692 BC). The families of Jerusalem underwent a similar fate (Jer. 39:9).

Ramah, five miles north of Jerusalem, is the dispatching point for exiles. Apparently in the confusion Jeremiah has been arrested again after being sent to Gedaliah's house (39:14). However, some hold that we have here a more detailed account of the story given in 39:11–14. The witness of the commander of the guard to God's action (40:2–4) seems unusual (but cf. Gen. 41:38; Matt. 27:54). Jeremiah chooses to stay with Gedaliah (40:1–6)—a patriotic gesture—even though he knows the future is with the exiles (Jer. 24:4–7).

Gedaliah, of the family of Shaphan the scribe (2 Kings 22:3–14), is appointed governor (40:7–12). He is cordial to Jeremiah; his policy of submission to the Babylonians echoes that of the prophet. Mizpah, headquarters for the new governor, is only a short distance from Ramah, the Babylonian command post. Officers with their men in the open country, guerrilla-like, have fought against Babylon. Likely they wished to know whether Gedaliah would be a "nationalist" or a Babylonian puppet. Gedaliah, in urging them to help in the harvest, is essentially calling for a return to normalcy.

Terrorist tactics are detailed in 40:13–41:10. Johanan, one of the guerrillas, emerges as spokesperson for the restless remnant. We can only guess at Baalis's motives (40:14). Did he wish for a leader in Judah sympathetic to a policy of

retaliation against the Babylonians? Did he wish to forestall any consolidation of survivors? Did he have personal ambitions? Johanan's counterplan points to the way of violence that prevailed after the loss of legitimate government. If the story beginning with 39:1 is continuous, then Gedaliah, assassinated by his own countrymen, governed less than five months.

The eighty men (41:5) come from three cities that were former worship centers. Shaved beards, torn clothes, and gashes indicate penitence and mourning. They are headed to the temple in Jerusalem, which, even if destroyed, is considered holy. They may have come to mourn its destruction.

Johanan leads a band that intercepts Ishmael at Gibeon, three miles south of Mizpah (41:11–18). The Ammonites, east of the Jordan, earlier were allies with Judah against Babylon. The murder of the Babylonian-appointed governor, along with the Babylonian soldiers, would be interpreted as insubordination. Babylon could be expected to bring quick reprisals. The motley group, having decided to head for Egypt, stops near Bethlehem. From there Johanan contacts Jeremiah for advice.

B. Trouble in Egypt (42:1–43:13). A remnant group goes off to Egypt, contrary to Jeremiah's advice. There, Jeremiah, who has gone with them, rebukes them for idolatry.

Johanan, active in rescuing his countrymen from Ishmael the assassin, has brought them on their way to Egypt as far as Bethlehem. Egypt, Judah's ally against the Babylonians, is not beset by the instability that plagues the Jews. Unsure of their next move, they seek guidance from the Lord through Jeremiah, as had Zedekiah's delegation earlier (42:1–6; 37:3).

Divine answers to prayer do not come on demand. God's word to the inquirers is to stay in the land and not go to Egypt (42:7–22). God's message allays the group's fear of the Babylonians' indiscriminate reprisal for Gedaliah's murder (41:1–3). Part of the message is the divine-assistance formula, "I am with you" (42:11).

Any decision to go to Egypt must calculate the consequences: death from a variety of causes—sword, famine, and plague (42:16–17). Verses 19–22 add Jeremiah's personal plea to the remnant not to proceed with their plans. The fatal mistake is not the request for guidance but their double-talk (literally "deceive yourselves"), whereby they promise to do what in their hearts they do not intend to do.

Jeremiah has accused others of lying (9:3–6); now the same charge is thrown into his face. Johanan and company go back on their word, as did Zedekiah earlier (chap. 34). They decide to go to Egypt (43:1–7).

The "remnant" (43:5) refers to those in Edom, Moab, Ammon, and other nearby countries who returned when they heard Gedaliah was appointed governor. Tahpanhes was an Egyptian fortress city in the eastern delta region of the Nile and thus the first Egyptian city they would reach.

At the Lord's command, Jeremiah engages in another sign act (43:8–13; cf. chaps. 13, 19, 32). The image of the shepherd's cloak suggests the speed with which Nebuchadnezzar will carry off the Egyptians' wealth. The word "wrap," as has been plausibly suggested, can mean "delouse." Nebuchadnezzar will systematically exterminate the Egyptians as so many pests. To what extent this prediction was fulfilled is not clear, since records are fragmentary. One text fragment now in the British Museum tells of an attack by Nebuchadnezzar against Pharaoh Amasis (Ahmoses II) in 568–567.

C. Failure to learn from history (44:1–45:5). Jeremiah's warnings against apostasy and his messages of doom continue in Egypt. The reason is that those emigrating from Judah to Egypt reinstate idolatrous worship. They have failed to learn from history.

Another catastrophe is in the offing (44:1–14). Some Jews who left Judah after Nebuchadnezzar's capture of Jerusalem settled in Egypt. Their religion is anything but a pure Yahweh religion. Burning incense and worshiping other gods are violations of the first commandment. God's fierce anger is unleashed only after his repeated calls for repentance have been spurned.

By adopting the gods of Egypt, the remnant Jews jeopardize their own welfare and that of future descendants. The accusation part of the judgment speech focuses first on sins committed (44:8–9) and then on things left undone: self-humiliation, reverence for God, and obedience to the law (44:10). The announcement is that only a few refugees will eventually return to the homeland. Most of the Jews who later resettle in the land are from Babylon, not Egypt.

"We will not listen" (44:15–19) characterizes the people's response; it was also the decision of the Jerusalemites earlier (6:17). The remnant's reading of history is that things used to be better, presumably during Manasseh's reign (before Josiah's), when the Mother Goddess was revered. The action of the families is united and deliberate. It is widespread and in defiance of the prophet's warnings.

Jeremiah offers a different interpretation of past history than that given by the remnant (44:20–30). It is their sin that has brought disaster. "Go ahead then" is said in irony. This is Jeremiah's last recorded speech, which is in keeping with his initial call.

The sign (44:29) that the threatened doom is indeed God's work is that Pharaoh Hophra will be handed over to the enemies, as was Zedekiah.

The year of the message to Baruch (605/4 BC) was also the year that Jeremiah reviewed his preaching (25:1–11) and prepared the scroll (chap. 36). If Baruch is the author of chapters 34–45, then he closes this section with a modest but frank note about himself.

Baruch's situation—one of sorrow, groaning, and pain—is reminiscent of Jeremiah's laments. The sorrow may be the consistent message of doom, or perhaps Jehoiakim's rejection of the word (chap. 36), or even Jeremiah's own endangered life (36:19). Even this personal oracle reaffirms God's decision to bring judgment.

8. Oracles about the Nations (46:1–51:64)

God, who has been named throughout as the "Lord of Hosts" (NIV "Lord Almighty"), will judge the nations. Egypt and Babylon were the two superpowers of that time. The other nations are for the most part geographically near to Israel. With these oracles Jeremiah fulfills in part his call to be a prophet to the nations.

A. Egypt (46:1–28). Both Egypt and Babylon were ancient empires, and both vied for the control of Palestine, Ammon, Moab, and other territories that lay between them.

Necho ruled in Egypt from 610 to 595. Carchemish, on the Euphrates, was on the east-west trade routes sixty miles west of Harran. Nebuchadnezzar's victory at Carchemish in 605 gave him access to the countries by the Mediterranean, including Judah. The long domination of Egypt over Syria-Palestine had ended.

In sarcasm Jeremiah calls on Egypt's military to prepare for battle (46:1–12). But at once he sees the Egyptians retreating. "Terror on every side" (46:5) may be a call to retreat when all is in confusion.

Verses 7–10 depict Egyptian ambitions, which crest like the surging Nile River. Verse 9 may describe a commander, or even the prophet himself, urging the troops on to make their dreams come true. Mercenary soldiers would have been recruited from Cush, Put, and Lydia, regions in Africa. "That day" (46:10) is the day of the Lord. God will unveil his power and demonstrate his complete control by dealing decisively and in vengeance with his foes. He will sacrifice them.

The setting is the Babylonian attack on the Egyptian home front (46:13–26). One such attack occurred in 601 BC, another in 568–567 BC. Mercenary soldiers, when overpowered, would consider escape to their home country. Pharaoh's "missed opportunity" (46:17) could be the chance to take advantage militarily of Nebuchadnezzar's return to Babylon after Carchemish.

The "one [who] will come" (46:18), the destroyer, is an oblique reference to Nebuchadnezzar, who is a towering figure. Mount Tabor in north-central Palestine rises 2,000 feet above the plain. The gadfly is Babylon (46:20). The mercenaries, who are her hope, will buckle under pressure. Those more numerous than the locusts (46:23) are the Babylonians.

The prose piece (46:25–26) is about Upper Egypt. The clash is basically with the sun god Amon, patron deity of Thebes. Thebes, the capital of Upper Egypt, was known for its large temple. The reasons for the disaster are not given, nor is a reason given for Egypt's promising future.

The salvation oracle of 46:27–28 is a repeat of 30:10–11. It underscores that the defeat of Egypt will mean salvation for Israel. For most of history Israel regarded Egypt as an enemy, though there were times when Egypt was Israel's ally.

B. Philistia (47:1–7). This oracle describes the agony of coastal cities—from Sidon in the north to Gaza in the south—ruthlessly attacked by a strong power, the foe from the north, Babylon. The Philistines occupied a strip of territory along the southern Mediterranean coast.

C. Moab (48:1–47). The Moabites, descendants of Lot (Gen. 19:37), were unfriendly to Israel at the time of the exodus (Numbers 22–24). In 601–600 BC Nebuchadnezzar sent Moabite groups to deal with Jehoiakim's revolt (2 Kings 24:2).

The language describing Moab's woes is pithy, picturesque, and liberally sprinkled with place-names. Cities will be destroyed; anguished cries will be heard everywhere. Refugees will seek escape, while Moab's god Chemosh stands by helplessly. Our knowledge of Moab's history is scant. Apparently, the Babylonians attacked both Moab and Ammon in 598 BC and, if Josephus is right, again in 582 BC.

A destroyer will ruthlessly invade the land (48:1–10), and Moab will be broken. The destroyer (48:8)—an unnamed enemy but presumably Nebuchadnezzar—is urged not to slacken in the massacre.

Moab was known for her vineyards. Wine on its dregs, if left too long, loses its flavor. So Moab, whose dependence for too long has been on Chemosh, has not been "poured out," but her exile will now improve her flavor (48:11–25). Embarrassment over the inadequacy of her god compares with Israel's embarrassment over the god Bethel, which was worshiped in Syria and, according to the records, also by the Jews in the Elephantine colony in Egypt. Yahweh, the Lord of Hosts, stands over Chemosh, Bethel, and all other gods.

It is the cup of the Lord's wrath that makes Moab drunk (48:26–39; cf. 25:15–21). The reasons for her destruction emerge: (1) she defied the Lord; (2) she ridiculed Israel; (3) she is extraordinarily proud. Much of the language in 48:28–32 is also found in Isaiah 16:6–12.

Verse 32 is best rendered, "I will weep for you more than I wept for Jazer" (NEB). Jazer, ten miles north of Heshbon, was in Ammonite territory but then was conquered by King Mesha of Moab. Some suggest that it was the center of the Tammuz cult, a feature of which was weeping for the dead. Visually, the shaved head and beard and the gash marks tell the story of woe (48.37).

Moab's precarious position compares to a creature about to be the victim of an eagle's swoop (48:40–47). So overpowering is the enemy that warriors will seem weak. Those trying to escape will be caught one way or another.

D. Ammon (49:1–6). Ammon lies in central Transjordan, opposite Shechem. The area was taken over by Israel after the exodus (Josh. 10:6–12:6; Num. 32:33–37) and assigned to Gad (Josh. 13:24–28). The region was lost to Israel when the Assyrian Tiglath-Pileser made war against Israel (1 Chron. 5:26). The Ammonites repossessed the region. Baalis, king of the Ammonites, was involved with Ishmael in the assassination of Gedaliah (40:14–41:10).

Molek (or Milkom) was the chief god of the Ammonites. At times Israel worshiped Molek and sacrificed children to him. In his name the Ammonites undertook their conquests.

God will bring the Ammonites terror because of their aggressive conquests and because of their trust in their wealth. The funeral lament, or dirge (49:3), underscores the extent of the destruction. Nebuchadnezzar destroyed Ammon in 582.

E. Edom (49:7–22). Edom, also known as Mount Seir, lies between the Dead Sea and the Gulf of Aqabah. It was inhabited by the descendants of Jacob's brother Esau (Gen. 36:1–17). Edom took advantage of Judah's plight in 586 and occupied southern Judah.

The cup (49:12) refers to the cup of wrath, which is also passed to Edom (25:17–28).

Edom, like Moab, is characterized by pride (49:16; 48:29). The root word for pride means "high." The concept is carried forward by the "heights of the hill" and the "nest as high as the eagle's." God will choose his agent to devastate Edom.

Verse 20, with its reference to the Lord's plans and counsel, returns to the theme of wisdom in verse 7. The language about a swooping eagle—likely Nebuchadnezzar—is traditional for depicting the speed and power of an attack. Other images to reinforce the theme of destruction are Sodom and Gomorrah (49:18; cf. Gen. 19:24–25) and the lion from Jordan's thickets (49:19).

F. Damascus (49:23–27). Damascus, north of Palestine on the Orontes River, was the capital of the Aramean state. The Babylonian king commissioned the Aramean state to deal with Jehoiakim's revolt (2 Kings 24:2–4).

Hamath and Arpad, each about one hundred miles north of Damascus, were two city-states allied with Damascus. Both lost their independence when they were overpowered by the Assyrians between 740 and 732. The acute distress, a result of the enemy attack, is the main theme of the oracle. Behind the combat stands God.

G. Kedar and Hazor (49:28–33). The Kedar were a nomadic tribal people in the Syrian-Arabian desert. Hazor is not the well-known town in Galilee but was another Arab tribe living in the eastern desert.

The war poem contains two summonses to attack (49:28, 31), each followed by a list of the plunder (49:29, 32) and the scattering of the fugitives (49:30, 32).

H. Elam (49:34–39). Elam, distant from Palestine, is east of Babylon and northeast of the Persian Gulf. After the overthrow of Babylon, in which Elam assisted, Elam was in turn absorbed by the Persian Empire. Its connections with Judah are unclear. Were there Elamite soldiers in the Babylonian forces? Was there a hope that rulers east of Babylon would break Babylon's grip and so shorten the captivity of the exiles? If so, this oracle squelches those dreams.

Bas-reliefs from Nineveh show the Elamites as bowmen. Their skill as archers was proverbial. The announcement to Elam is more general than to Hazor. Dispersion first, then annihilation is threatened against the Elamites. Along with Moab and Ammon, Elam will have its fortunes restored.

I. Babylon (50:1–51:64). God will punish Babylon. Her gods will be discredited, her city demolished. Other nations are repeatedly summoned to arms to completely destroy Babylon. Israel is called to escape, for this is God's deliverance for her. These three

themes—Babylon, the attacking foe, and Israel—like juggler's balls recur in the oracle.

The oracle is in two halves, with corresponding and contrasting features in each (50:4–44; 51:1–53). (See Aitken.) "I am against you" occurs in both halves (50:31; 51:25). Each half has a song about a weapon (50:35–38; 51:20–23); and in each there is a pun on Babylon (50:21; 51:41). Both halves announce Babylon's fall (50:46; 51:31). Her fall will have a far-reaching, even universal, impact (50:12). In the first half the figures of sheep, shepherd, and pasture dominate (50:6, 17, 45); in the second, harvest and drunkenness are frequent metaphors (51:7, 33, 39, 57).

The Babylonians (also called Chaldeans) were a tribe whose leader Nabopolassar took the Assyrian capital of Nineveh in 612 BC. Under Nebuchadnezzar they moved westward, defeated Egypt at Carchemish in 605 BC, and swooped down on Judah in 597 BC en route to Egypt. Bel is an older title for Marduk, a war-hero god and creator. He was Babylon's patron deity. The phrase "a nation from the north" (50:3) is stereotypical language for an invader. In the earlier part of the book the northerner coming against Israel was Babylon. Now the "northerner"—namely, the Medes and other allies of Cyrus (51:27–28)—will invade Babylon (50:1–3).

In the following verses Israel is basically told to move out (50:4–20). In bookend fashion, Israel is the subject of verses 4–7 and 17–20; Israel's foe is the subject of verses 8–10 and 14–16; and Babylon is the subject of the middle section (50:11–13).

Israel's physical return will put them in choice places. Spiritually, forgiveness will be in effect; it follows Israel's return to the covenant relationship. The image of a flock continues in verse 17, with a capsule review of history: Tiglath-Pileser of Assyria made war against Israel in 734 BC; in 722 BC Samaria, the capital of Israel, was taken; Babylon captured Jerusalem, capital of Judah, in 586 BC.

Israel's hope arose concretely out of a siege laid to Babylon by an alliance of peoples from the north. They would come with arrows and bows and swords. Reasons for the divine vengeance were that Babylon pillaged Judah and that she sinned against the Lord (specifically, in her pride). The city fell in October 539, when Cyrus the Persian, the commander of an alliance consisting of the Medes and other northern peoples, took the city.

The Hebrew words *meratayim* ("twofold rebellion"; NIV "Merathaim") and *peqod* ("punishment"; NIV "Pekod"), usually translated as proper nouns, are puns on Marratim, a district in southern Babylon, and Puqudu, a tribe east of Babylon. God will give the command to attack. The result of the battle is that Babylon, once a hammer shattering others, is herself broken (50:21–32).

Another reason for destroying Babylon, in addition to her destruction of Jerusalem's temple, is pride. To defy the Lord is to treat him insolently. The titles "Holy One of Israel"

The Ishtar gate, leading into the city of Babylon, the capital of the Neo-Babylonian Empire. This gate was built during the reign of Nebuchadnezzar (605–562 BC) and became the northern and most impressive entrance into the city.

(50:29) and "Lord Almighty" (50:31) underscore the presumption of Babylon's sin.

The Babylonian Empire will be devastated (50:33–46). Verse 33 echoes the theme of Israel's release as hostage from Babylon's grip. The Redeemer overpowers the opposition (as formerly in Egypt), and as an attorney, he takes over their case. His sword will cut into the political, religious, military, and economic segments of society.

The picture of a depopulated city inhabited by desert creatures is traditional (50:39; cf. Isa. 34:13–14). Sodom and Gomorrah are the classic instances of cities in ruin. "An army from the north" (50:41) is also standardized language. In addition to the primary foe, a distant alliance and an army of archers are arrayed against Babylon. Besides, God is the ultimate agent. Any resistance is futile.

The end has come (51:1–19). The destroyer includes the Medes and their allies. The theme of harvest, together with drunkenness, threads through the chapter (51:7, 33, 39, 57).

Figuratively speaking, the movie camera pans jerkily to Israel (her guilt is not minimized), and then to Babylon (her cup makes others drunk), and then back to Israel. Babylon's collapse is Israel's vindication. Attention then turns to the attackers, who are to take weapons and move in. Finally, it is all over.

Verses 15–19 are essentially a repetition of Jeremiah 10:12–16. The poem gives assurance that God will carry out his purpose. The Lord's vengeance is retaliation by the highest authority, God's settling of accounts with Babylon.

Forces are marshaled against Babylon (51:20–33). "You are my war club" (51:20) is God's address to the coming "destroyer," Cyrus the Persian. "Destroying mountain" (51:25), or towering destroyer, refers to Babylon; geographically it was situated on a plain, though it boasted a temple mountain or ziggurat. Militarily, she has been the greatest power in history, but her eruptive force, like an extinct volcano, will be neutralized.

Battle preparations are urged on the alliance that will attack. Ararat, ancient Urartu, is modern Armenia. Minni refers to a territory southeast of Lake Urmia settled by hill folk. Scythians occupied the region between the Black and Caspian seas; they were the Ashkenaz. The Medes conquered these early in the sixth century; together they become part of the force attacking Babylon. The Lord's purposes will be implemented. Babylon's chief military resource, her soldiers, is incapacitated. The threshing floor (51:33) is figurative, representing the place where God's further smashing with his war club will take place.

The next section (51:34–53) focuses on Babylon and Israel. Babylon has overstepped her bounds in destroying Jerusalem. Like an attorney, God again takes up Israel's case (51:36). Babylon will be reduced to rubble (51:37).

Israel is urged to seize the moment of Babylon's confusion and make her escape (51:45). Rumors of a Babylonian resurgence or of new leadership are not to be believed. God as scorekeeper will see that Babylon is treated as she has treated others.

The themes throughout the oracle are gathered up in its conclusion (51:54–58): the destroyer, the destruction, the motivation of God's retribution, drunkenness, death, and the futility of resistance. The "leveling" of the walls of Babylon is to be understood as a figure of speech for capitulation, for when the Persians attacked in 539 BC, surrender came quickly and without a battle. In 485 BC, however, Xerxes I laid waste to the walls.

The symbolic action (51:59–64; cf. chaps. 13, 19, 27, and 32) is a fitting conclusion to the oracle and to the entire book, even though the action is dated 594/3.

9. The Fall of Jerusalem (52:1–34)

Jeremiah's words end in 51:64. This account, which expands on the story in Jeremiah 39:1–10, is mostly taken from 2 Kings 24:18–25:30. It documents the historical fulfillment of much that is prophesied in the book and so adds to the credibility of Jeremiah's words.

Nebuchadnezzar's eighteen-month siege, begun in January 588 BC, came in response

to Zedekiah's rebellion (52:1–11). The famine conditions are further described in Lamentations 2:20–22; 4:1–20.

In August 587 BC, Nebuzaradan put the torch to the city (52:12–27a). His second assignment was to gather those destined for exile. Temple furnishings were dismantled; precious metals were salvaged.

Of the three Babylonian raids (597 BC, 587 BC, and 582 BC) the largest number of people were deported in 597 BC. Since 2 Kings 24:14–16 reports a total of eighteen thousand, presumably the list here (52:27b–34) is of men only. King Jehoiachin was in the first deportation. The sadness of the closing chapter is brightened by the glimmer of hope in Jehoiachin's improved condition. In 538 BC the exiles would return. It is because of Jeremiah's message that we know both the reason for sadness and the reason for hope.

> This relief from Nineveh shows Assyrian soldiers removing plunder from the captured city of Lachish, including two large incense stands (700–692 BC), similar to the valuables the Babylonians carried out of the Jerusalem temple (Jer. 52:17–19).

Select Bibliography

Aitken, Kenneth T. "The Oracles against Babylon in Jer. 50–51: Structures and Perspectives." *Tyndale Bulletin* 35 (1984): 35–63.

Brueggemann, Walter. *A Commentary on Jeremiah: Exile and Homecoming.* Grand Rapids: Eerdmans, 1998.

Craigie, Peter C., Page H. Kelley, and Joel F. Drinkard Jr. *Jeremiah 1–25.* Word Biblical Commentary. Dallas: Word, 1991.

Dearman, J. Andrew. *Jeremiah and Lamentations.* NIV Application Commentary. Grand Rapids: Zondervan, 2002.

Huey, F. B., Jr. *Jeremiah/Lamentations.* New American Commentary. Nashville: Broadman & Holman, 1993.

Keown, Gerald L., Pamela J. Scalise, and Thomas G. Smothers. *Jeremiah 26–52.* Word Biblical Commentary. Waco: Word, 1995.

Kidner, Derek. *The Message of Jeremiah: Against Wind and Tide.* The Bible Speaks Today. Downers Grove, IL: InterVarsity, 1987.

Martens, Elmer A. "Jeremiah and Lamentations." In *Cornerstone Biblical Commentary.* Edited by Philip W. Comfort. Vol. 8. Wheaton: Tyndale, 2005.

Stuhlman, Louis. *Jeremiah.* Abingdon Old Testament Commentaries. Nashville: Abingdon, 2005.

Thompson, J. A. *The Book of Jeremiah.* New International Commentary on the Old Testament. Grand Rapids: Eerdmans, 1979.

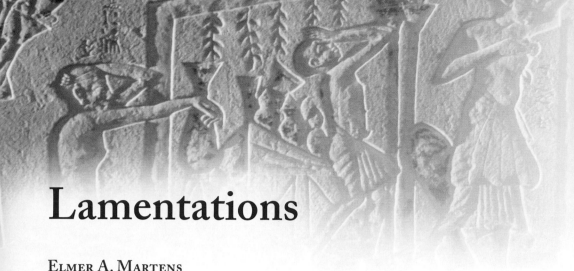

Lamentations

ELMER A. MARTENS

The circumstance that colors the book of Lamentations is the fall of Jerusalem in 597–587 BC. The prophet Jeremiah had foretold an invasion by an enemy from the north. The invaders would cause devastation; they were God's agents to punish Judah for its sin of breaking the covenant.

By the turn of the century (ca. 600 BC) the Babylonians (Jeremiah's enemy from the north) were in the region, and the power balance was decidedly shifting. In 597 BC they attacked Jerusalem, and Judah became a vassal state to the Babylonians. When the vassal king Zedekiah rebelled against Nebuchadnezzar, his Babylonian overlord, reprisal was immediate. Though the city maintained itself during an eighteen-month siege, Nebuchadnezzar's victory brought the burning of the city, including the Solomonic temple. The catastrophe—loss of temple, city, leadership, freedom, and land—was shocking. Many had become convinced that such a thing could never happen because Jerusalem and the temple were indestructible. This book laments the tragic collapse of a 350-year nation-state and the end of an era.

The poet wrestles in anguish with the contrast between Judah's status as God's covenant partner and her present collapse. Why had it all happened? Had God turned in anger against his people? How was one to deal with this traumatic experience? What interpretation was to

be put on events of such inexpressible horror? The book is about suffering. It can be compared to some of the psalms and parts of Isaiah 40–55.

Literary Features

The book, totally in poetry, is distinguished by three characteristics. First, much of the poetry is in the *qinah* meter, a rhythmic accent in a 3–2 pattern (the Hebrew word for "lament" is *qinah*). Poetic lines often consist of five words with a thought break after the third word. This 3–2 pattern, while not limited to use in lament literature, is characteristic of funeral dirges, for it gives the effect of a statement that, interrupted by a sob, is concluded with a shortened phrase. Characteristically, laments begin with "how" (1:1; Jer. 48:17). Often they contrast an earlier glory with present disarray.

A classic lament is David's song of grief upon the death of Jonathan (2 Sam. 1:19–27). The prophets effectively used laments or funeral dirges in order to portray coming disaster. Two kinds of laments are found in Lamentations: the individual lament (chap. 3) and the communal lament (chaps. 1–2, 4). The individual lament has an address to God, a complaint, a statement of confidence, a petition, and a word of praise. The communal lament has more flexibility and is designed for group use, usually in a worship setting (e.g., Psalms 44; 60; 74). It describes the distress and includes an appeal to God for help.

A second formal characteristic of the book is the acrostic pattern in which four of the five chapters are cast. In an acrostic, poetic lines or stanzas begin with the successive letters of the alphabet. In the first two chapters, each stanza of three couplets begins with the appropriate letter of the twenty-two-letter Hebrew alphabet—hence twenty-two verses. In the third poem (chap. 3) three successive lines each begin with the same alphabetical letter, the next three with the next letter, and so on, for a total of sixty-six verses. In chapter 4 the twenty-two stanzas consist of two couplets each; each stanza is in acrostic formation. The final poem is not an acrostic, but, like the Hebrew alphabet, has twenty-two lines.

The best-known acrostic in the Bible is Psalm 119, with eight verses to each of the Hebrew letters. Thirteen other acrostics have been identified.

Why follow an acrostic form when preparing a lament? It has been noted that a formal structure acts as a restraint on statements of grief, which would otherwise lack orderliness. Certainly it is a demanding task to pour emotion-filled material into a recipe-like form. A further reason for an acrostic would be its help in memorization. Finally, the acrostic by its form says what is to be said about suffering from *a* to *z*.

A third characteristic, formally speaking, is that of balance. The center poem is the longest. On either side of it are two poems, each with twenty-two stanzas, though of differing length. Moreover, as has been noted, the book itself is in *qinah* (3–2) pattern: three longer poems are followed by two shorter ones. Further, chapters 1 and 5 have a similar emphasis, an extended description of the tragic situation. Chapters 2 and 4 both deal with suffering, enemies, and God's wrath. This leaves chapter 3, an individual lament that concentrates on giving an explanation for the suffering. The effect is that the first two chapters lead up to the central chapter; more rapidly the final chapters lead away from the climax of chapter 3.

The tone of the book is one of sadness and deep sorrow. Essentially the book processes a community's grief. The poet tries to come to terms with the disaster. The writer does not give as a reason that the Babylonians were militarily superior. The Babylonians are not even mentioned by name. Nor does the poet consider that the gods of Babylon were stronger than the God of Israel.

Theological Themes

Specifically, the book leaves no doubt that the people's sin accounts for the tragic fall of Jerusalem. Each of the five poems makes clear that the event must be seen as God's punishment for sin. The book's message, therefore, is in keeping with what the earlier prophets proclaimed: sin will bring judgment. Such a message is also in keeping with the covenant terms, which listed destruction, loss of land, and dispersion as among the covenant curses (Deut. 28:15–64).

The fuller explanation, therefore, beyond the people's sin, is that God implemented the covenant curses—but not mechanically. The poem, especially in chapter 2, elaborates on God's wrath. It was God's anger against his people that precipitated such a horrendous event. That wrath is not capricious but is expressed in the context of God's righteousness. The tension of a good God even permitting such affliction is perhaps not resolvable, but chapter 3 is a wide-ranging attempt to respond to this tension.

The book is instructive in grief processing. First, a difficult situation is not denied or minimized. The poet's voice is heard pouring out grief and facing the ugliness of a crushed city and ruined dreams. Second, there is catharsis in explicitly stating the situation. The grimness of the event is not denied; rather, it is presented in detail. Sin is confessed. Third, the author wrestles over the assertion that God has brought on the disaster but that comfort and help can be only in him. The book is an illustration that in times of calamity one need not sink into despair. Fourth, for consolation the poet seizes on what is known of God, his goodness and his faithfulness (3:20–23). Fifth, in prayer the entire situation is rolled over on God himself.

Authorship

The author is not named but is popularly thought to be Jeremiah. Evidence for such a belief relies on Jewish and Christian tradition. Jeremiah is said to have composed complaints (2 Chron. 35:25), though these need not be the book of Lamentations. The Greek version of the Old Testament adds to the title of the book that it is by Jeremiah. While these are important considerations, other observations lead to a different conclusion: (1) there is nothing in the book of Jeremiah that suggests any

leaning to acrostic forms; (2) the assertion that they looked for help from allies (4:17) is altogether out of character for Jeremiah, who counseled submission to Babylon and objected to Israel's alliances with foreign powers (2:18); (3) the book has about it the mood of perplexity, whereas Jeremiah was certain about the reality of the coming disaster and its reason. The author was most likely a man, but may have been a woman. If the author was not Jeremiah, he (or she) was nevertheless an eyewitness of the events and wrote soon after 586 BC, probably before 570 BC.

Structure

The acrostic form plus the symmetrical and balanced arrangement nevertheless argue for a single author. Chapter 5, once claimed by scholars to be a later addition, is more and more thought to belong integrally to the whole. While we may not know the poet's name, we are the richer for the writer's frank statement of personal grief and faithful proclamation of the goodness of God.

Modern Application

Orthodox Jews read this book on the ninth of Ab to commemorate the destruction of both Solomon's temple (587 BC) and Herod's temple (AD 70). The Roman Catholic liturgy calls for a reading of the book during Holy Week. Persons and nations who fall into disastrous circumstances find a kinship here; together with the anonymous poet they can struggle through to commitment, even if not always to full clarity.

This tablet contains a poetic lament over the destruction of the city of Ur composed during the early second millennium BC.

Commentary

1. Lamenting a City in Shambles (1:1–22)

The city is Jerusalem. The date is after either 597 BC or 587 BC. In 598, provoked by Jehoiakim (609–598), Nebuchadnezzar of Babylon attacked Jerusalem, the capital of Judah. Less than ten years later Zedekiah rebelled against his overlord, Nebuchadnezzar. The Babylonian king laid siege to, captured, and burned the city. The acrostic poem depicts the result, notes the enemies' triumph, and acknowledges that God brought about the disaster because of Judah's sin. The absence of a comforter is a repeated note.

A. A lost splendor (1:1–6). "How" is a literary feature of a lament or dirge (cf. 2:1; 4:1–2; Jer. 48:17). The tone is at once affectionate and sympathetic, like a pastor coming to the bereaved. The city, once prestigious, has been reduced to slave status. Jerusalem's greatness under Solomon was world-renowned (1 Kings 10). Once this city was the hub of activity; now she is a "feeder" into the Babylonian system. Her lovers, namely her allies, such as Egypt or Moab, have deserted her.

The roads to Zion are without the pilgrims who would normally come to the worship feasts in Jerusalem. Religious, economic, and social life is nonexistent. The chief foe is Babylon, though ultimately the affliction is from the Lord. Jerusalem's collapse has come for moral reasons, the result of a breach of covenant (Deut. 28:15–68), rather than chiefly because of political misjudgment or military inadequacy.

Nor is it the enemies' god who has triumphed. The city is bereft of its dignity, its status, its leaders, and its allies.

B. Enemies mock and gloat (1:7–11). Now away from their home city, the citizens remember the wealth of the city—a wealth that included the temple and its prized furnishings. These the enemy, the Babylonians, have taken away (Jer. 27:19–22; 52:17–23). Contrary to God's law, which forbids foreigners to enter the temple (Ezek. 44:9), the Babylonians, a pagan people, have defiled the temple by entering it.

The enemies taunt Jerusalem by saying that her God is unable to defend her. The city is personified. Her nakedness, the depopulation of the city, is a disgrace; her "filthiness," menstrual uncleanness, is a telltale evil (1:9). She lives for the moment and does not consider her future.

C. In search of comforters (1:12–17). From a lament about Jerusalem by some onlooker, attention shifts to a lament by Jerusalem herself. Hurting people feel their hurt accentuated when others carry on as usual. She acknowledges the Lord's role in her affliction. Anger, like fire, consumes, and here consumes completely ("into my bones"). That God, like a hunter, has become Israel's adversary, is an additional disgrace. The winepress is figurative for judgment. In a trough hewn out of stone, grapes would be trampled to release the juice. Judah's dire plight is compounded by the lack of comforters.

D. Distressed and vengeful (1:18–22). In contrast to laments in other cultures, the righteousness of God is the setting for confession and lament here. Verses 18–20 review the main themes: Israel's sin, suffering, exile, worthless allies, and famine. Attention turns to the enemies, upon whom the poet calls down divine vengeance (1:21–22). Implicit is the argument that if God punishes sin, let him punish the enemy's excesses. Such a response at least takes seriously the verse, "Vengeance is mine, I [God] will repay" (Rom. 12:19 KJV, RSV; cf. Deut. 32:35).

2. An Angry God and an Awful Tragedy (2:1–22)

In the second poem, an acrostic like the first, the unprecedented tragedy of Jerusalem's destruction is explained as resulting from God's anger let loose against it. The tragedy is depicted; the mournful prayer of the victims is recorded.

A. God's anger unleashed (2:1–9). Once a cloud of glory filled the temple as a sign of God's favor (1 Kings 8:10). Now God's displeasure, like a dark cloud, stands over Jerusalem. God's strength is expressed anthropomorphically by the "right hand" (2:3, 4), his anger by the "hot nose" (NIV "fierce anger," 2:3). Of the five different words for "anger" here, several have to do with heat and fire; they denote an intense emotional disturbance. God's anger may be viewed as the expression of his justice, for here is not an impulsive emotional outburst, but a follow-through on a threat. By his anger God protects what he loves: justice. God's anger is against evil.

The effects of God's wrathful action are pictured in different ways. Overall, Israel has toppled from the splendor of her election. The ark of the covenant and even the temple are no longer important to God. Fields and fortresses, the land and its leaders, have been affected by God's anger. God's destroying action has taken the lives of the choice soldiers. Not only has God removed all outside resources, but worse, he has withdrawn his own offer for help. Even worse, he has, like an enemy, turned against Israel.

Jerusalem is in view in verse 6—first the temple, then the city. With the temple, God's dwelling and the place of meeting, destroyed, the festivals are no longer feasible. Specifically, God has rejected the altar. The altar of burnt offering stood in the courtyard; the altar of incense was inside the temple. Access to the temple is no longer monitored; the pagan Babylonians raise shouts of victory where pious Jews once raised shouts of praise to God. God directs the destruction of the city's fortifications. Finally, the leadership stratum—king, lawgiver, prophet—is annihilated. Tragedy occurs where there is no word from the Lord.

B. Widespread ruin (2:10–17). The remaining verses of the poem (2:10–22) depict the human reaction to God's destructive wrath, adding further details about the ruin. Dust and sackcloth were cultural expressions of grief, as was bowing to the ground, which denoted mourning and

An Egyptian relief showing women mourning (tomb of Horemheb, Saqqara, ca. 1330 BC). Some of the women are bowing down, similar to the description of mourning in Lamentations 2:10: "The young women of Jerusalem have bowed their heads to the ground."

repentance. Multiple age ranges are represented: elders, maidens, mothers, children, and infants who cry their hearts out. The collective group speaks in verse 10; but in verse 11 an individual, an inside observer who is deeply moved, speaks. Both questions of verse 13 suggest speechlessness. "Your wound is as deep as the sea" (2:13) conveys the notion not only that things could not be worse but that the catastrophe has no parallel.

Prophets, had they been true prophets, might have averted the disaster, or if not, could now be comforters. But false prophets are disqualified. A true prophet's function is to expose evil in society. Jeremiah reprimanded false prophets and those who listened to them (Jer. 14:14; 23:13; 27:9–10). Neither the prophets nor the "outsiders" can be comforters. Nor can God, who is the agent of the disaster. After the description of disaster (2:11–16) comes the interpretation (2:17). The word decreed long ago was God's warning that such disaster would come should Judah fail to follow God (Lev. 26:14–39; Deut. 28:15–68).

C. A prayer of anguish (2:18–22). The poet encourages Judah to meet her frustration and grief in the presence of the Lord and to pray on behalf of the children. The encouragement is addressed to the city walls, which are personified (2:18). The metaphor is apt in view of night watches maintained on the walls. In verses 20–22 the people offer prayer, or the poet prays on their behalf.

The appeal to the Lord is made on the basis of lack of precedent (whom have you ever treated like this?) and compassion. A report of starved women resorting to cannibalism is found in 2 Kings 6:25–29. The statement may be literal, of course, but since covenant curses projected such a situation (Deut. 28:53), reference to it could be a way of saying, "The worst has happened." Casualties of war are in the street, a war in which the Lord is the aggressor.

3. Processing Grief (3:1–66)

The form of chapter 3, while still an acrostic, is an individual lament (at least 3:1–20) and so differs from the communal laments that precede and follow it. Chapter 3 is the middle poem, with 3:1 exactly at the center of the book. In concept and intensity the first two chapters lead up to chapter 3, and the last two lead from it. As an individual lament it has the customary components of complaint, statement of confidence, and prayer. Although the summons to praise is absent, this individual lament can be compared with a similar genre in the psalms (e.g., Psalm 13) and Jeremiah 15:15–21. Yet the individual fades out; a group speaks in verses 40–47. Perhaps the poem was used as a responsive reading in worship. The individual lament becomes a prism through which to elaborate on the communal experience. Or the "I" may from the outset be understood as a collective pronoun.

A. Afflicted by God (3:1–18). One characteristic of a lament is the graphic depiction of the difficulty that called it forth. The ugliness of this scenario is God-caused. He (3:1 and throughout this section), though not named until 3:18, is the Lord. The speaker is the victim of the Lord's assaults. Verse 4 suggests that the problem is illness. To physical ailment is added psychological and spiritual isolation. Access to God has been stonewalled, blocked with huge boulders.

Other images follow to make graphic the individual's plight: wild animals mauling their victims (3:10–11); a hunter in target practice (3:12–13); a dietician administering bitterness (literally "poison") (3:15). Like Jeremiah, the individual is the object of ridicule. A Western idiom corresponding to 3:16 would be: "He made me eat dirt." The tension is severe. God, who might have been his hope, has become his adversary.

B. Confidence in God (3:19–42). Verses 19–20 provide a transition from the description of distress, of which God is the cause, to a statement of confidence, wherein God is the hope. Hope is implied by the lament as such; it looks for an answer from God. Hope in individual laments is usually made explicit in the "certainty of hearing," or confidence, statements.

The Lord's great love (3:22) follows through on covenant obligations. God's compassion cannot be exhausted. His faithfulness to his covenant is unfailing. Whereas the poet has earlier given up hope (3:18), he now determines that God will be his hope. Verses 21–26 have been called the theological high point of the book.

One of the poet's answers to suffering is to affirm God's goodness. For this reason the afflicted do well to wait even in silence. There is approval for turning over the yoke (responsibility?) to the younger generation (3:27). However, the context supports the view that yoke deals with suffering (cf. 3:1); the lesson of trust in God, when learned early, is orientation for the remainder of one's life.

Verses 28–30 once more picture the afflicted person in order to set the stage for verses 31–33. Despite the perception that the Lord brought on the affliction, faith affirms that it is not really in God's nature to afflict. More than that, his compassion and his unfailing love override whenever God does afflict. The poet is responding to an age-old problem: how can one reconcile belief in a God of goodness and power with the reality of suffering?

Verses 34–36 are further assertions of confidence by a victim of evil. A God of justice is obligated to redress evil. The Lord's power means that limits are enforced. God as the source of good and bad echoes Job 2:10. Suffering may be the result of sin (Deut. 28:15–68). It is not, however, the only reason for suffering. Still, ruthless honesty is necessary (3:40). Genuine repentance admits wrongdoing.

C. Beset with problems (3:43–54). The poet returns to complaints, but these are now of a communal nature. The complaint involves God, enemies, and personal suffering. Former themes are incorporated: covering with a cloud of anger (3:43–45; cf. 2:1), killing without mercy (3:43; cf. 2:17), inaccessibility (3:44; cf. 3:8), and humiliation (3:45; cf. 1:1, 6). Arguments for the Lord to pay attention to the situation arise from the humiliation of God's people, the suffering, and the threat of annihilation.

D. Calling on God (3:55–66). Prayers and report of prayers close the poem. The poet invokes previous experiences as reason for God to hear. Or, in a more likely interpretation, so sure is the poet of God's help, that talk proceeds in the past tense. Legal court language pervades verses 58–59. The enemies, in their glowering mood, though unidentified, will prompt the Lord to action. The prayer for vengeance (3:64), while in keeping with the Old Testament admonition to turn over all vengeance to God, falls far short of the New Testament exhortation to love one's enemies (Matt. 5:44).

4. Jerusalem's Humiliation (4:1–22)

Like the three preceding poems, this poem is an acrostic. Like chapter 2, it tells of Jerusalem's faded glory and reiterates the Lord's part, though not as sharply, in bringing about the disaster. One feature of the lament is the contrast between "then," a time of glory, and "now," a time of humiliation.

A. Jerusalem's faded glory (4:1–10). "How" is the recognizable introduction to a lament (1:1). Not Jerusalem only but the country's suffering populace is the subject. Jerusalem the golden has become very tarnished. Its pride, the sanctuary, is dismantled, and its stones are scattered about in the streets. However, with verse 2 as a clue, "gold" and "gems" may refer to the best of its citizens. The sons of Zion, either Jerusalem's citizenry generally or the temple functionaries, like currency, have become sharply devalued.

A new and ugly ethos prevails. People have become hardened, even heartless. Ostriches lay their eggs in the sand, thus putting the future of their young in jeopardy. Besides, they treat their young harshly. The rich have become poverty-stricken.

Sodom and Gomorrah are the classic symbols of catastrophe (Gen. 19:24–25, 29; Jer. 20:16; 23:14). Instead of "princes" (4:7), the Hebrew text reads "Nazirites." The Nazirites were a group that vowed self-discipline and devotion to the Lord's service (Num. 6:1–21). Perhaps the term suggests "the elite," who are described as the picture of health but because of famine have become scrawny and unrecognizable.

Sudden death seems preferable to slow death by famine. The reference to cannibalism, practiced by the sensitive women, may be a way of saying that the covenant curses have been implemented (Deut. 28:53). Still, famine drives people to bizarre actions, and the description may well be literal (2 Kings 6:25–29).

B. Jerusalem's dire plight (4:11–20). The Lord's anger is the theme of chapter 2. The doctrine of Zion and the temple as invincible had some theological support but was misleading in Judah's circumstance. As a fortification, Jerusalem was strategically placed, with valleys on three of her sides. Her fall was due to inside weaknesses. The sins of God's people as a reason for the disaster are noted in each of the four acrostic poems (Lam. 1:8; 2:14; 3:42; 4:13) and in the final chapter (5:7).

In a profound sense, the leaders' failure to be true spokespersons for God brought on the siege that resulted in the death of the "righteous" folk. These former leaders are now among the rejected. Those once honored are not shown respect.

As Sodom in its crisis had no helpers, so Judah is without assistance. Verse 17 is often cited as proof that Jeremiah is probably not the author of Lamentations. He counseled against

This scene portraying the siege of Lachish (Assyria, 700–692 BC), as the city is under attack and its citizens go into exile, is reminiscent of the fate of Jerusalem.

seeking foreign aid. Verse 19, it is almost certain, describes Zedekiah's attempt to escape (2 Kings 25:4–6; Jer. 39:4–7). Hopes were pinned on the king as the Lord's anointed. But he was captured.

C. A strange irony (4:21–22). "The cup" (4:21) is metaphorical language for the "wine" of God's judgment. Nations drinking this wine go into a stupor, stagger, and fall (Jer. 25:15–28). To be stripped naked is to be disgraced. Edom took advantage of the chaos after Babylon sacked Jerusalem; Judah was left without defenses. Edom then occupied parts of Judah, a circumstance that further fueled long-standing hostility.

5. A Summarizing Prayer (5:1–??)

This poem, unlike the four before it, is not an acrostic, though it has twenty-two lines, the number of letters in the Hebrew alphabet. The prayer reviews the distressing circumstances subsequent to the fall of Jerusalem and pleads for the Lord to grant restoration. In form the poem is a communal lament with an address to God, the listing of reasons for the lament, and a request to God for help.

A. Refugees in one's homeland (5:1–9). Jerusalem has been sacked and there is chaos. A large part of the tragedy is the loss of her land, her inheritance. The land was a keystone in her covenant relationship with God. Verse 3 may refer to a sense of abandonment by God, though the literal also holds true because of war casualties.

In the days of Jehoiakim (609–597 BC), Judah was a vassal to Pharaoh Necho of Egypt. In the early decades of the sixth century she was a vassal to Assyria. Marauding bandits were a hazard after Babylon's victory.

B. "Our hearts are faint" (5:10–18). Famine, sexual abuse, and violence make for very hard times. Life has taken a turn for the worse. Youth are put to hard labor. The collapse of society marks a reversal from what things have been.

C. "Restore us" (5:19–22). The communal prayer concludes by repeating a foundation of the faith: God's everlasting rule. The plaintive questions are rhetorical (5:20). The prayer for restoration is like Ephraim's prayer (Jer. 31:18–19). The poet accepts the fact that God punishes sin. Although the total case has been turned over to God, the closing note is sobering indeed (cf. Mal. 4:6).

Select Bibliography

Dobbs-Alsopp, F. W. *Lamentations.* Interpretation. Louisville: Westminster John Knox, 2002.

Gottwald, Norman K. *Studies in the Book of Lamentations.* Rev. ed. London: SCM, 1962.

Huey, F. B., Jr. *Jeremiah/Lamentations.* New American Commentary. Nashville: Broadman & Holman, 1993.

Martens, Elmer A. "Jeremiah and Lamentations." In *Cornerstone Biblical Commentary.* Edited by Philip W. Comfort. Vol. 8. Wheaton: Tyndale, 2005.

O'Connor, Kathleen. "Lamentations." In *The New Interpreter's Bible.* Edited by Leander E. Keck. Vol. 6. Nashville: Abingdon, 2001.

Provan, Iain W. *Lamentations.* New Century Bible Commentary. Grand Rapids: Eerdmans, 1991.

Ezekiel

Victor P. Hamilton

Ezekiel the Prophet

There are not many biographical details about Ezekiel in the book that bears his name. We know that the name of his father was Buzi (1:3). This is a strange name; the only Hebrew root we know of with which that name can be connected is "shame." Buzi means literally "my shame." But what parent would name a son "my shame"? Perhaps "Buzi" is related to another Semitic root that we cannot identify. Like Jeremiah (see Jer. 1:1), Ezekiel is a son of a priest but is called to be a prophet.

Unlike Jeremiah, however, Ezekiel's priestly heritage is prominent throughout his prophecy.

There are no such problems with Ezekiel's own name. It means either "El/God shall strengthen" (a statement) or "May El/God strengthen" (a prayer). In the opening chapters God reveals to the prophet why his name is Ezekiel.

We may safely surmise that Ezekiel belonged to the aristocracy. It was the policy of the Babylonians, when they invaded and conquered a country, to exile only the upper levels of leadership. This would deprive subjugated peoples of effective leaders. Hegemony was maintained by silencing (and exiling as necessary) outspoken leaders of the resistance movement.

Ezekiel is unique among the prophets in that his entire ministry was conducted outside of Palestine. Every date in Ezekiel (a total of thirteen), outside of the problematical "thirtieth year" of 1:1, is reckoned from the year in which Judah's king Jehoiachin was carried into Babylonian captivity. The earliest date we find in Ezekiel is 593 BC (1:2; 3:16). The latest date in the prophecy is 571 BC (29:17). Thus, Ezekiel's ministry spans approximately twenty-two years.

Ezekiel carries out his ministry while in captivity. He lives and preaches among his

A sculpture of Ezekiel from the facade of the cathedral of Notre Dame in Amiens, France

743

fellow exiles by the Kebar River. Ezekiel has his own parsonage ("Go, shut yourself inside *your* house," 3:24, emphasis added). On numerous occasions the elders in exile come to talk with him or watch him at his house (8:1; 14:1; 20:1; 33:21), indicating that Ezekiel more than likely was a religious leader in Jerusalem before 597 BC and carried that stature with him into exile.

Ezekiel was married (24:15–18), but we never hear of any children. In 4:14 he offers the protest "from my youth until now I have never eaten anything found dead." That Ezekiel would use such a phrase indicates that he is no youngster. He is definitely older than Jeremiah.

Structure

The arrangement of the prophecy of Ezekiel is clear. After a brief section describing Ezekiel's call (chaps. 1–3), we find prophecies/oracles of doom and destruction against Judah/Jerusalem (chaps. 4–24). These must have been spoken prior to the fall of Jerusalem, for every date provided by these chapters is before 587/6 BC (1:2, 593 BC; 8:1, 592 BC; 20:1, 591 BC; 24:1, 588 BC).

The second section comprises chapters 25–32, Ezekiel's prophecies/oracles to the nations. In so preaching, Ezekiel falls in line with Amos (1:1–2:5), Isaiah (chaps. 13–23), and Jeremiah (chaps. 46–51). The distinctive thing about Ezekiel's foreign oracles is his special focus on Tyre and Egypt. Seven of the thirteen dates in Ezekiel are in this section (26:1, 587 BC; 29:1, 587 BC; 29:17, 571 BC; 30:20, 587 BC; 31:1, 587 BC; 32:1, 585 BC; 32:17, 586 BC). Four of these dates refer to a day and month in 587 BC, very close to the time of Jerusalem's destruction.

The third section is prophecies/oracles of salvation directed to the exiles (chaps. 33–39). It is in this unit that Ezekiel is inspired by God to share with his exiled congregation the revivification, restoration, regeneration, and reunification of God's scattered people as they return to Israel from exile. It is Ezekiel's hearing of the fall of Jerusalem that allows him to

shift from prophecies of doom to prophecies of hope (33:21).

The fourth section (actually part of the third) is about the rebuilding of the city of Jerusalem, and especially the reconstruction of the temple (chaps. 40–48). There have been a number of different interpretations of how these chapters are to be understood. One view suggests that the nation of Israel will be reestablished in the messianic age along with all the accoutrements of temple and temple worship. Such interpreters still look for the building of the temple. A second line of interpretation treats chapters 40–48 symbolically and applies them to the Christian age and to the church. The first approach reads Ezekiel literally, and the second reads it symbolically. Perhaps between the two there is a mediating position that sees in Ezekiel a word of God to and for his people that has not yet transpired but does not insist on the implementation of all the data from *a* to *z*. Suffice it to say, the return and resettlement of postexilic times had virtually nothing in common with Ezekiel's vision and temple agenda. If anything, the rituals, personnel, and laws of that community were more Moses-like than Ezekiel-like.

Theological Themes

At three critical points Ezekiel sees the glory of God. First is his own personal experience of that glory (chap. 1), which nerves him with boldness for his own ministry. Second is his vision of the departure of that glory both from Jerusalem and from the temple (chaps. 8–11). Third is his vision of the return of the glory of God to Jerusalem and to the temple (chap. 43).

While it is the people's persistent sin that drives the Shekinah from the temple, it is not the people's return to righteousness and repentance that lures the Shekinah back. Surprisingly perhaps, a clarion call to repentance is minimal in Ezekiel. The reason is that for Ezekiel the fate of Jerusalem is sealed. This explains the reason for the many occasions (3:1–4:17; 5:1–4; 12:1–7; 12:17–20; 21:11–17; 21:18–20; 24:15–27) on which Ezekiel pantomimes Jerusalem's demise.

Ezekiel's major concern is to establish beyond a shadow of a doubt to the exiles the justice of God. What is about to happen, or has already happened, to Jerusalem is not due to the whim of an unpredictable God who one day on the spot decided to withdraw his favor from his people. At the same time, preaches Ezekiel, let not those in exile be infested with false confidence. Their survival in Babylon is not evidence of superior moral quality.

The most common phrase in Ezekiel is "They/You will know that I am the LORD." The "they/you" may be the survivors left in Jerusalem or the deportees in Babylon. The prophet's concern is that God's children, who are supposed to know him already, *really* know him. At one level this means that the exiles, when they see or hear about the catastrophe of 587/6 BC, will indeed know that the Lord is a God of power and is quite capable of fulfilling his promises and threats. At a deeper level, Ezekiel, through this phrase, yearns (and so does God) for a faithless and unknowing people to come to covenant allegiance and consciousness of their God's lordship.

We can be grateful that the last chapter in Ezekiel is not chapter 31 or chapter 32. There is a rabbinic tradition which holds that of the three Major Prophets the order should be Jeremiah, Ezekiel, Isaiah. Jeremiah was placed first because he is the prophet of destruction; Ezekiel follows because he begins with destruction but ends with comfort; Isaiah is last because he focuses entirely on comfort.

Obviously this is not an accurate summary of these three prophets. But it does indicate the major shift in Ezekiel's thought in chapters 1–32 and 33–48. Ezekiel may start in the black of night, but he ends in the glow of a morning dawn. For Ezekiel the most spectacular and precious thing is not the rebuilt city, the rebuilt temple, or even the reassembled people of God. These are good, but not the best. What makes it all so perfect is the presence of God in the midst of all this renovation: "the LORD is there" (48:35). That is the cause for Ezekiel's ecstasy.

Outline

Commentary

1. Prophecies of Doom and Judgment (1:1–24:27)

A. A vision of the glory of God (1:1–28). The significance of the thirtieth year (1:1) still eludes us. All other dates in Ezekiel are based on the year of Jehoiachin's captivity. Is it the thirtieth birthday of the prophet? An ancient Jewish tradition maintains that the thirty years refer to the number of years from the time King Josiah began his religious reforms in his twelfth year (628 BC) to Jehoiachin's captivity (598 BC).

Ezekiel is among the exiles in Babylon, having been taken there as a captive in 597. He is situated by the Kebar River/canal, which is near the ancient city of Nippur. It is here that he sees visions of God. Daniel also experienced God-given visions when standing by a body of water (Dan. 8:2; 10:4).

What these visions consist of is spelled out in verses 4–28. To begin with, Ezekiel sees a windstorm blowing from the north. In the midst of the storm he observes a chariot transported by four living creatures. These animal-like beings are cherubim, as chapter 10 makes abundantly clear. Each has four faces and four

The cherubim were composite winged creatures that guarded sacred space. Such composite creatures were a common motif in the ancient world, as seen in this Neo-Assyrian ivory piece (900–700 BC).

wings. The four faces are those of a man, a lion, an ox, and an eagle, which represent four dominant creatures. The four lordly creatures are, however, merely the bearers of the Lord of lords.

In the Old Testament, cherubim function as symbols of God's presence. For example, in the tabernacle, the dwelling place of God is in the Most Holy Place, above the mercy seat and between the cherubim. It is appropriate, and necessary, that Ezekiel receive a vision of something that symbolizes the presence of the living Lord. After all, Jerusalem will soon be destroyed and the temple will be razed. Everything looks bleak. Ezekiel is hundreds of miles from his home. Yet God is with him in Babylon too. His presence is with the prophet here as much as it could be anywhere else. For that reason Ezekiel is not in need of a promise from God that God will be with him, a promise that God gave to Moses (Exod. 3:12) and to Jeremiah (Jer. 1:8). The cherubim certify divine presence.

The second object Ezekiel sees, above the chariot, is an expanse (cf. Gen. 1:6) and above that expanse a throne. The expanse is obviously the platform on which the throne sits. The throne itself is made of sapphire. Seated on the throne is a man who is fiery from the waist up and fiery from the waist down. If cherubim stand for the presence of God, so does fire.

This is not just a vision of God but a vision of God seated on a throne. Thus in the visual symbolism we move from cherubim to throne. The first part of this vision suggests a God who is present, even in wicked Babylon. The second part of the vision suggests a God who is sovereign. He is on a throne. Certainly the prophet needs this reminder. About the only throne he can see is Nebuchadnezzar's. Has God been deposed? Is Nebuchadnezzar now in control? Indeed not. There might be an earthly throne, but beyond that there is the heavenly throne of God himself.

The third object Ezekiel sees is a rainbow in the midst of this fire. The rainbow immediately reminds us of Genesis 9, where it is a sign of the covenant that God will never again destroy the earth by a flood. So now we move from chariot to cherubim to throne to rainbow. Ezekiel is reminded not only of a God who is near and who reigns but also of a God who is a covenant-making and covenant-keeping God. Deportation to Babylon does not mean that God has dispossessed his people or that the covenant has been abrogated.

All that Ezekiel can do is fall facedown when he beholds the glory of the Lord. He does not say a word. He simply observes. Now we shift from something Ezekiel sees (1:4–28a) to something he is about to hear (1:28b).

B. Ezekiel's call (2:1–10). That Ezekiel is told to stand up on his feet indicates that he has control of himself. If a man is unconscious one cannot tell him to get up. Verse 2 supplies the first of many references to the Spirit of God both in the life and prophecy of Ezekiel. This is a theme he shares with Isaiah. By contrast, there is not one reference to the Spirit in conjunction with Jeremiah's life or ministry, but surely the Spirit of God was as active in and through his life as with his two colleagues.

The Spirit addresses Ezekiel as "son of man," an expression the NRSV renders regularly as "mortal." This title is used for the prophet about ninety times in the book and is used of no other prophet in the Old Testament. Possibly the repetition of this title is due to the fact that Ezekiel describes visions of the divine not found in any other prophecy.

Yet Ezekiel is still only a man, a mortal, nothing more.

The congregation to which Ezekiel is sent is described with two verbs: "rebelled" and "been in revolt." The first verb means "to refuse allegiance to, rise up against, a sovereign." The second verb is a political term and means something like "to violate covenant duties." The congregation is further described with two adjectives: "obstinate" (literally "hard-faced") and "stubborn." The first describes the people on the outside—their passive, emotionless faces. The second describes the people on the inside—hard-hearted. Obviously these are not upbeat, encouraging words for this exilic pastor. But they are accurate, and they delineate precisely the enormity of the task before the prophet. His congregation is not a promising one.

God says nothing about their response to Ezekiel. What God is concerned about is not the congregation's attitude but the prophet's attitude. Ezekiel is not to base or evaluate his ministry on their reaction. He is not to be results-oriented. Rather, he is to be obedience-oriented. He is to speak God's words to them.

There is no record that Ezekiel ever faced opposition, like Jeremiah did, even though his flock is far from inviting, encouraging, and supportive. Chapter 2 anticipates trouble, but it never emerges. But to be forewarned is to be forearmed anyway.

One thing Ezekiel must not do is lower himself to the people's spiritual level (2:8). His obedience must become a model and stimulus for them rather than their disobedience becoming a model and stimulus for him. Perhaps God is saying something like: "Do not try to get out of this like Jeremiah did" (cf. Jeremiah 1), if indeed Ezekiel knew Jeremiah.

Next Ezekiel is shown a scroll that has writing on both sides. Surely that the writing is on both sides indicates that the prophet's message is all from God. God does not write on one side, and Ezekiel on the other. It is the abundance of the divine message that is stressed. In our society "to eat words" is something negative, something unpleasant. In biblical thought "to eat words" is an agreeable experience.

Written on the scroll are "lament and mourning and woe." These are three fairly synonymous terms for lamentation, and putting three of them side by side suggests comprehensiveness. Unlike Jeremiah, who mingles prophecies of hope and doom, Ezekiel is all doom until chapter 33. That is the reason for the writing on this edible scroll.

C. Exhorter, sentry, and arbiter (3:1–27). Because God twice tells Ezekiel to eat the scroll (3:1, 3), it may be that there was some reluctance on Ezekiel's part. If so, he stands in the train of others such as Moses, Gideon, Jonah, and Jeremiah who were not initially euphoric about God's call. Only Isaiah is eager and receptive from the start (Isaiah 6). It is not enough for Ezekiel to take the scroll into his mouth (3:1); he must ingest it as well (3:3). To his surprise the scroll tastes as sweet as honey. This simile reminds us of Psalms 19:10 and 119:103. Ezekiel may even have borrowed the analogy from Jeremiah (Jer. 15:16). To find the word of the Lord sweet means that it is inherently desirable and attractive and has satisfactory effects.

Ezekiel is reminded that his message is not to foreigners (3:5). This is strange, however, in that chapters 25–32 are Ezekiel's oracles to the nations, which must mean that verse 5 refers only to the first part of the prophecy (chaps. 1–24). But if God had sent Ezekiel to them, their acceptance of his message would have been speedier than his own people's acceptance of his message (3:6). Jesus makes a similar point in Luke 10:13–15. Those you might not expect to listen, do listen. Those you assume will listen, do not listen.

If his congregation is tough, God will make Ezekiel tougher (3:8–9). A thick skin and a tender heart is a healthy combination in any of God's ministering servants.

It might sound strange that Ezekiel is told to go to his countrymen in exile—he is already there! Ezekiel is by himself at the river (1:1). He is now told to join his community of exiles

at Tel Aviv ("mound of the flood"). This place was formed over years by silt thrown up by storm floods. Ezekiel's bitterness and anger are either reflections of God's attitude toward his people or, more likely, a reflection of the prophet's realization that he has to pronounce doom on those he loves.

God further instructs Ezekiel to be a sentry (3:16–21). He is to warn his people of approaching danger, for danger is never far away from any community of faith. Silence on the prophet's part not only dooms the congregation but also makes the prophet himself culpable. The prophet's responsibility extends both to the wicked and to the backslidden righteous. In either case the prophet forfeits his life by neglecting his responsibility. This is a private communiqué to the prophet. So crucial is the sentry analogy that it resurfaces in chapter 33. Ezekiel has some input in the eternal destiny of the souls of humanity. As a matter of fact, he has much input! There is no other way for sidetracked believers to be restored to God's good graces apart from the involvement of the prophet.

In light of verses 16–21 the divine command of verse 24 is almost inexplicable: "Go, shut yourself inside your house." First he is commanded to be a sentry. Then he is ordered to confine himself to his house! And to complicate matters, God will make his tongue stick to the roof of his mouth. Ezekiel will lose his capacity for speech. How does a dumb, tongue-tied prophet under house confinement warn his people of impending danger?

To square verses 22–27 with verses 16–21, some have suggested that the dumbness did not begin after the prophet's call but only later, and even then it was intermittent. Others suggest that by dumbness is meant that Ezekiel will be immobile. He is to keep to his house, and the people are to come to him (8:1; 14:1; 20:1; 33:30–31). In verse 26 the Hebrew word translated "rebuke" in the NIV, some have asserted, means "arbitrate on behalf of, represent." Ezekiel will only represent God to the people; he cannot represent the people before God. Communication will go only one way. This explains why Ezekiel speaks only doom until the fall of Jerusalem. Standing before God on behalf of his congregation will be denied him.

D. The siege of Jerusalem symbolized (4:1–5:17). It is appropriate for Ezekiel to act out his message, as he does in chapters 4 and 5. For in the last paragraph of chapter 3 we are informed that Ezekiel was not able to talk. Conversation gives way to pantomiming.

In the first act (4:1–3) the prophet is told to take a clay tablet and to draw a siege of Jerusalem on it, complete with siege weaponry. Then he is to place an iron pan between himself and the inscribed city. This pan acts as a wall of separation between the prophet and the brick and symbolizes the impenetrable barrier between God and Jerusalem. The brick is a symbol of what is about to happen to Jerusalem. When Jeremiah raised this subject, it got him into hot water (see Jer. 7:1–15; 26:1–24). He was labeled a heretic and anti–Mount Zion. Ezekiel does not provoke such sentiment, perhaps because he is hundreds of miles away.

Ezekiel's second act (4:4–5) is to lie on his left side for 390 days, in which he bears the sin of the house of Israel. One day matches one year of sin by Israel. To what do the 390 days refer? If one adds this number to the date of Ezekiel's call, the number goes back to approximately 1000 BC (598 + 390), which is roughly the time of David and Solomon. But this is the period from the days of the united kingdom to Ezekiel. The Greek Septuagint reads "190 years," and this refers no doubt to the time of the northern kingdom, which began approximately 930 BC and lasted until 722/1 BC (around two hundred years). It appears, following the Hebrew text, that Ezekiel (or God) indicts the entire monarchy period of Israel.

Also, Ezekiel is to lie on his right side for forty days, in which he bears the sin of the house of Judah (4:6–8). The number forty is often used in the Old Testament as well as in the Christian tradition; in many instances it occurs in situations involving the removal of sin, such as Noah's flood, punishment on Egypt for forty years, forty days to the overthrow of Nineveh, forty days of Lent. The forty days here represent the exile of Judah, which lasted about forty years (587–539 BC). In both paragraphs (4:4, 6) Ezekiel is said "to bear the sin" of his people. It is most unlikely that this means that the prophet makes atonement for their sins. Priests may do this (Exod. 28:38; Lev. 10:17), the goat on the Day of Atonement does this (Lev. 16:21), and God does this (Exod. 34:7). Here, however, the prophet is burdened by the

> Similar to Ezekiel's drawing of the siege of Jerusalem (4:1–3), this Assyrian relief shows an attack on a city, including archers and a siege machine for battering down the walls (865–860 BC).

weight of the people's sin on him. The glory of the Lord makes him fall. The weight of sin flattens him.

Ezekiel's third act is to prepare various foods and make them into bread for himself (4:9–17). It is something that Ezekiel does while the siege is being enacted. The prophet's food is to consist of wheat, barley, beans, lentils, millet, and spelt. This is not designed to help Ezekiel put on weight. His daily intake of food is to be twenty shekels (eight or nine ounces). His only beverage is water, and of this he is to drink only one-sixth of a hin (two or three pints). This frugal diet symbolizes the minimal amount of food the people will have access to when Jerusalem is under siege.

Barley bread (4:12) was a staple of lower-income people, while the upper classes consumed wheat products. In this siege only food normally eaten by the poor will be available. Food, already in short supply, will also have to be rationed. That it is to be baked on human excrement means the food is not only meager but repulsive and unclean (4:12), leading Ezekiel to protest along the lines of Peter (cf. 4:14 with Acts 10:10–14).

It is crucial that the people before whom Ezekiel pantomimes, and who are already in exile, know the disaster about to visit the holy city, and more important, why it is visiting the city. It is impossible to sin and go against the divine order without the most serious of consequences. Jerusalem is God's chosen city, but if he leaves it, it becomes as vulnerable as any other city.

Ezekiel's final gesture is cutting off his hair and shaving his head (5:1–17). The common denominator in all these symbolic gestures is the affliction of Ezekiel: prolonged immobility and minimal food, which is defiled at that. The shaving of hair has the same impact. Shaving hair may symbolize mourning, and even disgrace and humiliation (2 Sam. 10:4). Samson lost his strength when he lost his hair. Leviticus 21:5 and Ezekiel 44:20 remind us that the priests were forbidden from shaving their

hair. Interestingly Ezekiel protested when he was told to eat unclean food, but he does not protest when he is told to shave his beard and head, even though he is a priest.

One-third of the hair he burns with fire inside the city he just drew on the tablet; one-third he strikes with the sword; and one-third he scatters to the wind. Death by catastrophe, war, and dispersion await the rebellious house of Israel. A few in this third group will be spared, but even some of the exiled will perish.

Being set in the center of the nations (5:5) makes Jerusalem more visible. Hence, her conduct ought to be more commendable. Yet just the opposite has taken place. She who has God's laws is acting at a lower moral level than those who do not have God's laws (5:7). What an indictment! The unbelievers have become a moral conscience for what is supposed to be the community of believers.

Because the people have committed unprecedented evil, God is going to unleash unprecedented judgment. Since Israel has not executed his judgments, God will execute his judgment. The famine will be so extensive and intense that society will be driven to cannibalism. Leviticus 26:29 holds out the possibility of filicidal cannibalism (fathers eating sons), but Ezekiel adds patricidal cannibalism (sons eating fathers).

How God's people have defiled his sanctuary will be spelled out in chapters 8–11. Here only the accusation is made. Verse 12 spells out the destiny of the "thirds" mentioned in verse 2. There is no indication that repentance will mitigate the divine judgment. Ezekiel, therefore, makes no room for exhortation. He gives only description. Only when punishment is complete will God's anger subside.

The remainder of the chapter (5:14–17) essentially repeats verses 8–12. Jerusalem will be destroyed. She will become a reproach, a taunt, and a warning to the nations. How far we have come from Genesis, where God's will was that his people be a blessing to the nations.

God the Creator of Israel has now become her annihilator. The iniquity of the Israelites is full, and the period of grace is ended. The language here is graphic, decisive, and thorough. The word pictures suggest catastrophe. And all because the chosen choose to live no longer like the chosen.

E. A further description of judgment (6:1–14). Ezekiel addresses the mountains (6:1). Perhaps the reason Ezekiel is told to speak to the mountains is that the majority of the people lived in the highlands rather than in the valleys. For a completely different emphasis (restoration), when for a second time Ezekiel prophesies to the mountains, see Ezekiel 36:1.

The high places God will destroy are not the mountains (though juxtaposition of the two is deliberate). They are sacrificial platforms on a natural height. They represent phenomena in Israel's religious praxis that originally may have been innocent and only later became blasphemous. Altars for sacrifice and altars for incense will also be destroyed, along with idols. This Hebrew word for "idols" is used thirty-nine times in Ezekiel. It may be that the Hebrew for "idols" is to be connected with another word meaning "dung pellet." In other words, the objects may be considered holy icons by the people, but they are actually nothing but excrement. There is some problem in connecting verse 5 with verse 4. If God is going to demolish their altars, how will he scatter the bones of the people around the altars? "Demolish" may mean "to make nonfunctional."

Note that the reasons for the people's destruction are not moral (e.g., for sexual sins). The people are condemned for illicit worship styles. They have introduced into their liturgical ceremonies customs unacceptable to their Lord; they have made worship an end in itself rather than a means to an end.

Some, however, will escape the sword (6:8). This is the remnant. (See the language of 5:3.) God judges his people, but he does not obliterate them. In captivity this remnant will remember the Lord they have grieved. God is quite certain that exile will bring the exiled to their senses. Thus we see that deportation is not a means by which God vents his rage. It has both a condemnatory aspect (sin has its consequences) and a salvific aspect (now they will return to me). These two thrusts must be seen in history's first deportation—the expulsion of Adam and Eve from the garden. Its purpose was to both judge them and reclaim them. The God who judges is the God who weeps.

Striking the hands and stamping the feet (6:11), if understood with the same expressions in 25:3, 6, indicate an expression of malicious glee. To see all this happening gives to somebody (the mountains? God? Ezekiel?) a sense of deep satisfaction.

Three scourges will visit the people: sword, famine, plague. These scourges will overrun people whether they are living in Jerusalem, near Jerusalem, or some distance from Jerusalem. Geography will neither condemn nor save a person. The situation of his heart, rather than his house, is the critical issue.

God's judgment will stretch from the desert to Diblah (6:14). The desert is the southern wilderness. Diblah (or Riblah?) is a town situated in Hamath, a country on the northern boundary of Israel (Ezek. 47:17; see 2 Kings 23:33).

What will be accomplished by all this? "They will know I am the LORD." This is not necessarily conversion, but it is admittance of God's power, his control of history, and his lordship over events.

F. The end of Jerusalem (7:1–27). In this chapter the prophet focuses on the termination of Jerusalem. He uses three crisp phrases to express this: "the end has come" (7:3, 6); "the day . . . comes" (7:10); "the time has come" (7:12). The Hebrew word for "end" is related to ripe summer fruit that is ready to be harvested (see Amos 8:1–3). Harvesting involves cutting down and clearing the fields. That is what the Lord is about to do, but it will not be a thanksgiving harvest.

Verses 5–9 repeat verses 3–4. Each time, three themes are prominent: what God is going to do ("I will . . ."); why he is going to do it ("for all your . . ."); the result ("then you will know that I am the LORD"). The botanical metaphors of verse 10 are appropriate. What is growing, however, is not wheat but arrogance and violence (7:11). The phrase "the rod has budded" recalls Aaron's rod (Numbers 17), but the similarity between the two stops at vocabulary. In Numbers it is of God; in Ezekiel it is of sin.

This time will be so bad that the purchaser will not be able to enjoy his acquisition for long, for it soon will be captured and ransacked by the enemy. The individual who has sold something should not be sullen at its loss or departure, for he would not have been able to keep it for long anyway, in light of the approaching enemy. If an individual sells his property, he will never recover that land as long as he lives (7:13). "Recovering land" sounds like Jubilee language (Leviticus 25). But there will be no more jubilee or jubilation. It is a time for war, indicated by the blowing of the trumpet, a sign of the critical nature of the times.

"Outside" and "inside" (7:15) refers to those inside and outside Jerusalem. Three different types of scourges will afflict the people: a sword for outsiders, plague and famine for insiders. The few who will escape will do so to the mountains, but they will moan like doves (7:16; for refugees compared to birds in the highlands, see Ps. 11:1; Isa. 16:2; Jer. 48:28). So frightened are the people they cannot control their bodily functions (7:17). They are like the very young or the very elderly.

Putting on sackcloth and shaving the head (7:18) are ostensibly mourning customs—mourning because of loss and humiliation. Even those things that normally give stability to life—silver and gold—will be abandoned. In fact, it was this silver and gold that partially got the people in trouble to start with (7:19). Long before Paul said it, Ezekiel shows that the love of money is the root of all evil. Silver and gold led to jewelry and jewelry led to idols.

In a time of deep crisis people will grab for anything, even a shoestring. Prophets who have visions, priests who give teachings, and elders who transmit counsel will be of no avail. Normally these are precisely the people to whom

one would turn in a time of difficulty. The three groups of would-be helpers are matched by three categories of would-be victims: king, prince, and people of the land (7:27). The latter three are those who carry influence in society, or who ought to carry influence. Few passages call attention to the connection between conduct/behavior and destiny as clearly as does Ezekiel 7. Note the repeated use of "conduct" in 7:3–4, 8–9, 27. God honors the right kind of conduct among his people; he is appalled by the wrong kind of behavior among them.

G. Idolatry in the temple (8:1–18). Mention was made earlier of defiling God's sanctuary with vile images (Ezek. 5:11). Chapters 8–11 will now spell this out in detail. The timing of this vision is specific: sixth year, sixth month, fifth day—that is, September 592. A problem of interpretation follows: is Ezekiel 8:1–18 a vision, or does it reflect what really happened? Ezekiel is shown at least four abominations that take place inside the temple. He sees these from hundreds of miles away in Babylon. Jeremiah is in Jerusalem around the same time preaching near the temple, but he never gives any hint of these abominations.

The first abomination Ezekiel sees is "the idol that provokes to jealousy" (8:3). While idolatry abounds throughout Israel's history, only one person (Manasseh) had the audacity to place an idol in the temple (see 2 Kings 21:7). Second Kings 23:6, however, tells us that Josiah (who is pre-Ezekiel) destroyed this idol. This indicates that the abominations Ezekiel sees are not necessarily current ones. He is taken on a voyage into the past. So serious is this that it drives God from his sanctuary.

Ezekiel observes the second abomination by looking through a hole in the temple's wall (8:10). What he sees are pictures of animals scratched on the walls, recalling the zoomorphic religion of the pagans, especially the Egyptians. In front of these pictures stand seventy elders. In Ezekiel's day even the national council is corrupt. The text names one of these elders: Jaazaniah son of Shaphan (8:11). He is from a distinguished family in the time of Josiah. Shaphan was secretary to Josiah (2 Kings 22:3). One of his sons (Ahikam) was a staunch supporter of Jeremiah (Jer. 26:24). Another son (Gedaliah) was appointed governor of Judah by Nebuchadnezzar (2 Kings 25:22). Jaazaniah is apparently the black sheep of the family. It is not clear why the people perform their acts of homage in the darkness (8:12), if they believe the Lord has forsaken the land. It makes the most sense to take darkness as part of the ritual rather than camouflage.

The third abomination Ezekiel observes is women mourning for Tammuz (8:14). Tammuz is the Hebrew equivalent of the Sumerian god Dumu-zi, whose name means "the faithful son." He was originally a human being who was deified and later banished to the underworld. That women are weeping for Tammuz reflects

the pagan ceremony observing Tammuz's annual death and descent into the netherworld. Normally this ceremony took place in the fourth month (June–July), but Ezekiel sees it in the sixth month (8:1).

The fourth abomination is twenty-five men facing the east and engaging in sun worship (8:16). This takes place between the portico and the altar, a sacred space.

The statement in verse 17c about putting the branch to their nose is interpreted by some as a fifth abomination, the significance of which escapes us. Note, however, that the phrase in question follows "they also fill the land with violence and continually arouse my anger." Verses 1–17a deal with temple idolatries. Verse 17b deals with social idolatries. It is likely that verse 17c connects with verse 17b and means something like "sneer at me" or "turn their noses up at me." Such brazen idolatries do not go ignored. On the contrary, they cause a major change in how God relates to the people (8:18). The God who lavishes pity now withholds it. The God who listens attentively now turns a deaf ear.

H. The execution of the idolaters (9:1–11). The six guards of the city that Ezekiel sees are really executioners. Together with the man clothed

This scene from the Book of the Dead picturing three Egyptian zoomorphic gods, with animal heads and human bodies, recalls the images of animals seen by Ezekiel in the temple (Ezek. 8:10). From left to right: Thoth with the head of an ibis, Horus with the head of a falcon, and Anubis with the head of a jackal (Ptolemaic Period, ca. 332–220 BC).

in linen (a heavenly scribe), the group numbers seven, the perfect number.

What makes their advancement necessary is the first stage of the departure of God's presence from the temple. He moves from the Most Holy Place to the threshold (9:3). The only thing that makes the temple a holy place is the presence of a holy God. When he leaves, the temple becomes like any other building. It surrenders its sanctity.

There were seven thousand in Elijah's day who did not bow the knee to Baal. And there are those in Ezekiel's day who grieve and lament over all the detestable things (9:4). The heavenly scribe is to put a mark on the foreheads of these faithful believers who have not compromised religious convictions. The Hebrew says: "put a *taw* on their foreheads." Taw is the last letter of the Hebrew alphabet, and in the original Hebrew script it was shaped like an *x*. We are reminded here of the mark on Cain (Genesis 4) that saved him from the wrath of his fellow man. Or one may think of the blood at the Passover on the doorposts that saved the occupants inside from the divine wrath. This concept is reflected in the seal placed on the foreheads of the faithful in Revelation 7:3.

Nobody except the godly remnant is exempted from divine judgment. Sex makes no difference and neither does age. The only thing that spares one is character and commitment.

Ezekiel is not exactly beside himself with joy as he observes these things. He intercedes for the people. Ezekiel 9:8 and 11:13 are the only instances in which Ezekiel intercedes on behalf of his people, a ministry God requested Jeremiah to avoid (Jer. 7:16; 11:14; 14:11; 15:1). The work of the prophet is to be both exhorter and intercessor. The Hebrew phrase for this second ministry is "to stand before the Lord." The prophet must be as good on his knees and his face as he is with his voice. Ezekiel has many models here. He follows Abraham, who prayed that God would not destroy all Sodom and Gomorrah if he found fifty to ten righteous

people in it (Gen. 18). Moses pleaded before God on behalf of the idol-making Israelites and even put his own life on the line in their behalf (Exodus 32).

God seems to ignore the prophet's question as to why God would kill both the righteous and the wicked. In God's response the phrase "the people of Israel and Judah" (9:9) is all-inclusive. This is why God's judgment is so far-reaching— because sin is so far-reaching. It touches not just Judah or Israel but both of them.

I. God's glory leaves the temple (10:1–22). God speaks again to the man in linen (10:2). In the Old Testament it is the priest who is clothed in linen (Exod. 28:39, 42). And only a priest had the prerogative to handle the holy fire of God.

The linen-dressed man in chapter 9 is a scribe. Here he takes coals from among the cherubim and strews them over the city. Here again, as in chapter 1, we encounter fire, which symbolizes either purification and cleansing or judgment. In chapter 10 it is clearly the latter, and reference may be made to the fire that falls on the wicked at Sodom and Gomorrah.

Again, as in 9:3, the initial stage of the Lord's departure from his house is mentioned. Understandably the cherubim are standing on the south side of the temple (10:3), for idolatrous acts take place on the north side (Ezek. 8:3, 5). God removes himself as far as possible from the iniquity. The cherubim are preparing to leave, pulling the heavenly chariot, which is why they are flapping their wings (10:5).

Verses 9–14 focus on the cherubim and the wheels of the chariot. Aside from minor differences, many of the details are similar to those in chapter 1. For instance, a cherub's face replaces a bull's face as one of the four faces. The bull was a popular feature of Canaanite religion, which might explain the substitution.

Verse 15a describes the original ascent of the cherubim, something Ezekiel refers to again in verse 19. Here (10:15b) he identifies them as living creatures. They fly to the east gate of the temple.

Reflection on what he sees makes Ezekiel realize that what is in front of him are cherubim (10:20). Ezekiel is the only person in the Old Testament to see the heavenly cherubim. It is hard to describe something one has never seen before, let alone even ascertain what it is.

The chapter is not really about cherubim or wheels. It is primarily about the departure of God from the temple; secondarily, it is concerned with the destruction of the city. (This last topic is confined to one verse—verse 2—and even there it is just the instructions, not the implementation of those instructions.)

Anything holy in the Old Testament is holy because of its relationship to God. Holiness is always relational, and never intrinsic—whether we are talking about people, land, days, or buildings. Without God's presence they become ordinary. The temple has been in existence for over four hundred years by Ezekiel's time. For all that, it may exist for another four hundred years, but without the divine presence it will be an empty symbol, a shell. It will be like a box, beautifully wrapped but empty.

J. Lost and saved (11:1–25). Again Ezekiel is transported in a vision to the temple. This time he sees twenty-five men, two of whom are named: Jaazaniah and Pelatiah. It is not known whether this is the same group as that mentioned in 8:16. Certainly the Jaazaniah of chapter 11 is different than the Jaazaniah of chapter 8, for they have different fathers. This group of men is not only lost but leading others astray with ill-conceived counsel (11:2). The misleading counsel the group is giving is that the ones who remained in Jerusalem after the deportation of 598/7 BC are the favored ones. Jerusalem is the cooking pot and they are the choice morsels. In verse 15 these people make a similarly false claim: "This land was given to us as our possession." Both of these sentiments (11:3, 15) are the diametric opposite of the truth. What they think is permanent is in fact transitory. Those who are not exiled are chaff. The exiled are redeemable. God directly repudiates the egocentrism of those in Jerusalem.

While this prophecy is being given, Pelatiah suddenly dies (11:13a), provoking a question from the prophet (really, a request for mercy) to God (11:13b; see 9:8).

How wrong the Jerusalemites are! In fact, God is not far away from the deportees. On the contrary, he has been a sanctuary for them even in their banishment. There is a wall around Jerusalem, but it is no wall that confines the Lord and restricts his movement. Even years of incarceration in Babylon can be as full of the glory of the Lord if he is there.

When the exiles are brought back to their homeland, they will eradicate idolatry. Following what they will do (11:18) is what God will do for them (11:19), and following that is what they will do (11:20). God will give an undivided heart (literally "one/single heart") and a new spirit. In other words, not only will there be a geographical change; there will be a spiritual change as well, resulting in new obedience. God will transform both their outer and inner circumstances.

In chapter 10 the divine glory leaves the temple. In chapter 11 the divine glory leaves the city. The temple has been abandoned, and now the city has been abandoned. Without the presence of God both have lost the real reason for their existence. The temple is but a building, and the city is but a site. It is not without significance that the vision of the divine exit follows the promise of return. Does this suggest that God is leaving to join those in exile? Interestingly, the divine glory stops above the mountain east of Jerusalem (11:23)—the Mount of Olives. God does not depart the city in a huff or in a rage, but, to use an anthropomorphism, with tears in his eyes.

The Spirit now brings Ezekiel back to Babylonia (11:24). This is the return portion of his visionary trip to Jerusalem. The screen has gone blank. Now it is time for Ezekiel to share the vision with his fellow exiles (11:25). He must not keep the good news to himself.

K. The exile symbolized (12:1–28). Once again the prophet acts out his message as in chapters 4 and 5. The people living in Jerusalem are using neither their eyes nor their ears. Accordingly, Ezekiel is told to pack his belongings, to dig through the wall of his house, to place his belongings on his shoulder, and to leave with his face covered. Why not leave through the door, as one normally does? Does this show a desperate attempt to escape, or an attempt to escape clandestinely? Covering the face may refer to shame, disgrace, or grief that the would-be escapees will feel.

Ezekiel carries out this pantomime, but apparently it has little effect on the people. So to the acted word (12:3–8) there is added the preached word (12:10–16). The leader in the flight will be none other than the prince himself, who leaves under cover of darkness with his face veiled. To have the prince be the first to run is like the captain of a sinking ship hitting the lifeboats first. But in his running he runs smack into God, snared by the net of the Divine (12:13). The prince and Jonah and Jacob are not the only ones who in their running encountered God right in the middle of their paths. This may be a specific reference to what happened to King Zedekiah (2 Kings 25:7; Jer. 39:7; 52:11). In these days of exile only a few will be spared. For the majority, however, their destiny is sealed. This is one major difference between Jeremiah's and Ezekiel's preaching. Doom for the people is inevitable for Ezekiel. At best a nucleus will be salvaged. This is not an easy or delightful message to preach, but it falls on Ezekiel's heart and shoulders as a divine mandate.

A second act Ezekiel carries out is trembling and shuddering as he eats (12:18). This is the second act of the prophet involving something he does with food (cf. Ezek. 4:9–17). The first one stressed scarcity of food. This one stresses the terror that will accompany food consumption. Mealtime, normally a relaxing, refreshing, reinvigorating time, will be shot through with panic. The people will not be able to "eat your food with gladness, and drink your wine with a joyful heart," as Ecclesiastes 9:7 urges.

A major part of the people's problem is their spiritual insensitivity (12:21–28). They are addicted to a snatch-and-grab mentality, an itch for the instantaneous. Since nothing has apparently happened, they deny the validity of the word of the Lord. The first proverb (12:22) emphasizes skepticism: "You prophets speak and nothing happens." This is an attitude that both Isaiah (5:19) and Jeremiah (17:15) had to face.

The second proverb (12:27) emphasizes irrelevance and postponement: "Ezekiel is not talking to us, but to someone down the road. Therefore we do not need to take anything he says personally." (For a parallel see Amos 6:3: "You put off the day of disaster.") The first saying makes Ezekiel a crackpot; the second makes him a futurist. But God will have the last say.

L. False prophets (13:1–23). Ezekiel's greatest opposition is not from "overt" sinners but from false prophets both in exile with Ezekiel and back in Jerusalem. Jeremiah too had an especially difficult time with them (see Jeremiah 23; 27–28).

The source of their prophesying is their own imagination and spirit. Their resources are all self-oriented. They are compared to jackals, which have a reputation for foraging among ruins (13:4). They show up after the damage has been done to feast on leftovers. Further, the false prophets shrink from the responsibility of being repairmen (13:5). By their philosophy nothing is seriously wrong; so why is there any need for one to "stand in the breach"?

Compounding their guilt is their (false) claim that they are speaking the word of the Lord (13:6–7). Theirs is a false hope: they expect their words to be fulfilled. The false prophets are absolutely sincere. Sincerity, however, is not synonymous with legitimacy.

Their message is peace when there is no peace (13:10). What makes a false prophet false is that his analysis of society is false. This may be due to several reasons. First, he may be paid by the establishment and therefore must say nothing to anger them. Accordingly, the false prophet will be content to be the voice of the people rather than the voice of God. Second, the false prophet may have a false view of God. God, he believes, keeps his promises to his people unconditionally and is favorably disposed to Israel. In either case, the false prophet engenders a feeling of false security among the people: "We have God on our side—always!"

The people build a flimsy wall (13:10) to keep out the rain. What kind of insulation do the false prophets add? Whitewash! But can such a wall and such a covering withstand the storm of God's wrath? The false prophets think so, for they have little room either in their theology or in their homiletics for the wrath of God.

The second group labeled here for condemnation is women who sew magic charms on their wrists and make veils for their heads (13:18). More than likely the reference here is to fortune-tellers. The law demanded the fastening of objects to the body (Deut. 6:8). But here is a prostitution of the custom. There are no copies of the Decalogue beneath these charms or veils. What these women do is ensnare people. The reference to barley and scraps of bread (13:19) may be a reference to the remuneration the fortune-tellers receive, and a pittance at that. Such gross sin for such meager wages! Or these items may well have been used in the magical process. Divination by

wheat (aleuromancy) and divination by barley (alphitomancy) are present in pagan literature.

God responds to these fortune-tellers as he does to the false prophets. Both groups present a false view of God. The pseudoprophets believe they have a monopoly on God's goodness and grace. The fortune-tellers believe they have access to a power other than God. God is nice, but not necessary. Both groups are guilty of a gross malfeasance: they have misled God's people. Most times God's people are to blame for their own sins. Sometimes, however, they are the victims of their leaders' sins.

M. Idolatry (14:1–23). We are not told why the elders come and sit down in front of Ezekiel. If they are anticipating a cozy fireside chat, they are about to be disappointed.

Three times God says that these elders have set up idols in their hearts and put wicked stumbling blocks before their faces (14:3–4, 7). This, however, refers to more than the practice of idolatry. Perhaps the elders have just heard Ezekiel's narration of the temple idolatries that he saw in a vision. "How awful, how blasphemous," they might have said among themselves. However, in seeing the sliver in the Jerusalemite's eye they have missed the plank in the deportee's eye.

If the exiled elders were practicing idolatry, the text would say so in straightforward

The Lord says to the false prophets, "I am against your magic charms with which you ensnare people like birds" (Ezek. 13:20). Such imagery is portrayed in this Egyptian relief, which shows birds, animals, and people ensnared in a large net (Edfu temple, Ptolemaic period).

language. By using the description it does, the text suggests that their sin is an inner idolatry, a mental idolatry, rather than an external one. Idolatry here does not mean prostration before busts of Baal or Marduk or any other god. It is a state of mind that is at cross-purposes with the will and being of God. It is out of the heart and mind that evil comes. God has a ways to go with these people if one day he is to give them "an undivided heart" (Ezek. 11:19). The truth is, they have a divided heart. God will go even so far as to mislead a prophet in giving counsel (14:9). The invitation to turn away from "idol-mindedness" is here (14:6), as is the promise of positive results from repentance (14:11). Behind God's punishment there are always God's efforts to produce redemption and restoration—here, to restore a healthy family relationship, to transform prodigals into the lost-and-found.

In verses 12–20 God parades four hypothetical cases before the exiles (14:12–14, 15–16, 17–18, 19–20). In each, God sends some kind of a scourge into a country because of the citizens' sins. Even if Noah, Daniel, and Job lived in that country, they would save only themselves and not even their children.

This is an odd triumvirate for several reasons. For one thing, Noah and Job are both Gentiles, while Daniel is a Hebrew. Noah and Job lived long before Ezekiel, but Daniel is Ezekiel's contemporary; hence Daniel's listing as the middle rather than the last of the three is unexpected. Noah and Job were married and had sons and daughters; Daniel, to the best of our knowledge, was celibate. Finally, we note that in all three references to Daniel in this chapter (and in Ezek. 28:3) Daniel is actually spelled "Danel" (see NIV note to 14:14). For these reasons some have suggested that this is a Daniel other than Daniel the prophet. But why would Ezekiel use an ancient, legendary, unknown, perhaps Canaanite person as a model of godly righteousness? It would not seem to chime with his message elsewhere about "outsiders."

A righteous nucleus could be the means of salvation for the unrighteous majority (Genesis

18–19). God would spare Sodom if he could find ten righteous people in it, but not here. No longer is vicarious salvation viable. So corrupt are these people that what was true for Sodom (the bastion of depravity) would not be true here.

N. A useless vine (15:1–8). The people still living in Jerusalem are compared to a wild vine that serves no function other than fuel for the fire (15:4). No doubt the mention of an initial burning followed by a second toss into the fire has a historical referent. The first "fire" was that involved in Jehoiachin's (and Ezekiel's) exile. Some, however, came out of that first fire. Their escape will be short-lived. The second fire—Nebuchadnezzar's invasion of 587/6 BC—will consume them.

It is not unusual for Israel to be referred to as a vine, and even as a choice vine. Both Isaiah (5:1–7) and Jeremiah (2:21) speak of God as a vinedresser who experiences keen disappointment over his vine's failure to bring forth good fruit.

Ezekiel, however, goes further than either Isaiah or Jeremiah. He suggests that a vine by its very nature is useless. For Ezekiel, uselessness is a congenital condition. He fails to see any future for the vine. What it is, it always will be. Hence, it is good only to be tossed onto the flames. No doubt, passages like this provide a background for Jesus's statement in John 15 that every unfruitful branch, every branch that does not abide in the vine, is "picked up, thrown into the fire and burned" (John 15:6).

O. A foundling turned harlot (16:1–63). Few chapters in the Bible provide a more forceful illustration of the love of God than this one, which, incidentally, is the longest chapter in the book. The Lord finds a female child abandoned by her parents, who are described in verse 3 as an Amorite and a Hittite. This may be understood as a reference to the pre-Israelite inhabitants of Jerusalem. This child the Lord rescues, raises, and eventually pledges his troth to in marriage. He lavishes great riches on her.

Instead of appreciating and loving her Lord, she squanders her dowry on fornication, engages in ritual filicide with her offspring, seeks other lovers (foreign alliances), and in the process becomes worse than all other harlots. Some twenty times in chapter 16, Jerusalem is connected with the words "prostitute," "prostitution," and "engage in prostitution."

For these sins the Lord sentences her (Jerusalem) to a bloody death. The punishment will be twofold. First, she will be stripped naked before her lovers (16:37), ironic in light of the fact that when she was much younger, the Lord found her naked and then covered her nakedness (16:6–7). Stripping designates public exposure and degradation. Second, God will deliver her to her paramours (16:37–41), who will stone her and finally burn her. Foreign nations will ravage Jerusalem. As in the book of Judges, God's form of punishment on his own is to remove his protective hedge around them and hand them over to an alien.

What makes Jerusalem's promiscuity so abominable is that she is more depraved than her sisters Sodom (to the south) and Samaria (to the north). Samaria is the "older" sister because Samaria is much larger than Jerusalem, Sodom is the "younger" sister because she is smaller than Jerusalem. Both of these analogies would touch a raw nerve, but the one referring to "sister Sodom" would be particularly upsetting. Not only is Jerusalem the worst of the three sisters, but she has done things that make Samaria and Sodom blush! How tragic and ironic it is when Sodomites, the epitome of iniquity, turn red when they gaze on the behavior of the citizens of the city of God!

To shame Jerusalem even further, the Lord promises the restoration of her two sinful sisters, and Jerusalem as well (16:53). God's love is not restricted to one citizenry and to one city. Jerusalem, who once could not even bring herself to say "Sodom," will now have to share the Lord's love with Sodom. After all, if Jerusalem can spread her love around in the wrong way, why cannot the Lord spread his love around in the right way?

Finally comes the announcement of unexpected grace (16:59–63). The Lord will remember and reestablish the covenant he made with Jerusalem in her youth. Further, he will reestablish Jerusalem's hegemony over her sisters ("I will give them to you as daughters," 16:61). God will do so because of his grace and faithfulness. Jerusalem, now shamed and contrite before the Lord, will again know him.

The movement in this chapter is from sin to judgment to restoration; from marriage to adultery to punishment to remarriage. This is a chapter about grace, God's grace, grace given abundantly, grace given gratuitously, grace that is greater than all our sin.

P. Two eagles and a vine (17:1–24). The Lord then instructs Ezekiel to tell the people an allegory and a parable. It is narrated in verses 1–10; verses 11–21 are the interpretation; and verses 22–24 are a prophecy of restoration.

In the story a great eagle comes to Lebanon, removes the top part of a cedar, and carries it away. He then plants the seed in fertile soil, where it turns into a vine. Then another great eagle comes, to which the vine is attracted. The second eagle does nothing. He is simply there. As a result of the vine's attraction to the second eagle, the first eagle will uproot the vine, causing it to wither. An east wind will finish it off.

There is little problem in interpreting the particulars of the message. The first eagle is Nebuchadnezzar, king of Babylon. Lebanon represents Jerusalem. The top of the cedar removed by the eagle and carried to another soil is King Jehoiachin and his fellow exiles. The vine that grows from the cedar crown is Jehoiachin's successor, Zedekiah, and the other great eagle to which the seedling is attracted is the king of Egypt, Psammeticus II (595–589 BC). The branches that stretch out to the second eagle are various parties and emissaries Zedekiah sent to Egypt to gain assistance and support in overthrowing the Babylonian presence in Israel.

For such malfeasance God condemned Zedekiah to execution in exile (17:16). Pharaoh (the second eagle) will be of little help to him then. Zedekiah's sin is that he despised the oath and broke the covenant with Nebuchadnezzar. A commitment should be a commitment. Zedekiah has put a ceiling on the reliability of his word and in the process has condemned himself.

God himself now makes an oath ("as surely as I live," 17:19). He will requite Zedekiah for his oath violation, either of Nebuchadnezzar's covenant with Zedekiah or of Yahweh's covenant with Israel, whose maintenance Zedekiah, as king, was to oversee. Verses 16–18 concentrate on the human agent of retribution; verses 19–21 concentrate on the divine agent. This does not mean that Zedekiah will get burned at two levels. Rather, it indicates that God uses human channels to implement his judgment.

The chapter climaxes with a prophecy of restoration, something King Nebuchadnezzar does not do with covenant breakers, but something King Yahweh does do with covenant breakers. There's the difference! Accordingly, Israel is doomed if she looks to either Eagle Egypt or Eagle Babylon for her well-being rather than to the one who said, "I carried you on eagles' wings" (Exod. 19:4).

Zedekiah is a gambler, one who attempts to play his cards as adroitly as possible. He knows how to shift gears in the game called political opportunism. Unfortunately such ambivalence extends into Zedekiah's relationship with God. His word is unpredictable, and he vacillates on the truth, which is not acceptable to Nebuchadnezzar and certainly not acceptable to the King of Kings.

Q. Individual responsibility (18:1–32). Through his prophet the Lord rebuts a popular proverb that God holds the succeeding generation accountable for the sins of the previous generation (18:2). If the children's teeth (those in exile?) are set on edge, it is because they have eaten sour grapes, and not their fathers.

After disposing of this misconception, Ezekiel constructs a theological/legal argument in support of the thesis of individual responsibility. To establish his case, he uses a three-generational model. The first generation is represented by the righteous father (18:5–9). He is characterized by no fewer than twelve virtues. He is free of cultic, sexual, and sociomoral sins.

Verses 10–13 deal with the second generation, the son. Unlike his father, he is a renegade. He defiantly breaks the laws of the Lord. In such a case, the son will not be able to ride on the coattails of his exemplary father. Instead, he will be put to death for his transgressions.

A discussion of the third generation (18:14–17) is absolutely necessary. This section deals with the sinner's son (in line with the proverb of 18:3). Just as his son rejected (for the wrong reasons) his father's example, so the grandson rejects (for right reasons) his father's example. He is like his grandfather. He does not share in the guilt of his father; he is not condemned because of his father's sins. He is saved because of his own righteousness.

Ezekiel is not creating a new doctrine. Actually, he is echoing Moses, who said: "Parents are not to be put to death for their children, nor children put to death for their parents; each will die for their own sin" (Deut. 24:16).

In verses 21–32 the argument turns to the principle of repentance. As in verses 5–20, a series of examples is provided. The first is that of the sinner who repents and is saved (18:21–23). The second is that of a righteous person who sins and is condemned (18:24–26). The first case affirms that repentance expunges past sins; the second case affirms that reversion expunges merits. Verses 27–28 return to the emphasis of the first example (18:21–23), showing preoccupation with repentance rather than with backsliding.

Verses 30–32 are a clarion call to repentance, for God takes no joy in the death of anyone. What Ezekiel is hoping to accomplish is that the people in exile will accept responsibility for their circumstances. Because their relationship to God is not an intractable or inherited fate, they can return to the Lord. And that is good news. Ezekiel's teaching in chapter 14 (no vicarious salvation) needs to be set alongside his teaching here (no vicarious punishment). You do not go into Abraham's bosom on the coattails of another, and you do not descend into Hades because of another's transgressions. The situation today is just the opposite of Ezekiel's day. Given our emphasis on the individual over the communal, we believe we completely control our own destiny. Given Israel's emphasis on the communal, they believed they could do nothing about their individual destiny.

R. A dirge for Israel's kings (19:1–14). Almost all of this chapter is poetic; it is a lament in two parts over the fall and collapse of monarchs in Judah, here styled as "princes of Israel." In the first part (19:2–9), reference is made to a lioness (Judah?) who sees two of her cubs captured and carried off. One of the cubs is taken to the land of Egypt, the other to the land of Babylon. It is more than likely that the two cubs represent Jehoahaz and Jehoiachin.

In the second part of the lament (19:10–14), the analogy is about a fruitful vine with strong branches, an image we have already encountered in chapters 15 and 17. The entire vine, though once lofty, is uprooted, tossed to the ground, and burned. The specific identification of the vine and its branches once again is not made.

By resorting to metaphors and avoiding personal names, Ezekiel shows a desire that his audience focus on the lesson of the lament and not on "who's who" in the lament. What it teaches is clear. The chapter may well have been titled "How the Mighty Have Fallen!" Kings have become prisoners, for they are rulers who have become

Ezekiel 19:3, 6 say of the monarchs of Judah, "He learned to tear the prey and he became a man-eater," illustrated by this Phoenician ivory plaque of a lioness devouring a man (900–700 BC).

misrulers. Once-powerful individuals have now been reduced to paupers. Glory has turned into disgrace. Riches have turned into ruin. This is all consonant with Ezekiel's earlier emphases. Jerusalem, once a city of sanctity, is now in ashes (or shortly to be so), abandoned by her God.

S. Rebelliousness (20:1–44). Like chapter 16, much of chapter 20 is a survey of Israel's past. This particular review is dated to the seventh year, fifth month, tenth day (August 591). This date is all the more ominous, for it is exactly five years to the day before Nebuchadnezzar torches the Jerusalem temple (Jer. 52:12–13). Again the elders come to Ezekiel for a spiritual message, only to be rebuffed.

Verses 5–29 are about the detestable practices of the exiles' fathers. This section is presented in four subunits. The first is verses 5–9 and covers the fathers in Egypt. Although chosen by God, the people still rebelled and held on to their images. Only for the sake of his reputation did the Lord restrain himself from destroying them.

The second subunit (20:10–17) covers the first wilderness generation. To these God gave his decrees and laws. But rebellion, started in Egypt, persisted in the wilderness. Again, for his name's sake God did not destroy them, but he disallowed entry into the promised land. Their children would be spared.

The third subunit (20:18–26) covers the second wilderness generation. It was much like the preceding. Guidelines were given but rejected. God's reputation restrained him a third time. What was novel here was the promise of exile, which is surprising given the fact that the people had not even entered the land. Also novel, and perhaps mysterious, is that God would mislead the people into sin by replacing genuine laws with statutes that were not good and laws they could not live by (20:25).

The fourth subunit is verses 27–29. The people had moved beyond Egypt (subunit 1) and the wilderness (subunits 2–3) and were now settled in the land of Canaan. Particularly they were charged with worshiping at high places (Bamah means "high place"). They imitated the Canaanites and other Gentile nations in their worship.

From a survey of the past Ezekiel shifts to the present, but only for three brief verses (20:30–32). Here he addresses his immediate audience. That generation continues in the way of its fathers, and therefore they will not get a response from God any more than their forefathers. To be informed that God is not available, that he disallows the seeking of his face, is reflective of the miserably unregenerate state of the people.

Fortunately the chapter does not conclude with a "closed" sign hung in the window of the heavenly office. What God has in mind is a new exodus, this time from Babylon (20:34). Part of this process of deliverance will consist of judgment in the desert, but only so that God may purge his people and sift out those who will accept the bond of the covenant (20:38).

The return of the people to the land will produce a sense of overwhelming shame (20:43) as they recall their impious behavior and that God acted toward them not on the basis of their merit but for his name's sake. Nothing is said here about repentance. Instead, God will do what he does, or not do what he could do, because of his own name (20:9, 14, 22), because of his reputation among the nations and because of his promise to the fathers. God's election of his people is irrevocable, their sins notwithstanding.

T. The sword of judgment (20:45–21:32). Ezekiel is told to set his face against Jerusalem and to preach against the sanctuary. Not only

does this sharpen the focus of chapter 21; it also indicates that the destruction of the city and temple have not yet occurred. Thus, the oracle must be prior to 587/6 BC.

The forest fire of 20:45–49 is now replaced by a sword (the word appears fifteen times in this chapter) as the symbol of destruction. We move from a natural-disaster analogy to a military analogy. In either case, the catastrophe will be far-reaching.

The phrase "I am going to cut off the righteous and the wicked" (21:4) is difficult. Has not Ezekiel, just three chapters back, said the opposite? Does character count for nothing? Granted that one's righteousness cannot save another person (chap. 14), now it seems that the righteous cannot even save themselves. Possibly, Ezekiel is intentionally employing hyperbole in speaking of undiscriminating calamity, all for the sake of persuading the whole community to return to God.

God once again calls on Ezekiel's thespian skills. He is to groan before the people with broken heart and bitter grief (21:6). This acting in turn prompts the people to inquire, and Ezekiel is only too happy to enlighten.

In verse 9 the repetition of the word "sword" is for emphasis. The sword is sharpened and burnished (21:10) and placed by God into somebody's hand (the king of Babylon's?). All power is God's power, and earthly power can terrify only as it is aroused by the wrath of God.

Ezekiel's act of striking his hands together (21:14), in which he is followed by God (21:17), is the triumphant gesture of the victor over the vanquished, thus making the sword oracle all the more frightening.

The last part of the chapter has an oracle against Israel (21:18–27) and an oracle against the Ammonites (21:28–32). It begins with another action by Ezekiel. This time he is told to mark out two roads, one of which heads for Rabbah in Ammonite country and one of which heads for Jerusalem. Both cities are capital cities.

It may seem strange that war strategies are determined through the use of magic, for

Nebuchadnezzar consults arrows/lots, idols, and the liver (21:21) in order to ascertain which of the two roads to follow. Jerusalem, the procedures indicate, is the direction to head. This idea is powerful and unorthodox. Through a magical, heathen operation, legitimate divine guidance is given. Nebuchadnezzar is on the correct road.

The prince of Israel (21:25) must be Zedekiah. He is on the verge of surrendering all the symbols of royalty. There will be no more kings after Zedekiah, "until he to whom it rightfully belongs shall come" (21:27). The messianic thrust is difficult to miss.

The chapter concludes with an oracle against the Ammonites, who gloated over Jerusalem's misfortunes, and perhaps notes judgment on the Babylonians as well. The Ammonites are not to rejoice in the fall of another, and the Babylonians must recognize that, although they are a superpower, there are limits to their aggression. God's ultimate will is that the sword be sheathed.

U. A city of blood (22:1–31). There are no fewer than eight references in this chapter to Jerusalem as a city filled with those who shed blood (22:2–4, 6, 9, 12–13, 27). That phrase is as old as Genesis 9:6. There are no new sins, just new sinners. It is a city marked by violence and brutality, with a soaring crime rate. All this is noted to justify God's intended annihilation of the city.

There are three sections in this oracle against Jerusalem. The first (22:1–16) begins with a challenge from God to the prophet to accuse the city. The city is one in which reverence for life is gone and attachment to idols has become popular. Both the shedding of blood and idolatry incur guilt. In the process, once mighty and glorious Jerusalem becomes an object of scorn and a laughingstock.

The princes of Israel (22:6) are the various individuals who have reigned on the throne in Jerusalem. As a lot, they are characterized as savage barbarians. Power has become a fetish for them. It has become a license to act insanely, even against those deserving highest respect.

Nor is there any reverence for holy things, especially Sabbaths. Sexual decency and propriety is a thing of the past. Social exploitation is rampant. Note that Ezekiel does not neatly divide acts of wrongdoing into the ethical and the ritual. They are all lumped together as "detestable practices" (22:2), whether it is shedding blood or desecrating Sabbaths.

The second unit in this chapter is verses 17–22. A new metaphor is introduced here. Israel has become dross to her God. Dross is, of course, the worthless material removed in the smelting process. In Moses's day God described Israel as "the apple of his eye" (Deut. 32:10). Here is an apple become dross. Dross is like chaff—both are good for nothing.

As silver is put into the fire, so Israel will go into the fire. There is no indication from Ezekiel that Jerusalem will emerge from this smelting process as refined silver. Again we observe a "no-hope" perspective.

The third unit is verses 23–31. Here the prophet rebukes successively the land (22:24), princes (22:25), priests (22:26), officials (22:27), prophets (22:28), and the people of the land (22:29). These are the "heavyweights" of the community, people with political, religious, and financial muscle. Nowhere in this list does Ezekiel confront aliens, children, slaves, or widows. It is one thing to have the political hierarchy go askew (princes and officials), but when it is joined by the religious hierarchy (priests and prophets), then all hopes for the preservation of a conscience in society are dashed. Instead of being loyal to their calling, they place popularity ahead of obedience.

What makes this so exasperating is that God is unable to find among these leadership groups one individual who, taking his life in his hands, will shout at the top of his lungs: "In God's name and for God's sake, stop!" (22:30). Elsewhere the phrase "stand before me" refers to intercessory praying (Gen. 18:22; Jer. 15:1).

V. Oholah and Oholibah (23:1–49). This lengthy chapter is about the sad history of Samaria and Jerusalem (cf. Ezek. 16:44–46 for another reference to these "sisters"). Oholah refers to northern Samaria and means "her tent." Oholibah refers to Jerusalem and the southern kingdom and means "my tent in her." The second name underscores the legitimacy of the Davidic kingdom ("my [i.e., God's] tent in her").

The discussion accorded Oholah, the older sister, is decidedly brief (23:5–10). Oholibah, the younger sister, is discussed rather extensively (23:11–35). The two sisters are presented simultaneously in verses 36–49, and thus the chapter ends as it began (23:1–4).

Using the metaphor of sexual infidelity, God pictures Samaria and Judah as harlots who have abandoned their true love (the Lord) and prostituted themselves to their paramours—really "clients" rather than lovers. In the case of Samaria this involves her attraction to the Assyrians (23:5) and to the Egyptians (23:8). The lovers are described as finely clad warriors. As in Ezekiel 16:37–39, the lovers turn out to be anything but lovers. Their lust now sated, they turn against and ravage the woman. What was supposed to be a tryst turns into a tragedy.

Oholibah tops her sister by one, for she has even a third lover—Chaldeans (23:14). What happened to her older sister fails to deter her from her own promiscuity. History as a great teacher is ignored. She even goes so far as to paint pictures or sketch drawings in red of her lover to be (23:14). Oholibah is so obsessed with lust that she is unable to fetch enough lovers.

Oholibah's lovers will turn against her as brutally as Oholah's did. What Oholibah thinks will be her enjoyment and salvation turns out to be her destroyer. Oholibah/Judah/Jerusalem made one very grave mistake. She looked for salvation in the wrong places. Political alliances with border superpowers, she thought, would save her. How blind! Since when do God's chosen people think they will find greater satisfaction and enjoyment in the nations of the earth than in the Lord of those nations?

To be sure, this is not an innovation of Ezekiel's contemporaries. Earlier prophets (Isa. 7:1–8:22; 30:1–31:9; Jer. 2:20–25; Hos. 7:11–13; 8:9) condemned their generation for fornicating with Gentiles, for pursuing alliances with foreign nations. God's people have become the Lord's unfaithful wife. As her husband, the Lord demands of Israel exclusive fidelity. That is what he has given her, and she needs to reciprocate. If she insists on multiple suitors, then God's only course of action will be to abandon her.

W. A steaming cauldron (24:1–27). Again the date is very precise. It is the ninth year, tenth month, tenth day (January 588 BC). It is the day on which Nebuchadnezzar laid siege to Jerusalem.

On this dark day the prophet is told to put a cooking pot on the fire and place water and choice pieces of meat in it. Already in Ezekiel 11:3 Jerusalemites have referred to their city as a cooking pot and to themselves as choice morsels. The pot provides protection and

Metal cauldrons can be seen along the top of this Assyrian relief depicting captured prisoners and plundered goods (865–860 BC).

insulation, they think. Not only are they wrong on that count; they are also incorrect in equating themselves with choice pieces of meat. In fact, their victims are the choice morsels (Ezek. 11:7).

Chapter 24 expands on chapter 11 by including the fire beneath the pot, something on which the metaphor makers of chapter 11 had not banked. The pot, far from being a shelter, will char and incinerate. In fact, the Lord himself will pile the wood under the cauldron. Once again, the message is sounded that those who survived the deportation of 597 BC are not thereby granted immunity from subsequent disaster. Their complacency is about to be shattered.

On the heels of this incident, Ezekiel is told that his wife will die (24:16). Ezekiel is not alone in weaving his familial experiences into his prophetic message (see Hos. 1:1–3:5; Isa. 7:3–9; 8:1–4). While Jeremiah is denied the normal enjoyments of life (with Jer. 16:2 supplying the only instance of a divine call to celibacy in the Old Testament), Ezekiel is denied the normal grieving process for his spouse (24:17).

Understandably, Ezekiel's stoicism throughout this ordeal provokes curiosity. Is Ezekiel incapable of remorse, is he superhuman, or is he subhuman?

The death of his wife gives the prophet an opportunity to apply her actual death to Jerusalem's impending death. It would be cruel and inhumane of God to take away the prophet's wife just to provide the residents of Jerusalem with an object lesson, and it is most unlikely that that is the case. Rather, the passing of Ezekiel's wife is an opportunity for the prophet, no doubt under heavy duress already, to make his message even that much more pungent.

The Jerusalem that Israel loves will be taken away, and the sanctuary will be desecrated. It is difficult for the modern reader to capture the horror of that dual announcement.

Only when the siege has taken place will Ezekiel have his mouth opened. This release from "dumbness" refers to what God said to Ezekiel in 3:26–27, and the prediction of that

release made here is fulfilled in 33:22. Ezekiel will have made his last dramatic presentation. The closing of Jerusalem will parallel the opening of his mouth.

2. Oracles against the Nations (25:1–32:32)

A. Ammon, Moab, Edom, Philistia (25:1–17). Ezekiel's message is not confined to Jerusalemites or to ex-Jerusalemites now living in captivity. He turns his attention in this chapter to four bordering nations.

Ezekiel first addresses the Ammonites (25:1–7; cf. Jer. 49:1–6), who were descendants of Lot. The main city of their territory was Rabbah (25:5). David annexed them during his reign (2 Sam. 12:26–31). At some subsequent point (post-Solomonic) Ammon regained her independence. Nebuchadnezzar used Ammonites to put down insurrections in Judah (2 Kings 24:2).

What Ezekiel chastises them for is their open mockery of the devastation that hit Jerusalem in 587 BC. They clapped their hands, stamped their feet, and rejoiced—all because of what happened to the sanctuary, to the land of Israel, to the people of Judah. As a result God will now turn them over to a foreign power.

Second, Ezekiel addresses Moab (25:8–11; cf. Jer. 48:1–47). Moab too has connections with Israel, going back to the patriarchs. Their taunt is that Judah has become like all the other nations (25:8). Moab fails to see how Judah's God is potent and able to save. Judah has fallen under Babylonian hegemony just like every other small country.

The third nation addressed is Edom (25:12–14; cf. Jer. 49:7–22), which traces its ancestry to Esau. Their sin is more venal than that of Ammon or Moab. They were not content with simply sneering remarks; they actually took revenge on the house of Judah. They will be judged, from Teman to Dedan (25:13). Teman was in the middle of Edomite territory, Dedan to the far south. Even Israel will participate in her judgment.

The fourth nation indicted is Philistia (25:15–17; cf. Jer. 47:1–7). Like the Edomites, they actively participated in Judah's and Jerusalem's demise. The Kerethites (Cretans) were a Philistine group.

All this invective against bordering nations who treated Judah with contempt, and in turn pay a price, finds its root in Genesis 12:3. We have in Ezekiel 25 an illustration of what happened to four nations who chose to be hostile toward Abraham's seed.

B. Tyre (26:1–28:26). Ezekiel squeezes four nations into the prophecy of chapter 25. By contrast, he devotes three whole chapters (26–28) to Tyre and four (29–32) to Egypt. One is a city, the other a nation. One is a powerful economic and trading community. The other is a regional power but was once a military superpower. Perhaps Ezekiel's extended treatment of these two nations is due to the fact that only these two were in revolt against Nebuchadnezzar at the time Judah was. They survived (for a while at least), while Judah/Jerusalem did not.

26:1–21. The most distinctive feature of Tyre was its physical location, a rocky island just off the Phoenician coast. The natural and artificial harbors provided Tyre with economic advantages and military security. Josephus tells us, in substantiation of this, that Nebuchadnezzar's siege of Tyre lasted for thirteen years (587–574 BC) and was somewhat inconclusive at that. This was a much longer period than the Babylonian siege of Jerusalem. Not until the late 300s was Tyre totally breached by Alexander the Great, who did so by building a causeway from the mainland. Tyre means "rock," which is to be understood both literally and metaphorically. Those who lived in Tyre had security and protection.

This prophecy has four sections to it. The first (26:1–6) identifies the sin of Tyre and the judgment to come on her. The date for this sermon, the eleventh year, first day, is 587 (or 586 if "eleventh month" is inserted). Tyre rejoices in Jerusalem's demise, as did Ammon and Moab. Her unusual name for Judah is "the gate to the nations," indicating that Tyre views Judah as a trading rival. Now she would have the market

to herself. God has something to say about this. He will bring nations against her "like the sea casting up its waves" (26:3). Here is the utter relentlessness of the ocean. No one wave will bring destruction, but the incessant pounding of the waves will destroy even the strongest rock. The phrase "I will scrape away her rubble" (26:4) suggests erosion. Tyre, the protecting rock, will become Tyre the bare rock.

The second section (26:7–14) describes the invasion of the king from the north (Nebuchadnezzar) against Tyre. This paragraph is a particularization of verse 3. The onslaught will be against both Tyre's mainland towns and Tyre herself. Destruction, plundering, and death will be the order of the day.

So devastating is this attack that even the neighboring princes will lament Tyre's overthrow. This is the third section of the chapter (26:15–18). The lament contrasts Tyre as she once was with what she now is and speaks of the tremors her fall has occasioned. If Tyre can be subjugated, what hope is there for anybody else?

The last section (26:19–21) describes Tyre's eclipse; she descends to the realm of the dead. The impossible has happened. Impregnable Tyre is not so impregnable after all. The protection she thought she had turns out to be illusory. Tyre has been "un-Tyred."

27:1–36. In chapter 26 Ezekiel uses the metaphor of an offshore rocky island to talk to and about Tyre. In chapter 27 he shifts the metaphor and compares Tyre to a ship. The appropriateness of these two back-to-back metaphors should be obvious. What an island and a ship have in common is that both are surrounded by water.

Tyre likes what she sees when she looks at herself: "I am perfect in beauty" (27:3). She will shortly learn that one consumed with self-congratulation and self-adulation will eventually come to naught.

Verses 4–7 elaborate on the precious materials brought from afar for the construction of the ship. It is not just the luxuriousness of these materials. Rather, they are products that

Tyre receives in trade, as the places of origin indicate. Ships are for trade, for transporting cargo from place to place. Since Tyre's wealth and status derived from trade, how right it is to refer to Tyre as a ship.

The cities surrounding Tyre provide not only materials for the ship's construction but also personnel for her maintenance, locomotion, and defense. In the process Tyre becomes a trading center, with representatives and merchants of all nations bringing their wares to Tyre for sale and exchange. The city rivals any modern commercial city for frenzied activity and busyness.

In 27:26, however, the ship Tyre leaves port and heads out into the open seas on her maiden voyage. The ship Tyre is about to become the first *Titanic*—the "unsinkable" ship that proves the experts wrong.

The source of Tyre's strength, the sea, becomes the source of her ruin. What once brought her fame now brings her infamy. The sea, once her source of power and pride, is now an instrument of the judgment of God. It is the blatant flaunting of prosperity, the look-what-I-have-done attitude that materialism often encourages. A gift of God, if misused and abused, can become an albatross around one's neck. That is what happened to Tyre and to many like her. And what is left after the ship sinks?

28:1–26. The concern of most of chapter 28 is an individual identified in verse 12 as the king of Tyre. There are two clear parts to this unit. The first is verses 1–10, an oracle of judgment. Verses 11–19, on the other hand, are a lament.

Verses 1–10 perpetuate the maritime connections of Tyre that chapters 26 and 27 emphasize, but verses 11–19 do not. The city is ruled by a monarch who fancies himself a god. Again the point is made, as in chapters 26 and 27, that Tyre's location confers on it an almost superhuman exemption from the vicissitudes most cities face and draws legendary wealth to it.

This feeling of "nobody can interfere with us" has infected the king with a noxious egocentrism. Note how "pride" and "proud" ring in verses 2–5. Possessions have become the yardstick by which the Tyrian king measures divinity.

Ezekiel, of course, is not a publicity agent for the king. He will attempt to be a conscience to him. The prophet announces that this "god" will be toppled—in fact, executed (28:6–10). The king of Tyre will become a "has-been." There has never been a shortage of pretentious gods. It started with Adam and Eve. They thought they could become like God. So did the prince of Tyre, caught up in his own little empire.

Verses 11–19 continue the message against the king of Tyre but in the form of a lament. What is extremely provocative here is Ezekiel's use of Genesis 2–3 in reference to the king of Tyre. Some commentators have suggested that verses 11–19 (along with Isa. 14:12–15) are indeed about Satan (Lucifer), who once walked among the angels of God but fell from paradise because of rebellion and insubordination. More probably Ezekiel presents the king of Tyre as an Adamic figure. The Genesis 2–3 antecedents seem clear in phrases like "you were in Eden, / the garden of God" (28:13); "the day you were created" (28:13); "a guardian cherub" (28:15–16); "I drove you . . . I expelled you" (28:16).

This may be Ezekiel's way of saying that Tyre, like Adam, owes all of her privileges, wealth, security, and power to God. It is not the sea that has made Tyre but the Lord of those seas. Or Ezekiel may be pointing out that those whom God once favored and blessed (Adam and this king) he may later have to punish.

In addition to Genesis analogies, the various stones the king wears (28:13) seem suspiciously close to the high priest's ephod, with its rows of precious stones (Exodus 28). The king of Tyre, in this analogy, was both Adamic and priestly, and both privileges he desecrated. As a result, the king lost what he had, and became what he never need become. His attempt to become deity, although at best a charade, cost him his existence.

C. Egypt (29:1–32:32). Egypt presented the greatest threat and challenge to Babylonian expansion in the Mediterranean world. For Ezekiel and Jeremiah, however, the Babylonians were God's instrument of judgment, and accordingly they advanced a policy of nonresistance. The Egyptian attempt to throttle the Babylonian advance is the antithesis of all they preached.

29:1–21. Verses 1–6a compare the Pharaoh (Hophra?) to the crocodile of the Nile. The king of Tyre deduced his divinity on the basis of the geography and topos of Tyre. The king of Egypt deduces his divinity on the basis of his exclusive ownership of the life-giving waters of the Nile.

God goes on a crocodile hunt. The fish that stick to his scales (29:4), as the monster is dragged

from the waters, represent the citizens of Egypt. They will suffer along with their leader.

Verses 6b–9a represent the second unit, and there is a shift in addressee and metaphor. All who live in Egypt are now spoken to, and not just the Pharaoh. The Egyptians are compared to a staff of reed for the house of Israel. This is not a new metaphor but goes back to Isaiah. The Assyrian Sennacherib sneered at Hezekiah for depending on "Egypt, that splintered reed of a staff" (Isa. 36:6), in a time of crisis.

The point here is not that Egypt failed to provide sufficient support and aid to Judah in her fight against the Babylonians. Quite the opposite. Her fault is that she even encouraged Israel to look on her as a source of confidence (29:16). She gave every impression of collaborating with Israel in her fight for independence from Babylon, and as such falsely pictured herself as a hope and a comfort. What good is it, Ezekiel protests, to offer drowning people straws?

In the third section (29:9b–16) there is an amazing word. God will punish Egypt for her hubris for forty years. But when the forty years are over, God will bring the Egyptians back from captivity. He will return them to Pathros (29:14), an Egyptian word meaning "land of the South." To be sure, she will not be restored to a position of international eminence, but she will be restored.

Ezekiel has no such hopeful word for any of the other nations (chaps. 25–28). Egypt is unique, then, in receiving some clemency, some ray of hope for her future. Might not such a word boost the hopes of the prophet's fellow exiles who hear this prophecy? If God will do it for Egypt, surely he will do it for us.

Verses 1–16 are dated to the tenth year, tenth month, twelfth day (January 587).

Egyptian pharaohs believed they received strength from their gods, such as Sobek, the crocodile god, represented here in a relief from Kom Ombo with a human body and crocodile head (Ptolemaic period).

Verses 17–21 are dated to the twenty-seventh year, first month, first day (571 BC), and represent the latest prophetic oracle in Ezekiel. Here Ezekiel is told that Nebuchadnezzar is to gain control over Egypt as compensation for his less than all-out victory over Tyre. If Egypt is a consolation prize for not obtaining Tyre, then it is a mighty big catch.

Judgment on Egypt means deliverance for Israel, and that is what is meant by "I will make a horn grow for the Israelites" (29:21). The misfortunes of one nation bespeak fortune for another. History is replete with examples.

30:1–26. Ezekiel predicts that a sword will come against Egypt (30:1–19). Egypt will take six of her supporters with her to her doom: Cush, Put, Lydia, Arabia, Libya, and the people of the covenant land. This last expression refers to foreign mercenaries serving in the Egyptian armies.

The general declaration of Egypt's demise (30:1–9) is followed by a specific announcement of how this demise will occur (30:10–12). Nebuchadnezzar will be the instrument of God's judgment. Verse 11 describes what the Babylonian king will do; verse 12 describes what the Lord will do, for he is the real author of judgment.

No explicit reason is given for the destruction of Egypt, except for the reference to "idols, images" (30:13) or "proud strength" (30:6). Some clue may be provided from the word "hordes," which occurs in verses 10 and 15. An alternate translation of "hordes" is "pomp." The Hebrew word occurs twenty-five times in Ezekiel, and sixteen of these are in chapters 29–32.

The second section of the chapter (30:20–26) is dated to the eleventh year, first month, seventh day (April 587 BC). God has broken the arm of Pharaoh, and there will be no healing to follow. This may refer to Necho's defeat at Carchemish in 605 BC or to Pharaoh Hophra's frustrated attempt to deliver Jerusalem from the Babylonians (588 BC). God has broken the arms of the Pharaoh, but he will strengthen the arms of the king of Babylon, enabling him to brandish the sword against Egypt.

Israel expects help from Egypt, but it will be help from a wounded, disabled ally. The prospects for real assistance from such a handicapped partner are bleak. If there are Jewish exiles in Babylon who still look to Egypt as a potential ally and not a threat (29:16), this word about Egypt's inevitable demise should put such feelings to rest permanently.

31:1–19. God gives a message to Ezekiel about the Pharaoh. The king of Egypt and his people are told to think about Assyria, which once was like a mighty, impressive cedar of Lebanon. Handed over to a greater power, the Babylonians, it fell. Ezekiel says to his people and to Egypt, "Look at Assyria and learn."

Ezekiel begins by addressing the cedar directly: Who can be compared with you? But from verse 3 on, the prophet shifts to the third person.

The tree is characterized by great height, lush verdure, and superb irrigation, which makes it fertile. It is so verdant that it offers shelter and nesting places for the birds. It is such a refuge that even animals bring forth their young beneath its branches (31:6). The tree represents a sanctuary. Any within its confines are unthreatened.

It is a tree with deep roots. In fact, the tree is incomparable. Not even the trees of paradise rival it. And all this beauty and majesty is due to God.

Unfortunately, the tree's height goes to its head. Majestic stature breeds arrogance. As a result, God hands the tree over to a ruthless nation. The Babylonians are ferocious woodcutters who quickly level the tree. As a result, the tree ceases to provide shelter for birds, animals, and people. All other trees are addressed with an implicit warning in verse 14. If this magnificent tree vaunted itself and perished all the same, what will happen to lesser trees (other empires) if they become enchanted with their own greatness?

The tree falls as low as the grave. It is not just toppled; it is buried.

Verse 18 returns to the second person of verse 2: Which of the trees can be compared with you? Although she is unique in stature, she is not unique in destruction. Assyria, however superhuman, has no immunity against collapse. Those who climb highest, when they fall, fall farthest.

32:1–32. The lament for Pharaoh (32:1–16) is dated to the twelfth year, twelfth month, first day (March 585 BC), after the capture and destruction of Jerusalem.

Two figures of speech in verse 2 describe the Pharaoh. He is compared to a lion and to a sea monster. God himself throws his net over the beast, rendering him immobile. Then he hurls him on the land and leaves him as food for the birds and animals. The blood and the remains of the carcass are so great that they fill the land. This is not just hyperbole, but a way of indicating the international stature and esteem of the fallen Pharaoh.

The demise of the Pharaoh is such that it sends shock waves into creation and the surrounding nations. Even the cattle will experience the effects of the divine judgment.

The second part of the chapter (32:17–31) is two weeks later than verses 1–16. In one rhetorical question (32:19), Ezekiel removes from anybody's imagination the thought that Egypt has special prerogatives, that she has a special corner on grace or blessing.

As Egypt enters the underworld she is spoken to by individuals already there (32:21). Three great nations, each with a glorious past, have already been interred in the underworld: Assyria (32:22–23), Elam (32:24–25), and Meshek and Tubal (32:26–27—Asia Minor). The dishonorable burial these powers suffered will be Egypt's experience too.

Two last groups are mentioned (32:30): princes of the north and the Sidonians. "Princes of the north" is probably a catchall term designating other nations to the north not previously spoken about in the chapter. The "Sidonians" are the Phoenicians.

The Pharaoh will be somewhat consoled when he discovers that he is not the lone occupant of Sheol (32:31). Misery indeed loves company. Verse 32 is a bit of a shocker. Pharaoh's capacity for belligerence was given him by the Lord. No man, however herculean, acts independently in God's world.

Why such an extended address to Egypt by Ezekiel (four chapters, 29–32)? First, it brings some consolation to the exiles. These Egyptians, who so harassed the exiles' forefathers and foremothers, now get their comeuppance. Second, it is a red flag in the face of the exiles: do not put your trust in those judged by God.

3. Restoration and Renewal (33:1–39:29)

A. Accepting responsibility (33:1–33). The first part of chapter 33 takes up verses 1–20. With its emphasis on Ezekiel as a watchman, the importance of one's present situation rather than the past, and individual responsibility, there are reverberations of Ezekiel 3:17–19 and 18:1–32.

In 33:2 God tells Ezekiel to speak to his countrymen, indicating that what follows is an object lesson about the usefulness of a sentry to the townspeople. Those who hear the sound of the trumpet but choose to ignore it do so at their own peril. A watchman who fails to perform his duties destroys both himself and his fellow citizens.

The watchman metaphor is applied to Ezekiel in verses 7–9, for while it is the priest who teaches, it is the prophet who warns. Ezekiel reveals to his fellow exiles his function as a lookout in order to motivate them to repent. The townspeople's appointment of a lookout parallels God sending his prophet. There is one difference, however. The townspeople appointed a lookout to take care of their own interests. God, on the other hand, has sent a prophet to them not for his interests but in their interests.

The people's lament that they are wasting away (33:10) is countered by the claim that God takes no pleasure in the death of the wicked (33:11). What he takes pleasure in is their turning (33:11). Among the prophets, "turn" is a key word for repentance, especially for Jeremiah, who uses it twenty-seven times, and Ezekiel, who uses it twenty-three times. Repentance of the backslidden is what brings God gratification. What follows is an impassioned appeal by God. The past does not save a person; the past does not condemn a person. Where a person is today in his or her relationship with God is what counts. Jesus seems to say the same thing about the Father when he tells of the two brothers, one who took pride in his past, and one who wished to renounce his past and throw himself on his father's mercy (Luke 15).

The second part of the chapter (33:21–33) is dated to the twelfth year, tenth month, fifth day (January 585 BC). About six months after the destruction of Jerusalem, a refugee informs Ezekiel of what has happened.

Once again Ezekiel addresses those who have survived the massacre of 587/6, those still living in the homeland. These survivors are impenitent and arrogant. Neither Abrahamic descent nor sheer numbers ("we are many") guarantee them possession of the land. They need to subordinate these false crutches to what will really save them, and that is full obedience to God and to his laws. Otherwise, God will turn them over to the treaty curses of sword, wild animals, and plague.

Verses 30–33 focus on Ezekiel and the exiles, whereas verses 23–29 focus on Ezekiel and the Jerusalemites. The sequel is probably deliberate. The deportees had best not say a precipitous "amen" to Ezekiel's words of verses 23–29, as if they are righteous and the Jerusalemites are wicked. Ezekiel is not a person to be listened to for an aesthetic experience. They love to listen to the prophet's words, but they do not put them into practice. They are hearers of the word but not doers. There are many religious platitudes in their mouths, but their hearts are greedy. Therefore, Ezekiel for his exilic congregation is only an entertainment piece. They want a performer but not a prophet; a composer but not a conscience; a musician but not a mandate. Ezekiel, thankfully, refuses to accept the role of a religious entertainer.

B. Shepherds and sheep (34:1–31). By the phrase "shepherds of Israel" (34:2) Ezekiel designates the leaders of the land. In the ancient Near East "shepherd" was a stock term for "king," and even gods could be so styled. Indeed, there are many parallels between this particular chapter in Ezekiel and Jeremiah 23:1–8, suggesting that Jeremiah 23 may have served as the stimulation for Ezekiel 34. The point

The crook symbolized the role of a leader as a shepherd over the people. In this statue, the pharaoh Rameses II holds a crook and a flail (thirteenth–fourteenth centuries BC).

made by the prophets, then, is that a society can be no better or rise no higher than its leaders.

What are the characteristics of these pseudoshepherds? First, they are concerned only about themselves and not about their flocks. Second, they allow the weak and sickly members of their flocks to fend for themselves. Third, they brutalize their sheep. As a result of such irresponsible lapses of duty, the flock has scattered and become prey for wild animals.

The Lord's response to this is twofold. He will relieve the bad shepherds of their duties (34:7–9), and he himself will become the shepherd of the sheep (34:10–16). Note the "I wills" in these seven verses.

Not all the problems lie with the shepherds, however. Blame is to be attached elsewhere. For that reason, in verses 17–24 Ezekiel speaks to the sheep. Among the flock are those sheep who are thoughtless, pushy, greedy, and belligerent. In such cases the Lord will render justice.

This is followed by the staggering announcement that God will raise up a future shepherd, and his name will be David (34:23–24). There are only two other references in the Old Testament to a post-David David (Jer. 30:9; Hos. 3:5). It may be that we should understand "my servant David will tend them/be their shepherd/be prince among them" to mean "one from the house of David" will expedite these ministries, rather than as reflecting a belief that David will return from the dead (cf. 1 Samuel 28; Matthew 17). Christians, of course, read the passage messianically, and properly so.

Verses 25–31 shift from the metaphor of sheep and shepherds to the imagery of prosperity and peace, which the restored people of Israel will enjoy once they are resettled in their own land. The "I wills" of this section may be profitably compared with the "I wills" of verses 10–16. The blessings with which God will visit his people read much like the rewards promised for obedience in the old covenant (see Lev. 26:1–13; Deut. 28:1–14). They are physical, immediate, and this-worldly. A David figure will shepherd God's flock (34:23–24), but

Yahweh himself will also care for his flock in the manner of a shepherd (34:25–31).

The emphasis in this chapter on good and bad shepherding surely provides a background for the New Testament's focus on the good shepherd (Luke 15:1–7; esp. John 10:1–21). Ezekiel would not have any need to fulminate against the good shepherd who lays down his life for the sheep, who knows his sheep, who calls his sheep by name, a shepherd who allows his sheep to feed off him instead of feeding off his sheep.

C. Edom (35:1–15). It may strike the reader as odd that Ezekiel would include an oracle against Edom at this point, because (1) Ezekiel has already addressed Edom (25:12–14) in the section of oracles to the nations (chaps. 25–32) and (2) the section now under discussion (chaps. 33–39) is one given over to hope and promise for Israel's future.

There is a good reason, however, for the inclusion of chapter 35 at this particular point. As we read through the chapter we discover that Edom has visions and intentions of taking over the land of Israel. The two "nations and countries" (35:10) are, of course, Israel and Judah. Once Israel has been destroyed, a vacuum will be created, a no-man's-land, and Edom will be more than delighted to incorporate that acreage into her own holdings.

The concern of chapters 33–39 is the restoration of Israel to her own land. But Israel cannot return to her land if it has been possessed by another. The function of chapter 35 is to demonstrate that no would-be usurpers of Israel's land will succeed in that enterprise. God will see to that. Here is an explicit illustration of the good shepherd of 34:25–31 looking out for his own. What he does with the wild beasts in chapter 34 he does with Edom in chapter 35.

Far from extending her borders by the annexation of Israel, Edom will in fact fall under divine doom. Mount Seir is the chief mountain range of the kingdom of Edom, situated to the southeast of Judah, between the southern tip of the Dead Sea and the Gulf of Aqaba. The mount stands for the kingdom. Because she delivered Israel to the sword, she herself will be delivered to the sword.

D. Restoration and regeneration (36:1–38). Exile is not God's last word for his people. Babylon will never become a permanent home away from home. Israel is not about to fade into the history books. It is God's intention to bring about for his elect both geographical salvation (36:1–15) and spiritual salvation (36:16–38)—in that order.

Ezekiel is told to prophesy to the mountains of Israel and to share the good news with them. This contrasts vividly with chapter 6, where Ezekiel is told to prophesy to the mountains of Israel and share with them the bad news—Israel will be scattered.

The enemies who have taunted Israel and attempted to move into her turf, especially Edom, will find themselves rebuffed. So committed is God to this that he swears with uplifted hand (36:7) to see that it is so. Verses 1–7 describe what God will do with Israel's enemies. Verses 8–16 describe what God is going to do with Israel. What is involved is the restoration of lushness and fertility to the land of Israel. Prosperity and fructification will return, as will people. Key phrases such as "more than before" (36:11), "never again" (36:12), and "no longer" (36:14–15) suggest a decided shift from what was to what will be, from the past to the present to the future.

God was fully justified in doing what he did to Israel in exiling them (36:16–21). Israel's defilement is likened to the impurity incurred by a menstruating woman (36:17). This analogy may reflect Ezekiel's priestly background, for ritual impurity induced by menstrual blood and other bodily emissions was a special concern of the priests.

In exiling his people and in restoring them, God does what he does for the sake of his holy name (36:21–22). It is not primarily the people's behavior, good or bad, that determines God's action, be it in judgment or in compassion. The point Ezekiel is making here is that whatever future Israel has comes from God. Neither the people's repentance nor their facile claims on God's mercy can regain the land. God's own character and sovereign purposes will be the determining factor. God must impress on his people that he is holy (36:23b) and that his name is holiness (36:23a).

God has a more profound interest than the geographical relocation of the exiles to Judah and Jerusalem. He desires for them an interior change once they are there (36:25–27). First, change their circumstances; then, change them. The God who "takes out" his people from the nations (36:24) also takes out everything in his people that is unlike him by sprinkling and cleansing them (36:25).

It may be no accident that the last "I will" in this list is the one about the divine Spirit. Unless there is an infusion of the Spirit into one's life that provides the resources for effective implementation of God's work of grace, then growth in that grace will be most unlikely. Note that the nations confess the power of God (36:36) not only when old towns are repopulated but when they see those former ghost towns repopulated by people with new hearts, with new spirits, with the Spirit.

Neither postexilic nor contemporary Judaism has manifested such interest in "new covenant" living. Ezra and Nehemiah did not lead a back-to-Jeremiah-Ezekiel movement but a back-to-Moses movement. It is the New Testament that finds its roots in prophets like Jeremiah and Ezekiel.

E. Resurrection and reunification (37:1–28). Chapter 37 divides clearly into two sections. The first (37:1–14) describes Ezekiel's vision of a valley full of dry bones that come to life. In the second unit (37:15–34) Ezekiel takes two pieces of wood, inscribed respectively with the names of the tribes of Judah and Ephraim, and brings them together, indicating the reunification of the two nations divided for hundreds of years.

One day the Spirit of the Lord transports Ezekiel to a valley full of bones, somewhere in Babylon. He is led on an inspection tour of the site by the Spirit and is given a close-up view of the horrendous extent of death.

The question put to Ezekiel—"can these bones live?"—is followed by Ezekiel's response—"Sovereign LORD, you alone know" (37:3). Some have interpreted this as an evasive reply. Ezekiel was fairly certain that the answer to the question was no but was reluctant to be that blunt about it. Others have suggested that his answer suggests: "Lord, you know perfectly well, so why ask me?" A third suggestion is that Ezekiel's response is a sign of wonder and trust: "Lord, I may not have the answer to this question, but I trust you, and I know that you know."

In these fourteen verses the Hebrew word *ruah* occurs no fewer than ten times. In verse 1 the word refers to the Spirit of the Lord, which transports and inspires Ezekiel. In verses 5–6 and 8–10 *ruah* is rendered (in the NIV) as "breath," that is, the life-giving breath from the Lord. In verse 9 the plural of *ruah* occurs, designating the four "winds" of heaven. Finally, in verse 14 *ruah* refers to God's Spirit as the life-giving Spirit. Although the metaphor is used for the first time, this is not the first place Ezekiel has spoken of the restoration of God's people to their land.

But what will God do with his people, once restored by the divine *ruah*? Verses 15–20 mandate Ezekiel's act of symbolism with the two sticks. Verses 21–28 then interpret that act to the people. God is going to join Joseph's stick

Ezekiel's vision of the dry bones (Ezek. 37:1–14), depicted on an epitaph (Austria, sixteenth century)

(Israel, the northern kingdom) with Judah's stick (the southern kingdom). David (37:24) will be king over a united people.

The important point here is that (northern) Israel is also involved in this redemption process. In so speaking, Ezekiel is announcing the cancellation of the stigma on the schismatic northern kingdom. There is no doubt that the biblical perspective from the days of Rehoboam and Jeroboam on is pro-Judean. This is reflected in passages of Scripture such as Psalm 78:67–72 ("he did not choose the tribe of Ephraim; but he chose the tribe of Judah").

The single kingdom that God will establish is Davidic but not Judean, for now membership will be extended even to the rebellious house of Israel. All exclusivistic and chauvinistic attitudes will have to go in this marvelous work of God's redemption of his own. For how can divisiveness continue to raise its ugly head where the cleansing, life-giving Spirit has been poured out?

To be sure, nothing approximating this sweet unification of God's people happened in postexilic days. On the contrary, feelings of acrimony were only exacerbated. Ezekiel envisions an age beyond the postexilic era to a messianic kingdom. At the practical level, the chapter speaks to the need of believers to let unity prevail over alienation.

F. Gog (38:1–39:29). Ezekiel has already devoted one section of his prophecy to oracles to the nations (chaps. 25–32). It is somewhat strange, then, that Ezekiel has two chapters (38–39) against another outsider (Gog/Magog) in the section comprising prophecies of hope and restoration. There are many instances in the prophetic books, and elsewhere, of nations invading Israel, but few of those instances are after Israel is resettled in her land (Ezekiel 38–39; Zechariah 14). Although the setting for Israel is ideal at the end of chapter 37, she is not to live happily ever after. A rude awakening at some undisclosed point in the future awaits her.

This particular oracle is directed to Gog of the land of Magog. This is unique in that in none of the oracles of chapters 25–32 is any specific individual named. Where Ezekiel uses names they are normally metaphorical, as in Oholah and Oholibah (chap. 23). It may be that Gog and Magog are "dummy" words. Commentators have frequently connected Gog with Gyges, king of Lydia, or with Gagaia, referred to in the cuneiform tablets from Tell el-Amarna in Egypt as a king of the barbarians. Magog is mentioned in the Old Testament only in Genesis 10:2 (= 1 Chron. 1:5), where he is listed as the second son of Japheth and grandson of Noah. In Revelation 20:8 Magog is a person.

Gog is further identified as the chief prince of Meshek and Tubal (38:2). A footnote to verse 3 in the NIV notes that the phrase may be read as "Gog, prince of Rosh, Meshek, and Tubal." It is this particular rendition that has given rise to the notion, popular in some evangelical circles, that Rosh represents Russia, Meshek represents Moscow, and Tubal represents Tobolsk. Thus, it is claimed, here is an explicit prophecy in Scripture of the now defunct Soviet Union and its belligerence against Israel. This can hardly be the case. Russia may indeed turn its hostilities on Israel, but not because Ezekiel prophesied it over two thousand years ago. Modern "futurists" are not alone in trying to equate Gog and Magog with some contemporary fierce and evil force. In the second century BC, Gog was thought to be Antiochus Epiphanes. Early Christians thought it was the Roman Empire. Luther thought Gog was the Turks of his day.

Maybe they are all right. Any threatening, militaristic, self-aggrandizing nation of any era has the potential to be Gog. But in any showdown of God versus Gog we know who will be the victor and who will be the victim.

While verses 3–9 describe Gog's preparations for invasion of Israel, the point is made that God is the stimulus behind the attack. It is he who incites the "Magogites" to invade. This is made clear by the phrases "I will turn you around, put hooks in your jaws and bring you out" (38:4); "you will be called to arms" (38:8). This is much like what Isaiah said about the Assyrians and what Jeremiah said about the Babylonians. The real mobilizer of the invasion is God. Phrases like "I will put hooks in your jaw" suggest that Gog needs to be dragged into the struggle. Nothing is said about any sin in Israel that prompts the attack. This is unlike any earlier occasion in the Bible when a foreign nation invades Israel.

In verses 10–13 Gog shifts from being a passive instrument to a belligerent, plundering aggressor. The subject of "I will" in verses 1–9 is God. The subject of "I will" in verses 10–13 is Gog.

In verses 14–16 God is the subject again. There is no inconsistency or contradiction in this, any more than there is in the statements that God/Satan told David to number the people (cf. 2 Sam. 24:1 with 1 Chron. 21:1). The Bible, in explaining phenomena, often distinguishes between a primary cause and a secondary cause. Here it is not a case of God *or* Gog, but God *and* Gog. One is the primary cause of invasion; one is the secondary cause.

Nothing in chapter 38 indicates the attack takes place or has taken place. It is all future. When Gog does attack Israel, he will have God to deal with. The judgment he will receive will be akin to that on Sodom and Gomorrah, or on Egypt in Moses's day. With the exception of the reference to a sword (38:21), all of the judgments are in nature (earthquake, plague, rain, hailstones, burning sulfur). How all these disturbances will miss Israel is not clear. Will

God put some kind of a shield around his people to protect them from these elements, as he protected Israel from hail (Exod. 9:26) and darkness (Exod. 10:23) in the time of Moses?

In many ways chapter 39 is like 38. For example, in chapter 38 Ezekiel is told to set his face against Gog. Here he is told to prophesy against Gog. In 38:3 and in 39:1 Gog is told that God is against him. Third, the emphasis is made that God will forcibly bring Gog against Jerusalem. Fourth, after Gog attacks Jerusalem God will bring destruction on Gog.

What is novel in chapter 39 is the description of the immediate post-Gog days in Israel. We are told that the weapons left behind by Gog and his troops will serve as fuel for the Israelites for seven years (39:9). This will save cutting the forest trees for firewood (39:10). The number of slain Magogites will be staggering. It will take Israel seven months to bury the dead of the enemy; the name of the burial site is the Valley of Hamon Gog (39:11; "the hordes of Gog"). In assonance, "Valley of Hamon" is very close to "Valley of Hinnom" (Gehennah). The Valley of Hamon is located east toward the Sea (39:11), probably a reference to an area east of the Dead Sea and thus outside Israelite boundaries. To make sure that not even a bone of a slain Magogite is missed, a commission is appointed to go through the land after the first seven months' work. It is important not only that the enemy be defeated but that he be removed and interred as well. Weapons must be not only captured but burned.

A further novel point here is the reference to the enormous feast that follows (39:17–20). Even the carrion birds and wild animals are invited. The menu, admittedly gruesome, lists flesh to eat and blood to drink. Such a cannibalistic metaphor is obviously just that—a metaphor. To interpret it literally would force a primitive crudity on the text. Further, we have to reconcile the burial of the enemy (39:11–16) with the subsequent feasting on the dead enemy (39:17–20). How does one eat what one has just buried? Strict chronological concerns have been subordinated to other concerns. What Ezekiel is portraying is the total annihilation of the enemy and Israel's radical elimination of them.

Note that Israel is not allowed to taunt the one who has fallen in her midst. Other nations found themselves in hot water for expressing such feelings against Israel when she was down and out. Ridicule, sarcasm, and taunting are illicit in anybody's mouth.

What is to be accomplished by this destruction of Gog? For one thing, God will display his glory among the nations. It is not his power or his wrath but his glory he displays. If word of what has happened goes no farther than Israel and Gog, then the ultimate purpose of it will have been missed. Now, Israel will know who the Lord is, and the nations will know why God exiled his people. In other words, God does not overlook in his own the sins he would condemn in an outsider. The election of Israel brings not only privileges but also, and primarily, heightened responsibilities, the subverting of which entails horrific judgment.

The climactic phrase is "I will pour out my Spirit on the people of Israel" (39:29). Wherever the Spirit is "poured out" (Acts 2:18; 10:45), the possibilities for spiritual growth, stability, and influence become almost incalculable.

4. The New Temple (40:1–48:35)

A. The temple area (40:1–49). The vision of the new temple comes to Ezekiel in the twenty-fifth year of his exile, at the beginning of the year, on the tenth of the month; this is fourteen years after the fall of Jerusalem. This is the latest date in the book except for 29:17–21. The year mentioned in verse 1 is 573 BC. The month designated as "the beginning of the year" could be either Nisan (spring) or Tishri (fall). The "tenth" day of each month is significant. The tenth of Nisan begins Passover observance (Exod. 12:3). The tenth of Tishri is the Day of Atonement (Lev. 16:29), and it inaugurates the year of Jubilee (Lev. 25:9). Liberation, renewal, and reconciliation are the themes of these days. Is there any possible connection with Ezekiel 40:1?

For a second time Ezekiel is transported in a vision to Jerusalem. The first excursion for the prophet was to witness Jerusalem's abominations and destruction (chaps. 8–11). This trip is for the purpose of viewing Jerusalem's and the temple's restoration.

Ezekiel is set down on the temple mount. There he sees what "[looks] like a city" (40:2), which is more than likely a reference to the walled complex of the temple (40:5). (The phrase "that looked like" recalls the prophet's vision of the heavenly chariot in chapter 1.) He then meets a man (some kind of celestial being) who will be the prophet's guide. This bronzelike man holds a measuring rod in his hand, and it measures six long cubits (10 feet 3 inches).

The first item shown to Ezekiel is a massive perimeter wall around the entire complex, giving the impression that the temple area is not unlike a fortress. This is followed by detailed information about the measurements of the east gate into the outer court (40:5–16). The gate is reached, first of all, by a seven-step staircase. Adding to the impression that Ezekiel sees a fortresslike structure is the fact that, once inside the gate, one observes three guard rooms (NIV "alcoves") flanking the passageway on each side. It is clearly stated that these rooms are for the guards.

Approximately the same information is given about the north gate (40:20–23) and the south gate

(40:24–26). These three gates all open into the outer court (40:17–19), in which there are thirty rooms.

Next, the prophet is shown the three gates that open into the inner court (40:28–37). These gates are much like those of verses 5–27, except they are eight steps (not seven) higher than the outer court. The inner court is a square of one hundred cubits.

In three of the rooms off the inner court and near the gateways there are installations for the slaughtering of the burnt offerings, sin offerings, and guilt offerings.

Finally, Ezekiel is shown two rooms off the inner court that serve as priestly chambers (40:44–47). One group of priests has charge of the temple, and one group has charge of the altar. These are described as the sons of Zadok, Levites. Again, it is guarding responsibilities that are noted, as the Hebrew expressions used here would indicate. Verses 48–49 continue the movement in this chapter from outside in, with a brief reference to the temple proper. It is

A tablet containing an architect's plan for a temple dedicated to the god Ningirsu is part of this statue of Gudea (2100 BC). The drawing may show the wall around Ningirsu's shrine.

reached by a stairway of ten steps (40:49 NIV note).

B. The temple proper (41:1–26). Ezekiel 40:5–47 describes the temple area (outer court/inner court). Ezekiel 40:48–41:26 turns to a description of the temple building. Like Solomon's temple, it has three parts on an east-west axis: (1) the vestibule/porch (NIV "portico") (40:48–49); (2) the outer sanctuary or the Holy Place (41:1–2); and (3) the inner sanctuary or the Most Holy Place (41:3–4).

Note here the increase in numbers. So far we have seen seven steps into the outer court, eight steps into the inner court, and ten steps into the temple proper. We have also witnessed a decrease in numbers. The entrance into the portico is fourteen cubits (40:48); the entrance into the Holy Place is ten cubits (41:2); the entrance into the Most Holy Place is six cubits (41:3). Each stage gets higher and higher. Each opening gets narrower and narrower.

Off three sides of the sanctuary (north, south, west) are a number of chambers (41:5–12). Nothing is said about the functions of these rooms, but they probably served as storerooms for equipment and furnishings, perhaps for tithes and offerings as well. Also there is an unidentified building at the back (west) of the temple (41:12).

The temple is one hundred cubits long (41:13a), and the inner courtyard is one hundred cubits square (41:13b–14). Also the yard/building behind the temple is one hundred cubits in length (41:15). The symmetry of these measurements is not coincidental. Everything in the temple fits perfectly and balances the whole.

Verses 15–26 describe the decorations and the woodwork of the temple. Impressive here are two-faced carved cherubim and palm trees. The wooden altar (41:22) may represent either the table of showbread or the small inner altar of incense.

C. Holy chambers (42:1–20). From 40:5 through 41:26 the movement, in the description of the temple, has been from outside to inside. Now the prophet is led back out to the outer court (42:1), where he is shown two sets of holy chambers (rooms for the priests), one on the north side of the outer court (42:2–9) and one on the south side of the outer court (42:10–12).

Verses 13–14 inform us of the functions of these rooms. They are, first of all, a place where the priests eat the most holy offerings. Second, they are changing rooms, in which the priests remove their sacred vestments before going into the outer court, where the laity are. It may appear to be a contradiction that these rooms are already in the outer court (42:1), and yet the priests must disrobe in these rooms before going into the outer court (42:14). The contradiction resolves itself if one understands these chambers to border on the inner court and to extend into the outer court, thus serving as a transition zone between the two.

Ezekiel is shown and told the external measurements of the entire temple complex (42:15–20). The complex is a square of five hundred cubits.

The purpose of the temple complex is to separate the holy from the common (42:20). Inside is holy; outside is profane. The opposite of "holy" in the Old Testament is not "sinful" but "common."

These three chapters (40–42) lay out the floor plan of this temple, and everything that follows (43–48) builds on them. While some interpreters look for a literal (millennial?) fulfillment of this vision, many believe that God was not giving his people the blueprint for a building project, which at some undisclosed time in the future they would implement. God is more likely speaking imaginatively than literally. The emphasis is not so much on bricks and mortar as on the return and permanent dwelling of the divine presence among his people. Interestingly, Jerusalem is never mentioned anywhere in these chapters 40–48. Nor is there mention of anybody who will be the construction supervisors and builders, as with Moses and the tabernacle and Solomon and the temple. When, however, the returning exiles come back to Jerusalem and turn their attention to rebuilding and restoring the ravaged temple, surely access to Ezekiel's vision will serve as a stimulus to them.

D. God's glory returns (43:1–27). Now outside the temple, Ezekiel is brought to the gate facing east to witness the return of the presence of God. It was through this gate that Ezekiel saw the divine glory leave the temple in 10:19. God returns through the gate by which he left. When he returns to his abode, God does not tiptoe back. He returns as a king (43:7, which refers to the only throne in this newly restored Jerusalem). With God's presence restored to the place of worship, religious apostasy becomes unlikely. Idolatry will be a thing of the past.

That Ezekiel is to make known to the people all the data about this new temple suggests that he is another Moses (43:10–11). God is the designer; Moses and Ezekiel are the transmitters of data.

The return of God's presence and God's directive to Ezekiel are followed by information about the altar in the temple (43:13–27).

Note the parallel here. The temple, although now finished, is not ready for service until the divine glory returns. Similarly, the altar, although completed, is not ready for use until it has been purified.

There are many notable omissions in Ezekiel's temple when it is compared either with the tabernacle in the desert or with Solomon's temple. Most obvious is the absence of any reference to the ark, the mercy seat, and the cherubim. The same may be said of the laver, the lampstand, and the bronze altar. The implications of these omissions are obscure.

But the altar is there, indicating that there will never be the possibility of legitimate worship without the presence of sacrifice. Two things are necessary for the reopening of the temple. One is the presence of the glory of God. Unless the Shekinah fills, the shell (i.e., building) fails. The second indispensable element is a purified altar.

E. Enterings and exitings (44:1–31). Once again Ezekiel is taken to the outer east gate,

which, he is told, is to be permanently locked, for that is the gate through which the Lord passed when he returned to the temple. The one exception is that the prince may use its vestibule when eating (44:3).

Next, Ezekiel is brought to the front of the temple by way of the north gate. Again Ezekiel sees the divine glory, and he falls on his face.

Ezekiel is told to look carefully, listen closely, and give attention to everything God is about to tell him (44:5). These imperatives sound much like 40:4, except that there they refer to what God is going to "show" Ezekiel.

God begins with a rebuke aimed particularly at the laity (the rebellious house of Israel) for allowing foreigners to guard the holy things. We cannot be sure of what Ezekiel/God speaks here. In the future, these laity will be replaced by Levites. They will slaughter the people's sacrifices, something that the laity themselves are supposed to do (Leviticus 1–4). It may be that, in transferring the responsibility for ritual sacrifice to the Levites, God is in effect punishing the people by barring them from the inner gates, where the sacrifice takes place.

Although the Levites are to fulfill certain functions, they are not to serve as priests. The priesthood is reserved exclusively for the descendants of Zadok (the hereditary priesthood of the Solomonic temple). They alone may enter the sanctuary.

The remainder of the chapter is devoted to the dos and don'ts of these Levite priests/sons of Zadok who serve at the altar. This includes their clerical clothing and "street clothing" (44:17–19), their hairstyle (44:20), their beverages (44:21), prospective spouses (44:22), their teaching ministry (44:23), their judicial obligations (44:24a), their responsibilities as guardians of holy days (44:24b), and their limitations on incurring corpse-impurity (44:25–27). The chapter concludes with data about the oblations to be given them by the Israelites (44:28–31). God is to be the only inheritance the priests have (44:28). In serving him they find their highest fulfillment and reward. Not possessions but obedience in ministry crowns the life of the altar-serving priest.

We noted in our discussion of chapters 40–43 the interesting absence from Ezekiel's temple of such standard items as the ark, cherubim, lampstand, and table of showbread. We note similarly in chapter 44 the absence from this temple of any high priest. The two omissions go together, for the inner area of the temple was the particular domain of the high priest.

F. Division of the land (45:1–25). The emphasis on priests and Levites in the previous chapter continues in chapter 45. Chapter 44 focused on the priest's responsibilities. At the end of the chapter notice was made about the food supply of the priests. Chapter 45 moves from food supply to land supply. This land supply is called a sacred district.

First of all, a portion of land twenty-five thousand cubits long and twenty thousand cubits wide is to be given to the priests. In the midst of this is the sanctuary, which is five hundred cubits square. There is a fifty-cubit "green belt" around this section (45:1–4).

Second, there is a portion for the Levites that is twenty-five thousand cubits long and ten thousand cubits wide. Distinction is made here between the priests, who minister in the sanctuary (45:4), and the Levites, who serve in the temple (45:5).

Third is an area designated as city land (45:6). Fourth is a reserve for the prince (future king) on the east and west sides of the sacred district and the city (45:7–8).

While Ezekiel is talking about the contribution and apportionment of land for the prince, he addresses a sermonette to the kings (45:9–12). They are to keep their hands off their subjects' holdings and are to be honest in the collection of taxes for the upkeep of the temple. Thus, the king is to be one who has "learned to be content whatever the circumstances" (Phil. 4:11) and who is impeccable in his business affairs.

With these collected portions the king can provide what is needed for the additional offerings on the feasts, the New Moon days, and the Sabbaths. Verses 18–25 speak of the annual sacrifices. Of special import here is the sacrifice of the first day and the seventh day of the first month. The purpose of these sacrifices is clearly the purification of the sanctuary (45:18), making atonement for the temple (45:20). It is God's own house that is to be purged. The two annual pilgrim feasts highlighted are Passover (45:21–24) and the Feast of Tabernacles (45:25).

G. Worship protocol (46:1–24). Ezekiel 45:18–25 lists the occasions of the annual sacrifices; 46:1–11 notes the occasions of the repeated sacrifices (i.e., the Sabbath day and the New Moon or first day of each month). Special emphasis is placed on how the prince and the laity are to enter and exit the place of worship.

In the prince's case, he approaches (but may not enter) the inner sanctuary by way of the eastern gate, on whose threshold he worships. He is to make certain that he enters and exits by the same gate on both Sabbaths and New Moons. In the laity's case and the prince's case, they are both to exit by the opposite gate they entered on the annual festivals. Thus they must traverse the entire outer court.

That the gate is left open until evening (46:2) probably indicates that the laity may look into the holy precinct while they worship by the exterior entrance.

After speaking of the prince's voluntary and daily offerings, Ezekiel takes up the matter of how the prince should give gifts of land to his sons or servants, and what limitations apply when those endowments of crown land are given to servants. Gifts the prince gives to his courtiers are to revert to the crown in the year of Jubilee.

The chapter concludes with Ezekiel being shown the temple kitchens, the place where the sacrifices are cooked or baked (46:19–24). There are two sets of kitchens. One is for the priests and the other is for the laity. This second set is located in the outer court. The more minor sacrifices are prepared here. Once again, the gradation of holiness is prominent even where kitchens are concerned.

H. The river of life (47:1–23). In the first twelve verses of chapter 47 Ezekiel is shown water coming out of the temple's south side. From there it flows for four thousand cubits through a desert and eventually empties into the Dead Sea. For this to happen, God must perform a geophysical miracle by making the temple site in Jerusalem a source of freshwater.

A celestial man leads the prophet on a tour of this river. At one thousand cubits it is ankle-deep. At another one thousand cubits it is knee-deep. At another one thousand cubits it is an unfordable river, deep enough to swim in. It is not explained how the river gets deeper as it flows farther. There is no mention of any tributaries that might explain the greater depth.

What makes this river so interesting is not only its increasing depth but the positive effects of its waters. The river desalts the Dead Sea, so the sea becomes a fisherman's paradise. Wherever the river flows and whatever it touches, the result is life.

Not only is the Dead Sea desalinized; the desert is fructified. Fruit trees of all kinds grow on both sides of this river. The fruit from these trees provides food and healing.

What is of interest here is that the vision of this river singles out for transformation the most barren tract of land (the Arabah) and the body of water most inhospitable to life (the Dead Sea). Moreover, the water flows from a temple built on solid rock!

This is surely a picture of the power of God's presence in his temple and among his people. It affects everything for good. There can be no doubt that Jesus had this chapter in mind when he said: "Whoever believes in me, as Scripture has said, rivers of living water will flow from within them" (John 7:38). That Jesus goes on in the next verse to connect these streams of living water with the Spirit is not without significance. The supply for the water from the temple (built on rock) is supernatural. The same is true of the follower of Jesus.

The vision of the temple river is followed by an outline of the boundaries of the land (47:13–23). We note with interest that these boundaries do not include land west of the Jordan. This must mean that the three Transjordanian tribes (Reuben, Gad, and half-Manasseh) are to be given different territories (see chap. 48). The boundaries also leave out Aramean territory to the north, once conquered by David, and Edomite territory to the south, once part of the Judahite kingdom.

Of particular import is the fact that verses 21–23 integrate the alien into the tribal structure and allow him to share in the patrimony of Israel. Earlier biblical injunctions had insisted on the humane and moral treatment of the alien (e.g., Exod. 22:21; Lev. 19:10; Deut. 14:29), but they still kept the alien outside of the tribal structure. Ezekiel's word is more radical than even that of the Torah. All of God's children, alien and native-born, will be part of this new community.

I. Division of the land (48:1–35). With the external boundaries now in hand, Ezekiel can turn to the matter of interior boundaries: how the land is to be divided among the tribes. The order of tribal allotments is unlike anything in any previous period of Israelite history.

The sequence from north to south is Dan, Asher, Naphtali, Manasseh, Ephraim, Reuben, Judah, priests/Levites, Benjamin, Simeon, Issachar, Zebulun, and Gad.

Tribal areas named after Jacob's sons by concubines are placed at the extremes (in the north, Dan and Naphtali by Bilhah, Asher by Zilpah; in the south, Gad by Zilpah). Tribal areas named after Jacob's sons by Leah and Rachel are placed closer to the center. Tribal areas always a part of the north are now shifted to the south: Zebulun and Issachar. Such repositioning allows the placement of the temple more perfectly in the center of the land. In fact, this city (never called "Jerusalem") is really an adjunct to the temple (rather than the other way around), what one might properly call a "temple city."

Most startling is that Judah and Benjamin are reversed. It is now Judah that is north of Benjamin and not vice versa. Is this Ezekiel's way, and God's way, of dampening sectionalism in the new order? No one tribe will be more sacrosanct than the other, or have pride of position.

Each tribal area is to be equal in size. To be sure, this is not stated explicitly, for chapter 48 provides only east-west determinants and not north-south boundaries. It is a legitimate inference, however. If the last few verses of chapter 47 deal with inequities between native-born and aliens, chapter 48 deals with inequities between tribal giants and tribal dwarfs. For Ezekiel, all such differences will be eradicated. Strong/weak, big/small will no longer be categories of distinction.

Between the seven tribes to the north and the five to the south is a special portion (48:8–22). It is a strip of land twenty-five thousand cubits long and wide and is divided into three east-west strips. The northernmost strip is for the priests (48:9–12); the middle strip is for the Levites (48:13–14). Both strips are designated holy. The lowest strip contains a centrally located city surrounded by land for grazing and flanked by farmland. Land outside of this square is crown land.

The last topic covered in the chapter is the reference to the four sides of the city, each of which has three gates bearing the names of three of the tribes (48:30–35). In this system the Ephraim and Manasseh of verses 4–5 have merged into Joseph, and Levi is counted as one of the twelve tribes. Leah's six sons (or the tribes bearing their names) are positioned at the northern and southern gates.

Finally, Ezekiel concludes his prophecy by identifying the name of this twelve-gate city. It is "THE LORD IS THERE." "Jerusalem" is conspicuous by its absence. What gives the city any kind of sanctity is not tradition, but the presence of the Lord. His glory is not confined to the temple. It spills into the whole land. In Ezekiel's city and John's city (Rev. 21:12–27) the climax is the same: God's dwelling is with people.

Select Bibliography

Allen, Leslie C. *Ezekiel.* 2 vols. Word Biblical Commentary. Dallas: Word, 1990, 1994.

Block, Daniel I. *The Book of Ezekiel.* 2 vols. New International Commentary on the Old Testament. Grand Rapids: Eerdmans, 1997, 1998.

Duguid, Iain M. *Ezekiel.* NIV Application Commentary. Grand Rapids: Zondervan, 1999.

Greenberg, Moshe. *Ezekiel.* 2 vols. Anchor Bible. New York: Doubleday, 1983, 1997.

Taylor, John B. *Ezekiel.* Tyndale Old Testament Commentaries. Downers Grove, IL: InterVarsity, 1969.

Wright, Christopher J. H. *The Message of Ezekiel.* The Bible Speaks Today. Downers Grove, IL: InterVarsity, 2001.

Daniel

Willem A. VanGemeren

Introduction

Authorship and Historical Context

According to the claims of the book itself (9:2; 10:2), the New Testament (Matt. 24:15), and Jewish and Christian tradition, Daniel is the author of the book that bears his name. Daniel, whose name means "God is judge," was carried into captivity from Jerusalem to Babylon in the third year of Jehoiakim (1:1), which, according to the Babylonian system of reckoning, was 605 BC. Apparently, he was of noble descent and was selected to become the king's courtier in a foreign land. He received special training in Babylon but was distinguished from his peers by a God-given ability to interpret dreams. Like Joseph in Egypt, God raised up Daniel to be his spokesperson in Babylon. He served under Nebuchadnezzar, Belshazzar, and Darius the Mede.

Authorship of the book has been contested since the time of Porphyry, a third-century-AD philosopher. Porphyry argued that the book reflects a second-century-BC background, recounting the actual historical circumstances of Antiochus Epiphanes. He denied the predictive element of prophecy and explained the book as a pious hoax. Unfortunately, this line of argument has had advocates throughout the history of interpretation, based on alleged historical errors, the denial of predictive prophecy, and the presence of Greek and Persian loanwords.

The book recounts Daniel's ministry from about 600 BC to 536 BC, the third year of Cyrus the Persian. The book must have been completed after the first Jewish migration to Judea. It records the transfer of authority from Babylon to Persia but is silent on affairs regarding the Jewish political nation.

Literary Features

The book of Daniel has two major divisions. The first six chapters consist of third-person narratives about Daniel and his friends in a

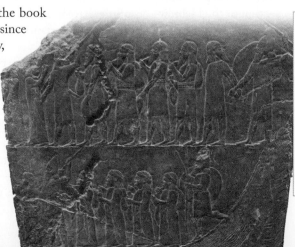

This scene from an Assyrian relief, showing prisoners being deported after the capture of their city during Ashurbanipal's campaign against Elam (653 BC), resembles the deportation of the inhabitants of Jerusalem by Babylon.

foreign court. Their response to the challenges posed by a pagan culture exemplifies loyalty to the covenant; even when their lives are threatened, they persevere in the faith. These stories are intertwined with dreams and interpretations of dreams. Chapters 7–12 are composed solely of visions and interpretations, written in the first person.

The book of Daniel belongs to the apocalyptic genre of literature. Apocalyptic literature flourished in Judaism from 200 BC to AD 100, but its roots were already present in the Old Testament prophets. The prophets—especially Ezekiel, Zechariah, and Daniel—employ visions and symbols. This in no way compromises the reliability of the historical information in the book of Daniel. At the same time, we must admit the difficulty in clearly distinguishing the historical from the symbolic.

The book of Daniel is written in both Hebrew (1:1–2:4a; 8:1–12:13) and Aramaic (2:4b–7:28). This reflects the historical situation, as Aramaic gradually became the official language of the Near East from 1000 BC until the time of Alexander the Great, when Greek supplanted it.

Daniel's position in the English Bible is different from that in the Hebrew Bible. In the Hebrew Bible it is placed in the third group—the Writings—after Esther and before Ezra-Nehemiah. Critics have argued that the book was not written until after the prophetic era, after the second section (the Prophets) was already closed, and that it could therefore only be included in the last section of the Hebrew Bible.

Others, contending that the spirit of prophecy does not operate outside Israel, have argued that Daniel was not a prophet. Against this view, however, it must be noted that Ezekiel's ministry took place wholly in exile, by the Kebar River. Yet it must be admitted that Daniel is a different kind of prophet. He does not quite fit the traditional definition, because he functions as a sage much like Joseph in a foreign land.

Theological Themes

The message of Daniel focuses on the sovereignty of the Creator-Redeemer over the kingdoms of this world (earthly power structures), the suffering and perseverance of the saints, and their deliverance when the kingdom of God triumphs over all human power structures. Difficult as it may be to fit all the pieces of the interpretive puzzles together, the message of Daniel, like that of Revelation, is clear. It is an encouragement to persevere in godliness in the hope of the final establishment of the everlasting kingdom of God and his Messiah.

The book of Daniel consists of revelations given over a seventy-year period, while the remnant of Judah and Israel were in exile. The people felt the absence of God, having been forcibly separated from their land and having witnessed the destruction of Jerusalem, including the temple. This period of isolation forced the people to look once again to the Lord as the source of grace and favor. In this context the Lord raised up Daniel. The words of Daniel, however, were not known to the people in exile. Apparently, he had little contact with the Jewish community. Daniel's role was that of a Babylonian statesman. Only after the exile did God's people receive the record of God's revelation to Daniel, giving them an interpretive framework. Notwithstanding the symbols, numbers, and ambiguous language, the message of Daniel is clear. The book is a powerful witness to the certainty that God's kingdom will be established. God's people throughout the centuries have been challenged to look beyond historical circumstances and to look to God for the ultimate reality.

The difficulty of interpreting Daniel and the variety of competing explanations function as a sober reminder not to seize upon any one interpretation. God holds the key to this and has given his authority to the Messiah. We do well to take our cue from Jesus, who saw in the prophecies of Daniel an intersection between the divine and the human—a world he stepped into in order to resolve the divine-human polarity and to vindicate the saints awaiting his redemption.

Commentary

1. The Preparation of Daniel and His Friends (1:1–21)

A. Background (1:1–2). Daniel was exiled in 605 BC, the fourth year of King Jehoiakim, together with a cross section of prominent citizens and craftsmen (Jer. 25:1; 46:2). Daniel's method of reckoning differs from that of the Palestinian system (cf. 2 Kings 23:36–24:2), as he writes "in the third year of the reign of Jehoiakim king of Judah, Nebuchadnezzar king of Babylon came to Jerusalem and besieged it" (1:1). It appears that this manner of reckoning is based on the Babylonian system, according to which the first year began with the New Year.

The tragedy of that hour was that "the Lord delivered" (1:2) Jehoiakim, articles from the temple, and prominent citizens into captivity. This was the beginning of the exile of Judah, spoken of by Isaiah, Micah, Zephaniah, and Habakkuk. The people had sinned, and the Lord had to discipline his rebellious children.

This was the first exile; a second followed, during which Ezekiel and King Jehoiachin were deported (597 BC). The third exile followed the desolation of Jerusalem and the destruction of the temple (586 BC).

B. Education (1:3–7). Nebuchadnezzar entrusts Ashpenaz, principal of the royal academy, with the instruction of young Jewish boys in the Babylonian culture, including cuneiform, Aramaic (the official language of the Babylonian Empire), astrology, and mathematics. All students at the royal academy were required to have no physical handicap, to be attractive in appearance, to show aptitude for learning, and to be well informed, quick to understand, and qualified to serve in the king's palace (1:4).

The royal academy is supported by the king, who supplies the students with a daily quota of food and wine (1:5). The curriculum lasted some three years, during which time the young men were to develop into competent statesmen to be used for the advance of the Babylonian kingdom. The royal grant was to perpetuate the Babylonian system of cultural, political, social, and economic values. The education was intended to brainwash the youths and to make them useful Babylonian subjects.

The process of cultural exchange is also evident in the change of names. Daniel ("my judge is God") becomes Belteshazzar ("may Nebo [Bel or Marduk] protect his life"). The names of his friends—Hananiah ("Yahweh has been gracious"), Mishael ("who is what God is"), and Azariah ("Yahweh has helped")—are also changed. Hananiah becomes Shadrach ("the command of Aku" [the Sumerian moon god]), Mishael becomes Meshach ("who is what Aku is"), and Azariah becomes Abednego ("servant of Nego" [or Nebo/Marduk]). Though it is clear that these names are reflections of Babylonian religious symbols, the youths do not object to them. They single out the important issues and do not pick quarrels over anything and everything that is different.

C. The challenge (1:8–20). The issue of food and drink is highly significant to Daniel and his friends. The Lord had clearly designated certain foods as unclean (Lev. 7:22–27; 11:1–47). Moreover, the royal court was closely associated with pagan temples, as food and drink were symbolically dedicated to the gods. Daniel humbly asks for permission not to eat the royal diet. The court official shows favor and sympathy to Daniel, even though he fears the wrath of the king. Again Daniel responds with courtesy and understanding regarding the official's predicament. He requests a test period, during which the power of God's presence could be made evident in the physical well-being of Daniel and his friends. The youths will eat only vegetables and drink only water for ten days. The Lord is with them; after ten days they look "healthier and better nourished than any of the young men who ate the royal food" (1:15). The youths

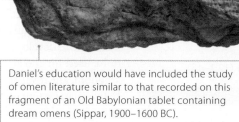

Daniel's education would have included the study of omen literature similar to that recorded on this fragment of an Old Babylonian tablet containing dream omens (Sippar, 1900–1600 BC).

distinguish themselves not only by their food but also by their wisdom (1:17). Daniel becomes prominent among his friends, as he can interpret dreams (1:17).

The king agrees with Ashpenaz's favorable assessment of the Judean youths and orders them into his service. Nebuchadnezzar finds them to be superior to his own courtiers in "every matter of wisdom and understanding" (1:20).

D. Daniel's service (1:21). The Lord is with this Judean prince in a foreign court. Daniel gains prominence in Babylon's court over a period of sixty-five years.

2. Nebuchadnezzar's Dream and Daniel's Interpretation: Part One (2:1–49)

A. The king and his astrologers (2:1–13). In Nebuchadnezzar's second year (2:1; 604 BC), he has a dream that disturbs him greatly. He turns to the traditional wisdom of his time by calling on his sages—"the magicians, enchanters, sorcerers and astrologers" (2:2)—to tell him what his dream means. They are all too ready to please the king, and ask for the particulars of the dream. Their request is "in Aramaic" (2:4), the official language of the Babylonian Empire. (Here begins the Aramaic section of Daniel, which continues until 7:28.)

The wise men are called to explain and interpret a dream but are unable to reconstruct the elements of it. The king repeatedly insists that they tell him both the dream and its interpretation (2:5–7). When the king refuses to change his mind but instead grows more and more agitated, the sages argue that the giving of dreams and their interpretation belongs to the gods (2:11). What the king demands is much more than they can handle. Finally, the king orders Arioch, chief of the royal guard, to have all the sages of Babylon executed as impostors and to have their houses destroyed.

B. The king and Daniel (2:14–19). Daniel deals tactfully with Arioch, goes to the king, and receives a delay in the execution. During this time he and his friends pray for God's mercy. They believe that only their God, "the God of heaven" (2:18)—a reference to God's spirituality and universal rule—can help them explain the "mystery." Daniel does not return to the king until the Lord has revealed the dream and its interpretation and until he has praised his God.

C. Daniel's praise (2:20–23). Daniel praises the Lord for his "wisdom and power" (2:20) in a prayer with hymnlike qualities. His wisdom and power advance his purposes, as he sovereignly rules over human affairs, even over kings and nations. He bestows insight on the wise. God's plan for the future lies hidden from man's scrutiny but is fully known to him. This God is no other than the "God of my ancestors," who is faithful to his servants in exile. Though Daniel refrains from using the divine name Yahweh, he intimates that the God of the fathers and the great king has a name and that this name will endure "for ever and ever" (2:20), even though it may seem to the Babylonians that their gods are victorious.

D. Daniel's interpretation (2:24–45). Daniel's request to be taken to Nebuchadnezzar by Arioch, the king's hatchet man, is granted. It is possible that Daniel already had a reputation for integrity and for God's being with him. The manner of Daniel's speech (2:24) shows his confidence, and Arioch's quick response reveals his trust in Daniel.

In the presence of the king Daniel gives God the glory, as, together with the sages, he admits that "no wise man, enchanter, magician or diviner can explain to the king the mystery he has asked about" (2:27). Only Daniel's God can and does reveal mysteries.

Daniel humbly admits that he is a mere instrument in God's hands and that his abilities should not be viewed as native but have been given to him by God. Then he proceeds to explain the dream.

According to Daniel, the king has seen a colossal statue, whose parts consisted of different materials. But to the king's amazement, he also saw a supernaturally cut rock (2:34). This rock struck the statue on its feet of iron and clay, smashing them, and made it appear as if the iron, the clay, the bronze, the silver, and the gold were little more than "chaff on a threshing floor" (2:35). Nothing remained of the statue. The rock became a huge mountain and filled the whole earth.

Through the dream of the colossal statue consisting of gold, silver, bronze, iron, and feet of iron mingled with clay, the Lord reveals how one empire will succeed another empire: Babylonia, Persia, Greece, and Rome. The resulting instability of the image is represented by the mixing of iron and clay. The image will be completely shattered by the rock, depicting the establishment of God's eternal kingdom. This vision would have given the exilic community great hope as this kingdom had been given to Israel as a theocratic nation. It was inaugurated more fully after the exile, in the coming of Christ and in the presence of the Spirit. But it will be gloriously established at the second coming of our Lord.

All sovereignty is derived from the Lord. He has given Nebuchadnezzar "dominion and power and might and glory" (2:37). Other kingdoms will arise, each inferior to the preceding one, but whatever the name of the kingdom, its authority is derived from God. In the end, however, no kingdom will fulfill God's will on earth. Therefore, he will establish the kingdom of God, "a kingdom that will never be destroyed, nor will it be left to another people. It will crush all those kingdoms and bring them to an end, but it will itself endure forever" (2:44).

E. Nebuchadnezzar's response (2:46–49). Nebuchadnezzar's response to the revelation signifies recognition of (not conversion to!) Daniel's God. His confession—"surely your God is the God of gods and the Lord of kings and a revealer of mysteries" (2:47)—while not insignificant, marks the king as a broad-minded man who willingly makes offering to any god who helps him.

Further, he gives Daniel the honor promised to any wise man who succeeded in telling the dream and in explaining it. Daniel receives a high office and many gifts. Through loyalty to the Lord, careful use of opportunity, and by choosing wisely in important issues, Daniel wins a place for himself as a counselor to the king.

3. The Fiery Furnace (3:1–30)

Soon after this experience the king has a colossal image made. It is overlaid with gold, ninety feet high, and nine feet wide. It probably was erected in honor of Nebo (or Nabu), the patron god of Nebuchadnezzar. The Valley of Dura, where the statue is set up, is unknown as a place-name. It simply may have been a place designated for the occasion.

Filled with pride, the king demands that all his officials worship the image. He calls on the satraps, prefects, governors, advisors, treasurers, judges, magistrates, and all provincial officials to join him in dedicating the image he has set up.

The king decrees that at the signal of the music, all his subjects proclaim allegiance to him, the Babylonian kingdom, and Nabu. Whoever disobeys will be thrown into a blazing furnace (3:6).

However, the Jews do not submit to this decree. Daniel's friends (Shadrach, Meshach, and Abednego) are readily singled out by the royal counselors, who may still have a vendetta with Daniel. The astrologers piously accuse the three Jewish leaders, acknowledging their own complete devotion to the king and thereby further implicating the Jews. They rightly assert that these Jews do not serve any of the Babylonian gods. The king's anger with the three is mitigated by his concern, which explains his giving them another chance.

The contest is actually between Yahweh and the god of Nebuchadnezzar. The Jews express their conviction that their God is able to deliver them. Their faith is so strong that they are determined not to submit to this act of state worship, even if the Lord does not miraculously deliver them.

So desperately does Nebuchadnezzar want his god and state to be victorious over the God of the Jews that, without any further ado, he changes his decree and requires that the oven be made "seven times" hotter. He then has some of his strongest men throw the Jews into the oven. The writer emphasizes the king's zeal, as everything moves toward the destruction of the three "radicals" from his empire. The god of Babylon must win! However, in his zeal to destroy the three Jews, he inadvertently causes his own soldiers, who throw the Jews into the fire, to be killed by the blazing heat of the oven.

Nebuchadnezzar again faces the superiority of Israel's God, as he suddenly sees four men walking in the fire. The narrative portrays the transformation of a powerful and rational emperor into an irrational and overzealous maniac. He has to recognize that these men are "servants of the Most High God" (3:26). He promotes Daniel's friends and promulgates a decree giving protection to Shadrach, Meshach, and Abednego.

4. Nebuchadnezzar's Dream and Daniel's Interpretation: Part Two (4:1–37)

A. Nebuchadnezzar's confession (4:1–3). Nebuchadnezzar's confession of God's sovereignty results from a series of events described in 4:4–37. The manner of expression is typical of Israelite poetry and probably reflects editorial reworking. The intent of this section of praise is to show that even a pagan king has to acknowledge that Yahweh is great, that his kingdom extends to all "nations and peoples of every language, who live in all the earth" (4:1), and that "his dominion endures from generation to generation" (4:3).

B. The dream and its interpretation (4:4–27). Nebuchadnezzar had reasons to be proud. In a short time he had consolidated the power of Babylon from the Persian Gulf to the Mediterranean and from the Amanus Mountains to the Sinai. He had spent many years on campaigns subduing and conquering. Finally he demonstrated his control in the operation of his administration, which ran smoothly by means of a tight network of officials and checks and balances. While resting at his palace, he has a dream that terrifies him. He calls on his trusted officials to interpret the dream, but this time he tells them the dream. Regardless of how hard they try, they cannot agree on a single interpretation. Then Nebuchadnezzar calls in Daniel, who is known as the "chief of the magicians" (4:9), trusting in his God-given ability. This time Nebuchadnezzar addresses Daniel with respect: "Belteshazzar, chief of the magicians, I know that the spirit of the holy gods is in you, and no mystery is too difficult for you" (4:9).

The king's dream is of a tree: it is enormous and strong, its top touching the sky; it is visible to the ends of the earth, with beautiful leaves and abundant fruit, providing sustenance and shelter for man and beast. Suddenly an angel decrees that this magnificent tree be cut down and its stump and roots "bound with iron and bronze" (4:15). Further, the angel explains that the king is to behave like an animal and be driven out to live with animals for a period of "seven times" (4:16).

The reason for the execution of this verdict lies in the fidelity of the angels to the great king and his sovereign rule over the kingdoms of this world; he does not put up with anyone who exalts himself to godhood.

Daniel's response reveals empathy for the king. When the king encourages him to explain the vision, Daniel responds graciously: "My lord, if only the dream applied to your enemies and its meaning to your adversaries!" (4:19). Then he proceeds with the explanation. The tree symbolizes the king and his kingdom. The messenger, who serves the decree of the Most High, forewarns Nebuchadnezzar that only the God of heaven "is sovereign over all kingdoms on earth and gives them to anyone he wishes" (4:25). Daniel (or Belteshazzar) is given to understand that the tree represents the pride and power of Nebuchadnezzar, which is to be cut down by divine decree until he acknowledges that God rules.

C. Nebuchadnezzar's humiliation (4:28–37). A year later the king prides himself on his accomplishments: "Is not this the great Babylon I have built as the royal residence, by my mighty power and for the glory of my majesty?" (4:30). Babylon was indeed a magnificent city: excellent fortifications, beautiful buildings, and hanging gardens. Its magnificence had become proverbial in a short time, and Nebuchadnezzar had

Nebuchadnezzar's various building projects and his desire to glorify the god Marduk are boasted in the cuneiform inscription on this stone block (known as the East India House Inscription). A portion of the inscription reads, "I am Nebuchadnezzar, king of Babylon, the exalted prince, the favorite of the god Marduk."

been the driving force behind the rejuvenation of this old kingdom. While he had reasons to be proud, in his pride he overstepped the boundary.

Suddenly he hears a voice and the decree of judgment. He begins to look like an animal. He eats grass like a bull and lives outdoors. Nebuchadnezzar may well have suffered from the disease known as boanthropy. During the time he suffers from the disease, he is not cared for and his appearance grows wild.

Only when he recognizes God's sovereignty and dominion is he restored to the throne. The king confesses that God's rule is far greater than his. The kingdom of God is an everlasting dominion, extends over all creation, and is absolutely sovereign. Though this public acknowledgment need not be interpreted as conversion from paganism to Yahwism, at least the king is forced to acknowledge Yahweh's sovereignty.

5. The Writing on the Wall (5:1–31)

Upon Nebuchadnezzar's death in 562, the ruling power changed hands in quick succession due to assassinations and court intrigues. While Nabonidus (556–539 BC) witnessed some growth of Persia on the east, he was unsuccessful in restraining Cyrus. Having been defeated in the field, he retreated, leaving the defense of Babylon to his son, Belshazzar ("May Bel protect the king"). In verse 22 Belshazzar is also known as the son of Nebuchadnezzar, which probably means in Semitic custom "any descendant" or even a "successor to the throne."

The spirit in the city is one of confidence. The banquet of Belshazzar reveals the self-assurance of the king and his nobles, as they drink from the vessels taken from the temple in Jerusalem. He is pagan not only in his drinking but also in his act of sacrilege, as he praises "the gods of gold and silver, of bronze, iron, wood and stone" (5:4).

The sudden appearance of mysterious writing on the wall greatly disturbs the king and his nobles. He calls in his sages to explain the writing. No one succeeds, even with the promise of being clothed in purple, having a gold chain placed around his neck, and being made the third highest ruler in the kingdom after Nabonidus and Belshazzar. This failure disturbs the king even more.

The queen—it is uncertain whether she is the grandmother or the queen mother—remembers Daniel, of whom she speaks highly, as Nebuchadnezzar has: "In the time of your father he was found to have insight and intelligence and wisdom like that of the gods" (5:11). She quickly reminds him of Daniel's ability to interpret dreams, explain riddles, and solve difficult problems (5:12).

Finally, Daniel is called in to interpret the enigmatic writing. The king repeats the offer of rewards and recognizes Daniel's past. But Daniel refuses the reward and freely reads and interprets the writing: *mene, mene, teqel, parsin* ("numbered, weighed, divided"), signifying that God's judgment will shortly fall on Babylon and that he has given the authority of Babylon over to Persia. The same God who gave dominion to Nebuchadnezzar has authority to give it to someone else. Daniel reviews some of the events that brought Nebuchadnezzar to the recognition of Daniel's God.

Part of this inscription from Ur, known as the Nabonidus Cylinder, is a prayer for Nabonidus and his son Belshazzar (555–539 BC).

Belshazzar is more arrogant than Nebuchadnezzar. Daniel presents God's case against Belshazzar: he is filled with pride; he has desecrated the temple vessels; he has rebelled against the God of heaven (5:22–23). Babylon's doom is sealed. Despite this oracle of doom Belshazzar keeps his promise, proclaiming Daniel to be the third highest ruler in the kingdom. The Persians invade the city that night, using the strategy of cutting off the water from the moat around Babylon. On the fifteenth of Tishri (September), 539 BC, Babylon falls without a siege. Darius (or Gubaru) becomes king of Babylon at the age of sixty-two.

6. The Lions' Den (6:1–28)

Darius reorganizes the former Babylonian Empire into 120 satrapies, administered by 120 satraps (6:1). The satraps were directly accountable to the king and to one of three administrative officers, among whom Daniel also served.

Daniel evokes the ire of the administrators and satraps. They make every effort to find fault with him, but Daniel is blameless. So the royal administrators, prefects, satraps, advisors, and governors come to Darius and ingratiate themselves to him with the request that Darius be the sole object of veneration for thirty days, with failure to do so resulting in penalty of death in the lions' den. They are successful.

They are able to trap Daniel in his habitual worship of the God of Israel. Daniel, who knows about the edict but relies on God to deliver him, regularly and openly prays three times a day at fixed times. He does not begin to pray when times are hard, but rather continues his habitual devotion to the Lord and to his temple, which now lay in ruins in Jerusalem. His only crime is prayer, "asking God for help" (6:11). Daniel's enemies hurriedly report him to the king, demand justice from Darius, and get it. Upon learning that Daniel is the victim of their plot, Darius understands the motivation for their flattery and is greatly outraged at this miscarriage of justice. But, trapping the king by his own decree, they demand Daniel's death, reminding him of the supremacy of law over loyalty and feelings.

His opponents persist until Daniel is thrown into the lions' den. Darius perceives at least something of the greatness of Daniel's God. The stone and royal seal ensure that Daniel's escape from the lions' den is impossible. Nevertheless, the king expresses hope that Daniel's God might deliver him. He spends a restless night full of anxiety. As soon as his decree permits, the king rushes to the den and with anxiety calls to see if Daniel is still alive.

Daniel speaks and gives glory to God: "My God sent his angel, and he shut the mouths of the lions. They have not hurt me, because I was found innocent in his sight. Nor have I ever done any wrong before you, Your Majesty" (6:22). Daniel's loyalty extends to both God and the king.

Hearing Daniel's voice, the king rejoices. He has Daniel brought out of the den and examined for wounds or scratches; he discovers that the lions have been kept from devouring this servant of God. He has the schemers and their families thrown into the lions' den, and they are quickly destroyed.

Further, the king decrees public recognition of Daniel's God as the God whose kingdom remains forever and whose power manifests itself in deliverance.

7. Vision of the Four Beasts (7:1–28)

A. The vision (7:1–14). In the first year of Belshazzar (ca. 553/2 BC), Daniel has a vision, whose message parallels that of the first dream of Nebuchadnezzar (chap. 2). Four beasts, symbolic of the nations (cf. Ps. 65:7), come out of "the great sea." The appearance of the beasts in each vision has both familiar and unusual features.

The lion with the wings of an eagle resembles the cherub, protecting the kingship of God above the ark. As it consolidated power, this kingdom believed that it was destined for eternity. But its power being human, it is forcibly removed: "Its wings were torn off and it was lifted from the ground so that it stood on two feet like a human being, and the mind of a human was given to it" (7:4). Though it appeared

A winged lion, perhaps resembling the griffin-lions found on the *Frieze of Griffins* decorating the palace of Darius I (Susa, ca. 510 BC), is among the creatures in Daniel's vision (Dan. 7:4).

to be the kingdom of the gods, the kingdom was as frail as any other human kingdom.

The bear with three ribs in its mouth represents the coalition of powers. The three ribs between its teeth and its readiness to eat its fill of flesh may symbolize the Persian conquest of Lydia (546 BC), Babylon (539 BC), and Egypt (525 BC).

The third animal has four heads. These suggest four kingdoms, or the extent of his rule (the proverbial four corners of the world).

The fourth and most terrifying is the beast that oppresses kingdoms. It has ten horns, from which comes another horn uprooting three of the original horns. This horn looks like a human face and is full of pride. Ten is a symbol of completion and need not be limited to a future kingdom consisting of "ten" nations, which some call a revival of the Roman Empire. This kingdom is to be more powerful, extensive, despotic, and awe-inspiring than the previous kingdoms.

Suddenly there arises "another horn, a little one" (7:8). This little horn comes naturally from the other horns but uproots three of the first horns in the process. It has the eyes of a man and a mouth that speaks boastfully (7:20).

Daniel momentarily interrupts the vision of the animals from the sea to reflect on the vision from heaven. The vision of the human kingdoms gives way to a vision of God ("the Ancient of Days"), enthroned on high as the great king. Daniel describes God in more detail than any of the prophets before or after him: his clothing is as white as snow; his hair is white like wool. The throne of God is flaming with fire and mobile like a chariot, with wheels ablaze with fire. The Lord is the great judge, who is seated to judge the kingdoms of this world. There is no escape from his judgment. A river of fire flows before him. He is the Lord of Hosts, with thousands upon thousands awaiting his command. The acts of men are recorded in his books.

Daniel returns to describe the acts and words of the little horn. The pride of this kingdom is self-evident by the boastful words of the horn. Despite its power and onslaught on God's kingdom, it comes to an end and is burned with fire from God's chariot. The other kingdoms are also stripped of their authority, though they are permitted to rule for a period of time.

The Ancient of Days gives authority over the remaining kingdoms to "one like a son of man" (7:13), who is permitted to approach the throne of the Ancient of Days without harm. In addition to authority, he is given glory and sovereign power and receives the worship of all nations and peoples of every language. His kingdom is not temporary or subject to God's judgment, but is an everlasting dominion.

B. Its interpretation (7:15–28). The visions of the beasts from the sea and the awe-inspiring vision of the glory of God and of his Messiah overwhelm Daniel. He is at a loss to explain what he has just seen. So he asks an angel for the interpretation. The four kingdoms symbolize the kingdoms of man, which are transitory; the everlasting kingdom belongs to "the holy people of the Most High" (7:18).

Daniel presses the angel concerning the disturbing vision of the fourth beast. Before the angel can explain, Daniel catches another aspect of the little horn. Not only does he speak boastfully; he also opposes and persecutes the saints. It appears that he is victorious over them until the Ancient of Days intervenes on their behalf and judges the horn. Then the righteous receive their reward, the kingdom.

The angel explains that the fourth beast differs from the others by the intensity of its disregard of the laws of God and man. It "will devour the whole earth" (7:23). The ten horns symbolize the succession of power. But the little horn will wrest power from three other kings/kingdoms and will have less regard for human rights and for the law of God than his predecessors. He will wage war with God and with his saints for "a time, times and half a time" (7:25; a cipher for three and a half years according to some interpreters). Then he too will be judged as he has judged others. By the power of God

his power will be taken away and completely destroyed. Then, the saints will rule with "sovereignty, power and greatness" (7:27). The kingdom of God and of his saints will last forever.

God will finally and victoriously crush the power of the fourth empire and all the kingdoms that arise out of it, including the king who will "speak against the Most High" and who will persecute the saints (7:25). This "king" may rule for a definite period (three and a half times), but his authority too will be removed. Then the everlasting kingdom of the Messiah will be established. Who is this "king"? Interpretations differ, depending on how one interprets the ten kings ("horns"). He may be the antichrist or the continuity and increase of evil in the end of days. Regardless of the identification of the little horn or of the length of his rule, the Messiah will cut him off suddenly and quickly.

Daniel is not relieved by what he has seen or by the interpretation given to him. He remains greatly disturbed and keeps the matter to himself.

8. Vision of the Kingdoms (8:1–27)

A. The vision (8:1–14). In the third year of Belshazzar (551/0 BC), Daniel sees himself in a vision in Susa, the Persian capital. There he observes a ram with two long horns standing by the Ulai Canal. The ram denotes the coalition of power. The ram pushes westward, northward, and southward, gaining greater control and augmenting its absolute power.

However, the ram's power is suddenly broken by a he-goat with a prominent horn between his eyes. The goat comes from the west, moves rapidly as if not touching the ground, and charges into the two-horned ram. The two-horned ram is powerless and easily overcome by the goat. The sovereignty of this kingdom is ended when its large horn is broken off, and in its place four prominent horns grow up toward the four winds of heaven.

Out of one of these four horns grows another horn, which exalts itself against God by turning against (NIV "toward," 8:9) "the Beautiful Land" (Canaan; cf. Jer. 3:19).

This prophecy, like Ezekiel 38–39 and Zechariah 12 and 14, reveals the drama of the opposition to the people of God by the powers of this world. Many read the text referentially as speaking of the invasion of the Seleucid (Syrian) king Antiochus IV Epiphanes into Judah, when, due to persecution and sacrilege in the temple for more than three years (1,150 days), the evening and morning sacrifices ("the 2,300 evenings and mornings") ceased (8:14). It is true that Antiochus had no regard for God, acted as "the Prince of the host" (8:11 NIV 1984, KJV), and required the Jews to worship the images of humans. It is true that the defeat of Antiochus marked the end of the suffering brought by this king. It is true that God miraculously gave victory to the Maccabees—the Jews still celebrate this miracle at Hanukkah, the Feast of the Rededication of the Temple (December 25, 165 BC). However, it is more true that the opposition continues to the very end. John makes this point in Revelation 11:2, where "forty-two months" symbolically stands for a period of intense persecution and wickedness.

B. Its interpretation (8:15–27). An angel asks Gabriel to further explain to Daniel the meaning of this vision. At the mention of Gabriel's name, Daniel falls down in worship, as Ezekiel did at the revelation of God's glory (Ezek. 1:28; 3:23). Daniel is addressed as "son of man." Gabriel explains that the vision pertains to "the time of the end" (8:17). Daniel is clearly in a visionary trance ("I was in a deep sleep," 8:18). The angel raises him up to his feet to make certain that Daniel will remember the import of the moment.

He explains that the two-horned ram represents the coalition of power under Persia, that the shaggy goat signifies the king of Greece, and that the large horn is the first king (i.e., Alexander the Great). He further explains that the four horns that supplanted the broken-off horn represent four kingdoms. From one of the kingdoms "a fierce-looking king, a master of intrigue, will arise" (8:23). This king will be powerful in his ability to destroy and especially

in his persecution of "the holy people" (8:24). Many take this to be a description of Antiochus IV Epiphanes, who was a master of deception. He opposed the principalities, the spiritual forces protecting God's interests in the nations, and even the "Prince of princes" (8:25). Yet his fate also lay in God's hands, as he came to a sudden end. Antiochus died at Tabae (Persia) in 163 BC. Because the vision of "the evenings and mornings" is the vision of the end and is to be properly sealed up—"for it concerns the distant future" (8:26)—a referential connection with Antiochus unnecessarily restricts the range of the prophecy.

Daniel is so exhausted from this vision that he is sick for several days. He has to excuse himself from doing the king's business. He does not understand the vision, but he preserves these words for later generations.

9. Daniel's Prayer and Vision of the Seventy Weeks (9:1–27)

A. Daniel's prayer (9:1–19). In the first year of Persian rule (539/8 BC), Darius, son of Xerxes (Hebrew, Ahasuerus) and a Mede by descent, becomes the governor of Babylon (9:1). Daniel is drawn to meditate on the prophecy of Jeremiah, who was one of the prophets predicting the era of restoration, consisting of covenant renewal, restoration of the people to the land, and the continuous service of the priesthood in the temple (Jeremiah 30–34). Jeremiah also predicted that the Babylonian kingdom was to last seventy years (Jer. 25:11–12) and that subsequently Jerusalem would be restored. Daniel longs for the era of restoration, for the establishment of the kingdom of God and of the messianic kingdom. To this end he fasts and prays for the restoration of his people to the land.

Daniel's prayer consists of confession and petition. In the confession he identifies with the history of his people, with their sin and punishment. The prayer of confession consists of a repetition of four themes: Israel's rebellious attitude to the law and the prophets, Yahweh's righteousness in judgment, the fulfillment of the curses, and the hope of renewal of divine mercy and grace. Daniel begins with an affirmation of God's mercy, inherent in Israel's confession of who Yahweh is: "Lord, the great and awesome God, who keeps his covenant of love with all who love him and obey his commands" (9:4). In contrast Israel has sinned against their covenant God: "We have been wicked and have rebelled; we have turned away from your commands and laws" (9:5). They have rejected the prophets. Therefore the Lord is righteous in his judgment. Yet the disgrace of Israel is apparent wherever they have been scattered. Their lot has changed by their own doing, but the Lord is still the same. Israel has received the curses of the covenant (Lev. 26:33; Deut. 28:63–67). The Lord has been faithful in judgment, even in bringing about the desolation of Jerusalem. Again Daniel affirms the righteousness of Yahweh.

Daniel throws himself on the mercy of God, as he prays for the restoration of Jerusalem, the temple, and God's presence among his people.

B. God's response (9:20–27). Daniel prays from the conviction that the Lord has decreed an end to the Babylonian rule. Now that this has taken place, Daniel prays for the speedy restoration of the people, the city, Jerusalem, and the temple. He has acknowledged the sin of Israel but trusts the Lord to be faithful to his promises.

Suddenly, the angel Gabriel appears to him in a vision. He was sent to explain God's plan as soon as Daniel had begun to pray (9:23)! This speedy response is an expression of God's special love for Daniel.

Building on the seventy-years motif, the angel reveals that the Lord has decreed "seventy 'sevens'" (9:24, perhaps seventy seven-year time periods according to some interpreters). The exact identification of this phrase is open to interpretation. But the purpose of the "seventy 'sevens'" is to finalize judgment on sin, to atone for sin and transgression, to bring in everlasting righteousness, to fulfill all the prophetic word, and to anoint the most holy (9:24). If we take it to refer to seventy periods of time, the periodization comes to the foreground, rather than the length of time. The reading of the first period raises the question of the number of the periods. Are there two or three? It is possible to read the text in two ways: 62 + 7 periods and 1 period, or 7, 62, and 1 periods.

The Hebrew text raises some other issues that are not so transparent in English. First, what is "the most holy" (cf. KJV)? It could be "the most holy one" (see NIV note) or a holy place (such as Jerusalem or the temple; cf. NIV, RSV, NASB). Second, what decree initiates the beginning of the restoration of Jerusalem? Opinions differ on when this took place: 596 BC (Jeremiah's writing), 538 BC (Cyrus's decree to restore the temple in Jerusalem), or 445 BC (Nehemiah's permission to restore the walls of Jerusalem). Third, what is the meaning of "the Anointed One"? While "Anointed" is capitalized in some English translations (NIV, NLT), Hebrew does not use capital letters to designate titles or proper names. Interpreters have connected the Anointed One with Cyrus, the antichrist, a Roman emperor, and Jesus Christ.

Fourth, who will "confirm a covenant with many for one 'seven'" (9:27)? Some hold that the Messiah is the subject of the sentence, but others see here a reference to a hostile foreign ruler, such as Antiochus, Titus, or the antichrist. Indeed, Antiochus and Titus brought an end to sacrifices and offerings and set up pagan symbols in the temple court. Opposition to the Lord is an act of "abomination that causes desolation" (9:27).

It is likely that the ambiguity in the expression translated as "seven" and in the number of periods, as well as the many other ambiguous expressions ("the most holy" [9:24], "the decree" or "word" [9:25], "the Anointed One" [9:25–26, capitalized in the NIV], the identity of the ruler [9:26], and the subject of the covenant [9:27]), projects a cartoonlike world that suggests a divine reality that cannot be captured by human interpretation.

The book of Daniel, like Revelation, has in view the eternal and complete establishment of God's kingdom, the glory of the saints, and the complete subjugation of the nations of this world. While the details of the prophecy defy a unified explanation, the purpose of the revelation was to encourage Daniel and the book's audience that the Lord purposed to bring sin and sinners to their just deserts and to explain that, while the opposition to God's purposes would increase, Yahweh planned to bring it to an end. God's redemption is an everlasting redemption.

10. Message of Encouragement (10:1–11:45)

A. Introduction (10:1–3). In the third year of Cyrus (536 BC) Daniel is standing by the banks of the Tigris, when suddenly he receives the revelation of a long period of suffering and persecution. He is so struck by the vision that he fasts and mourns for three weeks.

B. The angel (10:4–11:1). The vision comes shortly after the celebration of Passover and the Feast of Unleavened Bread. Daniel is so moved that the people around him are terrified by his appearance; they instantly flee, leaving Daniel alone.

Daniel is addressed by someone whom he describes in great detail (10:5–6). The angel has been trying to communicate with him for three weeks but has not been able to until Michael, one of the archangels,

The head of Antiochus IV Epiphanes on a silver tetradrachm coin (second century BC)

overcomes the spiritual power (a demon) over the Persian kingdom. The angelic visitor proclaims God's peace to Daniel and encourages him with a message pertaining to the end of Persia and the beginning of the rule of Greece. The kingdom of God is not established by flesh and blood but by spiritual powers.

The vision completely overwhelms Daniel. The angel touches him three times to wake him up. His face turns pale, he feels helpless, he is speechless, he is filled with anxiety, and he is ready to die. The angel strengthens him physically and assures him that the Lord loves him and wants to reveal to him his plan. The very resistance he has endured arises from spiritual warfare between the powers of darkness and the kingdom of God. The revelation comes from "the Book of Truth" (10:21), the record of God's plan for the progression of the redemption of his people. The angel together with Michael was sent to work out the restoration of the people of God from the moment Cyrus became king over Babylon and Darius was installed as governor (11:1).

C. The vision (11:2–45). The detailed description of the interrelationship between the kings of the south and the kings of the north in Daniel 11 has long challenged biblical scholars. The angel reveals to Daniel that three more kings (Cambyses, Smerdis, Darius Hystaspis?) will rule over Persia. The fourth (Xerxes I?) will try to incorporate Greece into the Persian Empire. Upon the death of Alexander the Great of Greece ("a mighty king," 11:3), his kingdom was divided into four parts: Macedonia, Thrace, Syria ("the king of the North," or the Seleucids), and Egypt ("the king of the South," or the Ptolemies). Verses 5–20 relate the rivalry and wars between the Ptolemies and Seleucids until the appearance of Antiochus Epiphanes.

The Seleucid Antiochus IV (nicknamed Epiphanes, or "madman") could be the "contemptible person" of verse 21. In his attempt to gain absolute control over Egypt, he was ruthless in his campaigns and encouraged his troops to loot and plunder. His mission against the Ptolemies also failed.

Finally, he aimed his anger at Jerusalem, the temple, and the Jewish people (11:30–35). He desecrated the altar in the temple, set up an image to Zeus (168 BC), and required the Jews to worship the gods of the Greeks. The Lord raised up "a little help" (11:34; Judas Maccabeus). The godly Mattathias led the Jews to resist the order to sacrifice to the gods. His son Judas Maccabeus led the insurrection and succeeded by the grace of God in cleansing the temple. The rededication of the altar took place in December 165. This event forms the background of the Hanukkah ("dedication") celebration (cf. John 10:22).

The power represented by Antiochus typifies the spirit of all kings who exalt themselves, doing whatever they please. The description of that king not only applies to Antiochus. It is symbolic of evil. The interpretive difficulty lies in the nature of apocalyptic language, which mixes historical details with a grand picture of opposition by the kingdoms of this world for the purpose of assuring the reader that in the end God's kingdom is victorious over all forms of evil. The problem of combining the historical with the eternal is characteristic of prophetic language as a whole. The apocalyptic features add to the complexity of interpretation. In spite of the disagreements in interpretation, the outcome is sure: evil "will come to his end" (11:45). The conflicts between the kingdom of God and that of this world will continue, but in the end the Lord will establish his glorious kingdom.

11. Troubles and Victory (12:1–13)

The victory will not come without persecution and perseverance. These words encourage the godly in any age to await the kingdom of God. The saints are promised life everlasting and joy, whereas the ungodly will experience everlasting disgrace. All who die will be raised to life, but not all who are raised in the body will enjoy lives of everlasting bliss—only those whose names are recorded in the book of life. The godly respond to God and will be accounted to be wise; their wisdom is like a tree of life,

as they will lead others to life, wisdom, and righteous living. Their future will be glorious, as they will share in the victory of the Lord.

The visions are to be closed, so that the wise might read them and gain understanding. Revelation of the future is for encouragement and the development of hope, faith, and love, rather than for speculation. The godly will always find comfort in the revelation made to Daniel.

Daniel receives assurance that these visions are true and will come to pass. He sees two witnesses on opposite banks of the river. In between the two is the angelic messenger, "the man clothed in linen," who is above the river. He swears by Yahweh's name that the fulfillment will take place "for a time, times and half a time" (12:7; cf. 7:25). Concerned about what he has heard, Daniel asks about the outcome. He does not receive much of an answer, but the angelic messenger does assure him that through the process of perseverance the Lord will always have a faithful remnant. This remnant will endure the process during which they "will be purified, made spotless and refined" (12:10). The wicked, however, will persevere in their evil. They will never come to understand their folly but will be cast out of the kingdom.

The calculation of the end is enigmatic. The Lord reveals to Daniel visions of the progression of redemption until the final and victorious establishment of his kingdom. These words are to encourage godliness in the face of evil. Though the oppression and persecution may be longer (1,335 days) than the tyranny of Antiochus Epiphanes (1,290 days), blessed is everyone who perseveres to the end.

Select Bibliography

Baldwin, Joyce G. *Daniel.* Tyndale Old Testament Commentaries. Downers Grove, IL: InterVarsity, 1978.

Gangel, Kenneth O. *Daniel.* Holman Old Testament Commentary. Nashville: Broadman & Holman, 2001.

Goldingay, John E. *Daniel*. Word Biblical Commentary. Dallas: Word, 1989.

Longman, Tremper, III. *Daniel*. NIV Application Commentary. Grand Rapids: Zondervan, 1999.

Lucas, Ernest C. *Daniel*. Apollos Old Testament Commentary. Downers Grove, IL: InterVarsity, 2002.

Seow, C. L. *Daniel*. Westminster Bible Companion. Louisville: Westminster John Knox, 2003.

Wallace, R. S. *The Lord Is King: The Message of Daniel*. Downers Grove, IL: InterVarsity, 1979.

Young, Edward J. *The Prophecy of Daniel: A Commentary*. Grand Rapids: Eerdmans, 1949.

Hosea

GARY V. SMITH

Introduction

Hosea the Prophet

Hosea's personal life was most unusual, for it almost appears that he married the wrong woman. His marriage fell apart when his wife became a prostitute, and eventually he had to buy his wife back from enslavement. One wonders how God can use a prophet with this kind of background. Wouldn't these kinds of personal problems disqualify a person from prophetic service, or was there a good reason why God allowed Hosea to go through these difficulties? Since 1:2 indicates that Hosea and Gomer are symbolic of God's relationship to Israel, it is evident that God was attempting to teach Hosea, as well as the people he spoke to, a powerful lesson about God's amazing love for sinful people. God does not give up on people just because they make a mistake; his love is steadfast, he is faithful to his plans, and he is willing to forgive all who repent of their sins.

The book says relatively little about the prophet himself. His father was named Beeri, but no one knows Hosea's occupation before the Lord spoke to him, how old he was, or even where he was born. He repeatedly refers to cities in Israel (Samaria in 7:1; 8:5–6; 10:5, 7; 13:16; Jezreel in 1:5; Gilgal in 4:15; Mizpah in 5:1; Gibeah in 5:8; 9:9; Bethel in 10:5), and he seems to write in a slightly different Hebrew dialect, so most conclude from this meager evidence

that he was born, was raised, and prophesied in and around the Israelite capital of Samaria. He claimed to be a prophet and God's watchman, but some considered him a fool or an inspired maniac (9:7–8).

Chapters 1–3 contain information about Hosea's wife, Gomer the daughter of Diblaim (1:3), his marriage, and his three children, who served as signs of the difficult relationship God had with Israel. In light of all the heartaches and troubles Gomer caused Hosea, it is puzzling why God would ask a godly prophet to marry a "woman of adultery/prostitution" (NIV "a promiscuous woman," 1:2). Because God never asks any other prophet to marry an impure woman like this, because everyone knows that God does not approve of such sinful activity, and because Gomer was unfaithful even after their marriage, some commentators suggest that these odd instructions and events should not be interpreted literally. Instead they hypothesize that chapters 1–3 report either (1) the spiritual prostitution of Gomer worshiping another god, (2) the report of a dream, (3) the teachings of a parable, or (4) a somewhat risqué drama that was reenacted over and over again in order to teach a spiritual truth. Nevertheless, the narrative report about Hosea's family reads like other historical events; there is no introductory notification informing the reader that this is just a parable or dream (which happens in other places), and there is no interpretation of this so-called parable. Thus it is best to accept this as an autobiographical account of what really happened in the life of Hosea.

Among those who take a literal interpretation of these events, some hypothesize that Gomer was actually pure at the time of her marriage; but the plain meaning of "marry a woman of prostitution" suggests that Hosea actually married a woman with loose morals who was sexually promiscuous both before and after her marriage. Although people in Hosea's day may have looked down on him because of his failed marriage, there is no indication that this disqualified him in God's eyes. At the very beginning when God instructs Hosea to marry Gomer (1:2), God explains the purpose, that Hosea's relationship with Gomer is to function as an analogy of God's relationship with Israel. There are in fact some benefits from this experience, for going through the painful events related to his wife's marital unfaithfulness helps Hosea understand God's terrible agony over the covenant unfaithfulness of his people. Hosea himself experiences a similar calamity. These difficult times also help Hosea comprehend the enormous depth of God's love for his sinful people, for Hosea is told to go love Gomer again, even though she was unfaithful after they were married (3:1). No one can read this story without realizing just how horribly destructive sin is (it is like prostitution in God's eyes). Of course this truth only magnifies the unbelievable greatness of God's marvelous love for all who are sinners.

Historical Context

Hosea initially ministered in Israel during the time of the Israelite king Jeroboam II (a few years after Amos's ministry, in 760 BC). The chronological information in 1:1 also indicates that Hosea prophesied in Israel while kings Uzziah, Ahaz, and Hezekiah were ruling in Judah. This means that the second part of Hosea's ministry in Israel was parallel to some of the years when Micah (1:1) and Isaiah (1:1) were preaching in Judah. Since Hosea never refers to the fall of Israel (721 BC) as something that has

already happened, it is safe to estimate that his prophetic career extended from approximately 755 to 725 BC.

This period of Hosea's ministry falls into three distinct political eras. During the time of King Jeroboam II, Israel was independent and prosperous and had a strong army. With this army Jeroboam II gained control of most if not all of the old Solomonic Empire, as Jonah prophesied he would (2 Kings 14:25; cf. Amos 6:14). Israel received a great deal of tribute from conquered lands and established a wealthy upper class to rule the land and grow the economy of the nation (Amos 3:15; 4:1; 6:1–7). Signs of the prosperity of Israel during these years are found in Hosea 1–3, especially those comments about there being abundant silver and gold, grain, wine, and flax (2:8–9) and great parties at festival times (2:11; cf. Amos 6:1–7). Both Amos and Hosea condemn the wealthy and powerful who have misused the blessings God gave them during the time of Jeroboam II (Amos 5:10–15; 6:1–14; 8:1–6; Hos. 2:8–13).

Later God directs Hosea to prophesy in Israel during the relatively weak reigns of the Israelite kings Menahem and Pekah (2 Kings 15:19–29). During these years there were several political assassinations (2 Kings 15:8–16, 23–25) before the Israelite king Pekah and the Syrian king Rezin formed a coalition to confront the strong Assyrian king Tiglath-Pileser III. When Ahaz the king of Judah refused to join this coalition, Pekah and Rezin declared war on Judah (the Syro-Ephraimite War of 734–732 BC). Instead of trusting in God (Isa. 7:1–10), Ahaz asked the Assyrian king Tiglath-Pileser III for help, and he responded by defeating both Syria and Israel and requiring tribute from them as well as from Judah (2 Kings 15:29; 16:8; 2 Chron. 28:20–21). These events are reflected in the messages in Hosea 4–11. Hosea predicts God's coming judgment on Israel (5:1, 14) and then warns of the blowing of the trumpets to rally the Israelite troops for war (5:8–11; 8:1, referring to either the Syro-Ephraimite War or the

Assyrian attack on Israel). Hosea warns the nation about a future military defeat, but there is no evidence that the people of Israel accept his message and repent. These must have been very difficult years for Hosea to minister in Israel. The economy, political stability, and social order were falling apart, and few were interested in the things he was preaching about.

The final era of Hosea's ministry coincides with the reign of Hoshea, the last king of Israel (2 Kings 17:3–6). Hoshea tried to survive politically by making secret alliances with both Assyria and Egypt (2 Kings 17:4), but when the Assyrian king Shalmaneser got wind of Hoshea's political deception, he invaded the land of Israel and besieged the capital city of Samaria. The next ruler, Sargon II, completed the conquest of Samaria in 721 BC and took thousands of Israelites into captivity in Assyria. Hosea was aware of Hoshea's political duplicity (8:9; 9:3; 12:1) and called the nation to repent or face the wrath of God. It appears that Hosea's prophecies end sometime before the defeat of Samaria and the exile of the people of Israel in 721 BC, but there is no information about whether Hosea was killed in this final battle, fled for safety into Judah sometime before the final battle, or was exiled with those who survived this conflict.

In many ways the social and economic situation in the northern nation of Israel mirrored the political situation. When Israel was strong in the days of Jeroboam II, the economy of the nation was flourishing (2:8–9, 11). During these years a strong social distinction developed between the wealthy upper class and the poor, oppressed lower class. In the second period of Hosea's ministry great political and economic instability engulfed the nation after the assassination of several Israelite kings and the failed attack on Judah in the Syro-Ephraimite War. The rise of the Assyrian king Tiglath-Pileser III brought great economic and social harm because Israel lost many people in battle, had fertile crops destroyed and barns raided by troops, and had to pay heavy tribute to Assyria after the war. Violence increased (4:2; 6:8–9; 7:1); God put a curse on their crops (9:2); and the general population suffered greatly (10:14–15). These conditions continued in the final years of Israel during the reign of Hoshea; God was allowing the nation to fall apart (13:15–16) because of her sins.

The Message of Hosea

The prophet Hosea focuses a good deal of his attention on the religious life of the people. Since the time of Ahab and Jezebel the nation of Israel was dominated by the worship of the Canaanite fertility god Baal (1 Kings 16:29–33). Although there were Israelite temples at Dan and Bethel, where Yahweh, the God of Israel, was worshiped in the form of a golden calf, Hosea condemns these practices as a perversion of true worship (8:5–6; 10:5; 13:2). Eventually the nation's worship of Baal and Yahweh became so intermixed that some people thought that these were just two different names for the same God, so they would call Israel's God by the name "my Baal" (2:16; see NIV note). Baal was the god of fertility

A stele showing Baal with a thunderbolt (Ras Shamra, Late Bronze Age)

who in Canaanite mythology would bring the people rain, fertility, and prosperity. Many were deceived into participating in the activities at these Baal temples because they wanted to become prosperous. Some mistakenly thought that Baal had given them abundant harvests of wine, oil, grain, and wool, so they gave their sacrifices and praise to Baal instead of Yahweh (2:8). Therefore, God decided to take away their material blessings (2:11–13) in order to bring an end to their false worship.

Hosea's sermons deal with three central issues brought on by this inappropriate Baal worship. First, the people do not really know God (4:6; 5:4; 6:3, 6) because the priests have not been teaching from the Scriptures (4:6) and because the people do not distinguish between the worship of Baal and Yahweh. Second, the people display no steadfast loyalty to the covenant God made with the nation but break the covenant in many different ways (8:1, 12). Instead of loving God with all the heart and fearing only him (Deut. 6:6; 10:12), they trust in alliances with foreign nations for their security (7:8, 11) and in their armies and fortresses (8:14; 10:13–14). Third, the people are not truthful in their relationship to God but are deceptive, just as their great forefather Jacob was (11:12–12:4). Like a wife who deceives her husband and loves two men, the Israelites claim one thing but actually do something else.

As the prophet Hosea addresses each of these issues, he structures his presentation on the general pattern of an ancient Near Eastern court case at the city gate. Just as a husband might accuse his wife of unfaithfulness, God brings a covenant lawsuit against Israel because she has been unfaithful to the covenant with God. The goal of this confrontation is to force the guilty party, Israel, to recognize her failures so that she might turn from her wicked ways and restore her covenant relationship with God. In order to do this, (1) God presents a series of accusations that describe the unfaithfulness of his people; (2) God presents a series of warnings and threats about the punishment he will inflict on the nation; and then (3) God offers the people the hope of restoring their covenant relationship with him if they will repent and turn back to him (6:1–3; 11:1–11; 14:1–9).

Authorship

Some critical commentators question if Hosea authored everything now found in the book of Hosea, suggesting specifically that the verses related to Judah (5:10, 14; 6:11; 8:14; 12:2) and the affirming promises of hope and restoration (1:10–11; 2:18–23; 6:1–3; 11:1–11; 14:1–9) were added by later editors to give Hosea's prophecies a more positive tone. Since most prophetic messages offer both negative warning of divine judgment and promises of hope for the future, the reader should not assume that Hosea was incapable of using hopeful promises as an effective tool to persuade his audience to turn back to God. The references to Judah indicate that the problems Hosea addressed were not problems that existed only in Israel; these were problems that also existed in Judah.

Literary Features

Hosea often legitimates his statements by alluding to earlier traditions in the Pentateuch (the books of the Law) or in other prophetic texts. For example, in 11:8 he mentions the destruction of the cities of Adam and Zeboyim (see Genesis 18–19), in 8:13; 9:3; 11:1, 5; 12:9 the exodus from Egypt (see Exodus 14–15), in 4:2 several of the Ten Commandments (see Exodus 20), in 2:15 Achan's sin at Jericho (see Joshua 7), in 12:3–4 the deceptive ways of the patriarch Jacob (see Genesis 25–35), and in 1:4–5 the story of Jehu's murder of Ahab's sons in the Valley of Jezreel (see 2 Kings 9–10). Hosea is explaining that God's actions in Hosea's day are similar to what God has done in the past and that many of Israel's sins are similar to the wicked things people did in the past. This emphasizes the need to break with their past sins in order to avoid another divine judgment.

Hosea expresses his messages in quite unique ways. He is very bold in his use of imagery of sin, of God's action, and of the future hope of the nation. He imagines God as a lion or a leopard (5:14; 13:7) or as a pine tree (14:8), or acting like rot or pus (5:12); Israel is compared to a stubborn heifer (4:16), an oven (7:4–7), wild grapes (9:10), a silly dove (11:11), or smoke (13:3), and her loyalty disappears as quickly as the dew (6:4). Hosea's imagery is initially somewhat shocking because it is so unusual, but his overall aim was to get his Israelite audience to understand how seriously God took their sinfulness. These images, and especially the picture of God and Israel as marriage partners (similar to Hosea and Gomer), enabled Hosea to present the problem of covenant unfaithfulness in a practical way that common people could understand. The emotional idea of an unfaithful wife, the shame this would bring to the family, and the loving expression of God's willingness to take his unfaithful partner back were moving emotional images that helped Hosea's audience understand how serious God viewed their sins to be. God was very angry at Israel's unfaithfulness and deceptive ways, but he also had a deep, abiding love for his people.

Theological Themes

In spite of the emotional tone of the book and the shocking imagery, the theology of Hosea's message is fairly straightforward and easy to understand. God has a covenant relationship with the people of Israel. God loves his people and has promised to bless them, but they must love God and be faithful to their covenant commitments. Hosea presents evidence throughout the accusation sections of the book that the people of Israel have failed to be faithful in their exclusive covenant love for God; they have acted like a prostitute by loving another god (Baal, 4:11–14). They do not even seem to know the difference between God and Baal (2:16), seem uninformed about God's law because the priests do not teach it (4:5–6), and are so steeped in their adulterous ways that it is almost impossible for them to repent and turn back to God (4:5). Nevertheless, God loves his people and wants them back, so he confronts them with their sins and makes them aware of the serious consequence their sin will have on their relationship to God. If they will repent of their sins, God will forgive them (14:1–7). Then they will again be his people (1:10–2:1), he will give them one king (the Messiah, 3:5), and God's rich blessings will be poured out on them when he establishes his final kingdom (2:16–23).

All these words are messages that come from the Lord through the prophet Hosea. On several occasions in the narration of chapters 1–3, the prophet inserts into the story words like, "the LORD began to speak though Hosea" (1:2) or "the LORD said to Hosea/me" (1:4, 6, 9; 3:1) in order to assure the reader that these unusual events have been commanded by God. The poetic sections in chapters 4–14 begin with the similar introductory clause, "hear the word of the LORD" (4:1). God's point of view remains consistent throughout the poetic messages in chapters 4–14, for whenever Hosea uses first-person terminology ("I, me, my"), his words represent the things that God wants Hosea to communicate to his covenant people.

Outline

1. Covenant Unfaithfulness in God's and Hosea's Family (1:1–3:5)
   A. Problems of Unfaithfulness in the Family (1:1–2:1)
   B. Confrontation of Unfaithfulness (2:2–15)
   C. God Will Bring Restoration to the Families (2:16–23)
   D. Love for the Unlovely (3:1–5)
2. God's Lawsuit because Israel Does Not Know God (4:1–6:6)
   A. Proof that Israel Does Not Know God (4:1–19)
   B. Punishment of War (5:1–14)
   C. Hope: Return and Know God (5:15–6:6)
3. God's Lawsuit because Israel Does Not Keep the Covenant (6:7–11:11)
   A. Proof of Israel's Lack of Covenant Love (6:7–7:16)
   B. Punishment of War and Captivity (8:1–10:15)

Commentary

1. Covenant Unfaithfulness in God's and Hosea's Family (1:1–3:5)

A. Problems of unfaithfulness in the family (1:1–2:1). The superscription in 1:1 verifies that Hosea received a divine revelation from God in the reign of Jeroboam II and during the reign of several Judean kings, basically from about 755 to 725 BC. Hosea records no dramatic call like Isaiah or Jeremiah (Isaiah 6; Jeremiah 1); his ministry simply begins when the Lord speaks to him concerning marrying Gomer (1:1–2). This paragraph can be divided into two parts. In the first part, Hosea marries Gomer, then Gomer's three children are given symbolic names. In the second part, God explains how the negative implications of the children's names will be reversed at some point in the future.

First, God instructs Hosea to marry the promiscuous Israelite woman Gomer (1:2–9).

Although people today may view this command as somewhat inappropriate or a detriment to the prophet's ministry, one should not try to rescue Hosea's reputation by interpreting this story as a parable or a dream. There is no doubt (see 1:2) that God wants the marriage of Hosea and the adulterous Gomer to represent God's covenant marriage with adulterous Israel. Hosea does not express any opposition to this instruction; he accepts God's direction and follows it even if it may seem a little odd. Remember that God also asks the prophet Ezekiel to illustrate God's message to his generation of exiles by lying on one side for 390 days and then on the other side for 40 days. God also instructs Ezekiel to cut off all his hair with his sword (Ezekiel 4–5), and he tells Isaiah to go naked for three years (Isa. 20:1–4). All of these unusual sign acts effectively communicate God's truth to audiences that are too stubborn to listen to any "normal" or traditional presentation of God's word.

The first child of Hosea and Gomer is a boy (1:3). God tells them to name the boy Jezreel because this will remind people of the massacre that King Jehu carried out many years ago in the Valley of Jezreel. When Jehu became the king of Israel, he killed all the sons of the wicked

The Valley of Jezreel, after which Hosea's son Jezreel is named (Hos. 1:4–5)

ruler Ahab and his wife Jezebel in the Valley of Jezreel (2 Kings 10:1–10). God approved the removal of this wicked family from power (2 Kings 10:30), but now the descendants of Jehu (meaning Jeroboam II) are no better than the children of Ahab. Hosea's son will symbolize what God is about to do in bringing an end to the rule of the sons of King Jehu, for God will break their military power, represented by the bow in 1:5. In practical terms the ending of the line of Jehu means that Jeroboam II and his son Zechariah will soon die (2 Kings 14:28–29; 15:8–10). The second child that Gomer has is a girl (1:6; the text does not say she is Hosea's child), and God instructs Hosea to name her Lo-Ruhamah, "No Compassion" (NIV "not loved"), because God will not have any compassion on the people in the nation of Israel. God will still have compassion on Judah and forgive them; it will be God's grace that delivers them, not the strength of their army. The third child Gomer has is a son (1:8; again the text does not say if Hosea is the father), and they name him Lo-Ammi, "Not My People," because the people of Israel are no longer acting like God's beloved covenant people.

This paragraph ends (1:10–2:1) with a surprising and astonishing complete reversal of the meaning of the names of the three children. How this change will come about is not really explained in these verses, but it will be an unbelievable act of divine grace. There will be a change in the relationship between God and his people. Apparently this will happen because of God's great love and because it is God's will. Although all three names initially represent God's curse on his people, which threatens to end the relationship between God and Israel, there will be a day sometime in the future when God will bless his people and fulfill his promises to Abram by multiplying their numbers to equal the sands of the sea (cf. Gen. 22:17; 32:12). This assures the listeners that the present judgment of God will last only so long. Later God will revive the nation in the land of Israel, multiply them exceedingly, have compassion on them

(calling them "Compassion"), take them back as his own people (calling them "My People"; see 2:23), and gather Judah and Israel together under one ruler. This sounds like a promise of the future messianic kingdom of God. This will be the positive day of Jezreel (meaning "God sows"), when he plants his own people back in the land he promised them.

B. Confrontation of unfaithfulness (2:2–15).

In order for God to reestablish a normal relationship with his people, there will need to be some dramatic changes in the hearts of the people of Israel. Initially chapter 2 appears to be a divorce court scene where Hosea is talking to his children about confronting their sinful mother Gomer, but after a few verses one realizes that the confrontation is not just about Hosea and Gomer; the text is also talking about God's confronting the sons of Israel. Although the marriage relationship is severely threatened by spousal unfaithfulness and prostitution, the major focus is on Hosea's and God's parallel attempts to get back their unfaithful partners. In order for the partners to fully renew their love relationship, the unfaithful spouse has to know how serious the situation is and must change her ways.

Several steps are taken to help the sinful spouse move forward in this restoration process. First, family members confront her about this serious problem. Then the husband proclaims that she is not acting like his faithful wife (2:1), a statement that reveals how destructive the situation is. She is exhorted to reject the lifestyle and look of a promiscuous woman. The threat to strip Gomer bare would be an act of shaming and humiliating her before the public, just as God's curse of stripping the land bare of all fertility and turning it into a dry desert would humiliate his people Israel and expose their shameful dependence on the useless power of the fertility god Baal. These wives must realize that they have acted in unfaithfulness to their covenant relationship and have done a very disgraceful thing. If the unfaithful wives weaken their resolve or are tempted to return to their old ways, their husbands will symbolically hedge their wives in to protect them from these other lovers (2:5–6). Some in Israel may have thought their lovers (other gods) would provide fertility for her crops, but it was actually God who sent the rain. If these Israelites find out that these false gods do not provide prosperity and fertility, then they will return and stay with their rightful husband. Therefore, to combat this misunderstanding God will remove all fertility, end all Baal festivals, expose Israel's foolishness, destroy her crops, and punish her for the days she worshiped Baal, who will be proven powerless; therefore, Israel will

finally realize that Yahweh is the God who provides all her needs (2:8–13).

After Israel has realized the impotence of Baal, God will win his wife back. Using bold sexual imagery of wooing, God explains his plans to whisper in her ear words of love so that Israel will know how much he cares for her (2:14). This will be a repetition of what God did in the past when he cared for his people in the wilderness of Sinai (Deut. 8:1–8; Jer. 2:2). Then Israel will respond positively like she did at the time of the exodus, when she sang about God's greatness (see Exodus 15). This implies a renewal of the covenant relationship originally confirmed at Mount Sinai. Then God will pour out his abundant covenant blessings and reverse the curse on the people resulting from Achan's sin (Joshua 7) in the Valley of Achor (meaning "valley of trouble") and turn their dwelling place into a blessed door of hope for the future.

C. God will bring restoration to the families (2:16–23). This paragraph has three "in that day" promises (2:16, 18, 21), which refer to the eschatological things God will accomplish for his people in the distant future when he establishes his kingdom on earth. These verses expand on the positive promises that were already introduced in 1:10–2:1. First, the people will no longer confuse the title "my husband," which belongs to God, with the name of the pagan god "my Baal" (Hebrew *baal* means "master" or "husband"); in fact, the god Baal will be so irrelevant to the people of Israel that his name will never be mentioned again (2:16–17). Second, "in that day" God will transform nature by making a covenant of peace between all people (there will be no war) and between people and animals (cf. Isa. 11:6–9). This suggests a return to a precurse setting like the Garden of Eden. God will also renew

The Lord condemns Israel for burning incense to Baal (Hos. 2:13; 11:2). Censers such as this terra-cotta stand were used to burn incense to the gods (Taanek, thirteenth–twelfth century BC).

his wedding vows of commitment with his people because he is a God who relates to his people on the basis of justice, love, faithfulness, and compassion (2:18–20). Third, "in that day" God's power will cause the sky to rain and the ground to produce crops abundantly; thus, all that was taken away through God's judgment because of sin will be restored through these blessings. At that time God will sow or plant (playing on the meaning of Jezreel, "God sows") his people in the land; he will have compassion on the people who were formerly called "No Compassion" (NIV "Not my loved one," 2:23). He will say to his people, "You are my people," thus reversing the curse of the earlier names of Hosea's children. Then the Israelites will also proclaim, "You are my God," indicating a restoration of the covenant relationship between God and his people (2:21–23).

D. Love for the unlovely (3:1–5). Although God's positive plans for Israel are already known (2:14–23), this paragraph helps one appreciate that a high price was required in order to bring about this change in God's and Hosea's families. The story provides no information about when this occurs, but God speaks directly to Hosea, telling him that he should show his love to his adulterous wife, even though another man loves her (3:1–3). This act will mirror God's deep love for adulterous Israel, who has been following other gods. This means that Hosea will have to buy Gomer, almost like having to pay a second bride-price for the woman who is already his wife. Apparently this is necessary because she is indebted to another man, possibly as his slave. Although one wonders about Hosea's emotional response to this news, the story is only interested in affirming that Hosea graciously pays the price to free his wife of this debt so that he can live with her. It is impossible to evaluate the fair value of the goods that Hosea pays, for the price relates more to her debt than to her value as a slave. Hosea does set down some restrictions on Gomer's activities in order for them to restore their relationship. There is no reference to any punishment on Gomer or any

comments about how their reunion goes, but Hosea does require that she stop all contact with her past sinful ways, thus restricting her from seeing other men. Hosea's action is in some ways parallel to God's dealings with Israel (3:4–5). Israel will be in exile for some time without a king or the ability to offer sacrifices (because the temple will be destroyed), but then at some point in the future God will return his people to their land, where they will reestablish their covenant relationship with God and have a Davidic Messianic king ruling over them (cf. 2 Sam. 7:11–16). This assures the audience that God's promise to establish a king on the throne of David forever will be fulfilled.

2. God's Lawsuit because Israel Does Not Know God (4:1–6:6)

A. Proof that Israel does not know God (4:1–19). This new section was likely presented to the people during the reign of Pekah, either just before or during the Syro-Ephraimite War (5:8–9). It appears that the people of Israel do not realize just how terrible their sins are or how their sins have made it impossible to maintain their covenant relationship with God, so Hosea explains the seriousness of this matter by presenting God's case against his unfaithful people in an imaginary court of law (4:1–3). In such a context the evidence can be fairly and fully presented and evaluated by a judge, and God can produce an unbiased verdict. God's initial charge is that the people of Israel do not know him and do not acknowledge him as their God. This has happened because the priests have not faithfully taught the covenant law of God to the people (4:6). They have forgotten to teach the people the words of God in the law of Moses. Consequently, the people are ignorant of the requirements of their covenant relationship with God. Instead of correcting the sinful people, the priests relish the people's involvement in various acts of wickedness (4:8).

Second, the worship of the Israelites is characterized by excessive drinking of wine, sacrificing at open-air Baal temples, worshiping wooden idols, and sacred prostitution by both men and women (4:10–14). This is not the kind of worship that God ordained in Leviticus; it is the kind of sexually perverted pagan worship widely practiced at Baal temples. The people should not participate in such worship, but both the men and women who are involved with these activities are so stubborn (like a stubborn heifer) that it is difficult to change them. They are so devoted to their idols, wine, and prostitution that they do not understand the seriousness of their sin. They seemingly cannot bring themselves to change and turn back to God (4:16–19). God rejects the priests and this vile worship by the people, for it will lead to their shame and destruction.

B. Punishment of war (5:1–14). In God's verdict against the nations, he holds the political leaders (the kings) and spiritual leaders (the priests) responsible for this terrible situation in Israel (5:1–7). They have allowed evil things to continue; in fact, they themselves are partially responsible for ensnaring the people at the pagan worship sites of Mizpah and Tabor, failing to stop the sacred prostitution going on at various temples, and refusing to acknowledge the true God as the only one worthy of worship. Because of their arrogant attitudes, a perverse spirit of prostitution controls the people. Because the leaders have so frequently repeated these acts of unfaithfulness to God, it is almost impossible for them to return to God (5:4–7). God will discipline them for these things, for he knows exactly what they have been doing. Things are so bad that if one might try to seek God by sacrificing a sheep, they will not find him; God has withdrawn from them because of their terrible sinfulness (5:6).

Consequently, the army trumpets will soon blow, and the nation will be at war (probably some part of the Syro-Ephraimite War in 734–732 BC and its aftermath). Israel will be laid to waste when God pours out his wrath on his people, and Judah will suffer too (5:8–14). No hope is given to Israel; instead, it is absolutely certain that Israel will be defeated when God's wrath falls on them. It will be futile at this time

for Israel to turn to Assyria for help (5:13), for God will attack both Israel and Judah like a fierce lion. He will rip them apart and carry some of them off into exile, and no one will be able to rescue them from his powerful hand (5:14).

C. Hope: Return and know God (5:15–6:6). Although the future seems certain and tragic, God surprisingly offers the possibility of hope if the people will admit their guilt and turn to seek him. God will allow them some time, so that they will come to the point where they are willing to confess their sins, want to know God, and long to experience his healing (5:15). They must earnestly seek God, acknowledge who God is, and desire to know him so that they can experience the material and spiritual blessings of his coming. Although God wounded them in the past, they can be sure that he will revive the wounded if they seek God. God will leave a blessing (rain and fertility) for his people, but they must first come and return to him (6:1–3). Immediately after this offer of hope is God's sad, lamenting response (6:4–6), indicating that relatively few people actually pray the prayer of repentance in 6:1–3. What can God do if the people do not respond to his offer of restoration? God has warned them and punished them, but nothing seems to work, for their covenant loyalty lasts about as long as the dew on the ground. They do not take God's severe judgment seriously, suggesting that they just do not understand that acknowledging God as their Lord is far more important than the ritual of offering sacrifices (6:6).

3. God's Lawsuit because Israel Does Not Keep the Covenant (6:7–11:11)

A. Proof of Israel's lack of covenant love (6:7–7:16). The second part of the covenant lawsuit discusses a second major charge against Israel. They have not been steadfast or consistent in their expression of covenant love to God. Hosea describes several ways in which the nation's actions demonstrate that they have not truly loved God with all their heart and soul.

First, the priests, who are supposed to live holy lives, have been unfaithful in demonstrating their love for God; they break God's covenant by murdering people in ambushes and promoting shameful acts of prostitution that defile the nation (6:7–10).

Second, although God wants to show his love by bringing restoration and healing to his people, this is impossible because their sinful deeds, such as deceit and robbery, have made them callously indifferent to God's love as well as his plan to judge their sins. Thus God must bring judgment instead of restoration (6:11–7:2).

Third, the kings and princes of Israel plot and scheme by deceit to overthrow one another (cf. 2 Kings 15). At one point they will appear to be a friend, and in the next moment they are ready to get involved with plots to assassinate the king (7:3–7). They are politically unfaithful (thus adulterers) and liars; like an oven, they get hot with passion and drunk with wine. So at a time when the king is supposed to be honored and people are supposed to be enjoying a festival, they join evil companions in talk about how to overthrow the reigning king. While all this is happening, no one ever bothers to consult God to see what his will is on these very important matters.

Fourth, instead of trusting God to protect them and defeat their enemies, Israel makes military alliances (7:8–12). These foreign alliances sap the strength of the nation, for such arrangements require tribute, a reduction in freedom, and many moral compromises. Although people may not realize the danger of these political arrangements at first, just like the slow process of the graying of a person's hair (7:9), these alliances will gradually undermine the integrity and purity of the nation of Israel. Unfortunately the arrogance of the leaders will not allow them to admit their mistakes and turn back to trusting God; instead,

they senselessly act like an indecisive dove by making alliances with one nation (Egypt) after another (Assyria). God will soon stop this silly dove's behavior by capturing it.

Finally, God laments the coming destruction of his people, who have strayed from giving their love to God (7:13–16). God laments because he has done everything he can (he trained them, made them strong, and redeemed them) to get these people to maintain their covenant faithfulness to him, but they have repeatedly rebelled, spoken lies about God, ignored God, and refused to depend on him. It seems like they are plotting against God, trying their best to undermine everything he wants them to do. If they continue in this way and do not turn upward to call on God, they will end up being destroyed in war, their kings will be killed, and other nations (like Egypt) will ridicule them for their political blunders.

B. Punishment of war and captivity (8:1–10:15). 8:1–14. This chapter describes how Israel's sinfulness is leading to the coming destruction of the nation. In the first section (8:1–7), the prophet Hosea indicates that God will bring a devastating war on Israel because they have worshiped a golden calf and because they have been politically unfaithful in their covenant relationship with God. The political judgment in 8:1 may refer to the attack of their enemy Assyria, which

Hosea 8:5 says, "Samaria, throw out your calf-idol!" This bull statuette is from Samaria (second half of second millennium BC).

brought an end to the Syro-Ephraimite War. The stipulations within God's covenant describe how Israel, God's covenant partner, is to relate to foreign nations in the political sphere, how people are to treat one another within just social relationships, and what people are to do to maintain their relationship with God. Although some have said that they acknowledge God and his covenant (8:2), in reality they have rebelled against almost every commandment in the law. In the area of politics, the Israelites anoint kings that God did not choose (8:4; cf. 2 Kings 15), but in the sphere of worship they make man-made idols of gold, such as the golden calves at the temples in Bethel and Dan (1 Kings 12:26–29). Since the Canaanite god Baal was pictured as a bull calf, it was easy for them to confuse the golden calf image of Yahweh from their exodus experience (Exod. 32:4) with the calf image of Baal. God's anger burns against the people of Israel for these sins; therefore, God will destroy these calf idols, which are not even real divine beings. The Israelites have sown sinfulness, so they will reap the rewards of their terrible sinfulness. The people have sold themselves to alliances with pagan nations and have become like an unclean or impure vessel (8:8). Although the Israelites might think that these political alliances will save them, God will cause all these alliances to weaken the nation because they will require the burden of paying a heavy tribute in taxes.

The prophet Hosea also condemns Israel's worship of God with sacrifices (8:11–14). Instead of worshiping at the one true temple in Jerusalem, the Israelites have multiplied altars for giving sacrifices throughout the country. Most of these are pagan altars, so instead of appearing more devoted to God, the people actually have become more sinful. Since they have adopted the Canaanites' rituals and their theological concepts of morality, many of the Israelites totally ignore God's laws (8:12; cf. 4:6). In fact, God's laws about sacrificing (Leviticus 1–5) seem very strange to them. When the people do not follow the ritual instructions in

Leviticus, the sacrifices that are supposed to be a sweet-smelling savor that pleases God (Lev. 1:9, 13, 17) become repugnant. Consequently, God will punish these people for their sins and take away their political independence, for these people have strayed so far away from God that they do not even know that it was God who created the nation of Israel many years earlier in Egypt (8:14a). The life and material security of the people in Judah and Israel are all wrapped up in their wonderful palaces, and their trust is founded on the strength of their well-fortified cities, but God's plan is to take away all of these false securities when he brings the fire of war on these cities and destroys everything in them (8:14b).

9:1–17. In another attempt to persuade his audience to repent and turn back to God, Hosea tells a group of people at harvest time that God will soon bring an end to the joyous harvest festivals in Israel (9:1–9). Instead of being a time to rejoice and praise God as they used to be (Deut. 16:14–15), the Israelite festivals reflect the influence of pagan festivals. The introduction of sacred prostitution into the festivals demonstrates that the people love Baal, the fertility god who they claim has brought fertility to their crops, more than they love Yahweh, the God of Israel. In order to demonstrate to the people that Baal does not bring prosperity, God will take away all fertility so that the nation will have poor harvests (9:2). Then God will send them out of his land and into the lands of Egypt and Assyria, where they will have to eat unclean food. In these pagan lands they will not be able to sacrifice to God. They will not be able to please or appease God; they will be defiled. So what will happen on future festival days that were designed to honor God? The people will not celebrate these days but will suffer desolation, live and die in Egypt, and not be able to enjoy all the things that silver and gold used to buy them (9:6). Hosea closes the first half of this chapter with a final reminder that the time of divine retribution is close at hand. Although some people think Hosea is a fool or a madman for saying these things, the truth is that he proclaims these messages simply because of the sinfulness of Israel (9:7–8).

The rest of the chapter compares two examples of past sins with the present situation in Israel (9:10–17). The first example begins back at the joyous time when God first found Israel's forefathers (9:10–14). They were wonderful, like sweet, juicy, fresh grapes at the beginning of the harvest season (cf. Isa. 28:4). But some years later, while the Israelites were passing through Moab, some of their forefathers got involved with the shameful events at Baal Peor (Num. 25:1–8), which resulted in the death of about twenty-four thousand people. Elsewhere Hosea accuses his audience of worshiping Baal, the god of fertility, so it is not surprising for him to suggest that the nation's glory will pass away, women will no longer get pregnant, and those children that are born will die. God's curse (Deut. 28:18, 41) will fall on the nation when God departs from them and no longer protects them. The people of Israel initially had a great advantage (comparable to the advantage of the people of Tyre), but soon they will be killed in a terrible war. Because of this terrible destiny Hosea sorrowfully prays for God to bring his just judgment and remove his blessings of fertility and many children (9:14).

The second example refers to Israel's sins at Gilgal (9:15–17). It is not clear what the sin was, but it is related either to the pagan place of worship there (4:15; 12:11; Amos 5:5) or to the fact that Saul was anointed king there (1 Sam. 11:15). Thus the terrible thing that God hates could relate to the political or to the religious institution at Gilgal. The punishment is harsh. God will drive these people out because he does not love the rotten fruit they produce. They will have no children and will suffer under God's curse. Like verse 14, verse 17 ends this example with a prayer that agrees with God's just decision to cast Israel out of the land and make them fugitives in exile. Under God's curse the nation has no hope and no prophet to intercede for them.

10:1–15. The last major sermon in this punishment section is divided into two paragraphs.

First, Hosea reminds his audience that because of their sins God will destroy all the detestable altars where the people worship (10:1–8). Hosea compares Israel to a vine that has produced much fruit, because for many years they were a prosperous nation. But the richer the people became, the more they built pagan altars and standing stones that represented pagan gods. Therefore, God will destroy all these pagan altars and standing stones to stop this unfaithful worship (10:1–3). This may be a prophetic prediction of the final fall of the nation in 721 BC. Verse 3 contains a quotation of some Israelites. When they say, "We have no king," they are probably referring to the fact that they do not consider God as their king; thus, this phrase is somewhat parallel to the statement that they do not fear or stand in awe of God and the comment that a king could do nothing to help them. After Hosea predicts the fall of the nation, one might expect the people to humble themselves and repent. Instead, they make many promises, oaths that they do not intend to honor, and therefore injustice sprouts up like weeds (10:4). One of the central deceptions in Israel is the worship of the golden calves at temples at Dan and Bethel (referred to as Beth Aven, which means "house of iniquity"; cf. NIV note). It appears that when the gold from the golden calf was used to pay the tribute owed to the Assyrians (10:6), both the priests who loved to serve at that temple and the people who worshiped there mourned because of the humiliating demise of this idol. People will be ashamed because this great idol of gold that they worshiped could not save them or even itself. With this Assyrian conquest will also come the end of the nation of Israel, its capital city of Samaria, its king, and its wicked high places. The people will be like twigs floating down the river, unable to resist the flow of captives meandering through the countryside toward Assyria. When the people are taken into captivity, the uncultivated land will revert to wild thistles and useless thornbushes (10:8). Nothing they have trusted in will rescue them;

everything they have will be taken away. People will be depressed and hopeless because their false gods will not save them. Some will rather die in a rockslide caused by an earthquake than have to suffer the indignity of going into exile.

The second paragraph in this chapter describes the devastating war that will end the nation (10:9–15). Hosea suggests that part of the nation's sinfulness goes back to their earlier sinful deeds at Gibeah (cf. Hos. 9:9; Judges 19–20), which resulted in violence and war. The problems of the past continue at Gibeah (cf. Hos. 5:8), and they are about to develop into further warfare for the nation of Israel. God's punishing judgment will come because of two sins, but they are not identified. Possibly Hosea is referring to the sin of worshiping the two golden calves, two sins at Gibeah, or possibly both idol worship and a false trust in their army. Hosea finds another creative way of expressing what is about to happen to Israel by comparing Israel to a heifer trained to do agricultural work (10:11). God put his covenant yoke on this heifer and asked her to work plowing the field. God wanted Israel to plant righteousness and to have faithful covenant love so that he could shower those who would seek him with his righteousness and blessings. Unfortunately things did not work out this way; his people planted evil seeds instead of righteous seeds, so naturally they have reaped evil results. Part of this is explained as their consumption of the poisonous fruit of lies, deception, and false beliefs. One cannot expect the blessings of God's wonderful fruit by depending on human strength or large armies instead of on God (10:13). The evil calamity that will come as the fruit of this false trust will be war and the defeat of the key military fortifications that protected the nation. One of the key events will have Shalman—the Assyrian king Shalmaneser V, who ruled from 727 to 722 BC—defeat the Israelites in a devastating battle at Beth Arbel (10:14). So far archaeologists have found no reference to this battle in ancient Near Eastern texts, and this is the only reference to it in the

Bible. It must have been a disastrous battle of hateful brutality, for even defenseless mothers and their small children were thrown off the high cliffs onto the rocks below. The destiny of Israel is military defeat; the nation and its king will die because of their great wickedness.

C. Hope: God loves you (11:1–11). This chapter brings the second section (6:7–11:11) of the covenant lawsuit to an end with a word of hope, just like the end of the first section of the lawsuit (5:15–6:6). The four brief paragraphs in this chapter contrast God's great love for his people and Israel's repeated rejection of his love. Israel deserves God's severe punishment, but God laments over his people and ends up promising salvation.

In the first paragraph, God is pictured as a loving father, and Israel is likened to a stubborn son (11:1–4). At the time of the exodus from Egypt, Israel was a young nation that God loved; in fact, God called Israel his son (Exod. 4:22). Although God expressed his love for the Israelites, they did not respond positively to God's love but went away after the fertility god Baal and offered sacrifices on altars at Baal temples. This was an act of ungratefulness, and it was astonishing because it was Yahweh the God of Israel who patiently taught his son Ephraim to walk, possibly a reference to God's care for the people while they were in the wilderness. God acted just like a parent who teaches a child by taking their hand and guiding them. God miraculously healed them (see Num. 21:1–9), but the nation seemed to ignore his miraculous grace in healing them. Finally, God is pictured as one who led them with love and kindness, lifted the heavy burden they were carrying, and fed them as a father might feed a young child. This must refer to God guiding them through the wilderness for forty years and his provision of manna and quail (Exodus 16; Numbers 11). These are all examples of God's tender care and expressions of his deep love for his people.

The second paragraph indicates that the nation's lack of repentance or turning to God will lead to divine judgment (11:5–7). These ungrateful people who inherited the wonderful land of milk and honey will end up exiled in the foreign land of Assyria (not in the more familiar land of Egypt) because they have stubbornly refused to repent and come back to God. This will happen because Assyria will send their army and destroy the gates, walls, and cities of Israel (11:6). The time for repentance has passed; it is now time for Israel to be held accountable for their actions. Though some might cry out to God in desperation in that final hour of judgment like a child pleading for mercy when facing punishment, it will do them no good.

Although God has determined to discipline these people he dearly loves, in the third paragraph he laments the thought of actually having to do this (11:8–9). Just as a loving father has internal struggles with how or whether to severely punish his son, so God cries out in distress over his decision to destroy his people. In these words to Hosea, God reveals that he is not a cold and heartless father; his heart goes out to his beloved children that he has to punish. This does not indicate that God is indecisive, does not know what to do, or is second-guessing himself. Because of his deep love for Israel he is in emotional anguish; he asks himself if it is really possible for him to give up on his children. In the past he was willing to punish the wicked cities of Sodom and Gomorrah, Admah and Zeboyim (Gen. 19:1–38; Deut. 29:23), but it is much more difficult to do something like this to the covenant people he loves so much. In many ways it is impossible to compare God's feelings to the emotional response of humans, but on the other hand, these kinds of human analogies are the only way God can explain to human beings his tender love for his people. God's heart is overcome with compassion for his people. Although God will discipline his children, he will not act in fierce anger against them; he will not completely destroy Israel off the face of the earth. He is a holy God; he does not act or respond like a man might react to betrayal (11:9). He operates on a different plane of existence that is higher than and somewhat

foreign to the thinking of most people (Isa. 55:8–9), so he is able to respond in ways that are far beyond anything that humans know (e.g., Jon. 3:10–4:2). Although the Bible reveals much about God's person and his actions, the dynamics of God's interaction are often inscrutable and exceed human comprehension (Eccles. 8:16–9:1). Nevertheless, one can be absolutely sure that God loves but also punishes sinners.

This message of hope ends in the fourth paragraph with a promise of restoration after the time of discipline (11:10–11). God's punishment was earlier compared to the attack of a lion (Hos. 5:14), but in this passage of hope God describes himself as a lion that roars in order to call his people back to himself. At that future time the Israelites will respond positively to God's call and turn back to him. The people of Israel will come trembling, humbly fearing him and following him in a new exodus from the lands of their captivity. Then God will resettle them in the land he originally promised them. God's loving forgiveness and gracious restoration will elicit a positive response from the Israelites. This indicates a major transformation of the hearts and minds of the Israelites. They will no longer be rebellious but will renew their covenant relationship to God.

4. God's Lawsuit because Israel Is Deceitful (11:12–14:9)

A. Proof of deceitful ways (11:12–13:3). In the final section of this long covenant lawsuit against Israel, the nation is accused of deceitfully lying about her love for God. The people claim to be committed to God, but in reality there is no truthfulness in these words. They do not do what they say they will do (11:12–12:2). This is not just a minor issue of a few people who on rare occasions become unfaithful to their commitments to live as the holy people of God. Instead, many people in both Israel and Judah repeatedly say deceptive things to God and practice undisciplined behavior that involves them with things that God rejects. While God is faithful and holy, the people of Israel are deceptive and untruthful in their relationship to God. To illustrate this problem God gives a specific example: Israel's deceptive behavior is like chasing the wind all day long. This suggests that she is trying to achieve something that is impossible to grasp. The Israelites try to gain political security by making deceptive promises to Assyria, and then they turn around and break these promises by sending gifts to Egypt to buy friendship and cooperation (11:1). Not only is Israel telling lies to other nations; the people's actions reveal the deceptive lies they make to God, for they really are not trusting him for their political welfare. Thus God brings this third charge in this covenant lawsuit against Israel (and it is also a problem for Judah). If the nation does not change her ways, God will justly punish his people based on their untruthful ways (11:2). There is a direct relationship between their rebellious, deceptive ways and their guilt. The punishment for these lies will fit the crime.

The problem of deception is traced back to Israel's ancient forefather, the patriarch Jacob (12:3–6); thus, this is not a new problem or new character defect that God has not seen before. Genesis 25:21–26 describes the birth of the twins Jacob and Esau as the beginning of Jacob's deceptive action. Esau was born first, but Jacob was "grasping" the heal of Esau (12:3a), an act that might be interpreted as a sign that Jacob wanted to be the firstborn child. Thus the second child was named Jacob ("the heel grasper"), a name that is also a pun on the

Hebrew word meaning "deceiver." Later Jacob's deceptive ways were fully revealed when he deceived his father by claiming that he was Esau; thus, he was able to steal the blessing of his father (Gen. 27:35–36). Another example that illustrates the character of Jacob was his wrestling with the angel of the Lord (12:3b–4a; Genesis 32). While Jacob was on his journey home from Laban's home in Paddan Aram, he met numerous angels from God at the Jabbok River, so he called the place where he was camping "the camp of God." But once he received word that Esau was coming to meet him with four hundred men (Gen. 32:6), Jacob seemed to forget about this angelic protection that God was providing. Fearing the worst and thinking that Esau was coming to take his revenge against him, Jacob initially committed himself to God's care and prayed for God's intervention (Gen. 32:9–12). Nevertheless, after he prayed, he immediately instructed his servants to prepare an enormous gift of cattle

Hosea 12:7 accuses the merchants of dishonest practices, which include the use of inaccurate weights and balances. This lion is a standardized weight from the palace of Shalmaneser V, king of Assyria (727–722 BC).

so that he could appease the wrath of Esau. Thus his deceptive action proved that he was not really trusting God at all. Later that night the angel of the Lord wrestled with Jacob all night (Gen. 32:24–30). Although Jacob could not overcome the angel's strength, Jacob did overcome the angel in the sense of begging a blessing from him. Hosea 12:4b describes yet another incident in Jacob's life: God talked to Jacob at Bethel (Gen. 28:10–22). No explicit interpretation is given to these last two illustrations from the life of Jacob, but Jacob's struggle with the angel may suggest that the people of Israel should not wrestle with or resist God like Jacob did but should listen to and accept the promises of God Almighty as Jacob did at Bethel. Verses 3–6 end with a call for the prophet's audience to repent and turn to God, to establish a steadfast covenant relationship of love with God, to practice justice in all their social relationships with others, and to trustingly wait for God to act on their behalf (12:6).

Additional acts of deception are cataloged against Israelite merchants to prove the guilt of the nation (12:7–10). As Amos has also mentioned (Amos 8:4–6), merchants in Israel are using two sets of weights (a light weight when they sell grain and a heavy weight when they buy grain) on their scales to deceive and defraud their customers of what they are justly owed. Thus a small group of upper class individuals has become quite wealthy and arrogantly flaunts their riches. To make the situation even worse, these rich merchants feel they are above the law of the land and will never be held accountable for their sins. These people trust in their wealth because through it they are able to bribe judges and buy their way out of any difficult situation. Thus, their hopes for the future are based on their confident trust in their money, not in God. This claim of self-sufficiency is put in direct contrast to God's claims (12:9–10) that he is God Almighty, the one who delivered them from Egyptian bondage and who is able to send them back to where they have next to nothing. They do

not determine the future of the nation with their riches; God is the one who controls their destiny. They may have enjoyed their appointed feasts of the past when they first came up out of Egypt (Passover; Feast of Tabernacles; Lev. 23:33–44; Deut. 16:13–17), but they will soon not enjoy them when God removes their riches and sends them back to the wilderness, where they have nothing (12:9). God has repeatedly warned the Israelites through the prophets, who deliver messages in visions and parables. Israel has been repeatedly told to trust God and not be unjust to the poor, so there is no excuse for this kind of behavior by the people of God. They know what God wants, and they know that he does not accept what they are doing.

The people choose to follow the ways of deception (12:11–14) in their worship at Gilgal (12:11), a place famous for various acts that God has rejected (Hos. 4:15; 6:8; 9:15). Their sacrifices there do not impress God, for he will soon allow this altar to become a useless pile of rocks. The next example of deception involves an ambiguous comparison between Jacob, who "kept" or "took care of" (NIV "tended," 12:12) Laban's sheep in order to pay the bride price for a wife (Genesis 27–29) and the unnamed Moses who "took care of" (NIV "cared for," 12:13) the Israelites when they came up out of Egypt. Although there are some similarities between these two men—in both situations people were in a foreign land, both men were unfairly enslaved, and both eventually escaped—the main point of comparison may be the different ways these two attained success. In light of the earlier negative example of Jacob, Hosea may be suggesting that the Israelites should not follow the negative example of Jacob, who schemed to gain more sheep and schemed against Laban when he left (he did not rely on God for these things). Instead the Israelites should look to the example of the prophet whose name is not even mentioned (Moses), for in the second example the "caring for" was accomplished by God's power, not by human deceptive cleverness. These verses end with a strong conclusion warning the nation about what will happen next. Israel has provoked God's fierce anger, so the Israelites can be absolutely sure that they will soon be repaid for all their sins.

The final accusation against Israel is a brief condemnation of their deceptive worship (13:1–3). Hosea provides a brief historical summary of Israel's past, present, and future. Earlier, in a time of strength and prosperity (probably since the era of Jeroboam I and later), the people were deceived, and they confused the worship of Yahweh and the god Baal. This may have happened because the people thought that the golden calf idol of Yahweh and the bull calf idol of Baal referred to the same divine being (13:1; 2:16). This confusion has led to the present political and economic decline of the nation after the death of Jeroboam II. But instead of turning back to Yahweh, the nation has fallen into greater devotion to Baal, kissing the calf idol made of gold and even offering human sacrifices. Drawing on three common experiences, Hosea describes what the future will bring to the nation of Israel (13:3). Israel (1) will fairly quickly evaporate, just as the morning mist and dew evaporate when the sun comes out, (2) will be scattered far and wide just as the chaff from a threshing floor is scattered abroad by the wind, and (3) will disappear just as smoke rising in the air is gradually diffused until it cannot be seen anymore. All the deceptions going on in the northern nation undermine the truthfulness of Israel's commitment to their covenant relationship with God, so if there is no change God will eventually act against his covenant people.

B. Punishment of destruction (13:4–16). This punishment is tragic because the God who will destroy the nation of Israel is the Almighty God, who years ago redeemed his helpless people from Egyptian slavery (Exodus 14–15) and chose them as his special holy people (13:4–8). There was no one who could save them from their terrible situation in Egypt, so God acted on their behalf. At Sinai God asked for their exclusive devotion to him within the covenant relationship and instructed them to worship no other gods because he alone was their Savior. He continued to care for his people by miraculously leading them through the hot and dry Sinai wilderness, giving them more manna and quail than they could eat (Exodus 16; Numbers 11). But when they came into the rich land of Canaan, they had everything one could desire. Although God had warned them not to become proud and forget him (Deut. 8:10–20), they became satisfied with their situation in the land and soon forgot that God gave it all to them. They became proud and self-sufficient and did not think they needed God's help. Consequently, God will turn against his people and attack them like a ferocious lion or an angry mother bear who has lost her cubs (13:7–8). Just like a wild beast rips open and tears apart the helpless body of its prey, so will God attack the people of Israel.

The people who are primarily responsible for the sins of the nation are the wicked political and religious leaders of the nation (13:9–11). God was their helper and Savior from the beginning, not their human kings or princes. After the disastrous years of the judges, the nation asked to have a king like the other nations (1 Samuel 8) because they rejected God as their king. God allowed the nation a king, but God set limits on the behavior of their king (Deut. 17:14–20; 1 Sam. 12:12–15). When king after king did not act within these divine parameters, God eventually removed these kings from power. In the future God will send another king (the Assyrian king), who will come and take Israel away into captivity.

The final paragraph on punishment (13:12–16) recognizes that death and destruction are coming soon, but this will not be the end of God's plans for his people Israel. God has a complete record of all the sins of Israel, so there is no question about her guilt or exactly what she has done. As a consequence, great inescapable pain (like the pain of childbirth) will fall on the nation. Israel has no wisdom and will be like a child who refuses to be born, God says, implying they will die. A second metaphor pictures God's intervention as a divine drought that will scorch the land and dry up all its springs. As a result an enemy nation will come and plunder the wealth of the nation (13:15). A third description drops the metaphorical language and describes a barbarous military conquest in which people are killed by the sword, children are mercilessly massacred, and helpless pregnant women have their wombs ripped open (13:16). This hopeless scene of total annihilation is interrupted by one short promise, which gives some hope for the future (13:14). This sliver of hope in the midst of judgment reminds one of similar statements in Hosea 6:4 and 11:8–9. In all three of these passages God is overcome by the thought of the total annihilation of his people, and consequently in great compassion he refuses to completely give up or to totally reject his people. In compassion God will ransom some from the power of death; therefore, God can taunt death and refuse to allow it to conquer his plans for his people. It is possible that the restoration of the nation in Ezekiel 37 picks up this same theme.

C. Hope: Repent and God will forgive (14:1–9). The third part of this lawsuit ends with a statement of hope just like the earlier sections in Hosea 5:15–6:3 and 11:1–11. Although the nation has repeatedly sinned and will surely be disciplined by God, there is still hope that the people will repent and return to God. God first calls them to repent (14:1–3). God wants to give his people life and the blessings of the covenant, but he is not able to do this until the problem of the nation's sin is dealt with. Sin is the stumbling block that has tripped up the nation, so they must turn from their sin (cf. Isa. 55:6–7), return to the Lord (cf. Deut. 30:2), prayerfully confess their sins, and seek God's gracious forgiveness so that they can once again praise him. They need to confess that their Assyrian alliance, a strong Israelite army, and dependence on false gods

will not save them. These man-made attempts to survive in this world provide no lasting answers to the trials and tribulations of life. Their only hope is to trust in God, whose strength is seen when people are weak and unable to save themselves. Only God is truly compassionate to the weak, the powerless, and the fatherless. He is able to bring true hope and comfort if only people will turn from their sinful ways and depend on him.

God next promises to forgive and restore his people when they trust in him (14:4–8). Although the text does not indicate who, if anyone, prayed the prayer in 14:2–3, God still promises that he will heal his people miraculously, love them freely, and no longer be angry with them (14:4). This love from God will be totally unearned and completely undeserved, so it expresses God's deep commitment to pour out his grace to a hopeless, unfaithful people.

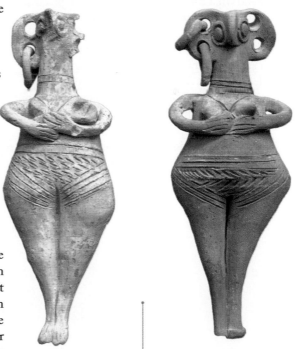

The source of Israel's fruitfulness is the Lord (Hos. 14:8), not fertility goddesses or charms like the ones pictured here (Cyprus, 1450–1200 BC).

His love will overpower their sinful tendencies, and then he will be able to bless them with fertility. The nation will metaphorically blossom like a beautiful flower and become deeply rooted like a grand tree in the soil of Israel. Eventually its splendor will match the beauty of an old olive tree that has deep roots, so many people will gather under its shade. God's people will be fruitful and multiply and be as many as the grains of wheat in a field. Fertility gods and their idols will no longer tempt these people because God will answer whenever he is called; he will watch over them. God will be the source of their fertility; they need not look to anyone else.

The book of Hosea ends with an unusual admonition to the reader of this collection of sermons by Hosea (14:9). The reader who is truly wise and discerning, like the wise people of Deuteronomy (4:6–8; 30:11–16), Psalms (1:1–6), and Proverbs (10:27–31), will understand what this book is about and what practical lessons to draw from the failures of Israel as well as the gracious promises of God. These words were not meant to entertain people with a sad story about a group of people who were destroyed. It does not philosophize about the viability of various metaphysical hypotheses or try to draw a hypothetical line in some moral gray area. It has plainly spoken about the failures of a blessed nation that was not faithful to the God who loved her. It is a practical book that describes what people should do to please God, and what people should not do (Deut. 10:12; 30:15–20). Therefore, the most obvious lesson of this book is to accept the fact that the ways of a holy and loving God are right and always just. The second lesson relates to how people should respond to what God says and does. Those who are righteous will listen to and follow what God says, but those who are foolish will rebel against God's instruction. The first group will enjoy God's blessings, but the second group will stumble and fall. Everyone has a decision to make, and the people who read this book will be held accountable to faithfully apply what they have heard.

Select Bibliography

Garrett, Duane A. *Hosea, Joel.* New American Commentary. Nashville: Broadman & Holman, 1997.

Hubbard, David Allan. *Hosea.* Tyndale Old Testament Commentaries. Downers Grove, IL: InterVarsity, 1981.

Kidner, Derek. *Love to the Loveless: The Message of Hosea.* The Bible Speaks Today. Downers Grove, IL: InterVarsity, 1981.

McComiskey, Thomas Edward. "Hosea." In *The Minor Prophets: An Exegetical and Expository Commentary.* Edited by Thomas Edward McComiskey. Grand Rapids: Baker Academic, 1992.

Smith, Gary V. *Hosea, Amos, Micah.* NIV Application Commentary. Grand Rapids: Zondervan, 2001.

Stuart, Douglas. *Hosea–Jonah.* Word Biblical Commentary. Waco: Word, 1987.

Joel

SHERI L. KLOUDA

Introduction

The book of Joel tells the story of Judah and her dramatic rescue, tracing her journey through pestilence, famine, exile, and restoration. Equally significant is the prophetic overview of God's ultimate victory and rule over his enemies embedded within Joel's oracles. Despite the book's brevity, the reader should not underestimate the eschatological significance of Joel's prophecies for the original audience as well as its contribution to New Testament revelation. Joel's frequent allusions to the Pentateuch, the five books of the Law, as the authoritative foundation for his prophecies, combined with his appeal to the work of his contemporaries, underscores the immediate historical relevance of his words to a nation in crisis. Joel describes current events as orchestrated by God, threatening rebellious Judah with divine chastisement while assuring her of eventual deliverance. The writer adeptly navigates the transitions between imminent fulfillment and the cosmological scope of a later, more complete realization of his prophecies. Incorporating apocalyptic imagery and language designed to incite hope for a devastated nation, Joel speaks in terms of visions, cosmic anomalies, and an ultimate final conflict between good and evil. Divine victory eradicates evil and establishes the cosmological reign of a messianic king. The citation of Joel 2:28–32 in Acts 2:17–21 associates this unique prophetic vision with the gift of the Holy Spirit at Pentecost, bridging the chasm between an ancient past and a glorious, unrealized future.

Joel the Prophet

The identities of Joel and his father, Pethuel, remain uncertain since 1 Chronicles mentions a number of individuals with the name Joel living during the period between the transition to Israel's monarchy and the postexilic return (e.g., 1 Chron. 4:35; 5:4, 8, 12; 6:21; 7:3; 15:7, 11; 27:20). The geographic references to Jerusalem, Judah, and Zion, as well as Joel's obvious familiarity with priestly practice and procedures, imply the prophet lived within the centralized temple community. While the majority of scholars affirm Joel as the author of the book, a few commentators doubt that the apocalyptic sections (1:15; 2:1–2, 10–11; 2:28–3:21) originated with the prophet.

Date

Scholarly opinions diverge widely concerning a date for the book. The superscription (1:1) does not specify the historical time period. Those who argue for a postexilic date for composition base their arguments on a number of criteria, suggesting that contextual evidence of regular sacrificial offerings and references to the priesthood point to the rebuilding of the temple, after 516 BC. In addition, the prophet does not specifically mention a king or the monarchy in his message. Allusions to Israel's and Judah's captivity and deportation appear to support a late date for the prophecies. Moreover, the transitional content of the book from prophecy to apocalyptic material leads some biblical experts to propose that it dates from the fourth century BC.

The same criteria used for a late date of the book, however, also support an eighth-century-BC composition. References to the temple and the priesthood could indicate a preexilic origin. The failure to mention Assyria, Babylon, or Persia as political threats, combined with the inclusion of the Phoenicians, Philistines, Egyptians, and Edomites (3:4, 19) as Israel's enemies, argues favorably for an origin before the exile. In addition, an eighth-century historical setting best reflects the relative autonomy of those foreign nations listed in chapter 3. The mention of a city wall (2:9) may also suggest either an early or a late date. The book's canonical position, situated with Hosea, Amos, and Jonah, presumes these works as contextual contemporaries, and the prophet's association of the "day of the Lord" with an earthquake harmonizes well with King Uzziah's reign and Amos's descriptions. Joel employs literary themes and events consistent with a preexilic composition, sharing dozens of terminological and linguistic links with early prophetic works. The evidence therefore favors a compositional origin sometime in the mid-eighth century (ca. 750–740 BC).

Literary Features

A devastating locust plague occasions the writing of the book, which describes an insect invasion so comprehensive in scope that it threatens the survival of Judah's population (1:2–12). Joel envisions the extent of the destruction by voracious locusts as equivalent to the widespread judgment of the day of the Lord. The prophetic warning in 2:1–11 uses the metaphor of a second, unparalleled locust plague, followed by drought, to characterize God's chastising Judah by means of an enemy invasion. While locusts never figuratively symbolize

armies in ancient Near Eastern literature or the biblical text, locusts are mentioned in Deuteronomy 28:38, 42 in light of future conquest and exile. The far-reaching consequences of the locust invasion that Joel emphasizes seem to extend beyond the realm of a literal swarm of pests to symbolize the wide-reaching effects of enemy attack and conquest of Judah. The connections between the two sections, offset by corresponding passages focusing on repentance (1:13–20; 2:12–17), reinforce the theological emphasis on the day of the Lord as a time of divine discipline and cleansing, followed by eventual restoration.

All the Hebrew manuscripts and ancient versions attest to the unity of the composition, although chapter-and-verse divisions vary. The Greek and Latin versions originally divided the text into three sections. The first rabbinic Bible as well as later Hebrew editions, including the modern standard edition (*Biblia Hebraica Stuttgartensia*), segment the book into four sections. Consequently, 3:1–5 in the Hebrew (Masoretic Text) corresponds to the English 2:28–32, and Hebrew 4:1–21 reflects its English counterpart, 3:1–21.

> Locusts, such as the one pictured in this Egyptian tomb painting, will swarm when environmental conditions are right, leaving devastation in their wake (Joel 1:4).

The allusive nature of Joel's prophecies becomes apparent in light of a generous number of shared literary links with eschatological or apocalyptic themes in other prophetic books, including several allusions to Isaiah (Joel 1:15 [Isa. 13:6]; 2:3 [Isa. 51:3]; 2:27 [Isa. 45:5–6, 18]; 3:2 [Isa. 66:18]), Jeremiah (Joel 3:1 [Jer. 33:15; 50:4, 20]), Ezekiel (Joel 1:15 [Ezek. 30:2–3]; 2:3 [Ezek. 36:35]; 2:28 [Ezek. 39:29]), and the Psalter (Joel 2:17 [Ps. 79:10]; 2:21 [Ps. 126:3]). These affinities reaffirm the continued theological struggle Israel experiences as she seeks to harmonize the merciful and compassionate disposition of God with the demands of his divine holiness, which punishes sin and requires restitution. In addition, Joel demonstrates a broad familiarity with other authoritative texts, interweaving motifs such as the exodus, the divine attributary formula (Exod. 34:6–7), and themes of judgment and restoration from Deuteronomy 32, along with mythological concepts, such as the sacred mountain or divine warrior imagery. In the process of drawing from authoritative, well-established texts recognized by the contemporary audience, Joel underscores the divine origin of his prophecies, validating his message as a continuation of previous revelation.

Theological Themes

The book of Joel has been recognized for its emphasis on eschatological themes, describing God's role and relationship to Israel. The Lord preserves a remnant of his people, pouring out his Spirit on all of them without class distinction. Supernatural visible signs, such as the eclipse of the sun (3:15; cf. Amos 5:18–20; 8:9; Zeph. 1:15) and the hail of blood and fire, attend the day of the Lord. God regathers and rescues Israel and leads her in triumphal procession back to the land, engaging and defeating the enemy nations in a great final battle.

Structure

The clever structure of the book reflects Joel's skillful use of repetition, in particular through the forty-seven instances of twice-repeated terms and phrases in the book. The two halves of the book correspond to one another, as reflected in the outline below.

Commentary

1. The Locust Invasion as the Lord's Judgment of Judah (1:1–20)

A. The devastating consequences of the locust invasion (1:1–12). Joel first addresses the general population and the elders (1:2), invoking the audience to "hear" his message. The nuance of the Hebrew root for "hear" implies that the audience understands the message and responds. The prophet also implores the people to recount this event to their descendants, in hopes that their children will learn that covenantal disobedience requires divine punishment. The incomparable catastrophe that plagues the inhabitants of the land in the form of a locust swarm will certainly produce a story of legendary proportions that will become part of the nation's history.

The prophet uses four different words for "locusts"in 1:4 and 2:25, perhaps reflecting the various stages of the development of locusts. He reinforces the totality of the devastation and emphasizes the long-range effects of the voracious insects on the productivity of the land and the subsequent starvation of the people. Joel commands the drunks to "wake up" and "weep"(1:5) because the locusts have destroyed the grapes, which produce wine. Most likely, he is addressing those who are oblivious to the consequences of widespread plague. The prophet compares the locusts to a "nation"(1:6), perhaps establishing the connection between a literal military invasion by Judah's enemies and the destruction of her food source, preparing the reader for the analogy in chapter 2. Not only have the locusts consumed food-producing crops and the grains to sustain cattle; they have stripped the bark from fruit trees, leaving them vulnerable to disease by removing their protection (1:7). Similarly, Judah's walls are breached and her defenses destroyed by the enemy (whether a reference to the Assyrian crisis or a foreshadowing of the Babylonian invasion and exile, 2:7–9).

The prophet then uses the analogy of a grieving bride, whose groom is unable to consummate the marriage because he lacks the bride-price normally paid to the bride's family in exchange for betrothal. She wears sackcloth as a sign of her mourning. The infestation also affects religious life, interfering with regular temple offerings by the priests (1:9) and threatening the ritual worship of the Lord.

After the source of food and prosperity for the Lord's people has been consumed by insects, a drought follows (1:10–12), robbing the land of necessary nutrients to feed and nurture subsequent crops. The onset of drought typically characterizes the Lord's judgment on his people (Isa. 42:15–16).

B. The Lord's call for Judah's repentance (1:13–14). The first of two formal calls for repentance is introduced with a command to the priests to don sackcloth in penitence and remorse for the absence of produce for sacrificial offerings (1:13). The lack of offerings signifies the breach in the relationship between the Lord and his people, who no longer have a means

> Joel 2:12 calls the people to return to the Lord "with fasting and weeping and mourning," which may have resembled the weeping and mourning displayed in this Egyptian funeral procession scene (Saqqara, 1550–1292 BC).

for repairing their sinfulness before God. The prophet instructs the priests to "declare a holy fast" and "summon the elders and all who live in the land" (1:14) so that they can cry out and petition the Lord to restore productivity to the land and deliver his people from their suffering. (The formula "declare a holy fast, call a sacred assembly" recurs in 2:15; however, the purpose of the fast and the assembly in chapter 2 focuses on rejoicing instead of mourning.) The locusts have not only devoured all the vegetation but consumed the seeds for future crops, endangering the livestock. The language is reminiscent of the great fast called by the king of Nineveh, in which the people and the animals wear sackcloth in repentance (Jon. 3:5–8).

C. Judah's appeal for the Lord's rescue (1:15–20). The "day of the LORD," an expression that recurs several times throughout the book (1:15; 2:1, 11, 31), typically denotes a time of divine wrath characterized by God's war against evil. Immediate events in Judah represent just a foretaste of a greater, cosmological judgment of the Lord against his enemies. A drought follows the locust attack, suggesting a relationship between the two. While the connections are not readily apparent, it is possible that the same winds that drive the locust plague also absorb the moisture from the ground. It is also plausible that the drought is simply another manifestation of the Lord's judgment, or a separate catastrophic event. Nevertheless, drought enhances the dangers of uncontrolled fires (1:19), which rage throughout the dry countryside. The nation calls out to the Lord with one voice, as if to call the Lord's attention to their plight and incite him to act on their behalf.

2. Military Conquest as the Lord's Judgment of Judah (2:1–17)

A. The devastating consequences of Judah's invasion by her enemies (2:1–11). The blowing of the trumpet, or shofar, an instrument made from a ram's horn, normally signifies a call of strength or victory. In addition, the priests sound the trumpet to mark the beginning of sacred festivals (Lev. 25:9; Ps. 81:3), to gather the community in anticipation of a theophany (an appearance by God; Exod. 19:16–19; 20:18; Zech. 9:14), or at the inauguration of a new king (2 Sam. 15:10; 1 Kings 1:34, 39; 2 Kings 9:13). The command to sound the trumpet here serves as a warning to the people of an approaching danger for which they should prepare (cf. Jer. 4:5, 19–21; 6:17; Isa. 18:3; Ezek. 33:3–6; Hos. 8:1). Joel announces the imminent arrival of "the day of the LORD" in ominous terms, as a large army converges on Judah from the north, obliterating the landscape and wreaking chaos and destruction in its wake. Similarly, the prophet Habakkuk predicts the Babylonian invasion of Judah (Hab. 1:5–11), highlighting the Lord's use of foreign nations as agents of judgment or discipline. The blowing of the shofar in Zephaniah (1:16) also heralds the infamous day of the Lord.

Even the forces of devastation fall under the authority of a sovereign God. The Lord employs the military power of first Assyria and later Babylonia as instruments through which he punishes Judah, allowing the contingency to carry away captives, destroy Jerusalem, and profane the temple. The divine-warrior language in 2:10 describes the upheaval of nature at the arrival of the Lord. Typically, natural catastrophes such as earthquakes attend the arrival of the Lord, whether in judgment or triumphal victory. Even the celestial bodies fail to provide light, reinforcing the unparalleled severity of the Lord's wrath toward his people.

While Joel's words have immediate relevance for his contemporary audience, the apocalyptic nature of his prophecies points forward to unrealized fulfillment following worldwide catastrophic events in the eschatological future, when the Messiah himself will render judgment on the nations and exercise dominion from his throne in Jerusalem.

B. The Lord's call for Judah's repentance (2:12–17). In a second appeal (cf. Joel 1:13–14), the Lord calls for Judah's repentance. The prophet instructs the people to rend their hearts rather than their garments. The ripping of garments publicly signified deep internal grief; however, the prophet asks not for outward expressions of mourning but for an internal response of true sorrow and penitence. In the prophetic address to the rebellious community, he adapts an abbreviated version of the formula in Exodus 34:6–7 describing divine attributes (originally recited by the Lord to Moses, who desired to see the presence of God). The formula reveals the inherent character of God, who forgives covenant misconduct and remains faithful to his commitments to Israel. The Lord not only demonstrates forbearance and patience in light of his people's continual transgression but also demonstrates his covenant love (Hebrew *hesed*) in his willingness to abide by the covenant despite Israel's unfaithfulness. In addition, the Lord's *hesed* manifests itself in the restraint of his wrath. While the Lord chastises his people, he does not exact the full measure of his judgment on them.

Joel argues on the basis of the Lord's character that the Lord may recognize true repentance and mitigate his wrath against Judah. If God is all-knowing, there is no human response he does not already anticipate, while God's immutability—or the fact that he does not change—means that God does not "change his mind" on the basis of human decision. Thus, when Joel suggests that the Lord will "relent," he is using human language to describe God's unfathomable will in refraining from immediate divine judgment (2:13). Similarly, the book of Jonah represents the prophet's struggle with God's character as compassionate and merciful in light of his apparent failure to judge Nineveh for its evil behavior. Joel reinforces the inscrutability of God's actions by the rhetorical expression, "Who knows?" (2:14). The text recalls the practice of gleaning, or allowing the poor to gather the remnants of harvest intentionally left behind out of pity for their circumstances. Joel suggests that the Lord may "bless" Judah by providing the means for offering temple sacrifices and reinstating her position of favor with God (2:14).

Once more, the prophet commands the priests to sound the shofar, this time for the purpose of a sacred assembly (2:15). The command extends to everyone, including nursing mothers, their children, and newlyweds, who are normally excluded from religious gatherings on the basis of purity laws (2:16). The Lord requires comprehensive repentance from a unified community, which is then instructed to plead for salvation and preservation from enemy invasion and oppression. Joel draws from language typically associated with a standard appeal for the Lord's favor, calling attention to the Lord's reputation among the nations, which is directly affected by whether he will preserve the nation associated with his name. What distinguish Israel and Judah from the Gentiles are the character and commitment of the Lord, his presence among them, and his covenant faithfulness toward them (Exod. 33:15–16). By allowing the nations to obliterate his people, the Lord brings reproach on himself. Joel employs the rhetorical question, "Why should they [the Gentiles] say . . . , 'Where is their God?'" The same expression appears in similar contexts that frame the people's lament from the perspective of the Lord's reputation (Ps. 42:3, 10; 79:10; 115:2). The first call for a sacred assembly (1:14) mirrors the second (2:15–16), since the purpose of both is community prayer and repentance. The assembly enjoins the Lord not to allow her to be ridiculed by the Gentiles, using a formulaic expression commonly found in laments that center on military threat and oppression (cf. Ps. 79:4).

3. The Lord's Response to Judah's Appeal (2:18–32)

God responds to the cries of his people by delivering them from the clutches of the enemy and exercising his divine anger on the nations that persecuted them. In many ways, Joel 2 resembles the structure of Psalm 79, a lament that traces the destruction of Jerusalem by the enemy, recalls the pleas of the captives, recounts the Lord's deliverance, and describes his subsequent victorious battle over the evil nations.

A. The Lord's conquest of the enemy restores productivity to the land (2:18–27). The jealousy of God provokes his desire for vengeance against the nations who have tormented his people. Deuteronomy describes the Lord's jealousy as his demand for exclusivity among the Israelites, depicting his wrathful response to the infidelity manifested in idolatry (Deut. 32:16, 21). God's jealousy and protectiveness toward his people are incited in battle toward their adversaries (Isa. 42:13; 59:17; Zech. 1:14). The Hebrew term for "to be jealous" (*qana*) is related to the verb meaning "to acquire (as property)" or "to purchase" (*qanah*). God envisions Israel as his "property," and those who encroach on them and seek to snatch them away from him arouse his fierce anger.

The Lord announces that he will restore their supplies of "grain, new wine and olive oil" (2:19), reversing the circumstances from 1:10, which depicts the ruin of grain, new wine, and oil as the result of the locust invasion. In addition, he promises to prevent his people from becoming the recipient of further ridicule by the nations (2:19), answering the community's plea in 2:17.

Joel prophesies concerning the hasty retreat of the invading army from the Lord and into the wilderness. Subsequently half are driven toward the Dead Sea in the east and the other half to the Mediterranean Sea in the west, where both groups seem to die. The imagery is reminiscent of the demise of Pharaoh's army in Egypt following the departure of the Israelites from Egypt. The prophet calls on the land (2:20), the animals (2:22), the vegetation (2:22), and the people of Zion (2:23) to rejoice in the Lord's rescue and restoration. The production of figs and olives as well as the ripening of grain and renewal of the grassy fields signifies the end of the Lord's chastisement and the favorable standing of his people before him. The normal cycle of autumn and spring rains once again nourishes the land. The nation will once again prosper and, more importantly, have the means to offer sacrifices to the Lord at the temple. The people eagerly celebrate the reinstitution of worship in the community.

Suffering and adversity provide the occasion for glorifying God and affirming his sovereignty. The Lord declares that he will "restore" or "make whole" (NIV "repay"; from the same Hebrew root as *shalom*) his people for the losses they have endured as a result of the drought, the insect invasion, and the Babylonian conquest (2:25). God does not punish his people out of malice but rather to chastise them and purify them so

The new oil that the Lord promises as he restores productivity to the land (Joel 2:19, 24) would come from olive presses like this one, which were used to extract olive oil (Hazor, eighth century BC).

they may once again enjoy a relationship with him. Consequently, the deliverance and restoration of Israel to her land and the renewed productivity and prosperity she enjoys testify to the benevolence and faithfulness of the Lord (2:26), providing another story of redemption to declare to future generations. The Lord's presence will once again inhabit Jerusalem (2:27), where he will reign in authority as God alone. Twice the oracle promises that Israel will not be ashamed again (2:26–27); instead, she will inhabit the land with pride and confidence.

B. The rescue of the Lord's people and his reign on Mount Zion (2:28–32). The apocalyptic themes represented in this section unquestionably point to future events not fully realized by the restoration of Judah and the return of God's people from Babylonian exile. While 3:1–5 centers on the day of the Lord as an age of salvation and vindication for Judah, 3:1–17 depicts the day of the Lord as a terrifying display of divine wrath toward God's adversaries.

Joel characterizes the day of the Lord as the "pouring out of the Spirit" on everyone, without distinction (2:28–29). The pouring out of the Spirit is normally associated with the advent of prophetic gifts (1 Sam. 10:6–10; 18:10; 1 Kings 22:22–23; Neh. 9:30; Zech. 7:12; 13:2); therefore, prophetic abilities will be poured out on all of Israel during this great age. Joel may also have the analogy of Amos 8:11 in mind, where Amos describes the failure to hear God's word in terms of thirst and drought. Consequently, Judah's reception of the Lord's counsel constitutes the reversal of that spiritual drought.

Joel 2:28–29 sustains a number of parallels to Numbers 11–12, suggesting the prophet deliberately invokes the earlier narrative. All of God's people will prophesy (Num. 11:25–29) through "dreams" and "visions" (Num. 12:6). The endowment of the Spirit follows famine in both passages (cf. Num. 11:4–6, 18–23, 31–34; Joel 1:1–2:32). Joel's announcement fulfills Moses's request that God would bestow his Spirit on all Israel (Num. 11:29). Joel, however, announces a radical innovation in his message; since cultural convention normally recognized prophecy as limited to men of elevated social standing, the expansion of prophetic gifts beyond gender and class distinction signifies a new age.

Perhaps the most familiar reference to the outpouring of the Spirit is Peter's citation of Joel 2:28–32 at the day of Pentecost in Acts 2:17–21. The pouring out of the Holy Spirit caused ecstatic behavior resembling that of Old Testament prophets (1 Sam. 1:13–14; Jer. 23:9). In addition, all believers are equally indwelled by the Holy Spirit, retaining equal status before God. Although Joel perceives the Spirit as a phenomenon limited to Israel, in Christ the distinctions between Jew and Gentile have been eliminated.

Darkness prevails during the impending day of the Lord, and natural aberrations, such as earthquakes, fire, smoke, and a bloodred moon signal the salvation of Judah and the doom of judgment (2:30–31; cf. Amos 8:9; Isa. 60:2). These cosmological disruptions evoke imagery associated with theophany—God's physical revelation to convey information—or epiphany—God's physical intervention as divine warrior to rescue and deliver his people. Physical manifestations of the Lord, such as the pillar of cloud and fire that served as a sign of God's presence among his people during the exodus, are replaced with immediate and personal access to the Lord as he reigns on earth. Only those who repent and rely solely on God will endure the day of the Lord (2:32).

4. The Day of the Lord as Victorious Rule and Reign (3:1–21)

Although the day of the Lord means salvation and restoration for Israel, the impending judgment of God awaits those who have tormented and abused the Lord's elect nation.

A. The Lord's defeat of Judah's enemies (3:1–16). The idiomatic expression "restore the fortunes" includes the concept of a release from imprisonment or debt combined with the return of the Lord's people to their homeland (Deut. 30:3; Ps. 14:7; 53:6; 126:4; Jer. 29:14; 30:3, 18; Hos. 6:11; Amos 9:14; Zeph. 2:7). The statement reiterates the context of 2:25, where the Lord promises to compensate Israel for her losses during the locust invasion and famine.

In a typical lawsuit format, the Lord gathers the adversaries in the "Valley of Jehoshaphat," which means "the Lord judges." The actual location defies identification, though some equate this valley with Kidron, a valley east of Jerusalem between the Mount of Olives and the temple, on the basis of other texts that refer to an area east of Jerusalem typically associated with visions and theophanies (Ezek. 10:19; 47:1–12). The fountain that flows from the Lord's temple (3:18) also travels through this valley.

The Lord accuses the nations of relocating and dispersing his people from their land and selling them on open market as prostitutes (3:2–3). The prophet mentions Tyre and Sidon, two groups of people who made most of their income through barter and trade. The precious metals, temple vessels, and slave cargo transported by ship will be returned to the Lord one day (cf. Isa. 60:4–14), while the merchants bow in obeisance before the very captives they traded. The mention of Tyre, Sidon, and Philistia, minor enemies of Israel in comparison to the Assyrians or Babylonians, may support an early date for the book as preceding the Assyrian captivity. Although the mention of the Greeks seems troubling at first, there is evidence for Greek trade in the Mediterranean region during the eighth century.

God's judgment, ironically, enacts a reversal of roles as the captors are exported as captives, and those who were enslaved become slave owners (3:8), receiving honor from their oppressors. The punishment hints at the laws of *lex talionis*, or equal recompense for injuries received from another (Exod. 21:24; Lev. 24:18; Deut. 19:21).

Joel 3:10 reuses familiar imagery from Isaiah 2:4 characteristic of an eschatological return of Messiah (cf. Mic. 4:3) in which implements of war are transformed into tools of peace ("swords into plowshares"), but Joel reverses the meaning of the expression by warning Israel's enemies to construct weapons of war from agricultural tools ("Beat your plowshares into swords"). The connections between the return of the Lord in Joel 2:28–32 and Isaiah 2:1–5 (Mic. 4:1–5) are hardly coincidental and appear to reflect the development of a unified theological understanding of the establishment of an ideal eschatological, messianic, worldwide kingdom.

The Lord's trampling of the nations like grapes in a winepress (3:13) finds correspondence in Isaiah 63:3–6, which describes the total annihilation of the nations and the bloodshed as staining the garments of the Lord. Joel draws on parallels from other prophetic texts to inform and clarify his metaphors while also reinforcing the divine authority of his declarations.

Once again, the prophet adapts divine-warrior language as a means to convey the frightening proportions of the Lord's wrath against the Gentiles (3:14–16). While the day of the Lord becomes a day of divine protection for Israel, the nations can only anticipate their demise in the face of an angry, vengeful God.

B. The Lord's establishment of a permanent kingdom in Jerusalem (3:17–21). The Lord resides on his holy mountain, Zion, as a witness to his sovereignty. The inviolability of Jerusalem becomes a reality in that future age, and the Lord's

The streams of water flowing from the vessel held by a Mesopotamian deity in this statue at the entrance of the Nabu temple in Khorsabad (eighth century BC) are reminiscent of the fountain that Joel describes flowing out of the Lord's house (3:18).

presence in his city as well as the productivity of the land provide abundance and peace for God's people. The reference to a fountain flowing from the temple of the Lord (3:18) recalls Zechariah 14:8 and Ezekiel 47:1–12, both contexts describing the establishment of an eternal kingdom following the conquest of evil (cf. Rev. 22:1–2). Threats from Egypt and Edom, two of Israel's most ferocious adversaries, have been eliminated (cf. Zech. 14:18–19), and the eternal safety and security of Jerusalem's inhabitants prevails under the authority of the Lord. The Lord's people finally experience the covenant rest God has promised. Such a rest prefigures an even greater rest, the security of salvation accomplished through the sacrifice of Christ for all believers.

Select Bibliography

Allen, Leslie C. *The Books of Joel, Obadiah, Jonah, and Micah*. New International Commentary on the Old Testament. Grand Rapids: Eerdmans, 1976.

Baker, David W. *Joel, Obadiah, Malachi*. NIV Application Commentary. Grand Rapids: Zondervan, 2006.

Barton, John. *Joel and Obadiah*. Old Testament Library. Louisville: Westminster John Knox, 2001.

Coggins, Richard J. "Joel." *Currents in Biblical Research* 2, no. 1 (2003): 85–103.

Crenshaw, James. *Joel*. Anchor Bible. New York: Doubleday, 1995.

Dillard, Raymond Bryan. "Joel." In *The Minor Prophets: An Exegetical and Expository Commentary*. Edited by Thomas Edward McComiskey. Grand Rapids: Baker Academic, 1992.

Garrett, Duane A. *Hosea, Joel*. New American Commentary. Nashville: Broadman & Holman, 1997.

Hubbard, David Allan. *Joel and Amos*. Tyndale Old Testament Commentaries. Downers Grove, IL: InterVarsity, 1989.

Sweeney, Marvin A. *The Twelve Prophets: Hosea, Joel, Amos, Obadiah, Jonah*. Berit Olam. Collegeville, MN: Liturgical Press, 2000.

Wolff, Hans. *Joel and Amos*. Hermeneia. Philadelphia: Fortress, 1977.

Amos

GARY V. SMITH

Introduction

Amos the Prophet

The first verse of the book of Amos informs the reader that this book contains the "words of Amos," indicating that he was the one who originally spoke the prophetic oracles collected together on this scroll. Amos is never mentioned elsewhere in the Hebrew Bible, so there is very limited information about his life and ministry. Amos grew up in Judah in the small village of Tekoa, which was approximately twelve miles south of Jerusalem. Tekoa was located high in the mountains along the ridge road that went from Hebron to Jerusalem. To the west of Tekoa were rocky hills where shepherds could tend their sheep, and to the east was a rugged, dry wasteland that sloped down toward the Dead Sea. This small village had a military outpost (2 Chron. 11:5–12) that was constructed to protect Judah's southern cities from invading armies. Since Amos lived relatively close to Jerusalem, one can assume that he periodically worshiped at the temple, heard stories about past military conflicts from soldiers at the fort in Tekoa, and was well acquainted with the sheep business.

Before Amos became a prophet, he worked as a shepherd (7:14). The unusual Hebrew word for "shepherd" in 1:1 indicates that he was a "manager of shepherds," a middle-class position that implies Amos must have had some education and good managerial abilities. Amos also cared for a grove of sycamore fig trees (7:14), but he never provides any explanation of what he did with these figs. His rural background comes through in the imagery he uses to describe the behavior of lions (3:4) and the requirements of shepherds when a lion kills one of their sheep (3:12). He knows about traps used to catch birds (3:5), the plagues that occasionally ruin crops (4:9), the lamenting of farmers (5:16), the foolishness of running horses over rocks (6:12), the damage swarms of locusts can afflict on crops (7:1–2), and how to use a sieve to separate out good grain from the straw and chaff at harvest time (9:9).

Historical Context

Amos 1:1 indicates that the prophet spoke these words during the reigns of Jeroboam II king of Israel (793–753 BC) and Uzziah king of Judah (791–740 BC). Amos lived in Judah during the long, prosperous, righteous, and strong military reign of King Uzziah (2 Chron. 26:1–5). Uzziah equipped a large elite army with the finest weapons, defeated the Philistines, and rebuilt the fortifications of Jerusalem; but later in his reign he proudly insisted on offering for himself a sacrifice in the temple, so the Lord punished him with leprosy (2 Chron. 26:6–23). Even though Amos lived in Judah, God called him to declare the word of God in the northern nation of Israel, where Jeroboam II ruled (7:15).

Second Kings 14:23–26 says little about the forty-one-year reign of Jeroboam II, except that he did evil in the eyes of the Lord and that he expanded the borders of Israel just as God had promised through the prophet Jonah. When Amos prophesied his message, the powerful army of Jeroboam II had already conquered the territory from Hamath in the north to the brook of the Arabah in the south (6:14); thus Amos's ministry should be dated in the second half of Jeroboam's reign, possibly around 760 BC. Uzziah and Jeroboam II expanded these kingdoms to equal the size of the large kingdom ruled by David and Solomon. All this military success made it difficult for the people in Israel to believe Amos's warnings of God's coming judgment, for everything was going well and they had a strong army. Israel had a strong economy based on tribute from defeated nations, trade, and the agricultural produce of the land, so Amos's talk about the defeat of the army, the destruction of cities, and exile seemed more like the ravings of a mad prophet. During Amos's ministry in Israel he got into a controversy with Amaziah, the priest at the temple in Bethel (7:10–17). After hearing Amos's prophecy, the priest sent king Jeroboam II a letter concerning the treasonous words of Amos (7:10), for Amos claimed that God would raise up a sword against the dynasty of Jeroboam (7:9).

Amos spends a fair bit of time talking about the deplorable social situation in Israel. Because of its strong economy, Israel had a wealthy upper class that lived like kings in large palatial homes (6:8, 11). According to Amos, some have winter homes in the Jordan Valley for the warmer climates and summer homes around Samaria in the cooler mountain elevations (3:15). These people enjoy lavish parties with the best music, wine, oils, and food (6:4–6), but they are totally unconcerned about the rampant oppression of the lower class (6:6–7). Amos condemns the wealthy people who are crushing the needy (4:1), the businessmen who are cheating the poor by using false weights (8:4–6), the landowners who

charge exorbitant rents (5:11), and those who bribe judges to win court cases (5:10, 12). The wealthy drive poor people into bankruptcy or slavery, sexually mistreat servant workers, and do not return pledged garments in the evening as the law stipulates (2:6–8).

Amos does not say a whole lot about the religious situation in Israel. He indicates that God has rejected their worship and hates their music because their hearts and actions do not demonstrate a transformed life guided by justice (5:21–24). Some of these people sacrifice often in order to impress God and brag about their generosity to impress their friends (4:4–5), but God can see what is really in their hearts. Amos condemns the worship going on at the temples in Bethel (including a golden calf), at Gilgal, and at Beersheba, then challenges his audience to truly seek the Lord if they want to live (5:4–6). There was some pagan worship in Israel (5:26; 8:14), but the prophet Hosea addresses this issue in much more detail. The people do know about God's election of Israel as his own special people (3:1–2), God's deliverance of Israel from Egypt (2:10; 9:7), his conquest of the Amorites and giving of the land to his people in the days of Joshua (2:10), and God's promise to save his people on the final day of the Lord (5:18–20); but these great acts of divine salvation only bring on a false impression of security instead of a deep commitment to fear God. The wealthy people enjoy God's blessings, but they fail to love and serve God with all their heart (Deut. 10:12).

Amos was called from his secular work of managing shepherds in Tekoa to persuasively speak God's message to the people of Israel (7:15). Before this divine call to action he was not a prophet and his father was not among the professional prophets who worked at temples for money (7:12–14; Mic. 3:5). His short ministry in Israel probably did not last even a year, but he did preach powerful messages both in the capital city of Samaria (3:9; 4:1; 6:1) and at the temple in the city of Bethel (7:1–17). Although no one organized the messages of

Nathan, Gad, Elijah, and Elisha into separate books in the Hebrew Bible, the oracles of Amos were gathered together to form one of the first prophetic writings. When the earthquake hit Israel about two years after Amos preached his messages (1:1), people seemed to realize that this was a fulfillment of the earthquake prophecies in 2:13; 8:8; 9:1, 5. This may be one of the key reasons why Amos's prophecies were widely accepted as divinely inspired and worthy of reproduction in written form.

Authorship

Some critical commentaries imagine a long writing process involving as many as four different stages of redactors or editors who gradually added verses and paragraphs to the original writings of Amos over the next three hundred years. They suggest that the superscription in 1:1; the oracles against Tyre and Edom in 1:9–12 and against Judah in 2:1–4; the hymns in 4:13; 5:8–9; and 9:5–6; and the final salvation oracle in 9:11–15 were not written by Amos. But other commentators have pointed out that most of the messages in Amos contain a similar style, common rhetorical and persuasive techniques, a balanced structure, and thematic continuity that point to the compilation of these oracles by one individual. These characteristics would probably not be present if multiple people over several generations added verses here and there to reflect the theological issues in later periods of history. It is better to view the book as a unit that portrays the conflicting tensions Amos faced in his ministry. Assigning passages to later authors robs the prophet of authentic parts of his message, denies him knowledge of so-called advanced theological themes, limits his ability to change his style of writing when introducing new genres of literature, and takes away his expression of words of comfort.

Literary Features

The style of most of Amos's oracles is poetry, though there are a few verses of narrative (e.g., 1:1; 5:1; 7:10–17). Amos uses rhetorical questions to get his audience to think about what they believe (3:3–6; 5:18, 20, 25; 6:2, 12; 7:8; 8:2; 9:7), employs numbered phrases ("for three sins . . . even for four" in 1:3–2:6), pairs oracles against the nations (1:3–2:16), and experiences visions (7:1–8:3). Five times in 4:6–11 he repeats, "you have not returned to me," there are five visions in 7:1–9:4, and there are five parallel conditional clauses in 9:2–4. Amos likes to prove his point by quoting his audience's own perspective on a topic (2:12; 4:1; 5:14; 6:13; 7:10, 11, 16; 8:5–6, 14; 9:10) and by quoting authoritative Hebrew traditions to back up a point (2:9–10; 3:1; 5:6, 14; 9:7). He persuades people by quoting from hymns (4:13; 5:8–9; 9:5–6), referring to legal and cultic requirements (2:6–8; 3:12; 4:4–5; 5:21–24; 8:5–6), and using wisdom sayings (3.3–6; 6:12). By skillfully working these factors into his arguments, Amos presents a powerfully logical case that should bring to repentance those who are humble enough to listen to what God is saying.

Theological Themes

The theological message embedded in Amos's oracles gives them authority as well as power. Foundational to everything else is Amos's belief that Yahweh, the God of Israel, is the sovereign power that rules the world. He is the "Lord of Hosts" (3:13; NIV "Lord God Almighty"), the ruler of the armies of heaven and earth, who testifies against his people and will come and destroy the wicked (5:9). He is the creator of the world (4:13) and controller of the stars (5:8), who lives in his magnificent heavenly palace (9:6). He can touch the earth and cause it to melt or call forth fire (7:4), plagues (7:1–2), and water (5:8; 9:6) to bring destruction on the earth. He is a holy God (2:7; 4:2), who will come in great power to establish his justice on the earth. He uses armies (3:11), nature (4:6–9), and his spoken word as his instruments to accomplish his will. He offers life, hope, and the possibility of his grace to those who will seek him (5:4, 6, 14–15). But not every Hebrew person will enter into God's blessed kingdom on the day of the Lord (5:18–20), for God will separate the righteous from the wicked (9:10) and then pour out his blessings on his faithful people as well as on the Gentiles that are called by the name of the Lord (9:12).

It is this God who speaks through Amos to reveal his will for Israel; he is the lion that roars to warn his people of grave impending danger (1:2; 3:8). God reminds them of his past grace in miraculously delivering them from the power of Egypt, his loving care while they were in the wilderness, his powerful grace that enabled them to defeat the Amorites in Canaan and take control of the land, and his grace that called some to be prophets and Nazirites (2:9–11; 3:1). He has chosen Israel out of all the families of the earth to be his people (3:2), but his grace does not give his people an absolute guarantee of divine blessings. Their election carries with it a great responsibility to love the Lord with all their hearts and to follow the stipulations of their covenant relationship. If they fail to walk in God's ways as defined in the covenant (2:6–8), if they do not stop acting unjustly toward others (8:4–6), and if they continue in their pride (6:8), God will punish them for their iniquities (3:2).

Commentary

1. God's War Oracles against the Nations (1:1–2:16)

A. The superscription (1:1–2). This book begins like most other prophetic books: by identifying the author of these words (Amos), his secular employment (a manager of shepherds), his location (Tekoa), his audience (the northern tribes in Israel), and his time (during the reign of Uzziah and Jeroboam II), probably around 765–760 BC. The words that he spoke he "saw" (NIV) or "envisioned" (NASB), a term that points to the prophet perceiving them through the medium of divine revelation.

Verse 2 introduces God's roaring voice as the source of the prophet's message. God speaks words of warning from his temple in Jerusalem; his voice is like that of a roaring lion that screams out as he leaps to capture his prey (cf. Amos 3:7–8). As a consequence of God's ferocious action, the land where the shepherds pasture their flocks will mourn, and even the fertile, green Mount Carmel will dry up. The drying up of these two symbols of fertility confirms that Amos's message is actually God's roar and summarizes what God is now doing (he is on the attack). These early warnings of worse times to come should have motivated the prophet's audience to listen to what Amos was saying.

B. God's judgment of the foreign nations (1:3–2:3). Although other prophets have oracles against other nations (Isaiah 13–23; Jeremiah 46–51; Ezekiel 25–32), the oracles by Amos are much shorter, structured with identical phrases, put in pairs, and serving as parts of a larger "war oracle." Before Israelite troops went to war, the commander would seek God's approval (1 Sam. 23:2, 4) by asking a prophet or priest to pray for divine guidance. Once God answered the prophet, he would pronounce a war oracle that usually explained how God would defeat their enemies and save his people. Since the Israelites in Samaria were involved in many wars during this period, Amos used the war oracle to get the people's attention, to gain their approval of him as a true prophet, and to cause them to realize exactly what God was planning to do in the near future.

First, Amos gives an oracle about the defeat of Syria and its capital city of Damascus (1:3–5). The prophet's Israelite audience would quickly agree with Amos that Syria had acted in rebellion against God. They had sinned "three . . . even four" times, a rhetorical expression that indicates repeated rebellion and legitimates God's punishment. It was just for God to bring his wrath against them, for recently they had inhumanly mistreated the Israelite people living in Gilead, the area east of the Sea of Galilee (2 Kings 13:1–7). Amos compares their immoral behavior to the harvesting of grain. Just as farmers drag heavy wooden threshing sledges with iron spikes over the grain to separate the grain from the stalk, so the Syrians brutalize the people of Gilead by running over them. Consequently, God will send the fire of war against the palaces of kings Hazael and Ben-Hadad, destroy the gates of Damascus, remove the people who live in the distant provinces of Syria, and exile the remaining people back to the place where they came from in Kir (cf. Amos 9:7).

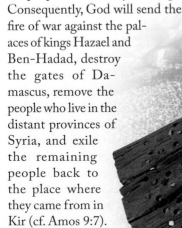

Using nearly identical terminology, the second oracle speaks out against the Philistines (1:6–8), who have also committed many rebellious acts. God will hold them accountable and pour out his wrath on them. Amos castigates Gaza for kidnapping the entire population of some unwalled villages and then selling them to the Edomites. These innocent people have been treated like animals, denied their freedom, and sold at the slave market. Consequently, God will bring fire on the palaces of Gaza and the other Philistine fortified cities. The common people, the rulers in these cities, and the remnant that remains will perish. Certainly the Israelite audience would have applauded the words of this courageous prophet from Judah and accepted him as a true prophet.

The next two oracles, addressing God's plans for the Phoenicians and the Edomites, use a slightly different pattern: the punishment statement is shorter, and there is no final "says the LORD." The Phoenicians from the cities of Tyre (and probably Sidon) have sinned repeatedly, so it is proper for God to send his wrath against them (1:9–10). Their sin is similar to that of the Philistines, in that both of these nations have sold people to Edom. But selling an entire village of innocent people (possibly

> Amos compares Syria to a threshing sledge (Amos 1:3), like the one seen here.

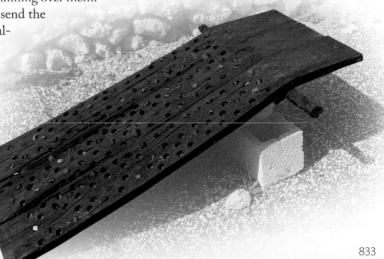

Israelites) is not their only fault, for the Phoenicians have kidnapped people from a country that they had a peace treaty with. Instead of respecting their treaty, the Phoenicians have betrayed this trust and broken their covenant. This may have happened because King Jehu killed the children of Ahab and Jezebel (she was a Phoenician; 2 Kings 10:1–11), although Amos never identifies this specifically. Amos's Israelite audience would naturally despise the treasonous acts of these former allies, so they would wholeheartedly agree that God should destroy Tyre with fire and ruin the king's palace.

Next Amos addresses the many sins of Edom (1:11–12), the descendants of Esau (Gen. 36:1). Although Jacob and Esau were blood brothers and should have had brotherly love for one another, the two nations that came from these brothers fought again and again (2 Sam. 8:11–14; 2 Kings 8:20–22; 14:7; 16:6). Amos concludes that it was just for God's wrath to fall on Edom because the Edomites have had absolutely no mercy on the sons of Jacob, but in great anger repeatedly have allowed the fire of their hatred to drive them to kill their brothers. Consequently, the audience would agree with God's plan to send the fires of war against the main Edomite city of Teman and destroy the palaces in Bozrah.

The last pair of oracles addresses the future of the Ammonites and Moabites, the two nations that came from Lot's two daughters (Gen. 19:30–38). God's word about the Ammonites (1:13–15) is that his determination will not vacillate, for he has decided to pour out his wrath on them because of their three and four acts of rebellion. Among their rebellious deeds is the specific sin of ripping open pregnant women from Gilead, a heinous atrocity in which the Ammonites killed innocent noncombatants, defenseless women and their unborn children, in a time of war (cf. 2 Kings 15:16). This heartless and senseless butchering terrorized those living in Gilead (probably Hebrews). These cold-blooded murderers did this simply to enlarge the borders of Ammon.

Certainly Amos's audience in Samaria would agree that God is just in kindling the fires of war on the capital city of Ammon (Rabbah), to destroy the palaces of the king who has ordered these atrocities, and to exile their rulers and princes to another land.

The sixth war oracle identifies Moab (2:1–3) as a very rebellious nation that God is determined to punish because the Moabites desecrated the body of the dead king of Edom, an act of vindictiveness and total disrespect for an enemy. All people in all cultures honor their dead and would view the desecration of a dead body as a morbid and perverted act. Especially heinous in this case is the burning of the corpse, thus depriving the king of a culturally appropriate burial. So God will send the fire of war on the chief cities of Moab, and many people will die, specifically those in power. ("Judge" [NASB; NIV: "ruler"] is another title for the king.)

C. God's judgment of his people (2:4–16). The final pair of oracles describes what God will do to Israel and Judah (2:4–6). The Israelites who were listening to Amos were probably a little surprised to hear that a prophet from Judah would condemn his own nation, but this adds to Amos's credibility and the persuasiveness of his message, for a true prophet must speak everything God says and not show any favoritism. Israel and Judah had lived as separate nations for about two hundred years, and the two nations fought several wars against each other (1 Kings 14:30; 15:7, 16–21; 2 Kings 14:8–14), so the Israelites in Samaria had little love for the people of Judah. Following the established pattern, Amos speaks about the many rebellious deeds of Judah and God's determination to hold them accountable. Two of Judah's acts of rebellion are recounted. First, they have not followed the covenant stipulations in the law of Moses. They agreed to follow God's instructions when they committed themselves to a covenant relationship with God, so now they will be held accountable for what they agreed to. One of the ways they have failed is that they have listened to the lies and deceptive ideas of their leaders and false prophets (cf. Isa. 3:12; 28:15; Mic. 3:5). These political and religious leaders have led the people astray after other gods and did not stop them from unjust practices toward the poor. Since Judah has sinned, fire will consume the palaces of its rulers in Jerusalem. It will be treated no differently than will the other nations. Of course when the Israelites in Amos's audience heartily agreed with God's punishment of Judah for breaking the covenant, they were admitting that it was legitimate to judge Israel with this standard, for they also had knowledge of God's covenant laws.

The climactic conclusion to this prophetic message is the extended oracle about Israel (2:6–16), the people Amos is talking to. Of course they are expecting this war oracle to end with the usual positive conclusion that God will save them and use Israel to defeat God's enemies. But Amos surprises them by using the exact same terminology of judgment against Israel because Israel too has sinned many times ("three . . . even four"). Thus, Israel is no better than any of these other nations and should be evaluated on exactly the same terms. They are guilty, so God will not rescind his decision to pour out his wrath on them. Instead of listing just one sin, Amos catalogs seven ways the people of Israel have rebelled against God (2:6–8). These rebellious acts involve the mistreatment of others (just like the other nations), but the difference is that Israel shamefully mistreats her own people, not foreigners.

First, poor and innocent Israelite debtors are not assisted with charity (Deut. 15:12–18) or given additional time to repay their debt. Instead, they are heartlessly forced to give up their land to a wealthy lender or are driven into slavery. Second, this is done even to people who cannot pay off a relatively small amount of debt (the price of a pair of sandals). Third, the powerful metaphorically trample the heads of the helpless into the dust (cf. Isa. 3:15), mercilessly humiliating them and treating them as the scum of the earth. Fourth, people in the upper class manipulate the weak to their own advantage and deprive them of their normal rights as God-created human beings. Fifth, contrary to the stipulations in the law of Moses (Exod. 21:7–11; Lev. 18:8, 15; 19:20–22), a wealthy father and his son have had sexual relations with the same servant girl. God claims that all these ugly deeds "profane my holy name" (2:7); they pollute and desecrate his reputation, and they defile his moral standards. Because of these acts other people will not see God's holiness reflected in his people. Sixth, wealthy people who have taken a garment as a pledge from a debtor are supposed to return it in the evening (Exod. 22:25–27; Deut. 24:12–13), but these heartless people refuse to return the garment so that the poor person can keep warm for the night. Instead, they take the stolen cloak to the temple with them, an act that does not please God at all. Finally, the seventh rebellious act is that judges steal the wine people have given to the state to pay a fine. These judges would take the wine with them to the temple to drink or to present as a drink offering to God. These acts demonstrate that the Israelites mistreat people just like the other nations, plus they break the laws of Moses, just like the people of Judah.

In order to emphasize the ungratefulness and perversity of the Israelites, Amos goes on to describe God's past acts of grace on behalf of the people of Israel, who are now rebelling against him (2:9–12). Many years ago God graciously defeated their enemies while they were enslaved in Egypt and enabled Joshua and the Israelite army to defeat the many nations (including their giants) living in Canaan. He also cared for them by providing everything they needed for forty years while they wandered in the wilderness, and he sent them prophets and Nazirites to reveal his will, but they forgot about his grace and rejected his prophets. Therefore God's judgment (Amos 1:13–16) will shake this nation and destroy its strong army. No one, no matter how strong they are, no matter how fast they can run, will be able to escape this horrible destiny. God's judgment on Israel will be severe.

2. The Reasons for God's Judgment of Israel (3:1–6:14)

A. For every effect there is a cause (3:1–8). Many Israelites would have questioned this word of divine judgment against them, for many thought that their election as God's special chosen people (Deut. 7:6–7) and God's powerful grace in delivering them from Egypt (Exodus 14–15) implied that God would never destroy them (3:1–2). Amos indicates that God makes no absolute promises to sinful people but will require much from those who have received his blessings. Therefore, God's plan is to punish sinful Israel, if there is no repentance. Although some were no doubt astonished by the announcement, Amos emphasizes that everything that happens in this world has a cause. Lions roar for a reason, birds get caught in a trap for a reason, trumpets are blown for a reason, destruction comes to a city for a reason, and God tells a prophet to warn a nation for a reason. This should cause the Israelites to fear God's roar and repent, for Amos is warning them of God's plan to destroy them.

When Israel's houses are destroyed, as Amos warns (Amos 3:15), not even their ornate furniture will be spared. Such beautiful furniture is illustrated in this Neo-Assyrian relief as it is carried by servants, possibly taken away as plunder (721–705 BC).

B. God will bring judgment on Israel (3:9–4:3). Since some Israelites doubt that God will judge them, Amos uses three judgment oracles to persuade them that this is true. First (3:9–12), God asserts that if some pagan people from the Philistine city of Ashdod and from Egypt were to watch what has been happening in the capital city of Samaria, they would testify that there is much oppression and violence, and that many people are acting like they do not know the difference between right from wrong. Because of this, God will have a foreign nation surround Israel, destroy its fortresses, and loot the large homes of the wealthy oppressors. As a lion devours everything but a few useless scraps and bones of the animal it is eating, so this enemy will devour everything from the homes of the upper class except a few worthless scraps of wood and a small piece of cloth (3:12). Second (3:13–15), Amos warns his audience that God will remove every security the people have, both objects of religious security, like the altar at the temple at Bethel, and objects of material security, like their wonderful winter and summer homes. Even their furniture with inlaid ivory decorations will be destroyed. Third (4:1–3), God swears an irreversible oath against the wealthy and powerful women of Samaria ("the cows of Bashan") who crush the poor and live for pleasure. These people will be forcibly led through the breaches in the walls of Samaria with meat hooks (being treated like cows) and will be sent far away. These three judgment speeches indicate that there is no question about God's plans, and his oath makes these plans absolutely sure.

C. Israel did not return to God when they worshiped (4:4–13). Some Israelites may think they are safe from any judgment because they regularly go to the temple to worship God. To counter this false conclusion, Amos imitates a priest calling the people of Israel to come to the temple (cf. Ps. 100:4; Joel 1:13–14). He sarcastically invites them to sin (4:4–5), because that is what they do when they go to their temples for worship. Instead of encouraging them to come once a year to sacrifice, which was the normal practice (cf. 1 Sam. 1:3), Amos sarcastically invites them to prove how superspiritual they are by coming every day. Does God want people to tithe every three days instead of every three years (Deut. 14:22, 28), or is he looking for righteous people with a pure heart? Is God glorified when people give large thank and free-will offerings and then brag about them? Are they actually glorifying God or themselves? To further his persuasive point that these people do not truly worship God, Amos reminds them of five trials God sent to cause them to turn to him (4:6–13): (1) God sent a famine and a lack of food, but they did not return to him. (2) God withheld the rain, and they still did not turn to him. Then God (3) ruined the crops in their gardens and vineyard, (4) sent plagues and caused men to die in battle, and (5) overthrew some of them just like he overthrew Sodom and Gomorrah, but still they did not return to God with all their hearts. Since the Israelites will not come to God and get right with him, God is coming to them, so they need to prepare to meet God (4.12). The Creator of the heavens and the earth, the one who knows everything and has the power to do anything, will meet them and hold each one of them accountable.

D. Lamenting the death of the nation (5:1–17). Having made very limited progress in persuading the Israelites to transform their lives, Amos begins to wail as he laments the death of the nation. Although it seems to most Israelites that Israel has a strong army and economy, God realizes that the nation is as good as dead because he knows what the future holds. Amos laments that the virgin Israel, a young nation in the prime of her life, is soon to be a fallen, deserted virgin that no one will help. He laments that her armies will go out strong but come back decimated, with few survivors (5:3). Her only hope is to seek God truly if she wants to live (5:4). It is useless to worship at Bethel or other sacred temples in the nation because all of those

temples will be destroyed with a fire that cannot be put out. God will bring destruction, because in Israel, violence is ruling over justice (5:7). The plain truth is that righteousness is dead and buried. In hymnic style (5:8–9) Amos reminds his audience that their only hope is in the true God, who put the stars in their constellations. This God can also bring great darkness over the earth, just like he did in the time of Noah (Genesis 7–8) or when he flashes his destructive power and destroys a strong, fortified city. Why would God do such a thing? As long as the upper class continues to manipulate decisions in court and deprive the weak of justice (5:10–11), God will do everything he can to prevent the rich from receiving the rewards of their injustice. They will not enjoy their homes built through oppression and injustice (5:12); instead, a dark day of calamity is coming when the prosperous will be forever silent, having received their just reward (5:13). Their only hope is to reject evil behavior and love justice; maybe God will be merciful (5:15). If they do not do this, the whole nation will experience a day of wailing and mourning like they have never known before. God's powerful presence will pass through the midst of Israel, just like he passed through the midst of Egypt at the time of the Passover, when he killed the firstborn children (Exod. 11:4–6).

E. Don't be deceived by false hopes (5:18–27). Lest anyone think that somehow the nation of Israel will escape God's wrath and not suffer judgment, Amos addresses three issues that might be false sources of hope for the people in Israel. First, the prophet questions the audience about their beliefs about the day of the Lord (5:18–20). Some Israelites doubt his prediction of doom; they think that on the day of the Lord, God will miraculously intervene in history, defeat his enemies, and invite his Hebrew people to enjoy his eternal kingdom, where the Messiah will reign as king forever. Amos announces that this is a deceptive hope, for that day will actually be a day of darkness for Israel. On that day the Israelites will be lumped together with God's enemies. Disaster after disaster will happen to them; it will be impossible to flee from God's judgment.

Second, Amos reminds his audience it would be deceptive to think that their worship will win them favor with God, for God hates their worship (5:21–24). He does not accept any of their sacrifices or any of their worship songs because righteous behavior does not rule their lives. If a person lives sinfully all week, God will see that and will not accept the ritualistic worship of such a person on the Sabbath. What they need to do is to let justice flow out of their lives like a river. This means that God wants to see the results of repentance in the way people live: the rich dealing honestly with the poor, justice in the courts, and no one selling people into slavery.

The third issue Amos addresses is the deceptive pagan worship that some people have followed (5:25–27). The question in 5:25 seems to ask if the people only brought sacrifices to God during their wilderness journey. The implied answer is no. Their covenant relationship with God is based on worshiping God with all their heart and soul (Deut. 6:5), not just on the

external act of sacrificing to God. So the people should not be deceived and think that God will be pleased with those who are worshiping the Assyrian star god, called Sikkuth or Kiyyun. One cannot bow down to other gods and still claim to be honoring the one true God. Because they have done these things, Amos warns his audience that God Almighty will send Israel into exile far beyond Damascus, into the land of Assyria (5:27).

F. Don't be deceived by size, affluence, or power (6:1–14). In another woe oracle Amos laments at an Israelite funeral banquet (cf. Jer. 16:5–9) because the foremost people of the capital city of Samaria feel so secure and carefree in their present situation. He challenges them to go visit the cities of Kalneh, Gath, and Hamath to see if those kingdoms are bigger than Israel. Are they living with a false sense of security like the people in Samaria? Since

Amos urges Israel to "maintain justice in the courts" (Amos 5:15). Justice was important throughout the ancient world, as this relief from Abydos illustrates. Pharaoh stands before the gods offering up Maat, the goddess of order and justice, to indicate that he upholds justice.

these cities are smaller, they have no false sense of security; they are vigilant and try to put off the day of their calamity, but the Israelites' smug attitude of indestructibility actually brings their end nearer. Next Amos describes the affluence displayed at this funeral banquet (6:4–6). Those attending sprawl out on the finest furniture, eat the best beef, enjoy great music, drink large amounts of wine, and have the finest lotions; but they ignore and do not grieve over the deterioration of the nation. God announces that the feasting days will soon be over, and these first-class citizens will go into exile first (6:7).

The Lord loathes the pride and arrogance of the wealthy who live securely in their large palaces (6:8), so God has determined to destroy the nation's fortified cities, to destroy the population through war so much that those who come to bury the dead will find no one alive in any of these houses (6:10). Then he will smash all the large and small houses to bits. Finally, the prophet asks a series of absurd questions like: "Do people run horses on rocks?" (6:12, author's translation). Obviously, only a crazy person would be dumb enough to try this, for soon the horse would fall and break a leg. So too, is it absurd that the Israelites have turned a good thing like justice into something as destructive as poison? Is it absurd for Israelites to brag about defeating the city of Lo Debar, which means "nothing"? Only God defeats cities; people do not have the "strength" to defeat the city of "Karnaim," which means "horns, strength" (see NIV note). In the end there is only one possible destiny for this sinful and deceived nation. God will send a powerful nation against them to defeat them, from the northern border at Hamath to the southern border by the Dead Sea.

3. Visions and Exhortations about the End (7:1–9:15)

It appears that chapters 7–9 were spoken while the prophet Amos was preaching in and around the temple at Bethel. The date is unknown, but Amaziah's later attempt to exclude Amos from preaching in the Bethel temple (7:12) suggests these sermons were given near the end of his ministry in Israel.

A. Two visions of destruction bring compassion (7:1–6). Amos's first vision is about a locust plague that God sends to destroy Israel's crops (7:1–3). Since the king has already had his share of the crops, this plague will hit hard the poor farmers, who would get the second crop. Because of Amos's love for these people, he intercedes by asking God to have compassion because these poor farmers could not survive the famine that such a severe event would bring. In response God stops the plague and provides the people with more time to repent of their sins.

In the second vision Amos sees a fire that is able to dry up the sea and destroy the farmland (7:4–6). The picture is not very clear, but this must be something like a gigantic volcanic eruption if it is able to destroy both the land and the sea. If part of the land is the farmland of Israel, one can understand why the prophet Amos would identify with the people living in that area. Although there is no evidence that the people of Israel have repented and turned to God, once again Amos briefly intercedes and asks God to stop this fire, and once again God has compassion.

B. Vision of destruction of king and temple (7:7–17). In the third vision the prophet observes God with a plumb line, standing on a wall (the exact wall is not identified) in order to determine if the wall is plumb (7:6–9). This symbolizes God's work of examining the nation of Israel to find out if it is upright or if it is falling over and in need of destruction. Does Israel meet God's specifications in the covenant: loving God with all their hearts? Are they holy as God is holy? Do the people live according to the instructions God has given them? It is evident that Israel is not plumb and does not meet God's standards, for the interpretation of the vision (7:9) indicates that God plans to bring some nation against Israel in order to destroy its pagan high places, their king Jeroboam II, and their sanctuaries at Bethel and Dan, for God has determined to spare them no longer. Thus the end of the nation is near.

In a brief historical interlude Amos reports what Amaziah the priest in charge of the temple at Bethel does when he hears this prophecy about the plumb line (7:10–17). He interprets the news in this vision as political treason, so he reports Amos's prophecy to king Jeroboam II. The text does not include any response from Jeroboam II, so no one knows if Amos actually had to leave Israel immediately. Because of this vision Amaziah confronts Amos and tells him to flee back to Judah, to leave the foreign affairs of Israel to the Israelite prophets, and to go make his money as a professional prophet in Jerusalem. Showing no fear of Amaziah, Amos denies being a professional prophet who works for money and states that he makes his living by caring for sheep. Amos explains that he is in Israel prophesying because of God's calling, so Amaziah's attempt to shut him up and send him out of Israel is an act that directly contradicts God's command. In a not so subtle way Amos is boldly condemning Amaziah, undermining his authority and raising questions about the priest's relationship with God. Amos concludes this tense confrontation by announcing that Amaziah's family will one day be disgraced and killed, his inheritance in Israel will be lost, and Amaziah will be exiled with the rest of Israel into a pagan land.

C. Vision and exhortation about the end (8:1–14). Like the preceding section, this portion has a vision followed by a related message about God's approaching judgment of Israel. In this vision the prophet notices a basket of ripe summer fruit, indicating that it is harvest time (8:1–3). The interpretation of the vision is that the time is ripe for God to harvest the fruit in the nation of Israel; thus its end is near. The statement "I will spare them no longer" (8:2) connects this vision with the earlier plumb line vision, which had the same warning. This evaluative statement indicates that there will be some dire consequences, because God's assessment of this fruit is very negative. Verse 3 explains

what will happen. God paints a word picture in which dead bodies are lying everywhere, even defiling the temple area, because the gods that were worshiped there will provide no protection. A few people will live, but some will be wailing for their dead family members while others will be stunned and shocked so severely that they will be dumbfounded and silent.

The rest of the chapter reflects on this terrible event in a judgment speech (8:4–14). Initially, the prophet provides an accusation (8:4–6) that gives one of the reasons why God will no longer have mercy. Earlier, in Samaria, Amos pointed to the violence and oppression of the poor (2:6–8; 3:9–10; 4:1; 5:11–13), so it is not surprising that he returns to this theme again when he preaches at a new location (the Bethel temple), where the people have not heard his earlier messages. This time he focuses on the deceptive actions of the scheming merchants as well as their attitudes about the Sabbath. Amos speaks about those who crush and trample the poor in the land of Israel. In previous oracles Amos talked about oppression by the wealthy upper class, but here it is the middle-class merchants who are abusing those who trade in the marketplace. In two different ways, they are cheating the buyers and sellers who come to trade with them. First, they take advantage of the poor by having two sets of weights for their scales: a heavy weight (1.1 shekels) for buying grain, so that the seller will have to provide more grain than is honestly required, and a light weight (0.9 shekel) for selling grain, so that they will have to part with less grain when people buy from them. Second, they use a larger bushel basket that has to be filled when the merchant is buying grain and a smaller bushel basket when the merchant is selling grain. Of course one could always add a little dust, dirt, and chaff when selling so that it does not cost so much grain to fill a bushel basket. These deceptive practices were contrary to God's requirement (Lev. 19:35–36; Deut. 25:13–15; Prov. 11:1; 16:1). Through dishonest means like these, the merchants were able to drive the poor into bankruptcy or slavery because they could not pay their debts. God, says Amos, will act against the nation of Israel because of this kind of unrighteous activity.

Part of the tragedy of this situation is that these devious merchants can hardly wait until the Sabbath or other religious feast days are over. They are anxious to get back to the business of cheating people. The Sabbath was to be a holy day (Exod. 20:8–11), and the celebration at the New Moon feast (Lev. 23:23–25; 1 Sam. 20:5; Isa. 1:13–14) was to be a day dedicated to God, so no work was to be done. Although the nation maintains the aura of orthodoxy by not having businesses open on holy days, the merchants are more interested in making more money than in worshiping God.

Elsewhere God swears by his own holiness (4:2) or by himself (6:8), but in Amos 8:7 he swears by his name, the "Majestic/Glorious one of Jacob" (NIV "Pride of Jacob"). Since God does not change, there is no doubt about whether God's judgment will fall on Israel. In almost hymnic fashion (8:8–9) God describes how his coming will affect their world. The earth will quake, moving up and then down like the mighty Nile River. Plates of solid rock will collide under the surface, and things on the surface will be destroyed, causing people to mourn and fear for their lives (cf. Isa. 24:1–6, 19–21). God's judgment will turn the present optimistic songs of joy in Israel into words of mourning. The few remaining people will lament in sackcloth and ashes. The severity of their bitter agony is expressed by comparing

their mourning to the wailing of a family that has lost its only son (8:10).

The final paragraph (8:11–14) indicates that during this period of divine judgment people will try to find a word of comfort from God or some direction about what they can do to survive this dark period, but none will be available. When there is a famine and there is no water or food, people go to great lengths to survive by rigorously searching from one end of the country to the other just to find something to eat. In a similar manner people will search for a prophetic message from God, but none will be found. They rejected Amos (7:10–17) and other prophets (2:11–12), so eventually God will reject them and will send no one to comfort them. Part of the reason may be implied in 8:14, for it appears that the prophet is saying that those who follow other gods will fall and never rise again. The phrase, "those who swear allegiance to the guilt of Samaria" (8:14, author's translation), probably refers to people who swear oaths at the Baal and Asherah temple built in Samaria (1 Kings 16:32); this is their "guilt." The reference to the god who lives at the city of Dan is to the golden calf that Jeroboam I put in a temple in Dan (1 Kings 12:29) just after the northern tribes declared their independence from Judah. The "way/custom of Beersheba" (see NASB, NRSV; the NIV has "god of Beersheba")

This high place at Dan (tenth century BC) functioned as a worship center. Archaeologists have uncovered incense burners, incense stands, and a horned incense altar; however, it is unclear if this is where Jeroboam I placed the golden calf, the "god" of Dan (Amos 8:14).

must also refer to the pagan religious practice at that city in the southern part of Judah. The people who worship at these syncretistic places will cease and never be seen again.

D. No one can escape from God's hand (9:1–10). The final chapter begins with another vision, a hymn, and a final warning. The fifth vision pictures the enactment of God's judgment on Israel by describing his destruction of Israel's temple (probably at Bethel) and by statements that God will not allow anyone in the nation to escape his wrath (9:1–4). In this vision God is standing beside an altar at a temple, commanding that the temple and the people in it be destroyed. The earth will shake, the pillars of the temple will buckle, and the falling roof and pillars will kill all those inside. Although this vision involves only one building and a few people inside it, one should assume that similar events will happen throughout the country, for five times God indicates that no one will escape from his hand. Using exaggerated terminology, Amos states that even if people try to hide in the depths of Sheol or climb up to heaven (both are impossible), they will not escape from God's wrath. Others may try to hide in caves at Mount Carmel or deep in the sea, but God will find them. Even the few that go into exile will not be safe from the sword, because God is determined to punish these sinners.

Having described the thoroughness and severity of God's judgment, Amos reminds his audience of the greatness of God's power by quoting from one of their hymns (9:5–6). God is able to bring about everything he has predicted because he is the commander in chief of the armies of heaven, the Lord of Hosts. When he touches the earth, his power has the ability to melt it, to make it move up and down (the earthquake), and to cause people to mourn. He is the glorious God who lives in the upper reaches of the heavens; he is the God who created the earth and who has already demonstrated at the time of Noah that he is able to destroy all flesh on earth with a flood. His name is Yahweh, the God of the people of Israel. This hymn confirms

to Amos's audience that God is able to carry out the judgment described in the vision in 9:1–4.

The third short paragraph in this section attempts to convince those who still question God's intention to punish his own special and chosen people (9:7–10). Although there were still some people who thought that "disaster will not overtake or meet us" (9:10), God reveals that his judgment is coming. It appears that these people believe that God's tremendous grace in bringing the Israelites from Egypt is a sure sign that God will never judge his people. But Amos argues that God also delivered other nations (the Philistines and Arameans) from difficult situations in other countries and brought them to new lands. Does this mean that God will never judge these nations? Obviously, no Israelite would say this. God also claims that he views the Cushites from southern Egypt as similar to Israel; thus, Israel is not the only nation God cares about. The real key to understanding God's future action is not to view it as an extension of God's past acts of grace. One of the main predictive factors that can indicate God's future action is the sinfulness of each nation. He will destroy every sinful nation. Yet within these dire predictions is the brief promise that God will not totally destroy all the people from Israel. There will always be a righteous remnant left (9:8). How will God distinguish the righteous from the wicked? He will separate the righteous from the wicked just like a farmer uses a sieve to separate the good grain from dust and rocks that get mixed in with the grain on the threshing floor.

E. The hope of final restoration (9:11–15). The scroll containing Amos's messages ends with a surprising vision of hope for the distant future. Maybe some Israelites will be reminded of what the future holds for the righteous people of God and will repent of their sins so that they will be able to enjoy this time of divine blessing. Some modern commentators doubt that Amos ever gave this message and argue that a later editor added it to Amos's messages, because it seems so foreign to the rest of his harsh messages, and because it could have provided a false hope for some in his audience. Since most other prophets speak messages of both judgment and hope, since this positive vision applies only to the distant future, and since this hope is not applied to sinful Israel but only to those who are called by God's name, this section should be viewed as a legitimate attempt to persuade Amos's audience to seek God now, so that they will not miss out on God's blessings in the future. This paragraph has two parts, one based on the introductory "in that day" phrase in 9:11, and the other based on the phrase "the days are coming" in 9:13.

God reminds the Israelites that his promises to his people have not changed; he will eventually establish his glorious kingdom (9:11–12) and restore the land and its people (9:13–15). Regarding the first promise, God's action is dramatically recounted in four "I will" clauses (9:11). Concerning the nation that he will soon judge, he says, "I will restore" it like it was in the past. God will restore the ruptured and dilapidated kingdom that was united under David (the fallen booth) but divided into two nations (Israel and Judah) after the death of Solomon (1 Kings 12). This future restoration will involve both Hebrews (9:11) and people from foreign nations (9:12). In addition God promises that "I will repair," "[I will] restore," and "[I will] rebuild" the ruined cities that will suffer destruction in the near future. Later prophetic writers will expand and speak more broadly about the conditions in the New Jerusalem and this restored nation, including information about a future Davidic king (the Messiah) who will rule forever in righteousness (Isa. 9:1–7; Ezek. 37:15–28; Hos. 3:5). Verse 12 indicates that other people who are called by God's name from Edom (a symbol of foreign nations, as in Isa. 34:1–8; 63:1–6) will be a part of this future kingdom. This verse became very important when the early Christian church was trying to decide if they should allow uncircumcised Gentiles into the church. James's quotation of Amos 9:12 resolved the issue (Acts 15:16–17), bringing a unified acceptance of Gentiles who bear God's name just as Amos prophesied. Although the history of Israel demonstrates great

hatred between Edom and Israel (1:11–12), through the witness of the seed of Abraham, God will extend his blessings to other people (Gen. 12:1–3; Isa. 2:1–4; 19:18–25; 42:6; 66:18–21). People from every tribe, language, and nation will be part of God's future kingdom (Dan. 7:14).

The second promise relates to the restoration of fertility to the land and the return of the people to the land of Israel (9:13–15). When God restores his kingdom, the land will produce so abundantly that those harvesting grain in the summer will not be able to finish their work before it is time to plow the fields for the next crop. The grapes will be so large and abundant that their juice will flow like a stream down the hills. Finally, the land of milk and honey will produce the kind of crops envisioned in the covenant blessings (Lev. 26:5). The land will then be like a restored Garden of Eden (Isa. 51:3; Ezek. 36:35). God will also cause some of his exiled people to return from their captivity so that they can rebuild their homes and enjoy the blessings of a fertile land. Once God plants them in his land, they will be like deep-rooted plants that cannot be uprooted. Since God has given this land to them, no other nation will ever remove them from this land. This will be that glorious time when God will fulfill many of his eschatological promises to his people.

Select Bibliography

Hubbard, David Allan. *Joel and Amos*. Tyndale Old Testament Commentaries. Downers Grove, IL: InterVarsity, 1989.

McComiskey, Thomas Edward. "Amos." In *The Minor Prophets: An Exegetical and Expository Commentary*. Edited by Thomas Edward McComiskey. Grand Rapids: Baker Academic, 1992.

Motyer, J. Alec. *The Day of the Lion: The Message of Amos*. Downers Grove, IL: InterVarsity, 1974.

Paul, Shalom. *A Commentary on the Book of Amos*. Hermeneia. Philadelphia: Fortress, 1991.

Smith, Gary V. *Hosea, Amos, Micah*. NIV Application Commentary. Grand Rapids: Zondervan, 2001.

Stuart, Douglas. *Hosea–Jonah*. Word Biblical Commentary. Waco: Word, 1987.

Obadiah

ANDREW E. HILL

Obadiah the Prophet

This shortest book of the Old Testament is ascribed to Obadiah the prophet (v. 1). His name means "servant (or worshiper) of Yahweh," and is one of the more common biblical names (cf. 1 Kings 18:3–16; 1 Chron. 3:21; 7:3; 8:38; 9:44; 12:9; 27:19; 2 Chron. 17:7; 34:12; Ezra 8:9; Neh. 10:5; 12:25). Aside from an unfounded tradition of the Babylonian Talmud (*Sanhedrin* 39b) that identifies Obadiah with Ahab's steward, a devout believer in the Lord (1 Kings 18:3–16), personal information about Obadiah is completely wanting.

Date

Obadiah's oracle has been dated variously to time periods ranging from 850 to 400 BC. The date of the prophecy can be ascertained only by assuming that verses 11–14 refer to a specific episode in the history of Israel. The two most likely referents are the attack of Jerusalem by the Philistines and Arabs (ca. 844 BC; cf. 2 Kings 8:20; 2 Chron. 21:16–17) during the reign of Jehoram (853–841 BC), or the destruction of Jerusalem by the Babylonians in 587 BC (2 Kings 25:1–12; cf. Ps. 137:7–9; Ezek. 25:1–3, 12–14). Dating Obadiah shortly after the fall of Jerusalem seems to be the more likely option, since the total conquest of the city described in verse 11 is best accounted for by Nebuchadnezzar's invasion, siege, and sack of the Judean capital.

Literary Features

The book of Obadiah is one of several oracles against Edom (Isa. 21:11–12; 34:5–17; Jer. 49:7–22; Ezek. 25:12–14; 35:1–15; Amos 1:11–12), and its literary form is generally identified as a national oracle, much like Nahum's prophecy against Assyria (cf. also the national oracles in Isa. 13:1–23:18; Jer. 46:1–51:64; Ezek. 25:1–32:32; Amos 1:3–2:16; Zeph. 2:4–15). This anti-Edomite polemic can be traced through the Old Testament, from the mixed blessing Isaac pronounces on Esau (Gen. 27:39–40) to the exilic imprecation of Edom for its part in the overthrow of Jerusalem (Ps. 137:7) right through Malachi's affirmation of Edom's obliteration (1:2–4).

Obadiah's oracle, like those of Isaiah (1:1), Daniel (8:1), and Nahum (1:1), is a "vision" or revelation. In its broader sense the word signifies a divine communication to God's prophet or spokesman, and it connotes the authority and authenticity of the prophetic message. More specifically, the word is a technical term associated with the seeing of a vision. Its use in the Old Testament is restricted almost exclusively to the preexilic prophets and often occurs in the context of impending judgment. That Obadiah's oracle is a "vision" helps account for the terseness of language, the vivid imagery, and the certain realization of the event seen in advance as the prophet makes known Yahweh's word.

Obadiah 1b–6 repeats practically verbatim the words of Jeremiah 49:14–16 and 49:9–10. Naturally this raises the question of priority. Three views have emerged in the scholarly literature, one defending Obadiah's priority, one positing Jeremiah as the original source with Obadiah drawing from it, and one arguing for a no-longer-extant source common to both prophets. A common anti-Edomite source is the most likely explanation for the similarities between the two prophecies, with Jeremiah drawing more loosely from it and Obadiah adhering more carefully to the received tradition.

Although the literary unity of Obadiah has been challenged by critical biblical scholars, there is a basic strophic pattern in the prophecy evidencing an overarching design. The repetition of "Yahweh" at the beginning and end of verses 1–4 and 15–21 marks out clear literary units. The formulas "declares the LORD" (vv. 4, 8) and "the Lord has spoken" (v. 18) are additional indicators of a deliberate structure.

The classic four-point outline, standard in Hebrew prophetic literature (i.e., charges against specific sins, pronouncement of divine judgment, call to repentance, promises of restoration to the remnant) is evident in Obadiah, minus the call to repentance (characteristic of the anti-Edomite oracles). This basic theology is underscored by the recurrent themes of the day of the Lord, Esau/Edom, Edom's sin in relation to Judah, and the eventual reversal of the divinely appointed roles for each.

Theological Themes

Obadiah, as Yahweh's envoy, proclaims a tripartite message to the nations. First, he condemns the pride and cruelty of the Edomites in their mistreatment of Judah during the sack of Jerusalem. This gross misconduct will not go unpunished, and Edom's doom is certain (vv. 2–9).

Second, the prophet addresses the remnant of Israel, assuring them of the ultimate triumph of Yahweh and righteousness over the wickedness of all the nations in the day of the Lord (vv. 15–16). That day brings the promise of deliverance and restoration for the people of God, a theme common to the prophets.

Finally, implicit throughout this brief prophecy is Yahweh's dominion over the nations. He is "the Sovereign LORD" (v. 1) who logs the iniquities of the peoples (vv. 10–14), administers

The mountainous terrain of the land of Edom, which figures prominently in the book of Obadiah's imagery

divine justice (vv. 4, 8, 15), and controls the destinies of the nations.

Obadiah's oracle of divine retribution against Edom for assisting in and gloating over Judah's day of misfortune clearly teaches God's sovereignty over the nations of the earth and his justice in punishing the guilty. It also serves as a warning to the nations that they too are in jeopardy of having their deeds returned on them as the day of God's wrath approaches (vv. 15–16).

More important for Israel, this prophetic statement of God's activity in history was designed to call to mind his covenant love for his people, thus bringing a word of encouragement for the present and a promise of hope for the future (cf. Ps. 111:2–9; Lam. 3:21–28).

Outline

1. Superscription (1a)
2. Yahweh's Message against Edom (1b–14)
    A. Edom's Judgment Pronounced and Reaffirmed (1b–9)
    B. Indictments (10–14)
3. The Day of the Lord (15–21)
    A. Universal Judgment (15–16)
    B. Zion Delivered (17–18)
    C. Yahweh's Kingdom Established (19–21)

Commentary

1. Superscription (1a)

Unlike other prophetic books, Obadiah's oracle contains no information about the time or place of its origin, nor does it include any autobiographical data about the prophet. The brevity of the superscription matches the brevity of the book, perhaps to focus attention on the message rather than on the prophet himself.

The word used to describe Obadiah's prophecy ("vision") is a technical term having to do with receiving a revelatory word from God. More than mere human sight, this visionary experience is the result of divine inspiration and implies that the prophet actually saw and heard the communication from Yahweh. This

gives him the insight and perception necessary to understand the unveiling of future events. The same expression occurs in Isaiah 1:1 and Nahum 1:1, and the ecstatic visionary experience the word connotes may help account for the graphic imagery and explicit detail of the language found in these prophecies.

2. Yahweh's Message against Edom (1b–14)

A. Edom's judgment pronounced and reaffirmed (1b–9). Edom (also called Hor, Seir, and Esau) and Israel were kin according to the ancestral traditions recorded in the Old Testament. The eponymous patriarchs of Edom and Israel were Esau and Jacob respectively, both sons of Isaac (Gen. 25:19–34; 27:1–28:9; 32:1–33:20). The country of Edom was located in the highlands and sandstone cliffs on the southeastern edge of the Dead Sea, from the Brook Zered in the north to the Gulf of Aqaba in the south. A strong tribal organization existed in Edom from patriarchal times (Gen. 36:1–30), and the Edomites had a form of monarchy before the Israelites (Gen. 36:31–43). Edom was well established as a nation by the time of Israel's exodus from Egypt, as they denied Israel passage to the east and threatened them with a show of force (Num. 20:14–21; 21:4). Edom and Israel coexisted peacefully until the reign of Saul (1 Sam. 14:47); David defeated the Edomites at the Valley of Salt (2 Sam. 8:13–14). Judah controlled Edom as a satellite state until the time of Jehoram, when the Edomites successfully revolted and reestablished autonomous rule (2 Kings 8:20–22; cf. 1 Kings 11:14–25; 22:47). Later victories by the Judean kings Amaziah (2 Kings 14:7) and Uzziah (2 Kings 14:22) were localized and temporary at best.

As early as 597 BC, the Babylonians wrested control of the Negev from Judah (cf. 2 Kings 24:8–17), and the Edomites moved into the area to fill the vacuum. In 587 BC Edom not only assisted Babylon in the sack of Jerusalem but also occupied Judean villages, and continued to live in them well into the Persian period (cf. 1 Esdras 4:50). The exact date of Edom's collapse remains imprecise, and the circumstances are uncertain.

By the time of Malachi's oracle (ca. 460 BC) the Edomite kingdom was in ruins (1:2–4). Edom apparently remained largely independent until a coalition of Arab tribes overpowered and displaced the Edomites sometime during the fifth century BC. By 312 BC inscriptional evidence indicates the Nabateans had overrun the region of Edom, making Petra their capital city. Remaining Edomites either moved to Idumea or were absorbed by the Nabatean Arabs.

Obadiah's first pronouncement begins and ends with the Yahweh word formula characteristic of Hebrew prophetic speech, marking verses 1b–4 as a distinct utterance. The use of the formula at once identifies the source and authority of the prophetic word (cf. Amos 3:8; Mic. 3:8), as well as the covenantal context of the message. (This divine name was revealed to Israel as part of the postexodus covenant experience constituting them as the people of God; Exod. 6:2–7; 19:1–24:18) The title "Lord Yahweh" underscores God's rule over heaven, earth, and human history and is best translated "Sovereign LORD" (NIV). Fittingly, even as Judah was decimated and made a byword among the nations (Ps. 44:13–14; Lam. 2:15–16), Edom too will be reduced (i.e., "cut down to size"), made desolate, and despised by her neighbors (v. 2). The self-deception induced by a sense of false security in the inaccessible heights of the surrounding terrain ironically will only compound the abasement Edom will experience once judgment comes. Like Assyria, who said, "I am the one! And there is none besides me," Edom too is destined for ruin and the scoffing of passersby (Zeph. 2:15). Like Babylon, Edom has not reckoned with God, and so calamity and unforeseen catastrophe will suddenly befall her (Isa. 47:8–11).

Despite the terseness of Obadiah's language, it is rich with puns, imagery, and surprise. The wordplay in verse 3 is striking, in that the term for rocks (Hebrew *sela*) is akin to the name of the Edomite capital, Sela. Edom's perceived invincibility, similar to that of the soaring eagle that nests high in the crags, takes no account of the fact that even the eagle can soar and nest only at the express command of God. Edom has miscalculated her strength, foolishly forgetting that

Ad-Deir (also called "The Monastery"), one of several buildings that the Nabateans carved into the rock in Petra, their capital, in the territory that once belonging to Edom

God's pleasure "is not in the strength of the horse, nor his delight in the legs of the warrior" (Ps. 147:10–11).

Obadiah's second pronouncement (vv. 5–9) expands the message of judgment introduced in the previous section. The degree of Edom's punishment is at issue in verses 5–6. Thieves steal only what they want (or can carry), and grape pickers may overlook a few grapes. However, on the day Edom is ransacked and pillaged, nothing will remain untouched by the looters. Even the most mundane of possessions will be pillaged by the ruthless invaders (cf. Jer. 49:9–10).

Interestingly, verse 6 begins with a variant form of the interrogative word that opens the book of Lamentations: "How?" The parallel to the lament over Judah is heightened by reference to the treachery of former allies (Lam. 1:2, 19). Judah had her "friends" too, but in the day of distress they were traitors and covenant breakers (Ps. 55:20; cf. Amos 1:9). Centuries before, the prophets had warned of the folly of political alliances (see Hos. 7:8–11). Those who once shared food at a common meal (i.e., those in economic or political union with Edom) will lay a snare and entrap Edom unawares. (The last phrase of verse 7 is obscure, as the variations in the English versions attest.)

It seems best to understand the reference to wisdom or knowledge as further irony. Edom is about to be deceived, in spite of all her wisdom. Pride distorts reality and blinds to the truth. This is why Edom is so easily deceived by treacherous allies. Edom's pride (v. 3) carries the seeds of its own destruction in that God has purposed to bring low and to disgrace all who boast in conceit and insolence (Prov. 11:2; 16:16–18; Isa. 16:6; 25:11). Babylon was vaunted for her wisdom, yet it proved impotent in the face of destruction (Isa. 47:8–15). Edom's reputation as a depot of wisdom tradition in the ancient world was also widespread (see Jer. 49:7). Yet it too will fall. Teman was an important city in Edom, and here it is used as an appellative for the whole (v. 9). Military prowess, like wisdom,

will prove useless in the day of God's wrath. Edom's defensive strategies will be confounded and her warriors routed. With the slaughter of the Edomites the jealous Lord has taken vengeance on his foes, punished the guilty, and restored faith and hope in the remnant of Judah for the fulfillment of covenant promises.

B. Indictments (10–14). The causal use of the Hebrew preposition *min* in verse 10 (NASB, NIV: "because"; NEB, RSV: "for") marks the beginning of the second stanza in this first division of Obadiah's oracle. This section of the prophecy explains why Yahweh has decreed divine judgment against the Edomites. The list of charges (labeled "violence," v. 10) levied against Edom is made more weighty by the fact that the wrongdoing has been perpetrated by a brother against a brother (see Gen. 25:24–34; Deut. 23:7). The charges include failure to ally with Judah in resisting a common foe (v. 11); delighting in Judah's calamity with vindictiveness, haughtiness, gloating, and mockery (v. 12); trespassing and looting the ruins of Jerusalem (v. 13); and ambushing fugitives fleeing east from the Babylonian onslaught and returning them to the enemy.

This catalog of Edomite crimes calls to mind the lawsuit oracle or judicial speech (e.g., Hos. 4:1–3; Mic. 6:1–2). Usually this prophetic speech form has three parts: the summons, the trial (with speeches by both prosecution and defense), and the sentence. The treachery and faithlessness of Edom has been so heinous that the sentence (Edom's humiliation and dissolution, vv. 2–10, 15) immediately follows the summons (v. 1b). The trial contains only the speech by the prosecution (i.e., the indictments), and this merely to underscore Edom's guilt and the justice of the verdict of Edom's death warrant.

3. The Day of the Lord (15–21)

A. Universal judgment (15–16). These verses mark the beginning of the second principal section of Obadiah's oracle. The specific indictment of Edom now gives way to a more general statement of the universal judgment that characterizes the day of the Lord. The shift to the broader themes of judgment on the nations and the restoration of Israel lends perspective to Obadiah's pressing concern for divine justice in view of Edom's role in Jerusalem's fall. It also bolsters future hope among the remnant of Jacob by validating the eschatological paradigm, often repeated by the prophets, of the final triumph of Yahweh in the world order (e.g., Isaiah 24–27; 32; Jeremiah 29–33; Ezekiel 33–34; Hosea 13–14; Amos 9).

This thematic alternation in verses 15–21 is heightened by the striking language variation in the Hebrew text, with the series of eight alephs (the first letter of the Hebrew alphabet, an unvoiced guttural sound) opening each of the lines in verses 12–14, abruptly interrupted by the fourfold repetition of the harsher palatal consonant *k* in verses 15–16 (in the prepositions *ki*, "for, because," and *kaasher*, "just as"; cf. NASB, RSV). The emphatic position of the causal preposition "for/because" sets the tone for this segment of the prophet's message and further explains the relationship between the pointed denunciation of Edom and the more indefinite pronouncement of God's wrath against the nations.

The notion that crime punishes itself ("your deeds will return upon your own head," v. 15), or the principle of retribution, is well founded in biblical teaching. The legislation of the Torah is rooted in the concept of *lex talionis*, or "an eye for an eye" (Exod. 21:24–25; Lev. 24:20; Deut. 19:21), meaning punishment will be exacted in a fashion commensurate with the crime. Israel's wisdom tradition echoes this belief (Prov. 26:27; cf. Ps. 7:15–16); and even Paul acknowledges that people reap what they sow (Gal. 6:7–8). Judah witnessed the surety of this truth when God used Assyria to punish Samaria, crushed the Assyrian Empire by the hand of Nebuchadnezzar, and tragically, used this same Babylonian king to destroy Judah because of her guilt (Jer. 25:8–14). Obadiah calls the remnant of Judah to observe the final destiny of the wicked and to rest in Yahweh as their portion and strength (Ps. 73:17–19, 23–28).

"You drank on my holy hill" (v. 16) is a cryptic expression for the cup of wrath God pours down the gullets of the nations as he defends his people Israel (Isa. 51:17–23; cf. Zech. 12:2). Ironically, the cup of wrath once tasted by Samaria is now passed on to Judah (Ezek. 23:31–34); finally, it will be drunk by the nations (v. 16). Like the staggering drunkard falling unconscious to the ground in his own vomit, the nations will drink themselves into oblivion with the wine of God's anger (Jer. 25:27, 32–33). Edom's offense is all the more abominable because it participated in the destruction and desecration of Jerusalem, the city that bears God's name.

B. Zion delivered (17–18). The adversative conjunction "but" introducing these lines of the oracle alerts the reader to the upcoming comparison, as the prophet contrasts the judgment and destruction pending for Edom (vv. 1b–14) with the future blessing and restoration of Israel (vv. 17–21). "Mount Zion" is a common reference in the Prophets and the Psalms to Jerusalem, the city of David (2 Sam. 5:7; 1 Kings 8:1). That Mount Zion will be "holy" (v. 17) is an indication of the extent of Jacob's salvation and restoration and the fullness of renewed relationship with Yahweh.

The use of the word pair "Jacob/Joseph" heightens the foil between Jacob and Esau, and may be more than a poetic echo, as the use of "Joseph" elsewhere in the Old Testament suggests the larger collection of Israelite tribes (Ps. 77:15; Zech. 10:6; cf. Ezek. 37:16–19). The holiness characteristic of the restored remnant in Zion transforms Israel into an instrument of Yahweh's judgment, confirming Ezekiel's word about God's vengeance on Edom (Ezek. 25:14). The consuming fire of God's wrath that devoured the "stubble of wickedness" during the exodus (Exod. 15:7) and toppled the haughty Assyrians (Isa. 10:12–19; 29:5–6) is now unleashed against the Edomites. Unlike Israel, where the Lord preserved a remnant from Mount Zion, not one survivor will escape from the mountain of Esau (vv. 9, 19). The juxtaposition of Jacob and Esau (v. 18) recalls the ancient narrative of fraternal rivalry and the prophecy Rebekah received concerning "two nations" in her womb (Gen. 25:21–27). It also lends perspective to the later declaration of Malachi, "Yet I have loved Jacob, but Esau I have hated" (Mal. 1:2–3). The concluding phrase "the LORD has spoken" serves as a sort of colophon, solemnizing the prophecy regarding the day of the Lord and emphasizing the certainty and finality of Esau's judgment.

C. Yahweh's kingdom established (19–21). Characteristic of prophetic literature, Obadiah's oracle concludes with the promise of restoration for the remnant of Israel. The promise of people moving to claim territories formerly occupied by enemies (vv. 19–20) enlarges the thought found in verse 17. Although the translation of verse 20a is difficult (here it seems best to read "the exiles of this army [or host], the sons of Israel, will have the Canaanites' land as far as Zarephath," following the NJB), there can be no doubt that the people referred to in verse 19 are indeed the house of Jacob. Zarephath was a town between Tyre and Sidon on the Phoenician coast, and Sepharad has been identified with Sardis in Asia Minor or Hesperides near Benghazi in North Africa. Regions in the south (the Negev and Edom), the west (Shephelah and the coastal plain of

The Edomites may have trusted in their gods and goddesses, like the three-horned deity pictured here, but they would not escape God's judgment.

Philistia), and the north and east (Zarephath, Samaria, and Gilead) will again be inhabited by the house of Jacob and Joseph. The prophet certainly intends to stir up memories of distant promises made to the Israelite forefathers concerning the land of Canaan as an inheritance, an everlasting possession (Gen. 17:1–8; Exod. 3:8; Josh. 1:1–9; 2 Sam. 7:10; cf. Deut. 1:6–8). The purpose of Obadiah's appeal to history is to instill hope in the Babylonian exiles (and those who remained in Jerusalem as vassals to Nebuchadnezzar) by reinforcing their faith in Yahweh as a covenant-keeping God. By beginning and ending these verses (vv. 19–20) with the Israelite possession of the Negev, the prophet indicates that the fall of Edom should be viewed as the trigger event setting in motion the fulfillment of all God's promises to Israel.

The culmination of Israel's restoration as predicted by Obadiah parallels the final outcome of human history, in that both consummate with the Lord's kingdom or sovereign rule in the created order (v. 21). This theme of Yahweh's ultimate dominion over the world through Israel as his signet occurs frequently in the Old Testament as part of the messianic expectation of the day of the Lord (e.g., Ezek. 37:24–28; Dan. 2:44–45; 7:21–27; 9:24–27; Zech. 12:3–4). The ongoing contrast between the destinies of Mount Zion and the mountains of Esau now reaches its climax. Israel will be saved and restored, while Edom will be judged for her crimes of injustice and oppression. The juxtaposition of the terms "deliverers" and "judge" (NIV "govern") is theologically significant given the close relationship of their meanings. The Hebrew judge was a divinely appointed savior for the people of Israel, the oppressed, and the socially disadvantaged (Judg. 3:9, 15; 2 Kings 13:5; Neh. 9:27). The Old Testament judge brought deliverance to the oppressed Israelites by renewing covenant faith (Judg. 6:19–32), establishing covenant justice in the community (Judg. 4:5), and judging oppressor nations through military action (Judg. 3:10; 4:6–16). By raising up these deliverers in Zion, God would not only accomplish the immediate goal of judging Edom's sin and avenging Israel but also achieve his larger objective of establishing his righteous dominion on earth and executing true justice among the nations.

Select Bibliography

Alexander, T. Desmond, David W. Baker, and Bruce Waltke. *Obadiah, Jonah, Micah*. Tyndale Old Testament Commentaries. Downers Grove, IL: InterVarsity, 1988.

Allen, Leslie C. *The Books of Joel, Obadiah, Jonah, and Micah*. New International Commentary on the Old Testament. Grand Rapids: Eerdmans, 1976.

Craigie, Peter C. *Twelve Prophets*. Vol. 1. Daily Study Bible. Philadelphia: Westminster, 1984.

Niehaus, Jeffrey J. "Obadiah." In *The Minor Prophets: An Exegetical and Expository Commentary*. Edited by Thomas Edward McComiskey. Grand Rapids: Baker Academic, 1992.

Raabe, Paul R. *Obadiah*. Anchor Bible. New York: Doubleday, 1996.

Stuart, Douglas. *Hosea–Jonah*. Word Biblical Commentary. Waco: Word, 1987.

Watts, John D. W. *Obadiah: A Critical Exegetical Commentary*. Grand Rapids: Eerdmans, 1969.

Jonah

SHERI L. KLOUDA

Introduction

The book of Jonah is one of the more dramatic narratives in the Old Testament. The human protagonist, the prophet Jonah, survives a savage ocean storm and entombment in a sea creature of mythic proportions, and is finally delivered from imminent death—all to witness the eleventh-hour reprieve of a wicked people and hated enemy. This biographical account of the prophet's experiences as he attempts to disobey God and flee from the Lord's presence resonates with the daily struggles of the faithful reader. Shedding practical theological insight on typical questions and concerns such as the measure of the Lord's compassion, the narrative emphasizes the sovereignty of God and his willingness to forgive the truly repentant. The story transcends the limits of human comprehension, reaffirming God's unfathomable nature while reasserting that no human can impede the divine will.

Authorship and Date

Although the text never mentions Jonah as the author, both Jewish and Christian traditions attribute authorship of the book to the eighth-century-BC prophet Jonah mentioned in 2 Kings 14:25. In this text Jonah predicts the restoration of Israel's borders to those originally associated with the Davidic dynasty. Jonah, the son of Amittai, came from Gath Hepher near Bethlehem and lived during the reign of Jeroboam II (782–753 BC) in the northern kingdom of Israel. While the book of Jonah is situated among the prophets, Jonah himself utters only five words of prophecy in the entire narrative.

A number of factors prompt some scholars to argue against Jonah as the writer, since most of the book is written in the third person. For example, the notion that God desires salvation for all of his people, including the Gentiles, reflects a late theological

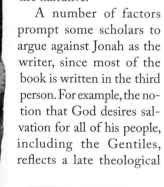

This stele shows Adad-Nirari III, king of Assyria, with the symbols of his gods. His sons were in power in Assyria during the time of Jonah son of Amittai.

development more comfortable in the postexilic period. Other arguments for a possible fifth- or sixth-century date include literary affinities with other biblical texts, such as the Psalter, and the presence of several potentially late Hebrew terms as well as possible Aramaic influence. While the text itself remains essentially preserved, a few late Hebrew forms may simply reflect scribal updating. Linguistic studies no longer assume that Aramaic terms must indicate late composition, since many Aramaic terms have been located in biblical literature normally associated with the northern kingdom. Consequently, linguistic evidence does not preclude a mid-eighth-century date for the narrative. Historically, Nineveh was not destroyed until 612 BC, so the setting of the book depicts a time before Nineveh's devastation.

Historical Context

Nineveh was the capital city of Assyria, whose people enjoyed a reputation for their severe cruelty, especially toward Israel. Often they impaled their captives or wore amulets around their necks created from human heads. Idolatry played a significant role in Nineveh; the city was home to a number of temples, dedicated to deities such as Ashur, the source of power and life over all the Assyrian gods, and Nabu, the god of scribes and wisdom. Located at the apex of a central trade route, Nineveh was a commercially vital city with a healthy population of at least 120,000 men.

Theological Themes

Many struggle to identify a single theological theme for the book, since what seems simple on the surface actually harbors a number of complexities.

Although there is widespread familiarity with the story of Jonah and the whale, the book's thematic diversity contains several intertwined theological threads, making it one of the most practical texts to teach and preach from. The overarching emphasis on God's sovereignty over his creation and his creatures (1:4, 9, 15, 17; 4:6–8) is developed in light of the compatibility of God's judgment of and his compassion toward sinners, particularly Gentiles (3:10; 4:2). In addition, the text addresses the nature of God's gracious response to national and individual repentance. Consequently, the book addresses the prejudice of national exclusivity, the concept that Israel considered her relationship with the Lord as unique, limited to only one nation and people (3:9–10; 4:11). The subtle contrasts between the righteous actions of the sailors in Jonah 1, the ethical and moral repentance of the Ninevites in Jonah 3, and the stubborn and unyielding character of Jonah function to highlight the ironic obedience of the ungodly Gentiles to the Lord in comparison with Jonah's refusal to comply with the Lord's commands and failure to understand his ways.

Structure

The underlying structure of the book reveals two major sections, which mirror each other both in content and in sequence of events (1:1–2:10; 3:1–4:11). The language describing the Lord's initial call to Jonah and Jonah's negative response (1:1–3) recurs in the Lord's second call to the prophet (3:1–4). Jonah 1:4–16 and 3:5–10 describe the repentance of the sailors and the unanticipated remorse of Nineveh's population to the Lord's impending judgment. Jonah emphasizes the Lord's sovereignty, as God "appoints" (NIV "provides") a great fish (1:17), a shading plant (4:6), a worm (4:7), and a hot wind (4:8). The first climactic episode begins with Jonah's brush with death and concludes the entire first section with the Lord's deliverance (1:17–2:10), while the second climactic episode (4:5–11) begins with Jonah's desire to die (4:1–4) and concludes with the Lord's deliverance of Nineveh. Repetition plays a significant role in the structure of the narrative, linking the parts contextually in the mind of the reader. The interplay between the Hebrew verbs meaning "rise" and "descend" mimics the rocking of the waves (1:2, 3 (2×), 5–6; 2:3, 6; 3:2–3, 6). These same words also figuratively trace Jonah's progressive distance from the Lord and his subsequent restoration.

Commentary

1. The Lord's First Commission to Jonah and Jonah's Disobedience (1:1–16)

A. The Lord's first commission to Jonah (1:1–3). While we cannot be certain exactly how God conveyed his message to Jonah, the initial phrase, "The word of the LORD came to Jonah," typically introduces divine communication in the Old Testament. The Lord commands Jonah literally to "rise and go to Nineveh," two commands that recur in Jonah's second commissioning from God (3:1). The text characterizes Nineveh as a great city, most notably as the capital of Assyria. Nineveh's inhabitants were well known for their barbaric and cruel treatment of their captives, specifically their mistreatment toward Israel; consequently, the

depth of Nineveh's moral decline draws God's attention. Other prophetic books also describe Ninevites as arrogant and godless (Zeph. 2:13; Nah. 3:19). Jonah's refusal to travel there underscores Israel's animosity toward Nineveh's population.

Jonah flees to the coast of Joppa, near Jerusalem. There he boards a ship headed to Tarshish, probably a seaport located on the west coast of the Mediterranean, in the opposite direction of Nineveh. Jonah seeks to escape Yahweh's presence, despite his subconscious knowledge that God is all-knowing and everywhere. Jonah literally "descends" to Joppa, "descends" into the ship, and later "descends" to the bottom of the sea (1:2–3, 5; 2:4, 7). The concept of descent figuratively represents Jonah's growing distance from the Lord.

B. The Lord's response to Jonah's refusal to obey (1:4–6). Yahweh makes the fact that he is all-present known through physical manifestations of his power. God "hurled a great wind" (1:4 NASB, RSV, ESV) toward the sea, rousting violent swells that threaten to capsize the ship full of pagan sailors. The polytheistic sailors, perhaps acknowledging that the sudden storm represents the active displeasure of a sea god, call out each to his own god, and when those prayers do not yield tangible results, they begin to hurl (ESV) cargo from the ship in an effort to lighten the load (1:5). The sailors attempt to avoid shipwreck, first by appealing to divine authority then taking matters into their own hands by throwing materials overboard. Meanwhile, the captain notes Jonah's visible absence and confronts him in the berth where he is sleeping deeply. Jonah's obvious lack of concern for the ship's predicament troubles the sailors, who roust Jonah from below deck and beseech him to call on his God for rescue (1:6). The writer contrasts the Gentiles' intuitional response to crisis by appealing to divine power with Jonah's

A model of a Canaanite merchant ship (ca. fourteenth century BC), which may be similar to the ship to Tarshish on which Jonah sailed failure to respond appropriately. The man of God seems oblivious to the consequences of his disobedience, nor does he appear to feel any responsibility for the sailors he has endangered.

C. The sailors' response to crisis at sea (1:7–16). The narrative never explicitly tells us that Jonah prays to Yahweh on behalf of the sailors. Frightened by the worsening conditions, the sailors once again seek a resolution to their impending destruction through drawing lots. Lots were often used as a means to seek divine direction in decision making. God's sovereignty is once again demonstrated, as the lots indicate Jonah is somehow responsible for the raging storm. In an effort to discover more about the origin of the threat, the sailors ask Jonah to identify his occupation, his birthplace, and his ethnicity (1:8). All three of these answers would help the sailors understand which god was angry with Jonah, and help them determine how to appease that god's anger. Jonah answers the question indirectly,

first identifying himself as a Hebrew, then launching into a short doxology praising the sovereignty of the Lord, the one God, dwelling in heaven, "who made the sea and the dry land" (1:9 NASB, RSV). The expression reinforces the Lord's control over all aspects of creation. The sailors grow even more frightened at Jonah's response, perhaps in light of Yahweh's reputation among the nations as a fierce and wrathful God and because Jonah has already told them he is fleeing from the Lord's presence (1:10).

The sailors demonstrate remarkable ethical and moral standards as they struggle to determine how to deal with Jonah's disobedience and the Lord's wrath. Jonah instructs the crew to hurl him into the sea, assuring certain death; however, the sailors do not want to risk intensifying the Lord's anger by killing one of his people, and make a final effort to wrestle the ship under their control (1:13). The narrative hints at the concept of human sacrifice as a means of appeasing the sea

god and depicts the sailors as morally upright in seeking other alternatives. It is interesting to note that while Jonah seems unaware of the conflict facing the sailors, he does not find anything wrong with the request. Finally, the men seek the Lord's mercy by asking him not to hold them responsible for shedding innocent blood as they hurl Jonah into the sea (1:15).

Following the immediate calming of the sea, the sailors offer sacrifices and make vows to the Lord in gratitude and allegiance. Clearly, the placid sea demonstrates that Jonah's disobedience was the cause of the storm. Scholars debate whether the sailors' actions constitute a genuine conversion or simply an acknowledgment of the Lord as one among their pantheon of gods. Religious syncretism was quite common in the ancient Near East, where people were willing to welcome additional gods into their pantheon. Furthermore, the adverse circumstances of the crew may have prompted them to appeal to God temporarily, out of desperation and the threat of imminent death rather than from religious conviction.

2. The Lord Protects and Rescues Jonah (1:17–2:10)

A. The Lord's provision of the fish (1:17–2:1). The Lord provides (literally "appoints") a "huge fish" or sea creature to swallow Jonah, in which Jonah remains alive for three days and nights (1:17). In the New Testament, Matthew (12:39–40) draws an analogy between the death and resurrection of Jesus Christ and the imprisonment of Jonah. Matthew identifies Jonah's salvation by a providentially provided creature as a miraculous sign that typifies God's provision of Christ as a means of salvation and depicts his resurrection from the dead. This is the first of only two occasions in which Jonah prays to God (2:1; 4:2).

B. Jonah's prayer for the Lord's deliverance (2:2–9). The prayer uttered by Jonah resembles the form of a typical thanksgiving psalm, and is linked to several psalms through similar language and themes (for example, Ps. 18:4–6; 30; 34; 40:1–12; 52; 56:13; 103:4). The unusually large number of affinities between psalm fragments and Jonah suggest that Jonah's prayer may have originated later; at the very least, the composition suggests the prophet's familiarity with temple worship songs. Jonah's psalm includes an introductory call (2:1–2), followed by a description of his former catastrophe (2:3–6), and concludes with gratitude to the Lord for his rescue from Sheol, or death (2:7–8). In response to his deliverance, Jonah promises to make sacrifices and fulfill a former vow (2:9).

Both the genre of the prayer and the poem's interruption of the flow of the narrative are what prompt some to argue that the passage is a later addition. However, other narratives contain mixed genres, and there is no reason to assume that a writer cannot vary in literary style. Others claim that the placement of a thanksgiving psalm before the text describing Jonah's salvation seems inappropriate. Obviously, though, Jonah did not write down the psalm while in the belly of the sea creature but in retrospection; this presents a logical explanation for the awkward placement of the prayer before the Lord formally delivers Jonah in the passage.

Jonah calls out to the Lord from "the belly of Sheol," a location normally associated with death (2:2; NIV "deep in the realm of the dead"), and observes that the bars of the earth restrain him (2:6). A number of texts mention the "bars" or "gates" of Sheol (Job 17:16; 38:17; Ps. 9:13; Isa. 38:10). The term designates a place of separation or removal from God, yet Jonah's poem affirms that somehow God hears his prayer even from the roots of the mountains (2:2) and that he has been rescued by the Lord from the "pit" (another synonym for death, 2:6). Jonah's submersion in the rough seas, combined with the choking mass of seaweed, threatens to drown the prophet (2:5). Although it seems as if Jonah has resigned himself to certain death and separation from God, he "remembers" the Lord, associating the presence of the Lord in the temple with the place where prayer is heard and answered (2:4, 7). Jonah's utterance in verse 9 does not fit well in the psalm, but perhaps it reflects an admonition toward the sailors from the ship, who place their trust in worthless gods.

C. The Lord delivers Jonah (2:10). Creation responds at the spoken word of the Lord. Jonah is deposited unceremoniously on the dry land, apparently in proximity to God's original destination. One can assume that the sailors thought Jonah had perished, and told the story of their voyage to others, so his reappearance, certainly very white and wrinkled as well as smelly, may have frightened the inhabitants of Nineveh, who could have perceived Jonah as a ghost or spirit.

3. Jonah's Second Commission and Nineveh's Response (3:1–10)

A. Jonah's proclamation of the Lord's message to Nineveh (3:1–4). The Lord's second commission to Jonah mirrors 1:1–3 almost verbatim, although in this instance Jonah obeys the Lord and travels to Nineveh. While in 1:2 the Lord states the reason for Jonah's visit to Nineveh, in 3:2 Jonah is simply told to proclaim the message the Lord is about to give him. The adjective "great" describes the city four times (1:2; 3:2, 3; 4:11), indicating its political, cultural, and geographic importance. Nineveh, located at the crossroads of two major trade routes, served as the capital of Assyria. While the text describes Jonah's journey as of three days' duration, we are uncertain whether it took three days to arrive at Nineveh or whether the prophet traveled around the eight-mile circumference of the city for three days. It is also possible that the three-day journey included visits to the entire district of Nineveh rather than just to the city itself. The use of "three days" alludes to the time Jonah spent in the sea creature and connects the preceding narrative with the events in Jonah 3. Nevertheless, since Nineveh has a population of at least 120,000 (4:11), God expresses divine concern over the degree of violence and evil rampant among the citizens (1:2).

Jonah's proclamation, the only prophetic oracle in the book, announces the imminence of judgment within forty days (3:4). The number forty occurs frequently in Scripture to describe the length of a divine encounter (Gen. 7:4; Exod. 24:18; 34:28; Num. 13:25; Deut. 9:9–10; 1 Sam. 17:16; 1 Kings 19:8; Ezek. 4:6). The threat of judgment is not implausible in light of a military threat against Assyria from an enemy to the north.

B. Nineveh's response to the Lord's message (3:5–9). Significantly, the peasants, believing the oracle from God, take the initiative and begin fasting as a result of Jonah's pronouncement (3:5). The practice of fasting as well as the donning of sackcloth, a fabric constructed from goat's hair and extremely irritating to human skin, typically represented mourning (Ezek. 7:18). Prophets often wore sackcloth and fasted, outwardly demonstrating their grief over the people's sinfulness (2 Kings 1:8; Zech. 13:4). The extent of the fast supersedes social strata and class distinction.

After hearing of Jonah's announcement, the king officially decrees a fast throughout the kingdom and steps down from his throne to sit on the ground in the dust, a gesture of great humility (3:7). The king instructs the inhabitants not to eat or drink anything, nor to feed and water their domesticated animals. The participation of animals in ritual mourning seems unparalleled in the ancient Near East, yet Jonah does not question the practice.

The king then follows his physical decree with an ethical command, beseeching the citizens to "turn" or "repent" (NIV "give up"; Hebrew *shub*) from their violent and evil behavior (3:8). A call to moral reform is unusual, since typical Assyrian practice sought to divert divine wrath through rituals. The king carefully phrases his words, acknowledging that God is free to act despite the nation's repentance, yet affirming the possibility that God could "turn" or "relent" (*shub*) and refrain from judgment (3:9).

C. The Lord relents from judgment (3:10). Significantly, the Lord recognizes not the outward expression of Nineveh's contrition but the city's willingness to renounce wickedness and evil (3:10). In his great compassion, the Lord "relents" (NASB; a different Hebrew verb from 3:9) and spares Nineveh from destruction. While some scholars believe this verse affirms that God can be swayed from a course of action by the repentance or the fervent prayer of creatures, such a claim would deny that God is all-knowing by suggesting that God cannot know for certain how a human being will respond. Consequently, the Lord's acts are dependent or contingent on the actions of his creatures, which subjugates the divine will to human will. In addition, this view, known as the "openness of God," assumes that God is not immutable or unchangeable and that, in fact, God can "change his mind." It would follow, then, that if God can change his will or mind on one occasion, we cannot with any certainty know if God will change his mind about other matters, such as the salvation of believers. But we can only understand the author's choice of words as an attempt to grapple with the inconceivability of God's restraint from judgment in light of his divine holiness. The incomprehensible nature and will of God is expressed in terms that ascribe human qualities to the divine being in order to explain God's actions within the limitations of human concepts.

4. Jonah's Unjustified Anger and God's Response (4:1–11)

A. Jonah's unjustified anger toward God's sparing of Nineveh (4:1–4). Jonah demonstrates his arrogance and his lack of understanding as he reacts with unjustified anger after the Lord revokes his judgment toward Assyria. The Hebrew term for "evil" in Jonah 3:8, 10 recurs

in 4:1, supporting the connection between God's earlier act and Jonah's presumptuous reaction to what he perceives as a great injustice or "evil" (NIV "to Jonah this seemed *very wrong*"). Ironically, God's compassion lessens his divine wrath in 3:9–10, while the anger of Jonah, a mere mortal, is further inflamed. Jonah affirms his knowledge of God's gracious and compassionate character, employing the formula in Exodus 34:6–7 describing divine attributes. The formula was first uttered in its fullest form to Moses; partial forms also occur in other texts (Num. 14:18; Ps. 103:8–13; Nah. 1:3; Mic. 7:18–19; Joel 2:13–14). Which part of the formula was quoted by a biblical writer depended on whether he wanted to emphasize the Lord's mercy or the longevity of God's anger. In some sense, Jonah believes that the Lord's mercy toward his creatures is exclusive to the nation of Israel and that the parameters of the Lord's grace should not extend to the Gentiles. Jonah concludes his outburst by telling God what he should do—that is, take Jonah's life (4:3). Jonah's request further clarifies his misunderstanding concerning the will of God, which is not constrained or dictated by his creatures. God questions Jonah's right to be angry, since God has also extended grace and compassion toward Jonah despite his disobedience to the Lord's commands (Jonah 1:4).

B. God's response to Jonah's unjustified anger (4:5–11). Jonah travels east of Nineveh and settles down to wait for Nineveh's demise, as if it is inconceivable that the city will be spared by God (4:5). In an expression of his divine mercy and

A late-Roman sarcophagus (ca. AD 300) with scenes from the story of Jonah

compassion, the Lord "appoints" or "provides" (4:6–8; cf. 1:17) a plant, probably a castor oil plant, to shade and cool Jonah as he sits in the desert. Jonah rejoices in God's merciful provision, an accommodation that Jonah does not deserve in light of his opposition to the Lord (4:6).

Then the Lord appoints a weevil to chew the roots of the plant so that it withers and dies, and finally the Lord appoints an east wind to blow on the vulnerable Jonah. At the height of summer, the desert temperature can reach 110 degrees and, combined with the sirocco, or east wind, can render the air and ground devoid of any moisture whatsoever. The effects of the sirocco are so severe that people normally seek sturdy, protective shelter from the fierce winds. Jonah remains unprotected except for a booth, a small, temporary three-sided shelter consisting of large branches or other materials. Jonah suffers in the blazing heat and, once again, pleads to die (4:8).

The Lord once again asks Jonah if he is justified in his anger concerning the destruction of the shade plant, but the prophet adamantly refuses to acknowledge his error (4:9). God aims to bring Jonah to the realization that none of his creatures deserve the mercy and compassion of God and that the grace of God is freely dispensed according to his divine purpose and will. The author contrasts Jonah's pleasure in God's provision of undeserved mercy on his behalf with Jonah's disappointment in God's compassionate response to Nineveh. The Lord poses a rhetorical question that highlights his sovereignty and care for the world, yet it remains uncertain whether Jonah reaches a full understanding of the nature of God. Regardless, the Lord employs the ministry of Jonah to Nineveh and Assyria to reinforce his covenant promise to bless the nations through the descendants of Abraham (Gen. 12:1–3).

Select Bibliography

Alexander, T. Desmond, David W. Baker, and Bruce Waltke. *Obadiah, Jonah, Micah*. Tyndale Old Testament Commentaries. Downers Grove, IL: InterVarsity, 1988.

Baldwin, Joyce. "Jonah." In *The Minor Prophets: An Exegetical and Expository Commentary*. Edited by Thomas Edward McComiskey. Grand Rapids: Baker Academic, 1992.

Bruckner, James K. *Jonah, Nahum, Habakkuk, Zephaniah*. NIV Application Commentary. Grand Rapids: Zondervan, 2004.

Fretheim, Terence. *The Message of Jonah*. Minneapolis: Augsburg, 1977.

Limburg, James. *Jonah*. Old Testament Library. Louisville: Westminster John Knox, 1993.

Magonet, Jonathan. *Form and Meaning: Studies in the Literary Techniques in the Book of Jonah*. Frankfurt, Germany: Peter Land, 1976.

Marcus, David. "Nineveh's 'Three Days' Walk' (Jonah 3:3): Another Interpretation." In *On the Way to Nineveh: Studies in Honor of George M. Landes*. Edited by Stephen L. Cook and S. C. Winter. Atlanta: Scholars Press, 1999.

Sasson, Jack. *Jonah: A New Translation with Commentary*. Anchor Bible. New York: Doubleday, 1990.

Simon, Uriel. *Jonah*. JPS Bible Commentary. Philadelphia: Jewish Publication Society, 1999.

Sweeney, Marvin A. *The Twelve Prophets: Hosea, Joel, Amos, Obadiah, Jonah*. Berit Olam. Collegeville, MN: Liturgical Press, 2000.

Willis, John T. "The 'Repentance' of God in the Books of Samuel, Jeremiah, and Jonah." *Horizons in Biblical Theology* 16 (1994): 156–75.

Micah

Tremper Longman III

Micah the Prophet

The first verse of the book of Micah names Micah of Moresheth as the one who received and communicated the vision concerning the future judgment and salvation of Samaria and Jerusalem. The name Micah is common in the Old Testament (a longer form of the name is Micaiah) and means, "Who is like Yahweh?"

Moresheth was a village approximately twenty-five miles southwest of Jerusalem. The village was located on the edge of the rolling hills of the Shephelah, near the coastal plain. Bruce Waltke speculates that "Micah's identification as a Moreshite implies that he was an outsider to the capitals" (Waltke, 3). Scholars are not certain why Micah's parentage is not mentioned, but it may be because his family was not prominent. He is identified by means of his hometown because his ministry took place at a different city (probably Jerusalem).

Micah is mentioned in only one other place in the Old Testament (Jer. 26:17–19). When Jehoiakim comes to the throne in Judah, the priests and the false prophets try to put Jeremiah to death. Some elders intercede for him and cite the ministry of Micah as a justification for Jeremiah's prophecy of judgment.

Authorship and Date

In the past, critical scholars have argued that the genuine oracles of Micah are restricted to the first three chapters. If one grants the possibility of predictive prophecy, however, there are no persuasive reasons for denying Micah the authorship of any part of the book.

The first verse, once again, is our source of information on the date of Micah's ministry. Three kings of Judah are listed to provide the period of time during which Micah preached threat and hope among the people: Jotham (750–732 BC), Ahaz (732–716), and Hezekiah (715–686). Since Micah's work may have begun toward the end of Jotham's reign and ended at the beginning of Hezekiah's, we cannot be certain about the actual length of his ministry.

The reference to the coming judgment of Samaria (1:6) indicates that Micah's preaching began well before 722 BC, the year in which Samaria fell to the forces of Assyria. Another oracle that may be fairly certainly dated is the lament in 1:8–16. The cities mentioned in this section coincide with the probable route of Sennacherib's army as he approached Jerusalem in 701 BC. Of course, the reference in Jeremiah 26:17–19 cites Micah 3:12 as an oracle delivered during the reign of Hezekiah.

Historical Context

A brief overview of the history of Israel and Judah that relates to the prophecy of Micah notes that the period before his ministry was a time of political and economic prosperity but spiritual dullness (particularly the reigns of Jeroboam II of Israel [786–746 BC] and Uzziah of Judah [783–742 BC]). Soon, God's judgment would lead to the downfall of Samaria at the hands of the Assyrian army under the leadership of Shalmaneser V (722 BC). The southern kingdom, Judah, was not absorbed into the Assyrian Empire but was forced to pay tribute. During the reign of Sargon II, Judah did not rebel, but upon this strong king's death and the accession of his son Sennacherib, Hezekiah, the king of Judah, joined a coalition led by a Babylonian rebel, Marduk-Baladan (2 Kings 18–19). In reaction Sennacherib threatened the independence of Jerusalem (701 BC), but through the ministry of Isaiah and Micah, Hezekiah repented of his sins and God spared the city. Nevertheless, it was not long after Hezekiah's death that the rulers of Judah turned against the Lord. Manasseh, his son, for instance, brought much grief to Judah. Micah's prophecy predicts the destruction of Judah at the hands of the Babylonians, which took place in 586 BC, and even further ahead to the restoration from captivity (539 BC).

The Assyrian king Sargon II faces a dignitary in this relief from Sargon's palace at Khorsabad (716–713 BC). Micah prophesied during the reign of King Hezekiah of Judah, who rebelled against Sargon's son, Sennacherib.

Structure

Much debate surrounds the structure of the book of Micah. Opinions vary radically. Some argue that the book has no overall structure and is simply a loose collection of prophetic oracles. Others identify extremely complex and sophisticated structures. A few points are certain:

1. Micah did not speak these oracles at one time. The book is best taken as an anthology of his prophetic messages over the years of his ministry.
2. Chronology is not the key to the structure of the book, though early in the book Micah does predict the capture of Samaria and Sennacherib's invasion, while at the conclusion of this book, he looks ahead to the Babylonian captivity and the restoration.
3. The prophecy is roughly structured on the basis of alternating messages of threat and hope. God through his prophet disputes with his people in two rounds. The first is found in chapters 1–5. There is a harsh message of judgment (1:2–3:19—2:12–13 may be an exception) but also a note of salvation (4:1–5:15—5:10–15 may be an exception). The second round (6:1–7:20) also begins with judgment (6:1–7:7) but concludes on a profound note of hope (7:8–20).

Theological Themes

The theology of Micah is largely concerned with divine judgment against sin. Yahweh commissioned Micah to bring this message of judgment against his people. Israel and Judah both departed from the way of the Lord and angered him by their sin. The sin is cultic (1:5–7) as well as social (2:1–2). Israel's civil (3:1–3) and religious leaders (2:6–11 [prophets]; 3:11 [priests]) have rejected the ways of God. They have a false security in the Lord.

The Lord, accordingly, presses his case against his people who have broken covenant with him. He reveals himself as a warrior against his people (1:3–4). The Lord desires that his people love him and act justly. He calls his people back to himself.

While judgment against sin is the dominant note of the book, hope is not lacking. As early as 2:12–13, Yahweh speaks in comforting tones of salvation after judgment. The final picture of God (7:18–20) shows him to be unprecedented in grace and true to his covenant promise to Abraham. The promises to David are not dead but will be fulfilled in the future (5:1–2).

Indeed, the authors of the New Testament believed that Micah's message was fulfilled in the coming of Jesus Christ. For example, the Gospel of Matthew cites Micah 4:2 in reference to Jesus's birth in Bethlehem (Matt. 2:5). Micah here looks forward to a future Davidic ruler, and Jesus Christ, a descendant of David, was appropriately born in Bethlehem.

Outline

Commentary

1. First Round of Judgment and Salvation (1:1–5:15)

A. God's judgment of apostasy and social sin in Samaria and Judah (1:1–3:12). 1:1–16. As with most other prophetic books, the book of Micah begins with an introductory verse (1:1) that gives the prophet's name, the time period in which he ministers, and the object of the message that God gives him.

Micah begins with an invocation, a call to listen to the Lord. The call goes out to the whole earth and all who are in it, but the message is specifically directed toward Samaria, the capital of the northern kingdom, and briefly toward Jerusalem, the capital of the southern kingdom. Micah announces that the Lord has a case against Israel. He will witness against Israel by exposing her evil deeds (1:2–7). The concept of the witness is connected to the covenant (Deut. 30:18; 31:19, 26; Josh. 24:27). After all, the witness was present at the time Israel agreed to obey the law and now comes forward to challenge the nation's integrity (see further commentary on 6:1–8).

The naming of the sin of Israel is preceded by the dramatic appearance of the Lord. He comes as a fearful judge, a mighty warrior (cf. the picture of God in the first part of the book of Nahum). God comes from his dwelling place, the temple, which is the earthly symbol of his true, heavenly dwelling place. He leaves it in order to destroy the high places. The high places were sites of false worship the Israelites built for the worship of other gods.

When God appears as judge or warrior, nature reacts violently (cf. Nah. 1:4–5; Zech. 14:3–11). The mountains, a well-known symbol of stability, will melt like wax before fire or water rushing down a slope (1:4).

Verse 5 points the finger at the guilty parties. They are none other than Samaria and Jerusalem, the capital cities of the northern and southern kingdoms respectively. Omri and his son Ahab (1 Kings 16:24), a pair known for their sympathy with the Baal cult in the north, built Samaria. Jerusalem, the city chosen by God for his earthly dwelling place, has time and time again been perverted with the worship of false gods. Even the temple itself has been polluted by the presence of pagan idols.

The accusation is followed immediately by God's judgment. Samaria will be devastated and turned into an empty field—a field with scattered rubble, which will be so empty that it will be used for agricultural purposes. Verse 7 directs God's judgment against the wicked religion that flourishes in Samaria. Deuteronomy 23:17–18 specifically prohibits both the practice (known among Israel's neighbors) of religious prostitution and the use of prostitutes' wages for gifts to the temple. For breaking this law and others, Samaria will be destroyed.

The second half of chapter 1 (1:8–16) gives the reaction to God's announcement of judgment. The first to react is the prophet himself, who is plunged into noisy mourning. His mourning will sound like the howl of a jackal and the moan of an owl, animals of the wilderness often mentioned in judgment oracles against cities (Isa. 13:21; 34:13; Jer. 50:39). His reaction reminds us of the later reaction of the author of Lamentations to the destruction of Jerusalem. Micah's mourning is not triggered by a concern for personal safety but rather by the destruction coming to God's people and the land he has given them. The prophet is distressed particularly by the danger that comes so near to Jerusalem. While it is difficult to precisely date these separate oracles of Micah, this oracle fits well with the various invasions of Samaria and Judah in the last quarter of the eighth century BC. It specifically predicts the incursion of Sennacherib in 701 BC. At this time, Sennacherib harassed many of the towns of Judah but was stopped just short of taking Jerusalem.

The bulk of this section, however, predicts the reaction of a number of cities (1:10–15). These cities were likely the ones subdued by Sennacherib as he made his way down the coast of Palestine toward Jerusalem. They are located in the southern foothills (Shephelah) as one moves from the coast toward Jerusalem. The prophet employs wordplay between the

Remains of the ancient city of Samaria

names of the cities and their reactions in order to make his point.

The wordplay begins with a vengence in verse 10. The wordplay in this instance is found in the similar sounds within each Hebrew clause. Although Micah tells Gath to "weep not at all," he urges those on the Israelite side of the Shephelah to express their mourning: "In Beth Ophrah [literally "house of dust"] roll in the dust."

The next four towns Micah mentions have either unknown or uncertain identifications. Nevertheless, the wordplays continue. The inhabitants of Shaphir (1:11), a name connected with a Hebrew word for "pleasant" or "beauty," will be naked and full of shame because of the coming judgment. The citizens of Zaanan (1:11), a city whose name probably comes from the Hebrew verb "to go out," will not come out, presumably due to fear of the invaders. The significance of the name Beth Ezel (1:11) is not obvious to the modern interpreter. Maroth (1:12) is a name related to the Hebrew word for "bitter." They waited for something sweet, but the bitter truth was the presence of the enemy at the very gate of the capital.

Lachish (1:13) is a well-known city in the Shephelah; it is singled out by the fact that a whole verse is given to it and by the content of that verse. The wordplay is based on the similarity in sound between the name Lachish and the Hebrew for "to the team of horses" (*larekesh*). The significance of Lachish in this oracle may be seen in the accusation that they began the sin that infected Jerusalem. Nothing in the text indicates clearly what that sin was. Many have guessed from the reference to chariots that the sin was an overreliance on military armaments.

The next three city names also involve wordplay. Moresheth Gath (1:14), Micah's hometown, located near Lachish, has a name similar to the Hebrew word for "betrothed." The parting gifts are specifically those gifts given by a father to his daughter as she leaves his home to go to that of her husband. Micah alludes to the deportation that will follow the defeat of his hometown. The town known as Akzib (1:14), related to the Hebrew word for "lie," will be a deception. Akzib was a city devoted

This Assyrian relief from Nimrud shows women mourning as they are led away into exile (865–860 BC).

to the production of materials that would bring in money for the support of the nation. It let Judah down in the moment of need. Mareshah (1:15) sounds like the word for "conqueror." The ironic twist is that a conqueror will come against the town named "conqueror." The last city named is Adullam (1:15), the location of the cave in which David sought refuge as he fled from Saul (2 Sam. 23:13).

The last verse in the chapter addresses all the inhabitants and tells them to cut off their hair (an ancient mourning rite), for God is about to separate them from their children through exile.

2:1–13. The second chapter begins with a woe oracle (2:1–5). The roots of the woe oracle genre are found in funeral laments, expressing sorrow over the loss of the deceased. The prophets, however, adapt the form to their own purposes. No sympathy may be heard in Micah's voice; rather, threat of sure judgment. The use of the woe threat signifies that the object of the oracle is as good as dead.

The object of the oracle is described in general terms in verse 1 and then more specifically in verse 2. They are those who stay up at night contemplating how to work evil and then rise early to perform their wicked deeds. Their specific evil that Micah pinpoints is the amassing of real estate at the expense of other people. The land-grabbers both covet (breaking the tenth commandment) and seize (breaking the eighth commandment) land belonging to others. This sin is particularly grievous since the land was given to the Israelites by the Lord, so that each family might possess some. Thus, certain laws were in effect to protect the ownership of the land by the original recipients (Leviticus 25). The story of Naboth and Ahab (1 Kings 21) provides a good historical example of this type of sin.

As happens so frequently in the Prophets, the Lord chooses an appropriate punishment for these greedy and selfish men. It is tit for tat. The evil men plan iniquity; the Lord plans disaster against them. They desire status and riches at the expense of others; the result will

be that men will ridicule them. Indeed, their own land will be taken away and given to others, even traitors. The reference in verse 5 may be an allusion to the future exile.

The false prophets come to the aid of the land-grabbers and confront Micah (2:6–11). This section is a dispute between the false prophets representing the interests of the wicked land-grabbers on the one hand and God and Micah on the other.

The false prophets attack Micah's message of doom, his message that God will punish their sin. They forbid Micah to prophesy. They do not believe judgment is coming their way. The attitude of confidence the false prophets express is similar to that found in Jeremiah 7, where the people trust in the temple as the sign of God's presence in Jerusalem. According to the false prophets, God will not do the things Micah is insisting on. Indeed, the special word for "prophesy" in verse 6 may have a negative connotation ("rant" or "dribble").

Micah exposes the deeds of social injustice current during his time period. The false prophets and their clients rob the shirts off the backs of defenseless travelers. They treat God's people like their enemy. They rob women and children of their possessions and God's blessing. Women and children were the weak in Israelite society and accordingly are the object of God's special protection.

Once again Micah alludes to exile, this time in verse 10. God will eject the wicked from the land because through their wickedness they have made the land unclean.

The section ends on a strongly sarcastic note. The false prophets are prophets who bring only good news. Micah is no doubt extremely unpopular because of the generally negative tone of his prophecy. These people would rather hear a prophet who prophesies plenty of wine and beer.

Suddenly the prophet speaks in positive tones (2:12–13). This abrupt transition has caused many to question the plain meaning or originality of this short oracle. However, we know so little about the prophecy's structure or history of development that it is safest to accept the text as it is.

Micah glimpses that beyond the punishment of the exile God will once again bring his people together. The two opening phrases—"I will surely gather" and "I will surely bring together"—emphasize the certainty of the future promise.

The image used is the familiar one of the people of God as the sheep and the Lord as the Shepherd. The Good Shepherd will gather the remnant into its pasture. He will once again, as at the time of the exodus, lead his people out of captivity.

3:1–12. The words "then I said" remind us that Micah is being used of God to bring his judgment against the people (3:1–4). This also indicates that what follows in chapter 3 is a continuation of what came before; indeed, we find the same hard-hitting judgment brought against powerful oppressors that we saw in the earlier chapters.

Once again (cf. 1:2) Micah calls for attention, this time the attention of the leaders and rulers of Israel. These men are accused of gross sin and dereliction of duty. They are the ones who should know justice (perhaps judges are specifically in mind), but they do not. They have rejected the admonition Amos (5:14) gave earlier, so that they hate good and love evil.

The image Micah then evokes in his hearers' minds is that of a cannibal who rends the flesh of his victim, cooks it, and then has a meal. In other words, the leaders, who should be serving and protecting the people whom God has entrusted to their care, are exploiting them. They use them to their own advantage and to the people's disadvantage.

The time, however, will come when these wicked leaders will turn to the Lord. They will cry out to the Lord (the language reminds one of a similar phrase that occurs frequently in the book of Judges). The Lord, however, will not respond to these individuals because their sin is too great.

The subject of God's judgment as spoken through the prophet Micah now switches to the prophets (3:5–8). In a word, they prophesy falsely and thus turn the people away from the Lord. Why do they do this? The Lord accuses them of loving payment more than him or his people. A positive oracle may be gained from these false prophets if the pay is high enough. On the other hand, if no payment is offered, they prepare (literally "sanctify") war.

Their judgment is appropriate (introduced by "therefore"). They sinned with the gift of prophecy, so that gift will now be removed from them. There will be no visions and no divination, only darkness. No answers will be forthcoming from God.

A strong contrast exists between these false prophets and Micah. The Lord has given Micah his Spirit. He has empowered him with his message, and his message is one of judgment.

The third judgment oracle of the chapter (3:9–12) once again (cf. 3:1) opens with a call to the leaders and rulers to heed the word of the Lord. They are again characterized as those who are enemies of justice and right. The additional description identifies them as leaders in Jerusalem, who bring progress to that city through oppression and violence.

Verse 11 highlights and compares the sin of the leaders, priests, and prophets. Their common sin is that they perform their duty not in God's power and for God's glory but rather for their own glory, specifically for money. Their confidence in the Lord is hollow. They trust in God's choice of Jerusalem as his place of special dwelling (that is, in the temple). If God's house is in Jerusalem, how can it be destroyed?

God himself will destroy this proud city. The destruction will be so complete that nothing will be left. Even the temple, which was the pinnacle of the hope that God's presence in Jerusalem would spare it from destruction, will be utterly destroyed and abandoned, so that weeds will overgrow it.

In Jeremiah 26:18–19 we get a unique glimpse of the initial reaction to Micah's oracle.

The word of judgment came to Hezekiah, and it reduced him to repentance, so that the "Lord relented." Jeremiah makes the same argument in chapter 26 (see also Jeremiah 7), that the leaders presume the Lord's presence in the city. However, Jehoiakim, the reigning king, does not respond in the same positive way as Hezekiah.

B. God's word of hope to Israel (4:1–5:15).
4:1–13. Another abrupt transition from threat to promise takes place between the end of the third chapter and the beginning of the fourth. An oracle of severe judgment (3:9–12) is followed by a contrastingly glorious picture of salvation.

Micah looks beyond the immediate future of Zion's punishment (as described in the preceding oracles) to the more distant future, in which Zion will be exalted (4:1–5). Isaiah (2:2) and Micah both speak of the day when Zion will be raised above all other mountains in preeminence. Zion's greatness has nothing to do with its present physical features (it is a relatively small mountain) but everything to do with God's choice of it as his place of earthly dwelling. When Zion is so exalted, it will be like a magnet for the nations. There will be a constant flow of people going to Jerusalem in order to learn God's law.

As the nations learn God's law and apply it to their lives, the world will be transformed. Warfare will be a thing of the past; nations will engage in constructive activities. Individuals will live out their lives in security and with satisfaction, reminiscent of the high point of security reached during the reign of Solomon (1 Kings 4:25).

The hope is real. It will be fulfilled; God has spoken it. Indeed, the prophecy began to be fulfilled with the building of the second temple. Nevertheless, complete fulfillment awaits the ushering in of the kingdom of God in its fullness (Revelation 21–22). Accordingly, the people of God must make their stand for the Lord in the present. Thus, Micah speaks for the people of God and reaffirms their commitment to trust and obey the Lord, even though the nations follow their own false gods.

The opening phrase "in that day" marks the beginning of a second oracle of hope (4:6–8), reminding the reader once again that Micah is focusing on the future. God will intervene and restore his people whom he has punished. They are weak (lame, exiled, grief stricken) because of God's punishment, but God brings strength out of weakness. The Lord will again establish his kingdom from Jerusalem. Further, the glories Jerusalem once knew in the days of David and Solomon will be known again.

With the next oracle (4:9–10), Micah seems to take a giant step backward. He refers to the future Babylonian exile. This oracle is connected to the preceding one by its reference to Zion and to the next two because each of them begins (in the Hebrew) with the word "now."

Micah begins the oracle with a satirical question—Why do you cry aloud?—addressed to the people. They are crying because they are under attack; they are in pain because the Babylonian army is pressing them and forcing them out of Jerusalem. They will be exiled to Babylon. Micah, however, does not stop there, but goes on to reveal that God will deliver them out of Babylon. Verse 9 also implies that they will lose the king. In Israel the king not only was the focus of the government but also was considered the Lord's anointed.

Many have trouble believing that Micah could speak of the Babylonian exile, which was more than one hundred years after his death, and the restoration, which was even later. God, however, reveals himself in the Bible as sovereign over history and as one who chooses to reveal his will to his prophets.

Once again Micah reverts to the time of distress (4:11–13). Jerusalem is pressed by many nations. Verse 11 may be profitably compared with Psalm 2:2 and Zechariah 14:2, both of which picture the nations gathering to wage war against God's people. God is behind the enemy's action even though they are unaware of it. Verse 12 makes this clear; the prophet reveals that God is in control of the situation and gathers the enemy against his people only so he may devastate the enemy. They are gathered like sheaves on the threshing floor. They will soon feel the hooves of the ox as Israel threshes them with particularly dangerous metallic hooves. Jerusalem will, in brief, wage holy war against their enemies and accordingly devote the spoils to God, who will provide the victory.

5:1–15. The next oracle (5:1–6) is similar to the previous two in that in Hebrew it also begins with the word "now." Further, like the others, this oracle begins by describing a time of distress for Israel from which she will be delivered. This third oracle, however, reverses priorities and concentrates on the positive note of deliverance.

The first line of the oracle is extremely difficult. Some versions translate it as, "Marshal your troops, O city of troops," but it is best to read it, along with many commentators, as, "Now gash yourself, daughter of marauder!" The act of cutting oneself was a well-known expression of mourning in the nations surrounding Israel. Israel, however, was forbidden to engage in this practice (Deut. 14:1); thus the command has a sarcastic tone.

The reason for mourning is clearly given. The Israelites are under siege, and the ruler has been publicly humiliated (slapped with a rod).

At this point, however, the mood of the oracle changes. Israel moves from the low point of humiliation to the high point of deliverance. That the deliverance will come from Bethlehem Ephrathah is a surprise. God uses the small and the weak of the world to accomplish his mighty purposes. Indeed, the choice of Bethlehem has further significance, in that David came from this small village (1 Samuel 16). The connection with David is explicit in the passage when Micah refers to the ancient pedigree of the coming ruler. That pedigree is Davidic, and the roots of the fulfillment predicted in verse 2 may be found in the Davidic covenant (2 Samuel 7).

However, a delay is anticipated in the fulfillment of this great hope. This is expressed in the metaphor of verse 3: the one in labor (a symbol of the distress of the siege) must give birth first (the distress must first end). At that point the promised deliverer from Bethlehem will come and establish a kingdom of peace. He will shepherd his people. Kings were frequently titled "shepherd" in the ancient Near East. This metaphor points to the king, the one who guides and protects his people. The king predicted in these verses will excel at his job. In fact, he will be their peace.

The connection of the next two verses to this oracle is not certain. It may be a separate oracle. However, it does continue the theme

| Area around the modern city of Bethlehem |

of the security of Israel in the face of her enemies. In these two verses an Assyrian invasion is anticipated and calmly considered. The defense will be sufficient ("seven, even eight" signifies that there will be more than enough). Assyria here may stand for any potential enemy of Israel.

Of course, readers of the New Testament are aware that these verses find their fulfillment in the coming of Jesus Christ, who comes out of Bethlehem (Matt. 2:6). He is the one "whose origins are from of old, from ancient times" (Mic. 5:2). He is the son of David (Rom. 1:3), our peace (Eph. 2:14).

At this time Israel is being mocked by surrounding nations. In the future, Israel will dominate them (5:7–9). God is the one who will reverse the situation.

Micah expresses this thought through two metaphors. The second one is clear (5:8). The remnant of Israel will be like a lion among the nations. The lion symbolized powerful and ruthless nations who were capable of devastating others. The first metaphor (5:7) is less clear. Often in the Old Testament, dew and showers signify blessing. Indeed, some scholars (e.g., Waltke, 317–18) take the image in a positive direction; Israel will be like dew bringing refreshment to the nations. However, this interpretation does not fit well with the parallel lion image. It is better to understand dew as a curse. In any case, verse 9 makes it clear that the hope in this oracle focuses on future military victory over present enemies.

The last oracle of the second section (5:10–15) begins with the formula "in that day," which again indicates that the prophet is looking into the future. God pronounces a series of purifying actions that he will bring against Israel. While it is true that the oracle never mentions Israel by name but rather addresses the object of the speech as "you," it is clear from the context that Israel is meant.

God informs Israel that he is going to remove the sources of wickedness and temptation from her midst. Specifically, he is going to abolish those objects that lead Israel to trust things other than him.

First, God will destroy the confidence Israel places in her military might. He will do this by removing horses, chariots, and fortified cities from the land. God has promised to protect obedient Israel from hostile attack and has proved through his numerous saving actions (the exodus is the most dramatic) that he can do so. Nevertheless, Israel constantly doubts his ability. She prefers to trust in military technology.

Second, God will destroy those objects by which Israel tries to manipulate the divine. These include magic and idolatry. Sorcery is a method for forcing God or gods to perform an act or reveal a message. Idolatry elevates a part of creation to the level of the Creator (Rom. 1:22–23). The Asherah pole (5:14) is a symbol of life and fertility associated with the worship of the goddess Asherah. These objects were prohibited, and their removal was demanded in the law of Moses (Exod. 34:13; Deut. 7:5; 12:3; 16:21).

The last verse shifts attention to the nations and presupposes that Israel has been purified. At the end time, God's judging action will turn against the nations. This is a note of hope concerning Israel's future.

2. Second Round of Judgment and Salvation (6:1–7:20)

A. God's dispute with Israel (6:1–8). God's dispute with Israel takes the form of a legal proceeding. It is as if God, calling on creation to serve as witness to his complaint against his people, has taken Israel to court. The background of this section is found in the covenant God established with his people. The covenant was like a treaty between God as king and Israel as his people. Before witnesses, the people responded to God's gracious acts of deliverance by receiving God's law and promising to obey it (Exodus 19–24). Now that the people have broken the law repeatedly, God calls on the witnesses of the covenant to attest to the people's wickedness.

Israel is called to account for her actions toward God. She has turned against him. Why? Not only has he done nothing against Israel; he has also done marvelous acts of salvation on her behalf. Specifically, God reminds the people of the exodus, Balaam's divinely inspired blessing when he was paid to curse Israel (Numbers 22–24), and his bringing Israel into the promised land by a miraculous crossing of the Jordan.

This leads to God's instruction to Israel concerning what response he desires from them. How will the Israelites make their relationship with God right again? Micah contrasts external religious acts (sacrifices) with inward religious attitudes (justice, mercy, humility). These verses have been distorted to say that Micah and the prophets in general detested the priestly sacrificial system. Most scholars now admit that Micah was not attacking the sacrificial system itself but the conviction that external religious acts without inward piety can establish a right relationship with God.

B. God's reproach for Israel's social sins (6:9–16). God once again pronounces judgment on his people. Micah calls the people's attention to the Lord ("Listen!" [6:9]). He adds a parenthetical comment directed to God that sounds familiar to those who know the book of Proverbs: to fear God's name is wisdom (Prov. 1:7; 9:10). As the people will soon learn, the opposite holds true as well; to treat God wrongly or indifferently is foolish and extremely dangerous.

God then addresses the people of the city (most likely Jerusalem) and forcefully informs them that he is well aware of their sins, specifically social oppression. They cheat and lie in order to prosper in business. They grow rich at the expense of others.

God will not permit this state of affairs to continue, so he will punish them. The punishment, once again, focuses on the nature of their sin. They cheated (by fraudulent business practices; compare Prov. 11:1; 16:11; 20:23; see also Lev. 19:35, 36; Deut. 25:13–16; Ezek. 45:10) in order to get rich and live a comfortable life. The Lord tells them, however, that they will be anything but comfortable. The Lord had blessed Israel with much material prosperity while they were faithful to him. At the time of the conquest, God told them that they would have cities, houses, vineyards, and olive groves

Remains of Ahab's palace in Samaria. Micah prophecies the downfall of those who follow "all the practices of Ahab's house" (6:16).

that they did not build or plant (Deut. 6:10–12). Now that they are disobedient, however, God tells them that no matter how much work they do, they will have no material prosperity.

The last verse of this section summarizes both the reason for punishment and the nature of that punishment. Israel has sinned by following Omri and Ahab. These kings were known for their importation of the worship of Baal into the northern kingdom. Furthermore, Ahab was renowned for his own evil business practices. Since they go in the way of Ahab rather than in the way of justice, mercy, and humility, they will be destroyed.

C. The prophet laments Israel's condition (7:1–7). Micah continues with a lament. He mourns the spiritual condition of his people. This section may be profitably compared with the many laments found in the book of Psalms. Two general types of laments are encountered in the Scriptures, individual and corporate. Though the latter are occasionally written in the first-person singular, the lament found in Micah 7 is best taken as an example of an individual lament, that is, as the prophet Micah's mournful cry.

Micah paints a dark picture of contemporary society. No one is left who desires to follow God. The only thing the people do well is evil. Micah is exceedingly distressed and likens his own reaction to that of a man who craves grapes and figs but arrives too late in the field to get any. In short, he is bitterly disappointed and frustrated. Even the most promising of his contemporaries are quite bad.

The sins of the people have caught up with them. Society has turned against itself; the situation has degenerated into chaos. Even the closest human relationships (wife, child, parents) are unreliable.

Micah realizes that hope is not to be found in human relationships. Hope may be found only in God, and Micah is confident in his God.

D. Psalms of hope and praise (7:8–20). The prophecy of Micah concludes with four sections (7:8–10, 11–15, 16–17, 18–20) united by their psalmlike style and their forward look to the time of restoration.

Micah continues to speak in the first-person singular, but now he stands for the whole nation. He envisions the time when Israel will be downtrodden and taunted by her enemies. He warns these nations not to rejoice too much, since God will deliver his people from their distress. The prophet proclaims that, though now the people of God are laid low, the Lord will bring salvation in the future.

This transformation of the Lord's attitude toward his people will come about due to the people's acknowledgment of their sin. When God reverses the fortunes of his people, he will lift them up and the taunting nations will become the object of judgment.

The prophet then addresses the people of Israel directly and informs them that the day of restoration will come. That future day will be a day in which the wall (probably of Jerusalem) will be restored. Such an allusion anticipates the future work of Nehemiah. People will then flock to Zion from such far-flung and normally hostile locations as Assyria and Egypt. The context does not make it clear whether the reference is to the return of exiled Israelites to the land or the conversion of foreign peoples. In any case, Israel's blessing once again coincides with the downfall of the rest of the world.

Micah addresses his next words to the Lord and presents the needs of the people before him. He asks God to once again shepherd the people. The shepherd metaphor emphasizes God's guidance and care of his people (see Psalm 23). The Lord will once again restore his love to his people and deliver them as in the days of old. For a third time the nations are mentioned as the objects of God's future punishment.

The prophecy concludes with a hymn that meditates on God's forgiveness and faithfulness to his people. The opening question, "Who is a God like you?" is a wordplay on the name Micah (in Hebrew Micah means "Who is like Yahweh?"). Micah is stirred to speak of God's incomparable forgiveness. He removes Israel's sin and throws it away. He does this because he is faithful to the covenant relationship, which he established with Abraham.

Select Bibliography

Allen, Leslie C. *The Books of Joel, Obadiah, Jonah, and Micah.* New International Commentary on the Old Testament. Grand Rapids: Eerdmans, 1976.

Andersen, Francis I., and David Noel Freedman. *Micah.* Anchor Bible. Garden City, NY: Doubleday, 2000.

Hill, Andrew. "Micah." In *Cornerstone Biblical Commentary.* Edited by Philip W. Comfort. Vol. 10. Wheaton: Tyndale, 2008.

Mays, James Luther. *Micah.* Philadelphia: Westminster, 1976.

Smith, Gary V. *Hosea, Amos, Micah.* NIV Application Commentary. Grand Rapids: Zondervan, 2001.

Smith, Ralph L. *Micah–Malachi.* Word Biblical Commentary. Waco: Word, 1984.

Waltke, Bruce K. *A Commentary on Micah.* Grand Rapids: Eerdmans, 2006.

Nahum

HERMANN J. AUSTEL

Introduction

Nahum the Prophet

The opening verse of the book of Nahum identifies the author as Nahum the Elkoshite. Apart from this, nothing certain is known of him. Suggestions as to his birthplace are largely conjectural and include Elkosi in Galilee, Al Qosh in Iraq, Capernaum ("Village of Nahum"), and Elcesei, a Judean village.

Structure

The three chapters can be divided into two parts. Chapter 1 describes the majesty and righteousness of God in his dealings with mankind, his kindness toward those who trust him, and his wrath toward those who reject him. Though Judah and Nineveh are clearly in view, the language is universally applicable. Chapters 2 and 3 describe the destruction of Nineveh and give the reasons for this.

Date

The book can be dated somewhere between 663 and 612 BC. According to 3:8 it was written after the destruction of Thebes (No Amon [NKJV; cf. NASB]), which was destroyed in 663 by Ashurbanipal. The other limit is 612, the year of the fall of Nineveh. There is no objective evidence that the book is not what it claims to be: an oracle announcing the coming destruction of Nineveh.

Theological Themes

Nahum forms a natural sequel to the book of Jonah in that it reveals the alternative to the grace of God. In the book of Jonah, Nineveh experiences the forgiving grace of God about 150 years before the cataclysmic destruction depicted so graphically by Nahum. In his resentment toward God's pardoning of Nineveh, Jonah (4:2) quotes Exodus 34:6, one of the basic texts of the Old Testament and one frequently quoted or alluded to by Old Testament writers. It is a grand pronouncement by the Lord himself that he is a gracious and merciful and forgiving God. It is for this very reason that Jonah initially refuses to preach to Nineveh, because he understands very well that this pronouncement, seen in its context, is an assurance of forgiveness to all who would repent of their sins, and he has no desire to see Nineveh spared. The sparing of the Ninevites is an outstanding example of the extent of God's forgiving love.

Nahum, writing possibly 100 to 125 years after Jonah, at the high point of the power and arrogance of Nineveh, vividly sets forth the calamitous downfall of a later, unrepentant generation. Nahum 1:3 quotes a portion of Exodus 34:6 ("slow to anger") and of Exodus 34:7 ("will not leave the guilty unpunished"). The point is clearly and unmistakably made that, though God is slow to anger, punishment is certain and sure for unrepentant sinners.

In a very real sense, then, Jonah and Nahum vividly illustrate the "kindness and sternness of God" (Rom. 11:22). He extends his grace freely to repentant sinners, but judgment is certain and final for those who continue in sin and rebellion.

Another prominent theme is that of comfort. The very name of the prophet indicates this (Nahum means "comfort"). This theme is carried out in two ways:

1. In a number of specific statements (1:7, 12–13, 15; 2:2) Nahum declares that God is a refuge for those who trust him, that he will remove the yoke and shackles of bondage from Judah, that Judah will again rejoice in true peace and security, and that her splendor will be restored. These statements are gems that shine brightly in the midst of the graphic portrayal of Nineveh's sin and downfall.

2. The fact that God judges Nineveh with such finality and so irrevocably cannot but be an unspeakably great relief for those who for years have lived under the dread domination of the cruel and vindictive Assyrians. It is no great wonder that Jonah resents the sparing of Nineveh. Yet, though Jonah is not able to see the whole picture, Nahum shows us how carefully and accurately God keeps his books and how surely and with what finality he closes the account in his own time and way. Nineveh lies a desolate and unmourned ruin with no future, while Judah will prosper again.

The downfall of Assyria is a demonstration of the principle that God's enemies, no matter how powerful, will in God's own time fall. This principle is clearly stated in chapter 1, and the fact that God passes sentence on an unnamed enemy (though Nineveh is certainly in view) makes it easy to see Nineveh as an example of what will happen to all evil kingdoms. It would seem that chapter 1 is deliberately general for this very reason. While God is indeed slow to anger, he is not lacking in either power or resolve (1:2–3), and he will surely bring judgment on the sinner. Chapters 2 and 3, then, graphically portray the carrying out of God's judgment.

That Assyria should fall was an incredible thought in Nahum's time, yet God carried out his promise to the letter.

Outline

1. The Zeal and Power of God (1:1–2:2)
   A. The Principle Underlying Divine Judgment (1:1–6)
   B. Destruction and Deliverance Contrasted (1:7–2:2)
2. The Siege and Destruction of Nineveh (2:3–13)
3. The Cause and Certainty of Nineveh's Downfall (3:1–19)

Commentary

1. The Zeal and Power of God (1:1–2:2)

A. The principle underlying divine judgment (1:1–6). The prophecy of Nahum is described as an oracle or "burden" (1:1 ASV, KJV). This word is regularly used of statements of a threatening nature. The fact that this prophecy is also designated as a vision points out that it is an official message from God, not spite on Nahum's part.

Though God has seemingly been overlooking Assyria's sins against him and Israel, this is not due to either weakness or lack of zeal on God's part (1:2–3a). The Hebrew word for "jealous" also means "zealous." God does not treat sin lightly; zeal is an essential part of his character. Not only is he holy, but he zealously carries out the requirements of this holiness. His zeal will neither allow his people to sin with impunity nor allow Gentiles to sin against his people or his purpose with impunity. Unrepentant Nineveh will be punished, and Israel will be saved. As an avenging God, he deals with injustice. Vengeance in the Old Testament is a juridical term involving the righting of wrongs that have been done. Earlier, Nineveh experienced God's grace because they had repented. Now they will experience his vengeance. The outpouring of God's wrath has been delayed, not because he does not care or because he was helpless to act, but because he is patient and slow to anger. The fact that Nineveh is not specifically mentioned in chapter 1, yet seems clearly to be in view, indicates that she serves as an example of the way God deals with his enemies in general. He will not leave the guilty unpunished. This is quoted from Exodus 34:7 and forms the necessary counterpoint to God's grace as described in Exodus 34:6. The nation or individual who rejects God's forgiving grace will of necessity experience the outpouring of his wrath. God will have the last word. A Jonah may be impatient with God for sparing a Nineveh for a time, but God's people may rest confidently in his determination and power to deal with sinners in his own time and way.

The awesome and irresistible power of God is displayed in nature (1:3b–6). If the most powerful forces of nature are at God's disposal to be used as his instrument of judgment, and if no area of creation is immune to the fierceness of God's wrath, how will any person or kingdom be able to withstand God's judgment? It must be carefully noted here, however, that judgment is not the only purpose of the manifestations of God in nature. Similar language is frequently employed to describe God's historical acts of redemptive activity, in which judgment on the enemy may be involved, or simply the removal of obstacles to that redemption (cf. Ps. 18:7–19; 106:9; Isa. 50:2). The same is true of future events, both near and eschatological. All of nature is at God's command. He uses the whirlwind and the storm to accomplish his purpose of judgment. He dries up the sea and makes rivers run dry if need be to remove them as obstacles to the deliverance of his people. Bashan, Carmel, and Lebanon were all noted for their fertility, the mighty oaks of Bashan and the beautiful cedars of Lebanon being proverbial expressions thereof. But when God chooses to pour out his wrath, even the most fertile and productive lands wither and fade. Even the solidity and the mass of the mountains and hills cannot stand before the power of God

when he chooses to act. How much less can humans, who are themselves subject to the forces of nature and who build their kingdoms on shaky ground, hope to withstand the searing blast of the judgment of God! The fact that mountains in the ancient Near Eastern world symbolized kingdoms allows the thought to move very naturally from quaking mountains to tottering kingdoms (1:5–14).

B. Destruction and deliverance contrasted (1:7–2:2). The Lord is good (1:7–8). This all-encompassing statement is one of the most frequently reiterated declarations about the character of God in the Old Testament. It stands in stark contrast to the fate awaiting God's enemies. To his own, God is goodness personified. Every need is met in him. He is the source of every blessing and benefit, from forgiveness for sin to abundant grace for daily needs, no matter how great the difficulty, to ultimate victory. In this context the goodness of God is specifically seen in terms of his being a refuge in times of trouble. God is the ultimate stronghold, the place of safety. When he sets out to judge, there is no place of safety or refuge for the sinner, but for those who trust in him there is peace and security. (Psalm 46 is especially appropriate in this context.) To trust in anything or anyone else can only bring bitter disappointment and loss. The NIV's "he cares for" (literally "knows" in Ps. 1:6) attempts to express that special concern God has for his own. For God's enemy there is only the prospect of sudden and overwhelming defeat described in terms of an overwhelming flood.

Though according to historical sources there was physical flooding of Nineveh at the time of its downfall, the force of the expression is to describe an overwhelming, crushing defeat as a huge wall of water wipes away all that lies before it. As if that sweeping defeat were not enough, God is said to pursue his foes into darkness. There is no possible escape. There is no place of refuge, no possibility of being overlooked. In the case of Nineveh, a few managed to escape when the city fell. They fled to Harran, but they were pursued there and were defeated in 609 BC, leaving no trace of the once mighty empire.

The downfall of Nineveh is a pointer to the future, serving as an example of the destruction that awaits the enemies of God and his people. This is indicated by the statement in 2:2 that Judah and Israel will have their splendor restored. This did not happen at the fall of Nineveh, but will happen in the day of the Lord after the enemies of God have been judged (cf. Zeph. 1:14–18; 3:8–20). The principle of Nahum 1:8 has been true throughout the ages; in Nahum's time it was relative to the destruction of Nineveh as the principal threat to Judah, and in the end times it will be applied to the final enemies of God.

The futility of opposing God is here vividly set forth (1:9–2:2; cf. Isa. 8:9–10). However grand and well-conceived the plans of Nineveh and other world powers might be, they are doomed to utter failure. As with the "little horn" in Daniel 7, there may be initial success, but the outcome is sure. The opponents of God will be so thoroughly routed that they and the trouble they bring to the saints of God will not be able to rise again. Verse 10 is a notoriously difficult verse, but it is clear that it also describes the futility of opposing God. His foes will be as ineffective as one who is caught in a thornbush, as futile as one who staggers in his drunkenness. Finally, they will be consumed as though they were overly dry stubble.

Though Nineveh is not specifically mentioned in verse 11, she is clearly in view. The

The destruction of Nineveh in 612 BC is recorded in this Babylonian cuneiform tablet chronicling the years 615–609 BC.

one plotting evil may be Sennacherib (2 Kings 18–19), or this may be a collective reference to the evil kings of Nineveh. In any case, Nineveh is seen as a center of evil and rebellion against God and as such stands in the line of world powers energized by Satan, culminating in the reign of the antichrist.

Verses 12–13 are addressed to Judah in the form of assurance that Nineveh's yoke will be removed. These verses look beyond the temporary relief brought about by Nineveh's downfall to the final eschatological deliverance of the Messiah. Verse 14 addresses Nineveh and announces its utter destruction. It is a historical fact that after the fall of Nineveh, no trace was left of the power and influence of the mighty kingdom. It was as though Nineveh had never existed. Though Nineveh's kings assumed that their kingdom would stand indefinitely because of the protection of their idols, God buries Nineveh with the words, "You are vile" (1:14).

Verse 15, addressed to Judah, declares the delight with which God's messenger will be received when he comes with the joyful news that God has redeemed his people. The enemy has fallen, and God alone reigns. The victory celebration gives the glory to God, who alone is worthy of praise.

Nahum 2:1–2 marks a transition and is the third in the series of contrasts in God's dealings with Nineveh and Judah. Verse 1 begins the description of the fall of Nineveh that is taken up again in verse 3 and then developed in the rest of the book. Verse 2 concludes the promises of the benefits that Israel will enjoy as a result of the defeat of her enemies. The result of the attack on Nineveh will be a scattering to the winds of her inhabitants (cf. Nah. 3:18). The words "Guard the fortress" (2:1) are likely words of irony uttered by God in order to emphasize the futility of any kind of defense, no matter how strong. Both the destruction of Nineveh and the restoration of Israel (2:2) are sure.

One can understand the reference to Israel only as referring to all twelve tribes. In Nahum's time this seemed very unlikely; the northern kingdom had already been scattered throughout the Assyrian Empire for more than sixty years. But now it is Nineveh's turn to be scattered and Israel's turn to be exalted.

If the question is raised as to the fulfillment of this prophecy, it may be suggested that this is an example of what is sometimes called "telescoping," in which the ultimate fulfillment is anticipated by one or more anticipatory fulfillments. The fall of Nineveh brought relief to Judah from the Assyrian threat (partial fulfillment), yet within seven years Judah fell under Babylonian domination and within twenty-six years Jerusalem was destroyed along with the temple. Then, about eighty years later, when Babylon had been defeated, Judah was restored to the land (but still under foreign domination). Yet the ultimate fulfillment is still to come, involving all Israel, not just Judah, and seeing the full establishment of glory in Israel, both material and spiritual. "Jacob" and "Israel" no doubt refer to the contrast between a self-seeking, conniving Jacob, a homeless wanderer desperate for God's help when he came to Peniel (Genesis 32), and Israel, the man that God intended Jacob should become, one who would receive God's blessing, not by self-effort, but by trusting God and on God's terms. So will the nation experience the fullness of God's promise.

2. The Siege and Destruction of Nineveh (2:3–13)

Nineveh has lived and prospered by the sword. It is now about to die by the sword. Nineveh is to be on the receiving end of the violence she has so freely meted out over the years (2:3–6). The assault on Nineveh is relentless, swift, fierce, and irresistible. Verse 3 describes the dread-inspiring appearance of the invader. The soldiers' shields are red, either stained with the blood of the battle or dyed red. This, along with the scarlet dress of warriors, when taken with Ezekiel 23:14, seems to indicate that red was a characteristic color of Babylonian armies at the time. The Medes, according to Xenophon, had a similar custom.

Verse 5 depicts the speed and the fury of the assault. There is no stopping the onrushing chariots. "The streets" and "the squares" (2:4) refer to the area outside the strongly fortified central city. The outer defenses have already been breached, and the assault on the inner city is now imminent. The subject of verse 5 is difficult to identify with certainty. Some see this as a reference to the commander in Nineveh in his last desperate measures to shore up the defenses of the city. "Yet they stumble on their way" is taken, by this view, as pointing to the ineffectual efforts of the defenders to prepare for the final onslaught. An alternative, and probably more satisfactory, view is to see this as referring to the actions of the attackers. Nahum 3:3 explains the stumbling: the corpses of the defenders are so numerous that the attackers stumble over them in their rapid forward progress as they dash to the city wall. The protective shield, or mantelet (2:5), is a shield put up for the protection of the attackers. The river gates are sluice gates used to control the flow of the Tebiltu and Khosr rivers to and through Nineveh. Apparently the gates were first shut to cut off drinking water; then when the reservoirs were full, they were opened so that the onrushing waters undermined part of the wall and even the palace, making it easier for the attackers to rout the defenders. Ancient tradition is in general accord with this. In light of this verse, 1:8 might well be a double entendre.

The city is emptied both of its inhabitants, by capture and by flight, and of its material wealth (2:7–10). God decrees that Nineveh will be plundered and destroyed. Verse 7 describes the captivity and grief of the inhabitants, verse 8 the precipitous flight of the defenders. The human suffering described here is an echo of the terrible suffering formerly inflicted on others by the conquering Assyrian armies. Nineveh has been a pool or reservoir, collecting people and wealth. Now the flow is reversed, and there is no stopping the rushing outflow. The pungency of expression and the terseness of this passage graphically capture the drastic, unexpected, and rapid turn of events. That the supply of plunder is endless is echoed in the description of the sack of Nineveh in the Babylonian Chronicle: the spoil that was taken was a quantity beyond counting (2:9).

Nineveh, similar to a lion's den, has been a place of security for its people as well as a repository filled with the plunder of conquered nations (2:11–13). Assyria has victimized other nations as a lion preying on helpless animals. Now Nineveh is itself to be destroyed and robbed of people and wealth. At the climax of this section comes the awful and unalterable declaration of the Lord of Hosts: "I am against you." This expression is found twenty-eight times in the Old Testament and is used when God is set to act against a people that has steadfastly refused to submit to him. No matter how powerful or numerous or wise the nation, no matter what precautions are taken, these words spell certain doom. But for those who trust God and seek refuge in him, the words of 1:7 apply: "The LORD is good, a refuge in times of trouble. He cares for those who trust in him." The voices of messengers, with their haughty and arrogant demands of submission and tribute, with their taunts and reproaches against God (cf. 2 Kings 18:28–35;

This Assyrian relief from the palace of Sennach-erib in Nineveh shows scribes recording the spoils of war being collected by Assyrian soldiers (640–620 BC). As Nahum prophesies, now it is Nineveh's turn to be plundered.

39:1–13), will never again be heard. God has the last word.

3. The Cause and Certainty of Nineveh's Downfall (3:1–19)

Nahum 3:1–7, with its terse, powerful phrases, depicts Nineveh in a typical battle, overwhelming yet another hapless victim. The woe is here a divine denunciation and pronouncement of judgment (3:1–4). Verse 1 masterfully depicts both the character of Nineveh and the source of its prosperity and greatness. It was built on bloodshed and deceit and can maintain itself and continue to grow only by ruthlessly devouring other cities and kingdoms. Its appetite for blood and plunder is insatiable. Nineveh was a great and powerful city, proud of its achievements. But now God gives his assessment.

The graphic, staccato phrases of verses 1–3 evoke the image of a ruthless, grinding military machine. Nineveh's means of empire building by the brutal subjugation and plundering of other cities is likened to the rapaciousness and greed of a harlot. Cruel, yet seductive, Assyria enslaved other nations, gaining permanent advantage for herself by offering temporary benefits to others. Many understand verses 2–3 as another description of the downfall of Nineveh in the form of an aside, yet it seems best to understand this passage as referring primarily to Nineveh's past conquests. The repetition of the words "I am against you" from 2:13 is important. Not only does it emphasize the implacability of God's purpose to destroy Nineveh, but it serves a structural purpose as well: in 2:13 the words relate to Nineveh as a predatory lion (2:11–13); in 3:5, they relate to the never-ending demands of the harlot Nineveh for more spoils of war. Secondarily, this passage serves the purpose of noting that Nineveh is now going to receive the same treatment she administered to others (cf. 2:3–10).

The further result of God's judgment (3:5–7) is that Nineveh will be exposed to public disgrace, just as in the case of the judicial exposure of the nakedness of a harlot (Ezek. 16:37–42;

Hos. 2:3; Mic. 1:11). Nineveh is no longer the proud queen of harlots (see a similar description of eschatological Babylon in Rev. 17:3–6), holding the lives and destinies of nations in her capricious hands. Now she has been made a public object of scorn and contempt. There will be no sorrow at Nineveh's passing, only rejoicing.

The remainder of the chapter is given over to the certainty of Nineveh's destruction. Thebes (Hebrew *no amon*, "City of the God Amon"), situated about 140 miles north of modern Aswan, was one of the greatest cities of the ancient world. It was often called simply "The City," and some of its remains can be seen in the impressive temple ruins of Luxor and Karnak and the funeral monuments of the kings on the other side of the Nile. The rhetorical question "Are you better than Thebes?" (3:8) has to do with strategic location rather than moral superiority. Ashurbanipal defeated Thebes in 663 and dealt with it in typically cruel Assyrian fashion, pillaging it and razing it to the ground, killing numerous inhabitants and enslaving others. This defeat of Thebes came about despite its favorable location, numerous allies, and strong defenses. Just as the seemingly impossible happened to Thebes, so it will be with Nineveh (3:8–11). It may be that the words "You too will become drunk" (3:11) refer to the drunken condition of many of the defenders of Nineveh, as described by some ancient Greek historians. But the expression is more likely used figuratively, as is often the case in Scripture. As such it describes Nineveh's helplessness in the face of the attackers in terms of the reeling, tottering, and ineffectiveness associated with drunkenness. She will seek refuge, but there will be no place to go, no help.

Nineveh will be a choice object of plunder, easy to take, ripe for the plucking (3:12–17). There may be a subtle allusion as well to the fact that the time has come for Nineveh to be judged. Fruit or grain being ripe for the harvest is frequently used metaphorically in Scripture as pertaining to readiness for judgment (e.g.,

Jer. 51:33; Joel 3:13). The weakness of Nineveh is depicted in terms of its defenders and fortifications. The formerly fierce and indomitable soldiers are all women. This reflects the standard Near Eastern expression of the loss of stalwart manliness due to loss of morale (cf. Isa. 19:16; Jer. 50:37; 51:30). Because of the collapse of the defenders' courage, the gates of the land are wide open. The outer defenses, including fortified cities guarding the way to Nineveh, will fall before the enemy, leaving Nineveh isolated and without protection. An ample water supply was important in preparation for a protracted siege. Though Sennacherib had made extensive provisions to ensure abundant water, special precautions were necessary to counteract the enemy's cutting off of the water supply to the city. Since stones were scarce in Mesopotamia, clay bricks were used for fortifications. During siege conditions extensive repairs would be necessary to fix breaches in the walls. The ravages of fire and sword are compared to the terrible impact of a plague of grasshoppers (or locusts) on a field. Assyria had a long history of the establishment of trading stations. But they are represented here as being not only as numerous as locusts but as harmful to the land, plundering then leaving without making any truly helpful contribution. The guards and officials of Nineveh are also compared to locusts: numerous for a short time, but then suddenly gone.

Nineveh fell in 612 BC. Though Ashuruballit II and his followers established a new capital at Harran, Assyria was already dead, the last remnant of the kingdom disappearing in 609, when Babylon forced the last holdouts to flee Harran.

Nahum closes with an epitaph for the king of Assyria (3:18–19). "Shepherd" is a common Old Testament and ancient Near Eastern designation for rulers. With the demise of rulers and nobles, Nineveh's people will be scattered on the mountains without a trace throughout the nations, without a hope of any healing, without a chance of recovering. Its passing will go unmourned. On the contrary, there will be great rejoicing by those who have felt the lash of Nineveh's endless cruelty.

The destruction of Nineveh was a major milestone in human history. With all the power and influence that Assyria wielded in its own time, nothing remained after its fall but a bad memory. Therefore, it serves well as an example of the lack of a future for the kingdoms of this world. By contrast, though God's people have been scattered, there is indeed a bright future as God raises up a Shepherd and gathers them to himself.

Select Bibliography

Baker, David. *Nahum, Habakkuk, Zephaniah.* Tyndale Old Testament Commentaries. Downers Grove, IL: InterVarsity, 1988.

Barker, Kenneth L., and Waylon Bailey. *Nahum, Habakkuk, Zephaniah.* New American Commentary. Nashville: Broadman & Holman, 1998.

Bennett, T. Miles. *The Books of Nahum and Zephaniah.* Grand Rapids: Baker, 1969.

Bruckner, James K. *Jonah, Nahum, Habakkuk, Zephaniah.* NIV Application Commentary. Grand Rapids: Zondervan, 2004.

Keil, C. F. *The Twelve Minor Prophets.* 2 vols. Biblical Commentary on the Old Testament. Grand Rapids: Eerdmans, 1949.

Kohlenberger, John R., III. *Jonah–Nahum.* Chicago: Moody, 1984.

Laetsch, Theodore. *The Minor Prophets.* St. Louis: Concordia, 1956.

Longman, Tremper, III. "Nahum." In *The Minor Prophets: An Exegetical and Expository Commentary.* Edited by Thomas Edward McComiskey. Grand Rapids: Baker Academic, 1992.

Maier, Walter Arthur. *The Book of Nahum.* Grand Rapids: Baker Books, 1959.

Orelli, C. von. *The Twelve Minor Prophets.* Reprint. Minneapolis: Klock & Klock, 1977.

Patterson, Richard D. *Nahum, Habakkuk, Zephaniah.* Chicago: Moody, 1991.

Smith, J. M. P., et al. *Micah, Zephaniah, Nahum, Obadiah and Joel.* International Critical Commentary. Edinburgh: T. & T. Clark, 1911.

Smith, Ralph L. *Micah–Malachi.* Word Biblical Commentary. Waco: Word, 1984.

Habakkuk

R. D. Patterson

Introduction

Habakkuk the Prophet

Scholars largely agree that this prophecy was written by the man whose name serves as the title of the book—the prophet Habakkuk. Very little is known about Habakkuk except that he plainly calls himself a prophet (1:1) and presents for his readers an oracle or burden that the Lord has given him. The name Habakkuk has been associated either with a Hebrew word meaning "embrace" or with an Assyrian plant name *hambaququ*. Accordingly, some Bible scholars have suggested that Habakkuk was the son of the Shunammite woman to whom Elisha gave the promise, "You will hold [embrace] a son" (2 Kings 4:16). Others, following the second etymology of the name, reason that Habakkuk must have lived and been educated in Nineveh before coming to Judah. Still others put forward the idea that he was Isaiah's successor by relating Habakkuk 2:1 with Isaiah 21:6. But none of these suggestions are certain. We do know that he was called of God to proclaim God's word to Judah, which he delivered with fine literary ability, as evidenced in his use of graphic imagery and striking similes. The fact that he uses certain musical terms in chapter 3 and adds a note that the psalm of that chapter is to be sung to the accompaniment of stringed instruments may also point to his having been a Levite (see 1 Chronicles 25).

Date

Evangelical commentators have suggested three different dates for Habakkuk's prophecy. Some suggest the time of Jehoiakim (609–597 BC), so that the conditions against which Habakkuk complains in the first chapter relate largely to the events of the first Neo-Babylonian invasion (ca. 605 BC; see 2 Kings 24:1–4; 2 Chron. 36:5–7). Others maintain that the desperate moral circumstances of chapter 1 reflect conditions that existed in Josiah's time before the copy of the law was found (621 BC). Still others associate the details of Habakkuk's prophecy with the time of Judah's most wicked king, Manasseh (686–643 BC).

The third position is to be preferred, for the following reasons. First, the circumstances that Habakkuk decries reflect the debased spiritual atmosphere of Manasseh's day (see 2 Kings 21:1–16; 2 Chron. 33:1–10), a time that was so evil that God promised he would bring a total "disaster on Jerusalem and Judah" (2 Kings 21:12). Second, the canonical position of Habakkuk between Nahum and Zephaniah, as well as the closeness of theological perspective among the three prophets, would favor the earlier date. Third, it may be that both Zephaniah and Jeremiah knew and utilized Habakkuk's prophecy (cf. 1:8 with Jer. 4:13; 5:6; cf. 2:10 with Jer. 51:58; cf. 2:12 with Jer. 22:13–17; cf. 2:20 with Zeph. 1:7). Finally, because Manasseh was carried into captivity in the latter part of his reign and subsequently repented and initiated several religious reforms, a date shortly before or after the western campaign of Ashurbanipal of Assyria in 652 BC cannot be far from wrong.

The occasion of this prophecy is rooted in Habakkuk's spiritual perplexities about God's seeming indifference to great moral decay and outright spiritual apostasy. Habakkuk agonizes over the immorality, inequities, and inequalities rampant in the society of his day. He cannot reconcile such conditions with the presence of a holy and just God. Therefore, he takes his soul-searching concerns to God himself. His prophecy describes his dialogue with God—his questions and God's assuring replies. God's answers also reveal something as to the nature of his person and work in Israel and with all people, so that this short book contributes greatly to Old Testament theology.

This portion of an Assyrian relief from Nineveh shows King Ashurbanipal in his chariot (ca. 645 BC).

Theological Themes

Theologically, the book of Habakkuk makes it clear that God is not only eternal and glorious but also sovereignly active in guiding all of earth's history to his desired end. God is revealed in his Word as a God of justice and mercy who has provided for the salvation of the faithful and the deliverance of his people, Israel. Experientially, Habakkuk's short prophecy reminds the believer of the possibility of intimate communion with God that can overcome the deepest depression and the darkest seasons of doubt.

Structure

Structurally, the third chapter of Habakkuk's prophecy displays such stunning literary and thematic differences that critical scholars have often assigned it to independent origin. Some scholars even consider 3:16–19 to be a further independent unit.

It is evident that a basic difference in thematic emphasis exists between the first two chapters (Habakkuk's perplexities and God's answers) and chapter 3 (the prophet's prayer and praise). Chapter 3 includes some old epic material (3:3–15) that had been passed down through generations of Israelites since Moses's day. These two portions also evince distinct literary styles, the first two chapters being written in a familiar prophetic style that makes use of oracles, laments, and woes all in classical Hebrew, whereas the epic material of 3:3–15 is written in an older poetic style that contains some very difficult grammatical constructions and rare words. Nevertheless, the unity and single authorship of Habakkuk can be demonstrated from at least three conclusive facts. First, a common theme runs throughout the prophecy, namely, that God sovereignly controls the affairs of history. Second, demonstrable points of internal dependence and relation exist between the various portions, such as Habakkuk's patient waiting on the Lord (2:1–3, 20; 3:2, 16–19), his consistent portrayal of the godless (1:4, 13; 3:13), his reception of the Lord's answer to his perplexities (1:5; 2:2; 3:2, 16), and his confidence that the

Lord will not utterly destroy his people (1:12; 3:1–2, 16–19). Finally, only with the closing verses of the third chapter is there a satisfactory answer to all of the prophet's uncertainties. Accordingly, the prophecy must be viewed as the product of one author, Habakkuk.

Commentary

1. The Prophet's Perplexities and God's Explanations (1:2–2:20)

Habakkuk introduces his prophecy by reporting that the words he will share with his readers are an oracle, which God has placed on his heart. A similar superscription introduces Habakkuk's great prayer and praise in 3:1.

A. First perplexity (1:2–4). Habakkuk cannot understand why God is ignoring the rampant corruption that Habukkuk sees all around him in Judah. He has often cried to God in anguish but has received no answer. Because the call-answer motif is used often in the Old Testament to express intimacy of communion between God and the believer, God's failure to answer the prophet's call may indicate Habakkuk's fear that perhaps he is out of fellowship with God.

The Hebrew words for Judah's sin that Habakkuk uses in verses 2–3 involve the ideas of malicious viciousness, utter wickedness, and perversity. They depict a general condition of oppression, strife, and contention. What little justice there is is perverted. The terrible conditions mentioned here are most applicable to the time of the wicked king Manasseh. According

to 2 Kings 21:1–18 and 2 Chronicles 33:1–20, Manasseh plunged into every sort of Canaanite religious debauchery, including the worship of Baal and Asherah and the establishment of a state astral cult. Even the temple in Jerusalem was desecrated with Canaanite altars and symbols. The king himself not only practiced witchcraft but even involved his own son in the loathsome rites of infant sacrifice. Because Manasseh rejected God's rightful sovereignty over his life, it is small wonder that Judah was filled with violence and immorality. For Judah's law ultimately resided in the revealed teaching of God, whose standards were to permeate every area of the believer's life. Accordingly, justice and righteousness, the twin expressions of God's legal and judicial holiness, were openly perverted.

Manasseh would not accept God's rebuke or instruction. Therefore, God brought judgment on him by allowing him to be carried off captive by the king of Assyria. This event probably is to be associated with the widespread revolts that plagued the reign of Ashurbanipal of Assyria in the mid-seventh century BC. Although 2 Chronicles 33:12–16 reports Manasseh's repentance and subsequent restoration of true worship, it came too late to have any permanent effect on the spiritual tenor of the people of Judah. Indeed, when his son, Amon, succeeded Manasseh, he not only reintroduced all of his father's wickedness but "increased his guilt" (2 Chron. 33:23). Because Zephaniah and Jeremiah appear to have used Habakkuk's prophecy, and because the conditions described here must have occurred before Manasseh's captivity, release, and repentance, Habakkuk probably penned his prophecy about 655–650 BC.

B. First explanation (1:5–11). God's reply to Habakkuk's perplexity is puzzling. He tells Habakkuk that he will punish wicked Judah by using the Babylonians (or Chaldeans). Since the Neo-Babylonian Empire would not be a force to be reckoned with until the latter part of the seventh century BC, such a threat seems totally unbelievable. In fact, although full judgment would not descend on Judah and Jerusalem for more than half a century, Habakkuk is being told that those forces that will spell their doom are already being set in motion. Whether Habakkuk lived to see the rise of the Chaldeans is not known, but Manasseh's summons to Babylon (2 Chron. 33:11) would doubtless serve as a harbinger of Babylon's later dealings with the people of God. The pronoun "your" with the noun "days" is plural and therefore does not indicate specifically Habakkuk's lifetime. The words are to be taken in a general way.

Verses 7–11 contain a description of the coming Babylonian army. God gives a detailed description of Judah's future foe so as to reinforce his dire pronouncement. They will be a formidable and fierce people who will be noted for both their cruelty and their arrogant spirit. Armed with a sizable cavalry, they will move swiftly across the land and with all the cunning of a ferocious wolf that uses the gathering twilight to attack the sheepfold.

The army covers vast distances with the speed of an eagle set for the prey. The image changes in verse 9 to depict the band of despoilers as a desert storm. Just as the east wind carried in its cyclonic winds untold amounts of sand, so the Chaldeans will gather numerous prisoners.

In verse 10 the audacity and rapacity of the coming Babylonian host are underscored. A description is given of the siege methods typically used by armies in the ancient Near East in capturing a fortified city (cf. 2 Sam. 20:15; 2 Kings 19:32; Jer. 32:24; Ezek. 17:17). In verse 11, Habakkuk turns his attention to the Babylonians' unbridled conceit. Elated by their successes, they will throw away all sense of propriety, their reckless pride thereby sowing the seeds of their own destruction.

Thus, God's reply to Habakkuk is one of assurance. He is already dealing with Judah's sin, but the full realization of his activity will come in God's own appointed time and way, however incredible his plan might seem to Habakkuk.

C. Second perplexity (1:12–17). Habakkuk has received God's answer to his questioning remarks. God is right. Habakkuk

Habakkuk 1:8 describes the cavalry of the Babylonians. Members of the Assyrian cavalry are shown in this relief from Nineveh (700–692 BC).

does not fully understand what God has said. He can understand Judah's coming punishment for sin, but he cannot reconcile the holiness of God with God's determination to use such a wicked people as the Babylonians to destroy the people of God. Throughout chapters 1 and 2 there is not only an indication of the prophet's perplexities with reconciling the nature of God and the circumstances of the world but a suggestion of presumption on Habakkuk's part. His own theological system is unable to cope with life's realities, so that rather than waiting patiently for God's purposes to unfold, he actually presumes to instruct God. He has charged God with negligence and indifference (1:2–4); he will now charge God with using evil to overcome evil. In so doing, he reminds God that, as far as Habakkuk can see, a holy God could not carry out such a plan.

In laying out his consternation at God's reply, Habakkuk diplomatically begins with the statement that he is sure Israel's God must do that which is right (1:12). He reaffirms his belief in God, who is the everlasting Lord, the Holy One, Israel's Rock, and his very own God.

Having made the point of his allegiance to God, Habakkuk quietly points out the paradox that a holy God could use such a wicked nation to execute his purposes (1:13–17). Yes, Judah is wicked, but the same can be said to an even greater degree of the people whom God himself has just described. In making his point Habakkuk utilizes some of the same Hebrew words used to describe Judah's sin. Can God not see the danger of using such a treacherous and wicked nation as Babylon?

Habakkuk complains to God that his plan will render Judah and the surrounding nations as helpless as fish and sea creatures, which fishermen catch with hooks, nets, or a dragnet. Unchecked by any foe, these Babylonian "fishermen" will know no god but their own nets. Although some commentators have found allusions to reports of the Scythian practice of sacrificing to a sword or to Alexander the Great's placing of a war machine in a Tyrian temple,

the figure is probably not intended to refer to any literal sacrifice, for such is not known from the practices of the Babylonians. Simply put, the analogy is one of fish (the conquered peoples), fishermen (the Babylonians), and the means of taking the fish (the mighty military forces of the Babylonians). What Habakkuk fears, then, is that the great success of the Neo-Babylonian army will cause them to have such pride that the Babylonians will live recklessly and riotously, believing only in themselves and raw power.

Habakkuk ends his second questioning on a note of lament. He wonders whether such arrogance and ferociousness, once unleashed, will go on mercilessly unchecked by any hand, including that of God. God has asked Habakkuk to "look at the nations" (1:5); having done so and having heard God's solution to his first perplexity, Habakkuk is only more deeply dismayed.

D. Second explanation (2:1–20). Having voiced his protest against God's explanation, Habakkuk assumes the position of a prophetic watchman (cf. Isa. 21:8; Jer. 6:17; Ezek. 3:17; 33:2–3). Habakkuk will wait in earnest anticipation for what God will say in response to his latest complaint (2:1–3). Again the language is figurative. As a watchman stands ready at his post to receive news from afar, so Habakkuk will prepare his soul for God's message to him.

The Lord's reply is not long in coming. As a preliminary instruction, Habakkuk is told to write down God's revelation. Just as men write important messages and information plainly on tablets or inscribe them on stelae so that passersby may read them, so the Lord's prophet is to record God's word for all to read. This is especially important because the fulfillment of the divine revelation will take some time. As the time approaches for its realization, however, it will be like a swift distance runner lunging with bursting lungs for the finish line. The Hebrew word translated here as "speaks" means literally to "blow out," "puff," or "pant." The verb is often used in contexts involving the giving of testimony (e.g., Prov. 6:19; 14:5, 25; 19:5,

9). Regardless of how slowly the fulfillment of God's word seems to move, it will truly come in God's appointed time, and that with sudden finality. Therefore, the words that Habakkuk is to record will bear witness to God's divine government truthfully: they "will not prove false." It is God who has said it! That ought to be enough for the person of faith.

God now discloses a great and hidden purpose in his ordered government (2:4–5). Behind the ebb and flow of earth's activities and the seemingly normal operations of human institutions, God is superintending the issues of the day. In doing so, he allows the two major classes of people, the righteous and the unrighteous, to be clearly distinguished. Despite the fact that God permits unrighteous people to thrive for a period and may even use them to execute his mysterious purposes, nonetheless the arrogance and self-will of the wicked will ultimately carry them to destruction. Habakkuk should see that the Babylonians certainly fit into this category. As is so often the case with the wicked, their success will produce an intellectual giddiness that will only be fed by the wine of their drink. The conquerors of Assyria will thus show themselves to be heedless of that which contributed so heavily to Nineveh's downfall. The Babylonians' riotous lifestyle will bring about an insatiable lust for power and plunder that will be as seemingly unquenchable as the thirst of death and the grave.

In clear distinction from the wicked are the righteous, for unlike the wicked, they are consumed by neither power nor greed nor pride. Rather, "the righteous person will live by his faithfulness" (2:4). The Hebrew noun translated "faithfulness" here is also often rendered as "faith" (see NIV note). It is based on a verbal root that means to "be firm," "be permanent," or "be secure," hence "be faithful." To the Hebrew mind no dichotomy existed between faith and faithfulness. The truly righteous person is the one whose faith is demonstrated in faithful deeds.

Habakkuk 2:4 is cited three times in the New Testament. Paul uses it in Galatians 3:11 to demonstrate that salvation is not achieved by keeping the works of the law but is entered into only on the basis of genuine faith. In Romans 1:17, Paul emphasizes the fact that the believer's salvation, acquired by faith, must also be lived out totally in faith. The writer of Hebrews (10:35–38) points out that the sure coming of Christ for his faithful ones makes living by faith a categorical necessity.

Having made clear the reasons for his patience with humanity over the long course of history, God now tells Habakkuk plainly that, despite the fact that he will allow the Babylonians' natural desires to be satisfied in order to bring Judah to judgment, the Babylonians will nevertheless reap the fruit of their unrighteousness (2:6–20). God presents the self-destruction of the Babylonians in a series of pithy taunt songs in the mouth of those whom they have oppressed. Five woes are pronounced, each consisting of three verses. Prophetic woe oracles were a type of announcement of judgment consisting of three elements: invective (or strong denunciation), threat, and reason(s) for the judgment.

In the first woe (2:6–8) God declares that the Babylonians will be despoiled. As the Babylonians plundered others, they too will be plundered. The long course of their rapacity will one day suddenly turn on them. Their accrued spoil will pile up like a debt they owe and that will surely and suddenly be recalled.

In the second woe (2:9–11) God reports that the Babylonians will be dishonored. Those who build their kingdoms by unjust gain will be brought to shame. Using the riches that the Babylonians had gained from the vast plunder that they had taken, Nebuchadnezzar would build up Babylon to be his own splendid city (cf. Dan. 4:29–30). The once-mighty Babylon would become a heap of ruins whose very stones bewail its former grandeur.

In the third woe (2:12–14) God states that the Babylonians will be devastated. The Babylonians had built their proud city with the blood-bought spoils of other nations. Although they gloated over the treasure hoards that they had gathered to aggrandize their capital, little did they realize that it would all be used eventually for their enemies' siege fires. Worldly-wise Babylon stands as a representative of all nations who serve self rather than God. Surely all those who oppose him, as did Babylon, will one day be destroyed by the Lord at his coming to set up his universal and everlasting kingdom on earth.

In the fourth woe (2:15–17) God announces that the Babylonians will be disgraced. In these verses Babylon is likened to a man who gives his neighbors intoxicating wine in order to make sport of them by denuding them. Babylon has taken many lands and formed many alliances only to despoil its neighbors. All of this will turn back on them; the ones who have caused disgrace will in turn be disgraced. The Babylonians will drink to the full from their own stupefying wine and be exposed to open shame.

All of this is nothing less than the Lord's judgment. For the wine will be found in a "cup from the LORD's right hand" (2:16). The cup is often used as a figure of that which God appoints for humanity, be it a blessing (Ps. 16:5; 23:5; 116:13) or a judgment (Ps. 75:8; Isa. 51:17, 22; Jer. 25:15–17; 49:12; 51:7; Ezek. 23:31–34; Rev. 14:10; 16:19). The right-hand imagery is used in Scripture where distinct emphasis, honor, or definiteness of act is intended. Therefore, Babylon's judgment is both certain and severe. Her vaunted glory will turn to disgrace. The force of the figure here yields a picture of one who is so overcome with drink that in his drunken stupor he lies naked in his own vomit.

Two further charges are laid against proud Babylon: she has greatly deforested Lebanon, whose cedars were prized in the ancient world, and has spilled the blood of man and animal alike in her insatiable thirst for world domination. Surely such violence will be repaid.

In the fifth woe (2:18–20) God proclaims that the Babylonians will be deserted. What little spiritual consciousness the Babylonians had was largely the result of thousands of years of pagan polytheism. They had foolishly followed their idolatrous predecessors in calling god that which was the product of their own hands. Worst of all, in the hour of God's judgment, Babylon will be forsaken by her idols and perish with none to help her. Had Babylon only surrendered to the will of God rather than living for self and taking her endless plunder and numberless captives, how different it all might have been. Now she must learn forcibly the full truth of the next verse.

Verse 20 stands both as a final word to the fifth woe and as a word for all humanity. It is better to pay homage to the one who inhabits the heavens than to trust in gods that are no gods.

Ruins of the ancient city of Babylon

2. The Prophet's Prayer and God's Exaltation (3:1–19)

A. The prophet's prayer (3:1–2). Habakkuk's prayer in this chapter is actually a prayer psalm. The Hebrew word for prayer used here designates five psalms (Psalms 17; 86; 90; 102; 142) and is also used of the collected psalms of David (Ps. 72:20). Habakkuk's prayer psalm is genuinely personal and yet designed for the sacred liturgy, as further indicated by the final footnote at the end of the chapter and the recurring use of the musical term *selah*, probably designating a musical interlude. The phrase "On *shigionoth*" is perhaps best understood as referring to a song that can be set to several tunes.

Habakkuk recalls God's past mighty deeds on Israel's behalf and pleads with God that, as he now brings Judah to judgment, he will nonetheless deal with his people in mercy.

B. The prophet's praise (3:3–15). After laying bare his soul's concerns before God, Habakkuk turns to praise the Lord as the only one who can meet that need. In so doing, he draws on a body of old (and exceedingly difficult) poetic material that had been handed down since the days of Moses. These epic poems told of God's deliverance of his people from Egypt, his preservation of them in their wilderness wanderings, and his triumphant leading of them into the land of promise. Actually, two poems are to be found here, the first describing God's leading of his redeemed people from the southland toward the place where they would cross the Jordan (3:3–7), and the second commemorating the exodus and early incidents within the promised land (3:8–15).

Habakkuk rehearses certain details concerned with the age-old account of God's deliverance of his people out of Egypt, the journey to Mount Sinai, and the movement from Sinai to the Jordan River. Habakkuk's first psalm joins the story at this latter stage. It may be that God gave to Habakkuk a vision of the things that he describes here.

The approach of God from the southland at the head of his people and in company with his heavenly train is detailed first. The two localities mentioned in verse 3 mark the Transjordanian southland. Teman is the name of the southernmost of Edom's two chief cities. The name comes from a grandson of Esau (Gen. 36:11, 15, 42; Jer. 49:7, 20) whose descendants entered into the area. Paran designates not only a mountain range west and south of Edom and northeast of Mount Sinai but also a broad desert area in the Sinai peninsula. The event described here is given in similar words in Deuteronomy 33:1–2 and Judges 5:4, where the term "Seir" is used in parallelism with Mount Paran and Edom, and the importance of Mount Sinai is underscored.

Israel's God comes filling heaven and earth with his radiant glory. Far greater than the brilliance of the rising sun or the glaring blaze of the sun at midday is the glory of the omnipotent God. This theophany of God's awesome majesty was also accompanied by a manifestation of his power in plague and pestilence. It may be that these effects of God's coming are here personified as though they are part of his heavenly army. However glorious God's coming for his people might have been, it was horrible for his enemies.

The first poem closes with a further discussion of the effects of God's powerful activity. A violent shaking convulsed the earth so that the mountains tumbled downward. God's age-old paths collapsed before his power. Likewise, the inhabitants of the area were struck with terror at the presence of Israel's delivering God.

In verses 8–15 a vivid description is given of God's further victories involving his use of natural forces. Several incidents come to mind here, such as the crossing of the Red Sea (Exodus 14–15), the crossing of the Jordan River (Joshua 3–4), and the victories at the Wadi Kishon (Judges 4–5) and Gibeon (Joshua 10). The whole imagery of verses 8–11 is somewhat difficult, but the point appears to be that God is the mighty warrior who uses his celestial weapons on behalf of his earthly people.

In verses 12–14 the great victory of Israel's almighty deliverer is portrayed. They focus on

God's redemption of his people out of Egypt at the time of the exodus. God is seen moving in great fury against the enemy, defeating him, disarming him, and destroying him with his own weapons. The poetic imagery implies that the evil leader of that enemy army was smashed with a blow to the head that crumpled him up like a heavy weight being delivered to the roof of a house and crushing it from top to bottom. Verse 14 is particularly picturesque. The enemy's self-confidence is compared to that of certain brigands who, expecting to realize their nefarious ends, lurk with eager anticipation in dark, secret places so as to set upon unsuspecting passersby. Israel's overconfident enemy, however, will be rudely disappointed.

In all of this God's purpose is to be seen not so much in the fury of nature or in his ferocious assault against the enemy but in his desire to save his people. The term "your anointed" (3:13) has been taken to refer to Israel itself, Israel's Davidic king, Moses, or the Messiah. The term is not used elsewhere of Israel, however, making those interpretations that take it to refer to some individual to be more likely. Since the setting of the psalm is the exodus, David does not seem a likely choice. Hence, a reference to Moses or to the Messiah seems to be the most likely possibility.

Habakkuk brings this psalm to a stinging close with a reminder that Pharaoh's ambitions sank in the waters of the Red Sea (cf. Exod. 15:1–12). The point of the double psalm is clear. Just as God led his people victoriously out of mighty Egypt, through the Red Sea, and on to Sinai, up from Sinai and through the wilderness, through the Jordan River and into the promised land, so he can and will yet lead his people in triumph over their enemies—but in his appointed time, way, and strength. The exodus, therefore, forms an oft-repeated biblical motif testifying to God's redemptive power, which reaches its culmination in a new spiritual exodus accomplished in Christ's saving redemption and completed kingdom.

C. The prophet's pledge (3:16–19). The prophet does not miss the point of the divinely delivered psalms. Having heard all of this (perhaps even having been shown the actual events in a supernatural vision), Habakkuk can feel his heart pounding (literally "my inward parts shook"). The further description in verse 16 makes it clear that such stark terror grips the prophet that he shakes convulsively, from quivering lips to trembling legs. The questioning prophet now stands silent before the Lord of all the earth (cf. Job 42:1–6). He will no longer question God's purposes; he will merely wait quietly and patiently for those purposes to be realized. Though judgment must come because of Judah's sin, though all of Judah's produce fail, Habakkuk will trust in God. More than economic issues are in view in verse 17, for each of the commodities speaks of deep spiritual principles upon which the basic covenant between God and his people has been established.

Habakkuk's closing words are vastly different than his opening ones. In contrast to his harsh questions and accusations, the prophet now surrenders to God's purposes for Israel and the nations. God's patient answers and the further revelation of God's person and power have been sufficient to humble the prophet. In yet another striking simile Habakkuk declares that he will live triumphantly and faithfully through it all. He will rest secure in the strength that God alone can supply.

Select Bibliography

Andersen, Francis I. *Habakkuk.* Anchor Bible. New York: Doubleday, 2001.

Armerding, C. E. "Nahum–Habakkuk." In *The Expositor's Bible Commentary.* Edited by Frank E. Gaebelein. Vol. 7. Grand Rapids: Zondervan, 1985.

Baker, David W. *Nahum, Habakkuk, Zephaniah.* Tyndale Old Testament Commentaries. Downers Grove, IL: InterVarsity, 1988.

Barker, Kenneth L., and Waylon Bailey. *Micah, Nahum, Habakkuk, Zephaniah.* New American

Commentary. Nashville: Broadman & Holman, 1998.

Bruce, F. F. "Habakkuk." In *The Minor Prophets: An Exegetical and Expository Commentary*. Edited by Thomas Edward McComiskey. Grand Rapids: Baker Academic, 1992.

Keil, C. F. *The Twelve Minor Prophets*. 2 vols. Biblical Commentary on the Old Testament. Grand Rapids: Eerdmans, 1949.

Patterson, Richard D. "Habakkuk." In *Cornerstone Biblical Commentary*. Edited by Philip W. Comfort. Vol. 10. Wheaton: Tyndale, 2008.

———. *Nahum, Habakkuk, Zephaniah*. Chicago: Moody, 1991.

Robertson, O. Palmer. *The Books of Nahum, Habakkuk, and Zephaniah*. New International Commentary on the Old Testament. Grand Rapids: Eerdmans, 1990.

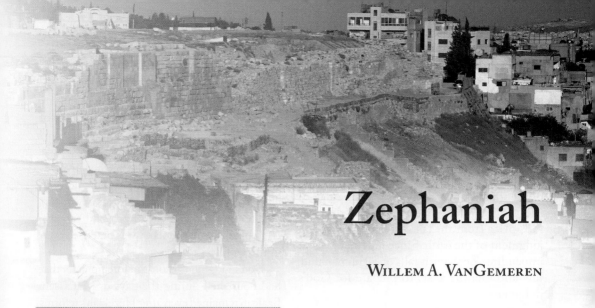

Zephaniah

WILLEM A. VANGEMEREN

Zephaniah the Prophet

The name Zephaniah (literally "Yah has hidden") means "the LORD has protected." In the opening verse, his genealogy is traced back four generations to Hezekiah, the great reforming king of Judah. He was the son of Cushi and a contemporary of Josiah, the greatest reforming king (641–609 BC). He probably made his home in Jerusalem, as he shows familiarity with the city's religious and social life (1:4–13; 3:3–4) and physical appearance (1:10–13). His ministry may be dated to Josiah's early rule because Jerusalem is still full of idolatrous practices (1:4–6) and Nineveh is not yet destroyed (2:13). Because Josiah's reforms took place in 621 BC, it is reasonable to assume that Zephaniah's ministry may have been a factor in the great revival that spread over Judah and extended to Samaria (2 Kings 22:3–23:25; 2 Chron. 34:3–35:19).

Zephaniah was born during the long rule of Manasseh (686–643 BC), the most wicked king in Judah's history. Manasseh had led Judah into an era of bloodshed, idolatry, and internationalism (2 Kings 21:1–18; 2 Chron. 33:1–20). The effects of his long reign were still felt in Jerusalem's religious and social life. The major political forces were Assyria and Babylonia.

Zephaniah lived through the transition of power from Manasseh to Josiah, who expressed a growing interest in Yahweh. Zephaniah seized the opportunity of calling on the aristocracy to join with Josiah in purging Jerusalem of idolatry, foreign customs, and political intrigues. Yahweh's anger had been aroused, and the day of judgment was sure to come. But the future of God's people was conditioned on her present response to God's word. Therefore, he encouraged the godly to pursue righteousness.

Literary Features

The book is composed of three judgment oracles (1:2–6; 1:7–2:3; 3:6–8), one woe oracle of judgment (3:1–5), four oracles against foreign nations (2:4–15), a promise of salvation (3:9–13), and one oracle of salvation (3:14–20).

Zephaniah's language is strikingly similar to that of Amos and Hosea. His literary style has much in common with the styles of earlier prophets: a play on the names of cities (2:4–6; cf. Mic. 1:10–15), assonance (2:9), the description of the day of the Lord (1:14–16; cf. Amos 5:18), and descriptions of the judgment. His outstanding contributions are the development of the day of the Lord (1:14–16) and the description of the leaders of Jerusalem (3:3–4).

Theological Themes

Zephaniah's message flows out of his view of God and the historical situation at hand. His view of God's attributes is simple but majestic. God is sovereign over his creation (1:2–3), jealous of his kingship (1:18), and righteous (3:5), and he is the king who loves and rejoices over those who humble themselves (3:14–17).

The time of God's judgment on Judah, the surrounding nations, and the world is near. *Now* is the time to seek the Lord, before it is too late (2:2–3). The prophet calls for a response from God's people. The abiding significance of Zephaniah lies in his view of the day of the Lord. He telescopes the events that will take place from the fall of Nineveh to God's judgment of the earth. Since judgment is still impending, Zephaniah calls on all humankind, Jew and Gentile alike, to prepare for God's judgment.

dwelling place. Yahweh's hand is stretched out with the intent to cut off all forms of paganism. The reason for Yahweh's anger is the lack of responsiveness by his own people. Idolatry is a flagrant breach of the covenant. For Zephaniah, idolatry is any expression that involves other deities, priests of non-Aaronic descent, illegitimate public and private forms of worship, double-mindedness, or apathy toward Yahweh. In Zephaniah's day idolatry was practiced even in the temple ("this place," 1:4).

God's judgment is on the foreign cults that had flourished during the days of Manasseh. Baalism remained even after Hezekiah's reforms

Outline

1. Oracles of Judgment (1:1–2:3)
   A. Universal Judgment (1:1–3)
   B. Judah's Idolatry (1:4–6)
   C. The Day of the Lord (1:7–18)
   D. The Call to Repentance (2:1–3)
2. Oracles of Judgment against the Nations (2:4–15)
   A. Philistia (2:4–7)
   B. Moab and Ammon (2:8–11)
   C. Cush (2:12)
   D. Assyria (2:13–15)
3. Oracles of Judgment against Jerusalem and the Nations (3:1–8)
4. Promises to Gentiles and Jews (3:9–20)

Commentary

1. Oracles of Judgment (1:1–2:3)

A. Universal judgment (1:1–3). Zephaniah's first oracle proclaims God's judgment on the earth, including nature and all humankind. His message is universal, as it extends beyond a primary focus on Judah to include all nations. The devastation coming on the earth will be on a much larger scale than that of God's judgment by flood in the days of Noah (Genesis 6–8). The catastrophic language dramatically illustrates God's great anger with the earth on account of the wicked.

B. Judah's idolatry (1:4–6). Yahweh's judgment extends first to his own people (Judah) and to Jerusalem, which he has chosen for his

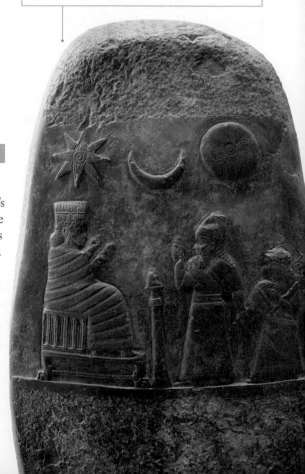

Zephaniah 1:5 condemns false worship, including "worship [of] the starry host." This boundary marker of King Meli-Shipak shows three astral deities whom God's people were not to worship: Ishtar (star), Sin (crescent moon), and Shamash (sun) (second–first millennium BC).

(2 Chron. 33:3). The prediction that Baalism together with all other forms of idolatry would be destroyed was to some extent fulfilled during the reforms of Josiah (2 Kings 22:3–23:25; 2 Chron. 33:1–20) and more fully in the period of the exile, when the land was purged of all forms of idolatry. Molek (1:5) was an Ammonite deity to whom children were sacrificed (1 Kings 11:5, 33; 2 Kings 23:10, 13; Jer. 32:35). In addition to these deities new gods had been added to the Judean pantheon, the astral deities introduced by the Assyrians, who encouraged the worship of the sun, moon, and stars (2 Kings 23:11; Jer. 19:13; 32:29; Ezek. 8:16). False worship was combined with the ministry of non-Aaronic priests ("pagan priests") and faithless priests of Aaronic descent ("idolatrous priests," 1:4 NIV 1984; NKJV).

Yahweh demands absolute loyalty from his people, and he is angry because they have devoted themselves to other deities and are hypocritical and apathetic. Zephaniah condemns all who do not seek the Lord.

C. The day of the Lord (1:7–18). Three oracles of judgment on Jerusalem's political and commercial centers of power set forth the effect of the day of Yahweh's judgment on the political and economic leaders of Judah: the aristocracy, the traders, and the wealthy. Yahweh himself will see to it that the abuses of power and social callousness will get their rewards.

In the first oracle (1:7–9), the prophet compares the day of Yahweh to a sacrificial feast. There are three parties: the host (Yahweh), the invited guests (enemies of Judah), and the sacrifice (Judah).

People must be prepared for the day of the Lord. Zephaniah's admonition of silence (1:7) is a prophetic call for people to recognize the difference between the Creator and his creatures. Humanity cannot justify itself before God, the master of the universe. The designation "Sovereign Lord" (NIV; literally "Lord Lord" or "Lord Yahweh") emphasizes the control of God. He who dwells in his holy place calls on humanity to be silent. The Judge of the universe has prepared a day of judgment.

Moreover, the people must be prepared because the day of Yahweh is "near." From the prophet's perspective, the judgment of God hovers over humanity and may come at any time. The day of the Lord is compared to a sacrificial banquet, to which the Lord has summoned the enemies of Judah as guests and has consecrated them as his instruments of judgment. The sacrificial language is a prophetic metaphor of the day of Yahweh. The guests have been consecrated to participate as priests in the sacrifice. The sacrifice consists of the leaders of Judah: the princes, the royal household, and the courtiers. The aristocracy of Judah has adopted a pagan way of life and idolatrous practices, symbolized by their being clothed in "foreign clothes" (1:8). The courtiers are those who "avoid stepping on the threshold" (1:9). Several interpretations of this phrase have been proposed: (1) they had accepted pagan superstitions (cf. 1 Sam. 5:1–5), (2) they were willing to please their masters (RSV, "who leaps over the threshold"), or (3) they served idols. The charge against them is not that they "fill the temple of their gods" (NIV) but that they fill their master's house with wealth obtained by illegitimate means.

In the second oracle (1:10–11), the traders and financiers, whether Judean or foreign, are warned about the impending judgment and its effects on the financial center of Judah. Through the Fish Gate, situated by the north wall, the wall most vulnerable to attack, one had access to the business center of Jerusalem. The new prosperity brought about the extension of the city beyond the old walls to include the New Quarter. But instead of traders, enemy forces will come, and the merchants with all of their merchandise will be no more. Instead of the sound of barter, a cry together with sounds of destruction will rise up from Jerusalem's market district. Jerusalem's center of trade, industry, and business will come to a violent end. Zephaniah exhorts people to prepare themselves by wailing in expectation of the judgment to come (cf. Isa. 13:6; Jer. 4:8; Joel 1:5; Amos 8:3).

In the third oracle (1:12–13), Yahweh's judgment is expressed against the wealthy, who are callous seekers of their own pleasures. Yahweh will carefully investigate and bring to judgment all of the wealthy. His searching is like that of a man tracking down an escapee with a searchlight. The wealthy are compared to wine left on its dregs. The figure is borrowed from the wine industry, where wine was transferred from vessel to vessel to remove the dregs and yeast. Wine left on its dregs became undrinkable. Zephaniah's metaphor may also contain some irony (cf. NEB, "who sit in stupor over the dregs of their wine"). The wealthy are so oblivious to the impending judgment that they think that God is powerless. They believe they hold the future in their hands and that God stands idly by. Yahweh's judgment reverses the fortunes of the wealthy. They have enriched themselves by having no regard for Yahweh, his covenant, his commandments, or their fellow citizens. Their aim is to build and to plant, but their goals will be frustrated by Yahweh's judgments.

Zephaniah's classic and moving poetic description of the day of Yahweh (1:14–18) is not original with him (Amos 5:18–20). Israel had expected that day to be victorious, marked by victory over enemies, with national glory reminiscent of the era of David and Solomon. God's judgment was thought to be limited to Israel's enemies and could not conceivably affect his covenant people. Amos had to dispel that illusion. He characterized the day as a time of judgment marked by adversities, anguish, and despair, a judgment from which no one could escape. Zephaniah further develops the poetic imagery into an apocalyptic vision of the dreaded day when Yahweh comes to war against his own people.

The first strophe (1:14–16) emphasizes the speed with which Yahweh moves against his people. The terrible day of Yahweh is "near—near and coming quickly."

The appearance of Yahweh will resemble his theophany at Mount Sinai, when he made his covenant with Israel (Exod. 19:16; 20:21; Deut. 4:11). On the day of Yahweh, however, there will be no revelation of his glory; no fire representative of his presence will appear. The day of the Lord instead will be a period of darkness, judgment, and alienation. Amos explained the day of darkness as a series of catastrophes from which there would be no escape (5:19), a time marked by sheer helplessness. Zephaniah intensifies Amos's explanation by heaping up words portraying an admixture of cause (war), emotion (the cry of despair), and results (ruin). The intent of the prophet is to so affect his hearers that they will respond with dread and repent.

The prophet shifts his description from the day of Yahweh to the effects of the Lord's judgment (1:17–18). Yahweh comes as a warrior against his own people to bring distress on them, to make them feel helpless, even to bring utter destruction. The reason for the severity of his judgment is that the people have sinned against his holiness. When his holiness has been desecrated, he responds with jealous anger. The jealousy of God is that attribute which defines Yahweh as the source of all, the only one worthy of humanity's loyalty, worship, and obedience. He is jealous of his rights as the king of the universe. The jealousy of God is therefore not an expression of suspicion but rather of precaution, so as not to permit his creatures to disregard his honor or to assume glory for themselves with little regard for him. The divine reaction of anger is an expression of his jealousy. His divine majesty has been wounded and demands retribution.

The prophet began his oracles with an oracle of judgment on the world, including humanity (1:2–3). He concludes by returning to the same motif, threatening judgment upon "all who live in the earth" (1:18). In view of the nature of the anger of Yahweh, his judgment extends to all the earth; it does not differentiate between covenant people and Gentiles; it is inescapable.

D. The call to repentance (2:1–3). The shameful nation of Judah is called to prepare themselves to be like chaff for the judgment of God, which will consume them like fire or blow them away like the wind.

Judah must do something before the terrible day of the Lord comes, for it will not be a day of peace and prosperity but an expression of the Lord's wrath. The repetition of the warning gives ground to the exhortation to seek Yahweh. The godless have been accused of not seeking Yahweh (1:6), and the judgment will not pass them by. For the godly, however, the day of Yahweh is a day that should not be feared. God holds out an encouragement not for the people as a whole but for the godly remnant, the "humble of the land" (literally "the poor of the earth"). The humble are not poor with regard to material possessions but are those who depend on God and walk in reliance on him. The pious remnant must continue to seek righteousness and humility. Election is not guaranteed by birth or by the sign of the covenant (circumcision). It is made evident by the fruits belonging to the life of faith.

2. Oracles of Judgment against the Nations (2:4–15)

On the international scene, Judah's political future was far from secure. Judah was surrounded by enemies: Philistia to the west, Assyria to the north, and Moab, Ammon, and Edom to the east. Zephaniah expresses the sentiment of the population of Judah in his oracles of judgment against the nations. Yet he has a grander purpose in view. He speaks of the establishment of God's kingdom, which the remnant of Judah and the nations will share together. Zephaniah's particular reference to the nations, therefore, is symbolic of all kingdoms that oppose the rule of God, whose purpose is to establish out of the remnant of Judah and the nations a people who will submit themselves to him and worship him wherever they may be found (2:11). Since the coming of our Lord Jesus Christ, the salvation of which the prophet speaks has become more real to all who believe on his name, whether Jew or Gentile (1 Pet. 1:10–12). Zephaniah predicts that the future of the kingdom of God is dependent on the way in which Yahweh deals with his enemies. Therefore, the salvation message is present in Zephaniah, but not with the same clarity as we find it in the New Testament. The way to read these oracles of judgment is to first focus on their historical context, then trace the fulfillment of the oracles as they apply to the ancient nations and to any foe of the kingdom of God.

A. Philistia (2:4–7). Philistia, situated to the west of Judah, receives first mention because of its long-standing hostility. No reason for the judgment of Philistia is given, because every Judean understood why Philistia should fall. Zephaniah shows no feeling of hostility or joy in the description of the fall of the Philistines. He moves from a description of the fall of four Philistine cities to a proclamation of woe on Philistia emphasizing how the Lord will bring blessing out of curse when the land of the Philistines is finally occupied by the remnant of his people. They will be the recipients of an era of peace and prosperity.

The judgment oracle against Philistia begins with a specific mention of four of the five major Philistine cities: Gaza, Ashkelon, Ashdod, and Ekron. Gath is not included because it had already been destroyed (see 2 Chron. 26:6).

The literary imagery is filled with pastoral associations. Zephaniah emphasizes the poetic effect and carefully chooses his words to heighten the emotive impact. This is also the case in the ordering of the cities: Gaza and Ekron both begin with the same Hebrew consonant (ayin) and form an envelope around Ashkelon and Ashdod, which both begin with an aleph. The judgment on the cities is singularly brief.

Philistia will be subjected to two judgments: desolation of the land and removal of her population by death or exile. The term "Kerethite" (2:5) is a reference to the Cretan origin of the Philistines and may also be an example of prophetic irony, since in Hebrew the word for "Kerethite" is related to the verb "to cut off." God's judgment lies on Philistia. The war-loving Kerethites will be cut off so that Canaan, the land of promise, will have no reminders of Judah's long-standing enemy.

Philistia will become a place for shepherds with their flocks. After the cities have been leveled and the orchards destroyed, weeds and thistles will take over. The cultivated and inhabited land will become a place for grazing and trampling of animals.

The remnant of Judah will inhabit the coastland of the Philistines. War will be over. The incessant rivalry between Judah and Philistia, necessitated by the limited territories and adjoining boundaries, will be past. These verses picture the devastation of Philistia and an era of peace and prosperity when God's people will live in the land without fear.

God's promise ultimately pertains to the era of restoration, which includes the finding of pasture and lying down (2:7). The verb "lie down" denotes the rest, provision, and protection Yahweh the great shepherd gives to his people. The language of remnant, shepherding, and lying down is further developed in 3:12–13. God's people will be able to enjoy the inheritance promised to them by Yahweh himself. The promise belongs to "the remnant"

(2:7), a term designating the faithful among the covenant people who seek Yahweh. The promise of the peaceful possession of this earth belongs to the godly. The Lord will "care" for them by bestowing his divine favor on them. The remnant receives the assurance that Yahweh has planned for the restoration of his own.

B. Moab and Ammon (2:8–11). Though the Israelites were related to the Moabites and Ammonites through Lot, a nephew of Abraham, their relations had always been bitter (cf. Num. 22:2–24:25; Deut. 23:3–6; Judg. 3:12–30; 1 Samuel 11; 2 Sam. 8:2; 10:1–19). The policy of Moab and Ammon was to ridicule Judah by scoffing at her precarious situation. When Judah needed political and military support against the Assyrians, Moab and Ammon did not come to her rescue but were intent on protecting their own delicate situation. Their concern for self-preservation and their offensive relations with Judah are the subject of the prophetic oracle of judgment. Yahweh has "heard the insults of Moab and the taunts of the Ammonites" (2:8). Even when God's people fall short of what he expects, he remains loyal to his covenant. The taunting, laughing, reviling, threats, and insults directed against his children affect Yahweh as a Father. The oracle against Moab and Ammon assures the remnant of God's care. The oracle becomes a source of hope and comfort to all of God's people.

Ashdod is listed among the Philistine cities that will be devastated (Zeph. 2:4). Today the area of ancient Ashdod, shown here, is covered with weeds and thistles.

Yahweh rises on behalf of his own. He is the Lord of Hosts. As the king of the universe, he commands innumerable hosts and will protect the future of his people. He is still the God of Israel, as he has promised to the patriarchs to be the God of their children. He assures the pious community that he will be with them, regardless of how the nations may rise up against them or boast over their own advantages. The assurance is guaranteed by an oath, "as surely as I live." Yahweh swears by himself that he will come to the aid of his people.

The judgment on the nations is poetically portrayed as a repetition of God's judgment on Sodom and Gomorrah, a favorite metaphor in the prophets (Isa. 1:9–10; 3:9; 13:19; Jer. 23:14; 49:18; 50:40; Amos 4:11). It is not unlikely that the prophet plays on the sound of the words "Moab" and "Sodom," "Ammon" and "Amorrah" (Hebrew "Gomorrah"). He further explains the nature of the reversal of the fortunes of these nations. They are likened to a plot of weeds and salt pits.

The future lies with the remnant. They are further identified as "my people." How this language must have spoken to the hearts of the godly community in exile! God's rule will be established, and the righteous will inherit the earth. The Jews, upon their return from exile, did not receive the complete fulfillment of this prophetic word, but the people of God in any age can look forward to the time when God's judgment will come to the kingdoms of this world, which will be overturned like Sodom and Gomorrah. Then the righteous will truly inherit the earth. The verb "inherit" signifies taking possession of the land (Exod. 23:30) as legal heirs. The enemies of God are not considered heirs of the world. In verse 10 the prophet explains why the fortunes of the nations will be reversed. They were filled with pride and insults. In their pride they mocked and taunted the people of the Lord. Because they have reviled the covenant people, they are subject to the curse: "Whoever curses you I will curse" (Gen. 12:3).

When the Lord acts on behalf of his own, he will appear as "awesome" or terrifying to the nations. Taunting will cease and their gloating words will not be heard anymore because of the presence of Yahweh, the God of Israel. The nations along with their national deities and idols will disappear from the earth. In place of paganism and idolatry the prophet looks forward to the universal worship of the Lord.

To some extent, this was fulfilled in the Judaism of the Diaspora, when Gentiles worshiped the Lord as God-fearers or proselytes in their local synagogues. Yet Zephaniah goes beyond the expectation of the central and universal worship of Yahweh. He anticipates Jesus's teaching that acceptable worship may take place *wherever* God's people assemble and worship him in spirit and truth (John 4:23).

C. Cush (2:12). Ethiopia (Cush) ruled Egypt as the twenty-fifth dynasty from 712 to 663 BC. Here the prophet may be making a sarcastic reference to Egypt by calling it "Cush" even though it was no longer ruled by the Ethiopians. Still, it is not clear from the context whether he has Ethiopia or Egypt in mind.

D. Assyria (2:13–15). Relations between Assyria and Judah went back more than one hundred years prior to the time of Zephaniah. Isaiah had predicted the victory of Assyria over the eastern Mediterranean region. By Zephaniah's time, the Aramean and Israelite kingdoms had been subjugated, and their populations exiled. Sennacherib had invaded Judah (701 BC), and Hezekiah had been forced to pay tribute. Hezekiah's son Manasseh spent time in Babylon as a part of a reform program to ensure his loyalties to Assyria (2 Chron. 33:11). Josiah had to decide where his loyalties lay. He could avoid political problems by pleasing Assyria, which had been the dominant power for over a century. Due to the length of Assyria's rule, the extent of its military power, and its proximity to Jerusalem, Assyrian influence on Israel's politics, culture, and religion was pervasive. It was difficult for Zephaniah's contemporaries to realize how close Assyria was to its demise.

Zephaniah strongly condemns Assyria's religious influence on Jerusalem as well as its tyrannical power. Yahweh proclaims to the people of Judah that they should neither rely on the superpowers (Ethiopia [= Egypt?] and Assyria) nor be worried by the coalition of the small nations (Philistia, Moab, and Ammon). All kingdoms, whether great or small, will fall.

The oracle against Assyria is in the form of a message of doom. The great Assyrian power will come to nothing. It will be like a "desolate" place, a "desert." Assyria's power will be dried up like a brook without water.

The presence of animals (2:14) indicates that life is possible in Assyria; its climate is not altered. Flocks, herds, and wild animals will inhabit Assyria's ruins.

The fall of Nineveh is sarcastically portrayed by a hyperbolic description of its greatness (2:15). By exaggerating the greatness of Nineveh, the prophet heightens the effect of its fall. Nineveh represents the Assyrian Empire. The treasures and plunder from conquered nations came to Nineveh and enriched the empire. Because Nineveh had been the capital of the Assyrian Empire for more than one hundred years, its citizens imagined the empire was secure. Zephaniah speaks of the city in its fancied security. Nineveh represented a totalitarian regime. The king, called the "shepherd" of his people, embodied the divine destiny of the empire. The unique position of the Assyrian king and the Assyrians' pride in their way of life were idolatrous from God's perspective. The prophet sarcastically personifies Nineveh by proclaiming its divine status. For Judah, the statement "I am the one! And there is none besides me" (2:15a) was a confession of the unique and exclusive claim of Yahweh (cf. Isa. 43:10; 44:6; 45:5, 18, 21–22; 46:9). The mood of the oracle changes rapidly. Sarcasm changes into lament (2:15b). The end of Assyria will be celebrated by all who pass the ruins of the city. The scoffing and the shaking of the fist are expressions of hatred mixed with joy. The hatred for Nineveh will be turned to joy because she will have received her just rewards.

3. Oracles of Judgment against Jerusalem and the Nations (3:1–8)

Though no direct reference is made to Jerusalem, it is clear that Zephaniah focuses on the capital city of Judah in chapter 3. As an insider familiar with the corrupt and tyrannical regimes of Manasseh and Jotham, Zephaniah charges Jerusalem with faithlessness. The oracle is a woe oracle of judgment. Jerusalem will fare no better than the surrounding nations. The charges are essentially three: Jerusalem is corrupt; it has forsaken Yahweh; its leaders are hopelessly evil.

Zephaniah paints a portrait of an incredibly evil city. Jerusalem is a "bloody" city where gangsters rule. Because of bloodshed, the city has become "defiled," suggesting ritual uncleanness (Ezra 2:62; Neh. 7:64; Mal. 1:7, 12).

At her very core, Jerusalem is a covenant-breaking city. Whatever one may say about her, she is not what she is supposed to be. Jerusalem is, moreover, a foolish city. She digs her own grave because she is unresponsive to the call of wisdom.

Zephaniah charges the leaders—the officials, rulers, prophets, and priests—with ruling like gangsters. The political, social, and religious climate of Jerusalem is corrupt. Their ferocious appetite for self-enrichment makes the officials behave like tyrants. They are like "roaring lions" (cf. Amos 3:8). The officials thwart justice by shedding innocent blood. Human life has been reduced to a material

Zephaniah 3:3 describes Jerusalem's corrupt officials as "roaring lions." The roaring lion seen here guarded the temple of Ishtar built by Ashurnasirpal II (Nimrud, 883–859 BC).

resource for the self-satisfaction of the city's leaders. The judges pervert justice in their pursuit of personal happiness. They are compared to "evening wolves." The prophets are unreliable, wanton impostors. They are "unprincipled" and "treacherous" (2:4). The combination of these terms heightens the impact. The priests, though consecrated, are not able to apply God's law to their society. They profane whatever is holy. The word "sanctuary" might also be translated "sacred" or "holy things." Zephaniah does not specify whether the offensive behavior of the priests pertains only to the sanctuary or extends to all that is sacred. Profanation, nonetheless, is a disregard of God's commands.

In an indirect way Zephaniah warns Josiah not to trust the officials and religious leaders of Jerusalem. If he is to break away from the perverse pattern set by his father and grandfather, he has to be willing to forgo the counsel of those in power and return to Yahweh. Yahweh's nature is radically different from that of the wicked leaders of Jerusalem. He is righteous, just, and faithful. Since he is unique in these qualities, he alone is qualified to judge his people. The generation of the exile, while fully aware of Yahweh's anger and judgment, can comfort themselves knowing that Yahweh has been faithful in his judgment and will continue to be faithful. Yahweh's intent is to remove all wickedness from *within* his people

(3:11) so that he may fully dwell in the *midst* of his people once more (3:15, 17).

The prophet affirms that God does no wrong. Wrong is the exact opposite of faithfulness and signifies perversity, wickedness, or lewdness. Instead, Yahweh dispenses justice. Morning by morning and day by day his justice and righteousness are evident. Yahweh the great king is here pictured dispensing justice without fail. In contrast to this righteous and just judge are the wicked, who have no sense of shame. They will not even come to be tried by the Lord until it is too late. In the end his judgment overtakes them.

These foolish people have not seen how Yahweh has shown his righteous judgment in the past by cutting off entire nations, reducing them to wastelands. The story of the Old Testament is the story of redemption in which Yahweh interacts with humankind and judges peoples and nations in his own time. The prophet has predicted the fall of Philistia, Moab, Ammon, and Assyria. Now he calls on his people to look at the record of the past and to learn from it.

With an apocalyptic tinge, Zephaniah portrays the judgment as lying just beyond the horizon. Yahweh will soon gather the nations together and witness against them. Because Judah is scarcely different from the nations, she too will attend the awesome judgment of the day of Yahweh. Yahweh acts as accuser, witness, and judge of the nations. On the day of the Lord the future of the kingdoms of the world will be determined. Before the fullness of the era of restoration, the judgment of the Lord must purify the nations.

4. Promises to Gentiles and Jews (3:9–20)

Yahweh's anger and love go together. On the day of Yahweh's anger, he will "purify the lips" of the peoples (3:9–11). This image is an expression of restoration. Zephaniah portrays the restoration as an era in which all languages are pure. The division of languages and cultural and religious differences will be over. The tower of Babel will no more be a symbol of human autonomy, because the nations will serve one

God. Scattered peoples will come to worship the Lord together and to present him offerings appropriate to the salvation they have experienced.

The day will be a day of grace for the nations. When God has removed autonomy, haughtiness, and wickedness, only the people of God will be left. The prophet anticipates the time when all wrongdoing and all causes for shame will be removed.

Grace is also shown to the remnant of Judah (3:12–13). The remnant motif was first introduced in the call to repentance (2:1–3). A glorious future belongs to those who demonstrate humility, trust in the Lord, and faithfulness. The "meek and humble" (3:12) are not only those who survived the Babylonian holocaust but all those who have opened their eyes to the reality of humanity's collision course with God. God thus assures the godly of every age that he looks for those who do not depend on themselves, that is, the poor in spirit. Those who are truly humble rely on the Lord. True humility is an expression of the fear of the Lord. The wicked do not respond to the call of wisdom (3:2, 7). In contrast, the righteous begin with trust in the Lord and commit all their ways to him.

The practical working out of godly wisdom is the expression of faithfulness to the Lord. Faithfulness is not only an attitude but a way of life. The essence of Old Testament piety is found here (cf. Ps. 15:2–5; 24:3–6; Mic. 6:8). The requirement is no different since the coming of Christ.

Zephaniah celebrates the joy of redemption (3:14–15). The imperatives "sing," "shout aloud," "be glad," and "rejoice" urgently convey the assurance that past troubles are over and that the new era of redemption has begun. The people must exult in the Lord their Redeemer. First, they are to rejoice in the great power of their king, who is able to put their enemies under his feet. Second, they must also rejoice in Yahweh's kingship. Yahweh alone has the authority to judge the nations, Judah, and Jerusalem. Third, they must rejoice because Yahweh their king is

in their midst. The prophet telescopes the whole progression of God's kingdom by focusing on the eschatological state in which all adversity, enemies, and evil will be removed. Yahweh alone will be king and will reside with his people. This picture of the future is the ground of the hope of God's people throughout the ages, because it assures the saints of Yahweh's sovereignty over the earth and of his loving purposes for his children.

The "Daughter Zion" (3:14) is a reference to either the inhabitants of Jerusalem (cf. Mic. 4:10, 13; Zech. 9:9) or the covenant people in general (cf. Isa. 52:2; 62:11; Zech. 2:10). The song of the redeemed is not a quiet musing but a loud and jubilant shouting.

The same Lord who removes pride and wickedness (3:11) will also remove the punishment of the people. The Lord will also deal with the enemies as the source of the troubles. He reveals himself as Yahweh, king over Israel, who voluntarily comes to live in the midst of his people. He is the Immanuel, the God who is with us. With his presence, there is no need to be afraid anymore.

The song of the redeemed is rephrased as a proclamation (3:16–17). Yahweh quietly rejoices over his people and the success of his plans. The ultimate assurance of the redeemed lies in Yahweh's quiet rejoicing because his plans will work out. He knows the end from the beginning.

The exhortation not to let "hands hang limp" (3:16) is a caution to the people not to become incapacitated by fear (see Neh. 6:9; Isa. 13:7; Jer. 6:24; 50:43; Ezek. 21:7). They need not fear, because Yahweh, the mighty warrior, will be with them. He has planned to save his people. The act of deliverance presupposes need. Those who will receive his salvation are the humble and needy. He will rejoice over his own people and quiet them with his love (3:17).

The glorious king will preserve a people for himself (3:18–20). He will search out and bring together the lost and scattered. The main thrust of the section lies in the future of the redeemed.

Zephaniah, by means of repetition, brings out the certainty of restoration and the glory of the people of God.

The return from exile marks in a unique way another beginning in the unfolding history of redemption. The major moments in that history include creation, dispersion, promise, a holy people, a royal nation. The restoration from exile will be a second exodus, when the promises given long ago are at last renewed.

Select Bibliography

Baker, David W. *Nahum, Habakkuk, Zephaniah.* Tyndale Old Testament Commentaries. Downers Grove, IL: InterVarsity, 1988.

Barker, Kenneth L., and Waylon Bailey. *Micah, Nahum, Habakkuk, Zephaniah.* New American Commentary. Nashville: Broadman & Holman, 1999.

Bruckner, James K. *Jonah, Nahum, Habakkuk, Zephaniah.* NIV Application Commentary. Grand Rapids: Zondervan, 2004.

Miller, Steven R. *Nahum–Malachi.* Holman Old Testament Commentary. Nashville: Broadman & Holman, 2004.

Motyer, J. Alec. "Zephaniah." In *The Minor Prophets: An Exegetical and Expository Commentary.* Edited by Thomas Edward McComiskey. Grand Rapids: Baker Academic, 1992.

Robertson, O. Palmer. *The Books of Nahum, Habakkuk, and Zephaniah.* New International Commentary on the Old Testament. Grand Rapids: Eerdmans, 1990.

Smith, Ralph L. *Micah–Malachi.* Word Biblical Commentary. Waco: Word, 1984.

Haggai

HERMANN J. AUSTEL

Introduction

Haggai the Prophet

The author of the book of Haggai is known simply as "the prophet Haggai." Apart from this book he is mentioned in Ezra 5:1 and 6:14. His name is usually associated with Zechariah, his contemporary, and he is generally thought to have been older than Zechariah, because his name always appears before that of Zechariah, and because of the possible (but not necessary) inference from 2:3 that he himself might have been old enough to have seen Solomon's temple.

Soon after the first band of exiles had returned from Babylon to Jerusalem (539 BC), they began to rebuild the temple (Ezra 3). It was not long, however, before various hindrances and waning enthusiasm brought a halt to the project. Haggai's mission was to rekindle the faith and courage of the people so that they would complete the temple. They responded almost immediately, and four years later (516 BC) the temple was completed and dedicated (Ezra 6:14–15).

Theological Themes

Haggai's message is extremely practical and down to earth: Build the temple! Several truths become clear in this book:

1. God's people must put God and his work first in their lives. Only in this way is God honored. Then God provides them with his blessed and enabling presence.
2. Putting personal or selfish interests ahead of God is self-defeating.
3. God calls his people to put his interests before their own.
4. The value of one's work should be measured by its conformity to God's will and purpose, not in comparison to the work of others.
5. God is faithful. He will keep his promises to restore Davidic kingship and establish his sovereign rule of the nations through Messiah.

Outline

1. First Message: A Call to Action—Build the Temple (1:1–15)
   A. Reproach: Their Priorities Are Wrong—Self before God (1:1–6)
   B. Admonition: Get Priorities Right— God before Self (1:7–11)
   C. Response: Obedience and the Will to Restart Building (1:12–15)
2. Second Message: A Word of Encouragement (2:1–9)
   A. The Problem: The Inferiority of Zerubbabel's Temple (2:1–3)
   B. The Encouragement: A Greater Glory Yet to Come (2:4–9)
3. Third Message: Confirmation of Blessing (2:10–19)

4. Fourth Message: The Restoration of the Davidic Kingdom (2:20–23)

Commentary

1. First Message: A Call to Action—Build the Temple (1:1–15)

Each of Haggai's messages is precisely dated, with the reign of Darius I as a reference point. The modern calendric equivalent of the first date is August 29, 520 BC. Haggai brings his first message on the day of the festival of the New Moon (Num. 10:10), when great numbers of worshipers regularly gathered in Jerusalem.

Darius here is Darius I ("the Great"), who reigned over the Persian Empire in 521–486 BC. Zerubbabel is the grandson of Jehoiachin, the king of Judah who was exiled to Babylon in 597 BC. As such he is of the royal line of David but holds an appointed office as governor of Judea under the generally benign Persians. The other person addressed is Joshua, the high priest. Joshua was among the first group to return from Babylon along with Zerubbabel (Ezra 2:1).

A. Reproach: Their priorities are wrong—self before God (1:1–6). Haggai's message is brief and to the point. It is also, more importantly, from the Lord, thus urgent and authoritative. "LORD Almighty" (1:2) is literally "Lord of Hosts." This designation for God is found frequently in the prophetic books, but is especially common in Haggai, Zechariah, and Malachi. It is a reminder of the fact that, whatever one's need, all the resources of heaven and earth are at God's command. Thus for God's people there can never be any cause to fear or hesitate when backed by God's promise. But while there is great comfort for Israel in this name, there is in it as well the reminder that God is the Lord of Israel's hosts. He is their commander in chief, and they are responsible to him.

The expression "these people" (1:2) instead of "my people" is used to draw attention to God's displeasure with Israel's spiritual apathy. Their attitude is summed up in the statement, "The time has not . . . come." Haggai describes a people who have lost their vision and have come to comfortable terms with leaving God's work undone. Contributing to this attitude are the following: (1) the fierce and persistent opposition of the Samaritans and other neighbors (Ezra 4); (2) the negative and disparaging reaction of the older priests at the laying of the foundations (Ezra 3:12–13); (3) a spirit of discouragement, making the people wonder if the end product will be worth all the difficulties and dangers; (4) a lack of vital trust in God; and (5) growing indifference and lukewarmness.

Haggai prophesies during "the second year of King Darius" (Hag. 1:1, 15; cf. 2:10). The ruins seen here are from Darius I's palace at Persepolis.

God's statement in verse 4 points clearly and unequivocally to Israel's wrong sense of values, a spirit diametrically opposed to that of David (2 Sam. 7:2; Ps. 132:1–5), who felt ill at ease in a luxurious house while the ark of God had only a tent as a covering. The term "paneled houses" (1:3) refers to the practice of laying wood paneling over the basic stone walls and indicates that the people had gone far beyond providing for their basic needs and were primarily concerned with personal luxury while totally neglecting the temple.

Haggai asks the people to give careful thought to the consequences of their misplaced priorities. This same admonition is given five times in the book (1:5, 7; 2:15, 18 [2×]) and is designed to shake the people out of their complacency. By taking careful stock of their physical situation they are led to realize how far they have strayed from the path of blessing. Verse 6 graphically draws attention to the realities of the situation. Though they have not been reduced to abject poverty, the fruit of their labor falls far short of expectation. On top of that, food, clothing, and money do not provide the normally expected benefits. The people bring in less than expected, and what they do bring in does not live up to expectations. God's blessing is not there.

B. Admonition: Get priorities right—God before self (1:7–11). As Haggai again calls on the people to consider their sin in neglecting the temple and the consequences in lost blessings, he now tells them what they must do. It is simply a matter of obeying God and starting once again to build the temple. By this act of obedience they will both please God and bring him honor.

To make sure his hearers do not lose sight of the cause-effect relationship between their poverty and their neglect of the temple, Haggai reminds them of the fact that their harvests have been consistently much poorer than expected and that what they do harvest does not last as it should. The reason for this is simply that each is busy with their own house (1:9), while the house of God remains in ruins. Because of their behavior all of nature is affected, not only the three basic crops (grain, grapes, olive oil), but also the productivity of people and cattle. The productivity of the land depended very much on adequate and timely rain and dew. When God withheld this and sent drought and excessive heat, the land, cattle, and people all suffered. Haggai uses an appropriate wordplay in stressing the reason for the drought. The temple remains a ruin (Hebrew *hareb*, 1:9); therefore, God calls for a drought (*horeb*, 1:11). Only as the people put God first can they experience his richest blessing.

C. Response: Obedience and the will to restart building (1:12–15). Haggai's message is simple and to the point. The response of the people is likewise prompt and unequivocal. They fear the Lord because they recognize the voice of God in Haggai's words (1:12). Then they begin to work on the house of the Lord. God's gracious working provokes both fear and obedience. As a result of their response, God can now promise renewed blessing: "I am with you" (1:13). These gracious words are repeated in 2:4 and, along with the other promises of blessing in 2:5 and 2:19, constitute a powerful source of encouragement. God's presence and enablement guarantee the successful outcome of the project, no matter how severe the opposition and various difficulties might be. There is a period of twenty-three days between Haggai's first message and the actual start of work. This time was no doubt required to organize work teams and to allow the workers to finish their harvesting activities.

2. Second Message: A Word of Encouragement (2:1–9)

A. The problem: The inferiority of Zerubbabel's temple (2:1–3). Not quite a month after the work has begun (cf. 1:15), Haggai speaks again to encourage the people, assuring them that their labor is not in vain, that what they are doing is indeed meaningful and pleasing to God. The problem is addressed in 2:3: "Who of you is left who saw this house in its former glory?" Those who had seen Solomon's temple fifty years prior to this disparaged the new temple now under construction. Ezra 3:10–13 recounts the laying of the foundation of the temple shortly after the return of the exiles. There was great rejoicing on this occasion by the younger people, but also loud weeping on the part of the older priests, Levites, and family heads. The reason for this weeping was that they had seen the glory of Solomon's temple and knew that the present effort would not come close by comparison. This negative attitude still had a harmful impact on the people in Haggai's time, making them wonder whether all their effort might not be in vain since the temple would be so poor by comparison to Solomon's. Their temple seemed to be "like nothing" (2:3).

B. The encouragement: A greater glory yet to come (2:4–9). The phrase "be strong" (repeated three times here) is reminiscent of God's admonition in other crucial situations (2:4–5). Joshua was encouraged with these words (Deut. 31:23; Josh. 1:6–9) when he faced the awesome responsibility of stepping into Moses's shoes and leading Israel in the conquest of Canaan. Again, in 1 Chronicles 22:13 and 28:20, David encourages young Solomon with respect to the great task of building the temple. When God has ordered a job to be done, he always does his part. It is for his servants to be strong and work. This admonition is here grounded on two promises: (1) "I am with you" (2:4); and (2) "I will fill this house with glory" (2:7). The first promise is a link to the past, to the covenant made at Sinai built on the covenant made with Abraham (Genesis 12). God is not going to abandon his promises or his people. The second is linked to the future, the glory that is yet to come, as promised again and again by the prophets. The fact that God is present with his people means that he approves of the work and that he will support and protect them. To God's people this makes all the difference between despair and rejoicing, defeat and victory.

The first reason they should not be discouraged at what seems so feeble an attempt to restore the temple to any semblance of its former glory is that God is with them in accordance with his promise. A second reason is now added. God relates their present activity to the coming surpassing glory of the temple (2:6–9). It was natural for the people to make comparisons between Solomon's temple and Zerubbabel's temple. But from God's perspective these temples are both his house, singular. These buildings are merely visible representations of the fact that God has seen fit to dwell among his people, whether in the tabernacle, the temple of Solomon or of Zerubbabel, or the millennial temple (Ezekiel 40–44; 47). The second temple, though less splendid than that of Solomon, is nevertheless God's house. Since God has acknowledged it and promised his presence, there is no reason for discouragement. Furthermore, the standard of excellence is not Solomon's temple but the future temple. The people's work, though seemingly insignificant, is nevertheless a part of God's overall program of establishing his presence on earth in such a way that not only Israel but ultimately all nations will be affected.

The principle of this message serves as a powerful incentive to believers of today. As long as we are doing the work God has given us to do in accordance with his will, we are valued participants in God's great program of making his salvation known to the lost, no matter how small our part may seem to be in comparison to the roles of others.

"In a little while" (2:6) is an expression sometimes used of eschatological events. It emphasizes imminency and perhaps the suddenness of the onset of the events described. As God has acted in mighty, earthshaking fashion in the past on behalf of his people, so will he do again. This future event is described as a shaking of "the heavens and the earth . . . and all nations" (2:6–7). Great upheavals, political, social, and cosmic, are in God's program. All that is false and impure, all that is in opposition to God, will be removed in preparation for the establishment of his kingdom. Here the direct result of this shaking is the filling of God's house with glory.

"What is desired of all nations will come" (2:7) has commonly been understood as a messianic reference. There are, however, compelling grammatical and contextual considerations that lead some translators and commentators to see this as a reference to the great wealth of the nations. That which they have highly treasured will be brought and will fill the temple. While other passages such as Ezekiel 43:1–5 stress the presence of the glory of God in the future temple, here its physical splendor is primarily in view. But the following words, "I will grant peace" (2:9), do point to the presence of God with his people (see Ezek. 34:25; 37:26–28). No more conflict, no more opposition. God will reign supreme.

3. Third Message: Confirmation of Blessing (2:10–19)

The legal question asked of the priests poses no difficulty for them. It is in two parts and makes the point that uncleanness defiles everything with which it comes into contact. The opposite, however, is not the case. If a priest were to carry a piece of consecrated meat in the folds of his robe, any item of food that came into contact with that fold would not thereby become ceremonially clean (though the garment itself would be clean, according to Lev. 6:27). On the other hand, a defiled person renders unclean anything he or she touches. Just so has the uncleanness of Judah's disobedience in neglecting the temple vitiated everything they touched. All areas of life are affected.

The date of the message in 2:15–19 is December 18, 520 BC. The people have been at work on the temple project for some three months now, and there are no doubt many indications of God's gracious presence. But they have not yet experienced the abundant harvests that result from God's blessing. This is due to the fact that they are between harvests. The fields are plowed and the new seed planted in anticipation of a rich harvest, but their barns and wine vats still show the effects of their former disobedience. They contain only half of what might normally be expected.

Nevertheless, the people are to mark this day, December 18, as the beginning of a new era. Verse 18 picks up the thought of verse 15a. Verses 15b–17 are a reminder of the past. The barns are still empty and the vine has not yet borne fruit. But from this day on they will begin to see the visible results of their obedience unfolding before them as their experienced eyes observe the beginnings of a new and abundant harvest. To a certain extent they have obeyed in faith up to this point, but from now on the words "I will bless you" will become a tangible reality.

4. Fourth Message: The Restoration of the Davidic Kingdom (2:20–23)

This is the second message on this date and is directed to Zerubbabel. The events described here are clearly eschatological. The phrase "I am going to shake" is the same as in 2:6–7 and refers to the great upheavals that will precede the establishment of God's kingdom. God will overturn royal thrones. The same Hebrew word is used of the destruction of Sodom and Gomorrah in such passages as Deuteronomy 29:23; Isaiah 13:19; Jeremiah 20:16; and Amos 4:11. As sudden and as final as Sodom's ruin was, so will it be with the Gentile thrones. Reformation is not in view here, but utter destruction. This is the fate of the "world powers." The overthrowing of chariots and their drivers is reminiscent of the description of the destruction of Pharaoh's army in the sea (Exod. 15:1, 5). The terror and confusion will be so great that men will fall by the sword of their brothers. Just when the might of the world powers seems to be unassailable, God will shake and overthrow them and establish his own kingdom. (See, e.g., Zech. 12:1–5; 14:1–9.)

Zerubbabel was in the royal line, but he never reigned as king; nor were there any aspirations on Haggai's part to make him king. The context is clearly eschatological, and Haggai uses Zerubbabel, the current representative of David's royal line, to point to the Messiah.

The reference to Zerubbabel as "my servant" and as the one whom God has chosen is reminiscent of the messianic "servant passages" of Isaiah 42, 49, 50, and 53. God's Messiah will successfully accomplish the task for which he was sent. The term "signet ring" (2:23) refers to the authority given to the Messiah. He will be God's personal representative. The designation is one of high honor and privilege. It is noteworthy that the curse on Zerubbabel's grandfather Jehoiachin (Coniah) is couched in language involving the signet ring. Though he was the signet ring on God's right hand, he was pulled off and cast to his enemies the Babylonians (Jer. 22:24). But now the Davidic line in the person of Messiah is restored to the place of authority and honor, God's signet ring. Thus the book ends on a note of encouragement. The labor of Zerubbabel is not in vain. There will be immediate blessing, but also future glory in a temple of surpassing splendor and a king who rules as God's personal representative on earth. There was every reason for Judah to be encouraged. Just as there is every reason for believers today to be encouraged in obeying and serving God.

The Lord promises to make Zerubbabel "like my signet ring" (Hag. 2:23), similar to this seventh-century-BC signet ring, which is inscribed with a name in Hebrew.

Select Bibliography

Alden, Robert L. "Haggai." In *The Expositor's Bible Commentary*. Edited by Frank E. Gaebelein. Vol. 7. Grand Rapids: Zondervan, 1985.

Baldwin, Joyce G. *Haggai, Zechariah, Malachi*. Tyndale Old Testament Commentaries. Downers Grove, IL: InterVarsity, 1972.

Boda, Mark J. *Haggai*. NIV Application Commentary. Grand Rapids: Zondervan, 2004.

Chisholm, Robert B., Jr. *Handbook on the Prophets*. Grand Rapids: Baker Academic, 2002.

Merrill, Eugene H. *Haggai, Zechariah, Malachi*. Chicago: Moody, 1994.

Meyers, Carol, and Eric Meyers. *Haggai, Zechariah 1–8*. Anchor Bible. New York: Doubleday, 1987.

Motyer, J. Alec. "Haggai." In *The Minor Prophets: An Exegetical and Expository Commentary*. Edited by Thomas Edward McComiskey. Grand Rapids: Baker Academic, 1992.

Orelli, C. von. *The Twelve Minor Prophets*. Reprint. Minneapolis: Klock & Klock, 1977.

Smith, Ralph L. *Micah–Malachi*. Word Biblical Commentary. Waco: Word, 1984.

Taylor, Richard A., and E. Ray Clendenen. *Haggai, Malachi*. New American Commentary. Nashville: Broadman & Holman, 2004.

Verhoef, Pieter A. *The Books of Haggai and Malachi*. New International Commentary on the Old Testament. Grand Rapids: Eerdmans, 1987.

Wolf, Herbert. *Haggai–Malachi*. Chicago: Moody, 1976.

Wolff, Richard. *The Book of Haggai*. Grand Rapids: Baker Books, 1967.

Zechariah

Hermann J. Austel

Introduction

Zechariah the Prophet

Zechariah was the son of Berekiah and the grandson of Iddo. The latter is named in Nehemiah 12:4, 16 as one of the heads of priestly families returning from Babylon to Judea. Thus we have in Zechariah another example (with Jeremiah and Ezekiel) of a priest serving as a prophet. He was a contemporary of Haggai (Ezra 5:1).

Date

Zechariah began his written ministry in October–November 520 BC. Two other dates are given: February 15, 519 BC (1:7) and December 7, 518 BC (7:1). The oracles of chapters 9–14 came after the completion of the temple in 516 BC. These last chapters are commonly held to be as late as 480 BC, but it is difficult to be certain.

Structure

The book has three major parts. The first gives encouragement for the rebuilding of the temple. After an introductory admonition, it consists of

a series of eight visions that relate the rebuilding of the temple to God's overall program for Israel. The second part deals with questions about the practice of fasting and mourning for the destruction of the temple. The third, not directly related to the temple, consists of two oracles concerning the future of Israel and the nations.

Some scholars maintain that chapters 9–14 were composed by a different author (or authors) than chapters 1–8. They commonly point to differences in subject matter, style, and vocabulary as supporting evidence. By way of brief reply it should be noted: (1) Ancient Jewish and Christian tradition supports the book's unity. (2) All existing manuscripts treat the book as a unified whole. (3) Though it is true that in part one the temple is of great concern, the whole book is truly

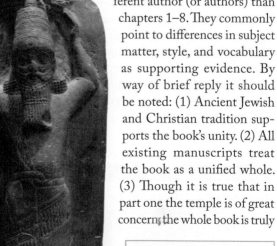

Temple building was an important activity in the ancient world. In this stele, Ashurbanipal is carrying a basket of earth for the first-brick ritual in the rebuilding of the temple to Nabu in Borsippa (668–655 BC).

eschatological in scope. In parts one and two current pressing needs and questions are dealt with in the light of the grand scope of God's purpose. This is practical eschatology. There are many other similarities in themes, such as the centrality of Jerusalem (2:4–5; 14:11) and the importance of spiritual cleansing (3:1–6; 12:10–13:6). (4) It would be unreasonable to demand that a writer maintain the same method of presentation throughout his work, especially when the concerns and needs of the people are different. When all is considered, there is no valid reason to reject the unity of the book.

Theological Themes

The scope of Zechariah's theological and eschatological vision is among the grandest in the Old Testament. Zechariah relates the past, present, and coming circumstances of Israel to God's great unfolding program for his people and to the fact that the Lord (identified with the coming king) will reign supreme over a chastened and cleansed world. Some of the dominant themes are (1) the destruction of Gentile world power; (2) the return of Israel to the land; (3) the future unity of Judah and Israel; (4) the necessity for repentance and cleansing; (5) the coming exaltation of Jerusalem and its people; (6) the joining of redeemed Gentiles in worship with Israel; (7) extensive descriptions of Messiah's person and ministry, especially in chapters 9–14; and (8) the certainty of the fulfillment of God's purpose.

Commentary

1. Call for a Return to the Lord (1:1–6)

The first message of Zechariah, coming during the eighth month of Darius's second year (October–November, 520 BC), falls between Haggai's second and third messages (Hag. 2:1–9 and 2:10–19, respectively). It adds a new dimension to Haggai's message of practical obedience—that of a personal relationship with the Lord.

Zechariah's opening message establishes a fitting foundation for the rest of the book, placing the matter of the rebuilding of the temple within the framework of God's overall purpose with regard to Israel and Jerusalem. It provides solid encouragement with regard to the ultimate destiny of Jerusalem and its inhabitants. Even after addressing the immediate matter of temple concerns, Zechariah goes on to present a magnificent panorama of future redemptive history, leading to the grand climax in which God's immutable purpose for Israel and the world, centered in his Messiah, is brought to a successful conclusion. Yet this brief introduction is a solemn reminder that the enjoyment of God's blessing is dependent on one's personal response to God. There are three major points: (1) their forefathers failed to respond to God's word—thus the tragedy of the destruction of Jerusalem and the exile. (2) God's purpose as declared in his word is unchanging. It has been, and will continue to be, fulfilled to the letter. (3) Therefore do not make the mistake your forefathers made. Turn to God with all your heart.

God was furious because of the way in which Israel's forefathers had "mocked God's messengers" and "despised his words" (2 Chron. 36:16). The inevitable result was that God's word "overtook" them (Zech. 1:6) as a fleeing thief might be apprehended by justice in pursuit. God warns Zechariah's audience against following the same tragic path, which involved outer conformity to prescribed ritual worship but lacked heart response to God. God desires that they should seek him. Even though the people have been at work on the temple for several months already, they need to be reminded that more than outward obedience is needed. The blessing of God's personal presence and fellowship is for those who seek him from the heart. People, whether evildoers or prophets, are mortal. But God's word stands forever. Whether threat or promise, that word will surely be fulfilled. God means what he says, and he has done exactly as he has said. This forms a warning to the current generation, lest they take God's word lightly. It serves also as an encouragement to those who seek God: his promise will unfailingly come to pass.

2. The Eight Night Visions (1:7–6:8)

Zechariah's visions relate the rebuilding of the temple to God's overall purpose with respect to Jerusalem, giving the assurance that there is a bright future for both city and people. Despite current and future opposition, God is going to prevail. His promise will be carried out, as already pointed out in 1:6.

Before we discuss the individual visions, it will be helpful to see them as a cohesive unit. They are structured in a chiastic a-b1-b2-c1-c2-b1'-b2'-a' pattern. That is to say, visions 1 and 8 correspond, and visions 2 and 3 together correspond to 6 and 7 as a unit. Visions 4 and

5 form the central core, around which the rest are structured.

> a First Vision: Problem—Gentiles Prospering, Jerusalem Ailing (1:7–17)
> b1 Second Vision: Gentile Oppressors Judged (1:18–21)
> b2 Third Vision: Exiles to Leave Babylon for Jerusalem (2:1–13)
> c1 Fourth Vision: Joshua Cleansed (3:1–10)
> c2 Fifth Vision: Zerubbabel Empowered (4:1–14)
> b1' Sixth Vision: Sinners in Jerusalem Judged (5:1–4)
> b2' Seventh Vision: Sin Moved from Jerusalem to Babylon (5:5–11)
> a' Eighth Vision: Resolution—Gentiles Judged, God at Rest (6:1–8)

Visions 1 and 8 (the two *a* units) provide the frame. In vision 1 God is displeased with the state of affairs of the world (a world in which the nations are prospering at the expense of Jerusalem). In vision 8 God's displeasure is resolved (6:8), because the nations that have opposed God and oppressed Israel have been appropriately dealt with, preliminary to the crowning of the Messiah (6:11–15).

Visions 2 and 3 correspond to 6 and 7 (the *b* units) and relate to Jerusalem's preparation for the kingdom age. The former speak of the defeat of its enemies and the reoccupation of the city by Israel; the latter, of the cleansing of Jerusalem by judging the sinners within and transferring wickedness as a pervasive presence to Babylon, with which it is appropriately identified.

Visions 4 and 5 (the *c* unit) form the central and focal point of the visions. Here God is not only working *on behalf of* his people; he is working *within* the people, to cleanse and then to empower them for the task at hand.

The goal is the reestablishment and cleansing of Jerusalem, followed by the crowning of the promised Messiah.

A. First vision (a): Problem—Gentiles prospering, Jerusalem ailing (1:7–17). The visions come three months after Zechariah's opening message and two months after Haggai's last two messages. The first and the eighth visions have much in common. However, the first records the situation at the time of writing, with God's promise of setting matters straight; the eighth records the actual carrying out of this promise.

The man riding a red horse (1:8) is identified in verse 11 as the angel of the Lord, who in turn is elsewhere identified as the Second Person of the Trinity. He has charge of the "fact-finding" patrol, receives its report, and then intercedes for Israel. He is to be distinguished from the angel who was talking with Zechariah (1:9, 13–14), who appears here and in other visions as an interpreter or spokesman for God. The significance of the various colors of the horses (1:8) is not given, though in Revelation 6 the red horse is associated with warfare and the white horse with victory. It is not until the eighth vision (6:1–8), however, that the horses go forth to battle. Here they do reconnaissance work. The report brought back (1:11) is that the whole world is at rest and in peace. The angel of the Lord's response indicates that this is a situation in which the Gentile nations are prospering while God's people (possibly represented by the myrtle trees in a ravine or low place, 1:8) are struggling under the dominion of foreign powers. The temple has not yet been rebuilt; consequently, full restoration from God's anger has not yet been accomplished.

God responds with kind and comforting words through the interpreting angel. His response encourages a people whom God has seemingly forgotten. God's zeal on behalf of Jerusalem will bring about the fulfillment of his promise of verses 16 and 17. At the same time the great anger that has been directed at Israel (1:2) is now (1:15) to be directed at the nations living in self-confident and smug security.

This is a common prophetic theme: the wicked, who for a time are able to run roughshod over God's people, will eventually be punished. The righteous, on the other hand, will ultimately be vindicated. The nations that were God's tools or means of chastising Israel went beyond what was called for in their treatment of Israel. They were arrogant and self-sufficient, refusing to acknowledge the handiwork of God in what was taking place. God will, however, once again deal graciously with Jerusalem; the temple and the city will be rebuilt. God's choice of Jerusalem as his dwelling place will once again be very evident.

B. Second vision (b1): Gentile oppressors judged (1:18–21). Visions 2 and 3 describe the removal of external hindrances, whereas visions 6 and 7 describe the removal of internal, spiritual hindrances. These are the corresponding *b* units.

In Scripture horns symbolize kings or kingdoms in their exercise of royal might and authority. The horns of cattle, particularly of the wild ox, were

The horns that Zechariah views during his second vision (1:18–21) may resemble the horns on the helmet of this statue of a winged lion with a human head. A pair of these statues guarded the entrance to the throne room of the Assyrian king Ashurnasirpal (865–860 BC).

used in the ancient world as symbols of invincible strength (cf. Deut. 33:17). The horns here described are kingdoms that scattered Judah, Israel, and Jerusalem (1:19). Judah has been at their mercy. But God will raise up craftsmen who will destroy the horns and the power they have over God's people. The horns are not identified. It is, however, difficult to avoid some connection with the fourfold succession of world empires described in Daniel 2 and 7. Zechariah and his hearers would have been familiar with the book of Daniel and would most likely have made such a connection. Whether these horns represent Gentile world powers as a whole or whether they build on Daniel's four kingdoms, the message is clear: these powers will be destroyed and then replaced by God's own kingdom established in Jerusalem.

C. Third vision (b2): Exiles to leave Babylon for Jerusalem (2:1–13). With the destruction of the world empires (four horns) described in the second vision, the stage is set for a marvelously resurgent Jerusalem. Both visions together expand on the words of the Lord in 1:14–16. God's zeal on behalf of Jerusalem is manifested first of all in his judging the nations that have oppressed Jerusalem (vision 2). The present vision enlarges on the statement of 1:16 with regard to the rebuilding of Jerusalem.

The man with the measuring line (2:1) answers to the statement in 1:16 that God will stretch out a measuring line over Jerusalem. A greatly enlarged city is in view here, grand in scope and glory since God himself is the architect and since it will be a place fit for the presence of his glory. There will be a great influx of people, necessitating a greatly enlarged city and making defensive walls impractical. This prophecy was not fulfilled in Zechariah's time. Even in the days of Nehemiah, some eighty years later, the city was largely empty and had to be filled by casting lots to determine who should be required to live in it (Neh. 7:4; 11:1–2). The complete fulfillment will not be realized until the messianic age. The message of these visions was nonetheless an encouragement for

Zerubbabel in that the work in which the people were presently engaged was part of God's great program for Jerusalem and Israel.

Jerusalem will have no walls of defense, but God himself will be a wall of fire around it (2:5) and its glory within. The presence of the glory of God both guarantees the safety of Jerusalem (cf. Exod. 14:19–20, 24–25) and attests to the favored status of Jerusalem and the renewed fellowship of Israel with God. In view of this, he admonishes those who are still in Babylon to flee from there and to participate in the new life in Jerusalem. (See also Isa. 48:20 and Jer. 51:6–10.) The fact that the same message occurs in Revelation 18:4, just before the destruction of eschatological Babylon, indicates that these Old Testament admonitions point forward particularly to the latter days.

There is a threefold message implicit in these words in the light of the context: (1) It is Israel's privilege to leave Babylon. They do not *have* to remain. Therefore, they should return and participate in that which God is doing in Jerusalem. (2) They are no longer to be identified with Babylon and its ways but with God and Jerusalem. (3) Babylon is doomed to terrible destruction (2:8–9; see Jeremiah 51 for a graphic description of Babylon's coming downfall, with repeated admonitions to flee). Therefore, Israel must not get caught up in Babylon's ways and in her fate. God is going to destroy those nations that have plundered Israel, of whom Babylon is the chief representative.

The speaker in 2:8–13 is the Lord Almighty (literally "the Lord of Hosts or Armies"). The natural reading of this passage is that the angel speaking to Zechariah calls himself the Lord of Hosts—yet he has been sent by God; while this may be puzzling from a purely Old Testament perspective, it becomes clear from the perspective of the New Testament teaching on the Trinity. Similar passages are found in Isaiah 48:16 and Zechariah 12:10.

The translation of the Hebrew underlying the words "after he has honored me" (2:8 NIV 1984; NIV "after the Glorious One") has been much debated. A translation that fits both the Hebrew and the context is "with glory he has sent me." That is, the Messiah's mission is carried out in the presence of, or in association with, the glory of God.

The reason given here for Babylon's destruction emphasizes the special status that Israel as the apple (or pupil) of his eye has before God. This knowledge certainly ought to put fresh spirit into a people who have experienced so many setbacks. With the fall of Babylon and the Gentile nations comes the rise of Israel. When all this has taken place, there can no longer be any doubt that God is in charge of the events that have transpired. Israel will then shout and be glad, for God will be at home in their midst. Not only Israel but many nations will be joined with the Lord, becoming God's people and participating in the glories of the new age. Nonetheless, it will be abundantly clear that Judah is God's portion, his special people (2:12). Jerusalem will once again be the place chosen by God for his presence on earth.

In visions 2 and 3 God judges the nations and prepares Jerusalem for his people and the presence of God. In visions 6 and 7 he judges sinners in Jerusalem and removes wickedness, as a pervasive presence, to Babylon, where it is enshrined. Thus these two sets of visions contrast.

The vision concludes with the striking admonition, "Be still before the LORD, all mankind, because he has roused himself from his holy dwelling" (2:13). Humans have had their say long enough, with complaints against God's ways, with mockery, with threats against God and his people. But now God comes forth to take action. All will be utterly silenced.

D. Fourth vision (c1): Joshua cleansed (3:1–10). The first three visions had to do with God's program regarding the establishment of Jerusalem as the center of God's glory on earth. It will be filled to overflowing with a people living in the peace and security of God's presence. Gentile dominion and oppression will have been removed. This is God's work *on behalf of* his people. In the next two visions (the *c* units)

the focus is on God's ministry *within* the people themselves. In this vision he cleanses them, making them fit to enter his presence; in the fifth vision he empowers them, enabling them to do his work. These two visions form the focal point of the whole, emphasizing the fact that this internal ministry of the Spirit of God is essential to God's purpose—a cleansed and empowered people.

Joshua the high priest (3:1) here serves as the representative of Israel. His cleansing symbolizes the future cleansing of Israel. God has called them to be a holy nation and a kingdom of priests (Exod. 19:6), a nation that has access to God and serves him in holiness. Here Joshua is seen standing before the angel of the Lord, ministering before God in his capacity as high priest (Deut. 10:8; Ezek. 44:15). But the place of worship, the temple, appointed by God as the means of access to him, is here invested with the characteristics of a courtroom.

Satan stands at Joshua's right side (the place of the accuser). There are just grounds for Satan's activity. Joshua's sinful uncleanness (3:3) renders him unfit to come into God's presence. The name Satan is in fact a transliteration of the Hebrew word meaning "the accuser, or adversary." It describes a fundamental characteristic of this fallen angel who not only hates God but does all in his power to keep humanity from fellowship with God. He may represent himself as humankind's friend and advocate, but his real character as opponent and accuser is here clearly seen. Job 1 and 2 record his cynical attempts to discredit Job before God and to cause Job to turn from God. The New Testament warns against his efforts to frustrate God's purpose (cf. 1 Pet. 5:8; Rev. 12:10).

But God himself intervenes on behalf of Joshua and his people. This speaks powerfully to the infinite grace of God and also to his unfailing adherence to his purpose with regard to Israel. God silences Satan with a double rebuke, as he also gives a twofold affirmation of support for Israel: (1) Satan is reminded that God has chosen Jerusalem and will not be deterred from carrying through with his sovereign electing love. (2) The burning stick taken out of a fire refers to Israel's recent deliverance from Babylon as well as to God's continued preservation of his people. Verse 3 describes both Joshua's unworthiness to stand before God and God's cleansing of Joshua, making him fit to come into God's presence and effectively stopping Satan's objections. Note that Joshua is dressed in filthy clothes as he stands before the angel of the Lord. The high priest was required to be holy and to wear special garments when he came into God's presence. But Joshua's garments are not only dirty—they are befouled as with vomit or excrement. He is most worthy of condemnation. What Joshua/Israel cannot do for himself, God does: "See, I have taken away your sin, and I will put fine garments on you" (3:4). With these brief words God's gracious saving activity is summarized. He replaces man's feeble and inadequate attempts to produce the kind of righteousness that will stand before God with righteousness that is perfect and adequate in every way. In the same way, God graciously replaced unworthy Adam's fig leaves with coats of skin (Gen. 3:7, 21; cf. also Isa. 61:10; Rev. 7:14; 22:14). The new garments are not only clean; they are rich, festal garments suitable to wear in God's presence.

Zechariah seems to be so emotionally involved in the scene before him that he anticipates what is to come next, the putting on of the turban to complete the high priest's attire. The word "turban" (3:5) here is closely related to the high-priestly "turban" in the Pentateuch (which had attached to it a plate engraved with the words "holy to the Lord"; Exod. 28:36–37). It is used in only two other passages, in figurative contexts. In Job 29:14, Job describes his righteousness: "I put on righteousness as my clothing; justice was . . . my turban." In Isaiah 62:3, Israel, restored to a righteousness evident to all, is a "crown of splendor" and a royal turban (NIV "royal diadem") in God's hand. So here also the turban gives public testimony to Joshua's new state of righteousness before God.

In verses 6 and 7 Joshua/Israel receives a twofold charge and a threefold promise. If he will now live a life of obedience and total commitment to God, consistent with his new righteous standing, he will have the privilege of an unhindered priestly ministry. As God's representative on earth, he will govern (literally "execute justice, act as judge") and have charge over the temple. He will also have totally unhindered access to God, as the angels have. Verse 8 continues to make it clear that Joshua's cleansing is representative of a spiritually restored Israel. He and his associates are symbolic of things to come. A brief but important statement follows, pointing to the one through whom Israel's cleansing and restoration will be made possible: "I am going to bring my servant, the Branch" (3:8). The term "servant" is a well-established designation of the Messiah in his capacity of successfully carrying out God's program of salvation (Isa. 42:1–7; 49:1–9; 50:4–9; 52:13–53:12). The term "Branch" designates the Messiah as Lord (Isa. 4:2), king (Jer. 23:5; 33:15), and man (Zech. 6:12). As the Branch (literally "shoot from the root"), the Messiah both brings about a new beginning and epitomizes the ideal that God intends for Israel. The stone of verse 9 is no doubt another reference to the Messiah (cf. Ps. 118:22; Isa. 28:16, where he is the chief cornerstone). Joshua and Zerubbabel were engaged in rebuilding the kingdom of Israel. This chapter makes it clear that the only validity for Israel's position as a royal priestly nation is through the cleansing ministry of the Messiah; and only as Joshua's work is built on the stone that God has given can there be any lasting results.

The seven eyes (3:9) may foreshadow the sevenfold spirit of God (Rev. 5:6). The seven eyes of God range throughout the earth (Zech. 4:10). They symbolize God's administrative activity in the affairs of his people.

The meaning of the inscription (literally "engraving") on the stone (3:9) is uncertain. If our identification of the stone with the Messiah (cornerstone) is correct, then it is possible that the engraving is a special distinction placed on him by God. At any rate this engraving is related to redemption: "I will remove the sin of this land in a single day." This verse summarizes the vision.

E. Fifth vision (c2): Zerubbabel empowered (4:1–14). This vision is linked to the previous vision as the focal point of God's work of cleansing and empowering his people. The task

The foundation or cornerstone of buildings in antiquity often contained relics or records, such as these inscribed foundation tablets of Ashurnasirpal II, discovered in this limestone box, which record the building of the temple to Mamu (883–859 BC).

before Zerubbabel and his associates must have seemed insurmountable, especially in view of God's descriptions of the coming glory of Jerusalem and the temple. This fifth vision is given to show Zerubbabel that God gives divine enablement for the work that he has ordained.

The vision contains two major objects. The first is a solid gold lampstand (4:2). The lampstand no doubt is intended to symbolize the bearing of witness or testimony. Isaiah 60:1–3 speaks of restored Israel as being a light to which the nations, in a world of darkness, will come. This will be possible because the light of God in the person of the Messiah has first come on Israel (Isa. 9:2; 60:1–2). Next Zechariah sees two olive trees (4:3) next to the lampstand, one on either side. The fact that the olive trees supply the oil that fuels the lamps suggests that what is in view here is the source of supply for the testimony symbolized by the lamps. Zechariah's question "What are these, my Lord?" (4:4) is a request regarding the significance of the lampstand and the trees. The answer is given to him in verse 6: "'Not by might nor by power, but by my Spirit,' says the Lord Almighty." These

oft-quoted words constitute the central and key message of the chapter and may be applied to anyone laboring for the Lord. This is universally true but is especially encouraging under seemingly impossible conditions.

These words are directed to Zerubbabel, who has been charged with leading the rebuilding program. There is here both encouragement and admonition. Zerubbabel need not fear the size or difficulty of the task. God's supply of power is sufficient for any and every situation. But Zerubbabel needs to rely on God rather than on personal skill, strength, or ingenuity. The word translated "might" is frequently used of armies, wealth, or influence. But God's work is accomplished by the power of his Spirit. This is symbolized by the oil of the olive trees that supplies the fuel for the lamps.

Verse 7 applies the truth of verse 6 to Zerubbabel's situation. The mighty mountain might refer to the opposition of Gentile political power, since this symbolism was common in the Near East (cf. Dan. 2:44). But it may well refer to difficulties and obstacles of any kind, no matter how great. What an encouragement and comfort to Zerubbabel, and indeed to anyone engaged in the work of God, to realize that it is by *God's* power, not by human strength, that impossibilities become actualities. No mountain is so solid and so huge that God cannot level it.

As to the specific matter at hand, the building of the temple, it will be completed. God will bring out the capstone, the last stone to be laid. This will be a particularly joyous occasion because of the difficulties and the length of time involved in the building. The joy will be so great that there will be spontaneous shouts of "God bless it! God bless it!" This is most likely an unqualified expression of approval, such as "Wonderful!" or "Bravo! Bravo!" It is also recognition of the fact that God's favor rests on the temple and that its completion is due to the working of God's power. This is to be compared to the mixed reaction of the people when the foundation was laid (Ezra 3:10–13).

Verses 8 and 9 give specific encouragement to Zerubbabel. The task is difficult, even mountainous, yet by God's enablement he will carry it out. God finishes what he starts. Verse 10 carries on the thought that there will be joyful acknowledgment of God's hand in the temple project, even by those who have despised "the day of small things." Many have minimized the rebuilding efforts as insignificant and futile. But now this negativism will be replaced by rejoicing. The message is clear and unequivocal: God, whose omniscient interest in man's activities spans the earth, has had his watchful and approving eyes on Zerubbabel's efforts.

Verses 11–14 take up again the matter of the two olive trees. More detail is given through Zechariah's questions. In addition to the olive trees, he wants to know about the two olive branches beside the two golden pipes that pour out golden oil. This question helps us see the connection between the trees and the lampstand. The oil flows from the trees through the branches to the pipes and through the pipes into the lampstand, supplying fuel for the lamps. The answer to the question as to what the two branches represent is given in verse 14. Both kings and priests were anointed; and Zerubbabel, in the kingly line, and Joshua the high priest were the current representatives of these two offices. The power and effectiveness of their ministries depended on the enabling power of the Holy Spirit. As they receive the empowering of the Spirit of God, the testimony and witness of God's people to the true God can shine brightly. The ultimate responsibility of these two officials is to serve the God of all the earth. God's lordship and sovereignty are thus affirmed, and the outworking of his program through his servants will demonstrate his absolute lordship. As most expositors recognize, there are clear messianic and eschatological implications in this chapter. In Jesus the Messiah the kingly and priestly offices are combined.

Chapters 3 and 4 form a unit in their emphasis on the internal work of God in his people. They also form a unit in looking forward to the Messiah, through whom the nation will be cleansed and restored, and through whom the kingdom and the temple of God will be rebuilt, thus reestablishing God's people as an effective light to the nations and witness to the saving power and sovereignty of God.

F. Sixth vision (b1′): Sinners in Jerusalem judged (5:1–4). The sixth and seventh visions have to do with God's purging the land of sin. Here are internal obstacles to the building of the kingdom, that is, the unrepentant sinners within the land. (Visions 2 and 3 deal with external obstacles: the nations that stand in inimical opposition to God and his people.) Chapter 3 promised cleansing for a penitent and responsive people. This chapter promises judgment for impenitent lawbreakers. God is gracious and forgiving to those who repent, but there is no place in God's kingdom for those who resist his grace. This vision, then, forms a contrast with that of chapter 3, which refers to the cleansing of those who truly seek God.

In the sixth vision Zechariah sees a flying scroll (5:1). The significance of the scroll is given in verse 3. It is a curse going out over the whole land. This curse brings together all the curses of the law. It is a flying scroll because it travels through the land seeking out unrepentant lawbreakers. Two sample transgressions are named in verses 3 and 4, thievery and swearing falsely. The first is a typical crime against one's neighbor, the other a crime against the holiness of God. No transgressor will be able to evade the curse. It will seek him out even in his house, destroying it utterly while he himself is banished. Being the seed of Abraham only in the physical sense does not qualify a person for a place in the kingdom. Vision 4 ends in blessing. This one ends in judgment.

G. Seventh vision (b2'): Sin moved from Jerusalem to Babylon (5:5–11). In the previous vision, unregenerate sinners are purged from the land. In this vision, wickedness as a pervasive principle is removed from the land and taken to Babylon, where it is enshrined.

The measuring basket of verse 6 is literally an ephah, a measure somewhat smaller than a bushel. The basket with the woman inside represents the iniquity of the people throughout the land. She is the personification of wickedness. The woman tries to escape, but the lid is placed firmly over the mouth of the basket. The two women of verse 9 are agents of God who whisk the basket away to the country of Babylonia. A house or temple is built for the basket and its contents, and it is placed there as an idol on a pedestal, to be worshiped by those who have rejected God. From the time

of the building of its tower in defiance of God to its ultimate destruction, Babylon appears in Scripture as the center of opposition to God. This, then, is the appropriate home of wickedness. Note that in 2:6–7 God's people are urged to flee from Babylon and to return to the "holy land," where God will dwell in their midst. An appropriate exchange is taking place. All this is preliminary to the final events yet to transpire: Babylon with all its wickedness will be utterly destroyed.

H. Eighth vision (a'): Resolution—Gentiles judged, God at rest (6:1–8). This vision brings to a fitting conclusion the series of night visions outlining God's program of rebuilding Jerusalem and revitalizing his people. It is clearly eschatological in scope, completing what was anticipated in the first vision. There are obvious similarities to the first vision in the presence of various colored horses being sent throughout the earth. There are some differences in the colors of the horses and in the fact that there are chariots in this last vision. But the most distinctive difference is that in the first vision the horses go out on reconnaissance, bringing back their report, whereas in this vision the horses go out to execute judgment. In the first vision the nations live in undisturbed quietness, and God is disturbed and angry with them. In this vision the nations are judged and the Spirit of God is satisfied and at rest because his purpose has been accomplished.

The vision opens with the appearance of four chariots (6:1). From the contents of this vision it becomes apparent that these are war chariots. Horses and chariots are logical symbols for the carrying out of divine judgment in war (Jer. 46:9–10; Joel 2:4–11; Nah. 3:1–7). These chariots come out from between two mountains of bronze, which are commonly identified with Mount Zion and Mount Olivet, with the Kidron Valley in between. What is important to recognize is that they come from the presence of God himself. Bronze is often associated with divine judgment (Num. 21:9), and this accords well with the symbolism of the passage.

The fact that there are four chariots relates to the universality of the judgment. All four corners of the earth (cf. Isa. 11:12) will be affected. Horses of varying colors are harnessed to the four chariots. The colors are not identical with those of chapter 1, nor are they explained. Whatever the individual colors might signify, these horses clearly mean terrible judgment on a rebellious and God-hating world. The horses with their chariots are identified in verse 5 as the four spirits (or "winds") of heaven. These are angelic beings, agents of God's justice, carrying out his sovereign purposes. The military defeats, the toppling of kingdoms, the plagues and "natural disasters," are not happenstance; they have been ordered by a God who has long been silent, giving people every opportunity to respond and repent.

God's title, "Lord of the whole world" (6:5), will no longer be questioned. Mesopotamian kings loved this and other similar grandiose titles. But now it will be clearly seen who is truly Lord. Note that this title is assumed by God in the last days, when he sets out to enforce his lordship (Ps. 97:5; Mic. 4:13; Zech. 4:14). The chariot with the black horses goes toward the north country (6:6). It is the north country again in verse 8 that is particularly singled out as the focal point of judgment. The reference is almost certainly to Babylon. Though it lay to the east of Jerusalem, the invasion route of Babylon (and Assyria) was always from the north (via the Fertile Crescent).

God's angels are eager to carry out the program of judgment, to snuff out the blasphemous and boastful rebelliousness of the nations. But all is in God's control, and judgment will take place only when he gives the command, not a moment before. If only people would realize that all their prideful achievements in opposition to God are due only to God's patience and tolerance! This passage makes it clear that the whole earth, not only north and south, is under judgment. Nevertheless, it is the land of the north, or Babylon, that is at the center of the world's opposition to God. The speaker is the angel of the Lord, the

Lord of all the earth. The judgment on Babylon, the land of the north, has given rest to God's Spirit. When God finished creating the world, he rested (Gen. 2:3), not from weariness but because what he had made was perfect and he was satisfied. But sin brought discord into the world, and God's "rest" was disturbed. In Zechariah 1:14–15, God's response to the world scene is one of strong emotion and anger. Now, with the destruction of Babylon along with the establishment of God's kingdom on earth and the enthronement of God's Messiah, all is right with the world and God's Spirit is once again at rest.

3. The Crowning of Joshua (6:9–15)

The book of Haggai, after giving assurances of immediate blessing and of the future glory of the temple, closes with a prophecy of a victorious Messiah, who will reign over Jerusalem (Hag. 2:20–23). In a similar way Zechariah caps off the eight visions with a remarkable and memorable symbolic action—the crowning of Joshua as a foretoken of the Messiah. The fact of the crowning is significant; it is a reminder that when God has dealt with Babylon and the other nations, he will establish his own king on the throne. This king will flourish and be clothed with majesty. The manner of the crowning is significant in two ways: (1) It sets forth in the clearest possible way that in the Messiah the two offices of king and of priest will be united. (Note that Joshua the *priest* receives the crown of a *king*. See also Jer. 30:21, where the future king will also act as priest.) (2) It underscores the fact that the visions involving Joshua and Zerubbabel (chaps. 3 and 4) reach out beyond these men to the Messiah himself. The unusual plural form of the Hebrew word for "crown" may be a pointer to this twofold office. In verses 10 and 11 Zechariah is instructed to take the silver and gold that have been brought as a gift from Babylon and to go to the house of Josiah. There he is to make a crown and set it on the head of Joshua. The significance of this crowning is given in verses 12–15: "Here is the man whose name is the Branch." Note that

Joshua the priest is here the type of Christ, but it is the *office* of Zerubbabel that is primarily in view. (In chapter 4 it is Zerubbabel who will build and complete the temple. Here it is Joshua who does the same thing. Together they are a type of the Messiah to come.) This passage, which clearly has reference to the future, serves to illustrate the far reach of the visions in chapters 3 and 4. Zerubbabel finished the temple as promised in 4:9. But the completion of that project served as the illustration of a far greater fulfillment yet to come. The words "It is he who will build the temple" (6:13) stress the fact that Christ the Branch, and no other, will accomplish this task.

Throughout the eight visions, the rebuilding of the temple is inseparably related to the restoration of Jerusalem and to the spiritual as well as the physical restoration of Israel. He who has been despised is now universally acknowledged as the king of kings. He reigns now as both king and priest, and there will be no conflict of interests between the two offices. As king he is able to rule in righteousness without having to condemn a sinful populace, because as priest he has cleansed them of sin and brought them into fellowship with God.

Verse 15 adds that Gentiles who are far away will come and help build the temple. This comports with many Old Testament passages that speak of the help and wealth that the nations will bring (Isa. 60:4–9; Hag. 2:7; Zech. 14:14).

4. The Observance of Fasts (7:1–8:23)

A. The question (7:1–3). About two years after the temple rebuilding had recommenced, the question arose regarding the necessity of continuing the annual fasts that commemorated the destruction of the temple. The delegation comes from Bethel. The word "entreat" (7:2) indicates that these people are not merely asking for a judicial decision from the priests and prophets. They are seeking a favor from God. The fasts have obviously become wearisome to them. Except for the fast of the Day of Atonement, God had not prescribed fasting as an annual ritual. It was appropriate on special occasions

such as when there was mourning for sin (cf. Joel 1:13–14). In the present case the fasts have become a burdensome ritual with no real spiritual motivation. God does not tell them what they *want* to hear, but rather what they *need* to hear. His answer is in four parts, each introduced by the expression, "And the word of the LORD came again to Zechariah." Their question is not answered directly, but the answer in its first two parts goes right to the heart of their spiritual condition. The second two parts point to the blessings of God in a renewed Jerusalem and to the festivals that will replace the fasts.

B. The rebuke (7:4–14). The answer, with both rebuke and promise, is extended to all the people and the priests. "Was it really for me that you fasted?" This probing question goes right to the core of their problem: self-interest. Neither their fasting after the loss of the temple nor their former feasting while the temple stood were really for God's sake. Thus God dismisses their fasts as self-serving and meaningless ritual. The prophets before the exile had also condemned the futility of ritual worship without a true change of heart. As the people ignored God's wishes in prosperous times (7:7), so they ignore his wishes now, not mourning for their sin but for their loss.

The people are concerned about fasting—whether or not it should be continued. God's concern is that they should truly listen to him for a change. What he says in these verses he has said many times in the past. His specific admonitions all relate to the essence of the commandment to "love your neighbor as yourself" (Lev. 19:18). These admonitions are stressed because they are tangible and more easily demonstrated than the admonition to "love God" (cf. 1 John 4:20–21).

Israel's persistent, stubborn refusal to listen to God has caused God to turn a deaf ear to their entreaties and pleas for deliverance. The result is their scattering as "with a whirlwind" (7:14). The desolation of the land is not a capricious action on God's part but a direct result of their disobedience. Thus God redirects their question from a concern about the observance of a ritual to the true need of their lives: a heart that responds to God's call.

C. The promise (8:1–23). Chapter 7 ends with a description of the desolation of the land brought about by Israel's disobedience. Now God takes it upon himself to bring about a change despite Israel's failure. This is the outworking of God's grace and his faithfulness to his promises.

The depth of God's emotion is very evident here. In 1:14 his zeal is aroused by the sight of a Gentile world that is secure and prosperous while Israel is in distress. There his zeal brings about the destruction of the godless nations and a restored Jerusalem. Here his zeal is aroused by the words of 7:13–14, and it effects spiritual as well as physical restoration. The fact that God will dwell in Jerusalem is the supreme blessing, and if God is there, what purpose does fasting serve?

The two names given to Jerusalem are more than names. They are now for the first time accurate representations of the new character with which Jerusalem is invested, names that reflect the very presence of God. In the word translated "Truth" (8:3 KJV, NASB) the concept of faithfulness is present as well (cf. NIV "Faithful City"). A related word occurs in Isaiah 1:26, where Jerusalem is called both "Faithful City" and "City of Righteousness." This latter name is paralleled by the term "Holy Mountain," used here. What a change from its former condition! Verses 4 and 5 describe the peaceful living conditions in this city where truth, faithfulness, and holiness reign. Fear and unrest are absent. To say such a thing to Zechariah's contemporaries seemed an incredible thing (8:6), but with God nothing is impossible.

Verse 7 describes a regathering of Israel from all countries of the world. The conditions described in these verses were certainly not realized to any large degree in Zechariah's time. As is so often the case in prophetic Scripture, Zechariah sees the return from Babylon and the limited peace of his own day as simply a

foretaste of the glory to come. In view of this, Israel's self-imposed fasts keep them looking back at past defeats instead of forward to what God will do for them. They will be restored physically and spiritually, living in close fellowship with God under the new covenant. God has always been true, faithful, and righteous, but now under the new covenant these attributes are displayed in a new way, and he can justly receive a people whose sins have been forgiven.

Zechariah continues to encourage the people to keep building the temple in anticipation of the future. Verses 10 and 11 point to an upturn in economic prosperity and in the peace and safety of the people. Verse 12 promises a remarkable fertility for the land along with ideal weather conditions. All this God will provide as an inheritance to the remnant of his people. The word "remnant" refers not only to survivors of past judgments but to a people whose heart is right with God—a redeemed people. The wording of 8:13 (as well as 8:20–23) makes it clear that this whole passage still awaits its ultimate fulfillment.

It was Israel's destiny according to the Abrahamic covenant not only to receive God's blessing but to be a channel of blessing to the world in turn. Verses 14 and 15 give added assurance that the blessings described here will indeed come true. The previous destruction of Jerusalem by Babylon provides the assurance that, just as God has been true to his threats (see the warnings in Jeremiah), so will he also be true to his promises. The remnant can confidently rely on God to fulfill his purpose, no matter how impossible the obstacles might appear to be.

The message of 8:16–17 is similar to that of 7:9–10, but the setting is different. In chapter 7 the admonition went unheeded, and Jerusalem was destroyed. Here Jerusalem is destined to be restored; therefore, the people should now conduct their lives in anticipation of this. Jerusalem will be called the City of Truth and Holiness. They ought now to live a life of truth and holiness.

In verses 18–23 the subject of fasting again comes to the foreground, though it has always been in view. Fasting will become passé, to be replaced by joyous festivals (8:19) because of the rich outpouring of God's blessing on Jerusalem. The admonition to love truth and peace again urges them to let their present conduct be molded by future realities.

Verses 20–23 build on Isaiah 2:1–5 and Micah 4:1–5, where Jerusalem is the focal point of the globe because the Lord is there to give direction to all peoples of the world. He will instruct multitudes of willing hearers who have come to learn his will and to do it. In the present passage the role of Israel is stressed. Contempt for and hatred of Jerusalem has been replaced by the recognition that it is a place of honor, where God dwells. The formerly small and despised nation will now be joined by "many peoples and powerful nations" in seeking God (8:22). The Jews also will be acknowledged to have special status with God. Taking hold of the edge of a robe is an act of supplication to a superior (cf. 1 Sam. 15:27). The testimony of God's marvelous working on behalf of Israel will not fail to have its effect on a watching world.

Chapter 7 began with men entreating God from self-centered motives. Chapter 8 ends with multitudes of Gentiles joining Israel in entreating God with honest and responsive hearts. Not only is Israel blessed, but through Israel God reaches out to bless the Gentiles as well.

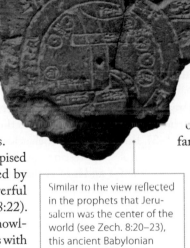

Similar to the view reflected in the prophets that Jerusalem was the center of the world (see Zech. 8:20–23), this ancient Babylonian map shows the world as a disc with Babylon at the center (700–500 BC).

5. The Coming of the Messiah (9:1–14:21)

A. The first coming and rejection (9:1–11:17). For Zechariah, the coming of the Messiah is central. This is clear in two oracles (chaps. 9–11 and 12–14) celebrating God's worldwide triumph through the king's advent. The salvation of Israel and God's judgment against the nations is clearly in view as well. The major thrust in both cases is the last days, often referred to elsewhere in Scripture as the day of the Lord. But there are also three major differences between the two oracles: (1) In the first, the Messiah is rejected; in the second, he is received by repentant hearts. (2) In the first, there is frequent alternation between near and far fulfillments, or telescoping, a frequent prophetic practice in which distant events are viewed from the standpoint of near events. The near and the far are often intermingled in such a way that they merge into one. The second oracle describes eschatological events almost entirely (13:7 being the exception, a "flashback" to the past, given as a reason for Israel's trials). (3) The first oracle is against the nations (9:1); the second concerns Israel (12:1). In the first, God judges the nations, but always with an eye on Israel's deliverance and blessing. In the second, God brings Israel to repentance and cleanses and protects her, while the nations are destroyed.

9:1–17. In the first oracle, the cities named are all north of Israel (9:1–8). Beginning with Hadrak and proceeding southward to Philistia, Zechariah portrays the defeat of these cities as a whirlwind military campaign (probably predicting Alexander's march down the Palestinian coast as a "near" fulfillment). When God makes his power felt as described in these chapters, people will see that it is God's hand at work, and many will turn to him. Zechariah provides a glimpse into the future with reference to various idolatrous and unclean customs practiced by the Philistines. God will effect a cleansing and transformation of these inveterate enemies of God's people. Here is another of many Old Testament passages speaking of the conversion of Gentiles. Not only will they become part of God's people; they will even become leaders in Judah, an indication of their complete acceptance by God and people alike. In this respect they will be like the Jebusites, the original inhabitants of Jerusalem, who were not destroyed when David captured their city. Rather, they were absorbed by Judah and became part of God's people.

Jerusalem stands out by contrast to other cities because of God's special care. In contrast to the fate of the other Palestinian cities, Jerusalem was unexpectedly spared. This fact brings about a natural telescoping into the future, when once again Jerusalem stands in contrast to other cities. It is clear that Jerusalem will later suffer defeat—Zechariah knows this (14:1–3). But when the final battle is over, when the smoke has cleared and city after city lies in ruins, Jerusalem will remain and will never again be overrun by an oppressor. No longer can Jerusalem say that God has forsaken her. Rather, his eyes are on her, to protect and provide for her. The word "now" signals a change to come through the advent of the Messiah.

Zechariah now directs Zion's attention to the long-awaited king, the Savior (9:9–10). He is righteous, in contrast to the many wicked kings who have preceded him. There will be absolute justice in his reign. He also comes with salvation, deliverance for his people. These ideal requirements for kingship are met in Christ in a unique way. Through his substitutionary death at his first advent he provided salvation from sin and imputed righteousness to all who

will receive him. As reigning king at his second advent he will redeem his people from their enemies and reign with righteousness.

The Messiah's humility at his first advent stands in contrast to the pomp and arrogance usually associated with kings. He rides on a donkey instead of a horse (which is associated with warfare). He comes not as a human conqueror but as God's servant. The removal of various instruments of war at his second advent is made possible by the Messiah's reign of righteousness and peace (cf. Isa. 2:4; 11:1–9). His presence guarantees the peace and security, not only of Jerusalem, but of all nations.

Zechariah again turns to Israel (9:11–17). The deliverance and blessing described in these verses is on the basis of Israel's covenant relationship with God, ratified by the blood of sacrifice. There is a place of refuge and security to which released prisoners may go, the fortress Zion, secured by God himself. The prisoners of hope are those who, though still in difficulty, hope in God and his promise. God promises to reward them abundantly. In verse 13 Judah and Ephraim are described as God's weapons—means of defeating his enemies. The victory over Greece points to the Maccabean victories over the Greek Seleucids after Antiochus Epiphanes' oppression and his desecration of the temple and is a foreshadowing of God's deliverance of Israel in the end times.

Israel's boundless joy, like a cup filled to overflowing, is compared to the bowl filled with the blood of sacrifice used in the sprinkling of the altar in worship. In their joy they recognize God as the author of their deliverance and the true object of praise. Verses 16–17 summarize their newly attained state of bliss and prosperity. They will be well cared for, as precious as jewels in God's crown, shining forth with the joy and glory of their newfound prosperity and standing with God. In place of poverty and humiliation there is prosperity and glory. What a future and what a blessed hope for God's people!

10:1–12. Zechariah 10:1 begins with an invitation and continues with a promise. The intent is to cause the reader's eyes to focus on God as the author of blessing and deliverance. There are two major aspects to the promise. First, God will shepherd his flock, replacing the false shepherds (10:2–3). The shepherd/flock theme has already been introduced in 9:16 and forms the major theme of chapter 11. Second, God is going to bring about change on behalf of Israel. This change is first of all an internal transformation of a weak, disoriented, captive people to brave, strong, and victorious heroes. The change is also external—deliverance from the power of the enemy.

Verse 1 provides an effective transition from the picture of a vigorous and prosperous people thriving on the produce of fertile soil to the admonition to seek the Lord, who is the author of that fertility and prosperity. It is God who sends the rain, and it is God who brings comfort and deliverance to his people. The message is clear: seek God and trust him. He will prosper and deliver his people. By failing to heed this admonition and by trusting in deceitful idols and lying diviners, Israel has fallen on hard times. They have wandered like sheep without a shepherd. They have been led astray, away from God and into suffering and exile; but in verse 3 God steps in. He deals with the false shepherds and leaders who abuse their authority and strength at the expense of the weak. He has long been silent, but now he will judge the wicked leaders and will care for his flock, providing for all their needs, physical and spiritual, delivering and protecting them from their enemies, providing them with the right leadership and making them strong.

From the last line of verse 3 through the first line of verse 5, Zechariah describes the strength and the leadership God will provide for Judah. The Jewish Targums correctly see a reference to the Messiah here. As promised repeatedly in Old Testament prophecy, beginning with Genesis 49:10, from Judah will come the true king, the source of able, stable, and victorious leadership, the one who exemplifies all the highest qualities of leadership—God's shepherd, the

Messiah. Judah also will be transformed into a power to be reckoned with (10:3, 6), as will Ephraim (10:7).

The cornerstone metaphor of verse 4 is clearly messianic in Isaiah 28:16 and in Psalm 118:22. Not only is stability in view here, but the cornerstone is the one on whom the whole structure of the kingdom of God is built. The tent-peg metaphor symbolizes one who both is prominent and carries on his shoulders the affairs of state. (See Isa. 22:22–24, where he carries the royal keys as a symbol of great authority.) The battle-bow metaphor obviously has a military reference. It is not used specifically of the Messiah elsewhere, but it is clearly a metaphor of military victory. "Every ruler" in this context is used simply of one who imposes his will on others (as described in 10:5). Though the whole of Judah has such power over the foe, the Messiah himself is the true source of this new power. Once again Judah and the house of Joseph (i.e., Ephraim) will be united. God, in his great compassion, will restore them again as one nation and as God's people in truth. In their newly exalted state it will be as though God has never rejected them. They will live in close fellowship with a responsive God, and there will be great rejoicing. God will signal for his people in the lands to which they have been exiled, will gather them in, and will multiply them in the land. Though Israel is widely scattered, their remembrance of God will not die out. They will no longer be a feeble nation but strong and numerous. The great powers of the past, Assyria and Egypt, will be subdued, but God will strengthen Israel. They will be strong politically, militarily, and numerically, but most importantly, spiritually.

11:1–17. Chapter 10 introduced the shepherd that God will raise up to care for his people. He will destroy the power of the enemy and deliver and restore Israel at his second coming. This anticipates a time when Israel will have accepted the shepherd to follow his leadership. In chapter 11 an earlier time is in view, the first advent of the Messiah, in which his own people tragically reject him, resulting in terrible consequences. The major portion of this chapter depicts this rejection by Israel of God's provision of the good shepherd. It is preceded and followed by a statement of the consequences of this rejection. The opening three verses are in the form of a lament for the devastation of the land from Lebanon through the Jordan Valley, resulting from Israel's rejection of their shepherd. The lament is not for a raging forest fire that devours first the cedars of Lebanon, then the pines, then sweeps down through Bashan to the Jordan Valley. The devouring fire is rather a symbol for judgment and portrays here a devastating military defeat. The cedars of Lebanon, stately trees, and oaks of Bashan are the nobles of the land, the shepherds are the leaders, and the lions are the choice men, the military leaders.

Images of the Good Shepherd, such as this one from the fourth century AD, were common in early Christian art.

In the body of the chapter, verses 4–14, Zechariah receives a commission to be a shepherd to God's flock. He represents the good shepherd appointed by God to care for his people. "Marked for slaughter" indicates the sorry status of this flock. Their shepherds have no care or concern for them; rather, they deal ruthlessly with them, using them as objects for personal profit.

It becomes clear as the passage unfolds that the abused flock has the option of receiving or rejecting God's shepherd. They decide to reject him. In rejecting God's shepherd, they reject God's help and salvation. They are left to suffer helplessly at the hands of their own countrymen and an oppressing king. This came true quite literally in the factionalism and civil strife of

AD 70, when Rome oppressed the land and destroyed Jerusalem. God did not intervene, for they had rejected his salvation.

As Zechariah symbolically tends the flock, his care is particularly for the oppressed—those who recognize the word of the Lord being fulfilled in the coming of the shepherd. They are a small, despised minority.

In caring for the sheep, Zechariah takes up two staffs, one called Favor, the other called Union. The first signifies God's special favor exercised on behalf of his people; the second signifies internal unity and cohesiveness within the nation, especially the two major factions, Judah and Israel. God's shepherd replaces the leadership of Israel (the three shepherds, symbolic of the three offices of prophet, priest, and king). He is the perfect leader, ideal in every way. Yet the flock detests him and rejects him. Therefore he leaves them to their fate, dying and consuming one another.

The breaking of the staff called Favor (11:10) symbolizes the revoking of the protective covenant keeping the nations from harming Israel. Only the faithful remnant recognizes the Messiah at his coming and sees in the judgment that results from his rejection the fulfillment of God's word (11:11).

The shepherd's pay—thirty pieces of silver—was the price to be paid for a gored slave (Exod. 21:32). For God's shepherd to be evaluated this way is a deliberate insult. God's response is, "Throw it to the potter" (11:13), evidently an act symbolizing rejection and contempt. This symbolic act was fulfilled by Judas when he threw the thirty shekels into the temple and when the priests used it to buy a potter's field for the burial of the poor (Matt. 27:3–10). Verse 14 describes the breaking of the second staff, Union, symbolizing the lack of internal cohesion within the nation.

Israel rejected the Good Shepherd provided by God for their benefit. There were immediate consequences, but much worse will be the time when they become subject to one whose qualities are opposite to those of the Good Shepherd (11:15–17). This is the antichrist, who will exercise terrible power during the tribulation (cf. Daniel 7; Revelation 13). He is a (spiritually) foolish (11:15) and worthless (11:17) shepherd. It will be a time of incredible hardship and suffering for Israel until God judges the false shepherd.

B. The second coming and reception (12:1–14:21). 12:1–14. As God sets out to unfold his great eschatological working in and on behalf of Israel (12:1–9), he reminds us that he is the Creator of heaven and earth and that he also formed man's spirit within him. Thus he has the absolute right and sovereign ability to do as he wishes. There is no power in heaven or earth that can deter him from accomplishing his purpose. Israel as a nation (not just the northern kingdom) will be restored, the nations will be judged, and God's kingdom will be established.

The expression "on [or "in"] that day" occurs sixteen times in the last three chapters of Zechariah. The setting is in the last days, when God judges the nations, restores Israel, and establishes his kingdom on earth. The particular setting of this paragraph is the last and climactic siege of Jerusalem by the forces of the enemies of God. It seems as though victory is in their grasp. But God intervenes, and it is not Jerusalem that is destroyed but the forces of the antichrist. The cup of reeling is a frequent prophetic metaphor describing the staggering effect God's judgment will have on the nations (cf. Jer. 25:15–28). Instead of being drunk with the wine of revelry, they will drink the cup of God's wrath. The nations view Jerusalem as a cup that will make them drunk with the joy

of victory, but they will find that they will go away staggering in utter defeat at God's hands.

Judah and Jerusalem are separated in verses 5–7. There is apparently some rift, or at least friction, between the two. Verse 7 seems to point to a spirit of elitism on the part of those in Jerusalem. Jerusalem will be a rock, apparently easy to deal with, but by God's intervention a rock so heavy that the nations will injure themselves. Both the cup of reeling and the immovable stone metaphors graphically illustrate the sudden and unexpected disaster that befalls the attackers. Verse 4 makes it clear that it is God's doing that saves Jerusalem. The three elements of panic, madness, and blindness are also present in the curse pronounced on a rebellious Israel (Deut. 28:28), but here the enemy is afflicted with these elements. At the same time that the enemy is struck with blindness, God will guard and protect Judah. The people of Jerusalem are strong because of their God. There seems to be an acknowledgment here not only of the power and reality of God but also of the fact that the people of Jerusalem have trusted God. At the very least their hearts are prepared for the appearance of the Messiah, their king. The leaders of Judah, encouraged and empowered by God, will overcome their enemies.

God's deliverance is twofold: he provides a shield for the people, and he gives them supernatural strength so that the feeblest will be as heroic as David, and the leaders will be like God, like the angel of the Lord (equated here as elsewhere with God), the invincible "commander of the army of the LORD" (Josh. 5:14). No more are God's people ready prey for their voracious enemies. God is their shield and strength. Verse 9 is a pointed summary of the whole paragraph. This eschatological attack against Jerusalem is God's means of bringing the nations to judgment. To the attackers victory seems assured (they even penetrate Jerusalem initially [14:2]), and to Jerusalem it might seem hopeless, but the victory is the Lord's.

Zechariah has described a great victory won on Israel's behalf by the powerful intervention of God. Now an even greater victory is won, this time an *internal* victory over sinful and rebellious hearts (12:10–13:1). This victory is likewise won because of God's gracious intervention. He takes the initiative and brings about a change in heart.

The outpouring of God's Spirit, like an abundant stream of water onto arid ground, will bring about a miraculous transformation in human hearts (Isa. 32:15; 44:3; Ezek. 36:25–27; 39:29; Joel 2:28–29). Not until God does this will Israel's blindness and hardness of heart be removed and will the people acknowledge and receive their Messiah. God's spirit of grace will convict their hearts and move them to true repentance. His spirit of supplication will move them to cry out to God. On this great day the working of God's Spirit will cause the scales to fall from Israel's eyes, and they will see the Lord Jesus as their Messiah.

Verse 10 gives remarkable information about the one to whom they will look. (1) Since God is speaking, the "me" to whom they look is clearly God. (2) The one they have pierced is God. This conforms to Jesus's claims to deity. (3) This passage links him with the Suffering Servant of Isaiah 53:5, who "was pierced for our transgressions." John 19:34–37 sees the piercing of Jesus's side by the spear as a fulfillment of this verse. (4) This passage clearly anticipates a twofold advent of the Messiah: the first when he was pierced; the second when they recognize him and trust in him. The result will be true repentance. The depth of their emotion and sense of loss because they have slain him instead of receiving him is vividly expressed. The mourning of that day is compared to the weeping of Hadad Rimmon in the plain of Megiddo. This most likely refers to the tradition of mourning for the death of Josiah in battle with Pharaoh Necho in the plains of Megiddo (2 Chron. 35:22–25). The loss of Josiah was keenly felt, particularly by the godly of the land, his death being a catastrophe. Thus the mourning of Israel described here is compared to that associated with great personal loss and terrible national catastrophe. The mourning is individualized to stress the fact that this is not a case of mass psychology or of ritual mourning. Each family and each individual, from the house of David on down, will grieve deeply for their sin.

13:1–9. God will respond to Israel's repentance (13:1). An abundance of forgiveness is available to them (an open fountain). There is cleansing for every sin and every impurity. The Hebrew word for sin describes humanity's missing the mark, falling short of God's requirements. Impurity has to do with ceremonial matters, those things that disqualify a person from coming into God's presence. After years of rejection, dispersion, and suffering, Israel now comes home, is united with her Savior, and finds glorious forgiveness and peace.

Zechariah 13:2–6 describes the love and loyalty of Israel for God in the kingdom age. Now that Israel is in right relationship to God through Jesus Christ, there is no room in the land for false prophets or idolatry.

Idolatry played an integral part in the sins of Israel leading to the destruction of Samaria and Jerusalem. It was not a problem as such after the exile. However, as the second coming of Christ approaches, it will once again increase in prominence, especially as people worship the antichrist and demons (Isa. 2:18, 20; Matt. 24:11, 15, 23–24; 2 Thess. 2:2–4; Rev. 9:20; 13:4–15). But in the messianic kingdom, the land will be purged of any form of idolatry. Christ alone will reign. The whole complex of idolatry, false prophets, and demon worship is spawned of Satan and will no longer be tolerated.

The convictions of redeemed Israel will be so firm and their love and loyalty to Christ will be so strong that parents will even put their own children to death for the sin of telling lies in the Lord's name. False prophets will attempt to conceal their true identity by claiming to be farmers. Accused prophets will claim innocence, attributing probably self-inflicted wounds (see 1 Kings 18:28) to mistreatment at the hands of so-called friends. The impression that Zechariah leaves is that in actual fact these prophets have been involved in idolatrous activity.

Zechariah returns to the theme of the rejected shepherd, but now from a different perspective (13:7–9). In chapter 11 the flock rejected its shepherd. Human responsibility is stressed. Here the shepherd is slain by God's decree. The result of the rejection of chapter 11 is that the flock becomes prey to the nations and ultimately comes under the rule of a false and worthless shepherd. Here, the flock is dispersed: two-thirds perish while the rest are refined and restored to fellowship with God. The resolution of the rejection of chapter 11 is seen in the repentance of 12:10 and the forgiveness of 13:1. The rejected shepherd is ultimately embraced. The final resolution of the smiting of the shepherd here is seen in the victorious return of the Lord and his reign over the whole earth.

God himself calls on the sword as the instrument of death to slay his shepherd. Though the redemptive reasons are not given here, the passage makes it clear that the rejection and slaying of the shepherd is no accident of history. He is the one whom God has appointed for his people, the one who alone can fully provide for all the needs of the flock. The remarkable designation "the man who is close to me" (13:7) identifies the shepherd as both man and "colleague" or "associate" of God. When the shepherd is struck, the sheep will be scattered. The term "little ones" emphasizes their helpless condition.

A great catastrophe is to come on Israel. The destruction of Jerusalem in AD 70 was but a foretaste of the tribulation to come. God will refine and purify as silver and gold the third of the flock that remains. As terrible as the coming tribulation will be, its purpose is to cleanse and prepare Israel to receive her Messiah. This is not punitive judgment but rather a means of drawing Israel back to God. As a result they will call on God's name in repentance and in trust. Their hearts will be entirely directed toward God. They have turned away from all that grieves him. God will forgive them and receive them

so that he can say "they are my people," and they will be able to say "the LORD is our God."

14:1–20. Chapter 14 returns to the final siege of Jerusalem. Besides adding some particulars omitted in chapter 12, chapter 14 has a different purpose. Both chapters show that much more is at stake than the defense of Jerusalem and the destruction of the enemy. In chapter 12 the impact of Christ's coming brings God's people to repentance and faith. In chapter 14 Christ's coming is seen in its impact on the world at large, in the establishment of a worldwide kingdom where Christ alone is king. The repentance of Israel in chapter 12 is a prerequisite for her proper role in the Messiah's world kingdom.

The king's coming will be victorious (14:1–7). "A day of the LORD" is literally "a day *for* the Lord." God is personally interested and involved in the events and their outcome. This day begins as a day of great darkness for Jerusalem (cf. Amos 5:18–20). The attacking nations will ransack Jerusalem. This is not a hit-and-run raid. Their intent is to impose the authority of the antichrist on Jerusalem completely. The attack on Jerusalem is brought about not by political or military considerations but by the satanically inspired motive of crushing the last major stronghold of resistance to the antichrist. But as in the case of the crucifixion of Christ, God is in control, using the ambition and malice of humans to accomplish his own ends (Acts 2:23). Initially the nations will have great success, capturing the city, ransacking the houses, raping the women. The attackers, however, will be suddenly and unexpectedly interrupted in their looting and pillaging. Just as they seem to have achieved final victory, the Lord himself will fight against them.

Some details of Christ's coming and victory are now given. His feet will stand on the Mount of Olives, the place from which the glory of God left Jerusalem before the destruction of the temple in 586 BC (Ezek. 11:23) and from which Christ ascended into glory (Acts 1:9–12). Here also will the glory of God (in the person

927

of Christ) return to Jerusalem (Ezek. 43:1–4). When the Lord touches the mountain, it will be split in two, forming a great valley running east to west. This is only one of a number of great, supernaturally caused changes that will take place (14:6–10). The people of Jerusalem will flee through this valley to Azel (a place east of the Mount of Olives, but not identified to date). Then the Lord will come. There is here a brief personal testimony of Zechariah's personal identification with, and loyalty to, God in this conflict. At first there will be no light, no daytime or nighttime. Then, when evening comes, there will be light again. Evidently this describes a unique and heretofore unknown state of darkness (semidarkness?), which is neither day nor night, while God's judging activity is going on. When evening comes the heavenly sources of light will resume their normal functioning. The

whole universe is involved in the display of God's power, heightening the terror of that day.

The physical rejuvenation of the land due to the perennial supply of living water flowing out of Jerusalem corresponds to the spiritual blessing and revitalization that the Lord effects in the lives of his people (14:8–11). No more will Israel rely on the leaky cistern of trust in false gods (Jer. 2:13). This abundant supply of water is as regular and plentiful in the dry summer season as in the wet winter. This is no wadi (intermittent stream) but a dependable, never-failing supply of water. This also serves as a wonderfully apt picture of the unfailing mercies and blessing of God to his own.

God will be king over the whole earth. His kingship will be universally acknowledged. Furthermore, there will be one Lord, and his name will be the only name. This both recalls and expounds the great Jewish Shema (Deut. 6:4). There is no longer any question as to who is Lord, who is to be worshiped. Now not only Israel but the whole world will recognize the truth: God is sovereign; he is the

Zechariah 14:4 describes the Lord standing on the Mount of Olives, which is seen here from the Kidron Valley.

Redeemer; he forgives those who repent but judges the unrepentant. Probably as a part of the same upheavals in verse 4, the land around Jerusalem will become like the Arabah, the broad depression of the Jordan Valley, while Jerusalem will be raised up as a large mesa dominating the whole area. It will be inhabited, never to be destroyed again. It will be secure and remain so.

The manner in which the Lord deals with the attackers is briefly described (14:12–15). The Hebrew word for "plague" means literally "a striking [by God]" and is used in Exodus 9:14 to describe the way God strikes Egypt. The method God will employ is not stated. What is clear is that he makes a distinction, as he did in Egypt, between his own people and his enemies. After the nations attack each other, Judah will participate in the "mop-up" phase of the battle. They, along with the people of Jerusalem, will share in the wealth of all the surrounding nations as it is collected at Jerusalem. Now Jerusalem is not being plundered but enriched.

The attacking armies are completely destroyed. But there will be those among the nations of the world who will repent and turn to the Lord (14:16–19). These will enter the millennial kingdom and will join Israel in worshiping and obeying the Lord (cf. Isa. 2:1–4; Zech. 8:20–23). They will go up yearly to worship and to celebrate the Feast of Tabernacles. The celebration of this festival during the millennium will be appropriate in that (1) it follows shortly after the great day of atonement, a day of national repentance and forgiveness for sins; (2) it is a thanksgiving festival commemorating the end of centuries of homeless exile; and (3) as a harvest festival it acknowledges the gracious providence of God in both the physical and the spiritual realms. The keeping of the Feast of Tabernacles and the worship of the Lord are equated in verses 17–18. Since this festival is in part an acknowledgment of God as king and as gracious provider, to refuse to participate is to refuse to acknowledge God. The punishment

fits the crime, since withholding rain results in crop failure. No amount of modern technology can counteract the withholding of God's blessing on the land.

There are several possible reasons why Egypt is singled out here: (1) It is a link to Israel's background as the land they left to journey to the land of promise. (2) Egypt was dependent on the Nile for the fertility of its land, but God can diminish and even dry up the Nile. (3) God had once before established the fact of his lordship by bringing Egypt to her knees. He can do it again. (See Isa. 19:18–23 for a remarkable description of the place Egypt will have among the redeemed in the millennial age.)

Jerusalem will for the first time truly be a "Holy City" (14:20–21). In the Mosaic economy the high priest had "Holy to the Lord" inscribed on his turban (Exod. 28:36). Now even the bells of the horses are so engraved. Ordinary cooking pots will be like the sacred bowls used for sprinkling blood on the altar. The distinction between sacred and profane is now eliminated, because all of Jerusalem is truly dedicated to the Lord. The priestly calling of Israel will become actuality. The term "Canaanite" (14:21) sometimes refers to traders or merchants (see Job 41:6; Prov. 31:24) and may refer to the fact that the need for traders (who sold holy utensils to pilgrim worshipers in the temple precincts) will no longer exist, since all that is in Jerusalem will be holy and suitable for temple worship. But more likely "Canaanites" are persons who are spiritually unclean and unfit to come into God's presence. No longer will anyone come unworthily before the Lord, because God will have sanctified his people, making them fit to worship him.

Thus this great prophecy concludes with God's having accomplished his intended program. Israel has been transformed into a people worthy of its calling, the hostile world powers have been judged, and the once-rejected Messiah now reigns supreme in a world of redeemed Jews and Gentiles that is blessed by his presence.

Select Bibliography

Baldwin, Joyce G. *Haggai, Zechariah, Malachi.* Tyndale Old Testament Commentaries. Downers Grove, IL: InterVarsity, 1972.

Barker, Kenneth L. "Zechariah." In *The Expositor's Bible Commentary.* Edited by Frank E. Gaebelein. Vol. 7. Grand Rapids: Zondervan, 1985.

Boda, Mark J. *Zechariah.* NIV Application Commentary. Grand Rapids: Zondervan, 2004.

Feinberg, Charles L. *The Minor Prophets.* Chicago: Moody, 1976.

Laney, J. Carl. *Zechariah.* Chicago: Moody, 1984.

McComiskey, Thomas Edward. "Zechariah." In *The Minor Prophets: An Exegetical and Expository Commentary.* Edited by Thomas Edward McComiskey. Grand Rapids: Baker Academic, 1992.

Merrill, Eugene H. *Haggai, Zechariah, Malachi.* Chicago: Moody, 1994.

Smith, Ralph L. *Micah–Malachi.* Word Biblical Commentary. Waco: Word, 1984.

Unger, Merrill F. *Zechariah: Prophet of Messiah's Glory.* Grand Rapids: Zondervan, 1962.

Webb, Barry G. *The Message of Zechariah: Your Kingdom Come.* The Bible Speaks Today. Downers Grove, IL: InterVarsity, 2003.

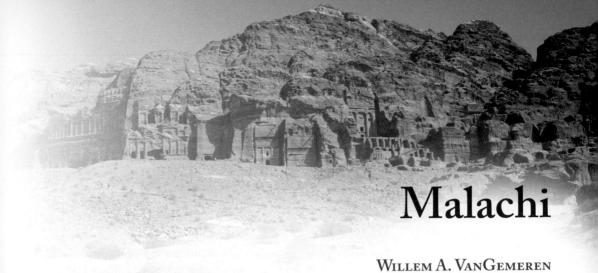

Malachi

WILLEM A. VANGEMEREN

Introduction

Malachi the Prophet

Nothing is known about Malachi, his ancestry, or his place of residence. According to the church fathers, Malachi was a Levite from the region of Zebulun. It is impossible to verify this assertion, but Malachi's concern with the corruption of worship, the glory of God, the corruption of the priesthood, and the tithe would support the priestly interests if not the background of the prophet.

Date

He lived after the exile in a world filled with shattered hopes. Scholars are in general agreement on the postexilic date of this book, and though there is some minor disagreement, his ministry is dated around 440 BC. This date fits the present archaeological evidence of the devastation of Edom by the Nabateans (1:3–4), the reference to the "governor" of the Persian province (1:8), the existence of the temple, and the moral and social problems portrayed in Ezra-Nehemiah.

Historical Context

Following Israel's return from exile, the prophetic promises were only partially fulfilled. The prophets had spoken about the renewal of the covenant, the restoration of the people to the land, the messianic kingdom of peace, the renewal of temple worship, the continuity of the priestly ministry, the rebuilding of a glorious temple, and a new era characterized by Isaiah as the New Jerusalem (65:17–25).

The religious enthusiasm characteristic of the returning exiles and the contemporaries of Haggai and Zechariah had waned. The restoration of which the prophets had spoken had not yet come. God had not "shaken" the nations, and the messianic kingdom had not yet been established. The Lord had not blessed his people as he had promised. The era of fulfillment had turned into a period of waiting. While waiting, some had exchanged their beliefs for the fast life (3:5, 15), while others were cynical about the value of organized religion. A minority remained faithful regardless of how bad the times were (3:16).

Theological Themes

God raised up Malachi to address the problems of cynicism, formalism, and unfaithfulness, and questions about the benefits of godliness. Malachi defends the love, honor, and justice of God. God's love is shown by his election and care for his own. God, Father of Israel and king of the universe, expects his children to respond to his love, honor, and justice.

The focus of the prophet is on the veracity of God and on humanity's responsibility. The Lord is faithful, even when it seems as if he does not respond. The prophecy encourages all who remain faithful to him to persevere. Malachi calls for responsibility in marriage, sacrifice, religion, social concerns, tithes, and observance of God's laws. He redefines the "godly" as those who persevere in godliness. Israel may no longer claim any automatic hold on God but must show that they have the Spirit of God. God is faithful to his own and will richly reward his children.

Literary Features

Malachi is the twelfth of the Minor Prophets. The placement of the book after Zechariah may not have been out of chronological considerations but because of the connecting phrase, "A prophecy: The word of the LORD" (1:1), also found in Zechariah 9:1; 12:1. The prophet uses a disputation form to move his audience from the presumptions that their relationship with Yahweh is good and that Yahweh is at fault to the conclusion that they all, priests and people, are under judgment. The Lord's favor rests on a small community within Israel and will extend to all who fear him, including people from the nations.

Outline

1. Introduction (1:1)
2. God's Love for His People (1:2–5)
3. The Honor of God (1:6–14)
4. The Knowledge of God (2:1–9)
5. Intermarriage and Divorce (2:10–16)
6. The Justice and Patience of God (2:17–3:6)
7. The Tithe (3:7–12)
8. God's Love for the Remnant (3:13–4:3)
9. Conclusion (4:4–6)

Commentary

1. Introduction (1:1)

The book of Malachi is an oracle, a word, from Yahweh. "Oracle" (or "burden") is a technical, prophetic term for a word of judgment on both the nations and Israel/Judah. The prophet functions as an ambassador whose duty is to proclaim the word, no matter how burdensome the message or how unresponsive the people. The prophet is appointed by God to discharge

his office, and in that appointment there is a sense of urgency (cf. Jer. 20:9). He *must* proclaim the oracle, because the oracle is the word of Yahweh.

2. God's Love for His People (1:2–5)

In the first disputation, Yahweh assures his people of his love. The structure is symmetric. The cynicism of the people (1:2) is symmetric with the expression of hope in God (1:5). The affirmation of God's "love" (1:2–3) is symmetric with an affirmation of his "greatness" (1:5). God's past acts against Edom (1:3) are symmetric with his promise to rid the land of all evil (1:4). The focus of the oracle is on the demonstrations of Yahweh's love for his people, which are the very reasons why the elect in Israel should put their faith in God and praise him (1:1–2).

Although the postexilic Jewish community was not living in the fullness of the messianic age, they had been loved. It had been nearly a century since their return from exile and the rebuilding of the temple. The priests were again serving God in the temple. God was reconciled to his people, and through the ministry of the prophets Haggai and Zechariah he had encouraged them to look forward to the messianic kingship that would bring peace, prosperity, and justice (cf. Hag. 2:20–23; Zech. 9:9; 13:1–14:21). Yet the prophetic assurance of God's love receives only a cynical response from God's people.

In response to the people's question, "How have you loved us?" Malachi turns to Israel's history. Yahweh loved Jacob more than Esau. His love is not based on Israel's righteousness (Deut. 9:4) or greatness (Deut. 7:7) but on his promise of blessing (Deut. 7:8) guaranteed by oath to Abraham, Isaac, and Jacob. Esau was bypassed. No human reasoning can fully explain God's choice. His love for Jacob was an act of love, election, and sovereignty (Rom. 9:1–29).

The people may have given Malachi a cynical look as he proclaimed God's love for them a second time. The Edomites, descendants of Esau, were supposed to have been wiped out, and their territory should have been given to Israel (Amos 9:11–12; Obadiah 8–10, 18–19, 21). Yet they still existed as a nation, and their territory now adjoined Judah!

God's judgment on Esau, however, is progressive, slowly moving toward completion (1:3–4). The Edomites had harassed the Judeans as they attempted to flee Judah and Jerusalem at the time of the fall of Jerusalem (586 BC). The books of Obadiah and Lamentations speak of the hatred shown by the Edomites, who did not help Judah in her time of need but instead rejoiced in her tragedy. Later, the Edomites were displaced by desert nomads who had destroyed the mountain strongholds and devastated the land, forcing them to flee into the northern Negev. Malachi confirms the prophetic word of God's judgment on the Edomites. Regardless of how long it may be, Yahweh himself will see to the end of the Edomites (1:4).

The rejection and judgment of Edom is without mercy. God promises to harass and judge the Edomites (Idumeans) until every trace of their evil scheming and activity is removed. His anger will rest on them until their land is emptied of Edomites. Malachi encourages God's people with the promise that evil will be dealt with in the day of the Lord.

In the Old Testament, Edom represents all the enemies of God's kingdom. The prophets point beyond the Edomites to the fall of all Gentile kingdoms. Since God's judgment rests on such a small nation (Edom), how much more will it extend to all kingdoms! If the Edomites, who are related to the Israelites, will not escape the judgment of God, how will other nations avoid the day of the Lord? It is in this context that we must understand God's response to Judah. He declares that he will so execrate and destroy evil that not a trace will be left. During the time of the postexilic restoration, the Jews remained subject to a foreign nation, the Persians. In the coming centuries they would be subject to the Greeks, the Ptolemies, the Seleucids, and the Romans. The Lord here affirms that he will judge all nations that oppress his people, thus purging all wickedness from his creation. History attests to the fulfillment of this promise: the Lord brought desolation to Edom and to the enemies of his people. The

> The land of Edom. The Lord says of this land belonging to the descendants of Esau, "I have turned his hill country into a wasteland" (Mal. 1:3).

Lord's anger still rests upon wickedness, and he will make an end to the rule of evil forever.

In anticipation of God's coming demonstration of his love for the elect, the people of God must now pray with hope that Yahweh be exalted beyond the territory of Israel (1:5). This prayer is often taken as a proclamation ("Great is the LORD"). However, the same phrase is translated correctly in the psalms as "The LORD be exalted" (40:16; 70:4 NIV 1984). The context is hope in the deliverance of the Lord. The eyes of faith already see his victory over the enemies of the kingdom and the full establishment of God's kingdom. The translation should be: "May Yahweh be exalted beyond the borders of Israel." The phrase "beyond the borders" has occasioned difficulty. The preposition may be translated as "over" or "beyond." In view of his universal interest (1:11, 14) and his concern that evil be removed, the reading "beyond" is preferable. Yahweh, the God of Israel, is not limited to Judah. His kingship will extend to the ends of the earth.

3. The Honor of God (1:6–14)

Even though the people are not certain of God's love (1:2), he expects a minimal response of honor and respect. Malachi likens the situation to that of a son's respect for his father or a servant's respect for his master. The people of God, however, are so self-centered that they cannot express

The Lord asks whether a governor would be happy if he were offered a lame or diseased animal (Mal. 1:8). This palace relief depicts the type of offering made to royalty: a servant is bringing a kid goat to be sacrificed for a royal banquet (Persepolis, fifth century BC).

themselves in love and devotion toward Yahweh. He affirms that he is Father and master. God is not only the Father of the faithful (1:6) but also the king whose kingdom is not limited to Jerusalem or the land of Judea. His name is feared among the nations. He is the great king.

These three grounds for honoring Yahweh (as Father, master, and king) provide the structure of the second disputation. Malachi's argument focuses on the priests' utter disregard for the God of Israel. They of all people should be expected to remain faithful. The job of the priests as cultic functionaries was to please God by presenting offerings and sacrifices and in teaching the law of God. They may not have been aware of their attitudes and hidden motives. This section is a warning for Christians, particularly ministers of the Word, to be careful not to "despise" or "show contempt for" the name of God by slovenly attitudes and shoddy service.

Malachi charges the priests with profaning the glorious name of the Lord (1:6–10). Since God is the Father of his people and the master of the universe, it is only fair that his servants, the priests, protect his "honor" ("glory") and give reason for the Gentiles to "respect" the God of Israel. Instead, they are irreverent and nurture a low view of God. Malachi cites their disregard of the sacrificial laws as evidence of their guilt. They show contempt for God by having no regard for the revealed priestly rules and regulations. His "table" (i.e., the tables on which the sacrifices were slaughtered; cf. Ezek. 40:39–43) is treated with contempt. In response to the twofold disputation ("How have we shown contempt for your name?" and "How have we defiled you?"), Yahweh charges the priests with defiling his altar by presenting offerings not in accordance with the priestly regulations. According to Leviticus 22:23–27, the priests were to inspect the offerings before they were consecrated to the Lord to see whether they were ritually clean. The priests, according to Malachi, disregard these regulations. They sacrifice anything presented to the Lord in the temple, whether blind, lame, or sickly. The prophet returns to the analogy with which he began by asking whether they present sickly animals as gifts to the governor, their political master. They must repent and ask God to restore his favor. However, if they continue their practices, the priests may as well close the temple down and extinguish the fires on the altar. The Lord looks for heartfelt honor, not mere formalism.

Certainly, Yahweh's kingship extends from east to west, because his name is great among the nations (1:11). Malachi concludes that this worship of God is more acceptable than worship in the Jerusalem temple. This does not mean that God is pleased with pagan sacrifices but that true worship is offered to him by Gentiles who come to him in faith (cf. Zeph. 2:11; 3:9). A note of expectation of a greater fulfillment may also be present, as his kingdom extends from "where the sun rises to where it sets," from east to west. When Jews worshiped the Lord in their various locations of the Diaspora (Persia, Babylonia, Egypt), Gentiles were drawn to his worship as God-fearers and proselytes. The prophetic word was already being fulfilled; Gentiles were joining with the Jews in the worship of Yahweh in increasing numbers. Truly, Yahweh's name was known and was becoming great among the nations. Thus, the prophet argues against the priests that, since Yahweh's name is great among the nations, how much more should the people of Jerusalem and Judea honor their God?

The prophet moves rapidly from charges and countercharges to judgment (1:12–14). He charges the people with profaning the Lord and his temple. The charge is a severe one. But they respond by asking what wrong they have done. They are bored with their vocation. By permitting injured, lame, and sickly animals to be brought into the temple, they demonstrate that they are more concerned about their own livelihood than about the honor of the Lord. Anyone who continues to bring sickly sacrifices, even in fulfillment of a vow, will be cursed because, regardless of the priestly attitudes, God is the great king. He will turn the priestly blessing into a curse.

4. The Knowledge of God (2:1–9)

In the second disputation, Malachi charges the priests with not giving honor to God; they offer defiled and blemished offerings and sacrifices. In this third disputation, focus shifts from their cultic function to their function as teachers of God's word. The key word is "warning" (literally "commandment," 2:1, 4). Malachi repeats the word and purposely builds up suspense so as to stimulate the question, what commandment has been broken that causes the Lord's curse to rest on the priests? It is not until verse 7 that the commandment is set forth in a straightforward manner: "For the lips of a priest ought to preserve knowledge, because he is the messenger of the LORD Almighty and people seek instruction from his mouth."

The knowledge of God is not knowledge about God or secrets pertaining to the priesthood. "Knowledge" is the ability to *know* and the desire to *do* the will of God on earth in accordance with his commandment. Knowledge is immensely practical, because it is in essence what could be called "godliness," "wise living," or "the way to holiness" (cf. Hos. 4:1, 6). The Lord has commanded the priests not only to oversee the offerings, sacrifices, and tabernacle but also to be the guardians of his revelation (Deut. 31:9). The priests were the teachers of the law of God. The failure of the priests before the exile had brought the judgment of God on

Israel and Judah. Malachi is concerned that their present insensitivity will renew God's judgment. His prophetic denunciation is an expression of his concern for the well-being of God's people.

Yahweh will not hesitate to curse his own priests (2:1–3). The curses are those enumerated in Deuteronomy 28:15, 20. The curses were applicable to all of God's people but particularly to the priests, because they had been instructed in "the commandment." The curse is explicated in a threefold formula, which is best translated as "I shall send a curse on you; and I shall curse your blessings. Indeed I shall curse them."

In verse 3, the nature of the curse is brought out more clearly. Yahweh will not limit his curse to the priests but will extend it to their children. He will also disregard their festivals, which were the occasions when the priests received food from the people; so when there was an economic depression, the priests were the first to suffer. At this time, the sacrifices being presented are unacceptable to the Lord. He puts them in the same class as dung (NIV 1984 "offal," 2:3), which was removed from the temple to be burned. The language is strong, but so is God's feeling about the priests.

The curse stands in contrast to the covenant God made with Levi (2:4–7). The original covenant was made with Phinehas, the grandson of Aaron, after he demonstrated his loyalty to the Lord (Num. 25:12–13). The purpose of the covenant was not curse but life and peace. However, "life and peace" were conditioned on the faithful performance of the priests. Malachi reminds the priests of their ancestry in order to evoke in them responsive hearts. In the early days of Israel, priests feared the Lord and respected him. They were the guardians of the law of God and did not betray Yahweh by improper speech and infidelity. Instead, they were characterized by godliness in that they walked in accordance with God's standards of fidelity, peace, and equity. When the priests were the guardians of the law, were godly, and walked in fellowship with the Lord, they were his human instruments in restoring many from

evil. The priests were the theocratic officers by whom the covenantal relationship was kept alive. It is at this point that Malachi explains the original "commandment" or "warning" to the priests (2:7).

The priests of Malachi's time have gone astray (2:8). They have departed from "the commandment" God originally gave them. Therefore, the Lord has withheld the fullness of blessing and will turn the blessings of "life and peace" into a curse. The problem is with the priests, who have turned away from glorifying the Lord, led people into sin, and disregarded their duties. The lives and teaching of the priests cause people to sin against the Lord. Thus, they breach the terms of the covenant. A breach in covenant fidelity evokes God's wrath, judgment, and curse.

Malachi 2:9 is a summary of 1:6–2:8. The repetition of the word translated "despise" or "show contempt for" (1:6; 2:9) forms an inclusio, for Yahweh has charged the priests with despising his name. They do not honor him as a Father and king in their sacred duty as priests. Their way of life and public instruction have led the people astray. The autonomy of the priests will incur God's judgment. Rather than being sought after as "messengers" of the Lord, the priests will be despised by the people. When this happens, the people will no longer be misled. The Lord does not annul the covenant with Levi but suspends the blessings of "life and peace." Because the priests have little regard for God's glory, he will utterly reject them—unless they learn to respond by following in the ways of the Lord and by studying the word of God. If the priests are to avert God's curse and judgment on them, they must return to the original commandment given to their forefathers. They may again become the "messengers" of the Lord by being the guardians of his law, faithful in their walk with God, and teachers of his people. Then the Lord's blessings of life and peace will attend his people.

5. Intermarriage and Divorce (2:10–16)

The fourth disputation, Malachi 2:10–12, opens abruptly. Who is speaking? Who is the

"Father"? It seems that the people contest something the prophet has said, or it may be that the prophet is quoting a proverb. Since Malachi, by the disputation method, portrays the spirit of the people as filled with cynicism and sarcasm, it is best to take verse 10 as an argument by the people. It is filled with self-righteousness and self-justification but is hollow from Malachi's perspective. The people's argument may be restated as, "Have we not all one Father? Has not one God created us? Why should we deal treacherously with one another? Why should we profane the covenant of the fathers?" Yahweh, who sees the heart, charges that they have dealt treacherously with each other and that they have broken the covenant. They have desecrated the "holy" institution of marriage by intermarriage and divorce. God is concerned with the purity of his people. The history of Israel before the exile was marked by idolatry, syncretism, and acculturation. Intermarriage was the way in which the people of Judah and Israel had accepted the cultures and gods of the nations (Judg. 2:11–13, 19; 1 Kings 11:1–8). Malachi's concerns, together with Ezra's and Nehemiah's (Ezra 9:1–2; Neh. 13:23–24), are with the identity of God's people. When any of God's people flout his law and break the covenant, they have no right to belong to the covenant community. They are to be disciplined. No offering can help the unrepentant sinner. Whoever tears down the covenant community by intermarriage has no right to be a part of that community.

In addition to intermarriage, God is concerned with divorce (2:13–17). If intermarriage is an affront to God's holy presence, how much more is he concerned with marital infidelity and divorce! Even if the people were to cry, bring offerings, and implore him to answer their prayers, he would have no regard for their rituals. The anticipated response to the prophetic judgment is a quick, spirited, indignant "Why?" The question receives a twofold response.

First, Malachi removes any pretense to innocence by stating that Yahweh will appear as witness to their faithlessness, which has manifested itself in divorce. The covenant relationship is characterized by fidelity, and the absence of marital fidelity is symptomatic of a deeper spiritual problem. The people are unreliable in their relationship with their peers, wives, and God. They are religious infidels.

Second, the severity of God's judgment is due to his intense hatred of divorce. The people have argued from the mistaken theological position that, since God is the Father of all Israel, they are safe from his judgment. Malachi replies that God's true children have the Spirit of God, which is manifested in faithfulness. The fruit of the Spirit of God is love and fidelity. The central verse (2:15), which is also one of the most difficult verses in the entire book, gives the theological ground for marital fidelity: (1) God has made "man" as one, namely male and female (Gen. 2:24); (2) man is "one," being both flesh and spirit; and (3) God's purpose is to raise up godly children through holy matrimony, which is characterized by a union of flesh with flesh and spirit with spirit. Therefore, not all may claim that God is their Father. The prophet has thus introduced the importance of the "spirituality" of God and of those who worship him. Since God has made human beings to have a spirit, they can relate to God only in the spirit. Only those who have the Spirit are his children, and they must respond by guarding their spirit. Covenant fidelity has a spiritual dimension that is expressed by marital fidelity.

6. The Justice and Patience of God (2:17–3:6)

The fifth disputation introduces a new element. The people have already questioned God's love, majesty, and fidelity. Now they raise the issue of his justice. Their argument, however, is wearing down because they have wearied the Lord (2:17). They have argued that they are all right and that the fault lies with God, but now they charge God with being unfair in all his dealings with humankind. They think that God does not discriminate between evil and good and that he even delights in those who do evil. Therefore, they ask, "Where is the God of justice?" The threefold charge against the Lord receives a threefold response (3:1–6).

First, the Lord will send his "messenger" who will prepare the way of the Lord. In Isaiah 40:3–4 the preparation of the Lord's coming is made by making ready a "way." His coming in Isaiah is to introduce judgment and to reward his children. Malachi also speaks of God's coming in judgment. The coming of God (3:5) is connected with the coming of the messenger of the covenant. The identity of this messenger is far from certain. The word for "messenger" in Hebrew is *malak*, and the Hebrew for "my messenger" is the same as the name Malachi. Is he, Malachi, the angel of the covenant or Elijah (4:5–6)? Jesus connects him with John the Baptist as having the spirit and power of Elijah (Luke 1:17; cf. Matt. 11:14). The purpose of the messenger is clear: he is to prepare the people for the coming of the Lord. In response to the first question, Malachi has introduced the "messenger" as God's means of announcing that his judgment rests on the wicked. The evil are *not* good in God's sight.

Second, the Lord will come to the temple. "The Lord" is further described as "the messenger of the covenant." Although some interpreters distinguish "the Lord" from "the messenger," the parallel construction argues for their synonymity. "The Lord" must be Yahweh, who has promised to fill the temple with his glory (Ezek. 43:1–5; Hag. 2:9). Yet he is also known as "the messenger of the covenant." A "messenger" was charged to guard Israel on

Malachi 3:2 uses the image of a refiner's fire. This relief from the tomb of Mere-Ruka shows craftsmen using blowpipes to increase the forge fire (Saqqara, Egypt, ca. 2300 BC).

the way to Canaan (Exod. 23:20–23), and it may well be that the identification of "the messenger" with "the Lord" is an Old Testament revelation anticipating God's fuller revelation in Jesus the Messiah. The Father sent John the Baptist and his Son to prepare humanity for the great judgment. The purpose of the messenger of the covenant is to "refine" the people of God.

The coming of the messenger is to introduce an era in which the restoration of the covenant will be ushered in in a new way. In response to the accusation that God is pleased with the wicked, Malachi has introduced the coming of the messenger of the covenant as God's means of purifying a people for himself. He compares the process of purification to the refining fire of the silversmith and the soap of a launderer. His purpose is to purge the people of God so that they will be like gold and silver.

God does not delight in evil but rather delights in "offerings in righteousness" (3:3). These can be offered only by those who have come through the process of purification. The righteous who lived before Christ looked forward to his coming and experienced the acceptance of their offerings in faith. The reference to the past is an expression of God's covenantal fidelity. God does not change. He has always expected his children to bring him offerings in the spirit of purity and righteousness. The opponents of the prophet's message have charged that God delights in evil; the prophet responds that God does not delight in evil but rather in righteousness.

Finally, the certainty of God's response is made sure by his coming in judgment. In response to their third question, "Where is the God of justice?" God comes in judgment. Even though this judgment may be delayed for millennia (2 Pet. 3:3–9), the judgment will certainly come on all who have broken his commandments.

Even though the commentaries and versions are not in agreement as to the extent of the argument, 3:6 could be the conclusion of 2:17–3:6. The Lord has charged his people with wearying him (2:17). They should be destroyed. Though the Lord is vexed by the words of his people, he does not change. His purposes stand. As an expression of his patience, forbearance, compassion, grace, and willingness to forgive, the Lord continues his plan of redemption. The fact that he does not yet come in judgment is an expression of grace. The people may change in that the righteous may join the wicked or may wonder whether God loves the wicked more than the righteous. The comfort of the godly is the revelation that the Lord does not change. Out of concern for his loved ones, the Lord will send the messenger and the messenger of the covenant to encourage them before his coming in judgment against all the wicked.

Since the coming of John the Baptist and Jesus Christ, a portion of the prophetic word of Malachi has been fulfilled. Jesus came as the "messenger of the covenant," by whom Jews and Gentiles find entrance into the covenant, by whom God accepts our offerings, and by whose Spirit we are purified. Because of God's grace we are not consumed.

7. The Tithe (3:7–12)

In the fifth disputation, Malachi argued that God would show his justice in judgment at his appointed time. The prophet, true to the prophetic tradition, calls for a response in preparation for the coming of the messenger and the messenger of the covenant. The appeal for a particular response links this section to the third disputation (3:10–16). In both sections, God is expecting a renewal of fidelity: in marriage (2:10–16) and in worship (3:7–12). The former is representative of our love for others and the latter of our love for God.

God remains faithful to his promise that he will return to those who seek him with all their heart. Israel's history is the story of a lack of responsiveness to God and his commandments. Even after the exile they were slow to respond. They were satisfied with their lack of commitment. The prophetic countercharge is quick. Malachi singles out one example of infidelity to God: the tithe.

Israel's failure to give the tithe exposes their failure to show loyalty to God in worship. The people have "robbed" God. The verb signifies a taking by force of what belongs to someone else. The tithe was God's divine right, specified in the law (Lev. 27:30; Num. 18:24–28; Deut. 14:28–29). From the tithes, Levites, priests, orphans, widows, and aliens were supported. The "offerings" were the portions of sacrifices that the priests were permitted to use for food (Exod. 29:27–28; Lev. 7:32; Num. 5:9). Support for the temple personnel and social programs is failing.

Greediness is not only a mark of selfishness; it is a token of infidelity and therefore of outright disobedience. The most severe penalty for failure to conform to God's will is "curse."

Malachi has demonstrated that Yahweh is not the Father of the descendants of Abraham but of those who have the Spirit of God. God is a good Father to responsive children. He promises to take care of their needs. The covenant king is concerned with extending his blessings to his people. For that reason, the prophet details how the Lord will grant his blessings (3:11–12): by taking care of all their needs, by protecting their possessions, by prospering their labor, and by keeping away the locusts. Since the people are reluctant, the prophet calls on them to test the Lord. This challenge to the people must be related to his call for them to return. By their repentance they will express their faith and dependence on him and will therefore be restored to covenant fellowship.

The Lord promises that his blessing will rest on his people so that they will be blessed in this life and in the life to come.

8. God's Love for the Remnant (3:13–4:3)

In the sixth disputation, Malachi sums up the argument of the book. In the first disputation (1:2–5), he argued that the Lord loves his people and that one day the faithful will recognize and see with their own eyes the establishment of the Lord's kingdom on earth. In the meantime, the hope of the faithful is in God, whose honor, fidelity, and justice are beyond question. The prophet sums up his argument by affirming that God will reward his loyal children who persevere to the end. This disputation is also related to the fifth (2:17–3:6), but is more direct and severe. The prophet does not give a general call for repentance. He makes it clear that many in the covenant community are too concerned with self but are incapable of establishing their own righteousness. Their feet are set on slippery paths, and they will perish. On the other hand, there is always a righteous remnant that does the will of God on earth, and they will receive a glorious reward.

The Lord charges the community of faith with speaking harshly against him (3:13–14). They say it is "futile" to serve God and that there is no "gain" in keeping God's commandments. The prophets have argued that it is vain to serve idols, but the people turn the argument around by claiming that allegiance to the Lord brings no benefit, no reward. The Hebrew word for "gain" or "reward" used here is not the usual word for reward, but signifies a bribe or a means of covering one's eyes toward injustice. Malachi uses the word sarcastically to reveal that the people are asking for undeserved favors. They expect God to do big things for them while they get by with injustice, improper sacrifices, divorce, and withholding tithes.

The people expect their religiosity to pay big dividends. They equate faithfulness to God with "going about like mourners" (3:14). Their hearts are not in their religion. They believe but do not have faith. Their lack of sincerity is brought out by their observation about the "arrogant." They make the bold claim that the arrogant, who are

> Malachi 4:2 describes "the sun of righteousness . . . with healing in its wings" (KJV, RSV, NASB), similar to the winged sun disk in this relief portraying the Zoroastrian god Ahuramazda (Persepolis, 550–330 BC).

filled with pride and live independently from the Lord, are the lucky ones. They set their own lifestyle, live practically without God, test him, and still prosper. Thus, they argue against the justice, love, and fidelity of God. The Lord has invited his own to test him and to see that he is good (3:10), but the people here respond skeptically and sarcastically that the arrogant put him to the test by flouting his commandments and get away with it. They have already come to the conclusion that God does not care what his children do. They have called into question God's fatherly concern for his children. God leaves their argument unanswered, shifting his attention to a group of godly people.

Within the covenant community, there is a group that has kept itself distinct from the arrogant, mockers, and cynics (3:16–18). They are variously called "those who feared the LORD" (3:16, twice), those who "honored his name" (3:16), "the righteous" (3:18), and "those who serve God" (3:18). The godly are thus characterized by their love for God and by their obedience to him. Malachi intends to let us into the discussions of two distinct groups. The complaints of the first group are loud and clear (3:14–15), but what are the godly saying? It does not seem to matter. Instead, Malachi emphasizes the various designations for the godly by drawing our immediate attention to God's responsiveness to his children, that God knows his own. It may be that the godly pray in the spirit of Psalm 73 for God to take care of their pains, while expressing trust in him:

> Surely God is good to Israel,
> to those who are pure in heart.
> But as for me, my feet had almost
> slipped;
> I had nearly lost my foothold.
> For I envied the arrogant
> when I saw the prosperity of
> the wicked. (Ps. 73:1–3)

In response, their names are written in "a scroll of remembrance" (cf. Exod. 32:32–33; Ps.

69:28; 87:6; Dan. 12:1). The Lord has marked a people for himself who will accept his tender care and the rewards of their labors. The greatest reward is to be a member of his "treasured possession" (Hebrew *segullah*). The word *segullah* is difficult to translate, since it connotes a people elected and loved by the Lord, who keep his commandments, and who make up a royal priesthood and a holy nation and who will share in a glorious future that God has prepared for his own (cf. Exod. 19:4–5; Deut. 7:6–9; 14:2; 26:17–19; Ps. 135:4). The prophet compares the Lord's care to a father's care for his son who has served him well. When the Lord shows his love for his people, then they will see the difference between the righteous and the wicked. The prophet indirectly addresses those who have argued against him, but he is directly addressing the godly community with words of comfort. They will see it with their own eyes. The day of the Lord will come upon mankind as a terrifying experience (4:1–3). The prophet compares it to the burning of a furnace and likens the wicked to stubble and shrubs that will be unable to stand the fire of that terrible day. They will be completely removed even as trees are destroyed by fire. Yet that day will bring its rewards for the righteous. The Lord will share with them the triumphs of his victory, expressed here metaphorically as "the sun of righteousness" and "healing in its wings."

The phrase "the sun of righteousness" is to be understood in the sense of Isaiah's prophecies. Righteousness represents the effects of God's righteousness on this earth: victory and glory (Isa. 51:6–7; 62:1–2). Yahweh shares his victory and glory with his people. They will experience the fullness of the restoration as a healing process. Regardless of their suffering in life, Yahweh guarantees that his victory and his restoration will be shared by his own. The light will dawn for his people in such a way that all the promises of the Law, the Prophets, our Lord, and the apostles will be fulfilled in them. That moment will mark the full establishment of his kingdom, which may come in gradually; and it may not always be apparent, but it will most certainly come. This will mark a time of great rejoicing. The joy and sense of fulfillment for God's children is likened to calves that, when released from the stable, paw at the ground. The arrogant and practical atheists will be unable to resist the renewal of the strength of God's children. A separation between the righteous and the self-righteous has taken place even within the community of faith. The one group will be marked for destruction while the other will be marked as God's possession.

9. Conclusion (4:4–6)

The conclusion to the book of Malachi includes a final appeal to observe the law of Moses in preparation for Elijah's return, to guard their spirit, and to return to the Lord. Malachi calls on the godly to love God and to love man. He emphasizes the practice of godliness in contrast to an intellectual knowledge of the Scriptures. Our Lord taught that John the Baptist came in the spirit and power of Elijah (Matt. 11:14; cf. Mal. 3:1). The new age will be characterized by a renewal of the covenant, and the sons of the covenant will enjoy a sense of continuity with their spiritual ancestors, Abraham, Isaac, and Jacob.

Select Bibliography

Alden, Robert L. "Malachi." In *The Expositor's Bible Commentary*. Edited by Frank E. Gaebelein. Vol. 7. Grand Rapids: Zondervan, 1985.

Baker, David W. *Joel, Obadiah, Malachi*. NIV Application Commentary. Grand Rapids: Zondervan, 2006.

Baldwin, Joyce G. *Haggai, Zechariah, Malachi*. Tyndale Old Testament Commentaries. Downers Grove, IL: InterVarsity, 1972.

Hill, Andrew E. *Malachi*. Anchor Bible. New York: Doubleday, 1998.

Kaiser, Walter C. *Malachi: God's Unchanging Love*. Grand Rapids: Baker Books, 1984.

Miller, Steven R. *Nahum–Malachi*. Holman Old Testament Commentary. Nashville: Broadman & Holman, 2004.

Smith, Ralph L. *Micah–Malachi*. Word Biblical Commentary. Waco: Word, 1984.

Stuart, D. "Malachi." In *The Minor Prophets: An Exegetical and Expository Commentary*. Edited by Thomas Edward McComiskey. Grand Rapids: Baker Academic, 1992.

Taylor, Richard A., and E. Ray Clendenen. *Haggai and Malachi*. New American Commentary. Nashville: Broadman & Holman, 2004.

Verhoef, Pieter A. *The Books of Haggai and Malachi*. New International Commentary on the Old Testament. Grand Rapids: Eerdmans, 1987.

What Happened between the Two Testaments?

When we open the New Testament it appears that a considerable amount of time has elapsed since we read the words of Malachi. Four centuries have passed. The Old Testament story ends with the prophets explaining the profound crisis of Israel's catastrophic exile and the hope that will come when God revisits and redeems their history. This is precisely the dramatic setting that sets the stage for the Judaism we meet in the New Testament.

After Israel returned to Judea following the Babylonian exile (586 BC), Jerusalem was rebuilt under the able leadership of Nehemiah and Ezra. Nevertheless, prophets such as Malachi called Israel to remain faithful to its covenant with God and to promote justice among its people (Mal. 4:1–2).

As the Jews returned to their homeland, they brought new ideas that would later influence the life of Judaism. During the exile they adopted the popular use of Aramaic, a language similar to Hebrew. By the first century this would be the common language of life in Israel and was likely Jesus's native tongue. Until the temple was rebuilt, the Jews also had to come to terms with practicing their faith without the temple and sacrifice. Faith was expressed through study, obedience, and prayer. This was possibly the origin of the synagogue, which began as a gathering of Jews who debated the Scriptures, prayed, and formed community centers. When the Jews rebuilt the temple, these village-based gathering places continued to flourish. We see this community innovation throughout the New Testament.

A major and permanent shift came to Israel's history in the fourth century BC with the fantastic character of Alexander the Great (356–323 BC). His first aim was the defeat of the Persians, which he accomplished through major battles from 334 to 332 BC. He freed Greek cities, defeated Persian outposts, and "liberated" provinces that had lived under Persian rule. However, he never released them to be free: they now lived under Greek rule.

Whereas the conquering empires of the east permitted the Jews to retain their cultural and religious identity, the coming of Greek culture—or Hellenism—in the fourth century would make a permanent mark on Israel's life. Greek culture was missionary by nature, sweeping up new peoples and converting them to a new, "modern" way of life. In the eastern provinces like Judea, the promises of Hellenism were intoxicating. Judaism soon found itself enticed to join the wider western Mediterranean world for the first time.

While Alexander and his successors were committed to conquest, their greatest legacy was this rapid spread of Hellenism to the lands they conquered. Above all was the spread of Greek, which became the new language of a new world that was uniting the cultures of Mesopotamia, Egypt, and the Mediterranean. The sustaining influence of Greek culture would dominate the eastern Mediterranean for almost 900 years and end only with the coming of Islam in the seventh century AD. Greek would naturally become the language of the early Christian communities and the language of the New Testament.

The greatest threat to Jewish life in this era was the gradual assimilation to Hellenistic culture. Greek theaters offered dramatic arts that were foreign to Jewish life. Gymnasium guilds enlisted young men at 18 to join their social and athletic centers, where sporting events were practiced nude. Jewish beards and flowing robes were replaced with broad-rimmed hats, short togas, and high-laced sandals (2 Maccabees 4:10–17). Indeed, Hellenistic life was eroding traditional Jewish culture. Jews began to use common Greek (or Koiné Greek) as their native language. This meant that the Hebrew Scriptures were no longer understandable in the Greek-speaking synagogues. Soon the New Testament itself (written by Jews) would be penned in Koiné Greek.

Throughout the Hellenistic period, the fledgling Roman Empire was expanding to the east. Two prizes were in its sights: Egypt and Syria. Egypt was famous for its wealth, its academies, and its agricultural produce. One day Roman galleys would ferry huge stores from Egypt back to Rome. Syria was the second prize. As gateway to the valleys of the Euphrates, Syria and its powerful city Antioch stood at the crossroads. The Roman Empire therefore devised a plan to claim these prizes.

One of Rome's most celebrated commanders in the first century BC was Pompey the Great (106–48 BC). He led Rome's campaign into the eastern Mediterranean. After he took Syrian Antioch, Judea was his next strategic goal. In 63 BC Pompey climbed the Judean mountains and took the city of Jerusalem. He organized the country under Roman rule, named it Judea, appointed his own high priest, stationed over 9,000 troops in the region, and then left.

For the next century and more, Judea lived under Roman control. Jewish aristocratic families tried to leverage power with Roman help, and occasionally Rome permitted the rise of "Jewish kings" such as Herod the Great (see Matt. 2:1). Roman governors often ruled the country on Rome's behalf. In the Gospels, we meet one of them: Pontius Pilate, the Roman ruler who crucified Jesus.

When we open the pages of the New Testament, we are in the midst of a story of political oppression and intrigue. Roman armies occupy the land. Jewish regional princes exert local control. Tax collection strips Judea of resources that are then transferred to Rome. And local Jewish resistance is everywhere. Jewish desire for God's intervention is growing.

Alexander the Great fighting the Persians at the Battle of Issus. This stone coffin, found near Sidon, Lebanon, is known as the Alexander Sarcophagus because of its reliefs (late fourth century BC).

A once dormant idea—that God would send his anointed messenger, the Messiah—is now alive and well. The emperor is claiming divine rights ("son of god" is on his coins), and he has declared that Rome's power has established a worldwide "peace" (the *pax Romana*).

Into this mix of politics and religious fervor, Jesus was born. When angels announced how his coming offered peace among people (Luke 2:14), any Roman could see the awkward comparison with Emperor Augustus. And when at his birth Jesus was hailed "king of the Jews" (Matt. 2:2), Herod the Great, Rome's local proxy king, was angered. When Jesus announced the inauguration of the "kingdom of God" (Mark 1:15), those who brokered the power of kings and kingdoms for Rome would wonder if a dangerous rival had just entered the stage of Jewish history. Jesus was all of these—and none of these—but his coming announced a shift in Jewish and world history that has never been reversed.

New Testament Introduction

The New Testament is a collection of twenty-seven books that were gathered together and, in time, used alongside the Old Testament by the early church. Written in Greek during the first century AD, the New Testament writings comprise four divisions: four Gospels telling the story of Jesus; the book of Acts, which records the history of the early church; a series of letters from writers such as Paul and Peter; and the book of Revelation.

Because Jesus was the full and final revelation of God, the early Christians treasured those things that were said by and about him, and as a result the books we call Gospels arose. Gospel writing began early, and apparently several such attempts were made, as Luke, who wrote one himself, says (Luke 1:1–4). Today we know that other gospels (such as the *Gospel of Thomas*; see photo) circulated for centuries, and some scholars have suggested that these ancient works should bear equal weight in telling the story of Jesus. But the early church was careful and discerning. It understood that writers who did not share the faith of the apostles might well exploit the story of Jesus for their own purposes. So, with care, the church ultimately accepted our four Gospels as authoritative, no doubt because they could be traced back in some fashion to those who had actually been with Jesus and represented the heart of apostolic teaching. In this way the authority of Jesus was extended to those books that were written about him and contained his remembered sayings.

Jesus's authority was conferred during his lifetime to a specially chosen group of twelve followers called "apostles." (See the commentary on Matt. 10:1–4.) Because they were to continue the work of Jesus after his death and resurrection, their lives—and to a certain extent their words—were recorded. The book of Acts is a follow-up to what Jesus *began* to do and teach while he was on earth (Acts 1:1); it is a record of what Jesus *continued* to do and teach through his church as it was guided by the Holy Spirit under the direction of the apostles.

Acts tells of how the gospel spread from Jerusalem ultimately to Rome, the capital of the Roman Empire at that time. This was accomplished through the efforts of the earliest apostles and disciples, who spread the gospel widely. Most of their stories remain untold, but some, such as the missionary work of Peter, were celebrated. Eventually a Jewish rabbi named Saul (also called Paul) was converted, discipled, and sent out as a missionary. His three extensive trips and final journey to Rome are described in some detail in the book of Acts.

Paul was counted as an apostle by the church even though he was not one of the Twelve. His acceptance was based on a direct call from Jesus himself that Paul received while on the road to Damascus; the experience is described three times in the book of Acts (9:1–6; 22:1–16; 26:12–18). Paul wrote many letters to the Gentile churches he founded; these letters were used for instruction by Paul's converts. Along with the other writings, they were collected and considered authoritative. Some scholars think that the gathering of these letters led to the formation of the New Testament. In any event, the growing collection was used as God's Word by the church.

In addition, the New Testament holds letters from a variety of other Christian leaders. In most cases, these are public letters written to churches about their beliefs and their efforts to form communities representing Christ. For this reason these writings are often called "general letters." Here we find the letters of Peter, James, Jude, and John. The book of Hebrews early on was included in the collection of Paul's letters, but a number of scholars, both ancient and modern, consider the author to be anonymous. So, for convenience it may be considered a general letter. These letters tell us of Christian life in the outposts of the Roman Empire. Life is depicted as difficult and challenging, but supported by the grace of God in Christ.

The book of Revelation is in a class by itself. It is a triumphant book that promises God's presence during the present suffering of his people and the ultimate victory of God at Christ's return. For Christians living during a period of severe opposition and persecution, it was a potent encouragement. For Christians living under parallel conditions today, it is the same.

The teaching of the New Testament is based on the fundamental teachings of the Old Testament. The idea of a personal God, who is Creator, Sustainer, and Redeemer; the responsibility of humanity to pursue moral behavior; the need for redemption from sin; the ultimate triumph of God over the evil forces of this world—these ideas each come from the Old Testament.

Yet the New Testament moves beyond the Old Testament framework in significant ways. The New Testament proclaims one foundational idea: God's promised messiah has arrived among us in Jesus Christ. And spinning out from that one idea is a whole host of new ways of thinking about ourselves, God's efforts in the world, and our tasks. The New Testament implies that in some ways the Old Testament has been eclipsed. A *new covenant* has been born. But the Old Testament is never dismissed. The Old Testament still forms the background of our thinking, and remains an invaluable source for understanding God.

A page from the *Gospel of Thomas*. This copy was discovered in 1945 near Nag Hammadi, Egypt, as part of a collection of manuscripts found stored in clay jars. The manuscripts are written in Coptic and contain some of the earliest Christian writings.

The Gospels and Acts

The New Testament properly begins with a small collection of books known as the Gospels. The Gospels contain the essence of the gospel—the good news—which is the life, death, and resurrection of Jesus Christ. Each of the Gospels has a different character or set of interests. Mark is the shortest Gospel. Matthew may well have read Mark and decided to fill out the story. Luke pursued his own research (see Luke 1:1–4) and pulled in yet more material. Thus we note that Matthew, Mark, and Luke (the Synoptic Gospels) are quite similar and in some cases tell the same stories. *These writers were aware of one another's Gospels and in some cases borrowed stories from each other's works.* The Gospel of John, on the other hand, is different. Most of John's Gospel (about 92 percent) cannot be found in the other three. John had his own profound relationship with Jesus, and in his book he tells stories of remarkable insight and inspiration that are unparalleled.

These books are not "lives of Jesus" or biographies in the modern sense. What they are designed to give us is the essence of what we need to know about Jesus as the Son of God and Savior of the world. Mark's Gospel, for instance, focuses over half of its verses on the last week of Jesus's life. This means that the Gospels' primary focus is on the disclosure of what Jesus's saving mission was and the facts surrounding the accomplishment of that mission. Clearly the center of Jesus's teaching was the "kingdom of God" that he inaugurated. And the center of Jesus's activity was his great sacrifice on the

cross. The earliest form of the gospel message was that Christ died for our sins, was buried, was raised on the third day, and appeared to his followers (1 Cor. 15:3–8). The Gospels fill that out by adding the events surrounding his birth and early life, his teachings, his ministry of healing, his trip to Jerusalem, and the events of his last days.

From the very beginning people had a good deal of interest in Jesus's life, and soon they wrote many small volumes to explain who he was. Some volumes contained authentic material; others, no doubt, were written to prove some point or other. In order to preserve the truth of what was remembered about Jesus, and under the guidance of the Holy Spirit, the four Gospels we now have were written, gathered together by the church, and given a special place in its corporate life. There is not necessarily a special reason why four were chosen; it is just that these particular books commended themselves to the earliest believers as being of supreme value and were retained as different and indispensable pictures of Jesus as God's Son and our Savior. (Note the introductory section to each of the Gospel commentaries. Our authors will carefully explain where the Gospel came from, who wrote it, and what its purposes were.)

Matthew describes Jesus as the new Moses, the fulfiller of Israel's hopes, the true Messiah, and the light of the world. Mark, the shortest and earliest of the four Gospels, emphasizes the last week of Jesus's life, devoting to this six of its sixteen chapters. Here we see Jesus as the divine servant of God who does God's will, even unto death. In Luke Jesus is presented as the ideal man, son of Adam, and the fullest embodiment of God's will for us as human beings. John's Gospel is a theologically nuanced book designed to show Jesus's true nature as fully divine and fully human. These four points of view combine to give us a composite picture of Jesus as God and man, Servant of God and Savior of all.

Acts

In the New Testament the book of Acts follows immediately after the four Gospels. The Gospels present the life of Jesus; the book of Acts invites us to read about the lives of Jesus's followers. Luke, the author of the third gospel, also wrote the book of Acts. Luke was a close friend of Paul and therefore recorded in great detail the life of this great disciple of Jesus. But Luke also tells us about the wider mission of the resurrected Jesus in the world. If in the Old Testament Israel was committed to establishing its life within the borders of the Holy Land, Acts boldly announces that this agenda is now gone: Jesus is making claim on the entire earth. His kingdom knows no border, no ethnicity, no nationality. The message of Jesus is not provincial—it is universal.

The Gospels and the book of Acts belong together. Combined they give us an account of Christian beginnings—Jesus and his church. Acts picks up where the Gospels leave off and carries us through those turbulent early days while Christianity is being established and believers are yet a tiny minority. But from these

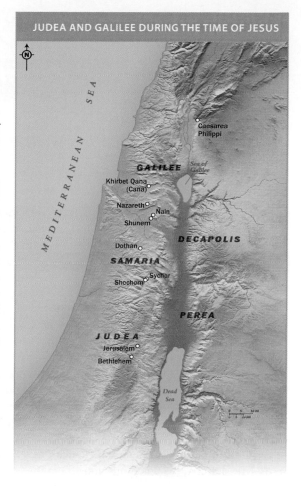

JUDEA AND GALILEE DURING THE TIME OF JESUS

persecuted, beleaguered few comes a power that will conquer the world in the form of God's saving truth. In the days after the crucifixion, the huddled, fearful group of Jesus's followers becomes a band of fearless leaders in the spread of the gospel, speaking boldly in prominent cities around the Roman Empire: Antioch, Ephesus, even Rome.

Matthew

Jeannine K. Brown

Jeannine K. Brown

Introduction

Purpose

The author of the Gospel of Matthew, writing to believers in Jesus in the latter part of the first century, portrays Jesus as God's chosen Messiah, who paradoxically ushers in the reign of God through his self-giving ministry and death. Matthew communicates that Jesus's messianic claims and mission are vindicated at his resurrection, when God grants him all authority. Matthew seeks to persuade his readers to respond in trust, loyalty, and obedience to Jesus Messiah and his teachings and to empower them to invite others to follow and obey Jesus through the promise of Jesus's presence with them.

A Narrative Reading

This commentary offers a narrative reading of Matthew, emphasizing its story features, internal coherence, and thematic development. Narrative criticism as a method for studying the Gospels analyzes a narrative at two levels—story and discourse. Analysis of the story level focuses on setting, character, and plot development. Discourse-level assessment focuses on the ways the implied author (implied within the narrative) tells the story to communicate with the implied audience. An author communicates on the discourse level through sequencing (see "Sources" below), structural devices (see

"Structure" below), thematic development, and authorial comments. (For a description of narrative analysis, including implied author and audience concepts, see Brown 2007, 157–63, also 40–42.) For example, Matthew narrates nine miracle stories in 8:1–9:34 in order to stress themes of Jesus's authority and the importance of faith. Thus, while attending to story and discourse levels, a narrative reading also seeks to understand the book of Matthew in light of its historical setting.

Author, Date, and Audience

Although the Gospel itself is anonymous, the title (added in the second century) specifies Matthew as the author. Church tradition also attributes it to Matthew the apostle (Eusebius, *Ecclesiastical History* 3.24.16, citing testimony from Papias, a second-century bishop). Modern scholarship has questioned these traditions, but certain scholars continue to support Matthew as the author of the first Gospel (see discussion in Keener, 38–41).

One difficulty for determining authorship is the nature of narratives, which point away from the author and toward the story being told. Matthew's author intends the audience to focus its attention on Jesus and the events and time frame of his life rather than on the author and the author's world. Yet reconstructing something about the author, audience, and date from the Gospel is possible by studying indirect references within the story (e.g., does 22:7 indicate Matthew writes after the destruction of Jerusalem?) and attending to direct authorial commentary where it occurs (e.g., 24:15; 28:15). Such reconstruction of the *implied* author, date, and audience (implied within the narrative) may be sketchy, since internal evidence can support contrasting reconstructions (as in the dating of Matthew).

The internal evidence of the first Gospel suggests that the author is a Jewish follower of Jesus (e.g., 1:2–17; Old Testament fulfillment themes), possibly from a scribal background (cf. 13:52; 23:1–2), who writes to a primarily Jewish audience (e.g., explanation of Pharisaic traditions from Mark 7:3–4 omitted in Matt. 15:1–2; also Gentile-inclusion theme), most likely between AD 68 and 85. In this commentary, "Matthew" will be used to refer to the Gospel's implied author.

Sources

Matthew's clearest source is the Jewish Scriptures (the Old Testament), which he cites and alludes to frequently (over seventy times by some counts). In fact, the Old Testament story is assumed and evoked throughout Matthew (e.g., Israel's exile and restoration in chapters 1–4; Psalm 22 in Matt. 27:32–50). Of the four evangelists, Matthew cites the Old Testament most often. Ten times he employs a formulaic introduction to highlight Jesus as fulfillment of the Old Testament (1:22–23; 2:15; 2:17–18; 2:23; 4:14–16; 8:17; 12:17–21; 13:35; 21:4–5; 27:9; cf. also 2:5; 3:3; 13:13–15). These fulfillment quotations typically connect at the story level (by connecting the Old Testament quotation with an event in Jesus's life) *and* function theologically (on the discourse level) to illuminate Jesus's fulfillment of Old Testament themes and contours in a more thematic way (see commentary on 2:1–23). Richard Beaton refers to the "bi-referentiality" of these citations (see Beaton, 5, 120; these two levels of narrative are described below). Matthew's use of the Old Testament sets Jesus's life and mission within the story and promises of Israel.

An icon of Matthew from a larger piece entitled *Christ and Twelve Apostles* (Antalya, Turkey, nineteenth century AD)

Modern Gospels scholarship has argued for a written dependence between Matthew, Mark, and Luke (the Synoptic Gospels), given their frequent overlap. Matthew most likely used Mark as a source for his Gospel, along with other oral and/or written Jesus traditions. Matthew begins making use of Mark at Matthew 3:3 (cf. Mark 1:3), continuing to borrow material throughout his Gospel. (About 90 percent of Mark is included in Matthew.) He omits some material from Mark (e.g., Mark 8:22–26), adds freely to it (e.g., blocks of Jesus's teachings), and sometimes rearranges passage order (e.g., Mark 4:35–5:43 lies behind Matt. 8:23–9:26 prior to material from Mark 2:23–4:34 in Matt. 12:1–13:58). Such freedom of arrangement would have fit ancient narrative practices. For example, Greco-Roman biographies were typically arranged by topic rather than strict chronology (e.g., eight kingdom parables clustered in Matthew 13).

Theological Themes

God's reign (the kingdom of God) as theological centerpiece. Studying a Gospel's theology involves exploring the author's presentation of God's person and activity, which in Matthew focuses on the kingdom of God (Matthew's "kingdom of heaven"; see commentary on 4:17–25). *A key assumption* in Matthew is that Israel's God has promised to restore them in faithfulness to covenant promises. God's rule will be fully established in this world when God comes to bring restoration (e.g., Isa. 52:1–10). *A central affirmation* in Matthew is that Jesus, the Davidic Messiah, inaugurates God's reign, as God's chosen king and Lord (28:18) and the manifestation of "God with us" (1:23; 28:20). Matthew also develops the kingdom theme by reference to Isaiah's motif of exile/return (e.g., Isa. 40:1–9; cf. Matt. 3:3). Jesus is portrayed as the one who both makes possible and enacts Israel's return from exile.

An "already/not yet" eschatology characterizes Matthew's kingdom theology. God has inaugurated the kingdom in Jesus, the Messiah-King; yet the consummation of God's reign is future, at "the end of the age" (a phrase Matthew uses; cf. 13:39, 40, 49; 24:3; 28:20). In line with the "not yet," Jesus's teaching highlights the present hidden nature of the kingdom, so that divine revelation and human faith are needed to perceive it (chap. 13). The hiddenness of the kingdom arises partly from the paradoxical way Jesus comes to be king—not through assertion of power but by willing and missional self-sacrifice (27:27–50). Yet Jesus's cross-shaped mission is authenticated and vindicated by his resurrection, when God grants Jesus all authority (28:18), showing him to be God's faithful and favored Son (3:17; 17:5).

In Old Testament prophetic expectation, God's reign and Israel's restoration would coincide with Gentile ingathering (e.g., Mic. 4:1–2; Isa. 25:1–12). Matthew emphasizes this aspect of God's kingdom throughout his narrative, beginning by highlighting Gentiles in Jesus's genealogy (1:3, 56) and concluding

with Jesus's mission to all nations (28:19; cf. also 2:1; 4:15; 8:5–13; 15:21–28; 21:43; 24:14; though also 10:5–6; 15:24). God's plan that Abraham's family would be a blessing to the earth's peoples (Gen. 12:3) comes to fruition as Jesus inaugurates the kingdom (see commentary on 28:1–20).

Christology. Matthew's portrait of Jesus is multifaceted and informed by various christological titles, Jesus's actions in the plot (e.g., healings; cf. 11:2–5), and key Old Testament story lines and texts tied to his identity. I sketch here four (overlapping) categories, which will emerge in this commentary: Jesus as Davidic Messiah who inaugurates the kingdom, as representative of Israel, as the embodiment of Yahweh in Israel's restoration, and as fulfiller of the Scriptures.

Matthew consistently portrays Jesus as *Davidic Messiah*, emphasizing his royal identity (1:1; 2:5–6; 21:1–11; with the Hebrew *mashiah* translated into Greek as *christos*). Though first-century messianic views were numerous and varied, the royal connotations of Davidic association would have been commonplace (e.g., *Psalms of Solomon* 17:5; cf. "Son of David" title in 9:27; 12:23; 15:22; 20:30, 31; 21:9, 15; 22:42). This association coheres with Matthew's theological emphasis on God's kingdom begun in Jesus, the royal Messiah. Yet Matthew also expands this category as Jesus speaks and enacts God's reign in ways that move outside Jewish messianic expectations, especially as he enacts the role of *servant of the Lord* from Isaiah (cf. Isa. 42:1–4 cited in Matt. 12:18–21; Isa. 53:4 cited in Matt. 8:17; also likely allusions to Isaiah 53 at Matt. 20:28 and 26:28). For Matthew, Isaiah's portrait of the servant, who willingly takes on suffering to bring justice and mercy to Israel and the nations, describes Jesus (though not in first-century Jewish expectations, since Isaiah's Suffering Servant was understood as referring to Israel, not the Messiah; e.g., Isa. 44:1).

Another messianic title Matthew uses is "Son of God" (e.g., 14:33; 16:16), easily heard by modern ears as a divine title. Yet the clearest

Old Testament examples of those called son by God are Israel (e.g., Exod. 4:22; Hos. 11:1; also *Jubilees* 1:25) and Israel's kings (2 Sam. 7:14; Ps. 2:1–12). Therefore, the term "Son of God" has messianic connotations (e.g., 2 Esdras 7:28–29; Dead Sea Scrolls, 4Q246 2.1) (Wright 1996, 485–86). In addition to evoking Jesus's role as Israel's representative (see below), Matthew uses the phrase as an alternate way to designate Jesus as Messiah (cf. 16:16; 26:63; alternate to "king" in 27:41–44), although with emphasis on Jesus's intimacy with the Father (e.g., 3:17; 11:25–27; 17:5).

Matthew highlights Jesus as the faithful *representative of Israel* in identity and mission, especially in chapters 1–4. Just as God brought Israel from exile in Egypt, God does the same for Jesus and his family (2:15, 19–21). In contrast to Israel's disobedience when tempted in the wilderness, Jesus proves his faithfulness to God when facing the same temptations (4:1–11) and demonstrates the covenant loyalty that God requires of Israel (cf. 3:17 with Isa. 42:1–4; cf. also Matthew's use of Psalm 22 in Matt. 27:27–50). Jesus's faithfulness even to death is vindicated by God in the resurrection, again at the temple's destruction in AD 70 as Jesus predicts, and finally at "the end of the age," when Jesus will judge all humanity. Matthew highlights vindication by repeated evocation of Daniel 7:13–14, which pictures a vindicated "son of man" approaching God's throne and receiving all authority (see 10:23; 16:27–28; 24:30–31; 26:64; see also 25:31 and 28:18). In Daniel's vision explained, it is "the holy people of the Most High" (i.e., Israel's faithful) who are represented by the son of man (cf. Dan. 7:18, 22, 27), so that Matthew's use of this vision connects the vindication of Jesus's faithfulness to his role as Israel's representative. Matthew's use of "Son of Man" is always a self-designation by Jesus. In many cases, it seems to be just that: a way that Jesus refers to himself, possibly in solidarity with Israel (see God's frequent reference to Ezekiel as "son of man," e.g., Ezek. 2:1). Yet when "Son of Man" occurs in allusions/ citations to Daniel 7:13–14, Matthew means to communicate Jesus's vindication to a position of universal authority.

A central christological affirmation implicit but crucial to Matthew's story is Jesus as the *embodiment of Yahweh* (Israel's God; cf. Exod. 3:14–15). For Matthew, Jesus enacts Israel's redemption (1:21), fulfilling God's promises that *God* will bring redemption (Wright 1996, 653). For example, Matthew affirms Jesus as "the Lord" for whom John prepares the way, citing Isaiah's prophecy that Yahweh ("Lord" translates the divine name; Isa. 40:3) will return to Zion (Matt. 3:3; Isa. 40:1–5), connecting Jesus intimately with Yahweh's mission and even identity (cf. also Matt. 22:41–46). Jesus is also granted the role of universal Lord and judge, a role reserved in the Old Testament Scriptures for God alone (11:27; 25:31; esp. 28:18; cf. Dan. 7:13–14). Jesus's lordship implicitly affirms Jesus's inclusion in the "unique divine identity" (Bauckham, viii). Appropriate to his lordship, Matthew portrays characters worshiping Jesus (Greek *proskyneō* is used ten times with Jesus as object, more than the combined total from Mark, Luke, and John). Matthew highlights worship of Jesus by beginning and ending with it (the Magi in 2:2, 11; Jesus's followers in 28:9, 17).

A final christological category Matthew emphasizes is Jesus as *fulfiller of the Scriptures*. This category arches over the others, since, according to Matthew, the covenant and promises of God find their fulfillment in Jesus (with "the Law and the Prophets" referring to the Old Testament Scriptures at 5:17; 7:12; 11:13; 22:40). Matthew highlights this category with his many Old Testament citations and allusions and his affirmation of Jesus's obedience to God's will (see above; also 12:12). Yet Matthew focuses particular attention on Jesus's relationship to the Jewish law (Hebrew *torah*). Jesus is shown to *fulfill* rather than abolish the law (the torah) by interpreting and teaching it rightly (5:17, with 5:21–48), because Jesus interprets the torah by its central qualities of mercy, justice, love, and faithfulness (9:13; 12:7; 22:24–40; 23:23). In this way, Jesus's torah interpretation is not burdensome (11:28–30), like some teaching he critiques (23:4). Yet Matthew's Jesus also *embodies* the torah by virtue of his messianic authority (e.g., 7:29; 11:25–30). It is Jesus's teaching (on the Law and the Prophets) that is authoritative for his followers (28:19).

Structure

While scholars debate Matthew's overarching structure, it is not for lack of discernible structural clues, which are abundant. The twofold "From that time on Jesus began to [preach/show] . . ." at 4:17 and 16:21 signals major turning points in Matthew's plot. Second, each of the five major blocks of Jesus's teaching concludes with the formulaic "After/When Jesus had finished . . ." (7:28–29; 11:1; 13:53; 19:1; 26:1), transitioning between Jesus's teaching and the subsequent story. Other structural signs include use of inclusio (a bookending device; cf. 4:23 // 9:35; 1:23 // 28:20) and a preference for groupings of three (e.g., 8:1–9:34—nine miracle stories in three groupings of three; 21:28–22:14—three parables).

Commentary

1. Jesus's Identity and Preparation for Ministry (1:1–4:16)

In the first major section of Matthew's Gospel, the author introduces Jesus of Nazareth by identifying him as the Jewish Messiah, son of David; the enactor of restoration from exile; hope for the Gentiles; the obedient Son who represents faithful Israel; and "God with us." Moving from Jesus's genealogy and his conception by the Spirit to the threat that his God-authenticated kingship poses to Herod, Matthew narrates God's protection and guidance of Jesus and his family in the face of societal and political threats. Decades elapse between Matthew 2 and 3, where we are introduced to John the Baptist and the adult Jesus. Matthew 3 narrates Jesus's preparation for ministry as he is baptized by John, signaling God's covenant faithfulness to Israel and affirming Jesus's faithfulness. Jesus's wilderness temptations in Matthew 4 affirm his identity as the faithful Son of God, fulfilling Israel's call to covenant faithfulness, which includes being a light to the Gentiles (4:13–16).

A. Birth and infancy (1:1–2:23). Matthew begins the infancy narrative of Jesus by emphasizing Jesus's lineage from Joseph (1:1–17) and Mary's conception of Jesus from the Holy Spirit. He resolves the tension between these two by narrating Joseph's adoption of Jesus (1:18–25). He highlights Jesus's Jewish and Davidic ancestry, the surprising presence of Gentiles in his lineage, and the themes of exile and restoration now enacted in Jesus the Messiah of Israel, who is Immanuel, "God with us." Matthew continues narrating Jesus's infancy (2:1–23) by describing the immediate threat that Jesus as Messiah-King is to Rome's client-king Herod, all the while affirming through Old Testament citations that Jesus is the legitimate, Davidic "king of the Jews." Once again, Gentiles make an entrance (the

Magi) and themes of exile's end and restoration now begun in Jesus are evoked in Matthew's Old Testament usage. Throughout the story, God's guidance comes through dreams, angel's voices, and even an eastern star.

1:1–17: Jesus's genealogy. Matthew begins his Gospel with a clear affirmation of the identity of this person Jesus, who will occupy the center of his narrative. From the opening title, the author highlights three aspects of Jesus's identity: Jesus is the Messiah ("Jesus Christ"), Jesus is a descendant of David ("son of David"), and Jesus is a descendant of Abraham ("son of Abraham"). These three affirmations will inform the rest of Matthew's story of Jesus; they also frame the genealogy of Jesus that follows 1:1. In fact, Matthew has carefully structured the genealogy to reflect these affirmations in reverse order, so that 1:1–16 forms a literary parallelism (A-B-C-C'-B'-A'):

Used to illustrate the genealogy of Jesus, a Jesse tree is an artistic representation of a shoot from the stump of Jesse (Isa. 11.1–2). Typically, Jesse reclines at the base with a branch coming out of his side. Side branches embrace figures that represent other ancestors of Jesus. Jesus is at the top, with Mary just beneath him. This portion of an ivory comb from Bavaria (1200 AD) shows a Jesse tree with prophets on either side of Mary and Jesus.

Jesus as
    A   Christ (1:1)
       B   Son of David (1:1)
          C   Son of Abraham (1:1)
          C′ Abraham (1:2)
       B′ David (1:6)
    A′ Christ (1:16)

Beginning with a genealogy is a natural way in Matthew's Jewish context to focus concerted attention on Jesus's identity. In ancient perspective, family line was intimately connected to identity. In addition to the inverted literary framework, Matthew structures Jesus's genealogy by arranging it in three groups of fourteen (1:17). This shaping coheres with the genre of ancient genealogy, in which the listing of generations could be condensed (i.e., generations skipped) for specific purposes.

Matthew indicates at 1:17 that the reader is to hear three movements of fourteen as important. The genealogy begins with Abraham, signaling the origins of Israel as a people. The first grouping ends (and the second begins) with David, the prototypical king of Israel. The second grouping ends (and the third begins) with the time of exile to Babylon, highlighting that time in Israel's history when there was no king in Israel and the people were exiled from the land. An exilic motif may also be signaled in the genealogy by the addition of "and his brothers" (1:11). The repetition of this phrase at 1:2 and 1:11 suggests that "and his brothers" marks Israel's two primary exiles, times when God's people are dislocated from the land God has promised them. The genealogy's final grouping ends with "Jesus, who is called the Christ" (1:16 KJV, RSV; Greek *christos* is the term that translates the Hebrew *mashiah*). The beginnings and ends of these three movements in Israel's history might be summarized as (1) the origin of Israel (Abraham); (2) kingship provided for Israel (David); (3) kingship and land lost (exile); and (4) kingship restored (Jesus, the Christ). In the genealogy, Matthew rehearses Israel's history to emphasize that Davidic kingship is restored in Jesus the Messiah.

Scholars have understood Matthew's emphasis on the number fourteen in various ways. Its significance might rest in the notion of seven as indicating completion, either fourteen as a doubled seven or three sets of fourteen indicating that six cycles of seven lead into the time of the Messiah—a seventh seven (e.g., Dan. 9:24). More likely, given David's prominence in the genealogy (1:1, 6, 17; cf. 1:20), fourteen is a *gematria* (the sum numeric value of Hebrew letters in a word) derived from David's name. The three Hebrew consonants in David's name (*dalet-vav-dalet*: D-V-D) total fourteen.

An intriguing aspect of Matthew's genealogy is the presence of four women in its early moments: Tamar, Rahab, Ruth, and Uriah's wife (1:3, 5–6). The inclusion of women in Jewish genealogies is atypical, since genealogies were patriarchal in form. The inclusion of these four women hints at an important theme to come: Gentile inclusion. Tamar and Rahab, both Canaanites (Tamar likely so: Gen. 38:1–6; Rahab: Josh. 2:1), and Ruth, a Moabite (Ruth 1:4), are surprising ancestors of Jesus, given their Gentile origins (see "Theological Themes" in the introduction). While there is no biblical evidence for the ethnic identity of Bathsheba, the fact that Matthew refers to her as "Uriah's wife" rather than by her name provides evidence that he is highlighting precisely her Gentile connection (Uriah the Hittite; 2 Sam. 11:3).

Through his carefully crafted genealogy, Matthew emphasizes Jesus as the Messiah, the long-awaited Davidic king who will restore the hopes of exiled Israel and will usher Gentiles into Israel's blessing (cf. Gen. 12:1–3). Yet, just as the author reaches the zenith of Jesus's genealogy, he introduces a crucial problem for understanding Jesus as belonging to this lineage. For at 1:16, it becomes clear that *Joseph's* lineage

is being rehearsed; yet Jesus is born of *Mary*, not Joseph ("of whom" [NKJV, RSV] translates a Greek relative pronoun that is singular and feminine, so it cannot refer to Joseph). Matthew answers this conundrum in 1:18–25.

1:18–25: Jesus's birth. The narration of Jesus's birth is closely tied to the preceding genealogy by the repeated Greek term *genesis*, translated as "genealogy" in 1:1 and "birth" in 1:18. Both accounts provide an important aspect of Jesus's "origin," another possible translation of *genesis*. These two passages provide the question and answer to Jesus's connection to Joseph's lineage, with Joseph as a focal character in 1:18–25.

Matthew narrates that Joseph is engaged to Mary when he discovers her pregnancy. Because of his righteous character (see commentary on 3:1–17), he plans to divorce her in a way that avoids drawing attention to the situation. Jewish engagements at this time were enacted by a marriage contract, although the wife would not move to her husband's household until a year after becoming engaged. If a breaking of the engagement was desired, a legal dissolution of the marriage contract was required. This provides the context for Joseph's plan to "divorce" Mary. (If later rabbinic writings indicate first-century marriage practices, Mary and Joseph were likely in their teens: Mary between the ages of twelve and fourteen with Joseph a bit older.)

Before Joseph is able to pursue this plan, however, an angel of the Lord appears and speaks to him in a dream. Angels and dreams will continue to guide Jesus's family in the days ahead (2:13, 19; cf. 2:12). Matthew draws on the plot features of angels and dreams to highlight the authority of the messages they communicate. The angel's message (1:20–21) emphasizes Joseph's expected response to wed Mary and name Jesus, the Holy Spirit's role in Jesus's conception (emphasized already at 1:18), and the salvific nature of Jesus's mission—"he will save his people from their sins" (1:21). The latter pronouncement fits the exilic motif already introduced in the genealogy (1:11–12). The Old Testament motif of Israel's exile and return is theologically connected to the forgiveness of Israel's sin that originally brought about exile (cf. Jer. 31:27–34).

In 1:18–25, Matthew emphasizes Joseph's naming of Jesus. The angel commands Joseph to name the child and explains the meaning of "Jesus" (1:21; Hebrew: Joshua, meaning "salvation"). At the passage's conclusion, Matthew confirms that Joseph does indeed name Jesus as instructed (1:25). The importance of this act becomes clear in light of ancient Jewish adoptive practices. For legal adoption to occur, all that Joseph needed to do was acknowledge Jesus as his own, which Joseph does by remaining with Mary and naming the child (Davies and Allison, 1:220). Joseph adopts Jesus into his family and so into his lineage (1:1–17). Matthew reemphasizes the importance of naming, since he also names Jesus. The author's first of many "fulfillment quotations," in which he cites the Old Testament as fulfilled by some aspect of Jesus's life, occurs here (1:22–23; see "Sources" in the introduction). The citation from Isaiah 7:14 provides Matthew's name for Jesus—Immanuel, "God with us." Jesus as God's presence with his people emerges as an important theme in Matthew, given its prominent placement by the author here and in Jesus's final words of the Gospel—"I am with you always" (28:20; cf. also 18:20). The importance of naming is also signaled by the bookending of Jesus's name in 1:18 (at the beginning of the Greek sentence) and as the final word of 1:25.

Having affirmed the identity of Jesus via his familial origins (Matthew 1), the author turns to the ways in which Jesus's messianic identity aligns with Jewish scriptural hopes and puts him at odds with the ruling powers of his day.

2:1–23: Jesus as long-awaited and rival king. The story in Matthew 2 is organized around four scriptural quotations (2:5–6, 15, 17–18, and 23) that ground Jesus's identity as king and bringer of restoration and authorize Jesus as true king of Israel. The chapter also serves to introduce a key conflict in Matthew's story. Jesus as Messiah-King, even in his infancy, is understood as a threat to the existing political structures represented by Herod (73–4 BC), king of Judea, Samaria, Galilee, Perea, and Near Eastern territories beyond Galilee. Herod, an Idumean by ethnicity, was granted rule over the Jews by Rome in 40 BC because of his allegiance. His position as king is emphasized at 2:1, 3, 9. The Jewish leaders ("chief priests and teachers of the law"; 2:4), whom Herod consults when he hears about a rival "king of the Jews," should be understood as religious/political leaders, given that their interests are generally aligned with those of Herod and Rome (and since religion and politics were virtually inseparable in the ancient world).

When Magi arrive in Jerusalem inquiring as to the anticipated birthplace of the "king of the Jews" (2:1–2), Herod is troubled and calls on those steeped in the Jewish Scriptures to answer their question. The reply by the teachers of the law comes from Micah 5:2, which references Bethlehem producing a shepherd-king for Israel (for the analogy of king to shepherd in the Old Testament, see Ps. 78:70–72; Jer. 23:1–6). Matthew, using this citation to communicate

The modern city of Bethlehem, the birthplace of Jesus (Matt. 2:1–8)

more directly with his audience, appears to draw from the context of Micah 5:2 to highlight restoration from exile through a shepherd-ruler (Matt. 2:6–7; cf. 1:11–12 for the theme of restoration from exile). This emphasis is supported by the immediate context of the Micah quotation, which points to a time in Israel's history when they were soon to be overrun and exiled by the Assyrians (Mic. 5:1, 5). The promise of the prophet's message is for a ruler who will bring about return from exile and restoration of God's people (5:2–4).

Once Herod knows the location and the timing of the star that the Magi have followed, he asks them to search out and alert him to the child's whereabouts so that he might join the Magi in worshiping this king (2:8). The reader has some hint that all is not right in Herod's request, since Matthew has indicated that Herod as king was disturbed by his original encounter with the Magi. Suspicion of Herod's motives is confirmed by a warning to the Magi in a dream not to return to Herod (2:12). Instead, after the star leads the Magi to Jesus, they give gifts and worship him (their purpose in coming; 2:2, 11); then they return home.

The Magi are a part of Matthew's literary landscape for only twelve verses, but their presence has had an influence that exceeds Matthew's brief reference to them. Church traditions have cast them as three kings. Yet no indication of their number is provided, and they were most likely royal servants or astrologers who came from the East, possibly Persia or Babylon (Powell 2001, 146–47). Matthew probably draws attention to them in chapter 2 to emphasize Gentile inclusion as he has already done by including Gentile women in his genealogy (1:3, 5–6). Though Jesus comes as the rightful king of the Jews, Gentiles unexpectedly show up in his lineage, and Gentiles are surprisingly the first worshipers at his feet.

Though the Magi have not told Herod the child's exact location, Jesus is still in danger. Once again, an angel of the Lord appears to Joseph in a dream (2:13; cf. 1:20), this time warning him to take Jesus and Mary to Egypt to avoid the treacherous reach of Herod. Joseph again obeys the Lord's command that comes through the angel and takes his family to Egypt. Matthew comments on the flight to Egypt with another Old Testament quotation: "And so was fulfilled what the Lord had said through the prophet: 'Out of Egypt I called my son'" (Matt. 2:15; citing Hos. 11:1).

Matthew's fulfillment quotations connect to two levels of his narrative. On the story level, the clear connection between Hosea 11:1 and the plot of Matthew 2 is the move to and return from Egypt. As God brought Israel, God's son, from Egypt (Hos. 11:1), so God will bring Jesus, God's son, out of Egypt. The typological nature of the connection between Hosea and Matthew is clear in the parallel actions of God in each. This connection highlights Matthew's interest in portraying Jesus as representative of Israel. The same connection will be picked up and developed further in Matthew 3–4 (on "Son of God," see 4:3 and "Theological Themes" in the introduction).

A second connection between the quotation from Hosea and Matthew 2 occurs on the level of the communication between author and reader—the *discourse level* of the narrative, where the Hosea quotation evokes the movement from exile to restoration (as did the Micah citation at Matt. 2:6). The immediate context of Hosea 11:1 is a recapitulation of this movement from Israel's sin and exile in Egypt and Assyria (11:2–7) to God's compassion and restoration in bringing Israel back from exile (11:8–11). Similarly, Matthew shows Jesus enacting a return from Egyptian exile (2:14–15; cf. also emphasis on return to "Israel" in 2:20–21).

Matthew's narration continues, with Herod reacting to the news that the Magi have outwitted him (2:16). Herod orders all boys two years and under in the environs of Bethlehem to be killed. Matthew then cites Jeremiah 31:15, which connects Rachel to Bethlehem on the story level (she was buried in Bethlehem according to Gen. 35:19) and speaks of her mourning for her lost children. On the discourse level, we again hear echoes of exile and restoration, since Jeremiah 31 is a chapter that explicitly promises Israel's restoration from exile (e.g., Jer. 31:10, 16–17). By drawing on Jewish biblical hopes, Matthew once again intimates that Jesus is the long-awaited restorer of Israel.

The author concludes the birth story of Jesus by narrating the return of Jesus and his family to "the land of Israel" (used twice; 2:20–21), and specifically to Nazareth in Galilee, after Herod's death (4 BC; 2:22–23). Once again, the Lord's guidance comes to Joseph through an angel in a dream, instructing him to return to Israel and then warning him about Herod's son Archelaus, now ruling in Judea. Joseph obeys, as he has at each instance of divine guidance (1:24; 2:14, 21–22). For Matthew, Jesus's return to the land mirrors Israel's return from Egypt (Exod. 14:1–15:27; Hos. 11:1) and begins Israel's return from their present exile (Matt. 1:11–12; 2:5–6, 15, 17–18).

The last fulfillment formula of Matthew 2 comes at the final moment of the birth narrative. "So was fulfilled what was said through the prophets, that he would be called a Nazarene [Greek *Nazōraios*]" (2:23). The interpretive difficulty at 2:23 is that this declaration cannot be found in the Old Testament or elsewhere. It is most likely that Matthew is relying here on a wordplay rather than a full quotation (intending the reader to connect *Nazōraios* to the location, Nazareth, in the previous line). Support for this comes from the general way he introduces the statement as coming from "the prophets" rather than a particular prophet. The precise wordplay is debated, with some scholars hearing a connection to the Nazirite vow (Hebrew *nazir*) in Numbers 6. In this case, the wordplay would be emphasizing Jesus as holy or set apart. More likely, *Nazōraios* plays on the Hebrew word *netser*, translated "branch." This Hebrew word occurs in Isaiah 11:1, where *netser* refers to a son of Jesse (David's father; cf. 1 Samuel 16): "from [Jesse's] roots a Branch will bear fruit." The

term *netser* was used to evoke messianic hopes in other Jewish writings of Matthew's day (e.g., Dead Sea Scrolls, *Thanksgiving Hymns* 7.19). Thus Matthew concludes the story of Jesus's birth just as he began it (1:1), by emphasizing Jesus as Messiah, son of David, the hope of Israel's restoration.

B. Baptism and temptation (3:1–4:16). Matthew moves from narrating the infancy stories to two preparatory events for the ministry of Jesus—his baptism and temptation. Both narratives are set in the wilderness ("desert"), tying Jesus's preparation for his ministry to the identity of the people of Israel as they prepared to enter the land promised to them. Both stories are also marked by the Spirit, signaling that the time of eschatological promise has begun. John the Baptist is introduced in Matthew 3 as the forerunner who signals Jesus's ministry by calling Israel and its leaders to repentance, announcing God's kingdom, and warning of judgment, while hinting at Gentile inclusion into God's restored people. Jesus's own baptism becomes both a sign of God's covenant faithfulness to Israel and an affirmation of Jesus's obedient, faithful sonship to God. The theme of Jesus as faithful Son continues in the temptation narrative (4:1–11). Using citations from Deuteronomy, Matthew contrasts Israel's disobedience in the wilderness with Jesus's obedient response in the face of temptation. In 4:12–16, Matthew transitions to Jesus's public ministry (4:17), highlighting Jesus's ministry in Galilee and hinting again at Gentile inclusion into the kingdom, which Jesus will soon announce.

3:1–17: Jesus's baptism. In Matthew 3, the author introduces John the Baptist, forerunner of Jesus Messiah. In his preparatory role, John is baptizing Jews in the wilderness near the Jordan River and calling God's people to "repent, for the kingdom of heaven has come near" (3:2). This message is identical to the message typifying Jesus's ministry to Israel soon to begin (4:17), thus emphasizing John's alignment with Jesus's message of the kingdom (see "Theological Themes" in the introduction).

It is possible that the origin of John's baptism is connected to (1) Jewish purification washings, either those indicated in the Old Testament (e.g., Num. 19:12) or first-century practices such as those from the Qumran community in the area of the Dead Sea; (2) Gentile baptism upon conversion to Judaism; or (3) some combination of these. Whatever the specific origin, it seems that John's baptism drew on expectations about washings or baptism but combined these with unexpected elements, such as his preaching of the kingdom (similar to the eschatological tone of Qumran). If John is drawing on the practice of baptizing Jewish converts but is now calling *Jews* to a "conversionist" baptism, then his message is an implicit indictment of Jewish disloyalty to God and so a call to return to covenant faithfulness. The latter comes through clearly in John's emphasis on repentance (3:2, 6, 11).

Matthew highlights John's continuity with the Old Testament story of God's covenant with Israel by means of an Old Testament fulfillment quotation (3:3) and by demonstrating John's connection to the Old Testament prophet Elijah (3:4). By quoting Isaiah 40:3 in relation to John, Matthew shows John as the one who prepares the way for the Lord. In Isaiah's context, the announcement of comfort to Israel focuses on the end of exile and the return of Yahweh, Israel's God, to Israel (40:1–5). The prophet goes on to speak of the *good news* of God's return to Israel (Isa. 40:9; the Greek Septuagint uses the term *euangelion* ["good news"], defined in Isa. 52:7 as the news of God's reign; see the use of the same Greek term in Matt. 4:23). Given this context of promise of God's presence and restoration from exile, the reader hears John as preparing the way for Jesus, who will bring God's restoration, a message already heard in Matthew 1–2.

Matthew's description of John's clothing evokes the picture of Elijah from 2 Kings 1:8. Picturing John as a kind of Elijah emphasizes John's role as forerunner of the coming of the Lord (cf. Mal. 4:5–6) as well as John's prophetic role. Like the prophets of old, John preaches a message of promise and warning. Matthew focuses attention on John's warnings particularly to the Jerusalem leaders, Pharisees and

The Jordan River, where John the Baptist baptized (Matt. 3:6). During the first century AD, the river would have been wider and the vegetation along the banks denser.

Sadducees, who come to the Jordan River either to observe John's baptism or to be baptized themselves (the Greek is ambiguous in this regard). John has strong words for these leaders who should be producing fruit in keeping with repentance—that is, in keeping with a return to covenant loyalty (3:8). The notion of bearing fruit is a common one in the Old Testament, focused especially on God's expectation that Israel would produce fruit (e.g., Isa. 5:1–7; 27:2–6; 37:31–32; cf. Matt. 7:15–19; 12:33; 21:43). Thus John warns Israel, especially its leaders, to live up to God's covenantal expectations for them.

For Matthew, the consequences of refusing to repent and to bear fruit are severe. John warns of the "coming wrath" (3:7) and, following the analogy of bearing fruit, warns of fruitless trees being destroyed (3:10). John warns against a presumption that Jewish ancestry will ensure vindication at the final judgment. Instead, his words hint at Matthew's prominent theme of Gentile inclusion, since if "out of these stones God can raise up children for Abraham" (3:9), then presumably he can make Gentiles into Abraham's children (cf. 8:11)!

The theme of judgment is a prominent one in Matthew (e.g., 12:33–37; 13:37–43, 47–50) and indicates both the punishment of the unfaithful and the vindication of the faithful righteous at the final judgment. Both strands are important in Matthew. Even though the former is the one emphasized here (3:7–12), Matthew's implication is that those who embrace repentance and produce fruit will be prepared for the kingdom and will receive the promised Holy Spirit (3:11), a signal of God's eschatological restoration (cf. Joel 2:28–29). John's warnings carry over into Jesus's role, as one who will baptize with fire—that is, purification or judgment—as well as with the Holy Spirit (3:11–12). John's subordinate role to Jesus's mission is emphasized in 3:11–12. John's baptism of repentance, though the first eschatological signal, is penultimate to and prepares for Jesus's baptism with fire and the Spirit.

When Jesus comes to be baptized by John (3:13–17), John demurs, indicating that Jesus should baptize him. Jesus's reply is intriguing: he must be baptized "to fulfill all righteousness" (3:15). Of all the Gospel writers, Matthew uses the noun "righteousness" (Greek *dikaiosynē*) most frequently (seven times in Matthew as compared with once in Luke and twice in John). The use of "righteousness" here likely evokes covenant faithfulness more broadly, not simply torah obedience, since how Jesus's baptism would fulfill the law is not obvious. In addition, in some instances Matthew uses *dikaiosynē* to refer to God's eschatological act of righting all things (e.g., the pairing of God's "kingdom and his righteousness" at 6:33; see also 21:32) (Hagner, 56). This understanding seems to fit best here: Jesus pursues John's eschatological baptism as a way of signaling the fulfillment of God's restoration in Jesus himself.

The Spirit of God descends on Jesus at his baptism, indicating that the time of God's restoration has begun (3:11, 16; cf. also 1:18, 20). The confirming word about Jesus comes from "a voice from heaven," a circumlocution for God's name (3:17). The climactic moment of the chapter occurs here in God's words affirming Jesus as faithful Son: "This is my Son, whom I love; with him I am well pleased" (cf. 17:5, where the same words occur). Though a number of Old Testament texts may possibly receive allusion here (Gen. 22:2; Ps. 2:7; with the most likely allusion being to Isaiah's obedient servant of Yahweh; Isa. 42:1; cf. Matt. 12:18), the story connection fostered is an affirmation of Jesus's identity as *obedient* son in line with Israel's calling to be faithful to God. This connection between Jesus and Israel has already been made via son language in Matthew 2:15. The explicit language of "Son of God" will be highlighted in 4:1–11, with a direct connection to obedience. Here, the focus at Jesus's baptism is God's affirmation of pleasure and love in the obedient son who has come to fulfill all righteousness.

4:1–11: Jesus's temptation. The temptation narrative follows Jesus's baptism and continues the focus on the preparation of Jesus for his public ministry. On the level of Matthew's communication with the reader, he continues to emphasize Jesus's identity as God's obedient Son—Jesus as Israel's representative.

God's Spirit has descended on Jesus at his baptism. Now the Spirit leads Jesus into the desert, where he will be tempted by the devil (also referred to here as the tempter and Satan). By indicating the setting of the temptations in the desert (4:1), Matthew ties Jesus's temptation to the testing of Israel in the wilderness. The parallel "forty days and forty nights" to Israel's forty-year wilderness wanderings confirms this connection, which Matthew highlights through Jesus's citation from Deuteronomy in response to each temptation.

Each of the first two temptations begins with the conditional "If you are the Son of God" (4:3, 6). So far, Matthew has used "Son of God" to (1) compare Jesus to Israel, God's son (cf. Hos. 11:1; Matt. 2:15), and (2) affirm Jesus's intimate relationship with God and obedience to God, especially if Isaiah 42:1 is the allusion behind God's affirmation of Jesus in 3:17 (cf. Isa. 42:3 for the faithfulness of Isaiah's

servant). Jewish understandings of "Son of God" language would likely have evoked messianic themes as well, since Israel's king—and subsequently Israel's anticipated Messiah—would have been the representative of Israel par excellence (2 Sam. 7:12–16; see "Theological Themes" in the introduction).

The first temptation centers on Jesus's hunger after fasting for forty days, with the devil tempting Jesus to turn stones into bread. Jesus answers, as he does in each case, with a scriptural text from Deuteronomy. The affirmation from Deuteronomy 8:3 prioritizes the sustenance of God's words over bread. In Deuteronomy, this affirmation comes as part of a call for Israel to remember their forty years in the desert as a time when God tested their obedience and humbled them. God fed them manna to teach them the true source of their sustenance (Deut. 8:2–3), with Deuteronomy 8:5 identifying Israel as God's son. The use of Deuteronomy 8:3 connects the wilderness testing of Jesus to that of Israel, contrasting Jesus's obedience by not pursuing bread with Israel's disobedience (8:3, 5; cf. Exod. 16:1–5).

In the second temptation, the devil entices Jesus to throw himself from the highest point of the Jerusalem temple, citing Psalm 91:11–12

The Judean wilderness, where Jesus fasted for forty days following his baptism (Matt. 4:1)

as evidence that God will send angels to protect anyone who "make[s] the Most High [their] dwelling" (Ps. 91:9). Jesus's reply again comes from Deuteronomy, this time 6:16: "Do not put the LORD your God to the test." The verse in Deuteronomy adds, "as you did at Massah," indicating the time when the Israelites questioned God's provision of water for them (Exod. 17:1–7). Jesus, in his refusal to heed the devil's temptation to test God, provides the contrast to the wilderness experience of Israel.

The final temptation consists of an implicit claim by the devil that all the kingdoms of the world belong to him and that he will give them to Jesus if Jesus will worship him (4:8–9). Matthew shows Jesus drawing from Deuteronomy 6 in his response: "Worship the Lord your God, and serve him only" (Matt. 4:10; Deut. 6:13). This call to exclusive allegiance to Yahweh is the positive side of the prohibition against testing the Lord that Jesus has already cited (Deut. 6:16). Though Israel failed the loyalty test in the wilderness, Matthew shows Jesus to be fully faithful to God through all three wilderness temptations. (Luke narrates the same three temptations but places the temple temptation last in order. By doing so, he emphasizes a temple motif that begins and ends his Gospel; see Luke 1:8; 24:53.)

An ironic note rings at the passage's end. Though Jesus has rejected the idea of asking God to send protecting angels (4:6), after he has sent the devil away angels care for him (4:11). God has provided for Jesus in the wilderness; and Jesus has proven himself the obedient Son, faithful representative of Israel.

4:12–16: Transition to Jesus's public ministry. Jesus's return to Galilee comes on the heels of news about John's imprisonment. With John's preparatory work accomplished, Matthew shows Jesus moving from Nazareth to Capernaum, on the sea (or lake) of Galilee, to begin his public ministry (4:17–16:20; cf. 8:5). Matthew includes another fulfillment quotation in 4:14–16. The connection between Isaiah 9:1–2 and Matthew 4:12 on the plot level

focuses on Jesus's relocation to Capernaum. For his readers, Matthew connects the redemption promised in Isaiah 9—the light dawning in darkness—to Jesus's ministry in Galilee about to be inaugurated (4:17). Galilee of the first century included both Jews and Gentiles, with a larger Jewish population in the lower Galilean region. Matthew, with Isaiah's reference to "Galilee of the Gentiles," hints at the inclusion of all nations in the redemption brought by Jesus (cf. 28:19; also 1:3, 5–6; 2:1–12; 3:9), though the explicit focus of his preresurrection ministry will be Israel (cf. 10:5–6; 15:24).

2. Jesus's Announcement of the Kingdom to Israel and Resulting Responses (4:17–16:20)

The second major section of Matthew focuses on Jesus's announcement and enactment of the reign of God and the responses it generates in Israel. The people have been prepared for Jesus's kingdom inauguration by John's call to repentance and announcement of the kingdom's impending arrival (identical to that of Jesus; cf. 3:2 and 4:17). In addition, Jesus's return to and relocation within Galilee sets up his Galilean ministry spanning 4:17–16:20.

Matthew 4:17–16:20 is structured by a number of formal and conceptual repetitions, the most overarching of which is the repeated formula at 4:17 and 16:21 ("from that time on Jesus began to . . ."; see "Structure" in the introduction). Three of Matthew's five great discourses sit within Matthew 4:17–16:20, each focused on announcing God's kingdom. In the first (chaps. 5–7), Jesus proclaims his manifesto of the kingdom. In the second (chap. 10), Jesus empowers and instructs his disciples for kingdom ministry. In the third (chap. 13), Jesus reveals more about God's kingdom, including its manifestation in two stages, so that its present expression has a hidden quality. This goes a long way to explain the growing rejection of Jesus's ministry by Jewish leaders and the ambivalence more generally from the crowds (11:2–16:20). Yet for those with ears to hear and eyes to see, Jesus is revealed to be the Messiah, the inaugurator of God's reign (cf. 16:16). In his teachings and miracles, human faith can see the authority and compassion of the God of Israel.

A. Proclamation of the kingdom in word and action (4:17–11:1). In this section of his Gospel, Matthew defines the center of Jesus's public ministry as the proclamation and enactment of God's kingdom. After summarizing Jesus's proclamation that the kingdom is about to arrive (4:17), Matthew turns to Jesus's teaching about the kingdom and its relation to covenantal loyalty in the Sermon on the Mount (5:1–7:29). Then Matthew shows Jesus enacting God's kingdom authority and mercy through his healings and other miracles with a wide range of responses to his ministry, from exceptional faith to unbelief (8:1–9:38). This section concludes with Jesus's instructions to his twelve disciples to participate in his mission (10:1–11:1).

4:17–25: Jesus's message and ministry. At 4:17, Matthew provides the centerpiece of Jesus's proclamation to Israel: "Repent, for the kingdom of heaven has come near" (for repentance theme, cf. 3:2). This summary of Jesus's message begins with an introductory phrase, "From that time on Jesus began to [preach]," which is repeated in 16:21, signaling its structural importance for defining the movement of Matthew's story.

For Matthew, Jesus's ministry can be summed up as proclamation of the soon-to-arrive kingdom, or reign, of God. Matthew's "kingdom of heaven" is conceptually the same as Mark's "kingdom of God" (cf. Mark 1:15 // Matt. 4:17; also Mark 10:14, 23 // Matt. 19:14, 23). Matthew probably follows the Jewish convention of circumlocution—avoiding reference to "God" when another construction can communicate the same idea (heaven as God's dwelling place). Though the reign of Israel's God is a regular Jewish affirmation (e.g., Ps. 93:1; 96:10; 99:1; 146:10), the Old Testament prophets also promise a day when God will reign fully over the heavens and the earth, making all things right (e.g., Mic. 4:1–8; Isa. 24:21–23; 52:1–10; Dan. 2:44; see also *Psalms of Solomon* 17). It is

the arrival of that day that is evoked with the kingdom language in Jesus's ministry. Most first-century Jewish believers longed for God's rule to come in redemption and vindication for the faithful of Israel, in judgment of idolatrous nations, and in restoration of the land and of Davidic kingship. When Jesus came on the scene preaching that the kingdom is near, the religious and political reverberations of such preaching would have ignited that hope.

Directly following this inaugural preaching summary, Matthew narrates the call of Jesus's disciples (4:18–22). Jesus issues a call for these four fishermen to follow him, making the analogy that their work will now involve fishing for people (4:19). The initiative that Jesus shows in this scene contrasts with the conventional practice of a would-be disciple attaching himself to a rabbi. Jesus initiates the relationship, and these fishermen leave their livelihood (4:19, 21) to follow Jesus (see 10:2–4 for the naming of all twelve disciples).

In Matthew 4:23–25, Matthew summarizes Jesus's ministry by describing his three primary activities: teaching, preaching, and healing (4:23). Preaching "the good news of the kingdom" connects with the summary of Jesus's preaching at 4:17, while subsequent chapters take up teaching (chaps. 5–7) and healing (chaps. 8–9). The summary statement in 4:23 is virtually repeated at 9:35, creating a bracket surrounding the narration of Jesus's Galilean ministry of teaching and healing (4:23–9:35). The crowds respond by bringing their sick to Jesus for healing (4:24), following him from the entire region of Galilee and Judea, including Jerusalem, and even Syria to the north and Perea to the east ("the region across the Jordan"; 4:25). The scope of the geographic description seems to indicate "the whole of the area that is populated with Jewish people" (Wilkins, 183).

5:1–7:29: Jesus's first discourse—the Sermon on the Mount. The first major section of 4:17–16:20 highlights Jesus's teaching ministry. It is no accident that Matthew begins his narration of Jesus's ministry with an extended teaching by Jesus. Matthew structures his Gospel in part by arranging most of Jesus's teaching into five major blocks, or "discourses" (see "Structure" in the introduction).

In this discourse, often called the Sermon on the Mount, Jesus teaches his disciples (along with the crowds; see 5:1–2 and 7:28–29) about the kingdom that he has announced in 4:17. The single consistent theme of the sermon is the imminent kingdom of God (5:3, 10, 19–20; 6:10, 33; 7:21; see "Theological Themes" in the introduction). Focused on Jesus's expectations for his disciples in light of the arrival of God's reign, the sermon centers on a call to covenantal faithfulness (e.g., 5:13–16, 17–20; 7:12) and provides a vision of how discipleship ought to look as God comes to make all things right (e.g., 5:7–10; 6:9–13, 25–34).

5:1–16. While much of this discourse consists of *exhortation*, its headlining passage *announces blessing* (5:3–12, with allusions to Isa. 61:1–11). These blessings, the great reversals that will happen with the arrival of God's reign, indicate that God's decisive act of restoration precedes and grounds the expectation for kingdom discipleship and enables the believing community to live it out. Thus, although the Sermon on the Mount has sometimes been viewed as idealistic and unattainable, Matthew

gives every indication that he expects his readers to hear it as an attainable ethic for believers in community with Jesus in their midst (18:20; 28:20).

With the first four beatitudes (5:3–6), Jesus pronounces a blessed condition on those who would not be considered blessed or fortunate in life: those who are spiritually poor or hopeless, those who mourn, those who are meek or oppressed, and those who are "starved for justice" (Powell 1996, 467). (The translation of "justice" for *dikaiosynē* here and in 5:10 fits a covenantal understanding of that term as God's commitment to making all things right; see commentary on 3:1–17.) These four blessings focus on those whose situation is most destitute, with the promise that they will find their situation reversed in God's coming kingdom. The reversal of situation is captured in each case by a specific blessing: the kingdom belongs to them (5:3), they will receive comfort (5:4), they will inherit the earth (5:5), and their longing for justice will be filled (5:6).

In the final four beatitudes (with the fourth expanded; 5:11–12), blessings are conferred on those who live in a way that signals their

The hills along the north shore of the Sea of Galilee where Jesus may have given the Sermon on the Mount

alignment with the values characterizing God's reign. As God's people show mercy and singular allegiance, enact peace and justice, and live with the resulting persecution, they show their alignment with God's care for those most destitute (5:3–6). The harmony between their actions and God's kingdom ensures they will receive mercy (5:7), see God (5:8), and be called God's children (5:9; cf. 12:50), and that they are already receiving the kingdom (5:10; note present tense of this blessing and at 5:3).

The beatitudes are followed by a declaration of the distinctive identity and mission of Jesus's followers. They are "the salt of the earth" (5:13) and "the light of the world" (5:14–16), indicating their distinctive identity within their environment for the sake of mission to the world. The light imagery evokes God's expectation for Israel to be a light to Gentiles (Isa. 60:1–3; see also 9:1–2; 49:6; Matt. 4:16). Matthew's Jesus uses this imagery to define his followers in relation to Israel's mission to the nations, setting their own mission in covenantal context.

5:17–48. The body of the Sermon on the Mount begins by highlighting the disposition of Jesus and his followers in relation to the Old Testament law, or torah (5:17–48). Jesus affirms his mission to fulfill the Law and the Prophets (the Old Testament Scriptures) rather than abolish them. He warns his followers against breaking or influencing others to break any of the torah's commands (5:19). In fact, their torah observance ("righteousness," Greek *dikaiosynē*), understood as an expression of covenantal loyalty, must surpass the covenant adherence of the Pharisees and teachers of the law (5:20; cf. 15:6; 23:1–4 for the latter's lack of obedience). As 5:21–48 makes clear, it is Jesus's interpretation and explanation of the torah that must guide his followers.

The often-termed "antitheses" of Matthew ("You have heard that it was said, . . . but I tell you . . ."; 5:21, 27, 31, 33, 38, 43) reflect Jesus's interpretation and intensification—rather than contradiction—of six Old Testament commands or cases. In each case, the expectation

for Jesus's followers is more stringent than its Old Testament counterpart (a surpassing righteousness; 5:20). This intensification fits the Jewish, rabbinic practice of "making a fence" around the torah in order to minimize the possibility of transgression (Mishnah *Avot* 1:1).

The Old Testament prohibition against murder is broadened to include anger (5:21–22; Exod. 20:13), with a related call to reconciliation (5:23–26). Jesus also expands the prohibition against adultery to include lust (5:31–32; Exod. 20:14). The third case involves the Old Testament prohibition of remarriage to a first spouse after a divorce and second marriage have occurred (Deut. 24:1–4). Jesus again commands a stricter ethic by limiting the allowable reason for divorce to *porneia* (a Greek term meaning sexual infidelity of some sort, though the specific connotation Matthew intends by this term is debated) rather than the broader circumstance of a husband's displeasure for something indecent (Deut. 24:1).

The fourth case raises the importance of keeping oaths made to the Lord (Deut. 23:21–23). Jesus narrows this to a prohibition against making oaths generally (5:33). Philo, a first-century Jewish writer, laments the "habit of swearing incessantly and thoughtlessly about ordinary matters" (Philo, *On the Decalogue* 92). This habit provides the context for Jesus's prohibition against making oaths. Instead, his followers ought to let their word alone rather than an oath guarantee their actions (5:34–37).

In its original context, "eye for eye" (the Old Testament *lex talionis*, or law of retribution; Exod. 21:24; Matt. 5:38) was likely a means of limiting personal revenge, leaving the exacting of fair retribution to a court. Once again, Jesus further limits an Old Testament prescription, this time disallowing all forms of retaliation to various insults to honor: a backhanded blow as an act to dishonor (5:39), legal removal of one's basic possessions (5:40), Roman conscription of a civilian to carry loads (5:41), and more general requests to borrow money or possessions (5:42). While in each of these illustrations commentators have recognized elements of hyperbole (e.g., removal of both tunic and cloak would leave a person naked), the exaggeration emphasizes nonresistance as a nonnegotiable for Jesus's disciples. In a context in which active political or social resistance has severe consequences, Jesus's radical ethic of nonretaliation moves beyond capitulation to one's oppressors to active self-sacrifice for others, even enemies.

The final "antithesis" has a summative function. By its emphasis on love of everyone, even one's enemies, it captures the spirit of the other five directives. While the Old Testament command to love one's neighbor derives from Leviticus 19:18, the coordinate "hate your enemy" is not an Old Testament quotation. It may be that the sentiment is an expression derived from texts such as Psalm 139:21–22. Jesus broadens the love command to explicitly include love of enemies and prayer for them (5:44). The rationale provided is that love of neighbor fulfills no greater ethic than that of tax collectors and pagans (5:46–47). Of the six cases of torah interpretation that Jesus has specified, only the final case includes a purpose. As Israel was to image God to the nations, Jesus's followers are called to be like their heavenly Father, morally complete or perfect (5:45, 48). They do this supremely by fulfilling the command to love, which sums and binds together all other commands (cf. 22:40).

6:1–18. From Jesus's interpretation of torah, Matthew turns to Jesus's teaching on Jewish religious practices (expressed as "righteousness" [Greek *dikaiosynē*]; 6:1; cf. 5:20) of giving to the poor (6:2–4), prayer (6:5–15), and fasting (6:16–18). These three practices are joined in Tobit 12:8, along with "righteousness," indicating their centrality in Jewish piety. The three sections are each structured by a prohibition, a command, and a promise. The common thread is a warning against doing acts of righteousness for human, instead of divine, approval (6:2, 5, 16). Jesus promises future reward to those who give, pray, and fast "in secret" rather than act to be seen by others (6:4, 6, 18).

The Lord's Prayer (6:9–13) falls within the section on prayer, extending that section beyond the formal symmetry of prohibition, command, and promise. Just preceding the Lord's Prayer is a call to avoid "babbling like pagans" in prayer (6:7), which likely refers to magical understandings of prayer in which repetitions would have been thought to compel the gods to action. In contrast, Jesus's followers are to cling to the truth that their Father knows and anticipates their prayers (6:8).

The Lord's Prayer provides a model prayer for disciples (6:9–13) and is thoroughly kingdom focused, looking ahead with longing for God's reign to be consummated. The address, "Our Father in heaven," indicates that the familial relationship to God that Jesus himself enjoys (see son language in Matthew 3 and 4) is shared in some way with Jesus's followers, who are God's children (cf. 5:16, 45, 48). After the address, three parallel petitions ask God to bring the kingdom, defined as universal recognition of God's holiness and accomplishment of God's will on earth:

> May your name be hallowed (revered as holy)
> May your kingdom come
> May your will be done. (author's translation; cf. NLT)

The final three petitions focus on daily needs (though the Greek term translated "daily" occurs nowhere else in Greek writings, so its meaning is unclear), forgiveness, and deliverance from temptation (6:11–13). Matthew's teaching that follows the Lord's Prayer presents forgiveness as an imperative for disciples (6:14–15; see commentary on 18:1–35).

6:19–7:12. The remainder of the body of the Sermon on the Mount covers various topics but fleshes out to some extent the ideas introduced in the Lord's Prayer: a call to singular loyalty to God (6:19–24) and trust for daily needs (6:27–34), a warning against judging others (7:1–6), and a call to prayer (7:7–11).

Jesus calls his followers to loyalty to God in contrast to storing up possessions (6:19–21) and money (6:24). The saying comparing the eye to a lamp (6:22–23), though not fully clear to today's readers, may draw on the ancient view that light goes out from a person's eyes, so that the person's body or self can be assessed by his or her eyes (cf. 5:16). The "healthy" eye might be better rendered "single-focused" (the Greek term frequently refers to singleness of purpose), since the context is about loyalty and the impossibility of serving two masters.

Jesus also calls the disciples to a life free from worry, a life defined by trusting in their God, who cares and provides daily needs of food and clothing (6:25–34). This exhortation was a weighty one in a cultural context where many people lived at a subsistence level (e.g., the day laborers of Matt. 20:1–15, who might have needed their end-of-day wage to feed their families). But for Jesus, life is to be free of worry, *even if* economically justifiable. His followers are to be characterized by focusing their first energies and priorities on the kingdom—God coming to make all things right (6:33). Trusting in God's righteousness eliminates worry and "little faith" (6:30; cf. 8:26 for this concept).

The final exhortations of the Sermon on the Mount include a warning against judging others (7:1), possibly focused on inappropriate eschatological judgments—determining about others what only God will decide at the end (cf. 13:27–30). Jesus goes on to warn against attending to the sins of others, while being oblivious to the gross sin in one's own life (7:3–5). The warnings against judging are tempered, however, by a call to discernment (7:6). Much speculation has gone into determining the referents for the "sacred" and "dogs/pigs." The "sacred" for Matthew would likely be related to the "good news of the kingdom" that Jesus brings (4:23; cf. 13:45). What we can say is that Jesus indicates that some will reject the sacred, and so his disciples are to be discerning as to their audience (cf. 10:14–15).

Also included at the end of the sermon is an encouragement to *ongoing* prayer (indicated by the Greek present tense in the imperatives to ask, seek, and knock; 7:7). The reason disciples can pray and expect an answer (7:8) is that they are children of a Father who gives good gifts when asked (7:9–11). The summative command of the Sermon on the Mount comes in 7:12, often called the golden rule: "So in everything, do to others what you would have them do to you." Jesus's ethical teachings in Matthew 5–7 come down to this motivation and its expression in action. In fact, the golden rule sums up "the Law and the Prophets" (7:12). This phrase hearkens back to the beginning of the body of the sermon, where Jesus affirms that he has come to fulfill the Law and the Prophets (5:17). Jesus as Messiah fulfills the Law and rightly interprets Scripture so that his followers hear self-giving for others at its center (e.g., 5:44; 7:12).

7:13–29. The conclusion to the Sermon on the Mount focuses on warnings about two paths (7:15–26). Jesus warns about the broad road leading to destruction, encouraging his disciples to take the narrow path leading to life (7:13–14). Jesus also warns of false prophets, who are recognizable by their evil fruits. A disciple is characterized by doing God's will (7:15–23). The two ways are illustrated by a closing parable in which a wise person and a foolish person build houses, one on rock, the other on sand (7:24–27). The wise person hears Jesus's words and enacts them; the foolish one hears but does not obey. The sermon's conclusion calls Jesus's disciples as well as Matthew's readers to obedience—to be the wise person who obeys Jesus's teachings.

Five times Matthew uses identical wording to transition from Jesus's teaching (in the five discourses) to Jesus's activity that follows: "When Jesus had finished [saying these things]" (7:28; cf. 11:1; 13:53; 19:1; 26:1). In this instance, Matthew narrates the response of the crowds to Jesus's teaching—amazement at his authority. While torah teachers usually gave instruction by referencing what former teachers had said, Jesus speaks with his own authority ("But I tell you . . ."; e.g., 5:22). Matthew introduces the theme of authority here and reiterates it throughout the story of Jesus's ministry in Matthew 8–10.

8:1–9:38: Jesus's enactment of the kingdom. After expressing Jesus's kingdom ministry in teaching (5:1–7:29), Matthew narrates Jesus's kingdom ministry in action (8:1–9:38). Matthew demonstrates Jesus's authority to heal the sick, cast out demons, forgive sins, and calm a storm. Other themes include Jesus's compassion in his role as Isaiah's servant of the Lord and the qualities of full allegiance and faith for those who would follow Jesus.

Matthew 8–9 is structured by three sets of three miracle stories (8:1–17; 8:23–9:8; 9:18–38) interwoven with teachings on kingdom discipleship (8:18–22; 9:9–17). The first set of miracle stories involves a leper (8:1–4), a servant of a Gentile centurion (8:5–13), and Peter's mother-in-law (8:14–15). The common factor in all three stories is Jesus's power over illness and his compassion for those in need.

8:1–17. Jesus willingly heals a leper (with "leprosy" being a term that could describe any number of skin diseases) upon hearing the leper's trust in Jesus's healing ability (8:2–3). Matthew emphasizes Jesus's authority and compassion as well as the importance of faith. Jesus touches the leper to heal him, a profound gesture to one who presumably rarely had physical contact during his illness (cf. Lev. 5:3 with Lev. 13:1–59). After healing him, Jesus commands him (1) to fulfill the requirements of the law for ritual cleansing with sacrifices, bodily washings, and purification rites (cf. Lev. 14:2–32); and (2) to refrain from speaking about the healing. The latter fits with other commands to silence in Matthew (e.g., 9:30; 12:16; 16:20), likely indicating the need for Jesus to conceal his messianic identity in the face of political ramifications until his own public declaration (at 21:1–11).

Capernaum (8:5) was the setting of a customs station and was near a trade route. Given this strategic location, the presence of Roman soldiers was likely. To hear of a centurion, a commander of eighty to one hundred soldiers and a representative of Rome's great military power, approaching Jesus in an attitude of submission (8:5–6), requesting healing for his servant (the Greek term may possibly be translated "son"), would have likely surprised Matthew's audience.

The healing of a centurion's servant is one of only two clear moments in Matthew where Jesus crosses the ethnic boundary between Jew and Gentile in his Galilean ministry (cf. also 15:21–28). On both occasions, it is the "great faith" of the Gentile supplicant on behalf of another that provides the impetus for the healing (8:10; 15:28). On both occasions, there is

The excavation of Capernaum, the ancient village on Galilee's north shore where Jesus was approached by a centurion (Matt. 8:5)

initial hesitation on Jesus's part (8:7; 15:23–24), in line with Matthew's explicit limitation of Jesus's ministry to Israel (10:5–6; 15:24). At Matthew 8:7, Jesus's first response to this Gentile is rendered best as a question, "Shall *I* come and heal him?" (8:7), given the emphatic "I" at the beginning of the clause.

The centurion's response, which recognizes Jesus's authority delegated to him by God (8:8–9), causes Jesus to be astonished and to commend his great faith (8:10). Matthew's theme of Gentile inclusion is highlighted in 8:11–12, where Jesus intimates that Gentiles will share in the kingdom (on feasting imagery; cf. Isa. 25:6) while some Jews would be excluded. Jesus heals the servant without even being present with him because of the centurion's faith (8:13).

The account of Jesus's healing of Peter's mother-in-law (8:14–15) emphasizes Jesus's power to heal by his touch (as with the leper; 8:3). Matthew sums up these first three miracles and Jesus's healing ministry generally (8:16) with a fulfillment quotation from Isaiah 53:4, emphasizing Jesus as the one who takes Israel's diseases upon himself (8:17). Readers have already heard a likely allusion tying Jesus to Isaiah's servant at Jesus's baptism (3:17). At 8:17, Matthew makes a clear connection between Isaiah's servant of the Lord and Jesus (cf. Isa. 53:4, 11).

8:18–22. Matthew includes here a teaching on discipleship. Although the identity of the two "would-be" disciples has been debated (is either a true disciple?), the account focuses on Jesus's expectations for his disciples in light of the arrival of God's kingdom: sacrifice and uncompromising allegiance (8:18–20), even in the face of family obligations (8:21–22; for "Son of Man" [8:20] as Jesus's self-designation, see "Theological Themes" in the introduction).

8:23–9:8. Matthew uses the next set of three miracle stories to demonstrate that Jesus's power not only is for healing but also extends over nature (8:23–27) and the demonic (8:28–34) and includes authority to forgive sins (9:1–8). Not only do these accounts show Jesus's authority,

but they also raise more deliberately the issue of Jesus's identity (e.g., 8:27), as well as show a range of responses to his ministry that includes faith, little faith, awe, and rejection.

When Jesus and his disciples are caught in a storm on the Galilean Sea, Jesus rebukes and calms the storm (8:23–26). Matthew emphasizes the disciples' inadequate faith (Greek *oligopistos*, "little faith," in 8:26; see also 6:30; 14:31; 16:8; and 17:20 for "little faith" used to characterize the disciples) and ties it to their inappropriate fear in light of Jesus's presence with them. Their little faith provides a contrast to the great faith exhibited by the Gentile centurion (8:10) and the faith implicit in the leper's affirmation of Jesus's healing power (8:2). The disciples' question at the end of the story raises the issue of Jesus's identity given his authority over nature itself—"What kind of man is this?" (8:27).

Matthew moves from Jesus's authority over nature to his power over the demonic (8:28–34). Jesus has crossed the lake and arrived in the region of Gadarenes, part of the Decapolis (cf. Matt. 4:25). (Manuscripts differ on the location name; some read "Gerasenes," an area thirty-three miles from the Galilean Sea [cf. Mark 5:1], others "Gergesenes," which was on the seashore, in addition to "Gadarenes," some six miles away.) This area was home to Gentiles as well as some Jews (Josephus, *Jewish War* 1.155; 3.51–58), which accounts for the presence of a herd of pigs (8:30; eating pork was forbidden by the law). Yet it is not at all clear that the two demon-possessed men healed by Jesus are Gentiles, since Jesus's mission in Matthew is to Israel (10:5–6; 15:24) and since Matthew otherwise explicitly names Gentiles who receive the benefit of Jesus's ministry (8:5–13; 15:21–28). After Jesus casts the demons into a herd of pigs, which then rush into the lake and drown, the townspeople beg Jesus to leave their region (8:31–34). With their rejection, Matthew continues to construct a continuum of responses to Jesus's ministry, ranging from rejection to inadequate faith to great faith.

Matthew's account of Jesus's healing a paralytic emphasizes his authority to forgive sin (9:1–8). In response to the faith of the paralytic's friends, Jesus unexpectedly grants the man forgiveness rather than healing (9:2; although in ancient context, it might be assumed that the two were connected; cf. John 5:14). Some teachers of the law privately assess that Jesus is blaspheming, presumably because only God can forgive sins (cf. Mark 2:7). Jesus intercepts their thoughts and raises the question of whether it is easier to forgive sin or to heal, implying that forgiving sin is the harder of the two. Yet he heals the paralytic to show that the forgiveness granted is genuine (9:6–7). The crowd's response contrasts with the response of the teachers of the law: the crowd is filled with awe and praises God for the authority to forgive sins that Jesus displays (9:8).

9:9–17. Between the second and third sets of miracles in chapters 8–9, Matthew again focuses on discipleship in light of the kingdom's arrival. The call of Matthew, a tax collector, to be a disciple of Jesus (9:9; cf. 4:18–22) is tied to Jesus's practice of eating with "sinners" (9:10–13). Tax collectors were those who had aligned their interests with the Roman occupation and would have been despised by their Jewish compatriots. "Sinners" is a broad category that would include tax collectors and any Jews judged as unfaithful to Israel's covenant with Yahweh. Faithful Jews would typically avoid eating with such people, since they might invite ritual defilement by doing so. By eating with them Jesus demonstrates that God welcomes "sinners" into the kingdom, for God is merciful (9:13). The citation from Hosea 6:6 signals Jesus's prophetic critique of obedience to purity regulations (sacrifice) without corresponding commitment to mercy, a key covenantal value (Greek *eleos*, which corresponds to the Hebrew covenantal term *hesed*). As Jesus will make clear later in Matthew, obedience to the law must be enacted with mercy and love at the center (12:7; 23:23; also 22:34–40).

After enacting mercy toward sinners as a signal of God's kingdom, Jesus responds to a question from John the Baptist's disciples by alluding to the kingdom's arrival. When asked why Jesus's disciples do not fast, Jesus answers that the time does not allow for it. Jesus's presence (as a sign of the kingdom's presence) is a time of joy and so is not appropriate to fasting (9:14–15). New wine calls for new wineskins (9:17). The arrival of the kingdom calls for a refocused (eschatological) interpretation of the "old" that aligns with God's kingship in Jesus.

9:18–38. The final set of three miracle stories again highlights Jesus's authority to heal and also focuses on faith that often precedes healing (9:22, 29) as well as Jesus's growing notoriety in the Galilean region (9:26, 31, 33). The first miracle story involves the healing of a bleeding woman and the raising of a dead girl. A ruler approaches Jesus, asking him to come to his daughter who has just died and expressing his faith in Jesus's ability to raise her (9:18). On his way to their home, a woman who has been subject to bleeding for twelve years approaches Jesus. Believing that contact with Jesus will heal her, she touches his cloak (9:20–21). Jesus declares that her faith has brought about her healing. The story ends with the raising of the ruler's daughter as Jesus takes her by the hand. Matthew ties the two stories into one, sandwiching the former within the latter (as Mark does; Mark 5:21–43; see "Sources" in the introduction). This connection serves to highlight the dual themes of faith and Jesus's authority and compassion.

The healing of two blind men occurs after they cry out to Jesus for mercy (cf. 9:13), recognizing him as "Son of David" (Messiah; see "Theological Themes" in the introduction). Jesus heals them "according to [their] faith" in his power to heal them (9:28–29). Matthew again highlights the faith of those coming for healing as well as Jesus's authority to heal simply by a touch of his hand (9:29). As he has done earlier (cf. 8:4), Matthew also indicates a certain level of secrecy that Jesus attempts to maintain (unsuccessfully here: 9:31), which parallels the notoriety that is accompanying his healing ministry (9:26, 33).

The final healing story involves Jesus's healing of a mute and demon-possessed man (9:32–33). On hearing the healed man speak, the crowd is amazed, exclaiming, "Nothing like this has ever been seen in Israel" (9:33). The Pharisees provide a contrasting response, attributing Jesus's power to demons (9:34). This final picture of Jesus's early Galilean ministry highlights the divided responses toward his enactment of the kingdom. While Jewish leaders question his authority (9:3, 34), the Galilean crowds follow Jesus as he ministers, expressing awe and amazement at his deeds and praising God (9:8, 33; cf. 7:28–29). The disciples, who have committed themselves to follow Jesus as their master (9:9; cf. 4:18–22), are described by Jesus as those of little or inadequate faith (8:26; cf. 6:30). Those who seek Jesus for healing often show faith in his power (8:2; 9:2, 18, 21–22, 28–29), with a Gentile supplicant being commended for his "great faith" (8:10). Matthew draws on this range of responses to encourage great faith in his reader as the proper response to Jesus's messianic authority (9:27).

Matthew concludes this section on Jesus's messianic teaching (chaps. 5–7) and kingdom enactment (Matthew 8–9) by summarizing Jesus's ministry to Israel in teaching, preaching, and healing (9:35; almost verbatim to 4:23). Upon seeing the crowds who have heard his teachings and brought their sick to him, Jesus is filled with compassion for the people of Israel, whom he likens to sheep without a shepherd. This response serves to indict Israel's leaders for not shepherding the people (cf. Ezekiel 34 for similar imagery in Ezekiel's critique of leaders in his day) and transitions between Jesus's ministry to Israel and his instructions to his disciples regarding their part in this ministry. The disciples are to be the answer to their own prayer for workers to join Jesus in kingdom mission (9:37–38).

10:1–11:1: Jesus's second discourse—the Mission Discourse. This extended discourse of Jesus is the second of five in Matthew and provides guidance for his disciples' mission to Israel. Matthew ties the Mission Discourse to Jesus's own mission by emphasizing their common activities: preaching, healing, raising the dead, cleansing lepers, and casting out demons (10:1, 7–8; cf. Jesus doing the same in chaps. 5–9). Matthew also revisits the comparison of Israel to sheep needing a shepherd (10:6: cf. 10:16). Jesus's disciples are called to be authentic shepherds of God's people in contrast to Israel's current leadership (9:36).

The Mission Discourse centers on the identification of the twelve disciples, their commission for ministry by Jesus, and his instructions for their mission. Matthew identifies the twelve disciples (called "apostles" only at 10:2) by name in 10:2–4. The choice of twelve followers is symbolic for Israel's twelve tribes and signals that Jesus is reconstituting or redefining Israel around himself and his enactment of God's kingdom. From this point on, Matthew will use the terms "the Twelve" and "the disciples" virtually interchangeably.

In the commissioning and empowering of the Twelve, Jesus grants them authority to heal and cast out demons (10:1) and limits their mission to Israel (10:5–6). The message they are to preach is virtually identical to the one Jesus (and John before him) has been preaching to the Jewish crowds (10:7; cf. 3:2; 4:17)—the soon-to-arrive reign of God.

The instructions that follow their commission to preach and heal (10:5–15) are quite specific to the mission of the Twelve. These instructions include relying on the hospitality of those within the towns they visit (so not bringing funds or extra supplies; 10:9–10), finding worthy hosts who will welcome them and their message (10:11–15), and symbolically renouncing those who reject their kingdom preaching: "Let your peace return to you" and, "Shake the dust off your feet" (10:13–14; paralleling how Jews might shake dust of foreign soil from their feet when returning to Judea [Keener, 320]). Jesus also warns the Twelve that they will be persecuted by some Jews and even arrested by Gentile leaders (10:17–18). They are not to worry about their defense, since Jesus promises that "the Spirit of [their] Father" will speak through them (10:19–20). Jesus calls them to stand firm in the face of betrayal and hatred, continuing their town-to-town ministry, since the coming of the Son of Man will precede the completion of their preaching (10:21–23).

Jesus's words, "You will not finish going through the towns of Israel before the Son of Man comes" (10:23), have often been understood as a reference to Jesus's second coming. Yet "comes" (Greek *erchomai*) is not the usual term Matthew uses for Jesus's reappearing (Greek *parousia* is nearly a technical term in the New Testament for the return of Jesus at the final judgment; see 24:3, 27, 37, 39). It is likely, instead, that Jesus's words in 10:23 intentionally echo Daniel 7, in which "one like a son of man, coming with the clouds of heaven" into God's presence, is vindicated and given power over all people and nations (Dan. 7:13–14). If so, Matthew indicates that the disciples' mission to Israel will still be ongoing at the time of his vindication and enthronement. (For Matthew, Jesus's vindication occurs at his resurrection [Matt. 28:18–20] and at the temple's destruction in AD 70 [see commentary on 24:1–51].)

Ivory book-binding plate illustrating the Mission Discourse, in Matthew 10:1–11:1 (Constantinople, tenth century AD)

In 10:24–42, the scope of the Mission Discourse broadens to include Jesus's followers beyond the Twelve (and Matthew's readers as well). Jesus's words in 10:24–42 begin by telling his followers that they will be maligned and persecuted as he has been (10:25; cf. 9:34). Yet he reassures them that they need not fear their persecutors; only God is worthy of such reverence (10:26, 28, 31). They can have boldness to speak "from the roofs," because God will make known the truth in the end (10:26–27) and cares for them deeply (10:29–31).

Jesus exhorts his followers to single-minded allegiance to him—an allegiance that freely acknowledges and aligns itself with Jesus (10:32–33), an allegiance that is greater than loyalties to one's family (10:34–37). This notion was quite countercultural in the first-century Jewish context, where family loyalties and obligations were paramount (cf. also 8:21–22). To be "worthy of [Jesus]" is to love Jesus more than all others and to take up one's cross and follow him (10:38). On the story level, which focuses on Jesus's teaching the Twelve, the metaphor of a cross poses a vision of discipleship as a path to death, since carrying one's cross was what Rome forced criminals to do on the way to execution. Matthew is also foreshadowing for his readers Jesus's own death by crucifixion. While it is possible to romanticize the cross today, the analogy of cross to discipleship would have been stark and sobering for Jesus's hearers.

Jesus's final words in the Mission Discourse (10:40–42) promise a reward for those who receive prophets, righteous persons, and "these little ones" who are disciples (see also the discussion of Greek *mikros*, "little one," in Matthew 18). These three terms refer to the Twelve and others like them sent out in mission, who travel without provisions or status but who go with Jesus's authority on his mission (10:1, 7–8). God will reward those who receive these "missionaries" and their message.

Matthew signals the end of this second discourse with the formulaic "After Jesus had finished [instructing his twelve disciples]" (cf. 7:28; see also "Structure" in the introduction). From 11:2 to 16:20, Jesus continues to teach and preach (11:1) but faces increasing hostility from Jewish leadership as his message and actions engender increasing attention and controversy.

B. Rejection by leaders and Jesus's withdrawal from conflict (11:2–16:20). In Matthew 11:2–16:20, Matthew narrates Jesus's ongoing ministry to Israel in the face of increased confrontation with and rejection by Jewish leaders. Faced with these controversies, Jesus withdraws from confrontation and instead turns to compassionate ministry focused on the Jewish crowds (12:15; 14:13; 15:21, 30). Matthew shows a range of responses to Jesus's emerging identity, from rejection by Jewish leaders and Jesus's hometown to the disciples' right confession of Jesus as Messiah–Son of God (cf. 14:33; 16:16; cf. chap. 13 for varied responses expressed in parable). Yet Matthew also narrates the struggle of Jesus's disciples to fully understand and embrace the truths about God's kingdom that Jesus both announces and embodies. The hidden nature of the kingdom means that divine revelation coupled with human faith is required to grasp its reality.

11:2–12:50: Rejection of Jesus as Messiah by Jewish leaders. This section of Matthew, between his second and third major discourses, focuses on Jesus's emerging messianic identity and the rejection he experiences as many,

particularly the Jewish leadership in Galilee, question his actions and become increasingly antagonistic. Matthew highlights Jesus's identity as an unexpected Messiah, especially Jesus as fulfiller of Isaiah's vision of restoration and Jesus as God's Wisdom (11:2–30). The unexpected nature of Jesus's messianic identity explains the divergent responses to his ministry. Stories of controversy, especially between the Pharisees and Jesus, cluster in Matthew 12 (12:1–8, 9–14, 22–32, 38–45), providing a vivid illustration of those who "stumble" over Jesus (or "fall away"; Greek *skandalizō*; 11:6).

11:2–30. This section of narrative begins with a question from John the Baptist that highlights concern over Jesus's identity (11:2–3). Reports of Jesus's messianic activity have reached John in prison. In context, the actions of the Messiah (11:2) refer to Jesus's healing, preaching, and teaching (see Matt. 4:23; 9:35). John's question demonstrates that Jesus's activity defies messianic expectations: "Are you the one who is to come?" (11:3). Though evidence from Jewish sources indicates that there was no single set of expectations about the Messiah, it is unlikely that central messianic acts would have included healing, especially within the trajectory of Davidic messianic expectation (see "Theological Themes" in the introduction). Instead, confrontation of pagan occupiers (Rome in the first century) would have ranked high on the list of things the Messiah would accomplish (cf. *Psalms of Solomon* 17:23–27). Jesus's early ministry according to Matthew shows no sign of this kind of direct political action. John's question allows Matthew to clarify what kind of Messiah Jesus is (with this section beginning with and ending on Jesus's messianic identity: 11:2; 16:16–20).

Jesus's answer, drawing language and ideas from Isaiah, indicates that his messianic ministry is characterized by signs of God's inbreaking kingdom—Israel's restoration—that include healing of the sick and preaching good news to the poor (Isa. 35:5–6; 61:1; also 26:19; 29:18). These are precisely the activities that

Matthew has used to characterize Jesus's ministry to Israel (Matt. 4:23–9:38). Jesus concludes his allusion to Isaiah by pronouncing blessing on all who do not "stumble" or "fall away" (*skandalizō*) because of Jesus. The Greek term *skandalizō* is used here metaphorically of the response of stumbling over the truth that Jesus is an unexpected Messiah. Matthew draws on this term elsewhere to express how people stumble over rather than embrace some part of Jesus's identity or message (e.g., 13:57; 15:12; cf. also 26:31). This blessing for those who receive Jesus sets the tone for various responses that will be highlighted in 11:2–12:50 and beyond.

Jesus's commentary about John (11:7–15) connects with the report of John's question about Jesus's identity, with Jesus confirming John's role as prophet and forerunner (citing Mal. 3:1; cf. Matt. 11:10). John's preparatory role is emphasized by Jesus's statement that even the "least in the kingdom" is greater than John (11:11). This is a temporal statement rather than an assessment of value: John is the one who prepares for Jesus, the enactor of the kingdom, and so John is not of the generation that sees the kingdom being inaugurated (11:13). He is imprisoned before Jesus announces the kingdom (4:12, 17) and dies in prison without seeing firsthand Jesus's ministry (14:3–12). Yet John has the unique role of "the Elijah who was to come" (11:14), preparing Israel for the Lord's (Yahweh's) coming (Mal. 4:5–6), which Matthew shows to be happening in Jesus's ministry.

Jesus's clarifying statement that John sits at the hinge of history (as precursor of the kingdom) also includes ambiguity (11:12). The verb might be intended to be read as a passive—"subjected to violence." The emphasis is then on the suffering that John and Jesus and those following them must endure as the kingdom arrives. On the other hand, if the verb is active—"forcefully advancing" (see NIV note)—the meaning would indicate that Jesus's kingdom

inauguration necessitates a clash between God and evil.

Jesus goes on to compare the general response to John with people's response to himself. Jesus claims that this generation—those who have been privy to Jesus's preaching and healing—is impossible to please (on "generation" language in this part of Matthew, see 12:39–45). They reject John's ascetic lifestyle consonant with kingdom preparation (repentance), but they also reject Jesus's celebratory and hospitable way of living in the inaugural days of the kingdom (11:15–19; cf. 9:9–13). In spite of rejection by this generation, Jesus claims that "wisdom is proved right by her deeds" (11:19). In context, it is Jesus who is proved right or vindicated (NASB) by his deeds, thus aligning himself with wisdom. Wisdom is personified in the Old Testament and Second Temple Jewish literature (e.g., Prov. 9:1–6; Wisdom of Solomon 6:11–16), and Matthew implies that Jesus is the embodiment of God's Wisdom. The bookending of the motif of Jesus's deeds in the first and last verses of this passage provides confirmation (11:2, 19). The "deeds of the Messiah" (11:2; see discussion above) are the deeds of Wisdom (11:19; cf. 11:28–30).

After focusing on Jesus's identity in relation to John and the petulant response of "this generation," Matthew 11 continues by emphasizing Jesus's judgment on the current generation that has seen the miracles Jesus has done but has not responded with appropriate repentance (11:20–24; for Jesus as judge, cf. 13:40–42; 25:31–33). Capernaum, Jesus's home base (8:5), and Chorazin (two miles from Capernaum) are judged as cities that have witnessed greater miracles than Tyre, Sidon, and Sodom (Old Testament cities receiving God's judgment; cf. Gen. 19:1–38; Zech. 9:2) and yet have not returned to God.

Matthew 11 concludes by returning to Jesus as the embodiment of the Wisdom of God (11:25–30; as in 11:1–19) as well as introducing the theme of revelation (11:25, 27). According

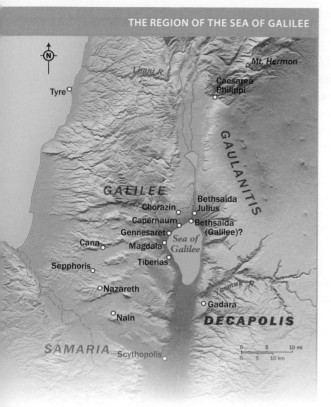

THE REGION OF THE SEA OF GALILEE

described as having a "yoke" (the same Greek term is used in Sirach 51:26 and Matt. 11:29), a word frequently associated with the torah; and (3) provides "rest" (in Sirach 6:28; 51:27; and Matt. 11:29) rather than causing one to be "weary" (in Wisdom of Solomon 6:14; Sirach 51:27; and Matt. 11:28). Jesus takes on the role of Wisdom, summoning to himself all who are weary from the heavy loads ("burden"; 11:28, 30) imposed by the teachers of the law (cf. Matt. 23:4). Jesus rightly interprets and fulfills the torah, because Jesus himself is the embodiment of the torah and the Wisdom of God (see "Theological Themes" in the introduction).

12:1–50. With the torah introduced, Matthew now narrates two controversies between Jesus and the Pharisees about the law; both controversies are focused on Jesus's practice of the Sabbath (12:1–8, 9–14). The Pharisees (12:2) were a Jewish sect considered to be experts in the law and were zealous in their obedience to it. An important part of their focus was adherence in everyday life to purity regulations intended to govern temple worship. Their desire was "to live out the rigor and piety of what was experienced at temple all year long" (Brown 2007, 209; cf. the description of the Pharisees on pp. 207–10). In the process, their prioritization of purity maintenance resulted in stricter boundaries between themselves and those people or activities that might make them ritually unclean for a period of time. Jesus's critique of the Pharisees, as we will see, is not of their commitment to purity regulations but of their prioritizing them over torah regulations focused on mercy, justice, and faithfulness (cf. 15:1–6; 23:23).

In the controversy stories of Matthew 12:1–8 and 12:9–14, the Pharisees accuse Jesus or his disciples of breaking Sabbath laws. For the first accusation, Jesus cites examples of David and Old Testament priests who were required to work on the Sabbath (e.g., Num. 28:9–10) to

to this prayer of Jesus, God has hidden the truth of the kingdom—what God is doing in Jesus—from the wise but has revealed it to "little children" (11:25), and the Son (Jesus, who has been described already as "Son of Man" and "Son of God") is the means of that revelation (11:27). This notion that God through Jesus reveals the nature of God's reign to some while it is hidden to others emerges more fully in the Parables Discourse of Matthew 13, as well as at Peter's climactic messianic declaration in 16:16–17.

Matthew communicates Jesus as God's Wisdom in the comforting words of 11:28–30, which evoke earlier Jewish writings about wisdom or torah, such as Sirach 6:18–27; 51:23–29 or Wisdom of Solomon 6:11–16. In these writings, personified Wisdom (1) invites people to come to her (compare Wisdom of Solomon 24:19 to Jesus's "Come to me"; 11:28); (2) is clear his disciples of the charge of lawbreaking when they glean grain to eat when hungry (12:1–5). Jesus also alludes to his own priority over the temple and its regulations and cites Hosea 6:6: "I desire mercy, not sacrifice" (cf. 9:13). While Jesus's words at 12:6–8 could be construed as abolishing the law, his use of Old Testament precedent to prove his disciples "innocent" (12:7) indicates that it is one's *interpretation of the law* that is again at issue rather than a superseding of it (cf. 5:17). Jesus views mercy as at the center of the law with the specific applicability of other regulations being governed by mercy (and justice, faithfulness; 23:23) as well as by the eschatological truth of the arrival of the Messiah (who is greater than the temple). In the second Sabbath incident, Jesus heals a man's shriveled hand and defends the action by an argument from lesser to greater: as anyone would rightly rescue a sheep from a pit on the Sabbath, it is even more in keeping with the law to do good to another human being on the Sabbath (12:11–12). Again, Jesus defends the action in question as lawful. Jesus and his disciples are faithful to the torah rather than lawbreakers.

Matthew narrates the Pharisees' response to Jesus's Sabbath healing: they plot to kill him (12:14). The conflict between Jesus and Jewish leadership intensifies, and as it does, Jesus withdraws, turning his attention to the Jewish crowds following him (12:15). Matthew will indicate in 14:13 and 15:21 this same response of Jesus's withdrawing after controversy. In this case, Jesus interacts with the crowds by healing their sick yet warns them not to reveal his identity (cf. 8:4; 9:30; 16:20). Matthew connects both of these actions to a citation from Isaiah 42:1–4, the longest of his fulfillment quotations (see "Sources" in the introduction). Jesus's compassionate healing ministry is alluded to in 12:20 (Isa. 42:3), and his warning of secrecy connects to 12:19 (Isa. 42:2). In addition, the Isaiah citation confirms that Jesus is Isaiah's servant of the Lord (also 8:17), who will bring justice not only to Israel but also to the Gentiles

("nations" in 12:18, 21, can be rendered alternately as "Gentiles"; cf. NRSV).

In Matthew 12:22–32, the healing of a demon-possessed man turns into a controversy over the source of Jesus's power. While the people respond by wondering whether Jesus might be the Messiah ("Son of David"; 12:23), the Pharisees ascribe his power to the prince of demons (as at 9:34). Jesus's response to this accusation centers on the impossibility of a kingdom warring against itself (so Satan could not drive out demons; 12:25–26). Instead, Jesus's exorcism of demons is an indication that his power comes from God's Spirit, a sign that "the kingdom of God has come upon you" (12:28; for the connection of God's Spirit and final restoration, see Joel 2:28–29). Jesus then claims through a parable that his power over demons proves that he has already bound Satan (12:29), so that it is one's response to Jesus that is all-important (12:30). The following saying (12:31–32) is difficult to decipher but likely indicates that, although God's forgiveness is wide (even sins against the Son of Man may be forgiven), the Pharisees' misattribution of the Spirit's power to Satan (12:24, 28) cannot be forgiven, since it signals a fundamental rejection of the work of God in Jesus.

In Matthew 12:33–37, Jesus intimately connects a person with their deeds ("fruit"; cf. 3:10; 7:16–20) and then highlights how speech arises from what is in the heart. While in Matthew 7:15–27 Jesus has emphasized the importance of actions (over words; 7:21), here he highlights the converse—that one's words will bring either acquittal or condemnation on the day of judgment (12:27). Two truths are emphasized: only one who is good can produce good words and actions; and one's words (as well as actions) will be the basis of final judgment (cf. 16:27). Jewish theology was quite able to hold together the notion of God's gracious salvation and a final accounting based on works (and words), since God's salvation preceded and provided the basis for God's covenant with Israel and Israel was called to remain faithful to that covenant to the end.

The controversies between Jesus and the Pharisees continue in 12:38–45, where Pharisees and teachers of the law ask Jesus to provide a miraculous sign, presumably to authenticate his words (cf. John 2:18; also Matt. 16:1). In the context of Matthew, this request is highly ironic, since Jesus has just provided a sign (cast out a demon to heal a man; 12:22) and the Pharisees have questioned its authenticity! Jesus condemns the request, judging them to be part of "a wicked and adulterous generation" (also 16:4). The only sign he will give them is a riddle: "As Jonah was three days and three nights in the belly of a huge fish, so the Son of Man will be three days and three nights in the heart of the earth" (12:40; cf. 16:4). This is the first allusion Jesus makes in Matthew to his own death (see 12:14 for the Pharisees' plot against him). The rest of this section focuses on Jesus's judgment of "this generation" for its lack of repentance in the presence of the one who is greater than Jonah and Solomon (12:41–42; cf. 11:20–24; 23:36). A parable about an evil spirit returning with multiple spirits to the person it has left indicates the final condition of wickedness that brings Jesus's judgment on this generation (12:43–45). Even after experiencing Jesus's miraculous works and kingdom message, the Pharisees of Matthew 12 epitomize all from that generation who do not respond to Jesus in repentance and faithfulness.

The final passage of Matthew 12 bridges to the Parables Discourse of Matthew 13 by introducing the motif of insiders and outsiders (12:46–50). Jesus is told that his family has arrived and is *outside* waiting to speak to him (12:46–47). Jesus responds by identifying his family with his disciples (who are *inside* the house; see 13:1) and everyone who "does the will of my Father in heaven" (12:49–50). In chapter 13, Matthew will develop this motif of insiders and outsiders (metaphorically, but using literal cues as signals to it; cf. 13:1, 36) in concert with the themes of revelation, parabolic teaching, and understanding (e.g., 13:11, 13, 34–35, 51).

13:1–53: Jesus's third discourse—the Parables Discourse. Having narrated the rejection of Jesus's messianic identity by Jewish leaders who represent "this generation" (11:16–24; 12:1–14, 22–45) as well as the wondering response of the Jewish crowds (12:23), Matthew follows up with an extended discourse by Jesus that comments on the varied responses to his kingdom message and also reveals more about the kingdom that Jesus is initiating. Called the Parables Discourse because it includes eight of Jesus's parables (or seven, depending on the status of 13:52), this discourse not only relies on the form of parable, but also highlights the effect of parables in hiding and revealing kingdom truths for their hearers (with each parable after the first introduced by "The kingdom of heaven is like . . ."; 13:24, 31, 33, 44, 45, 47; cf. 13:52).

Chapter 13 may be outlined to highlight the structural symmetry of pairs of parables and the two Old Testament quotations, as well as the focuses of the two halves of the chapter, one half on the crowds (13:1–35) and the other on the disciples (13:36–53).

13:1–9	Parable of the soils
13:10–17	Reason for parables: Isaiah quotation
13:18–23	Interpretation of parable of the soils
13:24–30	Parable of the wheat and weeds
13:31–32	Parable of the mustard seed
13:33	Parable of the yeast
13:34–35	Reason for parables: Psalm quotation
13:36–43	Interpretation of parable of the wheat and weeds
13:44	Parable of the treasure
13:45–46	Parable of the pearl
13:47–50	Parable of the fish and net
13:51–52	Response of the disciples and parable of the house owner
13:53	Conclusion to Parables Discourse

The first parable (13:1–9, 18–23) illustrates the variety of responses to the message about the kingdom by comparing people to kinds of soil receiving seed. Matthew has narrated a whole range of responses in chapters 8–9 and

11–12 (see commentary on 9:18–38), from great faith (8:5–13) to outright rejection (12:24). In this parable, the spectrum includes, on one end, those who lack any understanding about the kingdom Jesus preaches and brings (13:19) and, on the other, those who hear and understand Jesus's message and yield much fruit (cf. 3:10 for bearing-fruit motif).

Understanding emerges as an important theme in this first parable of Matthew 13 as well as in the two explanations for why Jesus speaks in parables (13:10–17, 34–35), with Scripture cited in both explanations. To answer the disciples' question of why he speaks to the crowd in parables (13:10), Jesus cites Isaiah 6:9–10 and distinguishes between three groups, the crowds (his audience in 13:1–35), the disciples who receive additional explanation of his parables (e.g., 13:37–43), and the earlier prophets and righteous ones who longed to hear what the disciples are now hearing (13:16–17). The Isaiah citation comes from that prophet's call to ministry, in which God indicates that Isaiah will prophesy to an obstinate people, who do not truly hear or see what God is doing (cf. Isa. 6:1–13). In similar fashion, Jesus's ministry also lands on ears that do not truly hear—that

do not understand (13:11–12). Teaching in parables both hides and reveals, depending on the kind of "soil" on the receiving end.

In Matthew 13:34–35, Matthew narrates the reason Jesus speaks in parables by citing Psalm 78:2. Here the reason for Jesus's speaking in parables to the crowds has to do with revealing what has previously been hidden—what is not easily understood. Parables in this case fit the nature of the truths of the kingdom being revealed, which are difficult to fully grasp (even the disciples do not always understand; 13:36). Once again, the reason for parables is about revelation (to those who are ready and willing to understand; 13:23) and obscurity (for those who are calloused; 13:15). This tension in the chapter is underscored in Jesus's invitation to the crowds and the disciples (and Matthew's invitation to his readers) at 13:9 and 13:43 (cf. also 11:15). Though the parables and their truths are difficult to comprehend and accept, anyone with ears among Jesus's listeners (and in Matthew's audience) is invited to hear and understand.

This area near Capernaum shows the rocky fields and hard paths that would have been familiar to the audience who heard Jesus tell the parable of the soils (Matt. 13:1–9).

In three clearly paired sets of parables, Jesus sets forth the mystery of the kingdom that he has already mentioned. The parables of the mustard seed and the yeast both indicate that, though the kingdom is seemingly insignificant or hidden at present, there will come a time when it will be unmistakable and all-encompassing. By these parables, Matthew's Jesus communicates the *already* (present in Jesus) and the *not yet* of God's reign. This same idea is expanded in the parables of the wheat and weeds and the fish and net, which indicate that judgment issuing in the separation of the righteous from the wicked will happen at "the end of the age" (a common phrase in Matthew; see 13:39–40, 49; 24:3; 28:20). The first of these two parables expressly indicates that judgment is withheld in the present (hidden) manifestation of the kingdom because it is not yet clear who is among the righteous (13:30, 38). The third pair of parables—those of the treasure and the pearl—illustrates the immeasurable worth of the kingdom in spite of its seeming insignificance and hiddenness (for language of the kingdom as hidden, see 13:35, 44; cf. 13:33 ESV). The kingdom, even in its present, hidden manifestation, is worth everything one has and brings great joy (13:44).

Two moments mark the end of the Parables Discourse. The first narrates Jesus's question to his disciples of whether they have understood his parables. Although *their* answer is an unqualified yes, Matthew will show their lack of understanding as the story progresses (e.g., 15:15; 16:22). The final saying or parable of Matthew 13 (13:52) calls the hearer to respond to the kingdom rightly, as did the first parable of the chapter. Jesus's parabolic instruction about the kingdom contains both new and old, expected and unexpected. Though the kingdom as Jesus conceives it has much in continuity with Old Testament and first-century Jewish expectations (e.g., God's rule reclaiming this world), it also has new elements not fully anticipated. The kingdom as presently hidden, with its clear manifestation still to come, is one of these surprising truths highlighted in Jesus's parabolic teaching of Matthew 13. (On the formulaic ending to Jesus's five major discourses, see "Structure" in the introduction; here 13:53.)

13:54–16:20: Conflict and identity. In this section, Matthew continues to narrate the growing conflict between the Jewish leaders and Jesus. As before (12:15), he withdraws from this conflict to engage in compassionate ministry to the crowds and interaction with his disciples (with withdrawal language at 12:15; 14:13; and 15:21). Jesus's identity is highlighted in this section of narrative, as the disciples come to confess Jesus as the Messiah (16:13–20) while others misunderstand (14:1–12) or reject his identity as the Messiah (13:54–58; 16:1–4).

13:54–14:36. Matthew's narration of the unbelief of Jesus's hometown (13:54–58) not only provides a vivid example of seed sown on unproductive soil (13:4, 19), but also frames the Parables Discourse by providing a point of contrast to Jesus's declaration that his true family are those who do God's will (12:46–50; cf. familial-language overlap at 12:49–50 and 13:55–56). Jesus's hometown is portrayed with the negative characterization given the Jewish leaders in Matthew 12: they distrust his authority, questioning its source. While the leaders have claimed Jesus's authority is demonic in origin (12:24), his hometown cannot overlook his family origins (13:54–56). In both cases, they stumble over Jesus's messianic identity (13:57; Greek *skandalizō* as "take offense" or "stumble"; cf. 11:6; also 15:12).

At the beginning of chapter 14, Matthew inserts a flashback to Herod's execution of John the Baptist (14:1–12). Herod the tetrarch (14:1; meaning "ruler of one-quarter") was a son of Herod the Great (2:1). After the latter's death, his kingdom was divided between three of his sons, with Galilee and Perea being assigned to Herod Antipas, who ruled these regions from 4 BC to AD 39. Herod Antipas, as a client-ruler of the occupation, represents Roman power and rule, as his father did (2:1). Matthew narrates in his story of Jesus how key leaders from Roman and Jewish quarters misconstrue Jesus's identity.

Herod's explanation for Jesus's powers differs from that of Jesus's hometown and the Jewish leaders, but it is similarly wrong. Herod believes Jesus to be John the Baptist back from the dead (14:2; cf. 11:2–5 for focus on John at the beginning of this section, where it is John who questions Jesus's identity). Herod is portrayed in 14:1–12 as superstitious (14:2), vindictive (14:3), fearful (14:5), and rash (14:6–7). In the end, he has John beheaded (14:10).

After hearing the news of John's death, Jesus withdraws to focus on compassionate ministry (14:13; cf. also 12:15; 15:21). A summary statement by Matthew emphasizes Jesus's compassionate healing of the crowds (14:14; cf. 9:36). What follows is the first of two miraculous feeding stories (14:15–21; cf. 15:32–39), illustrating Jesus's compassion toward the crowds and his miraculous power. Some have identified Jesus as a Moses figure in these feedings, with allusions to Moses feeding the people of Israel during their time in the wilderness (e.g., Exodus 16; see also Moses typology in Matthew 2 and 5–7). Matthew may also be connecting Jesus's miraculous feedings to Jewish expectation that provision of manna would return at the time of the Messiah (cf. *2 Baruch* 29:8). Matthew's reference to the large number of those fed (five thousand men, with women and children beyond that number) highlights Jesus's extraordinary power (14:21).

Jesus's authority is immediately reemphasized in Matthew's narration of Jesus's walking on water (14:22–33). The disciples are alone in the boat while Jesus has gone away by himself to pray (14:22–23). When the wind comes up on the lake, Jesus comes to the disciples "walking on the lake" (14:24–25; "the fourth watch of the night" [KJV, RSV] was 3:00–6:00 a.m.). When Jesus calls to them to allay their fears, Peter attempts to join Jesus (14:26–29). His fear of the wind, however, causes him to sink. Jesus rescues him, referring to Peter as one of "little faith" (14:30–31). Matthew has previously tied "little

faith" (Greek *oligopistos*) to anxiety about daily needs (6:30) and fear (8:26). Here he connects it to Peter's "doubt" or wavering (Greek *distazō*; attributed to the disciples generally at 28:17). In spite of inadequate trust in Jesus's power, the disciples recognize Jesus's identity as "Son of God," which points to their understanding of Jesus as the Messiah (see "Theological Themes" in the introduction). This is the first messianic confession from the disciples, and it mirrors Peter's confession at the climactic moment of this section of Matthew (16:16).

Matthew has framed Jesus's feeding of the five thousand and his walking on water with two summaries about Jesus's healing ministry (14:13–14, 34–36). The first highlights his compassion to heal; the second emphasizes his power to heal ("all who touched him were healed"; 14:36). Gennesaret (14:34) is a plain located on the northwest coast of the Sea of Galilee.

15:1–39. After narrating Jesus's interaction with the crowds and his disciples, Matthew again turns to controversy (15:1–20), this time between Jesus and Jewish teachers who have come to Galilee from Jerusalem. These Pharisees and teachers of the law confront Jesus over the lack of concern shown by his disciples in their table practices (15:1–2). The Pharisees follow the "tradition of the elders"; that is, they not only obey the torah but also observe teachings of past teachers (rabbis) on the torah (with many such teachings recorded in the Mishnah, ca. AD 200). In this particular case, hand washing to remove ritual impurity was required before eating. The likely background for this practice is the Old Testament command for priests to wash their hands (and feet) before entering the Tent of Meeting and before offering sacrifices (Exod. 30:17–21). Pharisees desired to bring the rigors of purity rites associated with the temple into everyday experience. Washing their hands before meals would have mirrored priestly temple practices.

Jesus's critique of the Pharisees' expectation that his disciples follow the oral tradition is not a direct criticism of that set of traditions. Instead, Jesus criticizes adherence to these traditions when adherence results in the breaking of the law itself! He claims that these Pharisees are breaking the command to honor parents by devoting to God resources that could and should provide for parents (15:3–6; cf. 23:3 for a similar indictment of law disobedience). Then Jesus cites Isaiah 29:13 (15:7–9), tying the hypocrisy of torah disobedience in the name of adherence to traditions to this same kind of hypocrisy that Isaiah saw in his day. Isaiah's complaint—empty worship drawn from human rules—fits Jesus's complaint against these Jewish teachers as well.

Jesus uses a parable of sorts to indicate that ritual cleansing before meals is unnecessary and misses the true source of impurity (15:10–11). Jesus's explanation of his parable or riddle (15:16–20) clarifies that it is the heart of a person (rather than hands) that ultimately produces what is unclean, for from the heart come intentions that result in disobedient actions (cf. list of 15:19). Here Matthew's Jesus is not invalidating the Jewish purity system; rather, he is providing an alternate interpretation of purity issues over against the tradition of the elders. (Mark's Gospel takes this story in a different direction, particularly in his extrapolation that all foods are clean [Mark 7:19]. Nevertheless, there is no Gospel evidence that Jesus or his disciples broke with kosher dietary practices.)

In response to Jesus's critique of the Pharisees and scribes, his disciples let him know that "the Pharisees were offended [*skandalizō*; cf. 11:6]" by his words (15:12). The language Matthew uses here, *skandalizō*, indicates that the Pharisees "stumble over" Jesus and his teaching. Jesus responds by picturing the judgment that will come to those who, like these Pharisees, not only are out of alignment with God (15:13) but also are leading others astray (15:14).

Peter, as representative of the Twelve (his frequent role in Matthew; cf. 16:16), asks Jesus to explain the parable (15:15). Jesus's response to his disciples indicates that he expects them to

have understood his teaching here (15:16–17). Despite their insider status in relation to Jesus's teaching in parables (13:11, 18–23, 36–43, 51), they do not fully understand Jesus's teachings. Jesus's words "Are you [plural] still so dull?" (15:16) demonstrate that they have fallen short of his expectations for understanding. Jesus's call to "listen and understand" (15:10) invites Matthew's audience to do what few characters in the story have done well—to hear Jesus and to understand his words (cf. 13:9, 43).

Engagement in controversy again leads to Jesus's withdrawing to compassionate ministry (15:21–31; cf. 12:15; 14:13), this time in the direction of Tyre and Sidon—Mediterranean coastal cities northwest of Galilee. In this location, Jesus is approached by a Gentile woman, a Canaanite, with the term evoking the Old Testament association of Israel's enemies (15:22; cf. Num. 21:1). Using the messianic title "Son of David," she cries out to him to heal her demon-possessed daughter (15:22). Yet Jesus speaks to her only after his disciples have entreated him to deal with her cries. His answer echoes the mission parameters he has already given to his disciples: "I was sent only to the lost sheep of Israel" (15:24; cf. 10:5–6). This initial scenario has much in common with the entreaty of the Gentile centurion on behalf of his servant who is ill (8:5–13), especially if 8:7 is understood as a question on Jesus's part. In both cases, which are the only instances in Matthew where a Gentile seeks out Jesus for a healing, Jesus hesitates to cross the boundaries of his God-established mission. Yet in both cases, it is the persistence of the Gentile supplicant, highlighting their "great faith" (8:10; 15:28), that convinces Jesus to minister outside Jewish parameters prior to the establishment of the Gentile mission at his resurrection (28:19; see "Theological Themes" in the introduction). The woman's exceptional faith provides the model for Matthew's readers, who have witnessed the lack of faith in Jewish leaders (12:24; cf. 15:12) and Jesus's hometown (13:58) and the "little faith" of the disciples (14:31).

Matthew provides another summary of Jesus's compassionate healing ministry at 15:29–31 (cf. earlier summaries at 12:15–21; 14:13–14; 14:34–36). The crowds respond with amazement, praising "the God of Israel" (a commonplace Old Testament phrase; e.g., Judg. 5:3). Matthew narrates next the feeding of the four thousand (15:32–39), which also emphasizes Jesus's compassion for the crowds (15:32) as well as his messianic power (see commentary on 13:54–14:36). Many have also noted the eucharistic overtones in the feeding miracles (e.g., breaking loaves, giving thanks; at 14:19 and 15:36; cf. 26:26).

16:1–20. In anticipation of the climactic scene of 11:2–16:20, Matthew returns to a number of motifs that he has developed. First, in Matthew 16:1–4, we see a challenge to Jesus by Pharisees and Sadducees that demonstrates their opposition to Jesus's ministry (16:1; cf. 12:14) in a request for a sign. (The analogy to weather signs in 16:2–3 is missing in some early manuscripts, presumably omitted by scribes in locations outside of Palestine where such signs did not forecast the same weather.) In their refusal to receive Jesus and the signs he has already displayed (cf. 11:20–24; 12:41–42), they epitomize the "wicked and adulterous generation" that rejects Jesus's enactment of God's kingdom (16:4; cf. 11:16; 12:39–45). Jesus leaves his opponents (16:4; cf. Jesus's withdrawals at 12:15; 14:13; 15:21), and they will not reappear in the narrative until 19:3.

As Matthew turns to Jesus with his disciples (16:5–12), a number of disciple-related themes resurface. Once again, Jesus refers to his disciples as "you of little faith" (16:8), this time in relation to their incomprehension of Jesus's power at the two miraculous feedings. Even though Jesus has demonstrated that he is able to provide food for large crowds, the disciples are concerned that they have forgotten to bring bread with them, in the process misunderstanding Jesus's warning about "the yeast of the Pharisees and Sadducees" (16:6–7; cf. the example of the Pharisees' teaching at

15:1–20). The disciples' little faith has been a motif in Matthew thus far both when Jesus describes them as having little faith (cf. 6:30; 8:26; 14:31) and in their inadequate appropriation of their own authority to participate in Jesus's ministry (10:1; cf. Jesus's expectation for their fuller participation in the miraculous feedings at 14:16–17; 15:32–33). The disciples are portrayed as those who understand at some level (cf. 13:11, 51; 14:33; 16:12) but lack fully adequate understanding of Jesus's authority (e.g., 15:16–17; 16:8–11). Because of their mixed portrayal, they are not ideal examples for Matthew's readers. Rather, Matthew intends his audience to sometimes emulate and sometimes distance themselves from the disciples' responses (Brown 2002, 128–33).

The climactic moment of Matthew 11:2–16:20 is Peter's confession that Jesus is the Messiah (16:16). In response to Jesus's question about his identity as perceived by others, the disciples provide a range of responses (16:13–14; including John the Baptist in line with Herod's belief at 14:2). Peter speaks on behalf of the disciples, rightly identifying Jesus as "the Messiah, the Son of the living God" (16:16). Although Matthew tells his readers that Jesus is the Messiah from the very beginning of the Gospel (1:1), this is the first occasion in which a character within the story identifies Jesus as the Messiah. The additional "Son of the living God" was likely understood as a messianic title within first-century Judaism (see "Theological Themes" in the introduction; also 26:63). Matthew's intention for this additional phrase includes the intimate relationship already demonstrated between Jesus and the Father (e.g., 3:17; 4:3; 11:25–27).

Jesus confirms that Peter's confession on behalf of the Twelve is true and has been given by divine revelation (16:17). Whether Jesus promises to build his church on Peter himself (as in Catholic interpretation, highlighting the wordplay between Peter's name and the Greek *petra* ["rock"]) or on the messianic confession Peter has made (the typical Protestant interpretation), it is clear that Matthew shows the binding and loosing authority of 16:19 to extend from Peter to the rest of Jesus's disciples and the church itself at 18:17–18. Given the use of binding and loosing terminology in Judaism of the time and Matthew's use of related language elsewhere (5:19; 23:4), these concepts likely focus on determining the applicability of particular laws in particular situations (something Jesus does at 12:1–12, for example) (Powell 2003, 438). Jesus promises this authority to interpret and apply commands (presumably, the "keys of the kingdom"; 16:19) to Peter and then the entire church (18:17). Though promised at this juncture, the fulfillment of these promised kingdom keys comes only at the end of Matthew's Gospel, where Jesus is given all authority (28:18). The disciples (and the church) receive their authority by derivation—by means of Jesus's presence with them (28:20).

After these promises, Jesus warns the Twelve against telling anyone of his identity as Messiah. Given the swiftness of Roman action against would-be Jewish messiahs of the first century, such concern for discretion (cf. 8:4; 9:30; 12:16) would be necessary and wise. (On the rise and fall of such would-be messiahs, see Josephus, *Jewish Antiquities* 17.10.4–7.) It is telling that the Romans crucify Jesus within a week of his public "debut" as Messiah (see commentary on 20:29–21:27).

Jesus hands Peter "the keys of the kingdom of heaven" (Matt. 16:19) in this illumination from *The Pericopes of Henry II* (eleventh century AD).

3. Jesus to Jerusalem: Kingdom Enactment through Death and Resurrection (16:21–28:20)

In 16:21–28:20, Matthew narrates Jesus's journey to Jerusalem to fulfill his mission to be "a ransom for many" (20:28). After repeated predictions of his death and extended teaching that his disciples are to follow his example of service without thought of personal status (16:21–20:28), Jesus rides into Jerusalem as Messiah, symbolically enacting Zechariah's vision of a peaceable king (21:1–11). He indicts the Jerusalem leadership for their mismanagement of the temple and demonstrates his authority to do so by virtue of his identity as Messiah and Lord (21:12–22:46). His predictions of the fall of the temple and about his reappearing and final judgment call his followers to live faithfully and mercifully in preparation for what is to come (23:1–25:46). Matthew narrates in detail the events leading up to Jesus's execution by Rome influenced by the Jerusalem elite. Jesus embodies his mission to be Israel's Messiah-King through self-sacrifice rather than assertion of his rightful authority (26:1–27:66). His identity and mission are vindicated at his resurrection, which sees him enthroned with authority over all and enacting his mission to reach all nations through his presence with his people (28:1–20).

A. Journey to the cross and teaching on discipleship (16:21–20:28). In this section, Matthew focuses on Jesus's journey from Galilee to Jerusalem, and he structures the section around three passion predictions—statements by Jesus that he will soon suffer and be crucified in Jerusalem (16:21; 17:22–23; 20:17–19). In the culminating moment, Matthew provides the purpose for Jesus's sacrificial journey—to become "a ransom for many" (20:28). Woven between these predictions and this purpose statement are teachings and object lessons for Jesus's disciples on the nature of discipleship. Jesus's relationship with the Twelve is the central plot element in this section. Even in the few passages that begin with other characters (e.g., 17:14–20; 19:3–12), their conclusions show Jesus "debriefing" with his disciples about discipleship (Brown 2002, 47–49).

16:21–17:27: Jesus discusses the cross and discipleship. Immediately after Peter rightly confesses Jesus to be the Messiah (16:16), Matthew narrates Jesus's first passion prediction (16:21). Jesus explains to his disciples the necessity of his impending suffering and death at the hands of Jerusalem leaders. In two subsequent passion predictions, Jesus indicates that he will be betrayed into human hands (17:22–23) and be crucified by Gentiles (20:17–19), demonstrating Matthew's emphasis on wide-ranging culpability for Jesus's execution (see 27:26).

In response to Jesus's prediction, Peter rebukes him, denying that execution will be Jesus's lot (16:22). Peter's response demonstrates two things. First, he has not heard Jesus's prediction of being "raised to life" in any meaningful way. This is understandable from the perspective of first-century Jewish expectations. Though a majority of first-century Jews would have believed in bodily resurrection, they would not have conceived of resurrection as a series of individual resurrections. Instead, Jewish hopes focused on a corporate resurrection of God's faithful people at the time of final restoration (e.g., Dan. 12:1–3; cf. 2 Maccabees 7:13–14, 20–23). So Jesus's reference to his resurrection

here was not likely heard as Christian readers of Matthew have (rightly) heard it since: as referring to Jesus's resurrection ahead of the final, general resurrection (cf. 1 Cor. 15:20–23).

Second, while Peter has rightly understood Jesus's identity as Messiah (16:16), he does not understand the kind of Messiah Jesus is. Since it is not clear that suffering was a part of first-century messianic configurations, Peter's response is understandable. Yet for Jesus (and Matthew), suffering and death are central for defining the kind of Messiah Jesus comes to be. Though Rome executed any number of would-be messiahs for their pretensions, Jesus is not predicting his death based on such likelihood but on necessity ("must"; 16:21). Peter's words, though probably well meaning, function as a stumbling block to the fulfillment of Jesus's mission; they do not represent the divine perspective (16:23).

Matthew follows this passion prediction with a teaching on discipleship that echoes the call to sacrifice that Jesus models (16:24–28). Self-denial and carrying one's cross provide the pattern for discipleship (16:24; cf. 10:38 for the connotations of a cross for first-century readers), just as they are definitional for Jesus's role as Messiah. Yet the paradox of discipleship is that losing one's life (Greek *psychē*) results in finding it. Since *psychē* can refer to both earthly and transcendent life (often translated as "soul" for the latter), a wordplay is operative in 16:25–26. Jesus defines losing one's life (and so self-denial) in terms of tangible actions (16:27), which Matthew will illustrate in subsequent chapters (Matthew 18 particularly).

Reference to "the Son of Man coming in his kingdom" (16:28) points ahead to the foretaste of Jesus as king at his transfiguration (17:1–9) as well as to his enthronement at his resurrection (chap. 28). The vision of the Son of Man coming in his kingdom derives from Daniel 7:13–14 and is a picture of Jesus's vindication of his claims and his mission (see 10:23; 24:30–31). When Matthew references Jesus's second coming, he uses a different, quite specific term, which occurs in Matthew 24:3, 27, 37, and 39. The transfiguration and the subsequent debriefing with Peter, James, and John reveal more clearly who Jesus is (17:1–13). Mountains are key locations for revelation, in Scripture generally and in Matthew specifically (cf. Matthew 5–7, 17, 24–25, 28). The central moment is when the divine voice affirms Jesus and his mission: "This is my Son, whom I love; with him I am well pleased" (17:5). These are the same words spoken by God at 3:17 (see commentary on 3:1–17 for possible Old Testament allusions), with only John privy to them. The disciples now learn of the intimate relationship between God and Jesus, the Son. The added words—"Listen to him!"—emphasize Jesus's teaching role with the disciples in this part of Matthew.

The appearance of Moses and Elijah with Jesus (17:3) precipitates the disciples' question about the scribal understanding that Elijah must "come first" (17:10). The teachers of the law reflect Malachi's prophecy that Elijah's appearance would precede the "day of the LORD" (4:5–6; cf. Sirach 48:10 for an expectation that Elijah would usher in Israel's restoration). Given the disciples' recent confirmation of Jesus's messianic identity and experience of him in glorified form, it is not at all difficult to see why they would be wondering about the imminent arrival of that final day (Matthew's "end of the age"; e.g., 13:39; 24:3; 28:20). Jesus affirms the truth of this expectation but with a twist: Elijah has already come and been rejected, as will the Son of Man (17:12). The disciples make the connection between this prophesied Elijah and John the Baptist (see 3:4; 11:7–14).

Matthew narrates the healing of a demon-possessed boy (17:14–20), whose father has sought his healing from the disciples while Jesus was away with Peter, James, and John.

When the disciples fail, the father comes to Jesus. Jesus's response echoes his words against "this generation" in 12:39–45, where Jewish leaders inappropriately ask Jesus for a miraculous sign. In this case, Jesus reacts against the general unbelief of the present generation as exemplified by the disciples' inability to heal the boy (17:17). After Jesus heals him, the disciples privately ask why they were unsuccessful (17:18–19). Jesus attributes their inability to their "little faith" (*oligopistia*; 17:20; see also 6:30; 8:26; 14:31; 16:8), distinguishing the disciples from and connecting them to the current generation, whom Jesus characterizes as lacking faith ("unbelieving"; 17:17). The disciples' little faith here corresponds to their inability to cast out a demon. They do not adequately trust in the authority Jesus has already given them (cf. 10:1). With faith as small as a mustard seed, the disciples could do miraculous things. Yet their little faith falls short of the small amount of faith necessary for doing the impossible (17:20). (The NIV omits 17:21, placing it in a

These Tyrian shekels are from the Ussfiyeh hoard, discovered on Mount Carmel in 1960. Originally minted in the city of Tyre, Tyrian shekels were worth four drachmas each; thus one was enough to cover the temple tax for Jesus and Peter (Matt. 17:27).

footnote, since it is most likely a copyist's addition in light of its parallel in Mark 9:29 and its omission in many manuscripts.)

Jesus predicts his execution and resurrection to his disciples a second time, yet they grieve at this news, indicating that they do not understand what Jesus means by "on the third day . . . raised to life" (17:22–23; see 16:21).

The final passage of 16:21–17:27 narrates Jesus's pronouncement on paying the temple tax while also introducing the motif of stumbling that will be explored in Matthew 18. The two-drachma temple tax (equivalent to the half-shekel of Exod. 30:11–16) was levied on all adult Jewish males annually, though there is debate on how rigidly this was followed in the first century. When questioned by the collectors of this tax whether his teacher pays it, Peter responds in the affirmative. Jesus then takes the situation as a teaching opportunity and uses the analogy of human kingship: while kings levy taxes, they do not tax their own offspring (17:25–26). In the same way, those who are children of the kingdom are exempt from taxation (17:27). Yet Jesus's teaching and practice goes further: he will pay the tax to avoid causing others to stumble (NIV "cause offense"; cf. 11:6). Kingdom freedoms are constrained by concern for others (cf. 18:6–7). The amount miraculously provided is just enough to pay for Peter and Jesus (a four-drachma coin for both two-drachma payments).

18:1–35: Jesus's fourth discourse—The Community Discourse. The messages of the Community Discourse—embedded in 16:21–20:28, with its focus on defining Messiah and discipleship—center on the need for the messianic community to renounce status concerns, care for their most vulnerable, and pursue restoration and forgiveness of those who stray. The community of disciples must deny self and live a cross-shaped existence (16:24) empowered by Jesus's presence within the community.

Though possessing a certain seamlessness, Matthew 18 may be divided into two sections, each beginning with a question posed to Jesus

(18:1, 21). These narrative moments lead into Jesus's extended answer in each case. The Community Discourse includes teachings of Jesus for the twelve disciples on the story level as well as addressing Matthew's audience quite directly (see "A Narrative Reading" in the introduction).

In Matthew 18:1–20, Jesus begins by addressing the disciples' question about who is greatest in God's kingdom (18:1). This is a status question—an understandable one in the context of ancient conventions that clearly spell out honor and status levels based on birth, family, title, wealth, and relationship with others. As their daily conventions revolve around attention to status concerns, the disciples assume that the inauguration of God's reign will set up a new set of status criteria. They are hopeful that they will rank higher in God's status system than in that of the Greco-Roman world (cf. 20:20–21).

Jesus's response indicates that the disciples' assumptions about God's kingdom are mistaken. He brings a child to them to signal their need for change regarding status concerns (18:2–3). Instead of being preoccupied with *their status in the kingdom*, they need to become like children to *enter the kingdom*. Jesus then indicates it is the humble status of children that the disciples should emulate (18:4). While today's readers of Matthew often hear "humble" (ESV, NASB) as an internal disposition, the original audience (and the disciples) would have understood this as a term indicating social status (see NIV). In that cultural context, children did not possess status inherently; they did not have the rights and honor that modern Western society gives them. Instead, they were considered weak and irrational and as possessing little status until they reached adulthood (Brown 2002, 70–71). As such, they are ideal examples for the disciples, who are preoccupied with status concerns. Jesus aligns himself with those marginalized in the status systems of his day, and he calls the disciples to do the same: anyone who welcomes a child welcomes Jesus (18:5)!

In Matthew 18:6–10, Jesus expands his discussion about those in the messianic community who, like children, possess little or no status. Jesus defends these "little ones" (*mikros*) against those who would cause them to sin (*skandalizō*: "stumble"; 18:6) or who look down on them (18:10). Warnings are given against bringing about the sin and stumbling of others (18:5–6) or of oneself (18:7–9). Using hyperbole to great effect ("cut [your hand] off"; "gouge [your eye] out"), Jesus teaches that it is better to lose hand, foot, or eye if it causes sin than to risk "eternal fire" (18:8). Jesus grounds the value of these persons of low status in their access to his Father and in God's concern for them. (The NIV places 18:11 in a footnote, since it is almost certainly a later scribal addition drawn from Luke 19:10.)

To illustrate God's deep care for little ones, especially those who stray, Jesus tells a parable of a shepherd who leaves his ninety-nine sheep in safety to seek and find the one that has strayed away (18:12–13). His joy is greater over the restoration of that single sheep than over the rest who never strayed. Jesus applies the parable (18:14) to the Father's great concern over losing even a single little one.

The theme of restoration initiated in the parable finds further emphasis and clarity in 18:15–20, where the restoration of a sinning community member is paramount. The goal of the process described in 18:15–20 is to win over one's brother or sister (18:15). The restorative process involves (1) bringing the purported sin to the person privately; (2) if the first action does not result in restoration, bringing one or two witnesses along in line with the Old Testament command to protect the accused from false testimony (18:16; not to aid the accuser; cf. Deut. 19:15); and (3) if neither action results in restoration, bringing in the church as a whole to advocate for restoration (18:17). As a last resort, the church is to treat the erring member as an outsider (with tax collectors and pagans connoting outsiders in Matthew's social context; cf. 5:46–47). Though it is not explicit, the reader is right to presume that this final action (as with the rest) is also for the purpose of restoration (cf. 1 Cor. 6:9–12 for a similar excluding action with the goal of restoration).

Jesus's words at 18:18 echo his earlier promise concerning binding and loosing (cf. 16:19). Jesus then uses language of "two or three" (from 18:16, reflecting Deut. 19:15) to promise that God will hear and answer when the Christian community agrees in prayer (18:19), based on Jesus's presence with them (18:20). The promise of Jesus's presence grounds the instructions for discipline not only in 18:15–19 but also in 18:1–14. At the thematic center of the Community Discourse, Matthew emphasizes Jesus's presence with his people as the hope for their common life (cf. 1:23; 28:20 for the bookended theme of Jesus's presence).

The second half of Matthew 18 is introduced by Peter's question regarding the appropriate number of times that forgiveness is warranted (18:21). Although generous in his suggestion, Peter's sevenfold forgiveness contrasts with Jesus's answer of "seventy-seven times" (18:22). His answer alludes to Genesis 4:24, where Cain's son Lamech claims that God will avenge him seventy-seven times (cf. Gen. 4:13–15). Jesus's call to his messianic community is to live out a reversal of escalating vengeance through unlimited forgiveness. To illustrate, Jesus tells a parable of a servant who is released from an astronomical debt of ten thousand talents by a compassionate king (with a talent being roughly equivalent to six thousand denarii) only to refuse release of a debt of one hundred denarii for a fellow servant (with a denarius representing about a day's wage). The king's reversal of debt forgiveness and his punishment of the servant at the parable's conclusion is compared to God's treatment of "each of you unless you forgive your brother or sister" (18:35). This teaching echoes Matthew 6:14–15, where God's forgiveness is predicated on one's forgiveness of others. The parable provides a helpful expansion, clarifying that the warning is issued to those who have *already experienced God's forgiveness*, so that human forgiveness is portrayed as arising organically and necessarily from an experience of God's forgiveness.

19:1–20:28: Illustrations of discipleship. *19:1–30.* Signaling the conclusion of the fourth discourse, Matthew includes the familiar formula, "When Jesus had finished [saying these things]" (19:1; repeated at 7:28; 11:1; 13:53; 26:1). The next section takes place to the east of Judea, across the Jordan River (19:1). After summarizing Jesus's ministry of healing to the crowds (19:2), Matthew narrates a legal debate between the Pharisees and Jesus (19:3–9; cf. 12:1–14). The Pharisees use a question about legal reasons for divorce to test Jesus ("for any and every reason?"). Jesus answers by citing Genesis 1:27 and 2:24, indicating the basis for the permanence of marriage in God's creational intention that husband and wife be "one flesh" (19:4–6). In turn, the Pharisees cite Deuteronomy 24:1, which may have been used in Jewish debates for both wide latitude and a narrow understanding of permissible divorce. Jesus argues that Deuteronomy provides a concession rather than a command. His own teaching on divorce, according to Matthew, allows for it only in cases of unfaithfulness, fitting the more conservative interpretation of Deuteronomy (19:9; cf. discussion of exception clause at 5:32; and Mark 10:11 for Jesus's divorce teaching without an exception clause).

The debate with the Pharisees recedes into the background as Jesus debriefs with his disciples, who misconstrue his teaching as a reason to avoid marriage altogether (19:10). Jesus takes the opportunity to teach that choosing celibacy for God's kingdom is the right course for those "to whom it has been given" (19:11), while not undermining the importance of marriage. Jesus's teaching affirms both "life-long marriage as one flesh according to the original intention of God and singleness for the sake of the kingdom according to the power of God" (Brown 2002, 79). Using this story, Matthew continues to subvert prevailing status expectations about the kingdom (cf. 18:1–5). Here, Jesus limits the power of husbands to divorce their wives "for

any and every reason" to only cases of marital unfaithfulness and, in a culture in which they were socially marginalized, elevates the status of eunuchs within kingdom perspective.

In 19:13–15, Matthew highlights status issues by reiterating Jesus's perspective on children (cf. 18:5). The disciples attempt to keep children from Jesus, showing that they have not assimilated Jesus's teaching at 18:1–5. Jesus corrects the disciples, inviting children to come to him and indicating the central place that children have in God's kingdom.

In counterpart, Matthew narrates a story illustrating how persons of great status, the rich, do not have priority in God's reign or kingdom (19:16–26). In fact, the story of the rich man who comes to Jesus asking the way to eternal life concludes with Jesus teaching his disciples the difficulty the rich will have entering God's kingdom (19:23–24). Jesus's initial response to the man's question is that obedience to God's commandments brings life (19:17–19; with his examples drawn from Deut. 5:6–21). The man says that he has kept these but indicates he still lacks something (19:20). Jesus calls him to complete loyalty (the Greek term may be rendered "perfect" or "complete") by selling his possessions, giving the proceeds to the poor, and then following Jesus (19:21). Jesus calls this man to give up precisely that which stands in the way of discipleship—his "great wealth" (19:22), something he is not yet willing to do.

Jesus's debriefing with his disciples (19:23–26) points to the great difficulty of the rich in entering God's kingdom (with the image of a camel going through a needle's eye emphasizing this difficulty). The disciples are astonished by this statement (19:25), indicating that they consider the rich to have great status and advantage in God's kingdom (as they do in ancient society). Jesus's concluding statement intimates the leveling of the playing field in God's scheme of things, since what is humanly impossible (salvation) is quite possible for God (19:26). God can save both rich and poor, though Matthew shows that those who are poor and of lesser status are closer to the kingdom than the rich and powerful (e.g., here and 5:3–6).

Peter's subsequent question provides opportunity for an extended teaching on status and reward (19:27–20:16). In contrast to the rich man, the disciples have "left everything to follow [Jesus]" (19:27). Peter's question about what they will have elicits Jesus's two-pronged answer. First, he assures his followers that their faithful discipleship will result in their vindication at the "renewal of all things" and a role in that final judgment ("thrones" likely connote a judging role; yet cf. 25:31–46 for disciples also being judged in that final day). All followers of Jesus who have left home and family (cf. 12:48–50) will be rewarded with blessing and eternal life (with hundredfold language used to indicate abundance of blessing; 19:29). Second, Jesus also warns against presuming on one's kingdom status or reward (19:30). With language that clearly connotes status (first/last), Jesus qualifies his promise of reward and status. This same warning is repeated at 20:16, after the parable of the workers, which addresses status presumption.

20:1–28. In the parable (20:1–15), Jesus compares God's reign to the payment of groups of day laborers working in a vineyard for a particular landowner. After hiring laborers throughout the day, the landowner pays those hired during the last hour a full day's wage (a denarius)—the same amount he has promised to those who began working in the early morning. Seeing this, those hired first expect to receive more than a denarius, yet they receive just what was promised them. They grumble to the landowner: "You have made them equal to us who have borne the burden of the work" (20:12). Their accusation is the inequity of equal pay for unequal work. The landowner counters that he paid them an agreed-on and fair wage. They resent not his fairness but his generosity (20:15). Jesus's parable warns against presuming reward and status in the kingdom (19:30; 20:16), especially for those who are "first" (in story context, the Twelve—who expect higher

status in the kingdom; cf. 18:1; 19:27; 20:20–21). The parable also hints at a surprising (and offensive!) equality within the kingdom.

In Matthew 20:17–19, Matthew provides Jesus's third passion prediction to his disciples, this time making explicit that Jesus's death will be crucifixion at the hands of the Gentiles (20:19). Without narrating a specific response of the disciples (as he does at 16:22 and 17:23), Matthew implies a continuing incomprehension on the part of the disciples as to what Jesus's mission is really about by telling the story of a bid for status in the kingdom by James and John.

The request for second and third positions in the coming kingdom (to sit at Jesus's right and left) comes through the mother of James and John (20:20–21). Yet it is clear that James and John are involved in the plan since they answer Jesus's question about drinking the cup he will drink (with cup language used in the Old Testament to signal God's judgment; e.g., Jer. 25:15; 49:12). That they think they will be able to drink that cup, which refers to Jesus's execution, indicates that they have not understood either Jesus's passion predictions (16:21; 17:22–23; 20:17–19) or his expectations for their role in his mission, which is rooted in self-sacrifice for others (16:24–26; 18:1–35). When the other disciples are angered by James and John's request, Jesus counters their perspectives on status with a series of sayings that culminate Jesus's kingdom teachings in 16:21–20:28. Jesus first contrasts their relationships within the believing community with the way rulers of the Gentiles take the role of absolute master over others (20:25). The disciples, by contrast, should take the position of servants and slaves in relation to one another (20:26–27). Living out the metaphor of a slave is much like living out the child analogy Jesus has used in 18:1–5. In both cases, Jesus holds up as an example one with little or no status. His disciples should emulate those of little status rather than one who holds and maintains power and status. Jesus corrects those who seek to be "greatest" (18:1;

see also 20:26) and "first" (19:30; 20:16, 27) in a kingdom that is not about status pursuit but status renunciation. Jesus in Matthew 20:26–27 "reinterpret[s] greatness and 'firstness' to such an extent that all sense of rank is removed from them" (Brown 2002, 91).

Jesus's own mission is the example to emulate: "The Son of Man did not come to be served, but to serve, and to give his life as a ransom for many" (20:28). Jesus's words very likely evoke Isaiah's servant of the Lord, described as "[the Lord's] righteous servant [who] will justify many" (Isa. 53:11–12; see "Theological Themes" in the introduction). Matthew signals here for the first time in his narrative that it is *Jesus's death* that will bring Israel's redemption (cf. 1:21; also 26:28) and God's kingdom. God's reign is inaugurated by God's servant, who pours out his life for others rather than dominates as the Gentiles do. An inversion of power redefines kingdom and discipleship to such an extent as to be almost unrecognizable.

B. Final proclamation, confrontation, and judgment in Jerusalem (20:29–25:46). In this section, Matthew narrates Jesus's arrival and early actions in Jerusalem, the ensuing controversies with the Jerusalem leaders regarding his authority, and Jesus's subsequent prophetic judgment of the temple and its leadership. Through these Jerusalem encounters, Matthew emphasizes Jesus's identity as Davidic Messiah and his rightful authority and lordship over the temple and its present leadership as well as all humanity at the end of the age. Matthew also highlights the importance of living out covenantal faithfulness, mercy, and justice for all who would follow Jesus as king.

20:29–22:46: Jesus in Jerusalem. *20:29–21:27.* Jesus's healing of two blind men (20:29–34) is a transitional story between Jesus's teaching of the disciples in 16:21–20:28 and his arrival in Jerusalem in 21:1–11. Links occur between the calls of the blind man to Jesus as "Son of David" (20:30, 31) and the cries of the Jerusalem crowds, "Hosanna to the Son of David!" (21:9), and the crowds are reintroduced to a central place in Matthew's story (20:31; 21:9, 11). The healing story emphasizes Jesus's messianic compassion and authority (20:34) and ends with the two men following Jesus—language used by Matthew to signal discipleship (e.g., 4:19; 16:24).

For Matthew, Jesus's entry into Jerusalem (21:1–11) enacts Zechariah's prophetic announcement that Israel's king would arrive in Jerusalem not as a warrior on his horse but on

Matthew 21:2 describes Jesus approaching Jerusalem from the Mount of Olives, which is in the upper right of this photo of the Kidron Valley. To enter Jerusalem, Jesus would have traveled down from the Mount of Olives, across the Kidron Valley, and then up into the city.

a donkey—as in times of peace (Zech. 9:9–10; also 1 Kings 1:33, 38). Just as Zechariah's prophecy anticipates a "gentle" king (21:5; see the Greek Septuagint of Zech. 9:9), Matthew's Jesus has already identified himself as "gentle" (11:29; see also 5:5 [NIV "meek"]). Matthew emphasizes Jesus's symbolic appropriation of the peaceable and gentle king by narrating Jesus's instructions to procure a donkey (21:1–3), by quoting Zechariah 9:9 as fulfilled in Jesus's arrival in Jerusalem (21:4–5), and by concluding with the response of the crowds to Jesus's royal entrance. The crowds accompanying Jesus hail him as "the Son of David"—a messianic title. They choose a blessing from Psalm 118, which may have been understood to have royal connotations (Ps. 118:26; Matt. 21:9). When questioned by the people of Jerusalem, these crowds who have followed Jesus from Galilee to Jerusalem identify him as "the prophet" (21:11; a possible reference to Deut. 18:15–19; cf. John 6:14).

Matthew immediately turns to Jesus's clearing the temple upon his arrival in Jerusalem (21:12–13). The selling of sacrificial animals was a necessary accommodation for pilgrims traveling long distances to Jerusalem for Passover (26:2), as was the changing of money from Greek and Roman currency (with their pagan images/inscriptions) to the prescribed temple currency of coins from Tyre in Phoenicia. Jesus's complaint in his symbolic action is likely about the location of such transactions within the temple confines (probably the Court of Gentiles, which accommodated large crowds during festivals) rather than a rejection of these practices altogether. He cites Isaiah (56:7; at Matt. 21:13) to indicate the temple's purpose as a house of prayer, not a "den of robbers" (an allusion to Jer. 7:11).

Jesus's action in the temple signals (implicitly but clearly) his messianic identity and anticipates his prophetic judgment on the temple in 23:37–24:35. "Those who had witnessed his overtly messianic arrival could hardly fail to read this [temple] action in the same light, as

an assertion of messianic authority" (France, 784; France discusses pertinent Jewish literature tying temple rebuilding or purification to the Messiah's arrival [784–85]). Jesus, as the Messiah, has the right to call the temple's leadership to account for its administration. Jesus demonstrates the purpose of the temple as a place of prayer, welcome, and healing (21:14). His identity as "Son of David" is reaffirmed in the shouts of children, to the consternation of the chief priests and teachers of the law (21:15–16; cf. Ps. 8:2).

In the third of three symbolic acts, Matthew's Jesus curses a fig tree that has no figs (21:18–22), evoking Old Testament prophetic critique of Israel's fruitlessness (Mic. 7:1; cf. Jer. 8:13). Matthew uses this account to emphasize Jesus's critique of the current temple administration (in combination with 21:12–13, with the most immediate referent for mountain in 21:21 being the temple mount) and to call disciples to faith without doubt (cf. 17:20).

The question the chief priests and elders raise about Jesus's authority (21:23) sets the terms for a series of controversies between Jesus and the Jerusalem leadership (chaps. 21 and 22). Jesus agrees to answer their question about the source of his authority for his recent actions if they will identify John's baptism as divine or human in origin (21:24–25). Their dilemma: if they say *divine*, they will have no excuse for rejecting his message; if they say *human*, they will antagonize the crowds, who believe John was God's prophet. They claim ignorance, and Jesus does not answer their question (21:27). Yet, in the ensuing controversies, Jesus asserts his God-given authority powerfully and effectively, so that, in the end, no one dares to ask him any more questions (22:46).

21:28–22:14. Jesus first addresses the Jerusalem leaders with three parables that indict them for abdicating their leadership role in guiding Israel in righteousness (21:32). In the parable of the two sons (21:28–32), Jesus contrasts the son who, though initially disobedient, repents (the Greek term is rendered variously as "changed his mind" and "repent" in 21:29 and 32) and obeys his father with the son who says he will obey but does not. In regard to believing John the Baptist's message, the tax collectors and prostitutes are like the first son, the chief priests and elders like the second (21:31–32). According to Jesus, the wayward of Israel enter God's kingdom ahead of its leaders, because the latter "did not repent and believe [John]" (21:32).

This harsh indictment leads into a parable of judgment on the same leaders (21:33–46). Jesus draws on the Old Testament portrayal of Israel as a vineyard (e.g., Isa. 5:1–7) and tells a story of a vineyard entrusted by a landowner to local tenants. When he sends his servants to collect the fruit, the tenants beat or kill them. Even when he sends his son, they do the same. The judgment on the tenants is the vineyard's removal from them and its transfer to other tenants (21:41). Jesus cites Psalm 118:22–23 to indicate God's vindication of the rejected one (cf. 28:18) and declares that God's kingdom will be taken away from Israel's current leaders and given "to a people who will produce its fruit" (21:43; with the singular noun "a people" likely referring to faithful Jews and Gentiles). The judgment of this parable and the previous one is aimed specifically at the Jewish leaders, who have failed to lead and care for the Jewish people as they ought. Their failure is seen precisely in their rejection of both John and Jesus (the son of the parable). The chief priests and Pharisees know that Jesus has referred to them in these two parables (21:45), so they seek to arrest him secretly (21:46).

The third parable Matthew includes (22:1–14) is likely also intended for the Jewish leadership, though the ending is not specific to them as at 21:31–32, 45. God's kingdom is likened to a wedding banquet held by a king for his son. Those invited refuse to come, even killing the king's servants who bring the invitation. In response, the king sends his army to destroy these murderers and burn their city (with a possible reference to the fall of Jerusalem in AD 70; see "Author, Date, and Audience" in the introduction). Since the original guests refuse the king's invitation, he opens the banquet to anyone his servants can find, "the bad as well as the good" (22:10; cf. 13:40–43, 49–50). Jesus's parable up to this point emphasizes the affront of refusing God's kingdom invitation and the judgment that will fall on those who reject that invitation, as the Jewish leadership has been doing. The final scene of the parable strikes closer to home. A man who is at the banquet is discovered without the proper wedding garments and thrown out. This scene warns those who have responded to the kingdom invitation (offered by Jesus) of judgment if they do not bear fruit (with "weeping and gnashing of teeth" being a common image for judgment in Matthew; cf. 8:12; 13:42, 50; 24:51; 25:30). Though the wedding garment is an ambiguous image, in context it seems best interpreted along an ethical line, since both good and bad enter the parable's banquet (22:10) and since the previous two parables emphasize ethical behavior (21:32, 43; for similar warnings to insiders, cf. 7:21–23; 16:27).

22:15–46. After Jesus's parables prophesying judgment on Jewish leadership, various groups of leaders go on the offensive by bringing difficult questions to Jesus. The first group is a coalition of Pharisees and Herodians (with the Herodians likely representing the interests of Herod and other clients of Rome within his circle) who ask Jesus whether it is "right to pay the imperial tax to Caesar" (22:17). Knowing that they intend to trap him, Jesus denounces their hypocrisy, possibly for bringing a coin with Caesar's image into the temple area (22:18–19; cf. 6:1–18). Jesus asks them to identify whose portrait and inscription are on the denarius they produce (22:18–20). When they reply, "Caesar's," Jesus gives an answer that defies the no-win situation they think they have created. "Give back to Caesar what is Caesar's, and to God what is God's" (22:21). Jesus appears to concede payment of the census tax (requiring a denarius per person) to Rome, while intimating

God's ownership of all things (a bedrock of Jewish theology; cf. Ps. 24:1). By a rather ambiguous answer, Jesus subverts the reach of the emperor—a reach that would claim to extend to all of life—by signaling that what belongs to God must be given to God. Jesus's questioners are rightly amazed at his answer (22:22).

The next group of leaders questioning Jesus is the Sadducees (22:23–33), who pose a question meant to reveal the absurdity of belief in bodily resurrection. They hypothesize a woman widowed seven times from the death of seven brothers. Their question: At the resurrection from the dead whose wife will she be? Jesus answers that they are (dead) wrong, because they are ignorant of both the Scriptures and God's power (22:29)! At the renewal of all things there will be no need for marriage as context for procreation, since the power of God will ensure that the resurrected faithful will never again die (in this, they will be like the angels; 22:30). Jesus argues from the Scriptures (Exod. 3:6) that the dead will be raised: if God can still be referred to as the God of Abraham, Isaac, and Jacob long after these men have died, then the implication is that God will raise them to life again at the final resurrection (22:31–32). In his defense of the promise of future resurrection, Matthew's Jesus implicitly affirms that God's rule will arrive in spite of the current Roman regime. As with his teaching on Roman taxation, Jesus's message here has a subversive element (Wright 2003, 419).

The final question asked of Jesus again comes from the Pharisees, who send one of their torah experts to ask Jesus about the greatest commandment (22:34–36). Matthew has already emphasized Jesus's torah interpretation through the lens of love and mercy (cf. 5:43–48; 9:13; 12:7), and Jesus's answer at 22:40 fits that theme: "All the Law and the Prophets hang on" the commands to love God (Deut. 6:5) and love neighbor (Lev. 19:18). Given previous accusations that Jesus was lax in his torah observance (cf. 12:1–14; 15:1–20), these Jerusalem Pharisees may have hoped to discover a problem with Jesus's torah interpretation. If so, Jesus gave them nothing to fault. His answer falls well within the parameters of Jewish teachings (e.g., *Testament of Dan* 5.3).

While the Pharisees remain assembled, Jesus turns the tables to ask his own question (22:41–46), which silences the entire Jewish leadership after their litany of questions (21:23–27; 22:15–40). His query answers their questions of his authority by addressing the issue of his messianic identity. When he asks them whose son the Messiah is, they answer in expected fashion: "The son of David" (22:42). While their answer is accurate (see Matthew's preference for this title for Jesus in 1:1; 12:23; 21:9), it is not fully adequate. Citing Psalm 110:1, Jesus asks how David could call his own son "Lord" in a psalm that clearly elevates and vindicates this "Lord" (22:44). Jesus concludes with a riddle: How can David's "Lord" be his son? (22:45). Although no one in the story can answer the riddle, the reader of Matthew knows its solution. Matthew has shown Jesus to be the Messiah and has defined Messiah both as Davidic in ancestry (1:1–17) and as "Lord"—a title used for Jesus throughout Matthew's Gospel (e.g., 7:22; 8:2, 25; 17:4; 20:30–31; 25:44), which signals Jesus's authority over all things (cf. 28:18). The riddle requires a double affirmative: Jesus as the Messiah is both David's son and his Lord. Matthew concludes this section in which Jesus's authority is questioned by affirming that Jesus derives his authority from his identity as Messiah and Lord (see "Theological Themes" in the introduction).

23:1–39: Judgment on Jewish leadership. The preliminary judgments issued by Jesus on the Jerusalem elite in Matthew 21–22 lead into a more extended section of judgment in Matthew 23–25, with chapter 23 focused on prophetic judgments leveled against teachers of the law and Pharisees specifically. Yet the story audience of these woes is the crowds and Jesus's disciples (23:1) rather than the teachers and Pharisees themselves. Matthew intends this chapter to shape the discipleship and leadership of the Christian community, focusing on themes of avoiding hypocrisy and right teaching of and adherence to the law.

Jesus begins by calling the crowds and disciples to respect the teaching role of these leaders (see the description of the Pharisees in the commentary on 12:1–14) but warns against following them in their actions since "they do not practice what they preach" (23:2–3; cf. 15:3–6; 23:23 for examples of Pharisaic disobedience). The indictment that these leaders put heavy loads on people in relation to the law provides the negative counterpoint to Jesus's claim that his "burden is light" (11:30). The second warning Jesus gives his followers is to avoid the example of the Pharisees and teachers of the law in seeking human attention and honor (23:5–7; cf. 6:1–18). Phylacteries were small leather boxes containing portions of Scripture that were bound to the upper arm and the forehead in literal observance of Exodus 13:9, while tassels were worn on the corners of one's outer garment to remind Jews of God's commands (Num. 15:37–39). Jesus's criticism of the Pharisees and teachers is that they increase the visibility of these symbols in order to gain recognition from others. In contrast, Jesus's followers are to humble themselves and serve others, rejecting the desire and pursuit of human exaltation and honor (23:11–12; cf. similar themes in 18:1–20:28).

After calling his followers to a contrasting way of discipleship, Jesus directs seven "woes" or judgments at the Pharisees and teachers of the law (23:13–36). The first six woes are arranged in thematic pairs, focused on mission (first and second woes), law (third and fourth), and incongruity between the outside and inside person (fifth and sixth), with the final woe culminating the other six.

The first (23:13) and second (23:15) woes condemn the Pharisees and teachers for their hypocrisy in closing the kingdom to others and themselves, even as they win converts. A convert who follows their lead in rejecting God's kingdom as announced and embodied in Jesus would become "a child of hell." (The NIV places 23:14 in a footnote, since it is very likely a later scribal addition drawn from Mark 12:40 or Luke 20:47.)

The third (23:16–22) and fourth (23:23–24) woes focus on hypocrisy in Pharisaic interpretation of the law and traditions associated with it. In the third woe, Jesus critiques any attempt to distinguish between binding and nonbinding oaths, since all are binding before God (though cf. Matt. 5:33–37). Jesus's interpretation is consistent with Old Testament teaching that oath making is not required but does bind any oath made as an oath to God (cf. Deut. 23:21–23). Jesus's interpretation critiques traditional commentary on the law when it abrogates the law itself (cf. 15:1–9). The fourth woe judges these teachers for their detailed obedience in tithing but their neglect of what Jesus calls "the more important matters of the law—justice, mercy and faithfulness" (23:23). These values are central to Jesus's torah interpretation in Matthew (e.g., 5:17; 9:13; 12:7, 20; see commentary on 12:1–50).

The fifth (23:25–26) and sixth (23:27–28) woes charge the Pharisees and teachers with the hypocrisy of an outward appearance of piety without a corresponding inward righteousness. The accusation is that inside they are full of greed, self-indulgence, hypocrisy, and wickedness (23:25, 28). The antidote is to "clean the inside" so that the outside can be clean (23:26).

The final woe (23:29–36) judges the hypocrisy of these leaders in commemorating martyrs of the past, claiming that they wouldn't have taken part in their deaths (23:29–30). Jesus accuses them of being descendants of those who murdered the prophets in two ways. First, they have called those murderers their "ancestors" (23:30) and have thus testified to their own complicity (23:31–32). Second, Jesus claims that they will persecute and murder those of his followers that he will send to them (23:34). Jesus sums up the Old Testament martyrs from the first (Abel, Gen. 4:8) to the last (if Zechariah of 2 Chron. 24:20–21 is being referred to. We possess no historical evidence for the martyrdom of Zechariah, son of Berekiah, mentioned in Zech. 1:1. If Zechariah of 2 Chronicles is meant, then he would be the last martyr of the Old Testament, with Chronicles being the final book in the order of the Hebrew Bible). Jesus indicts "this generation" in his conclusion to the woes to Pharisees and teachers of the law, as he has done earlier in Matthew (12:38–45).

In the conclusion of chapter 23, Matthew describes Jesus's lament over Jerusalem and his desire to gather the people of Jerusalem as a hen gathers her chicks. The unwillingness to be gathered by Jesus echoes the unfaithfulness of this generation that Jesus has already lamented (17:17). Jesus's prediction of judgment is that "your house is left to you desolate"—a reference to the Jerusalem temple (destroyed by Rome in AD 70; for "house" as temple, cf. Jer. 7:1–8; Lam. 2:7; also Matt. 21:13; 24:1–2).

Yet the final moment of this prophetic judgment offers a word of hope (23:39): "You will not see me again until you say, 'Blessed is he who comes in the name of the Lord'" (Ps. 118:26). The temple (and redemptive) overtones of Psalm 118 (cf. 118:19–20, 26–27), as well as the acclamation of Jesus by the Galilean crowds with these same words (21:9), suggest that the judgments predicted in this chapter need not be final. Matthew's Jesus envisions a time after the temple's desolation when his appearing may produce not only judgment but also possibly restoration if only Jerusalem will welcome him as the Lord's blessed one—the Messiah ("until" as conditional) (Davies and Allison, 3:323).

24:1–25:46: Jesus's fifth discourse—The Eschatological Discourse. Matthew's fifth and final extended section of Jesus's teaching continues with the theme of judgment on Jerusalem leaders and the temple begun in chapters 21–23. Matthew provides glimpses of Jesus's second coming or reappearing and the end of the age, with its final judgment of all peoples. Regarding the temple's destruction, Jesus warns his followers against confusing precursor signs with the events that will occur when it falls (24:4–35). The opposite warning is given for Jesus's reappearing: there will be no anticipatory signs, so the disciples should always be prepared (24:36–41). The last half of the discourse consists of five parables exhorting Jesus's disciples to be prepared by living lives of faithfulness and mercy (24:42–25:46).

24:1–51. Matthew 24:1–2 transitions between Jesus's prophecy of the temple's desolation (23:38–39) and the Eschatological Discourse, beginning with the disciples' questions (24:3). As Jesus departs from the temple to the Mount of Olives, he predicts, "Not one stone here will be left on another" (24:1–2). In response, the disciples ask two questions: (1) When will the destruction of the temple

Jesus predicted the fate of the temple as he left it on his way to the Mount of Olives (Matt. 24:1–3). In this photo of a staircase leading to the temple, the worn stairs seen to the lower left are original and were in use during the time of Jesus. The Mount of Olives is in the background in the upper right.

occur? and (2) What will be the sign of Jesus's reappearing (Greek *parousia*) and the end of the age? (with "coming" and "end" combined as one entity by a shared Greek article).

The rest of the chapter answers these two questions, although scholars do not agree where Matthew's Jesus turns from answering the first to the second or whether the two answers are fully distinct. Yet a number of signals indicate that 24:1–35 addresses the first question of the temple's destruction, with 24:36–51 (along with Matthew 25) turning to the question of Jesus's *parousia* and the end of the age (following France, 889–94). Matthew uses the Greek term *parousia* in a technical sense (as do other New Testament writers) to indicate Jesus's "reappearing" at the final consummation, or the "end of the age" in Matthew's language, at 24:3 (*parousia* at 24:3, 27, 37, 39; see also 1 Cor. 15:23; 1 Thess. 3:13; 4:15). The term *parousia* can be translated "coming"; but given the use of another word for a "coming" of Jesus in Matthew 24 (*erchomai*; cf. 24:30 and see discussion below), it is helpful to distinguish when Matthew chooses to use the technical term *parousia*, since at these points he is clearly referring to Jesus's "reappearing" (second coming).

Jesus's words concerning the temple's destruction (24:4–35) begin by warning his disciples that they will be tempted to misinterpret various events as signaling the temple's destruction when those signs are actually precursors to it. Matthew's reference to "the end" (Greek *telos*) at 24:6, 13–14 uses language distinct from his Greek phrase for "the end of the age" (24:3; also at 13:39–40, 49; 28:20), possibly indicating that with *telos* he is referring to a more immediate "end"—namely, the temple's destruction. Precursor signs of the temple's end include false messiahs (24:5; cf. 24:23–26); wars, famines, and earthquakes (24:6–7); and persecution of the disciples (24:9–13). The preaching of the gospel "in the whole world" (cf. Acts 11:28 and Col. 1:6, where this phrase delimits the Greco-Roman world) will be penultimate to the temple's destruction (24:14).

In 24:15–26, Jesus moves to describe the horror of the temple's (and Jerusalem's) destruction. The reference to "the abomination that causes desolation" derives from Daniel (Dan. 8:13; 9:27; 11:31; 12:11; Matt. 24:15) and refers generally to the transgressing of the temple confines by Gentiles (Romans, in the case of AD 70). When this occurs, there will be no more time for preparation, as was the case with the precursor signs of 24:4–14; it will be time to flee (24:16–20). Only the brevity of this time alleviates its horror: "For the sake of the elect those days will be shortened" (24:22).

In Matthew 24:27–28 Jesus briefly contrasts the destruction of the temple with Jesus's *parousia* ("reappearing"; NIV "coming" in 24:27). Matthew has just indicated that the temple's destruction will be accompanied by enticements to find the messiah in obscure places, such as the desert or inner rooms (24:23–26). In contrast, the "*parousia* of the Son of Man" will be as visible as lightning flashing across the breadth of the sky (24:27).

Matthew's Jesus gives three final pictures about the temple's destruction: the first from Old Testament prophets, a second from Daniel specifically, and a third from the image of a fig tree (24:29–35). The words of Matthew 24:29 echo common Old Testament cosmic language used to signal God's actions of judgment or salvation within human history (e.g., Isa. 13:10; 34:4; Ezek. 32:7; Hag. 2:6, 21). Therefore, the cosmic activity of 24:29 signals the "earth-shattering" future destruction of the temple as judgment from God (Wright 1996, 354–60).

The quotation of Daniel 7:13–14 in Matthew 24:30–31 pictures the vindicated Son of Man approaching ("coming" to) the heavenly throne of God and receiving glory (with "coming"—*erchomai*, not *parousia*—indicating a heavenward coming in Matthew as in Daniel). Matthew has already used this image of Jesus's vindication from Daniel 7 (Matt. 10:23; 16:28). For Matthew, Jesus in his message and mission will be vindicated first at his resurrection and again when his predictions concerning the temple come to pass. (For Matthew's application of Daniel 7 language to various moments of Jesus's own vindication, including his resurrection and the temple's destruction, see France, 396–97.) The NIV's "the peoples of the earth will mourn" (at the Son's vindication; 24:30) can also be rendered "the tribes of the earth," possibly indicating Israel's mourning at the temple's destruction (cf. Zech. 12:10–14). The final image of this section is that of a fig tree (24:32–33; cf. 21:18–22), used to emphasize that discernible signs will precede the temple's destruction and that Jesus's predictions about it will come true before the passing of "this generation" (in AD 70; 24:34).

Jesus's words in Matthew 24:36–41 turn to address his *parousia* or reappearing ("coming" in 24:37, 39 translates *parousia*). In contrast to the signs that will attend the destruction of the temple, Jesus's reappearing will be characterized by suddenness (24:37–41), with no one except the Father knowing its timing (24:36). The resulting admonition is to *be prepared*—the point of the two brief parables about a thief's unexpected arrival (24:42–44) and a servant at his master's delay and unexpected return (24:45–51).

25:1–46. This theme of preparedness for Jesus's reappearing at the end of the age is the center point of the parable of the ten virgins and the bridegroom (Matt. 25:1–13). Though not much is known about first-century Jewish wedding customs, it may be that these young, unmarried women leave the groom's home to welcome and accompany the couple back to the groom's household (Davies and Allison, 3:395). When the bridegroom is "a long time in coming" (25:5), five virgins run out of lamp oil because they neglected to bring extra. They miss the opportunity to join the bridegroom and enter the wedding banquet (25:10). Jesus's parable calls all his followers to be ready for his reappearing, since they "do not know the day or the hour" (25:13; cf. 24:36, 42).

The second parable of Matthew 25 illustrates what preparedness looks like (25:14–30). Three servants are entrusted with large sums of money (a "talent" equals approximately six thousand denarii, with a denarius being a day's wage; see NIV note to 25:15) from their master and expected to use it to gain more during his long absence (25:19). The first two do so (25:20–23), while the third servant simply buries the money and so makes no profit (25:24–27). The master takes away the money given to this third servant and commands that he be thrown into the darkness (25:28–30; for similar language of "weeping and gnashing of teeth" signaling final judgment, cf. 8:12; 13:42, 50; 22:13; 24:51). This parable points to faithfulness as the key to preparedness for Jesus's reappearing and final judgment.

The concluding parable of Jesus's final discourse illustrates what faithfulness should look like by painting a portrait of the final judgment of humanity (25:31–46). Though this teaching is often called a parable, its only parabolic aspects involve the image of a shepherd separating sheep from goats (25:32). Matthew draws on imagery from Daniel 7:13–14 again, indicating that the ultimate vindication of Jesus as God's chosen one will occur at the final judgment (with the picture of Jesus enthroned pointing to his judging role; cf. 19:28). At the final judgment, "all the nations" will appear before Jesus, the king (25:32, 34). Although the Greek term *ta ethnē* can refer to "the Gentiles" as well, here it most likely refers to all "nations" (all people) including Israel, given the universal scope of the scene. The criteria for judgment are not surprising in light of Matthew's earlier themes. Mercy and justice practiced on behalf of "the least of these" is what ultimately separates those who enter life and those who do not (25:40, 45). Matthew has demonstrated the importance of these qualities for Jesus's ministry (9:13, 27, 36; 12:7, 15, 18–21; 14:14; 15:32; 20:31, 34) and for his expectations of disciples (5:7, 10; 23:23).

At issue is the identity of the "least of these." They are described as brothers and sisters (25:40, though not at 25:45), which would indicate that they are the needy and least among Jesus's followers (cf. 12:49–50; also "least" is the superlative form of "little ones" [*mikros*], identified as Jesus's followers at 10:42; 18:6–10). Yet Jesus's clear teaching in Matthew on the solidarity between himself and his followers (10:40–42; 18:5, 20) does little to explain the surprise of the righteous that Jesus identifies himself with "the least" of his followers. The surprise may stem from Jesus's identification with all human need. "They have helped . . . not a Jesus recognized in his representatives, but a Jesus *incognito*" (France, 959).

C. Jesus's execution by Rome and resurrection/ vindication by God (26:1–28:20). In 26:1–28:20, Matthew narrates Jesus's final days and hours as he willingly suffers and goes to his execution to restore his people and usher in God's reign. Though the disciples desert him and Rome and the Jerusalem leaders crucify him as a criminal, God vindicates Jesus as Messiah and Lord at his resurrection.

26:1–56: Betrayal and desertion. Matthew signals the conclusion of the fifth discourse with the familiar formula, "When Jesus had finished [saying these things]," this time referencing "*all* these things" to signal the final of the five blocks of Jesus's teaching (26:1; see "Structure" in the introduction). Immediately afterward, Matthew narrates another passion prediction by Jesus (cf. 16:21; 17:22–23; 20:17–19) and the intensifying plot by the Jewish leadership against Jesus (26:3–5; cf. 21:46). Jesus's prediction connects his crucifixion—a Roman form of execution—to the Passover feast, which is two days away (26:2; cf. 26:17–29). Passover, one of three central Jewish festivals, celebrated Israelite freedom from bondage to Egypt. As such—and given the great numbers of Jewish pilgrims attending—Passover could become the locus of political foment, as the chief priests and elders fear (26:5; cf. 27:24 for Pilate's similar concern). No one in power—the Jerusalem leaders or Rome—wanted a messiah to arise during Passover! (For a historical example, see Josephus, *Jewish Antiquities* 17.9.3).

In 26:6–13 (set in Bethany, just east of Jerusalem), Matthew narrates how an unnamed woman anoints Jesus with expensive perfume—an act Jesus commends and the disciples decry. Jesus interprets her act as preparation for burial (with perfumes often used in embalming) and praises her deed as one that will be recounted along with the spread of the gospel itself (26:13). Her action contrasts Judas's act of betrayal in 26:14–16. As one of Jesus's inner circle ("one of the Twelve"), Judas will have opportunity to lead the chief priests to Jesus when he is away from the people, who might rise to Jesus's defense (cf. 26:5).

Matthew marks the beginning of the Passover celebration at 26:17 (with "the first day of the Festival of Unleavened Bread" signaling its inception or the day anticipating it, as in Mark 14:12; for the combining of the two festivals cf. Deut. 16:1–8; Philo, *On the Special Laws* 2.150). He tells his disciples to prepare their Passover meal by going into Jerusalem and meeting a man with whom Jesus has presumably made room arrangements. In the later evening, Jesus celebrates the Passover meal with his disciples (26:20). Matthew emphasizes two moments: Jesus's identification of Judas as his betrayer (26:21–25) and his interpretation of their Passover meal around himself and his forthcoming death (26:16–29; though little is known about pre–AD 70 Passover practices). The bread and wine of the Passover meal are reinterpreted to signify Jesus's sacrificial death "for the forgiveness of sins" (1:21) as the means of covenant renewal ("my blood of the covenant"; 26:28; cf. likely allusions to Exod. 24:8; Isa. 53:12—for "many"; Jer. 31:31–34). Jesus connects his enactment of the renewed covenant with the still future consummation of God's kingdom (26:29; cf. the kingship theme at 27:33–56).

After moving east from the city to the Mount of Olives (across the Kidron Valley from Jerusalem; 26:30), Jesus predicts that not only Judas but also all his disciples will fall away (*skandalizō*—"stumble"; cf. 11:6), citing Zechariah 13:7, concerning the scattering of the flock at the striking of the shepherd. Though Peter protests, Jesus predicts Peter will disown him before morning arrives (26:34; cf. 26:69–75).

Jesus and his disciples move to a nearby olive grove called Gethsemane (26:36–46), where Jesus prays repeatedly that the necessity of his impending death be removed (26:39, 42, 44; for cup language, see 20:22), though he submits to his Father's will (for obedience to God's will in Matthew, see 7:21; 12:48–50). The disciples, whom Jesus asks to keep watch as he prays, fall asleep at each turn. Although privy to Jesus's predictions and teaching about his imminent death, they continue to show that they do not understand the full import of his words. They do nothing to prepare for his death (26:6–13); they boldly protest Jesus's prediction about their falling away (26:31–35); and yet they succumb to sleep when they should be watching for Jesus's enemies and praying that they will resist temptation (26:38, 41). Jesus announces the arrival of his betrayer before they show any awareness of the danger (26:46).

Matthew's account of Jesus's arrest (26:47–56) begins with a kiss from Judas (26:49), who has brought an armed crowd gathered by the chief priests and Jewish elders (cf. 26:3), which includes their servants, who attempt to arrest Jesus (26:50–51). When one of Jesus's disciples strikes the high priest's servant, Jesus rebukes his violent response. Jesus, according to Matthew, is not the leader of a human rebellion (Greek *lēstēs*; 26:55) against Rome. Though he could call on angels to rescue him (26:53; cf. 4:6, 11), he will submit to the Father's will for his mission, in order that the Scriptures might be fulfilled (26:54, 56). Since Matthew does not cite a particular scriptural text but refers to "Scriptures" (plural; 26:54) and "the writings of the prophets" (26:56), these statements likely indicate Jesus's fulfillment of the Old Testament Scriptures generally. In contrast to Jesus's command of the situation, his disciples flee the scene, deserting him as predicted (26:31).

26:57–27:26: Jesus on trial. Upon arrest, Jesus is brought before the Sanhedrin, the Jewish ruling council that, according to Matthew, comprised chief priests, Jewish elders, and some teachers of the law (26:57–68)— in other words, the Jerusalem elite. The high

An olive grove in the Garden of Gethsemane, where Jesus prayed after the Last Supper and was arrested (Matt. 26:36–46)

priest Caiaphas (whose tenure spanned AD 18–36) leads the proceedings, which consist of a search for and examination of testimony against Jesus by others and by Jesus himself. Their intent is to bring charges against Jesus to Pilate, the Roman governor (the prefect of Judea; cf. 27:1–2). Evidence from later rabbinic sources indicates that those convening Jesus's "trial" did not follow the (ideal) legal parameters for Jewish trials before the Sanhedrin. This is not surprising, given the sudden nature of Jesus's arrest and the concern over arresting Jesus in Jerusalem during the Passover festival (26:5). This last-minute trial eventually produces two witnesses who agree with each other (a requirement from Deut. 19:15). Their testimony is that Jesus threatened, "I am able to destroy the temple of God and rebuild it in three days" (26:61), though Matthew has nowhere recorded these words (cf. John 2:19). Yet Jesus's temple action and his words of judgment against the temple and its current leadership (21:12–13; 23:37–39; 24:1–35) may have been conflated with Jesus's predictions of being killed and then raised in "three days" (12:40; 16:21; 17:23; 20:19), producing the misconception that Jesus was threatening to destroy the temple (with these accusations repeated at 27:40). Jesus does not respond to this accusation with its mix of truth and falsehood.

Caiaphas then asks Jesus the messianic question: "Tell us if you are the Messiah, the Son of God" (26:63; for "Son of God" as a messianic title, see "Theological Themes" in the introduction). His question is a logical follow-up to the errant testimony about Jesus destroying the temple (cf. 21:12–13; for an expectation that the Messiah would purify Jerusalem, see *Psalms of Solomon* 17:33). Jesus answers in the affirmative and adds the implicit claim of his vindication as Messiah by God via allusion to Daniel 7:13–14 (see commentary on 24:1–51). Jesus's claim of future vindication necessarily implies that Caiaphas and the Sanhedrin will be proved wrong in their assessment of Jesus. Between Jesus's silence concerning the temple

accusations, his claim to be Messiah and the future ruling one (Dan. 7:14), and the implication that those trying him will be proved utterly wrong, it is not surprising that Caiaphas declares Jesus's words blasphemy and the Sanhedrin calls for his death (26:65–66; 27:1), which will require Roman authorization.

Presumably during Jesus's hearing before the Sanhedrin, Peter denies knowing Jesus (26:58, 69–75). Three bystanders recognize Peter as one who was with Jesus, either by sight or by his Galilean accent. Peter in all three instances denies any association with Jesus. After his third denial, the rooster crows. Peter remembers Jesus's pointed prediction and weeps bitterly (26:34, 75). All twelve disciples have deserted Jesus.

After the brief interlude of Peter's denial, Matthew continues narrating Jesus's trial, with the Sanhedrin turning him over to Pilate, the Roman governor of Judea (27:1–2), presumably to authorize and enact the death sentence they have deemed appropriate to his claims and perceived threats (for Roman jurisdiction of capital cases, see John 18:31; Josephus, *Jewish War* 6.126). An important theme in the trial scene (and Judas's demise sandwiched within; 27:3–10) is that of innocence and culpability. Jesus alone is innocent (27:4, 19); but Matthew spreads the responsibility for his death broadly, so that Judas, the chief priests and elders, the crowd, and Pilate are implicated in Jesus's death (cf. 27:4, 20, 24–26; see discussion below).

The account of Judas's regret and his suicide (27:3–5) concludes with the chief priest using the money returned by Judas to buy a burial field (27:6–8). For Matthew, the connections between the details of Judas's demise and Zechariah 11:12–13 illustrate again Old Testament fulfillment in Jesus's story.

In Jesus's hearing before Pilate, the charge against him has undergone a cultural translation: Jesus's acknowledgment of his identity as the Messiah becomes a charge that he claims to be "the king of the Jews" (27:11). Yet what the Sanhedrin expects of the Messiah is essentially the same as what Pilate understands by "king of the Jews." Both claims are religious *and political*, although Pilate is presumably less versed in the religious nature of Jewish messianic hopes. So both charges imply sedition. They fear that this Jesus may be preparing to lead a rebellion against Rome, which both the Jerusalem elite and Rome (Pilate) would have been keen on suppressing. While Jesus acknowledges his kingship when asked by Pilate (27:11), he does not defend himself when the Jerusalem authorities bring charges against him (27:12–14).

Pilate offers to release one prisoner (according to his custom; 27:15) and gives the crowd the choice of either Jesus or Barabbas, whom Matthew describes as "a well-known prisoner" (according to Mark 15:7, a murderer and insurrectionist). Matthew indicates that Pilate offers this choice because of the Jewish leaders' envy of Jesus (27:18). The descriptor "called the Messiah" makes most sense with the inclusion of "Jesus Barabbas" present in some manuscripts, so that "Barabbas" and "Messiah" distinguish the two men, who both have the (common) name "Jesus." But the chief priests and elders incite the crowd to call for Jesus's death (and Barabbas's release; 27:20–23), which Pilate readily implements (27:26).

The issues of innocence and culpability are thematic and complex in this narrative. Most clearly expressed are Jesus's innocence (27:4, 19) and the culpability of Judas (27:4) and the Jewish leaders of Jerusalem (27:1, 20), with the latter fitting the emphasis in chapters 21–28 on the Jerusalem leaders as Jesus's primary antagonists (e.g., 21:15, 45–46; 23:1–39; 26:3–5; 28:11–12).

More ambiguous in light of Matthew's purposes are the Jewish crowds, who have been read at some points in history as primarily responsible for Jesus's death, especially with the words attributed to them at 27:25 ("His blood be on us and on our children!"). Yet there are problems with attaching primary blame here since the makeup of the "people" at 27:25 is ambiguous. They would seem to be identical to the "crowd" just mentioned at 27:20, 24, who

have been persuaded by the Jerusalem leaders to call for Jesus's execution and may be related to the handpicked "crowd" sent by those same leaders at Jesus's arrest (26:47). This places the greater culpability back on the Jewish leadership (27:20). In fact, the very "people" (Greek *laos*; 27:25) who presume to own responsibility for Jesus's death are the same people whom the Jerusalem leaders fear will be open to the deception of the resurrection (27:64) (Carter, 528).

The context of the people's words at 27:25 points to Pilate (along with the Jerusalem leaders) as primarily responsible for Jesus's death. The political reality is that only Rome can legally execute Jesus. Pilate, as Rome's representative in Jerusalem, authorizes Jesus's execution (27:1–2, 26). Though in 27:24 Pilate claims that he is innocent of Jesus's blood and transfers responsibility to the people, he is no more able to do this than the Jewish leaders who say the same words to Judas (27:4). Unless he transfers his authority to the people, Pilate cannot transfer his responsibility for using it. Innocent blood (27:4, 24; cf. 23:35) is not so easily washed away.

The warning from Pilate's wife regarding Jesus's innocence (27:19) heightens Pilate's culpability when he decides to crucify Jesus. That she has received revelation from God is affirmed by the mode of her knowledge: dreams have been used by Matthew to emphasize God's direction (cf. 1:20; 2:12, 19). Her presence in this narrative reminds the reader of other faithful Gentiles enfolded into Matthew's story of Jesus (see "Theological Themes" in the introduction) and contrasts with the injustice of Pilate's decision to crucify Jesus.

27:27–66: Jesus's crucifixion, death, and burial. The crucifixion scene begins with Pilate's soldiers mocking and humiliating Jesus as they dress him in "kingly" fashion (robe and crown of thorns; 27:28–29) and hail him as "king of the Jews" (27:29). They intend these royal accoutrements and words to show Jesus's messianic pretensions to be ridiculous. Matthew, however, wants his readers to hear irony. What the soldiers ridicule, Matthew shows to be utterly true—Jesus truly is king of the Jews.

The theme of Jesus's kingship permeates the crucifixion narrative (27:33–56), which takes place on Golgotha (from Aramaic, meaning "skull")—a location where other executions likely occurred. The charge written atop the cross reads, "This is Jesus, the King of the Jews" (27:37). He is mocked by the Jerusalem leaders, who claim that if he is "the King of Israel . . . the Son of God," he should be able to rescue himself from death (27:42–43). The title Son of God is used synonymously with king (Messiah), as elsewhere in Matthew (e.g., 27:40).

Matthew also draws on Psalm 22 in the crucifixion scene, a psalm that portrays the suffering of an afflicted man who nevertheless trusts God for rescue. The connections with Jesus's situation include the following: (1) Jesus is mocked by Roman soldiers, passersby, Jerusalem leaders, and two robbers crucified with him (27:31, 39, 41, 44; cf. Ps. 22:7); (2) Jesus is crucified (27:35): his hands and feet are "pierced" (Ps. 22:16); (3) Jesus's garments are divided by lot-casting (27:35; Ps. 22:18); (4) Jesus's trust in God is mocked using the words of Psalm 22:7 (Matt. 27:43); and (5) Jesus echoes the psalmist's despair, "My God, my God, why have you forsaken me?" (27:46; Ps. 22:1, Aramaic).

By interweaving motifs of Jesus's kingship and faithfulness in suffering, Matthew redefines kingship and kingdom in terms of suffering and sacrifice. Jesus as God's Messiah (and as "God with us"; 1:23) lives out his mission to Israel and the world in line with self-denial and willing sacrifice for others rather than in assertion of prerogatives and power.

According to Matthew, Jesus willingly dies (26:42; 27:50) as a ransom for God's covenant people (20:28; 26:28), to save them from their sin (1:21). He is the king—the Messiah—inaugurating God's kingdom by his life and death. Matthew confirms this vision of an inaugurated kingdom by his narration of events that follow Jesus's death (27:51–54). He writes of an earthquake accompanying the tearing of the temple curtain (27:51). Matthew likely refers to the inner curtain that separated the innermost, restricted area of the temple—the Most Holy Place—from the rest of the temple (cf. Exod. 26:31–36; though the term can describe the curtain separating the temple from its courts). If so, Matthew indicates through this apocalyptic sign that Jesus's death inaugurates a new kind of access to God's presence (1:23; 18:20; 28:20) not tied to the temple or limited to the covenant with Israel (as argued by Daniel Gurtner). Earthquakes are part of stock apocalyptic imagery used to confirm God's activity and so the cosmic significance of historical events (cf. Ps. 18:6–8; Isa. 29:5–6).

Matthew also connects Jesus's death to a resurrecting of "many holy people," who then make appearances in Jerusalem following Jesus's resurrection (27:52–53). This sign fits the

The Interior of a tomb in Jerusalem from the first century AD. Matthew 27:52–53 describes tombs, such as this one, breaking open and the bodies of holy people emerging to enter the holy city.

apocalyptic tone of 27:51–53, signaling the cosmic ramifications of Jesus's death. If 27:52 alludes to Ezekiel 37:11–14, Matthew is demonstrating that Jesus's death ushers in return from exile (cf. Matthew 1–4), anticipating the day when God will vanquish all enemies, including death. It is as if, with the raising of these holy ones, resurrection spills over into human experience prior to Jesus's own resurrection—the first and prototypical resurrection: "With the death of Jesus history has begun its final rush to the eschatological denouement" (Nolland, 1214).

The final response to Jesus's death and its accompanying signs comes from the Roman guards, who exclaim, "Surely he was the Son of God!" (27:54). Whatever these Gentile onlookers mean by "Son of God" (the title, with connotations of divinity, was common enough in the Greco-Roman world), Matthew wants his readers to hear this exclamation as affirming Jesus as God's Messiah and Israel's representative, as well as the favored Son in intimate relationship with the Father (see "Theological Themes" in the introduction).

Matthew concludes the crucifixion scene by portraying the many Galilean women who remain with Jesus, even as his twelve disciples have deserted him (27:55–56; cf. 26:56, 75). Some women continue attending Jesus after his death, holding vigil at the tomb (27:61; 28:1). The reader of Matthew's passion narrative has seen other women providing a faithful contrast to their male counterparts: the unnamed woman who anoints Jesus for burial (26:6–13) and Pilate's wife, who testifies to Jesus's innocence (27:19). Joining these faithful women is Joseph of Arimathea, who was discipled by Jesus and who buries him (27:57).

Matthew indicates that the day after Jesus's death and burial (which occurred on "Preparation Day"—the day preceding the Sabbath and/or Passover), the chief priests and Pharisees ask Pilate to post guards at the tomb to prevent theft of Jesus's body (27:62–66). They are concerned that Jesus's followers may, in line with Jesus's resurrection predictions, steal his body and deceive the people with such claims. This is Matthew's last word about "the people" (Greek *laos*; 27:64), a word that provides hope that they might still believe (see discussion at 27:25). Pilate grants their request, ordering Jesus's tomb to be secured and guarded.

28:1–20: Resurrection and commissioning. Once the Sabbath is over, Mary Magdalene and Mary the mother of James and Joses (cf. 27:56, 61) return to the tomb. Instead of finding it sealed and guarded, they experience an earthquake (cf. 27:51) and see an angel roll back the entrance stone (28:1–2). The guards faint in fear, while the angel comforts the two women and calms their fears with the news that Jesus has risen as predicted (28:4–6). They are invited to see the evidence—the empty tomb—and instructed to tell Jesus's (now eleven) disciples that Jesus has risen and will meet them in Galilee (28:6–7). Matthew's portrait of the two Marys as the first witnesses of the empty tomb (and the resurrection; 28:9) would have surprised his original audience. Ancient perspectives prioritized male testimony over female and would have tended to view women's testimony as less reliable (less rational and so less trustworthy; cf. Josephus, *Jewish Antiquities* 4.8.15; Origen, *Against Celsus* 2.55). Yet, according to Matthew, not only are these women the first witnesses of the resurrected Jesus, but they are also the first to worship him in his resurrected state (28:9; cf. 28:17) and are commissioned to tell the disciples the news.

The sparse resurrection account (only ten verses; compare this with the 125 verses devoted to Jesus's death) is followed by the "cover-up" by the chief priests and elders, who bribe the guards to say that Jesus's disciples stole his body (28:11–15). Matthew briefly steps from the story to indicate that this explanation continues to circulate when he writes his Gospel (28:15).

The Gospel's final story shows Jesus meeting with his disciples on a Galilean mountain (28:16–20; with mountains being locations of revelation in Matthew; cf. chaps. 5–7, 17,

24–25). One of the Twelve has betrayed Jesus, Peter has denied knowing him, and the others have fled at his arrest (26:56). Yet Jesus summons the eleven to meet him in Galilee and refers to them as his "brothers," signaling restoration of relationship (28:10). As they meet, they worship Jesus (as the women have already done; 28:9). Yet the disciples continue to "doubt" (Greek *distazō*; cf. 14:31–33 for the same combination of worship and wavering from the disciples). Matthew implicitly reintroduces the disciples' "little faith" at his story's end (with "doubt" and "little faith" as synonyms in 14:31). Fortunately, Jesus's mission does not depend on an exemplary response by the disciples but on Jesus's ongoing presence with them (28:20).

Matthew 28:18–20, often called the Great Commission, evokes Daniel's vision of a vindicated Son of Man enthroned beside the Ancient of Days and given "authority, glory, and sovereign power" (Dan. 7:14; for Matthew's frequent use of Dan. 7:13–14, see "Theological Themes" in the introduction). For Matthew, this enthronement and vindication occurs first and foremost at Jesus's resurrection, so that 28:18–20 establishes the significance of his resurrection narrated in 28:1–10. Although Jerusalem's political rulers have viewed Jesus's death as vindication of their own power, Jesus's resurrection demonstrates his vindication by God as rightful king (Messiah).

The final words of Matthew's Gospel are Jesus's commission to his disciples to make other disciples from all nations—Jew and non-Jew alike. Jesus's own mission, circumscribed during his ministry by the phrase "the lost sheep of Israel" (15:24; cf. 10:5–6), is expanded to all nations after his resurrection/vindication. Teaching and baptism are the two activities Jesus intends his disciples to accomplish "in the name of the Father and of the Son and of the Holy Spirit" (28:19–20; with the trinitarian formula distinguishing this baptism from John's baptism in Matthew 3). Disciples are to be taught "to obey everything [Jesus has]

commanded," continuing Matthew's pervasive theme of obedience (cf. 5:20; 7:15–27; 19:17–19; bearing-fruit motif).

The promise of Jesus's presence with his disciples (28:20) grounds this commission to make disciples. Though they are authorized to go out in mission (see the authority promised at 16:19; 18:18–19), their authority is derivative. It is Jesus who has been given all authority. Instead of explicitly granting that authority to his disciples here, Jesus promises his ongoing presence. They participate in his authority by participating in his presence with them. This promise of presence, echoing across Matthew's Gospel (at its beginning, middle, and end: 1:23; 18:20; 28:20), is the hope and power for the spread of Jesus's mission. Disciples may be those who waver between worship and doubt, but Jesus—the crucified, resurrected, and vindicated Messiah—will be with them until "the very end of the age." Matthew concludes his narrative with a vision for Christian discipleship and mission grounded on Jesus's sacrifice in death and vindication in resurrection and empowered by Jesus's promised presence with his followers.

Select Bibliography

Bauckham, Richard. *God Crucified: Monotheism and Christology in the New Testament*. Grand Rapids: Eerdmans, 1998.

Beaton, Richard. *Isaiah's Christ in Matthew's Gospel*. Society for New Testament Studies Monograph Series 123. Cambridge: Cambridge University Press, 2002.

Brown, Jeannine K. *The Disciples in Narrative Perspective: The Portrayal and Function of the Matthean Disciples*. Academia Biblica 9. Atlanta: Scholars Press, 2002.

———. *Scripture as Communication: Introducing Biblical Hermeneutics*. Grand Rapids: Baker Academic, 2007.

Carter, Warren. *Matthew and the Margins*. Maryknoll, NY: Orbis, 2000.

Davies, W. D., and Dale C. Allison. *Matthew*. 3 vols. International Critical Commentary. Edinburgh: T. & T. Clark, 1988–97.

France, R. T. *The Gospel of Matthew*. New International Commentary on the New Testament. Grand Rapids: Eerdmans, 2007.

Garland, David. *Reading Matthew: A Literary and Theological Commentary on the First Gospel*. New York: Crossroad, 1993.

Gurtner, Daniel M. *The Torn Veil: Matthew's Exposition of the Death of Jesus*. Society for New Testament Studies Monograph Series 139. Cambridge: Cambridge University Press, 2007.

Hagner, Donald A. *Matthew 1–13*. Word Biblical Commentary. Dallas: Word, 1993.

Keener, Craig S. *A Commentary on the Gospel of Matthew*. Grand Rapids: Eerdmans, 1999.

Nolland, John. *The Gospel of Matthew*. New International Greek Testament Commentary. Grand Rapids: Eerdmans, 2005.

Powell, Mark Allan. "Binding and Loosing: A Paradigm of Ethical Discernment from the Gospel of Matthew." *Currents in Theology and Mission* 30 (2003): 438–45.

———. *Chasing the Eastern Star: Adventures in Biblical Reader Response Criticism*. Louisville: Westminster John Knox, 2001.

———. *God with Us: A Pastoral Theology of Matthew's Gospel*. Minneapolis: Fortress, 1995.

———. "Matthew's Beatitudes: Reversals and Rewards of the Kingdom." *Catholic Biblical Quarterly* 58 (1996): 460–79.

Westerholm, Stephen. *Understanding Matthew: The Early Christian Worldview of the First Gospel*. Grand Rapids: Baker Academic, 2006.

Wilkins, Michael J. *Matthew*. NIV Application Commentary. Grand Rapids: Zondervan, 2004.

Wright, N. T. *Jesus and the Victory of God*. Minneapolis: Fortress, 1996.

———. *The Resurrection of the Son of God*. Minneapolis: Fortress, 2003.

Mark

JAMES R. EDWARDS

Introduction

For the first seventeen centuries of church history, Mark, the shortest of the four Gospels, was regarded as an inferior abbreviation of the Gospel of Matthew. Discussions of the Gospels in the early centuries of Christianity cite Matthew and John most frequently, Luke a distant third, and Mark last and only rarely. Until modern times, church lectionaries likewise included citations from Luke and Mark only when they differed from Matthew and John, which were regarded as the two most important Gospels. In the early nineteenth century, however, careful literary analyses of the first three Gospels led a majority of scholars to hypothesize that Mark was not a servile abbreviator of Matthew but rather the *earliest* of the Gospels, and the primary source for both Matthew and Luke. This radical reevaluation of Mark has resulted in two centuries of unprecedented attention and a flood of literature devoted to the Gospel of Mark.

Authorship, Date, Place of Composition, and Audience

Like the other canonical Gospels, Mark nowhere identifies its author, nor even, as is the case with Luke (1:1–4) and John (20:30–31), the occasion of writing. Early and reputable witnesses, however, including Papias, Eusebius, Clement of Alexandria, and Origen, attest that the second Gospel derives from John Mark,

who, although not an apostle, was a faithful interpreter of Peter, whose testimony was the chief source of Mark's Gospel. This John Mark, the son of Mary in whose house the early church gathered in Jerusalem (Acts 12:12), was an assistant on Paul's first missionary journey. Although he quit the journey at Perga (Acts 12:25; 13:4, 13), the New Testament indicates he later traveled with Barnabas (Acts 15:37–41), was reconciled with Paul (Col. 4:10; Philem. 24; 2 Tim. 4:11), and finally joined Peter in Rome (1 Pet. 5:13). The aforementioned church fathers state that Mark composed the Gospel in service of Peter's preaching in Rome, although he took liberties with the chronological order of some events. The Gospel must have been composed sometime after AD 64, when Peter arrived in Rome, but probably before the fall of Jerusalem in AD 70, for chapter 13, which reflects some aspects of the First Jewish Revolt, does not seem to reflect the fall of Jerusalem.

If Mark composed the Gospel in Rome and for Roman Christians, then his primary audience was Roman Gentiles. This is corroborated by the fact that Mark seldom quotes from the Old Testament, explains Jewish customs unfamiliar to Gentiles (7:3–4; 12:18; 14:12; 15:42), translates Aramaic and Hebrew phrases by their Greek equivalents (3:17; 5:41; 7:11, 34; 10:46; 14:36; 15:22, 34), and incorporates a number of Latinisms.

An icon of Mark from a larger piece entitled *Christ and Twelve Apostles* (Antalya, Turkey, nineteenth century AD)

Style

The second Gospel communicates meaning *implicitly* rather than explicitly. Readers are not told what things mean; rather, readers must enter the drama of the narrative to experience its meaning. Mark writes in an unadorned though vivid style, maintaining a vigorous tempo throughout by linking sentences with "and," "again," and "immediately." Mark rarely intrudes into the plot of the narrative with his own editorial comment, and he does so only when necessary to establish the meaning of an otherwise obscure point (e.g., 3:30; 7:19). Unlike the other Gospels, and especially John, which rely on long didactic units of Jesus's teachings and dialogues, the second Gospel is action packed, portraying who Jesus is by what he *does*. Mark's modest vocabulary range

is augmented by several very effective literary techniques. As master of the unexpected, Mark employs irony and paradox throughout the Gospel in order to challenge false preconceptions of Jesus and the kingdom of God so that readers may experience "a new teaching . . . with authority" (1:27) and learn that new wine requires new wineskins (2:22). The second Gospel also achieves meaning by its artful arrangement of material. Mark often places stories side by side in order to let them comment on each other (e.g., 4:35–41 // 5:1–20), and Mark is unique among the Gospels in employing the "sandwich technique"—inserting a seemingly unrelated story into the middle of a story in order to make a *third* point by implication.

Major Themes

Jesus is the unrivaled subject of every section in the Gospel with the exception of two sections about John the Baptizer (1:4–8; 6:14–29), both of which foreshadow Jesus. The characteristic of Jesus that left the most lasting impression on his followers and caused the most offense to his opponents was his *authority*, which Jesus received at his baptism (1:9–11), to teach, heal, minister, and even suffer as God's Son. Several episodes—particularly Jesus's presumption to forgive sins (2:10), redefine Sabbath (2:27–28), and subjugate nature (4:35–41)—depict Jesus doing what only *God* can do. Divine Sonship is most supremely expressed, however, through the motif of the servant of the Lord who "give[s] his life as a ransom for many" (10:45). Mark refers to Jesus by numerous titles, including teacher, rabbi, Son of David, Christ/Messiah, Lord, Son of Man, and Son of God, the last of which is the key to Mark's presentation of Jesus. The Gospel begins with the announcement of Jesus as God's Son (1:1); he is recognized as such by demons (1:24; 3:11; 5:7), and at the baptism (1:11) and transfiguration (9:7) is declared God's Son by the Father. He is not knowable to humanity as God's Son, however, until his suffering on the cross—and there first by a Gentile Roman centurion (15:39).

The major themes that interface with Jesus's divine Sonship in Mark include discipleship, faith, insiders-outsiders, and the journey. Regarding discipleship, Mark repeatedly emphasizes that Jesus's followers must share Jesus's fate: as Jesus is with the Father, so disciples are to be with Jesus (3:13); and as Jesus serves in humility and suffering, so too must his disciples deny themselves and take up their cross and follow him (8:34). The most difficult lesson for disciples to learn is faith and trust in Jesus, which comes not by a magical formula but only by repeated *hearing* of Jesus and by participation in his mission. Those who should understand and follow often do not (Jesus's family, 3:31–35; Jesus's hometown, 6:1–6; religious leaders, 11:27–33), whereas a host of unlikely outsiders (lepers, 1:40–42; the unclean, 5:34; foreigners, 7:24–30; the blind, 10:52; the poor, 12:41–44; and the centurion in charge of Jesus's crucifixion, 15:39) confess and follow Jesus. An "insider" is not defined by moral perfection but by being in Jesus's presence and doing the will of the Father (3:34–35; 4:11). Above all, the response of faith and discipleship is exemplified by following Jesus "on the way" to his passion in Jerusalem (8:31; 9:31; 10:32–34, 52). The "way" or journey thus describes the way Jesus must go and the way the disciples must follow if both are to fulfill God's plan.

Commentary

1. Ministry in Galilee (1:1–8:26)

A. Preparation for ministry (1:1–13). The first verse of Mark summarizes the content of the Gospel and functions as its de facto title. The opening word, "Beginning," recalls the opening word of Genesis (so too the book of Hosea and Gospel of John), implying that in the gospel of Jesus Christ a *new* creation is at hand. "Beginning" should probably be understood not as the first of several things in a sequence but rather first in terms of "source" or "essence." Mark's Gospel thus intends to set forth the *essence* of God's redemptive work in Jesus Christ. The word "gospel" does not mean a book but rather the story of salvation in Jesus. The Greek word for "gospel" means "good news." Several verses in the Greek Old Testament use the term in this sense (1 Sam. 31:9; 2 Sam. 1:20; 1 Chron. 10:9), and even in the Greco-Roman world the birthday of Caesar Augustus (63 BC–AD 14) was hailed as "good news." For Mark, the advent of Jesus is "good news" because it fulfills God's release from sin and oppression and the proclamation of peace foretold by the prophet Isaiah (52:7; 61:1–3). The name Jesus in Hebrew (*Yehoshua*) means "God is salvation"; the name Christ—Greek for "Messiah" (Hebrew *mashiah*)—is not a personal name but a title meaning "God's anointed." The offices of prophets, priests, and kings were conferred in the Old Testament by anointing. With reference to Jesus, "Christ" refers to the eschatological fulfillment of the kingly office of King David (2 Samuel 7; Psalm 2). The final term in Mark's opening line is "Son of God." Although this title is absent in the important fourth-century manuscript Codex Sinaiticus and in quotations of the verse by several church fathers, the many manuscripts that include the term offer support that it was part of the original text. "Son of God" is the most important and most complete title for Jesus in the Gospel of Mark, signifying the full deity of Jesus the Messiah. Thus, in his opening line, Mark announces that the essence of the good news of God's redemptive intrusion in the world is not a doctrine, teaching, or law, but a *person*, Jesus of Nazareth.

Surprisingly, Mark begins a Gospel intended for Roman Gentiles with a quotation from the Old Testament (1:2–3). The introduction to the quotation, "It is written," designates the authority of God. The quotation is a collage of three Old Testament texts: verse 2 comes from Exodus 23:20 and Malachi 3:1; and verse 3 comes from Isaiah 40:3. The whole is attributed to Isaiah—who was considered the greatest of Old Testament prophets—evidently because the third verse is the defining element. In Exodus 23:20, 23, the "messenger" who would lead God's people is a divine messenger of Yahweh, but here it applies to John, thus indicating his divinely ordained purpose. The references to "ahead of *you*" (literally "before *your* face"), "who will prepare *your* way," and "prepare the way for the *Lord*" all refer to Yahweh in the Old Testament, but here they refer to Jesus, whom Mark depicts as fulfilling the role of God. Thus, Mark employs the quotation to indicate that John the Baptizer is the divinely appointed messenger of Yahweh who does not simply herald the advent of the Messiah but of God himself appearing in Jesus of Nazareth. Mark's commencement of his Gospel with this Old Testament quotation signals not only that the advent of Jesus stands in continuity with the work of God in Israel but also that the mission of Jesus is not understandable apart from the Old Testament. The gospel is thus not separate from God's work in Israel but a completion of it. Finally, the references to Jesus's ministry as a "way" or "path" suggest that the mission of Jesus leads

not to escape from the world but to a practical and transforming way within the world.

John the Baptizer is immediately introduced in verse 4, but John's person and work are more restricted in Mark than in the other Gospels. In 1:4–8, Mark limits John's appearance to the single purpose of prefiguring Jesus, the More Powerful One (1:7). The origins of John's rite of baptism for the remission of sins are obscure and much debated. Jews practiced ritual washings before worship or in the reception of proselytes. These, however, were self-washings and were practiced repeatedly, whereas John's baptism was a once-for-all lustration administered by a second party. John's baptism thus signified an action of God rather than a human act. Moreover, proselyte baptism signified engrafting into a faith community, whereas John's baptism signified moral and spiritual regeneration necessary to enter into a covenant relationship with God in preparation for the coming of the Messiah.

The Greek word for "repentance" means "change of one's thinking" and connotes a willful act rather than an emotional feeling. Repentance, which must result in "fruit" (Matt. 3:8; Luke 3:8), is the single prerequisite necessary to prepare for the imminent in-breaking of God. Mark specifies that the inhabitants of Judea and Jerusalem, both centers of Jewish leadership and authority, "went out" to John, similar to the way the Israelites "went out" to Moses in order to seek the Lord (Exod. 33:7). John's camel-hair garment and leather belt, as unusual in his day as they would be in ours, signified the dress of a prophet (Zech. 13:4), and specifically of Elijah (2 Kings 1:8). In the Old Testament, Elijah was more than the forerunner of the Messiah; he was the forerunner of the Day of the Lord, God's eschatological kingdom (Mal. 3:1; Sirach 48:10). The in-breaking of God's kingdom is signified in 1:7 by John's reference to Jesus as the More Powerful One. In first-century Judaism, loosing of sandals and washing of feet were duties of Gentile slaves; the assumption of this role by John signifies his humility and subordination in relation to

Jesus. John's baptism in water was intended to symbolize Jesus's baptism in the Holy Spirit (1:8). In the Old Testament, bestowal of the Spirit belonged exclusively to God. John's attributing of this function to Jesus, the More Powerful One, again signifies that Jesus comes in the power and prerogative of God.

According to the early church (Acts 1:21–22), the event that inaugurated Jesus's ministry and endowed it with saving significance was his baptism (1:9–11). It is with this event that Mark commences the story of Jesus, rather than with his birth (Matthew and Luke) or preexistence (John). Mark's wording ("Jesus . . . was baptized by John," 1:9) portrays Jesus as the undisputed subject of the event, with John serving as mediator. Arising from the water, Jesus experiences three things that Jews associated with the advent of God's eschatological kingdom:

1. The tearing apart of the sky: According to Second Temple Judaism, the Spirit of God had stopped speaking directly to God's people after the cessation of the great Old Testament prophets. At the advent of the Messiah, however, the long-awaited Spirit would return and reveal God in an unprecedented manner (Isa. 64:1; *Testament of Levi* 18:6–8; *Testament of Judah* 24:1–3). The Greek word for "tear" appears again in Mark only at the tearing of the temple curtain at the crucifixion, where Jesus is again recognized as the Son of God.
2. The descent of the Spirit: The eschatological age would be verified and empowered by the descent of God's Spirit; here the Spirit does not merely rest on Jesus but enters *into* him.
3. The voice from heaven: Jesus is declared to be God's beloved Son. Jesus is not *made* God's Son at this point, but rather, his divine Sonship is *acknowledged* and *declared* at the baptism. The divine declaration of verse 11 combines Suffering Servant imagery (see Isa. 42:1; 49:3),

royal Sonship imagery (Ps. 2:7; Exod. 4:22–23), and beloved filial imagery (Gen. 22:2, 12, 16).

The three heavenly signs designate the baptism as the inaugural event of Jesus's ministry, in which he is empowered by God's Spirit to speak and act not simply *for* God, but *as* God.

Jesus's forty-day trial in the wilderness (1:12–13) may reflect God's testing of Israel in the wilderness for forty years (Deut. 8:2). The wilderness plays an important role in the Old Testament not only in the wilderness wandering after the Exodus but also in the prophets, as a place of Israel's refreshment with God and refinement for obedience to his call. Immediately after the baptism, the Spirit literally "drives" (NIV "sent") Jesus out into the wilderness, like the scapegoat of Leviticus 16:21. The same Spirit that descended on Jesus at the baptism has an appointment for him with God's adversary to determine whether Jesus will use his divine Sonship for his own advantage or in obedience to God's saving purpose for the world.

B. Summary of Jesus's message (1:14–15). The commencement of Jesus's public ministry in Galilee is announced in connection with the arrest of John the Baptizer. The same Greek word (*paradidōmi*, "hand over") for John's arrest (NIV "put in prison") will later be used for the handing over of the Son of Man (9:31; 10:33) and of Christian disciples (13:9, 11–12). This signifies that Jesus will proclaim the gospel, as it was proclaimed by John, in the face of adversity and suffering. "Good news" is thus costly news. The long-awaited eschatological era and the kingdom of God are fulfilled in Jesus's person and ministry; God's kingdom is not something the pious evoke from God but is the reign that God introduces in Jesus, and into which people enter by repentance and faith. Repentance (the Greek word means to change one's thinking) and faith (the Greek connotes trust) are active responses to the kingdom of God as proclaimed by Jesus.

C. Galilean ministry (1:16–7:23). 1:16–45. The call of the first four disciples—Peter,

Andrew, James, and John—occurs on the northwest shore of the Sea of Galilee (1:16–20). The sea is a picturesque lake seven miles wide and thirteen miles long that is surrounded by hills and that lies seven hundred feet below sea level. Unlike other rabbis, who called students to learn torah, Jesus entered into the world of the disciples and called them to *himself*. What they need to know they will learn as they follow him. In order to become "fishers of men"—that is, to participate in the mission of spreading the kingdom of God—the fishermen must leave their nets and even families and follow Jesus. Each fisherman must respond personally to the call of Jesus, but in so doing he enters into a new fellowship of others who also hear and obey the summons of Christ.

The first act of Jesus's public ministry in Mark is an exorcism (1:21–28), in which the More Powerful One (1:7) exercises the divine authority he received at baptism to free a man from demon possession and to prevail over the dominion of Satan (see 3:27). Although Jesus was raised in Nazareth, he chose Capernaum, propitiously situated on the northwest shore of the Sea of Galilee on the Via Maris, the main trade route leading from the Mediterranean

to Damascus, as his base of operations. The population of Capernaum was largely (though not entirely) Jewish, and on the Sabbath Jesus teaches in the synagogue, the Jewish assembly hall for teaching torah. The authority with which Jesus teaches surpasses even that of the scribes, torah experts who enjoyed legendary reputations and special privileges among Jews. Rather than noting the specific content of Jesus's preaching, Mark stresses the unique *authority* with which Jesus taught and healed a man of demon possession. The plea of the demoniac, "What do you want with us?" occurs a dozen times in Scripture, normally indicating that the two parties have nothing in common with each other. As a member of the spiritual realm, the demon recognizes Jesus's divine nature as "the Holy One of God" (1:24). The story begins and ends with the amazement of the crowd at Jesus's *authority*, which supersedes that of the scribes and rescues a man from the grip of Satan. Jesus teaches and heals with one and the same authority, by which Mark signifies that Jesus's word is deed.

The Greek word for "immediately" (1:29; NIV "as soon as")—which occurs eleven times in Mark 1—contributes to the sense of urgency in Mark's narrative: the time is at hand (1:15) for the authority of God's Son to bear witness to the gospel. Close to the synagogue is Peter's house, where Jesus heals Peter's mother-in-law of a fever (1:30–31). The Greek word for "wait

The north shore of the Sea of Galilee with its characteristic coves. This was the region of much of Jesus's public ministry and where he called his first disciples (Mark 1:16–20).

on" (1:31) is *diakoneō*, from which "deacon" is derived. Mark's use of this word to describe Peter's mother-in-law serving the company following her healing may have been included to remind the members of the church in Rome to which he is writing to use the gifts, health, and opportunities God gives each believer to serve the Christian community in tangible ways. What Jesus has done to one person in healing Peter's mother-in-law he now does to the whole community (1:32–34). After sunset on Saturday, Sabbath prohibitions against work and travel ceased, and Capernaum shows up en masse with people suffering from a host of physical and demonic maladies.

Mark closes the day's activities in Capernaum with a reference to Jesus's forbidding the demons to speak (1:34). This unexpected command seems to contradict Jesus's mission to proclaim and promote the kingdom of God. At least three reasons can be given for the command to silence. First, rumors of Jesus's messianic status were not to Jesus's advantage—and could invite Roman reprisals—since the popular understanding of "messiah" carried military connotations. Second and more important, the command to silence seems to derive from Jesus's conscious patterning of his ministry after Isaiah's servant of the Lord, for whom *hiddenness*, ironically, was paramount in achieving God's purpose. Finally and of ultimate importance, Jesus cannot be truly and fully known until his redemptive suffering on the cross. Until that time, all proclamations of him—at least from imperfectly informed humans and demonic opponents—are premature and must be silenced.

Mark 1:35–39 describes Jesus's itinerant ministry among the small villages along the northwest quadrant of the Sea of Galilee. Mark normally prefers to describe Jesus's encounters with specific persons and places, but general summaries like verses 35–39 remind readers of the broad reach and expanse of his ministry. Jesus was more than a private teacher and healer: he was a public figure in Galilee. This is the first of three times in Mark when Jesus seeks solitude in order to pray (also 6:46; 14:32–39), each of which is set within a context of either implied or expressed opposition. Here Peter and other, unnamed disciples pursue Jesus and seek to control his movements. The effect, whether intended or not, would prevent Jesus from fulfilling his wider ministry. In 8:32–33 Peter will pose a greater hindrance to Jesus's ministry. Jesus resists the intrusion of the disciples by reasserting his mission: to proclaim the gospel among the Jewish synagogues and to confront demonic oppression.

Jesus is then approached by a man with leprosy (1:40–45). Leprosy, a widespread and dreaded skin disease in the ancient world, robbed a victim of dignity as well as health. Fear of its contagion required lepers to make themselves physically repulsive and to be quarantined from society (Leviticus 13–14; Mishnah *Nega'im*), thus depriving them of their occupations, homes, families, and worshiping communities. Leprosy was often regarded as a divine punishment and hence required not simply healing but divine cleansing (a word that occurs four times here). In desperation, this leper breaks the fifty-pace buffer zone (Luke 17:12) to reach Jesus. Jesus responds not by reviling him but by declaring his desire to cleanse him. In *touching* the leper, Jesus demonstrates the power of "divine contagion" to heal disease contagion. Jesus sternly commands the cleansed leper to remain silent and to present himself to a priest, whose function it was to render a certificate of healing, thus allowing the leper to resume normal life. The leper, however, "spreads the news," and as a consequence Jesus needs to remain "outside in lonely places." Jesus and the leper, in other words, have traded places!

2:1–3:6. In this section, Mark narrates five stories in which Jesus exercises his unique authority as the Son of God. In each story, Jesus supersedes the authority of the law and rabbinic custom, and in each he incurs the opposition of Jewish leaders, especially the Pharisees and scribes. These five encounters demonstrate that Jesus is not the captive of any social or religious party; rather, he offers a word of both judgment and redemption to them all.

The first story, in 2:1–12, begins ostensibly as a healing story of four men who bring a paralytic to Jesus. So many people gather to hear Jesus "preach the word to them" that there is no room inside or outside the house. Finding the door to the house blocked by the crowd, the resourceful foursome digs through the mud plaster and thatch roof common to Palestinian dwellings and lowers the litter with the paralytic down to Jesus. The determination of the four friends, like that of the leper in the preceding story, illustrates that genuine faith (mentioned here in 2:5 for the first time in Mark) overcomes obstacles to get to Jesus. Just as intercessory prayer is efficacious for others, so here the faith of the four porters plays a role in the forgiveness of the paralytic's sins. Mention of forgiveness of sins shifts the story abruptly from the paralytic to the scribes. Offended by Jesus's pronouncement of forgiveness, the scribes accuse Jesus of blasphemy, for only God can forgive sins (Exod. 34:6–7; Ps. 103:3; Isa. 43:25; Mic. 7:18). Desiring the onlookers to *know* that "the Son of Man has authority on earth to forgive sins" (2:10), Jesus provides evidence of forgiveness of sins (which cannot be verified) by healing the paralytic (which can be verified). As in 1:21–28, the authority of Jesus in both spiritual and physical realms is the same authority. In answer to the scribe's question, "Who can forgive sins but God alone?" Mark invites us to supply the name of Jesus.

In the Gospels, "Son of Man" occurs only from the mouth of Jesus as a self-designation. It occurs fourteen times in Mark, where, in agreement with its uses in the other Gospels, it refers (1) to Jesus's future exaltation as judge (8:38; 13:26; 14:62), (2) to Jesus's earthly authority (2:10, 28), and most frequently (3) to Jesus's sufferings (nine times in Mark). Each use of the title refers to a divine attribute (or the fulfillment of one). "Son of Man," therefore, does not refer to Jesus's humanity, as might be supposed, but rather to his humiliation, authority, and exaltation in fulfillment of God's ordained way.

In 2:13, as occurs often in the first half of the Gospel, Mark describes Jesus teaching beside the Sea of Galilee. The frequent references to crowds going *out* to him (1:32, 45; 2:13; 3:8; 4:1) may symbolize that discipleship entails leaving behind some of life's comforts and securities. "Teaching," which occurs some fifteen times in Mark, indicates the essential role that instruction plays in Jesus's ministry, and the large crowds that attend it indicate the public nature of the gospel.

The Roman tax system functioned, in part, by renegade Jews like Levi (2:14–17) receiving a franchise to collect taxes in set regions. Whatever amount a tax collector obtained in addition to the contracted sum with Rome was his to keep. The Roman system of taxation thus attracted unscrupulous individuals and virtually required dishonesty in order for a tax collector to survive economically. That Jesus would call as a disciple a tax collector, who was detested because of his collaboration with the Roman occupation and ritually unclean because of it, was no less offensive than his touching of a leper (1:40–45). This story repeats and reinforces the truth of 2:1–12: there he forgave *sins*; here he demonstrates forgiveness of *sinners* by eating with them. The scandal of Jesus's eating with tax collectors consists in the fact that he does not make moral repentance a precondition of his acceptance and love of sinners.

That Jesus's disciples do not follow the examples of the disciples of John the Baptizer and the disciples of the Pharisees, both of whom were considered morally and ritually exemplary, is a further cause of offense to his contemporaries (2:18–22). The Pharisees, a lay movement that came into existence during the Maccabean revolt (168–146 BC), staunchly resisted the accommodation of Jewish life to prevailing Greco-Roman ideals. Pharisees, who constituted perhaps only 1 percent of the Jewish population in Jesus's day, exercised an influence far beyond their numbers because of their uncompromising allegiance to the sovereignty of God, their belief in the resurrection of the dead and in the existence of angels and demons, and their scrupulous adherence to both the written torah and the oral traditions founded on it. Jesus stood in formal agreement with most of the foundational beliefs of Pharisaism, although he emphasized fulfilling the *intent* rather than simply the letter of the law. It is not surprising, therefore, that the Gospels record more exchanges of Jesus with the Pharisees than with any other school of first-century Judaism.

Although fasting was technically required of Jews only on the Day of Atonement (Lev. 16:29–30; Mishnah *Yoma* 8:1), Pharisees typically fasted on Mondays and Thursdays of every week (*Didache* 8:1; Babylonian Talmud *Ta'anit* 12a). The Pharisees understood true religion to consist of fasting (i.e., what is *not* done), whereas in this story Jesus understands it as feasting (i.e., what *is* done). Indeed, Jesus depicts himself as the groom at a wedding feast. This imagery again implies divine Sonship, for in the Old Testament God is often considered the bridegroom and husband of Israel (Isa. 5:1; 54:5–6; 62:4–5; Ezek. 16:6–8, Hos. 2:19). While the bridegroom is present, fasting should be suspended, although it may be resumed when the bridegroom is "taken from them." The root of Mark's Greek verb here is used in the Greek version of Isaiah 53:8 to describe the vicarious death of the Suffering Servant.

The significance of Jesus as the bridegroom is conveyed in two crisp metaphors or parables about a new patch that shrinks and tears an old garment (2:21), and new wine that bursts old wineskins (2:22). Jesus is like the new patch and new wine: he cannot be merely integrated or appended to existing structures, including Judaism, torah, and synagogue. Like new wine, Jesus requires new "wineskins" of transformed hearts and transformed communities, such as the church.

Of the two observances most characteristic of Judaism, circumcision and Sabbath, the latter is the more important and the subject of the fourth conflict narrative, in Mark 2:23–28. The Sabbath commandment forbids Jews (as well as their slaves and animals) from beginning any work that would extend over the Sabbath—from sunset Friday to sunset Saturday—or from doing any work on the Sabbath that was not absolutely necessary ("necessary" work referred to work that preserved life). Thus, a person could be rescued from the mouth of a wild animal or retrieved from under a fallen tree on the Sabbath, but a dislocated foot or hand could not be set on the Sabbath. The preeminence of the Sabbath is signaled by two factors: it is the longest of the Ten Commandments (Exodus 20; Deuteronomy 5), and it is rooted in the order of creation—as God created six days and rested on the seventh (Gen. 1:1–2:4), Jews were divinely mandated to rest on the Sabbath.

When Jesus and the disciples walk through a field and eat grain, the Pharisees accuse them of "doing what is unlawful on the Sabbath" (2:24). The putative infractions are either traveling (walking more than 1,999 paces was considered a journey) or harvesting, or both. In defense, Jesus appeals to the precedent of when David and his companions ate from the twelve loaves of altar bread intended for the priests (1 Sam. 21:1–6; cf. Exod. 40:23; Lev. 24:5–9). The appeal to David hints at Jesus's messianic status, for David was both Israel's greatest king and precursor of the Messiah (2 Sam. 7:11–14; Ps. 110:1). In 2:27 Jesus clarifies the relationship of human life to Sabbath. In contrast to the Pharisees, who make human life subservient to the Sabbath, Jesus declares that people are not made for Sabbath rules, but rather the Sabbath is intended to bless and enhance human life. Second and more important, Jesus grounds this teaching in his own authority as Son of Man. In declaring that "the Son of Man is Lord even of the Sabbath" (2:28), Jesus once again puts himself unambiguously in the place of God.

Each of the five conflict stories in 2:1–3:6 portrays Jesus's sovereign authority as superseding all other authorities—whether of society, of scribes and Pharisees, or even of the law—in order to introduce God's kingdom to needy, alienated, and sinful people. In this fifth and final conflict story (3:1–6), all eyes are trained on Jesus to see if he will heal on the Sabbath. A shriveled hand is not life threatening and does not qualify as an exception to Jewish Sabbath rules. Mark places this story immediately after 2:27–28 in order to demonstrate Jesus's revolutionary teaching of *doing*—not refraining from—God's work on the Sabbath. Before healing the man, Jesus asks two questions. The first question, about doing good or evil, refers to healing the man; but the second, about saving life or killing, cannot refer to the man, since a shriveled hand is not fatal. The second question refers, rather, to the intentions of the Jewish religious leaders with regard to *Jesus*. Grieved and indignant about their hardness of heart, Jesus commands the man to stretch forth his hand. Only in exposing his malady to Jesus is he healed. But Jesus is thereby jeopardized (see also 1:45), for "the Pharisees went out and began to plot with the Herodians how they might kill Jesus" (3:6). Thus, early in his ministry, the shadow of the cross falls on Jesus.

3:7–35. In another narrative summary (3:1–12; also 1:35–39), Mark notifies readers of the wide geographical extent and ethnic diversity of Jesus's ministry. The distance from Sidon in the north to Idumea in the south is roughly two hundred miles, and the regions of Jordan extend fifty miles east of Galilee. The audience comes from Jewish (Galilee, Judea, and Jerusalem), mixed Jewish-Gentile (Transjordan and Idumea), and Gentile regions (Tyre, Sidon). A boat is made ready for Jesus as a refuge from the size and press of the crowd. The accent falls on the demons who, as spiritual forces, become the second party in addition to God to recognize Jesus's divine Sonship. By their subjection, the demons demonstrate Jesus's sovereignty over them.

From his entourage Jesus chooses twelve men to follow him as formal apprentices or

THE GEOGRAPHICAL EXTENT OF JESUS'S MINISTRY

apostles (3:13–19). The number twelve, not a common number in Judaism, suggests that the twelve apostles reconstitute the twelve tribes of Israel. The Greek of 3:13 emphasizes the solemnity and symbolism of the event: Jesus issues the call from a mountain (mountains were sites of divine revelation in Israel) and summons the Twelve to himself. Jesus calls the Twelve first to be with him, then to verbal proclamation of the gospel, and finally to cast out demons—that is, to oppose evil and demonic forces. Apostleship thus entails the whole person—the relational, verbal, and behavioral. All lists of the apostles in the New Testament give preeminence to Peter, James, and John as an inner circle among the Twelve. As far as we know, none of the Twelve was a Jewish religious leader. Rather, all were representative of the common and diverse extremes (e.g., a tax collector and a Zealot) in first-century Judaism. The inclusion of the name of Judas, Jesus's betrayer, reminds readers that the original Twelve were not a perfect fellowship; indeed, the worst betrayer came from *within* the chosen rank of Jesus's apostles.

The narrative in 3:20–35 is the first of Mark's signature "sandwich" units, in which a seemingly unrelated story is shoehorned into the middle of another story. The middle story determines the meaning of the flanking halves and succeeds in making an entirely new point of the A^1-B-A^2 sequence. Mark begins (A^1, 3:20–21) and ends (A^2, 3:31–35) the narrative with Jesus in a house surrounded by family and followers, into which he inserts the B-story of Jesus and Beelzebul (3:22–30).

The story begins with a house so besieged by a crowd that Jesus and the disciples are "not even able to eat." Evidently believing that Jesus is on a collision course with the Jewish religious establishment, his friends and followers ("his own people," 3:21 NASB, NKJV) conclude that Jesus "is out of his mind" (3:21) and attempt to "take charge of him." Leaving this episode momentarily in abeyance, Mark inserts the accusation of the scribes that Jesus is in league with Satan (3:22). The Greek reference to "Beelzeboul" (NIV "Beelzebul") appears to equate Satan with the pagan god Baal, who was ubiquitously detested in Israel. The contemptuous epithet, apparently meaning "Baal the prince," or "Baal's dominion," insinuates that Jesus derives his power to cast out demons from the archdemon himself. Jesus responds with a threefold refutation. Verses 23–26 appeal to *logic*: since the ministry of Jesus is diametrically opposed to Satan, if what the scribes say is true, then Satan is clearly working against himself and hastening his own downfall. Verse 27 refutes the accusation in a terse but trenchant *parable*: Jesus is the More Powerful One (1:7), who plunders the "strong man's [Satan's] house" and makes his possessions (those oppressed by Satan) his own. Finally, in 3:28–29 Jesus issues a solemn *warning* against blaspheming the work of God's Holy Spirit. The key to understanding this controversial admonition is Mark's editorial insertion, "They were saying, 'He has an impure spirit'" (3:30). Anyone who can call the ministry of Jesus evil can no longer judge between good and evil, light and darkness. Such a sin is eternal because loss of ability to differentiate between good and evil entails also the loss of ability to repent of evil.

Mark concludes the "sandwich" in verses 31–35 by completing the episode of Jesus and his followers that he introduced in verses 20–21. The whole sandwich is devoted to the theme of insiders and outsiders. Jesus's mother and brothers stand outside seeking him (3:32); that is, they intend to assert a claim on him. Ironically, those who would be expected to be on the inside (his own family and the Jewish religious establishment represented in the scribes) misjudge Jesus and remain outsiders. For Mark, there are only two positions in relation to Jesus: those who stand on the outside with false assumptions, or those unnamed and unexpected disciples "seated in a circle around [Jesus] . . . [who do] God's will" (3:34–35), who are his true "brother and sister and mother" (3:35).

4:1–34. Chapter 4, on parables, and chapter 13, on eschatology, are the only two chapters in Mark devoted entirely to Jesus's teaching. The parable of the sower (4:1–20) is another A-B-A sandwich construction, in which Jesus's teaching on the mystery of the kingdom of God (4:10–12) divides the parable of the sower (4:1–9) and its explanation (4:13–20).

The parable discourse takes place in the now familiar context of Jesus's teaching alongside the northwest quadrant of the Sea of Galilee.

Jewish rabbis did not typically teach in parables, but parables were the preferred form of Jesus's public teaching; the first three Gospels, in fact, contain some sixty of his parables. The word "parable" means something placed alongside something else as a means of clarification. Jesus employs ordinary experiences from fishing, farming, family life, and so forth to illustrate various aspects of the kingdom of God. Parables are not allegories,

wherein each element of the story, like a mathematical equation, represents a specific reality. Jesus's parables, rather, usually have only a single main point, and like stained glass windows in a cathedral, they reveal their brilliance only when hearers enter "into" the narrative. The summons to "listen" or "hear" begins and ends the parable of the sower (4:3, 9), by which Jesus teaches that active involvement or *heeding* is the way to engage a parable. A sower scatters seed widely on unpromising terrain in hopes of a harvest. Three-quarters of the seed is lost to hardpan, rocks, thorns, and parched ground. Despite these adversities, some seed lands on good soil, and the parable ends, surprisingly, with an extraordinary harvest of "thirty, sixty, or even a hundred times" the number of seeds sown. The harvest is no mere human harvest, in fact, but a metaphor of the kingdom of God: despite the opposition of religious leaders, fickle crowds, and obstinate disciples, the harvest of Jesus's ministry will be extraordinary.

The rationale for speaking in parables in verses 10–12 constitutes the B-part of the sandwich. In a private setting, Jesus teaches that the gospel is presented differently to different audiences. To "insiders" Jesus proclaims the mystery of God's kingdom openly. "Mystery" means the truth of God that is available only as a revelation of God. On the one hand, insiders consist of the disciples and the others "around him" (the same Greek phrase is used in 3:34)—that is, those who are in fellowship with Jesus and who do God's will. "Outsiders," on the other hand, are taught in parables. Surprisingly, parables *hide* the meaning of the kingdom from outsiders rather than open it to them (4:12). The point of the explanation in verses 10–12 is that parables, like the kingdom of God inaugurated in Jesus himself, cannot be understood by those who hear casually or carelessly from the outside, but only by those

Sunset over the northwest shore of the Sea of Galilee, where much of the Galilean ministry of Jesus occurred who hear in faith and fellowship with Jesus and in obedience to God's will.

Verses 13–20 complete the sandwich by returning to the parable of the sower. So important is the parable of the sower, in fact, that it contains the key to understanding all parables (4:13). Its explanation focuses on false and correct ways of hearing and responding to the gospel, which is represented by the seed. The seed that is eaten by birds, or falls on rocky soil, or is choked by thorns represents false ways. In each of these instances, Mark indicates by the aorist tense of the Greek verb for "hear" (4:15–16, 18) that the gospel is given only a brief, superficial, even careless hearing. As a result, it is lost. The people who represent good soil, by contrast, attend to the gospel with earnest and ongoing engagement, which Mark signals by the present tense of the Greek verb for "hear." The mark of a true disciple, an insider, is to "hear the word and accept it and bear fruit" (4:20 ESV, NASB). Those who genuinely hear and receive the mystery of the kingdom of God will, by the grace of its generative power, produce a harvest beyond belief.

Mark includes three additional, shorter parables in the parable medley of chapter 4 (4:21–34); the first is about an oil lamp on a stand (4:21–25). The NIV makes the lamp the object of the verse, but the Greek makes it the subject; that is, "Does the lamp come in order to be placed under the bowl or bed?" In the Old Testament, a lamp can be a metaphor for God (2 Sam. 22:29) or the Messiah (2 Kings 8:19; Ps. 132:17). The unusual wording of verse 21 implies that Jesus is the lamp of God who has come to bring light and revelation (e.g., John 1:5; 8:12). True, the lamp may appear hidden or insignificant, in the same way that Jesus, the gospel, and the kingdom of God at first seem hidden or inconsequential (4:22). Nevertheless, God brings to light what is hidden, and he does so once again by the admonition to *hear*, to which Mark appeals three times in verses 23–24. Those who hear, like the "insiders" of 4:11, will receive the kingdom of God

in greater measure, and those who do not will lose it altogether (4:24–25).

The final two parables once again liken the kingdom of God to seeds, the first parable (4:26–29) focusing on the process of growth. Who but Jesus would liken the sublime kingdom of God to the mundane subject of slow-growing seeds? A farmer plants a seed and then goes about life as usual. The seed grows imperceptibly, and even the farmer "does not know how" (4:27). The seed possesses a power of generation independent of the farmer, who can be absent and even ignorant, yet the seed grows. Humanity, likewise, goes about business as usual, but the kingdom of God is present and growing, even if small and unobserved. The kingdom is not dependent on human activity; indeed, apart from sowing, the only human activity noted in this parable is waiting in confidence that, in God's time and power, the gospel will grow into a fruitful harvest.

The final parable stresses the contrast between the insignificant beginning and inconceivable end of a mustard seed (4:30–32). The Old Testament celebrated the mighty cedar as a symbol of God's power and splendor (Ps. 80:10; Zech. 11:2; Jer. 22:23). Jesus, however, likens the kingdom of God to a mustard seed, so small that it is practically invisible. From insignificance and obscurity, God's kingdom grows into a bush or tree that provides refuge for "the birds of the air" (NASB, RSV)—which may imply the inclusion of all the nations in God's coming kingdom.

Mark's concluding explanation of parables in verses 33–34 resembles verses 10–12 and resumes the theme of insiders-outsiders. Jesus spoke "many similar parables," of which the parables of chapter 4 are but a sampling. By parables, Jesus spoke "as much as they [outsiders] could understand" (4:33)—and understanding depends on *hearing*, which Mark includes for the tenth and final time in the chapter. But in private, Jesus, who is himself the living parable of God, "explained everything" to insiders, his disciples (4:34).

4:35–5:20. Mark now places two stories adjacent to one another, each interpreting the other. The first, in 4:35–41, describes a storm on the Sea of Galilee, the fury of which threatens to sink the boat in which Jesus and the disciples are sailing. The following story, in 5:1–20, describes a demon-possessed man who wreaks havoc on himself and on all who come into contact with him. Both stories display Jesus's power to rescue lives from cataclysms and from the chaos of both nature and human nature.

The first account is replete with details reminiscent of eyewitness experience and is recounted in a way that recalls the storms of Jonah 1 and Psalm 107:23–32. The Sea of Galilee lies some 700 feet below sea level, surrounded by steep hills on the west and even more forbidding mountains on the east. Less than 30 miles to the north, Mount Hermon rises to 9,200 feet above sea level, and the confluence of cold air from Mount Hermon and hot air rising from the Sea of Galilee not infrequently produces squalls of hurricane force. As Jesus and the disciples proceed eastward across the lake, their boat is seized by such a storm. Fearing their impending deaths, the disciples rouse Jesus from sleep in the stern and reproach him, "Teacher, don't you care if we drown?" (4:38). Jesus then "rebuked the wind and said to the waves, 'Quiet! Be still!'" (4:39). The Greek words for "rebuke," "quiet," and "be still" frequently occur in Hellenistic exorcism accounts. By describing the quelling

of the storm in the language of exorcism, Mark portrays Jesus as the Strong One (1:7; 3:37) who vanquishes Satan and evil forces. Indeed, Jesus is the manifestation of God who does what only God can do. At the word of Jesus, calm replaces chaos. Ironically, the disciples are more terrified by the power of Jesus than by the terror of the storm. "Who is this?" they ask. "Even the wind and the waves obey him." This is the question not only before the disciples but also before Mark's readers: will their experience of Jesus lead to faith (4:40) or to fear and doubt?

The calming of a natural storm is immediately followed with an account of the calming of a violent storm in human nature (5:1–20). The encounter takes places on the east side of the lake in the Decapolis, although the exact location is disputed in the Greek textual tradition. Decapolis (literally "Ten Cities") was a loose description for the Gentile region east of the Jordan River where the Hasmoneans and later the Romans established showcase cities of pagan culture and ideals that were intended to surpass Jewish settlements west of the Jordan. The wretchedness of the demoniac, who even in life is consigned to the place of the dead, is described in more graphic detail in Mark 5:2–5 than in either Matthew 8:28 or Luke 8:27. From a Jewish perspective, everything in 5:1–20 reeks of uncleanness: Jesus meets a man with an unclean spirit living among unclean tombs surrounded by unclean herds of swine, all in unclean Gentile Decapolis. A legion in the Roman army consisted of nearly six thousand soldiers; the

This first-century fishing vessel, discovered in 1986 along the Sea of Galilee, is an example of the fishing boats used by Jesus's disciples (Mark 4:35–41).

attribution of "Legion" to the demoniac may suggest that his demonic oppression rivals the force and domination of the Roman army in the Decapolis. The superhuman strength and explosive terror of the demoniac are no contest for the Son of God, however, whom the demoniac recognizes in Jesus, and to whom he pleads for clemency.

The demons acquiesce to Jesus's superior authority but beg not to be banished from the region. There is a measure of grace even in Jesus's judgment of Satan's minions, for he consents to their plea. Entering a herd of swine, the demons trigger a stampede down a cliff, causing some two thousand pigs to drown in the lake. The moral question posed by the undeserved loss of the livestock is not considered in the story. Evidently, for Jesus (and Mark) the rescue and restoration of one human being is more important than even a large-scale economic catastrophe. The exercise of Jesus's miraculous power restores the demoniac to his "right mind" (5:15), just as it restored the lake to order and calm in the previous story; but it also results in fear (5:15) among the inhabitants of the region, as it did earlier among the disciples. The miraculous exorcism does not lead those in the Decapolis to believe; rather, it leads them to expel Jesus (5:17). Jesus refuses the demoniac's request to follow him, perhaps because a Gentile would have been a stumbling block in Jesus's mission to Israel. Jesus, however, sends the man to announce "how much Jesus had done for him" (5:20), which is always the heart of human testimony to the divine. In so doing, the healed demoniac becomes the first missionary to the Gentiles.

5:21–43. This healing story is another example of Mark's sandwich technique, in which the story of the healing of Jairus's daughter (5:21–24, 35–43) is interrupted by that of the woman with a hemorrhage (5:25–34). Having crossed the lake, Jesus and the disciples disembark on the western (Jewish) shore. A synagogue ruler named Jairus emerges from the crowd and begs Jesus to heal his daughter, who is deathly ill. A synagogue ruler was the president or head of a local Jewish worshiping community. His duties included general oversight and maintenance of the building, procuring Scripture scrolls, arranging Sabbath services, and perhaps education of Jewish children. Worship services were officiated, however, by scribes, rabbis, and trained laypersons rather than by the synagogue ruler. In going with Jairus (5:24), Jesus fulfills his mission declared in 1:38, "This is why I have come."

While Mark's Gospel is the shortest of the four, his stories, although fewer in number, are usually recounted in fuller detail. This is particularly true of his portrayal of human need. Mark's account of the woman's futile attempts to receive medical help and her desperate effort to reach Jesus (5:26–27) are omitted in Matthew and Luke. The description of the woman's recovery—the Greek word translated "suffering" (5:29) combines both physical affliction and shame—conveys that the woman's prospects for health were no better than the little girl's prospects for life. As was the case with leprosy, a protracted menstruation problem left a woman unclean throughout its duration. Like the leper (1:40), the woman risks defiling Jesus with her uncleanness, in the desperate hope of being healed. She acts on what she hears and knows of Jesus. Although it was a serious violation of Jewish law for her to approach Jesus in her state, Mark portrays her act as a sign of faith. Immediately she is healed from her long-incurable disease. Like the man in 3:1–6, in bringing her infirmity to Jesus, she is healed. The woman's intent to touch Jesus is rivaled by Jesus's desire, despite the disciples' remonstrations, to know who touched him. Not content simply to dispatch a miracle, Jesus wants to encounter the woman. For Jesus, miracle must lead to meeting. Jesus's tender response, "Daughter, your faith has healed you" (5:34), overcomes the woman's fear of social ostracism. The Greek word for "heal," *sōzō*, means both "to heal" and "to save"—both senses are appropriate in this instance.

The drama now intensifies as the interruption, so profitable to the woman, has cost the life of Jairus's daughter. "Why bother the teacher anymore?" ask Jairus's servants (5:35). In the Greek, Mark's description of Jesus's response is masterful. The word *parakouō* (NIV "overhearing") can mean (1) to overhear something not intended for one's ears, (2) to ignore (see NIV note), or (3) to discount the truth of something. All three meanings apply to Jesus's response in verse 36. In direct address to Jairus, Jesus commands, "Don't be afraid; just believe." The present tense of "believe" means to *keep* believing, just as in the parable of the sower it meant to *keep* hearing (4:20). The word for "believe" in verse 36 is the same Greek root as the word for the woman's faith in verse 34. Jesus thus bids Jairus to demonstrate the same trust that the hemorrhaging woman demonstrated. Arriving at Jairus's house, Jesus allows only Peter, James, and John, his inner circle of disciples, and the girl's parents to accompany him into her room. Jesus's figurative reference to the girl's death as "sleeping" is met with scorn by the professional mourners. The command *talitha koum* is Aramaic, meaning, "Little girl [literally 'little lamb'], arise." Immediately, reports Mark, the girl arises, to the amazement of all present. What does Mark achieve by sandwiching the story of the hemorrhaging woman into the story of Jairus and his daughter? Mark wants to show that Jairus, a man of reputation and respect, must learn the meaning of faith from an unnamed woman whose only identification is her shame. If Jairus can trust Jesus as the woman trusted Jesus, he need not fear. Faith means trusting in Jesus when all human hopes have been exhausted.

6:1–30. The itinerant ministry of Jesus and his disciples in Galilee includes a visit to Jesus's hometown of Nazareth, some twenty-five miles to the southwest of Capernaum (6:1–6a). Nazareth lacked both distinction and importance. It is not mentioned in the Old Testament or in Josephus or rabbinic literature; even in Christian literature it is not mentioned until two hundred years after Jesus's day. According to archaeological evidence, first-century Nazareth was an obscure hamlet of earthen dwellings cut into sixty acres of rocky hillside, with a population of no more than five hundred peasants. The reference to Jesus as a "carpenter" (6:3) is not overtly demeaning, for the majority of the people in Nazareth practiced occupations in the same social category. "Mary's son" (6:3), however, is disrespectful, at the least, and may even insinuate illegitimacy, for in Judaism a son was regularly identified in relation to his father, even if deceased. "Mary's son" can scarcely be allusion to the virgin birth (otherwise unmentioned in Mark), since the expression is disparaging rather than honoring. According to Jewish custom, Jesus's sisters are unnamed and unnumbered probably because they have married into other family units. Of Jesus's four named brothers, only James and Jude are mentioned again in the New Testament. Catholic and Orthodox traditions teach that Mary remained "ever virgin" and that Jesus's siblings were half brothers and sisters. The plain sense of verse 3, and of the New Testament in general, however, is that Jesus was the eldest sibling of five brothers and at least two sisters. Surprisingly, Jesus is not a celebrity in Nazareth as he is elsewhere in Galilee, but a "stumbling block" (6:3; NIV "offense"). This repeats Mark's insider-outsider motif: those we should expect to believe in Jesus do not, and those we should not expect to believe in him do. The return to Nazareth ends with Jesus "amazed at their lack of belief" (6:6). The greatest hindrance to faith is not sinfulness but hardness of heart.

Mark now develops the theme of discipleship by means of another sandwich unit (6:6b–30), in which the mission of the Twelve (6:6b–13, 30) is divided by the poignant account of the martyrdom of John the Baptizer (6:14–29). The Greek word for "witness" is *martyreō*, from which the English word "martyr" is derived. By sandwiching the death of John between the sending and return of the Twelve, Mark signifies that those who heed Jesus's summons to mission must be prepared for the ultimate witness of martyrdom.

Jesus "calls" and "sends" the disciples into mission in verse 7 with the same authority by which he himself ministers, and with which he commissioned them as apostles in 3:13–14. The sending into mission of disciples whose trust and understanding of Jesus is flawed (1:36–39; 3:21; 4:38; 5:31) is a reminder that service to Christ is rendered not by merit or perfection but by dependence on him. Mention that Jesus "gave them authority over impure spirits" (6:7) confirms that Jesus's disciples, like their master himself, are sent into the world to confront evil. The mission of the Twelve is not their own but is an extension of *Jesus's* ministry. The sending of the disciples with only staff, sandals, belt, and tunic (6:8–9) recalls the sending out of the Israelites from Egypt at the exodus (Exod. 12:11). Disciples are sent not in plenty but in *need*, thus ensuring both their dependence on their Lord and their receptivity to others. If disciples go with an elaborate support apparatus, then they need not go in faith; and if they do not go in faith, their proclamation is not believable. The command to remain where they are received (6:10) teaches that trust in the Jesus who sends them into mission includes trust in those whom he has designated to meet their needs. The command to shake the dust off their feet when they are not received (6:11) is tantamount to declaring a Jewish village *heathen*, since Jews were required to shake themselves free of dust when returning from Gentile regions, lest they pollute the Holy Land. The missionary outreach of the Twelve, like the ministry of Jesus, consists of the proclamation of repentance, exorcisms, and healings (6:12–13).

Before Mark reports the return of the Twelve in verse 30, he inserts the account of the martyrdom of John the Baptizer. There are only two stories in the Gospel of Mark that are neither from nor about Jesus. Both, however, are about John, and both foreshadow Jesus. The first, in 1:2–8, foreshadows Jesus's ministry, and the second, here in 6:14–29, foreshadows his death. Mark reported John's imprisonment in 1:14, and now in a flashback he recounts his death. Jesus's fame reaches King Herod, who fears that he is a reincarnation of John the Baptizer, whom he beheaded (6:14–16). "King Herod" was Herod Antipas, the son of Herod the Great, ruler of Galilee and Perea from 4 BC until AD 39. Herodias, the wife of Antipas's half brother Herod Philip (not the tetrarch Philip of Luke 3:1), was actually the granddaughter of Herod the Great and thus a niece of Antipas. The opinion of Antipas that Jesus is Elijah or the Baptizer returned to life or one of the ancient prophets (6:15) is widespread and is later voiced by Jesus's own disciples (8:28). Josephus, who also recounts the death of the Baptizer at the hands of Antipas (*Jewish Antiquities* 18.116–19), also attributes John's arrest to Antipas's fears of John's influence on the people, though Mark includes the additional reason of John's denunciation of the treacherous marriage between Antipas and Herodias (6:18).

A tentative ruler whose actions were determined by the influences of others, Herod Antipas cannot risk allowing John to remain at large, nor can he bring himself to eliminate him. Herodias, cunning and calculating, emerges as the prime mover in the story by exploiting Antipas's impotence and by sacrificing the honor of her daughter in order to eliminate the Baptizer. The daughter, whom Josephus identifies as Salome, inflames the celebrities, officials, and leaders of Galilee with an explicit dance at Antipas's birthday banquet. Desiring to impress his glittering guests, Antipas promises the girl "up to half my kingdom" (6:23) for her performance—a promise that Rome would not possibly allow. At the order of Herodias, the girl requests the head of John. Mark does not record whether John is executed at Antipas's palace at Machaerus, east of the Dead Sea (as reported by Josephus), or in Sepphoris, the capital of Galilee. John—who is not granted a word in the story—meets his end by a cold sword wielded by petty functionaries at the command of a treacherous ruler who seeks to please the crowd. By appending the return of the Twelve to the death of John in 6:30, Mark signals that, in following Jesus, one must reckon with the fate of John, as Jesus will teach in 8:34: "If anyone would come after me, he must deny himself and take up his cross and follow me."

6:31–56. Following Herod's sadistic banquet, Mark reports on a banquet of Jesus (6:31–44). The banquet of Herod was in a palace; Jesus's is in the open. Herod invited important people; Jesus receives all people. Herod bolstered his own reputation; Jesus ministers to peoples' hunger and needs. So memorable is Jesus's banquet that it is the only miracle recorded in all four Gospels.

After the return of the Twelve, and in fulfillment of the first prerequisite of apostleship (3:14), Jesus summons the Twelve away from the pursuit of the crowd to be with him in rest and solitude. The crowd anticipates their retreat, however, and precedes them to the destination. Despite the invasiveness of the crowd, Jesus looks on it with compassion and, according to custom, teaches the people. Given the remoteness of the region, lateness of the hour, and size of the crowd, the disciples recommend dismissing the crowd to the surrounding villages for provisions. Rather than accepting this reasonable solution, Jesus intensifies the impending crisis by ordering, "You give them something to eat" (6:37). The disciples look beyond themselves to solve the problem, whereas Jesus looks among them for the solution. "How many loaves do you have?" he asks (6:38). Despite the obvious inadequacy of this amount, Jesus orders the crowd to sit in groups of hundreds and fifties, perhaps in imitation of Moses's similar command to the Israelites in the wilderness (Exod. 18:25; Num. 31:14). The prayer with which Jesus receives and multiplies the bread and fish is similar to his prayer over the bread and wine at the institution of the Lord's Supper (14:22). In utilizing the Twelve to dispense the bread, Jesus ministers to the crowd *through* the disciples. Like the harvest in the parable of the sower (4:9, 20), the feeding of the five thousand results in a miracle of abundance: "All ate and were satisfied" (6:42), with twelve basketfuls remaining (6:43).

A mosaic of loaves and fishes, recalling the feeding of the five thousand (Mark 6:34–44), from the floor of a Byzantine church excavated on the north shore of the Sea of Galilee, near Capernaum

The feeding miracle takes place within sight of Gamala in Galilee, where the Zealot movement originated. The "many people [who] were coming and going" (6:31) in the region, and the reference to "sheep without a shepherd" (6:34), which in the Old Testament is normally a military image (Num. 27:17; 1 Kings 22:17; Ezek. 34:5; see also Judith 11:19), betray a revolutionary fervor among the wilderness crowd and the hope that Jesus might be a military Messiah against Rome. This is further supported by the reference to five thousand *men* (6:44; the Greek *andres* specifies men alone; see Matt. 14:21), and above all by John 6:15, which explicitly states that the people "intended to come and make [Jesus] king by force." Jesus, however, refuses the populist and militant sentiments of the crowd, and like Moses, who supplied the Israelites with manna in the wilderness, feeds the crowd with the multiplication of bread and fish as a foreshadowing of the eschatological banquet of God.

Two statements in 6:45–52 bear further witness to the potential of a messianic uprising during the wilderness banquet. Jesus quickly compels the disciples to sail to Bethsaida (the northeast shore of the lake, 6:45), ostensibly to prevent them from becoming swept up in the crowd's messianic fervor. He then repairs to the hills to pray (6:46). This is the second of three instances in Mark where Jesus prays (1:35; 6:45; 14:35–39). Each prayer is set at night in a lonely place, each finds the disciples removed from him and misunderstanding his mission, and in each Jesus faces a crisis. In this instance, the crisis may be the temptation to assume the populist messianic ideal.

From the hills, Jesus spies the disciples alone in the storm-tossed boat at night, "straining at the oars" (6:48). The Greek word implies "torment" and "distress," conditions that befall the disciples whenever they are separated from Jesus. During the fourth watch of the night (3:00–6:00 a.m.), Jesus walks to the disciples on the water. The Greek cannot mean to walk "beside" the water, or anything other than walking on the open water. Readers are assured it is not an optical illusion, for the disciples "all saw him" (6:50). The baffling reference to "passing by them" (6:48) appears to signal a self-revelation of God, recalling God "passing by" on the water (Job 9:8; NIV "treads on the waves of the sea"), or "passing by" Moses (Exod. 33:22) and Elijah (1 Kings 19:11) on Mount Sinai. As in the forgiveness of sins (2:10) and power over nature (4:39), in walking on the water Jesus does what only God can do. "It is I" (6:50) is identical with God's self-disclosure to Moses in Exodus 3:14, and may further evince Jesus's divinity. As in earlier calming of storms in nature (4:41) and in human nature (5:15), the revelation of Jesus's person and exhibition of his power causes fear, misunderstanding, and even hardness of heart in the disciples (6:49–50, 52). Mark reminds readers, however, that following Jesus is not measured by perfect or complete understanding, but by *being in the boat with him.*

Chapter 6 concludes with a summary report (6:53–56; see also 1:35–39; 3:7–12) of Jesus's healing throngs of needy people on the west side of the lake. "Gennesaret," the only proper noun in the account, refers to a densely populated region between Capernaum and Tiberias. In a flurry of commotion, nameless and faceless people who are identified only by their need and desperation swarm to Jesus from town and countryside simply to "touch even the edge of his cloak" (6:56). The account concludes with the assurance of Jesus's untiring goodness, for "all who touched it were healed" (6:56). The accent in the account remains on the blessings of Jesus's physical touch, however, for there is no mention of faith, discipleship, or understanding of Jesus's saving purpose.

7:1–23. Jesus's confrontation with the Pharisees and scribes over the question of uncleanness marks the end of his ministry in Galilee, which began in 1:14. Henceforth in Mark, Jesus will reappear in Galilee only intermittently, in 8:11 and 9:33. The Pharisees and scribes, last seen in chapter 3, come from Jerusalem, which throughout Mark is seen as the primary center of opposition to Jesus. The issue of ritual purity was the dominant trait of Pharisaism, and not surprisingly it is the issue at stake in 7:1–23, the longest conflict discourse in Mark. In accusing Jesus and the disciples of eating with unclean hands, the Pharisees are not primarily concerned with hygiene but with ritual and ceremonial observances instituted to maintain Jewish distinctiveness over against Gentile culture. The explanation of the observances in 7:2–4, which would be wholly unnecessary if Mark were writing for Jews, is one of many indications of a Gentile audience, and probably Roman Gentiles.

Quoting Isaiah 29:13 in Mark 7:6–7, Jesus accuses the Pharisees and scribes of cloaking evil intentions with pleasing words. The charge of "hypocrite" (7:6) implies the same, for "hypocrite," which is the Greek word for a theater performer, designated an actor who wore various masks to impersonate different roles. The "tradition of the elders" (7:3–4) refers to the unwritten oral tradition that would later be codified in the Mishnah (ca. AD 200). In contrast to Sadducees, Pharisees believed that the oral tradition was equally authoritative with the written torah. Pharisees affirmed that the written laws of torah declared *what* God required but that the oral tradition was necessary to determine *how* to fulfill God's requirements. Unfortunately, the focus on the *how* shifted attention away from the original intent of the law and onto an array of peripheral observances. Jesus expressly declares that the "tradition of the elders" does not clarify torah or assist in its fulfillment but actually skews its meaning, resulting in "nullifying" the commandments of God and replacing them with mere human traditions (7:8–9, 13). The instance of "Corban" (a Hebrew word meaning "offering") in verses 11–13 is a case in point. The fifth commandment requires honor of father and mother (7:10; Exod. 20:12), but the ritual of Corban allowed Israelites to take money that would otherwise be used for support of parents and dedicate it to God by investing it in the temple. Similar to deferred giving today, Corban allowed people to retain possession over their property, proceeds, or interest during their own lifetime, after which the money became temple property. The result was the evading of an explicit commandment—thereby the defrauding of one's parents—in the name of a higher obligation to God. Corban—and the many practices like it (7:13)—was a glaring distortion of the law, which actually *prevented* a person from fulfilling the law.

Summoning the crowds, Jesus commands them to *hear*, for hearing, as Jesus taught in the parable discourses of chapter 4, leads to understanding (7:14). "Nothing outside a person can defile them by going into them. Rather, it is what comes out of a person that defiles them" (7:15). Uncleanness, in other words, is not essentially related to external matters—foods, objects, customs, regulations, rituals, and rites—but to the inner intentions of heart and mind. The latter defile a person, and it was on account of them, rather than external observances, that torah was instituted. The importance of this teaching is reinforced by private instruction in a "house" (7:17), where, removed from the interference and influence of the crowd, the disciples commonly received revelation from Jesus. Not for the first or last time, the disciples are "dull" (7:18) and uncomprehending. Jesus illustrates the point by food, which does not come from within but from without, and simply passes through the body (7:18–19). Mark adds his own parenthetical remark at the end of verse 19, assuring readers that Jesus therefore "declared all foods clean." Christians, in other words, are free from kosher. What they are not free from—and this is the ultimate point of the discourse in 7:1–23—is the real source and nature of "uncleanness." "What comes out of a person is what defiles them" (7:20). From the "heart"—the depth and center of human personality—come forth "evil thoughts . . . sexual immorality, theft, murder, adultery, greed, malice, deceit, lewdness, envy, slander, arrogance and folly" (7:21–22). None of these behaviors and attitudes is the result of an external cause that can be regulated by the oral tradition. Rather, "these evils come from inside" (7:23). "Uncleanness" is not a property of objects or observances but of inner attitudes, a condition of the heart. Goodness—or evil—originates within the *will* of humanity, and the law was given by God to change the will, the *intent*, of the heart.

D. Jesus travels to Gentile regions (7:24–8:9). The story of a Gentile who was a "true Israelite" (7:24–30) is the first of three stories in Mark 7:24–8:9 in which Jesus extends his ministry to Gentile regions. Tyre lay thirty miles northwest of the Sea of Galilee along the Mediterranean and epitomized a long history of antagonism to Israel. The home of the infamous Jezebel of 1 Kings (16:31–32), as well as a staging ground for attacks on Israel during the Maccabean revolt (1 Maccabees 5:14–15), Tyre, in the words of the Jewish historian Josephus, was "a notoriously bitter enemy" of Israel (*Against Apion* 1.13). Mark does not specify why Jesus goes to Tyre, although he says that Jesus hopes to evade detection (7:24). It is not difficult to imagine that Jesus quit Galilee to escape the intrigues of the Pharisees (3:6; 7:1–23) and the ire of Herod Antipas, ruler of Galilee who killed John the Baptizer (6:14–30). A Gentile woman who belongs to the infamous pagans of Syria Phoenicia seeks out Jesus, begging him to relieve her daughter of a demon (7:26). No one with such notorious credentials surely ever presumed to approach an adherent to the "tradition of the elders." "First let the children eat all they want,' [Jesus] told her, 'for it is not right to take the children's bread and toss it to the dogs'" (7:27). Although Jews often spoke of Gentiles as "dogs," Jesus did not normally regard people in such stereotypes. His reference seems unnecessarily offensive—unless the woman presumed that in coming to Tyre Jesus was forsaking his ministry to Israel in favor of a mission solely to the Gentiles. If she presumed this—and it is difficult to account for Jesus's reference to her as a "dog" if she did not—Jesus may have employed this blunt stereotype to remind her

that Jews, despite their opposition, retained priority in his mission. This interpretation is supported by Mark 1:2–3, which affirms that the gospel comes from Israel, and that Gentiles participate in the gospel only insofar as they are engrafted into salvation history in Israel (see Rom. 11:11–32). In his response to the Syrophoenician woman, Jesus reminds her that there is no place for Gentile pride or arrogance over disobedient Israel (see Rom. 11:18–21). The woman's reply in verse 28 shows her understanding and acceptance of Israel's privilege. Indeed, this Gentile woman understands Jesus's mission better than most Jews, including his own disciples. Like Jacob, who "struggled with God and with humans" and prevailed (Gen. 32:28), this woman "took Christ at his own words," said Luther; "he then treated her not as a dog but as a child of Israel" (Bainton, 362).

A second story further expands the ministry of Jesus to the Gentiles (7:31–37). From Tyre, Jesus travels twenty miles north to Sidon, then southeast to the Gentile Decapolis east of the Sea of Galilee, following a horseshoe circuit of one hundred rugged miles. In the Decapolis a man "who was deaf and could hardly talk" (7:32) is brought to Jesus for healing. The description of the man's speech and hearing defects is a single word in Greek, a word that occurs only once elsewhere in the Greek Bible, in Isaiah 35:6. Use of this rare term indicates that Mark intends for readers to see the healing of verses 31–37 as a fulfillment of Isaiah 35, in which the glory of the Lord anoints the desert wastelands of Lebanon with joy. The regions of Tyre and Sidon are precisely the Lebanon of Isaiah 35, thus indicating that the eschatological redeemer of Zion promised to the Gentiles in Isaiah 35 is none other than Jesus. The removal of the man from the crowd may be Jesus's way of indicating his personal importance to him. Spittle, like other body excretions, normally fell under the category of defilements in Judaism, but in holy persons spittle was often considered a healing agent. The "tradition of the elders" (7:1–23) forbade Jews from contacting unclean objects or persons, but in his intimate contact with this man by touch and spittle, Jesus demonstrates his embrace of Gentiles. The empathy of Jesus's prayer in 7:34 and the concrete description of the healing in Greek ("the fetter of his tongue was broken" [NIV "his tongue was loosened," 7:35]) suggest release from demonic bondage as well as physical healing. The command to silence in verse 36—the only such command to Gentiles in Mark—indicates that, for all their differences, Jews and Gentiles were both equally prone to disobey Jesus. The concluding chorus in 7:37, "He has done everything well," may recall Genesis 1:31, reminding readers that the Son's work in redemption, like the Father's in creation, is *good*.

This section closes with a third story about Jesus's ministry to the Gentiles, the feeding of the four thousand (8:1–9). On the Gentile, east side of the Sea of Galilee—perhaps in the vicinity of the healing of the demoniac (5:1–20)—Jesus attracts a large crowd that remains with him for three days. The Greek word describing the presence of the crowd (8:2) connotes its special attachment to Jesus; ironically, Gentiles receive Jesus with a devotion that Jews do not. The "compassion" (8:2) Jesus feels for the persevering crowd is (according to the Greek word used) deep and powerful. Jesus does not want to dismiss the vulnerable multitude in the desolate region, and the disciples, sensing an impending crisis, ask where bread could be found for such a crowd in such a place (8:4). It may seem odd that the disciples, having witnessed the earlier feeding of the five thousand, would ask such a question. It should be remembered, however, that it is not unusual for even mature believers (and the disciples are not yet mature) to doubt the power of God after having experienced it. It is possible (though not certain) that Mark regards the seven loaves of bread produced as a symbol of the seven Gentile nations of the Old Testament (e.g., Deut. 7:1); but if so, the Gentile nations are not displaced or destroyed, but *fed* by Jesus. Although the feeding of the four thousand is similar to the feeding of the

five thousand in 6:31–44, and is sometimes thought to be a doublet of it, the second feeding differs specifically in the size of the crowd (four thousand *people* in 8:9 rather than five thousand *men* in 6:44), in the Greek words for "basketfuls" (8:8 and 6:43), and especially in the prominence of Jesus, who in the four thousand speaks in the first person, displays deeper compassion, perceives the impending crisis, and personally seats and attends to the crowd. Clearly, the feeding of the four thousand shows Jesus's compassion for Gentiles in the wilderness, as the feeding of the five thousand shows his compassion for Jews in the wilderness.

E. Opposition from Pharisees and disciples (8:10–26). Following the feeding of the four thousand, Jesus and the disciples cross to the west side of the Sea of Galilee, landing at Dalmanutha (8:10). This is the lone reference in all ancient literature to Dalmanutha, the location of which is uncertain. The implication of the story, however, is that it was either near to or identical with Magadan (Matt. 15:39), about three miles north of Tiberias. At Dalmanutha the Pharisees ask Jesus "for a sign from heaven" (8:11)—that is, for an outward and compelling proof of his authority. Several words in verses 11–12 ("dispute" [NIV "question"], "seek to control" [NIV "asked"], "attempt to discredit" [NIV "test"], and "sighed in exasperation" [NIV "sighed deeply"]) indicate the antagonism of the Pharisees. For Mark, the demand for a sign is an undisguised indication of unbelief. Jesus solemnly declares that unbelief will not be honored by a sign; he will not grant by empirical means what can be granted only by faith and trust. Jesus resolutely "left them, got back into the boat and crossed to the other side" (8:13).

The lack of understanding that Jesus encountered in Dalmanutha now accompanies him in the boat (8:14–21). Jesus warns the disciples, who have only one loaf of bread with them on the voyage, to "watch out for the yeast of the Pharisees and that of Herod" (8:15). "Yeast" is a leaven that ferments in dough, causing it to rise. In Jesus's warning, the "yeast" appears to signify the disbelief of the Pharisees and Herod fermenting among the disciples. The disciples, however, uncomprehending of Jesus's metaphor, remain fixed on "bread." In an attempt to overcome the disciples' obtuseness, Jesus presses them with seven rhetorical questions: Do you still not see? Do you still not understand? Are your hearts hardened? Can you not see? Can you not hear? Do you not remember? Do you still not understand? (8:17–21). Have the lessons of both miraculous feedings been lost on the disciples? asks Jesus. The conversation about bread in the boat marks a low point in the disciples' understanding of Jesus and his ministry.

Mark is fond of juxtaposing two stories in order to demonstrate an interrelationship between them (e.g., 4:35–41 // 5:1–20). The placement of the healing of a blind man in Bethsaida (8:22–26) immediately following the conversation about bread in the boat (8:14–21) is another example of such a juxtaposition. In Bethsaida, on the east side of the mouth of the Jordan River at the north end of the Sea of Galilee, a blind man is brought to Jesus (8:22). As with the healing of the deaf-mute in the Decapolis (7:31–37), Jesus conducts the man outside the village (to separate him from its unbelief [6:45]?), applies spittle to his eyes, and places his hands on him. Both acts enhance the personal nature of the encounter. Jesus then asks, "Do you see anything?" (8:23). His question echoes the pleading question to the disciples in the previous story, "Do you still not see?" (8:17). There are, moreover, seven references to "seeing" in the original Greek in verses 23–25, just as there were seven references to lack of understanding in the previous story. The healing of the blind man of Bethsaida is the only miracle in the Gospels that proceeds in stages (which is probably why Matthew and Luke omit it). Mark's inclusion of the story immediately following the failure of the disciples to understand signifies that faith is a process. Like the blind man, the disciples, who "have eyes but fail to see" (8:18), can also be made to see and understand, but not on their own. The ability to see, both physically and spiritually, is

a gift of God, made possible by the repeated touch of Jesus.

2. Journey to Jerusalem (8:27–16:20)

A. Peter's confession at Caesarea Philippi and the transfiguration (8:27–9:29). 8:27–9:1.

The Caesarea Philippi declaration is like a continental divide in the Gospel of Mark. Prior to Caesarea Philippi, Jesus randomly and repeatedly crisscrosses the Sea of Galilee; thereafter he sets his face to Jerusalem. In the first half of the Gospel, Jesus teaches the masses in Galilee, casts out demons, and forbids people from announcing his identity; thereafter he primarily instructs the disciples, with no further exorcisms (apart from 9:29) or commands to silence. The first half of the Gospel takes Jesus outside Israel to Tyre, Sidon, and the Decapolis; the second half takes him to its heart in Jerusalem. Both halves conclude with christological confessions, the first with a Jewish confession of Peter that Jesus is the Messiah (8:29), the second with a confession of the Gentile centurion that Jesus is the Son of God (15:39).

From Bethsaida, Jesus sets out with the disciples to Caesarea Philippi, twenty-five miles to the north at the foot of Mount Hermon. Founded by Herod Philip in honor of Caesar Augustus, "Philip's Caesarea" lay at the northernmost edge of his tetrarchy, at the source of the Jordan River and at the famous sanctuary of Pan, the pagan god of flocks and nature. "On the way" the party passed beneath the distinct camelback promontory of Gamala, where the Zealot movement was founded in AD 6 and where militant messianic fervor ran high. In Caesarea Philippi, a region rife with competing religious claims, Jesus for the first time solicits a claim about his identity. "Who do people say I am?" he asks the disciples (8:27). The disciples repeat the popular opinion earlier voiced by Antipas (6:14–15) that Jesus is John the Baptist, Elijah, or one of the prophets. Elijah, in particular, was reputed to have been taken bodily into heaven without dying (2 Kings 2:11), whence he would come as a herald of the great and terrible day of the Lord (Mal.

3:1; 4:5–6). Great as these figures were, they are inadequate analogies, for they imply that Jesus is merely a reappearance of something that happened before. Identifying Jesus with preexistent categories is like pouring "new wine into old wineskins" (Mark 2:22). Not content with the opinions of others, Jesus presses the disciples for a personal confession: "Who do *you* say I am?" (8:29). He has not rushed this moment; enough time has elapsed for the disciples to make a judgment based on personal experience. The answer cannot be supplied by collecting more data or evidence or by further discussion; it can be reached only by a decision of personal *faith*. Peter insightfully and courageously declares, "You are the Messiah" (8:29). The Greek word for Christ (*christos*) translates the Hebrew word for messiah (*mashiah*), which means "anointed one." In the Old Testament, "messiah" is an infrequent epithet of one who could come as a future eschatological king according to the

The Banias (or Paneas) Waterfall, near Caesarea Philippi. In this region, Peter confessed Jesus to be the Messiah (Mark 8:27–29).

model of the Davidic monarchy (2 Samuel 7; Psalm 2) to establish God's reign on earth. After the Maccabean revolt, however, and especially after the onset of the Roman occupation of Palestine in the early first century BC, the concept of messiah increasingly assumed military expectations. Indeed, in AD 132–35, the Jewish guerrilla warrior Bar Kokhba openly proclaimed himself messiah in his unsuccessful attempt to overthrow the Roman occupation of Palestine.

In declaring Jesus "Messiah," Peter supplies the right answer, but he has the wrong understanding. Rejecting Peter's militant messianic understanding, Jesus "began to teach them that the Son of Man must suffer many things and be rejected by the elders, the chief priests and the teachers of the law, and that he must be killed and after three days rise again" (8:31). Jesus's teaching is so contrary to the disciples' expectations that, as he repeatedly touched the blind man in 8:22–26, he will repeat it three times (8:31; 9:31; 10:33–34) "on the way" to Jerusalem (8:27). At last Peter and the disciples understand—and "rebuke [Jesus]" (8:32). Never was it heard in Israel that the Messiah would *suffer*, or by suffering expiate the sins of Israel. It is important to recall that the one figure in the Old Testament associated with suffering—the Suffering Servant of Isaiah (42, 49, 51, 52–53)—is nowhere in Jewish history or literature associated with the Messiah. Ironically, the suffering of God's Messiah will not come from humanity at its worst—the godless and wicked—but from humanity at its *best*—"the elders, the chief priests and the teachers of the law" (8:31). So essential is humiliation and suffering to the mission of Jesus that to attempt to divert Jesus from it— as Peter does in verse

32—is not to "have in mind the concerns of God, but merely human concerns" (8:33). To judge the work of God in any other light than the perspective of God is to become an "adversary" to God, which is the Hebrew meaning of "Satan" (1 Kings 11:14).

In 8:34, the subject shifts from Christology to discipleship. For Mark, these are not two separate matters but two sides of the same coin. A proper confession of Jesus is inevitably also a confession of what believers must become. In verse 34, Jesus teaches that discipleship consists of following him, denying self, and taking up one's cross. Today the cross is primarily an object of art or jewelry, but in Jesus's day it was a hated instrument of cruelty, suffering, dehumanization, and shame. Reserved for the lowest social classes, and particularly slaves, the cross was the extreme terror apparatus of the Roman totalitarian state. The depiction of discipleship by such a repugnant symbol may account for the fact that in the second half of Mark there are fewer and smaller crowds around Jesus than in the first half. The image of the cross signifies a total claim on the disciple's allegiance and a total relinquishment of his or her resources to Jesus.

This truth is reinforced in 8:35–37, each verse of which declares the total claim of the gospel on one's existence. To lose one's life for the gospel is, ironically, to save it (8:35); to gain the whole world at the cost of one's life would be a fatal bargain, for what could one give to regain one's life? (8:36–37). Concluding his solemn address to the disciples in the prophetic imagery of an "adulterous and sinful generation" (Isa. 57:3–13; Ezek. 16:32–41; Hos. 2:2–6), Jesus warns that whoever is ashamed of the way of the cross in this life will be looked on with equal shame by the Son of Man in the world to come. Mark concludes his climactic discourse on Christology and discipleship with a saying of Jesus that the kingdom of God will come in power in the lifetimes of "some who are standing here" (9:1). Mark strategically places this saying between the prediction of Jesus's death in 8:31 and the account of his transfiguration (9:2–9), which anticipates his resurrection. That "the kingdom of God has come with power" (9:1) must therefore be understood to refer to the resurrection of Jesus from the dead—which Jesus's hearers would indeed live to see.

9:2–29. The initial reference "after six days" (9:2), opening the transfiguration narrative (9:2–13), is unusual since Mark rarely gives specific time delimitations. The "six days" appears to link the transfiguration to Peter's confession, assuring the bewildered disciples of the divine confirmation of Jesus's way to the cross. Peter, James, and John appear elsewhere as Jesus's inner circle (Mark 5:37; 13:3; 14:33). The "high mountain" (9:2) probably refers to Mount Hermon, rising 9,200 feet above Caesarea Philippi; the glorification of Jesus on its summit, however, doubtless also recalls the epiphany of God to Moses on Mount Sinai (Exod. 34:35). The Greek word for "transfigured" (9:2) means to "change" or "transform," in this instance into dazzling light. The figures of Elijah and Moses, who epitomize the Old Testament prophets and law, appear in audience with Jesus, signifying that the law and prophets lead to and are fulfilled in Jesus. Peter's desire to erect three "shelters" (9:5) is not as foolish as is often supposed, for the Greek word *skēnē*, "tabernacle," recalls the tabernacle in the wilderness erected to the glory of God (Exod. 40:34–36; Tobit 13:11). The cloud that envelops the disciples, momentarily revealing the glory of Jesus as God incarnate (9:7), expressly recalls the presence and glory of God that enveloped the tabernacle (Exod. 24:15–16; 40:34–36). "This is my Son, whom I love" (9:7) recalls the divine words at the baptism of Jesus, though here it is directed not to Jesus (see 1:11) but to the disciples. "Listen to him" (9:7) designates Jesus as the prophet who would follow Moses (see Deut. 18:15–18), and it assures the bewildered disciples that Jesus's prediction of his suffering and death in Jerusalem (8:31) is not a mistake but God's providential will for him. Taking up one's cross and following Jesus (8:34) is a difficult teaching, to be sure, but the transfiguration does not end on an ominous note, for Jesus does not escape to heaven with Elijah and Moses but remains "with [the disciples]" (9:8) on the journey to Jerusalem.

On the descent from the mountain, Jesus commands the disciples to be silent for the final time, admonishing them to banish thoughts of messianic triumphalism and not to mention the transfiguration until the resurrection of the Son of Man (9:9). The Greek of verse 10 indicates that the disciples did not simply keep the secret but suppressed it. Their puzzlement is a further sign of their blindness (8:14–21), for among the Pharisees the doctrine of the resurrection had been an article of faith for two centuries. The disciples ask, "Why do the teachers of the law say that Elijah must come first?" (9:11). Their question, by suggesting that Elijah's return to restore all things (Mal. 4:5–6) should obviate the need for the Son of Man to suffer, indicates further resistance to the idea of suffering. Elijah will restore all things, affirms Jesus, but not before "the Son of Man must suffer much and be rejected" (9:12). This latter reference is an apparent allusion to the suffering of the servant of the Lord in Isaiah 53:3. Indeed, says Jesus, "They have done to [Elijah] everything they wished" (9:13). The fate of "Elijah" here refers to the fate of John the Baptizer (see Matt. 17:13). The suffering of Isaiah's servant of the Lord and the fate of Elijah (i.e., John the Baptizer) concur that the

> Mount Hermon, most likely the "high mountain" where Jesus was transfigured (Mark 9:2–8)

triumphant day of the Lord can be purchased only by the suffering of the Son of Man.

In the second-to-last miracle story in Mark (9:14–29), a desperate father struggles for the life of his son and the existence of his faith. While Jesus and the three principal apostles, Peter, James, and John, were on the Mount of Transfiguration, a man brought his son who was "possessed by a spirit that has robbed him of speech" (9:17) to the remaining disciples for healing. The boy's condition is identified by the parallel story in Matthew 17:15 as epilepsy, a diagnosis that Mark's further descriptions amply confirm (9:18, 20–22, 26). The disciples' inability to heal the boy is another instance of their inadequacies when Jesus is not with them (also 6:48). Jesus does not chastise the disciples, for inability is not a fault. His exasperation at the crowd (9:19), however, implies more serious problems of misunderstanding and hardness of heart. In recounting the boy's condition, the father declares his own heart. At the sight of Jesus, the malevolent spirit convulses the boy, while his father cries to Jesus, "If you can do anything, take pity on us and help us" (9:22). So inseparable is the father's desperation from his son's condition that he begs for help and compassion "on *us*" (9:22). "'If you can'?" replies Jesus in surprise (9:23). The problem is not one of God's unwillingness or inability but of human disbelief. True faith is always aware how small and insignificant it is. True faith stands in the gap between the promise of God and the weakness of the flesh. In complete vulnerability, the father brings both his faith and weakness to Jesus: "I do believe; help me overcome my

unbelief!" (9:24). Seeing the crowd converge and not wanting to make a display of his power, Jesus "rebukes" the spirit and commands it to leave the boy (9:25). If the boy's condition was epilepsy, Mark understands it in this instance to be demonically instigated. An encounter with Jesus can leave things initially worse than before, as indicated by the deathlike condition of the boy after the expulsion of the demon. Here too the father must trust Jesus rather than immediate and apparent circumstances. Stretching forth his hand, Jesus "lifted [the boy] to his feet, and he stood up" (9:27). This description echoes the raising of Jairus's daughter from the dead (Mark 5:41), emphasizing the miraculous authority of Jesus. Disappointed in their inability to heal the boy, the disciples ask Jesus privately, "Why couldn't we drive [the demon] out?" (9:28). Jesus directs the disciples to the necessity of prayer. Indeed, the very inadequacy of the disciples must drive them to prayer; for prayer, as one scholar says, is "faith turned to God"—that is, God's gift to the disciples in facing situations beyond their abilities.

B. "On the way" to Jerusalem (9:30–10:52).
9:30–50. As Jesus and the disciples are "on the way" from Caesarea Philippi to Jerusalem—a distance of two hundred miles as the crow flies—Mark includes four brief narratives on humility and suffering, each of which illustrates and reinforces Jesus's call to self denial and cross bearing (8:31–38).

Passing through Galilee for the final time, "Jesus did not want anyone to know where they were" (9:30). The anonymous journey may have been advised by the continued opposition of Antipas and the Jewish authorities, but above all because Jesus's face was set toward Jerusalem. "On the way," Jesus gives the second and shortest of three passion predictions (8:31; 9:31; 10:33–34). In the second prediction, Jesus does not attribute his death to the Jewish leaders, as in the first, but to all humanity. Moreover, the Greek word for "delivered" (9:31) is in the passive voice, which was a common way for Jews to avoid using the name of God (for fear

of defiling it). This implies that Jesus's impending suffering in Jerusalem is a fulfillment of the divine will. The disciples, however, "did not understand what [Jesus] meant and were afraid to ask" (9:32). Ironically, when the word of God is decisively spoken, the human response—and here from those with the greatest opportunity to understand—remains one of ignorance and fear.

The second of the four stories, in 9:33–37, takes place in Capernaum, Jesus's base of operations in the first half of Mark. Alone with the disciples, Jesus asks what they talked about "on the way." They meet his question with embarrassed silence, for they were arguing who was the greatest. The placement of this story after the second passion prediction accentuates the contrast between Jesus and the disciples: he embraces humility, they argue who is greatest; he surrenders his life in service, they desire recognition and distinction. The second passion prediction is thus followed by a second misunderstanding. "Sitting down, Jesus called the Twelve" (9:35). In sitting and summoning, Jesus assumes the role and authority of a rabbi. "Anyone who wants to be first must be the very last, and the servant of all" (9:35). At no point does the way of Jesus part more sharply from the world than in its understanding of greatness. Jesus redefines greatness in terms of giving rather than getting, and no vocation affords the opportunity of giving more than that of a servant. The most basic meaning of "servant" (Greek *diakonos*) is "waiting tables," a posture Jesus himself assumes (Luke 22:27). Worldly greatness is reserved for the gifted few, but in the kingdom of God anyone can be great because anyone can serve. Service is the primary way for believers to imitate and fulfill the mission of Jesus (10:43–45). Jesus then embraces a child and commands the disciples, as he teaches in Matthew 25:40, to embrace "the least of these brothers and sisters of mine."

The third narrative, in verses 38–41, reminds disciples not to judge others by their own standards but by Jesus's generosity. As a member of Jesus's inner circle, John, son of Zebedee, takes an elitist attitude toward an unnamed exorcist. Failing to learn the object lesson of the previous story, John regards his call as one of entitlement and exclusion; indeed, he speaks of following *us* rather than following Jesus (9:38). Ironically, John wants the exorcist to stop doing what he and the other disciples could not do (9:28). Jesus is more generous than the disciples. Faith no larger than a mustard seed is acceptable (Mark 4:30–32), as is a little child (9:36–37). Even a cup of cold water given in Christ's name will not go unrewarded (9:41). Jesus receives what is done to a follower of Jesus as done to himself.

The final narrative is a graphic warning against causing others to sin, or "stumble." Verse 42 asserts the inestimable value of the small and insignificant. Not causing "one of these little ones . . . to stumble" does not refer to children but to those "who believe in me"—that is, to disciples. Whatever is done to a follower of Jesus, whether good (9:41) or bad (9:42), is done to Jesus. Verses 43–48 shift the focus from jeopardizing others to endangering self. The instruction to cut off hands, feet, or eyes is not a command to literal physical mutilation. Like the millstone of verse 42, these are metaphors that are exaggerated for effect: let nothing—not even things as dear as hands, feet, and eyes—prevent you from entering the kingdom of God. Some ancient manuscripts insert the saying in verse 48 after the saying about hands (9:43) and feet (9:45). "Gehenna" (NIV "hell") is a Semitic word for the Hinnom Valley, southwest of Jerusalem, where human sacrifice was practiced under Ahaz and Manasseh (2 Kings 16:3; 21:6). Ever after Ahaz and Manasseh, the Hinnom Valley symbolized the divine wrath and punishment of hell, which was to be avoided at all costs. The concluding references to fire and salt—both of which accompanied temple sacrifices (Lev. 1:1–17; 2:13)—are probably further metaphors of the trials and cost of discipleship.

10:1–31. Chapter 10 entails the call to discipleship in three fundamental aspects of life: marriage (10:1–12), children (10:13–16), and possessions (10:17–31).

Near the end of the journey from the north and before entering Jerusalem, Jesus teaches in "the region of Judea and across the Jordan" in Perea (10:1). There the Pharisees question him about divorce (10:1–12). Divorce and marriage were burning questions in Jesus's day, as they are in ours. The question of whether it was lawful for a man to divorce his wife (10:2) was a "test," however; indeed, it was a *trap*, for Jewish law unambiguously permitted divorce (Deut. 24:1–3). The only question was *on what grounds.* Here opinions varied widely, from conservative rabbis like Shammai, who permitted divorce on the sole ground of adultery, to liberal rabbis like Hillel, who allowed divorce (at least in theory) for virtually any reason. In posing the question, the Pharisees desire both to maintain an easy divorce policy and to catch Jesus in violation of torah. Jesus asks what Moses (i.e., the law) commands (10:3). The Pharisees promptly quote from Deuteronomy 24:1–3, that "a man [may] write a certificate of divorce and send [his wife] away" (10:4). The law permits divorce, maintains Jesus, only "because your hearts were hard" (10:5)—that is, as a concession to human sin rather than as a true picture of God's will.

The Pharisees focus on exceptions to marriage; Jesus focuses on how to fulfill God's intentions for it. The purpose of Deuteronomy 24:1–3, according to Jesus, was to limit the consequences of sin by permitting divorce, but it does not reveal the divine intention for marriage. Going behind the authority of torah, Jesus cites the first and fundamental teaching on marriage: at creation God made them "male and female" (Gen. 1:27), and in marriage the two "become one flesh" (Gen. 2:24). God ordained marriage, in other words, to be a union of a man and a woman who become inseparably one. Unlike the Pharisees, who stacked the deck of divorce in favor of the male, Jesus portrays male *and female* as created mutually equal—and mutually responsible in the marriage union. The Pharisees considered the man the lord of marriage, but Jesus says *God* is the lord of marriage: "What God has joined together, let no one separate" (10:9). The mutual responsibility for marriage is accentuated in verses 10–12, when Jesus teaches the disciples in private that, in suing for divorce and contracting a second marriage thereafter, *both* men and women are guilty of adultery.

The next fundamental aspect of life to be addressed is children (10:13–16). When some children are brought to Jesus, the disciples "rebuked them" (10:13). "Rebuke," normally reserved in Mark for exorcisms (1:25; 3:12; 9:25), is a strong denunciation, implying an attitude toward children that the disciples earlier (9:38) displayed toward an independent exorcist. Seeing their exclusivism, Jesus is "indignant" (10:14)—the only passage in the Gospels apart from 1:41 where the anger of Jesus is so sharply aroused. "Let the little children come to me," he orders, "for the kingdom of God belongs to such as these" (10:14). Jesus's attitude toward children is remarkable—and unprecedented—in the ancient world. In Jewish and Roman societies, childhood was not regarded with the same tenderness as in modern Western societies. It was typically regarded, rather, as an unavoidable and uncelebrated interim between birth and adulthood. In blessing and *embracing* children, Jesus was not acknowledging their innocence, purity, or spontaneity—for that would imply their acceptance was based on some virtue in themselves. Rather, children are blessed for what they *lack*—size, power, and sophistication. Having nothing to bring to Jesus, they have everything to receive from him by grace. Neediness—not merit—is the prerequisite to entering the kingdom of God, which is present in Jesus.

In the third discussion of what is fundamental to life (10:17–31), the possessions and social standing of the rich man are a striking contrast with the deficiencies of the children in the previous story. The rich man approaches Jesus with great eagerness and apparent receptiveness; he is the first person in Mark to ask to inherit eternal life, and he receives a clearer picture of the kingdom than anyone yet

in Mark. Ironically, however, he turns away. Jesus deflects the address "good teacher" (10:17) perhaps because, like rabbis in general, he wished to avoid possible blasphemy against God, but more likely because he wished to redirect the man's thoughts to the commandments of God. To the prohibitions of murder, adultery, theft, false testimony, and dishonoring parents, Jesus adds a commandment, not found in the Decalogue, against defrauding the poor—perhaps because wealth is often gained at the expense of the poor (10:19). It is often supposed that the rich man cannot have been sincere in claiming to have kept all the commandments. We should remember, however, that the Ten Commandments speak of *acts* that could—and were meant to—be kept (even if one intended otherwise). We should doubtless accept the truthfulness of the rich man's claim, "All these [commandments] I have kept since I was a boy" (10:20), for (1) Jesus does not challenge his declaration, and (2) Jesus would scarcely look on insincerity with "love," as he does in verse 21. It is often imagined that if the law were perfectly kept, one would gain eternal life. To a man who has, in fact, kept the law, Jesus declares, "One thing you *lack*.... Go, sell everything you have ... give to the poor.... Then come, follow me" (10:21). Jesus offers himself as a substitute for the man's possessions. The man's full adherence to the law, good as it is, is no substitute for knowing and following Jesus. This offer, however, the man cannot accept. Standing on his own merits, he is self-confident; but when he is called to give up his security and follow Jesus, his "face fell, and he went away sad" (10:22 NLT).

Possessions pose a problem for the disciples as well as for the rich man, for Jesus "looked around" and *twice* warns, "How hard it is for the rich to enter the kingdom of God" (10:23–25). The famous statement in verse 25 about a camel going through the eye of a needle is humorous, to be sure, but also deadly earnest. The most common attempt to weaken it—that is, that "the eye of the needle" refers to a small Jerusalem gate through which camels might enter by kneeling (implying that the rich may enter the kingdom if they humble themselves!)—is far-fetched, for that gate lay nine centuries in the future when Jesus spoke. The intended offense of the analogy is not lost on the disciples, who, nearly as shocked as the rich man (10:22), ask, "Who then can be saved?" (10:26). Jesus's word does not comfort them, in other words, but convicts them of their utter insufficiency before God. This, at last, is the right frame of mind—which explains why Jesus answers their question and not the rich man's. "With man this is impossible, but not with God; all things are possible with God" (10:27). Only where things are no longer possible may the disciples receive all things from God. Peter asks whether the sacrifices the disciples have made to follow Jesus are then worthless (10:28). They have given up homes, families, and fields (10:29), their most essential relationships and allegiances. Jesus assures them that when all has been forsaken for him, he will return all a hundredfold—though not without trials—in this life, and he will give them eternal life in the world to come. Discipleship entails a deep irony: the "first will be last, and the last first" (10:31).

10:32–52. The final passion prediction, in 10:32–34, is the most explicit of the three, with many predictions fulfilled in chapters 14–15. Jewish leaders are responsible for Jesus's death in the first prediction (8:31); Gentiles in the second (9:31); but "the chief priests and the teachers of the law" and "Gentiles" (10:33)—that is, both Jews and Gentiles—in the third prediction. Discipleship is always following Jesus "on [the] way up to Jerusalem" (10:32). Nowhere else does Mark speak of Jesus "leading the way" except to his suffering and death. Peter has just boasted of having "left everything to follow" Jesus (10:28), but on the actual road to Jerusalem he and the disciples are reluctant and afraid.

The failure of the disciples to understand the way of Jesus is exposed with acid clarity in 10:35–45, where, immediately following Jesus's announcement of his impending humiliation,

James and John ask for fame. James and John think of God's kingdom in terms of benefits. Jesus, however, speaks of the costs of participating in it in terms of a "cup" and "baptism" (10:38), both metaphors of suffering. The brothers assure Jesus of their willingness to bear the costs of discipleship. Despite their assurance, Jesus declares that the rewards of glory are hidden in the eternal purpose of God (10:40). Disciples are not to follow Jesus because of future rewards but because they wish to be with Jesus—wherever he leads.

The other disciples are "indignant" with James and John for their request of special honor, perhaps because they secretly have hoped for it themselves (10:41). The dissension among the Twelve becomes the pretext for one of Jesus's most important lessons and self-revelations. Earthly rulers and officials, says Jesus, "exercise authority" (10:42)—and usually with severity. The beginning of verse 43 reads in Greek: "It is not this way among you"; that is, this is not the way the kingdom of God works. Repeating the lesson of 9:35, Jesus solemnly declares that the preeminent value of God's kingdom is not power, prestige, or authority, but *service* (10:43). The idea of a "slave"—a position of absolute inferiority in the ancient world—being "first" was as paradoxical as the idea of a camel going through the eye of a needle (10:25). Disciples must practice service rather than authority *because it is Jesus's posture*: "The Son of Man did not come to be served, but to serve, and to give his life as a ransom for many" (10:45). Jesus calls disciples not to an ethical system but to "the way of the Lord" (Mark 1:3), the very pattern of the incarnation. A servant is preeminent because a servant *gives*, and giving is the essence of God, who gave his Son for the sins of the world. In describing the Son of Man as giving "his life as a ransom for many" (10:45), Jesus appropriates the unique description of the servant of the Lord in Isaiah 53:10–11. The servant is the only figure in the Old Testament whose suffering is vicariously effective for others. Verse 45 attests to Jesus's supreme consciousness of his impending suffering and death in Jerusalem as a "ransom for many," a self-substitution *on behalf of* all humanity.

The healing of a blind man in Jericho concludes the journey to Jerusalem (10:46–52). Bartimaeus is the only person healed in the Synoptic Gospels who is named, and by concluding with a comment that he "followed [Jesus] on the way" (10:52 ESV), Mark designates him a model disciple. Jericho lies 20 miles northeast and 3,500 feet lower than Jerusalem. As Jesus, the disciples, and a large crowd leave Jericho, a blind beggar, whose name in Aramaic means "son of Timaeus," cries out, "Jesus, Son of David, have mercy on me" (10:47). What Bartimaeus lacks in eyesight he makes up for in insight. "Son of David" recalls the hopes of a promised deliverer like David (2 Sam. 7:11–14), thus indicating that Bartimaeus associates messianic expectations with Jesus. Refusing to be silenced by the crowd, Bartimaeus repeats the cry. Unlike the crowd, Jesus does not treat Bartimaeus as an annoying problem. He stops, summons him, and restores his dignity by asking, "What do you want me to do for you?" (10:51). It is the same question Jesus asked James and John in 10:36, but whereas they asked for superhuman glory, Bartimaeus simply asks for human eyesight. Jesus restores his sight with warm assurance: "Go . . . your faith has healed you" (10:52). The Greek word *sōzō*, which means both "heal" and "save," is doubly appropriate here, for the encounter with Jesus has changed Bartimaeus from a beggar beside the way to a disciple on the way.

C. Stories of conflict in the temple in Jerusalem (11:1–13:37). Mark 11–16 is commonly called the "passion narrative," the account of Jesus's suffering and death in Jerusalem. In devoting fully one-third of his narrative to the final week of Jesus's life, Mark indicates its importance for understanding Jesus and the gospel. All the material in Mark 11–13—and most of 14–15—is oriented around the focal point of the *temple.* Mark does not present Jesus as either a preserver or reformer of the temple, however, but as its replacement. The *locus Dei*—the dwelling place of God in the world—is no longer (and will never again be) the Jerusalem temple, but *Jesus himself.*

11:1–26. Jesus begins his final week by making his way to the temple in Jerusalem (11:1–11). Unlike the modern road to Jerusalem, which proceeds from Jericho to Bethany to Bethphage to Jerusalem, the Roman road in Jesus's day ran along the spine of the mountain

On the road outside Jericho, Jesus healed the blind man Bartimaeus (Mark 10:46–52). Most of ancient Jericho, as it was in Jesus's day, lies beneath the modern Arab oasis town. But the winter palace of Herod the Great (seen here) remains.

flank that led from Jericho up to Bethphage on the Mount of Olives, and from there either down to Bethany or to Jerusalem. It is this route that Mark describes in 11:1. The Mount of Olives runs on a north-south axis east of Jerusalem, and its summit, three hundred feet higher and less than a mile distant, affords a breathtaking view of the holy city. Mark, who seldom mentions place names, may mention the Mount of Olives because of its association in Judaism with the coming of the Messiah and the final judgment (Ezek. 11:23; Zech. 14:4; Josephus, *Jewish Antiquities* 20.169). From the summit of the Mount of Olives, Jesus sends two unnamed disciples to an unnamed village (Bethany?) to fetch a "colt" (the Greek means the young of either horse or donkey) on which to ride into Jerusalem. Jesus may have known about the colt because of his connections in Bethany (see John 11–12). The reference to "the *Lord*" needing the colt (11:3) and to the riding of an *unbroken* animal both suggest Jesus's divine authority. The preparation for the entry into Jerusalem demonstrates Jesus's precise foreknowledge and sovereignty over subsequent events.

Once the colt has been procured, the way is strewn with cloaks and branches as Jesus rides into Jerusalem. "Hosanna" (11:9) is a transliterated Hebrew word meaning, "Save, I pray." "Blessed is he who comes in the name of the Lord" is a quotation from Psalm 118:25–26, where it refers not to the Messiah but to pilgrims entering Jerusalem. "Blessed is the coming kingdom of our father David" (not a Scripture quotation) insinuates messianic overtones, however. Like modern military parades, triumphal processions were common throughout the ancient Near East as a means for rulers to exhibit their prowess and subjugate populations through displays of military might. This narrative is traditionally and rightly designated the triumphal entry according to Matthew 21:1–11 and John 12:12–19. Mark's narrative is scarcely triumphal, however, for the crowds vanish, Jesus enters the temple alone, and having looked around briefly, he returns to

Bethany, whence he came. This is the first of Mark's clues that the temple is not the habitation of God's Son.

The cursing of the fig tree (11:12–25) often offends readers, not only because it is the only miracle of destruction in the canonical Gospels, but also because Jesus curses a tree for not producing fruit out of season (10:13). The fig tree story is another of Mark's sandwich units, however, in which the cursing and withering of the tree is interrupted by the "cleansing of the temple" episode. The splicing of the two stories together signifies that the fate of the unfruitful fig tree foreshadows God's judgment on the unfruitful temple. Walking the roughly two miles from Bethany to Jerusalem, Jesus sees a fig tree in leaf and approaches it in hopes of finding figs to eat. In Judea fig trees produce immature green figs before coming to leaf, and once foliage appears one expects to find branches loaded with figs, which, though not mature, are edible (Hos. 9:10; Song 2:13). The statement, "It was not the season for figs" (11:13), must mean not the season for *ripe* figs. More important than botany, however, is the theological symbolism of the story. The fig tree is often a symbol of God's judgment in the Old Testament, and here as in the prophetic tradition (Isa. 34:4; Jer. 8:13; Hos. 2:12; Joel 1:7; Mic. 7:1) the curse of the fig tree symbolizes God's judgment on the temple.

In the central, B-part of the sandwich, Mark turns to the clearing of the temple in verses 15–19. Herod the Great commenced building the temple in Jerusalem in 20 BC, and it was still under construction in Jesus's day. The temple consisted of four majestic divisions, the first of which, the Court of Gentiles, an open-air rectangle of 500 × 325 yards (35 acres!) enclosed by a perimeter of massive porticoes, was accessible to both Jews and Gentiles. The Court of Gentiles, where animals were sold for sacrifice and currency exchanged for the Tyrian shekel (made of pure metal and with no image), is the setting of verses 15–19. Quoting Isaiah 56:7, Jesus overturns the tables of animal sellers and money changers in order to make the temple a place of prayer "for all nations" (11:17). The commercial interests associated with the Jewish sacrificial system have deprived the "nations" (Greek "Gentiles") of the one place where non-Jews could worship. The Messiah was popularly expected to "cleanse" the temple of Gentiles and restore it for exclusive Jewish rites and rituals. Jesus does not "cleanse" and restore the sacrificial system of the temple, but clears it *for* Gentiles. The chief priests and scribes—the two groups responsible for oversight of the temple—fully understand his intent and begin "looking for a way to kill him" (11:18; also 3:6). Jesus then abandons the temple to go "out of the city"—a second reminder (11:11) that the temple is not the habitation of God's Son. Mark completes the sandwich unit with the note that the next day the fig tree was "withered from the roots" (11:20–21). Something "withered from the roots" cannot be revived. That expression, which recalls the seed in the parable of the sower that had no depth of soil (4:6), signifies that the new covenant in Jesus's blood (14:24) has replaced the blood of animal sacrifices and that by his resurrection from the dead Jesus will raise a new temple not made by human hands (14:58). The saying in verses 23–25 is appended to the fig tree–temple sandwich in order to remind readers that Jesus, and not the temple, is the object of the believer's faith and prayer, and that faith and prayer make possible forgiveness, which is the epitome of the gospel.

11:27–12:44. Beginning with the episode in 11:27–33, and continuing through chapter 12, Mark reports a series of controversies and conflicts between Jesus and the Sanhedrin, the supreme judicatory that controlled the temple and extended its influence over Jewish life. Composed of chief priests, elders (both Pharisees and Sadducees), and scribes, and ideally totaling seventy-one members, the Sanhedrin was granted full authority over Jewish religious affairs and significant control over Jewish political life as a buffer organization between Rome and Palestine.

11:27–12:12. "The chief priests, the teachers of the law and the elders" (11:27)—in other words, a delegation of the Sanhedrin—confront Jesus in the temple with the question, "By what authority are you doing these things?" (11:28). By "these things" they are evidently recalling Jesus's presumption to forgive sins (2:10), supersession of torah and Sabbath (2:23–3:6), acceptance of sinners and tax collectors (2:16), disruption of temple operations (11:15–19), and other challenges to their authority. In Israel's most authoritative place, and by its most authoritative body, Jesus is summoned to give account of his own authority. The question, "Who *gave* you authority to do this?" (11:28), recognizes that no one possesses authority on his own to do what Jesus does. Such authority, presumably, comes only from God—and herein is the trap of the Sanhedrin's question. If Jesus claims such authority, he can be charged with blasphemy, which in Judaism was a capital offense. Jesus meets their question with a counterquestion: "John's baptism—was it from heaven, or of human origin?" (11:30). This is not a diversionary tactic but an attempt to direct the Sanhedrin to the proper answer. At John's baptism Jesus was declared God's Son and endowed with God's Spirit to do "these things." A decision about John can open a door to a decision about Jesus. The Sanhedrin weighs the political consequences before them and answers evasively, "We don't know" (11:33). That was not entirely true. They were, rather, unwilling to commit, and to those unwilling to commit, Jesus is unwilling to reveal himself.

The parable of the vineyard (12:1–12) retells the history of Israel in the well-known imagery of a vineyard (e.g., Isa. 5:1–7), though it is adapted to the widespread system of absentee landownership in first-century Palestine. The parable depicts the central purpose of Israel's history as leading to the landowner's beloved son (12:6), and Israel's failure to receive the son as grounds for its judgment. The placement of this parable as the final and only parable outside chapter 4 indicates its supreme importance for

Mark. Tenant farmers are entrusted with the oversight of a vineyard, but when the owner sends servants to collect his produce, the tenants maltreat some and kill others. In a final act of outrage, the tenants kill the owner's beloved son and throw his body to the birds, thinking the vineyard will be theirs. After every conceivable overture of clemency, the landowner intervenes and takes vengeance on the tenants. The landowner in the parable represents God. His judgment falls not on the vineyard

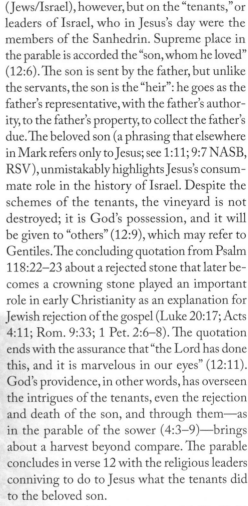

(Jews/Israel), however, but on the "tenants," or leaders of Israel, who in Jesus's day were the members of the Sanhedrin. Supreme place in the parable is accorded the "son, whom he loved" (12:6). The son is sent by the father, but unlike the servants, the son is the "heir": he goes as the father's representative, with the father's authority, to the father's property, to collect the father's due. The beloved son (a phrasing that elsewhere in Mark refers only to Jesus; see 1:11; 9:7 NASB, RSV), unmistakably highlights Jesus's consummate role in the history of Israel. Despite the schemes of the tenants, the vineyard is not destroyed; it is God's possession, and it will be given to "others" (12:9), which may refer to Gentiles. The concluding quotation from Psalm 118:22–23 about a rejected stone that later becomes a crowning stone played an important role in early Christianity as an explanation for Jewish rejection of the gospel (Luke 20:17; Acts 4:11; Rom. 9:33; 1 Pet. 2:6–8). The quotation ends with the assurance that "the Lord has done this, and it is marvelous in our eyes" (12:11). God's providence, in other words, has overseen the intrigues of the tenants, even the rejection and death of the son, and through them—as in the parable of the sower (4:3–9)—brings about a harvest beyond compare. The parable concludes in verse 12 with the religious leaders conniving to do to Jesus what the tenants did to the beloved son.

12:13–37. All the stories in 11:27–12:44 portray the opposition of the Sanhedrin to Jesus. The chief priests challenged Jesus in 11:27–33, and beginning in 12:13 the remaining constituents of the Sanhedrin—the Pharisees (12:13–17), Sadducees (12:18–27), and scribes (12:28–40)—challenge Jesus as well. The Pharisees are sent "to catch [Jesus] in his words" (12:13), and they begin by flattery (12:14). The Herodians appear to have been partisans of Herod the Great and his pervasive dynasty.

Vineyards, like this one, were common in Judea. Jesus used the vineyard and those who tend it as a vital metaphor for Israel (Mark 12:1–12).

Their coalition with the Pharisees, with whom they shared little in common, was surely based more on a common enemy in Jesus than on common values (see Mark 3:6). "Is it right to pay the imperial tax to Caesar or not?" (12:14), they ask. The imperial poll tax here referred to the required payment of a denarius (the average daily wage), stamped with the impression of Tiberius Caesar (Roman emperor AD 14–37). The question of the Pharisees and Herodians is designed to ensnare Jesus however he answers: support for taxation will discredit him in the eyes of the people, who detest Roman occupation; refusal to pay will invite Roman retaliation for insurrection. In a brilliant repartee, Jesus grants that the image and inscription are Caesar's; therefore, the coin belongs to Caesar. This answer acknowledges the legitimacy of human government. Jesus then adds, "And [give] to God what is God's" (12:17). This answer— which has not been asked of Jesus—indicates that the political question of the Pharisees and Herodians cannot be answered without answering the more fundamental theological question—namely, that government may not assert total claim over its citizens. Political and civil duties cannot be properly rendered until the ultimate claim of God is acknowledged. Humanity, which bears God's image (Gen. 1:26), belongs to God.

Following the test of the Pharisees comes Mark's lone challenge to Jesus from the Sadducees (12.18–27). The Sadducees and Pharisees both arose during the Maccabean revolt (second century BC). Although they differed greatly in outlook, the Sadducees and Pharisees dominated Jewish life, and especially the Sanhedrin. Pharisees believed in divine sovereignty; Sadducees attributed events to human free will. Pharisees accepted the authority of the Torah, Writings, and Prophets (the three divisions of the Hebrew Bible), and even oral tradition; Sadducees affirmed the authority of written torah alone. Pharisees affirmed the existence of angels, demons, and the resurrection from the dead; Sadducees denied all three. Theologically,

Pharisees were less restrictive and more tolerant than Sadducees, whose exclusive reliance on the Torah (the first five books of the Old Testament) and allegiance to Rome resulted in theological and political conservatism. Pharisaism on the one hand was a lay movement neither interested in political rule nor exclusively associated with the temple. Sadducees, on the other hand, constituted a clerical and lay aristocracy closely associated with the priesthood and temple, and although they were fewer in number than Pharisees, they dominated the high priesthood and Sanhedrin and collaborated with Rome for the privilege of power.

The Sadducees, who denied the resurrection of the dead (because it is not attested in the Torah), intended to discredit Jesus by devising an ingenious test case of a woman lawfully married to seven brothers. The idea is based on the custom of levirate marriage (Gen. 38:8; Deut. 25:5–6), whereby a man was obligated to marry a childless widow of his deceased brother in order to preserve the honor, name, and property of the deceased brother—and prevent the widow from marrying a Gentile. Assuming that resurrected existence is a mere extension of earthly life, the Sadducees reason that a woman who was married to seven husbands sequentially on earth could not be married to them simultaneously in heaven. In a summary rejection of their premise, Jesus declares the whole artifice is false "because you do not know the Scriptures or the power of God" (12:24) This is a bold indictment, for torah and power were the two *strong* suits of the Sadducees. The resurrected life, continues Jesus, is not a prolongation of earthly life, but an entirely new dimension of existence (1 Cor. 15:40–44), like the life of "the angels in heaven" (12:25). Indeed, even torah—which the Sadducees accept as God-given—presumes the resurrection of the dead, for the promise "I am the God of Abraham, the God of Isaac, and the God of Jacob" (12:26; Exod. 3:6) was not temporal (i.e., ended by death) but eternal.

The final test of Jesus from the constituents of the Sanhedrin comes from a scribe

(12:28–37). Scribes (NIV "teachers of the law") were torah experts of great erudition who both advised the Sanhedrin and enjoyed legendary reputations and privileges. Famous rabbis were often asked, as Jesus is asked here, to summarize the essence of all 613 commandments in the torah in a nutshell. According to the NIV (12:28), the scribe asks which is the greatest of the "commandments." The Greek, however, does not read "commandments" but something more absolute and unqualified: which commandment comes before *everything* and is incumbent on *everyone*? Jesus answers by quoting the Shema (12:29–30), the quintessential summary of the torah in Deuteronomy 6:4–5 recited morning and evening by every pious Jew. The word "all" occurs four times in the quotation, emphasizing the need for total love to God. The Shema commands believers to love God with heart, soul, and strength, but Mark records Jesus adding a fourth command, to love God "with all your *mind*" (12:30). The scribe asked for only one commandment, but as in his earlier response to the Pharisees and Herodians (12:17), Jesus appends a second, "Love your neighbor as yourself" (Lev. 19:18). Both of these commandments form a unity, encompassing the one will of God in a single "commandment greater" than everything else. No rabbi before Jesus brought love of God and love of others—theology and ethics—into such indivisible unity.

"Well said, teacher," replies the scribe (12:32). Of nineteen references to scribes in Mark, this is Jesus's only encounter with a nonadversarial scribe. The collage of Scripture texts in 12:32–33 indicates that this scribe—and perhaps not he alone—understands love (Greek *agapē*) to supersede "burnt offerings and sacrifices." As torah authorities, scribes presumed to speak the final word in religious matters. It is Jesus, however, who passes final judgment on the scribe, "You are not far from the kingdom of God" (12:34). The scribe's nearness to the kingdom is not due to his knowledge of torah but to his proximity to Jesus.

"From then on," notes Mark, "no one dared ask [Jesus] any more questions" (12:34). Jesus has survived interrogation from Sanhedrin (11:27–33), Pharisees (12:13–17), Sadducees (12:18–27), and scribes (12:28–34)—and prevailed over them. Now, at the end of the day, Jesus asks the question of the day. Why do the scribes say that "the Messiah is the son of David?" (12:35). As in the parable of the vineyard (12:1–12), Jesus chooses to raise the question of "the Son [of God]" at the heart of Israel and before the authorities of Israel. The issue of *identity*, which Jesus raised privately on the way to Caesarea Philippi, he now raises publicly in the precincts of the temple. Behind Jesus's question lay the common assumption that the Messiah would be a descendant of King David. Jesus challenges this assumption by quoting Psalm 110:1, "The Lord said to my Lord: 'Sit at my right hand'" (12:36). If David was the author of this psalm (as was widely accepted in Jesus's day), and if "Lord" refers to God and "my Lord" to the Messiah, then the Messiah is not David's descendant but his Lord and master. "How then can [the Messiah] be [David's] son?" asks Jesus (12:37). The Messiah is not an extension of David but his superior; not the fruit of David but the *root* of David (Rev. 22:16). The Messiah is not David's son, after all; he is God's Son!

12:38–44. In the final episode of Jesus's public teaching, Mark contrasts scribes, in their "flowing robes" and seats of honor (12:38–39), and a "poor widow" of no honor (12:42). The ostentation of scribes and their temptation to use their prestige for self-advancement ("they devour widows' houses" [12:40]) fall under Jesus's judgment, just as false prophets have fallen under the prophets' judgment (Isa. 10:2; Amos 2:1–16; Mic. 3:1–12). A widow, by contrast, deposits a mere pittance— "a few cents" (12:42)—into the temple treasury. In addition to being a place of worship, the temple functioned as a sacred bank by collecting and storing dues, taxes, donations of money and precious objects, and individual wealth. The "temple treasury" (12:41) was located in the Court of Women, the courtyard immediately inside the sanctuary, where Jews (including men, women, and children) were allowed, but not Gentiles. In contrast to the well-to-do scribes and crowds, "this poor widow" (12:43), declares Jesus, put "more into the treasury" because she gave out of her need, not out of her surplus. For Jesus, the value of a gift is not the amount given but the cost to the giver. The reference to the sacrifice of "all she had" (12:44) is a fitting final word for Jesus's public ministry, for the widow gave what all disciples must give in obeying the call to "come, follow me" (1:17).

13:1–37. Like the farewell discourses of major biblical figures (Jacob, Genesis 49; Moses, Deuteronomy 32–33; Joshua, Joshua 23; Samuel, 1 Samuel 12; Paul, Acts 20), Mark 13 attributes to Jesus a final discourse that constitutes the longest block of teaching in the Gospel. Some instructions occur in other contexts in other Gospels (compare Mark 13:9–13 with Matthew 10:17–22), suggesting that some of the teachings in chapter 13 were delivered at various times in Jesus's ministry. The organizing theme of the chapter is eschatology (from Greek *eschatos*, "last [things]"), in which future events, including some as distant as the second coming of the Son of Man, are prefigured by the destruction of the temple and fall of Jerusalem in AD 70. Mark places the whole eschatological discourse on the Mount of Olives, where Jesus sits "opposite the temple" (13:3), which

is symbolic as well as literal, for the chapter concludes Mark 11–13 (all of which is set in the temple) with the pronouncement of Jesus's judgment on the temple and prediction of its destruction.

Mark appears to divide Jesus's teaching on the future into two time frames. Events identified by "all these things" (13:2, 4, 8, 29, 30) relate to the immediate future and the destruction of the temple by Rome in AD 70. Events identified by "those days" (or "that day," 13:17, 19–20, 24, 32) concern the distant future and the second coming of the Son of Man in final judgment and glory. These two designations result in the following outline:

- A¹ End of temple and fall of Jerusalem (13:1–13)
- B¹ Tribulation and second coming of Son of Man (13:14–27)
- A² End of temple and fall of Jerusalem (13:28–31)

Mark 13 warns readers against attempts at constructing timetables and deciphering signs of the second coming. Disciples are admonished to be alert and watchful (13:5, 9, 23, 33, 35, 37), for neither they (13:33, 35) nor even Jesus (13:32) knows the time of the end. Disciples are not to be led astray by even the most obvious signs (13:5–6, 21–22), for the end is not yet (13:7, 13). Discipleship is not fulfilled by predicting future events but by *faithfulness in the present*, especially in trials, adversity, and suffering.

Construction of the Herodian temple began in 20 BC and was still in progress in Jesus's

A large scale model of the Herodian temple (Israel Museum, West Jerusalem). This view looks on from the east showing the Gentile courts surrounding the central holy places.

day. The temple was constructed on a scale of such magnitude that when it was completed in AD 66, it exceeded in size any other temple in the ancient world. On leaving the temple, the disciples draw Jesus's attention to the magnificence of its stones and buildings (13:1). Jesus warns the disciples not to be misled by its grandeur, for it will be like the "fig tree withered from the roots" (11:20): "Not one stone here will be left on another" (13:2). The Mount of Olives earlier commenced Jesus's triumphal entry into Jerusalem (11:1). Now, sitting in authority on its summit (13:3), from which the prophet Zechariah declared God's judgment on Jerusalem (Zech. 14:1–8), Jesus warns the disciples of two impending dangers. First, the disciples are to "watch out" (13:5) and "be on [their] guard" (13:9) against false teachers and messiahs. Such people will work "signs" (13:4—the word is used negatively here, as it was in 8:11–12); indeed, they "will come in [Jesus's] name, claiming 'I am he'" (13:6), but they nevertheless "deceive" and lead astray. The first and gravest future danger is not external but internal, inside the household of faith. Second, disciples are warned of external dangers—wars, natural calamities, famine—that will affect all people (13:5–8). Despite the severity of these disasters, they neither impede the spread of God's reign nor signal the end (13:7). They indeed subject the church to adversity, for believers will be accused, arrested, tried, and beaten (13:9–11). Most distressing, believers will be betrayed, hated, and even killed by fellow believers and family members "because of me" (13:13). Despite these hardships, however, "the gospel [will] be preached to all nations" (13:10). Adversity will afford believers unprecedented opportunities to declare their faith before authorities and rulers, and they need not be anxious about doing so, for the Holy Spirit will speak through them (13:11). In Jesus's depiction of the future, adversity is not an abnormality but the *norm* of Christian existence in the end times. Believers who "stand firm to the end will be saved" (13:13).

In 13:14 Jesus mentions a specific calamity ("the abomination that causes desolation") that appears to prefigure the end times, which are further profiled in verses 14–27. "Abomination" (see Dan. 9:27; 11:31; 12:11; 1 Maccabees 1:54) describes the outrage of Antiochus IV, the Seleucid king, who in 168 BC erected an altar to Zeus in the Jerusalem temple and sacrificed a sow on it. His intention was to exterminate Judaism, and his provocation ignited the Maccabean revolt of 166–142 BC. For Jesus, the "abomination" of Antiochus IV was a prefigurement of a blasphemous antichrist who in the end time would do a scandalous deed before the return of the Son of Man in judgment and glory. Scholars often regard the destruction of the temple by Titus in AD 70 as the realization of the "abomination," for some details in verses 14–18 recall the siege and destruction of Jerusalem by Titus. If this is correct, Mark warns readers ("let the reader understand," 13:14) that the catastrophic fall of Jerusalem in AD 70 is a foreshadowing of the disasters that will take place at the end of time, when "the man of lawlessness" will appear (2 Thess. 2:3–4), a blasphemous antichrist who will do horrors and outrages before the return of the Lord. "Those . . . days" (13:19)—now referring to the end time—will be so dire and unprecedented that unless God intervenes and shortens them, "no one [will] survive" (13:20). The true Messiah is sparing with signs and wonders in order not to coerce allegiance, but the last days will see many false prophets and messiahs perform many wonders and attract many followers (13:21–22). "Be on your guard" (13:23), warns Jesus, for the true disciple knows these deceptions in advance and is not distracted from faithful obedience to the Lord. In "those days" (13:24)—the end of time—earthly calamities will be mirrored by celestial portents—the darkening of sun and moon and shaking of stars and planets (13:24–25)—all foretold in the Old Testament prophets. Then the Son of Man, though now subjected to suffer in Jerusalem (8:31; 9:31; 10:33–34) and destined to be crucified as a common criminal (Phil. 2:8), will come "in clouds with great power and glory" (13:26). Jesus, who is now Son of God in humility, will be revealed as Son of God in power (Rom. 1:3–4) by fulfilling the prophecy of Daniel 7:13 and by vindicating the elect at the final judgment. The great assurance of the second coming is that the Creator and Redeemer of all will condemn evil, end suffering, and gather his "elect" to himself.

Verses 28–31 return to the impending fall of Jerusalem and thus the near future, which was the subject of verses 5–13. As with the fig tree (13:28), which blossoms when winter is past and summer has arrived, when "you see *these things* happening" (13:29)—that is, the fall of the temple (13:4)—you know that the end is "right at the door" (13:29). The generation to which Jesus speaks will witness the fall of Jerusalem, which itself is a preview of the end of the world. Jesus's statement that "heaven and earth will pass away, but my words will never pass away" (13:31) is a claim only God can make. In making this claim, Jesus assures his disciples that his words will outlive the cosmos and that the world to come is already present in his teaching.

The Olivet Discourse concludes in 13:32–37, on the subject of the distant future. "About that day or hour no one knows," says Jesus (13:32). "That day" reintroduces the theme of the second coming of verses 14–27. Remarkably, in this, the only passage in the Gospel of Mark where Jesus explicitly calls himself "the Son [of God]," he confesses what he does not know and cannot do! The Son relinquishes all claims concerning the future to the Father's plan. In the great mysteries of life, humans want signs; Jesus, however, wants only the Father. Given such mysteries, Jesus's concluding word—five times in verses 33–37—is "Be on guard," "Be alert," "Keep watch." When and how the end will come cannot be known, only *that* it will come—suddenly! Given that reality, the only sensible way to live, like a householder awaiting the uncertain time of the owner's return (13:34), is in constant readiness. "Watch!"

D. The abandonment of Jesus in Jerusalem (14:1–72). Mark 14 and 15 rehearse the betrayal, suffering, and crucifixion of Jesus, commonly known as the "passion" (from Latin *patior*, "suffering"). Chapter 14, the longest in the Gospel, commences the chain of events in Jesus's *abandonment*, first by Judas and the chief priests, then by the Sanhedrin and all his disciples, and finally by the crowds and even the Father (15:34). The passion commences with the betrayal of Jesus by Judas, into which Mark sandwiches a story of a woman who anoints Jesus with costly ointment. The key to Mark's sandwich construction is found in the middle episode, which in this instance is a costly sacrifice of faith *for* Jesus, whereas in the plot with the Sanhedrin Judas sacrifices his faith itself by the betrayal of his master.

14:1–16. The Jewish Passover was celebrated annually (Exodus 12) by ritually slaughtering a year-old male lamb or goat on the afternoon of the fourteenth of Nisan (March-April). The Passover meal, eaten in family gatherings after sunset (i.e., 15 Nisan), commenced the weeklong Feast of Unleavened Bread (Exod. 12:15–20). The plot of the "chief priests and the teachers of the law" (i.e., the Sanhedrin, 14:1) is described with blunt realism: they intend to seek out Jesus, arrest him by guile, and kill him. Jerusalem, the only place where Passover could be celebrated, drew enormous crowds for the festival; this increased the potential of an uprising as well as the need for security precautions on the part of the Romans. The Jewish authorities hope to seize Jesus without provoking his Galilean sympathizers (14:2). Mark now inserts the story of the anointing of Jesus by an unnamed woman, whose compassion stands in stark contrast to the plot of the religious authorities (14:3–11). It was normally a breach of etiquette for a woman to interrupt Jewish male fellowship, but Mark portrays the woman's intrusion as an act of faith (also Mark 5:34). Mark's profuse description of the ointment in verse 4, which amounted to the equivalent of a year's earnings, is an attempt to convey the value of the woman's sacrifice. Smashing the jar symbolizes the totality and irrevocability of the gift. No gift or act of generosity from either crowds or disciples approximates what this woman does. Some present regard the act as a "waste," a judgment that both demeans the woman and insinuates Jesus's unworthiness of it. Jesus accepts the gift as "a beautiful thing" (14:6), for the woman "did what she could" (14:8). In nearly the same words Jesus earlier commended the incomparably smaller gift of the poor widow in 12:44, indicating that the value of a gift consists not in amount but in giving what one is *able*. Jesus receives the anointing as a preparation for his burial, and he commemorates it because the woman somehow understands that the mystery of the gospel is revealed in Jesus's death (14:9). Mark closes the sandwich by returning to Judas. Identifying him as "one of the Twelve" may warn readers that closeness to Jesus does not guarantee faithfulness. Mark is silent about Judas's motives for betraying Jesus, although money played a role (14:11). Judas's betrayal is more premeditated, but all the disciples will defect as well (14:50).

The preparation of the Passover in verses 12–16 is reminiscent of the preparation of the entry into Jerusalem in 11:1–6; both show Jesus's foreknowledge and governance of events as his "hour" (14:35) approaches. "The first day of the Festival of Unleavened Bread" technically began at sundown on the fifteenth of Nisan (Thursday evening), but Mark appears to place the beginning of Passover on Thursday afternoon, the fourteenth of Nisan, when Passover lambs were slaughtered in the temple. The mood of expectancy and urgency produced by the great influx of Passover pilgrims in Jerusalem is reflected in the triple occurrence of the Greek word for "prepare" in verses 12–16. The disciples are given what appear to be undercover instructions to meet "a man carrying a jar of water" (14:13). This must locate the meeting place at or near the Pool of Siloam or the Gihon Spring, the two water sources of Jerusalem. Carrying water was normally women's

(or slaves') labor; a man carrying a water jug would have caught the eye of the disciples, suggesting perhaps that he was a member of the all-male Essene sect. Jerusalem residents customarily made spare rooms available for Passover pilgrims, and the target water bearer, perhaps in accordance with previous arrangements by Jesus, ushers the disciples to a well-appointed banquet room.

14:17–31. Mark sets the Last Supper (14:22–26) in another sandwich construction, placed between Jesus's predictions of the betrayal (14:17–21) and defection (14:27–31) of the disciples. The sandwich dramatically illustrates the self-sacrifice of Jesus in contrast to the infidelity of the disciples. Reclining was the customary position of feasting in the ancient world, and while Jesus is reclining with the disciples at Passover, he solemnly announces, "One of you will betray me" (14:18). The announcement of betrayal in a context of sacred feasting and intimacy is bitterly ironic. "One who is eating with me" (14:18), "who dips bread into the bowl with me" (14:20), does not limit the field of suspects but *expands* it to include all the disciples. Jesus's unsettling announcement provokes soul-searching—and self-justification—in the disciples. "Surely you don't mean me?" they reply (14:19). There was one traitor in the formal sense, but by dawn all the disciples will abandon Jesus, if not from greed (14:10–11), then from weakness (14:37–42), fear (14:50–52), or cowardice (14:66–72). In one of the most concise expressions in Scripture of the relationship between predestination and free will (16:21), Jesus says that the betrayal of the Son of Man is both foreordained ("it is written" implies divine purpose) and yet a free choice for which the culprit is responsible.

At the centerpiece of the sandwich, Mark places the Last Supper, narrated with liturgical form and brevity (14:22–26). The account is built on seven Greek verbs in verse 22 (eat, take, bless, break, give, say, take), signifying the gracious activity of Jesus on behalf of the disciples. In pronouncing the bread and wine his "body" and "blood," Jesus signifies the gift of *himself*, wholly and without reserve. Of the four Gospel writers, only Mark adds "and they all drank from it" (14:23). The Last Supper is a table of grace, not of merit, for the "all" who drink (14:23) and swear allegiance (14:31) also fall away (14:27) and flee (14:50). The "blood of the covenant" (14:24) recalls Exodus 24:3–8, the first covenant at Sinai, sealed with the blood of a sacrificial animal. Unlike in the first covenant, however, in the new covenant (Jer. 31:31–34) the blood of Jesus is not thrown *on* the community but imbibed *into* it. The "many" in verse 24 alludes to the Suffering Servant of Isaiah, who "bore the sin of many, and made intercession for the transgressors" (Isa. 53:12). Jesus concludes the supper by resuming the eschatological motif of chapter 13 (14:17, 19, 20, 24, 32): "until that day when I drink it new in the kingdom of God" (14:25). The Last Supper is intended as the interim feast of believers with their Lord until his return.

Mark closes the A-B-A sandwich construction with a conversation between Jesus and Peter (14:27–31) that recalls the theme of 14:17–21, where Jesus predicted "one of you will betray me" (14:18). Following the Passover, Jesus announces, "You will all fall away [Greek *skandalizō*]" (14:27). The Greek word is used in a passive sense, implying that the disciples will not willfully defect but fall away through weakness. Jesus supports his announcement by quoting Zechariah 13:7: "I will strike the shepherd, and the sheep will be scattered." The "I" refers to God, the shepherd to Jesus, and the sheep to the disciples. This quotation repeats the paradox of 14:21: evil is used by God to fulfill his greater purpose. The Zechariah quotation (like Isa. 53:10) also implies that Jesus understands his impending passion in Jerusalem not as an accident but as divinely ordained. Jesus announces that he will be reunited with the disciples after his resurrection, not in Jerusalem or the temple, but in Galilee, where their call to discipleship began (1:16). Until now, when Jesus announced his

impending suffering "on the way" to Jerusalem, the disciples often responded by claiming their position and privilege. Peter protests similarly here that he will not fall away (14:29–31), a protest echoed by all the disciples (14:31). Despite Peter's vociferous protests, Jesus sadly informs him that he will deny him not in a momentary lapse, but three times.

14:32–52. Following the Last Supper, Jesus goes to Gethsemane (Hebrew "olive press"), an olive grove in the valley between the Mount of Olives and the temple mount where he and the disciples often gathered (Luke 22:39; John 18:1–2). Commanding the disciples to remain, Jesus departs a few paces in order to pray (14:32–42). This is the third time in Mark that Jesus prays (cf. 1:35; 6:46); each prayer is set in a context of crisis and decision, this being the most traumatic. In all the Bible, no affliction or agony is described with the intensity of 14:34–35. According to Mark, the decision to submit to the Father's will in Gethsemane causes Jesus greater internal suffering than does the physical crucifixion of Golgotha. The "cup" and "hour" (14:35–36), reflecting apocalyptic imagery, do not refer to Jesus's arrest but to his messianic destiny. Jesus's distress is not the result of facing his own death but of giving his life as "a ransom for many" (10:45; Isa. 53:12). Jesus must become the sin-bearer of all humanity, which will result in his complete alienation, even from God (15:34). "Abba" (14:36; Aramaic "Papa"), an address of God seldom if ever used by rabbis, expresses Jesus's consciousness of being God's Son and his intimacy and trust with the Father. "Take this cup from me" reveals Jesus's human desire to avoid the cross, but his plea is finally resolved in submission to the Father's will: "Not what I will, but what you will" (14:36). Ironically, at the point where Jesus feels most distant from God's presence, he is closest to his will. Gethsemane is the prelude to Golgotha, for in the valley below Jerusalem his soul is crucified, and on a hill above Jerusalem he will relinquish his body. The three warnings of Jesus to the disciples to "watch" (14:34, 37–38) reveal their failure to fulfill the Olivet Discourse (13:36–37), and they prefigure Peter's three forthcoming denials. The admonition to the disciples, "Watch and pray," for "the spirit is willing, but the flesh is weak" (14:38), is a reminder that trust and obedience of God are always a struggle against temptation and weakness.

In contrast to the intensity and pathos of Gethsemane, the arrest is narrated in resigned objectivity (14:43–52). "My betrayer is at hand" (14:42 ESV, NKJV) immediately identifies Judas, who, as if to remind readers that disciples of Jesus can also be betrayers of Jesus, is again named as "one of the Twelve" (14:43; 14:10; 3:19). Judas's accomplices are the "chief priests, the teachers of the law, and the elders," the three constituent bodies of the Sanhedrin, now "armed with swords and clubs" (14:43). As a disciple, Judas knew Jesus's daytime movements and nighttime lodgings, and he gives a prearranged sign to the authorities, lest in the darkness of an olive grove at night they fall upon the wrong person. The sign is a kiss—a tender or passionate kiss, according to the Greek of 14:45. Why Judas chose this sign is unclear—although it had been similarly used at least twice in the Old Testament (Gen. 27:26; 2 Sam. 20:9–10). Betrayal by an intimate act of affection, and by an epithet of respect, "Rabbi" ("my great one"), is a profound mockery. Jesus is immediately "seized" by the soldiers, a term that repeatedly characterizes the arrest (14:44, 46, 49, 51). The disciple who cuts off the ear of the servant of the high priest is often thought to be Peter, but Mark simply identifies him as "one of those standing near" (14:47). Jesus reproaches the crowd for assaulting him as a "bandit" or "robber" (14:48; NIV "leading a rebellion"), the word in Greek (*lēstēs*) sometimes referring to an adherent of the Zealot movement. The reference to the fulfillment of Scriptures in 14:49 must recall Isaiah 53:12: he "was numbered with the transgressors." "Then everyone deserted him and fled" is Mark's bitter climax to the arrest. All have drunk the cup (14:23), all have pledged to die with him (14:31)—and all flee! The young man who flees the mayhem of the arrest is sometimes thought to be Mark himself, author of the Gospel. We have no certain knowledge that Mark was present in Jesus's earthly ministry; but if he was—and if he wished to confess his own flight at the arrest—would he have expressed it so opaquely? The lack of identity of the naked man more likely invites readers to examine their own readiness to abandon Jesus: "There is no one righteous, not even one. . . . All have turned away" (Rom. 3:10, 12).

14:53–72. For the third time in chapter 14 Mark employs the technique of sandwiching one story into the midst of another, thereby making a third point by implication. The present sandwich consists of Peter's denial (14:53–54; 14:66–72) divided by Jesus's trial before the Sanhedrin (14:55–65). The theme of the sandwich is bearing witness under persecution—the Greek word "witness" is mentioned seven times in this unit—by contrasting Jesus's faithful witness with Peter's false witness.

The sandwich begins with Peter following Jesus "at a distance, right into the courtyard of the high priest" (14:54). The distance will soon stretch into a denial. The focus then shifts to Jesus, who is hauled before the Sanhedrin on the heels of his arrest (14:53). The Sanhedrin normally met in the temple sanctuary, but "the courtyard of the high priest" suggests a meeting in the private dwelling of the high priest Caiaphas, whose house lay about a kilometer to the southwest of Gethsemane. Beneath the house of Caiaphas, now commemorated by the Church of Saint Peter in Gallicantu (Cockcrow), a warren of rock-hewn chambers provided maximum security for prisoners such as Jesus. The proceedings against Jesus in 14:55–65 egregiously violate Jewish jurisprudence set forth in the Mishnah. In particular, a verdict of guilty in capital cases required a second sitting the following day; both must be in the daytime, and neither on the eve of the Sabbath or a festival. A charge of blasphemy, moreover, could be sustained only if the accused cursed God publicly, resulting in death by stoning. The manifest departures from stipulated protocol suggest that the Sanhedrin proceeded in the fashion of a grand jury by hearing *and* condemning Jesus in a single sitting, and perhaps with less than a quorum. In "looking for evidence against Jesus" (14:55), the Sanhedrin produces "many" (14:56) false witnesses, though their testimonies disagree. The only specific accusation Mark records is that Jesus would "destroy this temple made with human hands and in three days . . . build

Ancient Roman steps leading from the area south of Jerusalem to the Kidron Valley and the Garden of Gethsemane, where Jesus was arrested. Following his capture, Jesus may well have walked these steps (or some nearby) to his interrogation.

another, not made with hands" (14:58). Given that the temple lay at the heart of Jewish worship and the power of the Sanhedrin, this was a serious charge. For Mark, the accusation again testifies that Jesus has replaced the temple as the place where humanity meets God.

The silence of Jesus throughout the trial—in this respect too John the Baptist was a forerunner of Jesus (Mark 6:14–29)—again reflects the Suffering Servant of Isaiah: "as a sheep before its shearers is silent, so he did not open his mouth" (Isa. 53:7). Jesus breaks silence only at the insistence of the high priest, "Are you the Messiah, the Son of the Blessed One?" (14:61). Ironically, Mark places the two most complete christological confessions from humans in the mouths of those responsible for Jesus's death: the high priest at the trial and the centurion at the cross (15:39). Throughout Mark, Jesus has remained silent about his divine Sonship and commanded the same of others, because until his suffering he cannot rightly be known as God's Son. Now that his execution is imminent, Jesus fully affirms, "I am [God's Son]" (14:62). Although he is presently Son of God in humility (Rom. 1:3), he will come in the future on the clouds of heaven, seated at the right hand of the Mighty One (14:62). The claim to be the messiah was not a crime in Judaism (on the term "messiah," see the commentary on 8:27–9:1). The charge of "blasphemy" (14:64) was limited to equating oneself to God, which indicates the high priest fully understood Jesus's claim to be God's Son. The tearing of the high priest's clothes (the Greek term indicates an inner garment) was a sign of profound consternation (2 Sam. 1:11; 2 Kings 18:37). The mockery of, spitting on, and beating of Jesus in verse 65 fulfill both the treatment of the Suffering Servant (Isa. 50:6) and the third passion prediction (10:33–34).

Mark concludes the sandwich unit by returning to Peter, who is warming himself by the fire in the courtyard of the high priest (14:54, 66). Verses 66–72 focus exclusively on Peter, who alone of the participants is named. Nights in Jerusalem in March-April require the warmth of a fire, the light from which allows Peter to be identified. While Jesus undergoes a trial by the high priest, Peter undergoes one by a mere servant girl. To her accusation that he was with "that Nazarene," Peter vociferously denies (according to the Greek) that he knows Jesus either in theory or practice (14:68). The statement that Peter "went out into the entryway" (14:68) is both factual and symbolic, for he is now farther from Jesus. Peter is identified by his Galilean accent and again accused of association with Jesus—to which he explodes in a volley of abuse and denial (14:71). Peter cannot bring himself to mention the name of Jesus, but he cannot forestall the cockcrow heralding the shattering truth of his denial. Mark concludes the abandonment of Jesus in chapter 14 on the bitter note of weeping (14:72).

E. The trial and crucifixion of Jesus in Jerusalem (15:1–47). 15:1–20. Following the sentence of the Sanhedrin, Jesus is transferred to Pontius Pilate, the Roman prefect of Judea, whose consent was necessary in cases of capital punishment (cf. John 18:31). Before Pilate, as before the Sanhedrin, Jesus is portrayed as submitting in silence. The events leading to the crucifixion, and the crucifixion itself, are narrated in Mark (as in all the Gospels) with utmost restraint; rather than exploiting the brutality and cruelty of crucifixion, or sentimentalizing it, the Gospels accentuate the shame and mockery to which Jesus was subjected. Pilate, fifth Roman governor of Palestine, who ruled from AD 26 to 37, normally resided at Caesarea Maritima. During festivals, when Jewish pilgrims thronged to the temple, Pilate's presence was required in Jerusalem, where he resided in Herod's palace, which is the probable site of the hearing of Jesus. Although Pilate was the longest-ruling Roman governor of Judea, his tenure ended in banishment. He was repeatedly

challenged by his Jewish subjects, and his insensitivity and inflexibility in dealing with their confrontations led to his eventual exile under the emperor Caligula.

Pilate asks Jesus the same question asked by the high priest in 14:61: "Are you the king of the Jews?" (15:2). In Greek it is a statement with a question implied, making Pilate also an unknowing confessor of Jesus. Although, as pointed out above, the claim to be the messiah was not a crime in Judaism, its political implications of earthly rule (see Luke 23:2) pose a potential threat for Pilate. Jesus's answer to Pilate's question in verse 2, neither an affirmation nor denial, could be rendered, "You would do well to consider the question." Jesus's remaining silence in the face of lies, hatred, and cruelty dominates Mark's subsequent passion narrative.

Evidently harboring doubts about the necessity of Jesus's execution, Pilate proposes releasing an insurrectionist, whose name "Barabbas" (in Aramaic) means "son of the father." The real "Son of the Father" will die in place of another "son of the father," who is a known criminal, "the righteous for the unrighteous" (1 Pet. 3:18). The proposed prisoner exchange misfires, however; the crowd "came up" (15:8) in protest against Pilate to Herod's palace, on the prominent western hill in Jerusalem. Mark explicitly states that the moving force behind Jesus's crucifixion is no longer the scribes and Pharisees as in Galilee, nor the Sanhedrin, but solely the "chief priests [who] stirred up the crowd" (15:11) against Jesus. Pilate makes three anemic appeals for Jesus's release (15:9, 12, 14), but his efforts are politically motivated ("wanting to satisfy the crowd," 15:15) rather than based on moral conviction. Facing mounting uproar—"Crucify him!" (15:13–14)—Pilate decides that Jesus is unworthy of defending on principle or by a show of force. In the end, he stands down and consigns Jesus to crucifixion. Although the chief priests appear to have instigated events leading to the crucifixion, Pilate bears final responsibility for it, for crucifixion was a Roman punishment requiring the approval of a Roman governor.

Jesus's trial before Pilate, like John's before Antipas (Mark 6:14–29), is profoundly ironic: Pilate first seeks amnesty for Jesus, then for himself; the Jewish subjects rule, and sovereign Pilate is increasingly subjected, whereas even in chains Jesus remains free in his divinely ordained purpose. Pilate becomes an impotent potentate; the chief priest an agent provocateur; and Jesus remains innocent, silent, defenseless.

In preparation for crucifixion, Jesus is stripped, bound to a post, and beaten an unspecified number of times with a short leather whip woven with bits of bone, metal, or stone. "Flogging" (15:15), or flagellation, lacerated and stripped flesh, often exposing bones and entrails. Its purpose was to shorten the duration of crucifixion, but it was so brutal that not a few prisoners died before being crucified. The mistreatment of Jesus by Pilate and the soldiers fulfills the final passion prediction—the "handing over" (10:33 // 15:15), "mockery" (10:34 // 15:20), "spitting" (10:34 // 15:19), and "flogging" (10:34 // 15:15)—to the detail. This took place in "the palace" (Praetorium; 15:16), most probably Herod's lavish residence on the western hill, which Josephus says contained "enough bedchambers for one-hundred guests" (*Jewish War* 5.177–83; *Jewish Antiquities* 15.318). In macabre sport, a "company of soldiers" mocks Jesus by draping him in purple (symbolizing royalty), crowning him with thorns, and lampooning Caesar's salute, "Hail, King of the Jews" (15:17–18). A "company" was one-tenth of a Roman legion, or about six hundred soldiers. Mockery leads to violence as they beat "him on the head with a staff" (15:19). Bespattered with blood and ridicule, the figure of Jesus recalls Isaiah's Suffering Servant:

> I offered my back to those who
>   beat me,
>   my cheeks to those who pulled
>   out my beard;
> I did not hide my face
>   from mocking and spitting.
>   (Isa. 50:6)

15:21–39. With restrained objectivity, and without sentimentality, sensationalism, or appealing to readers' emotions, Mark recounts the crucifixion in order to show what Jesus's death *accomplished*. Cicero described the hideous brutality of crucifixion as the "most cruel and horrifying punishment." Reserved for non-Roman citizens, crucifixion unleashed excessive and prolonged cruelty on the classes for which it was intended: slaves, violent criminals, and prisoners of war. As a rule, victims were crucified naked and in public in order to add shame and degradation to extreme suffering. The Jewish messiah was expected as a victorious conqueror; there is no certain evidence in any layer of Jewish tradition outside the New Testament of a messiah who would *suffer*. The concept of a messiah suffering on a cross of shame (Heb. 12:2) was so scandalous that some twenty-five years after Jesus's death Paul confessed that the preaching of a crucified messiah was "a stumbling block to Jews and foolishness to Gentiles" (1 Cor. 1:23). Some gnostic sects were so aghast at the idea of a crucified messiah that they put Simon of Cyrene, not Jesus, on the cross.

One of the realities of Roman occupation most detested by Jews was compulsory service. Exercising this privilege, soldiers force an unknown passerby, Simon of Cyrene, to carry the heavy crossbeam of Jesus's cross to the site of crucifixion. Simon's place of origin in Cyrene (North Africa) may indicate he was a man of color. Mark may mention the names of his sons Alexander and Rufus because they were known by or members of the church in Rome to which he was writing (see Rom. 16:13). Simon becomes the first person in Mark literally to take up his cross and follow Jesus (8:34). According to Jewish and Roman custom, victims were executed outside city limits (Lev. 24:14; Num. 15:35–36). Jesus is brought to a place called "Golgotha" (15:22; Aramaic "skull" or "scalp") for crucifixion. Both the oldest Christian tradition and the most recent archaeological excavations corroborate the Church of the Holy Sepulchre in Jerusalem as the site of the crucifixion. The administration of "wine mixed with myrrh" (15:23; see Ps. 69:21), a primitive narcotic, was intended to deaden pain. The dividing of Jesus's garments in verse 24 fulfills the same fate of the suffering righteous man in Psalm 22:18. Jews reckoned time beginning with sunrise at 6 a.m., so that the "third hour" (ESV, NASB) was "nine in the morning" (15:25). Roman and Jewish custom required the cause of execution to be affixed to the cross, which in this case reflects Pilate's accusation (15:2, 9, 12, 18), "king of the Jews." The crucifixion of Jesus between two robbers, "one on his right and one on his left" (15:27), is remarkably similar in wording to Mark 10:40: the two criminals, in other words, occupy the places requested by James and John! The sole point at which Mark departs from the reserve of the crucifixion narrative is in emphasizing the *mockery* of Jesus. Nondescript bystanders shook their heads and "hurled insults" (15:29; cf. 14:55–58); "the chief priests and the teachers of the law mocked him" (15:31); even the robbers "heaped insults on him" (15:32). Ironically, the derision of the chief priests makes them guilty of the charge of blasphemy, for which they condemned Jesus (14:64). The challenge to "come down now from the cross, that we may see and believe" (15:32), yet another appeal for a sign (8:11–13), is evidence of *unbelief*. The taunt that Jesus "can't save himself" (15:31) repeats the temptation in Gethsemane to avoid "this cup" of suffering (14:36). If Jesus submits to the temptation and comes down from the cross, he cannot be a "ransom for many" (10:45).

The crucifixion of Jesus is attended by several portents, the first being darkness from "noon . . . until three in the afternoon" (15:33). The darkness covers "the whole land," symbolizing the universal and cosmic rejection of Jesus. It appears to express God's eschatological judgment, "In that day . . . I will make the sun go down at noon and darken the earth in broad daylight" (Amos 8:9). Although Jesus was silent before the Sanhedrin and Pilate, he cries out from the cross, "My God, my God, why have you forsaken me?" (15:34; Ps. 22:1). His rejection by Rome, Israel, and even his own followers is so total that in his dying breath he senses separation from God. The bystanders mistake Jesus's cry "my God" (Aramaic *eloi*) for "Elijah" (Hebrew *eliyyahu*), the name of one who was taken bodily into heaven (2 Kings 2:11) and was popularly believed to be the rescuer of righteous Jews in times of crisis. The hope is further evidence that God will not let his Righteous One die. In order to ameliorate his suffering, a mixture of sour wine and vinegar (15:36; Ps. 69:21) is offered to Jesus.

With utter finality and objectivity, Mark reports that "Jesus breathed his last" (15:37). At his death two further portents occur that signal the climax of the Gospel of Mark. The first is the tearing of the temple curtain "from top to bottom" (15:38). Mark intends this to be a revelatory portent, for "tear" is the same word used of the tearing of the heavens at Jesus's baptism in 1:10 (the only other time the word is used in Mark). In both tearings, Jesus is declared the Son of God. There were two curtains in the temple, a larger embroidered tapestry depicting "a panorama of the heavens" (Josephus, *Jewish War* 5.213) before the Court of Israel (where Jewish males worshiped), and a smaller curtain before the inviolable Most Holy Place, into which the chief priest entered only on the Day of Atonement. Both curtains are rich in symbolism, although it is unclear which Mark intends. Mark's vocabulary may favor the smaller curtain, since the term he uses refers throughout the New Testament only to the curtain before the Most Holy Place. If this curtain is intended, then the cross of Jesus signifies the true and final Day of Atonement, allowing humanity access to the heart of God.

The second portent at the crucifixion is the confession of the centurion, "Surely this man was the Son of God" (15:39). "Son of God" is Mark's load-bearing christological title, which until this moment has been unconfessed by any human being. Heretofore in Mark, Jesus has commanded both demons and people to silence, for until the cross all declarations about Jesus are premature. The Son of God can be rightly known only in his suffering and death on the cross. The centurion—a Gentile in charge of the execution of Jesus—is the first person to confess Jesus as God's Son, thus embodying the scandal of grace: "While we were God's enemies, we were reconciled to him through the death of his Son" (Rom. 5:10).

15:40–47. The oldest ascertainable form of the Gospel of Mark ends with the story of Joseph of Arimathea (15:40–41, 47), which sandwiches the account of the women attending Jesus's crucifixion and empty tomb (15:42–46). In contrast to the women, who watch the crucifixion "from a distance" (15:40) and who are anxious, distressed, and fearful at the tomb (16:5, 8), Joseph acts with resolution and boldness in procuring the body of Jesus from Pilate and burying him honorably. The faithfulness of Joseph is thus contrasted to the fearfulness of the women.

The temple discourse (13:32–37) and the agony of Gethsemane (14:34, 38) ended with the command to "watch." The sandwich unit begins in 15:40 with the names of several women "watching" the crucifixion. The Greek word for "watch" is used by Mark to suggest watching in detachment rather than in solidarity. Mary Magdalene appears in all four Gospels as the first witness of the resurrection of Jesus. "Mary," "James the younger," and "Joseph" (15:40) are probably (although not certainly) Jesus's family members mentioned in 6:3. The names of these and the reference to "many other women" (15:41) indicate that Jesus was followed by more than the Twelve apostles. Ironically, *women* unmentioned before now remain to the bitter end at the cross. True, they stand at a "distance," but the distance of the women is better than the absence of the apostles. Into the report of the women's trepidation at the cross Mark inserts the story of Joseph of Arimathea, who on late Friday afternoon retrieves Jesus's body for burial. Arimathea is probably the Ramathaim of 1 Samuel 1:1 (see also Ramah in 1 Sam. 15:34),

about twenty miles northwest of Jerusalem. It took courage for a prominent member of the Sanhedrin to request from the governor the body of a man executed as an enemy of the Roman state. The description of Joseph as a man "waiting for the kingdom of God" (15:43) indicates he was a faithful Jew and perhaps a secret believer in Jesus. The ironies of the crucifixion abound: earlier a Roman centurion who crucified Jesus confessed him as the Son of God (15:39); now a member of the Jewish council that condemned Jesus gives him an honorable burial. Mark certifies the death of Jesus on the basis of three witnesses: Joseph (15:43), Pilate (15:44), and the centurion (15:45), two of whom have physical contact with the corpse. This grim fact is necessary and conclusive evidence that chapter 16 is about resurrection, not resuscitation. The body of Jesus was placed on a shelf cut into the side of a limestone cave, the mouth of which was sealed by a large, disk-shaped stone.

Mark completes the sandwich begun in verse 40 by returning to the story of the women in verse 47.

F. The resurrection (16:1–8). Following the Sabbath, Mary Magdalene and Mary the mother of Joses (probably Jesus's mother) visit the tomb of Jesus early on Sunday morning. Their ointments of oil mixed with myrrh and aloes (John 19:39), which they had not had time to buy or apply when Jesus was buried, were not intended for embalming (i.e., to prevent decay of the body) but to perfume the decaying corpse as an act of devotion. The naming of the women three times in connection with Jesus's death and resurrection (15:40, 47; 16:1) establishes the veracity of the resurrection on the basis of eyewitnesses. The names of *women* attest to the authenticity of the resurrection narrative, for had the early Christians fabricated the resurrection account they would scarcely have done so on the testimony of women, which was immaterial in Jewish legal proceedings. "Just after sunrise" (16:2) assures readers that the women had not mistaken the tomb in the darkness. The removal of the large stone from the tomb suggests that in all respects the resurrection of Jesus was God's work. The "white robe" (16:5) on the young man at the tomb, plus his knowledge of the errand of the women and the "alarm" (16:5) he evokes within them, all imply an angelic being rather than the young man mentioned in 14:51. The visit to the tomb is vintage Markan irony: the living are preoccupied with death; the angelic sentry at the tomb is a herald of life (16:6). The angel's invitation to inspect the "place where they laid him" (16:6) indicates that the tomb was empty; thus, the women are not to expect a vision or mystical experience, but a meeting with the resurrected Jesus. The empty tomb does not prove the resurrection, however, for the body of Jesus could have been stolen (see Matt. 27:64). Faith is not the result of a fact—even a fact as awesome as the empty tomb—but of an encounter with the resurrected Lord. The announcement, "Tell [Jesus's] disciples and Peter, 'He is going ahead of you into Galilee,'" (16:7) is both a fulfillment of 14:28 and a word of grace. Peter's denial has not been the final word; the final word belongs to the resurrected

This first-century-BC rolling-stone tomb, possibly the burial place for Herod's family, is similar to the tomb in which Jesus was buried.

Jesus, who promises to go "ahead of you" (16:7). Mark has warned that faith is not evoked by signs, miracles, and portents (8:11–13), and that includes even the resurrection, for the sandwich unit ends in 16:8 with the women silenced by fear and fleeing in bewilderment. In his earthly ministry, people disobeyed Jesus's command to silence; now at the empty tomb, the women disobey the command to proclaim the resurrection!

G. Later resurrection traditions (16:9–20). Verses 9–20 represent one of the most difficult textual problems in the New Testament. The two oldest and most important Greek manuscripts of the New Testament omit the longer ending of Mark, as do several early translations, versions, and testimonies of church fathers. The literary character of 16:9–20 also differs from that of the rest of the Gospel of Mark. Twenty-seven new words occur in the longer ending, plus several stylistic features otherwise absent from Mark. The role of signs in 16:17–18 contradicts Mark 8:11–13. These and other factors make it virtually certain that Mark did not write 16:9–20. This longer ending of Mark, which was added in the early decades of the second century, consists of a resurrection harmony excerpted from the other three Gospels. The various excerpts appear to have been selected and edited in the secondary ending in accordance with the theme of the unbelief of the disciples.

If the Gospel of Mark originally ended at 16:8, then readers, like the women, are left in a state requiring a response of faith, which must be elicited by hearing rather than by sight. This is the conclusion that a majority of modern scholars draw with regard to the oldest ascertainable ending of Mark. Although Mark *may* have ended his Gospel at 16:8, it is not certain—and perhaps even unlikely—that he did. It seems hard to imagine that Mark, who begins his Gospel with a direct and bold declaration of Jesus as God's Son and promised Messiah, would end his Gospel on a note of bewilderment (16:8). Very few ancient texts end as inconclusively as 16:8, which breaks off in mid-sentence. The addition of the longer ending at a later date is certain if artless evidence that the early church considered 16:8 a defective ending. It seems probable, therefore, that the Gospel of Mark originally concluded with a resurrection narrative, similar perhaps to that of the Gospel of Matthew. Not infrequently ancient manuscripts suffered the loss of first and last pages due to wear and tear, and this may have been the fate of the final leaf of Mark's original manuscript. Although Mark, most probably the earliest of the four Gospels, does not contain in its present form a resurrection appearance of Jesus, it should be remembered that the earliest written testimony to the resurrection occurs in 1 Corinthians 15, written a decade earlier by the apostle Paul.

The theme of the secondary ending is the call of the disciples from unbelief (16:11, 13, 14 [2×], 16) to belief (16:16–17). The first call of Jesus comes through Mary Magdalene, the first herald of the saving faith of the gospel (16:9–11). The reference to the exorcism of seven demons comes from Luke 8:2, and Mary's report to the despondent disciples reflects John 20:14, 18. The second call of Jesus comes through the story of two travelers in verses 12–13, which presupposes the walk to Emmaus (Luke 24:13–35). The third call comes from a personal appearance of Jesus to the eleven disciples in verse 14, who upbraids the disciples for disbelieving the two earlier witnesses. Verses 15–16, also from Jesus, reflect the Great Commission of Matthew 28:19. Salvation by faith, sealed by baptism, is ordained for "all creation." Salvation is accompanied by signs of power, according to verses 17–18, including exorcisms, glossolalia, healings, handling of snakes, and drinking of poison. The last two signs are nowhere else attested in Scripture and apparently derive from later sectarian Christian practices. The first three signs, however, indicate that the early Christian proclamation was undergirded—as

is true in many parts of the world today—by heavenly gifts of witness and ministry. Verses 19–20 conclude with the ascension of Jesus, which reflects Acts 1:9–11. The longer ending of Mark thus reflects some circumstances and themes, such as disbelief and dramatic signs, that appear to derive from a later period of the early church and that clearly differ from the Gospel of Mark. The longer ending reflects the chief characteristics of the early church in its emphasis on belief, mission, proclamation, and the saving significance of the gospel for all creation, and though it is not especially Markan, it is not unevangelical.

Select Bibliography

Bainton, Roland. *Here I Stand: A Life of Martin Luther*. Nashville: Abingdon, 1950.

Cranfield, C. E. B. *The Gospel according to Saint Mark*. Cambridge: Cambridge University Press, 1974.

Evans, Craig. *Mark 8:27–16:20*. Word Biblical Commentary. Dallas: Word, 2001.

France, Richard. *The Gospel of Mark*. New International Greek Testament Commentary. Grand Rapids: Eerdmans, 2002.

Guelich, Robert. *Mark 1–8:26*. Word Biblical Commentary. Dallas: Word, 1989.

Gundry, Robert. *Mark: A Commentary on His Apology for the Cross*. Grand Rapids: Eerdmans, 1993.

Hengel, Martin. *Studies in the Gospel of Mark*. Translated by J. Bowden. Philadelphia: Fortress, 1985.

Hooker, Morna D. *A Commentary on the Gospel according to St Mark*. London: A & C Black, 1991.

Hurtado, Larry W. *Mark*. New International Biblical Commentary. Peabody, MA: Hendrickson, 1989.

Lane, William. *The Gospel according to Mark*. New International Commentary on the New Testament. Grand Rapids: Eerdmans, 1974.

Martin, Ralph P. *Mark: Evangelist and Theologian*. Grand Rapids: Zondervan, 1973.

Schweizer, Eduard. *The Good News according to Mark*. Translated by D. Madvig. London: SPCK, 1971.

Swete, Henry Barclay. *The Gospel according to St Mark*. 3rd ed. London: Macmillan, 1909.

Taylor, Vincent. *The Gospel according to St. Mark*. 2nd ed. New York: St. Martin's Press, 1966.

Luke

THOMAS R. SCHREINER

Introduction

Authorship

Nowhere does the Gospel of Luke reveal its author's identity. To ascertain the author, therefore, one should first of all examine the Gospel's internal evidence to find clues about its authorship. Unfortunately, the Gospel does not supply the reader with much information. We do learn, however, that the author was not an eyewitness (Luke 1:2), and thus anyone who observed Jesus in his public ministry can be eliminated. Furthermore, the writer of Luke clearly was intelligent and well educated, for he displays an ability to write in excellent Greek and is well acquainted with the Old Testament.

Also, scholars almost universally agree that the author of the Gospel of Luke is the same person as the author of the Acts of the Apostles for the following reasons: (1) Both books are dedicated to the same person—Theophilus (Luke 1:3; Acts 1:1). (2) The author refers to "my former book," and says that the "former book" contains "all that Jesus began to do and to teach" (Acts 1:1). This former book is most naturally the Gospel of Luke. (3) Last, many of the themes with which Luke ends his Gospel (24:36–53) are picked up again in Acts 1:1–11, which suggests that the same author is continuing his former work, briefly tying together the two works so that the reader of Acts can pick up where the Gospel left off.

Clearly, then, the same author wrote both Luke and Acts. But Acts, unfortunately, is also anonymous. Are there any hints in Acts about the identity of the author? The chief clue is found in the "we sections" of Acts (Acts 16:10–17; 20:5–15; 21:1–18; 27:1–28:16). The careful reader notices that the author speaks of Paul and his companions as "they" (e.g., Acts 16:7–8), and then he suddenly starts using the first-person plural "we" (Acts 16:10–13, 16), probably because he is now participating in the Pauline mission. Indeed, in these sections he may be referring to a diary he kept of these events. By comparing these "we sections" with the rest of the book, the reader can begin to eliminate certain names from authorship (cf. Acts 20:4). Although other solutions are possible (e.g., that the author was Titus), it is most likely that the author of the Gospel was Paul's traveling companion—the physician Luke.

Luke is mentioned three times in Paul's letters. In Colossians 4:14 he is called "our dear friend Luke, the doctor." In Philemon 24 he is mentioned as one of Paul's fellow workers. In 2 Timothy 4:11 Paul says that "only Luke is with me." This reference to Luke's loyalty is especially poignant because the context of 2 Timothy 4 reveals that Paul is about to be executed by the Romans, and many of Paul's companions abandoned him in such a perilous situation. If Philemon and Colossians were written by Paul from Rome (and this theory is still the most probable), then the references to Luke in these letters fit with Acts 27:1–28:16, where the author of Acts accompanies Paul to Rome.

W. K. Hobart argued that Lukan authorship was supported by Luke's precise use of medical terminology, showing that the author was a physician (Col. 4:14). But H. J. Cadbury carefully tested Hobart's thesis and demonstrated that Luke's alleged medical terminology is often found in Greek writers who were not physicians; therefore, one should not claim that the language used in Luke-Acts clearly indicates that a physician wrote it. Cadbury's study, however, does not preclude Lukan authorship; it simply shows that one cannot argue for Lukan authorship from medical terminology. Colossians 4:14 also implies that Luke was a Gentile and not a Jew. In Colossians 4:10–11 Paul names Aristarchus, Mark, and Jesus Justus and says that they are his only companions of the circumcision, meaning presumably that they are his only Jewish companions. Then in Colossians 4:12–14 Paul names Epaphras, Luke, and Demas and says that they send their greetings. If the three listed in Colossians 4:10–11 are the only Jews with Paul, then the obvious conclusion is that Luke was a Gentile.

Even though the internal evidence may point to Lukan authorship, decisive evidence is lacking. But it is significant that the early tradition of the church is unanimous in positing Lukan authorship. For example, the early title of the Gospel—"Gospel according to Luke"—is attached to our earliest manuscript of the Gospel, from the late second century AD. Irenaeus, the Muratorian Canon, and an ancient prologue to the Gospel (all written near the end of the second century AD) also assert Lukan authorship. Tertullian, writing early in the third century AD, also held to Lukan authorship. Some scholars tend to doubt the tradition of the early church on these matters, and certainly the early church fathers were not infallible. Nevertheless, the ancient tradition is a serious witness, and since the church fathers were closer to the events

An icon of Luke from a larger piece entitled *Christ and Twelve Apostles* (Antalya, Turkey, nineteenth century AD)

than we are, we should put our trust in their conclusions unless there is compelling evidence for not doing so. Furthermore, those who doubt Lukan authorship do not adequately explain why the early church would attribute the work to Luke. After all, Luke is not a notable figure in the New Testament itself. The most probable reason for the tradition of Lukan authorship is that this tradition is accurate.

Scholars often question Lukan authorship because Luke's picture of Paul seems to contradict Paul's self-portrait in his letters. But the difference in the portrait of Paul is probably due to two different perspectives. Inevitably, there will be differences between the way a person describes him- or herself and the way an outsider views that person. In addition, it is also claimed that Luke's writing is subapostolic; a belief in the imminent return of Christ

(Greek *parousia*) has been abandoned, and the church has become an institution that grants salvation. The objection regarding the second coming is too simplistic. A careful reading of the Gospel accounts shows that there are three different types of sayings about the end: some stress the imminence of the end (Mark 13:30 and parallels), others a period of delay (Matt. 25:14–30), and others uncertainty regarding the end (Mark 13:32–37 and parallels). The Gospel of Luke displays the same tension (e.g., 21:9 and 21:33) and thus is in accord with the other Gospel accounts. The notion that the church has been institutionalized is also oversimplified, for it is obvious that any new movement must have some organization. The question is whether the Lukan organization is as advanced as the church of the second century AD. Even a cursory reading of the letters of Ignatius (d. ca. 107) shows that there are major differences, for there are no regional bishops in Luke as there are in the Ignatian letters. Neither of these objections, then, is decisive.

Date and Audience

The date and destination of the Gospel of Luke are also shrouded in uncertainty. Indeed, the problem is particularly knotty because the date of Luke usually depends on the dates of Mark and Acts (most scholars still hold to Markan priority). Two basic theories are favored in scholarship today: Luke was written in either the 80s or the 60s. Those who favor a date in the 80s maintain that Luke was written after Mark, and the latter was not written until circa AD 65–70. In addition, some scholars claim that Luke was probably written after the destruction of the temple in AD 70. Others think Luke was written in the early 60s because Acts ends (28:30–31) with Paul under house arrest, and no information is given on the outcome of his trial. According to this theory, such an abrupt ending in Acts shows that Luke finished Acts before Paul's case was resolved. In this instance Acts would be dated between AD 61 and 63. Since Luke was written before Acts, the Gospel would be placed in the

early 60s or late 50s. The same scholars would argue that the Gospel of Mark was written in the 50s. Other scholars date Luke between AD 65 and 70, arguing that it was probably written before the destruction of Jerusalem in AD 70. Certainty is impossible on such difficult matters, but a date before the destruction of Jerusalem in AD 70 seems probable.

Where was Luke when he wrote the Gospel? Early traditions suggest Achaia, Boeotia, or Rome. The latter is especially attractive because of the tradition that Mark wrote his Gospel in Rome; however, no one really knows where Luke was, but the matter is not crucial in the interpretation of the Gospel.

Almost all scholars agree that Luke wrote to Gentile Christians. The dedication of the two volumes to a person who has a Greek name (Theophilus), the excellent Greek of the prologue (1:1–4), the interest in Gentiles, and the elimination of certain Jewish customs and debates (e.g., the controversy on cleanness in Mark 7:1–23), and the substitution of Greek terms for Jewish terms all suggest a Gentile audience.

Sources

That Luke used sources is immediately evident from the prologue of the Gospel (1:1–4). He indicates that many others have written accounts of the Gospel traditions and that these traditions have been handed down to the church. Luke specifically states that he "carefully investigated everything from the beginning" (1:3), showing that he thoroughly sifted through the information that was available to him. What were the actual sources Luke used? This is a matter of speculation, of course, and so dogmatism is excluded.

Most New Testament scholars still agree that Luke used the Gospel of Mark when he composed his Gospel (although this theory is contested rather strongly by a significant number of scholars). The reason for this is that a substantial portion of Mark's Gospel, often including the exact words from Mark, is used in Luke's Gospel. Of course, the argument as it is stated above could support Lukan priority, but for a variety of complex reasons such a view is unlikely.

Also, both Luke and Matthew may have used a common source that was either a written document or consisted of oral tradition. This material is designated "Q" (from German *Quelle*, "source"). Unfortunately, Q has not survived and possibly never even existed in written form. Approximately 230 verses appear in both Matthew and Luke but not in Mark's Gospel. A common source is possible since the wording of this common tradition that Luke and Matthew share is remarkably similar and sometimes exactly the same. But if the wording is so similar, then perhaps Luke borrowed it directly from Matthew (very few scholars think Matthew borrowed from Luke). This is improbable, however, because Luke uses the same sayings that Matthew does and places them in completely different contexts. It is highly unlikely that Luke would transpose the same sayings or break up Matthew's tightly organized Sermon on the Mount (Matthew 5–7). Thus, the idea that Luke and Matthew both used and adapted a common source or sources, each without directly depending on the other's Gospel, is the most likely, though we cannot be sure if the source or sources were oral or written.

Last, any material in Luke's Gospel that is not dependent on Mark or Q is usually labeled "L." This is simply a convenient way of indicating that Luke had other sources of information. It is impossible to know how many.

We should also not rule out that Luke may have received information from Mary the mother of Jesus, the disciples of John the Baptist, Manaen (an early disciple; cf. Acts 13:1), Cleopas (Luke 24:18), and others. Many New Testament scholars would doubt that Luke depended on any of these persons. But it is quite probable that Luke would have spoken to living persons about what they had heard and seen of Jesus when he came into contact with them. Any twentieth-century researcher would have done the same, and in the ancient world such a procedure would have been prized just as highly, as the early church father Papias in the second century made clear.

Some scholars have maintained that Luke's use of his sources shows that his writing lacks historical reliability—that he was writing to edify the church and to propound his own theology and not to transmit what really happened. First, we should note that such a position contradicts Luke's own statement of his purpose in the prologue of the Gospel (1:1–4), where he indicates that accuracy in the work is one of his concerns. Second, it is methodologically flawed to pit edification and theology against history. All history writing is interpretive to some degree; the writer must select which themes he will emphasize. Clearly, Luke does have a distinctive theology, but it is not logically necessary to conclude that such interpretive selection and presentation by an author obviates historical reliability. The same point applies to edification; that is, what really happened could be edifying. Third, Luke's use of the Gospel of Mark (the most common theory) also shows that he was interested in historical accuracy. For example, the sayings of Jesus shared by Luke and Mark usually have only minor differences. The modern reader needs to remember that the ancient writer was not always interested in exactly what was said. Luke would naturally be content at times to paraphrase Jesus's words and actions. Such a paraphrase would be inaccurate only if it deceived a person about what actually happened. Luke was not recording on tape the words of Jesus, but neither was he freely inventing them; he clearly felt free to record in his own style what happened. Last, when Luke's account differs from the other Synoptics, we need to recall that none of the accounts claims to be exhaustive. Thus, one should not demand that any Gospel writer tell the whole story. All our questions about historicity will never be answered when reading the Gospels. But humility and the inspiration of Scripture suggest that we should give the writer the benefit of the doubt.

Theological Themes

When studying Luke's theology one must remember that he did not simply write a Gospel but that he also wrote the book of Acts. Both works must be taken into account in formulating a Lukan theology.

It is evident from the writing of both the Gospel and Acts that Luke is interested in the continuing history of the church. The prologue to the Gospel (1:1–4) clearly shows that Luke was interested in historical accuracy. More than any other Gospel writer Luke explains the relationship between the events he narrates and Roman and Palestinian history. Of course, Luke was not a disinterested historian; he wrote these books because he saw this period of history as the decisive in-breaking of God's salvation.

It is not surprising, therefore, that Luke is usually described as a theologian of salvation history. Luke sees what is happening in the ministry of Jesus and the ministry of the early church as the fulfillment of God's plan and purpose. This saving plan comes to realization as people experience salvation.

Luke also emphasizes that this salvation is for all people, even for the people considered to be outcasts or socially marginal. Thus, Jesus proclaims his saving message to tax collectors, sinners, the poor, women, and children. This theme continues in Acts, where the early church slowly grasps that God wants the gospel message to be proclaimed to both Samaritans and Gentiles. Jews and Gentiles are equal members in God's new community.

The power of the Spirit and the importance of prayer are also prominent themes in Lukan theology. In the Gospel of Luke Jesus conducts his ministry in the power of the Spirit. His messianic work can be accomplished only because "the Spirit of the Lord is on me" (4:18). After Jesus's resurrection and exaltation he becomes the dispenser of the Spirit (Acts 2:32–33) and pours the Spirit on his disciples. Then his disciples proclaim the gospel of salvation to the ends of the earth by the power of the Spirit. Prayer also plays a vital role in Jesus's ministry.

Luke emphasizes repeatedly that Jesus prayed before making important decisions or at key points in his ministry. The disciples in Acts follow the pattern of their master by continuing in prayer.

Luke also focuses on the importance of discipleship. Some of Jesus's strongest statements on the commitment demanded of those who would follow Jesus are found in this Gospel (9:57–62; 14:25–35). Also, Luke stresses in uncompromising terms the dangers of materialism. The love of riches ousts one's love for God, which is why Luke thinks it is a blessing to be poor, for the poor are dependent on God (6:20–26). In Acts, Luke portrays the ideal of Christian community (Acts 2:42–47; 4:32–37).

Unlike Paul, Luke does not fully explain the meaning of Christ's death on the cross. Luke views the death of Jesus as the fulfillment of God's plan (Luke 24:44), and he even connects the possibility of forgiveness with the death of Jesus (24:46–47). What Luke does not do, however, is attempt to explain in detail the relationship between Jesus's death and the forgiveness of sins.

The salvation that Luke centers on is available through Jesus of Nazareth. The significance of Jesus becomes apparent when one examines the titles Luke ascribes to him. Jesus is Messiah, Lord, the Son of God, the Son of Man, Savior, servant of the Lord, king, prophet, and the Son of David.

Outline

1. Prologue: A Reliable Account of Salvation History (1:1–4)
2. Preparation for Jesus's Ministry (1:5–4:13)
   A. Two Births Predicted (1:5–56)
   B. Two Sons Born (1:57–2:52)
   C. The Baptist's Ministry: Preparation for the Lord (3:1–20)
   D. Jesus: Endowed by the Spirit for Ministry (3:21–4:13)
3. Jesus Proclaims Salvation in Galilee by the Power of the Spirit (4:14–9:50)

Commentary

1. Prologue: A Reliable Account of Salvation History (1:1–4)

Luke's prologue is distinctive among the Gospel texts because it is written in excellent classical Greek, showing that Luke is consciously writing a literary work. Many have preceded Luke in composing Gospels, relying on the oral testimony of eyewitnesses who handed down the tradition. Luke has also decided to compose a Gospel; one cannot demonstrate from the text that he has decided to do this because he thought the previous Gospels were inadequate or inferior. Indeed, verse 2 implies that Luke trusted the reliability of the previous accounts. Luke then displays his credentials for writing a Gospel. His investigation was comprehensive ("from the beginning"), accurate ("carefully"), and well organized ("orderly"). The word "orderly" does not necessarily imply that Luke is writing in strict chronological order but only that the Gospel itself is organized in a literary way. The work is dedicated to Theophilus, although a wider readership is clearly expected. Theophilus cannot be identified with certainty. Some think he may have been a Roman official, but the words "most excellent" may simply suggest that he was a member of the higher class in Roman society. The purpose of the work is related in verse 4. Luke is writing so that Theophilus will be convinced of the reliability ("certainty") of the matters in which he has been instructed. The reference to eyewitness testimony and the careful nature of Luke's research (1:2–3) support the claim of reliability. Luke, however, was not simply writing a historical treatise; he was writing about the events of salvation history, about the events that "have been fulfilled" (1:1) through the person of Christ. Luke was not a dispassionate historian, but neither was he an inferior historian. He writes history from an interpretive standpoint, showing that God's saving purposes have been fulfilled in Christ.

2. Preparation for Jesus's Ministry (1:5–4:13)

A. Two births predicted (1:5–56). In the first part of this section of the Gospel, Luke describes the prediction of the birth of John the Baptist (1:5–25). In verses 5–7 Luke sets the background before writing of Zechariah's vision. The Herod who is mentioned is Herod the Great (cf. Matt. 2:1–19), who ruled over Palestine from 37 BC to 4 BC. Zechariah and Elizabeth were both from priestly stock, and Zechariah was from the "division of Abijah." The priestly tribe of Levi was divided into twenty-four divisions, and the division of Abijah was the eighth of the twenty-four (1 Chron. 24:7–18). Each division served in the temple at Jerusalem two weeks every year. To be childless was considered a great reproach among the Jews (cf. 1:25; Gen. 30:23; 1 Sam. 1:5–6), but verse 6 clearly shows that their failure to have children was not due to sin.

Zechariah was chosen by lot to offer incense in the temple (1:9). The number of men in the priestly ranks was so large that no person was permitted to offer incense more than once in his lifetime. In accordance with Exodus 30:7–8, incense was offered twice a day, both in the morning and evening. The parallels with Daniel 9 suggest that the vision occurred in the evening. The Greek word used for "temple" in this context refers to the Holy Place since only the high priest could enter the Most Holy Place (cf. Heb. 9:6–7). The sudden appearance of the angel Gabriel (1:19) arouses fear in Zechariah. The content of Zechariah's prayer (1:13) is problematic. Was Zechariah praying for a son (1:6–7) or was he praying for Israel's redemption? Perhaps he was praying for both since John's birth relates to both of these concerns. John's abstinence from alcohol reminds one of the Nazirites (Num. 6:3; Judg. 13:4). The filling of the Holy Spirit (1:15) in Luke is usually related to prophetic activity, indicating that John is a prophet. Verses 16–17 reveal John's function: to prepare the people for the Lord's advent. He will fulfill the role of Elijah, as was predicted in Malachi 3:1 and 4:5. Zechariah is punished for his doubt—clear Old Testament precedents show that children were born to childless couples (Genesis 16–21; Judges 13; 1 Samuel 1), and Zechariah as a priest knew these stories. In addition, Zechariah's muteness (1:21–22) functions to show the people that he has seen a vision.

The announcement of Jesus's birth (1:26–38) has many similarities to the previous story, but the significance and superiority of Jesus's birth are heightened because he will be born of a virgin (not just barren parents) and will sit on David's throne (unlike John, who will prepare the way of the Lord). The emphasis on Davidic sonship is first implied in verse 27, for by adoption Jesus becomes Joseph's son. Verses 32–33 plainly show that Jesus will be the promised Messiah from the line of David (cf. 2 Sam. 7:9–16). The text, of course, goes a step further: Jesus is not just the Son of David but also the Son of God (1:35; cf. 1:32). In Luke "Son of God" refers to Jesus's unique relation to Yahweh.

The angel Gabriel visited Mary in Nazareth of Galilee (Luke 1:26), which became Jesus's boyhood home. Nestled within a bowl formation in the Nazareth Range, Nazareth was then a very small village, but today it has grown into a large town.

Mary's favored status (1:28) does not imply any intrinsic worthiness; it merely means that she has been a recipient of God's gracious activity. Nevertheless, Mary's obedience and faith (1:38; cf. 1:45) are clearly a model for Luke's community.

Mary's question in verse 34 has engendered much controversy. Since she is engaged to Joseph, why does she even ask this question? (The verbs in 1:31 are future.) Some scholars have said that Mary had made a vow of perpetual virginity, but this is contradicted by her engagement to Joseph. Others claim that Mary knew from Isaiah 7:14 that the Messiah would be born of a virgin, and she was protesting because she was already engaged. But it is unlikely that Mary understood Isaiah 7:14 to refer to a virgin birth, and Luke never uses the passage. Still others take this to be a Lukan literary device. In other words, Mary never spoke these words, but the question advances the narrative to the great announcement; however, this solution impugns Luke's historical reliability. It is most likely that Mary understood the angel to be saying that the conception would be imminent, and Mary's marriage was still not consummated.

Naturally, the historicity of the virgin birth has been questioned. Some scholars have said that the story was borrowed from the pagan world, where heroes were born from the union of gods and human women. These accounts, however, are different from the Lukan and Matthean accounts, for nothing in the latter texts suggests that actual intercourse took place between God and Mary. The words "come on" and "overshadow" in verse 35 do not imply sexual relations, and Luke here describes with great delicacy an incomprehensible event. Others have questioned the veracity of the accounts because of the silence of the rest of the New Testament. The rest of the New Testament, however, does not contradict the present account. (For a detailed discussion, see Machen.)

The text of 1:39–56 can easily be divided into two sections: (1) Elizabeth pronounces a blessing on Mary as the mother of the Lord

(1:39–45); (2) Mary breaks forth in praise to God for his mighty works (1:46–56). The blessing of Elizabeth ties the narrative together; now the mothers of the two sons meet, and even in the womb John begins his ministry. In addition, Elizabeth's words in verse 43 confirm the promise that was made to Mary. Mary is blessed (1:42) not because she is incomparably holy but because she is the mother of the Lord and because she believes that the divine promise will be fulfilled (1:45). So once again Mary becomes a model for the Lukan community (cf. 1:38). The content of Mary's song is rather surprising, for only in verse 48 does Mary dwell on the personal benefits of being the mother of the Lord. The song stresses the exaltation of the humble, the humiliation of God's enemies (especially the proud and rich), and the fulfillment of God's promises to Abraham. Presumably the song celebrates what God will accomplish through the birth of Jesus, the Messiah. The song is typically Jewish (cf. particularly 1 Sam. 2:1–10, which contains numerous parallels). The prophecy, of course, is fulfilled in a way that surprises Mary, since Jesus suffers before he is exalted.

B. Two sons born (1:57–2:52). 1:57–80 The account of John's birth (1:57–66) continues the parallelism between John and Jesus, which is characteristic of the Lukan infancy narrative, although Jesus's birth is described in more detail (cf. 2:1–20). Circumcision on the eighth day (1:59) was in obedience to the Old Testament law (Lev. 12:3), indicating that John was incorporated into the covenant (Gen. 17:9–14). The controversy over the naming of the child is curious because this is the only early passage that indicates that a child was named at his circumcision. In the Old Testament a child was named at birth. Moreover, there is no clear evidence that the naming of a child after his father was common or expected, although the naming of a child after his grandfather was common. The name John means "God is gracious."

The text implies that Zechariah was deaf as well as mute (1:62), and presumably he had communicated previously in writing to Elizabeth what the name of the child should be (1:60). The main function of the story is to show that the Lord's hand is with John (1:66). This is communicated to the reader and the original participants in the events in two ways: (1) Elizabeth conceives and gives birth to a child long after her childbearing days are over; (2) Zechariah is suddenly given the ability to speak again after being deaf and mute for a period of time.

Structurally, Zechariah's hymn (1:67–80) can be divided into two parts. In the first part of the hymn Zechariah praises God for the redemption he has accomplished through the house of David (1:68–75). In the second part of the hymn he focuses on the role of John (1:76–79). Like the Magnificat, this hymn is full of Old Testament allusions, and the marginal references to the Old Testament should be consulted. Luke makes an editorial comment before the opening of the hymn (1:67), explaining that Zechariah's hymn is prophetic and Spirit-inspired. In addition, the hymn also answers the question in verse 66 about the role of John in salvation history.

Zechariah begins the hymn by praising God for his deliverance (1:68). The word "horn" (1:69) means strength, alluding to the horns of animals. This is a very common Old Testament expression (Deut. 33:17). The salvation God has accomplished is a fulfillment of the prophecies made to David (1:69–70). Clearly, Zechariah is thinking of God's promise to David that an heir would always sit on the throne (2 Sam. 7:12–16), and thus he is thinking of Mary's promised son. This may seem strange because John has just been born and Zechariah is praising God for Jesus. But we have already seen in Luke 1:11–17 that John's birth is linked with the fulfillment of God's saving purposes. The fulfillment of God's covenant (1:72) to Abraham (1:73) is also the object of Zechariah's praise. With the birth of John and the promised birth of Jesus, Zechariah sees the fulfillment of all the Old Testament promises. Zechariah

conceives of this fulfillment in nationalistic terms; the Jews will be rescued from the onslaughts of all enemy forces so that they will be able to serve God in peace and harmony (1:71, 74–75). The remainder of Luke demonstrates that the prophecy will be fulfilled in Jesus in an unexpected way.

In verses 76–77 Zechariah turns his attention to the role of John. He will be a prophet (cf. Isa. 40:3; Mal. 3:1) and will prepare the way for the Lord. Here the "Lord" is probably not a reference to God but to Jesus. John's ministry will be a spiritual one, for the people will learn the saving message that consists of the forgiveness of their sins (cf. Jer. 31:31–34). The last two verses (1:78–79) are particularly difficult. The salvation John proclaims is due to the tender mercy of our God, and that same mercy also explains the advent of the rising sun. The Greek word for "rising sun" may also be translated as "root" or "branch." In either case it probably expresses a messianic title (cf. Num. 24:17; Mal. 4:2 on rising sun, and Isa. 11:1; Jer. 23:5; Zech. 3:8 and 6:12 on root or branch). The Messiah will illumine those in darkness and bring in peace.

2:1–52. Luke's interest in history becomes evident as he dates the birth of Jesus in relationship to world history. Augustus (2:1) was officially the Roman emperor from 27 BC to AD 14, and under his reign the Roman world experienced unparalleled peace and prosperity. During the reign of Augustus censuses were conducted for the purposes of taxation. The main purpose of this incident is to show that Jesus was born in the town of David, which was Bethlehem (2:4; cf. Mic. 5:2; Matt. 2:4–6). Thus, God in his sovereignty used the decree of Augustus to accomplish his purposes (cf. Isa. 45:1–6). Verse 5 seems to indicate that Mary is now married to Joseph, although the marriage has not yet been consummated. The wrapping of Jesus in strips of cloth (2:7) was the usual way mothers took care of their children (cf. Ezek. 16:4). A second-century tradition places Jesus's birth in a cave, but there is no compelling evidence for that here. The newborn Jesus was laid in a manger—that is, a place where domesticated animals were fed. The inn in verse 7 was probably a public place where a number of travelers would spend the night under one roof. Possibly the manger was located under the open sky or in a barn somewhere, although the text says nothing about other animals being present. Another possibility is that Jesus was born in the small home of a Jewish peasant family who kept their animals indoors with them.

The historical accuracy of Luke's description of the census is plagued by various problems, the most serious being the date of Quirinius's governorship. Quirinius began his governorship of Syria in AD 6, and this is obviously too late to accord with the date of Jesus's birth, for Jesus was born before the death of Herod the Great in 4 BC. Scholars have suggested various solutions to the problem, but we will mention only two. (1) Quirinius conducted several military operations in the eastern part of the empire, and he may have had extraordinary authority to order a census during the governorship of

Saturninus (9–6 BC). (2) Perhaps the census began during the reign of Herod the Great and was not finished until the governorship of Quirinius. No easy resolution of this problem is available, and we must be content with some uncertainty since our historical records are incomplete.

The shepherds are not selected for the visitation (2:8–20) because they are sinners but because of their lowly status. The shepherds would take turns watching the flock at night to guard against wolves and thieves. The text does not indicate the time of year, although December would be an unusual time of year to be outside at night. The shepherds are told that the good news is for all the people (2:10), and by this Luke is probably indicating the inclusion of the Gentiles. The significance of the birth is plainly revealed to the shepherds, as Jesus is called Savior (Deliverer), Christ (Messiah), and Lord (2:11). The meaning of the last line of the angels' hymn in verse 14 has been construed in different ways. The translation of the NIV is correct: "Glory to God in the highest heaven, and on earth peace to those on whom his favor

The Church of the Nativity in Bethlehem. Tradition says this church is built upon the site where Jesus was born (Luke 2:6–7).

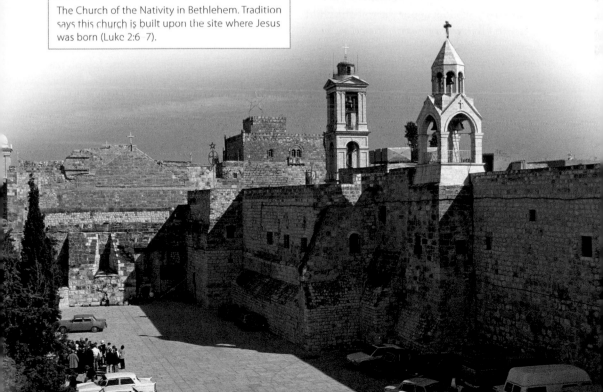

rests." The notion that God's peace extends to "men of good will" is a serious distortion of the doctrine of grace, and the King James Version rendering ("good will toward men") is based on an inferior text.

The story shows the spontaneous obedience of the shepherds (2:15), the amazement of those who hear the report of the shepherds (1:17–18), and Mary's careful reflection over the events that are occurring (1:19). The reference to Mary in verse 19 may indicate that she was a source of Luke's information for this story.

The theme that ties together 2:21–40 is the fulfillment of the law—that is, the fulfillment of Scripture. Jesus is circumcised in accord with the Old Testament law (Lev. 12:3), Mary is purified (2:22–24; cf. Lev. 12:4–8), and both Simeon and Anna prophesy, indicating that God is fulfilling his covenant promises. In verse 39 Luke reiterates the major theme of this section by noting that "Joseph and Mary had done everything required by the Law of the Lord." The parallelism between John the Baptist and Jesus continues, but the superiority of Jesus is again emphasized. At John's circumcision and naming many wonder about the role the child is going to fill (Luke 1:65–66). The greater significance of Jesus is indicated by the startling prophetic revelations in the temple concerning his ministry.

Luke has compressed together several themes in verses 22–24, and they need to be distinguished. (1) The purification of Mary was stipulated by Leviticus 12:1–8. A woman was considered to be unclean after the birth of a boy for forty days, and when her purification was finished she was to offer sacrifices for cleansing. Mary and Joseph offer either a pair of doves or two young pigeons (2:24; cf. Lev. 12:8) because they cannot afford to offer a lamb. (2) The Old Testament also required that the firstborn child should be redeemed by a payment of five shekels (Exod. 13:13; Num. 18:15–16). Such a redemption reflects the Old Testament tradition that the firstborn belongs to Yahweh. Luke does not say that the payment is made, perhaps because

he has combined this theme with the next one. (3) Interestingly, Luke combines the redemption of the firstborn with the presentation of Jesus to the Lord (2:22–23). Nowhere does the Old Testament require such a presentation, and the presentation of Jesus reminds the reader of Hannah's presentation of Samuel (1 Sam. 1:22–24, 28). Perhaps Luke's amalgamation of these three themes explains why he speaks of "their purification" (NASB, RSV) in verse 22, because according to the Old Testament law only Mary needed to be purified.

The Spirit had already revealed to Simeon that he would not die before he would see the Messiah of the Lord (2:26). "He was waiting for the consolation of Israel" (2:25), and this means that he was waiting for God to fulfill his covenant promises to Israel. The coming of the Spirit on a person in Luke (2:25) usually indicates prophetic activity, and thus it is not surprising that Simeon prophesies. Simeon is ready to die because he has seen God's salvation (2:29–30); the word "salvation" is just another way of describing Christ and his work in this context. When Simeon speaks of "all nations" (2:31), Gentiles are included, which verse 32 makes clear (cf. Isa. 49:6). The reference to the child's father and mother (2:33) does not contradict the virgin birth because Joseph has adopted Jesus into his family. After his positive oracle Simeon turns to a more ominous matter. Jesus will "cause the falling and rising of many in Israel" (2:34). Either two different groups are being described here—one group will rise and another will fall—or more probably Luke is referring to one group. Those who embrace the message of Jesus will fall before they rise. In other words, identification with Jesus will bring persecution. Such hostility to Jesus will reveal the thoughts of the heart (2:35); that is, it will reveal that some are opposed to Jesus. Simeon, then, adds that Mary herself will experience anguish from the rejection Jesus will encounter. Like Simeon, Anna proclaims redemption for Jerusalem (2:36–38; here "Jerusalem" refers to Israel as a whole), linking that redemption with

Jesus. One should not read the saying about her never leaving the temple too literally. Perhaps she resided in one of the many rooms adjacent to the temple.

In 2:41–52 Luke discusses the account of the young boy Jesus at the temple. According to the Old Testament all Jewish males were required to go to Jerusalem for the great festival of Passover (Exod. 23:14–17; Deut. 16:16). By New Testament times women also attended. Jesus would have been expected to fulfill this requirement after he reached the age of thirteen. It is not entirely surprising that Jesus's parents do not know that he is still in Jerusalem. It was common for pilgrims to travel in large caravans (2:44), and they could have easily concluded that Jesus was with relatives or friends. The account of Jesus's discussion with the religious leaders (2:46–47) does not imply that he is teaching them; rather, it implies that his knowledge of the law is penetrating and thorough. Joseph and Mary find Jesus after three days (2:46): the first day they depart for home, the second day they return to Jerusalem, and on the third day they find him. Jesus's answer (2:49) to his parents' question strikes the modern reader as odd, but Luke is not interested in the psychological dynamics of the story. The point of Jesus's answer is that obedience to his Father takes precedence over obedience to his parents. Thus, the center of the story is christological—Jesus is no ordinary son. Jesus's parents are perplexed (2:50), and Luke wants the reader to focus on who Jesus is. The story ends (2:51–52) with Jesus returning home; he submits himself to his parents and grows in grace and wisdom.

C. The Baptist's ministry: Preparation for the Lord (3:1–20). The historical introduction in 3:1 signifies the real beginning of the gospel story (cf. Acts 10:37). Luke is the only Gospel writer who clearly sets the events into the context of world history. Tiberius's reign extended from AD 14 to 37. The reference to Tiberius's fifteenth year (3:1) is not definitive because there were different ways of calculating chronology in the ancient world. One possible date is AD 28/29, though AD 26/27 could be correct as well. Pontius Pilate ruled as the governor of Judea (the correct technical term is prefect) from AD 26 to 36. Herod the tetrarch of Galilee is not Herod the Great but Herod Antipas, who reigned over Galilee and Perea from 4 BC to AD 39. Antipas was the son of Herod the Great and is the Herod referred to in the rest of the Gospel. Philip was also a son of Herod the Great and reigned from 4 BC to AD 34. Very little is known about Lysanias. Only one person could be high priest at a time in Israel (3:2). Annas functioned as high priest from AD 6 to 15, and Caiaphas was high priest from AD 18 to 36. Luke does not distinguish carefully between Annas and Caiaphas because the latter was the son-in-law of Annas, and hence Annas continued to exercise great power during the high priesthood of Caiaphas. The event Luke is placing into its historical context is the beginning of John the Baptist's ministry. John's ministry is conducted in the desert (3:2) near the Jordan River. He preaches "a baptism of repentance for the forgiveness of sins" (3:3). This was not merely ritual washing but involved a definite break with sin. Luke sees John's ministry as a fulfillment of Isaiah 40:3–5. Just as Isaiah predicted, Israel needed a "new exodus" to enter the land of promise. Spiritually Israel needed to come out of the wilderness, pass through the Jordan, and enter the land of promise. John is the transitional prophet between the old and new eras (cf. Luke 16:16), and he is preparing all people for God's salvation.

Verses 7–18 can be divided into three subsections: John preaches on (1) eschatology (3:7–9), (2) ethics (3:10–14), and (3) the Messiah (3:15–17). In verses 7–9 John warns that baptism without a change of lifestyle is worthless. Neither can the Jews rely on their heritage, for being a child of Abraham does not matter if one does not partake of the character of Abraham. John's ominous reference to "the coming wrath" confirms these warnings, for the ax of judgment is ready to fall. What is the "good fruit" (3:9) one should produce before judgment falls? In verses 10–14 Luke gives us a sample of John's ethical teaching. John does not call people to imitate his ascetic lifestyle, nor does he upset the existing social order, for he does not ask tax collectors or soldiers to leave their present jobs. Instead, he counsels those who are in these professions to be honest and content with their wages. The soldiers described here are probably not Romans but the soldiers of Herod. The common people are counseled to share their food and clothing with others (3:10). John's preaching on imminent judgment and his powerful ethical message stimulate the people to consider whether or not he is the Messiah (3:15). John clearly shows that he is not the Messiah for the following reasons: (1) one is coming who is "more powerful" (3:16) than John; (2) John is not even worthy to untie the thongs of his sandals, a task that was usually performed by non-Jewish slaves in Palestine; (3) John's baptism is only in water, but the coming one "will baptize . . . with the Holy Spirit and fire." Luke is thinking of the coming of the Spirit at Pentecost (Acts 2:1–4), and the reference to fire may refer either to the refining of the righteous or to judgment on the recalcitrant (3:17). Since Luke wants to focus on Jesus, he completes the story of the Baptist's ministry here and briefly relates the story of his imprisonment. Luke will return to the Baptist again for other reasons (cf. 7:18–35; 16:16).

D. Jesus: Endowed by the Spirit for ministry (3:21–4:13). Luke is not as interested in the actual baptism of Jesus (3:21–22) as he is in the events that accompany it. The descent of the Spirit indicates that Jesus is being anointed for his ministry (cf. Acts 10:37–38). The descent of the dove in bodily form, the opening of heaven, and the voice from God point perhaps to the inauguration of the new creation (Gen. 1:2; 8:8–12) and the reality of the Spirit's descent. It is characteristic of Luke to mention that Jesus was praying. The words of the heavenly voice contain allusions to Psalm 2:7, Isaiah 42:1, and Genesis 22:2, indicating that Jesus is God's Son and servant. This passage is not teaching that Jesus was adopted as God's Son, for Luke 1:35 shows that Luke considers Jesus to be God's Son from the beginning.

The inclusion of the genealogy of Jesus (3:23–38) here is explained by Luke's desire to give Jesus's ancestry before the onset of his ministry. In addition, there seems to be a link between 3:22 and 3:38, for Luke's genealogy is distinctive in that it ends not with a human being but with God. Obviously, the genealogy is not attempting to prove that Jesus was the Son of God in a physical sense, but Luke is making a literary and theological point in placing God at the very end of the genealogy. Indeed, the very first verse of the genealogy urges the reader to ask about the identity of Jesus's father, since Joseph is not really his father (3:23). The genealogy does not contradict the virgin birth, as verse 23 makes clear. Some scholars have expressed concern because of the differences between the genealogies of Matthew and Luke (cf. Matt. 1:1–17). For example, Matthew gives the names in forward order—from Abraham to Jesus—while Luke gives the names in reverse order—from Jesus to God. A number of problems could be listed, but the most serious are as follows: (1) Joseph's father is Heli in Luke (3:23) and Jacob in Matthew (Matt. 1:16); (2) in Luke Jesus's descent from David is traced through Nathan (Nathan the son of David not Nathan the prophet; cf. 2 Sam. 5:14), but in Matthew Jesus's descent from David is traced through Solomon (Matt. 1:6); (3) Luke's list is considerably longer between David and Jesus. One common solution has been that Luke is giving the genealogy from Mary, but this cannot be supported from the text of Luke. A more credible solution is that Matthew is giving the royal line of David (i.e., the legal heirs to the throne; Joseph belonged to this line via levirate marriage), and Luke is giving the actual family line of Joseph.

The last event before Jesus's public ministry begins is his temptation in the wilderness (4:1–13). Two themes tie this section together:

(1) Jesus by the power of the Spirit overcomes the devil by citing the Word of God; and (2) the devil is challenging Jesus's filial obedience as God's Son (4:3, 9). Jesus shows before his ministry begins that his trust and obedience are in his Father. Matthew and Luke have a different order in recording the temptations; the second and third temptations are reversed in Matthew.

Luke emphasizes that Jesus is full of the Spirit and led by the Spirit (4:1), implying that Jesus conquers the devil by the power of the Spirit. The devil attempts to seduce Jesus from obedience to his Father with three different temptations. In the first temptation (4:3–4) the devil tries to persuade Jesus to use his status as God's Son to satisfy his own physical desires, instead of trusting in the Father to provide his needs. Jesus's answer (from Deut. 8:3) implies that the satisfaction of physical desires cannot take precedence over faithful obedience. In the second temptation (4:5–7) the devil promises Jesus authority over all the kingdoms of the world if Jesus will consent to worship him. Jesus's answer (from Deut. 6:13) is that worship and service belong to God alone, and thus it is unthinkable for him to worship the devil in order to gain earthly power and glory. Last (4:9–11), the devil brings Jesus to the pinnacle of the temple and, while arguing from Scripture (Ps. 91:11–12) that the angels will protect Jesus, suggests that he should leap. Jesus does not reject the devil's scriptural argument (God does protect the godly), but he does refuse to perform such a whimsical act because it would involve testing God (see Deut. 6:16). Jesus is certainly referring to his Father rather than himself when he says, "Do not put the Lord your God to the test" (4:12).

3. Jesus Proclaims Salvation in Galilee by the Power of the Spirit (4:14–9:50)

A. Proclamation of good news in Galilee (4:14–5:16). Jesus's public ministry in Luke begins at 4:14–15. Luke emphasizes that Jesus is controlled by the Spirit, for he returns from his temptation "in the power of the Spirit" (4:14).

The scene is being set for Jesus's homecoming that follows. Evidently his teaching in the synagogues was wildly admired, and thus his popularity was spreading.

In 4:16–30 Luke has probably changed the chronology of Jesus's rejection at Nazareth and moved it up to the beginning of his Gospel because of its programmatic character (cf. Mark 6:1–6; Matt. 13:53–58). Jesus returns to his hometown of Nazareth and participates in a synagogue service. This is the oldest extant account of a synagogue service. Usually such a service included hymns, prayers, a reading from the Torah, a reading from the Prophets, and a sermon. The readings from the Torah may have been prescribed by a lectionary, but the prophetic readings were not set at this time, and so Jesus himself probably chose the passage from Isaiah. The quotation in verses 18–19 from Isaiah 61:1–2 also includes a phrase from Isaiah 58:6. Jesus draws attention to several things by using this passage from Isaiah. (1) The prophecy of Isaiah has now ("today") been fulfilled (4:21). (2) The fulfillment is Jesus himself; he is the one whom the Spirit has anointed. The reference to Isaiah 61 and the use of the word "anointed" suggest that Jesus is referring to himself as the Messiah and servant of Yahweh. (3) Jesus's ministry is directed to those in need—the poor, the prisoners, the blind, and the oppressed (4:18–19). In Luke these terms refer primarily to spiritual need, although a literal meaning is not excluded.

Significantly, Jesus does not continue reading Isaiah, for it also speaks of the day of God's vengeance. The point is that Jesus's ministry is one of good news and grace (4:18–19). Initially Jesus's gracious words impress the crowd, but they take offense when they reflect on Jesus's heritage; he is merely Joseph's son (4:22). Jesus responds with the principle that "no prophet is accepted in his hometown" (4:24). He then gives two examples from the Old Testament to illustrate his point (1 Kings 17:8–16; 2 Kings 5:1–14). Both Elijah and Elisha, who were also prophets, did not aid people from Israel—they aided Gentiles. Jesus implies, of course, that the Gentiles were more open to their prophetic ministry than the Jews. This incenses the people, and they try to kill Jesus, but Jesus walks "right through the crowd" (4:30). In this account Jesus reveals his messianic mission of grace and mercy. Nevertheless, the Jews reject him, and Jesus implies that the good news will then be proclaimed to the Gentiles (cf. Acts 13:44–48; 28:23–28).

Four different events are combined here to underline the authority of Jesus (4:31–41). (1) Jesus's teaching in Capernaum astonishes the populace because of its authority (4:31–32). (2) Jesus also manifests his authority over demons by expelling a demon from a man in the synagogue (4:33–37). Many people today discount the reality of the demonic and claim that what we have here is some form of mental illness; however, Jesus never discounted the reality of the demonic world, and oftentimes the rejection of the demonic is due to a rationalistic worldview that rejects any belief in the supernatural realm. One should not, however, rule out that, in some instances, a relationship exists between demonic possession and mental illness. (3) Jesus also reveals his authority over illness by healing Peter's mother-in-law of a fever (4:38–39). (4) In the last scene (4:40–41) numerous people come to Jesus, and he heals them of illness and demon possession. The distinction drawn between the ill and the demonized indicates that Luke did not think that all who were sick were controlled by demons. They came to Jesus at sunset because that was when the Sabbath ended, and people could then carry the sick. These stories also function christologically. The demons recognize Jesus as "the Holy One of God" (4:34), "the Son of God," and "the Messiah" (4:41). Jesus does not silence the demons because their words are false. Rather, the demons are trying to exercise control over Jesus by revealing his status; Jesus silences them and thereby reveals his superiority over them.

In 4:42–44 we see that Jesus's popularity continues to grow (cf. 4:37); however, Jesus does not take his directions from the populace but from his Father. He has been sent to "proclaim the good news of the kingdom of God" (4:43) throughout Palestine. The kingdom of God is central in Jesus's teaching, and it is probably best defined as the saving rule of God. In this chapter God's rule is effective in the teaching of Jesus and his miraculous works. The reference to Judea (4:44) seems strange (some manuscripts try to resolve the problem by substituting Galilee), but the word here refers to all of Palestine and includes Galilee.

The story of the disciples' call (the focus is on Peter) is placed later in Luke (5:1–11) than in Mark (cf. Mark 1:16–20). In contrast to Mark's account, Luke helps explain why the disciples follow Jesus, for they have already seen his

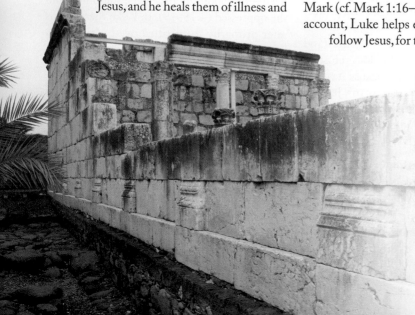

Beneath this white limestone synagogue in Capernaum that dates from the late 300s, archaeologists have located buildings from Jesus's day (in black basalt stone). The basalt subfloor beneath the synagogue may be the original building known to Jesus and the site of his first exorcism (Luke 4:33–37).

miracles (Luke 4:38–39) and heard his word. "Gennesaret" (5:1) is an alternative name for Galilee. Peter's query about letting down the nets (5:4–5) is understandable because the best fishing in deep water was done at night, and during the day they fished in shallow water. Nevertheless, Peter respects Jesus enough (cf. "Master" in 5:5) to do what he says. The tremendous quantity of the fish staggers Peter, and he is profoundly struck by his unworthiness (5:8), which reminds us of Isaiah's own consciousness of sin when he was in God's presence (Isa. 6:5). Luke adds that the incident has the same impact on Peter's partners, including James and John (5:9–10). Drawing an analogy from Simon's occupation, Jesus says that "from now on you will fish for people" (5:10). The story closes with the disciples leaving everything and following Jesus (5:11).

The story of the cleansing of the leper (5:12–16) precedes the controversy stories (5:17–6:11) because Luke shows that Jesus was obedient to the Mosaic law. In accordance with the law, he commands the man healed of leprosy to report to the priest (Lev. 14:1–32). The word "leprosy" in the Bible refers to various kinds of inflammatory skin diseases, and not necessarily to Hansen's disease. Jesus shows his compassion by touching one who is considered unclean. Jesus does not contract uncleanness by touching the leper. Instead, his touch makes the leper clean. The account also reflects Jesus's rising popularity, although he frequently spends time in communion with his Father (5:15–16).

B. Conflict with the Pharisees (5:17–6:11). The next five stories belong together since in each of them the Pharisees question Jesus (hence "conflict stories"), and he responds by defending the legitimacy of his behavior. The climax comes in 6:11, where Jesus's opponents fulminate against him.

The drama of the episode is apparent from Luke's introduction. Pharisees from every area of Palestine were present to investigate Jesus's teaching (5:17). The Pharisees were a popular religious party that emphasized obedience to both the written and unwritten law. The teachers of the law (or scribes) could come from any branch of the Jewish religion, but in this context they are probably Pharisees as well. Letting the paralytic down through a tiled roof (5:19) does not contradict Mark 2:4, for tiled roofs existed in Palestine at this date and Mark does not say what the roof was made of. Responding to the faith of the paralytic's helpers, Jesus penetrates to his deepest problem (the text does not say the illness is due to sin, although such a view is possible) and pronounces a verdict of forgiveness (5:20). The Pharisees conclude that such a statement is blasphemous because only God has the prerogative to forgive sin (5:21). A prophet could also forgive sin in God's name (2 Sam. 12:13), but Jesus's answer in verse 24 implies that on his own authority he is pronouncing forgiveness. Perceptively reading his opponents' thoughts, Jesus responds by arguing that the visible act of healing will function as proof that he can forgive sins. The performance of the miracle stuns the onlookers, and spontaneous praise is given to God (5:25–26). In addition to forgiving sins, Jesus also claims to be the "Son of Man" (5:24). The Son of Man in Jewish thought is a heavenly figure who will pronounce judgment on the last day (Dan. 7:13–22; Luke 9:26; 12:8).

Jesus's second controversy with the Pharisees stems from his call of Levi (5:27–32). Levi is a model of discipleship because he "left everything and followed [Jesus]" (5:27). But Levi is also a tax collector, and tax collectors were despised in Jewish society because they used the tax system to line their own pockets. The Pharisees and the scribes, who emphasized segregation from anything that would make one unclean, are surprised when Jesus goes to a banquet attended by tax collectors and sinners (5:30). In this context "sinners" refers to others who are ritually unclean. By eating with these people, Jesus himself would contract uncleanness. He defends his association with sinners by enunciating the principle that the doctor comes to aid the sick, not the healthy (5:31). In verse 32 Jesus explains the meaning of his illustration; his ministry is not for the righteous but for sinners. Here "the healthy" and "the righteous" refer to the Pharisees. The story does not teach that the Pharisees are actually righteous, only that they presume they are righteous. Jesus came to call those who were aware of their spiritual need.

Jews practiced fasting on the Day of Atonement. The Pharisees fasted twice a week, on Mondays and Thursdays, and apparently the disciples of the Baptist also fasted. Since fasting is a sign of one's religious devotion, Jesus is questioned because his disciples eat and drink (5:33). Jesus replies that fasting is as incomprehensible for his disciples as it would be for wedding guests to fast when the bridegroom is with them (5:34). Jesus clearly identifies himself as the bridegroom, insisting that his presence is a call for festivity. Fasting will commence when the bridegroom is absent, an allusion to Jesus's separation from his disciples at his death (5:35). Jesus does not reject fasting altogether (cf. Matt. 6:16–18; also Luke 4:2; 22:16, 18); however, the early church did not regularly practice fasting but reserved it for special occasions (see Acts 13:1–4; 14:23; cf. 9:9). Jesus then tells two parables that illustrate the incompatibility between Judaism and the new community. One cannot combine the new garment of the gospel with the old garment that focuses on religious practices. Any attempt to patch up the old garment will result in the tearing of the new one, and the new will not match with the old anyway (5:36). Jesus puts the same point another way. The new wine of the gospel cannot be poured into the old wineskins. Such an attempt would ruin both the new wine and the old wineskins. New wine continues to ferment and expand, bursting old wineskins, which are weakened by use (5:37). Jesus's point is that his gospel cannot be combined with Pharisaic practices; it is new, fresh, and spontaneous (5:38). However, Jesus recognizes (5:39) that most people find it difficult to embrace something new; they prefer their old, comfortable ways.

In the first (6:1–5) of the Sabbath controversies, the Pharisees accuse Jesus of doing that which is not lawful "on the Sabbath" (6:2). The law permitted the plucking of grain while walking through a field (Deut. 23:25), but the Pharisees prohibited such on the Sabbath because harvesting constituted work. Jesus responds to this criticism by recalling how David and his companions ate the "bread of the Presence" (1 Sam. 21:6), even though only priests were permitted to eat this bread (Lev. 24:5–9). Jesus's point is that David legitimately broke the technical requirements of the law when human need was present. The Pharisees may have been thinking, "But you are not David." Accordingly Jesus argues that he is greater than David, for as "the Son of Man," he is "Lord of the Sabbath." So Jesus authorizes the behavior of his disciples in this situation, and thus the first Sabbath controversy ends with Jesus making a bold statement about his person and authority.

The atmosphere in the second incident (6:6–11) is tense, for the Pharisees are looking for evidence to charge Jesus with disobedience to the law. Jesus confronts the issue openly and calls the man with the shriveled hand to come forward, asking all who are present about the real purpose for the Sabbath. Jesus's rhetorical question (6:9) and action of healing (6:10) show that doing good on the Sabbath is a positive duty. In other words, the failure to perform good deeds on the Sabbath is evil. Mark tells us that the religious leaders respond by plotting to kill Jesus (Mark 3:6), whereas Luke tells us of their fury and their uncertainty about what to do with him (6:11). In any case, the series of conflicts between Jesus and the Pharisees (Luke 5:17–6:11) ends with the latter being the implacable foes of Jesus.

C. Good news for the poor (6:12–8:3). 6:12–49. This section directly contrasts with the previous one. The religious leaders are rejecting Jesus, and he responds by choosing a faithful remnant (6:12–16) who will be responsible for communicating his message to others. The significance of the selection is indicated by verse 12: Jesus spends an entire night in prayer before choosing the Twelve. Simon Peter (6:14) heads up every list of the apostles in the New Testament. Bartholomew is sometimes equated with Nathanael (John 1:44–51). Matthew and Levi (Luke 5:27) are the same person (6:15). The Zealots (6:15) were members of a nationalistic religious party in Israel that led the revolt against Rome. Judas son of James (6:16) should be identified with Thaddaeus in Mark's list (Mark 3:18; cf. John 14:22). The meaning of "Iscariot" is disputed. Probably it means "a man from Kerioth," a city in southern Judea (Josh. 15:25). In any case, Judas's name evokes the memory of his betrayal.

The description of the geographical setting (6:17–19) of the Sermon on the Plain (6:17) does not necessarily contradict Matthew (Matt. 5:1), for Jesus could have delivered the sermon on a level place in the mountains. Luke prepares the reader for the sermon by noting that a vast array of people have gathered specifically to listen to Jesus (6:18). Jesus also heals many of those who have gathered to hear him.

The Sermon on the Plain (6:17–49) is considerably shorter than Matthew's Sermon on the Mount (cf. Matthew 5–7). The relationship between the two accounts is complex; one can probably explain some of the differences by the editorial work of the evangelists. Jesus opens the sermon by drawing radical contrasts between two kinds of people. Those who are poor, hungry, weeping, and hated are blessed. Although this happiness is a present experience ("yours is the kingdom," 6:20), it is primarily a future blessing: "you will be satisfied . . . you will laugh" (6:21), "your reward [is] in heaven" (6:23). Jesus does not say that God automatically blesses if one is poor, hungry, and sad. It should be noted that Jesus is speaking to disciples (6:20) who fall into these categories. Verse 22 makes it plain that being hated does not in and of itself bring a reward; the person who is rewarded is the one who is hated because of his allegiance to "the Son of Man." Clearly, then, these verses also have a spiritual dimension; Jesus is speaking to his disciples, whose longings and desires will not be fulfilled in this world. This does not mean that the literal meaning of the words should

be excluded, but one should not simplistically conclude that all the poor and the hungry of the world are blessed. Jesus is not teaching the virtue of poverty as such; he is saying that the poor, hungry, sad, and persecuted are blessed if they have given their allegiance to the Son of Man. The "woes" in verses 24–26 are directed toward the rich, the well fed, the happy, and the popular. Jesus's point is that these people derive all their satisfaction from this world. They feel no need of God, nor do they look forward to his future kingdom. This world is their heaven. Jesus pronounces a woe on such self-satisfied, prosperous, and smug people because a day is coming when fortunes will be reversed.

In the first part of the next section (6:27–36) Jesus describes the nature or position of people who are his disciples (cf. 6:20–26). In the rest of the sermon he focuses on the way disciples should live. Jesus begins with the radical message that disciples should love their enemies. The enemies in view are clearly those who persecute disciples (6:28–29). Love for enemies manifests itself in terms of actions: do good to them (6:27, 32–33, 35), bless and pray for them (6:28), and lend to them (6:34–35). Jesus gives two examples of the nature of this love; it is nonretaliatory (6:29) and generous (6:30). The cloak would be one's outer garment, and the tunic the garment that is worn next to the skin. In verses 29–30 Jesus does not suggest the capricious and arbitrary sharing of possessions with lazy people; rather, he emphasizes the spirit by which disciples should live—a revengeful, demanding, and grasping spirit is forbidden (6:31). Last, disciples should show a higher quality of love than sinners (6:32). The love of nonbelievers for one another is based on mutuality and repayment, but the love that marks the "children of the Most High" (6:35) gives without expecting anything in return. Such unselfish love will be rewarded at the end, and disciples will be imitating their Father, who is merciful and kind to all (6:35–36).

In the next section (6:37–45) Jesus addresses the theme of judging others. In verses

37–38 he forbids censorious and condemning judgment. Those who treat others with mercy will be treated mercifully by God. (The text is not saying that God will not judge believers at all but that he will judge with mercy if one shows mercy.) The picture of forgiveness in verse 38 is of a measuring jar in which the corn is pressed down so that the jar will hold more, shaken together so that every crack is filled, and poured over the top so that it overflows. Just as God has generously given to his own, so the disciple should give an overflowing amount to others. In verses 39–45 Jesus gives three exhortations. (1) The proverb on the blind man (6:39) is explained in the next verse (6:40). Students cannot surpass their teachers but will end up being just like them. This probably means that the disciples need to be careful how they teach others, for false teaching has potentially disastrous consequences. (2) The point of the humorous illustration of the speck and the log (6:41–42) is that those with the log think they are superior to those who have a speck in their eye and fail to see their own inadequacy and blindness. As in verses 37–38, Jesus attacks those who smugly and censoriously condemn others. Not judging others does not mean that one does not evaluate and use discrimination; Jesus is speaking against a superior and self-righteous attitude, not against careful evaluation. Those who are humbly aware of their own sin can help in removing the speck from another person's eye (6:42; cf. Gal. 6:1). (3) Verses 43–45 are a call to self-examination. Good conduct issues from a good heart, and evil conduct springs from an evil one. The behavior of a person is not an accident; it is a revelation of the innermost motives of the heart (6:45).

The sermon's call to obedience follows in 6:46–49. Hearing Jesus's words without obeying them is like building a house with no foundation. On the day of judgment that person will experience destruction. Those who hear and obey the words of Jesus are compared to one who builds a house on a secure foundation; the day of judgment holds no fear for the wise builder.

7:1–8:3. The events in this section of the Gospel show that even though the religious leaders reject Jesus's ministry, the members of society who are poor and looked down on— namely Gentiles and women—are receptive.

In Matthew 8:5–13 Jesus talks personally to the centurion, whereas in Luke 7:1–10 he speaks only to intermediaries. Matthew has probably abbreviated the account. In John the story of the healing of an official's son (John 4:46–53) is a different incident. The central point of this story is not the healing of the servant but the faith of the centurion (7:9). The centurion was probably a member of Herod Antipas's army since the Romans were not in Galilee before AD 44. From Jesus's statement in verse 9 it is also evident that the centurion is a Gentile; he thus becomes a symbol of Gentile belief in Jesus, a remarkable contrast to Israel's unbelief. The humility of the centurion is also apparent. The Jewish elders (community leaders in Capernaum) believe that he "deserves" (7:4) Jesus's help. But the centurion considers himself undeserving and unworthy (7:6–7). The centurion undoubtedly knew that a Jew would become "unclean" if he entered a Gentile's house.

Jesus's compassion on a widow (7:11–17) further illustrates his concern for the poor. By losing her only son (7:12), she would be deprived of her last means of support. The town of Nain was approximately six miles south of Nazareth. Not only is Jesus able to heal someone who is near death (7:14), but he also is able to resuscitate the dead by pronouncing the word, which provides the basis for his reply to John the Baptist (7:22). The resuscitation of the son of a widow undoubtedly reminded the people of Elijah (1 Kings 17:17–24; cf. also 2 Kings 4:18–37), which explains why the people immediately conclude that Jesus is "a great prophet" (Luke 7:16). Perhaps Luke expected his readers to think of the prophet of Deuteronomy 18:15–20 as well.

The next section (7:18–35) can be subdivided into three smaller units: (1) the Baptist's doubts about Jesus (7:18–23), (2) the role of John the Baptist (7:24–30), and (3) the fickleness of the religious leaders (7:31–35). It is not surprising that John begins to have doubts while in prison (cf. Matt. 11:2–19) about whether Jesus is the "one who is to come." (This phrase seems to be John's way of referring to the Messiah; cf. Luke 3:16.) Moreover, the judging aspect of Jesus's ministry is strangely lacking (cf. Luke 3:17). Jesus replies to the query of John's disciples by pointing to the wonders and signs he has performed (7:21–22). These miracles were particularly significant because in the Old Testament they point to the arrival of the era of salvation, the coming age when God would fulfill his promises (cf. Isa. 29:18–19; 35:5–6; 61:1). Jesus is indicating to John, then, that he is fulfilling the Old Testament Scriptures, albeit in a surprising way, which is why he ends this incident by pronouncing a blessing on one who does not stumble over the nature of his messianic ministry (7:23).

The text does not tell us how John responded (although Jesus's commendation implies that he responded positively); instead, Jesus launches

Luke 7:11–17 refers to a widow from Nain. Seen here, the modern village of Nain lies on the north side of Mount Moreh, near Nazareth. The biblical town has not been excavated, and the ancient town of Na'in was destroyed in war in 1948.

into a discussion on John's role in salvation history. He was not fickle, nor did he dress luxuriously (7:24–25); his role was prophetic. But, Jesus adds, he was "more than a prophet" (7:26), for he had the task of preparing the way for the Messiah (cf. Mal. 3:1). John's distinctive role made him the greatest of all the Old Testament saints (greatness being described here in terms of function, not of essence). Nevertheless, because John did not actually participate in the era of salvation, anyone who is a member of the kingdom "is greater than he" (7:28; greater again in function, not in essence). Luke adds in a parenthetical remark that "all the people" glorify God because Jesus's words are a vindication of John's ministry (7:29). But by rejecting John's baptism, the Pharisees fail to see that John and Jesus are the agents of God's saving purposes.

The Pharisees' rejection of God's purpose leads nicely into the topic of the fickleness of the present generation (7:31). Jesus compares the religious leaders to sulking children, for they think something demonic distinguishes the asceticism of John the Baptist, and something wild and unruly underscores Jesus's eating and drinking, not to mention his association with the lower class. Jesus's exaggerated description of John and himself makes the point that nothing will satisfy these people, and yet God's wisdom (7:35)—that is, his plan—is demonstrated to be right "by all her children" (namely by those

who have responded positively to the message of John and Jesus [cf. 7:29–30]).

The story of the forgiveness of a sinful woman (7:36–50) has sometimes been identified with the account in Mark 14:3–9 (and parallels), but it is clearly a different story. The link with the preceding context is the accusation leveled against Jesus in Luke 7:34. Jesus may have been invited to Simon's home after a synagogue service. No doubt Simon respected Jesus since he gives him the honorable title "teacher" (7:40; teacher = rabbi). Uninvited guests at a banquet in the Palestinian world were not an unusual feature, although the presence of a sinner (7:39; she was probably a prostitute) may have sparked some surprise. Those enjoying the banquet reclined with their feet extended behind them, resting their heads on their left hands and eating with their right. The woman enters behind Jesus and spontaneously begins to weep (7:38) because of either repentance or joy. Perhaps the two were commingled. When she sees that Jesus's feet are getting wet, she looses her hair (something a respectable woman would not do), drying his feet with her hair. She proceeds to kiss his feet and anoint them with expensive perfume (7:38).

Observing the activity, Simon concludes that Jesus cannot be a prophet (7:39) because a prophet would know what kind of woman this was. Moreover, a prophet would prevent a sinner from touching him because touching a sinful person would make one ritually unclean. (Thus the story has a twofold theme, revolving around the status of the woman and the status of Jesus.) Jesus responds to Simon's silent protest by telling him the parable of the two debtors (7:41–42). The point of the parable is plain—the one who is forgiven the larger amount will respond with more love and gratitude. A denarius was worth approximately a day's wages. Simon's reply (7:43) simply reflects a careful rabbinic answer. Jesus then applies the parable to the treatment that he has received from Simon and the woman (7:44–47). Jesus does not criticize Simon for being inhospitable, for these

courtesies were not necessarily an expected part of ordinary hospitality. Jesus's point is not that Simon was rude but that the woman showed "extraordinary" love. One would greet "friends" by kissing them on the head, but the woman kissed Jesus on the feet (7:46). On a special occasion one might put inexpensive oil on a guest's head, but the woman poured expensive perfume on Jesus's feet (7:46).

Verse 47 has been incorrectly interpreted at times to mean that the woman is forgiven *because* of her love for Jesus. But the point of the entire story is that her love is the *result* of her forgiveness. That love and gratitude flow from forgiveness is clearly the point of the parable (7:41–42), and the woman's actions of love toward Jesus stem from her experience of a forgiveness that has already been received. In verse 48 Jesus simply confirms the forgiveness of the woman. Indeed, verse 50 clearly shows that it is *faith* that has *saved* the woman. The phrase "whoever has been forgiven little loves little" (7:47) should not be taken too woodenly. In the application of the parable it applies to Simon and has an ironic twist. The meaning is not that righteous people cannot love much because they do not need much forgiveness (an argument for sinning more so that forgiveness can be deeper; cf. Romans 6). Rather, people who assume they are righteous will never experience much love for Jesus since they are so unaware of their sinfulness.

Luke summarizes Jesus's preaching ministry about the kingdom of God in 8:1–3, noting that he visits a number of towns. Contrary to Jewish custom Jesus had women followers, and they supported him financially (8:3). These women are carefully distinguished from the twelve apostles. There is no evidence that Mary Magdalene was the woman in the prior story. The number seven indicates the severity of Mary's state. The Herod mentioned here is Antipas (8:3).

D. Revelation and obedience (8:4–21). One of Jesus's distinguishing characteristics was teaching in parables, and some of the most memorable of Jesus's parables occur in Luke. Jesus addresses the parable of the sower (Luke 8:4–15; but cf. Mark 4:1–20; Matt. 13:1–23) to the crowd that was gathering (Luke 8:4–8), but he does not explain its significance to them. The sowing of seed on all kinds of soil would not be unusual in Palestine because plowing would follow sowing. In verse 8 he challenges his hearers to penetrate to the true meaning of the parable. The disciples are perplexed about the parable and inquire about its meaning (8:9). Jesus responds with a difficult saying, explaining the rationale behind parables (8:10). God reveals the secrets of the kingdom (the plans of God that were previously hidden but have now been made known) to the disciples, but the meaning of the parables is obscure to outsiders so that even though they hear the words they will not understand their true meaning (cf. Isa. 6:9). Jesus's hard words here cannot be applied to all the parables, for some of the parables were clearly understood even by Jesus's opponents (cf. Luke 10:25–37). Perhaps the obscurity of the parables is operative in those who have already responded negatively to Jesus's message. Jesus explains the meaning of the parable in verses 11–15. Some scholars have doubted whether Jesus would have allegorized the parables, but there is no a priori reason to exclude allegory. The modern reader, however, should not press the allegory beyond the limits indicated by the biblical writer. The different kinds of soils represent various ways of responding to the proclaimed word of God. Luke emphasizes that those who bring forth good fruit must persevere (8:15). The problem with those who are compared to the rocky soil is that they cannot endure persecution (8:13), and those who are compared to the thorny soil are squelched by the delights and worries of life (8:14). Thus the parable seems to have a twofold lesson: (1) those who hear the proclaimed word need to persevere in obedience, and (2) those who proclaim the word must realize that not everyone will respond positively. Why is this a "secret of the kingdom" (8:10)? Perhaps because the Jews never conceived of the kingdom message as having such limited success; they expected it to come in apocalyptic power and to rout their enemies.

In 8:16–18 we have three different sayings of Jesus that are combined. The main point is revealed in verse 18: "Consider carefully how you listen." In other words, this paragraph resembles the preceding one; Jesus stresses the need for faithful obedience to the preached word. The significance of putting one's lamp on the stand (8:16) is probably that the hearers must bear fruit in their listening, for a day will come when what they hear will not be secret any longer; it will shine for all to see. The last part of verse 18 supports our interpretation of verse 10 above. Receptive and obedient listening will lead to increased understanding, but rejection of the truth will lead to increased incomprehension of the word of God.

The next paragraph (8:19–21) fits nicely with the emphasis on obedience to the word of God that was stressed in the preceding parables. The arrival of Jesus's mother and brothers becomes an object lesson for the crowd; the true mother and brothers of Jesus are those who listen to and obey the word of God. Luke does not imply any criticism of Jesus's family members here. The brothers of Jesus are most likely the natural children of Mary and Joseph. Joseph's absence is probably due to his death.

E. The revelation of Jesus's identity (8:22–9:50). 8:22–56. Next Luke relates three miraculous works of Jesus, and the reader sees that Jesus has power over nature, demons, disease, and death. Hills and gorges surround the Sea of Galilee, and sudden windstorms would sweep down onto the lake. Fearing imminent death by drowning, the disciples arouse Jesus and implore his aid. At Jesus's command the storm ceases, and calm returns. Immediately Jesus communicates the lesson for the disciples: "Where is your faith?" (8:25). Their confidence should have been in Jesus and his saving power. Then the disciples pose a question: who is this one who has such astounding power over nature? Slowly the disciples begin to reflect on the identity of Jesus. The story ends this way because Luke wants the reader to contemplate the same question.

Jesus travels to the other side of the lake, which was largely Gentile territory. The precise location of the encounter with the Gerasene demoniac (8:26–39) is no longer certain, and the textual tradition reflects this uncertainty. Luke's description of the demonized man shows the severity of his condition (8:27–29). Jesus discovers that the man's malady is due to many demons (8:30). The demons beg Jesus not to send them into "the Abyss"; the abyss would be the realm of the underworld where some demons were confined (Rev. 9:1–11). The sending of the demons into the pigs seems strange, and many have questioned the wisdom of such an activity. Some have rightly pointed out that pigs were unclean animals for the Jews, but this is not a satisfactory explanation for Jesus's activity since he was in Gentile territory. Perhaps the

point of the story is that one man's deliverance is worth the destruction of many pigs. The neighboring townspeople arrive and are seized with fear, requesting Jesus to leave their region (8:37). The theme of Jesus's rejection continues. But Jesus bids the man who was delivered to proclaim his word in that region, showing that his healing is designed to lead to mission.

The next two stories are deliberately interwoven; Luke begins with the request of Jairus for his dying daughter, inserts the story of the bleeding woman, and then returns to the story of Jairus (8:40–56). The ruler of a synagogue (8:41) arranged synagogue services. The accomplishment of Jairus's request is delayed by the throng that surrounds Jesus and is then interrupted by the woman who "touched the edge of his cloak" (probably his tassel; cf. Num. 15:38–39). This woman has been hemorrhaging for twelve years, and such bleeding would make her ritually unclean (Lev. 15:25–30). Luke may tone down Mark's remark on how her many doctors have only made her condition worse (Mark 5:26), perhaps because of his profession. Jesus is aware that healing power has gone forth from him, and he explains that her deliverance is not due to superstition but to saving faith

The east side of the Sea of Galilee, seen here, was populated by many Gentiles in the first century AD. This region was the site of Jesus's expulsion of swine into the Sea of Galilee (Luke 8:26–39).

(8:46–48). While Jesus is healing the woman, the daughter of Jairus dies. The friends of Jairus think any further activity is futile (8:49), and they ridicule Jesus's naïveté in saying the girl is merely sleeping (8:53). But Jesus's words to Jairus are, "Don't be afraid; just believe, and she will be healed" (8:50). Thus, we see that the resuscitation of Jairus's daughter fits with the prior story; in both instances Jesus responds to faith. Jesus manifests his power over disease and death. His power over demons and nature also (8:22–39) causes the reader to reflect on Jesus's identity.

9:1–50. In the next episode (9:1–9) Jesus sends out the disciples to communicate the message of the kingdom of God (9:1). The kingdom message includes both the proclamation of good news and apostolic power over disease and demons (9:1–2). Jesus forbids the Twelve from bringing extensive provisions for the journey; he wants them to rely on God for sustenance. The disciples are to be content with the house that receives them (9:4), but if the people reject the message, the disciples are to shake the dust of the town off their feet, which symbolizes that the town is unclean and that they are severing fellowship with it. The preaching of Jesus and his followers comes to the attention of Herod Antipas (9:7). The key question Luke wants the reader to ask is, "Who is this Jesus?" By recording the current speculation on the identity of Jesus (Is he John the Baptist, Elijah, or one of the prophets?), and by placing the question on the lips of an important person like Herod, Luke brings the question of Jesus's identity to the center of attention.

The apostles return from their mission, withdrawing with Jesus to the area around Bethsaida for some rest; however, the multitudes learn of Jesus's destination and follow him. The feeding of the five thousand (9:10–17) is probably an object lesson for the disciples. They do not have the resources to feed the multitudes, but by depending on God they will have more than enough to satisfy the crowds. The story also continues to raise the question, who is this?

Peter answers that query in the next section (9:18–20). The account is suggestive, however, of Jesus's messiahship. He is the new Moses who gives manna from heaven (Exod. 16:1–36; Num. 11:1–35; cf. 2 Kings 4:42–44). The story may also evoke images of the messianic feast of the last days (Isa. 25:6–8). There is no compelling reason to doubt the historicity of the episode.

The preceding narratives have raised the question, who is this? Now Peter gives the decisive answer: you are the Messiah (9:18–20). The disciples see more clearly than those who identify Jesus with Elijah, John the Baptist, or one of the prophets. Of the Synoptic writers only Luke tells us that Jesus was praying (9:18).

Peter understands that Jesus is the Messiah, but the disciples also need to grasp what kind of messiah he will be (9:21–27). He does not fit the popular conception of a messiah who will triumph over Israel's enemies by using military power. He will suffer and die before he is vindicated by the resurrection (9:22). Jesus uses the title Son of Man. According to Daniel 7:9–22 the Son of Man is a heavenly figure who will participate in the judgment on the last day; however, Jesus pours new content into the title by claiming that the Son of Man must also suffer. Thus, Jesus links the Son of Man and the Suffering Servant (Isa. 52:13–53:12). Jesus's destiny is closely associated with the responsibility of his disciples. His disciples must be prepared to suffer and to lose their lives in this world for Jesus's sake. They will show that they are ashamed of Jesus and his words if they do not participate in his sufferings. If, however, the disciples share in Jesus's rejection, they will end up saving their very selves. The last verse (9:27) is difficult. It may mean that the disciples experience the kingdom in the events of the resurrection and Pentecost, or that the transfiguration itself is a manifestation of the kingdom.

The episode of the transfiguration (9:28–36) is closely connected with the preceding one ("about eight days after," 9:28; Mark 9:2 has "after six days"; the point is that it was about one week later). As Jesus prays, his face and clothes become gloriously radiant. Luke characteristically mentions that Jesus prays before an important event. Moses and Elijah appear and discuss with Jesus his "departure" (Greek *exodos*, from which the English word "exodus" is derived; see NIV note to 9:31) in Jerusalem. According to Jewish tradition Moses and Elijah were expected to return before the advent of the kingdom. The reference to Jesus's "exodus" shows that his passion is primarily in view (cf. 9:22), although the resurrection may also be implied. The story also focuses on who Jesus is. Peter suggests building three booths for the great men who are present. But Peter misses the significance of the event. The point is that Jesus is superior to Moses and Elijah. The story ends with Jesus alone, and Elijah and Moses are gone. In addition, the voice from the cloud (the cloud represents God's presence) says to listen to Jesus, stressing again that Jesus is God's final and definitive revelation. The scene is similar to Jesus's baptism (3:21–22), for Jesus is again called God's chosen Son. The purpose of the story is to confirm Jesus's sonship and glory. The disciples think that Jesus's passion rules out his glory, but actually the passion is the route to glory.

The juxtaposition of 9:37–43a with the transfiguration is striking because after his glorious manifestation Jesus encounters the unbelief and frailty of human beings (9:41). The father of a demonized boy is close to despair because no one can help his son. Luke's description emphasizes the severity of the boy's condition. The goal of the story, then, is to show that only Jesus can help him, and the crowd responds by remarking on God's greatness as manifested through Jesus.

People are marveling about Jesus's works (see the preceding exorcism), but Jesus says to the disciples that they should be focusing on his future suffering rather than his miracles (9:43b–50). Luke notes that the disciples cannot comprehend what Jesus is saying (9:45).

Perhaps the next two stories provide the reason for their incomprehension. The disciples cannot understand Jesus's suffering because they are consumed by rivalry and competition (9:46–48); however, Jesus says that true greatness comes when disciples forget about being great. Children were considered to be insignificant in ancient society. Nevertheless, a great person treats children with respect and consideration; such actions show that the person is not using acts of kindness merely to get ahead and also show that this person has received the Father. John also recounts how the disciples try to prevent a man from expelling demons in Jesus's name since he does not become one of Jesus's disciples (9:49–50). Jesus replies that whoever is not against him is on his side. This last saying seems to contradict 11:23, but the sayings are proverbial and not contradictory since they are in completely different contexts.

4. Galilee to Jerusalem: Discipleship (9:51–19:27)

A clear break occurs in the text here, indicating a major division in the Gospel. Luke may depart from using Mark as a source, for he does not recount a story from Mark until 18:15. Luke uses the motif of a travel narrative, but the reader should understand it primarily as a literary technique. As a travel narrative it gives very few details about where the events are taking place. Jesus is en route to Jerusalem so that he can fulfill the things that have been written about him. On the way he teaches his followers about discipleship.

A. The journey begins (9:51–13:21). **9:51–10:42.** The first account in this section (9:51–56) reminds us that the passion of Jesus lies ahead. The resolution of Jesus to go to Jerusalem is related to his suffering and death, and the hostility of the Samaritans foreshadows what he will experience in Jerusalem. (The Samaritans and Jews were enemies with a long history of hatred.) The phrase "taken up to heaven" (9:51) clearly refers to Jesus's ascension, but it probably also refers to all that will happen in Jerusalem, including Jesus's death, resurrection, and ascension. The refusal of the Samaritans to welcome Jesus provokes James and John to ask Jesus if he wants them to send fire on the Samaritans (like Elijah did in the Old Testament; 2 Kings 1:10, 12). Jesus rebukes his disciples, which shows them that nonretaliation is a better way and gives them a pattern to follow when they encounter opposition. The words of Jesus in verses 55–56 are not in the earliest manuscripts.

Jesus's encounter with three would-be followers indicates the stringency of discipleship (9:57–62). The first man is enthusiastic and pledges to follow Jesus anywhere (9:57). But Jesus responds by underlining the cost of following him (9:58). Even animals have a place to sleep, but Jesus experiences homelessness and rejection, as the preceding episode with the Samaritans shows. Jesus invites the second man to follow him (9:59). This man responds with a reasonable request. He wants to go home and bury his father first. In Judaism burial of dead relatives was a duty, and it was even considered more important than studying the law. Even priests were permitted to bury their relatives (Lev. 21:1–3); therefore, Jesus's answer is startling. He overturns social conventions, insisting that the kingdom of God has priority over family loyalties. When Jesus says to let the dead bury their own dead, he means leave the task of burying the "physically dead" to those who are "spiritually dead." Last, a man promises to follow Jesus after saying farewell to his family (9:61). Again, this is a reasonable request; Elijah let Elisha say farewell to his family before the latter followed the former (1 Kings 19:19–21). Nevertheless, Jesus's call is more radical. No one can plow effectively if he or she looks back, for the furrow will be crooked and the wooden plow tip might break. So too, no one can follow Jesus without making him the absolute and exclusive center of life.

Luke alone tells us that besides sending out the Twelve (Luke 9:1–6) Jesus also sends out the seventy (-two; 10:1–24). (The textual evidence is divided so that it is impossible to say whether Jesus sent out seventy or seventy-two.)

The disciples are like innocent lambs being sent out into a world full of hostility; yet workers are needed for the harvest (10:2–3). The instructions that are given to the seventy (-two) are very similar to the instructions that Jesus gave to the Twelve in Luke 9:1–6. The urgency of the task is underlined. There is no time for the long greetings characteristic of oriental culture (10:4). Financial support should come from the town in which the disciples reside, but they should be content with the food and shelter they receive from their hosts, instead of looking for a house that provides for them in a more luxurious way (10:4, 7–8). The greeting "peace to this house" (10:5) is not just a way of saying hello; it refers to the peace of salvation that Jesus is bringing. "Someone who promotes peace" is one who is willing to receive the saving message (10:6). The disciples are to proclaim the presence of the kingdom, and the sign of its presence is their healing ministry (10:9). Those who reject the message of the kingdom are to be warned of their solemn fate (10:10–12).

The warning of judgment reminds Jesus of the rejection he experienced in Galilee. Even though they saw his miracles, they refused to submit themselves to the kingdom message; therefore, they will certainly be judged. Jesus is not saying that Tyre and Sidon will not be judged, only that the judgment of the Galilean cities will be more severe because they have more evidence. Verse 16 shows that those who reject the message of the seventy (-two) are just as culpable as those who rejected Jesus, for those who reject Jesus's messengers reject Jesus and the Father.

The disciples return (10:17–20) with joy because they did not anticipate being able to expel demons (cf. 9:10). When Jesus says that he saw Satan fall from heaven (10:18), he is not speaking of Satan's prehistoric fall, nor is he referring to a vision he had during the disciples' ministry, nor is he predicting Satan's future fall. He is merely describing in symbolic terms the impact of the disciples' ministry. The kingdom of God is making inroads on Satan's domain.

The disciples were sharing in Jesus's authority over all forms of evil and destruction. "Snakes and scorpions" (10:19) does not refer to demonic powers but symbolizes all kinds of evil (cf. Deut. 8:15); however, Jesus cautions that the disciples are not to become enamored of the sensational. The crucial thing is not the expulsion of demons and power over evil but the assurance of having one's name written in God's book.

The joy of the disciples after returning from their mission stimulates Jesus to express his praise to the Father (10:21–24). The Father has not revealed the gospel of the kingdom ("these things," 10:21) to the wise and learned, probably because they were impressed with their own wisdom. But to the humble and childlike he has opened up the secrets of the kingdom. Jesus emphasizes that this is in accord with God's sovereign plan and gracious will (10:21). In verse 22 we have one of the most important verses in the Synoptic Gospels on the mutual relationship between the Father and the Son. Some scholars have questioned the authenticity of the verse, but the Jewish character of the saying shows its authenticity. When Jesus states that the Father has handed "all things" over to him, he means that the Father has given the Son authority to reveal the knowledge of the Father and Son to others. Then Jesus indicates that the Father and Son possess a mutual and exclusive knowledge of each other. The centrality and uniqueness of the Son is

affirmed because no one can know the Father apart from the Son's permission. Jesus's words show that the knowledge of God is a gift bestowed from above, and thus it follows that the disciples are privileged to see the revelation of the Father in the Son. Many Old Testament persons wanted to see this capstone of God's self-revelation, but it was not part of God's gracious purpose (10:24).

In the telling of the parable of the good Samaritan (10:25–37) the lawyer wants to involve Jesus in a theological argument over what is necessary for eternal life (10:25). Instead of answering the question, Jesus directly asks the lawyer for his point of view. The lawyer responds by citing Deuteronomy 6:5 and Leviticus 19:18; eternal life is inherited when one loves God with the totality of one's being and one's neighbor as oneself. Jesus agrees with this response (cf. Mark 12:28–33) but forces the discussion into the practical realm by saying, "Do this and you will live" (10:28). Some have thought that Jesus is speaking only hypothetically here because this answer would contradict salvation by faith. This is incorrect, for true faith always manifests itself in works (cf. James 2:14–26). The lawyer's attempt at self-justification (10:29) probably stems from his realization that he is

Remains of the ancient Roman road between Jerusalem and Jericho—the setting for the parable of the good Samaritan (Luke 10:25–37)—can still be seen in the desert of Judea. This road was used frequently by Galileans, such as Jesus, traveling to Jerusalem.

not fulfilling the twofold commandment, and his question leads into Jesus's parable. The road from Jerusalem to Jericho was 17 miles long, and a traveler would descend 3,300 feet. Jericho lies 770 feet below sea level. Lonely roads were a prime place for robbers to strike (10:30). Both a priest and a Levite pass by when they see the wounded man (10:31–32). The priest would probably be returning from his time of service in the Jerusalem temple. Levites aided priests in the temple by carrying out minor duties related to the temple and its cult. The priest and Levite may have avoided the man because they thought he was dead, and they did not want to become ritually unclean. More probably, they were fearful of the robbers attacking them also. Jesus surprises his listeners by saying that a Samaritan helps the wounded man, for Samaritans were implacable enemies of the Jews (cf. Luke 9:51–56; John 4:9). It is interesting that Jesus does not say in the parable that Jews ought to love all people, even Samaritans. Instead, he does a more shocking thing. He uses the "unclean" Samaritan as an example of what neighborly love is. The Samaritan demonstrates his love in a practical way (10:34–35). In the ancient world, oil and wine were commonly used to soften wounds and as an antiseptic. Jesus exposes the real issue in this parable (10:36). Who is my neighbor? is not the question, but rather, am I a neighbor? The lawyer asked a calculating question (10:29) designed to exclude some from love's grasp. Jesus's story shows that love does not have any calculable limits. It may be significant that the lawyer does not say "the Samaritan" (10:37).

The next story (10:38–42) may have occurred at some other time, and Luke may have inserted it here for topical reasons. Luke probably omits the name of the village (Bethany; John 11:1, 18; 12:1) because it was near Jerusalem, and Jesus does not arrive in Jerusalem for some time. Martha complains to Jesus about Mary's failure to help with the meal preparations. In fact, Martha seems to be blaming Jesus ("Lord, don't you care," 10:40) since Mary is not helping

because she is listening to Jesus teach. The point of the story is not that a life of contemplation is better than a life of service. Rather, Jesus gently chides Martha because her preparations are too elaborate; she is distracted "by all the preparations" (10:40; literally "much service"), and she is "worried and upset about many things" (10:41). Jesus says that "few things are needed—or indeed only one," and this stands for the better part that Mary has chosen, namely listening to the word of God. The implication is that Martha, if she would keep the preparations simple, could also listen to Jesus. The story is significant because Jesus, in contrast to most Jewish teachers of the day, encourages learning among women. Sitting at a teacher's feet (10:39) is the usual posture of a student, indicating that Mary is one of his pupils.

11:1–54. Next Jesus offers teaching on prayer (11:1–13). Prayer is an important part of Luke's Gospel, and Jesus's example of prayer and John's instructions on prayer stimulate the disciples to ask for help in praying (11:1). The Lukan form of the Lord's Prayer is shorter than the Matthean form. The differences between the two accounts may be due to editorial modification of the prayer by the authors of the different Gospels, but it is also likely that Jesus taught the prayer on more than one occasion. The word "Father" comes from the Aramaic *Abba*, which emphasizes the intimate relationship between the believer and God. Two requests follow that center on God's purposes. "Hallowed be your name" means that disciples are to pray that God's name (i.e., his person and character) is honored, exalted, and revered. "Your kingdom come" is a request that God bring his rule to fruition, which he will do in the days of messianic blessing and joy. The last three petitions in the prayer focus on human needs. First, the request for daily bread certainly refers to physical bread, although many commentators also see a reference to "spiritual" bread. The word "daily" is difficult. It could refer to (1) necessary bread, (2) daily bread (so NIV), or (3) bread for tomorrow. Second, the prayer contains a plea for forgiveness since believers manifest God's forgiveness to others. Third, believers should pray that God will shield them from temptation that would lead them into sin. Then, in a story about a person requesting provisions from a friend at midnight, Jesus tells a parable about prayer (11:5–8). The arrival of a friend at night would not be unusual in the Middle East because it would be too hot to travel by day. Moreover, no host would fail to offer food to a guest. The "friend" inside is reluctant to get up because he would wake up all his children, probably because he lived in a one-room house. Nevertheless, the persistence of the friend outside persuades the other to get up and supply his needs. Some have argued that the friend inside responds not because of the other's persistence but because of his fear of being embarrassed, for the next day everyone would learn of his lack of hospitality (the Greek word for "persistence" can be translated "shame-lessness"). However, such an interpretation fails because in verses 9–10 the lesson of persistence is drawn from the parable. That does not mean that one needs to be persistent because God is reluctant to give. The point of the parable is not that God, like the person in the house, must be persuaded to give. Just the opposite. One needs to be persistent because God longs to give good gifts to his children, and he is sure to answer (see 11:11–13). Clearly God is much more generous than any human father. A water snake in Palestine could be mistaken for a fish, and a scorpion could roll up to resemble an egg (11:11–12).

Many people conclude that Jesus's miracles demonstrate that he is from God (cf. 7:16), but an alternate explanation soon arises (11:14–26). Perhaps his ability to exorcise demons stems from his alignment with Beelzebul. A more convincing sign is requested to prove his authenticity (11:15–16); however, Jesus shows that the accusation of demonic collusion is sense-less. If Jesus expels demons with satanic power, then Satan is contributing to his own demise (11:17–18). If Jesus's adversaries claim that he

exorcises demons with satanic power, then it logically follows that exorcisms performed by their colleagues are accomplished by Satan as well (11:19). Instead, the exorcism of demons is a sign of God's power, an indication of the presence of the kingdom (11:20). Indeed, Jesus's exorcisms show that he has defeated the strong man (Satan), and that is why Jesus can plunder Satan's possessions (i.e., free those who are captive to Satan [11:21–22]). Opposition to Jesus on this issue, then, is an indication that one has joined the adversary (11:23). In verses 24–26 Jesus warns of the danger of a demon evacuating a person when nothing positive takes its place. Such a person opens him- or herself up to demonic possession that is even worse than the former state. It is not enough to expel demons if there is no acceptance of Jesus's kingdom message. An exorcist may make matters worse if he expels demons but does not fill the gap by taking sides with Jesus (cf. 11:23).

If we relate the next incident (11:27–28) to the preceding episode, Jesus is saying that his critics should focus on obedience instead of doubting his mighty works. A woman in the crowd, feeling rather sentimental, uses a Jewish expression that means, "How happy is the mother of such a son" (11:27). Jesus does not reject such an affirmation, but he points to something more fundamental. True happiness comes from hearing and obeying God's word (11:28).

The narrative here picks up from verse 16 the demand for a sign (11:29–32). Evidently people wanted a sign that was more convincing and definitive than exorcisms; however, Jesus says that the demand for a sign is wicked, for obedience to God's word is the real issue. The only sign that will be given to the people is the sign of Jonah. Some relate this to the preaching of Jonah, but the primary reference is probably to Jonah's deliverance from the whale, and thus we have an allusion to Jesus's resurrection (cf. Matt. 12:40). Both the Queen of Sheba, who came to test the wisdom of Solomon (1 Kings 10:1–10), and the men of Nineveh, who responded to the preaching of Jonah, will pronounce a sentence of guilty on the Jews of Jesus's day. After all, Jesus is greater than Solomon and Jonah, and his contemporaries should perceive this about Jesus by observing his ministry.

The paragraph in 11:33–36 is difficult to interpret. In this context the light that shines for all to see is Jesus and his message about the kingdom (11:33). Also, the eye functions as a lamp because it is the organ by which light enters the body; however, if one's eyes are unhealthy, then light cannot enter (11:34). The point is that those who are in darkness have refused to be illumined by Jesus. They may think they are illuminated by light, but actually they are in darkness because they have rejected the path of obedience (11:35). Only those who have responded obediently to Jesus's message will be fully illumined (11:36).

In 11:37–54 Jesus wages a full-scale attack on the practices of Pharisees and their scribes. A Pharisee is surprised that Jesus does not ritually wash himself before eating (11:38). The Old Testament did not require this ritual washing, but the Pharisees practiced it because of the defilement one would contract from Gentiles and unclean people. The Pharisees overly concerned themselves with outward matters of cleanliness, failing to see the importance of cleansing from inward sin, especially greed (11:39–40). By giving alms from the heart to the poor, the Pharisees would be moving in the right direction. By cleansing the inside they would be cleansing the outside as well. Jesus then exposes the faults of the Pharisees in three woes. (1) They focus on the minutiae of religion, such as tithing every plant in one's garden, but forget about what is really important, namely justice and love of God (11:42). Tithing should not be eliminated, but it should be placed in its proper perspective, for the Pharisees tithed even more than the Old Testament required. (2) The Pharisees are enamored of the glowing reputation they gain from being religious (11:43). (3) Indeed, they resemble "unmarked graves." Walking over an unmarked grave would

defile a person in Jewish culture. The point is that even though the wickedness of the Pharisees is not apparent or observable, it is defiling and contaminating (11:44). An objection from a scribe leads to three woes being pronounced against them also (11:45). (1) The lawyers with their many regulations make the practice of religion so burdensome and tiring, yet they are not willing to help those they burden (11:46). (2) In an ironic statement (11:47–48) Jesus says that by building the tombs of the prophets, the lawyers show their sympathy with those who killed them. They wanted to keep them in the grave! The lawyers' sympathy with those who killed the prophets of old is clear because they will kill the prophets and apostles who are now God's spokesmen (11:49–51). (3) Last, the interpretation of Scripture practiced by the lawyers blocks ordinary people from receiving knowledge about God and prevents them from entering the kingdom (11:52). After such a blistering attack it is not surprising that the Pharisees begin to plot against Jesus (11:53–54).

12:1–59. The next verses (12:1–3) follow naturally from the preceding discourse, in which Jesus has criticized Pharisaic religion. Here he warns his disciples to be on guard against "the yeast of the Pharisees, which is hypocrisy" (12:1). Such hypocrisy cannot be hidden forever; at the end it will be revealed for all to see (12:2–3). Verses 2–3 also blend in with the following exhortation (12:4–12) to the disciples. The disciples should not deny Jesus, because ultimately such a denial will be broadcast for all to see.

The disciples are encouraged to persevere under persecution (12:4–12) for the following reasons: (1) Those who buckle under persecution are afraid because of the pain and deprivation of physical death. Such fear needs to be conquered because bodily pain is all that their adversaries can inflict (12:4). (2) God, though, should be feared because he can cast a person into hell. A healthy fear of punishment will encourage the disciples to endure persecution (12:5). (3) From a proper fear of destruction the text moves to a fear that is to be avoided. Under persecution one may fear that God has forgotten him or her. But this is not the case. God even remembers sparrows, which are sold for less than a cent (12:6). In fact, every hair on a person's head is "numbered" by God (12:7). God remembers and cares for the person who is suffering persecution; God has not forgotten, and no suffering can touch a person without first passing through God's hands. (4) Verses 8–9 bring out what is implicit in verse 5. What should people fear when being persecuted? They should fear denying Christ, for such denial will mean that such a person is "disowned" by God. The person who confesses Christ publicly, however, will be rewarded. (5) Verse 10 is a qualification of verses 8–9. What really constitutes a denial of the Son? Apparently, forgiveness is possible if one "speaks a word against the Son of Man,"

but blasphemy "against the Holy Spirit will not be forgiven." What is the sin that will not bring forgiveness? Probably a persistent and stubborn refusal to submit to the gospel. It is not an occasional denial of Christ (as Peter did) but the hardness of heart that refuses to repent and turns completely against the witness of the Spirit. (6) Last, Jesus promises that when disciples are persecuted, the Spirit will give them wisdom to defend themselves (12:11–12).

The section on possessions (12:13–34) can be divided into three subsections: (1) warning against greed (12:13–15), (2) the parable of the rich fool (12:16–21), and (3) worry over possessions (12:22–34). In the first paragraph (12:13–15) a man wants Jesus to arbitrate in an inheritance dispute between his brother and himself. This would be typical work for a rabbi. But Jesus refuses, insisting that this is not his role. In verse 15 he warns of the root problem: greed. A greedy person thinks that the good life is found in things, but this is a distorted perspective (12:15). This discussion leads Jesus to relate the parable of the rich fool (12:16–21). The problem with the rich fool is not that he has bumper crops or that he decides to build more storage space (12:16–18). The problem

In Luke 12:5 Jesus refers to "hell," or in Greek, Gehenna. This is a translation of the Hebrew for "Valley of Hinnom," which is located on the west and south sides of Jerusalem. The expansive green area in this aerial is the southern part of the valley. Jerusalem burned its refuse here, so it was considered an unclean place and thus to be avoided.

is that he invests his entire life in his possessions (cf. 12:15). He draws all his security from his material goods (12:19) and fails to reckon with God. He is living as if he will never die and has forgotten the importance of spiritual riches (12:20–21). Such a shortsighted investment in temporal things is foolishness indeed. In the last section, Jesus gives his disciples the proper perspective on riches (12:22–34). Believers should avoid anxiety about food and clothing, for true life does not consist in material possessions (cf. 12:15, 21). And if God cares for ravens and adorns flowers with such beauty, then he will provide the fundamental physical needs of believers (12:24, 27–28). Jesus is not suggesting here that work is unnecessary; we need to remember that the problem being addressed here is worry, not laziness. Worry is also senseless because it does not accomplish anything (12:25–26). No one can live even a day longer by worrying. The root problem with worry is lack of faith (12:29). It is understandable that pagans are consumed with the desire for security, but believers need to remember that the Father knows what they need (12:30). If believers make the kingdom their consuming passion, then God will take care of other needs (12:31). Disciples, then, are not to fear but to trust God (12:32). They will not draw their security from possessions, and so they will be free to give their possessions to others. If their treasure (or security) is money, then that will be their consuming passion. Making money one's treasure is the path to insecurity, however, because it is always subject to the uncertainties of life (12:33).

From the proper attitude toward money Luke now turns to the way disciples should view the interval between Jesus's ascension and return (12:35–48). The parable of a master returning from a wedding party (12:35–38) shows that while the master is absent his servants should be ready and watching for his return, even if he comes at a time that is later than they expect. (The Jews split the night into three watches, so the second or third watch would be very late.)

Girding up the loins (12:35) was necessary in Palestine because men wore long, flowing robes that needed to be tied up with a belt when one wanted to run or engage in serious work. Verse 37 envisions a reversal of roles that was unheard of in Palestine. If the servants are faithful, then the master will serve them. The parable of the alert house owner (12:39–40) demonstrates that the disciples cannot predict with certainty when the Son of Man will come; therefore, they must always be ready. Peter inquires about whether Jesus is speaking specifically to the apostles/disciples or to all people (12:41). Jesus does not answer the question directly, although he implies that he is referring only to the apostles/disciples, because they possess authority over the other servants (12:42). In this third parable, Jesus focuses on the responsibility of managers to take care of their servants (12:43–46). He warns that the delay of the master should not lead the manager to abuse the servants. Irresponsible behavior will be punished, and responsible behavior will be rewarded; however, punishment will be based on the degree of knowledge. All punishment will not be equal because those who are entrusted with more responsibility and knowledge will pay a greater penalty (12:47–48). The central thrust of this section is that the daily obedience of disciples shows their readiness for the return of Jesus; disobedience will be punished and obedience will be rewarded.

The relationship of the next paragraph (12:49–53) to the preceding one may be the thought of judgment. The fire that Jesus wants to be "kindled" (12:49) is the fire of judgment that discriminates between the unrighteous and righteous. It probably does not refer to the Holy Spirit here (but cf. Luke 3:16). The purifying fire is also related to Jesus's imminent baptism (12:50). The baptism that Jesus must undergo is not a literal baptism; rather, it is a metaphor of some overwhelming catastrophe—clearly his death on the cross. The arrival of Jesus did bring peace on earth (Luke 2:14), but the fire of judgment also means the separation and division of families. That division stems from one's stance toward Jesus (cf. Mic. 7:6).

Discerning the signs of the times is the subject in 12:54–59. The purifying fire of God's judgment is imminent (12:49). Jesus warns his listeners that they need to see the urgency of the present time, because the eschatological crisis is at hand. His listeners are adept at detecting forecasts of coming weather (12:54–55), but they fail to see the forecast of the coming crisis that is implicit in Jesus's ministry (12:56). Jesus uses an illustration to convey the same point in another way (12:57–59). If a person were going to court, knowing he could lose the case and spend some time in jail (12:59), then he would certainly try to reconcile with his adversary on the way to the courthouse. So too a person who is under the threat of judgment should reconcile with God while there is still time.

13:1–21. In 13:1–9 the necessity of repentance before the coming judgment continues as Luke's theme. Pilate, probably at Passover, had some Galileans slaughtered while they were preparing their sacrifices (13:1). Apparently those who told Jesus about this incident thought that the Galileans were executed because of sin (13:2). Jesus does not focus on the sin of the Galileans; instead, he uses the occasion to warn everyone that they too will perish without repentance. Jesus seizes on another example to make the same point (13:4–5). The tower of Siloam was probably part of the old wall

in Jerusalem, near the juncture of the south and east walls. The accidental death of the eighteen was not due to any exceptional personal sin. (Jesus does not deny that the Galileans and those who died at Siloam were sinners; he denies that the manner of their death was due to any exceptional sin.) In the parable of the fig tree (13:6–9) the necessity of repentance before the crisis of the final judgment is underlined again. Executions and accidental deaths are not definitive signs of God's judgment (13:1–5); but if an individual is not bearing fruit, then judgment is certain. God, however, patiently waits for fruit to appear, giving people every possible chance to produce fruit. Nevertheless, people cannot put off the day of judgment forever, idly thinking that it will never come (13:8–9).

In the next section (13:10–17) we see the saving power of Jesus at work. Still, the synagogue ruler maintains that healing on the Sabbath is wrong. God made weekdays for work, never intending that work be done on the Sabbath (13:14). Using a typical rabbinic method of arguing from the lesser to the greater, Jesus accuses those who hold this position of hypocrisy. If one cares for the physical needs of animals on the Sabbath, then it follows that one *should* care for the physical needs of people (13:15). Indeed, the Sabbath is a particularly appropriate day to frustrate the work of Satan (13:16). Such actions and words silenced Jesus's opponents and delighted his supporters.

The parables of the mustard seed and the yeast (13:18–21) teach the same lesson. The rule of God has manifested itself in Jesus's ministry. The liberation from Satan of the crippled woman is one example (cf. 13:10–17). However, the kingdom has not been ushered in with apocalyptic power. It

In Luke 13:6 Jesus uses a fig tree, such as this one, to represent lives that are to bear fruit.

seems small and powerless—like the proverbially small mustard seed and the yeast hidden in flour. Nevertheless, the eventual spread of the kingdom is sure. As a mustard seed grows into a tree, and as yeast spreads through dough, so too the kingdom of God will rule over all. Some have said that "yeast" here represents evil, but such an interpretation overlooks the context of the parable in Luke.

B. The journey continues (13:22–17:10). **13:22–15:32.** The travel note in 13:22 (cf. Luke 17:11) suggests a major break here in the text. Luke introduces more instructions for disciples, focusing on the salvation available for the humble (13:22–15:32). But the divisions of the text are rather difficult at this point and somewhat arbitrary.

13:22–14:35. A question about the number of people who will be saved (13:23) becomes the occasion for Jesus's instruction (13:22–30). Jesus does not answer the question directly (13:24). Instead, he focuses on the necessity to expend every effort ("strive") to enter the door of salvation. The urgency of decision is also underlined because the day is coming when it will be too late to enter; the door will be closed (13:24–25). Those who are outside will object that they knew Jesus, that they even feasted with him and enjoyed his teaching (13:26), but such an association with Jesus is superficial; he recognizes and admits entry only to those who obeyed his message (13:27). Those who are excluded will feel remorse ("weeping") and fierce anger ("gnashing of teeth") because they will not be able to participate in the great eschatological banquet (cf. Isa. 25:6–8; Rev. 19:9). Indeed, the great saints of old will feast with the Gentiles in the kingdom, a warning to the Jews of Jesus's day that the roles of Jews and Gentiles can be reversed (13:28–30).

Some Pharisees then tell Jesus to leave Galilee or Perea (Herod's realm) because Herod wants to kill him (cf. 23:7–12). There is not enough evidence to show whether these Pharisees were friends or foes of Jesus. Jesus, however, is not impressed with Herod's threats. He compares Herod to a cunning fox, saying that in the days ahead he will continue to carry out his ministry (13:32). Nevertheless, Jesus will be leaving Herod's realm and will arrive in Jerusalem, not because he is afraid of Herod, but because as a prophet he must "reach [his] goal" and die in Jerusalem (13:32–33). The temporal references in verses 32–33 should not be taken literally; they are simply a way of describing a period of time before the end. (The end is "the third day.") The reference to Jesus's destination in Jerusalem reminds him that the city has rejected his message, as it has rejected the message of prophets in former times (13:34; it also implies that Jesus has spent some time in Jerusalem). Such a rejection fills Jesus with anguish (13:34). But Jerusalem's rejection also spells her future judgment; her house will be left desolate (13:35). Here "house" refers to either the city as a whole or the temple. Jerusalem will not see her Messiah again until the second advent, when her faith will be renewed (13:35; cf. Rom. 11:26). Others think this last phrase means Jerusalem will not see Jesus again until he comes as her judge.

All of the episodes in chapter 14 through verse 24 take place at a banquet in a prominent Pharisee's home (14:1). The precise nature of the Pharisee's position is uncertain. The first episode is another controversy story on the Sabbath (14:1–6; cf. 6:1–11; 13:10–17). Hostility continues to build against Jesus because of his healings on the Sabbath, and he is being watched suspiciously on this occasion (14:1). "Dropsy" (14:2 KJV, RSV) involves swelling due to excess fluids building up in tissues and cavities. Jesus forthrightly challenges the Pharisees on the legitimacy of healing on the Sabbath; their silence indicates that they cannot refute him (14:3–4). Jesus justifies his healing by referring to the practice of rescuing one's child or ox from a well on the Sabbath (14:5). Some manuscripts read "donkey" instead of "child," but the latter is a superior reading. The Pharisees were apparently more humane than the Qumran community, for the latter did not even allow rescuing a beast on the Sabbath. "Let no beast be helped to give birth on the Sabbath day; and if it fall into a cistern or into a pit, let it not be lifted out on the Sabbath" (*Damascus Document* 11:13–14). Jesus's actions are such that no criticism can be voiced (14:6).

Observing that people are clamoring for the places of status at the banquet, Jesus makes some remarks on humility (14:7–14) to the guests (14:8–11) and to the host (14:12–14). Luke says that Jesus tells a parable (14:7); however, the word "parable" can have various meanings, and here it refers to the "wisdom sayings" that Jesus utters. Jesus's advice in verses 8–10 could be understood as a sly way to get ahead. People who claim the reputable places at banquets end up being publicly humiliated when they are asked to take a lower seat. So if you really want to get ahead, pretend to be insignificant and take the lowest seat. The host will notice your humility and advance you to a higher seat, indicating your intrinsic superiority. But verse 11 shows that Jesus does not have such a cunning program in mind, for such clever and false self-humiliation is still diseased with the root problem of trying to advance oneself above others. Those who try to advance themselves in a clever or a blatant way will be humbled, but God will exalt those who genuinely humble themselves before him. Jesus's words to the host in verses 12–14 can be easily misunderstood as well. He is not saying that one should never invite friends over for dinner. The problem he is addressing is the expectation of recompense—that is, the calculating spirit that does good so that more benefits will accrue to oneself. He uses the vivid (and serious) example of inviting the handicapped, because such an invitation shows that one is not controlled by a spirit of repayment. Jesus promises a reward at the resurrection for those who live in such an unselfish manner. Rewards come to those who live for the sake of others.

The reference to "the resurrection of the righteous" (14:14) leads one guest into a reverie on the blessing of being part of the eschatological banquet (14:15). Jesus responds by telling the parable of the great banquet (14:15–24), puncturing the man's sentimentality and bringing him back to reality. The kingdom of God is like a banquet, but the people invited make excuses so that they do not have to participate. The excuses (14:18–20) given show that these are people for whom material goods and family take priority. Their rejection at this point is extremely rude because they have already accepted the initial invitation (14:16–17). Jesus is probably referring to the religious leaders here; we need to remember that he is eating in a Pharisee's house (14:1). The master responds in verse 21 by inviting those of the lower class (referring to tax collectors and sinners, lower-class Jews) from the town. Luke's concern for the poor and handicapped (cf. 14:13) continues. Even after those from the lower class are brought to the banquet, there is still room for more, so the master sends his servant to the countryside so that his "house will be full" (14:23). This seems to be a clear reference to the Gentile mission. The phrase "compel them to come in" does not imply that some will enter the kingdom against their will. In Palestine people politely refused an invitation until they were persuaded to accept (cf. Gen. 19:3). The point of the parable is that people may talk sentimentally about the blessings of the kingdom (14:15), but in reality many do not want to accept the invitation. Those who refuse the invitation will never enter the kingdom (14:24).

The scene changes. Jesus is no longer in the Pharisee's house; now a large crowd is following him (14:25). Jesus challenges the crowd to think carefully about the radical commitment that he demands (14:25–35). Jesus invites all to follow him (cf. 14:15–24). Yet following him is not easy but requires ruthless self-denial. The call to hate one's family members is startling (14:26). Obviously, Jesus is not speaking of "psychological hatred" (cf. 6:27–28). The use of hyperbolic language indicates that no one can take precedence over Jesus. One must renounce "even their own life" and be willing to follow Jesus in the way of death (14:26–27). Those who are not willing to follow Jesus in such a radical way cannot be his disciples. Two illustrations are given to show the need for counting the cost before embarking on the road to discipleship. Someone building a tower (14:28–30) would surely calculate the cost of the project before starting. A half-finished building would be the object of ridicule. So too no king would plan to wage war against an enemy without considering beforehand the possibilities of victory (14:31–32). The application from the two illustrations is drawn in verse 33. Before one embarks on the road to discipleship, one needs to recognize from the beginning that Jesus demands total and complete commitment. Only those who have such a radical commitment can be Jesus's disciples. The illustration of the salt makes a similar point (14:34–35). A disciple who is not salty is one who ceases to be radically committed. Such disciples are good for nothing.

15:1–32. The setting for all of the "lost" parables in chapter 15 is the Pharisaic complaint that Jesus associates and eats with tax collectors and sinners (15:1–2). By eating with defiled people, Jesus himself would contract uncleanness. Thus these parables all emerge from a controversial setting and need to be interpreted as parables in which Jesus defends his ministry to the "lost." Three different parables with the same basic theme are included here, the last one being the most detailed.

Jesus's association with sinners is justified because God is like a shepherd who searches diligently for any lost sheep (15:3–7). The retrieval of the lost sheep

The parable of the lost sheep (Luke 15:3–7) led to early Christian art portraying Jesus as the shepherd joyfully carrying the found sheep on his shoulders. This statuette of the Good Shepherd is from the fourth century AD.

brings joy to God ("heaven" [15:7] is another way of referring to God; cf. Matt. 18:14). Verse 7 adds a point not contained in the parable (cf. 15:4–6)—namely, that God's joy comes from the repentance of the lost. The statement about the "ninety-nine righteous persons who do not need to repent" may be an ironic poke at the Pharisees; Jesus is not saying that some do not need repentance, only that some do not know they need repentance (cf. the lost son in 15:11–32). Parables do not represent stories from real life. Hence, the reader is not supposed to worry about whether the ninety-nine other sheep were abandoned in the wilderness (15:4). Such a question reveals that we have forgotten Jesus is telling a parable!

The parable of the lost coin (15:8–10) makes the same point as the previous parable. A shepherd with one hundred sheep is fairly well off, but a woman who loses one coin and searches for it is probably poor. It is often said that the lost coin was part of her dowry, yet there is no evidence in the text for this. If a woman searches carefully for one lost coin and exults over finding it, then it stands to reason that God will search diligently for those who are lost, rejoicing greatly over their repentance (15:7). A lamp would be needed during the day in a peasant's house that had no windows (15:8).

Many themes are intertwined in the parable of the lost son (15:11–32), and one could easily label it a parable of the father's love, but the theme of being "lost" is consistent with the two previous parables. Without doubt this is one of the most compelling and memorable stories ever told. It was not uncommon for a father to divide the estate before his death. Immediately the younger son cashes in his assets (he would receive one-third of the property since he was the younger son). He goes abroad and lives wildly, ending up bankrupt. When a famine strikes, he desperately needs work and is hired to feed pigs, a shocking job for any Jew since pigs were unclean animals. Nevertheless, his degradation is not yet complete. He is so hungry that he longs to eat the food these unclean animals are eating. Such debasement stimulates him to reconsider and change his life. The depth of his repentance is profound, for he no longer feels worthy to be called his father's son; however, the father's love is spontaneous. Before hearing of any confession of guilt, he runs to embrace his son while the latter is still far away. The son confesses his inadequacy, but the father does not even let him finish the soliloquy he has prepared ("make me like one of your hired servants" [see 15:19]). Instead, he treats him like an honored guest, adorning him with the best robe, putting a ring on his finger, and giving him sandals. (Slaves did not wear sandals.) Indeed, he starts a celebration by having the fattened calf prepared (15:23). Meat was not often eaten in Palestinian culture, so this surely indicates a festive occasion. The occasion of the celebration is the return to life of the lost son.

The story could easily end here, but the older son (who is often forgotten in popular renditions of the story) now returns home. The older son is hurt by the special treatment that the younger son has received and refuses to participate in the party. Displaying his love, the father entreats him to come in. But the older son is scandalized by what he considers to be favoritism for his younger brother. A young goat (15:29) would not be near the value of a fattened calf. Indeed, he cannot even acknowledge that the younger son is his brother; instead

he says "this son of yours" (15:30). The father, however, continues to plead with his older son, noting that the entire remaining inheritance now belongs to him and reminding him of the closeness of their relationship ("You are always with me," 15:31). The father says that the celebration was a necessity because of the return to life of the lost younger son (15:32). Notice that the father reminds the older brother of his relationship to his kin by saying, "this brother of yours" (15:32). The parable ends up in the air. Will the older son enter the party?

Jesus is defending his association with tax collectors and sinners. The festive eating with them is a necessity, for it symbolizes God's joy over their repentance. And his acceptance of them indicates his forgiving grace. Like the older son, the Pharisees are invited to enter the party as well. This clearly indicates Jesus's heart toward the Pharisees, which is often conceived of in negative terms. The parable, then, is a beautiful description of the forgiving love of God, his grace, and the joys of repentance. We must not demand that the parable teach the whole of Christian theology, and hence we must not conclude from it that the atonement is unnecessary, for one cannot expect a parable's teaching to be exhaustive.

16:1–17:10. The focus on the salvation available for the humble ends at 15:32, marking a shift in the text. But the textual divisions in this unit remain a bit arbitrary.

16:1–13. The parable of the dishonest steward is one of the most difficult to interpret in Luke. Where does the parable end? Does it end with verse 7, 8a, 8b, or 9? Is the master in verse 8 Jesus or the master of the steward in the parable? Why does the master praise the dishonest manager (16:8)? And what is the message of the parable for the church? Before we begin to answer these questions, a few preliminary matters need attention. The manager is not merely an ordinary household servant, but an estate manager, the agent of his master. He probably handled all the economic affairs of the master. He is charged with dishonesty

(16:1), and the charge must be true because no self-defense is attempted (16:3). The master fires the manager and asks for a final accounting sheet so that his successor can conduct business (16:2). The manager realizes his predicament. He is a white-collar worker, and so he cannot handle manual labor. Also, it would be a blow to his pride to beg. By lowering the bills of the debtors, he will win their friendship, ensuring a future place for himself (16:4–7).

We cannot interpret this parable any further until we answer some of the previous questions. First, it is probable that the parable ends at 8a. Second, the "master" referred to in verse 8 is not Jesus but the master of the steward. Identifying the master as Jesus is problematic because then the parable ends suddenly and unexpectedly without any indication of how the master responded to the manager's dishonesty. The comment in verse 8b is probably from Jesus because it seems clear that a religious application is now being drawn from the story. Thus the parable ends in the middle of verse 8, closing with a comment from the manager's master. Third, almost all scholars agree that the master is not praising the dishonesty of the manager. Praise for dishonesty is inexplicable. Some scholars argue that the master is praising the manager because when the manager reduces the debts he is only eliminating the interest from the debts. According to the Old Testament the taking of interest was forbidden, but in this case the manager exacts interest so that he can line his own pockets. On this interpretation the master does not praise the manager for his dishonesty; instead, he commends the manager for renouncing the illegal practice of charging interest. This interpretation is attractive because it removes the problem of the master commending his steward for dishonesty, but it is not the most obvious meaning of the text. There is no indication in the text at all that the manager has decided not to charge interest. And the interest in verse 6 is improbably high—100 percent! Moreover, the master in verse 8 praises his dishonest employee, showing no indication

that he has just done something that is righteous. If the above analysis is correct, why does the master praise his manager? Not because of the employee's illegal and immoral behavior (although he does act immorally) but because he does something that is clever and prudent.

The lesson that Jesus draws from the parable, then, involves both comparison and contrast—use money wisely and prudently as the steward did, but do not use it dishonestly as he did (cf. 16:10–12). When Jesus refers to "unrighteous mammon" (so KJV; rightly translated in the NIV as "worldly wealth" [16:9, 11]), he is not saying that money is intrinsically evil, only that it is easily abused and used for evil. The lessons Jesus draws from this parable are as follows: (1) Use your money for kingdom purposes so that in the end your use of wealth will indicate that you are worthy of entering into heaven (16:9). This is not salvation *by* works, but salvation *with* works. (2) If one is faithful in handling a small amount of money, one will be faithful with large amounts (16:10). (3) One who cannot be trusted with money cannot be trusted with spiritual riches (16:11). (4) One who cannot handle his or her own affairs will not be called on to manage the affairs of another (16:12). In verse 13 Jesus penetrates to the root; no one can give exclusive service to both God *and* money.

16:14–31. Clearly the reproof of the greedy Pharisees (16:14–15) continues to focus on money, but it takes the discussion in a new direction. Apparently the Pharisees were ridiculing Jesus because they imagined some compatibility between serving God and serving money. Jesus replies that their attempt at self-defense is hollow because God penetrates to the true state of their hearts. An attempt to appear pious before people without being pious before God is detestable to God.

It is hard to see how the statements on the law (16:16–18) in this paragraph relate to the preceding paragraph. In verse 16 discontinuity is drawn between the period of the law and the period of the kingdom. "The Law and the Prophets" refers here to the Old Testament

Scriptures. Whether John the Baptist is to be included in the former or the latter is disputed. The main point of the text is that with Jesus the proclamation of the kingdom has arrived. What Luke means by "everyone is forcing their way into it" is problematic. It could mean (1) everyone is urgently invited to enter into the kingdom, or (2) everyone is trying hard to enter into the kingdom, or (3) everyone uses violence against the kingdom. The first view has the most to commend it, for the latter two have difficulty explaining the inclusion of the word "everyone." Verse 16 emphasizes the discontinuity between the law and the kingdom, but verse 17 qualifies that statement. Actually, the preaching of the kingdom does not invalidate a single part of the Old Testament law. The "stroke" here refers to the marks that distinguish Hebrew letters from one another. It is not referring to ornamental crowns found in some manuscripts of the Torah, for the latter are not found in first-century manuscripts. Obviously Jesus is not saying that the entire Old Testament law is still literally in force; this is a hyperbolic way of saying that the Old Testament law as Jesus has interpreted it is permanently valid. Verse 18 illustrates the principle of verse 17. The Old Testament nowhere forbids divorce altogether, but Jesus interprets the Old Testament in such a way that divorce is forbidden.

At this point the chapter returns to the theme of the proper use of riches (16:19–31). Verses 19–26 teach that there will be a reversal of fortunes after death. The rich man lives in great luxury during his life, but he is apparently unconcerned about the plight of the poor. Lazarus is abandoned at his gate, diseased and hungry. Dogs, which were considered to be unclean and a nuisance, lick the sores on his body. He is even denied the pleasure of eating the leftovers from the rich man's table; however, when the two men die, their roles are reversed. Lazarus goes to Abraham's bosom (16:22), perhaps another way of describing the messianic banquet. This expression occurs only here in the Bible. The rich man goes to Hades (16:23). *Hades* is the Greek translation of the Hebrew word *sheol* and usually indicates the realm of the dead. Here it clearly refers to a place of torment. Possibly this parable teaches that *sheol* is divided into two realms, one of blessing and one of punishment. But the parable should not be pressed too hard for such information since this is not the main point of the story. As Lazarus desired the crumbs from the rich man's table, now the rich man wants just a drop of water from Lazarus (16:24). But he is denied. A chasm exists between Lazarus and the rich man, and now the rich man is reaping what he sowed. There is a clear message to Christian disciples here; they need to use their money prudently and generously in order to enter eternal dwellings (cf. 16:9). In verses 27–31 the parable takes a different tack. The rich man realizes that it is too late for him, so he entreats Abraham to send Lazarus to warn his brothers of their imminent doom (16:27–28). (One should not use this detail of a parable to probe the self-consciousness of those who are being punished.) Abraham dismisses the suggestion because the brothers already have "Moses and the Prophets" (16:29). This also suggests that the message of Jesus does not invalidate Old Testament revelation (cf. 16:17). The rich man, however, protests that the Scriptures are not enough. They need the definitive proof that a resurrection would provide (16:30). Abraham retorts that this is incorrect. Those who do not put credence in the Scriptures will not be persuaded by a resurrection. Certainly Jesus's resurrection was in Luke's mind when he wrote this. The point of the last part of the parable is clear. No miracle can convince anyone of the credibility of the kingdom message. The Scriptures are sufficient for salvation, and those who reject their message will rationalize miraculous phenomena as well.

17:1–10. Four sets of sayings are combined here that have no obvious relationship to one another except that each one is about discipleship. (1) Jesus warns the disciples about the danger of causing others to stumble in their faith (17:1–3a). It would be better if a person were dead than that he would lead another into sin. (2) From the subject of leading others into sin, Jesus moves to the topic of forgiving those who fall into sin (17:3b–4). No matter how many times a person sins, if that person repents after being confronted, then he or she should be forgiven. The number seven here should not be taken literally; it symbolizes limitless forgiveness. (3) Perhaps the extent of forgiveness that is required of disciples leads them to say, "Increase our faith" (17:5); however, Jesus says that the problem is not the quantity of their faith but the reality of it. A small amount of faith can accomplish great things (17:6). (4) Last, obedient disciples cannot claim any reward or regard themselves as doing anything particularly notable (17:7–10). In the secular world a master expects the servant to serve the master before taking care of his or her own needs. The central point of the parable is not that God is ungrateful for the obedience of disciples because he expects such service anyway (17:9). Rather, the point is that disciples cannot boast before God about their service.

C. The last leg of the journey (17:11–19:27).
17:11 37. Another travel note in 17:11 in dicates a break in the narrative. The setting is Jesus traveling "along the border between Samaria and Galilee." The major thrust of the cleansing of the ten lepers (17:11 19) is that only one returns and praises God. Moreover, this one person is a foreigner—a Samaritan. By focusing on a Samaritan, Luke is stressing the universality of the gospel message. Verse 19 implies that the Samaritan has received more than just physical healing.

The connection of the paragraph on the coming of the kingdom (17:20–37) with the previous paragraph is not obvious. Some have suggested that both the nine lepers and the Pharisees fail to see the presence of the kingdom in Jesus. The Pharisees want to know when the kingdom will arrive (17:20). Jesus replies that the coming of the kingdom cannot be calculated by observing signs. And in one

sense the kingdom is present *now*—it is *within you* (17:21). This last comment does not mean that the kingdom was internally present in the Pharisees; rather, it means that the kingdom has arrived in the person and ministry of Jesus. Jesus's words to the Pharisees on the arrival of the kingdom lead into a discourse for the disciples on the coming of the Son of Man (17:22–37). Jesus begins by emphasizing that his followers will long to see the days of his future messianic reign (17:22), but such anticipation should not blind their critical faculties (17:23). They should not be misled by those who claim to know where he is, for his coming will be as sudden and obvious as lightning that flashes in the sky (17:24). Furthermore, before any of this can happen, the Son of Man must suffer death (17:25). Jesus compares the day of his coming to the days of Noah and Lot (17:26–30). Life was progressing in an ordinary way when the flood and the destruction of Sodom and Gomorrah occurred. There was no warning that an apocalyptic judgment was evident. All indications were that life was going on as usual. So too the coming of the Son of Man will be without warning. No apocalyptic signs will clearly herald his appearance.

The instructions in verses 31–33 must be metaphorical rather than literal. Verse 33 supplies a hint as to the meaning of the metaphor. Jesus is saying that one should not become attached to material possessions so that one is not ready for his arrival. The one who tries to preserve his or her life in this world will lose it in the next. Disciples must stay faithful to their master while waiting. Verses 34–35 show that the Son of Man will come suddenly and unexpectedly. People will be involved in the ordinary activities of sleeping and eating. However, there will be a separation among people who work closely together. "One will be taken" could mean one is taken for judgment or taken away from judgment. The latter is probable, for God took away Noah and Lot so that they would escape the judgment. Those who are left will face the full fury of the judgment. The disciples' question in verse 37 is strange. It probably indicates that they have not understood Jesus's discourse, for Jesus has already said (17:23) that this kind of question is irrelevant. Jesus answers that his coming will be as obvious and as unmistakable as the arrival of vultures over a corpse. No one will doubt what is happening.

18:1–43. The previous section focused on the unexpected coming of the Son of Man. The parable of the unjust judge (18:1–8) underlines the necessity of persistent prayer and faith until the Son of Man comes. Luke begins by giving the reader an editorial comment on the meaning of the parable (18:1). The difficulties of life may tempt one to give up on prayer, but one should continue in prayer until the end. The parable proper follows (18:2–5). The unscrupulous judge cares nothing about justice for the widow. Widows were helpless and weak members of society, having virtually no recourse to overcome oppression and exploitation. Even though the widow is at a disadvantage, she uses her strongest weapon: persistence. She "kept coming" (18:3), so that the judge reconsiders his habitual refusals (18:4). He is tired of her "bothering" him (18:5) and is afraid she will wear him out (see NASB, RSV). The last phrase in 18:5 literally means "give a black eye to" (NIV "come and attack me"). But the judge is not worried about a physical assault, nor is he worried about his reputation (he does not care what people think [18:2, 4]); he is tired of the bother. What is the meaning of the parable? Jesus asks his listeners to consider its meaning (18:6). Obviously it is not saying that God is like the unjust judge and that one has to pester him so that he will answer our requests even though he does not want to help us. Instead, it draws a contrast between God and the judge. Unlike the judge, God will quickly grant justice to those who call to him for it (18:7–8); however, there is a point of tension in the parable. If justice is received so quickly, why would anyone give up in prayer (18:1)? And why would anyone lose faith before the Son of Man comes (18:8)? Perhaps the vindication will not seem quick for people

on earth but will be agonizingly slow—so slow that they may give up on prayer, concluding that God is not just, that he does not punish the wicked and vindicate those who long for justice. The parable promises that God will answer, despite how long it may seem to take. Human beings may be asking, "Can God be trusted to vindicate the elect?" But the parable ends on a different note. No one can question God's faithfulness; the only question is whether human beings will be faithful to the end (18:8).

Again, it is hard to detect the relationship between the parable of the Pharisee and tax collector (18:9–14) and the preceding parable. Perhaps this parable illustrates the kind of faith (cf. 18:8) that God desires. Luke again begins the parable by making an editorial comment (18:9). This parable is addressed to the self-confident and self-righteous—those who look down on others with contemptuous disdain. On the one hand, the Pharisee, confident of his moral superiority, approaches the temple to pray. He praises God that he is not like other sinners and then lauds his own religious devotion. By fasting twice a week and tithing, he would be going beyond the requirement of the Old Testament law. On the other hand, the tax collector (see Luke 5:27–32) is deeply conscious of his own unworthiness. He stands far away, fearing even to raise his eyes. All he can ask for is mercy since he knows he is undeserving of God's forgiveness. Jesus concludes by saying that the tax collector, rather than the Pharisee, was justified in God's eyes. Here Luke is indicating that the Pauline doctrine of justification by faith apart from works has its roots in the teaching of Jesus. Verse 14b also teaches Christian humility. The beauty and power of this parable are inescapable. Modern-day readers identify with the tax collector, but in the process we have unconsciously uttered the prayer, "Thank God I am not like that Pharisee," showing that the heart of the Pharisee lives in all of us.

The disciples reprove those who bring children to Jesus, perhaps because they considered it to be a waste of time; however, Jesus compares the inhabitants of the kingdom to children (18:15–17), probably referring to the openness, spontaneity, and freshness of children. Indeed, all those who enter the kingdom need to become like children in exercising childlike humility. Like the prior parable, this paragraph emphasizes that it is the humble who will be exalted.

A rich ruler inquires about the pathway to eternal life (18:18–30). Jesus immediately questions the ruler about calling him good, stressing that only God is good. Jesus is not admitting sinfulness here, nor is he leading the ruler to the realization of his divinity. He is initially directing attention away from himself to God, reminding the ruler that all goodness comes from him. The five commandments cited focus on those that deal with social relationships (18:20). Jesus implies that eternal life comes from obedience to the law. There is no reason to doubt the truthfulness of the ruler's assertion of obedience to the law; Jesus does not accuse him of blatant hypocrisy. Instead, he probes deeper. The ruler has placed one thing above God, namely, his riches. If he really desires eternal life, he must sell all and follow Jesus. Obedience to the law does not merely consist in the ability to refrain from certain sins; it means that one has placed God above everything else in one's life. God is not supreme if one is not willing to follow Jesus in discipleship. Jesus has also removed any sense of respectability the ruler could derive from his obedience (cf. 18:11–12). The ruler's wealth prevents him from following Jesus, and Jesus responds by stressing how difficult it is for the rich to enter heaven. The picture of a camel going through the eye of a needle does not refer to a gate called by that name (no such gate has ever been found!), nor is the textual reading "rope" better than "camel" (18:25). Jesus draws a vivid and humorous picture of that which is impossible. The hearers are perplexed about Jesus's statement. If rich people cannot be saved (for they were highly respected), then who could be saved (18:26)? Jesus replies that humanly it is impossible for anyone to be saved, showing

that his picture in verse 25 is supposed to convey an impossibility. Salvation is possible only with God. In verses 28–30 Jesus does not criticize Peter for asking about future rewards; instead, he promises that they will be significant for those who have left everything to follow him. The leaving of a wife (18:29) should probably be understood as a renunciation of the privilege of marriage for the sake of the kingdom.

The third passion prediction (18:31–34) comes on the heels of the promise of rewards. There will be rewards, but the path to rewards is suffering. This passion prediction is distinctive because it stresses the fulfillment of Scripture, the role of the Gentiles, and the incomprehension of the disciples. We should not fail to see that the prediction of the resurrection is contained here as well.

The healing of the blind man (18:35–43) occurs while Jesus is leaving Jericho (cf. Mark 10:46–52). Jericho was near to the city of Jesus's destination, namely, Jerusalem. Despite being discouraged by the crowd, the blind man hails Jesus as the Son of David, referring to his messianic status as he begs him for help. The implication is that the blind man is one of his disciples since he puts his faith in Jesus and follows him on the road to the cross (Jerusalem). Is the blind man's recovery of sight contrasted with the failure of the Twelve to see (cf. 18:34)?

19:1–27. The episode with Zacchaeus (19:1–10) is notable because it contains many of the main themes of Luke's Gospel. A chief tax collector (19:2) was probably the head of a group of tax collectors. The grumbling starts again when Jesus decides to lodge at another tax collector's house (cf. Luke 5:27–32); however, Zacchaeus vindicates Jesus's decision by demonstrating the reality of his repentance. Half of what he owns he will give to the poor, and he will make fourfold restitution to those who have been cheated (19:8). The present tense of the verbs "give" and "pay back" should be understood as futuristic presents. Some scholars claim that Zacchaeus is not repenting of sin here but is defending himself. He has always (present tense) given half of his goods to the poor and repaid those who have been cheated. Such a view is incorrect, for it does not explain the word "today" in verse 9. Zacchaeus reforms his life the day he meets Jesus. Observing what has happened, Jesus says that "salvation has come to this house" (19:9). Salvation is a major Lukan theme, perhaps the central one in the book. We also see Luke's concern for the poor in this story; however, we should not fail to observe that here we have a rich man who is saved (cf. 18:18–30). The salvation of the rich is possible with God, for "the Son of Man came to seek and to save the lost" (19:10), both the rich and the poor, the clean and the unclean, the despised and the respectable.

The parable of the ten pounds (19:11–27) is similar to the parable of talents in Matthew 25:14–30, but there is no agreement on the literary relationship between the two parables. In Luke the context of the parable is the expectation that the

consummation of the kingdom is imminent (19:11). Luke has already taught that the kingdom is present in Jesus's ministry (Luke 11:20), but even though Jesus has inaugurated the kingdom, he has not completed it. Since he is "near Jerusalem," some think the completion of God's kingdom purposes is at hand. The parable implies an interval of time before the kingdom is consummated. The nobleman goes on a distant journey (19:12). Typically Jesus is not interested in speculating on the date of the kingdom's consummation; he focuses on the need for responsible work by his servants. In the parable, each of the ten servants is given one mina, which probably equaled about three months' wages. Each servant is expected to make a profit in the master's absence. The message to the disciples is that they are expected to bear fruit in the interval of time between Jesus's ascension and return. When the nobleman returns, he settles accounts. Seven of the ten servants fall out of the picture, and the master reckons with only three. The first two invest the money responsibly and are rewarded lavishly by the master (19:15–19). The point is that God graciously rewards his servants with far more than they deserve. The focus, however, is on the third servant (19:20–24). He does not invest his money and accuses the master of being cruel and exploitative. Perhaps he feared that if he made a profit the master would take it, and if he lost the money the master would demand repayment. The master retorts that the standard of judgment will be the servant's own words. If he as the master is so

A sycamore tree—such as this one in Ramat-gan, Israel—is a type of fig tree that, full grown, can reach a height of sixty feet. The low, thick branches would have made it easy for Zacchaeus to climb (Luke 19:4).

harsh and exploitative, then obviously he will harshly judge someone who did nothing. The point of the parable is not that God is harsh and cruel but that he will judge those who waste the resources he has given to them. The bystanders object to the transfer of the third servant's mina to the first servant, but the transfer intentionally teaches God's sovereign graciousness. The rewards are based not on merit but on grace. Another theme is woven into the parable. The citizens of the country do not want the nobleman to assume rule over them (19:14). When he gains the kingship, he executes those who resisted his rule (19:27). This clearly refers to the Jews who have rejected Jesus as their king. Their rejection of Jesus will ultimately lead to judgment. This theme is appropriate in Luke's Gospel because the final rejection of Jesus is on the horizon.

5. Arrival at Destiny: Death and Resurrection in Jerusalem (19:28–24:53)

A. Entrance into Jerusalem (19:28–48). The long journey to Jerusalem is over (cf. Luke 9:51). Jesus finally arrives in Jerusalem (19:28–40), and the culmination of his lifework is at hand. Verse 28 depicts Jesus traveling ahead of the disciples, which underlines his determination to go to Jerusalem. Perhaps the acquisition of the colt (19:29–34) was a matter that Jesus arranged beforehand. Jesus climbs on the colt, and his entry into Jerusalem is acclaimed in messianic terms. The riding of the colt symbolizes the humility of his entrance. The Pharisees object to the enthusiastic words of the crowd, but Jesus replies that if they are silent the stones will take up the shout.

The sight of Jerusalem moves Jesus to tears (19:41–44), not because of his own fate but because of the fate of the city. They have not recognized that in his person they have been visited by God, that the prospect of peace with God is being offered. Now it is too late. Judgment will come, and the city will be destroyed because they will have rejected God's messenger.

Luke's description of the cleansing of the temple (19:45–48) is brief and to the point.

Obviously Jesus thinks that the commercial activity going on in the temple is obscuring its function as a house of prayer. The cleansing would have occurred in the Court of Gentiles, not in the inner precincts. A cleansing of the temple was expected in the last times (Mal. 3:1), and Jesus's action may have also symbolized the future judgment of Jerusalem and destruction of the temple. The cleansed temple does not become the location of Jesus's teaching, and it probably solidified the opposition to Jesus, convincing the leaders that it was time to do away with Jesus. Nevertheless, the popularity of Jesus frustrates the immediate desire of the leadership.

B. Controversy between Jesus and leaders heightens (20:1–21:4). The conflict between Jesus and the religious leaders intensifies, and the debates in this chapter reflect the heightening tensions. An official group of religious leaders, probably commissioned by the Sanhedrin, approaches Jesus and asks about the source of his authority (20:1–8). "These things" (20:2) seems to refer to the teaching of Jesus, but it certainly includes the bold action of cleansing the temple. Jesus does not answer the question directly; instead, he poses a question about the legitimacy of the Baptist's ministry (20:3–4). This is not an attempt to escape from the controversy, nor is it a debating trick. It was the Baptist who proclaimed the coming of Jesus and baptized him. Before Jesus discusses his own status, he needs to know what their estimation is of the message of his forerunner. After all, the answer to their question is in John's preaching: Jesus derives his authority from God. The authorities, however, claim ignorance (20:5–7), fearing a rebuke from Jesus on the one hand and a violent reaction from the crowd on the other. Jesus responds by not giving a direct answer to their question (20:8), although the answer is really implied. Jesus leaves his listeners to draw their own conclusion.

Absentee landlords who rented out their land to tenant farmers were common in Palestine. In the parable of the wicked tenant farmers

(20:9–19) the obvious allegorical features are sometimes held to be a creation of the early church, but there is no reason why Jesus could not have used an allegory. The end of the parable (20:19) tells us that the parable is directed against the religious leaders. They have been given the responsibility to tend the vineyard (symbolizing Israel; cf. Isa. 5:1–7). When the owner of the vineyard desires to collect some of the fruit, he sends messengers (representing the prophets). In each case the messengers are wounded and ousted. The repetition of the same pattern three times is for rhetorical purposes, building the narrative to a climax. The owner of the vineyard is perplexed. The sending of his son will probably command the tenants' respect. Of course, the son here is Jesus, and instead of rejecting him the religious leaders put him to death, thinking they will inherit the vineyard. Commentators debate whether the thinking of the tenants on inheriting the vineyard is reasonable (20:14–15). Possibly some tenants did revolt against owners and try to take possession of the property in Jesus's day. But the parable is not necessarily attempting to reflect the culture and practices of that time. Here the action is irrational, for the owner of the vineyard will come and execute the tenant farmers and give the vineyard to others. The kingdom of God will be taken from the religious leaders and be given to the Gentiles. The people's response—"God forbid!" (20:16)—is an expression of horror. It was unthinkable that the kingdom would

be removed from Israel (though Jesus is not teaching that Israel has no future role in God's salvation plan). Jesus, however, solemnly assures them that this is precisely what the Scriptures foretold (Ps. 118:22). The builders (the religious leaders) have rejected the stone (Jesus), which "has become the cornerstone" (20:17). This is not a decorative stone but a stone placed at the corner of the building to bear the stress and weight of the two walls. Thus, it is *the* crucial stone in the building. Verse 18 expresses two thoughts: (1) those who stumble (probably in unbelief) over that stone will themselves be broken; (2) if the stone falls in judgment on anyone, that person will be pulverized. This parable of judgment only provokes the leaders' desire to do away with Jesus, but his popularity with the people holds firm (20:19).

The previous parable increased the opposition to Jesus, but since the religious leaders cannot yet arrest him, they try to entrap him. Their praise for Jesus's integrity is lavish but insincere and hypocritical. Paying taxes to Caesar (20:20–26) was a volatile issue in first-century Palestine. Some Jews thought that the payment of such a tax necessarily involved compromise of their religion. Moreover, the image of the emperor on the coin was thought to be a violation of the second commandment. The questioners were probably hoping either that Jesus would disavow paying taxes and incur trouble with Pilate or that he would advocate complete submission to the Roman government and alienate Jewish

Luke 20:17 refers to Jesus as a cornerstone. These Herodian cornerstones holding up the southeast corner of the temple mount average over seven feet long and three feet wide, and they weigh approximately eighty tons.

patriots. By calling for a denarius (20:24), Jesus shows that even pious Jews possessed coins with Caesar's image, clearly showing their submission to his jurisdiction. The first part of Jesus's answer (20:25) acknowledges the legitimacy of submission to Roman power insofar as that power is acting lawfully. But that is not the whole story. One is to give to God what belongs to him, and obviously his jurisdiction is total. Thus Jesus is not setting up two separate realms, for the authority of God takes precedence over the state (cf. Acts 5:29). However, one should obey the earthly ruler as one who is delegated by God to enforce justice (cf. Rom. 13:1–7). Jesus's answer was so impressive that it silenced his adversaries.

Jesus has given a deft answer to a controversial political question. Now Jesus is faced with a question about the resurrection from the Sadducees (20:27–40). The Sadducees were an aristocratic group who were the most powerful political faction in Palestine. They rejected both the oral tradition of the law, to which the Pharisees adhered, and belief in the resurrection and angels (cf. Acts 23:8). They relied only on the Old Testament Scriptures for their theology, focusing especially on the Torah. In this episode they try to show that the doctrine of the resurrection is ridiculous. Referring to the custom of levirate marriage (a man marries his deceased brother's wife who is childless to raise up children for his brother), they imply that a future resurrection is out of the question. If a wife had seven such husbands, to which husband would she be married in the resurrection? Jesus's answer has two parts. (1) The Sadducees fail to see the discontinuity between this age and the age to come. Marriage and procreation are a vital part of earthly life to preserve the human race, but in the coming kingdom there will be no institution of marriage. People will be like angels. This does not necessarily mean that sexual differences will be obliterated, nor does it mean that human beings and angels will be exactly alike. It means that human beings will be like angels in at least one way—neither group will marry. (2) What Jesus has said

weakens the Sadducean objection. But now he moves to the Scriptures to demonstrate his case. If Exodus 3:6 says that God is the God of Abraham, Isaac, and Jacob, then the patriarchs must continue to live. Some have said that this example does not prove the resurrection but only the immortality of the soul. Others have tried to argue that Jesus is speaking here only of a future resurrection, but this is not supported by verse 38. Jesus's argument seems to be this: if the patriarchs belong to God, then they are guaranteed a future resurrection. God is only the God of the living, not the nonexistent. Jesus's answer impresses some teachers, probably Pharisees who disagreed with the Sadducees (20:39). His prowess in answering questions again silences his opponents.

Now Jesus shows his superior understanding by posing a question that the religious leaders cannot answer (20:41–44). Quoting a messianic psalm (Ps. 110:1), he asks how the Messiah can be both the Son of David and the Lord of David. Jesus is not denying that the Messiah was to be David's son. Instead, he is implying that there is a mysterious way in which the Messiah is both David's son and Lord. A resolution of the paradox is not given here, although the reader of Luke's Gospel knows that Jesus is both the Son of David and the Son of God (cf. 1:32, 35).

Jesus has just criticized the theology of the religious leaders, and now he upbraids the religious practice of the scribes (20:45–47). They perform their religious duties for show and to garner respect, but at the same time they defraud widows of their money. Severe judgment will fall on such pretentious religiosity. We should not conclude that all scribes were hypocrites; Jesus merely focuses on the danger of religiosity (cf. Luke 11:37–52).

The widow's sacrificial gift (21:1–4) is a remarkable contrast to the pretentious religion of the scribes—who exploit widows (20:45–47)! On the one hand, others are giving substantial gifts to the temple, but the text suggests that the gifts are insignificant because they put no strain on the givers' budgets. On the other hand, the widow's gift is notable because of the extreme sacrifice it entails, even though the amount of money is negligible.

C. Apocalyptic discourse (21:5–38). The temple that elicited the admiration of his disciples was beautiful indeed. Herod the Great began to refurbish it in 20/19 BC, and the work was not completed until AD 63 or later. Jesus, however, predicts that the temple will be completely demolished (21:5–6). The Romans fulfilled this prophecy in AD 70. Some scholars have maintained that this saying was attributed to Jesus after the event occurred, but such a view reflects a bias against predictive prophecy.

Jesus now warns his disciples against eschatological enthusiasm and braces them for future persecution (21:7–19). The question of the disciples in verse 7 clearly refers to the date of the fall of Jerusalem, but it also seems to involve the date of the end of this age. The fall of Jerusalem becomes a type for the destruction that will occur in the end times. (Luke has distinguished more clearly than Matthew [Matthew 24] and Mark [Mark 13] the events that will take place in Jerusalem from the events of the end.) Jesus's answer indicates that the question in verse 7 relates to the last times. He warns his disciples not to be deceived because many will claim to be the Messiah or declare that the end has come. The arrival of the end cannot be calculated from wars, insurrections, famines, earthquakes, and disease (21:9–11). These events will occur before the end, and they may even signal the imminence of the end, but no certain calculation can be drawn from them. The disciples ought not to think the end will deliver them from suffering, because persecution will precede the end (21:12). They will be prosecuted by civil and religious authorities. But their defense will produce an opportunity to testify about the gospel, and they will receive the necessary words with which to defend themselves. The persecution may be bitter, perhaps even involving betrayal by family members and death. They must steel themselves

to face implacable hostility (21:17). To say "not a hair of your head will perish" (21:18) seems to contradict verse 16, where Jesus asserts that some will be put to death. The saying in verse 18 means that one will be spiritually preserved from any harm, since physical death does not damage one's essential self. All of this is encouragement to stand firm and persevere, because such perseverance is necessary for salvation (21:19). Again, this is not salvation by works. Such perseverance gives evidence of the genuineness of one's salvation.

In the next section Jesus specifically answers the question about the destruction of Jerusalem (21:20–24). One will know that Jerusalem's time of destruction has arrived when foreign armies surround it. This encirclement is a signal, not of the need for heroism, but the need to flee. God's avenging wrath will be poured out on the city, bringing distress to the entire populace. "The times of the Gentiles" (21:24) refers not to the Gentile mission but to Gentile authority over Jerusalem. Josephus's *Jewish War* contains a graphic commentary on the Roman conquest of Jerusalem in AD 70.

From the destruction of Jerusalem Luke moves to the coming of the Son of Man (21:25–28). Luke does not specify the temporal relationship between these events, but the former clearly functions as a correspondence or type of the latter. The emphasis on signs in this paragraph is in tension with Luke's claim elsewhere that no signs will precede the end (cf. 17:20–25). This is probably Luke's paradoxical way of saying that the end is not calculable, and yet certain signs precede it. The signs picture in dramatic terms the breakup of the natural world order, and the resulting terror and fear that seize the human race. The Son of Man will return during these troubled times. The message for believers is, when the world begins to convulse, take hope! Your redemption is imminent.

The parable of the fig tree (21:29–33) is easy to comprehend. Just as the appearance of leaves on a tree shows that summer is near, so too the signs previously described indicate that the coming of the Son of Man is near. The assertion that "this generation will certainly not pass away" (21:32) is difficult. It could refer to (1) the generation in which Jesus was living, (2) the Jewish race, (3) the human race, or (4) the end-time generation. It probably refers both to (1) and (4), for Jesus's generation experienced the razing of Jerusalem, and Jerusalem's destruction becomes a type of the end. In typical Jewish fashion Jesus combines in this discourse information about the destruction of Jerusalem and the end of the world.

The arrival of the Son of Man and the destruction of Jerusalem have a practical message for disciples. They should constantly be vigilant (21:34–36), not forgetting in the interval their purpose for living. The end will come suddenly, and the entire earth will be affected. When Jesus says pray to escape what will happen (21:36), he does not mean that people should pray that they will not be on earth. Rather, he means they should pray that they will not face the terrible judgment of God. By following the path of obedience, they will receive a favorable verdict from God and stand before the Son of Man with joy.

The verses on Jesus's ministry in Jerusalem (21:37–38) are not part of the apocalyptic discourse. Jesus continues his teaching ministry up until the end, and his popularity with the people continues.

D. Passover events (22:1–38). The Feast of Unleavened Bread was held during the fifteenth to the twenty-first of Nisan (March–April), and the Passover on the fourteenth and fifteenth days of the same month. Because the two feasts were so close together, Luke does not differentiate clearly between them. Members of the Sanhedrin ("chief priests and the teachers of the law") want to arrest Jesus, but they are afraid of a popular uprising among the people, for Jesus is greatly admired (cf. 19:28–40; 21:38). Judas Iscariot's decision to betray Jesus (22:1–6) is the crucial break that the religious leaders need. He discusses the matter and makes plans with the chief priests and the temple police. The only

explanation Luke gives for Judas's disloyalty is the work of Satan (cf. John 13:2, 27), and perhaps the desire for money (22:5). No crowd could be present when the transaction was carried out because the arrest of Jesus could have fomented a revolt among the people (22:6).

The next paragraph concerns the Passover preparations (22:7–13). All the Synoptic Gospels agree that Jesus ate a Passover meal with his disciples. The lambs would have been slain in the afternoon on the fourteenth day of Nisan, and the meal would be celebrated that evening (22:7). The evening would start a new day according to the Jewish reckoning. John seems to date the meal before the Passover (John 13:1; 18:28; 19:14), which would place Jesus's death on the fourteenth of Nisan, the day the lambs were sacrificed. The problem of the difference between John and the Synoptics is complex and cannot be treated adequately here. Some have argued that the Synoptic writers used the sectarian calendar from the Essenes, which would explain the variance in dating. It has also been suggested that the meal in the Synoptics is not actually the Passover but a Passover type of meal. The best solution is that the Gospel of John uses the terminology of "Passover" for the Feast of Unleavened Bread, which immediately followed the Passover, since the two feasts occurred at the same time. The account here suggests that Jesus secretly prearranged the location of the meal, probably so that Judas could not betray him before the celebration of the feast. "A man carrying a jar of water" (21:10) would be notable, for this was usually done by a woman.

A Passover meal (22:14–23) usually had the following order: (1) preliminary events—a blessing was said, then the first cup of wine and a dish of herbs were served; (2) the Passover liturgy was recited, the second cup was drunk, and a part of the Hallel (Psalms 113–18) was sung; (3) the meal was celebrated, a blessing was pronounced over the unleavened bread, the lamb was eaten with the unleavened bread and bitter herbs, and the third cup was drunk after the meal; (4) the rest of the Hallel psalms were sung. (There is disagreement over whether there was a fourth cup.)

Jesus expresses his intense desire to partake of the Passover with the disciples (22:15). Some scholars have said that Jesus abstained from the meal, but the most natural meaning of verse 15 is that Jesus did eat the Passover with the disciples. This Passover meal, however, is the last one Jesus will eat with his disciples. But the meal also takes on eschatological significance. Jesus will celebrate the Passover with the disciples again during the messianic banquet (22:16, 18). The first cup (22:17) is either the first or second cup of the Passover service. The Passover in the Old Testament represents the liberation of Israel from Egypt, but Jesus now begins to reinterpret the Passover. The bread he breaks symbolizes his broken body; that is, it represents his sacrificial death, which is vicarious in nature (22:19). The cup in verse 20 would be the third cup, after the main meal. This cup represents the new covenant (Jer. 31:31–32), and the wine represents his blood that establishes the new agreement and is poured out in a sacrificial way for others. Some manuscripts omit Luke 22:19b–20, but these verses should be included as part of the original text due to the strength of the manuscript evidence. Jesus continues his words, predicting that one of those eating with him will betray him (22:21). The fact that one of Jesus's closest associates, who even shared the Passover with him, would act with treachery is intended to evoke horror from the reader. Nevertheless, this betrayal accords with the divine plan.

The predicted betrayal causes the disciples to question who might be responsible (22:23). But the conversation quickly turns to which disciple is the greatest (22:24–30), for if one could be in the lowest position of a traitor,

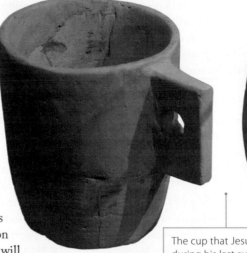

The cup that Jesus drank from during his last supper (Luke 22:17, 20) may have resembled these first-century-AD stone drinking vessels from Masada.

then presumably there must be some kind of rank. Jesus confronts the competitive spirit of his disciples, contrasting the secular meaning of greatness with his own perspective. Gentiles use power to dominate others and to acquire a reputation for themselves. The new community, however, should not be characterized by a quest for power or greatness, for true greatness consists in serving. Jesus uses his position not to demand service but to give service and aid to others. Nevertheless, the disciples will be rewarded for their service and endurance with Jesus in his trials (22:28). They will share with Jesus in the messianic banquet and the kingdom, having a responsibility to judge Israel.

In 22:31–34 Jesus foretells Peter's denial and restoration. Even though the disciples will eventually inherit the kingdom, their faith will be tested. In verse 31 "you" is plural, referring to all the disciples, and the sifting will involve the separation of the wheat from the chaff; that is, Satan wants to test the disciples so that they fall from the faith. Jesus directs the rest of his words to Peter. The test of fidelity will be severe, and despite his protestations to the contrary, Simon will even deny Jesus (22:33–34). Nevertheless,

Jesus's prayer for Peter will be efficacious. His faith will not permanently fail, and after his restoration he is to fortify the faith of the other disciples.

In this perplexing paragraph regarding the two swords (22:35–38), the nature of the testing that the disciples and Jesus will face is now explained more fully. On their previous mission the disciples lacked nothing, presumably because others met their needs. But now the time of opposition has set in. Jesus's words on acquiring a sword (22:36) should not be interpreted literally; they are a sign of the conflict and opposition the disciples will face. Indeed, Jesus himself will be considered a criminal (cf. 23:32–33), fulfilling Isaiah 53:12. The disciples mistakenly interpret Jesus's words on swords literally. Jesus rebukes their incomprehension (cf. 22:49–51) by saying, "That's enough" (22:38).

E. Arrest and trial (22:39–23:25). After the meal ends, Jesus and the disciples go to the Garden of Gethsemane at the foot of the Mount of Olives (22:39). The theme of testing continues from the preceding paragraphs. The account begins and ends with Jesus exhorting his disciples to pray that they will not enter into temptation (22:39–46). Jesus functions as the model. He naturally feels revulsion about his destiny, entreating his Father to take the cup away from him, for the cup represents God's wrath that will be poured out on him. But through prayer he overcomes the test, remaining faithful and fixed on his Father's will. The disciples function as a foil. They do not pray but sink into sleep at the hour of testing. Verses 43–44 are textually uncertain; although they may not be original, they may contain ancient and probably authentic tradition.

The text now moves to Jesus's betrayal and arrest (22:47–53). Judas betrays Jesus with a mark of friendship and affection, revealing the low point of his degradation (22:47–48). Still misunderstanding Jesus's words about swords (22:36–38), the disciples think that now is the time to put them to use. One disciple (Peter, according to John 18:10) severs the right ear of the high priest's servant. Jesus, however, rebukes his disciples for resorting to violence (22:51; cf. 22:38) and compassionately heals the servant's ear, demonstrating that even during his suffering his work is one of healing and restoration. Jesus then addresses his captors with irony. Do they think he is leading a violent revolution? Is that why they have equipped themselves with such weapons? And why do they not arrest him in public? Clearly their actions show that they are aligned with the powers of darkness.

Jesus is brought to the high priest's house. Mark tells us that Jesus was examined that night (cf. Mark 14:53–65), but Luke omits the nighttime meeting and tells us only about the examination the next morning. Peter's testing now becomes a reality (22:54–62). Just as Jesus predicted, Peter denies him three times, displaying a lack of courage even before a servant girl. The process of restoration begins with a poignant look from Jesus. Peter's remorse naturally must precede any restoration, when he must turn and strengthen his brothers (22:32).

Those guarding Jesus (nothing is said about Roman soldiers) ridicule him (22:63–65). This is part of the humiliation that Jesus predicted he would undergo.

Jesus's trial begins with an interrogation before the Sanhedrin (22:66–71). This council, which functioned as the official court of the Jews, meets to examine Jesus. They immediately address him with their central concern (22:67): does he claim to be the Christ? Jesus, however, refuses to answer the question, maintaining that it would be useless to give an answer to such an audience, presumably because they understand the messiah in a way different from Jesus. Nevertheless, Jesus proceeds to conflate Daniel 7:13 and Psalm 110:1, claiming that as the Son of Man he will sit (probably as judge) at God's right hand (22:69). Jesus's answer provokes the Sanhedrin to ask whether he considers himself to be the Son of God (22:70a). Son of God should not be equated with Messiah (cf. Luke 1:32–35) but goes beyond it, suggesting an intimate and unparalleled relationship with

God. Jesus's answer is again rather mysterious and guarded: "You say that I am" (22:70b). The answer is a kind of guarded affirmation, suggesting that Jesus would rather explain the same reality a different way. Nevertheless, the council concludes that the evidence is substantial enough to convict him (22:71).

The repudiation of Jesus by the religious leaders becomes official as they now accuse him before the Roman prefect Pontius Pilate (23:1–7). Pilate's normal residence was the city of Caesarea (cf. Acts 23:23), but he came to Jerusalem for Passover. The charges against Jesus are political (23:2), and the only one that arouses Pilate's interest is the idea that Jesus might be "the king of the Jews" (23:3). Jesus replies to Pilate's question with another ambiguous answer; the Greek literally says, "you say," which affirms that such is the charge raised against Jesus. The major point Luke wants to make is that Pilate is convinced of Jesus's innocence (23:4). When Pilate learns that Jesus hails from Galilee, he sends him to Herod Antipas, who had jurisdiction over that region. The reason Pilate sent Jesus to Herod may have been to satisfy the latter's curiosity, or he may have wanted to learn more about the case from someone who was familiar with the Jews, or perhaps he wanted to get rid of the case.

Now Jesus appears before Herod (23:8–12), who is thrilled about seeing Jesus, apparently expecting some kind of miracle show or at least an interesting theological discussion. But Jesus continues to show that he is in command of the situation by refusing to speak with Herod. Herod becomes disgusted with Jesus, joining his soldiers in ridiculing and mocking him. Why did Herod and Pilate become friends on this day (23:12)? Perhaps because they experienced a kinship in their reaction to Jesus. Both of them lacked the courage to set free a man who was clearly innocent; like Pilate, Herod sees no evidence of wrongdoing. Thereby Herod becomes the second witness of Jesus's innocence (cf. Deut. 19:15).

Luke continues to emphasize the innocence of Jesus. After Jesus returns from meeting with Herod, Pilate sums up the situation and sentences Jesus (23:13–25). Neither Pilate nor Herod has found Jesus guilty of any crime (23:15), but a flogging will be administered, probably to warn him not to run afoul of the authorities again (23:16). The crowd, however, pressures Pilate to release Barabbas—a murderer and a terrorist—rather than Jesus. Indeed, they now specify that crucifixion should be the means of Jesus's death (23:21). Pilate continues to protest that Jesus is innocent, but his good intentions collapse under pressure from the crowd. His cowardice and feebleness lead him to submit to the crowd's will. Thus, an innocent person is put up for execution while a guilty murderer is released.

F. Crucifixion and burial (23:26–56a). By custom the victim carried his own cross, so probably Simon was pressed into service because Jesus was breaking down under the weight of the cross. Some women who are present begin to weep for Jesus. Jesus warns that their tears should be reserved for their own fate. The judgment on Jerusalem will be so horrible that the unhappy state of barrenness will be preferred (cf. Luke 1:25). People will call to the mountains and hills to shield them from the impending judgment. Verse 31 probably is saying that if the judgment is severe on the innocent Jesus, then it will be incredibly harsh for guilty Jerusalem.

The prophecy (Isa. 53:12) that Jesus would be "numbered with the transgressors" (22:37) finds its fulfillment here as Jesus is crucified between two criminals (23:32–43). Jesus's words of forgiveness (23:34) are textually uncertain, although internal evidence suggests they should be included. Even though Jesus is treated as a criminal and is subjected to the humiliation of being stripped (23:34), he responds with forgiveness. The misunderstanding of Jesus's messiahship is revealed by the threefold mocking (23:34–39). The religious leaders, Roman soldiers, and one of the criminals ridicule Jesus, asserting that if he were really the Messiah and the king of the Jews he would extricate himself from death. They fail to see that Jesus is accomplishing salvation by his death. The other criminal (23:40–43), however, recognizes that Jesus is innocent, imploring him to remember him when he begins his reign. Jesus's answer goes beyond the man's request, for "today" the man will be with Jesus in the bliss of paradise.

In 23:44–49 Jesus expires, prompting the centurion to proclaim his innocence. The darkness that covers the land from "about noon . . . until three in the afternoon" could not have been caused by an eclipse, for during Passover there was a full moon. Some have speculated that the darkness was due to a sirocco stirring up the dust, but there is no clear scientific explanation for the phenomenon. The darkness suggests an ominous future for Jerusalem, while the splitting of the veil between the Most Holy Place and the Holy Place suggests that free access to God has been accomplished. Placing his confidence in his Father until the end, Jesus serenely commits himself to his Father's care. The centurion underlines the Lukan theme that

Jesus is innocent, while the onlookers display their regret for what happened by beating their breasts. The regret here should probably not be understood as repentance. Other followers of Jesus observe what happens from a distance.

Joseph, a member of the Sanhedrin, did not agree with the verdict against Jesus, and was obviously an admirer of Jesus. He sees to it that Jesus receives an honorable burial (23:50–56a), and that he is not thrown into a common grave with criminals. Instead, he is placed in a new tomb, which has never been used. The day of Preparation before the Sabbath would be Friday. The women do not have time to anoint Jesus in the proper manner before the Sabbath, so they note where the tomb is and prepare the spices before the Sabbath begins, waiting for the Sabbath to end before returning to the tomb.

The Church of the Holy Sepulchre. According to ancient Christian tradition, this church is built around the place where Jesus was buried (Luke 23:53).

G. Resurrection: Scripture fulfilled (23:56b–24:53). On Sunday, "the first day of the week," an unspecified number of women return to the tomb to anoint Jesus's body (23:56b–24:12). Luke does not tell us that they worried about removing the stone (cf. Mark 16:3), yet when they arrive, the stone has been rolled away and Jesus's body is no longer in the tomb. Instead, they see two angels dressed in dazzling apparel, who announce to them that Jesus has risen from the dead. Luke calls the angels "men" (24:5), not because he did not know they were angels (see 24:23), but because angels in the Bible always appear as men (cf. also Acts 10:3, 30). Mark refers to only one angel (Mark 16:5). This does not contradict Luke's account unless one assumes that Mark's narrative is an exhaustive account, for nowhere does Mark say there was *only* one angel. The angels remind the women that Jesus's death and resurrection were predicted by Jesus himself, stressing that these events were in accord with the divine plan. Women, then, receive the news of the resurrection first, even though they were not considered in Jewish society to be credible witnesses. Notice that Luke says nothing about an appearance of Jesus here; the tomb is empty and angels claim he is risen. The women report the news to the apostles, yet the apostles view these tales as "nonsense." Peter, however, is stimulated to investigate further. He sees the linen that was used to wrap Jesus's body lying on the ground, and leaves the scene mystified (24:12; cf. John 20:3–9). There are many difficult problems in harmonizing the different resurrection accounts, but such a harmonization is not impossible (see Wenham).

The first resurrection appearance recorded in Luke's Gospel is found here in 24:13–35. Two people are traveling to Emmaus from Jerusalem. The distance of sixty stadia is about seven miles. As they travel, they are discussing the events of the previous day, and Jesus catches up with them as they journey. They cannot recognize Jesus, not because he looks different, but because in God's sovereignty they are prevented from identifying him. When Jesus inquires about the topic of their conversation, Cleopas (cf. John 19:25, which may refer to the same person; the identity of Cleopas's partner is unknown, but perhaps it was his wife) responds by identifying Jesus as a prophet through whom God has worked in a mighty way. Nevertheless, he has been executed by the religious leaders, indicating that he could not have been the Messiah (24:21). To make matters worse, some women are saying that this Jesus is alive. They are right that the tomb is empty, but such a report could not be believed because no one has seen Jesus. The "unknown" Jesus counters the belief of these two by pointing to the Scriptures. The Old Testament Scriptures clearly teach that the Messiah must suffer before he enters into glory. For the texts that Jesus used, one should probably refer to the speeches in the book of Acts (Acts 2:14–39; 3:12–26; 13:16–41). The two persuade Jesus to spend the evening with them, and in a scene that recalls the Last Supper, they recognize him as he breaks bread and gives thanks. These two people, however, were probably not present at the Last Supper, and thus they may simply be recalling being with Jesus on other occasions when he gave thanks. Jesus immediately vanishes, and they decide to return to Jerusalem and tell the others the good news. But when they arrive the Eleven speak first, informing them that the Lord has arisen and has "appeared to Simon" (24:34). Then the two companions relate the story of their encounter with Jesus (24:35).

During this animated exchange about Jesus's resurrection, Jesus himself appears to the disciples (24:36–43), pronouncing the message of peace (cf. Luke 2:14). The disciples are taken aback, thinking that they are seeing a spirit. Some scholars have argued that this is improbable since they were just discussing the reality of the resurrection, but such a response is psychologically probable when an unexpected visitor suddenly appears in a room. Jesus counters their doubts with hard evidence. Do they think he is only a spirit, a hallucination, a mirage, or a vision? He encourages them to observe closely his hands and feet (24:39–40), presumably because of the nail prints in them (cf. John 20:24–28). Technically speaking, the nails were put through the wrists, but a reference to the hands would include the wrists as well. If observation of Jesus's body is not enough, then they should touch him as well, for no spirit has flesh and bones. Last, Jesus proves the reality of his resurrection by eating fish before his disciples, for no spirit could do that. It is important to realize that Jesus's body was not simply resuscitated. A resuscitated body is simply a return of the old body to physical life, but such a body must die again (cf. the resurrection of Lazarus in John 11). Jesus's body was a resurrected body, a glorious body that had embarked on a new level of existence. It was still a physical body, but a transformed and empowered physical body.

The end of Luke's Gospel does not clearly indicate that a forty-day interval separates Jesus's resurrection and ascension; instead, the end of Luke seems to put the resurrection and ascension on the same day. A reading of Acts 1:1–11 shows that Luke compresses the account in his Gospel, probably intending to give a summary of what Jesus taught in the forty-day interval. Again, Acts 1:1–11 provides a parallel but supplemental account. Here (24:44–49) Jesus emphasizes that the Old Testament Scriptures needed to find their fulfillment in his ministry. The threefold division that Jesus refers to in verse 44 is the division of the Hebrew canon into the Torah, Prophets, and Writings. Indeed, the Scriptures even predict (cf. Isa. 2:1–4; 49:6) that the message of forgiveness will be proclaimed to all nations "beginning at Jerusalem" (24:47). Here we have a foretaste of the message of Acts. Jesus's disciples will be the agents of this message since they are witnesses of the saving events (24:48). Nevertheless, they must abide in Jerusalem until they are empowered from above, a clear reference to the Holy Spirit (cf. Acts 1:8). Jesus, who is the bearer of the Spirit in Luke, will become the dispenser of the Spirit to his disciples.

The ascension (24:50–53) occurs in Bethany (24:50). This does not contradict Acts 1:12, which assigns the location to the Mount of Olives, because Bethany was located at the foot of that mountain. At the time of his departure Jesus gives his disciples a priestly blessing (cf. Num. 6:24–26). The ascension is described in spatial terms (24:51), which has sometimes been a stumbling block to those who are part of the scientific age. But what other way would Jesus use to communicate to his disciples that he would no longer be appearing to them? Clearly, one does not have to argue that heaven is "up there" to see that the act was an effective way of demonstrating that the resurrection appearances were at an end. Acts also informs us that Jesus must be exalted before the Spirit can descend (Acts 2:33). The exaltation of Jesus leads the disciples (for the first time in Luke!) to worship Jesus. They now recognize that he is truly the Son of God (cf. 1:35). Verse 53 should not be interpreted woodenly; the disciples were not in the temple every minute. The main point of the verse is the last phrase; they were "praising God" for the salvation that Jesus had accomplished. This is a fitting response for the believer today as well.

Select Bibliography

Bock, Darrell L. *Luke*. 2 vols. Baker Exegetical Commentary on the New Testament. Grand Rapids: Baker Academic, 1994–96.

Fitzmyer, Joseph A. *The Gospel according to Luke*. 2 vols. Garden City, NY: Doubleday, 1981–85.

Machen, J. Gresham. *The Virgin Birth of Christ*. Grand Rapids: Eerdmans, 1958.

Marshall, I. Howard. *The Gospel of Luke: A Commentary on the Greek Text*. Grand Rapids: Eerdmans, 1978.

Stein, Robert H. *Luke*. New American Commentary. Nashville: Broadman & Holman, 1990.

Wenham, John. *Easter Enigma: Are the Resurrection Accounts in Conflict?* Grand Rapids: Zondervan, 1984.

John

GARY M. BURGE

Introduction

Few books of the Bible have influenced the life and thought of the Christian church as has the Fourth Gospel. Its readers have always noted its profundity and literary energy. Here Christians have discovered a portrait of Christ that has been deeply satisfying. We are intrigued to witness how John joins intimacy of expression with penetrating insight. Scholars have poured so much energy into unraveling the Gospel's many enigmas that the flood of academic articles and books shows no sign of abating. Yet the Gospel seems to evade our grasp and as a result has become an inexhaustible subject of interest.

Until the eighteenth century, the Fourth Gospel was held to be the most accurate and valuable Gospel. But the rise of biblical criticism eclipsed John's prominence. Critics noted its differences from the Synoptic Gospels (Matthew, Mark, Luke). Lengthy discourses replaced parables and pithy sayings. John's language and theology seemed to indicate that here the story of Jesus had been refashioned for the Greek world. The result: the Fourth Gospel could no longer be viewed as contributing reliably to the history of Jesus's life. Critics looked on its early apostolic origin with grave doubt.

Today scholars hold a variety of opinions concerning this Gospel. They are constantly weighing textual, grammatical, historical, and theological issues. And there are few "agreed" results. This alone should caution us when yet another interpretative theory is ushered into view. But at least one trend can be charted in this mass of literature. Since the 1950s a fresh appreciation for John has become almost universal. While John does diverge from the Synoptic Gospels, its independent narratives are still to be valued. For instance, only John records Jesus's dialogue with Nicodemus, but this single witness in no way implies that the incident never happened. More importantly, John's cultural orientation is now viewed as heavily dependent on the Palestinian Judaism of Jesus's day. In other words, John's thought world does not have to be Greek. For example, important Jewish scrolls discovered near Israel's Dead Sea (Qumran) have proved that Judaism in Jesus's day was using language similar to that of the Fourth Gospel. Even archaeological finds have substantiated some of the specific narratives of the Gospel that formerly had weathered heavy criticism (e.g., the pool with five porticoes in 5:2).

This "new look" has reopened a number of old questions. If John's frame of reference is Jewish, then the Gospel's date *may* be early. And if it is early, it *may* have originated with the circle of apostles—even John the son of Zebedee. Now the possibility of apostolic authority behind the Gospel is a legitimate defensible alternative. Johannine study has indeed come full circle.

Above all, this new outlook on John demands that the interpreter seriously employ the Old Testament and all available Jewish materials. No longer will it suffice to interpret, for example, the miracle at Cana (2:1–11) in terms of the Hellenistic god Dionysus of Thrace, who also supposedly changed water into wine. On the contrary, John's *primary* reference is to Jesus's messianic announcement (using Old Testament and Synoptic imagery). This will be the approach used in this commentary. The message of the Fourth Gospel is clothed with allusions and metaphors that spring from first-century Judaism. Granted, this Judaism was complex and well acquainted with Greek influences, but still, the Gospel's text is elucidated best when seen as firmly rooted in the Old Testament and Palestinian Judaism.

Authorship

The Fourth Gospel provides no explicit internal evidence concerning its author. "John" is nowhere identified as such. But this silence is not unusual and is a feature found in the Synoptics as well. The Fourth Gospel may, however, provide us with clues concealed in the enigmatic figure of the "beloved disciple" (NIV "the disciple whom Jesus loved"). This title occurs in six passages in John (13:23; 19:26; 20:2; 21:7, 20). John 21:24 describes the beloved disciple as the one "who testifies to these things and who wrote them down." Therefore the origin of the Gospel must in some way be connected to this person. The Gospel of John may be a record of his eyewitness account of Jesus's life.

But who is this disciple? First, some have suggested that he is an idealized literary figure: the ideal Christian disciple. To a degree this is true (he is faithful and intimate in his knowledge of Jesus). But this hardly excludes the possibility of a genuine historical person. Second, Lazarus has sometimes been nominated. Lazarus is the only male figure said to be loved by Jesus (11:3, 5, 36). Further, the beloved disciple texts occur only after Lazarus is introduced in chapter 11. But this solution is unlikely. Why would Lazarus's name be mentioned in chapters

An icon of John from a larger piece entitled *Christ and Twelve Apostles* (Antalya, Turkey, nineteenth century AD)

11 and 12 but then left shrouded in subsequent accounts? Third, we know that a man named John Mark was a part of the early church (Acts 12:12) and that he was associated with Peter. If Mark was related to the Levite Barnabas (Col. 4:10), this may also explain how the beloved disciple knows the high priest in John 18:15. A strong patristic tradition, however, maintains that Mark wrote the second Gospel—and besides, the beloved disciple was certainly one of the Twelve (13:23), and John Mark was not.

The best solution may still be the traditional one: John the son of Zebedee (Mark 3:17; Acts 1:13). This man was one of the Twelve and along with James and Peter formed an inner circle around Jesus. This is the origin of his eyewitness testimony and penetrating insight. In the Synoptics John appears with Peter more than with any other, and in Acts they are companions in Jerusalem (Acts 3–4) as well as in

Samaria (Acts 8:14). This dovetails with the Peter/John connection in the Fourth Gospel. Raymond Brown has offered a novel theory to buttress this (Brown, 1:xcvii; 2:905–6). He suggests that John and Jesus may have been cousins (through their mothers). This explains two things. In John 19:25 Jesus entrusts Mary to John due to a natural family relation. (She may have been John's aunt.) And in 18:15–16 John is known by the high priest through Mary's priestly relatives (Luke 1:5, 36).

Patristic evidence points to the same conclusion. Writing at about AD 200, Irenaeus says that the beloved disciple was John the disciple of Jesus and that John originated the Gospel at Ephesus. Irenaeus even writes that when he was young, he knew another teacher, Polycarp, bishop of Smyrna (ca. 69–155), who claimed to have been tutored by John himself. The church historian Eusebius (ca. 300) records this John/Polycarp/Irenaeus connection in the same way. Further, Polycrates, bishop of Ephesus (189–198), refers to John's association with the Gospel in his letter to Victor the bishop of Rome. It is also confirmed by Clement of Alexandria (ca. 200) and the Latin Muratorian Canon (180–200).

Criticisms of this conclusion are commonplace, and we would do well to consider the most important ones. (1) Earlier in this century critics regularly pointed to John's inaccurate geographical details. They affirmed that this inaccuracy could hardly come from an eyewitness writer. But subsequent historical and archaeological study has if anything shown John's reliability. (See Craig Blomberg's volume *The Historical Reliability of John's Gospel*.) (2) Could a fisherman-turned-apostle have penned a work of such subtlety and insight? Could a Galilean such as this be acquainted with Greek thought? Of course. Recent study of Palestinian Judaism has shown a remarkable degree of Greek cultural penetration at all levels of society. And while the New Testament does affirm that John the apostle was a commoner (Acts 4:13), we still are unwise to predict what John could or

could not accomplish. Furthermore this fails to consider that John's disciples, an amanuensis (professional scribe), or John's community may have edited the final edition of the Gospel. (3) Finally, some lodge the complaint that John was not readily accepted in the early church. This is true. But we have to reckon with two facts. First, our evidence for John's neglect is not as weighty as it seems. Important early writers may not quote John or allude to him, but to note what a patristic writer *fails* to say is an argument from silence. Second, John found wide acceptance in heretical gnostic circles. This has been confirmed recently by the gnostic documents found at Nag Hammadi, where in the *Gospel of Truth* Johannine themes abound. The unorthodox on the fringes of the Greek church embraced John and provided the earliest widely known commentaries (Valentinus, Heracleon). Therefore, the church was cautious in its use of the Gospel because of its dangerous abuse elsewhere.

Date

All that we have been saying about the new appreciation for the Jewishness of the Fourth Gospel and the fact that John the son of Zebedee stands behind the Gospel's authority implies some conclusion about its date. The sources of John must be early and have their roots in first-generation Christianity. But fixing a certain date for the publication of the Gospel is difficult because objective data are slim. The latest possible date is AD 150. Not only do patristic references, allusions in apocryphal Gospels (*Gospel of Peter*), and Nag Hammadi point to this; but also recently in Egypt two papyrus fragments of John (Rylands Papyrus 457; Egerton Papyrus 2) have been dated at about AD 150. Allowing time for John to circulate, the Gospel could not have been completed long after 125.

The earliest possible date for the Gospel is more difficult. If John knows and employs the Synoptics (and this is disputed), then AD 70 or 80 is appropriate. In John 9:22, 12:42, and 16:2 we read about Jewish believers being excommunicated from the synagogues. In AD 85 the rabbis of Palestine instituted such expulsions for Christians (e.g., Rabbi Gamaliel II). Therefore we find a remarkable consensus of scholarly opinion that John was published somewhere between 80 and 100. Irenaeus says that the apostle lived to a great age—until the reign of Trajan (98–117). And Jerome, writing much later (ca. 375), argued that John died "in the sixty-eighth year" after Jesus's death: hence, about AD 98.

However, an earlier date may be within reach. Current research has challenged John's "dependence" on the Synoptics (especially Mark and Luke). If anything, John may know pre-Synoptic traditions. Above all, the way in which John describes the topography of Jerusalem, his knowledge of the geographical and political divisions in Judaism, and his use of metaphors all point to a date approximating that of the Synoptic writers. The great watershed date of AD 70 (when Jerusalem was destroyed by Rome) is critical: John presupposes a Judaism before this war. And with his critical disposition toward the temple (John 2:13–24; 4:21–24) and severe conflicts with Jewish leaders (cf. chaps. 5, 8, 10), we are surprised to find no reference to this catastrophic event. To paraphrase C. H. Dodd, much in John is barely intelligible outside of the context of pre-70 Judaism.

To sum up, the traditions about Jesus that John preserves most likely stem from the earliest apostolic period: perhaps AD 60–65. But the final edition of the Gospel may have been published later. John and/or his disciples may have edited the work, making additions and sharpening its message for later Christianity.

Tradition tells us that the place of writing was Ephesus, and no decisive reasons have been raised against it. There may even be biblical support for it. The Fourth Gospel entertains a polemic aimed at followers of John the Baptist (see 1:19–28, 35–42; 3:22–36; 10:40–42). Elsewhere in the book of Acts we learn about Paul encountering followers of John the Baptist with deficient beliefs. Surprisingly, they too are located in Ephesus. But it would be impossible to be certain.

Purpose

The interpretation of any biblical book is strengthened when we understand the deeper motives and concerns that have led the author to write. John's vigor and concentration reveal a remarkable intensity of purpose. It is as if a powerful truth had broken upon him and he was compelled to express it. To a greater extent than the Synoptics, each section of the Fourth Gospel contributes to a central theme: the appearance of the Son of God in human history. John explores two facets of this appearing: revelation and redemption.

John 1:5 underscores this revelation: "The light shines in the darkness, and the darkness has not overcome it" (RSV). Dualistic language describes this harsh invasion of the world by God. Offending every modern sensibility, John writes that in Christ we behold the glory of God—even though he has appeared in flesh. But this offense is an ancient one too. The darkness assails the light but cannot vanquish it. The world is in permanent enmity with the Son. But even though Jesus is persecuted, tried, and crucified, still John affirms that the light is not extinguished.

But the gift of Christ is not simply his revelation of the Father (14:9). John's second message concerns redemption: "In him was life, and the life was the light of men" (1:4 RSV). There is hope for us in the world. The message of this invasion of history is also a message of sacrifice and redemption. Those who embrace this revelation, who identify with the light, and who have faith shall gain eternal life. The life of the Son is poured out in sacrifice, thereby creating the community of the redeemed (John 17:6, 20–26). They bear Christ's Spirit, which sustains them because the hatred once extended toward the Son is now extended to them (15:12–27).

Thus John's purpose in writing is to explain this revelation and redemption and to explicate their possibilities. In John 20:31 the author makes clear this aim: "But these are written that you may believe that Jesus is the Messiah, the Son of God, and that by believing you may have life in his name." Here several major themes converge: belief, acknowledgment of Jesus's sonship, and the promise of life. But even here the mystery of John confronts us. An ancient manuscript discrepancy in the Greek word for "believe" places the meaning of the verse in doubt. One set of Greek manuscripts implies that John is evangelistic ("that you *might come to believe*"); the other implies encouragement ("that you *might continue believing*"). This latter reading has the best support and more helpfully explains the character of John. It is written for Christians who, already knowing the rudiments of Christ's life and Christian truth, now wish to go further. Not only is there an uncompromising maturity in this Gospel, but also its narratives imply that it was written to address certain practical circumstances in the church. On the one hand, some would say that John is engaged in a polemic—asserting Christian truth amid unsympathetic forces. On the other hand, John's purpose also includes the clarification of Christian doctrines at an early stage of church development.

Audience

Jewish audience. John's Gospel reflects Jewish concerns. The conflict between Jesus and the Pharisees that we meet in the Synoptics is given marked attention in John. A brief perusal of John 8:31–59 or 10:19–39 makes this clear. There is a sustained attack on the religious position of Judaism. For instance, "the Jews" virtually becomes a technical term in John for those who reject Jesus. In 9:22 (KJV, RSV) the parents of the blind man who are Jewish fear "the Jews." But this is not all. The messiahship of Jesus and his relationship to the festivals and institutions of Judaism are both emphasized.

What does this mean? Each Gospel was written not only to record the history of Jesus but also to address particular circumstances in the life of its first readers. Here the Christians of John's church may have needed encouragement due to persecution and hostilities. So John

buttresses Christian claims against Jewish unbelief. The historical fact of Jewish unbelief in Jesus's day is joined with Jewish opposition in John's day. But make no mistake. John's Gospel is not anti-Semitic, despite this intense debate with "the Jews." This Gospel bears witness to a harsh divorce that took place in the first century *within Judaism*: Jews who believed in Jesus were in full debate with Jews who did not. And as readers of this Gospel, we are listening in.

Christian audience. John's Gospel also reflects Christian concerns. At the time the Gospel was published, the early Christian church had grown and diversified considerably. Therefore, it is no surprise to find that John has included historical materials relevant to Christian needs in his generation. It would be a mistake, however, to think that any of these needs became the controlling force in John's literary design. On the contrary, they serve as subthemes that run through the Gospel and clarify John's situation. Scholars have identified an extensive list of topics, but we shall note in passing only four prominent motifs.

The significance of John the Baptist. Did the Baptist himself have followers who failed or refused to follow Jesus? Luke 3:15 and Acts 19:1–7 imply this, while later writings confirm it (see the Latin Pseudo-Clementine Recognitions). The Fourth Gospel takes pains to affirm that the Baptist was *not* the Messiah (John 1:20; 3:28), that he was *not* the light (1:8–9), and that Jesus is superior (1:30; 3:29–30; 10:41). We even witness disciples of John the Baptist becoming Jesus's first converts (1:35–42). Matthew, Mark, and Luke have no parallel motif.

The place of sacramentalism. Of course, John has a "sacramental" view of history inasmuch as the incarnation of Christ for him means the genuine appearance of God *in history*. Worship can affirm such genuine appearances when worship symbols (baptism, the Lord's Supper) take on the real properties of that which they depict. Hence such symbols are called sacraments. Scholars have identified a unique Johannine interest in the Christian sacraments, but there is little agreement about John's intention. Some note an absence of interest (e.g., the Lord's Supper is omitted), while others see allusions everywhere (baptism: John 3; 5; 9; Eucharist: John 2; 6; both: 19:34). It seems best to conclude that John's principal message about each is corrective (see 3:1–21; 6:52–65): without the Spirit these expressions of worship become powerless rituals void of their original purpose.

Our future hope: Eschatology. Many early Christians longed for the second coming of Christ and anticipated an imminent end to history. This explains the cherished sayings of Jesus about this in the Synoptics, where this future expectation is described (see Mark 13; Matthew 24; Luke 21). How did they cope when this hope was frustrated (cf. 2 Pet. 3:1–12)? John does not record Jesus's Synoptic eschatological discourses. He still maintains the future hope (5:25–30; 1 John 2:28) but introduces a fresh emphasis: the longed-for presence of Jesus is mediated to us now in the Spirit. In the upper room Jesus's announcement of the Spirit takes on eschatological tones (see 14:18–23). That is, in one vital way that we often overlook, Jesus *has* come back and is already with us in the Spirit. In technical terms, John emphasizes a *realized eschatology* in contrast to the apocalyptic hope of the Synoptics.

Christology. Irenaeus, the second-century church father, wrote that the Gospel of John was penned to refute the gnostic heretic Cerinthus. While this is not likely, Irenaeus nevertheless correctly observed that John's presentation of Christ was carefully considered. Questions about Jesus's nature, origin, and relation to the Father are examined in a fashion unparalleled by the Synoptics. For instance, John affirms the oneness of Jesus and the Father (10:30; 14:9–10), their distinction (14:28; 17:1–5), and their unity of purpose (5:17–18; 8:42). It is not surprising that in the formation of trinitarian doctrine, John's Gospel played a notable role (cf. Tertullian, *Against Praxeas*). This was particularly true at the Council of Nicea (325), when Arius denied the eternal nature of the Son. In later Arian debates, Athanasius was heavily dependent on the Fourth Gospel and found in the Greek term *logos*, a title for Jesus used in the Johannine prologue, a most serviceable tool for depicting the person of Christ (*On the Incarnation of the Word of God*).

John claims full divinity for Jesus. On the one hand, if anyone were inclined toward adoptionism (that Jesus was a divinely inspired man), John's Gospel gives an unrelenting argument to the contrary. On the other hand, the Greek world was comfortable with divinities and, if anything, hesitated to affirm Jesus's full humanity (docetism). Here John contends that Jesus is truly human, truly flesh (1:14; cf. 20:27). The brilliance and abiding value of John is that it strikes a middle path between these concerns. Jesus was eternally divine and fully incarnate, fully God and fully human.

But scholars have been quick to point out that this "balanced Christology" seems artificial. If one removes the prologue (1:1–18), the balance is tipped and, in the words of some, John becomes a "naive docetist" (see Käsemann). But this seems unfairly harsh (Morris 1978, 37–53). One solution has been to view John as having stages of development; the prologue may have been added to the Gospel at a later stage when the Epistles of John were published. The battle cry of 1 John is certainly against docetism (1 John 4:1–3), and if the high Christology of the Fourth Gospel had been fueling heretical docetic beliefs, then the addition of the hymnic prologue would have given the needed balance.

Nevertheless, it is vital to say that the humanity of Christ is intrinsic to the whole of the Gospel of John. "John portrays Jesus in a twofold light without reflection or speculation. He is equal to God; he is indeed God in the flesh; yet he is fully human" (Ladd, 289). This affirmation alone has rendered John valuable to the church and its creeds.

Outline

Commentary

1. The Prologue (1:1–18)

One reason why the Gospel of John was symbolized in the ancient church by the eagle is the lofty heights attained by its prologue. With skill and delicacy John handles issues of profound importance. It comes as no surprise, then, that this prologue has been foundational to the classic Christian formulation of the doctrine of Christ. Here divinity and humanity, preexistence and incarnation, revelation and sacrifice are each discussed with deceptive simplicity. This prologue may well have been an ancient Christian hymn. We know of other hymns from the early church, especially in Paul's writings, and here too is an artful flowing of language and theology.

The initial allusion to Genesis 1 cannot be missed (1:1). John begins by introducing Jesus as the Word (Greek *logos*). Here he builds on contemporary Jewish thought where the Word of God took on personal creative attributes (Gen. 1:1–30; Ps. 33:6, 9). In the New Testament period it was personified (Wisdom of Solomon 7:24–26; 18:15–16) and known by some (e.g., Philo) as the immanent power of God creatively at work in the world. John identifies Jesus Christ as this Word and therefore

This illustration from the Gospels of Saint Médard depicts John beneath his symbol, the eagle (Soissons, France, early ninth century AD).

can attribute to him various divine functions such as creation (1:3, 10) and the giving of life (1:4).

But John goes further. He is ready to infer some personal identity between the Logos and God. "And the Word *was* God" (1:1). Attempts to detract from this literal translation for grammatical reasons (e.g., "the word was a god," or "divine," etc.) run aground when we consider the number of other times such a divine ascription is given to Jesus: he employs the divine Old Testament title I AM (e.g., 8:24, 28, 58); he is one with God (10:30); and he is even addressed by Thomas in the Gospel's final scene as "my Lord and my God" (20:28).

The entry of the Logos into the world (the incarnation) is described as light shining in darkness (1:5). Even though John the Baptist's testimony is clear (1:6–9), still Jesus experiences rejection (1:10–11). But there is more.

The darkness is hostile. There is enmity. John 1:5 says that the "darkness has not overcome [the light]." The Greek term translated "overcome" (RSV; NIV note: "understood") means "seize with hostile intent" (cf. 8:3–4; Mark 9:18). The hostility of the darkness points to the cross. But as the Book of Glory (13:1–20:31) shows, the power of darkness will not prevail.

John indicates, however, that the light has its followers; Jesus has his disciples (1:12–13). Even though his own people—adherents to Judaism—spurn his message, those who do receive him obtain power to become God's children. Verses 12–13 anticipate the story of Nicodemus (3:1–21), in which this rebirth is explored. A careful reading of 1 John shows that "children of God" and "born of God" were commonplace terms describing Johannine disciples (1 John 3:2, 9; 4:4, 7, 12–13). In other words, there will be a powerful transformation of those who embrace this light. In the upper room Jesus will draw out the implications: this power will come about through the Spirit, who will quicken each believer (14:15–31).

The prologue's finale is found in verses 14–18. John sums up in fresh language what has already been said. Now the abstract thought of light and darkness gives way to concrete Old Testament images. John 1:14 is one of the most important verses in the Bible. The Word did not just appear to be human; *the Word became flesh.* This assertion would have stunned the Greek mind, for which the separation of the divine spirit and the mundane world (Greek *sarx*, "flesh") was an axiom of belief. But the second phrase is equally stunning for the Jew. This Word dwelt (Greek *skēnoō*) among us and revealed his glory. John uses Old Testament terms of the dwelling (literally "tabernacling") of God with his people. The tabernacle (cf. Exod. 25:8–9; Zech. 2:10) was the dwelling place of God. Now *Jesus* is the locus of God's dwelling. Hence, the glory of God, once restricted to the tabernacle (Exod. 40:34), is now visible in Christ. The Old Testament contrast with Jesus is extended to Moses (John 1:17–18), while the benefits of their covenants are compared. Moses gave law; Jesus brought grace. Moses's request to see God was denied (Exod. 33:20; cf. Deut. 4:12); but Jesus has come to us from the very heart of the Father (John 1:18). The authority of his revelation is that much greater (cf. Heb. 3:1–6).

2. The Book of Signs (1:19–12:50)

The Book of Signs chronicles Jesus's public ministry within Israel. It begins with the traditional Synoptic starting place (John the Baptist) and concludes with Jesus in Jerusalem at his final Passover. Throughout the narrative, Jesus presents himself to Judaism through a series of miracles and compelling discourses but in the end finds rejection. Messianic fulfillment is a prominent motif. Jesus's messiahship is shown to be the fulfillment of the principal festivals and institutions of Judaism. But since the Jews fail to grasp the message of Jesus's signs, John shows us who will: the Greeks. The book closes with Jesus's final plea to Judaism and a picture of eager Greeks imploring Philip, "Sir . . . we would like to see Jesus" (12:21).

A. The testimony of John the Baptist (1:19–51). The opening frame establishes two points: first, it clarifies the relation between Jesus and John the Baptist; second, it provides a study in the nature of conversion and true discipleship. It is, however, a literary unit, as the sequence of days makes clear (1:29, 35, 43). In each successive day, interest shifts from John to Jesus. John's disciples even become Jesus's disciples. The section is closely tied to the unit on the Baptist in 3:22–36, where again John is demoted and Jesus is elevated. The entire section may be, as 1:19 indicates, "John's testimony."

The Gospel assumes that we know something already about John the Baptist's ministry at the Jordan River. No introduction is given; instead, we listen as priests and Levites (specialists in ritual purification) question John about his identity and work (1:19–28). The Baptist makes three specific denials: he is not the Messiah (1:20; cf. Luke 3:15). Neither is he Elijah (1:21). Jesus elsewhere indicates that John does fulfill

Elijah's spiritual role as messianic forerunner (cf. Matt. 11:14 with Mal. 4:5). Apparently John needs to deny a material identification with Elijah in order to distinguish himself further from Christ. Last, John is not the prophet (1:21). This no doubt is the messianic prophet like Moses described in Deuteronomy 18:15–18. "Prophet" will later become a title for Jesus (John 6:14; 7:40).

But if John is none of these popular eschatological figures, who is he? What is he doing? The first question (1:22–23) is answered from Isaiah 40:3. He is a herald, a forerunner (cf. Mark 1:1–3). The second (1:24–27) is also anticipatory: his water baptism will be overshadowed by the appearance of a "greater one" who will baptize in the Spirit (1:33; cf. Mark 1:7–8 NLT).

The denials of the Baptist are now complete, and the way is clear for true testimony to Jesus to begin (1:29–34). Note that this is not a narrative of Jesus's baptism but a testimony, an account in John's own words confessing the identity of Jesus. That Jesus is announced as "the Lamb of God" is striking (1:29). This might refer to the daily sacrifice at the temple. But it is likely better to view it as the sacrificial Passover lamb of Exodus 12 (cf. Isa. 53:7). Later the Gospel will fully employ this imagery when Jesus is sacrificed on the cross at Passover (19:14, 36).

The chief announcement of John the Baptist centers on the eminence of Jesus. Jesus is superior to John inasmuch as he "was before [him]" (1:30; cf. 1:15). It would not be unlikely if this included the thought of Jesus's anointing with the Spirit (1:32–33). This was the principal event at the Jordan. John's account of this differs from the Synoptics in one respect: two times John remarks that the Spirit descends and *remains* on Jesus. This permanent anointing stands in stark contrast to the temporary anointing of the Old Testament prophets. This permanence was central to the Jewish depiction of the Messiah (Isa. 11:2; 42:1; cf. *Testament of Levi* 18:6–7).

The testimony of John continues, as he now directs his disciples to follow Jesus (1:35–42).

This section and the next model for us the true character of discipleship. First, disciples must follow Jesus (1:37–38, 43); they must "come and see" (1:39, 46), experiencing for themselves the truth of Christ. And then they must go and bring others: Andrew finds his brother Simon (1:41), and Philip finds Nathanael (1:45). Second, we read a roll call of titles for Jesus from 1:35–51—Lamb of God (1:36), Rabbi (1:38), Messiah/Christ (1:41), Jesus of Nazareth, son of Joseph (1:45), Son of God (1:49), King of Israel (1:49), and Son of Man (1:51). Disciples must know whom they follow.

In 1:35–42 John the Baptist sees Jesus and repeats the identification given at Jesus's baptism (1:36, repeating 1:29). He then ushers his disciples into Jesus's company. The language here is important. The first question of the disciples, "Where are you *staying*?" (1:38), employs a vital word for John. "Staying" or "abiding" (Greek *menō*) appears throughout the Gospel (forty times) and describes the union of the believer with Christ (see, e.g., 8:31, 35; 14:10; 15:4–17). Hence Andrew and an unnamed disciple (John?) abide with Christ.

On day three we meet the first apostles who follow Christ. Now we learn that Jesus has other followers who are not yet apostles and who share a similar intimate discipleship (1:43–51). From Perea Jesus moves to Galilee and calls more followers. Philip, a native of Bethsaida (east of Capernaum), discovers the Messiah, but the focus of the narrative turns to his immediate response. He finds Nathanael and extends to him the same words used by Jesus for Andrew in 1:39, "Come and see" (1:46). Disciples must therefore make more disciples in the manner of Jesus.

To be a disciple means coming under the authority of Jesus. In 1:42 Jesus renames Simon as Peter. Now in 1:47–50 Nathanael experiences Jesus's prophetic power over his life. But this power is minor in comparison to what Jesus will display. The description of Jesus in 1:51 may be based on Jacob's vision in Genesis 28:12. Jesus is the locus of God's self-revelation on earth. In this regard, this final verse reiterates the affirmation of the prologue: Jesus is the full revelation of the glory and presence of God.

B. Jesus and the institutions of Judaism (2:1–4:54). The stories that hallmark the beginning of Jesus's public ministry all share a similar theme: messianic replacement and abundance. In chapters 2–4 Jesus is compared with important institutions, and in each instance, his presence makes them obsolete. (The same will be true of 5:1–10:42. There Jesus will appear during the major Jewish festivals and demonstrate his authority.) This theme is similar to the Synoptic parables of replacement: new wine breaks old wineskins, and new patches cannot be affixed to old cloth (Matt. 9:16–17). So too the former institutions of Judaism cannot sustain the impact of Christ's coming.

The section has an interesting literary division. The first story is set in Cana of Galilee, and so is the final miracle (the healing of the

> The village of Cana was a half-day's walk north of Nazareth. While the ancient village has likely been located, little of it has been excavated. The village of Der Samet, seen here, which is near Hebron, may show the same building styles known in first-century Cana.

official's son). The wedding miracle is referred to as Jesus's first sign (2:11), while the closing healing miracle is Jesus's second sign (4:54). These literary indicators define the limits of the section. Then in 5:1 we at once learn that Jesus is on his way to "one of the Jewish festivals."

2:1–25. We know that Jesus is already in the region of Galilee (1:43), and the best identification for Cana is Khirbet Qana, nine miles north of Nazareth. John indicates that Jesus arrives here on "the third day" (2:1). This may refer to traveling time to Cana or fit the day sequence in chapter 1. In the latter case, some believe that John is chronicling the momentous first week of Jesus (a new week of creation?). Cana is a climax of sorts: here the disciples believe in him for the first time because Jesus manifests his glory (2:11).

Weddings (2:1–12) were festive events in first-century Judaism, and entire communities participated. Since Galilee is Jesus's home, it is not surprising that he is in attendance. When the wine fails (2:3), Jesus's mother draws him in. His response in verse 4 is not meant to give offense. "Woman" was a customary polite address (cf. Matt. 15:28; Luke 13:12). Jesus will use it again when he is on the cross (19:26).

In verse 4 "What have you to do with me?" (RSV) is an awkward English rendering of a Semitic idiom meaning, "How can this affair concern me?"

The miraculous solution is described in some detail (2:6–9), and as in Synoptic miracle stories, there is a climaxing testimony, in this case on the lips of the steward (2:10). Six stone jars each holding twenty or thirty gallons are filled with water, and this in turn supplies the wedding with an enormous quantity of wine (about 175 gallons).

Some degree of symbolism can be affirmed here without denigrating the historical character of the event. This is Jesus's first public sign, and the key to interpreting it is Jesus's messianic announcement and abundance. The wedding banquet was an Old Testament symbol of the Messiah's arrival (cf. Isa. 54:4–8; 62:4–5), which Jesus often employed (Matt. 22:1–14; Mark 2:19–20). The Old Testament also describes this messianic era with the image of an abundance of wine (Jer. 31:12; Hos. 14:7; Amos 9:13–14). Jewish apocalypticism taught that the vine would give its fruit ten thousandfold (*2 Baruch* 29:5; see also *1 Enoch* 10:19). Therefore Jesus announced himself with powerful eschatological metaphors.

But for the Messiah to come (and this is the unexpected news) the old institutions must pass away. Jesus enacts his first miracle on a religious device of Judaism. What were these jars? The Mishnah indicated that stone jars could be used as permanent vessels for purification (ritual washing). Jesus has transformed their contents. In the previous chapter John the Baptist offered a ritual washing, but he announced a more powerful baptism to come (1:33). Jesus has now taken up the necessary symbols as the fulfiller of Judaism.

Two remarkable statements frame the story: "They have no more wine" (2:3), and "You have saved the best [wine] till now" (2:10). This is a poignant commentary on the bankruptcy of Judaism and the arrival of Jesus. The new wine is abundantly superior to the old. But moreover, that which contained the old wine must pass away.

From here Jesus travels with his family (cf. Mark 6:3) to Capernaum, a village on the north shore of the Sea of Galilee. According to the Synoptics, this was an important center of activity for Jesus in Galilee.

Pilgrimage played an important role in the life of every Jewish family. Passover was one such pilgrimage festival in which Jewish families traveled to Jerusalem for worship. Hence Jesus travels from Galilee to Judea. The story of the temple cleansing (2:13–25) provides us with one of the closest Synoptic/Johannine parallels (cf. Matt. 21:12–13; Mark 11:15–17; Luke 19:45–46). Aside from its chronological placement (the Synoptics have it at the end of Jesus's ministry), the stories are strikingly alike. Some would argue that they narrate the same event.

Jesus is offended by two things that he witnesses. First, although the selling of sacrificial animals (2:14) was necessary for worship, it may be that this usually took place in the Jerusalem market area east of the city in the Kidron Valley. Obviously the high priest Caiaphas has brought the commercial enterprise into the Court of Gentiles. Second, money changers converted pagan coinage (with imperial images) to acceptable currency in order for Jewish men to pay their half-shekel annual tax (cf. Matt. 17:27). The cacophony of noise and the spirit of commercial self-interest had little to do with the purposes of the season. In response Jesus drives out these merchants with a whip (2:15), but John rightly adds that it is simply made of cord, for genuine weapons were prohibited by the temple police.

Again we find here the themes of messianic announcement and replacement. In the Old Testament, the prophets linked the ultimate renewal of the temple with the eschatological day of the Lord (Isa. 56:7; Mal. 3:1). Jesus's rebuke in John 2:16 reflects this and stems from Zechariah 14:21. This is why in 2:18 those who witness this demand a sign—some justification.

They recognize the messianic importance of the act. But Jesus's response picks up another line of Old Testament thought: in the day of the Lord a *new* temple would be built (Ezekiel 40–46; Tobit 14:5), and this temple would be Jesus's body (John 2:21). This reiterates what we have already seen (cf. 1:14, 51): this sacred Jewish institution would find a dramatic new replacement (cf. 4:21–24).

Of course it would be difficult for the citizens of Jerusalem to understand this. The Jews think that Jesus must mean a refurbishing of Herod's temple begun in 20 BC (2:20). Even the disciples' comprehension has to await the resurrection (2:22). Nevertheless, Jesus's words will be remembered, twisted, and used to condemn him at his trial (Mark 14:58).

It is interesting to compare these first two signs of Jesus in Cana and Jerusalem. In Galilee Jesus finds faith (2:11), but in Jerusalem, while some believe (2:23), the Jews there generally lack comprehension. Throughout the Gospel, Jesus will find faith in Galilee and conflict in Judea. Indeed, it will be in Jerusalem that he will be killed. Verses 23–25 describe the unsatisfactory nature of the Jerusalem reception and go on to generalize about the shortcomings of humanity (2:25). They also serve as a transitional section for the next chapter. Nicodemus will be one such man: he has witnessed the signs and come forward (3:2), but he fails to apprehend who Jesus is and to believe.

3:1–36. At first glance this section on Jesus and the new birth seems to consist of two disparate parts: the dialogue with Nicodemus (3:1–21) and the critical comparison of Jesus and the Baptist (3:22–36). Note, for instance, how in 3:22 Jesus moves "into the land of Judea" (NASB, NKJV) when he has just been in Jerusalem, a city of Judea (2:13, 23). While numerous plausible theories have offered to relocate 3:22–36 (generally after 1:19–34), they are difficult to support. In fact, a connecting thread may unite the chapter. On a literary level, Jesus now dislocates yet another office in Judaism, the rabbinate. Nicodemus's ability as a teacher is

faulty (3:10), while Jesus is addressed as "rabbi" (3:2). On another level, the subject the teacher Nicodemus cannot penetrate (rebirth, 3:3) is really center stage. In 1:33 we learned about a new baptism in the Spirit, which would come with the work of Jesus; in 3:1–21 it is explicated. If "born of water and the Spirit" (3:5) does refer to baptism (Jesus's baptism; Christian baptism), then the section on the relative merits of John's baptism (3:22–36) naturally follows. It extends the discussion broached in 1:33 in that Jesus's baptizing work exceeds that of John. In 4:1–3 we even find the only New Testament reference to Jesus baptizing. And here Jesus "was gaining and baptizing more disciples than John" (4:1).

While Jesus is in Jerusalem at Passover (2:13), a Pharisee named Nicodemus comes to him at night (3:1–21). His approach is well intentioned, but his spiritual perception is inadequate. (It may be that "night" in 3:2 is symbolic; for Nicodemus is not "of the light"; see, e.g., 1:4–5; 3:19–20; 9:4; 11:10; 13:30.) He reappears in 7:50 at a Sanhedrin meeting giving advice sympathetic to Jesus's case. And in 19:39 his sympathies become explicit: he joins Joseph of Arimathea in burying and anointing the body of Christ.

This passage introduces the first major discourse so typical of Jesus's teaching in the Fourth Gospel. In this and other such discourses, questions posed to Jesus enable him to transpose the topic to a higher plateau (e.g., chap. 14). Earthly understanding must give way to spiritual understanding. Here Nicodemus makes three comments (3:2, 4, 9), each of which Jesus greets with a response (3:3, 5–8, 10–15).

When Nicodemus inquires about the character of Jesus's signs, Jesus replies that rebirth is a prerequisite for seeing the kingdom of God (3:3, 7). Nicodemus's misunderstanding (3:4) turns on a literal understanding of the Greek phrase *gennēthē anōthen*, "born again." How can anyone be born twice? Yet *anōthen* can also mean "from above" (a spatial vs. a temporal rendering), and this is Jesus's intended meaning. Typically, the Johannine Jesus employs a play on words. *Anōthen* in John takes the spatial sense ("from above"), as is evident from its use in 3:31 (also 19:11, 23). In other words, entrants to the kingdom must be born from "above," that place from which Jesus originates. The Christian, as it were, must become like Jesus, who is "from above" (3:31). The theological language for this is brought out in 3:5–8. This birth must consist of water (repentance, baptism, or the ministration of John) and the Spirit (the eschatological endowment brought by Jesus; 7:39; 20:22). This experience cannot be quantified but, like the wind, emerges under the power of God (3:8).

The deficits in Nicodemus's understanding are common to those who cannot understand heavenly things (3:12; cf. 1 Cor. 2:1–16). Before Pentecost, this is true of the disciples too (cf. 2:22). But the key that will unlock the problem is the complex of events that includes Christ's death, resurrection, and ascension (3:13–15)—in Johannine language, Christ's glorification. It is the result of this work that will release the Spirit (7:37–39).

It is difficult to know whether 3:16–21 continues the words of Jesus or represents the comments of the evangelist (see NIV note on 3:15). The same holds for 3:31–36. Are these the words of the Baptist or the author? Some scholars argue that a certain symmetry should be seen: Jesus and John's statements are followed by the beloved disciple's additional remarks (3:16–21 follows 3:1–15 as 3:31–36 follows 3:22–30).

In 3:16–21 we learn how this gift of spiritual birth offered to Nicodemus might be appropriated. Belief in the Son gains eternal life (3:15–16, 18). Disbelief gains judgment and condemnation (3:18–19, 35). This sums up the worldview characteristic of John's Gospel: one is either attracted to or repulsed by the light (3:19–21); one pursues either truth or evil. There is no equivocation here. Yet the coming of the Son was not inspired by a desire to condemn—it stemmed from love (3:16–17). But judgment is an inevitable result. Light brings exposure (3:20): it reveals who we really are.

Is the prospect of Jesus truly better? Evidence from the New Testament and the first century indicates that John the Baptist had followers who did not go over to Jesus (cf. Acts 19:1–7). The scene now shifts to the work of the Baptist with his disciples (3:22–36), and it makes one point: Jesus's baptism *is* superior: "He must become greater; I must become less" (3:30).

The scene is set at the Jordan River, where John is at work (3:22–24). A minor crisis arises when it is observed that Jesus's following is exceeding that of John (3:26). The transition is breeding animosity, but John the Baptist responds with a series of testimonies: the providence of God determines the success of ministry (3:27), and as he made clear at the outset (1:29), Jesus is the Christ and bridegroom (3:28–29); John is merely his advocate.

These concrete expressions (echoing the Synoptic Gospels) now expand into abstract statements in 3:31–36. The superiority of Jesus is grounded in his superior heritage: he is from above (3:31). The Son has come from the Father, but the Baptist belongs to the earth. John the Baptist speaks "as one from the earth" (3:31), but the Son utters the words of God (3:34). Therefore, there is an inestimable difference. Once more, the Spirit provides the major difference: out of his love for his Son, God has given to him "the Spirit without limit" (3:34). Jesus's possession of the Spirit supplies him with superior authority and enables him to offer new birth to men like Nicodemus.

4:1–54. Jesus's departure from the Jordan River is prompted by his concern that the Pharisees are viewing him as supplanting John the Baptist's ministry (4:1; cf. 3:22–36). Would the hostility toward John now be aimed at Jesus? In the Synoptics, it is John's arrest that brings Jesus into Galilee (Mark 1:14). The same is true in the Fourth Gospel. Jesus avoids incrimination stemming from his association with John. To be sure, Jesus's ministry was similar to that of John: both men employed baptism (4:1–2). Even in Galilee after the death of John, Herod Antipas will fear that Jesus may be John come back from the dead (Mark 6:14–20).

The usual route from the Jordan River to Galilee traversed the rift valley to Scythopolis (Beth Shan) and then went northwest into the valleys of lower Galilee. Instead, Jesus climbs into the Judean mountains and follows the ridge route north through the tribal territories of Benjamin and Ephraim and on into Samaria (4:5–6). The precise location of the city of Sychar remains uncertain; however, it is probably Shechem (so identified by Jerome and the Syriac) inasmuch as the traditional site for Jacob's Well is 250 feet from there. Further, Shechem is on the road from Judea to Galilee.

Jesus's conversation with the woman of Samaria (4:1–42) is striking on several counts. First, the enmity between Jew and Samaritan is well established (see Luke 10:29–37) and stands behind the woman's words in 4:9. Moreover, few Jewish rabbis would initiate open conversations with women as Jesus does (see 4:27). Nevertheless, Jesus does so, and the ensuing dialogue harmonizes with the theological developments we have seen thus far: Jesus overturns the sanctity of an important religious institution. In this case it is the sacred well of Jacob. At Cana (2:1–11), Jerusalem (3:5), the Jordan (3:22–26), and here, water serves a symbolic role, depicting the older institution that needs the messianic gift of Christ. As water became wine (2:9) and John's baptism was replaced by that of Jesus (3:30; 4:1), so now well water will be replaced by living water. What is this gift that makes all else obsolete? It is the eschatological Spirit promised by Jesus (3:5). This is what will bring power to John's baptism. The same is true in Samaria. John's only other reference to living water is in 7:38–39, where it is defined as the Spirit. The Spirit is explicitly emphasized even as the dialogue develops (4:23–24).

The dialogue with the woman enjoys a literary structure much like that in chapter 3: inquiries by the woman based on a misunderstanding of Jesus's spiritual intent serve to transport the discussion to deeper levels of thought. But while Nicodemus never reenters the scene to issue his response (suggesting no faith in Jerusalem?), things are different in Samaria. We read a series of improving titles for Jesus ("Sir," 4:11, 15; "Prophet," 4:19; "Messiah," 4:25, 29; "Savior of the world," 4:42); the woman's testimony converts many in the village (4:39); and Jesus remains with them for two days before going north into Galilee (4:43).

In verses 7–15 Jesus discusses living water. This section (like the next) introduces an "earthly" subject and through the questions of the woman leads to a spiritual message. Jesus's request for a drink of water is rebuffed (4:9), but he issues a challenge to the woman: if she knew who Jesus was, she would see that he is the supplier of living water (4:10). A second round (4:11–15) turns on her misunderstanding: Jesus cannot supply water because he has no access to the well. But here at last Jesus's clarification unfolds his meaning. His water ends *all* thirst and provides eternal life (4:14). It is the Spirit. (Compare this discourse with that on living bread in John 6:35–59.) Marvelously the woman asks to drink.

In the next section Jesus's focus is on true worship (4:16–26). When the light enters the darkness of the world, it necessarily brings judgment (3:19–20). Before the gifts of God can be obtained, the soul must be cleansed of sin. Jesus probes the moral life of the woman (4:16–18), but she does not flee—she admits to Jesus's prophetic powers (4:19). She chooses to remain in the light; yet now she hopes that the religious institutions of her acquaintance will free her from Jesus's scrutiny. Mount Gerizim (a mountain towering over the well) was the Samaritan holy place; Jesus is obviously a Jew who venerates Jerusalem. But Jesus dismisses these institutions too (as he dismissed the well): again the new dimension that transcends these is the Spirit (4:23–24). This spiritual worship is not worship in the inner aesthetic recesses of a person: it is worship animated by God's own eschatological Spirit. Jesus's challenge and offer in each of these scenes is the same. Yet here we move a step further; worship must also be in "truth." It must affirm the realities of truth (Jesus is the truth, 14:6), be doctrinally informed (cf. 1 John 4:1–3), and be directed toward Jesus.

Now Jesus takes up the subject of true nourishment (4:27–38). When the disciples return from the village (see 4:8), the woman departs in haste, leaving her jar behind (4:28). In the light of Jesus's offer, is it now obsolete? Her positive report in Shechem ("Could this be the Messiah?") leads many to make their own inquiries at the well. (Note the parallel on evangelism and discipleship in 1:35–51 with Andrew and Philip.)

> The woman at the well tells Jesus, "Our ancestors worshiped on this mountain, but you Jews claim that the place where we must worship is in Jerusalem" (John 4:20). The Samaritans, neighboring rivals to the Jews in Judea, had their own temple and rejected Jewish worship. Seen here are the remains of the steps from the Samaritan temple on Mount Gerizim.

Not even the disciples are exempt from misunderstanding Jesus. Jesus sent them out for food (4:8), yet now when Jesus is encouraged to eat he says that he has food enough (4:32). The disciples' misunderstanding (4:33) propels the discourse forward (4:34–38). His nourishment is found in accomplishing his urgent mission.

The woman's testimony bears fruit (4:39–42). And yet those who are invited to come out to see Jesus for themselves (as were Peter and Nathanael in 1:35–50) must obtain their own faith. Jesus remains in Samaria for two days, and many in the village believe (4:42).

The miracle in which the official's son is healed (4:43–54) brings Jesus back to Cana, the town that introduced this section of the Gospel (2:1–12). In both instances the sign of Jesus is numbered (2:11; 4:54), and his work is greeted with belief. Notice how there is a progression as Jesus moves from Jerusalem (chap. 3) to Cana (chap. 4). In Jerusalem Jesus cannot trust men (2:24), and Nicodemus comes making secretive inquiries at night (3:1–2). Then in Samaria Jesus is received eagerly (4:39–42), while in Galilee the enthusiasm for him is

open (4:45). The transition from Jerusalem to Galilee is a transition from unbelief to belief, from darkness to light. The proverb of verse 44 (used in the Synoptics to refer to Nazareth; cf. Mark 6:4) is applied here to Jerusalem, the city that kills the prophets (Luke 13:33; cf. John 4:19; 6:14).

The healing miracle finds a close parallel in the Synoptic cure of the centurion's servant (Matt. 8:4–13) and the story of the Syrophoenician woman (Mark 7:24–30). Both are cures effected at a distance. In John the miracle serves to display the new life promised by Jesus in the preceding discourses (3:16; 4:14, 36). In Cana, as in Samaria, Jesus hopes to inspire belief (4:50), and in this case, the official's son is saved (4:51). The Johannine account underscores one feature of the miracle: Jesus's word is powerful and effectual. The very hour of healing is the hour of Jesus's utterance (4:52). This combination of miracle and belief (4:50, 53) is what distinguishes the Johannine term "sign." The powerful works of Jesus are designed to evoke a response, to reveal who Jesus is. They are signs that lead elsewhere—to faith. This is the intent of the signs in Cana, Jerusalem, Samaria, and again in Cana. This is the aim that John has even for his reader of the Book of Signs. "Many people saw the signs he was performing and believed in his name" (2:23).

C. Jesus and the festivals of Judaism (5:1–10:42). This major section now compares Jesus with the festivals of Judaism in much the same way that the earlier unit (2:1–4:54) focused on Jewish institutions. Again, themes of messianic replacement and abundance will appear. However, now the subtleties of the comparison will become vital. In each instance, Jesus is described in the context of the festival (Sabbath, Passover, Tabernacles, Dedication), and as his discourse expands, elements from the festival will be swept up and given fresh definition. Jesus is their replacement! Or better, veiled within the liturgical and theological themes of the festival are symbols that point to Jesus, symbols whose true meanings are satisfied in Christ.

All of the Book of Signs (chaps. 1–12) might be viewed as giving the reader evidence—judicial evidence—for the truth of Christ's claims. Indeed, the word "sign" (Greek *sēmeion*) may be a judicial term for evidence. So too we have been introduced to witnesses who substantiate Jesus's case: John the Baptist ("I testify," 1:34), the Spirit (1:33; 3:32–34), and the Samaritan woman ("Many . . . believed in him because of the woman's testimony," 4:39). In chapter 5 Jesus will be forced to itemize his witnesses (5:31–40).

This forensic motif will become prominent in chapters 5–10. The trial of Jesus, which officially commences in chapter 18, is begun already, as interrogators in Jerusalem approach Jesus, examining his case. In virtually every chapter the "Jews" play this role. They assess Jesus's case, weigh the evidence, and make a judgment. This fascinating literary format places readers in an interesting position. They are forced to evaluate the evidence and the testimony for themselves. The first witness is John the Baptist (1:19–35), and the section closes (10:40–42) with a final reference to the Baptist's testimony and the value of Jesus's signs. By 10:42 the majority of the witnesses, the evidence, and the signs are in. The jury (the reader) may deliberate.

5:1–47. Jesus and the Sabbath receive prominent attention in this section. A feast now prompts Jesus to return to Jerusalem (5:1). Three pilgrimage feasts were known at this time—Passover, Pentecost, and Tabernacles—and scholars debate which could be meant here. The text is unclear, but at least it serves to introduce us to the literary motif of Jewish feasts that will follow. In this chapter the festival is the weekly Sabbath, a day of worship and rest. Jesus works a healing miracle (5:2–9), conflict follows (5:10–18), and then Jesus provides a major discourse explaining the authority of his work and his divine identity (5:19–47).

The location of the pool (5:2) had a history of controversy until archaeologists excavated it in the courtyard of St. Anne's Church in Jerusalem. The pool's name, Bethesda (see NIV note), is still unclear since manuscripts reflect numerous readings (5:2). John notes that various people with infirmities waited at the pool hoping to benefit from healing power associated with the site. This has led some scholars to see in the archaeological remains evidence for a healing sanctuary near the pool. Jesus, however, ignores the pool's supposed powers and with a word heals the lame man (5:8–9). But as with so many other healing stories in the Synoptics (cf. Mark 3:1–6), it is the Sabbath, and this arouses objections among the Jewish leaders. (Note that the NIV omits 5:4, placing it in a footnote, since the verse does not appear in the best ancient Greek manuscripts.)

When the lame man carries his bed, he violates a well-known Sabbath prohibition (Mishnah *Shabbat* 7:2). But since he does not know Jesus (Matt. 5:11, 13), he cannot indicate to his accusers who directed him thus. This comes later in the temple (5:14), when Jesus and the man meet again. Does 5:14 teach that there was a connection between this man's sin and his infirmity? The New Testament elsewhere avoids this conclusion (see John 9:3; Luke 13:1–5). Although a causal relationship may not necessarily exist between personal suffering and sin, sin may result in human misery and penalties (see Rom. 1:27).

The importance of verses 16–18 cannot be missed. For the first time we learn of Jewish hostility toward Jesus and the plan to kill him (5:18). The judicial theme comes out in 5:16 in the word "persecute" (*diōkō*), the grammar of which indicates a protracted period of persecution. God and Jesus form the substance of the following discourse. Jesus justifies working on the Sabbath because of his special relation with God (5:17): if God can work, so can Jesus. This is a dangerous defense. Could it be proven?

Jesus's divine authority is the subject of one of the most exalted discourses in the Gospel (5:19–47). Here Jesus makes explicit claims to divinity inasmuch as he associates himself directly with God. The discourse consists of three units.

First, Jesus describes his work as continuing the work of the Father (5:19–30). While prohibiting human labor on the Sabbath, the rabbis agree that God sustains the natural processes of life (birth, death, rainfall, etc.). Sovereignty over life was chief among these divine tasks. Jesus justifies his labors by assuming divine prerogatives (5:21). (Note how in John 4:46–54 Jesus gave life to a young boy.) In addition, judgment (which condemns or justifies) belongs solely to God. This authority now belongs to Jesus too (5:22–24), who exercises it not only in the present age (5:24) but also in the future, eschatological age (5:25–30).

Second, Jesus buttresses his case by introducing witnesses for his defense (5:31–40). In Jewish law one witness (even a person witnessing of himself [5:30–31]) was insufficient either to condemn or confirm a charge (Deut. 17:6; Mishnah *Ketubbot* 2:9). Therefore, this section answers the legal complaint: four witnesses are ushered forward. John the Baptist (John 5:33–35), the mighty works or signs of Jesus (5:36), God the Father (5:37–38), and the Scriptures (5:39–40) all substantiate Jesus's claims.

But what is the root cause of Jesus's rejection? The third unit (5:41–47) provides an analysis and prophetic critique. The problem is not intellectual—it centers instead on inner disposition. "You do not have the love of God in your hearts" (5:42). Jesus is angered not because they refuse to glorify him (5:41) but because they refuse to glorify God (5:44). The desire for human praise, affirmation, and prestige has crippled them, and they cannot love God (5:44a). Human noteworthies are esteemed (5:43b), but the Son, who bears divine credentials, is rejected. The very Scripture used to condemn Jesus will soon bring the severest judgment on its possessors (5:45–47).

6:1–71. Jesus and Passover are the focus of chapter 6. The scene now shifts to Galilee, where in the springtime festival of Passover (6:4) Jesus miraculously feeds a multitude of five thousand people. This is the only miracle of Jesus that appears in all four Gospels; it must have been deemed very important by the early church (Matt. 14:13–21; Mark 6:31–44; Luke 9:10–17). John's Gospel follows the Synoptic account closely. But John also echoes Matthew and Mark in that the feeding miracle is followed by the story of Jesus walking on the sea (6:16–21; cf. Matt. 14:22–33; Mark 6:45–52).

But this is where the comparisons end. Two typically Johannine literary features that we have witnessed elsewhere stand out. First, the symbolic elements of the festival are emphasized in order to highlight their christological significance. Passover spoke of Moses, who not only fed the Israelites in the wilderness (Exod. 16:4–36) but also became the ideal messianic figure in Judaism. Jesus is therefore depicted as the prophet like Moses (6:14; cf. Deut. 18:15) who exceeds the manna miracle of Moses (6:30–34, 48–51). Second, the Johannine discourse is the vehicle used to advance this comparison. When questioned by the Jews, Jesus presses home the spiritual meaning of this event in what may be the longest public discourse in the Gospel (6:25–65).

The Sea of Galilee was often called the Sea of Tiberias, in honor of Herod Antipas's founding of the new provincial center of Tiberias in AD 26 (cf. John 21:1). The Passover is probably a year after the one mentioned in 2:13. During the intervening year, Mark notes, John

the Baptist was arrested, and by the time of the feeding of the five thousand he has been executed (Mark 6:14–29, where the Baptist is beheaded). This lapse of time explains Jesus's growing popularity (6:2–3).

Jesus's charge to Philip to feed the people (6:5) recalls the conversation of 4:31–38, in Samaria. Spiritual food is at issue. It is a test (6:6) because Jesus needs to elevate the disciples' consciousness as to the manner of his ministry. Nevertheless, misunderstanding ensues. (Note the motif already in 3:4; 4:11, 33.) Hence, Philip inventories their savings (eight months' wages, 6:7), and Andrew spots a boy with a few provisions (6:9). John alone records that the boy holds barley bread, which was the bread of the poor, but symbolically it may recall the great Old Testament feeding miracle of Elisha (2 Kings 4:42). John also notes that it is Jesus who distributes the bread (not the disciples) and that in his prayer of blessing, rather than using the Synoptic *eulogeō* ("to bless"), Jesus gives thanks (Greek *eucharisteō*; cf. 1 Cor. 11:24). Is this a veiled symbol of the Eucharist or the Lord's Supper? This use of symbolism seems

The hills above Tabgha, the traditional site where Jesus multiplied the loaves and fishes (John 6:5–13)

natural to Jesus's teaching in John, and in this chapter the eucharistic application will become more explicit (6:52–58).

The dangers of Jesus's popularity and the perils of misunderstandings are shown in the crowd's response (6:14). They have interpreted the sign: Jesus has enacted the "Moses miracle" of Passover. However, Jesus flees (6:15) because the crowd wishes to force on him a political definition of messiah ("make him king by force"). Mark records this same crisis: Jesus puts the disciples on a boat and personally disappears into the mountains (Mark 6:45–46).

The destination of the disciples is Capernaum, and after they have worked against the wind for hours heading to the fishing village of Peter and Andrew (6:16–19), Jesus joins them—walking on the sea. The fear of the disciples indicates the miraculous and incomprehensible nature of the event. Above all, Jesus reveals himself through yet another symbolic expression, "I am" (Greek *egō eimi*). In the Greek Old Testament the name of God revealed to Moses on Mount Sinai is *egō eimi*, or "I AM" (Exod. 3:13–14). John's use of this divine Old Testament title elsewhere for Jesus (8:58; 18:6) may imply its use here. Once the company arrives in Capernaum, Galileans from the earlier site of feeding follow him there and become suspicious because Jesus was not in the boat (6:22, 25). Jews from Tiberias likewise search for him and come to Capernaum (6:23). The zeal of the Galilean Jews is noteworthy (cf. 4:43–45).

In the Capernaum synagogue (6:59) Jesus provides a full discourse explaining his person and work. Again, the discourse is propelled forward by inquiries (6:25, 28, 30, 34, 41, 52), and at each level the revelation of Christ deepens.

Initially the crowds merely possess the surface apprehension of the miracle (6:25). They must go deeper and unveil the sign, for the signs are revelatory. Like the woman needing water (4:7), these people need imperishable food supplying eternal life (6:27; 4:14). For this food alone they must labor. What then is labor? Faith in Christ (6:29). But the human impulse is to

demand evidence so compelling that we *must* believe. If Jesus is making personal claims on the order of Moses, then his sign must exceed that of Moses (6:30). In John 6:31 Jesus's response is an intricate Jewish commentary (midrash) based on one or several Old Testament texts: "He gave them bread from heaven to eat" (cf. Exod. 16:4, 15; Ps. 78:24). The true bread they seek is not dependent on Moses (or Judaism): it is whatever God rains on humans as a gift, and which gives life (6:33). The Jews here resemble the Samaritan woman inasmuch as they are intrigued: "Sir, give us/me this bread/water" (6:34; 4:15).

The divine origin of Jesus is a favorite Johannine theme (3:13–31), and John often ironically presents it in innocent inquiries (e.g., 7:28, 34–36). So too the question of 6:25 about Jesus's mysterious appearance in Capernaum goes unanswered, because now a theological response is at hand. Jesus is the bread of life that has mysteriously descended (6:35, 38). The twin themes of hunger and thirst (cf. chaps. 4, 6) are now satisfied. Belief is still the key (6:36; cf. 6:29); however, now a new note is struck. God is sovereign over the ministry of Jesus (6:38) as well as its results (6:37, 39, 44). Those whom God calls are effectively called and securely preserved (6:39–40; cf. 10:14–18; 17:6). In other words, the work of Jesus and the gathering of disciples are both a result of God's perfect will.

From the crowd's point of view this revelation is hard to accept, and they murmur (6:41–43). Is Jesus not a commonplace citizen of Galilee (cf. Mark 6:1–6)? How can he descend from heaven? But Jesus knows that further explanation will not complete what is lacking. The gift of faith and the ability to apprehend who Christ really is—these are divine things (6:44–48). Faith is not merely rational persuasion: it includes God's drawing us (6:44). To stay in Judaism is death (6:49), but to consume the bread of life brings life (6:50–51).

But a deeper revelation is to come: the bread to be consumed is Jesus's flesh offered in sacrifice (6:51). Still, the discourse is urged forward through a literal misunderstanding. How can humans eat his flesh (6:52)? The following explanation (6:53–58) reinforces this thought and draws on sacrificial images (flesh and blood). If symbolism is still at work (as it likely is), the symbols inevitably suggest the elements of the Lord's Supper. It is not the sacrament that gives life; rather, salvation is found in the sacrifice behind it and the faith that it evokes (6:35, 40, 47). Outside the Eucharist an admonition to drink blood in any other Jewish setting would be incomprehensible.

But if the descent of Christ gives difficulty to the crowds (6:41–42), this deeper teaching causes the disciples to stumble (6:60). They too murmur (6:61). Jesus breaks the impasse by showing that literal flesh is not the key; rather, it is the Spirit who conveys life (6:63). If the Eucharist is still at issue, the message is clear: its physical element "counts for nothing" if the Spirit's power is not present.

But to understand this fully takes more than human minds can grasp (6:64, 66). Jesus repeats the exhortation given to the crowds in 6:44–47. Penetrating the mysteries of God is also a divine gift (6:64–65). The deeper realities offend, and here some disciples draw back and abandon Christ (6:66). But Peter knows that the greatest virtue is to continue embracing Jesus no matter where he might lead (6:68–70).

7:1–9:41. The third feast of Judaism to inspire Johannine interest is the autumn harvest of Tabernacles. It joined Passover and Pentecost as a pilgrimage feast and was celebrated on 15 Tishri (September-October), commemorating the end of the harvest field labor (Lev. 23:39). It also recalled Israel's wandering and life in booths (Lev. 23:42–43). Every Jewish male was obligated to attend sometime during the course of seven days of worship and sacrifice (Exod. 23:14–17; Deut. 16:16).

John's interest in the Feast of Tabernacles (John 7:2, 37) is specialized and builds on the symbolic ceremonies conducted at the temple. Two ceremonies in particular frame Jesus's self-disclosure. Water and light each play a ceremonial role based on eschatological prophecies in Zechariah (see below). In this context Jesus announces that he is the source of "living water" (7:38) and that he is the "light of the world" (8:12). The discourses that follow pick up prior themes (Jesus's authority and origin) and add to the judicial evidence for Jesus's case that the Book of Signs has been accumulating. Just as Sabbath (chap. 5) and Passover (chap. 6) became literary springboards to reveal who Jesus is, so now the Feast of Tabernacles becomes a place where Jesus unveils himself in Jewish imagery.

7:1–52. Jesus's reluctance to return to Judea (7:1–13) is understandable when we recall the events of his last visit. The subject of his death arose then (5:16), and it will arise again (7:1, 7, 19). In fact, this will be Jesus's last visit to Jerusalem; in the coming spring he will be crucified. Nevertheless, his brothers (cf. 2:12) urge him to go—to make his identity plain (7:3–4)—but their intentions are not in Jesus's interest since, as John states clearly, they "did not believe in him" (7:5).

Does Jesus deceive them when he says that he will not go to the feast (7:8) and then he does (7:10)? (See the note in the NIV.) The earliest interpreters of John viewed this as a classic case of Jesus's symbolism and its attendant misunderstanding. Jesus's brothers lack belief and do not have divine insight; not just anyone can fully comprehend the Son (cf. 6:44). "Going up" (Greek *anabainō*) elsewhere for Jesus means death, resurrection, and ascension (cf. 20:17). This is why Jesus's "time has not yet fully come" (7:6, 8)—Jesus is sovereign over his death and departure (so 10:17–18). He may attend the feast, but he alone will control the hour of death.

Jesus's arrival is marked by controversy (7:10–13). Judaism is divided (7:40–44). This echoes the Synoptic picture of Jesus's final days in Jerusalem, where Jesus's teachings find both a popular following and the concentrated hatred of the Jewish leadership. It is possible that the Johannine chronology gives the best picture of Jesus's final Judean visit: he comes to the city in the autumn, teaches in the region during the winter, and is crucified during Passover in the spring.

The now familiar form of the Johannine discourse meets us again at the Feast of Tabernacles. Questions that essentially misunderstand who Jesus is provoke him to respond. Irony is John's literary device throughout. Here two Jewish objections to Jesus are central to the debate: the authority of Jesus's teaching and the nature of his origin.

Educational standards for rabbis were well established in the first century. Advanced study under a rabbinic scholar (e.g., Paul under Gamaliel) in a school was common. Jesus possessed no such credentials. In effect, the Jews wish to see these, and Jesus complies: his diplomas are divine (7:14–24). The Synoptics attest to Jesus's uncanny sense of authority (Matt. 7:28–29). Here Jesus explains the source of that authority.

The Jewish notion of authority was specialized. No one possessed *inherent* authority; it was secondary and indirect. Authority was passed down and conferred to the rabbi through ordination. It was as if the authority of Moses was preserved through the generations. And if the chain was broken, authority might be lost. Jesus's problem was this: he was not ordained. On whose shoulders was he standing? What traditions were his? What was the source of his authority? Jesus's answer is clear: his authority stems directly from God (7:14–18). Jesus does answer the rabbis in their own categories: his authority was properly conferred to him—but his source of authority is unconventional to say the least.

In particular, Jesus demonstrates his authority by overturning traditional teaching on the Sabbath. Note how in 7:22 the rabbinic concept of tradition and authority is employed. Still, Jesus supplants this with his own instruction: doing good (e.g., healing [5:1–18]) is no violation of the Sabbath. Circumcision is the precedent (7:23).

In chapter 5 Jesus asserted his authority in the same way, and it led to speculation about destroying him (5:15–16) on the basis of his claims about himself (5:17–18). The same responses are evidenced here (7:25–36). Again an ironic misunderstanding (7:27) fuels the discourse. Popular Jewish belief held that the Messiah would be concealed until his surprise unveiling to Israel. But the crowds know Jesus's home—he is from Galilee. But this is wrong at a deeper level. Jesus comes from God (7:28–29). John employs the crowd's false perception of Jesus's origin in order to explain Jesus's true origin. In response, the listeners are divided (cf. 6:66–71). Some are hostile (7:30), but others step closer toward faith (7:31). The light either draws to itself or repels.

Once again the Jewish leadership misunderstands Jesus (7:32–36). Jesus is going where they cannot travel. This of course is his return to the Father, but they take it to mean his travel to prohibited Gentile lands (7:35). This illustrates once more the truth that access to divine revelation rests solely in God's sovereign hand (6:44–58).

On the last feast day, numerous ceremonies involving sacrifice and ritual water could be viewed at the temple. Reading Zechariah 9–14, we see the priests portray how in the last days everlasting fountains would flow from Jerusalem (Zech. 13:1; 14:8). Pitchers of water from the Gihon Spring were poured on the altar as the Hallel Psalms were sung (Psalms 113–18). This was especially meaningful since at this time of year water was scarce in Israel, and people feared drought.

In this setting (7:37–39) Jesus sweeps up this symbolism and announces that he is the source of true drink (cf. 4:10). John 7:38 has always posed difficulties for interpreters. The NIV makes the believer the one in whom living water is flowing. But the Greek can be punctuated another way: "If anyone thirsts, let him come to me; and let him drink, who believes in me." This reading is best. It means that Jesus is the source of the eschatological Feast of Tabernacles water. Jesus is the source of the Spirit

(7:39a). In 19:34 we may even have a symbol of this flowing when Jesus is glorified (7:39b).

At the middle of the feast (7:14) Jesus's revelation is met by a response from the people (7:25–31) and the Jewish leadership (7:32–36). On this last day the same applies: the people and the leaders are divided (7:40–52). Some express incipient faith (7:40–41, 46); others show contempt (7:41, 44, 47–49). In both cases the issue of Jesus's inferior Galilean origin is a problem (7:41–42, 52). In John 1:46 this same concern troubled Nathanael, but there was a difference. He had the courage to "come and see" Jesus for himself. This too is the counsel of Nicodemus in 7:51. A true verdict requires an assessment of the evidence—the facts. This applies to the Sanhedrin. But also in John's judicial literary format, this applies to the reader. The Book of Signs is submitting evidence for our inspection.

7:53–8:11. The section about the woman caught in adultery has always proved difficult. Three questions persist: (1) Is it an insertion into the text of John? Most scholars answer in the affirmative. The best Greek manuscripts do not have it, and when they do, it appears in a variety of places (e.g., after John 7:36; 21:25; Luke 21:38; or even Luke 24:53). It also has a style unlike that of John, and it interrupts the Feast of Tabernacles story (see 8:12). If it belonged here, 7:53–8:1 would imply that Jesus was at the Sanhedrin meeting in 7:45–52! (2) Is the story authentically from Jesus? Yes it is. It is similar to Synoptic stories of Jewish entrapment climaxed by Jesus's profound pronouncement (8:7). (3) Why was it located here in John? The surrounding discourse (esp. chap. 8) asserts themes that the story illustrates. Jesus judges no one (8:15), and his accusers cannot convict him of sin (8:46). (For a current study on the history of the text, see Burge 1984.)

But these concerns should not deter us from the power and authority of the story. The account has always been a favorite for good reason. The falsehood of the scribes and Pharisees is indicated in two ways. First, the Old Testament law on which they base their charges (8:5) required the punishment of both parties (Lev. 20:10; Deut. 22:22). The woman's partner is absent. Was she set up? Second, Jewish law carefully stipulated what evidence needed to be in hand. No execution was possible without a solid case. Hence Sanhedrin records indicate judges who would even demand to know the color of the sheets on the bed. The law even distinguished intercourse from preliminary sexual contact. This extensive demand for evidence made adultery charges rare in Judaism since couples would naturally take precautionary measures to conceal themselves. However, the law was aware of men who, rather than divorce their wives for an illicit affair, chose to have them "set up" with witnesses for execution. (If a man thus executed his wife, he became heir to her property; but not if he divorced her.) But this self-interest was deemed morally wrong. If witnesses viewed preliminary coition, they were obliged to interrupt the act and prevent the greater crime. If, as we suspect, a man has discharged his wife thus and engineered testimony ("caught in the act," 8:4) to execute her without warning her, the entire affair may appear legal but reeks of injustice. In Jesus's eyes the entire situation would have been reprehensible.

The woman is simply a pawn for the Jewish leaders who wish to play off Jesus's well-known compassion for sinners (even women sinners! cf. Luke 7:36–50) against the demands of the law. They wish to discredit Jesus (8:6). However, Jesus does not deny the woman's sin but draws her accusers into the circle of condemnation.

8:12–59. John 8:12 returns to the festival setting of Tabernacles (cf. 7:2). The discourse of 7:14–39 focused on one symbolic element: the everlasting temple water of Zechariah. Now Jesus employs a second ritual theme: everlasting light (8:12–20). Zechariah also predicted that light would shine forth perpetually from the temple in the last days (Zech. 14:6–7). This too was associated with Moses and the wilderness tabernacles: was not Israel led by a pillar of light (Exod. 13:21)? The Feast of Tabernacles was further celebrated during the autumn equinox, recognizing the failing summer sun.

Pilgrims to Jerusalem enjoyed the light ceremonies of the temple (see Mishnah *Sukkah* 5:2–4). Four enormous candlesticks were lit each night, illuminating the brilliant temple limestone. It is a tribute to the Jewishness of John that he records an incidental detail of importance. Just as Jesus spoke of messianic fulfillment at the height of the water ceremonies (7:37), now John says that Jesus is in the area of the temple treasury (8:20). The treasury was in the Court of Women, and this was the location of the festival lampstands! Beneath the ritual lights of the Feast of Tabernacles Jesus announces, "I am the light of the world."

"Light" is a frequent metaphor for Jesus in the Gospel (see 1:5; 3:19; 12:46; 1 John 1:5). As light, Jesus discloses the person of God for us; illumines life and gives us meaning and purpose; and also exposes sin, judging those who dwell in darkness. These are persistent themes in the Fourth Gospel. Here the pilgrims at the Feast of Tabernacles recognize something authoritative in Jesus's words but demand legal substantiation (8:13–19). This question was posed in chapter 5 at another festival. In the Old Testament (Deut. 17:6) and the Mishnah (*Ketubbot* 2:9) it was held that a person could not be condemned unless two witnesses were present (cf. Matt. 18:16; 2 Cor. 13:1). This was extended to self-testimony. Now, however, Jesus does not inventory his witnesses.

The seven-branched lampstand, or menorah, was a common decorative element in synagogues, such as the synagogue in Eshtemoa near Hebron (third–fourth century AD), where this lintel was excavated. The menorah was a symbol of the temple and the lampstands lit there each night.

He has done this already (5:30–47). The most acute witness to Jesus is the Father (8:18). Jesus's self-witness is also valid because Jesus can assume the authority of the Father, namely, that of judgment (5:22; 8:16). But since Jesus's opponents do not know the Father, they can hardly perceive the weight of his testimony.

The balance of the Tabernacles discourse now takes on the traditional format we have seen many times. Misunderstanding on the part of Jesus's questioners propels the discourse forward, leading Jesus to further self-revelations. Now, however, in Jerusalem, these revelations will become more profound than anything before, and the hostilities more direct. Here (8:59) and at the next feast (Dedication, 10:31, 33), violence seems imminent. If what Jesus says is true, he must be followed or destroyed.

Where is Jesus going (8:21–30)? This is the second time this question has been asked (cf. 7:32–36). Earlier Jesus volunteered no explanation. Now when his audience mistakenly thinks that he will commit suicide (8:22), Jesus unveils something of his true origins (8:23–24). Jesus is returning to the place from which he originated, "from above" (8:23; cf. 3:31). The divine implications of this are explicit in 8:24. Jesus uses the divine name (*egō eimi*) as a description of his identity. In this round (8:24, 28) and the next (8:58), this is the climax of Jesus's testimony. The Greek form of the Hebrew name Yahweh (Exod. 3:14) is applied to Christ in an absolute way. Jesus is the great I AM.

Again the crowd misunderstands. "Who are you?" (8:25). "I am" (8:24) usually requires a predicate. Still they fail to see. Jesus bears the full authority of God! But here at last Jesus indicates when they will perceive: at the cross (8:28). This is the second passion prediction in John (elsewhere 3:14 and 12:32–34; cf. the same triple prediction in the Synoptics: Mark 8:31; 9:31; 10:33–34). The metaphoric language in all three passion sayings is critical: the cross is the *lifting up* of Jesus (not his destruction). "Lifting up" (Greek *hypsoō*) is often used for exaltation (Acts 2:33; 5:31). His elevation on Calvary is the initial step in his departure. It is in this process that his divinity will be unmistakable. He will be exalted.

Jesus discusses Abraham's true descendants in 8:31–59. The implications of this radical teaching are clear, and controversy is sure to follow. Jesus is overturning the canons of Jewish religion in their entirety! Knowing him who bears this power and authority will bring true freedom (8:32). But again, the Jews understand this in earthly terms: they are free since they are not slaves (8:33). But Jesus is concerned with spiritual slavery (8:34–36), and this they cannot perceive.

From here Jesus is engaged in the harshest polemic in the Gospel (8:37–59; cf. Matt. 23:1–39). Verse 35 is key. If the Jews are not sons in God's household (as Jesus claims), two results follow: their tenure there is limited, and they have another father. Being a descendant of Abraham (8:37) and being a son (8:35, 38) are two different things. Jesus claims that lineage has no effect on spiritual status before God (so Paul, Rom. 2:25–29). But their desire to kill Jesus is telling: they have a spiritual father other than God (8:38–43). At once they see where Jesus is headed: at issue is not only Jewish lineage (8:39) but also their sonship. Jesus is challenging both. The lethal attack is launched in 8:44. The failure of Jesus's opponents to accept the truth and to hear God's word (8:47) has led them to desire Jesus's murder.

Jesus's spiritual critique is now turned back on him, and he is assailed with words not even found in the Synoptics (8:48–49). If the Jews here are children of the devil (8:44), then Jesus is demon possessed (7:20; 8:48). The nearest parallel to this is in Mark 3:22–27, where Jesus is said to be in league with Satan. But John 8:48 cuts deeper.

Despite this offense, Jesus presses home the implications of his divine status. This will bring the final crisis. Jesus and those who believe in him are free from the threat of death (cf. 8:31–33, 51). This is astounding. Does Jesus claim to be greater than Abraham and the other Old Testament heroes who died (8:52–53)? If this is Jesus's claim, he must be demon possessed (8:52). But Jesus takes up the challenge. In 8:56–58 the discourse comes to its climax: Jesus is indeed making personal divine claims as compared with Abraham. Two times in this discourse we hear the refrain, "Who are you?" (8:25), "Who do you think you are?" (8:53). Now the answer is given. Jesus's existence has been eternal—before Abraham—and he is the bearer of the divine name (8:24, 28, 58). His attackers understand him fully now and try to kill him for blasphemy, but he slips away (8:59; cf. 7:44; 8:20).

9:1–41. In chapter 9 Jesus brings light to a blind man. Cast in the form of so many Synoptic conflict stories, this narrative is closely connected with the previous chapter. We are still at the Feast of Tabernacles setting, and Jesus is still affirming that he is "the light of the world" (9:5; cf. 8:12). Here the light of Jesus is *parabolically* viewed in the service of a blind man who gains his vision. But those who live in darkness without this light (the Jewish opponents) cannot see. In the end, the Pharisees are described as blind since they do not possess the spiritual vision or the light of Christ. It is interesting to trace the attitudes of the blind man and the Pharisees here. The former makes three confessions of ignorance (9:12, 25, 36) but in the end is led to true vision and faith (9:34–38). The latter make numerous confident statements of knowledge (9:16, 24, 29) but are shown to be ignorant (9:41).

The story is symbolic, then, of spiritual vision and blindness complete with their attendant dispositions (cf. the similar blindness motif in Mark 8:14–30).

The healing in 9:1–34 and the one described in 5:1–18 have much in common (Sabbath, pool, interrogation, conflict). Here too the question of the origin of suffering arises (9:2; 5:14). And again, the link between sin and suffering is opaque. If we take the traditional punctuation, 9:3 implies that the purpose of the infirmity is the glory of God that will follow the healing. The man was born blind *so that* God could show his glory. However, some scholars have argued that the punctuation should stop at 9:3b, giving the following translation: "'Neither this man nor his parents sinned,' Jesus said. 'But so that the work of God may be displayed in his life—we must do the works of him who sent me.'" In this case, no comment is given as to the purpose of the man's blindness, but instead Jesus simply says that we need to get to work to correct it, thereby showing God's glory.

Healing with mud and saliva was well known among the ancients, and Jesus employed it often (cf. Mark 7:33; 8:23). The focus of the healing, however, is its symbolic element: the man is told to wash in the Pool of Siloam. This was the pool at the south end of the city filled by the Gihon Spring and was the source for the water ceremonies at the Feast of Tabernacles. But for John something deeper is at hand. We recall that Jesus replaced these Tabernacles waters in 7:37–39. Now the pool, which is their source, bears Christ's name. Siloam means "sent" (9:7), and the Fourth Gospel regularly refers to Jesus as one who is "sent" (e.g., 5:36–38; 8:16, 18, 26). The blind man finds his healing in Jesus both in symbol and in reality.

The judicial interest we have witnessed thus far in the Book of Signs takes a fresh turn. Rather than Jesus, the healed man goes on trial. Since it is the Sabbath (9:14), the Jewish leadership feels compelled to investigate a possible criminal violation. The interrogation has four steps, as various witnesses move to center

Stairs leading down to the Pool of Siloam (left), discovered at the south end of Jerusalem by Israeli archaeologists in 2004. This spring-fed pool, where Jesus told the blind man to go wash (John 9:7), was a source of water and ritual washing in Jesus's day.

stage. In much the same way that in John 4 the Samaritan woman revealed her developing faith by using a progression of titles for Christ, so here the narrative parades Christ's names ("Jesus," 9:11; "Siloam," 9:11; "prophet," 9:17; "Messiah," 9:22; "from God," 9:33; "Son of Man," 9:35; "Lord," 9:38).

Step one involves the interrogation of the man by his neighbors (9:8–12). They are witnesses to the miracle but remain incredulous. After this, Pharisees take over, and they examine the man and his family. Step two (9:13–17) confirms the Sabbath violation but uncovers a flaw of logic in the trial. If God listens to Jesus (e.g., he heals), how can Jesus be a Sabbath violator? Step three (9:18–23) shows how they choose to resolve the dilemma: God is consistent with his law; therefore, the miracle must be a fraud. God does not entertain sin and miracles at the same time. One element must go. But the man's parents are no use. They confirm that this is their son and that he was blind, but their fear of the authorities makes them reluctant to say more.

Step four is easily the most important (9:24–34). The man is recalled a second time in hope of finding a way to condemn Jesus's sin. The brute fact of the miracle cannot be ignored, and yet even with this tangible evidence in hand the religious leaders spurn both the man and Jesus. Their allegiance is set; they are intransigent. The language of 9:28 is important. The Pharisees have polarized everyone's commitments: you cannot be a disciple of Moses and a disciple of Jesus at the same time. The chasm between church and synagogue is at hand (cf. 8:39–47).

The blind man's final defense (9:30–33) supports the logic both of his own case and John's case in the Book of Signs. Are not the signs of Jesus compelling evidence? Why have these leaders rejected the man and Jesus? Because there is no acceptable excuse, the result is judgment (9:39, 41).

In an earlier story the lame man who was healed and who suffered abuse at the temple was found again by Jesus and encouraged (5:14).

So now, once this blind man is expelled from the synagogue (9:34), Jesus finds him again and commends his efforts. Since the man witnessed and accepted the signs, belief was an easy thing (9:38). His disposition to the sign was all-important. But for the Pharisees, whose minds were closed, the light could not penetrate. They became blind because they remained in the darkness (9:39). John 8:41 suggests we have personal responsibility for how we respond to the revelation we receive. To see the signs of God and reject them is a more serious matter than never having perceived them at all.

10:1–39. The Festival of Dedication now introduces us to the fourth festival of Judaism that Jesus attends and that, like the others, becomes a place of discourse and revelation. Unlike the other feasts, the Feast of Dedication was a minor, more recent celebration. It recalled the desecration of the temple in 168 BC by the Greek monarch Antiochus IV Epiphanes, the corrupt priests installed by him, and the Maccabean wars, which finally regained and purified the temple in 164 BC. A moving account of this is given in 1 Maccabees 4:36–58, which is followed by Judas Maccabeus's announcement that this dedication (Hanukkah) should be celebrated each winter on the twenty-fifth day of the Jewish month Kislev (November-December).

This Jewish background provides striking depth to the discourse of Jesus in chapter 10. As we have suggested, Jesus has been in Jerusalem since autumn (the Feast of Tabernacles, 7:2–3), and now his conflict with the Jerusalem leadership has reached a peak. Jesus will not publicly debate the Jews again after chapter 10. This final crisis tone is paralleled by the Synoptic account found, for instance, in Matthew 23, where Jesus's criticisms are extremely biting. The same is found in John 10. After the conflict with the Pharisees in chapter 9, which described them as blind (9:39–41), now they are depicted as false shepherds (10:1, 10, 12–13).

Because the literary division between this festival and the previous one is less clear (cf. 5:1;

6:1; 7:1), scholars are divided on the question of where 10:1–21 should fall. Does it apply to the foregoing (the subject of 10:21 implies this) or to the material in 10:22–39? We have chosen to unify all of chapter 10 under this final feast. There is a strict change of subject at 10:1, and the second half of the chapter still presupposes the sheep metaphor (see 10:26–27). Moreover, the subject of the discourse in 10:1–21 applies directly to the Feast of Dedication, which recalled the corrupt priests of the Greek era (Jason and Menelaus) and had in Jesus's day evolved into a ceremony of priestly rededication. Synagogues read aloud Ezekiel 34, in which false priests are described as false shepherds. Therefore in a season that studied religious leadership and its historic failings, Jesus gathers up the current metaphor from Ezekiel 34 and interprets it in light of his own mission.

The metaphoric teaching of Jesus in 10:1–21 closely resembles the parables of the Synoptics. The parable is given in 10:1–5, a note of incomprehension is recorded in verse 6, and then Jesus interprets the meaning of the parable (cf. the format of Mark 4).

The parable itself discusses the legitimate leaders of the sheep. Just as with the corrupt priests of the Maccabean era, Jesus suggests that there may still be false leaders of God's people whose intentions are malevolent. Two criteria set apart fraudulent leaders. First, their entry into authority is wrong (10:1). Sheepfolds were often protective stone fences with one access gate. If the gatekeeper (10:3) has not ordained the shepherd's entry, he is to be feared, not followed. Here Jesus indicates that he alone has true authority because he has obtained the gatekeeper's invitation. Second, the false leader's voice cannot be recognized. The intimacy between shepherd and sheep is a well-known Palestinian phenomenon. Sheep can even bear personal names! Here Jesus shows that he alone knows and is known by the sheep. In John this is a central feature of discipleship: discerning Jesus's voice and abiding in him.

As in other discourses, the failure of the listeners to understand Jesus's meaning (10:6) leads him to explain himself more fully (cf. 3:9–14; 7:35–39). Initially Jesus affirms that

In John 10:7, Jesus identifies himself as the gate to the sheepfold. As seen here, ancient sheepfolds were built of stone and had one access gate.

he is the way ("the gate," 10:7, 9) through which one finds salvation or pasture. This is an advance over the parable, wherein the shepherd is distinguished from the gatekeeper and the gate. Now we learn that Jesus distributes not simply access to leadership but life itself. If the parable has allegorical elements, note that now in the interpretation Jesus assumes a new sovereignty over the fold. Has he assumed divine tasks again? The sheepfold is designed to keep out those who would harm the sheep (10:10), and Jesus is their guardian. He refuses access to many, including those like the Pharisees. These leaders destroy, but God sent Christ so that those who believe might not be destroyed (3:16; 6:39; 17:12).

But Jesus is also the good shepherd (10:11, 14). God is often described as the shepherd of Israel (Gen. 49:24; Ps. 23; 78:52–53), and similarly, the patriarchs, Moses, and David were shepherds. Leadership in Israel meant shepherding, and thus impious Israelite kings were called false shepherds (1 Kings 22:17; Jer. 10:21; 23:1–2; Ezek. 34:1–31). In Mark's account of the feeding of the five thousand, Jesus is evidently using this same pastoral motif for himself (6:30–44, esp. vv. 34, 39–40). Here in 10:11–18 the superiority of Jesus's work is given. Not only is his devotion to the sheep such that he is willing to die for them while others flee from danger (10:11–13, 17); he also knows them deeply—so deeply that in 10:15 an appropriate analogy for this knowledge is Jesus's relationship to his Father. As Jesus is in the Father, so the disciple is in Christ (cf. 14:20, 24).

A variety of secondary themes emerges from these teachings. Is there only one flock of Jesus? Is Judaism the limit of his care? John 10:16 indicates the contrary: "other sheep" refers to members (Gentiles?) beyond Judaism. Is the death of the shepherd something tragic—beyond his control? Not at all. His power enables him voluntarily to die and regain his life (10:18). Elsewhere in the New Testament, God raises up Jesus (Acts 2:24; Rom. 4:24; Eph. 1:20; Heb. 11:19; 1 Pet. 1:21). But in Johannine thought

the Father and the Son possess the same powers (10:28–30). The Son controls the hour of death entirely (2:4; 7:6, 8; 8:20).

The responses to Jesus's discourses have followed a pattern that is seen again here. At Passover, Tabernacles, and now at Dedication, a division erupts among the listeners (6:41, 60; 7:25, 45; 10:19–21). There is no neutral position for one who is faced with Christ's revelation. Either hostility (10:20) or the seeds of faith (10:21) will follow. Those who believe are ready to cast off the extreme charge of demon possession lodged against Jesus at the Feast of Tabernacles (7:20; 8:48). Jesus's teachings and miracles (esp. 9:1–7) are confirming evidence for them.

With this encounter we reach a sort of crescendo in the Gospel. The evidences accumulating in the Book of Signs will shift following this chapter. No longer will Jesus discourse with the Jewish leaders. He will later be with friends in Bethany (11:1–12:8), supportive crowds (12:12–19), and Gentiles (12:20–36). Then Jesus will "hide himself" from all but his personal disciples (12:36). Here in chapter 10 the height of Jesus's self-revelation is completed: his identity with the Father is now explicit (10:30, 33) and centered on his claim to the title Son of God (10:34–36). Similarly, the hostilities are keen: twice attempts are made on his life, but he escapes (10:31, 39). This narrative epitomizes Jesus's ultimate claims about himself and the fateful Jewish reaction (10:22–39).

The temple courtyard was surrounded by colonnaded porches that gave shelter from the weather. Solomon's Porch was on the east. Since it is winter (the season of Dedication) Jesus is found there sheltered from the cold Jerusalem wind (10:22–23). If the judicial emphases that we are following are correct, here the christological inquiries take on new significance. The evidence has been displayed (10:25–26), and now Judaism aims its two charges that will reappear later at the formal trial: (1) Are you claiming to be the Christ (cf. Luke 22:67)? (2) Are you the Son of God (cf. John 19:7 and Luke 22:70)?

The way in which Jesus defends his claims and explains Jewish disbelief affirms that God is sovereign over who accepts revelation. The leaders are simply not of Jesus's fold and hence cannot hear his voice. This divine control over revelation has appeared elsewhere (6:37, 44, 65; cf. 17:6). Understanding the signs alone is a divine gift.

In 10:28–29 the sovereignty of Jesus and God over the flock is in exact parallel ("no one can snatch them out of *my*/*his* hand"). This operational or functional unity leads to the essential or "ontological" unity of 10:30: "I and the Father are one." These verses are crucial and have played a vital role in the formation of trinitarian doctrine. Christ has regularly assumed divine prerogatives, and he has emphasized his oneness with the Father. Now the doctrinal point is explicit. The authority of Jesus's messiahship rests above all on his unique relation with the Father.

The Jewish leaders judge it as blasphemy (10:31). Jesus in turn employs a defense that at first may seem peculiar to us today. He debates like a rabbi. First, he notes that the general ascription of "gods" was known in the Old Testament (Psalm 82) and used for those who were vehicles for the word of the Lord (10:34–35). Is Christ not at least this? Second, Christ is more. If the first premise is correct, what do we say of him who is a unique vehicle of the word of God—who *is* the Word (John 1:1)? Of course Psalm 82:6 does not mean that agents of God are divine, but the presence of the term "god" alone is sufficient for Jesus to make his point following rabbinic theological logic.

We have seen how in the various feasts of Sabbath, Passover, and Tabernacles messianic replacement was used to unveil Jesus's identity. Here only the most careful reader will catch the allusion. We have seen how the Feast of Dedication recalled the cleansing and rededication of the temple. Here one of the chief terms from 1 Maccabees 4 is used of Christ. In John 10:36 Jesus has been "set apart" (NIV) or "consecrated" (RSV) and sent into the world.

This term (Greek *hagiazō,* "to make holy") recalls the Maccabean story (1 Maccabees 4:48). Jesus is the truly consecrated temple of God (cf. John 1:14; 2:21).

The final appeal of Jesus, in 10:37–39, again rests on his works and their evidential value. The Jews of the Book of Signs have obtained the signs sufficient for belief. And these will point the way toward the conclusion of the unity of the Father and the Son (10:38; cf. 10:30). But just as the former revelation of this brought hostility (10:30–31), so now Jesus's opponents attempt to arrest him (10:39).

10:40–42. Jesus now withdraws before the crucial events of his final week. He knows the region of the Jordan and Perea well (Matt. 19:1; Mark 10:1), and this is his refuge. Soon he will climb the ascent from Jericho to Bethany and inaugurate the week of the passion.

In the literary format of John these verses indicate a major transition. Jesus has withdrawn from public purview. The public signs are over. The Book of Signs, which began with John the Baptist (1:18), now anticipates its completion with a second reference to him (10:40). The Fourth Evangelist even reminds us of the subject of these ten chapters. Although John worked no signs, Jesus did; and those who witnessed these and perceived their truth found faith (10:42).

More signs await those disciples of the inner circle (chaps. 11–12), and we as readers are privileged to view these. The final plea for belief, however, will come to us at 12:44–50, when we with the rest of the disciples will have viewed sufficient signs, sufficient evidences from which to reach a verdict about Jesus.

D. Foreshadowing death and resurrection (11:1–12:50). It has often been argued that 10:40–42 was at one time the conclusion of Jesus's public ministry in John's Gospel and that at some later stage the Gospel was edited to include chapters 11 and 12. For instance, the sequence of events here (movement to Perea, Bethany, Ephraim, and back) is difficult to reconcile with the Synoptics, as is the motive for

Jesus's arrest (11:45–53; 12:9–11). Further, the term "the Jews" now loses its harsh polemical tone so common to John (cf. 9:22 with 11:19, 45). But despite this, traditional Johannine elements abound: the use of *egō eimi* ("I am") in 11:25 and the literary device of misunderstanding (11:11–12, 23–24, 50–51). Nevertheless, the Synoptics know little of Mary and Martha—much less Lazarus—and this narrative is a unique (but not inauthentic) Johannine story.

What is the purpose of chapters 11–12? While the Synoptics at this point expand on Jesus's teachings in Jerusalem during his final spring visit (cf. Matthew 21–26), John has chosen a miracle story that epitomizes Christ's mission and fate. With superb dramatic form, the Lazarus story (11:1–44) sums up Jesus's career. It is the ultimate sign. Jesus, the source of life (10:28; 11:25), now gives life to one man. But even this ultimate revelation is condemned, leaving Jesus judged as worthy of death (11:50).

Moreover, woven into this story are hints of Jesus's own passion. He too will die and come forth. The Lord of life will lay down his life and return from the grave like Lazarus. Later in the same town of Bethany, Mary will anoint Jesus—figuratively preparing him for burial (12:3–8).

Therefore, chapters 11 and 12 provide a transition, preparing us for John's second book, the Book of Glory (chaps. 13–20). Jesus's signs are finished, and he is advancing toward "the hour"—the hour of death, resurrection, and glory.

11:1–57. The village of Bethany, two miles east of Jerusalem, was the regular residence of Jesus while he was in Judea (cf. Mark 11:11; 14:3). While Lazarus is not known in the Synoptics (but see Luke 16:20), Luke does refer to the sisters Mary and Martha (Luke 10:38–42). The profile of the two sisters in Luke (the compulsive Martha; the contemplative Mary) is paralleled in John (11:20; 12:2–3).

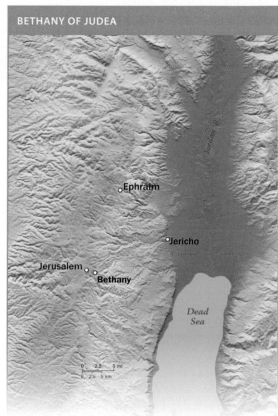

BETHANY OF JUDEA

While Jesus was in the Jordan Valley (John 10:40), his friends must have known his whereabouts, since Mary and Martha are able to contact him. Jesus's response to Lazarus's illness (11:1–44) is similar to his explanation of the blind man's infirmity in 9:3. Sometimes crises serve divine purposes so that God may be glorified when they are resolved.

That Jesus does not respond at once (11:6) in no way disparages his love for the family (11:5). There are problems with a return to the mountains of Judea, which the apostolic party fully realizes (11:8, 16). Threats of death have been known for over a year (5:18; 7:25), and some have even tried to kill Jesus already (8:59; 10:31). But the Lord feels the pressing need to depart. His time is short, and just as with the hours of daylight for the traveler, each hour must be used to maximum benefit (9:10; cf. 12:35–36). The spiritual light now present is even more valuable than this. Jesus is the light of the world (8:12), and while he is present and able to dispel darkness, his work must progress. The task at hand is the revival of Lazarus, who is now dead (11:11–14; note the familiar use of misunderstanding). A paradoxical exchange is thus at hand: Jesus chooses to risk death in Judea in order to save a man from death. He indeed is the good shepherd who is willing to lay down his own life for the life of his sheep (10:15).

It is a tribute to John's interest in historical detail that he mentions how long Lazarus has been dead (11:17, 39) and the exact location of Bethany. Because the ancient world did not have precise methods to monitor death or coma, most rabbis held theories about the impossibility of resuscitation after three or four days of death. Our story is making one point: Lazarus was fully dead by anyone's standards, and the miracle (11:43–44) involves resurrection, not resuscitation.

When Jesus enters the hill country, it is clear that the customary mourning is under way (11:18–19, 31). (Mark 5:38–39 provides an interesting parallel.) Although Martha is the first to greet Jesus on the road (11:20–27), Mary will come later (11:31–32), and John no doubt wants us to compare them. Both women express the same words: "Lord, if you had been here, my brother would not have died" (11:21, 32). Jesus is the Lord of life (11:25), but the women despair. Their hope is in a healing miracle because resurrection is so far beyond their comprehension (11:26–27). While Mary is overcome (11:35; cf. 12:3; Luke 10:39), Martha pursues a conversation. "Even now" in 11:22 implies faith—even now in death Jesus may be able to do something. But is the only comfort in the last days, the future resurrection? Ironic misunderstanding (11:23–24) gives the conversation its classic Johannine form and allows Jesus to elevate his meaning. The resurrection life is a present experience! Eternal life begins now for the person who trusts in Christ (11:25–26). The horror of death is gone (11:26a; cf. 3:16–21).

When pressed, Martha cannot affirm Jesus's powers to this extent (11:26b); but still she holds on to what she does know (11:27). Jesus is her Lord; knowledge of his powerful abilities will come with time.

One unique feature of this story is the way in which Jesus expresses his emotions over Lazarus's death (11:33, 35, 38; cf. Luke 19:41). He does not approach suffering and death dispassionately. He feels the pain. He knows tragedy and has feelings. In this case these emerge out of his love for his friend Lazarus (11:36).

Lazarus was buried in a typical first-century stone tomb (cf. Jesus's tomb, 20:1; Mark 15:46). Since these were designed for multiple burials, there would be no difficulty reopening it (11:39) if sufficient help was available. Again we are given a second confirmation that Lazarus is dead (11:39), this time in graphic terms. But this does not deter Jesus. As his feeding miracle demonstrated that he was the bread of life (6:35), and as his healing of the blind illustrated that he was the light of the world (8:12), so now he will prove that he is the resurrection and the life (11:25).

All that Jesus does has one aim: to promote the glory of God (11:40). His audible prayer heard here (11:41–42; cf. 12:27) serves this purpose. Jesus is no miracle worker with simple powerful feats at his disposal. His deeds are signs that promote belief. They reveal something of God's presence at work, and they illumine Christ as God's divine agent.

Burial cloths further confirm Lazarus's death (11:44) and provide another parallel to Jesus's burial (19:39–40; 20:5–7). The unusual reference to a face cloth appears only here and in 20:7. One interesting difference, however, is that Lazarus requires aid with his bindings—Jesus's grave clothes are noticeably left behind.

As with so many other signs of Jesus (e.g., 7:40–44), the onlookers immediately divide into two camps. Here at Bethany, too, the events compel some to believe, while others file a report with members of the Sanhedrin, who determine Jesus's fate (11:45–57). The deliberations of the Sanhedrin, now called to a formal meeting about Jesus, typify the drift of the Jewish leadership's reaction to Christ since chapter 9: Jesus's signs seem compelling, but the practical implications of this are more than they can bear. What if the masses start to follow him? Would it not upset the fragile political equilibrium with Rome (11:48)? Would Caesar tolerate a messiah? The Sanhedrin must choose either to follow the logic of Jesus's truth, regardless of the cost, or to retreat into the safety of their own nicely controlled religion.

Caiaphas chooses the latter (11:49–50)— that Jesus must die in order to save Israel's precarious freedoms—but John takes this as a prophecy that even the high priest himself misunderstands (11:51–53). Of course Jesus must die for the sake of the Jewish nation (and for that matter the Gentiles, 11:52) but in a sense the Sanhedrin will never understand.

Because of the high council's resolve to kill Jesus (11:53) he goes into seclusion in much the same way that he did after the Feast of Tabernacles (cf. 10:39–42). Ephraim's location (11:54) has proved perplexing. It may be the Old Testament village of Ophrah (Josh. 18:23) northeast of Bethel (modern et-Taiyibeh).

With the pilgrimage Feast of Passover at hand, everyone is expecting Jesus to appear. Questions are alive in both the crowds and the Sanhedrin (11:56–57), and for good reason. The last pilgrimage feast (Tabernacles, John 7–9) witnessed numerous conflicts with Jesus. The city is astir with anticipation (7:10–13, 25–26, 32–33). Therefore, precautions are taken: if Jesus appears in the city from his wilderness retreat, his whereabouts should be reported (cf. 11:46).

12:1–50. Both John (12:1–8) and the Synoptics (Matt. 26:6–13; Mark 14:3–9) record the anointing at Bethany, and since the settings are virtually identical, the narratives pose a textbook case in the difficulties of Synoptic/Johannine interdependence. Added to this is a Lukan story (Luke 7:36–38) with interesting parallels to both Mark and John.

Jesus's return from the wilderness (11:54) is prompted by another Feast of Passover, one year since the last festival, celebrated in Galilee (6:4). Jesus returns to Bethany, where Lazarus, Mary, and Martha live, and from here he will make his final visit to Jerusalem (12:12). If the Markan account is a true parallel, then this residence is also the home of Simon the leper (Mark 14:3).

Again Mary and Martha take up their usual roles (cf. Luke 10:38–42; John 11:20): Martha busies herself with the duties of a hostess, and Mary makes an unusual gesture of devotion to Jesus. Imported from North India, this perfume was precious indeed, and the anointing was extravagant. A denarius was one day's wage, and this was worth three hundred (Mark says more than three hundred denarii). When Mary lets down her hair (cf. Luke 7:38), she strictly breaks Jewish convention—women never did this in public. But this is simply more extravagance, justified because no devotion to Jesus can be excessive. Jesus's defense of her in Mark 14:6 makes this abundantly clear. Judas is the antithesis of all this. Money is his concern since he is the treasurer (John 12:6; 13:29). But his flaw is twofold: care of the poor cannot come before undiluted worship of Christ (12:8); and when this care springs from an impure heart (12:6), its spiritual value evaporates.

Jesus's final visit to Jerusalem is recorded in 12:9–50. Before long the presence of Jesus in Bethany becomes public knowledge, and crowds arrive to see both him and Lazarus. Although the Sanhedrin desired to seize him when he appeared (11:57), the crowds may have interfered with a clean arrest (cf. Luke 19:47–48). The Johannine account introduces a new element. Lazarus's death is planned too (12:10–11) because he has become a celebrity (12:17–19). It is this fame spreading from Bethany that greets Jesus as he rides into the city from the eastern hills (12:9–19). The triumphal entry into Jerusalem is narrated in each of the Gospels (Matt. 21:1–11; Mark 11:1–10; Luke 19:28–40), and John's differences stem chiefly from his abbreviated version. The crowd celebrates Jesus's arrival with festive displays and shouts. The Old Testament explanation in each account comes from Zechariah 9:9, although John amends Zechariah's "Rejoice greatly" to "Do not be afraid" (John 12:15). This may be a unique allusion to Zephaniah 3:14–17, in which the prophet dispels the fears of Israel, affirming that "the LORD is in your midst" (Zeph. 3:15 ESV). For John, Jesus's arrival is a fitting fulfillment.

The celebrations of the Jews are now echoed by an entirely unexpected interest among some Greeks in Jerusalem (12:20–36). This is unexpected because Greeks are Gentiles (though these may be proselytes) and unaccepted by Jews. John's irony cannot be missed: when Jesus's efforts to unveil himself to Israel have been exhausted, Greeks arrive, eager to see Jesus. Jewish reluctance is exceeded by Greek zeal. Mark's Gospel follows a similar structure. In Mark the watershed is in 8:27–30, and from then on Jesus devotes himself exclusively to his disciples. But prior to this revelation at Caesarea Philippi, Jesus finds an unprecedented response among the Greeks (Mark 7:24–30; 7:31–37; 8:1–10). Once Judaism fails to embrace the signs of Christ, Gentiles are given the opportunity (Matt. 21:41–44; Luke 2:32; 4:25–27; Rom. 1:16).

Jesus's response to Andrew and Philip's report is extremely important. The "hour" that has been put off for years (cf. John 2:4; 7:6; 8:20) has now arrived (12:23). Jesus recognizes the culmination of all that he has been attempting in Judaism. The cross and death are all that remain (12:24). But in John it is not a death of disgrace and shame; Jesus will be glorified, and this will mysteriously result in great things. The same is true of his followers (12:23–26). Self-effacement and self-denial are the only pathways to finding the company of Jesus or the honor of the Father (cf. Matt. 10:37–39; Mark 8:34–38). The humanity of Jesus can be seen in how even he wrestles with this truth (John 12:27; cf. Mark 14:36). Strength is found

here and later in Gethsemane, when he submits himself to God's higher purposes. The glory of God is manifest when his servants persevere in temptations such as this and in ultimate trials (12:28–29). The cross will be the ultimate test for Jesus, and here in the midst of God's glory Jesus himself will be glorified (17:1–5).

The crowds receive the confirming voice from heaven just as they received the signs (12:28–30). Throughout his Gospel, John's view of revelation has taken shape: a sign from God is revelatory only when it is greeted by faith. The Book of Signs will only speak to those whom the Father is already giving into the Shepherd's hand (6:44–45; 10:27–29).

It is now time for Jesus to define his hour of death and glory. It too will be a sign, but how will it be received? Can the average person accept that the world's judgment will be inaugurated when one man is crucified (12:31–32)? This crowd cannot (12:34)—but neither could the disciples at this point (Mark 8:31–33; 9:30–32; 10:32–34). But fortunately the crowd stays with Jesus; they keep inquiring. The last question posed to Jesus is in John 12:34: "Who is this 'Son of Man'?" In the previous chapter Martha could not comprehend all that Jesus revealed (11:21–27), but still she held on to the light she possessed. When confusion and uncertainty are at hand, John would not have us walk away in disbelief. Jesus now affirms the same (12:35–36). Continue to engage God! Embrace the light! Walk in it!

Jesus's disclosure of himself is finished (12:36). He now hides himself from public view because his signs are completed, and they are left for us to interpret.

John the evangelist, who has been the narrator of the story all along (2:22–25; 3:16–21, 31–36; 7:5), now sums up the meaning of Jesus's public ministry (12:37–43). John 12:37 makes plain what all of early Christianity was forced to acknowledge: Jesus's many signs fell on disbelief. John joins the other evangelists in drawing texts from Isaiah that must have been commonly used in the early church (Isa.

6:10; 53:1; cf. Matt. 13:14–17). Isaiah too found disbelief in Israel and attributed it to God's sovereignty over revelation. John, however, has woven this theme into the entirety of the Book of Signs. Hence the unbelievers are unable to believe (John 12:39); God affects their perception (12:40). John, however, does not probe the mystery of the interplay between human responsibility and divine sovereignty. In 12:41 Isaiah's words are interpreted as prophecies directed to Jesus because the glory Isaiah viewed (6:1–5) is Jesus's glory too. This closing frame in the Book of Signs repeats what we read in the prologue: Christ is the glory of the Father unveiled for human eyes (1:14).

But has no one believed the signs? Of course there are the disciples, but has not God opened the eyes and ears of some Jewish leaders? John has not neglected these: there are some who believe, but they fear persecution (12:42). Nicodemus typifies these men (3:1–21; 19:39), for when he did speak up (7:50–52), he was severely rebuked. Similarly the parents of the blind man feared expulsion from the synagogue (9:22). Nevertheless, the praise of God awaits those people of prominence and esteem who ignore the cost and make their faith visible (12:43).

The Book of Signs concludes with a harrowing cry from Jesus imploring Jews to believe (12:44–50). It reiterates much of what has gone before. Jesus is light; he reveals God and disperses the darkness (1:9; 8:12). Above all, he has not spoken on his own authority; he is God's agent in the world. Belief in Christ is belief in God. To see Christ is to see the Father (12:44–45; 14:9). Even the words of Jesus have not been his own but stem from what the Father has directed (12:49–50; 17:6–8). This truth, however, has serious implications inasmuch as there will be a divine accounting for all Jesus has said.

The signs are complete, and the Book of Signs may now close. Evidence for Jesus's case is public. The Sanhedrin has made its decision about him (11:53), but the crowd still asks, "Who is this 'Son of Man'?" For them and for us the Book of Signs is open for examination. From John's point of view, these signs will compel us to believe.

3. The Book of Glory (13:1–20:31)

With chapter 13 we move to another major literary division in the Fourth Gospel, which contrasts directly with the Book of Signs (1:19–12:50). The contrast is chiefly one of perspective. In the Book of Signs, for instance, Jesus addresses a public audience. His teaching provokes a crisis of faith, as some believe while others reject him. Here, though, the audience is narrowed to the circle of disciples who follow him to the cross. We noted how in chapter 12 Jesus "hid himself" (12:36), indicating an end to his public self-disclosure. Now his focus is on "his own" (13:1; 17:6–19). We could also point out that, while the interest of the first half of John is on the signs of Jesus, now the Gospel will concentrate on the coming of "the hour" (12:23, 27; 13:1)—that is, the hour of his glorification (13:31–32). It is not an hour of tragedy in this Gospel but one of victory that involves Christ's passion, crucifixion, resurrection, and ascension. Just as the many signs of Jesus were accompanied by discourses (cf. John 6, the feeding miracle and the bread-of-life discourse), so too this last sign of death and resurrection will be interpreted by lengthy teaching in the upper room (chaps. 13–16).

The Gospel imitates the arc of a pendulum: it begins at a high point, descends, and elevates again. The Johannine prologue reflects this too, as the Word is in God's presence (1:1), experiences rejection (1:10–11), and then returns to places of glory (1:18). With the Book of Glory we are in the upward swing of the arc, the descent having been chronicled by those chapters that describe Jesus's efforts to reveal himself (chaps. 1–12). The lowest point is reached when Judaism confirms Jesus's death (11:50), and John is forced to explain Jewish disbelief (12:37–50). The highest point comes with the return from the grave of the glorified Lord. Here, echoing the prologue again, the disciples are the recipients of life-giving power (1:12–13; 20:22).

A. The Passover meal (13:1–30). The Synoptics record that, during his last week of ministry, during the Passover festival, Jesus enjoys a final meal with his disciples (Mark 14:12–25). Each Synoptic writer terms this "the Passover" (Matt. 26:17; Mark 14:12; Luke 22:7–9), which is ordinarily served after dusk on the Jewish date of 15 Nisan (in March-April). John mentions such a meal (13:2, 26) and indicates through mention of the betrayal of Judas (13:21–30) that this meal is the Passover from the Synoptics (cf. Mark 14:17–21).

However, John's date seems not to be 15 Nisan (Passover), for later he will say that Jesus is crucified on 14 Nisan, when the temple lambs are being slaughtered (19:14). Hence John's story shows the meal to be on the day of Preparation, one night prior to the Passover feast.

Scholars have solved this riddle in a variety of ways. The easiest and most popular solution is simply to say that one Gospel tradition or the other is incorrect. But critics can find fault with each account: Would the Sanhedrin hold a trial on a feast day, as the Synoptics contend? Or has John moved the cross to 14 Nisan to develop a paschal emphasis for Jesus's death (cf. 19:32–37)? Others have pointed to competing calendars in the first century. Still others think that Jesus was simply offering an irregular Passover meal one day early.

But there is another solution that deserves consideration. It is clear that John understands this meal to be the same one as in the Synoptics. The reference to Judas Iscariot (13:21–30; cf. Matt. 26:20–25) solidly links the two. John also implies that this is indeed a Passover meal:

pilgrims must eat it in Jerusalem as the law requires (John 11:55; 12:12, 18, 20), it is a ceremonial meal with formal "reclining" (required at Passover), Jesus does not leave the precincts of Jerusalem after the meal (as the law required) but goes to Gethsemane, Passover alms are distributed (13:29), and the disciples are in a state of Levitical purity (13:10) required at Passover. Therefore John's meal clearly suggests a Passover meal. But what do we do with the passages that imply Jesus is crucified on the "day of Preparation"?

The argument that, according to John, Jesus was crucified on 14 Nisan (the day of Preparation) is anchored to five texts that imply the Passover has not yet happened when Jesus is crucified.

1. "Now before the feast of the Passover, when Jesus knew that his hour had come to depart out of this world to the Father . . . during supper . . ." (13:1–2 RSV).

This mosaic (Sepphoris, third–fourth century AD) depicts a triclinium, a Roman dining room featuring couches or benches that were placed in a "U" around a central table. Jesus and his disciples would have dined in a similar setting, reclining around the table (as the beloved disciple is described as doing in John 13:23).

2. "Some thought that, because Judas had the money box, Jesus was telling him, 'Buy what we need for the feast' . . ." (13:29 RSV).
3. "They themselves did not enter the praetorium, so that they might not be defiled, but might eat the passover" (18:28 RSV).
4. "Now it was the day of Preparation of the Passover; it was about the sixth hour" (19:14 RSV).
5. "Since it was the day of Preparation, in order to prevent the bodies from remaining on the cross on the sabbath (for that sabbath was a high day), the Jews asked Pilate that their legs might be broken, and that they might be taken away" (19:31 RSV).

We shall look at these verses in turn later in the commentary, but for now note that they do not necessarily imply that the meal in John 13 was *before* Passover. In 13:1 "before the Passover Festival" probably describes when Jesus knew his hour had come, and the meal mentioned in 13:2 refers to the Passover itself, described in 13:1. John 13:29 records that Judas must make a purchase for the feast, but this may well be something they need at the moment—or something needed for the next day. In 18:28 the authorities fear defilement from Gentile contact, but such ritual uncleanness would expire at sundown (if it were 14 Nisan). These men likely refer to eating an afternoon meal (the Jewish *hagigah*) on the day *following* the night of Passover (15 Nisan). Finally, the "day of Preparation" referred to in 19:14 and 19:31 does not necessarily refer to preparation for the Passover. It may refer to *preparation for the Sabbath*. In fact, 19:31 makes the connection with the Sabbath explicit. Mark 15:42 refers to Jesus's day of crucifixion (Friday) in this manner as well ("And when evening had come, since it was the day of Preparation, that is, the day before the Sabbath . . ." [RSV]). Furthermore, we have no extrabiblical evidence in Aramaic or Greek describing 14 Nisan as "the day of Preparation

of the Passover." Many scholars think the phrase may simply be an idiom meaning, "Friday of Passover week" (or, "the day of Sabbath preparation within the week of Passover").

If this line of reasoning is correct, John's chronology fits the Synoptic outline perfectly. Thursday evening begins the date 15 Nisan, when Jesus hosts a Passover meal; on Friday afternoon Jesus is crucified on the day of (Sabbath) Preparation during Passover. This explanation may appear complex, but it is important. In critical discussions of the historical reliability of John's Gospel, the problem of chronology and the Johannine passion narrative always comes up for examination.

The Synoptic emphasis is found in the words of institution during the meal (Luke 22:14–23). While it comes as a surprise that the Fourth Gospel does not record this (but see 6:52–58), we find that another event, the foot washing, is prominent (13:1–20). The theme of servanthood so central to the narrative, however, does appear in Luke in the upper room: Jesus rebukes the disciples' interest in greatness and authority as he instructs them about servanthood (Luke 22:24–27).

Foot washing was a common custom due to the wearing of sandals and the dry, dusty Palestinian roads. A good host would provide a servant who would work in this capacity, but if none were there he certainly would not take up the chore himself, as Jesus does (13:4–5). That which enables Jesus to serve like this may be described in 13:3. Jesus has perfect self-esteem: he knows of God's love expressed in his origin and destiny and therefore can relinquish human status to become a servant.

A variety of themes runs through the narrative. First, foot washing speaks of Jesus's death. Jesus's dialogue with Peter (13:6–11) explains that an understanding of this will come about only after Jesus's death (13:7; cf. 2:22; 12:16). Since this washing is the criterion for fellowship with Christ, Peter dare not object (13:7–8). Cleansing (through the cross; baptism?) speaks of cleansing from sin; hence it is not just any washing that is important: Jesus must cleanse his followers (13:8). As in other dialogues, misunderstanding follows. Peter's zeal for Christ leads him astray: if he supplements Jesus's provision, will he have more of Christ (13:9)? Verse 10 gives Jesus's reply, but it is difficult to interpret. The reference to bathing (which is new) is often seen as an allusion to baptism (see Greek *louō*; Acts 22:16; 1 Cor. 6:11; Eph. 5:26; Titus 3:5; Heb. 10:22), in which case Jesus may mean that once a disciple is cleansed of sin through conversion/baptism, only partial washing (confession) is needed for postbaptismal sin (cf. 1 John 1:8–2:6). This is the patristic interpretation, which may be right but is now complicated by some important ancient manuscripts omitting the key phrase "except for his feet" (13:10 ESV).

Second, impurities speak of Judas (13:10–11). The metaphor of cleansing and impurity shifts from Peter to the larger group of apostles at the end of 13:10 (the final "you" in 13:10 is plural). Not only is Peter partially clean, but so are the disciples (13:11) since Judas Iscariot is among them. This will be developed at length in verses 21–30.

Third, foot washing is a symbol of mutual service (13:12–17). In this sense Jesus has modeled behavior he wishes his followers to emulate. If service on this order is possible for him, then it cannot be beneath us (13:16). Here disciples are pressed beyond a mere knowledge of Jesus's will. Blessing follows faith expressed in deeds (13:17; cf. Matt. 7:24–27). But as in John 13:10–11, when Jesus's thoughts are interrupted by the imminent betrayal of Judas, so here service on this order is not possible for anyone who is not called (cf. 6:44; 10:29). This applies to Judas in particular (13:18–19).

While the Fourth Gospel does not explore the motives behind Judas's betrayal (13:21–30) nor the overtures of the Sanhedrin (see Matt. 26:14–16, 20–25; 27:3–10; Luke 22:3–6), it does provide us with the poignant account of the beloved disciple's inquiry. This is the first real introduction to the story of this disciple. When Jesus expresses his dismay concerning the betrayal (13:21), the disciples examine themselves (Luke 22:23), and Peter prompts the beloved disciple (John) to ask Jesus. The disciples are reclining on a couch around a low table. John is to the right of Jesus and hence in the best position for a confidential question (13:25–26).

Two times in this account (13:2, 27) we learn that Satan is the true power behind Judas. It is interesting that Satan's appearances are so few in this Gospel. It contains no exorcisms, and Satan's only role involves the efforts of those who are Jesus's fiercest opponents (the Jews, 8:44; Judas Iscariot, 6:70; 13:2, 27). Satan's chief work is in undermining Jesus's testimony and his glorification. No suspicions are raised when Judas departs (13:27) because he was the custodian of the group's funds (cf. 12:6) and he had tasks to do: acquire provisions for the festival and give special offerings to the poor on Passover night.

Verse 30 is crucial because it marks the time after which Jesus may instruct his chosen disciples privately and fully. Judas has departed, and the final sentence reads, "It was night." This motif has symbolic as well as literal value. The hour of death, pushed forward by Judas, is when the light of the world is extinguished (9:4). Darkness is the opposite of light and typifies those outside of Jesus's fold (3:19), who stumble without him (11:10). At the Gethsemane arrest, Luke records Jesus speaking of this period as a time "when darkness reigns" (Luke 22:53).

B. The Farewell Discourse (13:31–17:26). In the upper room, Jesus now turns to his faithful followers and instructs them at some length. The discourse runs from 13:31 to 16:33 without narrative interruption and then concludes with Jesus's prayer (17:1–26), which precedes the arrest (18:1–11). The literary form of this section is called the "farewell speech" and was well known in Judaism at this time. For example, one can turn to the *Testaments of the Twelve Patriarchs*, an intertestamental extracanonical work that records the final words of Israel's patriarchs. The *Assumption of Moses* (first century

AD) does the same for Israel's prophet-leader in Transjordan. Each Jewish farewell speech shows similar elements that are found in Jesus's farewell: (1) There is a plea for obedience to the law. Thus in 13:34 and 15:12 Jesus speaks of his new commandment of love. (2) Often writings are left behind (cf. *Assumption of Moses* 10:11; *4 Ezra*), and in the Fourth Gospel itself we have the chronicle of Jesus's life now deposited for his followers. (3) Spirit-filled representatives carry on the work, just as Joshua obtained the Spirit that rested on Moses (*Assumption of Moses* 10–12). Here Jesus promises the Spirit of truth (14:17), who anoints the disciples and particularly the beloved disciple for his work. (4) Finally, the anxiety of those left behind is relieved. So Jesus speaks of comfort, terming the Spirit "the Comforter" or "Paraclete" (Greek *paraklētos*; NIV "Advocate"; 14:16, 26; 15:26).

It is evident then that Jesus recognizes the importance of this evening and is making his formal farewell. He addresses his disciples' worries in light of his imminent death and departure. But above all he holds out a promise and hope centered on the coming of the Holy Spirit—one who will guide, teach, encourage, empower, and mediate to the believer the comforting presence of Christ.

13:31–14:31. The specific subject of the Farewell Discourse is Jesus's departure to the Father (13:31–14:3), and here we see John's technical language being employed. "Glorification" has been used to describe both Jesus's ministry (8:54; 11:4; 12:28) and his death (7:39; 12:16, 23). Now this latter specialized usage comes in full (13:31, 32; 17:1); the cross is another time in which Jesus is glorified, and in turn so is the Father (21:19). But glorification as a process is complex: it is not just Christ being lifted up on the cross; rather, it is the entire passion, from betrayal to empty tomb—a process that inaugurates his return to the Father. Hence 13:31 states that Jesus's glorification has *already* begun. The onset of "the hour" is behind him; his departure is under way (13:33).

In John 14:2, Jesus says, "My Father's house has many rooms." During the time of Jesus, extended families often lived in large compounds with many rooms that surrounded a common courtyard. Shown here are the remains of such a compound in Capernaum.

As Jesus mystified his Jewish audience at the Feast of Tabernacles with this teaching (7:33–36), so now Peter is perplexed (13:36–38). He presses the question about departure, and unlike the Jewish leaders in chapter 7, he knows that it may involve death (13:37–38; cf. 8:21–22). Nevertheless, Jesus answers now in full, and chapter 14 will seek to answer the question of Christ's departure, provision, and return. But Jesus is not simply intent on explaining this. In the meanwhile, the character of the surviving community (the church) is important (see 13:34–35). The command of love expressed in unity and fidelity to Jesus will be taken up in chapters 15 and 17.

In early Christianity, the problem of Jesus's departure was resolved by looking forward to his return, or second coming (Greek *parousia*). For some this was the only comfort. However, the discourse in chapter 14 is a carefully designed reassessment of this. It begins with a description of the traditional futurist hope (14:1–3). Jesus is preparing rooms in heaven (14:2) and someday will return to transport his followers there (14:3). The discourse then introduces three questioners (Thomas, 14:5; Philip, 14:8; Judas, 14:22) who ask leading questions so that Jesus's answer may be sharpened. In the end this futurist eschatology is refashioned into what is called realized eschatology. That is, hope and comfort are not in the future but can be realized now. Thus the coming of Jesus (14:3) shifts to the coming of the Spirit (14:23, 28). The "rooms" (Greek *monē*, 14:2) of heavenly dwelling become rooms (*monē*, 14:23; NIV "home") of divine indwelling.

The sequence of exchanges has an interesting thematic development. There are four interlocking steps:

1. *Jesus:* I am *going* and coming (Greek *erchomai*, 14:1–4). *Thomas:* We do not know the *way* you are *going* (14:5).
2. *Jesus:* I am the *way* to the *Father* (14:6). *Philip:* Show us the *Father* (14:8).
3. *Jesus:* You have seen the *Father* already. I will *manifest* him (and myself) to you

(14:9–11). *Judas:* How will you *manifest* yourself (14:22)?
4. *Jesus:* In the *Spirit*—by coming (Greek *erchomai*, 14:23) to you.

For Thomas (14:5–7) the chief concern is whether they will accompany Jesus. Note that it is not a moral or ethical way; it is salvific. The way to be found is the way of salvation leading to the Father (14:4–17). Two surprises come about: Jesus is both the means (14:6) and the end (14:7). There is no suspended hope, because the object of their faith (the Father) is now present in Christ. In him the Father is already present (cf. 8:19; 10:30, 38).

Philip now inquires about this Father-Son relationship (14:8–11), and Jesus makes himself explicit. It is the Father himself who is present in Jesus (hence John's full divinity of Jesus), and this validates both his words and works. Whenever the Father is present, he manifests himself. This pertains to Jesus's followers as well (14:12–14), who will be enabled to exhibit similar works. Running through these verses is a theological parallel between the Father's relation to the Son and the Spirit's relation to the disciple. As the Father abides in (Greek *menō*, 14:10) Jesus, so too the Spirit abides in (*menō*, 14:17) the believer. Thus the confidence of Christ can be ours: as the Father was committed to his Son, so Jesus through his Spirit will stand with us in every need (14:13–14). The point in these verses is not that every prayerful request will be granted but that the character of Christ's relationship with God at this level may be ours. But here we must recall Jesus's consistent submission to his Father's will (5:19, 30; 6:38; 7:16–17; 8:28–29) and his desire simply to glorify (12:28; 17:4) and please God (8:29).

The provision of Jesus that will bring about this relationship is declared to be the indwelling Spirit (14:15–17), who now bears two new names: the Paraclete (NIV "advocate," 14:16) and the Spirit of truth. Paraclete (Greek *paraklētos*) is unique to John (elsewhere, 14:26; 15:26; 16:7; 1 John 2:1) and expresses the Spirit's strengthening, equipping role. A *paraklētos* was a judicial advocate (cf. Matt. 10:16–20), and here Jesus says that Christians alone can enjoy his aid (John 14:17). As Jesus was alien to the world (1:10), so too his provision of the Spirit will be unknown and unrecognized. As Jesus was on trial in the world (cf. the Book of Signs), now his followers have a judicial aid to support them (15:18–27).

The continuation of Jesus's reassuring words now picks up the language of the second coming (14:18–24). Futurist eschatology imperceptibly blends with realized eschatology. In Judaism, disciples who had lost their rabbi were often called orphans (14:18), but this will not be the case for Jesus's followers—he will come back visibly (14:18–19). But what sort of return is this if the world cannot take part? Will there be no secular verification? Remarkably the description of the coming of the Paraclete in verses 15–17 parallels the coming of Jesus in verses 18–21. Note the stress on love and obedience (14:15, 21), the world (14:17, 19), personal recognition (14:17, 19), and indwelling (14:17, 20).

Judas (not Iscariot, 14:22) asks the question that brings the discourse to its climax. If the manifestation of Jesus mentioned in verse 21 is private, then it needs some explaining. Finally, Jesus says that the hope he has been describing here is not apocalyptic at all. Jesus's return can also be found in the inner experience of the Son and the Father within the believer. The room of dwelling (see 14:2) is now redefined and found in the disciple's heart (14:23).

Jesus provides further reassurance by predicting beforehand the impending crisis (14:29–31) and affirming that he will indeed return (14:28). But as we have seen, this is a redefined return. The chief attribute he desires for them is peace (similarly, Paul in Rom. 5:1; Eph. 2:17), and this will come about through the Spirit (John 14:26; cf. Eph. 2:18). On Easter Day, when Jesus appears to the disciples, "peace" is his first word (20:19, 21), and this is followed by their anointing with the Spirit (20:22).

This second Paraclete promise (14:25–31) contributes to our understanding of the roles of the Spirit (cf. 14:16). Here the emphasis is on revelation. The Paraclete will be a teacher (1 John 2:22–27), bringing back to memory the sayings of Jesus (John 14:26). Thus, here is practical equipment for the church! But we also have here a confirmation of the production of the Gospel record itself. The Spirit will be a preserving, conservative force in revelation. He will not primarily be creative but will reiterate Jesus's words. Once again we see the Spirit functioning like Jesus: as Jesus was dependent on the Father (14:10), so the Spirit depends on Christ.

15:1–16:4a. The vine metaphor (15:1–17) builds on the emphases of Jesus in chapter 14. There we saw that the answer to the disciples' anxiety concerning Jesus's death and departure is found in the Spirit. Christ in Spirit will indwell the believer. Jesus's new metaphor in chapter 15 affirms this again. The verb for indwelling (Greek *menō*; 14:17) appears numerous times (NIV "remain," 15:4–7, 9–10), but now it is viewed in terms of its results. Spiritual experiences must lead to fruit-bearing in the form of new obedience and love.

The vine/vineyard metaphor is used frequently in the Old Testament. Israel is often depicted as a vine transplanted from Egypt (Ps. 80:8–11) and brought to fertile soil (Ezek. 17:1–6). Enemies may trample the vineyard (Jer. 12:10–11), but God tends it carefully and looks for fruit (Isa. 5:1–7). The vineyard may be the preeminent biblical symbol of the locus of God's activity, his nurture, and his expectations (cf. Matt. 21:33–41).

Jesus's use of the metaphor is surprising. Rather than claiming to be the vinedresser and assuming the prerogatives of God (e.g., John 5), Jesus is the vine (which formerly stood for Israel). Union with Jesus means participation in the new Israel, the people of God (cf. Paul, who uses a similar metaphor in Rom. 11:17–24). This theological notion has appeared elsewhere, in John 10:7 ("I am the gate for the sheep") and in 14:6 ("I am the way"). Attachment to Jesus is the only means of access to God's household. In other words, Jesus marks the beginning of the new Israel.

Two themes dominate the section. First, the believer must have an inner apprehension of Christ (in Spirit; 14:23). Abiding or remaining (Greek *menō*) in Christ is a prerequisite Christian experience. Initially, Christ dwells in us (15:4–5), but this is no tribute to our merit; for our acceptability as vessels—our cleanliness— is his accomplishment (15:3). Conversely, we abide in Christ (15:4–5), and this is the origin of fruitful living. Just as branches are barren when they are not attached to the vine (15:4), the possibility of separation from the Vine is a dreadful prospect (15:2, 6).

Second, there should be outer evidence of Christ's indwelling. Note how carefully the passage balances our mutual participation with God. Our effort is necessary. For instance, on the one hand, we must devote ourselves to Jesus's words and be obedient (15:7, 10). But on the other hand, it is also the nurture of God that causes us to flourish and glorify him (15:8). "Apart from me you can do nothing" (15:5). Jesus describes God as a vinedresser who prunes with skill, knowing the benefits that will accrue to the branch in later seasons.

The results of this reciprocal abiding are given in 15:7–17. (1) *Prayer with confidence.* Jesus mentions twice the certainty that comes with prayer joined to spiritual union (15:7, 16; cf. 14:12–14). (2) *Assurance.* We acquire confidence in Jesus's love for us because it is modeled on God's love for him (15:9–10; 17:26). Assurance is closely related to our knowledge of Christ's love (see Rom. 8:35–39). (3) *Joy.* This is not mere happiness but a deeper tranquility that is free from worry about the affairs of living and that knows God's purposes are good (15:11; 16:20–24; 17:13). (4) *A new community.* Throughout the discourse, Jesus exhorts his followers to love one another (13:34; 15:12, 17; 17:21; see 1 John 2:7–11). As his love for us is modeled on God's divine love for him (15:9), now our love for one another should be modeled on his love and sacrifice (15:13, 17). Christlike love should be the hallmark of the church (see esp. 17:20–26; 1 John).

The remarkable summary of Jesus's offer and expectations appears in 15:14–17. What especially stands out is his offer of friendship. In Christ, disciples have unparalleled access to God. True friendship is always hallmarked by complete candor, honesty, and transparency between persons. Jesus has become that sort of friend because he has unveiled himself fully (15:15). Moreover, this is not a casual thing passed out indiscriminately: Christ has chosen us to be his friends (15:16)! The indwelling of Christ and his love are thoroughly individual and personal in these chapters. But Jesus's seriousness cannot be missed. If he has offered this qualitative relationship to us, we must extend it to one another (15:17).

Early Christianity was unanimous in its outlook on the world. Insofar as the church formed a radically new community, it experienced strife and conflict with society. Social divisions recur with marked frequency in the book of Acts. In his letters, Paul describes persecution as virtually a constituent part of the Christian experience (1 Cor. 4:11–13; 1 Thess. 2:13–16; 2 Tim. 3:10–13). This treatment was expected because the disciples of Christ had inherited the hostilities shown to their master.

Jesus predicted these conflicts in his final teachings (Matt. 10:17–25; 24:9–14; Mark 13:9–13), and here in the Farewell Discourse the subject is addressed in full (15:18–16:33). The conflicts are outlined, but in addition the provisions of Jesus are given.

Jesus explains that the precedent for this experience is his own (15:18, 20). Christ and his followers are alien to the world's values and therefore cannot obtain its affections (15:18–16:4a). Jesus has selectively created a new order—"I have chosen you" (15:19)—and this implies judgment on the old. The language here is strong: hatred will typify the division between church and world.

The world's guilt is based on its accountability before divine revelation. God in Christ has come, spoken, and acted on our behalf (15:22–24), and our response forms the basis of our judgment. This is a common Johannine theme. In 5:45 the disbelieving Jews will be held accountable to their own Scriptures, which speak of Christ. In 9:18 the judges of the blind man will themselves be judged because they rejected the sign. And in 12:37 John connects the disbelief of the Jews with a rejection of Jesus's revelatory signs.

Nevertheless, the disciples will not be alone in these conflicts. Jesus reminds them again of the Paraclete (cf. 14:16, 26), who will be their aid. This promise dovetails with similar promises in the Synoptics (Mark 13:11), but John has heightened the judicial setting. In the Book of Signs (John 1–12) we saw how Jesus's ministry was described in forensic terms: he was on trial before a world that was weighing the evidence (signs). Now this lifelong trial is promised for the disciples. This judicial-literary metaphor explains the origin of the Spirit's new title. A paraclete is a legal assistant or advocate who aids and counsels. He substantiates our witness (another legal term) as we too are placed on trial before the world. Jesus is quite specific about the extent of these hostilities (16:1–4a) in order to equip his followers for the near future (cf. 1 Pet. 4:12). In 16:1 the Greek word behind "fall away" (NIV) is *skandalizō*, which means to trip or stumble (a *skandalon* is a trap). In Johannine thought this term refers to anything that

In John 16:7, Jesus promises to his disciples the arrival of the Holy Spirit. The symbol of the Spirit has traditionally been a dove (cf. John 1:32–33), as featured here in the alabaster window above the Altar of the Chair of St. Peter at St. Peter's Basilica in Rome (designed by Bernini, seventeenth century).

causes the disciple to fall away or weaken in faith (6:61; 1 John 2:10; cf. Matt. 26:31).

16:4b–33. The further work of the Paraclete now receives attention. In 16:4b–15 we come to Jesus's fourth and fifth predictions (cf. 14:16, 26; 15:26). The closing subject of chapter 15 (the world) continues to be Jesus's concern. While sorrow may follow Jesus's departure (16:5–6), it is actually necessary for him to go, since the coming of the Spirit is dependent on his death/glorification (cf. 7:39). In some fashion the Spirit and Jesus are mutually exclusive; or, as we shall see in chapters 19 and 20, the Spirit comes in the midst of Christ's glorification. The Spirit is Jesus's Spirit and is released in his death (cf. 19:30, 34; 20:22).

The relation between the Spirit and the world has been gradually developing. In 14:15–16 we learned that the world cannot know the Spirit. In 15:26–27 we saw the Paraclete serving as a defense advocate before the world's hostilities. Now in 16:8–11 the Paraclete passes to the attack. This too is a judicial description, for in Jewish courts accusers could themselves be accused and convicted. In verse 8 the term "convict" (Greek *elenchō*; NIV "prove") is legal terminology for the trial. While the symmetry of the verses is difficult, their message is clear: the Paraclete will engage the world through the mission of the church. The Spirit will substantiate the church's voice, inwardly persuading the hearts of its hearers and strengthening its witnesses.

The final Spirit saying (16:12–15) turns to a new subject and should be compared with 14:25–26. In this earlier passage the Spirit's work was conservative, preserving the historical sayings of Christ. Now we learn that there are things to be revealed that are yet unknown (16:12). The Spirit will be a guide into truth, especially that which pertains to future disclosures (16:13). Thus Jesus is predicting a prophetic anointing similar to that known to Paul (1 Cor. 12:29; 14:21–23; Eph. 4:11; 1 Thess. 5:19–20). First John 2:26–27 implies that the Johannine churches used this gift as well. But note a very important limit on this "charismatic" activity: the Spirit will not diverge from the historical revelation of Jesus Christ (John 16:13–14). The Johannine church understood this necessary reflex back to its original moorings. Note the number of times that John points his readers back to what we knew "from the beginning" (1 John 1:1–3).

The picture so far has developed thus: Jesus must go away, but he will return; yet this return will be realized in a significant way through the Spirit's indwelling the Christian. The Spirit will instruct, defend, empower, and guide the disciple within the world. The remaining question—When will these events take place?—will point to Easter (16:16–33).

Seven times we find a reference to "a little while" (16:16–19), which indicates the disciples' worry about the interval between departure and return. Their concern is understandable, since in 16:10 Jesus said that they would see him no more; however, a time of "seeing him" (16:17, 19, 22) precedes this final removal, and it is not too distant. That this refers to Easter can be seen in two ways. First, joy will hallmark their attitude (16:20–22, 24), and on Easter Day, when they see Jesus, rejoicing is their response (20:22; Greek *chairō*). Second, "seeing" Jesus is a part of the Easter witness. In fact, Mary's exclamation in 20:18 is, "I have seen the Lord!" With this evidence it is no surprise to find that the coming of the Spirit, the anointing described throughout these chapters, is finally given on Easter (20:19–22).

Another advantage of this day besides joy is a deepened knowledge of God and his will (16:25–28). The era of misunderstanding will be over (see this motif in chaps. 1–12), and accurate perception will be ours (cf. 2:22; 12:16). John 16:25–28 parallels 16:12–15 inasmuch as it implies a gift of previously unknown insight into God. Hence access to the Father is direct (16:26–27) because Jesus and the Father will be united with us (14:9, 23; 17:21).

Proof that the disciples are not yet equipped—and need to be—can be seen in verses 29–33. They think they understand clearly (16:25, 29) and have full belief. But this cannot be theirs until the Spirit is on them. In fact, they will flee when the crisis of the cross is upon them (16:32). But Jesus understands the limitations of his people; when they grieve over their flight, their recollection of these words will bring comfort (16:33).

17:1–26. Having concluded his discourse, Jesus now turns to prayer. Each of the Synoptic Gospels records a time of prayer in the Garden of Gethsemane (Matt. 26:36–46; Mark 14:32–42; Luke 22:40–46), and no doubt John 17 should be compared with this. If John 14:31 was the terminus of the upper room teaching, then John may want us to consider this prayer to be at another location. Some think that Jesus is somewhere between the upper room and the garden (Kidron Valley; 18:1) and suggest that he is in the temple, since at Passover the city gates would remain open. If this is correct (and we cannot be certain), the prayer may be one of consecration, since the Greek term *hagiazō*, "to make holy" or "sanctify" (17:17, 19), appears elsewhere only at the temple (10:36). In this sense Jesus may be preparing himself for death as a holy sacrificial victim (cf. Deut. 15:19).

Just as the farewell discourse was a well-established literary custom in Judaism, the same can be said for a prayer of departure. The departure of Moses in Deuteronomy offers a good comparison. The great prophet's final words are spoken from the plains of Moab and recorded in Deuteronomy 1–31. This is followed by two prayers (Deuteronomy 32–33) and a closing account of Moses's death (Deuteronomy 34). In Moses's first prayer he blesses God and then he goes on to bless Israel, interceding for them as they go out to appropriate their tribal lands. In Jesus's prayer we find the same two interests. Jesus turns from his own concerns (17:1–8) to those of the church (17:9–26), just like Moses. In this latter role Jesus becomes a priest interceding for his people (see Rom. 8:34; Heb. 7:25). Note how in 1 John 2:1 another Johannine teaching even depicts Christ as our Paraclete (or advocate) in heaven.

The first words of the prayer in Greek bear a significant Johannine phrase: "the hour [NIV "time"] has come." This hour has been anticipated from the outset (2:4; 7:30; 8:20) and is described as the time of Jesus's glorification (12:23, 27; 13:1; cf. 19:14, 27). This glorification is a process culminating in Jesus's return to the Father by way of the cross. Now Jesus prays that his glory (and the Father's) might be evident (17:1–8). In the Book of Signs Jesus's works manifested glory (1:14; 2:11; 11:4, 40; 12:28). But if these signs were veiled, now he asks that his last great sign would speak powerfully. Note how in 12:32 Jesus predicted the true power of the sign of the cross.

In the prologue to the Gospel we learned how the arrival of God's Son made the glory of God visible (1:14). Now Jesus mentions that this effort has been successful (17:4). Those who are chosen, who have apprehended this glory, find life (17:3); but it is a salvation strictly mediated through the Son. The Son himself possesses glory—a glory shared with the Father—and this will be reappropriated upon Christ's return (17:5). This thought is important and draws us into the incarnational theology of John. Coming from the Father, he takes up our humanity at some expense, only to return once more to his original glory with the Father. This resembles Paul's thought in Philippians 2:5–11.

The glory of God has been visible in Christ in yet one more way. Jesus has revealed God's name (Greek *onoma*, "name"; NIV "you"; 17:6). Paul says the same: this Christ who emptied himself is the bearer of "the name that is above every name" (Phil. 2:9). The name of God is a vital Old Testament concept beginning with Moses's experience on Sinai (Exod. 3:13–15; Deut. 12:5; Isa. 52:6), and Jesus has given this throughout his public ministry in the great "I am" sayings (e.g., 8:28, 58). In the Old Testament, possessing God's name is precious; it implies relationship, obedience, and knowledge. Only Christians possess God's name in this Old Testament sense (17:6), and they alone draw the correct inference: the Son who bears this name has come from God and must be believed.

Jesus now prays exclusively for his followers (17:9–19) even though they have been on his mind all along (17:6–7). In one sense this prayer is a continuation of that prayer for glory in 17:1–5. Christ's glory is continually manifested through the lives of his people (17:10). But this will happen only if they, like him, are holy (17:19). Three petitions of Jesus for his people will achieve this end. (1) *Unity* (17:11–12). Christ prays that the unity shared between him and the Father might be realized in the church. But note the prerequisite that will facilitate this in verse 11: "Keep them in thy name" (literal). Christian unity stems from personal faithfulness in God's presence. Like the good shepherd of 10:7–18, Jesus has protected his sheep until now, but other provisions will soon be necessary. (2) *Joy and perseverance* (17:13–16). Conflict will hallmark the life of any who simultaneously live in the world and adhere to God's word. This was made clear in 15:18–16:4a. Jesus, however, asks not simply for spiritual protection (17:15) but for a new disposition: joy in the midst of suffering. (3) *Holiness* (17:17–19). This attribute reflects the presence of Christ because he, like God, is holy (17:19). Sanctification comes through sustained exposure to the truth found in God's word (17:17). It is not just a superior moral effort but something deriving from the holiness of Christ, in whose presence we are to live (17:19).

Once before Jesus hinted at the church, which would grow much later. The good shepherd has "other sheep that are not of this sheep pen" (10:16). Now Jesus turns directly to concerns for others who will believe as a result of his disciples' work (17:20–26). It is interesting that Jesus's chief concern in 17:20–23 is again for unity. The later church of John must have been torn by divisions if 1 John is evidence (cf. 1 John 2:7–11, 18–21). Again he asks that the Father-Son relation would be the model of this unity (John 17:21; cf. v. 11). And again it is facilitated only by a profound spiritual unity with God in Christ (17:21, 23). Unity is not merely a human achievement but flows from a mature walk with Christ.

Just as we noted the importance of Jesus's final public words (12:44–50), now we read his final private teachings for his disciples before his arrest. John 17:24–26 sweeps up subjects from the entire Farewell Discourse but emphasizes one central theme: Jesus desires that he and the Father indwell the believer, conveying to that person the certainty of God's love. While God's presence will be experienced at the end of time (17:24), the Holy Spirit will manifest the reality of Christ in us in this present world. Jesus's final prayer asks that two things be "in" us: God's love and Christ's presence. Later John will write the same thing. How do we know that we abide in him? We bear God's love (1 John 4:7, 16) and Christ's own Spirit (4:13).

C. The passion (18:1–19:42). The story of Jesus's trial, death, and resurrection provides us with an excellent opportunity to test historical tradition in the Fourth Gospel, since so much of

John's passion narrative overlaps with the Synoptics. The New Testament scholar C. H. Dodd even began his magisterial volume with a study of this section (see Dodd). Nevertheless, the Johannine account has had to weather various criticisms. Scholars have noted how John places all guilt on the Jews while leaving Pilate innocent. (In Luke, however, Pilate announces Jesus's innocence three times; see Luke 23:4, 14, 22.) Further, we can note how John theologically reshapes a story of agony into a story of victory and glory (note 18:36). John is no doubt emphasizing themes important to him when, for instance, the arresting party falls to the ground at the mention of the divine name (18:6). Yet it is not necessary to argue that John has dramatically embellished his account with no regard for history (Bruce 1980, 7–20). Incidental historical details abound, such as the name of the high priest's slave (18:10–11), his relation to Peter's questioner in 18:26, and the type of courtyard fire (charcoal, 18:18). When added to the harmony of this account with the Synoptics, these details lend significant credibility to John's independent account (cf. the interrogation before Annas, 18:13–14, 19–24).

The consistent sequence of events in the passion of Jesus both here and in the Synoptics shows how this story had an ancient, pre-Gospel history. It may have been the first narrative circulating among the early Christians who needed to answer the apologetic question, "If Jesus was the Messiah, why was he crucified?"

18:1–27. It was the custom of Jewish celebrants on Passover to spend the night after their meal in prayer and meditation. Jesus does the same, crossing the Kidron Valley east of Jerusalem and entering a garden. The place of the arrest (18:1–11) is apparently familiar to all, since Judas, who left during the meal (13:30), now arrives with the arresting party (18:2–3). The authorities have found exactly what they

The Kidron Valley, which Jesus crossed on his way from Jerusalem to an olive orchard known as the Garden of Gethsemane (John 18:1)

needed: a quiet place where Jesus can be arrested without public notice.

John and Matthew stress the armaments of the party and imply that they expect a fight. John 18:3, however, stands out in that it tells us that a detachment of Roman troops assists. Rather than record Judas's identifying kiss, John writes that Jesus takes the initiative to voluntarily identify himself (18:4–5). His hour has come, and he will instigate its advance. The emphases that follow are uniquely Johannine. When Jesus utters the divine name ("I am," 18:5), the party falls prostrate in awe. When they recover, he exchanges his life for the freedom of his followers (cf. 6:39; 17:12; and the shepherd, 10:11–18). Peter's zeal is misguided (18:10–11) since interfering with "the hour" is just as wrong as hastening its approach (7:6–9).

Once Jesus is bound he is taken for a preliminary interrogation before Annas, who served as high priest from AD 6 to 15. Even though he is deposed now, he still retains his title due to his weighty influence. In fact, all of his five sons became priests (cf. Luke 3:2; Acts 4:6). His son-in-law, Caiaphas, is featured in the Synoptic trial and given only passing reference in John (11:49; 18:13–14, 24).

Intertwined in the trial sequence (18:12–27) is the story of Peter's threefold denial (18:15–18, 25–27; cf. Mark 14:66–72). Jesus has predicted Peter's fear of identification in this crisis (John 13:36–38), and now it is fulfilled. John diverges, however, from the Synoptic story. He records that "another disciple" (likely John) who was acquainted with the priest let Peter into the courtyard (18:15–16). It is interesting that John records the specific type of fire (18:18). A charcoal fire (Greek *anthrakia*; NIV "fire") will appear once again in 21:9, when Jesus reunites with Peter.

The Jewish interrogation is briefly recorded in 18:19–23, but certainly extensive questioning occurred. The Fourth Gospel does not record the charges and countercharges well known to us in the Synoptics. Instead (as with the arrest) Jesus initiates and provides the substance of the dialogue. It is his hour of glorification. He is in control. His chief defense is that his teachings have been public—open to the inspection of all. In other words, no inquiry will uncover more than is already known. On a literary level, we might say that the Book of Signs has provided

exhaustive evidence for Jesus's trial. No more is required.

From the house of Caiaphas (often thought to be located on Jerusalem's western hill or "upper city") Jesus is led to the praetorium, or governor's palace. It was necessary to involve the Roman authorities in capital cases since the Roman subjugation of Palestine had eliminated numerous Jewish judicial powers (see 18:31). Since AD 6 Pilate was the fifth Roman governor (AD 26–36) to rule Judea. Based in Caesarea with numerous troops, Pilate came to Jerusalem occasionally to conduct his administrative duties with the Jews. The praetorium was his residence, although it is uncertain whether he chose Herod's palace in Jerusalem or the Antonia Fortress, with its garrison near the temple (the traditional site since Crusader times).

18:28–19:16. This entire narrative section bears the marks of a carefully written unit. Its dramatic suspense is second to none. Pilate moves in and out of the praetorium five times (18:29, 33, 38; 19:9, 13), establishing the innocence of Jesus and exploring his title of "king." In fact, kingship weaves continuously through the story, becoming the principal theme (18:33, 36–37, 39; 19:2–3, 12, 14–15, 19–22) until Pilate's caution turns to fear (19:8). Even when Jesus is crucified, Pilate insists on Jesus's title in death (19:19–22).

Pilate meets with the Jewish leadership outside his residence so that they might not become ritually unclean due to contact with Gentiles (18:28). The accusation that Jesus is a criminal is less clear than the Synoptic charges that bring political offenses to mind (especially Luke 23:2). Pilate is initially unmoved and prefers to leave the case in Jewish courts, but his audience reminds him of the Roman restriction prohibiting the Jews from carrying out capital punishment.

Pilate now goes inside (18:33) to Jesus, who is in custody and speaks with him. In this round Pilate's first inquiry is important: "king" was a political title that was enjoyed in Judea only by

Herod the Great. Is Jesus making a political challenge with this word? Jesus accepts the title but redefines it: his kingdom is otherworldly. He is not an insurrectionist of the sort that Rome fears. Pilate feels no threat and glibly dismisses Jesus, but his closing remark ("What is truth?") shows that he cannot be one who recognizes Jesus's voice (18:38). Soon, however, Pilate's interest will be piqued.

Jesus is innocent, and this judgment is conveyed outside (18:38). But since Pilate's generous overture is rejected (18:39–40), Jesus is flogged, a severe punishment often preliminary to crucifixion. However, the mocking of the soldiers serves another purpose: this is Jesus's symbolic coronation. He is hailed "king" and so arrayed (19:2–3), but Pilate hopes that the severity of Jesus's pitiful condition and profuse bleeding will permit him to be released. Instead, Pilate is met with calls for death, which would usually give a governor no hesitation. But now the crowd offers a new title for Jesus: Jesus claims to be the Son of God. The round closes differently than the previous one. Pilate is afraid (19:8).

When Pilate reenters the praetorium, it is evident that the glib tone of 18:38 has disappeared. "Son of God" was a metaphysical claim; it evoked a meaning not unknown among Romans. Pilate's initial question (19:9) shows that he is probing the identity of Jesus. Like Nicodemus earlier (3:1–21), Pilate is making a discreet inquiry. And like many who came to Jesus, he has to choose to follow the light or the darkness. Pilate's reflex to his own power (19:10) is completely demolished when Jesus explains how the governor actually derives his power from God. Furthermore, Pilate has been the unwitting pawn of other powers, the Jews, who have instigated this trial (19:11). The round ends with Pilate's earnest desire to release Jesus (cf. Matt. 27:18–19).

As Pilate readies himself to come outside, already voices meet him. But now a new threat is hurled at him, and his stamina collapses (19:12–16). "Friend of Caesar" (19:12) was a technical term meaning "loyal to Caesar," and it referred to people who had distinguished themselves in imperial service. It was the guarantee of a good career. Therefore Pilate must choose between this new king and Caesar. In two discourses, Jesus described the dangerous temptation to regard secular acclaim above divine approval (5:44; 12:43).

Pilate chooses the former (19:13–16) and goes through the motions of making a judicial edict. The "Stone Pavement" (Aramaic *gabbata*, "elevated place"?) may have been a visible platform for such pronouncements. (Archaeologists claim to have found this pavement in the remains of the Antonia Fortress.) The time of this announcement, "about noon," is indicated (19:14) because of a theme that will arise during the crucifixion. The hour of Jesus's condemnation is the hour when the temple began to slaughter the ritual lambs for Passover. Jesus is one such lamb (19:31–36).

The decision between Caesar and the king Jesus, weighed earlier by Pilate, is decided now by the chief priests (19:15). This is their irrevocable rejection of Christ: "We have no king but Caesar" (similarly, Matt. 27:24–25).

19:17–42. Each of the Gospels is content to give us a brief description of the crucifixion (19:17–37), thereby sparing us its gruesome details. It was despised by Jews and Romans alike and employed mainly in the provinces for slaves and criminals. Following a severe flogging with a metal- or bone-tipped whip, the victim was forced to march to the site of death carrying the crossbeam, even though often the individual was already fatally injured. Jesus had already been scourged thus (19:1; cf. Mark 15:16–20). The Synoptics mention that Jesus's condition is so serious that he cannot carry anything as he walks, but a passerby named Simon of Cyrene is forced into service (Mark 15:20–21).

Golgotha is the Aramaic word for skull or cranium (19:17), and may derive from the shape of a hill or simply be an apt metaphor for a place of death. It was certainly outside the city walls of Jerusalem, and if the northern courses of Herod's walls have been correctly determined then the traditional site of Jerusalem's Church of the Holy Sepulchre can be accepted.

The extended attention given to the title on the cross is strictly Johannine (19:19–22; cf. Mark 15:26). While it conveys historical information, its chief importance is theological. Jesus's death has been described as his glorification (e.g., John 7:39; 13:31). It has also been called his "lifting up" (3:14; 8:28; 12:32, 34) inasmuch as he is returning to the Father and to his previous glory (17:1–5). Therefore, the cross is not a place of defeat or humiliation in Johannine thought. It is a further revelatory sign since it will evoke faith and create followers (12:32). If we keep this in mind, then the place of regal language (kingship) becomes clear: Christ, already crowned (19:2), is now enthroned (19:19–22). The irony of the scene fits well the two-level understanding that has accompanied the signs and discourses throughout the Gospel (e.g., 3:3; 4:7–8). Pilate misunderstands the truth that he so valiantly defends. Only John mentions that the title is in three languages (19:20), and this underscores his interest in those outside of Judea who are also a part of Christ's fold (cf. 10:16; 12:20; 17:20).

The Romans customarily removed and confiscated the clothing of the crucified, thereby heightening his shame and giving the soldiers some benefit for their labors. This occurs at Golgotha (19:23–24; cf. Mark 15:24). John's narrative explains that Jesus's garments are divided four ways, but he focuses on a seamless undergarment valued by the guards. Its preservation is explained from Psalm 22:18, but its symbolic meaning may lie elsewhere. The garments of the high priest included this item (Exod. 28:4; 39:27), and it may suggest some priestly symbolism for Jesus (which is a common New Testament thought; see Heb. 4:14; Rev. 1:13); but this interpretation must remain uncertain.

The presence of women at the cross is striking (19:25–27). Unlike the apostles, who fled, the women would have been safe from incrimination because of ancient oriental chivalry giving them a protected status. We see that John attends as well but for one purpose: Jesus's first word from the cross makes provision for his mother's future. Mary is taken into the beloved disciple's care. A plethora of symbols is often attached to this act (e.g., does John represent the church to whom the heritage of Israel, Mary, is entrusted?), but few of these suggestions find any consensus.

The remaining activity on the cross (19:28–37) now emphasizes two dominant theological themes. First, Jesus is a Passover victim dying a sacrificial death. This motif already appeared in 19:14 (also 1:29) and again comes to mind here. Jesus's thirst (19:28) echoes Psalm 22:15, while the hyssop that satisfies his thirst reflects Exodus 12:22 and Passover symbolism. Hyssop was used with blood on Israel's doorposts in Egypt. This is a uniquely Johannine note (cf. Mark 15:36). John is also the only one of the evangelists who speaks of the Roman *crurifragium*, or breaking of legs (19:31–37). Again this serves Passover imagery in that the Passover lamb could have no broken bones (19:36; Exod. 12:46). Jesus was already dead (19:30), but if a man were not, a violent blow to the legs with a lance would hasten death since the body would no longer have leg support. Finally, we should refer to the blood from Jesus's side (19:34). (On the medical question see Zugibe, 118–31.) The sacrificial blood cannot be congealed—it must be a living victim—and here John has provided proof (see Mishnah *Pesahim* 5:3, 5).

Second, the hour of death ushers forward the Spirit. As Jesus discussed his departure in his Farewell Discourse (John 13:16), we saw how the Spirit was promised to replace the presence of Christ (14:16). The Spirit would turn grief to joy. Here on the cross two veiled allusions indicate the connection between the Spirit and the hour of glory. In 19:30 Jesus says, "It is finished," and bowing his head "he gave over the Spirit" (author's translation). The phrase is different from that in the Synoptics and is found nowhere in Greek literature for death. "Give over" (Greek *paradidōmi*) means handing something on (1 Cor. 15:3), and here Jesus directs himself *not* to the Father but to those followers below. Hence this is a symbolic act depicting an anointing about to come (John 20:22). The blood and water—especially the water—may be symbolic. John 7:37–39 states that living waters will flow from Christ; in the immediate context (7:39) this is related to the Spirit and the hour of glorification. Thus 19:34 may fulfill 7:37–39, indicating that at the hour of death Jesus's spirit is about to be released.

Since the Passover would officially begin at dusk, Joseph from Arimathea (a village of uncertain location) and Nicodemus remove the body of Jesus so that he can be buried before the feast (19:38–42). Mark notes that Joseph is a member of the Sanhedrin (Mark 15:43); Matthew mentions his wealth (Matt. 27:57). Along with Nicodemus (John 3:1–15; 7:50–52), Joseph exerts his influence on Pilate to obtain Jesus's body (19:38). The myrrh and aloes (19:39) along with linen cloths were commonly used in Jewish burials, but the amount of spices (about seventy-five pounds) seems extraordinary.

D. The resurrection (20:1–29). The final chapter of the Book of Glory concludes those elements that make up the hour of Christ's glorification. First, there is the account of the empty tomb, which records the evidence of the resurrection but emphasizes above all the faith of the beloved disciple (20:1–10). Second, Matthew's story of Jesus's appearance to various women (see Matt. 28:9–10) has a parallel in the account about Mary Magdalene, a woman who dramatizes the grief of the apostolic company and their joy upon seeing Jesus again (John 20:11–18). Finally, Jesus appears to his disciples and during his visit breathes on them the Holy Spirit (20:19–29).

Mary's arrival at the empty tomb (20:1–10) is before morning (20:1; on Mary see 19:25 and Luke 8:2), and although John mentions her alone, the Synoptic Gospels say that she is accompanied by other women (cf. Matt. 28:1;

Mark 16:1; Luke 24:10). Rolling-stone tombs were not impossible to reopen and were designed to offer future access to a tomb for secondary Jewish burial or for additional primary burials. Mary's surprise centers not so much on the fact that the stone is rolled back (for to her mind Joseph or Nicodemus might have reopened it) but on the absence of Jesus's body. The text gives no indication that she believes in his resurrection at this point (John 20:9). For her, Jesus's body has simply been reburied elsewhere.

Her report to the disciples introduces a complete shift in subject (20:3–10). While the story provides numerous accurate details about what they view (20:5–7), the story primarily emphasizes the relation between John (the beloved disciple) and Peter. In the Fourth Gospel, John always gains the upper hand. He outruns Peter to the tomb (20:4) and looks in first. Even though Peter goes in first, John *believes* when he enters (20:8; cf. 20:29). This theme appears elsewhere in the Gospel. At the Last Supper, for instance, Peter recognizes in John some unique access to Christ (13:23–24). In 18:15–16 the beloved disciple admits Peter to the high priest's home. And in 21:6–8 they are contrasted once again. Many scholars note

that John bears the remarkable title "beloved disciple" (NIV "the disciple whom Jesus loved") and conclude that to some degree the Fourth Gospel venerates him as a hero. No doubt the profundity of the Fourth Gospel and its penetration into the truth of Christ indicate John's depth of faith and experience, to which these narratives of contrast bear witness.

The story of Mary Magdalene and Jesus (20:11–18) bears some resemblance to two separate Synoptic narratives. Mary now witnesses two angels (20:12) and afterward meets Jesus and seeks to embrace him (20:16–17). In Luke two angels appear to the women when they arrive at the tomb (Luke 24:4–9), and in Matthew we read about women seeing Jesus near the tomb and worshiping him (Matt. 28:9–10). The Johannine account, while independent of these, has clear historical moorings. (Note that Mary Magdalene appears in both Synoptic stories: Matt. 28:1; Luke 24:10.)

With the hour of glory, what message does this passage convey? Weeping (Greek *klaiō*,

Rolling-stone tombs were common among the wealthy in first-century Judea. This tomb located in lower Galilee typifies the kind of tomb owned by Joseph of Arimathea and used for the burial of Jesus.

20:11, 13, 15) is a prominent theme here and has a special Johannine usage. Elsewhere it appears at Lazarus's funeral (11:31, 33), which is a paradigm of Jesus's death. But, moreover, it is found in Jesus's own prediction: "Very truly I tell you, you will weep and mourn" (16:20). Mary experiences the grief of being alone without Jesus. Yet in the Farewell Discourse, Jesus remarked that this mourning would become rejoicing (16:22).

But what will create this joy? The answer of the Farewell Discourse is now dramatized. Mary misunderstands Jesus's appearance, thinking him to be a gardener (20:14–15). But when he calls her by name, she at once recognizes his voice (see 10:3, "He calls his own sheep by name"). Yet now she misunderstands the meaning of Jesus's presence. Why does Jesus forbid her embrace (20:17) whereas in 20:27 he will invite Thomas to touch him? Mary is trying to hold on to the joy she has found in his resurrection. In effect Jesus is saying that his permanent presence with her will be in another form. This is precisely the message of the Farewell Discourse. Jesus's "coming" will also be in the Spirit Paraclete, who will indwell his followers individually (14:18–26).

The message she is to convey (20:17) is that the final steps of departure are at hand. "Ascending" (Greek *anabainō*) is referred to in both the perfect and the present tenses: it has begun and is still under way. And it is necessary that it continue this way, since the coming of the Spirit is directly dependent on Jesus's departure (16:7).

The story of Mary, therefore, is an interpretative vehicle that underscores the transition now under way. Jesus will not leave them as orphans (14:18) because as he moves through "the hour" he will give his Spirit. For this they must make ready. The gift of the Spirit will climax the events of "the hour."

On the evening of this Easter Sunday, Jesus appears to the disciples and provides confirmation of his resurrection (20:20). Twice he speaks of "peace" (20:19, 21), fulfilling that which he promised in his farewell: "Peace I leave with

you; my peace I give you" (14:27; 16:33). Seeing the Lord was also a part of this promise (16:16; thus for Mary, 20:18; the disciples, 20:20, 25; and Thomas, 20:25, 29), as was rejoicing (16:20; 20:20). In other words, Jesus is recalling his words from the upper room, and this must necessarily include the coming of the Spirit (20:19–29).

That this is a definitive gift of the Spirit and no symbolic event is clear. The comments in John 7:39 are satisfied: Christ has been glorified and the gift is given. The breathing of Jesus (Greek *emphysaō*) echoes Genesis 2:7, when God gives life to Adam. Jesus is such a creator (John 1:3), and the Spirit gives life (6:63). Thus, the gift of the Spirit is Christ's re-creation. Above all, Jesus has given his own breath, his own Spirit, and the personal dimensions of his indwelling are emphasized. (On the relation of this anointing with that in Acts 2 see Burge 1986.)

In this hour Jesus also transfers to his disciples his own mission. He sends them forth (20:21) in the same way the Father commissioned him (13:16, 20; 17:18). The basis of the church's authority is that it bears the commission of Christ. Furthermore, they will bear the divine Spirit, ensuring their success. The authority over sins (20:23) also reflects Jesus's ministry (3:19–20; 9:40–41). However, its meaning must be carefully understood. The judgment of Christ stemmed from his revelation of the light and the response of his listeners. When the light is unveiled, each one brings judgment on himself depending on his response. The mission of the church is to continue the revelatory work of Christ in the world.

When Jesus met with the disciples, Thomas (11:16; 14:5; 21:2) was absent. He receives the now familiar Easter greeting (20:25) but claims that unless he can acquire this certainty himself (i.e., "see the Lord") he will not believe. On the following Sunday the group is gathered again, and Jesus appears, offering to Thomas that which he seeks. Thomas provides the Gospel's final response to Jesus when he offers the ultimate title of divinity and lordship to him (20:28). Jesus's final words speak to Thomas and to the church together. While "seeing" forms the basis of the apostolic witness (Acts 1:21–22; 1 Cor. 15:3–8; 1 John 1:1–4), it cannot belong to all. Those who believe without seeing—without demanding signs (cf. John 4:48)—are more blessed still.

E. Conclusion (20:30–31). It is evident that this is a natural conclusion to the Gospel (see commentary on 21:1–25). The Fourth Evangelist stresses the purpose of his Gospel: that we might believe. (The verb has two readings, which the NIV calls attention to in a margin note: "to begin to believe" [aorist] and "to continue to believe" [present]; the former implies an evangelistic purpose, the latter a pastoral intent for those who already believe.) The Gospel is a record of signs—of evidences—that the reader must weigh. It stems from Jesus's disciples, who are trustworthy witnesses (see 19:35), and in particular from the testimony of John (21:24). Its aim is to lead us to faith in Christ because in him alone can we find life.

4. Epilogue (21:1–25)

The origin and placement of this final chapter has perplexed many. John 20:30–31 seems to be a natural ending to the Gospel, whereas chapter 21 seems to be an appendage. In 20:29 a blessing is given on those "who have not seen" and yet believe, and here we hardly expect another visit from the resurrected Christ. It is even possible that the editors who included this chapter identify themselves in 21:24 (see below).

That John's Gospel has experienced some editorial attention need not surprise us; hints to this effect have been seen all along. We noted the prologue already (1:1–18) and the account of the adulterous woman (7:53–8:11, which also raises manuscript variant problems). Each is a narrative with its own unique history. We even noted how some scholars would reverse chapters 5 and 6 for greater sequential clarity. And finally, some have pointed to chapters 11

and 12, suggesting an expansion to the Book of Signs.

But to note such features is not to say that these additions cannot be from the pen of the Fourth Evangelist. On the contrary, each narrative enjoys a striking unity with the rest of the Gospel. In chapter 21 these connections are numerous. In 21:14 the appearance of Jesus is numbered as his third, which presupposes his appearances in 20:19 and 20:26. Typical of the Fourth Gospel is the John/Peter rivalry in 21:7 (cf. 13:23–25; 20:3–9). There is also characteristic Johannine language, such as the charcoal fire in 21:9 (cf. 18:18), the word for "fish" in 21:9–10, 13 (Greek *opsarion*, 6:9, 11), the reference to Thomas and Nathanael in 21:2 (cf. 1:45–46; 11:16; 14:5; 20:24), the name of Simon's father in 21:15 (see 1:42), and the double use of "truly/amen" in 21:18 (see, e.g., 5:19; 6:26; 8:34).

This evidence suggests that chapter 21 is authentically Johannine but secondary to the original format of the Gospel (but see Smalley 1974). John 21:20–23 implies that John the apostle has died and that the community he founded is wrestling with his absence. Disciples who have survived their master identify themselves in 21:24 ("we know that his testimony is true"). No doubt they collected together John's teachings—including chapter 21—and gave the Gospel its final form. This may even be the origin of other editorial "seams," the testimonials such as that in 19:35, and the special title for John the son of Zebedee, "the beloved disciple."

A. The miracle of 153 fish (21:1–14). Both Mark and Matthew record a resurrection appearance to the apostles after Easter, and Matthew specifically identifies Galilee as the place (Matt. 28:16–20; Mark 16:12–20; 14:26–28). This is also the Johannine setting. The story of the miraculous catch of fish has close parallels with another miracle (Luke 5:1–11). (Some would urge that John's story is another rendering of that in Luke, but this conclusion is not necessary.) Here Jesus repeats the earlier fishing miracle, and this repetition becomes the vehicle of revelation. (The same is true of the meal in 21:9–14 as well as Peter's triple confession in 21:15–17, echoing his triple denial, 18:15–18, 25–27.) Jesus takes them through the same experience twice, and in this discloses his identity to them.

The Sea of Tiberias is an alternate name for the Sea of Galilee and comes from Herod Antipas's regional capital of Tiberias, on the western shore. The apostles and a number of additional disciples have returned to their native Galilee after Easter (cf. Matt. 28:16), some apparently assuming their former occupations. In Matthew and Mark a critical note is sounded: each mentions the disciples' lack of faith and records Jesus's call to go forth into the world (Matt. 28:17, 19; Mark 16:14, 15). Something apparently has failed in the men's resolve and conviction.

In the present story Jesus takes charge of Peter's fishing venture. Despite a night of fruitless toil (21:3; compare the earlier miracle, in Luke 5:5) they are obedient to the voice on the shore, even though they do not yet recognize Jesus (21:4; cf. 20:29). Just like in the earlier fishing miracle, the nets are filled (21:6; Luke 5:6), and just like before, Peter responds prominently in devotion to Christ (21:7; Luke 5:8). However, the familiar superiority of the beloved disciple appears even here (cf. 13:23–24; 20:3–4, 8). He recognizes Jesus first, and on his word Peter runs to the beach. It is interesting to think about the beloved disciple's response in light of this rivalry motif. He stays with the fish and brings them safely to shore.

Although Peter's despair is turned to jubilation at the size of the catch and the appearance of Jesus, the meaning of the miracle lies deeper. Johannine symbolism often produces two levels of meaning (e.g., 3:3–4; 4:7–8), and we should expect the same here. The fish and bread served by Christ recall the feeding miracle in 6:1–14. (Peter might even recall an earlier charcoal fire, 18:18.) Jesus is revealing himself by evoking memories of past activities.

But here the recently caught fish play a central role. The beloved disciple has not neglected them (21:8), and Jesus orders Peter to bring the net finally ashore (21:10–11). The number of fish (153) is striking and is not an accidental note. First-century writers enjoyed cryptic devices, especially numerical values that symbolized some word or thought (e.g., 666 in Rev. 13:18). Jerome says that 153 was the ancient number of known fish species. In effect John would be saying that all people are part of the church's mission. But evidence for this interpretation is slim. Some scholars suggest mathematical sums ($1 + 2 + 3 \ldots + 17 = 153$. And $17 = 10 + 7$, two numbers of perfection) (e.g., Barrett, 581–82). But the riddle remains unsolved.

Essentially Jesus is emphasizing the mission of the disciples. When Jesus directs their work, they will prosper. And the beloved disciple has indeed chosen the correct task: to remain with the fish so that none are lost (cf. Matt. 4:19). This is the same theme in John 21:15–19. Peter will be challenged to compare his devotion to Christ with his care for Christ's sheep.

B. Jesus and Peter (21:15–23). The exchange between Jesus and Peter is one of the most celebrated dialogues in the Bible (21:15–17). Its interpretation turns on our understanding of verse 15: "Do you love me more than these?" What is Jesus's comparison? ("These," Greek *toutōn*, being any gender, has no clear antecedent.) On the one hand, is Peter being asked if his love for Christ exceeds his love for fishing? This is plausible since it was Peter who instigated the trip to sea (21:3), and Jesus will challenge the apostle to recommit his efforts to ministry with the new sheep metaphor. On the other hand, "these" may refer to the other disciples. If Peter's love for Christ excels generally, then it should be followed by a coordinate care for God's flock.

Either way, Jesus's challenge to Peter is that he consider carefully his love for his Lord and take up the task of shepherding. The dialogue enjoys numerous interplays of Greek synonyms: two words for love (*agapaō*, *phileō*), the flock (*arnia*, *probata*), tending/caring (*boskō*, *poimainō*), and know (*oida, ginōskō*). Of these pairs of synonyms, the interplay of verbs for "love" has inspired most comment. (Jesus uses *agapaō* twice and then *phileō* in the final exchange; Peter uses *phileō* throughout.) This variation is either a feature of John's Greek style—the other synonym pairs suggest this—or it bears some meaning. If the latter is true then two options are possible. Either Jesus consents to Peter's verb and we find in *phileō* an affectionate love Peter desires to express, or *agapaō* is the greater love (a sacrificial love), and Jesus is challenging the quality of Peter's affection. In this sense Peter confesses some limit to his love. Above all it must be recalled that these verbs were interchangeable in the first century and that even John himself seems to use them as synonyms (cf. 3:35 with 5:20; 13:23; 19:26; 21:7, 20). This is the most common interpretation among modern commentators.

Jesus now turns to a description of the fate of Peter and John (21:18–23) and especially what it will mean for Peter to "follow" him (21:19). Peter once announced that he was willing to follow Jesus even to death (13:37). Jesus demurred, predicting Peter's denial (13:38). But now all things are changed. Jesus now predicts Peter's faithfulness even to death (21:18), and John, for fear that we might misunderstand, provides an explanatory note (21:19; so too 12:33). "Stretch out your hands" implies crucifixion. While we know that Peter was martyred in the 60s, Tertullian in the early third century AD explains that he died on a cross.

In 21:20–23 the discussion of Peter's martyrdom opens the subject of the beloved disciple's death. The nature of Jesus's comment (21:22) and the editorial notes of the writer (21:23) indicate that within the community of believers was a belief that John was going to survive until the second coming of Christ. But he did not. Here is evidence of the dismay that must have gripped the church during the eventual death of the apostles. Jesus's words are repeated: disciples should continue to follow and not be distracted by speculations about Christ's future will. For John's church the message is clear: John's survival may not have been Christ's will at all.

C. Appendix (21:24–25). These final notes assert the authority of the beloved disciple as a reliable eyewitness and as the originator of a trustworthy historical tradition. This same sort of confirmation is given in 19:35. From 1 John 1:1–4 we can see how John's connection with the historical events of Jesus's life was valued. Moreover, the Gospel bears eloquent testimony to the power of John's spiritual perception of Christ, and this too must have been deeply respected.

The disciples of John who penned these words identify themselves in the plural "we" of 21:24. They have survived their pastor and now have collected his teachings for

Along the Sea of Galilee's north shore, on the grounds of the Franciscan Catholic Church of St. Peter's Primacy, stands this modern statue commemorating Jesus's commissioning of Peter (see John 21:15–19). At this location, archaeologists have uncovered the remains of a fourth-century church, proving the sanctity of this site in antiquity.

the church. The process must have been difficult, for as 21:25 indicates, the amount of material at their disposal was voluminous.

Select Bibliography

Barrett, C. K. *The Gospel according to St. John.* 2nd ed. Philadelphia: Westminster, 1978.

Bauckham, Richard. *The Testimony of the Beloved Disciple: Narrative, History, and Theology in the Gospel of John.* Grand Rapids: Baker Academic, 2007.

Beasley-Murray, G. R. *John.* Word Biblical Commentary. Waco: Word, 1987.

Blomberg, Craig. *The Historical Reliability of John's Gospel: Issues and Commentary.* Downers Grove, IL: InterVarsity, 1998.

Brown, Raymond E. *The Gospel according to John.* 2 vols. New York: Doubleday, 1966–70.

Bruce, F. F. *The Gospel of John.* Grand Rapids: Eerdmans, 1984.

———. "The Trial of Jesus in the Fourth Gospel." In *Gospel Perspectives.* Vol. 1 of *Studies of History and Tradition in the Four Gospels.* Edited by R. T. France and D. Wenham. Sheffield: JSOT Press, 1980.

Burge, Gary M. *The Anointed Community: The Holy Spirit in the Johannine Tradition.* Grand Rapids: Eerdmans, 1986.

———. *John.* NIV Application Commentary. Grand Rapids: Zondervan, 2000.

———. "A Specific Problem in the New Testament Text and Canon: The Woman Caught in Adultery (John 7:53–8:11)." *Journal of the Evangelical Theological Society* 27 (1984): 141–48.

Carson, D. A. *The Gospel according to John.* Pillar New Testament Commentary. Grand Rapids: Eerdmans, 1991.

Dodd, C. H. *Historical Tradition in the Fourth Gospel.* Cambridge: Cambridge University Press, 1963.

Käsemann, Ernst. *The Testament of Jesus.* Philadelphia: Fortress, 1968.

Keener, Craig. *The Gospel of John: A Commentary.* 2 vols. Peabody, MA: Hendrickson, 2003.

Ladd, George Eldon. *A Theology of the New Testament.* Rev. ed. Grand Rapids: Eerdmans, 1993.

Milne, Bruce. *The Message of John.* The Bible Speaks Today. Downers Grove, IL: InterVarsity, 1993.

Morris, Leon. *The Gospel according to John.* New International Commentary on the New Testament. Grand Rapids: Eerdmans, 1971.

———. "The Jesus of St. John." In *Unity and Diversity in New Testament Theology.* Edited by Robert A. Guelich. Grand Rapids: Eerdmans, 1978.

Smalley, S. S. *John: Evangelist and Interpreter.* New York: Thomas Nelson, 1978.

———. "The Sign in John 21." *New Testament Studies* 20 (1974): 275–88.

Whitacre, Rodney A. *John.* IVP New Testament Commentary. Downers Grove, IL: InterVarsity, 1999.

Zugibe, F. T. *The Cross and the Shroud.* New York: Paragon, 1986.

Acts

DAVID W. PAO

Introduction

According to the modern versions of the New Testament, the Acts of the Apostles follows the four Gospels. This arrangement highlights the fact that Acts provides an account of the period following the life of Jesus the Messiah. As the second volume of the writings of Luke, however, Acts does not simply provide the historical account of growth of the church. It also testifies to the work of God through the apostles of Jesus, who continue to witness the power of the gospel as it fulfills the ancient promises made to Israel. In other words, instead of simply an appendix to the work of Jesus, this work points to yet another phase in the fulfillment of salvation history.

The Unity of Luke-Acts

Since the work of Henry Cadbury in the 1920s (*The Making of Luke-Acts*), most scholars recognize that Luke-Acts has to be read as two parts of a single work. This affirmation of the unity of Luke-Acts not only points to the need to interpret any one passage within the literary context of this wider narrative but also allows the reader to notice the numerous parallels between the two parts of the narrative. These parallels in turn reveal the theological emphases of the author, and these emphases often serve to address the needs of the church. In his Gospel, for example, Luke emphasizes the descent of the Holy Spirit on Jesus as he

began his ministries on earth (Luke 3:21–22). In Acts, Luke likewise draws attention to the descent of the Holy Spirit on the apostles as they began their ministries (Acts 2:1–13). Such parallelism addresses a practical concern of the church: Luke encourages the early Christians that, although Jesus is no longer with them in person, the Spirit, who works behind him, is the one who is working behind the church that bears his name.

Although some (e.g., Mikeal Parsons and Richard Pervo, *Rethinking the Unity of Luke and Acts*) have continued to question the unity of Luke-Acts, most see this as the basic assumption behind any informed reading of the Lukan writings. In terms of genre, these two works are not simply representatives of the ancient biographies and histories; together they point to the faithful God who fulfills his promises to Israel. In terms of narrative flow, several themes introduced in Luke (e.g., Holy Spirit, Gentiles, repentance, Samaria/Samaritans, temple, rejection of the prophet) are fully developed only in Acts; therefore, to read only one part would provide a partial picture. In terms of theological framework, one finds the same emphases on significant theological topics: identity of Jesus, the mission of the apostles, the progression of the kingdom of God, the universal relevance of the gospel message. In terms of the use of Old Testament paradigms, both works also draw from one prophetic tradition in the description of the climactic work of God at the dawn of the eschatological era.

The recognition of the unity of Luke-Acts also affects our consideration of several significant background issues for the reading of Acts: authorship, audience/recipients, date of writing, purpose, and literary structure.

Authorship

Who wrote the Gospel of Luke and Acts? Overwhelming external evidence points to Luke, the companion of Paul, as the author. The oldest manuscript (late second century AD) of the Gospel identifies Luke in the attached title. The roughly contemporary Muratorian Canon, as well as early church fathers beginning with Irenaeus, supports this identification. The internal evidence in the Lukan writings supports this. The "we-passages" in Acts, where the narrator includes himself in the story (16:10–17; 20:5–15; 21:1–18; 27:1–28:16), most naturally point to the author as a companion of Paul. According to the Pauline tradition, Luke was indeed a co-worker of Paul (Col. 4:14; Philem. 24; 2 Tim. 4:11).

Since Luke is identified as a medical doctor in Colossians 4:14, scholars in the nineteenth century sought to show that the "medical language" in Luke-Acts is sufficient to prove that the author is indeed a physician. Recent scholars, however, have noted that such "medical language" falls short of technical medical jargon. Nevertheless, features in the Lukan writings are consistent with the fact that the author is a medical doctor. First, the preface (Luke 1:1–4) reflects the affinity of this work with scientific writings (see Loveday Alexander, *The Preface to Luke's Gospel*). This indirectly points to an author who is aware of the scientific literature. Second, ancient documents testify to the fact that physicians had the need and luxury to travel extensively. This again can explain Luke's interest in the journey motif in both his Gospel (Luke 9–19) and Acts (Acts 8–28).

According to early traditions, Luke was a resident of Antioch. Noting that the we-passages begin with the account of Paul's travel in Macedonia (16:10–17; cf. 20:5–15), it is also possible that Luke came from Macedonia. Some have therefore suggested that Luke wrote from Antioch or Macedonia, while others, for various reasons, have pointed instead to Caesarea, Asia Minor, Greece, and even Rome. Most would agree, however, that knowing the exact location from which this work originated is not critical to our reading of this narrative.

Audience

The intended audience is equally difficult to identify. The prologues of both Luke (1:3) and Acts (1:1) mention Theophilus. The fact that Luke uses the phrase "most excellent" points to the elevated social status of this Theophilus (see Acts 23:26; 24:3; 26:25). One should not, however, assume that Luke is simply writing to one individual. First, Theophilus could serve as a sponsor of the work (cf. Josephus, *Against Apion* 1.50). If so, Theophilus would not even be the primary intended audience of this work. Second, ancient biographies and histories were always written to wider communities and not one individual. Therefore, Luke is most likely addressing a wider audience. Third, the content of Luke-Acts addresses a wide variety of issues. To limit the work to one individual seems inappropriate.

The content of Luke's writings shows that the audience was composed of believers at home in a Gentile environment while at the same time aware of Jewish culture. First, details in this narrative point to a Gentile audience: (1) emphasis on the salvation of the Gentiles (Luke 2:30–32; 3:4–6; Acts 1:8; 13:46–47); (2) portrayal of the Roman political system (Luke 2:1–2; 3:1–2; Acts 26:26); (3) use of Greco-Roman literature (Acts 17:28); (4) use of Greco-Roman literary conventions (Luke 1:1–4; Acts 1:1); and (5) lack of lengthy Jewish legal matters (cf. Matt. 5:21–48). Luke does, however, quote frequently from the Old Testament (e.g., Luke 3:4–6; 4:4, 8, 12, 18–19; 7:27; 20:17, 37, 43; 22:37; Acts 1:20; 2:17–21, 25–28, 34–35; 4:25–26; 7:42–43, 49–50; 8:32–33; 28:26–27), and the use of these quotes

This illumination from a tenth-century Byzantine manuscript depicts Luke writing.

assumes that the audience is well versed in the Old Testament. It seems likely, therefore, that these are Gentiles who have in some way been affiliated with Jewish synagogues.

These first-century Gentiles who may have worshiped in the synagogue but were not full proselytes were "God-fearers," and these God-fearers appear often in the pages of Acts (14:1; 16:13–14; 17:2–4, 10–11, 17; 18:4; 19:8). Moreover, the phrase "the things you have been taught" in the Lukan prologue (Luke 1:4) suggests that these God-fearers have already accepted the gospel. This work, therefore,

addresses concerns of an early Christian community dealing with issues related to their faith in Jesus the Messiah. The Lukan text does not allow us to be more precise in identifying this Christian community.

Date

The date of writing is yet another area of scholarly debate. The events in Acts 28 took

1167

place in the 60s, and Luke's writings were quoted as early as the mid-second century. Some have suggested that Luke wrote his works in the early second century, but the issues discussed in Luke-Acts point to the struggles of the first-century church, and the focus on the active work of the Spirit points to an earlier period. Most therefore have adopted a first-century dating instead.

Scholars who affirm a first-century dating are generally divided into two camps: those who argue for a pre-70 dating, and those who do not. Those who insist on a pre-70 dating point to the following observations: (1) Luke does not mention the death of Paul in the 60s; (2) Luke also fails to mention the fall of Jerusalem in 70; and (3) Luke does not mention the letters of Paul. Those who argue for a post-70 dating counter by pointing out that (1) Luke did not intend to write a biography of Paul but an account of the progression of the gospel; (2) other post-70 writings (e.g., Hebrews) also did not feel the need to explicitly mention the fall of Jerusalem; and (3) although Luke does not quote from the Pauline Epistles, his writings do reflect the influence of Pauline thought. These scholars also provide additional arguments for a post-70 dating: (1) assuming that Mark is among the sources of Luke's Gospel and that Mark was written in the 60s, the earliest Luke could have been written is the 70s; (2) Luke mentions that "many have undertaken to draw up an account of the things that have been fulfilled among us" (Luke 1:1), and this may point to a certain gap between Luke and the other, earlier Gospels. In light of these observations, it is difficult to insist on a pre-70 dating for the Lukan writings. Strong arguments are lacking, however, for a considerably later dating for these volumes. It is therefore reasonable to assume that Luke wrote his two-volume work around 70.

Purpose

Any reasonable reading has to assume that the author writes with a set of purposes in mind. To discern the purposes of Luke-Acts, one has to examine the literary and historical contexts of this work as well as the themes, motifs, and conceptual emphases embedded within the narrative. In light of the complexity of this two-volume work, many have acknowledged that Luke wrote his work to address a number of concerns, although some are less prominent than others.

1. In his prologue, Luke explicitly notes the purpose of his work: that the readers "may know the certainty of the things you have been taught" (Luke 1:4). In light of this note, it seems apparent that Luke intends to strengthen and confirm the faith of the readers. What aspects of the "things" that they have heard require affirmation remain unclear.

2. In his classic work *The Theology of St. Luke*, Hans Conzelmann argues that Luke includes a history of the church to deal with the problem created by the delay of Jesus's return. This history of the church provides meaning for the period between the first and second coming of Jesus. To Conzelmann, this "invention" of salvation history allows the readers to replace an eschatological urgency with the affirmation of the meaning of present existence between the times. While this proposal seeks to provide a firm historical rationale for Luke's work, contemporary works in the first and second century fail to confirm the significance of the problem created by the delay of Jesus's return. Moreover, eschatology remains a prominent topic in Luke-Acts (Luke 13:22–30; 17:22–37; 21:25–33; Acts 3:20–21).

3. Noting Luke's emphasis on the innocence of Jesus and his apostles in the eyes of Roman officials (Luke 23:1–5, 13–16; Acts 18:12–17; 19:35–41; 23:26–30; 24:24–27; 25:13–21; 26:30–32), some have suggested that Luke aims at convincing the Romans that Christianity should be considered a harmless and acceptable "movement." While this certainly explains a certain set of passages, others provide a rather negative picture of the Roman officials (see Luke 13:1; 22:24–30; Acts 4:27; 24:27). Moreover, much of the content of these two

volumes, such as the use of the Old Testament, cannot be explained by this proposal alone.

4. In light of the significance in both Luke and Acts of the gospel of salvation being proclaimed, this certainly should be considered as one of the main reasons for Luke's project. The first volume points to the foundation and center of the gospel, with the second volume depicting the power of this gospel to conquer the world. This focus on the proclamation of the gospel of salvation is able to explain the focus on both Jesus the Messiah and the church that builds on the ministry of the Messiah. Without further qualification, this proposal can suffer from the weakness of proposal 1 above in that it may fail to define the precise focus of Luke's work.

5. To specify which aspect of this gospel of salvation Luke is focusing on, one unique and constant concern throughout this two-volume work can be underscored: the universality of God's salvation and the impact of such a salvation on the identity of God's people. In every turning point in the development of the plot, Luke emphasizes that this gospel is not to be limited to ethnic Israel (Luke 2:30–32; 3:4–6; 4:16–30; 24:46–47; Acts 1:8, 13.46–47, 28.28). Moreover, in all these turning points, one finds Luke quoting or alluding to the Old Testament text, thus highlighting the emphasis he places on these passages. In Acts, the movement from Judea to Gentile territory is the driving force behind the development of the narrative. In terms of historical context, Paul, who has traveled with Luke (see discussion of we-passages above), shares Luke's concern as he also emphasizes the universality of the gospel message and the corresponding issue of the identity of Gentile believers as they relate to ethnic Israel (Rom. 9:1–11:21; 1 Cor. 1:10–17; 2 Cor. 8:1–9:15; Gal. 2:11–5:1; Eph. 2:22–3:20; Phil. 3:1–11; Col. 1:15–2:19). In this two-volume work, Luke aims to describe the powerful work of Jesus the Messiah, whose death and resurrection usher in a new era in salvation history, an era that witnesses the

powerful work of the gospel on both Jewish and Gentile soil. Through this lens one is able to read this historical work as theologically meaningful, as Luke is not content with the mere reproduction of historical records but is also presenting such material as a way to explain the powerful work of God in history.

Outline

1. Ascension and Commission (1:1–11)
2. Restoration of God's People in Jerusalem (1:12–7:60)
   A. Fulfillment of the Twelve (1:12–26)
   B. Descent of the Spirit (2:1–47)
   C. Opposition to the Apostles by Jewish Leadership (3:1–4:31)
   D. Unity and Division in the Early Church: Ananias and Sapphira (4:32–5:11)
   E. Continuing Opposition to the Apostles by Jewish Leadership (5:12–42)
   F. Unity and Division in the Early Church: Appointing the Seven (6:1–7)
   G. Stephen and the Preparation for Missions beyond Judea (6:8–7:60)
3. Reunification of God's People in Judea and Samaria (8:1–12:25)
   A. Saul and the Persecution of the Church (8:1–4)
   B. Ministries of Philip (8:5–40)
   C. Conversion and Call of Paul (9:1–31)
   D. Ministries of Peter (9:32–11:18)
   E. Church at Antioch (11:19–30)
   F. Persecution in Jerusalem (12:1–25)
4. Mission to the Gentiles (13:1–21:16)
   A. Paul's First Missionary Journey (13:1–14:28)
   B. Jerusalem Council and the Identity of Gentile Believers (15:1–35)
   C. Paul's Second Missionary Journey (15:36–18:22)
   D. Paul's Third Missionary Journey (18:23–21:16)
5. Appeal to Caesar and the Proclamation of God's Kingdom (21:17–28:31)
   A. Paul's Arrest and Imprisonment in Jerusalem (21:17–23:35)
   B. Paul's Imprisonment in Caesarea (24:1–26:32)

Commentary

1. Ascension and Commission (1:1–11)

Luke begins his second volume by referring back to his "former book" (1:1), that is, the
Gospel of Luke, which contains the words and
deeds of Jesus. This link is important because the
development of the church builds on the life and
work of Jesus. In the Gospel, the disciples failed
to understand and appreciate the mission and
identity of Jesus. In the beginning of this second volume, Luke emphasizes that the apostles
are now fully equipped to continue the earthly
ministries of Jesus. First, Luke mentions that
Jesus gave instructions "through the Holy Spirit
to the apostles he had chosen" (1:2). Affirming
the unique status of these apostles, the work of
the Holy Spirit also guarantees the ability of
these apostles to proclaim faithfully the gospel
of Jesus. Second, with "many convincing proofs"
(1:3) Jesus shows that he has truly risen from
the dead. This allows the apostles to be faithful
witnesses to Jesus as the risen Lord. Third, Luke
emphasizes that Jesus appeared to them for a
lengthy period of time ("forty days") and "spoke
about the kingdom of God" (1:3). This again
ensures that these apostles are fully qualified
to serve as the leaders for the first generation
of the early Christian movement.

The first words of the risen Lord in this
volume point to the difference between the
baptism of John and the baptism of the Holy
Spirit (1:5). This baptism of the Holy Spirit
signifies the arrival of the eschatological era (cf.
Isa. 11:1–3; 32:14–17; 44:1–4). With this note,
the disciples naturally think of the promises
concerning the restoration of Israel (1:6). Jesus's
response in 1:7 does not deny the fact of the
restoration, but it does qualify the timing of the
final restoration. Moreover, Jesus's response also
provides a radical reformulation of the expected
restoration program: the centripetal return of
the exiles toward Zion/Jerusalem is replaced by

the centrifugal diffusion of the gospel to the
world of the Gentiles (1:8).

Many have considered 1:8 as providing the
ground plan of Acts. In geographical terms,
this verse does point to the movement of the
gospel: from Jerusalem to Judea and Samaria,
and ultimately reaching "the ends of the earth."
Not to be missed, however, is the significance
of the language used in this verse. The phrase
"when the Holy Spirit comes on you" reflects
the language of Isaiah 32:15 (cf. Luke 24:49), a
passage that points to the eschatological restoration of Israel. The call to be Jesus's "witnesses"
also finds its closest parallels in the prophecies
of Isaiah (43:10, 12) where the eschatological
people of God will witness the powerful work
of God at the end of time.

In light of these references to Isaiah, the references to "Jerusalem," "all Judea and Samaria,"
and "to the ends of the earth" take on added
significance. According to the programmatic
statement in Isa. 40:1–11, the eschatological
era consists of a three-part program: (1) the
arrival of the salvation of God in Jerusalem (Isa.
40:1–2), (2) the restoration and reunification
of Israel (Isa. 40:9–11), and (3) the mission
to the Gentiles (Isa. 40:3–5). Here in Acts,
"Jerusalem" likewise points to the first step of
this program as God fulfills his promises to
Israel. The emphasis on "all" Judea and Samaria
points to the reunification of Israel, as "Judea"
becomes a symbol for the southern kingdom,
and "Samaria" for the northern kingdom. When
both "Judea and Samaria" accept the gospel
message, one witnesses the fulfillment of God's
promises (Isa. 11:13). Finally, the phrase "to
the ends of the earth" appears only four times
in the Old Testament (Septuagint), in Isaiah
(8:9; 48:20; 49:6; 62:11), where it points to
the Gentiles. Therefore, this phrase most likely
refers to this ethnic group rather than a precise
geographical locale such as Spain or Rome.
In the context of Isaiah, this phrase points
to yet another stage of God's work, when he
rebuilds his people in the messianic age. From
this discussion, it becomes clear that 1:8 not

only provides the geographical ground plan of Acts, but also points to the three stages of the fulfillment of God's promise to Israel. In this sense, then, Luke is not merely tracing the geographical expansion of the early Christian movement; he is also describing how the events that follow the ascension of Jesus are significant events in God's redemptive history.

Luke has already provided an account of Jesus's ascension in his first volume (Luke 24:50–53), but here in 1:9–11 he provides an account with slightly different emphases. The mentioning of "cloud" and the "two men dressed in white" highlights the significance of this event (cf. Luke 24:4), and the words these two men speak point to the return of Jesus in the future. Jesus's public ascension therefore becomes a promise of his return. Moreover, the emphasis on "looking" (1:11) also confirms the role of the apostles as witnesses. In the narrative that follows, Luke explains that the ascension of Jesus signifies his enthronement in heaven, when he becomes the Lord of all (2:34–35). By means of his lordship over all, he can grant forgiveness and salvation to both Jews (5:31) and Gentiles (10:34–36). Mission then becomes a call for all to submit to the universal sovereignty of this Lord.

2. Restoration of God's People in Jerusalem (1:12–7:60)

A. Fulfillment of the Twelve (1:12–26). After the disciples witnessed the ascension of Jesus, they "went upstairs to the room where they were staying" (1:13). This room may remind the readers of the "large room upstairs" (Luke 22:12) where Jesus

had his Last Supper with his disciples. After the Last Supper, Jesus went to the Mount of Olives to pray, but the disciples failed to be alert in prayers (Luke 22:45). After his ascension, however, these disciples also return from "the Mount of Olives" (1:12), but they are now "constantly in prayer" (1:14).

This section that describes the selection of Matthias to replace Judas is surprising in light of the fact that Matthias will never reappear in Luke's narrative. The focus of this episode is not, however, on Matthias the individual but on the need to establish the number of the apostles as "twelve." Luke emphasizes the significance of numbering (1:17) by concluding the description with the note that "Matthias . . . was added to the eleven apostles" (1:26). The note that this group numbered "about a hundred and twenty" (1:15) points to the significance of the symbol "twelve," and this was already emphasized by Luke earlier when he noted that the twelve disciples were to "sit on thrones, judging the twelve tribes of Israel" (Luke 22:30). This use of "twelve" as a symbol of Israel is common in Second Temple (i.e., "intertestamental") Jewish

Acts 1:12 indicates Jesus ascended into heaven from the Mount of Olives (see 1:9–11). Nearby, the Crusaders constructed a chapel (seen here) to commemorate the ascension. After Jerusalem fell in the twelfth century, the chapel was acquired by the Muslim ruler Saladin. The building became a mosque but was never used. Today its custodians are the Islamic Waqf (who also oversee the Dome of the Rock), and it is chiefly a pilgrimage site for Christians.

literature, and the organization of the community responsible for the Dead Sea Scrolls also builds on the principle of "twelve." In this context, Luke emphasizes that the election of Matthias completes the circle of the Twelve, and this signals the beginning of the restoration of God's people in an eschatological era (see also Acts 26:7). In this new era, the criterion for entering God's people is no longer one's ethnic identity but one's relationship to the "Lord Jesus" (1:21).

Embedded within 1:20 are two quotations from the Old Testament: Psalms 69:25 and 109:8. In their original contexts, both verses point to the failure of those who oppose God to succeed in their evil plans. Here not only does Peter cite these verses to justify the election of an apostle to replace Judas, but he is also affirming a wider theological principle. This becomes a significant theological introduction to Acts: the enemies of this word will not deter its progression. The fate of Judas then becomes an exemplary event that points to the fate of all those who oppose the plan of God (cf. Matt. 27:1–10).

B. Descent of the Spirit (2:1–47). After the establishment of the Twelve, Luke proceeds to describe the descent of the Spirit as a further sign of the dawn of the eschatological era (2:1–13). The dating of this event to "the day of Pentecost" (2:1) may be important for two reasons. First, "Pentecost" is by definition the fiftieth day after Passover (cf. Lev. 23:15–16). To locate this event at Pentecost is to provide a temporal marker for the events that followed Jesus's death and resurrection. Luke has noted earlier that Jesus appeared to his disciples for "forty days" (1:3) before he ascended into heaven. This places the descent of the Spirit within days of his ascension. Second, by the first century, Pentecost becomes a feast that celebrates the giving of the law on Mount Sinai during the time of the exodus (*Jubilees* 6:17–21; Tobit 2:1–2), and some authors even point to a voice from heaven that can be understood by people from all nations during this event

(Philo, *On the Decalogue* 46). If Luke intends to highlight this connection, then the descent of the Spirit at this critical moment would point to the establishment of the new constitution for the restored people of God.

The "sound" (2:2) of a blowing wind and the fact that the believers "saw" (2:3) what appeared to be tongues of fire point to the public nature of this event. This is not a private experience but a public manifestation of the Spirit announcing the arrival of a new era. In the Old Testament, "wind/spirit" (Greek *pneuma*), "fire," and ecstatic speech can point to the presence of the mighty acts of God and the accompanying prophetic spirit that interprets such acts. In this context, the arrival of this Spirit on God's people signifies that they are "clothed with power from on high" (Luke 24:49) as they serve as witnesses to the gospel of Jesus Christ (1:8). Later in his speech, Peter also makes it clear that the descent of the Spirit signals the arrival of the "last days" (2:17).

This is the first appearance of the phrase "filled with the Holy Spirit" (2:4) in Acts. Elsewhere in Acts, this phrase points to the power to proclaim the gospel message, not to one's superior status in the eyes of God or one's private spiritual development (see 4:8, 31; 9:17; 13:9). The fact that "all of them" experience this power of the Spirit is significant because it points to the entire people as corporate witnesses in this age of fulfillment. Moreover, this is also a fulfillment of Jesus's promise when he earlier announced that they would "be baptized with the Holy Spirit" (1:5).

The "other tongues" (2:4) that they speak in are probably foreign languages intelligible to residents of different parts of the Roman world (cf. 2:8), although some in the audience do mistakenly assume that these apostles "had too much wine" (2:13). While it is theoretically possible that this is a miracle of listening, this is not an aspect that Luke emphasizes. Moreover, a comparable phrase in the Old Testament also points to intelligible foreign languages (Isa. 28:11).

The ability to speak in other tongues has been interpreted as a divine confirmation of personal conversion or a sign of sanctification. Luke's emphasis does not rest on such individualistic reading, however. Most individuals in Acts do not speak in other tongues when they are converted, and when Luke does describe converts speaking in tongues, he does so to emphasize how a new people group becomes part of God's people (see 10:46; 19:6). Speaking in other tongues then becomes a confirmation of the inclusion of various people groups into God's elect.

The rather lengthy and detailed description of the audience (2:5–11) is often considered as providing merely background information, but a careful look at this section reveals yet another aspect of the significance of the Pentecost event. In these verses, Luke emphasizes the Jewish identity of the audience: they are Jews, proselytes, and half-proselytes who believe in God but have yet to be circumcised and join the synagogues as full converts (i.e., God-fearers). Although they come "from every nation under heaven" (2:5), Luke emphasizes their Jewish identity. In historical terms, their presence in Jerusalem during this major pilgrim festival is expected, but the descent of the Holy Spirit signifies that this is not simply yet another festival. In emphasizing that Jews from all nations witness God's mighty act in Jerusalem as he fulfills his promises to Israel, this account depicts the long-awaited ingathering of the exiles from the Jewish

At Pentecost, the Spirit descended on the gathered followers of Jesus like small flames (Acts 2:1–4). This description evokes images of the temple and instances in Jewish history where fire symbolizes the presence of God. Here the event is interpreted by the fourteenth-century artist Duccio di Buoninsegna of Siena.

Diaspora. Understanding the list of nations in verses 9–11 as pointing to the Jews living in exile is confirmed by a similar list in Isaiah 11:11, when the prophet promises that "in that day the Lord will reach out his hand a second time to reclaim the surviving remnant of his people from Assyria, from Lower Egypt, from Upper Egypt. . . ." In light of the prophecies of old, the presence of Jews "from every nation under heaven" becomes a significant step in the fulfillment of God's promises to Israel.

When the crowd accuses the apostles of drunkenness (2:13), Peter stands and addresses the crowd (2:14–40). This is the first of the major speeches in Acts, and these speeches provide critical commentary on the significance of the events that Luke is recording. In this speech, Peter first refutes the charges of drunkenness by emphasizing that what just happened points instead to the fulfillment of God's promises. Quoting from Joel 2:28–32 while inserting the phrase "in the last days" (2:17; cf. Isa. 2:2), he emphasizes that the outpouring of the Spirit points to the arrival of the eschatological era. Another insertion in this quotation ("and they will prophesy," 2:18) further identifies the early Christian community as the eschatological community that testifies to the work of God in the era of fulfillment.

The heart of the speech focuses on the role and significance of Jesus Christ. Jesus the man of God rejected by the Jews ("you," 2:23) has been raised by God. This not only fulfills the promise of David (2:25–28; see Ps. 16:8–11); Jesus's resurrection also ushers in the era that witnesses the work of the eschatological Spirit. With his resurrection, Jesus also proves to be "Lord and Messiah" (2:36), one who surpasses David himself (2:34–35; see Ps. 110:1). The lordship of Jesus has a number of implications. First, through his name, one's sins may be forgiven (2:38a). Second, because of his paradigmatic role in salvation history, those who are baptized in his name will receive the eschatological Spirit (2:38b–39a). Finally, because of his universal lordship, even those "who are far off" (2:39b) will be able to experience this eschatological salvation. The phrase "who are far off" reminds one of Isaiah's promises concerning the salvation to the Gentiles: "Peace, peace, to those far and near" (Isa. 57:19); the use of a similar phrase later in Acts also confirms this reference to the Gentiles (22:21). Jesus is not only the Lord of the Jews; he is also the Lord of the Gentiles. In Acts, this christological affirmation provides the firm basis for missions.

The many who respond to Peter's message become the foundation of the early Christian community (2:41–47). These believers' sharing "everything in common" (2:44) fulfills the Hellenistic ideal of a utopian community, and the fact that they gave to "anyone who had need" (2:45; cf. 4:34) also fulfills the Jewish ideal of the sabbatical/Jubilee era (cf. Deut. 15:4). This portrayal again reaffirms the location of this community at the end of time as they experience the renewed presence of God in this new era. The basis of this unity does not lie in an unrealistic vision of social harmony or a perverse sense of economic utility, but in the "apostles' teaching" (2:42) that points to the power of the work of Jesus Christ. Moreover, this practice is not to be universally imposed, as some believers still own personal property (cf. 4:37), and the perfect unity of the Christian community is a reality that is yet to be fulfilled (cf. 5:1–11).

Their practice of "breaking of bread" (2:42) provides continuity with the practice of the earthly Jesus (cf. Luke 5:27–32; 7:34; 9:10–17;

15:2; 19:7; cf. 14:8–24). This act points to the formation of a new community in the name of Jesus. Moreover, the breaking of bread "in their homes" (2:46) also marks a shift in the central meeting place of the early Christian community, as the households became the center where the presence of God could be experienced.

C. Opposition to the apostles by Jewish leadership (3:1–4:31). 3:1–26. Immediately following the Pentecost event, this section points to the powerful acts of the Holy Spirit through the hands of the apostles. The miracle performed by Peter provides the occasion for two speeches that define both the continuing role of the risen Jesus and the opposition by Jewish leadership.

Earlier, in his Pentecost speech, Peter pointed to the fulfillment of God's promise that he "will show wonders in the heavens above and signs on the earth below" (2:19; see Joel 2:30). In light of this miracle (3:1–10) Peter demonstrates the impact of such a fulfillment in the history of the church. The healing of "a man who was lame from birth" (3:2) reminds Luke's readers of Jesus's healing of a "paralyzed man" (Luke 5:17–26) at the beginning of his Galilean ministry. This points to the exemplary nature of the period of the church as it demonstrates the continuity between the ministries of Jesus and that of the apostles. Nevertheless, Luke makes it clear that Jesus is superior to the apostles because they are performing this miracle "in the name of Jesus Christ of Nazareth" (3:6).

On the one hand, the fact that "Peter and John were going up to the temple at the time of prayer" (3:1) could be taken as a sign of their faithfulness to Jewish religious practices. On the other hand, their act of healing in the temple precinct can also be considered a challenge to the temple leadership, as they are able to demonstrate the powerful presence of God apart from the temple practices. The exact location of this "Beautiful" gate (3:2) remains unclear, although it undoubtedly leads into the Court of Women and the Court of Gentiles. In light of the fact that the temple treasure was located in the Court of Women, those passing by this gate would have their offering ready. This is, therefore, an ideal place for the crippled man to ask for alms.

The significance of sight in this account is introduced when Luke tells us the crippled man "saw" Peter and John (3:3). Peter's command, "Look at us" (3:4), provided hope for this person as he "gave them his attention" (3:5). At the end, however, what people "saw" (3:9) was not the provision of financial help but the complete healing that leads to the praising of God. This again fulfills the prophetic note that was introduced at the beginning of Luke's writings: "All people will see God's salvation" (Luke 3:6; see also Isa. 40:5). Two details in Luke's description can further be illuminated by their Old Testament usages. First, while the crippled man expects to receive "alms" (eleēmosynē) from Peter and John, what he receives is the saving "mercy" (eleēmosynē) of the faithful God (cf. Isa. 38:18; 59:16). Second, the fact that this healed man "jumped" (3:8) may also allude to Isaiah 35:6, where a sign of the eschatological age is that "the lame leap like a deer" (cf. Luke 7:22).

In the speech that follows (3:11–26), Peter makes a number of significant points that pave the way for the understanding of the growth of the early Christian movement. First, Peter emphasizes that the healing is not accomplished by their "power or godliness" (3:12); instead, it is Jesus who is working through them. It is the mighty acts of the risen Lord that are recorded in this narrative, not accounts of the mighty deeds of the apostles. Within this speech alone, Jesus is called "his [God's] servant" (3:13, 26), "the Holy and Righteous One" (3:14), "the author of life" (3:15), "Messiah" (3:18, 20), "the Lord" (3:19), and "prophet" (3:22). The unique role of the risen Jesus in salvation history is thus clearly noted.

Second, Peter firmly situates this event within an age that witnesses both the continuity with the past and the uniqueness in its present eschatological moment. On the one hand, the Jesus who accomplishes this act is a servant of the "God of Abraham, Isaac and Jacob, the God of our fathers" (3:13), and his death and resurrection fulfilled what God "had foretold through all the prophets" (3:18); he is also the "prophet" that Moses had long promised (3:22; see Deut. 18:18). On the other hand, this event anticipates the final act of God. The "times of refreshing" (3:19) and the times when God will "restore everything" (3:21) can refer only to Jesus's return, but the plural "times" in these two verses could also point to a lengthy period of time when God begins to restore all things to himself. The "times of refreshing" (3:19) in particular should be understood as referring to the outpouring of the Holy Spirit (cf. Symmachus Septuagint Isa. 32:15), an event that points to the beginning of God's restoration of the universe. If so, then the miracle that was just performed becomes yet another sign of God's act of restoration.

Finally, Peter emphasizes that those witnessing this miracle and the events that are happening before their eyes have to repent of their sins. While the call of repentance figures prominently in the various speeches in Acts, its importance is laid out specifically in this speech. Transcending the immediate concerns surrounding the healing of the crippled man, Peter calls Israel to repent of their act of rejecting their Messiah (3:13). It is only through repentance that they can participate in God's acts of restoration in this eschatological age (3:19–20). As for those who refuse to repent, they will be "cut off" from this eschatological community of God's people (3:23). Moreover, their repentance will also pave the way for the Gentiles to be blessed (3:26). The salvation-historical and ecclesiological significance of individual acts of repentance explains the urgency of the subsequent repeated calls to repentance.

4:1–31. The different roles the people and their leaders played in the persecution of their Messiah (see 3:17) are again illustrated in the varied response to Peter's call to repentance (4:1–4). Instead of repenting of their rebellious acts, the Jewish leaders put Peter and John into jail (4:1–3). Many among the people "believed"

(4:4), however. This division of the people fulfills yet another prophecy concerning Jesus in Luke's first volume: "This child is destined to cause the falling and rising of many in Israel" (Luke 2:34).

When Peter stands before the Sanhedrin (4:5–22), he faces "the rulers, the elders and the teachers of the law" (4:5), the group that persecuted Jesus (cf. Luke 20:1; 22:66). The earlier reference to the Sadducees (4:1) also identifies a main opponent of the church in Acts, as they refuse to accept the reality of the resurrection (cf. 23:6–8). This sect is also connected with the priesthood, whose leaders are named in verse 6. In the Second Temple period, the high priest possessed significant political power, as he functioned as the intermediary between the provincial/imperial power and the local population. Annas was the high priest until AD 15, and his son-in-law Caiaphas took on such responsibilities from AD 18 to 36. Being in power for such a lengthy period of time, their family became the dominant political players of the time (cf. Luke 3:2). Together with other leaders of the people, they were the core members of the "Sanhedrin" (4:15), the council in charge of the local affairs of the people. In the first half of the first century, however, this "Sanhedrin" was probably no more than an ad hoc committee that convened only when there was a crisis at hand. For them, this crisis is created by the apostles' teaching and their ability to convince a large number of the people (4:4).

Peter's being "filled with the Holy Spirit" (4:8) again points back to the effects of the outpouring of the Holy Spirit (2:4). In this case, however, the power of the Spirit is manifested neither in the speaking of tongues nor in the performance of miracles but in the defense of the gospel message. Since these apostles are "unschooled, ordinary men," their "courage" impresses these Jewish leaders (4:13). Their willingness to stand firm in the midst of threats and warnings (4:19) proves that they are indeed filled with the Holy Spirit.

Peter's initial reply (4:8–12) repeats his earlier message (3:12–26) that focuses on their rejection of Jesus. Two details are further developed in this short speech, however. First, in verse 11 Peter uses Psalm 118:22 to show that Jesus the rejected one becomes the foundation of God's mighty acts in this new age. Psalm 118 has appeared numerous times in this two-volume work (cf. Luke 13:35; 19:38; 20:17), and this psalm undergirds one major line of argument throughout Luke's work: while Jesus will be rejected by his own people, this is part of God's salvific plan. Just as the Jewish leaders were not able to thwart God's plan when they persecuted Jesus, they will not be able to limit the power of the gospel message by threatening those extending his work.

Second, the unique lordship of Jesus is emphasized: "Salvation is found in no one else, for there is no other name under heaven given to mankind by which we must be saved" (4:12). The phrase "under heaven" underlines this exclusive and universal claim. Death is but the process through which Jesus can be enthroned as the king of all. This exclusive claim directly challenges the Jewish leaders, who see the temple cult as their base of power. Peter and John make it clear that one can no longer rely on the sacrificial system in seeking approval in the eyes of God. Moreover, as the "Lord of all" (10:36), he is able to save all those who believe in him.

Noting the impact of the miracle performed by these apostles, these Jewish leaders can only urge them not to preach this gospel (4:18). Peter and John's reply ("Which is right in God's eyes: to listen to you, or to him? You be the judges!" 4:19) turns their defense into a stern indictment, as they now directly claim that the Jewish leaders are working against the will of God. The struggle between the early Christian movement and the Jews becomes the struggle between God and the ones opposing him.

In the midst of persecution, the believers offer a prayer to God (4:23–31). Instead of being a desperate cry for help, this prayer confidently proclaims the sovereignty of God. As in Old Testament anti-idol polemic, this prayer contains (1) an appeal to God as the Lord over all creation and therefore the sovereign one, (2) a description of the peoples/nations as enemies of the Lord, (3) a reference to the futility of their acts against the God of Israel, and (4) an appeal for the Lord to "stretch out your hand" (4:30). Linguistically, this prayer finds its closest parallel in the prayer of Hezekiah (Isa. 37:15–20), where one also finds an appeal to God under the threat of enemies.

The believers first affirm God as Creator (4:24). In the conceptual world of the ancient Israelites, creation language is used to construct a power claim whereby the Creator can claim victory over the forces of evil or chaos (cf. Ps. 73:12–17; 89:9–13). In appealing to God the Creator, these believers are again placing their trust in him who has the power over all. The quotation that follows (4:25–26; see Ps. 2:1–2) is applied to those who oppose the plan of God. Both "the Gentiles" and "the people of Israel" (4:27) are identified as those who fight against God and his Anointed One, as noted in the Psalms, but all their acts are within the plan of God (4:28). In verse 29, the prayer shifts to the present concerns of the believers. It is here that one finds a striking redefinition of divine warfare. Instead of emphasizing the use of physical force against God's enemies, these believers are to proclaim the gospel "with great boldness" (4:29). It is the word of God that will assume the role of the conqueror in Acts. In the Greek Septuagint, the phrase "signs and wonders" (4:30) is most often used to refer to the work of the divine warrior in the Exodus tradition (cf. Exod. 7:3, 9; 11:9, 10; Deut. 4:34; 6:22; 7:19; 13:2; 28:46; 34:11). Here it is used in reference to the miracles performed in conjunction with the proclamation of the gospel message. In this eschatological era, one finds a different manifestation of God's power and might.

D. Unity and division in the early church: Ananias and Sapphira (4:32–5:11). Luke again provides a summary account of the harmonious life of the believers (4:32–37). This description can be compared with the earlier summary account (2:42–47), but a few details pave the way for the narrative that follows (5:1–11). First, the phrase "one in heart and mind" (4:32) emphasizes the unity of the early Christians, but this unity will soon be broken by those within the community. Second, the focus on the "apostles" (4:35) as the leaders of this community also prepares for the exercise of their authority in the next episode. Third, the honest offering of money by Barnabas (4:37) also sets up a contrast with the deception of Ananias and Sapphira.

While the early Christian community gathered and "shared everything they had" (4:32), Ananias and Sapphira disrupted this unity by keeping back part of the money they received from selling a piece of property (5:1–11). The account consists of two parallel parts. First, Peter confronts Ananias (5:3–6), which leads to his death. Then Sapphira suffers the same fate after her confrontation with Peter (5:7–10). Peter makes it explicit that their crime was not in keeping part of the money but in deceiving God (5:4) and testing the Holy Spirit (5:9). In doing so, they are not only unified in their attempts to break down the unity of the community, but they also reject the Holy Spirit, who creates and sustains this community of believers.

This account again evokes images and themes from the Old Testament and the wider literary contexts within the Lukan writings. The disruption of God's work among his people reminds one of Achan's deception and greed when his evil act led to Israel's defeat at Ai (Josh. 7:1–26). The conspiracy of a couple against God may point further back to the story of Adam and Eve, when they conspired and lied against God (Gen. 3:1–24). In both accounts, the work of Satan leads to the disruption of the state of harmony, and the responsible couple is cast out from the presence of God. If the idealistic picture of the community as provided in 2:42–47 and 4:32–37 points to the dawn of the eschatological reality, this account reminds the readers that the full consummation of this reality has yet to arrive. Within the narrative of Luke, this account that highlights the presence of Satan and the temptation of wealth also points back to the character of Judas in his betrayal of Jesus (Luke 22:1–6). As Jesus was betrayed by one of his disciples, this early Christian community is also threatened by two of its own.

The concluding statement (5:11) is important for two reasons. First, the mentioning of "great fear" points to the presence of God within this community. "Fear" is often the response of those who witness God's acts in history. In this context, the presence of God is manifested by his act of judgment, but in judging, God is able to show how this community truly is his elected people (cf. Lev. 10:1–5; Deut. 17:12–16). Second, it is probably by no accident that in Acts the word "church" first appears in this context. Through God's act of purification, this people becomes the community that will testify to the gospel throughout the world. Moreover, instead of an ideal community, this "church" is one that will struggle but will become victorious through the power of God.

E. Continuing opposition to the apostles by Jewish leadership (5:12–42). Luke here again provides a portrayal of the ministry of the apostles and the opposition from the Jewish leaders. The summary account of the miracles performed by the apostles (5:12–16) provides a different manifestation of the power of God. While the death of Ananias and Sapphira points to the powerful act of God in judgment, here

the mighty acts performed through the hands of the apostles point to the powerful saving acts of God. Throughout Luke's narrative, one finds both aspects of divine power manifested among those who encounter the apostles. This summary account also points to a return to a state of affairs prior to the disruption caused by Ananias and Sapphira: performance of "signs and wonders" (5:12; cf. 2:43), meeting in Solomon's Colonnade (5:12; cf. 3:11), significant increase in the number of believers (5:14; cf. 2:41, 47; 4:4), and healing of the sick (5:16; cf. 3:1–10).

The apparent tension between 5:13 and 5:14 can be resolved by recognizing that the word "join" in this context does not refer to "believed in the Lord" (cf. 5:14) but simply adhering to the group of believers (cf. 9:26; 10:28; 17:34). Other details in this account highlight the continuity between Jesus and his apostles. The power that is transmitted even through Peter's shadow (5:15) reminds one of Jesus's own magnificent power (Luke 8:44), and the presence of large crowds that gather from surrounding towns (5:16) likewise reminds one of Jesus's own popularity (Luke 7:16–17).

In light of the success of these apostles, the Jewish leaders decide to take action against them (5:17–42). This section repeats Peter's

A model of the Jerusalem temple at the Israel Museum. In this view looking toward the east, the columned porch on the far (east) side is Solomon's Colonnade. This area was a meeting place not only for Jesus but also later for his followers (Acts 5:12).

earlier statement that one "must obey God rather than human beings" (5:29; cf. 4:19), and the narrative itself also makes clear that the Jews are not standing on the side of God. After the Jews first arrest the apostles, "an angel of the Lord" comes to deliver them (5:19). This becomes an emphatic statement indicating that the Jews are opposing the work of God himself.

When the high priest and the Sadducees are considering ways to further punish these apostles, a Pharisee provides a more reasonable proposal. In Luke's first volume, the Pharisees are the primary opponents of the early Jesus (Luke 5:17–39; 6:1–11; 7:29–50; 11:37–54; 14:1–24; 16:14–31; 18:9–14). In Acts, however, the high priest and the Sadducees become the primary opponents of the word. When the Pharisees do appear on the scene, they are relatively benign characters, among them Paul (23:1–10; 26:1–8), who provides the model response of a Pharisee confronted by the risen Jesus. In this episode Gamaliel the Pharisee (5:34) is Rabban Gamaliel I, the student of the well-known Hillel. Paul later acknowledges him to be his former teacher (22:3).

Gamaliel suggests that Jesus may be no more than someone like Theudas (5:36) and Judas the Galilean (5:37), the leaders of two unsuccessful revolutionary movements. These two names do appear in the work of Josephus (*Jewish Antiquities* 20.97–98, 102; 18.1–10; *Jewish War* 2.117–18), although they may be common names, as Josephus dates Theudas to a later period of time (AD 44–46). Gamaliel's advice is that if the work of these Christians "is of human origin, it will fail" (5:38). In light of the narrative that follows, Luke has already proven that their work is not "of human origin." More importantly, Gamaliel further suggests that if they are from God, then the Jews who fight against them are "fighting against God" (5:39). The continued persecution of the Christians by the temple leadership also shows that they are indeed "fighting against God" (cf. 6:12–15; 7:59–8:3; 12:1–19; 13:45, 50; 14:2; 16:3; 18:12; 20:3).

F. Unity and division in the early church: Appointing the seven (6:1–7). After the portrayal of the unity of the Christians in the proclamation of the good news (5:42), Luke presents an urgent problem in the church that ultimately leads to another stage of the progression of the gospel message. The severity of the problem is highlighted by Luke's use of the term "complained" (6:1); the same Greek term often is used in the Septuagint in reference to the grumbling of the Israelites in the wilderness (Exod. 16:7–12; Num. 17:5, 10). In this context, God's people likewise face a crisis when the care of one group is neglected. The identity of the two parties involved has been debated. *The Message*'s rendering of the two Greek terms as "Greek-speaking believers" (*Hellēnistōn*; NIV "Hellenistic Jews") and "Hebrew-speaking believers" (*Hebraious*; NIV "Hebraic Jews") is likely on the right track in that these are Jews who speak different languages. Their differences are not to be limited to linguistic differences, however, since they also represent two communities with different cultural identities.

In light of the repeated call for the care of widows in the Mosaic law (Exod. 22:22–24; Deut. 10:18; 14:28–29; 16:11; 24:17–21; 26:12–13), the neglect of the "widows" is a pressing problem in a community that claims to have "no needy persons among them" (4:34). This explains why "the Twelve" (6:2) have to gather and appoint the seven and to lay their hands on them (6:6). These seven all have Greek names, and it is therefore possible that they are representing those "Hellenistic Jews." They are not called "deacons" (*diakonoi*) in this passage, but they are called to "wait on" (*diakoneō*, 6:2) tables.

The problem with this passage is twofold. First, it is puzzling as to why there is a need for those waiting on tables to be "full of the Spirit and wisdom" (6:3). Second, the job description of the seven seems to be contradicted by the actual account of at least two of them in the narrative that follows (6:8–8:40). These questions force the readers to rethink the main purpose of this account. Instead of simply focusing on the inner conflict within the early Christian community, this account draws one's attention to the need to include those who are often neglected in society. The speech of Stephen (7:1–53) and the ministries of Philip (8:1–40) extend this theme, as the outcasts are now to be included in this eschatological community. Moreover, to "wait on tables" is not simply a menial job. In Luke's Gospel, Jesus has already repeatedly evoked the imagery of table fellowship in the discussion of the inclusion of the outcasts and Gentiles in God's eschatological banquet (Luke 5:27–32; 7:34; 14:8–24; 19:7). In this account, therefore, when the seven are called to "wait on tables," they are to extend the work of the Twelve as they witness God's power beyond the confines of Judea.

This account concludes with a summary statement: "So the word of God spread" (6:7). Being the first of three similar summary statements that focus on the powerful word of God (cf. 12:24; 19:20), this statement concludes the first part of Acts, as the apostles minister in and around the Jerusalem area. This statement should be literally translated, "So the word of God grew." Despite the disagreement among the believers, the word of God continues to grow and become strong. The active role this powerful word plays in this narrative should not be ignored.

G. Stephen and the preparation for missions beyond Judea (6:8–7:60). After introducing the seven in the previous section, Luke focuses on the ministry of one of them. The description of the events surrounding Stephen (6:8–15) before his lengthy speech is significant not only to introduce Stephen the person but also to introduce the issues at the center of Stephen's speech. In introducing Stephen the person, Luke again points the readers back to his earlier portrayal of Jesus. Like Jesus, Stephen is "full of God's grace and power" (6:8; cf. Luke 2:40; 4:22), performing "great wonders and signs" (6:8; cf. 2:22), and is full of "wisdom" and the Spirit (6:10; cf. Luke 2:40, 52; 3:22). He debates with his opponents in the synagogue (6:9; Luke 4:16–27)

and is seized and brought before the Sanhedrin (6:12; Luke 22:66), being accused by "false witnesses" (6:13; cf. Luke 23:2). With the prospect of suffering under their hands, Stephen acquires "the face of an angel" (6:15; cf. Luke 9:29, 32). The connection between Stephen and Jesus is confirmed when, at the end of his speech, he sees "the Son of Man" (7:56), and his last prayer also resembles that of Jesus (7:59–60; cf. Luke 23:34, 46). The power of the risen Jesus is not limited to the Twelve; he is also present with Stephen and others who are to extend his work beyond the confines of Judea.

In introducing the issues involved, Luke notes that Stephen is accused of "speaking against this holy place and against the law" (6:13). This "holy place" can refer to the temple (1 Kings 7:50; Ps. 24:3; 28:2; 46:4; Isa. 63:18), but this "place" can also refer more generally to the promised land (Deut. 1:31; 9:7). In Judaism, the "law" is not just a set of commandments. It represents the covenant that God has made with his elected people (Exod. 24:7; 34:28; Deut. 4:13; 9:11). To speak against the "holy place" and the "law" is to challenge the gifts of God to Israel and their unique status in his plan. These issues are dealt with in Stephen's speech, and these are also questions that dominate the rest of Luke's narrative as he portrays God's work beyond the land of Israel and the people that he has elected in the past.

In response to these charges, Stephen gives a lengthy speech (7:1–53) that provides a recital of the history of Israel. He begins by emphasizing the active role of God in his covenant with Abraham (7:2–8). Then he moves to Joseph, where he depicts the rebellious nature of his brothers (7:9–16), and then provides an extensive treatment of Moses where the faithfulness of God is evident even when Israel rebels against her God (7:17–44). The final section focuses on the Jerusalem temple, as Stephen responds to the charges leveled against him (7:45–53).

The main themes of this speech emerge through the pattern that lies behind the precise selection of details and events. First, in response to those who focus on the unique status of the land, Stephen emphasizes the series of mighty acts of God that happened outside the land of Israel. The numerous geographical names clearly highlight this point: Abraham was called while he was in Mesopotamia (7:2); Joseph experienced the presence of God in Egypt (7:9), and his family was also delivered from the famine by following Joseph to Egypt (7:12); Moses grew up in Egypt (7:21–22) and was called by God "in the desert near Mount Sinai" (7:30); Israel experienced God's powerful hand as they left Egypt (7:36); and they received the law on Mount Sinai (7:38). The emphasis on God's mighty acts outside the land of Israel is heightened by the strikingly short summary statement in verse 45, which covers the period from Joshua to David. This short statement clearly points to the fact that nothing comparable happened after Israel entered the promised land. This emphasis challenges the very idea of a territorial religion, as reflected in the accusations launched against Stephen (cf. 6:13).

After dealing with the land, Stephen focuses on the temple. Unlike the tabernacle, which was built in the wilderness "according to the pattern" provided by God himself (7:44), this temple is considered one "made by human hands" (7:48), a phrase that was used to describe the construction of man-made idols (Lev. 26:1, 10; Isa. 10:11; 16:12; 19:1; 21:9; 31:7; 46:6; cf. Acts 17:24). Unlike the tabernacle, which traveled through the wilderness, this temple is considered one that seeks to limit the work of God (7:49–50; see Isa. 66:1–2). This polemic, however, is not directed against the temple itself but against those who consider the temple as the guarantee of God's presence among their community, and their community alone.

After responding to the charge concerning the "holy place," Stephen turns to the one concerning "the law" (cf. 6:13). Instead of emphasizing that he himself has been faithful to the law, he charges the ancestors of his accusers with being unfaithful to the law once it was delivered to them. Immediately after the provision of the torah on Mount Sinai (7:38), the people of Israel "made an idol in the form of a calf" (7:41). Stephen emphasizes that this is not an isolated incident, however. In the time of the patriarchs, the brothers of Joseph sold him into Egypt because of jealousy (7:9). When Moses first stood up for his fellow Israelites, they rejected him as their leader, a fact that Stephen repeats twice in this speech (7:27, 35). In the concluding section, Stephen accuses them of being "stiff-necked people," whose "hearts and ears are still uncircumcised," and of resisting the Holy Spirit (7:51). This statement not only identifies them as the enemies of the Holy Spirit (cf. Isa. 63:10), but also, by calling them "uncircumcised," denies them their covenantal rights as God's elect (cf. 7:8). Stephen further distances himself from them by shifting from "our ancestors" (7:11–12, 15, 38–39, 45) to "your ancestors" (7:51–52) in the conclusion of this speech (cf. 28:25). This final shift is most likely prompted by the most serious case of their rejection of God's plan, as they persecuted and killed the Messiah, whom God sent Israel. This violent act confirms that they have not obeyed "the law that was given through angels" (7:53).

Stephen also provides, embedded in the discussion of Israel's rejection of the plan of God, a significant discussion of the role and status of Jesus. In his discussion of Moses, Stephen cites Deuteronomy 18:15 in identifying Jesus as a "prophet" like Moses. This eschatological prophet is one who is able to once again reveal the mighty acts of deliverance among God's people. The second title, however, "the Righteous One" (7:52), appears in the context of persecution. This title alludes to the righteous sufferer in Isaiah (cf. Isa. 53:11) as Stephen points to how God has vindicated Jesus even when his own people have rejected him. The other two titles in the section that follows this speech, "Son of Man" (7:56) and "Lord" (7:60), point further to the vindication and glorification of this suffering Messiah. Through these titles Stephen's message is clear: although God's people rejected his Messiah, they are not able to thwart his plan.

This speech that focuses on the God who is not limited by a geographical region or a people who have rejected him provides a significant theology of mission. As God worked beyond the land of Israel in the past, he will be able to do so once again in this eschatological age. This speech, then, paves the way for the spread of the word beyond Judea after the death of Stephen (cf. 8:1).

The account of Stephen's martyrdom (7:54–60) provides a bridge between the past and the future of the gospel ministry. The continuity of Stephen's ministry with that of Jesus is highlighted not only by his final prayer (7:59–60) but also by his witness of "Jesus standing at the right hand of God" (7:55). Earlier reference to Jesus sitting at the right hand of God (cf. Acts 2:34; see also Ps. 110:1) points to the completion of God's salvific work in the death and resurrection of Jesus. "Jesus standing at the right hand of God" points, however, to the continuation of aspects of God's work through the risen Lord. In this context, not only does the risen Lord receive Stephen and vindicate

his work, but he is also "standing," which may indicate the beginning of yet another stage in the work of God in history when the gospel reaches beyond the region of Judea (cf. Acts 1:8).

This martyrdom account also points forward to the next episodes of Luke's narrative. The introduction of Saul (later referred to as Paul), who is among those who are stoning Stephen (7:58), points forward to his call and conversion in 9:1–19. This note may also point to Saul's affiliation with the Sanhedrin, as he plays the role of a witness in this trial narrative.

3. Reunification of God's People in Judea and Samaria (8:1–12:25)

A. Saul and the persecution of the church (8:1–4). The summary statement that comes after the account of Stephen's death provides a glimpse of the dire situation of the church, but it is precisely in such a situation that God is able to introduce the next stage of his plan. Being persecuted, "all except the apostles were scattered throughout Judea and Samaria" (8:1). This persecution then launches the next stage, as announced in 1:8, when believers are to be witnesses in "all Judea and Samaria." The apostles remained in Jerusalem probably because they felt the need to hold firm to the work that the Holy Spirit had established there. This also allows others to continue their work beyond the confines of the city of Jerusalem while they continue to minister to the Jews (cf. Gal. 2:9).

Luke again locates Saul among those who are persecuting the church (8:3). His failure to "destroy" the church again testifies to God's faithfulness to his own chosen ones.

B. Ministries of Philip (8:5–40). Introduced in chapter 6 as one of the seven, Philip becomes the first to bring the gospel to the region of Samaria (8:5–25). In Greek, verse 5 should be translated as "the city of Samaria." The fact that the city of Samaria no longer exists in the time of Philip can explain the omission of the definite article

The stoning of Stephen (nave of the Autun Cathedral, Burgundy, France, twelfth century)

("the") in some manuscripts, thus allowing modern translators to render the phrase as "a city in Samaria" (NIV). Nevertheless, the external support for the inclusion of this article is strong, and it should be retained. While "the city of Samaria" had been renamed "Sebaste" in the first century AD, it is apparent that Luke includes this name to highlight the symbolic significance of "Samaria" in this account. According to the Old Testament, the end of time shall witness the reconciliation of Judah and Samaria (cf. Isa. 11:13). By evoking the ancient city of Samaria, Luke is pointing to the significance of Philip's ministry in the reconciliation of the two parts of the divided kingdom. This emphasis on reconciliation explains the reason why the Jerusalem apostles send a delegate out to Samaria when they hear that the people there have accepted the word of God (8:14). The climactic manifestation of the reunification of Judea and Samaria appears when the people in Samaria "received the Holy Spirit" as Peter and John lay their hands on them (8:17).

Embedded within this narrative is the portrayal of Simon, the one who opposes the word. While Philip proclaims "the Messiah" (8:5), this Simon claims to be "someone great" (8:9). The appellation applied to him, "the Great Power" (8:10), may indicate that he is worshiped as a god, especially when the "Great Power" could be a Samaritan name for the God of Israel. The eventual acceptance of the word by the Samaritans (8:12) and by Simon himself (8:13) shows that "the name of Jesus Christ" is superior to other claims to divinity.

After his apparent conversion, Simon continues his attempts to gain possession of the divine power by offering money to the apostles (8:18–19). The expression "full of bitterness" (literally "gall of bitterness," 8:23) evokes the anti-idol language of Deuteronomy 29:18, and "captive to sin" alludes to Isaiah 58:6, a verse that has already appeared in the narrative (Luke 4:18; cf. Acts 10:38). The contrast between Jesus, who releases the chain of wickedness,

and Simon, who is condemned to such chains, cannot be missed.

When Philip leaves Samaria, "an angel of the Lord" leads him to the road that runs down from Jerusalem to Gaza (8:26), where he meets an Ethiopian eunuch (8:26–40). The conversion of this Ethiopian is puzzling because Luke makes it clear that Cornelius is the first Gentile to be converted (10:1–48). Nevertheless, Luke's focus here is not on the ethnic identity of the eunuch. He is designated once as an "Ethiopian" and an "important official" (8:27), but it is his status as a "eunuch" that is emphasized throughout this passage (8:27, 34, 36, 38–39). Luke's inclusion of the conversion story of this eunuch is best understood in light of the wider restoration program that he emphasizes throughout his narrative. His discussion of the eunuch recalls Isaiah 56:4–5, where one finds the promise to the "eunuchs" who are faithful to God's covenant that they will be included in his eschatological community. Within Isaiah's vision of the restoration of God's people, one finds an emphasis on the inclusion of the outcast. These "eunuchs" then become symbols of God's salvation that reaches beyond the traditional confines of the covenantal community. By placing emphasis on the conversion of this eunuch, Luke points to the fulfillment of this significant part of God's promises for the community of the end times.

The importance of Isaiah is confirmed by the lengthy quotation from Isaiah 53:7–8 in verses 32–33. Isaiah 53 presents God's servant who is rejected by his own people. This rejected servant becomes one who is able to save one who is also being rejected by his own community. In response to the eunuch who asks the identity of this rejected servant, Philip preaches the good news about Jesus, the one who fulfills the plan of God. The experience of being baptized allows this eunuch to participate in God's eschatological community, just as other Israelites are invited to do (Acts 2:38); his "rejoicing" (8:39) also testifies to the reality of this experience of God's salvation (cf. Luke 1:24; 6:23; 10:20; 15:5, 32).

C. Conversion and call of Paul (9:1–31).

Luke's portrayal of Saul (Paul) here is comparable to the previous descriptions: he is depicted as the enemy of the word, except that his involvement in the persecution against the church has intensified (9:1–2). An observer of the stoning of Stephen (7:58) and one who begins to "destroy the church" (8:3), here Saul is "breathing out murderous threats against the Lord's disciples" (9:1). He has also become a leader of a movement, as he requested letters from the high priest to capture disciples in Damascus. This introduction allows one to read this narrative as the confrontation between Saul and the work of God. As an enemy of the word, Saul should have suffered the same as Judas (1:18–19) or Ananias and Sapphira (5:1–11). Instead, this enemy of the word is to be transformed into one of the most significant leaders of the early Christian movement.

Damascus is about 135 miles northeast of Jerusalem. Archaeological evidence from the time of Saul's traveling to Damascus suggests that for a period of a few years Rome was unable to maintain firm control over this city. This would explain why the high priest in Jerusalem would be able to give permission to Saul to capture Jesus's disciples in that city. Notably, Luke describes these disciples as those "who belonged to the Way" (9:2). Luke is the only New Testament author who repeatedly calls the church "the Way" (cf. 19:9, 23; 22:4; 24:14, 22). As in the Qumran community, which used the same self-designation, this Way-terminology is most likely derived from Isaiah 40:3, a verse quoted in Luke 3:4. In Isaiah, this "way" points to the fulfillment of the eschatological salvation. In Acts, this Way-terminology likewise becomes a significant claim, as Luke indicates that this eschatological salvation can be found only in the gospel that these apostles are preaching. It is precisely in situations where Jesus's disciples are persecuted by the Jewish leadership that one finds the use of this label for the church.

In a sense then, this becomes an identity claim, and the polemic against competing claims to be God's faithful sons cannot be missed.

Saul's Damascus Road experience (9:3–9) contains a number of significant details. First, this is an encounter with the risen Jesus. The question, "Why do you persecute me" (9:4), makes it clear that Saul is not simply persecuting Jesus's disciples; he is opposing the work of the risen Jesus himself (cf. Luke 10:16). Facing this Jesus he has persecuted, he recognizes that this is the Lord to whom he needs to submit. It is therefore not surprising to find the lordship of Jesus emphasized more in this section than in any other in Acts (9:1, 5, 10–11, 13, 15, 17). Luke makes it clear that this is not simply a private vision, although Saul's companion "did not see anyone" (9:7). The appearance of "a light from heaven" (9:3) points rather to a theophany event not unlike those that appear in the Old Testament (Exod. 24:16; Isa. 9:2; 42:16). It is likely that Saul's companions did witness the light (cf. 26:13–14), although they fail to "see" the meaning behind such an event. Second, to Saul this encounter is undoubtedly a conversion experience, although not in the modern sense of changing religion. Instead of abandoning his past, he finds fulfillment of the torah that he cherishes in Jesus himself (24:14–16). This experience of encountering Christ affects both his behavior and his understanding of the God that he has attempted to serve. Third, this is also a call narrative, as through Ananias Saul is called to be God's "chosen instrument to proclaim [his] name to the Gentiles and their kings and to the people of Israel" (9:15).

While the focus of this section is on Saul, the surprisingly lengthy account of the appearance of the Lord to Ananias (9:10–19a) demands an explanation. Although Saul is ultimately the object of God's call, this account also emphasizes the call to Ananias as illustrated by the resemblance of this account to Old Testament call narratives (cf. Isa. 6:1–13; 49:1–6; Jer. 1:4–19): vision/encounter (9:10a), initial response (9:10b), call (9:12), obstacle/doubt

(9:13), reassurance (9:14), obedience (9:15). Ananias is called to approach Saul and to relay the message that he has received from the risen Jesus. The emphasis placed on this call to Ananias draws attention to the need of divine intervention for the early Christian community to accept God's amazing work through his servant Saul. The repeated mentioning of Saul's past in this chapter (9:1–2, 13–14, 21) highlights the resistance to accepting Saul's conversion, but Luke emphasizes the need to accept God's work and not be an obstacle to the unfolding of God's plan in history.

Jesus tells Ananias that Saul "must suffer" for his name (9:16), but when Ananias relays this message to Saul, he promises him that he will "be filled with the Holy Spirit" (9:17) instead. This apparent tension should be examined within the life of Jesus himself. In his Gospel, Luke records that Jesus "must suffer many things" (Luke 9:22) even when he is the one who has been anointed by the Spirit (Luke 3:22; 4:18). In this context, therefore, Ananias is not changing the message that he has received from Jesus. He is emphasizing the continuity between the mission of Jesus and that of Saul.

After his Damascus Road experience, Saul spends some time in Damascus before joining the disciples in Jerusalem (9:19b–31). With the only appearance of the phrase "Jesus is the Son of God" (9:20) in Acts, Luke points to the center of Saul's preaching as evidence of his significant realization during his encounter with the risen Lord. Moreover, the account of his rejection by his fellow Jews (9:23–25) also points to the dramatic reversal, in that the one who has persecuted Jesus is now being persecuted because of his name. This also provides an immediate fulfillment of Jesus's prophecy through Ananias (9:16).

Saul's visit to Jerusalem causes anxiety among those who have heard of his acts against the believers. His reception by Barnabas (9:27) confirms the meaning of Barnabas's name ("son of encouragement," Acts 4:36). This account also paves the way for their ministry together in Antioch (11:22–26). Saul's postconversion experience also appears in his own letters (Gal. 1:11–24 and 2 Cor. 11:32–33). There he also notes the opposition by King Aretas in Damascus, but Luke focuses on the persecution by the Jews.

D. Ministries of Peter (9:32–11:18). With this section, Luke shifts his attention back to Peter. The brief account of the healing of Aeneas (9:32–35) again points to "Jesus Christ" as

The Old City of Damascus still shows remnants of its ancient walls. This gate, adjacent to the Christian region of Damascus, is the traditional site of Paul's escape from the city (Acts 9:25).

the power behind the ministry of the apostles (9:34). The more detailed account of Peter's raising Dorcas from the dead (9:36–43) brings him to Joppa, the place where he will receive the significant vision concerning the conversion of Gentiles (10:9–23). These two miracles also remind readers of similar acts of healing during the earthly ministry of Jesus (Luke 5:17–26; 7:11–16). The powerful Peter portrayed in these two healing accounts is contrasted with a reluctant Peter in the next episode, when he must be convinced to reach out to the Gentiles. This further highlights the greater miracle that follows, as God shows that he is also the savior of the Gentiles.

The conversion of Cornelius is considered to be a major point in the progression of the word (10:1–11:18). The first part of the story (10:1–23) focuses on the visions of Cornelius and Peter, while the second part (10:24–48) provides an account of the preaching of Peter and the conversion of Cornelius and those with him. Peter then repeats this story in his report to the church at Jerusalem (11:1–18). The significance of this story is highlighted by the space it occupies in Luke's narrative.

The first part of the story begins with numerous references highlighting its very different geographical and cultural context (10:1). Caesarea is one of the most significant ports of the Mediterranean world. It was founded by Herod the Great and became a major Hellenistic city occupied mostly by Gentiles. Cornelius is introduced as a "centurion in what was known as the Italian Regiment." "Centurion," referring to a leader of about one hundred soldiers, has already appeared twice in Luke's work (Luke 7:1–10; 23:47) and has served as a symbol of the faith of a Gentile. Luke further describes Cornelius as "God-fearing" (10:2), a phrase that likely points to the Gentiles who worshiped the God of Israel in Jewish synagogues but refused to be circumcised and to be converted to Judaism as full proselytes (10:22, 35; 13:26). Cornelius's regular prayer life and his acts of charity (10:2–3) point to his devotion to God, which is not unlike the devotion of those Diaspora Jews

> Peter's vision at Joppa led him to travel north to the Roman city of Caesarea (Acts 10:24). This remarkable port built by Herod the Great was by this time the base of Roman military presence in the province of Judea.

who sought to be faithful to God in Gentile lands (cf. Tobit 1:16–20). Throughout the narrative, however, Luke firmly identifies Cornelius as a Gentile, one who has been excluded from God's covenantal people. It takes a vision for Cornelius to send his messengers to Peter, and it takes another vision for Peter to accept these messengers and follow them back to the house of Cornelius.

Luke's detailed account of Peter's vision, which happens three times (10:9–16), points to its significance. The vision involves the issue of unclean food (cf. Lev. 11:1–47) and reaches its climax with the declaration by a voice: "Do not call anything impure that God has made clean" (10:15). In context, this declaration is to be interpreted as referring to a new stage in salvation history when Gentiles are now no longer considered unacceptable to God. This reading is confirmed by Peter's statement later, in verse 28, in reference to the Gentiles. In Old Testament and Second Temple Judaism, the observance of clean and unclean laws is often used as an identity claim whereby Jews are publicly set apart from the Gentiles (cf. Dan. 1:8–12; 2 Maccabees 6:18–25). God's vision for Peter directly challenges this separatist claim, as God indicates that the Gentiles are now fully acceptable to him.

While Peter is still trying to discern the meaning of the vision, the messengers sent by Cornelius come to his house (10:17–23a). Realizing the connection between the vision and their visit, Peter goes to Cornelius's house and they exchange information concerning the visions that they have received (10:23b–33). Then Peter preaches and speaks to Cornelius and those around him about the death and resurrection of Jesus (10:34–43). This speech begins with a striking note: "I now realize how true it is that God does not show favoritism but accepts from every nation the one who fears him and does what is right" (10:34–35). Without denying the unique status of Israel, this statement provides a strong critique of the Jewish theology of election. The suggestion that "God does not

show favoritism" challenges the very foundation of the identity of Israel as God's unique instrument. This affirmation of the impartiality of God is unheard of in the contemporary Jewish literature, but it becomes the central article of faith in this account of God's work in the eschatological era. The dawn of this new era is possible because of the mighty acts of God through his Messiah, who is now the "Lord of all" (10:36).

As Peter challenges the Jewish theology of election, he proceeds to redefine the elect people of God. The criterion to join this people is no longer one's ethnic identity but "everyone who believes in him [Jesus]" (10:43). This gospel is to be spread through his "chosen" ones (10:41), but these "chosen" ones are now the witnesses who can testify to Jesus's life, death, and resurrection (10:41). God's acceptance of the Gentiles is confirmed by the outpouring of the Holy Spirit among these Gentiles (10:45). As in the Pentecost event, where God's people experienced the miracle of tongues, these Gentiles also receive this gift when they are accepted as equal to Jewish believers (10:46). In response to the manifestation of divine approval, Peter also has them baptized "in the name of Jesus Christ" (10:48).

Although this is undoubtedly a new era in God's salvific plan, Luke also emphasizes its continuity with the past. First, this salvation to the Gentiles originated with the gospel that "God sent to the people of Israel" (10:36). The priority of Israel even in this eschatological era is repeatedly affirmed in this narrative (cf. 13:5, 46; 14:1; 18:4). Second, Peter emphasizes that "all the prophets testify about him" (10:43), thus suggesting that the gospel of Jesus Christ that is now reaching to the Gentiles is not an accident in history. Finally, the fact that this gospel to the Gentiles is preached by a pillar in the Jerusalem church also points to the continuity between the Jewish and Gentile churches.

The surprising work of God among the Gentiles forces Peter to defend his acts, as he is accused by "the circumcised believers" (11:2) upon his return to Jerusalem. The accusation that Peter "went into the house of uncircumcised men and ate with them" (11:3) does not exactly repeat the earlier account of Peter's vision and his interaction with Cornelius, but it does point to the central issue of contention. Peter already realized that a Jew is not supposed to associate with a Gentile (10:28), but through a vision of unclean animals God forced Peter to realize that Gentiles are now considered "clean" in the eyes of God (10:15), and Peter is therefore urged to have table fellowship with the Gentiles.

Peter's reply (11:5–18) does not simply repeat the earlier account; he also highlights the role of certain characters. First, he points to the role of God throughout the entire event. God's role is already noted through the emphasis on visions (10:3, 17, 19), angels (10:3–4, 7, 22), and the powerful manifestation of the Holy Spirit (10:44–47). In this report, Peter again mentions a vision that contains a declaration from God (11:5–9) and the appearance of an angel (11:13), as well as guidance (11:12) and confirmation (11:15) by the Spirit. At the end, Peter explicitly notes that "God gave them the same gift he gave us" (11:17), and the crowd responds by praising the God who "has granted [the Gentiles] repentance that leads to life" (11:18). This recognition is important because the fact that God has even granted the Gentiles such privilege means that they are to be included into God's people as Gentiles.

Second, the active role of Cornelius is also emphasized in this report. The earlier account simply notes that Cornelius sent messengers to invite Peter to his house (10:4–8). Peter's report here makes it clear that Cornelius sent messengers to Peter so that "he will bring you a message through which you and all your household will be saved" (11:14). This explicit note not only points to the significance of Cornelius's request, but also highlights Cornelius's role as he accepts the angel's call so that he can be saved. While the emphasis on God underscores his sovereignty behind all these events, the focus

on Cornelius also points to his active role in the reception of this gift.

Third, this report again highlights the role of the Jerusalem apostles. The mere fact that Peter is the agent through which a Gentile can hear the gospel serves to highlight the central role the Jerusalem church plays in this important event (cf. Acts 8:14). The need for Peter to provide a detailed report to the Jerusalem church reinforces this point (11:2). The unity of the Jerusalem church and the church of the Gentiles is thus maintained.

Finally, the role of the word of God should not be missed. Earlier references to the word emphasize the progress of the word among the elect people of God (cf. Acts 6:7); in his speech to Cornelius and those around him, Peter also notes that this "word" (NIV "message"; Greek *logos*) was sent by God to "the people of Israel" (10:36). In his introduction to Peter's speech in Jerusalem, Luke announces that the Gentiles have finally "received the word of God" (11:1). This signifies yet another stage in the progression of this powerful word of God.

E. Church at Antioch (11:19–30). After describing the conversion of the Gentiles, Luke turns his attention to the situation in the church at Antioch. The notes concerning the scattering of the believers "by the persecution that broke out when Stephen was killed" (11:19) recall the earlier account after Stephen's death (8:1), but this section also picks up on the earlier mentioning of the relationship between Barnabas and Saul in 9:27 and places them now in Antioch (11:25–26). This paves the way for the later narrative, as the church in Antioch will send out Barnabas and Saul as the messengers of the word (13:1–3).

The preaching of the gospel in Phoenicia, Cyprus, and Antioch pushes the gospel beyond Judea, Samaria, and even the coastal area near Caesarea. The focus of this section is on Antioch, the third largest city in the Roman world (Josephus, *Jewish War* 3.29). Luke notes that some begin to speak to the "Greeks" (11:20). Instead of "Greeks" (*Hellēnas*), some Greek manuscripts read "Hellenists" (*Hellēnistas*, cf. NRSV), a word that could refer to Greek-speaking Jews (cf. 6:1). The earliest manuscripts support the reading "Greeks," and in light of the fact that this group is to be contrasted with "Jews" (11:19), Luke most likely intends to refer to Gentiles here.

The connections between the Jerusalem church and the Antioch church are emphasized in a number of ways, thus highlighting the unity between missions in Judea and missions in the Gentile lands. First, "the Lord's hand was with them" (11:21a) recalls God's mighty hand among the believers in Judea (Acts 4:30), and the report of an impressive growth (11:21b, 24) likewise points to earlier reports (2:41, 47; 4:4; 5:14). Second, the fact that Barnabas is sent to Antioch by the Jerusalem church (11:22) strengthens this connection. Third, the fact that "some prophets came down from Jerusalem to Antioch" (11:27) provides further evidence of the communication between the two churches. The relief help sent by the believers in Antioch to Jerusalem (11:29–30) in turn points to the unity behind these two churches.

The believers are first called "Christians" in Antioch (11:26), pointing to the distinct presence of this community in this significant city. The passive verb "called" probably indicates that outsiders applied this label to the believers. Other appearances of this term in the New Testament further point to the likelihood that this was originally a derogatory term applied by those opposed to this movement (26:28; 1 Pet. 4:16). In any case, this term points to the identity of believers as those who follow "Christ."

The mentioning of the "severe famine" that "happened during the reign of Claudius" (11:28) is confirmed by extrabiblical accounts that point to the existence of several famines during Claudius's reign (AD 41–54; cf. Josephus, *Jewish Antiquities* 3.320–21; 20.101; Suetonius, *Claudius* 19.2; Tacitus, *Annals* 12.43). It is possible that this famine relief effort is to

The modern city of Antakya, Turkey, was once known as Syrian Antioch. In Antioch, Jewish and Gentile Christians were first forced to think about how to overcome ethnic differences. The church in Antioch, which launched Paul into his missionary journeys, became hugely influential in the early Christian world.

be equated with the one mentioned by Paul in Galatians 2:1–10. Jesus himself had predicted the occurrence of famine (Luke 21:11), but Luke here does not focus on the eschatological nature of this event.

F. Persecution in Jerusalem (12:1–25). In the midst of the demonstration of the church's unity, one again finds the persecution of the church by the Jews. The first section of this account (12:1–19a) focuses on Herod's persecution of Peter and God's deliverance of Peter from prison. The second section (12:19b–25) focuses on the demise of Herod. Placed side by side, these two sections provide a stark contrast to one another as the work of God proceeds in the midst of persecution.

The "King Herod" (12:1) introduced here is Herod Agrippa I, the grandson of Herod the Great, who in AD 41 gained control of the entire reign of his grandfather. A popular ruler among the Jews (Josephus, *Jewish Antiquities* 19.328–31), he ruled until AD 44. His popularity was probably rooted in his constant desire to please the Jews; this is supported by Luke's statement that Herod persecuted the early apostles to strengthen his standing among the Jews (12:3). In listing the evil deeds of Herod, Luke mentions Herod's execution of James the brother of John (12:2). Since James was one of the Twelve (Luke 5:10; 6:14), his death signifies the martyrdom of the first apostle, one of the leaders of the Jerusalem church.

The miraculous deliverance of Peter from prison recalls a similar event in 5:17–24, but the details included here point back to the death and resurrection of Jesus. These include the appearance of a Herodian ruler (12:1; cf. Luke 23:6–16) during the Feast of Unleavened Bread and Passover (12:3–4; cf. Luke 22:1, 7), the arrest and the intended trial (12:4; cf. Luke 22:54–23:25), the appearance of an angel (12:7; cf. Luke 22:43), the call to "get up" (12:7; cf. Luke 24:7, 46), the presence of a woman witness (12:13; cf. Luke 24:1–8), the disbelief of other disciples (12:15; cf. Luke 24:11), and the assumption that Peter is only a disembodied

spirit (12:15; cf. Luke 24:37). Luke again points to the continuity between Jesus and his apostles. The mentioning of James (12:17) the brother of the Lord (cf. Acts 1:14) confirms the connection between Jesus and the apostolic church in that he was considered to be one of the "pillars" of the Jerusalem church (Gal. 2:9).

Other details point further back to the Exodus traditions. The summary statement concerning the evil deeds of Herod (12:1) recalls the description of the acts of Pharaoh in Exodus 3. The Passover reference (12:4) naturally evokes this significant event, and Peter's escape from prison also recalls the departure of the Israelites from Egypt in Exodus 12–14, 18. Even the command to put on "sandals" (12:8) reminds one of a similar command in Exodus 12:11. The death of Herod in 12:20–23 likewise recalls that of Pharaoh (Exodus 14–15). While a clear dependence cannot be proven, Luke is likely depicting the recapitulation of God's acts in history.

Luke's portrayal of Herod's death (12:19b–25) provides a strong contrast to the depiction of Peter's deliverance. Luke explicitly identifies the cause of Herod's death as his refusal to give glory to God (12:23), when the people declared, "This is the voice of a god, not of a man." The act of honoring Herod is therefore interpreted as an act of idolatry that cannot be tolerated. Herod's arrogance is contrasted with the humility of Peter, who, after escaping from prison, honors God as the one who has saved him (12:11). Herod's failure to recognize that Jesus is the only Lord of all led to his destruction by "an angel of the Lord" (12:23), the same agent that earlier delivered Peter from prison (12:11).

Josephus also provides a description of Herod Agrippa's demise (*Jewish Antiquities* 19.343–50). Josephus situates Herod in Caesarea, and he is hailed as god by the audience. In describing his cause of death, Josephus points to a sensation of pain in his heart and stomach that ultimately leads to his death. Although there are differences in the details emphasized in the two accounts, both accounts point to Herod's acceptance of the claim to be a divine being.

A king dressed in royal robes being killed by God in the presence of an audience consisting of people from Tyre (12:20) points one to the prophetic oracle against the King of Tyre in Ezekiel 28. In rebuking this ruler, the Lord reminds him that he is "a mere mortal and not a god" (Ezek. 28:2), and he "will die a violent death" (Ezek. 28:8). Other prophetic books contain similar warnings that those who claim to be "like the Most High" (Isa. 14:14)

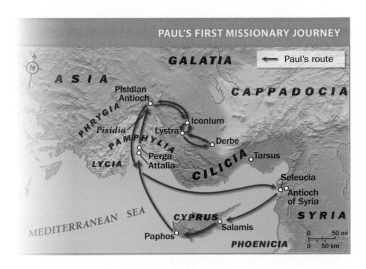

PAUL'S FIRST MISSIONARY JOURNEY

will fall from their exalted place of power (Isa. 14:12). In the context of Acts, anyone who challenges the sovereignty of the "Lord of all" (10:36) will be overcome by the power of God. This point is well illustrated by the summary statement at the end of this narrative: "But the word of God continued to spread and flourish" (12:24). As the second of the three similarly worded summary statements in Acts (cf. 6:7; 19:20), this statement points to the completion of the second stage in the progression of the word. The first summary statement concludes the preaching of the gospel in Jerusalem (6:7), and this statement points to the completion of the gospel preaching in Judea and Samaria. The full-blown mission to the Gentiles will only start in chapter 13, where one finds the first missionary journey of Paul. Verse 25 paves the way for this journey by bringing "Barnabas" and "John, also called Mark" back from Jerusalem to Antioch.

4. Mission to the Gentiles (13:1–21:16)

A. Paul's first missionary journey (13:1–14:28). 13:1–52. The third stage in Luke's portrayal of the progression of the word begins with the sending off of Saul and Barnabas by the church of Antioch (13:1–3). The list of prophets and teachers is important, as it points to the diversity of backgrounds of those who serve in Antioch (13:1). Although they are most

likely all Jews, they came from different parts of the Roman world. Barnabas was from Cyprus (4:36), while Saul was "born in Tarsus" (22:3). Judging from the Latin name "Niger," which means "black," it is possible that Simeon was from Africa, and Luke explicitly notes that "Lucius" is from Cyrene, in North Africa. Finally, Manaen's connection with "Herod the tetrarch" points to his social location, and he is to be counted among the aristocrats. It is perhaps not an accident that among such a group God would raise up two who will champion the first extensive mission trip.

The explicit guidance of the Holy Spirit at the beginning of this journey points to the significance of this event. The fact that Barnabas and Saul are "set apart" (13:2) for the work of God by his own initiative and that they receive the laying on of hands points to the account of the commissioning of the Levites in Numbers 8:5–11. This not only provides sufficient justification for their work beyond the land of the Jews; it also provides a redefinition of God's people, as these messengers will serve God's elect ones beyond the confines of Israel.

The account of their ministry on the island of Cyprus (13:4–12) begins with a note concerning the guidance of the Holy Spirit (13:4), not unlike the one found at the beginning of Jesus's ministry (Luke 4:1, 14). It is in this episode that Luke first calls "Saul" by his Roman name, "Paul" (13:9), thus indicating the shift that the gospel is now reaching an increasingly Gentile audience. While preaching to the proconsul Sergius Paulus in Paphos, Barnabas and Paul are met with opposition by the false prophet "Bar-Jesus" (13:6), who is also called Elymas (13:8). Paul's direct speech against Elymas reveals his true nature not only as a false prophet and a sorcerer but also as a "child of the devil" and "an enemy of everything that is right" (13:10). This is in contrast to Paul, who is "filled with the Holy Spirit" (13:9). The phrase "an enemy of everything that is right" can be literally rendered as "an enemy of all righteousness [Greek *dikaiosynē*]" (NRSV), and this directly identifies him as the enemy of the risen Lord, who is called "the Righteous One" (*ho dikaios*, 22:14; cf. 3:14; 7:52). Moreover, the description of Elymas's work as "perverting the straight

ways of the Lord" (literal translation, 13:10) is the exact reversal of the one who prepares for the eschatological work of God: "Prepare the way for the Lord, make straight paths for him" (Luke 3:4; cf. Isa. 40:3). The attempt of Elymas "to turn the proconsul from the faith" (13:8) is therefore an attempt to turn the proconsul from the true God to the false deity that Elymas himself represents.

The triumph of the word is manifested when the punishment uttered by Paul is fulfilled (13:11). This punishment of loss of sight is significant because it reverses the promises of the Old Testament prophet that "all people will see God's salvation" (Luke 3:6; cf. Isa. 40:5); this also counters Paul's aim in his preaching to the Gentiles as he seeks to "open their eyes and turn them from darkness to light" (Acts 26:18). The conversion of the proconsul also points to the power of the word of God as a governor of a Roman senatorial province subjects himself to the authority of the risen Lord.

The center of this account of the first missionary journey lies in Paul and Barnabas's experience in Pisidian Antioch, of the Roman

The remains of the Basilica of St. Paul at Pisidian Antioch. Foundation stones at the southern wall of the church (left) have been dated to the first century and may be the remains of the synagogue in which Paul preached (Acts 13:14–42).

province of Galatia (13:13–52). The account begins by locating them in a synagogue (13:13). As Jesus began his public ministry with a sermon in a Jewish synagogue (Luke 4:14–31), Paul also begins his public ministry as a missionary in a synagogue. As in the case of Jesus's Nazareth sermon, Paul's sermon also provides a unique glimpse into his preaching in a Jewish synagogue, because although Luke mentions Paul visiting the synagogue often (14:1; 17:1–2; 18:4–5; 19:8), only here does he provide the content of his synagogue preaching.

The content of this lengthy sermon occupies much of the first part of this section (13:16–41). The first section (13:16–25) presents a review of history that connects the mighty acts of God during the exodus event to the eschatological deliverance that comes through Jesus. Paul also directly identifies Jesus as the descendant of David, whom John the Baptist testified to be the one who fulfills God's promises. The second section (13:26–31) focuses on the climax of salvation history: although the people of God rejected the savior promised by God, God raised Jesus from the dead. The third section (13:32–37) lists three Old Testament promises that point to the resurrection of the Son of God (13:33 [Ps. 2:7]; 13:34 [Isa. 55:3]; 13:35 [Ps. 16:10]). These quotations pick up Paul's earlier claim as they point to Jesus as the fulfillment of the Davidic promise. Psalm 2:7 identifies Jesus, the descendant of David, as the Son of God. Isaiah 55:3 points to the faithfulness of God toward his own people as he fulfills his promises to David. Psalm 16:10 points to the resurrection as a sign for God's eternal blessings on his Son and his kingdom. The final section (13:38–41) calls the people of God to believe in Jesus and his gospel. This section ends with a quotation from Habakkuk 1:5, one that warns the audience not to follow their leaders in Jerusalem in rejecting God's mighty acts through his Son.

As in the case of Jesus's experience in Nazareth (Luke 4:22), the Jews' initial response to Paul's message is positive (13:42–43). Like Jesus (Luke 4:23–29), however, Paul is soon rejected by many who are jealous of him (13:44–45). In response to the Jewish opposition, Paul makes a striking proclamation: "Since you reject it [i.e., the word of God] and do not consider yourselves worthy of eternal life, we now turn to the Gentiles" (13:46). This statement seems to indicate that Paul will not continue to preach the gospel to the Jews, but the fact that he "went as usual into the Jewish synagogue" during his next stop in Iconium (14:1) argues against this conclusion. This statement should instead be compared to the prophetic critique offered by Old Testament prophets: the ultimate goal of such warning and critique is to urge the people of God to repent. Other, similar statements Paul will utter later in the narrative (cf. 18:6; 28:28) reflect similar intention. In this context, Paul's statement points clearly to the responsibility of the Jews for rejecting the gospel. Although God is faithful to his people, his people continue to reject him.

After this striking statement, Paul quotes from Isaiah 49:6 in justifying his turn to the Gentiles (13:47). This text from Isaiah has been alluded to a number of times in the Lukan narrative (Luke 24:47; Acts 1:8), but most striking is its connection with Luke 2:32, where the phrase "a light for revelation to the Gentiles" is applied to Jesus. In this context, however, the introductory note ("this is what the Lord has commanded us") indicates that the "light" is now referring to Paul and Barnabas, who are bringing the gospel to the Gentiles. The continuity between the mission of Jesus and that of his followers is therefore emphasized by the repeated use of Isaiah 49:6, a verse that describes God's work in an eschatological era.

This account concludes with a description of Gentile reception (13:48) and continued Jewish rejection (13:49–52) of the gospel. As they learned from Jesus's own instructions to his disciples (Luke 9:5), Paul and Barnabas "shook the dust from their feet" to signify how the Jews are to be responsible for their rejection of the gospel (13:51). In the midst of persecution, however, the disciples continue to be "filled with joy and with the Holy Spirit" (13:52).

14:1–28. The experience of Paul and Barnabas in Iconium (14:1–7) is comparable to their experience in Pisidian Antioch. Paul and Barnabas go "as usual into the Jewish synagogue," and initially they receive a positive response from those who are present (14:1). But some of the Jews again decide to oppose them and those who have believed (14:2). Luke's description concerning "a plot . . . among both Gentiles and Jews, together with their leaders [or "rulers"; Greek *tois archousin*], to mistreat them and stone them" (14:5) recalls the prayer by the believers who quote from Psalm 2:2 in describing the persecution suffered by the earthly Jesus: "The kings of the earth rise up and the rulers [*hoi archontes*] band together against the Lord and against his anointed one" (Acts 4:26). Therefore, the persecution they receive provides yet another confirmation that they are indeed walking in the steps of their Lord. This also fulfills the prophecy of Jesus when he called Paul: "I will show him how much he must suffer for my name" (Acts 9:16). In addition, the fact that Paul and Barnabas, in the midst of opposition, "spent considerable time there, speaking boldly [*parrēsiazomenoi*] for the Lord, who confirmed the message of his grace by enabling them to perform signs and wonders [*sēmeia kai terata*]" (14:3) also points to God's answer to that same prayer of the believers: "Now, Lord, consider their threats and enable your servants to speak your word with great boldness [*parrēsias*]. Stretch out your hand to heal and perform signs and wonders [*sēmeia kai terata*]" (Acts 4:29–30).

After leaving Iconium, Paul and Barnabas travel to Lystra (14:8–20). Their ministry in Lystra begins with the healing of a crippled man (14:8–10). In numerous ways, this account recalls the earlier miracle performed by Peter in 3:1–10: both men are crippled "from birth" (14:8; cf. 3:2), and in both accounts the apostle looks directly at the man (14:9; 3:4). After being commanded to stand, both men "jumped" up and "began to walk" (14:10; 3:8). Through this account, the connection between Paul and the

original Twelve is reaffirmed. It is perhaps not by accident that it is in their first missionary journey that Luke first calls Paul and Barnabas "apostles" (14:4, 14).

When the crowd sees what has happened, they shout, "The gods have come down to us in human form" (14:11). Barnabas they call Zeus, and Paul, Hermes (14:12), and the priest of Zeus and the crowd want to offer sacrifices to them (14:13). Archaeological remains testify to the worship of Zeus and Hermes in this region in the Roman period. The fact that Barnabas is called Zeus, the head of the Olympian Pantheon, points to the fact that he is not considered to be of a lower status than Paul. Hermes is the god of eloquence, and is probably considered to be a spokesperson for Zeus. This also points to the role of Paul as one who is primarily responsible for proclaiming the gospel.

The reaction of Paul and Barnabas to such response is noteworthy. Unlike Simon Magus (8:9–10) and Herod (12:21–23), Paul and Barnabas refuse to be honored as deities since they recognize that they are mere mortals, having the same nature as human beings (14:15). While rejecting such acclamations, they urge the crowd to turn from "worthless things," a phrase often used in reference to idols in the Septuagint (Lev. 17:7; Isa. 2:20; 30:15; cf. Isa. 44:9). With this phrase, Paul and Barnabas move beyond merely refusing to be worshiped as gods to a discussion of how the audience should turn from worshiping idols.

Instead of worshiping idols, they should worship "the living God" (14:15a). This peculiar description appears most often in contexts where one finds the affirmation of the sovereignty of God over against idols (and other powers) neither able to see nor hear, nor to save those who worship them (cf. Deut. 5:26; Josh. 3:10; 1 Sam. 17:26; Jer. 10:10; 23:36; Dan. 6:20, 26). Unlike these idols, which are created things, this living God is the Creator, "who made heaven and earth and sea and everything in them" (14:15b; cf. Exod. 20:11; Ps. 146:6). In light of the fact that he is the Creator of all, this

Lord is in control of all, including the nations and the rulers (cf. Isa. 37:16–20). This would explain the transition from the affirmation of the sovereignty of the Lord in verse 15 to the concern with "all nations" in verse 16. Although God's specific revelation has yet to be revealed to the nations, he has shown his kindness to them, thus testifying to his own existence. This speech, which is addressed to Gentiles, is very different from the one addressed to the Jews in the synagogue in Pisidian Antioch. There, Paul focused on Jesus as the fulfillment of Old Testament promises. Here, Paul argues from nature and creation that the God of Israel is the Lord of all. This address also paves the way for a more detailed and elaborate discussion in Paul's Areopagus speech in Athens (Acts 17:22–31).

As in Pisidian Antioch, the crowd is again turned against the apostles, at which point Paul and Barnabas leave for Derbe (15:20). Luke does not provide any description of their ministry in Derbe; instead, he focuses on their return trip to Antioch of Syria. This is an important trip because what Paul and Barnabas do when they revisit the churches in Lystra, Iconium, and Antioch is an important part of their ministry as apostles of Jesus Christ. Moving beyond mere conversion, they strengthen the disciples, encourage them to be faithful to the gospel (14:22a), and appoint leaders for the newly formed communities of believers (14:23). The direct statement, "We must go through many hardships to enter the kingdom of God" (14:22b), is an important one. First, it identifies suffering as an essential part of the growth of the believers. Second, the word "must" (Greek *dei*) points to the necessity that is grounded in the plan of God. Therefore, this statement should not be interpreted as, "We ought to go through many hardships so that we can enter the kingdom of God," but, "Going through many hardships as we enter the kingdom of God is part of the plan of God." Third, earlier the risen Lord revealed to Ananias that Paul "must [*dei*] suffer" for his name (9:16). Now Paul in turn expands this prophecy to include

all those who follow Jesus. As Jesus himself suffered, those who follow him will have the honor to suffer for his name.

B. Jerusalem council and the identity of Gentile believers (15:1–35). With the conversion of the Gentiles during the first missionary journey of Paul and Barnabas, the church is confronted with the question concerning the ethnic identity of Gentiles who enter the people of God (15:1–6). This issue is sharply raised by those believers who are Pharisees, as they insist, "Gentiles must be circumcised and required to obey the law of Moses" (15:5). When Paul and Barnabas, among others, go to Jerusalem, they meet with the leaders of the Jerusalem church. The meeting, often called "the Jerusalem council," provides an important occasion for the clarification of significant issues that touch on the heart of the gospel message. Luke's report of the meeting focuses on the speeches of Peter (15:7–12) and James (15:13–21), the latter of which concludes with the "apostolic decree" (15:19–20). Luke's emphasis on the significance of this event is reflected by the inclusion of the letter to be sent to the Gentile believers (15:22–35), a letter that summarizes the discussion in the Jerusalem council.

Peter's speech (15:7–12) recalls the conclusion reached in the Cornelius story in 11:12, when he again points to the implication of the vision from God (15:9). The reaffirmation of the equality between Jews and Gentiles in this eschatological era is made with this striking statement that there is no distinction "between us and them," a statement that once again challenges the Jewish theology of election. Significantly, this discussion of equality is tied to the issue of purity in the assertion that God is able to purify the hearts of the Gentiles. The Jews often emphasize their special status before God through their meticulous practice of the purity laws that aim at separating them from the unclean Gentiles. Peter's statement therefore focuses on the act of God, who takes the initiative to cleanse the Gentiles and erase the distinction between Jews and Gentiles. This active role of God in the cleansing of the Gentiles is called "grace," and Peter makes it clear that both Jews and Gentiles are saved through this "grace of our Lord Jesus" (15:11).

The speech of James (15:13–21) moves the discussion one step forward by noting that these Gentiles who are saved by grace are to be identified as part of the people of God. He states, "God first intervened to choose a people for his name from the Gentiles" (15:14). The fact that the word "people" (Greek *laos*) is applied to the "Gentiles" in this statement shows that Gentiles are now part of the people of God. James then quotes from Amos 9:11–12 in verses 16–18. In quoting from this passage, which deals with the renewal of the house of David and the restoration of the people of God, James is situating God's acceptance of the Gentiles within the wider restoration program that he promised. Not only is Jesus the Son of David, but the eschatological era that his death and resurrection introduce is one that fulfills God's promises to David.

James concludes his speech with a recommendation that Gentiles should observe a minimal set of requirements as they participate in the people of God: "Abstain from food polluted by idols, from sexual immorality, from the meat of strangled animals and from blood" (15:20). The exact nature and meaning of these prohibitions is a subject of intense debate. Some have considered this to be a selection of Mosaic commandments, but this is contrary to Peter's assertion that the "yoke" should not be placed on the neck of the Gentiles (15:10). Moreover, the precise selection of these commandments from within the Mosaic law cannot be explained by this reading. Others have pointed to the laws concerning the foreigners living in the land of Israel in Leviticus 17–18 as the possible context of the decree. These two chapters in Leviticus do address issues concerning idolatry, sexual immorality, and blood, and the purpose of that section in Leviticus is to facilitate the interaction between Israelites and foreigners within the same land and community. The apostolic

decree may well address the same sociological concern, as the prohibitions are meant to facilitate the practical interaction between Jews and Gentiles. These then should not be considered as requirements through which one can be saved.

A third option is to see this apostolic decree within the context of polemic against pagan worship. This would obviously explain the mentioning of "idols" in the first part of this decree. "Sexual immorality" may point to cultic prostitution or even a general criticism of the immorality of those who worship false gods. References to "strangled animals" and "blood" may also point to Gentile cultic practices. If so, what the decree focuses on is the call to the Gentiles to worship the one and only living God. This reading is preferable because the decree is addressed not to those living in the land of Israel, as in the case of Leviticus 17–18, but to those who are living in Gentile lands. Both the second and third reading point to the need to read this decree in its proper historical and cultural contexts. Rather than providing abstract and absolute laws for future Christians to observe, this decree calls the Gentiles to live as faithful followers of Jesus Christ.

This reading of the decree and the flow of the arguments presented by James and Peter force one to reconsider the meaning of the final statement of James's speech: "For the law of Moses has been preached in every city from the earliest times and is read in the synagogues on every Sabbath" (15:21). A surface reading may assume that James is suggesting that since many are familiar with the Mosaic law, then Gentiles should at least observe a part of it. This would be an unlikely concluding note to a discussion that emphasizes the "grace of our Lord Jesus" (15:11). In light of Peter's earlier rhetorical question, "Why do you try to test God by putting on the necks of Gentiles a yoke that neither we nor our ancestors have been able to bear?" (15:10), this statement requires a different reading: Moses has been preached and read in every city from the earliest times, but we still fail to observe his commandments; why then should we require the Gentiles to do that which we failed to do?

With the church adopting this recommendation, they send Judas and Silas, leaders of the Jerusalem church, with Paul and Barnabas to Antioch with a letter that outlines the decree (15:22–35). This letter emphasizes that this is not simply a decision reached by humans but is also affirmed by

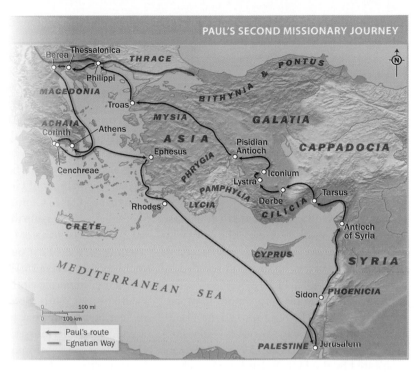

PAUL'S SECOND MISSIONARY JOURNEY

the "Holy Spirit" (15:28). Judas and Silas's ministry among those in Antioch (15:32), along with the "blessing of peace" they receive from these believers, once again points to the unity of the Jerusalem and Antioch churches.

***C. Paul's second missionary journey (15:36–18:22).* 15:36–16:40.** Luke's account of Paul's second missionary journey begins with a note concerning the disagreement between Paul and Barnabas because of John Mark, which leads to their parting of company (15:36–41). This surprising account of the argument between Barnabas and Paul points to the historicity of Luke's account, as he does not shy away from the problems among those proclaiming the gospel, although Paul's own writing points to his eventual reconciliation with John Mark (2 Tim. 4:11). In terms of literary function, this short paragraph explains the disappearance of Barnabas while introducing "Silas" (15:40), a leader of the Jerusalem church (15:27), as Paul's new missionary partner.

After arriving at Lystra and visiting the converts of his earlier missionary journey, Paul

decides to bring Timothy along as he travels farther west (16:1–5). Timothy is an important figure in Paul's second and third missionary journeys (cf. 17:14, 15; 18:5; 19:22; 20:4). He is considered by Paul to be his "co-worker" (Rom. 16:21; cf. 1 Thess. 3:2), his "brother" (1 Cor. 16:11; 2 Cor. 1:1; Col. 1:1; Philem. 1), and even his "son" (1 Cor. 4:17; Phil. 2:22; 1 Tim. 1:2, 18; 2 Tim. 1:2). In this account, Luke describes Timothy's mother as a Jew, his father a Greek (16:1). Paul's decision to circumcise him (16:3) is important for two reasons. First, Paul's ministry among the Gentiles has already generated some criticisms among "the circumcised believers" (11:2; 15:1), and these criticisms led to the convening of the Jerusalem council (15:6–29). Against those who argue that "the Gentiles must be circumcised" (15:5), the council decided that Gentiles did not have to be circumcised in order to be saved. While the council focused on the requirements for the Gentiles, Paul's act here focuses on the Jewish identity of Timothy. On the one hand, Paul's decision to circumcise Timothy shows that he is not opposed to the practices of the Jews. The mission to the Gentiles is therefore not an act to deny the significance of the history and traditions of the Jews. On the other hand, this act also anticipates the later accusation of the Jews that Paul tells "all the Jews who live among the Gentiles . . . not to circumcise their children" (Acts 21:21). In this account, Paul makes it clear that he does not aim at violating the customs of the Jews. Paul also makes it clear, however, that he circumcises Timothy not because this is a requirement for Timothy to participate in God's people, but rather because Paul does not want to offend "the Jews who lived in that area" (16:3). This brief account, then, only confirms the decision reached by the Jerusalem council (16:4).

When Paul and his companions move beyond "the region of Phrygia and Galatia" (16:6), an area that may refer to the places Paul visited in his first journey (Acts 13:15–14:20), they are prohibited by the Holy Spirit from preaching the word in both the province of Asia to the west and the province of Bithynia to the north (16:6–10). They then travel to Troas, where Paul has a vision in which a man of Macedonia begs them to come to Macedonia (16:9). In this account, which introduces a new direction of the Pauline mission, Luke emphasizes the role of God through the appearance of the "Holy Spirit" (16:6), the "Spirit of Jesus" (16:7), and a "vision" (16:10). The redirection through divine intervention recalls a similar description in the exodus event when God redirects his people according to his own plan (Exod. 13:17–18). In light of the emphasis on the work of God in this account, the call to "help" (16:9) may also point back to similar calls in the Old Testament when the mighty work of God is expected (Gen. 49:25; 1 Sam. 7:12; 1 Chron. 12:18; Ps. 10:14; 28:7). The sudden appearance of the first-person plural pronoun "we" in reference to the traveling of Paul and his companions introduces the first of a series of we-passages (16:10–17; 20:5–15; 21:1–18; 27:1–28:16). These passages can best be explained by the fact that Luke himself is

among the companions of Paul in these sections of his journeys. These passages also point to the significance of eyewitness reports in his narrative (cf. Luke 1:2).

After arriving in Macedonia, they travel to Philippi, where one finds the account of the first convert in Europe (16:11–15). The "place of prayer" (6:13) that Paul and his companions visit on the Sabbath may be a synagogue, and in this "place of prayer" one finds the conversion of Lydia, a "worshiper of God" (6:14), a description that applies to Gentile half-proselytes like Cornelius who worship the God of Israel (Acts 10:2). The social status of Lydia is emphasized in a number of ways. First, purple clothing belongs to the wealthy (Luke 16:19). The fact that Lydia is a "dealer in purple cloth" (16:14) reflects her exalted social status. Second, the mentioning of "her household" may point to her status as a widow, but her possession of a household shows that she is not a poor widow. Moreover, her invitation to Paul and his companions to stay with her also reflects that she is a person of means.

Lydia's status as a wealthy and independent woman is contrasted with that of the "female slave" who is manipulated by her owner (16:16–18). In this first explicit exorcism account in Acts, one finds a surprising confession by the evil spirit through this girl (16:17). While she is a slave of the evil spirit, she recognizes that the apostles are "servants of the Most High God," a title that points to the supreme authority of God and the risen Lord (cf. Acts 7:48). The word "way" in "way to be saved" also correctly points to the eschatological saving acts of God through Jesus Christ (cf. Luke 3:4). Among such acts is the releasing of those who are enslaved to the power of evil. This is precisely what this slave girl experiences when the evil spirit is cast out in the name of Jesus Christ (16:18).

In reaction to this demonstration of power, Paul and Silas are persecuted by the Jews and the magistrates under their influence (16:19–40). While they are in prison, they are once again delivered by the power of God. The connection with the previous episode cannot be missed. The deliverance of the slave girl from the power of the evil spirit and the deliverance of Paul and Silas from prison both testify to the liberating power of the work of God. Both events also point to the fulfillment of Isaiah's promise explicitly noted in Jesus's Nazareth sermon (Luke 4:18–19; see Isa. 58:6; 61:2). In the account of Paul and Silas's imprisonment, one finds yet another ironic twist. While Paul and Silas remain in prison even after the miraculous earthquake that forces open the prison doors, it is the jailer who realizes that he needs "to be saved" (16:30). The ones in physical chains are able to deliver a message that frees the jailer from the chains of darkness (16:31–33).

The relationship between Rome and the early Christian movement begins to take center stage when Luke introduces Philippi as "a Roman colony" (16:12), although other cities to which Paul has already been were also Roman colonies (e.g., Pisidian Antioch, Lystra). The significance of this fact is made clear when Paul and Silas later refuse to just walk out of the prison because they have been treated unfairly in light of their status as "Roman citizens" (16:37). Although they are accused of "advocating customs unlawful for . . . Romans to accept or practice" (16:21), they have proven to be law-abiding Roman citizens and are finally escorted from their unjust treatment (16:39). This account again points to the Jews as the ones who disturb the peace of the city while the apostles are simply proclaiming the gospel that leads to salvation.

17:1–34. After Paul and Silas leave Philippi, they pass through several cities on the *Via Egnatia* (Egnatian Way) and arrive at Thessalonica, the capital of the province of Macedonia (17:1–9). The fact that Paul goes into a Jewish synagogue and that this is "his custom" (17:2) shows that he still insists on preaching to the Jews even though he has constantly been persecuted by some of them. The summary statement of his preaching apparently presupposes the knowledge of his synagogue sermon elsewhere

(cf. Acts 13:16–41), but this summary itself is important in that it points to the death and resurrection of Jesus as the center of the gospel message. Moreover, his explanation that "the Messiah had to suffer" points again to the necessity of Christ's suffering, which is repeatedly noted in Luke's writings (cf. Luke 9:22; 13:33; 17:25; 24:7, 26, 44–46). When Paul was called to preach the gospel to the Gentiles, the risen Lord also referred to the necessity of Paul's own suffering (Acts 9:16). In this context, therefore, Paul's focus on the suffering of Jesus not only points to the center of the gospel message but provides the continuity between his mission and the ministry of the earthly Jesus.

As in the previous instances (cf. Acts 13:43–45; 14:1–2), Paul's preaching of the gospel also provokes a divided response (17:4–5). Neither the identity of the converts nor that of Jason, who welcomed the apostles into his house, is discussed further. The focus is rather on the charge against these apostles and their followers: "They are all defying Caesar's decrees, saying that there is another king, one called Jesus" (17:7). This accusation resembles those made against Jesus (Luke 23:2) during his trial. While Paul and his companions never preach the existence of an earthly political kingdom that challenges the Roman Empire, it is true that Jesus is indeed "the king," as Jesus himself admitted (Luke 23:3). This charge of subverting the claims of the Roman imperial system moves beyond the early accusations of the Jews at Philippi that these apostles advocate "customs unlawful for . . . Romans to accept or practice" (16:21). The Jews realize that while they have not been able to deter the growth of the early Christian movement, they can use the power and fears of the Roman provincial officials to oppose this movement.

Paul and Silas's experience in Berea is more pleasant, as many Jews and Gentiles accept the gospel (17:10–15). In the eyes of Luke, these Bereans are "of more noble character" (17:11); thus a lack of noble character is ascribed to those who oppose the gospel message. These

Bereans are noble because they have "examined the Scriptures every day to see if what Paul said was true" (17:11). This description points not only to their serious attitude when they receive the message but also to the intimate relationship between the gospel and the Old Testament Scriptures. Jesus fulfills the plan of God, and a proper understanding of the gospel requires a proper reading of the Scriptures of Israel. When the Jews from Thessalonica cause unrest, Paul is led out of the city and sent to Athens.

Paul's stay in Athens, a city with rich cultural and intellectual history, provides an occasion for him to preach directly to the Gentiles who are not affiliated with the Jewish synagogues (17:16–34). The theme of this major speech is introduced by a note that Paul "was greatly distressed to see that the city was full of idols" (17:16). In this city of cultural and historical significance, one finds Paul being confronted by "Epicurean and Stoic philosophers" (17:18). The Epicureans affirmed a thoroughly materialistic worldview and saw the acquisition of pleasure as the highest principle. The Stoics affirmed a pantheistic worldview and saw reason as the underlying principle of both society and the cosmos. While these two schools diverged in their understanding of the world and the place of humans in such a universe, they both wrestled with a way to explain reality. These attempts were deemed necessary in light of the diminishing influences of the classical Olympian deities and of the mythologies that sought to explain the cultic practices attached to the worship of these deities. When Paul preaches "the good news about Jesus and the resurrection" (17:18), these philosophers naturally find the need to question him, especially since this Jesus seems to be a foreign deity. They bring Paul to "a meeting of the Areopagus" (17:19), a phrase that could literally be rendered simply as "Areopagus" (i.e., Mars Hill), thus referring to a particular location. It is more likely, however, that Luke is referring to a council that meets there (thus the NIV's translation).

In his speech, Paul begins by referring to an altar "to an unknown God" (17:23) that is erected in Athens, one of the few such altars mentioned by Pausanias (*Description of Greece* 1.1.4) and Philostratus (*Life of Apollonius* 6.3.5). Then Paul draws on Old Testament anti-idol polemic in response to the religiosity of the Athenians. First, the description that God is the one "who made the world and everything in it" (17:24) alludes to Isaiah 42:5. Since God is the Creator of all, he "does not live in temples built by human hands" (cf. Lev. 26:1, 30; Isa. 10:11; 46:6; see also Acts 7:48). Moreover, the claim that "we should not think that the divine being is like gold or silver or stone" (17:29) recalls Deuteronomy 29:15–16, which describes the idols in the land of Egypt, and Isaiah 40:18–20, which provides a detailed description of the construction of idols. Finally, as in Old Testament anti-idol polemic, Paul's arguments in this speech are also accompanied by an affirmation of the authority and power of God over all the nations (17:26–27). This God of all nations "commands all people everywhere to repent" (17:30) because he will be the judge of all (17:31). At the end of the speech, Paul moves beyond the Old Testament in drawing attention to the climactic event in salvation history—the resurrection of Jesus. It is the mentioning of this event that caused the Athenians to sneer at him earlier (17:18), but Paul emphasizes that this is precisely the proof that all human beings will eventually be judged.

As Paul draws from the Old Testament traditions, one also finds phrases from the Greek writers. In verse 28, Paul explicitly points to the "poets" that they are familiar with. "We are his offspring" came from Aratus (*Phaenomena* 5; cf. Cleanthes, *Hymn to Zeus* 4), but the source of the earlier statement, "For in him we live and move and have our being," remains unknown, though it resembles a phrase from Epimenides' poem *Cretica*. Paul's knowledge of the Greek poets points to his educational background, which was not limited to the Jewish Scriptures. These quotations also show Paul's attempt to establish connecting points with an audience whose cultural background is not exactly identical to his.

18:1–22. Leaving Athens, Paul traveled west to the Roman city of Corinth (18:1–17), the capital city of Achaia, whose political and economic influence had surpassed that of Athens. As a city that boasted two significant harbors, Cenchreae, which led to the Greek East, and Lechaion, which led to Italy, Corinth was also a significant cultural center. This helps explain why Paul would spend a year and a half in this city (18:11). Verses 2–3 provide significant historical details for this narrative. First, Aquila is introduced as "a Jew" (18:2). This can refer to Aquila as part of the target of Paul's preaching (18:4), but in light of the second half of verse 2, this identification more likely aims at explaining Aquila and his wife Priscilla's move to Corinth. This note also introduces an important couple in the ministry of Paul as noted in the following narrative (18:18–19, 26) as well as in the letters of Paul (Rom. 16:3; 1 Cor. 16:19; 2 Tim. 4:19). Second, while explaining Aquila and Priscilla's presence in Corinth, Luke points to the edict of Claudius that forced "all Jews to leave Rome" (18:2). This edict is mentioned by Suetonius

(*Life of Claudius* 25.4), who notes that Jews were expelled from Rome because of *Chrestus*, a reference that probably points to the unrest caused by the preaching of the gospel of Jesus Christ. The fact that this edict can be dated to AD 49 also provides a key date to anchor the events of Acts within the wider historical setting of the first century. Third, this passage provides a description of Paul as a "tentmaker" (Greek *skēnopoios*), a term that can refer to a variety of occupations related to textiles. Paul is not "idle" when he visits the various communities (2 Thess. 3:11; cf. 1 Thess. 5:14; 2 Thess. 3:6–7), nor does he preach the gospel for his own profit and benefit.

Paul's experience in Corinth is consistent with his previous receptions, with the Jews rejecting the gospel and opposing him. That Paul "shook out his clothes in protest" (18:6) recalls Jesus's earlier instruction to his disciples (Luke 9:5; cf. 10:11) and Paul's earlier act in response

The Temple of Apollo in Corinth. Corinth was a trading town that connected north and south Greece as well as sea traffic between the Aegean and Adriatic seas. Paul visited here on his second tour and stayed for eighteen months to establish a church (Acts 18:11).

to Jewish opposition in Pisidian Antioch (Acts 13:51). Paul's statement that follows explains this act. "Your blood be on your own heads" evokes the language of the Old Testament (Josh. 9:24; 2 Sam. 1:16; 1 Kings 2:33), and "I am innocent of it" points to the responsibility of the Jews for their rejection of the gospel. Paul's claim to "go to the Gentiles" (18:6) likewise recalls his earlier statement in 13:46; as in the earlier episode, this is not an indication of his giving up on the Jews (cf. 18:19, 26; 19:8).

The vision from the risen Lord (18:9–10) provides an introduction to the judgment of Paul before Gallio (18:12), the proconsul of Achaia in AD 51–52. "Do not be afraid" (18:9) evokes the fear-not formula that is often used in divine war contexts when God promises to fight for his people (cf. Num. 21:34; Deut. 3:2; Josh. 8:1–2). The risen Lord promises Paul that he will be present with him as he struggles against those who oppose the work of God. The fact that Gallio dismisses the case the Jews have brought against Paul fulfills the promise made by the risen Lord (18:14–16). Gallio's verdict is important in that the early Christian movement is not to be considered a subversive sect but one related to Judaism, a religion approved by Rome. Luke's emphasis on this verdict shows that even the Roman officials are but an instrument of God as he reveals his glory to the ends of the earth (cf. Acts 4:28).

Luke's description of Paul's return to Antioch (18:18–22) provides the itinerary of Paul to Antioch through Ephesus, Caesarea, and Jerusalem. This brief account serves two additional functions. First, it emphasizes Paul's connection with the Jewish believers and the Jerusalem church. The "vow" (18:18) that Paul takes most likely refers to the Nazirite vow that Jews took when dedicating themselves to God for a period of time (Num. 6:1–21). Paul's cutting off his hair is probably an act prior to the observance of the vow that ends when he has his hair "shaved" (Acts 21:24; cf. Num. 6:18). Luke does not provide the specific occasion for this vow, but this brief note is sufficient in emphasizing Paul's adherence to Jewish traditions. The note that "he went up to Jerusalem and greeted the church" (18:22) also highlights his connection with the center of Jewish Christianity. Second, this account also aims at introducing Paul's return to Ephesus during his third missionary journey. In verse 21, he evokes his obedience to "God's will" in his plan to return to Ephesus. His eventual return to Ephesus (18:24–19:41) is therefore to be understood as dictated by the will of God.

D. Paul's third missionary journey (18:23–21:16). 18:23–19:41. The account of Paul's third missionary journey begins with a note on Paul's travels through the region of Galatia and Phrygia (18:23). The focus of the first episode in this section is, however, on a native of Alexandria who has moved to Ephesus (18:24–28). The description that Apollos is a "learned man" (18:24a) can also point to him being an "eloquent man" (NRSV), but the statement that follows, "with a thorough knowledge of the Scriptures" (18:24b), confirms that he is indeed a "learned man." The phrase "with great fervor" in verse 25 can also be translated as "with the zeal of the Spirit" (cf. Rom. 12:11), but "he knew only the baptism of John" argues against this latter reading. Nevertheless, the fact that he "had been instructed in the way of the Lord" and he "taught about Jesus accurately" suggests that he is at least a believer. Moreover, his not being baptized again shows that this is not a deficiency for a preacher of the word. Whatever is missing in his knowledge and experience is amended by the teaching ministries of Priscilla and Aquila.

When Paul himself arrives at Ephesus, he confronts a group of disciples who have not received the Holy Spirit (19:1–7). Paul then places his hands on them, and they receive the Holy Spirit, which is confirmed by their ability to speak in tongues and to prophesy (19:6). In this brief account, Luke provides a significant discussion of the role of Paul, the identity of these Gentile believers, and the message Paul preaches. First, the significance of Paul is revealed when this account is read in light of the earlier description of the Samaritans' reception of the Holy Spirit (Acts 8:19). The Samaritan believers did not receive the Spirit until the Jerusalem apostles placed their hands on them. In this account, Paul takes on the role of the Jerusalem apostles, as the Spirit descends on the believers through his placing his hands on them. The emphasis is not on the exalted role of one apostle, however, but on the continuation of the Jerusalem church and the mission to the Gentiles. This is reinforced by Luke's statement that "there were about twelve men in all" (19:7), a statement that again evokes the symbol of twelve (see 1:15–26). Under the leadership of the Twelve, the Jewish believers witness the dawn of the eschatological Spirit on the restored people of God. Here the presence of the Spirit among the twelve disciples in Gentile lands confirms that God has indeed taken "a people for his name from the Gentiles" (Acts 15:14). Finally, the message Paul preaches is also of significance. Because they did not receive the Holy Spirit (19:2), Paul preaches to them, and they are "baptized in the name of the Lord Jesus" (19:5), and then the Holy Spirit comes on them (19:6). Luke makes it clear that to receive the Spirit, one has to be "baptized in the name of the Lord Jesus." The reception of the Spirit is

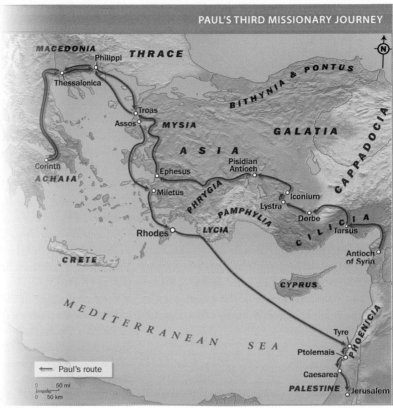

PAUL'S THIRD MISSIONARY JOURNEY

then equated with submission to the lordship of Jesus.

In the summary statement that follows (19:8–10), Paul again faces opposition from those who oppose "the Way" (19:9). Significantly, it is through his ministry in Ephesus that "all the Jews and Greeks who lived in the province of Asia heard the word of the Lord" (19:10). This statement points to the strategy of Paul's missions. He would often spend considerable time in key cities of the region (e.g., Antioch, Corinth, Ephesus), and his preaching would affect those living in the entire region. This note also signifies the reversal of the prohibition in Acts 16:6, in that the word has finally reached those who live in the province of Asia. The phrase "Jews and Greeks" also points to the universal focus of the eschatological gospel.

Luke's account of Paul's ministries in Ephesus focuses on two episodes, the first of which points to the superiority of the name of Jesus (19:11–22). Luke begins with a description of the work of God through Paul as he effortlessly heals the sick and casts out demons (19:11–12). Such acts of power attract the attention of the seven sons of the Jewish high priest Sceva, who have been trying to use the name of Jesus but have failed to produce any results (19:13–14). More important, the evil spirit admits that he only knows Jesus and Paul (19:15). While Luke has emphasized the continuity between the Jewish prophetic traditions and the mission of Jesus and his apostles, this episode draws a line between the Jews and the apostles. Even the sons of a Jewish high priest cannot compete with the apostles, who preach in the name of Jesus. The failure of these Jews even when they invoke "the name of the Lord Jesus" (19:13) also shows that the power of the apostles does not simply lie in the evocation of a magical formula, as the earlier description of Simon the Sorcerer demonstrates (cf. Acts 8:18–23).

The ministry of the apostles is also distinguished from the work of the pagan magicians. When these magicians "brought their scrolls together and burned them publicly" (19:19), they acknowledged that the apostles were not simply magicians like them. This episode, which focuses squarely on the exalted status of "the name of the Lord Jesus" (19:17), paves the way for the next event, which describes the demise of Artemis, the great goddess also called Diana and considered by the Romans to be a fertility goddess. This manifestation of the power of God among both Jews and Gentiles is but an example of how "all the Jews and Greeks who lived in the province of Asia" witness God's power (19:10).

The appearance of the last of the three similarly worded summary statements, in verse 20, is noteworthy. As the previous statements provided a conclusion to the stage of the mission of the apostles in Jerusalem (6:7) and Judea and Samaria (12:24), this statement provides a concluding note to the Gentile mission of Paul at the end of his third missionary journey. Not only is the statement concerning the growth of the

Ephesus was one of the most spectacular cities in western Asia Minor. The theater (shown here) could seat twenty-four thousand. Since Ephesus was a city of high cultural aspirations and thriving commerce, Paul knew it could become the base of an influential church (see Acts 19).

word noted, but the phrase "in power" (Greek *kata kratos*) also points to the nature of the journey of the word. The word "power" (*kratos*) is used only once more in the Lukan writings, in a context where war imagery cannot be missed (Luke 1:51). More importantly, the phrase "in power" (*kata kratos*) is most often employed in military contexts in Hellenistic literature, and its only occurrence in the Septuagint (Judg. 4:13) also confirms this militaristic emphasis. In summarizing the journey of the word, Luke employs this military metaphor to describe its victorious advance. In spite of opposition, the powerful word is able to conquer the world.

Sending Timothy and Erastus to Macedonia (19:21–22), Paul stays behind in Ephesus, where he witnesses a great disturbance caused by those who see Paul's message as a challenge to the cult of Artemis (19:23–41). In this second event in Ephesus that Luke chooses to focus on, one again finds a challenge to "the Way" (19:23; see comments on 9:2). Through the mouth of Demetrius, a silversmith who produces silver shrines of Artemis, the ministry of Paul in Ephesus and throughout Asia is described as one that is focused on undermining idols and foreign gods (19.26). The first part of verse 27 can be literally translated as "the temple of the great goddess Artemis will be regarded as nothing" (NET), and this claim again can be compared to the anti-idol polemic of the Old Testament prophets (cf. Isa. 40:17). Although the rest of the narrative in Acts 19 does not portray the collapse of the cult of Artemis, the assertion that through Paul's ministry the great goddess Artemis "will be robbed of her divine majesty" (19:27) points to the power of the word of God.

In the midst of this disturbance, "the Jews in the crowd pushed Alexander to the front" (19:33). Most commentators understand Alexander as a Jew who represents the Jewish community in an attempt to dissociate themselves from the Christians. Although both the Jews and the Christians opposed the worship of idols, the Jews feel the need to make a distinction between themselves and the Christians. The Romans, however, consider this too fine a distinction to make. Therefore, when they realize that Alexander is a Jew, they all ignore him and continue to shout praises to their goddess (19:34).

The response of the city clerk reflects his confidence in the strength of the Artemis cult (19:25–41). The statement that Artemis "fell from heaven" (19:35) is meant as a response to Paul's claim that Artemis is no more than a man-made object of worship, although this reference may also reflect the myths related to this goddess. The center of his argument lies in the political consequences this riot might have (19:38–40). Those who oppose Paul should bring their cases to the proper authorities because the continuation of such a riot will only lead to the intervention of the Romans. After all, one of the primary functions of a provincial governor is to secure the social and political stability of a region.

20:1–38. After the unrest in Ephesus, Paul travels through Macedonia and Greece and decides to travel back through Macedonia because of a plot against him (20:1–6). In this brief account, a considerable amount of space is spent on introducing those who accompany Paul on his journey back. These include Sopater from Berea, Aristarchus (Acts 19:29; 27:2; cf. Col. 4:10; Philem. 24) and Secundus from Thessalonica, Gaius from Derbe, Timothy from Lystra (Acts 16:1–3), Tychicus (cf. Eph. 6:21; Col. 4:7; 2 Tim. 4:12; Titus 3:12) and Trophimus (Acts 21:29; cf. 2 Tim. 4:20) from Asia. This list points not only to the success of Paul's missions but also to Paul's strategy as he trains up leaders from various locales. Moreover, the delegation from churches in different regions may represent the widespread concern of the Gentile churches for the saints in Jerusalem, underscored by the fact that this is a journey to bring back the collection from the Gentiles to the Jerusalem church (cf. Rom. 15:25–33).

The incident in Troas (20:7–12) provides a glimpse of a local worshiping community. Paul speaks to and breaks bread with a group that meets in a room "on the first day of the week" (cf. 1 Cor. 16:2). In its context, then, this account may serve as an introduction to Paul's farewell address that follows, as well as his journey back to Jerusalem. This function is made clear by a number of parallels with the account of Jesus with his disciples right before his arrest (Luke 22:7–46). Paul starts his journey back to Jerusalem after the "Festival of Unleavened Bread" (20:6), and the account of the Last Supper of Jesus with his disciples is situated during "the day of Unleavened Bread" (Luke 22:7). Eutychus sinks "into a deep sleep," and the disciples also fail to stay awake during a critical moment (Luke 22:45). Jesus travels to Jerusalem to suffer, and Paul also travels to Jerusalem with the full realization of his impending suffering (cf. Acts 21:4, 10–11). Jesus delivers his farewell address after breaking bread with his disciples (Luke 22:14–28), and Paul will also deliver his farewell address after the act of breaking bread (20:13–28). Paul's raising Eutychus from the dead "on the first day of the week" may also remind the audience of Jesus's own resurrection (cf. Luke 24:1). What is striking is that while Jesus—who has the power of resurrection—is willing to go to the cross, Paul—who is able to deliver Eutychus from the dead—is also willing to suffer at the hands of those who oppose the gospel of the risen Lord.

When Paul travels from Troas to Miletus (20:13–16), Luke again highlights the goal of the journey by noting that Paul decides to pass by Ephesus because "he was in a hurry to reach Jerusalem" (20:16).

In Miletus, however, Paul sends for the elders of the church of Ephesus and delivers a farewell speech (20:17–38). In this context, the speech not only provides a concluding note to Paul's ministry in Ephesus but also aims at introducing a different stage of his ministry, as he is transformed from a traveling missionary to a prisoner in the hands of the Roman officials. As in other farewell speeches (cf. Gen. 49:1–32; Luke 22:13–28), this speech provides a review

of the ministry of a central character. The focus is not on the individual, however, but on the community that will survive after the character passes from the scene.

In his review of his labors in the province of Asia (20:18–21), Paul points to his status as a slave (20:19). As a slave, he serves with "great humility" and "tears" (20:19). This "great humility," not simply an attitude, is the actual experience of being humiliated for the sake of the gospel. The connection between the preaching of the gospel and the suffering he endures not only evokes the call on his journey to Damascus (Acts 9:15–16) but also serves as an example to those who follow him. To fulfill his call, Paul will travel to Jerusalem with the full awareness of the "prison and hardships" awaiting him (20:22–24). Through such "prison and hardships," however, he will carry the name of Jesus "to the Gentiles and their kings" (9:15), as the narrative that follows testifies.

Shifting his focus to the community of believers, Paul warns them of the challenges they will face (20:25–31). He first urges them to be "shepherds" of their "flock," a set of metaphors often used in depicting the relationship between God and his people (cf. Ps. 80:1; 95:7; Isa. 40:11; Jer. 23:2–3; Ezek. 34:8, 12; Zech. 10:3). In this context, Paul is urging the elders to carry on the work that God has already accomplished through the death of his Son on the cross, as he notes that this "flock" is the "church of God, which he bought with his own blood" (20:28). Paul then warns them of the "wolves" that are to come (20:29). These "wolves" are the enemies of God (cf. Ezek. 22:27; Hab. 1:8; Zeph. 3:3); but what is striking is that some of these "wolves" are from among them. This prophetic note is again fulfilled, as Paul's own epistles testify.

Finally, Paul commends these elders to the power of God (20:32–35). Paul fully realizes that the power to protect one's flock does not reside in the inherent virtue and power of the elders. Paul points rather "to God and to the word of his grace" that can build up the church (20:32). In depicting "God" and his "word" in parallel terms, Paul is affirming that the powerful word that has conquered the world (cf. 19:20) will sustain the community that it creates. Moreover, "the word of his grace" points to the word of his power because "grace" can point to the power of God in Luke's writings (cf. Luke 4:22; Acts 6:8). As the mighty God in the past was able to lead his people into the promised land, the "inheritance" that had been promised to them (cf. Gen. 15:7; Exod. 6:8; 15:17; Deut. 1:8; Josh. 11:23), God and his powerful word will also be able to give them the "inheritance" that his prophets have prophesied (Isa. 49:8).

21:1–16. After his farewell speech, Paul continues his journey to Jerusalem. The first few verses provide yet another detailed itinerary, as Paul and his companions travel through Kos, Rhodes, Patara, and Phoenicia and arrive at Tyre. There disciples confirm what the Holy Spirit has already told Paul: he will face hardships in Jerusalem (21:4; cf. 20:23). In this context, it is best to understand the role of the Holy Spirit as revealing what is going to happen (cf. 21:11–15), and the disciples infer from what the Spirit has revealed that Paul should not go on to Jerusalem. Paul's decision to move forward is therefore not in defiance of the Spirit; on the contrary, he is following "the Lord's will" as he travels to Jerusalem (21:14). As he leaves Tyre, he prays with all the disciples, "including wives and children" (21:5), an act that highlights the significance of the event (Luke 3:21–22; 6:12; 9:28). As a prayer before his arrest, this prayer also resembles Jesus's Gethsemane prayer (Luke 22:39–46).

When they arrive at Caesarea, Luke and his companions stay "at the house of Philip" (21:8). Luke reminds readers of the earlier narrative of Philip by calling him an "evangelist" (Greek *euangelistēs*), a word whose verbal form has been used more than once in describing his ministries (Acts 8:12, 35, 40). Moreover, the phrase "one of the Seven" (21:8) also points back to the choosing of the "seven men" in Acts 6:3. The fact that Paul is now staying with Philip not only points to the unity of the missionaries who work in different regions but also testifies to the reconciliation between Paul and the ones he persecuted, especially as the ministries of Philip started, when the Jerusalem church suffered from the persecution carried out by Paul and other Jewish leaders in Jerusalem (8:1).

The prophecies of the four daughters of Philip and Agabus (21:9–11) point to the presence of the Holy Spirit with the church and with Paul in particular as he moves toward Jerusalem. Luke's calling the daughters of Philip "unmarried" (21:9; literally "virgins") may recall the "virgin" Mary (Luke 1:27), who likewise utters words of prophecy (Luke 1:46–55). In this context, however, the word "unmarried" most likely refers to their status as "daughters" of Philip, thus fulfilling the prophecy of Joel as noted in Peter's Pentecost speech: "In the last days . . . your sons and daughters will prophesy" (Acts 2:17; see Joel 2:28). The prophecy of Agabus also resembles that of Old Testament prophets, as he uses prophetic symbolic acts to demonstrate that which will happen to Paul in Jerusalem (21:11; cf. Jer. 19:1–15; Ezek. 5:1–12). In Old Testament prophetic tradition, these are efficacious acts that signify the beginning of a chain of events. The point is often to show that God is in control even in the midst of apparent chaos. In this context, Luke's account of Agabus's prophetic act is to emphasize that God is still in control even though his apostle is suffering at the hands of those who oppose him.

Paul's response also recalls the journey of Jesus to the cross. "I am ready . . . to die in Jerusalem for the name of the Lord Jesus" (21:13) recalls similar notes in Luke (Luke 9:21; 18:32). "The Lord's will be done" (21:14) also points back to Jesus's Gethsemane prayer (Luke 22:42). In light of such parallels, Luke is emphasizing that Paul's suffering is part of the plan of God.

5. Appeal to Caesar and the Proclamation of God's Kingdom (21:17–28:31)

A. Paul's arrest and imprisonment in Jerusalem (21:17–23:35). **21:17–22:29.** Luke's account of Paul's arrival at Jerusalem reflects both the warm welcome Paul receives and the tension that lies behind his reception (21:17–26). First, Luke emphasizes that "the brothers and sisters received [them] warmly" (21:17). As in the past, Paul and his companions go to James and the elders and report to them what God has done among the Gentiles (cf. Acts 14:27). These Jerusalem leaders respond by praising God, thus recognizing that what they have heard are indeed the mighty acts of God (Luke 5:25–26; 7:16; 13:13; 17:15; 18:43; 23:47; Acts 4:21; 11:18).

After such notes of welcome, the Jerusalem leaders then report that the many Jews who are "zealous for the law" have been informed that Paul teaches "all the Jews who live among the Gentiles to turn away from Moses" (21:21). Therefore, they request that Paul join four men in the purification rites in the temple and pay their expenses, to show that Paul is faithful to the Jewish customs. Two questions remain unclear in this account. First, the exact nature of the rites to fulfill the vows is unclear. The reason why Paul has to fulfill the vows with the other four men is also left unexplained. Because of the note on the shaving of heads (21:24), it seems possible that Luke is again referring to the Nazirite vow here (Num. 6:1–21). Although the Mosaic regulations concerning the Nazirite vow did not stipulate a purification rite, they do point to the need of remaining in a state of purity during the period of the vow (cf. Num. 6:9–12). Later regulations provide a detailed discussion of the ritual requirements for purification for those who are in contact with unclean objects/persons (Mishnah Nazir 6.5–8.2). Whether the Jerusalem leaders considered Paul unclean is not explicitly stated, but his act would at least show his observance of the Mosaic law.

The second question has to do with the position of the Jerusalem leaders. The fact that they do not stand up to defend Paul against false accusations may reflect their own doubt concerning the missionary practices of Paul. That none of these "many thousands" of Jewish believers (21:20) defend him when he is later arrested (cf. 21:27–36) only strengthens this suspicion. On the one hand, Luke's failure to mention the reception of the collection that Paul brings back to Jerusalem may confirm Paul's fear as reflected in his own writings just prior to his return to Jerusalem, when he asks for prayer that his "contribution . . . to Jerusalem may be favorably received by the Lord's people there" (Rom. 15:31). On the other hand, Luke has not discussed the collection at all in this narrative. Moreover, Luke apparently does not encourage readers to doubt the sincerity of the Jerusalem believers here. What he emphasizes are Paul's innocence and his willingness to follow the instructions for the sake of the gospel.

When the days of purification are nearly over, some Jews from Asia see Paul in the temple, stir up the crowd, and seize him (21:27–40). The accusation that Paul teaches people "against our people and our law and this place" (21:28) recalls the accusation against Stephen in 6:13, but it is ironic to accuse Paul of this offense precisely when he is fulfilling his vow in the temple area. The additional charge that he has brought a Gentile into the temple area is also one based on false assumptions (21:29), although a Gentile who steps beyond the Court of Gentiles is subject to death (Josephus, *Jewish War* 5.194; *Jewish Antiquities* 15.417). The crowd then goes against Paul, but he is delivered by and falls into the custody of the "commander of the Roman troops" (21:31), a Roman tribune of a cohort of a thousand soldiers. As this commander is trying to find out what Paul has done, the crowd shouts, "Get rid of him!" (21:36), as the Jewish crowd did when they were trying to have Jesus put to death (Luke 23:18).

> Gentiles were strictly prohibited from entering the inner sanctuaries of the Jerusalem temple (see Acts 21:28). A "dividing wall" with warning signs kept them out. Here one such sign, written in Greek, reads: "No intruder is allowed in the courtyard and within the wall surrounding the temple. Whoever enters will invite death for himself."

As Paul is taken by the soldiers, he is questioned whether he speaks Greek and whether he is the Egyptian who led a revolt in circa AD 54. This question implies that the soldiers have simply assumed him to be an uneducated rebel from the outlying regions of the Roman Empire. Paul identifies himself not only as a Jew but also a citizen of Tarsus (21:39; cf. 9:11, 30; 11:25). Being "a citizen of no ordinary city" allows him to defend himself, and being a Jew allows him to address the crowd to clarify the charges launched against him.

In his first defense after his arrest, Paul provides a detailed account of his background, conversion, call, and subsequent vision that brings him to the land of the Gentiles (22:1–22). His addressing the crowd as "brothers and fathers" (22:1) reminds the readers of the speech of Stephen (cf. Acts 7:2), one that is given under similar circumstances. As a "defense" (22:1), this becomes Paul's first formal defense speech in Acts. Paul begins by emphasizing his credentials as a pious Jew (22:3–5). Beyond merely growing up in Jerusalem and studying under the respected Gamaliel (cf. 5:34), he demonstrates his being "zealous for God" by his persecuting those who belong to the Way. While the Jews may be "zealous for the law" (21:20; cf. 2 Maccabees 4:2), Paul is equally zealous, but his zeal is directed toward God. In addition to the details contained in the earlier report in 9:1–2, Paul claims that he persecuted those belonging to

the Way "to their death" (22:4). His connection with Jewish authority is further secured by his connection with "the high priest" and "all the Council" (22:5).

Paul then describes his experience on the Damascus Road (22:6–16). Compared with his previous account (9:1–19), here Paul lays particular emphasis on the "bright light" able to impress him even during the "noon" time (22:6). In emphasizing the striking presence of the risen Lord, Paul aims at highlighting the significance of this experience as an epiphany. According to 9:7, Paul's companions "heard the sound but did not see anyone." Here, however, Paul notes that his companions "saw the light, but they did not understand the voice of him who was speaking to [him]" (22:9). Considering the two statements, it seems that Paul's companions saw the light but not the risen Lord, and they failed also to comprehend the significance of the event. The fact that Paul emphasizes here that they "saw the light" also highlights the public reality of this event.

Instead of the reluctant messenger described in 9:10–14, Ananias is portrayed here as "a devout observer of the law and highly respected by all the Jews living there" (22:12). The emphasis on the status of Ananias in the eyes of the Jews aims at situating both the conversion and call of Paul within the work of God among his people. In both accounts, however, Ananias is the messenger through whom Paul's mission is explained (22:14–16; cf. 9:15–17).

In this account, Paul inserts a report of the vision he had when he returned to Jerusalem (22:17–21). Significantly, he mentions Stephen, the one who has already been persecuted because of the name of Jesus. Paul calls Stephen a "martyr" (Greek *martys*, 22:20) here, a word that means "witness." Paul is

earlier called by the risen Lord to be his "witness" (*martys*, 22:15), and ironically his mission is to continue the work of one whose death he consented to (Acts 8:1).

The crowd is willing to listen to Paul's conversion account, and they do not even object immediately to calling "Jesus of Nazareth" (22:8) the "Righteous One" (22:14), but when Paul mentions that he was sent "to the Gentiles" (22:21), the crowd erupts with anger. For hundreds of years, Jews had lived under Gentile rule. To many Jews the mission of the Messiah was to punish the Gentiles and deliver the Jews from their hands (cf. *Psalms of Solomon* 17); instead of preaching a message against the Gentiles, however, Paul emphasizes that this Messiah is sending him to preach the good news among the Gentiles.

As the commander flogs and questions Paul (22:23–29), Paul again invokes his status as a Roman citizen (22:26; cf. 16:37). Luke does not explain the origin of his citizenship, but the fact that he was "born a citizen" (22:28b) may point to the contribution of his family to Rome or to the Roman army stationed near Tarsus. What Luke does emphasize is how Paul is in some way more honorable than the commander, who paid "a lot of money" (22:28a) for his own citizenship, a practice not unheard of in the time of Paul (Dio Cassius, *Roman History* 60.17). This claim of being a Roman citizen will pave the way for his later appeal to the Roman emperor (Acts 25:11).

22:30–23:35. To clarify the nature of the accusations made by the Jews, Paul is brought before the chief priests and the Sanhedrin (22:30–23:11). Paul's opening words are significant (23:1). In stating that he has fulfilled his "duty to God," Paul declares that he is directly responsible to God, not to those who claim to represent him. The note on his "good conscience" also highlights that he is only responsible to God. In Paul's letters and in other New Testament writings, this phrase does not refer to mere subjective feelings or an adherence to an abstract set of universal moral imperatives;

rather, this "good conscience" refers to submission to the will and sovereignty of God (cf. 1 Tim. 1:5, 19; 1 Pet. 3:21). Finally, "to this day" also points to the consistency and determination of Paul (cf. 2:29; 26:22) as he aims at fulfilling God's call. From this basis, Paul makes it clear that he is defending not merely himself but the God whom he preaches.

Apparently because of his claim in regard to his relationship with God, the high priest Ananias (AD 47–59) orders Paul to be struck on his mouth (23:2). In response, Paul says, "God will strike you," a phrase that evokes a curse on those who are disobedient to God (cf. Deut. 28:22). The label "whitewashed wall" points to his hypocrisy (Ezek. 13:10–16; Matt. 23:27–28; cf. Luke 11:37–44), a point made explicit when Paul further claims that Ananias violates the law he claims to uphold.

When Paul is accused of insulting "God's high priest" (23:4), he responds by claiming that he was ignorant of the fact that he was standing in the presence of the high priest. This statement cannot be taken literally as a reference to Paul's ignorance. Because it is difficult to see how Paul could have failed to notice the presence of the high priest in a Sanhedrin meeting, this statement should be understood as a veiled criticism of Ananias, who has failed to act as a faithful high priest of God. Similarly, though Paul's citation of Exodus 22:28 in his self-criticism (23:5) can be understood as expressing regrets, it can also point to his knowledge of and obedience to the Mosaic law, while the high priest himself is the one violating the law (cf. 23:3), thus not deserving to be treated as "the ruler of [God's] people" (23:5).

The center of Paul's defense lies in the issue of resurrection (23:6–10). While most of the council members would have been Sadducees (cf. 5:17), some Pharisees are also present because without them the common people would not support the decision of the council (Josephus, *Jewish Antiquities* 18.17). Being aware of the presence of these Pharisees, Paul brings up the issue of resurrection because he knows that the Pharisees believe in resurrection, angels, and spirits, though the Sadducees do not (Luke 20:27; cf. Josephus, *Jewish War* 2.164–65; *Jewish Antiquities* 18.16).

It is noteworthy how Luke repeatedly highlights the dissension that arises among the members of the council on the issue of resurrection (23:7, 9–10). The dissension among the Jews has been noted a number of times in the Acts section of Luke's narrative (2:12–13; 4:1–4; 5:12–18; 13:45–50; 14:1–7; 17:4–5, 12–14; 19:8–9), and such dissension is in stark contrast to the unity of the church (1:14; 2:43–47; 4:24, 32–35; 5:12; 8:6; 15:25). In Greco-Roman discussions, consensus can be considered to be a criterion of truth, and the lack thereof would therefore point to the lack of credibility of the argument of that particular party (Polybius, *Histories* 23.11.6–7; Philo, *On the Virtues* 35; Josephus, *Against Apion* 2.179–81, 242–43). In this context, the failure of the Jews to stand united in their interpretation of the law disqualifies them from judging Paul on the basis of the law, especially when the center of Paul's preaching is precisely on the resurrection of Jesus.

The appearance of the risen Lord (23.11) at this point affirms that God is present with Paul. The comforting words from the risen Lord also affirm that Paul is innocent in the eyes of God. The point of these trials is not, therefore, to determine Paul's innocence but to bring him to Rome. That Paul "must" (Greek *dei*) testify about Jesus in Rome further gives meaning to the events that are about to transpire (23:12–22). The plot against Paul is now to be understood as within God's plan in bringing Paul to Rome to testify to the power of the name of Jesus.

The conspiracy by the Jews to have Paul killed moves him one step closer on his way to Rome (23:12–22). In light of verse 11, the act of the Jews shows that they are indeed "fighting against God" (Acts 5:39). As Paul did earlier (9:1–2), these Jews also go "to the chief priests and the elders" and conspire with

them to oppose those belonging to the Way (23:14). Luke mentions the oath they take three times (23:12–14, 21), presumably to show their determination to kill Paul. Their assumed failure to fulfill the oath also shows that they are the ones who are not faithful to the law (cf. Num. 30:2). Paul, though, has already proved that he is a faithful Jew by fulfilling a vow that he himself did not make (21:20–26).

The commander then decides to transfer Paul to Caesarea, the capital of the province of Judea (23:23–35). The 470 soldiers that are sent to protect Paul are about half of the cohort under this commander. The size of this force not only points to the significance of Paul the Roman citizen but also reflects the opinion of this commander that Paul has not committed any crime worthy of death, a point made explicit in the letter he writes (23:29). This declaration of innocence parallels a similar claim by Pontius Pilate concerning the crimes brought against Jesus (Luke 23:4, 14–15, 22), and it is the first in a series of similar declarations in Acts (cf. 25:18, 25; 26:31–32).

The letter drafted by the commander identifies him as "Claudius Lysias" (23:26). Omitting any reference to his intention to flog him (cf. 22:25), Claudius Lysias writes instead that he has delivered Paul from the Jewish crowd because he knows of Paul's status as a Roman citizen (23:27). In sending Paul and his accusers to Felix, he also transfers the responsibility to deal with this case to another Roman provincial official. Antonius Felix is a Roman freedman, whose ascent to power reflects the opportunities available to slaves of the Roman aristocrats. He was sent by Claudius to be the procurator of Judea, Samaria, Galilee, and Perea in AD 52–60 (Josephus, *Jewish War* 2.247) before he was replaced by Festus (cf. 24:27).

B. Paul's imprisonment in Caesarea (24:1–26:32). 24:1–26. The trial before Felix (24:1–27) provides one of the most detailed accounts of the formal interaction between the plaintiff, the defendant, and the judge in Acts. The charges against Paul are presented by Tertullus, a legal advocate who represents Ananias and other elders of the council (24:2–9). Tertullus begins by praising Felix for his accomplishments and his care for the Jewish people. While such flattery is not unexpected in a speech of this nature, to credit Felix for "a long period of peace" and for his foresight that has "brought about reforms in this nation" (24:2) has moved beyond any reasonable perception of reality. Not only does one find revolutionary movements during his reign (Josephus, *Jewish War* 2.252–70), but Felix is also accused of being ruthless in his dealings with his subjects (Josephus, *Jewish Antiquities* 20.182).

The center of Tertullus's charge against Paul is that he stirs up riots everywhere (24:5a), he is the leader of "the Nazarene sect" (24:5b), and he "tried to desecrate the temple" (24:6). Like those who accused Jesus (Luke 23:2), Tertullus understands that Felix only cares about the maintenance of political stability. The threat of riots and the existence of a political "sect" that is influential everywhere certainly deserve serious consideration. Moreover, the charge of the desecration of the temple also threatens the stability of a state where the centrality of the temple as a political institution has long been recognized, even by the Roman governors. In the first-century context, the role of the temple as an instrument of Roman imperial power in Judea has to be recognized, especially when the high priests were often considered to be the puppets of the Roman provincial power. To challenge the status of the temple, then, is to challenge a significant link between the local people and their foreign overlord. In a brief paragraph, therefore, Tertullus is able to outline the threat Paul poses to Felix and his rule.

Coins minted under Procurator Antonius Felix (AD 52–58), before whom Paul went on trial in Acts 24

In response, Paul provides a defense that links his acts with the gospel he preaches (24:10–21). First, he begins by noting that Felix has been "for a number of years . . . a judge over this nation" (24:10). It is noteworthy that Paul does not mention any of Felix's deeds as a benefactor of the Jewish people. The reference to "a number of years" may be explained by a note in Tacitus, *Annals* 12.54, where Felix is said to have been involved in certain ways in the governing of the province when Cumanus was a procurator in AD 48–52. In appealing to his experience in this province, Paul attempts to reveal the weaknesses of Tertullus's argument.

The focus of Paul's speech is, however, a confession of a different sort (24:14–16). What he admits is that he worships the God of Israel, he is faithful to Israel's tradition, and he hopes for "a resurrection of both the righteous and the wicked" (24:15). In this way, Paul turns this defense speech into a testimony to the work of God through Jesus, who is the first one to be raised from the dead (cf. 24:21). In his Areopagus speech, which was also addressed to a Gentile audience (Acts 17:22–31), Paul raised the issue of resurrection when he noted that through this resurrected one God "will judge the world with justice" (17:31). In this speech before Felix, the phrase "a resurrection of both the righteous and the wicked" also alludes to the future judgment that is to come, where the role of God as ultimate judge is noted. In this sense, then, Paul is implying that although he is the one now being judged, the one who is accusing him and judging him will one day be judged by the God that Paul preaches.

In the final part of his speech, Paul returns to the matter of his innocence (24:17–21). In highlighting his faithfulness to his tradition,

Paul mentions that he came to Jerusalem "to bring my people gifts for the poor" (24:17). This may be a reference to the collection from the Gentiles for the believers in Jerusalem (Rom. 15:26; 1 Cor. 16:1–4; 2 Corinthians 8–9; Gal. 2:10). "To present offerings" (24:17) refers back to his presence in the temple to accompany others in fulfilling their vows (21:26). Paul then points to the "Jews from the province of Asia" (24:19) as responsible for stirring up the crowd. This section of the speech is linked with the previous section by yet another reference to "the resurrection of the dead" (24:21). Paul again admits that he is only guilty of one charge: preaching the resurrection of Jesus.

Felix's response reflects his weakness, as he refuses to declare Paul innocent (24:22–23). Luke describes Felix returning with his wife Drusilla. According to Josephus, Drusilla was a Jew who "was persuaded to transgress the ancestral laws" to leave her own husband and marry Felix (*Jewish Antiquities* 20.143). If Luke and his readers were aware of this, the sudden appearance of Drusilla may enhance the ironic effect: the one who has been unfaithful to the law is now the judge concerning matters of the law.

In this second meeting, Paul again testifies to his "faith in Christ Jesus" (24:24). Instead of depicting Paul's fear, Luke emphasizes that it is Felix who is "afraid" (24:25) when he realizes that he may one day be the one who is being judged. Luke concludes his depiction of Felix by noting that he is hoping for a bribe from Paul. In light of Luke's discussion of possessions elsewhere (cf. Luke 5:11; 11:39; 12:13–21; 16:1–31; 18:18–30; Acts 1:18; 5:1–11; 8:18–19), Felix's act is to be understood as a reflection on his character.

24:27–25:22. With Festus succeeding Felix (24:27), Paul finds himself being tried by yet another Roman procurator (25:1–22). Porcius Festus was the procurator in Judea for only two years (ca. AD 60–62) before his death. Josephus credits him with maintaining peace in Judea by controlling the activities of revolutionaries (*Jewish Antiquities* 20.185–88). The political

situation quickly deteriorated after Festus was replaced with others far less sensitive to Jewish law and custom. His ability to control his subjects is reflected in this brief account of his interaction with Jewish leadership (25:1–5), where he refuses to have Paul transferred to Jerusalem as suggested by the Jewish leaders who plan to kill him during the transfer. This account also points to the heightened tension between Paul and the Jews, as their leaders are now personally involved in the plot to have him murdered.

Luke's account of Paul's appearance before Festus (25:6–12) again emphasizes the failure of the Jews to prove their charges against him (25:7). Luke's summary of Paul's defense (25:8) repeats his earlier claims that he has not done anything "against the Jewish law" (cf. 22:23; 24:14) or "against the temple" (24:12). In this context, however, Paul adds that he has not done anything "against Caesar" (25:8).

The focus on Caesar in this account is enhanced by two other references in Paul's response to Felix's question as to whether he is willing to stand trial in Jerusalem. First, in describing his appearance before Festus, he claims that he is "now standing before Caesar's court" (25:10a). In other words, he recognizes the authority of Festus as an agent of the Roman imperial system, and he would rather be tried under this system than by those who claim to be faithful to the law of God. Moreover, the phrase "where I ought [*dei*] to be tried" (25:10b) again points to the plan of God to have Paul appear before "the Gentiles and their kings" (9:15). Second, and more important, it is in this context that he explicitly appeals to Caesar (25:11). This provision to appeal to the Roman emperor is available only to Roman citizens (see Pliny the Younger, *Letters* 10.96), and it is considered to be one of the provisions instituted by Augustus (Suetonius, *Augustus* 33.3; *Claudius* 14). When it was established as a formal legislation in 18 BC, this provision did not simply enhance the rights of individual Roman citizens; it also allowed the Roman emperor to have direct control of the provinces when provincial officials ceased to be considered the final authority to which citizens had to submit. Provincial officials who failed to acknowledge such rights of Roman citizens were liable to death. In this context, the emperor to whom Paul was appealing would have been Nero (AD 54–68), and Paul's appeal becomes one of the first uses of this provision in our extant historical sources.

Before Festus allows Paul to leave for Rome, however, he decides to first consult with King Agrippa (25:13–22). This Agrippa is Agrippa II, the son of King Herod Agrippa I (cf. Acts 12:1, 19–25). Agrippa rose in power during the reign of Claudius, and under Nero he gained control over areas surrounding Judea and Samaria. Traditions point to his incestuous relationship with his sister Bernice (Josephus, *Jewish Antiquities* 20.145; Juvenal, *Satire* 6.156–60).

In his report to Agrippa, Festus emphasizes his adherence to proper legal procedures as well as his effectiveness as a judge (25:16–17). Festus concludes that the charges have to do with "their own religion" (25:19). Significantly, while the issue of resurrection has already been brought up in Paul's defenses (23:6–8; 24:15, 21), Festus's report specifically points to "a dead man named Jesus who Paul claimed was alive" (25:19) as the center of Paul's dispute with the Jewish leaders. Little does he know that Paul's traveling to Rome allows him to continue to preach this gospel of the risen Lord at the center of the Roman Empire.

25:23–26:23. Paul's trial before Agrippa begins with Festus's presentation of Paul and the charges brought against him (25:23–27). This presentation makes three significant points. First, Paul is opposed by "the whole Jewish community" (25:24). This again is consistent with Luke's portrayal of these Jews as being like their ancestors in their opposition to the work of God and his prophets (cf. Acts 7:51–52). Second, Festus again emphasizes that Paul "had done nothing deserving of death" (25:25). Third, this presentation indicates that the purpose of Paul's appearance before Agrippa is to allow

Festus to know exactly what he should write to the emperor when Paul is transferred to Rome (25:26–27).

Paul responds with yet another defense speech that points to the heart of the gospel he preaches (26:1–23). The note on Agrippa's knowledge of "Jewish customs and controversies" (26:3) separates this ruler from the Roman procurators, who were often ignorant of and insensitive to the concerns of the Jews. In this speech, this note also suggests that Paul's trial is concerned mainly with matters of "Jewish customs and controversies." In other words, he is not guilty of any of the political crimes with which he has been charged.

Paul begins by establishing his faithfulness to Jewish traditions (26:4–8). He has led an impeccable life as a faithful Jew since he was a child (26:4), and he belongs to the sect of Pharisees, the "strictest sect of our religion" (26:5). Then he ties the gospel that he preaches to the hope of the twelve tribes of Israel (26:6–8). This claim is important for a number of reasons. First, Paul is claiming that the gospel is the fulfillment of God's promises to Israel, a point that has been made repeatedly in the Lukan narrative (cf. Luke 2:25, 29–31; 16:16; 24:27, 44–49; Acts 3:18–26). To reject this gospel is to reject God's promises to Israel. Second, the continuity with the traditions of Israel is emphasized by Luke's use of the term "twelve tribes" (26:7); this Greek word apparently is coined by Luke. Luke's conscious use of the connotation of the number twelve has already been noted (see comments on 1:12–26), and here it points again to the continuity of Israel and the church. Paul is not creating a new community but is testifying to the fulfillment of the destiny of Israel. Third, in claiming that he is on trial because of this "hope" of Israel (26:6; cf. 28:20), he is also accusing the Jews of misunderstanding the plan of God. This point is further developed in the following section (26:12–18). Fourth, Paul does not talk about the "hope" of Israel in abstract terms; instead, he locates this "hope" in the fact that "God raises the dead" (26:8). Paul also made this link between "hope" and "resurrection" in his earlier defense speeches (23:6; 24:15), and here it becomes a key to his argument. This connection between "hope" and "resurrection" may be drawn from Psalm 16:8–11, a passage quoted in Peter's Pentecost speech (2:25–28).

After noting his efforts in persecuting the Christians in different cities (26:9–11), Paul returns to his Damascus Road experience (26:12–18). Compared with the previous accounts (9:1–31; 22:6–16), this one emphasizes the role of God in Paul's conversion and call. The omission of Ananias in this account focuses on the direct revelation from God apart from any human agency. The use of the Greek verb meaning "I have appeared" (26:16) in the mouth of the risen Lord may evoke accounts of divine epiphanies, when God shows his presence among his people (cf. Luke 9:31; 22:43; Acts 7:2). Moreover, the phrase "It is hard for you to kick against the goads" (26:14), one that reminds the audience of similar proverbs in Greek literature (Aeschylus, *Agamemnon* 1624; Euripides, *On Bacchanals* 795), points to the futility of fighting against God. The point is clear: if Paul's mission is ordained by God, opposing his ministry is "fighting against God" (cf. Acts 5:39).

The continuity of Paul's mission with Old Testament promises is stressed by the concentration of Old Testament phrases and expressions in this account of his conversion: "servant" (26:16; cf. Isa. 41:9; 42:1; 52:13), "witness" (26:16; Isa. 43:10, 12; 44:8), "I will rescue you from your own people" (26:17; cf. Jer. 1:7–8, 19), "from darkness to light" (26:18; cf. Isa. 42:6; 49:6; Mic. 7:8–9), and "forgiveness of sins" (26:18; cf. Isa. 58:6; 61:1). This again shows that his encounter with the risen Lord only strengthens his desire to see the fulfillment of the hope of Israel.

The emphases on the role of God as well as the fulfillment of the Old Testament are extended through his description of his ministry after his encounter with the risen Lord (26:19–23). His preaching is to turn people "to God" (26:20), and he experiences God's help "to this very day" (26:22a). What he preaches is "nothing beyond what the prophets and Moses said would happen" (26:22b). What Jews may find surprising is, again, his emphasis on Christ's death and resurrection as the climax and fulfillment of God's promises to Israel (26:23).

26:24–32. In reaction to Paul's speech, both Festus and Agrippa reject his message, but both fail to find him guilty of the charges brought against him. In response to Festus, who ironically claims that he is "insane," probably because of his own failure to appreciate his "great learning" (26:24), Paul states that he can "speak freely" to him because all these things were "not done in a corner" (26:26). In this context, to "speak freely" demonstrates the courage of the one who proclaims the truth, and "not done in a corner" points to the public nature of the content of his preaching. It is possible that Paul is evoking the model of an ideal philosopher in expressing how Christianity is not a sect that is "stirring up riots among the Jews all over the world" (24:5).

In response to Agrippa, who rightly realizes that Paul's defense is a proclamation of the gospel (26:28), Paul also concedes that his concern is not with his freedom but with the spiritual state of his audience (26:29). While Agrippa's final comment that Paul could have been set free had he not appealed to Caesar (26:32) rightly affirms Paul's innocence, it also reflects Agrippa's ignorance of God's plan in that Paul's journey to Rome as a prisoner is indeed a way to fulfill Paul's role as the ambassador of the gospel even to the center of the Roman world.

C. Paul's voyage to Rome (27:1–28:16). The first part of this account brings Paul from Caesarea to Crete (27:1–12). The sudden reappearance of the "we" in this account (27:1; cf. 21:18) probably helps in explaining the details contained in the following narrative. Also important is Julius, the centurion who is introduced by name in verse 1, one who will serve as both a guard and a witness to all that happens in this fateful journey to Rome. Paul's companions also include

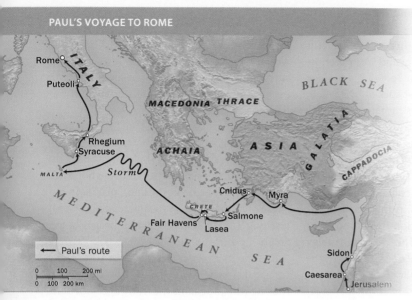

PAUL'S VOYAGE TO ROME

Rome
ITALY
Puteoli
BLACK SEA
MACEDONIA THRACE
Rhegium
Syracuse
ACHAIA
ASIA
GALATIA
CAPPADOCIA
MALTA
Storm
MEDITERRANEAN SEA
Cnidus
Myra
CRETE
Fair Havens
Salmone
Lasea
Sidon
Caesarea
Jerusalem

← Paul's route

0   100   200 mi
0 100 200 km

words of comfort from the mouth of the risen Lord (18:9). Instead of a promise to be freed from the chains, Paul was promised that he "must stand trial before Caesar" (27:24). The word "must" (*dei*) again points to the necessity of the plan of God to be fulfilled, and the words of promise are comforting only when one realizes that Paul's journey to Rome is not an accident in history but part of God's plan for him to proclaim the name of Jesus in Rome. For the rest of those traveling with him, the second part of the vision is probably more encouraging: "God has graciously given you the lives of all who sail with you" (27:24). The power of this word of prophecy lies in the fact that Paul's earlier prediction has already been fulfilled (27:21; cf. 27:10).

soldiers (27:31), sailors (27:27, 30), and other prisoners on board (cf. 27:1, 42).

After a difficult journey from Sidon (27:3), they land in Fair Havens on the southern coast of Crete (27:8). Luke notes that it was "after the Day of Atonement" (27:9), in September–October. Paul warns them of the impending disaster if they are to continue with their journey (27:10), but the centurion decides to follow the advice of others and insists on moving ahead (27:11). In the ancient Mediterranean region, late May to mid-September was considered a safe season for sea travel, and mid-November to mid-March was considered to be extremely dangerous. Paul's journey would have been just past the safe season for traveling, and the fact that this journey would last for months (cf. 28:11) points to the risk in setting sail from Crete. The "owner of the ship" (27:11) insists on setting sail, likely because his ship transported grains from Egypt to Rome and to delay the trip for months would incur incredible loss.

As Paul has predicted, they do encounter a storm as soon as they leave Crete (27:13–26). When those in the ship "finally gave up all hope of being saved" (27:20), Paul reveals to them the vision that he has had (27:23–24). "Do not be afraid" (27:24) recalls the earlier

As in the preceding account, Paul's prophecy that "only the ship will be destroyed" (27:22) is again fulfilled (27:27–44). The dire situation is dramatically illustrated by the attempt of the sailors to escape (27:30), but Paul stops them. Paul's statement, "Not one of you will lose a single hair from his head" (27:34), points to their deliverance from this storm. Elsewhere in Luke, however, other "hair" references point to the significance of the salvation of one's soul (cf. Luke 12:4–7; 21:16–19).

The significance of the meal scene (27:33–35) has been a subject of debate. The taking of bread, giving thanks to God, and breaking it and eating it (27:35) recalls the account of the Last Supper (Luke 22:19), but similar acts also appear in other Lukan meal scenes (cf. Luke 9:16; 24:30; cf. Acts 2:42, 46). Nevertheless, if the Last Supper is to serve as the key to understanding the other meal accounts, this meal may point specifically to the presence of

God. Moreover, considering that numerous parallels do exist between the trials of Jesus and those of Paul, this meal may recall Jesus's last meal with his disciples before his death on the cross. To call this a sacrament or even a singular reenactment of the Last Supper does, however, go beyond the description of the Lukan text.

After the ship runs aground, the soldiers are about to kill the prisoners, but the centurion stops them. Eventually, all the passengers on the ship are able to reach land safely. This again points to the fulfillment of the prophecy of Paul (27:22). These prophetic activities confirm Paul's earlier defense that he is constantly benefiting from God's help (26:22). If so, this would also point to his innocence. Throughout this shipwreck experience, however, Paul's innocence is not affirmed by political rulers but by God himself. This focus on Paul's innocence is explicitly noted in the next episode.

Coming on shore, Paul and those around him find themselves on Malta (28:1–10), an island about sixty miles south of Sicily. The account of their experience on this island centers on Paul being bitten by a viper. At first, the islanders think that he has been punished by "Justice" personified (28:4; cf. Hesiod, *Theogony* 901; Josephus, *Jewish War* 1.84). When Paul survives without injuries, the islanders realize that he must not be guilty because he has survived not only the storm of the sea but also the vicious attack of the viper. To Luke's readers familiar with Hellenistic literature that points to the manifestation of divine justice through one's fate in the midst of natural disasters (cf. *Greek*

Anthology 7.290; Heliodorus, *Ethiopian Story* 2.20), Paul's deliverance from such calamities proves that he is innocent in the eyes of God.

As in a previous account (14:8–20), Paul is considered to be a "god" (28:6). Luke again clarifies that Paul is simply the messenger of God by noting that Paul has to invoke the power of God through prayer (28:8) to heal those who are sick. Paul emerges, however, as one in chains to one who is able to free people from their chains of illness (28:9; cf. Luke 4:18–19). In light of the fact that Luke always uses the Greek word for "honor" or "value" in reference to material possessions (Acts 4:34; 5:2, 3; 7:16; 19:19; cf. Matt. 27:6, 9; often translated as "money"), the remark that these islanders "honored us in many ways" (28:10a) may point to their expression of gratitude through tangible gifts. The final phrase then should be read as an elaboration of the "honors" Paul and his companions receive: "They furnished us with the supplies we needed" (28:10b).

The final leg of the journey brings Paul from Malta to Rome (28:11–16). The note that the ship they are in has "the figurehead of the twin gods Castor and Pollux" (28:11) is noteworthy. Considered to be the sons of Zeus and Leda, these twin gods are venerated as the protectors on the sea. The previous account has made it

The Appian Way was a major road that led travelers into the city of Rome. Here remnants of it are visible. Paul would certainly have used this road in his travels to Rome.

clear, however, that it is the God Paul worships who has protected them. The note that "Paul thanked God" (28:15) recalls his earlier act of thanksgiving during the storm (27:35); in both situations, Paul acknowledges God to be his ultimate guide and protector.

D. Paul's proclamation of God's kingdom in Rome (28:17–31). After Paul has arrived in Rome, he calls together the leaders of the Jews and explains the false charges that have been launched against him (28:17–22). When they meet again "on a certain day" (28:23a), Paul again turns the defense of his own innocence into a defense of the gospel (28:23b). After noting their response, Paul utters a final word concerning the Jews who fail to receive the gospel (28:24–28). What is surprising about this sequence of events is that Paul no longer acts like a prisoner. Instead, he becomes the judge who summons people before him (28:17). His final word becomes the judgment against the Jews, who are found guilty before God. After Paul's long journey to stand trial before the Roman emperor, what Luke emphasizes is not the final trial of Paul but the final trial of the Jews. The opinion of the Roman emperor is no longer important, but the status of the Jews before God again becomes the center of Luke's attention.

In verses 24–25, Luke again focuses on the disagreement among the Jews (cf. comments on 23:5–10). The note that "some were convinced by what he said, but others would not believe" (28:24) is to emphasize that "they disagreed among themselves" (28:25a). This disagreement among the Jews points to their failure to stand on the side of truth, and significantly Paul's final word of judgment is directed against both groups as they are about to leave. Rather than focusing on the exact nature of the response of those who are said to have been "convinced," this account emphasizes the description of the Jews as divided.

The severity of this "final statement" is highlighted by Paul's evocation of "the Holy Spirit" and "Isaiah the prophet" (28:25b). Moreover, the change from "*our* ancestors" in the previous

speech (28:17) to "*your* ancestors" (28:25b) shows Paul's distancing himself from this disobedient people of God. Paul's use of Isaiah 6:9–10 in verses 26–27 points to the fact that these Jews are like their ancestors who refused to respond to God's call to repentance. Isaiah employs anti-idol language in describing God's people: as idols have eyes but do not see, have ears but do not hear, have mouths but do not speak, God's people have become like the idols that they worship (cf. Ps. 115:8; 135:15–18). Paul likewise accuses the Jews of their failure to worship the true God, who has sent his Messiah to suffer on the cross and to be raised from the dead. The quote from Isaiah is therefore not a curse but a statement of the consequence of their hardening of heart, rejecting God as their ancestors did.

The note that salvation will now go to the Gentiles (28:29) indicates the consequence of the Jewish rejection of the gospel. As in similar notes earlier in the narrative (Acts 13:46–47; 18:6), however, this does not aim at closing the door of salvation on the Jews. Just as Isaiah utters those harsh words in an attempt to urge God's people to repent, so too Paul's quote from Isaiah and his statement here in 28:29 should be considered a prophetic call for the people of God to repent.

Luke ends his narrative by noting that Paul "proclaimed the kingdom of God and taught about the Lord Jesus Christ—with all boldness and without hindrance" (28:31). At the center of the Roman Empire, where the emperor is honored as the Lord of all, Paul is proclaiming the existence of a different "kingdom" whose "Lord" is Jesus Christ himself. The gospel together with its claim of submission has finally reached the center of the world. Paul has also completed his call to carry the name of Jesus "to the Gentiles and their kings and to the people of Israel" (9:15).

Select Bibliography

Alexander, Loveday. *The Preface to Luke's Gospel: Literary Convention and Social Context in Luke 1.1–4 and Acts 1.1*. Society for New Testament Studies Monograph Series 78. Cambridge: Cambridge University Press, 1993.

Barrett, C. K. *A Critical and Exegetical Commentary on the Acts of the Apostles.* 2 vols. International Critical Commentary. Edinburgh: T. & T. Clark, 1994–98.

Bock, Darrell L. *Acts*. Baker Exegetical Commentary on the New Testament. Grand Rapids: Baker Academic, 2007.

Bruce, F. F. *The Acts of the Apostles*. 3rd ed. Grand Rapids: Eerdmans, 1990.

Cadbury, Henry. *The Making of Luke-Acts*. 1927. Reprint. Peabody, MA: Hendrickson, 1999.

Conzelmann, Hans. *The Theology of St. Luke*. New York: Harper & Brothers, 1960.

Gaventa, Beverly Roberts. *The Acts of the Apostles*. Abingdon New Testament Commentaries. Nashville: Abingdon, 2003.

Hemer, Colin J. *The Book of Acts in the Setting of Hellenistic History*. Wissenschaftliche Untersuchungen zum Neuen Testament 49. Tübingen: Mohr Siebeck, 1989.

Johnson, Luke Timothy. *The Acts of the Apostles*. Sacra Pagina 5. Collegeville, MN: Liturgical Press, 1992.

Marguerat, Daniel. *The First Christian Historian: Writing the "Acts of the Apostles."* Translated by Ken McKinney, Gregory J. Laughery, and Richard Bauckham. Society for New Testament Studies Monograph Series 121. Cambridge: Cambridge University Press, 2002.

Marshall, I. Howard. *The Acts of the Apostles*. Tyndale New Testament Commentaries. Grand Rapids: Eerdmans, 1980.

Pao, David W. *Acts and the Isaianic New Exodus*. Wissenschaftliche Untersuchungen zum Neuen Testament II.130. Tübingen: Mohr Siebeck, 2000. Reprint. Grand Rapids: Baker Academic, 2002.

Parsons, Mikeal, and Richard Pervo. *Rethinking the Unity of Luke and Acts*. Minneapolis: Fortress, 1993.

Spencer, F. Scott. *Journeying through Acts: A Literary-Cultural Reading*. Peabody, MA: Hendrickson, 2004.

Talbert, Charles H. *Reading Acts: A Literary and Theological Commentary on the Acts of the Apostles*. New York: Crossroad, 1997.

Tannehill, Robert C. *The Narrative Unity of Luke-Acts: A Literary Interpretation*. 2 vols. Foundations and Facets. Philadelphia: Fortress, 1986–90.

Witherington, Ben, III. *The Acts of the Apostles: A Socio-Rhetorical Commentary*. Grand Rapids: Eerdmans, 1998.

The Letters and Revelation

The letters of the New Testament (twenty-one in all) were written by Paul, John, Peter, James, Jude, and the anonymous author of Hebrews. (For hypotheses concerning the authorship of Hebrews, see the commentary introduction to that letter.) These letters were written over a span of approximately fifty years, the bulk of them during the years of Paul's active ministry (roughly AD 48–65). The known writers were all close associates of Jesus, with the exception of Paul, who argues for his place among them on the basis of his intimate knowledge of Jesus, his personal encounter with the risen Christ, and the instruction he received directly from the Lord. This, he felt, qualified him to be classed as one of the apostles, equal in authority and rank to the original twelve—including Peter, James, and John, the "inner circle" of those appointed by Jesus. In a poignant story in Acts 9, Paul tells about first meeting the apostles following his conversion. In Acts 15 (and Galatians 2) we read about the matured Paul now standing shoulder to shoulder with them.

These letters deal with the life of the church, and usually with its problems. A problem would arise, local solutions would fail, and so help would be sought from an acknowledged authority. Or perhaps one of the apostles would hear of a problem and write to correct it. Consequently the letters contain advice on difficulties in all areas of life—personal, ethical, doctrinal, liturgical, social, ecclesiastical, financial.

Because the New Testament letters were written to address specific questions, they contain little, if any, systematic thought. It is not that a systematic understanding did not lie behind the answers given, but the letters were not written as short treatises on systematic theology. The letters give us a glimpse of the actual lives and problems of the first Christians. We are thus able to see how the first generation of believers lived, and we are challenged to apply their insights to our own situation.

When we read these letters we need to think carefully about how we should employ them for our lives today. In some cases, the letter is *describing* some practice in the church that we simply do not use anymore. For instance, in 2 Timothy 2 Paul tells women not to braid their hair. As the commentary will explain, what is important here is not the braids but what they might mean in the culture of Paul's world. Therefore we must be alert that when a New Testament letter is describing a certain practice, it may simply be that Paul is trying to answer a problem in his ancient context using ancient forms. On the other hand, there are times when Paul is *prescribing* practices or beliefs that he considers to have a universal applicability. So, for instance, in Galatians 3:28 Paul is firm

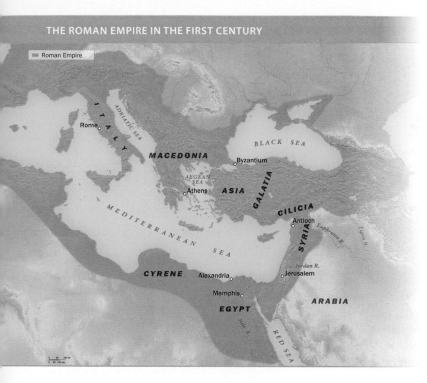

THE ROMAN EMPIRE IN THE FIRST CENTURY

Roman Empire

to Israel and to Jesus as the fulfillment of Israel's hopes. They also look at Jesus's life as he lived it at that time, and the Gospel writers are careful to locate it precisely in the days of Herod or Augustus or Pontius Pilate. The book of Acts and the Letters tell us of church life as lived by the early believers in Rome, Greece, or Asia Minor. Sometimes they are so specific that two quarreling individuals are mentioned by name (for example, Phil. 4:2).

about how in the church there should be no discrimination.

The challenge for us today is to discern what teachings of Paul are culturally *descriptive* and what teachings are universally *prescriptive*. For example, in 1 Corinthians 11:10–15 Paul argues that women should wear head coverings and long hair while men should wear short hair. Are these specific rules for us to follow today? Some people say yes, while others disagree. Commentary writers and theologians have wrestled with these questions for centuries, and we will see these debates within the pages that follow.

Revelation

The book of Revelation concludes the writings of the New Testament. It was put at the end because it looks beyond the confines of its own place in history into the future and to what God is yet to accomplish in and for his people. The other New Testament books also have this forward look, but they arise out of a specific context. So the Gospels look backward

The book of Revelation stands above history as well as in it. The great central vision of chapters 4 and 5 depicts the awesome throne of God as the central focus of the universe. History is important and time flows on, but always as the outworking of the will of the one whose eyes are like a flame of fire. God rules above the ages and will accomplish his purposes in this age and in the age to come.

Revelation ends with the extraordinary vision of the New Jerusalem, where heaven and earth have become one and where God is all in all. This is the grand future event toward which all creation moves and which concludes the New Testament. Its reassurance is profound: *God will be victorious despite the apparent powerlessness of his people and the soaring power of those who oppose him.* The arrival of Jesus-in-power at the end of the book describes the great final drama of human history that began in the book of Genesis. God's creation—so spoiled by human sin, so loved by God beyond measure—now is re-created and renewed.

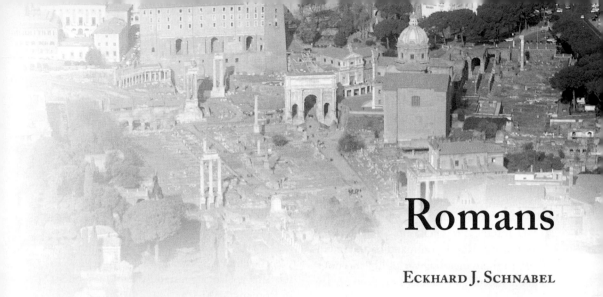

Romans

ECKHARD J. SCHNABEL

Introduction

Paul's letter to the Christians in the city of Rome is not only his longest letter but also arguably his most influential. While we do not know whether it achieved its purposes among the followers of Jesus who lived in the capital of the Roman Empire, we do know that for many Christians throughout the centuries, reading and understanding this letter proved life changing and, in some cases, history changing.

Date and Historical Context

Paul provides information that helps us situate the letter in its historical context. He informs the Roman Christians that he has brought to an end his work as a pioneer missionary among Gentiles in the eastern regions of the Mediterranean (15:18–23). He intends to visit them in Rome on the way to Spain, where he wants to open up a new region for the proclamation of the gospel (15:23–24, 28–29). Before coming to Rome, something he has wanted to do for some time (1:13), he will first travel to Jerusalem in order to hand over the funds that were collected in the churches he established in Macedonia and Achaia (15:25–28). He asks the Roman Christians to pray for him as he travels to Jerusalem, as both his safety and the acceptance of the collection funds are uncertain (15:30–32).

Paul wrote his letter to the Christians in Rome in the winter and early spring of AD 56–57 while staying in Corinth. After he completed his missionary work in Ephesus, where he had worked from AD 52 to 55 (Acts 19), he visited the churches in Macedonia and Achaia (Acts 19:21). He stayed in Corinth for three months (Acts 20:2–3), waiting for shipping on the Mediterranean Sea to resume in the spring (Acts 20:3), as he wanted to be in Jerusalem for the day of Pentecost (Acts 20:16). Paul's host during this time was Gaius (Rom. 16:23), presumably the same Christian whom he baptized when he established the church in Corinth (1 Cor. 1:14).

Audience

The addressees of the letter are the Christians in the city of Rome (1:6–7). The history of the church in the capital of the Roman Empire is known only in broad outline. Scholars agree that the origins of the church in Rome are connected with Jews living in Rome who were converted to faith in Jesus as Messiah. The questions of when and where Roman Jews first came into contact with the gospel of Jesus Christ have been answered in different ways. Jews of Rome who visited Jerusalem on the occasion of the Feast of Pentecost in AD 30 could have met Peter and the other apostles, been converted to faith in Jesus the Messiah, and taken the message of Jesus back to Rome. Luke mentions "visitors from Rome" among the pilgrims at Pentecost (Acts 2:10). Jews of Rome could also have come into contact with

Jewish Christians in other cities in the eastern Mediterranean at an early date, perhaps in Antioch in Syria. Peter might have traveled to Rome when he left Jerusalem because of the persecution instigated by Herod Agrippa I in AD 41/42 (Acts 12:17).

By the early 40s, there were Jewish Christians in Rome. The Roman historian Cassius Dio mentions an edict of Claudius issued in AD 41 intended to quell unrest in the Jewish community of Rome, commanding the Jews to adhere to their ancestral way of life and not to conduct meetings (Cassius Dio 60.6.6). This edict probably presupposes missionary activity of Jewish Christians in the synagogues of the city of Rome. The existence of Jewish Christians in Rome is probably the background for another edict of Claudius. In AD 49 the emperor ordered the expulsion of the Jews from Rome. Suetonius reports measures undertaken by Claudius against men of foreign birth, pointing out that "since the Jews constantly made disturbances at the instigation of Chrestus, he expelled them from Rome" (*Claudius* 25.3–4). The disturbances were probably provoked by the missionary outreach of Jewish Christians who preached Jesus as Messiah (Greek *christos*). Luke reports that in Corinth Paul met the Jewish couple Aquila and Priscilla, who had recently come from Italy because "Claudius had ordered all Jews to leave Rome" (Acts 18:2). Paul arrived in Corinth in AD 50, just after the expulsion of the Jews from Rome.

When Paul wrote to the Roman Christians in AD 56/57, seven years had passed since Claudius's edict of AD 49. By this time some of the expelled Jews had returned to the city, including some of the Jewish Christians who had had to leave, such as Aquila and Priscilla (Acts 18:2; Rom. 16:3). However, the expulsion of the Jews must have changed the composition of the church membership considerably. While the church originated among Jewish believers, and probably had a majority of Jewish believers before AD 49, it had become a predominantly Gentile church by the time Paul wrote his letter. This is also suggested by Paul's argument in Romans 11:17–24.

Why did Paul write to the Roman Christians? The answer to this question needs to take into account Paul's goal to recruit the Christians in Rome for his plan to begin missionary work in Spain (15:24). As a letter of introduction to the Christians in Rome, Paul's letter is rather long—Cicero's letters range from 22 to 2,530 words, Seneca's from 149 to 4,134 words, while Paul's letter to the Romans has 7,111 words (in the Greek text). We also must take into account that Paul was about to visit Jerusalem, where he would meet traditionalist Jewish Christians who believed that Gentile followers of Jesus should submit to Jewish law and to circumcision. The questions

The Roman emperor Claudius (AD 41–54). His expulsion of Jews from Rome greatly affected the social matrix of the Roman church.

about the gospel he preached are the same questions that were controversial during the previous two decades, in which he had been active as a missionary. Paul thus wrote a long letter in which he provided a synthesis of the gospel of Jesus Christ he had been preaching. He had been called by God on the road to Damascus to proclaim the crucified and risen Lord Jesus Christ among the Gentiles (Gal. 1:15–16). The fundamental convictions that Jesus Christ is the only source of salvation for both Gentiles and Jews (Rom. 1:16) and that Jesus Christ unites Jews and Gentiles in the one new community of the followers of Jesus (Gal. 3:28) are central elements of what Paul calls the "truth of the gospel" (Gal. 2:5, 14). These convictions raise questions about several matters: (1) how Jewish Christians should view Gentiles (and Gentile Christians) and how Gentile Christians should view Jews (and Jewish Christians); (2) the sin of Gentiles and the sin of Jews; (3) God's condemnation of sinners and God's salvation, which is now available to all through Jesus the Messiah; (4) the validity of the Mosaic law; (5) God's righteousness in terms of the reality of everyday life; and (6) God's righteousness in the context of the reality of his promises to Israel and of Israel's rejection of the Messiah. As Paul wrote to the Roman Christians, he wrote a synthesis of the gospel of Jesus Christ, which he had preached for many years.

Commentary

1. Introduction (1:1–17)

Paul begins his letter with an epistolary opening, which was customary for Greek Hellenistic letters (1:1–7), and an introductory section, in which he expresses thanksgiving to God, indicates the reason for writing the letter, and describes the background for his planned visit to Rome (1:8–15). In 1:16–17 Paul succinctly summarizes the main theme of the letter.

A. Sender, address, and salutation (1:1–7). The first word, typical for ancient letters, is the name of the sender. Paul introduces himself with his Latin name, *Paul(l)us* (Greek *Paulos*), which could be his personal name or his nickname; his Hebrew name was Saul (see Acts 7:58; 8:1, 3; 9:1, 4; 13:9). Paul underlines three realities that explain who he is. (1) Paul is a "slave" (NIV "servant") of Jesus Christ; his life totally belongs to Jesus Christ, to whom he thus owes total allegiance. (2) God called him to be an apostle who carries the gospel to others (Gal. 1:15–16; 1 Cor. 15:5–7). Paul's call to devote his entire life to serving Jesus Christ coincided with his conversion on the road to Damascus (Acts 9:1–19). It was God's gracious and effective call that brought him to faith in Jesus Christ and that caused him to work as an apostle. Paul is an apostle of Jesus Christ (see 1 Cor. 1:1; 2 Cor. 1:1), an envoy called by God to work on behalf of Jesus Christ, to whom he belongs. (3) Paul has been "set apart"—that is, consecrated and commissioned "for the gospel of God." The message he proclaims is the "good news" (Greek *euangelion*, generally translated as "gospel") of God's revelation in Jesus Christ for the salvation of Jews and Gentiles.

The reference to "the gospel of God" prompts Paul to describe the message he proclaims in 1:2–4. (1) The gospel, which has been promised by God through his prophets (1:2), is God's revelation in Jesus Christ, the fulfillment of God's promises, and authenticated by Scripture. (2) The gospel of God concerns Jesus Christ (1:3–4; most scholars assume that Paul quotes an early Jewish Christian creed, which would explain why Jesus's death is not mentioned). (3) As far as Jesus's human nature (literally "flesh") is concerned, he is of royal messianic descent (literally "born from the seed of David"). Jesus fulfills Old Testament promises and Jewish expectations (2 Sam. 7:16; Isa. 11:1, 10; Jer. 33:14–18; *Psalms of Solomon* 17:21). (4) Jesus was declared to be "Son of God in power"; that is, he was installed in the messianic office as God's Son who is invested with God's power (Ps. 2:7). (5) Jesus's resurrection from the dead marks the beginning of the new age of God's Spirit, who gives life and holiness (Ezek. 37:1–14). (6) Jesus the Messiah is Lord (Greek *kyrios*), exalted by God to be the ruler of the world.

The reference to Jesus Christ then prompts Paul to add a description of his apostolic ministry in 1:5–6. (1) He has received the grace of being an apostle through the mediation of the risen and exalted Lord Jesus Christ. The plural "we" is a writer's plural, not a reference to all Christians; the structure of the epistolary *prescript* ("*a* to *b*, greetings") clarifies that Paul still describes himself as the sender. (2) The goal of his work as God's envoy is to lead Gentiles to faith in the gospel and thus to faith in God himself and in his Son Jesus the Messiah and Lord. (3) Faith in the one true God and in his Son Jesus Christ involves, by its very nature, obedience—loyalty to God's sovereignty and submission to God's will. (4) The scope of his missionary work is focused on polytheists, pagans who worship other deities (Rom. 11:13–14; Gal. 2:8–9). The Roman believers

live among "all the Gentiles" and thus belong to the sphere of his divine apostolic commission.

The addressees are described in 1:7. They live in the city of Rome. They are loved by God. They have been called by the holy God of Israel. They are holy on account of the holiness of God, who both charges and enables them to live holy lives (1:7a). In the light of what Paul will say about human beings in 1:18–3:20, the statement that the recipients are "loved by God" expresses the miracle of salvation.

The epistolary opening ends with the salutation (1:7b). Paul transforms the ordinary Greek greeting, *chairein* ("greeting"; cf. Acts 15:23; 23:26; James 1:1), into a vehicle of blessing upon the Roman believers and a summary of his most central concerns. He blesses them with "grace" (*charis*), reminding them of the undeserved love of God revealed in Jesus Christ, which provides access to God for sinners who do not deserve it (3:24). He blesses them with "peace" (*eirēnē*; Hebrew *shalom*), the traditional Jewish greeting, which here in the context of "grace" refers to the peace with God that God himself has granted those who believe in Jesus Christ (5:1–11). The power to grant the content of the blessing derives "from God our Father and from the Lord Jesus Christ."

B. Thanksgiving and petition (1:8–15). Paul first expresses his thanksgiving to God (1:8), praying to God "through Jesus Christ." He continues to worship the one and only God, the God of Abraham and Israel. At the same time he is convinced that "now," when God's righteousness has been revealed in Jesus Christ (3:21–22), God can be approached only through faith in Jesus the Messiah.

In 1:9–12 Paul mentions the reasons for writing the letter. He solemnly asserts that he writes as a missionary who serves God, whose service is dependent on and made effective by the Spirit of God, whose sphere of service is the proclamation of the gospel of Jesus the Son of God, and whose service includes unceasing prayers for the churches (1:9). He informs his readers that he has been asking God for some time to make it possible to visit Rome, while acknowledging his uncertainty as to when and how his plans might be carried out (1:10). He longs to meet the Christians in Rome, and he is confident that God would use his presence in the Roman congregation to consolidate their obedience (1:11) and to encourage them in their faith, and he is certain that he would be encouraged and strengthened himself (1:12). But he recognizes that the fulfillment of his wishes has not been God's will so far (1:10). Paul the missionary strategizes future movements and projects, Paul the pastor desires to strengthen the believers in Rome, and Paul the believer prays that God would allow him to carry out his plans, while Paul the theologian rests assured that God's sovereign will determines what actually happens.

In 1:13–15 Paul describes the background for his plans. He reiterates the fact that he has repeatedly made plans to visit the Christians in Rome, plans that he has been unable to carry out since his missionary work has kept him in Asia Minor and in Greece (1:13; obstacles to following through with missionary plans are mentioned in Acts 16:6–7). The "harvest" that he intends to reap in Rome includes the strengthening of the faith of the Roman Christians (1:11–12, 15), one of the main features of apostolic service besides leading unbelievers to faith in Jesus Christ. According to 15:24, 28, Paul wants to visit the Roman Christians in order to involve them in his mission to Spain. This is most likely the "fruit" of 1:13 (NIV "harvest"; cf. 2 Cor. 11:8–9; Phil. 4:14–19). He asserts that he has been commissioned to proclaim the gospel to all people (1:14): to the Greeks, that is, to the elites of the Greco-Roman world; to the non-Greeks (*barbaroi*, from which the English word "barbarian" is derived), that is, to the people who have no Greek culture and do not speak Latin, the uncivilized whom the elites despise; to the wise, that is, those who are formally educated; to the foolish, that is, the uneducated and the uncultured, capable of mischief and incapable

of contributing to the welfare and progress of humankind. He preaches to all people.

C. Theme of the letter (1:16–17). Paul summarizes that his letter explains the gospel that he has preached in the past and that he will preach in Rome and in Spain. He asserts that he is not ashamed of the gospel (1:16). Paul knows from experience that the gospel is an embarrassing message because it is "the message of the cross" (1 Cor. 1:18). The message about a Jewish man who was executed by Roman authorities by crucifixion and yet who is, on account of his death, the messianic Savior of the world is a cause for revulsion to Jews and foolish nonsense to Gentiles (1 Cor. 1:23). Paul is not ashamed of the gospel because it is the power of God for salvation.

Paul summarizes in 1:16–17 the following convictions about the gospel of God concerning Jesus the Messiah. (1) The gospel has power; that is, it achieves what it promises. The gospel is effective, as it is the very power of God that convinces people of the truth of the "message of the cross." This means for Gentile believers among his readers that the emphasis on wisdom that characterizes orators is replaced by the effectiveness of the message about Jesus. (2) The gospel effects salvation. It rescues human beings from the wrath of God that consigns sinners to judgment (1:18–32; 5:9; 8:1). It restores the glory of God, which sinful human beings lack since Adam's rebellion (3:23; cf. 5:3; 8:23, 30); it integrates the Gentile believers into the people of God in fulfillment of God's promises to Abraham (4:11–12); it establishes peace with God and access to his grace (5:1–2); it leads to the reality of the personal experience of God's love (5:5); it secures the gift of the Holy Spirit (5:5; 7:6; 8:1–11); and it causes the believer's adoption into God's family (8:15–17). (3) The power of the gospel is effectively experienced by people who believe—that is, by people who come to faith in God's revelation in and through Jesus Christ. (4) The gospel is the power of God, who saves people irrespective of their ethnic background, "first to the Jew, then to the Gentile [literally "Greek"]." (5) The ongoing proclamation of the gospel reveals "the righteousness of God" (1:17). This expression describes God's action by which he brings people into right relationship with him. This means that God fulfills his covenant promises (cf. Isa. 46:13; 51:5–8; 62:1–12; Jer. 23:5–6). This means that God brings Jews and Gentiles into obedience to the lordship of Jesus Christ. This means that God graciously grants unrighteous sinners the status of being righteous (forensic, imputed righteousness). This means that God reconciles sinners with himself and believing Jews and Gentiles with each other. This also means that God leads the justified sinner to live a life of faith and obedience. The passive voice ("is revealed") clarifies that it is God himself who justifies sinners and who renders missionary work effective. The righteous status that God grants to the sinner is by faith alone ("through faith"), which is the purpose of God's plan of salvation ("for faith"; NIV "by faith from first to last"). Paul quotes Habakkuk 2:4 to confirm the truth that God's righteousness can be attained only on the basis of faith.

2. The Gospel as the Power of God for Salvation to Everyone Who Has Faith (1:18–15:13)

A. The justification of sinners on the basis of faith in Jesus Christ (1:18–5:21). In the first main section of the letter, Paul explains the gospel as the saving revelation of God's righteousness, which justifies sinners, whether pagans or Jews (1:18–3:20), on the basis of faith in Jesus Christ (3:21–5:21).

1:18–3:20: God's wrath against Gentiles and Jews. Paul begins his exposition of the gospel with a statement concerning the revelation of God's wrath on account of human sinfulness (1:18), followed by a description of the nature of human sin (1:19–23) and the consequences of sin (1:24–31), thus confirming the legitimacy, the severity, and the scope of God's judgment (1:32). He then argues why Jews are not exempt from the revelation of God's wrath (2:1–3:20).

1:18–32. Paul now answers the questions implicit in 1:16–17: Why has God manifested his righteousness in the gospel of Jesus Christ? Why can salvation be appropriated only through faith? The description of human sinfulness begins with the assertion that God's wrath, which brings judgment and condemnation, "is being revealed from heaven." In the Old Testament, wrath is God's response to sin (Exod. 15:7; 32:10–12; Num. 11:1; Jer. 21:3–7); it should not be confused with capricious or irrational passion. The prophets link God's wrath with a future day of judgment (Isa. 13:9, 13; Zeph. 1:15, 18; 2:2–3; 3:8; Dan. 8:19). The object of God's wrath is the universal failure to respect and honor the glory of God, and the universal reality of the violation of the standards of right conduct. People demonstrate their wickedness in the suppression of truth, universally refusing to acknowledge the truth about God the Creator, and they refuse to live according to God's standards. Paul asserts that the reality of God's anger is made manifest in the present ("is being revealed"). The gospel reveals the culpability of humankind and the consequences of unrighteousness, visible in the intellectual and moral decadence of human society.

In 1:19–23 Paul confirms the divine verdict of verse 18. The presupposition of sin is the knowledge of God, who has revealed himself

to humankind (1:19–20a). What can be known about God is his power and divine nature; these are invisible realities, but they are manifest in the works of creation (cf. Sirach 17:1–9; Wisdom 13:1–9; Philo, *On the Creation of the World* 8–9). Contemporary philosophers regarded this argument as plausible (cf. Cicero, *On the Nature of the Gods* 1.18, 44, 105; 2.44, 153). Paul's formulation "what may be known about God" is deliberately careful: the works of creation reveal God's eternal power and divine nature but not necessarily his intervention in history. Because humankind has seen God's power and divine nature in the works of creation, nobody has an excuse for suppressing this truth (1:20b). The reason why God reveals his wrath against the godlessness and the wickedness of the human race is the universal refusal to acknowledge God (1:21–23). People refuse to give God the Creator the glory that he deserves, and they refuse to be grateful to God for his good gifts (1:21a).

The result of this twofold refusal is unfolded in five statements that explain the present manifestation of God's wrath. (1) Human thinking has become "futile" and doomed to self-deception because people do not adequately take into account the reality of God (1:21b). (2) Human existence has become disabled and distorted in all its intellectual, emotional, and physical

dimensions (1:21c). (3) Human beings have a distorted and illusory self-image, as their claims to wisdom fail to recognize the truth that they have become fools (1:22). Some see here an echo of Adam's fall (Genesis 3): when he sought superior knowledge in ways that contradicted what he knew of the Creator, he was reduced to hiding, to shame, to lame excuses, and to an existence outside the glorious presence of God. (4) Human beings exchanged the glory of God for the copy of an "image" (1:23a). Instead of acknowledging God in worship and actions, they preferred the copy of a copy, an image twice removed, a distortion even of the proper form of the creatures that pagan idols depict. While Paul thinks here primarily of the pagans who worship idol images, his language also echoes the incident of the golden calf when the Israelites "exchanged their glorious God for an image of a bull, which eats grass" (Ps. 106:20). (5) People produce and then worship images that are likenesses of human beings and of animals (1:23b). They worship self-made creatures instead of the Creator (cf. the satire against the

The Roman Forum contained many temples devoted to pagan worship. The columns in this photograph mark the remains of the following temples (from left to right): in the left foreground, the Temple of Vespasian and the Temple of Saturn; in the right background, the Temple of Antoninus and Faustina, the Temple of Vesta, and the Temple of Castor and Pollux.

idol manufacturers in Isa. 44:9–20). The readers of Paul's letter were surrounded by examples of the idolatrous veneration of humans, birds, four-legged animals, and serpents, which were depicted in altars, temples, and statues, as well as in art and architecture and on coins.

God's reaction to the suppression of the truth is described in 1:24. God handed over the human race to the control of their own desires. They are thus forced to suffer the consequences of their willful distortion of the truth about God. The result of human beings left to their own resources is polluted behavior, which separates them from God, whom they have dishonored through idolatry, and which dishonors their own bodies through sexual perversions. In 1:25–27 Paul elaborates on the nature and the consequences of sin. As people venerated creatures rather than the Creator, they exchanged the truth about God for a lie. The suppression and distortion of the truth of God is intentional, not an inadvertent mistake. In 1:25 Paul interrupts his description of idolatry by a prayer in which he thanks God for the blessing of creation. The "amen" invites the readers to concur and join him in praising God. In 1:26–27 Paul explains for the second time God's response to humankind's assault on his honor and dignity. God delivered them up to dishonorable passions. When people reject God and worship a self-made substitute, they will also violate the divinely created order for humankind. The exchange of God the Creator for the worship of images of creatures results in the exchange of natural sexual relations with unnatural sexual relations among women and among men (homosexuality). God created man and woman, male and female (Gen. 1:27) to become "one flesh" (Gen. 2:24). Paul's language ("unnatural," "inflamed," "lust," "shameful") denies same-sex relationships any decency or dignity. (The question whether homosexuality is a genetic disposition or a "natural" and personal tendency does not come into view; Paul would surely argue that just as other patterns of sinful behavior—such as malice or deceit—represent

natural predispositions or personal preferences, the decisive question is not what people prefer and what their natural or genetic "makeup" is but whether God regards it as transgression of his will.)

In 1:28–32 Paul mentions for the fifth time humankind's suppression of the truth about God (after 1:18, 21, 23, 25). After people have assaulted God, they assault each other. Failure to acknowledge God leads to a mind that is worthless, not because it is uninformed or uncultured (which could be rectified through education), but because it perversely rejects truth about God and truth about nature. This is why people do things that are improper (1:28). The following catalog, which lists twenty-one types of evil behavior and characteristics of unrighteous people (1:29–31), explains that these evils are not described as problems of every individual but as the collective reality and experience of the human race. Paul concludes this depressing albeit realistic description of the human condition with a final affirmation of corporate and individual accountability (1:32).

2:1–16. Jewish readers agree with Paul's indictment of humankind in the previous paragraph. However, Jews believed that they had a privileged position before God. In 2:1 Paul shifts his style to employ diatribe, interacting with a dialogue partner. This interlocutor is not imaginary, since Paul had conversations with pious Jews who would have emphasized their exemption from God's judgment on account of their status as members of God's covenant people (cf. Wisdom of Solomon 15:2–3: "Even if we sin we are yours, knowing your power, but we will not sin, because we know that you acknowledge us as yours. For to know you is complete righteousness"). Paul does not clarify immediately the Jewish identity of his discussion partner (cf. Nathan's conversation with David in which the indictment, "You are the man" [2 Sam. 12:7], comes only later in the encounter). Paul initially addresses critics of the Gentiles in general. He asserts that those who condemn the Gentiles are doing the very same things they are doing. In 2:2 Paul asserts that what he says of God's judgment is in accordance with the facts: God judges those "who do such things" (1:19–32).

In 2:3–4 Paul refutes the objection that the connection between human wrongdoing and divine judgment does not apply to Jews. The rhetorical questions in 2:4 are designed to demonstrate to the Jewish critic of Gentile sinners his false assumptions. Pious Jews may indeed rely on God's kindness in delaying his judgment ("forbearance"), and they know about the importance of repentance. But they make the mistake of having little regard for the scope of God's kindness in view of the hopeless condition of humankind, unaware that they need as much repentance as the Gentiles do. In verse 5 Paul takes up verse 1 and explains why pious Jews are not exempt from judgment, despite the warning of Deuteronomy 10:16. They have failed to recognize that they have a hard and impenitent heart, a condition that will result in God's condemnation. In verse 6 Paul quotes the scriptural principle that God's judgment will be according to people's deeds (Ps. 62:12; Prov. 24:12; cf. Isa. 3:10–11; Jer. 17:10; Hos. 12:2). Jesus and the early Christians accepted this principle (Matt. 7:21; 16:27; 25:31–46; 2 Cor. 5:10; Col. 3:24–25; 1 Pet. 1:17; Rev. 2:23; 20:12–13; 22:12). The implication is that God has no favorites who are exempt from the application of this principle on the day of judgment. God treats all human beings the same—condemning sinners on judgment day as a result of their sinful acts, and saving sinners on judgment day on the basis of their faith in Jesus who died for their transgressions.

In 2:7–11 Paul clarifies the "doing" that leads either to eternal life or to eternal condemnation. He speaks not simply of a broad principle, or hypothetically, as some have argued. Paul explains the real eternal destinies of real people, whether they are Jews or Greeks (2:10). He asserts that people who persevere in good works seek glory and honor and immortality; these are the personal benefits of those for whom God's

glory and honor are priorities—they will receive eternal life (2:7, 10). Paul will clarify in verses 28–29 the identity of these people: they are Christian believers, in whom the promises of the prophets regarding obedience to God's law, empowered by the Spirit, have been fulfilled. In contrast to people who do good works and who receive from God eternal life, there are people who are selfish, who disobey the truth, and who are won over by unrighteousness; their destiny is God's wrath and judgment in the future and anguish and distress in the present (2:8–9a). All of this is true both for Jews and for Greeks because God the judge is impartial (2:11). The phrase "first for the Jew" (2:9b) clarifies the target of Paul's argument: the assumption of pious Jews is that they have privileges with regard to the day of judgment; this claim collapses in view of God's impartiality.

In 2:12–16 Paul introduces the law into the discussion for two reasons. The law records God's standards for the last judgment, which has been the topic since 1:18; and pious Jews appealed to the law as God's good gift that distinguished them from the pagans and that guaranteed their salvation. Paul argues that what determines the outcome of God's judgment is not the possession of the law as such but the sinfulness of people (2:12). Pagans who do not have the law will be condemned for their sin "apart from the law." Jews who live with the law (literally "in the law") yet disobey the law with their actions will be judged by the law. For the Jews who have heard the law read and explained in the synagogues, this means that they are deemed to be righteous in God's judgment *only* if they have actually been obedient to the law (2:13).

For Gentiles who do not have the law this means that, if they carry out the law, they will be justified on the day of judgment (2:14–15). Paul states the following about these Gentiles: (1) They "do not have the law by nature"; that is, they are not Jews, who have the law as a birthright, but Gentiles, who have never had the Mosaic law (NIV "who do not have the law, do by nature things required by the law" assumes a natural law that Gentiles obey; but this is not what Paul means). (2) They do "things required by the law"; that is, they show a comprehensive fulfillment of the law, thus fulfilling the conditions for justification. (3) They are "a law for themselves": even though they have not received the law as the Jews did, they obey its requirements and are thus considered to embody the law. (4) The first witness that testifies on their behalf for their justification on the day of God's judgment is their new heart, which is inscribed with the requirements of the law, promised in Jeremiah 31:31–34 for the time of the new covenant. (5) The second supporting witness is their conscience, perhaps to be understood in terms of the assurance from the presence and the work of the Holy Spirit in their lives (cf. Rom. 9:1). (6) The third supporting witness is "their thoughts," which are no longer subject to condemnation by God (as in 1:21) but constitute a defense for them, as their transformed hearts and their consciences are in accord with God's verdict. (7) This demonstration will take place in the future, on the day when God will judge humankind through Jesus Christ—that is, in view of the question of how Jews and Gentiles have responded to the gospel of Jesus Christ. Note that Paul makes similar statements about the Christian believer's obedience to the law in 2:25–29 and in 8:3–4. Paul does not simply accuse Israel of sin; as he points to the fulfillment of God's covenant promises, he seeks to provoke the Jews to jealousy (cf. Rom. 11:13–14).

2:17–29. Beginning in 2:17, Paul takes up the objections of his Jewish dialogue partner, who argues that Israel's covenant status places Jews in a different position from that of the Gentiles. Paul insists that the Jewish covenant privileges, which he does not deny (3:1–2; 9:4–5), do not exempt them from God's judgment. In verses 17–24 Paul evaluates the claim that the Mosaic law constitutes a fundamental advantage of Jews over Gentiles. First, he cites the claims of his Jewish dialogue partner (2:17–20). (1) He proudly calls himself a Jew,

identifying himself with the beliefs, rites, and customs of the adherents of Israel's Mosaic and prophetic tradition. (2) Jews rely on the law in the sense that it gives them comfort, support, and contentment. (3) Jews boast in God; that is, they are confident their special relationship with God will vindicate Israel on the day of judgment. (4) Jews know the will of God, as God has revealed in the law the proper ways in which his people should conduct themselves in everyday life. (5) Jews approve of what is superior; they know what really matters since they have been instructed in the law. (6) Pious Jews are convinced they are a guide to the blind (cf. Isa. 42:6–7), probably a reference to the attitude of many Jews that Israel has been called to be a leader of other nations (Josephus, *Against Apion* 2.291–95; Philo, *On the Life of Abraham* 98; Matt. 15:14; 23:16, 24). (7) Jews are convinced they are a light to those who are in darkness since they have been given the light of the law (Ps. 119:105). (8) Jews are instructors of the foolish; they can provide moral guidance to the Gentile world. (9) Jews are teachers of children—that is, the Gentiles who have an immature grasp of the will of truth. (10) Jews have "the embodiment of knowledge and truth" in the law, which explains the confidence expressed in verses 19–20—what the philosophers and the religions of the world long for and claim to offer, the Jews possess in the law.

In verses 21–24 Paul confronts the Jewish boast with reality. He first asks a series of four rhetorical questions. The (implied) positive answer to these questions explains "the same things" (2:1), which Jews practice but condemn in the Gentiles. Paul asserts that the Jews fail to teach themselves what they teach others. Just as the Gentiles will be condemned because of their idolatry and immorality (1:18–32), so Israel as a nation is subject to the same condemnation because of the three transgressions of stealing, adultery, and robbery of pagan temples. These charges are based on the Decalogue (Exod. 20: 4–5, 14, 15; Deut. 5: 8–9, 18, 19). The charge of temple robbery could refer to actual plunder of pagan temples (cf. Josephus, *Jewish Antiquities* 4.207) or to the use of objects taken from pagan shrines (in violation of Deut. 7:25–26). All three transgressions were certainly rare among the Jewish people. But Paul's accusation is not out of the ordinary when we compare it with charges of the prophets (Isa. 3:14–15; Jer. 7:8–11; Ezek. 22:6–12) and of Jesus (Matt. 23:1–39; Luke 11:39–52) and with Jewish literature of the time (*Psalms of Solomon* 8:8–14; Philo, *On the Confusion of Tongues* 163; *Testament of Levi* 14:4–8; *Damascus Document* 6:16–17). Paul does not target all Jews as individuals; rather, he addresses the Jewish claim that Israel has a privileged position over the Gentiles on account of her possession of the law. He argues in the proposition of verse 23 (which should not be understood as a question) that even though Israel takes pride in the law, she dishonors God by breaking the law. The empirical fact that there are Jews who do what the law forbids proves that Jews are just as guilty before God as Gentiles. The Jewish claim to covenant privileges is contradicted by the reality of Jewish actions. Paul argues, using the quotation from Isaiah 52:5, that just as Israel's disobedience in the past brought shame on God and the exile on Israel (cf. the larger context in Isa. 50:1–3), so now the Jewish people dishonor God by their disobedience.

In 2:25–29 Paul takes up the significance of circumcision, the mark of the covenant that was of central importance for Israel's self-understanding (Gen. 17:9–14). Paul does not deny the value of circumcision for the Jewish people but insists that it has value in the context of the final judgment only "if you observe the law" (2:25a). The criterion in God's court on judgment day is not the possession of the mark of circumcision but obedience to the law. Jews who break the law become non-Jews (2:25b). In verses 26–29 Paul shows again (cf. 2:14–15) how Gentiles (who believe the gospel of Jesus Christ) have become members of the people of God. When uncircumcised Gentiles keep

> In the ancient world, when a nation and therefore its gods were conquered, its temples were stripped of their wealth and precious things (cf. Rom. 2:22). This relief from the Arch of Titus shows men returning from the destruction of Jerusalem, carrying the spoils of war, particularly the contents of the Jewish temple (notice the menorah).

the just requirements of the law, they will be reckoned as circumcised (2:26), as legitimate members of God's people. There is a reversal that will become manifest on the day of judgment. The Gentile believers who are physically uncircumcised but keep the law will condemn the Jews who possess the law and have the mark of circumcision but break the law (2:27). Jews can forfeit their covenant relationship with God through wickedness, and non-Jews can be reckoned as members of God's (new) covenant people through their obedience. In verses 28–29 Paul describes the identity of these uncircumcised (non-Jewish) yet obedient people: they are incognito Jews (not "outwardly" but "inwardly") who have a circumcision of the heart, that is, who have experienced God dealing with their most basic spiritual problems. The circumcision of the heart was known in the Old Testament (Deut. 10:16; Jer. 4:4; 9:25–26; Ezek. 44:9); its reality was expected for the future (Deut. 30:6), in the time of the new covenant (Jer. 31:31–34), when God would place his Spirit in the hearts of his people (Ezek. 36:26–27), resulting in the removal of all uncleanness, in a new heart and a new spirit, and in full obedience to God's statutes. Paul asserts that this reality has arrived: Gentiles have received this true, inward circumcision of the heart, not because they have followed the written letter of the law, but because God has given them the promised Holy Spirit. They are true members of God's people, not because of the verdict of others, but because they have God's approval ("praise").

3:1–8. Paul knows that his argument in chapter 2 will provoke objections from Jews. He is willing to air these objections since he is dealing with serious questions, which have immense implications for the understanding of God, of salvation, and of who belongs to God's people.

In 3:1–4 Paul notes objections which insist that the privileges of the Jews cannot have been annulled. When the question is raised, "What advantage, then, is there in being a Jew, or what value is there in circumcision?" (3:1), Paul has

to grant that his dialogue partner has a point ("Much in every way!")—Jews have indeed an advantage over Gentiles. The reason for this answer is Paul's belief that the Jews have been given God's authentic self-revelation (3:2; the phrase "first of all" implies further privileges, which Paul will list in Rom. 9:4–5). The second argument of Paul's Jewish opponents, in verses 3–4, links the premise of Israel's divine election with Paul's argument in 2:17–29. The question is raised of whether the unfaithfulness of some Jews nullifies God's faithfulness to Israel. Paul protests against the suggestion that he holds such a view (see commentary on 9:1–11:36). He agrees with the theological principle his Jewish dialogue partner cites, quoting Psalm 51:4. God's truth is the reliability of his faithfulness, which stands in contrast to the falseness and sinfulness of every human being (the latter fact has been Paul's concern since 1:18).

In 3:5–8 Paul allows his opponent to voice the objection that his teaching turns God into an unrighteous judge and leads into libertinism. This is a direct attack on Paul's theology, which, if it can be sustained, has two serious consequences. In the first part of this attack (3:5–6) the opponent summarizes the opinion of Paul with a seemingly blasphemous proposition. The statement "our unrighteousness brings out God's righteousness more clearly" implies the apparently logical inference that if sinners by their unrighteousness provoke God to manifest his righteousness (God forgives sinners), then God cannot punish sinners for their unrighteousness. This argument is designed to draw out the conclusion that, if Paul is correct, God's righteousness stands in contradiction to God's judgment of wrath; in other words, if Paul is right, God is unjust. Parenthetically, Paul apologizes that he utters such a blasphemous thought. His answer to this attack against his theology is another vehement protest. The inference that his opponent suggests is totally absurd since God is the judge of the world. If his opponent were correct, it would lead to the further inference that God cannot be the judge of the world, which is an absurd suggestion.

The second part of the attack (3:7) intensifies the objection of verse 5 by relating it to verse 4—Paul's theology is blasphemy because he holds that lying to God (which is what sinners do) provokes not God's wrath but a demonstration of his truthfulness, which increases his glory. If this is the case, why are sinners still condemned as sinners? The implication is stark: if there is no difference between the righteous (the Jews) and sinners, any judgment must become meaningless. The final and decisive part of the attack (3:8) consists in the accusation that Paul has a blasphemous ethic. The dialogue partner argues that if Paul is correct, one might as well do evil so that good may come. If there is no theological possibility of a divine judgment, the ethical difference between good and evil becomes void. For Paul, at least for the time being, such a conclusion marks the end of any meaningful discussion: "Their condemnation is just!" The conclusion of the opponent is blasphemy since it turns the faithfulness of God's righteousness and the severity of God's wrath into a wicked farce. Paul will explain his answer to the questions of 3:1–8 in reverse order in chapters 6–8 and in chapters 9–11. After a further explanation of the sinfulness of the Jewish people in 3:9–20 and an exposition of the revelation of God's righteousness in Jesus Christ as the solution to the plight of humankind in 3:21–5:21, Paul expounds the reality of God's righteousness in the lives of Christian believers (6:1–8:39) and the reality of God's righteousness in the present and future history of Israel (9:1–11:36).

3:9–20. Paul summarizes his conclusion from chapter 2: Jews are not at all better off than the Gentiles, since both Jews (2:1–29) and Gentiles (1:18–32) are guilty of sin. They are "all under the power of sin"; that is, both Gentiles and Jews are controlled by the power of sin evident in their present behavior as well as in their destiny in God's judgment, in which nobody has any excuse. In 3:10–18 Paul provides

biblical evidence for his assertion that Jews have no advantage over Gentiles because they are sinners. In verses 10–12 he quotes Psalm 14:1–3 to confirm that the Jewish people are not righteous, as they disregard God. Psalm 14 laments the oppression of the righteous in Israel by evildoers within Israel (who say that "there is no God"). In verses 13–15 Paul shifts his attention from the abandonment of God to the wrongs done to the neighbor, citing a series of eight pronouncements against enemies of biblical authors. In verses 13–14 he cites Psalms 5:9, 140:3, and 10:7 for sins of human speech—deadly deceit, poison, cursing, and bitterness. In verses 15–18 he cites Isaiah 59:7–8 (Prov. 1:16), Isaiah 59:8, and Psalm 36:1 for sins of human conduct—murder, destruction, strife, and rejection of God.

In 3:19–20 Paul concludes his indictment of sinners. Verse 19 confirms that Paul has been addressing Jews in the preceding series of Old Testament quotations. It is Jews who are "in the law" (not "under the law," as NIV translates). Since 1:18 Paul has silenced "every mouth" by proving that the whole world is accountable to God. He established in 1:18–32 the sinfulness of the Gentiles, which needed no further proof. He established the sinfulness of the Jews in 2:1–3:18, against the objections of a Jewish dialogue partner whom he sought to silence with phenomenological and biblical evidence. Paul concludes in 3:20 with an allusion to Psalm 143:2 and perhaps Genesis 6:12, asserting that final justification by God does not take place on the basis of obedience to the works prescribed by the law. No "flesh" (NIV "no one") has the ability to obey the law. In 8:3–4 Paul will argue (as he did in 2:13–14 and in 2:25–29) that the Spirit provides for the Christian believer the power to fulfill the law. The law may have indeed provided various mechanisms for the atonement of sin; note the burnt offerings and the sin offerings described in Leviticus 1 and 4–5 (cf. Exod. 34:7; Num. 14:18–19). These provisions of the law can no longer compensate for sin, because God has provided a new place of atonement, as Paul will argue in the next section (3:21–5:21). Paul informs Jews who continue to rely on the law that the law merely leads to the knowledge of sin (3:20). In the new messianic age, in which the promised new covenant has become a reality, the law cannot justify sinners; it can only reveal their actions and efforts as sin.

3:21–5:21: God's saving righteousness for Gentiles and Jews. Paul describes how God "now"—at the time when Jesus the Messiah came—declares sinners justified as a result of Jesus's atoning death (3:21–31). Faith in Jesus Christ creates the universal people of God, consisting of Jews, the ethnic descendants of Abraham, and of Gentiles, the families of the earth whom God wanted to bless through Abraham (4:1–25). Jews and Gentiles who believe in Jesus Christ have peace with God, the hope of sharing the glory of God, the love of God, and the Holy Spirit (5:1–11). God's triumph over sin in and through Jesus Christ solves once and for all the fundamental problem of the power of sin, which, since the fall of Adam, brings condemnation and death on humankind (5:12–21).

3:21–26. Paul explains the revelation of God's saving righteousness through faith in Jesus Christ in two parts. In verses 21–26 he explains the significance of God's action in the death of Jesus Christ, providing atonement for sins and redemption. In verses 27–31 he describes the universality of justification by faith in Jesus Christ, which corresponds to the universality of the sinfulness of humankind described in 1:18–3:20.

Paul begins in 3:21 with the fundamental assertion, "But now apart from the law the righteousness of God has been made known." The phrase "but now" marks a contrast between the time of Gentile idolatry and immorality and God's provision of righteousness for sinners, a contrast between Jewish efforts to find salvation through the law in the old covenant and the revelation of God's righteousness in the new covenant. God's saving action took place

apart from the law, independently of the Mosaic law, both for Gentiles who do not have the law and for the Jews who do not obey the law. The disclosure of the righteousness of God is God's act of saving Gentile sinners and Jewish lawbreakers. God saves the ungodly and the disobedient, the very people who assaulted his glory and who did not obey his will. Paul clarifies that this new reality is scriptural: the Law and the Prophets bear witness to it (cf. Rom. 1:2; 4:1–25; 9:25–33; 10:6–13; 15:8–12). The gospel of God concerning Jesus Christ that Paul proclaims is the fulfillment of God's promises for the new covenant; it is not a new religion.

In 3:22–26 Paul explains the revelation of the saving righteousness of God as follows. The *means of salvation* is not the law but trust in Jesus the messianic Savior—faith in Jesus Christ (3:22). The Greek phrase, literally "faith *of* Jesus Christ," has a rich meaning. Some interpret the phrase in terms of the "faith" that Jesus himself had (subjective genitive); in other words, Jesus was faithful to accomplish the work that God had given him. Others interpret it in terms of Jesus Christ as the source of faith (the Greek genitive of source); that is, Paul writes about the faith given by Jesus Christ. The traditional interpretation sees Jesus Christ as the object of the faith of the sinners (objective genitive): Paul references the sinners' faith in Jesus Christ (see NIV).

The *scope of salvation* is universal ("to all"), without distinction between idolatrous polytheists and pious Jews, open to all who believe. The *target of salvation* is sinners (3:23), people whose behavior suppresses God's truth and ignores God's will, people who have lost the glory of living in God's presence (a reference to Adam's fall; in *Apocalypse of Moses* 21:6, Adam accuses Eve, "You have deprived me of the glory of God"). The *nature of salvation* through faith in Jesus Christ is justification (Greek *dikaioō*), God's acquittal of the sinner who faced condemnation on the day of judgment, but who now is declared righteous and thus set right with God (3:24). The *manner of salvation* is that of a free gift. The *motivation of salvation* is God's grace (*charis*), the undeserved love of God. The *means of salvation* is also redemption, deliverance from the hopeless human condition of 1:18–3:20. "Redemption" sometimes refers to a ransom that has been paid (cf. 1 Cor. 6:20; 7:23; also Mark 10:45); many see an allusion to the Old Testament motif of redemption in a new exodus, a new covenant, and a new creation (Isa. 43:14–21; 48:20–21; 52:1–2; Ezek. 20:33–38; Hos. 2:14–23). The *facilitation of salvation* is bound up with Jesus the Messiah. It is in and through Jesus's death and resurrection that the new epoch of salvation has been inaugurated and that both idolatrous pagans and lawbreaking Jews are delivered from sin and death. In 3:24, Paul uses for the first time in Romans the phrase "in Christ Jesus" (which occurs over eighty times in his letters), which describes the "location" or sphere of God's intervention in the history of humankind for the salvation of sinners.

The *locale of salvation* is the cross, where Jesus Christ became the new place of God's atoning presence (3:25). The Greek term *hilastērion* (NIV "sacrifice of atonement") is best understood against the background of its Old Testament usage, where it designates the gold plate on the ark of the covenant in the Most Holy Place (Exod. 25:17–22), above which God was thought to be present and where blood was sprinkled on the Day of Atonement to cleanse the temple from sin and thus to facilitate the atonement for Israel's sins (Leviticus 16; cf. the reference to "blood" in 3:25). Some interpreters translate *hilastērion* as "propitiation," a term that describes the elimination of God's punitive wrath; others translate it as "expiation," which emphasizes the removal of sin. The concepts of propitiation and expiation proceed from a more general Hellenistic understanding of the term *hilastērion*, which may well have been how Paul's sentence would have been understood by new Gentile converts who heard this passage read in the congregation. Paul emphasizes the consequences of Jesus's death for God's wrath (1:18–32), for humankind's sinfulness (1:18–3:20), and for the power of sin (3:9). Jesus's death redeems the unrighteous from God's wrath, cleanses sinners from sin, and breaks the power of sin. Because Jesus is the sinless sacrifice and dies in the place of sinners, the sinners live. The phrase "God presented Christ" describes Jesus's death as a public manifestation of God's grace. Jesus died in public, in full view of the citizens of Jerusalem.

The effects of Jesus's death are appropriated "by faith" in Jesus Christ (3:25–26)—that is, by responding with trust and confidence. Another effect of salvation is the demonstration of God's righteousness; God demonstrated his righteousness by providing Jesus as the sacrifice that fulfills the terms of his covenant with Israel. A further effect of Jesus's death is the final, ultimate forgiveness of sins. While in the past God's forbearance left the sins committed beforehand unpunished, Jesus's sacrificial death was God's final answer to the problem of sin, which the sacrificial system of the law was not.

3:27–31. In 3:27, Paul returns to the theme of Jewish boasting, drawing out what implications God's saving action in the sacrificial death of Jesus Christ has for the Jews' reliance on election (circumcision) and obedience (the law) as the basis for their expected vindication in God's judgment. He asserts that this boasting is made impossible (3:27). The question, "Because of what law?" should be understood in the sense of "What kind of understanding of the law is involved when we argue that the Jewish boasting is excluded?" Paul argues that when Jews understand the law as commanding obedience through works, which leads to justification on the day of judgment, the sequence "works → obedience → justification → boasting" is confirmed. If the law is understood in the context of faith (in the revelation of God's saving righteousness through Jesus Christ, 3:21–26), now faith being the means of justification, the sequence is "faith → justification." This means that the pattern that leads from works to boasting is abandoned. In verse 28 Paul contrasts two

While the Jews believed there was only one God (Rom. 3:30), the Gentiles came from polytheistic backgrounds. This altar to an unnamed god found on Palatine Hill in Rome (at the Velabrum) may have been part of the early city of Rome. The inscription reads in part, "Whether to a god or goddess sacred." It was believed that if the protecting deity was not named, the city could not be conquered.

basic confession of Jewish monotheism (Deut. 6:4). Since there is only one God, there can be only one means of justifying sinners. This is what Paul has argued in 3:21–26, read in the context of 1:18–3:20: members of God's covenant people (the circumcised Jews) are justified before God by faith in Jesus Christ, and idolatrous polytheists (the uncircumcised pagans) are justified "through that same faith" (3:30).

Paul asks in verse 31 whether his assertions about Gentile sinners and Jewish sinners, about circumcision and the law, and about God's revelation of righteousness in Jesus Christ appropriated by faith nullify the law. He assures that this is not so ("By no means!" [NIV "Not at all!"]). He does not abolish the law; rather, he "upholds" the law. Later passages show what Paul means: those who accept by faith the revelation of God's saving righteousness in Jesus Christ will keep the law, which contains God's holy, just, and good commandments (7:12). Believers in Jesus Christ encounter the law no longer as the law of sin and death—that is, as sinners who face eternal condemnation—but as the law of the Spirit of life in Christ Jesus—that is, as people who have received the Spirit of the new covenant and who have been given new hearts (8:2–4).

4:1–25. Paul links his rejection of boasting (3:27–31) with Abraham, whom he describes as the fundamental paradigm for God's people, the prototype of justification for both Gentiles and Jews. Paul argues in 4:1–16 that Abraham was justified by God not on the basis of works but on the basis of faith. Abraham was regarded as the first converted Gentile (from Ur of the Chaldeans, Gen. 15:7) and as the first Jew who was circumcised and received God's covenant (Genesis 15; 17). Contrary to the traditional Jewish understanding of Abraham, Paul argues that Abraham, as the Jews' ancestor according

ways of justification: sinners are justified on the day of judgment by faith in Jesus Christ without the involvement of the law (Paul's conviction); or sinners are justified by works prescribed by the law (the Jewish conviction). Paul has argued in 2:1–3:20 that the latter is not possible. The truth that justification before God is not by obedience to the law applies not only to Jews (who do not obey the law) but also to Gentiles (who do not have the law).

In verses 29–30 Paul gives a theological argument for his conviction. God's final solution to the problem of the reality of sin among Gentiles and among Jews is not justification through obedience to the law, because then only Jews could be saved (since only Jews possess the law). This is an unacceptable position since God is not only the God of the Jews but also the God of the Gentiles. The truth is that "there is only one God" (3:30). This formulation reflects the to the flesh (4:1; NIV "our forefather"), discovered that he was *not* justified on the basis of his works. His works provided him with claims for boasting before human beings "but not before God" (4:2).

Paul reestablishes the sequence of faith → justification → obedience for Abraham, reading Genesis 15:6 (quoted in 4:3) in the light of Genesis 12:1–4 (and not in the light of Genesis 17 and 22, where he proves his obedience by "works"). When Abraham was justified, he was an ungodly idolater who had no "works" God could reward (4:4–5). God justified the Abraham who believed, not the Abraham who "worked." This is also true with regard to David, whose sins were forgiven and who was reckoned by God as righteous apart from works (4:6–8, quoting Ps. 32:1–2). The blessing of justification God pronounces on sinners such as David is valid not only for Jews such as David but also for Gentiles such as Abraham before his circumcision (4:9–12). Abraham's circumcision was the "seal of the righteousness" God granted him on account of his faith in God's promises (4:11a). Abraham is thus the ancestor of the new people of God: the ancestor of the uncircumcised Gentiles who have come to faith and who are graciously granted righteousness by God on the basis of this faith (4:11b), and the ancestor of the circumcised Jews who have come to faith (in God's saving revelation in Jesus Christ; cf. 4:21–22). In verses 13–15 Paul explains that God's promise to Abraham regarding his blessing for the families of the earth—he was promised that he would be "heir of the world" (4:13; cf. Gen. 12:3)—was not fulfilled through the law. When Israel had the law, the promise that the nations would be blessed was not fulfilled. If the law encounters sinners, it can only bring God's wrath, which is particularly true for Gentiles, who do not have the law.

In 4:16–25 Paul provides a profile for the authentic faith of the people who belong to God's (new) covenant, using Abraham the converted Gentile as the prototype of all his offspring (4:16). Abraham is the father of all who have faith, whether we are Jews ("those who are of the law") or Gentiles ("not only"). Authentic faith trusts in God's promise (4:16, 21) and in God's power to create life out of nothing (4:17), defying human expectations (4:18), overcoming temptation to resort to human efforts (4:19) in the face of human impossibilities, growing by standing the test of unbelief (4:20), giving all glory to God. Paul concludes in 4:24–25 by linking saving faith with the almighty God, who raised Jesus from the dead, and with the work of Jesus the Lord, who died to accomplish the forgiveness of sins and who was raised from the dead in order to make the justification of sinners possible.

5:1–11. After the blessing of justification for sinners (3:21–31), and after the blessing of the Gentiles' becoming members of God's new covenant people (4:1–25), Paul mentions in 5:1–2a another consequence of the revelation of God's saving righteousness through Jesus Christ: peace with God. The godless and disobedient sinners of 1:18–3:30 have been granted peace with God, as they have come to faith in God and in his work of salvation in Jesus Christ. In verse 2 Paul clarifies that this peace is not a subjective feeling of peacefulness in the soul but the objective fact that God's wrath has been removed through Jesus's death and that sinners have now been granted access to God's grace, that is, to the realm in which God's redeeming love for sinners reigns (cf. 4:21). Having excluded boasting (3:27; cf. 2:17), Paul now introduces boasting again, redefined by God's grace, which justifies sinners. If boasting is indeed a basic factor of human existence, expressing the grounds of human confidence, Paul's exposition in 5:2b–11 is fundamental for understanding the life of the Christian believer.

Paul speaks about three boasts. (1) Christians have confidence in the hope of sharing the glory of God (5:2b). They exult in the hope that the glory of God, which has been forfeited as a result of sin (3:23), will be finally and fully restored on the day when believers will be in God's presence.

(2) Christians have confidence in their sufferings (5:3), because suffering for the sake of the gospel leads to endurance, which in turn develops Christian character, which in turn bolsters the hope of sharing the glory of God (5:3–4). This chain (hope → suffering → endurance → character → hope) is the basis for Paul's assertion that "hope does not put us to shame" (5:5). The believer's hope is unshakable because the grace of God, which grants this hope, is the power of the love of God. In verses 5–8 Paul explains the love of God. Sinners who have come to faith in God's saving righteousness through Jesus Christ have received from God not wrath but love. God's love is a gift of the Holy Spirit, who is the effective presence of God in the hearts of believers, a gift which demonstrates that they will be spared on the day of judgment, guaranteeing that their hope will not turn out to be an illusion. God granted his saving love at a time when the believers were helpless and ungodly sinners. The effective demonstration of God's love was in the past, when the miracle happened that Jesus Christ died for people who were neither righteous nor good but enemies (5:7, 10). Jesus's death guarantees the demonstration of God's love in the future day of judgment, when God will justify believers on account of the death of Jesus, who has been raised from the dead to life at the right hand of God.

(3) Christians have confidence in God himself. This boast is based on the work of Jesus Christ and is the result of the sinner's reconciliation, which they enjoy now, in the present (5:11).

5:12–21. This section concludes the first major part in Paul's letter, while preparing for the second part, in which Paul explains the reality of the revelation of God's saving righteousness in the life of believers. In this section, Adam stands for the sinfulness of all humanity (1:18–3:20), while Jesus Christ stands for God's solution to the problem of the human condition (3:21–5:11). In 5:12 Paul sets up a contrast between two men. One man is responsible for sin in the world, resulting in death, which has

spread to all people. Death is described as an unnatural state: it was not originally part of the world; it entered God's creation through Adam (whose name means "man"). Death is both physical and spiritual (cf. 5:16, 18, the reference to condemnation). When Adam sinned, he was separated from God's immediate presence (Genesis 3). Adam is responsible for the presence of sin in the world, and he is responsible for the presence of death.

The phrase "because [*eph' hō*] all sinned" (5:12) has provoked much discussion with regard to the connection between Adam's sin and the sinfulness of people born after Adam. Some relate the Greek phrase *eph' hō* to the law (all have sinned *on the basis of* the law), to death (death was *the result of* all sinning), or to "one man" ("*in* Adam all sinned"; interpreted in this manner by Augustine and the Latin Vulgate, this is the classical text for the doctrine of original sin). Most interpret the phrase as a causal conjunction (all people die "*because* all people have sinned"), some as consecutive ("*with the result that* all people have sinned"). Paul's concern is with original death. Adam's sin brought about a situation in which all people are separated from God and thus suffer death, and in which every human being without exception commits sins. The causal connection between Adam's sin and his death is repeated in the experience of all human beings: since nobody escapes the reality of sin, nobody escapes the reality of death. People are sinners because they sin (1:18–3:20), and they are sinners because they are Adam's descendants living in the time after Adam's rebellion against God.

Paul interrupts his contrasting comparison ("just as") at the end of verse 11 (until 5:18). He needs to clarify the significance of the law, which the Jews regard to be God's answer to the problem of sin. In 5:13–14 Paul addresses the relationship between sin and death in the time from Adam to Moses. He argues that sin existed in the world before the law was given, which is proven by the fact that the people who lived in the time between Adam and Moses died (death being the consequence of sin, 5:12). During this time, sin was not charged against anyone's account, the computation of the charge being death. Sin existed, but it could not be quantified and punished as transgression of the law. It was rebellion against God, albeit not in terms of breaking the Mosaic law, even if people did not violate a specific commandment, as Adam did. The point is that Adam provided a type of "the one to come"—Jesus Christ, the "second Adam" (1 Cor. 15:47–48). Adam is a pattern because he is the representative of the old epoch. He is the man who inaugurated the history of the human race as a history of idolatry and disobedience. His fate reveals the effective universality of sin. Before Paul explains that Adam prefigured Jesus Christ in his universal effectiveness for salvation (5:18–19), he clarifies in 5:15–17 the dissimilarity between Jesus Christ and Adam. The gift of justification through Jesus Christ cannot really be compared with the transgression of Adam. While the death of "the many" (all people) is the result of Adam's disobedience, the effect of Jesus's action is not the consequence of a human deed but the gift of God's unmerited grace (5:15). The reality of justification cannot really be compared with the sin of Adam. The effective power of God's saving justification granted to sinners who have committed countless sins is incomparably greater than the power of sin that resulted from a single transgression of one human being (5:16). While the descendants of Adam are controlled by the power of death, believers who belong to Jesus Christ receive the gift of grace, which they experience as righteousness and as dominion over the power of sin and death in this life and in the life to come (5:17).

In 5:18–19 Paul completes the contrasting comparison between Adam and Jesus Christ. Adam's sin led to the condemnation of every single human being, while Jesus's righteous act, his obedience to God's will on the cross (and throughout his life), leads to the justification of sinners who receive the life they have lost because of their sin (5:18). The phrase

"justification and life for all people" cannot mean that every single human being is saved as a result of Jesus's death (which is what the doctrine of universalism teaches). Paul does not argue that the groups affected by the action of Adam and of Christ are coextensive. The character of Jesus's obedience is universal in the sense that it affects all people who belong to him—that is, everybody who receives the gift of God's grace (5:17), who acknowledges Jesus as Lord (5:11), who is "in Christ" (3:24; 6:11; 8:1), just as Adam's disobedience is universal in the sense that it affects all people who belong to him, in other words, all his biological descendants. Verse 19 restates and explains verse 18: Adam's disobedience resulted in the sinfulness of humankind, while Jesus's obedience resulted in God's saving righteousness being extended to sinners. Paul's conclusion in 5:20–21 clarifies again the role of the law and summarizes God's purposes in the history of salvation. The Mosaic law was added to the already-existing nexus between sin and death, with the result that the trespass increased (5:20). The "excess" of sin, which the law caused, is the specific definition of sin as transgression of the will of God revealed in the law and the condemnation of the sinner who is punished with the death sentence on the day of judgment. As sin did its work with universal effectiveness, God's grace proved all the more powerful. The "excess" of grace, which results from Jesus's obedience, is the cancellation of the guilty verdict, which sin, multiplied on account of the existence of the law, pronounced against the sinners. Thus the history of humankind, seen as history governed by God, is a history of salvation in two stages. The time when sin ruled, consigning people to death, is followed by the time when grace rules, extending to sinners righteousness and eventually eternal life, on account of the work of Jesus Christ our Lord (5:21).

B. The reality of justification by faith in the life of the Christian (6:1–8:39). In the second main section of the letter, Paul explains the reality of God's saving righteousness in the life of the

Christian (6:1–8:39). Believers in Jesus Christ cannot possibly trivialize sin, since they have been freed from the slavery of sin (6:1–23). There has been a fundamental change from tolerating sin to being in the Spirit and living according to the will of God (7:1–8:17). While believers suffer in the present world, they suffer in hope (8:18–30), assured of their ultimate triumph on account of the love of God (8:31–39).

6:1–23: The new life of true righteousness. Paul argues that while sin has not yet been eliminated as a present reality, believers in Christ who have been declared righteous do not regard sin as something insignificant, because they have understood the implications of their conversion. When they came to faith they were united with Christ, who died because of sin and who was raised from the dead (6:1–14). The fact that believers are "not under the law but under grace" does not mean they tolerate sin. Rather, they have been freed from the slavery of sin, with the result that they are consistently devoted to righteousness and holy living (6:15–23).

6:1–14. In 6:1 Paul repeats the sacrilegious proposition of his Jewish dialogue partner (3:8), but as a question put forward by the justified sinner of 3:21–5:21. The suggestion that believers might continue to sin in order that grace may increase may have been an objection to Paul's theology voiced by Jews or by Jewish Christians. The objection is based on a false inference—namely, that Paul's teaching regarding the justification of sinners by God's grace implies that an increase in sin (which God forgives) leads to an increase in grace (God can forgive more sins). The question of the reality of God's saving grace in real life is of the highest importance for Christian believers. This is the reason why Paul raises this question, and why he answers it in the course of chapters 6–8, addressing Christians directly (not indirectly through a conversation with a dialogue partner). In 6:2 Paul protests against the suggestion that the reality of God's righteousness saving sinners by grace encourages people to go on sinning

("By no means!"). He answers the question of verse 1 with the assertion that believers in Jesus Christ, who died for sinners, will not continue to live in sin because they have "died to sin"—and dead people cannot sin.

In 6:3–10 Paul gives a theological explanation; in 6:11–14 he gives an ethical explanation. He begins in 6:3 with a reminder of a theological truth he expects the Roman Christians to know already. Faith in Christ establishes a union with Christ with respect to his death. While English versions translate the verb in verse 3 as "baptize," for speakers of the Greek language the term *baptizō* does not mean "baptize"—i.e., "to use water in a rite for the purpose of . . . establishing a relationship with God"—but "to put or go under water," as it is used for a ship that sinks, for a flooded city, or metaphorically for people who are immersed in debt (see BDAG, 164). Paul asserts that sinners who have come to faith were "immersed into" the Messiah Jesus, which means that they share his fate. (At the same time, believers would have been reminded by Paul's formulation of their immersion in water when they had come to faith in Jesus and became members of the congregation of believers.) Jesus is a representative figure—the Messiah, who is the second Adam and whose obedience affects those who belong to him (5:12–21). Since Jesus died on the cross—the place where God was graciously present to atone for their sins—their immersion into Jesus Christ is an immersion into his death. Faith in Christ therefore establishes a union with Jesus the Messiah that causes the believer's participation in his death (and resurrection, 6:5). If Paul's readers understood the apostle to refer to baptism, he would want to clarify that the union with Christ does not become a reality through water baptism understood as a purely ceremonial event but through faith in Jesus as the crucified Messiah and Savior (Rom. 1:16–17; 3:22, 25–28, 30; 4:5, 9, 12; 5:1). Participation in the death of Jesus the Messiah means participation in his burial (6:4).

Paul mentions burial because it confirms that death has occurred (1 Cor. 15:3–4).

Paul goes on to argue that since faith in Jesus Christ establishes a union with his death, it likewise establishes a union with his resurrection. As Jesus was raised from the dead through the glorious power of God the Father, so believers participate in his resurrection, which enables them to live a new life. And this is the reason why they cannot sin deliberately or live carelessly. The newness of the life of the Christian believers is the new life of the Spirit (7:6), the life of the new creation (2 Cor. 5:17; Gal. 6:15), the life of the new humanity (Eph. 2:15). Verse 5 explains: believers are united not only with Jesus's death but also with Jesus's resurrection. While the verse speaks of the believer's future resurrection, Paul asserts that believers are enabled to live a new life on account of the power of God, which was manifested in Jesus's resurrection and is at work in their lives by virtue of their union with Christ.

Paul restates in 6:6–10 what he said in verses 3–5, explaining why Christians cannot continue sinning. Since union with Christ is a union with his death, it is a union with Jesus's crucifixion (6:6). Since Jesus died on the cross for the sins of Adam's descendants ("our old self"), believers have been crucified with Christ by virtue of their union with the second Adam. The purpose of Jesus's death and the purpose of the believer's union with him is the destruction of the "body ruled by sin," the liberation from the power of sin that has enslaved Adam's descendants (1:18–3:20). Verse 7 explains why believers cannot be slaves to sin: dead people are no longer controlled by the power of sin, which means that believers who have been identified with Jesus's death and who died when Jesus died have been freed from the enslaving power of sin and its consequence, which is God's condemnation. This does not mean that Christians can no longer sin. We are united with Jesus's death and resurrection, but the resurrection of our body is still in the future. Believers have been freed from sin and its consequences, but they are not yet free from temptation, or from the possibility of sinning, or from the reality of committing sins. But sinning is not the state of affairs that believers consider to be normal and acceptable. In verses 8–10 Paul explains what the believer's union with Jesus's resurrection means. As they are incorporated into Christ's death, they will live with him in the future of God's ultimate triumph over death (6:8). The reason is that Christ, whom God raised from the dead, will not die a second time (6:9), which means that those who are united with Christ's death will not die a second time either. Death no longer has any power over Jesus, and thus death no longer has power over believers, as their death has already taken place (on the cross).

Baptistery from a sixth-century-AD church at Philippi. Paul says in Romans 6:3, "Or don't you know that all of us who were baptized into Christ Jesus were baptized into his death?"

Verse 10 explains why the power of death has been canceled: when Jesus died, he "died to sin"—that is, to break the power of sin, which owns sinners by imposing the death sentence (5:21; 7:9–11, 15–20). As the power of sin has been broken once for all, the risen Christ lives for the glory of God.

In 6:11–14 Paul explains his assertion in 6:2, that believers have died to sin and thus cannot go on sinning, with regard to the behavior of Christians in everyday life. Believers who are incorporated into Christ must consider themselves dead to sin and thus ready and enabled to live for the glory of God (6:11). This is possible as a result of the reality of being "in Christ Jesus." It is as the result of their union with Christ that they participate in the liberation from the power of sin through Jesus Christ and in the newness of life he lives for the glory of God. They must recognize that they are no longer controlled by sin, which always results in death. Now God is their master. The implications of this new reality are spelled out in verses 11–12. Believers must not allow sin and desire for sin to take over again. Paul acknowledges that sin can be tempting, that both temptations and acts of sin continue to be possibilities for believers, and that both sin and temptations are not ideas but realities that affect the person of the believer (and his body, which continues to be mortal, i.e., weak and finite). This is why Paul formulates an imperative—since Christ triumphed over sin and death, believers in Christ must not allow themselves to come under the enslaving power of sin again, as their union with Christ's resurrection enables them to resist sinful desires. Since sins are committed by the members of the human body, Paul challenges the believers not to allow their bodies to promote wickedness (6:13). They must realize that they have been promoted from death to life, that they placed themselves at the disposal of God, and that they must use their bodies to promote righteousness. Paul promises that sin will no longer rule over the believers (6:14). Since Christ has broken the power of sin, those

who are united with him cannot be controlled by sin (and its consequence, which is death). Sin can no longer be their lord, because they belong to the Lord Jesus Christ. Believers in Jesus Christ are "not under law"—they are not exposed to the death sentence of the Mosaic law, which condemns sinners. Rather, they are "under grace"—their life in the present and their life in the future are determined by the grace of God, who has forgiven their sins through Jesus Christ.

6:15–23. In verse 15 Paul restates the question of verse 1, suggesting that some might argue that living under grace gives permission to sin. Paul forcefully rejects such a conclusion and explains its fallacy in 6:16–18, emphasizing that there are only two options: obedience to sin or obedience to righteousness. Believers should know that they are slaves of the master whom they obey, which is either sin or God (6:16). If sin controls people, the result is death, eternal separation from God (Gen. 2:17; 3:24). If obedience to God controls people, the result is righteousness, the grace of God's gift through Jesus Christ, and life in the presence of God. Paul's thanksgiving (6:17) clarifies that believers do not occupy neutral ground in the battle between sin and righteousness. They were once enslaved to sin (1:18–3:20). Since they accepted the teaching of the apostles—the preaching of the gospel of God—and came to faith in Jesus Christ, they have become obedient to God. It was God himself who caused them to become obedient in their hearts to the gospel. It was God who liberated them from the power of sin and its death sentence and subjected them to the power of righteousness (6:18). When Paul uses the language of slavery with regard to God and righteousness, he speaks in human terms (6:19). In their past life, the believers were slaves to uncleanness and lawlessness. In their present new life they can and must be slaves to righteousness, which results in sanctification. They are committed to the process of becoming more and more holy, as God is holy. Christian believers have no choice: they either sin or they decide to live according to the will of God. There is no middle ground. People are either subject to the tyranny of sin and lacking in righteousness (6:20), not getting any benefit from their impure and wicked activities, which eventually result in God's death sentence (6:21), or people are subject to the lordship of God, liberated from the power of sin, with the benefit of a holy life and the confidence that they will have eternal life (6:22). Being slaves to sin has no advantage, while obedience to God and his righteousness yields the fruit of sanctification. Paul expresses this alternative in his concluding statement. The "wages of sin"—the compensation paid by sin for services rendered—is death, eternal separation from God. The free gift given by God is eternal life, made possible on account of the work of Jesus the Messiah and Lord.

7:1–8:17: From flesh to Spirit. Paul explains in this section the change in ownership of human beings, who are owned either by sin or by Jesus Christ (which is his argument in 6:15–23 for the assertion that believers cannot go on sinning). After a succinct introduction (7:1–6) he explains that, before their conversion, believers were ruled by sin and death (7:7–25). As the result of their being united with Christ, they are ruled by the Spirit of life, who helps them to live according to the will of God (8:1–17).

7:1–6. Paul begins with a reference to the legal principle of Jewish law: the law is binding on a person only during the lifetime of that person; once the person has died, he or she is free from the stipulations of the law (7:1). Paul illustrates this principle with the law of marriage. The law binds a married woman to her husband (according to Jewish law, women cannot divorce their husbands). In the case that her husband dies before she does, she is no longer bound to her husband (7:2). On the one hand, this means that if she lives with another man while her husband is alive, she will be identified and punished as an adulteress (7:3). On the other hand, if her husband dies, she is free from the law concerning her husband and

thus free to marry another man. The death of her husband releases the wife from the marriage bond and allows her to have relations with another man without these relations being classified as adultery.

Paul concludes from the legal axiom that the law has authority over a person only as long as the person lives that believers who are united with Jesus's death and who have therefore died are freed from the normative power of the law (7:4). The death of Jesus results in the death of the believers as they are incorporated into Christ. They have died to the law—as they have died in Christ, the law no longer has power over them. Christ's death broke the power of the law, which, when it encountered sin (which it always does), resulted in death. As believers in Christ have died to the law, they no longer belong to the law, and thus they are free to belong to someone else, namely, to God. As a result of their incorporation into Christ, whom God has raised from the dead, believers experience the power of resurrection in their lives, allowing them to bear fruit for God.

This reality is explained in verses 5–6. Before their conversion, believers lived in the "flesh" (Greek *sarx*). This means that their physical existence was conditioned by opposition to God and thus determined by sin—indeed, by "sinful passions," which were manifest in the actions of their body, resulting in condemnation (7:5). Paul's assertion that the sinful passions were "aroused by the law" was provocative for Jews, who believed that the role of the law was to curb sin, not to stimulate sin. Paul will explain in verses 7–11 what he means. When the fundamental self-centeredness of human beings encounters the law, which formulates God's will and which demands unconditional love for God and neighbor, the sinful ego reacts and asserts itself; and thus sinful passions are stimulated and sinful actions ensue. The phrase "but now" marks the change of ownership that has taken place (7:6). Believers have died with Christ; they are thus freed from the condemning power of the law. They have been released from being slaves of the law, which controlled their destiny as sinners. They are no longer governed by the "letter" of the law (NIV "the written code"), which pronounced the death sentence (cf. Gal. 3:13; 2 Cor. 3:6). Rather, believers are slaves (NIV "we serve" puts it mildly) in the newness of the Spirit. Their life changed ownership from belonging to the law (resulting in death, on account of the reality of sin) to belonging to Jesus Christ (resulting in new life, on account of the reality of the resurrection). This new reality is conditioned by the revelation of God's righteousness through Jesus Christ, by the presence of the Holy Spirit, by the fulfillment of the promises that in the new covenant God's Spirit will give to God's people the desire and the ability to keep the statutes of the law (Jer. 31:31–34; Ezek. 36:26–27). Paul explains 7:5–6 in the next two sections: the old life in the flesh (7:5) is explained in 7:7–25, and the new life in the Spirit (7:6) is explained in 8:1–17.

7:7–12. Paul next describes the rule of sin. The assertion in verse 5 (and the statements in 3:19–21; 5:20) may suggest to some readers that the law itself is sin (7:7). Paul energetically rejects such a conclusion. He explains his "By no means!" (RSV, ESV; NIV "Certainly not!") in verses 7–12: since the law condemns sinners and consigns them to death as the consequence of their sin, the law belongs on God's side and is thus opposed to sin. The problem is sin, not the law. Paul recounts the history of the encounter between the "I" and sin.

The identity of the "I" (Greek *egō*) is disputed. The main interpretations are autobiographical (Paul recounts his own experience), salvation-historical (Paul describes the experience of Israel), related to Adam (Paul recounts the experience of Adam), universal (Paul reflects on the experience of humankind). In view of the structure of Paul's argument in chapters 7–8 (as suggested by 7:5–6) in the context of his argument since 1:18, it is not plausible to assume that he would write a long text about his personal experience. Nor is it plausible to assume that Paul is describing the experience

of Jews only, considering that he has indicted both Gentiles and Jews for sinful disobedience (1:18–3:20), that he outlined God's solution of the problem of the sinfulness of both Jews and Gentiles in 3:21–5:21, and that he has described the reality of God's righteousness in the lives of both Gentile and Jewish believers since 6:1. It is best to combine the interpretation linked with Adam and the universal interpretation—all people without exception, all of Adam's descendants, both Jews and Gentiles, are subject to sin. Thus, Paul describes in this passage the encounter between human beings and the reality of sin, with the narrative of Adam's fall (Genesis 3) in the background.

The history of the "I" begins with the knowledge of sin (7:7). Knowledge of sin is possible only in the context of the law. Paul explains verse 5—the sinful passions became effective when "I" became acquainted with the desire for what was forbidden. The commandment "You shall not covet!" (Exod. 20:17) is not only the tenth commandment; it also points to God's prohibition of eating from the Tree of the Knowledge of Good and Evil in the Garden of Eden (with the punishment of death in case of noncompliance; Gen. 2:17; 3:3, 11). And it points to the biblical truth that uncontrolled desire is the manifestation of human self-centeredness and self-worship, and thus idolatry. As desire is operative in sin, the law is operative in the commandment not to covet. As "I" encountered the law in the commandment not to covet, and as "I" did not obey this commandment, "I" made the acquaintance of sin. This "coming" of the law cannot refer to the Mosaic law, since people knew about sin before Moses (5:13–14); it refers to the story of Adam in the Garden of Eden, whose story is told as the story of all human beings.

In 7:8–11 Paul describes how sin came from outside to the "I." Appearing as a personified being, Sin used the existence of the commandment as an opportunity to produce the desire for what is forbidden, which then became a base of operations for sin (7:8). The statement "apart from the law, sin was dead" formulates a principle that explains the function of the law. When there is no law or commandments, sin is inactive and powerless. God's enemy was able to attack Adam and Eve in Eden only because there was the commandment of Genesis 2:17. The potent power of Sin is death (7:9), an effect that takes place only when there is a law that represents the will of God and that thus defines

The Fall of Man by Hendrik Goltzius (1558–1617). Paul's discussion of sin and the law in Romans 7 echoes his thoughts about the fall of Adam and Eve developed in Romans 5.

what constitutes rebellion against God, the consequence of which is death. The time when "I" was alive in absence of the law (7:9) is the time in Paradise before the fall, when everything was "very good" (Gen. 1:28–31; 2:7–15), the time before the arrival of the commandment of Genesis 2:16–17. The great reversal in the history of the "I" happened "when the commandment came," which was used by sin to spring to life (7:9). The result of the encounter with the law, which was (mis)used by the sin of covetous self-absorption, was the death of the "I" (7:10). Human beings lost the life they had before this encounter. This result of the encounter is ironic, because the commandment that had been given to promote and protect life (Gen. 2:17; cf. Lev. 18:5; Deut. 30:15–20) in fact resulted in death of the "I."

Paul explains that the cause of the death of the "I" was not the commandment but Sin, which used the commandment for its own purposes (7:11). Sin's mode of operation is described with the word "deceive," which takes up Genesis 3:13, where Eve laments that the serpent has tricked her. When we interpret Genesis 3 not only as the story of the fall of

Adam and Eve but also as the fundamental narrative of human existence, we see that sin deceives in three ways. (1) Sin distorts the divine commandment by emphasizing seemingly negative aspects of God's will. (2) Sin lets humans believe that disobedience against God's commandment will not be punished with death. (3) Sin uses God's own law to cast doubt on the goodness of God and thus on the very identity of God, seeking to provide a reason for preferring self-determination over subjection to God. Genesis 3 demonstrates that the strategy of sin worked: Adam and Eve were deceived, as they believed the serpent; rather than improving their situation through their self-asserting action, they were driven from Paradise.

Paul highlights the deception of Sin with the statement that "I" was killed as a result of my doing what Sin suggested "I" do—to desire what God has forbidden and to actively disobey God (7:11). Paul formulates his preliminary conclusion as an answer to the objection of verse 7—the law is holy since it is the law of God, who is holy (7:12). To eliminate any doubt about what he means, Paul clarifies that he does not speak in generalities: the commandment, the voice of the law in its specific stipulations, is also holy. Paul pushes further: the commandment is not holy in some general sense; it is righteous because it formulates God's demands, which lead his people to righteousness, keep them from harmful and fatal desires, and thus protect them from sin. And it is good because it represents God's goodwill, which preserves and promotes life.

7:13–25. Paul clarifies the role of the law (which is good) and the character of sin (which deceives). He repeats the objection of verse 7: if the law is good, and if the law pronounces the death sentence, then the law is responsible for my death (7:13). Paul's protest clarifies again that it is not the law but the operation of sin that is responsible for my death. Paul shows that the divine purpose regarding the function of the law (after the encounter between the "I" and sin) is twofold. (1) The law reveals sin as sin. It proves that sin misuses God's good gift of the law. It uncovers sin's deception of human beings. It shows that following the desires suggested by sin leads to death, not to the fulfillment of the promises made by sin. (2) The law increases sin "beyond measure" (NIV "utterly"). As the law unmasks sin with regard to the consequences of sinning, the true character of sin is demonstrated—it always leads to death.

In verses 8–11 Paul has described how sin came from the outside, successfully subduing the "I." In verses 14–23 he describes the historical reality of the "I," which now belongs to sin and which is controlled by the death sentence of the law—a reality that is the effect of the history of verses 8–11 for humankind. Paul begins in 7:14–16 by describing the "I" as occupied by sin, as the place of conflict between sin and the law, between "what I want" and "what I do." The statement "the law is spiritual" (7:14) emphasizes the divine origin of the law in God's Spirit. However, God's holy law with

its just and good commandments does not have the intended effect in human beings. Since "I" belong to the sphere of the flesh, which opposes God, I am a slave living under the control of sin, helplessly doing what sin tells me to do. The conflict between the law, which has been usurped by sin, and the "I" is a conflict inside human beings—between what "I" want and what "I" do. This is an uncanny and sinister conflict, since "I" understand what "I" want, but "I" do not understand that "I" do what "I" hate (7:15). As God's creature made in God's image, "I" want to do the good that God reveals (and the law demands) and refrain from the evil that the law prohibits. Human beings, created by God, who is good and holy, feel aversion when they do the evil and impure things that the law prohibits. The voice of their guilty conscience confirms that the law is good (7:16).

In 7:17–20 Paul demonstrates that in the conflict between the "I" and sin, it is sin that dominates. "I" discover "sin living in me," as in a house (7:17). As human beings have been created in God's image, it is a grotesque situation that sin has established itself as a squatter, managing human beings who have been created in God's image. "I" am forced to acknowledge that "good itself does not dwell in me" (7:18). Human existence in the "flesh" or "sinful nature"—the life in opposition to God and his will—is not good, as humans were before the fall. "I" realize that I have only myself to blame: I know what is right, but I cannot do it. Doing good remains theory; doing evil is reality. Despite recognizing what is good and wanting to do it, we practice the evil in which we do not want to be involved (7:19). This historical reality demonstrates that my actions are not controlled by me but by sin, the occupying force controlling the "I" (7:20). The only freedom that "I" have is the freedom to sin.

The final description of the human predicament, in 7:21–23, reveals a contrast within the law itself. As the law has been usurped by sin, manipulated in pronouncing the death sentence rather than promoting life, "I" find this law active in my experience, unable to do good, but very much capable of doing evil (7:21). Having been created in God's image, "I" delight in God's law "in my inner being," which has not yet moved into action (7:22). However, I find "in the members of my body" (NASB; i.e., in my actions) that, rather than being obedient to the law, "I" am obedient to sin. The law of God has been manipulated by sin—when the law encounters sin, it pronounces the death sentence. Thus the law of God has become "another law," a law misused by sin that leads to death rather than to life (7:23).

The desperate cry "What a wretched man I am!" in 7:24 expresses the hopelessness of the human condition. "I" am controlled by sin and realize that my human body is owned by death. As a sinner "I" will suffer the death penalty stipulated by the law. The despondent question in verse 24 acknowledges that human beings cannot save themselves. In 7:25a Paul gives the answer to the question in verse 24—God himself has solved the problem of the sinful human condition through Jesus Christ our Lord for all the people who acknowledge the crucified and risen Jesus Christ as Savior and sovereign Lord. Romans 7:25b is a concluding summary of 7:14–24. Created in God's image, human beings want to serve God and obey his law. But as people who live in the flesh—that is, in opposition to God on account of their sinful actions—they are condemned to serve the law, which has been usurped by sin and which they therefore encounter as law that pronounces the death sentence.

8:1–17. After Paul has described the tragic and hopeless situation of human beings who live in opposition to God and his holy law, he now turns to a description of the life of Christian believers who are ruled by the Spirit of life, who helps them live according to the will of God. In 8:1–4 Paul explains his exclamation of thanksgiving in 7:25, elaborating what he has said in 7:6. Believers who have been incorporated into Christ and who have thus been freed from the control of the law, which leads

to death, are enabled to fulfill the law through the power of the Spirit. Verse 1 reminds the readers that believers who are "in Christ Jesus" are not under condemnation because they have died with Christ (Rom. 6:1–11), who atoned for their sins through his death (3:21–31). In verses 2–4 Paul describes the liberation from the tragically miserable situation of 7:7–24. God's condemnation, pronounced in the death sentence of the law, was canceled because God's Spirit freed believers from "the law of sin and death" (8:2)—that is, from the consequences of the law, which, when it encounters sin, leads to death (Rom. 7:13–23). The liberation God granted through his Spirit on account of the death and resurrection of Jesus Christ brought about a change in the law. The condemning law, which posted sin to the account of sinners, controlling their lives as an existence leading to death, has become the law of the new covenant, whose effect is determined by God's Spirit and that thus promotes and protects life.

God did what the law could not accomplish. When the law encountered human beings, who lived in opposition to God, it was unable to help the sinners, as it had to pronounce the death sentence (8:3). God saved human beings from their hopeless predicament when he sent Jesus, whose mission it was to die as a sin offering for the atonement of sins, into the world. The death of Christ, who died for sinners, marks God's condemnation of sin and its power over human existence. The result of Jesus's death and resurrection is the fulfillment of the law by believers who are "in Christ Jesus" and who are thus no longer dominated by the power of humankind's opposition to God (the "flesh") but by the power of God's Spirit (8:4). The passive verb ("might be fulfilled in us"; KJV, RSV) indicates that the obedience of the believers is the work of God, through the power of the Holy Spirit.

In 8:5–8 Paul describes two modes of existence. There are people who are dominated by opposition to God (the flesh), and there are people who are dominated by the presence of

God in their lives (the Spirit). People's lifestyle and values indicate to which group they belong (8:5). There is a stark contrast between the destinies of the two groups. People who are controlled by the values of living in opposition to God march toward eternal death. People who live in the power of the Holy Spirit have eternal life and peace with God, as the condemnation of God's judgment has been removed (8:6). People whose values are controlled by the flesh are hostile to God—they do not submit to the will of God revealed in the law; they cannot keep the law; and thus they cannot please God (8:7–8).

The application in 8:9–11 emphasizes the following four truths. (1) Believers are not in the flesh, as their values and lifestyles are no longer determined by the secular world, which opposes God. (2) Believers are "in the Spirit" as their values, lifestyles, and actions are determined by the Spirit of God, who lives in them and dominates their personality after sin, the squatter that has occupied human beings (7:17), has been evicted. The Spirit of God is the Spirit of Christ—that is, the Spirit of the new covenant, which has been inaugurated by the saving work of Jesus Christ—whom believers have received. (3) The presence of the Spirit has transferred believers from being owned by sin to being owned by Jesus Christ. (4) The presence of the Spirit, due to the presence of Christ in believers' lives, guarantees that they will not be burdened forever with their mortal bodies. The Spirit they have been given is a life-giving Spirit, who will grant them eternal life on account of God's saving righteousness and on account of the resurrection of Christ through the power of God.

The exhortation in 8:12–13 challenges Christians to grasp their new existence "in the Spirit" as ethical obligation. They have been liberated from the slavery of the values and actions of a life lived in opposition to God (8:12), an existence in which death was the inevitable result (8:13a). Since they have been transferred to the gracious dominion of Jesus Christ, who

has given them the Spirit of God, who is holy, they will and they can and they must resist and extirpate the sinful impulses of the body, with the result that they will obtain eternal life (8:13b). The battle against temptation and sin is the responsibility of the believer, while the reason for the victorious outcome is the power of the Holy Spirit.

Paul explains in 8:14–17 that God's Spirit bears witness to the believers that they truly belong to God's people. People who inherit eternal life belong to God's family; they are "children of God" (8:14). And people who are children of God are people who are led by God's Spirit. Being led by the Spirit does not refer to guidance in decision making but to the determination by the Spirit of the believer's values, lifestyle, and actions. The passive form of the verb emphasizes again that the primary force in Christian obedience is the Spirit of God. The Spirit whom the believers received when they came to faith in Jesus Christ is a Spirit who generates a new obedience in their hearts (8:15). People who have come to faith in Jesus Christ and who have received God's Spirit have been adopted into God's family, both Jews and Gentiles. The community of the Christian believers functions as God's adopted son when they are united with Jesus Christ the Son of God. This new reality is celebrated in prayer as believers praise God for their status as adopted sons and daughters.

The exclamation "Abba!" (8:15) expresses the dynamic intimacy and closeness of the believer's relationship with God. The Aramaic word means "father" and was used by Jesus when he addressed God his Father (Mark 14:36). Believers have the assured confidence that God is their loving Father (rather than their judge who condemns) because the Spirit bears witness together with their own spirit that they are God's children (8:16). Just as children are heirs of their father, Christians are "heirs of God" since they are "co-heirs with Christ" (8:17). The reality of the union between believers and Jesus Christ makes them "heirs of God"—they will inherit everything that God has promised, the supreme benefit being life in the very presence of God. The assertion at the end of verse 17 is surprising only at first sight: the condition of receiving God's inheritance in the glory of God's new world is faithfulness and perseverance in suffering. Christians are not there yet; they still live in a world where the flesh exerts influence through temptation to sin. Believers suffer until they experience future glorification.

8:18–39: Suffering in hope and ultimate triumph. In the concluding section of his description in chapters 6–8 of God's saving righteousness through Jesus Christ in the lives of the believers, Paul reflects first on believers' suffering in the present (8:18–30) and then on the triumph of God's grace in the future (8:31–39).

8:18–30. Paul points out that believers' present suffering is nothing in comparison with the future glory that awaits them (8:18). Paul knows that the life of a Christian is often accompanied by suffering—the distress of everyday living, the pain of illnesses, and the afflictions of discrimination and persecution resulting from being a follower of Jesus Christ. But these sufferings seem insignificant, and thus bearable, when we see them in the light of the glory of God's new world, which he will usher in before long.

Paul explains in 8:19–23 that the sufferings of believers should be understood in the context of a fallen creation in which distress, pain, and death are part and parcel of human existence (Gen. 3:14–19). Since Adam's fall, creation is no longer "very good" and waits for restoration and perfection. The promised consummation of God's salvation is not a restoration of paradise, however, but the glorification of the children of God in a new heaven and a new earth (8:19). Creation changed as it was impacted by the futility of human existence, which became the dominating reality on account of Adam's sin. The present state of creation is distressful, but there is hope because God promised the restoration of a perfect world (8:20). One day, when believers in Jesus Christ will be glorified

as God's children in the consummation, creation will be liberated from being subject to the control of decay and corruption (8:21). At the moment, creation is suffering pain, waiting for the birth of God's new world (8:22).

As human beings are part of creation, they participate in the distress and the pains of creation. This is true for Christian believers as well (8:23), precisely because they have the Spirit of God, who has given them insight into the causes of the distress of creation and into the deadly consequences of sin, which affects creation. Believers express their frustration with the present corrupting state of affairs by groaning "inwardly"—they are very much aware of what is going on, but they do not go around complaining to others. The presence of the Spirit does not distance believers from creation. On the contrary, the Spirit draws them into an even closer solidarity with creation, as they know that its restoration is connected with the consummation of their own salvation in the future. The presence of the Spirit is the "firstfruits" of the consummation, God's pledge that believers will indeed share the glory of Jesus Christ the Son of God, with the redeemed bodies of God's new and perfect world (1 Cor. 15:35–57). The anguished cry of Romans 7:24, in which the groaning of 8:23 finds expression, is answered in verse 23 with reference to the glory of the future consummation.

In 8:24–27 Paul elaborates on the situation of the believer. The salvation of believers is a reality because of the effect of the atoning death of Christ. But the physical completion of their salvation has yet to come. Believers are saved in hope (8:24). This hope stands in contrast to seeing, as it is directed toward the invisible reality of God's perfect world. This means that, as believers live in hope, they wait patiently for the consummation (8:25). Believers are not alone, even though they live in a world darkened by sin, waiting for God's future to arrive. They have God's Spirit, who helps them in their weakness (8:26). Here, weakness is not the fact that believers can still be tempted by sin but the inability to pray as they should be praying. Since believers have not yet seen what they will inherit as co-heirs of Christ, they do not fully know what terms like "salvation," "freedom," "glory," and "adoption as God's children" mean with reference to the unseen reality of God's new and perfect world. Christians experience salvation as "firstfruits" only (8:23), with the full harvest yet to come. Christians speak the language of hope. Even when they pray they do not use a language that truly corresponds to the glory and majesty of God. But God's Spirit helps believers to pray, as he translates their prayers into words that correspond to the glory of God (8:26–27).

Paul concludes in 8:28–30 by emphasizing that all things that may happen to believers, including the sufferings of the present time, assist their "good" (their salvation). This is a fact because those who love God have been called according to God's purpose (8:28). Nothing can harm believers; everything helps them on their path to future glory. Believers who love God are the people whom God has called in accordance with his gracious decision to save sinners. God's gracious decision to save sinners is succinctly explained in two steps in verse 29: God elected sinners to be saved, and God predestined the goal of the election of sinners. This goal is the glorification of the believers—they will share the glorious form of Jesus Christ, the

risen Son of God, and live as members of God's family. Sinners whom God predestined to share the glory of the risen Jesus Christ have been called by God to come to faith in Jesus Christ (8:30). As they responded to this call with faith, sinners received the unmerited gift of God's righteousness. And it is these justified sinners who will be glorified by God in the glorious future of his new world. This does not mean that believers in Jesus can live in any way they please, however, since their ultimate salvation is guaranteed; this is why Paul exhorts believers to "continue to work out your salvation with fear and trembling" (Phil. 2:12).

8:31–39. Paul now speaks of the future triumph of the believers. He begins with a rhetorical question: "If God is for us, who can be against us?" The implied answer underlines the conviction that God is for us. This is a basic summary of the good news of the revelation of God's saving righteousness for sinners, which Paul has been describing since Romans 3:21. The central assertion of the gospel is the certainty that God is "for us"—a reality that became effective for the salvation of sinners when he sacrificed his own Son for all of us in the incarnation and death of Jesus Christ (8:32). The consequence of the fact that God gave his Son into death for sinners is the guarantee that he will give to those who have identified with Jesus Christ "all things"—everything else necessary for the consummation of salvation and the attainment of his glory. In verses 33–34 Paul explains the conviction that nobody can be against us. He describes the future trial in God's court of law, in which a potential enemy might bring charges against believers. God and Christ appear as the believer's advocates whose actions

> The Circus Maximus, designed for the great chariot races in Rome, could seat about sixty thousand people. It became the site where many Christians were put to death for their faith. Nevertheless, Paul promises that nothing—not "trouble or hardship or persecution or famine or nakedness or danger or sword"—can separate us from the love of Christ (Rom. 8:35).

render the accusations null and void. Because God is the judge who pronounces believers in Jesus Christ to be righteous, having canceled their guilt and the death sentence of the law, there is nobody left who could effectively accuse God's children. Because Christ has taken believers' sins upon himself, and because he is at the right hand of God on account of his resurrection from the dead, interceding for all who have come to faith in him, there is nobody left to condemn the sinner. Romans 8:33–34 thus confirms the truth of 8:1.

In 8:35–39 Paul explains further why believers cannot be condemned on the day of judgment. He asks whether there is anyone or anything that might separate believers from the love of Christ—that is, from the love that Jesus Christ has for sinners, for whom he died on the cross and whom he protects through intercession before the throne of God (8:35). Powers that might separate believers from Jesus, with the result that they would be exposed to God's condemnation after all, are trials and experiences of suffering such as hardship, distress, persecution, famine, lack of clothing, peril, or mortal danger in war. Such trials are prophesied for the tribulation of the last days (Mark 13:8; Rev. 6:8). The quotation from Psalm 44:22 serves as confirmation that the people of God will indeed experience suffering and distress, which always characterize the lives of the righteous (8:36). Paul emphasizes that suffering and distress, particularly suffering that results from believers' faith in Jesus Christ, cannot separate them from Christ. On the contrary, suffering in union with Christ leads to glorification with Christ, to a triumphant victory, which means infinitely more than merely the end of suffering (8:37).

In the last two verses of the central section (chaps. 6–8) of his letter, Paul celebrates the believers' triumph over life and death as a result of their connection with the love of God in the Lord Jesus Christ. The power of the love of God and of Jesus Christ guarantees not only victory over suffering and tribulation but also,

and in a much more fundamental sense, victory over all forces that oppose God in this world (8:38–39). There is no power that can separate the believer, who is loved by God and protected by Christ, from God's final and glorious salvation—not even death, the most powerful force and the last enemy of believers (1 Cor. 15:26); not life in the flesh, which lives in opposition to God and seeks to entice believers to yield to temptation and sin; not demonic powers, which control the world, which has rebelled against God; not hostile forces that seek to control the earth; not hostile forces that seek to control the heavenly world; not supernatural beings of any kind. Paul asserts that since the hostile powers are part of God's creation (8:39), they are controlled by the power of God, who has triumphed over the mighty power of death through Christ's death and resurrection. Because believers are "in Christ Jesus," whom they acknowledge as Lord, they participate in God's triumph over the powers of evil, and they participate in God's triumph over sin and death. This is the reason why believers are assured of their glorification in the consummation of God's new world (8:30)—they have experienced God's love, they trust in Jesus the Messiah, and they are obedient to Jesus the Lord. Christian believers are justified sinners who join the praise of God's grace in the midst of the suffering and the distress of a sinful world.

C. The reality of justification by faith in salvation history (9:1–11:36). In the third main section of his letter, Paul explains the reality of justification by faith in salvation history, raising the question of Israel's rejection of the gospel. As the Jews have rejected the gospel, has God then rejected Israel (cf. Rom. 11:1)? After he emphasizes his intense concern for the salvation of the Jews (9:1–5), Paul first shows that the suggestion that the Jews' unbelief proves that God has failed to keep his promises to Israel is false (9:6–29). Second, Paul argues that the responsibility for Israel's unbelief lies with the Jews themselves, who insist on attaining righteousness through the law while rejecting Jesus the Messiah (9:30–10:21). Paul then rejects the conclusion that God has totally rejected Israel. There are indeed Jews who are believers, and Jews will continue to find salvation through faith in Jesus Christ in the future (11:1–32).

9:1–5: Paul's intercession for Israel. The present unbelief of the Jewish people pains the apostle to the utmost, a fact that Paul underscores with the solemn affirmation that he speaks the truth and that he does not lie (9:1). Paul emphasizes that the Jews' unbelief grieves him greatly (9:2). The cause for his grief is implied in verse 3 and apparent from Paul's argument in the larger context. His intense concern for the salvation of the Jews is expressed in verse 3 in dramatic fashion. Paul asserts that if it could lead to the salvation of his people, he would wish to be cursed and thus cut off from Jesus Christ (cf. 10:1). Paul's wish is similar to Moses's plea after the Israelites reject Yahweh and worship the golden calf (Exod. 32:32). He knows that such a wish cannot be fulfilled (cf. Rom. 8:35–39). The object of his intense sorrow is his unbelieving brothers, his fellow Jews, the "Israelites" (9:3–4). The theological significance of the Jews' refusal to believe in Jesus Christ becomes obvious in verses 4–5. Since Israel was God's chosen people, who had privileges that the Gentiles did not possess, Israel's unbelief raises the question of God's covenant faithfulness (9:6).

Paul mentions nine characteristics that constitute Israel's privileges. (1) They are Israelites; that is, they bear the name of honor that God gave to Jacob (Gen. 32:38–39). (2) They received the adoption; they are God's "firstborn son" (Exod. 4:22; Deut. 14:1; Hos. 11:1). As Abraham's descendants, Jews have a unique, special relationship with God. (3) They have glory, the manifestation of God's weighty presence in their midst, focused on the tabernacle and later the temple (Exod. 29:43–45; 40:34–35; 1 Kings 8:1–13). (4) They have the covenants, God's commitments in the time of Abraham (Gen. 15:1–21), Isaac (Gen. 26:4–5), Jacob (Gen. 28:4, 13–14; 35:11–12), Moses

at Sinai (Exod. 19:5), Joshua (Josh. 8:30–35), David (2 Sam. 23:5), Josiah (2 Kings 23:3), and Nehemiah (Neh. 9:1–10:39). (5) They have the law; they received the revelation of God's holy, good, and just will. (6) They have the "worship" (NIV "temple worship")—that is, access to God through the sacrificial system (Exod. 12:25–26; Josh. 22:27). (7) They have the promises God made to Abraham, Isaac, and Jacob, to Moses and to David and to other leaders of Israel, including the promises concerning salvation and eternal life. (8) They have the fathers, the patriarchs, the leaders of God's people since Abraham. (9) The Messiah comes from Israel, representing the fulfillment of the promises God made to the fathers. Paul ends this enumeration of Israel's privileges with a doxology directed at Jesus the Messiah (correct, e.g., is NIV: "the Messiah, who is God over all, forever praised!"; cf., with different punctuation, NRSV: "the Messiah, who is over all, God blessed forever," which is less likely).

It should be noted that Paul links the attributes of 9:4–5 with believers in Jesus Christ, whether they are ethnic Jews or converted Gentiles. Not all Israelites truly belong to Israel; rather, it is the children of the promise, those who believe as Abraham believed (Romans 4), who count as true descendants of Abraham (9:6–8). Believers in Jesus Christ have received God's Spirit, who grants them "adoption" into God's family as God's children (8:14–15, 23; cf. Gal. 4:5–7; Eph. 1:5). As a result of faith in Jesus Christ, the glory of God, which humankind has lost, is restored to all who believe (3:23–24; 5:1–2; 8:17–21). Believers in Jesus Christ experience the benefits of the new covenant (8:3–4; cf. 2 Cor. 3:6; Eph. 2:12). Believers have access to God on account of the saving work of Jesus Christ, worshiping God in everyday life (5:1–2; 12:1–2). The promises given to Abraham are fulfilled in all people who believe as Abraham believed (4:16; 15:8–9). Gentile believers are also counted among Abraham's descendants (4:16). Believers in Jesus acknowledge him as Messiah, whether Jews or Gentiles, while unbelieving Jews do not know him; this is perhaps the implied reference in the statement in 9:5 that "from them is traced the human ancestry of the Messiah." This does not mean that Israel's privileges have been transferred to "the church" (conceived of as consisting of Gentile believers). But these privileges do not guarantee the salvation of all Jewish people. Paul wants them to be saved, but this means that they must come to faith in Jesus Christ.

9:6–29: God's righteousness in the history of salvation. Israel's unbelief does not mean that the word of God has failed. God's promises for Israel have not been canceled, as the examples of Isaac and Jacob demonstrate. Being authentic descendants of Abraham is not determined by birth but by the sovereign will of God, who cannot be accused of being unjust, as he is the Creator. The basic assertion Paul confirms in the following discussion is verse 6: God's promises for Israel have not been abrogated.

9:6–13. Paul argues first that it is God's free election that determines true membership in Israel. The word of God has not been rendered invalid. The word of God is the word of the sovereign God who elects whom he chooses, a reality that characterized already the beginning of Israel's history at the

time of Abraham, Isaac, and Jacob. The point is that "not all who are descended from Israel are Israel" (9:6), and not all Abraham's descendants are "Abraham's children" (9:7a). In 9:7b–9 Paul proves this to be the case first with reference to the example of Isaac. From the two sons of Abraham (born of two different mothers), God chose Isaac, not Ishmael, as the person for whom his promise of offspring was fulfilled (Gen. 21:12). This means for the purpose of God's election that biological descendants of Abraham are not automatically children of God. Rather, it is God's promise that causes some of Abraham's natural descendants to be God's children (9:8). This is confirmed by Genesis 18:10, 14—Isaac was the promised son, not Ishmael (9:9). Paul's second proof, in 9:10–13, is the example of Jacob. From the two sons of Isaac (born of the same mother as twins), God chose Jacob, not Esau. Not all the sons of Isaac were sons of God's promise. The fact that God

The veneration of Abraham in Judaism was long-standing by the era of Paul. This structure in Hebron (West Bank), originally built by Herod the Great, is said to be the location of the burial of Abraham, Isaac, and Jacob. Underground tombs exist beneath the building, but they have not been excavated.

chose Jacob over Esau, the second-born over the firstborn—even before they were born—illustrates the purpose of God's election. Being loved by God is not dependent on works but on the gracious will of God, who calls individuals to be his people (9:11–12). The word of promise by which God made his choice is Genesis 25:23, confirmed by Malachi 1:2–3 (quoted in 9:12–13).

9:14–29. Second, Paul argues that it is God's free mercy that makes people members of the true people of God. In 9:14–21 Paul repudiates the conclusion that God is unjust because he seems to act in an arbitrary manner. This objection (9:14) follows naturally from what Paul has argued: if God elects people to be his children without regard for birth and merit—without regard for affiliation with Israel—does this not call into question God's covenant faithfulness? Is God not unjust? Paul dismisses this objection. God, who elects some and hardens others, is the sovereign Creator of the world. Paul's argument again proceeds in two stages. First, the freedom of God's mercy revealed to Moses (Exod. 33:19) demonstrates that affiliation with God's election is the result of God's mercy, not the result of human desire or effort (9:15–16). Second, the freedom of God's power and judgment visited on Pharaoh (Exod. 9:16) demonstrates that history is the work of God's sovereign omnipotence (9:17–18). God grants mercy to some, while he decides to harden the hearts of others. The objection of verse 14 is restated in verse 19: if God hardens whom he chooses, he has no right to judge anyone, because nobody can resist God's will. Paul counters with a fundamental theological truth: human beings are not competent to question God (9:20). Paul confirms this truth with the parable of the Creator and the creature (Isa. 29:16; 45:9). God is the almighty Creator; human beings are his creatures. It is absurd when creatures accuse their Creator. In verse 21 Paul confirms the same truth with the parable of the potter and the clay (cf. Jer. 18:6).

The potter has full control over the clay; the vessels he fashions cannot complain.

The application of this truth, in 9:22–29, is compelling. As God has acted in the past with complete sovereignty in his election of people, so he has chosen believers in Jesus Christ in the present. God's actions with regard to the "objects of his wrath" are linked with the unbelieving Jews: God has endured them with much patience, but they have been made for destruction (9:22). In Romans 1:18–3:20 Paul demonstrated that God's wrath against the Jewish people (as against the polytheists) is not arbitrary but the consequence of their own actions of disobedience. God's actions with regard to the "objects of his mercy" are linked with believers: God elected them for the glory of eternal life in the future, with the goal that the riches of God's glory are being proclaimed in the present (9:23). In verse 24 Paul identifies the "objects of [God]'s mercy" with "us"—that is, with believers in Jesus Christ, whether Jews or Gentiles. The final application of this truth in 9:25–29 confirms the reality of divine election with the authority of Scripture—Hosea 2:25 and 2:1 announced God's calling of the Gentile believers (9:25–26); Isaiah 10:22–23 and Isaiah 1:9 announced Israel's restriction to a remnant that will be saved (9:27–29).

9:30–10:21: Israel's resistance to God's righteousness. After evaluating God's responsibilities, Paul addresses the responsibility of Israel. The reason for Israel's unbelief rests squarely with Israel. The Jewish people insist on attaining righteousness through the law, rejecting Jesus Christ, while Gentiles believe in Jesus and thus receive righteousness (9:30–33). Israel's zeal is misguided, ignorant of the fact that God now grants righteousness through faith in Jesus Christ the Lord, who fulfills the ultimate purpose of the law and who is the end of the law (10:1–13). Israel has no excuse for her unbelief, as God has indeed sent messengers who proclaimed the good news of God's saving righteousness through Jesus the Messiah and Lord, a message that should have caused the Jewish people to hear and to come to faith (10:14–21).

9:30–33. Paul first comments on the Gentiles. They did not participate in the pursuit of righteousness, which God accepts by means of the law, because they did not have the law. And yet they have attained righteousness—through faith in Jesus Christ (9:30). The situation of the believing Gentiles is contrasted with the situation of the unbelieving Jews. The members of God's people according to the flesh (Israel) who pursued righteousness by observing the law did not attain righteousness. The reason for this failure is that they did not fulfill the law (9:31). Paul explains in verse 32: Israel insisted on expunging the curse of the law through observance of the law's stipulations rather than accepting God's righteousness by faith in Jesus Christ, as the Gentiles did. They thus stumbled over "the stone" promised by God, which is Jesus, the promised Savior (quotation of Isa. 28:16 and Isa. 8:14). Israel has rejected the stone that God placed in Zion, laying a foundation for a new "temple" (the new place of worship in the new covenant). The reason for Israel's exclusion from salvation is unbelief in Jesus Christ, who brings God's promised salvation (cf. Rom. 3:21–26; 10:4) and in whom all people are to trust, both Jews (Israelites) and Gentiles.

10:1–13. Paul asserts again that he desires and prays for the salvation of his fellow Jews (10:1; cf. 9:1–3). In 10:2–5 Paul explains why the Jewish people need salvation. He attests that they are zealous for God (10:2). They are passionately determined to do God's will and defend God's honor (cf. Elijah, 1 Kings 19:10, 14). But their zeal is "not based on knowledge" since they do not recognize that God revealed his righteousness in Jesus the Messiah. Paul was himself, before his conversion, extremely zealous (Gal. 1:14); he had a zeal for God's honor that manifested itself in his persecution of the followers of Jesus (Phil. 3:6). The tragedy is that, even though the Jewish people are eager to worship God and do his will, they have not accepted the truth that God grants righteousness through

the death and resurrection of Jesus the Messiah. They continue to establish and maintain righteousness through obedience to the law. Because God's righteousness now comes through faith in Jesus Christ, the righteousness they achieve through the law is their own righteousness and not God's righteousness (10:3). In 10:4 Paul reiterates how salvation is achieved in light of God's new revelation. Since God now grants righteousness through faith in the crucified and risen Jesus Christ, the righteousness he accepts on the day of judgment no longer comes through the law but through the Messiah. It is in this sense that Christ is the end (Greek *telos*) of the law (10:4). Another thought is present as well: the righteousness that was the goal (*telos*) of the law now comes through faith in Christ. Jesus Christ is both the end of the law (as a means of acquiring righteousness) and the goal of the law (as a description of the righteousness that God demands and accepts). Righteousness is granted to "everyone who believes"—but only to those who believe, whether they are Jews or Gentiles.

In 10:5–13 Paul confirms this truth through scriptural quotations. The principle of righteousness that comes through the law depends on obedience (10:5). Moses said that Israelites who obey the law will live (Lev. 18:5). The principle of righteousness that comes through faith depends on Jesus the Messiah (10:6–8). The Messiah has come, and he is present in the gospel that is being preached, as promised by the Scriptures (Deut. 9:4; 30:11–14; cf. Ps. 107:26). Jesus the Messiah has taken the place of God's revelation (Deut. 30:1–20) as well as the place of divine wisdom (cf. Baruch 3:29–30 on Deut. 30:1–20)—both were gifts God had given to Israel. The word of God that brings God's saving righteousness is the word of faith in Jesus Christ, which Paul proclaims (10:8). In verses 9–10 Paul explains the meaning of the expression "the word [that] is near you" in Deuteronomy 30:14 for believers in Jesus the Messiah. Saving faith, which receives God's righteousness as a gift, involves a twofold confession (10:9). The confession by mouth is the affirmation that the crucified, risen, and exalted Jesus is Lord (Greek *kyrios*). The confession by heart is the affirmation that God raised Jesus from the dead and thus vindicated him as the place of God's atonement for the sins of Jews and Gentiles (Rom. 3:25). The reference to the heart implies that Paul does not speak of the recitation of a creedal formula in Christian worship but of the deep persuasion of individual sinners who have come to faith in Jesus Christ and whose life is determined by God's gracious gift. In verses 11–13 Paul describes the new epoch of salvation through faith in Christ. Scripture confirms (Isa. 28:16; cf. Rom. 9:33) that it is believers who appear as righteous people before God (10:11). This principle has universal validity. The new order of salvation in which faith in Jesus the Messiah leads to righteousness applies both to Jews and to Greeks (Gentiles) since Jesus Christ is the Lord of all people who believe in him (10:12), a truth confirmed by Joel 2:32 (10:13).

10:14–21. Paul proceeds to survey possible explanations for Israel's unbelief that may excuse the Jewish people from culpability. In 10:14–17 he surveys the process of the proclamation of the gospel. The Christian confession presupposes faith in Jesus Christ; faith in Jesus Christ presupposes hearing the message about Jesus Christ; hearing about Jesus Christ presupposes preachers; preaching presupposes preachers who have been sent by God, which according to Isaiah 52:7 and Nahum 2:1 is a necessity (10:14–15). Paul argues that the Jewish people have no excuses (10:16). Israel has not believed the gospel despite the fact that preachers and God's message have reached the Israelites. This disbelief was prophesied by Isaiah, who lamented the fact that Israel had not believed the message of the suffering and the exaltation of the servant of the Lord (Isa. 53:1). Paul's summary in verse 17 asserts that saving faith comes from the apostolic message, a message specifically about the Messiah and his death and resurrection. In 10:18–19 Paul asks a series

of questions that may exonerate Israel. Perhaps Israel has never had a chance to hear the word of God. Paul dismisses this explanation of Israel's unbelief. Israel has indeed heard, because the words of God's messengers have been heard in the entire world (Ps. 19:5). Another explanation for Israel's unbelief may be that they did not comprehend the message they heard. Paul dismisses this explanation as well. The Jews have not only heard the message about Jesus the messianic Savior but also have indeed understood the message. The problem of Israel is that they are not obedient. Paul confirms that the Jewish people have understood the message of Jesus Christ with two witnesses, Moses (quotation of Deut. 32:21) and Isaiah (quotation of Isa. 65:1–2). Israel's rebellion against the Lord was (in Moses's days) and is (today) answered by God with a provocation to jealousy—he called a new people from among the Gentiles who have understood God's revelation (10:19). As in the prophecy of Isaiah, God is found by the Gentiles who did not ask for him (10:20). As in the days of Isaiah, God has extended an invitation to Israel that was rejected (10:21). It is Israel's fault alone, not God's, that the Gentiles have attained God's saving righteousness while Israel has failed to do so. The knowledge that Israel lacks (10:3) is due to their unwillingness to accept the apostolic message as God's word of salvation.

11:1–32: The salvation of Israel. Paul points out that it would be wrong to conclude that God has rejected Israel and that Jews cannot find salvation. There is a remnant of Jews who have come to faith (11:1–10). More importantly, Israel's unbelief has caused the gospel to be proclaimed among the Gentiles, whose experience of God's saving grace is meant to make Israel jealous (11:11–24), prompting Jews to repent and to find salvation as well, in fulfillment of God's promises (11:25–32).

11:1–10. In view of Paul's argument that only Israel is to be blamed for their failure to believe in God's revelation of saving righteousness through Jesus the Messiah (chaps.

9–10), the conclusion that God has rejected Israel (11:1) might seem plausible. Paul rejects such a conclusion. First, there are descendants of Abraham who have heard, understood, and accepted the gospel of Jesus Christ. Paul mentions himself as a case in point (11:1). The fact that he has received God's saving righteousness proves that God has not rejected his people (11:2). Paul uses the words of Psalm 94:14 and 1 Samuel 12:22 to make this point, which he highlights with a reference to the unmerited love of God for his covenant people. Second, God has maintained a remnant of believing Israelites whom he reserved for himself by his electing grace. Paul mentions Elijah and the seven thousand faithful Israelites who did not abandon Yahweh as a case in point (11:2–4; 1 Kings 19:10, 14). The conclusion is formulated in 10:5–6. God in his grace has chosen a remnant. It was always only a remnant of Israelites who remained faithful to God, and the salvation of this remnant is due to God's election, which is a gift. In other words, the reason why some Jews receive God's saving righteousness through faith in Jesus the Messiah is that God has graciously chosen them to be a part of his (new) covenant people. "Works" (obedience to the law) do not save the Jewish people in the new epoch of the Messiah Jesus.

The consequences for Israel are spelled out in 11:7–10. The nation as a whole has not attained the salvation that the Jewish people have been seeking. God's chosen remnant has found salvation, while God has hardened the rest (11:7). The truth that God hardened the majority of Jews is explained as conforming to the pattern of God's dealings with Israel in the past. Paul cites from all three parts of the Hebrew canon: from the Torah in verse 8 (Deut. 29:3), from the Prophets in verse 8 (Isa. 29:10, the phrase "spirit of slumber" [KJV; NIV: "spirit of stupor"]), and from the Writings in verses 9–10 (Ps. 69:23–24). Moses asserts that the people of Israel do not see and hear the word of God; they do not keep the law and thus face God's judgment of exile. There is, implicitly,

hope for future redemption; Moses speaks of a time when God will bring Israel back from exile, a time when he will circumcise their heart so that they will love the Lord their God with all their heart and soul (Deut. 30:6). The reference to the "spirit of slumber" suggests that there may be an awakening in the future. Paul refers to David in verses 9–10 to make the point that, as David once pronounced a curse on his enemies, so now Jesus the Son of David, the crucified and risen Messiah, a stumbling block for Jews (cf. 1 Cor. 1:23), brings judgment on unbelieving Israel. The "table" of the Jews (11:9) may be a reference to the table fellowship of pious Jews, which excluded the Gentiles (and Jewish sinners); what they failed to see and understand was that the revelation of God's saving righteousness through Jesus Christ has created a new people, consisting of believing Jews and believing Gentiles, with a new table at which Jesus's death and resurrection are remembered (1 Cor. 10:21).

11:11–24. Paul asks whether Israel's failure to believe in the gospel of Jesus the Messiah means that Jews have fallen from their state of election (11:11a, reformulating 11:1). In 11:11b–15 he explains why he rejects the conclusion that Israel's failure is permanent. Two arguments are important. First, Israel's disobedience has resulted in the salvation of the Gentiles (11.11). In Paul's ministry, the rejection of the gospel by local Jews often resulted in his turning to Gentiles, among whom a greater number of people believed (cf. Acts 13:45–48; 18:6; 28:24–28). Second, the salvation of the Gentiles is meant to provoke Israel to jealousy (11:11).

Paul explains these two arguments in verses 12–14. First, if Israel's fall leads to the salvation of the Gentiles, the salvation of Israel cannot be excluded as a possibility (11:12). God has not given up on the Jewish people—they are "Israel" and will be saved if and when they come to faith in Jesus as Israel's Messiah and Savior. Second, Paul's ministry also aims at the salvation of Israel (cf. 1:16). The salvation of the Gentiles is meant to provoke a yearning for salvation among the Jewish people so that some of them might be saved (11:13–14). Paul hopes that unbelieving Jews will become jealous when they see what happens when Jews (the remnant) and Gentiles come to faith in Jesus Christ, forming communities in which the new covenant people of God live together, with their lives transformed by the power of the Holy Spirit (expected to be poured out in the age to come). The unbelieving Jews would then realize that the followers of Jesus Christ have something they want but do not have and thus be provoked to acknowledge the truth of the revelation of God's saving righteousness through Jesus Christ. The ground for this hope is expressed in verse 15—if Israel's rejection of the gospel contributed to the reconciliation of the "world" (Greek *kosmos*; here, the Gentiles) with God, then the acceptance of the gospel by an increasing number of Jews will lead to an even more astounding benefit—the climactic event of the resurrection of the dead, which is expected at the juncture of this age and God's new world.

In 11:16–24 Paul applies these truths to the assembly of Gentile believers and Jewish believers. The example of the dough of the first-fruit offering, which renders the whole lump holy (11:16; Num. 15:17–21), demonstrates that Israel as a whole is consecrated to God on account of the election of the patriarchs and the promises given to them. The same point is made with the example of the roots and the branches (Jer. 11:16). If the roots of Israel (the patriarchs) are holy, then the branches are holy as well. All who belong to God's people participate in the election of the patriarchs. God has not totally rejected ethnic Israel. There will be more Jews who will come to faith in Jesus Christ and become members of the people of God's new covenant. In 11:17–21 Paul restates the illustration of the roots and the branches in terms of an allegory of the olive tree and wild shoot. The olive tree is Israel (Jer. 11:16–19; Hos. 14:6–7); the wild shoots are the Gentiles. The Gentile believers—probably the majority in the church in Rome at the time—must not boast over the unbelieving Jews; such boasting establishes a reverse national righteousness, which comes under the same verdict as Israel. If God removed some branches (unbelieving Jews) from the olive tree (Israel), and if God grafted wild shoots (the Gentile believers) into the olive tree, then they have no reason to boast (11:17–18). Without the promises given to Abraham, God would not have admitted the Gentiles

When Paul imagined the people of God as an olive tree (Rom. 11:17), he was drawing on one of the most familiar images in Israel. This ancient tree (with new shoots) is found east of Jerusalem at the Church of All Nations.

into his people. The decisive factor in the removal of the branches (the unbelieving Jews) and in the grafting in of the wild shoots (the believing Gentiles) is the Jews' unbelief on the one hand and faith and God's unmerited grace on the other hand (11:19–20). Faith leading to salvation excludes (ethnic) arrogance. The only proper response to what God has been doing is to stand in awe before God. Arrogance, which is unbelief, provokes God's judgment.

Paul summarizes his exhortation for Gentile believers in 11:22–24. God's kindness and severity are not possessions that can be taken for granted. God's kindness rests on the Gentile believers only if and when they acknowledge him. If they reject God's kindness, they will experience God's severity (11:22). There is always the possibility that Jews will come to faith in Jesus Messiah and will be grafted back into the olive tree, "if they do not persist in unbelief," because nothing is impossible in view of God's power (11:23). If God could graft wild shoots into the olive tree, then he can graft the original branches back into the olive tree (11:24). Gentile Christians who think that the unbelief of the Jewish people excludes them forever from God's saving grace, which is granted through Jesus Christ, are mistaken.

11:25–32. Paul now proceeds to explain the mystery of Israel's salvation. He begins by underlining the significance of the following explanation of God's sovereignty, warning the Gentile believers not to be proud (11:25). The "mystery" that Paul refers to is not a particular secret that only he knows and now reveals. Rather, it is a reference to the divine plan of salvation, which has been hidden but which God now has revealed to his people (cf. Dan. 2:18–19, 27–30; Dead Sea Scrolls, *Rule of the Community* 3:22–23; 11:3–5; *1 Enoch* 103:2; 104:10–12; for Paul see 1 Cor. 15:51; Eph. 1:9; 3:3–4, 9; 5:32; 6:19). The mystery is not a new revelation that Paul has received as he writes chapter 11 and that contradicts his exposition in chapters 9–10. Paul's exposition of God's plan of salvation in 11:25–26 focuses on three elements.

First, God has hardened a part of Israel (11:25). At present there are Jews who have refused to come to faith in Jesus the Messiah and who have not received God's salvation. This assertion is consistent with 9:27; 11:7, 14, 17. Paul's statement implies that God has not rejected the Jewish people as a whole as a result of Israel's failure to believe in Jesus the Messiah.

Second, the period of hardening comes to an end when the "full number of the Gentiles" has come in. The hardening of the Jewish people lasts until all Gentiles have been converted whom God elects to save by grace (11:25).

Third, the salvation of "all Israel" takes place in this manner (the Greek phrase *kai houtōs* is modal, meaning "and so" or "and in this manner").

Most commentators interpret the term "Israel" here as a reference to ethnic Jews. If this is correct, Paul asserts that "all Jews" will be saved. This can hardly mean "all Jews/Israelites throughout history" because it seems unlikely that Paul thinks the hardening is reversible (9:18, 21–23; 11:1–10). The suggestion that there is a separate path to salvation for Jews and for Gentiles, with the former being saved at the end through their faithfulness to the (old) covenant and their obedience to the law, is impossible in view of Paul's burning desire for the Jewish people to be saved (9:1–3; 10:1), which happens when they no longer stumble over Jesus the Messiah (9:32–33). Most suggest that "all Israel will be saved" means that there will be a large-scale conversion of Jews to faith in Christ at the end, with the word "all" referring to "Israel as a whole, as a people whose corporate identity and wholeness would not be lost even if in the event there were some (or indeed many) individual exceptions" (Dunn, 681). A strong minority position disagrees and argues that "all Israel" refers to believing Jews and believing Gentiles who have been integrated into the one people of God's new covenant on account of God's grace through Jesus Christ. (For this comprehensive meaning of "Israel" as designation of the people of God consisting of Jewish and Gentile believers in Jesus, see Gal. 6:16.)

These commentators point out that there is no indication that "all" should be restricted to "many"; that the expression *kai houtōs* refers back to Paul's conviction that the conversion of Gentiles is the means by which Jews are provoked to jealousy, resulting in more conversions among the Jewish people; that Paul emphasizes that both Gentile and Jewish believers are true Jews who are truly circumcised (2:28–29; cf. Phil. 3:3) and thus the "Israel of God" (Gal. 6:16); and that Paul links the privileges of ethnic Israel (9:4–5) with Gentile believers.

These main plausible interpretations that have been suggested all have a difficult element. Either "all" is reduced to "many," or "Israel" in verse 26 is given a different meaning than in verse 25. Either the timing of Israel's conversion is emphasized (after the last Gentile has been converted), while the phrase *kai houtōs*, which expresses a process, is downplayed, or the manner of the conversion of Jews is emphasized, while the meaning of "until," which expresses timing, is downplayed. Since all three elements of the mystery are already occurring—Jews are obtuse regarding the gospel, Gentiles are being converted, the Gentile mission has led to more conversions among the Jewish people—we should be cautious in describing definite stages in God's plan of salvation. There can be no doubt that Paul wants Jews to be saved now and that he reaches out to the Jewish people in his missionary work. Whether or not there will be a large-scale conversion of Jews in the future before the end does not change Paul's eagerness to evangelize in the synagogues of the cities in which he works as a missionary.

In 11:26–27 Paul provides scriptural confirmation from Isaiah 59:20–21 and Isaiah 59:21a + 27:9 (with allusions to other Old Testament passages). The first citation explains the means by which Jacob's ungodliness is removed. This will happen through the deliverer who comes from Zion; in other words, through Jesus Christ (11:26). Those who see in verse 25 a reference to a future conversion identify the coming of the deliverer with the risen Lord Jesus who comes "from Zion," who returns from the heavenly Jerusalem at the end of the present age. Those who see a reference to a process that takes place in the present and that culminates in future conversions of Jews identify the coming of the deliverer from Zion with the coming of the historical Jesus, on account of whose death in Jerusalem God grants redemption to Jews and Gentiles. The context of the Old Testament passages suggests that the new covenant, to which believing Gentiles and believing Jews belong, is not a covenant with a national righteousness but the promised covenant in which the problem of sin has been solved once and for all, something that the law could not do. This is why the going out of the law to the nations has been replaced by the coming of the deliverer. The second citation (11:27) emphasizes God's covenant that removes Israel's sins, recalling the promise of a new covenant in Jeremiah 31:31–34.

Paul's summary of God's plan of salvation in 11:28–32 begins with the assertion that, "as far as the gospel is concerned," the Jews are God's enemies, thus allowing the Gentiles to receive the chance to hear the gospel (11:28; cf. 11:11–12). Gentile believers should note that the Jews, as God's chosen people, are loved by God because of the promises given to the patriarchs (11:16–17). God's gracious gifts (9:4–5) and God's call to salvation cannot be revoked; this means that the Jewish people are not hopelessly lost. God's call is his effective call that justifies the godless (see the call of Abraham and Israel; Gen. 12:1–3; Deut. 7:6–7). In verses 30–31 Paul explains the mystery of verses 25–26, focusing on salvation. The Gentiles presently receive God's mercy; the time of disobedience was followed by a time of mercy due to the disobedience of the Jewish people, which brought the Christian missionaries to the Gentiles (11:30). The Jews are presently disobedient for the sake of extending mercy to the Gentiles, but the time of disobedience is followed by a time of mercy (11:31). If the last clause in verse 31 ("in order that they too may now receive mercy as a result of God's mercy to you") explains the phrase "and in this way all Israel will be saved" in verse 26, then Paul asserts that Israel receives salvation in the same manner in which Gentiles receive salvation—as mercy, if they do not persist in unbelief (cf. 11:23). Israel will receive God's mercy "now"—through the process in which the Gentiles receive salvation, which causes Jews to become jealous, which in turn leads them to faith in Jesus Christ. Paul concludes in verse 32 with the statement that God's saving action involves the inclusion of both Jews and Gentiles in the sin of disobedience (cf. Rom. 1:18–3:20) as well as in God's mercy (cf. Rom. 3:21–5:11). The basic characteristic of salvation history is the justification of the godless as the work of God's sovereign grace.

11:33–36: Praise of God's righteousness. The prospect of ever more Gentiles and Jews coming to faith in Jesus Christ prompts Paul to erupt in praise of God's righteousness. The first stanza (11:33) consists of two exclamations. Paul first praises the depths of God's riches (the salvation he grants to pagans and Gentiles), the depth of God's wisdom (his justification of sinners), and the depth of God's knowledge (his actions in salvation history). Then Paul praises God's mysterious actions. God's judgments are unsearchable, as he grants righteousness to the unrighteous. God's ways are inscrutable, as his mercy elects Jews and Gentiles to form the people of his new covenant. The second stanza (11:34–35) formulates three rhetorical questions, which take up the terms of verse 33 in reverse sequence. Nobody has comprehended the mind of God (Isa. 40:13a); nobody has advised God (Isa. 40:13b); nobody has ever given anything to God (Job 41:3). The third stanza (11:36) expresses the glorious sovereignty of God the Creator and Savior. Everything is from God since he is the cause of the old and the new creation; everything is through God since he is the power of the old and the new creation; and everything is to God since he is the goal of the old and the new creation. The paragraph ends in verse 36 with a doxology

praising God's glorious majesty, inviting the Christians in Rome to respond with "Amen."

D. The reality of justification in the Christian community (12:1–15:13). In the fourth main section of his letter, Paul returns to the reality of the life of the followers of Jesus. He expounds further on the believers' obedience, based on the power of love, in various areas of everyday life. The life of the believer is a life of self-sacrifice for God (12:1–2), made possible as a result of the ministry of the gifts of grace (12:3–8) and as a result of the reality of love (12:9–21). Christians continue to have obligations to civic authorities (13:1–7). They fulfill the law through love (13:8–10). They are motivated to be obedient to the Lord Jesus Christ by the imminent arrival of God's new world (13:11–14). Paul exhorts the believers in Rome not to quarrel about matters related to food (14:1–12). Everyone should be willing to renounce their freedom out of love for fellow believers (14:13–23), following the example of Jesus Christ (15:1–6), motivated by the fulfillment in the present of God's promises to the patriarchs (15:7–13).

12:1–2: Total commitment to God. Paul has formulated exhortations for believers throughout chapters 5–11. The beginning of verse 1 signals that here begins a longer section in which he draws out some of the consequences of the gospel for everyday living. He begins with the fundamental charge that believers in Jesus Christ must consecrate their whole person (here designated as "body") to God. That believers yield their entire life to God is a "reasonable act of worship" (NIV "true and proper worship"), the appropriate response to the mercies God extends to sinners. This total commitment is the "sacrifice" that believers offer to God, a reality in which they are alive (cf. Rom. 6:11, 13; 8:13) and holy (cf. Rom. 1:7; 11:16). They are thus acceptable to God again since his wrath has been removed and the failure to properly worship God (1:25) has been reversed through Jesus Christ. Worshiping the living and holy God in a life committed to holy living entails distance from the values of an unholy world where humankind is spiritually dead as a result of sin (cf. Rom. 7:10–11). Since the age to come penetrates into the present evil age due to the revelation of God's saving righteousness through Jesus Christ, the worship of Christians who live out the logic of the gospel in everyday living involves resistance to the values and thought patterns of the secular world, transformation of their values as God's Spirit renews their thinking, and discernment of the will of God for their everyday living.

12:3–13:14: The community of believers. Paul's exposition of the life of the believers and of the Christian community focuses on the church as the body of Christ (12:3–8), on love as the criterion of behavior (12:9–21), on believers' obligation to civic authorities (13:1–7), on the fulfillment of the law (13:8–10), and on the urgency of the present time in view of Christ's return (13:11–14).

12:3–8. Paul begins his discussion of life in the community of believers with an affirmation of his apostolic authority—what follows is not his personal opinion but the will of God. He urges believers to base their self-esteem not on secular values (such as social position, wealth, influence) but on the one faith God has given to every believer (12:3). The identity of Christians is not tied to one's personal preferences but to faith in Christ. The church is not an assembly of individuals who have their own personal interests, values, and claims but a corporate entity that can be compared with the human body, which consists of many members but is a unified whole (12:4–5). The identity of this body and the function of its members are determined by Jesus Christ (cf. 1 Corinthians 12; Eph. 4:1–32). Being a Christian is not a private affair but links the believers with fellow believers in a larger body, in which everyone serves the whole by serving one another. In verses 6–8 Paul lists seven gifts that God in his grace has given to the believers and with which they serve other believers. They are prophecy (spontaneous revelations received from God for the benefit

of the believers; cf. 1 Cor. 14:29–33), serving, teaching, encouraging, sharing, leading, and acts of mercy. Since there is overlap between the gifts (the last three gifts all constitute "service"), Paul does not describe a clearly defined set of ministries. This is confirmed by the diversity of the list of spiritual gifts in 1 Cor. 12:8–10, 28–30; 13:1–3, 8; 14:6, 26. Paul's point is that believers should respond to the promptings of God's grace in active participation in the fellowship of Christians, serving with humble and openhearted commitment to one another while maintaining the unity of the faith.

12:9–21. Paul clarifies in 12:9–13 that the diversity of believers and their ministries can constitute one body only if their lives are controlled by love (cf. 1 Corinthians 13). The gifts of the Spirit are functions of the body, while love determines how the members of the body function. Love is the esteem and affection believers have for each other as a result of having been saved by God's love (Rom. 5:5, 8; 8:39) and Christ's love (Rom. 8:35). Since all good gifts can be manipulated and devastated by human beings, Paul emphasizes that the love God has poured into our hearts (5:5) must be kept genuine, protected from evil, and focused on what is good, as an expression of affection and esteem for the other believers (12:9–10). The basic attitude and behavior of Christians must be determined by diligent discipline and earnest eagerness, by an enthusiastic spirituality, by the consistent commitment to serve Christ as Lord, by rejoicing in view of the hope of sharing the glory of God, by patient endurance in suffering, by perseverance in prayer, by helping to alleviate the practical needs of other believers, and by providing hospitality in their homes for strangers (12:11–13).

In 12:14–21 Paul moves from the internal relationships of believers within the congregation to the relationship with their secular contemporaries. The criterion of love applies not only to believers' behavior in the church but also to their behavior in general. If they are discriminated against and persecuted, the proper response is to bless, not to engage in payback or to take actions that are evil (12:14, 17, 19, 21). Since Gentile Christians have no official permission to meet regularly, Paul advises that Christians avoid trouble. These exhortations are not simply tactical, however. They are themes of Old Testament and Jewish tradition (Exod. 23:4–5; Prov. 20:22), and more specifically, the application of Jesus's teaching (cf. Matt. 5:44; Luke 6:27–28; for 12:18 cf. Mark 9:50; Matt. 5:9). Paul knows that life, including the life of Christians, is not free of trouble. He thus commands that believers have genuine empathy with others, whether they suffer or whether they have success (12:15). He calls believers to live in harmony with one another, which is possible if they banish pride, if they associate with people held in low esteem (as Jesus did and commanded; see Matt. 5:3–5; 11:29; 18:4; 23:12), and if they abandon feelings of superiority (12:16). Paul knows that it may not always be possible to live at peace with every person (12:18), as the hostility of people who reject the gospel is all too often an unfortunate reality. If they suffer from their neighbors, they must leave matters in the hands of God, who will repay any injustice on the day of judgment (12:19). However, Christian believers do not simply endure suffering passively. They seek to

transcend it by doing good to their oppressors, extending hospitality and kindness (12:20; Prov. 25:21–22). The heaping of "burning coals on [the] head" is probably a reference to God's judgment (cf. 2 Sam. 22:9, 13; Job 41:20–21; Ps. 140:10; Prov. 6:27–29; Ezek. 24:11); believers' loving behavior toward their enemies increases the enemies' guilt, which God will judge. Paul ends with the command not to let the evil that others inflict control them but to courageously commit to do good so that evil may be overcome (12:21).

13:1–7. Paul turns to exhortations regarding behavior toward the ruling civic authorities. This is the next logical step after the directions for behavior toward fellow believers (12:9–13) and the directions for behavior toward unbelievers (12:14–21), including those who persecute Christians. Paul gives three commands (13:1, 5, 7). (1) Believers must be "subject" to official government authorities; in other words, believers obey the edicts, rules, and regulations issued

In Romans 13:7, Paul tells Roman believers to pay to governing authorities whatever is due them, whether revenue or honor. The Roman Forum, seen here, was the main commercial thoroughfare in ancient Rome as well as the center for religious and political affairs.

by government officials. (2) Believers are faced with the "necessity" to submit to state authorities. (3) Believers must pay taxes; this is a specific example of submission to civic authorities.

In 13:1–5 Paul explains that the basic reason why Christians must submit to the authorities is the biblical truth that God has ordained and appointed all governing authorities (13:1; cf. Prov. 8:15–16; Isa. 45:1–7; Dan. 4:17, 25, 32). It follows that anyone who resists the divinely appointed authorities resists God himself and will incur God's (and the rulers') judgment (13:2). The divine institution of governing authorities is reflected in the fact that they promote good conduct and punish bad conduct (13:3–4). When they fulfill this function, they are "God's servants." (And when they don't, such as the Roman emperors who persecuted Christians, they are still accountable to God.) The praise for good behavior (13:3) is the public commendation of people who made extraordinary contributions to the city (e.g., financing of public works). Such commendations were recommended by the city magistrates and then inscribed in stone (honorary inscriptions). The sanction for bad behavior is punishment, meted out by police officials and other governmental powers. (In Egypt police officers are referred to as "sword-bearers.") Because it is God who institutes the authorities, obedience is a matter of theological principle. It is motivated not only by fear of being punished but also by the concern for a good conscience (13:5).

In antiquity, the vast majority of people were powerless. Paul does not address the possibilities that citizens have in a participatory democracy, and he does not address the problem of secular states that explicitly or implicitly reject any notion of the rulers' responsibility toward God (which both the Greeks and the pagans recognized). Paul is realistic, which is why he does not mention the Zealot option, which only ten years later led to the Jewish revolt against Roman rule and resulted in untold suffering and the destruction of Jerusalem in AD 70. The application of the principle of 13:1 is spelled out in

13:6–7 with regard to the payment of direct and indirect taxes (tribute and custom tax). These taxes must be paid, as they are demanded by the ruling authorities, whom God has instituted. The background of this astonishingly specific example is probably the unrest in the city of Rome at the time, caused by the increase in direct and indirect taxes under Nero. With the last two obligations—respect and honor—Paul returns to his admonition to acknowledge the legitimate jurisdiction of the divinely instituted governing authorities.

13:8–10. Paul returns to love as the fundamental criterion of behavior. Loving others—being actively concerned for others, having affectionate regard for and interest in others—is an obligation (13:8a). The people to be loved are Christians, but also the neighbor who is the enemy (12:14, 17, 21). The reason and motivation for loving others is given in verses 8b–10. Believers who love others have fulfilled the law; they have properly done what the law asks (Rom. 8:4; cf. Matt. 5:17–20). The commandments of the law, which establish human relationships—no adultery, no murder, no stealing, no envious desires (cf. Exod. 20:13–17; Deut. 5:17–21)—are summed up in the commandment to love others as much as one loves oneself (Lev. 19:18, the most frequently cited passage of the Pentateuch in the New Testament; see Matt. 5:43; 19:19; 22:29; Mark 12:31; 12:33; Luke 10:27; Gal. 5:14; James 2:8). Paul does not reduce the law to one single commandment; he formulates the substance of proper obedience to the will of God.

13:11–14. While the admonition to submit to governmental authorities and to pay taxes suggests that, in many ways, life goes on for Christians as it always has, Paul points out that the expected return of Jesus Christ is near. Final salvation is closer than it was a few years ago (13:11); the day of the revelation of God's glory and the day of God's judgment is near (13:12). Christians know that the last days have arrived (cf. Gal. 4:4; 1 Cor. 10:11; Heb. 1:1–2; 9:26; James 5:9; 1 Pet. 1:20). The nearness of the end, which is the beginning of the glorious inheritance of believers, who are united in Jesus Christ, should motivate them to live by the power of God, who raised Jesus from the dead. The present reality is described as night, works of darkness, and the evils of excessive feasting, drinking bouts, sexual promiscuity, violation of all bounds of what is socially acceptable, quarrels, jealousy, and the tendencies of the flesh. Christians live in the context of this reality, which they must confront (cf. 12:1–2). Paul calls them to be wide awake, to stop being involved in the evil practices and traditions of pagan society, to do battle with temptation and sinful values and lifestyles, to live honorably and transparently ("as in the daytime"), to be transformed by their union with Jesus Christ, who is Lord.

14:1–15:13: Unity in diversity. The believers in Rome are "holy people" (1:7), but they also have problems. In the final paragraph of his exhortation, Paul addresses the conflict that exists between believers who regard the Christian faith as an essentially Jewish movement and believers who do not pay attention to distinctive Jewish traditions—that is, between Jewish Christians and Gentile Christians (cf. 15:7–9). The critical debate is not about whether Gentile Christians must be circumcised (as in Galatians 2–4) or about the question of whether Christians can dine in pagan temples and eat food sacrificed to idols (as in 1 Corinthians 8–10). The controversy concerns dietary practices (14:2, 21) and the observance of certain days (14:5–6). Paul's discussion highlights, again, the nature of the people of God as the community of the new covenant, in which the old distinctions between Jews and Gentiles are no longer relevant. The controlling principle is not the specifics of obedience to the law but the reality of God's love, which believers need to apply to relationships within the church (14:15; cf. 12:3, 9–10, 14–17, 21; 13:8–10).

14:1–12. In his discussion of the divisions between the "weak" and the "strong," Paul first argues that Christians who are weak in their

faith (14:1) must stop condemning their fellow believers who are less scrupulous (14:3–5, 10, the strong of 15:1) because only God himself has the right to judge (14:10–12). Believers whose faith is weak place their trust in certain dietary practices: they eat only vegetables (14:2), they do not drink wine (14:21), and they observe certain days (14:5). They were Jewish believers (and Gentile Christians influenced by Jewish traditions) who practiced the dietary laws and who observed certain days (including probably the Sabbath). Eating meat and drinking wine are not prohibited in the law. However, Jews could eat only meat that was kosher, in other words, slaughtered according to the rules of the law (Israelites may not eat blood; cf. Deut. 12:15–16). When Claudius evicted the Jews from the city of Rome in AD 49, the Jewish slaughterhouses were probably shut down, prompting Jews who remained in the city (and Jews who later returned) to refrain from eating meat altogether in order to avoid any unclean meat. As wine may have been offered in ritual libations in pagan temples before it was sold in the market, a scrupulous observance of the law led some Jews to refrain from drinking wine altogether (cf. Daniel and his friends, Dan. 1:3–16; 10:3). Paul argues that those who observe these practices must not condemn those who do not, and that those who eat and drink anything must not despise those who have religious scruples regarding matters related to diet. Paul does not refrain from giving his opinion: those who have scruples concerning food or the observance of certain festival days are weak in their faith.

Paul emphasizes five concerns. (1) Believers must not judge each other, because only God judges people (14:10–12). (2) Believers must not despise others, because God has welcomed all believers (14:3, 10). (3) Believers must be convinced that the details of their personal behavior honor Jesus Christ the Lord and express their thankfulness to God (14:5–6), acknowledging that they are accountable to God (14:12). (4) Believers can have differences of opinion, which should be tolerated (14:1, 5–6; evidently the Jewish Christians did not argue that the observances they practiced were necessary for salvation and should be followed by "nonobservant" Christians as well). (5) The identity of Christian believers is not tied up with diet and religious holidays but with the Lord Jesus Christ, who died for sinners and who was raised from the dead. This means that believers who are united with Jesus Christ in his death and resurrection seek to please God in all things, having been liberated from the fundamental human sin of setting their own priorities and constructing their own values (14:8–9).

14:13–23. Second, Paul discusses renouncing one's freedom out of love. He argues that Christians who are strong in their faith have the responsibility not to damage the believers who continue to adhere to Jewish legal practices in the area of dietary law and Sabbath observance. Paul agrees theologically with the strong: no food, no beverage, no day of the calendar is ritually unclean (14:14, 20). They are right in believing that the kingdom of God, which has been inaugurated with the coming of Jesus Christ, is not linked with food and drink but established and present in righteousness, peace, and joy in the Holy Spirit (14:16–17). The strong have faith before God (14:22). However, they threaten to damage the weak,

who could stumble and lose their footing (14:13), be injured and ruined (14:15), be destroyed and fall (14:20), take offense (14:21), and be condemned (14:23). This happens if the strong eat and drink what the weak cannot eat or drink, thinking that such behavior makes them unclean (14:14). Paul refers to what happens when Gentile Christians share meals with Jewish Christians who still keep the dietary laws (for Christian meals cf. 1 Cor. 11:17–34). The behavior of the strong causes the weak to follow their example and eat food their faith does not allow them to eat. They consume food they regard as unclean, thereby violating their faith, a fact that damages them, as they are convinced that they have rebelled against the will of God (14:15). As a result of the damage that their faith repeatedly suffers in these situations, they doubt (14:23). Doubt is incompatible with faith (cf. Rom. 4:19–21), and everything that is not done from faith is sin (14:23).

Even though Paul implicitly challenges the weak to have a faith that is strong (he calls them "weak" and agrees with those who eat and drink anything), he calls

Marble statue of Dionysus (AD 40–60), known as Bacchus in Roman mythology, who was the god of wine and agricultural activity. Some Jewish Christians refused to drink wine because it might have been a libation offering in the pagan temples. Paul's criterion to refrain from drinking is when it may cause another believer to stumble (Rom. 14:21).

on the strong to change their behavior. His straightforward command, eventually formulated in verse 21, is not to eat meat or drink wine or do anything else that causes the Jewish believers to injure their faith. He asks them to resolve not to be a stumbling block for the weak (14:13), to show love for their fellow believers (14:15), to make sure that their behavior does not become grounds for irreverent comments about the gospel (14:16–17), to serve Christ and be acceptable to God (14:18), to act in such a manner that peace is maintained and that the fellowship of believers is being built up (14:19), and to keep the faith they have to themselves "before God" (14:22 NASB, NRSV; i.e., not to force their convictions on the weak, and to eat and drink what they wish in the privacy of their homes).

Paul mentions fundamental criteria for Christian behavior: acting out of love for fellow believers as a manifestation of God's love for justified sinners (14:15; cf. 5:5, 8); evaluating the importance of differences of personal behavior in the light of the righteousness God has given to sinners, in the light of the peace that Jesus Christ has obtained for believers, and in the light of the joy of the Holy Spirit (14:17); safeguarding the continued growth of the church (14:19; cf. 1 Cor. 14:1–5); and respecting the "work of God" (14:20), which is the faith of all believers, and the existence and the unity of the church.

15:1–6. Before Paul concludes his discussion of the controversy between the strong and the weak in 15:7–13, he reminds believers of the basis of their Christian identity. In verses 1–2 Paul summarizes the primary responsibility of the strong. Those who are strong in the faith can and must accept the scruples of the weak as their own burden (cf. Gal. 6:2) by not eating and drinking what the weak cannot eat and drink. They must not insist on indulging their personal self-interest. They must endeavor to give pleasure to their fellow Christians. They must keep in mind the purpose of being a body of believers, which is the continued growth of all

Christians. In verses 3–4 Paul explains the main reason for his advice to the strong: Jesus is their example. Jesus the Messiah did not live to please himself. Rather, he denied himself by submission to God's will, which took him to the cross (cf. 2 Cor. 8:9; Phil. 2:5–8). Psalm 69:9 confirms this: as the righteous person who is devoted to the Lord (69:10) is insulted by his enemies and also by his own family (69:8, 28), so Jesus was despised by the Roman authorities and by the Jewish leadership. In the same manner, as the Messiah was willing to be insulted for God's honor, the Gentile believers should be willing to give up the focus on their personal interests. They should be willing to be ridiculed by their pagan friends and neighbors who will despise them if they follow Jewish scruples in the area of food and drink. Paul asserts in verse 3 that the Scriptures are crucial for understanding both Jesus Christ and their own identity, because the Scriptures give the believers comfort in the midst of their trials, which result in hope (cf. Rom. 5:1–5; 8:25). Paul ends with a prayer wish in which he prays for the unity of the strong and the weak (15:5–6). This is a unity expressed in Gentile believers and Jewish believers living together, which requires perseverance and encouragement; the constant orientation by Jesus, the crucified and risen Messiah; and the desire to honor God with one voice.

15:7–13. Paul summarizes the section on the controversy between the strong and the weak, and at the same time, he concludes the main body of the letter. In verse 7 he asserts that mutual acceptance and unity are fundamental values for two reasons: all believers have been accepted by Christ, with whom they are united by faith; and the glory of God is the primary concern and reality of those who honor the Creator, as he must be honored by his creatures, who live in his presence. In verses 8–9 Paul explains how Christ accepted both Jews and Gentiles. Christ came as a servant for the Jews who waited for messianic salvation (Rom. 2:1–3:20); Jesus's death and resurrection have brought the salvation that confirms the promises of salvation given to the patriarchs (9:1–11:36). Since God's promises to the fathers included the families of the earth, the Gentiles also have benefited from the coming of Jesus Christ; they needed salvation, as they had rebelled against God in their assault on his glory (Rom. 1:18–32); they have received salvation on account of God's mercy, as have the Jews (3:21–5:21), with the result that they honor and glorify God. The truth of God, which has been abused by pagans and by Jews (Rom. 1:18, 25; 2:8; 3:7), has been vindicated through Jesus the Messiah. The promise given to the fathers has been fulfilled (Rom. 2:25–29; 4:9–22; 9:4, 8–9); the Gentiles have received God's mercy (1:16–17; 3:21–31; 9:15–18; 11:30–32); the failure of humankind to honor God (1:21) has been reversed. The following quotations from Psalm 18:49 // 2 Samuel 22:50, Deuteronomy 32:43, Psalm 117:1, and Isaiah 11:10 confirm God's promise that both Gentiles and Jews together would honor and glorify God. In his second prayer wish (after 15:5–6) Paul prays that the God who gives hope will fill both Jewish and Gentile believers with joy and peace, both of which result from faith (15:13). And he prays that the joy of the Lord and peace with God may result in an abundance of hope, which is the present desire for the future reality of life in the immediate presence of God (Rom. 5:2). The hope of sharing the glory of God, and the Christian life in general, is sustained not by the personal efforts of believers but by the power of the Holy Spirit.

3. Conclusion (15:14–16:27)

Paul concludes his letter with information about his travel plans (15:14–33), recommendations of Phoebe (16:1–2), greetings to co-workers in the Roman churches (16:3–16), and an admonition with regard to dangers facing the churches in Rome (16:17–20). The letter ends with additional greetings (16:21–24) and a doxology (16:25–27).

A. Paul's missionary work and future travel plans (15:14–33). Paul describes his missionary work as focused on outreach to pagans. This is

the reason why he wants to visit the churches in Rome, whom he hopes to involve in the mission to Spain, which he is planning.

15:14–21: Paul's missionary work. The apostle assures the Roman Christians that his long and, on occasion, bold letter does not question their spiritual maturity nor their independence. They are indeed capable of instructing one another (15:14–15). He writes to them because of the missionary commission he has received from God. Paul describes his missionary work as follows. (1) His calling and his work as a missionary are gifts from God, not the result of his will or ambition. (2) He is a servant who acts as directed by Jesus Christ, his superior authority. (3) He has been directed to focus his proclamation of the gospel on the pagans. (4) His missionary work is an act of sacrifice in which the converted Gentiles are offered as a sacrifice pleasing to God. (5) This priestly ministry takes place not in a sacred space (in a temple) but in the world, and it abandons the religious distinctions between Jews and Gentiles. (6) The goal of his missionary work is the conversion of pagans, who become acceptable to God. As they accept the saving righteousness of God through Jesus Christ and become obedient to the will of God, they glorify God, as they always should have done. (7) The process of missionary ministry is word and deed, both oral proclamation and hard work. (8) The power that makes his missionary proclamation effective is Jesus Christ and the power of the Holy Spirit. (9) Signs and wonders (which include conversions, healings, speaking in unlearned languages) testify to the presence of God in his ministry. (10) Paul has preached the gospel in a circle from Jerusalem to Illyricum. If we trace Paul's movements on an ancient world map—he preached in Jerusalem, Syria (Damascus, Arabia/Nabatea, Antioch), Cilicia, Galatia, Asia, Macedonia, Achaia, and apparently Illyricum (perhaps the travels described in Acts 20:1–3)—he moved in a circle from Jerusalem in a northerly, then westerly direction toward Rome and Spain. (11) Paul had decided at some point that he would work as a pioneer missionary in cities and regions where no missionaries had preached before, rather than help consolidate churches that others had established.

15:22–33: Paul's travel plans. Paul asserts that there are no places left in the regions of the eastern Mediterranean in which pioneer missionary work needs to be done (15:23). Paul's comment in 1 Corinthians 9:5, on the missionary travels of the other apostles, who take their wives along, and on the churches mentioned in Revelation 1:11, illustrates that there was much more missionary work in progress than Luke describes in the book of Acts. Paul plans to begin pioneer missionary work in Spain (15:24, 28). He informs the Christians in Rome that he wants to visit them, as he hopes that they will assist him, probably with logistical help—funds, information, letters of introduction, escorts, perhaps translators.

Paul informs the Roman believers that, rather than traveling from Corinth (from where he writes his letter) to Rome directly, he will first visit Jerusalem (15:25–28). In the churches of Macedonia and Achaia (and also Asia; see the list of Paul's travel companions in Acts 20:4), he has organized a collection for the poor Christians in Jerusalem. The Christians in Judea apparently still suffered from the effects of a severe famine in AD 46–48 (cf. Acts 11:27–30; Gal. 2:10). Paul gives more details about this collection in 1 Corinthians 16:1–4 and 2 Corinthians 8:1–9:15. Paul reports that the churches in Macedonia and Achaia gave joyfully, and he asserts that it was at the same time their duty to help the poor Christians in Jerusalem on account of the blessings they have received from them (15:27). Paul may have believed that the gifts he brought from the Gentile Christians to Jerusalem fulfilled Old Testament promises that the nations would bring their wealth to Zion (Isa. 2:2–3; 45:14; 60:5–17; 61:6; Mic. 4:1–2, 13). He may also have hoped that this demonstration of the Gentiles' inclusion into the people of God would provoke unbelieving Jews to jealousy and prompt them to come to faith in Jesus the Messiah. Paul anticipates that

his visit to Jerusalem will not be easy (15:30–31). He expects fierce opposition from unbelieving Jews, and he does not rule out the possibility that traditionalist Jewish Christians might reject gifts from Gentile Christians. He asks the Christians in Rome to pray that his life may be preserved. This prayer was answered. Despite several assaults on his life during his visit (Acts 21:26–36; 23:12–35), he survived, although only by being taken into custody by the Roman authorities. He asks the Roman Christians to pray that the gifts of the Gentile churches may be accepted, a prayer that may have been answered (see Acts 24:17). Paul ends by praying for the Roman Christians, asking God, who is the source of peace, to be with every one of them (15:33).

B. Greetings (16:1–24). Paul's greetings relate to Phoebe, co-workers who are presently in Rome, dangers facing the church, and further co-workers and friends.

16:1–2: Recommendation of Phoebe. Phoebe is a Christian sister who serves as a worker in the church in Cenchreae, one of the two ports of Corinth. The use of the Greek word *diakonos* does not suggest menial service only. Paul often uses it for missionary preaching and pastoral teaching (1 Cor. 3:5; 2 Cor. 3:6; 6:4). He asks the Roman Christians to welcome her as a fellow believer and to assist her in any matter in which she needs help. Some suggest that Paul has asked Phoebe to organize the logistical details of the mission to Spain and that he asks the Roman Christians to support her in these efforts. This is not impossible, given the fact that Phoebe was evidently wealthy: she had been a benefactor to Paul and to other Christians, which means that she had provided financial help to missionaries.

16:3–16: Greetings of co-workers and other believers. In the longest list of greetings in any of his letters (16:3–16), Paul greets twenty-six individuals and at least five house churches. These greetings express the affection that Paul has for his former co-workers and other believers in Rome, resulting from the new life they share. (Note the frequent "in Christ" or "in the Lord.") Many of the believers in Rome he knew personally. Some had been his co-workers for many years (e.g., Priscilla and Aquila). The list illustrates why Paul can be confident that there are experienced believers in the churches in Rome who can instruct the Christians responsibly and competently (15:14). The inclusion of eight women, whom Paul acknowledges with joy and thanksgiving, illustrates the importance of the ministry of women in the early church. The presence of Greek, Latin, Roman, and Jewish names and the presence of the names of slaves and freedmen (e.g., Ampliatus, Asyncritus, Junia, Tryphosa, Tryphena) attests to the cultural and social diversity of the house churches in Rome. The house churches met in the homes of Priscilla and Aquila (16:5), Aristobulus (16:10), Narcissus (16:11); the "brothers and sisters" in verse 14 and "the Lord's people" in verse 15 probably represent two further house churches.

Believers greeted each other by kissing (16:16; cf. 1 Cor. 16:20; 2 Cor. 13:12; 1 Thess. 5:26; 1 Pet. 5:14), a sign of familial affection—probably not only in church but also when they met in public. This was a potent expression of the transforming power of the gospel, particularly when wealthy believers

greeted Christian slaves. Paul sends greetings from "all the churches of Christ" (16:16)—that is, from all the churches that he has established and that know and support his ministry. This greeting expresses the universal scope of the gospel and the unity of the believers that results from the truth of the gospel.

16:17–20: Postscript: Dangers facing the church. Paul adds a postscript, perhaps in his own hand (cf. Gal. 6:11; Col. 4:18). He urges the believers to watch out—that is, to identify and evaluate people who cause dissensions and who question the gospel, and to keep away from them (16:17). These people are not interested in Jesus Christ. They are absorbed with their own appetites, and their smooth talk and eloquence can easily detract from the truth of the gospel (16:18). There is no agreement on the identity of these troublemakers. Probably Paul provides a general warning based on Jewish traditions that warn of apostasy and on his own experience (cf. 1 Cor. 1:10–17; 2:1–5; 2 Cor. 11:5–6; Phil. 3:19; Col. 2:4). He knows that the Roman Christians have become obedient to the gospel, which is cause for joy and at the same time the basis from which they can identify and avoid evil teachings (16:19). He assures them that the influence of Satan in the world in general, and in the activities of troublemakers in particular, will be short-lived because God will soon

These buildings in Ostia Antica, the ancient port city of Rome, were likely insulae (apartments). The Roman house churches greeted by Paul in Romans 16 may have met together in homes similar to these.

consummate his victory over the serpent (Gen. 3:15). The benediction in verse 20 prays for a continued experience of what they already have: grace from God, who has given them peace.

16:21–24: Additional greetings. Final greetings to the Christians in Rome are conveyed by co-workers in Corinth, prominent among them Timothy, who had worked with Paul in Macedonia, Achaia, and Asia. Paul had dictated the letter to Tertius, who was a secretary (16:22) and was perhaps one of the slaves of Gaius, Paul's host (16:23). Both send their greetings, indicating that they are both Christian believers and thus part of God's universal family and also of Paul's mission. Erastus, "the city's director of public works" or city treasurer, is probably the same Erastus who is mentioned in an inscription acknowledging his benefaction that paid for the pavement in front of the theater, given in gratitude for being appointed to the aedileship, a municipal office with wide-ranging administrative duties.

C. Final doxology (16:25–27). The letter concludes with a doxology, which ascribes glory to God. The long sentence summarizes the central themes of Paul's letter: the power of God (1:16), the gospel Paul proclaims (1:1–6; 2:16), the message of Jesus the Messiah (1:3, 9; 3:21–31), the nature and the consequences of the gospel as the mystery God promised in the prophets and that he has now revealed (1:16–17; 11:25), the importance of the Scriptures (1:2; 3:21), the present time ("now") as the time in which God saves Jews and Gentiles (3:21–5:21), the obedience to the will of God the Creator and the merciful Savior among Jews and Gentiles (1:5; 6:1–8:39), the wisdom of God's revelation of saving righteousness (1:18–5:21; 9:1–11:36), and the work of Jesus the Messiah, whose death atones for the sins of humankind and whose resurrection grants new life to pagans and Jews (3:21–8:39). These truths and realities confirm that all the glory of all the ages belongs to God. The "Amen" emphasizes Paul's commitment to these truths and invites the Roman Christians to join in the praise of God the Creator and the Savior.

Select Bibliography

Cranfield, C. E. B. *Romans: A Shorter Commentary.* Grand Rapids: Eerdmans, 1985.

Dunn, James D. G. *Romans.* 2 vols. Word Biblical Commentary. Dallas: Word, 1988.

Fitzmyer, Joseph A. *Romans.* Anchor Bible. New York: Doubleday, 1993.

Moo, Douglas J. *Encountering the Book of Romans.* Grand Rapids: Baker Academic, 2002.

———. *The Epistle to the Romans.* New International Commentary on the New Testament. Grand Rapids: Eerdmans, 1996.

Osborne, Grant R. *Romans.* IVP New Testament Commentary. Downers Grove, IL: InterVarsity, 2004.

Schreiner, Thomas R. *Romans.* Baker Exegetical Commentary on the New Testament. Grand Rapids: Baker Academic, 1998.

Seifrid, Mark A. "Romans." In *Commentary on the New Testament Use of the Old Testament.* Edited by G. K. Beale and D. A. Carson. Grand Rapids: Baker Academic, 2007.

Stott, John. *Romans: God's Good News for the World.* Downers Grove, IL: InterVarsity, 1994.

Stuhlmacher, Peter. *Paul's Letter to the Romans.* Louisville: Westminster John Knox, 1994.

1–2 Corinthians

James A. Davis

Among the letters of Paul, 1 and 2 Corinthians are perhaps most notable for their practical content and personal style. The first of these two features emerges as a consequence of the vital and often volatile nature of life in the church at Corinth. For it is certain that the practical questions that largely occupy the apostle in both epistles arise not at his initiative but rather at the insistence of his converts. It is in response to their circumstances and backgrounds that the practical and sometimes pointed counsel of these letters originates. The distinctly personal style of both is also largely, if not wholly, a product of the apostle's relationship to the church, and so, for that matter, are many of the stylistic peculiarities that have raised questions about the unity and integrity of 2 Corinthians. Thus it is necessary for the interpreter of these epistles to come to know, insofar as that is possible, the history of the circumstances that form the background to Paul's Corinthian correspondence.

Historical Background

The ancient history of the city of Corinth may, for the sake of convenience, be divided into four principal periods: the preclassical period (ca. 3500–1350 BC), the classical period (ca. 1350–338 BC), the Hellenistic period (338–146 BC), and the Roman period (146 BC–AD 395). For our purposes, we need concern ourselves with only a few of the major events in the last

of these four historical periods. In 146 BC a Roman army burned the ancient city of Corinth to the ground for its participation and leadership in the rebellion of the Achaian League (a group composed of the principal city-states located in Achaia, the southern peninsula of Greece). At that time, many of the citizens of Corinth were either killed or sold into slavery, and for a century afterward the city lay derelict.

In the year 44 BC, however, the city was refounded on the order of Julius Caesar, who sought to redeem the strategic and economic potential of the site with a new colonial population made up of freedmen (manumitted Roman slaves), army veterans, and former residents. Because of its location, near the narrowest part of the isthmus connecting Macedonia (the northern mainland of Greece) and Achaia, and because of the hazards associated with sea travel, particularly in the winter, when the possibility of conveying cargo across the narrow isthmus must have appeared as an exceedingly attractive alternative, the city quickly regained its former prosperity. Under Augustus in 27 BC it was made the capital of the senatorial province of Achaia.

Renowned for its metallurgists, who specialized in bronzework, and for its sponsorship of the biennial Isthmian games, which were second in popularity and prestige only to those of Olympia, the city rapidly attracted a variety of new residents, creating a cosmopolitan atmosphere dominated by economic stratification, cultural diversity, and religious pluralism. The reputation given to Corinth as an especially immoral place seems to have been largely created by the envy of other Greek city-states, which attempted to buttress their slander by pointing to the presence of the cult of Aphrodite in Corinth as an indication of the low morals of the populace, grossly exaggerating both the cult's size and its influence. The truth of the matter lies neither at this extreme (despite the repetition of such rumors in the literature of the time) nor at its opposite, but in the realization that Corinth was a large urban center, no richer or poorer in terms of morality than comparable cities, either ancient or modern.

Date

According to Acts 18:2, among the Jewish residents of Corinth in the middle of the first century AD were a husband and wife, Aquila, a native of Pontus (a Roman province in northeastern Asia Minor), and Priscilla (whose name suggests that she may have come from a Roman family). They had only recently come to Corinth as the result of a decree issued by the Roman emperor Claudius (AD 41–54) in which he expelled the Jewish population from Rome. Paul joined them shortly after his arrival in the city (Acts 18:3).

According to Orosius, a fifth-century Christian writer, the decree of Claudius was issued in the ninth year of his reign (AD 49). The first- and second-century Roman historians Suetonius and Dio Cassius (respectively) provide confirmation for the issue of the decree. But their accounts lack any reference to the year of the decree, as do the extant works of Josephus, upon which Orosius claims to depend. As a consequence, there is some debate among scholars concerning the precise date of the decree, but none with respect to the certainty of its issue.

Fortunately, Luke provides two other reference points that enable us to speak with more certainty about the chronological framework

> At the time of Paul, Corinth was a large and important city. Upon entering the city, visitors would have seen the Fountain of Peirene (shown here), which provided the city's water supply.

of Paul's initial ministry in Corinth. The first of these is his mention of a hearing granted by the proconsul Gallio to the Jews of Corinth in their attempt to prosecute Paul (Acts 18:12). The proconsular term of L. Junius Gallio to which Luke refers may be dated (with the help of an inscription discovered at Delphi in 1905 by the French archaeologist Emile Bourguet) as having occurred during AD 51–52. Thus, since Luke's account also makes reference to a period of ministry for "a year and a half" (Acts 18:11), it would appear probable that Paul's initial mission to Corinth began sometime early in AD 50 and finished in the latter half of AD 51.

The Church at Corinth

Thus, in a period that in duration exceeded all the other missions mentioned by Luke in conjunction with the apostle's second journey, the church at Corinth was brought into being by the grace of God and the labors of a man whom he had called (1 Cor. 1:1). Several further features of this founding mission should also be mentioned.

First, it is important to note that Paul's initial mission in the synagogue in Corinth seems to have lasted longer than his initial mission in many other cities and resulted in some significant conversions within the Jewish community (e.g., of "Crispus, the synagogue ruler" [Acts 18:8; see also 1 Cor. 1:14]; "his entire household" [Acts 18:8]; and perhaps of his successor Sosthenes [Acts 18:17; cf. 1 Cor. 1:1]). Thus, from the outset there was an important and influential Jewish Christian minority within the Corinthian church.

Second, though the truth of the apostle's generalization in 1 Corinthians 1:26 must be given its full weight, the Corinthian Christian community that constituted the fruit of the Pauline mission seems nonetheless to have had a significant number of socially, educationally, and economically privileged members. Among them were Crispus (whose status has just been mentioned), Gaius (whose means were sufficient to provide hospitality for the whole church; cf. Rom. 16:23), and Erastus, "the city's director of public works," whose name has also been

found on a dedicatory pavement at Corinth (cf. also Rom. 16:23).

Third, partially as a result of the success of the initial Pauline mission, the church that the apostle left was a church accustomed to persuasive preaching, to official tolerance, and to relative freedom from persecution (due no doubt to the reluctance of Gallio to consider Christianity a religion separate in any significant sense from the legally sanctioned Judaism [Acts 18:15]), and to the teaching of a variety of Christian leaders (one should consider, for example, the roles that may have been played by Silas and Timothy [2 Cor. 1:19] or by Aquila and Priscilla, whom Paul names as his co-workers [Rom. 16:3], as well, of course, as Apollos [1 Cor. 1:12; 3:4, 5, 6, 22; 4:6; 16:12]).

The Corinthian Correspondence

The book of Acts records in summary fashion that, following his departure from Corinth in the fall of AD 51, Paul returned to Antioch by way of Ephesus (where Priscilla and Aquila remained [Acts 18:26]) and Caesarea (Acts 18:18–22). However, after spending some time in Antioch, Paul decided to return to Ephesus and traveled overland back through Galatia and Phrygia, arriving in Ephesus again apparently toward the end of AD 52. According to Acts 19:1–10, 21–22, Paul subsequently spent more than two years in a mission to the Ephesians before deciding to return to Macedonia and Achaia to take up a collection for the church at Jerusalem. Linking this account of Paul's movements with 1 Corinthians 16:8 indicates that 1 Corinthians was written toward the end of Paul's stay in Ephesus, probably some months before Pentecost of AD 55.

First Corinthians itself, however, shows that there had been comparatively frequent communication between Paul and the church at Corinth for some time before the composition of this letter. From 1 Corinthians 5:9 one learns of an earlier letter from Paul to the Corinthians, from 1:11 of a report brought to Paul by members of Chloe's household, and from 16:17 of a subsequent delegation probably bearing a letter from the church that Paul had only just received. Given the regular trade between the cities of Corinth and Ephesus, such frequent contact should occasion no surprise, but it does point clearly to the fact that 1 Corinthians is itself a product, at least in part, of an ongoing dialogue between Paul and the church. The information that Paul received most recently, then, by way of a report and a letter, prompted him to write, responding in turn to both in 1:10–6:20 and 7:1–16:4, respectively.

From the report, Paul learned that the church was becoming increasingly polarized by serious divisions among its members as they attempted to locate wisdom and leadership that would enable them to develop appropriate standards for Christian conduct and spiritual maturity (1:10, 26; 2:6; 3:1–4, 18; 4:4; 5:1; 6:1). The situation, however, was further complicated by a high regard at Corinth for eloquent speech (2:1–5, 13; 4:18–20). Accordingly, differences in eloquence between teachers were apparently being taken as indicative of different degrees of inspiration, and this had led, in turn, to painful and divisive comparisons (1:12; 3:5–9, 21–23).

It is not odd, in light of this, that the Corinthians' letter should reflect their divergence of views even as they queried Paul about the propriety of marriage and divorce (7:1–40: Should one state be considered more spiritual than another?), the consumption of food sacrificed to idols (8:1–11:1: Should the practices of those with strong or weak consciences be followed?), the practice of authentic Christian worship (11:2–14:40: Should distinctions in gender, wealth, and gifts find expression, and if so, how?), the nature of the resurrection (15:1–58: Should one believe in an event that would involve the body as well as the spirit?), and the collection for God's people (16:1–4: When and how should it be gathered?).

At the time 1 Corinthians was sent, Paul's plan appears to have been to return within the year to Corinth as his final stop on a journey through Asia Minor, Macedonia, and Achaia (1 Cor. 4:18–21; 16:5–9). Shortly after

1 Corinthians was sent, however, the apostle changed his plans and decided to make his journey to Macedonia by beginning and ending with a visit to Corinth (2 Cor. 1:15–17). Intervening events made Paul modify his plans a third time following his visit to Corinth (the second visit of 2 Cor. 13:2), and on his subsequent journey through Macedonia, he did not return to Corinth as he had originally promised he would (2 Cor. 1:23).

At least two of the reasons for this final change of plans become apparent in 2 Corinthians. First, Paul's second visit to Corinth was not at all as he had hoped it would be. Instead, it had involved him in a number of exceedingly painful (2 Cor. 2:1) confrontations in which, according to Paul, both the Corinthians (2:2) and he himself (2:5) suffered grief. As a result, from somewhere along the way through Macedonia, Paul wrote a letter to pointedly express his "distress" and anguish of heart at the distance that had developed between him and some of the Corinthians, and sent it off with Titus.

Second, upon reaching Asia at the close of his journey, Paul was beset by "hardships" and "pressure" associated with a peril so deadly that he "despaired even of life" (2 Cor. 1:8–10). In the midst of such an experience, it would have been impossible for him to return to Corinth, even if he had desired to do so. Nevertheless, having been rescued from death by God's grace, and having reached Troas once more, Paul was anxious and without peace of mind apart from news of the Corinthian response to his last letter (2 Cor. 2:13). Accordingly, he pressed on into Macedonia, hoping to meet Titus. Their meeting took place a short time later, and, as its result, Paul wrote 2 Corinthians from somewhere in Macedonia (2 Cor. 7:5–7, 13–16).

The Literary Integrity of 2 Corinthians

Although the preceding reconstruction of events represents something of a consensus among interpreters, there is nonetheless a considerable diversity of opinion about the literary integrity of 2 Corinthians and the precise historical background that might have occasioned the composition of 2:14–7:4; 6:14–7:1; 8:1–9:15; and 10:1–13:14. Indications exist that suggest these texts may not have been written at the same time as the rest of 2 Corinthians.

With respect to 2 Corinthians 2:14–7:4 and 8:1–9:15, the evidence is slight. For while it is true to say that 2:14–7:4 represents something of an intrusion into the narrative account that begins with 1:8–2:13 and concludes with 7:5–16, such a parenthetical and digressive intrusion is not uncharacteristic of either Paul's literary style or his Corinthian correspondence. (One may compare, for example, 1 Cor. 9:1–27, which intrudes into an apostolic reply that begins with 8:1–11 and concludes with 10:1–11:1.) Similarly, it has often been noted that there is an abrupt transition in the flow of the letter as one moves from 7:16 to 8:1 and a surprising reiteration of subject as one moves from 8:24 to 9:1. Upon further reflection, it may be seen that the abrupt transition is related to an important change of topic, and that reiteration of a principal subject, in this case the "service to the Lord's people" (9:1), is once more a characteristic of Pauline literary style.

It is more difficult to make a definite decision about 2 Corinthians 6:14–7:1. The lack of any reference to the immediate historical situation, the logical and literary links—which are apparently restored when 7:2 is read immediately after 6:13—and the concepts and vocabulary that are used in the passage argue that this text may have been a part of the letter that Paul affirms he wrote to the church prior to 1 Corinthians in order to advise them "not to associate with sexually immoral people" (1 Cor. 5:9). If that is true, then perhaps an individual, unknown to us, collected and edited Paul's Corinthian correspondence and inserted this section into 2 Corinthians. That person may have been unsure of its proper place in the sequence of Paul's letters to Corinth, or perhaps it seemed appropriate, despite its historical origins, to read this text in conjunction with the message of 2 Corinthians. On the other hand, however,

it is possible that Paul may himself have felt a need at this point in the letter to remind the Corinthians of his previous counsel, and in doing so, chose to make use of thoughts and perhaps even words drawn from his memory of the earlier letter.

A decision in favor of literary integrity becomes most difficult, however, when one considers the evidence with respect to 2 Corinthians 10:1–13:14. For while earlier parts of the letter show clear signs of having been written in a conciliatory spirit, at a moment when Paul sought to commend the Corinthian Christians and gratefully acknowledge their renewed affection for him (1:7; 2:5–11; 6:11; 7:2–4, 7, 13), the spirit of 10:1–13:14 is profoundly critical. This section contains numerous indications that these chapters were not occasioned by an effort to effect harmony between the apostle and his converts, but instead were written by Paul in an attempt to defend his rightful apostolic authority against all those in Corinth who might attempt to deny it (10:5–8; 11:4–6, 12–16; 12:11–13; 13:1–3). Furthermore, on two occasions in the latter part of the letter (i.e., 12:14 and 13:1), Paul speaks about a third visit he is about to make, but in the earlier portion of the letter he fails to mention it even where one would expect such a reference (i.e., 1:15–2:13). Finally, in 12:18 Paul writes as though the mission of Titus announced in 8:16–24 has already been completed.

Given such evidence, one could propose a set of circumstances that might still enable one to maintain that 2 Corinthians 10:1–13:14 was written at the same time as 2 Corinthians 1:1–9:14; or one could construct a different set of circumstances that might enable one to conceive of 2 Corinthians 10:1–13:14 as a part, if not the whole, of the letter written "out of great distress and anguish of heart and with many tears" (2:4) immediately prior to 2 Corinthians 1:1–9:14; however, the simplest explanation of the scriptural evidence points to the conclusion that 2 Corinthians 10:1–13:14 is a part of a letter written sometime after the composition and dispatch of 2 Corinthians 1:1–9:14. Of the letter's reception, and of the subsequent relationship between Paul and the church at Corinth, we know far less than we might like. But, comparing Romans 16:23 with Acts 20:2–3 and 1 Corinthians 1:14, we may infer that once again the letter of the apostle had a salutary effect, enabling him to make his promised third visit to Corinth, at which time he composed his letter to the Romans while residing in the house of Gaius, his convert (Rom. 16:23).

Commentary

1. Epistolary Introduction (1:1–9)

As was customary, Paul opens his letter with a greeting, or salutation (1:1–3). This conforms to the normal compositional pattern for personal letters written during the Greco-Roman era. (For an excellent introduction to the pattern of Greco-Roman letters, see Doty.) A greeting of this type routinely contained the name of the sender(s) of the letter, joined on occasion by a short self-description; the name of the intended recipient(s) of the letter, again joined on occasion by some short descriptive comment; and a word of greeting.

In 1 Corinthians the senders are Paul, who describes himself as an apostle sent out by Christ Jesus and by the will of God (see also Rom. 1:1; 2 Cor. 1:1; Gal. 1:1), and Sosthenes (see Acts 18:17). The letter is addressed to the church at Corinth (that Paul addresses the church as a whole is significant; see 1:10–12).

The members of the church at Corinth lived in a city that was commercially prosperous due to the remarkable trade moving north-south as well as east-west. Ships could be pulled overland along a road called the Diolkos (shown here).

There follows a threefold description emphasizing that the church has been set apart or sanctified to be in relationship to Christ, called within that relationship to the pursuit of holiness as saints, and united in these distinctives with all believers "in every place [who] call on the name of our Lord Jesus Christ" (1:2 RSV).

The normal Greek word of greeting, *charein*, is, as in Paul's other letters, transformed into the Christian greeting, *charis* ("grace"), and is joined with the Hebrew greeting *shalom* (Greek *eirēnē*, "peace"; 1:3).

Next, in 1:4–9, Paul includes a section in which he gives thanks to God for the whole of the church at Corinth (again as in letters of this era, which began by showing deference to the god/gods of the sender/recipient of the letter). Such thanksgiving is warranted, according to Paul, first and foremost because the grace of God, his unmerited love, has been given to them all in Christ Jesus. Furthermore, God's initial gift of grace has led to an enrichment of the community in speaking and in knowledge, which has confirmed the apostolic testimony about Christ. Thus, at present, the church does "not lack any spiritual gift" as it eagerly waits with Paul "for our Lord Jesus Christ to be revealed" at his return (1:7).

The words that follow contain one of the strongest statements within Paul's letters of his conviction that his converts would be enabled to persevere in their faith until the time of our Lord's return. Paul does not base his confidence on the strength of his converts' faith or on his own ability to pastorally maintain them in the faith, but rather on the sustaining and atoning power of Christ and the faithfulness of God, both of which are constantly available to those who have been called into fellowship with the Son (1:8–9).

2. Paul's Response to Reports about the Community at Corinth (1:10–6:20)

A. A report of factions within the community (1:10–4:21). **1:10–2:5.** Having given thanks to God for those things that characterize the church as a whole, Paul now appeals (1:10–17) to the church "so that there may be no divisions" (none having apparently taken place to this point, though the danger is clearly present) and so that they may be completely "united in mind and thought" (1:10). Paul's appeal is more than a mere formality, as is shown by the fact that it is made "in the name of our Lord Jesus Christ," and by the following verses, which demonstrate the need for the appeal by referring to a report Paul has received from members of Chloe's "household" about actual conditions at Corinth. These people, sent probably on business by Chloe (a woman of apparent importance), had brought to Paul a report that disputes had broken out among various groups within the community (1:11).

The disputes seem to have revolved around two interrelated issues: (1) the search for wisdom (i.e., guidance about how one should live the Christian life after conversion—the term is used in a way that seems particularly analogous to the Old Testament concept of wisdom) and (2) comparisons that were being made between teachers with respect to their ability to impart such wisdom.

Three and perhaps four groups are mentioned (1:12). The first group has identified itself with Paul (though Paul does not reciprocate and identify himself with them, or distinguish them from the other parties). The second has aligned itself with Apollos. (See Acts 18:24–19:1, which reports a visit by Apollos, a Hellenized Jewish Christian, to Corinth, and characterizes his teaching as eloquent, based on the Old Testament Scriptures, bold, and powerful.) The third group looked to Peter for leadership, or to teachers who used his name (for though it is possible that Peter himself had been at Corinth, it is not necessary to think of this as being the only way a group associated with Peter's Jewish Christian views may have come into existence at Corinth). The final slogan, "I follow Christ," has always proved difficult to interpret. Although it seems to designate a fourth group (whose apparent claim was allegiance to Christ's teaching alone), it could denote the common claim of each of the three groups ("I am of Christ," "No, I am," etc.), or Paul's own retort to all ("You follow so and so, but I follow Christ").

With a series of rhetorical questions issuing out of passion and conviction, Paul responds to these misplaced allegiances. Do the Corinthians really suppose that the presence of Christ is somehow divided among them? Do they really mean to suggest that their allegiance is due to someone other than the one who has been crucified for them? Have they really forgotten that they were all baptized in one name? The last question leads Paul to recall (though he admits his recollection is not complete) that he did baptize Crispus (1:14; Acts 18:8), Gaius (1:14; probably the Corinthian who together with Paul sends greetings in Rom. 16:23), and Stephanas (1:16; one of the Corinthians with Paul as he was writing [1 Cor. 16:17]). But neither these nor anyone else "can say that you were baptized into my name" (1:15).

The last verse of this section provides a bridge to the next (which criticizes the wisdom of the Corinthians and commends a different kind of wisdom [1:18–3:20]). The transition is accomplished through the denial that "words of human wisdom" have ever played a role in the preaching of the gospel. Indeed, such words and wisdom are the antithesis of preaching that concentrates on the cross of Christ and its power.

Paul's criticism of the search for wisdom at Corinth (1:18–2:5) may be divided into three parts, in terms of its focus (1:18–25), its effects (1:26–31), and its claim to inspiration (2:1–5).

Paul begins with a corollary of the point made in the last verse. Those who are perishing because of their lack of perception may indeed regard the "message of the cross" as "foolishness" rather than wisdom. But for those who are being saved, the proclamation of the life, death, and resurrection of Christ with the cross as its focus is recognized as the central manifestation of God's power and wisdom (see 1:24).

The implication is that the "message of the cross" has been neglected in the Corinthians'

search for wisdom in favor of a different focus. This focus Paul now begins to criticize, employing a quotation drawn from the prophetic critique of wisdom in Isaiah 29:14. In its context in the Septuagint (the Greek translation of the Old Testament, which Paul often quotes), the citation promises to "hide" (see RSV) and in that sense destroy or do away with the wisdom of the wise and understanding. These words in context appear to look to a time beyond their original historical setting when the wisdom of the Old Testament law will be superseded by God's new action among his people. That this time has come is precisely Paul's point.

The wisdom of this age/world, whether it be the wisdom of the scribal scholar or the pagan philosopher, the wisdom of the Jews (which seeks confirming signs of one's knowledge of the Torah and of God's plan) or the wisdom of the Greeks (which searches for truth in the abstract; 1:22), has been superseded. It has been frustrated in its attempt to grasp God's plan by the revelation of a new part of the wisdom of God displayed in the life, death, and resurrection of Christ, and set forth in Paul's preaching (1:21–22). Thus, paradoxically, while the events proclaimed in the gospel may seem to be manifestations of foolishness and weakness when evaluated with the wisdom heretofore known to Jews or Greeks, it is only through belief in the saving wisdom of such apparent foolishness and weakness that any shall be saved (1:21, 24–25).

In criticizing the effects of the Corinthian search for wisdom, Paul next urges his readers to consider the circumstances surrounding their conversion. God's call came not because they possessed wisdom, influence, or noble birth. (Paul's statement implies that one effect of the search for wisdom has been that some at Corinth do indeed lay claim to these attributes either literally or figuratively. Jewish wisdom writings often ascribed to the wise man all the attributes mentioned here and others like them.) It came, instead, on the basis of their willingness to identify with things considered foolish, weak, lowly, and despised in this world, things that characterize the life and death of "Christ Jesus, who has become for us wisdom from God" (1:30). This took place "so that no one may boast before him" (i.e., God), but instead might "boast in the Lord" (i.e., in Christ), who is the focus of the wisdom, righteousness, holiness, and redemption that have come to us from God (1:29–31; cf. Jer. 9:23–24). It is illegitimate, therefore, to search for wisdom and then to use it to boast before God and distinguish ourselves at the expense of our brothers or sisters.

Finally, Paul concludes his critique of wisdom by referring to the way in which he initially "proclaimed the testimony about God" (i.e., God's activity in and through Jesus Christ and him crucified) among the Corinthians. Once more Paul draws a contrast, this time between the "demonstration of the Spirit's power" (2:4) evident in Paul's preaching despite his weakness, fear, and trembling (2:3), and eloquence, "persuasive words," and wisdom (2:1, 4–5). The contrast implies that those searching for wisdom at Corinth have begun to view eloquence and persuasive words as authenticating signs of divine inspiration, perhaps even judging Paul's teaching inferior on these criteria to that of others (see 1:12, 17). Paul, however, makes plain that the definitive "demonstration" (the word is a technical term used by both Jews and Greeks to denote a conclusive or compelling proof) of inspired speech lies not in its "form" but rather in its power to convince and convert (2:5; see 1 Thess. 1:5).

2:6–3:20. Having criticized the wisdom that some at Corinth value, Paul now turns to a wisdom he can commend. It is a wisdom that is different in focus (2:6–9), that differently authenticates itself and its possessors (2:10–3:4), and that is different in its purpose and effect within the Christian community (3:5–17). On the basis of these contrasts, Paul clearly differentiates the Christian wisdom he commends in this section from the wisdom that he has criticized in the preceding section.

This section begins with Paul's claim to "speak a message of wisdom among the mature"

(2:6). But he quickly and firmly asserts that such wisdom belongs to neither this age nor the rulers of this age who, in reliance on an obsolete understanding of God's wisdom and will, crucified the Lord of glory (2:6, 8).

It has long been debated whether by "rulers of this age" Paul means human religious and/or political authorities (e.g., Luke 23:35; Acts 3:17; 4:26; 13:27), supernatural demonic "powers" who are said to dominate the present world order (e.g., Eph. 3:10; 6:12), or a combination of these two groups in which the influence of demonic "powers" is judged to lie behind the actions of human authorities (Col. 2:15). Since Paul uses the word "rulers" in the plural on only one other occasion, where it unambiguously refers to human beings (Rom. 13:3); since in the rest of the New Testament the plural likewise always refers to human "rulers"; and since this usage matches Luke's account of early Christian preaching, it seems most likely that Paul is referring to those persons in authority, both Roman and Jewish, responsible for the crucifixion.

In contrast to the wisdom that guided their actions, Paul characterizes Christian wisdom as being God's wisdom (i.e., it comes from and belongs to God). It is also secret, or mysterious, in the sense that it is "a wisdom that has been hidden" in events "that God destined for our glory before time began" (2:7). Christian wisdom may be said to find its focus in the meaning of the Christ-event as proclaimed in the gospel. Indeed, that event, properly and fully understood, points in a way that the law alone or Greek philosophy cannot; it points to the direction of God's plan past, present, and future, to what God has prepared for those who love him.

Over against the demonstrated ignorance of the rulers with respect to true wisdom stands Paul's assertion that "God has revealed it to us by his Spirit" (2:10). The remainder of the section enlarges on this remarkable claim. Verses 10 and 11 establish the Spirit of God as an adequate guide to such wisdom. For the Spirit is able to understand all the aspects of the wise plan of God, even its deepest secrets, just as the same capacity to understand our own plans and intentions belongs only to the spirit within us. Verses 12–13 describe the process by which the Spirit's knowledge is communicated. As persons called into fellowship with God through faith in Christ, we have received "the Spirit who is from God" so that we may "understand what God has freely given us," namely, a knowledge of the divine intent, God's "thoughts" and plan for salvation, past, present, and future (2:12). This wisdom, says Paul, is "what we speak," and even the words in which it is conveyed are a product of the Spirit's inspiration (2:13; cf. 2:4).

The last and largest part of this section (2:14–3:4) carefully restricts Christian wisdom to the spiritual person, for the person without the Spirit cannot understand its importance or accept its validity, because it is spiritually discerned (2:14–15). However, the evaluation of the spiritual person's grasp of Christian wisdom is "not subject to any man's

judgment" (2:15), for since no one has fully known the mind of the Lord, judgment can belong only to the Lord himself (2:16a; cf. 4:3–4). Nonetheless, as recipients of God's Spirit, we have the assurance that we know at the very least the mind of Christ (2:16b).

Yet even the possession of the Spirit and the mind of Christ does not necessarily ensure growth in our understanding of divine wisdom, as the next four verses show; for the Corinthians, still much as they were when Paul left them, are "mere infants in Christ" (3:1), unready for any wisdom that passes beyond milk (the proclamation of the gospel) to solid food (the attempt to explore the implications of God's act in Christ for our present behavior, 3:2; cf. Heb. 5:12–14; 1 Pet. 2:2). Their "jealousy" and "quarreling" demonstrate that they are still under the influence of wisdom that is "worldly" (3:3–4).

Paul now uses three metaphors designed to illustrate the purpose and the effects of authentic Christian wisdom. In the first metaphor (3:5–9), using a familiar Old Testament image of the community as God's field or vineyard, Paul compares his own ministry at Corinth (in which he "planted the seed" of wisdom through the proclamation of the gospel) and the ministry of Apollos (who watered it through further preaching and teaching [cf. Acts 18:27–28]) to the work of God (who made it grow). Such a comparison clearly shows that "neither he who plants nor he who waters is anything" as over against

Bust of Herodes Atticus (AD 101–77), a wealthy and distinguished sophist who funded the building of a Corinthian theater and the remodeling of the Fountain of Peirene. The Corinthian church became enamored with Greco-Roman sophistry and rhetoric. Paul, on the other hand, speaks "not in words taught us by human wisdom" (1 Cor. 2:14) and resists proclaiming the message of the cross by any criteria of Greek rhetoric.

"God, who makes things grow" (3:7). It also shows that "the man who plants and the man who waters have one purpose" (3:8). They should not, therefore, be compared with one another by the community (though each "will be rewarded according to his own labor" by God's ultimate judgment). They should be regarded in the same way, as "co-workers in God's service," at work side by side in God's field, or on God's building (3:9).

This last phrase leads to the second image, the community as God's building (3:10–15). In this case, the metaphor further defines the Christian community that is growing in wisdom as one that has learned not only to value its teachers equally but also to see clearly that there is a need for continuity between the foundational proclamation of the gospel (laid, in this case, by Paul as an "expert builder") and the subsequent teaching of others (who seek now to build on Paul's initial preaching; 3:10). There can be no attempt to lay a new foundation. Instead, the superstructure must always be evaluated to see if its materials conform in kind to the original foundation. For on the "day" (a reference to the Old Testament day of the Lord), the quality of every builder's work will be revealed with fire, and the builder either rewarded or singed with the flames that consume his or her work.

The final two verses (3:16–17) of this section reveal the reason for this severe judgment in a third vivid image. The building on which Paul and others are at work, the church at Corinth, is God's temple (see 1 Pet. 2:5), for God's Spirit is alive in its midst. In a solemn statement of *lex talionis* (the law of punishment in kind), destruction is promised to anyone who brings about the destruction of God's temple by breaking it away from its foundation.

Paul's criticism of the inadequacies of the "wisdom of this world" and his definition and commendation of the "wisdom of God" are now drawn together and the teaching applied to the tendencies of some at Corinth toward self-deception, self-centered comparisons, and self-aggrandizement.

"Do not deceive yourselves," Paul writes, and then goes on to clarify the kind of self-deception that imperils the Christians at Corinth (3:18–20). His concern is the possibility of self-deception with respect to wisdom because some at Corinth tend to define wisdom and designate those who are wise "by the standards of this age." In response, alluding to 1:18–31 and applying the contrast developed there between the wisdom of the world and the "foolishness" of the gospel, Paul advises all who are wise by such standards to throw away their "wisdom" and embrace what "the wisdom of this age" regards as "foolishness"; for in reality, "the wisdom of this world [has become] foolishness in God's sight." This development, surprising as it may be to those who trust in the continuity of wisdom, was nonetheless anticipated in the Old Testament Scriptures (Job 5:13; Ps. 94:11).

3:21–4:21. Paul then turns to the situation that gave rise to his remarks on wisdom, the tendency of some at Corinth to make comparisons between their teachers, to boost their favorite above the others, and to boast of their allegiances (1:12–17). Alluding to 3:5–9, Paul again asks the Corinthians to recognize that the truth lies in precisely the opposite direction. It is not the Corinthians who "belong" to Paul, Apollos, or Cephas; rather, along with all things, life and death, the present and the future (Rom. 8:38–39), Paul, Apollos, and Cephas "belong" to them, as servants of Christ and "as those entrusted with the secret things of God" (4:1).

The mention of the word "servant" leads Paul to allude to 3:10–15, and in 4:2–5 he applies the teaching of the former passage to himself and the church at Corinth. As a teaching servant of Christ, Paul has been "given a trust" and, in order to fulfill it, "must prove faithful" (4:2). Yet his faithfulness cannot be judged either by the Corinthians or by Paul himself, for the judgment of his faithfulness belongs to the one who gave the trust. It is the Lord, Paul writes, who judges him. It is best, therefore, for both Paul and the Corinthians to "judge nothing before the appointed time," because faithfulness to the divine trust depends as much on "what is hidden" and imperceptible (including "the motives of men's hearts") as it does on that which is now in the light (4:5). Praise for Paul, Apollos, and the others who have taught the Corinthians will come not from them in the form of group allegiances but from God, who will give to each one the proper amount in reward for faithfulness to the divine commission.

Paul now concludes this section in which he has dealt with the tendency of the Corinthians to make self-centered comparisons between their teachers, and in particular between Paul and Apollos, with a saying that was probably in use at Corinth (4:6). Its reference to "what is written" is obscure, although most likely it is meant to allude to the Old Testament Scriptures, either in whole or in part. But its message is nonetheless generally clear, and the same as that of 3:5–9. The church is to learn "from us" (Paul and Apollos together) the "meaning of the saying" and is to apply it to their lives without taking "pride in one man over against another." Indeed, pride, the desire to be different and better and boast of what wisdom one has come to possess, seems to Paul to lie at the root of all the church's present difficulties.

"Already you have all you want! Already you have become rich! You have become kings—and that without us!" (4:8). The Corinthians in their willingness to attribute wisdom and honor to themselves and their readiness to discriminate between their teachers are acting as if the kingdom of Christ has already become complete (though whether this premise forms the actual basis for their actions or the hypothetical basis for Paul's critique is unclear). However, it has not (1 Cor. 15:23–28), and this observation, so evident in the lives of the apostles, Paul now uses ironically to negate the tendency of the Corinthians toward self-aggrandizement at the expense of others (4:8–21).

Both Paul and the other apostles have been "put on display" and held up to ridicule, "like men condemned to die," who indeed were brought into the arena "at the end of the procession" (4:9). Those to whom the apostles preach view them as a spectacle to be seen but not taken seriously. And so together they have become fools in the eyes of the world (but fools for Christ!), while the Corinthians prefer to be seen and regarded as wise. Similar contrasts are apparent between the apostles' real "weakness" and the Corinthians' self-designated "strength," or between the apostles' real "dishonor" and the Corinthians' self-conferred "honor."

In verse 11, however, Paul drops the ironic comparisons as he proceeds in his attempt to teach the Corinthians that "no servant is greater than his master, nor is a messenger greater than the one who sent him" (John 13:16). Like Christ, the apostles "go hungry and thirsty . . . [and] homeless" even now (4:11), and in obedience to his teaching, "when we are cursed, we bless; when we are persecuted, we endure it; when we are slandered, we answer kindly" (4:12; Matt. 5:11, 44). Thus, "to this moment," the light of the world (Matt. 5:14; John 8:12) continues to be regarded as "the scum of the earth" (4:13).

Such words must have stung the Corinthians' pride. But in spite of this, Paul's intention is not to exalt himself or humiliate them. Rather, as one who "in Christ Jesus . . . became your father through the gospel" (4:15), he has written in a fatherly act of compassionate correction to warn them of the dangers inherent in their self-centered attitudes and to urge them, as his children, to grow out of their immaturity by imitating their father. In order that they might learn to imitate in the way their father intends, Paul says, "I am sending to you Timothy, my son whom I love, who is faithful in the Lord." Like an older brother, he will remind his brothers and sisters of their father's "way of life in Christ Jesus," which agrees with the lifestyle he commends for all his children in every church that he teaches (4:17).

Lest the Corinthians interpret this action as reluctance to confront his children, Paul writes last of his own plans. He "will come again soon, if the Lord is willing" (cf. 16:5–7, where the timing of the visit is more thoroughly thought out). And when he comes, he will not be diverted by the Corinthians' own verbal claims but will look instead for signs of God's power evident in their midst. For the kingdom of God "is not a matter of talk but of power" (4:20; cf. 2:1–5). It is up to the Corinthians, therefore, to choose how they wish to see the love of their father expressed—through the corrective power of the "whip," or in a more "gentle spirit" (4:21).

B. A report of immorality, arrogance, and improper judgments (5:1–6:20). 5:1–6:11. Up to this point in the letter, Paul has dealt with a report about different allegiances resulting from a search for wisdom that has involved a considerable manifestation of pride. But Paul has also heard that Corinthian pride has expressed itself in an even more damaging way. It is actually reported that there is "sexual immorality among you, and of a kind that does not occur even among pagans." Clarification of the general term "sexual immorality" immediately follows: "A man has his father's wife." The words of the text indicate more than a single immoral act. In addition, we can perhaps infer, because Paul does not speak of adultery, that the man's father is deceased; from the lack of reference to incest we can infer that the woman is this man's stepmother; and from the failure to mention her in 5:5, we can infer that she is probably not a Christian (see also 5:12–13). Marriage or cohabitation with such a person was forbidden to Jews (Lev. 18:8; 20:11) and was also condemned by several prominent Greco-Roman moralists. Even before addressing himself to the question of proper discipline, however, Paul confronts the laissez-faire attitude of a prideful church that has failed, because of a self-centered and permissive individualism, to respond with appropriate grief and censure.

Then, counting on the Corinthians to act together with him when they "are assembled in the name of our Lord Jesus," making the word and the power of Christ manifest in the church in exactly the way that he would if physically there, Paul prescribes judgment (5:3–5). The

man is to be handed over to Satan by expulsion from the church (5:11), which will deliver him back into the kingdom of this world, which Satan rules (5:5; Eph. 2:2). The purpose of the action is not punitive, however, but in order that "the sinful nature [i.e., that which may be presumed to have fully taken over the man's body and enslaved him in bondage for life] may be destroyed and his spirit saved on the day of the Lord" (5:5).

Again, however, Paul's mind turns back to the church (5:6–8). A body of believers that can boast of its achievements and ignore its obvious failures clearly has not yet learned that "a little yeast works through the whole batch of dough." Paul employs a proverb he has used before (Gal. 5:9), and one commonly used in Jewish circles to denote the way in which any moral evil eventually permeates its host. On this occasion, however, the proverb prompts Paul to some further analogies between the preparations for Passover (part of the ritual involved the removal of leaven from the household prior to the beginning of the festival [Exod. 12:15, 19; Deut. 16:3–4]) and Christian existence (which involves for Paul the continual call to "put off" the old sinful nature as well as to "put on" the new [Eph. 4:22–24]). In this sense Christians are indeed to "keep the Festival," to "get rid of the old yeast . . . the yeast of malice and wickedness," and to become what they "really are," a "new batch without yeast . . . the bread of sincerity and truth" (5:7–8). Furthermore, this must be done quickly, for the festival is already in progress: Christ, "our Passover lamb," has already been sacrificed.

In 5:9–6:11 Paul reminds the Corinthians he has written to them before that they should not associate with "sexually immoral people" (5:9). His counsel, however, has been misunderstood by the church, which took it to apply to the advisability of contact with the "people of this world" (5:10) and therefore neglected it as an impossibly rigorous and impractical standard. Adherence to such a standard would involve the Christian community's complete withdrawal from the world, and this possibility Paul does not even pause to contemplate. Rather, he writes again, more fully and clearly, what he wrote before: "You must not associate with anyone who calls himself a brother but is," as the Greek text and the specific case indicate, habitually "sexually immoral or greedy, an idolater, or a slanderer, a drunkard, or a swindler" (5:11). And then, lest someone say that his judgment is unbalanced in its selectivity, Paul reminds his readers that his refusal "to judge those outside the church," while compelling judgment for those inside, stems from the sure promise that "God will judge those outside" and certainly impose on them a sentence that is both harsher and more permanent (2 Thess. 1:8–9) than that which he now imposes on his own.

In 1 Corinthians 5:1, Paul refers to the kind of sexual immorality that the pagans would tolerate. Artwork on Greek pottery, such as this depiction of a drunken banqueter and a musician (Attica, 510 BC), often included portrayals of drunkenness and sexual promiscuity.

However, when one seeks to bring judgment against a Christian brother or sister, the secular law court is hardly the appropriate setting (6:6). The place for such disputes, if they arise at all (6:7), should be "before the saints" (6:1; NIV "Lord's people"). Indeed, as before, the Corinthians have acted exactly contrary to what is true. The saints will judge the world and even the angels who have fallen (see also Matt. 19:28; 25:41; 2 Pet. 2:4; Rev. 20:4). Therefore, in light of their role in these ultimate judgments, they are certainly qualified to "judge" trivial cases

that concern "the things of this life" (6:2–3) without recourse to secular courts.

That is exactly what Paul calls on them to do in the next two verses, though his advice is full of irony. If even those of "little account" in the church are better qualified to render judgments than those outside, then surely there must be someone wise enough among the Corinthians—who value their wisdom so highly—"to judge a dispute between believers" (6:4–5). To fail to do so prolongs disputes and provokes lawsuits that completely defeat both the ideal of Christian community and the Christian witness. The fact that these disputes have been prolonged, however, also points to the self-centered behavior of some who refuse to be wronged in any way without rushing to their own defense and to the willingness of some Corinthians to knowingly cheat and wrong fellow believers.

Some of the Corinthians appear to have forgotten that to engage in sin routinely is to place themselves back among the "wicked," who will not inherit the kingdom of God. Paul urges them not to deceive themselves in this way. Neither those who are habitually sexually immoral (as Paul's list makes clear, the general term includes behavior other than that which has provoked judgment [5:1–13]) nor thieves (once more the list expands beyond the specific behavior condemned in 6:8) will inherit the kingdom of God. Therefore, such behaviors, despite their routine place in the pasts of some, must be left behind through the constant remembrance that the believers have been cleansed from sin's stain and set apart from its power so that they may live in relationship with the God who has justified them in the name of the Lord Jesus Christ and by the Spirit.

6:12–20. Having made clear again the reality of standards for Christian conduct, Paul now goes on to deal with the rationalizations that have led some of the Corinthians to standards of their own: "Everything is permissible for me" (6:12). Reasoning from the same axiomatic truths that Paul reiterates in verse 11, some at Corinth have concluded that their Christian faith gives them complete freedom to set their own standards according to their individual sense of propriety. Paul does not disagree in principle, but warns them of two dangers: that they may fall into conduct that is "beneficial" neither to themselves nor to others, and that they may become "mastered" again, this time by the very patterns of behavior that marked freedom for them initially. A more specific instance of the same kind of rationalization has produced among some of the Corinthians the saying, "Food for the stomach, and the stomach for food" (6:13). Again, Paul's point is not so much that he disagrees in principle, but that they should remember that the freedom to eat whatever one desires is inconsequential in light of the coming destruction and transformation of our bodies, and therefore is not a freedom one should cling to or defend at all costs.

A final rationalization, unrepeated by Paul, probably underlies the words that follow these and returns us again to the subject of sexual morality. For some of the Corinthians, it followed from their freedom to eat that they were also free to indulge their sexual appetites in prostitution. For Paul, however, this action and the logical analogy that lies behind it are fundamentally wrong, because they involve the believer's body as a physical, psychological, and spiritual whole in an action that unites the Christian (whose body in this sense belongs to the Lord [6:14] and, as such, is already "united" to Christ [6:15, 17; 12:27]) with the active presence and enslaving power of immorality.

Paul urges his converts to "flee" from this perilous rationalization and activity. All other sins are outside the body, in that they do not involve the entire personality (6:18). Our bodies are a temple of the Holy Spirit, who dwells within each of us, and we are, as a result, no longer free to use our bodies apart from a recognition of the presence of the Spirit within us. "Bought at a price," which God did not hesitate to pay in and through his Son, we must respond in gratitude by giving "honor" to God with our whole being.

3. Paul's Response to Questions from the Corinthians (7:1–16:9)

In the first verse of chapter 7, Paul moves from oral reports about the church and begins to address questions posed by the Corinthians themselves in a letter. The letter is now lost but originally was perhaps carried to Paul by the three Corinthians mentioned in 16:17. The recurring expression "now for" or "now about" introduces Corinthian questions throughout this section.

A. Questions about marriage, divorce, and celibacy (7:1–40). The questions to which Paul responds in 7:1–16 probably had something to do with the relative worth of marriage as compared to abstinence or celibacy. Furthermore, behind the questions probably lay the supposition that abstinence or celibacy promoted spiritual achievement.

In any case, in the first two verses Paul's words strike a balance that is characteristic of his response as a whole. "It is good for a man not to marry," but the benefit is not one that can be enjoyed apart from the constant temptations offered by a promiscuous society. As a result, it is better for each man (who has not been given the gift from God [7:7] to resist such temptation) to have one woman as wife and each woman to have one man as husband.

That the command is given reciprocally to both sexes is remarkable, as it transcends cultural norms and prepares for things to come later in the letter (see 1 Cor. 11:11–12).

Moreover, within a marriage, sexual relations should not be suppressed except (Paul is making a concession, not giving a command) by "mutual consent" (again, the idea of mutuality is remarkable) "and for a time" (lest prolongation lead to temptation) "so that you may devote yourselves [together] to prayer" (7:5). For the wife no longer has "authority over her own body but yields it to her husband," and (most remarkably of all), the husband "does not have authority over his own body but yields it to his wife" (7:4). Paul's desire is thus for all to be free from temptation as he is, whether through the gift of marriage or the gift of celibacy. So his counsel to the unmarried and the widows is the same. It is good for them to remain unmarried, but advisable for those to marry who might otherwise be consumed with passion.

Another set of questions concerns separation and divorce. This set relates to the preceding questions: if, as is supposed, celibacy was considered preferable to marriage, this could give sufficient grounds for separation or divorce. Paul, however, relies here on a "command" of the Lord. The pursuit of celibacy is an insufficient reason for a wife to separate from her husband or for a husband to divorce his wife. It is noteworthy that Paul addresses the woman first (perhaps this is the initial clue to a tendency among some women at Corinth toward the exercise and defense of an absolute liberty that transgressed the boundaries established for true Christian freedom [see also 1 Cor. 11:5; 14:34]). As a realist and not a legalist, Paul also provides for situations where separation still occurs (advising a woman in that case to remain unmarried or to be reconciled to her husband).

Paul's answers so far have been given to believers who are married to one another, but now he turns to the rest, and to questions (raised out of the same context of concern for a spiritual status) about mixed marriages. In doing so, Paul states openly that his instructions go beyond those of Jesus (see also 7:25). But this does not mean they lack inspiration (7:40) or authority (1 Cor. 1:1; 4:1). Again, the counsel is given to both the man and the woman whose spouse "is not a believer." If the unbelieving spouse is "willing" to live with the believer, they are not to seek divorce. But will such a marriage not associate the believer too closely with the influence of the world? No, responds Paul, because the unbeliever is "sanctified," set apart from the world's influence (though not completely, as are those "sanctified in Christ Jesus" [1 Cor. 1:2; 6:11]), through the choice of constant association with a believing spouse. If this were not so, then (as some at Corinth had perhaps said) their children would be unclean. But, together with their mother and father, they too are holy. On the other hand, "if the unbeliever leaves," choosing to abandon the association, then the believer is not bound to struggle to maintain the bond, because God has called us "to live in peace." There is still one other possibility, so far unmentioned, and that is the best of all. Perhaps, though one cannot know, the association will serve to draw the unbeliever to faith and so to salvation.

As elsewhere in this second half of his letter, Paul's response (7:17–27) now moves from ethics (7:1–16) to a statement of principles before turning back again to advice (7:28–40). Paul now states the basic conviction underlying his balanced counsel (the "rule I lay down in all the churches" [7:17]). Spiritual growth is not dependent on status (marital or otherwise) but on attention and obedience to God's call. Accordingly, Christians should not ordinarily seek to change their status; rather, as far as possible, they should retain the status God has assigned to them.

Paul reiterates the principle with reference to circumcision. Those who were circumcised before their call should not now seek to erase the marks of circumcision, nor should those who before were uncircumcised seek its imposition

(7:18; Acts 21:17–26; Gal. 5:2). Instead, each should remain as he was. For that which served before to promote a distinction in status, knowledge, and obedience between them has now been set aside; and both together will be enabled in Christ to know and obey God's intentions for them as they walk in obedience to the leading of the Spirit (Gal. 5:25; 1 Cor. 2:6–16).

A final example concerns the slave and the freedman. Here, however, the analogy is incomplete, for Paul admits that the slave should use the chance to gain freedom whenever it comes. Nonetheless, the main point remains intact. The distinction in status between slave and free is irrelevant to those who belong to the Lord, who makes the slave his freedman (Gal. 5:1) and the free one Christ's slave (Rom. 1:1).

All three categories now come back into the argument as the section is finished by way of summary. All, whether married or celibate, Jew or Gentile, slave or free, have been bought "at a price" and thus have been brought into the body of Christ, where distinctions of status have no place (7:23; 12:13; Gal. 3:28; Eph. 2:14–18; Col. 3:11). Therefore, Paul urges them not to become subject again to human standards that would make their status a basis for comparison, but to transcend those standards and find unity and equality in the body of Christ. Paul closes the section with a final repetition of the principle (7:24).

Chapter 7 began with words addressed to single persons and questions about the value of marriage. The subsequent discussion, however, has focused primarily on related questions posed by those already married. In 7:25–40 Paul completes his answer to the questions of the unmarried and the widowed.

The answer is made in light of the principles already given and reflects Paul's considered "judgment," which, though not binding as a command "from the Lord," is worthy of trust. It is based, at the same time, on a conviction that the present, unsettled state of this world reflects that the time of its existence has been shortened; it is already beginning to pass away.

Therefore, it is best if the unmarried remain, like the married, as they are. Not all, however, will reach this decision, and so Paul adds realistically that its opposite, a decision to marry, is no sin.

In light of the reality of the world's demise, however, Christians should live not with reference to its expectations but rather as those who already have begun to live in God's new kingdom. Those who have wives should remember that one day the caliber of fellowship to be enjoyed between everyone in the kingdom of God will match that which is now the exclusive possession of husbands and wives (Mark 12:25). Similarly, those who mourn should likewise recall that their mourning has already begun to call forth comfort (Matt. 5:4). And those who "are happy" in the present world should bear in mind that the age to come will reverse present fortunes (Luke 6:25). Finally, those who buy or "use the things of the world" must realize the transitory nature of their possessions and not become engrossed in the enterprise of attainment and use (Luke 12:16–21).

Those contemplating marriage must also consider a further factor, for their marriage will deservedly initiate a concern to give pleasure and comfort to the spouse in a present world full of pressure and trouble. This concern will be added to the valid concern they bear as individuals to please the Lord in response to the call to be about his business (see Mark 13:34–37; Acts 13:2; 1 Cor. 3:13; 15:58). All this Paul would have them consider "for [their] own good" before entering into marriage. This is said not to restrict those who would marry from doing so, but to remind all of the priority of devotion to the Lord.

A section of advice follows whose reference is obscure. In the NIV this gives rise to an extended footnote in which the Greek, which speaks about proper action by a man with respect to "his virgin," is interpreted as referring to the way in which a father treats his daughter. It may more likely refer to the way in which a man treats his betrothed. In either case, though, the general point is clear and largely repetitive;

if a man thinks he is "acting improperly" toward a woman in either of these relationships by unduly prolonging a condition that perpetuates singleness, then marriage is a legitimate choice. Conversely, if a man "has control over his own will" but decides not to marry, then this man also is doing the "right thing" and choosing what to Paul is the "better" of the two alternatives (7:37–38).

Last comes the apostle's answer to widows who have asked about marriage. He reminds them that the unique loyalty of the marriage bond, though it is lifelong (with 7:15 as the exception, not the rule), is terminated by death. Accordingly, they are as "free to marry" as any others, or to choose not to do so, with this choice, in Paul's judgment once again, the better.

B. Questions about food, idolatry, and freedom (8:1–11:1). 8:1–13. Paul introduces a second major topic with the words, "Now about food sacrificed to idols" (8:1). Under this topical heading, as in the previous chapter, Paul treats several different though related questions. Here they concern the propriety of Christians in their own homes eating food that may have previously passed before an idol (8:4–6; 10:23–26); of Christians eating such food in the home of an unbeliever (8:7–9; 10:27–29); and of Christians accepting an invitation to dine in a pagan temple (8:10–12; 10:14–22).

It would be hard, as all these issues indicate, for any Christian at Corinth not to ask questions. Invitations to dine at a temple were, as archaeology has shown, a common social convention among everyone except slaves, and virtually all the food sold in the marketplace would have passed through a pagan temple for symbolic purposes before its sale. But the questions here appear to have been asked by some in a way that defended their own conduct and challenged Paul's (9:3) in this matter and others (9:4–6) as either too bold in its exercise of Christian and apostolic rights (9:4–12a) or too timid in its restraint (9:12b–27), and in any case inconsistent with what they had come to expect of an apostle (9:1–2). Paul's reply alternates between instructions and his own example rather than between advice and principles.

In 8:1–13, as in 6:12 (and perhaps in 7:1), Paul begins by giving assent to a guideline advanced by some at Corinth, in this case the principle that possession of knowledge justifies any conduct that is consistent with it. As before, however, Paul quickly qualifies the guideline with a reminder that knowledge can blind its possessor to its own importance and lead him or her in isolation from others toward a false assurance. Love, on the other hand, is a far more reliable guide, for it leads its possessor toward personal maturity in fellowship with others, and when turned toward heaven, to communion with God. Consequently, it is important both to know the truth and yet to speak it in love (Eph. 4:15).

Paul proceeds to review, for those who have need of it, the basic truths that undergird Christian monotheism. The first of

This head of the goddess Tyche was found at Corinth (late first century AD). Tyche, who was believed to control the fortune and prosperity of the city, was one of many deities worshiped in the various temples throughout Corinth. In 1 Corinthians 8, Paul addresses the food used in such pagan worship.

these is that "an idol is nothing," having no real existence in the world except in the minds and hearts of its worshipers, who nonetheless by their ignorant devotion open themselves to the influence of real beings with demonic power (10:14, 19–22). The second, on which the first is founded, is that there is no God but one, who is the source of all creation, service to whom gives life meaning, and who is the Father of the one Lord Jesus Christ, his agent in the beginning of life and in its continuation and renewal. (Similar ideas expressed in Eph. 4:5–6 and Col. 1:15–16 are probably a fragment from an early Christian confession.)

Next, Paul reminds his readers that some among them do not yet trust the substance of this truth enough to know its power in experience beyond simple assent. Therefore they continue to have doubts about the nature of the food that they eat and the implications of doing so. Because of this, fellow believers, in their words (8:8 probably paraphrases some of them) and actions, need to "be careful" lest the "exercise of . . . freedom" and knowledge lead them to ignore the effect of their behavior on the faith of the weak.

Finally, Paul applies what he has said to the situation in Corinth. Some have already accepted invitations to dine in pagan temples in public view and are in danger of leading those with a weak conscience to disregard it and act insincerely. Thus the weak, for whom Christ died, will be led to abandon action that matches their convictions and perhaps even to depart from any attempt at morality, a path that leads to destruction (see 1 Cor. 5:5). When this happens, those who have encouraged it will be found to have sinned against both the weak and Christ, who cares for even the weakest believer (Mark 9:42). Therefore, Paul chooses, for himself, to restrict the actions that he might legitimately take according to the criteria of love and concern for his fellow believer.

9:1–27. The mention of restraint prompts Paul to recall that some at Corinth have begun to interpret his reserve as an indication that he is not free to act, as they presume an apostle would, without reference to the beliefs of others. The rhetorical questions he poses in response are not so much concerned with his defense as they are with the fact that this false supposition may cause the Corinthians to neglect his advice (9:1–27). So he must reestablish his apostolic authority through reference to his experience of having seen the risen Lord and to the results of his initial mission, which brought the Corinthian church into existence through the preaching of the gospel. Thus, though outsiders may question his status, Paul expects his own to remember that their life in Christ is the continuing seal of its authenticity.

But does not a true apostle ask his converts to provide him with food and drink and the financial support to enable him to travel with a "believing wife" (9:4–5)? Do not the "other apostles and the Lord's brothers and Cephas" request such things from those whom they serve (9:6)? Indeed they do, and so, too, can Paul, who now illustrates the legitimacy of this right by noting that a soldier has a recognized right to serve at the expense of others, that those who plant crops or tend livestock have a recognized right to share in the produce, and that this right of support is recognized not only in the sphere of human affairs but also in the law of Moses, which speaks (in Deut. 25:4) about the right of an ox that treads grain to do so without a muzzle, that he might eat as he works.

These last words Paul takes (employing a traditional rabbinic method; cf. Rom. 5:9–10, 15, 17) to refer just as much if not more to the reward deserved by himself and others like him (9:8–10). Confirmation is provided by the observation that those who have plowed or threshed the grain are also entitled to possess a "hope of sharing in the harvest." Thus Paul and the others who have "sown spiritual seed" among the Christians at Corinth are also entitled to share in the harvest of their ministry through the provision of their continuing material needs (9:11–12).

But Paul has indeed, as they know, made no use of this right. Yet this is not, as his words have shown, because he is not entitled to do so. Rather, it is because he has decided to avoid any hindrance to the reception of the gospel of Christ. For despite the right of "those who preach the gospel" to "receive their living from the gospel" (9:14), which is analogous to the right of those who work "in the temple" and serve at the altar to "share in what is offered on the altar" (9:13), Paul has chosen not to make use of this or any of his rights, and he is not corresponding with the Corinthians for the purpose of requesting them. He has elected instead to make his boast in a ministry that disavows any dependence on another except the one who compels him to preach. Thus it is an almost involuntary obedience to God's call, rather than a voluntary and carefully planned decision to take up a self-supporting career, that stands behind Paul's attempt to "discharg[e] the trust committed to [him]" (9:17; see also 1 Cor. 4:1–2). And the reward he receives for such service is precisely the ability to make good on the terms of his boast, to preach the gospel free of charge.

But given independence from all, Paul has freely subjugated himself again, not to their support but to their way of life, in order to win them to faith. Though no longer bound by the notion of the law as a covenant enabling maintenance of the righteousness necessary for fellowship with God, Paul is nonetheless willing to follow many of the customs that are indifferent to one justified by faith (see also Rom. 3:21–22; Acts 18:18; 21:26) when to do so means an opportunity to gain entrance for the gospel. Conversely, among those for whom the law was no guide, Paul is willing, to the extent permitted to him by "Christ's law" (Mark 12:28–34; Luke 10:25–37; Gal. 6:2), to loose himself from divine law as a point of reference if this leads to the fulfillment of the gospel's

The stadiums in Greek cities hosted footraces and other athletic events. The stadium shown here at Nemea, about eleven miles from Corinth, was the site of the Nemean Games, part of the Panhellenic game cycle. Winners would receive a crown of celery leaves. Paul tells the Corinthians, "Run in such a way as to get the prize" (1 Cor. 9:24).

objective. And so, at length, his reasons now plain, Paul repeats his readiness to abide by the standards of the weak, or even to become all things to all people if, in this way, it becomes possible for him to bring about their continuing allegiance to the saving gospel of Jesus Christ. For Paul, as their apostle, also shares in the blessing of their entrance into a growing faith (9:23; see also Col. 2:5).

A last illustration allows Paul to compare his restraint with that of a runner who gives up much in "strict training" to attempt to gain the winner's "crown" in "the games" (9:24–25). Paul does not renounce his rights to no purpose, like a halfhearted runner running aimlessly, or a casual boxer who is always punching the air. Rather, like the serious athlete, he beats back his physical needs until they conform with the priorities of his Christian ministry, lest after proclaiming to others Jesus's call to abandon all and follow him, Paul himself should be found seeking to retain some personal prerogative and so be "disqualified for the prize" (9:27; see also Phil. 3:13–16).

The figure of the casual athlete allows Paul to make a transition from himself (9:1–27) to those at Corinth who have taken a casual attitude to their behavior with respect to food dedicated to idols (8:10–12). Their exercise of freedom without restraint, exemplified by a casual acceptance of invitations to dine in pagan temples, endangers both them and the weak if it fails to take seriously the influence of evil behind idolatry (chap. 10).

10:1–22. The people of Israel had made similar presumptions as those who together had been under the cloud and had passed through the sea (10:1; Exod. 13:17–14:31). Indeed, their experience suggests to Paul that all Israel underwent a baptism into Moses analogous to Christian baptism into Christ (1 Cor. 12:13; Gal. 3:27). Furthermore, they all ate "spiritual food" and drank "spiritual drink" (10:3–4; see also Exod. 16:1–17:7; Num. 20:1–13), experiences corresponding even more closely to the Christian (John 4:10; 7:37). For the "spiritual rock," from which the drink came, continued

to appear throughout their journey (according to a common Jewish understanding that interpreted Israel's repeated ability to find water in the wilderness in this way). So Paul does not hesitate even to identify this saving action with the preincarnate work of God in Christ. Nevertheless, these experiences did not succeed in protecting most of the people from evil or from God's judgment when they failed to take their actions seriously.

This should now serve as an example to dissuade Christians from stubbornly refusing to acknowledge and give up what is evil. The temptation (as one eats, drinks, and indulges in the "revelry" of any pagan occasion) to stubbornly ignore evil and acquiesce in an act of idolatry should be rejected (1 Cor. 8:10–12; 10:14–22) if the Christians at Corinth are not simply to repeat in their own experience the experience of Israel (Exod. 32:6). In the same way, the temptation to "commit sexual immorality as some of them did" (Num. 25:1–9; the difference in the exact number of those who died is insignificant to the point of the argument) should also be refused. Persistence in behavior that might "test the Lord" (in his resolve either to provide or to punish) should be eschewed, as should every temptation to grumble (10:10; Num. 16:41–50; 1 Cor. 1:11; 3:3).

Thus the past still serves to provide typical examples of divine judgment and, in this case, gives "warnings" to those who now participate in the "fulfillment" toward which all God's action in the past was pointed (10:11). Christians who are entrenched in the firm defense of their conduct are especially urged to be careful. Yet no temptation, even of pride and stubbornness, is theirs alone. They are involved in something that has proved itself to be a common experience for all God's people before and since. And God can be trusted not to allow temptation to go beyond their ability to resist if they will seek and do not ignore the way of escape he will provide (10:13).

In this case, as Paul urges his "dear friends" to recognize, the way of escape lies in a flight from the site of idolatry (10:14). He appeals without qualification to their ability to reason and form judgments based on what they know, for Christians are "sensible people." Yet some of the Corinthians have failed to take into account all that needs to be considered before coming to a decision about how to respond when invited to a pagan temple. Paul has sketched out the potential implications of their conduct for others (8:9–12); now he invites them to consider the potentially harmful effects on themselves.

Once again the argument is by analogy. Just as the acceptance of the "cup of thanksgiving" and the "bread that we break" at the celebration of the Lord's Supper enables a corporate and real participation or communion (Greek *koinōnia*) with Christ (10:16; because though many are present with individual thoughts, all "partake of the one loaf" and thus become one body [10:17]), and just as the same sense of participation or communion in the sacrificial worship going on at the altar is experienced in the life of the "people of Israel" by all those who eat the sacrifices (10:18), so the "sacrifices of pagans" (i.e., the food and drink present in a pagan temple) likewise draw all who eat or drink them into corporate communion in a sphere where demonic presence is genuine and

demonic influence powerful (10:19–20). For despite the fact that an idol has no real or personal existence, neither the reality nor the personal character of the evil that perpetuates a false worship can ever be doubted. Thus a Christian cannot participate in a meal at a pagan temple. To do so disregards realities and the inherent contradiction of trying to drink the cups of both the Lord and demons. Such action can only provoke the Lord to a jealous defense of his own unique right to be worshiped (Exod. 20:3; Isa. 42:8; Rom. 1:18–31) or invite the ludicrous thought that we are somehow more able in our freedom than he in his holiness.

10:23–11:1. The discussion to this point has highlighted two principles, which Paul now summarizes. Paul has labored thus far to show

The last standing columns of the Temple of Apollo (sixth century BC), the largest temple in Corinth. Participation in temple activities, such as those Paul mentions in 1 Corinthians 10, was considered not merely a religious duty but a civic responsibility.

that Christian freedom is not absolute. It must be qualified through the exclusion of any attitude or action that is not "beneficial" to the development of the individual (10:1–23), or not "constructive" with respect to the growth of the community (8:1–13). Moreover, the two are tied together, because the goal for the Christian is to seek not simply one's own good but also the "good of others" (10:24; Phil. 2:4).

Abruptly Paul turns to those who have gone to the opposite extreme and placed more restrictions than necessary on their freedom of conscience and behavior. They should "eat anything sold in the meat market without raising questions of conscience" that are unnecessary outside the environs of a pagan temple. For beyond the confines where false worship is given and evil dwells, "the earth is the Lord's and everything in it" (10:26; Ps. 24:1). They may also accept an invitation to a meal at the home of an unbeliever and eat whatever is "put before" them (10:27). When they do, they should not raise questions of their own conscience, although they must respond to "anyone" (a Christian or not) who feels obliged to inform them that others present who are consuming this food both know and accept that it has been offered in sacrifice (10:28–29).

The next two questions are obviously intended to reinforce this advice, but the flow of thought is difficult. It may be, however, that the questions are intended to draw attention back to the basic advice of verse 27. If so, then the sense is that there is no need for Paul or any Christian to exercise restraint in deference to "another's conscience" unless that other person expresses his objections. For if he does not (given that our conduct should not rest on assumptions about another person's conscience), then Christians should be free to eat any meal with thankfulness and without fear of denunciation (10:30; Gal. 2:11–16).

This action or any other, however, should be construed as an opportunity to glorify God rather than an occasion to express our freedom. And the praise of God can only be diminished if our action causes anyone inside or outside the church to doubt the moral integrity of the gospel. So the Corinthians should follow the example of Paul, who attempted to follow the "example of Christ" (11:1) by conforming as far as possible to different standards (1 Cor. 9:19–23; Matt. 9:10–13; Luke 7:36–50) and neglecting the pursuit of his own good in favor of the good of many (10:24; cf. Mark 10:45) in order that they might continue in faith and so be saved.

C. Questions about worship, gifts, and order (11:2–14:40). **11:2–34.** A third topic provoking questions at Corinth concerned the proper expression and relative value of spiritual gifts, in particular the way in which certain gifts should be used in a worship service. Within this sphere of questions about worship, however, Paul takes time to deal first with two issues that have proved divisive in the worship of the church. These he has heard about, though the source of the report is not given.

The first issue is concerned with the different head coverings that appropriately distinguish women and men as they pray or prophesy in worship (11:2–16). The interpretation of the passage is complicated from the outset (so also to some extent is 11:17–34) by its dependence on prior teaching, which Paul has given to the church but which, of course, is unknown to us. However, by beginning with "praise," Paul hints that the church has not departed significantly from the substance of what he has previously taught.

The discussion of the issue then begins with a call for the church to acknowledge (again or anew) that the "head of every man is Christ, and the head of the woman is man, and the head of Christ is God" (11:3). However, the word "head" (Greek *kephalē*), used here and repeatedly throughout this section, has various meanings. It may be used (as in 11:4–5) to speak of a physical head. But from this literal meaning come two metaphorical ones, which allow the same word to denote rule and authority (the head of the church being in authority over the body [Eph. 1:22]) or source and origin (the head of the church being the source of its existence [Col. 1:18]).

Of course, the precise meaning intended here will greatly influence the interpretation of the principle being expressed, not to mention any attempt to apply it to different, broader questions about the roles appropriate to men and women in contemporary worship. It may be helpful, therefore, to note first that either meaning enables these words to support the instructions that follow. But it is also significant to observe that the second has the advantage of according greater continuity to the section as a whole (see 11:8–11).

If the second of the metaphorical meanings is Paul's here, then his principle will be a statement of the truth that the source of every man's existence (or perhaps "person's"; the Greek can be used generically) is Christ, "through whom all things were made" (the Nicene Creed; cf. John 1:3; Col. 1:16); the source of woman's existence is "the man" (the definite article in Greek is used with the word "man," not "woman" [see Gen. 2:22–23; 1 Tim. 2:13]); and the source of existence for the historical person of Christ is God (Luke 1:34–35; Gal. 4:4). Thus a man who prays or prophesies with his physical head covered (either, as the NIV text suggests, by some form of head covering or, as the footnote has it, with long hair) symbolically dishonors the source of his existence by obscuring that which was created in the image of God and designed to reflect that image to God's glory (11:7; Gen. 1:26). Similarly, a woman who prays or prophesies (a practice Paul affirms apart from these comments on proper dress) with her physical head uncovered symbolically refuses to honor the source of her existence (i.e., by trying to obscure the distinctions between woman and man) and so brings dishonor on her own head as surely as if it "were shaved." Thus, if a woman refuses to "cover her head," she may as well "have her hair cut off," for the latter state is no more or less dishonoring to her than the former.

The basis for this argument is now repeated and supplemented (11:9; Gen. 2:18) before Paul returns to the question of the woman's appearance. For the "reason" he has given (11:7–9), and because of the angels (who were present with God at creation [Job 38:4–7] and at the time the law was given to reveal and preserve the created order [Acts 7:53; Gal. 3:19]), the woman who prays or prophesies must "have a sign of authority on her head." This allows her to transcend her created distinction from man (without seeking to deny it) in the expression of her gift. For both now participate in worship in a new order in Christ (1 Cor. 12:13; 2 Cor. 5:17; Gal. 3:28; Col. 3:11). This does not mean, however, that in the Lord woman is free to disregard man, nor is man free to disregard woman. The truth is that they are dependent on each other, and both are dependent on God.

As before, the Corinthians are urged to form their own conclusions based on Paul's presentation (11:13). But they are reminded as they do that nature reveals this same order as surely as scriptural argument. Thus, "if anyone wants to be contentious," refusing to accept the evidence of either Scripture or nature, then Paul's practice (see also 1 Cor. 11:1) will have to provide sufficient grounds for their conformity to these instructions.

In contrast to the previous section, Paul has no praise for what he has heard about the Corinthians' demeanor when they gather in worship at the Lord's Supper (11:17–34). Indeed, as it is, their behavior does "more harm than good." For in the midst of a celebration of unity, there are divisions among fellow believers. And while some "differences" are needed to distinguish those who believe and act genuinely (receiving "God's approval" as a result) from those who do not, other differences are unnecessary; and if stubbornly or pridefully maintained, they are liable to result in judgment (11:34).

The division between those who remain hungry and those who get drunk at the Lord's table is one such unnecessary and dangerous difference. For when it exists, the disunity created means that "it is not the Lord's Supper" that is being eaten. Homes are settings in which one may eat and drink freely according to his or her own means, but to do so in the midst of others who are hungry is to despise the new order of the church of God, in which people, both slave and free, are united in their status in Christ (12:13; Gal. 3:28; Col. 3:11) and to humiliate Christian brothers and sisters. Paul's words imply that the Corinthian church celebrated the Lord's Supper at the end of a communal meal, and there is just enough evidence about the members of the church (see Theissen) to suggest that the division of which Paul has heard is the product of differences in social and economic status, which were a prominent feature of life in the first century.

Since Paul cannot praise the Corinthians for remembering what he has taught them about the Lord's Supper, he now reminds them of the words he received and "passed on" to them. (The two verbs are technical terms in Judaism for the deliberate preservation and careful transmission of a tradition as it was originally "received" from its source. Paul therefore provides what is probably the earliest account in the New Testament of this part of the tradition about Jesus's words and actions; cf. Luke 1:1–3.) Paul's testimony accords quite closely, though not exactly, with that of the Gospel records. Our Lord, on the night of his betrayal, took bread, gave thanks, broke it into pieces, and said, "This is my body, which is for you; do this in remembrance of me" (11:24). These words, precisely in contrast to their intent, have proven to be an abiding source of division among Christians. For whatever the relationship established between the body and the bread, both are given for the benefit of all (the "you" is plural in Greek), that all may share in one body and celebrate their unity together in this memorial. In the same way, Jesus took the cup at the end of the meal and said, "This cup is the new covenant [see Jer. 31:31–34] in my blood; do this, whenever you drink it, in remembrance of me" (11:25). Thus, whenever Christians together "eat this bread and

drink this cup" (in contrast to common food and drink), they proclaim the Lord's death, which is for all (2 Cor. 5:14–16), inaugurating the new age (2 Cor. 5:17; 10:11) that will be brought to its culmination when he returns.

Therefore, because of the significance invested in these elements, anyone who consumes them in a manner that is not in keeping with their purpose of uniting believers with each other and with their Lord "will be guilty of sinning against the body and blood of the Lord" (11:27). He will have failed to distinguish the consumption of these elements from that of ordinary food and drink. So all people, before they eat or drink, should examine their attitudes toward those with whom they are about to share in this most intimate fellowship. For if the Corinthians do not sense within themselves, or within their previous behavior toward those around them, a genuine affirmation of unity, or a willingness to affirm unity, then they have failed to "recognize the body of the Lord," which is made present in order to unite and celebrate the unity of all with Christ, and they eat and drink judgment on themselves. Furthermore (as Paul discerns from what he has heard), judgment has already begun to manifest itself in the weakness, sickness, and death of some within the church (though one should not presume that any of these symptoms are always associated with divine judgment [John 9:3]). But such signs of judgment would be unnecessary if the Corinthians would judge themselves in the manner Paul has indicated (11:31).

The conclusion to be reached is brief. When the Corinthians gather in worship to celebrate the Lord's Supper, they must "wait for each other" and come together to eat instead of going ahead as individuals with their own private provisions. If any are so hungry that they cannot wait, then they should eat at home first so as not to provoke judgment. Paul will provide more directions when he comes (11:34).

12:1–31. Paul passes on now to Corinthian questions about the spiritual gifts (12:1–14:40), for Christians should not be "ignorant" about them (12:1–3). Their pagan experience should show, however, how easy it is to get carried away in ecstatic worship and "influenced" toward speech, even speech uttered falsely in the name of a mute idol. Thus, it is important to realize that speech inspired by the Spirit of God will never produce the words "Jesus be cursed," despite any sense of ecstasy (which, if it were false, might explain this strange utterance) or any temptation under persecution to apostasy (an alternative context in which this cry might be comprehensible). Conversely, no one can say "Jesus is Lord," producing the content of the most basic Christian confession (Phil. 2:11), without openness to the inspiration of the Spirit.

In this section (12:4–31), the major topic of discussion comes more clearly into focus. It is the relative value of the various spiritual gifts that is at issue, and probably also speculation about the degree of inspiration (or the Spirit) associated with each gift. Since speech "in tongues" is mentioned repeatedly in this chapter and the next, becoming the main focus of discussion in chapter 14, it seems likely that this gift was highly regarded at Corinth and that its recipients tended to exercise a dominant role in worship.

In response to this situation, Paul stresses first (in an early expression of trinitarian thought) that all the "different gifts" are distributed by one Spirit, just as different services are allocated by the same Lord and different "kinds of working" are enabled by the same God. Thus in the same way that services and works are performed not primarily for the benefit of the individual but for that of others, "the manifestation of the Spirit is given for the common good" (12:7).

The list that follows is not intended to be exhaustive but is typical of the gifts that had been experienced at one time or another by Christians in Corinth (see also Rom. 12:6–8; Eph. 4:11). These gifts include the "message of wisdom" and "message of knowledge," faith and the gifts of healing, "miraculous powers," prophecy and "the ability to distinguish between spirits" (RSV), the ability to speak in "different kinds of tongues," and the interpretation of tongues. It is then repeated that all these are the product of the same Spirit, who distributes them not necessarily one by one but to each person "as he determines" is best for the good of all (12:11).

Paul now illustrates the unity (12:12–13), diversity (12:14–20), and integrity (12:21–26) produced at the Spirit's inspiration among those at Corinth who belong to the body of Christ. Though suggested by Jesus's words on the road to Damascus (Acts 9:4) and by its use in the Greek philosophical traditions of Stoicism (with which Paul shows passing familiarity elsewhere), this figure is used casually in the Pauline Letters (1 Cor. 6:15; 10:17; 11:29), with the exception of these verses.

Just as "the body is a unit though it is made up of many parts . . . so it is with Christ" (12:12). (The cult of Asclepius, the god of healing, and his daughter Hygeia was accorded a prominent place in Corinth, and those who sought healing for a part of the body would often leave a representation of it in the Asclepion. Perhaps Paul has this in mind as he reminds his readers that the body is a unit and not simply a

People would come to the Asclepion, built in honor of the deified Greek physician Asclepius, to be healed. Pictured here are votive offerings, usually representing the afflicted body part, given in gratitude to Asclepius.

collection of various parts.) The point is analogy, not identity. Christ dwells in the church after the resurrection but possesses his own body as well. The basis for comparison lies in the fact that all Christians, despite the inequities of their former existence, have now been brought into one body (see also Gal. 3:27–28) by a common experience of the Spirit in baptism.

This does not mean, however, that all will now be given exactly the same gifts, for a body is not constituted by a single part but by many. Thus the diversity among the parts of the body is no cause for concern about membership or status in the body. For, in fact, "God has arranged the parts in the body" with thought for the proper place and role of each, so that there are "many parts, but one body" (12:20).

Moreover, the unity of the body is not superficial but integral to its existence. Weaker parts of the body are indispensable, less honorable parts (i.e., those not usually receiving recognition) are given "special honor" (12:23), and "parts that are unpresentable" are accorded a modesty that witnesses to their importance. And all this is by design (12:18). For God has now given greater honor to those members who before their incorporation into the body of Christ had little honor outside it, so that no cause for a division of honor, attention, status, or concern might exist within the body. Thus, if any part of the body suffers in its ability to function within the body, "every part suffers with it," and when one part is honored, all will rejoice in the recognition of its capability (12:26).

Repeating the affirmation with which he began the analogy, Paul now moves to his conclusion. The gifts may be differentiated, but not on the basis of supposition about the degree of inspiration. Rather, those who are given gifts are to be set in order on the basis of their ability (via God's appointment) to serve and edify the body (1 Cor. 3:5–15). Thus apostles come first, prophets second, teachers third, then "miracle-workers," healers, helpers, administrators, and last those "speaking in different kinds of tongues" (12:28). The point is reinforced by

questions that treat the gifts in the same order. If all are not appointed and gifted to be apostles, it follows that all should not expect to receive any particular gift, including the ability to speak in tongues or interpret.

The discussion, however, is not allowed to conclude on this point. For neither the gifts nor the giver is static (12:11). Thus all may "eagerly desire" to someday sense the call and empowerment to use in service to the body those gifts that really are "greater" in the list Paul has outlined. But in the midst of this ambition (as they are encouraged to realize) they should know that these gifts are still not the "most excellent way" to serve (12:31).

13:1–13. Once more Paul pauses to insert a section that interrupts his direct reply in order to clarify the grounds on which his response rests. He has said that the gifts are given for the "common good" (12:7), but this goal will not be reached apart from a motive to guide and direct their exercise. Thus, if I speak in the tongues of men and of angels, and love does not motivate the control of my speech, "I am only a resounding gong or a clanging cymbal" (13:1; instruments used to produce a variety of sounds that command attention but only frustrate their audience unless accompanied by music or words that interpret their meaning). Similarly, to have "the gift of prophecy" (which conveys insight into the mysteries of God's activity [1 Cor. 2:7] and knowledge about God himself [1 Cor. 8:4]) or a "faith that can move mountains" (Mark 11:23) is of no value unless these abilities are motivated by love as they are used within the body of Christ (13:2). So also the offering of "all I possess" in sacrificial service to "the poor" or the offering of "my body to the flames" in the sacrifice of martyrdom is of no lasting benefit apart from the motivation of love (13:3).

This love comes to expression in different ways at different times, through patience and kindness that elevate others. It does not express itself through the envy, boastfulness, or pride that keeps attention centered on self. On the same basis the rudeness, the pursuit of self-gain, the anger, and the vindictiveness that express themselves at the expense of others are never characteristic of love. For love cannot be identified with the enjoyment that is achieved for ourselves by such means. Its enjoyment consists in acknowledging the truth, of which our perception and interest are only a part. Such love always protects the interests of others, always trusts in their intentions, always hopes for their good, and always perseveres in its attempt to do these things.

Such love also "never fails" to express itself—whether in the past, the present, or the future—among those who belong to God. It will continue to do so even after prophecies, tongues, and knowledge cease (13:8; there is no indication here that Paul thought any of these events likely before the time when God's kingdom is perfectly or completely manifested [13:10; 15:20–28]). For our knowledge of God and our words spoken in worship in the light of what we know (whether our knowledge is expressed in words of prophecy or in tongues) are only a part of what they should be, and when perfection in thought and expression arrives, the imperfect always "disappears" (13:9 10).

It is this way in our own experience, for childhood speech and thought inevitably give way to different patterns in adulthood. Similarly, the "poor reflection" of anything seen in a mirror (such as those manufactured in first-century Corinth) could not be compared to the experience of seeing the same thing face-to-face. For now, then, these analogies should caution us that our present knowledge of God (and, by implication, the worship such knowledge initiates) will change and pale when we come to know God as completely as he now knows us. In view of this, three things can be trusted to "remain" unaltered by the enlargement of our knowledge: "faith, hope, and love . . . but the greatest of these is love" (13:13).

14:1–40. If love motivates the exercise of the gifts, it should not be difficult, as Paul now shows (14:1–25), to determine which

gift should be accorded priority in worship. For while all the gifts are desirable, the "gift of prophecy" builds up or edifies the church to a greater extent than any other, and, in contrast to some at Corinth who thought otherwise, on this basis it is to be given priority over the exercise of the gift of speech in tongues. For speech in tongues is not directed in the first instance toward those present in worship but toward God. Indeed, the conversation concerning divine mysteries is private to the extent that it is unintelligible to others apart from interpretation (14:2; also 14:5). But prophecy (whether it explains the significance of God's actions and words for the present or reveals what God intends for the future) is given in language expressly to strengthen, encourage, and comfort other persons at worship. So the one who speaks in tongues edifies himself, but the one who prophesies edifies the church. Therefore, the ability to speak in tongues is not to be neglected, for it has value for everyone to whom the gift is given. But the exercise of prophecy in worship is preferable because it is of value not only to the individual but also to the church. This contrast holds unless the one who speaks in tongues also interprets, so that the church may be made aware of the contents of an otherwise private conversation.

Several illustrations reinforce the point. If Paul were to come to the Corinthians speaking in tongues, clearly his visit would do them no good unless he also communicated in the intelligible language associated with the other speaking gifts. Similarly, the sounds produced by musical instruments must be distinct and clear if they are intended to convey a tune or a message that is understandable. Language itself furnishes a final illustration. For even languages, all of which have meaning, cannot convey their meaning so long as the hearer remains a foreigner to the language of the one who speaks.

For the reason that has now been stated and illustrated, persons who speak in tongues in worship should pray that they may interpret this speech to the others present. This is true even when persons pray in tongues. For in such prayer, apart from interpretation, the individual may communicate with God in a way that brings satisfaction to the spirit without enabling the mind to comprehend its basis. However, prayer of this kind is not to be abandoned. Instead, it is to be supplemented by prayer that can be understood by the mind (just as the song that springs spontaneously from our spirit is to be supplemented by that which is composed purposefully by our mind), and recognized as a form of prayer that is less desirable in corporate worship because it does not allow others to join in its praise.

The weight of Paul's own practice is now thrown behind the argument. For even though Paul himself can give thanks to God for the ability to speak in tongues, a gift he has received with greater frequency than any at Corinth, he nonetheless prefers "in the church" to speak words that are few but meaningful to all as opposed to words that may be numerous but do not promote corporate understanding or response (14:18–19).

The Corinthians are exhorted to have a mature evaluation of the gifts by keeping in view a passage from Isaiah (Paul uses the term "law" as it was used among the rabbis, to refer to any part of the Old Testament). In context (Isa. 28:11–12) these words come in response to the mocking of the form of speech used by the prophet to convey God's message. In turn Isaiah promises that, since Israel will not listen to the Lord's word in their own language, they will hear the message that his judgment has come upon them spoken by men of strange tongues, and even then they will not listen readily. In this sense "tongues, then, are a sign, not for believers but for unbelievers" (14:22), as a display of God's power sent with the intention that when they are at last understood they may also convict. Prophecy's true purpose, however, is to instruct and speedily convict those who believe in its words.

Paul then applies this interpretative insight to the exercise of tongues and prophecy in the Corinthian worship service. If the church gathers and "everyone speaks in tongues," when others come in (whether they enter simply seeking an understanding of the faith or the confirmation of their disbelief), they will not readily listen to sounds they do not understand but attribute them instead to a temporary insanity (14:23; see also Acts 2:13–15). But if, in the same circumstances, prophecy is being exercised, then the message of conviction will be immediately understood and repentance, worship, and confession will surely follow.

In a series of instructions, Paul now spells out the practical consequences of all his teaching in this section (14:26–40). When the church gathers, "everyone" is to make the contribution that the Spirit inspires. Their ministries must be organized by their common commitment to structure the service of worship so as to promote the "strengthening of the church" (14:26). Thus, if those who have the ability to speak in tongues feel inspired to contribute, they must not be allowed to dominate the service. "Two—or at the most three—should speak, one at a time," and someone should be able to interpret to all present (14:27). If such interpretation is not made available by the Spirit, those who speak in tongues "should keep quiet" enough in the church to enable their speech to function as a private prayer (14:28).

Prophecy likewise, despite its value, is not a gift to be exercised in excess. "Two or three prophets should speak," and then there must be time allowed for the congregation to reflect on the significance of what it has heard (14:29). If a prophetic insight comes to a church member while another person is giving a prophetic message, the one who is speaking should give way temporarily to the other member. In this way all who are inspired can "prophesy in turn" and the church can receive the maximum amount of instruction and encouragement (14:31). Those with the gift of prophecy should not object that they cannot be interrupted, because it is within their control to remember and resume their message. In this way a peaceful order will be established that reflects God's character and brings the worship of the church at Corinth into the form found "in all the congregations of the Lord's people" (14:33; see also 1 Cor. 4:17; 7:17; 11:16). Verse 33 then probably forms the conclusion to this paragraph rather than the introduction to the next; note the otherwise unnecessary repetition of the phrase "in the churches" in verse 34.

To explain the meaning of the next two verses and remove any tension between them and the permission given (in 11:5) to women to pray and prophesy has always proved difficult. The difficulty might conceivably be removed by the observation that some early manuscripts of 1 Corinthians place these two verses after verse 40, indicating that they may have been added later to this letter (note how the words of verse 36 follow naturally those of verse 33), placed here by someone who failed to understand the different situations addressed by the two letters and who attempted to harmonize 1 Corinthians, at least in part, with the instructions found in 1 Timothy 2. Such observation and supposition, however, cannot be substantiated by the evidence available to us.

The explanation that seems most worthy of consideration takes its cue from the evidence of verse 35. The words "if they want to inquire about something" appear to point to a certain kind of speaking that was proving itself as disruptive within Corinthian worship as the unrestrained exercise of other kinds of speech and that was associated in this particular congregation with women. Perhaps it was simply the frustrated speech of wives whose soft-spoken questions were ignored by husbands, or the bolder speech of women who ignored their husbands entirely and interrupted to ask questions of the person who was speaking.

In any case, Paul's instruction (14:34) is that such women "should remain silent in the churches." (The Greek words here are more accurately translated "in the meetings of the church.") "They are not allowed to speak" (in the disrespectful and disruptive way that they are doing), but "must be in submission" (to their husbands; the word "submission" is one that Paul defines for his own use in terms of respect [Eph. 5:21–33]), "as the Law says." (Though there is no specific place in the Old Testament where such submission or obedience is commanded, this idea is indeed the presumption behind much of its content.) Instead "they should ask" their questions of their husbands at home (either before they disrupt the

> Paul wanted his churches to exhibit a modesty and propriety recognized by the surrounding culture, especially in worship (1 Corinthians 14). At Corinth he was particularly concerned about women's reputation. For women, modest draped clothing with a head covering was common (see 1 Cor. 11:2–16), as seen here in a sculpture from 300 BC (Tanagra, Greece).

speaker, or before they distract their husbands and those around them). For "it is disgraceful" (see 1 Cor. 11:7, where the same Greek word is used of women who refuse to cover their heads as a sign of respect) "for a woman to speak [in this way] in the church" (14:35).

The whole section is now brought to a close with two rhetorical questions, a statement of the possibilities left open by the argument, and a final exhortation. The questions are designed to deflect the Corinthian tendency toward a sense of their own inspiration and the stubbornly prideful maintenance of unhelpful and idiosyncratic customs. The statement sets forth Paul's expectation that any true "prophet" or "spiritually gifted" person will acknowledge the truth in what he has written (14:37). If stubborn ignorance is chosen, however, then it will also be safe to ignore the claims of such an individual to be led by the Spirit. The exhortation epitomizes Paul's advice. The ability to prophesy should be sought eagerly, and speaking in tongues should not be forbidden. But whatever form the worship service takes as a result of adherence to these directions, "everything should be done in a fitting and orderly way" (14:40).

D. Questions about the resurrection and life in the age to come (15:1–58). Whether this final section comes in reply to reports (15:12) or tentative questions that are just beginning to be asked (15:35), its principal purpose is clear. Paul writes to defend, to clarify, and to broaden his teaching concerning the resurrection (15:1–11). From the content of the statement attributed to some of the Christians at Corinth (15:12), it seems that their attitude was being shaped by a skeptical aversion similar to that of the Athenians whose attentiveness to Paul's preaching came to an end at his mention of the "resurrection of the dead" (Acts 17:32).

If this is so, then the crux of the issue was probably not a denial of the possibility of a life after death but an opposition (which was characteristic of Greeks and, on occasion, of Jews living in a Greek environment) to the notion of a bodily resurrection and the preference for

an idea of immortality of the soul. Added to this was likely a remembrance that when Paul had originally spoken about the resurrection, he had done so with words about believers already being "raised with Christ" (Eph. 2:6; Col. 2:12; 3:1; in contrast, 2 Tim. 2:17–18). In response, Paul seeks to demonstrate the validity of the idea of bodily resurrection (15:1–11), its necessity (15:12–19, 29–34), its futurity (15:20–28, 51–58), and its nature (15:35–50).

Paul begins by reminding the Corinthians "of the gospel I preached to you," which they received, in which they have placed their trust, and by which they are saved if they continue to "hold firmly" to their faith in its truth. For otherwise, if initial acceptance gives way to confirmed disbelief, they will "have believed in vain" (15:1–2).

The content of Paul's preaching is now crystallized in a creedal form that is introduced with the same technical terms for the careful transmission of tradition as were used before to demonstrate a link between Paul and others who provided sure access as witnesses to the events that are now described. The contents of this very early creed are composed from the facts of Jesus's death, interpreted (with probable reference to his teaching [Mark 10:45] and the scriptural figure of the Suffering Servant [Isa. 53:12]) as a death for our sins, burial (which meant he had actually died [Mark 15:44–46]), resurrection (which took place when God raised his Son in accordance with the Scriptures [Acts 2:24–32]), and appearance after death ("to Peter" [Luke 24:34]; then to the Twelve [as a group, not a number; Luke 24:36]).

The creed (whose elements are all joined to one another by the repetition of the word "that") is now supplemented by additions. They provide evidence for an appearance of the risen Christ to more than five hundred (15:6; otherwise unmentioned in the New Testament), to James (15:7; accounting apparently for his conversion and rapid rise to leadership in the Jerusalem church [Mark 3:20–21; John 7:5; Acts 12:17; 15:13]), to all the apostles (an appearance distinguished here from that of 15:5; cf. Acts 1:3), and last of all (in time only, not in importance) to Paul (in an appearance so long after the others as to make Paul an apostle "abnormally born"; see also Acts 9:5).

Nonetheless, though least among the apostles and undeserving of the title because, unlike the others, he had persecuted the church of God (15:9; Acts 9:1–2), Paul was still called by divine grace, which is "not without effect," to do the work of an apostle. In response, he expended more effort in travel and ministry and reaped more success (because of the "grace of God that was with me") in the founding of churches than any other (15:10). So whether the Corinthians wish to view Paul's preaching, or that of those whose witness formed the tradition behind his preaching, as the source for their knowledge of Jesus's death and resurrection, it makes no difference to the content of the gospel or the substance of their faith.

Paul next points out the implications of unbelief (15:12–19). The Corinthians had been reminded that the resurrection lay at the heart of the gospel that was proclaimed to them. But was it necessarily the center, or did the call to a spiritual life in union with the risen Christ demonstrate that, unlike Christ, Christians were called to be those who pursued and received spiritual immortality rather than resurrection from the dead? Some such question appears to have led various persons within the church to deny any connection between the fact "that Christ has been raised from the dead" and their idea "that there is no resurrection of the dead" (in general; 15:12).

But the disjunction is a false one, for if in fact there is no such thing as a "resurrection of the righteous" (Luke 14:14; Acts 24:15), then there is no reason to believe in the anomaly of Jesus's resurrection. But if he "has not been raised," then both to preach and to believe the resurrection is "useless" (15:14). Worse, such preaching would be tantamount to bearing "false witness" about God's actions. "For we have testified about God that he raised Christ

from the dead," and that cannot be true if "the dead are not raised" (15:15–16). Worse still, if Christ has not been raised, then apart from God's vindication made evident by the resurrection, faith in Christ's death as the sacrifice for our sins is futile, and those who have fallen asleep, or died, believing in Christ as their Savior "are lost" (15:18). Worst of all, if Christians have only a false hope in Christ for any life beyond the present, then "we are to be pitied more than all men" as self-deluded (15:19).

In fact, however, such consequences need be explored no more, as Paul gives the implications of a true understanding (15:20–28). "Christ has indeed been raised from the dead, the firstfruits of those who have fallen asleep" (15:20). By the term "firstfruits," Paul means to signify the first produce of a harvest. Such produce possessed special representative significance as a sign of what might be expected from the crop and was to be presented to God in the temple (Exod. 23:19). The thought of Christ's resurrection as a representative event triggers the comparisons that follow between Christ and Adam as representative persons. For just as death came into the world through a man whose actions were truly representative of the harvest of sin and death that has become characteristic of all who have come after him, so now the resurrection of the dead has come through a man whose destiny his progeny can also fully expect to share. For inasmuch as all who are united with Adam by birth and by sin die, all who are united with Christ by rebirth and faith will, like him, be made alive.

"But each [will be made alive] in turn"—first Christ, then "those who belong to him" at his coming (15:23; 15:52; 1 Thess. 4:14). Then "the end will come," the time when Christ hands over to the Father his kingly rule over all those who believe in him (15:23–24). This will not happen, however (Ps. 110:1; Mark 12:36; Acts 2:34–35), until all the other forces that exercise an alien power over Christ's people have been destroyed, including the last such enemy, which is death. But when all these have been destroyed, the God who has put them all under Christ's feet (Ps. 110:1; cf. Ps. 8:6) by destroying their power must not be expected to subject himself to Christ. Rather, just the opposite will happen. "The Son himself will be made subject" (or perhaps, as is suggested by the Greek, he "will subject himself") to the Father, who has given him his kingly authority so that God may be recognized as the true source of "all" that has happened "in all" these events (15:28).

A series of rhetorical questions presses home the practical implications of Paul's argument (15:29–34). The first, however, certainly raises more questions for us than simply the one asked. It is surely relevant to point out that there is no value in being "baptized for the dead" if the dead are not raised (15:29). But when and where was such a baptism practiced, and why? Paul's words most naturally suggest a baptism undertaken by Christians for Christians who died in faith without having been baptized, because of a deathbed conversion. Or perhaps they refer to some who converted and were baptized in order to be reunited with their dead Christian loved ones. In any event, Paul does not recommend the practice but only states that it takes place.

Paul's own life is the subject of the next question. For if there is no resurrection, then to repeatedly "endanger" one's life on behalf of the gospel is foolish (15:30). Why expend the effort that brings him unnecessarily closer to death every day? And what possible benefit could there have been in allowing himself to be put in the arena with "wild beasts" at Ephesus for the cause of Christ (an event otherwise unmentioned in the New Testament)? For if the dead are not raised, then it is much more prudent to enjoy the pleasures of life for as long as possible (15:32; Isa. 22:13).

As they reflect on their answers to these questions, the Corinthians are not to be "misled" by the opinions of those outside the church, for as even the pagan playwright Menander said, "Bad company corrupts good character" (15:33). Instead of a life lived in sin, which results from

an excessive pursuit of the pleasures of the body, prompted perhaps by the notion that a spiritual union with Christ after the death of the body is assured, the Corinthians are called back from such shameful ignorance of the truth to the Christian use of right reason.

The argument could certainly have been ended at this point, but a question about the nature of the resurrection prompts further discussion (15:35–50). If there really is a resurrection, "How are the dead raised? With what kind of body will they come?" (15:35). The second question explains the sense of the first. The Corinthians are not asking about the way in which God's power could make possible a resurrection but are questioning the implications of the idea. To ask the latter question, however, is foolish if the former is already answered with reference to God. The use of analogy will demonstrate this.

Paul begins with a biological analogy in common use among rabbis of the first century (John 12:24). A seed that is sown does not come to life in the form of a plant unless its first form, its bodily shell, dies. Furthermore, the form of the seed that is sown says nothing about the nature of the plant that will sprout.

The form of the seed and that of the plant differ because God gives the latter a bodily form according to his own plan, and that he is able to do this is demonstrated repeatedly in the present by his power to give each kind of seed its own body. Similarly, divine activity in the present also explains why "all flesh is not the same" (15:39). But just as "earthly bodies" now manifest God's splendor differently than do "heavenly bodies" (15:40), "so will it be with the resurrection of the dead" (15:42).

The body that now displays God's glory is perishable. The body that will be raised will display God's glory in an imperishable form. The body whose glory is now partially obscured in the dishonor of sin and death will be raised to reflect fully and completely God's glory. The body that dies in weakness will be raised to share in the power that comes from God himself. And finally, most comprehensively, the one who dies in a "natural body" will be raised to life in a spiritual body (15:44a; note, however, that it is still a body, which is both like and unlike ours).

Thus the plausibility of a spiritual body, and something of its nature, is demonstrated from the fact of a "natural body" (15:44b). It may also be demonstrated from Scripture. For in the same way that Adam as a living being represents the first of his species, so Christ, the last Adam, as a spiritual being, gives life to a new race of persons whose bodily form is now represented only by his own. The point, however, is that full spiritual existence in a glorified body does not come until natural existence in a physical body is ended. But when it does, we shall share in the same kind of spiritual existence as our Lord, as surely as we now share in the same kind of physical existence as Adam. And the resemblance will extend even to our appearance.

But if the end of our natural life is a prerequisite to the transformation that allows our participation in the eternal kingdom of God, then what will happen to those who are left alive at the time of Christ's coming and this world's demise? The answer is part of the mysterious wisdom of God's plan. "We will not all sleep, but we will all be changed" (15:51). In the same moment that the dead are raised, those who are alive will also be changed. Their perishable physical existence will be cloaked by the imperishable existence and immortality of a body transformed by God's power, just as with those who have died and been resurrected.

And so the prophetic words of Isaiah 25:8 and Hosea 13:14 will be fulfilled. For, together with those who have been resurrected,

First Corinthians 15:52 says, "For the trumpet will sound, the dead will be raised imperishable, and we will be changed." This stained glass window (Sainte-Chapelle, Paris, ca. 1200) portrays the resurrection of the dead at the trumpet's sound.

those who have not passed through death and resurrection and yet have been transformed will also be able to celebrate their victory in Christ over the sting of death (15:54–55). For death's power over a sinful humanity has been destroyed by Christ, and he gives to all his own, whether living or dead, his victory over death in which they may gratefully share. Consequently, Paul encourages the Corinthians to remain true to their trust in Christ's promise to share with them his victory over death and to devote themselves fully and without fear to the work of the Lord (15:58).

E. Questions about the collection and Paul's plans (16:1–9). A final Corinthian question remains about "the collection for God's people" (see also Rom. 15:25–28; Gal. 2:10). From the content of Paul's reply, their questions seem to have been more concerned with the nature and timing of their own participation than with the collection itself or the rationale behind it. The Corinthians are advised to do as Paul has already directed the "Galatian churches" to do. (Paul's reference must be to a message sent orally or in writing; the Letter to the Galatians contains no explicit reference to the collection or directions for contributors.) Each person is to save up a weekly contribution "in keeping with his income."

Paul neither specifies a level for the gift nor directs that it be collected and held by the church but asks simply that it be set aside weekly in order that he may not have to make a special appeal and so work a special hardship on any member of the church at the time of his arrival. When he arrives, he will give those appointed by the church the appropriate letters of introduction and "send them with your gift to Jerusalem" (16:3; Acts 20:4). Whether Paul will accompany them himself is uncertain as he writes this letter (though it seems almost certain that he did, and that the collection is the reason for a journey to Jerusalem [Acts 20–21]).

Paul now coordinates the instructions for the collection with his own plans. At this point (though as 2 Cor. 1:15–17 indicates, his plans were modified), Paul's hope is to come to Corinth after passing through Macedonia, to stay at Corinth (perhaps even for the winter), and then to continue his journey wherever that may take him. But he does not intend to begin his journey or leave Ephesus (from where this letter is written) until Pentecost; the opportunity for ministry, despite opposition, is simply too great to be abandoned too quickly (16:8–9).

4. The Recommendation of Others (16:10–18)

Paul's response to the Corinthians' questions is now concluded, but his mention of his own plans leads him to relay to his readers what news he has of other persons with whom he and his readers are acquainted. They can expect a visit from Timothy, and when he arrives, they should give him no cause for fear to act and speak openly. Instead, they are to overcome his fears with their acceptance of his ministry and send him back to Paul in peace. (Whether "the brothers" mentioned here are traveling with Timothy or waiting for him with Paul is uncertain.)

Next Paul writes to the Corinthians about Apollos. Paul has indeed seen him and strongly urged him to visit them again (whether on his own initiative or at the Corinthians' request is unclear). But, at least at the time Paul last saw him, "he was quite unwilling to go," and so they must not expect him until a later opportunity presents itself. (Whether Apollos ever returned to Corinth is not known.) Perhaps, however, it is not too much to conjecture that the words of exhortation that immediately follow are meant to reflect Apollos's agreement with the substance of Paul's letter and his own greeting to the church.

Third, Paul commends to his readers those from the household of Stephanas, the first converts in Achaia. They have devoted themselves to the service of the Lord's people and consequently deserve the same submissive respect as others from outside the church who function as teachers and leaders or anyone else who "joins in the work, and labors at it" (16:16).

Finally, Paul conveys to the church that Stephanas, Fortunatus, and Achaicus have arrived, and he gladly commends their service in supplying him with the information that has allowed him to respond more fully to the church's needs. Such men "deserve recognition" for their ministry of keeping the apostle and the church in touch with one another (16:18).

5. Final Greetings and Formal Closing (16:19–24)

As in the opening of this letter, Paul now reverts to the elements that were customary in the closing of a letter in his era. First are closing greetings sent by Paul and by others. The others mentioned include "the churches in the province of Asia" (among which Paul is now working), Aquila and Priscilla (who earlier hosted Paul and worked alongside him in his initial mission in Corinth, departing and journeying with him to Ephesus, where they chose to remain), "the church [at Ephesus] that meets at their house," and "all the brothers" (either the rest of the Ephesian believers or Paul's fellow workers in the Ephesian ministry—in either case the word must be understood as a generic rather than a gender-specific term). The warmth of their greeting to the Corinthians is to be conveyed symbolically with the Corinthians embracing one another in the way that these others would embrace them if they were present. Paul's final greeting in his own hand serves a double purpose: authenticating this letter as his own (Gal. 6:11; Col. 4:18; 2 Thess. 3:17) and indicating that it was probably composed, as was customary, by dictation (Rom. 16:22).

Next, again as was usual, one finds a final short message. Originating perhaps as part of an early Christian worship service (in which the response to the words found here may have been, "If anyone loves the Lord, let him be blessed"), these words seem meant to remind the readers that in the end "love for the Lord" (RSV) is the paramount quality of Christian faith and as such should unite all believers. Similarly the cry "Come, O Lord" (reflecting the Aramaic expression *marana tha*) is also probably cited from the liturgical context of worship that was meant to unite all believers.

Finally, as was normal, a formal closing concludes the letter. Paul's closing ends the letter as it began—with the recognition of God's grace given in Jesus and with the conveyance of his own abiding love for all in Christ.

Outline—2 Corinthians

Commentary

1. Epistolary Introduction (1:1–11)

Paul again opens his letter with a customary greeting (see 1 Cor. 1:1–3). After naming himself as the sender of the letter together with Timothy, he describes himself to the church in words almost identical to those used in his earlier letter. The letter's address indicates that Christians elsewhere in Achaia, probably principally at Cenchreae (Acts 18:18; Rom. 16:1) and Athens (Acts 17:34), have been affected by the recent affairs in the church at Corinth (likely the largest in Achaia). The salutation concludes with Paul's usual Christian greeting.

Thanksgiving typically follows the greeting (see 1 Cor. 1:4–9), but Paul's thanksgiving here is not given over to God for his grace and love at work in the church. Instead, Paul praises God for his comfort made manifest in a particular experience of suffering in Paul's life. The experience itself, which he compares in kind to the "suffering of Christ" as one involving distress, "hardships," "great pressure," despair, the imminence of death, and "deadly peril" (1:5–10), remains unmentioned (perhaps indicating that the Corinthians knew the facts well enough, including the part their own failure to honor Paul and his gospel had played in the apostle's sufferings). Paul chooses rather to extol the "Father of compassion and the God of all comfort" (1:3), from whom he has received the strength to sustain himself in suffering.

Furthermore, precisely because of his experience, which forced him to rely exclusively on God in a situation in which he had given himself up for dead, Paul has become uniquely equipped to minister to "those in any trouble," bringing to them the "comfort we ourselves have received from God" (1:4). In the light of his own experience, Paul seeks to minister comfort and conciliation to the church at Corinth, and he begins by asking for their prayers.

2. Paul's Explanation of His Conduct in Recent Matters (1:12–2:13)

A. The basis for Paul's behavior and an appeal for understanding (1:12–14). Having asked for their prayers, Paul next appeals to the Corinthians in conciliation to reassess their estimation of him and his ministry. Boasting and the kind of criticism that belittles one in order to exalt another had consistently troubled the church and severely complicated its relationship with Paul (1 Cor. 3:21; 4:7; 5:6). Such boasting and criticism were also no doubt responsible in large measure for the pain that Paul had experienced on his last visit to Corinth, pain which led him, in turn, to compose a letter that struck back severely in anguished self-defense (2 Cor. 2:1–4).

But now Paul seeks to clear away the selfish boasting of the past and to make a boast in which he invites the Corinthians to share, a boast in the Lord. In conduct, Paul has always sought to relate to the church "in the holiness and sincerity that are from God" (1:12a). In speech and writing he has similarly shunned the attempt to present a wisdom that invites comparisons between his message and those of others, in favor of a simplicity of thought and advice rooted in "God's grace" (1:12b–13). It is Paul's hope, therefore,

that the Corinthians will come to understand that the only boast to be made among Christians is a boast that unites them with their leaders, a mutual boast in God's holiness, sincerity, and grace at work in their lives.

B. The cause for Paul's change of plans (1:15–2:2). In 1 Corinthians 16:2–8 and at the beginning of this section (1:15–16) are found two different itineraries relating to Paul's plans to revisit the Corinthian church. However, as 2:1 indicates, neither plan was carried through. Thus, it appeared as though Paul was at best not truly concerned with his relationship to the church and at worst a fickle person who made promises "lightly" (1:17) and constantly went back on his word.

Once more Paul meets this obstacle to reconciliation squarely and clarifies the reasons for his conduct by relating his actions to the conviction he shares with the Corinthians concerning God's faithfulness. Paul, Silas, and Timothy preached Christ with consistency in such a way as to emphasize that all God's promises were faithfully fulfilled in him. No matter their number or the length of time taken in mercy to bring them to fulfillment or the manner, expected or unexpected, in which they are fulfilled, the eventual fulfillment of God's promises demonstrates his glorious faithfulness. Those who are in Christ place their hope for what is yet to come on this kind of faithfulness, demonstrated especially in the receipt of the Holy Spirit.

But it is also just this kind of faithfulness that has motivated Paul to change the manner in which his plans should come to pass. Not out of a faithless, fickle sense of self-importance, but out of a merciful desire not to grieve the church (2:2), Paul has changed his plans; his desire is to work with the Corinthians rather than to act based purely on his own original agenda (1:24). This goal has led Paul to set aside his previous plans and to work out a different schedule for their eventual fulfillment.

C. The purpose of Paul's last letter (2:3–11). As a part of his altered agenda, Paul wrote a third letter to the church (for reference to the first, see 1 Cor. 5:9; the second is our canonical 1 Corinthians), the purpose of which he now seeks to explain. It was written so that on his next return to Corinth he might not "be distressed by those who ought to make me rejoice," in confidence and trust that such distress could be avoided so as to produce a joyful visit for all (2:3). But in order to achieve its end, Paul's letter had first to deal openly and honestly with the source of the problem. To write such a letter was certainly not easy, for its purpose was not simply to rebuke but to share with the church the anguish of an unrequited love.

The letter seems to have achieved its intent (2:9), and with reconciliation now possible, Paul hastens to make sure that it is accomplished. He urges the cessation of the punishment inflicted on the individual who opposed his authority, causing distress both for Paul and for the church, and counsels forgiveness, granting it freely himself in concert with the rest of the church (2:5, 7, 10). Then, with particular pastoral sensitivity to the needs of the offender as well as those of the body and himself, Paul encourages the community not only to forgive the offender but also to comfort him and to reaffirm its love for him. This they should do lest he be "overwhelmed with excessive sorrow" and the discipline that was meant to be remedial become simply retributive, thus allowing Satan yet another entrance into the situation (2:7–8, 11).

D. The motive for Paul's movement from Troas to Macedonia (2:12–13). In this, the final segment of Paul's explanation of his recent conduct, he seeks to acquaint the church with events in his ministry from the time of his last

letter until the present moment of composition. In all probability Paul's "painful" letter had been dispatched to Corinth with Titus from Ephesus. But from there, before receiving a reply, Paul departed to Troas. Despite the open door for the gospel of Christ that presented itself to Paul in Troas, he had been unable to feel at peace without news from Titus, and so in an attempt to meet Titus on the route of his return, he had gone on to Macedonia.

3. Paul's Reflection on His Ministry (2:14–5:21)

A. The source and character of Paul's ministry (2:14–3:6a). Surprisingly, the conclusion to the account of Paul's anxious attempt to meet the returning Titus is not immediately related. Instead, we are made to wait until 7:5 to receive the conclusion of the narrative. In the interim, Paul gives us the opportunity to share in some of his own reflections on the nature of his ministry. The catalyst for these reflections is clearly the relationship between Paul and the church at Corinth in general, and the return of Titus to Paul with news of his recent visit to Corinth in particular. But in their breadth and scope Paul's words within this section describe, perhaps better than any other part of the Pauline correspondence, the apostle's own sense of mission and ministry.

Paul begins his reflections, accordingly, by giving thanks to God, for in its essence his apostolic ministry is simply a part of "Christ's triumphal procession," which is directed and

A "triumphal procession" (2 Cor. 2:14) was the conclusion to a military victory when the conquerors returned home. This first-century-AD chalice displays a procession by the emperor Tiberius.

guided by God (2:14). The verbal imagery used here is intended to allude to a Roman triumph, a procession carefully orchestrated by a Roman military commander to display the results of a significant military victory. As a part of some of these processions, fragrant spices, perfumes, and incense were used along the way, and it may be that this inspires the description of Paul's ministry as a conveyance for the aroma of Christ. The image, however, is mixed here with another drawn from the Old Testament (where a pleasing aroma is said to result from a ritual sacrifice [Lev. 1:9, 13, 17]). The aroma of Paul's ministry, as a part of the aroma of Christ, can be said to ascend to God at the same time that it diffuses among men and women, both those who are being saved and those who are perishing (2:15–16a; 1 Cor. 1:18).

To be the bearer of an aroma so potent as to lead to life for its recipients and death for those who reject its fragrance is a heavy responsibility. To be "equal to such a task" seems overwhelming (2:16b). But, at the same time, it is important to Paul to note that, unlike many who "peddle the word of God for profit," he has made a conscientious attempt to bring himself to the task with sincerity and a sense that the proclamation of the gospel is always made before God as well as a human audience (2:17).

His words, however, in the context of the competition for ecclesiastical leadership that had been going on at Corinth (1 Cor. 1:12; 2 Cor. 10:1–13:13), needed careful clarification on two counts. First, there was the possibility that they might be read by some as a purely subjective self-commendation, and second, there was the likelihood that they might prompt an immediate comparison between Paul and others who carried formal letters of recommendation.

Paul takes up the latter point by first claiming the Corinthians themselves as the recommendation for his ministry (3:2). And unlike a letter that Paul or anyone else might write, the testimony commending the faithful work of the apostle has been permanently written by the Spirit of the living God in their lives. Then,

moving back to the former point, Paul reminds his readers that his confidence is a product not of self-analysis but of his relationship with God through Christ. Therefore, only God can give persons the competence that makes them equal to the task of functioning as ministers of a new covenant.

B. The message of Paul's ministry (3:6b–4:6). But, as is so often the case in Paul's writings, the terms that are used to conclude one argument lead inevitably to the opening of another. (This is also commonplace in Jewish literary style in general.) Here the mention of a new covenant (see Jer. 31:31–34) inspires a transition in thought from discussion about the source and character of Paul's ministry to a consideration of its message. Paul presents it in terms of a comparison between the ministry that carried as its essence the written covenant "of the letter" (Exod. 24:3–8) and the ministry that proclaims the new covenant of the Spirit (the nature of the comparison suggests, as does 11:22, that the distress in the church at Corinth has come from some who pressured the whole of the church toward a strict allegiance to the law and customs of Judaism).

The comparison does not proceed, however, by way of deprecation, describing the latter ministry as glorious and the former as inglorious. Rather, Paul makes a comparison between the recognized and authentic "glory" of the former covenant (3:7, 9a, 11a) and the "surpassing glory" of the latter (3:8, 9b, 10, 11b). The argument is strengthened by allusion to the account of the gift of the law (Exod. 34:29–35). Paul provides an interpretative commentary on the meaning of this passage, inferring from the Septuagintal text that the glory radiating from Moses's face when he brought the gift of the law down from the mount was a fading rather than a permanent possession, one perpetuated only by Moses's frequent reentrance into God's presence. The glory of Moses's ministry in bringing to Israel the covenant of the law was therefore real but transitory. The glory of Christian ministry in proclaiming the new covenant is greater, for it "lasts" (3:11).

In this context of comparison Paul proceeds to set forth a contrast between the two ministries, a contrast between the effect of the "letter" and that of the Spirit (3:6). The contrast, however, is marked. For the letter, being lifeless, had no power to effect the way of life it commanded, and consequently it became that which "condemned" and "brought death" rather than life (3:7, 9). But the Spirit, a living and active part of God's being, has precisely that power which the law lacked, the power that effectively "brings righteousness" (3:7; not only a knowledge of righteousness) and gives life. Thus the conclusion follows by contrast, as well as comparison, that a ministry in service of the new covenant surpasses one in service of the old.

This perspective on the value of Christian ministry then motivates Paul to bold proclamation. He has put no veil on his message in an attempt to shield the surpassing glory of the gospel from his fellow Jews (as had Moses, who had hidden the glow of God's glory behind a veil [Exod. 34:33–35]). Instead, it was quite the other way around. If Paul's message was veiled, that was only because the law and its traditional interpretation (given "when the old covenant is read") had veiled and dulled Jewish minds to the truth of the gospel. But, as experience has shown, whenever they turn to the Lord, that veil "is taken away" (3:16; Exod. 34:34), and it is removed (according to Paul's interpretation of Exod. 34:34) under the inspiration of the Spirit. For the Spirit brings freedom from the systematic adherence of Judaism to the law and its traditional interpretation; the Spirit actually enables the transformation of existence that was the intention behind the letter of the law (3:17–18).

And so, transformed "through God's mercy," Paul has been given the ministry of bearing the message that transforms its recipients. Because he has been sent from God, his proclamation can embrace neither "deception" nor the distortion of anything that God has said in the past (4:2).

Thus, where the message remains obscure, one may be sure that such obscurity is not a result of the proclamation but a result of the work of the enemy, the god of this age (cf. John 12:31), who has blinded the minds of those who persist in unbelief to the light of the gospel. Neither can the proclamation promote its bearer but only its subject, Jesus Christ, the Lord who is the very image of God (and therefore the true and second Adam, the beginning of a new creation [see 2 Cor. 5:17]). Only through Christ can the full light of God's glory become known.

C. The cost of Paul's ministry (4:7–5:10). A change of metaphor signals the beginning of a new thought, though it is closely related to all that Paul has just said. For the light of the gospel may also be described as that which has been placed within the minds and hearts of its human bearers as a treasure placed within "jars of clay" (cf. Matt. 13:44). The power that transforms belongs to the treasure, not to its receptacle. But the receptacle, though remaining frail, is itself measurably changed by its contents.

Abandoning metaphorical language, Paul proceeds now to describe the change that has come about since the placement of the treasure within him. It is not a change in the conditions or circumstances of his life (for pressure and perplexity continue to be a part of his experience, together with persecution and physical beatings that have come more recently, since the beginning of his ministry). Instead it is a change in the attitude and fortitude of the apostle, which has enabled him to bear suffering and even to triumph in the midst of it.

For the power of the treasure is clearly "revealed" through the weakness and frailty of its mortal receptacle (4:10–11). So even while death is at work on Paul, "life is at work" through him for the "benefit" of those to whom he ministers, and this provides Paul with compensation for the cost of his ministry (4:12, 15). Moreover, a sure confidence provides Paul with further compensation. It is the confidence that even should death prevail, "the one who raised the Lord Jesus from the dead will also raise us with

Jesus and present us with you in his presence" (4:14). Such compensatory thoughts, kept ever more securely in view because of the inexorable renewal of his inner self, prevent Paul from despair and provide him with a new perspective on his present afflictions.

Paul, of course, has spoken to the Corinthians before about the hope of resurrection, but now he sees an opportunity to develop his thoughts further. So, in a passage that has given rise to a wealth of interpretation, Paul proceeds to reveal what he expects for himself beyond death. He employs a metaphorical description of the body as an earthly tent (5:1), in terms of his own experience (Acts 18:3) and the cultural background of his audience (the physical body having been described as a "tent" in Greek literature since the time of Plato and Pythagoras).

Paul begins by restating his confidence (built on the experience of Christ) in the reality of the resurrection (5:1; cf. 4:14; 1 Cor. 15:4, 12–20). Then, taking his teaching one step beyond its formulation in 1 Corinthians 15:35–53, Paul attempts to explain more fully how our earthly tent will be transformed like that of our Lord into "an eternal house in heaven" (5:1; cf. John 2:19–22) to become "our heavenly dwelling" (5:4). The transformation will take place when

our bodies receive a new "clothing" (5:2; see also 1 Cor. 15:53). But rather than suggest that such a "clothing" implies the death of the mortal body and the "unclothing" of the immortal soul (a view that appears to have been favored by some at Corinth [5:3; 1 Cor. 15:12, 35]), Paul asserts that the "clothing" process of resurrection takes place when our current "clothing" is "overclothed" "so that what is mortal may be swallowed up by life" (5:4). "For this very purpose" God created both the body and the soul: not for the destruction of either but for the redemption of both. For this reason also the Spirit of the immortal God has already entered our bodies, as a "deposit guaranteeing what is to come" (5:5).

Thus Paul is "confident," as one who lives by faith and not by sight, that when at last he leaves his home in the body, he will be transformed in a way that will allow him to be at home with the Lord. But then as now the "goal" will be to

This stone structure found in Corinth was known as a bema, or speaker's platform. It was where orators spoke and officials made their formal judicial rulings. When Paul refers to the "judgment seat" (Greek *bēma*) of Christ (2 Cor. 5:10), this may have been the image he held in mind.

give the pleasure of a returned love and service to the Lord who loved us and laid down his life for us. Against the standard of his love for us the adequacy of our response will be measured (5:6–10).

D. The perspective of Paul's ministry (5:11–21). Paul's mission proceeds with these expectations, and as they are known to God, so now they have been made known to God's people at Corinth. In making his hopes and fears known, however, Paul is not "trying to commend" himself, but only sharing with the Corinthians in a way that will allow them to take the measure of his apostleship in truth apart from appearances. For all that Paul has done has been in response to the compulsion of Christ's love, demonstrated in Christ's willingness to die for all and include all in his death (5:14; cf. Rom. 6:5–11; 1 Cor. 15:22; Gal. 2:20; Col. 3:3). No longer then can those who belong to Christ live for themselves; they must live instead at the direction of "him who died for them and was raised again" (5:15).

Furthermore, if Christ has died for all, then a purely human perspective can no longer form the basis for judgments about the worth of his actions or the value in his plan for any man or woman. Anyone who is in Christ (i.e., who belongs to him through incorporation into his body) has already become a part of a new creation (i.e., a part of the transformation of human existence that has begun in Christ and will culminate in the re-creation of heaven and earth [Rom. 8:19–23; 1 Cor. 15:22; 2 Pet. 3:10, 13; Rev. 21:1]). They have passed beyond the point of living solely as a part of the old creation (though a part of that which is "old" has been left both within and without, in our bodies and our world) and have begun to live as a part of the new created order.

Moreover, the source of such new creation is God, whose work, as in the creation accounts of the Old Testament, forms the decisive beginning for it. For "God was reconciling the world to himself in Christ" (5:19; the order of words within this Greek clause is ambiguous and has produced a variety of translations). The achievement of the work, however, depended on Christ. For the new creation was allowed to proceed without counting the "sins" of the old only because "God made him who had no sin to be sin for us" (5:19, 21). And now the extension of the work rests on those to whom have been entrusted the ministry and the message of reconciliation. For God has chosen to extend his work in Christ through "Christ's ambassadors," through them making his appeal to be reconciled to God to those who do not yet participate in the new creation (5:20).

4. Paul's Appeal to the Corinthians (6:1–13:10)

A. An appeal for complete reconciliation (6:1–7:4). As one of "God's co-workers," chosen to bear the message of reconciliation, Paul now presents the Corinthians with the first in a series of appeals, urging them "not to receive God's grace" in vain (6:1). In context these words seem meant to spur the Corinthians to respond to Paul's attempt at reconciliation with the church. The citation (from Isa. 49:8) and its interpretation may then be seen as reinforcement to the appeal, entreating the church to respond without delay. Paul reminds them of what he has already written in an attempt to remove any "stumbling block" that might impede the progress of reconciliation (6:3) and then seeks to persuade the church to look again at what he has done for them as one of the servants of God.

A statement summarizing the sufferings that the apostle has endured on behalf of the church now ensues. If one follows the suggestions of Murray J. Harris, the nine items are a list of general, humanly inflicted, and self-imposed trials that Paul associated with his apostleship (Harris 1976, 357). Under the first heading come "troubles, hardships and distresses" (6:4); under the second, "beatings, imprisonments and riots" (6:5a); and under the third, "hard work, sleepless nights and hunger" (6:5b).

Next comes a corresponding list of Christian virtues that have marked Paul's apostolic ministry (6:6–7). These include "purity" (the moral uprightness that gave credence to the witness of Paul's life and mission [1 Thess. 2:10–12]), "understanding" (which balanced the apostolic commitment to holiness among believers with a godly compassion and forgiveness [Eph. 4:32; 1 Thess. 2:7]), and the "patience" and "kindness" associated with a "sincere love" inspired by the Holy Spirit (1 Cor. 13:4). Also mentioned among the marks of Paul's ministry are truthful speech (see also 2 Cor. 4:2; 11:31; 13:8), the power of God (Rom. 15:19; 1 Cor. 2:4; 4:20; Eph. 3:20; Jesus's own ministry is characterized by the conjoining of proclamation and power [Luke 7:22–23]), and the weapons of righteousness (2 Cor. 10:4; Eph. 6:14).

Then, in a series of contrasts, Paul brings the paradoxical experience of the apostle fully and realistically into view. In external appearance Paul's apostolic ministry may indeed at times have seemed to some, not the least of whom were Paul's opponents, to be characterized by marks of ineffectiveness and failure. But Paul makes his appeal with the eye of faith, with a perspective that looks through appearances and perceives the realities of God's power at work in his ministry.

Having "spoken freely" in an attempt to lay open

his ministry before them and make himself fully vulnerable in love and "affection," Paul brings his appeal for reconciliation to its legitimate close by entreating the Corinthians in "fair exchange" to open their hearts to his ministry (6:11–12). A part of such openness, however, entailed the church giving heed to his apostolic authority. Accordingly, in order to effect a full reconciliation, Paul urges the Corinthians not to "be yoked together with unbelievers" (6:14).

The source for such metaphorical language is undoubtedly Deuteronomy 22:10, which prohibits the yoking together of an ox and a donkey for purposes of plowing, but the precise application intended by the apostle is elusive. Clearly all association is not forbidden, and so it is probably best to understand Paul's injunction here to prohibit only those relationships in which the degree of association entails an inevitable compromise with Christian standards

Participation in pagan idolatry was an ongoing problem in the Corinthian church (2 Cor. 6:14–7:1). The remains of the Temple of Octavia (shown here) indicate that the imperial cult had a strong foothold in Corinth.

of conduct. The injunction is accordingly followed by a series of five rhetorical questions, all of which point to crucial differences between the believer and unbeliever. The fifth question epitomizes the contrast "between the temple of God and idols" (6:16), which is reminiscent of 1 Corinthians and probably represents the best clue to the apostle's intent in this passage (see 1 Cor. 8:10–11; 10:14, 19–21).

This question also affords Paul the opportunity to reiterate that together Christians form the temple of the living God, a truth that has brought to fulfillment the divine vow that was made at various points throughout the history of Israel (Exod. 25:8; 29:45; Lev. 26:11–12; 1 Kings 6:13; Jer. 32:38; Ezek. 37:27). In light of this, Paul, adapting the words of Isaiah 52:11 and Ezekiel 20:34, 41, urges the Corinthians to separate themselves from unbelievers and from practices that involve the use of "unclean things" (6:17; his words do not refer to the separations inaugurated by Christians because of doctrinal differences). As a conclusion to this series of scriptural citations, Paul returns to the thought with which he began and underlines his principal point in personal terms. As sons and daughters (the reference to women here is noteworthy and probably reflects a deliberate attempt to speak to a congregation in which women played an active, vital, and respected part [1 Cor. 7:3–4; 11:5]), Christians belong in association with the Lord almighty, who has promised to be a Father to each of them. Simultaneously, it is necessary for all who possess such promises to keep both body and spirit free from those associations that undermine their central commitment to the holiness that shows their "reverence for God" (7:1).

Having urged upon the church actions appropriate to reconciliation, Paul concludes his appeal with a reiteration of his own readiness for reconciliation. What he has said has been to show, contrary apparently to the claims of his detractors, that no one has been wronged, corrupted, or "exploited" by Paul's ministry (7:2). Furthermore, in making an attempt at reconciliation that urges a change in the associations of some within the church, it has not been Paul's intent to condemn. Instead, as one devoted to their service, Paul has sought to convey his confidence and pride in their ability to conform themselves to his apostolic counsel.

B. A new basis for appeal (7:5–16). In this section Paul resumes the autobiographical narrative that was broken off in 2:13 to allow for the inclusion of the reflective apologetic of 2:14–5:19 and the appeals for reconciliation found in 5:20–7:4. The break in the narrative may reflect Paul's desire, having heard the "comforting" news Titus brought back from Corinth, to convey to the church both his immediate and his considered reaction to their new attitude toward him. Furthermore, upon consideration, it may have seemed more important to present the latter before the former. In any case, he resumes the story as he left off, with himself in Macedonia struggling against external adversities and inner "fears" (7:5).

Within the context of such need and the humility imposed by it, God habitually acts to comfort the downcast (Isa. 40:1; Matt. 5:4; James 4:6–10; 1 Pet. 5:5–6). In his own case, therefore, Paul interpreted the coming of Titus, and the news he brought of the Corinthians' renewed "concern" for their apostle, as a real and divinely wrought comfort (7:6–7). But it was not only Paul who had suffered through the events of the recent past. The church had also experienced remorse upon their receipt of his last letter. Thus, while it had not been Paul's intention to inflict sorrow on those who had caused him to be sorrowful, in this instance, through God's working, an unintended effect led to an unexpectedly quick and thorough "repentance," leaving neither Paul nor the church with any sense of regret (7:9–10).

Quite to the contrary, the sorrow that was divinely inspired had produced an eagerness within the majority at Corinth to clear themselves and an eagerness within Paul to recognize the "innocence" that belonged to the majority of those within the church (7:11–13).

Moreover, Titus himself had been uplifted and had become enthusiastic in his "affection" for the congregation (7:14–15). Such an unexpectedly rich outcome from a letter sent with such hesitation was indeed an occasion for gladness and for an expression of renewed confidence in the church's ability to pay heed to future apostolic appeals.

C. An appeal for full response to the collection (8:1–9:15).
Having expressed renewed confidence in the Corinthian church, Paul now proceeds to a further appeal concerning "service to the Lord's people" (8:4). The service the apostle has in mind involves the collection of an offering intended to supply the "needs of God's people" and to be a manifest "expression of thanks to God" (9:12). There seems no doubt that this is the same gift for Jerusalem that was first mentioned in 1 Corinthians 16:3 (see also Rom. 15:26–27). Obviously, in the period between the writing of our two canonical letters, the subject had been put aside because of the strained relationship between Paul and the church. But now it recurs, for the receipt of the collection is a project in which Paul is presently engaged among the "Macedonian churches" (8:1).

Indeed, it is the "rich generosity" (8:2) of the Macedonian Christians that Paul holds up as he urges the Corinthians to renew their involvement in this endeavor. The Macedonians' generous giving (8:1–5), however, has not sprung from human nature. It is a tangible expression of the grace of God at work in the lives of those who have given themselves to the Lord. It has originated without effort by Paul,

continued despite the "most severe trial" and extreme poverty (8:2), and produced joy among all those who have contributed "as much as they were able" (8:3; cf. Mark 12:41–44).

It is such giving, inspired by grace, that Paul seeks from the church at Corinth (8:6–15), and with good reason. Titus has already been able to report that a new beginning was made during his visit. However, in order that the church might be given full opportunity to excel in "this grace of giving" (8:7), Paul has urged Titus to return to Corinth and "bring also to completion this act of grace" (8:6). In accordance with the nature of the collection, giving is not commanded, but Paul does confess to an attempt to put the "sincerity" of the church's love for others to the test of a comparison (8:8). To do this is only to recognize that the Corinthian church contains persons much more able to give than their Macedonian sisters and brothers. Accordingly, Paul urges the Corinthians to imitate Christ, who though he was rich yet agreed willingly to become poor "so that you through his poverty might become rich" (8:9; cf. Phil. 2:5–11).

Paul is unwilling, however, to conclude his appeal apart from the provision of some specific advice with respect to response. As this is

This inscription, which says, "Erastus, the city treasurer, greets you," is likely speaking of the same person as Paul mentioned in Romans 16:23. A portion of the church in Corinth was quite wealthy, and Paul exhorted them to follow the lead of the poorer churches of Macedonia to give to the support of the Lord's people (2 Cor. 8:1–15).

now the third time an appeal is being made to the church (1 Cor. 16:1–4; 2 Cor. 8:6), Paul's primary counsel to the church is to "finish the work," so that the "willingness" to respond, which has been commendably evident from the inception of the collection, may at last be matched by the "completion" of a corporate gift that is "according to [their] means" (8:11). The principle behind Paul's advice thus becomes clear. It is the free decision to give that renders the gift acceptable. Accordingly, one should give joyfully, "according to what one has," and not attempt out of a sense of zeal or pious duty to give what one "does not have" (8:12).

Paul drives home the principle. His "desire" is not to pressure the Corinthians but instead to urge on them a uniquely biblical notion of equality that regards the "plenty" of one as that which exists to supply the "need" of another (8:13–14). The idea is then illustrated, in a fashion characteristic of the Corinthian letters, by an appeal to Scripture (8:15, based on Exod. 16:18).

Prior, however, to the use of gifts in an effort to "honor the Lord" and demonstrate an "eagerness to help" (8:19), there remained the problem of the actual collection at Corinth. Apparently, as Paul was pondering precisely how to handle this task, Titus took the "initiative" (8:16–17). Paul, in turn, seeks in this section to commend Titus to the church.

But Titus is not to be commended and sent on alone (8:16–24). So that no one may suspect Paul's motives, and in order to avoid "criticism," Titus is to be accompanied by an unnamed brother whose reputation is beyond reproach, and who has been "chosen" by the common consent of the churches (presumably all the churches associated with the collection) to "carry the offering" (8:18–21).

Moreover, Paul is sending a third brother (who is either a Corinthian or a man whose confidence in them derives from some other background [see 8:22]) in order, Paul implies, to inspire the church with his own zeal. Nonetheless, it is Titus whom Paul commends most

warmly as his personal partner and co-worker in the ministry. The other brothers come as "representatives of the churches" and as an "honor to Christ" (8:23). It is therefore both to Paul and to the churches that the Corinthians are asked to demonstrate the "proof of [their] love" (8:24).

Though the appeal might naturally have been concluded at the end of the previous chapter, Paul again brings up the "eagerness" of the Corinthians "to help" (9:2), suggesting that the preceding section is somewhat parenthetical. The resumption of discussion about the Corinthians' contribution to the collection, however, allows the apostle to stress to the Christians at Corinth that there is a need for their actual readiness to contribute as well as their willingness to do so (9:1–5), and affords him an opportunity to carry further his advice to the church about the way in which contributions should be decided on.

Once more Paul seeks to motivate the church by referring to the initial response to his appeal. Indeed, the apostle has been using the example of their readiness as a model in urging the Macedonians to give to the collection (9:2). Consequently, it is in the interest of both Paul's integrity ("that our boasting about you . . . should not prove hollow" [9:3]) and the Corinthians' honor that all who have promised to give be urged to bring the collection of their contributions to completion, lest they be "unprepared" for the arrival of any Macedonians who might accompany Paul, and be "ashamed" at their failure (9:4). A purpose for the parenthetical section in the previous chapter thus becomes clear. In order that the work might be finished and the contributions ready and waiting as an authentic gift, all the brothers, including Titus, are being sent.

Paul closes his appeal (9:6–15) by way of reminder, either seeking to recall his own previous teaching or perhaps referring to some portion of the Gospel tradition (Luke 6:38; 19:11–27). In either case, however, the saying about sowing and reaping serves to decisively correlate giving with a Christian's financial welfare. Accordingly, each person should feel free to decide in faith on the amount of a gift. The emotion that accompanies a Christian's gift should be one of joy rather than any sense of compulsion or reluctance.

This will be facilitated if the Corinthians will also remember that God has promised to care abundantly for their needs (Matt. 6:25–34). Thus at "all times" they may confidently step forward and contribute to every good work (9:8). For, in accordance with the Scripture (Ps. 112:9), the person who does so will acquire an enduring sense of having done what is right. Such a person may also rest assured that God will continually and generously resupply the resources that have been expended "so that [he or she] can be generous on every occasion," enabling both righteousness and thanksgiving to increase (9:10–11).

Thus the service of giving may be seen not only as an offering to meet human "needs" but also as a way to make possible the increased worship of God. "Expressions of thanks" and "praise" will undoubtedly result, witness to the transforming power of the gospel of Christ will be eloquently and effectively rendered, and "prayers" will be offered in sincerity for the continued growth of the church in the grace that is part of God's "indescribable" gift (9:12–15).

D. An appeal for full allegiance to apostolic authority (10:1–18). There is a perceptible change in the tone of Paul's letter beginning at this point and continuing until its end. But the degree of difference, and the reasons for it, are much less clear. In any event, some continuity with the previous context is afforded by the repetition of a formal appeal (10:1–6); in this case, the appeal concerns apostolic authority.

The appeal is sounded in the midst of apparent doubt among some at Corinth about Paul's ability to exercise apostolic authority in a clear and compelling way, especially when face-to-face with his audience, as over against his ability and willingness to write in a bold way from a distance. For his own part, Paul refuses, in imitation of the meekness and gentleness of Christ (see also 1 Cor. 4:12; 1 Pet. 2:23), to be moved to a demonstration of his authority simply by the challenge to do so (cf. Matt. 4:3, 6). Instead, before the necessity for authoritative action imposes itself, he chooses to beg that the challenge be withdrawn.

If it is not, then a demonstration will indeed take place. But it will not be a demonstration of Paul's deficiencies, as his opponents anticipate. It will be instead a show of the divine power that operates through the Lord's chosen apostles without regard to the criteria of authority that are recognized and accorded weight in this world (see Acts 4:13; 1 Cor. 2:1–5). For God has empowered those whom he has commissioned with weapons that "demolish arguments" about authority and "every pretension" of those who set their own perceptions about the ability to exercise power against the knowledge that comes from God (10:5). Accordingly, should it be necessary, Paul will not hesitate to take action that will "take captive every thought to make it obedient to Christ," nor neglect the punishment due "every act of disobedience" once order and respect have been restored (10:5–6).

Paul's appeal has been made necessary because of the appearance of some at Corinth who have tried to dissuade the church from continuing allegiance to Paul as a primary apostolic authority (10:7–18). Their attempt to undermine Paul's rightful claim to authority has had two thrusts.

On the one hand, they seek to belittle Paul by drawing a distinction between the frightening authority with which he gave instructions to the church when absent and his inability to manifest a similar authority through speech and the power of his person when actually present. In reply, Paul reminds his readers that as long as they look simply at the "surface" of such an allegation it may seem to have the appearance of the truth, especially when promoted by Christians who confidently proclaim that in offering this observation they "belong to Christ" (10:7). But the claim of allegiance to Christ is not an exclusive possession, and if it legitimately belongs to anyone, it certainly belongs to Paul as much as his detractors. Consequently, though the apostle will admit to a more open use of the authority that the Lord has given to him when writing, he will permit no one to think that he is embarrassed to assert such authority when seeking to build up the body of Christ with either letters or "actions" (10:8–11).

On the other hand, those who oppose Paul attempt to elevate their own authority by making a boast that their credentials and associations commend them as persons who enjoy a higher status than Paul in the eyes of many other churches. Paul, however, refuses to respond to the challenge of comparison directly. Instead, he draws attention more subtly to the fact that the terms of measurement and comparison employed by his opponents are largely self-serving, allowing them only to "compare themselves with themselves" (10:12). Similarly, they refuse to recognize that the limits of Paul's work and reputation are not due to any lack of eminence but rather to the fact that he has devoted himself exclusively to the field that "God has assigned" him, including the church at Corinth (10:13–14).

Accordingly, because he has received his own divine commission (Acts 9:6, 15; 26:16–18; Gal. 2:11–17), Paul does not attempt to bolster his authority by "boasting" of associations between his work and that "done by others" (10:15), as do his opponents. Instead, he simply expresses the hope that his labor in trying to build up the church at Corinth will eventually lead to the preaching of the gospel in "regions beyond" Corinth (10:16). For it is only through mission beyond the churches that are already established, and not through repeated incursions into territory that has already been evangelized, that the Lord's commission will be accomplished (Matt. 28:19–20; Acts 1:8). Commendation, therefore, belongs not to the "one who commends himself" but to the one who answers the call of the Lord and makes his "boast" in the divine commission (10:17–18).

E. Support for the appeal (11:1–12:13). Having made his appeal, countering both the criticism and the self-commendation of his opponents, Paul proceeds to support it by pointing to several subsidiary issues (in 11:1–6, that of faithfulness to the gospel) at stake in this contest for authority. To do this, however, he must engage in the foolishness of an apology in defense of himself and his preaching. But because of his jealous love for the Corinthians, and his desire as their "father" to present the church to Christ as a "pure virgin" bride, untainted by the errors of others, Paul is willing to make his appeal on any terms (11:2).

Paul's chief concern, however, is not his own status but the minds of his converts (men or women), which "may somehow be led astray" by arguments about authority and deceived about truth in this matter as effectively as was Eve (11:3; Gen. 3:1–7). The crux of his concern is the immaturity of the Corinthians' faith and their consequent childlike acceptance of those who claim authority in the name of the Lord but whose views about Jesus, the nature of the gospel, and the experience of the Spirit are significantly different from those that were originally proclaimed at Corinth. Consequently, since the comprehension of the gospel is at issue, Paul will not permit the church to entertain even for a moment the idea that his credentials as an apostle are at all inferior to those of anyone his detractors put above him. And no one, Paul trusts, will be blinded to this by the fallacious argument that his knowledge about the faith is somehow inadequate because his self-expression is ineloquent.

Another issue in the contest for authority concerned proper apostolic practice with respect to the receipt of financial support (11:7–15). As was the case with the issue of faithfulness to the gospel, the Corinthians were apparently poised to accept a twisting of the truth that Paul had already taught them about the freedom of an apostle to make use, or not to make use, of financial support from his converts (see 1 Cor. 9:3–18). His opponents apparently charged that Paul's stance demonstrated he had only an imperfect knowledge of the Lord's will for an apostle and that his refusal to accept support from his converts during his initial mission at Corinth indicated lack of love for the church.

Paul, however, adamantly refuses to accept either that he has sinned against the Lord's will by "preaching the gospel . . . free of charge" (11:7) or that his rejection of Corinthian support demonstrates any lack of love. He reminds them that he acted as he did not because of any lack of knowledge about the propriety of the principle of support (for while he was with them he was "receiving support" from "other churches") but out of a pastoral desire not to burden his converts immediately with the necessity of his financial welfare (11:8–9). Thus he vows to continue his practice of not accepting support from his converts during an initial mission and to make such a practice a part of his distinctive apostolic boast.

As for those who have come to Corinth to contest his authority to act as he has, Paul charges that they themselves cannot make any truthful claim to be apostles. Insofar then as they have claimed apostolic authority for their mistaken teaching, they are deceitful workmen and servants of Satan, who characteristically promotes falsehood by "masquerading" as a bearer of the light of true knowledge (11:13–15a). If these people do not desist, "their end will be what their actions deserve" (11:15b).

A third issue raised in the struggle for authority at Corinth involved the respective credentials of Paul and his opponents (11:16–32). If an inspection were made, charged Paul's detractors, then his inferiority to them, or if not to them then to those they claimed as sponsors, would be clearly seen. But contrary to his adversaries' expectations, and perhaps to those of some of the Corinthians, Paul takes up the challenge to compare his background and service with his rivals', refusing to be written off by anyone as a foolish inferior.

The real foolishness, he charges, belongs to those at Corinth who consider themselves wise

enough to make decisions about the possessors of apostolic authority. In putting up with the boasting of Paul's opponents and evaluating their claim according to "the way" of "the world," they have ignored the truth that persons who resort to boasting to establish their authority are "not talking as the Lord would" (11:17–19). To such Corinthians also belongs (as Paul seeks to emphasize through ridicule) an illogical tolerance of teaching that aims to "enslave" or "exploit," and a ludicrous willingness to accept as an authority anyone who attempts to dominate them (11:20). Accordingly, in words full of irony, Paul observes that with such criteria sensitivity may justly be construed as weakness, and he laments his lack of strength. Nevertheless, in an attempt to redeem his own, Paul is ready to descend to whatever type of comparison they might find persuasive and to match any kind of boast.

If some Corinthians are awed by the fact that Paul's rivals are Hebrews, Israelites, or descendants of Abraham (whether there is a distinction between these terms is of little consequence), then Paul is equally entitled to such respect. If, on the other hand, the claim that has captured the Corinthians' admiration is the boast that Paul's opponents have been greater servants of Christ, then clearly the evidence should tip any scale of comparison in Paul's favor (though it is truly senseless to think of making such comparative evaluations of the Lord's servants [1 Cor. 3:5–7; 4:1–5]).

To substantiate his case, Paul now presents a summary (which goes beyond the record of Acts in completeness while demonstrating at the same time its essential trustworthiness) of his apostolic service. However, in laying claim to the title "servant of Christ," as it has become necessary for Paul to do in the face of opposition, he submits for primary consideration incidents that display his moments of weakness and vulnerability rather than those that demonstrate accomplishments won as a result of his personal strengths.

In an effort to bear the gospel to the world, Paul has repeatedly suffered the lashes of the Jews, beatings inflicted by the "rods" of Gentiles (Acts 16:22), and the stones cast at him by both (Acts 14:19). He has been willing to expose himself to the physical dangers associated with travel on land and sea, and to the emotional stress of recurrent conflicts with "false brothers" (11:24–26). He has uncomplainingly endured countless personal deprivations, including nights "without sleep," hunger and thirst, exposure to the cold without clothing, and the kind of hard labor and toil that might more naturally have been done by persons below his station in life. Finally, he has daily faced the inner "pressure of concern" for those in the churches he has left behind who have found their faith weak in moments of crisis or who have fallen away from faith and back into "sin" (11:27–29).

To verify his testimony, Paul takes an oath, solemnly swearing its truth in the name of the God and Father of the Lord Jesus. Then, as a last example typifying much of what he has said about facing danger, opposition, and hardship, Paul relates how he was forced to flee the city of Damascus in secret (11:32–33; Acts 9:23–25). It is in demonstrations of divine power at work to support him in such moments of human vulnerability that Paul urges his audience to seek confirmation of his right to be called an apostle.

A final issue, closely related to the third, apparently pertained to the ability to recount previous personal experiences of revelatory visions (12:1–13). Once again, though there is really nothing to be gained by an attempt to supplement the record of divine support that he has already presented, Paul consents, as before, to "go on boasting" in an attempt to win the wayward Corinthians back to his side (12:1). But once more he does so in a way that shows his reticence to cooperate fully in any contest of credentials proposed by his opponents, speaking modestly of his own experience as only that of a man in Christ.

Proceeding, Paul relates an experience that happened to him some fourteen years earlier (placing it in the period between his first visit

St. Paul's Bay (seen here) is the site of Paul's shipwreck in Malta (Acts 27). Paul refers to this shipwreck in 2 Corinthians 11:25 as one example of the high price he paid for representing Christ in his work.

to Jerusalem following his conversion and his arrival in Antioch [Acts 9:23–30; 11:19–26]). During this experience, while completely unaware of the whereabouts of his body, Paul was nonetheless brought to a form of consciousness in paradise and enabled to see and hear "things that man is not permitted to tell" (12:4). From the point of view of Paul's opponents, it is entirely proper for "a man like that" to boast about the privilege of receiving such a vision (12:5). But Paul is unwilling to take this view, or to allow the Corinthians to think that this experience constitutes the real basis for his claim to be an apostle. And so he continues to present a claim that offers a clearer indication of apostolic vocation, a boast in the weakness of what he has done and said in Christ's service.

Furthermore, the Corinthians should know that following the experience of exaltation there came still further moments of weakness as "a thorn in my flesh, a messenger of Satan, to torment me" (12:7). Paul's picturesque description has led to a wide range of interpretations concerning the nature of his thorn, but in the end, little more can be said with certainty than what Paul in fact tells us; namely, that the thorn began to affect him only after his experience, that it was painful for him, and that it had enabled Satan and the thought of sin to gain entrance to his mind. Paul had "pleaded with the Lord" to remove it (12:8). But in response, he received instead divine power that finds its perfect completion when it enables the overcoming of such weakness.

Paul's experience itself then illustrates his message to the church. The true boast of an apostle, of one sent out by the Lord on a mission (for that is what the title truly means), is that in the course of such a mission, the Lord has faithfully provided power in moments of necessity so that the apostle may claim, "When I am weak, then I am strong" (12:10). Accordingly, though he regrets having "made a fool" of himself with a different boast, Paul has shown through it that he deserves to be commended rather than written off as the inferior of his

opponents or those whose apostolic authority they might claim as superior to Paul's. All the manifestations of divine power—"signs, wonders and miracles"—have been demonstrated at necessary points in the mission to Corinth, along with a kind of "perseverance" that convinced the Corinthians these were more than the tricks of a charlatan seeking some temporary converts (12:12). Indeed, they have received from Paul all that the other churches have except for the request that they share in the burden of his support.

F. The conclusion of the appeal (12:14–13:10). Paul concludes his appeal for Corinthian allegiance to his apostolic authority by informing the church that he is preparing to come to them a third time and urging them in advance to think over what he has said. If they do, they will surely see that his reluctance to accept their support is no more difficult to explain than the reluctance of parents to accept their children's support or to give up the privilege of spending their resources on behalf of those whom they love. It is just this kind of parental love that Paul has lavished on the church. They can scarcely love him less for it, or for refusing for any reason to burden them with his support.

Nor can anyone seriously imagine (as Paul's sarcasm is meant to show) that he has sought to "exploit" them belatedly by sending Titus and others (including a brother known to both the Corinthians and the apostle) to visit the church on his behalf (12:17). If they admit that "Titus did not exploit" them in any way after his arrival, then neither can the apostle who sent him be justly accused of motives or actions contrary to those of his emissary (12:18).

Paul reiterates, however, that his primary purpose is not his own defense. Instead, he has written in an attempt to bring the truth—which alone can be spoken in the sight of God—plainly into view, and to strengthen its hold on the minds of the Corinthians. The apostle's fear is that upon his return, both he and his converts may find that the lies of his detractors have worked so well that neither of them will be happy to learn the truth. Indeed, for his part, Paul suspects that as a result of the work of his rivals, there may already be sufficient "quarreling, jealousy, outbursts of anger, factions, slander, gossip, arrogance and disorder" at Corinth to humble the apostolic pride that he previously took in the origins and growth of the church. As a result, he is afraid that he will grieve over many who have "indulged" in the kinds of sin about which he previously warned them and who have, as a sign of disbelief in Paul's authority, made no attempt at repentance (12:21).

However, such people have already received a warning in person and now by letter (13:2). Paul's "third visit" will be for them a time of confirmation of their sins "by the testimony of two or three witnesses" (Deut. 19:15) and fulfillment of Paul's solemn promise not to spare any of those who have sinned from the authoritative apostolic judgment and discipline that will prove that Christ is speaking "through me" (13:1–2). For Christ, even though he once was crucified in weakness, now lives in and through "God's power." Consequently, as the Corinthians have had occasion to learn before, he is neither weak nor powerless to deal with those who stubbornly persist in sin (13:3–4). Indeed, he has given power to those who live with him so that, though they often find themselves weak in

him, they may nonetheless have strength for discipline as a part of their faithful service to others in his name.

In light of this, Paul urges the Corinthians to sincerely examine themselves, to take a test designed to evaluate the degree to which their recent words and deeds witness to the presence of Christ as Lord within. Failure to note any degree of correlation would, of course, suggest the complete absence of faith. Much more likely is the discovery, despite Paul's prayer to the contrary, of a relative or partial lack of correspondence between faith and action, of something that is wrong, indicating the need for repentance and a return to what is right. Paul confidently encourages his audience to apply the test to him as well as to themselves, so that they may not only reflect on the measure of their own recent faithfulness but also rediscover the measure of his. Yet his chief hope is not that the Corinthians "will see that we have stood the test," but rather that they will come face-to-face with their need for repentance (13:7). For Paul is persuaded that neither he nor his converts will ultimately be able to continue doing anything against the truth if it is known within.

In 2 Corinthians 12:14; 13:1, Paul indicates that he is ready to make a third visit to Corinth. The Lechaion Road (shown here) was the main thoroughfare leading into the city and was likely the road Paul would have traveled to make that visit.

Furthermore, because his primary concern is for the Corinthians, Paul is glad to admit both his own weaknesses and their strengths. Indeed, his "prayer" is not primarily for himself but for the increasing "perfection" of his converts in actions that accord with the truth (13:9). And the same motive explains why he writes. For Paul would rather make timely use in a letter of the authority that the Lord has given him for "building up" if the alternative is to lose communication with his converts and to be forced to use his authority belatedly for "tearing down" (13:10 RSV).

5. Epistolary Conclusion (13:11–14)

The conclusion of the letter begins with an affectionate personal farewell, indicating that despite all that Paul has written, including some biting and pointed sarcasm, he nonetheless continues to regard his audience at Corinth with a genuine love as fellow members of the family of faith. Accordingly, as the father of their faith, he continues to urge them to "aim for perfection," to "listen to [his] appeal," to "be of one mind," and to "live in peace" (13:11). He also encourages the Corinthians to imitate his love for them by openly manifesting a familial affection for one another.

Paul conveys the "greetings" of the remainder of the family and adds a closing prayer (as was also usual) for the welfare of those who will be receiving the letter. However, as might be expected, Paul's closing prayer is distinctly Christian in content and comes intriguingly close to providing an affirmation of trinitarian theology in its form as it draws the name of the Lord Jesus Christ together with that of God and the Holy Spirit in a threefold petition for the continual outpouring of the divine blessings of grace, love, and fellowship in the lives of its readers.

Select Bibliography

Davis, James A. *Wisdom and Spirit*. Lanham, MD: University Press of America, 1984.

Doty, William G. *Letters in Primitive Christianity*. Philadelphia: Fortress, 1973.

Dunn, James D. G. *1 Corinthians*. T. & T. Clark Study Guides. New York: T. & T. Clark, 2004.

Fee, Gordon D. *I Corinthians*. New International Commentary on the New Testament. Grand Rapids: Eerdmans, 1987.

Furnish, Victor P. *II Corinthians*. Anchor Bible. Garden City, NY: Doubleday, 1984.

Garland, David E. *1 Corinthians*. Baker Exegetical Commentary on the New Testament. Grand Rapids: Baker Academic, 2003.

Harris, Murray J. "2 Corinthians." In *The Expositor's Bible Commentary*. Edited by Frank E. Gaebelein. Vol. 10. Grand Rapids: Zondervan, 1976.

———. *The Second Epistle to the Corinthians*. New International Greek Testament Commentary. Grand Rapids: Eerdmans, 2005.

Martin, Ralph P. *2 Corinthians*. Word Biblical Commentary. Waco: Word, 1985.

Mitchell, Margaret M. *Paul and the Rhetoric of Reconciliation: An Exegetical Investigation of the Language and Correspondence of 1 Corinthians*. Louisville: Westminster John Knox, 1991.

Murphy-O'Connor, Jerome. *St. Paul's Corinth: Texts and Archaeology*. Wilmington, DE: Michael Glazier, 1983.

Theissen, Gerd. *The Social Setting of Pauline Christianity: Essays on Corinth*. Edited and translated by John H. Schütz. Philadelphia: Fortress, 1982.

Thiselton, Anthony C. *The First Epistle to the Corinthians*. New International Greek Testament Commentary. Grand Rapids: Eerdmans, 2000.

Welborn, L. L. *Politics and Rhetoric in the Corinthian Epistles*. Macon, GA: Mercer University Press, 1997.

Witherington, Ben, III. *Conflict and Community in Corinth: A Socio-Rhetorical Commentary on 1 and 2 Corinthians*. Grand Rapids: Eerdmans, 1995.

Galatians

SCOTT E. MCCLELLAND

Introduction

Authorship

The vast majority of scholarly opinion has affirmed the apostle Paul as the author of the Epistle to the Galatians. The characteristic opening line, which identifies his name and apostolic claim, the personal final greeting, and the theological focus all point to the historical Paul. Only a few scholars, mostly in the nineteenth century, have questioned this rather universal acceptance through two millennia of church tradition.

The majority of the letter (epistle) was likely generated through the process of dictation to an amanuensis (secretary), as was common in first-century letter writing of this size and importance. The appearance of two anacolutha (unfinished sentences) in 2:6 gives further credence to this view, while also displaying the emotional intensity of the words there. His reference to the "large letters" he writes "with my own hand" (6:11) points to where Paul personally took up the pen to provide his authenticating mark and final exhortations. (Compare 2 Thess. 3:17, ironically a widely disputed letter.)

Text

It should also be noted that the text of this epistle appears to have been copied and handed down with little variation. The relatively constant agreement between some of the most respected and diverse Greek manuscripts provides us great assurance as to the "purity" of the text we have received.

Occasion, Purpose, and Destination

While broad agreements exist on many of these questions, there are few more difficult issues for the student of the New Testament than those associated with fitting the actual writing of Galatians (and indeed many of Paul's letters) into the historical outline supplied by the book of Acts. The occasion (the reasons why a letter was written when it was) and the purpose (what Paul sought to accomplish) of each letter are crucial components for proper interpretation of a letter's meaning. We need to navigate through some of the discussion surrounding these issues before the reader can sufficiently weigh the evidence regarding the historical context of Galatians.

The difficulties begin even with the name of the epistle and the people Paul intends to address. The term "Galatia" referred to one of the Roman provinces of Asia Minor (modern-day Turkey). This province cut in a north-south direction across the middle of the peninsula, encompassing a number of diverse peoples, cultures, and languages.

Beyond reference to the territory, however, the term "Galatian" could be used to designate certain groups of ethnic people within that province. These people would be the descendants of

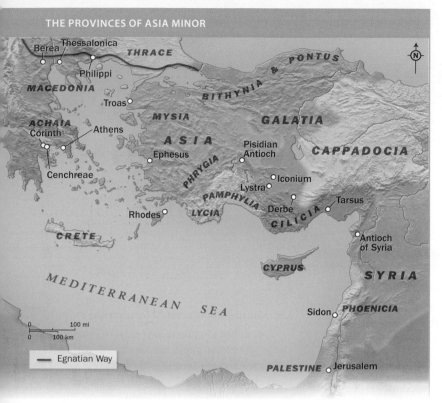

THE PROVINCES OF ASIA MINOR

These theories are based on the premise that Galatians was written to a group Paul visited, among whom he also founded a church during one of his missionary journeys recorded in the book of Acts. The decision one makes regarding the destination of the letter governs one's view of its date and, possibly, its purpose.

If Paul used the term "Galatia" to designate the Roman province, the first missionary journey recorded for Paul and Bar-nabas in Acts would likely be the time when he initially made contact with these Galatian people. This aligns with the southern Galatian theory. The destination of the letter is believed, then, to be the churches at Pisidian Antioch, Iconium, Lystra, and Derbe (Acts 13–14). Such a position allows for (but does not necessitate) Galatians to be one of the earliest written, if not the very first, of Paul's letters.

the ancient Gauls, likely a barbaric tribal group from northwestern Europe. They settled in the northern part of the territory that would subsequently bear their name around 278 BC. The ancient cities of Ancyra (Ankara, the modern Turkish capital), Tavium, and Pessinus would be associated with the settled areas of the ethnic Gauls prior to, and at the time of, this letter. Once conquered by the Romans, after 189 BC this land, as well as more southern areas, was incorporated under the provincial name of Galatia.

Thus, when Paul uses the term "Galatians" (especially in a derogatory way in Gal. 3:1), it is difficult to know whether he has a provincial or ethnic designation in mind. Those who have attempted to answer this question often use their position as a starting point to adopt a view on the destination of the letter, usually calling it either a "northern Galatian" or a "southern Galatian" theory.

The alternative, northern Galatian theory is now not generally as popular as the southern theory. Those who hold this position believe Paul would not refer to the church members of the south as "Galatians" if they were not racially associated with that tribe. The major difficulty of holding to this position is the lack of any specific mention in Acts of Paul's travels in the northern part of the province. Possible visits could have been in this area on one of his journeys from Antioch to Ephesus (Acts 16:6; 19:1). However, the passages in view make no mention of the founding of churches during any presumed time in these areas. Holding this view forces the date of the letter's writing to a much later time period than that of the southern theory.

Certainty on this issue is impossible, but there are a number of reasons to favor the southern Galatian theory: (1) the churches of the south became important and strong communities in apostolic times, though we know nothing about any northern churches (providing motivation for the preservation of the letter); (2) two of Paul's major companions came from this area (Timothy and Gaius), and they appear to represent Galatia (1 Corinthians 16) in the collection taken for Jerusalem; (3) Galatians 4:13 may well imply more than one visit by Paul to these churches, a fact verified by the book of Acts (Acts 13–14; 16); (4) the repeated mention of Barnabas without further elaboration seems to suppose acquaintance with him—we know that Barnabas accompanied Paul to the cities in the south during the first missionary journey.

Date

A further major difficulty in harmonizing this letter with the book of Acts is Paul's description of his contact with the church in Jerusalem, and its leadership, in the first section of the letter. While Paul records two visits to the city after his conversion experience, Acts records three.

Most scholars agree that Paul's first postconversion visit (Gal. 1:18) is identical to the visit mentioned in Acts 9:26. Difficulties arise as to the alignment of the visit described in Galatians 2:1 with either Acts 11:30 or 15:1–4. The decision made on this issue brings with it some major implications for the determination of date, occasion, and destination of the letter.

The proposal that Acts 11 corresponds to Galatians 2 appears most natural since the book of Acts records one more visit than does Paul. It would seem likely, then, that Galatians was written after the second and prior to the third visit recorded in Acts.

This alignment is strengthened by the basic apologetic nature of the early chapters of Galatians. Principally the argument is that Paul, in defending his independent and equal apostolic status compared to that of the apostles in Jerusalem, must report on any and all interactions he has had with the church at Jerusalem.

Under this scheme, Galatians would have been written very early in Paul's ministry, at least before the Jerusalem council of Acts 15 (AD 49–50), and very close to his return from the first missionary journey (Acts 13–14). This view helps place in perspective his surprise at his readers' desertion from the gospel "so quickly" (1:6), since he would have been through the region of Galatia in the very recent past.

The evidence, however, seems to favor a different alignment. There is a noticeable similarity of style, vocabulary choice, theological development, and, most importantly, the type of opposition faced by Paul in this letter with that found in his letter to the Romans and the Corinthian correspondence. Thus, many scholars have made a strong case that Galatians belongs to the same time frame as do these others (AD 54–56). This would place the writing of Galatians after the Jerusalem council.

The decision on this matter turns on how much it is believed Paul would have felt it unnecessary to mention the famine relief visit of Acts 11 in recounting his past contact with Jerusalem. Scholars are divided as to how crucial it would be to Paul's credibility if he did not mention every visit to Jerusalem.

This criticism is mitigated by pointing to Paul's main purpose in recounting his visits to Jerusalem. It may not have been to cite every visit to the city but rather to indicate those occasions upon which he personally met with the main apostles in Jerusalem. Since the question at issue was how much he relied on their permission for his work, recounting a visit where he did not encounter the leaders there would be unnecessary. Thus, he would not need to mention the famine relief visit of Acts 11:30

since he apparently met with no apostles during his time there.

When all is considered, the alignment of Galatians 2 with Acts 15 appears to have more strength, and is the position adopted in this commentary.

Opponents

Throughout the letter, Paul makes reference to a group of opponents to his work in Galatia. Over the years, scholars have often used the term "Judaizers" to describe a group of conservative Jewish Christians who mandated that a Gentile must first obey the precepts of Judaism, particularly symbolized by submission to the rite of circumcision, prior to being accepted as a full member of the Christian church.

The conflict Paul had with these opponents represents a pivotal point in the history of the early Christian movement theologically as well as ecclesiastically. The outcome would determine whether the faith would retain the exclusivist character of orthodox Judaism or, as Jesus himself seemed to command (Matt. 28:19), would be made available to all of humankind with equal accessibility.

Both Paul's letters and the book of Acts evidence a considerable difference of opinion among the Jewish members of the early Christian movement as to how to integrate the numbers of Gentiles who seemed attracted to the faith. This difference reflected a long-standing animosity between the Jewish and Gentile communities of the ancient world.

A principal issue of distinction between these believers was the practice of circumcision. This rite, performed on every male Jew shortly after birth, was seen to be both a loathsome rite for adult Gentile converts to follow and a culturally disdained practice in the Hellenistic world. It also had an implied retention of male privilege in the new community (compare Gal. 3:28). Perhaps because it revealed a strong measure of commitment, many Jewish followers in the early church were adamant about its continued practice for all those who followed Christ. While they recognized that the message

of Jesus was not universally accepted among their own people, they did not consider the Christian movement to be outside orthodox Judaism.

Thus, the Epistle to the Galatians represents the collision of those two ideologies. We gain from the Pauline perspective an appreciation of the issues (as well as the personalities) involved. We also gain an understanding of the viewpoint that eventually won the day and went on to characterize the Christian church.

Inherent Limitations

Common to all the Pauline Letters is the fact that Paul is, first and foremost, a "task theologian." His letters are primarily written to address certain concerns that were troubling the church(es) involved. Thus, we look in vain for any full systematic treatment of theological issues. Rather, we usually hear Paul give only as much theological material as is needed to correct a crisis situation or to maintain a church's resolve until he can personally be on the scene.

This is quite evident when we look at Galatians, as he seems to touch on those issues at stake in the Judaizer controversy and little else. Yet what we can glean from the letter is the overall sense of how Paul emphasized the completely new reality inaugurated for each believer as he or she accepted Jesus Christ as the risen Lord and Savior.

New Life in Christ

Permeating the incredulity that Paul has at the behavior of the Galatians, who seem willing to submit to the circumcision "party," is the sense that they have missed the most important aspect of their new life of following Christ. Whereas formerly, as Gentiles, they were often considered to be outside the realm of God's covenant promises, they have now been, through God's great initiative in Christ, fully embraced into the fullness of that covenant. Rather than joining an already existing "system" of proper approach to God (Judaism), the Galatians have been included in the reality that Judaism has longed for: life in the Spirit. This new reality was of a nature so superior to everything that had gone before that it completely changed all social and religious categories used to value human persons. The basis for acceptance before God was not found in ethnic, sexual, or social status but in an individual's possession of God's Holy Spirit.

Paul's advocacy of this new reality struck at the very heart of established Judaism's exclusivity. Paul portrays the Mosaic law (and its traditional interpretations) as the guardian against human immorality. It is the tutor that pointed toward the holiness of God while revealing the imperfect state of each person and their inability to achieve righteousness through it. In the new reality found in Christ, it has been superseded by the appropriation of God's own Spirit into the life of each person aligned with Christ. Thus, rather than humans standing as an "outsider" to God's will and ways, the new reality brought humankind into an "insider" position, where the Spirit would interact directly with each person's own nature. This interaction called for no mediator or ceremonial signs of inclusion. In response to this new reality, followers are to "keep in step with the Spirit" (5:25) while they also continually "test" themselves (6:4) as to the constancy of their walk by comparing their actions and attitudes with both the "fruit of the Spirit" (5:22) and the "acts of the flesh" (5:19). Bearing spiritual "fruit," not circumcising the flesh, has now become the tangible sign of one's inclusion into this new reality of God's kingdom.

Galatians, most likely written in the same time frame as 2 Corinthians, gives further explanation to that letter's great proclamation in 5:17: "If anyone is in Christ, the new creation has come: The old has gone, the new is here!"

Outline

Commentary

1. Introduction (1:1–10)

A. Salutation (1:1–5). The apostle Paul followed the normal Greek letter-writing form in composing his letters. The normal form was characterized by an introduction that cited the name of the author and those addressed. This would normally be followed by a greeting varying in length and usually determined by the degree of warmth felt between the author and the recipients. We notice here, contrary to his other letters, that Paul gives only the briefest of greetings (1:3). His style is proper and a bit curt and immediately evidences a defense of his apostolic origin. Clearly, Paul perceives himself to be under attack as he writes. He wastes no time in rising to his own defense.

The attacks against him appear to have revolved around the origin of his apostleship and, with it, the basis of his authority in that role. Paul may have been the primary author to develop this otherwise common term in its verbal form, *apostellō* ("to send out," as designating an ambassador), into an official noun of distinction *apostolos*. Accompanying authority claims would not come simply from the use of the term itself but from the overall understanding of who it was that had commissioned the apostle. Greater authority would be given to one sent out personally by Jesus (as Paul claims for himself) than to one who was sent out by church authorities. Unfortunately for him, his claim to the same apostolic authority as that of the original disciples of Jesus (Gal. 2:6–10; 1 Cor. 9:1–27) was one that could not be independently verified. (See Acts 9 for the story of his conversion.) Throughout Paul's ministry, the uniqueness of his calling, with its lack of objective proofs, provided ammunition for those who disagreed with his positions (see, e.g., 1 Corinthians 5; 9; 2 Corinthians 10–13).

Here in the opening words of the letter, Paul defends the source of his apostolic calling (1:1). The key factor for him was viewing his apostleship as divinely appointed and not a product of human decision ("sent not with a human

commission nor by human authority" [TNIV]). Paul appears to be referring to his conversion experience and his belief that Jesus appeared to him, then, personally. Thus, Paul lists "Jesus Christ" first as the one through whom the commissioning was made, with "God the Father" as the ultimate source of the appointment.

Though he acknowledges the greetings of others to the Galatians (1:2), Paul seems to have little time or desire for pleasantries. The brevity of his greeting is an unmistakable mark of his deep concern, perhaps even his anger at the present circumstances. His stock, yet sincere, wish for "grace and peace" to them leads him into a further enunciation of the good news of redemption found in Christ (1:3–5).

Paul briefly and effectively reminds the Galatians that redemption is solely the work of God in Jesus Christ. Jesus is the one who sacrificially gave himself "for our sins" (see Rom. 5:6, 8; 1 Cor. 15:3), resulting in our rescue from "the present evil age" (1:4). This rescue does not remove the recipient from the present world. Rather, the use of the term "age" is similar to other references Paul makes to the distinction

The region around Pisidian Antioch, part of the imperial province of Galatia

between the wickedness of the fallen world and the newness of life afforded by redemption and the infusion of God's presence into our lives (see 1 Cor. 1:20; Eph. 2:2; 6:12).

The effect of this opening review is to establish the ground on which Paul will argue his grace-focused gospel. The recognition of the completed work of God in redemption would be undermined by any claim to human activity in conjunction with it. The unusually early doxology found here (1:5) has the effect of placing his detractors in the precarious position of lessening the glory attributable to God if they affirm any human aspect to the redemption process.

B. Occasion for writing (1:6–9). Paul moves quickly to express condemnation for the Galatians' recent actions in a paragraph that is noteworthy for its emotional intensity. He is "astonished" not only by the apparent departure of the Galatians from what he will argue is the core of the gospel but also by their lack of endurance with the truth (1:6). Such a desertion is understood not simply as a differing point of view but as a rejection of God himself ("the one who called you to live in the grace of Christ"; 1:6)! While the use of the term "so quickly" may relate to Paul's recent visits there, he may also be referring to their desertion from the gospel upon its very first challenge since the establishment of their churches.

In describing this desertion, Paul uses two different terms to refer to the unwelcomed "gospel" to which the Galatians were attracted. The term translated as "different" (1:6) denotes a "difference in kind" (from one unrelated thing to another) rather than a difference between related things. To mark off this difference in kind, he uses a contrasting term, "another" (KJV, RSV; NIV: "no gospel at all") indicating his is not simply a disagreement with a point of view or an equally possible approach to following Christ.

We receive our first hint that the difficulties are the results of a special interest group here (1:7). The agitators are described as those wishing to confuse the Galatians by perverting

the gospel. Paul will provide further insight into their motives later in the letter (see 4:17; 6:12–13).

The seriousness of the situation is established by the two "curse" (Greek *anathema*) statements (1:8–9). There are few other terms that could be so reflective of the vehemence with which Paul opposes these false teachings. The use of *anathema* reflects the concept of eternal damnation. (Literally it referred to the dedication of an object, usually in pagan temples, for the purpose of its destruction.) Paul is not venting anger from the perspective of a wounded ego; he merely states the fact that those who are found to be advocating a false view of the work of Christ are not just mistaken; they are lost.

Quite simply, nothing and/or no one had the authority to override the truth of the gospel (including Paul himself or even angels; 1:8). Paul's concern is to place the issue of authority and the discussion of apostolic origins into a proper perspective. Ultimately it is not to the messenger that one gives allegiance but to the message. There is only one gospel. Anything else, Paul asserts, is perverted and false.

C. Review of accusations (1:10). Because most of Paul's letters were occasional letters (prompted in response to problems existing in the churches addressed), we are placed in a position similar to that of one who eavesdrops on one side of a telephone conversation. Often we must reconstruct the sense of the whole conversation with only a few clues on which to proceed. Such is the difficulty here. Paul asks a series of rhetorical questions, each (because of their construction in Greek) with an intended negative answer. They give us an indication of the types of accusations being made by those who discredited Paul's view of the gospel and/or his apostolic authority.

The Greek grammar of verse 10, with the use of "for" (KJV, ESV) as a connection from the previous thought, indicates that Paul's questions are prompted by his previous pronouncement of *anathema*. Paul appears to be reviewing accusations, presumably from the agitators (1:7), that his preaching of free grace was motivated by an attempt to win a vast following for his ministry. Those who held a view that gave an important place to a righteousness based on good works would quite understandably have believed such a "do-nothing" gospel to have been formulated by a desire to be popular among the Gentiles.

Paul's previous *anathema*s (which could potentially include himself; 1:8) were designed to show that it was not popularity he sought but faithfulness to the gospel as he understood it. The final statement of the verse indicates that if pleasing humanity was his goal, being a "servant of Christ" would not be the most logical way to proceed (1:10). His words are reminiscent of the warning, spoken by Jesus, regarding the serving of two masters (see Matt. 6:24).

2. Paul and the Nature of His Apostleship (1:11–2:21)

Apparently part of the process used to sway the Galatians from Paul's influence was to cast doubt on his credentials as an apostle (or at least as one "above" the authority of the agitators or the leaders they claimed to represent). The opponents of Paul seemed to claim for themselves a direct line of authority to someone, or some group, associated with the church in Jerusalem. While we have no way of evaluating the possibility that a countermission to Paul may have been authorized by an official or officials of that church, such a claim was apparently believed by the Galatians.

Paul's defense of the mysterious conversion experience he claimed, then, had to center on the only objective evidence he had: his changed life from a persecutor of the church to an effective minister of the gospel. In order to reestablish his right to direct the Galatians in their spiritual affairs, Paul not only had to recount his own claim to apostleship, but he also had to establish that the apostles in Jerusalem recognized the equality of his apostolic standing with them.

A. Preconversion days (1:11–14). As when he denied human agency in his apostolic calling (1:1), Paul makes it clear that no one was

involved in his own understanding of the gospel (1:11–12). This denial involves three specific areas that may have been alleged sources for the gospel Paul represented: (1) it was not "of human origin" (from him or anyone else); (2) it was not handed down by tradition; (3) he was not instructed in it.

What Paul appears to be saying is that the ultimate triumph of Jesus as Redeemer through an act of free grace (the core of the gospel as specified earlier; 1:4) came to him through the very revelation of Jesus's presence during the Damascus Road postresurrection appearance (1:12; see Acts 9). Paul seems not to have specific declarations of doctrine in mind (see 1 Cor. 11:23–32; 15:1–8). Rather, the reality of the victory of Jesus over death, signifying God's acceptance of his sacrifice, allowed everything Paul knew of God to fall into proper perspective. This, presumably, is what Paul means by "the gospel" in Galatians 1:11. The specifics of the history and doctrine were secondary to the reality revealed in him (1:16) at his conversion.

Paul appeals to their own knowledge of his former superior standing in Judaism and his own attempts to "destroy" the church (1:13–14). As a conscientious Pharisee, Paul was highly acclaimed among his peers and was able to name the revered rabbi Gamaliel as his mentor (revealed to us in Acts 22:3). He mentions his advancement in the "traditions of my fathers" (1:14), which would have involved intense study of the Scriptures and the teachings of the rabbinical sages.

B. Conversion (1:15–17). What becomes clear is Paul's emphasis on the full agency of God in his conversion. Paul reflects his belief that though his change in life appeared dramatically abrupt to him and to all who heard of it, such was not the case with God, who had prepared this very step as early as his appearance in his mother's womb (1:15). Paul expresses this calling in terms reminiscent of the callings of the prophets Isaiah (Isa. 49:1) and Jeremiah (Jer. 1:5). Such terminology would, no doubt, sting his Jewish-oriented opponents.

The revelation of God's Son *in* Paul (1:16) had as its purpose the consecration of an individual to preach the gospel to the Gentiles. This is a decisive calling for Paul, one that allowed him to claim an equality of apostolic standing with the leader of the disciples, Peter, who in Paul's view was specifically chosen to lead the mission to the Jews (2:8). Acts 26:17 fully records God's commissioning of Paul to the Gentile mission.

His response to this dramatic change was not to seek counsel or explanation from Jerusalem or from anyone else (1:17). There was no need to interpret the experience as if it were unclear. Rather, Paul headed into the region of Arabia (a large kingdom similar to the area of Syria, Jordan, and Saudi Arabia today, ruled then by the Nabateans). The text does not specify what he did while in that area. The reason he mentions it is not to explain what he did as much as to show what he did not do (i.e., consult with Jerusalem). After a stay of some undetermined time, he returned to Damascus (1:17), where presumably the incident of escape from the city took place (see additional details in 2 Cor. 11:30–33).

C. First meeting with Jerusalem leadership (1:18–24). Paul's desire was to show that he did not owe allegiance to Jerusalem (and thus would not have to agree with or submit to the opponents who claimed to be from there). Further, he wanted to show that it was the opponents who would have to submit to his authority in Galatia, since he had been recognized by the major Jerusalem apostles as holding the lead position over the Gentile missionary enterprise. To do this he needed to show that he owed nothing to Jerusalem for the authority he had received to proclaim the gospel.

His first visit to Jerusalem is said to have occurred "after three years" (1:18). This reference and the one in 2:1 to "fourteen years"

have proved to be problematic in understanding Pauline chronology. The reference here could take either his conversion or his return to Damascus as its starting point. The time referred to in 2:1 may be subsequent to these three years, or could just as well be the time of his conversion. The grammar gives us very little aid in determining these issues conclusively. In general, many scholars prefer to see Paul's conversion to be the operative starting point (with AD 32–33 as a likely date for it) and AD 35–36 as the date of the visit Paul mentions here. This occasion most likely aligns with the reference in Acts 9:26–30.

The three years between his conversion and the meeting of any of the Jerusalem officials emphasizes the independent nature of Paul's work. When he did go up to Jerusalem, he had the opportunity to visit (the Greek term means "to get to know"; 1:18) only Cephas (Aramaic name for Peter—likely the nickname Jesus actually used for him; see Matt. 16:18) and James (1:18–19). The visit did not last long (fifteen

On this portion of the ivory carving known as the *Harbaville Triptych* (tenth century AD), Paul is pictured (second from the right) as one of the apostles, along with (from left to right) James, John, Peter, and Andrew. On his first visit to Jerusalem, Paul met with only Peter and James (Gal. 1:18–19).

days; 1:18). No time of instruction or of commissioning is implied.

In stressing that he "saw none of the other apostles—only James" (1:19), Paul apparently counted the "Lord's brother" (likely half brother, the son of Joseph and Mary after the birth of Jesus) among the apostles. While some scholars have sought to deny this, it does seem that the traditional designation of only the Twelve plus Paul as apostles is far too limited.

This seems to be a crucial point for Paul. In all this time of being a Christian, he had extremely limited contact with the Jerusalem leadership. He certainly makes it clear that he and Barnabas undertook the ambitious first missionary journey without being supervised in any way by Jerusalem. This display of independence would serve to so deflate the opponents' accusations that Paul felt compelled to offer a guarantee of its truthfulness (1:20).

After Jerusalem, it was on to the regions of Syria and Cilicia (Antioch was in Syria, Tarsus in Cilicia), with no further contact with Jerusalem, or anywhere else in Judea (1:21). The good news about his changed life was known in Judea only by reputation (1:22–23). While that evoked glory to God (1:24), it brought no formal relationship between Paul and Jerusalem. Clearly, then, Paul was not serving under the leaders of Jerusalem in any way.

D. Second meeting with Jerusalem leadership (2:1–10). The second meeting with Jerusalem is fraught with far more problems for Paul, as he attempts to indicate his degree of independence from that power base of the early church (2:1–5). If we are correct in assuming that this section represents the same visit as that detailed in Acts 15 (which then causes us to understand "after fourteen years" [Gal. 2:1] as referring to a time period subsequent to the "three years" of 1:18), then Paul has the task of explaining why he went to Jerusalem at all if he did not need to appear for the purpose of defending his ministry before those who had the power to direct it.

Paul's explanation emphasizes a few points concerning his encounter with Jerusalem on that occasion. He begins, not coincidentally, with the impression that his arrival had the air of one who was the leader of a delegation from the Gentile missionary enterprise (2:1). The mention of his fellow traveler Barnabas and the taking along of Titus (a representative of the harvest won in the Gentile lands) serve to place Paul in the position of one who arrives as an independent expert consultant on Jewish-Gentile relations. He adds that his coming also had an element of compulsion to it. His visit was initiated by revelation (2:2). Such an inclusion further proves that his directions come from his relationship to God and not from the authority of the Jerusalem leadership. (He was not "summoned.")

Paul also indicates that he had his own purpose for attending the conference (2:2). It was imperative for the leader of the Gentile mission to have the trust and support of the Jerusalem church or to face the threat of continual schismatic strife. Though the early church seemed to be learning that the same Holy Spirit was given to all individuals upon their acceptance of Christ (see Acts 10:34–38; 11:18), the animosity characterizing Jewish-Gentile relations was not going to be eradicated easily. Paul must settle this issue early in the history of the Gentile outreach, or he would face ongoing feelings of prejudice throughout the areas in which he would be working.

Thus, when Paul mentions that he submitted the content of his preaching to "those esteemed as leaders," he is not saying that he sought their correction. Rather, he explains that they met in private in order to be sure that they could bring a united front to the conference. It is unstated if Paul knew that the Jerusalem apostles would agree with him; he describes these things from hindsight. Through everything else he has written, however, it is evident that Jerusalem agreement was not a prerequisite to the continuance of his ministry. Disagreement on these issues, however, would certainly have led to a split and weakened church. This is likely what he had in mind when he added that he was concerned about "running . . . in vain" (2:2).

Paul uses the Greek term *dokeō* in verse 2 to describe the ones to whom he submitted his preaching (literally, the ones who "seem" or "have an appearance," with the idea of holding a recognized position). Verses 6 and 9 will elaborate on the individuals he has in mind, including James, Cephas, and John.

Verses 3–5 have been difficult for interpreters to agree on. The Greek manuscripts vary slightly, but significantly, in verse 5. The difficulties are further complicated by the awkward grammatical connections of these verses. Obviously, the emotional tone of the moment is reflected in Paul's recounting of it. Paul may have been so emotionally involved in describing the events that his secretary was hard pressed to put into written words the apostle's swift-flowing descriptions.

The most likely meaning of the text, backed by the best manuscript evidence and the context of the passage, would appear to picture a confrontation precipitated by those demanding circumcision for Gentiles, which was further complicated by the presence of Titus. Paul firmly makes it known to his readers that there was no compromise of his position, either by himself or by Titus (2:3).

It is hard to know the identity of the "compeller" in verse 3. Though Paul goes on to state that the whole matter was initiated by those he describes as "false believers" (2:4), most likely they would not have had the authority to compel Titus to be circumcised. It is quite possible, then, that Paul has the Jerusalem leadership in mind here. Despite the arguments of the legalists, the leadership refused to compel Titus (and, by implication, any Gentile) to add any additional qualifications for Gentile fellowship in the church beyond an individual's faith in Jesus Christ. Thus, Paul would seem to be describing, in remarkably little detail, the deliberations of the leadership on this issue. They are pictured as in full agreement with Paul's position.

It is interesting to notice the final remark in verse 3, "even though he was a Greek" (i.e., Gentile). Is Paul simply informing the Galatians why it was significant that Titus was under discussion for circumcision? Doubtless they were well aware of his being a Gentile. Rather, it is likely that Paul is dramatically emphasizing the new status of Gentiles in Christ. Even though Titus was among a conference full of Jews, he was treated as having a fully legitimate right to fellowship among them by virtue of his faith alone. It is likely that the Galatians were struck by this. All those important Jewish believers, and they placed no further requirements on Titus? Why then are these others demanding more?

As if to answer such a question, Paul momentarily interrupts his narrative of the events of the conference, digressing to the type of opponents he encountered there (2:4). The Galatians are to see that the ones described as the infiltrating "false believers" who had come "to spy on the freedom we have in Christ Jesus" with the purpose "to make us slaves" (2:4) are the same type of characters troubling them. The Greek terms for "infiltrated" (see also 2 Pet. 2:1) and "spy" (see 2 Kings 10:3; 1 Chron. 19:3 in the Septuagint) are usually found in descriptions of secret military operations designed to conduct subversive activities to undermine an enemy's defenses.

Are these opponents even Christians? Paul's use of "false believers" in verse 4 and in a similar context in 2 Corinthians 11:26 suggests he is indicating that the nature of the doctrine taught by such opponents excludes their membership in the faith. This view is further enhanced by Paul's disclaimer in Galatians 2:5 that his delegation (and, possibly, he is including the Jerusalem leadership here as well) never even gave a moment's hesitation on the matter "so that the truth of the gospel might be preserved for you." Surely Paul viewed the issue that plagued Jerusalem then, and is plaguing Galatia as Paul writes, to be pivotal in one's inclusion or exclusion from the faith. Clearly, in Paul's view, these opponents are at least in danger of exclusion.

While Paul was satisfied by the decision of the Jerusalem council, he is just as concerned to show the Galatians that the leadership in Jerusalem made a specific point of also recognizing the apostolic authority he possessed. The point is that Paul gave them no more recognition than they deserved, while they finally gave to him all the recognition that he deserved (2:6–10).

The use of the phrase "those who were held in high esteem" (2:6) recalls for Paul's readers the individuals with whom he met prior to the confrontation with Titus (2:2). He repeats the vague reference to their authority four times (2:2, 6 [twice], 9). Each use of the term appears to refer to the same three leaders, James, Cephas, and John, who are also identified by the term "pillars" in verse 9.

Verse 6 has a curious mixture of Greek tenses. Paul uses the imperfect in referring to the pillars ("whatever they were"). Then he utilizes the present tense ("makes no difference") in referring to his reaction to them. It seems clear that the imperfect is referring to their reputation as being part of Jesus's inner circle. Yet Paul is making the point that no group's past performance is going to dictate the direction of his ministry.

His digression about God's not showing partiality (2:6), which reflects a Hebrew idiom of not "looking at the face" (i.e., looking on outward appearances; Deut. 10:17; 1 Sam. 16:7; James 2:1), provides a theologically based reason for his behavior. Presumably one would expect Paul to show some deference to these men (at least to Cephas and John), since they followed Jesus even before his resurrection. While such diplomatic niceties might avoid conflict, they could also be devastating, especially since, as Paul desires to show, such submission would cause him to follow men who may not be as correct as he on this important issue. When it is a question of either being consistent with

the gospel or following the dictates of "church politics," Paul leaves no doubt what he will do.

The results of this meeting with the "pillars" are important for Paul's purposes, and he discusses them carefully. While Paul is pleased that these men recognized his authority, he wants to be very sure that such recognition does not appear as a type of commissioning. Paul arrived with the same status with which he departed; nothing was added (2:6) to him. The real change occurs in the minds of the pillars. The results are well worth noting: (1) They recognized that Paul was entrusted by God with the Gentile missionary enterprise (2:7). (2) The authority of Peter and Paul was equated, each in his own sphere of operation (2:8–9). This was as a consequence of their perception of the leading of God on the matter (2:8) and was not simply an administrative decision. (3) They parted as equal partners in the overall enterprise of evangelization (2:9). (4) The one additional comment made by the Jerusalem leaders, concerning sensitivity to the poor, really did not need to be stated since Paul already had that area of need in mind (2:10). Even on this rather trivial point, Paul does not waver from his previous statement in verse 6 that the "pillars" added nothing to his ministry!

Verses 7–8 could be regarded as a type of semiquotation of an official document, or of an oral agreement that was reached at the council. The recognition of various spheres of responsibility is stated in terms Paul probably would not use (see Gal. 1:7–9; he would likely avoid any implications that two gospels were being preached). Yet the statement would be, nonetheless, sufficient for the purpose of showing his equal status with Peter. The change in Peter's name may reflect the fact that such an agreement would be framed both in Aramaic, the common language in Judea, and in Greek. In quoting the Greek for his readers, Paul utilizes the Greek translation for Cephas, which is Peter.

If this view is correct, it may be significant that the "quotation" uses the term "apostle" (2:8) in referring to Peter's status, but the term is not repeated in reference to Paul. There is debate as to whether the parallel construction in the Greek implies the word's presence or if it was consciously left out. It may well be that Paul assumed it and the "pillars" did not, for even with regard to the spheres of responsibility there may have been some ambiguity, since we know that Peter ministered in Rome and possibly elsewhere (Corinth? See 1 Cor. 1:12; 9:5).

E. Correcting Cephas (2:11–21). The incident related in this section (2:11–14) indicates that in spite of the basic agreement reached at the Jerusalem council, certain ambiguities continued to exist. The incident at Antioch is significant, for it moves us on to the next logical step in Paul's argument regarding his authority on the matters troubling the Galatians. We need to take careful note of the situation as Paul has developed it. The authorities in Jerusalem had recognized Paul's equal status relative to them, but in Paul's view they also acknowledged his priority over matters dealing with Gentiles.

Thus, when Paul confronted the erring Peter at Antioch, he did so in rightful exercise of his authority in that sphere. Peter was wrong in regard to his treatment of Gentile believers in Antioch. The implication is clear for the Galatians. Those who are appealing to Jerusalem as the ground for their authority should recognize that Jerusalem has relinquished its authority over such matters to Paul, since, when they have dealt with the matter in the past, they have shown themselves (as represented by Peter) not to have the proper sensitivity or theological insight. All this, of course, is Paul's own view of the matter. Unfortunately we do not have the reactions of Peter to the confrontation.

Placed as it is after the presentation of agreement on the issue of Gentile circumcision, this incident reveals what Paul believed was truly behind Jewish demands for continued segregation. For, as Paul shows, Peter theoretically agreed with the equal status of Gentiles, even to the point of eating with them (dining at the same table was a cultural sign of acceptance and fellowship). Verse 12 is skillfully constructed to indicate reactions of both acceptance and hesitancy by Peter to the practice of having full fellowship with the Gentile believers.

The inconsistency in Peter's actions is blamed solely on the arrival of a group alternately described as "certain men . . . from James" and as "those who belonged to the circumcision group" (literally "those out of the circumcision"; v. 12). Clearly Peter gave in to the ethnic bias of the arriving Jewish contingent. It is doubtful that he actually changed his theological view as to the status of Gentiles before God. Obviously he had not fully thought through the implications of his theology for his relations with all persons, in spite of the continued

This is the rebuilt (1863) facade of Saint Peter's Church in Syrian Antioch. The natural cave that forms the interior of the church was, according to tradition, the place where the first Christians met and prayed. In Galatians 2:11–21, Paul describes his confrontation with Peter at Antioch.

bias of some. Peter, it seems, was not alone in this problem of integrating faith with living, since even Barnabas followed his example, as well as other Jews present (2:13).

From Paul's description of the actions of the ones who deserted the table fellowship, it is clear that he places the blame squarely on the shoulders of Peter for initiating the response. The actions of the rest of the Jews and Barnabas, described in the passive voice, indicate how Peter's action influenced their similar response. Paul describes their departure from the Gentile table fellowship with the term "hypocrisy" (Greek *hypokrisis*; 2:13).

Paul notes that his public rebuke ("in front of them all"; 2:14) of Peter came because Peter's action appeared to have been the culmination of a series of indiscretions that indicated a continuing bias against Gentiles by the Jewish members of the church. (See the charge concerning Peter's attempt to "force Gentiles to follow Jewish customs" in 2:14.) Paul's statement has the ring of irony. We might do well to paraphrase Paul's point: "If you, one of the sacred, live secularly, and not sacredly, how do you suppose the secular will become sacred?" Other terms might be inserted, but the idea is clear: Jews took great advantage of their heritage, yet they still had not understood that the new covenant did not allow for any human advantage.

Paul had not confronted Peter on a trivial issue. He describes Peter's actions as "not acting in line [literally "walking straight"] with the truth of the gospel" (2:14). Peter's indiscretion, then, was not just a diplomatic mistake but was related to the very heart of the good news itself. Paul often represented the uniqueness of the gospel he preached as contained in the new reality of equal status for all persons saved by Christ (cf. Gal. 3:28; Eph. 2:11–22; one wonders, after twenty centuries, have we learned this lesson even today?).

As Paul relates this story, it seems that he has concluded his personal apologetic. Is Paul an apostle? Yes. The Galatians have heard his testimony of seeing Jesus personally and having his status confirmed by the Jerusalem leadership. Does he have equal authority with Jerusalem? Yes. In fact, they recognize not only his equality but his primacy over matters concerning the Gentiles. Is it important that the Galatians follow him and not the opponents? Yes. Look what happened at Antioch. The lack of calling, knowledge, and sensitivity of the Jerusalem leadership in Gentile affairs has shown itself to be not only insulting to Gentile believers but also inconsistent with the full truth of the gospel. The opponents will only continue this practice.

In this section Paul has shown why the gospel is compromised through ethnic favoritism and that with his leadership the Galatians can progress in the gospel. Moving toward the opponents' position is nothing more than a giant step backward.

Many commentators have debated where Paul ceases his address to the erring Peter (and the other Jews involved in the Antioch incident) and where he begins to address the Galatians once again. The present writer agrees with the NIV, which includes 2:15–21 with the rest of Paul's Antioch address to Peter. This new section appears particularly directed to Jewish Christians yet provides the foundation on which Gentiles also find their place in God's family: justification by faith. It provides the groundwork for Paul's condemnation of the Galatians' attraction to adding works of law to their Christian experience.

The argument here, and in the remainder of the letter, reminds one of the arguments found in Romans (esp. chaps. 3, 6–8). Such parallels have influenced many, including this writer, to view these two epistles as written at about the same time.

Paul uses terminology appropriate to a Jewish audience and reflects the universal division of the human race from a Jewish perspective: "Jews by birth" and "sinful Gentiles" (2:15). This division will be seen to have an ironic ring to it, since Paul will show later in the letter that the work of Christ has destroyed all previously imagined divisions among humankind (see Gal. 3:28).

Paul acknowledges his own position among the "Jews by birth" but goes on to explain that this "advantage" (see Romans 2–3) only allows Jews to be even more sensitive to the need for God's justification because of their own inability to perfectly follow the torah (i.e., the biblical law). Paul, then, has not denied the Jewish advantage; he only shows that the advantage in itself is not enough to provide a right standing with God.

The key verse of the section is verse 16. We find a repetitive treatment of the doctrine of justification by faith here. Paul logically progresses to the next step of a Jewish Christian's understanding. At some point in time there had to be the realization that no one, not even the Jew who attempted it, was "justified by the works of the law, but [instead] by faith in Jesus Christ" (2:16). Jewish Christianity could not exist if it were not for the recognition of these facts. It is also the foundation on which Paul will build his argument for the equality of Jews and Gentiles in Christ (see Gal. 3:26–29; see also Rom. 3:9–18, 22–26).

Paul concludes verse 16 with a paraphrase of Psalm 143:2 ("by the works of the law no one will be justified"), giving what he sees to be a scriptural anticipation of the failure of works of the law to gain justification. Thus, both by experience and on the basis of Scripture, the act of placing one's faith in Jesus Christ has become for the Jew the only proper way to obtain justification. Paul, not incidentally, has also introduced the two categories (experience and Scripture) that he will utilize in addressing the Galatians concerning their own basis of justification (3:1–18).

Verse 16 also introduces some powerful concepts to be considered. The idea of justification (Greek *dikaiosynē*) was utilized in legal proceedings in pronouncing someone innocent of the charges brought against him or her. In Paul's twenty-two uses of the term in the New

Testament, it has the dual effect of affirming that someone is not to be condemned (see Rom. 3:26; 8:1–4) and declaring that a person is viewed as righteous in God's sight (Rom. 3:24). Both benefits are appropriated through faith in Jesus Christ.

In addition, Paul uses "faith" (Greek *pistis*) to denote the channel through which believers obtain justification by Christ. It is not described as the cause of justification, only the channel by which justification is appropriated. While *pistis* itself means simply "confidence" or "trust," it always has specific content in the New Testament: confidence or trust in Christ (i.e., in the sacrificial act of Christ's death on the cross; see Rom. 3:22, 26; Gal. 2:20; Phil. 3:9). This concept of faith in Christ, in Romans and Galatians especially, is contrasted with the ineffective works of law as vehicles to deliver the benefits of justification to humankind.

"Law" here is not the villain of the story. Rather, it is a person's inappropriate use of the law that is in view. Paul, in the more elaborate argument found in Romans (esp. 2:12–15; 7:7–25), establishes the validity of the Mosaic law as a fundamental expression of the righteousness of God. Yet, too, the law displays itself as the accuser of persons (see Gal. 3:10–13) and the vehicle through which they recognize their own sin and sinful inclinations (Rom. 7:13–14). It is the works of law that are condemned by Paul (see Gal. 3:10) as insufficient. When opposing faith and law, Paul is indicating the difference between one's acceptance of Christ's death on his or her behalf and one's determination to reject that death and seek self-justification.

For many, the problem with Paul's radical justification doctrine was in pressing fully the implication that a believer no longer had to work to obey the Mosaic law. If Gentiles, who have no conception of righteous living (i.e., living according to the law), accept Christ and do as they please, does that then mean "that Christ promotes sin" (2:17; literally "Christ, servant of sin"; likely an opponent's slogan)?

Paul strongly answers with his characteristic "Absolutely not!" (2:17). The reason is quite clear. If the law, as a standard for making one righteous, has been supplanted, its continued use as a measurement of personal righteousness is illegitimate. Thus, if Paul (note the change from the plural "we" to the singular "I" in 2:18–21, placing himself as representative of those following this position) were to reestablish the law's legitimacy as a proper channel of justification after it has been annulled (literally "set aside"; NIV "destroyed," 2:18) by Christ's work, he could legitimately be viewed as a lawbreaker. But he is not doing this. Indeed, such a charge reflects a misunderstanding of the full reality of being "in Christ." Rather than just being an additional piece of the theological puzzle, faith in Christ results in an entirely new realm of being for the believer (see 2 Cor. 5:17).

First, using a death-life scenario in verses 19–21, Paul sums up the effect of the law on his former life without Christ: "Through the law I died to the law" (2:19). Here we find the proper understanding of the function of the law. It points out the rightful condemnation of humanity by God (see Romans 7). This realization is the first step in one's appreciation of the work of God through Christ. Thus, this death had to occur, "so that I might live for God" (2:19).

Second, by attaching the Greek preposition *syn*, "together," to the verb *stauroō*, "crucify," Paul effectively shows that in Christ the believer was also crucified in Jesus's substitutionary death (2:20; the Greek New Testament and some modern translations include this expression at the beginning of 2:19; see also Gal. 5:24). Thus, Christ's experience, when appropriated in faith, becomes the experience of the believer. The consequent benefits of Christ's death and newness of life are also those of the believer.

Thus, the believer's new life is forever wedded to that of Christ and characterized by the nature of Christ (2:20). Paul describes the mystical union of the believer with Christ, here and throughout the New Testament, by such expressions as "living in Christ" or "Christ living in me" (see, e.g., Rom. 6:4–8; 8:2–11; 2 Cor. 5:17; Col. 2:12–14). Life in Christ is not an identification of Christ and the believer to the exclusion of the individuality of either. It is, however, the acknowledgment of the source of life: Christ the living Lord. This is at once the reason for and the guarantee of the believer's moral lifestyle. With the reality that "I no longer live, but Christ lives in me" (2:20), the power to live righteously resides in the believer. Further, the believer is no longer motivated by an external, accusing law but by an internal motivation to serve "the Son of God, who loved me and gave himself for me" (2:20; the verb tense refers to the decisive act of love and sacrifice at the cross).

Concluding this section, Paul appears to reflect a charge his opponents likely used against him. In viewing him as one who has rejected the law of God for a form of antinomianism (the belief that one is governed by no laws), they believe he has nullified the gracious acts of God in revealing himself to Israel through the law (see also Acts 21:20–26). However, as Paul indicates, their conclusion is based on the false assumption that righteousness comes through the vehicle of the law. In one of the most dramatic statements found in the New Testament, Paul carries their position to its logical—and devastating—conclusion: "If righteousness could be gained through the law, Christ died for nothing!" (2:21). Allowing legalistic restrictions or ethnic differences and customs to mix with grace results in a perversion of the grace offered at the cross and mocks the very death of Christ.

The Galatians have been made to see that those opponents who have been attempting to institute the law into their lives are actually in danger of nullifying the cross of Christ. The so-called Jewish advantage has actually become a hindrance to the full appreciation of the new life to be found in Christ.

3. Treatise: The Efficacy of Grace over Law (3:1–4:7)

A. The argument from experience (3:1–5). The transition from a recitation of Paul's past activities to present circumstances seems abrupt, but actually it punctuates the incredible final assertion of chapter 2, which was the logical conclusion of the opponents' "gospel": "Christ died for nothing" (2:21). Paul refers to them as "You foolish Galatians!" (3:1), since the very idea of being attracted to a viewpoint that had as its ultimate result the utter rejection of the necessity of Christ's death must be ridiculed as sheer folly. In verse 1 Paul uses the Greek term *anoētos* (NIV "foolish") to denote the improper thinking of those who, otherwise, should be expected to perceive things correctly. They are not incapable of proper thought. Thus, their uncharacteristic foolishness must be the result of some "magical spell" (as indicated in the sarcastic rhetorical question, "Who has bewitched you?").

Paul's outburst is related to what he perceived to be a very successful initial ministry among them. He reminds them that "Jesus Christ was clearly portrayed as crucified" before their "very eyes" (3:1). It is also likely that he is being quite literal here, since it was not at all unusual for those who preached religious or philosophical messages to actually act them out in dramatic forms before their audiences.

The second rhetorical question of this section is a key to understanding Paul's definition of authentic Christian experience. As to whether they have really attained the goal of being in Christ (see 2:20), Paul wants to hear from the Galatians just one thing: "Did you receive the Spirit by the works of the law, or by believing what you heard [literally "out of hearing faithfully"]?" (3:2).

Receiving the Spirit (i.e., the Spirit of Christ, the Holy Spirit) was the fundamental mark of authentic inclusion in the body of Christ (Rom. 8:9–11, where the verses following represent a very close parallel to Gal. 2:20). The reception of the Holy Spirit was an eschatological promise associated with the unique ministry of Jesus himself and a fulfillment of the covenantal promises of God made throughout the Old Testament (see also Joel 2:28–32; John 1:33; Acts 2:17). Jesus encouraged his disciples to look forward to the time of receiving the Spirit (John 20:22) and commanded them to remain in Jerusalem until they did receive the Spirit (Acts 1:5). The Spirit provides the new life of the believer (Rom. 8:9; Gal. 2:20), reveals the will of God (1 Cor. 2:10), and aids in prayer (Rom. 8:26; Gal. 4:6). Thus the Spirit is a necessity for one to become, and remain, a Christian.

In many ways the rhetorical question of verse 2 highlights the problem with the Galatians and, possibly, with Christian experience. So many other experiences of life are progressive and gradual. Even then, only a very few ever reach the highest goal. In many ways this was the Galatian (and Judaizer) misunderstanding. In contrast, immediately upon "believing what [they] heard," people received the very presence of the Spirit of God in their lives. While

The hill, or tell, in the background, Kerti Huyuk, is the location of ancient Derbe. Derbe was situated in the province of Galatia, so the church there was likely among the recipients of Paul's letter to the Galatians.

growth would still be mandated, there was no higher level left to achieve. Paul's unstated but nevertheless implied question throughout the remainder of the letter is simply, "After receiving the Spirit of God, what more is there to receive? What more could you want?"

Thus Paul launches into an elaboration as to why he calls them foolish. After receiving the goal (the Spirit) by faith, are the Galatians now going to attempt to receive it by their own effort (3:3)? The foolishness is, of course, in the folly of embarking on an impossible course that seeks as its goal something they have already received!

Verse 4 appears to relate to some experiences otherwise unknown to us. Asking if they have "experienced so much in vain" may well relate to the common opposition that believers in Christ received from their fellow countrymen and from non-Christian Jewish zealots (cf. Paul's own persecutions during his first missionary journey, especially in southern Galatia; Acts 13:50; 14:5, 19). Paul's hopeful addition to this question, "if it really was in vain," indicates that under the present series of questions lies a questioner who would not even allow the possibility of failure to be the result of his work in Galatia (see Gal. 1:7).

Paul returns again to a contrast between the effectiveness of observing the law and that of believing what one hears (3:5). This time the effect of such belief is the outward manifestation of miracles, a visible sign of the Spirit's reception. The book of Acts repeatedly calls our attention to the fact that certain visible manifestations of the Spirit's presence were often given in order to indicate an authentic reception of the gospel in areas that were new to the message (see Gal. 8:6, 17; 10:44–46; 11:17; 19:6). Thus, when Paul asks questions (here, and 3:2) concerning the initial appearance of the Spirit in the Galatians' experience, he is reminding them of a measurable event, undeniable by anyone who was present at that time.

B. The argument from Scripture (3:6–18). Paul links the undeniable experience of the Galatians with undeniable Scripture (3:6–9). Yet his turning to the example of Abraham was most likely not coincidental. Rather, it is probable that the Jewish opponents used Abraham as the prototypical saint of God, who received the Old Testament covenant, which had circumcision as its sign. Their argument surely was that if Gentiles wished to receive the benefits of that covenant, then they also must accept its accompanying sign and legal prescriptions.

Paul's utilization of the Abraham story is basically designed to make two major points: (1) Abraham's righteous standing before God occurred prior to the institution of circumcision and the Mosaic law; (2) Abraham's righteous standing before God was made possible through a gracious declaration of God, in acceptance of Abraham's belief. Thus, the prototypical Jew is to be viewed as one who received a place in sacred history by grace through faith.

Using a quotation from Genesis 15:6 (found in the Septuagint), Paul recites what he believes to be the most explicit statement concerning God's means for justifying humankind: Abraham "believed God, and it was credited to him as righteousness" (3:6). The faith of Abraham is interpreted to be that which operated on the premise that God was who he said he was and was worthy of trust (see Rom. 4:17).

On the basis of the proposition in verse 6, Paul concludes that, contrary to the opponents' views, the true children of Abraham must be those who enter into peace with God in the same way as Abraham (3:7). Abraham becomes the prime example of the effectiveness of faith since his justification occurred prior to the ceremonial rite of circumcision and centuries before the revealing of the law (see Gal. 3:17). In the old covenant as well as the new, it is faith in the promise of God that is the operative element (see Rom. 4:14, 16, 18–25). The implication for the Galatians is obvious: whoever is not among "those who have faith" (3:7; as opposed to those who observe the law, 3:2, 5) is neither a child of Abraham nor a child of God.

Finishing these thoughts, Paul uses an unusual expression, which personifies Scripture as being able to foresee the future when it declared concerning Abraham, "All nations will be blessed through you" (3:8). This quotation of the covenantal promise of Genesis 12:3 directs our attention to how closely Paul links the recorded words of Scripture with the actual words of God. God's promise to Abraham, which included participation by more than merely those of his physical line, presents Paul with one of the major motivating factors to carry on with his mission to the Gentiles (Col. 1:25–27). Verse 9 summarizes the foregoing section showing that faith, not ethnic background, is humanity's only way to appropriate the same covenantal blessings announced to Abraham.

To show the other side of the argument, Paul conducts a review of Scripture passages that deal specifically with the fallacy of pleasing God through legal obedience (3:10–14). It is interesting to consider whether this was only a review for the church or was the first time they had heard of these passages. Paul's initial missionary preaching may not have dealt extensively with Old Testament concerns, possibly because of a lack of familiarity with them among most Gentiles.

It is Paul's wish to indicate that the law (the Mosaic covenant) was a unified standard, no part of which could be violated (3.10). Thus, any believers finding themselves to be violators of that law would not be pleasing at all to God but would be under the curse contained in that covenant (3:10–12).

Thus, contrary to the opponents' beliefs, Paul shows that Christ does not make a person able to obey the law but accepts the curse of the Mosaic covenant (and, in effect, removes it from the covenant) in his own death (3:13–14). Such a removal of the curse opens the way for all who have been released from the demands of the old Mosaic covenant to, in turn, receive the benefits of the promises for blessing, which were given in the older Abrahamic covenant (i.e., blessings that were made prior to the law and appropriated by faith, 3:14).

Now Paul attempts to show that one subsequent covenant cannot violate the provisions of a previous covenant (3:15–18). Specifically,

another agreement, made some 430 years later (3:17), cannot alter the provisions of the covenant made earlier with Abraham. The NIV's "let me take an example from everyday life" (3:15) is a rather free rendering of the Greek "I speak as a man"; yet the idea that Paul is drawing an illustration from human relationships is a valid description of these verses. Covenantal agreements were made under the most sober circumstances, calling for a life-and-death commitment from the participants. They were not easily entered into or easily altered.

Simply put, Paul is arguing that no one acquainted with the Abrahamic covenant could mistake the Mosaic law as its fulfillment. The very terminology of the older pact, "and to your seed" (3:16), precludes the idea that the Israelites, even if they had been capable of following the Mosaic law, would have been the earlier covenant's fulfillment. (This is what Paul means when he points out that a multifaceted fulfillment was never in view as would be implied if the covenant had specified "and to seeds" [3:16].) The apostle is not being overly literal with the term "seed." He only wishes to remind his readers of what they, and the opponents, have come to know, namely, that the Abrahamic covenant would be fulfilled by a personal deliverer and not by a legal code followed by many.

C. The purpose of the law (3:19–25). Paul proceeds with a characteristic style of arguing his case by presenting the presumed objections of a hypothetical opponent (see, e.g., Rom. 3:9, 27; 6:1, 15; 7:7; 11:1). Here he does not wish to imply that the Mosaic law was either unnecessary or without a place in salvation history. His arguments further call for an understanding of the proper place of the law as a vehicle for pointing to God's grace, not as a path of righteousness in and of itself.

Verse 19 clearly points out the temporary and limited purpose of the law as an indicator of sin. Presumably, once this fact was pointed out, the need for the promised seed to come would be clear. Paul implies that once the seed had come, this function for the law would be ended.

Coming abruptly into the argument is the highly unusual expression of verse 20, which the NIV has tried to clarify with "a mediator, however, implies more than one party; but God is one." Historically, this has been a most perplexing verse with many differing interpretations.

It appears that Paul is trying to make some distinction between the covenant of God with Abraham and the acceptance of the law by the people of Israel through the agency of angels (Acts 7:53) and Moses. While Abraham entered into a full covenant with God, Israel simply ratified an existing legal code accepted by their representative head, Moses. Thus, the superiority of the promise over the law may be in view as well as an additional support to the assertion of verse 17 that the law could not negate the promise. Further, the promised seed of verse 16, which was emphasized to be singular, may be in view here to show that only Christ, and not Moses, could be properly declared to be that "one party."

Paul places the law in a position secondary to the promise, awaiting its fulfillment through that promise, with the rhetorical question of verse 21 ("Is the law, therefore, opposed to the promises of God?"). The grammar reveals the expectation of a negative answer. The effect of these questions places the law in right perspective as thoroughly God's righteous standard, which, also thoroughly, reveals that all things (the Greek term means "the entire creation") have fallen under the power of sin.

This relief from the sarcophagus of a physician named Ioannes shows God giving the law to Moses (Constantinople, fifth century AD).

The point of the law, then, was to prepare humankind to receive the gift of Jesus Christ, the promised seed, with an attitude of need and gratitude. Paul seals such imagery with a short discussion of the role of the law as a "household attendant" (NIV "guardian"). At "the coming of this faith" (3:23, referring specifically to faith in Jesus Christ) the need and the appropriateness of the attendant's task had ended (3:25). The attendant's whole task was to point the way to faith in Christ (3:24).

D. The results of faith (3:26–29). No statements in the Pauline corpus reveal more readily than these the radical newness of human experience Paul believed to be a direct result of a personal encounter with Jesus Christ. In the cultural and religious context of first-century Galatia, where distinctions of national origin, gender, and economic status were the defining tools for human interaction, Paul's words here declare the inauguration of a new paradigm of human value.

Paul switches back to the second-person plural from the first-person singular (3:15–25) to state his conclusion. If the Galatians are being pressured to become something more than they believe they already are, they should note with care the fact that once they have been joined to Christ (3:26), all temporal distinctions become meaningless; all of them are already "children of Abraham" (see 3:7). This is where the opponents have missed the radical nature of faith in Christ. Access to God through Christ is open to all, and once access has been appropriated, the unity of humanity that began prior to the fall is restored, with the resultant loss of distinctions, which were simply echoes of the fall.

It should be noted that the main emphasis of these statements is on the reality of kinship (or sonship) in the covenantal family of Abraham as a result of faith in Christ. Paul's elaboration of this fact in verses 27–28 is a timeless truth, but in the context of a first-century Gentile church led to feel its experience is inferior to a Jewish experience in Christ, these words would make a far greater impact than we may be capable of imagining. Paul specifies the accompanying full rights of this new intimate relationship, showing that Gentiles in Christ are also "heirs according to the promise" (3:29). Such statements leave no doubt that the opponents' position not only fails to add anything to the Galatians but in fact will negate that which they already have received.

While much has been made of the fact that Paul uses baptismal imagery here (see Betz, 181–85), it is too much to say with certainty that he reflects this wording from an existing ceremony. Nevertheless, with the image of being "clothed" in Christ, Paul might very well have a baptismal ceremony in mind. Many early Christian baptisms utilized white robes for the participants to display the overall newness of life in Christ (with the effect of also reducing any visible human distinctions of status or even gender).

The three couplets in verse 28 may reflect an ordering by Paul devised to contradict existing prayers found in Jewish and Gentile circles that gave thanks to God for an individual's superiority over supposed inferiors (Betz, 184n26). In any case, Paul's elaboration on the oneness found in Christ leaves no room for those in Galatia (or for modern readers) to allow for any prejudicial treatment of fellow believers in light of ethnic, economic, or gender particularities. Rather than an exhaustive list, the apostle provides enough elaboration to show that absolutely no distinction can be carried over into the Christ experience.

We should also note, as do many, that the couplets Jew/Greek and slave/free are not exactly like male/female. While the two former couplets eradicate any distinction whatsoever, the latter one, linked by the conjunction *kai* ("and"), indicates that while the complementarity of gender difference remains, such difference no longer represents any barrier to full participation in the newness of life found in Christ (see Snodgrass, 167).

E. Maturing into sonship (4:1–7). Paul builds on the dual images of kinship and covenantal inheritance from the previous climactic section (3:26–29) to point out an important truth in his view of salvation history. Just as the kinship of a child in a wealthy family is never in dispute, although that one must await the time of maturity to assume the control of the estate, so also the kinship of the Gentiles has never been in dispute. Though they were not God's people until the coming of Christ, it was always God's plan to include them (all of humankind) under God's grace.

The use of the symbol of guardianship appears to be applicable to both Jews and Greeks (notice the first-person plural in 4:3, 5). Prior to Christ, Paul asserts, everyone is assessed as having been under the "basic principles" (Greek *stoicheia*; NIV "elemental spiritual forces") of the world. While there has been much discussion as to what Paul includes under this term, it appears that he considers all religious expressions (including the law!) as having been only the basic foundation of that which was to come in Christ.

Verses 4–7 show clearly the redeeming work of God in securing the available kinship for humanity. In a repetition of the Greek verb, God is shown to have "sent his Son" (4:4) and "sent [his] Spirit" (4:6). Thus, it is totally a work of God that has occurred in the fullness of time (4:4), with the result that each Galatian follower of Christ is "no longer a slave, but God's child" (4:7). As if to certify this fact of kinship as being received, Paul describes the Spirit as crying out through the heart of each redeemed person, "Abba" (4:6), which is literally the cry of a small child to a loving father.

While Paul's presentation appears to be designed to show the Gentiles that they are positionally equal with the prejudiced opponents, he has moved far beyond just that fact. In addition, he has shown that, by the gracious work of God in Christ, they actually have received the type of intensely personal relationship that most religious Jews would never have dared to assert for themselves (see Boice, 474n6).

4. An Appeal to the Galatians (4:8–31)

A. An appeal to maturity (4:8–11). Appealing specifically to the Galatian Gentiles, Paul reminds them of their former enslavement to polytheism. He confronts them also with the inappropriateness of turning toward any other religious expressions designed to add to the saving work of Christ. His purpose seems to be to point out that whether they embrace Gentile religious notions or the ancient and holy traditions of Judaism, all of them are "weak and miserable forces [*stoicheia*; NIV note: "principles"]" (4:9; see 4:3), which have now been superseded by their position in Christ.

Referring to the fact that they have already begun to observe certain (presumably Jewish) regulations (4:10), Paul asserts that such actions threaten to negate all that he has done among them (4:11). Such actions suggest that they have made no progress since Paul's visits. In their attempt to mature through legalism, the Galatians have actually indulged in a childish flirtation with danger.

B. An appeal to their personal relationship (4:12–20). The apostle turns to offer the Galatians an objective measure by which to judge his arguments and

motives. He refers back to their first meeting (4:13; the Greek term for "first" would normally refer to the first in a series, possibly giving some weight to the southern Galatian theory). His tone is now more personal (use of "brothers and sisters," 4:12, and "my dear children," 4:19). He calls on them to imitate him, based on the integrity of his former work among them (4:12).

Because of some illness, which he does not pause to detail here (perhaps his "thorn in my flesh"; see 2 Cor. 12:7), Paul's initial visit caused him to come under obligation to the Galatians. He recalls for them their former touching and sympathetic response (4:15) to his needs and appeals to the strong personal relationship (4:14) to press them to reject those who would attempt to drive a wedge between them and their founder (4:17).

He applauds them for their concern to be zealous yet immediately asks them to be very careful to judge if the object of their zeal is worthy (4:17–18). Referring to them as his "children" (4:19), Paul takes the loving tack of a parent who wants to encourage the first steps of their child, stumbling though they may be. His wish is that his readers not only grow but also be capable of discerning which direction is appropriate for their growth (4:18).

Here Paul's frustration becomes visible. He was thinking that his relationship with these churches was secure enough to withstand any adversity, but

In Galatians 4:14, Paul recalls how the Galatians "welcomed me as if I were an angel of God." Acts 14:12 recounts that in Lystra, Paul was called Hermes, who was the messenger of the gods in Greek mythology. Hermes is depicted on this Greek pottery (480–470 BC), wearing the winged sandals of a divine messenger.

now he finds that he is treated with contempt. He wishes his tone could be less anxious and stern (4:20). The fact that he has had to deal roughly with them points out the severity of the situation.

C. An allegorical appeal (4:21–31). His final appeal has perplexed many commentators. The use of the historical narrative concerning Hagar and Sarah coupled with the prophetic utterance of Isaiah (Isa. 54:1) appears to make Paul guilty of some specious scriptural interpretation. This may be an instance when our lack of specific acquaintance with all the dynamics of the Galatian situation hinders our ability to understand. (Possibly Paul's approach discredits interpretations offered by the opponents?)

The "allegory" (4:24; NIV "figuratively") stresses the main points of Paul's previous arguments and thus stands as a good, if somewhat ironic, summation of the opponents' errors. Utilizing an incident revolving around Abraham (likely one of the opponents' favorite figures because of the institution of circumcision), Paul shows that, like the covenants of law and grace, Hagar and Sarah can be compared (literally "stand in the same line") yet have some very different characteristics.

Hagar	Sarah
slave woman	free woman
son, physically born	son, born according to promise
Mount Sinai (old covenant)	(new covenant?)
present Jerusalem, enslaved	Jerusalem above, free

The major difference between the two is of "kind," not circumstance. Paul appears to be relying on the Galatians' acquaintance with the historical narrative to point out the major factors in the story. One factor, which is unstated but certainly in view, is that the Hagar incident was not a necessary part of God's plan and had not been included in the promise to Abraham (see Genesis 16). So also, the covenantal promises to Abraham had not included the law (which he already stated to have become necessary only because of human sin; see Gal. 3:19; Rom. 5:20).

Thus, rather than being discontinuous with the promises of Abraham, the gospel of grace is fully aligned with those original promises. As if to further enhance the point, Paul recites a prophecy of Isaiah concerning Israel's restoration from the captivity of Babylon (Isa. 54:1). While the Israelites were few in number then (as the Gentile Christians are, relative to Jewish believers, at the time of writing), miraculous, God-ordained growth was promised.

Finally, then, as in their situation, the son under slavery persecuted the son of promise (Gal. 4:29). The opponents are clearly portrayed as operating outside the covenantal promises of God. Sarah's statement in Genesis 21:10 conveniently allows Paul to imply not only that the opponents' position should be rejected but also that the opponents themselves should be cast out (4:30), since the enslaved cannot inherit the promises with the free. Paul indicates that rather than being seen as second-class citizens of the Mosaic covenant, the Galatian Gentile Christians have been fully accepted as children and heirs (they are Isaac; 4:28; see Gal. 3:7) of the Abrahamic covenant.

5. Freedom in Christ (5:1–6:10)

A. Thesis (5:1). Grammatically, verse 1 of chapter 5 is related to the previous paragraph, yet it also provides both a summary and a transition point to the letter. While the manuscript evidence varies on points of grammatical connectives, the sense of the statement is not endangered. In fact, this statement provides the thesis for Paul's insistence on the Galatians' rejection of the opponents.

The NIV's rendering of the verse into two sentences appears to be quite correct (against the KJV). The first sentence stands as the declaration of purpose for Christ's redeeming work (literally "Christ set us free to freedom"), emphasizing the decisive event, which changed the believer's condition from one of slavery (under the law and other elemental principles; see Gal. 4:3, 9) to freedom (see Gal. 2:4; John 8:32–36; Rom. 7:4, 6; 1 Cor. 9:1, 21; 11:29).

The second part of the verse encourages the Galatians to hold to their position against those who would return them again to slavery. This encouragement will be given practical substance in verses 13–26. But Paul digresses for a moment, providing specific warnings against any Galatian hesitancy on this point (5:2–12).

B. Warnings and reproof (5:2–12). This digression serves to provide the last and most pointed set of warnings concerning the seriousness of the Galatians' consideration of the opponents' position. Beginning with an emphatically personal appeal (literally "Behold, I, Paul, say to you"), he expands on the fact that the very act of circumcision, rather than being a safeguard for those who are unsure of which position is correct, actually serves to negate the power of Christ in their lives (5:2). The fact that Paul seems to restate this very same proposition in a slightly altered manner in verses 3–4 reminds us of his double curse against this teaching in Galatians 1:8–9.

The call from Paul is for them to declare their allegiance. To attempt to be justified through law is to forsake the grace offered in Christ and to forsake Christ himself (5:4). If they are under the power of faith, then they join him (note the switch from "you" [plural], 5:2–4, to "we," 5:5) in awaiting the completion of the salvation begun in Christ. In this statement, one of the few about the end times, it is of crucial importance to note that the follower of the promise receives God's declaration of righteousness (see Gal. 3:6), while the follower of the law is incessantly and futilely working to keep the law (5:4; see Gal. 3:10–12) in order to gain that declaration.

In summing up the ineffectiveness of the rite of circumcision, Paul needs to make the point that may well be an overriding consideration in the minds of the opponents and wavering Gentiles: without circumcision, or without the legal requirements, does the Christ

follower fall hopelessly into antinomianism (thus believing they are governed by no laws)? Paul assures them in verse 6 that the physical act of circumcision, or even the lack of it, guarantees nothing as to the type of life one will lead. Rather, contrary to following legal requirements, proper faith will express a person's relationship to God through loving action, motivated more by gratitude than obligation. Paul will pick up on this theme again in the next section of the letter (5:13–26).

An evident shift in tone takes place in verse 7 and continues throughout the rest of the letter as if to signal Paul's satisfaction that his argument should have the effect of restoring his "founder's status" among his readers. He now questions how the rift in their relationship could have taken place. The contrast now is clearly between Paul and the one (singular in 5:10) or ones who have been hindering the Galatians. Certainly God, "the one who calls you" (5:8; see Rom. 8:28, 30), is not the cause for their defection. The blame seems to sit squarely on the shoulders of the opponents among them. Paul's expression of confidence in the Galatians for moving forward again arises from his professed knowledge of their shared faith in Christ (5:10).

The final, somewhat inconsequential objection to which he addresses his remarks apparently came from those opponents who knew that Paul had appeared at times to allow circumcision to coexist with his gospel of grace (5:11). This may be a reference to his actions relative to Timothy (Acts 16:3). If so, it lends further credence to a dating for this letter after the Jerusalem council (Acts 15). In any case, Paul makes it known that even his allowance of circumcision does not contradict his present position that the opponents are attempting to attribute to such rites (and the accompanying obligation to keep the law) something that Paul had never allowed. His action toward Timothy, for example, was one of simple expediency (cf. 1 Cor. 9:19–23). The opponents, on the contrary, make circumcision a necessity for covenantal inclusion.

He ridicules the opponents' charge that he preached circumcision. Why then would he be attacked so vigorously? Instead, he points to such a charge as a mere distraction from the opponents' real conflict with him. He represents the "offense" of the cross (5:11; Greek *skandalon*; literally a "trap" or "snare"), which overturns their entire human approach to righteousness.

Apparently the surfacing of such attacks against Paul's ministry so frustrated him that he allowed a sarcastic remark to finalize his disgust with the opponents' preoccupation with the outward rite of circumcision (5:12). While some commentators appear reluctant to believe Paul would utter such a condemnation, this would actually be a better fate for these opponents than the one he calls for in Galatians 1:8–9. (See Mark 9:43, where Jesus uses similar terminology in reference to something that is a *skandalon*.)

C. Proof of one's grounding (5:13–26). Paul has now thoroughly analyzed the opponents' position and has found it wanting. Paul has defended his position as an apostle and his rejection of the additional requirements of Jewish conversion for Gentiles who want to come into the covenantal relationship with God through faith in Christ. Yet one might ask, "What's left? If you take away law, by what standard will a person live?"

In addressing this type of question, Paul reasserts his view of the purpose of redemption in Christ (see Gal. 5:1) with the emphatic "You, my brothers and sisters, were called to be free" (5:13). This freedom does not induce license (indulging the sinful nature, 5:13), since it is not the absence of law, but was the goal of the law (5:14; see Jer. 31:31–34). Paul shows that the proper expression of the law comes from a heart full of grateful love rather than anxious self-centeredness and is shown through mutual service (5:13; literally "becoming slaves to one another") and the love of neighbor (5:13–18).

This is an especially attractive and pointed picture of the results of true freedom, since it appears to be in complete contrast to the character of their congregational relationships at that time (5:15). Rather than being the guarantor of righteous actions among these former pagans, the inclusion of the law into their lives has only given vent to competitiveness and lack of concern for each other. You can almost hear Paul say, "Precisely!" Their way shows that they use the law inappropriately, since they do not gain the results through it that all recognize to be crucial for those who desire to be found in God's righteousness (5:14; see Lev. 19:18; Luke 10:27 and parallels).

As a counterbalance to the possibility of expressing one's "sinful nature" or "flesh" (5:13) through freedom, Paul asserts that living "by the Spirit" (5:16) will characterize true freedom. The contrast of flesh (Greek *sarx*) and Spirit (Greek *pneuma*) is found throughout the Pauline Epistles, as well as other parts of the New Testament. Rather than pointing to two different parts of the same individual, the terminology relates to an orientation that motivates the course of life a person will take. These two orientations conflict in the most basic sense (5:17; see Rom. 7:15–23). Paul seems to assert that in spite of a person's will to do right (i.e., follow the law), the flesh orientation makes that will ineffective and dooms the person to failure (5:17). This assertion reveals the utter fruitlessness of the righteousness-through-law approach.

The great emancipation for the Christ follower is to be "led by the Spirit" (5:18), a leading that takes away our subjugation to the law and to the sinful nature the law appeals to (see Rom. 6:11–14).

The next two sections (5:19–26) provide a practical contrast of attitudes and actions, which can be a personal test for the Galatians' present orientation. By finding oneself on the list of either vices or virtues, one could also identify whether or not one was led by the Spirit.

Fifteen acts of the flesh are specified (5:19–21), with the insistence that the list is not exhaustive ("and the like," 5:21; see other lists in 1 Cor. 6:9–10; Eph. 5:5; Rev. 22:15). While they may have been grouped according to various schemes, the list includes sins that many would expect ("sexual immorality, impurity and debauchery";

Gal. 5:19) and others that might be unexpected ("discord,... fits of rage, selfish ambition"; 5:20). Some of the sins appear to relate directly to the pagan lifestyles the readers once practiced ("idolatry and witchcraft;... orgies"; 5:20–21), while others could even be associated with the type of "biting and devouring" (5:15) that appeared to be a result of their new legalistic lifestyle ("jealousy, ... dissensions, factions"; 5:20).

Paul asserts that it does not take great spiritual insight ("the acts of the flesh are obvious"; 5:19) to spot the inappropriateness of these activities and attitudes among believers. In fact, he reminds them that he spoke to them about this before (5:21) and told them that such acts revealed a person who would "not inherit the kingdom of God" (5:21).

In contrast to the multiple "acts" of the flesh, the singular "fruit" (likely denoting a harmonious unity) promotes a God-oriented expression of activities and attitudes that enhance one's relationship to God and fellow men and women. The nine attributes found here (5:22–26) are clearly indicative of the Holy Spirit in the believer's life, and come as a composite whole, not as individual items that some have and others do not (5:22–23; for other lists of virtues, see 2 Cor. 6:6; Eph. 4:2; 5:9; Col. 3:12–15).

Three sets are discernible in the list. The first, "love, joy, peace" (5:22), reflects the resultant attitude of one who has been endowed with the Spirit of the God, who is identified as love (1 John 4:8), who brings complete satisfaction (John 3:29), who is declared to bring "on earth peace" (Luke 2:14), and who is identified as the "Prince of Peace" (Isa. 9:6).

The second set, "forbearance, kindness, goodness" (5:22), reflects how a Spirit-led individual will conduct interpersonal relationships. The third set, "faithfulness, gentleness and self-control" (5:22–23), seems to focus primarily on a person's inner life when under the control of the Spirit. (For a full treatment of such terms, see Barclay, 63–127.)

Paul concludes the list in verse 23 with the pronouncement, "Against such things there is no law." Certainly his remarks are not just indicating that the foregoing list of "fruit" is permitted under the law. Rather, his point seems to answer those who feel that the call to move beyond the law would leave the Galatians without any foundation on which to measure their actions. Paul maintains that the work of the Spirit in one's life provides an internal motivation and proper orientation to participate in the attitudes and actions that are consistent with the character of Christ. Thus, with the freedom afforded through Christ (5:1, 13), the believer crucifies the sinful nature and becomes a new person (5:24) who by nature *is* the righteousness demanded by the law and granted through the Spirit (see 2 Cor. 3:6).

The final exhortations of the chapter indicate that while the reality of the fruit is a gift from the Spirit, the believer's responsibility is to actively "live by the Spirit" and "keep in step with the Spirit" (Gal. 5:25).

The follower of Jesus (and Paul includes himself here) does not sit idly by with the power of the Spirit within. We are, instead, called to active participation, in accordance with the new reality of our kinship. The tension of positional and experiential reality of the new creation is evident throughout all Paul's letters (see especially Phil. 2:12).

The final statement of the chapter may introduce the next, more practical section of exhortations. In any case, Paul's focus moves from theory (5:1, 13–25) to practice (5:26; 6:1–10). Possibly the particular statement of verse 26 is put in close proximity to the encouragement to live by the Spirit since some of the Galatians might begin to develop a new set of hierarchical stages related to their manifestation of fruit. This Paul will not allow.

D. Practical ethics (6:1–10). It is not unusual for Paul to conclude his letters with a section on practical living, which emphasizes some of the themes he addressed in the heart of the letter (see Rom. 12:9–21; 1 Cor. 16:13–14; 2 Cor. 13:5). A pervasive problem for the gospel of grace was for the attitude of hierarchy to invade the Spirit-led life (cf. Rom. 12:3–8;

1 Cor. 1:10–17; 2 Cor. 10:1–18, esp. v. 12). It may well be that this was the chief attraction of legalism—the opportunity to measure oneself relative to another and to appear superior. As Paul indicates, such an attitude is completely foreign to the gospel (Eph. 2:8–10).

In areas particularly open to the temptation of hierarchical appraisal (e.g., the awareness of another's sin, 6:1, and the awareness of another's burden, 6:2), Paul exhorts the Galatians to "live by the Spirit" (6:1, referring back to the previous chapter regarding the fruit that defines such a person). The Spirit-led individual will work toward restoration (6:1), which has the effect of obliterating the wrong that could be used to strengthen one's claim of superiority against the erring sister or brother.

Paul completes these exhortations with an appeal for each person to seriously assess their own condition, as one whose only concern is to test their own level of responsibility in the Lord (6:3–5), without falling into an attitude of conceit (6:3). The Galatians are to see that their faithful actions in this area do fulfill a law, namely, the law of Christ (6:3). It is interesting to note that Paul seems to regard such practical areas of personal relationships among believers as the benchmark of which type of law they follow: the one leading to acts of the flesh or the one exhibiting the fruit of the Spirit.

In the area of financial responsibility, the Galatians are exhorted to share with those who instruct them "in the word" (6:6). Why Paul adds this concern here is open to interpretation. He may be including a concern that related to a particular injustice done to a fellow worker. However, the following statements (6:7–10) seem more than coincidentally related to issues discussed in 2 Corinthians 9:6–15, where this particular sowing-reaping proverb (see Job 4:8; Hos. 8:7) is stated in a similar context. Very likely, the same type of oppositional elements found in Galatia were present in Corinth as well (2 Cor. 11:22–23). The group there, as here, denounced Paul's apostolic credentials (2 Cor. 10:2, 4, 10–15; 11:5, 7–8, 13, 15, 18). Given this interpreter's position as to the dating of this epistle, it is also likely that these opponents attempted to discredit Paul's collection for the church at Jerusalem (Rom. 15:25–27; 1 Cor. 16:1–4, especially v. 2; 2 Cor. 8:1–9:15).

Thus, this final section is provided in answer to the opponents' objections that participation in Paul's collection is unwise, giving a pretender the chance to defraud them (see 2 Cor. 11:8). Paul's word is to appeal to God's judgment of the matter (6:7). Their participation is called for as a manifestation of the Spirit in their lives, an active "doing good" (6:9), which is especially appropriate when it benefits the "family of believers" (i.e., the Jerusalem church; 6:10).

6. Conclusion with Personal Appeal (6:11–18)

Confirming the belief that most of the letter was dictated is the notification in verse 11 that Paul writes the remainder of the letter "with my own hand." In drawing attention to the "large letters" with which he writes, Paul may give us the final clue as to why, upon his initial visit, the Galatians were willing to tear out their own eyes for him (4:15). The "thorn in my flesh" of 2 Corinthians 12:7 and the ailment that plagued him in Galatia may well be attributed to some

As was customary, Paul used an amanuensis (a secretary) to write his epistles. In Galatians 6:11, Paul picks up the pen and exclaims that he writes with "large letters." The parchment pages shown here, from a Coptic codex containing portions of the Gospel of John and the Psalms, are an example of ancient writing (Upper Egypt, fifth century AD).

form of eye disease. His handwriting may have been awkward, but it authenticated his letters. (See 2 Thess. 3:17, where the expression, "This is how I write," may also be explained by such a theory.)

Here Paul takes the opportunity to personally emphasize the main point of his letter. The ones who trouble the Galatians are considered to be hypocritical opportunists, attempting to build their own misguided view of spirituality (6:12–13) by forcing the Galatians into a dependent relationship. The opponents' motivation in all this is considered to be fear—a desire not to be persecuted (6:12), presumably by their own nonbelieving brethren (the same who have persecuted Paul).

In ridiculing his opponents' motives, Paul sets forth his own motive. It is found in the pivotal experience of the "cross of our Lord Jesus Christ" (6:14). This event has the effect, for Paul, of causing the death of the world to him (6:14, referring to the world's system, especially with regard to its values).

As if to leave them with one final, decisive word, he declares that the rite the opponents assert as being crucial becomes meaningless in relation to the gracious work of the Spirit in making a "new creation" (6:15; see 5:6; 2 Cor. 5:17). Even the benediction, so characteristic of the final words of the Pauline Epistles, carries this message. Peace and mercy are reserved only for those who "follow this rule." Only these people can be properly identified as "*the* Israel of God" (6:16; see Rom. 9:6; 11:7; Eph. 3:6). Therefore, in Paul's view, to be admitted as a member of the *old* covenant people of God, one must adhere to the provisions of the *new* covenant, which was promised as part of the *old*.

Paul's last words alert us to the toll such battles exacted from him. The constant harassment concerning his apostolic credentials and the problem of legalism as an excuse for Jewish prejudice toward Gentiles were exhausting him. His authenticity was really not a matter of speculation; it should be a matter of evidence, the physical marks (Greek *stigmata*; literally a "brand mark" on an animal or slave) of a man scarred by a world that persecuted him as it did his Lord. Is there really any other, more convincing evidence they would need to see (see 2 Cor. 11:22–30)?

The benediction is characteristic of Paul, though unusually short (see Rom. 16:25–27). Particularly poignant for this epistle is the inclusion of the title "brothers and sisters" (6:18). He sends off the letter with a prayer that such a designation might still be appropriate.

Select Bibliography

Barclay, William. *Flesh and Spirit*. Grand Rapids: Baker, 1976.

Betz, Hans Dieter. *Galatians*. Hermeneia. Philadelphia: Fortress, 1979.

Boice, James Montgomery. "Galatians." In *Expositor's Bible Commentary*. Edited by Frank E. Gaebelein. Vol. 10. Grand Rapids: Zondervan, 1976.

Bruce, F. F. *The Epistle to the Galatians*. New International Greek Testament Commentary. Grand Rapids: Eerdmans, 1982.

Carson, D. A., Peter T. O'Brien, and Mark A. Seifrid, eds. *The Paradoxes of Paul*. Vol. 2 of *Justification and Variegated Nomism*. Grand Rapids: Baker Academic, 2004.

Guthrie, Donald. *Galatians*. New Century Bible Commentary. Greenwood, SC: Attic, 1977.

Jervis, L. Ann. *Galatians*. New International Biblical Commentary. Peabody, MA: Hendrickson, 1999.

Morris, Leon. *Galatians: Paul's Charter of Christian Freedom*. Downers Grove, IL: InterVarsity, 1996.

Nanos, Mark D., ed. *The Galatians Debate*. Peabody, MA: Hendrickson, 2002.

Silva, Moisés. *Interpreting Galatians: Explorations in Exegetical Method*. 2nd ed. Grand Rapids: Baker Academic, 2001.

Snodgrass, Klyne R. "Galatians 3:28: Conundrum or Solution?" In *Women, Authority and the Bible*. Edited by Alvera Mickelson. Downers Grove, IL: InterVarsity, 1984.

Tenney, Merrill C. *Galatians: The Charter of Christian Liberty*. Grand Rapids: Eerdmans, 1950.

Witherington, Ben, III. *Grace in Galatia: A Commentary on Paul's Letter to the Galatians*. Grand Rapids: Eerdmans, 1998.

Ephesians

RICHARD J. ERICKSON

Introduction

Authorship

Ephesians claims unambiguously to come from Paul's hand, both in the very first word of the letter and in various other personal references. Yet doubts about this arise for several reasons. The author's obviously limited acquaintance with his readers (1:15; 3:2) is highly puzzling if Paul is writing to his friends in Ephesus, where he spent nearly three years. Likewise, the literary relationship between Ephesians and Colossians shows that if the same person did not write both letters at the same time, then one was modeled on the other. But the letters differ markedly in vocabulary and style, suggesting that the same person did *not* author both documents. Furthermore, the teaching of Ephesians appears in some cases to reflect situations in the early church that postdate Paul's death by several decades (see references to "apostles and prophets" in 2:20; 3:5). These factors add up to the possibility that Paul did not write Ephesians.

Still, if Paul did write Ephesians, it predates his death in Rome under Nero, around AD 65. References to chains and imprisonment would place composition in the early 60s, probably at Rome. But to whom was it written? Clearly, the author is not well acquainted with the intended readers, which would be strange if they were Paul's congregation at Ephesus. Oddly, certain important and early Greek manuscripts lack the words "in Ephesus" (1:1), suggesting that the document was never meant for that congregation, but for some other or others that Paul had never visited. Perhaps it was a circular letter sent to several churches in Roman Asia, including Ephesus. At any rate, the real destination (if not Ephesus) and the origin of the insertion "in Ephesus" remain conjectural.

Taken one by one, the separate pieces of evidence against Pauline authorship can perhaps be explained away. Their cumulative effect is what carries the greatest weight against authenticity. The evidence is not airtight either way. Objections to the "inspired lie" perpetrated by another author's calling himself "Paul" dismiss the idea that pseudepigraphy may have functioned in the first century like footnoting does today. We may then with good conscience treat Ephesians either as written by Paul or as written by one of his associates. Meanwhile, for simplicity's sake, we can refer to the author as Paul.

Content

Central to the message of Ephesians is God's re-creation of the human family according to his originally intended design. This new creation shatters the Jewish community's long-standing opinion that God accepts Jews and rejects non-Jews. The traditional criterion of distinction between the Jew and the non-Jew is obedience to the law, but this criterion, fostering pride and exclusivism, was abolished in Christ's sacrificial death. Consequently, nothing hinders reuniting all humanity as the people of God, with Christ as the head. The fact that even within the church, let alone outside the church, this reunification is not fully in effect is the result of the advance arrival of the new age of God's rule. Even now God endows his new family with the power of the Spirit, enabling them to live out here and now their future new life. Thus Ephesians focuses on God's people united in Christ through the power of the Spirit.

Outline

Commentary

1. Opening and Greetings (1:1–2)

The author identifies himself by name and calling and greets his readers in the manner typical in the Pauline Epistles, but without the usual companions. Whether the addressees live specifically in Ephesus is unclear.

2. Re-creating the Human Family: What God *Has* Done (1:3–3:21)

A. The mystery of God's will and God's threefold blessing (1:3–14). This opening section, setting the agenda for the rest of the letter, is itself opened in verses 3–6. God, who in Jesus Christ originated the solution to the dilemma of our sin, is praised (blessed) for blessing us in Christ with every spiritual blessing (1:3). The word "bless" carries here two different senses, depending on whether God or a human being is the one who blesses. "In the heavenly realms" implies that God's blessings are secured in the very character of God and are not subject to the uncertainties of earthly life. This is repeatedly confirmed in this section by emphasis on God's decision, will, and purpose.

God made his choice before the creation of the world: we, the human race, were created to be holy and blameless before him (1:4). Because he loved us and simply because it pleased him to do so, he predestined us to be his own adopted family (1:5), perhaps from among all other creatures. The purpose of this sovereignly independent choice was that we might praise the glorious grace God has freely given us (1:6). He is no egotistical God, but one who knows better than we do that if his creatures concentrate their praise and attention on him, all their creaturely potential will be realized.

This predestination applies to all humanity, not to some elect portion. It does not refer to Christians only but to the entire race. It was God's plan for creation that we humans would be his special delight, able to commune with him and praise him forever. It is this original design, marred and corrupted by human rebellion, which God has now restored in Christ Jesus. The concept of predestination (or election) emphasizes God's initiative, God's choice in creating—and now in re-creating. There is no hint here of his choosing some people and rejecting others.

Threaded throughout this tone-setting passage is the key to the entire argument of the letter: all this is done for us "through Jesus Christ," "in the One he loves," "in Christ," "in him" (1:3–6). The solution to the human dilemma resides in Christ the Lord, whose Father is none other than the blessed God.

In Christ three spiritual blessings are ours: redemption, adoption, and sealing with the Spirit (1:7, 11, 13). Together they amount to a whole new God-determined existence. Paul begins with redemption, made available to us through the payment of a price—the blood, or death, of Christ (1:7). It consists in the forgiveness of sins, the necessary first step toward the re-creation of a truly holy, blameless family. God's blessing us with redemption implies that his original intentions (1:4–6) have been momentarily frustrated; sin has spoiled creation. Redemption then is the foundation of God's re-creative work on behalf of humanity. Without redemption, nothing else could be done.

We have this redemption, this new standing with our Creator, not because of our own worthiness, but simply according to the wealth of his grace—another assurance of the security of God's provision (1:7–8). He has heaped grace on us beyond measure (according to his own wise understanding), having made known to us what he wanted to do all along, something that gives him pleasure, something that he decided to accomplish at the proper time in Christ, namely, the "mystery of his will" (1:9). This mystery, hidden in God's will but now revealed to us, is nothing less than that everything in creation, heavenly and earthly, human and nonhuman, will be gathered and united in Christ (1:10).

The first blessing's negative orientation is balanced by the second blessing's positive orientation. In Christ we have been appointed to participate (1:11). The purpose is that we may praise God's glory and so be enabled to fulfill our proper destiny as those who belong to a holy God (1:12). The place we have been allotted was hinted at already in verses 5 and 10. It is a place in God's new family, whose head is Christ. Again, God himself is the author, decider, planner, and accomplisher of this; he has desired it when we did not. And desiring it, he can and will do it. Indeed, he has already done it.

Up to this point, Paul has been speaking in the first person plural, meaning that he includes his readers—or possibly, contrasting them instead with some other group to which

Ephesus was the major city of Asia Minor. This photograph of Ephesus shows the ancient columns ringing the agora, the commercial center of the city, and the theater just behind it. The church of Ephesus had high status throughout the first several centuries of the common era.

he himself belongs. This other group he has called "we, who were the first to put our hope in Christ" (1:12). Now he draws the readers into the picture by centering the third blessing on them. They have heard the "message of truth," the true message, the gospel that brought them, too, into God's salvation once they believed it (1:13). This gospel is the proclamation that Jesus of Nazareth, the Jewish messiah, has been declared king of all creation by his resurrection from the dead (Rom. 1:2–6), with the implication that all humanity, not just Israel, belongs to him.

Thus these Gentiles, too, are "in Christ" and in him have received the third blessing—the "*seal*, the promised Holy Spirit" (1:13). This at least portrays the Spirit as a down payment, a "deposit guaranteeing our inheritance" (1:14; the word translated "inheritance" is related to the word translated "chosen" in 1:11) while we await the full redemption of God's possession. As will be seen in 3:14–19, however, the presence of the Spirit implies far more than a passive guarantee; it also means the power necessary to live out now in this doomed age the ethic of the new age to come, which in Christ has already entered the scene. This new ethic, good for us and for everyone else, is rooted in the praise of the glorious Creator.

B. Prayer for enlightenment (1:15–23). The immense significance of this threefold work of God on behalf of humanity makes it imperative that people understand it. For the more they do so, the greater their ability will be to live and grow in their new relationship with God and each other. Therefore ("for this reason"), Paul prays for his readers, whose faith he has heard about, that they may increase in understanding. Their two-dimensional faith encapsulates the sort of life the epistle promotes. It consists of faith in the Lord Jesus and love toward all the saints. In other words, it involves a confidence in God's work through Christ, which then issues in loving concern for fellow members of the new family, no matter who they may be, acted out in attitudes and concrete deeds (1:15). The

epistle in fact divides in half, treating these twin aspects of the faith. That Paul never stops giving thanks for this church or praying for it is not to be taken literally. He simply means that they are now a regular concern of his; he loves them this way, just as they love all the saints (1:16).

He prays for these people, that God would foster their understanding by giving them the Spirit of wisdom and revelation and enlightened hearts (1:17–18). The expression "glorious Father" (literally "Father of glory") may allude to the indwelling Spirit as God's Shekinah glory, as in the temple. Either way, it is unlikely that Paul contemplates here the readers' need to receive the Holy Spirit, since in verse 13 he already declared that they do have the Spirit. What is meant, rather, is that they need to receive *from* the Spirit a revealing of the divine wisdom, so that they might themselves know God (or perhaps Christ). The phrase "eyes of your heart" refers to the spirit of the community—the mind, the inner soul—in its power to grasp ideas (1:18a). The implication is that if God does not give this illumination, it cannot be had. It is also important to keep in mind that the concern is for health of the entire community and not merely for the spirituality of individuals.

Paul specifies what he wants the believing community to understand with their enlightened heart: (1) the hope to which God has called them, (2) the glorious abundance of God's inheritance, and (3) God's more than sufficient power for those who believe (1:18b–19). These three concepts bear a striking similarity to the three spiritual blessings that Paul enumerated earlier. That they are not precisely parallel simply begins to unfold their significance. Paul's prayer that the believers better understand these three concepts is not left dangling; in the course of the next two chapters, indeed over the remainder of the letter, Paul himself elaborates their meaning.

Before beginning to do so, however, he makes an important connection between these ethereal, abstract concepts (and blessings) on the one hand, and down-to-earth history on the other. The power that God has in such abundance for his people is the very same power he exercised in raising Christ from the dead (1:20). It may be difficult to grasp the truth of one's membership in the redeemed, Spirit-sealed family of God, newly re-created on earth. Emotionally and mentally, perhaps, we are too weak to hold on to these things in the onslaught of reasons to doubt their reliability. But God has anchored them in a concrete historical event—the physical resurrection of Jesus from the tomb. These truths, then, are no less secure and reliable than the fact that Christ is no longer dead; indeed, they could not be true apart from that event.

Moreover, the exercise of this power that raised Christ from the dead and secured for us our hope and inheritance has also seated Christ at the place of supreme honor in the universe, the right hand of God (1:20); this is what the gospel is about. Consequently, whether viewed from below or above, Christ supersedes all competitors, potential or real, for power (1:21). Rule and authority, power and dominion, and titles upon titles are given both in this doomed evil age and in the glorious, unending age to come. But neither they nor their possessors take precedence over God's Messiah. The fact that rebellious creatures (including all of us in our fallen natures) are permitted to compete with Christ and with each other is characteristic of this present age. The future age has already been initiated, however, in the life, death, resurrection, and exaltation of Jesus Christ, for all things *have been* subjected to him (1:22, a quotation from Ps. 8:6), whether they know it or not. Christ has already been made head over all things, uniting in himself the restored universe, for the sake of the church, his body, the new, all-encompassing family of God (1:23; see 1:10b).

C. Redemption: Clearing the ground (2:1–10). Returning to the first blessing, redemption, Paul elaborates what is implied in it. Through the work of Christ, by divine fiat, God has swept clear the ground on which he re-creates the spoiled creation. The word "redeem/redemption" does not occur in this portion of the letter, but the theme pervades it.

The human predicament is described first from the Gentiles' perspective (2:1–2; cf. 2:3). They were formerly dead, in the estimation of God, since they previously lived in transgressions and sins. Their lifestyle conformed to this present worldly age, to the competitive values underlying all cultures and all political and economic systems. Behind that worldly system stands the satanic "ruler of the kingdom of the air" ("air" referring to the presumed dwelling place of the spirit world), who even now drives both groups and individuals to disobey God.

Among such disobedient people Paul now includes the Jews (2:3). Jews, too, live under the influence of their fleshly, sinful human desires. Existence on earth consists of a continual struggle to satisfy the selfish demands

A statue of Ephesian Artemis (first century AD), who was worshiped as a fertility goddess. Ephesians 2:2 says that the recipients once "followed the ways of this world," which likely included the worship of other gods, a common part of the world around them.

of body and soul. Consequently, the Jews are by nature under the wrath of God, just like the rest of humanity, namely, the Gentiles.

This is no insignificant remark! First, it clearly precludes any human beings from supposing that they are exempt from judgment. From a Jewish point of view, the entire human race is either Jewish or Gentile, and both groups are by nature condemned. Second, this statement of a redeemed Jew to Gentiles embodies the humility characteristic of the newly created family of God (see Eph. 2:11–22).

The human predicament is absolute; there is no escape. "Dead" people, already condemned, cannot avoid condemnation. Only from the outside can any effective solution come. Paul introduces that outside solution in 2:4: "But . . . God." God's character as one who is boundlessly merciful and who loves human beings with a "great love" has changed the picture. He remedied the hopeless situation in three ways with one sweeping act in Christ.

First, he brought these dead Jews and Gentiles back to life *together with Christ* (the "us/we" in 2:5 now includes the Gentile readers). Anticipating the sum of the matter (stated in 2:8–10), Paul suddenly asserts that this salvation from death is wholly God's doing, an act of his grace (2:5). He then returns immediately to the point to state the two remaining ways in which God has interfered. Second, God raised us *together with Christ*, and third, he seated us *together with Christ* in that same heavenly place of honor that Christ himself now occupies (2:6). In other words, just as Christ is the manifestation of God to humanity, so Christ, as the head of his body, the church, is the manifestation of humanity to God. In Christ, God and humanity meet and are at peace.

God's purpose in restoring and honoring humanity, in being kind to his rebellious creatures, is to demonstrate for all time the surpassing bounty of his forgiving grace (2:7). The point is not that God needs to flaunt it but that creation needs to see it.

Paul now draws the obvious conclusion: if we were dead and therefore helpless, and if

God intervened and by his own will revived us in Christ, then it is an act of his grace alone, a gift (2:8). It is important to hear that the objects of God's attention are all *dead*; their only qualification for his gracious favor is their hopelessly sinful rebellion. They need not clean up first; in fact, being dead, they cannot. The worst person imaginable is for that very reason eligible. We receive grace, says Paul, not by producing anything to exchange for it but simply by succumbing to God's gracious mercy, by entrusting our fate to him. In short, we are saved by grace.

This free salvation has a twofold relation to human works. First, works have no part in the acquiring of salvation. Recent exegetical discussion suggests that by "works" Paul means the various marks of Judaism: circumcision, Sabbath keeping, kosher food, and the like, as if ethnicity were the issue. It is possible, however, that Ephesians broadens the idea to include any sort of self-aggrandizing behavior. Either way, our works cannot place God in our control; we would in fact destroy ourselves in our boasting (2:9). Second, however, truly good works realize our God-intended potential. God has prepared a way of life for which we as his creatures are ideally adapted. We were made to function best and to be happiest as a united community, living as God originally created us, and now is re-creating us, to live. Paul describes that lifestyle with detail in Ephesians 4–6.

Thus at the heart of redemption is a return to the pristine, predestined (1:4) relationship between God and humanity: total acceptance on the part of God and total dependence on the part of humanity, all embraced in a framework of love and community. On this cleared ground God now reestablishes his family.

D. Adoption: Removing the barriers (2:11–22). Paul turns next to the second spiritual blessing: adoption. Just as the word "redemption" does not occur in 2:1–10, although redemption is its theme, so now the words "adoption" and "inheritance" do not appear in this text, but those themes predominate.

One of the deepest yearnings of the human soul is to belong. We instinctively draw circles that include ourselves and exclude others, giving us coveted membership in a group others wish they belonged to. There can be no "inner ring," in C. S. Lewis's terms, unless there are despised outsiders. The Jewish nation, God's "inner ring" in their own view, drew the circle at the law, epitomized in marks of Jewishness. Jews stigmatized Gentiles as the "uncircumcised," often in self-exaltation (2:11). Without the despised Gentiles, Jews would have failed to be distinctive in their own nationalist perspective. Romans felt the same way toward non-Romans.

Paul reminds his Gentile readers that, under such circumstances, they were without Christ (who came through the Jewish nation); they had no part in the true family of God and thus no access to the promises God had made to that family; in short, they were hopelessly alienated from their Creator. Ironically, the particular people through whom God intended to show his grace to all humanity became the chief obstacle to that goal, erecting a barrier between themselves and their mission. The universal, natural (2:3) enmity toward God results in enmity between groups of human beings and indeed between individuals within groups (2:12).

But those outsiders, formerly excluded and far off, have now been brought near, within the circle, by the sacrificial death of Christ (2:13). Bringing the Gentiles "near" implies the establishment of peace, and Christ Jesus himself is the peace. By removing the criterion of judgment, the law, Christ has demolished the barrier separating the two groups, making the two into one united group (2:14). The allusion is to the balustrade or wall in the Jerusalem temple separating the inner Court of Jews from the outer Court of Gentiles. Inscriptions in the wall, warning of instant death to Gentiles crossing the barrier, have been recovered in the rubble from the destruction of Jerusalem in AD 70.

With his physical body Jesus removed the barrier, the law as used by its ancient guardians,

the law understood as a list of individual commandments and ordinances distinguishing Jews from non-Jews. His death fully satisfied the law once and for all and thereby eliminated it as a means of separation between people (2:15).

Christ's dual purpose in this was (1) to create in himself one new humanity out of the two hostile groups, making peace between them, and (2) to reconcile both groups to God in this one united body by obliterating in himself their hatred toward God and toward one another (2:16). Thus, not only Jews and Gentiles, but any two (or more) groups or individuals are deprived of all grounds for rejecting each other and are brought to peace both with each other and with God. This is precisely the two-directional restoration alluded to in 1:15.

So as not to let this grace go unknown to those it was intended to benefit, Christ preached peace both to the outsiders and to the insiders (Isa. 52:7; 57:19). Because the ground of the insiders' security (namely, the law, the "wall") had been taken away from them, they needed to have peace preached to them no less than the outsiders did (Eph. 2:17). Both Gentile and Jew have access to the Father, the goal of all human striving, only through Christ and by the same Spirit. Contrary to all expectation, God views the entire human race as one and deals with it all at one time, by grace, in one person.

In verse 19 Paul sums up: the Gentile Christians are no longer shut out from the family of God. They have been given a place within the ring. In fact, "ringism" has been abolished. Gentiles are part of the household, part of the citizenry of God's own people; they belong. God hosts the premiere family reunion. In a metaphor echoing the allusion to the temple in 2:14, Paul describes the situation as the construction of a new temple (2:20–22), a new dwelling place for God on the earth among his people. Founded on the "apostles and prophets" (i.e., on the promises God has made), and with Christ himself as the cornerstone holding the whole structure together, this new building grows continually as people of all kinds are added to it. The fact that God lives in this new temple "by his Spirit" implies the Shekinah glory familiar from the Old Testament (Exodus 40; 1 Kings 8; Ezekiel 10; 44).

The whole message of Ephesians pivots on this passage. The re-creation of the family of God as the place where God dwells on the earth is part of the central purpose in Christ's coming to reclaim creation. This new temple of humanity is rebuilt on the ground of redeemed men, women, and children, ground cleared in Christ by divine fiat. It is brought to concrete reality in the lives of real, everyday people by the power of God's Spirit working in them. This working of the Spirit's power, the third spiritual blessing, is the subject, after a digression, of the next stage in Paul's argument.

Before moving on to the digression, however, it is important to observe the implication of this passage for contemporary churches. Paul spoke to a group of Gentile Christians who had been made to feel inferior by those who felt themselves religiously privileged because of their own relationship to God through the law. We who make up the church of Jesus Christ today must be ready to recognize ourselves as counterparts to the Jews of Paul's day. Whenever we assume that our code of behavior, our heritage, our music, our habits (or lack of them), our attendance at one particular church rather than another, our work ethic, our political opinions, or any other distinction we may enjoy makes us more acceptable to God than other people are, we have taken upon ourselves the role, and the condemnation (Gal. 3:10), of the destroyers of God's family, the family we are called to model.

E. Digression: Paul, outsiders, and God's glory (3:1–13). Paul now takes up the third spiritual blessing, that of the Spirit's influence on the church. Through Christ, God has renewed the human family "in the heavenly realms" (see Eph. 1:3) by eliminating all cause of division. This brings Paul to pray that the Spirit will bring about this new unity in the church's life here and now (see Eph. 3:14–19). But first, having mentioned the Gentile mission, for which he

suffers imprisonment, he stops midsentence to explain that mission more fully.

God has seen fit to entrust Paul with a message for the readers, the mystery of what God has done for them in Jesus Christ (3:2). Reviewing what Paul already mentioned (3:3; also Eph. 1:9–10?) will convince the readers of Paul's grasp of this long-hidden plan, now made known by the Spirit to (and through) God's chosen instruments, the apostles and prophets (3:4–5; see Eph. 2:20).

From the viewpoint of the mission to the Gentile world, the essence of the mystery is this: by virtue of Jesus Christ, non-Jews have a place among God's people alongside Jews, partaking in every way in the inheritance, the unity, and the covenant promises (3:6; see Eph. 2:5–6 for three similar "together-with" descriptors). Astonishingly from the Jewish perspective, there is no mention of needing a proper relationship to the law for such participation. It is solely a matter of being "in Christ." Neither moral effort nor ethnicity is any longer part of the prerequisites, if either ever was.

By the grace and power of God, in spite of his own sins, Paul became a servant of this gospel, this royal proclamation announcing Jesus as king of all creation (3:7). The honor came to him who in his own mind was the least (deserving?) of all God's people—probably a reference to his former persecution of the very body to which he now belongs (3:8; of course, with grace, what one deserves is irrelevant!). It is now his privilege to announce to the Gentiles the news of the inexhaustible wealth in Christ the king and to make everyone possible aware that this mystery, hitherto concealed in the heart of God, is now available for all to know (3:9). Paul emphasizes the universality of the good news by highlighting God's having "created all things"; it is not just about humanity.

God's purpose in revealing the mystery is that, through the unlikely instrument of rebellious humanity now transformed into his own people in the form of the church, he might make known his multifaceted wisdom to the entire universe (3:10). This age-old, unanticipated plan he carried out in the person and work of Christ, Lord of the universe (3:11), in whom we have full confidence, by faith, to come freely and boldly into the presence of God (3:12).

In view of all this, Paul begs them not to be disheartened about his incarceration and other afflictions. As a servant of the gospel (3:7), he obeys its purposes whatever the cost. Moreover, it is for their benefit that he suffers; it leads to their glory (3:13) no less than, consequently, to God's (3:21). Imprisonment is a small price to pay for such a prize.

F. Empowerment: Realizing the future (3:14–19). Paul resumes his prayer, interrupted in verse 2, addressing the Father (3:14), who himself unifies the new humanity and all creation. He is the universal God of family (3:15) and therefore is rightly petitioned to promote the present outworking of humanity's new unity in Christ. Accordingly Paul asks his gloriously resourceful God to provide the readers with inward strength through the power of the Holy Spirit (3:16). This is the same Spirit of the third blessing (Eph. 1:13–14) and the same power that Paul connects with it in his earlier prayer (Eph. 1:18–19). The Spirit provided inner power parallels (or realizes) Christ's indwelling of human hearts open to him in trusting submission (3:17). The present, outward expression of this inward, heaven-based unity will be realized only through Christ's progressive influence over the Christian community in its daily attitudes, decisions, and deeds, both private and communal.

Paul describes this unity as "being rooted and established in love" (3:17); the church's solid foundation and nourishment for life together is found nowhere else than in the indwelling Christ. The consequence and indeed the purpose of this inward work of grace is that the readers be empowered to know and experience what otherwise cannot be known or experienced, namely, the love that Christ has for them. Paul wants these Gentile Christians as well as all other members of God's family

to grasp the full dimensions of this incomprehensible love (3:18).

Here is the final purpose of all the foregoing purposes, the supreme goal of the family-minded God: that the readers be filled with all the fullness of God (3:19). Redemption, adoption, and empowerment all aim at one and the same object: to have at last on the earth a race of human beings who truly love each other and their Creator, and not only in the future coming age (Eph. 1:21), but right now in this present evil age ("world"; Eph. 2:2). For with the coming of Christ and by the power of the Spirit, the new age has arrived, invading and overlapping with this doomed age of death and sin.

On the foundation of the profound change in the affairs of God and humanity, Paul now builds in the second half of the epistle a demanding ethic for the church to live by. Yet it is really God who builds it through Paul, and it is really Christ who lives it out in the church by the Spirit's power. This ethic describes in fact *what God is now doing*, in Christ, on the basis of *what God has already done*, in Christ.

G. Doxology (3:20–21). On the message of this threefold work of God in Christ on creation's behalf, Paul now pronounces a benediction. He glorifies the God who is able to do all this, who is in fact able to do far more than we would ever think of asking him to do, so small is our own vision of our need and so comprehensive and bountiful is his (3:20). Whatever he delights to do he does according to the same power that Paul knows is already at work within us. What God does so immeasurably is what Paul is now about to describe. To God, says Paul, be glory forever.

And God's glory is forever found in the context of humanity: both in the church and in Jesus Christ, that form in which God himself assumed human shape (3:21).

3. Re-creating the Human Family: What God *Is* Doing (4:1–6:20)

The "imperative" second half of the letter is structured around five occurrences of some form of the phrase "therefore walk" (4:1, 17;

5:1–2, 7–8, 15). Each of the five presupposes the "indicative" first half of the letter ("therefore") and specifies walking in a particular way. All five may relate individually to chapters 1–3, or perhaps the first is unpacked by the following four.

A. Therefore walk in unity (4:1–16). On the solid ground of God's completed work in Christ, Paul urges readers to live a life of unity, worthy of their calling (4:1). As a prisoner himself, he knows what he is asking his readers to risk. The *worthy* life manifests (1) humility, proper self-estimate—both positive and negative; (2) gentleness, genuine concern for people's need for love, acceptance, and respect; and (3) patience (4:2). Patience produces a loving tolerance of people's weaknesses and foibles (including one's own) but without encouraging such shortcomings. Patience also displays a strong desire to keep the unity of the Spirit in the bond of peace (4:3). This is not the same thing as keeping the peace, which often leads to complicity. Fostering true unity requires endless patience as insecure personalities come closer to Christ and therefore to each other.

The foundation of the unity of the new family of God lies in eternal realities (4:4–6). There is one body; the church is one church regardless of local manifestations (including traditions or, today, denominations). There is one Spirit of God and not a separate Spirit for every competing group. There is only one world future, now already here in part. There is only one Lord, Jesus Christ—no other lord or Caesar takes precedence over him (1:20–22)— one common message to be believed, and one common rite of initiation belonging to the entire church (4:5). And it all comes back to, and indeed issues from, the fact that there is only one God in the universe; he has created it all, and his presence and power pervade it all (4:6). Only on this monotheistic foundation can the unity of God's family possibly come to reality.

By the same token, the members of the body, unified in theory but fragmented by nature, could never become one, as God wishes, without tools and enablement. But God has given grace to them all (4:7), endowing each one differently as Christ has liberally apportioned (no sense of stinginess here in the word "apportion"). Paul quotes Psalm 68:18 to make his point, oddly substituting the verb "gave" for the original "received" found in both the Hebrew Old Testament and the Septuagint. Such free treatment of a biblical text (and the following interpretation) may sound strange to modern readers, but Paul likely follows here an early Jewish Targum that applied it to Moses at Sinai. Taking the term "ascended" as key, Paul instead applies the whole passage to the ascending and (at Pentecost?) descending, gift-bearing Christ, the Christ who fills the universe (4:9–10; 1:23).

The gifts he has given his people (4:11) promote the unity of the church (4:13). They include apostles and prophets, those specially gifted and authoritative communicators of God's message to humanity. The category of "apostle" may have been temporary, while that of prophet continues in God's spokespersons to particular times, cultures, and situations. Evangelists traveled from place to place with the gospel, announcing like royal heralds the good news of Jesus's accession. Pastors and teachers, or perhaps pastor-teachers, nurtured the flocks submitting to the evangelists' message. These are not the only gifts Christ gives the church (cf., e.g., 1 Corinthians 12), nor are individuals necessarily excused from services for which they are "ungifted." Some pastors, for example, could and presumably did do the work of evangelism (cf. 2 Tim. 4:5).

The purpose of endowing the church with these gifts of grace is to equip the individual members for service to all (4:12). Future, potential members are doubtless among those benefiting from such service. Christ's goal clearly is to build up the church, so that the believers all attain to unity of faith and knowledge of God's Son, which will make them truly mature, fully human—by God's standard, not their own (4:13). That standard is the fullness of Christ, humanity perfected (see Eph. 3:19). In short, the goal is that we do what Christ himself does. The corresponding immaturity is susceptible to the cunning and appeal of human opinions, especially regarding relations between God and humanity (4:14). Instead, by living the truth in love—even when it hurts, but always with compassion—we are called in all things to grow into the likeness and person of Christ, who is the unifying head of the body (4:15).

This section closes with a metaphorical model of unity. Like the human body, held together by design, the church grows through the coordinated and cooperative work of its many members, who out of love for the whole contribute their individual efforts toward the good of the whole. But the plan and the energy are drawn from the head, which watches over and provides for his body. Indeed, he lives out his own life through it (4:16).

B. Therefore walk in newness (4:17–32). Efforts to walk in unity succeed to the degree to which they reflect the indwelling influence of Christ. Confident that he communicates the very counsel of the Lord, Paul negatively urges his Gentile readers to conduct their lives no longer as their fellow unconverted Gentiles do (4:17). This does not imply that Paul recommends a "Jewish" lifestyle; by "Gentile" here he means "pagan," "Christless." That is, he warns against living life apart from Christ, according to the old, or natural (2:3), walk. The contrast between the old and the new does not become explicit until 4:22–24, but Paul characterizes the old now in 4:17–19.

In 1:15–23 Paul stressed the importance of human thought for appropriating the message. Now he returns to the role of the mind, this time in regard to successfully (or unsuccessfully) living a life worthy of the calling inherent in that message. The unacceptable lifestyle he describes results from a futile, vain mind, focused on concerns that in the end come to nothing. Such a mind does not understand what God's true values and standards are; it has no light from the mind of God. In matters of everlasting consequence, it is full of ignorance brought about by hardened refusal to acquiesce where the truth is available (4:18; there is no real distinction between "heart" and "mind" or "understanding" here, as if they refer to separate compartments in a human being). The natural result of such a state is alienation from the life of God. The progression is downward. Out of basic human need for sensitivity and tenderness, those with hardened minds turn to sensuality. Rejecting the one in favor of the other, and with calloused sensitivity, they practice incredibly inventive impurity, with neither end nor satisfaction in view (4:19).

This pagan lifestyle formerly followed by the readers does not resemble the Christ they have learned to know (4:20). In saying this, Paul assumes that what they have heard and been taught about Jesus corresponds with what is actually the case (4:21). The "truth that is in Jesus," as it concerns inward change, he sums up as a three-step progression, in which the focus is on newness.

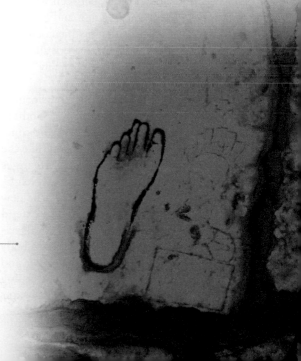

This footprint points the way to a brothel in Ephesus (first century AD). Ephesians 4:19 describes the Gentiles as giving "themselves over to sensuality so as to indulge in every kind of impurity."

First, with respect to their previous habits of life (4:17–19), they are to *lay aside* the "old self," the ignorant, insecure, self-centered ego rotting away from entanglement in the deceitful (futile) values of this world (4:22). Removing the old, dying self is nothing less than the act of repentance, the death of the sinful nature, repeated again and again throughout life whenever conviction of sin is worked by the power of the Spirit through the message. Second, upon the (daily) death of the old nature, the mind is made new, furnished with the light of God's mind, enabled to see as God sees and to make godly decisions (4:23). Third, to make such decisions and actually to live a Christlike lifestyle is to *put on* the new self, a creature not of one's own making but designed by God according to true righteousness and genuine dedication to the purposes of his eternal will (4:24). Thus the ongoing change from a godless and selfish deathbound life to the Christlike, eternal life of God involves newness, renewal, an inward change of mind wrought by God himself in bringing the new creation to present reality.

Paul writes these things to believers, people who are already Christians. Thus, we must distinguish between becoming Christian and becoming *a* Christian, between what are sometimes called sanctification and justification. The implication is that justified believers are gradually transformed into Christlikeness, and this transformation consists of many "small" considerations.

Paul's instructions for being transformed outwardly into the earthly family of God fall into five categories (4:25–32). First, he commands readers to "put off" falsehood (like the old self) and, quoting Zechariah 8:16, urges truthfulness with neighbors (4:25). "Neighbor" probably applies to members of the new covenant community, but it can also extend to nonbelievers. The startlingly practical reason for this is that members of Christ's body injure themselves by lying to each other and conversely benefit the community by telling the truth. Second, citing Psalm 4:4, Paul warns

against uncontrolled anger. While useful and appropriate (indeed commanded), anger must not be permitted to fester and thus to overpower the angry person (4:27). To "lose it" is to be diabolically selfish. Third, those accustomed to stealing should, as new creatures, do so no longer but by their own labor should make themselves useful (4:28). Remarkably, the reason for this admonishment is not a matter of independently earning one's own living. The purpose for avoiding theft and for working with one's own hands is to provide for the needs of other people, an entirely fitting purpose in a new community. Fourth, Paul cautions the readers against obscene and worthless talk, enjoining them instead to speak in ways that meet hurting people in their need, to speak words that ultimately encourage and strengthen the whole group (4:29). Fifth and finally, in this new life of Christlikeness believers must forgive one another in imitation of God's having forgiven them in Christ (4:31–32). Forgiveness springs from kindness and compassion and has nothing to do with bitterness, anger (4:26), or malicious and vindictive cruelty. Cattiness and a vengeful spirit have no place in God's new family.

Attending to these injunctions prevents grieving God's Holy Spirit (4:30). This does not mean that the Spirit becomes sad at our failings. It means that an offense against any human being is an offense against the Father's newly adopted community and against the Spirit, who has been set as a seal on that newly united humanity (Eph. 1:13). Attending to these injunctions is what it means to put on the new self, to walk in newness.

C. Therefore walk in love (5:1–6). Were it not for the intrusion of the phrase "therefore . . . walk" in 5:1–2, it would be natural to assume an unbroken connection between 4:32 and 5:1–2, in view of their shared emphasis on imitating God. The break, however, introduces a third way of walking, or perhaps a second way of promoting the unity of the Spirit in the bond of peace (4:3). Paul now directs readers to imitate God as children imitate their parents (5:1). They are loved by their Father; "therefore," they can "walk in the way of love" toward one another. The definition of this lifestyle of love is the self-sacrificial love of Christ for us, says Paul. Because of Christ's giving himself up in love for us, we are secure in our position and future with God. We are secure enough to sacrifice our own interests as an offering to God on behalf of the interests of other people (5:2). It is uncomfortably threatening both to forgive without guarantee of a favorable response and to give up personal anxieties without assurance of provision. But once we realize that our ultimate worth and final provision rest with a God who has been more than favorably disposed all along—and always will be—the threat evaporates (cf. John 13:3–5).

The loving lifestyle that fosters unity within the family can take any number of forms; for the moment, Paul focuses on what might be called "appropriate conversation," both in the sense of interpersonal relations and in the usual sense of speech (5:3–6). Sexually immoral behavior and any sort of impurity of life are absolutely prohibited. The same is true of greed, classified here with "impurity." Whereas in most modern congregations greed may be far less frowned on than sexual misbehavior, Paul prohibits them both in the same breath, as if they were identical at root: *loveless*. Likewise, incongruous with God's new human family is any ugly coarseness in the form of foul-mouthed joking and foolish talk. Believers' speech must instead be filled with the natural overflow of thankful hearts (5:4), something they can scarcely avoid when they keep their minds on what God has *lovingly* done for them.

Paul warns that those who practice such sins have no part in the kingdom of Christ and God (5:5; the lists in 5:3, 5 correspond); worshiping their own lusts, they cannot enjoy the peaceable rule of God. This of course includes all human beings in their fallen state, and that deceitful "old self" (4:22) misleads them even here. Because verse 5 is phrased somewhat elliptically, readers can get the impression that idolaters have no part in the kingdom *because of* their

idolatry. Fallen nature instantly assumes the reverse as well, namely, that living a moral life guarantees participation in the kingdom. But participation in the kingdom, in the new family of God, is a free gift of God's grace, bestowed on idolaters, on those who do *not* deserve it. That is the point of chapters 1–3.

Thus 5:5 means that persons having no part in God's family are also idolaters, and for the same reason: they do not receive the grace of God in Christ but insist on worshiping and protecting the independent old nature. Yet putting to death the old nature, laying off the old self in repentance, is the only way by which people enter the life of God. Thinking otherwise, assuming that God is either obligated to reward morality or too gracious to mind about idolatry, is stupid. God's wrath is real; whatever it is, the disobedient are promised it (5:6).

D. Therefore walk as light (5:7–14). Because of the serious dangers facing the disobedient, Paul warns his readers not to be led astray by worthless talk (5:6) into participation in the deeds of such persons (5:7). Disobedience works against God's design for unity in his re-created family and is thus characterized as darkness, the opposite of the light of the Lord. Outside Christ, Paul's readers "were once darkness," but no longer. In the Lord, they now "are light" (5:8). The metaphor depicts human beings as bearing enormous influence in either direction. As light, they conduct themselves in correspondence to the goodness, righteousness, and truth of God's nature (contrast 5:3), seeking to know what pleases Christ, which is indispensable for living this way (5:9–10).

In addition, enlightened living refuses to share in what does not please the Lord. In fact, avoiding participation in evil exposes it, both negatively by rejecting it and positively by doing what Christ would do. Enlightened living means being a light in dark places (5:11–12), which has the effect of transforming darkness into light. The light of Christ shining out from his light-filled followers exposes hidden dark deeds for what they are (5:13–14a).

Finally, living as light means continuously receiving the light. Quoting perhaps from an early Christian baptismal hymn, Paul states that the dispersing of darkness is an ongoing process even for the believer, analogous to the resurrection from the dead (5:14b). Death to one's former, sinful self gives way each new "morning" to a new life of walking in the light of Christ. Likely these words are directed to the believing readers, but they describe exactly the process of divine initiative that wakens all those "dead in [their] transgressions and sin" (Eph. 2:1). Re-created life is *response*—to forgiveness (4:32), love (5:2), and now light. This hymn fragment encapsulates the "therefore walk" structure of the entire letter.

E. Therefore walk in wisdom (5:15–21). In the fifth and final instruction on walking in unity, Paul enjoins wisdom-guided behavior. The contrasts between wise and unwise and between foolishness and understanding (5:15, 17) echo Old Testament wisdom literature, as does the reference to "evil" days (5:16). Psalm 37:19, for example, speaks of "evil times" (NIV "times of disaster") in which God's people foolishly fret over the prosperity of the wicked. Walking in wisdom, says Paul, implies understanding "what the Lord's will is." God will take care of the wicked; the readers need not worry about it. After all, as members of God's new family in Christ, they are already members and representatives of the new age to come.

Instead, readers must be Spirit-filled, busy with what the Lord has given *them* to do and not forfeiting precious opportunities by wallowing in self-pity like those drunk with wine. It is the Spirit who, as God's seal on the church, implements Christlike behavior in the lives of the family members (5:18). The Spirit-filled life manifests at least four representative characteristics (5:19–21; the list is not exhaustive). Various translations, including the NIV, obscure the original parallel structure that ties all four of these characteristics together. First, the Spirit-filled life fosters mutual encouragement and edification through believers speaking and singing to each other the promises of God and truths of the faith. Second, it includes spontaneous, heart-generated praise to the Lord Jesus. Third, Spirit-filled believers continually thank God the Father for everything he has given them in Christ. Fourth, mutual submission out of reverence for Christ marks the Spirit's

The Library of Celsus in Ephesus, built in AD 117 to honor the governor Gaius Julius Celsus Polemaeanus. Four statues representing Wisdom, Knowlege, Valor, and Intelligence—Celsus's virtues—occupy the lower niches in the facade. Paul likewise instructs the Ephesians to be known for their virtues, to live "not as unwise but as wise" (Eph. 5:15).

presence in the life of the new family. The personal security found in Christ frees believers to prefer one another in the daily affairs of living. In the following text, three sample situations explain what this means. The structural implication is that Eph. 5:15–6:9 constitutes one long section, parallel to the other four "therefore walk" texts. But because of the special significance of 5:21–6:9, it has its own section in the commentary.

F. Wisdom as mutual submission (5:21–6:9). Using the culturally familiar format of the household code (and Christianizing it in the process), Paul explains mutual submission in three domestic relationships as a mark of Spirit-filled living.

In each of the three parallel domestic relationships, the "weaker" party is addressed first. Thus in the first set (5:21–33), wives are instructed to submit to their (own) husbands in everything, as they would to the Lord Jesus (5:22). Paul's rationale is that just as Christ is head and savior of the church, so the husband is head of the wife (5:23–24). There is nothing surprising here; it is standard cultural wisdom. Yet with tragic irony this text has served for centuries to sanctify the abuse of women within Christ's church, a travesty occurring in part because interpreters stop interpreting at verse 24.

Paul Christianizes the marital section of the household code not only by introducing the model of Christ and the church but also through what he proceeds to say to husbands. His instructions to them (5:25–33) occupy three times the space he uses for wives, with obvious implications. The entire section is still governed by verse 21: husbands are to submit to their wives. As if that were not enough, the manner of submission, also modeled on Christ and the church, requires a husband to love his wife by giving himself up for her. How this self-sacrifice might look in a particular situation Paul leaves to the imagination.

He also describes the Christlike motivation for husbandly self-giving. As with Christ and the church, the purpose is to foster the

wife's full potential as God's creation. The entire explanation (5:26–27) revolves around Christ's plans for humanity's perfection, but the principle applies equally to how husbands aim to enhance the humanly glory of the person to whom each has joined himself. It is as if a husband's wife is an extension of his own body (5:28–29), again just as the church is Christ's body (5:30). This bodily, dual-person identity is already anchored in Genesis 2:24, but Paul regards Christ's identity with the church as superseding even the law (5:32). Correspondingly implicit in this is the perfecting of husbands: they become Christlike themselves when they, like Christ, die for another.

Whether women have been divinely programmed to submit to a self-denying husband, as if by natural default, is highly debatable. It is just as likely that Paul's instructions in verses 22–24 are intended to make the best of the sin-warped culture he lived in. In terms of mutual submission, a husband is perhaps just as likely to submit willingly to a wife who genuinely "dies" for him as a wife is to a husband who loves her like this. However that may be, Paul has called for *mutual* submission (5:33), which at least implies that husbands die to themselves for the sake of their wives, and probably that wives die to themselves for the sake of respecting their husbands. There could hardly be a more profound way to express the home-based lifestyle that promotes "the unity of the Spirit through the bond of peace" (4:3).

The same call to mutual submission applies to the relationship between children and their parents (6:1–4). Once more, Paul speaks first to the dependent party in the matched pair: children are to obey their parents as their role in the call to mutual submission (6:1). And once more, this comes as no surprise; Paul's appeal to Exodus 20:12 affirms the ancient expectation (6:2–3). His observation that this commandment is the first to incorporate a promise raises the question of why some obedient children die young. But this commandment belongs to a complex community ethic. Yahweh's people are called to a lifestyle reflecting his will. If they obey, they will live long as his people in the land he will give them. The instruction to children to obey their parents is not simply a word to this or that specific child but a word to the entire nation about raising children among God's people.

The idea of submissive parents probably sounded as bizarre to Paul's readers as did the idea of submissive husbands. Nonetheless, he calls parents to submit to their children in two ways (6:4). First, they must treat their children with dignity and respect, avoiding unnecessarily provoking them to anger through capricious and unkind treatment. The point is not the children's anger but the parents' provocation. Children only gradually learn the meaning of mature behavior from loving and submissive parents; they learn it neither untaught nor badly taught. Second, parents submit to their children by carrying out the high privilege and frequently frustrating task of bringing up children in Christian discipline and instruction. It requires every bit as much self-denial as what Paul recommended for married couples toward each other. We could conceivably read this text to say that the parents themselves are to be disciplined and instructed in the Lord as they bring up their children. Even if that is not what Paul meant in this text, it is not difficult to imagine that he might have agreed.

Finally, Paul calls for mutual submission between slaves and masters (6:5–9). The dependent party is again addressed first, as is the pattern. Slaves submit to their masters by rendering sincere, honest work, without pretense and with all goodwill (6:5–7). Where this might seem unreasonable because of the abusive character of some masters, Paul recommends a kind of theological fiction. In three different ways (6:5, 6, 7), he recommends slaves regard their masters (or mistresses) as if each were actually Christ. It scarcely needs elaboration, although Paul does elaborate briefly. For it is the Lord ultimately who rewards good and faithful service (6:8). Evidently, the Lord himself rewards all good

service, even what is offered to undeserving masters.

The usual surprising counterinstruction requires that masters submit to their slaves (6:9). Contrary to how he dealt with husbands (5:25–33) but similarly to how he dealt with parents (6:4), Paul now puts it to masters in as simple a form as he can: "Masters, do likewise to your slaves!" This can only mean that believing masters must entertain the appalling idea that Jesus himself is their slave. How would they treat him if he were? Ironically, he actually is their slave, as we see elsewhere in Scripture—in the hymn in Philippians 2:6–11, for example. In his many words about those who are first in the kingdom being slaves to all, Jesus hardly excluded himself.

On the other hand, Jesus the "slave" is also the master and impartial rewarder of both slave and free (6:8–9). The ironic interplay among the themes of Lord, master, and slave, in which all three categories exchange roles, eventually undermines all forms of the institution of slavery, of sweatshops, of enforced labor and crippling interest rates. In due time, it will utterly change the world, as it already is in the process of doing, if only haltingly. There is no reason that this teaching should not apply to all forms of labor relations.

G. Holy war: Fighting right the right fight (6:10–20). Paul's argument has reached its final stage. God has redeemed, adopted, and sealed the readers as members of his new creation. They can now live together in unity, newness, love, light, and wisdom—essential characteristics of that new creation. Yet Paul is fully aware that believers in their current context face fierce resistance to living out this new lifestyle of God's future. They are engaged in a holy war. As he closes the letter, Paul reassures the beleaguered readers that they are not left alone and unequipped to face their enemies. They have a dynamic leader, stout armor, and clear rules of engagement as their support in fighting right the right fight.

Paul begins by urging the readers to "be strong in the Lord and in his mighty power," not in any other person or power (6:10). The text then falls into two main sections, one devoted to the armor that believers have for making a firm stand (6:11–17) and the other explaining what they should do in their new armor (6:18–20) in order to be strong in the Lord.

The resistance that the armored readers struggle against is from the devil and his schemes (6:11). The struggle is *not* against "flesh and blood" (Greek "blood and flesh"), that is, against other human beings. Paul emphasizes this because even believers readily identify their foes as other people who resist *their* schemes. The church is as prone to infighting as the world is, which perhaps implies that Paul's reference to "blood and flesh" is not limited to Christians but extends to all humanity. The real enemy is the devil, active in the rulers, powers, and forces of darkness and wickedness he has at his disposal (6:12), human and inhuman.

The earlier reference to "evil" days (Eph. 5:16) alludes apparently to despair over the *prosperity* of the wicked. In 6:13, however, the idea relates to any circumstance in which God's people face *resistance* of the wicked against the new creation. Paul thus admonishes them to resist this resistance! Three times he urges them to "stand firm" (6:11, 13, 14), almost as a refrain in a battle hymn. Missing from his instruction, however, is any violent, offensive maneuver. There is another tactic.

A carved relief from Ephesus of the equipment for a Roman soldier. In Ephesians 6:10–17, Paul uses the metaphor of Roman body armor to describe how Christians should arm themselves against the devil.

Paul's description of God's armor is full of irony. The metaphor of military armor clashes with the qualities represented by the metaphor (6:14–17; the images come mostly from Isaiah 11; 52; 59). The equipment for struggling against the devil, his schemes, and his pawns reflects the very nature of God and his redeemed people: truth, righteousness, peace, faith, salvation, and the Spirit's word. These are the unweapons with which believers stand firm. They amount to the new person Paul urges the readers to "put on" (Eph. 4:24); only now he speaks of it as "putting on" the full armor of God. The same verb appears in both cases. This is a holy war, a Christlike jihad. Jesus waged this same war against evil, standing firm in truth and righteousness, in peace, faith, salvation, and the word of God. It led him to crucifixion, and before he died he prayed that the Father would forgive his persecutors, for they were mere pawns. His struggle was not against other human beings.

Prayer constitutes the rule of engagement for this war (6:18–20), one lone tactic. What Paul evidently has in mind is diligent, persistent prayer for perseverance, for enduring strength, for the ability to stand firm no matter what comes. He asks believers to pray this way not just for themselves but also for all the saints, including Paul. Holy warfare is not a quest for individualized spirituality; it is a community matter. Of course, personal discipleship is entailed in the struggle for genuine unity and social justice. But individualized discipleship, even among Christians, is a means to an end and not an end in itself. God's great plan is to sum up all humanity together in Christ into a divinely designed *society* (Eph. 1:9–10).

In an oxymoron, Paul refers to himself as "an ambassador in chains" (6:20), probably for effect. As an ambassador for the gospel, he proclaims the good news that by the resurrection from the dead, Jesus the Jewish Messiah has now been made king of the entire world, including Rome (Rom. 1:2–6). And this is why Paul asks for prayers on his own behalf, that he might speak boldly as an ambassador with a message from the king of creation. Yet Paul's calling is really no different from the calling all followers of Jesus have received. Their very adherence to the lifestyle described so powerfully in the preceding three chapters loudly proclaims that a new king has arrived on the scene, establishing a new and permanent rule over humanity, establishing in fact a new humanity. The overhaul of broken creation is under way. Naturally, the resistance is fierce on the part of those who have no wish to abandon their power and presumed autonomy. They are capable of persecuting the new family of God even unto death, let alone putting them in chains. In the face of all that can and will be done against these ambassadors, Paul urges them to pray for one another to persevere, to stand firm, to resist the devil's schemes in the evil day. And they will if they seek to be strong in the Lord and in the strength of *his* might, and in no one else's, not even Paul's.

Thus ends the sustained argument of Ephesians: God has *already* re-created humanity and all creation through what he has accomplished in Christ; yet God is also currently *in the process of* re-creating humanity and all creation through the good works he has prepared for his people to do. God has provided all they need for carrying out here and now their little part in his ongoing plan to sum up all creation in Christ. Thus, they may stand firmly obedient and faithful in the power of the Lord, no matter what happens, for they now know what will happen last: they shall be summed up in Christ together with all things, all things in heaven and all things on earth.

4. Closing Remarks (6:21–24)

Except for three minor variations, the text of verses 21–22 is identical with that at Colossians 4:7–8. Paul deputizes his fellow worker Tychicus both to deliver news of Paul's situation and to encourage the readers. He closes with a blessing of peace, love, and faith, as well as grace, which, as he is careful to point out, originates with God and Christ and is enjoyed by those who love the Lord Jesus (6:23–24).

Select Bibliography

Best, Ernest. *Ephesians: A Shorter Commentary.* New York: T. & T. Clark, 2003.

Bruce, F. F. *The Epistles to the Colossians, to Philemon, and to the Ephesians.* New International Commentary on the New Testament. Grand Rapids: Eerdmans, 1984.

Houlden, J. L. *Paul's Letters from Prison.* Westminster Pelican Commentary. Philadelphia: Westminster, 1970.

Lincoln, Andrew T., and A. J. M. Wedderburn. "The Theology of Ephesians." Part 2 of *The Theology of the Later Pauline Letters.* Cambridge: Cambridge University Press, 1993.

Mitton, C. Leslie. *Ephesians.* New Century Bible Commentary. Grand Rapids: Eerdmans, 1976.

Patzia, Arthur G. *Colossians, Philemon, Ephesians.* Good News Commentary. New York: Harper and Row, 1984.

Stott, John R. W. *The Message of Ephesians: God's New Society.* The Bible Speaks Today. Downers Grove, IL: InterVarsity, 1979.

Philippians

JANET MEYER EVERTS

Introduction

Toward the end of his life, Paul wrote the Letter to the Philippians to the first congregation he had established in Europe. In it Paul reveals his passion for the gospel and his love for his fellow believers in Christ. In Philippians 4:15, Paul writes about the special relation that he shares with the Philippian church. This is a church close to Paul's heart, one with which he shares true partnership in the gospel of Christ. When the Philippian church heard about Paul's imprisonment in Rome, they responded by sending Epaphroditus with a generous gift. Paul apparently wrote the Letter to the Philippians in response to this gift and the news of the church he received from Epaphroditus. This is one of Paul's letters that was not occasioned by problems in a church but by gratitude and deep friendship with a congregation.

Date, Authorship, and Place of Origin

The traditional view is that Paul wrote the Letter to the Philippians from prison in Rome around the year AD 60. There is little reason to challenge this tradition, although several alternative locations have been suggested for the origin of the letter and for the city of Paul's imprisonment, suggestions that will be discussed below.

Few scholars have questioned Paul's authorship of Philippians. The letter opens with the greeting from "Paul and Timothy," but it is clearly Paul alone who has actually written the letter. Timothy might have been Paul's secretary or companion, but he is not a coauthor. His name appears again only in 2:19, whereas the first-person singular pronouns "I," "me," and "my" appear over fifty times. Both the biographical section and the theology are consistent with what we know of Paul's theology elsewhere in the New Testament, and from the earliest church fathers on, Paul has been considered the author of Philippians.

The date of Philippians is dependent on the decision about the letter's place of origin. It is clearly written from prison, so the question becomes, During which of Paul's imprisonments did he write the Letter to the Philippians? Although several locations have been suggested, only two deserve serious consideration, since Acts records only two places where Paul was imprisoned: Caesarea (58–59) and Rome (60–62).

The text of Philippians offers several clues about where and why Paul was imprisoned: it appears that Paul was in prison facing a trial that could end in death or acquittal (1:19–24; 2:23–24), that he planned to visit Philippi upon his acquittal, that there were members of the "praetorian guard" (1:13 NASB, RSV; NIV: "palace guard") and "Caesar's household" (4:22) where he was being held, that Timothy was with Paul, that trips were being made between Philippi and the place where Paul was being held, and that extensive evangelistic efforts were being carried out in the city where Paul was being held.

Acts 23–24 records Paul's two-year imprisonment in Herod's praetorium in Caesarea, so the praetorian guard of Philippians 1:13 could refer to Herod's soldiers. But in the first century a reference to the praetorian guard more often referred to the emperor's elite troops stationed in Rome. Although anyone in imperial service can be called a member of Caesar's household, it would be far more likely that this term would be used of the emperor's household in Rome. There is also little evidence in Acts of life-threatening circumstances or imminent release while Paul was held in Caesarea. In Acts 23:11, Paul is told that he "must also testify in Rome," and Paul himself seems to know his rights as a Roman citizen when he appeals to Caesar. So it is doubtful that his life would be in danger in a Roman court until he reached Rome.

The traditional view that Paul wrote Philippians from Rome in the early 60s fits all the data found in Acts 28 and Philippians. Acts ends with Paul preaching the gospel in Rome as he awaits his trial, the very picture Paul presents of himself at the beginning of Philippians. A location in Rome is the simplest explanation of references to the praetorian guard and Caesar's household. This is a case where the traditional view is still the best.

Philippi: The City and the Church

Acts 16:12 calls Philippi "the leading city of that district of Macedonia." Situated at the eastern end of a large and fertile plain on the road that connected Europe to Asia Minor, it had a strategic position that ensured its importance as a Greek city and a Roman colony. It was named after Philip of Macedon, Alexander the Great's father, in 356 BC and came under Roman control in 168 BC. In 42 BC Octavian, later Augustus Caesar, won two great military victories near Philippi and honored Philippi by refounding it as a Roman military colony. This gave every resident Roman citizenship and populated the town and surrounding areas with discharged military veterans, thereby ensuring the allegiance of this strategically located town to the emperor of Rome. By the time Paul came to the city in 49, Philippi was the political center of the area and both Greek and Latin were spoken in the city. Despite the tremendous advantages in the Roman world of being a citizen of Philippi, Paul does not hesitate to remind the Philippians that as Christians they are now citizens of a heavenly kingdom. Their Lord is not Caesar but Jesus Christ, their Savior, who has everything, even the Roman Empire, under his control.

While on his second missionary journey, Paul received a vision of a man of Macedonia who begged him, "Come over to Macedonia and help us" (Acts 16:9). So Paul journeyed to Macedonia, and the church

The Krenides River and the remains of the Roman road that led across it. This is a possible location for Lydia's baptism and the beginning of the church at Philippi (Acts 16:11–15).

at Philippi was founded as the first Christian community in Europe. The well-known story of the founding of the church is told in Acts 16:11–40. Paul found a devout worshiper of God named Lydia, a seller of purple goods, who with her household formed the nucleus of the church at Philippi. "Given the prominent place of women in Macedonian life in general, it is not surprising that the core group of first converts were women, nor that the location of its first house church was in the home of a woman merchant" (Fee, 27). Although Acts does not indicate how long Paul actually stayed in Philippi, it was long enough for him to establish a close relationship with this church. Paul and Silas left Philippi after Paul was imprisoned for casting a spirit of divination out of a slave girl but not before the entire household of his Roman jailer had converted to Christianity. We know first from 1 Corinthians 16:5 and 2 Corinthians 1:16 and second from 2 Corinthians 2:13 and 2 Corinthians 7:5 that he visited Philippi at least two more times, and in 2 Corinthians 8:1–5 he wrote them a glowing commendation for generous giving.

Literary Unity

The Greek manuscript evidence clearly indicates that Philippians originally circulated as the complete letter we have today. Some scholars have, however, questioned the unity of the letter on other grounds, mainly the use of the word "finally" in the beginning of Philippians 3:1 (KJV, RSV; NIV: "further") and the change of tone and subject matter that follows. Such scholars suggest that our Philippians is really two letters combined. Since the same word for "finally" is used in Philippians 4:8, some have even suggested that the end of Philippians 4 is a third letter of thanks.

But these objections to the unity of Philippians can be answered readily. The Greek expression *to loipon*, often translated as "finally," is actually a phrase that indicates more follows and can be used as a transition between sections. It might be better translated "in addition" or "still" in order to avoid giving the impression of

a break in Paul's thought. Given the complete lack of manuscript evidence for more than one letter and the strong thematic unity of the letter, there is little reason to question the original unity of the Epistle to the Philippians.

Theological Themes

Two terms are so characteristic of this letter that they clearly summarize its major theological themes: *koinōnia*, which can be translated "fellowship" or "participation," and *euangelion*, the word for "gospel." From beginning to end, Philippians is a letter about what it means to fully participate in the gospel of Jesus Christ. However, Paul says very little about the content of the gospel or the saving work of Christ in this letter. Instead, Christ himself is presented as the embodiment of the gospel and the model of the Christian life for the Philippians. According to the "Christ hymn" of Philippians 2:6–11, Christ emptied himself by becoming a servant, and as a result, he was glorified by God. The pattern of emptying oneself and then being glorified is referred to as "kenosis theology" (from the Greek word *kenōsis*, meaning "an emptying") and is considered important for understanding Christ's incarnation.

Other leaders in the Christian community also model this dynamic of the gospel for the Philippians. Timothy and Epaphroditus do not look out for their own interests; they are willing to pour out their own lives for the work of the gospel. Paul is willing to share in Christ's sufferings, that he might also know the power of his resurrection (Phil. 3:10). This imitation of Christ in his humiliation and exaltation is important not just for leaders in the Christian community. Christ's servanthood is the model for every Christian, and Paul urges the Philippians to have the same mind in this matter as Christ Jesus. For as they participate in the dynamic of humiliation and exaltation that characterizes the gospel, they participate in Christ's sufferings and resurrection. This participation produces true joy and peace even in suffering, one of the great themes of the Epistle to the Philippians. Like Paul, the Philippians do not need to fear persecution or death for the sake of Christ and the gospel, for "to live is Christ and to die is gain" (Phil. 1:21). Christlike humility is also the key to true Christian community and brings unity for the sake of the gospel. The great enduring message of Philippians is that the Christian life is a life lived in conformity to the image of Christ as he is presented in the gospel.

Outline

Commentary

1. Paul's Apostolic Salutation and Prayer (1:1–11)

The opening verses of Paul's letters often introduce the major themes of the epistle that follows, and Philippians is no exception. Although Paul follows the letter-writing conventions of his time, he is not limited by them and uses them to further his purposes in writing. So in the opening sentences of the Letter to the Philippians, Paul presents the great theme of the Philippians' partnership with him in the gospel that will characterize the entire epistle. He also introduces the idea of humble service for the sake of the gospel, which is one aspect of true partnership in the gospel.

A. Address and salutation (1:1–2). Paul begins the letter with a standard epistolary greeting: he introduces himself as the writer, names the recipients of the letter, and then adds a short personal note. But even in this standard introduction Paul manages to introduce a strong sense of Christian purpose and a warm and joyous tone with his blessing: "Grace and peace to you from God our Father and the Lord Jesus Christ" (1:2).

In this introduction, Paul lists Timothy along with himself, not as a coauthor but as a companion (see Phil. 2:19–23). Timothy was probably with Paul in Rome at the time this letter was written. By mentioning Timothy's name with his own, Paul both gives honor to Timothy and shows the Philippians how important they are to him and the church in Rome. Not only does Paul himself love the Philippians, but he is also closely associated with others who care for them (see Phil. 2:20). Paul also mentions Timothy and himself because he intends to use both as examples of true gospel workers later in the letter. Unlike in most of his other letters to churches, Paul does not refer to himself as an apostle but as a "servant." Here Paul presents himself and Timothy as those who are "servants of Christ," who became a servant for the sake of the church (see Phil. 2:6–11). There is no indication in this letter that there is a dispute over whether Paul is an apostle or whether or not he has authority to instruct and rebuke the Philippian church. His relationship with this church and his authority are assumed. By calling himself and Timothy "servants," Paul is also calling the Philippians to be servants and is setting the stage for his call for humility in the Philippian church. This is a call for unity that is rooted in service to Christ and will later be demonstrated by the examples of Christ, Paul, Timothy, and Epaphroditus (2:6–3:21).

Paul then proceeds to address the congregation, calling them "saints [NIV "holy people"] in Christ Jesus" (1:1). Calling them "saints" also marks them as God's people. The use of "in Christ Jesus" reminds them that it was not through their own strength and holiness that they became God's people but because of what God has done in Christ. Paul then addresses two groups of people within the Philippian church: the overseers and deacons. Neither of these terms is uniquely Christian; Paul borrowed them from the Greco-Roman world and redefined them. The term "overseers" is often translated as "bishops." These "overseers" were not bishops in the sense that we know them today. There were multiple "bishops" in each church who functioned as leaders within the church. The word "deacon" was often used in the Greco-Roman world to refer to those responsible for distributing food and goods. Paul uses the term here to refer to those within the Philippian congregation who are responsible for managing and distributing food and goods to the poor and needy. It is likely that Paul is thanking these people because they helped organize the aid sent to him with Epaphroditus (see Phil. 2:25).

Paul concludes his greeting by wishing the Philippians "grace" and "peace" (1:2). He first wishes them "grace," which is the unmerited favor of God, and then "peace," which is the result of God's grace at work in the lives of the believers. Paul's blessing is a reminder that "grace" and "peace" come not from him but from God the Father through Jesus Christ.

B. Paul's thanksgiving and confidence (1:3–8). Paul moves from his customary greeting to a time of thanksgiving and prayer. He not only thanks God when thinking of the Philippians but prays for them with joy in spite of his position in prison. Paul claims that the reason for his joyful prayer and thanks to God is that the church at Philippi has partnered with Paul in the work of the gospel (1:5). This "partnering" is best understood in terms of their fellowship with Paul in his proclamation of the gospel. The Philippians have joined Paul in the mission of the gospel with their words, their hearts, and their deeds. Thus, Paul is thankful for their love and for their financial support in his imprisonment. This fellowship that Paul shares with the Philippians has been long and fruitful. In fact, Paul states that they were in fellowship from "the first day."

While Paul is still in chains and standing trial, he is confident about the future of the Philippian congregation. He is confident not only because of their desire to proclaim the gospel but also because neither the church worldwide nor the church in Philippi is dependent solely on Paul. They are part of God's church, and Paul is confident that God, who is faithful, will continue to work in the hearts of the Philippians and transform them, regardless of whether or not Paul is present. Since God "began a good work" (1:6), Paul trusts in God's faithfulness to continue the work. This attitude is a clear expression of Paul's humility in the face of his situation. He does not puff himself up as important and irreplaceable in the mission of the gospel. He is first and foremost confident in God's plan and in God's power, not in his own importance in God's plan. God's work in the Philippian church will continue until it is completed on the day Christ returns (1:6); because God is in control, he has a plan, and he is always faithful.

Paul goes on to open his heart to the Philippians, telling them how much he cares and how he holds them deeply within his heart (1:7). Not only does he feel this way, but his affection for them is understandable because they are sharing in God's grace with him. This verse is a reference to the gifts of aid the church at Philippi sent to Paul. Paul is imprisoned in Rome, yet the Philippians are sharing in his suffering through their prayers, love, and financial aid. By sharing in Paul's suffering, they also share in the grace Paul is receiving from God as a result of that suffering. Here Paul begins to offer himself as an example to the Philippians, an example that he will fully delineate in 3:1–21. Paul's life and word proclaim the gospel, even from behind bars, as he continues "defending and confirming the gospel" (1:7). Paul is fighting for the sake of the gospel when he is on trial; but regardless of what he is doing, the Philippians have been there for him, and he holds them in his heart no matter the physical distance between them. Paul ends with an oath testifying to his compassion and desire to be present with the congregation (1:8).

C. Paul's apostolic prayer (1:9–11). After telling of his love for the Philippians and of his thankfulness for their generosity, Paul proceeds to pray for them. Although such prayers are standard features of first-century letters, Paul uses this prayer to advance his pastoral concerns for the Philippians. He begins his prayer for the Philippians with a supplication for the congregation to grow in love and discernment and then states the purpose of this love: a life of holiness. He first prays that the Philippians abound in love and the truth of the gospel (1:9). Love and discernment go together for Paul. He calls the Philippians to love in such a way that their love is founded on truth and understanding. Paul desires for the Philippians to have this love and discernment so that they may live a life of holiness and obedience to God, so that they may "be pure and blameless for the day of Christ" (1:10). This life of holiness is itself a proclamation of the truth of the gospel, and Paul calls the Philippians to live up to that calling. In the final part of his prayer, Paul tells us the characteristics of this holy life. It is first and foremost filled with the "fruit of righteousness" (1:11). This fruit is the outworking of love, which finds its ultimate source in communion with Jesus Christ. He is the source of the fruit that will show itself in the Philippians' lives if they abound in love. More than that, Christ is the supreme example to follow on their path to holy living. One hallmark of a holy life is that it gives glory and praise to God (1:11). Praise and glorification of God is the goal of right discernment and correct conduct.

2. Paul's Ambition and Joy Is the Gospel of Christ (1:12–26)

In this section, Paul addresses the anxiety of the Philippians on his behalf. He knows that they care for him, as evidenced by their aid and the message sent through Epaphroditus (2:25). Paul also knows that his imprisonment is distressing to them and that they consider it a detriment to the advancement of the gospel. Paul desires to dispel their worries and correct their wrong thinking about what constitutes the true proclamation of the gospel.

A. The condition and mission of the gospel (1:12–18a). First and foremost, Paul wants to help the Philippians understand that his condition will not hurt the mission of the gospel, but benefit it (1:12). While it may seem that his physical condition and the possibility of his execution would be the most pressing concern, Paul focuses first on what is most important to him: the gospel of Jesus Christ. The good news of the life, death, and resurrection of Jesus Christ and its proclamation was the central fixture upon which Paul hung all his hopes and to which he had devoted his life. It might appear that, as a prisoner in Rome, Paul was not in a situation where he could carry out his life's mission and would therefore be in deep despair. However, Paul tells the Philippians that the opposite has proved true in two ways. First, people are beginning to understand the reason for Paul's imprisonment, and therefore, the gospel is being "preached" because of his imprisonment. The way Paul phrases his condition, "in chains for Christ," denotes something beyond the legal reason for his imprisonment. Paul is in chains not merely *because* of Christ, but *for* Christ (1:13). Those around Paul see that he sits in prison as a service to Christ. As a result they are curious about the gospel for which Paul suffers so willingly. Second, Paul's suffering for Christ has inspired many in the church in Rome to preach God's Word with boldness and fearlessness (1:14). Paul is an inspiration and an example for them. His suffering has turned out to have the exact opposite result of what one would expect. Instead of his imprisonment inciting fear in Christians and eliciting disgust from his guards, the church has been inspired to further preaching, and the guards have been exposed to the truth of the gospel in Paul's life.

Next, while still discussing the mission of the gospel, Paul anticipates an objection. He claims that his witness is inspiring the Roman church to preach the gospel, yet what about those in the church who dislike him? He recognizes that people in the Roman community might be preaching the gospel for less than noble reasons (1:15), reasons that he thinks are

incompatible with true Christian humility as he will identify it in 2:4. But here Paul does not worry about people's motives; he simply rejoices in the proclamation of the gospel. Those who proclaim the gospel "out of envy and rivalry" (1:15) are still preaching the gospel, and that is really all that matters to Paul (1:18). This statement is the center of this entire section and reflects Paul's position on his imprisonment. It does not matter whether Paul is liked or not, whether he is suffering or not; it matters only that God's work is being done and that the cause of the gospel is moving forward. Earlier in the epistle, Paul talks about seeing God's work being done in the lives of the Philippians, and he rejoices (1:3–6). Paul recognizes that the success of the gospel and God's work is not dependent on him. In this humility, Paul recognizes that, whether he is with the Philippians or not, God is faithful and will continue to work. Whether

This underground prison cell in the Mamertine Prison (dating back to the seventh century BC) is the traditional location where both Peter and Paul were imprisoned in Rome. Above this now stands the Church of San Giuseppe dei Falegnami, and the cell has been converted into a chapel honoring the two apostles

Paul is in prison or free, God is faithful, and the message of the gospel will continue to spread.

B. Paul's own condition (1:18b–26). After affirming the triumphant condition of the gospel, Paul moves to discuss his own condition. Although the Philippians are concerned about Paul, he rejoices because he is not without help. He is supported by the prayers of the Philippians and the help of the Holy Spirit. Thus, Paul is confident that his condition will turn out not only for the benefit of the gospel but also for his own benefit (1:19). He claims that, through the help he has received, he will be delivered. In 1:20, Paul details how he was helped and the nature of his deliverance. Ultimately, Paul's goal for his life is to continually exalt Christ in his body (1:20). He desires the courage to glorify God no matter the circumstances. Just as Paul has recognized his role as an example for the Philippians, he reminds them that his life is the result of following the supreme example of Jesus Christ.

Paul goes on to add the short and powerful statement, "whether by life or by death." These words split the path that Paul's deliverance might take. As a prisoner who is about to stand trial, Paul could be delivered by being released from prison. In that outcome, he would praise God and preach the gospel, thus glorifying Christ. Yet, it is also possible that he could be executed for the cause of Christ. If executed, Paul is confident that his martyrdom would glorify God, because of his faithful witness to the gospel. While these two paths seem polar opposites, they actually lead to the same end of glorifying God, just as the different reasons that people preach the gospel both lead to its advance. It is in this context that 1:21 can be understood. While Paul is alive, all that he strives for and the strength by which he lives and moves is found in Christ. While he lives he will continue to serve God and preach the gospel. Yet there is also something to be gained if Paul dies. Paul will then be with Christ, which, as Paul poignantly states, "is better by far" (1:23). There is also gain for the faithful witness to the

gospel and the glorification of God if Paul is executed.

Paul knows both of the alternatives that he faces: life and death. He knows that either will bring glory to God and that dying and being with Christ will be better for him. Paul is stuck between these two alternatives but privileges his pastoral responsibility and love for the Philippians over his personal desires and his love for himself (1:24). It is clear that Paul prefers not martyrdom but service to the church. In this he is following the example of Christ, who became a servant (2:7). Like Christ, he would choose martyrdom only if service to the gospel and the church demanded it, not because it would be better for him. Because they know Paul's attitude of humble service to them in the gospel, the Philippians do not need to worry that Paul will rush headlong into martyrdom and abandon them. Paul is confident he will be there to see them grow in Christ and to rejoice with them (1:25–26).

3. The Great Example of Christ and Life Lived according to the Truth of the Gospel (1:27–2:18)

Confident of the Philippians' partnership in the gospel, Paul now calls them to lead a life worthy of the gospel and sets the great example of Christ before them. Only by modeling their lives on Christ's life can a Christian community hope to achieve true unity and proclaim the gospel in humility and righteousness. The great Christ hymn of Philippians 2:6–11 is one of the most famous passages of the New Testament, and more has been written about it than any other part of Philippians. But it is important to see it in its context in the epistle. The supreme example of Christ is part of Paul's pastoral exhortation to the Philippian church, and he expects those who follow Christ to embody the same characteristics as the Lord they serve. Any theological conclusions based on this hymn need to be understood in this pastoral context. This section is primarily an exhortation to Christian unity and humility in the service of others, following the example of Christ. When the Philippians live in this way, they will become Paul's true partners in the service of the gospel.

A. An exhortation to a life worthy of the gospel (1:27–30). Although Paul is confident that he will see the Philippians again, this confidence comes from Paul's love for the congregation and the fact that he knows that they still need him as their pastor, not from any prophetic certainty. Thus, Paul begins his section of pastoral instruction with "Whatever happens . . ." (1:27). Paul recognizes that he is not in control of the situation but humbly acknowledges God's sovereignty. Paul acknowledges that he may come to see them or he may only hear about them (either in prison or in death), but he nonetheless desires that they live lives worthy of the gospel of Christ (1:27). A life modeled after the gospel of Christ has both internal and external manifestations. The internal aspect of this gospel life is stated here as unity but also contains the important virtue of humility. Paul calls the Philippians to stand in one spirit and as one body (1:27). They are to stand in unity as the body of Christ, the church. This is the important internal evidence of a life worthy of the gospel. The external aspect of this life is seen in the effect that a true Christian community has on the pagan world around it. Paul is calling the Philippians to stand for the faith of the gospel (1:27). Yet this effect on the world outside the church can only take place once the church is true to its calling to unity and faith in the gospel.

In 1:27–30, Paul hints at the similarities between the situation of the Philippians and his own situation in Rome. The Philippian church is meeting opposition in Philippi and is being tried and tested. Though some in the congregation have become afraid, Paul calls them to remember that their salvation is found in God (1:29). Not only do they have the promise of salvation and the destruction of those who persecute them, but their situation is a gift from God. While most Christians are granted faith enough to believe in Christ, the Philippians

have been given the honor of suffering for the sake of Christ, even going through the same situation as Paul himself. Paul calls their struggle the "same" in order to remind them of what he said in 1:7, namely that by sharing in his suffering they share in the grace that God is pouring out on him. By equating their suffering with his own, Paul reminds the Philippians of the grace of God that will strengthen them through any trial.

B. A call to corporate life in Christ (2:1–4). After calling the Philippians to an authentic Christian life and reminding them that he shares in their trials and sufferings, Paul makes a series of rhetorical remarks in order to comment on the character of the Philippians and remind them of the character of Christ. These four remarks all begin with the word "if," but this does not mean that Paul doubts that they are true. It is better to understand the "if" as meaning "since." Paul knows the Philippian congregation well. He knows these statements are true about this congregation, but he phrases them as "if" in order to catch their attention. With these remarks, Paul is telling the Philippians to pay attention. Paul both looks back and presses forward at this point. He constantly has his eyes on 1:27 and the call to a life worthy of the gospel. But he also presses forward and begins to set the great example of Christ before them—an example that defines and creates the gospel. Only those who truly model their lives on the life of Christ can live a life worthy of the gospel. Christ is the source of encouragement, comfort, love, fellowship with the Spirit, tenderness, and compassion.

The apostle begins his appeal by asking the Philippians to make his joy complete not only by continuing to live out those characteristics they have received from Christ but also by "being like-minded, having the same love, being one in spirit and of one mind" (2:2). While being united with Christ, being comforted by God's love, fellowshiping with the Spirit, and having tenderness and compassion are exceedingly important in the Christian life, they all can be considered *individual* Christian virtues. Unity with Christ is seen through personal godly behavior. Each Christian is individually comforted by the love of God. Each Christian has an individual relationship with the Holy Spirit. Tenderness and compassion are demonstrated to others, but they can still be something one *individual* does for another.

However, Paul is calling the Christian community at Philippi to be a Christian *community* instead of merely being a collection of Christian people. It is this true community spirit and unity that is the first important virtue of the gospel life. As a community, they are to be like-minded (2:2), meaning that they hold to the same truths about who God is, what he has done, and what he calls Christians to do in this world. They must be united in and under the authority of the Word of God. God's truth must unite their minds on that which is most important in the life of the Christian community and God's mission in the world. As a community, the Philippians are to have the same love (2:2), meaning that they are to show the love of Christ, tenderness and compassion (2:1), both as individuals and as a community. As a community, they are to be one in spirit and purpose, meaning that there should be a definitive end to any factions and groups formed by personal interests. The cause of the church is never the cause of any one person but is the cause of Jesus Christ. While individuals could exhibit the characteristics of 2:1, no community could have the characteristics of 2:2 and remain divided.

In 2:3–4, Paul moves on to the second important virtue in a life worthy of the gospel: humility. The Christian life is centered outside oneself. It is for that reason that Paul uses the same term (translated here as "selfish ambition or vain conceit") as he used to talk about those who preached the gospel in order to frustrate him in 1:16. Paul does not want such an attitude to prevail among the Philippians. In humility, they are to live a life in which their focus is on God and others. It is not necessary for them to ignore their own lives and interests, but they, like Paul in relation to his execution, are to put

The forum at Philippi, which was rebuilt during the time of Marcus Aurelius (second century AD). Paul founded the church at Philippi on his second missionary journey (Acts 16). In Philippians 2, Paul teaches the church how to maintain their unity.

the needs and interests of others above their own. It is a life of humility and unity that truly demonstrates the Christian life.

C. The supreme example of Christ (2:5–11). At this point, Paul is still attempting to help the Philippians understand the character of a life worthy of the gospel. A mere list of virtues or an explanation of concepts is not enough to truly understand what it means to follow Christ as both an individual and a community. So Paul begins a series of examples in order to illustrate the life he calls them to in 1:27. The first and primary example is Christ, which he introduces through an explicit call to follow Christ's example in 2:5.

The section that follows, 2:6–11, is organized in a poetic pattern and is often referred to as "the Christ hymn." Whether these lines were from an earlier Christian liturgy or were composed by Paul for this letter is difficult to tell. Paul uses these verses to display the prime example of the Christian life—Jesus Christ. The Christ hymn follows a pattern of increasing humiliation followed by increasing exaltation. Paul refers to Christ's preincarnate state, "being in very nature God," in 2:6. Jesus, as the Second Person of the Trinity, had the appearance of or was in the form of God before his incarnation. Yet the term "very nature" denotes more than a mere physical appearance. When Paul says that Christ was God in his very nature, he is talking about both the appearance of God (glory, power, majesty) and the true essence of God. Paul continues by saying that Christ, who was God in appearance and truth, did not consider his rights as needing to be asserted. This statement is both a truth about Christ and also a directive to the Philippians in how they are to have the attitude of Christ Jesus.

Paul is paralleling Christ with Adam. Adam was created in the image of God and chose a life of disobedience and self-exaltation ("you will be like God" [Gen. 3:5]). Jesus resisted the temptation to take what was his by right and chose instead to obey the Father and submit himself to the Father's will. Jesus Christ, as

Paul puts it, made himself nothing and took upon himself the nature of a servant, a human (2:7). This statement is not only an important claim about the incarnation but also a telling statement about human nature itself. "Made himself nothing" is often translated as "emptied himself," which better captures the action in the verse. Christ set aside the glory that was his right in order to become human. It is an emptying in that Christ remains divine yet sets aside the glory that is due to God. The rest of 2:7 emphasizes that Christ took on human flesh completely, with all its weaknesses and restrictions. He lived not merely within a human body but as a human, dealing with all the trials and pains of life; yet he was without sin. "Servant" also refers to the very nature of humanity. Paul is telling the Philippians that not only are they to follow Christ in humility, but also they, as humans, are in essence servants to both God and others. That is who they are. Paul is, by pointing out Christ's servant nature, calling the Philippians to a life of service in response.

Although becoming human humbled Christ from his divine status and glory, his path of humiliation did not end there. Christ, as God, could have easily been a king among the people of the earth, yet he chose to humble himself and become the least of humans. Even after he became incarnate, "he humbled himself" (2:8). Paul does not merely say at this point that Christ was crucified but points out that Christ was "obedient to death—even death on a cross" (2:8). This is *the* example that both Paul and the Philippians are to turn to in their lives. Paul was under persecution, as was the Philippian church. It was possible that they would be faced with death, but they should remember that their savior was obedient and was crucified. Yet the word "obedient" is used not only to remind them that they may face martyrdom but also to remind the Philippians that suffering for Christ is only to be done in obedience to God, not through self-assertion. They should not chase after martyrdom but should submit to God's will as Christ did, allowing themselves to be humbled, even if it means to the point of death.

The hymn does not end with Christ's death, as no true story about Christ can. Paul inserts the all-important "therefore" to show that what follows is a result of what came before. It was not a mere foregone conclusion that Christ would be exalted again to the glory he left, but because of his obedience, "God exalted him to the highest place" (2:9). After descending to the depths, Christ was brought up to the highest heights. Not only is the name Jesus above all other names, but it also has been so exalted by the Father that it will cause every knee to bow and every tongue to confess Christ's lordship (see Isa. 45:23). These are things of which only God is worthy. When Paul says that Jesus is exalted to this level, he is saying that he was restored to his greater glory as the Son of God. Jesus's path was traced from his preincarnate status as the Son of God to the depths of the cross and back to the exaltation given to Jesus by the Father. This path is the example that Paul sets before the Philippians. Their lives are to be ones of humility and service, true, but they are also to be lives that center on God and God's will, not on themselves. While Adam was self-assertive and self-centered, Christ allowed God to exalt him and lived his life in service to God and others. Paul calls them to follow the path that Christ set, which, to echo Paul's prayer in 1:11, brings glory to God the Father (2:11).

D. A call to Christlike obedience (2:12–18). After ending the hymn, Paul continues with another "therefore." In light of the example of Christ, Paul explicitly calls the Philippians to a life of obedience following the example of Christ. In light of his current situation of imprisonment, Paul calls them to obey while he is away, as he has known them to obey when he is there (2:12). Yet this obedience is even more important because Paul is not there. When Paul is there with them in Philippi, the Philippians may have obeyed only out of respect for Paul, not out of a genuine desire to obey God

in all things. Thus, when Paul is absent, their obedience is a greater indication of their true character. This obedience is to be seen in their following Paul's instruction: "Continue to work out your salvation with fear and trembling" (2:12). This is an often misinterpreted passage. First of all, it refers to salvation in the sense of the whole community. Paul has been calling the Philippians to unity and a life lived for others, so he would not then call them to think only of working out their own individual salvation. Here he is concerned about the spiritual life and health of the community, which they are to "work at" (which is a better understanding of the phrase "work out," just as two people "work out" their differences) until all factionalism, disunity, and selfishness are uprooted and overthrown. The phrase "with fear and trembling" is meant to emphasize that even this act of obedience is to be done in humility and reliance on God. In 2:13 the claim that God is the one who works on their will and desires crushes any interpretation of 2:12 that allows people to earn their salvation.

Paul continues his call to the Philippians to have an attitude like Christ in 2:14. Not only does Paul call the Philippians to humility and service, but he also warns them against spreading disunity in the Christian community. Paul's call to cease complaining is connected to his prayer in 1:10–11. He wants them to be pure and blameless, living out the Christian life with inner unity and outward holiness in spite of the condition of the world around them ("warped and crooked generation" is an allusion to Deut. 32:5). The purpose of their outward holiness and Christian life of humility, unity, and obedience is to shine the light of Christ into the world (Matt. 5:14–16) as they hold to the truth of the gospel and present the gospel to the world in both word and deed. Paul calls for their Christian lives to be true for their own sakes and also so that Paul may rejoice and boast in the Philippians. Paul has worked and labored in love for this congregation, and he greatly desires at the final day to boast in all that they have become. He does not want all the love he has given to end up being for nothing.

Paul's next sentence suggests the possibility of martyrdom. Even though his life would be sacrificed, the Philippians' faith would be a part of that sacrifice. They have offered their love and support to Paul and have genuinely shared in his pain and suffering (see Phil. 1:7; 4:14). Even in talking about his possible death, Paul is full of joy because of their faith and the hope he has for God's work in that community. Thus, he rejoices. And if Paul can rejoice in the face of death and remain hopeful, then the Philippians should be able to rejoice along with him (2:17–18).

4. Judge Those Who Work among You by the Truth of the Gospel (2:19–30)

After illuminating the supreme example of Jesus Christ for the Christian life, Paul moves on to the example of Christian leaders. Just as Christ is an example of a leader who is willing to sacrifice self for the sake of unity, true Christian leaders model this same self-sacrificing dedication to the cause of Christian unity. In this section, Paul discusses Timothy and Epaphroditus as examples and resolves to send them to the Philippians as living examples of the Christian life of self-sacrificing unity. Both Timothy and Epaphroditus put the needs of the church and the gospel ahead of their own interests and have a genuine concern for the welfare of the Philippian church.

Paul begins with Timothy, Paul's close companion mentioned in the opening of the letter. Paul is sending Timothy to the Philippians for at least two purposes. Paul is eager to receive news about how the congregation is doing, whether they are living in a manner worthy of the gospel, and he wants to encourage them about his own situation in Rome. Timothy is Paul's "son" in the gospel and can represent Paul in a special way to the Philippian congregation. But Timothy is also an outstanding example of a true Christlike leader who is not concerned with himself but looks to the interests of others, especially the Philippians (2:20–21). Just

as Paul called the Philippians to look to others' interests (2:4), he is going to send to them someone who exemplifies this important aspect of the Christian life. Timothy is an example for the Philippians primarily because of his humble heart. Not only has Timothy shown his heart for others, but he has proved his worth by serving closely with Paul in spreading the message of the gospel. Paul's chief concern, and therefore his primary reason for writing the Letter to the Philippians, is the progress of the gospel in Philippi. Because of his character and adherence to the gospel, Timothy can represent Paul as his forerunner, even as Paul hopes that he himself will be able to follow soon.

The Egnatian Way, a major Roman road that ran through Philippi, was probably the route Timothy and Epaphroditus followed in their travels to and from the city (see Phil. 2:19–30).

Paul then moves on to the example of Epaphroditus. Epaphroditus, as the messenger the Philippians sent to Paul (2:25), most likely delivered their financial aid to the apostle. Paul also appeals to Epaphroditus as an example because of his humble heart. Epaphroditus had a heart for the Philippians to the degree that he longed for them just as Paul did (1:8). Epaphroditus's heart was filled with love for the Philippians, and as a co-worker and fellow soldier with Paul, Epaphroditus was obedient to God in working for the gospel. Through his work with Paul and the delivery of financial aid, Epaphroditus gave what the Philippians themselves could not give (2:30). Yet his greatest act of obedience came in continuing to serve despite his illness. Paul commends him as a man worthy of honor, since he "almost died for the work of Christ" (2:30). Just as Christ was obedient unto death, so was Epaphroditus. Yet God had mercy on him for the sake of Paul and the Philippian community. It is as an honored example that Paul sends Epaphroditus back to the Philippians, most likely carrying this very epistle with him. Paul seems just as concerned that the Philippians honor Epaphroditus for what he has done on their behalf as that they honor Paul as their apostle. All those who serve the gospel and suffer for the sake of Christ prove their worth to the people of God.

5. Paul's Life as an Example of the Truth of the Gospel (3:1–21)

The word "finally" or "further," which begins this chapter (see "Literary Unity" in introduction), might lead Paul's readers to expect some concluding remarks, especially since the exhortation to "rejoice in the Lord" appears to be such an apt summary of what Paul has previously written. But the whole tone of the letter changes abruptly in 3:2, and a new subject is introduced rather unexpectedly. This change of tone and subject has led several scholars to suggest that Philippians 3 is actually a fragment of an earlier letter that has been grafted into the main body of the epistle. There is, however, no manuscript evidence to support such a claim, and although

the change of tone is striking, there is a basic similarity in theme between Philippians 3 and the rest of the letter. Paul still has the gospel at the center of his thinking, and the change in tone can be explained by his concern for the truth of the gospel. In 1:18, Paul rejoiced that the true gospel was being preached, even if it was being preached from false motives. But faced with the danger of those who insist on circumcision in addition to Christ, he cannot rejoice, because he must warn the Philippians about those who do not preach the true gospel. In the same way that he used others as examples of what it means to live the truth of the gospel, Paul will now use his own life to show that in Christ circumcision is no longer necessary. He can do this because those who preach the gospel should also be living examples of it.

A. Beware of those who oppose the truth of the gospel (3:1–3). The Greek expression *to loipon*, which is often translated "finally," might be better translated as "in addition," to avoid giving the impression that Paul is concluding the letter. Paul is really using this expression to draw his readers' attention to what follows: he wants to warn them to be watchful in the face of a recurring danger. There is little in the rest of Philippians to prepare the reader for this sudden denunciation of "those evildoers." But Paul does say that he is writing "the same things to you again" and gives several clues as to the nature of this threat.

In 3:2, Paul obliquely names those who threaten the church and almost certainly points to either Jews or Judaizing Christians. He calls his opponents "dogs," a term Jews often used to refer to impure Gentiles, and "those evildoers." He then uses the term "mutilators," which comes from a word used to describe mutilation forbidden by Mosaic law, to describe these people. Paul appears to be turning the claims of his opponents against them: their circumcision is really mutilation; they are ceremonially defiled, and their righteousness is evil. All these terms are rather oblique and therefore not too useful in identifying a specific group in Philippi that Paul might see as opponents of the gospel. In fact, there is no actual sense that this danger is immediately present at Philippi, as it was in Galatia. Paul gives no indication of being concerned with doctrinal errors or irregularities of practice in the Philippian church. The purpose of Paul's warning is a general one, issued in the face of something he sees as a constant menace to the churches he established.

Philippians 3:3 leaves little doubt that circumcision is the central issue in his debate with these opponents and that Paul's derogatory language in Philippians 3:2 refers to those who uphold the ceremonial laws of Judaism. Here he contrasts the "mutilators of the flesh" with those who are "the circumcision," among whom he includes himself. Those who have the right to the title of "the circumcision" are characterized by three things. The first is that they worship in a spirit given by God. The word "worship" (NIV "serve") refers to the service rendered to God by Israel. Paul claims that true worship, as well as true circumcision, is found in Christ. This is a clear reference to the humble and obedient servanthood of Christ in 2:6–11. So it is no surprise that the second characteristic of those who are truly of "the circumcision" is that they boast only of Christ and show his humility and servanthood in their lives. In addition, those of the true circumcision "put no confidence in the flesh"; this is the negative aspect of what it means to "boast in Christ Jesus." They trust only in Christ, not in fleshly circumcision.

B. Paul's life illustrates the truth of the gospel (3:4–14). Paul now proceeds to offer his own life as an example of what it means to "boast in Christ Jesus" and "put no confidence in the flesh" (3:3). True participation in the gospel of Christ means that one's life should show forth the truth of the gospel, and Paul is supremely confident that his own life shows that fleshly circumcision is something that needs to be put aside so that Christ can be fully glorified. The same pattern of giving up privilege and voluntary humiliation that characterized Christ's life characterizes Paul's life as he enters into an

intimate relationship with Christ. This union with Christ in no way depends on circumcision or any other human accomplishment. Instead, it demands that Paul give up everything in order to "be found in him" (3:9), just as Christ gave up everything in order to be "found in appearance as a man" (2:8).

The clear statement of the contrast between "mutilation" and "circumcision" in 3:2–3 sets the stage for Paul's autobiographical defense of the gospel. Paul has experienced the meaning of circumcision in the flesh and what it means to glory in Christ Jesus. So in Philippians 3:4–6, he can meet those who are preaching circumcision, whether they are Jews or Judaizers, on their own terms. Paul is willing to compare himself with anyone who "thinks they have reasons to put confidence in the flesh" (3:4), because he has more. Three of the reasons Paul gives are hereditary: he was born a Jew of the tribe of Benjamin; he was circumcised according to Jewish law; he was raised as a culturally pure, Hebrew-speaking Jew. These are hereditary distinctions of which many Jews could not boast. Paul's personal convictions while a Jew also gave him reason to boast of his Jewish distinctives: his attitude toward the law was that of the strict sect of the Pharisees; he was a zealous persecutor of the church; he was faultless in his strict observance of the law. Few Jews could match Paul's claims, and Paul's Jewish credentials show that he is fully competent by Jewish standards to judge any issue involving Jewish law or "confidence in the flesh." Paul's opposition to those who wish to add circumcision to the gospel does not come from ignorance about the law.

But "knowing Christ Jesus my Lord" has brought about a complete change in Paul's life. He describes this change in Philippians 3:7–8 and makes it clear that this change could never have been brought about by adherence to Jewish law. In fact, Paul now considers all his former advantages as a Jew, the things that he used to consider "gains," to be a total "loss" for the sake of knowing Christ. The word translated as "what is more," which begins 3:8, is an extremely strong expression in Greek, which indicates the complete reversal of Paul's former values, and the perfect tense of the verb "consider" in this verse indicates the continuing effects of this reversal. Even the meaning of the words "gains" and "loss" is reversed—what were "gains" according to the Jewish law are now considered "loss for the sake of Christ." Jews used the word translated as "garbage" to refer to the Gentile's portion at the banqueting table of God, but Paul now uses it to refer to everything that he used to consider gain under the Jewish law. The earnest repetition of key words like "confidence," "loss," "gain," and "consider" expresses the intensity of Paul's new convictions and the total reversal that has taken place in his life. This reversal in Paul's life

has occurred because of the "surpassing worth of knowing Christ Jesus my Lord" (3:8). It is the greatness of this revelation, not a deficiency in the Jewish law or Paul's righteousness, that makes his former life appear as "loss." Living for the Jewish law would be having a goal other than that of knowing Christ Jesus. All Paul's former gains are superseded by and lose their value before the single perspective that now controls his life: to know Christ, to gain him, to be found in him.

In Philippians 3:9–11 Paul draws out the implications of what it means to have "knowing Christ Jesus my Lord" as the single purpose of his life. One of these implications has already been made clear: in order to gain Christ, to be found in him, and to know him, Paul has counted everything else as loss, especially his former life under the Jewish law. Here he makes it clear that being found in Christ excludes "having a righteousness of my own that comes from the law" (3:9). As a Jew, Paul had a righteousness *in* the law (3:6); now that he is found *in* Christ, he can no longer have a

The remains of the bema (speaker's platform) at Philippi. This platform may be where Paul and Silas stood when they were dragged before the magistrates and subsequently beaten and thrown into prison (Acts 16:19–21). In light of his many beatings and imprisonments, Paul can declare that he knows what it is to participate in the sufferings of Christ (Phil. 3:10).

righteousness that comes *from* the law (3:9). The change in preposition (which is quite obvious in the Greek text but somewhat obscured in most translations) is highly significant. Being found *in* Christ means that Paul can no longer be found *in* the Jewish law—the two are mutually exclusive conditions. And if they are mutually exclusive for Paul, then they are mutually exclusive for all other Christians, including the Philippians. Now Paul's righteousness, and the righteousness of all who follow Christ along with Paul, comes *from* God through faith *in* Christ. Paul reminds the Philippians that, for a Christian, accepting circumcision and embracing the Jewish law as a way of righteousness is a rejection of one's position *in* Christ and "the surpassing worth of knowing Christ Jesus."

But this new position *in* Christ has also brought tremendous gain to Paul's life. His new knowledge of Christ is marked by the experience of "the power of his resurrection and participation in his sufferings." Here Paul affirms the intimate relationship that now exists between himself and Christ as he participates in the dynamic of the gospel. There are two aspects to this relationship with Christ. The first is the vivifying power of Christ, which has made Paul's new life *in* Christ possible. Inseparable from this experience of power, however, is Paul's participation in the sufferings of Christ. This is true participation in the gospel—one enters into the experience of suffering as one knows the power of the new life in Christ. For Paul, as for all Christians, the purpose of this suffering is determined by the death and resurrection of Christ. Suffering in Christ is an extension of Christ's death on the cross, and its purpose is that Paul might become "like him in his death" and therefore also "attaining to the resurrection from the dead." In the light of the resurrection, all suffering in the present age is embraced by God's purpose and points to the future significance of the resurrection. So as Paul participates in Christ's sufferings and is conformed to Christ's death, he always looks forward to the experience of "the resurrection

from the dead." What Paul meant in 1:21 by "to live is Christ and to die is gain" receives a fuller explication here. The death and resurrection of Christ are representative acts in which his people share; conformity to the death of Christ is the gateway to the experience of the resurrection.

In Philippians 3:12–14 Paul continues to stress the purpose toward which his whole life is oriented. One of the most striking aspects of this account of Paul's life is that Paul sees "knowing Christ Jesus" (3:8) not only as something in which he already participates but also as a goal he continues to pursue. This double sense of purpose, Christ as both motivation and goal, is explained in these verses: Christ has grasped Paul, so Paul presses on to grasp Christ, the goal of his life. Paul is fully aware that he has not yet reached this goal, nor is he "perfect" (3:12; NIV "arrived at my goal"). The Greek word here translated "perfect" could also be translated "finished" and fits well with the metaphor Paul uses in these verses of running a race. He forgets all that lies behind. Those things he now counts as "loss," and he looks only at the goal that lies ahead—the "prize for which God has called me heavenward *in* Christ Jesus" (3:14). Christ is the basis of this call as well as the prize, and the divine call *in* Christ provides the power Paul needs to attain the goal. Being *in* Christ means being shaped by Christ's death and resurrection, so the events of the Christ hymn of Philippians 2:6–11 find their counterpart in the way Paul presents his experience in Philippians 3:4–14. As Paul empties himself of all but Christ and becomes "like him in his death," he shows that what is *in* Christ is now *in* Paul, who has become a true embodiment of the gospel he preaches.

C. Follow the example of Paul as he follows the example of Christ (3:15–21). Christ has so claimed Paul's life that he can offer himself to the Philippians as a model of what it means to live a life conformed to the truth of the gospel, and here he urges them to join him in allowing Christ to claim their lives. The Greek phrase *touto phroneō* of 2:5, translated as "your attitude should be the same," is echoed in the *touto phroneō* of 3:15, translated as "all . . . should take such a view of things." This echo is not accidental. Paul wants the Philippians to have the mind of Christ and is so certain that his message and his life exhibit the truth of the gospel that he can confidently exhort them to join in imitating him as he imitates Christ.

Paul has expounded, in the form of personal testimony, the true position of the believer *in* Christ, and in Philippians 3:15–16, he urges the Philippians to persevere in this situation with him. Here he contrasts "all of us . . . who are mature" with those who "think differently." The word used for "mature" has the idea of a goal toward which one is striving; those who are mature have in mind the same goal as Paul. Yet Paul does not seem to be particularly concerned about those who might be less mature or think differently, since he is so confident of the truth he has stated that he can invoke the aid of God to illumine the minds and correct the behavior of those who do not share his convictions. So he merely urges the Philippians to "live up to what we have already attained" (3:16). Since the Philippians are already following the standard Paul has set, all they need to do is keep walking in the same way.

In Philippians 3:18, Paul refers to the enemies of the cross, possibly including those who worship pagan gods. At Philippi, inscriptions mentioning gods such as Liber and Hercules have been excavated, suggesting the presence of a sanctuary where they were worshiped. This head of Hercules is a Roman copy of an earlier Hellenistic original from the Imperial Roman Period.

To any who might object, Paul answers that the standard of conduct he urges is clear by the living pattern of behavior he has set forth: "Join together in following my example, brothers and sisters, and just as you have us as a model, keep your eyes on those who live as we do" (3:17). Here Paul holds up his life to the Philippians as a pattern to be imitated. But why does Paul do this and in what sense is his life to be imitated? This question really cannot be answered until the negative example of the "enemies of the cross of Christ" in 3:18–19 is considered. Those who pass by the cross have completely missed the heart of the gospel and its true meaning. Paul's goal is "to know Christ . . . and participation in his sufferings" (3:10); "their destiny is destruction" (3:19). The other phrases Paul uses to characterize these "enemies of the cross" can be interpreted in various ways and understood as referring to several different types of opponents of the gospel. These people set their minds on earthly things; their God is their belly, and the things in which they glory are actually their shame. This description could apply to much of the pagan world or the Judaizing enemies of the cross similar to those described in Philippians 3:2. This open-ended description of "the enemies of the cross" invites a comparison between the example set by Paul and anyone whose purpose is something other than "knowing Christ Jesus" (3:8). This seems to be Paul's intention, for he uses this description to contrast those who set their minds on earthly things with those who have the mind of Christ.

In Philippians 3:20–21, Paul reminds his readers that those who have the mind of Christ and are mature enough to join in imitating Paul as he imitates Christ have their citizenship in heaven. Their minds are not set on earthly things, for they "eagerly await a Savior" from heaven and the resurrection power that he brings. Those who embrace the crucified Christ and "becoming like him in his death" (3:10) will be made "like his glorious body" (3:21) when he brings all things under his control. This conforming of the believer to the image of Christ both in death and in glory is accomplished by the enabling power at work in him. One day the image of Christ will be revealed in all who have experienced the heavenward call of God in Christ Jesus. In light of this future glory, understanding Paul's call to imitate him as mere exhortation to Christian living hardly does justice to the text. Paul wants the Philippians to have this goal in mind so that God's power can be manifested in their lives as well as his. Fundamental to Paul's thinking is the conviction that the destiny of the believer involves sharing the likeness of the Lord Jesus. The power that accomplishes this is already at work in the lives of all who seek to imitate Paul as he follows the heavenly call of God in Jesus Christ.

6. Encouragements, Appreciations, and Greetings (4:1–23)

Having reminded the Philippians of their heavenly citizenship and their glorious destiny, Paul returns to the pastoral concerns of the present. The Philippian church needs to have the mind of Christ and stand firm in the unity of the gospel as they face those who are the "enemies of the cross of Christ." Then they can truly live in joy and contentment and experience the fullness of the grace of God in their community.

A. Encouragements to steadfastness and unity (4:1–3). Paul begins this section with another "therefore" (4:1) as he gathers all of what he has told the Philippians into a single restatement of his message: the Philippians, whom Paul loves, are to remain faithful to the Lord. Paul emphatically states that he not only loves the Philippians but also longs to be with them. Paul longs for them because they are his joy and his crown as a result of their partnership with Paul in the mission of the gospel. They are his joy because they have accepted the gospel that Paul preaches, and his crown because they, like a laurel crown in an athletic event, are the result of his calling as an apostle and his many labors in the gospel. In calling them his "crown," Paul may even be implying that they are part of "the prize for which God has called me heavenward in Christ Jesus" (3:14). Their faith brings both joy and honor to Paul, and out of his deep love for them, he calls them to stand firm in their faith in God.

Paul then addresses two women, Euodia and Syntyche. He identifies these women as more than mere members of the Philippian community; he calls them "co-workers" who have labored beside him in the mission of the gospel. Paul uses the same term for his professional colleagues such as Timothy and Silas. But it is certain that these women, along with Clement, have a leadership role in the Philippian community and should be demonstrating the unity of the gospel, not living in strife and dissension. Here Paul continues his theme of using Christian leaders to demonstrate the truth of the gospel as he exhorts Euodia and Syntyche to "be of the same mind" (4:2; this echoes Paul's exhortation in Phil. 2:2, where the same Greek phrase is translated as "being like-minded"). This disagreement was most likely a personal quarrel over a matter of leadership, not the message of the gospel; otherwise Paul would have weighed in and given his opinion on the issue. Paul suggests that they resolve their disagreement through agreeing "in the Lord" (4:2) because it is the Lord's interests and opinion that are ultimately important, not those of either woman. The love with which Paul treats them suggests their closeness to the apostle, as Paul reminds them that they are sisters in the Lord and that through their bond of faith they can truly resolve this and all disagreements.

In addition, Paul invokes the help of a "loyal companion" (4:3; NIV "true companion") to aid the sisters in the resolution of their issue. The identity of this individual is uncertain, but Paul assuredly uses the term "companion" in order to remind this person of his or her relationship to Paul, the gospel of Christ, and the community of faith. In this reminder, Paul empowers this person to resolve the dispute along with the help of Clement and other leaders who labor in the gospel. Paul claims that because of their service to the cause of the gospel, both these women and those who help them in their strife have their names written in the book of life, where the names of the faithful are written (see Exod. 32:32; Ps. 69:28; Luke 10:20). While their actions may go unnoticed in this world, Paul reminds the Philippians that God is paying attention and is pleased.

B. Encouragements to prayer and noble-mindedness (4:4–9). While external conflicts and anxieties may be present in the community, the Philippians are still called to rejoice because they belong to the Lord and he is watching over them (4:4). This joy is not empty but rests on the assurance of God's goodness and grace. It is their faith "in the Lord" (see 4:4) that allows them to rejoice in their trials. Paul calls them to this joy with authority because he himself is faced with troubles (Phil. 1:30) yet rejoices whether he is in prison or free. The Philippians are further called to let their "gentleness" be expressed to all people (4:5). This outward expression of grace is a natural result of their inward state of joy. Being "gentle" means that they must respond to their trials with love and peace, not retaliation. Paul then reminds them that "the Lord is near" and will rescue them from all their troubles. This reference to the coming Savior echoes Philippians 3:20 and reminds the Philippians again to live as citizens of heaven.

Knowing their current adversity, Paul calls the Philippians to prayer as a response to their condition. They do not need to be anxious, because God is with them even now. They have a present promise as well as a future hope. They are to trust in God and his provision instead of worrying about how they will provide for themselves. They are called to entrust God with all their concerns through prayer by presenting specific requests before God. These requests are not to be made with a self-serving attitude but with an attitude of thanksgiving, remembering what God has done and believing that he will continue to save them in the future. As a result of these faithful petitions, they will receive the peace that comes from God so that they may remain faithful and joyful regardless of their circumstances. This peace is one of the kingdom blessings of the Old Testament, which is made available now to those who are the citizens of heaven. In heaven God already reigns and his foes are already defeated, as the end of the Christ hymn in 2:9–11 reminds believers. Those who are citizens of heaven and live *in* Christ are given "the peace of God, which transcends all understanding." God will guard both the hearts and minds of the Philippians from the attacks they face and the effects of their long trial because they remain "in Christ Jesus" (4:6–7).

Paul concludes this section with a list of ethical terms that connect with the "peace of God" in 4:7. If the peace they receive from God is to continue working itself out in rejoicing and action in the community, as Paul hopes, then the Philippians need to set their minds on heavenly things and not "on earthly things" (3:19–20). They must "think" about these heavenly virtues, or better yet, allow these virtues to shape the way they view and move through the world even now. Paul calls them not only to ponder these concepts but to put them into action. Instead of giving an exhaustive list of virtues, Paul just gives the Philippians examples of what it would mean to set their minds on heavenly things, concluding that they must be "excellent or praiseworthy" (4:8). While this list could be understood as virtues that were common to moral philosophy in Paul's time, the apostle states that the virtues they must follow are not to be found in the world but in Paul's example and teaching and the teaching and example of Christ. If these virtues are put into practice, not only will the peace of God be with the Philippians, but the God of peace will be with them as well.

C. Appreciation of the Philippians' gift (4:10–20). As he approaches the conclusion of the letter, Paul reveals his personal reasons for sending this letter to the Philippians. The Philippian congregation sent financial aid to Paul through Epaphroditus, and Paul wishes to thank them for their generous gift. Paul rejoices not only for the gift that he has received but also for the love and care that this gift allows the Philippians to show. Paul does not admit to having any need but only rejoices in their ability to care for him. Paul states that he is content no matter the circumstances, which is a reference to his situation in prison. Paul is not affected by outward circumstances, because they are not the focus of his life. He concentrates on what is truly important: the preaching of the gospel, the imitation of Christ, and what it means to live as a citizen of heaven. As long as the gospel is being advanced and Christ is exalted, Paul is content with life in prison, martyrdom, or freedom, a theme he first introduced in 1:15–20. Plenty and poverty do not affect Paul's ability to rejoice because God's strength gives him contentment. It is Paul's deep personal "knowing Christ Jesus" and being "found in him" (Phil. 3:8–9) that makes this contentment possible. He wants to remind the Philippians that he lives not by his own ability to provide for himself or even because of their generosity but because of God's grace and goodness in Christ Jesus. Indeed, for Paul, "to live is Christ and to die is gain" (1:21) in every aspect of his life. This is the secret of his contentment and the model he offers the Philippians for dealing with any situation in which they might find themselves.

Those who know Christ and his strength can indeed do everything through Christ.

Paul's contentment is not meant to discourage the Philippians. Their giving is still a good thing. In fact, he reminds them of all they have done for him and the great degree to which he appreciates it. From the beginning of his ministry to them, the Philippians have constantly supported Paul, even when others refused and persecuted him. Here there is no indication that Paul accepted financial support from the Philippians when he was actually at Philippi. Their support came after he had departed and went on to establish other churches. Paul mentions Thessalonica here, but he also mentions the support of the Philippians in 2 Corinthians 8:1–5, where they are characterized as extremely generous givers. In this sense they became his partners and co-workers in the mission of the gospel, and Paul says that they have given aid "more than once" (4:16). Their gift provides for Paul's physical needs, and because he can see how God is working in the community, it gives him great spiritual joy as well.

Paul continues to use commercial language as he claims that what the Philippians gave has now been "credited to [their] account" (4:17). While Paul has given them much, he says that the Philippians have paid him back—or possibly overpaid him. He uses the terminology of "credit" and "account" not to imply that the Philippians gave for selfish reasons but to show that their gift to him is like an investment that continues to accrue interest even as it furthers the mission of the gospel. The fact that their gift is leading to the progress of the gospel's mission far outweighs any monetary sum.

Paul also sees this gift as a sacrifice on the part of the Philippian congregation and one that is pleasing to God. He uses the image of "fragrant offering" to remind the Philippians of the offerings made by priests in the Old Testament to cover sins and show devotion to God. Because of their generosity, Paul claims that *his* God will provide for *their* needs. This is not *Paul's* God in the sense that Paul worshiped a different God from the Philippians. The use of the personal pronoun shows Paul's closeness to God and his dependence on God for the provision of both his physical and spiritual needs. Paul claims that this same God will fulfill all the Philippians' needs because God lacks nothing and indeed is overflowing in "the riches of his glory" (4:19). Paul ends this section with a benediction. He reminds the congregation that, in all their gifts and in all Paul's contentment, ultimate glory is given to God.

D. Greetings and benediction (4:21–23). Paul concludes his letter the same way he opened it—by greeting God's people and commending them to God's grace. In his benediction he shows the same concerns and pastoral sensibilities that he has maintained throughout the letter. He greets "all God's people," emphasizing the entire Philippian community, not mere individuals. This statement emphasizes the theme of unity that has been addressed throughout the letter. Paul then reminds them that while they are a community of believers who are praying and caring for him, Paul himself is within a community of believers who share that same love. So Paul sends greetings from the Christian community in Rome and particularly the imperial members and servants of "Caesar's household" (4:22) who have come to faith in Christ through interaction with Paul. These Christians are further evidence of the success of the gospel, which has occurred because of Paul's imprisonment. He is bringing people to Christ by virtue of his proximity to the very center of power in the Roman Empire—not only in the city of Rome but also in the very household of Caesar. Exactly who from the household of Caesar has come to Christ cannot be assumed from Paul's reference. It would probably not

include members of the imperial family but might well have included the praetorian guard mentioned in Philippians 1:13 and those from far higher classes than imperial slaves, as well as household servants. But it does seem to indicate that Paul is encouraging Christians in the imperial colony of Philippi by reminding them that they have allies in the heart of the imperial household in Rome. Last, Paul wishes that the grace of Christ be with the Philippians' spirit. Even in his final greeting, Paul calls the Philippians to focus on Christ and rely on his grace to unify and strengthen them.

Select Bibliography

Barth, Karl. *The Epistle to the Philippians.* Translated by James W. Leitch. London: SCM, 1962.

Craddock, Fred B. *Philippians.* Interpretation. Atlanta: John Knox, 1985.

Fee, Gordon D. *Paul's Letter to the Philippians.* New International Commentary on the New Testament. Grand Rapids: Eerdmans, 1995.

Martin, Ralph P. *The Epistle of Paul to the Philippians.* Tyndale New Testament Commentaries. Grand Rapids: Eerdmans, 1959.

Motyer, J. A. *The Message of Philippians: Jesus Our Joy.* The Bible Speaks Today. Downers Grove, IL: InterVarsity, 1991.

Osiek, Carolyn. *Philippians, Philemon.* Abingdon New Testament Commentaries. Nashville: Abingdon, 2000.

Silva, Moisés. *Philippians.* Baker Exegetical Commentary on the New Testament. Grand Rapids: Baker Academic, 2005.

Thurston, Bonnie B. *Philippians.* Sacra Pagina 10. Collegeville, MN: Liturgical Press, 2005.

Witherington, Ben, III. *Friendship and Finances in Philippi: The Letter of Paul to the Philippians.* Valley Forge, PA: Trinity Press International, 1994.

Colossians

LYNN H. COHICK

Introduction

Located strategically in the Lycus Valley near the Meander River in western Anatolia (modern Turkey), Colossae facilitated trade with its two larger neighbors, Laodicea and Hierapolis. Though the city had seen grander days, in the first century AD it lived in the shadow of its nearby rivals. The wealth of Laodicea and Hierapolis no doubt helped the Colossian economy, which continued to be known for its wool industry. The prosperity of all three cities was severely shaken with a major earthquake in AD 60/61 (Tacitus, *Annals* 14.27.1). Laodicea rebuilt itself without help from Rome. Perhaps Colossae also regained some of its earlier strength, but evidence is sparse, and no excavations have been done of the city.

Even before Colossae was stirred up by the earthquake, not all was calm within the city's young Christian community. The church was not in imminent danger of casting off their faith, but the situation was sufficiently worrisome that Paul dispatched a letter to address the brewing unrest. What exactly was the trouble? Paul's letter reveals growing tensions caused by what he calls an errant "philosophy" (Col. 2:8). The term "philosophy" calls to modern minds ivory-tower ruminations about abstract theoretical principles of human existence and the cosmos. In the first century, however, philosophy was closely coupled with ethics; it promoted rational thought over superstitions and carried positive connotations of an educated person and a well-run society. The term's use in Colossians probably carries the ironic sense that though its adherents see it as wisdom, Paul discounts it as mere human musing.

Paul warns the mostly Gentile church against the individualism underpinning this philosophy, which focuses on visions and asceticism and is rooted in their particular application of the law of Moses. Paul emphasizes two points: first, being in Christ means being in a community of which Christ is the head; and second, living in this community does not include, for Gentiles, following Jewish cultic practices or esoteric pursuits, such as a quest for visions.

The authorship and date of Colossians are both hotly contested and tied tightly to questions about the philosophy. Therefore, before we can address authorship questions, we must discover *why* the letter was written and *what* was involved in the philosophy. As we explore the reason for the letter's existence, a strong case for Pauline authorship will emerge.

Content

Colossian philosophy as syncretistic. One theory about the philosophy Paul refers to is that it was a syncretistic movement that drew on folk religious beliefs and magic, as well as conventional Jewish thinking and practices, as a way to confront the supernatural powers controlling the world. In this view, the philosophy had not abandoned monotheism but lined up with certain pagan assessments about how to control the forces of nature and fate.

To support this theory, several pieces of data are put forth. One is a type of Jewish expression that emphasized magic and astrology. Colossians 2:8 uses the Greek term for "tradition," which was also used in magical spells. The spells, it was believed, helped protect against hostile spirits, who influenced heavenly bodies and sought to dominate humans. Moreover, the philosophy's preoccupation with festivals, New Moon celebrations, and Sabbath shows an interest in astrology. Astrology seems to have played a role in defining Sabbath celebrations among some Jewish communities.

The syncretistic position does not place Judaism at the center of the philosophy's identity but puts it on equal footing with aspects of pagan religious beliefs and practices. Parallels to mystery cults are also discovered in a number of places, such as in the term translated as "goes into great detail" (2:18), which has connections with mystery cult initiations. Moreover, the emphasis on visions mirrors the mystery cults' promises of a mystical union. The word "honor" (NIV "value"; 2:23) is said to carry "technical significance in local religions for privilege someone experienced of being chosen by a deity and going through a mystery initiation rite" (Arnold, 220).

In this view, the promoters of the philosophy came from within the church and were most likely Gentile, although a few might have been Jewish (Arnold, 228–32). They did not teach a different gospel as much as fail to give Christ his due. They focused on the present dangers created by spiritual forces and local gods and looked to angels for protection. They represented the general population, which drew on organized religion and folk beliefs to manage their precarious existence. The philosophy sought security in visions that served as initiation into a full Christian life.

Colossian philosophy as Jewish. As intriguing as these connections are between the Jewish and

pagan worlds, many scholars are unconvinced by the syncretistic explanation. Some of the characteristics labeled as pagan, such as the interest in food and drink and religious festivals (2:16), could easily fit with Jewish practices. Again, the syncretistic theory fails to adequately account for the references to circumcision (2:11, 13; 3:11) and the written code (2:14). Circumcision is stressed as an important part of the Colossians' self-identity in Christ, which implies that the philosophy addressed this rite.

While a few characteristics of the philosophy clearly speak of Judaism—for example, the mention of Sabbath (2:16)—other characteristics sound ambiguous. A primary question is whether Paul, or any Jew, would describe the law as part of the powers and principalities (2:20), as human tradition and "hollow and deceptive" (2:8). Paul connects the law to human tradition when describing his life before his call to be an apostle. He tells the Galatians that he was well advanced in Judaism and zealous for the traditions of his fathers (Gal. 1:14). Again, the Gospel of Mark (7:5, 8) places on the lips of Pharisees a question to Jesus concerning the traditions of the elders. Here the term is understood positively by the speakers, but it is judged insufficient by Jesus.

Perhaps more disturbing is the possible link made between the law and the basic principles of this world, or *stoicheia* (Col. 2:8, 20). The term can refer to the ordinary basic elements of the earth, such as water and air and fire (see 2 Pet. 3:10, 12). But it can also indicate those spirits that rule over the elements. Paul uses the term in Galatians 4:8–9 (see also 4:3), where he draws a parallel between those "who by nature are not gods" and "those weak and miserable forces [*stoicheia*]." He connects the law with *stoicheia* through the metaphor of slavery. He suggests both that the law played the same role of enslaving Gentiles as did their pagan idolatry and that for Jews it was the power set in charge over Israel. Interestingly, in both Galatians and Colossians, the *stoicheia* are mentioned next to comments about the attraction of special Jewish observances and festivals and interest in angels (Gal. 3:19; Col. 2:18). This intimates a common thought trajectory behind both the Galatian Judaizers and the Colossian philosophers.

Much of this discussion hinges on a historical situation that included Gentile-Jewish interaction. Asia Minor incorporated large numbers of Jews, such as the Jews from Asia and Phrygia who traveled to Jerusalem for Pentecost (Acts 2:9–10) and Philip the apostle (or evangelist; Acts 21:8–9) and his virgin daughters, who settled in Hierapolis (Eusebius, *Ecclesiastical History* 3.31.2–5). Is a robust, confident, and self-assured Jewish community the target of the letter's argument? One view suggests that these Jews were neither actively seeking to undermine the Christian church nor attempting to convert them to Judaism; nevertheless, their argument was persuasive, and hence threatening, to the newly formed Christian community (Dunn, 35). This analysis, however, fails to explain adequately why these Gentiles would now be particularly vulnerable to Jewish influence, especially if the Jews are not actively seeking to bring them into the synagogue.

In conclusion, the philosophy is best understood as a Christian group that emphasized Gentiles must fulfill the Jewish law (i.e., be circumcised) to be full members of the community. The philosophy's particular slant on obedience to the law included an ascetic component, with an interest in visions. To combat the philosophy, the Letter to the Colossians elevates Christ by speaking of creation, including all powers and authorities, as coming through the Son (1:16). The same language is used to describe the Colossians' previous status as being uncircumcised and dead in their flesh but made alive when Christ on the cross "disarmed the powers and authorities" (2:13–15). At some level, then, these powers and authorities are connected to or synonyms for the Jewish law.

The philosophy and the hymn to Christ. While the philosophy is not mentioned directly until chapter 2, the "hymn" in Colossians 1:15–20 is often seen as a counterbalance to the philosophy.

Those who see the philosophy as syncretistic suggest that the hymn presents Christ as above the astral powers, gods, and fate, which torment humans. The philosophy turned to folk remedies such as magic and astrology, while the hymn declares that Christ has the power to combat those cosmic forces. The syncretistic position interprets the hymn as a frontal assault on the philosophy's inadequate understanding of Christ.

This approach, however, de-emphasizes the hymn's concern with the church as Christ's body and as God's people sharing their inheritance of the kingdom of the Son (1:12–13). The hymn is rooted in the salvation story of God, it flows naturally from the liturgical language of 1:12–14, and its claims echo throughout the letter. The forgiveness of sins and the triumph over powers and authorities are repeated in 2:13–15, and themes of creation and new creation in 3:10. The exalted picture of the Son as the image of the invisible God champions the majesty of God's plan of reconciling through Christ (1:23).

The imperial cult and the hymn to Christ. The hymn also reminds the Gentile Christians to resist another persistent voice: the imperial cult. The emperor and his military sought to convince all peoples of the omniscience and omnipotence of Rome. Coins, statues, military triumphal parades, and, not least, the imperial cult proclaimed loud and clear Caesar's divine status as the savior of the world and Rome's role as the keeper of moral order and goodness. The imperial cult's tentacles reached deep into city life: "In Rome imperial images, painted and sculpted, were on display in almost every shop" (Price, 120). Imperial temples provided space to erect statues dedicated by local associations or people. Time itself was marked by the emperor, with Augustus's birthday starting the new year. The imperial cult pervaded all life; it was not relegated to public lip service or privatized as individually chosen, personal piety. Therefore, any claim by Christians that Christ was the image of God and held full supremacy affected not simply an individual's personal political views but also the very roots of his or her social network and worldview.

Authorship

Colossians announces its author as the apostle Paul (and Timothy; 1:1), but recent scholarship has called that into question. Many scholars conclude that the differing cadence, style, and language add up to a literary style that may imitate Paul. Here we see not the varying hand of the secretary but the deeper evidence of authorial (unconscious) mannerisms in speech and thought patterns. Absent is the acerbic tone of Galatians, the sharp dialogical style of Romans, or the sarcasm of the Corinthian correspondence (Dunn, 35).

If it were only at the literary level, however, many scholars would probably explain the unique qualities as a more developed Paul, a different secretary, or the influence of Timothy. But the differences extend to theological categories, which are said to stand at odds with Paul's undisputed letters. For example, the Christology

found in 1:15–20 and 2:9–10 is argued to be more fully developed than what would be expected in the first-generation church. Likewise, the ecclesiology seems further along the historical trajectory of the early church than what would be current in Paul's time. This includes understanding Christ as the head of the church (1:18), which expands on the image of the church as the body of Christ (hands, feet, ears, eyes, and *head*; see 1 Cor. 12:15–27. "The problem is not that Colossians fails to treat a typically Pauline theme but that Colossians fails to treat this theme in a typically Pauline manner" (Thompson, 3).

Moreover, some argue that standard Pauline topics are missing. For example, in the vision of the church there is no mention of the Spirit (as in Galatians 5), guiding and empowering believers in their lives of holiness. Instead, we have household codes (3:18–4:1), rules supporting the Greco-Roman social status quo. Absent is the eschatological stress on the future; instead, a strong realized eschatology permeates the letter. For example, in Colossians 2:11–12, the author speaks in the past tense of being raised with Christ through faith, in contrast to Romans 6:4, which concludes that believers were buried with Christ and now "may live a new life" (see also Rom. 8:11).

Imperial temples, such as this Temple of Augustus at Pisidian Antioch (early first century AD), were erected in many Roman cities for worship of Roman emperors upon their deification.

Also missing is a robust use of the Old Testament as seen, for example, in 1 Corinthians 10 or Romans 3. Abraham and his example, so important in Romans and Galatians, are absent from Colossians. No mention is made of justification, the bedrock of Paul's thought.

Finally, Colossians is remarkably similar to Ephesians, a letter many scholars consider post-Pauline. Some argue that Colossians served as a template for Ephesians, but even so, the fact that Colossians was used calls its own status as Pauline into question. That is, Colossians was appealing as a model for Ephesians precisely because it represented a step beyond the authentic Paul and could be a guide for how to interpret and configure Paul for the next generation of readers. Timothy has been put forward as a possible author. Some qualify this by surmising that Paul empowered Timothy to write Colossians and approved the finished product. In this case, the scholarly label "deutero-Pauline" is unhelpful, as the letter met with Paul's approval. Complicating matters are the connections between Colossians and Philemon, a letter that most regard as genuinely Pauline.

A growing number of scholars are dissatisfied with this debate. They argue that the style, sentence structure, and theological outlook could well fit the range of Paul's expressions. Moreover, they suggest that the personal details (4:7–18) make sense only if it were written by Paul. While the tone of the letter is softer and less direct, this is due to Paul's "outsider" role; though Epaphras established the church directly, Paul felt an oversight responsibility toward the Colossian congregation because Epaphras was part of Paul's team. Again, the letter's structure matches what is found in the undisputed Pauline Letters: themes are briefly or poetically stated and then developed more deeply in subsequent paragraphs (for example, Philippians 2).

Those who believe Paul authored Colossians claim that theological differences are overstated. As is characteristic of Pauline authorship, allusions to the Old Testament abound (such as the "exodus" described in 1:12–13). Other Pauline themes appear. For example, Judaism is described as a potential snare for Gentile Christians (cf. Rom. 2:17–29; Galatians 3–4; 2 Corinthians 3). The church is presented as the people of God and the body of Christ (cf. 1 Corinthians 12). Although Paul varies the metaphor slightly in designating Christ as the head in Colossians, this does not change the underlying argument that the church is Christ's body. Suffering is promoted as a key component of the Christian's life (1:24; cf. 2 Cor. 1:3–11; 4:7–18; Rom. 8:17–25). The church is to put to death evil desires and passions (Col. 3:10–11; cf. Rom. 6:11–14; Gal. 3:26–28). The cross, which is central to Paul's thought, is emphasized in Colossians 1:20 and 2:14 (cf. 1 Cor. 1:17–18; Rom. 6:6; Gal. 2:20).

Some scholars view the Christology and eschatology expressed in Colossians as well within the range of Paul's thought (see, e.g., Still, 125–38). The hymn is matched by the Christology expressed in Philippians 2:6–11; 1 Corinthians 8:6; and 2 Corinthians 4:4; 8:9. The charge that Colossians expresses only realized eschatology also falls short of the mark. Colossians makes clear that future glory awaits the Christian when Christ appears (3:4). The intensity of the imminent expectation of the second coming is not as high as in 1 Thessalonians 4:15–5:4 or 1 Corinthians 15:51–52; instead, it is similar to the level in Philippians and Galatians. Central to Paul's thought is the unity of Gentiles with Jews as the new people of God, inaugurating the new age of the Spirit (Col. 1:8, 20, 27; cf. Gal. 3:28; 1 Cor. 12:13; Phil. 1:27–28).

The personal material of 4:7–17 also is hard to explain in any other way than that Paul wrote it. The section contains not detached personal details but an intimate narrative suggesting direct and personal knowledge of the Colossians. One can hardly imagine any church receiving this letter in AD 70 or 75 being impressed with this level of personal detail, knowing all the while that Paul has been dead for a decade or so.

Two figures play an important role in this discussion: Philemon and Onesimus. Most scholars note the significant overlap between Colossians and Philemon. Both letters are sent from prison and claim to be from Paul and Timothy. Both contain an almost identical list of people, including three who traveled with Paul to Jerusalem before his arrest—Aristarchus, Timothy, and Mark—as well as Onesimus, Luke, Demas, and Epaphras (the founder of the Colossian church). Ironically, however, Philemon himself is not mentioned in Colossians. This seems odd if (as some suggest) the Letter to Philemon was used as a template for Colossians by a later imitator of Paul. Why not then mention Philemon? Why use such a short, personal letter as a template at all? The most reasonable explanation of the data is that Paul authored the letter.

Date

Of course, dating the letter depends on one's decision about authorship. We have an added factor to consider when dating this epistle: Colossians is part of a group of four letters from Paul called the "prison epistles" because all refer to Paul as a prisoner of Jesus Christ (Phil. 1:12–14 describes in detail his imprisonment by the imperial guard). Scholars suggest three primary imprisonments as possible places and times for Paul's communications. While it is possible that Paul wrote these four letters while languishing at Caesarea (see Acts 24:27), most scholars suggest either Ephesus (Dunn, 40; see also Wright, 34–39; an Ephesus setting for composing the epistle would date the letter to the early 50s [52–55 or 53–56]) or Rome as the most likely site.

Evidence pointing to a Roman imprisonment includes the direct documentation in Acts 28:13–31; we can be certain that Paul did indeed suffer imprisonment in Rome toward the end of his ministry. Second, the nuanced and distinctive style of the letter is better explained as coming at the end rather than the

middle of Paul's ministry. This is especially relevant when taking into account Colossians' similarity to Ephesians, for most date Ephesians to the end of Paul's ministry, if not considering it post-Pauline. Paul's imprisonment in Rome detailed at the end of Acts probably occurred in the early 60s, placing Colossians about this time. But we can be even more specific. In AD 60–61, when the nearby cities of Laodicea and Hierapolis were destroyed by a severe earthquake, it is most likely that Colossae was also heavily damaged. Because Paul gives no hint in his letter of such devastation, we can assume that the calamity had yet to occur. Finally, in suggesting Colossians and Philemon were dispatched at the same time, we explain the fact that Philemon does not mention Tychicus, while Colossians does not mention Philemon—both men were present to deliver the letters. Probably Onesimus left Rome with the Letter to Philemon in the company of Tychicus, who carried the Letter to the Colossians. Paul indicates that Tychicus and Onesimus traveled together (Col. 4:9).

Outline

1. Greetings from Paul and Timothy to the Colossians (1:1–2)
2. Thanksgiving (1:3–12)
3. The Hymn to Christ (1:13–27)
   A. The Father Rescues His People (1:13–14)
   B. The Son Offers Reconciliation (1:15–20)
   C. The Colossians Stand Firm in Faith and Hope (1:21–23)
   D. The Example of Paul's Suffering (1:24–27)
4. The Call to Christian Maturity (1:28–4:6)
   A. Paul Contends for the Colossians (1:28–2:7)
   B. Christ Is over Every Power and Authority (2:8–15)
   C. Reject False Teachings (2:16–23)
   D. Set Your Heart and Mind on Things Above (3:1–4:6)
5. Final Greetings (4:7–18)

1. Greetings from Paul and Timothy to the Colossians (1:1–2)

Colossians begins with Paul's standard address, identifying himself as an apostle of Christ Jesus by the will of God. First Corinthians 1:1 and Romans 1:1 stipulate that Paul was "called" to be an apostle of Christ Jesus by the will of God, and 1 Corinthians includes the cosender and brother, Sosthenes. He includes the name of his coauthor, Timothy. Philippians is addressed by both Paul and Timothy, though here they are described not as apostle and brother but as servants (slaves) of Christ Jesus (see also Rom. 1:1). Paul usually identifies himself as an apostle, which in general means emissary or messenger but in the early church carried with it a special status of one especially chosen or gifted to speak authoritatively to the church. Paul greets the Colossians as "holy people" (or saints), a typical designation for believers in Paul's letters. By identifying them as holy, Paul draws on the ancient Jewish conviction that God's people are set apart and devoted wholly to him. Paul reinforces his conviction that, in Christ, Gentiles, too, are full members of God's

kingdom (see 1:12–13; 3:11). Moreover, Paul calls the Colossians "faithful," a term rarely used by Paul to describe humans (though he identifies Timothy as such in 1 Cor. 4:17). His letter will continue to build on this identity by encouraging the Colossians to "continue in [their] faith" and hold fast to the "hope held out in the gospel" (1:23).

2. Thanksgiving (1:3–12)

In these nine verses, Paul begins and ends with thanksgiving for the Colossians' being in Christ. The descriptions in 1:3–4 and 1:12 parallel each other, the latter expanding on the former to speak of their faith in terms of the inheritance of God's kingdom and their love in terms of being part of God's people. In a similar fashion, 1:9–11 builds on 1:5–6. After establishing their faith and love in Christ, Paul adds another of his favorite terms—"hope" (see 1 Cor. 13:13; 1 Thess. 1:3; 5:8). The terms "faith," "love," and "hope" are dynamic and active for Paul (see also 1 Thess. 1:3). Faith is rooted in Christ; it is not simply a strongly

This tell, or archaeological mound, of the ancient city of Colossae has not yet been excavated.

held religious belief. It involves personal trust and acts based on that trust. Love is not an emotional attachment to certain like-minded folk but a commitment to the well-being of all believers and then to the world. Hope is not merely the mental state of hopefulness (as in "I hope it does not rain for our picnic") but the clear vision of that which is hoped for. In 1:27 we find the focus of hope, "Christ in you," and its expected outcome, "glory."

The center of this section introduces the term "gospel," described here in organic terms—it is growing both within their community and throughout the entire world; it is bearing fruit in all places. In 1:21–23 Paul expands on what the gospel message is. He explains that Christ's physical body was put to death, which results in humans being reconciled to God and being made holy. This gospel is accessed by faith held confidently to the end.

Paul offers high praise to Epaphras (a diminutive form of Epaphroditus, though we should not confuse Epaphras of Colossae with Epaphroditus of Philippi [Phil. 2:5; 4:18]), a fellow worker with Paul who faithfully presented the gospel of Christ to the Colossians (1:7–8). A native son of Colossae, he learned the gospel from Paul either during the latter's first journey, perhaps meeting him in Pisidian Antioch, or during Paul's stay in Ephesus on his third journey. Epaphras is with Paul when he writes the letter. In Philemon 23 (written at the same time as Colossians), he is identified as Paul's fellow prisoner. In Colossians 4:10, Aristarchus is called "fellow prisoner." The term is also used of Andronicus and Junia in Romans 16:7. This is probably not an honorific title, and it likely indicates that while Paul wrote Philemon, Epaphras stayed with him in prison, and when he wrote Colossians, Aristarchus was at his side (see Dunn, 347–48; Wright, 191). In Colossians 4:12–13, Paul describes Epaphras as wrestling or contending in prayer for the Colossians and those believers in Laodicea and Hierapolis. Paul uses the same verb when describing his own commitment to the Colossians in 1:29–2:1. Paul

clearly had the utmost respect and admiration for Epaphras and considered the churches in the Lycus Valley to be well served by him.

3. The Hymn to Christ (1:13–27)

A. The Father rescues his people (1:13–14). Verse 12 prepares the reader for a further discussion of God's kingdom with its insistence on the church's rightful inheritance of it. (On the kingdom of God in Paul, see also Rom. 14:17; 1 Cor. 4:20; 6:9; 15:24–28.) Verses 13–14 explain how this inheritance has been accomplished. Paul makes clear that the Colossians had lived in darkness, that is, in sinfulness. God rescued them through his beloved Son, and now they are in the light (see Luke 16:8; John 12:36; 1 Thess. 5:15). Paul describes forgiveness in terms of release from captivity, a theme he will develop more fully later in the argument, when he speaks of Christ's overcoming the powers and authorities (1:16; 2:10, 15).

B. The Son offers reconciliation (1:15–20). Verses 15–20 contain some of the most poignant and provocative Christology in the New Testament. The passage sounds like a poem or hymn, prompting scholars to wonder whether Paul authored this section (Wright, 64) or appropriated it from the church (Dunn, 83). Yet most agree that the hymn fits the context well and that Paul used it to expand on key themes of God's kingdom, creation, and Christ's power in reconciling humans to God. Christology informs cosmology by declaring that creation is going somewhere—the goal of creation is new creation rooted in Christ (Col. 3:10). Again, Christology validates soteriology (theology dealing with salvation), for the new people of God are reconciled to him and each other through the cross of Christ (Col. 2:13–14). Christology corroborates eschatology in its insistence that Christ's resurrection is but the first fruits of a believer's eternal life in glory (Col. 3:4).

In declaring that Christ is the image of the *invisible* God, Paul asserts that pagan idols are not representative of God, for God is invisible, except through the Son (see John 1:18).

Moreover, as the image of God, Christ reflects the Godhead in its divine nature. Christ being the source of all things, Paul concludes that all things are held together and function for Christ. He is the firstborn—not only in terms of rank but also in a temporal sense, as indicated in 1:18 ("the firstborn from among the dead"). Paul does not mean that Christ is the first created being—in response to Arius, Athanasius writes, "But if all the creatures were created in him, he is other than the creatures, and is not a creature, but the Creator of the creatures" (*Orations against the Arians* 2.62)—but rather that Christ is the exalted preexistent one who was with God at creation, though he was not preexistent in his human form. These key ideas play out in Colossians 3:9–10, wherein Paul admonishes the Colossians to live in their new self, "which is being renewed in knowledge in the image of its Creator." Christ is the means through which creation was made and is sustained. He brings the new creation into being; and the Colossians have entered into it, as their lives are now "hidden with Christ in God" (3:3).

In Christ all things were created, including thrones and powers and rulers and authorities. Paul may be thinking of magic, astrology, or the oppressive political powers holding sway in his day. He may be thinking of paganism and/or the Jewish law as it functioned within the Gentile church. Most likely, Paul is speaking in the broadest terms of anything that claims ultimate authority or precedence in a believer's life—anything that is feared or honored above Christ.

The fact that Christ is preeminent over creation has consequences for humanity. Specifically, Christ is the head (*kephalē*) of the church, which Paul identifies as his body. And Christ is the beginning (*archē*). Both of the terms in Greek carry the sense of source, creative initiative, or first principle as well as leader. N. T. Wright (104) says, "The word 'head' was as flexible and evocative in Hebrew or Greek as it is in English, and we should not squeeze all Paul's uses of it into exactly the same mould"

(see also Wright, 74). In the ancient world, it was common to speak of the cosmos or the state as a body (Plato, *Timaeus* 31b, 32a; Livy, *Histories* 2.32.9–12; Epictetus, *Discourses* 2.10.4–5). Philo, a first-century Jew, declares that divine Reason (Logos) is the head of the cosmos (*On Dreams* 1.128; *Questions and Answers on Exodus* 2.117). Paul may be drawing on all these nuances when he expresses that Christ is the head of the church—Christ is the source, the leader, and the mind of the church.

It is Christ's resurrection that secures his supremacy. Christ has always had preeminence in principle, but the resurrection made that supremacy actual in time by defeating sin on the cross. The reward is not only authority over all things but also the resurrection of his body (literally and figuratively as the church).

The purpose behind Christ's death and resurrection, as 1:20 makes clear, is to reconcile all things to God. Christ is fully God (1:19) and as such is able to carry out the redemption plan, which redeems and reconciles all creation—his creation—to God. The cross made peace between God and his creation; it reconciled all things, which suggests that its power was not limited to human sin but covered the ramifications of sin throughout all creation. This reconciliation is available to all by faith. Paul is not claiming a universal salvation here; rather, he is emphasizing the scope of Christ's redemptive work—all people can be reconciled, through faith (1:23; see also 2 Cor. 5:10).

C. The Colossians stand firm in faith and hope (1:21–23). After finishing the great hymn of praise to Christ, Paul now presents the implications of his Christology. He explains that in the past the Colossians were alienated from God. From God's perspective, the situation that created their alienation has been fixed on the cross. Does Paul imply that this "fix" is conditional, when he adds "*if* you continue in your faith" (1:23)? He is not suggesting that every once in a while the cross is ineffectual in atoning for sin or declaring that God might decide at some point to reject the cross as sufficient remedy for all sin. Paul is not insinuating that the Colossians are to muddle along as best they can and hope that their faith manages in the end to carry them to heaven. The point Paul makes is that the Colossians must stay the course, both in mind and in behavior. They must remain connected to the head, Christ, for the body cannot live without its head. Paul gives no hint that he is worried they might not reach this goal.

D. The example of Paul's suffering (1:24–27). Paul declared himself a servant of Christ in 1:23 and in the next few verses fleshes out what that means in terms of Christ's sacrifice and the growth of the church. He uses terms such as "flesh" and "body" (1:24) that carry a range of meaning and impact. In 1:22, Paul declared that Christ conquered sin with his death (on the cross) in his fleshly body, and in verse 24, Paul expands the connotations of Christ's body to include the church. He has both meanings in mind when he declares that he suffers physically (in his flesh) for the church, following Christ's example for the church (metaphorically, Christ's body).

Paul states that he rejoices *in* his sufferings. We might be tempted to tone down this claim by assuming Paul means that he rejoices in the midst of or in spite of his sufferings. But Paul probably expresses the Jewish conviction that, at the end of the present age, there will be terrible sufferings for the people of God, referred to as the messianic woes. Paul's suffering is indicative of the end of the present evil age and the start of the new age in Christ, which will be consummated when Christ returns (Col. 3:4). The suffering is confirmation that Paul is part of the new people of God, and in that light he can rejoice.

What does Paul mean when he declares that his sufferings "fill up . . . what is still lacking" in terms of Christ's afflictions? Given the magnificent hymn recounted a few verses earlier, Paul is certainly not implying that Christ's death was somehow insufficient. Indeed, Paul never uses the term "affliction" to describe the suffering of Christ on the cross. Instead, Paul probably

is referring to the ongoing work of Christ's servants who are commissioned to preach the gospel and who, in doing so, encounter great struggles (Rom. 8:17). Writing from jail, Paul feels this truth brought home to him with great force. In another prison epistle, Paul declares that he desires to participate in Christ's sufferings, "becoming like him in his death, and so, somehow, attaining to the resurrection from the dead" (Phil. 3:10–11). As an apostle, Paul knows well that tribulations are part of his work (see 1 Cor. 4:8–13; 2 Cor. 11:23–33). And he is convinced that the church, as Christ's body, will experience suffering as it lives out the gospel's truth. These sufferings might include overt physical afflictions or illness or painful broken relationships or the mental struggles against doubt and perceived failure that haunt the faithful. The list is long, but the sufficiency of Christ is greater.

Paul describes the gospel's power as bearing fruit and expanding across the whole world (1:6, 23). Now he adds a new descriptor to the Word of God—mystery, which refers to the new activity of God in Christ in creating a new people for God (see also Rom. 11:25–26; 16:25–26; Eph. 3:3–6). The mystery revealed is that Gentiles are full members of God's family through Christ. Now Jews and Gentiles equally partake of the riches of God through faith in Christ. The mystery is Christ himself (2:2) and his work on the cross creating a body (church) for himself. Mystery has the connotation of divine superabundance that the human mind cannot fathom (see also Rom. 9:23–24). Paul proclaims the future certain hope of glory enjoyed by all believers who participate in the mystery, that is, "Christ in you." (The Greek could read "Christ among you," as the "you" is plural. If so, then the verse would indicate the continued presence of Christ within the church; see also Rom. 8:10.)

4. The Call to Christian Maturity (1:28–4:6)

A. Paul contends for the Colossians (1:28–2:7). In 1:28, Paul reveals his overriding concern for the Colossians, namely, their maturity in Christ, which consists of discerning true wisdom (found in Christ alone) and then living that truth consistently to the end. The term "mature" carries the connotation of completeness and realized potential. It suggests an understanding of basic facts about God and his salvation plan as well as an ethical lifestyle. Jesus uses the same Greek term in the Sermon on the Mount: "Be *perfect*, therefore, as your heavenly Father is *perfect*" (Matt. 5:48).

Twice Paul uses an athletic image to stress his fervent efforts on behalf of the Colossians and their neighbors in Laodicea. He "contends" for them, using a term that draws on the rich imagery of the stadium games. Paul invites them to compare his diligence in serving the church with that of athletes who train fiercely for clan honor and pride.

The final two verses in this section summarize in more detail what Paul has in mind in encouraging them to full maturity. The foundation laid must be Christ Jesus as Lord. Paul speaks of the Colossians having *received* this truth, the verb here carrying a technical sense of tradition being passed on by a qualified teacher. Paul uses the same language in 1 Corinthians 11:23, when speaking about the Eucharist, and in 1 Corinthians 15:1, 3, when he summarizes the gospel message. In proclaiming Jesus as Lord, Paul draws on the church's ancient claims about Christ, as evidenced in the baptismal confession of Romans 10:9 and the Christ hymn in Philippians 2:6–11. Paul enjoins them to gain a better understanding of their faith that they might live strong and with joyous thankfulness (see 1:12; 3:15). So armed, they will be well prepared to face down the "philosophy" that threatens (2:8).

B. Christ is over every power and authority (2:8–15). The identity of this "philosophy" has been discussed extensively above, where I suggested that it encouraged Gentiles to take up the law in addition to their faith in Christ for full attainment of the Christian life. Paul warns the Colossians of this potential threat by using a rare verb, translated as "take captive," found only here in the New Testament (though Paul uses a similar term in 2 Cor. 11:8). The

Paul says, "I am contending for you and for those at Laodicea" (Col. 2:1), as an athlete would contend in the stadium. These are the remains of the unexcavated stadium at Laodicea (built ca. AD 69–79). Paul's letter was also meant to be read to the church at Laodicea (see Col. 4:16).

dangerous teaching, which has yet to infect the community, is characterized by human tradition, not the wisdom of God. Moreover, it relies on the *stoicheia* (elemental forces, basic principles of the world, or the gods of this world; see also Gal. 4:3, 8–9) rather than Christ, who represents the fullness of God (2:9). *Stoicheia* is repeated in 2:20, in the context of specific piety or purity rules (2:21), suggesting that it refers primarily to the Jewish purity rites, which when applied to Gentiles lead them away from Christ.

Arguing against the philosophy, Paul stresses the fullness of God in Christ. Paul provides a strong defense for the incarnation: that in Jesus Christ's life and death we see the fullness of God. This fullness lives on in the community because Christ has been raised and is alive and has made believers alive in him (2:13). The insistence that Christ is head over all powers and authorities anticipates Paul's later charge that though the philosophy seeks visions (access to or control over powers of the cosmos perhaps), such pursuit severs them from Christ, the head (2:18–19).

The importance of circumcision in this section suggests we are on the right track in proposing that the philosophy is connected with synagogue teachings. Even as circumcision was the key identifier for Jews, so baptism served as the initiation for Christians. The central question becomes, Who makes up the people of God—those who are circumcised or those who are baptized in Christ? Paul declares that the Colossian Gentiles and Jews are made alive and have their sins forgiven through Christ. Paul uses past-tense verbs to describe both their burial in baptism and their having been raised with Christ. The significance of the past tense here is to emphasize the reality of their new life in Christ, the power of the resurrection that lives in them through Christ. It allows Paul to highlight the efficacy of the cross in the following verses.

Through the cross of Christ, God defeated sin, disarmed powers, and gave believers life. Through Christ's death, God blotted off the page, so to speak, the condemning verdict. The canceled charge probably refers to the Mosaic law, judging by the qualifier "legal" (2:14 RSV, ESV; see also 2:20), referring to Jewish rites listed in 2:16–22. In canceling the debt of sin, God in Christ thereby rendered impotent those powers and authorities, including the Jewish law. When Paul speaks of these powers being made a public spectacle, he likely draws on the image of a triumphant general who has returned from battle displaying his conquered captives.

C. Reject false teachings (2:16–23). Having established the forgiven status of the believer in Christ and having shown Christ's triumph over the powers and authorities, Paul warns the Colossians to resist the philosophy's condemning influence (2:16, 18). In describing the discrete components of the philosophy, Paul highlights its Jewish character, including focus on Sabbath, New Moon celebrations, and food laws. (The relationship of Jewish law to the church created numerous debates and conflicts within the early church. See Acts 15:1–35; Gal. 2:1–12; 1 Cor. 8:1–13; 10:1–33; and Rom. 14:3–6, 17, where the language is similar to that found in Colossians.) The description "Do not handle! Do not taste! Do not touch!" (2:21) suggests Jewish piety, here relegated to the present age, which works off human tradition and its limited wisdom (see also Matt. 15:9, citing Isa. 29:13). Paul does not claim that Jews were legalistic. By observing the law, Jews expressed their status as God's chosen people. Paul does not dismiss these practices outright but rather relegates them to a secondary status in light of the surpassing greatness of Christ. Paul is speaking from an eschatological perspective: in Christ the new age for Jews and Gentiles has begun. The law was part of the old age and as such is a precursor to the reality in Christ.

Paul speaks about the philosophy's "worship of angels" (2:18), a difficult phrase to interpret. Some suggest that the phrase implies direct worship of spiritual beings, but it is difficult to imagine a first-century monotheistic Jew who followed Christ promoting the worship of created beings. Instead, Paul might be speaking ironically, implying that the philosophy was so interested in the law, mediated by angels (Gal. 3:19), that its devotion looked like actual worship of angels. However, the phrase probably refers to worship with angels, suggesting that the worshipers are taken up (perhaps in an ecstatic state) into the heavens and there worship God along with the angels. This interpretation is supported by Paul's claim in the next sentence that these people describe their visions in detail. Such bragging further condemns them (see also 1 Cor. 4:6, 18–19; 5:2; 8:1; 13:4).

Paul labels their behavior as false humility, although the term "false" is not found in the Greek; it must be added to communicate the context. The word implies ascetic behavior, especially fasting. In both Judaism and paganism, fasting was often linked to obtaining visions. Paul declares that the philosophy's detailed visions and ascetic fasts fail to bring its followers close to God. Paul condemns them as disconnected from Christ, the head of the body, the church. For Paul, the philosophy's regulations fail to deliver a holy life.

Paul has no patience for such teachings—he enjoins the Colossians to resist. The Colossians must own their true selves: they have died to this world and now live in Christ (see also Rom. 6:8–11; 7:4–6; Gal. 2:19). The world's traditions

Colossians 3:1 describes Christ as "seated at the right hand of God," enthroned in heaven. Early Christian art often depicted Christ on his throne ruling the world. This reproduction of a painting on parchment by Haregarius shows Christ in majesty (AD 844–51).

and expectations need no longer control them because they have entered into Christ's new life through baptism (2:12–15). At this point in the letter, Paul leaves the discussion of the philosophy to explore what life in Christ should look like among the Colossians.

D. Set your heart and mind on things above (3:1–4:6). 3:1–4. Paul described the death and resurrection of Christ in 2:12, and in 2:20–23 he detailed the ramifications of Christ's death for believers. Now in 3:1–4 he expands on the implications of Christ's resurrection. Both 2:20 and 3:1 begin with the same Greek phrase translated "if" or "since," suggesting that the instructions are two sides of the same coin. Just as the death of Christ demolished once and for all the world's wisdom and values, so, too, the resurrection of Christ confirms the future glory awaiting the saints. The gospel message must embrace both aspects of the cross—its past victory over sin and the future glory when Christ returns. Flanked by these two realities, the believer perseveres faithfully. Paul now turns his attention to this present, in-between time with instructions on life as God's chosen people (see 3:12).

Paul pushes the believers to make Christ's return and future glory a beacon that guides their steps in the dark and depraved world. The vision that should capture the Colossians' imagination is one of Christ now seated at God's right hand. This picture has deep roots in earliest Christianity, drawing on Psalm 110:1: "The LORD says to my lord: 'Sit at my right hand until I make your enemies a footstool for your feet.'" Mark 12:36 (and parallel passages); Acts 2:34–35; and Hebrews 1:13 cite it directly. Allusions to the verse are numerous. The force of the verb "to set" that Paul uses in 3:2 carries the sense of forging a perspective, permanently reshaping a mindset, and fixing a sustained opinion. The Colossians have died in Christ (in baptism 2:12) to the nonsense promoted by the philosophy and now must go forward daily living out that new reality. In Christ, believers have confidence that they will enjoy glory with Christ (see Col. 4:4; see also Rom. 8:18).

3:5–9. Paul exhorts the Colossians to "put to death" all that is connected to this world (3:5). Does this statement contradict what he insisted on in 3:3, that they have died, and their life is now hidden in Christ? No, for in 3:5 Paul elaborates how this death in Christ can be actualized in their daily lives. What died in Christ was the power of sin, the irresistibleness of it that hooks people like a fish on a line and then reels them in. Paul declares that as Christians, the Colossians no longer need take the bait of sin. Freed from that compulsion, believers can reject all those behaviors that alienate them from each other and from God.

The first grouping of sins (3:5) spotlights sexual improprieties, listed in order from the most to the least visible. He begins with public sexual immorality, rampant in the ancient pagan world. He moves from behaviors to attitudes, including greed, which focuses on satiating physical desires. Paul concludes that if you trace back from the behavior to the mindset that led to it, you will find idolatry at the core. Paul argues that the inward focus on satisfying physical passions amounts to placing oneself at the center instead of God. Paul insists that to effect a change at the public, behavioral level, one has to ultimately kill that which led to

it all—idolatry. As with weeds in the garden, merely snapping off the shoots will not make permanent changes. The gardener must dig out the roots for any lasting results.

A second list of sins pivots on anger. Once again Paul moves from the most public demonstration of anger—rage—to the more subtle forms of anger, such as slander. In all cases, what comes from the mouth sullies the person. Paul is quite concerned about lying. We talk about "little white lies" not hurting anyone, but for Paul truth telling should be characteristic of those who live in Christ, who is God's truth to us. Since we image Christ, the fully human being, we must be truthful. By following his charge against lying with the emphatic claim that social, racial, and ethnic differences should not divide the people of God, Paul reveals that lying is not simply a private matter but could infect the entire community. It denies the reality that believers have removed (a one-time act) their old self and put on (again, a one-time act) their new self. Paul is probably referring to their baptism (see Col. 2:12).

3:10–17. Paul promises that the believer's new self is being renewed "in knowledge in the image of its Creator" (3:10). A similar sentiment is expressed in Romans 12:2, where the believers are to renounce this world and be transformed by renewing their minds (see also 2 Cor. 4:16). Genesis 1:26–27 speaks of humankind being made in God's image, but later sin destroys that perfection (Gen. 3:6–19). Colossians 1:15 insists that Christ is the image of the invisible God, and Paul's claim in 3:10 indicates that, in Christ, humanity has been restored to fullness and completeness. Today we tend to read such passages as referring primarily to the individual, but Paul was clearly thinking of the entire church, because he goes on to describe the body of Christ as one, not disparate ethnic and social groups. Unlike the philosophy, which stressed private visions and competitive asceticism, Paul stresses the unity of the Christian community.

3:18–4:1. After the eloquent charge to the church to live in peace and in knowledge of the gospel, this section looking at the ancient household seems a letdown to modern ears. The shift appears so abrupt to some scholars that they suggest this list was inserted later. Yet read in context, the passage supports and fills out Paul's previous explanation of life in the church.

It might be possible to fool the public, but your family knows you well. Paul realizes this common human trait, and so after encouraging the Colossians to pursue peace in their community, he applies the truth of the gospel to the household. What one does in the privacy of one's most intimate relationships will reveal whether the "new self" is living up to its full potential.

The family in the ancient world was highly structured and hierarchical. The husband/father was the undisputed lord of his family, including grown sons (and their wives). The wife/mother also had significant authority in the raising of the children, and if she had a substantial dowry, she wielded economic influence as well. Slaves fulfilled many occupations: some were quite learned; most did manual labor. They could earn their freedom or be freed by their master's will. (Slaves made up about 10 percent of the total population, except in Rome, where slaves made up about 33 percent of the inhabitants.) It was possible for a household slave to have a better quality of life in terms of shelter, food, and clothing than a poor freeborn person.

A well-ordered home was sought by Gentiles and Jews alike. Aristotle's views carried the day—the home was the foundation of the state, and the home must be organized hierarchically and harmoniously (*Politics* 1.5). The vested interests of those at the top of the hierarchy—husbands, fathers, slave owners—were protected and increased. A few dissenters, such as the Cynics and the Essenes at Qumran, called for a radical restructuring of society, or chose to isolate themselves from society altogether. But the church lived in the midst of the world and sought to redeem through Christ's love the cultural structures that regulated social interaction.

Into this setting Paul applies the gospel message. We cannot conclude that Paul condoned the social and institutional structures of his day (patriarchy and slavery). Nor is Paul abandoning his claims about believers being hidden in Christ and having a new self. He is emphatic that essentialist categories such as race or ethnic identity—things a person cannot change—are completely unimportant within the household of God. No Gentile or Jew, no barbarian or Scythian—these cultural categories are de-emphasized in Christ. (Paul declares the gender category is made obsolete under Christ in a similar phrase in Gal. 3:28.) In his argument, Paul expresses a key outworking of the incarnation—Christ as the perfect, complete, fully human being offers to his body, the church, that same fullness. Such completeness comes, however, at a cultural price: one loses one's cultural or ethnic (or gender) bragging rights to being better than another. Christ is now the focus, the "all" (3:11).

When Paul speaks about social roles and obligations, he does not jettison his previous emphatic stance that all are one in Christ. Rather, his aim is to discuss how certain common and important social roles, such as husband and wife, parent and child, master and slave, can be played in that culture with fidelity to Christ. Paul recognizes the legal and cultural power that husbands have over wives, fathers over children (of any age), and masters (male and female) over slaves. He wants those who have been given power through social norms to exercise that rule in Christ-honoring ways. And he wants those who are under such power to respect those wielding it but also to remember that such authority is mediated, for only Christ has ultimate authority. Paul is not concerned about social and legal codes but about relationships lived in the covenant of love in Christ.

Therefore, the wife is asked to submit herself to her husband, not because Caesar has mandated that wives submit but because submission is a Christian character trait that can be lived out in marriage. Notice that Paul does not forbid the wife from loving her husband! All the Christian character traits noted in the preceding verses—peace, wisdom, knowledge, forgiveness, compassion, and so on—should be part of her Christian behavior at home. The Colossians likely were aware of the picture of Christ preserved in the hymn of Philippians 2:6–11, which poignantly portrayed the submission of Christ to the Father. They probably knew of Jesus's words on the Mount of Olives: "Father, if you are willing, take this cup from me; yet not my will, but yours be done" (Luke 22:42). Jesus Christ practiced perfect submission to the Father (1 Cor. 15:28); wives have a similar opportunity to practice this sort of submission. The phrase "fitting in the Lord" (3:18) is an important qualifier. The verb carries the sense of duty. For example, the Stoics used the term to describe a behavior that was in harmony with the natural order. But rather than tell the Colossians to follow what seems "natural," Paul qualifies the verb with "in the Lord." Some see this as establishing the "natural" hierarchy between husband and wife, but the phrase more likely means that the wife submits only to the degree that is countenanced in the Lord (see 1 Cor. 7:15).

Paul turns to husbands with the command to love their wives. Several points are worth noting. It appears at first reading that Paul did not mention the Lord's example when speaking to the husbands (unlike in Eph. 5:25). However, Paul's choice of verb, *agapaō* (related to *agapē*), alerted his readers that he was speaking of the type of love characterized by Christ's self-giving on the cross (Rom. 8:37). Paul's recipe for harmony in the marriage is that the powerful love which unites the church should be used to bind husband and wife. The Colossians might have expected him to say something like, "Husbands should rule their wives wisely and kindly." Anticipating this, Paul speaks to husbands to resist bitterness. Translations often read, "Do not be harsh," but that fails to do justice to the passive tense of the verb. It is the husbands who might feel cheated by having to love their wives

sacrificially. The society taught that they were owed respect and devotion apart from their attitude or actions toward their wives. Paul insists that they resist becoming bitter against their wives if such cultural expectations are not met.

Paul's charge to children echoes the fifth commandment (Exod. 20:12), which promises that those who honor parents will have a long life. In the ancient world (and in many cultures today) the child's obedience and honor due his or her parents continued until the parents' death. Given that, Paul is careful to warn fathers against abusing their authority. Perhaps Paul has in mind particularly his warnings against abusive speech in 3:8.

The most extensive discussion is left to last, that of slave and master. Even as children are to obey their parents in all things, so, too, slaves are to obey their masters. Of course, Paul would not expect either children or slaves to obey an order that contradicted God's teachings (see Acts 5:29). Nor is Paul condoning the institution of slavery. Rather, he is explaining to slaves how they can be faithful in the midst of their servitude. Paul declares that they are slaves of Christ (3:24), a label he uses for himself. (In fact, Paul teaches that every person is a slave—either to sin or to God [Rom. 6:16].) Ironically, Christians are also truly free in Christ, no matter their social status. However, Paul is not unaware of the complexities of slave life. He enjoins them to work as though the Lord himself is their master, and such efforts will be rewarded with an inheritance, something no slave could expect from a human master. Moreover, justice will be meted out; the Lord (implied) will fairly judge situations and render appropriate rewards and punishment. This is comforting news to those whose situation might render them voiceless (1 Pet. 2:19–20; Gen. 39:11–20).

To conclude this section, Paul writes one verse to slave masters, who, it should be noted, could be male or female. Why only one verse? In part it may be that there were few slave owners among the congregation. Also, Paul has been speaking twice to the paterfamilias (the family head) as husband and father. As in those important roles, so here, the male slave owner must wield his responsibility mindful of the Lord's own claims on his life. The master is enjoined to be just even as Christ will judge fairly. Finally, Paul is sending an entire letter to a slave owner, Philemon, in their midst, where he more fully expresses his opinions on Christians owning Christians. While there is no hint in Colossians that Paul expects Christian masters to free all their slaves or that Christians should denounce publicly the institution of slavery, Paul's letter to Philemon makes clear that, in the long term, slave ownership is not compatible with the Christian life.

4:2–6. The remaining call to faithful prayer includes several key terms from Colossians. Paul repeats his concern that the Colossians continue to be thankful (1:12; 2:6; 3:15). He speaks again of the mystery of Christ, having explained God's salvation plan in Christ to bring all people into the family of God (1:26; 2:2). Paul connects his imprisonment with his preaching, much as he did in 1:24. And he invites the Colossians to enter into that ministry by living and speaking the gospel to everyone.

5. Final Greetings (4:7–18)

Paul mentions ten names at the end of his letter, all companions in the ministry of the gospel. Tychicus is the bearer of the letter; he is joined by Onesimus, the slave of Philemon. Most likely these two carried that letter as well. Paul depended on such messengers to communicate his personal greetings and encouragement to his churches (2 Cor. 7:6; 8:17). Paul mentions three Jewish believers, Aristarchus, Mark (cousin of Barnabas), and Jesus called Justus, who stood by him faithfully. Paul asks that the Colossians welcome Mark if he comes, implying that the Colossians knew of the fallout between Paul and Barnabas (Acts 15:36–40). Paul assures them that the rift has been mended. Paul sends greetings from two

> Epaphras, founder of the Colossian church (Col. 1:7; cf. 4:12), may have brought the gospel to the city of Hierapolis since it was closely connected to Colossae and Laodicea. Pictured here are a gate and city street from Hierapolis, built during the reconstruction of the city by Domitian (AD 84–85) after its destruction by an earthquake.

other (presumably Gentile) believers, Luke and Demas. He asks that a special greeting be given to Nympha and her house church; it is unclear whether this house is in Colossae or Laodicea. And he gives a message for Archippus to complete the work he began in the Lord. A special commendation is given to Epaphras, the founder of the Colossian church (cf. Col. 1:7). We find intriguing overlap in the names here and in Philemon. Both letters include greetings from Epaphras, Aristarchus, Mark, Demas, Luke, and Archippus. Both letters include Onesimus, in Colossians as Paul's messenger, and in Philemon as the main subject of the letter.

Paul concludes with a signature statement explaining that he writes the final remarks in his own hand (1 Cor. 16:21; 2 Thess. 3:17). One has the sense that he is impeded from elaborating the final blessing, for normally he writes "the grace of the Lord Jesus Christ be with your spirit" (Phil. 4:23; Gal. 6:18) or even more expansive closings (2 Cor. 13:14; 1 Cor. 16:23–24; Rom. 16:25–27). He asks the Colossians to uphold him because of his chains (4:3). Not only does he desire their prayers but perhaps also their active (financial?) support. The Philippians, for example, sent Epaphroditus

to help Paul in prison (Phil. 2:25–30; 4:18). As Paul closes, the Colossians are left in no doubt about his chains, nor his love for Christ and his church.

Select Bibliography

Arnold, Clinton E. *The Colossian Syncretism*. Grand Rapids: Baker Books, 1996.

Dunn, James D. G. *The Epistles to the Colossians and to Philemon*. New International Greek Testament Commentary. Grand Rapids: Eerdmans, 1996.

Martin, Troy W. *By Philosophy and Empty Deceit: Colossians as Response to a Cynic Critique*. Journal for the Study of the New Testament Supplement Series 118. Sheffield: Sheffield Academic Press, 1996.

Price, S. R. F. *Rituals and Power: The Roman Imperial Cult in Asia Minor*. Cambridge: Cambridge University Press, 1984.

Still, Todd D. "Eschatology in Colossians: How Realized Is It?" *New Testament Studies* 50 (2004): 125–38.

Thompson, Marianne Meye. *Colossians and Philemon*. Two Horizons New Testament Commentary. Grand Rapids: Eerdmans, 2005.

Wright, N. T. *Colossians and Philemon*. Tyndale New Testament Commentaries. Grand Rapids: Eerdmans, 1986.

1–2 Thessalonians

GENE L. GREEN

Introduction

Thessalonica

The history of Thessalonica. When Cassander the king of Macedonia founded the city of Thessalonica in 316 BC, he named it after his wife, Thessaloniki, the half sister of Alexander the Great. The kingdom of Macedonia needed a port on the Aegean Sea. Cassander established Thessalonica at the head of the Thermaic Gulf. The city's location gave it excellent access to the cities of the wider Mediterranean world. Thessalonica's situation also provided easy access to the surrounding territory in Macedonia and beyond, since it was located at the intersection of the main north-south and east-west routes. Thessalonica quickly became a hub for government and commerce. Antipater of Thessalonica called it "The Mother of Macedonia."

Rome began to expand as a world power beginning in the third century BC. Rome's eastward expansion precipitated three Macedonian wars, fought between 214 and 168 BC. In the last of these conflicts, the Roman general Aemilius Paulus defeated the last king of Macedonia, Perseus, at the Battle of Pydna. Soon thereafter, the city of Thessalonica fell to the Roman army. Rome guaranteed that the Macedonian kingdom would never rise again.

Rome withdrew her troops and allowed Macedonia to continue as a vassal. At that time, Thessalonica became capital of the second district (some Greek manuscripts of Acts 16:12 note that Philippi was "of the first district"). A rebellion against Rome led to Macedonia's being reconquered and organized into a Roman province in 148 BC. In 146 BC, the Romans named Thessalonica as the capital of the province, since the city had not joined the rebellion. Some twenty-five years later, the Romans built one of the great east-west highways, the Via Egnatia, which traversed Macedonia and extended from Dyrrachium in Illyricum on the Adriatic (Rom. 15:19) to Byzantium, passing through Thessalonica (Acts 17:1) and Philippi (Acts 16:11–12).

Thessalonica was at the heart of Roman power. During the wars between Julius Caesar and Pompey (49–48 BC), the city became a second Rome, as two hundred senators gathered

Thessalonica was named after Thessaloniki, daughter of Philip II. The inscription on this base, which once held her statue, reads: "Queen Thessaloniki, [daughter] of Philip."

there. A few years afterward, Julius Caesar was assassinated by Brutus and Cassius, who afterward fled to Macedonia. Mark Antony and Octavian (later titled "Augustus") pursued them and defeated the assassins at the Battle of Philippi (42 BC). In this conflict, Thessalonica sided with Antony and Octavian. As a result, Antony granted Thessalonica the honor of being a "free city," which meant exemption from taxation to Rome, freedom to mint coins, liberty to govern according to ancient custom, and exclusion of Roman troops garrisoned within the city walls. Later, when Antony struggled with Octavian for control of the empire, Thessalonica remained loyal to Octavian, who defeated Antony at the Battle of Actium (31 BC). The city erased Antony's name from all honorary inscriptions previously dedicated to him.

Rome remembered Thessalonica's fidelity, and the city responded by honoring the Romans, even establishing a priesthood dedicated to Dea Roma (the goddess Rome) and the Roman benefactors. The city erected an imperial temple to honor Julius Caesar and Augustus, the adopted son of the "deified" Julius. Bilingual inscriptions from the city in Latin and Greek bear witness to the Roman presence. Moreover, an inscription from the Vardar Gate includes both Roman and Macedonian names among the principal "city officials," the politarchs (Acts 17:6, 8). Thessalonica reaped economic and political benefits from its loyalty to Rome.

The gospel comes to Thessalonica. The Acts of the Apostles and Paul's letters to the Thessalonians provide parts of the story of the evangelization of the city and Paul's continuing relationship with the newly founded church. Some scholars question whether or not the accounts in Acts and the epistles can be harmonized. The underlying question is whether Luke is a faithful historian. However, the convergence of the stories in Acts 17–18 and 1 Thessalonians is strong enough to encourage a more positive assessment of Luke's record at this point, despite the apparent tensions.

On his second missionary journey, Paul received his well-known "Macedonian call" (Acts 16:6–10). The first church he established was in Philippi (Acts 16:11–40), a congregation that later supported him (Phil. 4:16). Acts 17:1 suggests that Paul only spent the night in Amphipolis and Apollonia as he traveled the Via Egnatia to Thessalonica. Although Amphipolis was a significant city, there was no Jewish presence there as in Thessalonica. The gospel was "first to the Jew, then to the Gentile" (Rom. 1:16; cf. Acts 13:5, 14; 14:1; 18:5–6; 19:8–10). Not only Silas (Greek for the Latin name Silvanus; see 1 Pet. 5:12 and Acts 15:40) but also Timothy accompanied him (Acts 16:1, 3; 17:14–15; implied in 1 Thess. 1:1, 9; 2:1, 6). Despite having suffered in Philippi (1 Thess. 2:2; Acts 16:16–40), Paul and Silas boldly preached the gospel in Thessalonica. They spent three Sabbaths in the synagogue dialoguing about the gospel (Acts 17:2). Paul discussed Scripture with the Jews and "God-fearing Greeks" (Gentile sympathizers with Judaism; Acts 17:4), interpreting and presenting evidence from it to convince them of the core claims of the gospel: "The Messiah had to suffer and rise from the dead" (cf. Luke 24:45–46; 1 Cor. 1:23; 15:3–4), and "Jesus . . . is the Messiah" (Acts 17:2–3; cf. 9:22; 18:5, 28; Matt. 16:16).

The response among the Jews was very moderate, whereas the Gentile God-fearers, including many principal women, were eager to embrace the message (Acts 17:4). First and Second Thessalonians show little trace of a Jewish presence in the newly formed church. First Thessalonians 1:9 implies that Paul and his companions engaged in a wider mission to the Gentiles beyond that described in Acts.

Those from the synagogue who remained unpersuaded stirred up mob action against the preachers. The mob that formed was made up of day laborers who, when unemployed, gathered in the central plaza of town. The crowd went after Paul and Silas. Not finding them, they dragged out Jason (the messengers' patron) and other new believers and accused them before the city's chief magistrates (politarchs; 17:5–6; 18:14–15). The charge was that Paul and his associates had promoted civil unrest (17:6–7; 28:22). Later Roman opinion of Christians was similarly negative. Suetonius called the Christians "a class of people of a new and damaging superstition" (*Life of Nero* 16.2), and Tacitus spoke of them as a people who were "hated for their vices, which the multitude calls 'Christians'" (*Annals* 15.44).

The accusation was heightened by the charge that "they are all defying Caesar's decrees, saying that there is another king, one called Jesus" (Acts 17:7). Paul had proclaimed the kingdom of God wherever he went (see Acts 19:8; 20:25; 28:30–31), and unsurprisingly, his gospel was understood as a threat to Caesar's rule. He heralded Jesus as the king, the one whose authority and glory surpassed that of any ruler. Moreover, imperial decrees emitted under Augustus and Tiberius had made it illegal to enquire about or predict by divination the death of anyone, especially the emperor. The apostolic prediction of the advent of another sovereign would have been regarded as an audacious violation of those decrees (1 Thess. 4:16; 5:2–3; 2 Thess. 2:3–8; also Luke 23:2; John 18:36–37). The accusation provoked an uproar, and Jason was obliged to give a security, likely as an assurance that he, the other believers, and Jason's guests would cause no trouble (Acts 17:8–9). As a result, Paul and his companions were obliged to leave the city (Acts 17:10). They fled forty-five miles to Berea. The proclamation of Jesus as king had challenged the Roman imperial claims, and Thessalonica's politarchs needed to take action in order to preserve the city's favored status with Rome and their attendant economic security.

After the foreshortened ministry in Berea (Acts 17:10–15), Paul left for Athens, but Silas and Timothy stayed on in Macedonia. Apparently Silas and Timothy came to Athens, a trip that Acts does not record, and from there Timothy went back to Thessalonica (1 Thess. 3:1–2, 5). Paul prayed to be able to return to the city himself (3:10–11). He attempted repeatedly

to travel to Thessalonica, but somehow Satan overturned his plans (2:17–18). The persecution that had started against the apostles poured over to the new converts (1:6; 2:14; 3:3–4), and Paul's fear was that Satan had tempted the believers to apostatize (see 3:5 and comments). The wait for Timothy's return must have been agonizing. The church, composed of recent converts, was left without leadership. Its members suffered for the faith and experienced the dishonor of social ostracism. Would they remain firm? What news would Timothy bring back?

During the time that Paul's own plans to visit Thessalonica were blocked, he sent Timothy to the church, wrote two letters to encourage and instruct the congregation, and prayed for them over and over again. Later, on his third missionary journey, Paul was able to pass again through Macedonia (Acts 19:21–22; 20:1–6) and stop in Thessalonica, perhaps even twice (20:1–3).

Occasion and Purpose

The First Letter to the Thessalonians. After Paul had traveled onward from Athens to Corinth, Timothy rejoined him (Acts 18:1, 5), bringing good news about the church in Thessalonica (1 Thess. 3:6–8). The Thessalonians were indeed standing firm and exhibiting the virtues of genuine Christianity: faith, love, and steadfastness, the product of hope (1:3). Paul is unable to express adequately his gratefulness to God. The letter explodes with the thanksgiving and joy he experienced upon receiving this good news (3:9–10).

Paul wrote 1 Thessalonians at this point with a variety of purposes in mind, the first being to thank God for the faith of the Thessalonians (1:3; 2:13; 3:6–10). Paul was at a difficult point in his own ministry while in Corinth, so the good report about the Thessalonians encouraged him greatly (3:7; Acts 18:9–10; 1 Cor. 2:3).

Second, the document was a defense of Paul and his companions' sincerity and pure motives and an explanation about why they did not return to the church after leaving so abruptly. As evidence of his genuine love, Paul explains his attempts to return (2:17–18), how Timothy was then sent and was prevented from reaching them (3:1–5), and how Paul desired to return to the congregation and prayed to that end (3:6, 10). Under this reading, 2:1–12 should be understood as a defense of the character of the apostles' ministry. Other scholars, however, understand this section as showing their character as moral examples that the Thessalonians should imitate.

Third, the epistle encourages the Thessalonians as they face hostility from the other inhabitants of the city. The apostles explain that suffering is part of the Christian life (3:3–4) and that in their sufferings they "imitate" the churches of Judea (2:14–16), the apostles, and the Lord himself (1:6). Paul recognizes their firmness in faith (1:3; 3:8) and that in their sufferings the Thessalonians have even become an example for other congregations (1:7). At the same time, the letter emphasizes God's wrath (1:10; 2:14–16; 5:9). The time of God's judgment, the day of the Lord, will come, and those who assail the church will not escape (5:1–11).

Fourth, the letter responds to questions the Thessalonians put to Paul, possibly via a letter that Timothy conveyed (see 1 Cor. 7:1). The church had asked about fraternal love (4:9–12), the destiny of the dead in Christ (4:13–18), and when the day of the Lord would come (5:1–11).

Fifth, not all the news from the church was good. While the Thessalonians had learned basic Christian morality (4:1–2), there were serious lapses regarding sexual purity (4:3–8). In addition, some were not working, acting as dependent clients. The epistle addresses this issue, which needed to be emphasized more forcefully when Paul wrote 2 Thessalonians (1 Thess. 4:11–12; 5:14; 2 Thess. 3:6–15). Some had rejected prophetic utterances in the church (1 Thess. 5:19–20), and the Thessalonians were not responding properly to their new leadership (5:12–13).

The Second Letter to the Thessalonians. We do not know who carried the first letter to the Thessalonian church, nor do we have any indication

regarding how Paul received further news about the congregation. Given the similarity of the themes in the two letters, we may assume that Paul wrote this second letter not long after the first, during his eighteen-month stay in Corinth (Acts 18:11) on his second missionary journey.

While 2 Thessalonians does not echo all the concerns that motivated Paul to write the first epistle, such as the apostolic defense (1 Thess. 2:1–3:13) and the admonishment regarding sexual immorality (1 Thess. 4:3–8), it does betray a heightened concern regarding other major issues previously addressed. After relating his thanks for and boasting about the church (1:3–5; 3:6–8), Paul returns to the issue of the believers' suffering (1 Thess. 1:6; 2:14; 3:3–4). The persecution continued to be severe (2 Thess. 1:4–5; 2:14). He explains that their sufferings are intended to *prove* (note the translation) them "worthy of the kingdom of God" (1:5). Here, as in 1:10, he reminds them of the final destiny and vindication of the believers. He graphically describes the severity of the final judgment for unbelievers (1:8–9). In contrast, the Thessalonian Christians will be vindicated "because you believed our testimony to you" (1:10). The great event that separates those who believe from those who do not is the revelation and coming of our Lord Jesus (1:7, 10), which heralds the day of the Lord (2:1–3, 8).

Second Thessalonians also addresses the church's understanding of the last things, or eschatology (as 1 Thess. 1:10; 3:13; 4:13–5:11, 23). A false and destabilizing teaching had infiltrated the church: the day of the Lord, some were saying, had already come or was at hand (2 Thess. 2:2). This deception (2:3) found fertile soil in the Thessalonian church because of their concerns about this day (1 Thess. 5:1–11) and the persecutions they endured (2 Thess. 1:5–12). Paul and his associates remind them that two events will precede the day of the Lord: (1) the rebellion and (2) the revelation of the "man of lawlessness" (2:3). Paul presents an extensive discourse about the coming of this figure and God's judgment on him and his followers

(2:4–12). While Paul's argument was quite comprehensible to them due to this prior teaching (2:5), the middle section of chapter two remains difficult for us to interpret. What is the "rebellion," who is this lawless one (2:3), what force "holds it back," and who will be "taken out of the way" so that the "man of lawlessness" may be revealed (2:7–8)? What is clear to us is that the revelation of Christ will come soon after the revealing of the lawless one and Christ will destroy him.

The third chapter begins with a request for prayer (3:1–2) and the assurance that God will strengthen and guard them from the evil one, Satan himself (3:3–5). After this, Paul takes up the third major issue, regarding the conduct of certain disorderly members, a topic previously addressed (1 Thess. 4:11–12; 5:14). He warns those who are not working but have remained dependent clients of their patrons (2 Thess. 3:6–15). On the other hand, he calls the Thessalonians to continue practicing benefaction toward those who are in need (3:13). The problem surrounding work does not appear to be tied to their eschatological concerns, as some have supposed.

Authorship

In 1 Thessalonians 1:1 Paul appears as the author of the letter alongside his associates Silas and Timothy (see also 2:18). From antiquity, the church has regarded the letter as authentic and not pseudonymous. Eusebius (d. 341/342) included 1 Thessalonians among the authentic Pauline Letters. The *Didache* (late first or early second century), Ignatius (d. ca. 107), the *Shepherd* of Hermas (beginning of the second century), and Tertullian (207/208) use it, while even Marcion regarded it as authentic. The Muratorian Canon (second part of the second century) includes 1 Thessalonians, and Irenaeus (end of the second century) cites it as Paul's work.

What role did Silvanus and Timothy play in composing the letter (1:1)? The letter uses the first-person plural instead of the singular throughout, save in three passages (2:18; 3:5;

5:27; 2 Thess. 2:5; 3:17) where Paul underscores his own perspective. Silvanus and Timothy helped found the church and may have served as joint authors. Writing with others was a known practice (Cicero, *Letters to Atticus* 11.5.1, speaks of letters that "you wrote in conjunction with others and the one you wrote in your own name"; cf. Acts 15:23–29).

Second Thessalonians 1:1 names Paul as the author, along with Silvanus and Timothy. Paul includes a final greeting at the end, written in his own hand (3:17), a common practice when an author employed the services of a scribe. However, first-person plural verbs dominate throughout the letter (singular verbs appear in 2:5; 3:17). Paul wrote the letter in collaboration with his associates, though he is the principal author.

The evidence from the ancient church for the authenticity of this letter is even stronger than for 1 Thessalonians. An impressive list of authors refer to it: Ignatius (d. ca. 107), Polycarp (d. 155/160), and Justin (d. 165). Irenaeus (end of the second century) and Clement of Alexandria (d. 220) attribute their quotes from this letter to Paul. Tertullian (d. 215/220) uses it and even refers to the author as "the apostle." The Muratorian Canon classifies it as a book accepted by all.

Some contemporary scholars, however, have questioned the authenticity of 2 Thessalonians. For example, they point to the similarity of the vocabulary and style of 1 and 2 Thessalonians, saying this betrays the hand of a copyist. But why not understand this similarity as a mark of authenticity? In the same way, the form of the heading in 1 and 2 Thessalonians is nearly identical, something not found in other Pauline Letters. But could not Paul use the same opening in two letters written near the same time? The eschatology of the two letters appears distinct, since the joy and expectancy found in 1 Thessalonians are absent from the second letter. But the solemn tone of 2 Thessalonians is due to the acute persecution the Thessalonians were suffering (1:5–12) and the error that had entered the church regarding the day of the Lord. Major commentators on these letters discuss the arguments against authenticity but do not find them convincing.

Date

Paul and his associates composed 1 Thessalonians when Timothy came to Corinth from Thessalonica (1 Thess. 3:2, 6; Acts 18:5). Paul was in Corinth during the reign of Claudius (AD 41–54; see Acts 18:1–2) and when Gallio was the proconsul (Roman governor) of Achaia (Acts 18:12–17). Gallio took his post on July 1 of AD 51 (as indicated in an inscription from Delphi) and stayed in the city for just under a year. Paul was tried before him and then remained in the city for some time (Acts 18:18). Paul's total visit lasted eighteen months (Acts 18:11). If the movement against Paul began when Gallio was named proconsul, and if Paul left some time later around the end of AD 51, we estimate that he arrived in the city near the start of AD 50. Not long after that, Timothy

arrived and Paul wrote 1 Thessalonians, making this one of the earliest of Paul's letters that have survived.

We do not have the same historical markers for dating 2 Thessalonians. The problems addressed in this letter are similar to those addressed in 1 Thessalonians, which suggests that the second letter was written not long after the first. Taking into account the time needed to carry the first correspondence to Thessalonica and the travel time for news to arrive from Thessalonica to Corinth, the date of the letter might be as early as late AD 50.

> **Outline—1 Thessalonians**
>
> 1. Epistolary Greeting (1:1)
> 2. Opening Thanksgiving: The Coming of the Gospel and Its Reception (1:2–10)
>   A. Faith, Love, and Hope (1:2–3)
>   B. The Coming of the Gospel and Its Reception (1:4–10)
> 3. The Body of the Letter (2:1–5:22)
>   A. The Gospel Arrives in Thessalonica (2:1–3:13)
>   B. The Apostolic Instruction: The Life That Pleases God (4:1–5:22)
> 4. Final Prayer, Greetings, and Blessing (5:23–28)

Paul wrote his two letters to the church at Thessalonica while he resided in Corinth. This view of Corinth shows the agora, the main marketplace of the city.

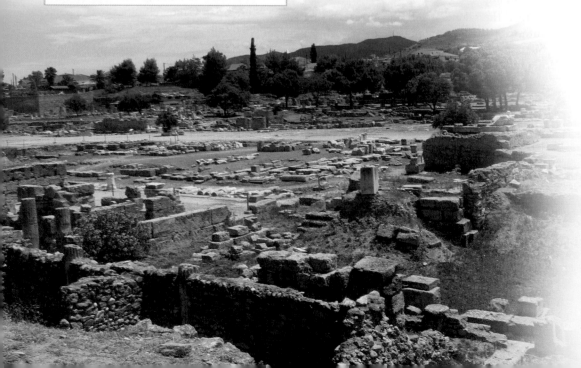

A. Prayer for Sanctification (5:23–25)
B. Call to Greet and Read to One An-
other (5:26–27)
C. Final Blessing (5:28)

Commentary

1. Epistolary Greeting (1:1)

In the ancient world, people believed that letters brought one into the presence of an absent person. Seneca (*Moral Epistles* 75.1) said, "I never receive a letter from you without being forthwith in your presence." First Thessalonians and other apostolic letters fill the gap left by the separation of the founders from the church (2:17–18; 3:6, 10–11). Greek letters began with the name of the author, followed by a greeting and a prayer or thanksgiving. Although the form of 1 Thessalonians is similar to that of ancient letters, it is substantially longer, as were Cicero's letter-essays. Letters were commonly read aloud when received (1 Thess. 5:27).

The authors are "Paul, Silas and Timothy," the founders of the church, whom Paul later identifies as "apostles" (2:6). The recipients of the letter were "the church of the Thessalonians." An *ekklēsia* ("church") was the assembly of free citizens in a Greek city (see Acts 19:32, 39, 41), although the Septuagint, the Greek translation of the Old Testament, also used it to translate Hebrew *qahal*, the assembly of the people of God (cf. Acts 7:38). To distinguish this *ekklēsia* from all the others in Greek cities, Paul clarifies that this one finds its source and identity "in God the Father and the Lord Jesus Christ." The Father and Son are regarded as being on the same level, evidence of Paul's high Christology. The opening verse defines the Christians' identity in relation to God and each other.

Paul Christianizes the common greeting in Greek letters (*chairein*) by changing it to "grace" (*charis*), which summarizes the saving work of God through Jesus Christ (Rom. 3:24; 5:15; Eph. 2:8; 2 Thess. 2:16). To "grace" he adds "peace," a common greeting among the Jews. This "peace" is not an emotional disposition but describes the relational status of a person

or people reconciled with God (Rom. 5:1). The combined greeting is more than a formality; it is a blessing that embraces the totality of the divine benefits the authors desire for these believers.

2. Opening Thanksgiving: The Coming of the Gospel and Its Reception (1:2–10)

Ancient letters sometimes included a thanksgiving after the opening greeting. Giving thanks to one's benefactors, whether human or divine, was a social obligation that the apostles observed. This thanksgiving anticipates the letter's major topics, such as the coming of the gospel to Thessalonica (1:5a, 9), the character of the missionaries (1:5b), the conversion of the Thessalonians (1:6, 9–10), the results of their conversion (1:3, 7–8), the sufferings that they endured (1:6), the mission of the church (1:8), and the eschatological hope (1:10).

A. Faith, love, and hope (1:2–3). The apostles' thanksgivings to God for the church (1:2) are frequent ("always") and inclusive ("for all of you"). The context of these thank offerings was likely their corporate prayer times ("mention you in our prayers"). They also pray for the Thessalonians "continually" (see 5:17, where the same adverb appears). Paul commonly uses this adverb to describe the life of prayer (1 Thess. 5:17; Rom. 1:9; 2 Tim. 1:3) or thanksgiving (1 Thess. 2:13). "Continually" thus suggests their persistence in prayer for the Thessalonians (see Luke 18:1).

The motivation for their thanks is the Christian virtues that the Thessalonians exhibited (1:3). The apostles bring to mind and mention before God ("We remember") the fundamental Christian virtues of "faith," "love," and "hope," which the believers have demonstrated. The authors' prayers are made in the presence of God: "before our God and Father" (1 Thess. 3:9–10). Although these words often speak of coming before God and Christ in the final consummation of all things (2 Cor. 5:10; 1 Thess. 2:19; 3:13), here that hope is a present reality in the prayers of the apostles. In the Greek, these words appear at the end of 1:3, which may imply that the Thessalonians lived out the virtues of faith, love, and hope "before our God and Father" (NKJV, NASB). However, the thought here is that their prayers are made before God, as in 3:9–10.

This trilogy of virtues characterizes true Christianity (1 Thess. 5:8; Rom. 5:1–5; 1 Cor. 13:13; Gal. 5:5–6; Col. 1:4–5; 1 Pet. 1:21–22; Heb. 10:22–24). Timothy has brought news to Paul of the church's "faith and love" (1 Thess. 3:6) and their perseverance (3:8), the fruit of "hope" (1:3). Paul and the others also remember the Thessalonians' "work produced by faith" (1:3; cf. Eph. 2:8–10; Gal. 5:6; 2 Thess. 1:11). Faith produces action, though the type of "work" is not specified. The word could indicate manual (1 Thess. 2:9; 4:11; 2 Thess. 3:8, 10) or ministerial labor (1 Thess. 5:12–13; Rom. 15:23). But here Paul likely refers to their "good works" (2 Thess. 1:11; 2 Cor. 9:8; Eph. 2:10). Among the Jewish people, acts of charity, visitation of the sick, hospitality toward strangers, and helping those who had been forsaken were considered to be good works. The Greek idea of "good works" embraced doing good to others without distinction, whoever the others might be (see 1 Thess. 3:12). It included any acts and donations that benefited a community.

The apostles also recalled the Thessalonians' "labor prompted by love." The objects of this love were the other members of the congregation (2 Thess. 1:3), their leadership (1 Thess. 5:13), other Christians in Macedonia (4:9–10), and even those outside the community (3:12). "Labor" implies hard and exhausting work. Love seeks the welfare of others and labors hard for their benefit.

Paul and his associates also recall the Thessalonians' "endurance inspired by hope in our Lord Jesus Christ." Endurance, one of the most highly valued virtues in the church, is the ability to stand firm and persevere in the face of suffering or temptation (Luke 21:19; Rom. 5:3–4; 2 Cor. 1:6; 6:4; Col. 1:11; 2 Thess. 1:4; 1 Tim. 6:11; Titus 2:2; Heb. 12:1; James 1:3–4; Rev. 2:2–3). In the face of persecution and the temptation to abandon the faith (1 Thess. 1:6; 2:14; 3:1–5; cf. 2 Tim. 2:11–12), the Thessalonians stood firm (3:8). The reason for this was their "hope in our Lord Jesus Christ," that is, hope in the coming of the Lord (1 Thess. 1:10; 2:19; 3:13; 4:16; 5:23; 2 Thess. 1:7–10; 2:1; and see 1 Thess. 5:8). Hope was not a virtue that marked the Gentile world (1 Thess. 4:13; Eph. 2:12). According to Greek philosophy, the only ones who did not err in their hope were the gods, whereas people's hopes were considered uncertain. The Christian perspective puts hope on a certain foundation since the object is sure: "our Lord Jesus Christ" in his coming.

B. The coming of the gospel and its reception (1:4–10). Paul now moves to the deepest motivation for their thanksgiving, the election of the believers: "For we know, brothers and sisters loved by God, that he has chosen you" (1:4). The Greek grammar connects this verse with the preceding thoughts, so there should be no paragraph break here (see NRSV, ESV). The source of the believers' election is the love of God ("loved by God"; cf. Deut. 4:37; 7:7–8; 10:15; Ps. 47:4; 78:68; Isa. 42:1; Matt. 12:18; Rom. 11:28; Eph. 1:4; Col. 3:12). Whereas the placement of political or military leaders in Paul's time had to do with the merit or character of those chosen, divine election finds its center in the one who chooses (Rom. 5:6–8). The implied result of election is the formation of the Christian community, the brothers and sisters "loved by God" (cf. 2 Thess. 2:13).

Having expressed confidence that the Thessalonians are elect, Paul underscores the first evidence of their election: "because our gospel came to you not simply with words but also with power, with the Holy Spirit and deep conviction" (1:5a). "Gospel" was a familiar term in the Roman world, often appearing in association with the imperial (ruler) cult. Announcements about significant moments in the emperor's life as well as his decrees and discourse were published far and wide as his "gospel." The apostolic announcement was about the true ruler, Jesus Christ, whose authority supersedes that of the emperor (cf. Mark 1:1). Also, in Israel the "gospel" was the culmination of the hopes of the people of God, which centered on God's victory and sovereignty (Isa. 52:7; 61:1). The "gospel" has to do with the proclamation of those events that inaugurate this new era.

In 1 Corinthians 2:1–5 Paul contrasts persuasion via rhetorical methodology with the proclamation of the gospel. In 1 Thessalonians 1:5, however, Paul simply states that the message of the gospel (the "words" as in 1:6, 8; 2:13; 2 Thess. 3:1) came to the Thessalonians accompanied by divine power (cf. Rom. 15:18–19; 1 Cor. 1:6–7; 2 Cor. 6:7; 12:12; Heb. 2:3–4; and note the result in 1 Thess. 2:13). "Power" refers to the miracles God performed (Mark 6:5; Acts 2:22; 1 Cor. 2:4; 2 Cor. 12:12; Heb. 2:4). The Holy Spirit worked through the preaching and convicted the hearers of the truth of the message (Luke 24:46–49; Acts 1:8; 5:32; 1 Cor. 2:2–4; 1 Pet. 1:12). The "deep conviction" could refer to the apostles' certainty about the message but likely points to the fullness or totality of God's working. The proclamation was also powerful in that the gospel message was reinforced by the conduct of the messengers: "You know how we lived among you for your sake" (1:5b, see 1 Thess. 2:1–12). There was complete harmony between the character of the apostles and the message they preached.

The way the Thessalonians received the gospel was additional evidence of their election (1:6–10): "You became imitators of us and of the Lord, for you welcomed the message in the midst of severe suffering with the joy given by the Holy Spirit" (1:6). Imitation is not a well-recognized form of instruction today in the West, but the ancients appreciated the value of imitating people who served as models, as do people in other cultures today. The New Testament often calls believers to imitate Christian leadership (1 Cor. 4:16; 11:1; Gal. 4:12; Phil. 3:17; 4:9; 2 Thess. 3:7, 9; 1 Tim. 4:12; Titus 2:7; 1 Pet. 5:3), other members of the community (Phil. 3:17; Heb. 6:12; 13:7), and God the Father and Jesus Christ (Eph. 5:1; 1 Cor.

11:1). In 1:6 the focus is on how the Thessalonians followed the example of the apostles and the Lord in their intense or "severe" sufferings. Paul well understood that suffering was an element of the Christian life (see Acts 9:15–16; 14:21–22; Rom. 8:17; 2 Cor. 1:5; Phil. 3:10; 1 Pet. 2:21). The miracle of the Thessalonians' conversion was that they received the message of Christ crucified amid the great hostility shown toward this new faith that had recently arrived in Thessalonica.

They also had "joy given by the Holy Spirit" in the midst of this suffering. Joy in suffering was a theme in Jewish literature that filtered into the church through Jesus's teaching (Matt. 5:11–12; Luke 6:22–23; 21:28). The first Christians, like many believers today, suffered intensely but found joy in sharing in the sufferings and the shame of Christ (Acts 5:41; Rom. 12:12; 2 Cor. 4:8–10; 7:4; Phil. 2:17; 1 Pet. 1:6; 4:13–14). Their source of this joy was the Holy Spirit (cf. Gal. 5:22; Rom. 14:17; 1 Pet. 4:13–14). The ones who imitated Christ's and the apostles' model of suffering in turn became a model for other churches (1:7). The influence and ministry of this church, located in the city known as "The Mother of Macedonia," spread far and wide (1:8; 4:10). Indeed, the church spread the gospel throughout the province of Macedonia and beyond (1:8). The Lord's message or word is the gospel itself (2 Thess. 3:1), which "rang out," a word elsewhere used to describe a loud noise like a clap of thunder, the cry of a multitude, the sound of the trumpet, or a rumor that runs everywhere. So great were their efforts to spread the gospel that Paul remarks, "Therefore we do not need to say anything about it." The final words ("about it") do not appear in the Greek text. The point is simply that Paul and his companions did not need to proclaim the gospel (the verb translated "say" appears again in 2:2, 4, 16) in certain parts due to the Thessalonians' efforts.

Paul and his associates had received reports from others who had encountered the Thessalonian believers (1:9). The Greek for "reception," which is the same word translated "visit" in 2:1, is best understood as an "entry." The entry of an orator into an ancient city was an important event. Aristides spoke of his entry into Smyrna: "Before I even entered the city, there were people coming to meet me because they had heard about me, the most distinguished of the young men were giving themselves to me, and there was already a definite plan for a lecture" (*Oration* 51.29). In the following chapter (1 Thess. 2:1–12) Paul describes the character of his entry into the city. The effects of the apostles' entry were impressive, evidenced by the Thessalonians' conversion (1:9; Acts 14:11–18; 17:22–31; 19:23–41). The early church condemned idolatry, as people were called to turn to the only "living and true God" in contrast with the dead and false idols (Rom. 1:22–25; 1 Cor. 5:11; 6:9; 10:14–22; Gal. 5:20–21; Eph. 5:5; Col. 3:5; 1 John 5:21; Rev. 21:8; 22:15). Conversion to God not only entailed abandoning practices associated with idolatry (1 Pet. 4:3) but also included worship and moral service to God (Rom. 6:6, 16–19).

Turning to God included embracing the Christian expectation regarding the end, "to wait for his Son from heaven, whom he raised from the dead" (1:10). "To wait" was used in the Greek translation of the Old Testament to signify the hope God's people held for divine salvation and mercy (Isa. 59:11; see also Ps. 25:3; 27:14). The object of this waiting is Jesus, the one risen and slated to return (1 Thess. 4:13–18). Among the Greeks there was no belief in a resurrection. Pliny the Elder even says there are some things the gods cannot do, such as raise the dead (*Natural History* 2.5.27). But God did indeed raise Christ from the dead, and the risen one will return as the one "who rescues us from the coming wrath" (1 Thess. 1:10; 5:9). The wrath of God is the execution of his judgment against sin (Matt. 3:7; Luke 3:7; Rom. 2:5; Eph. 5:6; Col. 3:6; Rev. 6:16–17; 11:18; 16:19; 19:15), not an outburst of emotion. It is an eschatological event directed toward those who do not know or obey God (2 Thess. 1:6–10; Rom. 1:18). Christ's death and resurrection deliver the believer from this wrath (cf. Rom. 5:9).

The odeum at Thessalonica (third century AD). Although primarily used for poetry contests and musical performances, an odeum could serve as a venue for visiting orators and philosophical debates. When Paul entered a new city, he preferred to begin his preaching at the local synagogue.

3. The Body of the Letter (2:1–5:22)

A. The gospel arrives in Thessalonica (2:1–3:13). Having finished the initial thanksgiving (1:2–10), Paul now begins the body of the letter. The themes of the thanksgiving are now taken up again and elaborated, with 2:1–12 explaining the character of the apostles and their entry while 2:13–16 reminds the church of their reception of the gospel in the midst of great persecution. The following section (2:17–3:13) recalls the story of the apostles' absence from the church and their continued care and concern for the Thessalonians.

2:1–12: The apostolic entrance. At first glance, this section appears to be a defense against criticisms levied against the character of the apostles. The critique of their character may have originated with the unconverted Thessalonians (2:14) or perhaps members of the church itself who questioned why the apostles came, left, but then did not return. What kind of people were these men? But the relationship with the church was warm and strong (3:6), and moreover, we have no indication that the critique came from outside the church. Some scholars, however, argue that this section is not a defense. Rather, the language is similar to that of Cynic philosophers who distinguished themselves from other, less honorable philosophers. On this reading, Paul presents himself as a moral example that others should follow, as did those philosophers. However, although philosophers used personal examples as a means to teach ethics, in 2:1–12 the apostles do not exhort the believers to imitate their character. What, then, motivated Paul to include this teaching? The most likely reason was that the situation itself called for it: the apostles left soon after the church was founded, and Paul had not returned. This explains the long discourse regarding Paul's attempts to return in 2:17–20, the rehearsal of the motivations for sending Timothy in 3:1–6, and the notes about a future visit in 3:7–12. The question that arose was about the apostles' character and concern for the church. First Thessalonians 2:1–12 is the beginning of a response that spans chapters 2 and 3.

In 2:1, Paul speaks about his coming to Thessalonica as his "entry" (NIV "visit"; see comments on 1:9). While Paul may refer either to the *character* of the apostolic mission or its *results* among the Thessalonians (as 1 Thess. 3:5), the emphasis in this section (2:1–12) is on the character of the ministers. However, character and results cannot be neatly separated.

Paul and Silas had suffered by being beaten and jailed before coming to Thessalonica (2:2a; see Acts 16:19–40; Phil. 1:30). Not only were they stripped, beaten with rods, and jailed, but they were also publicly dishonored and insulted by this treatment. Aristotle said of this type of dishonor, "The insult consists of the injury and pain by which the one who suffers is dishonored" (*Rhetoric* 2.2.5–6). Despite this socially weakened position, Paul says, "But with the help of our God we dared to tell you his gospel" (2:2b). The Cynics highly prized the ability to speak with boldness in spite of opposition and criticism, but the source of Paul's boldness was God. Paul adds (2:2c) that when preaching in Thessalonica he and his companions faced continued opposition, yet they still preached the gospel.

The gospel proclamation was not simply a presentation of facts but a call to respond to the divine initiative (cf. Luke 3:18; Acts 2:40). The apostles' exhortation or summons was not based on a false message ("error"), nor was it preached with impure or immoral motives such as greed or glory (2:3–6). Neither did they use deceitful methods, employing rhetorical trickery to persuade their audience (cf. 1 Cor. 2:4). Their character was such that they had been tested and approved by God for the mission of preaching the gospel (2:4a). Leadership in the church was to be examined and approved (Rom. 14:18; 2 Cor. 13:7; 1 Tim. 3:10), but the most important examination and approval comes from God (Rom. 16:10; 2 Cor. 10:18; 2 Tim. 2:15). Inscriptions from the era indicate that those who served in public office should be approved by others. Since the apostles were commissioned by God, they seek to please him (1 Thess. 2:4b; Gal. 1:10; 2 Tim. 2:4). The verb translated "please" appears in inscriptions to designate the good service of citizens and officials on behalf of a city or its people, communicating the idea of service rendered in the interests of others. The apostles served the Lord and were not seeking glory from people (2:6). God continued to test their character and motives.

In 2:5 Paul invokes two witnesses, the Thessalonians and God himself, to attest to the apostles' character (see also 2:10; Deut. 17:6; 2 Cor. 13:1; 1 Tim. 5:19; Heb. 10:28). Aristotle, distinguishing between flatterers, who want something out of you, and true friends, said: "The man who always joins in the pleasures of his companions . . . [and] does so for the sake of getting something by it in the shape of money or money's worth . . . is a Flatterer" (*Nicomachean Ethics* 1127a). The apostles were the Thessalonians' true friends and not flatterers who sought their own gain. Nor were they out for glory (2:6a). "Praise" or "glory" is the honor, prestige, or fame that a person might receive, which was sought diligently by the sophists of the era. Epictetus (*Discourse* 3.23.23–24) caricatured those who wanted nothing more than to hear the praise of others: "'But praise me.' What do you mean by 'praise'? 'Cry out to me, "Bravo!" or "Marvelous!"'" The apostles would have nothing of this public adulation.

On the contrary, the apostles' care for the Thessalonians was like that of a nurse for a child (2:6b–7). Here Paul, Silas, and Timothy are "apostles." Although the term "burden" could refer to a financial obligation placed on someone (as in 2:9), here as in other contexts it suggests a weight of authority that some important person exercises over others. They did not impose their apostolic authority when they ministered to the Thessalonians (see 2 Cor. 10:8; 13:10; 1 Pet. 5:3). Rather, they were "gentle among you," as a wet nurse. (See NIV note; instead of "gentle," some Greek manuscripts read: "infants" [NIV "young children"].) A wet nurse (Greek *trophos*; NIV

"nursing mother") was a woman hired under contract to breast-feed another person's baby, but she could also be in charge of the child and his or her education. As such, she was a person of great confidence and affection. But here Paul compares his nurture of the Thessalonians with the tenderness of a wet nurse who feeds and cares for her own children, not those of another.

The apostles shared their lives with the Thessalonians because of their care for them (2:8). They longed deeply for the Thessalonians and committed themselves to them (cf. 3:1). They shared the gospel of God (see 1 Thess. 1:5; 2:2, 4, 9; 2 Thess. 2:14). Unlike those sophists who would come to town just for gain or glory, the apostles gave both the message and themselves to their hearers. Indeed, they made sure that their presence would not be a financial burden for these new believers: "Surely you remember, brothers and sisters, our toil and hardship; we worked night and day in order not to be a burden to anyone while we preached the gospel of God to you" (2:9). The apostles also received gifts from the Philippian church during this time (Phil. 4:15–16), although they worked to sustain themselves (2 Thess. 3:8–9). Paul's trade was tentmaking (Acts 18:1–5), and he may have even been up before dawn working ("night and day" [2:9]). This verse may reflect the economic realities of the church (2 Cor. 8:1–2).

Paul once again invokes the Thessalonians and God as two witnesses (2:5) who can testify to the character of the apostles' conduct (2:10). The messengers' conduct had been holy or pure (the Greek word describes actions that conform to what is permitted or ordained by the divine). They had also behaved righteously or justly; that is, their conduct conformed to human and divine norms. Marcus Aurelius said that Socrates "could be satisfied with being just in his relationships with men and pious in his attitude towards the gods" (*Meditations* 7.66). The apostles acted in conformity with both divine and human law and fulfilled all their obligations to both ("blameless" [2:10]).

Paul's care for them was like that of a wet nurse with her own children but also like that of a father (2:11). He and his associates acted as an ancient father would by training them in the moral life. Philo said the father should teach the law to his children and instruct them "concerning what they should choose and avoid, that is to say, to choose virtues and avoid vices and the activities to which these lead" (*On the Special Laws* 2.228). So Paul adds, "encouraging, comforting and urging you to live lives worthy of God, who calls you into his kingdom and glory" (2:12). "Encouraging" is a strong word, frequently used to refer to moral exhortation (Rom. 12:1; 1 Cor. 1:10; and 1 Thess. 3:2; 4:1, 10; 5:11, 14; 2 Thess. 3:12). "Comforting" can mean "consoling," but also, as here, it can speak of encouraging and persuading a person to take a certain course of action. "Urging" is the strongest of the three, meaning "insisting" or "requiring." The three together underscore the apostles' insistence in their moral instruction. The goal was that the Thessalonians "live lives worthy of God" (2:12; cf. Eph. 4:1; Phil. 1:27; Col. 1:10). The idea of living a life worthy of God is found in Jewish moral instruction (Wisdom of Solomon 3:5; 7:15; Sirach 14·11) as well as Jesus's teaching (Matt. 10:37–38). Greek inscriptions sometimes speak of those who lived lives worthy of a deity, the idea being that the person conducted him- or herself in conformity with the standards demanded by the relationship with the exalted figure. Here that figure is God himself, the one who called the person to his kingdom and glory. This calling was both an honor and an obligation.

2:13–16: Second thanksgiving. This section opens with the epistle's second thanksgiving (cf. 1 Thess. 1:2–10). The apostles leave the explanation of the apostolic mission (2:1–12), focus on the Thessalonians' response (2:13), and then move to reflect on their sufferings (2:14). This final note leads the authors to compare the sufferings of the Thessalonians with those of the churches of Judea at the hands of the Jewish community there. Paul follows with a severe critique of his Jewish contemporaries (2:15–16), which some have suggested is a non-Pauline addition to the epistle since it seems foreign to the rest of the letter and appears to contradict Paul's positive attitude regarding his own people in Romans 9–11. But Paul's critique stands within the Jewish prophetic tradition. God has not rejected his people (Rom. 11:1–5), and there is hope of a national salvation (Rom. 11:23–26). Far from being anti-Semitic, Paul loved his people (Rom. 9:1–5; 10:1; 11:13–16). The strong polemic in these verses stems from the repeated encounters Paul had with those of his people who opposed the gospel. These verses do not justify any form of anti-Semitic attitudes or actions.

The thanksgiving begins with the recognition that the Thessalonians received the gospel as a divine and not simply human message (2:13). To give thanks to one's benefactor was one of the most important social obligations in antiquity, whether the benefactor was human or divine. The Thessalonians received the divine teaching as it truly is, the word of God (cf. Gal. 1:11–12), since it came in divine power (1 Thess. 1:5). God spoke to them and called them through this proclamation (2 Thess. 2:14; 2 Cor. 5:20), and their reception of that message was the moment of their conversion (Acts 8:14; 1 Thess. 1:5). Paul highlights the continued divine activity through this word—it "is indeed at work in you who believe" (2:13). The message of the gospel has the power to transform people's lives.

Paul introduces one of the evidences that demonstrated their true reception of the gospel: their suffering persecution (2:14; 1 Thess. 3:3–4): "For you, brothers and sisters, became imitators of God's churches in Judea, which are in Christ Jesus: You suffered from your own people the same things those churches suffered from the Jews" (2:14). While many early congregations suffered for their adherence to the gospel (Acts 14:22; 1 Pet. 5:9), the churches in Judea were recognized as the first fruits of God's work in the new covenant (Rom. 15:26–27; Gal. 1:17–24;

2:1–10) and enjoyed high honor among the other churches (cf. the Jerusalem council in Acts 15). Paul at one time had been a perpetrator of the sufferings of those churches (Acts 8:3; Gal. 1:22–23; 1 Tim. 1:13). Persecution against them broke out with the death of Stephen (Acts 8:1–3; 9:1) and again under Herod Antipas (Acts 12:1–5). It is no surprise that those congregations are presented as a model for Christian suffering. Although the persecution was initiated by the Jewish community in Thessalonica, the Gentiles carried it out (Acts 17:5–9).

Paul begins the litany of the sins of his own people, saying that they "killed the Lord Jesus and the prophets and also drove us out" (2:15a). He passes over Roman responsibility for Jesus's death (1 Tim. 6:13) as he focuses on his own people's role (Acts 2:23, 36; 3:13–15; 4:10; 5:30; 7:52), since they acted as had their ancestors in slaying the prophets (1 Kings 19:10, 14; Matt. 23:31, 34, 37; Acts 7:52; Rom. 11:3). Paul understands the persecution of the Christian messengers within this same frame, since he and his associates were driven out of city after city, including Thessalonica. Paul sees the unbelieving Jews as in opposition to God and others: "They displease God and are hostile to everyone" (2:15b). Their rebellion against God (cf. Rom. 8:8) was evidenced by their opposition to the messengers of God (2:15a, 16a) and their sin (2:16b). Paul regards their opposition to the spread of the gospel as hostility to humanity "in their effort to keep us from speaking to the Gentiles" (2:16a; see Acts 13:48–51; 14:2, 19).

Paul's final indictment is severe: "In this way they always heap up their sins to the limit. The wrath of God has come upon them at last" (2:16b). His claim is that his people have always resisted the divine initiative. The sentence echoes a familiar theme in the biblical and extracanonical literature concerning the sins of a people that come to their full measure before they are judged by God (Gen. 15:16; 6:11–13; Dan. 8:23; 2 Maccabees 6:14), though the direct source here is Jesus's teaching (Matt. 23:32). Paul comments that the unbelieving Jews have already begun to experience God's wrath (cf. Rom. 1:18), which may be an allusion to the multiple sufferings his people were already enduring. These denunciations resonate with themes already found within the prophets. This text does not justify anti-Semitism. God is the one who deals with all humanity and their sins (Romans 1–3) and offers to all the hope of salvation.

2:17–20: Exit of the founders. The founders of the church were torn away from the new converts in Thessalonica, an experience Luke describes in Acts 17:5–10 and Paul recalls here (2:17). The Greek text indicates that the apostles were "made orphans," an expression that in Paul's day could indicate a child's loss of parents or the tragedy of losing one's children. The separation, however, was only physical—not mental. The longing for the Thessalonians prompted great, even extreme, efforts to return. The desire was there to see the Thessalonians, and Paul expresses his own repeated attempts to do so: "For we wanted to come to you—certainly I, Paul, did, again and again" (2:18). The question on the table was why he had not returned to the church he founded. Paul explains, "but Satan blocked our way." The verb comes from a military context. To hinder the advance of an enemy, soldiers would break up and destroy the highway to impede their progress. The one who did this was Satan (see 1 Thess. 3:5; 1 Pet. 5:8), who is in constant battle against the people of God (Rom. 16:20; 1 Cor. 7:5; 2 Cor. 2:11; 11:14; 12:7; 2 Thess. 2:9). Paul does not state how Satan accomplished this. It may have been through sickness (2 Cor. 12:7), by means of the opposition mentioned previously (1 Thess. 2:15–16), or possibly through the bond that Jason was forced to post (Acts 17:9). Eventually Timothy and then Paul himself returned.

So that there would be no question with regard to the sincerity of the apostles' intentions, Paul explains in 2:19–20 the reasons why they wanted to return and see the Thessalonian believers. The church is the source of their joy not only in the present (2:20; 3:9) but also for the future when the Lord returns (2:19): "For what is our hope, our joy, or the crown in which we will glory in the presence of our Lord Jesus when he comes? Is it not you?" A crown or wreath of laurel, pine, or, in Macedonia, oak leaves was given to those who received great civic honors. Paul anticipates this joy and honor at Christ's coming (Greek *parousia*). The term *parousia* was used to describe the coming of a deity (as the god Asclepius to a sick person) or the advent of a dignitary, especially the emperor, to a city. New eras were inaugurated, coins minted, special arches and buildings constructed to commemorate such occasions. The source of the apostles' glory and honor is not the recognition of their accomplishments, however, but the Thessalonian converts themselves: "Is it not you?" They are the apostles' source of honor and of the extreme joy that comes with it (2:20).

3:1–5: Timothy's mission. This section should be read in the light of Paul's painful separation from the Thessalonians and his unfruitful attempts to return to the church (2:17–18; Acts 17:5–10). When he and his companions could no longer bear the agony and the weight of worry, they took action, with Paul in the lead (3:1; cf. 3:5): "So when we could stand it no longer, we thought it best to be left by ourselves in Athens." This verse presupposes an unknown visit of Timothy and Silas to Athens while Paul was preaching there. Acts only indicates that Silas and Timothy were left in Berea, with instructions to join Paul quickly, as Paul traveled on to Athens (Acts 17:14–15). Apparently Silas and Timothy did indeed meet up with Paul in that city, but then Timothy was sent to Thessalonica, and Silas was also sent to Macedonia (implied in Acts 18:5). Paul commonly worked with a team, and traveling with others provided extra security. In this case, however, Paul thought it better to be left alone than to leave the Thessalonians alone.

Paul asks, "What is . . . the crown in which we will glory?" (1 Thess. 2:19). In Rome, to receive an oak leaf wreath or crown was a high honor given to those who had saved the life of a Roman soldier in battle by an unusual act of courage. This gold oak wreath was found in Turkey (350–300 BC).

So, "We sent Timothy, our brother and God's fellow worker in the gospel of Christ, to strengthen and encourage you as to your faith" (3:2 NASB). Timothy was later sent on missions to Corinth (1 Cor. 4:17; 16:10–11) and Philippi (Phil. 2:19–24), and then to pastor in Ephesus (1 Tim. 1:3). Paul underscores his confidence in Timothy in this brief note of commendation. Some scribes apparently balked at calling Timothy "God's fellow worker" (3:2), and so readings such as "God's servant" or "God's servant and our fellow worker" are found in some Greek manuscripts (cf. NIV "co-worker in God's service"). Timothy's mission was to "strengthen" or establish the church. This verb appears frequently in contexts where someone is in danger of falling or being moved in one way or another (Sirach 13:21; *2 Clement* 2.6). In the New Testament it refers to being established in the faith, especially in the face of persecution and possible apostasy (Luke 22:43; Acts 18:23; Rom. 16:25; 1 Thess. 3:13; 2 Thess.

3:3; 1 Pet. 5:10; 2 Pet. 1:12; Rev. 3:2; and with new converts in Acts 14:22; 15:32, 41). In the same way "encourage" appears in contexts where new converts are exhorted to persevere in the faith (Acts 14:22; and 11:23; 16:40; 20:1; and see 2 Thess. 2:17).

Timothy's mission was prompted by concerns Paul had about the Thessalonians' stability in the midst of persecution (3:3). "Unsettled" in 3:3 could mean a profound emotional agitation but also may suggest the idea of being "shaken" or "moved." This latter concept is in mind, and for this reason Paul sent Timothy to "establish" or "strengthen" them (3:2). Paul's concern was not their emotional well-being but rather their continuance in the faith. Apostasy was a real possibility (3:5). Paul adds that they were "destined" for persecution. The basic instruction given in the early church included a theology of suffering. Those who followed the crucified one would suffer as he did (Acts 14:22), and Paul repeated this teaching over and over again while he was with the Thessalonians (3:4). As the Messiah had to suffer (Luke 24:26; Acts 17:3; 1 Pet. 1:10–11), so too his disciples must suffer (Rom. 8:17; 2 Cor. 1:5; 1 Pet. 4:12; 1 Thess. 2:14). The promise of persecution appears in 2 Timothy 3:12, and Peter, as does Paul, highlights its necessity (1 Pet. 1:6).

In 3:5, as in 2:18, Paul lifts his own voice above that of his companions (note the first-person singular): "For this reason, when I could stand it no longer, I sent [Timothy] to find out about your faith." He reveals an additional purpose for Timothy's mission to the church (3:2). Paul always carried deep concern for the churches (see, e.g., 2 Cor. 11:28–29). Had some succumbed under the pressure of persecution and given up the faith? Paul also recognized that the opposition to the church was spiritual and not only social: "I was afraid that in some way the tempter had tempted you and that our labors might have been in vain." The "tempter" is Satan, the demonic power behind this persecution (cf. Eph. 6:11–12) who also blocked the apostle's attempts to return to the city (2:18).

The purpose of the "tempter" was not simply to provoke the Thessalonians to sin but also to get them to embrace the sin—apostasy (Luke 8:12; 1 Pet. 5:8). Hence Paul's concern for their stability and continuance in the faith (1 Thess. 3:2–3, 6, 8). Had his labors in establishing a church in the city been rendered futile, considering the persecution and satanic opposition these new believers faced? What would Timothy find when he arrived in Thessalonica?

3:6–10: Timothy's return. The event that prompted Paul to pen this letter was Timothy's return from his trip to Thessalonica (see 1 Thess. 3:1–2). He had departed from Athens, and upon his return from the Thessalonian church, he caught up with Paul in Corinth (Acts 18:5). We can only guess how he traveled (by road or sea?) and how long the trip and stay with the church lasted (up to a month or so?). The wait must have been agonizing for Paul. "But Timothy has just now come to us from you" and, contrary to fears, "has brought good news about your faith and love" (3:6). Timothy's report was "good news," with this being one of the few places in the New Testament where this verb is not used of the preaching of the gospel (cf. Luke 1:19). In his report, Timothy pointed out the Thessalonians' "faith and love," the distinctive virtues of those who are true members of the redeemed community (Gal. 5:6; Eph. 1:15; Col. 1:4–5; 1 Tim. 1:14; Philem. 5; 1 Thess. 1:3; 2 Thess. 1:3). Their relationship with God and with one another was intact. Presently Paul will comment on their steadfastness (3:8), which is the fruit of their hope (1 Thess. 1:3). Faith, love, and hope marked this church, and these virtues were proof positive that Paul's labors among them had indeed not been in vain (3:5). But the Thessalonians also had "pleasant memories" of the apostles, and Timothy noted that they truly did "long to see us, just as we long to see you." There were no hostile feelings or bad memories, but rather their memories of the apostles were "pleasant" in the sense of "good," "friendly," or "tender." The longing for reunion was mutual. Friendly letters often included a comment that the separation was only physical and not emotional, and also expressed the desire to be reunited (1 Thess. 2:17; cf. 2 Cor. 1:16; Philem. 22; 2 John 12; 3 John 14). Such reciprocity marked true friendship.

The mutuality of friendship (cf. Rom. 1:10–11; 2 Cor. 1:7) finds expression in 3:7 as well: "Therefore, brothers and sisters, in all our distress and persecution we were encouraged about you because of your faith." As Timothy was sent to encourage the believers (3:2), so now Paul is encouraged because of them (as we may understand "about you") due to the report about their faith, love, and longing to see him (3:6). Paul was in Corinth at this time during a difficult stretch in his ministry. The sufferings, persecution, and mocking he endured in Philippi, Thessalonica, and Athens (Acts 17), plus the rough character of Corinth, left him with considerable fear (Acts 18:9–11; 1 Cor. 2:3). Paul speaks here of his "distress," the afflictions and calamities he and his associates endured (2 Cor. 6:4; 12:10), and "persecution," those direct attacks that came because of their proclamation of the gospel (Acts 14:22; Rom. 5:3; 8:35; 12:12). The Thessalonians' faith, love, and steadfastness were like renewed life for Paul: "For now we really live, since you are standing firm in the Lord" (3:8). Paul uses "live," perhaps suggesting "recover" (Mark 5:23; John 4:50–51, 53), in the figurative sense. Oppressed by circumstances, he and his associates "recovered" with hope and encouragement because of the Thessalonians' firm stance in the gospel. But we should not lose sight of the way Paul was repeatedly in danger of death (1 Cor. 15:31; 2 Cor. 4:10–11, 16). Under such pressures we can well understand how the verb "live" would come to mind. "Standing firm" suggests constancy and stability in the faith (1 Cor. 16:13), in the community of faith (Phil. 1:27), in the received doctrine (2 Thess. 2:15), or, as here, "in the Lord" (Phil. 4:1). The Thessalonians maintained their solidarity with the Lord despite the persecution (1 Thess. 2:14) and satanic attacks to lead them

into apostasy (3:5). This was the fruit of their hope (1 Thess. 1:3).

At this point the letter explodes into thanksgiving and joy: "How can we thank God enough for you in return for all the joy we have in the presence of our God because of you?" (3:9). This is the third thanksgiving in the letter (see 1 Thess. 1:2; 2:13). The thanksgiving implies that, though Timothy did his job (3:2) and the Thessalonians continued in faith, love, and hope (3:6, 8), God was the one who produced the believers' stability in the face of adversity. The way Paul poses the question recalls Psalm 116:12. Here, as in the psalm, thanksgiving to God is regarded as a debt to be paid, yet one impossible to pay in full. The principle of reciprocity is at the heart of the thanksgiving: to return thanks for a benefit received was an essential social obligation. So here the apostles received a great gift from God—the continuance in the faith of the Thessalonians. In response they want to offer thanks, but they cannot find a way that is adequate or equal to the gift. Paul speaks of "the joy we have" or, as the Greek, "the joy with which we rejoice," a rejoicing that exceeds measure. The joy is expressed "in the presence of our God," likely at their times of prayer (1 Thess. 1:3). Prayer was not just for petitioning God (3:10).

Paul attempted to return to the church (2:17–18) and now prays to be reunited with them. "Night and day we pray most earnestly that we may see you again and supply what is lacking in your faith" (3:10). The prayers are constant, even reaching into the night hours. The verb "pray" means to implore, and their prayers are intense beyond measure (suggested by the term translated "earnestly"). Timothy's visit and this letter were not enough (see 2 Cor. 1:16; Philem. 22; 2 John 12; 3 John 14). Paul was able to return later, in answer to these prayers (Acts 19:21–22; 20:1–6; 1 Cor. 16:5; 2 Cor. 1:16; 1 Tim. 1:3). The reason he wanted to return was to make their faith complete ("supply"; Luke 6:40; Heb. 13:21). The verb appears in educational contexts that refer to the process of training and completing the education a student receives. The Thessalonians were ignorant of certain fundamental theological tenets (1 Thess. 4:13) and had forgotten some teaching they had already received (5:1–2). They had not appropriated all of the apostles' moral teaching (4:3–8). A visit would help put all this right.

3:11–13: Prayer to return to Thessalonica. The apostles now voice their prayer in the letter: "Now may our God and Father himself and our Lord Jesus clear the way for us to come to you" (3:11). The prayer is addressed to "our God and Father," echoing Jesus when he taught the disciples to pray (Matt. 6:9; and see Rom. 8:15; Gal. 4:6). But the prayer is also directed to our Lord Jesus, who is elevated to the same level as the Father. Paul's high Christology is evident here as in 2 Thessalonians 2:16–17, where the Lord Jesus Christ is addressed before God our Father. The prayer is that their Father and Lord will "clear the way" for them to return. The verb means "to make straight" and alludes to the few straight paths that one could traverse. The use is metaphorical, as in both Jewish (1 Sam. 6:12; Ps. 5:8; Prov. 4:26–27) and Greek literature and communicates the idea of heading straight on without diverting. Here they pray that God would facilitate their return to the city without any impediment or diversion (1 Thess. 2:18).

They follow with a petition regarding the church's love: "May the Lord make your love increase and overflow for each other and for everyone else, just as ours does for you" (3:12). The Thessalonians are the objects of God's love (1 Thess. 1:4; 2 Thess. 2:13, 16), and God himself has infused love into the community (1 Thess. 4:9). Their love for each other is noteworthy (3:6), and they express that love toward other congregations in Macedonia (4:9–10). Timothy had reported this love, and in this the Thessalonians became a model for other congregations (1:7; 2 Thess. 1:3–4). This mutual love was the counterpoint to the hostility and social ostracism that the church experienced from without. This "love" has to do with group attachment and solidarity. Love places the interests of the other first and is not the same as

feelings of affection and emotional warmth. Even though the Thessalonians already show mutual love, the apostles pray that their love might increase abundantly and even overflow. And the prayer is answered (2 Thess. 1:3). The objects of this love are the other members of the Christian community. Here Paul echoes Jesus's love command (John 13:34–35; 15:12, 17; Rom. 12:10; 13:8; 1 Pet. 1:22; 4:8; 1 John 3:11, 23; 4:7, 11–12). The prayer is also that their love would abound "for everyone else," that is, those outside the community of faith (see 1 Thess. 5:15; cf. Gal. 6:10; 2 Tim. 2:24; Titus 3:2). The apostles are concerned about the relationships within the church but also about the church's relationship with outsiders (4:12; Col. 4:5; cf. 1 Cor. 5:12–13). The roots here are embedded in Jesus's teaching (Matt. 5:43–48; 22:39; Mark 12:31–33; Luke 10:27–37).

The final portion of the prayer focuses on the church's existence in light of its eschatological hope: "May he strengthen your hearts so that you will be blameless and holy in the presence of our God and Father" (3:13). The prayer is that their hearts, or persons, be established (the same verb appears in 3:2) blameless in holiness. "Hearts" can refer to the inner life of a person (see 2:4, 17) but in other contexts, as here, may focus on the center of someone's life and moral decisions (Matt. 5:8; Acts 15:9; Heb. 10:22). "Blameless" appears frequently with regard to the moral life of a person as well, especially focusing on the final outcome of one's life. So it appears often in funeral epitaphs as well as in judicial contexts where the verdict is pronounced over the accused. The hope is that the Thessalonians will not be found guilty in any way. "Holiness" denotes the condition of sanctification, a principal concern of the apostles regarding this congregation (1 Thess. 4:3–4, 7; 5:23; 2 Thess. 2:13). The term has to do with the consecration of one's life to God and the separation from sin that happens at the same time. The process of sanctification began at conversion (1 Thess. 1:9), was the will of God for their lives in the present (4:3a), included the separation from immoral practices that characterized their previous life (4:3b), and was enabled by the activity of God in their lives (5:23).

The prayer is that this moral purity will be theirs in the last judgment, "in the presence of our God and Father when our Lord Jesus comes" (3:13b). Their God and Father (3:11) is also their judge, and the prayer is that they be found blameless before him. In this last time, the Lord Jesus will come "with all his holy ones." These may be deceased Christians (1 Thess. 4:16) or angels (2 Thess. 1:7). The verse is an allusion to Zechariah 14:5, where celestial beings are in view (see Deut. 33:2; Ps. 89:5, 7; Job 5:1; 15:15; Dan. 4:13; 8:13). The New Testament often speaks of the angels or the saints who will accompany the Lord in his coming (Matt. 13:41; Mark 8:38; 13:27; 2 Thess. 1:7; Jude 14–15).

B. The apostolic instruction: The life that pleases God (4:1–5:22). Paul, Silas, and Timothy here transition to the second section of the body of the letter, which addresses both ethical and theological concerns. The teaching they have delivered to the new church includes moral orientation, and now they stimulate the new converts to grow in what they know and put the teaching into practice. The section responds to concerns regarding the church's sexual ethics (4:3–8) and the issue of labor (4:11–12). But it is also a response to the questions the church had put to Paul, perhaps via letter, about love among the members (4:9–10), the destiny of the dead in Christ (4:13–18), and the time of the day of the Lord (5:1–11). The section concludes with a series of exhortations centered on relationships with the church's emerging leadership (5:12–13) and among members of the congregation (5:14–22).

4:1–2: Introduction. The first verses of the section on living to please God serve as an introduction to both the teaching on sexual ethics (4:3–8) and the rest of the moral teaching of the letter. Topics in this introduction appear in the following argument, such as the repetition of the principal verbs ("ask" and "urge" in 4:1;

cf. 4:10; 5:12; see also 5:11, 14), the affirmation that the Thessalonians have, in part, put into practice the moral teaching (4:1; cf. 4:10; 5:11), the encouragement to grow in morality (4:2; cf. 4:10), and the exhortation to remember the moral teaching they have already received (4:2; cf. 4:9; 5:1–2).

The authors mark the transition to a new section saying, "As for other matters, brothers and sisters, we instructed you how to live in order to please God, as in fact you are living. Now we ask you and urge you in the Lord Jesus to do this more and more" (4:1). The principal verbs in the Greek are "ask" and "urge." The first is not simply a request but, in moral contexts, should be understood as "beseech" (Phil. 4:3; 1 Thess. 5:12; 2 Thess. 2:1; 2 John 5). The second verb means "exhort" and is also found in moral contexts, at times with the first verb, "ask" (1 Thess. 5:12, 14). The way Paul structures this initial exhortation echoes official documents of the era that authorities sent to those who were subject to them. The apostles' authority in these matters is derived from the Lord ("in the Lord Jesus").

The exhortation proper is that the Thessalonians "do this more and more" (see 1 Thess. 3:12 and 4:10), that is, excel and be outstanding to an ever greater degree in that which they have learned and are doing. The apostles have "instructed" them, a word in the Greek that speaks of what the Thessalonians received from the apostles. The term appeared in contexts of receiving authoritative and sacred tradition. They received teaching regarding "how to live in order to please God" (see 1 Thess. 2:4; 2:15). The authors speak of the moral life as the way one must walk. They underscore the obligation to walk this way by including a Greek term that means, "it is necessary." Paul and his associates leave no room for the Thessalonians to place the moral instruction to one side.

A commonplace in ancient letters was to remind the reader of what he or she already knew. In the same way, the apostles remind the Thessalonians of the fundamental teaching that has been handed over to them, which is not only doctrinal but moral: "For you know what instructions we gave you by the authority of the Lord Jesus" (4:2). "Instructions" should be translated "commandments" or "orders" and suggests the authoritative nature of the apostolic instruction. The authority behind this teaching is that of "the Lord Jesus."

4:3–8: Sanctification. In the next verses, the apostles address the problem of sexual immorality. Evidently some church members who received the teaching regarding their sexuality (4:1–2, 6) have rejected it (4:8). They responded to their passions as those who were unconverted (4:5), and they have not separated themselves from sexual immorality (4:3). So the apostles remind them that sanctification, here understood as sexual purity, is the will of God (4:3–4, 7–8) and that God will judge those who hand themselves over to such passions (4:6). However, the Christian has the power, through the Holy Spirit, to live according to the will of God (4:8).

Not a few religions celebrated in Thessalonica promoted sexual immorality. It would therefore have been difficult for new converts to understand the connection between faith and ethics. Moreover, social norms of the day permitted that which was prohibited within the church. Cicero, for example, argued in favor of sexual liberty for the youth, saying, "Pleasures should not always be prohibited. . . . At times pleasure should triumph over reason" (*In Defense of Caelius* 18.42). The only concern was that the pleasures not harm others. When voices were raised against extramarital relationships, the concern centered on the possibility of begetting children from these unions. But the norms for men and women were different. Plutarch, the moralist, said that the wife should not be upset if her husband sought sexual pleasure with another woman (*Morals* 140B). What was condemned was entering into a sexual relationship with another man's wife. On the other hand, the woman was prohibited from sexual encounters outside marriage. One marriage contract stipulated, "Isidora should not sleep apart nor be absent for a day from the house of Dionysus without his knowledge and should not ruin her house nor live with another man." Such dissimilar norms existed in both Roman and Greek society.

Paul encourages the Thessalonian believers to live holy lives in the midst of a pagan culture (1 Thess. 4:1–12). This votive relief (fourth century BC), possibly associated with the founding of Thessalonica, includes images of Athena, Zeus, and Hera and is a reminder of the city's pagan heritage.

Though his report about the church was good (3:6), Timothy brought other news about sexual misconduct in the church. Paul begins by affirming that "it is God's will that you should be sanctified: that you should avoid sexual immorality" (4:3). While Greek ethics were organized around a collection of ideals or virtues, Christian and Jewish ethics centered on the will of God (Rom. 12:2; Eph. 6:6). The passage contrasts the life oriented around God's will with that guided by passions (4:5). Here the will of God is their sanctification, or holy living (1 Pet. 1:15–16). Sanctification is the principal concern of this passage (4:3–4, 7), while the particular manifestation of it has to do with sexual purity (4:7). In language that echoes the Jerusalem decree (cf. Acts 15:20, 29), the apostles call the readers to avoid sexual immorality. "Sexual immorality" is a broad term that can include any sexual relationship outside marriage, including adultery, homosexuality, incest, prostitution, bestiality, and sexual relationships between singles. At times it is used in a more restricted sense (fornication, not adultery, as in Matt. 15:19; Mark 7:21), but here it indicates all forms of sexual immorality, including adultery (Matt. 5:32; 19:9).

The concern is "that each of you should learn to control his own body in a way that is holy and honorable" (4:4). The term translated "body" literally means "vessel" and may refer to the person's own body or the person's wife (see 1 Pet. 3:7 ESV). Some have suggested that it may even refer to male genitalia. The other problematic term is the verb. Does it mean "control" (oneself) or "obtain, acquire" (a spouse)? Most likely the NIV understands the passage correctly—the text is one of the many that call Christians to self-control (Acts 15:20, 29; 21:25; 1 Cor. 6:12–20; Eph. 5:3; Col. 3:5; and especially 2 Tim. 2:21–22, which also speaks of the body as a "vessel" [see ESV, NRSV] used in "honor" and "sanctification" instead of being dominated by passions). A person is to keep control of his or her body in holiness before God and honor before the community (Rom. 12:10) and God

(Rom. 2:7; 9:21; 1 Pet. 1:7; 2:7). Paul starkly contrasts the life of sexual self-control that leads to honor and holiness with the life defined by passion due to ignorance of God: "not in passionate lust like the pagans, who do not know God" (4:5; see Rom. 1:18–32; Eph. 4:17–18). The implication for the readers of this letter is clear: you know God—don't live that way! What determines the sexual conduct of the Christian is his or her relationship with God, not the passions that lead others in society.

The focus of this section is on adultery: "and that in this matter no one should wrong or take advantage of a brother or sister" (4:6). The first verb, "to wrong," came to mean "transgress" or "infringe" laws or commandments and appears in various contexts in combination with the verb "to sin." Some had transgressed the divine law by entering into a sexual relationship with a fellow Christian's spouse. In this act, the person "takes advantage" of another believer, the verb suggesting a form of exploitation (in other contexts it refers to political, economic, and military, as well as sexual exploitation). Such acts are not casually dismissed. The apostles remind the church that "the Lord will punish all those who commit such sins, as we told you and warned you before." They were not ignorant of what God required, nor were they unaware of the consequences. Paul refers to God as an "avenger" (KJV, RSV), a legal term used of officials and others who punished those who violated laws (Rom. 13:4). Elsewhere, as here, it was used to refer to God's judgment (Deut. 32:35; Ps. 94:1; cf. 2 Thess. 1:8–9). God will not tolerate sexual immorality in his community (1 Cor. 6:9–10; 10:1–13).

Paul reminds the Thessalonians of God's claim on their lives: "For God did not call us to be impure, but to live a holy life" (4:7). The believers in Thessalonica were chosen by God (1 Thess. 1:4) and called through the apostolic proclamation of the gospel to "share in the glory of our Lord Jesus Christ" (2 Thess. 2:14; see 1 Thess. 2:12). This election and calling included the call to sanctification (1 Pet. 1:15–16) and not impurity, here understood as sexual impurity (Rom. 1:24; 2 Cor. 12:21; Eph. 5:3). The Thessalonians were engaged by God to live according to his will with regard to their sexuality (4:7; cf. 4:1–3). Just as the gospel is a divine message (1 Thess. 1:5; 2:13), so too is the moral teaching that the apostles delivered. Paul therefore concludes, "anyone who rejects this instruction does not reject a human being but God" (4:8a). He adds that God "gives you his Holy Spirit" (4:8b), the one who enables them to live according to the will of God in sanctification (Rom. 8:4; Gal. 5:16; 1 John 3:24; 1 Thess. 5:23).

4:9–5:11: Responses to questions. Paul next appears to answer a series of questions put to him by the Thessalonians (see 4:9, 13; 5:1; cf. 1 Cor. 7:1, 25; 8:1; 12:1; 16:1), communicated orally or more likely by letter sent via Timothy. Likely the Thessalonians took advantage of the messenger at hand (there was no public postal system during this era). The questions they put to Paul were about fraternal love (4:9–10), the destiny of the dead in Christ (4:13–18), and the time of the day of the Lord (5:1–11).

4:9–12. If 4:9 is indeed a response to a query about familial love among the believers, what would have provoked the question? Perhaps the question arose from tensions generated by sexual misconduct, problems in accepting the emerging leadership (1 Thess. 5:12–13), and the way some refused to work (5:14). The social rejection the church experienced made the issue all the more important (2:14). Families, the fundamental unit of society, were affected by these believers who turned from community and familial deities (1:9). Building family bonds in the church similar to those that exist between brothers and sisters therefore became an urgent necessity.

The response begins, "Now about your love for one another we do not need to write to you, for you yourselves have been taught by God to love each other" (4:9). Various ancient authors spoke about love among siblings, emphasizing the way brothers and sisters collaborate and enjoy solidarity and harmony while also recognizing familial tensions. This love is the paradigm for the community known as "brothers and sisters." The Thessalonians, however, needed no teaching on the matter. Paul recognizes that they have already been taught by God how to love one another, this being through God's example in sending Christ (John 3:16; Rom. 5:8; Eph. 5:1–2), through the Holy Spirit (Gal. 5:22; Rom. 5:5), and through Jesus's teaching (John 13:34–35; 15:12, 17), which the apostles echoed in their instruction (Rom. 12:10; Gal. 6:2; 1 Pet. 1:22). Indeed, the Thessalonians have already learned lessons of love, as demonstrated by their love for all the churches in Macedonia (such as Philippi and Berea; 4:10). This love is something they have demonstrated (see 1 Thess. 1:3), possibly through hospitality (Rom. 16:1–2) or acting as benefactors by helping those in need (2 Cor. 8:1–5, 8–11, 24). As in 4:1, he urges them to excel in what they are already doing.

Having touched on the issue of being benefactors for others (4:10), Paul now fixes his attention on those members of the church who are receiving aid from their patrons, whether inside or outside the church. This passage, like 2 Thessalonians 3:6–15, demonstrates that the apostles were opposed to the social and economic dependency that characterized the client-patron relationships, likely due to its social entailments. High-status patrons would have multiple clients who expected food, money, and public representation to protect their rights, while they reciprocated by giving patrons honor by supporting their causes in public assembly, following them through town, and showing up at their homes for the morning greeting. Paul exhorts the church, "Make it your ambition to lead a quiet life: You should mind your own business and work with your hands, just as we told you" (4:11). Ancient authors sometimes discussed those who led the "quiet life" as people who were respectable and did not cause problems in the community. These discussions sometimes include the note that such people mind their own business by not causing public disturbance. The exhortation to work with their hands not only indicates that the members of the church were of the artisan class but also suggests that some Thessalonians were clients of prominent patrons and supported the cause of the patrons in the popular assembly. Paul calls them to labor, following his example (1 Thess. 2:9; 2 Thess. 3:7–8), "so that your daily life may win the respect of outsiders and so that you will not be dependent on anybody" (4:12). The type of decent conduct Paul prescribes was admired by the Greeks. The language he uses describes those in a community who conducted themselves in a worthy and noble manner and who received public recognition for their conduct. Living in an orderly manner and with decorum was one of the highest ideals of life.

4:13–18. In this section the apostles respond to the second inquiry of the Thessalonian believers. They were ignorant about the destiny of believers who had died before the Lord's advent. Verse 13 implies that between the time Paul left and Timothy's visit some members of the church had passed away. The believers' grief prompts Paul to orient them theologically and encourage them to comfort one another (4:18). This section picks up many of the themes found in ancient letters of consolation, such as the call to minimize grief (4:13), the discourse regarding the state of the dead (4:14–17), and the exhortation to comfort one another (4:18). Such ancient letters, however, focus on the way death is inevitable, the common fate of all, so one should not grieve too much in the face of fate's dictates. Paul's comfort, however, is firmly rooted in the resurrection of Christ (4:14). He offers hope where the rest offer none (4:13).

The exhortation begins, "Brothers and sisters, we do not want you to be uninformed about those who sleep in death, so that you do not grieve like the rest of mankind, who have no hope" (4:13). "Sleep," a common euphemism for death (see 4:16, "the *dead* in Christ") in both Jewish and Christian literature, implies nothing about the intermediate state between death and resurrection (cf. Luke 23:42–43; Acts

7:59–60; 2 Cor. 5:6–8; Phil. 1:20–23). However, at times "sleep" describes death in the light of the anticipated resurrection (Dan. 12:2; 1 Cor. 15:20). Paul seeks to minimize the grief of the church in the face of death, though he does not prohibit grief (John 16:6; Acts 8:2; Phil. 2:27). His and his companions' concern is simply that the Christians' grief not be like that of nonbelievers, who have no hope in the face of death (Eph. 2:12). Gentile hopelessness was expressed frequently in funeral epitaphs, some of which read, "I was not, I was, I am not, it doesn't matter" (see Green, 218).

In response to the grief the Thessalonians experience in the face of death, Paul and his associates return to the creed of the church (cf. Acts 17:3): "We believe that Jesus died and rose again, and so we believe that God will bring with Jesus those who have fallen asleep in him" (4:14). Paul presents the resurrection of Jesus as the guarantee of the resurrection of the believers, a denial of which was, in Paul's eyes, a virtual denial of the resurrection of Christ (1 Cor. 15:12–28). The resurrection is the focus of Christian hope, an emphasis often lacking in our reflections on death. Some have rightly argued that the verb translated "bring" should be understood as "take." Paul draws the parallel between Christ's experience of death and resurrection and the believer's experience of death ("fallen asleep") and resurrection ("take with Jesus"). The point is not that Jesus will return with the dead in Christ but that the dead in Christ will be raised as he was (see 4:16).

Paul traces his teaching back to Jesus: "According to the Lord's word, we tell you that we who are still alive, who are left until the coming of the Lord, will certainly not precede those who have fallen asleep" (4:15). "The Lord's word" does not here refer to a prophetic oracle (as Isa. 1:10), but either to the message of the gospel (1 Thess. 1:8; 2 Thess. 3:1) or, more likely here, to a teaching that came from the Lord Jesus (Acts 20:35). Since 4:15–17 conforms in many details to Matthew 24:29–31, 40–41, the source appears to be Jesus's last-days discourse. Paul's argument is simply that the dead in Christ will rise first and then, according to 4:17, the living and the resurrected dead will be taken up together to meet the Lord. The "coming of the Lord" is his *parousia*, a Greek term that was used to describe the glorious coming of a deity or the official visit of the emperor, himself honored as a god. An imperial visit was an event of great pomp and celebrations (1 Thess. 2:19), and the custom was for the officials of the city to go out to meet the coming sovereign and accompany him back to the city (4:17).

Verse 16 describes the dramatic events that occur at the Lord's coming: "For the Lord himself will come down from heaven [see 1 Thess. 1:10], with a loud command, with the voice of the archangel and with the trumpet call of God, and the dead in Christ will rise first." In a similar way, Philo of Alexandria spoke of the command of God by which he could bring together all the exiles of Israel from any part of the earth (*On Rewards and Punishments* 117; cf. Matt. 24:31). We may suppose that with this, God calls the dead to life. Christ also will come with the voice of the archangel (cf. Matt. 24:31) and the trumpet call of God. The trumpet was not a musical but a military instrument (1 Cor. 14:8) that was used in religious ceremonies and funeral processions as well. Here it not only is heard by the dead but also calls them forth (cf. 1 Cor. 15:52; Matt. 24:31; see also Isa. 27:13; Zech. 9:14–16). The result is that the dead in Christ will rise first, giving them the place of preeminence and honor.

Then, "After that, we who are still alive and are left will be caught up together with them in the clouds to meet the Lord in the air" (4:17). This event is commonly referred to as the "rapture" of the church, which occurs at the time of Christ's coming after the dead in Christ are raised. "Caught up" denotes taking something or someone by force or violence and at times is used of taking a person up to celestial places (Acts 8:39; 2 Cor. 12:2, 4; Rev. 12:5). Clouds often accompany times when God shows himself (Matt. 17:5), such as in Christ's second coming (Matt. 24:30; 26:64). The purpose of this event is "to meet the Lord." Paul uses a verb that describes the custom of sending an official delegation outside a city to meet a visiting dignitary (Acts 28:15). In formal receptions for dignitaries like the emperor, the leaders of the city, along with the whole population, would go out to meet him, and then upon his return to the city there would be a great reception with songs, cries, and

Paul says that a trumpet will accompany the coming of the Lord (1 Thess. 4:16). On this bas-relief from the Arch of Marcus Aurelius in Rome, a trumpet announces the triumphal return of the victorious emperor, Marcus Aurelius, in AD 176.

sacrifices. The pomp and ceremony at Christ's coming (*parousia*) is beyond compare. The end result is that we will be with the Lord forever. Paul does not state where we will be with the Lord, but the previous argument implies that the believers, living and resurrected, will return with him to this earth (cf. Matt. 6:10).

This embedded letter of consolation concludes, "Therefore encourage one another with these words" (4:18), a common topic in such ancient letters (see 4:13). This teaching was not just for the leadership but was to be used in the ministry each of the members exercised toward others (4:9; 5:11, 14–15).

5:1–11. This section constitutes a response to the third question of the Thessalonian believers (4:9, 13), which was about the time of the day of the Lord (5:1–2), a continuing concern of the church (2 Thess. 2:1–2). The persecution they suffered likely provoked the question. The response also suggests that they had questions regarding how to be prepared for that day (5:4–10). In response, the apostles affirm that maintaining a life characterized by faith, love, and hope will give them the assurance that the day of the Lord will not surprise them like a thief (5:4). While the unbelievers will not escape (5:3), the church will not experience divine wrath (5:9). The apostles' focus, as in the previous section, is pastoral and not speculative (5:11).

As in 4:9, Paul begins the section by reminding the Thessalonians about what they already know: "Now, brothers and sisters, about times and dates we do not need to write to you" (5:1). The question they had was about the time when the day of the Lord would arrive (5:2), an ancient query among God's people (Hab. 2:1–4; Matt. 24:3; Acts 1:6; 1 Pet. 1:10–11; and note the common responses found in Matt. 24:36; Mark 13:32; Acts 1:7). He reminds them that "the day of the Lord will come like a thief in the night" (5:2). This day is not only the time when God will come to judge the inhabitants of the earth (Isa. 13:6, 9; Ezek. 13:5; Joel 1:15; 2:1, 11; 3:14) but also when God will deliver his people (Joel 2:21–32; 3:18; Obad. 15–21; Zech. 14:1–21). That day will come like a thief in the night, that is, suddenly and at a moment when it is not expected. Paul's teaching is derived from Jesus (Matt. 24:43–44; cf. 2 Pet. 3:10; Rev. 3:3; 16:15).

Paul graphically describes how that day will come: "While people are saying, 'Peace and safety,' destruction will come on

Reassembled statue of Augustus from Thessalonica (first century AD). Augustus initiated the idea of *pax Romana*, the peace and security of the Roman Empire. Paul warns, however, "While people are saying, 'Peace and safety,' destruction will come on them suddenly" (1 Thess. 5:3).

them suddenly, as labor pains on a pregnant woman, and they will not escape" (5:3). Once again, Paul draws from Jesus's teaching (Luke 21:34–36). The Roman Empire and its rulers offered "peace and safety" or "security" since the establishment of the *pax Romana* (Roman peace) by the emperor Augustus. But at the very time of greatest political and social promise, divine judgment will come. This event will arrive like labor pains on a pregnant woman, from which there is no escape. Inscriptions from the era testify that many women died giving birth, making this an apt, though dreadful, metaphor.

Paul contrasts how believers will face that day: "But you, brothers and sisters, are not in darkness so that this day should surprise you like a thief" (5:4). While they do not know when the day of the Lord will come (5:2), they will be prepared for it since they are "not in darkness." The association of "darkness" with the life of sin is common in the Old Testament and Jewish literature (as Ps. 74:20; 82:5). Christian salvation is a transition from the realm of moral darkness to light (Acts 26:18; Eph. 5:8; Col. 1:13; 1 Pet. 2:9; and see Heb. 6:4; 10:32). Paul's point is that living the moral life in the light assures the believers that the day of the Lord will not surprise them, since they will be ready for it. Preparedness does not come by speculations about when that day will arrive. The believers are children of the light and day, not of the night and darkness (5:5). These participate in the light; that is, they belong to the sphere of light and are saved (Acts 26:18; Eph. 5:8; 1 Pet. 2:9). Being of the day means that they belong to the dawning new age (Rom. 13:12), which will shine completely when the Lord Jesus returns (1 Thess. 5:2, 8; 2 Thess. 1:10).

Paul exhorts them to act according to who they are: "So, then, let us not be like others, who are asleep [here in the moral sense, unlike 4:13], but let us be awake and sober" (5:6). To be "awake" signifies being spiritually and morally alert and vigilant (Matt. 24:42–44; 25:13) so that they do not enter into temptation (Matt. 26:40–41). To be "sober" means to

avoid drunkenness, although here the meaning is figurative, denoting self-control (2 Tim. 4:5; 1 Pet. 1:13; 4:7; 5:8). So the believer does not embrace the night with its sin (5:7). Since there was little nighttime illumination during this era, nights were considered horrible and sinister (see Matt. 26:34; John 13:30). Paul urges his readers that since they are of the day, "let us be sober, putting on faith and love as a breastplate, and the hope of salvation as a helmet" (5:8). Paul occasionally employs military metaphors when describing Christian conduct (Rom. 13:12; 2 Cor. 6:7; 10:3–5; Eph. 6:11–17; Phil. 2:25; 2 Tim. 2:3–4). Here he draws from Isaiah 59:17, where God himself is compared to a soldier, as also in Ephesians 6:11–17. The symbolic references of the armament are not the same as in Ephesians 6. In Ephesians 6:14 the breastplate is justice, but here it is faith and love; and in Ephesians 6:17 the helmet is salvation, while here it is the hope of salvation. The trilogy of faith, love, and hope (see 1:3; 3:6–8) is the vital element of the armor, which will ensure that the Christian is prepared for that day, whenever it comes.

Up to this point the contrast has been between the character of the Christians and the character of the unbelievers in light of the coming day of the Lord. But in 5:9 the focus changes to their ultimate destiny: "For God did not appoint us to suffer wrath but to receive salvation through our Lord Jesus Christ." Paul graphically describes God's wrath in 2 Thessalonians 1:6–10 and 2:8–12. This is the lot of those who do not obey the gospel. Because of God's election, the believers' destiny is to obtain salvation (5:8), the liberation from the wrath of God (see 1 Thess. 1:10), which comes through Christ's death. Paul links this salvation with Christ's crucifixion by stating that "he died for us so that, whether we are awake or asleep, we may live together with him" (5:10). This is one of the few texts in the Thessalonian epistles that expressly speaks of the death of Christ (2:15; 4:14) and the only one in which the purpose of his death is expressly stated. His death was substitutionary ("for us"; cf. 1 Cor. 1:30). Both the living ("awake") and deceased ("asleep," as in 4:13–15) believers "live together with him," an allusion to the resurrection of the dead and their rapture along with the living (4:16–17).

5:12–13: Community leadership. After responding to the Thessalonians' questions (4:9–5:11), the apostles take up a variety of issues, starting with the church's relationship with their emerging leadership: "Now we ask you, brothers and sisters, to acknowledge those who work hard among you, who care for you in the Lord and who admonish you" (5:12a). In calling the church to respect the new leaders, the apostles literally call the church "to know" them, which means they should "recognize" who the legitimate leaders are (cf. 1 Cor. 16:15–16). What legitimized the Thessalonian leadership was not their status or social rank, as was common in Greek and Roman society, but the hard work they undertook on behalf of the congregation (5:12b; see 1:3; 1 Cor. 3:8; 15:58; 2 Cor. 6:5; 11:23, 27). They are also those who "care for you," a term that may mean "to lead" or "to direct" (1 Tim. 3:4–5, 12; 5:17) but also "to protect" and "to give aid" (Titus 3:8, 14). It was commonly used to speak of those who were leaders of communities, the guardians and leaders of groups. Those who led communities were often their benefactors (Rom. 12:8; 16:1–2), but these leaders' authority was derived from the Lord. They also "admonish you," correcting the congregation's moral and doctrinal errors. Ministerial responsibility includes teaching but also changing conduct (5:14; 2 Thess. 3:15).

The following verse (5:13) calls the Thessalonians to honor their leaders and to live in harmony with one another. Leaders should be respected to the highest degree and loved, just as the members of the church love other believers (1 Thess. 4:9–10). They are not honored due to their high social rank but because of "their work." There should also be community harmony among the believers, a teaching given by Jesus (Mark 9:50). This call to community harmony reverberates through the epistles, as the believers are called to live in peace with those both inside and outside the community of faith (Rom. 12:18; 2 Cor. 13:11; Heb. 12:14). To live in peace meant the absence of discord and the maintenance of harmony between people, a virtue of special importance as these new believers experienced social rejection (1 Thess. 2:14).

5:14: Life in community. Leaving the theme of community loyalty, the apostles now instruct the believers about their response to various groups within the church: "And we urge you, brothers and sisters, warn those who are idle and disruptive, encourage the disheartened, help the weak, be patient with everyone" (5:14). This ministerial responsibility is placed not on the leadership alone but on all (1 Thess. 4:18; 5:11). They should admonish (see 5:12) the "idle." These are not "the lazy" but those who are "out of line" or "undisciplined." The term is found in the gymnasiarch law of Berea, which, among other things, prescribes disciplinary measures that need to be taken to correct the conduct of those who do not follow the rules of the gymnasium. In Thessalonica, they are believers who have rejected the apostolic teaching by refusing to work and maintaining their position as dependent clients (see 2 Thess. 3:6–15). The "disheartened" in need of encouragement are the discouraged, those in danger of giving up. There were likely many in this category due to the persecutions that the church endured (1:6; 2:14; 3:3–4) and the deaths of beloved believers (4:13–18). The "weak" who needed help may have been the physically weak, perhaps due to illness (1 Cor. 11:30), or those who had no social status or power, such as slaves, freedmen/women, or others who had no economic and social power (1 Cor. 1:26–29). The Greeks despised weakness in any form, but God accomplishes his greatest works in the midst of weakness (2 Cor. 13:4; 12:5, 9). The church should therefore help, and not despise, the weak. Finally, they should exercise patience toward everyone, not being irritable due to others' foibles. The diverse social mix in the church would provide innumerable opportunities to exercise this virtue.

5:15: Nonretaliation. Teaching about non-retaliation was part of the basic moral instruction for new Christians (Rom. 12:17–21; 1 Pet. 3:9), an important topic given the tensions with the surrounding community and the internal problems of the congregation: "Make sure that nobody pays back wrong for wrong, but always strive to do what is good for each other and for everyone else." Everyone recognized vengeance as the common way to respond to evil. In fact, one could never hope to maintain their social status if vengeance did not follow some offense that dishonored the person. In this environment, Jesus's teaching sounded exceedingly strange (Matt. 5:45, 48; Luke 6:35–36). Paul, like Jesus, counsels the church to do good to the one who has caused the offense (see 1 Thess. 3:12; Gal. 6:10).

5:16–18: Communion with God. In this group of three exhortations, the apostles move on to the characteristic traits of believers, joy (5:16), prayer (5:17), and thanksgiving (5:18), which should mark their lives at all times and in every situation. This is God's will. Though the Thessalonians already have joy in suffering (1 Thess. 1:6), a fruit of the Spirit in their lives, they are called to a life of joy that is constant (5:16; Phil. 4:4; 3:1). In the midst of agonizing situations, the presence of God by the Spirit fills the soul with hope and the heart with joy. Paul also calls them to "pray continually" (5:17), not an exhortation to pray at every moment (see the word in 1:3) but consistently and without fail (Luke 18:1; Rom. 12:12; Eph. 6:18; Col. 4:2). Unlike pagan prayer, which was based on a system of exchange with the gods ("You do this for me and I'll do that for you"), Christian prayer begins with the assumption that God, our Father, is disposed to hear and answer prayer (Matt. 6:9–13; 7:7–11).

The third exhortation of this trilogy is to "give thanks in all circumstances" (5:18a). Thanksgiving is offered to God, though the object of thanks is only implied, not stated. Giving thanks was an important social obligation, and deities were considered to be proper objects of thanksgiving because of the benefits they conferred. The call is not to give thanks *for* every situation but rather *in* every situation. Paul does not embrace fatalism, which says that what happens is what is supposed to happen. Rather, the Christian affirms that God can use any situation for his or her own good (Rom. 8:28) and that one can triumph in the midst of any circumstance, even adversity (Rom. 8:31–39). All the preceding exhortations are God's will for them (5:18b).

5:19–22: Prophecy. This last group of exhortations has to do with the use and control of prophecy in the church: "Do not quench the Spirit. Do not treat prophecies with contempt" (5:19–20). Paul speaks of the "Spirit" as the agent in prophecy (Luke 1:67; Acts 2:17; 19:6; 28:25; Eph. 3:5; Rev. 22:6), and here he responds to attempts to curtail this gift. Occasionally in Israel prophetic utterances were questioned and prohibited (Num. 11:26–29; Amos 2:12; Mic. 2:6). During the New Testament era Epicurean questions about prophecy, based on a rejection of divine providence, were well known. Such influences likely entered the church. Some prophesied in the church, but others rejected and despised these prophetic oracles. While there were abuses of the gifts in the churches, the apostolic teaching was not to eliminate them but to use them under proper control (1 Cor. 12:10; 14:29; 1 John 4:1–3; cf. 1 Cor. 14:39).

The following verses are connected with the previous two: "Test them all; hold on to what is good, reject every kind of evil" (5:21–22). "Test" is the same verb found in 1 John 4:1, which likewise talks of testing prophecy. The presence of false prophecies made such testing necessary (Matt. 24:24; 1 John 4:1–3; 1 Cor. 12:3; 2 Thess. 2:2). The basis for testing was apostolic doctrine, which carried authority that superseded that of prophecies. Having examined all prophecies, the Thessalonians are to "hold on to what is good." Those prophecies considered to be authentic should be retained and taken seriously. The verb "hold on" often refers to holding firm to received authoritative traditions (Luke 8:15; 1 Cor. 11:2; 15:2; Heb. 3:6, 14; 10:23). Finally, after examining all prophecies and holding firmly to that which is true revelation, the church should reject inauthentic revelations.

4. Final Prayer, Greetings, and Blessing (5:23–28)

A. Prayer for sanctification (5:23–25). The first part of the letter's closing contains a blessing expressed in the form of a prayer (5:23), the assurance that God is faithful to complete the work of grace in the Thessalonians' lives (5:24), and an appeal that they pray for the apostles (5:25). The apostles' prayer for the church is, "May God himself, the God of peace, sanctify you through and through. May your whole spirit, soul and body be kept blameless at the coming of our Lord Jesus Christ" (5:23). God is the ultimate source of their sanctification (1 Thess. 3:13). They must conform to the will of God in their sanctification (4:3), but never are they left on their own to attain this goal. God is the one who has called them and accomplishes this work through the Holy Spirit (4:7–8; 5:24). God is here described as "the God of peace," a name Paul uses frequently in benedictions (Rom. 15:33; 16:20; 2 Cor. 13:11; Phil. 4:9). "Peace" is practically a synonym for "salvation" (1 Thess. 1:1; Acts 10:36; Rom. 2:10; 5:1; 8:6; 14:17; Eph. 6:15).

The prayer is that God would "sanctify" (see 1 Thess. 3:13; 4:3–4, 7–8) them entirely, a thought clarified in the following clause. The apostles wish them to have complete health in spirit, soul, and body, which, according to the context, would mean moral health (blamelessness). So that the Thessalonians will understand that sanctification takes in all their being, the apostles include the terms "spirit, soul and body." There was a debate going on in this era regarding whether a person had three or two parts. We should not, on the basis of this text, conclude that Paul had aligned himself with the tripartite position, for in 1 Corinthians 7:34 he summarizes the totality of human nature in the terms "body and spirit." Jesus, on the other hand, spoke of human nature as body and soul (Matt. 10:28) but elsewhere as heart, soul, mind, and strength (Mark 12:30; Matt. 22:37; Luke 10:27). These terms describe different *aspects* of human nature, and in this present context the three simply strengthen the prayer that sanctification extend to the entirety of the Thessalonians' being so that they might appear "blameless" before the Lord in his coming (1 Thess. 3:13). Paul affirms, "The one who calls you is faithful and he will do it" (5:24). What God began in the election and calling of the Thessalonians (1:4; 2:12; 4:7; 2 Thess. 2:13–14) will be brought to completion at the time of the coming of the Lord (Phil. 1:6).

Paul also calls the church to pray for him and its other founders: "Brothers and sisters, pray for us." Paul frequently mentioned the reciprocity between him and churches, especially in prayers (Rom. 15:30–32; 2 Cor. 1:11; Eph. 6:19–20) but not limited to prayer (Rom. 1:11–12; 1 Thess. 3:8–9).

B. Call to greet and read to one another (5:26–27). This letter would have been read aloud in a gathering of the church where all, even the illiterate, could hear the message (Col. 4:16; 1 Tim. 4:13). After the reading, there would be time to greet each other "with a holy kiss" (5:26; cf. Rom. 16:16; 1 Cor. 16:20; 2 Cor. 13:12). The kiss signified a variety of things, such as the love between members of a family, honor and respect, and friendship (Mark 14:44–45; Luke 7:36–45; 15:20; Acts 20:37). Most well known was the kiss given on the forehead or cheek in greetings or departures between family members, friends, and respected persons.

C. Final blessing (5:28). As in all the Pauline Epistles, 1 Thessalonians ends with a blessing of grace. This blessing was a modification of the normal letter closing of the time, which said either "be strong" or "prosper." The apostles do not want them simply to be strong but rather to have the grace that comes from the Lord Jesus Christ. This desire, sounded in the opening prayer of the letter (1:1), summarizes the heart of the faith, which the Thessalonians had received.

Commentary

1. Epistolary Salutation (1:1–2)

This second epistle begins exactly as 1 Thessalonians did, using nearly identical wording. The only difference between this text and 1 Thessalonians 1:1 is that God is here called "*our* Father" (cf. Rom. 1:7; 1 Cor. 1:3; 2 Cor. 1:2; Gal. 1:3–4; Eph. 1:2; Phil. 1:2; 4:20; Col. 1:2; 1 Thess. 1:3; 3:11–12; 2 Thess. 2:16; Philem. 3), echoing the prayer Jesus taught the disciples (Matt. 6:9). Paul and his associates also add

here that grace and peace come "from God the Father and the Lord Jesus Christ," placing the Lord Jesus along with the Father as the agent of salvation.

2. Thanksgiving and Prayers for the Faith, Love, and Steadfastness of the Persecuted Thessalonians (1:3–12)

The apostles begin the second epistle with a thanksgiving to God for the church (1:3–5), then discuss the final judgment of the persecutors and the relief the Lord will give to his afflicted (1:6–10). This introduction ends with a report regarding their prayers for the church (1:11–12).

A. The first thanksgiving (1:3–5). As in 1 Thessalonians, the second letter begins with a thanksgiving to God for the congregation (cf. 1 Thess. 1:3–10). The first words of this thanksgiving are almost identical to 1 Thessalonians 1:3. Here the authors see their thanksgiving as an obligation. The language echoes Jewish reflection on prayer. Philo, for example, spoke of the "necessary obligation" to offer to God "hymns and blessings and prayers and sacrifices and the other expressions of thanksgiving" (*On the Special Laws* 1.224). It is also "right"

Underneath the remains of this second-century-AD agora in Thessalonica lies an earlier agora, the marketplace most likely used by the recipients of Paul's letters to the Thessalonians.

or "proper" as a duty. While we may affirm our rights, the emphasis here is on Christian duties. The reason the apostles thank God is that they understand him to be the agent in the Thessalonians' moral growth: "because your faith is growing more and more, and the love all of you have for one another is increasing" (1:3). Paul mentions their progress in "faith" and "love" (cf. 1 Thess. 1:3), while their hope is implicit in their "perseverance" (2 Thess. 1:4; see 1 Thess. 1:3; 3:6, 8). The members of this church were noted for their active "faith" in the midst of persecutions (1 Thess. 1:3; 3:2, 5–7; 5:8; 2 Thess. 1:10–11), and "love" characterized the relations among the believers (1 Thess. 1:3; 3:6, 12; 4:9–10; 5:8, 13). However, the apostles had exhorted them to love each other more and more (1 Thess. 4:10) and had prayed for an increase of love among them (1 Thess. 3:12). Clearly the Thessalonians had responded to the exhortation, and God had answered the prayer. There was reciprocity in this love. No member was excluded from either giving or receiving love.

Paul comments on their growing faith and love among other congregations: "Therefore, among God's churches we boast about your perseverance and faith in all the persecutions and trials you are enduring" (1:4). The news of this boasting would have given the Thessalonians much encouragement. Those who suffered dishonor in their town were being honored among the churches. They were tenacious, and their perseverance, or steadfastness, in the face of suffering and temptation flowed out of their firm hope in the coming of the Lord Jesus (1 Thess. 1:3; see Luke 21:19; Rom. 5:3–4; 2 Cor. 1:6; 6:4; Col. 1:11; 1 Tim. 6:11; Titus 2:2; Heb. 12:1; James 1:3–4; Rev. 2:2–3). Perseverance was one of the most valued virtues in the early church. The Thessalonians endured, but unlike Stoics whose creed was "endure and abstain" in the face of uncontrollable fate, they had an endurance that sprang from their faith in God.

The following verse (1:5) is a transition from the thanksgiving to the following exposition on the destiny of the persecutors and the Christians: "All this is evidence that God's judgment is right, and as a result you will be counted worthy of the kingdom of God, for which you are suffering." The evidence that God's judgment is right can be found precisely in the persecutions themselves (1:4). According to Jewish literature, the judgments of God are just because God will change the fortunes of both his persecuted people and the oppressors. Persecution is not a sign of God's rejection but rather of his acceptance (1 Pet. 4:17–19; Heb. 12:5–8). This type of perspective is the opposite of ancient history writing, which understood ill fortune as a sign of divine disfavor. God's judgment is right (Ps. 19:9; 119:137; Rom. 2:5; 2 Tim. 4:8; 1 Pet. 2:23; Rev. 16:7; 19:2) because at the end he gives to each his or her due (2 Thess. 1:6–10). In the city of Thessalonica, the believers had suffered reproach and dishonor due to their faith (1 Thess. 2:14), but God counted them worthy of the kingdom of God, like those considered worthy to be citizens of a great city such as Alexandria in Egypt (3 Maccabees 3:21; Luke 20:35; Acts 5:41). The kingdom and sufferings were intimately connected. Paul taught new believers that sufferings were a necessary prelude to entrance into the kingdom (Acts 14:22).

B. The destiny of the persecutors (1:6–10). The authors add additional information about how God's judgment is righteous, saying, "God is just: He will pay back trouble to those who trouble you" (1:6). In the eyes of God it is right to recompense the persecutors with affliction (1:6, 8–9) and give the Thessalonians relief (1:7). Scripture repeatedly affirms that God judges in accordance with his justice (Gen. 18:25; 1 Kings 8:31–32; 2 Chron. 6:22–23; Ps. 7:8–9; 2 Tim. 4:8; Rev. 18:6–7; 19:1–2). It would be unjust to allow the persecutors to escape the recompense for their actions (Ps. 137:8; Isa. 66:4, 6; Rom. 12:19; Heb. 10:30). God is not unmindful of his people or their persecutors.

Paul assures the church that God will "give relief to you who are troubled, and to us as well. This will happen when the Lord Jesus is revealed from heaven in blazing fire with his powerful angels" (1:7). The church will share relief (2 Cor. 8:13; 2:13; 7:5) with the apostles in the same way that they, like the apostles, have shared in suffering for Christ (1 Thess. 2:2, 16; 3:7; 2 Thess. 3:2). The relief in mind is the resurrection and rapture of the church (1 Thess. 4:13–18) and its glorification (2 Thess. 2:14). This will occur at the time of Christ's revelation (1 Cor. 1:7; 1 Pet. 1:7, 13). The angels of his power (cf. 2 Pet. 2:11) will accompany him in this moment (Zech. 14:5; Matt. 16:27; 24:30–31; Mark 8:38; 1 Thess. 3:13). The words "in blazing fire" are part of 1:8 in the Greek (see NRSV), although they are linked grammatically with the preceding sentence, in 1:7. Flames were a sign of God's presence (Exod. 3:2–3) but also repeatedly appear as a symbol of his judgment (Deut. 32:22; Isa. 29:6; 30:27, 30, 33; 33:14; 66:15–16). The crucified and despised Christ is God's agent in both salvation and judgment.

Paul affirms that Christ "will punish those who do not know God and do not obey the gospel of our Lord Jesus" (1:8). The language, taken from the Greek translation of Isaiah 66:15 and 66:4, speaks of Christ's vengeance, which is not an emotional outburst but the result of his righteous judgment (Luke 18:3, 5; 21:22; Acts 7:24; Rom. 12:19). Those who experience his vengeance are those who do not know God (Ps. 79:6; Jer. 10:25); they are not simply ignorant of him but have rejected him (Rom. 1:18–32; 1 Thess. 4:5). And as the knowledge of God results in obedience to his law (Ps. 36:10), so the ignorance of God is linked to disobedience to the call of the gospel (Rom. 2:8; 1 Pet. 4:17). Conversion is often described as an act of obedience to the gospel (Acts 6:7; Rom. 1:5; 6:17; 15:18; 16:26; Heb. 5:9; 1 Pet. 1:2, 14, 22).

Paul underscores the horrors of divine vengeance in 1:9. As the guilty party in judicial proceedings, the condemned will be punished "with everlasting destruction" (as 1 Thess. 5:3), "destruction" being a term that appears frequently with reference to eschatological ruin

and loss (Jer. 25:31; 48:3; Hag. 2:22; 1 Tim. 6:9). This destruction is "eternal" (Matt. 18:8; 25:41, 46; Jude 7). This does not imply annihilation but rather that the chastisement will endure and will not end. The following statement, drawn from the Greek version of Isaiah 2:10, 19, 21, makes the association between God's presence and judgment (Num. 16:46; Judg. 5:5; Ps. 34:16; 96:13; Jer. 4:26; Ezek. 38:20; Rev. 6:16; 20:11). The thought is not that they will be separated from the "presence" but that this judgment will come forth from God's presence as well as from "the glory of his might." The glory is his visible presence (Rom. 1:23; Jude 24), which is at times associated with God's power or might (Rom. 6:4; Col. 1:11). The discussion about judgment aims to encourage the believers in their affliction (1:4), letting them know that God will act in justice in favor of the community and against their persecutors.

The time of this judgment will be "on the day he comes to be glorified in his holy people and to be marveled at among all those who have believed. This includes you, because you believed our testimony" (1:10). Not only will the Lord Jesus come to judge, but also in that day his people will glorify and honor this one who was despised and rejected. His people will marvel at him, meaning they will view him with astonishment and thereby admire or honor him (see Luke 8:25; 11:14; John 7:21; Acts 3:12; Rev. 13:3). The "day" (see Isa. 2:11, 17) is the "day of the Lord" (1 Thess. 5:2, 4; 2 Thess. 2:2), the time when God will be exalted and the idolaters will be humbled according to the prophecy of Isaiah. The Thessalonians will take part in honoring him because they believed the apostles' testimony, the preaching of the gospel (Matt. 24:14; Luke 21:13; Acts 4:33; 1 Cor. 1:6; 2 Tim. 1:8). Their reaction to the divine message is in contrast with that of those who "do not obey the gospel" (1:8).

C. The remembrance of prayers (1:11–12). Having given thanks to God for the church at the start of the previous section (1:3–10), the apostles now offer up prayer for them (1:11–12).

This prayer is linked specifically with the teaching in 1:6–10 concerning the revelation of the Lord Jesus and the implications of this event for the church and her persecutors. The future promise for the believers brings with it obligations in the present, and these become the theme of the prayer. Paul and his associates pray "that our God may make you worthy of his calling" (1:11a). The verb does not mean "make worthy" but rather "consider worthy" (Luke 7:7; 1 Tim. 5:17; Heb. 3:3; 10:29) and appears in texts that speak of those who are evaluated and found worthy of some kind of honor. In the end it is God who will make them worthy of the call, giving them the ability to do his will (1 Thess. 5:23–24), but the apostles have also exhorted them to live a life worthy of God, who called them (1 Thess. 2:12; cf. Eph. 4:1; Phil. 1:27; Col. 1:10). Paul anticipates that God will evaluate their conduct in light of his call (cf. 1 Thess. 2:12; 4:7; 5:24; 2 Thess. 2:13–14), which brings with it great responsibilities. The second part of the prayer is that God "by his power" will "bring to fruition your every desire for goodness and your every deed prompted by faith" (1:11b). "Desire for goodness" (Rom. 10:1), or "goodwill" (see Phil. 1:15), is their desire to do that which is good, or, alternately, the good may be the source of their desire or goodwill. This second interpretation is preferable, as it parallels the following phrase, "deed prompted by faith" (literally "work of faith"). The idea is then that the goodwill that the Thessalonians demonstrated to others is the fruit of the good that characterizes them as Christians (Rom. 15:14; Gal. 5:22; Eph. 5:9). Their faith produced good works (see 1 Thess. 1:3). The way that this goodwill and work come to fruition is through the enabling "power" of God (Rom. 15:13; Col. 1:29).

The prayer ends by emphasizing honor: "We pray this so that the name of our Lord Jesus may be glorified in you, and you in him, according to the grace of our God and the Lord Jesus Christ" (1:12). The first part of the prayer echoes Isaiah 66:5 (see 2 Thess. 1:8–9). The Lord Jesus had been rejected and dishonored by the unbelieving Thessalonians, but this very one will be glorified (see 1:10). Paul links this glorification to the conduct of the Thessalonian believers. The glorification of a deity was a theme that appeared in the literature of the era. In this sense, "glorified" means "to be honored or respected." The worshiper honors the deity, and, in turn, the deity honors the worshiper. The worshipers of Jesus were despised, as was the Lord himself, but there is coming a time when both the Lord and his followers will be honored—and it will be mutual glorification, he in them and they in him. This glorification is the fruit of "the grace of our God and the Lord Jesus Christ." This grace is the source of their salvation and hope (1:2; 2:16; 3:18; 1 Thess. 1:1; 5:28) as well as their glorification. The grammar of the final words may be understood as an ascription of "God and Lord" to "Jesus Christ" ("our God and Lord, Jesus Christ").

3. The Body of the Letter (2:1–3:15)

The introduction of the letter included both a thanksgiving and digression concerning the revelation of the Lord (1:3–10) and a prayer for the church (1:11–12). The authors now introduce the eschatological and moral themes that constitute the body of the letter (2:1–3:15).

A. The time of the day of the Lord (2:1–17). The first section of the body (2:1–17) is a discourse concerning the time of the day of the Lord (2:1–12) and a thanksgiving for the divine election of the Thessalonians (2:13–14), followed by an exhortation and blessing centered on concerns regarding the stability of the congregation (2:15–17).

2:1–12: False teaching. Paul and his associates introduce the first section of the body of the letter with an exhortation not to "become easily unsettled or alarmed by the teaching allegedly from us—whether by a prophecy or by word of mouth or by letter—asserting that the day of the Lord has already come" (2:2). Paul links the day of the Lord with both Christ's "coming" and "our being gathered to him" (2:1; as 1 Thess. 4:15–5:2). We may assume that the false teaching about the day of the Lord muddled the Thessalonians' thinking about Christ's coming and the believers' gathering to him. This caused so much anxiety precisely because the teaching distorted their view of the second coming (Greek *parousia*) and the resurrection/rapture of the church. Christ's *parousia* (1 Thess. 2:19; 3:13; 4:15; 5:23; 2 Thess. 2:8) is the counterpoint to the coming of "the lawless one" (2:9). A *parousia* was the glorious coming of a deity or the official visit of the sovereign (emperor), who himself was honored as a god, to a city (for example, one inscription is dated "the sixty-ninth year of the first *parousia* of the god Hadrian in Greece"). Such events pale in comparison to Christ's royal *parousia*. The gathering of the believers, both the resurrected dead and the living, will occur at this time (1 Thess. 4:13–18). The gathering of the dispersed people of God was an eschatological hope (Ps. 106:47; 147:2; Isa. 52:12; Matt. 24:31; Mark 13:27). At Christ's coming, the hope will be realized.

The Thessalonians had become shaken and terrified due to the false teaching that entered by some means unknown to Paul. It could have been by "prophecy" (literally "spirit"; 1 Cor. 12:10; 1 John 4:1–3) or by a

"word," that is, by a message preached or taught by someone (2:15; Luke 4:32; 10:39; John 4:41; 17:20; Acts 2:41; 4:4; 10:44; 15:32; 20:2). On the other hand, the teaching may have come via a pseudonymous letter (see Paul's response in 3:17). However it came, the teaching was that "the day of the Lord has already come" (2:2; on the day of the Lord, see 1 Thess. 5:2, 4; 2 Thess. 1:10), a theology that affirmed that the end of all things had fully arrived (cf. Rom. 8:38; 1 Cor. 3:22; Gal. 1:4; Heb. 9:9; 2 Tim. 2:18). This teaching found fertile ground given the Thessalonians' confusion about the time of this event (1 Thess. 5:1–11). However, the verb translated "has come" could also mean "has drawn near" (1 Cor. 7:26; 2 Tim. 3:1). In this case, the unsettling teaching would have been that the day of the Lord was right at hand.

In light of the false teaching, the apostles exhort the church, saying, "Don't let anyone deceive you in any way" (2:3a), that is, by any of the means previously mentioned. The deception came through a source of supposed confidence. Certain events will precede the day of the Lord, and the fact that they have not happened is evidence that the Thessalonians are not at the very door of this event. The day of the Lord will not come "until the rebellion occurs and the man of lawlessness is revealed, the man doomed to destruction" (2:3b). "Rebellion" refers to the rejection of an established authority, whether political or religious. In this case, the

Bust of the Roman emperor Caligula, who reigned from AD 37 to 41. Paul says in 2 Thessalonians 2:4 that the man of lawlessness "sets himself up in God's temple, proclaiming himself to be God," similar to what Caligula attempted to do in the Jerusalem temple.

rebellion is against God (as in 2 Chron. 29:19; 33:19; Acts 21:21; 1 Tim. 4:1; Heb. 3:12). As here, in 1 Timothy 4:1 Paul speaks of this desertion from God as one of the signs of the end times (Matt. 24:10–13). The apostles expect that the Thessalonian believers will not participate in this rebellion (2 Thess. 2:13–14). The other event that will occur before the day of the Lord is that the man of lawlessness is revealed (2:3b; see 2:6–8). The name is a variant of the title found in Psalm 89:22 and Isaiah 57:3–4. This person is characterized as one without law and whose character is therefore the personification of sin. "Lawlessness" could refer to a lack of the law or opposition to the law but became a synonym for "sin" or "iniquity" (Rom. 4:7; 2 Cor. 6:14; Titus 2:14; Heb. 1:9; 10:17). As soon as he is mentioned, Paul points to his end: "the man doomed to destruction" (literally "the son of destruction"; cf. John 17:12). The one who incarnates sin, powerful as he might be, will meet his end when the Lord comes (2:8). He is elsewhere identified as the antichrist (1 John 2:18, 22; 4:3).

Paul states that this figure "will oppose and will exalt himself over everything that is called God or is worshiped, so that he sets himself up in God's temple, proclaiming himself to be God" (2:4). What captures the attention of the apostles is the unbridled pride of the lawless one. As an adversary (1 Tim. 5:14; 1 Pet. 5:8), he opposes every other deity ("called God," a phrase that refers to those who are ascribed divinity but are not divine) (1 Cor. 8:4; see Dan. 11:36–37). The following phrase, "object of worship" (NRSV), refers to any sanctuary, idol, or person who receives adoration (Acts 17:23). In 27 BC, Octavian received the name Augustus, which is the Latin equivalent of the word here, a name replete with religious and divine associations. A temple in Thessalonica was built to honor him and his father, the (supposedly) divine Julius. The man of lawlessness is so audacious that he establishes his own cult, taking his place in the temple reserved for images of the deity, and declares himself

divine (see Ezek. 28:2–10). The identification of "God's temple" is problematic. It may be the Jerusalem temple. Paul may be echoing how Antiochus Epiphanes profaned it in 169 BC (Dan. 9:27; 11:31; 12:11; 1 Maccabees 1:54; see Matt. 24:15; Mark 13:14). He was proclaimed as divine (a tetradrachma bore the inscription, "of the king Antiochus, god manifest and victorious"). However, he never placed himself in the temple as a deity but only identified the God of Israel with Dionysus and sacrificed pigs on the altar. Caligula (Gaius) tried to put up his image in the Jerusalem temple in AD 40 (Josephus, *Jewish Antiquities* 18.261–309) and attempted to convert the temple in Jerusalem into a sanctuary of his own cult, having named himself "the new Zeus manifest." He was assassinated in AD 41 before the image was erected. However, it is not necessary to identify "God's temple" in 2:4 as the Jerusalem shrine. It is likely not the heavenly sanctuary of God or the church, as neither could be described as a place where this figure declares himself to be god over all other deities. Alternatively, Paul may have in mind the imperial cult that flourished in Thessalonica during this period and that served as the prototype for the event Paul describes in this passage. In this case, we could translate 2:4b "in the temple of the god," that is, of the one who calls himself god. The Thessalonians should have remembered this teaching (2:5). Again and again the apostles have reminded the church of what they already knew (1 Thess. 2:9; 3:4; 4:1; 5:1–2; 2 Thess. 3:10) and affirmed the truths already learned (1 Thess. 1:5; 2:1–2, 5, 11; 3:3–4; 4:2; 5:2; 2 Thess. 3:7).

In 2:6, Paul and his associates again appeal to what the Thessalonians know: "And now you know what is holding him back, so that he may be revealed at the proper time." Most interpreters understand that a power or personage (2:7a) opposes the man of lawlessness (2:4, 6–8). What is the identity of this person or power? The Roman Empire, some other institution that represents law and order in society, the emperor (Acts 18:12; 21:27–26:32; Rom. 13:1–7), the apostolic preaching, or the apostle Paul, God himself, or his Holy Spirit? The identification is not certain, but in any case this verse does not suggest that the church will be raptured before the man of lawlessness is revealed. However, the term translated "hold back" may also mean "lay hold of" or "seize," being sometimes used of those possessed by a supernatural power, such as that of the god Dionysus (see 1 Cor. 12:2). This type of seizure may be exactly what Paul had in mind, and, understood this way, the one who seizes would be aligned with the lawless one rather than in opposition to him. This is "the secret power of lawlessness" that "is already at work" and therefore anticipates the revelation of the lawless one. As the Lord has his revelation (1:7), so too will the lawless one. The power that previews the coming of the lawless one will be "taken out of the way" (2:7b) as part of the final process of judgment (2:8).

As soon as the lawless one is revealed, he will meet his doom (2:8). Paul alludes to Isaiah 11:4 (11:1 predicts the coming ruler of the line of David). The conquest will occur at the time of Christ's coming (2:1), the counterpoint to the coming of the lawless one (2:9). Christ's "splendor" means doom for the lawless one (cf. Zeph. 2:11). The power of the lawless one is satanically inspired (2:9). The word "works" in 2:9 suggests supernatural activity (2:11; 1 Thess. 2:13; 2 Thess. 2:7) that comes from Satan (1 Thess. 2:18; 3:5) and accredits the lawless one in the eyes of many (2:10–11; cf. Mark 13:22; Rev. 13:13–15). Paul seeks to guard the Thessalonians from deception that can come when people see this figure's "signs and wonders" (cf. Acts 2:22; 2 Cor. 12:12; Heb. 2:4), which are false ("that serve the lie"). False miracles were part of a number of religions, including the imperial cult (cf. Rev. 13:13–14; 19:20).

The end goal of the lawless one is to deceive, and the counterpoint to his deception is the truth of the gospel. He comes using "all the ways that wickedness deceives those who are perishing. They perish because they refused to love the truth and so be saved" (2:10). Those who are perishing are those who have not been saved (1 Cor. 1:18; 2 Cor. 2:15; 4:3) since they did not respond in obedience to the summons of the gospel (2 Thess. 1:8), which is here called "the truth" (2:14; Eph. 1:13; Col. 1:5). Eternal destiny is dependent on one's response to the gospel of Christ, and refusing this truth opens a person to deception. Paul adds, "For this reason God sends them a powerful delusion so that they will believe the lie" (2:11). "Powerful" is the same word translated "work" in 2:9 and again speaks of a supernatural activity that is satanic and, according to 2:10, deceives those who do not receive the truth of the gospel. God, in his judgment, sometimes gives people over to the very sin and error they embrace (Ps. 81:11–12; Rom. 1:24, 26, 28; 11:8; 2 Tim. 4:4). In a way similar to this verse, some Old Testament texts note how God may use malignant spirits in his judgment (2 Sam. 24:1; 1 Kings 22:19–23; 1 Chron. 21:1; Ezek. 14:9). The end result is "that all will be condemned who have not believed the truth but have delighted in wickedness" (2:12). The choice is between the truth of the gospel, with all its moral implications, and disobedience (Rom. 2:8; 1 Cor. 13:6; 2 Thess. 1:8). Paul has moved from speaking of the judgment of the lawless one in 2:8 to the judgment of those who have rejected the gospel and embraced the error.

2:13–14: The second thanksgiving. The second thanksgiving begins almost identically to 1:3: "But we ought always to thank God for you, brothers and sisters loved by the Lord" (2:13a). In this verse, Paul draws a sharp contrast between them and the ones who reject the truth and perish (2:10–12). The readers are "loved by the Lord," the love of God being the foundation of their election (Deut. 4:37; 7:7–8; 10:15; Ps. 47:4; 78:68; Isa. 42:1; Matt. 12:18; Rom. 11:28; Eph. 1:4–5; Col. 3:12; 1 Thess. 1:4). The cause of the thanksgiving is this divine selection: "because God chose you as firstfruits to be saved through the sanctifying work of the Spirit and through belief in the truth" (2:13b). Calling them "firstfruits" alludes to the first portion of a harvest or the firstborn of animals, which were consecrated exclusively to God (Exod. 23:19; Num. 15:17–21; Deut. 12:6, 17). The election of God is that they might be saved instead of experiencing the divine wrath (1 Thess. 5:9) and perishing (2 Thess. 2:10, 12). God accomplishes his salvation through sanctifying them, a state differentiated from those who reject the truth of the gospel (2:12). The process of sanctification begins at conversion (1 Pet. 1:2) but continues throughout the life of the believer (Rom. 15:16; 1 Cor. 6:11; 1 Thess. 5:23). The Thessalonians became recipients of God's salvation as they responded in faith to the truth (compare 2:10 with 2:13), that is, the gospel of Christ (2 Thess. 1:10; Eph. 1:13; Col. 1:5).

God's election (2:13) is linked with his call (Rom. 9:12; Gal. 5:8; 1 Thess. 2:12; 4:7; 5:24), which came to the Thessalonians through the preaching of the gospel: "He called you to this through our gospel, that you might share in the glory of our Lord Jesus Christ" (2:14). The calling was not simply an invitation but rather a summons, to which they responded in obedient faith. This divine summons came via the proclamation of the gospel. God engaged them as they heard the message and responded to it as God's word (1 Thess. 2:13). God's purpose in this is that they might receive honor, or glory, which comes from the Lord Jesus Christ and which he possesses (cf. 1 Thess. 2:12). While glory is the final outcome of salvation (Rom. 8:17–21; 1 Cor. 2:7; Heb. 2:10; 1 Pet. 5:1, 4), this statement also has sociological implications. It is the fame, renown, or honor that a person receives, and for the Thessalonians this glory becomes the counterpoint to the dishonor they endure in their city.

2:15: Exhortation to be steadfast. The Thessalonians are called to "stand firm and hold fast to the teachings" they have received (2:15), through both the preaching they heard and the letter the apostles previously sent them (that is, 1 Thessalonians). The verse reflects a common exhortation given to new converts (see Rom. 14:4; 1 Cor. 16:13; Gal. 5:1; Phil. 1:27; 4:1) to stay stable and faithful to the Lord in the face of opposition (see 1 Thess. 3:8). The particular concern here is their continued adherence to the teaching they received (2:2, 5; cf. 1 Thess. 4:1–2). The teachings were the sacred apostolic tradition handed down to them in the gospel (Rom. 6:17; 1 Cor. 11:23; 15:3; Jude 3). These traditions were not of human but divine origin and, therefore, authoritative (1 Thess. 2:13).

2:16–17: The first prayer. These verses constitute the first prayer of the letter, directed equally to the Lord Jesus Christ and the Father (2 Thess. 1:2, 8, 12; 3:5): "May our Lord Jesus Christ himself and God our Father, who loved us and by his grace gave us eternal encouragement and good hope . . ." (2:16). They are loved (2:13) by Christ and the Father, the ones who give them comfort, or rather, encouragement in light of their persecutions (Acts 11:23; 14:22; 15:32; 16:40; 20:1; 1 Thess. 3:2). The aid God gives is not just for the moment but is eternal. The hope, a constant theme in these epistles (see 1 Thess. 1:3; 2:19; 5:8), is described as "good." This was far from Greek hopes, which were often no more than foreboding about the future. The Christian's hope is good.

The prayer is that the Lord Jesus Christ and the Father would "encourage your hearts and strengthen you in every good deed and word" (2:17; see 1 Thess. 3:13). The first verb, "encourage," in combination with "strengthen," describes the ministry to those facing opposition for their faith (Acts 15:32; 1 Thess. 3:2). God engages in this very ministry, which enables them "in every good deed and word" (2 Cor. 9:8; 2 Thess. 1:11). Their words and deeds are inspired by their encouragement and stability (Col. 3:17; cf. Luke 24:19; Rom. 15:18), the concern being for their mission as well as their continuance in the faith.

B. The final instructions (3:1–15). At the beginning of the final part of the letter, the apostles request prayer (3:1–2). Their concern is not simply for their personal needs but for the mission of the church. This and the following wish prayer (3:5) and intervening material

(3:3–4) form the transition to the section of the letter containing Paul's principal exhortations (3:6–15).

3:1–5: Request for prayer and the second prayer. The exhortation in 3:1 is the same as in 1 Thessalonians 5:25, but here with more specifics about the needs of the apostles. Paul frequently solicited such prayers from the churches (e.g., Rom. 15:30–32; 2 Cor. 1:11; Eph. 6:19–20). He and his companions ask for prayer "that the message of the Lord may spread rapidly and be honored, just as it was with you." The message of the Lord is the gospel (see Acts 8:25; 13:44, 48–49; 15:35–36; 19:10; 1 Thess. 1:8), which they want to "run" (taken from Ps. 147:15), making rapid progress in its extension through the world. The prayer is also that this message might be held in honor (Acts 13:48) instead of being dishonored and despised, as it was in so many communities (Acts 28:22). To hold that message in honor would imply its acceptance, as it was received and honored by the Thessalonians (1 Thess. 1:6; 2:13). The imagery is drawn from a race where the athlete is victorious and is honored. Paul follows the prayer request for gospel victory with the request "that we may be delivered from wicked and evil people, for not everyone has faith" (3:2). In 1 Thessalonians Paul occasionally speaks of the sufferings that he has endured in his ministry (1 Thess. 1:6; 2:2, 15–16). He is looking for deliverance or rescue (2 Cor. 1:10; 2 Tim. 3:11; 4:17–18) from "wicked and evil" people (Luke 23:41; 1 Thess. 5:22; 2 Thess. 3:3). Their opposition to the apostles is a sign that they do not have faith.

Paul and his companions remember the Thessalonians' sufferings: "But the Lord is faithful, and he will strengthen you and protect you from the evil one" (3:3). In the ancient world, patrons brought clients into their care, so to be "in the *fides* [Latin for "faith"]" of a patron meant to be under their protection. Here the Lord is viewed as the protecting patron who will strengthen his people in the face of opposition (see Luke 22:32; Acts 18:23; Rom. 16:25;

1 Thess. 3:2, 13; 1 Pet. 5:10; 2 Pet. 1:12; Rev. 3:2), which is satanically motivated. The verse echoes the Lord's Prayer, in which Satan is called "the evil one" (Matt. 6:13; 13:19; John 17:15; Eph. 6:16; 1 John 2:13–14). As in 2:13–15, Paul follows the statement about God's care with a word about their responsibility: "We have confidence in the Lord that you are doing and will continue to do the things we command" (3:4). Within this indicative sentence about God's work of strengthening and guarding them, we find the implicit exhortation to carry on doing what they are already doing. Paul's confidence is in the Lord (see 2 Cor. 2:3; 7:16; Gal. 5:10; Philem. 21), who enables them as they face grave danger.

Paul's second prayer for them (see 2:16–17) says: "May the Lord direct your hearts into God's love and Christ's perseverance" (3:5; echoing 1 Chron. 29:18; Prov. 21:1). The idea is to lead or direct someone's steps or way (1 Thess. 3:11) in divine moral guidance. These were loved by the Lord (2:13, 16). "The love of God" may be understood as either an objective genitive ("love for God") or a possessive genitive ("God's love," as in NIV). The prayer is either that they, too, will love God (as John 5:42; 1 John 3:17) or that this love from God (Rom. 5:5; 8:39) would motivate them. "Christ's perseverance" may be the steadfastness that looks to Christ (as opposed to turning away from him), or the prayer may be that they follow the example of Christ in his perseverance (Rom. 15:4–5; Heb. 12:2–3).

3:6–15: The disorderly. Some within the Thessalonian church were not working and had become dependent on others to sustain them (3:10–12). They were "disorderly" (KJV; NIV: "idle and disruptive") in that they did not heed the apostles' example (3:7–9) and verbal instruction (3:10). Some suggest that the reason the Thessalonians were not working to earn their bread was that they believed that the day of the Lord had come or was at hand (2 Thess. 2:1–2). Paul, however, does not directly link the present discussion with the church's confusion about the end times. More likely, these believers had, from the beginning, resisted the apostolic instruction to abandon their status as dependent clients of rich patrons (see 1 Thess. 4:11–12; 5:14). Paul's teaching here does not, however, absolve the church from its responsibilities toward those in true need (1 Thess. 4:9–10).

This relief from a funerary monument (50 BC) depicts the family prominently in the foreground while placing their slaves in the background, to show the difference in social status. These family members of high status may represent the type of wealthy patrons upon whom some believers in Thessalonica had become dependent (see 2 Thess. 3:6–15).

The first apostolic exhortation (3:6) echoes the weighty authority found in 1 Thessalonians 4:1–8: "In the name of the Lord Jesus Christ, we command you, brothers and sisters, to keep away from every believer who is idle and disruptive and does not live according to the teaching you received from us." Separation from disobedient members was a principal form of church discipline (Matt. 18:17; Rom. 16:17; 1 Cor. 5:9–13), though here it is not exercised as excommunication (3:14–15). In a collectivist society where honor is bound up with membership in the group, separation from the group would be a source of great shame and motivation to correct one's conduct. The exhortation regards those who are idle (as in 1 Thess. 5:14), a term that does not mean "lazy" but rather "out of line," "disorderly," or "undisciplined." Certain Thessalonians did not live according to the apostolic teaching or tradition (see 2:15) given them through deed and word (3:7–10).

Here, as elsewhere, Paul calls the believers to imitate his and the others' conduct (3:7). Learning by imitation was prescribed by the ancients, especially in the sphere of moral teaching about virtue and vice (3:9; Phil. 3:17; 1 Tim. 4:12; Titus 2:7; 1 Pet. 5:3). Examples were considered more persuasive than words. Paul reminds the church that he and his associates were not idle, that is, they did not lead a disorderly life with

regard to work. As 3:8 says, "nor did we eat anyone's food without paying for it. On the contrary, we worked night and day, laboring and toiling so that we would not be a burden to any of you." Previously the apostles reminded the church that they were not greedy and did not place any financial burden on them (1 Thess. 2:7, 9). Paul also raised his voice against any who were motivated by greed (1 Tim. 3:3, 8; Titus 1:7; Acts 20:33; 1 Tim. 6:9–10; Heb. 13:5; 1 Pet. 5:2; 2 Pet. 2:3). Though the apostles labored hard (Acts 18:1–5; 1 Thess. 2:9) and paid for their own food, they also received support from the Philippian congregation (Phil. 4:15–16).

Paul taught that payment for Christian ministry was acceptable (1 Cor. 9:7–14; 1 Tim. 5:17–18; Gal. 6:6; see also Matt. 10:10), though in order to become a model for the church to follow he did not take advantage of that privilege (3:9; 1 Cor. 9:15). Paul distanced himself from the practices of many itinerant philosophers of the era whose public speaking was motivated by greed for gain. His example matched his repeated exhortation to the church, "For even when we were with you, we gave you this rule: 'The one who is unwilling to work shall not eat'" (3:10). The rule given was an authoritative command (3:4, 12), backed by divine authority (3:6). Paul's exhortation was about a person who is able to work and yet "is unwilling," not those who, for whatever reason, could not work to earn their bread. Teaching about labor was part of the ethical instruction of the church (Eph. 4:28; 1 Thess. 4:11–12). Paul also absolves patrons of their obligations toward their clients. The teaching, however, does not absolve the church of its responsibility toward the needy (see also 1 John 3:17; James 2:14–17).

Next follows a second exhortation (3:11–12). Paul and his companions somehow heard that some members of the church were disorderly, not following the apostolic example and teaching (3:11a). They finally state how they were disorderly: "They are not busy; they are busybodies" (3:11b). "Not busy" is better translated "not working." In a play on words in the Greek, Paul says they are busybodies, which suggests that they were meddlesome in other people's affairs, perhaps as they took up the causes of their patrons (see 1 Thess. 4:11–12). Paul again buttresses his exhortation with an appeal to divine authority (as 3:6; 1 Thess. 4:1–8): "Such people we command and urge in the Lord Jesus Christ to settle down and earn the food they eat" (3:12). The call to quietness ("to settle down") appears also in 1 Thessalonians 4:11. In the literature of the era it described people who were respectable and did not cause problems in the community, in contrast to those who were socially disruptive. Paul wants the believers to earn their own bread as he showed them in his example (3:7–8). This means of support causes no social scandal.

On the other hand, the church should continue to do good and support those in genuine need, never flagging in this responsibility. A third exhortation is thus offered: "And as for you, brothers and sisters, never tire of doing what is good" (3:13; cf. Gal. 6:9–10; 1 Thess. 4:9–10). Continuing to support those in need, as well as the mission, is what is good (Phil. 4:14–15). They should not become weary and abandon their efforts (Luke 18:1; 2 Cor. 4:1, 16; Gal. 6:9; Eph. 3:13) in helping these.

Finally, Paul calls on the community to take disciplinary action: "Take special note of anyone who does not obey our instruction in this letter. Do not associate with them, in order that they may feel ashamed" (3:14). The verb "take special note" suggests disapproval and not just recognition of the problem. Such disorderly members, who had received repeated instruction and warning, were to be excluded even from the common meal of the church. These would be fully disenfranchised, and in a collectivist society the impact would have been devastating. The hope was that they would experience social shame (1 Cor. 4:14; Titus 2:8), which, in a society that valued honor above all else, would have been a very effective means of social control. The church bears a responsibility to guide the conduct of its members as the group supports the common Christian virtues and helps each to avoid vice.

The situation here is not exactly parallel to 1 Corinthians 5:9–11. Here the disorderly person remains a member of the community of salvation: "Yet do not regard them as an enemy, but warn them as you would a fellow believer" (3:15). Enemies were not simply tolerated during this era but rather became the object of ill will and action. Unruly members should be admonished (1 Thess. 5:12, 14) as those who are part of the family of God. Such counsel and warning aims to change the conduct of a person (Acts 20:31; Rom. 15:14; 1 Cor. 4:14; Eph. 6:4; Col. 1:28). There was a corporate responsibility toward the errant member.

4. The Third Prayer and Final Greetings (3:16–18)

The letter closes with a prayer for the church: "Now may the Lord of peace himself give you peace at all times and in every way" (3:16a). The peace they pray for from the Lord of peace

(John 14:27; Rom. 15:33; Phil. 4:9; 1 Thess. 5:23) is not an inward emotion but a social virtue that defines how they are to live together in community (2 Cor. 13:11; 1 Thess. 5:13) and how they are to live in relation to the unbelievers around them (Rom. 12:18; 1 Cor. 7:15; Heb. 12:14). This blessing flows from the character of God. The apostles also bless the church, saying, "The Lord be with all of you" (3:16b; Rom. 15:33; Phil. 4:9). The Lord is the one who is ever present with his people (Matt. 28:20; Acts 18:10). In the midst of their troubles and confusion, they are not left alone.

Though Paul wrote the letter with the collaboration of his companions, he gives a final greeting in his own handwriting (3:17). Ancient authors commonly used secretaries to write letters for them but then would add a final note in their own hand (1 Cor. 16:21; Gal. 6:11; Col. 4:18; Philem. 19). Some ancient letters include an obvious change in penmanship without there being any indication in the text that the pen has passed from scribe to author. Paul's greeting would serve as a seal of authenticity (see 2:2).

The letter ends as did the first: "The grace of our Lord Jesus Christ be with you all" (3:18).

Select Bibliography

Beale, G. K. *1–2 Thessalonians.* IVP New Testament Commentary. Downers Grove, IL: InterVarsity, 2003.

Bruce, F. F. *1 and 2 Thessalonians.* Word Biblical Commentary. Nashville: Thomas Nelson, 1982.

Green, Gene L. *1 and 2 Thessalonians.* Pillar Commentary. Grand Rapids: Eerdmans, 2002.

Holmes, Michael. *1 & 2 Thessalonians.* NIV Application Commentary. Grand Rapids: Zondervan, 1998.

Malherbe, Abraham. *1 Thessalonians.* Anchor Bible. New Haven: Yale University Press, 2004.

Marshall, I. Howard. *1 and 2 Thessalonians.* New Century Bible Commentary. Grand Rapids: Eerdmans, 1983.

Morris, Leon. *The First and Second Epistles to the Thessalonians.* New International Commentary on the New Testament. Grand Rapids: Eerdmans, 1991.

Stott, John R. W. *The Message of 1 and 2 Thessalonians.* The Bible Speaks Today. Downers Grove, IL: InterVarsity, 1991.

Wanamaker, Charles. *The Epistles to the Thessalonians.* New International Greek Testament Commentary. Grand Rapids: Eerdmans, 1990.

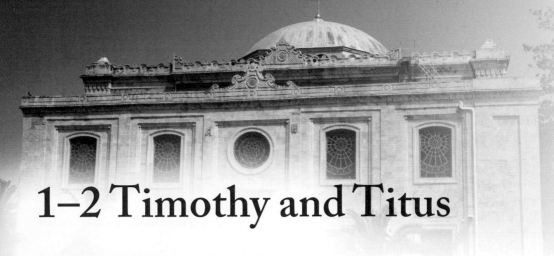

1–2 Timothy and Titus

Reggie M. Kidd

Introduction

The letters to Timothy and Titus, called the Pastoral Epistles, raise questions about the legacy of the apostle Paul. Evangelical scholars and some mainstream conservative scholars believe these writings provide Paul's own ideas and applications for the next generation of church leaders. Other mainstream scholars tend to think the Pastorals came from the second or third generation of the Pauline movement and represent a falling away from Paul's original vision.

This commentary treats the Pastoral Epistles as Paul's own explanation of his main theological values, which he designs to reflect the culture of his heirs in ministry.

Distinctive Features

The Pastorals share a range of common features with the earlier letters of Paul but stand apart in several respects.

First, they are letters written to Paul's co-workers as individuals instead of to a church or house church. (Philemon, by contrast, was written to a house church—see Philem. 2). Further, the Pastorals were written to perhaps the most "Greek" of Paul's protégés: though half Jewish, Timothy had not even been circumcised at infancy; and the Gentile Titus was pointedly never circumcised (Gal. 2:3).

Second, the Pastorals show a distinctive writing style, marked by a smoother flow of sentences and less complicated grammar.

Third, the vocabulary shows more Greek influence. A third of the Pastorals' vocabulary does not appear in the earlier writings of Paul. Words otherwise not used in the New Testament occur at the rate of about four to five per page in the earlier letters, but at the rate of about thirteen per page in the Pastorals. Some of this vocabulary is common to Greek moral and theological writings. Worthy of mention are the following: "godliness/piety," "appearance" (instead of Paul's more characteristic "presence"), and "healthy/sound." Jewish writers like Philo of Alexandria, aiming at a Greek readership, had already begun using many of the terms that distinguish the Pastorals from Paul's earlier letters.

It is interesting to note that Luke (Paul's traveling companion, lone associate during the writing of 2 Timothy, and author of Luke-Acts) shares much of this vocabulary, lending support to the possibility that Luke assisted Paul with these letters. Two examples: first, Paul's earlier letters denounce "greed" (1 Cor. 6:10; 1 Thess. 2:5), but the Pastorals and Luke denounce "love of money" (1 Tim. 6:10; 2 Tim. 3:2; cf. Luke 12:15; 16:14). Second, of the other New Testament writers, only Luke ("the beloved physician") uses the Greek term from which we get "hygienic" to refer to the spiritual aspect of Jesus's healing ministry (Luke 5:17; 15:27). The Pastorals use the same term to stress that doctrine should be not merely correct but also "healthy" or "sound" (1 Tim. 1:10; 2 Tim. 4:3; Titus 1:9; 2:1).

Fourth, while Paul mentions "overseers" (sometimes called "bishops") and "deacons" in Philippians 1:1, in 1 Timothy and Titus he gives much greater focus to church office (in the case of 1 Timothy and Titus) and to the character required for office (when 2 Timothy is added).

Fifth, a different strategy for dealing with troublesome teaching or behavior emerges. Instead of making his case with the community (as in most earlier letters) or even praying his case before the communities (as in Ephesians 1–3), Paul reminds his co-workers of the basic truths they are to press home. He does so in condensed creedlike statements (1 Tim. 2:3–7; 3:16; 2 Tim. 1:8–10; Titus 2:11–14; 3:4–7). He is not instructing churches in things they do not know. Rather, he is reminding protégés of how to apply teaching with which they are quite familiar.

Sixth, the Pastorals amplify values from the earlier letters. For instance, Paul's "let us do good to all, especially to those who are of the household of faith" (Gal. 6:10 NKJV) expands to "be ready to do whatever is good" in public life (Titus 3:1). Strikingly, earlier arguments against "works of the law" give way to an encouragement to do "good works." In Galatians and Romans, "works" (plural) are almost always "works of the law" and are almost always bad (Rom. 2:6 is controversial). In those earlier letters Paul does say "faith working through love" is good (Gal. 5:6 RSV, NASB), and he can use the singular noun "work" in a positive way (e.g., "work of faith"; 1 Thess. 1:3 KJV, RSV). By Ephesians (written during Paul's first imprisonment), Paul first reminds readers that salvation is "not by works" and then opens new ground by affirming that believers have been (re-)created in Christ Jesus "for good works" (Eph. 2:8–10 RSV, NASB). The Pastorals repeat Paul's principle of "not by works" (Titus 3:5 KJV; cf. 2 Tim. 1:9) and extend Ephesians' commendation of "good works" or "noble works" (1 Tim. 5:10, 25; 6:18; Titus 2:7, 14; 3:8, 14 KJV, ESV); but these letters accentuate the role of "good works" more than any of the earlier letters (see comments on 1 Tim. 3:14–16; Titus 2:1–10).

The Pastorals in the Early Church

Although the Pastorals show some differences from Paul's earlier letters, the early church received them, almost unanimously, as being written by Paul. When Peter acknowledges the authority of the writings of "our dear brother Paul," he does so in view of the way Paul expounded the Lord's "patience" unto "salvation" (2 Pet. 3:15–16), terms that are joined in Paul's writings only at 1 Timothy 1:15–16. The theology in the writings of Clement, Ignatius, and Polycarp shows evidence of influence from the Pastorals. The single curiosity from the early church is the Pastorals' apparent exclusion from the earliest manuscript of Paul's letters, the Chester Beatty Papyrus 46 (ca. AD 200). Because of its own writer's preference for asceticism, the forged apocryphal *Acts of Paul and Thecla* took dead aim at the Pastorals. The heretic Marcion, teaching that there was a split between an evil creator God of the Old Testament and a good redeemer God of the New Testament, eliminated the Pastorals because they affirmed creation. Gnostics ignored them because the Pastorals' opposition to "falsely called knowledge" hit close to home (1 Tim. 6:20–21).

Accounting for the Differences

Evangelical scholarship has resisted approaches that diminish the Pastorals' voice and authorship. Older advocates of the theory of a different author maintained that the Pastorals' author sought to honor Paul by employing an innocent, even transparent literary device by writing under Paul's name. However, evangelical scholarship has noted that Christian, Jewish, and pagan writers at the time consistently denounced forgeries, especially when it came to letters. More recent advocates of a different author frankly maintain the Pastorals were a deliberate fabrication. Evangelical scholarship balks at the notion that such an amoral conscience would lie behind accepted scriptural documents that claim to speak for "God, who does not lie" (Titus 1:2), in advocating "sound doctrine" (1 Tim. 1:10; 2 Tim. 4:3). Moreover, evangelical scholars doubt that readers close to the events and at home with the language would have fallen for such a ruse. The tendency, then, among evangelicals is to accept the similarities to the earlier letters to be a signal of the genuineness of Paul's authorship. They believe either that the differences are attributable to the fact that Paul was not under the burden (the way a fabricator would doubtless have been) of trying to sound like himself at every turn, or that some of the distinctive wording comes from a secretary.

If these letters are authentic, it is probably reasonable to assume that Paul was released from the house arrest of Acts 28 and ministered in the eastern Mediterranean, during which time he wrote 1 Timothy and Titus. Arrested again, he was sent to Rome, where he was martyred (per *1 Clement* 5.7), but not before he wrote 2 Timothy.

The principal question advocates of Paul's authorship have had to answer is, Has Paul lost some of the intensity evident in his earlier letters? The rejoinder is, Can we assume what Paul might say under the circumstances presented in these letters? If the apostle recognizes that his own course is near its end and that his gospel has established a toehold in European culture, letters precisely like these are altogether suitable advice to his closest—and most "European"—protégés for carrying on his legacy.

Outline—1 Timothy

Commentary

In 1 Timothy, Paul addresses the challenges facing an established church. He directs Timothy to put down false teaching from rivals—perhaps even leaders—within the church (see Acts 20:30). The letter does not deal with the heresy directly. Paul's interest, rather, lies in structuring the community in such a way as to promote true godliness. The church is the "pillar and foundation of the truth" (3:15).

1. Salutation (1:1–2)

Timothy is under attack. Appropriately, then, Paul begins by calling attention to the fact that it is only by the command of God that he himself is an apostle. In so doing, Paul underlines not only his but also Timothy's authority. Paul's primary purpose in this letter (see 1 Tim. 3:14–15) is to bring the church together as God's family. Thus he begins by recognizing Timothy as his own true son in the faith. (For Paul's becoming "father" to Timothy, see Acts 16:1–3.)

Three times Paul stresses that we are to place our hope in God alone and not in human devices (4:1–10, not in harsh regimens of self-denial; 5:5, not in our human family structures; 6:17, not in wealth). Significantly, Paul calls Christ Jesus our hope. God alone saves, and he does that through his divine Son.

Paul normally begins his letters, as he does here, by substituting "grace" for the typical Hellenistic "Greetings" and by offering the Jewish blessing: "peace." Distinctive of his two letters to Timothy is his insertion of "mercy," anticipating the way he says his own life demonstrates God's mercy (1:15–16).

2. Law and Grace (1:3–20)

A. Love over law (1:3–7). Timothy's mission is to make sure that side issues ("myths and endless genealogies . . . meaningless talk" [1:4, 6]) or contradictory teachings (law keeping, sexual and dietary restrictions) do not dilute the good news of God's saving mercy. For Paul, it is almost as bad to go beyond Scripture (1 Cor. 4:6) as to contradict it. Thus, his instructions are twofold: to put down "false doctrines" (literally "different teaching") and to advance "God's work—which is by faith" (1:4). The work Paul has in mind consists of two things: first, the way God has brought redemption through his Son (Eph. 1:10; 1 Tim. 2:3–6; 2 Tim. 1:9–10;

Titus 3:4–7), and second, the way the church as God's household displays that redemption through right relationships (1 Tim. 3:14–16; Titus 1:1–10).

Timothy is to contend for the faith so that *love* may flourish. While the opponents promote teaching that appeals to intellectual pride and moral rule keeping, Paul teaches a gospel that gives people a new inner nature. When the incarnated and vindicated Jesus is believed on (1 Tim. 3:16), he enables people to live generously, out of a "pure heart and a good conscience and a sincere faith" (1:5).

B. The point of the law (1:8–11). The law is good but cannot replace conscience as a guide to behavior. It can neither cover every situation in which love must be expressed, nor, as Paul taught the Galatians, enable the obedience it requires. As Paul will teach in verses 12–17, the inward transformation necessary for living according to God's will begins with an experience

Curetes Street, one of the main thoroughfares in ancient Ephesus, near the ruins of the Memmius Monument. Paul urges Timothy to stay in Ephesus in order to "command certain people not to teach false doctrines any longer" (1 Tim. 1:3).

of his mercy. Paul will build on this, teaching in subsequent chapters that the place where the Spirit shapes our moral responsiveness is within a well-ordered and rightly governed community of faith.

How then may one use the law "properly" (literally "lawfully," an artful wordplay)? The law informs the conscience by clarifying the kind of people we are not to be. People who need the law are outside its limits: "not for the righteous but for lawbreakers and rebels" (1:9). Paul lists four terms invoking the first four of the Ten Commandments, then three terms invoking the commandment against murder, two terms covering the commandment against sexual immorality, one term covering theft, and two covering false witness. The way Paul uses what would be to him extreme examples of law violation is striking: not just murderers but patricides and matricides; not just those who engage in sex outside marriage but males who have sex with males; not just thieves but "man-stealers" (either the NIV's "slave traders" or the NASB's generic "kidnappers"). Instead of the concluding "you shall not covet" (which covers the heart), Paul closes with a sweeping "whatever else is contrary to the sound doctrine" (1:10). The law reveals the sickness of the soul; sound doctrine promotes the health of the soul. Gospel-centered teaching points us to "the gospel concerning the glory of the blessed God" (1:11), preparing us, as Paul says elsewhere, to take on "an eternal weight of glory" (2 Cor. 4:17 RSV, NASB). The law's purpose is to drive us to God's mercy. Paul next uses his own life as an example.

C. Paul as trophy of grace (1:12–17). Refusing at first to believe that Jesus was the living personification of Israel's hopes ("I acted in ignorance and unbelief" [1:13]), Paul showed himself to be among those who were not righteous. Despite his claim to zeal for God (see Gal. 1:13–14), his hatred for Jesus had numbered him among those the law condemned. His language of self-condemnation here is exceptionally strong. His opposition to Jesus made him a "blasphemer" against God. He calls himself "a violent man," using a term suggesting insolence and arrogance.

Solemnly, Paul names himself "worst of sinners" (1:16). When writing his early, "great epistles," Paul felt it sufficient to acknowledge himself "least of the apostles" (1 Cor. 15:9). Writing later from prison and meditating on the comprehensive lordship of Christ, Paul moves himself further down the ladder: "I am less than the least of all the Lord's people" (Eph. 3:8). Now, urging radical grace over proud speculation and moralism, he points to himself as exhibit A in God's program of reclaiming a hopelessly ruined race.

In chapter 2, Paul will refer to the process by which Christ became our ransom (2:5). Here at 1:14, however, Paul emphasizes that the personal qualities of Jesus (the "faith" in God and "love" toward others that are "in Christ Jesus") subsequently become ours by grace.

Because Paul sees himself as a trophy of God's grace, not only does love follow but so does worship—thus, his doxology in verse 17.

D. What is at stake (1:18–20). Paul follows his brief doxology by returning to his commandment to Timothy (see 1:5), putting it in terms of a call to arms: "fight the good fight" (NIV "fight the battle well"). As 2 Timothy will make clear to us, courage will be necessary for Paul's young co-worker (see especially 2 Tim. 1:7).

Timothy would do well to keep in mind his own need for the same "faith and a good conscience" (1:19) he is to commend to others. Moreover, he should keep before himself the vivid image of two false teachers, Hymenaeus and Alexander, who "have suffered shipwreck with regard to the faith" and whom Paul has put under discipline (1:20).

3. Prayer and Worship (2:1–15)

A. The prayer of all for all (2:1–7). When Paul thinks of the church gathered, he thinks of its being a praying community. He calls for prayer for all people and for those in authority. The short-term goal of the prayer for authorities is that "we may live peaceful and quiet lives" (2:2). However, this is not the "peace and quiet" of middle-class complacency. Paul wants the best platform possible for pressing upon all people that God "wants" them "to be saved and to come to a knowledge of the truth" (2:4). As inevitable as persecution is (2 Tim. 3:12), Paul nonetheless believes that a better climate for the church's witness is one of political and social peace.

Paul differs from his opponents in seeing the scope of Christ's mission, and thus the church's, as being worldwide. That difference comes to elegant expression in the theological support Paul provides for his prayer for all people: "one God and one mediator" (2:5a). Paul means all people (see also Rom. 3:29–30) have access to God's salvation (note: 3:1, believers pray for all; 3:4, God wants all to be saved; 3:6, Christ gave his life for all). There are hints in the Old Testament that God would save the world through a single individual (see "a man" in the Greek Old Testament at Num. 24:7, 17; Isa. 19:20). This offer of salvation is finally available through Christ's incarnation ("the man Christ Jesus" [2:5b]) and his redemptive death ("who gave himself as a ransom" [2:6]—see also Matt. 20:28; Gal. 2:20). Paul closes this section by noting that Jesus is God's own witness to his love for humanity, a witness that has come at the fulfillment of God's timetable. Thus, Paul calls the church at Ephesus to take up its part in his ministry to the Gentiles through prayer and proclamation, aligning themselves with God's purposes to save people of every race.

B. Men and women at worship (2:8–15). Having issued his appeal for prayer,

Paul turns to specific behaviors in worship. The statements about salvation have been for all people. The directives that follow are gender specific, though, clearly, some instructions apply equally to all (e.g., "holy hands" and "good deeds"). Throughout, Paul's concern is that believers support the church's mission by living "peaceful and quiet lives in all godliness and holiness" (2:2).

Men are called to holiness and peace (2:8). A picture of men raising angry fists at one another over who is to teach and what is to be taught needs to yield to a picture of men lifting cleansed and peaceful hands in prayer. The picture recalls Psalm 134:2, with its call for temple servants to bless the Lord in the night. But a reference to Malachi 1:11's "in every place" sets the men's prayers in the new context of God's promise to bring salvation to the nations.

Women are called to modesty and to good deeds (2:9–10). The "also" of verse 9 indicates that women no less than men participate in the praying church's continuation of the mediator's work in reclaiming the earth for God. But no less disruptive—and thus subversive—of the church's mission than some men's quarrelsomeness is some Ephesian women's flashy attire.

Paul seems to speak here to an incursion into the church of a fairly widespread phenomenon in his day, referred to in recent scholarship as the rise of "the new Roman woman." Contemporary sources (literature such as Seneca, Plutarch, Epictetus, Philo; nonliterary indicators like statues, frescoes, coins) indicate many women in the Roman Empire were gaining economic independence, assuming greater roles in the public sector, and overthrowing traditional sexual taboos and domestic arrangements (including practicing contraception and abortion). Lavish hairstyles,

The head from a statue of Julia Titi (AD 61–91), daughter of the emperor Titus and mistress to her uncle Domitian. Notice the elaborate hairstyle. The diadem may have contained precious gems, and the complete statue would have been adorned with earrings and a necklace. Paul instructs women believers not to follow this trend in fashion but to dress "with decency and propriety" (1 Tim. 2:9).

jewelry, and self-promoting attire were emblems of the new stance (see Winter). Deftly, Paul invites Christian women to participate in nobler virtues.

Verse 11's injunction to silence is a readily understandable requirement for all students of the Word—male as well as female. Evangelicals have taken verse 12's prohibition of women's speech in a number of ways.

Some evangelicals believe the prohibition is absolute. The difficulty with this view is that Paul seems to endorse women ministering through speech in the congregation in 1 Corinthians 11:5; moreover, from Acts 2:17 and 21:9 it appears that the New Testament church was familiar with the prophetic ministry of women.

Other evangelicals believe Paul teaches as a basic principle that in Christ's new creation there is no "male and female" (2 Cor. 5:17; Gal. 3:28). They claim that Paul's prohibition here is secondary or temporary. Noting that in verse 12 Paul employs a Greek verb (*authenteō*) that until this time is exceedingly rare, these evangelicals interpret him as forbidding teaching "in a domineering way." (The verb *authenteō* is controversial. Some commentators think it has the sense of "to domineer"; others argue it simply means "to have authority.") They argue that Paul excludes wealthy and pushy women, who, in this particular situation (1) declare themselves beyond domestic responsibilities, (2) wrongly interpret Scripture, and (3) contradict Paul's teachings.

The difficulty with this view is that Paul's argument is not primarily situational but theological. It is altogether apparent that in his estimation some sort of unholy convergence of factors has emerged in Ephesus. Though specifics of the situation remain elusive, the problem Paul addresses involves a combination of the misinterpretation of Scripture (1:3–11), wealthy women (2:8–9), teachers who preach freedom from domesticity (4:1–5), and a teaching that the resurrection has already happened (2 Tim. 2:18). Important as these factors are, Paul nonetheless bases his reserve on his narrative

understanding of creation and the lingering effects of the fall in the era of redemption (1 Tim. 2:13–14).

Still other evangelicals believe that Paul extends to women permission to participate as sharers in the priesthood of all believers in the ministry of the Word in the congregation (Col. 3:16, including the praying and prophesying of 1 Cor. 11:5; see also Philip, who had seven prophesying daughters). However, they hold that when it comes to deliberating over what has been taught in a mixed-gender setting (1 Cor. 14:31–35) or to setting forth something like a formal teaching of the church, Paul stipulates male leadership. (These commentators interpret 1 Tim. 2:12's *authenteō* to mean "to have authority." See the comment on *authenteō* above.)

The difficulty with this view lies in understanding how in practice to embody an ethic that values and distinguishes women's gifts for public ministry. Overall, it seems that the difficulties of this view are the least formidable. If this view is correct, it will be understandable that some evangelical communities will struggle with accommodating the following aspects of Paul's theology: he teaches that there is no male and female, embraces women's prophesying in the assembly, names two women among those co-workers who have struggled alongside him in gospel ministry (Euodia and Syntyche), calls one woman a minister or deacon (Phoebe), and (perhaps) another an apostle (Junia). Different aspects of Paul's thinking will challenge other communities: in view of creation and the fall, he specifies certain conditions under which women should demur.

Though the NIV begins verse 15, "But women," the Greek is actually, "But she," and probably refers to Eve, who was the subject of the previous two verses. Counterpart to Adam in Romans, Eve here serves as a representative woman who "became a sinner" (the phrase is "came to be in transgression"). In Ephesus, some women have followed her example and have "already turned away to follow Satan" (1 Tim. 5:15) under the influence of "deceiving spirits and things taught by demons" (4:1). The Ephesian women must decide to whom they will listen: lying spirits and demons or the Lord himself (thus the emphasis in 2:11–12 on a quiet demeanor). Paul points women to a salvation that comes "through childbearing." Some interpreters believe that Paul promises women that if they return to the faith, the Lord will be with them as a part of their childbearing. However, the Greek actually includes a definite article ("through the childbearing"); thus, other interpreters believe that Paul has in mind one particular instance of childbearing: Mary's giving birth to Jesus. This reading has much to commend it: Paul seems to be asking women to take their bearings in their relationship with God, not from Eve's deception by Satan, but from Mary's receptivity to God's promise. Mary's faithful "May it be according to your word" brought about the human race's salvation "through (the) childbearing"—and established a model for "faith, love and holiness with propriety."

4. Leadership (3:1–13)

A. Overseers or bishops (3:1–7). Church leadership had become problematic in Ephesus. Charges were being brought against some church officers (1 Tim. 5:17–22), and disputes had erupted about who should be teaching (1:4–7). Immature believers had unwisely been elevated to spiritual leadership (3:6; 5:22), resulting in the scenario Paul had predicted for the church at Ephesus: "Even from your own number men will arise and distort the truth in order to draw away disciples after them" (Acts 20:30). Holding office in the church is no longer attractive to those who are genuinely qualified. Since those qualifications include being "not quarrelsome" and managing one's own affairs rather than meddling in others' for the sake of gain, the very people who are competent to serve have little inclination to be involved in the church's leadership. Paul writes to encourage service to the Christian community at a time when prominent people in provincial cities are abandoning civic service for the sake of a quiet

and undisturbed life. It is no coincidence that there is a large overlap between the virtues Paul requires of overseers and the virtues secular sources praise in community leaders.

Paul urges those who should be leaders to rise to the task: the one who aspires to be "an overseer" (or "bishop," KJV, RSV, NRSV) "desires a noble task" (3:1). At the same time, Paul urges the church to reevaluate the criteria by which they have been selecting their leaders. The qualification list opens and closes with traits that have an eye to outsiders' opinions: "above reproach," "a good reputation with outsiders" (3:2, 7). This alone indicates that leaders who lack character have damaged the reputation of the believing community. Because church leadership, like household management (3:4–5), involves authoritative oversight, Paul looks for traits for preventing an abuse of power. Paul carefully describes the kind of person who should be put in authority over God's household. It is a person who is faithful to his wife and who therefore can be expected to respect sexual boundaries. It is one who is temperate in sex, drink, and wealth and who will therefore offer judgments that are not corrupted by pleasure, addictions, or ambition. It is one whom the gospel has made "gentle" and who is therefore neither "violent" nor "quarrelsome."

Paul's list merely hints at the twofold role an overseer plays (that twofold role is repeated in 5:17, indicating that Paul is not distinguishing "overseers" or "bishops" from "elders" but rather discussing the same individuals from different aspects). One aspect of the leadership role is administrative and governing: he likens the task to household management and calls for hospitality. The other is educational: "able to teach" (3:2).

Paul warned in 2:14 that Eve had been deceived by the (there unnamed) devil and in this passage warns against a premature entry to office for those who will be susceptible to diabolic, arrogant pride.

B. Deacons (3:8–13). As at Philippians 1:1, Paul mentions a second kind of leadership role, "deacons." Not anticipating questions later readers might ask, Paul assumes his readers know what deacons do, so he does not describe their tasks. Some think he means assistant overseers or overseers in training. Some think he means officers who care for the material needs of the congregation—see Acts 6:1–6, where the Jerusalem elders' ability to attend to "prayer and the ministry [Greek *diakonia*] of the word" is protected by assigning others to "wait on tables" (*diakoneō*) for the church's widows. Even there, though, there must be some flexibility of thought, since one of those "table waiters" is Stephen, who is known preeminently for his verbal defense of the gospel (Acts 6:5; 6:8–7:60). As the Acts passage shows, the *diakon-* word group is flexible. In the Pastorals alone it can cover both Paul's and Timothy's gospel ministry (1 Tim. 1:12; 4:6), as well as the general assistance Onesiphorus and Mark provide Paul in his ministry (2 Tim. 1:18; 4:11).

In Acts and other epistles written by Paul, *diakon-* terminology clusters around financial matters (Acts 12:25; Rom. 15:25, 31; 2 Cor. 8:4; 9:1). First Timothy shows concern for how the church should allot its resources to relief for the poor (5:1–16) and for how various groups within the community should regard and employ their riches (6:1–19). Perhaps, as Acts 6 suggests, a central role of deacons is to assist overseers by supervising the church's finances and relief for the poor.

Character is required of deacons as well as for overseers. If deacons are to be trusted go-betweens, it is especially important that they be "sincere" (the Greek term is "not double-worded" or "not duplicitous"). If widows (see 1 Timothy 5) are under their care, it is particularly important that deacons are "not pursuing dishonest gain" (3:8).

Sandwiched between verses 10 and 12 is a discussion of women. The Greek text says, "In the same way, the women are to be worthy of respect" (the Greek word *gynē* means "woman" or "wife," depending entirely on context). Paul refers either to "deacons' wives" or to "women who are deacons." Unfortunately, the context is not clear here. Paul could mean that deacons' wives ought to conduct themselves in ways that befit their husbands' callings, and it is not difficult to imagine him writing to that effect. If so, however, it is puzzling that Paul would not have first commented on overseers' wives (especially since overseers are expected to be hospitable). On the other hand, it may be worth noting that at this point in the Greek language no separate word for "deaconess" had emerged; thus, Paul uses the masculine *diakonos* to refer to Phoebe, a ministerial assistant in Cenchreae, when he sends her to the church at Rome (Rom. 16:1–2). His opening of 3:11 ("In the same way") probably indicates Paul envisions women as well as men being tested for service as deacons, to "gain an excellent standing and great assurance in their faith in Christ Jesus" (3:13).

5. True and False Religion (3:14–5:2)

A. True religion (3:14–16). In Paul's absence, he expects Timothy to minister under his authority (see 1 Cor. 4:17, 19; 16:10–11; 1 Thess. 3:1–6). The gospel should be expressed visibly in the life of the church, and Paul wants Timothy's life (like his own) to exemplify that.

The Bible calls God "the living God" when comparing him with dead, false gods. That is especially the case here. Ephesus was the site of a huge temple to the "great" Greek goddess Artemis (one of the seven wonders of the ancient world). Located just outside the city limits, this was an open-air structure in which the "mysteries" of Artemis were celebrated. Its 127 towering marble columns, each 60 feet tall, supported a massive roof structure beneath which the elaborately decorated statue of the goddess was visible to those outside. Not Artemis, counters Paul, but "the mystery from which true godliness springs is great." That mystery is not a statue in a physical temple but Jesus, whose story (3:16) is revealed in the lives of his people ("the church of the living God, the pillar and foundation of the truth" [3:15]). The church is a countertemple—and is why it is so important to Paul that believers learn how "to conduct themselves in God's household."

The first two lines of the Christ poem in verse 16 cover Christ's earthly ministry in terms of incarnation and resurrection (much like Rom. 1:3–4). The last four lines outline four ways his ministry continues because of his resurrection.

B. False religion (4:1–5). Paul senses a dark, demonic conspiracy against the church. Satanic forces are frustrating the calling to live and teach the mystery of godliness. Distrust of the gospel's ability to teach inner control has led to a desire to be governed by the law (1 Tim. 1:3–10). A denial of the one God's love for all people has led to prayer for only local concerns (2:1–7). A refusal to be informed by the creation-fall account has produced disorder in the church's authority and leadership (2:1–15). Now, at the beginning of chapter 4, Paul expresses a surprisingly strong concern: demons are teaching the rejection of God-created food and marriage.

First Timothy 4:1–5 takes its place within the drama Paul sees in Christ's coming in the middle of time to effect redemption at Satan's expense (esp. Gal. 1:1–4; Col. 2:15; Eph. 1:3–23;

Only one tall pillar remains standing at the ruins of the Temple of Artemis in Ephesus. Paul tells Timothy that it is the church that is "the pillar and foundation of the truth" (1 Tim. 3:15).

2:1–10; 3:7–10; 6:12–20). This redemption has prompted an ultimately doomed response by Satan: the unleashing of a "secret power of lawlessness" (2 Thess. 2:7), masked, ironically, by teachers who promote phony lawfulness, a piety-pretending denial with respect to food and sex (the situation finds a parallel in Col. 2:8–23). Paul sets the opponents' theology and practice within a specific framework: Satan's "latter days" rebellion against the reconciliation of all things in Christ.

Paul responds to the false teachers by pointing to the teaching in Genesis 1 that creation is good. Evil lies not in a thing itself but in its misuse. Evil is an intrusion into creation, not a part of creation itself. It is not sexual activity that must be avoided but its corrupt misuse. Food is not the problem but rather the evil disordering of appetite. Part of what is restored in Christ is a prudence that allows believers to receive things for what they are, gifts God intended "to be received with thanksgiving" (4:3–4). In the Garden of Eden, the human race tragically exchanged the truth of God for a lie. A posture of grateful acceptance of creation and its gifts was traded for one of ingratitude and idolatry. Accordingly, God gave the race over to the corruption of conscience (Rom. 1:18–31). Now, in Christ, "those who believe and who know the truth" have had consciences re-informed

by prayers of consecration and by the Word of God (see Gen. 1:31; Matt. 15:11; Mark 10:9).

C. Timothy's responsibility for true religion (4:6–5:2). Paul compares the false teachers' asceticism with a long-standing teaching offered by Greek moralists about the moral virtue that comes from athletic training. It is not noble philosophizing, counters Paul, but "old wives'" storytelling that promotes physical discipline as being the key to inner balance. The point of Paul's "physical training is of some value" is that such training is of little benefit when compared with "godliness" that "has value for all things, holding promise for both the present life and the life to come" (4:8). What is really worth the effort (see verse 10, "we labor and strive," both athletic terms) is the process Paul puts before Timothy, a set of disciplines that will lead to his salvation and that of those in his care.

The pursuit of godliness has as its aim the salvation of all, not a select minority of the selfishly motivated hyperdisciplined. Paul's salvation is a full restoration of what it is to be human. It is available to all. Part of the guiding thought in the Pastorals is that the gospel empowers a kind of life that was envisioned in Greek thinking (see Titus 2:12). Paul notes that the source of the gospel's life-giving power does not lie down the path of external conformity to the law (1 Tim. 1:8–11) or down the path of what is, in reality, ungodly self-denial (4:1–5). It is, in sum, the life of faith that Paul referred to in 1:4 as "God's work—which is by faith." Timothy's life is to be an example in terms of godliness ("in conduct . . . in faith"—4:12), justice ("in love," "an older man . . . as if he were your father. Treat younger men as brothers, older women as mothers, and younger women as sisters"—4:12; 5:1–2), courage ("Don't let anyone look down on you because you are young"—4:12), and temperance ("in purity," "with absolute purity"—4:12; 5:2). Godliness is promoted in the context of Christian community, not in isolation from it: "public reading of Scripture . . . preaching . . . teaching" (4:13). At the same time, godliness is intensely personal,

as Paul urges Timothy: "Be diligent in these matters; give yourself wholly to them" (4:15). If the whole church is to provide visible proof of the truth of the gospel (3:16), Timothy's life is to be first in being the "pillar and foundation of the truth" (3:15).

6. Widows, Elders, and Slaves (5:3–6:2)

A. Widows and female benefactors (5:3–16). The first part of this section (5:3–8) treats widows whose poverty qualifies them to come under the care of the church. Even though the church is to think of itself as a family (see 3:15, "God's household"), the church is not a substitute for families. If there are "children or grandchildren" of a widow, these family members show their godliness ("put their religion into practice" [5:4a]; this is also the sense of 5:8) and their sense of justice ("repaying their parents and grandparents" [5:4b]) by providing for their own widowed grandmothers and mothers. However, if there is no family or if a family has insufficient resources to keep widows from sliding into poverty, Paul expects Christians to practice the relief for widows called for in the Old Testament (Exod. 22:22; Deut. 26:12) and famously characteristic of Jewish communities. Anna, the widowed prophetess who lived in the temple precincts, provides an example of the destitute widow of 1 Timothy 5:3–5 (see Luke 2:36–38). Paul maintains that care for elders is a divine and social obligation.

The second part of this section (5:9–16) treats widows whose record of ministry qualifies them for something like an office parallel to that of overseer or deacon (see 1 Tim. 3:1–7, 8–13). Like deacons, who are to be tested (3:10), these widows are to be installed after it has been established that their lives consist in "good deeds"—notably, "showing hospitality, washing the feet of the Lord's people, helping those in trouble" (5:10). This is the kind of faithful woman who, even in her own widowhood, "has widows in her care." Dorcas (known as Tabitha), the patroness of widows in Joppa, is an example of the care-providing woman that Paul envisions in this passage (see Acts 9:36);

she is one who has extended rather than received "good works and acts of mercy" (NIV "always doing good and helping the poor"). The grief at Dorcas's death by the widows who benefited from her kindness (Acts 9:39) is testimony to how important this role was in the early church. Paul wants to make sure that only suitably mature women are enrolled to this office. Younger widows are encouraged, instead, to take up new families rather than to risk reneging on their commitment to Christ and to those who would be dependent on them.

B. Elders (5:17–25). Having clarified which women are eligible for relief for widows (5:3–8) and which are to be supported as ministering widows, Paul now takes up the matters of paying and disciplining elders. Paul expects the church to find some of its leadership from the municipal elite and the independently wealthy. These are the kind of people who would readily recognize their own community values in the overseers list in 3:1–7. Paul mentions these wealthy individuals directly at 6:17–19. In addition, Paul expects some leaders will need to be paid for their service to the church (these, in the opinion of most interpreters, are in view in 6:8–10).

Skill in administration is vital to the life of God's household, and Paul's placing this section next to the widows' passage suggests that some of the difficulties in Ephesus were a result of a breakdown in administration. However, even more necessary is the ability to teach. Thus, special priority ("double honor") is put on "those whose work is preaching and teaching" (5:17). Paul quotes both the Old Testament (Deut. 25:4) and Jesus himself (Luke 10:7) to underline the importance of the church's support of a leadership that is independent of secular social, economic, and political clout.

Even though the church in Ephesus is in a major Hellenistic city, Paul expects it to take its bearings from the Old Testament and from Jewish community life. Paul has just cited the Old Testament in support of the idea that spiritual leaders should be paid. Now he invokes

the Old Testament (Deut. 19:15) to protect elders from false accusations. There is no way to be certain about the charges that have been brought. What is important is that Paul is concerned about due process (5:19) and avoiding favoritism (5:20–21).

Paul requires that mature believers, not recent converts, be placed in leadership in the church at Ephesus (unlike the church in Crete, which was a missionary setting). The temptation is to elevate too quickly either people whose secular power and prestige mask hidden agendas, or people whose glib tongues mask spiritual infancy or sinister motives. As if the stress that the relatively young Timothy is under in confronting an entrenched and socially powerful opposition isn't enough, Timothy has developed stomach problems and is frequently ill, for which Paul prescribes "a little wine" (5:23; see Prov. 31:6). Of even more comfort to Timothy must have been Paul's closing words in this chapter, assuring him that though the difference between good and evil sometimes comes to view in this life and sometimes only in the next, God will nonetheless ultimately make all things right.

C. Slaves and masters (6:1–2). Christian slaves are wondering what, in view of their redemption, they still owe their masters. In the Letter to Philemon, we see how diplomatically yet persuasively Paul can approach a Christian master about relating to a converted slave who is now a Christian brother. In that letter, he hints that Philemon should release his slave Onesimus to aid Paul in ministry. In 1 Timothy 6, by contrast, Paul urges slaves not only to consider how their continued—indeed, heightened—service can serve the gospel but also how disrespect toward their masters will not lead to a more consistent Christianity. Instead, it will lead to a slandering of God's name by those outside the church. Paul instructs slaves of Christian masters not to "show them disrespect just because they are fellow believers" (6:2) but rather to "serve them even better." In the Letter to Titus, he will say much the same, calling slaves to "adorn" the gospel through their service (Titus 2:10 KJV, RSV).

The phrase "those who benefit by their service" (RSV, NRSV; see NIV note; NIV "their masters") is in dispute. If this translation is correct, Paul is turning contemporary values upside down by inviting slaves to become their masters' benefactors through their ungrudging service. However, a more normal treatment of the language suggests Paul has in mind masters who "devote themselves to service." In this case Paul would be asking Christian slaves to recognize that those masters who serve the community (who live out 6:17–19, for instance) are themselves doing so as brothers. Paul—like Jesus—will expect these masters to give up the normal benefits of their liberality and generosity (such as honorific statues and inscriptions, "front row" treatment like that sought in Luke 14:7–11). Household dependents should accord such masters a brotherly respect. Regardless of which reading is correct, Paul calls Christian slaves to a new way of thinking.

7. Money and Wealth (6:3–19)

A. False teaching and love of money (6:3–10). Paul begins this section with a warning against false teaching that recalls the opening of the letter. He is returning to his concern about aspiring but confused teachers. In chapter 1, Paul addressed their speculations and their wrong use of the law. In chapter 4, he addressed their nonbiblical self-denial. Here in chapter 6, he speaks to the ill effects of their teaching and to the teachers' unworthy motives.

The false teaching creates a climate of spiritual disease that has three elements: godlessness, social strife, and a corrupt inner life (see Titus 1:12; 2:12). First, the teaching is contrary to true godliness, pointing people to a focus on something other than Jesus Christ (6:3–4). Second, the teaching promotes "envy, strife, malicious talk, evil suspicions and constant friction." Third, the teaching flows from people who are deluded about their own importance (they are "conceited" [6:4]) and are driven by an appetite for gain (6:5): "who think that godliness is a means to financial gain."

Modern interpreters often dismiss this last statement as a mere rhetorical flourish. But in many respects Paul seems to get to the heart of the issue here. Confusion about wealth is a huge

The beautiful mosaic floors and frescoed walls in these ancient terraced houses in Ephesus (occupied first century BC–seventh century AD) attest to the wealth that some individuals possessed. Paul addresses the dangers of wealth: "Those who want to get rich fall into temptation" (1 Tim. 6:9).

problem in this prosperous church. It is wealthy women who usurp teaching authority (chap. 2). It is prosperous household heads whom Paul urges to aspire to spiritual leadership (3:1). It is confusion over how families' and the church's resources should be managed in relief to widows that Paul addresses in chapter 5. The denunciation of greed among aspiring teachers (6:8–10) follows directly on the heels of instruction to provide "double honor"—that is, "twice the pay"—for elders who are especially apt at teaching and governing. The section will close with the only paragraph Paul ever addresses, at least in the writings that have come to us, to the rich about how they are to fit into the household of faith (6:17–19).

Greed is deadly to the soul and ruinous to community. Those who do not have money and those who do have money are equally susceptible to the vice of "love of money." Those who do not have money dream about what it would be like to have it. (The NET's "who long to be rich" is a better rendering of the Greek than the NIV's "who want to get rich.") Those who do have money find there is never enough (Luke 12:13–21, and the comments below on 1 Tim. 6:17–19). In the strongest terms, Paul instructs Timothy to look for would-be leaders whose godliness produces "contentment," drawing on a rich layer of wisdom teaching from the Old Testament (with 6:7–8, cf. Job 1:21; Eccles. 5:14). As an adage, "the love of money is a root of all kinds of evil" can sound irrelevant and overused. However, in the case of the Ephesian church, the love of money has indeed created a host of pastoral problems.

A bust of Tiberius, the Roman emperor from AD 14 to 37. In spite of the elevated status of the Roman emperors, Paul describes God as "the blessed and only Ruler . . . who alone is immortal" (1 Tim. 6:15–16).

B. What makes Timothy wealthy (6:11–16). As far back as the Letter to the Philippians, Paul expressed his trust in Timothy's ability to model Christian truth (2:19–24). Certainly Paul is worried about whether Timothy will have the boldness to fight the powerful—some in social status, some in eloquence—opponents in Ephesus. Nonetheless, Paul's instructions to Timothy about the life he is to lead indicate his confidence that in Timothy's character, the Ephesian church will find an antidote to the greed and power-grabbing that is plaguing them. Paul tells Timothy to flee the entrapment of greed that is crippling the Ephesian church. He instructs Timothy to pursue a range of virtues to display what "godliness with contentment" (see 6:6)—in a word, what living in Christ looks like (6:11).

Timothy himself is to be the opposite of those who desire the short-term gain that ministry could bring: money and influence. A minister's wealth and influence are to be found in the virtues traditionally associated with Paul's teachings: "faith, love," and hope (expressed as "endurance. . . . Take hold of the eternal life to which you were called. . . . Keep this command without spot or blame until the appearing of our Lord Jesus Christ" [6:11–12, 14]); and also in the virtues that being in Christ empowers: "righteousness [= justice], godliness," temperance (here expressed in terms of demeanor: "gentleness" rather than harshness—more on this at 2 Tim. 2:24–26—and "without spot or blame"), and courage ("Fight the good fight" [6:12]—again, more in 2 Timothy).

The theological values that are to be made transparent in Timothy's life are notable: creation ("God, who gives life to everything"), redemption (note the way Paul appeals to the narrative of Christ's suffering and to the promise of his return), and the majesty of God, the doxology of 6:15–16 nicely mirroring the doxology of 1:17.

C. How the wealthy can invest (6:17–19). Paul turns finally to those from whom the most serious issues at Ephesus have emerged: "those who are rich in this present world" (6:17). The women usurpers are rich (2:9–15). Prosperous household heads need to learn what is worthy of aspiring to and how to do so (3:1–10). Those with means must learn not to hoard for themselves but to care for family members (5:1–9) and for the church's poor (5:9–16).

Wealth presents both dangers and opportunities. Paul leads with the dangers. First, the rich must not be "arrogant" (literally "high-minded"). They must not think of themselves as morally superior or more deserving than others. Second, they must not "put their hope in wealth." It is easy to be seduced into thinking that power and possessions are permanent, or even that they can bestow a kind of immortality. (The ancient world was filled with memorials by which benefactors sought to have their largesse remembered forever.) But, Paul warns, wealth is "uncertain." The only one worth putting hope in is God himself (compare 6:17 with 4:10; 5:5), who alone, as Paul has just noted, possesses immortality (6:15).

Wealth offers opportunities as well as dangers. First, while goods cannot substitute for God, they nonetheless should be seen as gifts from God. Though it is difficult to discern details about the false teaching in Ephesus, it is characterized by one thing specifically: contempt for creation (see especially 1 Tim. 4:1–5). Paul's high view of creation comes into view nowhere better than here, where he argues that God "richly provides us with everything for our enjoyment" (6:17). God's generosity is revealed not just at the cross where our sins are forgiven (though it is), not just in the outpouring of the Holy Spirit for gospel ministry (though it is). God's generosity is revealed in every benefit of

creation, from food and marriage and possessions all the way to his Son's taking on a human body for our benefit. (Note the way Paul refers in 1 Tim. 2:5 to God's Son as "the man Christ Jesus," and in Titus 2:11; 3:4 as "the grace of God," and, "the kindness and love of God.") By saying that God gives things "for our enjoyment" (6:17), Paul underscores the Bible's view of the absolute, and therefore redeemable, good of all God's creation.

Second, wealth creates possibilities for cultivating virtue and for benefiting one's community. Paul asks the Christian rich to be as generous with their resources as their pagan counterparts: "to do good, to be rich in good deeds, and to be generous and willing to share" (6:18). Wealth lies not in possessions but in relationships, for wealth creates the ability to benefit others.

The primary difference between the Christian rich and the pagan rich lies in the return they expect. Aristotle taught, "Hidden wealth kept buried" does you no good; rather, you should use it to gain friends and to attain honor. Benefactors gave so they might receive "liquid IOUs" and concrete things like (summarizing a list in Aristotle's *Rhetoric* 1361a39–43) sacrifices in their honor, memorials in verse and prose, privileges, grants of land, front seats, public burial, state maintenance, "and among the barbarians, prostration and giving place, and all gifts which are prized in each country." Instead, Paul, sounding much like his master, maintains that Christians "lay up treasure for themselves as a firm foundation for the coming age," that is, for the day when they hope to hear their master's "Well done" (see Matt. 6:20; 19:21; 25:21, 23; Luke 16:10).

8. Closing Admonition: Opposing Spurious "Knowledge" (6:20–21)

Paul closes 1 Timothy with one of his shortest letter-endings, perhaps itself a commentary on the folly of arguing over myths, endless genealogies, and controversial speculations (1:3–4). With his denunciation of "what is falsely called knowledge," Paul almost prophetically provides the rallying cry for the second-century church's battle with gnosticism.

Commentary

In 2 Timothy, Paul calls Timothy to his side as he faces probable martyrdom (4:9, 13, 21) and at the same time urges his young protégé to be courageous in ministry in his teacher's absence.

1. Salutation (1:1–2)

The apostle discerns that Timothy needs fortification beyond the words of 1 Timothy. The distinctive terms of this second greeting provide further strengthening for Paul's protégé. Paul's own call is by "the will of God" himself,

and his call, like Timothy's, serves the "promise of life that is in Christ Jesus." In addition, here Paul calls Timothy "my dear son" (literally "my beloved son"). Timothy is thus reminded, first, that he ministers under an authority that he ought not to ignore; second, that he ministers for the sake of a goal (the promotion of God's life-giving promises) that is worth living and dying for; and third, that he does not do so alone—he is much loved.

2. Thanksgiving and Appeal (1:3–7)

A. Thanksgiving (1:3–5). In his first letter, Paul wrote without the normal prayer of thanks that he and other Hellenistic letter writers usually included. In that first letter, Paul seemed simply to want to get down to business. Now, sensing that Timothy's position is more fragile and his resolve less solid than he originally thought, Paul prays. Paul thus describes Timothy's ministry in the context of gratitude for the grand story line of covenant faithfulness that God has been working throughout the history of redemption. This includes Paul and Paul's own family (now including Timothy) and Timothy's own family. Timothy does not minister alone and in isolation. He stands in a long line of saints, and Paul's nonstop prayers support him as well. Moreover, though Timothy seems to be crippled by his own fears, Paul wants to encourage him with what he finds touching about Timothy's rich inward life: the tears he has shed in Paul's presence and the knowledge that their reunion will bring Paul great joy. Paul has seen evidence of great faith at work in Timothy. He now appeals for more.

B. First appeal: Rekindle the gift and be courageous (1:6–7). Timothy's ministry in Ephesus is challenging. He is a young man (1 Tim. 4:12) charged with the oversight of one of the largest and best-established churches in Paul's mission. Paul has warned that strong, erring would-be leaders could emerge (Acts 20:30). Though Paul has written off by name two false teachers as being shipwrecked in faith (1 Tim. 1:19–20), at least one of those two is still in Ephesus teaching that the resurrection has already taken place

(2 Tim. 2:17). Because Timothy is cowering at this challenge, Paul wants to strengthen his student's faith to do battle.

Thus, Paul reminds Timothy of the gift of the Spirit that came to him from God when he was set aside for ministry. If, as Paul says elsewhere, the Spirit's flow in us can be quenched (1 Thess. 5:19), so, too, can its fire be rekindled. Paul encourages Timothy to draw on the resource that is already within. God's Spirit is not marked by timidity but by "power, love and self-discipline" (1:7).

In both biblical and extrabiblical literature, "timidity" (often translated "cowardice") is an antonym of "courage" (see Josh. 1:9; Dio Chrysostom, *Oration* 23.8). While the other three Greek virtues (godliness, temperance, and justice) are stressed elsewhere in the Pastorals, the military virtue of "courage" dominates in 2 Timothy. Paul begins by telling Timothy not to play the coward. Paul challenges him instead to be a "good soldier of Christ Jesus" (2:3), recalling a theme he introduced at 1 Timothy 1:18: "wage the noble warfare" (NIV "fight the battle well"; cf. 1 Tim. 6:12; 2 Tim. 4:7). He explains cowardice's opposite in several terms: first, "power" (God's rule that will be manifest on the last day [2 Tim. 4:1] and is on display now when God converts sinners [see 1:8 and 2:25]); second, "love" (the goal of ministry—1 Tim. 1:5; 2 Tim. 1:13); and third, "self-discipline" (the kind of self-restraint that gives God room to grant repentance—see 2:22–26).

3. Examples to Emulate and to Teach Others (1:8–2:13)

A. Christ's victory: A gospel worth suffering for (1:8–10). Courage will enable Timothy to join Paul and Jesus in standing for the truth. Just as the Lord himself testified before Pilate (despite the NIV's "testimony about our Lord," this "testimony of our Lord" is the same notion Paul described in 1 Tim. 6:13), so must Timothy be ready to testify and suffer. Nor should Timothy be ashamed of his own spiritual mentor, despite Paul's having to minister from a Roman prison. The apostle stresses the

power of God on display in the gospel (1:8). Verses 9 and 10 virtually sing of the glory of the story he and Timothy have been given to tell. Paul highlights three things: God's salvation comes from his own purpose and grace; this salvation has been designed according to God's own timetable; and finally, Christ has destroyed death and brought to light life and immortality.

B. Paul's life: A life worth emulating (1:11–14). Paul has been called to serve this gospel as "a herald and an apostle and a teacher" (1:11). As a herald, he announces Christ's lordship of the universe by virtue of his victory over sin and death. As an apostle, he establishes the foundation of Christian community. As a teacher, he instructs believers how to live in Christ (see also 1 Tim. 2:7). Paul exposes himself to physical suffering and emotional humiliation because he knows God's resolve to see salvation through to "that day": the day of Christ's triumphal return to complete the restoration of all things (see Phil. 1:6).

Paul has delivered a "good deposit" that Timothy is to preserve by his own life of faith and love in Christ. This deposit is the sum of a "pattern of sound teaching" that Timothy is to teach others (see chap. 2), with the indwelling Holy Spirit's help.

C. One other life to emulate, contrasted with counterexamples (1:15–18). Sadly, not everyone in Paul's circle is staying true to the apostle. Though there is surely some exaggeration in Paul's saying that "everyone in the province of Asia" (where Ephesus is situated, and where Timothy is ministering) "has deserted me," it certainly means that Timothy is serving a church with little backing from Paul's supporters. Paul is offended enough by two of them to name them, Phygelus (who is otherwise unknown) and Hermogenes (who may be the person identified in the noncanonical, late-second-century *Acts of Paul and Thecla* as a coppersmith and Paul's opponent).

Paul is keen to present to Timothy the faithfulness of Ephesus's own Onesiphorus.

Paul prays God's mercy for Onesiphorus, who has recently found the apostle in his Roman jail and ministered to him there. Paul reminds Timothy of the way Onesiphorus has served them in Ephesus. Onesiphorus's lack of shame at Paul's chains (the Greek phrase is a clever understatement) becomes yet another example for Timothy to follow.

D. Second appeal: Teach others (2:1–7). Paul solidifies his appeal to Timothy with an emphatic, "You then, my son." The positive, flip side of Paul's earlier negative warning against timidity (2 Tim. 1:7) lies here in his "be strong in the grace that is in Christ Jesus" (2:1). In these verses Paul comes to the point: Paul has taught Timothy so that Timothy can teach others, who in their turn can teach still others. Paul has carefully built the case for the urgency of the task: Timothy must fortify himself to fortify the church in Ephesus so that it can be a self-sustaining community. It becomes increasingly clear that Paul looks ahead to his own martyrdom and desires that Timothy come to him in Rome to comfort him. Thus, it is vital that Timothy rise to the urgent need: teach others who can tend the body in Ephesus.

With considerable skill, Paul appeals to three familiar Hellenistic metaphors: soldier, athlete, and farmer (cf. 1 Cor. 9:7, 24—see also, for example, Epictetus, *Discourses* 3.22.51–69; 4.8.35–40). Soldiers are loyal, athletes know their game, and farmers work hard. Crisply, Paul exhorts Timothy to apply these truths to his situation: Listen to me! Care about those who need you! Get to it!

E. Remember Christ Jesus (2:8–13). First and last, the church's message is "Jesus Christ, raised from the dead" as the initiator of a new age, and "descended from David" as the sum of all

This relief of a Roman soldier from his grave stele is dated to the Roman Period (30 BC–AD 395). Paul exhorts Timothy to be "like a good soldier of Christ Jesus" (2 Tim. 2:3).

God's promises in the past (2:8). God reclaims the whole universe through Christ and does so by way of Israel's story.

In the Greek, verses 8–10 make up a single sentence, beginning with Jesus's resurrection and climaxing in believers' final salvation in glory. To combat the false notion that the only resurrection to take place has already occurred (2:18), Paul reminds Timothy that Jesus's resurrection brings the promise of his people's resurrection. Between the beginning and end of this three-verse sentence, however, is language of suffering. Paul describes his chains, his ignoble status as a criminal (no longer under mere house arrest), but also his willingness to "endure everything."

The reality of Christ's resurrection in the past and the certainty of believers' resurrection in the future create in Paul a confidence that though his body may be "chained . . . God's word is not chained" (2:9; the NIV nicely brings out the similar Greek words translated "chain"). Because God's word is unstoppable, Paul's imprisonment provides another opportunity for God's power to bring salvation to his people.

Paul hopes that Timothy will let his life take the same shape as Jesus's and Paul's. To that end, he invokes the last of the Pastoral Epistles' five "trustworthy sayings." Verses 11–13 are matchless in their poetic or hymnlike quality. Union with Christ in his death will bring life with him in resurrection (2:11; see also Rom. 6:8): now a cross, later a crown (2:12a; cf. Matt. 19:28).

However, if on the last day we deny Christ, he will deny us (2:12b; see also Matt. 10:33). Paul uses an unusual and emotionally charged future tense in the "if" clause that begins, "If we disown him" (literally "if we will disown him"), indicating the unthinkability of the act. Paul is remembering those who have abandoned him in prison (2 Tim. 1:15; 4:10). Others have abandoned Paul's teaching (2:17–18). Paul fears the sum of their careers will amount to a fatal denial of Christ himself.

Verse 13 contains the poetic punch line. Paul's deepest hope is that Timothy will choose a different path from those faithless ones. He is most confident, though, that regardless of anyone else's faithfulness or faithlessness, God himself will remain faithful. The poem's last line about God's not being able to disown himself has puzzled commentators. The effect is to ask Timothy and subsequent readers to ask themselves hard questions. Those whose ongoing faithlessness leads to final denial of the Savior will discover that it will be impossible for the Lord to acknowledge them. Those who repent, however, can take solace in knowing that God faithfully forgives his people's failings.

4. False Teaching (2:14–3:9)

A. Why to resist false teachers: Their influence is corrupting (2:14–21). Paul continues his discussion from 2:2 about how to train leaders. It is they especially who must learn that "quarreling about words" will only bring ruin to "those who listen." The warning against quarrelsomeness is important. Paul does not want his militant

call ("wage the noble warfare" [1 Tim. 1:18; NIV "fight the battle well"], "no one serving as a soldier" [2:4]) to be taken the wrong way.

By contrast with those who distract with "quarreling about words" (2:14) and "godless chatter" (2:16), and those who confuse with error (2:18), Timothy is to show competence as one who "correctly handles the word of truth" (2:15). The only other places this verb occurs in the Bible are in the Septuagint at Proverbs 3:6 and 11:5, where it refers to clearing a straight road. Timothy is to focus on forthrightness of speech and correctness of meaning. His own approval before God is at stake, and so is the health of his (and their) hearers. Paul compares the ungodliness that the false teachers promote with flesh-decaying and foul-smelling gangrene—an image that fits the theme of "sound [i.e., healthy] doctrine" in the Pastorals (1 Tim. 1:10; 6:3; 2 Tim. 1:13; 4:3; Titus 1:9, 13; 2:1–2).

Paul believes it is critical to handle the word of truth correctly when it comes to the timeline of redemption (see also 1 Corinthians). It is folly of the worst sort to believe that you have arrived at your final goal when you are still merely on the way. Thus, it is a fatal error to teach—as Hymenaeus and Philetus (otherwise unknown to us) do—that the only resurrection that is to take place has already happened. Wrongly applying teachings like those in John 5:24 and Ephesians 2:4–7, they probably believed that our new birth or regeneration is our final resurrection.

With his "nevertheless" at verse 19, Paul assures Timothy that the danger in the church is more than matched by God's provision, as illustrated by Israel's history (Num. 16:5; Isa. 28:16; 26:13; 52:11). Likewise now, God is invested in his "large house" (2:20; cf. the image at 1 Tim. 3:15). All those in the house—but Paul is especially thinking of those who would teach—must cleanse themselves of that which is impure so that what they have to offer is noble, holy, and useful to the house's master.

B. How to resist false teachers: With mature gentleness (2:22–26). Given the severity of Paul's words about the peril in which the false teaching places the church, it is worth noting that Timothy is to conduct his campaign for the truth with a gentleness that keeps the door open for his opponents to repent.

The commandment to flee "the evil desires of youth" (2:22) is probably aimed, in the first place, at sexual temptations. (The same Greek term translated "evil desires" here Paul elsewhere associates with sexual sin; see Col. 3:5; 1 Thess. 4:5.) Intriguingly, Paul notes that individual purity of heart (see Matt. 5:8) is experienced in the fellowship of "those who call on the Lord."

However, verse 23 suggests Paul's greater concern is that Timothy might overcompensate for his youthful timidity by responding to his opponents with an immature harshness. Secure in his ability to teach, Timothy is to show kindness to all, friend and foe alike. He is to resist the temptation to be quarrelsome with or resentful of his opponents. The effect of a mature and measured response will be to give God room to grant repentance. Timothy needs to lead with what Paul calls elsewhere "the humility and gentleness of Christ" (2 Cor. 10:1) and leave the convicting to God himself.

C. The false teachers put in their last-days context (3:1–5). Paul has just given Timothy one reason why he need not take opposition personally: God is in control of all things and all hearts (see also Acts 13:48; 16:14; Rom. 8:28–30). Now he offers a second reason: opposition has a place in God's timetable. Paul thus reintroduces the Satan-prompted opposition to Christ's redemption he referred to at 1 Timothy 4:1–5.

In 1 Timothy, legalism and asceticism were Paul's target. In 2 Timothy, Paul aims at a range of ethical failings flowing from an overrealized eschatology (the mistaken notion that the resurrection is "already," and there is no "not-yet"). To deny that sin must die one last death at Jesus's return is, ironically, to open the floodgates to an unbridled religion of self. It is not accidental that Paul's list of vices opens with "lovers of themselves" (3:2) and closes with

"lovers of pleasure rather than lovers of God" (3:4). Everything in between is about building up oneself and destroying others. Religion stressing only the already with no room for the not-yet cannot help but produce a narcissistic and abusive lifestyle. Whatever appearance of godliness such teaching maintains, it has nothing of the Spirit of God about it—the only power it knows is Satan's.

Though he is to be gentle, Timothy is called to be a skillful surgeon of the soul, courageously cutting out a range of ailments that bespeak sickness of soul.

Second Timothy parallels 1 Corinthians in three striking ways. In both churches, believers' final resurrection was being denied. In both churches, Paul warned against excesses of the flesh. In both cases, Paul says "courage"—at 1 Corinthians 16:13 through the direct command, "be courageous"; and at 2 Timothy 1:7 through the indirect observation of what God's Spirit does and does not produce in us.

D. The false teachers and the gullible women (3:6–9). Paul indicates that a large part of the problem in Ephesus is that religious charlatans have found an audience among undiscerning women. This passage sheds significant light on gender relationships in 1 Timothy as well—see 1 Timothy 2:9–15; 3:11; 4:7; 5:3–16. Literature of the period provides numerous examples of women who are easy prey to religious frauds (for example, Lucian, *Alexander the False Prophet* 6). Unlike Timothy's mother and grandmother (2 Tim. 1:5), some women in the Ephesian congregation do not have the grounding in the Scriptures to see the implications of the opponents' teaching. Paul traces these women's gullibility to their being "loaded down with sins" and being "swayed by all kinds of evil desires." It is unclear whether he means simply that they have tender consciences making them vulnerable to wrong solutions (e.g., the asceticism of 1 Timothy) or, more sinisterly, that they are involved in illicit relations with the false teachers (the latter may explain Paul's concern with sexual purity in these two letters—see 1 Tim.

2:9–10; 3:2; 5:2, 11–15). Regardless, these women have an insatiable religious hunger, and this hunger perfectly complements the false teachers and their manipulative speculations.

Paul likens the false teachers to the magicians who opposed Moses and produced lying miracles before Pharaoh (Exod. 7:11–12, 22; 8:7—Paul uses names supplied by Jewish tradition). Further, Paul refers to them in verse 13 with a term that often means "magicians," but here is translated "imposters"—Paul likely means "charlatans." It is not so much that the false teachers perform miracles but that their spurious ideas about the resurrection and their empty promises of godliness cast a spell over undiscerning listeners. Paul is confident that their falsehoods will eventually be found out.

5. Paul's Teaching (3:10–4:8)

A. Third appeal, part one: Stay with what you know . . . (3:10–17). The false teaching being circulated among the Ephesians is that the resurrection is entirely "now." In his controversy with the Corinthians over whether there was still a resurrection to come, Paul pointed to his own sufferings as proof that "we have not yet begun to reign" (1 Cor. 4:8–13). Here in 2 Timothy, Paul reminds Timothy of the normalcy of suffering by taking him back to the events of Acts 13–14, when Paul ministered in Lystra, Timothy's hometown. After being stoned and left for dead, Paul insisted on returning in order to teach: "We must go through many hardships to enter the kingdom of God" (Acts 14:22). Timothy must courageously recommit himself to living and to teaching the same pattern, regardless of an increasingly fierce opposition.

Timothy can trust the lives of the people whose experiences have been shaped by Scripture. Of greater benefit, however, are the Scriptures themselves (by which Paul means our Old Testament). The Scriptures are entirely trustworthy. They are the very breath of God, and they find their coherence ("make you wise for salvation through faith") in Christ Jesus. In 3:16 Paul characterizes the Old Testament's benefit using four terms that have been much discussed.

It is probably best to understand them as a Jewish Christian's use of the traditional categories of Scripture. First, "teaching": the law told the story of God's redemption of his people and spelled out implications for life in covenant with him. Second, "rebuking": the prophets brought God's covenantal lawsuit against his rebellious people; the prophets wrote in such a way as to convict an erring people of their waywardness, pointing them to one in whose sufferings and glory their hope lay. Third, "correcting": in the so-called Writings (the Psalms and the wisdom literature), God provided songs and sayings designed to realign his people's hearts with his own heart, teaching them to lament and rejoice and live in accordance with his wisdom. Finally, there is "training in righteousness": an all-encompassing term for education and spiritual formation in Paul's world. With this last phrase, Paul indicates that the world's highest aspirations for wisdom are more than met in the account of redemption in Christ anticipated and embedded in Israel's Scriptures.

B. Third appeal, part two: . . . and preach the gospel (4:1–5). In an ultimate effort to strengthen his timid protégé's resolve, Paul brings Timothy before "the presence of God and of Christ Jesus, who will judge the living and the dead" (4:1; for Christ's role in future judgment, see Acts 17:31; Rom. 2:16; 1 Cor. 4:5; 2 Cor. 5:10). He puts Timothy under oath and defines his duty with crisp verbs, five in verse 2 and four in verse 5. The overarching command comes first: "Preach the word"—Timothy is the herald of God's restoration of creation and pardon for sinners through Christ. Second, Timothy is to be "prepared in season and out of season." Contemporary teachers wrote about the need to accommodate the disposition of their audience. Accordingly, Paul tells Timothy that in view of the urgency of the moment and the dire need of the church in Ephesus, he is to be ready to "correct, rebuke and encourage—with great patience and careful instruction."

Paul resumes the sober "latter day" thoughts of 1 Timothy 3:1–5, 12–13. Timothy should expect to encounter people who become discontent with sound teaching and who seek teachers who merely satisfy spiritual lusts. The false teachers specialize in ego-gratifying, speculative storytelling. "Itching ears" (4:3), it would seem, are eager to hear that resurrection life is all in the "now."

In contrast with all counterfeit gospels and all false approaches to what it is for God to refashion us in his image, Timothy is to offer himself as one who is sober ("keep your head in all situations"), courageous ("endure hardship"), godly ("do the work of an evangelist"), and just ("discharge all the duties of your ministry"; 4:5).

C. Paul's final testimony (4:6–8). Chief among the reasons that Timothy must get over his timidity (1:7) is that, to anticipate Paul's athletic imagery, the baton is being passed. Paul sees his present imprisonment ending in martyrdom. He offers this final testimony as the reason for the appeal he has just given and as one last summary of the type of life he has lived and urges on Timothy (see 2 Tim. 1:11–12; 2:9–10; 3:10–11). Paul mixes Old Testament sacrificial imagery (the fulfillment of the Old Testament practice of a drink offering poured out in gratitude for God's gift of redemption [see Num. 15:5, 7, 10; 28:7; Phil. 2:17]) with contemporary athletic imagery of a race well run (4:6–7; and see Acts 20:24). Because of the successful completion of his ministry, Paul

anticipates a victory wreath—"the crown of righteousness" (4:8; see also 2:5; 1 Cor. 9:25; James 1:12; Rev. 2:10; 3:11). Such expectation is consistent with Jesus's promise of "Well done!" to those who serve him honorably and faithfully (Matt. 25:21, 23; Luke 19:17; see also Rom. 2:8–10).

6. Final Greetings (4:9–22)

The pathos of this letter lies in Paul's urgent, heartfelt request that Timothy join him. He appears to have sent Tychicus to relieve Timothy of his duties in Ephesus at least temporarily (4:5) so he can join Paul, awaiting martyrdom in Rome. Along the way—and this is one of the great stories of reconciliation in the New Testament—Timothy should bring along the once-estranged Mark (with 4:11; cf. Acts 13:5, 13; 15:36–41; Col. 4:10; Philem. 24). Paul's situation is dire; he has survived a preliminary hearing before the Roman authorities, but he has dim prospects for acquittal in the upcoming final hearing. He is not under the comfortable house arrest with which the book of Acts concluded and that had permitted the writing of Philippians, Philemon, Colossians, and Ephesians. Paul is familiar enough with imprisonment; but it is only here in 2 Timothy that he refers to his being treated "like a criminal" (2:9). Not only that, but all his companions except Luke have left him, some for ignoble reasons, some for reasons unknown.

Still, the tone of confident faith is remarkable. Paul seems to be interpreting his situation through the lens of Psalm 22, the song with which Jesus expressed the anguish of sufferings on the cross and by which the writer to the Hebrews speaks of the risen Jesus as

A bronze statue of a boxer (third–second century BC). In 2 Timothy 4:7, Paul tells Timothy, "I have fought the good fight."

the church's worship leader (see Heb. 2:12; 7:25; 8:1–2). As Jesus was abandoned on the cross (Matt. 27:46; Ps. 22:1), so Paul has been abandoned by Demas. As the psalmist looked to God for "rescue" from lions (Ps. 22:20–21), Paul has experienced "rescue" at his preliminary hearing and expects, even at death, "rescue" into God's heavenly kingdom. Paul continues to see his life as a union with Christ in his sufferings and glory (Phil. 3:10–11).

Further, Paul still focuses on the work to which God has called him; he is grateful his duress has meant that "the message might be fully proclaimed and all the Gentiles might hear it" (4:17). His request for manuscripts has prompted much guesswork: he may mean copies of Scriptures he had to leave behind at his arrest; he may mean his own collected writings; he may mean writings he is still preparing. In any event, his request means he is still working. He continues to warn about those who oppose him and will no doubt oppose Timothy as well. Paul does not specify the "great deal of harm" Alexander the metalworker did to him. The likelihood is that Alexander was the cause of Paul's arrest (thus his mention right after the cloak and parchments Paul had to leave behind in Troas). Even the greetings he sends indicate Paul is still on the job. He undergirds supporters in Ephesus (Priscilla and Aquila and the household of Onesiphorus; 4:19); he notes that Corinth's city treasurer Erastus is still there (see Rom. 16:23); he has left Trophimus in charge in Miletus despite the latter's illness; he completes his greetings with four named and with unnumbered and unnamed individuals from Rome. Though Paul is left without any ministerial assistance there besides Luke's, God's work goes on in the empire's capital city.

Additionally, even if he expects his death in the near future, the apostle will not despair and simply wait for it: he asks for a cloak in case he lasts the winter.

Paul closes with two phrases—one an ascription, the other a benediction—that are fine capstones to his writing career.

First, the ascription: "To him be glory for ever and ever. Amen" (4:18). Paul has a passion for promoting the majesty of God. The insult to God's dignity by Adam's disobedience has been more than turned aside by the second man's obedience. Christ has "destroyed death and has brought life and immortality to light" (2 Tim. 1:10), restoring God's creation to its original design of reflecting his glory. Paul's sufferings have done nothing but contribute to the reestablishment of God's splendor.

Second, the benediction: "The Lord be with your spirit. Grace be with you all" (4:22). Paul continues to assure Timothy of the kindhearted nearness of God to his people. Paul endures the ignobility of being known as a criminal because his own Savior's love took him to a criminal's cross. In life or in death, God's people can know that he is close by them and that he cherishes them.

Outline—Titus

1. Salutation (1:1–4)
2. Leaders and Rebels (1:5–16)
   A. Identifying and Appointing Leaders (1:5–9)
   B. Silencing Rebels (1:10–16)
3. A Lifestyle in Accord with Sound Doctrine (2:1–15)
   A. Relationships among Believers (2:1–10)
   B. Theological Grounding: God's Grace and Glory (2:11–15)
4. A Lifestyle Appropriate to Sound Doctrine (3:1–7)
   A. Responsibilities in State and Society (3:1–2)
   B. Theological Grounding: God's Kindness and Benevolence (3:3–7)
5. Summary: "Good Works" versus Foolish Controversies (3:8–11)
6. Personal Instructions (3:12–15)

Commentary

The Letter to Titus addresses a "missionary" or "church-planting" situation. Paul's delegate has been left behind in Crete to (1) put in place leaders who can refute false teaching and

(2) install a pattern of teaching that establishes the right fit between lifestyle and truth. Paul addresses the issue of Christians' relation to "culture" more directly here than in any other place in his writings: living "sensibly, righteously [or "justly"] and godly in the present age" (2:12 NASB). Paul's teachings contain the seedbed for what French commentator Ceslas Spicq dubbed a "Christian humanism" (ideas latent in Gal. 6:10; Rom. 12:17–18; Phil. 4:8).

1. Salutation (1:1–4)

Titus is one of the most trusted—and most "Greek"—of Paul's protégés. Paul charges him with establishing church life on an island that is home to some of Greek civilization's most ancient memories. Moreover, Titus is a veteran of Paul's battle over Jewish custom and teaching in Gentile churches (Gal. 2:3). Paul considers him the perfect emissary for dealing with a situation in which teachers "of the circumcision" (1:10) complicate these new converts' situation.

In this salutation, Paul deliberately emphasizes the purpose of his apostleship rather than its source. God's elect people should be characterized by faith in Christ rather than by empty "Jewish myths" (see 1:14). In addition, "knowledge of the truth that leads to godliness" (1:1) stands in distinct contrast to popular pagan legends about Zeus's origins as a man born and eventually buried on Crete (Kidd 1999, 185–209). Even Paul's note about God not lying (1:2; the only assertion of this fact in the New Testament) stands in contrast with "divine"

Zeus, who in fact did lie to have sexual relations with a human woman (taking the human form of her husband). The only hope for "eternal life" lies in what the true and living God promised "before the beginning of time" about executing his drama of creation, fall, redemption, and consummation. That promise has been fulfilled "at his appointed season" through Jesus Christ's coming (which Paul discusses at Titus 2:11 and 3:4) and in the "preaching entrusted to me," says the apostle (1:1–3).

Paul greets Titus, "my true son in our common faith," with the standard "Grace and peace" (1:3) from the earlier letters (minus the addition of "mercy" as in 1 and 2 Timothy), suggesting to many commentators that this epistle was the first of the three Pastoral Epistles.

2. Leaders and Rebels (1:5–16)

A. Identifying and appointing leaders (1:5–9). As a prisoner journeying to Rome, Paul had made a brief stopover in a Cretan port city (Acts 27:7–13), but it is impossible to determine the impact of that encounter. The Letter to Titus appears to have been written after a missionary venture to the island following Paul's first Roman imprisonment. Paul reminds Titus he has left him on Crete to finish their work by

> Crete is the fifth-largest island in the Mediterranean Sea. Paul explains to Titus why "I left you in Crete" (Titus 1:5) and advises him on the continuing ministry there.

completing the organization of the churches (1:6–9), by dispatching the false teachers (1:10–15), and by laying out sound doctrine and ethics (chaps. 2–3).

The terms "elder" and "overseer" appear interchangeable, since Paul uses the latter term (1:7) to describe the attributes of those to be appointed to a role (that of "elder") that could otherwise be thought of as merely honorific. Elders are to teach, both through lifestyle (1:6–8) and in word (1:9). Their verbal teaching will have aspects both positive ("encourage others by sound doctrine") and negative ("and refute those who oppose it").

In this missionary setting, elders model God's plan to rehumanize a humanity that tells lies about God, destroys one another, and lives with uncontrolled passions (see 1:12). Christ has come to restore knowledge of God, rightness in relationships, and integrity of persons (see 2:12). Elders exemplify all three. The second half of verse 8 is especially revealing: elders are to be "self-controlled" (that is, rightly related to themselves), "upright" (that is, just in their dealings with others), "holy" (that is, rightly related to God), "and disciplined" (a synonym for "self-controlled"). Since it will be their task to encourage piety, justice, and self-control within the churches, the leaders' impact is looked for first on their most immediate circle of influence: their children (1:6). Paul wants to ensure that the Cretan leaders' children "believe" (that is, are pious), and do not leave themselves liable to a charge either of prodigality (the word the NIV translates as "being wild" has to do with personal dissipation, a lack of self-control—it's an ironic synonym for "idle bellies") or of being "disobedient" (that is, being "vicious beasts," the opposite of living justly).

B. Silencing rebels (1:10–16). Paul orders the silencing of certain teachers. He faults their teaching in three ways: its theology, its social ethics, and its personal morality.

Paul considers the instruction of certain Jewish teachers to be theologically deceptive. They are lifting Old Testament characters out of the divine drama of redemption, making them nothing more than heroes in pointless yarns (see the apocryphal *Testament of Abraham*). To Paul, such teachers are "full of meaningless talk and deception" (1:10). Second, Paul regards the teachers as being relationally disruptive: they are themselves "rebellious" (1:10) and are "disrupting whole households" (1:11). To the extent that they promote any sort of ethic, they declare merely human "commands of those who reject the truth" (1:14), not rich biblical teaching. Third, Paul regards the teachers' motives as corrupt (they teach "for the sake of dishonest gain" [1:11]) and their impact as corrupting. Rather than offer a genuine prescription for personal purity, these teachers locate the problem of cleanness in things rather than in the human heart itself (1:15; cf. Matt. 15:10–20), and their conscience-corrupted actions deny the God they claim to represent (1:16; cf. 1 Tim. 5:8; 2 Tim. 3:5).

Paul's condemnation is so strong because he fears Cretan culture is receptive to a counterfeit gospel. Thus, he offers from "one of their own prophets" (traditionally, Epimenides of the sixth century BC) a probing self-critique about Crete's distortion of theology, social ethics, and personal morality: "Cretans are always liars, evil brutes, lazy gluttons" (1:12). One of the Bible's most delightful moments of irony lies in Paul's literary wink: "This testimony is true" (1:13). Cretan Christians minister in a culture that confesses that when it comes to honoring the divine, promoting justice, and governing the self, there is a gap between aspiration and realization.

The Cretan prophet's saying provides the keynote for Paul's message to Crete's Christians. This becomes clear when we get to Titus 2:11–12: "The grace of God . . . has appeared. . . . It teaches us . . . to live self-controlled, upright and godly lives." Christ came to teach, and his followers are called to embody, the opposite of the Cretan prophet's three phrases. Christ and his followers promote godliness, not religious lies. Christ and his followers display justice, not ethical viciousness. Christ and his followers embody self-control, not corrupt motives.

3. A Lifestyle in Accord with Sound Doctrine (2:1–15)

A. Relationships among believers (2:1–10). Paul indicates that, if the false teachers deny God by their actions (1:16), the faithful teacher must see to the confirming of God's character in the lives of Christ's followers—that is what he means by "what is in accord with sound doctrine" (2:1). The antidote for the sickness of soul Paul just diagnosed in Cretan culture and in the false teachers lies in the gospel's power to reshape human lives. God's character is visible where Christ creates people marked by "self-control" (2:2, 5–6, 12), where relationships bear these marks of God's character (2:2–10), and where the story of Christ's incarnation and redemptive work forms a people "zealous for good works" (2:11–14 NKJV, ESV). Throughout this section Paul has a missionary perspective, as is evident in his three "so that" phrases (2:5, 8, 10)—the first two having to do with the silencing of opposition and the last having to do with the furtherance of the gospel. The most profound argument Christians have that theirs is the true God "who does not lie" (see 1:2) is the lives they lead.

Older men are to exhibit confirmed integrity of character, and they are to display the gifts and virtues Paul urged in his earlier letters: "sound in faith, in love, and in endurance" (2:2; the practical outworking of hope).

Paul wishes older women to be prime examples of Jesus Christ's power to reshape impiety into godliness ("reverent in the way they live"—the phrase carries priestly connotations), social viciousness into justice ("not to be slanderers . . ."), and intemperance into self-control (". . . or addicted to much wine") (2:3). The instruction would have particular meaning on Crete. Traditionally, Cretan women knew greater political independence and sexual freedom than their mainland sisters. That heritage has met with the rise of "the new Roman woman" (see the discussion at 1 Tim. 2:8–15),

and Paul seems to be concerned about the abusive conversations and sexual adventures associated with Roman dinner parties. Paul calls the older women of the congregation to a brave—and not necessarily welcome—service to their younger sisters. They are to urge younger women to honor their responsibilities to their husbands and children, especially in showing sexual faithfulness to their husbands and in educating their children (Winter, 141–69).

To younger men, Paul addresses but one command: control yourselves. As unoriginal as the instruction may appear to us, it would have been altogether countercultural—and exceptionally community-formative—for Cretan young men to commit themselves to control over bodily appetites, avarice, ambition, temper, and tongue. What older women are to be to their younger sisters, Titus is to be to his younger brothers. In the whole of his behavior he is to be an example to them. In both the manner with which he teaches ("integrity, seriousness"; 2:7) and the theological accuracy with which he teaches ("and soundness of speech"; 2:8), Titus is to point younger men to an intersection of life and doctrine, robbing detractors of a potent point of critique.

In verse 10, Paul loads slaves' faithfulness in the most basic behaviors (not back-talking and not pilfering) with the weightiest of freight: "they will make the teaching about God our Savior attractive" (2:10). Thus, Paul joins ranks with Jesus in embracing the radically countercultural notion that the most eloquent pulpit is a towel and a basin (John 13).

B. Theological grounding: God's grace and glory (2:11–15). Paul transitions now to the idea that God came not to punish but to save us from our "ungodliness and worldly passions." Thus he "has appeared" once in "grace" (2:11). There will also be a future "appearing of the glory of our great God and Savior, Jesus Christ" (2:13). Paul chooses his terms carefully, referring to Christ's incarnation here and in 3:4 with abstract nouns: "grace," "glory," "kindness," and "love of God." To counter the Cretan religious lie that god emerged from humanity, Paul stresses that deity has come down to humanity. Further, it is as one who is already fully divine that Jesus bestows saving benefits—deity is not something conferred on him after the fact. Moreover, Paul describes Christ's coming as bringing salvation "to all people," a salvation that is defined in terms of Israel's exodus ("redeem . . . a people that are his very own" [2:14; see Exod. 19:5]) and God's promises for a restored Israel ("purify for himself" [1:14; see Ezek. 37:23]). A singular biblical story of creation, fall, redemption, and consummation is being played out in the world's history.

In this paragraph, Paul demonstrates that for him "salvation" is an immensely dense complex of realities. In the first place, Jesus's coming has educative value, answering Hellenistic culture's deepest desire for a school of truth (for some Greeks "piety," for others "prudence"), justice, and temperance. Second, as a work of "redemption" and "purification," Jesus's coming—like the exodus that had prefigured it in biblical history—breaks powers that hold humans in the control of alien domination—whether of "ungodliness" or "worldly passions" (2:12) or "all wickedness" (2:14; literally "lawlessness"). Third, Jesus's coming provides redemption and

purification precisely because and to the extent that his coming was one in which he "gave himself for us"—that is, to provide atonement (see 1 Tim. 2:6; Gal. 1:4; 2:20; 4:25; 8:1–4).

4. A Lifestyle Appropriate to Sound Doctrine (3:1–7)

A. Responsibilities in state and society (3:1–2). In 1 Timothy 2:2 Paul urges prayer for civil authorities. Now—as at Romans 13:1–7—Paul provides instruction for living under civil authority. The instructions in Romans 13 are simply to submit and be willing to pay taxes. Here the instructions are more active. The Greek term translated "be obedient" (3:1) indicates readiness of persuasion—an attitude of cooperation. In an age when municipal leaders often begged off when asked to help their communities, Paul tells Christians: "Be ready to do whatever is good." Moreover, when Crete's Christians step into the political arena, their demeanor should belie the Cretan prophet's saying that

> In Titus 3:1, Paul says, "Remind the people to be subject to rulers and authorities." One local ruler was the praetor, a Roman governor stationed in Gortyna, Crete's capital. Shown here are the ruins of his residence and of the government complex known as the praetorium (second century AD).

Cretans are "vicious beasts" (Titus 1:12; NIV "evil brutes"). Christians in the public square are to be winsome and conciliatory: "to slander no one, to be peaceable and considerate, and always to be gentle toward everyone" (3:2).

B. Theological grounding: God's kindness and benevolence (3:3–7). Without the grace of God, all people—not just Cretans!—show their incapacity for sobriety, justice, and piety. Thus Paul now includes himself in the confession of the misanthropic vices of humankind. As he did at 1 Corinthians 6:9–11, Paul here describes the turning point in terms of washing, justification, and the Holy Spirit.

Following verse 3's stinging indictment, verses 4–7 (a single sentence in the Greek) offer a robust theology of personal transformation. This statement completes and elaborates thoughts begun in 2:11–14.

In 2:11, Paul called the incarnation a personification of "grace." (At 2 Cor. 13:14, Paul indicates his association of Christ with "grace.") Now in 3:4 he introduces two notable terms. The Greek word for "kindness" (*chrēstotēs*) sounds similar to the title Christ. Paul uses a distinctive Greek word for "love" (*philanthrōpia*). Its first appearance in Greek literature refers to the fact that Prometheus had so "loved humans" that he raised the ire of Zeus. Here Paul stresses God is not a Zeus-like, selfish misanthrope who actually hates humankind. The incarnation is proof of God's *philanthrōpia*, his love for humankind.

Christ's appearing "that offers salvation" in 2:11 (a virtually untranslatable Greek expression that means something like "with the capacity to save") is completed by 3:5's stronger statement: when Christ appeared, "he saved us."

Christ's work extrinsic to us in 2:11–14 finds its complement in the Holy Spirit's work intrinsic to us in 3:4–7. What Christ accomplished for us, the Holy Spirit now makes active in us. Verses 4–7 not only move the discussion from the outside to the inside and from Christ's work to the Holy Spirit's; they also go one more step by including reference to the Father, making the discussion fully about the Trinity. For while it is

altogether true that Christ is called Savior here (because he is the embodiment of God's "kindness and love" and because it is through him that the Holy Spirit is outpoured), nonetheless it is the (implied) Father who is the subject of the main verb of the whole sentence: "he saved" (3:5). Moreover, it is the (implied) Father who pours out the Holy Spirit.

Finally, these verses sweep Paul's use of Hellenistic aspirations (to sobriety, justice, and piety) and Hebrew narrative (exodus and covenant community) into his familiar theology of baptismal washing, justification "not because of righteous things we had done," and inward "rebirth and renewal by the Holy Spirit."

5. Summary: "Good Works" versus Foolish Controversies (3:8–11)

Titus is to teach with such authority (2:15) and so strongly to emphasize correct doctrine (3:8) because Paul wants the teaching to take visible shape through believers' being "careful to devote themselves to doing what is good." As those marked by a turning from irreligion, social viciousness, and personal dissolution (1:12; 3:3), believers display a life of gospel-shaped justice and self-control that is "excellent and profitable for everyone" (3:8; cf. Matt. 5:16).

Paul closes the body of the letter by repeating his warning about the false teachers (see 1:10–16). He adds here the provision to avoid those who are so divisive that they tear the fabric of the Christian community (cf. Rom. 16:17–20; 1 Cor. 5:1–13; 2 Cor. 2:5–11).

6. Personal Instructions (3:12–15)

The closing notes seem straightforward but are relevant in the question of Paul's authorship of this letter. Mentioned here are names familiar in other letters of Paul (Tychicus and Apollos). However, there also appear two individuals (Artemas and Zenas) and a place (Nicopolis, apparently on the west coast of the Greek mainland) that are otherwise unattested in Paul. The unfamiliar names seem unlikely from the hand of someone posing as the apostle. In fact, the references seem implicitly to confirm that Paul was released and went to new places unrecorded in Acts.

Just before his final greetings, Paul reasserts his dominant concern: that believers on Crete show the proof of their teaching in their lives.

Select Bibliography

Fee, Gordon D. *1 and 2 Timothy, Titus*. New International Biblical Commentary. Peabody, MA: Hendrickson, 1988.

Johnson, Luke Timothy. *Letters to Paul's Delegates: 1 Timothy, 2 Timothy, Titus*. New Testament in Context. Valley Forge, PA: Trinity Press International, 1996.

Kelly, J. N. D. *A Commentary on the Pastoral Epistles*. Grand Rapids: Baker, 1963, 1981.

Kidd, Reggie M. "Titus as Apologia: Grace for Liars, Beasts, and Bellies." *Horizons in Biblical Theology* 21, no. 2 (December 1999): 185–209.

———. *Wealth and Beneficence in the Pastoral Epistles: A "Bourgeois" Form of Early Christianity?* Atlanta: Scholars Press, 1990.

Knight, George W., III. *The Pastoral Epistles: A Commentary on the Greek Text*. New International Greek Testament Commentary. Grand Rapids: Eerdmans, 1992.

Marshall, I. Howard, and Philip H. Towner. *A Critical and Exegetical Commentary on the Pastoral Epistles*. International Critical Commentary. New York: T. & T. Clark, 1999, 2004.

Stott, John R. W. *Guard the Gospel: The Message of 2 Timothy*. The Bible Speaks Today. Downers Grove, IL: InterVarsity, 1973.

———. *Guard the Truth: The Message of 1 Timothy and Titus*. The Bible Speaks Today. Downers Grove, IL: InterVarsity, 1996.

Towner, Philip H. *The Letters to Timothy and Titus*. New International Commentary on the New Testament. Grand Rapids: Eerdmans, 2006.

Winter, Bruce W. *Roman Wives, Roman Widows: The Appearance of New Women and the Pauline Communities*. Grand Rapids: Eerdmans, 2003.

Witherington, Ben, III. *A Socio-Rhetorical Commentary on Titus, 1–2 Timothy and 1–3 John*. Vol. 1 of *Letters and Homilies for Hellenized Christians*. Downers Grove, IL: InterVarsity, 2006.

Philemon

V. Henry T. Nguyen

Introduction

Paul's brief letter to Philemon is a fascinating work that provides an illustration of how the gospel transforms the lives of Christians and the way they treat one another. There are two features that make this epistle distinct among the New Testament writings. First, it is the shortest of Paul's letters, consisting of 335 words in 25 verses in the Greek text. Second, it is one of the few letters addressed to an individual rather than to a church or a number of churches; however, Paul does include other addressees in his opening and closing greetings (vv. 2, 23–24), which suggests that on another level the personal letter was to be read in the wider church community.

The details in the epistle provide us with a rough sketch of the story behind the letter. Paul, who is in prison, writes to Philemon, his "dear friend" (literally "beloved one") and "fellow worker" (v. 1). Philemon is apparently wealthy, since he is a slave owner and has a large house that is able to accommodate a church gathering (v. 2). The letter is accompanied by Onesimus, Philemon's slave, who has been away from Philemon and with Paul for some time due to a breach in their slave-master relationship. Paul returns Onesimus—who has become a Christian while with Paul (v. 10)—to Philemon and appeals for restoration between Philemon and Onesimus. Despite these details of the three-way relationship between Paul, Philemon, and Onesimus, many essential aspects of the epistle are open to debate—including the letter's occasion and purpose, the specifics of Paul's request, the historical situation behind the letter, and his attitude toward slavery.

Authorship, Date, and Place of Origin

There has been no major challenge to Paul's authorship of the letter (v. 1) or to the letter's literary integrity. The letter indicates that Paul is imprisoned (vv. 1, 9–10), but the location of his imprisonment remains unclear. Scholars have put forward three main proposals: Ephesus in the mid-50s, Rome in the early 60s, and Caesarea Maritima in the late 50s. Of the three proposals, the two more plausible options are Rome and Ephesus. Since Rome is the traditional location for Paul's "prison epistles" (Ephesians, Philippians, and Colossians), it could be the location of his imprisonment in this letter given the close link between Paul's epistles to the Colossians and to Philemon (e.g., see the similar lists of Paul's companions in Col. 4:10–14 and Philem. 23–24). However, the long distance from Rome to Philemon's house in Colossae makes Onesimus's travel to Philemon seem unrealistic. Ephesus, on the other hand, is in close proximity to Colossae, thus making Onesimus's journey to Philemon more feasible. Unfortunately, the book of Acts and Paul's letters do not mention an Ephesian imprisonment. In the end, the location of Paul's imprisonment remains uncertain.

Occasion and Purpose

Why did Paul write this letter? As early as the end of the fourth century, the "traditional" explanation has been that Paul writes the letter to Philemon appealing on behalf of Onesimus, who is a runaway slave of Philemon. Since Paul finds himself in a delicate position of harboring a "fugitive" and being legally obligated to return Onesimus to Philemon, he sends him back to Philemon with a request for clemency on behalf of Onesimus. Proponents of this theory speculate that verse 18—"If he [Onesimus] has done you any wrong or owes you anything, charge it to me"—means Onesimus has defrauded Philemon or stolen from him, which has propelled him to flee. Those who affirm this view also perceive Paul as willing to repay Philemon for what Onesimus has done, or more specifically, what he has taken. Paul's request, then, is for Philemon to readmit Onesimus into his household, clear his debt, and possibly grant him freedom (manumission).

Despite the popularity of the runaway interpretation, there are problems with it. In fact, there has been a widespread challenge to this view. One problem is the difficulty of accounting for why Onesimus, having defrauded or stolen from Philemon, would seek to obtain help from Philemon's friend Paul. It is doubtful that Onesimus

Paul sent his letter to Philemon via Philemon's slave, Onesimus. The delivery of the letter may have resembled the scene on this gravestone (ca. 50 BC), in which a slave holding a scroll stands before Caius Popillius (the deceased).

would risk being captured and punished by seeking out an apostle in prison. And it might be too great a coincidence if the two met by chance in the same prison. Also unlikely is the suggestion that Onesimus was captured and put into the same prison as Paul, since a runaway slave would not be placed with a Roman citizen under "house arrest," and Paul would not be able to send a fellow prisoner to Colossae. Another difficulty of this interpretation is that, if Onesimus was a "fugitive," Paul as a Roman citizen would have been obligated by Roman law to return Onesimus to Philemon. As a fugitive, Onesimus could suffer severe punishment, anywhere from beating to execution. In light of this severity, critics of the traditional interpretation have pointed out that if Paul writes that he will repay Philemon for what Onesimus has done (v. 18), then Paul is primarily concerned with some other matter than Onesimus's running away. Moreover, if Onesimus was indeed a runaway slave, it is strange that Paul fails to mention Onesimus's regret or sorrow, which we would expect to find in the letter. Thus, there is no clear evidence in the epistle that Onesimus is a runaway slave who has found Paul in prison.

Some interpreters have posited the scenario of Onesimus's leaving Philemon due to his poor working conditions and possible abuse by Philemon. However, if Onesimus did seek Paul out regarding unfavorable conditions, we would expect Paul in the letter to make a reference to Philemon's mistreatment and to ask him to treat Onesimus more favorably (cf. Col. 4:1). Furthermore, this interpretation places the blame primarily on Philemon, but Paul seems to admit that Onesimus, rather than Philemon, is at fault.

One strong proposal, which has a growing number of supporters, provides a scenario and corroboration of the text's details better than the runaway theory. This interpretation contends that Onesimus did not defraud Philemon or steal from him but committed an error that financially burdened Philemon and probably aroused his anger. Onesimus, then, seeks out Paul as a mediator in this matter. There was a legal custom during that time that allowed Onesimus to seek out a friendly third party to advocate and intercede on his behalf. Pliny the Younger's letter to Sabinianus (*Letter* 9.21) is a frequently cited ancient text that provides some striking parallels to the situation and to Paul's strategy in the Letter to Philemon. This scenario, then, regards Onesimus as not having run away but having sought Paul's intercession for the goal of returning to his master in more favorable circumstances.

In spite of the uncertainty surrounding the letter's occasion, these views all recognize that Paul implores Philemon to be reconciled with Onesimus, given their new relationship in Christ. By coming to the defense of Onesimus, Paul follows Jesus's pattern of self-giving love that embraces those who are weak and helpless. Furthermore, the major theme underlying the letter is the demonstration of how the gospel challenges the status quo of relationships by transforming and uniting believers in Christ as brothers and sisters, regardless of their social identity.

Philemon and Slavery

Many people have approached the Letter to Philemon as a Christian treatise on slavery, given that the letter involves an apostle, a slave owner, and a slave. (See Thompson, 229–66, for theological insights into the issue of Christianity and slavery.) The letter was especially important in the eighteenth and nineteenth centuries during the efforts to abolish slavery. Interestingly, it was used to support both the sanctioning and abolishment of slavery; for instance, proponents of slavery regarded Paul as condoning slavery since he sends a slave back to his owner. A careful reading of the text, however, reveals the complexity of this issue and points to a more prominent (though still related) issue of how the gospel transforms Christian relationships.

Although it does provide a social commentary on the realities of ancient society and the church, the letter does not provide a systematic treatment of slavery. In fact, it is difficult to ascertain Paul's attitude toward slavery in general and whether he protests this established social institution and accepted way of life in the ancient world. It must be kept in mind that slavery in the ancient world was different from the slave trade in the modern era in North America and Europe, especially since the latter came to be viewed as morally abhorrent while the former was not. Again, Paul's ultimate concern in the letter is that the gospel radically alters how Christians treat one another, regardless of their social positions and status. In Colossians 3:11 he momentously declares that "there is no Gentile or Jew, circumcised or uncircumcised, barbarian, Scythian, *slave or free*, but Christ is all, and is in all." In regard to Philemon and Onesimus, then, Paul affirms how the gospel alters their relationship from master-slave to brothers in Christ: "no longer as a slave, but better than a slave, as a dear brother" (v. 16). Therefore, the gospel transforms and enhances any social relationship, regardless of its shape (e.g., master-slave), and breaks down barriers of inequality between brothers and sisters in Christ. It should be said, however, that in the case of Onesimus, Paul seems to expect that Philemon will liberate Onesimus from slavery (vv. 16, 21)—thus opposing the view that Paul simply accepted (and even endorsed) the realities of slavery.

Commentary

1. Greetings (1–3)

In his typical fashion Paul opens the letter according to the standard conventions of the time. Before giving his usual greeting of "grace" and "peace" (v. 3), he indicates that the letter is sent from himself and Timothy and is addressed to Philemon and other members in the church. There are four notable features in this opening greeting. First, Paul identifies himself as a "prisoner of Christ," which is unusual since he typically describes himself in his letters as an "apostle" or "slave" of Christ. With the use of "prisoner" here Paul is probably (1) reminding his readers of his imprisonment, which results from his identification with Christ and his work for Christ, (2) evoking some emotional sympathy from Philemon and church members, (3) appealing to Philemon not based on his apostolic authority, and (4) identifying with Onesimus in a similarly humble status. Second, Timothy is included as a cosender (similar to Col. 1:1), probably because he was a close intimate of Paul and possibly knew Philemon. Third, although Philemon is the primary addressee, Paul also greets Apphia (Philemon's wife?), Archippus (his son?), and the church that meets in Philemon's home. This greeting highlights the public nature of this "personal" letter, since it would have been read aloud before the church. The inclusion of the church community in this private matter not only applies pressure on Philemon to act on Paul's appeal but also underscores that the church has a right to be involved in the personal affairs of its members. So Paul is not merely concerned about Philemon and Onesimus but also about the unity and love of the church community. Finally, in the greeting Paul uses familial imagery of "brother" and "sister"—and also "dear friend" (literally "beloved one")—which not only underscores the intimacy of the church but also prepares Philemon for the appeal to accept Onesimus as a "dear brother" (v. 16).

2. Prayer of Thanksgiving (4–7)

At this point, Paul is personally addressing Philemon, since the "you, your" are singular throughout verses 4–22. Paul asserts in verse 5 that he constantly thanks God: "I have heard of your love and faith, which you have for the Lord Jesus and for all the saints" (literal translation). Interpreters have often been puzzled by how the saints and Jesus could be the objects of both "love and faith." For Paul, however, both ideas are intertwined—love and faith toward Christ result in love and faith unto others.

Verse 6 is one of the most obscure verses in the epistle and poses many problems for interpreters. Some have understood the phrase "the sharing [*koinōnia*] of your faith" (NKJV, RSV) as a reference to Philemon's evangelistic work; however, the phrase more likely refers to Philemon's sharing of the same faith with other Christ followers. Paul explains that this "active" (or "effective") shared experience of faith in Christ will lead to the knowledge of every "good" that is ours, and for Christ, who is the origin and goal of the Christian life. In verse 7, by esteeming Philemon's love and faith for the saints and his "refreshing" of their "hearts" (cf. v. 20), Paul intimates that Philemon should continue to show his love for the saints by extending it toward another saint, Onesimus.

It is important to bear in mind that in Paul's epistles, the prayer of thanksgiving often hints to the issues that will be addressed in the remainder of the letter. In this letter, some key words in the thanksgiving that are taken up in the body of the letter are "love" (vv. 5, 9), "sharing, welcome" (vv. 6, 17), "good, favor" (vv. 6, 14), "heart" (vv. 7, 12, 20), "refresh" (vv. 7, 20), and "brother" (vv. 7, 20).

3. Paul's Appeal (8–22)

Although Paul is bold enough in Christ to command Philemon to do what he ought (v. 8), he appeals on the basis of love (v. 9). For Paul, the love believers share in Christ bonds them and solidifies Christ's work of reconciliation on the cross (Col. 1:20–23; 3:11). In other words, this love breaks down social barriers and places all three individuals (Paul, Philemon, and Onesimus) on common ground in Christ. Paul, moreover, in his appeal to Philemon, refers to himself as an "old [or elderly] man" and as a "prisoner of Christ Jesus" (v. 9), two descriptors that would elicit compassion and respect from Philemon and the members of the church.

Paul then explains that his request to Philemon is for Paul's "son," Onesimus, whom Paul "fathered" (i.e., converted to Christ) while in prison (v. 10). In verse 11 Paul makes a play on the name "Onesimus," which literally means "useful" and was a very common name during that era for slaves and those of servile origins. He asserts that even though Onesimus was once "useless," he is now "useful" to both Paul and Philemon. And Paul makes another pun by using *achrēstos* ("useless"), which would be pronounced exactly like *achristos* ("Christless"), to articulate that Onesimus is now no longer "Christless" but indeed "useful" (*euchrēstos*) to Paul and Philemon.

While telling Philemon that he is sending Onesimus back to him, Paul expresses that it is not easy for him to do so because Onesimus has become so dear to him—being Paul's "very heart" (v. 12). Paul further explains that although he wanted to keep Onesimus with him, he would not do so without Philemon's

initiation or consent (vv. 13–14). Paul then suggests that perhaps there was a bigger, divine purpose behind Onesimus's brief separation from Philemon, for Philemon might now "have him back for good" (v. 15). To be specific, Philemon will have Onesimus back "no longer as a slave, but better than a slave, as a dear brother" (v. 16). As noted above, in verses 1–2 Paul employed familial language, which prepares Philemon for the request here to accept Onesimus also as a "brother." In fact, Paul stresses the common relationship that he, Philemon, *and* Onesimus share as brothers in the Lord. Thus, in verse 16 Paul accentuates a transformation in social relations for those in Christ by urging Philemon to embrace Onesimus first and foremost as a brother. Furthermore, it is quite possible to grasp Paul's words "no longer as a slave" as an appeal for Onesimus's manumission, since it could explain the new relationship "in the flesh and in the Lord" (literal translation). Regardless of whether Paul is appealing for Onesimus's freedom here, he does spotlight this new kinship as the paramount relationship

> The freeing of slaves (manumission) by their owners was a frequent event in the Roman world. Many male slaves were freed prior to their thirtieth birthdays, and female slaves would be freed so they could marry. The Greek inscription on this relief commemorates the freeing of a female slave by her mistress (first century AD)

between Philemon and Onesimus rather than the master-slave relationship.

Having conveyed the emotional basis of his appeal (vv. 8–16), Paul now, in the climax of the letter, articulates his specific request to Philemon. After imploring Philemon to receive and embrace Onesimus based on their new kin relationship in Christ, Paul identifies with Onesimus by taking on the status of an indebted slave and asking Philemon to accept Onesimus as though he were accepting Paul—that is, as a "partner" (v. 17). Paul, in fact, strengthens his appeal by enjoining Philemon to reckon any of Onesimus's debts to Paul (vv. 18–19). Although Onesimus's fault and debt are not explained in the text, it is possible that Onesimus has wronged Philemon in some financial matter and consequently owes money to him. In extending an IOU (written with "my [Paul's] own hand" [v. 19]) to Philemon, Paul asserts that he will not even mention the incredible debt and obligation that Philemon owes him (v. 19), which is probably a reference to Philemon's conversion under Paul's ministry. In verse 20 Paul makes another pun on Onesimus's name by using its verb form (*oninēmi*) in his request to "have some benefit" (*onaimēn*) from Philemon, a request similar to the request for a "favor" (or "good work") in verse 14. The benefit "in the Lord" that Paul is asking Philemon for is probably what was mentioned in verses 10–14: to accept Onesimus back, to clear any of his debts, possibly to grant him freedom, and to return him to Paul for further service in the work of the gospel, a work in which Onesimus has proven to be "useful" (vv. 11, 13).

Paul further requests Philemon, "Refresh my heart in Christ" (v. 20), which is an encouragement for him to "refresh" Onesimus—Paul's "very heart" (v. 12)—according to their shared bond "in the Lord," "in Christ" (v. 20). Paul, moreover, expects Philemon to be able to refresh his heart, since he earlier thanked God for Philemon's refreshing of the saints' hearts (v. 7). In fact, Paul states that he has no doubt about

Philemon's "obedience" (v. 21), which is interesting since Paul asserted earlier that he is not going to give Philemon any commands (v. 8). This confidence in Philemon's obedience to an appeal based on love (v. 9) implies that Paul's requests in the letter signify what the gospel requires rather than what Paul thinks Philemon should do. Paul even points out the extent of Philemon's obedience, which is "even more" than what Paul asks for (v. 21). This degree of "even more" insinuates that Philemon should grant Onesimus his freedom from slavery and return Onesimus to Paul.

Before concluding the letter, Paul includes a request for a guest room to be prepared for him (v. 22). Paul apparently is confident that he will soon be released from imprisonment and be able to visit Philemon. Also, in the last clause of this verse, the "you, your" are plural, which means that Paul is again addressing the wider church community.

4. Closing Greetings (23–25)

Paul closes the letter with a list of individuals who send their greetings to Philemon (again, the "you" in reference to Philemon is singular). This list (vv. 23–24) resembles the one in Colossians (4:10–14), except for some notable differences: there is an interchange between Epaphras and Aristarchus as "fellow prisoner," the ordering of the names is different, and Jesus Justus is not included here. Though the two lists are not identical, the strong resemblance between them suggests that the epistles to Philemon and to the Colossians were written within a short time of each other. Finally, Paul's closing benediction (v. 25), which addresses the members of the church (the "your" is plural), is in typical Pauline fashion and exhibits the distinct Christian substance of the letter (see the distinct Christian greeting in v. 3).

Select Bibliography

Dunn, James D. G. *The Epistles to the Colossians and to Philemon.* New International Greek Testament Commentary. Grand Rapids: Eerdmans, 1996.

Garland, David E. *Colossians and Philemon*. NIV Application Commentary. Grand Rapids: Zondervan, 1998.

O'Brien, Peter T. *Colossians, Philemon*. Word Biblical Commentary. Waco: Word, 1982.

Patzia, Arthur. "Philemon, Letter to." In *Dictionary of Paul and His Letters*. Edited by Gerald F.

Hawthorne, Ralph P. Martin, and Daniel G. Reid. Downers Grove, IL: InterVarsity, 1993.

Thompson, Marianne Meye. *Colossians and Philemon*. Two Horizons New Testament Commentary. Grand Rapids: Eerdmans, 2005.

Wright, N. T. *Colossians and Philemon*. Tyndale New Testament Commentaries. Grand Rapids: Eerdmans, 1986.

Hebrews

Robert S. Rayburn

Introduction

Authorship

Although the Letter to the Hebrews was clearly written to address a spiritual crisis in a specific community of Christians by one well known to them, one cannot determine with certainty the identity of the author, the specific recipients or the location of their community, or the precise date of the letter's composition.

Though the letter has been ascribed to Paul from at least the end of the second century in the Eastern church and nearly universally in Christendom from Augustine to the Reformation, the arguments against Pauline authorship now appear to be decisive. Chief among them are the following: (1) the letter is anonymous, which is uncharacteristic of Paul; (2) the style of Greek is significantly different from that of Paul's letters; (3) the statement of Hebrews 2:3 seems impossible to reconcile with Galatians 1:12; and (4) the ambiguous testimony of the early fathers: Clement of Alexandria and Origen accepted Hebrews as Pauline but with major qualifications; Tertullian named Barnabas as the author and gave no hint of a controversy on that point—difficult to explain if the author were none other than the great apostle to the Gentiles.

The reference to Timothy (Heb. 13:23) and the ancient but inconsistent testimony to Pauline authorship have led to the widespread opinion that the author was at least a member of the Pauline circle. Origen suggested that he was a pupil of Paul who wrote what he had learned from the apostle. Others have proposed Luke either as the author or, as Clement of Alexandria supposed, the translator of Paul's Hebrew original. Most modern scholarly opinion, however, is divided between Barnabas and Apollos. Barnabas was a Hellenistic Jew, a Levite in fact, a prominent member of the apostolic circle (even called an apostle in Acts 14:14; cf. 1 Cor. 9:5–6), and has the considerable support of Tertullian's unqualified assertion that Barnabas was the author of Hebrews (*On Modesty* 20). Likewise Apollos, a highly educated Alexandrian Jew, a gifted controversialist, and a participant in the apostolic ministry (1 Cor. 1:12; 3:6), could well have written a work such as Hebrews, with its sophisticated use of Scripture and its elegant Greek. If the author of Hebrews was neither of these men, he was surely like them, "a good man, full of the Holy Spirit and faith" (Acts 11:24) and "a learned man, with a thorough knowledge of the Scriptures" (Acts 18:24; cf. 18:28). Plausible arguments can be advanced in favor of either of these and some others, but presently a firm conclusion remains unobtainable.

Certainly apostolicity was a prerequisite of canonicity, but this requirement could be satisfied by authorship by a member of the apostolic circle, as in the case of Mark or Luke-Acts. In any case, canonicity does not depend on the church's present certainty as to the authorship of a particular biblical work (e.g., Judges, 1–2 Chronicles). Furthermore, the author of Hebrews would be among the first to insist that the human authorship of Scripture is of secondary importance, being only the instrumentality of its divine inspiration. As he reminds his readers (3:7; 4:7), David may have written Psalm 95, but the Holy Spirit was the primary author and the one who speaks to us in it.

Occasion, Purpose, and Audience

The author's purpose in writing is quite clear, for he reiterates it regularly. He writes to arrest an incipient apostasy and to strengthen wavering faith. Perhaps some members of this community had already deserted the faith, turning their backs on the way of salvation and the Savior they had once acknowledged (6:4–6; 10:26–31). In any case, tempted to evade the persecution they were suffering on account of their faith and to find some way less costly than the discipleship to which Christ calls his people, many were trifling with apostasy by compromising their former beliefs (2:3, 18; 3:6, 12–15; 4:1, 11, 14; 6:4–6, 9–12; 10:19–29, 35–39; 12:1–3, 14–17, 25; 13:9, 13). With a keen appreciation of the fearful implications

of such a spiritual defection and with a deep personal interest in the outcome, the author writes this often severe, always affectionate, intensely sympathetic, and practical "word of exhortation" (13:22).

Those addressed are a community of converts from Judaism who, encountering stiff opposition from their former brethren and finding difficult the pioneering demanded of them by their new faith, were tempted to return to the comfortable security of the old ways. In recent times some scholars have maintained that the recipients of the letter were Gentiles or Christians irrespective of race and that the title "To the Hebrews" is only the by-product of a later and erroneous interpretation of the letter. However, the evidence of the epistle itself conclusively favors a Jewish Christian audience, and this remains the conclusion of a majority of scholars. Admittedly, it cannot be demonstrated that the title was attached to the letter prior to the last quarter of the second century AD, and its vagueness may appear not to comport well with a letter obviously addressed to a particular community (10:32–34; 13:18–19, 22–23) and not to Jewish Christians generally. Nevertheless, the title is very old and, so far as anyone knows, "To the Hebrews" is the only title the letter has ever had.

Further, the author throughout assumes on the part of his readers both an exact acquaintance

The ruins of the Jewish synagogue at Kefar Baram in Upper Galilee (third century AD). The Letter to the Hebrews was written to Jewish Christians who were tempted to return to Judaism.

with the Scriptures and an unshaken and unshakable conviction of their divine authority. Of course, Gentile converts acknowledged the Old Testament as the Word of God, but if their commitment to Christianity was weakened, so too would be their confidence in the Scriptures.

Finally, and decisively, a Jewish Christian audience is demanded by the central argument of the letter, which is designed to counter the opinion that the Levitical institutions were God's definitive provision for the salvation of humankind. The argument is constructed around three contrary-to-fact conditional statements (7:11; 8:7; 10:1–2), that is, statements in which the protasis (the "if" clause) is assumed to be false. The three statements and the massive argumentation marshaled in their support presuppose a real inclination on the part of the readers to assume the contrary, namely, that perfection could be attained through the Levitical priesthood, that the covenant life of Israel was and remains the ideal, and that the sacrifices could indeed make the worshiper perfect—thus rendering Christ and his work superfluous. Such assumptions were not a temptation for Gentile believers; and addressed to a Gentile audience, the great argument of the letter becomes what it definitely is not, a colorless examination of largely hypothetical questions. Rather, the letter is an impassioned plea to make complete and permanent the separation from Judaism (13:13).

One can possibly identify this community with some further precision. The Dead Sea Scrolls have greatly enlarged our knowledge of nonconformist Judaism in this period, that is, Judaism that was not primarily shaped by the rabbinical tradition and not represented by the Pharisees and Sadducees. Chief among representatives of such a separatist Judaism were the Essenes; it is widely believed that a community of Essenes was located at Qumran, where the Dead Sea Scrolls were found. Among the distinctives of this sect are a number that appear to bear some relation to the argument of Hebrews. These Jews looked for the fulfillment of Jeremiah's new covenant but

in the form of the restoration and purification of the Aaronic priesthood, with its system of ceremonies (cf. Heb. 7:11–28; 9:1–10); they anticipated the appearance of a great prophet, the second Moses of Deuteronomy 18:18 (*Rule of the Community* 9:11; 4QTestimonia; cf. Heb. 1:1–2), and sought a manner of life patterned after that of Israel in the wilderness (cf. Heb. 3:7–19; 4:1–11; 8:6–12; 12:18–21); they fostered extravagant speculations concerning angels, even expecting that in the coming kingdom the archangel Michael would play a more decisive role than the Messiah (*War Scroll* 17:6–7; cf. Heb. 1:4–2:18); they cast Melchizedek in the role of an eschatological deliverer (11QMelchizedek; cf. Heb. 7:1–17); and in their ritual they placed special emphasis on ceremonial washings (*Damascus Document* 10:10–13; *War Scroll* 14:2–3; cf. Heb. 6:2; 9:13). Though the evidence is by no means conclusive, a plausible case can be made for understanding Hebrews as a point-by-point refutation of the doctrines of a Jewish community of the Essene-Qumran variety; if correct, this would indicate that the recipients of the letter were originally converts from such a nonconformist Judaism and were now inclined to return to it.

Little more than this can be said about them. They were second-generation Christians. Never having seen or heard Jesus themselves, they had been evangelized by eyewitnesses (2:3). They were presumably Hellenistic (Greek-speaking) Jews, as the author cites the Greek version of the Old Testament, the Septuagint. They had suffered persecution but not yet martyrdom (10:32–34; 12:4). It may be that they were a distinct party or group that had separated itself from the larger believing community in their locality (10:25; 13:17, 24). Where they lived is impossible to determine. Jerusalem and Rome figure prominently in scholarly speculations, but the evidence is meager. Similarly, the place of the letter's composition remains uncertain. The only evidence in the letter itself is ambiguous (13:24), and the tradition that it was written from Rome is quite late.

Date

Clement of Rome makes use of Hebrews in his first letter, which is ordinarily dated around AD 95, though possibly earlier. A first-century date is further required by the facts that the recipients of the letter had learned the gospel from eyewitnesses of the Lord and that Timothy was still alive (2:3; 13:23). Other evidence supports a date of composition prior to AD 70. The absence of any mention of the destruction of the temple in Jerusalem furnishes a virtually unanswerable argument that the letter was written beforehand, inasmuch as mention of the demise of the temple ritual would seem so well suited to the author's purpose (8:13; 10:2). Further, the consistent use of the present tense in reference to the Levitical priesthood and ritual surely favors, though it does not demand, a date prior to the cessation of that ritual. Without knowing the location of this community of Jewish Christians, it is impossible to say more than this.

Theological Themes

The author describes his work as a "word of exhortation" (13:22), that is, a sermon, as appears from the use of the same phrase in Acts 13:15. Hebrews is a letter only secondarily, by reason of the few personal remarks at its conclusion and the fact that it was written in one place and dispatched to another. The sermonic form appears in the repeated reference to the author's speech (Heb. 2:5; 5:11; 6:9; 8:1; 9:5; 11:32); in his method, which is the citation, exposition, and application of Scripture; and in his singleness of purpose. Hebrews vies only with Galatians for the distinction of being the most single-minded work in the New Testament. It is a discourse on the absolute necessity of perseverance in the Christian faith. The arguments enlisted on behalf of this proposition are those precisely suited to allay the doubts and to unmask the errors that were undermining the faith of the author's readers.

However, the letter's specific destination and pointed applications notwithstanding, Hebrews is not at all provincial or dated as might be expected of a long-ago sermon to a long-forgotten community of Christians. The danger of apostasy being always present (Matt. 24:10; 1 Cor. 10:12; 1 Tim. 4:1), Hebrews' emphatic and solemn warning is always timely. The author supports his exhortation by appeal to some of the most fundamental elements of the good news, in particular those that have immediately to do with the nature and practicalities of the Christian's life of faith in the world. In addressing his readers' spiritual peril, he provides a scriptural elaboration of Christ's supremacy as the incarnate Son of God; his mediatorial work as intercessor, priest, and sacrifice; the nature of the Christian faith and hope; the method of God's dealing in mercy and judgment with his people; and the unity of the people of God and the gospel in the history of salvation. From these doctrines the author draws applications as profound and urgent for any believer today as for those to whom the sermon was first sent.

Like any good preacher, the author never loses sight of his readers' pressing need or his own purpose. He returns to his exhortation regularly, so that what one encounters in Hebrews is a repeated alternation between scriptural or doctrinal exposition and its application to the great question of his readers' perseverance in faith. (Note the recurring "therefore" in 2:1; 3:1; 4:1, 11, 14; 6:1; 10:19; 12:1, 28; cf. "the main point of what we are saying is this" [8:1].)

Two special features of the argument, crucial to a proper interpretation of the letter, require comment. First, the author's purpose is to correct his readers' ideas, derived from the principles and forms of the Judaism whence they came, that are incompatible with true faith and participation in the salvation of God. It is imperative that this purpose be given its due in the interpretation of the letter. Too often commentators have understood the author's central argument (chaps. 3–12) to be contrasting Christianity with the provisional religion of the Mosaic administration. It is then supposed that he sustains his exhortation to persevere in the faith and to make the break with

Judaism permanent by demonstrating that Judaism, embodying the temporary and imperfect economy of the Old Testament, has been superseded by and fulfilled in the religio-historical economy introduced by Christ and the apostles. Indeed, understood in this way, Hebrews is often thought to provide the New Testament's most thoroughgoing elaboration of the historical relationship between the Old Testament and the New Testament and the most complete explanation of the superiority of the latter.

This understanding of Hebrews, though very common, is quite contrary to the author's fundamental assumptions and clear statements. His contrast is never between a supposedly inferior faith, spirituality, and system of worship that prevailed in the age before Christ and their fulfillment in the Christian era. He says nothing about the difference between the religion or spiritual privileges of believers before and after Christ. On the contrary, at every point he identifies the situation of his readers with that of the ancient people of God: the gospel preached to them was preached to Israel in the wilderness (4:2); the promise, rest, and inheritance that pious Israelites grasped from afar is nothing other than that which is set before the believers to whom he writes and which they, likewise, will obtain only in the world to come and only if they endure in faith to the end (3:4, 19; 4:1; 6:11–12; 10:35–39; 11:10, 16, 35, 39–40; 12:1; 13:14); and the danger of apostasy and the enormity of its consequences are no less now that Christ has appeared (3:12; 4:11; 6:4–6; 10:26–31, 38–39; 12:25). It is striking and very important how completely this author identifies the situation that prevailed prior to the incarnation with that of the present and how readily he finds Christ present and active in the life of the Old Testament community (3:2–6; 11:26).

The contrast the author does draw is the radical contrast between unbelief and faith, apostasy and perseverance, the forfeiture of salvation and the eternal inheritance, and the wrath of God and his forgiveness. No doubt belonging to the church in the Christian era has advantages, but the author of Hebrews does not enumerate them. Indeed, although this letter is frequently claimed to be an assertion of the supremacy of the New Testament and the obsolescence of the Old Testament, on careful examination it proves instead to be the Bible's most thorough demonstration of the unity of the covenant of grace, the church of God, and true spirituality and faith throughout all eras of the history of salvation. Crucial to the

Few archaeological remains exist to help us imagine the magnificent second temple reconstructed by Herod the Great (first century BC). This large scale model (Israel Museum) helps us picture the place where observant Jews during the first century AD brought their sacrifices and offerings.

proper interpretation of the letter is how little interested this author is in distinguishing between the opportunities, privileges, responsibilities, and blessings of the saints before and after Christ and how completely he identifies them.

The failure to appreciate Hebrews' sustained emphasis on the unity of the administration of divine grace throughout the history of salvation has bedeviled the interpretation of the letter and muted its warnings. The author fashions his exhortation on the assumption of this unity. The recognition of this is vital; otherwise it is impossible to rightly understand the severe criticism that the author levels against the Old Testament covenant and worship. An appreciation of his consistent assumption of the unity of the gospel and the life of faith before and after the incarnation opens the way to the following recognition. In his criticism the author does not have in view the Old Testament economy per se, but rather that economy which eventuated when the gospel was not combined with faith, when the covenant was shorn of all but its outward forms, that is, the Old Testament economy as it was understood and practiced by the unbelieving Judaism of the author's day. This Judaism—not the true faith of the Old Testament—threatened his readers.

The great contrast drawn by this author is not between the old and new administrations, or between believers before and after the incarnation, but rather between two ways of salvation, one false and one true, and between two destinies, the one obtained by those who deny the faith and the other by those who patiently endure in faith and hope. In each case the former is illustrated in the letter chiefly by unbelieving Israel, the latter by the saints of that former era. One cannot overemphasize that the author treats the Mosaic administration, with its Levitical institutions, under the false view of them entertained in the Judaism of that day, a Judaism that had by this time so completely lost sight of the true meaning of the covenant, priesthood, and sacrifice that it no longer had

any place for a redeemer who would die for the sins of the world. In the letter's criticism of the Levitical institutions, therefore, one looks in vain for the author's admission of the proper and holy purpose of the sacrifices to signify and to confirm God's covenant, of the joy and peace that pious Israelites obtained in their evangelical use of them, and of their splendid and rightful place as an important part of covenant life. He does no justice to their rightful purpose but condemns them as utterly ineffectual to save sinners. "Weak and useless" is his scathing verdict (7:18–19). Indeed, to hear him tell it, it is hard to imagine what significant purpose was ever served by all these carnal regulations and performances (9:9–10; 10:11). The severely negative tone of his criticism of the Old Testament cultus is very impressive, and it is in no way mitigated by the author's description of the shadowy, provisional character of these institutions, by any external efficacy he attributes to them, or by the fact that he declares them fulfilled in the sacrifice of Christ; for in this way he does not intend to pay tribute to the cultus but only further to demonstrate its worthlessness in comparison with the priesthood and sacrifice of Christ.

In this criticism of the Levitical institutions, then, the author places himself squarely in the tradition of the Old Testament prophets who were similarly scornful of that worship as it was practiced by a people who, without living faith in God or submission to his law, trusted instead in the efficacy of external ordinances (Isa. 1:10–20; Jer. 7:21–23; Amos 5:21–25). It is imperative to remember that almost certainly Hebrews was written when the sacrifices were still being offered and when Jewish Christians were still participating, and properly so, in temple worship (Acts 21:20–26; cf. 1 Cor. 7:18). The author does not call for the abolition of the sacrificial ritual and the priesthood any more than the prophets before him. But like them he condemns the confidence that faithless and disobedient people are investing in mere ceremonies.

In sum, this author describes the Levitical ritual in much the same way as a preacher today might speak scornfully of the Lord's Supper to a congregation that imagines that one obtains the forgiveness of sins by the mere partaking of bread and wine. Interestingly, there is no mention of the Lord's Supper in Hebrews. The author has no intention of calling the attention of his readers, in their present state of mind, to another ceremony. Their growing confidence in externals could only too easily be transferred from the Levitical rites to those of the apostolic church—a danger to which the whole course of church history from that day to this bears sad but eloquent testimony.

Second, until relatively recent times the interpretation of Hebrews was heavily influenced by the widespread opinion that the author was a product of the Alexandrian school of biblical exegesis and, in particular, deeply indebted to Philo for his conceptual framework, his hermeneutics, and his manner of statement. The most significant consequence of this opinion was the eclipse of the eschatological perspective of the letter, a casualty of the assumption that the author shared Philo's conception of the timeless duality of the material and spiritual worlds. While there are certain affinities between Hebrews and the writings of Philo, the differences are profound and important. Recent scholarship has tended to discredit the alleged dependence on Philo, and the happy result of this has been a marked resurgence of interest in the eschatology of Hebrews. This is a great step forward, for in truth hardly any other book of the Bible more consistently throws the attention of the reader forward to the world to come.

Remarkably, the author is little interested in the present fulfillment of Old Testament prophecy. Indeed, the idea of fulfillment plays almost no role in the argument. For this author, the Old Testament is not a collection of prophecies now fulfilled in Christ so much as a contemporary word of God to be heard, believed, and obeyed. Expectation *not* fulfilled rather than unfulfilled

animates the letter and drives its argument. The rest of God, the eternal country and city, the resurrection, the receiving of the promise and inheritance, and even salvation itself (1:14; 9:28) were the hope of the saints of ancient days and must be no less so for every generation of believers (4:11; 10:36–37; 11:39–40; 13:14). The author's exhortation is always firmly fixed in his eschatology: the reason one must continue in the faith, holding fast to Christ, is not for fear of present consequences but because by shrinking back one forfeits the eternal rest and exposes oneself eventually to God's fearful judgment and consuming fire. The sustained emphasis of Hebrews on the futurity of salvation is a corrective to an unbiblical preoccupation with the present benefits of faith in Christ. Further, it is a reminder that the obligations of faith and obedience will never weigh on the church as they must until the specter of eternity is fixed before her mind's eye.

Outline

Commentary

1. The Superiority of the Christian Faith (1:1–10:18)

A. Jesus Christ superior to the prophets (1:1–4). The dramatic exordium is less an introduction than a thunderous opening salvo. This written sermon goes forth precisely to arrest a waning of conviction regarding the divine supremacy of Christ and the decisiveness of his work as the redeemer of sinners (1:1–2). The assertion of the Son's preeminence among the prophets and the finality of his revelation is possibly intended to correct the expectation of an eschatological prophet within the circle of Judaism from which these readers had come and to which they were now tempted to return. Note that no distinction is made between the message spoken formerly and "in these last days." It is not the message but the dignity of the messengers and the times and circumstances of their revelation that differ. God spoke then and now, and indeed continues to speak, through the ancient prophets as through his Son (e.g., 3:7; 10:37–38). One needs to remember that the living and active word of God (4:12) was for this author largely what is now called the Old Testament.

"These last days" (literally "at the end of these days") is taken from the Septuagint, which literally rendered the Hebrew phrase used in the Old Testament to designate the prophetic future (cf. Gen. 49:1; Deut. 4:30; Isa. 2:2; Ezek. 38:16). "These" refers to the future days prophesied in the Old Testament, or some of those days, or the beginning of them (cf. Heb. 9:26).

In verse 3, "radiance" indicates the Son's sharing of the divine attributes (cf. John 1:14; 2 Cor. 4:6), and "exact representation" indicates the correspondence of his nature with the Father's (cf. Col. 1:15). "Sustaining all things" refers to his government by which he brings the course of history to its appointed end. "Sat down" signifies the completion of the atonement (10:12–14) and suggests Christ's present activity as priest (4:14–16) and king (12:2). It is self-evident that if the Son's person and work are as described, any religion that does not place them at its center, in which he is not the hope and joy of sinners and the chief object of faith and worship, stands self-condemned.

B. Jesus Christ superior to angels (1:5–2:18). The superiority of the Son to the angels is now distinctly stated and furnished with an impressive biblical demonstration (1:5–14). The author's evident interest in providing conclusive proof of this point surely indicates that this was a matter of dispute. Possibly his readership attributed an unwarranted eminence to angels as a consequence of their function as mediators through whom God revealed the law (2:2; cf. Acts 7:53; Gal. 3:19). If the hypothesis of the readers' background in nonconformist Judaism is granted, they knew well an eschatology in which an angel played a more decisive role than the Messiah himself. Since they were Jews and Christians, their retreat from Christianity was resulting in a growing hesitance to ascribe divinity to Jesus while yet wishing to revere him, leaving him as less than God but more than man—that is, an angel. That his superior name is inherited indicates that Jesus Christ is here being considered not in his eternal and essential dignity as the Son of God but as the mediator, the "man Christ Jesus" (1 Tim. 2:5), who by his humiliation became superior to the angels (Heb. 2:9).

The fact that the author has the incarnate Son of God (1:5) in view helps in understanding Psalm 2:7, the first of the seven citations from Scripture, which figures prominently in the New Testament as a prophecy of the incarnation, the messianic ministry, and especially the resurrection (Mark 1:11; Luke 1:32; Acts 13:33; Heb. 5:5; cf. Rom. 1:4). The eternal Son could be said to become or to "be begotten" as the Son of God only with reference to the exaltation of the human nature he took to himself when he came into the world.

The second citation (2 Sam. 7:14), God's promise to David concerning Solomon, was extended in Old Testament prophecy and became the basis of the expectation of the messianic king of Davidic descent who would usher in God's everlasting kingdom (Ps. 72:1–20; Isa. 9:7; 11:1–9; Jer. 23:5–6; Luke 1:32–33).

In verse 6, the third citation (Deut. 32:43, from the longer text of the Septuagint and Dead Sea Scrolls; cf. Ps. 97:7) verifies that when the Son of God came into the world as a man, he was worshiped as divine. Perhaps the specific allusion is to Luke 2:13. "Firstborn" is another messianic title (Ps. 89:27). It suggests his consecration to God (Exod. 13:2) and his precedence as an heir. The application of this text to Christ is an instance of the attribution of the divine name Yahweh to Jesus.

The contrasting citations in verses 7–9 (Ps. 45:6–7; 104:4) establish that the superiority of the Son to the angels is as clear and great as that of a king to those who do his bidding, indeed, as that of God to his creatures. Psalm 45, a wedding song for an Israelite king, is properly applied to the one who establishes the reign of which the Old Testament kingship was but a foreshadowing. The ascription of this text to Christ results in one of the few places in the New Testament where Christ is directly referred to as God (cf. John 1:1; 20:28; Rom. 9:5).

In verses 10–12, the sixth citation (Ps. 102:25–27) serves to recapitulate the divine dignity of the incarnate Son of God as the Creator (1:2) and his majesty as the eternal Yahweh. (The divine name is missing in the Hebrew text, but the Septuagint's "O Lord" may bear witness to an earlier form of the Hebrew text. In any case, Yahweh is unmistakably being addressed, as the entire psalm demonstrates.)

The final citation, which occurs in verses 13–14, is from Psalm 110 and climactically reiterates the divine honor bestowed on Christ, the royal status he presently enjoys, and the inheritance soon to be his. On the other hand, the angels are but servants (cf. Ps. 103:20–21); some stand (Luke 1:19), but none sit in Christ's seat of honor. Their special ministry is to those who will share in Christ's inheritance. In his first mention of salvation, the author characteristically views it as yet future (2:5; 9:28).

The preceding exposition is now applied (2:1–4) in the first of many exhortatory sections that punctuate the letter and demonstrate its true purpose. The readers had no reservations concerning the legitimacy and severity of the sanctions of the Mosaic law, though it was mediated by angels (cf. Deut. 33:2 in the Septuagint; Acts 7:53; Gal. 3:19). How much more, then, ought they to fear the consequences of slighting a revelation communicated immediately by one far greater than angels, attested by eyewitnesses, and confirmed by miraculous signs of various kinds? The author is not belittling the law. It too was a revelation of God attested with marvelous signs (Heb. 12:18–27). But that only serves to heighten the sanction that attaches to the Son's own announcement of God's salvation. "Drift away" and "ignore" (2:1, 3) suggest less a deliberate repudiation of the faith than a squandering of salvation through an unwillingness to meet its stern requirements (3:12–13).

In the next section (2:5–18) the contrast between Christ and the angels continues. The assertion of the sovereignty of the Son over the world to come may be a direct rebuttal of such speculation regarding the role of angels in the coming kingdom now known to have been entertained among the Essenes. "The world to come" is the author's theme and thus may be identified with the salvation just mentioned in 2:3 (cf. 9:28). Throughout Hebrews, the author views salvation in terms of its future consummation. Its present dimensions are not emphasized, since they are not immediately relevant to the author's purpose, which is to call his readers to that persevering faith which alone obtains entrance to the heavenly country (Heb. 10:35–39).

The citation of Psalm 8:4–6 in verses 6–9 is introduced with an expression of striking indifference to the human authorship of Scripture. The psalm itself harks back to Genesis 1:26 and the supreme dignity bestowed on humanity, God's unique image bearer and vice regent. Elsewhere in the New Testament (Matt. 21:16;

1 Cor. 15:27; Eph. 1:22) it receives a messianic interpretation. Jesus is the perfect fulfillment of that dignity as *the* Son of man and last Adam. The incarnate Son's history has two periods: that of his humiliation and that of his eternal exaltation. Those in Christ recapitulate his history—they too, though lower now, will one day rule over angels (1 Cor. 6:3). Though the subjection of all things to Christ awaits the consummation, it is guaranteed by his exaltation to God's right hand, a reward for his self-sacrifice for sinners (Heb. 10:13–14; 12:2; Phil. 2:6–11).

In the following paragraph (2:10–18) the author explains why the Son had to become a man and suffer and die as a man. As the larger subject of the comparison of the Son to angels is not forgotten (2:16), it may be assumed that this explanation is offered in part to allay the suspicion of his readers that Jesus's reputation, on account of his humanity and humiliation at the hands of mere men, suffers in comparison with that of such purely spiritual and mighty beings.

The reason that the Son became a man and incurred such ignominy was precisely that in no other way could God save his people from their sins (2:10; 5:8–9; 9:15). The incarnation was not a pageant but a tragic necessity, for a salvation that would meet the exigencies of sinful humans and a just God required such suffering as only a divine-human Savior could endure. The Father is identified both as the original source of salvation in Christ and the ultimate beneficiary (cf. 1 Cor. 15:24, 28; 2 Cor. 5:18–21). "Pioneer," or "trailblazer" (Greek *archēgos*, as in Heb. 12:2), is a better translation than "author" (NASB), since the term refers to one who opens the way that others might follow (2:10; cf. Heb. 6:20).

In Hebrews the sanctification that results from Christ's sacrifice is not the moral renewal of the believer's life, which flows from and follows on his justification (as in Paul), but rather his reconciliation to God (2:11; 10:10, 14, 29). What makes Christ one with the beneficiaries of his sacrifice is not that they have the same Father (both being sons of God) but that they share a common humanity. "Is not ashamed"

(2:11) is an affirmation of the compassionate identification of Christ with his unworthy people, which led him to empty himself. It closely approximates Paul's statement in Philippians 2:6–8.

Three citations are now offered to demonstrate the Son's solidarity with the people of God (2:12–13). The first, from the unmistakably messianic Psalm 22, attests Christ's brotherhood with the redeemed. The second and third are from Isaiah 8:17–18, the prophet's cry of the heart interpreted messianically, especially on the strength of verse 14—"a stone that causes people to stumble" (cf. Rom. 9:33; 1 Pet. 2:8). Jesus is so much a man that he too must trust in God, and the people of God are his fellows not only as his brethren but also as his offspring (cf. Isa. 53:10).

The point of Christ's sharing humanity is recapitulated and elaborated in 2:14–15. It was necessary that the Son of God become a man, since a human death was required for the sin that separated humankind from God and rendered humankind subject to the devil. Only a man could die and only the God-man could die for the sins of the world (Gal. 4:4–5). The breaking of the devil's grip is accomplished precisely by the breaking of the grip of sin (Eph. 2:1–5), and liberation from the fear of death is nothing else but liberation from the guilt of sin or liability to God's wrath (1 Cor. 15:54–57).

In 2:16–18, the author further develops the rationale for the incarnation. Because Christ's purpose was to "help" (literally "take hold of"; the same Greek word occurs in Heb. 8:9) the people of God rather than angels, he had to become a man. Abraham's descendants are characteristically viewed as a spiritual rather than a racial entity—the elect of God (Rom. 9:6; 11:1–8; Gal. 3:29). There are elect angels (1 Tim. 5:21), but God's grace toward humankind is far more excellent than his grace to such angels, as it was a far more costly and heroic work to redeem sinners than to preserve angels in their original holiness. To deliver humankind required that Christ become his people's High

Priest, to represent them in offering himself as their substitute, and in dying for them to appease God's holy wrath against their sin. The glory of Christ shines more brightly in his redeeming of one unworthy sinner than in his preserving the whole vast company of elect angels. "Make atonement for" (Greek *hilaskomai*) is better rendered "make propitiation for," "placate," or "pacify wrath for." Propitiation is one of the main categories by which the Bible sets forth the nature and significance of Christ's sacrifice of himself for sinners (Rom. 3:24–25; 1 John 2:2). Christ's atonement is at once the gift of God's love and the requirement of his justice. Further, the experience of suffering temptation gained during his life in the world equipped him to help his people now in their temptations, an especially relevant point in this sermon to a people under temptation and one to which the author will return (4:15). Heroes are usually either sympathetic or strong. Christ is both, offering understanding, which misery craves, and relief, which misery craves even more.

C. Jesus Christ superior to Moses (3:1–4:13). The author draws together his previous themes in a striking exhortation (3:1) that concludes the previous section and introduces the next. The readers' failure to give Christ the place in their minds and hearts that his divine supremacy, mediatorial work, and human sympathy deserve has led to their crisis of faith. The holy direction and management of the heart and its thoughts is fundamental to sturdy faith and holy living (Prov. 4:23; Col. 3:1–2). Only in Hebrews is Jesus called an apostle, though the fact that Jesus was sent by God to act on his behalf is commonplace in the New Testament (cf. John 5:36).

The author now compares Jesus with Moses (3:1–6), again perhaps to counter an unhealthy veneration of Moses at the expense of Christ in his readers' minds. At this point, interpretations of the letter frequently begin to go seriously astray. Commentators often allege that these verses amount to a contrast of the inferior Mosaic order with the superior religio-historical economy introduced by Christ and his apostles. But the order of thought gives another sense altogether: there is but one house of God in which Moses served but which Christ built, and that house includes us (3:6). Hebrews refers repeatedly to the people of God but never in order to distinguish parts or epochs. The continuity of God's people or the church in all ages is a fundamental assumption of the author. That Christ should have built (the Greek word employed may also suggest administration) the house of God in former days is in keeping with the perspective of this author (Heb. 11:26; 13:8) and of the New Testament generally (1 Cor. 3:10; Jude 5). The Son is the builder (Heb. 3:4) only as the executor of the Father's will (1:2), unless, as a number of commentators have thought, the author intends here to call Jesus God. The true superiority of Jesus to Moses will be adequately measured only in this way: Moses was never anything more than a member of the house that Christ was building and a servant in that house over which Christ ruled as God's Son (3:5–6). Further, as a prophet, Moses pointed away from himself to Christ; his message was of salvation in Christ (cf. John 5:46; Rom. 10:6–10). Believers today belong to that house, as did Moses and the faithful before and after him (Heb. 11:1–40), if they hold fast to Christ and to no one and nothing else for salvation.

The warning of Hebrews 3:6 that membership in God's household is suspended on a living and persevering faith introduces a long exhortatory section (3:7–4:13) in which the danger of apostasy and the necessity of an enduring faith are illustrated from the history of Israel. In 3:7–11, the author cites the warning of Psalm 95:7–11 as the living and active word of God (Heb. 4:12) demanding to be heard and obeyed now as then. It is introduced as the word of the Holy Spirit, though later it is ascribed to David (4:7), an example of the consistent assumption of the writers of the New Testament that what the Scripture says, God says (cf. Rom. 9:15, 17;

Gal. 3:8; Heb. 9:8; 10:15). The cited portion of the psalm is an admonition not to imitate the wilderness generation in its faithlessness, only one particular instance of which is recollected in verse 8: rebellion and testing (Exod. 17:1–7; cf. Num. 20:1–13; 1 Cor. 10:1–11; Jude 5). The burden of the citation is the judgment pronounced on unbelief in the last verse. As the argument proceeds, it becomes clear that the failure to enter God's rest means nothing less than the failure to obtain eternal life, of which entrance into the promised land was only a figure.

The point of the citation is driven home as the author reminds his readers that in this fundamental respect nothing has changed since the wilderness (3:12–14): it is still possible for those numbered outwardly among the people of God to forfeit the eternal country; it still requires nothing more than spiritual neglect to harden a heart to the point that it will turn away from God; and it is still as vitally necessary to stand fast in faith all of one's life ("as long as it is called 'Today,'" 3:13) and to help one another stand (10:23–25).

As throughout the letter, the subject is not unbelief per se but apostasy, the rejection of Christ and the faith by one who professed to believe and was considered to belong to the church of God (cf. "brothers and sisters," 3:12). The warning in no way contradicts the massive biblical witness to the security of the elect, rooted as it is in the merits of Christ and the eternal and immutable love of God (John 10:27–29; Rom. 8:28–39). But the elect are kept by the power of God through faith (1 Pet. 1:5), which is quickened and strengthened by warnings such as these. Further, many who claim to believe in fact do not. Some manifest the falseness of their faith by apostasy (1 John 2:19), while others remain undetected until the day of Christ (Matt. 7:21–23; 13:36–43).

For a readership that was inclined to consider the life of Israel in the wilderness as a paradigm for their own (3:15–19), it was particularly necessary to emphasize that it was precisely that generation, the generation lifted out of Egypt on eagles' wings, that was rejected by God for unbelief. The exhortation of 3:12–14 is thus reinforced by this explicit recollection of Israel's forfeiture of the rest of God.

The desert of Sinai, "where your ancestors tested and tried me" (Heb. 3:9; see Ps. 95:9). Hebrews 3 warns against having hard hearts as did the Israelites during the exodus. Because of their rebellion, they perished in the wilderness instead of entering God's rest.

That the alternatives Israel faced in the wilderness are the same ones believers face today is demonstrated by the use of the terms "promise" (4:1; cf. 6:12; 9:15; 10:36; 11:39–40) and "good news" (4:2; see also the verbal form in 4:6, *euangelizō*, "to evangelize"; cf. Rom. 10:16; Gal. 3:8) and by the striking inversion of order—not "they also," but "we also" (Heb. 4:2). This serves as an impressive verification of the author's consistent assumption that the gospel and its demands have remained unchanged from the beginning and that the spiritual world of the ancient people of God with its conditions, blessings, and powers is identical to that in which his readers now live. He commands them to take care (literally "fear") and together to take care on each other's behalf (Heb. 10:24–25). Eternal salvation must never be taken for granted but must be worked out in fear and trembling (Phil. 2:12–13), all the more as it is possible to belong to the people of God in an outward way and yet, for want of a genuine and enduring faith, fail to obtain eternal life. The rest that faithless Israel failed to obtain but that believers will obtain is now identified as participation in God's own rest that began after the creation of the world (4:3–5; cf. Gen. 2:2–3). The present tense in verse 3 expresses a principle or rule and so looks to the future (cf. Acts 14:22). Israel, therefore, failed to obtain the rest not because the rest itself was not yet available but solely because of her unbelief. Further, Israel's forfeiture of the rest is at issue (4:6–8), not her failure to enter Canaan, as if the rest were one thing in the Old Testament and another today. Canaan was only a symbol of the eternal inheritance that faith obtains (Heb. 11:9–10, 13–16). Joshua brought Israel into the land, and generations of Israelites had lived in the promised land when God issued the warning of Psalm 95. It was quite possible to inhabit Canaan and yet forfeit the rest of God.

So the rest of God has always been available to women and men and remains so today. The sole question is whether we will exercise that persevering faith that alone obtains rest. For it is a rest that no one enters in this life but only in the world to come, when the believer has rested from work (10:36). The author speaks of a "Sabbath-rest" (4:9) to connect the rest that the believer will obtain with the rest of God (4:4; cf. Gen. 2:2–3). It does not refer directly to the weekly Sabbath but to eternal salvation as different from and following this life of work. The use of this unusual word, "Sabbath-rest," a word the author himself may have coined, suggests that the weekly Sabbath, or Lord's day, is an eschatological sign pointing to a fulfillment still to come. It should not be thought that this rest is inactivity, however, for God's rest is not (John 5:17). Again, note the author's characteristic emphasis on the futurity of salvation. The consideration of this future blessedness concludes with another summary exhortation to eschew the example of Israel, to fear the wrath of God that befell Israel, to set mind and heart on the life to come, and to strive to live by faith.

This appeal is enforced by a consideration of the character of the word of God, which confronted Israel and confronts us still today (4:12–13). It is the living voice of God, which is never disobeyed with impunity. Here the word is thought of as an instrument of God's judgment, discerning the secrets and motives of the heart (cf. 1 Cor. 4:5). The author's readers must not suppose that they will obtain the rest of God because they are accepted by human beings or are counted as members of the people of God. The faith required is to be exercised and will be measured in the day of Christ as much in the thoughts of the heart as in outward conformity to the will of God. The phrases "soul and spirit, joints and marrow" (4:12) denote the inner life of humankind in all its aspects. The terms no more prove that human persons are composed of three parts (spirit, soul, and body) than Matthew 22:37 proves that they are composed of four.

D. Jesus Christ superior to Aaron (4:14–10:18). 4:14–5:10. The author now discusses Jesus Christ's qualifications as our great High Priest, picking up the thread of his earlier statement that Christ is the High Priest of his people (2:17–3:1) and reiterating points made previously regarding his exaltation (2:9) and his experience of the trials of human life (2:18). After the stern warnings and the threat of God's searching judgment in the previous verses, consolation and encouragement are offered to those who have discovered that the life of faith is full of painful difficulties and severe temptations. Jesus, true God and true human being, is the High Priest who is both fully willing to help (as his suffering for sinners demonstrates) and fully able, for he combines perfect understanding of and sympathy with the struggling believer's lot in this world of sin ("in every way" [4:15]) with his unlimited ability to help. He knows how to deliver the godly from temptation, having been victorious himself in every moment of his sorely tested life. That he is now seated on a heavenly throne signifies both that his sacrifice for sin has been accepted by God (Heb. 1:3; 10:12–14) and that his perfect sympathy as a fellow man and brother of the saints is joined with divine omnipotence. Therefore, the believer who addresses Jesus should not doubt that he or she will receive both forgiveness for past sins and strength to bear up under present trials. "Approach" (4:16) translates the Greek term *proserchomai*, which the Septuagint often employs for the priest's approach to God in the sacrificial ritual (e.g., Lev. 21:17, 21). The author's meaning is not that access to God (limited in the Old Testament to the priest) is now extended to all believers, for the saints of the former age also came near to God (Heb. 11:6), as the psalms and other portions of the Old Testament emphatically demonstrate (e.g., Ps. 73:28). Rather, he means that the sinner must rely on Jesus, not on sacrificial ritual, for mercy and grace (Heb. 10:1–3).

The author now takes care to establish in the minds of his readers, steeped as they are in Levitical regulations, that Jesus is in every way qualified to be the believer's great High Priest (5:1–10). First, as a representative of humanity, a priest must be a man with fellow feeling for those he represents to God (5:1–3). As one who offers sacrifices for sin, he must know what it is to do battle with sin. In the Levitical ritual, this was emphatically expressed in the requirement that even the high priest must offer sacrifice for his own sins (Lev. 16:6). Second, the high priest must be appointed to his office (Heb. 5:4; cf. Num. 20:23–28).

Now the author demonstrates in reverse order that Jesus meets both requirements (5:5–6). The two citations from the Psalter, both in the form of an address by the Father to the Son, establish that Jesus has his priestly office by divine appointment. Psalm 110:4 introduces the theme to which the author will return in 6:20–7:28. Jesus also meets the requirement of sympathy with those he represents (5:7–10). It is true that he did not sin and needed no sacrifice for his own sins (5:3), but he was tempted more severely than any other person, and only the one who has resisted to the end knows the full weight of any temptation. The point made twice before (2:17–18; 4:15) is now elaborated. Christ as a man discovered what it is to cry out to God in fear and distress. The allusion to Gethsemane (Matt. 26:36–46) is unmistakable. He learned to say, "Thy will be done" (Matt 26:42 KJV), when the will of God was the way of the cross. In answer to his prayer he was enabled to bear his trial just as he will enable believers to bear theirs (4:15–16). This statement serves to demonstrate how completely and unqualifiedly the Son of God became a man like other men, though without sin. Though he was the Son of God and a sinless man, he was not exempt from the principle that it is through suffering that a person discovers the true nature and cost of obedience (5:8–10; cf. 2:10). He was "a man of suffering, and familiar with pain" (Isa. 53:3), and it is precisely that suffering and perfect obedience in suffering that make him fit for his roles as Savior and High Priest. The necessity of obedience to Christ is not in contrast to the necessity of faith, for true faith and obedience are always found together, the latter the product and the sign of the former (Heb. 3:18–19; 4:2,

6). The reference to Melchizedek anticipates the exposition to come in 6:20–7:28.

5:11–6:8. The exposition of Christ's high priesthood is interrupted in the interest of another exhortation to persevere in faith. This section begins with a rebuke and is more severe in tone. The author intends to say more of Christ's priesthood but must first prepare the audience to listen with understanding and appreciation. Their spiritual childishness shows itself in a disposition to content themselves with their theological and spiritual status quo, apparently since by further progress they would only put greater distance between themselves and their Jewish past and sharpen the opposition they were already suffering. But such spiritual stagnation is dangerous; spiritual life is sustained by the solid food of sound doctrine, and it is protected by that spiritual and ethical discernment that is the fruit of an ever-deepening knowledge and constant exercise of faith.

Though in their present state of spiritual immaturity the process of digestion will be more painful, solid food is urgently required to invigorate their flagging faith. Each of the elementary teachings (6:1–2) mentioned had a place in Judaism but had been invested with new significance in Christian preaching. These basics are not to be discarded, but neither are they sufficient. This sentence amounts to a ringing affirmation both of the obligation laid on believers to cultivate their spiritual lives and of the importance of doctrine to sanctification. Knowledge feeds faith. "Acts that lead to death" (literally "dead works") are not, as some have supposed, attempts to gain righteousness by means of works of the law or cultic performances but simply sins in general, all evil thoughts and actions from which the conscience must be cleansed (Heb. 9:14; cf. Rom. 6:21).

Though the believer is obliged to pursue maturity, God's grace and action are necessary (6:1 reads, literally, "let us be carried to perfection"). The NIV omits the "for" with which verse 4 begins and which indicates that in the case of apostates, God is unwilling and not permitting

(6:3). Perhaps some in this community had already apostatized; others were alarmingly near to doing so, prompting the author to warn of the grim and irrevocable effects of deserting the faith.

The severity of this warning and the gravity of the situation contemplated must not be mitigated. Scripture is not silent regarding the hopeless condition of those who, having been numbered among the people of God, professed faith in Christ, received instruction in the Word of God, and experienced some measure of the blessing of the Holy Spirit's ministry and the reality of the unseen world, then deliberately repudiate Christ's lordship and salvation (cf. Num. 15:30–31; Matt. 12:31–32; 1 John 5:16–17; Heb. 10:26–27). Of course, it is imperative to maintain that, appearances notwithstanding, such people were never born again or made genuine partakers of the redemption purchased by Christ (John 6:39; 10:27–29; Rom. 9:29–30; 1 Pet. 1:3–5, 23). The brief parable in verses 7–8, similar to others in the Bible (Isa. 5:1–7; Matt. 13:1–9, 18–30, 36–43), reminds us of the impossibility of distinguishing infallibly between the truly converted and the hypocrite and that spiritual fruit is the evidence of living faith. It also illustrates the righteousness of God's condemnation of those who spurn his favor.

6:9–20. In the next section, the author encourages his readers to press on. As a matter of fact, the author has good hopes that his warnings will be taken to heart and be God's instrument to invigorate his readers' flagging faith. His confidence rests on his acquaintance with the genuinely faithful lives they have lived as Christians, especially in the early days of their faith in Jesus Christ (10:32–34). Such faith, love, and obedience, however, must continue as long as they live in the world. In exhorting his readers to imitate the faithful of the former epoch (as appears from the following verses), the author characteristically anticipates a theme he will subsequently enlarge on (11:1–12:1).

Abraham, to whom all Jews look as their father, is mentioned as a man of faith deserving of their emulation (6:13–15; cf. 2:16; 11:8–19), but the theme now is not Abraham's faith but the certainty of God's promise. Since faith must wait so long for its reward, the believer may be sorely tempted to grow weary and lose heart. The wait cannot be shortened, but hope can be revived by a reminder that hope in God will never be disappointed. Abraham had to wait many years for even the beginning of the fulfillment of the promise God made to him (Gen. 12:2; 17:5, 19, 21), but he did not wait in vain. The Lord added a solemn oath to his promise (Gen. 22:15–18) to strengthen Abraham's faith during the lengthy wait when all appearances would have been contrary to God's promise.

Significantly, the incident in Genesis 22 followed not only the birth of Isaac but the trial of Abraham's faith when God commanded him to offer his son as a sacrifice. In speaking of Abraham's obtaining the promise, then, the author seems to be thinking not of what Abraham obtained in this life but of the fulfillment of the age to come (Heb. 11:13–16, 39–40). The birth of Isaac and the receiving of him back from the dead (11:19) are rather a pledge of the promise that Abraham would be a father of a great nation. As in Hebrews 3 and 4, the author assumes that the principles

Abraham's faith enabled him to wait patiently for the fulfillment of God's promises (Heb. 6:13–15). This painting of Abraham is from the Dura Europos synagogue (Syria, AD 245).

of life and salvation that applied in the days of Abraham and Israel are fundamentally the same as those that apply today. The promise was offered then as now (4:1) and is obtained by a patient and enduring faith now as then.

The oath God swore was a condescension on his part to his people's frailty (6:16–18). His word needs no confirmation (John 17:17; Titus 1:2), but humankind's faith is weak, the wait is long, and God takes pity on his children. Christ's exaltation to the right hand of God (Heb. 1:3; 2:9; 4:14) only further confirms the certainty of the eventual fulfillment of God's promise of eternal rest for those who trust in him. These readers were no more secure than Abraham had been, resting as he did on the immutable promise of God, but they had further cause to be encouraged and less excuse for a wavering faith now that Christ had appeared and accomplished eternal redemption. "The inner sanctuary" (6:19), a reference to the innermost chamber of the tabernacle and temple, anticipates the exposition of 9:6–14 and the contrast drawn there between the ineffectuality of the Levitical ritual and the power of Christ's sacrifice to save to the uttermost.

7:1–28. The author now turns to discuss Melchizedek the priest. The few details about

Melchizedek (7:1–3) are taken from Genesis 14:18–20. In distinction to the necessity of Aaronic ancestry as a prerequisite for Levitical priestly service (Heb. 7:14), nothing is said either of Melchizedek's birth and ancestry or his death and posterity. For the author's purpose, this fact demonstrates the existence in Scripture of another order of priesthood wholly separate from the Levitical. In this, Melchizedek serves as a type or embodied prophecy of Christ's non-Levitical and eternal priesthood, which is confirmed not only directly in Psalm 110:4 (already cited in Heb. 5:6) but also by his name ("king of righteousness") and his title ("king of peace"), both redolent of Christ's messianic office and dignity (7:2; cf. Isa. 9:6; Jer. 23:6; Zech. 9:9–10).

Attention is now drawn to the fact that, according to Genesis 14, Abraham, though the heir of the promise and even in his hour of triumph, clearly behaves as Melchizedek's inferior, in both paying him tithes and receiving his blessing. Abraham was under no legal obligation to pay tithes to Melchizedek as Israelites would later be required by God's law to pay a tithe to the Levitical priesthood; hence, his paying of a tithe amounted to a voluntary recognition of Melchizedek's inherent dignity as a priest of God (Heb. 7:16). "Who is declared to be living" (literally "it is testified," i.e., in Scripture; 7:8) looks back to verse 3 and the silence of the record regarding Melchizedek's birth and death. By the absence of this information, the type is perfected and more perfectly foreshadows Christ's eternal priesthood. This argument, a minor afterthought, may gain importance by reason of the preoccupation with the Levitical ancestry among the Essenes, who repudiated the established priesthood of their time precisely because it was no longer occupied by descendants of Aaron.

With the ground thus laid, the author sets out to show that, of the two priesthoods reported in the Scripture, Jesus's is superior (7:11–28) and the only source of salvation (see Heb. 5:9). Of great importance to the interpretation

of Hebrews is the contrary-to-fact conditional statement in 7:11, together with two other such statements that figure prominently as the argument unfolds (8:7; 10:2). These clearly indicate that the readers of the letter, tempted to return to the comfortable paths of their former faith and associations, were inclined to precisely the opposite conclusions, namely, that perfection *could* come through the Levitical priesthood and that the sacrifices *could* make perfect those who offered them. The grammatical form of these statements favors the conclusion that the time reference is present—that is, "if perfection could now be obtained. . . ." Further, these conditional statements demonstrate that the author is criticizing the Levitical institutions precisely for failing to provide in themselves the forgiveness of sins and the perfection of the conscience (7:18–19; 9:13–14). The fact that they were never intended to do either (10:4; the blood of bulls and goats *cannot* take away sins) is immaterial because the author is dealing with these institutions under his readers' view of them.

The statements frequently encountered in commentaries to the effect that the author is contrasting the provisional and ineffectual religious forms of the Old Testament with the fulfillment enjoyed by believers of the new era utterly overturn the historical-theological perspective of the Letter to the Hebrews and fail to account for the letter's commonplaces: the nature and condition of salvation are not different now than formerly; the church in the new age is no less threatened by the specter of apostasy; salvation (perfection) is no more the present possession of believers now than it was of the faithful in the former epoch; and nothing is more necessary than that these readers imitate the saints of old. The contrast drawn is not between some supposed primitive and inadequate religious form with its merely provisional forgiveness and severely limited access to God on the one hand, and the free access and effective forms of New Testament Christianity, on the other. The contrast is rather between two ways of salvation—one by ritual performance and the other by the sacrifice of Jesus Christ. The argument advanced is designed to correct a misplaced confidence in rituals and to confirm the conviction that salvation is and could only be in Christ alone. The argument could be turned with equal effect on Christian ritualism and on the sacraments of the Christian church when they are conceived intrinsically as possessing saving efficacy.

The author rejects the argument that since the inauguration of the Levitical priesthood came later, it superseded Melchizedek's order; for long after Aaron, the Word of God (Ps. 110:4) speaks of another priest in the order of Melchizedek (7:12–17). The law was served by the priesthood that upheld it, and the priesthood was, in turn, regulated by the law. But the law made no provision for a priesthood outside the tribe of Levi, and Jesus was of Judah. Christ's appointment as priest and all the more as an eternal priest of a wholly different order thus constitutes a superseding of the Levitical institutions and a further demonstration that they were by no means God's definitive provision for the salvation of humankind. That point is now repeated in a striking statement of the ineffectuality of that ritual. The author heaps scorn on it precisely for its failure to bring the sinner near to God (7:18–19).

Though at the time of writing the temple ritual continued, the author seems to have gathered that it was near to its demise, perhaps from the fact that the burgeoning Gentile church was doing without it altogether (Heb. 8:13; 9:10). But it is crucial to recognize that the Levitical cultus is being attacked for failing to provide what it was never intended to provide, a fact pious Israelites well understood (Ps. 51:16–17). It is being caricatured here because this caricature is precisely the view of the letter's recipients. They viewed the ritual (or were severely tempted to view it) as a way of salvation, separated from the true covenant of God, from faith, from Christ and his work of which these rituals and institutions, like baptism and the Lord's Supper after them, were but signs and seals. In this the readers were but following in the steps of their forefathers (Ps. 50:7–15; Jer. 7:1–26). All thought of the true and evangelical significance of that priesthood and sacrifice and of the joy and spiritual benefit that was the fruit of the believer's participation in this ritual is set aside in order to pour contempt on these bare ceremonies as utterly incapable of making sinners right with God. In this, the author simply imitates the technique and the argument of the great prophets before him (Isa. 1:10–20; Amos 5:21–25; cf. 1 Cor. 10:1–5). The author's intention is certainly not to contrast believing life and experience in the Old Testament with that of the New Testament, for the exact counterpart of the sacrifice is not the priesthood and sacrifice of Christ but the Lord's Supper; and more significantly, while he states that those sacrifices could not save sinners, it is fundamental to his whole outlook and argument that sinners of the old epoch were saved just as sinners are now: by Christ, through the gospel and faith. This is underscored by his reference to the better hope. "Better" is an important term in Hebrews and refers not to some supposed but unmentioned comparative advantage enjoyed by New Testament believers but rather to the blessings of God's eternal salvation, grasped by faith by the saints of all ages, in comparison with the false and worldly hopes of sinful humanity (7:19, 22; 8:6; 9:3; 10:34; 11:16, 35, 40; 12:24).

The superiority of Christ's priesthood is further confirmed by its enactment through divine oath (7:20–22). Characteristically, the author anticipates the development of his argument in 8:6–13. It is noteworthy that in this first reference to the new covenant, Jesus is said to be its guarantor. In keeping with the author's already well-established perspective, the new covenant, the fulfillment of subjective redemption or salvation, is not something the faithful of the former epoch awaited in hope but that Christians today enjoy as a present possession. One does not require a guarantor for what one already has (6:17–20). The new covenant, the rest of God, the promise, even salvation itself are presented in Hebrews as different aspects of the future consummation and the fulfillment of the world to come.

The permanence of Christ's priesthood sets it above the Levitical (7:23–25). Christ's priesthood does not need to be replaced generation after generation, which lends a continual efficacy to all aspects of his priestly work, including his intercession (Isa. 53:12; John 17:8–9; Rom. 8:34).

Finally, Christ's priesthood excels the Levitical by reason of his personal perfection (7:26–28). The eternally holy Son of God lived a sinless life as a man (4:15) and advanced through suffering to the full-orbed perfection of human maturity (5:8–9). Unlike Levitical priests, then, he had no need to offer sacrifices for his own sin. His sacrifice of himself—the eternal Son of God and the true and perfectly obedient man (2:17–18)—thus has unlimited potency. Verses 26–28 serve to recapitulate the argument so far presented.

8:1–13. The heavenly sphere of Jesus Christ's priesthood is the subject of 8:1–6. The intricate comparison of the two priesthoods being completed, the author advances his argument by comparing the two priestly works. The point is that Jesus's priesthood is exercised in heaven, in the very presence of God, and its effectuality is therefore neither earthly nor temporary but spiritual and eternal (8:1–2; cf. 4:14). He exercises his priesthood not at some distance from God but in God's immediate presence (see 9:24). The point is reiterated to allay the suspicions of his Jewish readership (8:3–5). Although Christ is not now visible to his people as a priest, his priestly work is no less authentic inasmuch as it involves the offering of sacrifice (Heb. 5:1)—that of himself, not that of the law (7:27; 9:14). The recipients of the letter are attracted to the rites of the temple, but this earthly round of ritual and its setting are but a copy of the real, heavenly sacrifice, which Christ offered once and for all and on the basis of which he now intercedes for his people. The detailed instruction God gave to Moses concerning the construction of the tabernacle (Exodus 25–40) demonstrates that the tabernacle and, by implication, the temple were not the reality but only copies of it. The author's readership is in danger of preferring the copy to the genuine article, of accepting an imitation as the true principle of salvation.

Moses was warned to build the tabernacle "according to the pattern shown you on the mountain," because the sanctuary is "a copy and shadow of what is in heaven" (Heb. 8:5; see Exod. 25:40). Shown here is a life-size model of the tabernacle (Timnah, Israel).

Now the author presents Jesus Christ as the guarantor of a better covenant (8:7–13). The argument now introduced in verse 7 parallels that of 7:11 and 10:2. Hebrews was written to a community inclined to regard the covenant life and experience of Israel, especially the wilderness period, as a paradigm for her own. These Jewish Christians were disposed to feel that they required nothing more than to duplicate the pattern of life with its outward forms established by their forebears. That pattern, in their minds, was the Mosaic covenant, but in fact, they conceived of that covenant not as the proclamation of the gospel (Heb. 4:1) but in legalistic and ritualistic terms. The author has already pointed out, in correcting the error of these ritualistically minded people, that the wilderness generation perished and forfeited the promise for lack of faith and thus is not at all to be emulated. In a similar way, he now argues that the very fact that another covenant was promised to replace the covenant with the fathers ipso facto demonstrates that the former covenant is obsolete and cannot serve as a paradigm for believers today (see another instance of this form of argument in Heb. 4:8).

But what are these two covenants? Commentaries are often singularly unhelpful at this point. It is usually asserted that the former covenant is the Mosaic administration per se and the new covenant is the superior administration introduced by Christ and the apostles. The contrast then is between a relatively inferior Old Testament revelation, faith, and spirituality and the fulfillment of the new epoch. But such an interpretation falls foul of the plain facts of the case and of the radical character of the distinction drawn between the two covenants (8:8–12). It does so in five ways.

First, the old covenant represents not Israel's life of faith but her culpable and damning unbelief in the gospel, as the author emphasizes with his own striking introduction to the citation: "But God found fault with the people and said . . ." (8:8). The difference between the old covenant and the new is the difference between the forfeiture of salvation ("I turned away from them," 8:9) and subjective redemption ("I will be their God," 8:10), between death and eternal life.

Second, the fulfillment of the promises of the better covenant is not to be found in some comparative advantage enjoyed by believers in the new epoch but rather in the consummation. These better promises are only the ancient verities of Old Testament faith, which elsewhere in Hebrews are called "the good news," "the inheritance," the "rest" of God, "a better country," and a "better resurrection." Believers in the time before the incarnation claimed these promises from afar (Heb. 11:1–38), precisely as believers must today. The popular notion that the law of God was but some external ordinance in the Old Testament but now in the new era has been inscribed on the heart is not only generally unbiblical (Deut. 4:8–9; 6:5–6; 30:6, 14; Ps. 40:8; Prov. 3:1, 3; Isa. 51:7; Jer. 24:4–7) but wholly without support in this letter. It is very important to recognize that the author's exhortation is *never* in the form a fortiori (from the lesser to the greater; for example, "if they could persevere in the old covenant, how much more ought we to do so in the new . . .").

Third, the specific promises of Jeremiah's prophecy of the new covenant are not considered by this author to have been fulfilled and cannot be so considered. Indeed, it would be highly ironic had the author understood that the expectation had now been fulfilled of a time when "no longer will they teach their neighbor, or say to one another, 'Know the Lord,' because they will all know me" (8:11) but then proceeded anyway to write Hebrews, which is nothing less than an impassioned plea to his brethren to "know the Lord" in the face of an incipient apostasy in principle no different than that of the fathers in the wilderness or of that against which Jeremiah protested.

Fourth, taken at face value, Jeremiah's prophecy is not a prophecy of the New Testament epoch, in which Israel's failure of faith would be repeated many times and on a far more terrible scale, but a prophecy of the final triumph of the grace of God, when the church will no more be a mixture of true and false sons or pass through periods of domination by unbelief as in the wilderness, in Jeremiah's day, and not infrequently since. The prophecy has many affinities with other prophetic texts that portray the triumph and consummation of the kingdom of God in the world (e.g., Isa. 11:6–9; 54:11–15; 59:20–21; Ezek. 16:59–63; Jer. 32:36–41; 33:14–26; Rom. 11:26–27).

Fifth, as the argument is presented in 8:7, 13 and unfolds subsequently, the author seems interested in but two features of Jeremiah's prophecy: the covenant guaranteed by Jesus promises forgiveness, and the very fact of such a promise of the new covenant constitutes a condemnation of the old. Indeed, if by "new covenant" the author means the new dispensation and by its blessings the comparative advantages believers enjoy today, he fails altogether to make that clear.

The old covenant is the broken relationship with God that resulted from Israel's response of unbelief and disobedience. Such a situation prevailed when the gospel was not combined with faith (Heb. 4:2). Of course, in principle it can be repeated today; indeed, the threat of repeating a breaking of the covenant is what calls forth this letter. The old covenant is not the Mosaic administration except where that system was perverted by unbelief into an occasion of apostasy. The new covenant, contrarily, is the living relationship God creates with his people by means of his gracious and powerful working within them, calling them to faith and obedience. This covenant of grace is contemplated in Jeremiah's prophecy from the vantage point of its consummation at the end of the history of the world, but, of course, it embraces all the people of God as one (11:39–40). This covenant, which is simply the divine application of the redemption which is in Christ to those who are being saved, mediates the heavenly realities of eternal life that have always been the hope of the faithful. In saying that the old covenant is

soon to disappear, the author means that the entire ritual system of Israel—the contrast of the two covenants is presented in terms of that ritual (8:1–6)—is about to disappear (7:18). That system stands under divine judgment because it has been denatured by its separation from the gospel.

9:1–10. The tabernacle and its ritual frame the author's discussion in 9:1–10. He continues his demonstration of the ineffectuality of the Levitical institutions to deal with sin and of his contention that forgiveness can be found only in Christ. Returning to the argument of 8:1–5, the author describes the earthly sanctuary and its furniture (9:1–5). He describes the tabernacle, not the similar plan of the temple, perhaps because of his readership's fascination with the wilderness period of Israel's history. The altar of incense appears to have been located in the Holy Place (Exod. 30:6; Lev. 16:12, 18), not the Most Holy Place. The wording here recalls that of 1 Kings 6:22 and perhaps is intended to suggest the intimate connection between this altar and the ark of the covenant in the priestly ritual. The activity of the priests and of the high priest on the Day of Atonement is described in 9:6–10 but now in the present tense (contra the NIV), furnishing an argument that Hebrews was written before the destruction of the temple and the cessation of its ritual in AD 70 and serving as a reminder that Jewish Christians were still participating without prejudice in that ritual (Acts 21:20–26). The fact that the divinely appointed order so severely restricted access to the Most Holy Place was an enacted lesson that the true, decisive ransom, of which the Levitical sacrifices were but a figure, had not yet been paid and that those sacrifices could not remove guilt. Under discussion is the single question of what sacrifice is the basis of salvation—the Levitical sacrifice or the sacrifice of Christ. The author ought not to be understood as suggesting that believers in the former era did not have direct access to God and full forgiveness through Christ, a notion against which the whole of Scripture rises in protest (e.g.,

Ps. 32:1–11; 103:1–22; Mic. 7:18–19; Rom. 4:1–8) and which is particularly impossible to reconcile with the perspective of the author of Hebrews (11:4–38). Again, he is belittling his readers' view of the Levitical rites, separated as they were from Christ and from living faith, as mere externalities and, what is more, only temporary.

9:11–10:18. The next major subsection focuses on the sufficiency of the redemption obtained by Jesus Christ. The imagery continues to be that of the Day of Atonement, but Christ's offering of himself is a transaction that transcends the earthly sphere and the potentialities of mere humans and their rituals. Though he died on a cross near Jerusalem (Heb. 13:12), his sacrifice is thought of as being offered in heaven (9:11). Text-critical considerations in 9:11 together with the author's sustained emphasis on the futurity of salvation make the reading "the good things that are to come" (cf. 10:1) more likely than "the good things that are now already here." Offering himself once and for all, Christ thus secured eternal redemption for his people (9:12). Redemption, along with propitiation and reconciliation, is a key concept in the Bible for the representation of the character and effect of Christ's saving work. Redemption is deliverance from some bondage by the payment of a price or ransom (Exod. 6:6; 13:13–15; Lev. 25:25 27, 47–54, Mark 10:45; Rom. 3:24; Eph. 1:7). The bondage here contemplated is that of sinners to death, to the devil, and to divine wrath; the ransom is the death of Christ in the sinner's place (Gal. 3:13; Heb. 2:14–17). Having obtained this eternal redemption, he entered heaven and sat down there to represent his people to God as their great High Priest and to await the consummation (Heb. 9:24, 28; 10:12–13).

The Levitical sacrifices and other rituals did avail to remove ceremonial defilement (9:13–14; the allusion to the ritual of sprinkling water containing the ashes of a heifer [Numbers 19] could be due to the significance attached to such ceremonies of cleansing in nonconformist

Judaism; cf. Dead Sea Scrolls, *Rule of the Community* 2:25–3:12). But the sacrifice of the incarnate Son of God, infinite in his perfection as a substitute for his guilty people (Heb. 2:9–10), actually satisfied the demands of God's justice on their behalf and turned away his holy wrath from them (Heb. 1:3; 2:17; 9:27, 28); it thus provided the removal of sin and guilt and established a living communion with God. "Eternal Spirit" refers either to the divine enablement of the Third Person of the Godhead by which Jesus performed his mission (Isa. 42:1; Mark 1:10) or, less probably, to his own eternal and spiritual life, by reason of which his sacrifice and priesthood are of everlasting value and effect (Heb. 7:16, 24).

The eternally effective sacrifice of himself constituted Christ the mediator, or better, guarantor of the new covenant, that is, of the eternal salvation that the gospel promises, which faith embraces, but the fulfillment of which awaits the consummation (Heb. 7:22). Verse 15 is often thought to mean that Christ, by his death, retroactively satisfied for the sins of those who lived before the incarnation. That Christ's death had such a retroactive effect and was the basis of gospel forgiveness in the Old Testament is unquestionably true. But as an interpretation of the author's statement it does grave injustice to a text as programmatic in scope as John 3:16. "The sins committed under the first covenant" are not the individual transgressions committed by those who lived before the incarnation but rather the sins connected with that covenant, that is, Israel's broken relationship with God, namely, unbelief and disobedience (Heb. 3:18–19; 4:1, 6), which are conceived to be the fundamental sins and root of every actual transgression. The proof of this is that Christ's dying for these old covenant sins guarantees the inheritance of this community of second-generation Christians (9:14; "our consciences"). Similarly, "those who are called" can hardly be restricted, as some commentators have supposed, to saints of the pre-Christian epoch. The phrase is thoroughly comprehensive in scope and intended to include the entire company of the elect, as appears from parallel statements elsewhere ("everyone," "many sons"; Heb. 2:9–10; "many"; 9:28). The sins for which Christ suffered punishment in his people's place are the sins that prevented Israel (and anyone) from sharing in the eternal inheritance. By the payment of his own life, Christ has delivered those whom God is calling to salvation from the guilt and the power of unbelief and disobedience, which alienate them from God.

The mention of inheritance in verse 15 perhaps prompted the author to draw an illustration in verses 16–22 from everyday life, made easier by the fact that *diathēkē*, which ordinarily means "covenant" in biblical Greek, commonly meant "last will and testament" in the Greek of the author's day. Of course, a will takes effect only after the death of the testator. The new covenant (i.e., the living relationship that God has established with the called and the promise of eternal life) is made effectual by Christ's death, a principle illustrated in the inauguration of the covenant at Sinai with blood. Several additional details not mentioned in Exodus 24:4–8 and the silence of the Pentateuch regarding any such sprinkling of the tabernacle suggest that the author was aware of sources no longer extant or drew from some authentic but now unattested tradition.

Recapitulating 7:27–28; 8:1–5; and 9:1–14, the author distinguishes the earthly ceremonies and sanctuary from the sacrifice of the Son and the spiritual and heavenly sphere of his priestly work (9:23–28). The principle of true salvation is not the oft-repeated Levitical rituals but the once-for-all, eternally effective self-sacrifice of Christ, sufficient to cover all the sins of all the called for all time. "Culmination of the ages" (9:26; NEB "the climax of history") suggests that human destiny and the purpose of history pivots on this single event. As humans die but once, so he who took their place (Heb. 2:14, 17) dies but once, but with eternal effect; however, the full manifestation and development of this await Christ's return.

The Levitical sacrifices are portrayed as inadequate in 10:1–4. They only foreshadowed the true salvation, which Christ has guaranteed and will someday bring to completion. This is the third and last of the contrary-to-fact conditional statements around which the central argument of this sermon is constructed. The appeal to the repetitive character of Levitical worship and its inability to cleanse the conscience (9:13–14) indicates that the author has not deviated from his original purpose. He is determined to persuade his readers that for salvation they must trust in Christ and his sacrifice and not in the rituals of Judaism. As is often supposed, he is not conceiving of the Old Testament order as a more primitive state of revelation and spirituality than the Christian era. He says nothing about that but instead compares a false theory of salvation with the fact of salvation in Christ alone. At the time Hebrews was written, a Christian might still have participated in the temple ritual (Acts 21:26) but could not think that such externalities were the substance of salvation any more than the faithful of the former epoch did (Ps. 51:16–17) or than a believer today should think of baptism or the Lord's Supper as having in themselves, separated from Christ and faith, justifying or sanctifying efficacy. The coming of Christ is decisive to the author not because it lifts the religious experience of believers to a somewhat higher plane than that enjoyed by the saints of the former epoch but because Christ secured the salvation that all God's people—past, present, and future—grasp by faith in this world and will enjoy in fullness in the next (Heb. 11:39–40). Believers in the former era rejoiced in the freedom from guilt that God's grace provided (Exod. 34:6–7; Ps. 32:1–2; 103:10–12; 130:1–8; Isa. 38:17; Mic. 7:18–19). For that matter, the Lord's Supper perpetually reminds the church today of her sin, for which she must constantly mourn, confess, and ask forgiveness (Matt. 5:3–6; 1 Cor. 11:27–32; 1 John 1:8–10).

Unwilling to leave a single stone unturned in his attempt to demonstrate to the satisfaction of his readers that the Levitical rituals are an insubstantial foundation on which to rest one's hope of salvation, the author launches into another argument that adds some new points and recapitulates others (10:5–18).

The author understands Psalm 40:6–8, cited in verses 5–7, to be prophetic of Christ. The author takes the phrase "a body you prepared for me," from the Septuagint rather than the Hebrew Masoretic Text, as referring to the body the Son of God assumed at his incarnation, the human nature in which he obeyed God and died in his people's place (Heb. 2:14; 5:8; cf. John 6:38; Phil. 2:7–8). The citation is perfectly suited because it compares the Levitical sacrifices unfavorably with the work of Christ.

Hebrews 10:11 describes the religious duties performed by every priest at the Jerusalem temple: "again and again he offers the same sacrifices." The Gentile readers of Hebrews could identify through their own experience of the repeated offerings given to Greco-Roman deities. This Roman relief shows a man offering incense to his gods (first century AD).

It was a truism of the Old Testament revelation that the Levitical ritual served no good purpose without faith and obedience on the part of the worshiper (10:8; 1 Sam. 15:22; Ps. 51:16–19; Isa. 1:11–17; Amos 5:21–24). This is the simple meaning of David's words in Psalm 40:6–8. Further, the faithful of the former era did offer such willing obedience, and their sacrifices were pleasing to God (Heb. 11:4; cf. Lev. 1:9). But the author is dealing with sacrifice or, as the four different terms indicate, the whole Levitical ritual in itself, which obviously had no intrinsic power to save from sin. The individual to whom the author is addressing himself is not the person whose sacrificial worship merely gives expression to his trust in God the Redeemer and to the glad consecration of his life to God, but the one who hopes that the act of sacrifice itself will cleanse him of guilt.

But Christ and his sacrifice have just that saving efficacy in themselves that the Levitical ritual lacks (10:9–10). The contrast drawn between the alternatives of the psalm citation is intended to nullify any idea that the sacrificial ritual could ever be the substance of salvation. This holiness or perfection has both present and future aspects (6:1; 10:14; 12:23).

The point made earlier (10:1–4) is recapitulated in verses 11–14. The ineffectuality of sacrifices that must be performed repeatedly is contrasted with the once-for-all sacrifice of Christ, the effectuality of which is attested by the singular honor of a place at God's right hand. The priests continue to stand (cf. Deut. 10:8; Ps. 134:1); the great High Priest has sat, a sign both of the ultimacy of his single sacrifice for sin (Heb. 1:3–4; 2:9) and of his royal dominion, now hidden but soon to be revealed (Heb. 1:13; 2:7–8). It is to Christ, therefore, not to Levitical priests and rituals, that sinners must come. In nonconformist Judaism of the Essene variety, likely the form of Judaism exerting the greatest influence on this community, there was an expectation of the restoration of the Aaronic priesthood, but it was never imagined that this would involve anything other than standing priests offering sacrifices repeatedly.

In verses 15–18 the author returns to the citation from Jeremiah 31:31–34 (cf. Heb. 8:8–12) for the dramatic conclusion to his great demonstration begun at 4:14 of the superiority of Christ's priesthood and sacrifice. The true salvation in Christ that God promises and applies to the hearts of those he calls eventuates in a full and permanent absolution. Looking to some regularly repeated sacrificial ritual as the basis of forgiveness, as his readership is tempted to do, amounts to a repudiation of the glorious gospel of salvation by the grace of God (Heb. 13:9).

2. Exhortations to Persevere in Christian Faith (10:19–12:29)

A. The danger of apostasy (10:19–31). The author has completed his demonstration that salvation is to be found in Christ and is based on his sacrifice and not the Levitical rituals. Now he explicitly states and applies the purpose of that lengthy argument to the present crisis of faith in the particular community to which Hebrews is addressed. The exhortation that follows recapitulates the earlier exhortatory sections (2:1–2; 3:7–13; 4:1–11; 6:1–12) and confirms that the author has had a single purpose throughout: to reverse an incipient apostasy and to strengthen flagging faith.

First, he passes his just-completed argument briefly in review (10:19–21). Christ's death for sin and his abiding priesthood provide free access to God (4:15–16; 6:19–20; 7:23–25; 9:8, 12–15). The "new and living way" does not suggest that believers of the former age were somehow fettered in their access to God, for neither the Old Testament nor Hebrews will tolerate the notion that those saints did not have full access to the Lord or confidence in laying claim to his forgiveness (see "draw near" in both 10:22 and 11:6). The old-new contrast in the Bible is absolute, not relative, and is never merely chronological. It always possesses an ethical-spiritual dimension. "Old" signifies the situation of humankind in sin,

"new" the experience of God's salvation (Ps. 98:1; Rom. 6:4, 6; 7:6; 1 Cor. 5:7, 8; 2 Cor. 3:6, 14; 5:17; Eph. 4:22–23; Col. 3:9, 10; Rev. 2:17; 5:9; 21:1, 5). It is not a question of varying access to God but of access where before there was none (Heb. 7:18–19). Believers of all ages have enjoyed this boldness of approach, but it has always been founded on Christ and his sacrifice, not on external rituals. "The curtain, that is, his body" is perhaps best understood as a comparison between the curtain through which the high priest gained access to the Most Holy Place (cf. Heb. 9:3; Mark 15:38) and Christ's bodily sacrifice, by which believers gain access to God.

In verses 22–25 the exhortation is fourfold. The first two reiterate the author's previous admonitions to persevere in faith with eyes fixed firmly on Christ (3:6, 14; 4:14). But such endurance requires the encouragement of others, and that is given and received chiefly in the life of the congregation. That the exhortation is in the first person throughout expresses the author's personal interest in his readers, his hopes for their restoration, and his solidarity with them in the good fight of faith (cf. Heb. 6:9; on "hearts sprinkled" [10:22] see 9:13–14; Lev. 14:6–7; Ps. 51:7, 10). "Bodies washed" is no doubt a reference to baptism but in its spiritual signification (cf. Ezek. 36:25; John 3:5; Eph. 5:26; 1 Pet. 3:21).

Exhortation is now reinforced with solemn warnings (10:26–31), similar to that of 6:4–8, regarding the horrifying and irremediable consequences of apostasy (cf. Heb. 2:2–3; 2 Pet. 2:20–22). "Deliberately keep on sinning" refers not to the immense sinfulness that remains in every believer's life, over which one mourns, of which one repents, and for which one turns to Christ (Heb. 4:15–5:12), but to the renunciation of the faith (3:12; 6:6). If, having once become acquainted with and having laid claim to the final and perfect sacrifice of Christ, one rejects it as the hope of salvation, all hope is forever lost. The Levitical sacrifices that this readership is tempted to prefer cannot make anyone perfect, and God will not grant repentance to apostates. This striking and grim definition of apostasy is a reminder of how differently the same thing may appear to a human and to God. What the apostate defends as a calculated step to serve his or her best interests, God regards as contempt for his beloved Son, as disdain for the terrible suffering and death he endured, and as an outrage against the Holy Spirit, impeaching his testimony to Christ's lordship (Heb. 6:4; 1 John 5:6, 10). The certainty and ferocity of God's wrath toward his enemies (Heb. 10:27), especially among his own highly favored people (Amos 3:2), is as unmistakable a datum of divine revelation (here Deut. 32:35–36) as his mercy toward those who repent and believe. That God is living renders his judgment inescapable by mere mortals. The author will return to this thought of God's fierce judgment in 12:18–29.

B. Encouragements to press on (10:32–39). As in 6:9–12, warning is followed by encouragement, as the author reminds his readers of their noble steadfastness in the days of their first love. They have endured public scorn, willingly identified themselves with those already in prison for faith in Christ (and so exposed themselves to the possibility of a similar fate), and suffered the loss of their property by looting or as a legal penalty, which happened frequently when Christians became the objects of a community's wrath. They suffered all but martyrdom (12:4) courageously, even gladly, confident that they would reap an eternal harvest if they did not give up (Gal. 6:9; cf. Matt. 5:11–12; Acts 5:41; 1 Pet. 4:13). They must not lose heart now and have no excuse to do so (10:35–36). The Lord helped them before to resist the opposition that now unnerves them, and he will do so again. Defection now would be tantamount to Israel's irrational sin of losing confidence in the Almighty, who had lifted them out of Egypt on eagles' wings, when they were within sight of the promised land (Heb. 4:16; Deut. 32:15; Ps. 78:9–55). The living faith that alone obtains the eternal inheritance expresses itself in a tenacity in the face of all manner of worldly opposition

and temptation and the long waiting made necessary by the futurity of the consummation.

The citation of Habakkuk 2:3–4 in Hebrews 10:37–38 derives from the Septuagint, which has interpreted the original "it" (the revelation of divine judgment) as "he" (a personal deliverer), an interpretation that is ratified by the author of Hebrews, who adds the definite article to the Septuagint's "he will surely come," yielding "he who is coming" or "the one who is coming," virtually a messianic title (cf. Matt. 11:3), though now with reference to Christ's coming again. The two lines of Habakkuk 2:4 are transposed simply to clarify the author's application of the citation to his own readership. There are but two alternatives and two destinies, and the author is confident that at least most of his readers, having flirted with danger, will at last stand fast (10:39).

C. Faith defined and exemplified (11:1–40). As a stronger faith is the need of the hour, the author sets before his readers the example of the heroes of faith (11:1–3). It is comforting to be reminded that the temptations one faces are neither unique nor even as severe as others have courageously endured, and the stirring examples of faith under trial will strengthen one's determination to be equally worthy of God's approval. In a statement similar to Romans 8:24–25, faith is defined as the unshakable confidence in the reality of the yet unseen world and the certainty of God's yet unfulfilled promises. This definition of faith is illustrated by reference to the nature of creation by divine fiat.

The succession of heroes of faith begins with three from before the flood (11:4–7). The author does not explain in what way Abel's sacrifice was superior, only that it was due to his faith. Abel was murdered, but he still speaks, crying out for the vindication that God will bring in due time (see Heb. 12:24; Gen. 4:10; Rev. 6:9–11). The signal honor afforded Enoch is the divine answer to his faith because he was commended as one who pleased God, which is impossible apart from faith. Noah's faith is demonstrated in the remarkable building project he undertook solely on the strength of his confidence in God's promise. Noah's faith was vindicated, while the world that did not heed God's warning was destroyed (cf. 2 Pet. 3:3–7).

The next set of exemplars of faith hail from the patriarchal period (11:8–22). Naturally Abraham occupies the largest place in this chapter, as Scripture itself singles out his faith (Gen. 15:6; Rom. 4:1–25; Gal. 3:6–9). On the strength of God's promise alone, Abraham left his homeland for parts unknown, considered his inheritance a land that neither in his own lifetime nor in that of his son and grandson would actually belong to him (apart from a burial plot he purchased, Gen. 25:9–10), and expected God to give him a son though he was advanced in years and married to an aged and barren woman. Abraham understood both that God's promises are indefectible and that their true fulfillment would be found not in this world but in the next. He understood that God had promised him vastly more than real estate for his descendants, indeed, nothing less than an inheritance with Enoch. Abraham's obedient faith and perseverance remind us that

faith must withstand not only the waiting until the promise is fulfilled but also appearances that seem directly to contradict the believer's hope. Events have so far vindicated Abraham's trust in God (11:12). The patriarchs all died with most of God's promises to them yet unfulfilled (11:13–16); still they died in the sure hope of their eventual realization (11:20–21), which further confirms the assertion of verse 10. Canaan was no more the true homeland they sought than it was the true rest of God for Israel (Heb. 4:8–9). God "is not ashamed" to be called the God of Abraham, Isaac, and Jacob, that is, not of the dead but of the living who wait in hope (Matt. 22:31–32). The supreme illustration of Abraham's faith as an invincible confidence in the promise of God and in God's ability to fulfill it in defiance of appearances is his obedience in offering Isaac

Hebrews 11:30 says that "by faith" the walls of Jericho fell. The archaeological site of the Jericho mentioned in the Old Testament is very eroded, and its excavation has been challenging. The walls uncovered here are from the Middle Bronze period, earlier than the time of Joshua.

as a sacrifice (11:17–18). That such indeed was Abraham's reasoning appears to be suggested in Genesis 22:5. One generation after another dies in the certainty that God's promise will not fail (Heb. 11:19–22).

The third general section on the heroes of faith covers the period of the exodus and the conquest of the promised land (11:23–31). Moses's faith first lived in his parents (cf. 2 Tim. 1:5). Apparently the author assumes that some divine communication was given to Moses's parents of God's purpose for their son, and their courage in the face of Pharaoh's edict (Exod. 1:22) resulted in greater security and station for their son than they had thought possible. Moses later turned his back on the exalted status he enjoyed to identify himself with the downtrodden people of God (11:24–26). The short-lived pleasures of the Egyptian court were not to be compared with the eternal inheritance that God bestows on those who will deny themselves to follow him. The striking reference to Moses's "disgrace for the sake of Christ" must not be minimized, as if "Christ" should be rendered "anointed one" and taken as a reference to the people of God or as if Christ is in some way to be understood as suffering in his people's suffering, which then Moses shared. The phrase is not taken from the Old Testament; it is the author's own. It agrees with his perspective that Christ was at work in the former epoch and already the object of faith (1:2; 3:2–3; 8:8; 12:2, 25; 13:8; cf. 1 Cor. 10:4; John 5:46; 8:56; Jude 5), and the parallel in 13:13 suggests that bearing disgrace for Christ's sake is something done for Christ himself. Christ was building the house in which Moses was a servant, and Moses gladly bore his master's reproach in confident expectation of his eternal glory. "He left Egypt" (11:27) probably refers to Moses's flight to Midian, which is viewed as an act of discretion, not panic (Exod. 2:14–15), and his forty-year sojourn there as a time of patient waiting for the Lord's call. Time after time Israel's deliverance was accomplished in defiance of seemingly insurmountable obstacles, when people took God

at his word and acted accordingly (11:28–30). The mention of a Gentile prostitute's faith and courageous action verifies that faith alone and not natural identity or personal history obtains salvation. This may also be an implied rebuke of this Jewish readership (11:31).

Space allows for but a summary of the remainder of the history of faith in the former epoch, from the time of the judges through the heroic resistance of the Maccabean period (11:32–38; compare 11:35 with 2 Maccabees 6:18–31). Some of the historical references are unmistakable ("shut the mouths of lions" [Dan. 6:22]; "quenched the fury of the flames" [Dan. 3:19–27]; "women received back their dead" [1 Kings 17:17–22; 2 Kings 4:18–37]), others less clear. The inclusion of such figures as Samson and Jephthah is a reminder that the living faith can coexist with massive imperfection. The mention of "women," "others," and "some" indicates that this faith was as much the pattern of life of many humble people as it was of the heroes of biblical history.

Verses 39–40 are frequently understood to mean that what the faithful of the former era did not receive, Christians have. Believers today live in the age of fulfillment. "Something better" (11:40) then is taken to refer to the superior state of religious life introduced by Christ and his apostles. But such an interpretation utterly overturns the author's argument. His readers have *not* received the promise (see Heb. 10:36) and will not unless they persevere in faith to the end as their forefathers did. The "something better" is surely not something other than the above-mentioned "better and lasting possessions" (10:34), "better country" (11:16), and "better resurrection" (11:35), which are no more the present possession of believers today than they were of Abraham or Moses. The entire chapter has been offered as encouragement to persevere in view of the fact that God's promise remains unfulfilled, and the verses that immediately follow reiterate the same thought: one must persevere to the end if one is to receive. The thought is explicitly *not* a fortiori (from the lesser to the greater), as if the author were saying: "If they could endure with the promise unfulfilled, how much more we who have received it." The comparison is not between the situation of believers in the old economy and that of Christians today but between what all believers enjoy on earth and what they will receive—after a lifetime of patient waiting—in the heavenly country. The basis of the author's exhortation is not some dissimilarity but rather the correspondence between the circumstances of believers before and after the incarnation. The object of Abraham's hope lay beyond the grave, and it is no different today. Verse 40 then means simply that the consummation was delayed, the ancients had to wait patiently for it, because God intended many more to share in his salvation ("planned"; literally "foreseen," in the sense of election and predestination). In the same way, believers today must wait until the whole company of the called is gathered in (cf. Matt. 24:14; Heb. 9:15).

D. Jesus, the superior example of faith (12:1–4). The author now imagines the ancient heroes of faith as a great company of spectators ready to cheer on his readers in a race the former have already completed but which the latter must yet run (12:1–2). The Christian athlete must divest himself of anything that will hamper him in this spiritual race, which is another way of saying that a chief principle of Christian spirituality is self-denial or self-discipline (cf. Matt. 19:27–29; 1 Cor. 9:24–27). Further, it will greatly help to avoid a harmful distraction or a loss of heart if believers concentrate their attention on the prize they are to obtain at the end, which is Jesus himself (cf. Phil. 3:8; Col. 3:1–4; Heb. 11:26–27; 12:24). Jesus is to be looked to as the one on whom every believer's faith "depends from start to finish" (NEB; cf. Heb. 4:14–16). But his life is also the perfect paradigm for the believer, who also will find strength to endure hardship in the prospect of heavenly joy. In verses 3–4 the recipients of this written sermon are reminded that their present suffering—the opposition they are encountering on account

of their faith in Christ—is not to be compared with what Christ endured for them, nor even with the trials of many of their spiritual forebears (11:37), and thus provides no excuse for their present faintheartedness.

E. The meaning and merit of discipline (12:5–13). The testing of their faith is intended by the Lord to benefit them and indicates his love for them. Any true father disciplines his children, corrects them when they err, and cultivates their maturity by requiring the endurance of adversity. In this, Christians are only following in their master's footsteps (Heb. 5:8). Though painful at the time, the heavenly Father's discipline will yield its perfect fruit if believers humbly submit to it as from the Lord, trusting him to help them endure it (1 Cor. 10:13; James 1:2–4). In the confidence that such trials inevitably and necessarily litter the straight and narrow road that leads to life, the readers must press on (12:12–13; cf. Isa. 35:3–4 and Prov. 4:25–27, the language of which the author borrows).

F. Warning not to turn away from God (12:14–29). Each person must study holiness, as the gospel requires, and help others to do the same, taking special care to nip sin in the bud when it arises within the community (12:14–17; cf. Deut. 29:18; 1 Cor. 5:6). Esau exemplifies the person who exchanges the unseen and future inheritance for the sensible and immediate pleasures of this world and, consequently, "falls short of the grace of God," that is, squanders irrevocably the blessing that was in one's grasp (Heb. 6:4–6; 10:26–31). Esau's tears showed remorse for the consequences of his folly, not godly sorrow that brings true repentance (cf. Gen. 27:34–40).

Verses 18–21 are commonly understood as setting forth a contrast: the old revelation and dispensation is earthly, menacing, and morbid in its concentration on law and judgment, while the new is spiritual, heavenly, and happy. But these verses present Israel not as a paradigm of Old Testament spirituality but of unbelief that leads to death in any epoch. That Israel "begged that no further word be spoken to them" was, in the judgment of this author, a culpable act of rebellion against God. The word the NIV translates "begged" in verse 19 is the same word it translates "refuse" in verse 25. Moreover, after all that has already been said of the unbelief of the wilderness generation (3:7–4:5), it is surely unlikely that here it is held up as exemplifying godly fear. The author correctly understands Israel's request (cf. Deut. 5:23–29), though not in itself sinful, as neither genuine nor indicative of future commitments. Further, as the citation of Deuteronomy 9:19 confirms, Moses's fear was not of the awesome manifestations of the divine holiness—he had already walked into that fire and gloom to the top of the mountain—but of the prospect of divine judgment against the people for the sin with the golden calf. These verses, then, depict the terror of the apostate face-to-face with the wrath of God, a terror no less the destiny of those who forsake the Lord today (Heb. 12:25, 29; see also 10:27, 30–31).

Contrarily, the author is confident of better things concerning his readers, the things that are obtained by a living faith (12:22–24). The thought is similar to that of 6:9–10 and 10:39. He is persuaded that his readers are genuinely converted (the probable interpretation of Greek *proserchomai*, NIV "you have come to"; cf. Heb. 11:6), and thus that their situation is different

from Israel's in the same way it is unlike Esau's. This confidence is the basis of his appeal to them to persevere. Of course, the blessings enumerated are not peculiar to the new epoch; they are the better things of the heavenly country that believers have always grasped from afar by faith (Heb. 11:10, 13–16, 26–27) and must so grasp by faith today. Hebrews was written to warn this community of believers that it would, like Israel, forfeit these very blessings if it chose to mimic Israel's apostasy. "Church of the firstborn" (12:23) refers to the privileged station of the saints as set apart to God (Exod. 4:22; 13:2) and heirs of all things, the very privileges that Esau squandered (Heb. 12:16–17).

The admonition in verses 25–27 reiterates 3:7–12 and 4:1–2. The readers must not imitate faithless Israel in the wilderness. The threat of divine judgment is no less serious today. In view of the connection of thought between verses 24 and 25 ("that speaks . . . who speaks"), it is reasonable to assume that Jesus is to be understood as the one who thundered his law at

Pictured here is Jebel Katerina, a peak in the mountains of Sinai. Hebrews 12:18–24 says that believers in Christ have not come to a terrifying sight such as happened at Sinai during the exodus. Rather, Christians have come to the heavenly city and to Jesus, the perfect mediator.

Sinai and who utters the promise of Haggai 2:6. Believers have not yet taken possession of the better things, but soon they will, and that forever (12:28–29). That prospect ought to awaken them to glad thanksgiving and to a new determination to work out their salvation in fear and trembling so as not to be found at last among those who miss the grace of God (12:15) and instead must face God's wrath. The warning reiterates Deuteronomy 4:23–24 and indicates that the word of God is no less menacing to the unbeliever and the disobedient today than it was in Moses's day.

3. Concluding Exhortations (13:1–19)

In what amounts to a postscript to his sermon, the author takes care to specify particular ways in which this true and living faith expresses and evidences itself. As elsewhere in the Bible, the believer is not left to work out the ethical implications of faith in Christ; the particular obedience required is carefully defined. Pride of place goes to brotherly love (13:1–3), a costly virtue by which these believers have already distinguished themselves, especially in regard to prisoners (Heb. 6:10; 10:33–34). Abraham is again invoked as an example, this time of hospitality (Gen. 18:1–16; cf. 1 Pet. 4:9) and of the blessing that attends the gracious host. Christian sympathy and fellow feeling (cf. Rom. 14:15; 1 Cor. 12:26) will not be satisfied with the simpler forms of charity but will extend itself to those who cannot be brought into the home (Matt. 25:35–36).

Sexual impurity and the love of money (13:4–6) are linked elsewhere (1 Cor. 6:9–10; Eph. 5:6) as sins of dissatisfaction with God's provision and thus sins of unbelief, as the citations from Deuteronomy 31:6 and Psalm 118:6–7 demonstrate. Neither the Lord's threatened judgment of the worldly nor his promise to provide adequately for his children is taken seriously. For both sins, the antidote is contentment and fulfillment in what God has given (Prov. 5:15–20; 1 Tim. 6:6–11, 17, 19).

The leaders mentioned in Hebrews 13:7 are not, as in verses 17 and 24, the present elders but those who previously evangelized this community (Heb. 2:3), provided its initial instruction in the Christian life, and marvelously adorned their doctrine by the holiness of their lives (cf. Titus 2:10). As valuable as the examples of heroic faith from the distant past may be (Heb. 11:4–38), there is yet more reason to imitate the sturdy faith of those one has known in the flesh and to whom one is greatly indebted. Whether "outcome" suggests martyrdom or, as is probable, simply the righteous character of their lives, they are apparently now numbered among the "spirits of the righteous made perfect" (12:23) and thus serve as examples of those who have persevered to the end.

Amid all the uncertainties of life in this world, the character and word of Jesus Christ stand firm (13:8; see also 1:12; 7:24–25; 10:23). He who sustained the faith of the saints of old (11:26) and of their former leaders just mentioned will not forsake them.

In verse 9 the author returns one last time to the great interest of his letter: to warn his readers of the fatal error of pursuing a compromise with Judaism. Since salvation is by grace through faith in Christ, putting confidence once again in the saving virtue of ceremonial regulations regarding food and drink would amount to a repudiation of the gospel (Heb. 9:9–10; cf. 1 Cor. 8:8). The argument is in principle very similar to Paul's protestation against the inroads of ritualistic legalism in the churches of Galatia and Colossae (Gal. 4:8–11; Col. 2:13–23).

The reference in verses 10–11 is again to the ritual of the Day of Atonement, which included the sin offering, the flesh of which the priests were not permitted to eat (Lev. 4:11–12; 16:15–27). The author has already demonstrated that this ritual typified the sacrifice of Christ (Heb. 9:6–12, 23–28). The superiority of the antitype (what the type foreshadows) is demonstrated in the fact that the believer has an altar—the sacrifice or sin offering of Christ, from which he is welcome always to partake (cf. John 6:53–56; 1 Cor. 5:7–8; 10:16). No doubt the readership is being swayed by the charge that Christianity suffers by comparison with Judaism for want of an altar. The church throughout the ages has never been immune from the temptation to gather confidence from the outward trappings of religion: altars, buildings, and impressive rites. The author's rejoinder is that the church's invisible altar is the reality of which the ceremonies of Judaism are but pale imitations (Heb. 8:1–5), and the church's food is the eternal and spiritual benefits of the Son of God's once-for-all sacrifice of himself for sin, for which beef or lamb, however impressively and ceremonially prepared, is no substitute.

The author notes a further parallel between type and antitype (13:12–14): the carcasses of the sin offerings were burned outside the camp, while Jesus was crucified outside the city of Jerusalem. The significance of the latter fact seems chiefly to lie in its suggestion that Judaism as a whole had rejected Jesus. As once before in Israel's history, when God

> Jesus was crucified outside the city, a sign of his disgrace that Christians must be willing to bear in his name (Heb. 13:11–12). This chapel in the Church of the Holy Sepulchre is the traditional site of Calvary, where Jesus was crucified.

left the camp of Israel after her sin with the golden calf and took up station outside the camp (Exod. 33:7–11), Christ's sacrifice of himself outside the gate represented divine judgment on the people's unbelief. To make peace with the Judaism that rejected Christ would be to make common cause with God's enemies whom he has demonstrated to be objects of his wrath. Instead, the readers must make the break with that apostate people and their strange teachings of salvation through the blood and the flesh of bulls and goats. These remarks would be particularly appropriate directed to a community influenced by a form of Judaism like that given expression at Qumran, where great care was taken to organize the sect as a reproduction of the camp of Israel in the wilderness.

No doubt such a separation will be intensely painful for these believers, all the more because they will be marked by their former brethren with the stigma of a betrayal of the ancient faith. But loyalty to Christ demands it, and the prospect of the eternal city should lessen the sting of the severing of earthly associations. In any case, such a pilgrimage from the comfortable scenes of the past to the heavenly country

would be a living up to their spiritual heritage as the descendants of Abraham and Moses (Heb. 11:8–10, 25–27). Those who call Jesus Lord are the true Israel (Rom. 9:1–9; Phil. 3:3).

They may no longer have animal sacrifices to offer to God, but there are yet more acceptable sacrifices than these: worship and good works (13:15–16). The superiority of such sacrifices of the heart was a truism of the Old Testament (1 Sam. 15:22; Ps. 50:13–14; 51:17; Hos. 14:2) reiterated in the New Testament (Rom. 12:1; Phil. 4:18; 1 Pet. 2:10).

It is likely that this group of Jewish Christians had been, by reason of their drift back toward Judaism, estranged from the larger Christian community. Perhaps en masse they had begun to separate themselves (Heb. 10:25) and in other ways make life difficult for the elders. In any case, the author expresses confidence that the present leadership would, if able to exercise its authority, steer his readers in the right direction. Texts such as Hebrews 13:17 provide a needed corrective to democratic or, worse, anarchic tendencies in the church. The church is a kingdom ruled by a king who exercises his dominion through officers (Matt. 16:18–19; 1 Thess. 5:12–13). This sacred authority should be prevented from degenerating into an authoritarianism by the genuine interest in the well-being of the people of God required of elders and by the prospect of accounting for their ministry at the judgment seat of Christ (cf. James 3:1). The spiritual prosperity of the church and the honor of Christ are best served when elders fulfill their stewardship in love and truth and when the saints submit to them as to the Lord.

Like Paul, the author writes his stern and likely painful admonition with a clear conscience and with the humble recognition that he needs God's grace and help fully as much as those to whom he writes (Heb. 13:18–19; cf. 2 Cor. 1:10–14). No doubt he wishes to assess the situation in

person and to deal with it in a more thorough fashion than he can in a written sermon, brief as it is (13:22). Evidently he has had a close association with these believers previously, has been separated from them for some time, and has been prevented for some reason from returning to them.

4. Benediction and Greetings (13:20–25)

The beautiful benediction in verses 20–21 forms an exquisite conclusion to the entire work, especially in its concentration on the centrality of Christ in God's grand program of restoring sinners to himself and to a life pleasing to him.

The personal notes in verses 23–24 do little more than tantalize. Nothing else is known of Timothy's imprisonment, and further references are hopelessly speculative. "Those from Italy" is ambiguous and could suggest either that the author is writing from Italy or that he is writing from some other place to a community of believers in Italy and naturally includes the greetings of expatriate Italian believers who are with him.

The salutation (13:25) is profound in its simplicity (cf. Titus 3:15) and expresses both the

CHRISTIAN COMMUNITIES IN FIRST-CENTURY ITALY

author's desire for and his confident expectation of the Lord's restoring his readers to their once sturdy faith in Christ Jesus.

Select Bibliography

Bruce, F. F. *The Epistle to the Hebrews.* New International Commentary on the New Testament. Grand Rapids: Eerdmans, 1964.

Ellingworth, Paul. *The Epistle to the Hebrews: A Commentary on the Greek Text.* New International Greek Testament Commentary. Grand Rapids: Eerdmans, 1993.

Guthrie, Donald. *The Epistle to the Hebrews.* Tyndale New Testament Commentaries. Grand Rapids: Eerdmans, 1983.

Hagner, Donald A. *Hebrews.* New International Biblical Commentary. San Francisco: Harper & Row, 1983.

Hughes, Philip Edgcumbe. *A Commentary on the Epistle to the Hebrews.* Grand Rapids: Eerdmans, 1977.

Lane, William L. *Hebrews.* 2 vols. Word Biblical Commentary. Dallas: Word, 1991.

Moffat, J. *A Critical and Exegetical Commentary on the Epistle to the Hebrews.* International Critical Commentary. Edinburgh: T. & T. Clark, 1924.

Montefiore, Hugh. *A Commentary on the Epistle to the Hebrews.* London: Allenson, 1964.

Vos, Geerhardus. *The Teaching of the Epistle to the Hebrews.* Nutley, NJ: Presbyterian & Reformed, 1974.

James

Douglas J. Moo

Introduction

Author

The writer of the letter identifies himself simply as "James, a servant of God and of the Lord Jesus Christ" (1:1). Who is this James? Of the four men with this name mentioned in the New Testament, only two are significant enough to have identified themselves as simply as does the author of this letter: James the son of Zebedee, who was one of the twelve apostles (Mark 1:19), and James "the Lord's brother" (Gal. 1:19), who early on became the leader of the Jerusalem church (cf. Acts 15:13; 21:18; Gal. 2:9). Although a few scholars have thought that the son of Zebedee could be the author, his early martyrdom (AD 44; cf. Acts 12:2) probably removes him from consideration. Still others think that the good, almost literary Greek of the letter, along with the way the author handles the topic of justification (2:14–26), makes it likely that someone toward the end of the first century wrote the letter and ascribed it to James. But this theory is unnecessary and calls into question the honesty of the writer. There is every reason to accept the widespread opinion of the early church that James the brother of the Lord wrote this letter.

Although this view is contested, it is probable that James was a younger brother of Jesus, born to Joseph and Mary after the birth of Jesus. Not a believer during Jesus's earthly ministry

(cf. John 7:5), James was probably converted as a result of a postresurrection appearance (1 Cor. 15:7). His wise leadership of the Jewish Christian church (see Acts 15:6–22), along with his piety and respect for ancestral traditions, earned him the title "the Just" in both Jewish and Christian history.

Audience, Date, and Occasion

James is classed among the General Epistles of the New Testament, those letters that are not addressed to specific churches (e.g., 1 Corinthians) or individuals (e.g., 1 Timothy). But this does not mean that James had no definite readers in mind as he wrote. The letter is addressed to "the twelve tribes scattered among the nations" (1:1). From its original application, the phrase "twelve tribes" came to designate the complete regathering of God's people that would take place in the messianic age (cf. Isa. 49:6; Ezek. 47:13). James, then, uses this title to remind his readers that they belong to that new creation, the church, that God has brought into being on the basis of faith in his Son (cf. Matt. 16:18). These "twelve tribes" have been "scattered" or "dispersed" among the nations. What is meant by this? In one sense, all God's people, as aliens and exiles, living apart from our true heavenly home, have been "scattered" in this world (cf. 1 Pet. 1:1). But the word "scatter" and its noun form, "those scattered," or "dispersion," was often used to designate Jews living outside

Palestine. It may be that James uses the word with this more specific meaning. Suggestive here is the reference in Acts 11:19 to those early Jewish Christians in Jerusalem who were forced to flee the city because of persecution and engaged in evangelism among Jews "as far as Phoenicia, Cyprus and Antioch." Could this not furnish a plausible background for the circumstances of the Letter of James?

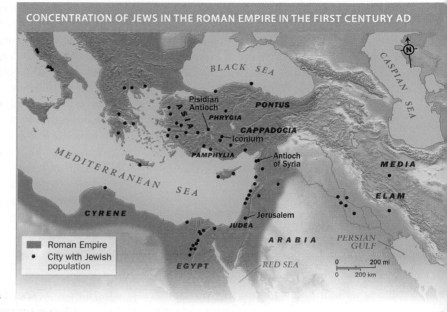

CONCENTRATION OF JEWS IN THE ROMAN EMPIRE IN THE FIRST CENTURY AD

Roman Empire
City with Jewish population

Forced to live away from their home church, these scattered parishioners required exhortation and advice on issues they were facing. What is more natural than that their spiritual guide send them a pastoral letter?

If this reconstruction of the circumstances of the letter is accepted, it would make James probably the earliest New Testament book to be written—sometime in the middle 40s of the first century. Also suggestive of an early date are the reference to the synagogue as the place of meeting (2:2) and the fact that the sharp debates over the place of the law in Christianity, so prevalent from the latter 40s on, are not reflected in the letter. The way in which James deals with justification in 2:14–26 also fits nicely into this early time period: James's teaching implies that he has heard of Paul's slogan "justification by faith" but that he has no firsthand knowledge of what Paul really meant by it. Such a situation would exist only before the Jerusalem council of AD 48 or 49 (see Acts 15).

We understand James, then, to be a letter of pastoral encouragement and exhortation written to Jewish Christians living outside Palestine in the middle 40s of the first century.

Structure and Sources

As a pastoral letter, James reads like a sermon, or a series of sermonettes. The purpose of these homilies is almost always to command and exhort: it is indicative of the tone of the letter that James has a greater frequency of imperative verbs than any other New Testament book.

James has structured loosely his series of sermonic exhortations. The letter may be divided into five major sections (see the outline), but there is no clear logical progression from one section to another, and even within the sections James often jumps quickly and without explanation from one aspect of his topic to another. This manner of moving from topic to topic is reminiscent of the wisdom books of the Old Testament and Judaism (e.g., Proverbs, Sirach).

Another interesting feature of the letter is James's habit of borrowing from other sources. Most prominent among these is the teaching of Jesus. Not only does James come close to quoting Jesus on one occasion (5:12; cf. Matt. 5:34–37); he also infuses his letter with themes, images, and emphases characteristic of Jesus. Other writings with which James has much in common are 1 Peter in the New Testament;

Proverbs in the Old Testament; Sirach, the works of Philo, and the *Testaments of the Twelve Patriarchs* among Jewish literature; and the early Christian books the *Shepherd* of Hermas and *1 Clement*. The parallels between James and these other sources do not, except in the case of the teaching of Jesus, suggest that James has borrowed directly from them. Rather, it would seem that some of the themes and language found in these books were known to James and he used them to make his own points.

Theological Themes

The Letter of James, it is sometimes said, has no theology. If by this it is meant that James does not present a systematic exposition of the faith or that his main intention is not to teach theology, then the statement is true enough. But in another sense, it is misleading. James approaches the practical issues he deals with from a profound knowledge of who God is and what he has done in Christ—theology indeed! And James also makes an important contribution to our understanding of several theological issues. Among these is theology proper—the doctrine of God. James emphasizes God's generous nature (1:5, 17), his total separation from evil (1:13), his jealousy (4:5), and his grace (4:6). Eschatology receives attention in 5:1–11, where James sounds the characteristic New Testament note of fulfillment without consummation: the "last days" have come, and we must now live in that knowledge (5:3, 5); however, we also wait for that day when our Savior and judge will appear in glory (5:7–11). Also prominent in James is the problem of poverty and wealth. Most of James's readers are poor, and they need to be encouraged to find solace in their spiritual wealth (1:9) and to be reminded that God will judge their wicked rich oppressors (5:1–6).

Of greatest interest theologically is James's teaching on justification in 2:14–26—teaching that many think to be in conflict with Paul. Does not Paul stress that "a person is justified by faith apart from the works of the law" (Rom. 3:28)? How, then, can James assert that "a person is justified by what he does and not by faith alone" (2:24)? A careful study of the ways in which James and Paul use the crucial word "justify" will show that the conflict is only apparent. While Paul uses the word to designate the person's initial acceptance before God, James uses it of the believer's final vindication before God in the judgment. Thus Paul emphasizes, combating the typically Jewish emphasis on doing the law, that a person can "get right" with God only through faith in Jesus Christ. James, criticizing Christians who were neglecting to live out their faith, reminds them that God does take works into account when we stand before him in the judgment.

It is, of course, this plea for working faith, for a belief that is so deep and vital that it *has* to spill over into all our lives, that characterizes the message of James. He encourages his readers, both in the first century and today, to live out their faith, to abandon any spiritual double-mindedness, and to press on to full Christian maturity. John Wesley's description in *A Plain Account of Christian Perfection* captures perfectly the goal that James encourages us to pursue: "In one view it is purity of intention, dedicating all the life to God. It is the giving God all our heart; it is one desire and design ruling all our tempers. It is the devoting, not a part, but all our soul, body, and substance to God."

Outline

1. Address and Greeting (1:1)
2. Trials and Temptation (1:2–18)
   A. Overcoming Trials (1:2–12)
   B. The Source of Temptation (1:13–18)
3. Putting the Word into Practice (1:19–2:26)
   A. Anger and the Tongue (1:19–20)
   B. "Be Doers of the Word" (1:21–27)
   C. The Sin of Favoritism (2:1–13)
   D. True Christian Faith Seen in Its Works (2:14–26)
4. Worldliness in the Church (3:1–4:12)
   A. The Taming of the Tongue (3:1–12)
   B. Peaceable Relations among Christians (3:13–4:3)
   C. A Call for Repentance (4:4–10)

Commentary

1. Address and Greeting (1:1)

Although James could claim to be a brother of the Lord and a leader in the early Jerusalem church, he is content to call himself a "servant." Indeed, like Moses (Deut. 34:5) and David (Ezek. 37:24) before him, James recognizes that there is no higher honor than being called to serve the living God. James's readers are also honored to belong to the people of God of the last day—"the twelve tribes." As I suggested in the introduction, these readers are probably Jewish Christians who had to flee from Jerusalem and take up new lives in lands outside Palestine.

2. Trials and Temptation (1:2–18)

A. Overcoming trials (1:2–12). As James's readers establish themselves in their new surroundings, they have to face many trials. Poverty and persecution appear to have been the biggest trials faced by these early Christians, but James has in mind all kinds of difficulties that can pose threats to our faith in God—sickness, the death of loved ones, a rebellious child, a hated job. Whatever the trial, James commands Christians to rejoice (1:2). How is this possible? By recognizing that God can use these problems and tribulations to produce Christians who are "mature and complete" (1:4). Trials, which test us as fire refines ore (see also 1 Pet. 1:7), lead to a more settled, stable Christian character; and as we continue taking a Christian viewpoint on trials, this perseverance will be able to finish its work of producing strong, mature, unshakable believers. Right at the beginning of his letter, James sounds a note that he will repeat throughout the letter in different ways: Christians must take a distinctively Christian perspective on life.

James sometimes links his topics by repeating a word: here he joins verses 4 and 5 with the verb "lack." A more substantive link may also exist, however. Wisdom may be that quality that is needed if the believer is to face trials in the appropriate Christian manner. Wisdom in the Bible is a practical, down-to-earth virtue that provides its possessor with insight into the will and ways of God. Like the book of Proverbs, James emphasizes that wisdom can be gained only by asking God. And as an encouragement to ask, James reminds us that God gives "simply," "with a single, unwavering intent" (the probable meaning of the Greek word here; NIV "generously"), and without holding our past failures against us (1:5). But not every asking, even if imploring and sincere, receives an answer from God. We must ask in faith, without doubting. In an expressive image, James compares the doubter to the constantly varied surface of the sea—forever in motion, never stable, up one day, down the next (1:6). Such a person is literally, James says, "double-souled"—divided at the very root of their being, a spiritual schizophrenic. That kind of person must not expect that God will respond to their prayers (1:7–8). What James criticizes in these verses is not the person who has occasional doubts about his or her faith, or lapses into sin now and again—few indeed would ever have prayers answered were that the case! Rather, James castigates the person who is basically insincere in seeking for things like wisdom from God, the person who is seeking to serve two different masters at the same time (see Matt. 6:24; James 4:4).

The discussion of poverty and wealth in verses 9–11 may be connected to verses 2–4 (if we recognize poverty as one of the most difficult of trials) or to verses 5–8 (considering that wealth has great potential for dividing our loyalties). James contrasts two people in these verses: poor Christians (1:9) and "the rich" (1:10–11). This latter phrase is ambiguous. If James has in mind rich non-Christians, then his contrast is between poor Christians, who are to rejoice in their heavenly calling, and rich unbelievers, who have nothing to boast about except their ultimate judgment for their wicked use of money. That James elsewhere uses "rich" to designate non-Christians (5:1) favors this interpretation. On the other hand, "the rich" could be Christians. In this case, James would be contrasting Christians from very different socioeconomic spheres and encouraging all believers to focus not on that worldly status but on their relationship to Christ. Poor believers should not despair because of their poverty but rejoice because they are "rich in faith and [heirs to] the kingdom" (2:5). Rich believers, on the other hand, must be careful not to take pride in their worldly possessions—for their wealth will quickly perish—but to boast in their "low position" (NIV "humiliation"), their relationship to Jesus, the servant who was "despised and rejected" (Isa. 53:3). Either interpretation makes sense of the verses, but the second alternative explains more naturally the order of the Greek words in verse 9 (literally "the brother, the humble one").

James concludes the opening section of the letter by returning explicitly to the theme of trials (1:12). Remaining faithful to God during trials brings God's blessing: the reward of life eternal that God has promised to those who belong to him. The risen Jesus similarly encouraged suffering Christians: "Be faithful, even to the point of death, and I will give you life as your victor's crown" (Rev. 2:10).

B. The source of temptation (1:13–18). The connection between James's discussion of trials in verses 2–12 and temptation in verses 13–15 is more explicit in the Greek text than in the English because a single Greek root does duty for both these concepts. In meaning, however, the two are to be carefully distinguished. A trial is an outward circumstance that can pose difficulties

to our faith. A temptation is the inner enticement to sin. What James is concerned about is that his readers will confuse these two and attribute temptation to God. Scripture indicates that God does "test" or put his people through trials (cf. Gen. 22:1). But, James emphatically asserts, God never tempts his people (1:13). He never entices them to sin or desires that they fail in the trials he may bring. Believers must never excuse their sin by blaming God for the temptation. Rather, James points out, believers need look no further than within themselves for the problem. It is our own "evil desire" that is the real source of temptation (1:14). Like the bait that lures the fish and the hook that snares it, sin entices and seeks to entrap us. That James does not here mention Satan does not mean that he ignores the power of the tempter (see 4:7). His point is to lay responsibility for sin clearly at the door of each individual. And, as J. A. Bengel remarks, "Even the suggestions of the devil do not occasion danger, before they are made 'our own'" (Bengel, 5:7). Shifting his imagery, James traces the terrible process by which temptation becomes spiritual death: the impulse to sin, alive in all of us, conceives sin when we succumb to temptation; if we do nothing to cut off the growth and maturation of sin, death is the inevitable result (1:15).

After issuing a warning not to be deceived (1:16), James provides a positive counterpart to verses 13–15: far from being responsible for temptation, or anything evil, God gives good gifts to his children. And that God will continue to do so can be depended on, for he is unchangeable. Unlike the sun, moon, stars, and planets ("the heavenly lights"; cf. Ps. 136:7–9), which regularly move and change their appearance, God never changes (1:17). As an outstanding example of God's good gifts, James cites the new, spiritual birth that Christians have experienced (1:18). This "new birth," or regeneration, is motivated solely by the will of God. It is accomplished through the instrument of "the word of truth," the gospel (cf. 2 Cor. 6:7; Eph. 1:13; Col. 1:5; 2 Tim. 2:15), and it has as its purpose the bringing into being of "firstfruits," the first harvest of the fruits produced by God's eternal plan of redemption.

3. Putting the Word into Practice (1:19–2:26)

The mention of the "word of truth" in verse 18 leads James to devote a lengthy section to a matter close to his heart—the appropriate Christian response to God's word. James stresses that the word's purpose is to be obeyed (1:21–27), gives an example of how that word should be obeyed in practice (2:1–13), and ties that doing of the word inextricably to genuine faith (2:14–26).

A. Anger and the tongue (1:19–20). Before launching into this major topic, James interjects a warning about the misuse of the tongue—the first of several that occur in his letter (1:26; 3:1–12; 4:11–12; 5:12). James echoes a theme sounded often in Proverbs (see 10:19; 15:1; 17:27–28): the righteous will listen well and consider carefully before they speak and will restrain their anger lest it lead to hasty, nasty, irretrievable words (1:19). James does not prohibit all anger but exhorts his readers to be slow and careful about allowing anger to develop. Anger, James reminds us, "does not produce the righteousness that God desires" (1:20).

B. "Be doers of the word" (1:21–27). Many translations and commentaries take verse 21 with verses 19–20, but it really introduces the main topic of the next paragraph: the right response to God's word. James commands us to receive the word (1:21). Elsewhere in the New Testament, this expression describes conversion, but this cannot be the meaning here, since James addresses people who already are Christian. What he means is well illustrated in Jesus's parable of the sower (Mark 4:1–9): believers have to provide the right climate for the growth

of God's word in their lives—they have to be fertile soil. Thus there is need to clear out the weeds of moral filth and evil. James's reference to the word as being "planted in" us may allude to Jesus's parable but probably also hints at the fulfillment of Jeremiah's famous prophecy about the new covenant, in which God promised to "put [his] law in their minds and write it on their hearts" (Jer. 31:33). Becoming more specific, James now tells us how we are to receive the word: by doing it ("Be doers of the word"; 1:22 RSV, NKJV). Hearing, or listening to, the word is absolutely essential; but if hearing does not lead to doing, if study does not result in obedience, if attendance at worship service does not lead to a righteous life—then the word of God has been mistreated and we are deceiving ourselves about the reality of our relationship to God (1:22). Jesus pronounced a blessing on "those who hear the word of God and obey it" (Luke 11:28). People who hear the word without doing it are compared to people who look into a mirror at their faces but immediately forget what they have seen (1:23–24). In other words, no lasting impression is made; the word has not really penetrated the heart

James talks about the tongue several times in his letter, beginning in 1:26 (see 1:19–20). Later, in James 3:4–5, he says that the tongue steers the whole body just as a small rudder steers a large ship. This marble relief (second century AD) shows a corbita, a two-masted trading vessel that sailed close to the coast as it traveled from port to port.

and life of the person who has heard. But the person who carefully listens to God's word and continues to put it into practice, not forgetting it—this person receives God's approval (1:25). It should be noted that the "word" of verse 22 has become in verse 25 "the perfect law that gives freedom." This is indicative of James's holistic understanding of God's word: the "word of truth" (1:18) that regenerates us is also God's law that demands our heartfelt obedience. For James this "law" clearly involves some Old Testament commands (2:10–12), but only as they have been made a part of "the royal law" that Jesus proclaimed (2:8).

James becomes more specific still. What does it mean to "do" the word? Three areas of obedience are singled out by James: personal behavior, social concern, and inner values. James again shows his concern about sins of speech by highlighting careful speech habits as an example of the religion that God accepts (1:26). Another characteristic emphasis in James is mentioned in verse 27 for the first time: concern for the poor and needy. "Orphans and widows" became in the Old Testament a stock description of the helpless in the world. God himself is "a father to the fatherless, a defender of widows" (Ps. 68:5), and his people are to show the same concern (cf. Isa. 1:10–17). Finally, and lest obedience to God's word seem entirely a matter of external behavior, James stresses the need for an inner attitude and value system distinct from that of the world in which we live.

C. The sin of favoritism (2:1–13). This section of the letter has one central purpose: to condemn any practice of favoritism in the church. "Favoritism" translates a rare word that is used by the New Testament writers to render the Old Testament Hebrew expression "receiving the face." It connotes the treatment of any person on the basis of an external consideration—be it race, nationality, wealth, or manner of dress. Such favoritism is foreign to the nature of God (cf. Rom. 2:11) and should also be unknown among believers in Christ (2:1). James's lofty description of Jesus as the Messiah of Israel

(Christ), the Lord, and the glorious one (or, less probably, "the glory," alluding to the Shekinah, the presence of God) shows just how exalted is his conception of Jesus. The illustration James uses in verses 2–3 need not refer to an actual situation but certainly implies that this kind of behavior was a real problem. Poor people were being discriminated against; and in doing so, James says, the believers manifest their evil thoughts (2:4). James's use of the word "synagogue" (NIV "meeting," 2:2) may imply that he is thinking of a nonworship gathering of the church (perhaps for the purpose of judging between believers; see Ward), but it is more likely that this is a primitive Jewish-Christian term for the church's gathering for worship.

James gives several reasons for his condemnation of favoritism against the poor. The first is that it stands in contradiction to God's own attitude and actions. He has chosen the poor in the world to receive the blessings of his kingdom (2:5). Note that James does not say that God has chosen *all* the poor or *only* the poor but that God has a special concern for the poor (cf. Luke 6:20). It seems to be the case that most of the early Christians were, in fact, poor (1 Cor. 1:26). The second reason James gives for condemning this favoritism has to do with the actual situation. The rich people were exploiting and persecuting the fledgling church. How ironic that the church should mistreat those from whom most of them were drawn in order to curry favor with the wealthy and powerful (2:6–7).

The third basis on which favoritism is criticized is also the most important: it violates the "royal law" of love for the neighbor. Jesus himself cited Leviticus 19:18, along with the requirement to love God, when asked to give a summary of the law (Matt. 22:34–40), and it is probably for this reason that James calls it the *royal* law: it was highlighted by Jesus, the king, as a crucial law for the kingdom of God (2:5). Favoritism, then, by mistreating "your neighbor," involves a clear violation of the law (2:9). Significantly, favoritism at the expense of the poor is also condemned in the context of Leviticus 19:18 (cf. 19:15). Verses 10–11 support the conclusion reached in verse 9, that those who show favoritism are convicted as lawbreakers, by arguing that the infringement of any one law incurs the penalty for the breaking of the whole law. This is so because the law is the expression of God's demand; ultimately, one either meets or fails to meet that demand—there can be no partial perfection. Therefore, James concludes, we had better speak and act with the realization that our conduct will be measured by the standard of "the law that gives freedom" (2:12). James's Christian understanding of the law is implied here again by this description (see also James 1:25). There is law in the Christian life, but it is not identical with the Old Testament law, which itself was fulfilled by Christ (Matt. 5:17) and can no longer condemn the believer (Rom. 8:1–3). The "royal law" will, however, judge the believer in the sense that we will appear before Christ for an evaluation of our earthly behavior (cf. 2 Cor. 5:10). On that day, mercy will be an important evidence of the reality of our relationship to God, even as Jesus stressed in his parable of the unmerciful servant (2:13; cf. Matt. 18:21–35).

D. True Christian faith seen in its works (2:14–26). James has firmly upheld the doing of the word as absolutely essential to valid religion. He has even warned that what we *do* will be taken into account in the judgment (2:12–13). How, one might ask, does all this square with the crucial role given to faith throughout the New Testament (and by James himself; see 1:6–8)? Is James replacing faith with works? In this passage he answers that question with a decisive no by showing that true Christian faith necessarily and of its very nature produces those works pleasing to God.

In a teaching style James frequently uses, he broaches the issue with a question, or, to be more precise, two questions (2:14). In the Greek, it is clear that the assumed answer to these questions is no—*this faith*, the faith that certain people *claim* to have but that is without deeds,

cannot save them from the judgment of God. The illustration in verses 15–16 drives home this point. What good have we done the fellow Christian who lacks the essentials of life if we simply dismiss him or her with words? Not that words are unimportant or that there will not be occasions when words are all we can offer. But the real test of our words is actions that back them up. Isaiah exhorted his contemporaries to put meaning into their religious rituals by sharing bread with the hungry and covering the naked (58:7–9), and Jesus promised the kingdom to those who feed and clothe "the least of these" (Matt. 25:31–46). Thus, James draws the conclusion (2:17): faith by itself is "dead"—not just in the sense that it is not doing what it should but that it is not even really what it claims to be.

In the ancient world, writers often used a sort of argumentative style to carry along their discussion. Paul uses it frequently in Romans, and James uses it here. He has an imaginary opponent object, "You have faith; I have deeds" (2:18a). The force of this objection has been understood in a great number of ways, but the simplest interpretation is to assume that the objector is arguing for the principle "different people, different gifts": Why cannot one believer be especially gifted with faith while another has the ability to perform good deeds? James answers this objection with a challenge (2:18b–19, author's translation): "Give me evidence, apart from deeds, that you have faith. You can't do it, can you? But I can point to my deeds as the clear evidence of the reality of my faith. Why, faith without deeds is no better than the intellectual 'faith' of demons; they have a perfectly correct 'theology' but do not have the commitment to what they believe—their faith has affected their minds, but not their wills. So a faith without deeds is also a less than Christian faith, a bogus faith."

This "foolish person" (2:20), the imaginary objector James uses to make his point, is now given evidence from the Old Testament that faith must be accompanied by works to be considered valid before God. James cites two very different people to make his point: Abraham, the honored father of the Jewish people, and Rahab, the immoral pagan. Abraham, James claims, illustrates the intimate relationship of faith and works. In going so far as to offer his son Isaac in obedience to the Lord (Genesis 22), Abraham showed that his faith was deep and strong (see also Heb. 11:17–19). His faith and his actions "were working together" in close partnership (2:22). Indeed, it was the exercise of his faith through works that brought his faith to full maturity. But James goes even further than this. It was on the basis of his works that Abraham was "considered righteous," or "justified" (the two English words translate the same Greek root; 2:21). And although God declared Abraham righteous by faith (2:23; cf. Gen. 15:6), this pronouncement was itself brought to its fullness of meaning ("made complete") when his works completed his faith.

These statements of James about being justified by works present a problem to the person who is aware that Paul claimed that a person "is justified by faith apart from observing the law [or "works of the law"]" (Rom. 3:28). Indeed, Paul even quotes the same passage that James has cited (Gen. 15:6) in favor of *his* point of view. To be sure, the problems being dealt with are quite different—Paul is attacking people who think that salvation is tied to doing the Jewish law; James addresses people who think that salvation brings no responsibility. But Paul's "works of the law" is simply a subset of James's "works," and so a formal contradiction remains. To put it simply, Paul says, "justified by faith alone"; James says, "justified by faith plus works." What is vital, then, is to see that Paul and James are using the key word "justify" with different meanings. When Paul uses the word "justify," he designates the initial acceptance of the sinner before God—the solely gracious act whereby God, the judge of all the world, considers us "right" before him because of our identification with Christ (see Rom. 4:5). James, on the other hand, uses "justify," as was typical

in Judaism, of the ultimate verdict of acquittal rendered over our lives. Jesus used the term in this way when he said, "By your words you will be acquitted, and by your words you will be condemned" (Matt. 12:37). While Paul, then, asserts that a person is initially declared righteous only through faith, James insists that our ultimate acquittal in the judgment depends on the evidence of true faith—works. And, as James makes clear, true faith will, by its very nature, produce those works that will acquit us at the judgment. A careful theological balance is therefore needed: Paul insists that faith and works are different things and must be kept separate when we think about our standing before God; but James likewise insists that faith and works are inseparable.

In verse 24, James summarizes his position for his readers. Again, it is important to see that James's "faith alone" is far from being genuine Christian faith: this "faith alone" is mere talk without action (2:15–16) or head knowledge without heart knowledge (2:19). This is *not* Christian faith. And with this Paul would have had no argument; he also stressed that it is faith "expressing itself through love" that counts (Gal. 5:6).

James's second Old Testament example is set forth in close parallelism to the first (2:25; cf. 2:21). Rahab too was "considered righteous" because of her actions. On the basis of reports about the power of the Lord, she committed the fate of herself and her family to him by helping the Israelite spies (Joshua 2). In doing this, she manifested the reality of her faith (see Heb. 11:31).

The main point of the paragraph is reiterated in its concluding verse: just as a body without the invigorating spirit is dead, so faith without works is dead—barren and useless. Rather ironically, in light of his criticisms of James, Martin Luther in his preface to Romans describes this dynamic nature of Christian faith as well as anyone: "O it is a living, busy, active mighty thing, this faith. It is impossible for it not to be doing good things incessantly."

4. Worldliness in the Church (3:1–4:12)

The heart of this section, and in many ways the heart of the whole letter, is 4:4–10, with its radical call for repentance from flirtation with the world. The worldliness plaguing the Christians to whom James writes has taken the form of a bitter jealousy and has led to quarrels (3:13–4:3) and harmful, critical speech (3:1–12; 4:11–12).

A. The taming of the tongue (3:1–12). The concern James has already shown about sins of speech (1:19, 26) is given full exposure in this paragraph. He introduces his topic by first warning people not to be too eager to become teachers (3:1). A particularly honored position among the Jews was occupied by the rabbi, and some of this prestige undoubtedly rubbed off on the teacher in the church. James does not want to discourage those who have the calling and the gift for teaching, but he does want to warn people about the heavy responsibility involved in teaching others about spiritual matters (see also Matt. 5:19; Acts 20:26–27). One of the reasons the teaching ministry is very difficult is that it makes use of the most dangerous, untamable member of the body: the tongue. So difficult is the tongue to control and subordinate to godly purposes that James calls the person "perfect" who is able to subdue it (3:2).

The power of the tongue may seem to be out of proportion to its size. But James reminds us with two pointed illustrations that small objects can have great power. The skillful rider uses a small piece of metal or leather to direct the motions of a powerful horse (3:3); the pilot controls the direction and speed of a huge sailing vessel with the touch of a hand on the rudder (3:4). So also the tongue, though a relatively small member of the body, possesses great potential for good or for evil. It can be used to encourage, evangelize, and endear; it can also be used to criticize, mock, and curse. The destructive potential of the tongue is highlighted in verses 5–6. Like a "spark" that sets ablaze a massive forest fire, the tongue

can set on fire "the whole course" of a person's life. (James shows his broad background here again by picking up a phrase, literally "the wheel of existence," that was current in certain Greek religions.) The tongue, James says, is a veritable "world of evil," the very sum and essence of the world as fallen and hostile to God, within a person's life. A power so potentially destructive of the spiritual life can only be explained as having its origin in the influence of Satan himself.

James has described the power and destructive potential of the tongue; now he reminds us how difficult it is to tame and how inconsistent is its nature. God gave to humankind dominion over the animal world at creation (Gen. 1:26; cf. Philo, *On the Special Laws* 4.110–16); but dominion

This spring at Dan is one of the sources of the Jordan River. James notes that out of the same mouth praise of God and cursing of fellow people cannot coexist, just as fresh water and salt water cannot come from the same spring (James 3:9–12).

over the tongue has been much more difficult to attain (3:7–8). In stressing that no one has been able to tame the tongue, James may imply that "when it is tamed we confess that this is brought about by the pity, the help, the grace of God" (Augustine, *Of Nature and Grace* 15). With a further allusion to Genesis, James highlights the "doubleness" of the tongue: we bless God with it, but we also curse people "made in God's likeness" (3:9). This inconsistency in the tongue should not be (3:10)—any more than a single spring should pour forth good, sweet, drinkable water one day and foul, brackish water the next (3:11). Like Jesus before him (Matt. 7:16), James uses the image of the plant that produces according to its nature to demonstrate the fundamental incompatibility of a renewed, sanctified heart pouring forth harmful, filthy, evil words (3:12). Although James does not specify in this paragraph the particular forms of evil speech that he has in mind, he elsewhere singles out the kind of criticism of others that springs from a judgmental attitude (4:11–12). And perhaps James would include in his strictures all those manifold sins of speech that are cataloged in Proverbs: lying, gossiping, criticizing, thoughtless and careless speaking, too much speaking.

B. Peaceable relations among Christians (3:13–4:3). Although a chapter break occurs in the middle of this section, 3:13–18 and 4:1–3 are closely related. They both analyze and condemn the bickering that is apparently all too common among James's readers. The first paragraph approaches the problem by contrasting two kinds of wisdom. There is, on the one hand, the "wisdom" that is "earthly, unspiritual, demonic" (3:15). It is characterized by "bitter envy" and "selfish ambition" (3:14). The word "envy" could also be translated "jealousy" and probably connotes here the prideful spirit of competition for favor and honor that so often disturbs our churches. "Selfish ambition" translates a single Greek word that can best be defined by noting its apparently only pre-Christian usage: Aristotle uses it to describe and condemn the selfishly motivated "party politics" in the Athens of his day (*Politics*

5.3.1302b4; 1303a14; cf. Rom. 2:8; 2 Cor. 12:20; Gal. 5:20; Phil. 1:17; 2:3). Where these attitudes exist, "disorder" and all kinds of evil will be the result (3:16). On the other hand, there is the wisdom from above. It is characterized not by a selfish desire to have one's own way but by "humility" (3:13). And, like genuine faith, it manifests itself in deeds, producing a godly and loving lifestyle. Most of all, James suggests, true wisdom brings peace. This is the focus of the list of virtues attributed to true wisdom in verse 17. And verse 18, with its promise of "a harvest of righteousness" to those who are peacemakers, underscores the point. Jesus likewise commended the peacemakers and promised them that they would be called "children of God" (Matt. 5:9). People who have true biblical wisdom will not be proud, arrogant, or quarrelsome but humble, unselfish, and peaceable.

Continuing his analysis of the quarrels that have broken out among his readers, James now traces the source of these bitter disputes to evil "desires." Sin, James has reminded us, comes from within, from our "own evil desire" (1:14); so too the specific sin of quarrelsomeness. These desires are fighting within us, waging "war against your soul," as Peter puts it (1 Pet. 2:11), and this fighting within also results in fighting without (4:1). The precise meaning of verse 2 depends entirely on how we punctuate the verse. (The earliest copies of the New Testament had no punctuation at all.) Some versions (KJV and HCSB, for instance) separate the relevant words into three separate sentences:

1. You want something but do not get it.
2. You kill and covet, but you cannot have what you want.
3. You quarrel and fight.

However, most contemporary versions (including the NIV and ESV) divide this material into two sentences:

1. You desire and do not have; so you kill.
2. And you covet and cannot obtain; so you fight and wage war.

Although the "and" beginning the second sentence is a bit of a problem, this second alternative should be accepted. It results in a neat parallelism, with each statement connecting an inner attitude to an outward consequence. Furthermore, this sequence fits a popular style of moral analysis in the ancient world (see Johnson 1983). But does James seriously mean to accuse his readers of committing murder? While it is possible that indeed he does (some of his readers may have been Jewish Zealots, who believed that violence should be used to usher in the kingdom of God), it is better to think that he is pointing to the ultimate consequence of unrestrained desire. Rather than becoming frustrated through the attempt to gain things on our own, we should ask God in prayer for what we need. If we still do not find ourselves receiving what we ask for, then we should check our motives: perhaps our prayers are oriented too much around our own selfish pleasures and not enough around the will of God and the needs of others (4:3).

C. A call for repentance (4:4–10). In a startling change of tone, James abandons his customary "my brothers and sisters" to address his readers as "you adulterous people." This change signals a shift in focus. James has been analyzing the sin of envy and its resultant quarrelsomeness; now he calls for a radical departure from that sin. In the Greek, "adulterous people" is feminine because James is making use of the Old Testament tradition according to which God's people are pictured as the "bride of the Lord" in the intimate spiritual union that he has brought into being through his electing love (see Isa. 54:1–6; Jer. 2:2; and esp. Hos. 1:1–3:5). To flirt with the world, then, is to commit spiritual adultery against the Lord (4:4). It is this background that provides the clue to the interpretation of verse 5. Many translations (NIV 1984, HCSB, NET, NLT) take the scriptural quotation as a warning about the tendency of the human spirit to be envious. There is much to be said for this interpretation, since the word for "envy" or "jealousy" that James uses here has

a negative nuance elsewhere. But the context suggests that James might rather be referring to the Old Testament teaching about God's jealousy for his people (see NIV, ESV, NRSV): "he [God] jealously longs for the spirit he has caused to dwell in us" (cf. Exod. 20:5; 34:14; Zech. 8:2). Our tendency to succumb to the allure of the world (4:4) is so serious just because our God demands that we serve him and him alone (4:5).

But while God's demand is all-encompassing, his grace is more than sufficient to meet the need. Proverbs 3:34 promises grace to those who are humble (4:6). Consequently, we need to "submit [ourselves] to God" (4:7) and "humble [ourselves] before the Lord" (4:10). These commands frame three pairs of imperatives in verses 7–9. First, we are to "resist the devil" and "come near to God." Each is accompanied by a promise: the devil will flee and God will draw near to us (see also 1 Pet. 5:5–9, which has many parallels to James 4:6–10). Second, like Old Testament priests, we are to "wash [our] hands"—to seek forgiveness for, and put away from us, outward sins. And at the same time, the inner attitude must be made right—our hearts are to be purified. Third, using the language of the Old Testament prophets (see Joel 2:12), James commands us to mourn deeply and sincerely for the sin that separates us from God (4:9). True Christian joy comes not with the ignoring of sin but with the experience of the forgiveness of sin; and we have to see the serious effects of our sin before we can truly turn from it and find forgiveness. Jesus similarly pronounced a blessing on "those who mourn" (Matt. 5:4) and warned, "Woe to you who laugh now, for you will mourn and weep" (Luke 6:25).

D. Arrogance and the critical tongue (4:11–12). In a short paragraph, James turns once again to sins of speech. He condemns "slander," a word used elsewhere in Scripture to denote rebellion against God's authority (Num. 21:5), slandering people in secret (Ps. 101:5), and bringing false accusations against people (1 Pet. 2:12; 3:16). From the stress in verse

12 on judging, it is probable that James has particularly in mind the judgmental criticism of others that was doubtless accompanying the quarrels and arguments in the church. This kind of criticism is wrong because it assumes that we are in a position to render ultimate verdicts over people, a prerogative that is God's alone (4:12). By criticizing others, we do not fulfill the law of love of neighbor (see James 2:8) but break it.

5. Looking at Life from a Christian Perspective (4:13–5:11)

The paragraphs in this section focus on the way we should look at ourselves (4:13–17), our material possessions (5:1–6), and our present difficulties (5:7–11) in the light of God's person and purposes.

A. Recognizing who we are before God (4:13–17). James addresses self-confident businesspeople in 4:13—whether Christian or non-Christian is unclear. These businesspeople have decided where they are going, how long they will stay, what they will do there, and even what the outcome of their efforts will be. James has nothing against making plans, but he does condemn the arrogance of those who think they can make their plans without reference to God. We must recognize that we do not control what will happen tomorrow and that our very lives are nothing more than "a mist," or smoke, that quickly vanishes (4:14). When we recognize who we are before God, we will see the need to consider the Lord's will in everything we do. The very continuation of our lives depends on his will (4:15). When James encourages us to *say*, "if it is the Lord's will," he does not mean, of course, that the simple repetition of these words in our prayers takes care of the need. Rather, we are to consciously place all our plans and hopes under the lordship of Christ, recognizing that he is the one who prospers or brings to grief those plans. At heart, the sin these businesspeople are committing is the sin of arrogance, of thinking that they, rather than God, are in the driver's seat (5:16). With a principle that has wide application, James concludes the paragraph by reminding us that

sin consists not just in doing those things we should not but also in failing to do those things that we should. Similarly, James's readers are now responsible for putting into practice the attitude he has just set forth.

B. The dangers of wealth (5:1–6). The "rich people" whom James addresses in this paragraph are clearly the wicked rich. The Old Testament often uses "poor" and "rich" almost as synonyms for the righteous and the wicked, respectively (see Prov. 10:15–16; 14:20; Ps. 37:1–40; and also the intertestamental book *1 Enoch* 94–105). Jesus reflected this usage when he blessed the poor and condemned the rich (Luke 6:20, 24). Thus, while the people addressed in this passage are clearly materially wealthy, they are not condemned for their wealth per se but for their selfish accumulation and abuse of their wealth. Why does James send a denunciation of wicked, wealthy unbelievers to Christians? John Calvin pertinently isolates two main reasons: James "has a regard to the faithful, that they, hearing of the miserable end of the rich, might not envy their fortune, and also that knowing that God would be the avenger of the wrongs they suffered, they might with calm and resigned mind bear them" (342).

Weeping and wailing are typical ways of describing the reaction of evil people to the judgment of the day of the Lord (Isa. 13:6; 15:3; Amos 8:3). These rich people will suffer condemnation on that day for four specific sins. First, they have hoarded their wealth and failed to use it to help the poor (5:2–3). James pictures their wealth rotting and corroding—evidence that it has neither done them any good nor benefited the needy. They have failed to follow Jesus's advice: "Sell your possessions and give to the poor. Provide purses for yourselves that will not wear out, a treasure in heaven that will never fail, where no thief comes near and no moth destroys" (Luke 12:33; see also, for the connection between the decay of wealth and failure to help the poor, Sirach 29:9–11). This selfish hoarding of wealth is all the worse in that it is being done "in the last days." The New

Testament consistently portrays the last days, the time of God's intervention to save and to judge, as having begun with the work of Christ (Acts 2:17; 2 Tim. 3:1; Heb. 1:2; 2 Pet. 3:3; Jude 18). All the more reason to use wealth in a way that will please God!

The second reason for the condemnation of these rich people is their failure to pay their laborers what is owed them (5:4). The Old Testament singled out the prompt payment of wages as a prominent requirement of the law (Lev. 19:13; Deut. 24:14–24; Mal. 3:5). James assures the rich that God, "the Lord Almighty," the judge, is well aware of their sin against those who depend on them for daily bread. A luxurious, self-indulgent lifestyle is the third basis for God's judgment (5:5). Like the people of Sodom, who lived in prosperous ease while the "poor and needy" went without (Ezek. 16:49), the rich people of James's day are preparing themselves for the judgment. James uses the image of cattle being fattened for the slaughter to illustrate this storing up of wrath for the day of judgment. Finally, James condemns the rich for using their influential social and political positions to condemn and murder the "innocent one" (5:6). Some interpreters think this is a reference to Jesus and that James has in mind the Jews' complicity in the execution of Jesus. But it is more likely that the singular is generic and that James describes the combination of economic and religious persecution that many early Christians suffered at the hand of the upper classes. Such persecution had long been practiced in Israel (cf. Amos 2:6; 5:12; Mic. 2:2, 6–9) and was all the worse in that the innocent had little ability to resist the machinations of the rich.

C. Waiting on the Lord (5:7–11). Much as Psalm 37 both pronounces judgment on the wicked oppressors of the "poor" and godly and encourages the righteous to "be still before the Lord" while they wait for God's vindication, James 5:1–11 encourages Christians to recognize that judgment will come upon the wicked rich and to wait patiently for the day of that judgment. Christians need to exhibit the patience of the farmer as they wait for "the Lord's coming" (5:7–8). (The rains crucial to Palestinian agriculture fell in the late autumn and early spring [cf. Deut. 11:14].) This coming is "near." Some people think that James must have been wrong to think that Jesus's return could have been near; almost two thousand years have gone by since. But when the New Testament speaks of the nearness or the imminence of the Lord's return, it does not mean that it has to take place within a short period of time. What is meant is that Christ's coming (Greek *parousia*) is the very next event in God's timetable of redemption and that it *could* take place within a short period of time. Every generation of believers lives in the eager expectancy of that return. As we wait, and as we suffer the difficulties of economic deprivation and other trials, we must be careful not to take out our frustrations on one another by grumbling against one another (5:9). The Lord who is coming to deliver us from sin and want is also coming to evaluate the lives of his people.

In their patient endurance of difficulties, Christians are to imitate the prophets and Job (5:10–11). At first glance, Job would seem to be a curious choice to hold up for imitation, for he frequently expressed his exasperation with the Lord. But what James wants us to emulate in Job is his perseverance: despite the disasters he faced, and the relentless attack of his "friends," Job kept his faith and did not abandon his trust in God. As a result, the Lord "finally brought about" the restoration of Job's fortune (Job 42:10–17).

6. Concluding Exhortations (5:12–20)

A. Oaths (5:12). James introduces his final section with a typical literary device: "above all" (cf. 1 Pet. 4:8 and Paul's use of "finally" in this way). James's prohibition of oaths is similar in wording and content to Jesus's prohibition in Matthew 5:34–37. Many think that Jesus and James intended to forbid all oaths; hence some Christians will refuse to take an oath in a court of law, for instance. But it is doubtful that such a situation is envisaged. From the emphasis on telling the truth in both contexts, it is more likely that any oath that in any way compromises our absolute truthfulness is what is forbidden.

B. Prayer (5:13–18). Prayer is often mentioned in the last section of New Testament letters: James is no exception. He begins by encouraging us to pray in any circumstance we might face. When "in trouble" we should turn to God for help; when things are going well, we should turn to God with praise (5:13). In the specific trouble of illness also, prayer is the main remedy. Here, however, James gives lengthier advice. He encourages the person who is sick to call for "the elders of the church," who should come to "pray over" the individual and to "anoint them with oil." The elders were the spiritual leaders in individual local churches (see Acts 14:23; 20:17; 1 Tim. 5:17; Titus 1:5; 1 Pet. 5:1). It is not at all surprising, then, that they should be called to pray for a believer who is sick. But why are they to anoint with oil (see also Mark 6:13)? Although some Roman

Catholic theologians find the sacrament of extreme unction "promulgated" in this text (Council of Trent 15.1), there is no basis for the identification. Since oil was a well-known medicinal agent in the ancient world (as the ancient physician Galen recognized; and see Luke 10:34), the anointing may have a physical purpose. But it would be unusual to single out the use of oil as applicable for *any* illness and strange that the elders of the church should apply it. More likely, the anointing has a symbolic purpose. Anointing with oil is frequently mentioned in the Old Testament as a symbolic action according to which what is anointed is set apart for God's service or blessing. (While the Greek word *chriō* was more often used for this, the word *aleiphō*, found here in James, also occurs [Exod. 40:15; Num. 3:3].) By anointing the sick person with oil, then, the elders are symbolically setting that person aside for the Lord's special attention as they pray. And since it is prayer to which James returns in verse 15, it is clear that it, not the anointing, is the main agent of healing.

By stressing that the prayer of faith is what brings healing, James has carefully qualified the apparently absolute nature of the promise in verse 15. For only prayers that are offered in accordance with the will of God can truly be uttered in faith. When praying for the healing of a person, the elders will often not be sure whether their specific petition is in accord with God's will. As another aspect of the healing process, the sick person is also encouraged to seek forgiveness for sins (5:15). The New Testament makes clear that some illnesses (1 Cor. 11:30), though by no means all (John 9), are the result of sin and that sin will need to be taken care of before healing can come. While James has focused on the role of the elders in healing, he makes clear in verse 16 that

In James 5:14, those who are sick are to "call the elders of the church to pray over them and anoint them with oil." The ointment bottles seen here were found in graves near Akko, Israel (first century AD).

all believers can be active in the ministry of healing as we confess our sins to one another and pray for one another.

As an encouragement to pray, James stresses the great effect of the prayer offered by a "righteous person" (5:16). By this James does not mean to confine effective prayer to a select group of "super saints"; "righteous" designates anyone in a right relationship with God. And even Elijah is cited not because he was a prophet or because he had a special spiritual gift. He was "a human being, even as we are," yet he was able to stop and start the rain by his prayers (5:17–18; cf. 1 Kings 17:1; 18:41–45).

C. Responsibility for fellow believers (5:19–20). In keeping with its literary, sermonic nature, the Letter of James closes not with a series of greetings or personal notes but with a call for action. James has given many commands in the course of his appeal. Now he encourages every reader to intervene to help others obey these commands. When we see a brother or sister who has "wander[ed] from the truth," we are to "bring that person back" (5:19). In doing so, we will be saving that sinner from spiritual death, the ultimate destination on that road that the sinner has chosen to follow (see 1:15). We will also "cover over a multitude of sins" (cf. Prov. 10:12; 1 Pet. 4:8). It is possible that this phrase refers to the sins of the one who does the turning back—an idea that is not unbiblical. But it is more likely that this is a further description of the forgiveness of sins granted to the sinner who has turned back from their way.

Select Bibliography

Bengel, J. A. *Gnomon of the New Testament.* 5 vols. Edinburgh: T. & T. Clark, 1860.

Calvin, John. *Commentaries on the Catholic Epistles.* Translated by John Owen. Grand Rapids: Eerdmans, 1948.

Davids, Peter H. *The Epistle of James.* New International Greek Testament Commentary. Grand Rapids: Eerdmans, 1982.

Dibelius, Martin. *A Commentary on the Epistle of James.* Rev. ed. Hermeneia. Philadelphia: Fortress, 1976.

Johnson, Luke Timothy. "James 3:13–4:10 and the Topos Peri Phthonou." *Novum Testamentum* 25 (1983): 327–47.

———. *The Letter of James.* Anchor Bible. New York: Doubleday, 1995.

Laws, Sophie. *The Epistle of James.* San Francisco: Harper & Row, 1981.

Martin, Ralph P. *James.* Word Biblical Commentary. Waco: Word, 1988.

Mitton, C. Leslie. *The Epistle of James.* Grand Rapids: Eerdmans, 1966.

Moo, Douglas J. *James: An Introduction and Commentary.* Tyndale New Testament Commentaries. Grand Rapids: Eerdmans, 1985.

———. *The Letter of James.* Pillar New Testament Commentary. Grand Rapids: Eerdmans, 2000.

Ropes, James Hardy. *A Critical and Exegetical Commentary on the Epistle of St. James.* Edinburgh: T. & T. Clark, 1916.

Tasker, R. V. G. *The General Epistle of James.* Grand Rapids: Eerdmans, 1956.

Ward, R. B. "Partiality in the Assembly; James 2:2–4." *Harvard Theological Review* 62 (1969): 87–97.

1 Peter

STEPHEN MOTYER

Audience and Occasion

Peter's first letter is called a "General Epistle" in that it was written not to one person or church but to all the churches greeted in 1:1. The precise regions listed are uncertain, for the terms could refer either to the Roman provinces so named or to the old ethnic groups and their associated areas, from which the Romans later adopted their official province names. It is most likely that the names are being used in their "official" sense, so the letter was probably addressed to all the churches in the northern half of Asia Minor (modern Turkey).

It is clear that Peter's readers were facing persecution for their faith, and this has occasioned debate among scholars on several counts. Who instigated this persecution, and why? Was it official or unofficial? Was the persecution merely a threat, or was it already a reality? The answers to these questions are not easy to determine, but the following seems to be most likely. The persecution was probably unofficial and local, instigated by pagan neighbors of the Christian believers, perhaps with the support of minor local officials. It was certainly a present reality for some, if not all, of Peter's readers. While the Roman Empire had an ambivalent attitude toward Christianity, and persecution was occasionally launched officially, this was rare compared with spasmodic local outbursts of hatred. And in this letter, the reasons given for the persecution are purely local. Peter mentions, for example, the annoyance caused by the Christians' refusal to join in riotous festivals (4:4).

Because of this setting, 1 Peter has been called "the Job of the New Testament"—the New Testament book that handles the theme of suffering most directly and intensely.

Authorship and Date

Few scholars today hold that the letter was actually written by the apostle Peter, largely on the grounds of style and language. First Peter is one of the finest examples of Greek prose in the New Testament, and scholars argue that Peter, who was an "unschooled" fisherman (Acts 4:13), could not possibly have produced such a work. In addition, the letter shows close affinities with Paul's writings, particularly the Letter to the Romans, and this too weighs against Petrine authorship. Alternative suggestions are that Silas drafted it as Peter's secretary (see 5:12), so that the style is his but the substance Peter's, or that it was written by another individual after Peter's death and then attributed to him out of respect for his memory.

Yet why should it have been impossible for Peter to compose a letter in Greek? Growing up in Galilee, Peter would have spoken both Greek and Aramaic. And if the letter was written from Rome, as 5:13 suggests, the influence of the Letter to the Romans is hardly surprising. The ascription to Peter is universal in the manuscript tradition and attested early by the church fathers.

Granted Peter's authorship, this letter was probably written from Rome toward the end of his life, perhaps in AD 64–65, when the persecution under the emperor Nero was looming, or had already broken out.

An icon of Peter from a larger piece entitled *Christ and Twelve Apostles* (Antalya, Turkey, nineteenth century AD)

Commentary

1. Suffering as a Christian (1:1–2:10)

A. The hidden inheritance, the hidden Lord (1:1–9). Peter begins his letter like any other in the world of his day, with a greeting, a prayer, and an expression of thanks. But his delight at the wonderful message he has to impart is so great that, like Paul, he fills out these bare, formal "bones" with the glories of the Christian gospel.

He is not simply Peter, but an apostle who writes with the authority of Jesus Christ. His recipients are not just the Christians of northern Asia Minor, but God's elect, whose earthly address is only temporary. His prayer is not the usual "peace be yours in abundance" (see Dan. 4:1), but includes "grace." Instead of the usual expression of thanks for something quite ordinary, like the good health of his recipients, Peter launches into a shout of thanks and praise to God for all the heavenly blessings he has stored up for those who are his.

The themes of this opening greeting and doxology set the tone for the whole letter. Peter brings up the three persons of the Trinity before us again in the very next section (1:10–21) and thus picks up the trinitarian blessing of verse 2. But this opening section is particularly balanced by 2:4–10, which brings to a close the first part of the letter. There Peter returns to the theme that above all thrills him here: the hidden things that are gloriously true of his readers even if all the world should shout a different message at them. Whether they feel like it or not, they are a royal priesthood, a holy nation (2:9).

Doubtless they felt more like his description of them in his greeting (1:1): "strangers in the world" (NIV 1984), "scattered," tiny, persecuted congregations spread across the huge expanse of half of Asia Minor, struggling to keep their faith alive against the pressure of a vastly pagan environment. But Peter will not let them dwell on what they look like from the world's point of view. He wants them to see how *God* looks at them. And from God's viewpoint, their scatteredness is his election. God has plucked them out of their paganism to be his own (1:1). He has foreknown them (1:2). Before they ever existed, the Father knew and loved them and made them his. God has sent his Spirit to sanctify them—that is, precisely to create the distinction between them and the world that causes them so much trouble, by leading them into a life of obedience to Jesus Christ, sheltered under the forgiveness won by his blood.

At the moment they are facing all kinds of trials (1:6) and are tempted to hopelessness and despair. But here too Peter will not let them—or us—believe what the eye sees. The reality is unseen: there is an inheritance that can never perish, which is kept in heaven for us (1:4), as a result of Jesus's resurrection and our new birth through him (1:3). And there is no possibility of losing it, for however weak we may feel, we are shielded by God's power until the moment of salvation comes. Our present experiences are all preparatory, making us fit for glory. Jesus too is unseen: but even so, with our eyes fixed on hidden realities, we will love him and our hearts will sparkle with a joy that surpasses language and even now partakes of the glory that is yet to be (1:8). We already hear the strains of heavenly praise and share in heavenly joy, because we are already "receiving . . . the salvation of your souls" (1:9), even in the midst of suffering and pain.

These inspiring opening verses contain the whole message of 1 Peter in a nutshell. The rest of the letter unpacks and applies this vision in greater and more practical detail.

B. Preparation for action (1:10–2:3). The exhortation of 1:13 provides the keynote of this section, as Peter tackles the unspoken question, How can I have a faith like that? He mentions faith four times in 1:3–9, and it would be very possible for an oppressed, isolated believer to feel that the faith described is too high to attain. Peter sets out in this section to show what the roots of such a faith are—and it turns out that the way we think is absolutely vital.

Peter's sudden introduction of "the prophets" (1:10–12)—probably shorthand for the whole Old Testament—is at first sight surprising. But there are two excellent reasons for their appearance. First, the prophets back up what Peter writes about the foreknowledge of God the Father in 1:2. God announced centuries ago his intention to save the followers of Jesus. It was in fact the Spirit of Christ who spoke in the prophets (1:11). Second, from the prophets we can learn the Christian faith, which Peter has just so eloquently and movingly summarized. Even though they wrote long before Christ came, they realized that they were writing about a grace to be given to someone else and eagerly sought to learn about the time and circumstances of its coming, the sufferings of the Christ, and his glories. The prophets became aware that they were writing for someone else, so that the gospel only needed to be "announced" (NIV "told," 1:12) when the time came. The prophets had already testified to it. See how Paul puts the same idea in Romans 15:4 and 1 Corinthians 10:11.

This is tremendously important for Peter. His letter contains no fewer than twenty-five direct quotations from the Old Testament, and many allusions to it besides. It is the basis of the Christian gospel, for without it we would not understand Christ. And so, in practice, a mind well fed by the Scriptures is the basic prerequisite for the experience of joy in suffering described in 1:3–9.

The existence of such a prophetic word is a summons to prepare the mind for action (1:13–21). The proper response to the Scriptures is to get thinking. The Greek for "minds that are alert and fully sober" means "make sure you keep all your faculties fully operational" (Peter repeats the exhortation "be alert and of sober mind" in 4:7 and 5:8). The mind that is girded up, redirected by the Scriptures, will begin to think in a new way.

However threatening the present, the fully girded-up mind will set its hope "perfectly" or "fully" on God's grace. The redirected mind will focus on God's priority, holiness. At its heart holiness means separateness: God calls us to be different, because he is different. Peter's readers must not worry about their distinctiveness that provokes such hostility from others. It is inevitable! If we are God's, we will begin to bear his likeness in every aspect of life.

The renewed mind knows that life will end with judgment (1:17). We must therefore live each moment under the scrutiny of the judge. We may rejoice to know God as Father, but there must also be reverent fear. Every moment matters, eternally. The thought that we are to be judged according to our work could lead to despair; but our eternal salvation is not jeopardized by our moral feebleness. It rests on nothing that we can produce, not even on our silver and gold (1:18): even our best perishes before God's judgment. But our salvation rests on "the precious blood of Christ" (1:19), just as the blood of the Passover lamb saved the Israelites. Christ was chosen (literally "foreknown") before the foundation of the world (1:20): it was no sudden whim on God's part that made him the sacrifice for sin. And as a result we may place sure faith and hope in God, who though our judge is also our Savior and Father. The resurrection seals the security of those who so believe and hope (1:21). In the midst of earthly insecurity, *here* is true confidence and security!

How may we be sure of knowing joy in suffering? In the next two paragraphs, Peter picks up what he wrote about the prophetic word in 1:10–12 and applies it practically: if our hearts and lives are truly being fed by the word of God, then we will be increasingly transformed within.

First, the word of God gives new life (1:22–25). When we obey God's truth, love will be born in us. God's word has a vital, life-giving power because of who speaks it. Peter quotes Isaiah 40:6–8, which contrasts the permanence

of God's word with the transitory nature of all earthly life. The gospel that Peter's readers have heard, and the Scriptures they now read, are alike "the word of the living and lasting God" (1:23; in the Greek, "living and enduring" could also describe the word rather than God; see NIV).

Second, the word of God nourishes new life (2:1–3). Every newborn infant needs a healthy appetite and proper food or it will not grow. The pure "spiritual" milk that will produce healthy Christian growth is God's own word.

C. The hidden spiritual house (2:4–10). Peter began his letter with the themes of God's elect and his mercy (1:1, 3). He ends this first section on the same note (2:9–10). He also returns to his central theme of hiddenness, though his treatment is different here. In 1:3–9 his thought was angled entirely toward the future, to the coming inheritance and the coming Lord, both now veiled, yet objects of love and joy. But now Peter turns to the past and the present. The hidden but coming Lord was rejected by humankind (2:4), who did not see the estimation God placed on him. In their present rejection, therefore, Peter's readers are sharing the fate of Jesus himself. He was like the stone the builders rejected (2:7).

Through this paragraph, Peter continues his focus on Scripture by quoting three "stone" passages that were applied to Jesus from a very early date (the tradition seems, in fact, to originate with Jesus himself; Matt. 21:42): Psalm 118:22–23; Isaiah 8:14; 28:16 (cf. Rom. 9:33). A stone can look most unimpressive—but it can perform a vital function if made the cornerstone of a large building; or it can bring a person tumbling to the ground if he or she trips over it. Jesus has become the cornerstone of God's spiritual temple, and there are two possible responses. We can either take our own angle and position from the cornerstone and line ourselves up on him, or we can refuse to live by reference to him and stumble over him instead. It is a vivid picture.

Peter urges his readers to see that they are being built in line with Christ: sharing all the angles of his life, experiencing his rejection as well as his glory. His opponents stumble fatally, but those joined to Christ are a chosen people, a royal priesthood (2:9), contrary to all appearances. In verses 9 and 10 Peter piles up phrases from the Old Testament (Exod. 19:6; Isa. 42:12; 43:20; Hos. 1:10; 2:23) to show how all that is true of God's chosen covenant people is true for those who believe in Jesus, however rejected and weak they may seem.

2. At Home, but Not in This World (2:11–3:12)

In the second section of his letter, Peter tackles the question that arises at the end of the first. If Christians must reckon themselves to be gloriously different from what they *appear* to be, if they must look beyond their scatteredness and suffering and see themselves as God's chosen people, then what should their attitude be toward their earthly circumstances? Peter's readers must have been tempted to respond to persecution by adopting an antiworld attitude and withdrawing as much as possible into the comforting warmth of Christian fellowship.

But Peter will not let them do this, even though he has underlined so powerfully their new and hidden status as God's people and the life and love that binds them. Withdrawal from the world is not an option for Christians. Rather, their difference must be expressed through the distinctiveness of their life *within* their earthly callings.

A. The Christian's inner life (2:11–12). In verse 11 Peter reaffirms the general attitude toward the world that ran through the first section of his letter. His readers are "foreigners and exiles" in the world; their home and their roots are elsewhere. It is natural, therefore, that he should go on to urge them to abstain from sinful (literally "fleshly") desires. This world is not our true home, and the flesh seeks to stifle the life of the Spirit within us.

However, although we may be citizens of another world, we still have to "live . . . among the pagans" (2:12) and do so in a way that testifies clearly to the existence and power of that new world. Our declaration depends not so much on words (Peter is remarkably silent about verbal witnessing), as on behavior. Non-Christians watch what we do. The word translated "see" means to watch over a period of time, implying prolonged observation. We must see to it that, even though we may be mocked (or apparently disregarded), the evidence of our lives will speak so loudly that, on the day of judgment, non-Christians will glorify God because they will have to concede that the testimony was laid before them quite unambiguously, even if they failed to heed it. What we are on the inside (2:11) will become obvious on the outside (2:12).

B. A life of submission (2:13–3:7). Romans 13:1–7 is a close parallel to 2:13–17. Paul and Peter agree that respect for and obedience to worldly authority are important because they are an expression of *God's* authority. Peter begins and ends by mentioning the Roman emperor as the one who embodies all the different forms of secular authority under which Christians find themselves.

In theory, worldly authorities exist "to punish those who do wrong and to commend those who do right" (2:14; cf. Rom. 13:3–4), but Peter is as aware as we are today of the possibility of corruption in high places. He even calls Rome "Babylon" in his closing greeting (5:13). Yet, just as we abstain from fleshly desires and still remain committed to ordinary human society (2:11–12), so we submit to worldly authority even though it is to pass away under the judgment of God. We know that God's world is fallen, but we submit to his ordering of it, keen to testify by our lives to what is to come. Simply by doing good we might silence (literally "muzzle") people inclined to revile us (2:15). Peter emphasizes this by the verbs he uses in verse 17. The proper attitudes are timely respect for all people (i.e., we are to take every opportunity to show honor to fellow men and women), love for fellow believers, fear of God (full devotion of heart, mind, and soul), and continuing respect for the emperor.

Peter next homes in on a group for whom a very particular application of the principle of submission to authority is necessary: slaves (2:18–25). Unrest among slaves was widespread at this time, and undoubtedly some Christian slaves believed that, having been "bought" by Christ, they had been set free from their earthly masters! Later on, there were actually Christian groups that encouraged slaves to run away from their masters on these very grounds. But Peter will not allow it. The same principle of *nonwithdrawal from the world* means that slaves must not stop being slaves but instead become better ones—even when their masters are harsh. If they suffer, they must make sure that they suffer unjustly, because it will not do their Lord credit if they deserve the beatings they get!

Then Peter attaches to this straightforward teaching a marvelous passage about the servant Jesus (2:21–25). In fact, it is likely that this is an adaptation of an early Christian hymn about Christ. It suits Peter's theme beautifully as, in close dependence on Isaiah 53, it describes how Jesus, the Suffering Servant of the Lord, submitted to suffering in this world because of his obedience to his heavenly master. Belonging to his Lord did not deliver him from suffering but led him straight to it. And through his suffering we have found forgiveness (2:24). To suffer, therefore, is simply to walk in his footsteps (2:21), and we can be sure that, whatever happens, he is a caring shepherd (2:25).

Peter has deliberately placed this hymn in the middle of this section so that it has a central place: Jesus is our example, not just in the way he suffered, but in his obedient submission to the powers of this world.

The zoom lens now focuses in on another, still more intimate relationship from which Christians were tempted to withdraw because of their new, otherworldly faith: marriage (3:1–7). Should Christian husbands or wives leave their partners if they do not share their faith? Again, some Christians answered yes. But Peter insists that they should not. He devotes more space to wives (3:1–6) because they could more easily be made to suffer from their husbands than vice versa. He eloquently teaches that the greatest beauty is that of character and that the loveliness of Christian character speaks far more powerfully than a hundred sermons. The word "see" in verse 2 is the same as that in 2:12, implying extended observation. The incident in mind in verse 6 is probably that of Genesis 12:11–20, where Sarah submits to some very unkind treatment from her husband, and in that context her beauty is emphasized. Abraham tried the same trick again later (Genesis 20), insisting that Sarah must show her love for him in this improper way, and she again submits. (She calls him "lord" in Gen. 18:12.) The Christian calling is patient submission to suffering within the structures of this world.

A Roman woman with braided hair (early second century AD). First Peter 3:3 exhorts women not to adorn themselves with such elaborate hairstyles, as do pagan women.

What about the Christian husband with the unbelieving wife? Verse 7 summarizes it beautifully. No separation! Even if they cannot share on the deepest spiritual level, they are still together "heirs . . . of the gracious gift of life" (i.e., ordinary human existence). The husband must show all the respect and care due to a weaker partner; and in so doing his own bond with the Lord will not be weakened.

It is vital to bear in mind the first-century cultural setting of 3:1–7. The normal expectation was that, if the male head of a household changed his religion, the whole household would follow (see Acts 16:31–34). It was strongly against this culture for a wife to change her religion apart from her husband. This helps us to see that Peter is not telling wives to be all-accepting doormats here. They have already stepped out and become different by believing in Christ for themselves. Now they must show that their "rebellion" deepens their love.

Similarly, a man becoming a Christian would have a culturally endorsed right to expect his wife to believe too. But in verse 7 Peter remarkably tells Christian husbands not to insist on this. Their wives must have the freedom *not* to believe! That's what honoring them demands.

C. The Christian's corporate life (3:8–12). "Everyone will know that you are my disciples, if you love one another" (John 13:35): this is the principle underlying these verses, with which Peter summarizes the whole section. Christians treasure their fellowship with one another. When they are faced with persecution, their common joy in their Lord becomes all the more precious. But Peter wants to impress on them that their relationship with each other is not entirely inward-looking. People will notice what they say to each other about the injustices they suffer (3:9). Consequently, the Lord must be their model. The quotation from Psalm 34:12–16 in verses 10–12 contains the key word of this entire section: "Do good." It also highlights the use of the tongue, just as the end of the last section did (2:9; see also 2:1): the way we speak will reveal the shape of our whole life.

3. Suffering—The Road to Glory (3:13–4:19)

In this section Peter focuses more precisely on the subject of suffering. The last section laid down the basic principle of submission to the structures of this world. Peter now shows how suffering fits into that submission. Once again, this section begins and ends on the same note: *doing good* (a favorite theme of Peter's) and suffering for God's sake or for what is right.

A. Suffering for doing good (3:13–22). These verses are among the most difficult in the whole New Testament, because Peter refers to traditions and stories obviously familiar to his readers, but unfortunately not to us. Yet the overall message is clear. Peter tells us that if we are called to suffer for what is right, we must look to Jesus, who suffered for our sins and through that suffering has come to a place of supreme authority, raised over all the powers of evil that seem so overwhelming to the persecuted Asian Christians. Jesus suffered, though he was righteous, and if we will now set apart Christ as Lord in our hearts and follow in his footsteps, we can be delivered from the fear of our persecutors, confident that through suffering we will share his victory. In the meantime we must bear witness to our hope by both word and deed, remembering that our baptism was our pledge to God, to live with good consciences before him.

Peter shares with Paul, and early Christians generally, the belief that authority and power in this world are earthly expressions of unseen fallen spiritual entities. Therefore, submission to secular authority as well as submission to all the constraints of earthly existence is a form of bondage to the powers of evil. Having told us to submit, Peter must touch on the spiritual implications of his teaching.

The "imprisoned spirits" (3:19) are not the souls of dead human beings but fallen angels (2 Pet. 2:4; Jude 6). According to Jewish tradition (*1 Enoch* 6–20), they deceived and corrupted the generation who lived before the flood, teaching them the arts of sin (see Gen.

6:1–4). As a result they were locked up in prison at the time of the flood, "to be held for judgment" (2 Pet. 2:4). They were the counterparts of the angels, authorities, and powers (3:22) still active today.

Jesus's preaching to these spirits was not an offer of salvation but a proclamation of his victory—in fact, the announcement of the judgment hanging over them. The spiritual forces behind the greatest corruption the world has ever seen have received their final condemnation at Jesus's hands! Having dealt with them, he finished his journey to heaven and took his place at God's right hand, in full authority over the powers behind the suffering experienced by Peter's readers. However much they may feel themselves to be victims, Christ is the victor!

The refusal of the angels to submit to their Creator was matched by the mockery of Noah's contemporaries, who did not respond to God's warning of impending judgment given by Noah's preaching (cf. 2 Pet. 2:5) and by the slow construction of the ark miles from the sea (3:20). The water in which they died was, paradoxically, the very medium of Noah's salvation. In this respect the flood foreshadows Christian baptism, for that too pictures death but leads to life. When they were baptized, Peter's readers pledged themselves to live for God and embraced the hope of resurrection through Jesus Christ. But in so doing they actually brought suffering upon themselves, just as Noah did by his obedience to God's command to build an ark and to warn his generation. Yet in their suffering, symbolized by their baptismal "death," they follow the path already trodden by their Savior on the way to glory.

Peter thus seeks to minister to his suffering brethren in the deepest possible way: not by simply pointing them to compensation in the world to come, nor by painting vividly the judgment in store for their enemies, but by showing them that, *precisely in their suffering*, already pictured in the baptism that united them with Christ, they are sharing with their Lord in his victory over all the powers of evil in the universe.

B. Living for God (4:1–11). There is no break in the flow of thought at 4:1. Although Noah is not mentioned in 4:1–6, we will best grasp Peter's meaning if we keep him in mind. For what Peter says in essence in verses 3–5 is, "You are in the same position as Noah, who refused to join in the profligate and licentious behavior of his contemporaries, even though they thought him peculiar for his refusal. Hold yourselves aloof from such practices, for God is about to act in judgment now as he did then." Peter actually uses the word "flood" in verse 4, where a literal translation would be "they curse you when you don't join the same flood of dissipation." The outpourings of vice around them are horribly reminiscent of the flood of God's wrath about to break.

It is especially helpful to read the difficult verse 6 with the story of Noah in mind. Noah was revered as a "preacher of righteousness" (2 Pet. 2:5), and by "the dead" Peter is probably referring to the people who died in the flood, the "dead" who ignored Noah's passionate message about the coming judgment. Who knows what God's purpose may have been? Yes, they died in the flood; but those waters symbolized baptism, because baptism is likewise about doing away with the flesh. Who knows whether their death in the flood might not have been a baptism for them, an entry into life?

Peter has his readers' persecutors in mind as he writes this. They may heap abuse on the Christians (4:4), but no one is so far gone as to be beyond the reach of God's life-giving power. They, too, could "live in the Spirit as God does" (4:6 NRSV) because of the faithful, suffering witness of the believers, who lovingly live and speak in God, as Noah did.

The basic principle holds true for all: "Whoever suffers in the body [literally "in the flesh"] is done with sin" (4:1). This was supremely true for Christ, who through death has conquered sin in all its manifestations; it is necessarily true for his followers, who through their suffering learn to dethrone evil desires and live for the will of God (4:2); and possibly it is even true for the persecutors of the church, who might come to life through the judgment of death and must therefore be the objects of patient testimony, in word and deed.

The flood was a partial judgment, a foreshadowing of the total winding up, which is now near. If Noah prepared with such diligence for the flood, how much more should we seek to be ready for the end (4:7–11)? Peter outlines the vital features of a life lived with an eye to the coming judgment.

In the privacy of heart and home, Christians need minds that think straight and hearts that pray straight. In ordinary social relationships, Christians must love one another and offer hospitality. In undertaking Christian ministry, each must put into active service whatever gift God's grace has bestowed, whether it is teaching or more practical forms of service. The believer must draw on God's resources and provision, and not for personal gain or glory. Rather, the object of life this side of the end must be the praise of God.

C. Sharing the sufferings of Christ (4:12–19). In this final subsection, Peter draws together the threads. His readers must not be surprised at the painful (literally "fiery") trial they are experiencing, because suffering is not something foreign as far as Christians are concerned. Rather, it lies at the very heart of our existence. Peter gives three reasons why we should not be surprised.

First, we are participating in the sufferings of Christ (4:13). We must expect to receive the same treatment as our master, simply because we are his servants (John 15:20). Suffering is woven into human experience as part of a fallen creation, but Jesus has blasted a way through death to eternal life. And so we should rejoice as we participate in this great saving movement, looking ahead to glory!

Second, because Jesus is already victorious, our suffering is a foretaste of that coming glory, a blessedness that comes to us as God's Spirit rests on us. What a revolutionary understanding!

Finally, our sufferings are the opening phase of God's winding-up operation, the beginning

of his judgment. Peter deliberately calls the tribulation "judgment," partly for theological reasons (because he understands all suffering and death as part of the curse laid by God on a fallen world), but also because he will not let his readers relax their guard. Their suffering is a trial (4:12), and they must make sure that they do not suffer deservedly (4:15)! But if we suffer according to God's will (4:19; i.e., with our hearts set on God's will, even in the midst of our suffering), then God will uphold us.

4. Final Exhortations and Greetings (5:1–14)

The final chapter begins with a resounding "therefore," which both NIV and NRSV have failed to translate. This makes the connection clear: in times of suffering and trial, special responsibility rests on the leaders of the churches to support and be shepherds of God's flock (5:2). Peter turns to this vital practical concern to round off his letter. But in fact his concern is not just pastoral, for there remains a theological question, raised by what he has said about submission to earthly powers and Christ's victory over them, which needs to be tackled as well. If, as he has told us, we must submit to earthly authorities even though Christ has proclaimed his victory over them, if we must continue to live as loyal citizens of Babylon (5:13) even though we know her satanic power has been broken, then what about authority structures within the church? What kinds of leadership and submission are appropriate for those who are already touched by the glory of the coming age?

Peter's pastoral concern predominates in 5:1–5. His self-designation in verse 1 hints at this deeper concern. He is a "fellow elder" (NRSV omits this)—not an exalted apostle—and with them a witness of (better, "to") Christ's sufferings. He therefore enters into all that that means, sharing those sufferings himself and thus participating in the glory to be revealed. His readers are not alone in their suffering. Peter stands beside them.

He urges the elders to be aware of their special responsibility as shepherds. The imperative has an urgency about it—get on with the job! Then in three pairs of balancing phrases ("not . . . but," 5:2–3) Peter tells them how they should exercise their pastoral care as far as *inner motivation* ("not because you must, but because you are willing") and *outward incentive* ("not pursuing dishonest gain") are concerned.

With the third "not . . . but" (5:3), Peter's second theological concern surfaces clearly. He uses here the same word that Mark records Jesus as having used when discussing this very issue with his disciples (Mark 10:42–43). Even if the church seems to possess a conventional, earthly authority structure, it actually reverses the normal pattern, modeling its vertical relationships on the Son of Man, who "did not come to be served, but to serve, and to give his life" (Mark 10:45). This is the style of leadership that will bring the full realization of the glory known now but in part (5:4). Peter drives this point home beautifully in verse 5 by using the single word "likewise" (NIV "in the same way"). He implies that the young men must be submissive to the "elders" in the same way as the elders are submissive to the young men! On both sides there is a "submission" that recognizes the distinctive gifts and ministry of the other and seeks to serve for Christ's sake. Verse 5b puts it in a nutshell: they must all tie humility

around them like a robe, so that they may enjoy God's grace in all their relationships. For God himself does not lord it over his creatures, but by his grace reaches out to us and suffers with us, in Christ.

Now Peter summarizes everything that he desires for his readers (5:6–11). Here is the framework on which he wants the house of our Christian life to be founded. For all that he has urged us to submit to our earthly circumstances, however trying, it is really to God himself that we submit (5:6), in hope of his deliverance. We humble ourselves before him not as before an earthly master, awaiting instructions, but so as to feel the burden of anxiety lifted from our shoulders (5:7)!

His readers may be consumed with anxiety about their earthly enemies, but Peter tells them that the spiritual foe is far more deadly (5:8–9). And we feel his pressure on us not just through our earthly trials but especially through the temptation not to face those trials with faith.

For all our seeking of stability and strength in this life, Peter reminds us in his closing blessing (5:10–11) that these are things that God

A modern Middle Eastern shepherd leading his sheep. First Peter 5:2 encourages the church elders to be "shepherds of God's flock" so that they will be rewarded when the Chief Shepherd appears (5:4).

reserves for the age to come. After the suffering of this age, in which we already trace his grace, he will finally complete us, strengthen us, and set us on a sure foundation.

In his final greeting, Peter associates with himself not just his two closest helpers, Silas and Mark, but also the whole church to which he belongs. "Babylon" (5:13) is almost certainly a reference to Rome, which was increasingly called "Babylon" by both Jews and Christians at this time. Using this term here fits beautifully with Peter's theme. It reminds us of the true (satanic) nature of secular power. Christ, however, has conquered it. But also—and more particularly, at this point—it reminds us of the place of Israel's exile and of the fact that we too are aliens and strangers in the world. The letter thus ends on the same note with which it began, when Peter saluted his readers as God's elect, strangers in the world, scattered. For though exiles, we are yet God's chosen, his elect people, destined for glory.

Select Bibliography

Dalton, William J. *Christ's Proclamation to the Spirits.* Analecta Biblica 23. Rome: Pontifical Biblical Institute, 1989.

Grudem, Wayne. *1 Peter.* Tyndale New Testament Commentaries. Grand Rapids: Eerdmans, 1988.

Horrell, David G. *The Epistles of Peter and Jude.* Epworth Commentary. Peterborough: Epworth, 1998.

Jobes, Karen H. *1 Peter.* Baker Exegetical Commentary on the New Testament. Grand Rapids: Baker Academic, 2005.

Marshall, I. Howard. *1 Peter.* IVP New Testament Commentary. Downers Grove, IL: InterVarsity, 1991.

Michaels, J. Ramsey. *1 Peter.* Word Biblical Commentary. Waco: Word, 1988.

Mounce, Robert H. *A Living Hope: A Commentary on 1 and 2 Peter.* Grand Rapids: Eerdmans, 1982.

2 Peter

Peter H. Davids

Introduction

Authorship, Audience, and Date

The Letter of 2 Peter had a more difficult time joining the canon than did any other New Testament letter. It was disputed into the fourth century, mainly due to its significant differences in style and methodology from 1 Peter, and perhaps due to its very Greek way of expressing ideas. Both issues made it difficult for third- and fourth-century church leaders to believe that 2 Peter was actually written by Peter.

Second Peter states that it was written by "Simon Peter" who is an "apostle of Jesus Christ," Simon being Peter's actual name and Peter, or "Rock," being the nickname Jesus gave to him. Given that we have only one other letter attributed to Peter, that the authorship of this letter is also disputed (although not as hotly as that of 2 Peter), and that we do not know much about the early life and education of Peter, there is no body of literature against which we can test this claim of authorship nor sufficient information about Peter to indicate whether or not he could have written the letter. What we do have is what the letter reveals about the author, which is the data from which scholars draw their conclusions.

The author of 2 Peter is very much at home with the Greek language, for he has at least some secondary rhetorical education (the letter is written in the "grand style" associated with the rhetoric of Asia Minor rather than the simpler style of Attic rhetoric), and with Greek philosophy, for he appears to be opposing some type of Epicurean influence and he uses Greek concepts expertly (e.g., 2 Peter 1:3–11). The author is also very much at home with the Letter of Jude, for he incorporates an edited version of most of that letter into 2 Peter 2:1–3:7. This, of course, means that he is writing after Jude and is the first witness to the existence of Jude. Given his use of Jude, the author is also familiar with stories that originated in the Old Testament. Yet, like Jude, he does not show that he knows these stories directly from the Old Testament but rather in the form in which they circulated

Extrabiblical stories referred to in 2 Peter were known to first-century Jews from texts like the book of *Jubilees*. The Hebrew version of *Jubilees* exists today only in fragments, such as the ones shown here (Qumran, second century BC).

in Second Temple Jewish literature (e.g., the book of *Jubilees*).

Our author seems to be writing to Gentile believers in Jesus, not to Jewish believers. In this, 2 Peter is similar to 1 Peter. While these first recipients are familiar with stories that modern Christians know from the Old Testament, this group of ancient auditors ("auditors," or "hearers," because the majority of the recipients would never read the book but rather hear the book read to them as if it were a sermon) does not seem to have been as widely acquainted with Second Temple Jewish literature as that of Jude, for 2 Peter edits both the direct quotation of *1 Enoch* and the story taken from the *Testament of Moses* out of the material he takes from Jude. We know that these recipients have received a previous letter from the same author (2 Pet. 3:1), but that letter is not necessarily 1 Peter. As Paul shows, New Testament authors could write numerous letters, many of which have not been preserved. The believing community that the auditors are members of is old enough that the missionaries who founded it ("your apostles"; 2 Pet. 3:2) are no longer there, having either moved on or died. It is also old enough that it was possible for believers to be taunted with the question, "Where is this 'coming' he [Jesus] promised?" (3:4).

Assuming that *1 Clement* does in fact refer to 2 Peter (which can be debated), 2 Peter must have been written before AD 96. It had to be written before the *Apocalypse of Peter* (dated AD 110–40), for that work uses 2 Peter. Simon Peter was probably martyred before AD 68 (the death of Nero), so the question one must answer is whether the letter could have been written this early and, if so, whether it was the type of letter that a person like Simon Peter would have or could have written.

Structure and Occasion

The letter is structured as follows. It opens with a salutation (1:1–2) and opening argument (1:3–11). The body of the letter contains a series of arguments in support of the author's position (1:16–3:13). The letter then closes with a final encouragement (3:14–18). Notice that the letter does not have a typical letter ending but merely a simple doxology in 3:18, leading some to believe that it is more a homily that was sent out with a letter opening (and an inserted resumptive address in 3:1) than an actual letter.

As noted above, the letter appears to have been written to oppose Epicurean influence. The Epicureans believed that everything (the world as a whole, including the gods) was made of atoms, that everything was heading toward final dissolution, that it followed that there was no individual future after death and certainly no final judgment, and that the best life was therefore lived for the present by maximizing pleasure. They were observant enough to realize that unbridled hedonism was not pleasant (as anyone who has eaten or drunk too much can testify), so they called for people to live according to the "golden mean," that level of self-indulgence that maximized pleasure without leading to negative consequences. Some version of such teaching has apparently infiltrated the community of those who follow Jesus, and the author of 2 Peter is not impressed by this wisdom, for it means a life lived without regard to the imperial rule of Jesus and his coming judgment.

Outline

1. Salutation (1:1–2)
2. Opening Statement (1:3–11)
3. Purpose Statement (1:12–15)
4. Arguments in Support of His Position (1:16–3:13)
   A. Apostolic Eyewitness (1:16–18)
   B. Prophetic Witness (1:19–21)
   C. Certainty of Judgment (2:1–10a)
   D. Denunciation of the False Teachers (2:10b–22)
   E. Recapitulation and Introduction of the Second Part of the Argument (3:1–2)
   F. Mockers Shown to Be Illogical (3:3–7)
   G. Delay of the Still Certain Final Judgment (3:8–13)

5. Final Encouragement to Stability
   (3:14–18)

Commentary

1. Salutation (1:1–2)

The letter opens with the identification of the author as "Simeon Peter" (RSV; NIV: "Simon Peter")—this work uses the more original form of the name, Simeon (as in Acts 15:14), rather than the shortened version Simon. He is writing to those with "a faith as precious as ours"—so, to faithful believers. The expression "our God and Savior Jesus Christ" is unusual and unlike similar expressions later in the letter. If our author is following the normal rules of Greek, he is talking about a single person, which makes this one of the clearer New Testament statements identifying Jesus as God.

2. Opening Statement (1:3–11)

The opening statement consists of two parts. The first part (1:3–4) uses Hellenistic concepts and unusual language to point out that Jesus took the initiative in delivering us and that this deliverance was accomplished through "our knowledge of" him (meaning personal knowledge and commitment, not just knowing about him). This enables us, on the one hand, to "participate in the divine nature" (a bold statement that we can become like Jesus/God) and, on the other, to "escape the corruption in the world" that is caused by desire. ("Evil" is not in the Greek text; for the Hellenistic world *all* desire was problematic and is the root of evil.) One cannot participate in the divine nature without escaping from the corruption in the world.

Therefore, the second part (1:5–11) is about the virtues (not listed in any particular order) that will make us more like Jesus. Pursuing these virtues (many of them community-preserving virtues) does not only make one's commitment to Jesus better; it also makes it more secure, preventing one from falling away. If we are moving toward the center, Jesus, we are in no danger of slipping back into the pit from which we were rescued. Thus, this action will make sure

not only that we are warmly welcomed when Jesus returns as emperor of this world (1:11) but also that we do not fall away and miss out on the rule of Jesus altogether, as the author of 2 Peter believes that some have done (1:9, picked up in 2:1–22).

3. Purpose Statement (1:12–15)

The purpose of the letter is testamental (similar to the purpose of other biblical [e.g., Gen. 49:1–28; Deut. 33:1–29] and extrabiblical testaments [e.g., the *Testaments of the Twelve Patriarchs*])—namely, that after his death the addressees will have a written record of Peter's teaching and so always be able to remember it. The reason this is necessary is that (1) Peter is mortal (he refers to his mortal body as a tent, as Paul does in 2 Cor. 5:1, where the resurrection body is a "house"—in other words, permanent), and (2) he believes that his death (as predicted by Jesus in either John 13:36 or 21:18–19) is impending (although he does not tell us why he believes this). This letter is to "remind" his addressees and to "refresh [their] memory" since they are "firmly established in the truth" (1:12–13), which is a rhetorically polite statement that assumes the best about them. However, the fact that he is writing this letter indicates his fear that they could be vulnerable to the new teaching of those he labels "false teachers."

4. Arguments in Support of His Position (1:16–3:13)

Given 2 Peter's thesis (1) that God has intervened by means of Jesus to free human beings from the power of evil that is rooted in desire and (2) that in order to live in this deliverance one needs to pursue virtue, one would then expect support for this assertion. The author does this by means of a series of arguments, which he introduces by his polite assertion that his addressees know and are practicing all this but that, given his impending death, it is his duty to "remind" them (1:12). It is clear from what follows in chapter 2 that he believes they are under threat; but in the Hellenistic world it was polite to phrase your instruction as a reminder, so this is rhetorically effective. Furthermore, since his impending death casts this letter into the form of a final testament, this also lends weight to his arguments as the "last words" of a revered leader.

A. Apostolic eyewitness (1:16–18). The first argument refers to the transfiguration, also found in Mark 9:2–8 and its parallels. Second Peter presents this as an eyewitness account of the enthronement of Jesus, describing it by terms like "majesty" and "honor and glory" with a voice coming from the "Majestic Glory," designating Jesus as God's Son. Jesus's reign has already been inaugurated, and if Jesus already reigns, trifling with his leadership and teaching and denying his "coming" are unwise indeed.

B. Prophetic witness (1:19–21). The experience of the transfiguration confirms what the prophets said. That is, Peter is not basing his argument on his religious experience alone but sees that experience as in continuity with the ancient prophets. We do not know which prophets he refers to (although there is an apparent allusion to Num. 24:17), but the author of 2 Peter wants to make clear that the prophets recorded in Scripture received not only the visions that they had from the Spirit but also the interpretation of those visions; so the prophets' interpretation of their visions were not "the prophet's own interpretation" but were just as directed by the Holy Spirit as were the visions. Did the teachers whom the author of 2 Peter opposes perhaps argue that, while inspired, the ancient prophets misinterpreted their visions and that they themselves had the right interpretation?

C. Certainty of judgment (2:1–10a). At this point our author reveals his central concern, as he incorporates the material he takes from Jude. There were false prophets in the past, and there are false teachers now. In Jude the others are outsiders, never named, and never said to be teachers. Here they are insiders ("among you") who are "false teachers," and it is only the new ideas that come from outside. (They "introduce"

them.) The phrase "destructive heresies" means not so much false doctrine (the denial of the return of Jesus is a secondary issue and so left to last) as ideas that lead to divisions in the community. ("Heresy" indicates they separated into a party or sect.) It is also clear that these ideas lead to "depraved conduct" (some form of promiscuity) that even those in the larger pagan community around the believers would condemn ("bring the way of truth into disrepute") and that these teachers based this teaching on "fabricated stories" (perhaps stories about spiritual experiences or visions), unlike the story of the transfiguration and the words of the prophets.

God, of course, is not fooled and will not be slow to judge them. The author gives a series of examples drawn from Jude, which he edits to stress that God can judge and at the same time save the righteous, rather than having to remove the righteous first or being prevented from judging because of the presence of the righteous. (Was this the teaching opposed by the author of 2 Peter?) The first example (2:4) is a reading of Genesis 6:1–8 through the lens of works like *1 Enoch*, in which the sinning beings are angels who are subsequently imprisoned. (Second Peter uses the term "Tartarus" [see NIV note], the prison of the Titans in Greek mythology.) But while the "ungodly people" influenced by the angels perished, Noah, "a preacher of righteousness" (an idea drawn from extrabiblical Jewish stories about Noah), was saved. The same is true about Sodom and Gomorrah and the rescue of Lot (2:7), whose "tormented" soul is also an idea drawn from extrabiblical Jewish traditions, although his righteousness may be implied from Genesis 18. The author's conclusion is that it is no problem for God to distinguish between the "godly" and the "unrighteous" in judgment (he does not have to remove the righteous first, and he does not worry that in judging the unrighteous he will accidentally harm the righteous) and that his judgment falls in particular on those following their natural desires (again, it is desire that is the culprit) and despising divine authority.

D. Denunciation of the false teachers (2:10b–22). The thesis that God distinguishes in judgment leads into a denunciation of the false teachers. Unlike the holy angels, these teachers slander celestial beings. (The clear reference found in Jude to the *Testament of Moses* has been removed.) But such behavior is simply emotional reaction and thus from what we would call the "animal brain"—so these teachers will die like animals.

The author charges these teachers with carousing (and not even trying to hide it) at the Lord's Supper ("while they feast with you"), adultery, and greed (financially exploiting the community). The last charge makes them like Balaam (also mentioned in Jude), who prophesied or taught for money (both practices—especially prophecy for money—were rejected in the early church). Balaam's action (and, by implication, that of the teachers) was so shameful that a dumb animal rebuked him verbally! (In Num. 22:30 the donkey speaks, but in 22:32–33 it is the angel who rebukes Balaam; however, in Second Temple Jewish literature the eloquent rebuke is in the donkey's mouth.)

These teachers promise much but deliver little (2:17–18). They have been and still claim to be followers of Jesus and, as pointed out in 2 Peter 1:3–5, have therefore been delivered from the power of desire. But now they are enslaved to it again

(so the "freedom" from conventional morality that they promise is a sham, since they are not truly free themselves). Therefore, they are worse off than if they had never become believers (2:20–21), presumably because they will receive harsher judgment than those who have never accepted the good news. This shocking conclusion is capped off with the citation of two proverbs, one Jewish and one pagan (2 Pet. 2:22).

E. Recapitulation and introduction of the second part of the argument (3:1–2). Our author pauses to recapitulate: this is a second letter (the first is not necessarily 1 Peter), and both simply remind the addressees what they already know from the Scriptures ("holy prophets") and those evangelizing them ("your apostles").

F. Mockers shown to be illogical (3:3–7). These teachers are the "scoffers" predicted to come in the "last days." (Many in the early church believed they were in the "last days.") Obviously, if one is living immorally, one can hardly believe in a judgment in which one will be called to account. These teachers therefore deny that there will be a "coming" of Jesus and that "he will judge the living and the dead" (to quote the later Apostles' Creed). Perhaps they thought that all judgment had been taken care of on the cross or in the fall of Jerusalem, and so it was past. The world, so they argued, goes on steadily.

The author again points to Noah. The earth, pictured as rising in creation out of the seas and with waters in the firmament above it, was destroyed by that very water; God will do it again, but this time by fire rather than water. The idea that the world is indissoluble forgets biblical history.

G. Delay of the still certain final judgment (3:8–13). But what about that "coming"? Jesus manifestly had not returned, and it had been

> The "Balaam inscription" found at Deir 'Alla (800 BC) is so named because it mentions Balaam son of Beor (see Numbers 22–24). In 2 Peter 2:15–16, the false teachers are accused of following the way of Balaam, who had to be rebuked by his donkey.

decades since his resurrection. The author argues that (1) God's sense of time is not the human sense (which, although not his point, is the understanding of the psalmist in Ps. 90:4 and was a common Jewish understanding), (2) God is not slow, but patient, and (3) God will in fact bring judgment at an unexpected time. (The image of the thief is drawn from Jesus [Matt. 6:19; Luke 12:39] and used by Paul [1 Thess. 5:2].) Our author admits that God has delayed the return of Jesus but insists it is for a purpose: God does not want "anyone to perish, but everyone to come to repentance" (2 Pet. 3:9). Presumably, then, when the judgment comes, God will have decided that he cannot deliver any more people through continued delay.

The sudden judgment, when it comes, will mean the removal of heaven (the firmament that is between where God is and the earth) and the heavenly bodies (the "elements"—as the term is used in a number of ancient texts—that hang in or from the firmament and thus will be destroyed with it). This will leave the earth "laid bare" (not destroyed) so all is open to the divine eye and easily judged.

Since even the heavens above (thought by ancients to control life on earth) are impermanent, believers should be living for the permanent, the renewed earth, purged of all evil, with, of course, a new heaven (since the old was destroyed in the course of judgment), which God has promised. The way one lives for this is not by talking about it but by living "holy and godly lives" (3:11).

5. Final Encouragement to Stability (3:14–18)

Our author sums up. (1) Live holy lives (3:14). (2) Think of the delay in the coming of Jesus as "our Lord's patience," which means "salvation"—perhaps the recipients' salvation,

for Christ could have come before they came to know and commit to him. Then our author notes (3) that Paul agrees with this teaching in at least three of his letters (the Greek form indicates that the author of 2 Peter knows of more than two letters, but we do not know how many of Paul's letters he knows), although, as was already clear in 1 Corinthians 5–6, some took Paul's teaching on grace to mean that licentious living would not be punished. Such distortion of Paul would lead to the destruction of the distorters.

The final reminder (3:17) is to "be on your guard" and thus not to be deceived and fall themselves, for the holy lives they are now living in obedience to Jesus are a "secure position." The letter (or perhaps sermon with a letter opening) ends with a blessing and doxology: the blessing is a summary of 2 Peter 1:5–8 and focuses on our imperial ruler and deliverer, Jesus, God's anointed king (to put our author's titles into more modern form). And certainly he will indeed have all honor (i.e., "glory") now and forever.

Select Bibliography

Bauckham, Richard J. *Jude, 2 Peter*. Word Biblical Commentary. Waco: Word, 1983.

Davids, Peter H. *The Letters of 2 Peter and Jude*. Pillar New Testament Commentary. Grand Rapids: Eerdmans, 2006.

Green, Gene L. *Jude and 2 Peter*. Baker Exegetical Commentary on the New Testament. Grand Rapids: Baker Academic, 2008.

Neyrey, Jerome H. *2 Peter, Jude: A New Translation with Introduction and Commentary*. Anchor Bible. New York: Doubleday, 1993.

Reese, Ruth Anne. *2 Peter and Jude*. Two Horizons New Testament Commentary. Grand Rapids: Eerdmans, 2007.

1–3 John

PAUL N. ANDERSON

Introduction

Date, Author, and Audience

The three epistles of John appear to have been written in the last decade and a half of the first century AD (85–95), and they fit within the larger set of Johannine writings ("Johannine" means "pertaining to John"), which includes the Gospel of John (finalized around 100) and Revelation (finalized around 90).

The author of these epistles does not give his name directly in the text (unlike Revelation), but the author of 2 and 3 John calls himself "the elder." Given the fact that 1 John is especially close to 2 John in style and content, and that 2 and 3 John were associated together traditionally, the author of all three Johannine Epistles may be called John the elder. Interestingly, Irenaeus mentions the graves of two Christian leaders in Ephesus as those of John the elder and John the apostle. Some confusion of the two is apparent, in that both may have been disciples of the Lord and both may have been called an "elder." Papias claims not to have known any of the Twelve but does claim to be a disciple of John the elder. Irenaeus claims to have been a disciple of Polycarp, who in turn claims to have sat at the feet of John the apostle. Least speculative is the likelihood of several Christian leaders in the Johannine situation between 70 and 100, of whom John the elder, the author of the epistles, is one.

While historical-critical scholars have argued that the first clear connecting of John the apostle with the Gospel bearing his name is Irenaeus (around 180), this is not the case. There is no second-century opinion as to who might be associated with the Johannine Gospel and Epistles other than the apostle and the elder, and one can understand their being referred to by their appellations ("the beloved disciple" and "the elder") if indeed they had the same first name and were ministering within the same general context. An overlooked clue to John's authorship, though, may be found in Acts 4:19–20, where Luke attributes a Petrine saying to Peter (we must obey God rather than man; Acts 4:19; 5:29; 11:17) and a typically Johannine saying to John (we cannot help testifying to what we have seen and heard; John 3:32; Acts 4:20; 1 John 1:3). It may have been wrong or misguided, but Luke connects the apostle John with a Johannine saying a *full century before Irenaeus.*

The three epistles of John are uneven in length, and they also differ in terms of their audiences. First John, which is four times as long as the other two combined, is written as a circular to several churches in Asia Minor. Second John is written to "the lady chosen by God and to her children," which is a reference to either a church or a female congregation leader and thus is addressed to a particular community and its leadership. Third John is written to a particular leader, Gaius, whose community members had been denied hospitality by Diotrephes.

Relationship to the Gospel of John

The relation of the Johannine Epistles to the Gospel is questioned. By the middle of the third century they were associated together as by the same author. Debates as to which preceded the other abound, but if an earlier edition of John was finalized around 85, the epistles may have followed the first edition *and* preceded the final edition around 100. While the vocabulary of 1 and 2 John is most similar to that of the Gospel, some differences of emphasis and approach are apparent—especially the epistles' more dogmatic and less dialectical mode of thought and their appeals to other sources of authority. Because the Gospel of John appears to have been finalized after the death of the beloved disciple (Jesus never said he would not die; John 21:18–24), the final editor appeals to his authority; and the material apparently added to the Gospel (John 1:1–18; chaps. 6, 15–17, and 21, plus "eyewitness" and beloved disciple references) seems very similar to the form and thrust of the epistles.

Therefore, a likely composition scenario envisions (1) a first edition of the Gospel around 80–85 (hence, it was the second Gospel written, as an augmentation of Mark, possibly before the completion of Matthew and Luke) preserving the testimony of John the apostle as the beloved disciple; (2) the composition of the Johannine Epistles between 85 and 95 by John the elder—accompanied by the ongoing ministry of John the apostle until his death during the reign of Trajan (beginning in AD 98); and (3) a finalization and circulation of the Fourth Gospel around 100 by John the elder, who declared in third-person reference, "his testimony is true" (John 19:35; 21:24). Revelation fits in here somewhere, although despite many similarities with the Gospel and epistles, it is the most grammatically and stylistically different among the Johannine writings. Then again, if John the elder (or another scribe) was involved also in the writing of the beloved disciple's narrative, even for its first edition, the distinctive style and vocabulary might be more closely connected to John the apostle than the literary evidence suggests.

Occasion and Content

The main concern of the Johannine Epistles is church unity. Here the exhortation to "love one another" is advanced repeatedly, as the original commandment of Jesus (John 13:34–35) finds its application as the key to Christian unity in the late-first-century church (1 John 3:10–23; 4:7–12, 16–21; 5:2–3; 2 John 5–6). The need for unity is apparent in the many crises addressed by the epistles: questions of ethics, defections, temptations from the world, tensions within the community, false teachers, struggles over authority, and a brief mention of idolatry.

A common approach to identifying the adversaries in the Johannine Epistles is to see them as gnostics; after all, the antichrists in 1 John 4:1–3 and 2 John 7 refuse to believe that Jesus came in the flesh—the docetist heresy. While all gnostics were docetists, not all docetists were gnostics. Further, the antichrists of 1 John 2:18–25 are secessionists, who have recently left the church, denying Jesus's messiahship in clinging to the Father, so there may have been more than one antichristic threat. (The Greek term *antichristos* is found nowhere in Revelation, only in 1 and 2 John.) Therefore, a less speculative approach is to acknowledge more than one set of likely adversaries within the Johannine situation rather than to laden Cerinthus and his kin with multiple imagined heretical fallacies.

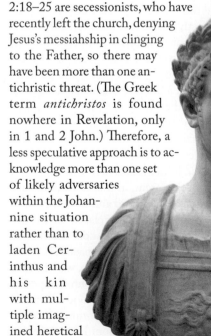

Through the Johannine Gospel and Revelation, as well as the letters of Ignatius and Clement of Rome, several largely sequential yet somewhat overlapping crises appear to have confronted members of the Johannine situation between 70 and 100. These include (1) coming apart from the customs of "the world" within a largely Gentile (pagan) setting; (2) tensions with local Jewish family and friends over the law of Moses and how Jesus represents the will of the Father as the Messiah/Christ; (3) tensions with pagan worship—especially emperor worship, which had increased in its expectations and celebrations under the reign of Domitian (AD 81–96); (4) Gentile Christians' teaching a doctrine of assimilation within pagan cultic settings—including an occasional defense of participating in the cultic honoring of the emperor, legitimated by a docetist teaching of a nonsuffering Jesus; (5) struggles with institutionalizing tendencies in the early church, designed to defend against docetist influences by appealing to a centralized form of hierarchical leadership. It is incorrect to think that only one crisis lay behind the struggles faced within the Johannine situation over three decades.

In the light of these issues, the ethical concerns of the elder come to the fore and present themselves for consideration in every generation. They include such issues as (1) debates over sin and what it means to be "without sin"; (2) living in the world but not of the world; (3) who the antichrists were and how their first-century threats relate to other adversaries in later generations; (4) the call to love one another as a means of providing a way to Christian unity; (5) warnings against idolatry; (6) exhortations to extend hospitality to other believers; and (7) warnings against leadership styles resorting to intimidation and self-assertion rather than the liberating command of truth. In these and other ways, the Johannine Epistles continue

to be relevant to readers in every generation, especially as their content communicates from one context to another.

Domitian, emperor of Rome AD 81–96, required emperor worship, which was one of the crises faced by the Johannine community.

Outline—1 John

7. The Victory That Overcomes the World (5:1–21)
   A. Belief in Jesus as the Christ Is Victory (5:1–3)
   B. The Life-Producing Testimony (5:4–12)
   C. The Boldness of Faith (5:13–15)
   D. Keep from Mortal Sins—in Particular, Idols! (5:16–21)

Commentary

1. The Prologue of 1 John—from Witness to Fellowship (1:1–4)

The first Johannine Epistle appears to have been written as a circular to one or more Christian communities in Asia Minor. The author names himself as "the elder" in the second and third Epistles (2 John 1; 3 John 3), but in his first and fullest communication he simply begins with a worship piece that is very similar in vocabulary and form to the prologue of the Johannine Gospel. Note the use of first-person plural references ("we," 1:1–5) as a means of including the audiences with the community of the elder. Appeals to corporate solidarity draw the hearers and readers into fellowship with the author and other Johannine leaders (cf. John 1:14, 16; 21:24), and the first epistle draws squarely on familiar themes developed in the first edition of the Gospel.

Like the prologue of the Gospel (John 1:1–18), the prologue of the first epistle (1 John 1:1–4) begins with a declaration of that which was from "the beginning." Rather than the beginning of the world, though, this prologue highlights the beginning of the Christian movement, harkening back to the ministry of Jesus. The testimony of what has been heard, seen, touched, and beheld connects the firsthand experience with the ministry of Jesus with second- and third-generation believers (John 20:29). Not only do the Gospel, the works and words of Jesus, the testimony of John the Baptist, and the Scriptures declare the Word of Life, but now the elder also does so with the witness of his letter.

The author here stands with the firsthand experience of the apostles and others who encountered the ministry of Jesus some five decades earlier. Links are drawn between firsthand encounter with the earthly ministry of Jesus and the firsthand encounter with the spiritual ministry of the risen Christ, imparted through the Holy Spirit to authentic believers (John 1:1–18 and chaps. 6, 15–17, 21). Even the testimony to "what we have seen and heard" (1:3) becomes an explicit Johannine association in Luke's rendering of the testimony of Peter and John in Acts 4:19–20. Luke connects this Johannine phrase with John the apostle a full century before Irenaeus, and the Johannine elder does the same, independently. Jesus declares what he has seen and heard from the Father (John 3:32), and his apostolic followers (John 20:21–23) do the same.

The goal of the elder's sharing is *koinōnia*, "fellowship," extended from one generation and sector of the Jesus movement to others. This is not, however, a mere expression of the desire for fellowship; Christian unity is rooted in the same unity that the Son has enjoyed with the Father from the beginning (John 17:20–26). This unity is both spiritual and missional. The loving fellowship between the Father and the Son and between Christ and his followers has a name: the Holy Spirit now avails without measure. This spiritual unity is experienced in fullness where believers gather in the name of Jesus (Matt. 18:18–20). And yet, authentic *koinōnia* is also a factor of sharing a sense of agency. The Son is one with the Father because he knows what the Father is doing and because he carries out the Father's mission (John 3:31–36); likewise, believers share unity with the Son, as he does with the Father (John 17:20–26), as his partners and friends because they know and do his will (John 15:14–15). True Christian fellowship then inevitably leads to joy (John 15:11; 16:20–24; 17:13), which is why the elder writes his letters (2 John 12).

2. The Question of Sin and the Commandment to Love (1:5–2:17)

The question of those claiming to be "without sin" is an intriguing one in 1 John. On one hand, it might appear that we have an alien gnostic group claiming perfectionism as a factor of direct access to God without need of the atonement. After all, the first commentary on John was written by Heracleon, a second-century gnostic, and the flesh-denying antichrists of 1 John 4:1–3 might point in that direction. This view has several problems to it, however. (1) The elder also speaks of the impossibility of sinning for anyone who is born of God (1 John 3:9), so this may be a simple extension of the elder's own teaching. (2) Just because the second antichrists are docetists (Jesus just appeared to suffer and die—as fully divine, he did not), this does not mean they are gnostic heretics; they may have simply been Gentile believers with a Hellenistic worldview. (3) Being "without sin" may be a particular reference to something in particular not being wrong, *not* a reference to sinlessness proper. (4) The emphasis on the atoning work of Christ is asserted in order to get people to abandon the sin that he came to remove (1 John 3:1–10) and to love one another. Therefore, those claiming to be "without sin" in John's audience are challenged with the commandment of the Lord to love one another (John 13:34–45).

A. Those claiming not to be sinning (1:5–2:2). Like any good teacher, the elder employs the inclusive "we" as a way of addressing his second-person audience, "you." He does this in verse 5 just as he has in each of the first four verses. Verse 6, however, turns the use of "we" to others. "If we say . . ." (NASB, RSV) is a way of confronting the claims of others, either in his immediate audience or among those his audience are having to engage. In listing the claims of some, the inclinations of all are addressed. While some of these claims are challenged as false in and of themselves, other admirable claims are confronted if they are not also accompanied by congruent behaviors. The first citation of what some might be claiming fits within this category.

In verse 6, those who claim to have fellowship with God but walk in darkness lie and do not practice the truth. Walking in darkness is not spelled out, but it likely refers to particular moral practices that are out of step with the elder and at least some leaders within the community. Conversely, the life-producing way forward involves "walking in the light" just as God is in the light, which avails the believer Christian fellowship and the cleansing blood of God's Son, delivering believers from sin. Such an appeal, though, was apparently rejected on two accounts: those confronted probably were not convinced that their behavior amounted to walking in darkness, and therefore they claimed not to be sinning. This leads to the elder's challenging of their defensive statements.

The next two statements regarding what "we say," which are challenged by the elder, include claiming to "be without sin" (1:8) and claiming that "we have not sinned" (1:10). The elder challenges these assertions directly: if we claim to have no sin, "we deceive ourselves and the truth is not in us." To confess our sins, though, is to acknowledge the

> In ancient times small oil lamps, such as this one from the Roman Period, were used for light. Olive oil was poured into the central cavity, and a wick placed in the hole at the pointed end would be lit. The imagery of "walking in the light" is used several times in 1 John.

authenticity of our condition and to avail ourselves of God's forgiveness and cleansing power (1:9). More pointedly, to claim that we have not sinned is "to make him [God] out to be a liar," and to expose the fact that God's word is not abiding in us (1:10). Again, the confronted might not have been claiming sinlessness proper, but the elder certainly raises the bar in hopes of getting them to acknowledge the darkness of their ways that they might be persuaded to walk in the true light of ways pleasing to God.

In the next sentence (2:1) the elder extends his ethical appeal to the entire audience: "My little children, I am writing these things to you so that you may not sin" (NRSV); at the same time he emphasizes the availability of grace for any who might. He employs a word used for the Holy Spirit in the Gospel of John—"helper," or "advocate"—but here he uses it in reference to Jesus. This is a familiar Johannine term, and while the Holy Spirit is "another" counselor and advocate (John 14:16), Jesus is the original. Conversely, he then employs an unusual reference to the atoning sacrifice (Greek *hilasmos*; see also 1 John 4:10) of Jesus Christ the righteous one, which seems more Pauline than Johannine. In fact, the word never occurs in the Gospel of John. Of course, the redeeming work of Christ is not simply for the community's benefit; it extends to the entire world, and that is the power of the gospel being proclaimed (2:2).

B. The old commandment of the Lord: "Love your brothers and sisters!" (2:3–11). The true evidence of knowing Christ is incarnational: obeying his commandments, the chief of which is to love one another. To obey the original commandment of Jesus is to experience God's love being perfected within (2:5). The elder now moves to the third-person singular in confronting the problematic community member. "Whoever says . . ." is the hook, and the three laudable statements listed are that one has come to know him (2:4), to abide in him (2:6), and to be in the light (2:9). To these positive claims to a believing relationship with Christ, the elder

poses the true evidence of authenticity. Such a person will obey Christ's commandments (2:4), will walk as Christ walked (2:6), and will not hate his or her brother or sister (2:9). Therefore, the true and outward evidence of the vertical relationship is the horizontal; the clearest measure of one's abiding in the love of Christ is the demonstration of loving consideration for others. Anything short of that is darkness, blindness, and death.

C. Love not the world! (2:12–17). Lest particular members of his audience feel singled out or left out, the elder now targets specific demographic groups in his audiences, covering the range of ages and relationships. To the "little children" (NIV "dear children") he announces forgiveness in the name of Christ (2:12); to the fathers, he affirms their knowing of "him who is from the beginning" (2:13; cf. John 1:1–3); to the youth, he extols their conquering the evil one (2:13). This triad is followed, then, by a second. To the children, he writes to affirm their knowledge of the Father; to the fathers, he writes because they know "him who is from the beginning"; and to the youth he writes because they are strong and indwelt by the word of God, and because they have overcome the evil one (2:14). The repetition and the parallel references add emphasis to his affirming message: "Do not love the world or anything in the world" (2:15). Rather than spell out particular sins, however, the elder is content to leave the sins of worldliness general: the desire of the flesh, the desire of the eyes, and pride in wealth (2:16) cover the territory effectively. These drives do not come from the Father but from the world. And the world, along with its desires, is a fleeting reality, not an enduring one. Doing the will of God, however, leads to eternal life (2:17).

3. The Antichrist Has Come! The Secessionists Deny Jesus's Messiahship (2:18–29)

Christian speculation about the identity and advent of the antichrist has been a major pastime from the second century until today. In order to stay close to the text and its original meaning, however, we should be aware of several facts. (1) The Greek word *antichristos* does not appear in Revelation, but only in 1 and 2 John. While "the beast," "666," and other biblical villains might seem likely prospects for speculating about contemporary threats, each of these subjects must be investigated on its own. The antichrist passages may have had nothing to do with "the beast" in Revelation. (2) Rather than pointing to a single person as "the antichrist," the three antichristic passages in the Johannine Epistles are primarily plural: *they* did this or that. (3) Rather than a futuristic threat, the first antichristic passage points to an event in the recent past—a church split. Therefore, "antichrists" is the term used within this Christ-centered community to explain the fact that family and friends have left John's church and perhaps joined another religious community. (4) The antichrists of 1 John 4:1–3 and 2 John 7 are not former schismatic threats but present and impending invasive threats. They are false teachers, not community-abandoning schismatics. (5) The problematic theological content of the two antichristic groups is entirely different, and the groups probably represent two threats, not one. The first refuses to believe that Jesus was the Messiah; the second refuses to believe that Jesus came in the flesh. The anti-Messiah predictions of long ago have now come to rest on the Johannine community, but the warnings of the elder are contemporary—addressed to his immediate audience, *literally*—not futuristic predictions.

A. The departure of the antichrists shows their inauthenticity (2:18–20). Indeed, the schismatic crisis this Johannine community has experienced fulfills the prediction of old that an adversary to the Messiah would come. This shows that it is the last hour, calling for a special measure of faith and faithfulness. Many antichrists have come, and their advent is marked by community members' having left John's church and abandoned fellowship with their brothers and sisters in Christ. Further, their departure shows they never were convinced of the truth to begin

with, which reflects the elder's own thoughts on why some are able to remain with Christ and his fellowship and some are not. Is schism and abandoning the fellowship of believers the "sin" that was mentioned earlier? Perhaps, although there may have been more than one. As the departure of the faith-wavering shows their lack of belonging to the true community, those who remain are encouraged by the elder's affirming their anointing by the Holy One and their abiding in true knowledge. Community defection is the mark of their antichristic actions, but the elder goes on, then, to address their root problems resulting from their inadequate beliefs.

B. Those who deny Jesus as the Christ lose the Father (2:21–25). In declaring again why he is writing (1 John 1:4; 2:1, 7–8, 12, 13–14, 21, 26; 5:13; 2 John 5, 12; 3 John 13), the elder affirms what he hopes for in his audience as though it were an actualized reality: their knowing and abiding in the truth. The "liar," though, is the one who denies that Jesus is the Messiah. *This* is the antichrist, the one who denies the Father and the Son. To deny the Son is to forfeit the Father, but to confess the Son is to receive the Father. Given that the Johannine situation was probably in its third decade of dialectical engagement with local Jewish family and friends, the temptation of the first secessionists was to affirm Jewish monotheism (holding to the Father) so as not to be thought guilty of either blasphemy or ditheism (having two Gods), which was the growing charge against the Jesus movement in the 70s and 80s. Rather, to hold to the Son is to receive the Father, promises the Johannine elder, and this leads to receiving the promise of eternal life (2:25).

The larger set of dialogues between the Jesus movement and its parent Jewish family in Asia Minor probably experienced something of the following elements. (1) Paul and other traveling ministers came through Asia Minor reaching Jewish and Gentile audiences alike. This probably caused some tension between the Jesus movement and local Jewish leaders; it certainly did among pagan temple keepers and religious artisans. (2) After the destruction of Jerusalem in AD 70, Jewish religious identity was reorganized into more of a biblical religion than a cultic one. Sacrifices were no longer offered, but keeping the law of Moses was central to being Jewish, and the heart of the law was the worship of one God. (3) As Christian confession of Jesus's messiahship developed into higher Christologies, both in worship practices and in evangelistic emphases, this evoked accusations of "ditheism." At Jamnia, on the western coast of Israel, a blessing against the heretics (the *Birkat ha-Minim*) was codified, which was the twelfth of eighteen benedictions. It cursed the followers of "the Nazarene," and scholars have recently come to see these tensions as explaining the references in John that even back then those who confessed Jesus openly were put "out of the synagogue" (John 9:22; 12:42; 16:2). While there probably was not anything like a universal ban or excommunication of Jesus followers, these pressures against confessing Jesus as the Christ, and especially as the Son of God, caused at least some defections of Jesus adherents from local synagogues. (4) Once they had departed from the synagogue, however, their Jewish family and friends likely sought to draw them back into the more established faith community, with its more supportive religious practices—the way of Moses, the truth of the torah, and the life afforded the children of Abraham. This might explain the reason for the first antichristic crisis. Jewish Christians had abandoned the Jesus movement to return to the religious security of the synagogue with its monotheism and religious certainty. (5) This would explain the elder's positing of holding to Jesus as the Christ as integral to the approval of the Father. To deny the Son is to forfeit the Father, but to embrace the Son is to receive the Father, who sent him.

C. Abide in Christ and his anointing (2:26–29). Here the deceivers would be appealing to the hallmarks of Jewish faith and practice at the expense of the Jesus movement. Consider

the appeals of the religious leaders in the Gospel: "We are disciples of Moses!" (John 9:28). "We are Abraham's descendants" (John 8:33). They claimed that whoever speaks of himself is a presumptuous prophet, not a true prophet. Therefore, Jesus in the Gospel is presented as addressing those claims with his authentic mission from the Father (see Deut. 18:15–22). Here the emphasis is placed on the spiritual anointing that believers have received from the one who abides in him and in whom they abide. Reminding them of the words of Jesus about God's direct instruction through the Spirit (John 6:45; 14:26; 15:26; 16:1–15), the elder affirms the importance of abiding in Christ as the present teacher (2:27; cf. John 15:1–15). This will strengthen them in their time of trial, and it inspires them to live in the righteousness they have received as a result of being born anew in the life of Christ.

4. To Abide in Christ Is to Attain Victory over Sin (3:1–24)

In chapter 3 of 1 John, the elder moves from concern over further defections and schisms, and he challenges conventional examples of sin. While the author does not spell things out with particularity, he does mention seeing a brother or sister in need and not helping them by sharing the means one has (3:17). Is this the sin mentioned in the first chapter? Perhaps; then again, not treating community members lovingly may take a variety of forms, so it is easier to include a matter for ethical consideration than to exclude one. Whatever the case, to abide in Christ is to attain victory over sin, and this is the central thrust of this section.

A. Christ removes our sins . . . and our sinning (3:1–6). Now the elder emphasizes the benefits of faith in Christ, leading with the privilege of being called the children of God (3:1). The community hymn celebrating the conviction that as many as received him received the power to become the children of God (John 1:12–13) is here developed as a benefit of abiding in Christ and his community. From the perspective of this-worldly existence, however, the prospect of next-worldly glory is extolled. We see now only in part, but when the fullness of God is revealed, believers shall be like him and will see him as he really is. This hope in God's glory in the future emboldens faithfulness to his ways in the present. In that sense, a vision of God's purity becomes the motivator of purified living in the present (3:4). Finally, the elder emphasizes Christ's taking away the sins of believers, implying both the power of his sacrifice and the capacity of his work to deliver the one abiding in him from the power of sin. No one who abides in Christ sins, and the one who sins has neither seen him nor known him. Relationship with Christ involves transformation and deliverance from sin; this is central to the power of the gospel.

B. Those who sin, not loving brothers and sisters, are not from God (3:7–10). Now the elder moves back to countering the seditious influence of those who would deceive them or lead them astray (3:7). Motivating his audience to live in righteous ways if they hope to be righteous, he also links the committing of sin to being a child of the devil. With this polarizing of options, he seeks to bolster believers' commitments to right living commensurate with their right believing. Those who are born of God do not sin because the "seed" of God abides in them (3:9). To be born of God is to eradicate the human bent toward sinning. Parallel to the stories in the Gospel, where a person's response to the revealer exposed whether one was rooted in light or darkness (John 3:18–21), here the measure of one's spiritual condition is whether that person does what is right. More specifically, to not love one's brothers and sisters betrays a lack of rootedness in God (3:10). This rhetorical move marks an interesting contrast to the Gospel. In John's Gospel, rootedness in God is exposed by a person's response to the one who not only speaks the words of God but who *is* the Word of God. In John's first epistle, rootedness in God is indicated by one's loving regard for members of the fledgling Christian community, as authentic righteousness is ultimately relational.

C. The party of Cain—the brother killers—includes the indifferent (3:11–17). Appealing again to the original teachings of Jesus, commanding his followers to love one another (John 13:34–35), the elder leverages the worst of fratricidal archetypes: Cain, the brother killer (3:12; Genesis 4). Would any in his audience relish the idea of being numbered among members of "the Cain Party"? Of course not! The threat of being labeled a brother killer becomes a negative incentive used to motivate the opposite: loving regard for members of the community. This ploy is followed by a positive reference to loving one another as the true measure of having passed from death to life (3:14). Back to negative intensification in verse 15, to hate a brother or sister in the community is to be guilty of murder (Matt. 5:21–22), and to be guilty of murder is to forfeit eternal life. By veering back and forth between negative and positive means of motivation, the elder seeks to steer his audiences toward right practice as well as righteous faith.

In verse 16 the example of Jesus is used climactically as the one who laid down his life for others as the ultimate example of love. Here the teaching of Jesus in John 15:13 becomes applied as an example for others to emulate. If Jesus was willing to lay down his life for his friends, and if the Johannine community is indeed inhabited by friends of Jesus, they ought also to be willing readily to lay down their lives for one another. On one hand, this parallel bears associations with martyrdom. To ingest the flesh and blood of Jesus (John 6:51–58) is to be willing to share in his sufferings on the cross. Only those willing to share in the Lord's crucifixion are worthy of participating with him in his resurrection (Rom. 6:5; Phil. 3:10–11; Mark 8:34–38).

The association with martyrdom here seems to point to persecution under Domitian, who required emperor worship of his subjects and punished severely (sometimes capitally) any who did not reverence the idols of Rome. Construction for Domitian's temple to himself in

Ephesus began in AD 82 and was finished about seven years later. At the entrance of the temple stood a large statue of Domitian with a raised, clenched fist, and the altar of his temple bore carvings of subjugated peoples being humbled at the hand of the Romans. Two decades later, Pliny, the governor of nearby Bithynia, wrote to the emperor Trajan asking if he should continue to kill Christians who refused to deny Christ or to worship Trajan's image. Pliny had just put to death two young Christian women, who, despite being warned three times, had refused to do either. In reply, the emperor advises him not to seek out Christians to persecute them, but if they are duly warned and refuse to worship Caesar, they must of course be put to death, implying a standing policy (Pliny the Younger, *Letter* 10.96–97).

Therefore, the willingness to suffer for Christ may have been more than an abstract consideration. It may indeed have been a measure of one's ultimate love and dedication to the Lord

Ruins of the ancient temple of Domitian at Ephesus. First John 3:16 refers to laying down one's life, which may have been necessary for Christians who refused to worship Domitian.

and his community. Pliny mentions those who have been accused of being Christians but were found to be "innocent" of the name. All they were guilty of was meeting together before the dawn, eating some common food, and singing a hymn to Christ "as though he were a god." Pliny declares that any such person, of course, could not be found "guilty" of being a Christian. If that is how the pagan governor saw it, how might fellow Christians have felt if someone who had denied them and their Lord in order to escape Roman persecution showed up for worship and expected to continue in fellowship with other believers? Was *this* the sin mentioned in the early part of the epistle, and were Gentile Christians claiming it was not a sin, therefore claiming to be without sin for participating in Roman civic life?

Following this appeal to willingly suffer the ultimate of sacrifices for the love of Christ and his beloved, however, the elder swings to the most mundane of considerations. Verse 17 emphasizes the issue of those having physical means and refusing to share with brothers and sisters in need. Is this the "sin" addressed in the early part of the epistle? Perhaps the appeal to

love one another as motivated by the love of Christ simply had to do with caring for the sustenance of fellow believers—sharing. After all, if this was the mark of the true fellowship of believers after the Holy Spirit had come upon them (Acts 2:42–47; 4:32–37), why was it not more evident within this community? The love of Christ also delivers us from the most insidious of sins: indifference.

D. On loving in truth and in deed (3:18–24). The elder concludes his exhortation to love others with an appeal to human integrity. Love should not be in word only but also in truth and in action. Congruity between word and deed reassures the believer's heart, but even if one's heart feels condemning, the good news is that God is greater than one's heart. Better yet, if one's heart is not condemning but confirming, the believer has boldness before God and receives what is asked for because of obeying God's commandments and doing what is pleasing to him (3:21–22; John 14:13–17; 15:7, 16; 16:23–27; James 4:2–3). Notice again the vertical and horizontal components of the commandments of God: to "believe in the name of his Son, Jesus Christ, and to love one another" (3:23). Just as abiding in him leads to fruitful discipleship (John 15:1–5), to obey his commandments is to abide in Christ and he in the believer (3:24; John 15:8–10). Knowing this to be true is conveyed as a gift by the Spirit (John 14:15–17). To abide in Christ is to attain victory, even victory over the power of sin itself.

5. The Antichrists Are Coming! They Deny Jesus Came in the Flesh (4:1–6)

While the first antichristic passage (1 John 2:18–25) describes a church split in which so-called believers abandoned the Johannine fellowship and likely rejoined the local Jewish community, the second antichristic passage describes a threat in the impending future that is not a schism but an invasion. False teachers are about, and the way they are discerned is also by considering their Christology. In contrast to the first group, however, which refused to believe that Jesus was the Jewish Messiah,

this second threat probably involved Gentile Christian teachers who refused to believe Jesus had come in the flesh. Indeed, the differences are several: one crisis is largely in the past, the other largely in the future; one crisis involves a departure, the other a visitation; and the first group denied Jesus's messiahship, the next his fleshly humanity. These appear to be very different threats indeed. The second threat continues on, then, in 2 John 7, as docetist teachers (Greek *dokeō* means "seem," "appear"—Jesus just *seemed* to be suffering) preached a nonsuffering Jesus.

A. Those who deny Jesus's humanity are false prophets and antichrists (4:1–3). While the first antichristic threat involved the splitting off of Johannine Christians, the second antichristic threat involved the crisis of false prophets coming to their church with a troubling message. In these and other situations, it is often the threat of problematic actions that leads to the discussion of problematic beliefs. The schismatic defections of Jewish Christians were challenged on the basis of their flawed (from John's perspective) understanding of monotheism, leading them to diminish Jesus's messiahship and his relation to the Father. If Jesus was indeed, however, sent from the Father as the prophet-Messiah predicted by Moses (Deut. 18:15–22; John 5:17–47), to receive him is to receive the Father, but to deny him is to forfeit the Father's pleasure. Likewise, the teachings and actions of Gentile preachers are "tested" to see if they stand up to righteous scrutiny.

A likely scenario is that the teachings of these traveling Gentile-Christian ministers sought to negotiate a middle path between the Jewish-Christian rejection of "worldly" behavior and an accommodation of standard religious, political, and moral practices within pagan Asia Minor and across the Greco-Roman world. Other than the last verse of 1 John (stay away from idols; 5:21), the elder does not mention the specifics. Standard practices, however, would have involved participation in religious-cultural festivals, which sometimes involved offerings to the gods, the eating of foods offered to idols, and engaging in cultic prostitution (Rev. 2:12–29). Especially under the reign of Domitian (81–96), when subjects of the empire were expected to at least offer incense to "the divine emperor" or to confess Caesar as Lord and God (note the direct challenge in John 20:28), the refusal to participate may have borne negative consequences.

This was especially a problem for a metropolis such as Ephesus if non-Jewish civic leaders began forgoing cultural festivals in honor of the emperor and pagan gods as a result of their newfound Christian faith. Not only would Christian leaders be put on trial now and then (Antipas, according to tradition, was roasted to death in a kettle [Rev. 2:13]; John was banished to Patmos in 84; Ignatius, bishop of Antioch, was put to death by Emperor Trajan around 115), but also common Christians would have been pressured to participate in cultural festivities as marks of support for the empire. If residents and civic leaders diminished their participation in holiday events—especially on the emperor's birthday and during imperial visits—because such events were "worldly" and unfit for followers of Christ, this posed a civic problem. Ephesus might lose Roman financial support for building projects and for being an official "keeper of the temple"—a highly sought-after status. Ephesus had received this award twice and was in stiff competition with Pergamum for many decades in vying for Roman favor in exchange for imperial honor. Therefore, pressure was social as well as political. And some Gentile Christians may have felt that some of these practices were not a problem, including worshiping the emperor. Therefore,

a nonsuffering Jesus legitimated nonsuffering discipleship. If Jesus did not suffer, his followers need not suffer either; worldly living was thus excused by a docetic Christology.

Therefore, the way to test false prophets is to examine their christological claims. While their assimilative teachings might have excused social and religious compromise in the name of "abundant life" or prosperous living in the world, costly grace implies costly discipleship. Docetic preachers (the full-blown gnostic threat was more of a second-century phenomenon) could be distinguished from suitable traveling ministers, however, by testing their beliefs and asking whether they believed Jesus Christ actually came in the flesh. If so, they could be warmly received; if not, they should be kept away from the community and rejected as perpetuating the spirit of the antichrist (4:3), which destroys Christian fellowship.

B. Greater is he that is in you than he that is in the world (4:4–6). At the entrance to the temple of Domitian in Ephesus is a large carving of the goddess Nike. (*Nikē* in Greek means "victory.") In Greek mythology this winged deity was drawn into assisting Zeus in the battle against the Titans, but the use of its image here reminded subjects of the

empire that they were conquered by the "divine emperor." Amidst other reminders of Roman domination, the author here assures his audience that "greater is he that is in you, than he that is in the world" (4:4 KJV). The worldly origin of the adversaries explains why the worldly listen to them, but the elder contrasts himself and his audience with the antichrists and their cohorts. Claiming to be from God, those who heed the elder show themselves also to be knowers of God; conversely, those who are not rooted in God turn a deaf ear to the Johannine leadership. The parallel to the interpretive reflection on the reception of Jesus here is clear. Just as the response of Jesus's audiences to him and his message exposed the degree to which they were "of the truth" and "knowers of God," the same measure is now extended to the elder's audiences. The spirit of truth and the spirit of error are distinguished, from the elder's perspective, in the telling response to his corrective word (4:6). Those who do not heed his word do not know God; the responsive ones, however, do.

6. Let Us Love One Another! (4:7–21)

Organizing a community effectively can happen in many ways. Rules may be laid down, with the rewarding of the compliant and the punishing of those committing infractions; incentives may be posed as an approach to reinforcing some behaviors and discouraging others; distant goals may be identified with means of attaining them being explored; values may be clarified and extolled as a means of motivating adherence; and leaders may be delegated authority, serving as determiners of standards and arbiters of conflict. The elder obviously has attained a good deal of personal authority, but whether it comes from positional or personal status is impossible to know. Whatever the case, he casts all his influence

A relief of the goddess Nike, uncovered during the excavations at Ephesus

into the appeal for his audiences to "love one another" as a means of motivating righteous living, right belief, and right relationship with other believers. Therefore, amid the centrifugal forces of worldly temptations, community defections, and false teachings, the appeal to follow the loving commandment of the Lord becomes the centripetal force levied to create relational harmony and corporate solidarity. This love-producing agenda is conveyed by means of three strategic appeals.

A. We love because God has first loved us (4:7–10). The first appeal to love one another roots its persuasion in the essential character of God, which from beginning to end is *love*. Not to love is not to know God, and everyone who loves is born of God and knows God (4:7–8). God's love, of course, must be extended, and the means by which God has done so is the sending of his Son so that the world might live through him (4:9). The very character of love, however, is defined as a factor of God's initiative, not human ingenuity. God's favor cannot be garnered by human merit or evoked as a consequence of human initiative. In contrast to the conditional covenant of the Mosaic law, and in diametric opposition to the patronage systems of the Greco-Roman world, the loving work of God is granted unconditionally and freely. Sacrifices offered by humans can in no way compare with the ultimate atoning sacrifice offered by God (4:10; see also 2:2). That is the perfect sacrifice, which eclipses all other approaches to justification (Heb. 10:1–39), and this is why it requires a revelation from God to be understood. Human attempts to garner divine favor can never suffice, for God's love is essentially undeserved. Revelation will ever be an affront to religion, and its central content is the first-initiated love of God made manifest in his Son. This is the pivotal introduction of grace to the cosmos, and the history of salvation has never been the same.

B. The perfecting of love in us (4:11–17). The elder's second appeal for his audiences to love one another moves the locus of the revelation of God's love through Jesus as the Son of God to the lives of believers. The perfecting of God's love in the Christian life becomes the locus of the ongoing revelation of God's love in the world, and it thereby is of world-changing significance. Our love for one another is a direct implication of God's love for us, and it becomes the truest evidence of the believer's mutual abiding in God (4:13, 16). Evidence of abiding in God is also manifested in the believer's confessing Jesus as the Son of God (4:15), and this becomes the believer's testimony to the world about its savior (4:14). Therefore, the perfection of God's love in the life of the believer is a factor of boldness on the day of judgment (4:17). Is this a reference to the judgment at the end of time, or is it a reference to the trial believers face in the world as witnesses to what they have seen and heard? Whatever the case, the perfection of love in the life of the believer becomes an eschatological witness to God's love in the world, just as Christ revealed God's love from the beginning. Incarnation happens again as the believer abides in the love of God and as God's love is perfected in the changed and changing life of the believer.

C. To love God is to love brothers and sisters (4:18–21). The third strategic attempt to motivate loving action and character among the elder's audience involves an appeal to the believer's aspirations and identity. The human-divine relationship is not rooted in fear but in love; after all, perfect love casts out all fear (4:18). Again, our love as a response to God's love is emphasized (4:19) as an echo of verse 10. While the saving initiative of God's love is the central hope of the gospel, that reality evokes an irresistible human response of love for God. As in the countered statements of particular targets in his audience in the first two chapters, the elder once more quotes the ones he aims to correct. Those who say, "I love God," but hate their brothers and sisters are liars. Is this the sin referred to in the early verses of the book—hypocrisy? How can one claim to love God, whom one has not seen, without loving

one's brothers and sisters in faith, whom one has seen? The appeal to the believer's identity and aspiration is a winsome move. One cannot authentically claim to love God without also loving those God loves—brothers and sisters within the beloved community of believers. This makes the original commandment of the Lord that much more compelling: those who love God *must* love Christian brothers and sisters. They have no choice. To refuse to embrace the beloved of God is to deny, in effect, one's love for the Father. Again, the incarnated message drowns out the verbal utterance. The clearest "word" is one's life; so it was with the original incarnation, and so it continues to be in the lives of Jesus's followers.

7. The Victory That Overcomes the World (5:1–21)

In contrast to the violent victories of Zeus and Nike, and in opposition to the myth of redemptive violence propounded by Domitian and the Romans, the victory of Christ Jesus overcomes the world once and for all. Unlike sacrifices that need to be repeated at every festival, the sacrifice of Christ has put an end to all human attempts to attain divine favor. As an affront to the garnering of favor within systems of social honor and patronage whereby accolades granted are motivated by the hope of procuring rewards and avoiding punishment, God's loving grace is undeserved and received through faith alone. And yet, while grace is received by faith, it is manifested in the world through faithfulness. In the final chapter of 1 John as a circular read among the Asia Minor churches, both faith and faithfulness are lifted up as a response to, and an implication of, that victory of God which overcomes the world.

A. Belief in Jesus as the Christ is victory (5:1–3). Just as the original ending of the Gospel of John (John 20:31) is written in order that hearers and readers might believe that Jesus is the Christ, the Son of God, and in believing have life in his name, the promise of this message concludes the final chapter of the first Johannine epistle. To believe that Jesus is the

Christ implies the content of Christian faith, but the loving regard for his followers is again declared as its authentic measure. Especially as an antidote to Johannine Christians who might yet be tempted to abandon the community and their belief in Jesus as the Christ, returning to the religious and cultural security of the local synagogue, the elder emphasizes that believing "Jesus is the Christ" (5:1) is the center of spiritual birth.

Those tempted to remain "underground" among Jewish family and friends, like Nicodemus, who came to Jesus "at night" (John 3:2), would especially be confronted by this reminder of saving faith. For those refusing to risk synagogue expulsion (John 9:22; 12:42; 16:2) by confessing belief in Jesus's messiahship openly, this reminder was a targeted appeal to bolster their courage. And, in contrast to the first antichrists, who split off from the church and denied their fellowship with brothers and sisters in Christ, obeying God's commandments and abiding in his love is measured by love for one another. While loving one another above implies sharing with those in need and getting along with others, the implied meaning here is for corporate solidarity with Christ and his community. Thus, Christian faith is the victory that overcomes the world and all of its temptations.

B. The life-producing testimony (5:4–12). To believe in Jesus as the Christ is also to believe in him as the Son of God (John 20:31), and Gentile believers are thus included in the confessional formula, as well as Jewish believers. Not only is it the Christian *faith* that overcomes the world (5:4), but so do the Christian *faithful* (5:5) by their trust and obedience. Jesus's coming by water and by blood likely refers to one or more of the following: the physical birth process emphasizing Jesus's humanity, martyrological associations with the sacramental themes of baptism and communion, or the water and blood that flowed from the side of Jesus in John 19:34. Whatever the case, the emphasis is on the suffering humanity of Jesus and its implications

for discipleship: if Jesus indeed suffered and died, we must be willing to do the same (John 6:27, 51–58, 63). To this emphasis is added testimony of the Spirit, and these three testify to Jesus's authenticity as the Son of God. As the Johannine Jesus emphasizes three witnesses, not just his own (John 5:31–38; 8:13–19; Deut. 17:6; 19:15), so the Johannine elder emphasizes three witnesses—the water, the blood, and the Spirit—which bear final testimony in the hearts of believers (5:10). These are ultimately the testimony of God (5:9), which outweighs human testimony on all accounts.

While some ancient manuscripts preface this threefold witness with a trinitarian formula (adding "in heaven: the Father, the Word and the Holy Spirit, and these three are one. And there are three that testify on earth"; see NIV note) in verses 7–8, that addition to the text clearly represents a later development in Christian theology. Since the early church came to associate the three witnesses of the Father, Son, and Holy Spirit with this passage in preaching and interpreting the passage, one can understand how such a "clarification" of the more obscure meaning might have been added. The central emphasis of the original threefold association, however, is not simply "earthly" as opposed to "heavenly"; it is antidocetic. It elevates pointedly the importance of Jesus's fleshly humanity. In so doing, not only are the false teachings of the second antichrists being challenged, but so are their implications. Believers must be willing to suffer for their faith, in solidarity with the Lord. To deny him before humanity is to risk denial by the Son of Man before the Father (Mark 8:34–38), and authentic believers must count the cost of faithful discipleship (John 6:51–63). Parallel to "making God a liar" in 1 John 1:8–10 by denying one's sin, one here makes God a liar by not receiving God's testimony about Jesus's fleshly humanity (5:10). Might there be a connection here? If claiming to be without sin is less a matter of asserting flawless perfection and more a matter of arguing that cultural and religious assimilation (participating in pagan festivals, worshiping Caesar, maintaining guild memberships with their votive inductions, etc.) are *not* sinful, these liberties were likely challenged by the docetic teaching that Jesus was so divine that he could not have suffered and died. Therefore, one cannot expect believers to risk suffering and loss; if Jesus did not suffer, we need not do so either. Just as hope for the resurrection can only come by means of the cross, the only way to life is through the dead and risen Son of God (5:12).

C. The boldness of faith (5:13–15). For the sixth time in this epistle (5:13; see 2:14, 21, 26) the elder declares his purpose in writing, and this time he explicitly echoes the evangelistic purpose of the Fourth Gospel (John 20:31): that his hearers/readers might believe in the name of the Son of God and thereby know that they have eternal life. The elder then reminds them of the promise of Jesus that anything asked in his name will be granted by the Father (John 14:13–14; 15:16) and that by asking in his name is the world overcome (John 16:23–32). Just as the purpose of Jesus is to further the will of the Father who sent him (John 4:34; 5:30; 6:40), the purpose of his followers should be the furthering of his will in the world (John 15:14–15) as his partners and friends. Even Jewish religious leaders believe that those who further the will of God receive their requests in partnership with God (John 9:32), and here the believer is reminded that anything one asks in the name of Jesus will be granted (5:14). But what does that involve? Is it simply a matter of concluding a petition with the words, "in Jesus's name," or "if it be thy will"? If so, any boldness related to asking according to his will as a recipe for effective praying, or as an inferred proper form, misses the point entirely.

For prayer to be effective according to the will of God or the will of Jesus, the believer must first discern the divine will. Mutual abiding implies intimate relationship and dialogue. God hears the believer's petitions because the believer has heard and discerned the will of God. Therefore, for the believer to pray according to the will of the Son, who seeks to do only what is the will of the Father (John 8:28), involves first becoming attuned to his will. Laying down one's own will and embracing the will of the Lord reorients one's life and reformats one's prayers. While God is not dependent on human assistance to accomplish his will in the world, he invites us into partnership as his followers. And, if the believer has indeed discerned the divine will and is offering it back to God as an earnest request, how can God not also grant what God has desired? *This* is the confidence and boldness of the believer's prayer: not in the right words or proper forms, but in the will of the Lord, which we offer back in our petitions and which we further with our willingness to lay down our lives for his friends and the beloved world for which he died.

D. Keep from mortal sins—in particular, idols! (5:16–21). The elder's concluding paragraph picks up again the main topic outlined in the second paragraph of the epistle: *sin*—its identification and its consequences. Here he distinguishes between mortal sins and venial ones. But what is meant by a sin leading or not leading to death? Would his audience have understood the distinction in particular? If not, they are not given much help in distinguishing the two, unless verse 21 is added as a means of clarifying what death-producing sins might have involved. The practical importance of the distinction, however, involves prayerful graciousness and discernment regarding some sins but the stern rejection of death-producing ones. The fact that there was apparent disagreement on which category some practices fit into casts some light on the claim to be "without sin" in 1 John 1:8–10. If the Johannine leadership were challenging some sins as mortal sins, to be rejected and disavowed on pain of spiritual death, and if some Gentile Christian—whose tendencies may have been bolstered by the false teachings of docetizing antichrists—were claiming that some practices were neither sinful nor a problem, that likely reflects an acute crisis faced by the elder and the communities he was addressing. Of course, all wrongdoing is sin (5:17), although not all sins lead to death. The root and the stock of the tree, however, determine the character of its fruit.

Therefore, the one who is truly begotten of God does not sin, and he or she is protected by the Only Begotten Son of God (John 1:14, 18), who has overcome the evil one (5:18). The elder thus concludes his letter with three corporate affirmations of what "we know" as bases for Christian faith and practice. First, *we know* that those who are really born of God do not sin, and this serves as an exhortation for authentic believers to live with integrity, ensuring their outward deeds match their spiritual commitments. Second, *we know* that believers are "of God," while the whole world is rooted in the evil one (5:19). This should account for the disparity between the way of life and the way of death, which creates tensions in every context and generation. Third, *we know* that the Son of God is come and has given us understanding to know the one who is true, and to do so authentically (5:20). The Son of the true one is Jesus Christ, and he is even the "true God and eternal life" (see John 1:18). To worship him alone is to refuse the appeals—political, societal, and material—to worship false gods and programs. All of this comes clear, then, in the last sentence: "Little children, *stay away from idols*!" (author's translation).

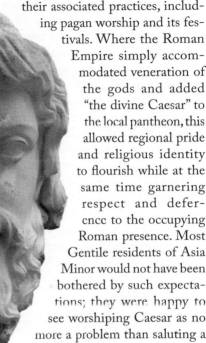

Statues of Zeus, such as this one from Ephesus (first century AD), as well as altars and temples to this chief deity have been unearthed in Asia Minor and were a part of the culture of the day. First John ends with the admonition, "keep yourselves from idols" (5:21).

On one hand, verse 21 seems out of place; perhaps it was tagged on by a distant editorial hand, some scholars might venture. What if, however, it is added as a crystallization of the central spiritual and moral thrust of the entire epistle? To commit oneself to Christ as the Only Begotten Son of the living God is to deny and disavow all idolatries and their associated practices, including pagan worship and its festivals. Where the Roman Empire simply accommodated veneration of the gods and added "the divine Caesar" to the local pantheon, this allowed regional pride and religious identity to flourish while at the same time garnering respect and deference to the occupying Roman presence. Most Gentile residents of Asia Minor would not have been bothered by such expectations; they were happy to see worshiping Caesar as no more a problem than saluting a flag or pledging allegiance to one's homeland. Jewish Christians, however, called for a higher commitment. In the worship of one God and his Son Jesus Christ, to live under his lordship means to displace all others. For those claiming that casual emperor laud and participation in cultic festivals were not a problem, and thus claiming to be "without sin," the elder's message is clear. There is one Lord—Christ Jesus—and just as he laid down his life for his friends, so should his followers be willing to do on behalf of others. So staying away from idols becomes a leading measure of one's love for Christ *and* for one another.

This being the case, the elder's struggle was not against gnostic perfectionists, who claimed to have "arrived" spiritually and thus to be beyond reproach. Rather, just community members of Jewish background were tempted to rejoin the synagogue, with its familiar traditions and religious certainty, excusing their abandonment of John's community and their Lord by diminishing his place as the Messiah and the Son of God. Conversely, community members of Gentile backgrounds were tempted to "love the world" (2:15) in assimilative ways: joining in with civic celebrations, emperor worship, and pagan moral practices, and excusing such compromises by teaching a nonsuffering Jesus who did not come in the flesh. The elder challenges both of these tendencies as the denial of community values going back to the teachings of Jesus himself—the command to love one another and not to abandon the community of faith or its values. Thus the teachings of Jesus in the Johannine Gospel find their timely application in the first Johannine Epistle, which was circulated and read in meetings for worship among the churches of Asia Minor. The members' love for one another is a direct measure of their love for God.

Outline—2 John

1. Greetings to the Chosen Lady and Her Children (1–3)
2. Let Us Love One Another (4–6)
3. Beware the Deceivers and the Antichrists, Who Deny the Flesh of Jesus! (7–11)
4. Final Greetings (12–13)

Commentary

While the first Johannine epistle was likely a circular to be read among the churches of Asia Minor, the second is written to "the lady chosen by God and to her children," probably around 90. The author names himself as "the elder," and the emphases on loving one another, truth, abiding, the Father-Son relationship, and joy mark this clearly as being written by the same leader. The phrase "lady chosen by God" may refer to women leaders in this sector of

early Christianity, especially as the woman in whose home a house church met would have had special authority in offering hospitality and in guiding community life. A larger home would have been a more likely place to hold worship than a smaller one; and within such settings the man of the home would have taken leadership in the public sphere, but the woman of the home would have taken leadership domestically, managing servants and welcoming guests. Her responsibilities would likely have extended to the leading of worship. The high place of women in the Gospel of John, featuring the Samaritan woman as the apostle to the Samaritans, Martha as uttering a climactic christological confession, her sister Mary as the anointer of Jesus's feet, the mother of Jesus and other women as faithful to Jesus at the cross, and Mary Magdalene as the apostle to the apostles, this featuring of women in leadership and ministry reflects a more primitive epoch in the history of the early church than the more patriarchal developments soon to follow. The Second Epistle of John appears to follow this pattern as an established one. Then again, the reference to the chosen lady's "sister" in verse 13 could suggest a feminine reference to a connected church community, as the reference to "the children of your elect sister" sending their greetings also (2 John 13 NKJV, RSV) seems to refer to a community if not another female Christian leader. The pointed message of 2 John, however, is to call for loving one another and also to reject the false teachings of docetic teachers, labeled "antichrists," for the sake of Christian unity.

1. Greetings to the Chosen Lady and Her Children (1–3)

The greeting of this letter compliments the chosen lady and her children, and the elder not only expresses his love for her in the truth but also emphasizes that all who know the truth do so as well (v. 1). He claims the truth "abides in us and will be with us forever" (v. 2 NASB) as a means of supporting his compliment and continues with a blessing reminiscent of Paul's letters. "Grace, mercy and peace from God the Father and from Jesus Christ, the Father's Son" is bestowed on his audience in truth and love (v. 3). In that sense, the elder's greeting extends lovingly not only to a fellow leader within the Johannine situation but also to her congregation.

2. Let Us Love One Another (4–6)

The elder expresses his joy at finding "some of your children walking in the truth" (v. 4), which suggests meaningful contact with her community. The elder emphasizes here, as in his first epistle, the formerly "new commandment" (NIV "new command") that they had known "from the beginning" (v. 5), challenging them to love one another. He then defines love as walking according to the Father's commandments. This familiar style and content connects 2 John with 1 John, and both are connected to the love command of Jesus in John 13:34–35. To walk in the truth is also to love one another within community relationship. This implies staying in the community and not leaving, as did the first antichristic threat (1 John 2:18–25), and it also implies addressing new threats as they present themselves.

3. Beware the Deceivers and the Antichrists, Who Deny the Flesh of Jesus! (7–11)

In contrast to the first antichristic threat, which involved a community defection resulting from refusing to believe Jesus was the Jewish Messiah, the second antichristic threat involved the advent of false teachers who refused to believe Jesus had come in the flesh. In verse 7, the docetic threat warned about in 1 John 4:1–3 is now trumpeted with a stark warning: any who do not confess that Jesus Christ has come in the flesh are the "deceiver and the antichrist" (v. 7). The audience is warned to be on their guard, lest they lose what they have worked for. Where the emphasis in the Gospel is on abiding *in* Christ (John 15:1–8), here it is placed on abiding in the teaching *about* Christ (v. 9). One difference between the beloved disciple's teaching and the

elder's emphasis might be suggested here. The one who goes beyond the teaching does not have God, but the one who abides in it has both the Father and the Son (v. 10). False teachers are to be denied hospitality, as welcoming them is akin to participating in their evil deeds (v. 11).

4. Final Greetings (12–13)

The elder extends final greetings, sending also greetings from the children of the elect sister of the elect lady (vv. 12–13). Again, the feminine reference could be a reference to women leaders in the church, or it could be a feminine reference to the church and its leadership. Either way, the elder's endearing relationship with these leaders is clear. He expresses his desire to come as an incarnated message—in person, so that their joy might be complete—rather than simply writing with pen and ink. In so doing he exemplifies and communicates the same quality of loving concern to which he calls his audience.

Outline—3 John

1. Greetings to the Beloved Gaius (1–2)
2. Joy at Believers' Walking in the Truth (3–8)
3. Diotrephes the Primacy-Lover (9–10)
4. Imitate Not Evil but Good (11–12)
5. Final Greetings among Friends (13–15)

Commentary

1. Greetings to the Beloved Gaius (1–2)

While 1 John was a circular, and 2 John was an epistle to a leader and her church, 3 John is a letter to an individual, Gaius, whom the elder loves in the truth. Referring to him as "beloved" (NIV "my dear friend"), the elder says that he prays that all would go well with him and that his physical health would match his spiritual health.

2. Joy at Believers' Walking in the Truth (3–8)

The elder shares his joy at the testimony of some of "the friends" (NRSV; NIV: "believers") regarding Gaius's faithfulness to the truth and how he has walked in it. He extols Gaius's loving hospitality extended to "the friends," which appears to be a reference to Johannine Christians (v. 5). Hospitality was apparently extended to traveling ministers, even though they were unknown to their host. They have, in turn, testified to the gracious hospitality they received, and they have testified of Gaius's love before the church (v. 6). Which church is meant here is not clear. It could represent a local community, but it more likely represents an emerging center of Christian authority (such as Antioch) that sends out traveling ministers and also supports them. Their travels draw support from fellow believers rather than from nonbelievers, and the elder exhorts Gaius to also support other such traveling ministers as co-workers in the truth.

3. Diotrephes the Primacy-Lover (9–10)

The elder claims to have written something to "the church," but then he claims that "Diotrephes the primacy-lover does not receive us" (v. 9, author's translation). One question relates to what is meant by "the church." Was it the local church under which Diotrephes served as a local leader, or was it a centralized ecclesial body from which Diotrephes was deriving his authority? The second question relates to what is meant by the Greek term *philoprōteuōn*, "primacy-lover." Does "loves to be first" suggest selfishness or egoistic focus on himself, or does it refer to his clinging to positional authority (cf. Peter in Matt. 10:2, who is called "first," *prōtos*, among the disciples)? A third question relates to why Diotrephes might not have received the elder and his associates. Did he think they were heretical (perhaps associating them with docetizing antichrists), or was he threatened by their approach to authority, perceiving it as challenging his own?

In verse 10 the elder addresses the issue with personal accountability; he poses the likelihood of paying Diotrephes and his community a visit in order to challenge the false charges Diotrephes is spreading about the Johannine leadership. Apparently not only is he speaking disparagingly of Johannine believers, but he also refuses to welcome them and casts out of his own church any who are willing to grant them hospitality. This point makes it hard to believe that he was simply a local leader with a bad temper. More likely is a parallel to the teachings of Ignatius in his letters to the churches: Diotrephes represents a means of dealing with the challenges of docetism and church discipline in the third Christian generation. Just as Ignatius, bishop of Antioch, advocated appointing one bishop in every church in Asia Minor (an application of Peter's receiving keys to the kingdom in Matt. 16:17–19?) and raising the value of staying within the walls of the church community, Diotrephes appears to be implementing this sort of advice. In that sense, he and the elder are trying to do the same sort of thing by different means: working to hold their communities together in the face of internal and external pressures. The elder approaches the matter by calling for loving one another and for solidarity with the community in relational terms; Diotrephes seeks to establish and maintain unity by structural means, including clear lines of authority and its hierarchical exercise.

This being the case, the following scenario is likely. First, in response to Judaizing pressures, empire-worship expectations, and docetizing threats among the churches of Asia Minor in the last two or three decades of the first century, Diotrephes was appointed bishop of his church, receiving an endorsement from a mother church (such as Antioch) as a means of holding his community together. Second, as Johannine Christians traveled in ministry among the churches, some of these were denied hospitality by Diotrephes and his community. They may have been associated with docetist teachers, or perhaps Diotrephes was simply returning the inhospitable treatment advocated by the elder in his first two letters, if some of those who were denied Johannine hospitality were from *his* church (2 John 9–11). Third, the elder writes to the centralizing church whence Diotrephes is deriving his authority, but he still refuses to welcome the Johannine traveling ministers.

Therefore, the elder is willing to come and reason with him personally (cf. Matt. 18:15–17). Fourth, perhaps Diotrephes was threatened by Johannine egalitarianism, exercise of inclusive ministry, and emphasis on the Holy Spirit's accessibility to all believers (John 14–16). It may even be in response to Diotrephes and his kin that the elder was motivated to gather the beloved disciple's witness into a finalized Gospel and circulate it as a reminder of Jesus's original intention for the church.

If indeed the elder has added material to an earlier edition of the Gospel, adding the prologue (John 1:1–18); eyewitness and beloved-disciple references (John 13:23; 19:26, 34–35; 20:2; 21:7, 20); and chapters 6, 15–17, and 21, several things become apparent. This later material has most of the Gospel's incarnational material (John 1:14; 6:51–58; 16:32–33; 19:34; 21:18–24), emphases on church unity (chaps. 6 and 17), and teachings on the present leadership of the Holy Spirit (chaps. 15–16). Therefore, while the first edition of John emphasizes that Jesus fulfills the Moses and Elijah typologies of the Jewish Messiah in order that people might come to believe in Jesus as the Christ, the Son of God (John 20:31), the later material emphasizes (with the epistles) the importance of abiding with Jesus and his community against imperial and docetizing pressures in the world. It is also in this later Gospel material that the juxtaposition of Peter and the beloved disciple occurs, highlighting Peter's affirmation of Jesus's sole authority (John 6:68–69) and the beloved disciple's intimacy with the Lord as exemplary for Christian leadership (John 13:23; 21:20–24). The later material in the Gospel and the rhetorical thrust of 3 John both correct the institutionalizing tendencies of Diotrephes and his kin. The risen Christ's leadership in the church may be assisted by human leaders, but it is never supplanted by them; as in authentic worship, the Lord leads his followers in spirit and in truth, and all who attend his leading can discern it and obey.

4. Imitate Not Evil but Good (11–12)

The primary emphasis of 3 John is the elder's exhortation of Gaius to extend hospitality to

> The issue of hospitality is discussed several times in 3 John. Seen here is the living area of a first-century-AD home in the Palestinian town of Taybeh, with stairs leading up to a storage/guest room.

others despite having been denied it himself. Demetrius is featured as a good example of someone whom others testify about favorably (v. 12), and the elder advocates imitating not what is evil but what is good (v. 11). Does this imply that the inhospitality resulting from Diotrephes' primacy-loving leadership is presented as evil? If so, the assertion that "anyone who does what is evil has not seen God" becomes problematic. Claiming that Jewish-Christian deserters "never were a part of us" (1 John 2:19; NIV "they did not really belong to us") and that loving the flesh comes from the world and not from God (1 John 2:16) is understandable, but to say a neighboring church leader has not seen God because of his autocratic style of leadership is another matter. Therefore, verse 11 may simply be a general reference, perhaps still about the value of extending hospitality, rather than a reference to Diotrephes in particular. Then again, the denial of hospitality and the propping up of one's primacy (like that of Peter in Matt. 10:2) may indeed have smacked of denying the loving and serving way of the Lord, so a reference to a leadership style moving toward centralized hierarchical authority—apparently what Diotrephes was doing—is not an implausible inference.

5. Final Greetings among Friends (13–15)

Parallel to the ending of 2 John, the conclusion of this personal letter also expresses the elder's desire to come as an incarnational letter—hoping to see them in person and to talk together face-to-face rather than simply writing with pen and ink. From one group of "the friends" to another (John 15:14–15), the elder asks his greetings to be shared with each, by name. Just as the Johannine Jesus imparted peace to his followers after the resurrection (John 20:19, 21, 26), so the Johannine elder imparts peace to Diotrephes in 3 John 14. His next venture, then, was likely to compile and finalize the testimony of the beloved disciple after his death (Jesus never said he would not *die*; he simply said to Peter, "If I want him to remain alive until I return, what is that to you?" [see John 21:22]),

claiming he "wrote [these things] down" and that "we know that his testimony is true" (John 21:24). Just as *our* testimony is true (3 John 12), so was his (John 21:24).

Select Bibliography

Anderson, Paul N. *The Christology of the Fourth Gospel: Its Unity and Disunity in the Light of John 6.* Rev. ed. Eugene, OR: Cascade, 2009.

Barclay, William. *The Letters of John and Jude.* Daily Study Bible. Philadelphia: Westminster, 1976.

Brown, Raymond E. *The Community of the Beloved Disciple.* New York: Paulist, 1979.

———. *The Epistles of John.* Anchor Bible. Garden City, NY: Doubleday, 1982.

Bruce, F. F. *The Epistles of John: Introduction, Exposition, and Notes.* Grand Rapids: Eerdmans, 1979.

Burge, Gary M. *The Letters of John: From Biblical Text to Contemporary Life.* NIV Application Commentary. Grand Rapids: Zondervan, 1996.

Dodd, C. H. *The Johannine Epistles.* Moffat New Testament Commentary. New York: Harper, 1946.

Grayston, Kenneth. *Johannine Epistles.* New Century Bible Commentary. Grand Rapids: Eerdmans, 1984.

Houlden, J. L. *A Commentary on the Johannine Epistles.* 2nd ed. Black's New Testament Commentary. London: A & C Black, 1994.

Kysar, Robert. *I, II, III John.* Augsburg Commentary on the New Testament. Minneapolis: Augsburg, 1986.

Lieu, Judith. *The Theology of the Johannine Epistles.* New Testament Theology. New York: Cambridge University Press, 1991.

Marshall, I. Howard. *The Epistles of John.* New International Commentary on the New Testament. Grand Rapids: Eerdmans, 1978.

Painter, John. *1, 2, and 3 John.* Sacra Pagina 18. Collegeville, MN: Liturgical Press, 2002.

Rensberger, David K. *1 John, 2 John, 3 John.* Abingdon New Testament Commentaries. Nashville: Abingdon, 1997.

Schnackenburg, Rudolf. *The Johannine Epistles: Introduction and Commentary.* Translated by Reginald and Ilse Fuller. New York: Crossroad, 1992.

Smalley, Stephen S. *1, 2, 3 John.* Word Biblical Commentary. Waco: Word, 1984.

Smith, D. Moody. *First, Second, and Third John*. Interpretation. Louisville: Westminster John Knox, 1991.

Stott, John R. W. *The Letters of John: An Introduction and Commentary*. 2nd ed. Tyndale New Testament Commentaries. Grand Rapids: Eerdmans, 1988.

Thompson, Marianne Meye. *1–3 John*. IVP New Testament Commentary. Downers Grove, IL: InterVarsity, 1992.

Von Wahlde, Urban C. *The Johannine Commandments*. New York: Paulist, 1990.

Jude

PETER H. DAVIDS

Author

The Letter of Jude identifies the author as "Jude . . . brother of James." The Jude (or Judah or Judas, which are all transliterations of the same name) intended here is the younger brother of the James (Jacob) to whom the Letter of James is attributed. This James in turn was the leader of the followers of Jesus in Jerusalem from at least AD 44 to 61 and the James whom Mark 6:3 identifies as a younger brother of Jesus himself. That would make Jude Jesus's youngest (Matt. 13:55) or second-youngest (Mark 6:3) brother. Much later, the canonical arrangement of the seven Catholic Epistles, or General Letters, put James as the first letter in the collection and Jude, written by the brother of James, as the last, bracketing the works of the others with letters attributed to brothers of Jesus.

We know nothing about Jude's life or his role in the Jesus movement after Jesus's resurrection. It is clear, though, that the writer believes he has authority to speak to those whom he addresses, not least because he is the brother of James, but also because he is "a servant [slave] of Jesus Christ." Thus, as a servant, while not having any rank of his own, he speaks with the authority of his master, as Moses did for God and slaves of Caesar did for Caesar.

A number of scholars question whether the traditional author did write Jude. In reality, there is no way to prove or disprove whether or not Jude the brother of James wrote this work or whether it was written in his name, for we know nothing of his education (the author of the letter has at least a good Greek primary education), nor do we have other work by him to indicate his writing style and theology. All one can say about the author is that he is very familiar with Second Temple Jewish literature, that he has an excellent Greek vocabulary and decent Hellenistic education, and that it is not clear whether or not he knows either Hebrew or Aramaic—Richard Bauckham believes he does, while others question this. If one doubts that this author is Jude, then one must ask why someone would write in the name of such an "unknown" rather than pick the name of a more famous leader in the Jesus movement.

Audience and Date

No information is given about either those to whom the letter is addressed or the historical circumstances of Jude's composition, except that the author expects the recipients to be familiar with Second Temple Jewish literature. Furthermore, any extrabiblical traditions we have about the brothers of Jesus connect their lives and descendants with Palestine, so that would be consistent with a Palestinian provenance for the letter and would perhaps indicate that the addressees were not too far away (although far enough from the author that a letter was needed). It is also clear that the letter is not really a "general," or "catholic," epistle since it is clearly written to a specific group of followers of Jesus whom the author knows and who know the author (e.g., he refers to them as "dear friends"; v. 3). The author views his addressees as at risk because of a group of others (they are never given a name) who have entered the community and are introducing destructive practices, probably on the authority of their prophetic dreams (they are called "dreamers"; v. 8 KJV, NRSV).

We therefore do not know when Jude was written. If it had a Palestinian origin, then it was probably written before 66, the outbreak of the war against Rome, although a date a decade or so later—when life was becoming more normal after the destruction of Jerusalem—is possible. Knowing that 2 Peter made use of Jude's letter only helps to place Jude in the first century, for 2 Peter has been variously dated from 64 to 90 (though sometimes much later). Given the reference to James, who was martyred in 61, a date after James's death and before the war with Rome may be as likely as any.

Jude was valued early in its history, because, as noted above, it was used as the basis of 2 Peter 2:1–3:3; the fact that the same topics are discussed in the same order, that some phrases and illustrations are identical, and that the issues addressed are similar indicates that this conclusion is well established. But after that we do not hear of Jude for over a century. In the third and fourth centuries, the work was disputed, but we are not told the reasons, although it is speculated that Jude's use of noncanonical literature may have been part of the reason. Jude does appear in fourth-century biblical collections, and by the end of the century it is included in canon lists. However, despite official acceptance, the work has been neglected for much of its history.

Structure and Content

The structure of the work is relatively clear. The letter opens with a salutation (vv. 1–2), then the body consists of an opening to the main topic (vv. 3–4), a discussion of the intruding teachers (vv. 5–16), and a conclusion (vv. 17–23). A benediction closes the letter (vv. 24–25).

The short letter is a contrast between those "dear friends" who are faithful ("kept for/by" [cf. NIV note] or "kept safe" [NRSV], v. 1), whose job it is to build themselves up in the faith (v. 20), and those others who have left the faith, their departure meaning that by word and action they are living in opposition to the ethical teaching of Jesus.

Outline

1. Salutation (1–2)
2. Letter Body (3–23)
   A. Opening: Reason for Writing (3–4)
   B. Main Discussion: Denunciation of the Intruding Teachers (5–16)
   C. Conclusion: Response of the Believers (17–23)
3. Benediction (24–25)

Commentary

1. Salutation (1–2)

The salutation is brief, identifying the author, as we have noted, and then identifying the recipients as people who have been "called," "loved," and "kept" by God the Father and Jesus Christ. There is no criticism of these "dear friends" stated anywhere in the letter.

2. Letter Body (3–23)

A. Opening: Reason for writing (3–4). After the salutation comes the reason for writing. While about to write in another vein, Jude has received information that means he must instead exhort the community he addresses to "contend for the faith," which will be defined in 22–23 as holding fast to what they are committed to and rescuing those who are deceived (i.e., the others and any they have influenced). The reason this is necessary is that these others have entered the congregation and are presently functioning within the community (Jude 12). Jude makes two related charges: they pervert grace into "a license for immorality" and they thereby deny "Jesus Christ our only Sovereign and Lord" (v. 4). In other words, living in disobedience to Jesus is a form of apostasy.

B. Main discussion: Denunciation of the intruding teachers (5–16). In the main section of the letter body, the author denounces the others, using groups-of-three illustrations originally from the Old Testament but now read through the lens of Second Temple Jewish literature. The first group (vv. 5–7) is the people saved in the exodus, the angels of Genesis 6:1–8, and Sodom and Gomorrah. Two of the three were once saved or had a dwelling with God, while all three were finally destroyed. The Genesis 6 story, read through the lens of *1 Enoch*, and Sodom are put last because each refers to sexual relations across a forbidden boundary (i.e., angel/human; in Jude 7 literally "strange flesh"). The others in the community are apparently crossing some type of sexual boundary, doing things that were not approved of even in the culture surrounding the believing community (perhaps like the man in 1 Cor. 5:1).

These "dreamers" (possibly indicating the source of their "revelation" [v. 8]; NIV "on the strength of their dreams these ungodly people") not only cross such boundaries but they also "reject authority," slandering the good angels ("celestial beings" or "the glorious ones"), perhaps

Icon of the archangel Michael (tenth century). Jude 9 holds up Michael as an example, referring to an account from the *Testament of Moses*.

those who were thought to have brought the law (and thereby ethical rules) to Moses (vv. 8–10). Unlike the archangel Michael, who in the *Testament of Moses* argued respectfully with the devil over whether or not Moses deserved burial (the devil accused Moses of having been a murderer in Egypt) and who left judgment to God ("The Lord rebuke you!"), these others, lacking the propriety of Michael, are like animals in that they do not understand what they slander. They are also like animals in that they follow their instincts, not realizing that these impulses will in the end destroy them.

The reference to the *Testament of Moses*, then, gives way to the second group of three: Cain, Balaam, and Korah (v. 11). This woe oracle sounds like it was pulled out of Old Testament prophecy. While the first and last of the group were rebels, all three were viewed in Jewish tradition as having taught evil. There is a crescendo in the descriptions: "taken the way of," "rushed for profit into," "been destroyed in." Only the spiritually suicidal would emulate them.

These others are a part of the local community of believers (vv. 12–13), for they participate in the Lord's Supper, which in that period was a full meal, a "love feast." Yet they are a defilement of that meal. Furthermore, they are there for their own gain, not for worship or building up others. Thus they are like Balaam or like the shepherds of Ezekiel 34:2. Four images create a vivid warning about them: (1) waterless clouds and (2) fruitless autumn trees indicate they promise much but do not deliver; (3) waves seem impressive, but these stir up "shame"; and (4) stars (believed by ancients to be angelic powers) that are wandering rather than in their proper courses (which parallels the clouds being "blown along") are doomed. Such stars will be destroyed, as was the case with the angels of Genesis 6:1–8.

The message of destruction is underlined by the quotation from *1 Enoch* 1:9 (vv. 14–17). As we noted above, our author is familiar with Second Temple Jewish literature such as the *Testament of Moses* and *1 Enoch*. Furthermore, the way he refers to a number of Old Testament stories shows that he is influenced by how these stories were retold in Second Temple literature. Here we find the only quotation of a "scripture" in the whole work, and it is the quotation of a "prophecy" that Jude attributes to Enoch (just as Matt. 13:14 refers to the "prophecy" of Isaiah and Matt. 15:7 says, "Isaiah . . . prophesied"). We now know the quotation as part of the opening chapter of *1 Enoch* (which is probably a composite book). Jude cites this work in an unself-conscious manner. He is, of course, not aware that there would later be canonical discussions and that *1 Enoch* would not form part of the eventual canon. For him it is simply an authoritative prophecy that he knows is appropriate for his topic, and he cites it as freely as he might have cited other prophets such as Isaiah or Jeremiah. The point of the prophecy is straightforward: final judgment is coming. Those for whom this judgment is a danger include not just the "sinners" named in the prophecy but also the others in the community, who are accused of grumbling (a term found only here, but the idea is also in James 5:9), being driven by their desires, and buttering up others. These sins were important to Jude but are sometimes forgotten about or downplayed today.

C. Conclusion: Response of the believers (17–23). The final section of the letter counsels the readers what to do about this situation. It is here that Jude surprises the modern reader the most, for he does not instruct them to throw the others out.

First, the "dear friends" are not to be surprised but rather to remember apostolic predictions (which were not passed down beyond that age, for they are not found elsewhere in the New Testament or church tradition) that this rejection of Jesus's morality is precisely what would happen in "the last times" (or "at the end of time"). Such people are members of the community of believers in which they cause divisions, but in fact they are totally of this age ("follow mere natural instincts" or "are soulish") and "do not have the Spirit."

Second, in contrast to such people, the dear friends are to strengthen themselves in their holy commitment (NIV "holy faith"; but it is not doctrine but commitment that is intended), to pray in the Spirit (which they clearly have and which the others, who do not have it, claim is leading them), and especially to look expectantly toward the final judgment, when they will receive mercy from "our Lord Jesus Christ." Thus they are to keep on being faithful as they have been doing.

Third, they are to rescue everyone they can from the false teaching, exercising mercy rather than judgment yet being careful that in the process they themselves are not sucked in. In fact, a better translation of Jude 22 is, "Be merciful to those who dispute," that is, the others. There is not a word about attacking and expelling the others who have come into the community; rather, the faithful are to live the truth themselves and rescue those trapped in desire. Verse 23 probably speaks of two actions toward one group: snatch them from the fire and show them mercy—but do so in a manner in which you are not yourselves contaminated.

3. Benediction (24–25)

The benediction is an elaborate blessing of God, who is first described as the one who can keep the readers stable and bring them successfully to his presence, which should relieve any fear that may have been engendered by this letter, including fear of being contaminated in the course of trying to rescue the others. Thus, he is "God our Savior," an unusual expression for God, although his saving acts are frequently celebrated in Scripture. This is done through Jesus Christ our Lord, for the believer (unlike the others) lives under the lordship of Jesus, and it is only in this way that he or she is related to "God our Savior." Finally, this culminates in ascribing eternal honor and authority to this God, as would be fitting in the court of such a king.

Select Bibliography

Bauckham, Richard J. *Jude, 2 Peter.* Word Biblical Commentary. Waco: Word, 1983.

———. *Jude and the Relatives of Jesus in the Early Church.* Edinburgh: T. & T. Clark, 1990.

Davids, Peter H. *The Letters of 2 Peter and Jude.* Pillar New Testament Commentary. Grand Rapids: Eerdmans, 2006.

Davids, Peter H., and Robert L. Webb, eds. *Reading Jude with New Eyes: Methodological Reassessments of the Letter of Jude.* Library of New Testament Studies. London: T. & T. Clark, 2007.

Green, Gene L. *Jude and 2 Peter.* Baker Exegetical Commentary on the New Testament. Grand Rapids: Baker Academic, 2008.

Neyrey, Jerome H. *2 Peter, Jude: A New Translation with Introduction and Commentary.* Anchor Bible. New York: Doubleday, 1993.

Reese, Ruth Anne. *2 Peter and Jude.* Two Horizons New Testament Commentary. Grand Rapids: Eerdmans, 2007.

Revelation

MAX J. LEE

Introduction

No other book has stirred the imagination and emotions of its readers as much as the Apocalypse of John. It has been the source of inspiration for classic works of literature like Milton's *Paradise Lost* and Dante's *Divine Comedy*, for timeless symphonies like Handel's *Messiah*, for masterpieces of art like Michelangelo's Sistine Chapel fresco *The Last Judgment*, and for such adored hymns as "Holy, Holy, Holy," "Crown Him with Many Crowns," and "Come, Thou Almighty King." Imagine, if you will, the rise of the curtain to an epic drama. The eternal God of the universe rips open the sky. An angel of the Lord flies down and sweeps you up to the highest part of the cosmos. This same angel gives you a personal tour of the heavens. You hear a litany of saints sing until the foundations of the earth shake. At their song's zenith, God appears on a fiery chariot and unveils to you the intimate details of his divine plan for all humanity. If you can envision these scenes, then you can grasp something of the power and grandeur of Revelation.

Revelation is also one of the most controversial texts of the New Testament. Ever since the publication of Hal Lindsey and Carole Carlson's *Late Great Planet Earth* (1970), Revelation has been wrongly read as a horoscope to the future. Lindsey popularized a (dispensationalist) way of reading Revelation in the twentieth century that continues to have a cultural influence on American evangelicalism today. Typically this method attempts to connect the narrative episodes in the biblical texts with the real-time events reported by the local news. Many, for instance, have tried to identify "the beast" (Rev. 13:1–10) with the world leaders of their day. Their guesses have ranged from the pope to Nazi Germany's Adolf Hitler to every modern US president. The ten horns of the beast have been likened to the United Nations and the European League (17:7–14), the number 666 to a barcode tattooed on the forehead or hand and used like a credit card (13:17–18), and the natural catastrophes of the seven seals, trumpets, and bowls to global warming (6:12–14; 8:7–12; 16:3–12). All these connections are fallacious. None are based on a historically informed reading of the biblical text. Yet these ideas endure and never seem to be left behind.

Interpretative Approaches to Revelation

The method of reading the Bible in one hand and the daily newspaper in the other is the poorer representative of the *futurist* approach. Futurists believe that most of the visions in Revelation (especially Revelation 4–22) point to events in the future that directly precede the second coming of Christ. Some like Lindsey think that from its pages a road map to the future can be charted out. Other nondispensational futurists are critical of correlating biblical prophecy with the evening

1585

news but still believe that Revelation mainly describes events that will occur at Jesus's impending return. But Christian interpreters throughout the centuries have exercised other approaches. The *preterist* approach (from the Latin word *praeteritus*, meaning "past" or "gone by") insists that Revelation reflects the historical conditions of the first-century church alone and that it speaks to the persecuted communities of Asia Minor in John's day. The *historicist* approach believes that Revelation offers an overview of the church's entire history and Revelation's chapters can be divided between the apostolic, patristic, medieval, Reformation, and post-Reformation periods. The *idealist* approach argues that the visions are symbolic of eternal realities and they cannot be tied to any specific historical event. It is probably best, however, not to limit oneself to any particular approach but to remain eclectic. The *eclectic* approach appreciates the contributions of each previous approach but limits itself to none of them.

Literary Genre(s)

The Greek word *apocalypsis*, literally "an apocalypse," is frequently translated as "a revelation." As a literary genre, apocalyptic literature was as widespread in the Roman world as biographies, histories, novels, and poetry are today. Several Jewish apocalypses were already in circulation in the first and second centuries AD, including *1–2 Enoch*, the *Apocalypse of Zephaniah*, *4 Ezra*, *2 Baruch*, the *Apocalypse of Abraham*, and the *Apocalypse of Adam*, to name a few. The Old Testament includes one canonical example: Daniel.

Apocalyptic literature is an intensified form of prophecy. If prophetic literature saw repentance as the ideal solution to the problem of sin and apostasy, then apocalyptic literature addressed a situation so dire and a people so enslaved to evil that repentance no longer seemed possible unless God broke into history to create new possibilities for humanity. The way apocalypses show how God operates in our world is through visionary experiences. God lifts the curtain behind the events of human history

and shows how he is working in the spiritual realm to carry out his redemptive plan.

It was the practice of the early church to have seers report their visions and share them as a word of prophecy during a public time of Christian worship (1 Cor. 14:29–33; *Shepherd* of Hermas, *Visions* 1–4; cf. Acts 10:9–11:18). The prophetic word was subject to the discernment of the church, but if it was found authentic, the congregation was then accountable to hear and obey it (Rev. 1:3; 22:7). Because the author of Revelation was exiled on the island of Patmos, his particular vision was written down in the form of a letter, circulated to the seven churches of Asia Minor, and read aloud in a liturgical setting (1:3–4).

Revelation is actually a threefold genre. It is part apocalypse (1:1), part prophecy (1:3; 22:7), and part letter (1:4–5; 22:21). These literary genres were never meant to be read as a road map to the future. Neither do they restrict the relevance of Revelation only to those Christians living near the time of Christ's return. Rather, whenever the author of Revelation discusses the future, its purpose is to encourage a response from the reader in the *immediate* moment. In the same way Jonah foretold a future judgment against the citizens of Nineveh in order to evoke an immediate repentance from them (Jonah 3:4–10), the prophet John even when describing far-off judgments expects his contemporary readers to respond now, not later. The readers of this apocalypse are asked to repent, make costly commitments, and with haste join God in what he is doing to rescue the world from sin. Revelation cannot be treated as a note stuffed in a bottle, lost in the sea of time, only to be opened and deciphered by those on shore who live within proximity of Jesus's return. Whatever John the seer observed in his visions, it must have been understandable to the original audience who first received its message.

Date and Authorship

The author of Revelation identifies himself as John (1:1, 4, 9; 22:8), a servant of Christ (1:1), and a prophet to the churches in Roman

Asia (1:3; 22:7). John was exiled by Rome on an island called Patmos in the Aegean Sea because of his Christian witness (1:9). Beyond these details, little else is said about him. Patristic traditions claim that this John was none other than the apostle, one of the Twelve, the son of Zebedee (e.g., Justin Martyr, *Dialogue with Trypho* 81.4). Those skeptical of apostolic authorship note the differences between Revelation and the Gospel of John (which is also believed to be written by the apostle). They point out, for example, variations in language and writing style. The Gospel's Greek is refined, but Revelation's contains a number of grammatical irregularities (see the note to Rev. 1:4b). There are also differences in theology. John's Gospel has a realized or inaugurated eschatology (i.e., the "last days" began with Jesus's ministry, and rebirth is evidence for the kingdom's arrival; John 3:15–16; 4:13–14; 5:24), while Revelation has a final eschatology (i.e., Revelation focuses not on the present invasion of the kingdom but on its consummation at Jesus's return; 19:1–22:5). Yet many of these variances can be explained. John may have had an amanuensis, or secretary, who helped him compose the Gospel but no such assistance with Revelation, and hence the changes in grammar and style. Theological divergence could be due to different emphases and not content. John's Gospel does speak about final eschatological events (e.g., John 5:28–29; 14:2–4) as well as realized ones, though focusing on the latter, while Revelation records John's immediate ecstatic encounters with the Spirit (1:10; 4:2; 17:3; 21:10), though emphasizing the final flooding of the Spirit at history's end (22:1–5). Although alternative Johns have been suggested throughout the centuries, none of them (e.g., John Mark, John the Baptist, John the elder, a pseudonymous or anonymous John) have been so convincing as to rule out apostle John as the author.

The date of composition for Revelation is near the end of Emperor Domitian's reign (81–96) around the year 95, though a minority number of commentators have suggested dates as early as the 60s during Nero's administration or as late as the second century under Trajan. Domitian has been characterized as a cruel despot by many Roman historians (e.g., Pliny the Younger, *Panegyric* 48–49), but accounts of his villainy were probably exaggerated. Roman historians at that time condemned Domitian's reign as a propagandistic foil by which his successor Trajan's new rule could appear benevolent and successful. It is also incorrect to think that Domitian launched a large-scale systematic persecution of all Christians throughout the entire empire (see Eusebius, *Ecclesiastical History* 3.14–20). Based on a more balanced reconstruction of Domitian's reign and from the internal evidence found within Revelation 2–3, we can surmise that the hostilities against Christians were indeed real, at times intense (e.g., Antipas's martyrdom at Pergamum; 2:13), but localized and part of a spectrum of other issues that challenged the believing community. What threatened the church the most was not persecution but moral compromise with the idolatrous values of Roman culture.

The Historical and Social Setting of John's Churches

Asia Minor was a Roman province where the imperial cult was popular and politically influential. When Asia Minor came under Roman rule in 133 BC, it was natural for the inhabitants to honor the Roman emperor as part of their ongoing practice of worshiping living monarchs. Veneration was a sign of loyalty and gratitude to those who brought unified peace and political stability to the land. Although in Rome only dead emperors could be deified by the Senate, it appears that *outside* of Rome, Caesar could be honored as a *living* deity. Domitian, for example, accepted the divine title "Our lord and god" from Ephesus and other cities. He even used it himself when making imperial pronouncements (Suetonius, *Domitian* 13.2).

The seven churches to which the book of Revelation is addressed (1:11) were all located in major urban centers. Faithful Christians who

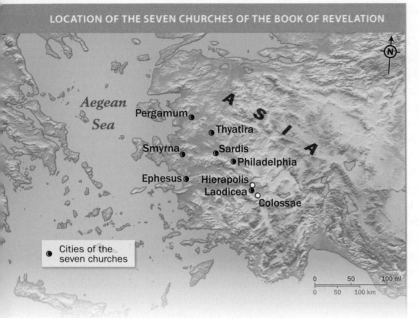

LOCATION OF THE SEVEN CHURCHES OF THE BOOK OF REVELATION

Aegean Sea

Pergamum

Thyatira

Smyrna

Sardis

Philadelphia

Ephesus

Hierapolis

Laodicea

Colossae

A S I A

N

Cities of the seven churches

0   50   100 mi
0   50   100 km

erupted over the identity of Jesus as the Messiah, it appears that the synagogue might have pressed the distinction between Judaism and Christianity publicly. The Christians, now seen as non-Jews, were expected to participate in the imperial cult. When the churches at Smyrna (2:9) and Philadelphia (3:9) refused, there were social and economic sanctions lodged against them by city officials based on the testimony of the Jews.

These cultic festivals often meant that an abundance of quality meat sacrificed to idols was available to all at the temples and at the markets. Idol food was a particular point of controversy for John's communities. Apparently some false Christian prophets taught the permissibility of eating idol meat and joining the cultic feasts despite the dangers of idolatry (2:2; 2:6; 2:14–17; 2:20–25). In Revelation it appears that cultural accommodation, Roman luxury, exotic entertainment, wealth, and economic prosperity posed greater threats to the integrity of the Christian community than outside persecution did.

were committed to monotheism and worshiped Christ, not Caesar, as Lord and God faced a crisis as they were pressured to participate in the cultic life of the city. Trade guilds (cf. Acts 19:24–25) would sponsor imperial festivals to enhance the status of their city before Rome and to compete for political favors. A lack of support for the cult often meant exclusion from the guild, economic hardship, and sometimes even confiscation of property, imprisonment, or death (Rev. 2:9–10; 2:13; 3:8).

Hostility came not only from the Roman government, the local city magistrates, and trade guilds but also from the Diaspora Jews. The Jewish people were among the few in the Roman Empire who were exempt from mandatory participation in the imperial cult. Jews were obligated to make daily sacrifices to God on behalf of the emperor but were not required to worship Caesar himself (Josephus, *Jewish War* 2.409; *Against Apion* 2.73; cf. Tacitus, *Annals* 5.5.4). Early Christianity, considered a "Nazarene sect" (Acts 24:5) of Judaism, was thus protected under this provision. However, as hostilities between the synagogue and church

The Golden Rule for the Interpretative Task

Reading a composition according to its literary genre is essential for the interpreter. No one reads poetry, for example, as if it were prose. Likewise, the early Christian communities that received Revelation knew what an apocalypse was and how to interpret it for its central message. Though we are at a disadvantage since we do not share the same literary and cultural instincts of the first-century reader, there is a simple guideline, or "golden rule" that all interpreters of Revelation can practice. *Readers should look to the Old Testament and the historical setting of John's churches for the source material of his visions.*

In the series of seven trumpet judgments, it is doubtful, for example, that John was given a glimpse into a dark future and, upon seeing unmanned air reconnaissance vehicles with machine guns, started to describe them as armored locusts with scorpion stingers (Rev. 9:1–12). John indeed saw locusts, but they appear as an intensified version of the eighth Egyptian plague (Exod. 10:12–20). The locusts symbolize God's judgment against idolatrous empires like Egypt and Rome. John expected his audience to recognize the exodus imagery and to use the entire Old Testament as a literary resource for interpreting the remaining visions. The author knew well the Scriptures of Israel and presumed anyone reading his apocalypse would refer to them frequently.

The Central Message of Revelation

John's goal was to help his first-century readers understand the significance of *their own present events* in the larger scheme of God's redemptive plan for humanity. True to the way the apocalyptic and prophetic genres operated in his day, Revelation gave a glimpse of what God had done in the past and was doing then in John's current time and place to undo evil (Revelation 1–18). The seer is also transported into the future to witness the ultimate destiny of God's people (but not until Revelation 19–22) so that he can view the present from the perspective of eternity. When sin and suffering run rampant, it is difficult to see God at work in our world. So the visions of John function to lift the veil and display the hidden dimensions of God's immediate invasion of time and space. Revelation is therefore not a playbook for how the future will unfold, although it does announce evil's demise and humankind's redemption as the ultimate outcome of history. John's visions speak to the reality of God for his day and what the ancient churches of Asia Minor could do to cooperate with the Spirit's activity among them. Yet to relegate the significance of Revelation to the past would be a mistake.

The message of Revelation has an enduring relevance for Christians of our century as well as the first. It is a profoundly theological book that uses symbols, metaphor, and figurative language from the Old Testament Scriptures and the cultural traditions of the Greco-Roman world to speak about God and salvation. Though much of Revelation unveils how the Roman Empire perpetuates evil through its military, its social patronage system, and the imperial cult, these very same issues of violence, economic injustice, and idolatrous religious practice are just as cogent for the modern church that engages evil today as it was for the ancient Christian movement.

When confronted with the three cycles of seven seals, trumpets, and bowls, ancient and modern readers alike cannot help but wrestle with the perennial question of theodicy (i.e., why a good and powerful God does not act immediately to stop evil) that is asked by all generations of Christians. During the seals, human sin and suffering are allowed to run their course to the point where the martyrs of the fifth seal cry out, "How long, Sovereign Lord . . . until you judge?" (6:10). Divine agency has been masked by silence, and the saints are asked to endure, trust, pray, witness, and worship their God even in moments of hardship and doubt (7:1–8:5). During the trumpets, the people of God are surprised to see that their very prayers for divine justice on earth and their witness to the nations contribute, in part, to the unleashing of the plagues that judge the idolatrous values of human society (8:1–5). Here divine power and human agency cooperate to dismantle the structures of evil (10:1–11:14). During the bowls, the initiative for the judgments comes directly from God himself (16:1). At last, God intervenes but with a finality that is frightening (16:2–21). From the seals to the bowls, the faithful begin to distinguish a divine purpose behind the chaos of our world. God does not cancel out sinful actions taken by people in an instant, for to do so would mean releasing a final form of judgment that would destroy all sinners.

No one would survive. He instead maximizes the possibility for all people to repent by making the cross his principal means for exacting justice in our world (5:1–13; 12:11; 15:2–4).

The bowls that bring blood stand in utter contrast to the life-giving blood of the slain Lamb (1:5; 5:9; 7:14; 12:11; 15:3; 17:14; 19:17–19), whose sacrificial death promises freedom and not torment, forgiveness and not judgment, eternal life and not death to those who faithfully follow him. Revelation presents evil in all its ugliness and power, but it also demonstrates that the way of the cross can dismantle sin and liberate the sinner. As we journey with the first-century church's titanic struggle against evil and the cost they bore to join God in his liberating work, modern believers cannot help but be challenged to live sacrificially and meet the challenges of life with an enduring faith.

The Literary Structure of Revelation as a Heavenly Liturgy

John saw visions, but we read about them. We are the beneficiaries of the author's tireless hours of reflection, writing, and rewriting so that the final literary form by which we receive these visions best communicates what he saw on Patmos two millennia ago. But what did John see as his spirit was taken from Patmos and was swept up to the highest heights of heaven (1:9–10)? As John received his tour of the heavenly realm, he saw God's courtroom illuminated by burning lampstands (1:12–20), the throne of God as a fiery chariot mounted on the wings of cherubim (4:1–11; 5:6–7; cf. Num. 7:89), a sanctuary door or gate (4:1), an altar for the burnt offering and incense (6:9; 8:3–5), libation bowls (15:7–8; 16:1–21), the ark of the covenant and Tent of Meeting (11:19; 15:5; 21:3), a brazen sea made clear like glass (15:2), and a large courtyard (11:2–3). His vision is a stunning rendition of heaven as the eschatological temple of the Lord. The earthly tabernacle built by Moses (Exod. 25:9–40) and the first temple built by Solomon (1 Chron. 28:11–19) were but crude copies of it. Although some Old Testament prophets had partial glimpses of this heavenly temple (cf. Ezek. 1:4–28; Isa. 6:1–7; Dan. 7:9–14; Zech. 4:1–9), John catches sight of the entire sanctuary and walks through it at the height of its splendor, transcendence, and glory.

What is more, this heavenly temple is not empty. It is buzzing with life and activity. All of heaven is worshiping the Triune God. Angels, fantastic creatures, resurrected elders, the saints of history, and a dumbstruck John participate in an eternal liturgy that finds an earthly equivalent in the Jewish morning worship service for the daily sacrifices at the Jerusalem temple. Although not exact, the heavenly liturgy roughly follows the same order of worship used during the Second Temple era (as outlined in the Mishnah tractate *Tamid*). At dawn, the ashes from the altars were cleared and the candles on the menorah prepared (Rev. 1:12–20). Then the sacrificial lamb was slaughtered and its blood poured out at the base of the altar (Rev. 5:6–9; 6:9–11). A blessing, the Ten Commandments, the Shema ("Hear, O Israel"; Deut. 6:4–9), and other Torah texts were read from scrolls (Rev. 5:2–7; 6:1–8:1). Meanwhile, another procession of priests walked from the inner court through the gate (cf. Rev. 4:1) into the Holy Place to make the incense offerings and pray in silence (Rev. 8:1–5). The burnt offering was made, the temple trumpets were blown (cf. Rev. 8:6–11:19), the cups of libation were poured out (cf. Rev. 16:1–21), the Levites broke out in song and music, and the people prostrated themselves in homage to God (Rev. 5:9–14; 14:3–4; 15:3–4). All these liturgical elements have been incorporated by the author of Revelation to describe his visionary experience. It comes as no surprise, then, that the heavenly liturgy, the eschatological temple, and its glorious furnishings form the literary backbone of John's Apocalypse.

Interwoven within the narrative framework of the heavenly temple is the theme of cosmic warfare. When the next element of the liturgy begins, the temple imagery fades out and a cosmic battle scene fades in. The seals on the Torah scrolls that are read as a blessing (Deut.

17:18; Neh. 9:38) turn into the seals on the royal decrees of a reigning monarch (1 Kings 21:8; Esther 8:8; cf. Rev. 6:1–8:1), temple trumpets blown over the sacrifices (Lev. 23:24; 25:9; Ps. 150:3) turn into war trumpets that herald an attack (Josh. 6:16–21; cf. Rev. 8:2–11:19), bowls of libation (Exod. 25:29; 1 Chron. 28:17) turn into bowls of divine wrath (Jer. 25:15–17; cf. Rev. 15:1–16:21), the angelic hosts who worship the Lord and the Lamb (Rev. 5:11–14) become the army of God (Rev. 19:11–14). As each segment of the worship service unfolds, different episodes in God's titanic war against the forces of evil are unveiled. The armies of God led by the Lamb wage war against Satan and his beasts (Rev. 12:1–14:20; 17:1–19:21). At stake in this struggle between good and evil are the redemption of humanity and the vindication of God. The liturgy is always the background and binding literary structure of Revelation, but it uses the imaging technique of fading out and fading in to forefront selectively the secondary theme of cosmological combat. The oscillation between liturgy and cosmic warfare brings together the key theological emphases of Revelation: the problem of suffering and God's providential action in the world, the identity of Christ as part of the Godhead, salvation and the perseverance of the saints, the mission of the church, eschatology, and the new creative order at Jesus's return. What John has left us is nothing less than a literary symphony.

Outline

1. Heaven as the Throne Room and the Royal Court of God (1:1–3:22)
   A. Prologue: An Apocalypse from God and a Letter from John (1:1–6)
   B. The Epiphany of the Glorious Son (1:7–20)
   C. The Seven Churches before the Divine Judge (2:1–3:22)
2. Heaven as the Eschatological Temple and the Theater for Cosmic Warfare (4:1–19:21)
   A. The Heavenly Liturgy Begins (4:1–5:15)

   B. The Seven Seals: Where Is God When His People Suffer? (6:1–8:1)
   C. The Seven Trumpets: Why History Belongs to the Intercessors (8:2–11:19)
   D. The Empire Unveiled as an Agent of Satan (12:1–15:4)
   E. The Seven Bowls: Why God Delays Ultimate Justice until the End (15:5–16:21)
   F. The End of the Empire (17:1–19:10)
   G. The Return of the King (19:11–21)
3. Heaven as a New City and the Earth as a New Eden (20:1–22:21)
   A. The Vindication of God and His People (20:1–15)
   B. Eternity (21:1–22:5)
   C. Benediction (22:6–21)

Commentary

1. Heaven as the Throne Room and the Royal Court of God (1:1–3:22)

The opening vision of Revelation takes place within the theater of a heavenly court, with the Lord Almighty seated on his throne, the Son as his royal viceroy, and the Holy Spirit in the form of seven spirits (1:4–6). The courtiers are the angels of the Lord, one of whom is sent to John. Though John is exiled on the island of Patmos, he is nevertheless taken up in his spirit to this heavenly courtroom and commissioned as a scribe to write what he sees (1:9–11). Christ appears as the glorified Son of Man and divine judge (1:12–20), the seven churches of Asia Minor are put on trial, and John records their judgment in the form of seven letters (2:1–3:22).

A. Prologue: An apocalypse from God and a letter from John (1:1–6). The first three words of the Greek text in Revelation are *apocalypsis Iēsou Christou*, literally "a revelation of Jesus Christ" (1:1). (Scholars differ on how to translate this Greek phrase. Some translate it as "a revelation *about* Jesus." Others translate it as "a revelation *from* Jesus," i.e., "what Jesus reveals." It is best read as "a revelation *of* Jesus," which allows for both interpretations.) *Apocalypsis* literally means an "unveiling" or an "uncovering," but in the context of other Jewish apocalypses and even later Christian ones (see the introduction), it is more accurately defined as "the dramatic disclosure of God's will." God lifts the curtain from the theater of history to unveil how he is working behind the scenes to redeem humanity and to set right all wrongs in our fallen world.

There is an explicit chain of agents through which the apocalypse is delivered. God and Jesus are the source of the revelation (1:1a), the angel is a heavenly intermediary (1:1b), and John is both seer and scribe (1:2, 4, 11). Each church would read the "words of this prophecy" aloud to the whole congregation during a public time of worship. The revelatory chain moves from God, to Jesus, to his angel, to John, to the churches, and finally to us, the readers; and a special blessing or beatitude (1:3; cf. 22:7; Matt. 5:3–11) is pronounced to all those who hear and obey. Since the events that God "signified" (KJV) or encoded in these visions are "the things that must soon take place" (1:1 ESV), and since "the time is near" for their fulfillment (1:3), readers should be wary of any interpretation that relegates the relevancy of Revelation to the distant future.

John moves from the revelation of Jesus and its prophetic urgency to an epistolary greeting (1:4a). From the highest height of heaven, where God's throne resides (Isa. 6:1; *1 Enoch* 14:18, 22), grace and peace pour forth from the one "who is, and who was, and who is to come," a divine title meant to be read as a single name and a theological reflection on Exodus 3:14, when Yahweh revealed himself as "I AM WHO I AM" (1:4b; a rabbinic commentary on this text [*Exodus Rabbah* 3.14] expands the name to: "I am he who was, and I am he now, and I am he forever. So it is said three times, I am."). Before the throne is the Holy Spirit in the form of seven spirits, an allusion to the sevenfold ministry in Isaiah 11:2–3. The Hebrew text of Isaiah 11:2–3 only mentions six spirits, but its Greek translation (i.e., the Septuagint) lists seven. The final person of the Godhead is Jesus,

whose atoning death and victory over sin has freed humanity (1:5–6).

B. The epiphany of the glorious Son (1:7–20). The two Old Testament figures, the Son of Man who "is coming with the clouds" (Dan. 7:13) like a king riding a chariot (cf. Isa. 19:1; Ps. 104:3) and the messenger of God who is pierced and rejected by Israel (Zech. 12:10) are now unveiled as being the same person. Jesus is the one whom "every eye will see," and "all the tribes of the earth will beat their breasts and mourn because of him" (Rev. 1:7, author's translation; cf. Matt. 24:30). The very sight of a pierced and risen Christ will convince all people of their own wickedness.

Old Testament theophanies (i.e., epiphanies or appearances of God in his glory) typically feature human observers struck by their sinfulness in the presence of the Holy One (Isa. 6:5–7; Job 42:5–6; cf. Rev. 1:17). The vision of Christ pierced and crucified is proleptic; it is a present glimpse for John and his readers of what will happen when Christ returns. We too will weep at the sight of Jesus because we will realize then, more deeply than we do now, that it was our sin that crucified the Lord of glory (cf. Acts 2:36–37). To the double "Yes!" and "Amen!" (1:7 NLT), God adds his own affirming guarantee: his title. "The Alpha and Omega" are the first and last letters of the Greek alphabet, meaning from beginning to end; he will providentially guide all history according to his sovereign plan (1:8; cf. Isa. 41:4; 48:12).

John tells the reader that he was on the island of Patmos, some thirty-five miles from the mainland. Other islands in the Aegean Sea were used as places of banishment by the Roman court (Tacitus, *Annals* 3.68; 4.30), so it is likely that Patmos (a rocky, volcanic, barren islet) was also used for that same purpose. John was exiled because he preached God's word and remained true to his testimony (1:9). He was a brother and "partner" (ESV; NIV: "companion") in affliction with God's family. (The Greek word translated as "partner" refers to a person with whom we share a deep communion or fellowship.) Together they have experienced not only the depths of tribulation but also the heights of the kingdom, and the power to endure. We are reminded that to be Christian is to share this common call to suffering (1:9; cf. 1 Pet. 2:21; 2 Tim. 3:12).

It is on "the Lord's Day" (i.e., Sunday) when John has an ecstatic experience that sweeps his spirit into the heavenly realm (1:10; cf. 2 Cor. 12:2). With imagery that anticipates the heavenly liturgy to come (Revelation 4–5), a great voice like a temple trumpet (see Lev. 23:24) resounds and commissions John to write what he sees on a scroll. A messenger will then take the scroll from Patmos to the mainland and travel a circular route from Ephesus to Smyrna, Pergamum, Thyatira, Sardis, Philadelphia, and finally Laodicea (1:11).

When John turns to see who is speaking to him (1:12), he is stunned by the blinding sight of Christ. He is the "one like the Son of Man" (NRSV; cf. Dan. 7:13) who stands among the seven golden lampstands of God's heavenly temple (1:12–13). Lampstands, or menorahs, were furnishings in the earthly tabernacle (Exod. 25:31–40), Solomon's temple (1 Chron.

28:15), and Herod's (Josephus, *Jewish Antiquities* 3.199). However, these earthly versions were pale imitations of the seven glorious lampstands seen by John (Heb. 8:5).

Even though the divine origin of "one like the son of man" is ambiguous in the Aramaic text of Daniel 7:9–14, it is clear in Revelation that this Son of Man is part of the Godhead, since he shares divine features ascribed to the Lord Almighty. In Daniel, it was God, as the "Ancient of Days" who judged the enemies of Israel, whose clothing was white as snow, whose hair was like wool, and whose throne was like a fiery chariot with wheels of flame (Dan. 7:9; cf. Ezek. 1:13–21). But in Revelation, the one on fire is not Daniel's Ancient of Days but the Son of Man, whose "eyes were like blazing fire," whose hair is white as wool and snow (1:14), and who holds the stars in his hands (1:16; cf. Dan. 12:3) and acts as judge (1:16). The seven stars in the Son's right hand are a reference to the sun, moon, and the five planets that a person

Patmos (shown here) is a Greek island located off the western coast of Turkey. John was in exile on Patmos due to his testimony about Jesus (Rev. 1:9).

could see with the naked eye (Saturn, Jupiter, Mars, Venus, and Mercury). Ancient astrologers thought the future was written in the stars, but here it is the Son of Man who holds the destiny of his people. The double-edged sword protruding from Christ's mouth is the Roman longsword used for penetrating armor. Here it is a metaphor for the power of God's Word to pierce our souls (1:16; cf. 2:12, 16; 19:15, 21; Ps. 52:2; 57:4; Heb. 4:12).

In 1:12–16, Jesus is also described as the angelic "man dressed in linen" from Daniel 10:5–9. Both Christ and the angelic messenger have divine robes, golden belts, feet as burnished bronze, eyes like torches, and shining faces (as lightning in Dan. 10:6, but brighter in Rev. 1:16, like the sun). Although in Daniel this man might be the archangel Gabriel (see Dan. 8:16; 9:21; 12:6–7), in Revelation he is the representation of God himself.

Like the prophets of other call narratives in the Old Testament (Isa. 6:1–10; Ezek. 1:28–2:3; Dan. 8:15–18; 10:4–21), John at first reacts to the divine epiphany with terror (1:17), because no sinner can stand before a holy God and live. Also like earlier prophets, John is reassured with the words "Do not be afraid!" (1:17; cf. Dan. 10:12, 19; Isa. 41:13) and strengthened by the Son's right hand (cf. Dan. 10:18). In this final scene, a mystery is unveiled. The stars in the right hand of the Son have turned into angels, and the lampstands into the seven churches of Asia Minor. In Daniel, heavenly bodies can symbolize God's people and their angelic representatives (Dan. 12:1–3; cf. Phil. 2:15). In Revelation, the stars and lampstands represent the church of God, whose light and witness will never fade because Jesus is ever in their midst (1:13, 20).

C. The seven churches before the divine judge (2:1–3:22). In Revelation 2–3, Christ lays bare the true spiritual condition of John's seven churches. In a dramatic reversal of the Old Testament expectations concerning Daniel's Son of Man, the Son does not put God's enemies on trial (as he does in Dan. 7:10–12, 26–27) but

rather God's people (cf. 2 Cor. 5:10; Heb. 12:5–11). Some historicist and futurist interpreters have tried to link the seven churches with successive periods of church history (e.g., Ephesus is the apostolic age, Smyrna the second- and third-century church, Pergamum the Constantinian era, Thyatira the medieval church, etc.), but such attempts ignore how closely each letter is situated within the geographical and cultural location of its first-century hearers.

2:1–7: The letter to Ephesus. Ephesus, whose harbor, roads, location, wealth, and special privileges with Rome made it an axis of trade in the Mediterranean, was the most cosmopolitan of the seven cities. Home to the imperial cult, it boasted magnificent temples dedicated to the emperors Domitian and Hadrian. It was also the site for one of the seven wonders of the ancient world: the Artemision, the temple of Artemis (goddess of the hunt and fertility). The Artemision was famous for its size, with a platform spanning over one hundred thousand square feet, and for its tree shrine at the center. The temple functioned as a place of asylum for fleeing criminals and symbolized abundant life. It also served as a bank that could receive huge monetary deposits.

On the surface, the Ephesian church appeared as zealous and productive as the city. In 2:2–3, Christ commends the Ephesian believers for their works, intensive labor, and perseverance. Under fire from several fronts (2:2, 6), they did not stumble or grow weary in their ministry. Yet Christ has one thing against them: they have abandoned "the love [they] had at first" (2:4; cf. Jer. 2:2; Ezek. 16:8). There is a sense of tragic irony as Christ walks intimately among the churches (2:1) yet is lost in the busyness of the Ephesian congregation.

Three verbs, each in the form of a command, unveil the process by which Christians recapture their first love: remember, repent, and do (the first things). "Remember *from where* you have fallen," says Christ (2:5a NASB). The first step toward restoration is to remember the starting point where one's heart began to drift from

God. Reconciliation involves *remembering correctly* how the offender has hurt the offended, since the wrongdoer must confess the offense and seek forgiveness. Second, one must repent and *completely turn away* from the pattern of behavior that hurt the offended. Last, the forgiven should do the kind of good works that characterized the love he or she first shared with the forgiver (2:5b).

There are no shortcuts to repentance, and sometimes the initial task of remembering accurately when one's faith began to stray can be a Herculean feat since time and sin distort a person's memory (cf. Num. 11:18–20; 14:2–4). But if the Ephesians do not repent, they will lose the light of their witness (2:5b). If they repent, Christ will give them the right to eat from the Tree of Life in the paradise of God (2:7). This final image not only points to paradise regained (Gen. 2:8–15) but also directly challenges the Artemis cult. The true refuge for the sinner is not the tree of Artemis but the cross. The common word for "tree" in Greek is *dendron*, but 2:7 uses *xylon*, referring to cut wood, things

made of wood, or a nonliving tree. So the "tree of life" in 2:7 is literally the "dead wood of life," or the cross (e.g., "cursed is everyone who hangs on a tree [*xylon*]," Gal. 3:13 NASB, NRSV [= Deut. 21:23]; cf. Acts 10:39; 1 Pet. 2:24). What a powerful invitation! Return to the cross and regain your first love.

2:8–11: The letter to Smyrna. Smyrna was a large port city known for its architectural achievements and aesthetic appeal. Its coins read: "Smyrna, first in Asia . . . for its beauty and splendor." Smyrna was known for its magnificent buildings and numerous temples (including one to the imperial cult). When viewed from a distance, Smyrna looked like a crown resting on the summit of a hill (Aelius Aristides, *Orations* 21.437; 22.443). In the sixth century BC, the city had been destroyed by the king of Lydia but was later rebuilt to its former glory in 290

The columns of the western stoa bordering the agora in Smyrna (second century AD). The city of Smyrna is located on the Aegean Sea on the western coast of Asia Minor. John writes to the suffering church of Smyrna so that they may remain faithful in the midst of persecution.

BC. Because of its death and rebirth, Smyrna was likened to the legendary phoenix, which dies in flame and reincarnates from its ashes. In contrast to the beauty of Smyrna, its faux resurrection, and its crowning summit, Christ appears as the truly beautiful and glorious one, the true resurrection (2:8), and the bestower of an imperishable crown for the faithful (2:11). As the one who orchestrates history from first to last, Christ addresses a church under pressure and reassures them that their faith is not in vain.

The tribulation of the church in Smyrna originated from vicious slander (2:9) by the local Jewish community, who had rejected the Nazarene sect as heretical (cf. Acts 25:5) and advised the city's officials to suppress the Christian movement. In doing so, the Jews were unwittingly becoming instruments of evil, a "synagogue of Satan." The fact that Christ addresses this group as "those who say they are Jews" and yet "are not" foreshadows the final parting of ways between Judaism and Christianity in the second century.

Instead of offering immediate relief, Christ actually warns them that their situation will worsen. Many early Christians experienced exclusion from the trade guilds, property loss, and poverty. Some will be thrown into prison, while others will suffer a martyr's death (2:10). The apostolic father Polycarp, bishop of Smyrna, was executed in this city by fire and sword (*Martyrdom of Polycarp* 4.1–3). Christians should not be surprised if their obedience leads to further persecution (cf. 2 Tim. 3:12). Yet the residents of Smyrna are actually abundantly rich in their present faith toward God (cf. Luke 12:21; James 2:5). A "crown of life" or athlete's laurel (Greek *stephanos*), which was a symbol of endurance and honor, awaits all those who finish the race of life with faithfulness (cf. 2 Tim. 4:7).

2:12–17: The letter to Pergamum. Pergamum was situated on a plateau some one thousand feet above the Caicus River valley and stood prominently in the expanse of the Mysian hills. The city was known for its great libraries, parchment materials, large theater, and many shrines (including the ones to Zeus, Athena, Asclepius, Hygeia, and Apollo). The temple of the *Sebastoi* (Greek for "the venerated ones," referring to Augustus Caesar and his successors) in Pergamum was the first imperial temple erected in Asia Minor (29 BC). Of the three greatest cities in Roman Asia (i.e., Ephesus, Smyrna, and Pergamum; Dio Chrysostom, *Orations* 34.48), the imperial cult was the most influential in Pergamum. Every five years or so, the Pergamene games were held in honor of the imperial family. It was a circus of epic proportions.

A Christian living in Pergamum could not avoid participating in the festivals or eating idol food without severe repercussions. Believers who refused to promote the imperial cult were ostracized from the trade guilds and even experienced confiscation of property, prison, and possibly death. Pergamum was one of the few cities that received from Rome the "right of the sword," enabling it to execute criminals at its discretion. The anonymous Antipas, whom Christ praises as "my faithful witness" (2:13), was the first of the Christian martyrs in this city.

Next John identifies someone in the church as the false prophet Balaam (2:14; cf. Num. 22:5–24:25). According to Jewish legend, Balaam advised King Balak to send Moabite women into the Israelite camp to seduce them into idolatry (Num. 25:1–5). Similarly, Christians who *eat* idol food (2:14), particularly during the cultic feasts, are guilty of the same spiritual adultery as Israel (2:14; cf. Jer. 3:6–9; Ezek. 23:35–38; Hos. 2:1–14). Those who *teach* idol food's permissibility are guilty of the same kind of false prophecy as Balaam (cf. Jude 11; 2 Pet. 2:15–16). The Balaam sect at Pergamum was probably a local manifestation of the wider Nicolaitan movement (2:15; cf. 2:6). It is possible they justified their participation in the imperial festivals on the theological basis that an idol is nothing (cf. 1 Cor. 8:4) and thus cultic feasting was harmless (cf. 1 Cor. 10:19–22).

Christ's appearance as one "who has the sharp, double-edged sword" (2:12; cf. 1:16) is a direct challenge to "the right of sword" exercised by Pergamum. No one has the authority to judge God's people except Christ (2:16). As judge, Christ warns the Balaam group that he will wage war against them with the sword of God's word (2:16b). He also calls *all* the house churches to repent (2:16a) for their corporate sin of neglect. To those who overcome, Christ promises manna (Exod. 16:12–31) and will sustain them through their desertlike circumstances (2:17; cf. Deut. 8:3). The white stone was a pebble cast as a vote of acquittal during a trial. This stone is also an admission pass to a special feast: the eschatological wedding banquet with Christ (Rev. 19:7–9; cf. Matt. 22:11–13).

2:18–29: The letter to Thyatira. Thyatira, unlike the other cities of Asia Minor, lay on almost level ground and was bordered by rising hills. Its landscape and location made the city vulnerable to constant invasion, but its

The restored and reconstructed Altar to Zeus from Pergamum (second century BC). This altar may be what John refers to in Revelation 2:13.

exporting business prospered because of the various roads that ran through the city and connected it to the Greek East. The first Christian convert in Macedonia—Lydia, a merchant of purple linens—was originally from Thyatira (Acts 16:14–15). Thyatira's guild of dyers was prominent, along with its clothiers, linen workers, and coppersmiths. It is possible that the Greek word roughly rendered "burnished bronze" (the term does not translate easily into English) may have referred to a special metal alloy of copper and a silverlike zinc produced only in Thyatira. This metal is used to describe the luminous quality of the divine Son of Man (2:18).

To a church whose city had a history of reconquest, Christ describes himself as "the Son of God" (2:18; cf. 2 Sam. 7:12–16; Ps. 110:1–2), the conquering Davidic king who would crush all of Israel's enemies with an iron rod (2:26–28; cf. Ps. 2:8–9). The Thyatiran believers also faced the same temptation to participate in cultic feasts (2:14). A false prophetess whom John pejoratively calls Jezebel deceived the church into idolatrous behavior (2:20). Jezebel in the Old Testament was the infamous wife of King Ahab, who promoted Baal worship, murdered God's prophets, and persecuted Elijah (2 Kings 9:22; 1 Kings 18–21). The Jezebel of Thyatira was a leader (probably a patroness of a house church) who shared "Satan's so-called deep secrets" (a wordplay on her claim that she taught the deep things of God; 2:24; cf. 1 Cor. 2:10; 8:1, 4) and taught the permissibility of idol food. To Jezebel and her disciples (2:23; cf. 1 Cor. 4:7), Christ warns that he will throw her and those who are spiritually united with her onto a sickbed (2:22; cf. Matt. 9:2). He will strike them with a deadly disease leading to death unless they repent (2:22–23; cf. 1 Cor. 11:29–30; Acts 5:3–10).

But Christ also tells the faithful in Thyatira to repent. In one of the most theologically striking texts of all seven letters, he warns the church, "You are *forgiving* [Greek *aphiēmi*] the woman Jezebel," when she should not be forgiven (2:20; both the NIV and NRSV translate the Greek verb as "you tolerate," but "you are forgiving" is to be preferred). With words reminiscent of the Johannine commission, "If you *forgive* [Greek *aphiēmi*] the sins of any, they are forgiven" (John 20:23 ESV), Christ calls the church to the priestly duty of discerning whether members have truly repented (2:21–22). It is the church's duty *not* to forgive until they take sin seriously (cf. Matt. 18:15–18). The one who searches the heart cannot be fooled by shallow repentance but will instead judge all according to their works (2:23). But to those who persevere, the son of David will share the right to rule the nations with him (2:27–28; cf. Ps. 2:9; Isa. 14:12).

3:1–6: The letter to Sardis. The city of Sardis had a reputation for wealth that exceeded its reality. According to an early Greek legend, King Midas washed off the cursed touch that turned everything into gold by bathing in the Pactolus River, which ran through Sardis. Sardis in its early history prospered through gold deposits discovered in the river. During the Roman era, however, Sardis became prosperous through its textile industry, its important trade routes, and its fertile plains. It had at least two temples on site, one to Augustus and the other to Artemis. In AD 17, Sardis suffered from a sudden earthquake, called the greatest disaster in local memory by Pliny the Elder (*Natural History* 2.86). With help from the emperors Tiberius and Claudius, Sardis was rebuilt. It quickly regained part of its former prosperity and sought the right to renew the imperial cult.

To the church in Sardis, Christ appears as the divine judge, the Son of Man, holding the seven spirits and stars (Rev. 1:12–16). Perhaps to outsiders the church looked like the epitome of success. But when Christ lifts the veil, John is horrified to see a congregation that is on the brink of spiritual death (3:1). Their works always fall short of genuine sacrifice (3:3). Though Sardis was known for its booming garment and textile trade, these believers wear soiled clothing (3:4), a poignant symbol of moral compromise with their surrounding culture. Christ warns them to wake up, strengthen what little faith remains, remember what they first heard, and obey (3:3–4). If they do not heed this warning, when the Son of Man returns (cf. Matt. 24:42–44; 1 Thess. 5:1–6), they will be caught off guard (as they were when the earthquake hit in AD 17) and shocked to find themselves on the wrong side of eternity. But to the faithful, Christ promises to dress them gloriously in white (a symbol of purity and victory) and never to blot out their names from the book of life (a heavenly register; see Exod. 32:32–33).

3:7–13: The letter to Philadelphia. Legend has it that Philadelphia was named after two rulers of the Attalid dynasty, the brothers Eumenes II and Attalus II Philadelphus. Philadelphia was known as the "gate" or "door" because it stood at the juncture of two major road systems. One road ran north from Ephesus and through a pass above the Cogamis Valley, while the other road ran east of Philadelphia through the Phrygian province. Philadelphia experienced the benefits and burdens of living in a volcanic area called the *Katakaumenē* (literally "burned over"), which provided rich, fertile soil for the city's large vineyards but because of frequent tremors also sent citizens fleeing from the city. Philadelphia, along with Sardis and Laodicea, experienced the infamous earthquake of AD 17 that leveled all three urban centers. When Philadelphia was rebuilt with Roman aid, the city was renamed "Neocaesarea" to honor the imperial family, and later "Philadelphia Flavia" to honor the Flavian emperor Vespasian.

The Philadelphian church had "little strength" (3:8a). Nevertheless, a church that seems weak to the outside world is where God can display his glory (cf. 1 Cor. 1:26–29; 2 Cor. 12:8–10). As in Smyrna (Rev. 2:8–11), the church at Philadelphia was experiencing hostilities from the Jewish synagogue (3:9) but did not deny Jesus's name (3:8b). Because of their perseverance (3:10) and works (3:8a), the holy and true one gives three promises. First, Christ tells the Philadelphians that the door

to the church's mission and ministry (cf. 1 Cor. 16:9; 2 Cor. 2:12; Col. 4:3) will stay open. No one can shut it. Second, he promises to vindicate the church before the Jewish community (3:9; cf. Isa. 60:14; Rom. 11:11). Last, the one who holds the keys to David's kingdom (3:7; cf. Isa. 22:2) promises them a place in David's new city, the New Jerusalem (3:12; cf. 21:2, 10; Jer. 3:17). Unlike the earthly Philadelphia, whose name changed twice, the heavenly Jerusalem and its citizens have a permanent name (i.e., the name of God) and with it the assurance that they belong to Christ. Believers will be a pillar in the portico of God's eschatological temple, which no earthquake can shake (cf. Ezek. 40:49), and they will receive the power to remain steadfast (3:12; cf. 1 Cor. 15:48).

3:14–22: The letter to Laodicea. The city of Laodicea, compared with Hierapolis and Colossae, was the most prominent of the three cities in the Lycus River valley. A trade route that connected Laodicea with Ephesus, along with lesser roads north to Hierapolis and east to Colossae, allowed for a prosperous exporting business. The city was a central hub between the three regions of Lydia, Phrygia, and Caria. Laodicea's textile industry was known for a fine, dark wool. The city was also a banking center, exchanging Roman coinage, gold, and other items of deposit for local currency. Laodicea was so wealthy that when the infamous earthquake of AD 17 struck, it was the only city that refused Roman aid. It was home to a medical school that prized among its other healing drugs an ointment for burns. Laodicea receives a scathing rebuke from Christ, who attacks these points of civic pride.

The Laodicean church was completely unaware of its true spiritual condition. Christ tells them: "I know your deeds, that you are neither cold nor hot. . . . Because you are lukewarm . . . I am about to spit you out of my mouth" (3:15–16). While neighboring Hierapolis was famous for its hot (95 degrees Fahrenheit) medicinal water springs, and Colossae for its pure, cold water, Laodicea had a poor water supply and imported water from five miles out through an aqueduct. The water was tepid on arrival. Christ laments that Laodicea is neither hot nor cold but rather disgusting (in the spiritual sense) like its lukewarm waters. Though they think highly of themselves (3:17a), they are actually wretched, pitiful, morally bankrupt, blind, and naked (3:17b).

Referencing their wealth, Christ admonishes the church to buy what really matters (3:18): purity of heart (like gold refined by fire), forgiveness and holiness (like white garments; 7:14; cf. Lev. 16:14–16), and moral discernment (like eyes healed by medicinal ointments). The purpose of this rebuke and accompanying discipline (perhaps in the form of the trials to come; 6:1–8:1; cf. Heb. 12:5–11) is repentance. Christ loves the church and has not given up on it. Yet in a heart-wrenching image, he stands outside knocking at the church's door (3:20; cf. Song of Sol. 5:2; Luke 12:36–37). To those who let Jesus in, Christ promises an intimate and restored fellowship (symbolized by the shared meal; 3:20).

> The aqueduct system at Laodicea, seen here, brought lukewarm water into the city. This water that is "neither hot nor cold" is alluded to in Revelation 3:15–16.

2. Heaven as the Eschatological Temple and the Theater for Cosmic Warfare (4:1–19:21)

In Revelation 1–3, John saw the throne room of God from which the divine Son of Man judges the seven churches in Asia. This theophany, specifically a throne-chariot theophany, is described with even greater detail in Revelation 4–5, which continues the image of heaven as the throne room and royal court of God, but also introduces the central composite vision that forms the backbone of the entire book of Revelation. When John receives his tour of heaven from the various members of God's court, he begins at the throne but steps out to discover that the throne room is part of a larger magnificent structure, namely, the eschatological temple of the Lord. For the most part (Revelation 4–19), John's central vision takes place in the true heavenly temple, after which the earthly tabernacle built by Moses, the first temple of Solomon, and the second temple renovated by Herod the Great were modeled (Exod. 25:9–40; 2 Chron. 28:11–19; Josephus, *Jewish War* 5.212–18).

A. The heavenly liturgy begins (4:1–5:15). **4:1–11: Praise the Creator.** The first thing John sees is the open door to the gates of the

heavenly temple (4:1; cf. 11:19; 15:5), and his spirit is immediately swept up into the inner sanctuary, where the throne of God resides (Rev. 7:15). The blowing of a temple trumpet usually heralds the next part of a Jewish liturgy (cf. Lev. 23:24), and so the familiar "voice like a trumpet" that commissioned John as a scribe in his first vision (1:10) now issues a new call to worship. A heavenly liturgy of epic proportions begins.

The object of worship is the Lord God Almighty in his full glory. In the throne-chariot epiphany traditions of Ezekiel 1–2, Isaiah 6, Daniel 7, and later Jewish apocalypses (e.g., *1 Enoch* 55; 61), God appears as a divine ruler seated on his heavenly throne (4:2) whose glorious splendor is depicted with the most luminous terms possible. Semiprecious stones like jasper and carnelian are worn like a tunic by God, and a rainbow of emerald is worn like a belt (4:3; cf. Exod. 28:13; Ezek. 1:16, 26–28; 28:13). Reminiscent of the Sinai theophany, where God appears before Israel in the form of a storm cloud (Exod. 19:17–18), flashes of lightning and peals of thunder roar from the throne (4:5; cf. Ezek. 1:13–14). The flaming torches from the menorah in the temple are the seven spirits, or the Holy Spirit (Rev. 1:4; cf. Isa. 11:2–3), whose light burns constantly and whose presence sustains the churches (4:5). A sea of glasslike crystal covers the temple floor. The sea is a symbol of chaos and sin in the Old Testament (Ps. 74:13–17), but its calm state before the throne means that chaos has clearly been subdued by God (4:6; cf. Ezek. 1:22; Gen. 1:8).

In a series of concentric circles surrounding God's throne, the different members of his heavenly council are identified. In the first outer circle are the twenty-four elders, who are similar to the elders at the Sinai theophany (Exod. 24:9–18) but also likened to the divisions of twenty-four priests, gatekeepers, and Levites of the earthly temple (1 Chron. 24:3–19; 26:17–19; 25:6–31). The elders of John's vision represent the entire people of God in their appointed priestly duties (4:4a). Their thrones

refer to the multiple-thrones scene of Daniel 7, where the resurrected saints or "holy ones" are given the right to cojudge with the Ancient of Days (Dan. 7:9–10, 18, 27; cf. 1 Cor. 6:3). The elders are dressed in white, a testimony to their pure faith, and are also wearing golden athlete wreaths, a symbol of their perseverance (4:4b).

In the second concentric circle (moving toward the center) are the four living creatures with six wings that resemble the cherubim of Ezekiel 1:4–25, with the faces of a lion, an ox, a man, and an eagle (4:6–7). The four angelic beings embody the entire created order from the four corners of the earth (7:1; 20:8): land animals, birds, human beings, and the like. The eyes of the cherubim "all around" signify divine omniscience and their role as agents of God's will (4:8a). In an endless chorus, they sing a hymn identical to the one sung by the seraphim of Isaiah: "Holy, holy, holy is the Lord God, the All Powerful and Mighty One" (4:8b, author's translation; cf. Isa. 6:3); thus the reader is reminded that God is wholly separate from us and that only out of his mercy does the Creator meddle in the lives of sinful human beings.

The twenty-four elders join the litany of the four cherubim with their own acts of worship. They fall prostrate and throw down their laurels before the enthroned one (4:9–10). In the ancient world, it was a common ritual for magistrates to surrender their crowns to pay homage to the emperor. Here the elders offer their crowns not to Caesar but to the Creator. At stake is the question: Who is the real Lord of the universe? Who has true power? In a hymn of their own, the elders proclaim, "Our Lord and God! You alone are worthy of worship, honor and glory. It was your life-giving power that created the world and continues to sustain all creation" (4:11, author's translation).

5:1–15: Praise the slain Lamb. As though the second movement in a symphony, the celebration in the eschatological temple of God continues, with a reading of a scroll. Typically, in a Jewish synagogue liturgy, the seals on a Torah scroll are broken so that God's Word may be read to the whole congregation. However, this scroll in the right hand of the enthroned Creator cannot be opened or read (5:1). Even a being as powerful as the angel with the great voice must ask, "Who is worthy to break the seals and open the scroll?" (5:2). The silence that follows (5:3) and the godly lament of John (5:4; cf. Ezra 10:1, 6; Neh. 1:3–6) demonstrate that no living creature can read or execute the contents of the scroll. Since there is writing on the inside and the back (5:1), the scroll type is undoubtedly an *opistograph* ("written on both sides"), which was used with legal documents. Most likely this scroll is a last will and testament (cf. Ezek. 2:9–10; Dan. 8:26; 12:9; *1 Enoch* 81:2–3). When legal documents were sealed in the ancient world, though the internal contents were hidden, often a shorter summary was given on the back of a rolled-up scroll. Only the executor of the will, that is, the one who could accomplish the instructions of the author, was eligible to break open the scroll and read from it. It is possible, then, that on the inside of God's scroll is written his full plan of redemption, and on the back is a description of God's will as it was revealed partially over time in the history of Israel.

Who, then, is worthy of executing God's divine plan? Could it be the Lion from the tribe of Judah (Gen. 49:9) who is the Root of David (Isa. 11:1, 10; Jer. 23:5; cf. Rev. 22:16)? These two royal titles emphasize the authority of the Messiah to conquer and judge Israel's enemies. Perhaps he can read the scroll. Then suddenly the scene shifts from the Lion of Judah to the slain Lamb (5:6). Though "standing as if it had been slaughtered" (5:6 NRSV), this Lamb is paradoxically described as having "seven horns" (a symbol of perfect power) and "seven eyes" (a symbol of perfect omniscience through the Spirit). The Lamb shares the position of axis mundi, or "the cosmic center," with the Creator himself (5:6). In a radical redefinition of true power, the slain Lamb, not the Lion, is the one who actually takes the scroll (5:7) and one by one breaks its seals (6:1–8:1).

In response, the whole court falls prostrate before the Lord and the Lamb (5:8). The elders each hold a lyre (cf. Ps. 33:2–3; 43:4) and a golden bowl of incense (a temple utensil, but here a symbol of the saints' prayers), and with them they continue worshiping the Creator (4:8–11) by worshiping the Lamb (5:9–14). The new song is first sung by the elders (5:9–10). Then comes a chorus of countless angels with their own refrain (5:11–12), and finally the entire creative order joins with a doxology (5:13). The Lamb is exalted for his redemptive work on the cross. His death provides atonement for every tribe, language, people, and nation (5:9; cf. 1:5; 7:9).

The arrangement of God's heavenly court in concentric circles (that is, the throne at the center, followed by the circles of cherubim, the twenty-four elders, countless angels, and all creation) resembles the Greek amphitheater and parodies the Roman imperial court, which focused on the emperor and his surrounding entourage of advisors, courtiers, and friends. The collective visions of Revelation 4–5 function to directly challenge Rome's definition of power as empire and domination. In the first liturgical movement (4:1–11), power is defined as creative: it is life-giving (not life-destroying) and brings order (rather than causing chaos). In the second (5:1–15), power is defined as redemptive. The way of the Lamb is *faithful suffering*. It stands in stark contrast with the coercive, violent, and manipulative use of force, which characterizes the military might of Rome. True power belongs to the Lord, the Creator of the universe, and his Son, the Lamb, who takes away the sins of the world, and to those who worship them both.

B. The seven seals: Where is God when his people suffer? (6:1–8:1). 6:1–8: The Four Horsemen of the Apocalypse. In this next set of visions, the slain Lamb breaks the seals on the scroll (6:1) one by one to unveil the contents of God's redemptive plan. The breaking of the first four seals follows a set pattern: the Lamb opens a seal, the cherubim issue the command,

"Come," and a demonic rider on a colored horse proceeds to carry out the scroll's contents. Revelation's portrayal of riders on white, red, black, and pale green horses is taken from Zechariah 1:8–15 and 6:1–8. The Zechariah texts describe four riders on similarly colored horses or chariots who patrol the four corners of the earth and report to God that the empires of the world feel falsely secure. The four horsemen of Revelation, however, take on a much more direct role in the judgment of falsely secure nations. The riders represent evil forces that God allows to have some limited influence on human history.

The first rider, on a white horse, is a symbol of empire (6:2). The color white has so far been associated with the purity and victory of God's people (1:14; 2:17; 3:4; 4:4), but here the rider is a satanic parody of false conquest (the Greek verb for "conquer" is emphatically used twice in the same sentence: literally "He rode out to conquer as one who conquers") and of false endurance (the latter signified by the *stephanos*, "athlete's wreath"). The bow that the rider carries is a distinctly non-Roman weapon used in Greece, Anatolia, and the eastern Mediterranean, though most infamously among the Parthians, who bordered the Roman Empire's eastern frontier and whose cavalries had excellent archers. There was always a potential danger that the Parthians would break through the

Roman lines of defense and invade the western part of the empire. The vision of the first rider is a stark warning against those who put their hope in Rome or any other government for national security. Empires rise and empires fall. The only enduring kingdom is the one established by the slain Lamb (5:10).

The second rider, on a fiery red horse, is a symbol of violence, war, and bloodshed (6:3–4). The great (Roman) sword that he carries and his charge to "take away peace from the earth" is a blistering critique of the *pax Romana* (Latin for "Roman peace"). The Roman peace was both policy and ideology. Augustus Caesar boasted that the Roman military machine had established a peaceful order to disparate lands and united the entire civilized world. But peace enforced by the sword is no true peace, and the civil unrest that ensued under Rome's iron hand had been cataloged case after case by its own historians. One notorious example is the scandalous year (AD 69) of four succeeding emperors (Galba, Otho, Vitellius, and ultimately Vespasian) that almost tore the empire apart from within.

The third rider, on a black horse, is a symbol of economic crisis and injustice (6:5–6). The measuring scale and the inflated prices for wheat and barley (eight and five times the expected cost) signal a food shortage. A denarius, a day's wages, for either a quart of wheat or three quarts of barley would hardly feed a small family, and there would be no money left to buy olive oil and (cheap) wine (which

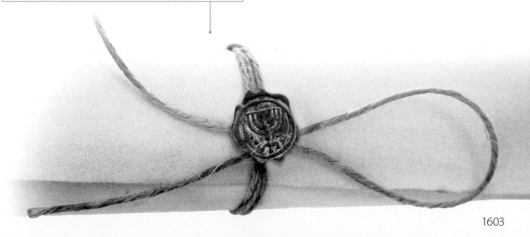

A lead bulla, or seal, with a menorah impression (Byzantine period). Beginning in Revelation 6:1, the Lamb opens a series of seven seals.

often replaced drinking water) despite their affordability. Even though through international trade the Roman economy made available all kinds of goods and services (see, e.g., the list of items in Rev. 18:11–14), access to them was disproportionate between the rich and poor. The former had easy access to luxury items, while the latter were unable to purchase basic staple foods. Both New Testament writers and Roman historians record several famines that devastated local grain supplies throughout the empire (Acts 11:28; Suetonius, *Claudius* 19; Tacitus, *Annals* 12.43), which could account for some economic woes of that day.

The fourth rider, on the pale green horse (6:7–8), unlike his predecessors actually has a name, "Death," and a sinister partner who comes right after him: "Hades" (the place of the dead). The last rider epitomizes the aftereffects of the first three cavaliers: wherever there is empire, violence, and economic crisis, death is sure to follow. The earthly beasts or wild animals, which probably fed off the carrion of bodies left in the wake of previous riders, complete the picture of chaos and divine judgment (cf. Ezek. 14:21; Jer. 15:3). Yet these forces of evil are not allowed to run amok. There is a constraint to the anarchy. The reach of the four riders is limited (by God) to a fourth of the world for this first cycle of judgments (6:8). So one by one, with each passing rider, God allows these false sources of security (i.e., government, warfare, a prosperous economy, and good health) to be the very means through which God judges the wicked but in the process also exposes the corrupt and fragile idols for what they are.

6:9–17: The fifth and sixth seals. The next two seals represent two different human responses to suffering. When the Lamb breaks open the fifth seal (6:9–11), John is astonished to see the souls of slaughtered martyrs under the altar of the heavenly temple, as if their blood were mixed in, and a part of, the sacrificial offering (Lev. 4:18; 8:15). These martyrs were killed because they proclaimed God's word and bore witness to Jesus (Rev. 1:9). From the cry

of Abel's blood spilled on the ground by Cain (Gen. 4:10) to the cries of Christians crucified and burned alive in the gardens of Nero, God's people have prayed, "How long, Sovereign Lord . . . until you judge [our enemies] and avenge [us]?" (6:10). Why has God not acted? This scene reveals God's answer to their prayers for justice (cf. Ps. 6:3; 35:17; 80:4). First, the altar tells us that God considers their sacrifice an act of true worship (cf. Rom. 12:1; Phil. 2:17). Moreover, their suffering has not been wasted but has a purpose; it is integral to a divine plan that will include even more joining their ranks until a certain number is reached (6:11). He has given them white robes of victory to reward their endurance and affirm their priestly roles (cf. Lev. 16:32).

When the Lamb opens the sixth seal (6:12–17), the scene shifts from the perennial problems of human history to the cosmic events that signal the final consummation of God's kingdom. A great earthquake, the sun turning dark as sackcloth, the moon becoming like blood, the stars falling from the sky, the sky splitting apart, and every mountain being thrown from its place (6:12–14) are examples of figurative language John borrows from apocalyptic traditions to describe creation under decay (Isa. 13:10–13; Joel 2:10, 30–31; Hab. 3:6; cf. Rom. 8:19–22). These "last days" began with the resurrection of Christ (Acts 2:17; Heb. 1:2) and reach their conclusion at his imminent return (Mark 13:24–27). Even then, human beings can remain unrepentant. From every segment of society, from kings to lowly slaves, there are people who would rather pray to the mountains to fall down and cover them or hide in the caves than cry out to the Lord and be saved (6:15–16; cf. Joel 2:32).

7:1–8:1: Worship interlude and the seventh seal. After the sixth seal is broken, there is an interlude of worship. The eschatological end is delayed by four angels (7:1), who—symbolizing a restraining force on lawlessness (2 Thess. 2:7)—hold back the winds on which the four demonic cavaliers ride (cf. Zech. 6:5). These angels also operate in conjunction with the worship and witness of the church. When the veil is lifted, we see that the church's presence in human history has had a sanctifying effect on the world. The angel who rises with the sun commands the other four not to harm creation (i.e., the earth, the sea, and even the trees; cf. Gen. 1:9–13) until every servant of God receives a signet seal (7:2). It was believed that Yahweh, like all kings, had a signet ring by which he authenticated decrees and marked what was his (Esther 8:8; Job 9:7; Sirach 17:22). God reins in the chaos for his sealed ones so that their mission can continue.

The 144,000 represent all saints from both the Old and the New Testament (see the introduction) and are listed here in a tribal census (7:4–7). Unlike other Old Testament lists of Israel's twelve tribes (Num. 1:5–15; 1 Chron. 2:1–2), conspicuously missing from Revelation's roster is Dan. The absence of Dan, who had a history and reputation for apostasy (1 Kings 12:28–30; *Testament of Dan* 5:6), serves as a warning that only those who persevere to the end will be saved (Rev. 2:7; 2:10–11). Sadly not all who start off in the Christian life finish it.

When the 144,000 appear again, they stand as a countless multitude whose diversity is evident, since individual persons can still be distinguished by nation, tribe, culture, and language and yet all are perfectly united in their litany to the Lord (7:9–10). This picture of the church triumphant provides hope for today's divided congregation. Here the people of God are one voice, dressed in white priestly robes (Rev. 6:11), holding palm branches (a symbol of homage to a king during his coronation; cf. Mark 11:8; 2 Maccabees 10:7). They shake the heavens by shouting, "Salvation belongs to our God, who is [both] the One seated on the throne and the Lamb!" (7:10, author's translation). Joining in the liturgy are the four cherubim, the twenty-four elders, and the myriad of angels of Revelation 4–5, who fall prostrate and sing their own doxology (7:11–12). Those robed in white who "come out of" the great tribulation

are not a persecuted group belonging to the distant future of a war-torn world (7:14). The grammar of this verse suggests that John and his readers are viewing this event as an ongoing situation that has already begun. The "great tribulation" that the Jewish apocalypses and Jesus himself said would happen in the last days (Dan. 12:1; Matt. 24:21) began with the resurrection of Christ and refers to the immediate trials faced by the church universal (Rev. 2:9–11). Believers who wash and whiten their robes are those who let suffering purify their faith and refine their character.

The next liturgical segment evokes images from the Festival of Booths (Lev. 23:34; Zech. 14:16; John 7:2), a weeklong holiday when Jews eat their meals in temporary booths or huts to commemorate how the tabernacle accompanied the Israelites through their wilderness wanderings during the exodus. God promises the faithful that he will permanently "dwell" with them (7:15 KJV; NIV "shelter them with his presence"; Greek *skēnoō* means literally "pitch a tent" over them; cf. Ezek. 37:26–28) and never let them go hungry or thirsty again, nor let the sun's heat fall on them (Isa. 49:10). Christ will shepherd (Ezek. 34:16, 23) and lead them to a place with living water (a symbol of eternal life; cf. John 4:14) where there is no more death or tears (Isa. 25:8). All will find perfect peace in the presence of the Lamb (7:17).

When the seventh seal breaks, appropriately there is silence (8:1). The eschatological hour and a half denotes a limited period of time before divine judgment can commence (Dan. 7:25; 9:27; Hab. 2:20), but here, as part of the liturgy, the silence is also a moment of reverent awe. Heaven is telling us, Be still and know the Godness of God (cf. Ps. 46:10).

Taken as a whole, the seven seals give a partial answer to the problem of theodicy (i.e., why a good and powerful God does not act immediately to end human suffering). They demonstrate that the origin of suffering and evil is complex. There are several degrees of separation from God, who once held the scroll

(4:1); to the slain Lamb, who takes it and breaks the seals (5:7; 6:1, 3, 5, 7, 9, 12; 8:1); to the cherubim, who give the command, "Come" (6:1, 3, 5, 7); to the four summoned riders who unleash each disaster (6:2, 4–5, 8); to the human agents who perpetuate the suffering caused by empire, violence, economic injustice, and death (6:15–16). In one sense, the seals affirm that God is in control of human history, that nothing happens outside his authority, and that suffering cannot affect our world unless he allows for it. On the other hand, to say that God is directly punishing sinners by causing them to become blind (cf. John 9:2–3) or receive cancer or lose their jobs and homes is to fail to understand the complexities of evil, much like Job's friends do (Job 2:11; 4:7–11; 8:3–6; 11:10–15). The degrees of separation in the agency of the seals demonstrate that God is *not* the direct cause of suffering. By his providential will, he allows sin to run its course, but for a redemptive purpose. His hope is that when people experience the consequences of sin, whether directly because of their personal actions or indirectly because we live in a fallen world where bad things happen, all will turn to Christ for deliverance. Mysteriously, God does not stop evil by suspending human freedom that contributes to it but rather turns evil into an unwitting actor of his design.

C. The seven trumpets: Why history belongs to the intercessors (8:2–11:19). **8:2–5: Prelude of prayer.** During a time of silence and prayer, the priest usually made an incense offering as part of the daily sacrifices of the Jerusalem temple (Mishnah *Tamid* 5.1–6; 6.1–3; 7.3). The priests typically sprinkled sacrificial blood on the altars of the outer temple courts (cf. Lev. 1:5) and later entered into the inner sanctuary to burn the incense on a separate altar before the Most Holy Place (cf. Exod. 30:1–9; Luke 1:8–12). In John's vision of the heavenly temple, there is only one altar, which fulfills both functions. For the fifth seal, John saw the slain martyrs at the base of the altar cry out: "How long . . . ?" (6:9–10). Here those same cries for justice and vindication rise up like incense and mix together with

prayers from all the saints (8:3). These prayers go directly to the Most Holy Place, where the throne of God resides, and God hears their every word (8:4). Not one prayer is wasted. Like the incense, each prayer is a fragrant offering to the Lord (cf. Ps. 141:2). The whole world feels the power of prayer when the angel ("of his presence"; Isa. 63:9) takes the golden censer, or thurible, and flings it on the earth (8:5). The crashes of thunder, flashes of lightning, and the earthquake are characteristics of the Sinai theophany (Exod. 19:16–17; 20:18–21) and tell the readers that as a result of prayer, God is making his presence known to all.

8:6–13: The first four trumpets. The seven angels who stand before God at the throne (8:2, 6) are arguably the same seven angels who represent the churches in Revelation 2–3. What does it mean, then, that these heavenly representatives of God's people are the ones who blow the trumpets and set loose the cataclysmic events to follow? As the church prays for and works toward God's kingdom on earth (cf. Matt. 6:10; Luke 11:2), it also contributes to that part of God's redemptive plan that allows for sin to run its course. Our prayers and witness open the possibility for divine judgment to break into our present reality, expose evil, and urge evildoers toward repentance. Sometimes people will simply not repent until they experience the pain of a world without God (cf. Rom. 1:24–32). But God can use suffering as an opportunity for unbelievers to repent and for believers to refine their faith.

With the blowing of the first trumpet, the heavenly liturgy moves forward with greater drama. John and his readers brace themselves for the next set of divine judgments. The account of the first four trumpets employs imagery from the Exodus plagues, which historically forced Pharaoh to release the Israelites from their captivity in Egypt. The ten plagues (Exodus 7–12) were designed to attack the various gods of the Egyptian pantheon, from the Nile River to Pharaoh himself, who was considered to be a living deity. One by one God defeated the idols of the Egyptian Empire and demonstrated once and for all that Yahweh is Lord over Egypt, the one true Creator, and the Redeemer of Israel (Exod. 9:14–16; 10:1–2). With the four trumpets, the same Creator and Redeemer exposes the idolatrous values of the Roman world.

The first trumpet unleashes hail and fire mixed with blood, which rain from heaven and burn up a third of the earth, a third of the trees, and all green grass (8:7). The disaster is reminiscent of the seventh Egyptian plague (hail and thunderstorm; Exod. 9:22–26) and the first (the Nile to blood; Exod. 7:17–21), which devastated the food and water supply. The Nile, with its irrigation canals and reservoirs, made Egypt the breadbasket of the Mediterranean and its economy prosperous. The Nile was turned to blood and the land judged to make Egypt experience its vulnerability and need for God. The Roman Empire was founded on bloodshed, and it could only reap more blood as it burned up the lands with its wars (Josephus, *Jewish War* 6.404–7). There are numerous other examples of how the land was devastated and the food supply cut short in the first century. (See the discussion on the third seal above.) Whatever material losses we experience in life, they should awaken our dependency on God.

The second trumpet features a burning mountain being thrown into the sea, which turns a third of the sea to blood, kills a third of the sea creatures, and destroys a third of the ships (8:8). This disaster evokes again the first Egyptian plague (the

Nile to blood) and especially the aftermath, in which all the fish die (Exod. 7:21). We are also reminded of Jeremiah 51:25, where God promises to make the "destroying mountain," Babylon, into a "burned-out mountain." Here the burning mountain is Rome, which the Jewish people considered a second Babylon (Dead Sea Scrolls, *Pesher Habakkuk* 1.6, 12–13; Rev. 18:8). The destruction of the ships in the sea is a symbol of Rome's decline as an economic power (Rev. 18:19), since the sea was a means for prosperous trade and international commerce. Those remembering the eruption of Mount Vesuvius in AD 79 and the scorched lands and dead life in its wake would find this vision especially terrifying.

The third trumpet focuses on a huge burning star falling from heaven and into a third of the earth's rivers and springs (8:10). The star's name is Wormwood (a particularly bitter herb

The type of trumpet introduced in Revelation 8:6 may be either a shofar made from a ram's horn or a long metal horn like the two in this relief that are being blown to announce the victor of a gladiator contest (first century BC).

used medicinally, of which one ounce can treat up to 524 gallons of water [Theophrastus, *History of Plants* 1.12.1]), and it has the effect of poisoning the water supply (8:11). As with the previous two, this disaster evokes the first Egyptian plague, but in this case the aftermath, in which the smell of the Nile makes the water undrinkable (Exod. 7:21). The event is also a reversal of the miracle at Marah (which means "bitter" in Hebrew), when Moses—because Israel was grumbling—threw a piece of wood into the region's bitter waters and turned them sweet (Exod. 15:23–25). The third trumpet vision assures the church that Rome's political power is in decline (like a star falling from its exalted place; cf. Isa. 14:12–15) yet also warns that with political decline often comes moral decadence. The Roman lifestyle of luxury can still pollute the church and lead it to the kind of ethical compromises that were taught by Balaam, Jezebel, and the Nicolaitans of Revelation 2–3. Also, not all people are happy with Rome. Those crushed by the Roman military machine are embittered, grumbling, and dying, and this spirit of bitterness can also infect the church.

The fourth trumpet strikes a third of the sun, moon, and stars with darkness to such an extent that there is no light for a third of the day and night (8:12). This catastrophe recalls the ninth Egyptian plague (darkness; Exod. 10:21–29), which blotted out the supreme god of Egypt, Amon-Re (the sun deity), as well as Pharaoh, his divine son and earthly representative. The plague of darkness demonstrated that Egypt does not rule the world. It also crushed the pride of Pharaoh's court magicians, who claimed that they could read the stars and from them discern Egypt's destiny. John's community would have understood the fourth trumpet as an indictment against the imperial cult and its inability to save, guide, or help its devotees to manage their destiny. Despite legends surrounding the birth and death of Augustus Caesar with celestial signs (Suetonius, *Augustus* 94.4; 100.4), God, not the emperor, is the author of all history.

He alone has the power to judge the Roman Empire and cover it in darkness (cf. Amos 8:9; Mark 13:24).

This vision is suddenly interrupted by the sight of an eagle flying overhead (8:13). The eagle symbolizes God's imminent judgment swooping down on Israel's enemies (Jer. 48:40–42), but it was also the insignia of Rome (2 Esdras 11:1–12:39; Josephus, *Jewish War* 5.48). The eagle's interruption places some restraint on the reach of the previous trumpet visions. Before God judges Rome completely, he will use Rome as an agent of divine justice to the world (cf. how God used Babylon to judge the nations like a vulture or eagle in Hab. 1:8). But the eagle inspires both dread (for the unrepentant) and hope (for God's people). In the midst of judging a sinful world, God will strengthen his people through the trials to come. He will mount them up on eagle's wings and sustain them with the winds of his Spirit (Exod. 19:4; Isa. 40:31).

9:1–21: The fifth and sixth trumpets. The fifth trumpet is the first of three "woes" (8:13), or laments, that signal a heightened intensity in the cycle of plagues. If the first four plagues affected the natural world—the earth and trees, the sea, the rivers, and the sky—the last three plagues will attack humanity more directly. When the fifth trumpet is blown, a chain of events starts but centers on the actions of a dense swarm of demonic locusts unleashed from a bottomless pit or abyss (i.e., a prison for evil spirits; Luke 8:31; 2 Pet. 2:4; *1 Enoch* 10:4–14). The swarm is reminiscent of the eighth Egyptian plague (locusts; Exod. 10:12–20) but also possibly the third (gnats; 8:16–19) and fourth (flies; 8:20–24), since locusts, gnats, and flies were all insects thought to originate in the belly of the earth and could cover the land like a blanket of darkness (Exod. 10:15; Joel 2:2, 10; cf. Rev. 8:12). The demonic locusts of Revelation, unlike the locusts that devastated Egypt's farming lands, are not allowed to damage the grass, trees, or any vegetation (9:3). But like the flies and gnats that bit the Egyptians, the locusts are given the power to torment (9:5) unbelieving humanity for a limited time (symbolized by the nonliteral five months; 9:5, 10). But they cannot kill. Meanwhile, God's faithful who have his seal of protection (9:4; 7:3–4; Ezek. 9:3–6) are not harmed, much as Israel was spared from certain plagues against Egypt (Exod. 9:4, 26; 10:23; 11:7; 12:23).

So what are we to make of this nightmarish vision? Certainly these are no ordinary locusts, since they are described with the combined features of animals, human beings, weapons of war, and other fantastic images from the apocalyptic imagination (9:7–10; cf. Joel 2:4–7). The angel of the abyss, whose name is Abaddon (Hebrew for "destruction"; cf. Job 26:6; Prov. 15:11) and Apollyon (Greek for "destroyer"), commands the army. This is a spiritual battle. Deuteronomy 28 warns that in the last days God's people will suffer through the Egyptian plagues because of their idolatry (28:27, 38–39, 42, 60), but Revelation has applied this text to the world at large and the idolatrous values that Roman society propagates. The pain the demonic locusts inflict is due to the unseen and hidden consequences of sin (Deut. 28:27). Evil and suffering, like the locusts, have a human face (Rev. 9:7–8). When the veil is lifted on the destiny of rebellious humankind, John sees how those who embrace the fallen values of the secular world are tortured from within by the very greed, corruption, lust, bitterness, anger, loneliness, and inner turmoil that are generated from life apart from God. According to Deuteronomy 28, the plagues cause "madness, blindness and confusion of mind" (28:28). Idolaters will have no rest and tremble in despair; they will be filled with constant dread, with life suspended in doubt (Deut. 28:65–66). The emotional, psychological, and spiritual torment is so great that people seek and long for death but cannot die (Rev. 9:6). Any life that shuts out God, even one as potentially comfortable and luxurious as what Rome had to offer, cannot satisfy, but instead makes people slaves to a much wider evil (cf. Deut. 28:68).

The sixth trumpet, or second woe (9:13–21), brings John and his readers closer to the final judgment of the unredeemed. The account of the sixth trumpet evokes several images: the tenth and most devastating Egyptian plague (the death of the firstborn; Exod. 12:29–32), the attempt by Pharaoh to rout Israel's escape with his chariot army (Exod. 14:7–14), and his unrepentant response to God's judgments (Exod. 8:15, 32). There is also a strong literary and theological connection between the fifth and sixth trumpets. The fifth trumpet's swarm of countless demonic locusts (9:7–10) shares characteristics with the sixth trumpet's demonic armies of 200 million riders (9:17–19). Both armies are composed of fantastic monsters with hybrid animal-human traits; both draw on horses and riders as symbols of power; both are released by fallen angelic beings (9:1–2, 14–15); both have tails that inflict injury (though the locusts cannot kill, while the demonic horses can); and both function as agents of judgment against idolatry (9:20). Also, the sixth trumpet vision consummates the process of inner spiritual decay described by the fifth. What began as moral corruption and material excess in the fifth trumpet culminates in the sixth, with the wages of sin leading to actual death (cf. Rom. 3:23). The fire, smoke, and sulfur—whose red, dark blue, and yellow hues parallel the breastplate colors of the cavaliers (9:17)—are Old Testament metaphors for the fatal judgment of the ungodly and their eternal separation from God (Gen. 19:24; Isa. 34:9–10; Ezek. 38:22).

The infinite wave of demonic hordes invading westward from the Euphrates River (9:14) would have undoubtedly stirred up the deep-seated Roman fears of a potential Parthian invasion (see Rev. 6:2). Though John was not predicting the future conquest of Rome by the Parthians, he was nevertheless taking the political anxieties of the Roman world and using them to produce a scene of horror. John's readers would have also noted that the Euphrates was traditionally the place of Israel's enemies. The Old Testament prophets warned that God would use the Assyrians (Isa. 7:20; 8:5–8), the Babylonians (2 Kings 24:7; Jer. 46:2), and the Persians (Dan. 5:28; 11:1–2) from "beyond the river" or "from the north" to bring divine judgment to the world. However, when the veil is lifted, Rome's demise is not due to a military invasion from enemies on its external eastern border but rather from the inner moral corrosion of its leading citizens.

First-century Jewish reflections on the exodus event posited another purpose of the plagues: to bring Pharaoh and the Egyptians to repentance (Philo, *Life of Moses* 1.95; cf. Josephus, *Jewish Antiquities* 2.293–95). But, tragically, instead of repenting, "he [Pharaoh] hardened his heart" against God (Exod. 7:13, 22; 8:15, 19, 32; 9:7). John sees this tragedy of hardened hearts repeated in the human response to the seven trumpet plagues. Nonbelievers continue to worship idols that can neither see nor hear nor truly help them in their hour of need (Rev. 9:20). As God strips away every idol through the plagues until no alternative sources of security are left, we witness the ultimate expression of pride and human sinfulness: people, even in outright misery (9:6), would rather die than turn to God for deliverance (9:21).

10:1–11:19: Witness interlude and the seventh trumpet. There is a two-part interlude of witness between the sixth and seventh trumpets that keeps John's audience in further suspense.

In the first part (10:1–11), a powerful angel descends from heaven and stands on the earth. He is immense, with one foot on the sea and the other on land (10:1–2; cf. Dan. 12:5–7). Unlike the other angels mentioned in Revelation so far, this angel shares divine characteristics associated only with God and the Son of Man (9:1). The angel is clothed with a cloud and has legs of fire (10:1; cf. Exod. 13:20–22; Dan. 7:13), his face is like the sun (Rev. 1:16; cf. Dan. 10:6), a rainbow hangs over his head (cf. Gen. 9:13–16; Ezek. 1:26–28), and his voice is thunderous like a roaring lion (cf. Amos 3:7; 10:7; Exod. 19:16–17; 20:18–21). The being is likely "the angel of Yahweh" (NIV "angel of the LORD") who acted as a representative of God himself (Exod. 3:2–12; Acts 7:35, 38).

Just when we would expect that this godlike titan will command the seventh trumpet to be blown and human history as we know it will end, he instead seals up the seven thunders (cf. Dan. 12:4) and reverses their impending judgments (Rev. 10:4).

Before the seventh trumpet heralds a new age when "time will be no more" (10:6; NIV "There will be no more delay!"), the church has a mission. The angel gives a "little scroll" to John, and he is asked to eat the scroll—that is, completely identify with its contents—and proclaim its message to the world (10:9–10). It tastes as sweet as honey but is bitter in the stomach (10:9; cf. Ezek. 2:8–3:3; 3:14). In the same way that Ezekiel received God's word with joy but also an impossible mission to proclaim judgment to a hardened people, John and his churches are called to preach a sweet and bitter gospel that offers grace yet demands repentance. In light of the Roman Empire's increasing hostility against Christianity, theirs will be a mission embittered by suffering and even death. The trumpets by themselves cannot bring people to repentance. The trumpets only provide the context for people to see sin in its ugliest form. To repent, the world needs the church to be a prophetic witness (cf. Ezek. 3:16–21).

In the second part of the interlude (11:1–14), we hear the same message as in the first but with increased drama. The two witnesses (11:3; cf. Deut. 17:6; 19:15), who are given authority to prophesy against many peoples, languages, and even kings (11:11), represent the entire prophetic tradition in the history of God's people, from Israel (symbolized by the olive trees; 11:4; cf. Hos. 14:5–6; Rom. 11:24–25) to the church (symbolized by the menorahs; 1:20). The prophets of both Testaments received heavy persecution and died in martyrdom (11:7–10; cf. Heb. 11:32–40). God's people, however, refuse to use the same tools of violence that their enemies employ. Proclamation and witness are the weapons of choice for the church (1:16; 2:12, 16), which uses the fire of God's preached word to consume evildoers (11:5; cf. Jer. 5:14; 1 Kings 18.36). The ministry of the church can bring judgment to the unrepentant (11:6), much like the ten plagues did against Egypt, or the drought against Ahab's rule during the days of Elijah (1 Kings 17:1; James 5:17–18). The 1,260 days (which equal 42 months, or 3.5 years) are not literal (cf. Dan. 7:25; 12:7). These numbers are a symbolic reminder that the time of the empire (i.e., the time of the beast; see Rev. 11:7; 13:1–18) and the period of the church's persecution are fixed. God will not let his people suffer indefinitely and without purpose. Instead, God knows his own, for he has John measure the temple, the altar, and the worshipers to demarcate the truly faithful (11:1). Only those at the altar, who genuinely sacrifice and serve the Lord, will be vindicated at the resurrection (11:11–12). The rest, who are in the outer courts, away from the inner sanctuary, are fakes (11:2). These apostates will

be judged along with the rest of the sinning city (11:13). As the second woe passes (11:14), and with the third about to come, the interlude ends with the wicked having to give glory to God (Dan. 4:37).

The seventh trumpet gives John, the readers, and all Christians a partial glimpse of history's end and God's eternal reign over the entire cosmos (11:15–19; cf. Matt. 24:31; 1 Cor. 15:52–58). The kingdom of the Lord God Almighty and of his Son, the Messiah, is shown in its fullest and most glorious splendor (11:15, 17). God's kingdom, which has been moving throughout the mission of Israel and the church to recapture what was lost to sin, has finally swallowed up the kingdom of the world (11:15). Like the rising of the sun after a long and painful night, the years of endurance and faithful witness by God's people have reached their reward: the saints will be raised to eternal life, the wicked judged, and God's glory, which once was confined to an earthly temple and ark (11:19), is finally opened for the entire universe to bask in its light (11:19). The darkness has ended forever. This is God's future promise to the church and our present source of thanksgiving as we preach the gospel until our Lord's return (11:17).

D. The empire unveiled as an agent of Satan (12:1–15:4). 12:1–18: The celestial woman and the dragon. The scene opens with a great sign. a woman pregnant with a son (12:2). This child will become the messianic savior of humankind (12:5; cf. Ps. 2:9). The reader familiar with the nativity story may be tempted to identify this woman as Mary the mother of Jesus (Luke 1:26–35). But a closer reading shows that the woman is a heavenly personification of all God's people throughout the history of Israel and the church. Clothed with the sun, moon, and twelve stars, the cosmic woman represents Jacob, Rachel, and his twelve sons (12:1; cf. Gen. 37:9). She is also captive Israel, whose sufferings, like the birth pangs of a pregnant mother, anticipate the apocalyptic arrival of God's kingdom (12:2; cf. Isa. 13:6, 8; Jer. 6:24). She is ultimately the church, who bears witness to Jesus even in the face of death (12:17). It is through the lineage, history, and faithfulness of God's people that the Lord's Messiah was born.

Now enters the celestial dragon (12:3). This one is gigantic, fiery red (a symbol of bloodshed and violence; Rev. 6:4), with seven heads (a symbol of mock perfection), having ten horns (a symbol of false power; cf. Dan. 7:7–8), and wearing seven royal crowns (symbols of political authority, unlike the *stephanos*, or athlete's laurel, worn by the woman; 12:1). The dragon is the anticreator, who disrupts the order of the heavens with chaos by flinging a third of the stars to the earth (12:4; Gen. 1:14–19). As the ancient serpent in the Garden of Eden (Gen. 3:1–6), it deceives (2:9) human agents to do its dirty work (13:1–18). As Satan (2:9, 13; 3:9), the devil, he accuses the saints within the heavenly courtroom of God (12:10; cf. Job 1:6–12). But with Christ's triumph of the cross and resurrection (12:5), the accuser has been forced out of God's heavenly court (12:7) and is no longer able to prosecute believers, since the blood of the Lamb atones for sins (12:10–11). He fails to devour the messianic child (12:4–5) and cannot stop the church (12:13–18). Defeat is inevitable, and the dragon knows it! (12:12).

The account of the dragon, the woman, and her son bears a literary resemblance to other combat myths in the ancient world. (For further reading, see Collins, 53–85.) The Egyptian saga tells of the mother goddess Isis, who, pursued by the red dragon Set, escapes to an island and bears the sun god Horus. In the Babylonian epic *Enuma Elish* (literally "When On High," which are the first words of the text), Marduk, god of light, kills the seven-headed dragon Tiamat in a heavenly war. But the most familiar combat myth for John's readers was that of the Greek and Roman goddess Leto, who, while pregnant, is pursued by the dragon Python. After Poseidon hides her on an island, Leto gives birth to Apollo. Apollo grows into a formidable warrior, vanquishes Python, and becomes a paradigmatic deity for the Roman emperors Augustus, Nero,

and Domitian. All these stories share a common climactic end: the hero defeats evil by violently slaying the monster.

Unlike these ancient heroes, however, Christ and the church do *not* use weapons of violence to conquer the enemy. They overcome the dragon through the sword of God's word (Rev. 1:16; 2:12, 16), by the blood of the Lamb, and by faithful suffering (12:11, 17). They defeat the dragon by freeing its human agents from sin's control and helping humanity to repent (Rev. 9:20–21; 16:9–11). The church is called to return evil with good (Rom. 12:14–21). Like the Israelites who were rescued from the Red Sea (12:15–16; cf. Exod. 14:26–29; 15:19), like the wilderness generation who were nourished in the desert (12:6, 14; cf. Exod. 16:12–13; Ps. 105:40–41), and like the returning exiles who were carried on eagles' wings back to Zion (12:14; Isa. 40:31; cf. Exod. 25:20), God's people are completely sustained and empowered by the Spirit in their battle with the dragon. Because they are not afraid to die (12:11), God can use them to do his work. John and his communities have joined the fray *midstory*, and this vision ends with the dragon poised defiantly on the shores of the sea, frustrated at its inability to kill the woman and the messianic son, and determined to destroy the woman's next generation of offspring (12:17–18).

13:1–18: The beasts of the sea and earth. In Revelation 12, Satan was unveiled as *the* force of evil in our world, the phantom menace behind human history who wages war against God's people. In Revelation 13, the dragon calls forth two legendary creatures, Leviathan from the sea (13:1) and Behemoth from the earth (13:11), as its agents of suffering and sin. According to Jewish tradition, these beasts were created on the fifth day, and their separation between the sea and the land was symbolic of God's establishing order to the primordial chaos (Gen. 1:21; Job 40:15–19; 41:1–2; 4 Ezra 6:49–52). Here, however, we have a sinister reversal, as the dragon summons both creatures from their domains to unleash chaos onto the created world.

The beast from the sea clearly resembles the dragon and likewise has seven heads and ten horns, but more diadem crowns (i.e., ten on its horns compared with the seven on the dragon's heads, emphasizing the beast's political might; 13:1; 12:3). Its resemblance to and commissioning by the dragon (13:2) suggest that the beast serves Satan. This beast combines the qualities of the four separate monsters of Daniel 7:1–8 into one: the body of a leopard, the feet of a bear, and the mouth of a lion, and ten horns (13:2). In Daniel's visions, each represents an earthly empire (possibly Babylonians, Medes, Persians, and Greeks) that occupied and persecuted Israel at various points in history. The horn of Daniel's fourth beast, which boasts "great things" (Dan. 7:20 KJV, RSV), is the Seleucid Antiochus IV Epiphanes, whose program to outlaw Judaism and Hellenize the Jews (1 Maccabees 1:41–64; 2 Maccabees 6:1–11) ignited a war for Judean independence that lasted approximately three and a half years, or forty-two months (168–65 BC; cf. Dan. 7:25).

This amalgamated monster symbolizes Roman imperial rule. The heads represent the imperial family, and the head that has a "fatal wound" (13:3, 12) is an allusion to the "revival of Nero" myth (Latin *Nero redivivus*), an urban legend that the slain Nero (who committed suicide by stabbing a sword into his throat; 13:14) would rise again to reconquer the Roman world. Despite the lethal wound to one of the heads, it is the *entire* beast that is healed (13:3, 12, 14; the distinction between part and whole—i.e., the head's fatal injury and the entire beast's recovery—is clearer in the Greek). Thus, after Nero's suicide (AD 68), Rome survived four emperors (Galba, Otho, Vitellius, and Vespasian) who vied for power. What looked like anarchy and a mortal blow would be followed by a remarkable recovery when Vespasian established the Flavian dynasty. Roman civilization would flourish again. Rome had united the known world by the sword and maintained civic order despite internal conflict. The empire must

have seemed like an unstoppable juggernaut. No wonder the ancient world worshiped Rome and wondered, "Who is like the beast? Who can wage war against it?" (13:4).

Like the mouth of the beast that bragged "great things" (13:5 KJV; cf. the little horn of Dan. 7:20) and blasphemed against God (13:6), emperors promoted their own glory by establishing the imperial cult in almost every major city throughout the Mediterranean. Caesars were given divine names like Apollo, Zeus, "our lord and god," "son of god," and "savior," and were praised for bringing a "gospel of peace" to newly annexed lands. Christians who refused to participate in emperor worship were persecuted (13:15; cf. 11:7–8). But just like Antiochus's tyrannical reign over Judea was limited to forty-two months (Dan. 7:25), the days of Roman dominance over God's people are numbered

The Roman emperor Nero, who died in AD 68. Legends surrounding Nero's return may be in the background of John's description of the beast in Revelation 13.

(13:5). Meanwhile, God does not bring an immediate end to suffering (13:10a; cf. Jer. 15:2) but calls for endurance and faithfulness from among the elect (13:10b).

The second beast speaks with the authority of the dragon and promotes the worldwide veneration of the first beast (13:11–12). The second beast symbolizes the wealthy social elite of Asia Minor, its magistrates, city officials, and trade guilds, who not only held political office but were also priests in the imperial cult. They erected imperial temples, set up "the image" of the emperor on statues and other icons (13:15; cf. Exod. 32:1–35), and sponsored extravagant festivals. Since the success of the festivals guaranteed political favors from Rome, those who refused to participate in the imperial cult (like the churches of Smyrna, Pergamum, and Philadelphia; 2:8–17; 3:7–13) "could not buy or sell," since they were ostracized by the trade guilds (13:17).

The "mark," or slave brand (13:17), of 666 on the right hand or forehead of the beast parodies the signet seal (7:3; 9:4; 14:1) on God's people. Contrary to popular notions that 666 is a physical tattoo, the mark of the beast is figurative. It means that God knows who belongs to Satan. The number 666 is an example of the ancient practice *gematria*, which assigns a number to a person by adding the numerical equivalent of each letter in his or her name. For instance, "Jesus" in Greek (*Iēsous*) adds up to 888 (see *Sibylline Oracles* 1.324–30). John writes that the number or name (3:17) of the beast is a man's and that it requires wisdom to decode it (13:18). The best candidate is Emperor Nero, whose name transliterated into the Hebrew *Neron Caesar* (*nrwn qsr*) adds up to 666. Nero infamously had Christians crucified, burnt alive, and torn by wild animals (Tacitus, *Annals* 15.44.2–8; cf. Heb. 11:36–38). Those with Nero's number would be citizens loyal to Rome who carried on his legacy of corruption, persecution, and vainglory. Alternatively, the number 666 could simply designate sinful humanity. Six is one short of seven, perfection. Therefore, 666

would be complete or utter imperfection and sinfulness (Irenaeus, *Against Heresies* 5.28.2–3).

Although the word "antichrist" is not used anywhere in the book of Revelation, many Christians have thought of the first beast as an antichrist figure, importing the term from John's letters (1 John 2:18, 22; 4:3; 2 John 1:7). This is appropriate as long as one remembers that an antichrist is anyone or anything that takes the place of Christ as Lord. There were many antichrists in John's day, and he expected more (1 John 2:18). The beast of the sea has parodied the death and resurrection of Christ, with its fatal head wound and miraculous recovery. The beast of the earth appears as a lamb with two horns. They try to imitate the slain Lamb, but fail. The empire had its gospel (the *pax Romana*). It claimed to be the world's savior, and the world believed it. But the peace that Rome brought to disparate lands was wrought by slaughter and violence; its prosperity was at the cost of poverty and injustice for others. Roman luxury led to moral decay and decadence. Any good that humanity attempts outside the agency and authority of God easily turns demonic.

14:1–5: Mount Zion descending. It often seems that the dragon and his beasts are winning the war against the saints (13:7). But in Revelation 14, we are asked to take a sacred pause and place our immediate disheartening experiences within a larger, more epic story. The church has been riding the ripple effects of the cross and resurrection for the past two millennia, and this victorious journey will reach its zenith when the followers of the slain Lamb celebrate the end of evil and the beginning of eternity.

The Lamb standing on Mount Zion with the army of 144,000 is a fulfillment of Old Testament messianic expectations that God would install Israel's king, his Son, on the throne in Jerusalem, and his Anointed One would bring decisive victory over Israel's enemies (Ps. 2:1–12; Isa. 24:23; *4 Ezra* 13:29–50). Mount Zion was the southern mountainous area of Jerusalem, site of Solomon's temple, and eventually represented the dwelling place of the Lord and his people (Ps. 132:13–18; 135:21). In Revelation, Zion is a new and heavenly Jerusalem (cf. Heb. 12:22–23) that descends on the earth in glorious splendor (3:12; 21:2). The 144,000 (as in Rev. 7:4) represent the entire people of God in both Testaments. They are *not* modern Israel. The kingdom that is consummated from Mount Zion is eschatological and transcendent. The new song is sung not on earth but from heaven (14:3) and by all God's angelic courtiers (cf. 5:9). The song celebrates the redemptive sacrifice of the slain Lamb and his rightful coronation as part of the Godhead (14:3; cf. 5:12–14). The church is invited to learn and join this new song. Like the pure bride on the day of her wedding (21:2; cf. Isa. 37:22) and like ritually pure warriors on the eve of battle (14:4; cf. Lev. 15:16–18; 1 Sam. 21:5), God's people are ready to worship because they have lived out their lives in holiness, moral purity, and complete fidelity to Christ.

14:6–13: Gospel of repentance. The next set of visions is three angelic pronouncements. The first angel proclaims an eternal gospel that is good news to some and bad news to others (14:6). For those who respond to the gospel (14:7; cf. 5:9; 7:9), their long-awaited vindication is indeed good news. For those who refuse to repent, a terrifying judgment ensues (11:9–14). The second angel announces proleptically that Rome has fallen (14:8a; cf. 18:1–24). Babylon was a symbol for Rome (cf. 1 Pet. 5:13; Dead Sea Scrolls, *Pesher Habakkuk* 2.11–12); both nations had been not only *agents* of God's judgment (cf. Jer. 25:8–11) but also *objects* of judgment (cf. Jer. 25:12–14). God is now stopping the wine of immoral passion (14:8b; cf. 17:2) that stemmed from the Roman lifestyle of wealth and luxury. The city will be judged; its horrific end is described in greater detail in 17:1–18.

The third angel declares that those who participate in the imperial cult and embrace the idolatrous values of the world will experience "the wine of God's fury," or God's just response to evil (14:9–10; cf. Jer. 25:15–29). Wine was often diluted with water to reduce its potency so people could drink and revel further. But the cup of God's wrath is undiluted, his final judgment unmitigated (14:10). For those who drink of this cup, there will be no Sabbath rest, no true *shalom*, no peace (14:11; cf. Heb. 3:10–19). Thus, the godly should remain "faithful to Jesus" (the Greek phrase can also be translated as "faith in Jesus"; 14:12).

14:14–16: Grain harvest of the righteous. When Christ appears again as the one like the Son of Man (14:14; cf. 1:12–20; Dan. 7:13–14), he comes as a victor (symbolized by the golden laurel; cf. 1 Cor. 9:24–27), as a divine figure (symbolized by the cloud theophany; cf. Exod. 24:15–18), and as a judge for the eschatological harvest (symbolized by the sickle; cf. Joel 3:13). Jesus promised that he would return to gather the elect as a farmer reaps a grain harvest (Matt. 13:36–43; Mark 13:26–27). The command to reap comes from the inner sanctuary (14:15; cf. 1 Thess. 4:16), which stands for God himself, since no one in heaven except the Father, not even the Son, knows the day and hour of final judgment (Matt. 24:36; Mark 13:32). The harvesting of the righteous is an image of final salvation, where seeds of the gospel sown by the church (11:3–13; 14:6) bear fruit over the entire earth (14:16; cf. John 4:36).

14:17–20: Grape harvest of the wicked. The fate of the wicked evokes Old Testament judgment oracles where the armies of the Lord trample over their enemies like those who tread over grapes (Isa. 18:5–7; Jer. 25:30; 51:33; cf. Lam. 1:15). The ripeness of the grapes demonstrates that sin has run its course (Joel 3:13) and the time for repentance has passed (Amos 8:2). Before chaos can consume all creation (Gen. 6:5–7; 19:12–13), God breaks into history to end evil's reign. The unrepentant are pictured as harvested grapes, cast into "the great winepress of God's wrath" (14:19–20). The juices are the blood of the wicked (cf. Isa. 63:2–6). Ancient winepresses in Israel were made of stone and built into the ground. Grapes were pressed by foot, and their juices flowed downward through grooves into a collecting vat. This vat is overflowing to cover 1,600 stadia, or about 184 miles. The area bathed in blood would cover all of Palestine (from Tyre in the north to Egypt in the south) and immerse a person as high as their chest ("as high as the horses' bridles"; 14:20). It is a gruesome scene; yet God is neither sadistic nor cruel. The scene speaks more to the revulsion of sin than to the violence of God. Such horror serves as a warning to the Christian community, that to side with the beast is to abandon God and resign oneself to a fate worse than death. The winepress is outside the Holy City (cf. Zech. 14:2–5), that is, outside the reach of God's grace and salvation. Those who are caught in the winepress are reaping the consequences of their violent rejection of the gospel.

15:1–4: Song of the new exodus. The celestial opera that began with two great signs in heaven—the cosmic woman (12:1) and the red dragon (12:3)—ends here with a third great sign: seven angels with seven plagues (15:1). The seven angels represent the churches in Asia Minor (1:20), and they also symbolize the church universal, whose prayers and witness play a key role in unveiling God's judgments on the world (8:2, 6). Those who have conquered the beast with their faithful suffering are about to sing the anthem of the Lamb (15:2).

With one voice, the saints from every generation praise both the all-powerful Creator and the slain Redeemer for their great works of salvation (15:3; cf. 5:9–14). The song of the Lamb is modeled after the Song of Moses (cf. Exod. 15:1–18) but not limited to it, for the Lamb's is a composite of several Old Testament texts (Deut. 32:4; Ps. 98:1–2; 111:2–9; Jer. 10:7; 16:19; Amos 4:13) celebrating the entire redemptive history of God. Just as the Lord delivered the Israelites from Pharaoh (likened to Leviathan in Isa. 30:7; 51:9–10) at the Red Sea (Exod. 14:26–30), God has saved his people forever by defeating the dragon, the beast, and their minions. In the old exodus, the faithful passed through the sea, but in the new, God has completely subdued the sea (often a symbol of cosmic evil) (Rev. 4:6; cf. Ezek. 1:22). The fire alludes to the wheels of flame and the fiery rivers that flow from God's chariot-throne (Dan. 7:9–10). Together the crystal sea and fire testify to the Spirit's reordering of creation (cf. Gen. 1:1–2, 6–8; Ps. 74:13–14).

E. The seven bowls: Why God delays ultimate justice until the end (15:5–16:21). **15:5–8: Tabernacle prelude.** John's attention is now drawn to that part of the heavenly temple called "the tabernacle of the covenant law" (15:5). If the earthly tabernacle represented for Israel a better way of meeting God than previously, in the burning bush, the pillar of fire, a cloud of thunder, or an unapproachable mountain (Exod. 25:8–9), then the heavenly tabernacle, with its curtains open so that the ark is visible (Rev. 15:5; cf. 11:19), anticipates a further step. A revolutionary new way for believers to commune with God is the resurrection (21:1–5). But before this can take place, God's ultimate justice for the world must be executed through the last cycle of bowl judgments (15:8). Seven angels dressed in priestly, ceremonially clean, bright linen robes (15:6; cf. Exod. 28:40–43) receive the libation bowls from the cherubim within the tabernacle (cf. Exod. 29:40). When the angels pour out the wine offering, it becomes the wine of God's wrath (15:7; 16:19; cf. Jer. 25:15–29).

16:1–9: The first four bowls. The seven bowls recapitulate the events unleashed by the previous cycles of the seven seals (6:1–8:1) and the seven trumpets (8:2–11:19). Yet the bowls have closer parallels with the trumpets than with the seals. Like the seven trumpets, the bowls modify the Egyptian plagues to fit the Roman context. Like the trumpet sequence, the first bowl judgment is unleashed on earth (16:1; cf. 8:7), the second in the sea (16:3; cf. 8:8), the third in the rivers and fountains (16:4; cf. 8:10), the fourth in the sky, affecting celestial bodies (16:8; cf. 8:12), the fifth in the demonic realm (16:10; cf. 9:1), the sixth beyond the Euphrates River (16:12; cf. 9:14), and the seventh at the eschatological end of human history (16:17; cf. 11:15).

The seven bowls of God's wrath are poured out at the command of a loud voice from the inner sanctuary of the temple (16:1). This is God's voice (cf. Isa. 66:6) issuing commands to the seven angels from the throne room. The key to understanding the bowls is the principle of *lex talionis* (the law of retribution), illustrated in Jeremiah 14:16: to those who spill or pour out blood, God says, "I will pour out their own wickedness on them" (NLT). As the unrepentant are heading to their final destiny, they begin to reap the same sins that they have sown in others.

The first libation bowl that is poured out inflicts "ugly, festering" sores on the earth's inhabitants (16:1–2). It is reminiscent of the sixth Egyptian plague, which unleashed boils on the Egyptians and their livestock (Exod. 9:8–12) but not on the Israelites. Here the sores torment only those who receive the mark of the beast (16:2). There is a wordplay in the Greek: "ugly, festering" can also be translated as "bad and evil" sores (16:2). These are spiritual wounds that disfigure, scar, and bring unbearable pain on the souls of all idolaters who worship false images (9:1–12; cf. Deut. 28:1–68).

The second (16:3) and third bowls (16:4–7) intensify the first Egyptian plague, which turned the Nile into blood, made it undrinkable, and killed the fish within it (Exod. 7:17–21). Here the second bowl turns the entire sea into blood, and every living sea creature dies from its polluted waters. The added detail that the blood is "like the blood of a corpse" (16:3, ESV, NRSV) reminds the readers that sin not only torments; *sin kills* and leads to both physical and spiritual death (cf. Rev. 20:14; 21:8; Rom. 5:12–20; 6:23).

The third bowl continues the plague so that it transforms the rivers and springs of (living) water into dead cesspools of blood (16:4). The vision inspires a heavenly hymn from the angel of the waters (cf. Gen. 7:17–24; *1 Enoch* 66:1), reminding that despite the severity of the judgments, God is just. His ways, though mysterious at times, are true (16:5; cf. 15:3;

19:2; Dan. 4:37). It is only fitting that those who spilled the blood of God's saints receive, in turn, a judgment of blood (16:6). With the choir from the altar (composed of the martyrs in 6:9–11), the readers are asked to trust in God's promises and sing with them: "Yes, O Lord God the Almighty, your judgments are true and just!" (16:7 NLT).

The fourth bowl unleashes a plague on the sun and scorches the earth with fire (16:8–9). This is a reversal of the ninth Egyptian plague, darkness (Exod. 10:21–29). Here the bowl plague intensifies the sun rather than blots it out. Again, there is law of retribution at work: the Roman Empire, whose military conquests left burned lands and devastation in their wake (Josephus, *Jewish War* 6.404–7), is now experiencing the fires of war and violence within its own borders (Rev. 8:7). Yet despite the severity of the plague, humanity is unrepentant and hard of heart (16:9), like Pharaoh (Exod. 7:13, 22; 8:15, 19, 32; 9:7).

16:10–21: The fifth through seventh bowls. The more intense the judgment, the more humanity seems to clench a defiant fist at God. With the fifth bowl comes a plague of darkness (16:10–11), which is reminiscent of both the Egyptian equivalent (Exod. 10:21–29) and the eighth plague, which sent a blanket of locusts to blacken the land (Exod. 10:12–20). This is a spiritual darkness inflicting agony to the point where people bite their tongues desperately (Rev. 16:10; cf. gnashing of teeth in Matt. 8:12; 22:13; 25:30). Sin has the power to blind, dull, and blacken the soul. Since the throne of the beast, that is, the imperial cult (cf. the throne of Satan in Rev. 2:13) darkened people's hearts, God rightly brings a judgment of darkness on Rome. Ironically, the wicked blame God for their suffering, although their own idolatry is the cause (16:11).

The sixth bowl (16:12–16) features unclean, foul-spirited, demonic frogs, which protrude from the mouths of the anti-Trinity: the dragon, the beast (of the sea), and the false prophet (16:12). Intensifying the second Egyptian plague of frogs (Exod. 8:1–15), the demonic frogs of Revelation are heralds of false ideologies and lies (e.g., the *pax Romana*). These false powers can duplicate the miraculous (cf. Exod. 7:11, 22), but their primary weapon of choice is deception. Fooled by evil, the kings of earth align themselves with the beast to their own destruction.

Armageddon, which means "the hill of Megiddo" in Hebrew (16:16), is sixty miles north of Jerusalem, on the southwest edge of the Jezreel Valley, and historically was the place where major battles between Israel and enemy nations took place (e.g., Judg. 4:4–16; 6:19–25; 2 Kings 23:28–30). It is symbolic of the final defiance of humanity against God. Even on the day when human history ends and Jesus returns like "a thief" in the night (16:15; cf. Matt. 24:43–44; 1 Thess. 5:2), the wicked will still gather their forces for one last stand against the Lord rather than repent (16:16; cf. Ps. 2:1–2; Zech. 14:1–15; Joel 3:2). In contrast, a beatitude or blessing is pronounced for those saints who are dressed in moral purity and righteous deeds (Rev. 3:4–5, 18; 6:11; 7:9, 14) and are ready for the coming of the bridegroom (cf. Matt. 25:1–13).

The seventh bowl (16:17–21) is an intensification of the seventh Egyptian plague, thunder and hail (Exod. 9:22–26). These hailstones are gigantic and weigh a talent each (about one hundred pounds). A tremendous earthquake (16:19–20) splits "the great city," that is, Babylon, into three parts. There is no place where anyone can hide. God's epiphany is a recapitulation of the Sinai theophany (cf. Exod. 19:16–25). Just by showing up, God has passed judgment. No sinner can stand in his presence. God's voice from the throne room of the temple cries out, "It is done!" (16:17). At last God exacts justice, but with a finality that is both welcoming and terrifying at the same time.

From the seals to the bowls (Revelation 6–16), the faithful begin to distinguish a divine purpose behind suffering. Until the seventh bowl, God does not cancel out evil, for to do so would mean the instantaneous condemnation of all sinners. All creation would be destroyed, since it too is tainted with sin. Instead, God maximizes the possibility for all people to repent by delaying his final justice until the very end of human history. In the interim, the church is called to endure, trust, pray, witness, and worship their God.

F. The end of the empire (17:1–19:10). **17:1–18: The Babylonian whore.** The next three chapters (Revelation 17–19) are an expansion of the sixth and seventh bowl judgments against "Babylon," which has stood for Rome throughout Revelation (14:8; 16:19; 17:5; 18:2, 10, 21). The dissolution of Roman power, which was anticipated in 14:8 ("Fallen is Babylon the Great!") and 16:19 (God "gave her [Babylon] the cup filled with the wine of the fury of his wrath"), is elaborated on in 17:1–19:10, as Rome's entire

Aerial view of the tell (archaeological mound) at Megiddo, with the Jezreel Valley spreading out beyond it in the background. This is the site that Revelation 16:16 refers to as Armageddon.

domination system of military might, economic exploitation, and religious idolatry crumbles under the justice of God.

In the first of two metaphors of Roman power (the other being "the great city"; 18:1–24), a great whore sits like a queen on the waters (18:7), riding a scarlet beast having seven heads and ten horns and covered with blasphemous names (17:1, 3). On her forehead is the title "Babylon the Great" (17:5), whose mystery will be unveiled and interpreted by one of the angels from the bowl judgments (17:1, 7; cf. Dan. 4:9–28; 5:24–30). The angel divides his interpretation into three parts. First, the beast (of the sea; Revelation 13) represents the Roman Empire but especially its political and military power base (17:8–14). Second, the waters on which the prostitute sits are the many nations that follow Roman rule (17:15–17). Last, the great whore is herself unveiled as the city of Rome, the epitome of wealth and luxury, which has seduced the world at large (17:18).

From a distance, the woman seated on the beast's seven heads (which represent seven mountains or hills; 17:9) looks like a royal figure. She is dressed in purple and scarlet clothing and adorned with gold, precious stones, and pearls (17:4). She is a parody of *Dea Roma*, the patron goddess of the city of Rome, featured on imperial coins as sitting on Rome's seven hills (Suetonius, *Domitian* 4.5; Strabo, *Geography* 5.3.7; cf. Rev. 17:9). But seen up close, the woman is actually a drunken courtesan sporting gaudy jewelry and clothes exacted from the kings of the earth with whom she has sexual relations (17:2). These suitors will later ravage her, strip her naked, murder her, consume her flesh, and burn her remains with fire (17:16–17). So gruesome is this scene that feminist commentators have called Revelation 17 the "ultimate misogynist fantasy" because this woman becomes the scapegoat for all that is evil in the world. (See Pippin, 57–58, for a now classic feminist reading of Revelation 17.) However, the Babylonian whore is a *corporate personality* and represents

both men and women. The prostitute as a symbol of vice and moral decadence was familiar among Greco-Roman moralists (Seneca, *On the Good Life* 7.3.1–3; Plutarch, *Pericles* 12.2) and Jewish readers alike (Isa. 23:15–18; Nah. 3:4–5). It is a familiar caricature (despite its patriarchal origins) and illustrates the exploitive nature of Rome's relations with her vassal states.

The empire's success was dependent on the patron-client relationships between Rome and the major urban centers of the empire. Cities received emergency funds from Rome to rebuild in times of crisis (e.g., Philadelphia; see commentary on Rev. 3:7–13), lobbied for wardenship of the imperial cult to sponsor festivals, which brought prestige and income to their local guilds (e.g., the Pergamum games; Rev. 2:12–17), and bid competitively to establish lucrative trading routes (e.g., the seaport of Ephesus; Rev. 2:1–7). In return for political favors from Rome, these cities and others around the world paid annual taxes and worshiped the emperor. Rome plays the harlot: she is given tribute from her client kings only because she services them (17:2). But as soon as the whore has nothing more to offer, the multitudes will unite to dismember her and consume any remaining resources for themselves (17:15–16). The entire set of relations between Rome and her clients is idolatrous. The empire seduces people with its power and wealth, and the people give their loyalty and worship to Caesar (cf. Isa. 23:15–18; Ezek. 16:1–36; Hos. 4:11–12).

The description that the beast "was and is not and is to come" (17:8 RSV) mocks God "who is, and who was, and who is to come" (1:4, 8; 4:8) and is a false claim to permanence. Only God is eternal. Rome will fall from its own internal violence and moral decadence. There is also an echo of the revival of Nero myth from the epitaph, but only in a corporate sense (see the commentary on 13:1–18). Just as the head was slaughtered but the entire beast was healed (13:3), there was a time when the empire was (the golden age of Augustus; *The Deeds of the Divine Augustus* 34), was almost not (the year of four emperors; Tacitus, *Histories* 1–3), and was to come (the Flavian dynasty; Suetonius, *Domitian* 13.2).

There has been endless speculation on the identity of the beast's seven heads, which are seven kings or Roman emperors (17:9); five have fallen, one is currently reigning, and the other has not yet come (17:10). With reasonable certainty, the living emperor is Domitian (Irenaeus, *Against Heresies* 5.30.4; see the introduction), but beyond this identification, caution is urged. Rather than searching through the annals of past emperors in an attempt to discover which of them are the preceding five (there are eleven from Augustus to Domitian), it is best to see the five kings as representative of all previous Roman rulers. The seventh king following Domitian (whose reign is cut short) and the succeeding eighth king (17:11) could be another allusion to the revival of Nero, but it is more likely a reminder that there will always be those in power who oppose the kingdom of God. Emperors rise, fall, and rise again, but it is God's will that prevails in the end (17:14).

The ten horns on the heads of the beast (cf. Dan. 7:23–24) are allies of Rome who give their support and power to the empire (17:13) within the same network of exploitive relationships as the whore and the kings of the earth. They foolishly join the war against the Lamb (17:14). Unlike them, Christians are called to resist the temptations of empire, its wealth and luxury (17:2). We are called to stand faithful to the Lamb despite the violence of the beast (17:6). We are reminded that any system based on the abuse of power, the exploitation of human beings, and the false ideologies of prosperity and peace should be directly opposed by the church and will inevitably self-destruct by God's providential hand (17:14).

18:1–24: Roman economy. Revelation 18 continues narrating the destruction of the Roman Empire due to its own political corruption, economic injustice, moral decadence, and idolatrous values. In the second of two complex metaphors on Roman power, the once-great city

of Babylon is in complete ruin. The readers are not told exactly how the city falls, only that it does ("She fell! Babylon the Great fell!" [18:2, author's translation]; cf. 14:8; Isa. 21:9), and what follows is a detailed description of the grisly aftermath of Rome's collapse.

The scene opens with the words of an unidentified angel (18:1; cf. Ezek. 43:1–3) whose speech against Rome resembles the taunt songs of Isaiah 23–24, Jeremiah 50–51, and Ezekiel 26–28 against the historic cities of Babylon and Tyre. The angel describes Rome as a completely desolate and empty place, uninhabitable to human beings (18:22–23), a lair for demons, and a haunt for unclean animals (i.e., scavengers who eat carrion, like ravens, vultures, and jackals; cf. Lev. 11:1–47; Zeph. 2:13–15; Luke 11:24–26). Rome has been judged (18:8). Its past sins have not gone unnoticed by God (18:5). Since widows in ancient times were considered weak, helpless, and completely dependent on God (Deut. 10:18; Ps. 146:9), the city's boast, "I sit enthroned as queen; I am not a widow" (18:7; cf. Isa. 47:7–8), is a shameless claim to self-sufficiency. To say one does not need God is the ultimate form of idolatry (cf. Isa. 14:4, 12–15; Dan. 4:29–32). In the Old Testament, the city was often a false source of security for the person who has left the domain of God (e.g., Cain in Gen. 4:16–17).

In luring the nations away from God and to herself as the source of material security, Rome has played the spiritual harlot (18:3, 7, 9; cf. Isa. 23:13–18; Nah. 3:1–7). Because she has intoxicated the kings of the earth with the wine of her immoral passion and merchants with the power of luxury (18:3), God has mixed a doubly potent cup filled with the wine of his wrath, poured it out against the city, stripped her of all wealth, sent a cycle of plagues, and judged her with fire (18:6–8; cf. 16:1–21). The double payment for her sins is neither vindictive nor unjust but rather a statement that the painful consequences of sin always outweigh its fleeting pleasures.

In 18:9–19, we hear the terrified lament of kings, merchants, and sailors for Rome (18:10, 15). They are stunned by the sudden collapse of the economic system that made them rich (18:4, 15). Rome was the center of international trade across the Mediterranean and a ravenous consumer of exotic goods from around the world. Of the twenty-eight types of merchandise listed in 18:12–13 (cf. Ezek. 27:12–24), most are luxury items that were imported by Rome from Spain, Greece, Asia Minor, Arabia, Egypt, Africa, Parthia, and even China. These included precious metals (gold, silver, high-quality bronze, and iron), jewels and rare materials for elaborate furnishings (pearls, precious stones, ivory, scented wood, and marble), expensive textiles (fine linens, purple and scarlet cloths, silk), spices and perfumes (cinnamon, amomum, myrrh, frankincense), high-quality foods or breeders' livestock (fine flour, cattle, sheep, horses), and chariots. Trade on even one luxury item could mean large profits for both the merchants who sold it and the sailors who delivered it. On the import of silk alone, Rome spent an estimated one hundred million *sestertii* per year for trade with India, China, and Arabia (Pliny the Elder, *Natural History* 12.41.84), which is roughly the amount needed to pay the annual salaries for eighty-five thousand Roman legionnaires. The remaining nonluxury items in the list—wine, olive oil, and wheat—were traded in bulk. Rome, for example, consumed some eighty thousand tons of grain annually and required a thousand ships to import it. The scope of John's cargo list for Rome speaks to the greed, consumption, excess, and waste of the city.

Worst yet is the final item of cargo: slaves. This industry received its stock in the most dehumanizing way: from prisoners of war, criminals, children sold by poor families, the indebted, piracy, and kidnapping. Beneath the veneer of dainty luxuries and glittering trinkets (18:14) lies the stark reality that the empire's economy was fueled by exploitive slave labor. John reminds his readers that slaves are not just bodies but living human souls (18:13).

How then are the people of God to respond? The voice from heaven (presumably God from his throne room; 16:1) says simply: "Come out of her, my people" (18:4a; cf. Jer. 51:45). This is not a command to withdraw from urban life (cf. 1 Cor. 5:10) or from our suffering witness in places like Rome, but a call to holiness, a commitment "not to be yoked with her sins" (18:4b, author's translation; cf. 2 Cor. 6:14–18), and a mission to dismantle the structures of evil, which enslave others, even at the cost of our own blood (18:24). In contrast to those who mourn, we are invited to rejoice that Babylon is falling (18:20). The stumbling block of the world has been thrown into the sea like a millstone (18:21; cf. Jer. 51:63–64; Mark 9:42) to make room for God's just kingdom. Rejoice!

19:1–10: Hymns and wedding song. The stunned silence from Rome's musicians at the sight of the burning city (18:22) is broken with the roar of "Hallelujah!" from heaven above (19:1). *Hallelujah* (transliterated into Greek as *hallēlouia* or into Latin as *alleluia*) means "Praise the Lord" in Hebrew and is used four times throughout two separate hymns in 19:1–8. (These hymns, incidentally, later became an inspiration for Handel's *Messiah*.) The first hymn is from a vast angelic assembly (19:1–4; cf. 5:11–12) and attributes salvation, glory, and power to God alone (19:2). It lauds God's judgment over the great whore, insists his ways are always just and true, and affirms his sovereign power by evoking a response of "Amen! Hallelujah" from the twenty-four elders and the four cherubim who encircle his throne (19:4).

The second hymn (19:5–8) begins with a call to worship for the entire church on earth. Though the empire seemed invincible, and though our world is still fraught with suffering and injustice, the angelic chorus nevertheless challenges all servants of Christ, small and great, to "praise our God" (19:5). Hymns in the book of Revelation (there are nine: 4:8–11; 5:9–14; 7:9–12; 11:5–8; 11:17–18; 15:3–4; 16:4–6; 19:1–4; 19:5–8) do more than just ratify the events in the narrative. They are acts of resistance, in worship to a transcendent God, against immanent evil. In the same way that African American slaves interpreted biblical texts on the exodus liberation, set them to music as spirituals, and "sang about the ways they could endure oppression, escape it, or even . . . fight against it" (Blount, 94), the hymns sung by the early church were weapons of worship against their Roman oppressors. Hymns enable worshipers to express—with the full range of human emotions, volume of voice, mental acuity, and spiritual freedom—theological truths that speak to the reality of God in a sinful world. No matter how much Rome or any other power wants to stop the church's witness, a church that sings out resistance to evil and absolute faith in Christ cannot be silenced (cf. Acts 16:25). Our joy is unstoppable because we anticipate a day when Jesus returns as the bridegroom and welcomes us as his bride (19:7–8; 21:2, 9; cf. Isa. 61:10; Matt. 25:1–12; 2 Cor. 11:2).

G. The return of the king (19:11–21). From this point onward (19:11–22:5), John narrates eschatological events surrounding the *parousia* of Jesus Christ. The Greek term *parousia* can be translated "return" but literally means "coming" or "advent" (see Matt. 24:36–42; 1 Cor. 15:21–28; 1 Thess. 4:14–17). In 19:11–16, John focuses on a particular aspect of the *parousia*, that is, the final defeat of God's enemies.

When the skies split apart and heaven opens up (19:11; cf. 4:1), a glorious rider appears on a white horse. This rider, with eyes "like a fiery flame" (19:12 HCSB; cf. 1:14), who is "Faithful and True" (19:11; cf. 3:14), who judges with justice (19:11; cf. 1:7; Dan. 7:13), who is called the "Word of God" (cf. John 1:1–14), from whose mouth extends the sword (of God's word) and who wears his name like a sword on his thigh (19:13, 15–16; cf. 1:17; Exod. 32:27; Ps. 45:3) is none other than Jesus, the Davidic Messiah who has come to rule the nations (1:15; cf. Ps. 2:9) and execute God's wrath (1:16; cf. 15:19–20). John catalogs titles upon titles so that the readers know beyond doubt that the white rider of Revelation 19 (who is nothing like the pale demonic parody of Rev. 6:2) is Christ, our king and Lord (1:16; 17:14).

Jesus returns with all the power, majesty, and splendor of a triumphant Roman emperor (Latin *triumphator*). On the occasion of a major victory, kings would often enter the capital city in a triumphal procession wearing a decorated white tunic and toga with gold-threaded designs, a golden crown (cf. the diadems of Christ, which signify his royal identity; 19:12), and riding on a chariot drawn by white

> Constructed by Domitian around AD 82, the Arch of Titus commemorates Titus's military victories. This panel shows his triumphal procession, with Titus wearing his toga and riding in his chariot. Revelation 19 depicts Jesus returning as a triumphant king.

horses (19:11). The king was accompanied by his armies, magistrates, senators, captive prisoners of war, and the spoils of his victory (19:14). He was greeted with the shouts of praise and divine accolades (19:16) from the citizens of the city. This *triumphator* tradition has been adapted by John to describe Christ's complete victory over the beast and his allies (19:19), but with some important (theological) differences.

The clothes of Christ are not the ceremonially elaborate royal tunic and toga but the ritually clean, fine *priestly* linens (19:8, 13; cf. the Son of Man in glorious linens in 1:12–16; Dan. 10:5–9). Priests would sprinkle the blood of the sacrifice on their own clothes for ritual purity (Exod. 29:21; Lev. 8:30), but the blood on Christ's priestly robes is his own (19:13; cf. 5:12; Heb. 9:20–28). The only weapons of war Christ uses to judge the nations and defeat the beast (cf. Isa. 63:2–4) are his own atoning blood and the sword of God's word (19:13, 15; cf. Isa. 49:2). He expects his church to use the same weapons as he.

The next scene borrows its savage imagery from the judgment oracles of Ezekiel, who spoke against Gog, Magog, and other enemy nations who mocked Israel during her exile. In Ezekiel 39:17–20, God invites the birds and wild animals to eat the flesh and drink the blood of Gog's armies. In Revelation 19, we are shown an equally gory feast, when God invites the birds that fly in mid-heaven (either vultures, hawks, or eagles; Rev. 8:13) to consume the flesh of all wicked people (19:17–18; 20:8). The gory feast is a bloodcurdling inversion of the wedding banquet of the Lamb (18:7–8; 21:1–2). Those who have refused the invitation to join the eschatological wedding celebration (9:20–21; 16:9; 16:11; cf. Matt. 22:2–8) are seen here experiencing the consequences of their refusal. The grisly menu of flesh from kings to slaves, from great to small, demonstrates that final judgment is a state of torment from which no unrepentant person can escape. The scene ends with the beast and the false prophet being thrown into a "fiery lake of burning sulfur"

(19:20). The fiery lake (cf. the "river of fire" in Dan. 7:9–11), or hell, is the final destination for the unrepentant. It is a place of eternal suffering and punishment for the godless (Rev. 20:14).

3. Heaven as a New City and the Earth as a New Eden (20:1–22:21)

In Revelation 20–22, John journeys outside the temple and discovers a glorious city, the New Jerusalem, within a new heaven and new earth (21:1–2). There is no sea, no sun, and no temple in this new created realm (21:22–27), because the presence of God and the Lamb dwells with the community of faith permanently and gloriously. The vision concludes with the assurance of Christ's return and a benediction of grace (22:6–21).

A. The vindication of God and his people (20:1–15). **20:1–10: The millennium.** In Revelation 20, the narrative spotlight on the defeat of Satan is a reminder that Rome is not the chief enemy but rather the powers of sin and death (cf. 1 Cor. 15:25, 55–57). An angel of the Lord has bound the dragon and sealed it in the abyss (20:1–3) for a thousand years, during which Christ and his risen saints reign together over the earth (20:4–5). Then, Satan is unexpectedly loosed again and, attempting one last coup d'état against God, is defeated. He is then thrown into the fiery lake forever (20:7–10; cf. 19:20).

The thousand-year (Latin *millennium*) interim reign is just one of five major end-time events described in the New Testament that interpreters have struggled to sequence: the rapture (not mentioned in Revelation but in 1 Thess. 4:13–18, though some dispensationalists argue that the command, "Come up here," in Rev. 4:1 refers to the rapture; see Walvoord, 103), the tribulation (Rev. 3:10; 7:14), the millennium (Rev. 20:2–7), the return of Christ (Rev. 19:11–21), and the new heaven and new earth (Rev. 21:1–2). Three major schemes have emerged, the most popular among American evangelicals being premillennialism. (For further discussion on each millennial scheme, see Grenz.)

Premillennialism argues that Christ returns *before* the millennium. Dispensational premillennialists argue that when Christ returns, he raptures (or "snatches up") living Christians into heaven before they die. Meanwhile, a world dictator (the beast or antichrist) rises to power and heavily persecutes the few who convert to Christianity (mostly ethnic Jews) for seven years (Rev. 4:1–19:10). After this tribulation, Christ returns a second time to conquer the beast and its armies (19:11–21), bind Satan in the abyss (20:1–3), resurrect believers (20:4–5), and begin a literal one-thousand-year reign of peace on earth (20:6).

Postmillennialism insists that Christ's return will happen only *after* the church establishes the millennium, defined as an ideal political state that the church achieves over time. The triumphal procession of Christ on a white horse (19:11–21), therefore, is a symbol of his victorious presence within the church. Proclaiming the gospel binds Satan (20:1–3). When the gospel has reached every nation (cf. John 12:31–32), the millennium is realized and Satan becomes completely bound (20:4–6). When the millennium has ended, Christ returns to stop the devil decisively (20:7–10) and launch eternity (21:1–2).

Amillennialism, as adopted by this commentary, argues that the millennium (like almost all numbers in Revelation) is *symbolic*. Ten is the number of power and authority (2:10; 12:3; 13:1; 17:3; cf. Dan. 7:7, 20, 24), and multiples of ten symbolize an immeasurable amount (5:11; 7:4; cf. Dan. 7:10). A thousand years refers to an indefinite period of time when the church lives under the agency of the Spirit (cf. Rom. 8:37). The millennium began when Jesus was raised from the dead (20:1–3; cf. 12:7–11), which is the first resurrection (20:5–6; cf. 1 Cor. 15:20), and continues today. When Christians remain faithful, Satan is bound (12:1–6; cf. Mark 3:23–28; Matt. 16:16–19; Luke 10:17–19); but when they compromise, Satan is loosed (20:7–9; cf. 2 Cor. 4:3–4; Eph. 2:2). The tribulation is not a future event but a present call for Christians to endure suffering and persecution (13:10; 14:12; cf. 2 Tim. 3:12). Satan seeks to destroy the city of God (20:9; cf. Matt. 5:14–16) by deceiving human agents like Gog and Magog (representative of all nations) into doing his evil work (20:8–9; cf. 19:17–21; Ezek. 38:22; 39:6). But because believers share in the life and power of the first resurrection (i.e., Christ's), they overcome (20:6; cf. 2 Tim. 2:12; Heb. 12:23). The millennium continues until Christ's return, when the wicked are judged (20:9–10; cf. Gen. 19:24; 2 Kings 1:9–12; Zeph. 3:8) and death and Hades give way to a new eternal age (20:14–21:1).

20:11–15: The resurrection. Regardless of the millennial scheme, all advocate the reality of final judgment and the resurrection of the dead (20:11–12; cf. Isa. 26:19–21; Dan. 12:2; John 5:28–29). The "great white throne" in Rev. 20:11 borrows its imagery from the throne occupied by the Ancient of Days in Daniel 7:9. At the resurrection of the dead, both believers and nonbelievers will be called to account (Matt. 16:27; 1 Cor. 3:12; 2 Cor. 5:10) as their works are read from the ledgers of the king (20:12; Esther 6:1; *1 Enoch* 90:20; *4 Ezra* 6:20). Final judgment is a *corporate* event. Our earthly life will be eternally present before God and the whole community of faith. All our sin will be exposed, yet forgiveness is also given. Christ has already made atonement (Rev. 5:9; 14:4) for those whose names are in the "book of life" (20:12, 15; cf. Exod. 32:32; Ps. 69:28; Dan. 12:1). Tragically, the unrepentant must face eternal torment or the "second death" (20:14). Hades, the temporary abode for the dead, is no longer needed after judgment is passed, and so it and death are thrown in the lake of fire forever (20:15).

B. Eternity (21:1–22:5). 21:1–8: The new genesis. In Isaiah 64:17–19, God uses the language of a new heaven and a new earth to assure the Jewish exiles in the Babylonian captivity that he will bring them home to the land of their ancestral birth. He promises to restore the city of Jerusalem, rebuild the ruined temple, and reestablish Israel as a sovereign nation. Creation language and Israel's restoration as the people of God are combined in Isaiah's prophecy to give a message of hope to the exiles. Likewise, the text of Revelation speaks of the eternal realm after the general resurrection as both a new genesis and a New Jerusalem (21:1–2).

Creation is renewed not by destroying the old and starting over but by transforming the old into something different, better, and transcendent (21:15; cf. Isa. 65:27). Creation's renewal is modeled after the transformation and resurrection of believers (1 Cor. 15:35–53). In the same way that sinners become a "new creation" because the old "has passed away" (NIV "has gone") and the new has come (2 Cor. 5:17), the first heaven and first earth "have passed away" (the Greek verb *parelthon* ["passed away"] in 2 Cor. 5:17 is virtually identical to the term *apelthon* ["passed away"] used in Rev. 21:1)—that is, they have discontinued in their current condition because God is restructuring the old created order into a new state of glory (cf. Rom. 8:19–22; Gal. 6:15; Col. 1:15–18). Creation changes without losing its former identity and becomes "a new heaven and a new earth" (21:1). God has not abandoned this world, and neither should we. Because God plans on transforming the old created order, the church should be faithful stewards of the planet and not exploit its resources.

In earlier visions, John saw "a sea of glass" as a part of God's heavenly court (Rev. 4:6; 15:2). Since the sea was a symbol of chaos and sin in the Old Testament (Ps. 74:13–17), its calm state before God's throne meant that he restrained sin (cf. Gen. 1:8; Ezek. 1:22). In the new heaven and new earth, the sea is not subdued; rather, it is *no longer* there (21:1). The very existence of

Woven in the fourteenth century AD, the Apocalypse Tapestries illustrate scenes from the book of Revelation. This tapestry shows the New Jerusalem coming down out of heaven (Revelation 21).

sin has been completely extinguished by God. Without the chaos of the sea, the new heaven and new earth become the perfect environment to receive the resurrected saints (21:7).

The New Jerusalem descending from heaven is the community of faith (21:2; see commentary on 21.9–22.5). The promises that God gave to Israel in Isaiah 25:8 to wipe away her tears, protect her from suffering, and keep her safe from death find a deeper fulfillment in an eternal home where there is no death at all, pain is gone, the old rule of sin is broken, and God himself will comfort his people with his *tabernacling* presence (21:3–4; cf. Lev. 26:11; Ezek. 37:27; 43:7). Joy will abound for the bride of Christ! (cf. Isa. 49:18; 52:1; 61:10; Eph. 5:22–27). The Alpha and Omega, the one who governs history from beginning to end, assures the reader, "It is done!" and promises the faithful that a sinless new world shall be their inheritance (21:6–7).

21:9–22:5: The New Jerusalem. Glimpses of the New Jerusalem have been shown to John throughout his heavenly tour (3:12; 21:2), but no detailed exposition of the city's import and meaning has been given until now. The epiphany of God's city has three major movements:

(1) the initial descent of the city and its summary description (21:9–14), (2) the measurements and materials of the city (21:15–21), and (3) the internal content and landscape of the city (21:22–22:5).

John the seer is taken up in his spirit to an unidentified mountain. If the old Jerusalem rests on Mount Zion, the New Jerusalem arrives at a locale of a grander height to signify its superiority to the older city (Isa. 2:2–3; 4:1–5; Mic. 4:1–2; Ezek. 40:2). As John witnesses the descent of a new and more glorious Jerusalem on the earth, he is reminded by the angelic intermediary that the city is the bride of the Lamb. Despite the complexity of the building metaphors used to describe the New Jerusalem, it is not a place but a people (21:9–10; cf. Isa. 64:17–19). John's panoramic overview of the whole city has one central theme: the deep and permanent communion of God with the church.

The dimensions of the *city* are an allusion to Ezekiel's vision of a restored *temple* in which God's glory is manifested as rivers of living water flowing from the sanctuary's foundation and each of its twelve gates is named after one of the twelve tribes of Israel (21:15–17; cf. Ezek. 40:1–4; 43:1–5; 47:1–12; 48:30–35). Just as Ezekiel's dimensions make the temple a perfect cube, so do the bowl angel's measurements of the New Jerusalem make it a cube. Yet everything about the New Jerusalem surpasses the eschatological temple, which Ezekiel surveys. The New Jerusalem is twelve thousand stadia in length, height, and width (about fifteen hundred miles), while the dimensions of the Ezekiel temple only amount to approximately one and a half miles. Since twelve is the number of God's apostles and his tribes, and one thousand is a multiple of ten (i.e., the number of power and vastness), the dimensions of the New Jerusalem are a spatial metaphor for a numberless multitude, the entire people of God from both Testaments, believers from every nation, tribe, and language (7:9) gathered around in perfect communion with each other and with God, whose glory the city reflects.

The material description of the city (21:18–21) focuses on its jewels (e.g., jasper, sapphire, chalcedony, emerald, sardonyx, carnelian, chrysolite, beryl, topaz, chrysoprase, jacinth, amethyst, pearls, and other precious materials). The stones have a twofold function. First, they highlight the glorified and transcendent nature (cf. Isa. 54:11) of the church at the resurrection. Second, they indicate the priestly role of the community since Jerusalem is dressed like a high priest. The listed jewels on the breastplate of the high priest (Exod. 28:17–20) resemble those embedded on the city walls, foundations, and gates. Each stone in the Exodus text represents a tribe of Israel. The stones in the New Jerusalem, therefore, could be another way of signifying the diverse membership of God's people in the same way that the different names around the city signify it (cf. Isa. 54:11–12; Josephus, *Jewish Antiquities* 3.8–9, 216–17).

In 21:22–27, John catalogs the content and occupants of the city. But the question, What is in the city? is not as important as, What is *not* in the city? or rather, What is no longer needed? There is *no* temple (22:22). There is *no* sun or moon (22:23). The Lord God Almighty and the Lamb have become the temple of the New Jerusalem; and their glory, abiding presence, and splendor so fill every corner, street, room, gate, wall, and quarter that there is no part of the universe a person can travel without basking in the light of God. The reach of the Lamb's lamp knows no bounds. This is a universal theophany of epic proportions (Isa. 6:1–10; Ezek. 1:28–2:3; Dan. 8:15–18; 10:4–21).

John's attention turns to the surroundings and landscape of the city (22:1–5). He beholds a glorious paradise of overflowing streams and fruit-bearing trees where there is no longer any curse. Like the Garden of Eden (Gen. 2:5–6) prior to the fall of Adam, this new Eden is unblemished by sin or the curse of suffering, toil, and death (Gen. 3:4–19). Yet the new Eden is much more than a return to a prefall state; it exceeds the old garden in glory and splendor.

The rivers of life are not only an echo of the Pishon, Havilah, Tigris, and Euphrates rivers of old Eden (Gen. 2:10–14); they are also an allusion to Ezekiel's temple vision of the waters that flowed from the foundation of the inner sanctuary (Ezek. 47:1–5). At first the water level rises to Ezekiel's knees, then his waist, and finally so high that he could swim in it. These living waters are a metaphor for the work and ministry of the Holy Spirit. Ezekiel envisions a time when the Spirit will flood human reality to such an extent as to take full control of God's people. That moment described by Ezekiel is now an eternal reality for those who reside in the city of God.

C. Benediction (22:6–21). Appropriately, the Apocalypse of John ends with worship. John is commissioned one last time to record a final benediction given by Jesus Christ himself, as the heavenly liturgy that began in 4:1 draws to a close. The structure of the liturgical elements in the vision focuses on the aspect of promise. Is it enough that God gives us his word? Will we trust in the promises of God even when we might not see God at work in our midst? On center stage is Jesus, who gives us the ultimate promise: "Look, I am coming soon!" (22:7; 22:12). With the assurance that the Son of Man will one day bring God's people home into glory, beatitudes are also given: "Blessed is the one who keeps the words of the prophecy written in this scroll" (22:7), and "Blessed are those who wash their robes" (22:14). From promise to blessing, the focus of these liturgical elements is to inspire commitment. We are challenged to obey God's prophetic word (22:7), to live righteously in an idolatrous world (22:11), and to serve as priests even if our blood is spilled in the name of ministering to others (22:14). We are invited to the table of presence to receive the Spirit's sustaining gifts. "Come!" says the Spirit and the bride. The Spirit is ready to flood, empower, and guide the life of the church (22:16–17). Once again Christ our king

promises, "Yes, I am coming soon" (22:20). Like the faithful bride who awaits the coming of the Lamb, we respond, "Amen. Come, Lord Jesus" (22:20). As the liturgy ends, God's grace remains with John, the churches, and all those who have journeyed with them through Revelation (22:21).

Select Bibliography

Aune, David. *Revelation*. 3 vols. Word Biblical Commentary. Nashville: Thomas Nelson, 1997–98.

Bauckham, Richard. *The Climax of Prophecy*. Edinburgh: T. & T. Clark, 1993.

———. *The Theology of the Book of Revelation*. Cambridge: Cambridge University Press, 1993.

Beale, G. K. *The Book of Revelation*. New International Greek Testament Commentary. Grand Rapids: Eerdmans, 1999.

Blount, Brian. *Can I Get a Witness? Reading Revelation through African American Culture*. Louisville: Westminster John Knox, 2005.

Boxall, Ian. *The Revelation of Saint John*. Black's New Testament Commentary. Peabody, MA: Hendrickson, 2006.

Caird, G. B. *A Commentary on the Revelation of St. John the Divine*. New York: Harper & Row, 1966.

Collins, Adela Yarbro. *The Combat Myth in the Book of Revelation*. Missoula, MT: Scholars Press, 1976.

Grenz, Stanley. *The Millennial Maze*. Downers Grove, IL: InterVarsity, 1992.

Hemer, Colin. *The Letters to the Seven Churches of Asia in Their Local Setting*. Sheffield: JSOT Press, 1986.

Keener, Craig. *Revelation*. NIV Application Commentary. Grand Rapids: Zondervan, 2000.

Osbourne, Grant. *Revelation*. Baker Exegetical Commentary on the New Testament. Grand Rapids: Baker Academic, 2002.

Pippin, Tina. *Death and Desire: The Rhetoric of Gender in the Apocalypse of John*. Louisville: Westminster John Knox, 1992.

Reddish, Mitchell. *Revelation*. Smyth & Helwys Bible Commentary. Macon, GA: Smyth & Helwys, 2001.

Walvoord, John. *The Revelation of Jesus Christ*. Chicago: Moody, 1966.

Timelines

Old Testament Chronology

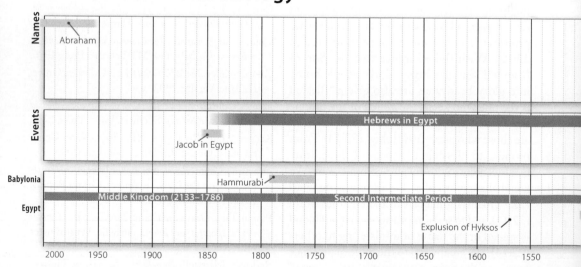

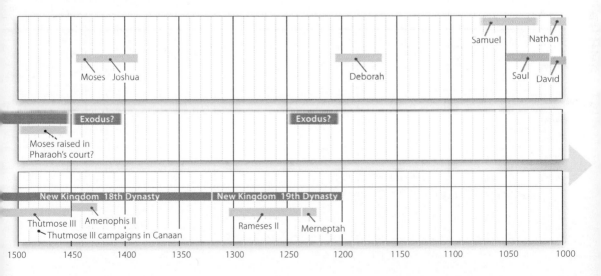

Old Testament Chronology

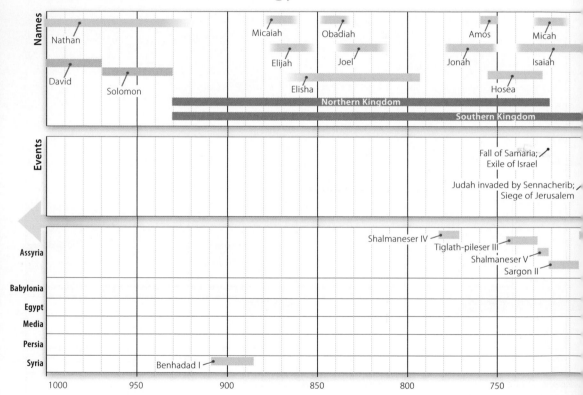

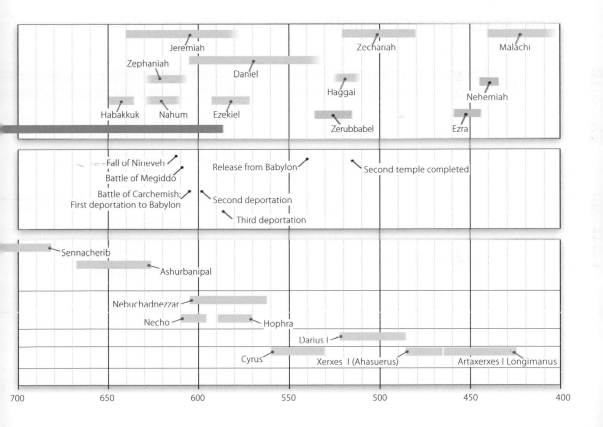

Jeremiah

Zechariah

Malachi

Zephaniah

Daniel

Haggai

Nehemiah

Habakkuk   Nahum   Ezekiel

Zerubbabel

Ezra

Fall of Nineveh

Release from Babylon

Second temple completed

Battle of Megiddo

Battle of Carchemish;
First deportation to Babylon

Second deportation

Third deportation

Sennacherib

Ashurbanipal

Nebuchadnezzar

Necho

Hophra

Darius I

Cyrus

Xerxes I (Ahasuerus)

Artaxerxes I Longimanus

700   650   600   550   500   450   400

New Testament Chronology

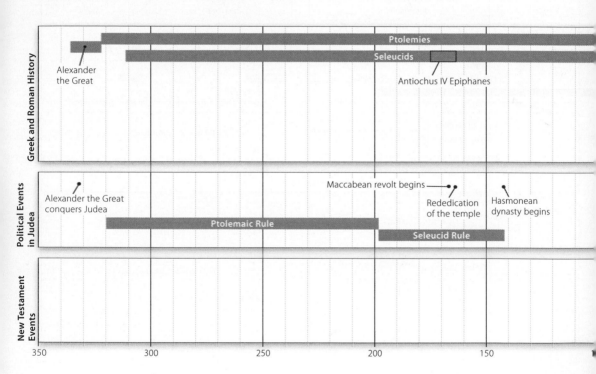

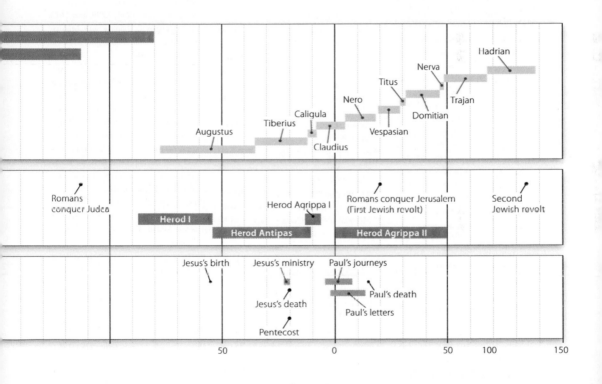

Hadrian

Nerva

Titus

Nero

Trajan

Caligula

Tiberius

Domitian

Augustus

Vespasian

Claudius

Romans
conquer Judea

Herod Agrippa I

Romans conquer Jerusalem
(First Jewish revolt)

Second
Jewish revolt

Herod I

Herod Antipas

Herod Agrippa II

Jesus's birth

Jesus's ministry

Paul's journeys

Jesus's death

Paul's death

Paul's letters

Pentecost

50   0   50   100   150

Illustration Credits

Unless otherwise indicated, photos, illustrations, and maps are copyright © Baker Photo Archive.

Look for
The Baker Illustrated Bible Handbook!

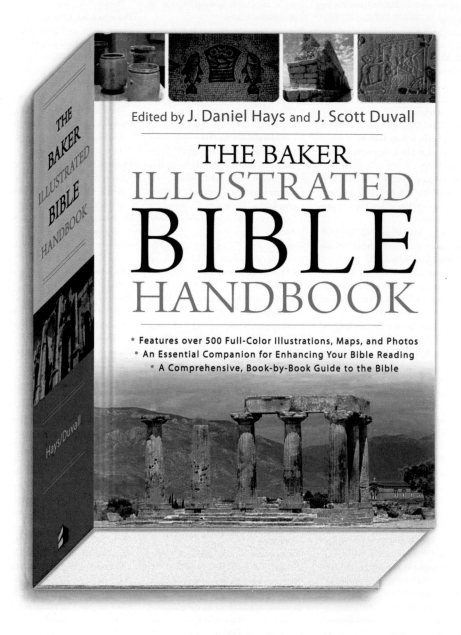

New Testament Chronology

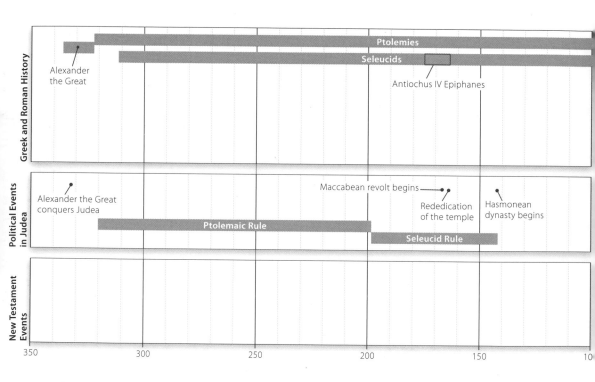